Case Directory

Small Animal Clinical Nutrition

4th Edition

MARK MORRIS INSTITUTE

Hand
Thatcher
Remillard
Roudebush

Small Animal Clinical Nutrition

4th Edition

Small Animal Clinical Nutrition

ISBN 0-945837-05-4

Printed in the United States of America by Walsworth Publishing Company, Marceline, Missouri.

For more information about this book contact:
Mark Morris Institute
P.O. Box 2097
Topeka, Kansas 66601-2097
Phone 785-286-8101
Facsimile 785-286-8173

Last digit is the print number: 9 8 7 6 5 4 3 2 1

Dedicated To

Mark L. Morris, Sr., DVM
Practitioner, Pioneer, Innovator and
Father of Small Animal Clinical Nutrition

Mark L. Morris, Jr., DVM, PhD
Innovator, Educator, Researcher and
Father of Small Animal Wellness Nutrition

Louise W. Morris
Bette M. Morris
Organizers, Stabilizers and Facilitators
of these Endeavors

Editors

Michael S. Hand, DVM, PhD
Diplomate, American College of Veterinary Nutrition
Vice President of Research, Hill's Science and Technology Center, Topeka, Kansas
Adjunct Professor, Department of Anatomy and Physiology, College of Veterinary Medicine,
    Kansas State University, Manhattan
Chair, Board of Directors, Mark Morris Institute, Topeka, Kansas

Craig D. Thatcher, DVM, MS, PhD
Diplomate, American College of Veterinary Nutrition
Professor and Head, Department of Large Animal Clinical Sciences,
    Virginia-Maryland Regional College of Veterinary Medicine,
    Virginia Polytechnic Institute and State University, Blacksburg, Virginia

Rebecca L. Remillard, PhD, DVM
Diplomate, American College of Veterinary Nutrition
Staff Nutritionist, Angell Memorial Animal Hospital, Boston, Massachusetts
Clinical Assistant Professor, School of Veterinary Medicine, Tufts University, North Grafton, Massachusetts

Philip Roudebush, DVM
Diplomate, American College of Veterinary Internal Medicine (Internal Medicine)
Veterinary Fellow, Hill's Science and Technology Center, Topeka, Kansas
Adjunct Professor, Department of Clinical Sciences, College of Veterinary Medicine,
    Kansas State University, Manhattan
Associate, Mark Morris Institute, Topeka, Kansas

Consulting Editors

Mark L. Morris, Jr., DVM, PhD
Diplomate, American College of Veterinary Nutrition
Topeka, Kansas

Bruce J. Novotny, DVM
Helios Communications, LLC, Shawnee, Kansas

Contributors

LARRY G. ADAMS, DVM, PhD, Diplomate, American College of Veterinary Internal Medicine (Internal Medicine) Associate Professor, Small Animal Internal Medicine, Department of Veterinary Clinical Sciences, School of Veterinary Medicine, Purdue University, West Lafayette, Indiana
Renal Disease

TIMOTHY A. ALLEN, DVM, Diplomate, American College of Veterinary Medicine (Internal Medicine)
Research Fellow, Hill's Science and Technology Center, Topeka, Kansas; Affiliate Faculty Member, Department of Clinical Sciences, College of Veterinary Medicine and Biomedical Sciences, Colorado State University, Fort Collins; Adjunct Professor, Department of Clinical Sciences, College of Veterinary Medicine, Kansas State University, Manhattan; Associate, Mark Morris Institute, Topeka, Kansas
Renal Disease, Feline Lower Urinary Tract Disease, Canine Urolithiasis

P. JANE ARMSTRONG, DVM, MS, Diplomate, American College of Veterinary Internal Medicine (Internal Medicine) Professor, Internal Medicine/Clinical Nutrition, College of Veterinary Medicine, University of Minnesota, St. Paul
Normal Cats, Assisted Feeding in Hospitalized Patients: Enteral and Parenteral Nutrition

LAWRENCE H. ARP, DVM, PhD, Diplomate, American College of Veterinary Pathologists, Diplomate, American College of Veterinary Microbiologists
Research Director, Discovery Pathology, Department of Biology, Hoffmann La Roche Inc., Nutley, New Jersey; Collaborator, Department of Veterinary Pathology, Iowa State University, Ames
Food Safety (case)

JOSEPH W. BARTGES, BS, DVM, PhD, Diplomate, American College of Veterinary Internal Medicine (Internal Medicine), Diplomate, American College of Veterinary Nutrition
Associate Professor, Department of Small Animal Clinical Sciences, University of Tennessee, Knoxville
Canine Urolithiasis

MARK BRINKMANN, BS, MBA
General Manager, Diamond Pet Foods, Meta, Missouri
Making Commercial Pet Foods

R. GLENN BROWN, PhD
Professor of Animal Nutrition, Department of Veterinary and Animal Science, University of Massachusetts, Amherst; Nutrition Advisor, Canadian Veterinary Medical Association, Ottawa, Ontario, Canada
Pet Food Labels

DOUGLAS E. BRUM, DVM
Angell Memorial Animal Hospital, Boston, Massachusetts
Gastrointestinal and Exocrine Pancreatic Disease (case)

WILLIAM J. BURKHOLDER, DVM, PhD, Diplomate, American College of Veterinary Nutrition
Assistant Professor, Department of Small Animal Medicine and Surgery, College of Veterinary Medicine, Texas A&M University, College Station
Obesity

KEVIN P. BYRNE, DVM, Diplomate, American College of Veterinary Dermatology
Lecturer in Dermatology, School of Veterinary Medicine, University of Pennsylvania, Philadelphia
Use of Fatty Acids in Inflammatory Disease (case)

JAMES W. CARPENTER, MS, DVM, Diplomate, American College of Zoological Medicine
Professor, Exotic Animal, Wildlife and Zoo Animal Medicine Service, Department of Clinical Sciences, College of Veterinary Medicine, Kansas State University, Manhattan
Feeding Small Exotic Mammals

LAINE COWAN, DVM, MS, Diplomate, American College of Veterinary Internal Medicine (Internal Medicine)
Small Animal Internist, Phoenix Central Laboratory, Everett, Washington
Food Safety (case)

CHRISTOPHER S. COWELL, MS
Principal Nutritionist, Hill's Science and Technology Center, Topeka, Kansas; Adjunct Professor, Department of Animal Science and Industry, College of Agriculture, Kansas State University, Manhattan; Associate, Mark Morris Institute, Topeka, Kansas
Nutrients, Making Commercial Pet Foods, Making Pet Foods at Home

STEPHEN W. CRANE, DVM, Diplomate, American College of Veterinary Surgeons, Diplomate, American Board of Laser Surgery
Executive Director, Western Veterinary Conference; Adjunct Professor, Department of Companion Animal, Las Vegas, Nevada and Special Species Medicine, College of Veterinary Medicine, North Carolina State University, Raleigh; Associate, Mark Morris Institute, Topeka, Kansas
Introduction to Commercial Pet Foods, Making Commercial Pet Foods, Making Pet Foods at Home

JAMES S. CULLOR, DVM, PhD
Director, Veterinary Medicine Teaching and Research
Center, University of California, Tulare
Food Safety

DEBORAH J. DAVENPORT, DVM, MS, Diplomate,
American College of Veterinary Internal Medicine
(Internal Medicine)
Veterinary Fellow, Hill's Science and Technology Center,
Topeka, Kansas; Adjunct Professor, Department of
Clinical Sciences, College of Veterinary Medicine, Kansas
State University, Manhattan; Associate, Mark Morris
Institute, Topeka, Kansas
*Assisted Feeding in Hospitalized Patients: Enteral and
Parenteral Nutrition, Gastrointestinal and Exocrine
Pancreatic Disease, Hepatobiliary Disease*

JACQUES DEBRAEKELEER, DVM
Associate Director, Regulatory and Scientific Affairs, Hill's
Science and Technology Europe, Etten-Leur, The
Netherlands; Adjunct Professor of Small Animal Clinical
Nutrition, Veterinary Faculty of the State University Gent,
Belgium; Associate, Mark Morris Institute, Topeka, Kansas
*Nutrients, Pet Food Labels, Making Pet Foods at Home,
Normal Dogs, Normal Cats, Appendices*

DONNA S. DIMSKI, DVM, MS, Diplomate, American
College of Veterinary Internal Medicine (Internal Medicine)
Oregon Veterinary Referral Associates, Corvallis, Oregon
Hepatobiliary Disease

SUSAN DONOGHUE, MS, VMD, Diplomate, American
College of Veterinary Nutrition
President, Nutrition Support Services, Pembroke, Virginia
Feeding Pet Reptiles

DAVID A. DZANIS, DVM, PhD, Diplomate, American
College of Veterinary Nutrition
Dzanis Consulting and Collaborations, Santa Clarita,
California
Pet Food Labels

MARTIN J. FETTMAN, DVM, PhD, Diplomate,
American College of Veterinary Pathologists
(Clinical Pathology)
Professor and Mark L. Morris Chair in Clinical Nutrition,
Department of Pathology, College of Veterinary Medicine
and Biomedical Sciences, Colorado State University, Fort
Collins
Dietary Effects on Drug Metabolism

RICHARD B. FORD, DVM, MS, Diplomate, American
College of Veterinary Internal Medicine (Internal Medicine)
Professor, Department of Companion Animal and Special
Species Medicine, College of Veterinary Medicine, North
Carolina State University, Raleigh
Endocrine and Lipid Disorders

LISA M. FREEMAN, DVM, PhD, Diplomate, American
College of Veterinary Nutrition
Assistant Professor, Department of Clinical Sciences,
School of Veterinary Medicine, Tufts University, North
Grafton, Massachusetts; Appointment with Scientist, Jean
Mayer, USDA Human Nutrition Research, Center for
Aging, Boston, Massachusetts
Cardiovascular Disease (case)

RUSSELL A. FREY, DVM, PhD, Diplomate, American
College of Veterinary Nutrition
Professor, Department of Anatomy and Physiology,
College of Veterinary Medicine, Kansas State University,
Manhattan
Nutrients

STEPHEN D. GILSON, DVM, Diplomate, American
College of Veterinary Surgeons
Associate, Sonora Veterinary Specialists, Scottsdale,
Arizona
*Assisted Feeding in Hospitalized Patients: Enteral and
Parenteral Nutrition (case)*

RICHARD T. (BILL) GOLDSTON, DVM, Diplomate,
American College of Veterinary Internal Medicine
(Internal Medicine)
Consulting Companion Animal Gerontologist, Veterinary
Centers of America, Santa Monica, California
Health Maintenance Programs for Dogs and Cats

ROBERT W. GRIFFIN, PhD
Principal, RW Griffin and Associates, Topeka, Kansas;
Adjunct Research Fellow, University of Massachusetts;
Professional Member, Institute of Food Technologists;
Member, Sensory Evaluation Division of Institute of Food
Technologists
Introduction to Commercial Pet Foods

KATHY L. GROSS, PhD, MS, Diplomate, American
College of Animal Nutrition
Principal Nutritionist, Hill's Science and Technology
Center, Topeka, Kansas; Adjunct Faculty, Department of
Animal Science and Industry, College of Agriculture,
Kansas State University, Manhattan; Associate, Mark
Morris Institute, Topeka, Kansas
Nutrients, Normal Dogs

W. GRANT GUILFORD, BPhil, BVSc, PhD, Diplomate,
American College of Veterinary Internal Medicine (Internal
Medicine), Fellow, Australian College of Veterinary Scientists
Head, Institute of Veterinary Animal and Biomedical
Sciences, Massey University, Palmerston North, New Zealand
Adverse Reactions to Food

MICHAEL S. HAND, DVM, PhD, Diplomate, American
College of Veterinary Nutrition
Vice President of Research, Hill's Science and Technology
Center, Topeka, Kansas; Adjunct Professor, Department
of Anatomy and Physiology, College of Veterinary
Medicine, Kansas State University, Manhattan; Chair,
Board of Directors, Mark Morris Institute,
Topeka, Kansas
Small Animal Clinical Nutrition: An Iterative Process

HERMAN A. W. HAZEWINKEL, DVM, PhD, Diplomate,
Royal Netherlands Veterinary Association (Companion
Animal Surgery), Diplomate, European College of
Veterinary Surgeons
Associate Professor, Companion Animal Orthopedics,
Department of Clinical Sciences in Companion Animals,
Utrecht University, The Netherlands
Developmental Orthopedic Disease of Dogs

JOHN J. HEFFERREN, PhD
Research Professor, Center for Biomedical Research, Higuchi Biosciences Center, University of Kansas, Lawrence; Adjunct Professor, Department of Pharmaceutical Chemistry, University of Kansas, Lawrence; Adjunct Professor, Department of Community Dentistry, University of Texas, Health Science Center, San Antonio; Clinical Professor, Department of Periodontics, School of Dentistry, University of Missouri, Kansas City
Dental Disease

M. ANNE HICKMAN, DVM, PhD, Diplomate, American College of Veterinary Nutrition
Senior Research Scientist, Animal Health Discovery, Pfizer, Inc., Groton, Connecticut
Normal Cats (case)

DENNIS E. JEWELL, PhD, Diplomate, American College of Animal Nutrition
Principal Nutrition Scientist, Hill's Science and Technology Center, Topeka, Kansas; Adjunct Faculty, Department of Animal Sciences and Industry, College of Agriculture, Kansas State University, Manhattan; Associate, Mark Morris Institute, Topeka, Kansas
Nutrients

BRUCE W. KEENE, DVM, MSc, Diplomate, American College of Veterinary Internal Medicine (Cardiology)
Associate Professor of Cardiology, Department of Companion Animal and Special Species Medicine, College of Veterinary Medicine, North Carolina State University, Raleigh
Cardiovascular Disease

CLAUDIA A. KIRK, DVM, PhD, Diplomate, American College of Veterinary Nutrition, Diplomate, American College of Veterinary Internal Medicine (Internal Medicine)
Veterinary Clinical Nutritionist, Hill's Science and Technology Center, Topeka, Kansas; Adjunct Faculty Clinical Nutritionist, Department of Clinical Sciences, College of Veterinary Medicine, Kansas State University, Manhattan; Associate, Mark Morris Institute, Topeka, Kansas
Normal Cats, Endocrine and Lipid Disorders

GEORGE V. KOLLIAS, DVM, PhD, Diplomate, American College of Zoological Medicine
J. Hyman Professor of Wildlife Medicine, Department of Clinical Sciences, College of Veterinary Medicine, Cornell University, Ithaca, New York
Feeding Pet Birds

HEIDI WEARNE KOLLIAS, MS
Research Assistant, Wildlife Health Laboratory, Department of Clinical Sciences, College of Veterinary Medicine, Cornell University, Ithaca, New York
Feeding Pet Birds

CHRISTINE KOLMSTETTER, MS, DVM
Clinical Veterinarian, Park Animal Hospital, Las Vegas, Nevada
Feeding Small Exotic Mammals

JOHN M. KRUGER, DVM, PhD, Diplomate, American College of Veterinary Internal Medicine (Internal Medicine)
Associate Professor, Department of Small Animal Clinical Sciences, College of Veterinary Medicine, Michigan State University, East Lansing
Feline Lower Urinary Tract Disease

ELLEN I. LOGAN, DVM, PhD
Senior Scientist, Oral Care, Hill's Science and Technology Center, Topeka, Kansas; Adjunct Associate Research Professor, University of Kansas, Lawrence; Adjunct Assistant Clinical Professor, College of Veterinary Medicine, Kansas State University, Manhattan; Veterinary Consultant, Odontex, Inc, Lawrence, Kansas; Associate, Mark Morris Institute, Topeka, Kansas
Dental Disease

DAWN E. LOGAS, DVM, Diplomate, American College of Veterinary Dermatology
Visiting Assistant Professor, College of Veterinary Medicine, University of Florida, Gainesville; Staff Dermatologist, Veterinary Dermatology Center, Winter Park, Florida
Skin and Hair Disorders

JODY P. LULICH, DVM, PhD, Diplomate, American College of Veterinary Internal Medicine (Internal Medicine)
Associate Professor, Department of Small Animal Clinical Sciences, College of Veterinary Medicine, University of Minnesota, St. Paul
Canine Urolithiasis

STANLEY L. MARKS, BVSc, PhD, Diplomate, American College of Veterinary Internal Medicine (Internal Medicine, Oncology), Diplomate, American College of Veterinary Nutrition
Assistant Professor, Department of Medicine and Epidemiology; Chief, Nutrition Support Service, School of Veterinary Medicine, University of California, Davis
Cancer

PETER R. MESSENT, MA, DPhil
Director, Research and Development, Pet Food Partners BV, Etten-Leur, The Netherlands
Introduction to Commercial Pet Foods

KATHRYN E. MICHEL, DVM, MS, Diplomate, American College of Veterinary Nutrition
Clinical Assistant Professor of Nutrition, Department of Clinical Sciences, School of Veterinary Medicine, University of Pennsylvania, Philadelphia
Assisted Feeding in Hospitalized Patients: Enteral and Parenteral Nutrition (case)

E. PHILLIP MILLER, DVM, MS, Diplomate, American Board of Toxicology, Diplomate, American Board of Veterinary Toxicology
Director, Product Safety and Efficacy, Hill's Science and Technology Center, Topeka, Kansas; Associate, Mark Morris Institute, Topeka, Kansas
Food Safety

H. LELAND MIZELLE, PhD
Assistant Professor, Department of Physiology and Biophysics, University of Mississippi Medical Center, Jackson
Cardiovascular Disease

EDWARD A. (NED) MOSER, MS, VMD, Diplomate, American College of Veterinary Nutrition
Veterinary Nutrition Consultant, Selinsgrove, Pennsylvania; Adjunct Assistant Professor of Comparative Nutrition, School of Veterinary Medicine, University of Pennsylvania, Philadelphia
Making Commercial Pet Foods

RICHARD W. NELSON, DVM, Diplomate, American College of Veterinary Internal Medicine (Internal Medicine)
Professor, Department of Medicine and Epidemiology, School of Veterinary Medicine, University of California, Davis
Endocrine and Lipid Disorders

GREGORY K. OGILVIE, DVM, Diplomate, American College of Veterinary Internal Medicine (Internal Medicine, Oncology)
Professor and Head of Medical Oncology, Comparative Oncology Unit, Department of Clinical Sciences, College of Veterinary Medicine and Biomedical Sciences, Colorado State University, Fort Collins
Cancer

CONNIE J. ORCUTT, DVM, Diplomate, American Board of Veterinary Practitioners (Avian Practice)
Staff Clinician/Service Head—Avian and Exotic Pet Medicine, Angell Memorial Animal Hospital, Boston, Massachusetts; Associate Editor, Journal of Avian Medicine and Surgery
Feeding Pet Reptiles (case)

CARL A. OSBORNE, DVM, PhD, Diplomate, American College of Veterinary Internal Medicine (Internal Medicine)
Professor, Department of Small Animal Clinical Sciences, College of Veterinary Medicine, University of Minnesota, St. Paul
Canine Urolithiasis

BERNARD-MARIE PARAGON, DVM, Prof Agrege
Professor, National Veterinary School of Alfort, France; Chief of the Animal Nutrition Laboratory and Clinical Nutrition Unit, Maisons-Alfort, France
Making Pet Foods at Home

ROBERT W. PHILLIPS, DVM, PhD, Diplomate, American College of Veterinary Nutrition
Professor Emeritus, Department of Physiology, College of Veterinary Medicine and Biomedical Sciences, Colorado State University, Fort Collins
Dietary Effects on Drug Metabolism

GUY L. PIDGEON, DVM, Diplomate, American College of Veterinary Internal Medicine (Internal Medicine)
Chief of Staff, The Animal Medical Center, New York, New York
Gastrointestinal and Exocrine Pancreatic Disease

DAVID J. POLZIN, DVM, PhD, Diplomate, American College of Veterinary Internal Medicine (Internal Medicine)
Professor, Department of Small Animal Clinical Sciences, College of Veterinary Medicine, University of Minnesota, St. Paul
Renal Disease, Canine Urolithiasis

REBECCA L. REMILLARD, PhD, DVM, Diplomate, American College of Veterinary Nutrition
Staff Nutritionist, Angell Memorial Animal Hospital, Boston, Massachusetts; Clinical Assistant Professor, School of Veterinary Medicine, Tufts University, North Grafton, Massachusetts
Small Animal Clinical Nutrition: An Iterative Process, Making Pet Foods at Home, Assisted Feeding in Hospitalized Patients: Enteral and Parenteral Nutrition, Gastrointestinal and Exocrine Pancreatic Disease

ARLEIGH J. REYNOLDS, DVM, PhD, Diplomate, American College of Veterinary Nutrition
Assistant Professor of Clinical Nutrition, Department of Clinical Sciences, College of Veterinary Medicine, Cornell University, Ithaca, New York; Board of Directors, International Sled Dog Veterinary Medical Society
The Canine Athlete

DANIEL C. RICHARDSON, DVM, Diplomate, American College of Veterinary Surgeons
Director of Research, Hill's Science and Technology Center, Topeka, Kansas; Adjunct Professor, Orthopedic Surgery, Department of Companion Animal and Special Species Medicine, College of Veterinary Medicine, North Carolina State University, Raleigh; Adjunct Professor, Surgery, Department of Clinical Sciences, College of Veterinary Medicine, Kansas State University, Manhattan; Associate, Mark Morris Institute, Topeka, Kansas
Developmental Orthopedic Disease of Dogs

PHILIP ROUDEBUSH, DVM, Diplomate, American College of Veterinary Internal Medicine (Internal Medicine)
Veterinary Fellow, Hill's Science and Technology Center, Topeka, Kansas; Adjunct Professor, Department of Clinical Sciences, College of Veterinary Medicine, Kansas State University, Manhattan; Associate, Mark Morris Institute, Topeka, Kansas
Pet Food Labels, Health Maintenance Programs for Dogs and Cats, Adverse Reactions to Food, Skin and Hair Disorders, Cardiovascular Disease, Hepatobiliary Disease, Use of Fatty Acids in Inflammatory Disease, Glossary

KORINN E. SAKER, DVM
Assistant Professor, Department of Large Animal Clinical Sciences, Virginia-Maryland Regional College of Veterinary Medicine, Virginia Polytechnic Institute and State University, Blacksburg, Virginia
Assisted Feeding in Hospitalized Patients: Enteral and Parenteral Nutrition (case)

WILLIAM D. SCHOENHERR, PhD, MS
Principal Nutritionist, Hill's Science and Technology Center, Topeka, Kansas; Associate, Mark Morris Institute, Topeka, Kansas
Nutrients, Use of Fatty Acids in Inflammatory Disease

KEVIN J. SHANLEY, DVM, Diplomate, American College of Veterinary Dermatology
Staff Dermatologist, Metropolitan Veterinary Associates, Valley Forge, Pennsylvania; Staff Dermatologist, Delaware Veterinary Specialty Group, Newark Animal Hospital, Newark, Delaware
Adverse Reactions to Food

KENNY W. SIMPSON, BVM&S, PhD, MRCVS, Diplomate, American College of Veterinary Internal Medicine (Internal Medicine), Diplomate, European College of Veterinary Internal Medicine (Companion Animals)
Assistant Professor of Medicine, Small Animal Medicine and Gastroenterology, Department of Clinical Sciences, College of Veterinary Medicine, Cornell University, Ithaca, New York
Gastrointestinal and Exocrine Pancreatic Disease

CANDACE A. SOUSA, DVM, Diplomate, American Board of Veterinary Practitioners (Canine and Feline Practice), Diplomate, American College of Veterinary Dermatology
Animal Dermatology Clinic, Sacramento, California
Skin and Hair Disorders

SCOTT J. STAHL, DVM, Diplomate, American Board of Veterinary Practitioners (Avian Practice)
Avian/Exotic Animal Clinician, Fairfax, Virginia; Adjunct Professor, Virginia-Maryland Regional College of Veterinary Medicine, Virginia Polytechnic Institute and State University, Blacksburg, Virginia
Feeding Pet Reptiles

JÖRG M. STEINER, Dr med vet, Diplomate, American College of Veterinary Med Vet, Internal Medicine (Internal Medicine), Diplomate, European College of Veterinary Internal Medicine (Companion Animal)
Clinical Investigator, GI Laboratory, College of Veterinary Medicine, Texas A&M University, College Station
Gastrointestinal and Exocrine Pancreatic Disease (case)

NEIL P. STOUT, BS
Director, Hill's Science and Technology Europe, Etten-Leur, The Netherlands
Making Commercial Pet Foods

WILLIAM S. SWECKER, Jr, DVM, PhD, Diplomate, American College of Veterinary Nutrition
Associate Professor, Production Management Medicine; Director, Clinical Nutrition Consultation Service, Virginia-Maryland Regional College of Veterinary Medicine, Virginia Polytechnic Institute and State University, Blacksburg, Virginia
Use of Fatty Acids in Inflammatory Disease

CRAIG D. THATCHER, DVM, PhD, Diplomate, American College of Veterinary Nutrition
Professor and Head, Department of Large Animal Clinical Sciences, Virginia-Maryland Regional College of Veterinary Medicine, Virginia Polytechnic Institute and State University, Blacksburg, Virginia
Small Animal Clinical Nutrition: An Iterative Process

PHILIP W. TOLL, DVM, MS
Principal Scientist, Hill's Science and Technology Center, Topeka, Kansas; Adjunct Faculty, Department of Anatomy and Physiology, College of Veterinary Medicine, Kansas State University, Manhattan; Associate, Mark Morris Institute, Topeka, Kansas
The Canine Athlete, Obesity, Developmental Orthopedic Disease of Dogs

LAUREN A. TREPANIER, DVM, PhD, Diplomate, American College of Veterinary Internal Medicine (Internal Medicine)
Assistant Professor of Small Animal Internal Medicine, Department of Medical Sciences, School of Veterinary Medicine, University of Wisconsin-Madison
Dietary Effects on Drug Metabolism (case)

DAVID C. TWEDT, DVM, Diplomate, American College of Veterinary Internal Medicine (Internal Medicine)
Professor, Department of Clinical Sciences, College of Veterinary Medicine and Biomedical Sciences, Colorado State University, Fort Collins
Hepatobiliary Disease (case)

KAREN J. WEDEKIND, PhD, MS
Senior Nutritionist, Hill's Science and Technology Center, Topeka, Kansas; Adjunct Faculty, Department of Animal Science and Industry, College of Agriculture, Kansas State University, Manhattan; Associate, Mark Morris Institute, Topeka, Kansas
Nutrients

ROBERT B. WIGGS, DVM, Diplomate, American Veterinary Dental College
Owner, Coit Road Animal Hospital, Dallas, Texas; Adjunct Associate Professor, Baylor College of Dentistry, Dallas, Texas
Dental Disease

JURGEN ZENTEK, Dr med vet
Privatdozent, Veterinary Specialist for Animal Nutrition and Dietetics; Lecturer in Department for Animal Nutrition, Tierarztliche Hochschule, Hannover, Germany
Developmental Orthopedic Disease of Dogs

KARL ZETNER, DVM, Diplomate, European Veterinary Dental College, Fellow of the Academy of Veterinary Dentistry
Professor of Surgery, Ophthalmology and Veterinary Dentistry; Head, Dental Department, University of Veterinary Medicine, Vienna, Austria
Dental Disease

STEVEN C. ZICKER, DVM, PhD, Diplomate, American College of Veterinary Internal Medicine (Internal Medicine), Diplomate, American College of Veterinary Nutrition
Veterinary Clinical Nutritionist, Hill's Science and Technology Center, Topeka, Kansas; Adjunct Faculty, Department of Clinical Sciences, College of Veterinary Medicine, Kansas State University, Manhattan; Associate, Mark Morris Institute, Topeka, Kansas
Nutrients, Normal Dogs, Developmental Orthopedic Disease of Dogs, Endocrine and Lipid Disorders

Preface

As veterinarians, we have all become more aware of the importance of pets to society. Relating and bonding to pets adds quality to our lives and improves longevity. Children who interact with pets are better students and function better in society. Interacting with dogs and cats reduces some of the risk factors for cardiovascular disease. Interactions with pets lower systolic blood pressure, decrease plasma cholesterol and triglyceride concentrations and reduce anxiety. Dog owners experience fewer minor health problems and require fewer physician visits than do non-owners. Pets are more than surrogate children; to many people they are very special companions. Pets deserve high-quality health care that will support their longevity and quality of life. Optimal nutrition is an important part of achieving these goals. Pet owners themselves have become increasingly aware of the importance of nutrition to health and expect state-of-the-art nutritional services from their veterinarian.

Much has happened in the field of small animal clinical nutrition since the publication of *Small Animal Clinical Nutrition III* in 1987. Today, veterinarians better appreciate the importance of nutrition and, in fact, have established a specialty in veterinary nutrition, the American College of Veterinary Nutrition (ACVN). The ACVN was organized in 1988 and received full accreditation by the American Veterinary Medical Association in 1997. The chief objective of the ACVN is to advance the practice of veterinary nutrition. This objective is achieved primarily through enhanced veterinary nutrition education. By 1999, more than 45 veterinarians were certified by the ACVN; most diplomates occupy positions in veterinary schools, private practice or industry. Many of these specialists have contributed to the fourth edition of *Small Animal Clinical Nutrition* and the book is intended to support the goals of the ACVN.

Clinical nutrition in veterinary medicine is relatively new and continues to evolve. Clinical nutrition integrates the science of nutrition with the practice of medicine and surgery to optimize health. Beyond the science, however, it is the art of clinical nutrition that successfully combines the knowledge of nutrient metabolism, disease processes and problematic logistics into the practical day-to-day feeding of our patients. This is truly an exciting time for those involved in the discipline of clinical nutrition because of the veterinary profession's increased understanding of the role of nutrition in health and disease management, pet owners' continued interest in receiving the best nutritional information for their pets and the recent proliferation of commercially available therapeutic foods. Our ability to improve the quality of life for pets and their owners is great.

In human clinical nutrition, dietitians provide food and nutrient guidelines, but the patient is ultimately in control and must correctly choose from a variety of foods. With veterinary clinical nutrition, the potential for compliance is better because there are readily available, highly palatable, convenient pet foods specifically designed to treat or prevent specific diseases. These products are powerful tools in the feeding management of dog and cats. Hence, there are many opportunities for veterinarians to positively affect the long-term health of pets and to assist in the medical and surgical management of numerous diseases.

There are opportunities to expand the role of nutrition in veterinary medicine, and, in the process, improve patient care. Research shows that fewer than 5% of the dogs and cats that visit veterinary hospitals are fed veterinarian-dispensed therapeutic or wellness foods. This is true even though clinical and epidemiologic evidence shows that three-fourths of adult dogs and cats have periodontal disease and one-fourth of the pet population is overweight or obese. Nutritional answers exist for these and other clinical problems. When veterinarians and their health care teams (veterinary technicians, receptionists, assistants) understand the process of clinical nutrition and conscientiously apply it, their patients, clients and practices all benefit.

New nutritional information has led to improved commercial veterinary therapeutic and wellness foods. These foods are readily available to veterinarians; it is important that veterinarians and their health care teams understand the benefits and shortcomings of specific foods and judiciously select the best food for each patient. The authors and editors have attempted to list a wide variety of commercial foods dictated by market share and availability of published nutrient information. The thousands of commercial foods and homemade recipes that are available preclude a complete listing.

The authors and editors have done their best to integrate the latest research in nutrition and understanding of clinical nutrition into this textbook. We hope that this information will stimulate continued interest and research in small animal clinical nutrition to benefit pets and ultimately society.

The Publisher

The Mark Morris Institute is a nonprofit educational foundation and publisher of this book. The mission of the institute is to improve companion animal health by enhancing the practice of veterinary nutrition. The institute currently has two key programs: 1) publication and distribution of the *Small Animal Clinical Nutrition* textbook and 2) provision of a curriculum of companion animal nutrition case studies, lectures and laboratories for veterinary schools and colleges. The faculty team who provides these lectures are prominent educators from academia and industry.

Acknowledgments

The editors thank the North American veterinary students who have provided valuable comments and feedback over the past decade. More than 30,000 veterinary students from the United States and Canada have reviewed various aspects of the first three editions of this book. The magnitude and quality of their feedback on a veterinary textbook is unprecedented. Many of the suggestions and ideas from this review process have been incorporated into this fourth edition.

We also thank the many people and organizations who contributed to the writing and publication of this book: Kathy Bumgardner, David Cumpton, Janette Funk and Jennifer Gaumnitz for their considerable contributions to design, style and creation of all text elements; Beth Harrison, Carol Unruh Ingenthron and Judy Rodman for administrative support, arranging innumerable editorial conference calls and meetings and fact checking; Visible Productions for graphics support; Dr. Lon D. Lewis for laying the foundation for this work by authoring and editing large portions of the three previous editions; Walsworth Publishing Company for their high-quality work and patience; and the Board of Directors of the Mark Morris Institute for supporting this multi-year project and providing insight along the way.

Of course, the fourth edition would not have been possible without the enormous effort on the part of an exemplary team of authors. We are truly indebted to them. The format was new and difficult, and the editors demanding. The fourth edition of *Small Animal Clinical Nutrition* is completely new; all chapters are new contributions to veterinary nutrition. Sincere thanks again to all of you.

We would like to extend special acknowledgment to Dr. Mark L. Morris, Sr., Dr. Mark L Morris, Jr. and their families. Their contributions to small animal clinical nutrition and veterinary medicine are unparalleled.

Finally, we are grateful to our families and friends who supported and endured us during the development of *Small Animal Clinical Nutrition*, fourth edition.

THE EDITORS

NOTICE

Companion animal practice, clinical nutrition and the commercial pet food industry change continuously. The authors and editors of this textbook have carefully checked the trade names and nutrient levels of commercial pet foods and verified food and drug dosages to ensure that information is precise and in accordance with standards accepted at the time of publication. Readers are advised, however, to check the product information currently provided by the manufacturer of each food and drug to be administered to ensure that changes have not been made in the nutrient profile, recommended feeding guide or in the contraindications for administration. This caution is particularly important for new and infrequently used foods and drugs. It is the responsibility of those recommending a food or administering a drug, relying on their professional skill and experience, to determine the best treatment for the patient and the appropriate food and food dosage. The publisher and editors cannot be responsible for misuse or misapplication of the material in this book.

Commercial pet foods mentioned in this text are often listed by market category: grocery foods, specialty foods and veterinary therapeutic foods with emphasis on products distributed in North America, Europe and Japan. For the purposes of this text, grocery foods refer to those commercial pet foods primarily marketed in grocery stores, feed stores and mass merchandise outlets. Examples of grocery foods include such brands as Alpo, President's Choice, Fancy Feast, Friskies, Ken-L-Ration Gravy Train, Pedigree Mealtime and Purina Dog Chow. Specialty foods refer to those commercial pet foods primarily marketed in pet stores, veterinary practices and large-format retailers. Examples of specialty foods include such brands as Eukanuba, Hill's Science Diet, Iams, NutroMax and Purina ProPlan. Veterinary therapeutic foods refer to those commercial pet foods marketed through veterinary practices for disease prevention and treatment. Examples of veterinary therapeutic foods include such brands as Hill's Prescription Diet, Eukanuba Veterinary Diets, Innovative Veterinary Diets (IVD), Leo Specific, Purina Clinical Nutrition Management (CNM), Veterinary Medical Diets (VMD) MediCal and Waltham Veterinarium. Names and nutrient information of commercial pet foods in this book are based on manufacturers' published information or product analyses. Readers are advised, however, to check product information currently provided by the manufacturer. Individual products listed in the chapters and appendices are based on overall market share and availability of product information.

THE EDITORS

Book Features

Unique features of this book and how to use it

Philip Roudebush

The chief goal of this book is to provide basic and applied information about small animal clinical nutrition to veterinary students and practicing veterinarians worldwide. Although research and new information regarding small animal nutrition continues to be published and publicized, there is often a lack of understanding about how to apply that information to clinical patients and animal owners. This book is organized not only to deliver the latest information about small animal clinical nutrition but to teach and reinforce the process of clinical nutrition; that is, how clinical nutrition is done.

Organization of the Book

The book is organized into six sections. *Section I (Principles of Small Animal Clinical Nutrition)* begins with an overview of the iterative process of clinical nutrition with emphasis on animal assessment, development of a comprehensive feeding plan and reassessment or monitoring the patient. The iterative process outlined in the first chapter is the foundation upon which the other chapters are built. Those chapters that directly apply to patients begin with the figure that summarizes the clinical nutrition process (Figure 1). The figure and subsequent organization of the chapters emphasize the importance of the process in addition to the clinical and nutritional information necessary to manage patients. The other chapter in Section I reviews basic information about nutrients and nutrient requirements of dogs and cats.

Section II (Pet Foods) covers a wide range of topics about commercial and homemade pet foods. This section ends with a unique chapter on pet food safety, which is an important topic in this era of increased concerns and public debate about safety of human foods.

Section III (Nutritional Management of Normal Pets) begins with an overview of health maintenance or wellness programs for dogs and cats followed by chapters that discuss in detail the key nutritional factors and feeding plans for normal dogs, normal cats and canine athletes. *Section IV (Nutritional Management of Clinical Patients)* covers a wide variety of topics from management of anorexia and obesity to cardiovascular disease and lipid disorders. Unique chapters in this section discuss dietary effects on drug metabolism, and the role of nutrition and diet in preventing dental disease and treating patients with cancer.

Table 1 shows the general format for most chapters in Sections III and IV that deal with nutrition of normal animals and those with clinical problems. Most chapters follow the two-step clinical nutrition process. Each chapter begins with an introduction and discussion about the ▯rtance of the particular animal or clinical entity. This ▯owed by a discussion of the first step (**Assessment**) ▯cludes assessing the animal, food(s) and feeding ▯. The second step (**Feeding Plan**) is then discussed

with emphasis on choosing an appropriate food(s) and feeding method. The iterative process is then completed with discussion of reassessment or monitoring plans.

Section V (Feeding Small Mammals, Reptiles and Birds) is included in response to numerous requests from veterinary students for practical feeding information for these patients. Birds, rodents, ferrets, rabbits and reptiles were once considered exotic pets but are becoming common veterinary patients. Section VI (*Appendices, Glossary and*

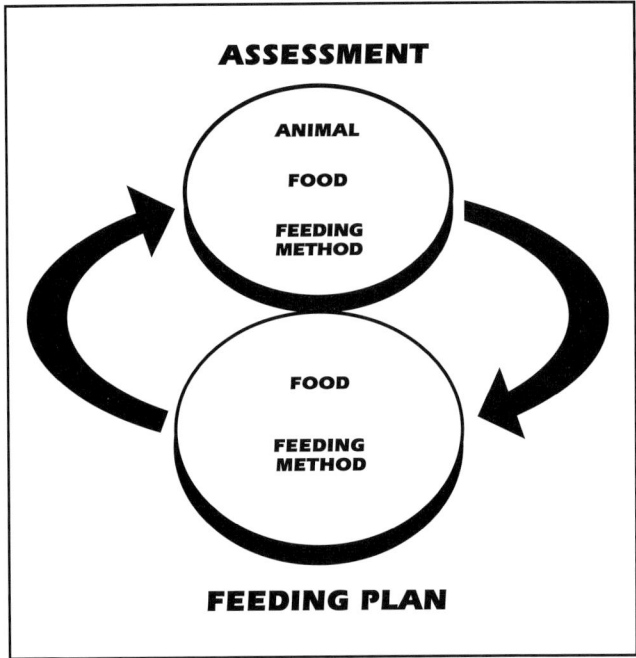

Figure 1. The iterative process of clinical nutrition.

Table 1. General format for most chapters.

Introduction/clinical importance

Assessment
    Assess the animal
        History and physical examination
        Laboratory and other clinical information
        Risk factors
        Etiopathogenesis
        Key nutritional factors
    Assess the food(s)
    Assess the feeding method

Feeding plan
    Select a food(s)
    Determine a feeding method

Reassessment

Endnotes and references

Cases

Index) summarizes a broad range of useful nutritional and dietary information that supports the concepts found throughout the book.

Features to Promote Learning and Ease of Use

Several features have been incorporated to aid and guide the reader's comprehension and make the book easier to use, including the following:

- Tabs with abbreviated chapter titles are printed on the outer edge of right-hand pages to ease finding the appropriate chapter.
- The diagram of the two-step iterative process is found at the beginning of those chapters that have direct application to clinical patients. The reader can find the appropriate pages for each step of the process beneath the figure on the first page of each chapter.
- The second page of each chapter includes a list of key words and terms. These words and terms are considered essential to understanding the material in the chapter and definitions are given in the glossary.
- The second page of every chapter includes a list of key points that summarize the most important concepts to understand about that particular topic.
- The third page of most chapters includes a table that lists specific dietary recommendations for the key nutritional factors (key nutrients and other key factors such as digestibility, food texture, urinary pH, etc.) for a particular animal's lifestage or clinical condition.
- Sidebars that discuss various topics of interest are included in most chapters.
- Nutrient profiles are included for a broad range of commercial pet foods. Commercial foods for prevention or treatment of clinical conditions are listed in the appropriate chapter, whereas selected commercial foods and treats for normal pets are listed in Appendices L and M. This information will help the reader select appropriate foods for patients. Lists of veterinary therapeutic products represent the global market.
- Actual clinical cases (more than 100 throughout the text) are described at the end of most chapters and sometimes within sidebars. These cases emphasize and teach the key concepts outlined in the chapters through use of the two-step iterative process, guiding questions and focused discussion. A comprehensive list of cases is found inside the front cover.
- The names of journals in reference lists are spelled out in full rather than using abbreviations.

- An extensive glossary is included as a mini-dictionary to define key terms and words used throughout the book.
- For the global audience, energy values are usually expressed as kilocalories and kilo- or megajoules.

How to Use This Book

Chapter 1 provides the foundation for understanding the process of clinical nutrition and the key skills necessary to implement an appropriate feeding plan. The reader who masters the information in the first chapter and understands the clinical nutrition process will find the other chapters easier to comprehend.

Each chapter contains a list of key words and terms on the second page. The reader is encouraged to read this list before reading the chapter. Definitions can be found in the glossary if words or terms are unfamiliar. The reader should also read the key points and key nutritional factors on the second and third page of each chapter. This will focus attention on the concepts, nutrients and food factors that are most important.

The clinical case discussions are self-contained learning units. They should be read after finishing the chapter to emphasize the clinical importance and relevance of the material. The cases may also be read before starting the chapter to obtain an overview and clinical perspective about the chapter topic.

Detailed information about number conversions, energy calculations, feeding guides, appropriate body weights, milk and milk replacers, nutrient profiles of commercial pet foods and treats, nutrient content of human foods, feeding orphaned and injured wildlife, analytical laboratories and assisted-feeding techniques is found in the appendices. The reader should consult these important sources of information.

Feedback to the Editors

During the past 15 years, more than 30,000 veterinary students in the United States and Canada have reviewed various aspects of the first three editions of this book. The collection of this type and quantity of feedback about a veterinary textbook is unprecedented. The feedback, suggestions and ideas from this review process have been incorporated in this book. The editors will continue to solicit feedback from veterinary students and practicing veterinarians—the primary audience for this book. Comments and suggestions can be sent to the Mark Morris Institute, P.O. Box 2097, Topeka, KS 66601-2097, USA.

Contents

Contents

Principles of Small Animal Clinical Nutrition

CHAPTER 1

Small Animal Clinical Nutrition: An Iterative Process

Craig D. Thatcher
Michael S. Hand
Rebecca L. Remillard

"Things should be made as simple as possible, but not simpler."
Albert Einstein

CLINICAL IMPORTANCE

The public has become more aware of the importance of nutrition to health during the past two decades as a result of the growing recognition that food is associated with disease processes such as coronary artery disease, hypertension, obesity, diabetes mellitus and cancer. The 1988 *Surgeon General's Report on Nutrition and Health* noted, "For the two out of three adult Americans who do not smoke and do not drink excessively, one personal choice seems to influence long-term health prospects more than any other: what we eat."[1] The 1989 National Research Council report titled *Diet and Health* confirmed the surgeon general's conclusions.[2] Improved awareness and attitudes about nutrition and health probably have also contributed to the public's demand for optimal nutrition for their pets.

The discipline of veterinary nutrition and its relationship to the practice of veterinary medicine have benefited from these changes. Food animal veterinarians have long recognized that no aspect of the production enterprise has more impact on health and production than nutrition; many health problems are associated with inadequate feeding programs. Food animal veterinarians recognize that optimizing feeding programs improves food animal health and productivity and, as a result, the economic status of producers. Food animal veterinarians who provide their clients with high-quality production medicine programs become unbiased nutritional consultants.

Similarly, small animal practitioners must improve their nutritional counseling skills because they cannot truly meet their patients' health needs without optimizing nutrition. Small animal veterinarians can improve the quality of medicine delivered to their patients by knowledgeably and systematically addressing the nutritional aspects of each case, whether the goal is treating disease or preventing disease. Veterinarians must emphasize health maintenance and disease prevention strategies for companion animals to provide the most beneficial service. Total disease prevention requires lifelong dedication to proper nutrition, immunizations, dental care and parasite control programs. Nutritional factors are a cornerstone in maximizing health, performance, longevity and disease prevention. Nutritional counseling and intervention, however, are beneficial only if done properly.

Veterinarians have a strong influence on the foods clients feed their pets. A study conducted by *Veterinary Economics* in 1990 found that 87% of veterinarians felt that offering nutritional services improved their practices.[3] Ninety-four percent of these veterinarians said that their clients were somewhat or very receptive to nutrition-related information. A 1995 study conducted by the American Animal Hospital Association found that 54% of pet owners interviewed sought veterinary advice on pet foods at least once and 43% had received a recommendation from their veterinarian on which manufacturer's pet food to feed their puppies or kittens. Seventy percent of the latter group fed the brand of food recommended by their veterinarian.[4]

The word *recommend* means to counsel or advise (American Heritage Dictionary). The implication is that the advice proceeds from actual knowledge of the subject. Veterinarians should know how food needs vary with each lifestage, with mental, physical and environmental stresses and with diseases. Causes and effects of dietary imbal-

KEY WORDS & TERMS—AN ITERATIVE PROCESS*

Absolute basis
Ad libitum feeding
Anabolic
As fed basis
Association of American Feed
    Control Officials (AAFCO)
Atwater values
Balanced food, ration or diet
Body condition scoring
Catabolic
Dry matter

Dry matter basis
Dry matter, energy density defined
Energy basis
Energy density
Food dosage
Food-restricted meal feeding
Free-choice feeding
Iterative Process
Key nutritional factors
Labile proteins
Malnutrition

Metabolizable energy
Minimum nutrient requirements
Modified Atwater values
Nutrient
Nutrient allowances
Nutrients of concern
Pearson square
Recommended dietary allowances
    (RDAs)
Self feeding
Time-restricted meal feeding

* Key words and terms are defined in the Glossary.

KEY POINTS—AN ITERATIVE PROCESS

1. The public has become more aware of the importance of nutrition to health during the past two decades as a result of the association of food with coronary artery disease, hypertension, obesity, diabetes mellitus and cancer.
2. Nutrition is a cornerstone in maximizing health, performance, longevity and disease prevention.
3. Veterinarians have a strong influence on the foods clients feed their pets.
4. The American College of Veterinary Nutrition has recommended that nutrition problem solving include assessment of the patient, the food and the feeding method. This assessment process is step one. Development of a feeding plan is step two and includes recommendations for food and feeding methods. After a suitable period of time, the two-step process is repeated to determine the appropriateness or effectiveness of the new feeding plan.
5. The primary goal of animal assessment is to establish the patient's nutrient needs, particularly for key nutritional factors.
6. Assessment of dogs and cats should include a review of the history and medical record, physical examination, laboratory tests and other diagnostics and estimation of the target levels for the key nutritional factors based on the animal's physiologic state and medical diagnosis.
7. Body condition scores and body weights should be routinely recorded in the medical record.
8. AAFCO nutrient profiles are adequate to meet the known nutrient needs of almost all healthy dogs and cats and are a better source of feeding recommendations for most dogs and cats than are minimum requirements.
9. AAFCO prescribes upper limits for certain nutrients with the obvious implication that some nutrient excesses can be harmful. As with RDAs for people, AAFCO allowances for pet food nutrient profiles are not necessarily optimums.
10. Key nutritional factors encompass nutrients of concern and other food characteristics.

11. Nutrients of concern encompass nutritional risk factors for disease treatment and prevention as well as nutrients that are key to optimizing normal physiologic processes such as growth, gestation, lactation and physical work.
12. The concept of nutrients of concern greatly simplifies the approach to clinical nutrition because most commercial pet foods sold in the United States provide at least AAFCO allowances of all nutrients.
13. Besides nutrients, other food characteristics are sometimes important to consider, including the food's influence on systemic acid-base balance and urinary pH, the food's texture, digestibility and osmolality and whether or not it contains few/novel protein sources or unique ingredients.
14. The three most useful components of food assessment are: ensuring that the food has been tested or fed to animals, determining the food's nutrient content (especially for the key nutritional factors) and comparing the food's nutrient content with the animal's nutrient needs (again, especially for the key nutritional factors).
15. Comparing the food's nutrient content with the animal's nutrient needs may identify significant nutritional imbalances in the food being fed. This comparison is fundamental to determining whether or not a different food should be fed.
16. There are at least three things to consider regarding feeding methods: the feeding route, the amount fed and how the food is offered.
17. A feeding plan should be based on realistic and quantifiable nutritional objectives, after the animal, food and feeding method have been assessed.
18. Owners should change their pet's food over the course of three to seven days. Some animals require even longer transition periods.
19. Veterinarians and their health care teams should actively involve clients in the formulation of the feeding plan to ensure compliance.
20. Reassessment of the animal should be performed at appropriate intervals to evaluate the effectiveness of the feeding plan.

hould be considered so that the resulting disorders
prevented or diagnosed and treated. Veterinarians
so be familiar with the various pet foods available
clients choose the most appropriate ones.

Veterinarians also need to understand the benefits and shortcomings of various feeding methods. Once a feeding plan has been instituted, veterinarians need the skills to monitor the program in order to assess and reassess outcomes and to modify the feeding plan when necessary. The primary goal of this chapter is to provide practicing veterinarians, veterinary technicians and students with the basic problem-solving processes needed to successfully manage the nutrition of companion animal patients.

The Two-Step Iterative Process of Clinical Nutrition

A brief review of instructional systems design (ISD) is in order to better understand iterative (repetitive) processes. ISD emerged after World War II as a set of recognized standard procedures used to develop well-structured materials in response to the need for more efficient training techniques.[5] ISD embodies various perspectives on learning, teaching, systems theory, behavioral psychology, communications and information theory. The ISD model breaks instruction into a series of phases or steps with defined procedures; a defined service or product must be delivered at each step. Steps include: 1) design, 2) development, 3) implementation, 4) evaluation and 5) analysis. Then the process repeats itself as a continuous loop and may involve many cycles.

Figure 1-1 depicts the two-step clinical nutrition process. The process is based on the ISD model. The American College of Veterinary Nutrition (ACVN) has recommended that nutrition problem solving include assessment of the patient, the food and the feeding method.[6] This assessment process is step one. Development of a feeding plan is step two and includes recommendations for food and feeding methods. If the assessment process indicates that the current food and feeding method are appropriate, the current feeding plan can remain in place. However, if the assessment indicates otherwise, a new feeding plan should be formulated and implemented.

After a suitable period of time (the length of which depends on the patient's condition), the two-step process is repeated to determine the appropriateness or effectiveness of the new feeding plan. Thus, the patient is reassessed and, if its status has changed, a new feeding plan is implemented. This is the iterative or repetitive part of the process. Any number of iterations or repetitions of the two-step process can occur, depending on the needs of each patient. A critically ill patient may need to be reassessed every few hours, whereas a normal adult dog or cat may be reassessed annually. The subsequent reassessment of the patient at each cycle is also referred to as monitoring.

▮ ASSESSMENT

Assess the Animal

The goal of animal assessment is to establish a dog's or cat's nutrient needs and feeding goals in light of its physiologic or disease condition. The animal's nutrient needs are the benchmark for assessing the animal's food. Assessment of dogs and cats to determine their nutritional status should be a structured process that includes:[7] 1) review of the history and medical record, 2) physical examination, 3) laboratory tests and other diagnostic procedures and 4) estimation of the target levels for the key nutritional factors based on the patient's physiologic state and medical diagnosis.

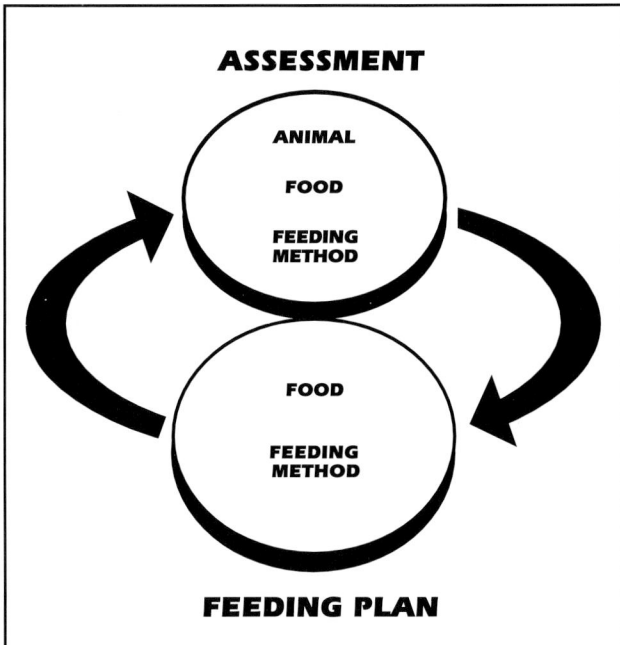

Figure 1-1. The two-step process of veterinary clinical nutrition.

Obtain an Accurate History and Review the Medical Record

Obtaining the animal's history and reviewing the medical record help determine the nutritional status of the patient. The signalment is part of the history and defines the patient's physiologic state and includes: 1) species, 2) breed, 3) age, 4) gender, 5) reproductive status, 6) activity level and 7) environment.

A complete history should also include questions about the pet's weight and therapies (medical, surgical, etc.) that may affect appetite, nutrient metabolism or both. An accurate description of the current feeding plan, including the animal's food, eating and drinking habits and feeding methods should be obtained from the client. Intakes of treats and nutritional supplements should be recorded.

Malnutrition

Malnutrition is defined as any disorder of nutrition with inadequate or unbalanced nutrition. Many veterinarians and animal owners think only of nutritional deficiencies when they hear the term malnutrition. Muscle wasting and a distended abdomen in a starving third-world child or a heavily parasitized puppy is often our first mental image of malnutrition. In first-world societies, however, malnutrition is usually due to overnutrition or excessive intake of nutrients. Obesity due to consumption of excessive levels of fat and calories is a common example of malnutrition in both people and their pets. Another example of malnutrition due to unbalanced nutrition is the developmental orthopedic disease seen in rapidly growing large- and giant-breed puppies as a result of excessive calcium and energy intake. Malnutrition due to either nutrient deficiencies or nutrient excesses can be harmful to dogs and cats.

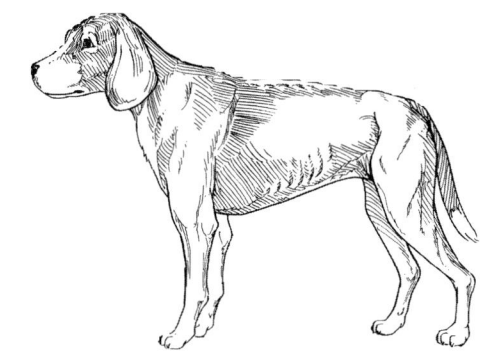

BCS 1. Very thin ▶

The ribs are easily palpable with no fat cover. The tailbase has a prominent raised bony structure with no tissue between the skin and bone. The bony prominences are easily felt with no overlying fat. Dogs over six months of age have a severe abdominal tuck when viewed from the side and an accentuated hourglass shape when viewed from above.

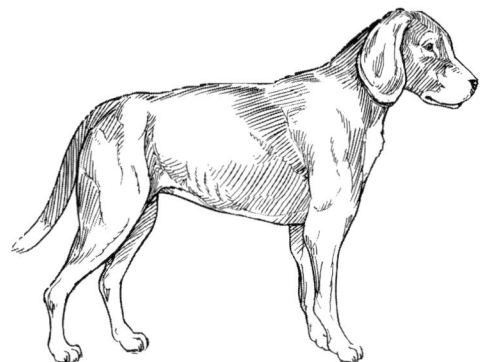

◀ BCS 2. Underweight

The ribs are easily palpable with minimal fat cover. The tailbase has a raised bony structure with little tissue between the skin and bone. The bony prominences are easily felt with minimal overlying fat. Dogs over six months of age have an abdominal tuck when viewed from the side and a marked hourglass shape when viewed from above.

BCS 3. Ideal ▶

The ribs are palpable with a slight fat cover. The tailbase has a smooth contour or some thickening. The bony structures are palpable under a thin layer of fat between the skin and bone. The bony prominences are easily felt under minimal amounts of overlying fat. Dogs over six months of age have a slight abdominal tuck when viewed from the side and a well-proportioned lumbar waist when viewed from above.

◀ BCS 4. Overweight

The ribs are difficult to feel with moderate fat cover. The tailbase has some thickening with moderate amounts of tissue between the skin and bone. The bony structures can still be palpated. The bony prominences are covered by a moderate layer of fat. Dogs over six months of age have little or no abdominal tuck or waist when viewed from the side. The back is slightly broadened when viewed from above.

BCS 5. Obese ▶

The ribs are very difficult to feel under a thick fat cover. The tailbase appears thickened and is difficult to feel under a prominent layer of fat. The bony prominences are covered by a moderate to thick layer of fat. Dogs over six months of age have a pendulous ventral bulge and no waist when viewed from the side due to extensive fat deposits. The back is markedly broadened when viewed from above. A trough may form when epaxial areas bulge dorsally.

2. Body condition score (BCS) descriptors for dogs in a five-point system.

BCS 1. Very thin ▶

The ribs are easily palpable with no fat cover. The bony prominences are easily felt with no overlying fat. Cats over six months of age have a severe abdominal tuck when viewed from the side and an accentuated hourglass shape when viewed from above.

◀ BCS 2. Underweight

The ribs are easily palpable with minimal fat cover. The bony prominences are easily felt with minimal overlying fat. Cats over six months of age have an abdominal tuck when viewed from the side and a marked hourglass shape when viewed from above.

BCS 3. Ideal ▶

The ribs are palpable with a slight fat cover. The bony prominences are easily felt under a slight amount of overlying fat. Cats over six months of age have an abdominal tuck when viewed from the side and a well-proportioned lumbar waist when viewed from above.

◀ BCS 4. Overweight

The ribs are difficult to feel with moderate fat cover. The bony structures can still be palpated. The bony prominences are covered by a moderate layer of fat. Cats over six months of age have little or no abdominal tuck or waist when viewed from the side. The back is slightly broadened when viewed from above. A moderate abdominal fat pad is present.

BCS 5. Obese ▶

The ribs are very difficult to feel under a thick fat cover. The bony prominences are covered by a moderate to thick layer of fat. Cats over six months of age have a pendulous ventral bulge and no waist when viewed from the side due to extensive fat deposits. The back is markedly broadened when viewed from above. A marked abdominal fat pad is present. Fat deposits may be found on the limbs and face.

Figure 1-3. Body condition score (BCS) descriptors for cats in a five-point system.

Table 1-1. How to convert from as fed basis to dry matter basis.

Step 1. Obtain the food's dry matter content by subtracting the water content from the as fed amount of the food.
  Example A: If a moist food contains 75% water, 25% of the food is dry matter:
    100% as fed − 75% water = 25% food dry matter
  Example B: If a dry food contains 10% water, 90% of the food is dry matter:
    100% as fed − 10% water = 90% food dry matter

Step 2. Convert the percentage as fed nutrient content of the food to a dry matter basis by dividing the percentage of the nutrient content on an as fed basis by the percentage dry matter.
  Example A: If the moist food above contained 10% protein on an as fed basis, on a dry matter basis it would contain 40% protein:
    10% protein as fed basis ÷ 25% dry matter = 40% protein dry matter basis
  Example B: If the dry food above contained 18% protein on an as fed basis, on a dry matter basis, it would contain 20% protein:
    18% protein as fed basis ÷ 90% dry matter = 20% protein dry matter basis

Table 1-2. Shorthand method for converting from as fed basis to dry matter basis.

A less accurate, shorthand method for converting from an as fed basis to a dry matter basis (Table 1-1) is to simply multiply the percentage nutrient content on an as fed basis by four for moist foods or add 10% for dry foods. This method is based on the assumption that moist foods contain approximately 75% water and dry foods contain approximately 10% water. Check the guaranteed analysis on the product label.
  Example A: If a moist food contains 10% protein on an as fed basis, on a dry matter basis it would contain 40% protein:
    10% protein as fed basis x 4 (factor for moist foods) = 40% protein dry matter basis*
  Example B: If a dry food contains 18% protein on an as fed basis, on a dry matter basis it would contain 20% protein:
    18% protein as fed basis + 10% (factor for dry food) = approximately 20% protein dry matter basis*

*Compare these results with those obtained in Table 1-1 for moist and dry foods with the same moisture content.

Table 1-3. How to determine the protein, fat and carbohydrate content as a percent of the food's total energy content.

Practically speaking, the available energy in foods for dogs and cats is provided by soluble carbohydrates, protein and fat; dietary fiber provides little if any energy to these species. Occasionally an animal's need for, or a food's content of, any or all of these three nutrients is expressed in terms of the fraction of the total energy they provide. The method is simply another way to express the relative amounts of these three nutrients. The following example demonstrates how to calculate the percentage of kcal and kJ from protein, fat and soluble carbohydrate of a pet food.

Nutrient	%	kcal/g of nutrient	kJ/g of nutrient	kcal/g of food**	kJ/g of food**
Protein	22	3.5*	14.64*	0.77	3.22
Fat	9	8.5*	35.56*	0.70	2.93
Soluble carbohydrate	51	3.5*	14.64*	1.79	7.47
Total				3.32	13.89

% kcal from protein = 0.77 ÷ 3.32 = 23.2%
% kJ from protein = 3.22 ÷ 13.89 = 23.2%
% kcal from fat = 0.77 ÷ 3.32 = 21.1%
% kʲ from fat = 2.93 ÷ 13.89 = 21.1%.
    ⅃l from soluble carbohydrate = 1.79 ÷ 3.32 = 53.9%
    ⁻om soluble carbohydrate = 7.47 ÷ 13.89 = 53.8%

  ᵈⁱ Atwater values.
    ᵗⁱe 1-9 for a more detailed explanation for calculation of energy
    pet foods.

Review of the medical record provides objective historical information and documents the pet's previous health status, health maintenance procedures that were performed and medications that were prescribed. Veterinarians should evaluate this information to determine if any of these factors are related to the animal's current nutritional status. This review permits early nutritional intervention in the treatment of established malnutrition (under- or overnutrition) and in the prevention of malnutrition in individuals at risk. (See sidebar "Malnutrition.")

A patient's food is usually changed because of altered requirements or alterations in nutrient intake, digestion, absorption, metabolism, excretion or a combination of these factors. Knowledge of normal nutritional physiology and of diseases and their nutritional pathophysiology is important in identifying patients at risk for malnutrition. The history and medical record are tools to help identify these risks.

Conduct a Physical Examination

A thorough physical examination can help define an animal's nutritional status as well as identify diseases that may have a nutritional component. Physical findings should be recorded in the patient's medical record. Veterinarians should examine each body system for problems that are responsive to nutritional intervention. An animal's body condition will likely reflect abnormalities of major organ systems.

Body condition can be subjectively assessed by a process called body condition scoring. In general, this process assesses a patient's fat stores and, to a lesser extent, muscle mass. Fat cover is evaluated over the ribs, down the topline, around the tailbase and ventrally along the abdomen. Body condition score (BCS) descriptors have been developed with respect to the species (dogs and cats) and age of the patient (Figures 1-2 and 1-3). Score descriptors vary due to the structural differences between species and between young and adult pets. The scores range from 1 to 5 with 1 being very thin, 5 being grossly obese and 3 being ideal.

Body condition scoring reasonably estimates an animal's body composition. Studies assessing scorer repeatability and variations between scorers have found agreement between 80 to 90% of the measurements.[8-11] Research with cats found a correlation of 0.9 or higher between BCS and body composition predicted from morphometry.[12] Veterinarians should routinely assign BCSs, obtain body weights and record both in the medical record.

The patient's body weight can be compared with breed standards (See Appendix H.) or with the animal's previous body weight from the medical record. The patient's pre-illness body weight or usual body weight during health can serve as a standard for determining the effect of illness on body weight. A history of rapid weight loss and a reduced BCS may indicate a catabolic condition with a marked loss of lean tissue, dehydration or both. A history of progressive weight gain and an increased BCS may indicate an anabolic condition with an excessive accumulation of fat, water or both.

Conduct Necessary Laboratory Tests and Other Diagnostics

No single laboratory test or other diagnostic procedure can accurately assess a patient's nutritional status. Routine complete blood counts, urinalyses and biochemistry profiles, however, can provide insight into the presence of metabolic disorders and other diseases. Albumin concentration, lymphocyte count, packed cell volume and serum total protein values may serve as general indicators of nutritional status. Other chapters in this textbook will discuss specific laboratory tests and other diagnostic procedures that may help assess healthy and sick patients.

Serum protein concentrations in people provide an estimate of long- and short-term changes in nutritional status and correlate with morbidity and mortality.[13] For example, low serum albumin concentrations may indicate protein depletion due to chronic undernutrition or protein loss. Shorter half-life serum protein concentrations such as prealbumin, transferrin, retinol-binding protein and fibronectin are used in human medicine to assess short-term changes in nutritional status. However, these tests have not been routinely available in veterinary medicine. Although not used widely, serum creatine kinase concentrations are elevated in anorectic cats and decline after 48 hours of nutritional support. Serum creatine kinase concentrations may become a useful marker for assessing and monitoring nutritional status in animals.[14]

Results of a single measurement or test must be interpreted cautiously, because over- or underhydration can alter concentrations of these proteins. Diagnostics such as radiography and ultrasonography, including echocardiography, may be indicated to further characterize the health status of patients. Results of laboratory and diagnostic tests should always be viewed in the context of the findings from the history, physical examination and the patient's medical record.

Determine the Key Nutritional Factors and Their Target Levels

The concept of key nutritional factors is fundamental to the practical application of clinical nutrition. However, to better understand the basis for this concept, a brief review of nutrient requirements vs. nutrient allowances precedes the description of key nutritional factors.

Researchers traditionally have used normal dogs and cats to determine nutrient requirements. In the United States, the primary sources for minimum nutrient requirements of healthy dogs and cats are the National Research Council (NRC) Nutrient Requirement bulletins published in 1985 and 1986, respectively.[15,16] These requirements were determined by feeding dogs and cats purified diets rather than commercially available foods.[17,18] The NRC values, therefore, are minimum nutrient requirements that have to be extrapolated to the types of foods that are normally fed to dogs and cats. In 1992 and 1993, the Association of American Feed Control Officials (AAFCO) published recommended nutrient profiles for dog and cat foods, respectively.[17,18] These nutrient profiles have been republished yearly and have replaced the NRC bulletins as the official source for nutrient profiles for dog and cat foods in the United States.

Four Ways to Determine the Nutrient Content of a Food

The nutrient content of a food can be determined one of four ways:

1. Obtain the target values from the manufacturers of commercially prepared foods.
2. Order a laboratory analysis.
3. Calculate the content based on the published values for the ingredients.
4. Use the information found in the label guaranteed analysis and typical analysis. (See Chapter 5.)

Only the first three are recommended because of the severe limitations of label guarantees and typical analyses.

Most pet food manufacturers, upon request, will supply target values for the nutrient content of their products. This approach is simple and inexpensive. Although these values usually reflect actual average nutrient levels, occasionally they vary significantly from actual values, thus this method is not always accurate. No laws govern the accuracy of target nutrient levels. In most instances, however, these values will be adequate.

The basic laboratory analysis is the proximate analysis (See Figure 2-3.), which provides the percentage moisture, crude protein, crude fat, ash and crude fiber in a food and allows calculation of the soluble carbohydrate fraction (also referred to as the nitrogen-free extract [NFE]). Most commercial laboratories will also conduct more expansive nutrient analyses including amino acids, fatty acids, minerals, vitamins and various fiber fractions. (See Appendix U for a partial listing of commercial laboratories.) Analysis of food samples for nutrient content is very straightforward and usually accurate. Limitations include proper sampling, the potential issue of analytical variance for certain nutrients and the expense and time involved for a complete analysis.

Calculations require nutrient contents of ingredients and a formula for the food in question. Published average nutrient contents of ingredients can be obtained from NRC nutrient requirement booklets and listings of average nutrient contents of human foods. (See Appendix T.) This approach would likely be used for determining the nutrient content of a homemade food. One limitation of this method is the time and knowledge required to do such calculations. Another limitation is accuracy (i.e., how closely the published average nutrient content of the ingredients represents the ingredient's actual nutrient content). Values can vary markedly.

The use of guaranteed analyses (United States and Canada) or typical analyses (Europe) listed on the label of commercially prepared foods as a means of establishing nutrient content has severe limitations:

1. In the case of guaranteed analysis, the quantities listed are minimums or maximums only.
2. Only a fraction of the nutrients in the food is required to be listed (e.g., guaranteed analysis only requires crude protein, crude fat, crude fiber and moisture; typical analysis only requires crude protein, crude fat, crude fiber, ash and moisture if more than 14%).

Guaranteed analysis values are not the nutrient content of the food. They are a guarantee by the manufacturer that the food contains not more, or less, than the stated amount. Label guarantees can provide a general idea of the nutrient content for a limited number of nutrients and the classification of the food (growth-type food, maintenance food, etc.).

Use caution when using guaranteed and typical analyses to compare specific nutrient levels between foods. When such comparisons are made, be sure to compare similar forms of foods (i.e., dry to dry or moist to moist). Label guarantees are listed on an as fed basis. Different forms of food can be compared if the foods are converted to the same moisture or energy content. (See Tables 1-1, 1-2 and 1-6.)

The AAFCO nutrient profiles include safety factors similar to those in the recommended dietary allowances (RDAs) that have been established for people.[19] These safety factors compensate for changes in a food's nutrient availability due to ingredient and processing variables and for individual differences in nutrient requirements within dog and cat populations. Because of these safety factors, the term "allowance" is better suited to describe AAFCO values than "requirements." AAFCO values are adequate to meet the known nutrient needs of almost all healthy dogs and cats and are a better source of feeding recommendations for most dogs and cats than are minimum requirements. The earlier NRC bulletins published for dogs and cats in 1974[20] and 1978,[21] respectively, also included safety factors and therefore were actually "allowances." Besides recommendations for lower limits, AAFCO prescribes upper limits for certain nutrients with the obvious implication that some nutrient excesses can be harmful. As with RDAs for people, AAFCO allowances for pet food nutrient profiles are not necessarily optimums. Appendix J lists NRC minimum nutrient requirements and AAFCO allowances for dogs and cats. No nutrient profiles have been established by NRC or AAFCO for geriatric dogs or cats or those with specific disease processes.

Limitations of Using Dry Matter Basis, Energy Density Defined and Energy Basis Units

Animals require less food to meet their energy requirements when foods with higher energy densities are fed. Under these circumstances, the concentrations of the other nutrients in the food need to be increased proportionately, to ensure the animal receives the needed nutrients in a smaller amount of food.

When foods with lower energy densities are fed, a lower concentration of the other nutrients should be required, assuming the dog or cat could eat, or would be fed, enough of the food to meet its energy requirement. In these instances, the nutrient levels need to be decreased proportionately, so that the animal would receive the needed amount of nutrients in a larger amount of food.

Foods of low energy density, particularly those low in fat and high in fiber, are usually intended for animals that have a tendency to be overweight. These animals should be fed fewer calories than animals with normal body weights and body condition scores. The nutrient content of foods in this category should not be corrected for their lower energy density because there is a disproportionately lower need for energy relative to the nonenergy nutrients. Although these animals require fewer calories, as far as is known, their requirement for other nutrients has not changed. Thus, they are essentially being fed the same amount of dry matter but fewer calories. On an energy basis, the food's nutrient values should be higher than if the animal had normal energy requirements.

On the other end of the spectrum are situations where foods of high energy density are fed to animals with an unusually high need for energy-providing nutrients relative to nonenergy nutrients. An example would be a working dog. In this case, on an energy basis, the food's nonenergy nutrient content could be lower than if the animal had normal energy needs.

Key nutritional factors encompass nutrients of concern and other food characteristics. The concept of nutrients of concern greatly simplifies the approach to clinical nutrition because most commercial pet foods sold in the United States provide at least AAFCO allowances of all nutrients. Thus, if a commercial food is fed, veterinarians and their health care teams need only to understand and focus on delivering the target levels for a few nutrients (nutrients of concern) rather than all 43 nutrients currently recognized for cats[18] and all 36 nutrients currently recognized for dogs.[17]

Nutrients of concern encompass nutritional risk factors for disease treatment and prevention as well as nutrients that are key to optimizing normal physiologic processes such as growth, gestation, lactation and physical work. The following elements must be considered in determining key nutritional factors and their target levels: 1) the patient's lifestage and physiologic state, 2) environmental conditions such as temperature, housing and pet-to-pet competition, 3) the nature of any disease or injury, 4) the known nutrient losses through skin, urine and intestinal tract, 5) the interactions of medications and nutrients, if applicable, 6) the known capacity of the body to store certain nutrients and 7) the interrelationships of various nutrients.

Depending on the patient's needs, food characteristics other than the nutrient content may be important to consider. These characteristics include the food's influence on systemic acid-base balance and urinary pH, the food's texture, digestibility, osmolality and whether or not it contains few/novel protein sources or unique ingredients.

Chapters 9 to 11 and Appendix J list key nutritional factors and their target levels for healthy dogs and cats. The key nutritional factors and their target levels for dogs and cats with specific disease complexes can be found in Chapters 12 through 26. Regardless of which nutrients are considered, the reader must understand how nutrient needs are expressed.

The three methods for expressing an animal's nutrient needs are: 1) absolute basis, 2) dry matter, energy density defined and 3) energy basis.

Absolute basis refers to the unit measure (usually weight) of a nutrient that is needed by an animal in a 24-hour period. These needs are expressed as quantities per kg of body weight per day.

Dry matter basis, energy density defined is the percentage or quantity of a nutrient in the food's dry matter that is needed by the animal. This measure describes what is required in a food and indicates an animal's nutrient needs. Dry matter refers to that weight of the food remaining when the water content is subtracted. (Tables 1-1 and 1-2 demonstrate methods of calculating dry matter.) Dry matter values are most meaningful if the energy density of the food's dry matter is specified because most animals eat, or are fed, to meet their energy requirements.

Energy basis refers to the quantities of nutrients per animal's energy requirement. Units of measure are typically nutrient amounts per 100 kcal or 1 MJ metabolizable energy (ME). Occasionally an animal's protein, fat and soluble carbohydrate needs are expressed as a percentage of the animal's total energy needs (Table 1-3).

In summary, the primary goal of animal assessment is to establish the patient's nutrient needs, particularly for the key nutritional factors. The animal's nutrient needs are the benchmark for assessing the adequacy of the animal's food. Additionally, as discussed above, other food characteristics are important in some cases.

Assess the Food(s)

After the nutritional status of the patient has been assessed and the key nutritional factors and their target levels determined, the adequacy of the food is assessed. The components to food assessment include: 1) physical evaluation of the food, 2) evaluation of the product label, including the ingredients used and whether or not feeding tests were conducted, 3) evaluation of the food's nutrient content relative to the animal's nutrient needs (key nutritional factors) and 4) determination of the presence or absence of specific food characteristics.

Physical Evaluation

Physical evaluation of the food can provide information about package quality (which may or may not reflect product quality), consistency and presence or absence of extraneous materials. Physical evaluation of the food is probably most useful for assessing whether or not the food has spoiled. (See Chapter 7.)

Label Evaluation

Evaluation of the product label is also of limited value. (See Chapter 5.) The ingredient panel of the pet food label provides general information about which ingredients were used and their relative amounts. The ingredients used in the product are listed in descending order by weight in many countries. The ingredient panel can be useful if specific ingredients are contraindicated for certain animals or an owner has an ingredient concern. However, the quality of the ingredients cannot be determined from the label and there is much misinformation about pet food ingredients. (See Chapter 4.)

The three most useful components when assessing food are to: 1) ensure that the food has been tested or fed to animals, 2) determine the food's nutrient content (especially for the key nutritional factors) and 3) compare the food's nutrient content with the animal's nutrient needs (again, paying particular attention to the key nutritional factors).

FEEDING TESTS

Although not considered feeding tests, the personal observations of veterinarians and pet owners about the performance of specific foods or recipes can be valuable. Such experiences are, in a sense, uncontrolled feeding tests. Through experience, veterinarians and pet owners form impressions about a food's value in disease management, its ability to support various lifestages and work, its palatability, resultant stool quality and skin and coat benefits. Limitations of personal observations include the lack of controls and the length of time it takes (months to years) to gather sufficient information about a wide variety of products. Also, some commercial products are continuously improved; therefore, yesterday's product does not necessarily reflect the capabilities of the "same" product today. However, personal observations can augment controlled feeding tests such as published clinical trials and regulatory agency prescribed feeding protocols for healthy pets.

Whether or not commercial foods for healthy pets have been animal tested can usually be determined from the nutritional adequacy statement on the product's label. (See Chapter 5, Table 5-6 for examples of such statements.) Few, if any, homemade recipes have been animal tested according to prescribed feeding protocols. Published clinical trials and case reports for commercial veterinary therapeutic foods can be obtained from the product's manufacturer. Manufacturers' addresses and toll-free phone numbers are found on pet food labels. Some brands of these products have passed regulatory agency (AAFCO) prescribed feeding tests although the product label may not include such information.

Commercial pet foods that have undergone AAFCO-prescribed or similar feeding tests provide reasonable assurance of nutrient availability and sufficient palatability to ensure acceptability (i.e., food intake sufficient to meet nutrient needs). Feeding tests also provide some assurance that a product will adequately support certain functions such as gestation, lactation and growth. However, even controlled animal testing is not infallible.

In the United States, the AAFCO testing protocol for adult maintenance lasts six months, requires only eight animals per group and monitors a limited number of parameters. (See Chapter 5 and Appendix J.) Passing such tests does not ensure the food will be effective in preventing long-term nutrition/health problems or detect problems with prevalence rates less than 15%. Likewise, these protocols are not intended to ensure optimal growth or maximize physical activity. Thus, in addition to having passed AAFCO tests, the food should be evaluated to ensure that key nutritional factors are at levels appropriate for treatment of disease, for promotion of long-term health or for optimal performance.

Determine the Food's Nutrient Content

Appendices L and M provide partial nutrient profiles for selected commercial foods and treats sold in the United States, Canada and Europe. The levels of the nutrients of concern for most of the commonly used commercial foods are listed in tables in the individual chapters. In most instances, these profiles will provide the necessary food nutrient content information. If the food in question cannot be found in this book, refer to sidebar "Four Ways to Determine the Nutrient Content of a Food" for other ways to determine its nutrient content.

Although there are three methods for expressing an animal's nutrient needs (See Animal Assessment above.), there are four methods of expressing a food's nutrient content: 1) as fed basis, 2) dry matter basis, 3) dry matter basis, energy density defined and 4) energy basis.

Table 1-4. Comparisons of methods to express food nutrient content and animal requirements/allowances for nutritional assessment of food.

Food nutrient content (units)
As fed basis (% or amount of nutrient/kg food)
Dry matter basis (% or amount of nutrient/kg of food dry matter)
Dry matter basis, energy density defined (% or amount of nutrient/kg of food dry matter, at a specified energy density)
Energy basis (amount of nutrient/100 kcal or 1 megajoule ME of food's energy content)

Animal requirements/allowances (units)
Absolute basis (amount of nutrient/kg animal)
Dry matter basis, energy density defined (% or amount of nutrient/kg of food dry matter, at a specified energy density)
Energy basis (amount of nutrient/100 kcal or 1 megajoule ME of animal's energy requirement)

As fed basis simply refers to the quantity of nutrients in a food as it is fed. This method ignores moisture and energy content. The units of measure are percentages or quantities of nutrients per unit weight (kg) of food.

Dry matter is that weight of the food remaining after the water content has been subtracted from the as fed amount. Dry matter basis, therefore, is the amount of nutrients in the food's dry matter. It accounts for variability in water content but not variability in energy density. The units of measure are percentages or quantities of nutrients per unit weight (kg) of food dry matter. The usefulness of dry matter basis is limited because the energy density of individual foods can vary widely. This consideration will be further explained below (dry matter basis, energy density defined). Tables 1-1 and 1-2 show the conversion from as fed basis to dry matter basis.

Dry matter basis, energy density defined is the same as dry matter but specifies a food's energy density, thus accounting for potential variability. The units of measure are the same as those used with dry matter basis but are further qualified by expressing the energy density of the food. For example, recommended nutrient values for canine and feline foods (Appendix J) are based on an energy density of 3.5 and 4.0 kcal ME/g of food dry matter, respectively (14.64 and 16.74 kJ ME/g). Dry matter basis, energy density defined is probably the most widely used method of expressing a food's nutrient content.

Energy basis refers simply to the amount of nutrients per 100 kcal or 1 megajoule ME of food. Occasionally, a food's protein, fat and soluble carbohydrate content is expressed as a percentage of the food's total energy content (Table 1-3).

Both dry matter basis, energy density defined and energy basis are reasonably accurate methods of expressing a food's nutrient content. However, even these methods have limitations. (See sidebar "Limitations of Using Dry Matter Basis, Energy Density Defined and Energy Basis Units.")

Compare the Food's Nutrient Content with the Animal's Nutrient Needs

When comparing a food's nutrient content with an animal's nutrient needs, methods of expressing nutrient content and nutrient/requirements (same units) must be compatible, as shown in Table 1-4.

Comparing food on an as fed basis to an animal's requirement on an absolute basis requires: 1) mathematical calculation and 2) either the energy density of the food or the amounts of the energy-supplying nutrients in the food. Table 1-5 provides an example of such a calculation.

When using dry matter basis, energy density defined to compare foods or to compare foods with animal requirements, the energy densities must be the same for the comparisons to be meaningful. Table 1-6 shows how to con-

---

Table 1-5. Example illustrating the mathematical process required to compare a food's nutrient content on an as fed basis to an animal's needs on an absolute basis.

Example: If an intact male cat weighing 4.5 kg requires 31 mg of magnesium (Mg) per day (recommended allowance) and the cat's food as fed contains 0.12% Mg, 20% fat, 35% protein and 27% soluble carbohydrate, does the cat receive adequate amounts of Mg? The answer is calculated as follows:

1) First find out how much food is to be fed. Because animals are fed to meet their energy requirements, the first step is to determine the energy density of the food, if it is unknown. This is done by calculating the amount of energy provided by each of the energy-supplying nutrients. Using the "modified Atwater" energy values of 3.5, 8.5 and 3.5 kcal ME/g (14.64, 35.56 and 14.64 kJ ME/g) for protein, fat and soluble carbohydrate respectively (See Table 1-8), multiply the percentage of each nutrient in the food (as fed basis) by 1 g of food. Then multiply the answer by the energy density of each nutrient. The sum of the three separate energy values is the energy density of the food.

In kcal ME/g of food:
35% protein x 1 g food x 3.5 kcal ME/g   = 1.23 kcal ME/g from protein
20% fat x 1 g food x 8.5 kcal ME/g   = 1.70 kcal ME/g from fat
27% soluble carbohydrate x 1 g food x 3.5 kcal ME/g   = 0.95 kcal ME/g from carbohydrate
                           3.88 kcal ME/g food (total)

In kJ ME/g food:
35% protein x 1 g food x 14.64 kJ ME/g   = 5.12 kJ ME/g from protein
20% fat x 1 g food x 35.56 kJ ME/g   = 7.11 kJ ME/g from fat
27% soluble carbohydrate x 1 g food x 14.64 kJ ME/g   = 3.95 kJ ME/g from carbohydrate
                           16.18 kJ ME/g food (total)

2) The next step is to determine the daily energy requirement (DER) of the animal. Multiply the formula for resting energy requirement (RER) by the appropriate modifier for maintenance of an adult cat. (See Table 1-7.)

RER (kcal ME/day) = 70(BW$_{kg}$)$^{0.75}$
= 70(4.5 BW$_{kg}$)$^{0.75}$ = 216 kcal ME/day
Modifier for feline adult maintenance = 1.4 x RER = DER
DER (kcal ME/day) = 1.4 x 216 kcal ME = 302 kcal ME

RER (kJ ME/day) = 293(BW$_{kg}$)$^{0.75}$
= 293(4.5 BW$_{kg}$)$^{0.75}$ = 904 kJ ME/day
Modifier for feline adult maintenance = 1.4 x RER = DER
DER (kJ ME/day) = 1.4 x 904 kJ ME = 1,266 kJ ME

3) Determine the amount of food to be fed by dividing the cat's energy requirement by the energy density of the food.
   302 kcal ME/day ÷ 3.88 kcal ME/g = 78 g food/day
   1,266 kJ ME/day ÷ 16.18 kJ ME/g = 78 g food/day

4) Determine the amount of Mg provided by the food by multiplying the amount of food fed by the percentage of Mg in the food.
   78 g food x 0.12% Mg = 0.090 g (90 mg) Mg

The amount of Mg provided by the food (90 mg) compared with the animal's requirement of 31 mg indicates more than an adequate (threefold) amount of Mg.

vert to the same energy density. In some cases it will be desirable to convert food nutrient content on an as fed basis to dry matter basis, energy density defined. (See Case 1-1.)

Comparing a food's nutrient content with the animal's nutrient needs will help identify any significant nutritional imbalances in the food being fed. This comparison is fundamental to determining whether or not to feed a different food.

Compare Specific Food Characteristics with the Animal's Needs

Besides requiring specific levels of certain nutrients, some patients have other food-related needs. These needs might include management of acute or chronic acidosis, maintenance of a specific urinary pH range, certain kibble texture, a specific range of digestibility or osmolality, specific ingredients and avoidance of certain protein sources. As mentioned earlier, the presence or absence of specific protein sources or other ingredients in a food can be obtained from the product label. Other information about food characteristics should be available from product manufacturers. Pet food labels contain addresses and toll-free phone numbers of the manufacturer. When available and where applicable, this information is included in the individual chapters and Appendices L and M.

Assess the Feeding Method

Feeding methods relate directly to the physiologic or disease state of the animal and the food or foods being fed. Thus, the information obtained by assessing the animal and the food is fundamental to assessing the feeding method. There are at least three things to consider regarding feeding methods: 1) feeding route, 2) amount fed and 3) how the food is offered (when, where, by whom and how often).

Feeding Route

Whether or not the feeding route is appropriate depends on the animal's condition. Although most animals are able

Table 1-6. How to convert to the same energy density.

Correcting energy densities in order to make valid nutrient comparisons, either between foods or between a food and an animal's requirement, is based on the assumption that the relationship between nutrient content and energy density is directly proportional. A simple ratio can be established to generate a multiplier that converts the units of the animal's requirements to those of the food; then the animal's requirement and the food's nutrient content can be compared. The multiplier is obtained by dividing the energy density of the food by the requirement energy density.

Example: Is a food that provides 0.72% potassium and 4 kcal (16.74 kJ)/g, on a dry matter basis, adequate for canine adult maintenance?
1) The requirement for potassium is 0.6% (dry matter basis) in an adult dog food that provides 3.5 kcal (14.64 kJ)/g.

2) Convert the requirement to the same energy density as the food by generating the multiplier.
Multiplier
= food energy density ÷ requirement energy density
= 4.0 kcal (16.74 kJ)/g dry matter ÷ 3.5 kcal (14.64 kJ)/g dry matter
= 1.14

3) To obtain the equivalent nutrient requirement for a food providing 4 kcal (14.74 kJ)/g, on a dry matter basis, multiply the requirement by the multiplier.
Equivalent nutrient requirement
= 1.14 x 0.06% potassium
= 0.68% potassium, 4 kcal (14.74 kJ)/g, on a dry matter basis

4) The amount of potassium in the food (0.72%) is compared to the animal's equivalent nutrient requirement (0.68%) and is found to be adequate.

5) The multiplier obtained above (1.14) can be used to convert the other nutrient requirements to the same basis as the food to compare the adequacy of their levels, if desired.

Once the energy densities of the food and the animal's needs are converted to the same units, the comparison is simple as shown in the following example.

If a cat food supplies 0.27% magnesium on a dry matter basis (4.0 kcal [16.74 kJ] ME/g food dry matter) and the cat requires 0.04% magnesium on a dry matter basis (4.0 kcal [16.74 kJ] ME/g food dry matter), the food contains excess magnesium.

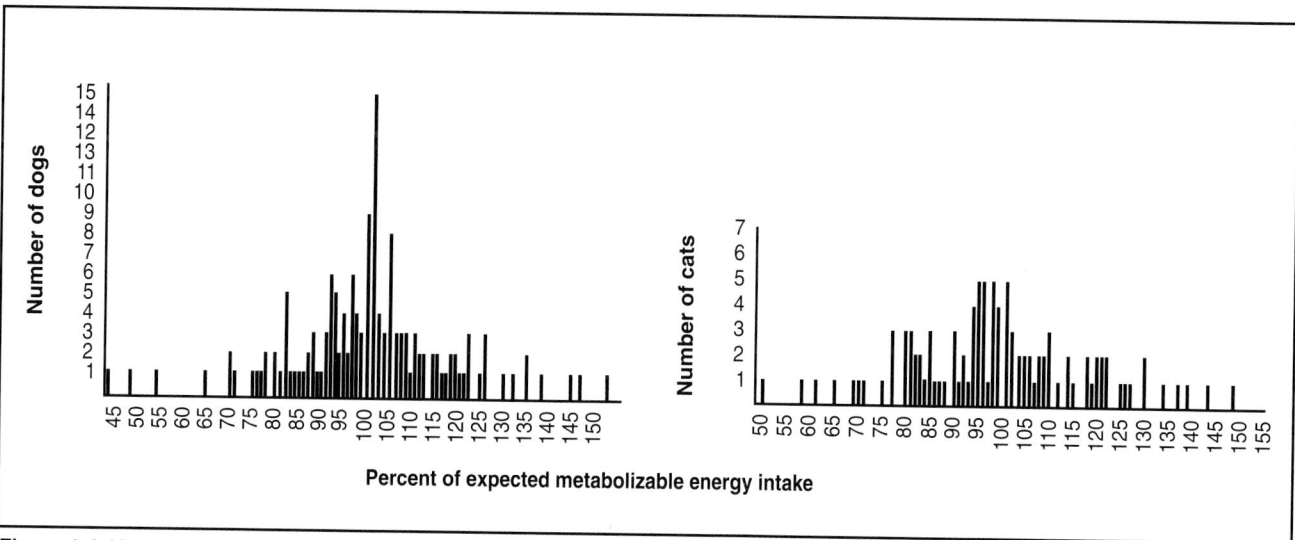

Figure 1-4. Variation in expected energy intake required to maintain optimal body weight in dogs and cats. Data were collected from 120 dogs and 76 cats kept under similar conditions and fed the amount of a variety of commercial pet foods necessary to maintain body weight. (Adapted from Lewis LD, Morris ML Jr, Hand MS. Small Animal Clinical Nutrition III. Topeka, KS: Mark Morris Associates, 1987; 1–10.)

Table 1-7. Calculation of energy requirements.

Calculation of daily energy requirement (DER) is based on the resting energy requirement (RER) for the animal modified by a factor to account for normal activity or production (e.g., growth, gestation, lactation, work). RER is a function of metabolic body size. RER is calculated by raising the animal's body weight in kg to the 0.75 power. The average RER for mammals is about 70 kcal/day/kg metabolic body size: RER (kcal/day) = $70(BW_{kg})^{0.75}$ or $30(BW_{kg})$ + 70 (if the animal weighs between 2 and 45 kg). Expressed in kJ, the average RER for mammals is about $293(BW_{kg})^{0.75}$. These energy requirements should be used as guidelines, starting points or estimates of energy requirements for individual animals and not as absolute requirements.

Feline DER

Maintenance (0.8 to 1.6 x RER)

Neutered adult	= 1.2 x RER
Intact adult	= 1.4 x RER
Active adult	= 1.6 x RER
Obese prone	= 1.0 x RER
Weight loss	= 0.8 x RER
Critical care	= 1.0 x RER
Weight gain	= 1.2-1.4 x RER at ideal weight

Gestation
Energy requirement increases linearly during gestation in cats.
Energy intake should be increased to 1.6 x RER at breeding and gradually increased through gestation to 2 x RER at parturition.
Free-choice feeding of pregnant queens is also recommended.

Lactation
Lactation is nutritionally demanding and the physiologic and nutritional equivalent of heavy work.
Recommend 2 to 6 x RER (depending on number of kittens nursing) or free-choice feeding.

Growth
Daily energy intake for growing kittens should be about 2.5 x RER.
Free-choice feeding is recommended.

Canine DER

Maintenance (1.0 to 1.8 x RER)

Neutered adult	= 1.6 x RER
Intact adult	= 1.8 x RER
Obese prone	= 1.4 x RER
Weight loss	= 1.0 x RER
Critical care	= 1.0 x RER
Weight gain	= 1.2-1.4 x RER at ideal weight

Work

Light work	= 2 x RER
Moderate work	= 3 x RER
Heavy work	= 4-8 x RER

Gestation
First 42 days: feed as an intact adult.
Last 21 days: use 3 x RER. (This quantity may need to be increased to maintain normal body condition for some dogs, especially larger breeds.)

Lactation
Lactation is nutritionally demanding and the physiologic and nutritional equivalent of heavy work.
Recommend 4 to 8 x RER (depending on number of puppies nursing) or free-choice feeding.

Growth
Daily energy intake for growing puppies should be 3 x RER from weaning until four months of age.
At four months of age energy intake should be reduced to 2 x RER until the puppy reaches adult size.

to feed themselves, orphans and some critical care patients may require assistance. Assisted-feeding methods are described in detail in Chapter 12 and Appendix V. Assisted-feeding methods include enteral feeding by syringe or tube (several approaches) and parenteral feeding.

Amount Fed

The nutrient needs of an animal are met by a combination of the nutrient levels in the food and the amount of food fed. Even if a food has an appropriate nutrient profile, significant over- or undernutrition could result if too much or too little is consumed. Thus, it is important to know if the amount being consumed is appropriate.

The amount of food being fed should have been determined when the history of the animal was obtained. Although many animals are fed free choice, owners should still be able to provide a reasonable estimate of the actual amount being consumed. The owner may need to return home and measure the amount the pet consumes before reporting this. The amount actually being consumed can then be compared with the amount that should be fed. If the animal in question has a normal BCS (3/5) and no history of weight changes, the amount fed is probably appropriate. Exceptions to this generalization include growing animals, animals that are gestating or lactating and hunting dogs and other canine athletes early in the athletic event season.

The appropriate amount to feed can be difficult to determine precisely, but can be estimated. For most commercial pet foods, food dosage estimates can be found in the feeding guidelines on the product label. However, food dosages can be calculated if guidelines are not available. The precision of feeding guidelines or calculated food dosages is limited because the efficiency of food use varies among individuals because of differences in physical activity, metabolism, body condition, insulative characteristics of the coat and external environment. Even when environmental conditions and physical activity are similar, sizable individual differences can exist.

Figure 1-4 was generated from data from several controlled studies on the amount of food (energy content standardized) consumed by mature, nonreproducing dogs and cats kept in kennels or runs under similar environmental conditions while maintaining body weight. The total amount of energy needed by dogs and cats for maintenance, even under similar environmental conditions varied threefold. Even when the extremes are excluded (the top and bottom 2.5%), the amount of energy needed varied more than twofold.[22] Therefore, a calculated food dosage should only be considered an estimate or a starting point that may have to be adjusted.

Calculations to estimate food dosage are based on the assumption that if a food contains the proper proportions of nutrients relative to its energy density, and is fed to meet an animal's energy requirement, then the animal's requirements for nonenergy nutrients will automatically be met. Food dosage estimation has four steps:

1) Estimate the energy requirement of the animal (Table 1-7).
2) Determine the appropriate category of food to be fed. Select a food that is suitable for the intended application (i.e., growth, gestation/lactation, maintenance, weight control [increasing or decreasing weight], old

age, physical work or a specific disease). If you are unsure whether the food is balanced for the intended application, evaluate it yourself as described above under food evaluation.

3) Determine the energy density of the food (kcal or kJ ME/g food, as fed basis). Sources include product labels, product literature, company personnel and calculation using modified Atwater values (Tables 1-8 and 1-9).

4) Divide the energy requirement of the animal by the energy density of the food to determine the daily amount to feed (food dosage). Case 1-2 includes an example of a food dosage problem.

How the Food is Offered

The amount fed is usually offered one of three ways: 1) free-choice feeding (dogs and cats), 2) food-restricted meal feeding (dogs and cats) and 3) time-restricted meal feeding (dogs). The number of feedings per day must be considered when the last two methods are used.

Free-choice feeding (also referred to as ad libitum or self feeding) is a method in which more food than the dog or cat will consume is always available; therefore, the animal can eat as much as it wants, whenever it chooses. The major advantage of free-choice feeding is that it is quick and easy. All that is necessary is to ensure that reasonably fresh food is always available. Free-choice feeding is the method of choice during lactation. Free-choice feeding also has a quieting effect in a kennel and timid dogs have a better chance of getting their share if dogs are fed in a group.

Disadvantages include: 1) anorectic animals may not be noticed for several days, especially if two or more animals are fed together, 2) if food is always available, some dogs and cats will continuously overeat and may become obese (such animals should be meal fed) and 3) moist foods and moistened dry foods left at room temperature for prolonged periods can spoil and are not appropriate for free-choice feeding. (See Chapter 7, Case 7-3.)

When changing a dog from meal feeding to free-choice feeding, first feed it the amount of the food it is used to receiving at a meal. After this food has been consumed and the dog's appetite has been somewhat satisfied, set out the food to be fed free choice. This transitioning method helps prevent engorgement by dogs unaccustomed to free-choice feeding. Engorgement is generally not a problem when transitioning cats to free-choice feeding. Although dogs and cats unaccustomed to free-choice feeding may overeat initially, they generally stop doing so within a few days, once they learn that food is always available. Avoid taking the food away at any time during this transition period. Each time food is taken away increases the difficulty in changing the animals to a free-choice feeding regimen.

With food-restricted meal feeding, the dog or cat is given a specific, but lesser, amount of food than it would eat if the amount fed were not restricted. Time-restricted meal feeding is a method in which the animal is given more food than it will consume within a specified period of time, generally five to 15 minutes. Time-restricted meal feeding is of limited usefulness with dogs and has little if any practical application in cats. Many dogs can eat an entire meal in less than two to three minutes. Both types of meal feeding are repeated at a specific frequency such as

one or more times a day. Some people combine feeding methods, such as free-choice feeding a dry or semi-moist food and meal feeding a moist food or other foods such as meat or table scraps.

Frequent food consumption resulting from frequent meal and free-choice feeding has several advantages. Feeding

---

Computerized Food Evaluation/Balancing Programs

There are three basic computer software approaches for food evaluation/balancing: 1) spread sheets, 2) linear programs and 3) stochastic programs.

Spread sheet programs automate the various basic mathematical calculations but optimize formulas through operator-managed trial and error.

Linear programs, in addition to automating various basic mathematical calculations, calculate simultaneous equations and optimize formulas via linear algorithms. They do not require trial and error management by program operators to optimize formulas; they do it automatically.

Stochastic programs accomplish everything that linear programs can do plus they can manage nonlinear algorithms relating to both animal and ingredient variability. These are the most sophisticated of the software programs available.

A cautionary reminder: computer programs are tools intended to make the mathematical work of food evaluation/balancing/formulation easier and faster. Their accuracy depends entirely on the accuracy of the databases from which they are working and they do not account for nutrient availability regarding ingredient sourcing and cooking, nor do they ensure a palatable food.

Formulation Software Programs

Company	Software program
Agri-Data Systems, Inc. 21620 N. 19th Ave., Suite #A-10 Phoenix, AZ 85027 Phone: (602) 582-3888, Fax: (602) 582-2916 E-mail: adsmwest@agri-data.com http://www.agri-data.com	Agri-Data
Agricultural Software Consultants, Inc. 2728-600 Shelter Island Drive San Diego, CA 92106 Phone: (619) 226-2600, Fax: (619) 226-7900 http://www.asc.mixit.com	Mixit
The Brill Corporation 6525 The Corners Parkway Suite 214 Norcross, GA 30092 Phone: (770) 662-5588, Fax: (770) 662-5601 E-mail: brill@brillcorp.com	Brill
Format International Format House, Poole Road Woking, Surrey England GU21 1DY Phone: 011 441 483 726 081 Fax: 011 441 483 722 827	Format
Optimal Consultants, Inc. 2020 W. McNab Road, Suite 108 Ft. Lauderdale, FL 33309 Phone: (954) 972-6544, Fax: (954) 972-0005 E-mail: optimal-soft@worldnet.att.net	Optimal

small meals frequently throughout the day results in a greater loss of energy as a result of an increase in daily meal-induced heat production. Also, it generally results in greater total food intake than does less frequent feeding.[23] Frequent feeding of small meals benefits animals with dysfunctional ingestion, digestion, absorption or use of nutrients.

Table 1-8. Energy available from protein, fat and soluble carbohydrate (nitrogen-free extract).

Metabolizable energy (kcal/g)			
Species	Crude protein	Crude fat	Soluble carbohydrate
All*	4.4 x digestibility*	9.4 x digestibility*	4.15 x digestibility*
Dogs and cats**	3.5**	8.5**	3.5**

Metabolizable energy (kJ/g)			
Species	Crude protein	Crude fat	Soluble carbohydrate
All*	18.41 x digestibility*	39.33 x digestibility*	17.36 x digestibility*
Dogs and cats**	14.64**	35.56**	14.64**

*The most accurate value to use when the digestibility of the three nutrients is known. Adapted from Lewis LD, Morris ML Jr, Hand MS. Small Animal Clinical Nutrition III. Topeka, KS: Mark Morris Associates, 1987; 1-8.
**"Modified Atwater" values (Dog Food Nutrient Profiles and Cat Food Nutrient Profiles). Association of American Feed Control Officials 1998.

Table 1-9. Example calculation of caloric density of a pet food.*

Analysis			Metabolizable energy (kcal)	
	%		kcal/g of nutrient**	kcal/g of food
Protein	22	x	3.5	= 0.77
Fat	9	x	8.5	= 0.77
Fiber***	3	x	0	= 0
Moisture	10	x	0	= 0
Ash***	5	x	0	= 0
Soluble carbohydrate†	51	x	3.5	= 1.79
Total				3.32††

Analysis			Metabolizable energy (kJ)	
	%		kJ/g of nutrient**	kJ/g of food
Protein	22	x	14.64	= 3.22
Fat	9	x	35.56	= 3.20
Fiber***	3	x	0	= 0
Moisture	10	x	0	= 0
Ash***	5	x	0	= 0
Soluble carbohydrate†	51	x	14.54	= 7.47
Total				13.89††

3.315 kcal/g (13.89 kJ/g) x amount of food/measuring cup = kcal/measuring cup††††

*As fed basis.
**From Table 1-8.
***If not available these may be estimated as 3% fiber and 9% ash in dry foods, 1% fiber and 6% ash in soft-moist foods and 1% fiber and 2.5% ash in moist foods.
†Percent soluble carbohydrate (nitrogen free extract) usually is not stated but can be calculated by subtracting the percent protein, fat, fiber, moisture and ash from 100.
††If the nutrient percentages were obtained from the label guarantee, multiply the food's caloric density by 1.2 for moist pet foods and 1.1 for semi-moist and dry pet foods. In this example, 3.32 (13.89 kJ) x 1.1 = 3.65 kcal (15.28 kJ)/g of dry food.
†††An 8-oz. (volume) measuring cup holds 3 to 3.5 oz. by weight (85 to 100 g) of most dry pet foods or 3.5 to 5 oz. by weight (100 to 150 g) of most semi-moist pet foods. It is more accurate to use the average weight of three individual measuring cups of food in determining kcal or kJ/cup.

Frequent feeding is also desirable in normal animals that require a high food intake. Puppies less than six months old, some dogs engaged in heavy work (high levels of physical activity), dogs and cats experiencing ambient temperature extremes, bitches and queens during the last month of gestation and bitches and queens that are lactating should be fed at least three times per day to ensure that their nutritional needs are met. These animals may require one and one-half to four times as much food per unit of body weight than most normal adult dogs and cats. A reduced frequency might limit total food intake in these situations. Also, more frequent feeding during periods of variable appetite suppression, such as occurs with psychologic stress or high ambient temperatures, helps ensure adequate food intake.

Most clinically normal adult dogs that are not lactating, working or experiencing stress will have a sufficient appetite and physical capacity to consume all of the food required daily in a single 10-minute period (assuming food of typical nutrient density [about 3.5 kcal/g or 14.64 kJ/g dry matter]). Cats are less likely to eat their entire meal in one 10-minute sitting, but once-a-day feeding is adequate for most healthy adults. Although many dogs and cats are fed once daily without noticeable detrimental effects, at least twice daily feeding is generally recommended.

FEEDING PLAN

A feeding plan should be formulated based on realistic and quantifiable nutritional objectives after the animal, food and feeding method have been assessed. The feeding plan will guide the veterinarian's selection of food or foods and the feeding method. The two steps to formulating the feeding plan are to determine: 1) what food or foods to feed and 2) the feeding method.

Determine What Food to Feed

As explained above (See Assessment.), comparing the food's levels of key nutritional factors with the animal's needs allows the veterinarian to determine whether nutrient excesses or deficiencies exist. If the animal's current food is adequate (key nutritional factors in balance with the animal's needs) then the food currently being fed can continue to be fed. The animal's current food must be modified or "balanced" if significant nutrient excesses or deficiencies exist.

There are numerous approaches to balancing foods. Some are rather extensive. (See sidebar "Food Formulation and Extensive Food Balancing" and also sidebar "Computerized Food Evaluation/Balancing Programs.") This section will review the most practical methods, including: 1) food replacement and 2) simple mathematical ration balancing (Pearson square). Alternatively, veterinarians can contact a person who specializes in veterinary nutrition.

Food Replacement

If food assessment indicates that an animal's nutrient requirements are not being met, the most practical way to balance a food is to simply select a different food (i.e., one that does a better job of meeting the animal's requirements). The most likely application of this method occurs

Table 1-10. Recommended short- and long-term food transition schedules for dogs and cats.

Short schedule*	Long schedule**		Food percentages	
Dogs and cats (days)	Dogs (days)	Cats (weeks)	Previous food	New food
1,2	1-3	1	75%	25%
3,4	4-6	2	50%	50%
5,6	7-9	3	25%	75%
7	10	4	0%	100%

*Recommended for most healthy dogs and cats.
**Recommended for situations in which the food change is known to be significant, the dog or cat has demonstrated low tolerance to such changes in the past or food refusal is anticipated.

when one commercial food is substituted for another. One homemade food can be replaced by another if the nutrient profiles of both recipes are available. (See Chapter 6.)

The process is straightforward and simple. The nutrient contents of other foods are evaluated to see which food most closely meets the animal's requirements. Assuming acceptable palatability, the "winner" of this comparison replaces the previous food. Case 1-3 shows an example of food replacement.

Changing foods for most healthy dogs and cats is of minor consequence. Some owners switch their pets from one food to another daily. Most dogs and cats tolerate these changes. However, vomiting, diarrhea, belching, flatulence or a combination of signs may occur with sudden, rapid switching of foods, probably because of ingredient differences. It is prudent, therefore, to recommend that owners change their pet's food over the course of at least three days. A seven-day period is even better, as owners increase the proportion of new food and decrease the proportion of old food (Table 1-10). Nearly all pets readily tolerate a seven-day transition period. A much longer transitional period is recommended in cases in which the food change is known to be significant, the pet has demonstrated a poor tolerance to such changes in the past or food refusal is expected (Table 1-10). For example, a long transition schedule is likely to be needed for an old cat recently diagnosed with kidney disease when the food must be switched from a highly palatable grocery "gourmet" food to an appropriate veterinary therapeutic food.

Simple Mathematical Ration Balancing (Pearson Square)

The Pearson square is another useful diet balancing tool. This handy method can be used to combine any two foods, supplements or ingredients to yield a mixture with a desired nutrient content. Figure 1-5 shows how the Pearson square method is used to balance a diet. Here's how to use the Pearson square:

1) A small square is drawn and the desired nutrient concentration of the proposed mixture is written in the middle of the square.
2) The nutrient concentration of one component of the mixture is written at the upper left corner of the square.
3) The nutrient concentration of the other component of the mixture is written at the lower left corner of the square.
4) The nutrient values at the corners are subtracted from those in the center of the square. The smaller number is always subtracted from the larger and the differences written diagonally at the right corners of the square.
5) The differences are added together and the sum is written below each difference as the denominator of a fraction.

6) The fractions are converted to percentages. These percentages are the proportion of each component of the mixture in the corners directly to the left. When combined in those percentages, the constituent components will yield a mixture having the same concentration as the number in the center of the square.

Determine the Feeding Method

As mentioned above, veterinarians and their health care teams should consider several aspects of feeding methods. These include the feeding route, the amount to be fed and how the amount fed is provided. In addition, feeding factors that affect compliance should be considered, such as whether or not the animal has access to other foods and who provides the food.

The feeding route will depend on the ability of the animal to self feed. Animals unable to self feed will need assistance such as syringe feeding, tube feeding or parenteral feeding.

Estimates of the amount of a new food to feed can be obtained from product information such as feeding guidelines on the product label. The food dosage estimate can also be calculated as shown above. (See Assess the Feeding Method.) Recall that individual variability is large and that either method is, at best, an estimate. The amount fed

---

As an example, the Pearson square can be used to solve the following problem: How much calcium carbonate containing 36% calcium must be added to a meat-based food to increase its calcium content from 0.01% to 0.3% on an as fed basis? Assume you are making 5 kg of the mixture. The problem is set up and worked as follows:

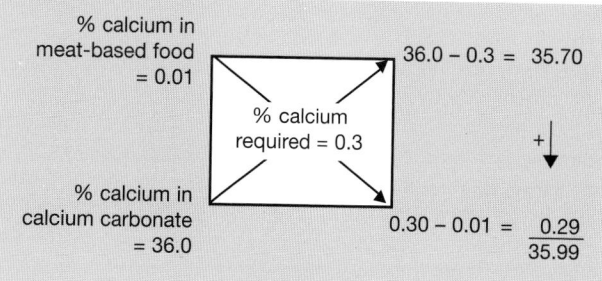

The final step converts fraction to percentages by dividing the numerator of the fractions by the denominator and multiplying by 100.
  Meat-based food: (35.70 ÷ 35.99) x 100 = 99.19%
  Calcium carbonate: (0.29 ÷ 35.99) x 100 = 0.81%
If the total mixture is 5 kg, then 99.19% (4.96 kg) should be a meat-based food and 0.81% (0.04 kg, or 40 g) should be calcium carbonate.

Figure 1-5. Example of how to use the Pearson square.

Food Formulation and Extensive Food Balancing

It is not the intention of this book to teach complete food formulation or extensive food balancing. Few practitioners need to know how to formulate balanced foods from scratch. Nutrient requirement information is readily available; however, accurate/relevant ingredient nutrient databases, an understanding of the availability of nutrients in various ingredients, knowledge of the effect of cooking on nutrient availability and knowledge of all of these variables on palatability are complex issues. Such information is not readily available, and usually requires assimilation by a team of experts, including veterinarians, nutritionists and food scientists to ensure proper formulation of complete and balanced foods.

Fortunately, numerous complete pet food options are readily available from commercial pet food manufacturers. (See Appendix L.) Many homemade food recipes have also been published. Be sure to obtain homemade food recipes from reliable sources as discussed in Chapter 6.

should be adjusted to ensure a normal body condition score (3/5) and to avoid intolerance (vomiting or diarrhea in the case of enteral feeding or metabolic complications with parenteral feeding).

As mentioned earlier in the chapter, how the food is provided and how often it is provided depend on the animal's condition and in some cases the lifestyle of the owner. Each animal's situation will dictate which feeding method is most desirable (free choice, time-restricted meal feeding or food-restricted meal feeding). For many physiologic and disease conditions this consideration will not be important. For others it will be very important. Recommendations for the best method of providing the food and the number of times per day the food is offered are included in each individual chapter.

Owner compliance is necessary for effective clinical nutrition. Feeding methods should reinforce or enable compliance. Enabling compliance includes limiting access to other foods and knowing who provides the food. An animal from a multi-pet household may have access to the other pets' food. If so, such access needs to be denied or limited. Restriction can be difficult in some homes. In such cases the veterinary health care team and pet owner may need to compromise.

Compliance can be eroded if everyone in the family is not supportive of the feeding plan. Whoever feeds the pet must understand the consequences when the wrong foods are fed or even the right foods are fed in the wrong amounts. Client education is essential for the successful outcome of any feeding plan. Specific client education must be provided for feeding healthy pets and for those with specific disease problems. Both oral and written instructions encourage compliance with feeding plans.

Veterinarians and their health care teams should actively involve clients in the formulation of the feeding plan to ensure commitment to the plan. The hospital staff should strive to uncover issues that clients may have about the feeding plan and negotiate mutually acceptable solutions. Open communication about the client's and the hospital's objectives, concerns and shared responsibilities is necessary for successful implementation of the feeding plan. Authoritarian approaches are unlikely to be effective because they discount the high degree of independent decision making that clients have based on their own perceptions of nutrition. Veterinarians and their health care teams can guide clients and enable them to make informed decisions.

REASSESSMENT

Finally, monitoring, or reassessment of the animal, should be performed at appropriate intervals to evaluate the effectiveness of the feeding plan. For patients undergoing intensive care, reassessment may need to be done every few hours, whereas pets in a health maintenance program could be reassessed annually. Reassessment signals the initiation of the iterative step of the clinical nutrition process. Involving the client in a plan of action is an essential component of the veterinarian-client relationship. The reader is referred to the remaining chapters of this book for information about specific feeding plans and practices according to pet nutritional needs in health and in specific diseases.

REFERENCES

1. United States Department of Health and Human Services. The Surgeon General's Report on Nutrition and Health. Public Health Service, DHHS (PHS) Publication No. 88-50210, 1988.
2. Diet and Health: Implications for Reducing Chronic Disease Risk. National Research Council. Washington, DC: National Academy Press, 1989.
3. Gants R. Are your clients ready for nutrition? Veterinary Economics May 1990: 40-48.
4. American Animal Hospital Association. The 1995 AAHA Report. Trends Magazine 1995; 11(4).
5. Bauer JE, Buffington CA, Olson WG. ACVN Highlights Common Principles of Nutrition. Veterinary Forum 1995; 12(10): 55-58.
6. Moore MG, Kearsley G. Distance Education: A Systems View. Belmont, CA: Wadsworth Publishing Co, 1996; 101-107.
7. Remillard RL, Thatcher CD. Dietary and nutritional management of gastrointestinal diseases. Veterinary Clinics of North America: Small Animal Practice 1989; 19: 795-816.
8. LaFlamme DP, Kealy RD, Schmidt DA. Estimation of body fat by body condition score. In: Proceedings. Twelfth Annual Veterinary Medical Forum, American College of Veterinary Internal Medicine, San Francisco, CA, 1994: 985.
9. Graham JF, Clark AJ, Spiker SA. The repeatability and accuracy of condition scoring beef cattle. In: Proceedings. Australian Society for Animal Production 1982; 15: 684.
10. Croxton D, Stollard RJ. Use of body condition scoring as a management aid in dairy and beef herds. Animal Production 1976; 22: 146-147.
11. Burkholder WJ. Body composition of dogs determined by carcass composition analysis, deuterium oxide dilution, subjective and objective morphometry and bioelectrical impedance. PhD dissertation. Virginia Poly Technic Institute and State University. May 1994.
12. LaFlamme DP. Body condition scoring and weight maintenance. In: Proceedings. North American Veterinary Conference, Orlando, FL, 1993: 290-291.
13. Giner M, Laviano A, Meguid MM, et al. A correlation between malnutrition and poor outcome in critically ill patients still exists. Nutrition 1996; 12(1): 23-29.
14. Fascetti AJ, Mauldin GE, Mauldin GN. Correlation between serum creatine kinase activities and anorexia in cats. Journal of Veterinary Internal Medicine 1997; 11: 9-13.

15. National Research Council. Nutrient Requirements of Dogs. Washington, DC: National Academy Press, 1985.

16. National Research Council. Nutrient Requirements of Cats. Washington, DC: National Academy Press, 1986.

17. Nutrient Profiles for Dog Foods. Official Publication. Association of American Feed Control Officials 1993; 93-99.

18. Nutrient Profiles for Cat Foods. Official Publication. Association of American Feed Control Officials 1994; 117-118.

19. National Research Council. Recommended Dietary Allowances. Washington, DC: National Academy Press, 1989; 10-23.

20. National Research Council. Nutrient Requirements of Dogs. Washington, DC: National Academy Press, 1974.

21. National Research Council. Nutrient Requirements of Cats. Washington, DC: National Academy Press, 1978.

22. Lewis LD, Morris ML Jr., Hand MS. Nutrients. In: Small Animal Clinical Nutrition III. Topeka, KS: Mark Morris Associates, 1987; 1-9–1-10.

23. Mugford RA, Thorne C. Comparative studies of meal patterns in pet and laboratory housed dogs and cats. In: Anderson RS, ed. Nutrition of the Dog and Cat. Oxford, UK: Permagon Press, 1980; 145-156.

■ CASE 1-1

Calcium Supplementation in a Great Dane Puppy

Michael S. Hand, DVM, PhD
Diplomate ACVN
Hill's Science and Technology Center
Topeka, Kansas, USA

Assess the Animal

A 10-week-old male Great Dane puppy weighing 15 kg was examined as part of its routine health maintenance procedures. The results of a physical examination were normal. The puppy's body condition score was 3/5.

Assess the Food and Feeding Method

The puppy is fed a dry lamb and rice-based commercial food. The owner feeds the puppy four 8-oz. measuring cups of food daily. The owner also provides eight calcium tablets daily as a supplement to "ensure enough calcium." A phone call to the pet food company's customer service department determined that the food's calcium content is 2.3% and that it provides 3.6 kcal/g (15.06 kJ/g) on an as fed basis (10% moisture). The customer service department also indicates that the food density is 94 g per cup. Product literature included with the calcium tablets indicates that each tablet provides 0.5 g of calcium carbonate, and that calcium carbonate contains 36% calcium (0% moisture). The owner asked if this is enough calcium for the puppy.

Questions

1. How many g of food and how many g of calcium carbonate were being fed on a dry matter basis?
2. Determine the total amount of calcium (dry matter basis) provided by the food and supplement.
3. Determine the percentage of calcium in the dry matter of the combined food and supplement.
4. Convert the energy density on an as fed basis to a dry matter basis.
5. Does the combination of the food and supplement meet the calcium requirement for a giant-breed puppy?

Answers and Discussion

1. Four cups x 94 g/cup = 376 g of food. Because the two components being evaluated have differing moisture contents (food = 90% dry matter and calcium carbonate tablets = 100% dry matter), it is advisable to convert the food to dry matter at this point: 376 g of food on an as fed basis x 90% dry matter = 338 g food dry matter.

   The owner said that eight calcium tablets are fed daily. The calcium carbonate source has no moisture so as fed basis equals dry matter basis: eight calcium tablets x 0.5 g calcium carbonate per tablet = 4 g calcium carbonate (as fed and dry matter basis).

2. According to the manufacturer, the food provides 2.3% calcium on an as fed basis. To convert this to a dry matter basis, divide the as fed percentage by the dry matter percentage: 2.3% calcium as fed basis ÷ 90% dry matter = 2.6% calcium on a dry matter basis.

   We have already determined that the calcium tablets provide 4 g calcium carbonate and that calcium carbonate contains 36% calcium. To determine how much calcium is provided by each component, multiply the amount of each component being fed by the amount of calcium in each component and add them:

   338 g food dry matter x 2.6% calcium = 8.8 g calcium
   4 g calcium carbonate x 36% calcium = <u>1.4 g calcium</u>
           10.2 g total calcium (dry matter basis)

3. Total food dry matter is the sum of the two components:

   338 g food dry matter + 4 g calcium carbonate dry matter = 342 g total food dry matter

   10.2 g total calcium (dry matter basis) ÷ 342 g total food dry matter = 3.0% calcium

4. We need to consider the effect of the supplemental calcium source on the energy density of the food and convert the energy density to a dry matter basis. In this case, we ignore any dilutional effect the 4 g of calcium carbonate has on the energy density of the food because it would be inconsequential (4 g ÷ 342 g ≈ 1%). To convert 3.6 kcal ME/g (15.06 kJ ME/g) as fed to dry matter basis, as described previously, divide the as fed basis by the dry matter percentage:

   3.6 kcal ME/g as fed ÷ 90% dry matter = 4 kcal ME/g (dry matter basis), or

   15.06 kJ ME/g as fed ÷ 90% dry matter = 16.74 kJ ME/g (dry matter basis)

   Thus, the total food contains 3.0% calcium on a dry matter basis and provides 4 kcal ME/g (16.74 kJ) dry matter.

5. To compare a food's nutrient content with a recommended target level requires that the energy density of

the food and that specified for the target level be similar or the same. Calcium is a key nutritional factor (nutrient of concern) for large- and giant-breed puppies. Calcium levels in foods intended for large- and giant-breed growth should not exceed 1.5% dry matter in foods that provide <3.8 kcal ME/g (<15.90 kJ). (See Chapter 17.) As described above, the conversion is made by generating a multiplier that converts the requirement to the same energy density as the food. This is done by dividing the food energy density by the requirement energy density

and multiplying the requirement by the multiplier: 4 kcal ME/g ÷ 3.6 kcal ME/g = 1.1 (multiplier), or 16.74 kJ ME/g ÷ 15.06 kJ ME/g = 1.11

$$1.1 \times 1.5\% \text{ maximum} = 1.67\% \text{ maximum.}$$

In this case, the combined food and supplement are providing excessive calcium for this giant-breed puppy. (See Chapter 17.)

CASE 1-2

Food Dosage Estimate for a Lactating Queen

Michael S. Hand, DVM, PhD
Diplomate ACVN
Hill's Science and Technology Center
Topeka, Kansas, USA

Assess the Animal

A 4-kg, three-year-old queen is presented for weight loss. The cat is nursing five three-week-old kittens. The queen's body condition score is 2/5 and the patient record indicates that the cat has lost 1 kg since its postpartum checkup.

Assess the Food and Feeding Method

The cat is being fed one cup of a commercial dry food daily, free-choice. The food is suitably balanced for feline lactation. The energy density of the food is 535 kcal ME/cup (2,238 kJ ME/cup) on a as fed basis.

Questions

1. What is this queen's estimated daily energy requirement (DER)?
2. What should the food dosage be based on this queen's DER?

Answers and Discussion

1. Resting energy requirement (RER) (kcal ME/day) = $70(BW_{kg})^{0.75}$
   = $70(4 \text{ kg})^{0.75}$ = 70(2.83) = 198 kcal ME/day or
   = $293(4 \text{ kg})^{0.75}$ = 293(2.83) = 829 kJ ME/day
   Modifier for adult feline = 1.5 x RER = DER
   DER = 1.5 x 198 kcal ME/day = 297 kcal ME/day,
   or 1.5 x 829 kJ ME/day = 1,243.5 kJ ME/day
   Modifier for feline lactation = (1 + 0.25[number kittens nursing]) x DER
   = [1 + 0.25(5)] x 297 kcal ME/day
   = 2.25 x 297 kcal ME/day = 668 kcal ME/day, or
   2.25 x 1,243.5 kJ ME/day = 2,798 kJ ME/day

2. The food being fed has a nutrient profile that is satisfactory for feline lactation. The energy density of the food is 535 kcal (2,238 kJ) ME/cup. Divide the energy requirement by the energy density of the food to determine how much to feed the cat:
   668 kcal ME/day requirement ÷ 535 kcal ME/cup = 1.25 cups/day, or
   2,798 kJ ME/day requirement ÷ 2,238 kJ ME/cup = 1.25 cups/day
   According to these calculations the cat is being underfed. The amount offered free choice should be increased by at least 25%.

CASE 1-3

Altering the Food and Feeding Method for a Young Rottweiler

Rebecca L. Remillard, PhD, DVM
Diplomate ACVN
Angell Memorial Animal Hospital
Boston, Massachusetts, USA

Assess the Animal

A four-month-old female Rottweiler was examined for diarrhea of five days' duration. The puppy had escaped from a fenced yard on trash pickup day and the owners suspected it had eaten garbage. The puppy appeared bright and alert, weighed 18 kg and had a body condition score of 3/5. The results of the physical examination were normal except for fluid-filled intestines on abdominal palpation. The owners described the stools as being small volume but frequent (eight

to 10/day) and liquid with some bright red blood and mucus. A fecal examination was negative for intestinal parasites.

Assess the Food and Feeding Method

The puppy was fed a commercial dry puppy food three times per day until its escape. The puppy still had a good appetite, but seemed to be drinking more than usual amounts of water. On Day 1 of the diarrheic episode, another veterinarian examined the puppy and asked the owner to feed a moist commercial veterinary therapeutic food (poultry, egg and rice based) with moderate fat (13%) and low fiber (<1%)(Prescription Diet Canine i/d[a]). However, the diarrhea had not resolved after feeding the food for three days.

Question

1. What is the appropriate food and feeding method for this patient with large bowel diarrhea?

Answer and Discussion

1. The food was replaced with a canned commercial veterinary therapeutic food that contained 12% fat and 13% crude fiber (Prescription Diet Canine w/d[a]). The owners were instructed to feed the puppy at its estimated resting energy requirement (805 kcal [3,368 kJ]/day) with two cans of the new food divided into four meals per day for one to two days; then to feed at the estimated daily energy requirement (1,600 kcal/day [6,694 kJ]) with four cans of the new food divided into three to four meals per day for another two days. The owners were instructed to return for a recheck if the puppy did not have a normal stool by the fourth day. If the puppy's stool was normal, the owners were instructed to slowly change the food back to the original puppy food.

Progress Notes

No stool was produced within the first 24 hours of feeding the higher fiber food. By the end of the second day the dog had a normal bowel movement with no blood or mucus. The owners continued to feed the higher fiber food for another two days as instructed. The puppy was then gradually switched back to the dry puppy food with no problems.

Endnote

a. Hill's Pet Nutrition Inc, Topeka, KS, USA.

Nutrients

Kathy L. Gross

Karen J. Wedekind

Christopher S. Cowell

William D. Schoenherr

Dennis E. Jewell

Steven C. Zicker

Jacques Debraekeleer

Russell A. Frey

"Nutriment is both food and poison. The dosage makes it either poison or remedy."
T. B. von Hohenheim

INTRODUCTION

Proper nutrition is among the more important considerations in maintenance of health and is key to the management of many diseases. A basic knowledge of nutrients, requirements, availability and consequences of deficiencies or excesses is important in order to feed animals correctly and give advice about feeding.

A nutrient is any food constituent that helps support life. Numerous essential nutrients have been discovered over the course of history. Nutrients are essential in that they are involved in all the basic functions of the body including: 1) acting as structural components, 2) enhancing or being involved in chemical reactions of metabolism, 3) transporting substances into, throughout or out of the body, 4) maintaining temperature and 5) supplying energy.

Nutrients are divided into six basic categories (Figure 2-1). Some nutrients fulfill a number of functions. For example, water and several minerals are needed for all the functions described above except supplying energy. Carbohydrates, fats and proteins may be used for energy but they can serve as structural components as well. Vitamins are involved primarily with metabolic functions.

Figure 2-2 shows how an individual nutrient can affect the health of an animal. The minimum dietary requirement has been established for most nutrients. Clinical signs of deficiency may result if a food doesn't provide this nutrient level. Similarly, the maximum tolerable levels of certain nutrients are known and toxicity may result if a food exceeds these levels. The area between deficiency and excess represents the range of safe and adequate nutrient intake. The extent of this area will change depending on the individual nutrient and overall composition of the food. What is less well known is how exposure to marginal deficiencies and excesses affects an animal over time.

The most common method of determining the nutrient content of food is the proximate analysis, which provides the percentage moisture, protein, fat, ash and crude fiber. Soluble carbohydrate or nitrogen-free extract (NFE) can then be calculated. Figure 2-3 shows how the determination is conducted. Many commercial laboratories conduct proximate analyses of foods. (See Appendix U.)

This chapter is organized into seven sections. The nutrients will be covered in the order shown in Figure 2-1, beginning at the base of the pyramid. Energy, a non-nutrient, but nonetheless essential for life will be covered after water.

WATER

Definition and Function

Chemically, water is the combination of hydrogen and oxygen, which are joined in the ratio of two hydrogen atoms to one oxygen (H_2O). Water is vital to life and is considered the most important nutrient. Water performs the following important functions in animals:

1. Water is the solvent in which substances are dissolved and transported around the body. The number of chemical compounds that can be put into aqueous solution is quite large.
2. Water is necessary for the chemical reactions that involve hydrolysis (e.g., enzymatic digestion of carbohydrates, proteins and fats).

KEY WORDS & TERMS—NUTRIENTS*

Absorption	Essential fatty acid(s)	Nonessential amino acid(s)
Amino acid(s)	Fat	Nutrient allowances
Availability (bioavailability)	Fatty acid(s)	Nutrient requirements
Basal energy requirement (BER)	Fermentation	Oligosaccharides
Beta-oxidation	Fiber	Protein(s)
Carbohydrate	Gross energy (GE)	Provitamin
Coenzyme	Homeostasis	Resistant starch
Cofactor	Kilocalorie (kcal)	Resting energy requirement (RER)
Conditionally essential nutrient	Kilojoule (kJ)	Short-chain fatty acid(s)
Crude fiber	Kjeldahl's method (test)	Starch
Daily energy requirement (DER)	Macromineral	Total dietary fiber
Deficiency	Maintenance energy requirement (MER)	Toxicity
Digestible energy (DE)	Metabolic body size	Triacylglyceride (TAG)
Dry matter	Metabolic water	Vitamer
Energy	Metabolizable energy (ME)	Vitamin
Essential amino acid(s)	Micromineral	Water

Key words and terms are defined in the Glossary.

KEY POINTS—NUTRIENTS

1. A basic knowledge of nutrients, requirements, availability and consequences of deficiencies and excesses is important to feed animals correctly and give advice about feeding.
2. Nutrients are divided into six basic categories: water, proteins, fats, carbohydrates, vitamins and minerals. Proteins, fats and carbohydrates are the energy-supplying nutrients.
3. A biologic dose-response curve exists for each nutrient. Physiologic function is consistently impaired at low concentrations of the nutrient. In contrast, toxic effects may occur at excessive concentrations.
4. Knowledge of daily energy requirement (DER) is needed to determine how much to feed an animal. Standard equations predict resting energy requirements (RER); DER is calculated by multiplying RER by appropriate factors.
5. Estimates of DER are starting points only. Amounts fed should be adjusted as needed to maintain optimal body weight and condition.
6. Carbohydrates are important in pet food processing.
7. Nitrogen-free extract (NFE) is the carbohydrate fraction of a proximate analysis. NFE is calculated by summing the percentages of water, crude protein, crude fat, ash and crude fiber and subtracting from 100.
8. In studies, starch from extruded corn, barley, rice and oats was nearly 100% digested in the small intestine of dogs.
9. Dogs and cats do not have an absolute dietary requirement for carbohydrates. However, carbohydrates are conditionally essential during growth, gestation and lactation.
10. Unlike starches, fibers resist enzymatic digestion in the small intestine, and are therefore fermented by microbes in the colon.
11. Fiber provides short-chain fatty acids for intestinal tract health, normalizes gastrointestinal motility, improves bowel function and increases the water content of feces.
12. In general, foods containing slowly fermentable fiber sources have lower overall dry matter digestibility than foods without fiber or those containing rapidly fermentable fiber sources.
13. Ten amino acids are essential for dogs and 11 for cats. Although nonessential amino acids can be synthesized from carbon and nitrogen by the body, they are critical for protein assimilation in the body and essential for metabolic reactions as essential amino acids. Animals don't have a protein requirement per se, but amino acid requirements.
14. Trauma, infection, severe sepsis and burns increase protein turnover and nitrogen losses.
15. Taurine is an essential amino acid for cats. Cats have minimal ability to synthesize taurine and have obligatory losses due to the necessity for conjugating bile acids to taurine.
16. Protein excesses are found in pet foods for several reasons. Some pet food companies perpetuate the myth that dogs are carnivores and that meat-based, high-protein foods are somehow more natural and better for dogs than lower protein foods or ones that contain both plant and animal sources of protein. Foods with higher protein content don't build more muscle in animals or result in a better coat. The excess protein is simply used as an expensive source of energy.
17. Lipids supply energy and essential fatty acids and are critical for absorption of fat-soluble vitamins.
18. On a per weight basis, the energy value of dietary fat is approximately 2.25 times that of protein or carbohydrate.
19. Deficiencies of essential fatty acids impair wound healing, cause a dry lusterless coat and scaly skin and change the lipid film on the skin, which may predispose the animal to skin infection.
20. Minerals are structural components of organs and tissues, constituents of body fluids and tissues (electrolytes) and catalysts and cofactors in enzymes.
21. In general, different forms of trace minerals differ in availability, i.e., sulfate and chloride forms are more available than carbonate forms, which are more available than oxides. Iron oxide and copper oxide are poorly available.
22. Vitamins are fat or water soluble and have many diverse functions including cofactors in enzymatic reactions, DNA synthesis, bone development, blood clotting, nutrient metabolism and release of energy.
23. Clinically, multiple B-vitamin deficiencies occur more often than single vitamin deficiencies. Therefore, B-vitamin deficiencies are often treated as a group.
24. Commercial pet foods are fortified to meet an animal's vitamin requirement for a given lifestage and to overcome processing and storage losses.

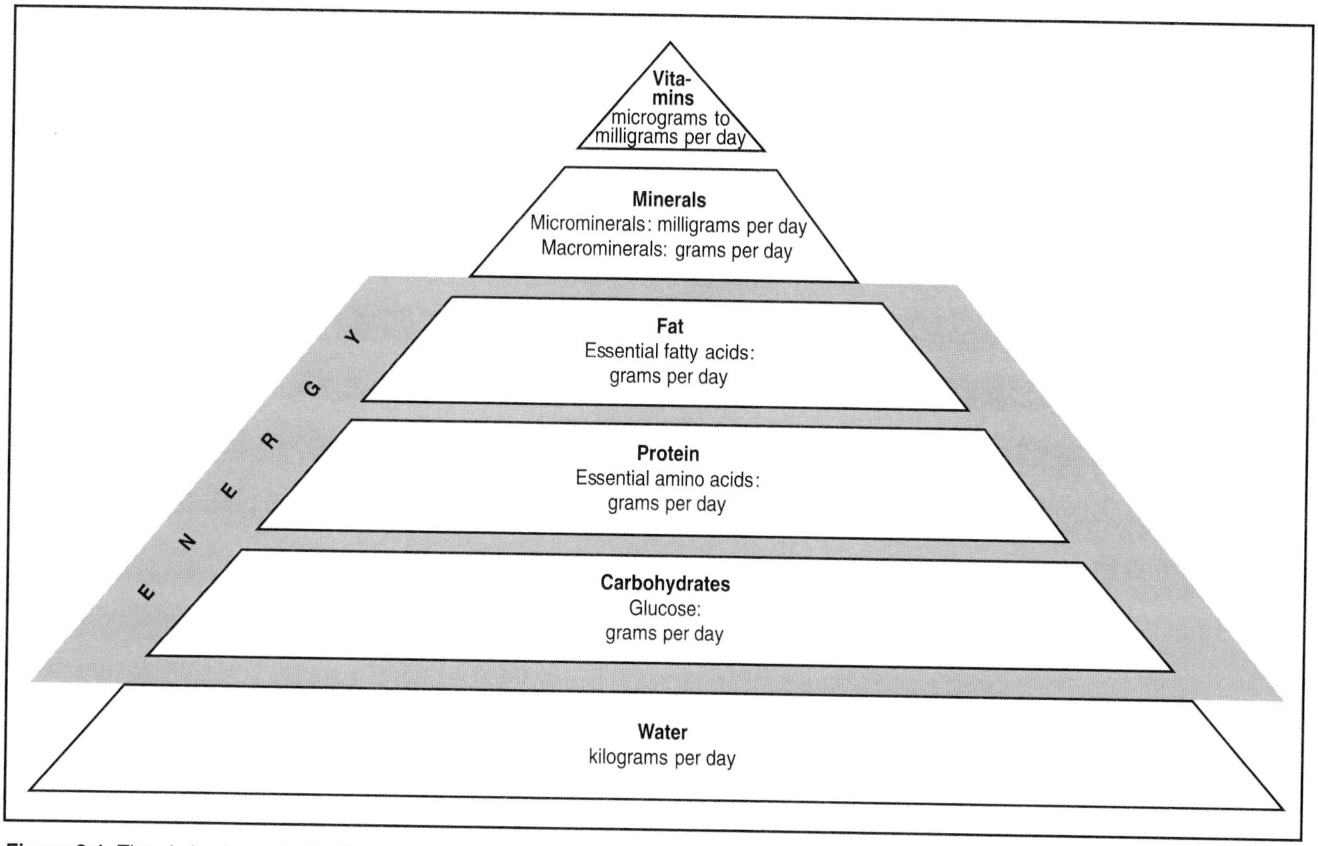

Vitamins
micrograms to milligrams per day
Minerals
Microminerals: milligrams per day
Macrominerals: grams per day
ENERGY
Fat
Essential fatty acids:
grams per day
Protein
Essential amino acids:
grams per day
Carbohydrates
Glucose:
grams per day
Water
kilograms per day

Figure 2-1. The six basic nutrients. Carbohydrates, fats and proteins may be used for energy but also serve as structural components.

3. Water assists in the regulation of body temperature. Water has a high specific heat (specific heat = amount of heat necessary to raise 1 g of water 1°C. Specific heat of water = 1). Large changes in heat production can take place within an animal with very little change in body temperature. This property also allows for heat to be circulated. Water has a high latent heat of vaporization. Water helps regulate body temperature when it is evaporated from the skin and respiratory tract. Large amounts of heat are required to evaporate small amounts of water; therefore, much heat can be lost with little loss of water.
4. Water provides shape and resilience to the body. Significant negative water balance can result in clinical dehydration. One manifestation of dehydration is loss of skin elasticity. As a major constituent of body fluids, water helps lubricate the joints and eyes, provides protective cushioning for the nervous system and aids in gas exchange in respiration by keeping the alveoli of the lungs moist and expanded.

Water is one of the largest constituents of the animal body, varying from 40 to greater than 80% of the total. The percentage of water in the body of animals varies with species, condition and age. Generally, lean body mass contains 70 to 80% water and 20 to 25% protein, whereas adipose tissue contains 10 to 15% water and 75 to 80% fat. The younger and leaner the animal, the more water it contains. Conversely, the fatter the animal, the lower its water content.

As animals become adults, they require proportionately less water on a weight basis because they consume less food per unit of body weight, thus, there is less urinary water loss. In addition, adult animals have less surface area per unit of body weight resulting in less evaporation from the skin.

Function/performance
Reduced intake
High intake
Optimal range
Deficiency
Toxicity
Minimum requirement
Nutrient intake

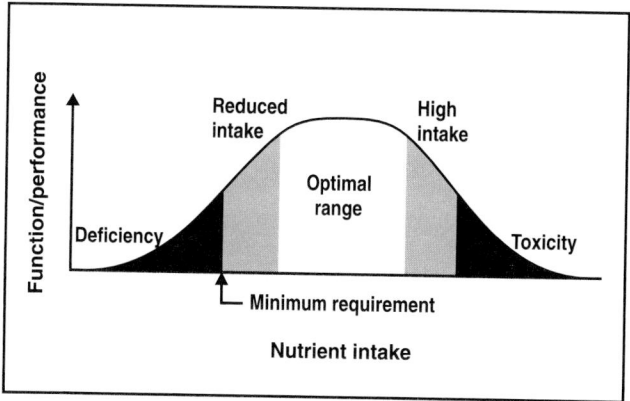

Figure 2-2. Total biologic dose-response curve. This response curve spans intakes ranging from deficiency to adequacy to toxicity. The intakes at which these three phases reside, and the width of the range between deficiency and toxicity vary widely among nutrients. (Adapted from Underwood EJ, Mertz W. Introduction. In: Mertz W, ed. Trace Elements in Human and Animal Nutrition, 5th ed. San Diego, CA: Academic Press Inc, 1987; 1.)

Water Quality

Water quality can be affected by salinity, nitrates and nitrites, toxic organic and inorganic chemicals and microbial contamination. A routine measurement of water quality is the concentration of all constituents dissolved in water, referred

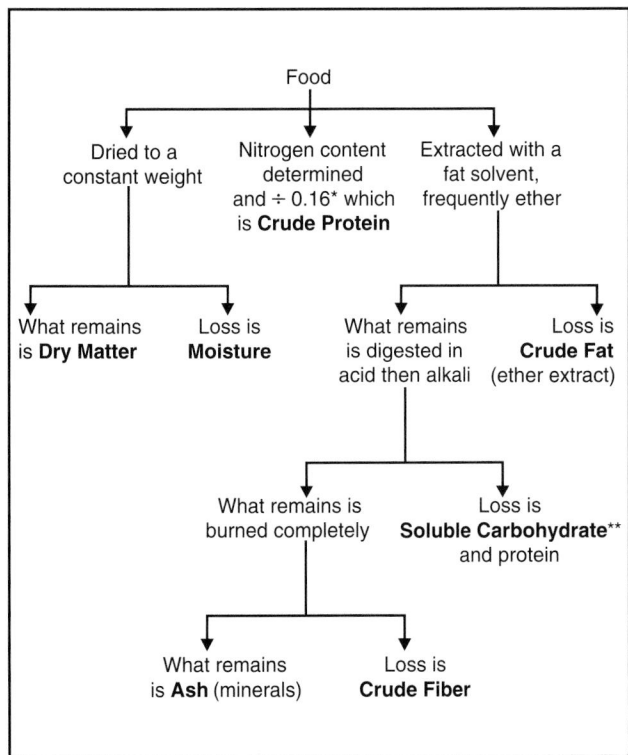

Figure 2-3. Proximate analysis of foods.
*Proteins contain 16 ± 2% nitrogen. Crude protein = nitrogen x 6.25 or nitrogen ÷ 0.16. Protein levels determined by this method will be erroneously high if the food contains non-protein nitrogen such as urea or ammonia.
**Frequently called nitrogen-free extract (NFE). NFE is determined as the difference between 100% and the amount of everything else in the food (i.e., 100% – % moisture – % crude protein – % fat – % crude fiber – % ash.) Any errors in these analyses also will appear in the NFE value.

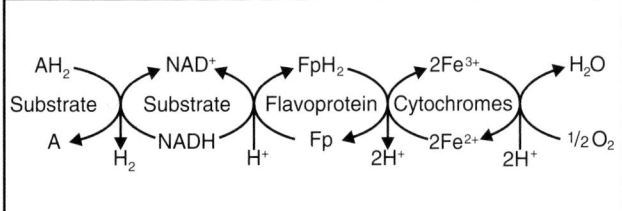

Figure 2-4. Electron transport chain and metabolic water production. Key: NAD = nicotinamide-adenine dinucleotide, NADH = the reduced form of NAD, Fe = iron, H_2O = water, O_2 = oxygen, H/H_2 = hydrogen, A = metabolite, Fp = flavoprotein.

to as "total dissolved solids" (TDS). Salinity (salt content of water) is synonymous with TDS as an indication of the total ionic concentration in fresh water. Water containing less than 5,000 parts per million (ppm or mg/liter) TDS is generally considered acceptable for consumption, whereas water containing more than 7,000 ppm is considered unsuitable for livestock or poultry.[1] Although the livestock and poultry TDS values are assumed to apply to dogs and cats, water containing less than 500 ppm TDS is considered acceptable for human drinking water and is a better recommendation for dogs and cats.[2]

Standard water quality testing (e.g., nitrates, sulfates, bacterial contamination) typically can be addressed

through local public health departments because the source of water consumed by dogs and cats is often the same as that consumed by people. Serious concerns about water quality (toxic inorganic chemicals or pesticides) need to be addressed through testing at commercial analytical laboratories capable of screening water for pesticide residues and other chemicals.

Mineral Content

Water "hardness," or the sum of calcium and magnesium salts in relation to calcium carbonate, has little effect on dog or cat well-being. High levels of magnesium in hard water have been implicated as a cause of urolithiasis in cats; however, the amount of magnesium consumed in drinking water is insignificant when compared with the amount consumed in food (i.e., usually a 10,000-fold difference).[3] Cats prone to urolithiasis may benefit from consumption of distilled water rather than hard water that has been softened with a sodium chloride water softener.

Nitrates

Nitrates are widely dispersed in the environment and can be a health hazard for all animals when significant amounts are present in drinking water. Although the concentration of nitrate ions (NO_3) commonly found in drinking water is well-tolerated by dogs and cats, nitrite (NO_2, the reduced form of nitrate) is readily absorbed and can be toxic. At toxic levels, nitrites oxidize the iron in hemoglobin to form methemoglobin, thus reducing the oxygen-carrying capacity of blood.

Frequently, nitrates in the water supply indicate bacterial contamination. Bacterial reduction of nitrate to nitrite is promoted as the pH increases in the intestinal tract. Bacteria in contaminated water sources can convert nitrate to nitrite. The safe upper limits for nitrate and nitrite determined for livestock drinking water are 1,320 ppm and 33 ppm, respectively. For human drinking water, the safe upper limit is based on the total amount of nitrogen derived from the combination of nitrate (30.4% nitrogen) and nitrite (22.6% nitrogen) and is 10 ppm of nitrogen. No safe upper limits have been established for dogs or cats. The livestock limits should be used until studies are conducted to determine the upper limits for dogs and cats.

Bacteria

The accepted criterion of the sanitary quality of water for people has been the absence of the coliform group of bacteria. Although all coliform bacteria are not pathogens, many possess this potential; their presence indicates water is able to support infectious bacteria or viruses. The presence of bacteria also can be predicted through results of other qualitative tests made on water samples. Bacteria proportionally accompany chemical compounds such as nitrites, nitrates and phosphates. Generally, if levels of these chemical compounds are high, the bacterial level will also be high.

Water Requirements

Water requirements are related to maintaining water balance in the animal. Body water lost by urination, defecation, evaporation and perspiration is replaced by one of two sources: 1) water derived from metabolism of nutrients and 2) water consumed as a liquid or as a portion of the food.

Oxygen is the final acceptor of hydrogen ions cleaved from energy-supplying nutrients (carbohydrates, fats and proteins) during the generation of ATP (Figure 2-4). This combination of hydrogen and oxygen is called metabolic water. Metabolic water can account for 5 to 10% of the total water requirement. An average of 13 ml of water is produced per 100 kcal of metabolizable energy (ME) ingested.[4] Oxidation of 1 g of glucose, fat and protein results in the production of 0.556, 1.071 and 0.396 g of metabolic water, respectively.[5] Glycogen also contains large amounts of water (3 to 4 g water/g of glycogen) that are released as glycogen is used.[6]

Dogs and cats meet most of their water requirement through water ingested as food or drink. Animals consuming commercial moist foods will drink less liquid than those fed dry foods because of the higher water content of moist foods (>75% water). This finding may have important diagnostic implications. (See sidebar "The Effect of Fasting on Water Intake: Diagnostic Implications.") As a general guideline, the daily water requirement of dogs and cats, expressed in ml/day, is roughly equivalent to the daily energy requirement (DER) in kcal/day (for dogs 1.6 x resting energy requirement [RER], for cats 1.2 x RER).[7,8] The amount of water consumed by mature, healthy, nonreproducing dogs and cats at a comfortable environmental temperature is about 2.5 times the amount of dry matter consumed as food.

Domestic cats, descendants of desert animals, normally form a more concentrated urine than dogs. Thus, water requirements for cats may be less than that for dogs. The need for water can be met by supplying clean, fresh water to pets at all times. (See sidebar "Measuring Water Intake in Dogs and Cats.")

Factors Affecting Water Requirements

Although the daily water requirements of dogs and cats are well-defined, practical estimates of daily water intake are less clearly understood. In addition to metabolic needs, animals of all sizes consume water to meet a variety of needs, including physical and social. Factors such as body size (surface area), lactation, ambient temperature, type and amount of food ingested, general state of health, stress, water losses through excretion or evaporation and individual animal differences influence the absolute requirement for water.

Water Deficiency and Excess

Deficits of more than a few percent of total body water are incompatible with health, and large water deficits (i.e., 15 to 20% of body weight) lead to death. Water deprivation can lead to death within days, whereas animals may survive for weeks without food. Under normal circumstances, thirst ensures that water intake meets or exceeds the requirement for water. Inadequate water intake reduces food intake, which reduces production in dogs and cats (growth, lactation, reproduction and physical activity). Decreased water intake may result from reduced availability, water temperature extremes or poor quality. Water intoxication (overconsumption) is extremely rare in normal, healthy dogs and cats but can be induced in animals offered water free choice after prolonged dehydration.

The Effect of Fasting on Water Intake: Diagnostic Implications

Fasting eliminates water available from food, alters the amount an animal drinks and decreases total water intake. Figure 1 shows the effect of fasting on drinking water intake, water intake from food and total water intake for dogs previously consuming moist or dry food. Total water intake decreased dramatically in both groups; however, the change in the amount consumed as drinking water was quite different. Figure 1, Panel A shows the response of dogs previously fed a moist food. Because most water intake for these dogs previously was from the food, only a small amount was supplied by drinking water. During fasting, water supplied by food was no longer available, thus the amount drunk increased. Figure 1, Panel B shows the response of dogs previously eating a dry food. Because these dogs obtained little water from the food, a large amount was supplied from drinking water. During fasting, less water was needed and the amount of drinking water consumed decreased.

The influence of the water content of the previous food on the amount of water consumed as drinking water may become important diagnostically. An owner who reports that a dog is not eating but is drinking twice as much water may be describing the normal response of a dog that has stopped eating a moist food, rather than a dog that is truly polydipsic. Conversely, dogs that had been eating dry food may appear to nearly stop drinking during periods of anorexia. These effects emphasize the importance of accurately assessing the food(s) and feeding method.

BIBLIOGRAPHY
Lewis LD, Morris ML Jr. Small Animal Clinical Nutrition. Topeka, KS: Mark Morris Associates, 1983; 5-6–5-7.

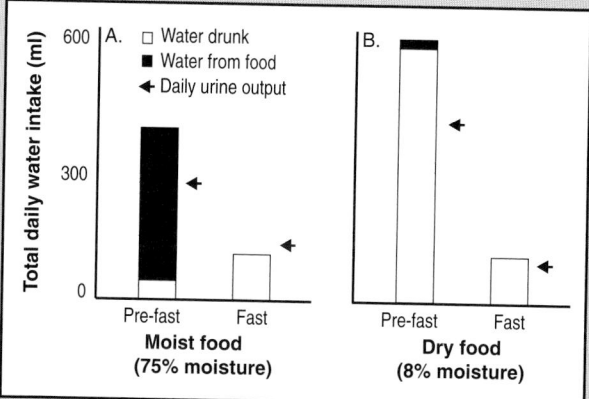

Figure 1. Effect of fasting on the amount of water consumed in the food and drunk by beagles previously consuming moist or dry foods.

ENERGY

Definition

Living organisms need energy to fuel all body functions. The ultimate source of all energy is the sun, which enables plants to make energy-containing nutrients from carbon dioxide and water through photosynthesis (Figure

Measuring Water Intake in Dogs and Cats

Daily water intake in dogs and cats can be measured easily with common household tools. The following steps should allow pet owners to obtain a reasonable estimate of daily water intake.
1. Determine daily water intake requirements (in ml) by calculating RER of the animal and multiplying by 1.6 for dogs and 1.2 for cats.
2. Using a fluid cup measure (1 cup = 227 ml), measure the amount of water to offer the animal throughout the day in a single container.
3. Fill the water bowl with an appropriate amount of water from the single container throughout the day, ensuring fresh water is available at all times.
4. Eliminate the animal's access to other sources of water (e.g., toilet bowls, sinks, etc.).
5. If more water is needed beyond the calculated amount, carefully measure more water into the container and account for the additional amount when making intake calculations.
6. Measure the water remaining at the end of the day (sum of that remaining in the water bowl and container) and determine the amount of water consumed by subtracting the remaining water from the total amount measured during the day.

2-5). Animals eat plants or other animals that have eaten plants. Although energy itself is not a nutrient, fats, carbohydrates and amino acids contain energy in the form of chemical bonds and are the energy-containing nutrients in food. Once eaten, these nutrients are digested, absorbed and transported to body cells where they are used to generate energy.

The energy content of nutrients can be determined by burning and measuring the amount of heat that is released. The body obtains the energy from nutrients by oxidation to carbon dioxide and water, but does not use heat for fuel directly, although heat is used for body temperature regulation. Instead, the body captures nutrient energy in energy-containing compounds through a series of enzymatic biochemical reactions. The most important energy-containing compound is adenosine triphosphate (ATP).

In nutrition, the joule is the internationally agreed upon unit of measure for energy.[1,2] The joule expresses the daily energy requirement (DER) of an animal by its power needs or watts. One watt equals one joule per second. In the United States, a more commonly used energy measure is the calorie, which expresses energy in terms of heat. A calorie is the amount of heat required to raise the temperature of 1 g of water from 14.5°C to 15.5°C. A kilocalorie (kcal) is 1,000 calories and a kilojoule (kJ) is 1,000 joules. Kilocalories and joules can be interconverted using the formula 1 kcal = 4.184 kJ.

Function

The biochemical reactions that take place in the body either use or release energy. Anabolic reactions require energy and, conversely, catabolic reactions release energy. ATP and other energy-trapping compounds pick up part of the energy released from one process and transfer it to the other process. For example, in the process of oxidation of nutrients (glucose, fatty acids and amino acids), the chemical reactions in the biochemical pathways of glycolysis, β-oxidation, deamination, tricarboxylic acid (TCA) cycle and oxidative phosphorylation simultaneously generate and consume ATP. However, the net effect of these reactions is the generation of ATP. Biochemical reactions that occur in glycogen synthesis, fatty acid synthesis, protein synthesis, gluconeogenesis, protein turnover, Cori cycle, sodium-potassium ion pump, ureagenesis and muscular contractions all require ATP.

In summary, animals use energy for pumping ions, molecular synthesis and to activate contractile proteins (Figure 2-5). These three processes essentially describe the total use of energy by an animal. Without energy supplied by food, these reactions would rapidly cease and death would occur.

Importance of Energy in the Diet of Dogs and Cats

The energy content of a food ultimately determines the quantity of food that is eaten each day and therefore affects the amount of all other nutrients that an animal ingests. Animals should be fed enough food to meet their energy requirements and the non-energy nutrients in the food should be balanced relative to energy density to ensure adequate nutrient intake. Animals eating an energy-dense food consume less of the food to meet energy needs; therefore, the concentration of other critical nutrients must be higher to ensure sufficient intake. Conversely, animals must consume more of a low-energy food to meet energy needs. Therefore, the concentration of non-energy nutrients should be lower to avoid excessive intake and maintain nutrient balance. If the energy density of the food is too low, food intake may be restricted by the physical limitations of the gastrointestinal (GI) tract. Such a food is referred to as being "bulk limited." Low-energy, bulk-limited foods designed for weight loss (See Chapter 13.) can be formulated to provide adequate intake of non-energy nutrients.

Energy Metabolism

Digestion, Absorption and Excretion

Digestion and absorption of the energy-supplying nutrients (protein, carbohydrate and fat) are discussed in other sections of this chapter. The total amount of potential energy in food is termed gross energy (GE). GE in food is determined by burning the food and measuring the heat produced in a bomb calorimeter. Animals are not able to use 100% of the GE in foods because some of the food energy is lost in the form of solid, liquid and gaseous excretions as well as radiant heat.

Nutritionists have partitioned dietary energy based on the losses that occur (Figure 2-6). Digestible energy (DE) refers to the GE content of food minus energy lost in feces (FE). Metabolizable energy (ME) is DE minus energy lost in urine and as intestinal gaseous products of digestion. Animals continuously produce heat as a result of basal metabolism and physical work. Heat production increases after a meal. This increase in heat due to food ingestion is called the heat increment of food (HI). HI consists of the heat of intestinal microbial fermentation and heat produced in intermediary metabolism as a result of using nutrients. The energy of HI is wasted except when the environmental temperature is below an animal's critical temperature. In this situation, the HI is used to keep the body warm.

Subtracting the HI from the ME of food gives the net energy (NE) of food. NE can also be partitioned into the amount used for maintenance (NE_m) and the amount used for production (NE_p: growth, pregnancy, lactation, exercise). NE values of foods and ingredients are typically used when discussing livestock nutrition (beef cattle, dairy cattle, swine), whereas DE and ME are more typically used in canine and feline nutrition. Although not commonly measured and used, the NE principles of partitioning energy for maintenance and production separately hold true for dogs and cats.

Energy Use

The initial biochemical reactions by which energy is derived from carbohydrates, fats and amino acids are different. However, all three nutrients eventually go through a final common pathway for energy generation called the TCA cycle. Glucose derived from dietary carbohydrates is first oxidized through the glycolysis pathway to yield pyruvate and then acetyl-CoA. Acetyl-CoA is oxidized in the TCA cycle producing carbon dioxide, and electrons, which are captured by important heme-containing compounds called cytochromes (Figure 2-7). Electrons produced in the TCA cycle are shuttled by nicotinamide-adenine dinucleotide (NAD) and flavin adenine dinucleotide (FAD) to the electron transport chain where the cytochromes participate in electron transfer through valence changes in their heme iron (Figure 2-4). NAD and FAD are synthesized from the vitamins niacin and riboflavin, respectively. The electrons are passed between successive oxidation/reduction reactions to the end of the chain where oxygen accepts the final electrons and is converted to water. ATP is formed as the electrons are passed down the chain (oxidative phosphorylation). A net of 36 ATP is generated for each molecule of glucose that is oxidized to carbon dioxide and water.

Fatty acids and glycerol from dietary fats are initially oxidized to acetyl-CoA by the β-oxidation pathway (Fig-

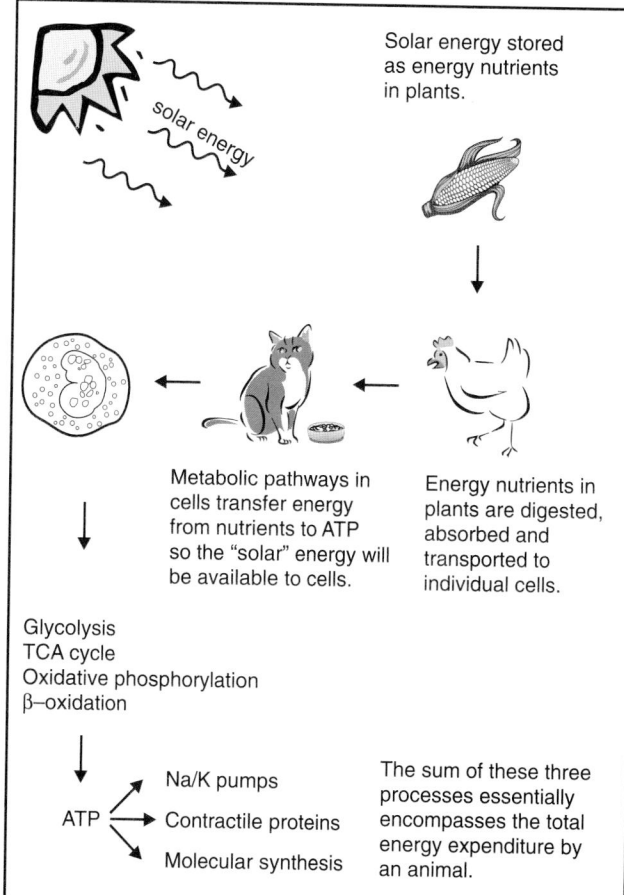

Figure 2-5. Schematic of how animals obtain and use energy. Plants use solar energy to produce energy-containing nutrients (i.e., proteins, fats and carbohydrates) via photosynthesis. Animals eat the energy-containing plant nutrients and other animals. Once eaten, energy-containing nutrients are digested, absorbed and metabolized by body cells to release energy that fuels the processes that sustain life.

ure 2-8). Acetyl-CoA is then oxidized in the TCA cycle and ATP is generated via oxidative phosphorylation in the electron transport chain. The number of ATP generated from fatty acid oxidation depends on the length of the carbon chain and degree of unsaturation. For example, myristic acid (C14:0) yields 112 ATP, palmitic acid

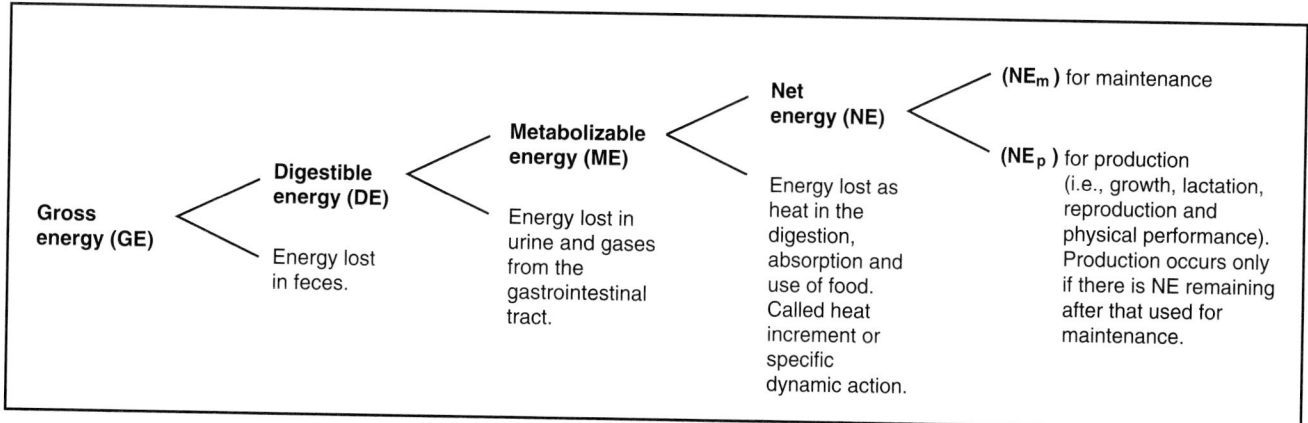

Figure 2-6. Schematic of how total gross energy of a food is partitioned into digestible energy, metabolizable energy and net energy. Net energy can be further partitioned into energy used for maintenance (NE_m) and production (NE_p).

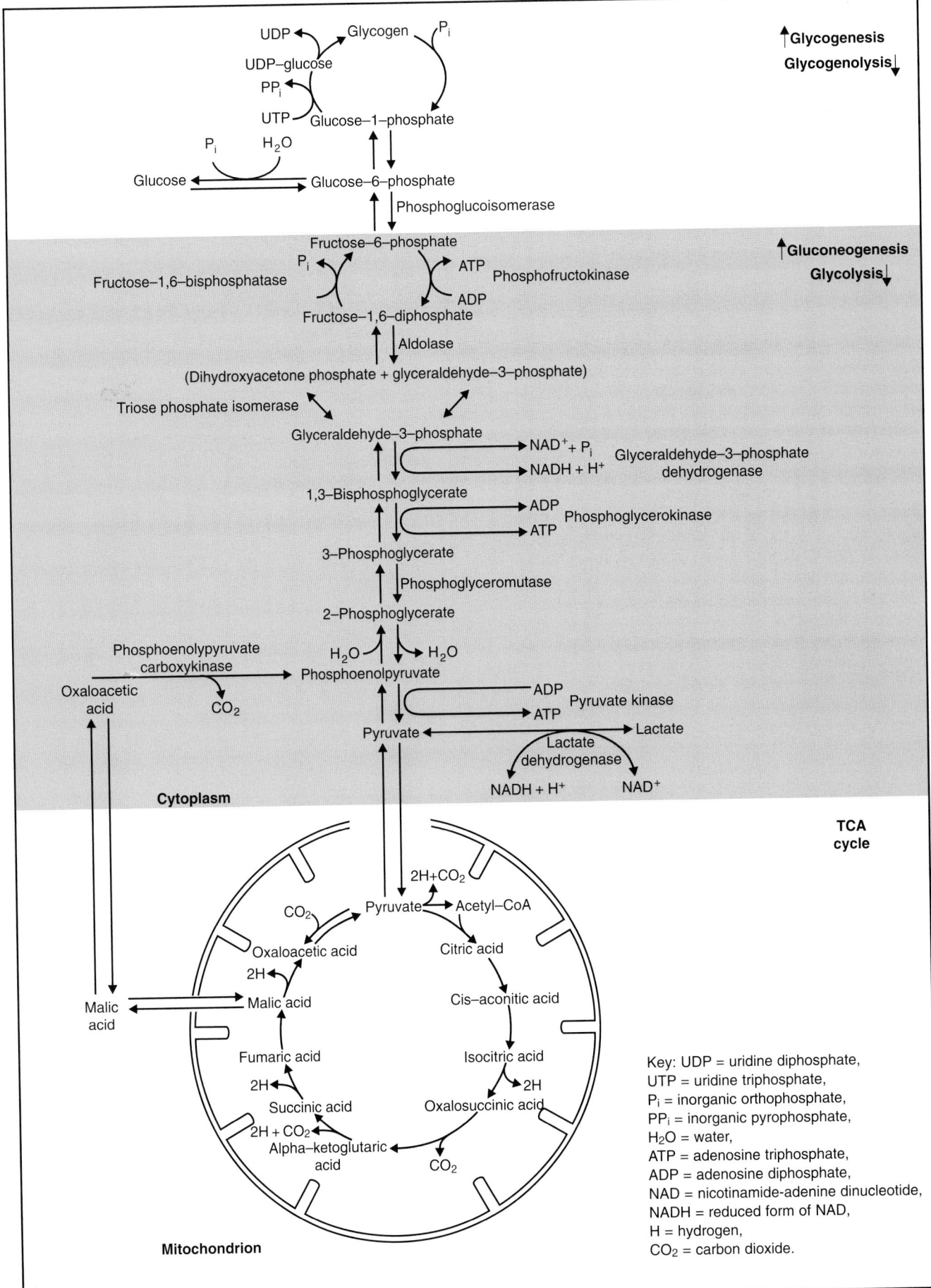

Figure 2-7. Biochemical pathways of glycogenesis, glycogenolysis, gluconeogenesis, glycolysis and the tricarboxylic acid (TCA) cycle.

(C16:0) 129 ATP, palmitoleic acid (C16:1) 127 ATP, stearic acid (C18:0) 146 ATP and oleic acid (C18:1) 144 ATP.

Amino acids used for energy are deaminated or transaminated to yield a carbohydrate moiety and ammonia, which is converted to urea. The carbon skeleton enters the TCA cycle and ATP is formed in the electron transport chain. The number of ATP generated from oxidation of amino acids to water, carbon dioxide and urea varies, but ranges from six ATP from glycine to 42 ATP from tryptophan.

Energy Storage

ATP is the usable form of energy for body cells, but not a good energy storage molecule because it is used quickly after being formed. Glycogen and triacylglycerides are better storage forms of energy. Production and use of ATP are equally balanced through a series of control mechanisms that monitor the amount of ATP available. After a meal containing adequate energy, the total body metabolism is generally anabolic; the body uses energy for synthetic reactions and tissue accretion (e.g., growth, reproduction). After the body has enough energy to meet demands, the pathways of glycolysis, β-oxidation, transamination, deamination and the TCA cycle are slowed. The pathways of glycogen and fat synthesis are simultaneously accelerated and excess dietary energy is stored as glycogen and body fat. These energy stores can then be used to generate ATP later when needed. Generally, in fasting animals, when the body needs energy, it uses glycogen first, fat stores second and finally, as a last resort, amino acids from body protein. (See Chapter 12.) In fed animals, food energy is primarily used for meeting body energy needs, thus preserving body tissues by preventing catabolism. Further discussions of use and control of body energy stores during exercise can be found in Chapter 10.

Differences in the amount of energy consumed and that expended by the body can clearly result in changes in body weight, growth rate and body composition (especially body fat). Excess energy intake and storage relative to energy expenditure is a common problem in pet dogs and cats (e.g., obesity). Obese pets are at increased risk for developing a variety of health problems. (See Chapter 13.) Excess energy intake in growing large- and giant-breed puppies may be related to developmental skeletal abnormalities. (See Chapter 17.) Conversely, inadequate energy intake relative to expenditure may occur in animals with heart disease and cancer resulting in cachexia (See Chapters 18 and 25.) and in vigorously exercising dogs such as sled dogs. (See Chapter 10.)

Energy Analyses

The energy content of food (Figure 2-6) is most reliably based on data collected in feeding studies.[3,4] ME determinations use direct measurement of energy intake and energy lost in feces and urine obtained from digestion or metabolism studies. Energy lost as expired gases is usually accounted for by standard assumptions based on published research.

Measuring ME in animals can be expensive and time-consuming. Therefore, standard equations have been developed based on proximate analyses of foods that yield reasonably good average ME values for pet foods.[4-8] (See Chapter 1.) The Association of American Feed Control Officials (AAFCO) has published accepted protocols for the determination of

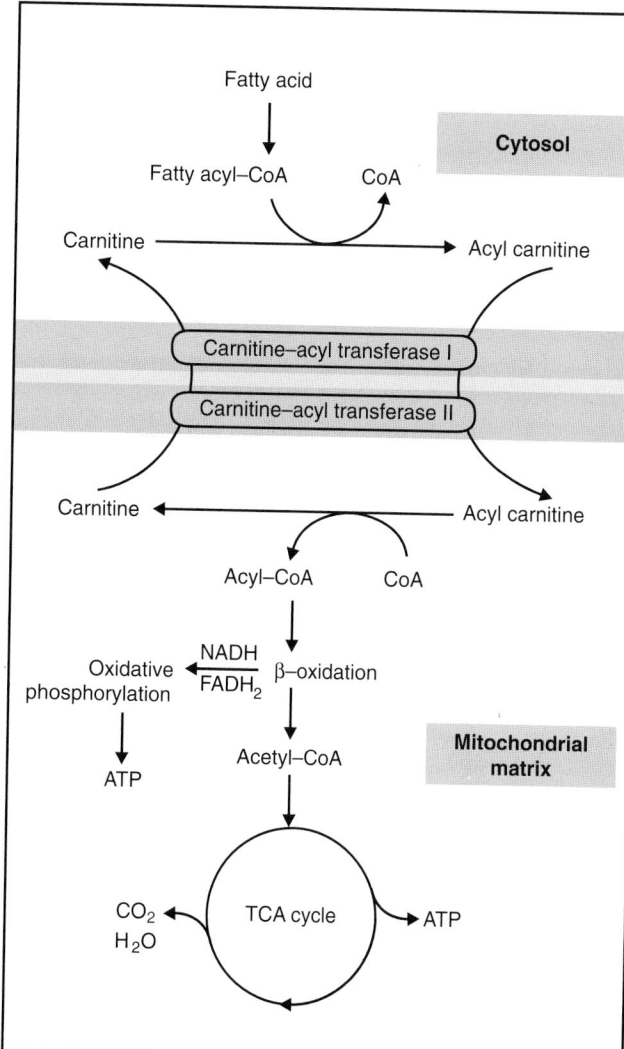

Figure 2-8. This diagram depicts metabolism of long-chain fatty acids for energy production. Entry of long-chain fatty acids into mitochondria is facilitated by carnitine-acyl transferase enzymes. Medium-chain and short-chain fatty acids bypass this important regulatory step and enter the mitochondria unaided. β-oxidation is an energy-yielding catabolic process involving fatty acids that occurs within the mitochondrial matrix. The resultant products are acetyl-CoA, which enters the TCA cycle for further metabolism (to CO_2, water and ATP) and reduced coenzymes (NADH/FADH$_2$) for ATP production by oxidative phosphorylation.

ME of dogs and cat foods.[4] (See sidebar "AAFCO Protocol for Determination of Metabolizable Energy of Dog and Cat Foods.") The AAFCO method of ME calculation can be applied to cat and dog foods and assumes an average apparent digestibility of 80% for protein, 90% for crude fat and 84% for carbohydrate. The digestion coefficients are then multiplied by energy values of 4.4, 9.4 and 4.15 kcal/g for protein, fat and carbohydrate, respectively. The resulting values of 3.5, 8.5 and 3.5 kcal/g are reasonable estimates of the ME derived from protein, fat and carbohydrate in typical commercial pet foods. (See Appendix C.) The method assumes no energy is derived from crude fiber, water or ash. This method overestimates the ME content of foods high in fiber or ash or foods with very low protein, fat and carbohydrate digestibility. Likewise, the equation underestimates the ME content of highly digestible and low-fiber foods.

AAFCO Protocol for Determination of Metabolizable Energy of Dog and Cat Foods

Animal feeding studies are the most desirable means for measuring the metabolizable energy (ME) of a food. The following steps summarize what is involved when investigators conduct a ME study using dogs or cats, according to protocols established by the Association of American Feed Control Officials (AAFCO).

1. Feed a group of animals a known amount of food each day for a given number of days (typically five to seven days for dogs and between five and 15 days for cats).
2. Collect and record the weight of feces excreted on the same days as food measurements were made.
3. Analyze the gross energy content of samples of the food (GE) and feces (FE) by bomb calorimetry. Bomb calorimetry involves placing a known amount of the food or feces into a bomb compartment submerged in a water bath. Oxygen is added to the compartment and ignited with an electrical spark and the increase in water temperature that surrounds the bomb is measured as the sample burns. Urinary energy (UE) can be measured directly by collecting urine and then determining the GE of the urine. Alternatively, UE can be estimated by measuring protein digestibility and then using a factor that predicts the energy content of the urine. Energy from intestinal gases is typically ignored because it constitutes a very small proportion of energy lost in dogs and cats.
4. ME of the food is then calculated as GE minus FE and UE.

BIBLIOGRAPHY

Association of American Feed Control Officials. Official Publication, 1998; 143-147.

Nott HMR, Rigby SI, Johnson JV, et al. Design of digestibility trials for dogs and cats. Journal of Nutrition 1994; 124: 2582S-2583S.

Shields RG, Kigin PD, Izquierdo JA, et al. Counting calories. Caloric claims: Measuring digestibility and metabolizable energy. Petfood Industry 1994; Jan/Feb(1): 4-10.

Estimation of the NE of a food requires measurement of the heat lost. Heat production can be measured directly using an animal calorimeter (direct calorimetry) or estimated indirectly from the exchange of oxygen and carbon dioxide (indirect or respiratory calorimetry).[2,3] (See sidebar "Calorimetry.") Partitioning NE into NE_m and NE_p involves estimating the energy retained by the animal and will be discussed below.

Energy Requirements

Knowledge of energy requirements is needed to determine how much food to feed to an animal. Determining energy requirements involves measuring energy expenditure of an animal under a defined set of physiologic and environmental conditions. Energy expenditure studies typically involve carefully accounting for all components of the energy budget of an animal including: 1) energy consumed in food, 2) energy losses from the body via urine, feces and intestinal gases, 3) heat produced by metabolism and/or physical work, 4) retention of energy as tissue accretion and 5) secretion of energy as milk.[2] Because the first law of thermodynamics states that energy is conserved, energy intake by the animal minus all energy lost must equal the energy retained or secreted as shown by the following equation:

$$RE = GE - FE - UE - GPD - HP$$

where GE = gross energy intake, FE = fecal energy excreted, UE = urine energy excreted, GPD = gaseous products of digestion, HP = heat production and RE = retained energy primarily in the form of lean and fat tissues or energy secreted in milk. The above equation can be simplified to three terms by substituting metabolizable energy (ME) for the GE – FE – UE – GPD portion of the equation. The simplified energy budget equation is now:

$$RE = ME - HP$$

Heat production is the sum of heat lost through radiation, convection, conduction and evaporation and heat stored in the body as exemplified by an increase in body temperature. Heat is lost when food is metabolized and when physical work is performed. When no food is given, no physical work is done and an animal is in a thermoneutral environment, heat production results from basal cellular metabolism. In this case, the term basal energy expenditure can be used as an alternative to heat production. Thus, when heat production is measured, we are measuring energy expenditure, and then energy expenditure is equated with energy requirements. Also, if energy retention is zero, then an animal is in energy equilibrium where HP equals ME. In this case, ME equals NE_m. The third term can be derived if two of the three terms of the energy budget equation are known. Alternatively, if all three components are measured then there is added confidence in the energy requirement estimate.

Laboratory protocols and specialized equipment have been developed to measure the three major components of the energy budget. ME determinations have been discussed previously. See sidebar "Calorimetry" for information about whole animal calorimetry used to estimate HI. The primary forms of RE in animals are protein and fat, although a small and relatively constant proportion of carbohydrate is stored as glycogen. The gold standard method for measuring RE in farm animals is the comparative slaughter method in which the energy content of an animal is determined by bomb calorimetry on ground carcass samples.[3] Other methods have been developed that are noninvasive, less costly and allow for repeat measurements on the same subject. Underwater weighing, bioelectrical impedance, anthropometric measurements (triceps skin-fold thickness, upper arm muscle area, body mass index) and dual energy x-ray absorptiometry (DEXA) are commonly used to estimate body fat and lean proportions of people. Some of these methods have been adapted for use in dogs and cats. In recent years, DEXA technology has become popular and has been used to provide rapid and repeatable estimates of body composition of dogs and cats.[9,10]

For animals under maintenance conditions, when no tissue is accreted or milk secreted, the RE component of the energy balance equation is theoretically zero; therefore, the HI is the estimate of the energy expended for maintenance of adult animals. In growing, pregnant or lactating animals, the RE portion of the energy budget is not zero; therefore, both the RE and HI should be measured to

Calorimetry

Calorimetry is the measurement of heat. Calorimetry has been used to understand how the body metabolizes food energy for hundreds of years. The discovery by Lavoiser and LaPlace in 1783 that heat produced by animals was related to oxygen consumption and carbon dioxide formation and was analogous to burning of a candle was revolutionary and signaled the beginning of the study of energy use by calorimetry. Because animals do not store heat, the quantity of heat lost from the animal is equal to the quantity produced. Calorimetry allows measurement of the heat lost (heat production, HP).

HP is one of the terms in the energy balance equation: HP = ME – RE. Because HP has been equated with energy expenditure and energy requirements, the measurement of heat really means measurement of energy requirements. Heat production can be measured directly (direct calorimetry) or estimated from respiratory exchange (indirect or respiratory calorimetry).

DIRECT CALORIMETRY

In direct calorimetry, an animal is placed in an airtight, insulated chamber. The heat lost from the body includes that lost by radiation, conduction and convection and by evaporation of water from skin and respiratory surfaces (e.g., lungs). The heat produced by the animal is measured as the difference in temperature between inside and outside of the chamber over time.

There are several different designs for chambers and ways to measure heat that give rise to various methods of determining heat production directly. Most direct calorimetry systems are relatively expensive to construct and operate, somewhat complex to operate, require confinement of the subjects, but are very accurate and reliable.

Direct calorimetry is suited to energy expenditure measurements for research purposes and, in the clinical setting, for well patients and moderately sick patients. Direct calorimetry with an enclosed chamber is not feasible for very sick patients that are attached to ventilators or those requiring constant supervision and intervention.

INDIRECT CALORIMETRY

Indirect calorimetry involves calculation of heat production by measuring respiratory exchange of oxygen and carbon dioxide. Food carbohydrates and fats are oxidized by the body to yield heat, water and carbon dioxide as shown in these example equations.

Glucose $(C_6H_{12}O_6) + 6O_2 \rightarrow 6CO_2 + 6H_2O + heat$ (2.82MJ)
Triglyceride tripalmitin $C_3H_5O_3(C_{16}H_{31})_3 + 74O_2 \rightarrow 51CO_2 + 49H_2O + heat$ (32.02MJ)

The amount of heat generated from the consumption of one liter of oxygen is exactly known if only glucose or a single fat is oxidized, as well as for mixtures of the two. These thermal equivalents of oxygen are used to estimate heat production from oxygen consumption. Protein is incompletely oxidized because the body cannot use the nitrogen. Animals typically do not obtain energy exclusively from carbohydrate, fat or protein; rather, they oxidize mixtures. Because the ratio of the volume of carbon dioxide produced for each volume of oxygen used is different for carbohydrate, fat and protein, this ratio, known as the respiratory quotient (RQ) can be used to determine the proportions of each nutrient oxidized. The RQ is 1 $(6CO_2/6O_2)$ for carbohydrate, 0.7 $(51CO_2/72.5O_2)$ for fat, and 0.8 for protein. Some food energy is metabolized to hydrogen and methane by gut microflora.

The apparatus used to measure the respiratory exchange is called a respiratory chamber. As with direct calorimetry, there are several different methods for constructing chambers and measuring gas flow (oxygen and carbon dioxide) into and out of the chamber. Indirect calorimetry chambers typically are less complex and less costly to construct and maintain compared with direct calorimetry chambers. Energy expenditure calculated from indirect calorimetry measurements can be just as reliable and accurate as direct measures.

Oxygen and carbon dioxide exchange can be measured with a simple hood, canopy or expiratory collection device instead of a chamber. These systems are portable and are easier to use in clinical situations and in animals and people as they perform their daily activities. These more portable systems may not be as accurate as the chamber systems, but are less costly and highly flexible. Energy expenditure can be measured in very sick patients using a hood system when other methods are not suitable.

Knowledge of energy use is important to make accurate estimates of energy requirements to optimize the health of animals. Energy requirements vary with nutritional, genetic and environmental influences; interactions among the factors are complex. Therefore, it is easiest to isolate and measure the specific factors that alter energy expenditure (e.g., resting energy expenditure, thermic effect of food, breed, age, gender, energy expenditure due to growth, pregnancy, lactation and work) and then develop prediction equations for total energy requirements of the animal, taking into account all the relevant factors. Although both methods of calorimetry, direct and indirect, have technical challenges, each technique is useful in research and clinical practice. Calorimetry is important to build an understanding of factors that influence energy requirements.

BIBLIOGRAPHY

Blaxter K. In: Energy Metabolism in Animals and Man. Cambridge, UK: Cambridge University Press, 1989.

Levine JA, Morgan MY. Measurement of energy expenditure in man: A review of available methods. Journal of Nutritional Medicine 1990; 1: 325-343.

---

accurately predict the energy requirements for animals undergoing these production parameters.

Energy requirements have been given different names depending on the physiologic and environmental conditions under which the measurements were made (Table 2-1). Basal energy requirement (BER) represents energy needs for a normal, awake, fasting, resting animal in a thermoneutral environment. For dogs and cats, fasting overnight or for 12 hours is usually considered adequate. BER includes the energy needed to maintain cellular activity, respiration and circulation. BER is determined by measuring the energy expenditure under the stated conditions. Thus the terms BER and basal energy expenditure (BEE) are synonymous.

RER represents the energy requirement for a normal animal at rest under thermoneutral but not fasted conditions.[2] The amount of time between a meal and when measurements are made can affect the estimate of RER; therefore, they should be standardized between animals and experiments. RER also differs from BER because it includes energy expended for recovery from physical activity. Depending on the level of activity and time between cessation of activity and the energy expenditure determination, RER may range from almost the same value as BER to as much as 25% higher.[11] Therefore, the differences between BER and RER include energy needed for: 1) digestion, absorption and metabolism of food (heat

Table 2-1. Commonly used measurements of energy.

Basal energy requirement (BER): BER represents the energy requirement for a normal animal in a thermoneutral environment, awake but resting and in postabsorptive (fasting) state. Other names: fasting heat production (FHP), basal metabolic rate (BMR), basal energy expenditure (BEE).

Resting energy requirement (RER): RER represents the energy requirement for a normal but fed animal at rest in a thermoneutral environment. RER differs from BER in that it includes energy expended for recovery from physical activity and feeding. Therefore, the difference between BER and RER includes energy needed for digestion, absorption and metabolism of food (heat increment) and recovery from previous physical activity. Other names: resting energy expenditure (REE).

Maintenance energy requirement (MER): MER represents the energy requirement of a moderately active adult animal in a thermoneutral environment. It includes energy needed for obtaining, digesting and absorbing food in amounts to maintain body weight, as well as energy for spontaneous activity. MER does not include energy needed to support additional activity (work, gestation, lactation and growth). Other names: maintenance energy expenditure (MEE).

Daily energy requirement (DER): DER represents the average daily energy expenditure of any animal, dependent on lifestage and activity. DER differs from MER in that it includes activity necessary for work, gestation, lactation and growth, as well as energy needed to maintain normal body temperature.

Heat production (HP): HP is the sum of heat loss through radiation, convection, conduction and evaporation and heat stored in the body as exemplified by an increase in body temperature. Heat is lost when food is metabolized (heat increment) and when physical work is performed.

Heat increment (HI): HI is heat produced from the digestion, absorption and metabolism of food. Other names: specific dynamic action (SDA), thermic effect of food, diet-induced thermogenesis.

Gross energy (GE): GE is the total heat produced by burning a food in a bomb calorimeter.

Digestible energy (DE): DE is the energy remaining after the energy lost from feces is subtracted from GE.

Metabolizable energy (ME): ME is energy available to the animal after energy from feces, urine and combustible gases has been subtracted.

Kilocalorie (kcal): One calorie is the energy needed to raise the temperature of 1 g water from 14.5 to 15.5°C. 1 kcal = 1,000 calories = 4.184 kJ.

Kilojoule (kJ): One kilojoule equals 107 ergs, or the energy expended when 1 kg is moved 1 m by 1 newton. 1 kJ = 0.239 kcal.

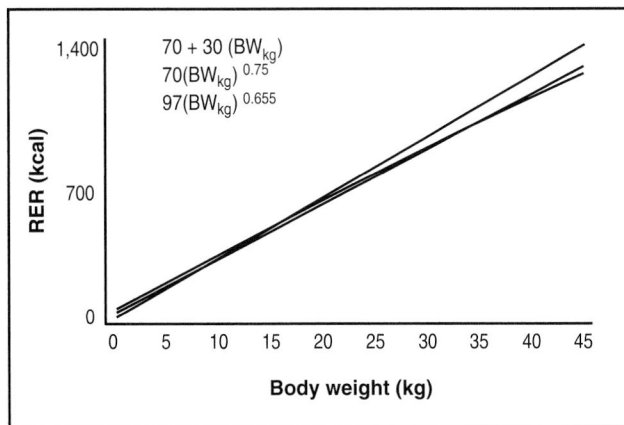

Figure 2-9. Comparison of three methods for calculating resting energy requirements (RER). (See Appendix D for more information.)

increment) and 2) recovery from previous physical activity. An animal in a state of maintenance has no net change in body composition, it produces no products and does not perform work.

Maintenance energy requirement (MER) is the energy required to keep an animal in a maintenance state. MER includes energy needed for: 1) basal metabolism, 2) obtaining, digesting and absorbing food in amounts to maintain body composition and 3) spontaneous voluntary activity (standing up, lying down, moving about to eat, drink and void feces and urine). MER does not include energy need-

ed to support additional physical activity (e.g., exercise or work) and production (e.g., gestation, lactation, growth).

DER represents the average daily energy requirement of any animal. DER depends on lifestage and activity. It differs from MER in that it includes activity necessary for work, gestation, lactation or growth. DER equals RER plus energy needed for physical activity and production. DER will be used throughout this text because it offers a practical and immediately usable energy requirement value for veterinarians and their health care teams. Table 2-2 summarizes energy requirements for cats and dogs.

Daily Energy Requirements

Measuring the energy expenditure of an individual animal is impractical for practicing veterinarians and pet owners. Therefore, researchers have developed prediction equations that may be used to estimate DER. Most of the equations predict RER based on the easily measured parameter of body weight. Once the RER is estimated, one can calculate DER by multiplying RER by an appropriate factor. The DER for growing, pregnant, lactating and exercising animals includes energy needed for maintenance plus the additional energy for work and production, thus different multiplication factors are used for each situation (Table 2-2). Similarly, deviations from the RER due to breed, gender, neuter status, presence of disease and environmental conditions can be included in the multiplication factor to improve the accuracy of predicting the DER for an individual animal. In routine veterinary practice, these energy requirement equations should be used as guidelines, starting points or estimates of energy requirements for individual animals and not as absolute requirements.

SIZE

It was known as early as the eighteenth century that large animals produced more heat than small animals. Research in the nineteenth century, however, showed that small animals produced more heat per unit of body weight (body surface area) than large animals.[2,11,12] Body surface area became the standard way of expressing energy metabolism within a species and makes sense because rate of heat loss from a body to the environment is proportional to the area of its surface.

Although use of surface area makes sense, it is not easily determined in animals. Equations to predict body surface area from body weight were developed $(BW_{kg})^{0.67}$; however, because of different body shapes, calculated surface area did not vary with body weight to the 0.67 power in some animals (e.g., compare a Labrador retriever weighing 30 kg with an Irish setter of the same weight, or a French bulldog with a whippet).[2] In the early 1930s, Kleiber and Brody ignored the concept of body surface area and through numerous animal experiments showed that energy requirements for a variety of different species are more closely represented as metabolic rate (kcal/day) = $73.3(BW_{kg})^{0.74}$ or $70.5(BW_{kg})^{0.734}$. In an effort to simplify calculations, researchers have proposed and used modifications of Kleiber-Brody equations using different exponents or converting exponential formulas to linear formulas.[13-17]

The debate about whether to use an exponential equation based on body surface area or metabolic body size or a linear formula to predict energy requirements for dogs and cats is largely academic.[18-22] Figure 2-9 compares energy requirements calculated using several different published methods. These equations yield similar estimates, especially at intermediate weight ranges. To practicing veterinarians, the differences in the energy requirement predicted by using one exponent or another or a linear equation vs. an exponential equation are small. For example, Figure 2-10 demonstrates results among dogs and cats when the average energy consumed is set at 100%. In 95% of 120 dogs, the energy consumed varied from 65 to 135% (range 43 to 152%); in 95% of 76 cats, it varied from 61 to 139% (range 50 to 146%). Thus, the amount of food needed by dogs and cats for maintenance, even under similar environmental conditions and when kept in cages or runs, varied threefold. Even when the extremes are excluded (the top and bottom 2.5%), the amount of energy needed varied more than twofold.

The following sections discuss differences in energy requirements for different physiologic and environmental conditions. The energy values expressed in this text are based on the exponent $(BW_{kg})^{0.75}$ because: 1) there is greater size diversity among dogs than for other species (e.g., 1 kg for a Chihuahua to 90 kg or more for a St. Bernard), 2) changes in lean body mass are of primary interest, 3) this equation works well for other mammals and 4) it can be easily calculated by cubing BW in kg and then taking its square root twice.

LIFESTAGE

Adult Maintenance

Estimates of the DER of dogs range between 100 to 200 kcal (440 to 850 kJ) of digestible energy (DE) per

$(BW_{kg})^{0.75}$ per day,[22-25] which represents a surprisingly wide range. Differences in activity levels of dogs account for much of this range. Other factors that contribute to differences in energy requirements include differences in breed, temperament, skin and coat insulation, age, social

---

Table 2-2. Calculation of energy requirements.

Calculation of daily energy requirement (DER) is based on the resting energy requirement (RER) for the animal modified by a factor to account for normal activity or production (e.g., growth, gestation, lactation, work). RER is a function of metabolic body size. RER is calculated by raising the animal's body weight in kg to the 0.75 power. The average RER for mammals is about 70 kcal/day/kg metabolic body size: RER (kcal/day) = $70(BW_{kg})^{0.75}$ or $30(BW_{kg})$ + 70 (if the animal weighs between 2 and 45 kg). Expressed in kJ, the average RER for mammals is about $293(BW_{kg})^{0.75}$. These energy requirements should be used as guidelines, starting points or estimates of energy requirements for individual animals and not as absolute requirements.

Feline DER
Maintenance (0.8 to 1.6 x RER)

Neutered adult	= 1.2 x RER
Intact adult	= 1.4 x RER
Active adult	= 1.6 x RER
Obese prone	= 1.0 x RER
Weight loss	= 0.8 x RER
Critical care	= 1.0 x RER
Weight gain	= 1.2-1.4 x RER at ideal weight

Gestation
Energy requirement increases linearly during gestation in cats. Energy intake should be increased to 1.6 x RER at breeding and gradually increased through gestation to 2 x RER at parturition.
Free-choice feeding of pregnant queens is also recommended.

Lactation
Lactation is nutritionally demanding and the physiologic and nutritional equivalent of heavy work.
Recommend 2 to 6 x RER (depending on number of kittens nursing) or free-choice feeding.

Growth
Daily energy intake for growing kittens should be about 2.5 x RER.
Free-choice feeding is recommended.

Canine DER
Maintenance (1.0 to 1.8 x RER)

Neutered adult	= 1.6 x RER
Intact adult	= 1.8 x RER
Obese prone	= 1.4 x RER
Weight loss	= 1.0 x RER
Critical care	= 1.0 x RER
Weight gain	= 1.2-1.4 x RER at ideal weight

Work

Light work	= 2 x RER
Moderate work	= 3 x RER
Heavy work	= 4-8 x RER

Gestation
First 42 days: feed as an intact adult.
Last 21 days: use 3 x RER. (This quantity may need to be increased to maintain normal body condition for some dogs, especially larger breeds.)

Lactation
Lactation is nutritionally demanding and the physiologic and nutritional equivalent of heavy work.
Recommend 4 to 8 x RER (depending on number of puppies nursing) or free-choice feeding.

Growth
Daily energy intake for growing puppies should be 3 x RER from weaning until four months of age.
At four months of age energy intake should be reduced to 2 x RER until the puppy reaches adult size.

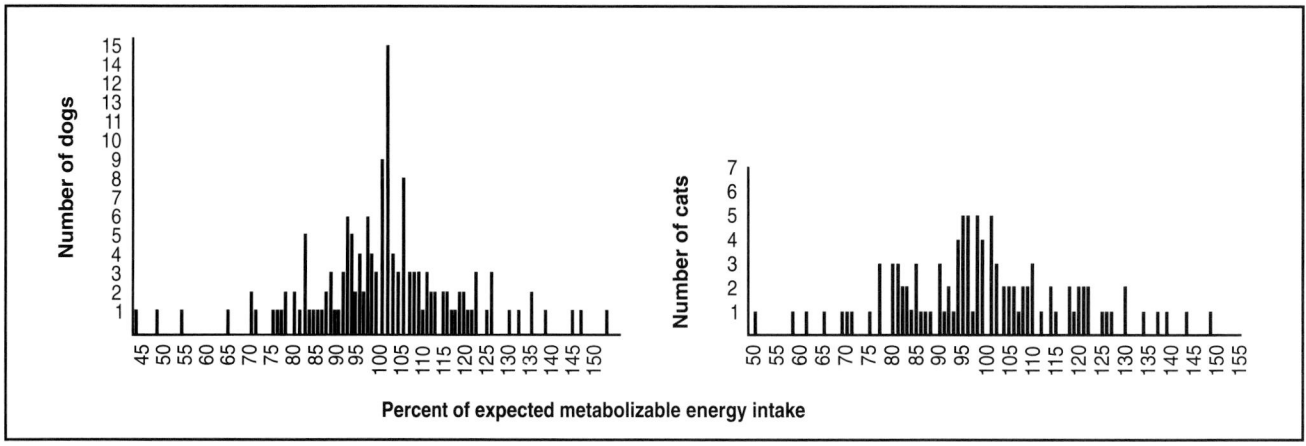

Figure 2-10. Variation in expected energy intake required to maintain optimal body weight in dogs and cats. Data were collected from 120 dogs and 76 cats kept under similar conditions and fed the amount of a variety of commercial pet foods necessary to maintain body weight. (Adapted from Lewis LD, Morris ML Jr, Hand MS. Small Animal Clinical Nutrition III. Topeka, KS: Mark Morris Associates, 1987; 1–10.)

environment and differences in methodology used to estimate the requirement. For the average sexually intact healthy adult dog, the DER approximates 1.8 x RER.

Non-obese adult domestic cats vary in body weight from approximately 2.5 to 6.5 kg, which is a much smaller range of weight extremes than exists for dogs. The National Research Council recommends a DER for adult cats of 70 to 90 kcal/BW_{kg} (290 to 380 kJ/BW_{kg}).[26] However, Earle and Smith reported that inactive cats required less energy (39 to 66 kcal/BW_{kg} or 162 to 278 kJ/BW_{kg}) and, similar to what is seen in dogs, they found that the energy intake per unit body weight was lower in heavier cats.[16] Generally, the DER for adult intact cats is about 1.4 x RER. Energy requirements are lower for neutered animals (discussed below).

Growth

Energy needs for growth are increased above maintenance because energy is needed to form new tissue. However, growth is a dynamic process; its rate declines as animals approach maturity. Therefore, the amount of energy needed also declines during growth. The time taken to reach maturity in dogs increases with increasing mature body weight. The highest energy requirement for puppies occurs at weaning. Growing puppies require 3 x RER from weaning until four months of age and 2 x RER from four months of age until the puppy reaches adult size.

Much research has been done in mammals to evaluate how food energy intake affects the composition of growth (i.e., body composition, fat vs. lean). Energy consumed during growth influences the proportion of lean and fat gain during growth. The metabolic efficiency of converting dietary fat to body fat for storage is higher than the efficiency of converting dietary carbohydrate or protein to body fat. This finding has been reported to occur in puppies when comparing the effects of high-fat and low-fat foods.[27] Puppies consuming a high-fat food had similar growth in lean body mass compared with that of puppies fed foods lower in fat, but deposited more body fat.[27] The prioritization of growth results in energy being preferentially used for protein growth and secondarily for fat gain. Excess energy with resulting obesity has been incriminated as a factor contributing to degenerative joint disease.

growing large- and giant-breed puppies is a frequently encountered problem. (See Chapter 17.)

The energy requirements of growing kittens follow a similar pattern as that for puppies. The highest energy requirement per unit of body weight occurs at about five weeks of age.[28] Energy recommendations for growing kittens approximate 2.5 x RER.

Reproduction (Gestation and Lactation)

In dogs, most of the fetal weight gain occurs in the last third of pregnancy; therefore, the energy requirement of the bitch does not increase markedly until this time. DER during gestation approximates 3 x RER for most breeds, although larger breeds may require more energy than this to maintain normal body condition. In cats, energy intake increases incrementally from the start of gestation and continues up to parturition.[29]

Lactation is one of the most energy-demanding life-stages for animals. Depending on the size and age of the litter, DER can increase as much as 6 x RER for cats and 8 x RER for dogs. Lactation lasts approximately six weeks in dogs and cats. The energy intakes for dogs and cats during reproduction are summarized in Chapters 9 and 11.

Age

Apart from lactation and imposed activity during work or sport, age may be the single most important factor influencing DER of adult pet dogs.[21] Three groups of adult dogs can be distinguished: 1) young (one to two years old), 2) middle aged (three to seven years old) and 3) older (more than seven years of age).[20,21,30] Older animals typically need fewer calories to maintain body weight and condition, primarily because of decreased activity.[25,31,32] This effect may also be due to increased body fat and less lean body mass resulting in reduced RER. In studies, dogs above seven years of age required 10 to 15% less energy than those three to seven years of age.[20,21]

One study in cats ranging from one to nine years showed no apparent correlation between increasing age and changes in body composition.[33] Burger found no significant effect of age on energy requirements of cats.[34] Although these data indicate that energy requirements of cats do not decline with age as with dogs, the greatest proportion of overweight cats are older than four and less than 11 years.[35-37]

Generally, because older animals are likely to be less active than younger animals, they should be fed less energy or food to avoid obesity.

Dogs and cats over 11 years of age tend to be thinner and have less body fat than animals between seven and 11 years old. In people, and most likely in dogs and cats, lean body mass declines with age.[35,38] Because energy requirements are related to lean body mass, reduced activity and reduced lean body mass may contribute to reduced energy requirements.

ACTIVITY

Activity significantly influences energy requirements (i.e., standing up requires 40% more energy than lying down),[25] yet recommendations for MER do not always mention the degree of activity included. Most of the disparities in the literature for MER and RER are attributed to the different activity levels of the animals under study. Short bouts of intense physical exercise may cause only a small increase in DER, but prolonged exercise can increase energy requirements four- to eightfold over RER. The DER for dogs of normal activity is 1.6 to 1.8 x RER. This requirement increases to 2 x RER for dogs doing light work, 3 x RER for dogs doing moderate work and 4 to 8 x RER for dogs doing heavy work.

THERMOREGULATION

The influence of housing and climate should not be neglected when evaluating energy requirements. When kept outside in cold weather, dogs may need 10 to 90% more calories than during optimal weather conditions (Table 2-3). Heat losses are minimal at a temperature range called the thermoneutral zone. The environmental temperature range at which dogs reach their minimum metabolic rate is breed specific and is lower when the thermic insulation (e.g., coat density and length, skin insulation) is better.[11,19,25,31,39] The thermoneutral zone was estimated at 15 to 20°C for longhaired and 20 to 25°C for shorthaired breeds.[11,19,25,31] For Alaskan sled dogs, it may be as low as 10 to 15°C.[25,31]

At temperatures above the thermoneutral zone, energy is expended to dissipate heat. Conversely, at temperatures below the thermoneutral zone, energy is used to maintain core body temperature. The degree to which environmental temperature affects energy needs of an animal also depends on air movement (wind chill factor), air humidity[25] and the degree of acclimatization.[22] Animal factors including insulative characteristics of skin and coat (subcutaneous fat, hair length and coat density)[22,25,32,40] and differences in stature, behavior and activity[32,40] interact and affect the DER.

NEUTER STATUS

There is a paucity of information in the literature regarding the effect of neuter status on energy requirements. Neutering (castration, ovariohysterectomy) of animals is thought to be associated with the development of obesity because of a combination of factors including reduced activity and changes in basal energy requirements. Data suggest that intact cats have higher energy requirements than those that have been neutered.[41,42] Neutered cats may be less able to self-regulate food intake than intact cats and thus are predisposed to eat more food and to become obese.[41]

In dogs, it is unknown whether increases in body weight after neutering result from increases in appetite

Table 2-3. Influence of low environmental temperatures on daily energy requirement (DER).

Breed	Increase in DER (%)	Environmental temperature Low	Normal
Labrador retrievers and beagles	25 (12-43)*	8.5°C (47.3°F)	15°C (59°F)
Great Danes	22**	Winter	Summer
Shorthaired dogs	95***	7.6°C (46°F)	25°C (77°F)
Longhaired dogs	59.5***	7.6°C (46°F)	25°C (77°F)
Beagles	70.5†	-17°C (1.4°F)	17°C (62.6°F)
Alaskan sled dogs	61.5†	-17°C (1.4°F)	17°C (62.6°F)

*Blaza SE. Energy requirements of dogs in cool conditions. Canine Practice 1982; 9: 10-15.
**Zentek J, Meyer H. Energieaufnahme adulter Deutscher Doggen. Berliner und Münchner Tierärztliche Wochenschrift 1992; 105: 325-327.
***Meyer H. Energie und Nährstoffe–Stoffwechsel und Bedarf. In: Ernährung des Hundes. Stuttgart, Germany: Eugen Ulmer, 1990; 99.
†Durrer JL, Hannon JP. Seasonal variations in caloric intake of dogs living in an arctic environment. American Journal of Physiology 1962; 202: 375-378.

and thus food intake or a reduction in energy expenditure or both. In a study of six dogs, the fasting energy expenditure was reduced from 37.1 kcal/BW$_{kg}$/day (155 kJ) to 33.9 (142 kJ) and 35.3 (148 kJ) at 30 and 90 days post-neutering, respectively.[43]

BREED

Some breeds such as Newfoundlands and huskies have relatively lower energy requirements, whereas Great Danes have energy requirements above the average.[20,30,39] Breed-specific needs probably reflect differences in: 1) temperament (resulting in higher or lower activity), 2) stature, 3) insulative capacity of skin and coat (which influence the degree of heat loss) and 4) lean body mass. However, when data are corrected for age, interbreed differences become less important.[21]

GENDER

In people, gender has a significant effect on energy requirement because of the proportionately greater muscle mass of men. (Women have a greater proportion of body fat.) No effect of gender, however, has been found in dogs[19,20] or reported to occur in cats.

DISEASE, INJURY, INFECTION AND CANCER

As a result of metabolic and physiologic changes, animals must recover from trauma, repair wounds, mount an immune response or compete with cancer in order to survive. These processes involve cellular work that requires energy. Energy-supplying nutrients must be provided in sufficient amounts to prevent catabolism of body tissues with resultant loss of function. However, most sick animals are inactive and anorectic and, therefore, their energy requirement is reduced. Thus, energy requirements for diseased animals logically lie somewhere between RER and DER. Although mathematical factors have been reported to multiply times RER (or MER) to estimate energy requirements for diseased dogs and cats,[13,14,44,45] very few studies have verified their validity by measuring the actual energy requirements of hospitalized dogs and cats under various disease conditions. (See Chapter 12.)

Burkholder has recommended a practical approach in which the RER and DER are used as references to assess whether a sick animal's voluntary food consumption is adequate or inadequate.[46] Forced nutritional intervention is recommended if food consumption is less than the calculated RER. If food intake approaches DER for adult maintenance, additional nutritional support is probably not needed. Regardless of whether a sick animal consumes food voluntarily or is forced, the food should have a nutrient composition that is optimized for recovery as discussed in Chapter 12.

WEIGHT LOSS/UNDERWEIGHT

The prevalence of suboptimal body condition begins to increase at about 11 years of age and rises sharply in very old animals, especially cats.[35] Anorexia is common in elderly people and can also occur in older cats and dogs. Changes in appetite can be influenced by many factors including decline in acuity of taste and smell, dental problems, physical disabilities, acute or chronic diseases, drugs and other therapies including dietary modifications. Prolonged reductions in food intake ultimately lead to chronic energy deficiency. As a result, loss of body weight occurs as body energy stores are diminished (fat and muscle protein).

In people, data show that reductions in body weight are linearly related to reductions in RER and are described by the regression equation REE (kcal/day) = -78.8 + 11.9 x weight change (kg).[47] Decreases in lean tissue lead to decreased protein turnover, which reduces energy expenditure. Thus, reductions in RER are due in part to reductions in body protein turnover and reduced body size. Other factors such as changes in Na-K ATPase activity, hormonal changes affecting nutrient metabolism and alterations in sympathetic nervous system activity may also reduce overall RER in weight loss.[47] Data from obese dogs suggest that RER may be reduced by up to 25% following a weight loss of 17%.[48] It is unknown whether similar reductions in RER occur in animals with normal body condition or older animals that lose weight.

WEIGHT GAIN

Weight gain occurs in growth; the energy requirements during growth have been discussed previously. Weight gain that occurs in nongrowing animals results in changes in energy requirements needed to maintain the increase in body weight. Research in people shows that REE linearly increases with increases in body weight and gains in lean body mass.[47] Theoretical calculations of increased energy expenditure due to weight gain and actual measurements agree closely and can be described by the regression equation REE (kcal/day) = 55.6 + 16.9 x weight change (kg).[47]

The composition of the weight gain averaged 63% body fat and 37% lean tissue in a summary of six studies involving 89 adult people.[47] The additional energy needed to support weight gain is mainly due to the amount of lean body mass that is gained and the energy required to support the increased protein turnover in the newly deposited protein.

There are no estimates supported by research using dogs and cats to correlate composition of weight gain in adults with changes in energy requirements. Therefore, in practice, dogs and cats that need to gain weight are usually fed more food, or a food with a higher energy density, until the desired weight has been achieved. The new target body weight is then used to calculate DER, and the pet is fed the amount of food necessary to maintain the new desired body weight. This method is effective, but it is difficult to predict how much of a food increase is truly needed or to estimate how long it will take for the animal to gain the needed weight. Suggested energy calculations for weight gain are summarized in Table 2-2.

■ CARBOHYDRATES INCLUDING FIBER

Simple Carbohydrates and Starches

Definition

Carbohydrates are composed of carbon, hydrogen and oxygen in the general formula $(CH_2O)_n$ (Figure 2-11). Carbohydrates encompass: 1) simple sugars such as monosaccharides (e.g., glucose) and disaccharides (e.g., sucrose), 2) oligosaccharides (three to nine sugar units; e.g., raffinose, stachyose) and 3) polysaccharides (more than nine sugar units). Examples of polysaccharides include starches (amylose, amylopectin, glycogen), hemicellulose, cellulose, pectins, gums, etc.

In a nutritional sense, polysaccharides, or as they are more commonly known, complex carbohydrates, can be further defined based on digestibility (Table 2-4). Complex carbohydrates that are digested by the animal's endogenous digestive enzymes are designated starches, whereas those polysaccharides that are resistant to enzymatic digestion and thus are fermented by intestinal microbes are labeled fibers. Starches and fibers differ chemically in that sugars in starches are linked with α-glycosidic bonds, whereas sugars in fibers are linked by β-glycosidic bonds. This small difference is important; mammalian enzymes can break α bonds but only microbial enzymes can break β bonds (Figure 2-11).

Structure

Simple sugars are divided into subgroups depending on the number of carbon atoms they contain. Three-carbon sugars (saccharides) are: 1) trioses $(C_3H_6O_3)$ such as glyceraldehyde, 2) four-carbon sugars are tetroses $(C_4H_8O_4)$, 3) five-carbon sugars are pentoses $(C_5H_{10}O_5)$ such as ribose and xylose, 4) six-carbon sugars are hexoses $(C_6H_{12}O_6)$ such as glucose, galactose and fructose and 5) seven-carbon sugars are called heptoses $(C_7H_{14}O_7)$. Only one disaccharide has been found in mammals (i.e., lactose), whereas the most common plant disaccharide is sucrose. Many oligosaccharides are commonly found in plants. The trisaccharide raffinose and the tetrasaccharide stachyose are the two most common oligosaccharides found in plants (e.g., soybeans and other legume seeds, sugar beets, root crops and sugar beet molasses). Longer chain oligosaccharides can be found in a variety of plants used as food.

Starch is made up of glucose units in straight chains with α1,4 bonds (amylose) and with α1,6 bonds that form branches (Figure 2-11). The α1,4 and α1,6 bonds can be broken by small intestinal digestive enzymes. Starches in plants are called amylopectins whereas animal starch is called glycogen. Plant starches exist as semicrystalline granules that vary in size, shape and amount of other compounds (proteins) associated with the granule.

The granular structure of starch affects the ease with which it is digested (Table 2-5). Most starches in cooked

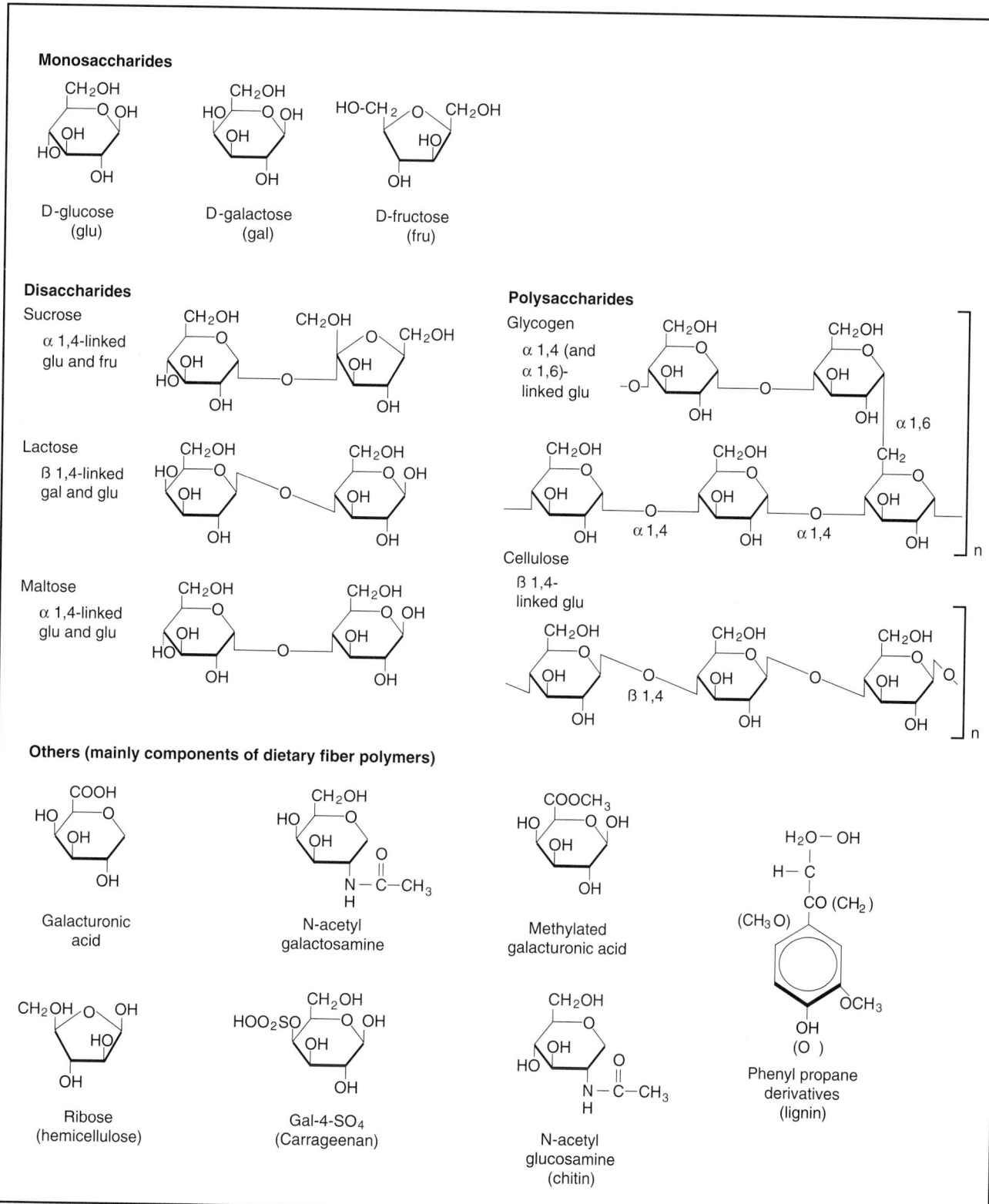

Figure 2-11. Components and classification of dietary carbohydrates. Dietary carbohydrates are usually classified as monosaccharides, disaccharides (sugars that yield two monosaccharides on hydrolysis) and polysaccharides (carbohydrates that yield nine or more monosaccharides when hydrolyzed). Other carbohydrates are primarily components of dietary fiber.

and extruded pet foods are easily and rapidly digested. Raw or uncooked starch is typically digested more slowly than cooked starch. Some plant starches resist enzymatic digestion in the small intestine[1] and have been named resistant starch. Resistant starch, by definition, is not enzy-

matically digested in the small intestine, thus it becomes available for microbial fermentation in the colon.

The amounts of rapidly digestible, slowly digestible and resistant starch in foods are highly variable and depend on the starch source, type and extent of processing.[2] Table 2-5

Table 2-4. Classification and digestion of complex carbohydrates.[*]

Complex carbohydrate type	Function	Digestion site	Digestion products
Starch, glycogen	Storage polysaccharide in plants and animals	Small intestine (enzymatic)	Mono- and disaccharides (glucose, maltose)
Hemicellulose, cellulose	Structural parts of plant cell walls	Large intestine (microbial fermentation)	Volatile fatty acids (acetate, propionate, butyrate)
Lignins, cutins, waxes	Associated cell wall substances	Not digested or fermented	Excreted in feces
Gums, mucilages, pectins	Naturally occurring polysaccharides in plants	Large intestine (microbial fermentation)	Carbon dioxide, methane, hydrogen, volatile fatty acids

[*]Adapted from the British Nutrition Foundation. Complex Carbohydrates in Foods. New York, NY: Van Nostrand Reinhold, 1990.

shows a nutritional classification of the types of starch that are found in foods.

Function

Simple carbohydrates and starches in foods are used by the body as a source of glucose. As such, they have several major functions. First, they provide energy (ATP) via glycolysis and the TCA cycle. Second, when metabolized for energy to carbon dioxide and water, they are a source of heat for the body. Third, as they proceed through metabolic pathways, certain products can be used as building blocks for other nutrients, such as nonessential amino acids, glycoproteins, glycolipids, lactose, vitamin C, etc. Finally, simple carbohydrates and starches in excess of the body's immediate energy needs are stored as glycogen or converted to fat.

IMPORTANCE OF CARBOHYDRATES

The primary purpose for adding carbohydrates and starches to pet foods is to supply energy. Generally, assuming an average digestibility (84%), carbohydrates supply about 3.5 kcal/g. Although there is no minimum dietary requirement for simple carbohydrates or starches per se, certain organs and tissues (e.g., brain and red blood cells) require glucose for energy. Glucose can be obtained from precursor nutrients such as glucogenic amino acids or glycerol from fats via gluconeogenic pathways. The body always maintains glucose supply to key tissues; thus, if adequate dietary carbohydrates are not available, amino acids will be shunted away from muscle growth, fetal growth and milk production to be used for glucose synthesis.

When energy needs are high and tissue accretion is occurring (e.g., during growth, gestation and lactation), adequate dietary carbohydrates or glucose precursors are necessary to maintain metabolic processes.[3-6] In these situations, carbohydrates become conditionally essential; therefore, foods fed to growing animals and those with high-energy needs should contain at least 20% carbohydrates.

In addition to nutritional reasons for adding carbohydrates to pet foods, carbohydrates also are important in pet food processing. See Chapters 3 and 4 for detailed information.

Metabolism

DIGESTION

Digestion of simple carbohydrates and starches occurs throughout the digestive tract and involves mechanical, enzymatic and microbial processes. Mechanical breakdown occurs primarily in the oral cavity. Because dogs and cats lack salivary α-amylase, enzymatic digestion of starch is not initiated in the mouth. In the stomach, food is mixed with gastric juices (i.e., hydrochloric acid and proteolytic enzymes). Although the stomach plays an important role in protein digestion, little carbohydrate digestion occurs here. Simple carbohydrates and starches are digested and absorbed in the small intestine. Enzymes secreted from the pancreas digest the majority of starches and sugars in the lumen of the small intestine, whereas enzymes at the small intestinal mucosal brush border are important in the final stages of carbohydrate digestion and absorption.

Starch is initially cleaved by the enzyme α-amylase, which creates branched oligosaccharides, the disaccharide maltose and the trisaccharide maltotriose. The brush border enzymes maltase, sucrase and isomaltase cleave the larger glucose chains into single glucose molecules that are then absorbed. Sucrase also splits the disaccharide sucrose into glucose and fructose units. Lactase, another brush border enzyme, splits lactose, the sugar found in milk, into glucose and galactose. Lactase activity is usually high in young, suckling animals but often declines in adults. Conversely, amylase, maltase and isomaltase display a reverse temporal pattern; concentrations of these enzymes are low in suckling animals and higher in adults.[5,7]

Starch is made up of glucose units in straight chains (amylose) and with branches (amylopectin) linked with α-bonds (Figure 2-11). Starches are contained within granules in plants in a highly crystalline formation. As foods containing starches are heated or cooked with water, the starch crystals are melted and hydrated, a process called gelatinization.[8] The extent to which starch granules are disrupted and the extent of gelatinization depend on many factors including grinding, moisture, cooking time and temperature. For most starches, the greater the degree of gelatinization, the higher the digestibility. Extrusion cooking, a process used in dry pet food production, increases overall digestibility of starches in grains by causing starch to gelatinize. The canning process also results in gelatinization of starch.

Several reports indicate that dogs and cats readily digest starches in commercial pet foods.[5,9-11] In studies, dogs were fed foods in which 30 to 57% of the food came from extruded corn, barley, rice or oats. The starch from all grains was nearly 100% digested in the small intestine; essentially no starch passed into the colon.[10]

Other studies compared the digestibility of isolated raw corn starch, tapioca and potato starches and cooked rice

Table 2-5. Nutritional classification of starch.*

Type of starch	Example of occurrence	Probable digestion in the small intestine
Rapidly digestible starch	Freshly cooked starchy food	Rapid and complete
Slowly digestible starch	Most raw cereals	Slow and complete
Resistant starch		
Physically inaccessible starch	Partly milled grain and seeds	Resistant
Resistant starch granules	Raw potato and banana	Resistant
Recrystallized starch	Cooled, cooked potato, bread and cornflakes	Resistant

*Adapted from the British Nutrition Foundation. Complex Carbohydrates in Foods. New York, NY: Von Nostrand Reinhold, 1990.

starch.[5,11] In these studies, isolated starches contributed 40% of the dry matter of the food. By the time the starch reached the colon, uncooked corn starch was digested to the same degree as cooked rice starch (more than 94% digested); however, uncooked potato (0%) and tapioca starches (<70%) were poorly digested in the small intestine. The uncooked tapioca starch subsequently resulted in increased bacterial fermentation rates as evidenced by high volatile fatty acid concentrations in the feces. Large amounts of easily fermentable carbohydrates (e.g., tapioca starch) in the colon increase the risk of excessive fermentation causing gas and flatulence and upsetting the balance of microflora.

In recent feeding trials with cats, investigators demonstrated that cooked corn starch was nearly 100% digested when consumed by cats at 4.7 g per kg body weight per day.[5,12,13] Raw corn starch was only 60 to 70% digested and raw potato starch was 40% or less digested when consumed at 8.8 and 8.9 g per kg body weight per day. Most commercial cat foods contain approximately 30 to 35% carbohydrate on a dry matter basis. This level provides approximately 5 to 8 g of starch per kg body weight per day, which should pose no digestive or metabolic problems for cats.[5]

ABSORPTION

Glucose and galactose are absorbed through an active transport mechanism using specific carrier proteins and a sodium gradient. Fructose is absorbed by a separate carrier system that appears not to be sodium dependent. Absorption occurs across the small intestinal mucosa through finger-like projections called villi. The cells covering the villi are called enterocytes and contain the carbohydrate-digesting enzymes, transport proteins and other enzymes used to synthesize triacylglycerides and chylomicrons. Absorbed sugars can be used by enterocytes as a source of energy or released into portal blood for transport to the liver and beyond.

Carbohydrate intolerance or malabsorption may result from deficiency of digestive enzymes or failure of the energy-dependent transport system. Many disaccharidase deficiencies result from intestinal mucosal damage induced by infections and other diseases. The resulting colonization of the lower small intestine by colonic bacteria may result in bacterial proteolysis of carbohydrate-digesting enzymes.

Unabsorbed carbohydrates in the intestinal lumen create high osmotic pressure, reduce water and mineral absorption and may result in small bowel diarrhea. In addition, excessive fermentation of unabsorbed carbohydrates leads to bacterial overgrowth, production of gas (carbon dioxide, hydrogen and methane) and short-chain fatty acids. Excessive carbohydrate fermentation can lead to flatulence, abdominal distention and diarrhea. Carbohydrate intolerance may be diagnosed by finding increased concentrations of hydrogen in the breath (breath hydrogen analysis) as a result of bacterial fermentation.[14]

USAGE

Glucose and other sugars derived from food arrive at the liver via the portal blood. The liver plays a central role in synthesizing, storing, converting and releasing glucose for use by other organs. The concentration of glucose in blood is finely controlled by insulin and glucagon.

The central nervous system and erythrocytes require glucose for their energy needs, whereas other tissues can use other substrates (e.g., muscle uses fatty acids). Glucose is metabolized via glycolysis followed by the TCA cycle (Figure 2-7). Complete oxidation of glucose to carbon dioxide, water, ATP and heat requires oxygen and is termed aerobic metabolism. The final transfer of energy from carbohydrate to ATP occurs via the electron transport chain (Figure 2-4). If there is a shortage of oxygen in tissues, such as occurs with intense exercise, some ATP can be derived from glucose via anaerobic metabolism in which glucose is partially metabolized to pyruvate (via glycolysis) and then converted to lactic acid.

Glucose consumed in excess of immediate needs may be stored as glycogen. The enzyme glycogen synthetase synthesizes glycogen from glucose units. This enzyme is particularly active in liver and muscles. Endurance athletes have used carbohydrate loading (i.e., eating large amounts of carbohydrate several days before competition) to maximize muscle glycogen stores. Carbohydrate loading in canine athletes has been practiced, but has not been widely researched. (See Chapter 10.) After glycogen stores are filled, additional dietary carbohydrates are converted to long-chain fatty acids and stored as triacylglycerides in adipose tissue.

In the hours following digestion and absorption of a carbohydrate-containing meal, the liver and other body tissues switch from glycogen storage to glycogenolysis under the influence of an increased glucagon to insulin ratio. This ratio also stimulates lipolysis, thus overall body metabolism switches toward lipid use for energy. Glucose is synthesized from carbon skeletons of amino acids, glycerol and lactic acid (gluconeogenesis) to maintain plasma glucose concentration. This function is critical to provide an adequate glucose supply to the brain (Figure 2-7). The liver and kidneys, but not muscles, are the sites of gluconeogenesis; therefore, muscle cannot supply glucose to the bloodstream.

STORAGE

The body stores sugar as glycogen, a glucose polysaccharide. Its highest concentration is in the liver, but muscle tissue, because of its greater mass, stores the most glycogen.

Ribose, although not a true carbohydrate store readily available for oxidation, is found as part of nucleic acids, ATP and guanosine triphosphate (GTP). The body also has stores of sugar-protein complexes (glycoproteins, mucus and proteoglycans) and sugar-lipid complexes (glycolipids).

EXCRETION

Excreted products resulting from normal carbohydrate metabolism include carbon dioxide in the breath, heat radiating from the body and water. In cases of malabsorption of simple sugars and starches, increased intestinal fermentation may lead to more hydrogen in expired breath and flatus and short-chain fatty acids in stools. Animals with deranged carbohydrate metabolism (diabetes mellitus, ketosis, glycogen storage diseases, fructose, galactose and pyruvate enzyme deficiencies) may have elevated urinary or plasma levels of the metabolic intermediates related to the specific disease (glucose, ketones, lactic acid, oxalate, etc.). Chapter 24 discusses treatment of the most common disease of abnormal carbohydrate metabolism, diabetes mellitus.

Carbohydrates of Special Importance

XYLOSE

Xylose is a five-carbon sugar used in clinical veterinary medicine to assess intestinal absorptive capacity, alterations in GI emptying, exocrine pancreatic insufficiency and bacterial overgrowth, as discussed in Chapter 22. When xylose is administered orally, approximately 48% is expected to be absorbed into the bloodstream and excreted into the urine.[15] Altered xylose absorption can be diagnostic for certain diseases. The xylose absorption test is typically only recommended for use in dogs; there is too much individual variability in the results from cats.[15]

LACTULOSE

Lactulose is a synthetic disaccharide containing galactose and fructose connected by a $\beta 1,4$ bond. Lactulose is formed when lactose (galactose and glucose) is subjected to isomerization in aqueous alkaline solutions. Lactulose is not hydrolyzed by mammalian enzymes, but can be digested by microbial enzymes; thus, it is fermented in the colon. Lactulose enhances the growth of specific types of bacteria (*Lactobacillus bifidus*), has laxative effects and acidifies the colon to aid in ammonia trapping. Fermentation of excessive amounts of lactulose may worsen flatulence and cause diarrhea. Clinically, lactulose is often given to help manage hepatic encephalopathy. (See Chapter 23.) It is also sometimes administered before breath hydrogen collection and used along with a xylose absorption test to differentiate among small intestinal disease, exocrine pancreatic insufficiency and bacterial overgrowth. (See Chapter 22.)

GLYCOSAMINOGLYCANS

Glycosaminoglycans are complex polysaccharides associated with proteins. They form integral parts of the interstitial fluid, cartilage, skin and tendons. The primary glycosaminoglycans are chondroitin sulfate and hyaluronic acid. Chondroitin sulfate is a polymer of two alternating sugar units, glucuronic acid and N-acetylgalactosamine. Hyaluronic acid is a linear polymer of two sugars: glucuronic acid and N-acetylglucosamine. Chondroitin sulfate and other glycosaminoglycans are available as dietary supplements with alleged benefits for arthritic conditions, degenerative joint diseases and geriatric patients in general.

RESISTANT STARCH

Resistant starch (Table 2-5) is a fraction of starch found in foods that potentially resists digestion in the small intestine.[1] Resistant starch is classified according to the rapidity with which glucose is released from a starch source and is a fraction of the total amount of starch that remains after a sample is incubated for 100 minutes with the enzymes pancreatin and amyloglucosidase. Three types of resistant starches have been identified:

RS_1 = starch physically trapped within the starch granule that is released during processing and chewing.

RS_2 = starch granular structures (e.g., those found in raw potato, bananas and tapioca).

RS_3 = recrystallized starch formed after cooking, when the starch cools or is dried.

RS_1 and RS_2 represent the residues of starches that are digested very slowly and incompletely in the small intestine. RS_3 is highly resistant to digestion by intestinal enzymes and is fermented by bacteria in the colon. The amount of resistant starch in pet foods and the extent and site of digestibility and fermentation have not been determined.

FRUCTOOLIGOSACCHARIDES

Oligosaccharides are polymers that contain up to nine sugars. Oligosaccharides that contain fructose are termed fructooligosaccharides (FOS). FOS resist digestion by enzymes in the small intestine and enter the colon intact. In the colon, certain bacteria (bifidobacteria and *Lactobacillus* spp) readily ferment FOS, which enhances the bacterial growth rate.[16-18] Increased numbers of these bacterial species may benefit the overall health of people and other animals, including pigs, rabbits and rats.[19-21]

Bifidobacteria produce short-chain fatty acids that decrease the intestinal pH and inhibit the growth of pathogenic bacteria. FOS reduce fasting blood glucose levels, cholesterol and low-density lipoproteins in people with diabetes mellitus.[22] The benefits of FOS in pigs, rabbits and rats include improved intestinal flora (i.e., reduced numbers of pathogens), reduced mortality, improved feed efficiency, improved weight gain, increased nitrogen digestion and retention, reduced body fat, improved stool quality and reduced odor of feces.[19,20,23,24] The value of FOS for dogs and cats has not been researched thoroughly. At the time of this writing, no published data exist detailing use of FOS in cats and no proven benefits of FOS have emerged for dogs.

Analyses

The total carbohydrate content of pet foods and ingredients is not typically determined directly by analysis but indirectly by difference. Nitrogen-free extract (NFE) is the carbohydrate fraction of a proximate analysis. NFE is determined by adding the percentages of water, crude protein, crude fat, ash and crude fiber and subtracting from 100%. NFE is primarily made up of readily digestible carbohydrates (e.g., sugars and starches) (Figure 2-3).

Techniques such as gas-liquid chromatography and high-performance liquid chromatography can be used to separate and analyze different monosaccharides. In addition, colorimetric enzymatic assays specific for each sugar are available. The starch content of foods can be determined by heating the sample to gelatinize the starch followed by incubation with starch-digesting enzymes (amyloglucosidase and pancreatin). The amount of glucose liberated by enzymatic hydrolysis is analyzed and converted to starch content.[25]

Requirements, Deficiencies and Excesses

Dogs and cats do not have an absolute dietary requirement for carbohydrates in the same way that essential amino acids or fatty acids must be provided. They do, however, have a requirement for adequate glucose or glucose precursors to provide essential fuel for the central nervous system. When energy needs are high and anabolic processes are proceeding at an active rate (e.g., during growth, gestation and lactation), it is best to supply a food containing readily digestible carbohydrates and starches. Without dietary carbohydrates, there is added strain on lipid and protein metabolic pathways to supply glucose precursors.[26] Lipolysis must be increased to provide energy and glycerol units for gluconeogenesis. Similarly, glucogenic amino acids from dietary protein must be used for glucose formation; therefore, these amino acids are not available to meet body protein synthesis requirements.

From a practical standpoint, whether carbohydrate is essential in the food or not is of little importance because most commercially prepared pet foods contain carbohydrates well in excess of glucose requirements. Grains such as corn, rice, wheat, barley and oats provide the bulk of starch in commercial pet foods and are well-digested and absorbed due to the cooking and extrusion processes used to make pet foods.

CANINE CARBOHYDRATE REQUIREMENTS

Gestation and lactation increase the need for glucose to support fetal growth and lactose synthesis in milk. In one study, pregnant bitches were fed a high-fat but carbohydrate-free (0% of energy from carbohydrate) food with 26% of ME from protein. They developed hypoglycemia the week before whelping and had reduced plasma concentrations of lactate and alanine, a reduced number of live births, lethargy and reduced mothering ability compared with bitches fed a food containing 44% of ME as starch.[3] In another study using 51% of ME as protein, pregnant bitches fed either a starch-free or starch-containing diet performed similarly.[6]

Extensive research in dogs indicates that a starch-free food containing at least 33% of ME from protein is necessary to supply needed glucose precursors.[4] Fetal abnormalities, embryo resorption, ketosis and reduced milk production are other possible adverse effects of providing inadequate carbohydrate during gestation and lactation.[26]

Overall, a minimum of 23% carbohydrate is recommended in foods for gestating and lactating bitches. Excess starch in the food typically does not cause health problems in dogs. Dry extruded dog foods typically contain 30 to 60% carbohydrate, mostly starch, and cause no adverse effects. Excesses of simple sugars in commercial pet foods are also not a practical concern because sugar levels are usually low. On the other hand, carbohydrate intolerances may occur in some animals as a result of primary or secondary disaccharidase deficiencies.

Table 2-6. Sources of dietary carbohydrates.

Carbohydrate	Sources
D-Glucose (dextrose)	Fruits; traces in most plant foods; honey; maple sugar
D-Fructose	Fruits; traces in most plant foods; honey; maple sugar
D-Galactose	Component of lactose; produced during digestion
Sucrose	Cane sugar; beet sugar; fruits; maple sugar
Lactose	Milk; dairy products (milk sugar)
Maltose	Sprouted grain; produced during digestion of starches
Amylose (plant starch)	Starchy plants; grains
Amylopectin (plant starch)	Starchy plants; grains; used as thickener in processed foods
Glycogen (animal starch)	Liver; muscle
Cellulose	Substituent of plant cell walls; major component of wheat bran
Hemicellulose	Substituent of plant cell walls
Pectins	Fruits
Carrageenan	Red seaweed; used in candies and some processed foods
Raffinose, stachyose, verbacose	Plant "antifreeze"
Dextrins	Used in processed foods
Corn syrup	Used in processed foods
High-fructose corn syrup	Used in processed foods
Lignin	Substituent of plant cell walls

FELINE CARBOHYDRATE REQUIREMENTS

Normal cats can maintain adequate blood glucose levels when fed low-carbohydrate, high-protein foods.[27] Cats also have some unique metabolic differences that limit their ability to efficiently use large amounts of absorbed dietary carbohydrate. For example, cats have low activities of the intestinal disaccharidases sucrase and lactase;[28] further, the sugar transportation system in the feline intestine does not adapt to various levels of dietary carbohydrates. Cats produce only 5% of the pancreatic amylase that dogs produce.[12] Unlike dogs, cats lack hepatic glucokinase activity, which limits their ability to metabolize large amounts of simple carbohydrates.[28,29] Glucokinase is responsible for phosphorylating glucose to G-6-P in the pathway of glucose oxidation. Feline liver is also thought to lack fructokinase.[29]

The metabolic differences between cats and dogs support the classification of cats as strict carnivores, adapted to a low-carbohydrate diet, and dogs as omnivores. If large amounts of carbohydrates are fed to cats (e.g., more than 40% of the food DMB), signs of maldigestion occur (e.g., diarrhea, bloating and gas)[5] and adverse metabolic effects can occur (e.g., hyperglycemia and excretion of significant amounts of glucose in urine). Despite the limitations of digestive capacity and metabolism, the starch levels found in commercial cat foods (up to 35% of the food DMB) are well-tolerated.

Sources

Starches are the primary carbohydrates found in corn, wheat, rice, barley, oats and potatoes (Table 2-6). Meat is a poor carbohydrate source. Commercial extruded pet foods use the starches in grains to give structure, texture and form to extruded kibbles. In addition, the extrusion process gelatinizes starch, which makes it easily and rapidly digested in the small intestine of dogs and cats. Most starches from grains are easily digested in the small intestine, when fed uncooked (raw) or cooked to dogs and cats.[5,9,10] Potato starch is an exception. Raw potato starch is contained in granules that have a crystalline structure that is not easily digested by people, dogs and cats.[5,30] Freshly cooked potato starch is highly digestible; however, starch begins to recrystallize when cooled or dried. In vitro digestion studies and studies in people show that up to 13% of the recrystallized potato starch resists digestion by pancreatic amylase and thus will be fermented in the colon.[30,31]

Some legumes (e.g., soybeans) contain significant quantities of raffinose and stachyose, which can be digested by gut microflora but not by canine and feline enzymes. These sugars allegedly cause digestive abnormalities (e.g., flatulence) due to the gaseous waste products produced by bacterial fermentation. Other longer chain oligosaccharides may have beneficial effects on health due to changes in the gut microflora (e.g., FOS).

Sugar is sometimes added to enhance palatability of foods for dogs. Commercial semi-moist cat foods use mono- and disaccharides as functional ingredients to achieve texture and moistness and to prevent spoilage. Pet food with gravies and sauces may contain dextrins, corn syrup and other starches for texture and appearance. Sucrose does not enhance palatability of foods for cats because cats have few sucrose-sensitive taste buds.[26,32] A dog's ability to taste sweetness is different from a person's because of differences in the number and type of sweetness receptors on taste buds.[32,33] Therefore, the sweetness rankings of different sugars developed for people are not applicable to cats and dogs. Unlike in people and other primates, dietary sugars do not present a risk for dental caries in dogs and cats. (See Chapter 16.)

Fiber

Definition

Fiber refers to a multitude of compounds categorized as complex carbohydrates (Table 2-4). Fibers differ from starches in that fibers resist enzymatic digestion in the small intestine. As a result, fibers are usually fermented by microbes in the colon. Fibers include cellulose, hemicellulose, pectin, gums and resistant starches (See previous discussion.) and are unique because of the types of sugars they contain and the resultant chemical bonds.

Chemical Structure

Unlike starches, cellulose is a polymer of glucose units bonded by β1,4-linkages (rather than α linkages) that are only broken by microbial enzymes (Figure 2-11). Cellulose is the most abundant polysaccharide in plants, forming the structure of plant cell walls. In plants, hydrogen bonds closely hold straight cellulose chains to one another forming orderly and compact aggregates called fibrils. Cellulose fibrils contain regions that are highly crystalline and other regions that are more random and amorphous. Cellulose is usually associated with hemicelluloses and lignins within plant cell walls. Water-soluble chemical derivatives of cellulose, including carboxymethylcellulose, methylcellulose and hydroxypropylcellulose, are used as stabilizers, thickeners and emulsifiers in pet foods and human foods such

as ice cream, gravies, soups and beverages. Cellulose is also added to weight-reduction foods for people and pets to dilute calories and provide bulk. Cellulose is not very water soluble but can have significant water-holding capacity and is slowly fermented by microbes in the colon.

Hemicelluloses are composed primarily of glucose, galactose, mannose, xylose, arabinose and uronic acids joined together in different combinations and various linkages. Hemicelluloses are closely associated with the cellulose in the cell walls of plants. Most hemicelluloses are not water soluble because of their various structures and composition.

Pectin is a linear chain of galacturonic acid linked by α1,4-glycosidic bonds found in cell walls and intercellular regions of plants. The linear galacturonic chain of most pectins is interrupted by other sugars (e.g., galactose, arabinose and rhamnose) to form branches and kinks. Pectins are found in high levels in fruits and vegetables such as apples, strawberries, raspberries, carrots, broccoli, potatoes, sugar beet pulp and the skins of citrus fruits. Commercially, pectin is extracted from either apple or citrus waste after the manufacture of juice. Pectins are water soluble, form viscous gels and are rapidly fermented by intestinal bacteria.

Gum is a general term for the diverse group of viscous and sticky polysaccharides found in the seeds and exudates of plants. The sugars that make up gums are diverse, and precise structural information for some of the gums is unknown. Gum arabic, guar gum, carrageenan gum, psyllium gum, xanthan gum, carob gum, gum ghatti and gum tragacanth are just a few of the gums used as thickening agents, water binders, stabilizers, emulsifiers and gelling agents in jams, pie fillings, confectionery products, sauces, salad dressings, canned meat products and moist pet foods. Depending on their source and processing, gums have variable viscosity and solubility in water and thus have variable fermentation rates. Most gums are moderately to rapidly fermented by intestinal bacteria.

Lignin is not a carbohydrate in the strictest chemical definition; however, it is often considered a fiber because it makes up the structural part of plant cell walls and is not digested by mammalian intestinal enzymes. Lignin is not a single chemical compound but a series of compounds made from derivatives of phenylpropane associated in complex cross-linked structures. Lignin is highly resistant to enzymatic (intestinal and bacterial) digestion and chemical degradation. Strong chemical bonds between lignin and plant cell wall fibers, proteins and other compounds make lignins unavailable during digestion.

Other plant polysaccharides can also be considered as fibers. These include fructans (inulin), galactans, mannans, mucilages and β-glucans with β1,3- and β1,2-glucose bonds. Amounts of these fibers in foods are usually quite low.

Other Classifications of Fiber

In addition to classifying fibers by their structure as described above, fibers have been classified by their rate of fermentation, digestible and indigestible fractions, solubility in water, water-holding capacity and viscosity (Figure 2-12). The different ways of classifying fibers allow the important physiologic functions and diverse effects of fiber in animals to be highlighted and understood.

Carbohydrate and fiber fractions	Method	Fiber solubility	Total dietary fiber analysis	Crude fiber analysis
Fructans, galactans, mannans, mucilages	Rapidly fermentable	Soluble fiber	Total dietary fiber	
Pectin	Moderately fermentable			
Hemicellulose				
Cellulose	Slowly fermentable	Insoluble fiber		Crude fiber
Lignin	Not digested or fermented			
Resistant starch	Moderately fermentable			
Starch	Enzymatically digested			
Mono- and disaccharides	Absorbed			

Figure 2-12. Physiochemical and analytical properties of dietary fiber components.

Fiber sources can be described as rapidly to slowly fermentable (Figure 2-13). Rapidly fermented fibers produce more short-chain fatty acids and gases in a shorter period of time vs. fiber sources that are fermented more slowly.[34,35] Slowly fermentable fiber sources used in pet foods contain primarily celluloses and hemicelluloses including purified cellulose and peanut hulls. Citrus and apple pectins and most gums are rapidly fermented. Fiber sources that contain mixtures of pectins, hemicelluloses and celluloses (e.g., rice bran, oat bran, wheat bran, soy fibers, soy hulls and beet pulp) are moderately fermentable. The rate and extent of fiber fermentation are important distinguishing characteristics when discussing physiologic functions of fiber. As the fermentation rate of fiber increases, GI transit time decreases, fecal bulk decreases and fecal bile acid excretion increases.

Fiber is also classified according to solubility, or the ability of a fiber to disperse in water. Most rapidly fermentable fibers such as pectins and gums are "soluble." Lignin and the slowly fermentable fibers such as cellulose and most hemicelluloses are "insoluble." All fibers hold water to some degree; however, the soluble fibers have a greater water-holding capacity and may form gels and viscous solutions within the GI tract.

Viscosity of fibers in water is affected by fiber concentration, ionic concentration, pH, particle size and the hydrophobic and hydrophilic properties of polysaccharide structures. An increase in viscosity in the GI tract can slow nutrient absorption, reduce postprandial glycemia, slow gastric emptying, delay mouth to cecum transit and reduce interactions of food particles with digestive enzymes and epithelial surfaces. The rate of fermentation of a fiber interacts with water-holding capacity and viscosity to affect the degree of fecal bulking (volume). For moderately and slowly fermentable fibers, the degree of fecal bulking is related to water-holding capacity. Slowly fermented fibers (e.g., cellulose) are the most effective stool bulking agents because they retain their structure longer and are thus able to bind water. For rapidly fermentable

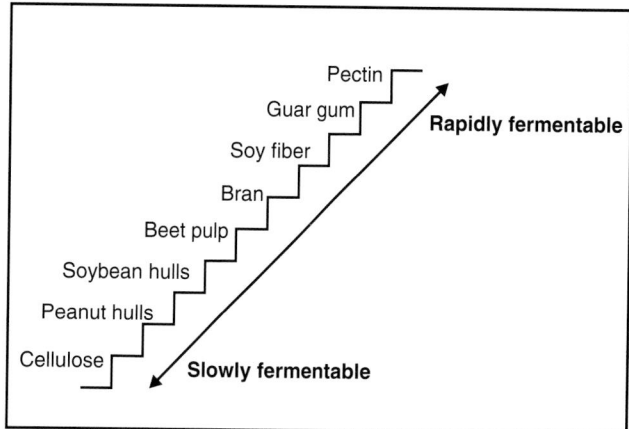

Figure 2-13. Relative degree of fermentation of various dietary fiber sources in the gastrointestinal tract of dogs and cats. At the extremes are pectin and gums, which are rapidly fermentable, and cellulose, which is slowly fermentable. Other fiber sources such as soy hulls and beet pulp are intermediate and termed moderately fermentable.

fibers, the increased bound water reduces fecal bulk. In fact, most fermentable fibers have laxative effects and may produce diarrhea if fed at high levels. An increase in fecal bulk has been advocated for the treatment and prevention of irritable bowel syndrome, constipation and other GI disorders. (See Chapter 22.)

Function

The primary function and benefit of adequate dietary fiber are to increase bulk and water in the intestinal contents.[36-38] Fiber appears to shorten intestinal transit rate in dogs with normal or slow transit time and prolongs it in dogs with rapid transit rate.[39] Together, these factors help to promote and regulate normal bowel function. In addition, the typical end products of microbial fermentation of fiber (acetate, propionate and butyrate) are important in maintaining the health of the colon. Fiber decreases luminal pH through production of short-chain fatty acids and increases the population of the anaerobic flora. The antibacterial properties of short-chain fatty acids may decrease pathogenic intestinal bacteria, increase resistance of the gut to colonization by pathogenic bacteria and may be important in prevention of and recovery from intestinal disorders and cancer.[37-40]

Colonocytes preferentially use butyrate, an end product of fiber fermentation, as their energy source rather than glucose or amino acids.[41] In addition, short-chain fatty acids facilitate the absorption of sodium, chloride and water in the colon. The gut microflora produce an array of compounds in addition to short-chain fatty acids, including biotin, vitamin K, carbon dioxide and methane. In cases where short-chain fatty acids are absent (parenteral nutrition, partial bowel resection), colonic mucosa atrophies, becomes inflamed and has decreased resistance to bacterial translocation. However, excessive fermentation and production of short-chain fatty acids may be accompanied by flatulence, abdominal distention and diarrhea. The rate and extent of fiber fermentation in the large intestine are important aspects of overall digestion and absorption of ingested nutrients. Short-chain fatty acids are an important energy source for cattle and horses (i.e., supply up to 75% of DER); however, they provide less than 5% of the energy needs of dogs and cats because of the short intestinal tract and relatively fast transit time in these species.[42]

Importance of Fiber in Foods for Dogs and Cats

Research results demonstrate the need for some fiber in foods to maintain health and optimal function of the entire GI tract, but especially for colonocytes.[2] In people, fiber in the diet has been used to help manage diabetes mellitus, obesity, gallstones, hypercholesterolemia, irritable bowel syndrome, constipation, colonic diverticulosis, colorectal cancer, celiac disease, Crohn's disease, migraine headaches, hyperactivity in children and dental caries.[2] Different types and specific levels of dietary fiber can be important in overall therapeutic management of specific disease conditions in dogs and cats.

OBESITY AND BODY WEIGHT MANAGEMENT

A pet food containing slowly fermentable fiber can be very effective for controlling body weight and treating obesity. (See Chapter 13.) Slowly fermentable fibers, such as cellulose or peanut hulls, increase bulk in the stomach and intestines and help promote a feeling of satiety when fewer calories are consumed.[43] Pets in weight-control programs can eat more total food when the calories are diluted by fiber; thus, the animal eats fewer calories and loses weight. The amount of slowly fermentable fiber in weight-control foods is also important. If rapidly fermentable fibers are included in the food at high enough levels to promote satiety, adverse effects such as loose stools and excessive gas may occur.[44]

DIARRHEA AND CONSTIPATION

Fiber normalizes intestinal water content; fiber absorbs water in cases of diarrhea and adds moisture in cases of constipation. (See Case 2-1 "Soft Feces in a Young Giant Schnauzer.") Moderate amounts of either slowly fermentable or rapidly fermentable fiber possess this water-modulating feature. The more fermentable fibers (e.g.,

gums and soy fibers) can help pets with diarrhea and constipation by moderating the water content of the stool, thereby making a watery stool drier and a dry stool moister.

The binding and gelling properties of fiber also assist in management of diarrhea. In constipated pets, the fermentable fibers increase stool weight and moisture content, making the stool softer.

DIABETES MELLITUS

Management of diabetes mellitus in people, dogs and cats includes dietary changes. Both slowly and rapidly fermentable fiber types help control blood glucose levels in diabetic animals.[45] Clinically, pet foods that contain cellulose, soybean hulls or peanut hulls minimize blood glucose fluctuations, which can reduce or eliminate the need for insulin therapy. (See Chapter 24.)

Metabolism

Fiber is enzymatically degraded by intestinal microbes, including bacteria, fungi and protozoa but not by intrinsic mucosal digestive enzymes of the intestine. These microbes normally reside in the lower small intestine and large intestine and are referred to as anaerobes or facultative anaerobes because they can live without oxygen. They survive by producing energy through fermentation. Microorganisms colonizing the lower GI tract are similar to those found in the rumen. The proportion of different bacterial species is related to the type of fermentable substrate available. Different substrates facilitate the growth of different species. Some substrates promote acetate and butyrate formation, whereas others enhance propionate formation or gases such as hydrogen or methane as end products.

Fermentation is the energy-yielding breakdown of nutrients such as sugar, starch and fiber in an environment with little or no oxygen. In this process, the microbes only partially use the total energy available. Smaller energy-containing compounds, called short-chain fatty acids (acetic, propionic and butyric), and gases (carbon dioxide, hydrogen and methane) are microbial waste products; however, short-chain fatty acids are valuable substrates for the host animal. Microbes contain enzymes that can break the chemical bonds in different fibers. For example, microbial enzymes that digest cellulose are called cellulases and common pectin-digesting enzymes include pectin esterase and pectic lyases.[46] Figure 2-14 shows the major microbial pathways for fermentation of fibers through pyruvate to short-chain fatty acids.

Fermentation of fiber in the colon affects nitrogen metabolism. Fiber fermentation by bacteria increases bacterial numbers. Bacteria use ammonia as a source of nitrogen to build amino acids, proteins and DNA for reproduction. Small amounts of urea diffuse from the bloodstream into the colon where it is hydrolyzed to form ammonia.[2,47,48]

FIBER INTERACTIONS WITH NUTRIENT DIGESTIBILITY AND AVAILABILITY

The amount and type of fiber in a pet food have the greatest overall effect on digestibility of all the nutrients. In general, foods containing slowly fermentable fiber sources will have lower overall dry matter digestibility than foods without fiber or those containing rapidly fermentable fiber sources. Also, as the level of fiber in the food increases, the dry matter digestibility of the food decreases. Apparent and true digestibility of fats, starch and energy are unaffected by the type and amount of fiber in the food.[49,50]

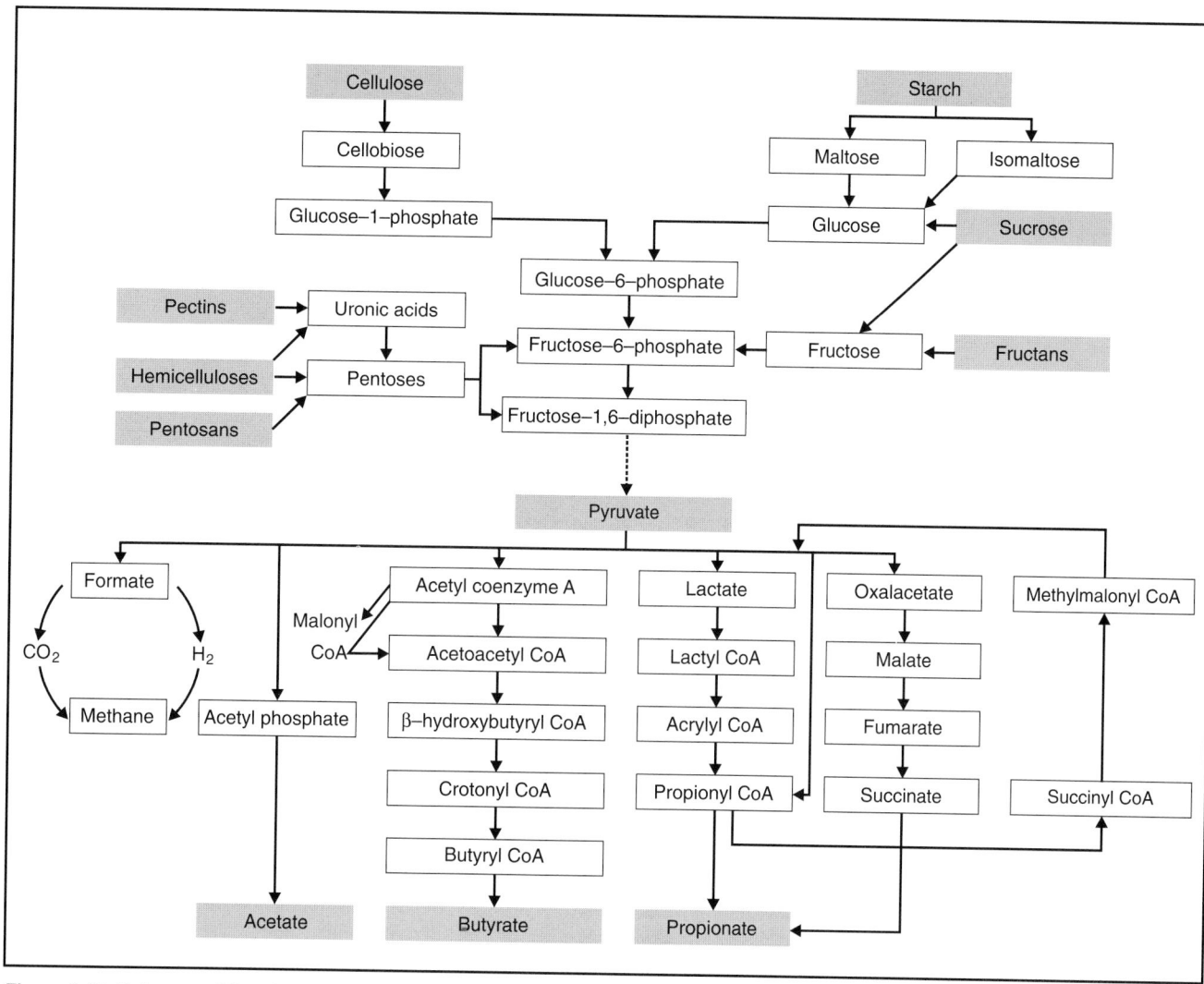

Figure 2-14. Pathways of fiber fermentation. Fibers (e.g., cellulose, pectins, hemicelluloses), starches and sugars are metabolized by intestinal microbes through various pathways to a common endpoint of pyruvate. The pyruvate is then further metabolized to yield energy for the microbe and waste products of short-chain fatty acids (e.g., acetate, propionate, butyrate) and gases (e.g., carbon dioxide, hydrogen and methane). Short-chain fatty acids are valuable substrates for the host animal that help maintain gastrointestinal tract health.

Apparent digestibility of protein is lower in foods containing fiber because of increased nitrogen in feces from the increased fecal biomass. Recent research using ileal-cannulated dogs has shown that true digestibility of protein is unaffected by dietary fiber type or content.[49,50] The discrepancy between the results obtained with total tract apparent digestibility and true digestibility can be explained by taking into account fermentation in the colon. One of the assumptions when calculating digestibility across the entire GI tract is that all material in the feces is of dietary origin. Fermentation of nutrients that pass into the large intestine, however, results in significant amounts of bacterial protein in the feces. Bacterial protein is then confounded with undigested dietary protein resulting in lower apparent digestibility. Therefore, it is best to use true protein digestibility to obtain an unbiased evaluation of pet foods containing fiber. When evaluating protein digestibility data, it is essential that fiber content of the food be known, and care must be taken when interpreting and comparing results among foods.

The main excretory product of fiber digestion is additional bacterial protein in the feces. It is typically analyzed as additional fecal nitrogen content and can confound protein digestibility measurements made using total fecal collections. Intestinal fermentation of fiber accounts for hydrogen, methane and other gases in expired breath. Some short-chain fatty acids are excreted in the stool.

Fiber affects mineral availability.[2] Some fiber types reduce and others enhance mineral absorption and use (Table 2-7). It is not clear what factors in fiber are responsible for the effects on mineral availability. Water-holding capacity, viscosity, cation exchange capacity, particle size, tannin content, oxalate content and presence of phytates, uronic acid and phenolic groups are among the properties of fibers that have been evaluated to predict effects on mineral availability.[2,46,51] Unfortunately, a direct relationship appears not to exist between these physiochemical properties measured on fibers in vitro and mineral availability measured in vivo. This disparity reflects the complex nature of the absorption processes within the intestine and interactions that occur with other food components.

Analyses

The fiber content of pet foods or ingredients can be measured by several different laboratory methods; the

Table 2-7. Mineral availability as affected by different fiber sources fed at 5% total dietary fiber.*

Fiber source	Zinc (%)**	Calcium (%)**	Iron (%)***	Phosphorus (%)†
Beet pulp	24[a]	44[a]	29[a]	67[a]
Corn bran	94	92	100	ND
Pea fiber	41	58[a]	ND	ND
Peanut hulls	30[a]	100	67	58[a]
Cellulose	88	100	100	100
Sunflower hulls	54	100	100	ND
Soy hulls	78	100	ND	64[a]
Wheat middlings	70	100	51[a]	ND
Apple pectin	ND	ND	55[a]	75
Citrus pulp cells	ND	ND	49[a]	75
Soy cotyledon fiber	ND	ND	86	66[a]
Gum arabic	ND	ND	81	100
Guar gum	ND	ND	100	35[a]

*Availability (%) of the mineral in a food with 5% iso-total dietary fiber relative to the same food with no fiber.
**Adapted from Wedekind K, Walker L, Hancock J, et al. Bioavailability of zinc and calcium is affected by certain fiber sources. Federation of American Societies for Experimental Biology Journal 1995; 9: A450.
***Adapted from Wedekind K, Beyer S, Titgemeyer E. Bioavailability of phosphorus is affected by certain fiber sources. Federation of American Societies for Experimental Biology Journal 1996; 10: A524.
†Adapted from Wedekind K, Walker L, Beyer S, et al. Bioavailability of iron is affected by certain fiber sources in chicks and puppies. Ninth International Symposium on Trace Elements in Man and Animals (TEMA-9) 1996; A20.
[a]Within the same mineral, a superscript "a" indicates significant reductions (p <0.10) relative to the no-fiber standard.
ND = not determined.

most common is the crude fiber method (Figure 2-12). In the United States, regulations require that the maximum amount of crude fiber be listed on the label of all pet foods. (See Chapter 5.) Determination of crude fiber adequately represents total fiber in a pet food when most of the fiber is slowly fermentable; however, the analysis excludes the more rapidly fermentable pectins and gums. Because the crude fiber analysis underestimates fermentable fiber, it does not accurately represent the total fiber in a pet food.

Fiber can also be measured by the total dietary fiber method[52] (Figure 2-12). This analysis is used to determine total fiber and is commonly used for measuring fiber content of human foods. In the total dietary fiber method, lipids are first extracted with ethanol and then the sample is digested with α-amylases to convert readily digestible starches to soluble sugars. All the water-soluble components (sugars, degraded starch, pectin, gums and most of the hemicellulose) are separated from the water-insoluble components or insoluble fibers (cellulose, lignin and a small fraction of hemicelluloses). The water-soluble components are further extracted with ethanol to remove the sugars and degraded starch. The residue that remains is termed soluble fiber, which includes pectins and gums.

The Van Soest fiber analysis system was developed as an improvement to the crude fiber method.[53] The Van Soest analysis uses detergents to more accurately estimate the different types of fiber and fractionate them into relatively digestible and indigestible fractions (Figure 2-12). Neutral detergent fiber (NDF) is the residue remaining after samples are boiled in a solution containing neutral pH detergent and EDTA. The residue that remains is mostly plant cell walls including hemicellulose, cellulose and lignin; however, the pectins are lost. Acid detergent fiber (ADF) is determined by boiling the analytical sample in an acidic detergent solution. The fraction remaining contains cellulose and lignin. The result of subtracting the amounts of ADF and NDF in a particular food or ingredient approximates the hemicellulose content. Like the limitations of crude fiber determinations, NDF and ADF do not measure the more soluble fiber fractions of pectins and gums;

therefore, they are not widely used to determine fiber in pet foods.

Requirements

Fiber is not considered essential in the diets of cats and dogs, although it is often included in commercial foods. Overall, dogs and cats do not derive much energy from absorbing the typical end products of bacterial fermentation; however, short-chain fatty acids are important in maintaining the health of the colon. Therefore, a small amount of fiber (less than 5%) that contains both rapidly and slowly fermentable fibers is recommended in foods for healthy pets. (See Chapters 9 and 11.) Today, much interest exists in human and veterinary nutrition about the role of "pharmacologic doses" of certain nutrients (e.g., fiber) in preventing chronic diseases. Undoubtedly, this interest will increase in the future. (See sidebar "Adequate vs. Optimal Nutrient Intake.")

Fiber also aids in the management of diseases such as obesity, diabetes mellitus, diarrhea, colitis and constipation. The types and amounts of dietary fiber required to assist in the management of these diseases can be found in Chapters 13, 22 and 24.

Deficiencies

Total deficiency of fiber in typical pet foods is not a practical problem because many ingredients used contain some fiber. Homemade foods, veterinary therapeutic foods made with more refined ingredients and purified diets used in research studies can be extremely low in fiber. Some dietary fiber that produces short-chain fatty acids is usually recommended.

Excess/Toxicity

Excess fiber may have undesirable effects. For instance, certain fiber types decrease the absorption of minerals. The effects on mineral absorption vary by type of fiber and the mineral. It appears that more rapidly fermentable fibers (e.g., pectins and guar gum) decrease availability of some minerals, whereas fibers that contain more cellulose have little effect on mineral absorption.

Adequate vs. Optimal Nutrient Intake*

NUTRITIONAL ESSENTIALITY

Nutritional essentiality describes those factors in the external chemical environments of organisms specifically required for normal physiologic functions. At least 40 such factors (e.g., vitamins, minerals, amino acids, fatty acids, water) are generally considered to be nutritionally essential. Foods are considered nutritionally "adequate" if they contain amounts of each of these essential nutrients that meet or exceed known needs.

The science of nutrition has functioned for a century under the nutritional essentiality paradigm that holds nutrients are essential to prevent ill-health in very specific ways. Specific prevention of nutrient deficiency diseases has been used to define nutrient essentiality and to establish dietary recommendations. Indeed, unless a clinical disease has been related specifically to the deprivation of a certain nutrient, then that nutrient has not been considered "essential."

Investigators have been able to estimate nutrient requirements quantitatively based on the specific deficiency disease connotation of the nutritional essentiality paradigm. The term "required" is generally used in reference to the lowest intake that prevents disease. Such minimum requirements, while seemingly physiologically relevant, are difficult to define or measure with any reasonable precision due to inter-individual variation, which is also difficult to estimate.

Reference levels of intake ("adequate levels") are set to exceed such minimums, and thus to have acceptably low risk of deficiency. Because risk is the probability of events occurring within populations, allowances relate to populations with their characteristic food habits and inherent inter-individual variations in minimum requirements. Thus, the recommended dietary allowances (RDAs) and the new reference (recommended) dietary intakes (RDIs) are implicitly intended to relate to the United States population (human) just as the Association of American Feed Control Officials (AAFCO) Dog Food and Cat Food Nutrient Profiles relate to pet populations.

CONDITIONALLY ESSENTIAL?

The nutritional essentiality paradigm does not pertain to cases in which nutrient needs of an individual or minority subgroup differ markedly from those of the general population. Under certain conditions, a dietary source of a "nonessential" nutrient can be needed to prevent physiologic dysfunction. For example, glutamine can reduce nitrogen loss and infection rate of bone marrow transplant patients. Carnitine can improve weight gain and nitrogen balance of parenterally fed infants, and helps maintain lean muscle mass in animals undergoing weight loss. The nutritional roles of these nutrients are simply not addressed by the nutritional essentiality paradigm.

NON-SPECIFIC EFFECTS?

The specific deficiency disease connotation of the nutritional essentiality paradigm has become a growing problem in dealing with issues of diet and health. This is because the paradigm does not pertain to functions of nutrients that are either nonspecific or nontraditional (i.e., outside the known functions of nutrients). Such functions have been suggested by recent epidemiology, which has produced evidence linking the consumption of several nutrients (e.g., high intakes of vitamin A-containing foods, relatively high intakes or high plasma levels of vitamin E and supranutritional dietary supplements of selenium) with reduced risks of chronic diseases.

In these cases, nutrient effects do not appear to have the specificity connoted by the nutritional essentiality paradigm. For example, the complementary natures of the antioxidant functions of vitamin E, vitamin C and selenium suggest that any one "spares" the need for the others in protecting against lipid peroxidation. Thus, the antioxidant nutrients appear to be risk modifiers of disease rather than primary agents in their etiologies.

ARE NON-NUTRIENTS REQUIRED?

The nutritional essentiality paradigm relates only to nutrients (i.e., dietary factors that are absorbed and function in normal host metabolism). Yet, it has become evident that some such non-nutrients (e.g., fiber) can positively affect health through functions that are technically external to the body. Several positive physiologic responses have been associated with the consumption of isolated fiber fractions or fiber-containing foods. Epidemiology has revealed associations of fiber-rich diets with reduced risks of cancer, coronary heart disease, diabetes mellitus, diverticulosis, hypertension and gallstone formation in people. Yet, under the nutritional essentiality paradigm, these effects are not easily described.

NEW PARADIGM

A new paradigm for nutrition is emerging out of the limitations of the essentiality paradigm. It takes an individualized view of organisms. It recognizes both endogenous and exogenous conditions as determinants of the dietary needs for definable health outcomes. These outcomes are not necessarily specifically associated with single nutrients. It recognizes these factors as nutrients if their activities benefit the metabolism and/or gastrointestinal function of the host. It recognizes various outcomes as appropriate for various individuals, both within a species/population, as well as between species.

Freedom from overt physiologic dysfunction, and reduced risk of chronic diseases, have become important outcomes in human and pet nutrition. Nutritional needs will be based on individual genetic and metabolic characteristics to the end that foods can be prescribed on an individual basis.

That the nutritional essentiality paradigm has been outgrown is indicated by its having become rather elastic in its application: Nutrients have come to be described as being required/essential for particular functions. Some are called dispensable/indispensable under certain conditions. Several are recognized as beneficial at levels greater than may be required.

Outgrowth of the old paradigm is occurring at an increasing pace with the development of the modern field of molecular biology. It is now clear that some nutrients function as gene regulators and that genetic bases can predispose to disease. The time is quickly approaching when it will be possible to identify disease predisposition, metabolic characteristics and specific dietary needs on an individual basis. Then, the population-based paradigm will be defunct and a new way of thinking about dietary needs will emerge.

*Excerpted from an article by the author originally published by *PetFood Industry* in July/August 1998, pages 31-43.

G.F. Combs, Jr.
Division of Nutritional Services
Cornell University
Ithaca, NY, USA

Table 2-8. Characteristics of selected fiber ingredients.

Fiber ingredient	Crude fiber (%)*	Total dietary fiber (%)*	Solubility in water	Fermentability rate
Apple pectin	0	95	Soluble	Rapid
Beet pulp	20	66	Insoluble	Moderate
Cellulose	80	98	Insoluble	Slow
Citrus pulp	12	77	Soluble	Rapid
Corn bran	19	90	Insoluble	Moderate
Guar gum	0	81	Soluble	Rapid
Gum arabic	0	91	Soluble	Rapid
Pea fiber	30	92	Insoluble	Moderate
Peanut hulls	57	76	Insoluble	Slow
Rice bran	44	13	Insoluble	Moderate
Soy fiber	20	83	Soluble	Rapid
Soy hulls	34	69	Insoluble	Moderate/slow
Sunflower hulls	54	80	Insoluble	Slow
Wheat bran	10	43	Insoluble	Moderate
Wheat middlings	7	46	Insoluble	Moderate

*As is basis.

Excess fiber can dilute the energy and nutrient content of the food to such an extent that an animal may have difficulty eating enough of the food to meet its needs. Controlled levels of fiber are advantageous in weight-reducing foods for dogs and cats; however, such foods are fortified so that only total energy intake is low and other nutrients are present in adequate amounts to meet daily requirements.

Sources

The maximum crude fiber content of pet foods must be listed in the guaranteed analysis section of pet food labels in the United States. Most dog and cat foods have crude fiber contents of less than 5% DM. The fiber in most pet foods comes from a variety of ingredients. Grains such as whole corn and brown rice are sources of fiber in dry extruded foods. Some pet foods contain specific ingredients added to provide fiber. Fiber sources commonly used in pet foods today include the hulls from rice, soybeans, peanuts and oats, dried beet pulp, various vegetable gums, corn bran, wheat bran, rice bran, oat bran and more purified fiber sources such as cellulose and soy fiber. AAFCO publishes official definitions of fiber ingredients.[54] Table 2-8 shows common fiber ingredients with fiber content and general classifications of solubility and fermentability.

■ PROTEIN/AMINO ACIDS

Definition

Proteins are large, complex molecules composed of hundreds to thousands of amino acids. Amino acids are composed of carbon, hydrogen, oxygen, nitrogen and sometimes sulfur and phosphorus. Four chemical groups covalently bonded to a carbon atom form the general structure of amino acids. The four groups include a hydrogen atom, a carboxyl group (COOH), an α-amino group (NH$_2$) and another chemical group specific for each amino acid (Table 2-9). Although hundreds of amino acids exist in nature, only 20 are commonly found as protein components. The amino acids found in mammalian proteins are the L-isomer of α-amino acids, which means the side chain unique to each amino acid is linked to the α-carbon atom in the L (levorotatory) position.

Structure

Proteins are linear polymers of amino acids in which the amino group of one amino acid and the carboxyl group of another amino acid are coupled together (peptide bond) (Figure 2-15). Amino acids arranged in chains are referred to as peptides. Two bonded amino acids form a dipeptide, three a tripeptide and more than three a polypeptide.

Proteins can be described as having a primary, secondary, tertiary or quaternary structure. The primary structure of proteins refers to the sequence (order) of amino acids along the polypeptide chain. The secondary structure of proteins refers to the configuration of the polypeptide chains resulting from hydrogen bonds between adjacent amino acids. Alpha-helices, β-pleated sheets or random coils are formed by these hydrogen bonds. The tertiary structure describes how further interactions of the amino acids cause folding and bending of the polypeptide chain giving the protein its biological activity. Proteins have a quaternary structure if they contain more than one polypeptide chain. Hydrogen bonds, electrostatic bonds and ionic bonds form between the polypeptide chains and stabilize the aggregates. The primary structure of proteins is responsible for the secondary, tertiary and quaternary structures that are formed.

Proteins may also be classified by other compounds bound to peptides. Simple proteins are made up of only amino acids. Simple proteins are subclassified into fibrous or globular proteins according to shape, solubility and chemical composition. Fibrous proteins include collagens, elastins and keratins, which are the major structural proteins in the body. Collagens are the main proteins of connective tissues and make up about 30% of the total proteins in the body. Elastin is the protein found in tendons and arteries. Keratins are the main proteins in hair. All enzymes, hormones and antibodies that are proteins have a globular structure. Subgroups of globular proteins include the albumins, histones, globulins and protamines.

Conjugated proteins contain amino acids and carbohydrates (glycoproteins), lipids (lipoproteins) or minerals (phosphoproteins, chromoproteins). Glycoproteins are commonly found as components of cell membranes and function to modulate enzymes, receptors and immune function and to recognize cells (antigen and blood types). Glycoproteins are also components of mucous secretions that act as lubricants in many parts of the body, myelin

Table 2-9. Amino acids.

Name	Structural formula	Abbreviations 3-letter	1-letter	Side chain	Essentiality
Alanine		Ala	A	Aliphatic	Nonessential
Arginine		Arg	R	Basic	Essential
Asparagine		Asn	N	Acidic	Nonessential
Aspartate		Asp	D	Acidic	Nonessential
Cysteine		Cys	C	Sulfur containing	Nonessential but can provide for up to 50% of methionine requirements
Glutamate		Glu	E	Acidic	Nonessential
Glutamine		Gln	Q	Acidic	Conditionally essential
Glycine		Gly	G	Aliphatic	Nonessential
Histidine		His	H	Basic and aromatic	Essential
Isoleucine		Ile	I	Aliphatic branched chain	Essential
Leucine		Leu	L	Aliphatic branched chain	Essential

Continued on next page.

Table 2-9. Amino acids (continued).

Name	Structural formula	Abbreviations 3-letter	Abbreviations 1-letter	Side chain	Essentiality
Lysine		Lys	K	Basic	Essential
Methionine		Met	M	Sulfur containing	Essential
Phenylalanine		Phe	F	Aromatic	Essential
Proline		Pro	P	Imino acid	Nonessential
Serine		Ser	S	Aliphatic	Nonessential
Taurine		Tau		Beta-amino acid and sulfonic acid group	Essential for cats, possibly conditionally essential for dogs
Threonine		Thr	T	Aliphatic	Essential
Tryptophan		Trp	W	Aromatic	Essential
Tyrosine		Tyr	Y	Aromatic	Nonessential but can provide for up to 50% of phenylalanine requirements
Valine		Val	V	Aliphatic branched chain	Essential

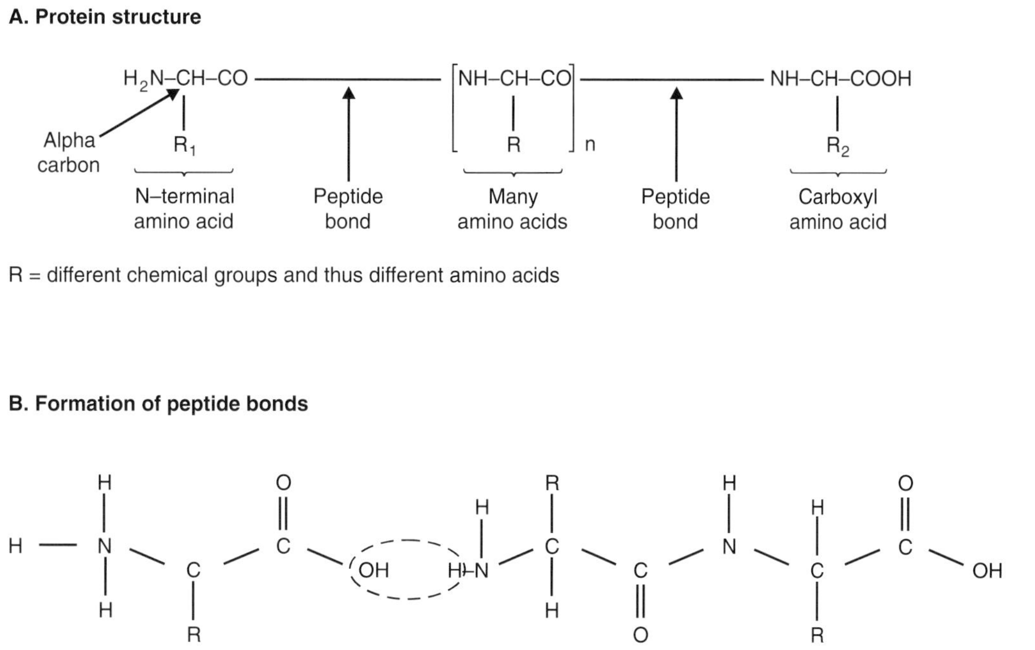

A. Protein structure

R = different chemical groups and thus different amino acids

B. Formation of peptide bonds

Figure 2-15. Protein structure (A) and formation of peptide bonds (B). The dotted lines show how the peptide bonds are formed, with the production of water. R = the remainder of amino acids. For example, in glycine, R = $(CH_2)_2$–COOH.

that surrounds nervous tissues and as part of lipoproteins. Lipoproteins transport lipids in the bloodstream in a water-miscible form to tissues. Lipoproteins are typically classified into four main categories according to their density: 1) chylomicrons, 2) very low-density lipoproteins (VLDL), 3) low-density lipoproteins (LDL) and 4) high-density lipoproteins (HDL). (See Chapter 24.) Proteins that contain minerals include hemoglobin (iron), cytochromes (copper) and caseins (phosphorus).

Some proteins in the body contain special amino acids that are derived from common amino acids. Collagen contains hydroxyproline and hydroxylysine, which are derivatives of proline and lysine, respectively. Triiodothyronine and tetraiodothyronine (thyroxine) are derived from tyrosine and function as hormones and part of the protein thyroglobulin. Gamma-carboxyglutamic acid is derived from glutamic acid and is key for the function of calcium binding in thrombin, which functions in blood clotting. Other amino acids such as taurine (a β-amino acid) and γ-aminobutyric acid function in specific roles in the body, but are not found as part of proteins.

Purines (adenine and guanine) and pyrimidines (cytosine, thymine, uracil) are other nitrogen-containing molecules that form nucleic acids. Nucleic acids (RNA and DNA) carry the genetic information that codes for the primary structure of proteins (the amino acid sequence).

Function

Proteins are the principal structural constituents of body organs and tissues including: 1) collagen and elastin found in cartilage, tendons and ligaments, 2) the contractile proteins actin and myosin in muscles, 3) keratin proteins in skin, hair and nails and 4) blood proteins including hemoglobin, transferrin, albumin and globulin. Proteins also function as enzymes, hormones (e.g., insulin)

and antibodies. Amino acids can serve as a source of energy after the nitrogen-containing amino group is removed by deamination or transamination.

Importance of Amino Acids

Several amino acids are classified as essential or indispensable (10 for dogs and 11 for cats). These amino acids cannot be synthesized by the body in sufficient quantities and therefore must be supplied by food. The carbon skeletons of these essential amino acids are the critical component that the body cannot synthesize. Many of the remaining amino acids are nonessential or dispensable; they can be synthesized in the body from carbon and nitrogen building blocks and need not be present in the food if adequate nitrogen and energy are available. Some amino acids are conditionally essential. These amino acids ordinarily are not required in the food except during certain physiologic or pathologic conditions when they may not be synthesized in adequate quantities.

Although nonessential amino acids can be made from precursor carbon skeletons, they are just as critical to the makeup of proteins and are just as essential for metabolic reactions in the body as essential amino acids. Protein is also necessary to provide the body with a source of nitrogen for synthesis of other nitrogen-containing compounds including purines, pyrimidines, nucleotides, nucleic acids, creatinine, nitric oxide and some neurotransmitters.

Metabolism

Digestion and Absorption

Dietary proteins must be digested to be absorbed from the GI tract. Protein digestion begins in the stomach with the action of the enzyme pepsin in the presence of hydrochloric acid. The main end products of gastric protein digestion are mixtures of large polypeptides; however, little or no absorption of these molecules occurs. In the small intestine, other enzymes (endopeptidases and exopeptidases) are secreted by the pancreas and the cells lining the small intestine. These enzymes break the bonds between the amino acids of large polypeptides resulting in free amino acids, dipeptides and tripeptides that can be absorbed across the intestinal wall.[1] Some proteins are less readily digested than others. The rapidity of digestion is influenced by many factors, including protein structure, processing effects, other nutrients in the meal and presence of enzyme inhibitory factors.

Absorption of amino acids is a sodium-dependent, active-transport process that requires energy (ATP). This process is mediated by four different carrier systems that transport neutral amino acids, basic amino acids, dicarboxylic amino acids and imino acids. These separate carrier systems help ensure transport of a well-balanced mixture of amino acids from the intestinal lumen to the portal vein.

Protein Usage

Absorbed amino acids and small di- and tripeptides are reassembled into "new" proteins by the liver and other tissues of the body. Amino acids from food are transported from the liver to other tissues by serum albumin or as free amino acids. The fate of amino acids after absorption falls into three general categories: 1) tissue protein synthesis, especially in muscles and liver, 2) synthesis of enzymes, albumin, hormones and other nitrogen-containing compounds and 3) deamination and use of the remaining carbon skeletons for energy.

A high rate of protein synthesis occurs in production of red and white blood cells, epithelial cells of the skin and those lining the GI tract (i.e., intestinal mucosa, which produces exocrine secretions, such as digestive enzymes and mucus) and the pancreas. In addition, all body proteins are continuously broken down and resynthesized, a process known as protein turnover. Some proteins (muscle proteins and some plasma proteins such as albumin) have a relatively long lifetime (days to weeks). Other proteins (cytokines and enzymes) have relatively short lives (minutes to hours).

Muscle protein composes nearly 50% of total body protein, but only accounts for 30% of new protein synthesized, whereas visceral and organ proteins compose a smaller portion of total body protein but account for 50% of new proteins synthesized. Because protein turnover is the sum total of the continuous degradation and synthesis cycles of specific proteins, a measure of protein turnover is only a "snapshot" in time of protein metabolism. In addition, rates of protein synthesis and degradation for any particular protein can change under different physiologic conditions.

The body is able to synthesize new proteins and enzymes provided all the necessary amino acids are available. The source of amino acids is not important. Cells use amino acids from a variety of sources including those derived from food proteins, single amino acids added to the food and amino acids synthesized by the body. In addition, cells synthesizing new protein cannot distinguish between amino acids from grains (e.g., corn and rice) and those from meats (e.g., chicken and beef). The only criterion is that all the amino acids needed to synthesize a particular protein be present in sufficient quantities when necessary. Protein synthesis will be limited when certain amino acids are not present or available in the quantities needed.

During protein turnover, a fraction of amino acids enter catabolic pathways that lead to their permanent loss. The amount of nitrogen lost every day as a result of the body's continuous breakdown process is called obligatory nitrogen loss. Dietary protein must be consumed each day to replace amino acids lost to catabolism. Trauma, infection, severe sepsis and burns increase protein turnover and nitrogen losses, whereas nitrogen losses are reduced during long-term fasting and starvation. Nitrogen is normally lost from the body in feces (nitrogen, proteins, cells), in urine and through skin desquamation and loss of hair.

Nitrogen balance is the net difference between nitrogen consumed and nitrogen lost; however, the determination is fraught with technical difficulties. Most commonly, nitrogen losses are underestimated through incomplete collection of feces, urine, hair and sloughed cells of the skin; whereas, nitrogen intake is routinely overestimated. Thus, nitrogen balance should only be regarded as a crude estimate of body protein status and not be used to distinguish among subtleties in protein and nitrogen metabolism.

Protein Storage

Although, in effect, there is some storage of excess amino acids, they are not stored to the same degree that extra fat and carbohydrates are stored. Structural proteins in all tissues, especially in muscles and liver and serum albumin, can be considered as amino acid stores. Muscle protein represents the largest reserve from which amino acids may be drawn in times of need. Too much loss of body protein impairs muscle function. Liver and muscle protein and serum albumin synthesis increase after consumption of a protein-containing meal. Once protein synthesis is maximized, excess amino acids are deaminated and transaminated to yield amino groups and carbon skeletons. The carbon skeletons can be used for many purposes including glucose precursors, which can be stored as glycogen or converted to fatty acids and acetyl-CoA, which can be used for fuel immediately. In the hours after consumption of a meal containing protein, body protein synthesis gradually declines as the amino acids from the meal are used. Because protein turnover and obligatory nitrogen losses continue to occur, muscles must convert from net uptake of amino acids to net release of amino acids as fasting becomes dominant. Although glycogen and lipids are the preferred short-term and long-term energy stores, protein catabolism can supply carbon skeletons needed to maintain glucose pools and supply the body with energy (ATP). Protein degradation continues until the next meal, after which protein synthesis exceeds protein breakdown.

The carbon skeletons of catabolized amino acids can be completely oxidized to carbon dioxide or converted by the liver to glucose or ketone bodies. Thus, amino acids can be glucogenic or ketogenic. Glucogenic amino acids can be converted to glucose through pyruvate or any of the TCA cycle intermediates. Ketogenic amino acids are those that can be converted to acetyl-CoA or ketone bodies but cannot be metabolized to glucose. Some catabolized amino acids yield two different carbon skeletons, one ketogenic and the other glucogenic (Table 2-10).

Protein Excretion

Amino acid catabolism produces waste nitrogen, if it is not used for purine or pyrimidine synthesis. Catabolism of amino acids typically leads to formation of ammonia, which is toxic to body cells. Ammonia must be converted to a less toxic form that can be transported in blood and excreted. Ammonia formation occurs in all tissues, but is especially prevalent in the liver and kidneys during gluconeogenesis. More than 90% of the nitrogen resulting from protein degradation is converted to urea in the liver and kidneys and then excreted in the urine. A smaller fraction of nitrogen is lost as ammonia, creatinine and nitrate. Hepatic and renal detoxification of ammonia via the urea cycle is a critical function. The amino acids ornithine, citrulline and arginine are key intermediates. Other amino acids (e.g., glutamate, aspartate, alanine and the amide group of glutamine) carry excess amino groups from other tissues to the liver and kidneys for conversion to urea. Catabolism of other nitrogen-containing metabolites also contributes to the waste nitrogen pool.

CLINICAL PROBLEMS ASSOCIATED WITH NITROGEN DISPOSAL

Hyperammonemia may result if any of the enzymes involved in the urea cycle are lacking or have impaired activity. Part of the therapy for any disease (e.g., liver disease) in which urea cycle function is reduced is to decrease plasma concentrations of ammonia. Reducing total protein intake, reducing intake of nonessential amino acids and substituting keto analogues of some amino acids may help reduce the ammonia load. Other measures (e.g., dialysis, transfusion, administration of drugs and other compounds that trap nitrogenous metabolites) can be used to prevent an ammonia encephalopathy crisis. (See Chapter 23.)

Reduced renal function may also impair nitrogen disposal (i.e., urea may not be excreted efficiently). Reducing waste products of protein catabolism through dietary manipulation aids therapy for chronic renal failure. (See Chapter 19.)

Catabolism of purines (adenine and guanine from nucleotides, ATP and GTP, RNA and DNA) may also create nitrogen disposal problems. Uric acid is the end product of purine catabolism in people, nonhuman primates, birds and Dalmatian dogs; allantoin is produced in all other mammals. Uric acid and allantoin are excreted in urine and feces. Accumulation of uric acid in serum can lead to gout (uric acid crystals in joints) and uric acid uroliths. Hyperuricemia can be treated with drugs (allopurinol) and with dietary intervention. Reducing total protein intake and reducing or eliminating dietary ingredients containing high levels of purines (organ meats, glandular meats, fish such as mackerel and sardines) have been successful in some dogs with urolithiasis. (See Chapter 20.)

Protein-losing enteropathy (PLE) and protein-losing nephropathy (PLN) are two syndromes in which excessive amounts of protein are lost from the body. PLE is a group of diseases characterized by excessive loss of serum protein into the intestinal tract. Causes of PLE include lymphatic disorders (lymphangiectasia, neoplasia, congestive heart failure) and diseases associated with increased mucosal permeability or mucosal ulceration (intestinal neoplasia, granulomatous enteritis, lymphocytic-plasmacytic enteritis, intestinal parasitism, etc.).

PLN is characterized by excessive loss of serum protein into the urine. Causes of PLN include glomerulonephritis and amyloidosis that develop secondary to chronic inflammatory conditions such as neoplasia, heartworm disease, ehrlichiosis, systemic mycosis, brucellosis, osteomyelitis and immune-mediated disease.

Analyses of Protein

Chemical Analyses of Protein

Protein concentration in foods (crude protein content) is typically calculated from the nitrogen content by the Kjeldahl method. In this method, the food sample is digested with sulfuric acid, which converts all nitrogen in amino acids to ammonia. The ammonia is distilled, collected and quantitated using a colorimetric titration procedure. Two assumptions are made in calculating crude protein from nitrogen. First, that all nitrogen in the food sample is present as protein and second, that all protein contains 16% nitrogen. The crude protein content of the food is then calculated: crude protein in food (g/kg) = g nitrogen in food/kg x 6.25.

Neither assumption is always true. Not all nitrogen in food is present as protein; some nitrogen is present as free amino acids, amides, glycosides, alkaloids and ammonium salts. Other nitrogen is complexed with lipids. Different protein ingredients in food also have different nitrogen contents and, therefore, different conversion factors (Table 2-11). The use of an average conversion factor (i.e., 6.25) for all proteins in food simplifies calculations and can be rationalized by keeping in mind that most pet foods are mixtures of protein-containing ingredients. In addition, animal protein requirements are typically calculated from determination of individual amino acid requirements that are converted to nitrogen requirements and then expressed as a protein requirement by multiplying nitrogen by 6.25.

Protein Quality

The crude protein content of pet foods gives a measure of the amount of nitrogen available to the animal but provides little information about the nutritional value. Crude protein digestibility is determined by calculating the difference

Table 2-10. Glucogenic and ketogenic amino acids.

Exclusively ketogenic	Leucine, lysine
Exclusively glucogenic	Alanine, serine, glycine, cysteine, aspartate, asparagine, glutamate, glutamine, arginine, histidine, valine, threonine, methionine, proline
Ketogenic and glucogenic	Isoleucine, phenylalanine, tyrosine, tryptophan

Table 2-11. Factors for converting nitrogen to crude protein.

Food protein	Nitrogen (g/kg)	Conversion factor
Soybeans	175.1	5.71
Barley, oats, wheat	171.5	5.83
Corn, eggs, meat	160.0	6.25
Milk	156.8	6.38

Methods for Assessing Protein Quality

In vivo methods for assessing protein quality (Table 1) involve feeding the test protein to animals and measuring a response such as nitrogen retention (biological value [BV]), weight gain (protein efficiency ratio [PER], net protein ratio [NPR], relative protein value [RPV], relative nutritive value [RNV]) or whole body nitrogen content (net protein utilization [NPU]). In vivo tests to determine protein quality are typically expensive and time-consuming. The methods that involve growth responses are of limited value in determining the value of a protein for nongrowing adult animals. The true amino acid digestibility is considered the best method for predicting nutritional value of a protein.

The in vitro methods of determining protein quality (Table 1) are simpler and less expensive than the in vivo tests. Most methods predict the quality of the protein by evaluating its amino acid profile. The amino acid score or chemical score method compares the amino acid most limiting in the test protein with the quantity of that same amino acid in the reference protein. Egg protein is typically used as a reference protein and given a score of 100. All other protein sources are given a score as a percentage relative to egg. The chemical score method only rates a protein based on its most limiting amino acid and does not take into account all the other essential amino acids in the protein.

The essential amino acid index (EAAI) method calculates a mean amino acid ratio for all the essential amino acids based on their individual ratios compared with the reference protein. The total essential amino acid content (E/T) calculates the proportion of essential amino acids of the total nitrogen in the protein. Although in vitro methods predict the quality of the protein based on the amino acid patterns, they do not account for digestibility and processing effects.

BIBLIOGRAPHY

Zapsalis C, Beck RA. Proteins: Sources and nutritional evaluation. In: Food Chemistry and Nutritional Biochemistry. New York, NY: John Wiley & Sons, 1985; 93-128.

Oser BL. An integrated essential amino acid index for predicting the biological value of proteins. In: Protein and Amino Acid Nutrition. New York, NY: Academic Press Inc, 1959; 281-295.

Table 1. Methods for assessing protein quality.

In vivo methods	Description
Biological value (BV)	Based on nitrogen balance when fed a test protein
	$$BV = \frac{food\ N - (fecal\ N + urinary\ N)}{food\ N - fecal\ N} \times 100$$
Protein efficiency ratio (PER)	Based on weight gain in growing rats fed a test protein compared with weight gain when fed a casein-based food
	$$PER = \frac{weight\ gain\ (g)}{protein\ intake\ (g)}$$
Net protein ratio (NPR)	Similar to PER but protein-free food is also fed
	$$NPR = \frac{weight\ gain\ in\ test\ group + weight\ loss\ in\ group\ fed\ protein\text{-}free\ food}{protein\ intake}$$
Net protein utilization (NPU)	Similar to NPR except total body N is determined instead of weight gain
	$$NPU = \frac{body\ N\ of\ animals\ fed\ test\ protein - body\ N\ of\ animals\ fed\ protein\text{-}free\ food}{N\ intake}$$
Relative protein value (RPV) Relative nutritive value (RNV)	Graded amounts of test and control proteins are fed and weight gain measured
	$$RPV\ or\ RNV = \frac{slope\ of\ weight\ gain\ curve\ for\ animals\ fed\ the\ test\ protein}{slope\ of\ weight\ gain\ curve\ for\ animals\ fed\ the\ control\ protein}$$ (slope ratio)
True amino acid digestibility	Small intestinal digestibility of each amino acid in a test protein is determined in animal fitted with an ileal cannula; removes confounding effects of large intestinal microbial population
In vitro methods	**Description**
Amino acid score (chemical score)	Comparison of the limiting amino acid content of test protein with that of an established standard
	$$AA\ score = \frac{mg\ amino\ acid/g\ test\ protein}{mg\ amino\ acid/g\ reference\ proteins}$$
Essential amino acid index (EAAI)	Mean amino acid ratio for all the essential amino acids based on their individual ratios compared with amino acid ratios of the reference protein
Total essential amino acid content (E/T)	Proportion of essential amino acids of the total nitrogen in the protein

between quantities of crude protein eaten and that present in the feces. Protein digestibility coefficients determined by digestibility tests in which nitrogen intake is measured along with nitrogen excreted in feces are termed apparent protein digestibility. Protein digestibility coefficients based on collection and analyses of digesta from the terminal ileum give a more accurate measure of protein nitrogen absorbed than those based on fecal collections. Values determined from terminal ileal digesta exclude endogenous protein secretion from the GI tract and contributions from the intestinal microflora. Ileal collection eliminates the large intestine and bacterial fermentation as a source of errors. Values obtained here are termed true protein digestibility coefficients. Apparent and true digestibility values can be determined similarly for each ingested amino acid.

Digestibility coefficients for protein and amino acids are not completely satisfactory for measuring the value of a protein for animals because the efficiency with which amino acids are used varies among protein sources. Several methods have been used to determine the quality of protein sources for animals. Some methods involve testing the protein source by feeding it to animals (in vivo methods), whereas other methods evaluate the protein's quality by chemically analyzing its amino acid composition (in vitro methods). (See sidebar "Methods for Assessing Protein Quality.")

Because protein-containing ingredients are added to pet foods to supply required amino acids, the amino acid composition and digestibility of the protein ingredients are important considerations. The quality of the protein affects the amount that must be provided to meet an animal's protein requirement. The amino acids of proteins that are easily digested are readily available for absorption. Such proteins have high nutritional value and less of them are needed to meet an animal's amino acid requirement. As protein quality increases, the amount of the protein required in the pet food decreases.

Another important factor contributing to protein value is the balance of essential amino acids. Even proteins that are easily digested can have low nutritional value if they have imbalances or deficiencies of essential amino acids. For example, gelatin is a protein source derived from animal collagen. Although gelatin is highly digestible it is a very poor quality protein because it is deficient in the essential amino acid tryptophan.

PROCESSING EFFECTS

Maillard reactions (nonenzymatic browning reactions) can cause deterioration of nutritional quality during processing or storage by affecting availability of some amino acids.[2] These reactions occur when reducing sugars, such as glucose, fructose, lactose or maltose, covalently bond with free amino groups such as those on lysine. Heat accelerates the reaction. Digestive enzymes do not cleave peptide bonds adjacent to an amino acid with an attached sugar. Lysine can be made unavailable through Maillard reactions with the reducing sugars found in most pet foods.[3] Maillard reaction products may increase microbial taurine degradation in the colon. Maillard reaction products are generally not absorbed, or if they are absorbed, they are excreted in the urine and are of no nutritional value to the animal.[4] Alternatively, controlled Maillard reactions can be used during cooking to produce desirable flavors, colors or aromas of foods. (See Chapter 4.)

Heat and alkaline pH may result in unusual crosslinking of certain amino acids and peptides that are not found in nature.[3] Examples include lysinoalanine (lysine linked with alanine), lanthionine (cysteine linked with alanine) and ornithoalanine (ornithine linked with alanine). Because these compounds are not well-used by animals, they reduce the protein quality of the food.[5] This type of amino acid crosslinking may occur during the processing of ingredients often used in pet foods, such as dried meat meals.

Protein/Amino Acid Requirements

Factors Affecting Requirements

New proteins can be synthesized from dietary amino acids or nonessential amino acids that were previously synthesized by the body. By definition, essential amino acids used in protein synthesis must be provided by food. Therefore, animals do not have a requirement for protein per se but have an amino acid requirement. The amount of each amino acid that an animal requires varies based on factors such as growth, pregnancy, lactation and some disease states. In addition to requiring specific essential amino acids, dogs and cats have a requirement for building blocks (carbon skeletons and nitrogen) for nonessential amino acids. The building blocks for nonessential amino acids can either be derived from excess essential amino acids that are broken down and reassembled into nonessential amino acids or from other nonessential amino acids in food. Thus, a complete statement of amino acid requirements should include all the essential amino acids and an amount of amino nitrogen that can be used for synthesis of nonessential amino acids.

Practically speaking, because most foods contain whole proteins and not individual amino acids, and because exact individual amino acid requirements are not known for every situation, it is fair to consider a protein requirement instead of individual amino acid requirements in most instances when discussing companion animal nutrition.

The amount of protein that must be included in a pet food also depends on how much food the animal consumes. It is easy to understand why animals that are growing, pregnant or lactating require dietary protein to support new tissue growth and milk production. If an animal only consumes small quantities of food to meet its energy requirement then the food needs to have a greater protein concentration to meet the animal's protein requirement. For example, high-calorie pet foods should have more protein as a percentage of the food than low-calorie foods. The opposite is also true. Larger portions of low-calorie foods are typically consumed; therefore, animals can adequately meet their daily requirements with a food that has a lower percentage of protein.

Adult animals also need dietary protein to replace the amino acids that enter pathways of amino acid catabolism and are permanently lost. Healthy adults also have a daily requirement for protein to replace nitrogen lost as urea, ammonia, creatinine, nitrate in urine and feces, sloughing of epithelial cells in skin and the GI tract, sweat, hair, nasal secretions, semen from males and secretions due to reproductive cycles in females. Dietary protein that must be consumed each day to replace the obligatory nitrogen loss is termed the maintenance protein requirement.

Adult and growing animals have maintenance requirements for protein, but only growing animals have the additional requirement of protein for growth. The additional protein required by pregnant and lactating animals really supports growth. An animal's physiologic state also may result in increased or decreased protein catabolism and nitrogen losses. For example, patients with cancer, burns and trauma may have increased daily protein requirements.

Nitrogen balance is the difference between the nitrogen consumed and the amount lost each day. Growing animals, pregnant females and any animals that are replenishing or rebuilding tissue are in positive nitrogen balance. Zero nitrogen balance occurs in normal healthy adults receiving minimally adequate or more than adequate dietary protein when nitrogen output equals nitrogen intake. Negative nitrogen balance can occur during lactation, starvation or fasting when there is inadequate or no protein intake. Excessive body protein catabolism due to burns, injury, fever, infections, hormonal imbalance or psychological causes can also cause negative nitrogen balance. Amino acid imbalances and antagonisms can cause negative nitrogen balance even when adequate amounts of protein are being consumed.

IMBALANCE AND ANTAGONISM

Essential amino acids must be provided in adequate amounts and in proper balance. When amino acids are used for protein synthesis, all the amino acids necessary to synthesize each protein must be present. The amino acid in shortest supply relative to demand is called the "first limiting amino acid." An imbalance occurs when one or more amino acids needed for protein synthesis are not available in the quantity needed, but at least one other amino acid is provided in excess.[6] Amino acid antagonism occurs when amino acids have similar chemical structures.[6] Typically, an excess of one of these amino acids increases the requirement of one or more chemically similar amino acids (antagonism). Neither amino acid imbalance nor amino acid antagonism occurs in pets eating typical commercial pet foods.

Protein Requirements for Dogs and Cats

The absolute minimum dietary protein requirement can be estimated by feeding extremely high-quality protein or commonly used protein sources. If the estimate is based on feeding high-quality protein (e.g., lactalbumin), a growing dog requires approximately 9.5% protein on a DMB[7,8] and an adult dog about 6.0% protein on a DMB.[9] AAFCO has established that foods for growth should contain at least 22% protein, and foods for adult maintenance should contain at least 18% protein, both on a DMB, for dog foods containing commonly used protein ingredients.[10] It is important to note that AAFCO recommendations should be interpreted as daily allowances, not as absolute minimum requirements.

Growing kittens and adult cats have higher protein requirements than most other domestic species. The minimum requirement has been estimated to be about 24% (DMB) for kittens and 14% (DMB) for adult cats, assuming use of extremely high-quality protein sources.[11] For commercial foods using commonly available protein sources, AAFCO has recommended that foods for kittens and adult cats contain at least 30 and 26% protein on a DMB, respectively.[10] Again, AAFCO recommendations for protein are meant to be interpreted as a daily allowance of protein, not as an absolute minimum requirement.

Amino Acids of Special Importance

Several amino acids have important roles in the nutrition and health of dogs and cats. Among these are taurine, arginine and glutamine/glutamate.

Taurine

Taurine is a sulfur-containing β-amino acid. The amino group resides on the second (β) carbon rather than the first (α) carbon as with other amino acids. Taurine also has a sulfonic acid (SOOH) rather than a carboxylic acid group. Taurine is not incorporated into proteins synthesized by the body because of its structure. Rather, taurine is found as a free amino acid in many tissues, including brain, retina, myocardium, skeletal muscle, liver, platelets, leukocytes, in fluids such as milk and in complexes with bile salts.[12]

Taurine is conjugated to bile acids to form water-soluble bile salts that assist in the absorption of dietary fats. Taurine also serves as a neurotransmitter and neuromodulator in the central nervous system and is involved with body temperature regulation, brain development, maintenance of normal retinal structure and normal heart function.[12] Taurine is also speculated to conjugate toxic compounds, serve as an antioxidant, stabilize cell membranes and regulate cell volume and osmolarity.[12]

Taurine is an essential amino acid for cats because cats have minimal ability to synthesize taurine and have obligatory losses due to the necessity for conjugating bile acids to taurine. Unlike other animals, cats conjugate bile acids only to taurine and not to glycine. Further, cats have an obligatory loss of taurine in the feces due to bacterial degradation in the intestine and intestinal losses of taurine through enterohepatic circulation. This obligatory loss coupled with a minimal capacity for cats to synthesize taurine makes taurine an essential nutrient for this species.

Documented signs of taurine deficiency include reproductive failure in queens, developmental abnormalities in kittens, central retinal degeneration and dilated cardiomyopathy.[13,14] Taurine deficiency is more likely to occur in cats that are fed dog foods, homemade foods and vegetarian foods that are not supplemented with taurine.

Taurine requirements in cats are highly dependent on ingredient sources and processing. The requirement increases slightly with increased dietary protein. Certain proteins (e.g., isolated soya protein) and the canning process increase the dietary taurine allowance compared with freezing or using casein as the protein source. Processing neither destroys nor binds appreciable quantities of taurine; however, processing apparently alters food so that enhanced numbers of intestinal bacteria degrade taurine. The specific biochemical alteration of food responsible for this change has not been described. Current recommendations are to include at least 1 g of purified crystalline taurine/kg (0.1% DM) in dry foods and at least 2 g of purified crystalline taurine/kg for moist foods (0.2% DM).[10]

There is no evidence that taurine is an essential amino acid for dogs; however, research indicates that it may be conditionally essential. In one study, investigators showed that feeding a high-fat food (24% DM) significantly reduced plasma taurine concentrations, with values from some dogs becoming marginally deficient.[15] Dilated cardiomyopathy in

American cocker spaniels and golden retrievers has also been associated with plasma taurine deficiency and low myocardial taurine concentrations.[16] (See Chapter 18.)

Arginine

Arginine is a basic amino acid that is essential for kittens, cats, puppies and dogs. Cats develop signs of deficiency rapidly. Within three hours of consuming a meal devoid of arginine, cats develop hyperammonemia, vomiting, ataxia, vocalization (moaning) and hyperactivity; death may occur. Similar signs of ammonia toxicity such as tremors, vomiting, profuse salivation and hyperglycemia appear quickly in dogs following a meal that lacks arginine. Arginine is a key intermediate in the urea cycle, which is the major metabolic pathway that detoxifies nitrogenous wastes, such as ammonia.[17] Ornithine and citrulline can substitute for arginine and prevent hyperammonemia because they are also urea cycle intermediates. However, they cannot restore growth rates.[18] Ornithine and citrulline are not present in high enough quantities to substitute for arginine in typical commercial foods for dogs and cats.

Most protein sources provide adequate arginine; therefore, most commercial pet foods are not supplemented with arginine. Supplements, such as milk replacers, or products intended for other species, such as some human enteral products, should be evaluated carefully for their arginine content before being administered to dogs and cats. In studies, the minimum arginine content of food that maximized growth in kittens was 0.83% (DMB).[19-21] AAFCO recommends that foods for growing kittens and adult cats contain at least 1.25 and 1.04% arginine (DMB), respectively.[10]

For growing puppies, a dietary arginine content of 0.4 to 0.56% (DMB) supported maximum weight gain;[22] however, 0.56% supported optimal growth and nitrogen balance.[23] AAFCO recommends that foods for growing puppies and adult dogs contain at least 0.62 and 0.51% arginine (DMB), respectively.[10]

The role of arginine in the formation of nitric oxide in the body has been investigated. Nitric oxide is classified as a hormone that helps regulate blood flow through blood vessels and is thought to be involved with blood pressure regulation. Nitric oxide is synthesized by the endothelial cells lining blood vessels and by macrophages to assist in infection control.

Glutamine/Glutamate

Glutamine and glutamate are five-carbon amino acids that are structurally similar and play key metabolic roles in the citric acid cycle, transamination reactions, generation of NADPH, γ-aminobutyric acid (GABA), the antioxidant glutathione and as folic acid cofactors. The carboxyl group of glutamate is replaced by an amide nitrogen in glutamine. The two amino acids are interconverted by the enzymes glutaminase (glutamine to glutamate + ammonia) and glutamine synthetase (glutamate + ammonia to glutamine).

For many years, glutamine and glutamate were considered nonessential amino acids; however, numerous studies have demonstrated that endogenous glutamine storage and synthesis may not be adequate to meet the body's needs in certain situations, such as critical illness, infection, cancer chemotherapy, low birth weight infants, diarrhea, human immunodeficiency virus (HIV) infection, bone marrow transplantation and cardiac surgery.[24-28] Glu-

tamine is also the preferred fuel of the small intestinal mucosa. Therefore, glutamine has been reclassified as a conditionally essential amino acid.[24,28]

Supplementation of pet foods or any food product with L-glutamine is difficult because the amino acid is unstable through heating and cooking processes. Glutamine breaks down into glutamate and ammonia. The latter can be toxic when ingested. L-glutamine can be added safely to powdered amino acid mixtures that are reconstituted with water and administered immediately to the animal. In complete pet foods, glutamine is best supplied by a high-quality, high-protein food.

Protein Deficiency

Clinical signs of protein deficiency include reduced growth rate, anorexia, anemia, infertility, reduced milk production, alopecia, brittle hair and a poor coat.[6] (See Case 2-2 "Lethargy and Weight Loss in a Mixed-Breed Dog.") If specific essential amino acids are deficient, the clinical signs can be similar to those of general protein deficiency. A deficiency of calories (energy) and essential amino acids (protein-energy malnutrition) increases catabolism of muscle and other body proteins (e.g., albumin and immunoglobulins). Continued failure to consume protein results in muscle atrophy and decreased blood levels of albumin, transferrin, thyroxine-binding protein and retinol-binding protein because carbon skeletons from these proteins are used as an energy source to supply glucose through gluconeogenesis.

Albumin concentrations in serum are not a particularly sensitive indicator of short-term protein malnutrition because the turnover rate is relatively long. Fatty liver can also be a sign of protein deficiency because specific apolipoproteins needed by VLDL to package and export fat from the liver are not synthesized in adequate quantities or at all during protein deficiency.

Protein Toxicity/Excess

Although not a practical problem, amino acid toxicity can occur if any amino acid is fed at a very high level. It is very hard to create an amino acid toxicity by feeding protein sources from plants or animals; however, synthetic amino acids mistakenly added to foods at very high levels can cause toxicity.[6] Synthetic amino acids that currently are added to some pet foods include L-methionine or D,L-methionine, L-lysine, L-arginine and taurine.

The minimum dietary protein requirement for healthy adult dogs is about 6% (DMB);[9] however, AAFCO recommends that dog foods contain a minimum of 18% protein (DMB).[10] Healthy adult cats require a minimum of 14% protein (DMB);[11] however, AAFCO recommends that foods contain at least 26% (DMB).[10] Commercial dog foods contain three to seven times the minimum required protein. Some commercial cat foods contain two to four times the minimum protein requirement. (See Appendix L.)

Excess dietary protein can be problematic for dogs and cats with specific disease conditions. For example, any disease that affects organs involved with conversion of ammonia to urea and waste nitrogen disposal can result in accumulation of toxic by-products of protein metabolism. In particular, protein intake above requirement has to be carefully monitored in any animal with impaired renal or liver function. (See Chapters 19 and 23.) In other situa-

Table 2-12. Protein quality of common pet food ingredients.

Ingredient	Protein (%)*	Amino acid (protein) quality**	Other comments
Egg (dried)	45-49	Good High quality, the standard to which many other sources are compared CS = 100, BV = 94, NPU = 94, PER = 3.92	Also contains lecithin
Casein	80	Good High tryptophan, lysine CS = 58, BV = 80, NPU = 72, PER = 2.86	
Whey	12	Good High lysine, isoleucine, threonine, tryptophan	
Beef, lamb, pork, chicken	29	Good Low tryptophan CS = 69, BV = 74, NPU = 67, PER = 2.30	May be variable in fat and connective tissue content
Liver	20	Good	Also a good source of vitamin A
Fish meal	59	Good High tryptophan, lysine, methionine	Highly variable
Meat and bone meal	45-50	Good	Highly variable, may contain high levels of bone that contribute to excess calcium, phosphorus and magnesium in food
Lamb meal	55	Good	Highly variable, may contain high levels of bone that contribute to excess calcium, phosphorus and magnesium in food
Chicken/poultry by-product meal	58	Good High lysine, methionine	Mineral levels can be variable
Soybean meal	48	Good High tryptophan, lysine CS = 47, BV = 73, NPU = 61, PER = 2.32	Good complementary protein source for meats, fish meal and corn
Corn gluten meal	60	Adequate	Good complementary protein source for meats and fish meal
Corn (whole)	8	Adequate Low tryptophan, lysine, methionine CS = 41, BV = 59, NPU = 51, PER = 1.12	Also good source of linoleic acid
Rice (white)	7	Adequate CS = 56, BV = 64, NPU = 57, PER = 2.18	Low-mineral levels
Wheat	14	Adequate Low tryptophan, lysine CS = 43, BV = 65, NPU = 40, PER = 1.53	Contains gliadin
Barley	12	Adequate Low tryptophan, methionine	Contains gliadin
Collagen (gelatin)	88	Poor Totally deficient in tryptophan CS = 0, BV = 0, NPU = 0, PER = 0	

Key: CS = chemical score, BV = biological value, NPU = net protein utilization, PER = protein efficiency ratio.
*Feedstuffs Ingredient Analysis Table: 1996 Edition. (As is basis.)
**Adapted from Brody T. Protein. In: Nutritional Biochemistry. San Diego, CA: Academic Press Inc, 1994; 295-352. Jurgens MH, Animal Feeding and Nutrition, 6th ed. Dubuque, IA: Kendall/Hunt Co, 1988; 172. National Research Council. Improvement of Protein Nutrition. Committee on Amino Acids, Food and Nutrition Board. National Academy of Sciences, Washington, DC, 1974; 70. Robinson DS. The nutritional value of food proteins. In: Food Biochemistry and Nutritional Value. New York, NY: Wiley & Sons Inc, 1987; 117-151.

tions, such as struvite urolith dissolution in dogs and adverse food reactions in cats and dogs, minimizing excesses of dietary protein is a beneficial part of therapy. (See Chapters 14 and 20.) In these cases, excess dietary protein could be considered "conditionally toxic."

Feeding protein above requirements or recommendations for healthy dogs and cats does not result in a true toxicity because the excess amino acids from the protein are catabolized and the waste nitrogen is excreted. However, not all dogs and cats that appear healthy are free of disease. Dogs and cats with chronic renal disease are usually subclinical until the disease has progressed to the point that two-thirds or more of functional renal tissue is lost.[29] Protein excess may contribute to progression of the disease. In addition to any direct effects protein excess might have on the progression of subclinical renal disease,[30] excess protein may contribute to

acidemia. (See Chapter 19.) This development is especially important in older cats with marginal renal function. Thus, even in apparently healthy dogs and cats, excess dietary protein may at times be conditionally toxic.

Excess dietary protein may contribute to fear-related territorial aggression in dogs. Excess dietary protein intake is theorized to interfere with the transport of tryptophan across the blood-brain barrier, resulting in a decrease in serotonin formation. Low concentrations of serotonin in the brain have been implicated in aggression in human studies.[31] Investigators noted a reduction of fear-related territorial aggression when dogs were fed 17 and 25% dietary protein levels (DMB); however, no reduction in aggression was noted when dogs were fed 32% dietary protein.[32]

Protein excesses are found in pet foods for several reasons. Cats are strict carnivores (See Chapter 11.) and have a higher protein requirement than dogs, which are omnivores. (See Chapter 9.) However, some pet food companies have perpetuated the myth that dogs are carnivores and that meat-based, high-protein foods are more natural and thus better than lower protein foods that contain both animal and plant sources of protein. Other fallacies, such as high levels of dietary protein build more muscle or a thicker coat, have contributed to pet owners' mistaken perception that higher protein is indicative of a higher quality pet food.

Excess protein adds unnecessary cost to foods. Excess protein is used for energy. As an energy source, protein is no better than soluble carbohydrate; however, protein is a more expensive energy source. The increased costs associated with increased dietary protein are invariably passed on to pet owners.

There are no nutritional reasons that support providing excessive amounts of dietary protein. After the protein/amino acid requirements are met, additional protein provides no additional benefits. Thus, dog foods for adult maintenance should not exceed 30% protein (DMB). Cat foods for adult maintenance should not exceed 45% protein (DMB).

Sources

Many ingredients supply protein/amino acids to pet foods (Table 2-12). Typical pet food ingredients that have high-protein concentrations are animal tissues from chicken, turkey, fish, beef and lamb and viscera such as livers, lungs and spleens. Grains also supply protein to pet foods. In fact, a large portion of the protein in cereal-based dry pet foods typically comes from grains, including rice, corn, wheat and barley. Some plant products (e.g., soybean meal and corn gluten meal) are concentrated sources of plant protein.

Multiple protein sources are often combined to improve the overall quality and amino acid profile when foods are formulated. This method of improving protein quality is termed protein complementation.[2] Protein sources are combined based on their amino acid excesses and deficiencies so that the nutritional weaknesses of each source will be counterbalanced by the strengths of other sources, resulting in a food with high-quality protein. Corn and soybean meal are typically used in animal food formulations to take advantage of protein complementation. Corn protein is low in lysine and tryptophan, whereas soybean meal is adequate in both amino acids. When used together in one food, these two protein sources provide a well-balanced amino acid profile.

Amino acid fortification is another method for improving the protein quality of foods.[2] In this method, one or more individual amino acids are added to a food when the main protein source of the food may be limiting. Methionine and lysine are typically used to fortify pet foods.

LIPIDS

Introduction

Definition

Lipids encompass a wide range of compounds that fulfill nutritional and functional requirements in mammalian systems. Generally, lipids share the physiochemical property of being insoluble (hydrophobic) in polar solvents such as water. Lipids that are solid at room temperature are commonly called fats whereas those that are liquid at room temperature are referred to as oils. In a nutrient analysis, the ether extract of a food contains primarily lipids and represents the crude fat content (Figure 2-3).

Table 2-13. Classification, structure and function of general lipids.

Classification	Structure	Function
Hydrocarbons	$-CH_3$, $-CH_2$, $-CH$	Building blocks
Nonesterified fatty acids	$CH_3(CH_2)_n(CH_1)_nCOOH$	
Saturated	Stearic, palmitic	Energy, membrane fluidity
Monounsaturated	Oleic, palmitoleic	Energy, membrane fluidity
Polyunsaturated (PUFA)	n-3, n-6	Precursors of eicosanoids and prostaglandins
Simple lipids	Fatty acid + alcohol in ester bond	
Triacylglycerides (TAG)	Glycerol + three fatty acids	Energy storage, insulation
Complex lipids		
Phospholipids	Diacyl glycerol 3' phosphate	Membrane lipids
Lecithin	3' phosphocholine	Emulsifying agent
Cephalin	3' phosphoserine/ethanolamine	CNS membrane
Inositol	Carbohydrate (3' phosphoinositol)	2nd messenger
Ceramide	Sphingosine + fatty acid	CNS membrane
Sphingomyelin	Ceramide + phosphocholine	Myelin
Glycolipids	Sphingomyelin + carbohydrate	CNS membrane/recognition
Cerebroside	Ceramide + monosaccharide	
Ganglioside	Ceramide + oligosaccharide	
Prostaglandins	20-carbon PUFA	Paracrine and autocrine action
Sterols and steroids	Four-ring hydrocarbon structures	Bile acids, hormones, membranes, lipoproteins, cholesterol, cholesterol esters
Fat-soluble vitamins	See vitamins	See vitamins

Structure

The structure of lipids ranges from simple to complex although any one classification scheme is difficult to impose. The basic subunits of lipids are hydrocarbon molecules linked by covalent bonds in various manners to themselves and other molecules in a vast assortment of permutations that result in the myriad of functions and structures observed in nature. Table 2-13 and Figures 2-16 and 2-17 will be helpful for reference throughout this chapter and the text.

Function

Intake of lipids benefits the animal by supplying energy, essential fatty acids (EFA) and a positive environment for fat-soluble vitamin absorption. Dietary lipid may be assimilated and stored as fat in adipocytes, incorporated into functional lipid or catabolized for fuel, depending on the energy status of the animal. The majority of fat found in adipocytes is triacylglycerides (TAG), which may be synthesized de novo from nonfat precursors such as carbohydrate or protein during periods of positive energy balance.

Some lipids required for adequate physiologic function, such as certain long-chain fatty acids, cannot be synthesized de novo and are thus required in food. These fatty acids are called EFA because a lack of them in foods results in classic signs of deficiency. A small amount of lipid (1 to 2% of total food) of no specific structure is also required in foods for proper absorption of fat-soluble vitamins (A, D, E and K).

Fatty Acids

Structure

Nonesterified fatty acids (NEFA) consist of hydrocarbon chains ranging from two to 24 carbons or more, with a carboxylic acid group on one terminus and a methyl group on the opposite terminus. NEFA that contain 14 to 24 carbons are classified as long chain, eight to 12 medium chain and two to six short chain. Figure 2-16 shows fatty acid chemistry and structure.

Lipid may be either in liquid or solid state depending on temperature and fatty acid composition. A more unsaturated (increased number of double bonds) fatty acid makeup results in fats that have lower melting points compared with those of fats made from more saturated (decreased number or no double bonds) fatty acids. The length of the carbon chains in the fatty acids making up a fat also changes the melting point. Fats that contain fatty acids of shorter carbon chain length have lower melting points than do fats that contain longer fatty acids. Animals take advantage of these differences in physical characteristics to synthesize phospholipids containing appropriate classes of fatty acids that allow for membrane fluidity at physiologic temperatures.

n-3, n-6 and n-9 Fatty Acid Families

Fatty acids with the first double bond between the third and fourth carbon are in the n-3 family, sixth and seventh carbon the n-6 family and ninth and tenth carbon the n-9 family. The n-3 and n-6 fatty acid families are EFA because they cannot be synthesized de novo in mammals; lack of EFA in foods results in suboptimal physiologic activity.[1] Mammals are capable of de novo synthesis of saturated fatty acids and fatty acids of the n-9 series up to 18 carbons.[2] Subsequently, mammals may elongate and desaturate de novo or dietary fatty acids of all classes via enzymes specific for certain carbons in the hydrocarbon chain (Figure 2-18). However, mammals cannot desatu-

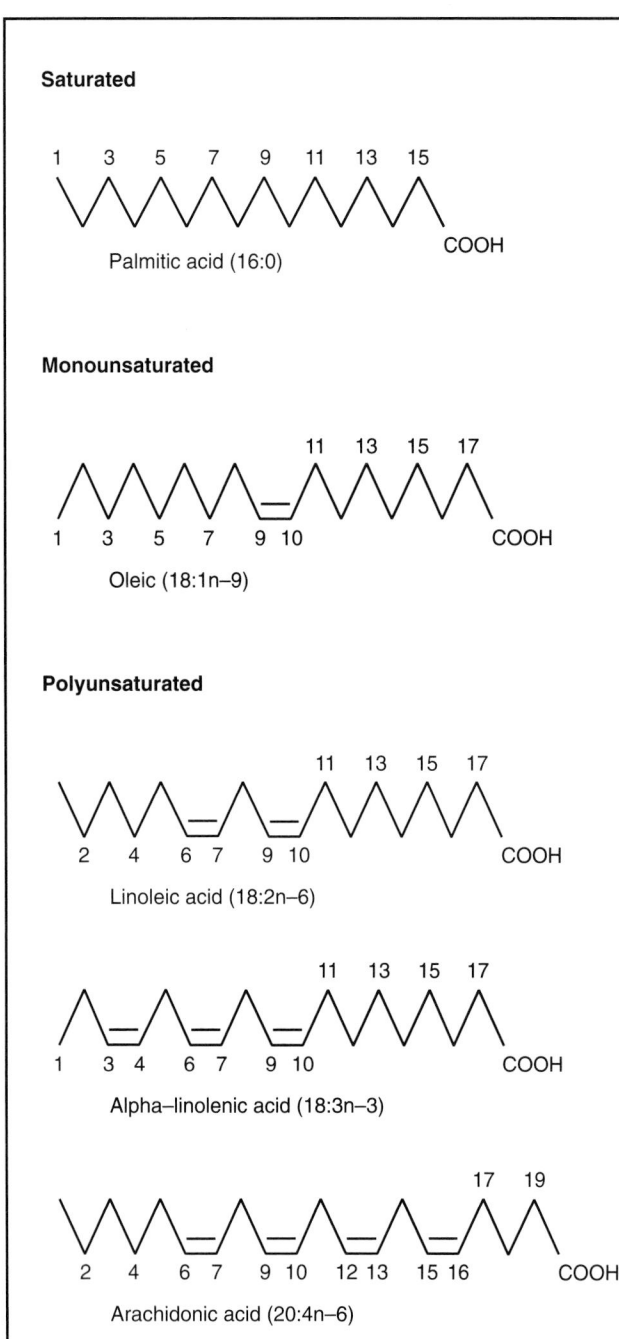

Figure 2-16. Fatty acids consist of hydrocarbon chains with a carboxylic acid group (COOH) on one terminus and a methyl group on the opposite terminus. Fatty acids with no double bonds in the hydrocarbon chain are referred to as saturated, one double bond as monounsaturated and more than one double bond, polyunsaturated. The carbon on the opposite terminus from the carboxylic acid group is designated the number one carbon and given the symbol n-1. Nomenclature specifies the number of carbons and the location and number of double bonds. For example, an 18-carbon polyunsaturated fat with three double bonds, the first of which is between carbons 6 to 7 is designated 18:3n-6 (γ-linolenic).

rate fatty acids between the n-1 carbon and the n-3, n-6 or n-9 double bond. Because of the specificity of these enzyme systems, unsaturated fatty acids cannot be converted between families (e.g., n-6 or n-9 to n-3). Also, because of limitations and specificity in metabolism, monounsaturated and saturated fatty acids cannot be converted to EFA (e.g., n-9 or stearate to n-6).

Members of the n-6 family include linoleic acid (18:2n-6), γ-linolenic acid (18:3n-6) and arachidonic acid (20:4n-6). Dogs, but not cats, are able to elongate and desaturate linoleic acid to form arachidonic acid.[3-5] The n-6 fatty acid family is required for growth, reproduction and precursors of eicosanoid and prostaglandin synthesis.

Members of the n-3 family include α-linolenic (18:3n-3), eicosapentaenoic (20:5n-3) and docosahexaenoic (22:6n-3) acids. The n-3 fatty acid family, especially 22:6n-3, is required for brain and retinal function.[6,7] Both fatty acid families contribute to cell membrane fluidity and skin health. Processing EFA in pet foods may affect their biologic activity. (See sidebar "Cis and Trans Fatty Acids.") Table 2-14 summarizes the families, common names and biologic use of several fatty acids found in nature.

Lipid Metabolism

GI Handling of Dietary Lipid

Lipids in foods include TAG, phospholipids, cholesterol, cholesteryl esters and fat-soluble vitamins. Long-chain NEFA make up a very small percentage of dietary lipid and will not be discussed here. Dogs and cats are efficient at digesting dietary lipids, with apparent lipid digestibility normally ranging between 80 and 95%. Increased levels of saturated and trans fatty acids reduce lipid digestibility. (See sidebar "Cis and Trans Fatty Acids.")

Fats and oils must undergo digestion via enzymatic and physical processes before they can be absorbed from the lumen of the gut. The following steps are involved in lipid digestion, absorption and initial metabolism (Figure 2-19):[8]

- Gastric lipase in the stomach and duodenum degrades TAG of intact lipid micelles
- Bile salts emulsify lipid micelles to form mixed micelles and coactivate pancreatic lipase
- Pancreatic lipase and colipase hydrolyze TAG in mixed micelles
- Gastric and pancreatic lipase activity results in 2-monoacylglyceride + 2 nonesterified fatty acids
- Nonesterified fatty acids and 2-monoacylglyceride are absorbed into enterocytes
- TAG are reformed in enterocytes from long-chain nonesterified fatty acids and 2-monoacylglyceride
- Apolipoproteins + TAG + cholesterol form chylomicrons in enterocytes and enter lymphatics
- Chylomicrons in lymphatics enter general circulation via thoracic duct
- Chylomicrons are partially metabolized and remnants attach to liver receptors

TAG containing medium-chain fatty acids undergo similar processing until they enter the enterocyte at which point they are not re-esterified, but transported via albumin directly to the liver for metabolism. (See sidebar "Long-Chain vs. Medium-Chain Fatty Acid Metabolism.")

Short-chain fatty acids (particularly butyrate) resulting from fiber fermentation in the large intestine are an impor-

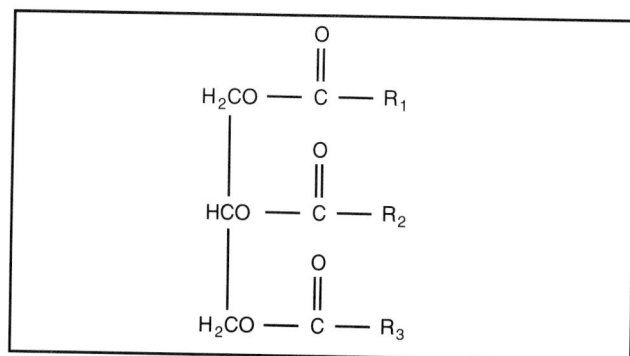

Figure 2-17. Triacylglycerides are the main storage forms of fatty acids, each molecule of which is composed of a three-carbon glycerol nucleus and three fatty acids (R_1, R_2, R_3).

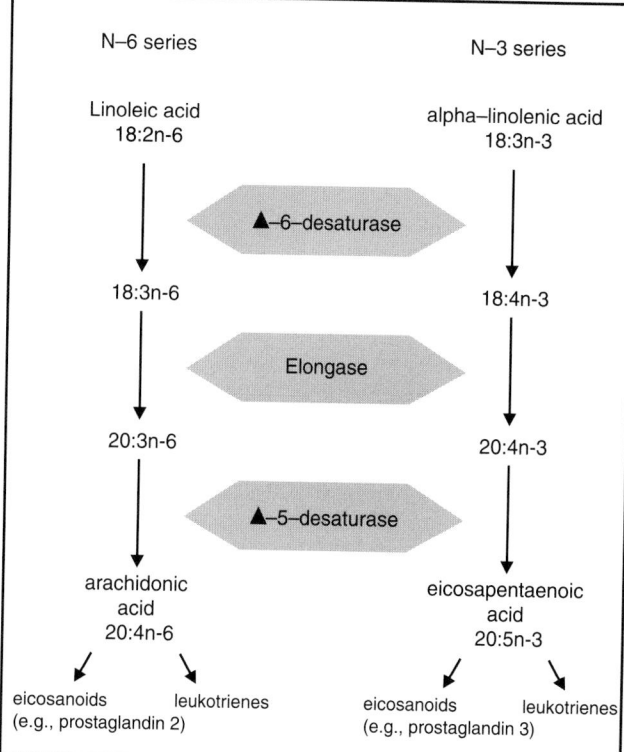

Figure 2-18. Diagram of metabolic pathways (elongation and desaturation) for essential fatty acids.

Cis and Trans Fatty Acids

When carbons are connected by a double bond, rotation around the bond is not possible resulting in fatty acids that are either cis (with the carbons being on the same side) or trans (with the carbons being on the opposite side). Most polyunsaturated fatty acids are in the cis configuration. Fatty acids can be converted, however, to the trans configuration during excessive heating or through partial hydrogenation (i.e., the production of margarine from oil). Although trans fatty acids are metabolized for energy and incorporated into storage lipid, similar to the cis isomers, they are not further metabolized to eicosanoids. Nutritionally, trans isomers are in many ways like saturated fatty acids in that they are used for energy but cannot function as essential fatty acids.

Table 2-14. Essentiality and biological function of common fatty acids.

Structure	Common name	Essential	Biologic function
14:0	Myristic	No	Energy use and storage, acylation of proteins
16:0	Palmitic	No	Energy use and storage, acylation of proteins
16:1	Palmitoleic	No	Energy use and storage
18:0	Stearic	No	Energy use and storage, membrane fluidity
18:1n-9	Oleic	No	Energy use and storage, phospholipid structure
18:2n-6	Linoleic	Yes	Energy use and storage, arachidonic acid precursor (20:4n-6)
18:3n-3	Alpha-linolenic	Yes	Energy use and storage, eicosapentaenoic acid precursor (20:5n-3)
18:3n-6	Gamma-linolenic	Yes	Energy use and storage, arachidonic acid precursor
20:4n-6	Arachidonic	Yes (cat) No (dog)	Energy use and storage, synthesis of cytokines and eicosanoids, synthesis of steroid hormones, membrane fluidity, competitor of eicosapentaenoic acid (20:5n-3)
20:5n-3	Eicosapentaenoic	Probably	Energy use and storage, synthesis of cytokines and eicosanoids, retinal and nervous tissue development, membrane fluidity, competitor of arachidonic acid (20:4n-6)
22:6n-3	Docosahexaenoic	Probably	Energy use and storage, retinal and nervous tissue development, membrane fluidity, competitor of n-6 fatty acids

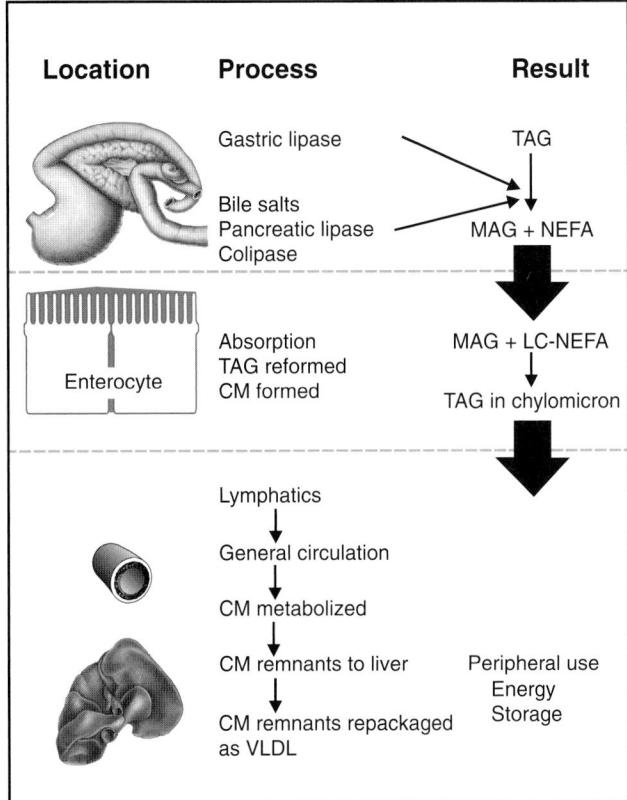

Figure 2-19. Digestion, absorption and fate of dietary triacylglycerides in mammals. See text for details. Key: TAG = triacylglyceride, MAG = monoacylglyceride, NEFA = nonesterified fatty acid, LC-NEFA = Long-chain NEFA, CM = chylomicron, VLDL = very low-density lipoprotein.

Table 2-15. Composition of general lipoprotein classes in mammals.

Lipoprotein	Acronym	Protein:lipid (%)
Chylomicron	CM	1:99
Very low-density lipoprotein	VLDL	10:90
Low-density lipoprotein	LDL	25:75
High-density lipoprotein	HDL	50:50

tant source of fuel for colonocytes. Excess short-chain fatty acids enter the portal circulation for metabolism by the liver.

Hepatic Handling of Dietary Lipid

The liver determines the fate of dietary lipid under the direction of hormonal signals related to energy balance. The primary fuel source for hepatocytes is provided via β-oxidation of nonesterified fatty acids whether dietary or endogenous in origin. (See Figure 2-8.) The fate of dietary lipid from chylomicron origin can be traced as follows (Figure 2-19):[9]

- Chylomicron remnants attach to receptors on liver cells.
- TAG are hydrolyzed to glycerol and CoA esterified fatty acids.
- CoA esterified fatty acids may be either shunted to β-oxidation in mitochondria or repackaged into TAG and then VLDL for use by peripheral tissues (storage or fuel). Their fate depends on the energy status of the animal.
- Glycerol is converted to 3-P-glycerol (only in liver) and enters the carbohydrate metabolic pathway.

Although fat storage is easily accomplished by de novo synthesis (the production of fat from carbohydrate or protein), it is more energy efficient for animals to deposit dietary fat than to synthesize it. When fat is deposited from foods, the fatty acid profile tends to reflect the type of fat consumed. When fat is synthesized, stored fat composition reflects the fat synthetic enzyme activity of the animal.

Lipoprotein Metabolism

Lipoproteins are relatively large conglomerates of protein and lipid that are necessary to transport hydrophobic lipids effectively through the aqueous medium of physiologic solutions. Table 2-15 gives a generic relative composition of the different lipoprotein classes observed in mammals. (See Chapter 24.) As the protein component increases, the relative density of the lipoprotein increases reflecting dilution of the buoyant density of fat. Lipoproteins are made only in the liver (VLDL, HDL) and enterocytes (chylomicrons). The protein fraction, before it is integrated with the lipid component, is termed apolipoprotein.

Lipoprotein metabolism is very complex and displays variation between species. However, a general introduction is necessary in order to understand lipoprotein metabolism disorders discussed in later chapters. An important point to remember is lipoprotein structure is not static and each class of lipoprotein has characteristics that may overlap with other classes. The following outline and Figure 2-20 depict lipoprotein metabolism from the origin of lipoproteins in enterocytes or hepatocytes:[9]

- Chylomicrons are formed in enterocytes
- HDL transfers apolipoprotein C-II and E (lipoprotein lipase cofactors) to chylomicrons and VLDL
- Lipoprotein lipase in peripheral tissue hydrolyzes TAG in chylomicrons (See sidebar "Lipoprotein Lipase.")
- Chylomicron remnants bind to receptors in the liver
- Liver hydrolyzes, reforms TAG and combines new apolipoproteins to form VLDL or HDL
- VLDL TAG are hydrolyzed by lipoprotein lipase in the periphery to form VLDL remnants
- VLDL remnants are taken up by liver or converted to LDL for uptake by peripheral tissues
- HDL made in liver (major) and enterocytes (minor) transport excess cholesterol from the periphery to the liver for excretion in bile salts (See sidebar "Good and Bad Cholesterol.")

Storage

Excess energy intake is stored in adipocytes as TAG. The TAG in adipocytes are formed directly from excess dietary fat or from de novo synthesis of fat in the liver under appropriate metabolic signals. The fat energy store in human adipocytes is capable of supporting life for one to two months. The key enzyme for release of energy from adipocytes is hormone sensitive lipase (HSL), which is under the control of hormonal signals. (See sidebar "Hormone Sensitive Lipase.")

Lipid Function

Energy

Although providing dietary fat is an excellent way to meet an animal's energy requirement, this requirement can also be theoretically met by the protein and carbohydrate content of a food. On a per weight basis, the energy value of dietary fat is approximately 2.25 times that of protein or carbohydrate. Additionally, direct use of dietary fat for storage in adipocytes or use in functional lipid requires less energy for assimilation and storage when compared with de

Long-Chain vs. Medium-Chain Fatty Acid Metabolism

Medium-chain fatty acids (mcFFA eight to 12 carbon lengths) are a minor component of natural compounds such as triacylglycerides (TAG) from mother's milk or coconut milk. TAG containing medium-chain fatty acids are assigned the name medium-chain triglycerides (MCT). Even in foods "rich" with MCT, the overall contribution to the fat component of those foods is minor, compared with long-chain TAG. However, because MCT are subject to different metabolic regulation they may prove useful in certain disease states and have been included in some foods formulated for specific diseases (Table 1).

BIBLIOGRAPHY
Brody T, ed. Regulation of energy metabolism. In: Nutritional Biochemistry. San Diego, CA: Academic Press Inc., 1994; 125-220.

Table 1. Comparison between medium-chain trigylcerides (MCT) and triacylglycerides (TAG).

Process	MCT	TAG
Gut hydrolysis	Rapid, 5x TAG	Slower rate than MCT
Absorption	2x faster than TAG	Slower rate than MCT
Enterocyte processing	Free fatty acid not reassembled in TAG	Free fatty acid reassembled in TAG
Transport	Portal vein, albumin bound	Chylomicrons, lymphatics and then general circulation
Hepatocyte Esterification	Not esterified to CoA	Esterified to CoA
Carnitine	Not bound to carnitine	Bound to carnitine
Beta-oxidation	Unregulated	Regulated

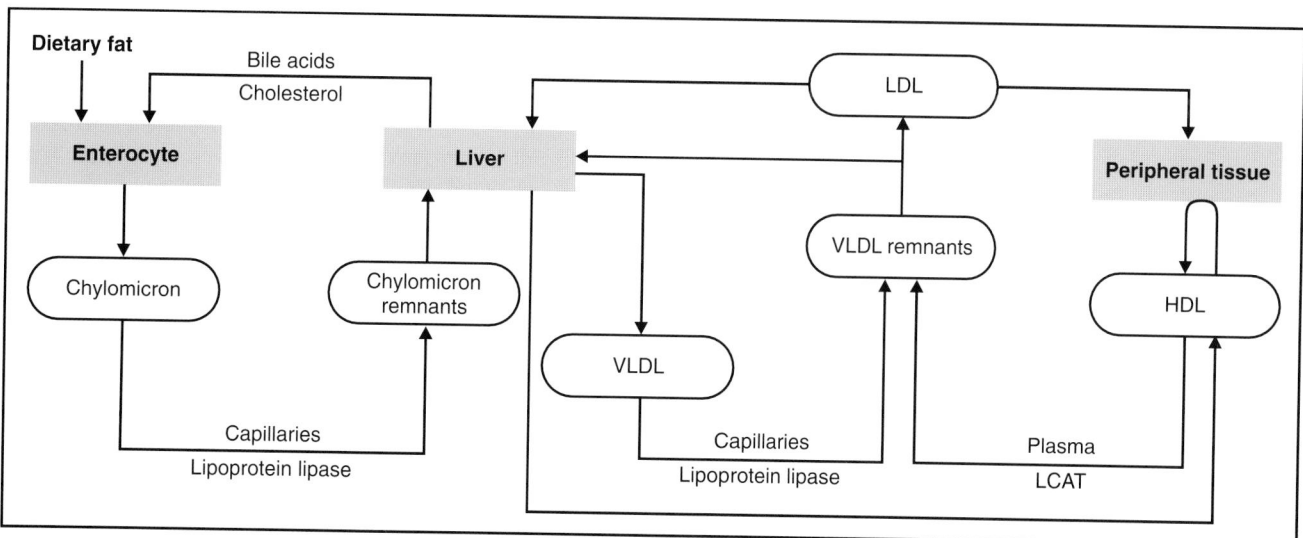

Figure 2-20. Lipoprotein metabolism. See text for details. Key: LDL = low-density lipoprotein, HDL = high-density lipoprotein, VLDL = very low-density lipoprotein, LCAT = lecithin cholesterol acyltransferase.

Lipoprotein Lipase

Lipoprotein lipase is an enzyme that hydrolyzes triacyl-glycerides (TAG) into nonesterified fatty acids (NEFA) and glycerol. Lipoprotein lipase is located within the cell and is under hormonal control, specifically insulin. In its inactive state, lipoprotein lipase lies underneath the cell membranes that surround blood vessels. It is attached to the inner surface of the cell via a rope-like protein connection. Under the influence of insulin, this connection is loosened and the lipoprotein lipase is allowed to "float" to the cell surface where it can hydrolyze TAG in lipoproteins. Apo-CII is required as a coenzyme for lipoprotein lipase. The resulting NEFA diffuse into the cell for metabolism and glycerol is transported back to the liver for metabolism.

Some lines of domestic cats have a genetic defect that results in absence of lipoprotein lipase activity.

Good and Bad Cholesterol

High-density lipoprotein (HDL) is the smallest of the lipoprotein molecules and is synthesized primarily in the liver and to a lesser degree in enterocytes. HDL are involved in reverse cholesterol transport. HDL transfer free cholesterol from cell membranes to the HDL molecule as cholesterol esters via an enzyme lecithin: cholesterol acyl transferase. The cholesterol esters may be transferred to very low-density lipoproteins (VLDL) by cholesterol ester transfer protein to eventually form low-density lipoprotein (LDL), which provides cholesterol to peripheral cells. Alternatively, the cholesterol esters may be delivered to the liver in HDL for excretion as bile salts. Because HDL are capable of transporting cholesterol from the periphery to the liver for disposal, they are said to contain "good cholesterol." LDL, on the other hand, are said to contain "bad cholesterol" because they transport cholesterol to the periphery where excess may result in arterial plaque and cardiovascular disease.

novo synthesis from protein or carbohydrate in food. In other words, fat that is stored directly from dietary fat has 10 to 15% more energy than fat that is made from excess dietary carbohydrate or protein because of the inherent loss of efficiency in de novo fat synthesis. This increased efficiency of fat use results in an increased energy value for dietary fat that animals may use to meet energy requirements or store as adipose tissue.

Essentiality

Fatty acids of the n-6 family have functionally distinct effects compared with those of fatty acids of the n-3 family. The addition of lipid-containing arachidonic acid (20:4n-6) to foods containing no arachidonic acid results in increased feed efficiency during growth and enhanced skin condition including reduced epidermal water loss. Arachidonic acid also allows processes requiring eicosanoids to occur such as reproduction and platelet aggregation.[3,4] Because dogs can

convert linoleic acid (18:2n-6) to arachidonic acid (20:4n6), linoleic acid is usually listed as an EFA for dogs. A concentration of 1% of the food dry matter as linoleic acid is a safe and effective concentration for dogs.[10-12]

Because linoleic acid corrected many clinical signs of fatty acid deficiency in cats, it also is listed as an EFA for cats.[1] Some of the signs of EFA deficiency in cats, however, were not ameliorated by linoleic acid but rather improvement depended on arachidonic supplementation. One group of investigators concluded that cats cannot convert linoleic acid to arachidonic acid in sufficient quantities for platelet aggregation and prevention of mild mineralization of the kidneys.[3] Arachidonic acid supplementation allows normal reproduction in female cats.[4] Male reproduction (spermatogenesis), unlike female reproduction, does not require dietary arachidonate because of the testes' ability to elongate and desaturate linoleate.[4] These studies show arachidonate to be an EFA for cats. Foods for cats should contain at least 0.5% linoleic acid and at least 0.02% arachidonic acid (DMB).

Studies with primates have shown that 22:6n-3 (docosahexaenoic acid) is essential for the normal development of nervous tissue and the retina.[6] Studies with piglets have shown that developing brain and retina are influenced by dietary n-3 fatty acids.[7] The eicosanoids resulting from n-3 fatty acid metabolism are less immunologically stimulating than those resulting from n-6 fatty acids (Figure 2-18). Thus, feeding n-3 fatty acids has been recommended in situations in which a reduced inflammatory response is desired such as: 1) before and after surgery, 2) after trauma, injury, burns and some types of cancer and 3) to assist in control of dermatitis, arthritis, inflammatory bowel disease and colitis.[13-15]

Fatty acids of the n-3 family, when compared with those in the n-6 family, have been shown, in some cases, to decrease platelet aggregation and increase bleeding time.[16] Dietary n-3 fatty acids slightly depressed platelet activity in rats and people; however, this finding is usually not a practical problem in healthy animals.[17] Healthy adult dogs fed 7% of the food dry matter as n-3 fatty acids from fish oil, over a period of two months, showed no problems with activated partial thromboplastin time, prothrombin time, buccal mucosal bleeding time clotting or platelet aggregation.[18]

Although more research with n-3 fatty acids in companion animals needs to be done, it is prudent to conclude that n-3 fatty acids will be shown to be essential for normal function of the retina and brain as well as for physiologic homeostasis. At this time there are no conclusive data proving the optimal level or relationship of n-3 fatty acids to n-6 fatty acids for any species at any specific lifestage. The optimal relationship will likely depend on many individual parameters and differ depending on individual physiologic function. (See sidebar "Adequate vs. Optimal Nutrient Intake.")

Fat-Soluble Vitamin Absorption

Dogs and cats have a "requirement" for lipid to enhance the absorption of the fat-soluble vitamins A, D, E and K. Dietary fat provides a physical environment in the gut that enhances the absorption of fat-soluble vitamins. This requirement is in the range of 1 to 2% of the food and is not specific for any type of fat.

Lipid Requirements

Although not required for health, calories supplied by fat can be more beneficial than those provided by carbohydrate or protein. In cases of high-energy demand, the energy concentration of the food can limit total caloric intake. When the total bulk of the food is a limiting factor, increasing dietary fat allows for increased energy consumption. Increased aerobic capacity during exercise is supported by increased fat consumption because of the enhanced use of fat calories when compared with calories from carbohydrate. (See Chapter 10.)

Lipid Deficiency

Deficiencies of fatty acids impair wound healing, cause a dry lusterless coat and scaly skin and change the lipid film on the skin, which may predispose the animal to pyoderma. (See Chapter 15.) If deficiency persists, alopecia, edema and moist dermatitis may develop. Lesions of moist dermatitis, associated with EFA deficiency, are most common in the external ear canals and between the toes. However, these lesions may develop anywhere on the body. Emaciation can result from severe, persistent EFA deficiency. An EFA deficiency can also impair reproductive performance (i.e., neonatal abnormalities and death may result if pregnancy occurs).

Lipid Excess

Increased dietary lipid is often associated with increased energy intake, because increasing the dietary lipid content of a food is nearly always associated with an increase in the food's caloric density. This relationship results from increased available energy. Changes in body composition result from changes in energy balance. Energy intake may be influenced by dietary fat; however, the energy balance controls adiposity not the lipid intake.

Increasing the fat concentration of foods generally enhances palatability for dogs and cats. Fatty acid composition is an important aspect of palatability and influences acceptance through flavor and mouth feel. Dietary fat also influences subsequent food selection,[19] an effect mediated through serotonin, a neurotransmitter involved in control of food intake.[20]

Interactions with Other Nutrients

High dietary fat concentration requires increased antioxidant protection, such as added vitamin E. In the absence of

Hormone Sensitive Lipase

Hormone sensitive lipase (HSL) catalyzes the reaction of triacylglycerides (TAG) to nonesterified fatty acids (NEFA) and glycerol in adipocytes. Under the influence of insulin (following a meal), HSL is modified to a very low activity, which favors deposition of TAG in adipose tissue. Under the influence of glucagon (fasting) or epinephrine (flight or fight mechanism), HSL is highly active and the result is an efflux of NEFA and glycerol into the blood (bound to albumin) for transport to other tissues as an energy source. The NEFA that arrive back at the liver are catabolized or repackaged to TAG. In some pathologic conditions, TAG may accumulate in the liver (feline hepatic lipidosis) because the necessary repackaging materials for very low-density lipoprotein synthesis are not available in the liver.

adequate antioxidants, dietary lipids will become rancid. (See Chapter 4.) Rancidity adversely affects the animal through reduced palatability, reduced vitamin activity and possibly subsequent oxidation of body fat. Because polyunsaturated n-3 fatty acids are more susceptible to peroxidation than are most n-6 fatty acids, the need for antioxidants in foods high in n-3 fatty acids is increased.

Excessive dietary unsaturated fat in conjunction with inadequate antioxidants may result in pansteatitis or "yellow fat disease." The end products of rancidification in adipose tissue cause a yellow, brown or orange discoloration of body fat. Affected animals are anorectic, depressed, febrile and lethargic. They move stiffly and generally show signs of cutaneous pain upon handling as the result of inflamed subcutaneous fat. Treatment involves dietary correction and oral vitamin E administration (30 mg/day) until clinical signs disappear.[21,22]

Lipid Sources

An array of animal and vegetable fats and oils in many combinations are currently used in commercial pet food production. Consumption of a specific fat results in a specific fatty acid profile that influences subsequent storage and metabolism. Because fatty acid intake strongly influ-

Table 2-16. Fatty acid composition of commercial fats and oils.*

Fatty acid	Name	Butter**	Tallow**	Lard*** (porcine)	Chicken fat***	Fish oil***	Corn oil**	Sunflower oil**	Soybean oil**	Olive oil**
14:0	Myristic	8.4	2.6	1.4	0.5	4.2	<0.1	0.1	0.1	<0.1
16:0	Palmitic	21.3	7.4	24.1	20.4	16.2	9.9	6.3	10.1	11.4
16:1	Palmitoleic	1.1	1.9	3.5	7.6	11.6	0.1	0.1	<0.1	0.1
18:0	Stearic	8.9	24.2	12.2	4.4	2.4	2.1	3.8	1.4	2.4
18:1n-9	Oleic	18.8	13.8	42.8	37.6	10.9	25.6	20.9	20.4	65.5
18:2n-6	Linoleic	1.0	3.9	11.7	12.3	1.2	53.1	62.3	51.8	10.4
18:3n-3	Alpha-linolenic	0.4	0.5	0.5	0.5	1.2	1.0	0.1	7.3	0.5
18:3n-6	Gamma-linolenic	0.2	<0.1	0.1	0.2	0.4	<0.1	<0.1	<0.1	<0.1
20:4n-6	Arachidonic	0.7	0.6	0.1	0.2	0.4	<0.1	<0.1	<0.1	<0.1
20:5n-3	Eicosapentaenoic	<0.1	<0.1	<0.1	<0.1	14.1	<0.1	<0.1	<0.1	<0.1
22:6n-3	Docosahexaenoic	<0.1	<0.1	<0.1	<0.1	11.9	<0.1	<0.1	<0.1	<0.1

*All values are expressed as g/100 g.
**Adapted from Hyvonen L, Lampi AM, Varo P, et al. Fatty acid analysis, TAG equivalents as net fat value, and nutritional attributes of commercial fats and oils. Journal of Food Composition and Analysis 1993; 6: 24-40.
***Unpublished data, generally in agreement with published standards (Handbook 8, USDA, Washington, DC).

ences what type of fat is stored and which end products of fatty acid metabolism will occur, "you are what you eat" applies to fat more than any other macronutrient. Table 2-16 shows the fatty acid compositions of different fat sources. Fatty acid composition of dietary fat within a single source varies for a number of reasons; therefore, the information in Table 2-16 should be considered indicative of the fatty acid profiles possible within these specific types of fats and oils.

Fatty acid profiles in body fat change because of changes in fat consumption. For example, pigs consuming soybean oil had a 70% increase in linoleic (18:2n6) acid in depot lipid when compared with pigs fed diets containing tallow.[23] An equally large change in fatty acid composition can be found in plants due to changes in varieties within a species. An extreme example of this is safflower oil, which can vary from approximately 80% linoleic (18:2n6) to approximately 80% oleic (18:1n9), depending on the individual variety.

Fish oils have recently garnered the attention of nutritionists and veterinarians for their purported positive effects in management of a variety of disease processes. The oils most commonly associated with fish are those of the n-3 and n-6 families. The primary fish oil supplement is derived from menhaden and is very high in the n-3/n-6 families, compared with animal fat. The n-3 family usually predominates over the n-6 family in fish and shellfish, whereas polyunsaturated fatty acids (PUFA) from vegetable sources are usually higher in the n-6 family. Threefold differences in fatty acid composition may occur in fish depending on season and geographic locale of the catch. Fish oil compositional profiles depend on dietary intake, type of fish (carnivore vs. plankton eater), warm vs. fresh water and season of catch. Unfortunately, data about specific variations based on the above factors are unavailable.[24]

MINERALS

Introduction

Definition

The term mineral is generally used to denote all inorganic elements in a food. These inorganic elements constitute the majority of ash that remains after combustion of all organic matter. Ash analysis is of little value either for expressing mineral requirements or for indicating the useful mineral content of foods for two basic reasons: 1) body requirements are specific for certain inorganic elements (e.g., calcium, zinc, etc.) and 2) ash may not be a measure of total inorganic matter present, because some organic carbon may be bound as carbonate, and some inorganic elements (e.g., sulfur, selenium, iodine, fluorine and even sodium) may be lost during combustion.

The most important reason to determine total ash is to calculate the nitrogen-free extract by difference, as is required in the proximate analysis of foodstuffs. Specific minerals of interest can then be assayed (if not volatilized) from the ash component.

More than 18 mineral elements are believed to be essential for mammals.[1] By definition, macrominerals are required by the animal in the diet in percentage amounts,

whereas microminerals or "trace" minerals are required at the parts per million (ppm) level. There are seven macrominerals: calcium, phosphorus, sodium, magnesium, potassium, chloride and sulfur. There are at least 11 trace elements or micronutrient minerals: iron, zinc, copper, iodine, selenium, manganese, cobalt, molybdenum, fluorine, boron and chromium. The last six are assumed to be essential for dogs and cats by analogy with other species. Calcium, phosphorus, magnesium, potassium, sodium and chloride are discussed in the following text. Neither AAFCO nor NRC lists a sulfur requirement for dogs or cats.[2-4] Generally, there isn't a dietary need for sulfur per se, if a food is formulated to meet the sulfur-containing amino acid requirements of simple stomached animals.

Of the microminerals, only iron, zinc, copper, manganese, iodine and selenium will be discussed here. These trace minerals have been deemed essential for dogs and cats (although clinical cases of manganese deficiency have never been reported to occur in dogs or cats).[2] Cobalt and molybdenum are clearly important minerals in ruminant nutrition, but are not considered essential in monogastric species. Information about chromium and boron, two ultra-trace minerals, is included because of the potential importance these nutrients may have in companion animal nutrition. Other new trace elements discovered since 1970 include arsenic, lead, lithium, nickel, silicon, tin and vanadium. The essentiality of these minerals has not been elucidated in all species and under practical conditions may not be essential in the diet.

Function

Minerals are fundamental as: 1) structural components of body organs and tissues, such as calcium, phosphorus and magnesium in bones and teeth, 2) constituents of body fluids and tissues such as electrolytes concerned with the maintenance of osmotic pressure, acid-base balance, muscle contraction, membrane permeability and tissue irritability (e.g., sodium, potassium, chloride, calcium and magnesium in blood, cerebrospinal fluid and gastric juice) and 3) catalysts/cofactors in enzyme and hormone systems, as integral and specific components of the structure of metalloenzymes, or as less specific activators within those systems. Table 2-17 lists specific functions of each mineral.

Homeostasis

Specific concentrations and functional forms of minerals must be maintained within certain limits for optimal growth, health and fertility. Higher organisms possess homeostatic mechanisms that attempt to maintain concentrations of minerals at their active sites within narrow physiologic limits despite over- or under-ingestion. Such mechanisms include control of intestinal absorption or excretion, the availability of specific stores for individual elements and the use of "chemical sinks" such as metallothionein that can bind potentially toxic amounts of elements in an innocuous form.[5]

The degree of homeostatic control varies from one element to another. Continued ingestion of diets or continued exposure to environments that are severely deficient, imbalanced or excessively high in a particular trace element, or in an interfering substance such as phytate or certain fibers, can induce changes in functioning forms, activ-

Table 2-17. Mineral functions and effects of deficiencies and excesses.

Mineral	Function	Deficiency	Excess
Calcium	Constituent of bone and teeth, blood clotting, muscle function, nerve transmission, membrane permeability	Decreased growth, decreased appetite, decreased bone mineralization, lameness, spontaneous fractures, loose teeth, tetany, convulsions, rickets (osteomalacia in adults)	Decreased feed efficiency and feed intake, nephrosis, lameness, enlarged costochondral junctions. Increased calcium intake is a risk factor for calcium-containing urinary precipi-tates; however, moderate- to high-calcium levels may be protective against calcium oxalate precipitates. Calcium in meals may bind with oxalate in the gut decreasing the risk.
Phosphorus	Constituent of bone and teeth, muscle formation, fat, carbo-hydrate and protein metabolism, phospholipids and energy production, reproduction	Depraved appetite, pica, decreased feed efficiency, decreased growth, dull coat, decreased fertility, spontaneous fractures, rickets	Bone loss, uroliths, decreased weight gain, decreased feed intake, calcification of soft tissues, secondary hyperparathyroidism
Potassium	Muscle contraction, transmission of nerve impulses, acid-base balance, osmotic balance, enzyme cofactor (energy transfer)	Anorexia, decreased growth, lethargy, locomotive problems, hypokalemia, heart and kidney lesions, emaciation	Rare. Paresis, bradycardia
Sodium and chloride	Osmotic pressure, acid-base balance, transmission of nerve impulses, nutrient uptake, waste excretion, water metabolism	Inability to maintain water balance, decreased growth, anorexia, fatigue, exhaustion, hair loss	Occurs only if there is inadequate good-quality water available. Thirst, pruritus, constipation, seizures and death
Magnesium	Component of bone and intracellular fluids, neuromuscular transmission, active component of several enzymes, carbohydrate and lipid metabolism	Muscular weakness, hyperirritability, convulsions, anorexia, vomiting, decreased mineralization of bone, decreased body weight, calcification of aorta	Uroliths, flaccid paralysis
Iron	Enzyme constituent, activation of O_2 (oxidases and oxygenases), oxygen transport (hemoglobin, myoglobin)	Anemia, rough coat, listlessness, decreased growth	Anorexia, weight loss, decreased serum albumin concentrations, hepatic dysfunction, hemosiderosis
Zinc	Constituent or activator of 200 known enzymes (nucleic acid metabolism, protein synthesis, carbohydrate metabolism), skin and wound healing, immune response, fetal development, growth rate	Anorexia, decreased growth, alopecia, parakeratosis, impaired reproduction, vomiting, hair depigmentation, conjunctivitis	Relatively nontoxic. Reported cases of zinc toxicity from consumption of die-cast zinc nuts or pennies
Copper	Component of several enzymes (oxidases), catalyst in hemoglobin formation, cardiac function, cellular respiration, connective tissue development, pigmentation, bone formation, myelin formation, immune function	Anemia, decreased growth, hair depigmentation, bone lesions, neuromuscular disorders, reproductive failure	Hepatitis, increased liver enzyme activity
Manganese	Component and activator of enzymes (glycosyl transferases), lipid and carbohydrate metabolism, bone development (organic matrix), reproduction, cell membrane integrity (mitochondria)	Impaired reproduction, fatty liver, crooked legs, decreased growth	Relatively nontoxic
Selenium	Constituent of glutathione peroxidase and iodothyronine 5'-deiodinase, immune function, reproduction	Muscular dystrophy, reproductive failure, decreased feed intake, subcutaneous edema, renal mineralization	Vomiting, spasms, staggered gait, salivation, decreased appetite, dyspnea, oral malodor, nail loss
Iodine	Constituent of thyroxine and triiodothyronine	Goiter, fetal resorption, rough coat, enlarged thyroid glands, alopecia, apathy, myxedema, lethargy	Similar to those caused by deficiency, Decreased appetite, listlessness, rough coat, decreased immunity, decreased weight gain, goiter, fever
Boron	Regulates parathyroid hormone; influences metabolism of calcium, phosphorus, magnesium and cholecalciferol	Decreased growth, decreased hematocrit, hemoglobin and alkaline phosphatase values	Similar to those caused by deficiency
Chromium	Potentiates insulin action, therefore improves glucose tolerance	Impaired glucose tolerance, increased serum triacylglyceride and cholesterol concentrations	Trivalent form less toxic than hexavalent. Dermatitis, respiratory irritation, lung cancer

ities or concentrations of that element in body tissues and fluids so that they fall below or rise above the desired limits. Altered metabolism develops in these circumstances, which may affect physiologic function. Structural disorders may also arise in ways that differ with various elements, with the degree and duration of the dietary deficiency or toxicity and with the age, gender and species of the animal involved.

Deficiency/Adequacy/Toxicity

Traditionally, minerals were classified as "essential" or "toxic," but as more information was gathered, elements shifted from the latter to the former category (e.g., selenium). However, toxicity may occur with all elements. A "biologic dose-response curve" exists for each element.[5] This curve (Figure 2-2) identifies a range of concentrations that spans three primary areas: 1) at low concentrations, physiologic function is consistently and reproducibly impaired (defined as deficiency), 2) at optimal concentrations, the nutrient is provided at levels necessary to meet the requirements of the animal and 3) at excessive concentrations, pharmacotoxicologic effects occur (toxicity). The intakes or dose levels at which these phases become evident and the width of the optimal plateau vary widely among minerals and can be markedly affected by the extent to which various other elements and compounds are present in the animal's body and in the food consumed. (See sidebar "Mineral Balance Studies.") Table 2-17 lists specific signs of mineral deficiency and toxicity.

Several nutrients have specific therapeutic uses at high dosages (e.g., zinc is fed at growth-promoting levels in swine to prevent diarrhea). However, high doses may result in detrimental side effects after prolonged use. The pharmacologic actions of nutrients differ in several ways from their physiologic functions: 1) doses greatly exceeding the amount of a nutrient present in foods are usually needed to obtain a therapeutic response, 2) the specificity of the pharmacologic action is often different from the physiologic function and 3) chemical analogues of the nutrient that are often most effective pharmacologically may have little or no nutritional activity.[6] (See sidebar "Adequate vs. Optimal Nutrient Intake.")

Claims of nutritional adequacy of pet foods are based on the current AAFCO nutrient allowances ("profiles"). These levels are neither minimal requirements nor necessarily optimal levels of intake. It isn't possible to establish optimal levels without additional information about nutrient requirements for all lifestages and information concerning the availability of nutrients from pet food ingredients and complete diets. In some cases, insufficient margins of safety have been given to account for population variation, product diversity, processing effects and potentially low nutrient availabilities of certain pet food ingredients. In the case of trace minerals, the ratio between dietary allowance and absolute requirement can be as large as 100:1 (e.g., chromium) because of incomplete absorption, or can approach unity (e.g., iodine) when absorption is high.[5] The nature of typical diets consumed strongly influences dietary allowances because numerous interactions among dietary components and different chemical forms in individual foods determine biologic availability. Thus, it is important to understand the limitations of AAFCO nutrient profiles.

Mineral Interactions

A tremendous number of mineral-mineral interactions exist (Figure 2-21). In general, these interactions can be antagonistic (the presence of one mineral reduces the transport or biologic efficacy of the other) or synergistic (the two minerals act in a complementary fashion either by sparing or substituting for the other mineral or the two together enhance a biologic function). Most mineral interactions are antagonistic and can occur via a number of different mechanisms that include interactions:[7] 1) in the food during processing, before consumption, 2) in the digestive tract, where there is competition for uptake sites or intracellular-level mechanisms, 3) at the tissue level, either at storage sites or inhibition of enzyme activity, 4) at the time of transport and 5) in the excretory pathway.

The rigors of processing can affect the availability of minerals either positively or negatively via changes in solubility, pH, reduction potential and charge density and creation of complexes.[8] Charge density refers to the valence state and size of a metal. For example, the cations in the periodic table in groups 6B to 2B, with a relatively high ionic charge (+2, +3) and small size, form a large number of stable complex ions, whereas the large alkali metal cations, such as Na^+ and K^+, with a small charge are much less likely to form complexes with proteins or carbohydrate moieties via ionic, coordinate or covalent bonds. Further, among the transition metals, which may form more than one cation, complexes formed by the +3 valence state (e.g., Cr^{+3}, Co^{+3}) are more numerous and more stable than com-

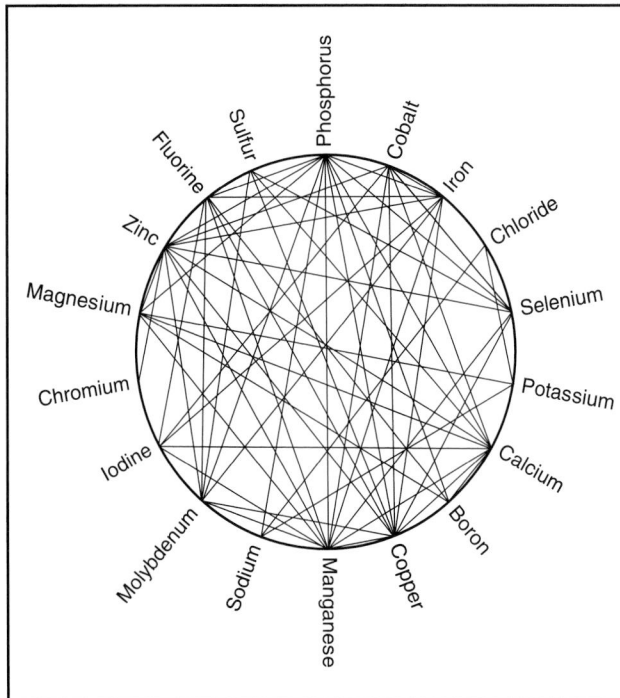

Figure 2-21. Mineral interrelationships. Minerals connected by a line have been shown clinically or experimentally to interact with the other mineral. This interaction may be bidirectional (each mineral affects the use of the other) or unidirectional (one mineral affects the use of the second mineral but not vice versa). (Adapted from Puls R. Mineral Levels in Animal Health. Clearbrook, British Columbia: Diagnostic Data Sherpa International, 1990; 19.)

Mineral Balance Studies

The requirements for most nutrients are derived from experimental and clinical evidence of deficiency and the amount of nutrient needed to prevent signs of deficiency. When balance studies are used to estimate requirements, the requirement is defined as the intake at which zero balance is attained, or when intake is equal to excretion in urine and feces. However, the zero balance point will underestimate the requirement, if the measurement does not account for endogenous losses and losses in sweat.

Mineral balance studies have been criticized as inadequate and erroneous measures of body requirements. Small percentage errors in determining intakes and excretion can result in significant differences in balance calculations. One of the biggest problems in conducting balance studies is separating feces into time intervals that can be related to intake. Fecal markers aid in separation, but peristaltic reflux may still confound results. In addition, one animal's rate of passage can vary markedly. Adaptation to a different level of intake may occur in a few days or weeks. Some adaptations, however, take several months or even years to occur. Thus, the adaptation period and collection period need to be sufficiently long to take into account animal adjustments to new foods, rates of passage and homeostatic adaptation.

Balance studies are probably more reliable when the mineral is excreted in the urine, rather than in the feces. This finding is true for sodium, potassium and selenium. When absorption of a nutrient is low, as is the case for a number of minerals, the amount of fecal mineral is large compared with the amount absorbed (e.g., the mineral concentration in feces is attributed to unabsorbed mineral and endogenous secretion). Failure to measure endogenous secretion may markedly underestimate the true amount of absorbed mineral. However, if radioisotopes or stable isotopes are used in conjunction with a balance study, the endogenous secretions can be distinguished from unabsorbed mineral and a measure of true absorption attained (as opposed to "apparent" absorption, which does not account for endogenous losses). Balance studies without the use of isotopes are fraught with inaccuracy and variability. Few analytical methods give a coefficient of variation as good as 5%, especially in complex matrices such as food, urine and feces. Thus, balance studies will not detect nutritionally important mineral differences when absorption efficiencies are low and radioisotopes or stable isotopes are not used.

Probably the biggest criticism of balance studies is that balance studies better reflect habitual intake than a requirement or zero balance. For example, an intake of 1 µg of selenium/kg body weight maintains a zero balance in Americans. Approximately one-tenth of that intake maintains a balance in people living in China; China is an area in which the risk of selenium deficiency is high and prevalence of Keshan disease is significant. Thus, zero balance does not necessarily indicate absence of disease. In New Zealand, selenium balance is maintained on an intake of one-third the amount required by Americans.

Analogous situations also exist worldwide for calcium balance. Widely different intakes of calcium result in zero balances in different countries. Thus, the previous dietary intake exerts a significant effect on the nutrient level that results in a zero balance and is more a reflection of the intake required to maintain an existing mineral pool size.

Balance studies should be evaluated with caution when attempting to determine requirements. A summary of their limitations follows:

- Prior long-term habitual intake influences whether positive, negative or equilibrium balance occurs at a particular intake.
- The duration of the study may not be long enough to allow for homeostatic adaptation.
- Cumulative errors occur from environmental contamination, individual variability and analytical methods. Thus, balance studies that demonstrate no treatment differences, may in fact be a result of the insensitivity and imprecision of the balance method.

BIBLIOGRAPHY

Kelsay JL. Interpretation of mineral balance data in estimating requirements. In: Trace Elements in Man and Animals (TEMA-5). Mills DF, Bremner I, Chesters JK, eds. Farnham Royal, UK: Commonwealth Agricultural Bureaux, 1985; 879-881.

Mertz W. Use and misuse of balance studies. Journal of Nutrition 1987; 117: 1811-1813.

plexes formed by their respective +2 ions. Charge is also involved with cell permeability and ion solubility before ions enter cells. Solubility varies tremendously depending on ion size and degree of polarity or charge.

Solubility is of obvious importance; a mineral must come in contact with the intestinal mucosa if it is to be absorbed. Charge density is less obvious but important for its effect on complex formation and membrane permeability. Solubility as it refers to mineral availability includes the solubility of an ion, salt, hydrate or complex, and to the type and strength of chemical bonds within these molecules. Inhibition of mineral absorption by a food can be overcome by the use of mineral enhancers, such as ascorbate, meat, citric acid and other ligands (e.g., ascorbate enhances iron absorption but negatively affects copper uptake; both effects are brought about by a change in pH and reduction in valence state).

Mineral-mineral interactions that occur in the digestive tract result from chemically similar minerals sharing "channels" for absorption. In this situation, simultaneous ingestion of two or more such minerals will result in competition for absorption.[7] In other words, when the dietary supply of a nutrient and/or the body reserves of a mineral are low, the intestine adapts to improve the efficiency of uptake and transfer. When the adaptation is nonspecific, other similar minerals have enhanced absorption. In iron deficiency, an upregulation of iron also increases uptake of lead.[7] Other examples of interactions occurring in the digestive tract include the formation of insoluble mineral complexes (e.g., foods containing phytate and excessive calcium will form an insoluble calcium/phytate/zinc complex that reduces zinc availability).

Mineral-mineral interactions can also occur at the tissue storage level. High levels of dietary iron, for example, reduce hepatic copper stores. In studies, when ratios of iron to copper exceeded 20:1, hepatic copper levels were reduced to less than 50% of control values.[7] Likewise, trace minerals such as zinc can be mobilized when calcium is deficient because co-mobilization of both minerals takes place from the skeleton, making both available for use.

Mineral-mineral interactions can also occur at the time of transport. Transferrin is a serum transport protein for iron. Transferrin is generally less than 50% saturated with iron in its transit from site to site.[7] Transferrin can also transport chromium and manganese; therefore, these

Organic vs. Inorganic Minerals

There is some debate about whether organic forms of trace minerals are more available than inorganic forms. The answer depends on the specific mineral, the dietary conditions and the physiologic state of the animal. Clearly, the organic forms of certain minerals (e.g., selenium, chromium, iron) are better used than inorganic forms. (See the selenium, chromium and iron sections of this chapter.) Which form is better used is less clear for other minerals (e.g., zinc, copper). For example, there are as many studies that have failed to show increased availability with zinc/copper organic forms as there are studies demonstrating improved availability.

A number of factors influence the outcome of availability studies, including: 1) the presence of non-nutritional factors (e.g., phytate, fiber, goitrogens), 2) nutrient interactions (e.g., excesses of other minerals) and 3) physiologic state (e.g., demand for certain minerals increases with reproduction and growth compared to that of maintenance, thus in these situations, the differences in availability are magnified between organic and inorganic sources).

Results of studies in puppies showed that as calcium levels increased from 1.0 to 1.5%, zinc usage (as measured by changes in plasma zinc concentrations) decreased, irrespective of whether the source was organic (zinc propionate) or inorganic (zinc oxide). Zinc from zinc propionate was approximately 1.8 to 2 times more available than from zinc oxide.

Other investigators likewise noted increased zinc retention (as measured by zinc deposition in hair and fecal zinc excretion) for adult dogs fed a zinc-amino acid chelate compared with the same dogs fed zinc polysaccharide or zinc oxide. Increasing calcium from 1.2 to 3.2% reduced zinc retention when dogs were fed zinc polysaccharide or zinc oxide, but not the zinc-amino acid chelate.

Similarly, researchers have demonstrated in livestock and fish that growth rate and calcium and phytate levels are factors that significantly affect zinc use. Thus, these factors determine whether the use of organic zinc sources is beneficial. Together, these data suggest little or no benefit to using organic zinc in foods low in phytate and calcium (e.g., low calcium is defined as calcium levels approximating NRC recommendations for respective species). However, as phytate and/or calcium levels increase, or demand for zinc increases (e.g., rapid growth rate), there is greater zinc use from organic zinc sources (parameters used to assess zinc availability included bone zinc, immune response and/or growth rate). Further, the more rapidly the animal grows, the greater the benefit demonstrated for organic zinc (e.g., fish >chicks [broiler breeds >leghorn-type] >puppies >pigs). The efficacy decreased as the animal matured, suggesting organic zinc sources in foods may be less beneficial for adult animals.

In summary, organic forms of minerals may be beneficial when dietary or physiologic conditions limit mineral availability. These conditions include: 1) mineral antagonisms caused by phytate, fiber and imbalances/excesses of other minerals and 2) increased metabolic demand such as rapid growth rate, reproduction and immune challenge.

BIBLIOGRAPHY

Wedekind KJ, Lowry SR. Effects of zinc source, calcium level and fiber on zinc bioavailability in puppies. Waltham International Symposium, 1997. (Abstract submitted).

Lowe JA, Wiseman J, Cole DJA. Zinc source influences zinc retention in hair and hair growth in the dog. Journal of Nutrition 1994; 124: 2575S-2576S.

Wedekind KJ, Hortin AE, Baker DH. Methodology for assessing zinc bioavailability: Efficacy estimates for zinc-methionine, zinc sulfate and zinc oxide. Journal of Animal Science 1992; 70:178-187.

Wedekind KJ, Collings G, Hancock J, et al. The bioavailability of zinc-methionine relative to zinc sulfate is affected by calcium level. Poultry Science 1994; 73 (Suppl. 1): 114.

Wedekind KJ, Lewis AJ, Giesemann MA, et al. Bioavailability of zinc from inorganic and organic sources for pigs fed corn-soybean meal diets. Journal of Animal Science 1994; 72: 2681-2689.

Paripatananont T. Comparison of bioefficacy of organic zinc (zinc methionine) with inorganic zinc (zinc sulfate) in diets of channel catfish. PhD Thesis. Auburn University, 1994.

minerals may compete for binding sites contained in transferrin.

Finally, mineral-mineral interactions can also occur within pathways of excretion. For example, levels of circulating ionized calcium govern the release of parathyroid hormone (PTH) from the parathyroid gland. PTH status, in turn, influences renal tubular handling of filtered phosphate. Recent evidence also points to an interaction between calcium and magnesium at the level of renal excretion.[7]

Availability

Evaluation of feeds as sources of minerals depends not only on what the feed contains (i.e., the analyzed nutrient content), but also on how much of the mineral can be used by the animal. The adequacy of a food, as determined by its analytical mineral concentration, can be misleading because a number of factors can influence the mineral availability. These include: 1) the chemical form (which influences solubility), 2) the amounts and proportions of other dietary components with which it interacts metabolically, 3) the age, gender and species of the animal, 4) intake of the mineral and the need (body stores) and 5) environmental factors.[5] (See sidebar "Organic vs. Inorganic Minerals.")

Few studies have been completed in dogs and cats to evaluate the availability of minerals in foodstuffs used in commercial pet foods. Thus, there are many unknowns about the availability of nutrients in pet foods and whether a given food is truly adequate for a given lifestage. The availability of different forms of a mineral can vary widely even among inorganic mineral supplements. In general, different forms of trace minerals (iron, zinc, manganese and copper) differ in availability as follows: sulfate and chloride forms >carbonates >oxides.[9-12] The oxides of iron and copper are poorly available and should not be used as mineral supplements in pet food.[11,13]

In general, meat-derived foodstuffs are considered a more available source of certain minerals than plant-derived foodstuffs. The organic forms of minerals found in meats are often more available or as available as those from inorganic mineral supplements, whereas the minerals in plants are often less available.[14,15] This finding is more true for iron, zinc and copper than for selenium.

Although the mechanism has not been fully delineated, one theory has been suggested to explain why organic

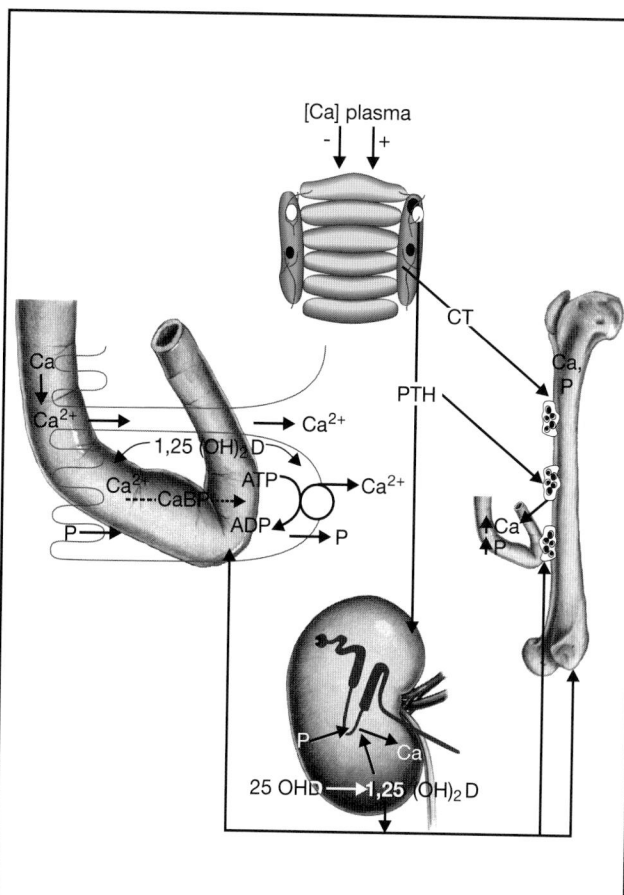

Figure 2-22. Calcium absorption by the intestine and bone resorption and reabsorption in the kidney are closely regulated by calcium-regulating hormones: parathyroid hormone, calcitonin and 1,25-dihydroxycholecalciferol. See text for details.

forms of minerals are better used than inorganic forms. This theory postulates that chelates or complexes provide the mineral in a protected form,[16] analogous to the iron contained in heme, wherein the iron is complexed to a protoporphyrin ring. Because the metal is complexed or bound, it is protected from being sequestered by other dietary components (e.g., phytate, fiber and sugars) and is less likely to compete with mineral excesses.

Regardless of whether the molecular species is plant- or animal-derived, the complex must be able to be absorbed by mucosal cells or be cleaved to release the mineral in a soluble form or have stability constants that allow the mineral to be transferred to mucosal or serosal acceptors for availability.[8] Other explanations for why animal products are generally more available forms of certain minerals than plants include the "meat-factor" effect, wherein meat provides an available form of the mineral and enhances the absorption of the mineral supplied by the rest of the food.[17,18] In addition, meats, unlike plants, do not contain anti-nutritional factors, such as phytate, oxalate, goitrogens and fiber, which reduce mineral availability.

Not all fiber sources negatively affect mineral availability. Research in chicks[19,20] and puppies[21] indicated marked differences about how fiber sources affect mineral availability (Table 2-7). In these studies, beet pulp consistently reduced the availability of minerals (zinc, calcium, phosphorus and iron); however, cellulose, corn bran and sun-

flower hulls had negligible effects. Pea fiber, peanut hulls and soy hulls inhibited availability of some but not all of the minerals evaluated. Additional mineral supplementation is warranted for foods known to have reduced mineral availability.

In the text that follows, research on nutrient requirements is only discussed when findings differ from current AAFCO or NRC recommendations. See Appendix J for AAFCO and NRC information.[2-4]

Macrominerals

Calcium

Calcium serves two important functions: 1) as a structural component in bones and teeth and 2) as an intracellular second messenger that enables cells to respond to stimuli such as hormones and neurotransmitters. Calcium's two major physiologic functions in bone are to serve as a structural material and as an ion reservoir. When calcium in bone acts as an ion reservoir, it is in equilibrium with serum ionized calcium and under tight homeostatic control.

The mechanism of calcium homeostasis in blood is complex and involves several organs. Blood concentrations of ionized (or free) calcium is the major initiator of calcium regulatory mechanisms in the body. Calcium in blood is in equilibrium between a free or ionized state (~50%), a protein-bound state (~40 to 45%) and a complexed or chelated state (~5 to 10%). The effects of changing ionized calcium concentration in blood are highlighted below (Figure 2-22).[22]

Low concentrations of ionized calcium:
- Stimulate PTH secretion, which stimulates conversion of 25-hydroxycholecalciferol to the biologically more potent 1,25-dihydroxycholecalciferol in the kidneys
- 1,25-dihydroxycholecalciferol stimulates calcium uptake in the gut via receptor-mediated mechanisms
- 1,25-dihydroxycholecalciferol, in conjunction with PTH, stimulates bone resorption
- PTH induces phosphaturia.

High or normal concentrations of ionized calcium:
- Stimulate calcitonin secretion, which does not stimulate 1,25-dihydroxycholecalciferol production
- 24,25-dihydroxycholecalciferol is now produced in the kidneys, which is considered biologically less active
- No stimulation of gut absorption or bone resorption occurs
- Increased renal calcium excretion results
- Calcitonin decreases osteoclastic activity.

PTH, calcitonin and 1,25-dihydroxycholecalciferol act together to maintain calcium homeostasis in the face of variable dietary intakes and changing calcium requirements during growth, pregnancy and lactation.

The amount of true calcium absorption may range from 25 to 90%, depending upon calcium status, calcium form or intake.[22] This exchangeable pool consists of the small amount of calcium in blood, lymph and other body fluids, and accounts for 1% of the total body calcium. The remaining 99% is located in bones and teeth. There are three routes of calcium absorption in the intestine. One is an active, saturable, transcellular process that occurs primarily in the duodenum and proximal jejunum. The process is regulated by vitamin D and involves a vitamin D-dependent, calcium-binding protein (CaBP or cal-

Calcium-Phosphorus Ratios

The "ideal" calcium-phosphorus ratio recommended for simple stomached animals is generally considered to be between 1:1 and 2:1. A number of factors, however, influence the importance of this ratio. Increasing levels of vitamin D reduce the significance of adverse calcium-phosphorus ratios. Further, the ratio can differ markedly with the form and availability of the calcium and phosphorus supplied in the diet. For example, animals eating foods high in phytate phosphorus require greater phosphorus intake to meet their needs. Thus, the ideal calcium-phosphorus ratio would be lower when foods with these dietary characteristics are fed vs. foods composed of mostly meat ingredients.

Investigators sometimes debate whether the calcium-phosphorus ratio is more important than absolute calcium and phosphorus levels (Table 1). For all practical purposes, however, if a food is formulated to meet or slightly exceed an animal's requirement for calcium and phosphorus, it would by default provide an optimal calcium-phosphorus ratio. The more rapid the growth rate (e.g., large- and giant-breed puppies >small-breed puppies >adult dogs), the more critical it is to optimize calcium and phosphorus levels. (See Chapter 17.) Increasing energy density increases the calcium and phosphorus requirement; the younger the animal the more critical it is that calcium and phosphorus be optimal.

Calcium-phosphorus ratios less than one have been evaluated in cats. Kealy et al compared the effects of feeding two foods with different calcium: phosphorus ratios to adult cats for 52 weeks. (The foods had 1:1 vs. 0.6:1 ratios; calcium and phosphorus levels were 1.27% calcium, 1.29% phosphorus and 0.75% calcium and 1.24% phosphorus, respectively, all on a DMB.) Serum concentrations of total calcium, ionized calcium, phosphorus, PTH, alkaline phosphatase and vitamin D analogs did not differ between cats fed the two different foods at any sampling time and no signs of orthopedic diseases or bone loss developed during the study.

Likewise, Morris and Earle evaluated the effects of feeding foods containing calcium-phosphorus ratios as low as 0.65:1 to kittens and found no adverse effects, provided calcium and phosphorus levels exceeded 0.5 and 0.63% (DMB), respectively. Morris and Earle determined these calcium and phosphorus levels to be the calcium and phosphorus requirements for kittens. Results showed that this ratio (0.65:1) was well-tolerated by kittens. Feed consumption, body weight gain, hematologic parameters and concentrations of plasma total and ionized calcium, total phosphorus, alkaline phosphatase, PTH, creatine phosphokinase, total plasma protein and albumin and plasma 25-OH-D did not differ from values in kittens fed foods with higher calcium-phosphorus ratios. Investigators noted significant changes in ionizable calcium concentrations; however, at 18 weeks in kittens fed foods with a calcium-phosphorus ratio of 0.38. These studies indicate that cats may tolerate wider dietary calcium-phosphorus ratios than the previously recommended ratios between 1:1 and 2:1.

BIBLIOGRAPHY

Kealy RD, Lawler DF, Ballam JM. Dietary calcium:phosphorus ratios for adult cats. Veterinary Clinical Nutrition 1996; 3: 28.

Morris JG, Earle KE. Vitamin D and calcium requirements of kittens. Veterinary Clinical Nutrition 1996; 3: 93-96.

Table 1. Examples of calcium-phosphorus percentages and ratios.

Examples	% calcium/% phosphorus (calcium:phosphorus ratio)
AAFCO adult allowance for calcium and phosphorus in dogs	0.6/0.5 (1.2:1)
AAFCO growth allowance for calcium and phosphorus in dogs	1.0/0.8 (1.25:1)
Example of why tuna is a poor source of calcium and has a poor calcium: phosphorus ratio	0.157/1.28 (0.12:1)
Example of a correct ratio, but excessive calcium and phosphorus levels	2/1.6 (1.2:1)

bindin). Active calcium absorption is affected by the physiology of the host—that is, calcium and vitamin D status, age, pregnancy and lactation.

The other pathways of calcium absorption are facilitated and passive absorption, which are important in the distal GI tract. Passive absorption is a nonsaturable, paracellular route that is independent of vitamin D regulation. The amount of calcium absorbed in this way depends primarily on quantity and availability of calcium in the food. No matter where absorption takes place, vitamin D is the most important regulator of calcium absorption.[23] Renal handling of calcium is also modulated by PTH and calcitonin but not as much by vitamin D.

Deficiencies and excesses of calcium, as well as calcium-phosphorus imbalances, should be avoided in dogs and cats. (See sidebar "Calcium-Phosphorus Ratios.") A food grossly deficient in calcium, but adequate in phosphorus can cause secondary hyperparathyroidism. An all-meat diet devoid of bones, for example, is a very poor source of calcium. Inadequate calcium intake produces hypocalcemia, which stimulates release of PTH, which in turn stimulates production of 1,25-dihydroxycholecalciferol, resulting in a higher fractional absorption of calcium and phosphate, and lower calcium but higher phosphate concentration in urine. PTH acts with vitamin D to promote bone resorption and turnover, which may lead to pathologic fractures. Hypocalcemia is a common problem in diseased states (chronic or acute renal failure, pancreatitis, eclampsia, etc.), and parenteral supplementation of calcium and/or calcitriol (1,25-dihydroxycholecalciferol) is sometimes warranted.[24] Calcium excess is probably more detrimental in rapidly growing animals than in adults, especially large- and giant-breed puppies. (See Chapter 17.) Table 2-17 describes signs of calcium deficiency and excess.

Pastoor et al conducted a balance study to determine the calcium requirement of adult cats.[25] Four levels of calcium ($CaCO_3$) ranging from 0.27 to 1.62% (DMB) were evaluated. The minimum level evaluated (0.27% calcium) resulted in positive mineral balance with no adverse effect on serum phosphorus, calcium, magnesium and alkaline phosphatase concentrations. This level is less than half that of current AAFCO recommendations (i.e., 0.6% calcium).[2] Likewise, two groups of investigators conducting studies in kittens demonstrated lower calcium and phosphorus requirements than those currently recommended

Table 2-18. Common mineral sources.*

Mineral	Source	Chemical formula	Mineral content**			
Calcium	Calcium carbonate		39% Ca	0.02% Na		
	Limestone	$CaCO_3$	38% Ca	0.05% Na	0.01% F	
	Calcium citrate		24% Ca			
	Calcium sulfate	$CaSO_4$	23% Ca			
	Calcium chloride	$CaCl_2$	35% Ca	64% Cl		
Calcium and phosphorus	Bone meal		24% Ca	12.6% P	0.37% Na	0.05% F
	Phosphate, curacao		36% Ca	14% P	0.3% Na	0.54% F
	Defluorinated		30-34% Ca	18% P	5.7% Na	0.16% F
	Dicalcium		18-24% Ca	18.5% P	0.6% Na	0.14% F
	Mono and dicalcium		16-19% Ca	21% P	0.6% Na	0.20% F
	Soft rock		17% Ca	9% P	0.1% Na	1.2% F
	Sodium tripolyphosphate		0% Ca	25% P	31% Na	0.03% F
Phosphorus	Phosphoric acid	H_3PO_4	0% Ca	23% P		
	Tricalcium phosphate	Ca_3PO_4	31-34% Ca	18% P		
Magnesium	Magnesium oxide	MgO	54% Mg			
	Magnesium sulfate	$MgSO_4$	9% Mg			
Potassium	Potassium citrate		36% K			
	Potassium chloride	KCl	50% K			
	Potassium sulfate	K_2SO_4	42% K			
Sodium and chloride	Sodium chloride	$NaCl$	39% Na	61% Cl		
	Sodium acetate		28% Na			
	Sodium tripolyphosphate		32% Na	25% P		
Iron	Ferrous sulfate	$FeSO_4 \cdot H_2O$	33% Fe			
	Ferrous sulfate	$FeSO_4 \cdot 7H_2O$	20% Fe			
	Ferric ammonium citrate		16.5-18.5% Fe			
	Ferrous fumarate	$FeC_4 \cdot H_2O_4$	32.9% Fe			
	Ferric chloride	$FeCl_3 \cdot 6H_2O$	20.7% Fe			
	Ferrous carbonate	$FeCO_3$	48.2% Fe			
	Ferric oxide	Fe_2O_3	69.9% Fe			
	Ferrous oxide	FeO	77.8% Fe			
Copper	Cupric carbonate	$CuCO_3 \cdot Cu(OH)_2$	57.5% Cu			
	Cupric chloride	$CuCl_2 \cdot 2H_2O$	37.3% Cu			
	Cupric hydroxide	$Cu(OH)_2$	65.1% Cu			
	Cupric oxide	CuO	79.9% Cu			
	Cupric sulfate	$CuSO_4 \cdot 5H_2O$	25.4% Cu			
Manganese	Manganese carbonate	$MnCO_3$	47.8% Mn			
	Manganous chloride	$MnCl_2 \cdot 4H_2O$	27.8% Mn			
	Manganese oxide	MnO	77.4% Mn			
	Manganese sulfate	$MnSO_4 \cdot 5H_2O$	22.7% Mn			
	Manganous sulfate	$MnSO_4 \cdot H_2O$	32.5% Mn			
Zinc	Zinc carbonate	$5ZnO \cdot 2CO_3 \cdot 4H_2O$	56.0% Zn			
	Zinc chloride	$ZnCl_2$	48.0% Zn			
	Zinc oxide	ZnO	72.0% Zn			
	Zinc sulfate	$ZnSO_4 \cdot 7H_2O$	22.7% Zn			
	Zinc sulfate	$ZnSO_4 \cdot H_2O$	36.4% Zn			
Iodine	Calcium iodate	$Ca(IO_3)_2$	65.1% I			
	Potassium iodide	KI	76.4% I			
	Cuprous iodide	CuI	66.6% I			
	Iodized salt		48.2 ppm I			
Selenium	Sodium selenite	Na_2SeO_3	45.6% Se	26.6% Na		
	Sodium selenate	Na_2SeO_4	41.8% Se	24.3% Na		

*Adapted from National Research Council. Nutrient Requirements of Cats. Washington, DC: National Academy of Sciences, 1986.
**Actual mineral levels in technical grade sources may vary.

by AAFCO for growth (i.e., requirements for calcium and phosphorus were 0.5 and 0.63%[26] and 0.36 and 0.28%, respectively.[27]) These investigators concluded that the 1% DM calcium recommended by AAFCO for kittens is excessive and that the NRC recommendation[4] of 0.8% DM calcium was a more defensible allowance for kittens fed typical moist foods. The current AAFCO canine and feline recommendations for calcium are 1.0% for growth/reproduction and 0.6% for adult maintenance (DMB for both values).[2] For dogs, this calcium requirement is based on an energy density of 3.5 kcal/g ME, whereas an energy density of 4.0 kcal/g ME is assumed for cats.[2] Foods with increased energy densities should have a proportionally increased amount of calcium to account for decreased food consumption.

The following meat meals are rich sources of calcium because of their bone content: poultry by-product meal, lamb meal and fish meal. Grains (corn, rice, etc.), on the other hand, are generally poor sources of calcium. Soybean meal and flaxseed have calcium contents between those of meat meals and grains. Meats without bone are poor sources of calcium. The most common calcium supplements used in pet foods are limestone (calcium carbonate), calcium sulfate, calcium chloride, calcium phosphate and bone meal, ranging in calcium from 16 to 39% (Table 2-18).

Phosphorus

Phosphorus is a vital participant in a number of tissues and functions. After calcium, phosphorus is the second largest constituent of bone and teeth. Phosphorus is a structural component of RNA and DNA, high-energy phosphate compounds such as ATP and cell membranes composed largely of phospholipids. As a component of nucleic acids, high-energy phosphate compounds and cell membranes, phosphorus is essential in cell growth and differentiation, energy use and transfer, fatty acid transport and amino acid and protein formation.

About 60 to 70% of phosphorus is absorbed from a typical diet.[28] In general, phosphorus availability is greater from animal-based ingredients than from plant-based ingredients. Phosphorus in meat is found mainly in the organic form, whereas in plants, phosphorus is in the form of phytic acid. Phytate phosphorus is only about one-third available to monogastric animals but availability from different grains can vary markedly.[1] Intestinal phosphorus absorption represents the sum of a saturable, carrier-mediated component and a nonsaturable, concentration-dependent component. Regulation of total body phosphorus requires the coordinated efforts of the kidneys and intestine. Under conditions of low dietary phosphorus intake, the intestine increases its absorptive efficiency to maximize phosphorus absorption and the kidneys increase renal phosphorus transport or minimize urinary phosphorus losses. Hormonally, these adaptations result from changes in plasma levels of 1,25-dihydroxycholecalciferol and PTH. Conversely, under conditions of dietary excess, the kidneys increase excretion of minerals. Avoiding excess dietary phosphorus slows progression of kidney disease. (See Chapter 19.) Table 2-17 describes effects of deficiency and excess.

Similar to the study design for calcium, Pastoor et al also evaluated the minimum phosphorus requirement for adult cats.[29] Four levels of phosphorus (provided as $NaH_2PO_4 \cdot 2H_2O$) ranging from 0.3 to 1.8% (DMB) were evaluated. The minimum level evaluated (0.3% phosphorus) resulted in positive mineral balance with no adverse effect on serum phosphorus, calcium, magnesium and alkaline phosphatase concentrations. Again, this level is lower than the 0.5% phosphorus value currently recommended by AAFCO. Levels of phosphorus exceeding 0.6% (DMB) were associated with lower plasma phosphorus concentrations, reduced creatinine clearance and decreased magnesium absorption. Thus, the authors concluded continued feeding of high levels of dietary phosphorus may be detrimental to renal function. The AAFCO recommendation for phosphorus, for both dogs and cats, is 0.8% for growth and reproduction and 0.5% for adult maintenance (DMB for both values).[2]

In general, meat tissue (poultry, lamb, fish, beef) is high in phosphorus. Eggs and milk products are also relatively rich in phosphorus. Oilseeds, protein supplements and grains likewise contribute significant amounts of phosphorus to pet foods, due more to their high inclusion rate than to high-phosphorus concentrations. A number of phosphorus supplements (Table 2-18) are used in pet foods, including calcium phosphate (monocalcium, dicalcium and tricalcium phosphate, defluorinated rock phosphate), sodium phosphates and phosphoric acid.

Magnesium

Magnesium is the third largest mineral constituent of bone, after calcium and phosphorus. Magnesium is involved in the metabolism of carbohydrates and lipids and acts as a catalyst for a wide array of enzymes. It is required for cellular oxidation (e.g., ATP production), it catalyzes most phosphate transfers (e.g., alkaline phosphatase, hexokinase and deoxyribonuclease) and it exerts a potent influence on neuromuscular activity. In light of these functions, it is not surprising that magnesium deficiency in animals is manifested clinically in a wide range of disorders, which include retarded growth, hyperirritability and tetany, peripheral vasodilatation, anorexia, muscle incoordination and convulsions. Other metabolic aberrations that may occur in magnesium-deficient animals include calcification of the kidneys and liver, a decrease in blood pressure and body temperature and decreased thiamin concentrations in tissues.[5]

From 20 to 70% of dietary magnesium is absorbed.[30] Intestinal magnesium absorption represents the sum of both a carrier-mediated system at low intraluminal concentrations, and simple diffusion at higher concentrations. A number of dietary and physiologic factors negatively influence magnesium absorption, including high levels of dietary phosphorus, calcium, potassium, fat and protein.

The kidneys play a critical role in magnesium homeostasis. Approximately 70% of serum magnesium is filtered by glomeruli; healthy kidneys reabsorb about 95% of the filtered magnesium.[31] Magnesium reabsorption in nephrons is influenced by several physiologic and metabolic factors, drugs and disease states. Certain drugs, such as diuretics, aminoglycosides, cisplatin, cyclosporin, amphotericin and methotrexate, can cause increased renal wasting of magnesium.[32]

Avoiding excess dietary magnesium is recommended for the prevention of struvite urinary precipitates in cats and dogs; however, magnesium deficiency is reported to increase the risk of calcium oxalate urolithiasis in rats.[33] Further, magnesium supplementation has been advocated to prevent calcium oxalate urolithiasis in people. However, this practice is very controversial because clinical trials have demonstrated mixed efficacy. The relationship of magnesium to feline and canine urinary calcium oxalate precipitates is unknown; however, ensuring magnesium concentrations above the minimum requirement is considered safe. (See Chapters 20 and 21.)

Conversely, increased magnesium supplementation may be warranted under certain clinical conditions in which magnesium stores are depleted. The GI tract and kidneys are the primary potential routes for magnesium excretion. Magnesium deficiencies may also result from renal losses secondary to renal tubular acidosis, hypercalcemia, hyperthyroidism, hypoparathyroidism and use of diuretics. Additionally, epidemiologic data and rat studies suggest that low urinary magnesium to calcium ratios may increase the risk for calcium oxalate formation.[33] Table 2-17 describes signs of deficiency and excess.

Pastoor et al evaluated the minimum requirement for magnesium in adult cats.[27] Four levels of magnesium ($MgCO_3$) were compared. Positive mineral balance was observed even at the lowest magnesium level (0.02% DMB) and no adverse effects were noted in serum magnesium and alkaline phosphatase concentrations. This magnesium level is half of the current NRC[4] and AAFCO recommendation.[2] Extrapolation of these results, which were obtained by feeding semi-purified diets, to commercial foods should be made cautiously because of the differences in ingredients used and the greater potential for mineral antagonisms and decreased availability that may occur in practical diets. AAFCO recommends 0.08% magnesium for growth and reproduction and 0.04% magnesium for adult maintenance (DMB for both values) for cats.[2] The AAFCO magnesium recommendation for dogs is 0.04% (DMB) for both lifestages.[2]

Ingredients containing bone (bone meal, lamb meal), oilseed/protein supplements (flaxseed, soybean meal) and unrefined grains and fiber sources (wheat bran, oat bran, beet pulp, soymill run) are rich in magnesium. Common magnesium supplements include magnesium oxide and magnesium sulfate.

Potassium

Potassium is the most abundant intracellular cation and the third most abundant mineral in the body. Potassium is involved in a number of functions, including: 1) maintaining acid-base balance, 2) maintaining osmotic balance, 3) transmitting nerve impulses, 4) facilitating muscle contractility and 5) serving as a cofactor in several enzyme systems (energy transfer and use, protein synthesis and carbohydrate metabolism).

Potassium is absorbed primarily by simple diffusion from the upper small intestine, though some absorption also occurs in the lower small intestine and large intestine. Potassium availability is relatively high (95% or higher) for most foodstuffs.[1] Yet, in contrast to most minerals, potassium is not readily stored and must be supplied daily in the diet. Thus, it is important that foods for dogs and cats contain adequate potassium. Increased intake of potassium is unlikely to cause sustained hyperkalemia unless renal excretion of potassium is impaired. Administration of certain drugs predisposes the patient to hyperkalemia (e.g., nonspecific β-adrenergic blockers and angiotensin-converting enzyme inhibitors).

Table 2-17 describes signs of deficiency and excess. The requirement for potassium is increased by increasing protein, energy density or chloride, and other factors such as stress (heat and exercise) and milk production. AAFCO recommends 0.6% potassium (DMB) for both dogs and cats for all lifestages.[2]

Rich sources of potassium include soybean meal, unrefined grains and fiber sources (soymill run, sunflower hulls, rice bran, wheat bran) and yeast. Potassium supplements commonly added to pet foods include potassium citrate, potassium chloride and potassium sulfate.

Sodium and Chloride

Sodium and chloride, in addition to potassium, are important for maintaining osmotic pressure, regulating acid-base equilibrium and transmitting nerve impulses and muscle contractions via Na-K-ATPase (sodium pump). In addition, sodium and chloride control the passage of nutrients into cells. Sodium ions must be present in the lumen of the small intestine for absorption of sugars and amino acids. Insufficient sodium concentrations decrease the use of digested protein and energy. Sodium also influences calcium absorption and mobilization and may affect absorption of several water-soluble vitamins (e.g., riboflavin, thiamin and ascorbic acid) that are sodium coupled.[1]

Sodium and chloride are readily absorbed, principally from the upper small intestine, and excreted predominantly in the urine with smaller amounts in feces and perspiration. Marked losses of salt can occur through perspiration in some species, secretion in milk, vomiting and diarrhea. When sodium intake is inadequate, the body has a remarkable capacity for conserving sodium by excreting extremely low levels in the urine. Chloride metabolism is controlled in relation to sodium. For example, excess urinary excretion of sodium is accompanied by urinary excretion of chloride.

Sodium concentrations in the body are regulated by hormones acting to maintain a constant sodium/potassium ratio in extracellular fluid. Aldosterone, secreted from the adrenal cortex, regulates the reabsorption of sodium from the renal tubules. Antidiuretic hormone from the posterior pituitary responds to osmotic pressure changes in the extracellular fluid. Both hormones maintain a constant sodium/potassium ratio.

The sodium requirement is influenced by a number of factors. The requirement is increased during reproduction, lactation, rapid growth and heat stress and with high dietary potassium levels. In people, the average sodium intake exceeds the recommended requirement by 15-fold.[34] Likewise, typical sodium content of pet foods exceeds the recommended level by four- to 15-fold. (See Chapter 18.) Yu and Morris determined the sodium requirement of kittens to be 0.16% (DMB or 0.30 mg Na/kcal ME) based upon aldosterone concentration in plasma.[35] The same investigators determined the requirement for adult cats was 0.08% sodium (DMB) or 0.15 mg Na/kcal ME.[36] The AAFCO recommendation for sodium in cats is 0.2% (DMB) for both lifestages, whereas in dogs, the recommendation is 0.3% for growth and reproduction (DMB) and 0.06% for adult maintenance (DMB).[2]

In the absence of studies establishing chloride requirements for dogs or cats, the recommendation for chloride is 1.5 times that of sodium. This value is comparable to the Na:Cl requirement ratio for other species. Thus, the chloride recommendation for dogs is 0.45% (growth/reproduction) and 0.09% (adult maintenance) and for cats 0.3% (DMB for all lifestages).[2] Table 2-17 describes signs of deficiency and excess. (See Case 2-3 "Seizures in an Airedale Terrier.")

The effect of dietary sodium chloride on blood pressure has generally been attributed to the sodium ion. However, it is clear from a number of studies that both sodium and chloride are necessary to inhibit renin production.[37,38] Salts such as sodium chloride, potassium chloride, lysine hydrochloride (but not lysine glutamate, sodium bicarbonate, potassium bicarbonate) inhibited renin production in sodium chloride-deprived rats and people.

Fish, eggs, dried whey, poultry by-product meal and soy isolate are ingredients high in sodium and chloride. Sodium and/or chloride supplements typically added to pet foods include salt, sodium phosphates, calcium chloride, choline chloride, potassium chloride and sodium acetate.

Microminerals

Iron

Iron is present in several enzymes and other proteins responsible for oxygen activation (oxidases and oxygenases), for electron transport (cytochromes) and for oxygen transport (hemoglobin, myoglobin). Because of the limited capacity of the body to excrete iron, iron homeostasis is maintained primarily by adjusting iron absorption. Iron in foods exists in two forms: 1) heme iron present in hemoglobin and myoglobin and 2) nonheme iron present in grains and plant sources.

Heme iron absorption is not greatly affected by iron status or other dietary factors. (Two exceptions are meat, which enhances heme iron absorption, and calcium, which inhibits heme and nonheme iron absorption.) In contrast to absorption of heme iron, absorption of nonheme iron is markedly influenced by iron status and by several dietary factors such as phytate, tannins and excesses of calcium, phosphorus, manganese, zinc, copper and ascorbic acid.[39]

The amount of iron absorbed from food is thus determined by three factors: 1) iron status of the body, 2) availability of dietary iron (as affected by other ingredients/nutrients) and 3) amounts of heme and nonheme iron in food.[39]

Iron is transported by plasma and is taken up by the bone marrow for hemoglobin synthesis. Although a small amount of hemoglobin circulates in plasma, by far the greatest amount of plasma iron is complexed to the specific iron-binding β_1-globulin transferrin. The degree of saturation of transferrin affects deposition of iron in liver stores and the supply of iron to red blood cell precursors. At saturation levels above 60%, much of the iron is deposited in the liver. Under normal conditions, only 30 to 40% of the transferrin is saturated; the remaining 60 to 70% represents an unbound or latent reserve.[40]

Iron is stored predominantly as ferritin and hemosiderin in liver, bone marrow and spleen. Normally, iron is stored primarily as ferritin. As tissue iron concentrations increase, however, the concentration of hemosiderin increases more than that of ferritin. Excretion of iron is limited. Only negligible amounts of iron appear in urine; the iron appearing in feces is predominantly unabsorbed iron. Iron is continuously lost in sweat, hair and nails.

Chausow and Czarnecki-Maulden determined that the iron requirement of kittens and puppies fed a phytate-free purified diet is 80 mg iron/kg of food (DMB).[41] This requirement is the AAFCO recommendation for iron for dogs and cats, for both growth/reproduction and adult maintenance lifestages.[2] Most pet foods are high in iron because of the high-iron concentrations found in meat ingredients, especially organ meats. Further, studies have shown the availability of iron to be relatively high from liver, muscle and animal by-products.[42,43] Consequently, iron deficiency is not of practical concern with most pet foods.

Although iron levels may be high in pet foods (levels sometimes exceed the requirement by 15-fold without supplementation), AAFCO has set a maximum level of 3,000 mg iron/kg of food for dogs (no maximum is established for cats), which clearly exceeds dietary concentrations of iron in most typical pet foods. Iron excesses should be avoided because of potential antagonisms with other minerals (e.g., zinc and copper). Table 2-17 lists signs of deficiency and excess. Chronic blood loss eventually depletes iron reserves and causes a microcytic, hypochromic anemia. The most common chronic blood loss in dogs and cats occurs with blood-sucking intestinal (hookworms) and external (fleas, ticks) parasites. Young puppies and kittens are especially vulnerable because of the low-iron content of milk.

Iron concentrations are high in most meat ingredients, especially organ meats such as liver, spleen and lungs. Other ingredients rich in iron include dicalcium phosphate and fiber sources such as beet pulp, soymill run and peanut hulls. In fact, poultry studies have shown that the iron contained in dicalcium phosphate alone can meet a chick's requirement for iron.[44]

Typical iron sources include ferrous sulfate, ferric chloride, ferrous fumarate, ferrous carbonate and iron oxide. The iron in iron oxide, however, is not biologically available. Iron oxide is often added to pet foods to impart a "meaty red" color. A relatively high level of iron oxide is added (up to 0.04%) when iron oxide is used as a pigment in pet foods. Analytically, a pet food containing iron oxide will appear to be high in iron, but may not be high in available iron. Thus, the contribution of iron from iron oxide should be considered when evaluating the iron adequacy of foods containing iron oxide (e.g., 0.04% iron oxide in a moist food contributes 933 mg iron/kg of food on a DMB).

Zinc

Zinc is a constituent or activator of more than 200 enzymes, so it is involved in a number of diverse physiologic functions. Some of zinc's primary functions include: 1) nucleic acid metabolism, 2) protein synthesis, 3) carbohydrate metabolism, 4) immunocompetence, 5) skin and wound healing, 6) cell replication and differentiation, 7) growth and 8) reproduction. Zinc also interacts with hormone production, most notably testosterone, adrenal corticosteroids and insulin. Zinc homeostasis is controlled through absorption and excretion.

The mechanism and control of zinc absorption are still not fully understood. Zinc absorption occurs primarily in the duodenum, jejunum and ileum. Only small amounts are absorbed from the stomach. Zinc absorption is markedly affected by other dietary components. Phytate, for example, decreases zinc absorption, whereas low molecular weight binding ligands such as citrate, picolinate, ethylenediaminetetraacetic acid (EDTA) and amino acids such as histidine and glutamate enhance zinc absorption.[45] The liver is the primary organ involved in zinc metabolism. When hepatic zinc content is increased above normal levels, additional zinc is associated with metallothionein, a metal-binding protein thought to have a role in storage and detoxification of zinc, copper, cadmium and other metals.

Zinc in plasma is bound to protein in two forms: 1) firmly bound zinc that appears to bind to globulin (approximately 33% of total plasma zinc) and 2) loosely bound zinc complexed with albumin (66% of total plasma zinc).[1] Storage of zinc is limited except in bone; stores increase only slightly as dietary zinc increases. Zinc concentration in bone has been used as a measure of zinc absorption and/or zinc status in young growing animals, whereas plasma zinc is only a reliable index under controlled experimental conditions.

Zinc is excreted primarily in the feces as unabsorbed and endogenous zinc (pancreatic juice, bile, other digestive secretions). Excretion of endogenous zinc in feces varies according to the balance between true absorption and metabolic needs. Variable excretion is one of the primary mechanisms used to maintain zinc homeostasis. Thus, both absorption and excretion are important in regulating zinc balance.

Zinc deficiency is probably more of a practical concern with pet foods than is toxicity, because: 1) zinc is relatively nontoxic and 2) its availability is decreased by a number of factors (phytate, high dietary levels of calcium, phosphate, copper, iron, cadmium and chromium). The antagonistic effects of calcium are greatest when phytate is also present, resulting in the formation of a highly insoluble complex of calcium, phytate and zinc. Signs of zinc deficiency have been reported to occur in dogs fed cereal-based dry foods (e.g., grains may contain significant concentrations of phytate), even when the zinc content of the food exceeded NRC minimum requirements.[3,13]

AAFCO recommends 120 ppm zinc (DMB) for dogs and 75 ppm zinc for cats (DMB).[2] For trace minerals, AAFCO makes the same recommendations for adult maintenance and growth/reproduction foods. In livestock, however, the requirement for zinc is greatly increased during growth and reproduction. Signs of zinc deficiency include anorexia, decreased growth rate, alopecia, parakeratosis, impaired reproduction, depressed immune function and growth disorders of the skeleton. (See Chapter 17.) Naturally occurring zinc-responsive dermatoses have been described. (See Chapter 15.)

Although relatively nontoxic, excess dietary zinc can interfere with other minerals (iron and copper), thus excesses should be avoided. The only reported cases of zinc toxicosis in dogs or cats have been due to dietary indiscretion (e.g., consumption of die-case nuts from animal carriers or pennies). (See Case 2-4 "Vomiting and Diarrhea in a Yorkshire Terrier.") Table 2-17 describes effects of zinc deficiency and excess. Ingredients naturally high in zinc include most meats, fiber sources and dicalcium phosphate. Zinc supplements most commonly used in pet foods are zinc oxide, zinc sulfate, zinc chloride and zinc carbonate.

Copper

Of the many copper-containing proteins, four enzyme systems may play key roles in the clinical signs associated with copper deficiency: 1) the ferroxidase activity of ceruloplasmin explains in part the disturbances of hematopoiesis in copper deficiency, 2) the monoamine oxidase enzymes may account for the role of copper in pigmentation and control of neurotransmitters and neuropeptides, 3) lysyl oxidase is essential for maintaining the integrity of connective tissue, a function that explains disturbances in lungs, bones and the cardiovascular system and 4) the copper enzymes cytochrome C oxidase and superoxide dismutase (SOD) play a central role in the terminal steps of oxidative metabolism and the defense against the superoxide radicals, respectively. These functions have been postulated to account for the disturbances of the nervous system as seen in neonatal ataxia in several animal species with copper deficiency.[46]

In most species, copper can be absorbed in all segments of the GI tract; however, the small intestine is the major site of absorption.[46] Although the biochemical mechanisms are not fully understood, there is good evidence that intestinal absorption of copper is regulated by the need of the animal and that metallothionein (a metal-binding protein) plays a key role in regulation. Copper appears to be absorbed by two mechanisms, one saturable, suggesting active transport at low dietary copper concentrations and the other unsaturable, suggesting simple diffusion at high dietary copper levels.

Most copper in plasma is bound to ceruloplasmin, a copper-binding protein. Newly absorbed copper, however, may be transported from the intestine loosely bound to albumin or certain amino acids. In this form, the element is readily available to the liver and other tissues, in contrast to the much more tightly regulated distribution of ceruloplasmin-bound copper. This difference in availability may explain the tissue damage caused by copper accumulation in hepatotoxicosis seen in Bedlington terriers and people with Wilson's disease, in which the ceruloplasmin transport protein is lacking.

The liver is the central organ of copper metabolism. Hepatic concentrations reflect an animal's intake and copper status. Copper is excreted primarily through the feces. Most fecal copper is unabsorbed, but active excretion also occurs via the bile. Copper homeostasis is maintained primarily through absorption.

Dietary copper deficiency has been reported in dogs and cats and thus is of practical concern.[13] (See Case 2-5 "Reproductive Problems in a Group of Cats.") Availability of copper from different foods and supplements can vary greatly, so the requirement for copper is difficult to define. The requirement can vary several-fold depending on the source of copper in the food and the level of other ingredients/nutrients/non-nutrients (e.g., interactions with phytate, calcium, zinc and iron). The AAFCO recommendation for copper in dogs is 7.3 ppm (DMB).[2]

Separate copper requirements are recommended for extruded cat foods (15 ppm) vs. moist cat foods (5 ppm) during growth/reproduction. The recommended AAFCO copper level for maintenance of adult cats is 5 ppm, regardless of the food form. The rationale for separate copper requirements for cats is based on unpublished data.[a] These investigators demonstrated increased needs for copper during reproduction in queens fed extruded foods. Separate requirements for extruded and canned foods were recommended in the absence of reproduction data for cats fed moist foods.

Researchers studied chicks to evaluate the availability of copper from feed ingredients typically used in pet foods.[14] Results showed that availability of copper was essentially zero from copper oxide and pork liver. Beef, sheep and turkey liver, however, were highly available sources of copper. AAFCO[2] has recommended that pet food companies discontinue the use of copper oxide as a copper source based on studies of swine, poultry and dogs and unpublished data for cats in which researchers have demonstrated the poor availability of copper from copper oxide.[9,47,48]

Signs of copper deficiency in cats include poor reproductive performance, early fetal loss, fetal deformities, cannibalism, coat hypopigmentation, kinked tails and inverted carpi.[b] Clinical signs in dogs include hair depigmentation and hyperextension of the distal fore-limbs.[49] Table 2-17 lists signs of deficiency and excess.

Copper excess in dogs and cats with normal metabolism is of much less practical concern than copper deficiency, but can interfere with iron and zinc use. Bedlington terriers, however, are predisposed to hereditary autosomal recessive disease resulting in copper hepatoxicosis. (See Chapter 23.)

Most meat ingredients, especially organ meats, are rich in copper. Ruminant livers are extremely high in copper;

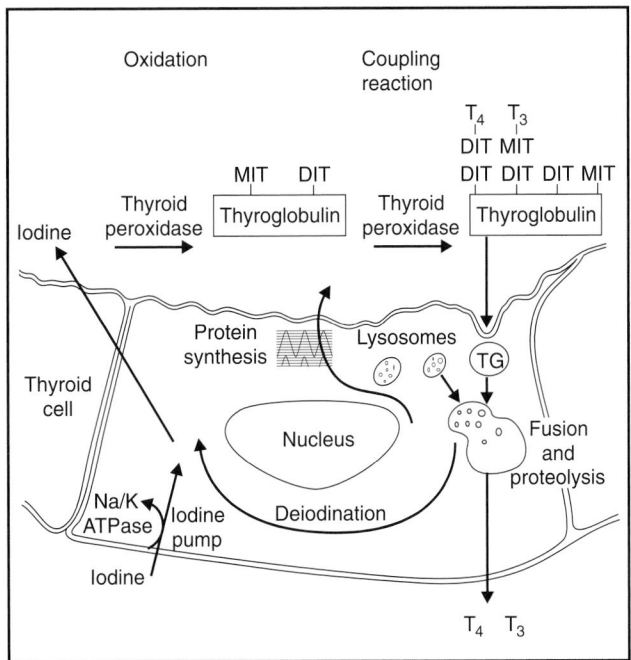

Figure 2-23. Diagram showing pathways of thyroid-hormone synthesis from iodine within the thyroid gland. (Adapted with permission from Hetzel BS, Maberly GF. Iodine. In: Mertz W, ed. Trace Elements in Human and Animal Nutrition, 5th ed. San Diego, CA: Academic Press Inc, 1986; 147.) See text for details.

concentrations are five to 10 times higher than in monogastric livers.[c] Typical copper supplements include cupric sulfate, cupric carbonate and cupric chloride.

Manganese

Manganese deficiency is of little practical relevance to dogs and cats, but is of practical relevance to birds. AAFCO recommends 5 ppm manganese for dogs and 7.5 ppm for cats.[2] The manganese requirement for birds is 10 to 12 times higher than that for people, pigs, dogs and cats.[1] Manganese functions as an enzyme activator or as a constituent of metalloenzymes. Although there are only a few manganese-containing metalloenzymes (e.g., arginase, pyruvate carboxylase and manganese-superoxide dismutase), many enzymes are activated by manganese, including hydrolases, kinases, decarboxylases and transferases. Other cations (especially magnesium), however, can partially substitute for manganese with little or no loss in enzymatic activity, thus manganese deficiency may not adversely affect physiologic or metabolic function.[1]

Manganese is also essential in bone and cartilage development because it activates glycosyltransferases (i.e., enzymes important for polysaccharide and glycoprotein synthesis). In addition, manganese is involved in reproduction and lipid metabolism (e.g., manganese is involved in the biosynthesis of choline and cholesterol).

Manganese homeostasis is maintained through regulation of absorption and excretion. Manganese is absorbed throughout the small intestine in a rapidly saturable process. Low molecular weight ligands, such as L-histidine and citrate, enhance absorption, whereas excessive concentrations of phosphorus, iron and cobalt can reduce absorption. Manganese is excreted via several routes that combine to provide an efficient homeostatic mechanism to regulate manganese levels in tissues. Bile flow is the primary route of excretion, but manganese is also excreted in pancreatic juice and in the small intestine.

Table 2-17 lists signs of deficiency and excess. Ingredients rich in manganese include fiber sources, menhaden fish meal and dicalcium phosphate. Manganese supplements include manganese oxide, manganese sulfate, manganous chloride and manganese carbonate.

Iodine

Iodine is a constituent of the thyroid hormones 3,5,3',5'-tetraiodothyronine (thyroxine, T_4) and 3,5,3'-triiodothyronine (T_3). Thyroid hormones have an active role in thermoregulation, intermediary metabolism, reproduction, growth and development, circulation and muscle function. Thyroid hormones also: 1) influence physical and mental growth and differentiation and maturation of tissues, 2) affect other endocrine glands, especially the hypophysis and the gonads, 3) influence neuromuscular functioning and 4) have an effect on the integument, hair and fur.[1]

The thyroid glands actively trap iodine daily to ensure an adequate supply of thyroid hormone. This trapping mechanism regulates a more or less constant iodine supply to the thyroid glands over a wide range of plasma iodide levels. Figure 2-23 outlines the steps of thyroid-hormone biosynthesis.[50] Iodine-trapping is an active transport mechanism linked to Na^+/K^+-ATPase activity. This mechanism is also regulated by thyroid-stimulating hormone, which is released from the pituitary gland to regulate thyroid activity. Iodide, released from thyroid cells into the colloid space, is oxidized by a thyroid-peroxidase enzyme. Iodine then combines with tyrosine residues associated with thyroglobulin protein to form monoiodotyrosine (MIT) and diiodotyrosine (DIT). The oxidation process proceeds further under the influence of the thyroid-peroxidase enzyme to couple MIT and DIT to form various iodothyronines (e.g., T_3 and T_4). Finally, iodinated thyroglobulin and thyroid hormones are reabsorbed into the thyroid cells and exposed to proteolytic enzymes. Much of the protein and iodinated tyrosines are lysed and returned as substrates to repeat the process. At the same time, some thyroid hormones are released into the circulation. Regulating the action of thyroid hormones is a complex process involving interaction among neurotransmitters, hormones and enzymes in the central nervous system, the pituitary gland, the thyroid glands, the circulation and peripheral tissues.

Belshaw et al estimated the iodine requirement for adult dogs to be 0.59 ppm.[51] AAFCO recommends an iodine level of 1.5 ppm (DMB) for dogs.[2] This margin of safety is necessary in practical foods to overcome effects of goitrogens and negative mineral antagonisms. The iodine requirement for cats has been extrapolated from other species. AAFCO recommends 0.35 ppm iodine for cats.[2] Recent work has demonstrated that the iodine requirement for adult cats may be higher than the minimum iodine requirement currently recommended by NRC or AAFCO.[52] These investigators evaluated serum iodine kinetics and thyroidal uptake. Their findings suggest that levels less than 2.4 ppm iodine may be deficient. However, no clinical or histologic signs of iodine deficiency were observed in any of the cats, regardless of the iodine levels fed.

The iodine requirement is influenced by physiologic state and diet. Lactating animals require more dietary iodine because about 10% of the iodine intake is normally excreted in milk.[1] Likewise, the presence of goitrogenic substances and nutrient excesses such as calcium and potassium increase the need for iodine. Potential sources of goitrogens in pet foods include peas, peanuts, soybeans and flaxseed. Fish, eggs, iodized salt and poultry by-product meal are rich sources of iodine. Iodine supplements typically used in pet foods include calcium iodate, potassium iodide and cuprous iodide.

Since the late 1970s, feline hyperthyroidism has become a more frequently diagnosed condition. However, much remains to be learned about this endocrinopathy (e.g., prevalence and cause). (See Chapter 24.) Hypothyroidism is a much more prevalent thyroid disorder in dogs. Both iodide excess and deficiency may result in subclinical or overt hypothyroidism. Table 2-17 lists signs of deficiency and excess.

Selenium

Selenium is an essential constituent of glutathione peroxidase, which helps protect cellular and subcellular membranes from oxidative damage. Glutathione peroxidase and vitamin E work synergistically to reduce the destructive effects of peroxidative reactions on living cells. Selenium spares vitamin E in at least three ways: 1) preserves the integrity of the pancreas, which allows normal fat digestion, and thus normal vitamin E absorption, 2) reduces the amount of vitamin E required to maintain integrity of lipid membranes via glutathione peroxidase and 3) aids retention of vitamin E in the blood plasma in some unknown way.

Vitamin E reduces the selenium requirement in at least two ways: 1) maintains body selenium in an active form, or prevents losses from the body and 2) prevents destruction of lipids within membranes, thereby inhibiting production of hydroperoxides and reducing the amount of the selenium-dependent enzyme needed to destroy peroxides formed in cells.[53] Selenium also has a vital role in maintaining normal thyroid hormone and iodine metabolism, particularly through the control of deiodinase enzymes that regulate conversion of T_4 to T_3.[54]

The duodenum is the main site of selenium absorption. There is no homeostatic control of selenium absorption regardless of the dietary selenium concentration. Likewise, selenium status also appears to have little effect on selenium uptake. Excretion of selenium, however, is homeostatically regulated. Urinary excretion of selenium is closely related to dietary intake in rats and people.[55] A dietary threshold is reached at low-selenium intakes, wherein excretion is shut down, thus conserving selenium. Urinary selenium increases proportionally at higher selenium intakes. Fecal excretion, on the other hand, remains constant over a wide range of selenium intakes.

Although selenium deficiency has been observed experimentally in dogs,[56] the incidence of selenium deficiency has not been reported for dogs and cats. Likewise, selenium toxicity has not been noted in dogs and cats, despite high concentrations (greater than 4 mg selenium/kg food) in seafood and fish-containing cat foods. AAFCO selenium recommendations are 0.11 mg/kg of food (DMB) for dogs and 0.1 mg/kg of food for cats (DMB).[2] Recent research in puppies has determined that the level of selenium needed to maximize sera glutathione peroxidase and selenium concentrations is 0.21 ppm, which is two times current AAFCO recommendations.[d]

Selenium availability is highly influenced by the chemical form of selenium (supplied as a supplement or from foodstuffs). Further, the requirement for selenium can be partially replaced by vitamin E. Selenium in animal feeds is highly variable primarily due to the variable selenium status of soils. Studies with pigs demonstrated that inorganic selenium (sodium selenite) and organic selenium (selenium yeast) were equally effective in supporting glutathione peroxidase activity, but that selenium stores in tissues (liver and muscle) were greater when organic selenium was fed.[57] Selenium content in milk is also higher when selenium is supplied in the organic form. Selenium concentrations in some commercial pet foods may not be adequate due to low availability of selenium in pet food ingredients. Recent studies conducted with chicks assessed the availability of selenium in pet food ingredients and some pet foods.[58,59] Relative to sodium selenite, the availability of selenium from feed ingredients and pet foods was low, averaging only 30% for ingredients of animal origin and 50% for ingredients of plant origin. These results suggest that selenium supplementation of certain foods is warranted.

Fish products are very rich in selenium (1 to 6 mg selenium/kg), but selenium availability in these ingredients is low.[58-60] Selenium levels exceeding 2 mg selenium/kg of food (DMB) are considered toxic for most livestock, but have not been reported to be toxic for cats. (See Case 2-6 "Sudden Death in a Chihuahua.") Table 2-17 lists signs of deficiency and excess. Cats may be able to tolerate higher selenium levels because the high-protein foods typically fed to cats are protective against high-selenium levels,[61] or because the availability of selenium in pet foods is generally low.[58,59] Fish, eggs and liver are ingredients rich in selenium. Typical selenium supplements include sodium selenite and sodium selenate.

Ultra-Trace Minerals

The minimum dietary requirements for ultra-trace elements in dogs and cats have not been determined. Based on research in other species, it is probable that supplemental micronutrients, such as chromium and boron, may be beneficial under certain physiologic and dietary circumstances.

Chromium

In 1957, Schwarz and Mertz identified a compound they called glucose tolerance factor (GTF) that restored impaired glucose tolerance in rats. Chromium was identified as the active component.[62] Chromium is ubiquitous in water, soil and living matter; however, tissue levels in animals are very low because of limited uptake by plants and absorption by animals. Further, many forms of chromium are poorly available. Therefore, supplementation with an available form may be warranted. Chromium in an organically bound form (e.g., GTF) is absorbed better, has a different tissue distribution and is more available to the fetus than inorganic chromium.[63]

Several studies in people and other animals have demonstrated beneficial effects of chromium supplementation (in chromium deficiency or diabetics) including: 1) improved glucose tolerance, 2) reversed hyperglycemia and glycosuria, 3) decreased circulating insulin concentrations, 4) decreased plasma lipid concentrations, 5) decreased body fat, 6) increased protein accretion, 7) improved immune response and 8) reduced cortisol production in response to heat and transport stress.[64-66] Not all studies have shown improvements in these variables. This lack of consistent response may be accounted for by an adequate chromium nutriture for some individuals or some factor other than chromium deficiency that may have compromised the variable (impaired glucose tolerance, etc.). Few tests are available to specifically diagnose chromium status. The glucose tolerance test has been most commonly used to evaluate chromium deficiency. Table 2-17 lists signs of deficiency and excess.

Boron

Boron indirectly influences PTH activity, thus it influences calcium, phosphorus, magnesium and cholecalciferol (vitamin D_3) metabolism. Hunt et al demonstrated that boron acts by at least three different mechanisms:[67] 1) it compensates for perturbations in energy substrate use induced by vitamin D deficiency, 2) it enhances macromineral content in normal bone and 3) it enhances some indices of growth and cartilage maturation, independent of vitamin D. Boron has a role in the control of urolithiasis. It decreases oxalate production in women fed magnesium-deficient diets.[68] Boron also decreases calcium loss and bone demineralization in postmenopausal women.[69] Table 2-17 lists signs of deficiency and excess.

■ VITAMINS

Definition

The term "vitamine" was coined by Casmir Funk in 1912 when he described a class of nitrogen-containing compounds that were "vital-amines" (i.e., being vital to life). This term was later changed to vitamin when it was found that not all of these compounds contained nitrogen. The discovery, isolation and synthesis of vitamins has occurred in the last 100 years, although the effects of vitamin deficiency, specifically scurvy, have been recorded since about 1150 B.C.[1]

A vitamin can be defined by its physical and physiologic characteristics. In order for a substance to be classified as a vitamin it must have five basic characteristics: 1) it must be an organic compound different from fat, protein and carbohydrate, 2) it must be a component of the diet, 3) it must be essential in minute amounts for normal physiologic function, 4) its absence must cause a deficiency syndrome and 5) it must not be synthesized in quantities sufficient to support normal physiologic function.

These definitions are important to note because not all vitamins are essential for every species. For example, vitamin C is essential for primates, guinea pigs and some species of fish, but not for most other animal species. Lack of the enzyme L-gulonolactone oxidase prevents those species from synthesizing vitamin C from glucose, thereby, making ascorbic acid a required vitamin. Under certain conditions of disease or increased metabolism, however, vitamin C may be "conditionally essential" in those species that have de novo synthesis.

Two other terms warrant definition: vitamers and provitamins. A vitamer is chemically the same compound as a vitamin, but may exert varying physiologic effects because it is an isomer. Vitamin E is a good example of vitamers, because of its many forms. α-tocopherol is the most biologically active form, whereas γ-tocopherol has little biologic function, but acts as an in vitro antioxidant. A provitamin is a compound that requires an activation step before it becomes biologically active. β-carotene, for example, is cleaved by enzymatic processes to release two molecules of retinol (vitamin A).

Function

The two main categories of vitamins are distinguished by their miscibility in either lipids (fat soluble) or water (water soluble). There are four fat-soluble vitamins (A, D, E and K) and 10 generally recognized water-soluble vitamins (thiamin [B_1], riboflavin [B_2], niacin, pyridoxine [B_6], pantothenic acid, folic acid, cobalamin [B_{12}], choline, biotin and vitamin C). AAFCO only recognizes three fat-soluble and eight water-soluble vitamins for dogs (vitamin K, biotin and vitamin C are not recognized), and four fat-soluble and nine water-soluble vitamins for cats (vitamin C is not included).[2] There are also a number of compounds that are classified as "vitamin-like compounds" or "quasi-vitamins," which will also be discussed later in this section.

Vitamins have incredibly diverse physiologic functions. Vitamins act as potentiators or cofactors in enzymatic reactions (Figure 2-24). They also play a significant role in DNA synthesis, energy release from nutrient substrates, bone development, calcium homeostasis, normal eye function, cell membrane integrity, blood clotting, free radical scavenging, amino acid and protein metabolism and nerve impulse transduction (Table 2-19).

Because of the differences between fat and water solubility and in chemical structure, vitamins are absorbed in the body through a variety of means. Fat-soluble vitamins require bile salts and fat to form micelles for absorption. They are then passively absorbed, usually in the duodenum and ileum, and transported in conjunction with chylomicrons to the liver via the lymph system. In contrast, most of the water-soluble vitamins are absorbed via active transport. Some vitamins (e.g., cobalamin) require a carrier protein called "intrinsic factor" whereas others need a sodium-dependent, carrier-mediated absorption pump.

Deficiency/Adequacy/Toxicity

Similar to other essential trace or micronutrients, differences in ingestion levels of vitamins create deficiency, adequacy or toxicity. The biologic dose-response curve (Figure 2-2) is appropriate for vitamins. (See sidebar "Adequate vs. Optimal Nutrient Intake.") A deficiency is a lack of the vitamin in quantities required for normal physiologic function. In general, fat-soluble vitamins are stored in the lipid depots of all tissues, making them more resistant to deficiency, but also more likely to cause toxicity. Conversely, water-soluble vitamins are depleted at a faster rate because

Table 2-19. Summary of names, functions and clinical syndromes associated with deficiency and toxicity of vitamins.

Vitamin	Function	Deficiency	Toxicity
Vitamin A	Component of visual proteins, (rhodopsin, iodopsin), differentiation of epithelial cells, spermatogenesis, immune function, bone resorption	Anorexia, retarded growth, poor coat, weakness, xerophthalmia, nyctalopia, increased CSF pressure, aspermatogenesis, fetal resorption	Cervical spondylosis (cats), tooth loss (cats), retarded growth, anorexia, erythema, long-bone fractures
Vitamin D	Calcium and phosphorus homeostasis, bone mineralization, bone resorption, insulin synthesis, immune function	Rickets, enlarged costochondral junctions, osteomalacia, osteoporosis	Hypercalcemia, calcinosis, anorexia, lameness
Vitamin E	Biologic antioxidant, membrane integrity through free radical scavenging	Sterility (males), steatitis, dermatosis, immunodeficiency, anorexia, myopathy	Minimally toxic, fat-soluble vitamin antagonism, increased clotting time (reversed with vitamin K)
Vitamin K	Carboxylation of clotting proteins II (prothrombin), VII, IX, X and other proteins, cofactor of the bone protein osteocalcin	Prolonged clotting time, hypoprothrombinemia, hemorrhage	Minimally toxic, anemia (dogs)
Thiamin (B$_1$)	Component of thiamin pyrophosphate (TPP), cofactor in decarboxylase enzyme reactions in the TCA cycle, nervous system	Anorexia, weight loss, ataxia, polyneuritis, ventriflexion (cats), paresis (dogs), cardiac hypertrophy (dogs), bradycardia	Decreased blood pressure, bradycardia, respiratory arrhythmia
Riboflavin (B$_2$)	Component of flavin adenine dinucleotide (FAD) and flavin mononucleotide (FMN) coenzymes, electron transport in oxidase and dehydrogenase enzymes	Retarded growth, ataxia, collapse syndrome (dogs), dermatitis, purulent ocular discharge, vomition, conjunctivitis, coma, corneal vascularization, bradycardia, fatty liver (cats)	Minimally toxic
Niacin (B$_3$)	Component of nicotinamide-adenine dinucleotide (NAD) and adenine dinucleotide phosphate (NADP) coenzymes, hydrogen donor/acceptor in energy-releasing dehydrogenase reactions	Anorexia, diarrhea, retarded growth, ulceration of soft palate and buccal mucosa, necrosis of the tongue (dogs), reddened ulcerated tongue (cats), cheilosis, uncontrolled drooling	Low toxicity, bloody feces, convulsions
Pyridoxine (B$_6$)	Coenzyme in amino acid reactions (transaminases and decarboxylases), neurotransmitter synthesis, niacin synthesis from tryptophan, heme synthesis, taurine synthesis, carnitine synthesis	Anorexia, retarded growth, weight loss, microcytic hypochromic anemia, convulsions, renal tubular atrophy, calcium oxalate crystalluria	Low toxicity, anorexia, ataxia (dogs)
Pantothenic acid	Precursor to coenzyme A (CoA), protein, fat and carbohydrate metabolism in the TCA cycle, cholesterol synthesis, triacylglyceride synthesis	Emaciation, fatty liver, depressed growth, decreased serum cholesterol and total lipids, tachycardia, coma, lowered antibody response	No toxicity established in dogs and cats
Folic acid	Methionine synthesis from homocysteine (vitamin B$_{12}$ dependent), purine synthesis, DNA synthesis	Anorexia, weight loss, glossitis, leukopenia, hypochromic anemia, increased clotting time, elevated plasma iron, megaloblastic anemia (cats), sulfa drugs interfere with gut synthesis, cancer drugs (methotrexate) are antagonistic	Nontoxic
Biotin	Component of four carboxylase enzymes: pyruvate carboxylase, acetyl-CoA carboxylase, propionyl-CoA carboxylase and 3-methylcrotonyl CoA carboxylase	Hyperkeratosis, alopecia (cats), dry secretions around eyes, nose and mouth (cats), hypersalivation, anorexia, bloody diarrhea	No toxicity established in dogs and cats
Cobalamin (B$_{12}$)	Coenzyme functions in propionate metabolism, aids tetrahydrofolate-containing enzymes in methionine synthesis, leucine synthesis/degradation	Cessation of growth (cats), methylmalonic aciduria, anemia	Altered reflexes (reduction in vascular conditioned reflexes and an exaggeration of unconditioned reflexes)
Vitamin C	Cofactor in hydroxylase enzyme reactions, synthesis of collagen proteins, synthesis of carnitine, enhances iron absorption, free radical scavenging, antioxidant/pro-oxidant functionality	Liver synthesis precludes dietary requirement, no signs of deficiency have been described in normal cats and dogs	No toxicity established in dogs and cats
Choline	Component of phosphatidylcholine found in membranes, neurotransmitter acetylcholine, methyl group donor	Fatty liver (puppies), increased blood prothrombin times, thymic atrophy, decreased growth rate, anorexia, perilobular infiltration of the liver (cats)	None described for cats and dogs
Carnitine*	Transport long-chain fatty acids into the mitochondria for use in β-oxidation	Hyperlipidemia, cardiomyopathy, muscle asthenia	None described for cats and dogs

*Carnitine is a vitamin-like substance.

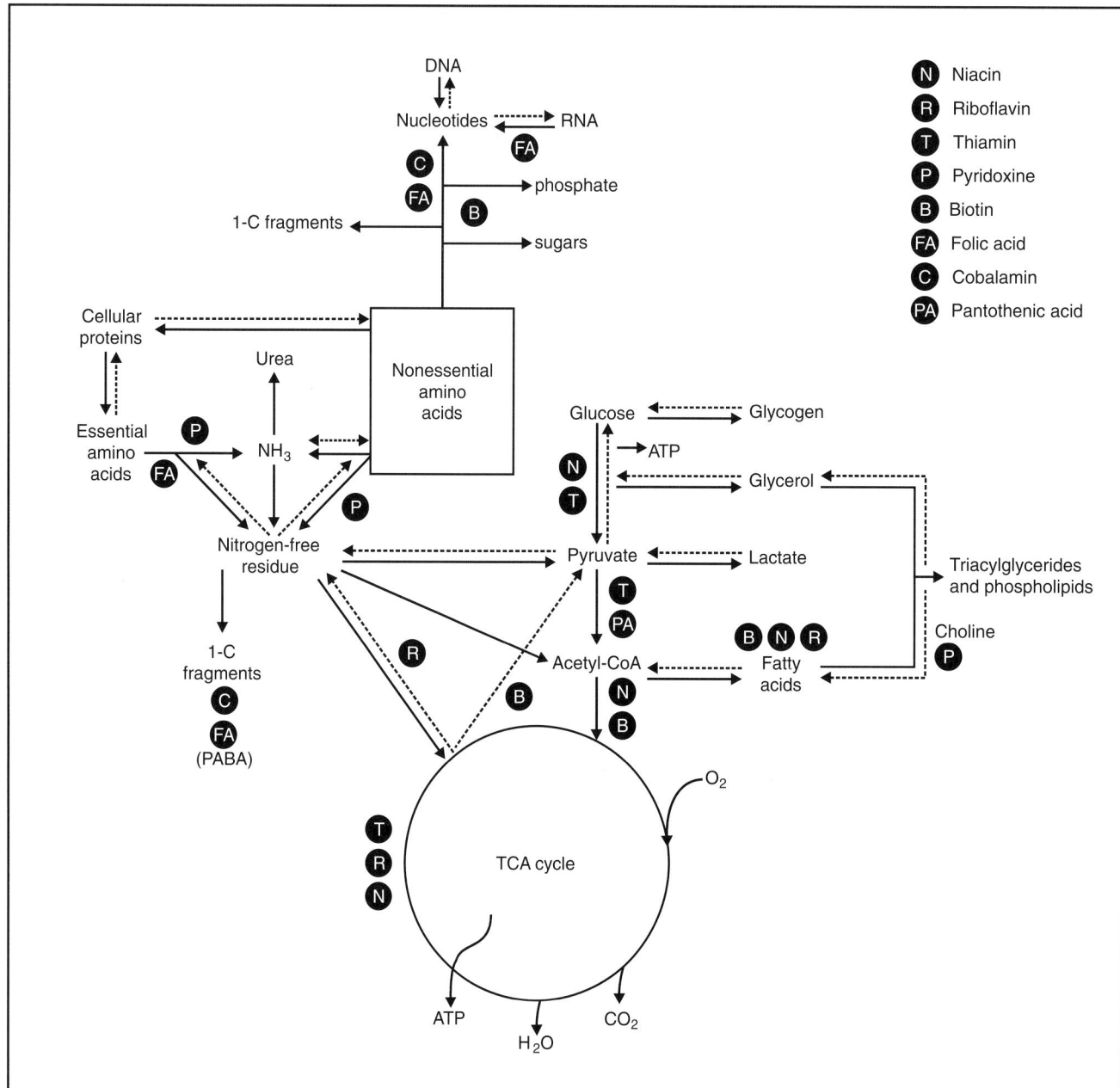

Figure 2-24. The role of B vitamins in intermediary metabolism.

of limited storage; therefore, they are less likely to cause toxicity and more likely to be acutely deficient.

Within the range of adequate intake, requirements are met for each lifestage and tissue stores are maximized. Consuming more vitamins than is required to maximize stores can, in many cases, lead to clinical signs of toxicity if the ingestion period is prolonged and the body cannot excrete excesses. It is, therefore, prudent to provide vitamins in the appropriate balance for each lifestage to meet requirements and build tissue stores, but not to over-supplement in the pharmacotoxicologic range.

Factors Affecting Requirements

Different lifestages of animals affect vitamin requirements. Growing and reproducing animals accrete tissues and therefore require higher levels of vitamins, minerals,

protein and energy for optimal performance. Over-supplementation, however, is still contraindicated because these animals are also more susceptible to toxicity. As animals age, metabolic and physiologic changes may increase the requirement for vitamins.

Various disease conditions also affect vitamin status. Prolonged anorexia deprives animals of vitamins and other nutrients and depletes vitamin stores. Polyuric diseases such as diabetes mellitus and chronic renal failure may increase the excretion of water-soluble vitamins. Renal failure can also lead to a secondary vitamin D deficiency by reducing the final hydroxylation step converting 25-hydroxyvitamin D_3 to 1,25-dihydroxyvitamin D_3, which occurs in the proximal tubules of the kidneys.

In addition, certain drugs (e.g., antibiotics) may decrease the intestinal microflora responsible for vitamin

K synthesis. Also, diuretic therapy may increase excretion of water-soluble vitamins.

Some vitamin requirements depend on levels of other nutrients. The amount of cobalamin required is related to the amount of folic acid, choline and methionine present because these nutrients interact metabolically and are dependent on each other. In addition, the amount of tryptophan influences niacin requirements because tryptophan is the precursor for that vitamin.

Feeding scientifically based formulas that specifically target the lifestage, nutrient interaction and disease condition will address changing vitamin requirements.

Vitamin Interactions

Much of the experimental work with vitamin deficiency disease has focused on the deficiency of a single vitamin. However, multiple deficiencies occur more frequently than a single-vitamin deficiency in patients. Pellagra is the classic example, in which deficiencies of niacin and tryptophan are usually accompanied by deficiencies of vitamin B_6 and riboflavin.

Many critical pathways require the concerted action of several B-complex vitamins (Figure 2-24). For example, one of the key reactions of metabolism is the conversion of pyruvate to acetyl-CoA. It is a key reaction because it occurs at the intersection of glycolysis and the TCA cycle. This pathway point is critical in the production of energy and the synthesis of fat and protein. Four different vitamins (niacin, thiamin, pantothenic acid and biotin) act as coenzymes in this one enzymatic conversion. Thus, a deficiency of any one of these four vitamins compromises the efficiency of the other three.

The interactions between vitamins may involve the processes of absorption, metabolism, catabolism and excretion. Some vitamins may spare the requirements of others, whereas others may have potentially adverse effects. Even the marginal deficiency of one vitamin can exacerbate a deficiency or increase the requirement of another vitamin. Some examples of vitamin-vitamin interactions appear in Table 2-20.

Availability

Estimating the vitamin content of foods and foodstuffs and ultimately the adequacy of a given food is difficult at best because of cumulative errors made in estimating vitamin content and availability. These errors include: 1) analytical errors in sampling and determination of the vitamin, 2) variation in the actual amount of the vitamin (e.g., lot-to-lot variation, seasonal effects, demographics, different cultivars), 3) the presence of vitamins in bound forms in many foodstuffs and foods, 4) storage losses and 5) processing losses. All of these factors make it difficult to define what vitamin level is optimal for a given lifestage and food. To account for potential errors, references recommend that analytical values in databases be discounted by 10 to 25%.[1]

Supplementation

All commercial pet foods contain added vitamins. Formulating a ration to meet vitamin requirements entirely from ingredient sources is extremely difficult and poses risks for the animal. Synthetic and naturally formed vitamins are used by the body in the same way, although they

Table 2-20. Examples of vitamin-vitamin interactions.*

One vitamin needed for optimal absorption of another
  Vitamin B_6 for vitamin B_{12}
  Folate for thiamin

A high level of one vitamin may interfere with absorption or metabolism of another
  Vitamin E interferes with vitamin K
  Vitamin B_6 interferes with niacin
  Thiamin interferes with riboflavin

One vitamin needed for metabolism of another
  Riboflavin needed for vitamin B_6 and niacin
  Vitamin B_6 needed for niacin

One vitamin protects against excess catabolism or urinary losses of another
  Vitamin C spares vitamin B_6

One vitamin protects against oxidative destruction of another
  Vitamin E spares vitamin A
  Vitamin C spares vitamin E

A high level of one vitamin can obscure the diagnosis of deficiency of another
  Folate deficiency obscures vitamin B_{12} deficiency

*Adapted from Machlin LJ, Langseth L. Vitamin-vitamin interactions. In: Bodwell LE, Erdman JW Jr, eds. Nutrient Interactions. New York, NY: Marcel Dekker Inc, 1988; 287-306.

may have different availabilities. The effects of processing on vitamin stability, availability in conjunction with disputed requirement levels in complex foods make fortification necessary. (See Chapter 4.)

Commercial pet foods, therefore, are fortified to meet an animal's vitamin requirement for a given lifestage, overcome processing and storage losses and avoid toxicity. Because pet foods are fortified with vitamins, it is usually unnecessary, and perhaps contraindicated, to concurrently give multi-purpose vitamin supplements. Supplementation may be warranted in the management of diseases that affect vitamin metabolism, but should be monitored if long-term treatment is planned.

Fat-Soluble Vitamins

Vitamin A

From a practical standpoint, vitamin A is perhaps the most important vitamin nutritionally. Vitamin A is added almost universally to animal foods. Plants do not contain vitamin A per se, but instead contain a provitamin in the form of carotenes (α, β, γ carotenes and cryptoxanthin are considered to be the most potent of the carotenoids). The vitamin A activity of β-carotene is markedly greater than that of other carotenoids, but it has only half the potency of pure vitamin A. Concentrations of carotenoids in plants vary widely according to geographic location, maturity, method of harvest, amount and type of processing, length and conditions of storage and exposure to high temperature, sunlight and air. As a result, vitamin A is among the most variable nutrients in the diet.

The vitamin A content in animal tissues can also be variable; concentrations can be very high in certain tissues such as liver. Levels of vitamin A in animal tissue vary depending on either the level of vitamin A or carotenoid present in the diet.

Nutritionally, vitamin A is also important because it is essential for a number of distinct biologic functions. It is necessary for normal vision, bone and muscle growth, reproduction and maintenance of healthy epithelial tissue.

STRUCTURE

Most of the preformed vitamin A in food is in the form of retinyl esters, whereas the source of vitamin A from plants is in the form of provitamin A carotenoids. Retinyl esters are hydrolyzed by hydrolases from the pancreas and the mucosal brush border to yield retinol. Retinyl esters and carotenoids are hydrophobic, thus their dispersion into the aqueous environment of the small intestinal lumen requires bile salts for micellar solubilization. This process allows access of hydrolytic enzymes to retinyl esters and exposes retinol to the mucosal surface, allowing free retinol and intact β-carotene to diffuse passively into mucosal epithelial cells. Absorption of vitamin A esters appears to be high (80 to 90%), but absorption may vary depending on the level and type of dietary fat and protein, which exert surfactant effects.[1]

β-carotene 15,15'-dioxygenase cleaves the provitamins (e.g., carotenes) into retinals. This enzyme is found in intestinal mucosa, liver and the corpus luteum. Enzymatic cleavage of β-carotene yields two molecules of retinal. Dietary carotenoids are only absorbed half as well as preformed dietary vitamin A. As the amount of carotenoids in the food increases, however, the absorption efficiency decreases. The intestinal absorption of carotenoids is much more critically dependent on the presence of bile salts than is absorption of vitamin A. Retinal produced by carotene cleavage is then reduced to retinol by a second enzyme, retinaldehyde reductase.

METABOLISM

Vitamin A is absorbed almost exclusively as the free alcohol retinol. Within mucosal cells, retinol is re-esterified mostly to palmitate, is incorporated into the chylomicrons of the mucosa and diffuses into the lymph. A small amount of retinol may be oxidized first to retinal and then to retinoic acid, which may form a compound (glucuronide) that passes into the portal blood. Vitamin A is transported through the lymphatic system with LDL to the liver, where it is deposited mainly in hepatocytes and stellate and parenchymal cells.

Some vitamin A derivatives are re-excreted into the intestinal lumen via the bile. This is true for much of the retinoic acid and some retinol. The major vitamin A components of bile are vitamin A glucuronides, many of which are reabsorbed. Thus, enterohepatic circulation may provide an important means of conserving vitamin A.

When vitamin A is mobilized from the liver, stored vitamin A ester is hydrolyzed before it is released into the bloodstream. Vitamin A retinol is transported to tissues in the bloodstream by a specific transport protein called retinol-binding protein (RBP). RBP is synthesized and secreted by hepatic parenchymal cells.

In contrast with most other species, dogs and cats have a unique way of metabolizing vitamin A. Cats require preformed vitamin A because they lack the dioxygenase enzyme necessary for β-carotene cleavage. In addition, studies have shown that cats and dogs do not depend on RBP to transport vitamin A in plasma.[3-6] Cats and dogs transport vitamin A as retinyl esters (mostly retinyl stearate) bound to LDL and VLDL in amounts 10 to 50 times those of other mammals.[3] This is of interest because free circulating retinyl esters are a sign of hypervitaminosis A in almost all other animal species, including people.

Recognizing that dogs are more tolerant of vitamin A toxicosis than other animals are and prompted by recent research,[7] the Canine Nutrition Expert/Feline Nutrition Expert (CNE/FNE) Panels increased the maximum vitamin A allowance for dogs from 50,000 to 250,000 IU/kg of food. For cats, the maximum dietary allowance for vitamin A is 750,000 IU/kg of food.[2]

The vitamin A content in foodstuffs can be highly variable and is subject to processing/storage losses. Thus, it is important when supplementing to build in a safety margin to ensure against nutrient losses and variability. Vitamin A requirements increase with pregnancy and lactation. Unlike dogs, cats cannot meet any of their vitamin A requirement from carotenoids. The AAFCO recommendation for vitamin A is 5,000 IU/kg of food (DMB) for dogs (growth/reproduction and maintenance requirements are the same) and 9,000 and 5,000 IU/kg of food (DMB) for growth/ reproduction and maintenance in cats, respectively.[2] Little is known about the vitamin A requirements during gestation and lactation. However, a minimum vitamin A allowance has been established for cats at 6,000 IU/kg of food (DMB), which is approximately double the requirement for growth (3,333 IU/kg of food) (DMB).[8]

DEFICIENCY AND TOXICITY

The appreciable stores of vitamin A in the body are mobilized as needed to mitigate against the effects of low dietary intakes of the vitamin. The only unequivocal signs of vitamin A deficiency are the ocular lesions nyctalopia (night blindness) and xerophthalmia (extreme dryness of the conjunctiva). Other signs include anorexia, weight loss, ataxia, skin lesions, increased susceptibility to infection, retinal degeneration, poor coat, weakness, increased cerebrospinal fluid pressure, nephritis, skeletal defects (periosteal overgrowth and narrowing of foramina) and impaired reproduction.[9]

Vitamin A toxicities have been encountered in numerous species. The most characteristic signs of hypervitaminosis A are skeletal malformation, spontaneous fractures and internal hemorrhage. (See Case 2-7 "Cervical Rigidity in a Cat.") Other signs include anorexia, slow growth, weight loss, skin thickening, suppressed keratinization, increased blood clotting time, reduced erythrocyte count, enteritis, congenital abnormalities, conjunctivitis, fatty infiltration of the liver and reduced function of liver and kidneys.

SOURCES

Naturally rich sources of vitamin A include fish oil, liver, egg and dairy products. The most common vitamin A supplements used in pet foods include vitamin A esters (all trans retinyl palmitate, acetate or propionate or vitamin A provided as fish oils [cod liver, salmon, menhaden, herring, etc.]). Because of stability issues, vitamin A sources are often coated, beaded, prilled or spray dried with antioxidants and emulsifying agents.

Vitamin D

Vitamin D exists in two forms: cholecalciferol (vitamin D_3, which occurs in animals) and ergocalciferol (vitamin D_2, which occurs predominantly in plants). Cholecalciferol can be produced in the skin of most mammals from the provitamin 7-dehydrocholesterol via activation with ultraviolet-B light. Both D_2 and D_3 forms can also be ingested and further metabolized to 25-hydroxyvitamin D through hydroxylation first by the liver, and then again to 1,25-dihydroxyvitamin D in the kidneys. It has generally been assumed that D_2 (plant form) and D_3 (animal form) are equally potent for all but a few species.

FUNCTION

The primary function of vitamin D is to enhance intestinal absorption and mobilization, as well as retention and bone deposition of calcium and phosphorus. This function is manifested through its activity as a hormone (i.e., 1,25-dihydroxyvitamin D_3).

METABOLISM

Vitamin D is absorbed from the small intestine by nonsaturable, passive diffusion, which depends on bile salts. Vitamin D then enters the lymphatic circulation primarily (~90%) in association with chylomicrons; the remainder of vitamin D is associated with an α-globulin fraction.[1] Like other steroids, vitamin D is transported in association with proteins. In most species, the binding protein is vitamin D-binding protein (DBP) or "transcalciferin." The concentration of DBP greatly exceeds the concentration of the vitamin D metabolites in blood. This concentration difference, in conjunction with the binding affinity, results in less than 5% of the available binding sites being occupied by vitamin D compounds. The distribution between bound and free vitamin D compounds greatly favors the bound form. In this fashion, DBP facilitates peripheral distribution of vitamin D from dietary origin and mobilizes endogenously produced vitamin D from the skin.

Vitamin D is distributed relatively evenly among the various tissues where it resides in lipid depots. Vitamin D can be found in fatty tissues such as adipose, kidneys, liver, lungs, aorta and heart. The primary circulating form of vitamin D is the parent vitamin D (~50%), with the next most abundant form (i.e., 25-hydroxyvitamin D_3 [also called calcidiol]) accounting for approximately 20% of the total.[1] In mammals, the liver produces 25-hydroxyvitamin D_3 via vitamin D-25-hydroxylase. (In birds, the liver and kidneys produce 25-hydroxyvitamin D_3.) At normal plasma concentrations, only small amounts of 25-hydroxyvitamin D_3 are released from this pool to enter tissues. Thus, circulating levels of 25-hydroxyvitamin D_3 are a good indicator of vitamin D status. Further hydroxylation occurs in the kidneys to yield 1,25-dihydroxyvitamin D_3 (also called calcitriol) via 25-hydroxyvitamin D_3 1-hydroxylase, the metabolically active form of vitamin D.

Several factors tightly regulate the vitamin D endocrine system: 1,25-dihydroxyvitamin D_3, PTH, calcitonin, several other hormones and circulating levels of calcium and phosphate. The vitamin D-dependent homeostatic system responds to perturbations in calcium concentration. For example, when serum calcium falls below a given level, PTH is secreted by the parathyroid glands, which function to detect hypocalcemia. The kidney responds to PTH, resulting in phosphate diuresis and stimulation of 25-hydroxyvitamin D_3 1-hydroxylase. The latter effect increases production of 1,25-dihydroxyvitamin D_3, which acts to increase enteric absorption of calcium and phosphate. In addition, 1,25-dihydroxyvitamin D_3 acts jointly with PTH in bone to promote mobilization of calcium and

phosphate. The combined result of these responses is to increase plasma concentration of calcium and phosphate. Calcitonin is secreted by the thyroid gland ("C" cells) when circulating concentrations of calcium are increased. Calcitonin suppresses bone mobilization and may increase the renal excretion of calcium and phosphate. In that situation, 25-hydroxyvitamin D_3 1-hydroxylase may be inhibited by 1,25-dihydroxyvitamin D_3, and may actually be converted to 24,25-dihydroxyvitamin D_3.

These events tightly regulate hydroxylase activity and maintain nearly constant plasma concentrations of 1,25-dihydroxyvitamin D_3, calcium and phosphorus. Once formed, 1,25-dihydroxyvitamin D_3 binds to specific receptors on the enterocyte nucleus and initiates events that stimulate calcium and phosphorus absorption. In addition, 1,25-dihydroxyvitamin D_3, acting with PTH, mediates resorption of bone with the release of calcium and phosphorus.

Many metabolites of vitamin D circulate in plasma other than 25-hydroxyvitamin D_3 and 1,25-dihydroxyvitamin D_3. One metabolite, 24,25-dihydroxyvitamin D_3, may also be biologically active, whereas other metabolites are generally considered physiologically inactive excretory forms.[1]

Requirements for vitamin D depend on: 1) environmental conditions (e.g., exposure to ultraviolet-B light), 2) dietary concentrations (ratio and forms) of calcium and phosphorus, 3) physiologic stage of development and 4) perhaps gender and breed. The AAFCO allowance for vitamin D is 500 IU/kg of food (DMB) for dogs (growth/reproduction and maintenance allowances are the same), and 750 and 500 IU/kg of food (DMB) for cats for growth/reproduction and maintenance, respectively.[2] Research has shown, however, that the vitamin D requirement for growing kittens is markedly lower (250 IU D_3/kg of food) than current AAFCO recommendations.[10]

DEFICIENCY AND TOXICITY

Signs of vitamin D deficiency are frequently confounded by a simultaneous deficiency or imbalance of calcium and phosphorus. Clinical signs generally include rickets (young animals), enlarged costochondral junctions, osteomalacia (adult animals), osteoporosis (adult animals) and decreased serum calcium and inorganic phosphorus concentrations. Experimental vitamin D deficiency has been produced in cats, resulting in neurologic abnormalities associated with degeneration of the cervical spinal cord.[11] Other signs included hypocalcemia, elevated PTH concentrations, posterior paralysis, ataxia and eventual quadriparesis.

Excessive intake of vitamin D is associated with increases in 25-hydroxyvitamin D_3 levels; with the D_3 form being more toxic than the D_2 form (i.e., the D_3 form produces higher serum levels of the 25-hydroxyvitamin D_3 metabolite than does comparable intake of D_2). When circulating at very high concentrations, 25-hydroxyvitamin D_3 can compete effectively with 1,25-dihydroxyvitamin D_3 for receptors in the intestine and bone. Therefore, during vitamin D toxicosis, 25-hydroxyvitamin D_3 can induce actions usually attributed to 1,25-dihydroxyvitamin D_3. Thus, 25-hydroxyvitamin D_3 is believed to be the critical factor in vitamin D intoxication.[12] Excessive vitamin D concentrations may result in hypercalcemia, soft-tissue calcification and ultimately death. (See Case 2-8

"Vomiting and Anorexia in a German Shepherd Mixed-Breed Dog.")

Recent research has suggested that cats and dogs have a low activation of 7-dehydrocholesterol by ultraviolet-B light, primarily because of the very low concentrations of the provitamin in skin.[11,13] Thus, it may be necessary to supplement vitamin D_3 or D_2 in dog and cat foods.

SOURCES

Marine fish and fish oils are the richest natural sources of vitamin D in foodstuffs but they may pose a risk for toxicity. One group of investigators found that moist foods generally contained higher levels of vitamin D than extruded foods and that some moist foods exceeded the AAFCO maximal allowance of 10,000 IU/kg of food.[11] Other sources of vitamin D include fresh water fish and eggs (especially yolks). Beef, liver and dairy products contain smaller amounts of vitamin D. The most common synthetic sources of vitamin D in pet foods include deactivated animal sterol (cholecalciferol), vitamin D_3 supplement, deactivated plant sterol (ergocalciferol) and vitamin D_2 supplement.

Vitamin E

FUNCTION

Vitamin E functions as an antioxidant in vivo and in vitro. α-tocopherol is the most active biologic form. The γ isomer is the most active in vitro form and is widely used in pet food manufacturing to prevent lipid oxidation in products. (See Chapter 4.) Because synthetic antioxidants, such as ethoxyquin, diphenyl-p-phenylenediamine (DPPD), butylated hydroxytoluene (BHT) and butylated hydroxyanisole (BHA) prevent many vitamin E deficiency syndromes, early investigators hypothesized vitamin E acted as a biologic antioxidant.

It was later learned that vitamin E worked in conjunction with glutathione peroxidase to protect cells against the adverse effects of reactive oxygen and other free radicals that initiate the oxidation of polyunsaturated membrane phospholipids, a function that could not be replaced by synthetic antioxidants. Thus, the role of vitamin E as an antioxidant was expanded. It now appears that vitamin E in cellular and subcellular membranes is the first line of defense against peroxidation of vital phospholipids. However, some peroxides are formed even when adequate levels of vitamin E are present.

Selenium, as part of the enzyme glutathione peroxidase, is a second line of defense that destroys peroxides before they damage membranes. Therefore, selenium, vitamin E and sulfur-containing amino acids, through different biochemical mechanisms, are capable of preventing some of the same nutritional diseases.[14] Vitamin E prevents fatty acid hydroperoxide formation, sulfur-containing amino acids are precursors of glutathione peroxidase and selenium is a component of glutathione peroxidase.

STRUCTURE

Eight isomeric forms of vitamin E are widely distributed in nature (four tocopherols [α, β, γ, δ] and four tocotrienols [α, β, γ, δ]). The vitamin E activity of foods depends on the chemical form and storage conditions of the products. Activity is highly variable in commonly used foodstuffs. The most biopotent form of vitamin E is α-tocopherol. In general, the relative biopotencies of vitamin E isomers are as follows: α >β >δ >γ.[15] Also, tocopherols are generally more available than tocotrienols.[1] Some vitamin E forms have little biologic activity; thus, total vitamin E analysis is not a reliable means of determining vitamin E activity.

METABOLISM

Vitamin E is absorbed from the small intestine by non-saturable, passive diffusion, which depends on micellar solubilization. Whether presented as free alcohol or as esters, most vitamin E is absorbed as the alcohol. Esters are largely hydrolyzed in the gut wall before absorption, probably by a duodenal mucosal esterase. The free alcohol enters the intestinal lacteals and is transported via lymph to the general circulation.

The efficiency of vitamin E absorption is low and variable (35 to 50%); the absorption efficiency is much lower than that of vitamin A.[1] Absorption of vitamin E is enhanced by the simultaneous digestion and absorption of dietary lipids. Transfer of vitamin E across epithelial cells may require several stages, most of them poorly understood. In mammals, vitamin E is transported from the intestine to lymphatic capillaries in association with chylomicrons. Conversely, in birds, tocopherol is transported via the portal vein directly to the liver. Unlike cholesterol or vitamin A, α-tocopherol is not re-esterified during the absorption process.

Vitamin E circulates in the lymph and blood bound to all of the lipoproteins. There is a very high correlation between tocopherol levels and the total lipid or cholesterol concentration in serum.

All tissues show linear increases in tocopherol concentrations with increases in tocopherol intake. This relationship differs from that of most other vitamins, which usually have distinct deposition thresholds in tissues other than the liver, and may provide an explanation for the pharmacologic effects of vitamin E. Vitamin E levels in tissues vary markedly with no consistent relationship to lipid parameters. The vitamin is most concentrated in membrane-rich cell fractions such as mitochondria and microsomes.

Vitamin E undergoes very little metabolism. Usually less than 1% of orally ingested vitamin E is excreted in the urine.[1] The major route of excretion is fecal elimination.

The need for vitamin E in the diet is markedly influenced by dietary composition. The requirement increases with increasing levels of PUFA, oxidizing agents, vitamin A, carotenoids and trace minerals and decreases with increasing levels of fat-soluble antioxidants, sulfur-containing amino acids and selenium. Various researchers have recommended up to 60 mg of α-tocopherol per g of PUFA; however, there is no consensus among experts about the quantitation of this relationship.[1] The AAFCO allowance for vitamin E is 50 IU/kg of food (DMB) for dogs and 30 IU/kg of food (DMB) for cats, no matter what lifestage.[2] For foods containing fish oils, AAFCO recommends an addition (i.e., above the minimum level) of 10 IU vitamin E/g of fish oil/kg of food.[2]

DEFICIENCY AND TOXICITY

The clinical manifestations of vitamin E deficiency vary markedly between species. In general, however, the neuromuscular, vascular and reproductive systems are affected most commonly. Signs of vitamin E deficiency are mostly attributed to membrane dysfunction as a result of the oxidative degradation of polyunsaturated membrane phospholipids and disruption of other critical cellular processes. Clinical findings of vitamin E deficiency in dogs include degenerative skeletal muscle disease associated with muscle weakness, degeneration of testicular germinal epithelium and impaired spermatogenesis, failure of gestation, brown pigmentation (lipofuscinosis) of intestinal smooth muscle and decreased plasma tocopherol concentrations. In cats, deficiency signs include steatitis, focal interstitial myocarditis, focal myositis of skeletal muscle and periportal mononuclear infiltration in the liver. (See Case 2-9 "Subcutaneous Nodules in a Young Cat.")

Vitamin E is one of the least toxic vitamins. Animals and people apparently tolerate high levels without adverse effects (i.e., at least two orders of magnitude above nutritional requirements [1,000 to 2,000 IU/kg of food]). However, at very high doses, antagonism with other fat-soluble vitamins may occur, resulting in impaired bone mineralization, reduced hepatic storage of vitamin A and coagulopathies as a result of decreasing absorption of vitamins D, A and K, respectively. A maximum of 1,000 IU/kg diet was set by AAFCO for dogs;[2] however, there is no evidence that levels above this are toxic to dogs and may even be beneficial.[16] A number of inflammatory dermatoses in animals have been treated with oral vitamin E. (See Chapter 15.) People have been given much higher dietary concentrations of vitamin E without adverse clinical signs.

SOURCES

Vitamin E is synthesized only by plants. The richest sources of vitamin E are vegetable oils and, to a lesser extent, seeds and cereal grains. Tocopherol concentrations are highest in green leaves. Tocotrienols are not found in green leaves, but instead are found in the bran and germ fractions of certain plants. Animal tissues tend to be low in vitamin E, with the highest levels occurring in fatty tissues. Common vitamin E supplements used in pet foods include α-tocopherol and α-tocopherol acetate (d,dl forms).

Vitamin K

Phylloquinone (K_1) and menaquinone (K_2) are the natural forms of vitamin K. Both forms are reduced to dihydrovitamin K upon digestion. Green leafy vegetables are the primary sources of K_1 whereas K_2 is produced from actinomycete bacteria found in normal intestinal microflora. Menadione (K_3) and its various forms, including menadione sodium bisulfite complex and menadione pyridinol bisulfite, represent the common chemically synthesized forms of vitamin K.

FUNCTION

Vitamin K plays a major role in the carboxylation of proteins (factors II, VII, IX, X and proteins C and S) to convert prothrombin to thrombin for normal blood clotting. Vitamin K is also involved in the synthesis of osteocalcin, a protein that regulates the incorporation of calcium phosphates in growing bone.[1]

METABOLISM

Any food can be expected to contain a mixture of menaquinones and phylloquinones. In general, such mixtures appear to be absorbed with 40 to 70% efficiency.[1]

Ingested phylloquinone is absorbed from the proximal small intestine into the lymphatic system (or portal circulation in birds, fishes and reptiles) by an energy-dependent process. Menaquinone is absorbed from the small intestine by a passive noncarrier-mediated process. Conditions that impair lipid absorption also adversely affect vitamin K absorption. Upon absorption, vitamin K is transported to the liver in chylomicrons. The vitamin is rapidly concentrated in the liver, but in contrast to other fat-soluble vitamins, vitamin K has a very rapid turnover in this organ. No specific carriers have been identified for any of the K vitamers.

Although phylloquinones and menaquinones are ingested, much of the vitamin K in tissues is from bacterial origin. Menadione (synthetic form) is rapidly excreted in the urine as the phosphate, sulfate or glucuronide form of menadiol. However, catabolism of phylloquinones and menaquinones is much slower than that of menadione and they are primarily excreted in feces as a glucuronide conjugate.

Because microbially synthesized K_2 is readily absorbed by passive diffusion in the colon in most mammalian species, dietary supplementation is unnecessary for most cats and dogs. Coprophagy increases vitamin K absorption in dogs. AAFCO lists no recommendations for vitamin K for dogs, but does recommend supplementation in feline foods containing more than 25% fish (0.1 ppm for all lifestages, DMB).[2] This recommendation is warranted because vitamin K deficiency has been observed in cats fed certain commercial foods containing high levels of salmon or tuna. (See Case 2-10 "Hemorrhagic Diathesis in a Group of Kittens.")

DEFICIENCY AND TOXICITY

Malabsorption diseases, ingestion of coagulant antagonists (e.g., coumarin, indanedione), destruction of gut microflora by antibiotic therapy (sulfonamides and broad-spectrum antibiotics) and congenital defects may influence vitamin K requirements. Vitamin K_3 (menadione) has lower lipid solubility and is the most effective form of vitamin K for cases of malabsorption. Vitamin K_1 is the only form of vitamin K effective in anticoagulant antagonism.[17]

Phylloquinone produces no adverse effects when administered to animals in massive doses by any route. The menaquinones are similarly thought to have negligible toxicity. Menadione, however, can produce fatal anemia, hyperbilirubinemia and severe jaundice. The intoxicating doses appear to be at least three orders of magnitude above those levels required for normal physiologic function.[1] The only reported case of toxicity in dogs occurred when warfarin was ingested, followed by intravenous treatment with 30 mg vitamin K_1 in 5% dextrose and lactated Ringer's solution.[9]

SOURCES

Data for vitamin K contents of foods are limited by the lack of good analytical methods. Nevertheless, because dietary needs for vitamin K are low, most foods contribute significantly to those needs. Rich sources of vitamin K in pet foods include alfalfa meal, oilseed meals, liver and fish meals.

Water-Soluble Vitamins

Deficiency of B vitamins occurs in veterinary medicine but may be difficult to specifically diagnose because analytical tests are not readily available. Therefore, diagnosis

Table 2-21. Thiaminase activity in fish products.[*]

Food	Thiaminase activity[**]
Marlin	0
Yellowfin tuna	265
Red snapper	265
Skipjack tuna	1,000
Dolphin (mahi mahi)	120
Ladyfish	35
Clam	2,640

[*]Adapted from Hilker DM, Peter OF. Anti-thiamin activity in Hawaii fish. Journal of Nutrition 1966; 89: 419-421.
[**]mg thiamin destroyed/100 g fish per hour.

relies almost entirely upon clinical signs and nutrient intake history.

B vitamins are relatively nontoxic and may be supplied to veterinarians in individual or combination forms. Because many of the B-vitamin deficiencies present with overlapping clinical signs, it may be prudent to treat deficiency with vitamin-B complex. If signs are specific for a particular B-vitamin deficiency, and if the single preparation form of the vitamin is available, individual targeted treatment may be initiated. However, individual preparations of B vitamins are often more expensive, and the relative nontoxic levels of B vitamins warrant treatment with the combination form.

Thiamin

Thiamin (vitamin B_1) is considered one of the "oldest" vitamins; description of clinical deficiency in dogs predates the discovery of the vitamin.[18] The trail to discovery of thiamin began in 1911 when Funk found that a crystalline compound isolated from rice polishings could alleviate signs of beriberi (i.e., anorexia, neuritis, paralysis and edema).[1] The structure of thiamin was not elucidated until 1936.

STRUCTURE

Thiamin consists of one pyrimidine ring and one thiazole ring linked via a methylene group. Thiamin may exist as free thiamin or in the mono-, di-(pyro), or triphosphate configuration. Thiamin pyrophosphate (80%) is the major form found in tissues; the other three forms are found in lesser amounts.[19,20]

FUNCTION

Thiamin pyrophosphate (TPP) is the major coenzymatic form of thiamin and is required for only a small number of enzymatic reactions. TPP is involved in the following general scheme of reactions: 1) nonoxidative decarboxylation of alpha-ketoacids, 2) oxidative decarboxylation of alpha-ketoacids and 3) transketolation reactions. Thiamin may also have a function unrelated to coenzyme activity. Thiamin triphosphate is concentrated in neuronal cells and may affect chloride permeability by controlling the number of functional channels, possibly by phosphorylation.

METABOLISM

Dietary thiamin may be present in any of the four forms mentioned above or may be of synthetic origin. Whatever the form, thiamin is hydrolyzed to free thiamin by intestinal phosphatases before absorption by intestinal cells. Absorption takes place primarily in the jejunum, by an active, carrier-mediated transport that also phosphorylates the vitamin. Passive diffusion becomes an important mode of absorption when dietary thiamin intake is high.

The absorbed thiamin is then transported in erythrocytes, which contain free thiamin and its phosphorylated forms, and in plasma, which only contains free thiamin and its monophosphate form. Tissues take up thiamin and may interconvert it between any of its four forms. The liver, heart and kidneys have the highest concentration of thiamin. Table 2-22 lists AAFCO allowances for dogs and cats.

DEFICIENCY AND TOXICITY

Thiamin deficiency may result from inadequate intake of thiamin, attributable to foods with low-thiamin content or processing losses, or high intake of thiamin antagonists. The processing conditions used to prepare commercial pet foods are destructive to thiamin. However, this anticipated loss may be overcome by adding synthetic thiamin before processing. (See Case 2-11 "Weight Loss in a Group of Cats.")

Thiamin antagonists may be synthetic or natural compounds that modify the thiamin structure rendering it inactive. The natural antagonists include thiaminases (enzymes that degrade thiamin), and polyhydroxyphenols (caffeic acid, chlorogenic acid, tannins), which inactivate thiamin by an oxyreductive process. Thiaminases are found in high concentrations in raw fish, shellfish, bacteria, yeast and fungi (Table 2-21). Thiaminases are estroyed by cooking.

Clinical thiamin deficiency is rarely observed in dogs and cats because most commercial pet foods have adequate supplementation. Signs of deficiency include anorexia, failure to grow, muscle weakness and neurologic dysfunction such as ventriflexion of the head in cats with paresis, and cardiac hypertrophy and ataxia in dogs.

Thiamin deficiency may be diagnosed by measuring erythrocyte transketolase activity or thiamin metabolites in blood directly. Table 2-22 lists concentrations of thiamin in blood for cats and dogs.[21] Activity of erythrocyte transketolase is an excellent indicator of thiamin status, if determined in a laboratory familiar with the analysis. Thiamin toxicosis is virtually unheard of via the oral route.

SOURCES

Thiamin occurs in animal tissues almost entirely in phosphorylated forms, whereas it occurs mostly as free thiamin in plants. Thiamin is widely distributed in foods, but is mostly present at low concentrations. The richest sources are whole grains, yeast and liver (especially pork liver). Meat products may also supply significant amounts of thiamin in foods. Thiamin is very labile, being susceptible to neutral and alkaline conditions, heat, oxidation and ionizing radiation. As a result, thiamin contributions from the ingredients used in pet foods are considered negligible, and extensive losses (up to 90%) may occur as a result of processing.[16] Thiamin hydrochloride and thiamin mononitrate are the most commonly used supplements in pet foods.

Riboflavin

Riboflavin (vitamin B_2) is the precursor to a group of enzymatic cofactors called flavins. Flavins linked to protein are called flavoproteins. The two major coenzymes derived from riboflavin are flavin mononucleotide (FMN) and flavin adenine dinucleotide (FAD).

STRUCTURE

Chemically, riboflavin belongs to the class of isoalloxazines. Riboflavin has a planar structure and has limited solubility in water. This property has clinical significance because it is difficult to deliver massive doses of the vitamin via intravenous solutions. Riboflavin is heat stabile, but very sensitive to acidic and alkaline conditions, especially in the presence of light.

FUNCTION

Flavins are used as coenzymes in about 50 enzymes in mammals. Flavins participate in intermediary energy metabolism and function mainly in oxidoreductase types of reactions (Figure 2-24).

METABOLISM

Most riboflavin found in food sources is in the form of free coenzyme derivatives that are not readily absorbed unless hydrolyzed, and covalently bound riboflavin, which is not well-used. The free flavin compounds are hydrolyzed before they are absorbed in the upper GI tract. After absorption, about 50% of the riboflavin in blood is bound to albumin and the other half to globulins.[20,22] Tissues requiring riboflavin convert it to FMN by phosphorylation (via flavokinase) and subsequently to FAD (via FAD synthase). Excess vitamin B_2 is eliminated largely as riboflavin via the kidneys. Table 2-22 lists AAFCO allowances for dogs and cats.

DEFICIENCY AND TOXICITY

Deficiency of riboflavin in dogs and cats is uncommon but may manifest as dermatitis, erythema, weight loss, cataracts, impaired reproduction, neurologic changes and anorexia.[9,23-25] Table 2-22 lists riboflavin blood values for dogs and cats. Recently, the requirement of riboflavin for adult dogs at maintenance has been suggested to be approximately 20 to 33% higher than values currently recommended by AAFCO (2.7 mg/kg vs. 2.2 mg/kg of food).[26] Most commercial pet foods are supplemented with synthetic riboflavin. Toxicity has not been reported in dogs and cats.

SOURCES

There appears to be little storage of riboflavin in the body, thus it is critical to supply the vitamin in the daily diet. Levels of riboflavin in excess of the requirement do not appear to be well-absorbed. Riboflavin is widely distributed in foods, primarily bound to proteins as FMN and FAD. Rich sources include dairy products, organ meats (e.g., liver, heart, kidney), muscle meats, eggs, green plants and yeast. Cereal grains are poor sources of vitamin B_2. Riboflavin is stable to heat, but exposure to light can result in marked losses. The supplemental form for addition to foods is usually riboflavin.

Niacin

Niacin is the generic term used to describe compounds that exhibit vitamin B_3 activity (i.e., nicotinamide and nicotinic acid). Nicotinic acid was isolated in 1867. It was not until 1937, however, that niacin was established as the specific chemical factor that cured black tongue (pellagra) in dogs consuming a niacin-deficient diet. Before 1937, pellagra was thought to be caused by tryptophan deficiency. Tryptophan metabolism is intrinsically linked to niacin requirements and may even affect niacin requirements when both tryptophan and niacin are limiting in food.[20,27]

STRUCTURE

Nicotinic acid and nicotinamide are substituted pyridine ring structures (pyridine 3-carboxylic acid and nicotinic acid amide). Niacin must be converted to either nicotinamide-adenine dinucleotide (NADH) or nicotinamide-adenine dinucleotide phosphate (NADPH) to participate in enzymatic reactions or protein modification.

FUNCTION

Niacin, in its cofactor form, is essential to several physiologic reactions: 1) oxidoreductive reactions, 2) nonredox reactions, 3) cleavage of β-N-glycosidic bonds with transfer of ADP-ribose to proteins (post-translational modification) and 4) formation of cyclic ADP-ribose (mobilizes intracellular calcium).

Oxidoreductive reactions are the primary function, but the others are significant in proper cell function. Generally, NAD/NADH is involved in catabolic reactions and transfers the reducing power (electrons) acquired from intermediary metabolites to the electron transport chain to ultimately produce ATP. NADP/NADPH, on the other hand, is generally involved in biosynthetic reactions that transfer reducing power (electrons) to macromolecules such as fat, protein and carbohydrate.

METABOLISM

Niacin in foods is found mainly as NADH and NADPH, which may be free or bound to other macromolecules. After ingestion, NADH and NADPH undergo hydrolysis by the intestinal mucosa to release free nicotinamide, which is readily absorbed.[20] Dietary niacin (nicotinic acid and nicotinamide) is absorbed readily through the gastric and small intestinal mucosa. Both free nicotinic acid and nicotinamide are found in blood. Tissues readily take up these compounds to synthesize required cofactors, which also trap the compound in the cell. Excess niacin is methylated and excreted in the urine.

Niacin may also be synthesized from tryptophan via the kynurenin pathway, which results in formation of nicotinic acid ribonucleotide. Some enzymes in this pathway require vitamin B_6 and iron as cofactors. In most mammals, foods high in tryptophan can alleviate signs of niacin deficiency. Cats have the enzymatic machinery to efficiently make niacin from tryptophan; however, one of the intermediates is rapidly siphoned away by another pathway. Thus, cats do not synthesize substantial amounts of niacin from tryptophan and have a strict dietary requirement for preformed niacin.[28] Table 2-22 lists AAFCO allowances for dogs and cats.

DEFICIENCY AND TOXICITY

Niacin is a fairly stable vitamin and processing conditions may actually release some bound niacin, which increases availability. Niacin deficiency may occur when foods with low amounts of niacin and tryptophan (e.g., corn and other grains) are ingested. Deficiency of niacin results in pellagra with its classic 4D signs: dermatitis, diarrhea, dementia and death. Clinical deficiency is not common in dogs because most commercial foods are supplemented with niacin. Cats, however, are more likely to develop signs of deficiency because of their strict requirement.

Measurement of methylated nicotinamide levels in urine best substantiates niacin deficiency. Niacin metabolites in whole blood have been reported for dogs and cats (Table 2-22), but these values generally have not been useful markers of deficiency in other species.[21,27]

Table 2-22. Blood levels, allowances and tests for B-complex vitamins.

Vitamin	Blood level	Cat Allowance*	Best test
Thiamin	20-90 ng/ml (WB)	5 mg/kg	Erythrocyte transketolase activity
Riboflavin	196-660 ng/ml (WB)	4 mg/kg	Erythrocyte glutathione reductase**
			Urine riboflavin
Niacin	1.8-5.8 µg/ml (WB)	60 mg/kg	Urine methyl nicotinamide or
			methyl-pyridones**
Pantothenic acid	104-270 ng/ml (WB)	5 mg/kg	Urinary excretion of pantothenate
Pyridoxine	86-350 ng/ml (P)	4 mg/kg	Blood levels of pyridoxine
			Urinary metabolites of pathway
			intermediates
Folate	3.2-34 ng/ml (P)	0.8 mg/kg	Serum folate
Cobalamin	120-1,200 pg/ml (WB)	20 µg/kg	Blood levels of cobalamin
			Serum and urine methylmalonic acid
Biotin	1,000-3,000 pg/ml (WB)	70 µg/kg	Urinary biotin
			Urinary organic acids
Choline	180-490 µg/ml (P)	2,400 mg/kg	Plasma choline and phosphatidycholine

Vitamin	Blood level	Dog Allowance*	Best test
Thiamin	46-112 ng/ml (WB)	1.0 mg/kg	Erythrocyte transketolase activity
Riboflavin	185-420 ng/ml (WB)	2.2 mg/kg***	Erythrocyte glutathione reductase**
			Urine riboflavin
Niacin	2.7-12 µg/ml (WB)	11.4 mg/kg	Urine methyl nicotinamide or
			methyl-pyridones**
Pantothenic acid	120-380 ng/ml (WB)	10 mg/kg	Urinary excretion of pantothenate
Pyridoxine	40-270 ng/ml (P)	1 mg/kg	Blood levels of pyridoxine
			Urinary metabolites of pathway
			intermediates
Folate	4-26 ng/ml (P)	0.18 mg/kg	Serum folate
Cobalamin	135-950 pg/ml (WB)	22 µg/kg	Holotranscobalamin II**
Biotin	530-5,000 pg/ml (WB)	None established	Urinary biotin
			Urinary organic acids
Choline	235-800 µg/ml (P)	1,200 mg/kg	Plasma choline and phosphatidycholine

Key: WB = whole blood, P = plasma.

*Allowances are similar for growth and adult maintenance and are expressed on dry matter basis (AAFCO Official Publication, 1998.)

**Not currently available in veterinary medicine.

***Investigators have shown a riboflavin requirement approximately 20-33% higher than the AAFCO allowance listed here. (Cline JL, Odle J, Easter RA. The riboflavin requirement of adult dogs at maintenance is greater than previous estimates. Journal of Nutrition 1996; 126: 984-988.)

SOURCES

Niacin is a very stable vitamin that is found in a variety of foodstuffs. The greatest amounts of niacin are found in yeast, animal/fish by-products, cereals, legumes and oilseeds. Niacin occurs in animal tissues as NAD and NADP and in plants mostly as protein-bound forms. Niacin is generally added to most pet foods as nicotinic acid or nicotinamide.

Pyridoxine

FUNCTION

The biologically active forms of pyridoxine (vitamin B_6) are the coenzymes pyridoxal phosphate (PLP) and pyridoxamine phosphate (PMP). PLP is involved in most reactions of amino acid metabolism, including transamination, decarboxylation, desulfhydration and nonoxidative deamination. PLP is also involved in the catabolism of glycogen and metabolism of lipids. As a coenzyme for decarboxylase enzymes, PLP functions in the synthesis of serotonin, epinephrine, norepinephrine and γ-aminobutyric acid (GABA). Pyridoxine is involved in vasodilatation through the production of histamine and is required in the pathway where niacin is produced from tryptophan. Pyridoxine helps catalyze the synthesis of taurine from cysteine and participates with ascorbic acid and NAD in the synthesis of carnitine from the amino acid lysine. Pyridoxine is also involved with the synthesis of the heme precursor porphyrin (as a coenzyme for δ-aminolevulinate synthase).

METABOLISM

The various forms of vitamin B_6 (pyridoxine, pyridoxal, pyridoxamine, PLP, PMP) are freely absorbed via passive diffusion in the small intestine. The glucuronide form is not absorbed.

The predominant form of vitamin B_6 in the blood is PLP, which is tightly bound to proteins. Pyridoxal crosses cell membranes more readily than PLP does. After uptake by cells, the vitamin is again phosphorylated by pyridoxal kinase to yield the predominant tissue form, PLP, which is considered to be the most active vitamin B_6 form.

The vitamin B_6 forms are readily interconverted metabolically by reactions involving phosphorylation/dephosphorylation, oxidation/reduction and amination/deamination. Phosphorylation appears to be an important means of retaining the vitamin intracellularly.

Only small quantities of vitamin B_6 are stored in the body. The products of vitamin B_6 metabolism are excreted in the urine; pyridoxic acid is the predominant metabolic product.

Because pyridoxic acid is not detected in the urine of vitamin B_6-deficient subjects, this metabolite is useful in the clinical assessment of vitamin B_6 status. Measurement of xanthurenic acid excretion after a tryptophan load, however, is a more sensitive indicator of vitamin B_6 status. When vitamin B_6 is deficient, the conversion of tryptophan to niacin is impaired, resulting in increased production of xanthurenic acid. Other indices of vitamin B_6 status are plasma concentrations of PLP and erythrocyte transaminase.

The dietary requirement for vitamin B_6 is influenced by a number of factors including lifestage, dietary composition and microbial synthesis. AAFCO recommends 4 mg vitamin B_6/kg of food (DMB) for cats and 1 mg vitamin B_6/kg of food (DMB) for dogs.[2] The requirement is the same for growth/reproduction and maintenance for dogs and cats.

DEFICIENCY AND TOXICITY

Reduced growth, muscle weakness, neurologic signs, (e.g., hyperirritability and seizures), mild microcytic anemia, irreversible kidney lesions and anorexia are signs of pyridoxine deficiency. Oxalate crystalluria is also a notable sign in pyridoxine-deficient cats.[8] Table 2-22 lists normal plasma levels of pyridoxine for cats and dogs.[21]

The prevalence of vitamin B_6 toxicity appears to be low. Earliest detectable signs include ataxia and loss of small motor control. Many of the signs of toxicity resemble those of vitamin B_6 deficiency: ataxia, muscle weakness and loss of balance. Histologic examination of tissues from dogs fed more than 200 mg pyridoxine hydrochloride/kg body weight/day revealed bilateral loss of myelin and axons in the dorsal funiculi and loss of myelin in the dorsal nerve roots.[29]

SOURCES

Vitamin B_6 is widely distributed in foods, occurring in greatest concentrations in meats, whole-grain products, vegetables and nuts. The chemical forms of vitamin B_6 tend to vary among foods of plant and animal origin; plant tissues contain mostly pyridoxine, whereas animal tissues contain mostly pyridoxal and pyridoxamine. Pyridoxine is far more stable than either pyridoxal or pyridoxamine, thus processing losses are greatest in foods containing animal products. Losses can be as high as 70% (average losses from 0 to 40%).[15] Pyridoxine hydrochloride is most often used for supplementation because it is relatively stable.

Pantothenic Acid

FUNCTION

"Pantothenic acid" is derived from the Greek word "pantos" meaning "found everywhere." Although this vitamin is found in practically all foodstuffs, the quantity present is generally insufficient for most monogastric species. Pantothenic acid occurs mainly in bound form (i.e., acetyl-CoA and acyl carrier protein). Acetyl-CoA is found in all tissues and is one of the most important coenzymes for tissue metabolism. Acetyl-CoA is a major substrate in the TCA cycle for production of ATP from fat (glycerol and fatty acids), glucose and amino acids. Acetyl-CoA is also involved in the synthesis of fatty acids, steroid hormones and cholesterol. Acetyl-CoA is necessary for oxidation of fatty acids, pyruvate and ketoglutarate.[30]

METABOLISM

Acetyl-CoA and acyl carrier protein are the predominant forms of pantothenic acid in foods and foodstuffs.

Thus, hydrolytic digestion of these protein complexes is the first step in metabolism of this vitamin. Both forms are degraded to pantothenic acid in the lumen of the intestine in a series of steps. Absorption occurs via a saturable, sodium-dependent, energy-requiring process. At high concentrations, simple diffusion occurs throughout the small intestine. Pantothenic acid is transported in the free acid form in plasma. Erythrocytes, which carry most of the vitamin, contain predominantly acetyl-CoA.

The requirement for pantothenic acid is affected by dietary composition and lifestage. Less pantothenic acid is apparently required to optimize growth when high-protein foods are fed, whereas high-fat diets may increase the requirement for pantothenic acid.[15] AAFCO recommends 10 ppm and 5 ppm (DMB) per day for dogs and cats, respectively.[2]

DEFICIENCY AND TOXICITY

Dogs with pantothenic acid deficiency have erratic appetites, depressed growth, fatty livers, decreased antibody response, hypocholesterolemia and coma, in later stages.[9] Pantothenic acid-deficient cats developed fatty livers and became emaciated.[8] Normal whole blood concentrations of pantothenic acid for dogs and cats are listed in Table 2-22.[21]

Pantothenic acid is generally regarded as nontoxic. No adverse reactions or clinical signs other than gastric upset have been observed in any species following ingestion of large doses.

SOURCES

Pantothenic acid is widely distributed in nature and occurs primarily in bound forms as acetyl-CoA and acyl carrier protein. The most important sources are meats (especially liver and heart), rice and wheat bran, alfalfa, peanut meal, yeast and fish solubles. Pantothenic acid in foods is fairly stable to cooking and storage. However, appreciable losses (up to 50%) have been reported during canning and storage of some foods at pH values greater than 7 and less than 5.1 Calcium pantothenate is the predominant form added to vitamin premixes.

Folic Acid

Folic acid is the name commonly used to designate a family of vitamers with related biologic activity.[20,31] Other common designations are folate, folates and folacin. Folic acid was first discovered in 1943 and was classified as vitamin B_{10} and B_{11}. Folic acid metabolism is closely linked with vitamin B_{12}, which will be discussed later in this section.

STRUCTURE

Folic acid may be subdivided into three functional components: the middle group is para-aminobenzoic acid (PABA), flanked on one side by a pteridine ring, and on the other side by a polyglutamic acid chain.

FUNCTION

Folic acid functions as a one-carbon (methylene, methenyl, methyl) donor and acceptor molecule in intermediary metabolism. Specific pathways include nucleotide biosynthesis, phospholipid synthesis, amino acid metabolism, neurotransmitter production and creatinine formation. In addition, vitamin B_{12} is closely paired with folate in the production of methionine from homocysteine.

METABOLISM

Natural sources of folic acid undergo hydrolysis by the intestinal enzyme γ-glutamyl hydrolase to form folyl-monoglutamate, which is subsequently absorbed by enterocytes. Thus the major form of folic acid vitamers in blood is the monoglutamate form. After folylmonoglutamate is absorbed by target cells, additional glutamates are added to the tail, which trap the molecule within cells.

Folic acid must be in the reduced form (i.e., dihydro or tetrahydro) to participate in one-carbon metabolic reactions. The enzyme dihydrofolate reductase (DHFR) interconverts dihydrofolates to tetrahydrofolates. Inhibition of this enzyme interferes with intermediary pathways that require reduced folates for coenzymes. Table 2-22 lists AAFCO allowances for dogs and cats.

DEFICIENCY AND TOXICITY

Folate is required in the diet daily; no reserves are kept in the body. Table 2-22 lists plasma levels for healthy cats and dogs.[21] Folate deficiency is characterized by poor weight gain, megaloblastic anemia, anorexia, leukopenia, glossitis and decreased immune function. Folate levels in blood may be measured to confirm a deficiency suggested by clinical signs. There have been no reported cases of folate toxicity.

SOURCES

Folates are found in several foods, but are not stable in a variety of conditions. Liver, egg yolks and green vegetables are good sources of folates. The vitamin is destroyed by heating, prolonged freezing and during storage in water. Commercial pet foods use pre-made vitamin mix with supplemental folate to overcome the effects of processing and storage.

Biotin

Biotin was originally know as the "bios" factor. It was first shown to be required for some yeast and bacteria; much later, researchers proved a requirement for mammals. Adding egg whites to the diet to induce signs of deficiency led to the original disease complex being called "egg-white injury," which was later identified as biotin deficiency.

STRUCTURE

Biotin is a bi-cyclic compound with eight possible stereoisomers in nature. Only D (+) biotin is physiologically active and it is usually denoted as D-biotin. Biotin, in its active form, is always found covalently bound to a protein (apoenzyme). The epsilon amino group is bound to a specific lysine residue via an amide linkage.

FUNCTION

Biotin is an essential cofactor for four different carboxylase reactions in mammals. These carboxylases have important functions in the metabolism of lipids, glucose, some amino acids and energy.

METABOLISM

The majority of biotin in food sources is thought to be covalently bound to protein. After ingestion, biotin must be hydrolyzed from protein by the enzyme biotinidase to be absorbed in the intestine.[20,32] After hydrolysis, free biotin is absorbed through the gut via unknown mechanisms and transported through the blood to tissues. Biotin is then transported to the required tissues where it is linked to its target apoenzyme by the enzyme holocarboxylase syn-

thetase. Excess biotin is eliminated by the kidneys. Table 2-22 lists AAFCO allowances for dogs and cats.

DEFICIENCY AND TOXICITY

Naturally occurring biotin deficiency is very rare in dogs and cats.[9] Feeding raw egg whites or oral antimicrobials are probably the two must common causes. Raw egg whites contain the glycoprotein avidin, which binds biotin rendering it unavailable for absorption. Feeding avidin to cats may result in signs of biotin deficiency that include dermatitis, alopecia and a dull coat.[33] Because half of the biotin requirement is thought to be met by gut microbial synthesis, antimicrobials that decrease the population of the intestinal microflora may also result in signs of biotin deficiency. Table 2-22 lists biotin blood values for dogs and cats.[21] Clinical signs include poor growth, dermatitis, lethargy and neurologic abnormalities. (See Case 2-12 "Skin and Coat Disorders in a Group of Kittens.") Biotin toxicity has not been reported.

Although assessment of biotin status is difficult, several methods have been developed including bioassays, avidin-binding assays and fluorescent derivative assays. Assay of biotin directly has not uniformly resulted in diagnosis of biotin deficiency.

SOURCES

Mammalian tissues are incapable of synthesizing biotin. The biotin requirement is thought to be met by two sources: diet and microbes (microbes in the intestine are thought to produce enough biotin to meet one-half of the daily requirement).[20,32] Biotin is widely distributed in foods, but mostly in very low, highly variable concentrations. Oilseeds, egg yolks, alfalfa meal, liver and yeast are the most important natural sources of biotin. Marked losses of biotin may occur as a result of oxidation, canning, heat and solvent extraction of foodstuffs. Less than one-half of the biotin in various foodstuffs is biologically available.[15] Most commercial pet foods are supplemented with synthetic biotin.

Cobalamin

Although cobalamin (vitamin B_{12}) was the last of the B vitamins to have its structure determined, the effects of deficiency have been noted since the 1820s. The term cobalamin is also used to denote the group of compounds with vitamin B_{12} activity. Vitamin B_{12} is intrinsically linked with folate metabolism.

STRUCTURE

Vitamin B_{12} is the largest and most complex B vitamin and the only one to contain a metal ion, cobalt. The structure consists of four pyrrole rings linked to form a macrocyclic ring designated as corrin, which is similar to hemoglobin. Substitutions on the corrin ring account for the different recognized forms of vitamin B_{12}. The active forms of B_{12}, 5'deoxyadenosylcobalamin and methylcobalamin, are very unstable.[20,34] Substituted forms of B_{12} are much more stable and may be used as pharmaceutical supplements (cyanocobalamin, hydroxocobalamin, nitritocobalamin).

FUNCTION

The cobalamins are important in one-carbon metabolism. Methylcobalamin, which contains cobalt in the 1+ state, is a coenzyme for methionine synthase. 5'deoxyadenosylmethionine, which contains cobalt in the 2+ state, is a coenzyme for methylmalonyl-CoA mutase. Vitamin B_{12} is required by the enzyme (methionine synthase) that removes a methyl group from methyl tetrahydrofolate (THF) to regenerate THF, which is needed for pyrimidine biosynthesis. This intimate relationship may result in folate trapping in B_{12} deficiency and the resultant megaloblastic anemia of folate deficiency.

METABOLISM

Vitamin B_{12} absorption depends on dietary intake and adequate GI function. Dietary vitamin B_{12} undergoes the following steps in order to be absorbed:[34] 1) hydrolysis (gastric and pancreatic) from food peptides, 2) binding to intrinsic factor (a glycoprotein essential for vitamin B_{12} absorption) from gastric parietal cells, 3) absorption in the ileum via cell surface specific receptors, 4) transport in blood by holo-transcobalamin II protein (20%) to all DNA-synthesizing cells, 5) storage in blood (80%) by the serum protein haptocorrin and 6) tissue uptake via cell surface specific receptors. Table 2-22 lists AAFCO allowances for dogs and cats.

DEFICIENCY AND TOXICITY

Vitamin B_{12} deficiency is very rare but may result in poor growth and neuropathies. (See Case 2-13 "Cachexia in a Young Giant Schnauzer.") Because vitamin B_{12} is only made by microbes and found in animal tissue, a vegetarian diet may lead to deficiency.

Vitamin B_{12} may be directly assessed by determination of serum B_{12} levels or indirectly by determination of serum or urine methylmalonic acid (MMA).[20] MMA levels in serum and urine increase with B_{12} deficiency. A new test, serum holotranscobalamin II, may prove useful in the future to detect early B_{12} deficiency.[34] Whole blood levels of cobalamin for dogs and cats are listed in Table 2-22.[21]

Toxicity of vitamin B_{12} has not reported to occur in dogs and cats unless excessive amounts are given parenterally.

SOURCES

Microbes and yeast can make vitamin B_{12} for absorption by animals. Plants generally contain very low amounts of vitamin B_{12}. Meat and, to some degree, milk products are good sources of vitamin B_{12}. Most commercial pet foods are supplemented with stable, pharmaceutical grade vitamin B_{12}.

Choline

Choline is classified as one of the B-complex vitamins though it does not entirely satisfy the strict definition of a vitamin. Choline, unlike other B vitamins, can be synthesized in the liver, and is required in the body in substantially greater amounts than the other B vitamins (i.e., 1,200 to 2,400 ppm vs. only 0.02 to 60 ppm). Thus, although choline is an essential nutrient for all animals, not all animals require it as a dietary supplement (e.g., no requirement is established for people and adult rats). Further, choline does not function as a coenzyme or cofactor as do most other vitamins.

FUNCTION

Choline has four basic functions in metabolism:[1] 1) as phosphatidylcholine, it is a structural element of biologic membranes, 2) as phosphatidylcholine, it promotes lipid transport (as a "lipotrope"), 3) as acetylcholine, it is a neurotransmitter and 4) after conversion to betaine, it is a source of labile methyl groups for transmethylation reactions (e.g., the formation of methionine from homocysteine, or creatine from guanidoacetic acid).

METABOLISM

Choline is present in the diet predominantly as lecithin (phosphatidylcholine); less than 10% is present as either the free base or sphingomyelin.[1] Choline is released from lecithin and sphingomyelin by digestive enzymes of the GI tract. Choline is absorbed from the jejunum and ileum mainly by a carrier-mediated process. When free choline or one of its salts is consumed, only one-third of the ingested choline appears to be absorbed intact. The remaining two-thirds are metabolized by intestinal microorganisms to trimethylamine, which is excreted in the urine. Phosphatidylcholine is not subject to such extensive microbial metabolism; therefore, the metabolism of phosphatidylcholine results in less urinary trimethylamine. Once absorbed, choline is transported in the lymphatic circulation primarily in the form of phosphatidylcholine bound to chylomicrons.

Most species can synthesize choline, as phosphatidylcholine, by the sequential methylation of phosphatidylethanolamine. The activity is greatest in the liver, but is also found in many other tissues. In most species, the choline requirement is greater for younger animals than for adults. Choline may not be required in some adult species.

The requirement for choline is affected greatly by dietary factors such as methionine, betaine, myo-inositol, folate, and vitamin B_{12}, as well as the combination of different levels and composition of fat, carbohydrate and protein in the diet. In addition, age, gender, caloric intake and growth rate influence the lipotrophic action of choline and thereby its requirement.

Vitamin B_{12} and folate are required for the synthesis of methyl groups and metabolism of the one-carbon unit. Biosynthesis of labile methyl from a formate carbon requires folate, whereas B_{12} plays a role in regulated transfer of the methyl group to tetrahydrofolic acid. Therefore, a deficiency of one or both of these vitamins increases the requirement for choline. Choline and methionine are the two principal methyl donors in transmethylation. Therefore, dietary adequacy of methionine and choline directly affects the requirements of the other. Excess dietary protein and/or high-fat foods increase the choline requirement. AAFCO recommends 1,200 ppm choline (DMB) for dogs and 2,400 ppm for cats (DMB).[2] Methionine can completely replace choline as a methyl donor. For example, in cat foods, if dietary methionine exceeds 0.62% DMB, then choline supplementation is not required.[2]

DEFICIENCY AND TOXICITY

Choline deficiency in most animal species is characterized by depressed growth, hepatic steatosis and hemorrhagic renal degeneration. Additional signs of choline deficiency in dogs include thymic atrophy and elevated plasma phosphatase values and increased blood prothrombin time. Table 2-22 lists normal plasma levels of choline for cats and dogs.[21]

Choline and phosphatidylcholine levels in blood may be measured to confirm deficiency suggested by clinical signs. Studies with dogs suggested a low tolerance to lecithin (phosphatidylcholine). Reduced erythrocytes resulted from daily oral administration of lecithin (equivalent to 150 mg of choline).[12] Adverse effects have been reported to occur in dogs receiving levels of choline equivalent to three times the apparent choline requirement.

SOURCES

All natural fats contain some choline, so choline is widely distributed in foods and foodstuffs. Lecithin has also been shown to be an effective emulsifying agent in foods and is the form of choline ingested in most foods. Egg yolks, glandular meals and fish are the richest animal sources and cereal germs, legumes and oilseed meals are the best plant sources. Choline is added to most pet foods as choline chloride and is added separately from the vitamin premix because of its hygroscopic nature and propensity to reduce the stability of other vitamins if added in the premix.

Vitamin C

Because of de novo synthesis, vitamin C is not technically a vitamin for healthy dogs and cats. (See vitamin definition.) However, it is included here because of its biochemical functions, including in vivo and in vitro antioxidant properties.

FUNCTION

Vitamin C, or specifically L-ascorbic acid, is a very labile compound that is readily oxidized to dehydroascorbic acid. It requires a reducing enzyme (dehydroascorbic acid reductase) to transform it back to the active form. Vitamin C primarily functions in the body as an antioxidant and free radical scavenger. Ascorbic acid is best known for its role in collagen synthesis, where it is involved in hydroxylation of prolyl and lysyl residues of procollagen.[1] It is also involved in drug, steroid and tyrosine metabolism,[15] and electron transport in cells. Ascorbic acid is also necessary for synthesis of carnitine, an important carrier of acyl groups across mitochondrial membranes. Normal circulating plasma levels are 4 μg/ml in dogs and 3 μg/ml in cats.[21]

More recently, research into the role of ascorbic acid has shifted from prevention of deficiency to the treatment and prevention of disease. Because ascorbic acid protects against free-radical damage induced by the "oxidative burst" of neutrophils,[1,35] and stimulates the phagocytic effect of leukocytes, it plays a role in immune function.[15] Larger doses may play a protective role against carcinogenesis. Ascorbic acid acts as a nitrate scavenger, thereby reducing nitrosamine-induced carcinogenesis. Vitamin C has been associated with a reduced risk for gastric cancer, oral cancer and perhaps lung cancer, but had no effect on cancer of the pancreas, colon and prostate gland.[36]

Ascorbate may even play a role in the prevention of gingival and periodontal disease. Studies with people have shown that 600 mg/day (10x the recommended dietary allowance) significantly reduced gingival bleeding upon probing.[37] Whether this effect can be demonstrated in species that synthesize their own ascorbate (i.e., cats and dogs) remains to be seen.

Ascorbic acid may have some benefit in exercise stress recovery.[38] However, megadose supplementation to prevent hip dysplasia has not proved effective.[39]

METABOLISM

Most higher animals can synthesize vitamin C from glucose via the glucuronic acid pathway. Animals that cannot synthesize vitamin C include people, guinea pigs, fish, fruit-eating bats, insects and some birds. Species that cannot synthesize ascorbic acid absorb the vitamin by a saturable, carrier-mediated, active-transport mechanism that is sodium-dependent. Species that can synthesize ascorbic acid absorb it strictly by passive diffusion. In either case, absorption efficiency of physiologic doses is high (i.e., 80 to 90%).[1]

Vitamin C is transported in the plasma in association with albumin, mostly in a reduced form. Under physiologic conditions, vitamin C exists as ascorbate, which cannot cross most membranes readily. Cellular uptake of vitamin C involves dehydroascorbic acid in erythrocytes, lymphocytes and neutrophils. Once inside the cell, dehydroascorbic acid is quickly reduced to ascorbic acid by an intracellular enzyme (dehydroascorbic acid reductase), which uses reduced glutathione (GSH) as the source of reducing equivalents. Ascorbic acid is widely distributed throughout the tissues, both in animals capable of synthesizing ascorbic acid as well as in those that depend on dietary vitamin C. The pituitary and adrenal glands have the highest concentrations of vitamin C; high levels are also found in the liver, spleen, brain and pancreas. Ascorbic acid is excreted in urine, sweat and feces. Losses in feces and sweat are usually minimal.

There are no AAFCO recommendations for vitamin C for dogs or cats.

DEFICIENCY AND TOXICITY

Acute vitamin C deficiency results in scurvy (in animals unable to synthesize the vitamin). In general, high intake of vitamin C is considered to be of low toxicity.

SOURCES

Fruits, vegetables and organ meats are generally the best sources of vitamin C. The vitamin C content of most foods decreases dramatically during storage and processing. Polyphosphorylated forms of vitamin C are available that can survive processing conditions.

Vitamin-Like Substances

Vitamin-like substances are substances that exhibit properties similar to those of vitamins, but that do not fit the strict definition of a vitamin. They have physiologic functionality, but questionable essentiality. These compounds can be "conditionally essential" depending upon the metabolic capacity of the animal.

Carnitine

L-carnitine is one of the most well-known vitamin-like substances. L-carnitine is a natural component of all animal cells.[40,41] Its primary function is to transport long-chain fatty acids across the inner mitochondrial membrane into the mitochondrial matrix for β-oxidation.[40,42] Skeletal and cardiac muscle contain 95 to 98% of the L-carnitine in the body and are significant storage sites.[43]

The biosynthesis of L-carnitine requires five enzymatic steps that occur in many cells in the body.[40] The final step in which γ–butyrobetaine is converted to L-carnitine is rate-limiting and occurs primarily in the liver.[40] Lysine, methionine, ascorbic acid, ferrous ions, vitamin B_6 and niacin are important in L-carnitine metabolism; these nutrients are required substrates and cofactors for the enzymes involved in L-carnitine biosynthesis.[44]

Clinical signs of L-carnitine deficiency include chronic muscle weakness, fasting hypoglycemia, cardiomyopathy, hepatomegaly and dicarboxylic aciduria.[45] In many cases of L-carnitine deficiency, no clinical signs are apparent.[44]

Carotenoids

A group of pigments called carotenoids also exhibit vitamin-like activity. More than 600 different compounds are classified as carotenoids, but fewer than 10% can be metabolized into vitamin A. (See vitamin A.) The carotenoids found in greatest abundance in a variety of foodstuffs are β-carotene, α-carotene, lutein, lycopene, β-cryptoxanin, zeaxanthin, canxanthin and astaxanthin. A primary characteristic of the carotenoids is their conjugated polyene structure.

ABSORPTION AND TRANSPORT

Carotenoids are digested and absorbed into the body using a mechanism similar to that used by vitamin A. Bile salts are necessary for carotenoid absorption. Carotenoids are incorporated into micelles where they are absorbed by the duodenal mucosa via passive diffusion with an approximate 50 to 60% efficiency.

After transportation in chylomicrons via the lymphatic system, carotenoids are bound to lipoproteins and transported in the bloodstream.

FUNCTION

Although carotenoids do not strictly fit the definition of a vitamin for mammalian species, they have biologic activity beyond their provitamin A role. Carotenoids with nine or more double bonds function as antioxidants by squelching singlet oxygen and other reactive oxygen species such as hydroxyl radicals, superoxide anion radicals and hydrogen peroxide, which are produced in normal metabolism.[46,47] This function is accomplished by the carotenoids sacrificing highly reactive multiple double bonds to the free radicals via hydrogen donation, thereby stabilizing the reactive products. Carotenoids also protect cell membranes by stabilizing the oxygen radicals produced when phagocytic granulocytes undergo respiratory bursts that destroy intracellular pathogens.[47]

SOURCES

Carotenoids are found abundantly in orange and green vegetables, highly pigmented fruits and some species of fish.

Bioflavonoids

The bioflavonoids are another group of red, blue and yellow pigments (noncarotenoids) that have vitamin-like activity. This class of compounds was originally mistaken for vitamin C because crude extracts of lemon juice and yellow peppers had antiscorbutic effects. Originally called citrin (mixture of eriodictyol and hesperidin), vitamin P or vitamin C_2, these compounds were reclassified as bioflavonoids in 1950.[1,30,48] More than 4,000 bioflavonoids have been identified.[48]

ABSORPTION AND TRANSPORT

Flavonoids are usually found naturally as glycosides linked to sugars. Mammalian enzymatic systems are unable to hydrolyze flavonoids, but the necessary glycosidases are present in the gut microflora. After hydrolysis and absorption in the small intestine, flavonoids are bound in the liver as glucuronides or sulfate conjugates.[30] Most of the flavonoids are further metabolized into phenolic compounds and rapidly excreted, usually within 24 hours.

FUNCTION

Although many different flavonoids exist with many different physiologic effects, this class of compounds shares some similar functions. The most notable is the sparing effect that flavonoids have upon vitamin C. Flavonoids have the ability to perform similarly to vitamin C: reduce capillary fragility and permeability and chelate the divalent metal ions copper and iron.[1] (See vitamin C.) Flavonoid reactions are involved in the antioxidant system for lipid and aqueous environments. Flavonoids have been reported to influence several critical enzyme systems.

SOURCES

Bioflavonoids are ubiquitous in the plant kingdom, but dietary sources are found most notably in the peels and skins of colored fruits and vegetables.

Other Vitamin-Like Substances

Some other substances with vitamin-like activity include ubiquinones, orotic acid inositol and para-aminobenzoic acid (PABA). Animals synthesize most of these compounds, which are important metabolic intermediates. They function: 1) in the metabolism of fatty acids, 2) in the electron transport chain, 3) as antioxidants and 4) as growth factors. Continued research in "conditionally essential" nutrients may lead to vitamin classification for many of these compounds.

■ ENDNOTES & REFERENCES

Water References

1. National Research Council. Nutrients and Toxic Substances in Water for Livestock and Poultry. Washington, DC: National Academy of Sciences, National Academy Press, 1974; 1-93.
2. United States Environmental Protection Agency. Quality Criteria for Water. Washington, DC: U.S. Environmental Protection Agency, 1976.
3. Kirk CA, Ling GA, Franti CE, et al. Evaluation of factors associated with development of calcium oxalate urolithiasis in cats. Journal of the American Veterinary Medical Association 1995; 207: 1429-1434.
4. Anderson RS. Water balance in the dog and cat. Journal of Small Animal Practice 1982; 23: 588-598.
5. Schmidt-Nielsen K. Desert animals. In: Physiological Problems of Heat and Water. New York, NY: Oxford University Press, 1964.
6. Gosolfi CV. Water and electrolyte metabolism in exercise. In: Fox EL, ed. Ross Symposium on Nutrient Utilization During Exercise. Columbus, OH: Ross Laboratories, 1983; 21-25.
7. Harrison JB, Sussman HH, Pickering DE. Fluid and electrolyte therapy in small animals. Journal of the American Veterinary Medical Association 1960; 137: 637-645.
8. Haskins SC. Fluid and electrolyte therapy. Compendium on Continuing Education for the Practicing Veterinarian 1984; 6: 244-257.

Energy References

1. Kleiber M. Joules vs. calories in nutrition. Journal of Nutrition 1972; 102: 309-312.
2. Blaxter K. In: Energy Metabolism in Animals and Man. Cambridge, UK: Cambridge University Press, 1989.
3. McDonald P, Edwards RA, Greenhalgh JFD, et al. Evaluation of foods. In: Animal Nutrition, 5th ed. Essex, UK: Longman Scientific & Technical, 1995; 238-265.
4. Association of American Feed Control Officials. Official Publication, 1998; 143-147.
5. Kendall PT, Holme DW, Smith PM. Methods of prediction of the digestible energy content of dog foods from gross energy value, proximate analysis and digestive nutrient content. Journal of Science in Food and Agriculture 1982; 33: 823-831.
6. Kendall PT, Burger IH, Smith PM. Methods of estimating the metabolizable energy content of cat foods. Feline Practice 1985; 15(2): 38-44.

7. Kuhlman G, Laflamme DP, Ballam JM. A simple method for estimating the metabolizable energy content of dry cat foods. Feline Practice 1993; 21(2): 16-20.

8. Opitz B. Untersuchungen zur Energiebewertung von Futtermitteln für Hund und Katze. Thesis. Veterinary Faculty, University of Munich, Germany, 1996.

9. Wedekind K, Toll PW, Richardson D, et al. Validation of dual energy x-ray absorptiometry as a quantitative measure of body composition in small subjects. Journal of Bone Mineral Research 1992; 7: S256.

10. Toll PW, Gross KL, Berryhill SA, et al. Usefulness of dual energy x-ray absorptiometry for body composition measurement in adult dogs. Journal of Nutrition 1994; 124: 2601S-2603S.

11. Kleiber M. Animal temperature regulation. In: The Fire of Life: An Introduction to Animal Energetics. Davis, CA: John Wiley & Sons Inc, Publishers, 1961; 146-174.

12. Schmidt-Neilson K. Metabolic rate and body size. In: Scaling: Why is Animal Size so Important? Cambridge, UK: Cambridge University Press, 1984.

13. Kronfeld DS. Protein and energy estimates for hospitalized dogs and cats. In: Proceedings. Purina International Nutrition Symposium, Orlando, FL, 1991: 5-12.

14. Hill RC. A rapid method of estimating maintenance energy requirement from body surface area in inactive dogs and in cats. Journal of the American Veterinary Medical Association 1993; 202: 1814-1816.

15. Burger IH, Johnson JV. Dogs large and small: The allometry of energy requirements within a single species. Journal of Nutrition 1991; 121: S18-S21.

16. Earle KE, Smith PM. Digestible energy requirements of adult cats at maintenance. Journal of Nutrition 1991; 121: S45-S46.

17. Allen T, Hand MS. Quantitative nutrition for internists. In: Proceedings. Eighth Annual Veterinary Medical Forum, American College of Veterinary Internal Medicine, Washington, DC, 1990: 333-336.

18. Männer K, Bronsch K, Wagner W. Energiewechselmessungen bei Beaglehunden im Erhaltungsstoffwechsel und während der Laktation. In: Proceedings. Ernährung, Fehlernährung und Diätetik bei Hund und Katze, Hannover, Germany 1987: 77-83.

19. Männer K. Energy requirement for maintenance of adult dogs. Journal of Nutrition 1991; 121: S37-S38.

20. Kienzle E, Rainbird A. Maintenance energy requirement of dogs: What is the correct value for the calculation of metabolic body weight in dogs? Journal of Nutrition 1991; 121: S39-S40.

21. Finke MD. Evaluation of the energy requirements of adult kennel dogs. Journal of Nutrition 1994; 124: 2604S-2608S.

22. National Research Council. Nutrient Requirements of Dogs. Washington, DC: National Academy Press, 1985; 2-5.

23. Durrer JL, Hannon JP. Seasonal variations in caloric intake of dogs living in an arctic environment. American Journal of Physiology 1962; 202: 375-378.

24. Leibetseder J. Erfahrungen Uber den langfristigen Einsatz von Fertigfuttern bei Hunden. Arch. F. Tierarztl Fortbildung 1978; 5: 37-48.

25. Meyer H, ed. Energie und Nährstoffe–Stofwechsel und Bedarf. In: Ernährung des Hundes. Stuttgart, Germany: Eugen Ulmer, 1983; 92-174.

26. National Research Council. Nutrient Requirements of Cats. Washington, DC: National Academy Press, 1986; 3-5.

27. Romsos DR, Belo PS, Bennink MR et al. Influence of dietary carbohydrates, fat and protein on growth, body composition and blood metabolite levels in the dog. Journal of Nutrition 1976; 106: 1452-1464.

28. Miller SA, Allison JB. The dietary nitrogen requirements of the cat. Journal of Nutrition 1958; 64: 493-499.

29. Loveridge GG. Body weight changes and energy intakes of cats during gestation and lactation. Animal Technology 1986; 37: 7-15.

30. Rainbird AL, Kienzle E. Untersuchungen zum Energiebedarf des Hundes in Abhängigkeit von Rassezugehörigkeit und Alter. Kleintierpraxis 1990; 35: 149-158.

31. Meyer H, ed. Energie und Nährstoffe–Stofwechsel und Bedarf. In: Ernährung des Hundes, 2nd ed. Stuttgart, Germany: Eugen Ulmer, 1990; 67-125.

32. Finke MD. Energy requirements of adult female beagles. Journal of Nutrition 1991; 121: S22-S28.

33. Munday HS, Earle KE, Anderson P. Changes in the body composition of the domestic shorthaired cat during growth and development. Journal of Nutrition 1994; 124: 2622S-2623S.

34. Burger IH. Energy needs of companion animals: Matching food intakes to requirements throughout the life cycle. Journal of Nutrition 1994; 124: 2584S-2593S.

35. Armstrong PJ, Lund EM. Changes in body composition and energy balance with aging. In: Proceedings. Symposium on Health and Nutrition of Geriatric Cats and Dogs. Hill's Pet Nutrition, Inc, Orlando, FL, 1996: 11-15.

36. Kronfeld DS, Donoghue S, Glickman LT. Body condition of cats. Journal of Nutrition 1994; 124: 2683S-2684S.

37. Scarlett JM, Donoghue S, Saidla J, et al. Overweight cats: Prevalence and risk factors. International Journal of Obesity 1994; 18: S22-S28.

38. Jewell DE, Kirk CA, Berryhill SA, et al. The effect of age on body composition in dogs and cats. In: Proceedings. Symposium on Health and Nutrition of Geriatric Cats and Dogs. Hill's Pet Nutrition, Inc, Orlando, FL, 1996: 52.

39. Zentek J, Meyer H. Energieaufnahme adulter Deutscher Doggen. Berliner Müncher Tierärztliche Wochenschrift 1992, 105: 325-327.

40. Meyer H, Heckötter E, eds. Empfehlungen zur Versorgung des Hundes mit Energie und Nährstoffen. In: Futterwerttabellen für Hunde und Katzen. Hannover, Germany: Schlütersche Verlagsanstalt und Druckeri, 1986; 9-12.

41. Flynn MF, Hardie EM, Armstrong PJ. Effect of ovariohysterectomy on maintenance energy requirement in cats. Journal of the American Veterinary Medical Association 1996; 209: 1572-1581.

42. Root MV, Johnston SD, Olson PN. Effect of prepuberal and postpuberal gonadectomy on heat production measured by indirect calorimetry in male and female domestic cats. American Journal of Veterinary Research 1996; 57: 371-374.

43. Anantharanman-Barr G. The effect of ovariohysterectomy on energy metabolism in dogs. Veterinary International 1990; 2: 19-20.

44. Donoghue S. Nutritional support of hospitalized patients. Veterinary Clinics of North America: Small Animal Practice 1989; 19: 475-495.

45. Remillard RL, Thatcher CD. Parenteral nutritional support in the small animal patient. Veterinary Clinics of North America: Small Animal Practice 1989; 19: 1287-1306.

46. Burkholder WJ. Metabolic rates and nutrient requirements of sick dogs and cats. Journal of the American Veterinary Medical Association 1995; 206: 614-618.

47. Saltzman E, Roberts SB. The role of energy expenditure in energy regulation: Findings from a decade of research. Nutrition Reviews 1995; 53: 209-220.

48. Brown RC. The effect of weight loss on the resting metabolic rate in the obese dog. Federation of American Societies for Experimental Biology Journal 1991; 5: A961.

Carbohydrate/Fiber References

1. Englyst HN, Cummings JH. Resistant starch, a "new" food component: A classification of starch for nutritional purposes. In: Morton ID, ed. Cereals in a European Context. First European Conference on Food Science and Technology. Chichester, UK: Ellis Horwood, 1987; 221-233.

2. British Nutrition Foundation. Complex Carbohydrates in Foods. New York, NY: Van Nostrand Reinhold, 1990.

3. Romsos DR, Belo PS, Bennink MR, et al. Influence of a low carbohydrate diet on performance of pregnant and lactating dogs. Journal of Nutrition 1981; 111: 678-689.

4. Kienzle E, Meyer H, Lohrie H. Influence of carbohydrate free rations with various protein/energy relationships on foetal development, viability of newborn puppies and milk composition. Advances in Animal Physiology and Animal Nutrition 1985; 73-99.

5. Meyer H, Kienzle E. Dietary protein and carbohydrates: Relationship to clinical disease. In: Proceedings. Purina International Nutrition Symposium, Orlando, FL, 1991: 13-26.

6. Blaza SE, Booles D, Burger IH. Is carbohydrate essential for pregnancy and lactation in dogs? In: Burger IH, Rivers JPW, eds. Nutrition of the Dog and Cat. Cambridge, UK: Cambridge University Press, 1989; 229-242.

7. Kienzle E. Enzymaktivitat in Pancreas, Darmwand und Chymus des Hundes in Abhangigkeit von Alter und Fetterart. Journal of Animal Physiology and Animal Nutrition 1988; 60: 276-278.

8. Camire ME, Camire A, Krumhar K. Chemical and nutritional changes in foods during extrusion. Critical Reviews in Food Science and Nutrition 1990; 29: 35-57.

9. Gross KL, Burchett S, Harmon DL, et al. Effect of altering starch cook and resistant starch content of extruded food products on nutrient digestibility in the dog (abstract). Journal of Veterinary Internal Medicine 1998; 12: 241.

10. Walker JA, Harmon DL, Gross KL, et al. Evaluation of nutrient utilization in the canine using the ileal cannulation technique. Journal of Nutrition 1994; 124: 2672S-2676S.

11. Schunemann C, Muhlum A, Junker S, et al. Prececal and postileal digestibility of various starches in the dog and pH values and concentration of organic acids in colonic chyme and feces. Advances in Animal Physiology and Nutrition 1989; 19: 44-57.

12. Kienzle E. Carbohydrate metabolism of the cat. 1. Activity of amylase in the gastrointestinal tract of the cat. Journal of Animal Physiology and Animal Nutrition 1993; 69: 92-101.

13. Kienzle E. Carbohydrate metabolism of the cat. 2. Digestion of starch. Journal of Animal Physiology and Animal Nutrition 1993; 69: 102-114.

14. Bissett SA, Guilford WG, Lawoko CR, et al. Effect of food particle size on carbohydrate assimilation assessed by breath hydrogen testing in dogs. Veterinary Clinical Nutrition 1997; 4: 82-88.

15. Williams DA, Guilford WG. Procedures for the evaluation of pancreatic and gastrointestinal tract diseases. In: Guilford WG, Center SA, Strombeck DR, et al, eds. Strombeck's Small Animal Gastroenterology, 3rd ed. Philadelphia, PA: WB Saunders Co, 1996; 77-113.

16. Gibson GR, Roberfroid MB. Dietary modulation of human colonic microbiota: Introducing the concept of prebiotics. Journal of Nutrition 1995; 125: 1401-1412.

17. Roberfoid M, Gibson GR, Delzenne N. The biochemistry of oligofructose, a nondigestible fiber: An approach to calculate its caloric value. Nutrition Reviews 1993; 51: 137-146.

18. Hidaka H, Eida T, Takizawa T, et al. Effects of fructooligsaccharides on intestinal flora and human health. Bifidobacteria Microflora 1986; 5: 37-50.

19. Bunce TJ, Kerley MS, Allee GL, et al. Feeding fructooligosaccharide to the weaned pig improves nitrogen metabolism and reduces odor metabolite excretion (abstract). Journal of Animal Science 1995; 73 (Suppl. 1): 70.

20. Willard MD, Simpson RB, Fossum TW, et al. Characterization of naturally developing small intestinal bacterial overgrowth in 16 German Shepherd dogs. Journal of the American Veterinary Medical Association 1994; 205: 405-407.

21. Howard MD, Gordon DT, Garleb KA, et al. Dietary fructooligosaccharide, xylooligosaccharide and gum arabic have variable effects on cecal and colonic microbiota and epithelial cell proliferation in mice and rats. Journal of Nutrition 1995; 125: 2604-2609.

22. Yamashita K, Kawai K, Itakura M. Effects of fructo-oligosaccharides on blood glucose and serum lipids in diabetic subjects. Nutrition Research 1984; 4: 961-966.

23. Delzenne N, Kok N, Fiordaliso MF, et al. Dietary fructooligosaccharides modify lipid metabolism in the rat. American Journal of Clinical Nutrition 1993; 57: 820S.

24. Morissee JP, Maurisse R, Boilletot E, et al. Assessment of the activity of a fructooligosaccharide on different caecal parameters in rabbits experimentally infected with E. coli 0.103. Publication Centre National d'etudes Veterinaires et Alimentaires, B P 53.22440 Ploufragan, France, 1992.

25. Herrera-Saldana R, Huber JT. Influence of varying protein and starch digestibilities on performance of lactating cows. Journal of Dairy Science 1989; 72: 1477-1483.

26. National Research Council. Nutrient Requirements of Dogs. Washington, DC: National Academy Press, 1985.

27. Kittlehut IC, Foss MC, Miglioini RH. Glucose homeostasis in a carnivorous animal (cat) and in rats fed a high protein diet. American Journal of Physiology 1978; 239: R115-R121.

28. Kienzle E. Carbohydrate metabolism of the cat. 4. Activity of maltase, isomaltase, sucrase and lactase in the gastrointestinal tract in relation to age and diet. Journal of Animal Physiology and Animal Nutrition 1993; 70: 89-96.

29. MacDonald ML, Rogers QR, Morris JG. Nutrition of the domestic cat, a mammalian carnivore. Annual Reviews in Nutrition 1984; 4: 521-562.

30. Englyst HN, Cummings JH. Digestion of polysaccharides of potato in the small intestine of man. American Journal of Clinical Nutrition 1987; 45: 423-431.

31. Cummings JH, Englyst HN. Gastrointestinal effects of food carbohydrate. American Journal of Clinical Nutrition 1995; 61: 938S-945S.

32. Boudreau JC, White TD. Flavor chemistry of carnivore taste systems. In: Bullard RW, ed. Flavor Chemistry of Animal Foods. Washington, DC: American Chemical Society Symposium 67, 1978; 102-128.

33. Boudreau JC. Neurophysiology and stimulus chemistry of mammalian taste systems. In: Flavor Chemistry: Trends and Developments. Washington, DC: American Chemical Society, 1989; 122-137.

34. Sunvold GD, Fahey GC, Merchen NR, et al. Fermentability of selected fibrous substrates by dog fecal microflora as influenced by diet. Journal of Nutrition 1994; 124: 2719S-2720S.

35. Sunvold GD, Titgemeyer EC, Bourquin D, et al. Fermentability of selected fibrous substrates by cat fecal microflora. Journal of Nutrition 1994; 124: 2721S-2722S.

36. Leib MS. Fiber-responsive large bowel diarrhea. In: Proceedings. Eighth Annual Veterinary Medical Forum, American College of Veterinary Internal Medicine, Washington, DC, 1990: 817-819.

37. Twedt DC. Dietary fiber in gastrointestinal disease. In: Proceedings. Eleventh Annual Veterinary Medical Forum, American College of Veterinary Internal Medicine, Washington, DC, 1993: 225-229.

38. Gurr MI, Asp N-G. In: Dietary Fibre. Washington, DC: ILSI, 1994.

39. Burrows CF, Kronfeld DS, Banta CA, et al. Effects of fiber on digestibility and transit time in dogs. Journal of Nutrition 1982; 112: 1726-1732.

40. Salter K, Davenport DJ, Twedt DC, et al. Dietary fiber effects on fecal pH, fecal cytology, stool quality, and fecal flora in dogs. In: Proceedings. Waltham Symposium on the Nutrition of Companion Animals, Adelaide, Australia, 1993: 89.

41. Roediger WE. Utilization of nutrients by isolated epithelial cells of the rat colon. Gastroenterology 1982; 83: 424-429.

42. Brody T, ed. Regulation of energy metabolism. In: Nutritional Biochemistry. San Diego, CA: Academic Press Inc, 1994; 125-220.

43. Jewell DE, Toll PW. Effect of fiber on food intake in dogs. Veterinary Clinical Nutrition 1996; 3: 115-118.

44. Fahey GC, Merchen NR, Corbin JE, et al. Dietary fiber for dogs: 1. Effect of graded levels of dietary beet pulp on nutrient intake, digestibility, metabolizable energy and digesta mean retention time. Journal of Animal Science 1990; 68: 4221-4228.

45. Nelson RW, Ihle SL, Lewis LD, et al. Effects of dietary fiber supplementation on glycemic control in dogs with alloxan-induced diabetes mellitus. American Journal of Veterinary Research 1991; 52: 2060-2066.

46. Robinson DS. Fiber. In: Food Biochemistry and Nutritional Value. New York, NY: John Wiley & Sons, 1987.

47. Mortensen PB. Effect of oral-administered lactulose on colonic nitrogen metabolism and excretion. Hepatology 1992; 16; 1350-1356.

48. Younes H, Garleb K, Behr S, et al. Fermentable fibers or oligosaccharides reduce urinary nitrogen excretion by increasing urea disposal in the rat cecum. Journal of Nutrition 1995; 125: 1010-1016.

49. Silvio JS, Harmon DL, Gross KL, et al. Nutrient digestibility in dogs fed differing fiber types (abstract). Journal of Animal Science 1996; 74 (Suppl.): 187.

50. Muir HE, Murray SM, Fahey GC Jr, et al. Nutrient digestion by ileal cannulated dogs as affected by dietary fibers with various fermentation characteristics. Journal of Animal Science 1996; 74: 1641-1648.

51. Southgate DAT. Minerals, trace elements and potential hazards. American Journal of Clinical Nutrition 1987; 45: 1256-1266.

52. Prosky L, Asp N-G, Furda I, et al. Determination of total dietary fiber in foods, food products and total diets: Interlaboratory study. Journal of the Association of Official Analytical Chemists 1984; 67: 1044-1052.

53. Van Soest PJ. Use of detergents in the analysis of fibrous feeds. II. A rapid method for the determination of fiber and lignin. Journal of the Association of Official Analytical Chemists 1963; 46: 829-835.

54. Association of American Feed Control Officials. Official Publication, 1998.

Protein References

1. Mathews DM. Protein digestion and absorption. In: Protein Absorption, Development and Present State of the Subject. New York, NY: Wiley-Liss, Inc, 1991; 119-145.

2. Zapsalis C, Beck RA. Proteins: Sources and nutritional evaluation. In: Food Chemistry and Nutritional Biochemistry. New York, NY: John Wiley & Sons, 1985; 93-128.

3. Camire ME, Camire A, Krumhar K. Chemical and nutritional changes in foods during extrusion. Food Science and Nutrition 1990; 29: 35-57.

4. Ebersdobler HF, Gross A, Klusman U, et al. Absorption and metabolism of heated protein-carbohydrate mixtures in humans. In: Friedman M, ed. Absorption and Utilization of Amino Acids, vol. III. Boca Raton, FL: CRC Press Inc, 1989; 91-102.

5. Knipfel JE. Nitrogen and energy availabilities in foods and feeds subjected to heating. Progress in Food Nutrition Science 1981; 5: 177-192.

6. Harper AE, Benevenga NJ, Wohlhueter RM. Effects of ingestion of disproportionate amounts of amino acids. Physiological Reviews 1970; 50: 428-558.

7. Miller DS, Payne PR. A theory of protein metabolism. Journal of Theoretical Biology 1963; 5: 398-411.

8. Payne PR. Assessment of the protein values of diets in relation to the requirements of the growing dog. In: Graham-Jones O, ed. Canine and Feline Nutritional Requirements. London, UK: Pergamon Press, 1965; 19-31.

9. National Research Council. Nutrient Requirements of Dogs. Washington, DC: National Academy Press, 1985.

10. Association of American Feed Control Officials. Official Publication, 1998.

11. National Research Council. Nutrient Requirements of Cats. Washington, DC: National Academy Press, 1986.

12. Zelikovic I, Chesney RW. Taurine in biology and nutrition. In: Friedman M, ed. Absorption and Utilization of Amino Acids, vol. I. Boca Raton, FL: CRC Press Inc, 1989; 199-228.

13. Pion PD, Kittleson MD, Rogers QR, et al. Myocardial failure in cats associated with low plasma taurine: A reversible cardiomyopathy. Science 1987; 237: 764-768.

14. Morris JG, Rogers QR, Kim SW, et al. Dietary taurine requirement of cats is determined by microbial degradation of taurine in the gut. Veterinary Clinical Nutrition 1994; 1: 118-127.

15. Sanderson S, Gross KL, Osborne CA, et al. Dogs fed a high fat diet have reduced plasma taurine concentrations. Federation of American Societies for Experimental Biology Journal 1996; 10: A506.

16. Kramer GA, Kittleson MD, Fox PR, et al. Plasma taurine concentrations in normal dogs and dogs with heart disease. Journal of Veterinary Internal Medicine 1995; 9: 253-258.

17. Milner JA. Arginine: A dietary modifier of ammonia detoxification and pyrimidine biosynthesis. In: Friedman M, ed. Absorption and Utilization of Amino Acids, vol. II. Boca Raton, FL: CRC Press Inc, 1989; 25-40.

18. Morris JG, Rogers QR, Winterrowd DL, et al. The utilization of ornithine and citrulline by the growing kitten. Journal of Nutrition 1979; 109: 724-729.

19. Anderson PA, Baker DH, Corbin JE. Lysine and arginine requirements of the domestic cat. Journal of Nutrition 1979; 109: 1368-1372.

20. Morris JG, Rogers QR. Arginine: An essential amino acid for the cat. Journal of Nutrition 1978; 108: 1944-1953.

21. Costello MJ, Morris JG, Rogers QR. Effect of dietary arginine level on urinary orotic acid excretion and citrate excretion in growing kittens. Journal of Nutrition 1980; 110: 1204-1208.

22. Czarnecki GL, Baker DH. Urea cycle function in the dog with emphasis on the role of arginine. Journal of Nutrition 1984; 114: 581-590.

23. Ha YH, Milner JA, Corbin JE. Arginine requirements in immature dogs. Journal of Nutrition 1978; 108: 203-210.

24. Neu J, Shenoy V, Chakrabarti R. Glutamine nutrition and metabolism: Where do we go from here? Federation of American Societies for Experimental Biology Journal 1996; 10: 829-837.

25. Souba WW, Klimberg VS, Plumley DA, et al. The role of glutamine in maintaining a healthy gut and supporting the metabolic response to injury and infection. Journal of Surgical Research 1990; 48: 383-391.

26. Klimberg VS, Souba WW, Salloum RM, et al. Glutamine-enriched diets support muscle glutamine metabolism without stimulating tumor growth. Journal of Surgical Research 1990; 48: 319-323.

27. Furst P, Albers S, Stehle P. Evidence for a nutritional need for glutamine in catabolic patients. Kidney International 1989; 36: 287-292.

28. Lacy JA, Yost M. A key to the literature of nutrition and immunology. Nutrition in Clinical Practice 1990; 5: 200-206.

29. Osborne CA, Stevens B. Handbook of Canine and Feline Urinalysis, 1981; 47.

30. Klahr S. Effects of protein intake on the progression of renal disease. Annual Reviews in Nutrition 1989; 9: 87-108.

31. Dodman NH, Miller HL, Delgado PL, et al. Acute tryptophan depletion: A method of studying antidepressant action. Journal of Clinical Psychiatry 1992; 53: 28-35.

32. Dodman NH, Reisner I, Shuster L, et al. Effect of dietary protein content on behavior in dogs. Journal of the American Veterinary Medical Association 1996; 208: 376-379.

Lipid References

1. MacDonald ML, Anderson BC, Rogers QR, et al. Essential fatty acid requirements of cats: Pathology of essential fatty acid deficiency. American Journal of Veterinary Research 1984; 45: 1310-1317.

2. McGarry JD. Lipid metabolism I: Utilization and storage of energy in lipid form. In: Devlin TM, ed. Textbook of Chemistry with Clinical Correlations, 2nd ed. New York, NY: John Wiley & Sons, 1986; 355-389.

3. MacDonald ML, Rogers QR, Morris JG. Effects of dietary arachidonate deficiency on the aggregation of cat platelets. Comparative Biochemistry and Physiology 1984; 78: 123-126.

4. MacDonald ML, Rogers QR, Morris JG, et al. Effects of linoleate and arachidonate deficiencies on reproduction and spermatogenesis in the cat. Journal of Nutrition 1984; 114: 719-726.

5. McLean JG, Monger EA. Factors determining the essential fatty acid requirements of the cat. In: Proceedings. Burger IH, Rivers JW, eds. Nutrition of the Dog and Cat. Waltham Symposium No. 7. Cambridge, UK: Cambridge University Press, 1989: 329-342.

6. Neuringer M, Connor WE, Van Petten C, et al. Dietary omega-3 fatty acid deficiency and visual loss in infant rhesus monkeys. Journal of Clinical Investigation 1984; 73: 272-276.

7. Arbuckle LD, Innis SM. Docosahexaenoic acid in developing brain and retina of piglets fed high or low alpha linolenate formula with and without fish oil. Lipids 1992; 27: 89-93.

8. Brody T, ed. Digestion and absorption. In: Nutritional Biochemistry. San Diego, CA: Academic Press Inc, 1994; 41-106.

9. Brody T, ed. Lipids. In: Nutritional Biochemistry. San Diego, CA: Academic Press Inc, 1994; 249-293.

10. Wiese HF, Hansen AE, Coon E. Influence of high and low caloric intakes on fat-deficiency of dogs. Journal of Nutrition 1962; 76: 73-81.

11. Wiese HF, Bennett MJ, Coon E, et al. Lipid metabolism of puppies as affected by kind and amount of fat and of dietary carbohydrate. Journal of Nutrition 1965; 86: 271-280.

12. Wiese HF, Yamananka W, Coon E, et al. Skin lipids of puppies as affected by kind and amount of dietary fat. Journal of Nutrition 1966; 89: 113-122.

13. Hansen RA, Ogilvie GK, Salman MD, et al. N-3 therapy: N-3,6 levels in canine lymphomas and controls. In: Proceedings. Fifteenth Annual Conference, Veterinary Cancer Society, Tucson, AZ, 1995: 64.

14. Ogilvie GK, Salman MD, Fettman MJ, et al. Omega-3 fatty acids improve hyperlactatemia and hyperinsulinemia. In: Proceedings. Fifteenth Annual Conference, Veterinary Cancer Society, Tucson, AZ, 1995: 62.

15. Kinsella JE, Lokesh B. Dietary lipids, eicosanoids, and the immune system. Critical Care Medicine 1990; 18: S94-S113.

16. Leaf A, Weber PC. Cardiovascular effects of n-3 fatty acids. New England Journal of Medicine 1988; 318: 549-557.

17. Goodnight SH. The effects of omega-3 fatty acids on thrombosis and atherogenesis. Hematologic Pathology 1989; 3: 1-9.

18. Myers N, Gross K, Armstead E, et al. The effect of dietary n-6:n-3 fatty acid ratio on hemostatic parameters and platelet aggregation in the dog (abstract). Journal of Veterinary Internal Medicine 1996; 10: 171.

19. Mullen BJ, Martin RJ. Macronutrient selection in rats: Effect of fat type and level. Journal of Nutrition 1990; 120: 1418-1425.

20. Mullen BJ, Martin RJ. The effect of dietary fat on diet selection may involve central serotonin. American Journal of Physiology 1992; 263: R559-R563.

21. Cordy DR. Experimental production of steatitis (yellow fat disease) in kittens fed a commercial canned cat food and prevention of the condition by vitamin E. Cornell Veterinarian 1954; 44: 310-318.

22. Collins DR. Nutrition. In: Pratt PW, ed. Feline Medicine. Santa Barbara, CA: American Veterinary Publications, 1983; 15-29.

23. Leszczynski DE, Pikul J, Easter RA, et al Characterization of lipid in loin and bacon from finishing pigs fed full-fat soybeans or tallow. Journal of Animal Science 1992; 70: 2175-2181.

24. Stansby ME, Schlenk H, Gruger EH. Fatty acid composition of fish. In: Stansby ME, ed. Fish Oils in Nutrition. New York, NY: Van Nostrand Reinhold, 1990; 6-39.

Mineral Endnotes & References

ENDNOTES

a. Morris JG, Rogers QR. University of California, Davis, USA. Personal communication, 1997.

b. Kirk CA. Hill's Science and Technology Center, Topeka, KS, USA. Personal communication, 1997.

c. Wedekind KJ. Unpublished data, 1997.

d. Wedekind KJ. Unpublished data, 1998.

REFERENCES

1. McDowell LR, ed. In: Minerals in Animal and Human Nutrition. San Diego, CA: Academic Press Inc, 1992.

2. Association of American Feed Control Officials. Official Publication, 1998.

3. National Research Council. Nutrient Requirements of Dogs. Washington, DC: National Academy Press, 1985.

4. National Research Council. Nutrient Requirements of Cats. Washington, DC: National Academy Press, 1986.

5. Underwood EJ, Mertz W. Introduction. In: Mertz W, ed. Trace Elements in Human and Animal Nutrition, 5th ed. San Diego, CA: Academic Press Inc, 1987; 1-17.

6. RDA (Recommended Dietary Allowances), 10th ed. Washington, DC: National Academy Press, 1989; 14.

7. Solomons NW. Physiological interaction of minerals. In: Bodwell CE, Erdman JW Jr, eds. Nutrient Interactions. Institute of Food Technologists. New York, NY: Marcel Dekker Inc, 1988; 115-141.

8. Clydesdale FM. Mineral interactions in foods. In: Bodwell CE, Erdman JW Jr., eds. Nutrient Interactions. Institute of Food Technologists. New York, NY: Marcel Dekker Inc, 1988; 73-107.

9. Aoyagi S, Baker DH. Bioavailability of copper in analytical-grade and feed-grade inorganic copper sources when fed to provide copper at levels below the chick's requirement. Poultry Science 1993; 72: 1075-1083.

10. Wedekind KJ, Baker DH. Zinc bioavailability in feed-grade sources of zinc. Journal of Animal Science 1990; 68: 684-689.

11. McDowell LR. Proper mineral supplementation of livestock diets is essential. Feedstuffs 1992; 17(23): 11-13.

12. Henry PR, Ammerman CB, Miles RD. Bioavailability of manganese sulfate and manganese oxide in chicks as measured by tissue uptake of manganese from conventional dietary levels. Poultry Science 1986; 65: 983-986.

13. Morris JG, Rogers QR. Assessment of the nutritional adequacy of pet food through the life cycle. Journal of Nutrition 1994; 124: 2520S-2534S.

14. Aoyagi S, Wedekind KJ, Baker DH. Estimates of copper bioavailability from liver of different animal species and from feed ingredients derived from plants and animals. Poultry Science 1993; 72: 1746-1755.

15. Hortin AE, Oduho G, Han Y, et al. Bioavailability of zinc in ground beef. Journal of Animal Science 1993; 71: 119-123.

16. Kratzer FH, Vohra P. Chelates in Nutrition. Boca Raton, FL: CRC Press Inc, 1986; 3.

17. Kapsokefalou M, Miller DD. Lean beef and beef fat interact to enhance nonheme iron absorption in rats. Journal of Nutrition 1993; 123: 1429-1434.

18. Turnlund JR, Swanson CA, King JC. Copper absorption and retention in pregnant women fed diets based on animal and plant proteins. Journal of Nutrition 1983; 113: 2346-2352.

19. Wedekind KJ, Walker L, Hancock J, et al. Bioavailability of zinc and calcium is affected by certain fiber sources (abstract). Federation of American Societies for Experimental Biology Journal 1995; 9: A450.

20. Wedekind KJ, Beyer S, Titgemeyer E. Bioavailability of phosphorus is affected by certain fiber sources (abstract). Federation of American Societies for Experimental Biology Journal 1996; 10: A524.

21. Wedekind KJ, Walker L, Beyer S, et al. Bioavailability of iron is affected by certain fiber sources in chicks and puppies (abstract). In: Proceedings. Ninth International Symposium on Trace Elements in Man and Animals (TEMA-9), Banff, Alberta, Canada, 1996: A20.

22. Nap RC, Hazewinkel HAW. Growth and skeletal development in the dog in relation to nutrition; A review. Veterinary Quarterly 1994; 16: 50-59.

23. Birge SJ, Avioli LV. Pathophysiology of calcium and phosphate disorders. In: Avioli LV, Krane SM, eds. Metabolic Bone Disease and Clinically Related Disorders. Philadelphia, PA: WB Saunders Co, 1990; 196-221.

24. Chew DJ, Carothers MA. Disorders of calcium: Hypocalcemia and hypercalcemia. In. Proceedings. Thirteenth Annual Veterinary Medical Forum, American College of Veterinary Internal Medicine, Lake Buena Vista, FL, 1995: 632-636.

25. Pastoor FJH, Van 't Klooster ATh, Mathot JNJJ, et al. Increasing calcium intakes lower urinary concentrations of phosphorus and magnesium in adult ovariectomized cats. Journal of Nutrition 1994; 124: 299-304.

26. Morris JG, Earle KE. Vitamin D and calcium requirements of kittens. Veterinary Clinical Nutrition 1996; 3: 93-96.

27. Pastoor FJH. Interaction of dietary minerals in the cat. PhD Thesis, Universiteit Utrecht, Netherlands, 1993.

28. Allen LH, Wood RJ. Calcium and phosphorus. In: Shils ME, Olson JA, Shike M, eds. Modern Nutrition in Health and Disease, 8th ed. Malvern, PA: Lea & Febiger 1994; 157.

29. Pastoor FJH, Van 't Klooster ATh, Mathot JNJJ, et al. Increasing phosphorus intake reduces urinary concentrations of magnesium and calcium in adult ovariectomized cats fed purified diets. Journal of Nutrition 1995; 125: 1334-1341.

30. Brody T, ed. Magnesium. In: Nutritional Biochemistry. San Diego, CA: Academic Press Inc, 1994; 573.

31. Shils ME. Magnesium. In: Ziegler EE, Filer LJ Jr, eds. Present Knowledge in Nutrition, 7th ed. Washington, DC: ILSI Press, 1996; 257.

32. Freeman LM. Magnesium in feline hypertrophic cardiomyopathy. In: Proceedings. Thirteenth Annual Veterinary Medical Forum, American College of Veterinary Internal Medicine, Lake Buena Vista, FL, 1995: 323-324.

33. Driessens FCM, Verbeeck RMH, eds. Nephro- and cystolithiasis. In: Biominerals. Boca Raton, FL: CRC Press Inc, 1990; 307-324.

34. Stamler J. Adverse effects of habitual high dietary salt on health and longevity. Perspectives in Applied Nutrition 1995; 3: 116-120.

35. Yu S, Morris JG. The minimum sodium requirement of growing kittens defined on the basis of plasma aldosterone concentration. Journal of Nutrition 1997; 127: 494-501.

36. Yu S, Morris JG. Sodium requirement of adult cats for maintenance based on plasma aldosterone concentration. Journal of Nutrition 1999; 129: 419-423.

37. Kotchen TA, Galla JH, Luke RG. Contribution of chloride to the inhibition of plasma renin activity by NaCl in the rat. Kidney International 1978; 13: 201-207.

38. Kurtz TW, Al-Bander HA, Morris RC. "Salt-sensitive" essential hypertension in men. New England Journal of Medicine 1987; 317: 1043-1048.

39. Hallberg L, Rossander-Hulthen L. Factors influencing the bioavailability of iron in man. In: Schlemmer U, ed. Bioavailability '93-Nutritional, Chemical and Food Processing Implications of Nutrient Availability. Federal Republic of Germany: Ettlingen, 1993; 23-32.

40. Morris ER. Iron. In: Mertz W, ed. Trace Elements in Human and Animal Nutrition, 5th ed. San Diego, CA: Academic Press Inc, 1987; 82.

41. Chausow DG, Czarnecki-Maulden GL. Estimation of the dietary iron requirement for the weanling puppy and kitten. Journal of Nutrition 1987; 117: 928-932.

42. Elvehjem CA, Hart EB, Sherman WC. The availability of iron from different sources for hemoglobin formation. Journal of Biological Chemistry 1933; 103: 61-70.

43. Conrad HR, Zimmerman DR, Combs GF Jr. Literature Review on Iron in Animal and Poultry Nutrition. West Des Moines, IA: National Feed Ingredients Association, 1980.

44. Deming JG, Czarnecki-Mauldin GL. Iron bioavailability in calcium and phosphorus sources (abstract). Journal of Animal Science 1989; 67 (Suppl. 1): 253.

45. Hambidge KM, Casey CE, Krebs NF. Zinc. In: Mertz W, ed. Trace Elements in Human and Animal Nutrition, 5th ed. San Diego, CA: Academic Press Inc, 1986; 24.

46. Davis GK, Mertz W. Copper. In: Mertz W, ed. Trace Elements in Human and Animal Nutrition, 5th ed. San Diego, CA: Academic Press Inc, 1987; 301-364.

47. Cromwell GL, Stahly TS, Monegue HJ. Effects of source and level of copper on performance and liver copper stores in weanling pigs. Journal of Animal Science 1989; 67: 2996-3002.

48. Czarnecki-Maulden GL, Rudnick RC, Chausow DG. Copper bioavailability and requirement in the dog: Comparison of copper oxide and copper sulfate. Federation of American Societies for Experimental Biology Journal 1993; 7: A305.

49. Zentek J, Meyer H. Investigations on copper deficiency in growing dogs. Journal of Nutrition 1991; 121: S83-S84.

50. Hetzel BS, Maberly GF. Iodine. In: Mertz W, ed. Trace Elements in Human and Animal Nutrition, 5th ed. San Diego, CA: Academic Press Inc, 1986; 2: 146-148.

51. Belshaw FE, Cooper TB, Becker DV. The iodine requirement and influence of iodine intake on iodine metabolism and thyroid function in the adult beagle. Endocrinology 1975; 96: 1280-1291.

52. Smith TA. Establishment of the minimum iodine requirement in the adult cat. MS Thesis. Kansas State University, Manhattan, KS, 1996.

53. Scott ML, Nesheim MC, Young RJ. Nutrition of the Chicken. Ithaca, NY: ML Scott and Associates, 1982.

54. Arthur JR. The Biochemical Functions of Selenium Relationships to Thyroid Metabolism and Antioxidant Systems. Bucksburn, Aberdeen, UK: Rowett Research Institute Annual Report, 1993.

55. Levander OA. Selenium. In: Mertz W, ed. Trace Elements in Human and Animal Nutrition, vol. 2. San Diego, CA: Academic Press Inc, 1986; 209-279.

56. Van Vleet JF. Experimentally induced vitamin E–selenium deficiency in the growing dog. Journal of the American Veterinary Medical Association 1975; 166: 769-774.

57. Mahan DC. Selenium metabolism in animals: What role does selenium yeast have? In: Proceedings. Alltech's Eleventh Annual Symposium, 1995: 257-267.

58. Wedekind KJ, Cowell C, Combs GF Jr. Bioavailability of selenium in pet food ingredients. Federation of American Societies for Experimental Biology Journal, 1997; 11: A360.

59. Wedekind KJ, Beyer RS, Combs GF Jr. Is selenium addition necessary in pet foods? Federation of American Societies for Experimental Biology Journal 1998; 12: A823.

60. Combs GF Jr, Combs SB. The Role of Selenium in Nutrition. New York, NY: Academic Press Inc, 1986.

61. Puls R. Mineral levels in animal health. In: Diagnostic Data. Clearbrook, British Columbia: Sherpa International, 1990; 193.

62. Schwarz K, Mertz W. Cr (III) and the glucose tolerance factor. Archives of Biochemistry and Biophysics 1959; 85: 292-296.

63. Mertz W, Roginski EE. Newer Trace Elements in Nutrition. New York, NY: Dekker, 1971; 123.

64. Anderson RA. Chromium. In: Mertz W. ed. Trace Elements in Human and Animal Nutrition, 5th ed. San Diego, CA: Academic Press Inc, 1987; 1: 225-244.

65. Page TG, Southern LL, Ward TL, et al. Effect of chromium picolinate on growth and serum and carcass traits of growing finishing pigs. Journal of Animal Science 1993; 71: 656-662.

66. Moonsie-Shageer S, Mowat DN. Effect of level of supplemental chromium on performance, serum constituents and immune status of stressed feeder calves. Journal of Animal Science 1993; 71: 232-238.

67. Hunt CD, Herbel JL, Idso JP. Dietary boron modifies the effect of vitamin D3 nutrition on indices of energy substrate utilization and mineral metabolism in the chick. Journal of Bone and Mineral Research 1994; 9: 171-182.

68. Hunt CD, Herbel JL, Nielsen FH. Physiological amounts of dietary boron influence magnesium and calcium metabolism in the postmenopausal woman. Federation of American Societies for Experimental Biology Journal 1994; 8: A430.

69. Nielsen FH, Hunt CD, Mullen LM, et al. Effect of dietary boron on mineral, estrogen, and testosterone metabolism in postmenopausal women. Federation of American Societies for Experimental Biology Journal 1987; 1: 394-397.

Vitamin References

1. Combs GF, ed. The Vitamins, Fundamental Aspects in Nutrition and Health. San Diego, CA: Academic Press Inc, 1992.

2. Association of American Feed Control Officials. Official Publication, 1998.

3. Schweigert FJ. Insensitivity of dogs to the effects of nonspecific bound vitamin A in plasma. International Journal of Vitamin Nutrition Research 1988; 58: 23-25.

4. Wilson DE, Hejazi J, Elstad NL, et al. Novel aspects of vitamin A metabolism in the dog: Distribution of lipoprotein retinyl esters in vitamin A-deprived and cholesterol-fed animals. Biochimica et Biophysica Acta 1987; 922: 247-258.

5. Schweigert FJ, Ryder OA, Rambeck WA, et al. The majority of vitamin A is transported as retinyl esters in blood of most carnivores. Compendium of Biochemical Physiology 1990; 95A: 573-578.

6. Schweigert FJ, Uehlein-Harrell S, Zucker H. Effect of feeding on vitamin A concentrations in blood plasma of dogs. Journal of Veterinary Medicine 1990; A37: 605-609.

7. Cline JL, Czarnecki-Mauldin GL, Odle J, et al. Effect of vitamin A intake on serum retinyl esters in dogs. In: Proceedings. Federation of American Societies for Experimental Biology 1995; No. 975: A167.

8. National Research Council. Nutrient Requirements of Cats. Washington, DC: National Academy Press, 1986.

9. National Research Council. Nutrient Requirement of Dogs. Washington, DC: National Academy Press, 1985.

10. Morris JG, Earle KE. Vitamin D and calcium requirements of kittens. Veterinary Clinical Nutrition 1996; 3: 93-96.

11. Morris JG. Vitamin D synthesis by kittens. Veterinary Clinical Nutrition 1996; 3: 88-92.

12. National Research Council. Vitamin Tolerance of Animals. Committee on Animal Nutrition. Washington, DC: National Academy Press, 1987.

13. How KL, Hazewinkel HAW, Mol JA. Dietary vitamin D dependence of cats and dogs due to inadequate cutaneous synthesis of vitamin D. General and Comparative Endocrinology 1994; 96: 12-18.

14. McDowell LR, ed. In: Minerals in Animal and Human Nutrition. San Diego, CA: Academic Press Inc, 1992; 300.

15. McDowell LR, ed. In: Vitamins in Animal Nutrition, Comparative Aspects to Human Nutrition. San Diego, CA: Academic Press Inc, 1989; 365-387.

16. Morris JG, Rogers QR. Assessment of the nutritional adequacy of pet foods through the life cycle. Journal of Nutrition 1994; 124: 2520S-2534S.

17. Edwards DF, Russell RG. Probable vitamin K-deficient bleeding in two cats with malabsorption syndrome secondary to lymphocytic-plasmacytic enteritis. Journal of Veterinary Internal Medicine 1987; 1: 97-101.

18. Voegtlin C, Lake GC. Experimental mammalian polyneuritis produced by a deficient diet. American Journal of Physiology 1919; 47: 558-589.

19. Rindi G. Thiamin. In: Ziegler EE, Filer LJ, eds. Present Knowledge in Nutrition, 7th ed. Washington, DC: ILSI Press, 1996; 160-166.

20. Brody T, ed. Vitamins. In: Nutritional Biochemistry. San Diego, CA: Academic Press Inc, 1994; 355-484.

21. Baker H, Schor SM, Murphy BD, et al. Blood vitamin and choline concentrations in healthy domestic cats, dogs and horses. American Journal of Veterinary Research 1986; 47: 1468-1471.

22. Rivlin RS. Riboflavin. In: Ziegler EE, Filer LJ, eds. Present Knowledge in Nutrition, 7th ed. Washington, DC: ILSI Press, 1996; 167-173.

23. Cowell CS. Riboflavin. In: Nutrition and Management of Dogs and Cats, 3rd ed. St. Louis, MO: Ralston Purina, Co, 1987; N-7i, 1-2.

24. Street HR, Cowgill GR. Acute riboflavin deficiency in the dog. American Journal of Physiology 1939; 125: 323-334.

25. Street HR, Cowgill GR, Zimmerman HM. Further observations of riboflavin deficiency in the dog. Journal of Nutrition 1941; 22: 7-24.

26. Cline JL, Odle J, Easter RA. The riboflavin requirement of adult dogs at maintenance is greater than previous estimates. Journal of Nutrition 1996; 126: 984-988.

27. Jacob RA, Swendseid ME. Niacin. In: Ziegler EE, Filer LJ, eds; Present Knowledge in Nutrition, 7th ed. Washington, DC: ILSI Press, 1996; 184-190.

28. Baker DH, Czarnecki-Maulden GL. Comparative nutrition of cats and dogs. Annual Reviews in Nutrition 1991; 11: 239-263.

29. Phillips WEJ, Mills JHL, Charbonneau SM, et al. Subacute toxicity of pyridoxine hydrochloride in the beagle dog. Toxicology and Applied Pharmacology 1978; 44: 323-333.

30. Machlin LJ, ed. Handbook of Vitamins. New York, NY: Marcel Dekker Inc, 1991.

31. Selhub J, Rosenberg IH. Folic acid. In: Ziegler EE, Filer LJ, eds. Present Knowledge in Nutrition, 7th ed. Washington, DC: ILSI Press, 1996; 206-219.

32. Mock DM. Biotin. In: Ziegler EE, Filer LJ, eds. Present Knowledge in Nutrition, 7th ed. Washington, DC: ILSI Press, 1996; 220-235.

33. Pastoor FJH, Van Herck H, Van 't Klooster ATh, et al. Biotin deficiency in young cats fed diets containing dried egg white. Journal of Veterinary Nutrition 1993: 2: 37-41.

34. Herbert V. Vitamin B12. In: Ziegler EE, Filer LJ, eds. Present Knowledge in Nutrition, 7th ed. Washington, DC: ILSI Press, 1996; 191-205.

35. Levine M, Welch RW, Wang Y, et al. Ascorbic acid in human neutrophils. In: Proceedings. Second International Conference on Antioxidant Vitamins and Beta-Carotene in Disease Prevention, 1994: 15.

36. Sauberlich HE. Vitamin C and cancer. In: Evaluation of Publicly Available Scientific Evidence Regarding Certain Nutrient-Disease Relationships. Bethesda, MD: Federation of American Societies for Experimental Biology, 1991: 1-32.

37. Leggott PJ, Roberston PB, Rothman DL, et al. The effect of controlled ascorbic acid depletion and supplementation on periodontal health. Journal of Periodontology 1986; 57: 480-485.

38. Kronfeld DS. Stress supplements: Protein and vitamin C. Pure Bred Dogs/Kennel Gazette 1983; 100: 8-9.

39. Richardson DC. The role of nutrition in canine hip dysplasia. Veterinary Clinics of North America: Small Animal Practice 1992; 22: 529-540.

40. Bremer J. Carnitine—Metabolism and functions. Physiological Reviews 1983; 63: 1420-1480.

41. Rebouche CJ, Paulson DJ. Carnitine metabolism and function in humans. Annual Reviews in Nutrition 1986; 6: 41-66.

42. Fritz IB. Action of carnitine on long chain fatty acid oxidation by liver. American Journal of Physiology 1958; 197: 297-304.

43. Rebouche CJ, Engel AG. Kinetic compartmental analysis of carnitine metabolism in the dog. Archives in Biochemistry and Biophysiology 1983; 220: 60-70.

44. Borum PR. Carnitine–Who needs It? Nutrition Today 1986; Nov/Dec: 4-6.

45. Stanley CA. New genetic defects in mitochondrial fatty acid oxidation and carnitine deficiency. American Pediatrics 1987; 34: 59-88.

46. Chew BP. Antioxidant vitamins affect food animal immunity and health. Journal of Nutrition 1995; 125: 1804S-1808S.

47. Bendich A. Carotenoids and the immune response. Journal of Nutrition 1989; 119: 112-115.

48. Harborne JB, ed. The Flavonoids. London, UK: Chapman & Hall, 1994.

CASE 2-1

Soft Feces in a Young Giant Schnauzer

Assess the Animal

A 10-month-old giant schnauzer weighing 44 kg was examined for persistently soft mushy feces. An extensive diagnostic evaluation, including multiple fecal cultures, did not reveal a cause for the poor stool quality. The dog's body condition score was 3/5.

Assess the Food(s) and Feeding Method

The owners had been feeding the dog a homemade food recommended by the breeder who sold them the dog. The food consisted of unspecified quantities of raw meat, liver, eggs, cooked brown rice, a few vegetables and approximately 100 g of various supplements.

The food was changed to a highly digestible commercial veterinary therapeutic food (Prescription Diet Canine i/dᵃ). The dog was fed a mixture of moist and dry food that provided approximately 1,440 kcal (6.02 MJ) per day.

Feeding Plan

The dog's stool quality improved somewhat with the change from the homemade food to the veterinary therapeutic food, but the feces were still not formed. The owners continued to feed the dry form of the veterinary therapeutic food supplemented with a high-fiber cereal (Post All Branᵇ cereal [33% fiber]) to yield approximately a 10% fiber intake. (See Pearson square calculations in Chapter 1.) The final feeding recommendation was one cup of the cereal with 2.5 cups of dry Prescription Diet Canine i/d.

Two weeks later, the owner reported the dog's feces were normal. The food was subsequently changed to a veterinary therapeutic food that contained moderate levels of dietary fiber (Prescription Diet Canine w/dᵃ).

Endnotes

a. Hill's Pet Nutrition, Inc., Topeka, KS, USA.
b. Kraft Foods, Inc., Rye Brook, NY, USA.

CASE 2-2

Lethargy and Weight Loss in a Mixed-Breed Dog

Assess the Animal

A five-year-old male dog of mixed breeding was admitted for lethargy, a dull coat and weight loss. The dog weighed 8 kg. Physical examination was normal except for a lusterless coat and a subnormal body condition score (2/5). Hypoproteinemia (total protein 4.1 g/dl, normal 5.0 to 7.5 g/dl) and hypoalbuminemia (albumin 1.2 g/dl, normal 2.2 to 3.5 g/dl) were noted on the serum biochemistry profile. The dog had had several struvite urocystoliths surgically removed two years earlier.

Assess the Food(s) and Feeding Method

For the past two years, the dog had been fed a veterinary therapeutic food (Prescription Diet Canine s/dᵃ) that contained reduced levels of protein (7.6% dry matter), calcium, phosphorus and magnesium, and resulted in production of an acidic urine. These nutritional characteristics have been shown to help dissolve struvite urocystoliths. (See Chapter 20.) The dog had been fed one can (620 kcal [2.6 MJ]) daily.

Because of the low-protein content and other nutritional characteristics of this food, it is not recommended for long-term maintenance of adult dogs. The manufacturer recommends that Prescription Diet Canine s/d be fed for no more than six months. Because no other causes of hypoproteinemia and hypoalbuminemia were found, protein malnutrition was tentatively diagnosed.

Feeding Plan

The dog's food was changed to a different veterinary therapeutic food (Prescription Diet Canine c/d[a]). This food contains reduced levels of struvite precursor substances and produces an acidic urinary pH; however, it has a higher protein content (22.8% dry matter). This food is also nutritionally adequate for long-term maintenance of adult dogs. The dog was fed 1.5 cans (700 kcal [2.9 MJ]) daily until it reached optimal body condition.

Endnote

a. Hill's Pet Nutrition, Inc., Topeka, KS, USA.

CASE 2-3

Seizures in an Airedale Terrier

Assess the Animal

A 20-kg, eight-year-old, neutered male Airedale terrier was admitted to an emergency clinic after a 45-minute episode of continuous seizure activity. The dog was moribund at presentation. Thirty-six hours before the onset of seizures, the dog had ingested a salt-flour figurine, weighing approximately 100 g. The dog vomited a clear fluid three times within 12 hours after ingesting the figurine and became progressively more polydipsic and polyuric. The dog then consumed an unknown additional volume of uncooked salt-flour dough. Within an hour after ingesting this mixture, the dog developed generalized, fine-muscular fasciculations, which rapidly progressed to clonic-tonic motor activity.

The moribund dog was unresponsive to painful stimuli, pyrectic (41.6°C [106.9°F]), tachypneic and had an irregular heart rhythm. A generalized seizure occurred during the examination. Serum electrolyte and blood gas analysis revealed severe hypernatremia (serum sodium 211 mEq/l, normal 145 to 158), hyperchloremia (serum chloride 180 mEq/l, normal 105 to 122) and metabolic acidosis (serum pH 7.135, normal 7.32 to 7.38).

Treatment Plan

Treatment was initiated with intravenous fluids (5% dextrose in water), sodium bicarbonate, diazepam, phenobarbital and furosemide. The dog was also cooled with ice-water wraps and electric fans. The dog suffered cardiopulmonary arrest five hours later and died.

Further Assessment

At postmortem examination, 1 liter of putty-like, grayish-white material and clear, watery fluid were found in the stomach. Hemorrhage was noted throughout the stomach and the proximal two-thirds of the small intestine. Acute renal and hepatic necrosis were found histopathologically. Sodium and chloride levels in tissues were higher than normal. The brain sodium level was 108 mEq/l, which is greater than the 80 mEq/l considered indicative of sodium salt toxicosis. Analysis of the liquid portion of the gastric contents showed that a minimum of 20 g of sodium chloride remained in the stomach.

Bibliography

Khanna C, Boermans HJ, Wilcock B. Fatal hypernatremia in a dog from salt ingestion. Journal of the American Animal Hospital Association 1997; 33: 113-117.

CASE 2-4

Vomiting and Diarrhea in a Yorkshire Terrier

Assess the Animal

A one-year-old, intact female Yorkshire terrier weighing 2.7 kg had a sudden onset of lethargy, watery diarrhea, vomiting, icterus and red-colored urine. Abnormal laboratory findings included hemolyzed plasma, anemia, azotemia, leukocytosis, hemoglobinuria and an elevated total bilirubin concentration. Abdominal radiographs revealed a metal object at the pylorus. The object was recognized by the owner as a nut that had been missing for two weeks from an air freight kennel used to house the dog. Serum zinc concentration was 32 mg/kg, compared with 1.1 mg/kg in serum obtained from a clinically normal dog at the same time.

Assess the Food(s) and Feeding Method

No dietary history was available. The manufacturer of the kennel indicated that the nut was made of pure zinc.

Treatment Plan

The nut was removed from the stomach using a fiberoptic endoscope. Additional therapy included intravenous fluids and a blood transfusion.

Reassessment

The dog stopped vomiting but remained depressed and continued to have profuse watery diarrhea. Semi-solid feces were passed on Day 5 after removal of the nut. The dog's appetite returned on Day 6 and the dog steadily improved until discharge seven days later. Serum zinc concentrations on Days 11 and 21 were 8.5 mg/kg and 1.0 mg/kg respectively (values for a clinically normal dog were 0.7 mg/kg). The owner reported that the dog seemed completely normal three months after discharge.

On analysis, the nut contained 97% zinc, 2% aluminum and other elements. The nut removed from the stomach was highly corroded and, on comparison of its weight with that of a new nut of the same design, it appeared that the dog received a total dose of 703 mg zinc/kg body weight.

Bibliography

Torrance AG, Fulton RB. Zinc-induced hemolytic anemia in a dog. Journal of the American Veterinary Medical Association 1987; 191: 443-444.

CASE 2-5

Reproductive Problems in a Group of Cats

Assess the Animals

A group of breeding domestic shorthair cats, ranging in age from two to five years and weighing from 3 to 4.5 kg, were presented for poor reproductive performance, including failure to conceive, fetal resorptions, small weak kittens and cannibalism. Neonatal kittens from these queens had graying of hair, dry and curled coat texture and skeletal abnormalities including inverted carpi and metatarsi, "kinked" tails and fused digits.

Physical examinations of the unbred queens were unremarkable. Some pregnant queens appeared slightly underweight for their date of gestation but were otherwise normal when examined. Newborn litters contained several small kittens, weighing less than 70 g or kittens with gray-to-whitish coats over the caudal one-half to three-fourths of the body. The coat color over the head and feet was unaffected. The coat texture of kittens less than three days old was somewhat dry and had a slightly curled appearance. Several newborn kittens had kinked tails and inverted carpi. Kittens older than three weeks had normal coats and improvements in carpal and tarsal malformations, but normal function or structure did not return in many kittens. Kittens with kinked tails and fused toes did not improve with age.

Reproductive problems included a decline in conception rate from 100% to between 0 to 50% over an eight-month period. In utero monitoring of pregnant queens through biweekly ultrasound examinations showed that the fetal loss rate was 67% and occurred between 25 to 30 days of gestation. Food intake was only about two-thirds of that expected for the queens.

The initial evaluation included complete blood counts and serum biochemistry profiles for many of the queens and serum trace mineral analyses and heavy metal toxicity screens for queens and affected kittens. The hemogram results included normal hematocrit and hemoglobin values with low mean corpuscular hemoglobin concentrations (hypochromasia) in four of six queens evaluated. Heavy metal toxicity screens of affected kittens were unremarkable with the exception of high-hepatic zinc level in one kitten and a single low-hepatic iron value. Serum copper concentrations for queens were normal, but hepatic copper values were not determined because queens were in active reproduction. In one- to two-week-old affected kittens, hepatic copper concentra-

tions ranged from 26.6 to 35.7 ppm and serum copper values from 0.3 to 0.4 ppm, which were deemed borderline low based on literature values.

Assess the Food(s) and Feeding Method

A commercial dry cat food that had passed an AAFCO feeding trial for feline growth and maintenance had been fed for approximately eight months to cats in this colony before any abnormalities were noted. The food was plant-based; the first four ingredients were corn, corn gluten meal, soybean meal and poultry by-product meal. In addition to containing typical vitamin and mineral supplements, the food also included copper oxide as a copper source and iron oxide as a colorant.

Analysis of the food disclosed no deficiencies when compared with recommended levels established for growing kittens. However, high levels of zinc and iron were noted in the food. High levels of dietary phytates, which can reduce mineral absorption, were expected to be in the food because of the plant ingredients it contained.

Feeding Plan

A dietary copper deficiency was considered the most likely cause of the reproductive failure noted in these queens. Although food analysis revealed that dietary copper levels were more than adequate, the copper oxide used in the food is a completely unavailable copper source for animals. Additionally, factors that impair copper absorption by chelation (phytates in plants) or transport competition (zinc and iron) were found in high concentrations in the food and would further impair absorption of available copper.

The cat food was supplemented with 15 ppm copper from an available source, copper sulfate.

Reassessment

After the food was supplemented with copper sulfate, the conception rate increased to 80% of breedings and in utero fetal death rates decreased to 12.5%. Food intake increased to expected levels. Three months after feeding the supplemented food, coat pigmentation abnormalities and limb and tail deformities again became evident in newborn kittens. Serum samples were again collected from pregnant queens for copper analysis. Copper values were low in four of nine queens, indicating continuing copper deficiency. An additional 10 ppm of dietary copper as copper sulfate were added for a total of 25 ppm supplemental copper. No abnormal kittens were born during the next five months.

Some less severe clinical signs of copper deficiency in kittens not consuming copper-supplemented food (i.e., queen's milk only) were reversible. Pigmentation and coat texture returned to normal and improved carpal flexion was observed with skeletal maturation.

Bibliography

Morris JG, Rogers QR. Copper oxide is an ineffective source of copper in queen diets. In: Proceedings. Pet Food Forum, Chicago, IL, 1995: 107-108.

CASE 2-6

Sudden Death in a Chihuahua

Assess the Animal

A three-year-old female Chihuahua was found dead one hour after being given 1.5 ml of a vitamin E preparation by intramuscular injection. The owner routinely administered the vitamin preparation twice yearly to all dogs of breeding age in his kennel. One week earlier, a similar incident occurred with a two-year-old female Yorkshire terrier. The owner had purchased the vitamin E product from the same veterinarian for several years. The Chihuahua and the vitamin E preparation were delivered to a diagnostic laboratory for examination.

At necropsy, the lungs were wet, glistening and mottled pink. White foam was found in the trachea and bronchi. All other internal organs appeared normal. Histopathologic examination of the lungs showed congested capillaries, perivascular edema and abundant proteinaceous fluid in the alveolar lumina. Liver and kidney specimens from the dog contained 12.9 and 12.1 mg selenium/kg, respectively (normal values <3 mg/kg).

Assess the Food(s) and Feeding Method

No food was available for evaluation. When contacted, the veterinarian suggested that the bottle of vitamin preparation might also contain selenium. Selenium had been added to a bottle of vitamin E intended for use in calves, but the mixture had not been dispensed. The veterinarian was concerned that the bottle might have been sold inadvertently to the owner of the dog.

Two liquid phases, one oily and the other watery, were visible in the vitamin preparation bottle. The water-base liquid from the bottle contained 5,317 mg selenium/l. Subcutaneous tissue at the injection site contained 129 mg of selenium/kg. The calculated dose of selenium that had been administered to the dog was 2.5 mg/kg. The minimal lethal dose of selenium administered by intramuscular injection in dogs is 2.0 mg/kg.

Comments

Selenium toxicosis in cattle, sheep, horses, swine and poultry has been documented and usually develops as a subacute to chronic disease resulting from ingestion of seleniferous plants or feeds that contain high concentrations of selenium because of errors in ration formulation. Lesions of subacute to chronic selenium toxicosis have also been produced in dogs by long-term parenteral selenium administration. Acute selenium toxicosis causes increased vascular permeability, which is manifested as hemorrhages and edema in many tissues.

Bibliography

Janke BH. Acute selenium toxicosis in a dog. Journal of the American Veterinary Medical Association 1989; 195: 1114-1115.

CASE 2-7

Cervical Rigidity in a Cat

Assess the Animal

A 10-year-old, castrated domestic shorthair cat weighing 7 kg was examined for lethargy, decreased appetite and weight loss of several months' duration. Weight loss of 2 kg over the preceding 12 months was evident from the medical record.

The cat appeared depressed, had a matted, unkempt coat and extended its cervical region and held its head low and directly in front of its body. The cat was afebrile, obese and dehydrated. On palpation, the cervical region was rigidly extended with tense musculature. A hard mass was palpable in the midcervical region. The rigidly extended neck was the only neurologic abnormality.

Evaluation included a complete blood count (mild leukocytosis with mature neutrophilia), serum biochemistry analysis (mild hyperglycemia and hypercholesterolemia), feline leukemia virus antigen test (negative) and cervical and thoracic radiographs. Radiography revealed a bone-dense, cervical mass ventral to the C_1-C_2 intervertebral space. Much of the normal vertebral architecture appeared to be obliterated and the trachea and soft tissues were deviated ventrally and laterally. Thoracic radiography revealed ventral, bony proliferations extending from thoracic vertebrae T_2 through T_7. Marked bony proliferation was evident along the sternum and several of the costal cartilages.

The cat's serum vitamin A concentration was markedly high (315 µg/dl, normal 20 to 80 µg/dl).

Assess the Food(s) and Feeding Method

The cat was fed a commercial dry cat food ad libitum supplemented with fresh beef liver daily.

Treatment and Feeding Plan

A tentative diagnosis of hypervitaminosis A was made based on the dietary history, clinical signs and radiographic lesions. The daily liver supplementation was considered the source of the excess dietary vitamin A. The cat was given a single intramuscular injection of dexamethasone and an oral analgesic was prescribed. The owner was advised to discontinue feeding beef liver and to feed only a balanced commercial cat food. The owner was further advised to encourage the cat to eat with hand-feeding.

Reassessment

Six months later, the cat was euthanatized for reasons unrelated to the hypervitaminosis A. The cat had been eating fairly well, although its stiff-necked posture remained.

Bibliography

Goldman AL. Hypervitaminosis A in a cat. Journal of the American Veterinary Medical Association 1992; 200: 1970-1972.

CASE 2-8

Vomiting and Anorexia in a German Shepherd Mixed-Breed Dog

Assess the Animal

A five-year-old, 10.6-kg, neutered female German shepherd mix was examined after three days of vomiting, anorexia and lethargy. The owners reported the dog was allowed free access to the neighborhood, which included a radiator machine shop where cholecalciferol-based rodenticides were used. The dog appeared depressed and moderately dehydrated.

Abnormal laboratory findings included moderate hypercalcemia, mild azotemia, proteinuria and isosthenuria. These results suggested vitamin D_3 toxicosis.

Assess the Food(s) and Feeding Method

No dietary history was available.

Treatment and Feeding Plan

Treatment consisted of intravenous 0.9% saline solution, diuretics, salmon calcitonin and corticosteroids. Hypercalcemia persisted throughout hospitalization. Further diagnostic testing did not identify a cause for persistent hypercalcemia. After seven days of hospitalization, the dog improved markedly and was discharged to the owners' care. Oral prednisone (at tapering dosages) and a veterinary therapeutic food formulated for renal patients were given at home.

Reassessment

The dog was evaluated several times during the next four weeks and appeared normal despite persistent hypercalcemia. The dog became normocalcemic five weeks after discharge from the hospital and remained normocalcemic when examined at two and three months.

Bibliography

Livezey KL, Dorman DC, Hooser SB, et al. Hypercalcemia induced by vitamin D3 toxicosis in two dogs. Canine Practice 1991; 16: 26-32.

CASE 2-9

Subcutaneous Nodules in a Young Cat

Assess the Animal

A five-month-old female domestic shorthair cat was examined for depression, anorexia, firm nodular subcutaneous fat in the groin region and abdominal hyperesthesia of one week's duration. The cat was normally docile and tractable but began to resist being handled and petted. Body condition was normal (3/5).

Hematologic abnormalities included a neutrophilic leukocytosis and a normocytic, normochromic, nonregenerative anemia. Urinalysis and fecal examination results were normal. Biopsy specimens were obtained from the affected subcutaneous tissue. The biopsy specimens were firm, nodular and brownish-orange when examined grossly. Serosanguineous fluid oozed from the biopsy sites. Histopathologic examination revealed pyogranulomatous panniculitis, ceroid pigment and multifocal areas of fat necrosis and mineralization.

Assess the Food(s) and Feeding Method

Since weaning, the cat had only been fed sardines, anchovies and mackerel ad libitum.

Treatment and Feeding Plan

A diagnosis of pansteatitis was made based on the dietary history and histopathologic lesions. Treatment included α-tocopherol (50 mg/kg body weight) once daily per os for two months and prednisolone for 15 days in a decreasing dosage schedule. A fish-free, complete and balanced moist cat food was offered. Because the cat was anorectic and unaccustomed to commercial cat food, it was initially force fed.

Reassessment

Marked clinical improvement occurred within one week and the cat appeared clinically normal within one month.

Comments

Vitamin E protects cells against lipid peroxidation. α-tocopherol appears to localize within cell membranes to prevent or inhibit initiation of lipid peroxidation. Animals fed oily fish and fish oils containing high levels of unsaturated fat require greater amounts of vitamin E to limit fat oxidation.

Bibliography

Koutinas AF, Miller WH, Kritsepi M, et al. Pansteatitis (steatitis, "yellow fat disease") in the cat: A review article and report of four spontaneous cases. Veterinary Dermatology 1993; 3: 101-106.

CASE 2-10

Hemorrhagic Diathesis in a Group of Kittens

Assess the Animals

A group of adult intact female cats and their kittens were involved in an AAFCO feeding trial to establish nutritional adequacy for gestation, lactation and growth. Necropsy of four kittens that died during the feeding trial revealed hepatic or GI hemorrhages. Fourteen of the surviving kittens were divided into two groups. Blood samples were taken on Days 1, 3, 4 and 6. After the Day 3 blood samples were taken, seven of the kittens were subcutaneously injected with a vitamin K preparation (200 µg K_1), and the other seven were left untreated. Clotting times were determined for each sample.

The mean clotting time for kittens not receiving vitamin K treatment was 50 ± 9 seconds (values for normal kittens 22 ± 0.1 seconds). Mean clotting times for kittens receiving treatment decreased significantly from 59 ± 10 seconds for Days 1 and 3 to 22 ± 0.4 seconds for Days 4 and 6.

Assess the Food(s) and Feeding Method

Queens and kittens were fed a commercial feline food formulated primarily from tuna, free choice. Individual food intake measurements were not available for the kittens because they were group housed for the AAFCO feeding protocol.

Feeding Plan

Further studies using purified diets did not identify the specific cause of vitamin K deficiency in kittens eating this fish-based food. These studies led to a recommendation that pet food companies include a supplemental source of vitamin K in moist fish-based foods for cats.

Bibliography

Strieker MJ, Morris JG, Feldman BF, et al. Vitamin K deficiency in cats fed commercial fish-based diets. Journal of Small Animal Practice 1996; 37: 322-326.

CASE 2-11

Weight Loss in a Group of Cats

Assess the Animals

Twenty-eight cats in a humane shelter in England developed lethargy, a mild decrease in food consumption and weight loss. Analysis of blood samples taken from three of the cats revealed a normocytic, normochromic anemia.

Three days after the onset of clinical signs, 13 of the cats rapidly lost body condition and developed an uncoordinated gait. Within eight to 12 hours, these cats developed ventriflexion of the head and had fully dilated pupils with no light reflex. Five of the cats subsequently developed seizures and died despite treatment with anticonvulsant drugs. A diagnosis of thiamin deficiency was made based on necropsy results.

Assess the Food(s) and Feeding Method

The cats were fed a commercial moist cat food for six months. The food was not a complete and balanced prod-

uct but was designed as a "complementary" food to be mixed with other complete dry foods. Two different lots of the moist food contained 0.56 and 0.04 mg thiamin/kg food. Assuming the food contained 75% water and had a metabolizable energy content of 1.25 kcal/g as fed, the food should contain at least 1.25 mg/kg food of thiamin for kittens and 0.5 mg/kg food of thiamin for adult cats.

Treatment and Feeding Plan

The other severely affected cats were treated with intravenous fluids and intramuscular injections of vitamin B complex for five days. These cats responded to therapy within 12 hours and were clinically normal five days later. No other cases have occurred since the humane shelter switched to a complete and balanced moist cat food.

Bibliography

Davidson MG. Thiamin deficiency in a colony of cats. Veterinary Record 1992; 130: 94-97.

Finke MD. Alpo Viewpoints in Veterinary Medicine 1993; 3(1).

CASE 2-12

Skin and Hair Disorders in a Group of Kittens

Assess the Animals

Twenty female kittens were involved in a feeding trial to evaluate dietary phosphorus requirements. The kittens were eight weeks old at the beginning of the trial. After eating the experimental food for 11 weeks, most kittens developed

dried secretions around the eyes, mouth, nose and feet, focal dermatitis of the lips near the canine teeth, alopecia along the back, neck and tail, achromotrichia, dull fur and a brownish appearance of the skin. Growth of the kittens was not impaired. Results of hemograms and urinalyses were normal.

Assess the Food(s) and Feeding Method

The food was a purified diet that contained dried egg whites, fish meal, beef tallow, corn oil, glucose, cooked starch, cellulose, taurine, vitamins and minerals. Food and demineralized water were provided ad libitum.

Feeding Plan

A tentative diagnosis of biotin deficiency was made based on the dietary history and clinical signs. The biotin content of the food was increased from 0.066 mg/kg to 3.0 mg/kg of food.

Reassessment

The kittens were markedly improved after eating the biotin-supplemented food for 10 weeks. Serum biotin concentrations of kittens fed unsupplemented food was about one-fifth of that of adult female cats fed a commercial complete and balanced dry cat food. Serum biotin concentrations responded to increased biotin intake.

Comments

Biotin deficiency induced by avidin in raw egg whites is a classic example of vitamin deficiency in experimental nutrition. Avidin is a glycoprotein that irreversibly binds biotin and renders it unavailable. Biotin deficiency was an unwanted side effect in this group of research cats due to egg whites in the formulation. The researchers ordered ovalbumin expecting to receive a purified fraction of egg protein. However, they received dried total egg whites, which contained avidin.

Bibliography

Pastoor FJH, Van Herck H, Van 't Klooster ATh, et al. Biotin deficiency in cats as induced by feeding a purified diet containing egg white (expanded abstract). Journal of Nutrition 1991; 121: S73-S74.

CASE 2-13

Cachexia in a Young Giant Schnauzer

Assess the Animal

A five-month-old female giant schnauzer was admitted for lethargy, depression and cachexia (body condition score 1/5). The dog weighed 7.8 kg and was 47 cm high at the shoulder. It had gained no weight in the previous eight weeks. The dog's four normal female litter mates weighed 20.5 to 22.5 kg and were 48 to 52 cm high at the shoulder.

Hematologic abnormalities included chronic nonregenerative anemia and neutropenia. Peripheral blood smears revealed marked erythrocyte anisocytosis and poikilocytosis, occasional hypersegmented neutrophils and large platelets. Analysis of bone marrow aspirates revealed decreased to normal cellularity with adequate iron stores. Serum iron and total iron binding capacity were normal. Serum biochemistry analyses were within normal limits for age-matched controls.

Intestinal maldigestion and malabsorption were ruled out based on normal GI contrast radiography, normal absorption of starch and fat and normal serum trypsin-like immunoreactivity. Normal hepatic function was documented by ammonia tolerance and BSP retention tests.

A urine sample was submitted for metabolic screening. Analysis revealed methylmalonic aciduria, which is a sign of vitamin B_{12} deficiency. Two serum samples had vitamin B_{12} concentrations of 21 and 36 pg/ml (values for normal dogs 209 to 483 pg/ml). Results of a test to measure intestinal absorption of an orally administered dose of vitamin B_{12} were suboptimal.

Assess the Food(s) and Feeding Method

The puppy was fed a variety of homemade and commercial dog foods ad libitum, supplemented with an oral liquid hematinic.

Treatment and Feeding Plan

Vitamin B_{12} (1 mg) was administered intramuscularly once daily for seven days. A complete and balanced commercial dry growth dog food was offered ad libitum.

Reassessment

Within 12 hours of the vitamin B_{12} injection, the puppy became bright and alert and developed a voracious appetite. Two weeks after treatment, the puppy had gained 7 kg; six weeks after treatment the puppy weighed 25 kg. Reticulocytosis occurred five days after parenteral vitamin B_{12} therapy was started. Neutrophil counts increased within 10 days and all hematologic abnormalities resolved within two months. The dog remained clinically normal when given 1 mg vitamin B_{12} intramuscularly every four to five months.

Subsequent testing of this puppy's mother documented an inborn error of vitamin B_{12} metabolism leading to selective vitamin B_{12} malabsorption. Inherited selective malabsorption of vitamin B_{12} has been described in other giant schnauzer puppies and in a cat.

Bibliography

Fyfe JC, Jezyk PF, Giger U, et al. Inherited selective malabsorption of vitamin B_{12} in giant schnauzers. Journal of the American Animal Hospital Association 1989; 25: 533-539.

Vaden SL, Wood PA, Ledley FD, et al. Cobalamin deficiency associated with methylmalonic acidemia in a cat. Journal of the American Veterinary Medical Association 1992; 200: 1101-1103.

Pet Foods

CHAPTER 3

Introduction to Commercial Pet Foods

Stephen W. Crane

Robert W. Griffin

Peter R. Messent

"The greatest obstacle to discovery is not ignorance—it is the illusion of knowledge."
Daniel J. Boorstin

INTRODUCTION

Fulfilling the nutrient requirements of pet animals with commercially prepared pet foods has proved successful and economical for many years. Prepared pet foods account for more than 90% of the calories consumed by pets in North America, Japan, Northern Europe, Australia and New Zealand.[1] In other parts of Europe, Latin America and the Pacific rim, commercially prepared pet foods account for 35 to 50% of the calories consumed by dogs and cats.[1]

The popularity of commercial pet foods and their potential impact on pet wellness make understanding their features, benefits and applications highly relevant to companion animal veterinarians and their health care teams. In addition, foods formulated specifically for disease prevention and treatment are important adjuncts to medicine and surgery in daily veterinary practice.

Clients recognize veterinary practitioners and technicians as authorities on nutritional matters. Veterinarians have a strong influence on the foods clients choose to feed their pets. A 1995 study conducted by the American Animal Hospital Association found that 54% of pet owners interviewed sought veterinary advice on pet foods at least once, and 43% had received a recommendation from their veterinarian about which manufacturer's pet food to feed their puppies or kittens.[2] Seventy percent of the latter group fed the brand of food recommended by their veterinarian.[2] Clients frequently seek more detailed information than "feed any good commercial food" and also inquire about the relevance of new human nutritional information to their pets.

This chapter provides general information about commercial pet food forms, pet food marketing concepts and pet food segments. It also includes ways of measuring features and benefits of pet foods. The content is necessarily general as there are an estimated 4,000 pet foods made by more than 260 manufacturers in North America alone.[3] Methods for assessing specific pet foods are described in Chapter 1.

PET FOOD FORMS

Commercial pet foods are available in three basic forms: dry, semi-moist and moist. As suggested by the category names, water content differs markedly among the three forms. Other differences include the typical nutrient profile and the advantages and disadvantages of each form. Pet food quality is independent of form; high-quality foods can be found in all three categories. Consumer preferences also vary. North Americans favor dry foods whereas Europeans feed a higher percentage of moist (usually canned) foods. The global trend is toward use of dry pet foods, especially for dogs.

Moist Foods

The moisture content of moist foods varies from 60 to more than 87%. The dry matter portion of the food contains all the nonwater nutrients: protein, fat, carbohydrate, vitamins and minerals (Figure 3-1). Small differences in moisture content greatly affect a moist food's dry matter content. For example, if the moisture contents of Food A,

KEY WORDS & TERMS—INTRODUCTION TO COMMERCIAL PET FOODS*

Acceptability (acceptance)	Grocery pet food	Nutrient profile
Anosmia	Gustation	Palatability
Anthropomorphic	Hedonics	Preference feeding test
Digestibility	Ingredient	Premium pet food
Feeding trial	Learned aversion	Private label pet food
Finicky	Monadic feeding test	Specialty pet food
Flavor rotation	Mouth feel	Supplement
Food addiction	Neophobia	Treat
Generic pet food	Nutrient	Veterinary therapeutic pet food

Key words and terms are defined in the Glossary.

KEY POINTS—INTRODUCTION TO COMMERCIAL PET FOODS

1. Commercial pet foods are available in three basic forms: dry, semi-moist and moist.
2. Small differences in moisture content greatly affect a moist food's dry matter content.
3. In some markets, moist foods serve as primary protein and fat modules in complementary feeding systems.
4. Dry foods cost approximately one-third as much as moist foods on a cost per calorie basis.
5. Semi-moist foods are often used as high flavor "bits" in soft-dry pet foods.
6. Generally, nutritional balance is maintained when less than 10% of the dietary intake consists of table scraps or treats.
7. Although treats are nutritionally trivial, supplements are very concentrated nutrient modules.
8. Routine vitamin-mineral supplementation is not necessary when pets are fed typical commercial pet foods.
9. Specific-purpose foods are divided into lifestage and special needs groups.
10. The all-purpose marketing concept is based on the premise that one product satisfies all nutritional needs at all times.
11. True feeding costs are best reflected by cost of the food per day or cost per calorie rather than unit price (cost per container or cost per weight).
12. The nutrient profile of a commercial pet food is important to animals and should be the primary focus rather than concern for specific ingredients.
13. The term "natural" is not legally defined or legally regulated and is, therefore, open to interpretation.
14. Commercial pet food marketing segments include grocery brands, private label brands, generic foods, specialty brands and veterinary therapeutic/wellness foods.
15. Two-pan palatability tests are widely used in the pet food industry to assess comparative food preferences.
16. The primary sensory modalities for canine and feline food acceptance and preference are smell, taste and texture.
17. The serving temperature of pet food modifies olfactory cues and mouth feel; dogs and cats generally prefer food served at body temperature.
18. Apparent digestibility is quantified by measuring the difference between the dry matter content of an individual nutrient or dry matter in the food and the quantity in the feces.
19. The primary determinants of digestibility are differences in ingredient selection and processing.
20. Fecal volume and consistency are of concern to many pet owners.
21. A nutraceutical is "a substance that is produced in purified or extracted form and administered orally to patients to provide agents required for normal body structure and function and administered with the intent of improving the health and well-being of animals."

Food B and Food C are 72, 78 and 82%, respectively, the dry matter percentage differs markedly.

Dry matter in Food A = (100 – 72) = 28%
Dry matter in Food B = (100 – 78) = 22%
Dry matter in Food C = (100 – 82) = 18%

The % dry matter difference = (28 – 22)/22 = 6/22 x 100 = 27% more nutrients in Food A than in Food B and (28 – 18)/18 = 10/18 x 100 = 56% more nutrients in Food A than in Food C.

Gums and gelling agents are often used to solidify the loaf and imbibe water in high-moisture foods to preclude "free" water in the container. Many moist pet foods contain high levels of meat and meat by-products. These foods are also characterized by higher levels of protein, phosphorus, sodium and fat than semi-moist or dry forms. A food with a very high meat content will require a source of calcium to balance the high endogenous phosphorus content brought by animal source tissues. Some moist foods are stated to be

"meaty" or having "meaty pieces" to fulfill the needs of "naturally carnivorous" pets. However, "meaty" is used as an adjective ("meat-like") and many meaty pieces are actually extruded soy or wheat flour (textured vegetable protein), starches, gum and meat meal combinations.

The high palatability of moist foods is a primary reason this form is fed. The high preference that animals express for moist foods requires portion-controlled feeding to prevent overconsumption.

Moist foods in North America are usually sold as "complete" with all nutrients present. A few moist foods are not complete and are usually intended as either treats or palatability enhancement modules for dry foods. In the United States, moist foods are rarely fed as the sole food source (less than 10%). Rather, moist foods are used as a supplement to the dry main meal as the pet owners' way to treat or pamper their pet.[a] This behavior has fueled the growth of the "gourmet" moist food category, which is defined by its taste appeal and aesthetic attributes. The segment has seen a proliferation of flavor offerings as well as an increasing number of textures (pâté, ground, flaked, chunks, stews, slices, etc.).

In some international markets, moist foods serve as primary protein and fat modules in a complementary feeding system. In complementary feeding systems, pet owners mix the protein-fat source of the moist module with a "mixer," which is a high-carbohydrate dry food. When mixing the complementary components, pet owners have the latitude to modify the recommended quantity of moist and dry feeding components. Whether mixing occurs for treatment purposes or as part of a complementary feeding system, the variation in nutrient intake may complicate obtaining an accurate dietary history.

Moist foods have a low caloric density as fed and typically yield 0.7 to 1.4 kcal (2.93 to 5.86 kJ) metabolizable energy/g food. The lower caloric density and higher packaging costs translate to a higher cost per calorie. Correspondingly, moist foods have the highest daily feeding cost.

Moist foods are preserved with heat sterilization and vacuum preservation in an anaerobic environment. (See Chapter 4.) An enamel liner insulates moist pet foods from their container. Nutrient stability is excellent. A shelf life of at least 18 months is anticipated, provided the mechanical integrity of the seams and lid seals is maintained. All moist foods are seriously damaged by even a single freeze-thaw cycle. Thus, care must be taken to store cans at nonfreezing temperatures.

Moist foods are packaged in a variety of containers including paper trays, plastic pots and stuffed plastic tubes ("chubs"), in addition to the more popular steel cans and aluminum trays (Figures 3-2 and 3-3). The food in chubs often is incomplete, is unbalanced, contains excess mineral levels and does not have an extended shelf life (must be used within 48 hours after opening the package). Chub contents are often added to dry food or high-carbohydrate mixers, or are used as protein and fat modules in making homemade foods.

Dry Foods

Dry pet foods contain 3 to 11% water. The high dry-matter content of these foods allows the expression of different formulation concepts. Dry food has been produced with a caloric density of 2.7 to more than 7.1 kcal (11.3 to 29.7 kJ) metabolizable energy/g food. The average dry pet food is lower in protein, fat and most minerals on a dry matter basis than the average moist pet food. Packaging and freight costs of dry pet foods are lower than those of moist products because water is not shipped in cans. Thus, dry foods cost about one-third as much as moist foods on a cost-per-calorie basis. Dry food particles are usually formed through extrusion; however, baking, flaking, pelleting, crumbling and dry meals are other possible manufacturing methods. (See Chapter 4.)

Dry foods are usually acceptable to most pets, but have reduced average preference when compared with moist or semi-moist foods. Dry foods are often perceived as providing dental hygiene benefits. However, the perception that dry foods are superior for dental hygiene is a generalization. An epidemiologic study of progressive periodontitis in poodles found no correlation between food form and disease progression.[4] Readers should consult Chapter 16 for more details about the relationship between food and oral health.

Figure 3-1. This cat food has a guaranteed analysis of 83% moisture. The food is shown after it has been removed from the package (left). Another specimen of the same food (right) was dried to constant weight in an oven. The dry matter portion of the food contains all the nonwater nutrients: protein, fat, carbohydrate, vitamins and minerals. Gums and other hydrocolloids are added to high-moisture pet foods to imbibe water, which helps maintain the product's shape. The low percentage of dry matter in this pet food means that feeding costs are high. (See sidebar "Cost of Feeding.")

Figure 3-2. Moist pet foods are available in a variety of packages, including multiple sizes of traditional steel cans, aluminum and plastic trays, chubs and compressed tubes.

Figure 3-3. Chubs are plastic tubes used to package high-protein, high-fat moist foods. A chub's contents are usually mixed with dry pet food or high-carbohydrate modules.

Semi-Moist and Soft-Dry Foods

Semi-moist pet foods have an intermediate water content (25 to 35%), falling in between moist and dry pet foods. Semi-moist foods use humectants and acidification

Nutraceuticals

Confusion exists about an emerging area of food and food technology called nutraceuticals. Part of the confusion surrounds terminology. (See Definitions of functional foods and related terms.) Manufacturers of these foods or of components in these foods purport the potential role they may play in preventing or treating disease.

A true veterinary nutraceutical is "a substance that is produced in purified or extracted form and administered orally to patients to provide agents required for normal body structure and function and administered with the intent of improving the health and well-being of animals." Most nutraceuticals must be considered as having potential rather than established benefits.

A nonprofit scientific organization was formed in 1996 to recommend guidelines for defining, labeling and manufacturing veterinary nutraceuticals. This 12-member North American Veterinary Nutraceutical Council plans to establish scientifically valid guidelines for manufacturers developing and conducting nutraceutical safety and efficacy studies. Eventually, the council hopes to work with regulatory agencies to create a separate and distinct classification for veterinary nutraceuticals, rather than group them with dietary health supplements or drugs. Currently, there are no laws or regulations that directly apply to the manufacture and sale of nutraceuticals.

It is beyond the scope of this textbook to list and discuss all the potential nutraceuticals and their purported uses and benefits. The following information is a general overview of some of the more commonly used products.

HERBS

Garlic (*Allium sativum*) is a member of the onion family that contains volatile oils with allyl disulfides such as allicin. Extracts of garlic have been reported to have bactericidal, insecticidal, antiviral and fungicidal activity; to decrease serum lipids; to prolong bleeding; to inhibit platelet aggregation and to increase fibrinolytic activity.

Ginger (*Zingiber officinale*) contains a volatile oil that is used as a stimulant, antiemetic and carminative (to reduce flatulence).

Ginseng is the common name for deciduous plants of the genus *Panax* that contain triterpenoidal saponins called ginsenosides. Metabolic effects include decreased serum glucose and cholesterol concentrations, increased erythropoiesis and hemoglobin production, central nervous system stimulation, increased blood pressure and increased gastrointestinal motility.

IMMUNOMODULATORY AGENTS

Polyunsaturated fatty acids of the omega-6 or omega-3 families are used in supraphysiologic doses for various dermatologic, cardiovascular, musculoskeletal and renal diseases. The basis for fatty acid therapy is discussed in more detail in Chapter 26.

Methylsulfonylmethane (MSM) is a metabolite of dimethyl sulfoxide (DMSO) and provides a supplemental source of dietary sulfur (34% available sulfur). Potential uses of MSM include management of inflammatory musculoskeletal disease.

VITAMINS

Vitamin A and synthetic vitamin A analogs (retinoids) are used to manage primary keratinization disorders of the skin surface or follicular epithelium and abnormalities of the sebaceous glands. (See Chapter 15.) Vitamin A affects differentiation and proliferation of epithelial cells by binding to and activating specific cell nuclear receptors.

Vitamin E is used as primary or adjunctive therapy for inflammatory dermatoses including discoid lupus erythematosus, pemphigus erythematosus, sterile panniculitis, dermatomyositis and ear margin vasculitis. (See Chapter 15.)

The anti-inflammatory effects of large doses of vitamin E may be related to: 1) stabilization of cell and lysosomal membranes against damage induced by free radicals and peroxides, 2) modulation of arachidonic acid and prostaglandin metabolism, 3) inhibition of proteolytic enzymes, 4) enhancement of phagocytic activity 5) enhancement of humoral and cellular immunity or 6) a combination of the above.

Beta carotene, vitamin C, vitamin E and certain enzymes are involved in complex defense systems that protect cell membranes against free radical damage. These nutrients may also have beneficial effects on the immune system.

PERFORMANCE ENHANCERS (ERGOGENIC AGENTS)

Dimethylglycine (DMG, vitamin B_{15}, calcium pangamate) is an intermediate metabolite (vitamin-like substance) that functions in oxygen transport and as an indirect methyl donor (may function as a "methionine pump" by converting excess homocysteine to methionine). Potential benefits include improved oxygen delivery in oxygen debt situations, reduction of lactic acid accumulation, faster race times and recovery times in athletic animals and potentiation of the immune response including enhanced vaccine response, lymphocyte proliferation and increased interferon production.

Octosanol is a long-chain waxy alcohol found in wheat germ oil and various nutrient supplements. Potential benefits include increased oxygen transport, improved neuromuscular function (reaction time) and improved race times and stamina.

Chromium picolinate is an ultratrace element for which specific requirements have not yet been established. Chromium was initially identified as "glucose tolerance factor" and may affect glycemic control by increasing the number of insulin receptors. It may also affect body composition by promoting lean body mass.

Coenzyme Q10 (CoQ10), ubiquinone, is a cofactor in the mitochondrial electron transport chain, the biochemical pathway in cellular respiration from which ATP and metabolic energy are derived. CoQ10 is a naturally occurring antioxidant that retards free radical formation. CoQ10 may protect against myocardial ischemia and aid in treatment of dilated cardiomyopathy and other diseases.

Yeast cultures are dried materials from fermentation of nonpathogenic strains of microorganisms such as *Saccharomyces cerevisiae*. Yeast fermentation products improve palatability of food and contain "nutrilites," which are metabolites that function as microbial growth enhancers. Yeast cultures are purported to: 1) promote rumen bacterial growth and fermentation, 2) increase milk fat and milk production, 3) improve mineral use, 4) increase packed cell volume, 5) increase protein digestibility and nitrogen retention and 6) increase aerobic capacity and stamina by reducing blood lactic acid accumulation during exercise.

Creatine (N-methyl guanidoacetate) is an important reservoir of high-energy phosphate groups in skeletal muscle and to a lesser extent in other tissues. Creatine is normally synthesized in the body from the amino acids arginine and glycine. Creatine is lost from the metabolic pool when it is converted to creatinine, which is excreted in the urine. Creatine supplementation is purported to improve athletic performance, shorten recovery time and reduce the risk of musculoskeletal injury. *Continued on next page.*

Continued from previous page.

CHONDROPROTECTIVE AGENTS

Chondroprotective agents are compounds that: 1) support or enhance macromolecular synthesis by chondrocytes, 2) support or enhance synthesis of hyaluronic acid by synoviocytes in synovial fluid, 3) inhibit degradative enzymes (collagenase, hyaluronidase) and inflammatory mediators and 4) remove or prevent formation of fibrin, thrombin and plaque in synovium, subchondral blood vessels or both.

Glycosaminoglycans (GAG) are complex carbohydrates, glycoproteins or both that include hyaluronic acid, chondroitin sulfate, dermatan sulfate, heparan sulfate (heparin) or keratan sulfate. They are important constituents of hyaline cartilage. Polysulfated glycosaminoglycan is a highly sulfated mixture of GAG made up primarily of chondroitin sulfate extracted from bovine trachea and lungs. Polysulfated GAG is available for parenteral and intra-articular administration.

Hyaluronic acid (hyaluronate) is a long-chain polymer of a repeating disaccharide unit, each containing one residue of acetylglucosamine and glucuronic acid. Hyaluronate is one of four molecules that form proteoglycans of hyaline cartilage and is also one of the major components of synovial fluid. Hyaluronic acid is usually extracted from rooster combs or bacteria and is available as injectable preparations.

Chondroitin sulfates are long-chain polymers of a repeating disaccharide unit, each containing one residue of galactosamine sulfate and glucuronic acid. Quantitatively they are the major glycosaminoglycans found in cartilage.

Chondroitin sulfates are isolated from bovine cartilage, shark and ray skeletons, seaweed and green-lipped mussels. They are available as injectable and oral preparations.

Glucosamine salts are precursors of hyaluronic acid and other glycosaminoglycans and are key "up regulators" of glycosaminoglycan synthesis. Glucosamine salts (glucosamine HCl, glucosamine sulfate, N-acetyl glucosamine) are available as oral preparations and in combination with chondroitin sulfate.

BIBLIOGRAPHY

Anonymous. Council defines "nutraceutical." Journal of the American Veterinary Medical Association 1996; 209: 1986.

Bayley AJ. Compendium of Veterinary Products. Port Huron, MI: North American Compendiums, Inc. 1995.

Bloch A, Thomson CA. Position of the American Dietetic Association: Phytochemicals and functional foods. Journal of Nutraceuticals, Functional and Medical Foods 1997; 1: 33-45.

Childs NM, ed. Journal of Nutraceuticals, Functional and Medical Foods. Binghamton, NY: The Haworth Press Inc. (published quarterly).

Goldberg I, ed. Functional Foods: Designer Foods, Pharmafoods, Nutraceuticals. New York, NY: Chapman & Hall, 1994.

Hanson RR. Mode of action of oral chondroprotective agents in feline practice. Feline Practice 1996; 24(5): 8.

Poppenga RH. Risks associated with herbal remedies. In: Bonagura JD, ed. Current Veterinary Therapy XII. Philadelphia, PA: WB Saunders Co, 1995; 222-226.

Bisset NG, ed. Herbal Drugs and Phytopharmaceuticals. Boca Raton, FL: CRC Press Inc, 1994.

Definitions of functional foods and related terms

Chemopreventive agent	Nutritive or nonnutritive food component being scientifically investigated as a potential inhibitor of carcinogenesis for primary and secondary cancer prevention.
Designer food	Processed foods that are supplemented with food ingredients naturally rich in disease-preventing substances. This may involve genetic engineering of food.
Functional food	Any modified food or food ingredient that may provide a health benefit beyond the traditional nutrients it contains.
Nutraceutical	Any substance that may be considered a food or part of a food and provides medical or health benefits, including the prevention and treatment of disease.
Pharmafood	Foods or nutrients that claims medical or health benefits, including the prevention and treatment of disease.
Phytochemical	Substances found in edible fruits and vegetables that may be ingested by people daily in gram quantities and that exhibit a potential for modulating human metabolism in a manner favorable for cancer prevention.

with simple organic acids to control water activity and inhibit mold growth. Semi-moist foods often contain meat meals and artificial flavors and provide a sweet, savory flavor to dogs and an acidic note for cats. This pet food form is highly palatable and has an average intermediate preference between moist and dry pet foods.

Semi-moist foods are often packed in cellophane pouches or wrappers that have an apparent appeal for consistency and convenience in food dosage. Although patients requiring weight control and management of diabetes mellitus benefit from a consistent food dose, the higher sugar content and lower fiber content of semi-moist foods make them ill-suited for these feeding applications. Once very popular, semi-moist pet foods experienced a greatly reduced market acceptance in the 1990s. However, this form continues to be important as the high-flavor "bits"

component of some popular soft-dry pet foods. In the soft-dry form, the semi-moist component may look like burger pieces, cheese, pasta or vegetables and provide anthropomorphic appeal to pet owners because of the appearance of ingredient variety (Figure 3-4).

Treats

Treats are small food rewards that owners use for reinforcement of their bonding with pets, as training aids and just for fun. A survey of 1,000 United States households revealed that 80% of dog owners fed human foods or table scraps as treats and almost nine of 10 respondents had fed commercially prepared treats or snacks.[5] A second survey conducted by veterinary epidemiologists concluded that about 60% of dogs received treats in some form and 30% were also given meat or meat juice.[6] Market research indi-

Figure 3-4. Semi-moist pet foods are no longer popular in the United States, although semi-moist foods are frequently blended with dry pet foods to make soft-dry combinations. The soft-dry pet food shown here contains two different dry foods and two different semi-moist foods. The semi-moist food improves palatability and provides anthropomorphic appeal by simulating pieces of meat and

Figure 3-5. Dried animal tissues are popular pet treats. Examples shown here include bovine penis, porcine penis, porcine tail, ovine lung, beef kidney, porcine ear, bovine liver, porcine nose, bovine trachea, turkey feet, bovine chin tissue and whole fish.

cates that more than 90% of dog owners who purchase specialty dog food brands give their dogs treats.[a] Sixty-five percent purchase biscuits, 45% buy "bones" and 40% buy chews. About half of these dog owners give their dogs treats every day; on average these respondents provide treats for their dogs five to six times per week. The pet typically receives two treats per treating occasion.

The variable contribution of treats to the daily nutrient intake is easily ignored by pet owners and those taking and interpreting a dietary history. As a generalization, dietary balance is maintained when less than 10% of the daily intake consists of table scraps or treats and the remainder is a prepared food that is complete and balanced. At low levels, treats can be considered nutritionally trivial except in certain medical conditions. However, excess treat intake interferes with normal appetite and dietary balance and can contribute to obesity. Inappropriate use of treats might include when: 1) the quantity consumed exceeds the manufacturer's recom-

mendation, 2) the pet has a high intake of cream, meat, organ tissues and processed human foods, and 3) up to 20% of the daily energy requirement is provided by treats used for dental benefits.

The nutritional content of commercial pet treats and human foods used as treats is found in Appendix M. An increasingly popular treat form is dried animal tissues (e.g., bovine penis, tail, tendon, or hoof and pig's ears) (Figure 3-5). Dried animal tissue treats are more than 85% protein, which often are characterized by a high-collagen content of low biologic value.

Chocolate is not recommended as a treat because the half-life of theobromine is prolonged in dogs. Fatality has occurred when toy or small dogs ingest as little as 20 g of baker's chocolate.[7] Unfortunately, treats that look like chocolate are commonly encountered in pet stores. This treat category may foster the dangerous and erroneous notion that it is safe to feed pets real chocolate or chocolate-containing candy.

Treats can be part of the dietary management of obesity, diabetes mellitus, urolithiasis, cardiac failure, renal failure and adverse reactions to foods when used under medical supervision.

Supplements

Supplements are different from treats, although the two are sometimes confused. Treats are nutritionally trivial, but supplements are very concentrated nutrient modules. The proper role of a supplement is to correct a diagnosed nutrient deficiency. Unfortunately, many supplements are overprescribed and present some risk for abuse and toxicosis.

The most common form of veterinary supplements is a wide variety of vitamin and vitamin-mineral combinations that are used by 10% of animal owners.[6] Mineral and electrolyte supplements include calcium, phosphorus, sodium, potassium, magnesium, iron and zinc. Protein and amino acid supplements (including taurine) are also common but should only complement the base food in situations of repletion feeding.

Routine use of vitamin-mineral supplements is not needed when a dog or cat eats typical commercial pet food. One set of authors evaluated the daily calcium and phosphorus intake of adult dogs and cats consuming an average dry commercial pet food compared with the daily recommended allowance (Table 3-1).[8] In dogs, average calcium and phosphorus intakes were almost three times the daily allowance, whereas in cats, intakes were 65 to 75% above the allowance. This finding suggests that supplementation of normal commercial rations with calcium and phosphorus is unnecessary. Similarly, these authors compared levels of daily vitamin intake (Table 3-1).[8] They found that dogs and cats consuming commercial dry rations were ingesting from two to five times the daily allowance of vitamins. Thus, the need for routine supplemental vitamins is questionable at best when dogs and cats eat a typical commercial pet food. For pregnancy, lactation and growth, all-purpose or specific-purpose growth pet foods contain adequate nutrient levels; supplementation will not benefit these conditions.

Fat supplements provide a concentrated source of calories and essential fatty acids. Corn, safflower, canola and sunflower oils mix easily with food and provide a cost-effective source of additional linoleic acid. Commercially available fatty acid supplements emphasize linoleic acid, gamma-linolenic acid and mixtures of various omega-3 fatty acids (eicosapentaenoic and docosahexaenoic acid). The usual objective for fat or fatty acid supplementation is to increase caloric intake or to manage seborrhea sicca, pruritus or keratinization disorders. (See Chapter 15.)

Various herbs and yeasts have been advocated for flea control but these products have no demonstrated efficacy.[9] Human health foods are also used to supplement pet foods. These items include sea salt, kelp, algae, lecithin, chelated minerals, enzymes and probiotic digestants of enteric microorganisms. (See sidebar "Nutraceuticals.") These items may be used in homemade foods or by owners who take these supplements themselves.

The correct use of supplements is based on a diagnosis of a nutrient deficiency. Unfortunately, supplements are commonly used as "insurance" against suspected deficient intake. They may also be used when super-supplementation of a particular nutrient is perceived as a need. In the first case, a more effective, less costly and safer approach is to simply exchange the suspect food and its corrective supplement for a food that is nutritionally adequate. The super-supplementation approach creates risk for toxicosis or dietary imbalance and can violate the treatment principle of "Above All, Do No Harm."

PET FOOD MARKETING CONCEPTS

Marketing concepts identify how a product will be advertised and sold. Understanding basic marketing concepts helps veterinarians and their health care teams evaluate advertising and answer questions from pet owners who are influenced by such advertising. Most clients know little about their pet's nutritional needs and are understandably susceptible to advertising claims. (See sidebar "Product Claims.") Basic marketing concepts for pet food include: 1) specific-purpose foods, 2) all-purpose foods, 3) low price, 4) people food, 5) flavors and varieties, 6) presence of an ingredient, 7) absence of an ingredient, 8) more is better, 9) product name and 10) natural foods. There may be modifications, combinations and cross-over among these basic categories. Additionally, more than one concept may be used by the same company for different brands so that if one feature does not appeal to a pet owner, perhaps another will.

Specific-Purpose Foods

The objective of the specific-purpose concept is to provide a specialized nutrient profile for a particular feeding application. When owners select a specific-purpose product it is often because they have been educated to understand the points of difference between all-purpose and specific-purpose products.

Many specific-purpose foods are sold from value-added environments such as veterinary hospitals, where educational opportunities often occur. Some grocery store brands also offer specific-purpose products and rely on advertising and packaging to communicate their purpose. Even though a product is named or marketed as fulfilling a specific application, it may or may not actually deliver the expected benefit.

Specific-purpose foods can be divided into lifestage and special needs groups. Lifestage products are formulated to provide appropriate nutrition based on pet age or "lifestage." The primary lifestage types are: 1) growth or puppy/kitten foods, 2) adult or maintenance foods and 3) senior/geriatric foods.

Table 3-1. Daily intake of calcium, phosphorus, vitamin A and vitamin D by an adult dog or cat consuming a typical commercial dry pet food.*

Dog	MDR**	Average intake
Calcium (mg/kg/day)	25	74
Phosphorus (mg/kg/day)	19	54
Vitamin A (IU/kg/day)	23	67
Vitamin D (IU/kg/day)	2.3	11
Cat		
Calcium (mg/kg/day)	41	70
Phosphorus (mg/kg/day)	36	67
Vitamin A (IU/kg/day)	46	121
Vitamin D (IU/kg/day)	4.5	9.1

*Adapted from Kallfelz FA, Dzanis DA. Overnutrition: An epidemic problem in pet animal practice? Veterinary Clinics of North America: Small Animal Practice 1989; 19: 433-446.
**MDR = Minimum daily requirements. From Nutrient Requirements of Dogs and Nutrient Requirements of Cats. National Academy of Sciences, Washington, DC: National Academy Press, 1985, 1986.

Special needs products provide specialized nutrition for individual pet needs. For example, rapidly growing puppies of the large and giant breeds have increased risk for developmental orthopedic disorders. (See Chapter 17.) Therefore, these puppies may benefit from a growth-type food specially modified to control nutritional risk factors such as excess calcium and energy intake. Other examples are light products for overweight animals and active products for animals with higher caloric requirements.

All-Purpose Foods

The all-purpose marketing concept is based on the premise that one product satisfies all nutritional needs at all times. These products must provide adequate nutrients to support the most demanding lifestages, which are growth and lactation. The advantage of all-purpose pet foods is that they require little explanation for use. Thus, they are suited for a grocery store-type distribution. Many national-brand, regional-brand, private label and generic foods use the all-purpose approach.

All-purpose foods are often assumed to be manufactured for adult animals. This assumption is based on the fact they are not called puppy or kitten foods and have pictures of adult animals on the package. However, these foods must be balanced to support the nutritional requirements for growth and lactation, even if they are fed to adult or geriatric animals. Thus, all-purpose foods provide nutrients in excess of allowances for adult and geriatric pets.

Low Price

For many pet owners, low cost is an important criterion for selecting pet foods. The unit price (cost per weight) is the most obvious way for consumers to compare cost but may be a poor method of judging value. Value-for-money is best evaluated by actually measuring feeding costs (cost per calorie or cost per day or year). Actual feeding cost evaluation may reveal that there are only small price differences between pet foods perceived as "inexpensive" and those perceived as "expensive." Additionally, many manufacturers of low-priced foods base their claims of nutritional adequacy on nutrient profiles rather than on test feeding of dogs or cats.

Product Claims

A claim promotes the relationship between a product and a desired attribute or result. Claims are important because they help pet food manufacturers (human food manufacturers, pharmaceutical manufacturers, etc.) differentiate their products from those of competitors, and in some cases, demonstrate product superiority. In the process, companies spend thousands to millions of dollars substantiating claims.

Pet food manufacturers make several types of claims, including: 1) nutritional adequacy, 2) light or reduced fat, 3) low magnesium, 4) palatability, 5) urinary pH, 6) metabolizable energy, 7) skin and coat benefits and 8) dental benefits (e.g., reduces plaque and calculus accumulation).

Claims appear in several product sites and on promotional materials. A claim may appear as part of a product name (e.g., "light formula") or as part of a product's labeling. Labeling is a broad term that includes the product's packaging (See Chapter 5.), print or television advertising and promotional literature (brochures, third-party articles, etc.).

CLAIM REGULATION

In general, pet food claims in the United States are regulated for legality, truthfulness, accuracy and fairness by the Center for Veterinary Medicine in the Food and Drug Administration (FDA) and by the individual states. In addition, the Federal Trade Commission has regulatory authority over media advertising (print, radio and television). Frequently, companies will choose to keep claims and/or advertising disputes out of the regulatory arena by mediating them with the National Advertising Division of the Better Business Bureau, a voluntary self-regulating industry body. When all else fails, these disputes enter the judicial system for final resolution. The Lanham Act is often the basis for these legal actions.

TYPES OF CLAIMS

Several types of claims exist: 1) general, 2) nutritional adequacy, 3) descriptive, 4) structure/function, 5) therapeutic foods, 6) health and 7) drug.

General Claims

General claims describe unique product attributes such as composition or ingredients, flavors and varieties, palatability and digestibility. These claims must be truthful and are often called "marketing" claims. Palatability claims are a frequently used type of general claim. These claims have a life span of about one year or until one of the products is changed before they must be resubstantiated.

Nutritional Adequacy Claims

For all practical purposes, nutritional adequacy claims are primarily regulated in the United States using the procedures and protocols established by the Association of American Feed Control Officials (AAFCO). To make a "complete and balanced" nutritional adequacy claim, pet food manufacturers must either conduct a feeding test (AAFCO protocol) or meet the minimum AAFCO nutrient profile. (See Chapter 5.) Lifestage claims are included as a subset of the nutritional adequacy claim.

Descriptive Claims

Descriptive claims must meet FDA/AAFCO requirements. Examples of descriptive claims include "light" or "low-calorie" foods. Low-calorie canine and feline foods must contain fewer than 3,100 and 3,250 kcal/kg of food, respectively. Another commonly used descriptive claim is "low magnesium" in feline foods for prevention of struvite urolithiasis. Low-magnesium foods must contain either less than 25 mg of magnesium/100 kcal of food or less than 0.12% magnesium on a dry matter basis. The amount of metabolizable energy in a food expressed on a kcal/kg basis is also a descriptive claim.

Structure/Function Claims

FDA approved structure/function claims include such things as, "Contains extra calcium for strong bones and teeth" and "Taurine is essential to the good health of your cat." Skin and coat claims are also generally considered structure/function claims.

Therapeutic Food Claims

Therapeutic food claims are regulated at the discretion of the FDA. Manufacturers who make therapeutic food claims formulate foods for the nutritional management of a condition or disease. Such claims must be backed by accepted scientific facts or data, and veterinary supervision is required for the administration of such foods. Examples of therapeutic food claims include, "Helps control the clinical signs associated with sodium and fluid retention," "An aid in the dissolution of struvite uroliths" and "A nutritional aid for dogs with dental stain, plaque or calculus."

Health Claims

Health claims state or imply a positive relationship between food and disease. Health claims require FDA approval; controlled studies must prove efficacy and long-term safety studies must also be conducted. Label claim wording must also meet FDA restrictions. The only FDA approved health claim for pet food involves feline lower urinary tract health. Examples of specific claim wording include, "Maintains feline urinary tract health" and "Reduces the risk of feline urinary tract disease."

Drug Claims

Drug claims are highly regulated by the FDA under the authority of the Federal Food, Drug and Cosmetic Act (FFDCA), specifically sections 501 and 512. These claims deal with the cure or prevention of a disease. Such claims require pre-market approval by the FDA, and require extensive resources to document safety and efficacy. Such research takes years to conduct, but, if the research leads to FDA approval, the product usually has market exclusivity. Drug claims are rarely made for pet foods.

E. Phillip Miller, DVM, MS
Diplomate ABVT (Veterinary Toxicology)
Diplomate ABT (Toxicology)
Hill's Science and Technology Center
Topeka, KS, USA

People Food

The concept behind "people-food" marketing is that a number of pet owners think their pets like and need the same foods people eat. Additionally, some people believe that human foods are inherently superior to pet foods. Some dogs and cats do like human foods, particularly meat-type foods. But, animals also voraciously eat items with no appeal to their owners (e.g., pet food, grass, vomitus, garbage and even feces and carrion). The concept of human food being superior to pet food is relative. First, people and pets have different nutrient requirements. Second, most pet foods are better balanced to meet the needs of dogs and cats than are diets for people.

Indeed, there is widespread public-health concern for human nutritional health in First World countries including inadequate intake of calcium, complex starches and fiber and excess intake of fat, saturated fat, cholesterol, salt and calories. For pet owners to feed their pet in duplicate could be a nutritional step backward for the animal. The desirability of feeding human food to pets is largely based on advertising themes designed to create anthropomorphic appeal. As a result, pet foods are often branded with recognizable human food names (chops, burgers, stews, pasta and gravy). This discussion is not intended to imply that pet foods that promote the people food concept are either good or bad, but simply to point out that the basis for the concept is not valid.

Flavors and Varieties

Flavor and variety marketing concepts are also based on anthropomorphic appeal because they fulfill the pet owner's assumption of the need for variety. From a pet food manufacturer's standpoint, offering many flavors and varieties increases the brand's potential shelf presence and exposes the shopper to more opportunities for purchase. However, in the wild, the diets of dogs and particularly cats, are somewhat monotonous.

Ingredients

Although flavor/variety descriptors often use ingredient names, ingredient-based marketing generally implies that the highlighted ingredients provide unique benefits to pets. However, fundamentally, ingredients and nutrients are not the same; the nutrient profile is important to animals and should be the primary focus rather than concern for specific ingredients.

In addition, products marketed on ingredient appeal usually contain other primary ingredients that may not be suggested by the ingredient name. If the veterinarian's objective is to restrict or exclude an antigen source, the ingredient list should be regarded as a better source of information than the product name. For example, most "lamb and rice" foods contain several protein sources in addition to lamb.[10]

Two variations on the ingredient-based marketing concept are "presence" of an ingredient and "absence" of an ingredient.

Presence of an Ingredient

Promoting the presence of a particular component in a pet food is a common marketing concept. An ingredient frequently promoted as beneficial for dogs is meat. The implied corollary is that meat is a high-protein food that is natural and enhances performance. The theme of "meat as desirable" is extended to "meaty" and "animal-protein" advertising themes. Manufacturers of dry dog foods that make a "meat-based" claim imply the presence of a high-meat content, which is not the case.

Likewise, fish is an excellent protein source for cats, but is not a natural food for most wild cats. Promotion of fish as desirable has historical roots in the low cost and availability of fish by-products from fish canning and filleting operations. Purported benefits have also been made for lecithin, wheat germ meal, mineral chelates, yucca extracts, herbs and probiotic bacterial cultures.

Absence of an Ingredient

Advertising the absence of a food component implies that a problem or danger may be associated with the ingredient. The marketplace example of "No Corn—Only Wheat!," or a competitor's reversed message, "Contains Corn—No Wheat!," creates consumer confusion and insecurity about both cereal sources. Although there are nutritional differences among grains (See Chapters 2 and 4.), no specific grain commonly used in pet foods is harmful or deserves fear-mongering. Other examples of negative marketing include denigration of the following ingredients: soy (bloating and gastric dilatation-volvulus), by-products (inferior fillers), "synthetics" (non-natural) and ethoxyquin (poison).

In pet food advertising, "no fillers" is used by manufacturers to prey on pet owner misconceptions. Consumers call almost every pet food ingredient other than meat and vitamins "filler," including grains, fiber sources and animal by-products, which are excellent nutrient sources.

More Is Better

A variant on the presence of an ingredient theme is "more is better." For example, some pet owners believe a "high-protein" content in a pet food benefits exercise and is necessary for hard-working dogs. In reality, prolonged hard work only slightly increases the essential amino acid requirements of dogs. More energy—not more protein—is the primary need in athletics. (See Chapter 10.) Therefore, specific-purpose foods for dogs with increased work levels should be energy dense and highly digestible and should contain adequate but not excessive levels of a high-quality protein. "Enough is best" is a better concept than "more is better."

Product Name

The product or brand name can become a marketing tool when it is amusing, easy to remember or authoritative. Brand names such as Happy Cat, Cycle 3, Bow-Wow, Eukanuba, Vet's, Vet's Choice, James Well-Beloved, Prescription Diet and Dr. Ballard's are examples. Product and brand names can also help identify and appropriately reinforce the food's application. Kitten Chow, Feline Maintenance and Canine Senior are examples.

Natural Foods

Sales of natural pet food products have increased markedly in the 1990s. However, the term "natural" is not legally defined or legally regulated and is, therefore, open to interpretation. The term has been applied to a wide range of pet foods with a variety of ingredients and characteristics. The current market definition of "natural" usually indicates a pet food that contains or does not contain certain ingredients or additives.[11]

Research has identified several factors that consumers seek in natural pet foods. To pet owners, a natural pet food is nutritious and free of artificial preservatives and colors.[a] The absence of artificial preservatives appears to be the most important feature of natural pet foods to pet owners in the United States.[a]

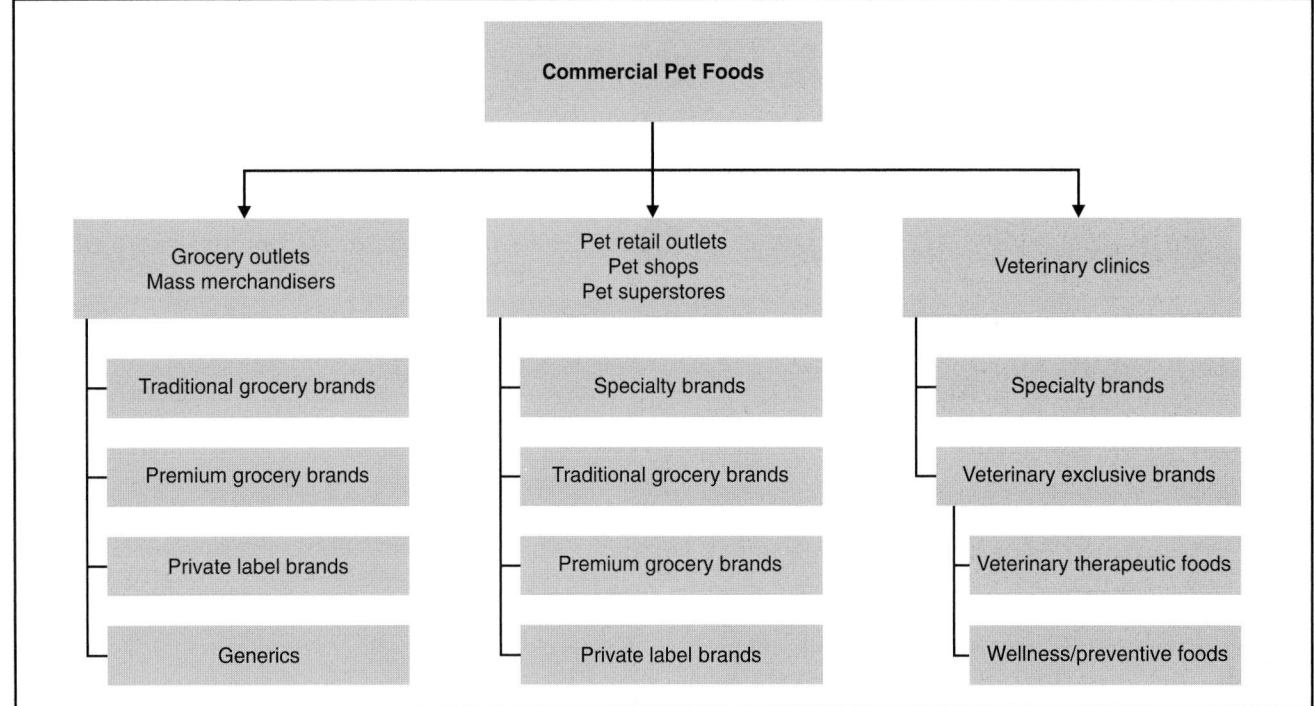

Figure 3-6. This diagram shows the market segments and usual distribution outlets of commercial pet foods.

PET FOOD SEGMENTS

Pet food brands have proliferated during the 1980s and 1990s, each attempting to carve out a new "segment" in the market (Figure 3-6). The following discussion will provide a broad overview of the various segments, as well as, general definitions of the product types that fall in each.

Grocery Brands

Traditionally, pet food was sold in grocery stores, and the brands that were sold in this outlet were called "grocery" brands. Grocery brands are national in scope. Many are well-recognized "household words" with high exposure levels due to large-scale advertising and wide distribution. Grocery outlets are the primary source of commercially prepared pet foods globally. Most grocery brands are "all-purpose" foods, balanced for growth/lactation. However, there has been a trend toward specific-purpose foods (lifestage and special needs) among traditional grocery dry brands.

The usual marketing theme for this segment combines a warm, friendly image with high palatability, flavor variety and moderate pricing. Palatability receives overwhelming attention in grocery brands through advertising that associates eating with gusto and rapid, voracious ingestion of food with pet satisfaction. In this context, pet owners feel that they are being "good" to their pets by providing a food that is enthusiastically consumed. "Gourmet" foods are a marketing subniche that further escalates the palatability message to accommodate "finicky" tastes.

"Premium" grocery brands are a relatively new set of brands sold in grocery outlets with a more nutritional focus. These foods are almost always specific-purpose foods with limited flavor offerings and a slightly higher price.

Private Label Brands

Private label or "store" brands are increasingly popular in larger national or regional supermarket chains and pet retail outlets. These foods are usually manufactured by a third party according to specifications established by the customer (e.g., chain or pet retail outlet). Private label brands can be identified by the label, which will state "Distributed by ____" or "Manufactured for ____" instead of "Manufactured by ____." These brands may be formulated, packaged and priced similarly to traditional grocery and premium brands. Ingredient selection and quality varies from good to poor. Many private label brands use a least-cost formulation. Although private label brands lack advertising saturation, their higher profit margin provokes favorable in-store merchandising, making them increasingly competitive with other brands in their segment.

Generic Pet Foods

Generic pet foods are nonbranded products (packaging often includes white or yellow boxes with black lettering). Their primary selling point is low price, which is achieved through the use of the lowest cost ingredients, manufacturing processes and packaging. Generic pet foods are usually produced locally or regionally to reduce transportation costs. Poor growth performance and zinc deficiency have been described in dogs eating generic foods. A jargon expression of "generic pet food syndrome" has been developed to describe some of the pathologic conditions that result from feeding certain generic pet foods. (See Case 15-2.)

Specialty Brands

Specialty brands are also called "premium" and "super-premium" foods and, like premium grocery brands, are more likely to emphasize superior ingredients and nutrition as a guiding philosophy. Specialty brands are distinguished from premium grocery brands by the outlets from which they can be purchased: pet stores, pet superstores, veterinary hospitals and some farm/feed and garden center outlets.

Most of these brands use the lifestage and special needs (specific-purpose) approach. Specialty pet foods are likely to confirm ingredient and final product quality by regular analytical testing and nutritional adequacy through feeding trials. Although there are points of similarity between brands, manufacturers in this segment are also likely to maintain differing nutritional management philosophies for particular feeding applications.

The growth of the specialty pet food segment has been robust because many pet owners realize that daily feeding costs are reasonable despite higher unit costs. The distinction between premium and super-premium is ill-defined, although ingredient choice and quality may be factors. Price is the primary differentiating factor.

Veterinary exclusive wellness brands are an additional subsegment within the specialty market. These products largely conform to the same descriptor as specialty brands except they are available only through veterinary hospitals. Manufacturers of these brands generally place a greater emphasis on the role that nutrition plays in disease prevention.

Veterinary Therapeutic Foods

Although veterinary therapeutic foods represent a very small market segment of the overall pet food industry, they have disproportionate importance to veterinarians. These foods have unique nutrient profiles that provide therapeutic synergy with medical and surgical modalities for a wide variety of disease conditions (Table 3-2). These foods usually have a specific purpose and should only be used under professional supervision. (See sidebar "FDA Perspective: Veterinary Medical Foods.")

■ MEASURING PET FOOD FEATURES AND BENEFITS

Veterinarians are frequently asked by pet owners to recommend or compare various commercial pet foods. Palatability, digestibility, stool quality and feeding costs are often mentioned as important pet food features by animal owners and are often highlighted in advertising and promotional materials by pet food manufacturers. It is important for members of the veterinary health care team to understand these pet food features and benefits in order to make informed recommendations to clients and interpret advertising and other promotional materials.

Pet Food Preference and Acceptability

Measuring the sensory aspects of eating evaluates the sum of the pleasant and unpleasant sensations that arise from the presentation and ingestion of food. Although "taste" is obviously important, the gustatory attributes of a food are only one of the variables involved. Olfaction, texture and eating experience also influence intake.

Table 3-2. Examples of signs and disorders often managed with veterinary therapeutic foods.

Adverse reactions to food (food allergy or food intolerance)
Anemia
Anorexia
Ascites/edema
Cardiovascular disease
Colitis
Constipation
Convalescence
Dental plaque, calculus and stain
Diabetes mellitus
Diarrhea
Exocrine pancreatic insufficiency
Feline hepatic lipidosis
Feline lower urinary tract disease
Gastroenteritis
Gingivitis
Heart failure
Hepatic disease
Hyperlipidemia
Hypermetabolic states
Hypertension
Obesity
Oral malodor
Pancreatitis
Renal failure
Surgical recovery
Urolithiasis

Preference and Acceptance Testing

"Preference" and "acceptance" are specific measurement techniques to assist in the investigation of alleged pleasant or unpleasant sensations of food intake. Obviously, investigators must infer these sensations indirectly in nonverbal animals. The measurement methods used in such tests must be of sufficient statistical power to reduce bias errors. Testing should also incorporate controls for potentially confounding variables such as high or low caloric density, hunger, preference for a single-feeding pan position and environmental distractions.

The two primary assessment tools are the one-pan acceptance (monadic) test and the two-pan preference test. The one-pan test measures acceptability; that is, it simply determines if a given food is palatable enough to be eaten in sufficient quantity to maintain the subject's body weight in a neutral state. The two-pan preference test measures "choice" between a pair of test foods that are fed simultaneously side by side. In application, the results of a two-pan preference test may indicate that animals distinctly prefer one of the foods, thus the preferred food would be termed more "palatable." However, the "losing" food could still be quite palatable and could be consumed in sufficient quantity to support body weight.

PREFERENCE TESTS

Two-pan palatability tests are broadly used in the pet food industry to assess comparative food preferences. During the test, animals have simultaneous access to an excess quantity of the test foods. This allows the animal to eat all of one of the foods and none of the second, or some of each food and not become hungry. The total food consumed from each pan is measured after a timed interval. At each successive meal, the position of the food pans is alternated within the animal's enclosure to cancel any bias for a favored or habitual eating location.

FDA Perspective:
Veterinary Medical Foods

A "medical food" is defined as "a food that is formulated to be consumed or administered enterally under the supervision of a physician and is intended for the specific dietary management of a disease or condition for which distinctive nutritional requirements, based on sound scientific principles, are established by medical evaluation." Although the definition is only in reference to foods for human consumption, it could also be adapted to apply to "veterinary medical foods," which are generally intended to be offered as the sole source of nutrition to animals with specific medical conditions, and usually contain restricted amounts of certain nutrients to aid in the mitigation of some disease processes.

These products are often identified on the market by the label bearing the phrase "use under the direction of a veterinarian" or some similar wording. As foods, veterinary medical foods are subject to the same labeling requirements as are any other nonmedicated pet food. As such, labels may not bear drug claims. This restriction also applies to product names. Thus, these products are often given names that would not be easily recognized by the average consumer, such as initials or numbers. Also, veterinary medical food labels must meet the same criteria for substantiation of nutritional adequacy by meeting the AAFCO nutrient profile or passing an AAFCO feeding trial protocol or include the phrase "for intermittent or supplemental use." Because directions for use are presumed to be given to the owner by the veterinarian, veterinary medical food labels are exempt from the requirement to include feeding directions.

Despite label restrictions, companies often establish the intended use of their veterinary medical food products as "drugs" through brochures, advertisements or other promotional materials. However, FDA recognizes that there are scientifically sound reasons for use of these products in some cases of disease in dogs and cats; thus these products serve a purpose for veterinarians, their clients and their patients. Also, veterinarians obviously must be informed of the indications, contraindications and directions for use of the products. Thus, FDA generally exercises regulatory discretion with respect to distribution of truthful information on diet and disease to veterinarians.

The same information distributed to pet owners; however, is of more concern. Proper use of these types of products requires adequate veterinary supervision. An owner who feeds a product for its desired therapeutic effect solely on the basis of labeling or advertising claims may cause harm resulting from improper diagnosis or treatment.

David A. Dzanis, DVM, PhD, Diplomate ACVN
Center for Veterinary Medicine
United States Food and Drug Administration

Although there are several methods of quantifying and expressing preference results, the only bias-free method is based on the intake ratio (IR):[12] IR = A/(A + B), where A and B are an individual animal's daily food consumption of each of two different foods. As an example, an animal ingests 200 g of Food A and 110 g of Food B. Using the equation, IR = 200/(200 + 110) = 200/310 = 0.65. Thus, 65% of the food consumed by this animal was Food A. Ratios greater than 0.50 indicate the animal ate more Food A than Food B, ratios below 0.50 indicate more of Food B was consumed, and ratios equal to 0.50 mean equal amounts of Food A and Food B were consumed.

For groups of test animals, the ratio can be summarized in two ways. First, any animal with a ratio greater than 0.51 can be classified as preferring Food A, whereas animals with ratios less than 0.49 can be classified as preferring Food B. Those animals whose ratios fall between 0.49 and 0.51 would be classified as having no preference. The result for the group can then be expressed as the percentage of animals preferring Food A, preferring Food B or having no preference. Although this "percent preferring" measure tends to be statistically insensitive (e.g., either large sample sizes or large differences are required to achieve statistically significant results), it substantiates advertising claims that are "consumer friendly" (e.g., seven out of 10 dogs preferred Food A to Food B).

The ratio can also be summarized for a group of animals by simply reporting the average intake ratio. Average daily intake ratios should not be confused with average consumption ratios. Only the former ratio is free from measurement bias, is more statistically sensitive and is, therefore, recommended to guide product development.

ACCEPTANCE TESTS

The one-pan or monadic method quantifies food acceptance. In most cases, this technique is less sensitive than the two-pan method. Although two-pan differences do not reliably produce one-pan differences, one-pan differences almost always produce two-pan differences.

Thirty animals (15 in each of the subgroups shown below) provide a reliable test platform as follows:

Group	Days 1-5	Days 6-7
A-B	Feed Food A	Feed Food B
B-A	Feed Food B	Feed Food A

Assuming consumption is stable after Day 3, the data collected across Days 4 to 7 are calculated and interpreted in the manner described above for two-pan preference tests.

Sensory Aspects of Preference

The primary sensory modalities for canine and feline food acceptance and preference are smell, taste and texture. The relative roles played by each modality in animals has been studied and debated.

SMELL

The olfactory system of dogs and cats is very highly developed. People have about 3 to 4 cm² of olfactory epithelia. Cats have about 21 cm² and dogs have 18 to 150 cm², with a high density of central nervous system neurons related to olfaction.[13] This highly developed olfactory system gives some dogs their legendary ability to detect extremely low concentrations (1 x 10^{-11} molar) of some solutions and to discriminate between the scents of identical twins.[14] Anosmic dogs have a greatly reduced ability

The duration and number of animals required for a preference test depend on the animal days necessary to yield the statistical power requisite for test objectives. Sixty animal test days (30 animals for two days) provide a stable and repeatable assessment platform for screening purposes. However, 120 to 240 animal test days are commonly used for more statistically rigorous preference examinations.

to distinguish different foods. Despite the clear importance of olfaction to dogs and cats, foods must also provide taste for animals to show a sustained interest.[15]

TASTE

In people, taste is confined to four basic groups: sweet, salty, bitter and acidic. Dogs and cats extend the range of taste sensitivity by detecting and responding to several amino acids that are only weakly bitter or acidic to people (Table 3-3). Some amino acids and peptides contribute to meaty and savory aromas. These effects can be intensified by complexing selected amino acids to selected sugars in Maillard ("browning") reactions.

Dogs and cats also respond to selected nucleotides and fatty acids that appear to increase the meaty taste perception. A nucleotide accumulates in decomposing animal tissue that cats dislike but not dogs, which may help explain the canine fascination with carrion.[15] Dogs respond to some simple monosaccharide and disaccharide sugars whereas cats have a weak interest or no interest in sugar or sugar solutions (Table 3-3). However, foods acidified with phosphoric or citric acid appeal to cats. These acids have been used in some brands of dry and semi-moist cat foods for many years. However, an acid taste is less preferred in moist cat foods and the general effect of any pH change is less marked in dogs.

TEXTURE/MOUTH FEEL

There is a significant oral-touch or mouth feel component to canine and feline food hedonics. Neither cats nor dogs like sticky foods. The size of ground cereal particles in dry foods, and the particulates in wet foods affect preference. The size and shape of expanded particles can be important; some dogs prefer an identical formula as an extruded chunk over a loose burger presentation. Contrary to owner perceptions, dogs also like larger kibbles of the same formula. Some cats prefer one shape of an identical formula to another and may develop strong preferences for mouth feel and the surface-to-volume ratio of certain shapes of dry kibbles.

VISION

Vision is important to the hunting and prey-seeking behavior of wild animals. However, any relationship between the limited color vision of dogs and cats and their preference for a food's color is unknown. Thus, the degree to which visual stimuli influence food preference is speculative. Highly manipulated food colorings are common, but are probably more appealing to pet owners than to pets.

Factors Affecting Food Preferences

WATER CONTENT

Dog and cat food preferences and moisture content correlate positively. On average, moist foods are preferred to semi-moist foods and semi-moist foods to dry foods. This effect is maintained but less clear cut when intake is adjusted for caloric consumption. Adding water to dry food increases preference for some pets. On the other hand, some animals refuse to eat dry kibbles softened with water. Some dogs and cats strongly prefer or are "addicted" to one food form.

Making a self-originating "gravy" is another way of adding moisture to food. "Gravy making" occurs when water is added to kibbles that are coated with a combina-

Table 3-3. Taste chemosensory neural groups that have been identified in dogs and cats.*

Neural group	Substances that stimulate the neural group
Dogs	
Group A	L-proline, L-cysteine, NaCl, fructose, sucrose
Group B	Malic acid, HCl, quinine hydrochloride
Group C	Nucleotides
Group D	Butyl chloride, phytic acid
Cats	
Group I	Malic acid, HCl
Group II	L-proline, L-cysteine, inorganic salts
Group III	Nucleotides

*Adapted from Boudreau JC, White TD. Flavor chemistry of carnivore taste systems. In: Bullard RW, ed. Flavor Chemistry of Animal Foods (ACS Symposium Series 67). Washington, DC: American Chemical Society, 1978; 102-128.

tion of gums, carboxymethylcellulose and digest. Adding warm water rehydrates the coating and releases savory volatiles. The act of making a gravy adds anthropomorphic appeal for owners who desire an element of home cooking for their pet. However, food safety concerns may arise when water is added to dry pet foods. (See Case 7-3.)

NUTRIENT CONTENT AND INGREDIENT SELECTION

In studies in which semi-purified foods were fed to cats, the food's protein content had little effect on preference levels.[16] However, increasing protein levels in typical pet foods has a positive effect on preference for dogs and cats. Savory characteristics may be especially strong for cats; cats seem to prefer the inclusion of some liver in their foods. Cats prefer liver to muscle meats and muscle meats to lung tissue. Dogs prefer beef, pork and lamb to chicken and liver. Horse meat is highly palatable to dogs.[17] Both species prefer fish as a protein source in moist foods, but the quality of fish is critically important to preference. The type of fish (white vs. "oily" species), the season of the catch and the cut and freshness of the fish are important variables. Other animal-source proteins some pets prefer include whey, cheese and egg.

Although dogs and cats prefer a high-meat content to a high-cereal content, cereal-based foods are acceptable to many animals. Dry foods must be cereal-based for manufacturing purposes. The specific cereal grain(s) and quality and processing parameters affect the olfactory and gustatory characteristics of dry pet foods.

Gelling agents include alginates, carboxymethylcellulose, pectin and gum combinations. These agents imbibe water in the course of forming aspic and gravy loaves and increase a food's palatability through increased water content. Gels have a neutral taste unless they are hydrated with meat juices. Additionally, pets may prefer a gelled food to a non-gelled form of the same formula if gelling eliminates a sticky texture. Breaking a gelled loaf into chunks increases the anthropomorphic appeal for owners and provides positive oral-touch impressions for cats. The advertising theme of flesh tearing as "natural" for cats is prevalent in some markets.

Dry foods have a lower total animal tissue content than moist foods, and the origin of animal source ingredients appears relatively less important than for moist foods. This effect may be due to the dilution effect of a higher cereal content or the loss of savory volatiles during processing. Higher fat levels in foods increase energy density and usually increase preference. Both animal and vegetable fat sources are palatable. Dry pet food formulas often combine some of each. Fatty acid aldehydes indicate oxidation damage and rancidity. These negative palatability factors usually occur in food inadequately protected with antioxidants.

COOKING EFFECTS AND FOOD TEMPERATURE

Dogs and cats prefer cooked meats to fresh meats. However, overcooking decreases preference, which is especially important if a "burned" flavor permeates moist cat foods. The controlled cooking of cereal starches during extrusion of dry foods is important to starch digestibility and the pet's preference for the final food. The serving temperature of pet food modifies olfactory cues and mouth feel. Dogs and cats prefer food served at body temperature (Figure 3-7). Rewarming refrigerated moist foods in a microwave oven can produce "hot spots." Learned aversions to foods may occur following accidental mouth burning.

PALATABILITY ENHANCERS

Most dry pet food particles are coated with flavor-enhancing agents such as "digests" of animal tissues. Digests are animal tissues enzymatically altered by proteolytic enzymes. When the tissue digestion process produces a desired amino acid and peptide content, sterilization and acidification of the proteolyzed slurry stop the enzymatic action. The digest is then applied to kibbles as a topical liquid or a coating powder.

Other palatability enhancers include salt, topically or internally applied fats, L-lysine, L-cysteine, monosodium glutamate, sugar and soy sauce. Blood and feather meals, nucleotides, yeasts, whey, cheese powder, fermented meats and yeasts, meat slurries injected at extrusion, hydrolyzed vegetable protein, egg and onion and garlic powders have all been used by various manufacturers to enhance palatability. Artificial flavor technology is becoming increasingly

evident; people may detect the odor of bacon, cheese and liquid hickory smoke in some pet foods and treats.

EFFECTS OF PAST FEEDING PATTERNS ON CURRENT FOOD INTAKE

Food experiences appear to influence canine and feline food acceptance and preference patterns. "Imprinting" is the preference for a familiar food as influenced by an animal's early ingestion experiences.[18] While puppies and kittens imprint on the inherent flavor cues found in mother's milk and preweaning solids delivered by their mother, they learn these flavors are "safe." Imprinting may be one way puppies and kittens learn what is to be hunted in addition to what is safe and nutritious.[18]

Aversion to new and unfamiliar foods and flavors occurs most commonly when animals receive a single food from an early age. "Novelty" is the behavior of enjoying new foods and flavors. In studies, dogs preferred novel foods and flavor changes when exposed to food rotation from weaning to two years of age.[1,18] Experience-based ingestive imprinting, aversion and novelty behaviors may help wild animals survive by allowing them to adapt to foods they are unaccustomed to when their typical food becomes scarce.

The surroundings in which a pet eats may also influence conditioned ingestive behaviors. Cats preferred a novel food when fed in their normal housing, but became aversive when the same food was presented in an unfamiliar environment.[19] Additionally, preference tests can differ between a laboratory setting and a home-feeding environment.[12] One effect of presenting a new food is a measurable, transitory increase in food intake.[20] This novelty response may occur even if the old flavor is preferred to the new one. The pet owner's anthropomorphic inference is that flavor boredom is a problem and the experience prompts more frequent flavor rotations. These events may set the stage for pets becoming "finicky."

FINICKY BEHAVIOR

Finickiness is defined as excessively particular or fastidious behavior. This behavior is commonly described as a human-caused problem resulting from a pet's conditioned expectations for frequent changes in food variety or flavor. Supermarket shelves contain a proliferating number of varieties and flavors. Some pet owners take advantage of this phenomenon and rotate the flavor they feed daily. Clearly, the emphasis given by many owners to satisfying the food preference(s) of their pets is a strong indication of how much pets are viewed as human surrogates.

Finicky can also be an intermittent, slow or "picky" eating pattern. In these circumstances, pet health care providers should consider the possibility that the pet is simply being overfed or the owner is confusing an appropriate autoregulation of food consumption with food refusal or flavor boredom. In either case, pet owners may be concerned when their pets' consumption doesn't match the high consumption/gusto portrayed by television advertising.

The pets' body condition score will need to be evaluated when helping clients deal with finicky pets. If the body condition score is normal (3/5) or the pet is overweight (4/5 to 5/5), the finicky behavior was probably acquired from excessive flavor rotation. Behavior modification, or gradually weaning the pet from a high-frequency flavor rotation to a more stable platform of less frequent changes, may correct the problem. Ritualizing the feeding routine to the same time, place, quantity and brand of food may also help.

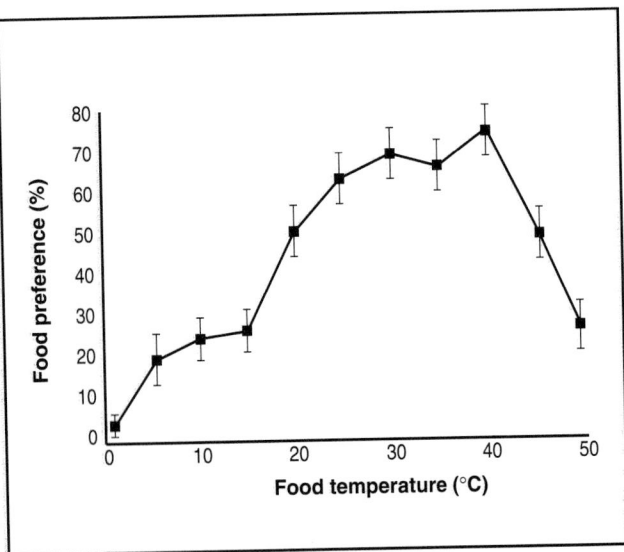

Figure 3-7. This graph demonstrates the influence of food temperature on food preference in cats. Data show the mean food preference of 23 cats fed moist food at various temperatures. Food preference was highest when food temperature approached the cats' body temperature. (Adapted from Sohail MA. The ingestive behavior of the domestic cat–A review. Nutritional Abstracts and Reviews—Series B, 1983; 53: 177-186.)

FOOD ADDICTIONS

Single-ingredient food addictions almost always cause compositional incompleteness or an imbalance in the nutrient profile, leading to nutritional deficiency, or toxicity syndromes. Progressive counter-conditioning (adding dilute pepper sauce to the addicting ingredient) while concurrently offering a complete and balanced pet food of the same general flavor as the addicting substance can be successful. In 14 separate single-food addiction cases, one of the authors successfully used this technique in all but three cats and one dog.[b]

Digestibility

Digestion is the various mechanical, chemical and bacteriologic degradation processes that reduce a complex food substance into absorbable entities such as amino acids, peptides, fatty acids and disaccharide and monosaccharide sugars. Digestibility is an important pet food feature. Although simple in concept, the integrated physiologic aspects of digestion are highly complex with numerous neuroendocrine control mechanisms operating at systemic and local levels.

Two measurable aspects are "apparent" and "true" digestibility. Apparent digestibility is quantified by measuring the difference between the dry matter content of an individual nutrient in the food and the quantity in the feces.[21] As an example, the % apparent protein digestibility is calculated:

$$\frac{\text{Protein food} - \text{Protein feces}}{\text{Protein food}} \times 100$$

Some fecal nutrient levels may be influenced by nondietary features. An example would be the protein or other sources of nitrogen in the feces contributed by sloughing intestinal cells, bacteria, mucus, blood, ammonia and urea. Nondietary factors that increase the fecal protein level reduce apparent digestibility.

True digestibility is a calculated value that must be established by first measuring the baseline value of endogenous output when a food devoid of a given nutrient is fed.[22] As an example, the % true protein digestibility is calculated as follows:

$$\frac{\text{Protein food} - (\text{Protein feces} - \text{Endogenous fecal protein})}{\text{Protein food}} \times 100$$

High digestibility yields more available nutrients for passive or active transport in intestinal absorption. Another benefit of increased digestibility is less food is needed to meet a pet's energy and nutrient requirements. Accordingly, high digestibility reduces food costs such that a pet food that appears more expensive to purchase on a unit price basis may actually be a better value than less expensive foods with lower digestibility and caloric density.

The primary determinants of digestibility are differences in ingredient selection and processing. For example, undercooked carbohydrates markedly reduce digestibility. The undigested residue can also alter the pH of intestinal chyme and may produce osmotic effects expressed as decreased stool quality and diarrhea.[23] Additionally, interbreed anatomic differences influence food digestibility in some dogs. In one study, Great Dane dogs had reduced relative gastrointestinal tract mass (weight) when compared with beagles. Giant-breed dogs also had more rapid oral-colon transit times, more voluminous feces and a higher content of fecal water and electrolytes. These effects were independent of food composition and form.[23-25] These findings suggest that, compared with smaller dogs, some large dog breeds are more prone to loose stools and may benefit more from highly digestible foods.

The results of testing for apparent digestibility are commonly used in pet food marketing as a measure of quality. This is often advertised under the "More is Better" concept. However, digestibility trial protocols permit either ad libitum or meal feeding of food quantities to maintain a neutral weight. If ad libitum feeding is chosen to test a more palatable food against a less palatable one, the more palatable food will probably be overconsumed and apparent digestibility will decline. Thus, the less palatable brand would appear more digestible.

Digestibility is one feature that can be altered to support specific applications in veterinary therapeutic foods.

Stool Quality

Fecal volume and consistency are of concern to many pet owners. In normal animals, fecal volume correlates with overall dry matter digestibility of the food, whereas the consistency of feces is affected by overall gastrointestinal motility and colonic function. Higher digestibility influences the quantity and quality of feces. Reduced dry matter intake reduces stool volume and may also improve the form and texture attributes relating to easy "clean-up" (Figure 3-8). Fecal volume, water content and firmness are especially important to owners of urban dogs who must pick up feces from gutters and curbs. These fecal attributes are also important to animal caretakers who care for dogs and cats in kennels and colonies where sanitation may be facilitated by washing elimination areas with high-pressure water sprayers. House-training puppies will also be easier if fecal volume is small and bowel movements are infrequent.

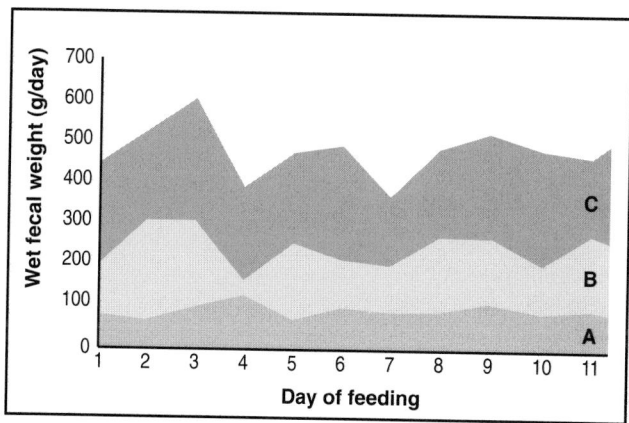

Figure 3-8. This graph shows the volume of feces (wet stool weight; grams per day) produced by the same group of laboratory beagles fed three different foods at quantities to maintain body weight. Food A is a commercial dry product formulated to provide concentrated calories and high digestibility for dogs with high-caloric requirements and those that have difficulty maintaining optimal body weight. Food A has a caloric density of 4.2 kcal/g (17.57 kJ/g) of food and energy digestibility of 88.5%. Foods B and C are commercial products. Food C has a caloric density of 3.5 kcal/g (14.64 kJ/g) and an energy digestibility of 80% Food B was formulated with a caloric density of 4.0 kcal/g (16.74 kJ/g) and an energy digestibility of 85%. Dogs need to eat greater quantities of these foods to maintain body weight. Note the inverse relationship between dry matter intake and fecal volume within the same group of dogs. These effects may be even more profound in large-breed dogs.

Cost of Feeding

Pet owners usually compare the cost of pet foods on the price per unit (e.g., price per bag or price per can) rather than the true cost of feeding (cost per day or cost per year). It is easy to compare the price per unit when evaluating two different pet foods, but more difficult to compare the true cost of feeding. The following example demonstrates that veterinarians and their health care team members need to discuss the true cost of feeding with pet owners when clients are concerned about the price of a particular food.

MOIST CAT FOOD

A 4.5-kg, three-year-old neutered male cat is diagnosed with lower urinary tract disease due to struvite urolithiasis. A moist veterinary therapeutic food (Food A) is recommended to help prevent further episodes of struvite urolithiasis. The cat's owner is concerned about the "high cost" of the veterinary therapeutic food, but would be willing to use Food A if it costs the same as what she now feeds her cat (Food B, a gourmet grocery brand). This calculation shows that the veterinary therapeutic food costs markedly less to feed than the cat's current food.

	Food A	Food B
Cost/can	$1.46	$0.50
Size of container	425 g	100 g
Cost/gram	$0.003	$0.005
Feeding amount (300 kcal/1,255 kJ)	214 g	350 g
Cost/day	$0.74	$1.75
Cost/year	$270	$639

Energy Content and Feeding Costs

The energy content and digestibility of a pet food directly affect feeding costs. The methods by which energy content can be determined and stated are regulated to ensure standardized reporting, which supports fairness to consumers. In the United States, any label statement for energy content must be limited to kcal of metabolizable energy per kg food and familiar measuring units (per can or measuring cup).

Feeding costs are directly related to the energy provided by a given volume of food and the cost of that food volume. True costs of feeding are best reflected by the cost of the food per day or year or the cost per calorie. (See sidebar "Cost of Feeding.")

■ ENDNOTES & REFERENCES

ENDNOTES
a. Laurie D. Hill's Pet Nutrition Inc., Topeka, KS, USA. Personal communication. October 1996.
b. Crane S. Personal observation. April 1996.

REFERENCES
1. Corbin J. Pros and cons of palatability enhancers available: Then and now. In: Proceedings. Focus on Palatability, Petfood Industry, Chicago, IL, 1995: 48-55.
2. American Animal Hospital Association. The 1995 AAHA Report. Trends Magazine 1995; 11(4).
3. McKey E. New study examines pet food trends. Pet Business 1993; 19: 270-300.
4. Hoffman T, Gaengler P. Epidemiology of periodontal disease in poodles. Journal of Small Animal Practice 1996; 37: 309-316.
5. Better Homes and Gardens Consumer Panel. Results of a survey. 1991.
6. Slater MR, Robinson LE, Zoran DL, et al. Diet and exercise patterns in pet dogs. Journal of the American Veterinary Medical Association 1995; 207: 187.
7. Hooser SB, Beasley VR. Methylxanthine poisoning (chocolate and caffeine toxicosis). In: Kirk RW, ed. Current Veterinary Therapy IX. Philadelphia, PA: WB Saunders Co, 1986; 191-192.
8. Kallfelz FA, Dzanis DA. Overnutrition: An epidemic problem in pet animal practice. Veterinary Clinics of North America: Small Animal Practice 1989; 19: 433-446.
9. Baker NF, Farver TB. Failure of brewer's yeast as a repellent to fleas on dogs. Journal of the American Veterinary Medical Association 1983; 183: 212-214.
10. Brown CM, Armstrong PJ, Globus H. Nutritional management of food allergy in dogs and cats. Compendium on Continuing Education for the Practicing Veterinarian 1995; 17: 637-658.
11. Kallfelz FA. Schools of nutrition: Processed foods. Veterinary Medicine Reports 1988; 1: 111-115.
12. Griffin R. Palatability testing: Lab versus home setting. In: Proceedings. Focus on Palatability, Petfood Industry, Chicago, IL, 1995: 124-145.
13. Dodd GH, Squirrell DJ. Structure and mechanism of the mammalian olfactory system. Symposia of the Zoological Society of London 1980; 445: 35-58.
14. Kalmus H. The discrimination by the nose of the dog of individual human odours and in particular of the odours of twins. British Journal of Animal Behaviour 1955; 3: 25-31.
15. Houpt DA, Hintz HA, Shepherd P. The role of olfaction in canine food preferences. Chemical Senses and Flavor 1978; 3: 281-290.
16. Morris JG. Nutrient content and dietary choice. In: Proceedings. Focus on Palatability, Petfood Industry, Chicago, IL, 1995: 36-42.
17. Heinicke HR. Factors affecting the palatability of canned and semimoist pet foods. In. Proceedings. Focus on Palatability, Petfood Industry, Chicago, IL, 1995: 57-68.
18. Thorne CJ. Understanding pet response: Behavioural aspects of palatability. In: Proceedings. Focus on Palatability, Petfood Industry, Chicago, IL, 1995: 17-34.
19. Boudreau JC, Slvalumar L, Do LT, et al. Neurophysiology of geniculate ganglion (facial nerve) taste systems; Species comparisons. Chemical Senses 1985; 10: 89-127.
20. Mugford RA. Comparative and developmental studies of feeding dogs and cats. British Veterinary Journal 1977; 133: 97.
21. Lewis LD, Morris ML Jr, Hand MS. Small Animal Clinical Nutrition III. Topeka, KS: Mark Morris Associates, 1987; 1-1–1-14.
22. Kendall PT, Blaza SE, Holme DW. Assessment of endogenous nitrogen output in adult dogs of contrasting size using a protein-free diet. Journal of Nutrition 1982; 112: 1281-1286.
23. Schunemann C, et al. Praecaecale und postileale verdaulichkeit verschiedener starken sowie pH-werte und gehalte an organischen sauren in darmchumus und faeces. Advances in Animal Physiology and Animal Nutrition 1989; 19: 44-57.
24. Meyer H, Kienzle K, Zentek J. Relation between body weight and the relative mass of the gastrointestinal tract. Journal of Veterinary Nutrition 1993; 2: 31-35.
25. Zentek J, Meyer H. Normal handling of diets–Are all dogs created equal? Journal of Small Animal Practice 1995; 36: 354-359.

CHAPTER 4

Making Commercial Pet Foods

Christopher S. Cowell

Neil P. Stout

Mark F. Brinkmann

Edward A. Moser

Stephen W. Crane

"Here shall you trace in flowing operation, in every state of practical, busy movement, the rills of civilization, materials here under your eye shall change their shape as if by magic . . . You shall see hands at work at all the old processes and all the new ones."
Walt Whitman, *Leaves of Grass*

INTRODUCTION

According to a 1996 report, there are 54.9 million dogs and 65.8 million cats in the United States.[1] Accordingly, 37.6% of households have at least one dog, and 32.9% have at least one cat.[1] Most pet owners in the United States feed commercially prepared pet foods daily. (See sidebar "History of Pet Food Manufacturing in the United States.") In 1995, pet food sales in the United States were reported to be $9.3 billion, up 6% from the previous year.[1] In 1986, pet food sales in the United States were $5.1 billion;[2] thus pet food sales have increased phenomenally in the United States during the past decade.

European and Asian countries have followed this trend towards commercially prepared pet foods. North America is the largest market followed by Western Europe and Asia. In the United Kingdom, for example, 90% of pet owners purchase commercially prepared pet foods at least once a week.[3] Pet food sales totaled $10.5 billion in Europe and $4.3 billion in Asia during 1992.[4]

This chapter describes the manufacturing processes used to prepare commercial pet food. The chapter is organized to follow the process of pet food manufacturing sequentially. The Extrusion section describes the processes of dry and semi-moist production including raw ingredient batching and mixing, extruding, drying, cooling and coating and packaging. The Canning section describes the process of canning, which includes meat grinding, mixing, can filling and sealing, sterilization and labeling. The Ingredient section covers common ingredients used in commercial pet foods, including their selection and nutritional and palatability contributions. Finally, the Quality Manufacturing section describes the processes of quality control, statistical process control, vendor selection and shelf-life maintenance.

COMMERCIAL PET FOOD MANUFACTURING

Principles of Extrusion/Dry Manufacturing

Most commercially prepared dry pet food is manufactured using a batch system (Figure 4-1). This system grinds and blends raw ingredients in predetermined amounts ranging from 1,000 to 5,000 kg, depending on capacity, then transports the resulting matrix to an extruder where it is cooked and formed into kibbles. After extrusion, the kibbles are transported to a

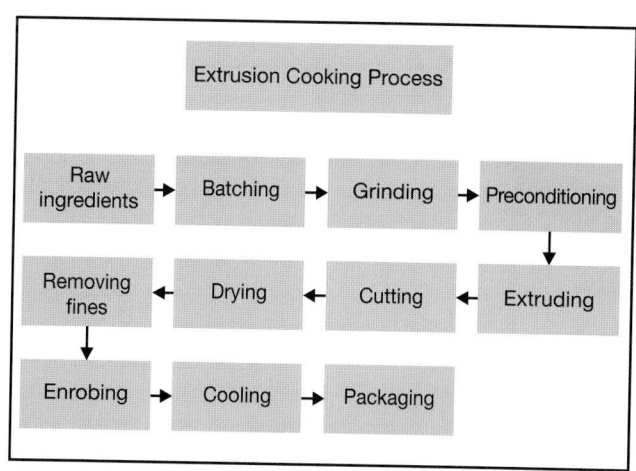

Figure 4-1. Process flow diagram for dry commercial pet food production.

KEY WORDS & TERMS—MAKING COMMERCIAL PET FOODS*

Antioxidant	Dry mix	Headspace
Aspic	Dryer	Humectant
Bring-down/cooling leg	Enrobe	Hygroscopic
Bring-up leg	Enrober	Kibble
Bulk ingredients	Ethoxyquin	Oxidative potential
Canning	Extrudate	Rancidity
Clostridium botulinum	Extruder	Retort
Commercial sterility	Filler/sealer	Shelf life
Compounding	Fines	Spin-out
Cooker/mixer	Gelatinization	Sterilization leg
Digest	Grease out	

* Key words and terms are defined in the Glossary.

KEY POINTS—MAKING COMMERCIAL PET FOODS

1. Commercial pet foods are a global multi-billion dollar per year business.
2. Good compounding (physically combining all of the dry mix ingredients) and mixing are essential to making a consistent, nutritionally adequate product. Improper manufacturing control or mis-compounding may result in unequal distribution of essential nutrients or lack of key ingredients in a product.
3. Extrusion is the most common processing method used to manufacture dry and semi-moist pet foods.
4. Extrusion uses a high-temperature short-time approach to fully cook and shape kibbles, which leads to improved digestibility, increased palatability and destruction of microorganisms and anti-nutritional factors.
5. Enrobing is the process by which liquid or dry coatings are applied to kibbles in the final step before packaging.
6. Water activity, not moisture content, is important in semi-moist foods. Most semi-moist foods have high moisture contents, but relatively low-water activity values because added humectants bind free water making it unavailable for microbial growth.
7. Hydrostatic or batch retorts are used to achieve commercial sterility (the absence of pathogenic microorganisms) in the production of canned pet foods.
8. The main pathogen of concern in manufacturing moist pet foods is *Clostridium botulinum*, a rod-shaped, spore-forming thermophilic anaerobe that produces a neuroparalytic exotoxin that causes botulism. *C. botulinum* is destroyed by temperatures greater than 116°C and will not grow when pH values are less than 4.6.
9. Although corn, rice, barley and oats have nearly identical ileal and total tract carbohydrate digestibility (all >98%), whole grains have differing dry matter digestibilities (rice >corn >barley >oats) due to differing fiber levels.
10. The protein-to-ash ratio is a good indicator of an ingredient's dry matter digestibility and efficiency in providing protein. The higher an ingredient's ash content, the lower the digestibility.
11. Fiber can be classified as soluble or insoluble. Each class has distinct advantages and disadvantages and should be chosen to fulfill a particular purpose. Soluble fibers are fermentable and important for gut health, but bind minerals. Insoluble fibers are excellent calorie diluents and are relatively inert.
12. Each type of fat has several different grades of quality as measured by peroxide value and free fatty acids, which indicate rancidity.
13. Modern factories use statistical process control in the manufacturing process to ensure the most consistent finished product quality.
14. Shelf life is the amount of time a product maintains nutritional, microbial, physical and organoleptic (sensory) integrity.
15. Antioxidants are compounds that function as one or more of the following: electron donors, oxygen scavengers, free radical scavengers or hydrogen donors.
16. The oxidation cascade creates rancidity with objectionable odors and flavors and functionally destroys the fat-soluble vitamins: A, D, E and K.

dryer where they are dried to target moisture, and then transported again by air or vibratory or conveyor belts to sites where fat and flavor enhancers are sprayed or dusted on the surface. The kibbles may or may not be sent through a cooler. The finished product is then transported to packaging machines that place it in containers for shipment and distribution. The entire process is usually automated and computer controlled.

Raw Materials

Ingredients used to manufacture pet foods often are received in bulk (90,000 kg by train cars; 25,000 kg by truckload) as in the case of grains or meat meals, which are the primary ingredients of any dry product, or in 25- to 50-kg bags for ingredients used in small proportions (e.g., trace minerals, crystalline amino acids and vitamins). Ingredients received in bulk are usually stored in silos until needed. Generally, the form in which a manufacturer receives ingredients depends on the physical makeup of the manufacturing plant and how much and what kind of storage units are available. Most ingredient suppliers offer multiple shipment options to best suit the manufacturer.

Grinding

Grinding changes the particle size of ingredients to enhance their nutritional and process characteristics. Ingredients supplied as large particles may need to be ground before mixing.

History of Pet Food Manufacturing in the United States

Domestication of cats and dogs was probably influenced by the enticement of food. Formation of a mutually beneficial association between Egyptians who cultivated and stored grains and wild cats that found abundant rodent species in Egyptian homes and food storage areas likely affected feline domestication. In any case, feeding domestic cats and dogs with table scraps and supplemental scavenging was the method of feeding until the mid 1800s.

The first commercially available pet food was created in 1860 by James Spratt, an American living in the United Kingdom, who was unimpressed with shipboard biscuits given to his dog on the passage across the Atlantic Ocean. Spratt developed a dry "dog cake" or kibble that he sold to English huntsmen. Spratt's United States company continued to manufacture pet food until it was purchased by General Mills in the late 1950s.

The next influential figure in the pet food industry was an Englishman named F. H. Bennett. In 1907, Bennett's company was formed in New York City and introduced Milk-Bone dog biscuits, which were marketed as a complete dog food.

Spratt and Bennett were the two primary manufacturers of commercial pet food until the early 1920s when the Chappel brothers of Rockford, IL, began canning horsemeat for dogs under the Ken-L-Ration brand name. By the mid 1920s, Clarence Gaines of Gaines Food Co., Sherburne, NY, began selling dog meal in 100-lb bags thus creating "Gaines Dog Meal."

In the 1930s, new dog food brands including Cadet and Snappy helped make canned pet food more popular than dry foods. In 1941, canned pet food represented 91% of the market. World War II changed that picture drastically as pet foods were classified as "nonessential" and the tin used to manufacture the cans was of great value to the war effort. By 1946, dry foods represented 85% of the market.

In Raritan, NJ, Dr. Mark Morris, Sr., began manufacturing small batches of specialized foods for dogs with kidney disease in his small animal hospital. In 1948, Dr. Morris signed a manufacturing agreement with Burton Hill of Hill's Packing Co., Topeka, KS, to manufacture Raritan Ration B, later known as Prescription Diet Canine k/d for sale in veterinary hospitals, thus creating a new category of pet foods designed to aid in the dietary management of disease.

The modern era of dry pet food manufacturing began in 1957 and continued through the 1960s when the Ralston Purina Company, St. Louis, MO, introduced the first extruded dog and cat foods called Dog Chow and Cat Chow. Moist cat foods, predominantly canned fish varieties in single-serving 6-oz. cans, were the top sellers at this time. During this time frame, General Foods created Gaines Burger, a new food that incorporated the convenience of dry food with the palatability of canned foods. It was the first semi-moist dog product. Tender Vittles, the first semi-moist cat food, was created by Ralston Purina in the early 1970s.

Originally produced as a consistent high-quality food for research kennels, Science Diet, manufactured by Hill's Pet Nutrition, Inc., Topeka, KS, became the first specialty product line designed for different lifestages in 1968.

Commercial pet food sales continued to grow from the 1970s to the present with many new product introductions every year including moist, semi-moist, soft-dry and dry pet foods, treats, beverages and edible toys.

BIBLIOGRAPHY

Serpell JA. The domestication and history of the cat. In: Turner DC, Bateson P, eds. The Domestic Cat: The Biology of Its Behavior. Cambridge, UK: Cambridge University Press, 1988; 151-158.

Gruber G. The exciting history of the pet food industry. Petfood Industry 1975; 17(1): 43-49.

Generally, the larger the particle size, the more likely that pre-grinding is necessary. A good example of this type of ingredient is whole yellow corn. A milling device known as a hammer mill is most often used to grind raw materials and the final dry mix. The hammer mill is a large capacity milling machine that contains multiple free-swinging steel hammers and a sieve or screen that can be changed to create the desired particle size. Centrifugal force spins the hammers against the screen, pulverizing whole grains to 1,000 microns or less.[5]

The entire dry mix is usually ground to achieve the desired uniform particle size (e.g., usually the consistency of coarse flour). A uniform size is critical for proper water absorption, optimal passage through the extruder and thorough cooking by the extruder.[5] Large uncooked particles may clog the extruder die and may reduce palatability, product appearance and digestibility.

Compounding and Mixing

Good compounding (physically combining all of the dry mix ingredients) and mixing are essential to delivering a consistent, nutritionally adequate product. Improper compounding will result in unequal distribution of essential nutrients or lack of key ingredients in a product.

Ground bulk ingredients are usually stored in large bins. From here, they are blown, via negative air flow, into mixing hoppers. Ingredients that form a smaller percentage of the product can be added by hand and combined with bulk ingredients. Computer-controlled scales weigh dry mix ingredients to ensure they are present in desired quantities.

After a "batch" of dry mix is compounded it must be properly mixed. Mixer types and times are carefully selected based on the flow characteristics of the ingredients that compose the mixture. Because particle size, density and shape influence flow characteristics, a ribbon blender is often used for thorough mixing.[6] A ribbon blender is a horizontal blending machine that has a shaft running through the middle of the mixer. A ribbon of steel attached to the shaft is the mixing element. A ribbon blender is able to thoroughly mix large quantities of dry ingredients (up to 5,000 kg) and is the most commonly used mixing device. After the finished dry mix is ground for the last time, it is transferred to the extrusion process area and stored in a bin.

Extrusion

Extrusion is the primary processing method for commercially prepared dry and semi-moist pet foods. The

Baking and Pelleting Technology

The first commercial pet foods were produced using baking technology. Currently, the baking process is used primarily for the manufacture of treats. The baking process uses equipment similar to that used for extrusion in the initial phases. Raw materials need to be finely ground and mixed before they are combined with water to form a "dough." The dough is then flattened by rollers as it proceeds to the forming stage called a rotary molding. The dough flows along a conveyor belt where it passes underneath a cylindrical rotor that contains the desired product shape outlines, similar to a large multi-shape cookie cutter. As the dough is "molded" into shapes, the rotor turns and releases the product now cut into shapes. An oven then bakes the product and in the final stages cools it so that it can be packaged.

Shape and product definition in baking are almost always superior to that of extrusion. Because the rotor can be tooled to make any detailed outline with little product expansion, the baked treat can have detail that extruded foods cannot achieve. The baking process, however, is less flexible than extrusion. High-gluten formulations (mostly wheat) are necessary to provide product shape and rigidity. Fat levels must be contained in a relatively small range. Too much fat will inhibit the molding process and too little will cause the newly formed pieces to stick in the rotor. Leavening agents must be used to expand the product and maintain texture.

The pelleting process, which is mainly used to make livestock feeds, is similar to extrusion, but has notable differences. The dry mix must be even more finely ground because the pellet mill has less flexibility in particle size than an extruder. The preconditioning phase is also longer in pelleting because most of the starch gelatinization must occur before product enters the pellet mill. Pressure from pressing the dry mix into the multi-hole die translates to cooking the mix and forming pellets.

The pelleting process is markedly slower and has a lower output than extrusion. Ingredient selection and process flexibility are limited in pelleting; the extruder can generate much more cooking energy, thereby allowing addition of internal fat and liquid that is incompatible with pelleting. Because pelleting uses less cooking time than extrusion (two to 16 seconds at 71 to 82°C vs. 10 to 270 seconds at 80 to 200°C), there is a greater risk for microbial growth and production of a non-commercially sterile product. In addition, extruded products are more digestible than pelleted products. The benefit of the pelleting process is its lower cost.

BIBLIOGRAPHY

Crane FM, Hansen M, Yoder R, et al. Effect of processing feeds on molds, *Salmonella*, and other harmful substances in feeds. In: Proceedings. Effect of Processing on the Nutritional Value of Feeds. National Academy of Sciences, Washington, DC, 1973: 72-90.

Ferket P. Technological advances could make extrusion an economically feasible alternative to pelleting. Feedstuffs 1991; 63(9): 19-21.

---

process itself can be thought of in terms of bread making: mixing, kneading, proofing (rising of the dough), shaping, rising and slicing (Figure 4-2). The first step in extrusion cooking is proper preconditioning of the dry mix to start gelatinization of the starches.

The dry mix is fed into the preconditioner by a weighing system that accurately maintains a constant feed rate. The preconditioner contains mixing/conveying paddles (Figure 4-3) that mix the dry mix and liquid additions (fat, meat slurries, etc.), along with water and steam to increase the moisture content and prepare the mixture for cooking and forming. Generally, the dry mix and any liquid additions are retained in the preconditioner for about 45 seconds. The preconditioner achieves a 20 to 25% cook of the starch (a measure of the completeness of extrusion cooking). Extrusion provides much more flexibility in processing different formulations than do pelleting or baking technologies. (See sidebar "Baking and Pelleting Technology.")

SINGLE-SCREW EXTRUDERS

Single-screw extruders were originally used in the plastics industry and later converted to all types of food applications and are used by approximately 90% of pet food manufacturers.[5] Extruders come in a variety of sizes from pilot plant prototype machines to large volume machines capable of extruding 12 to 15 tons of food per hour. Single-screw extruders consist of a cylindrical multi-segmented barrel with a single screw that propels, mixes and cooks the material and forces it through a multi-holed die where it is cut to the desired length by a rotating knife (Figures 4-4 to 4-6). This type of extruder operates on the principle of friction. The desired cooking of the dough is achieved when the material comes in contact with the barrel wall.[7] The most common type of single-screw extruder used in the pet food industry is called a high shear cooker extruder.[8]

The process conditions of the single-screw extruder can be adjusted to produce different types of products. For example, a high-fiber, low-fat formula produces significantly more friction, and is therefore more prone to overcooking than more conventional formulas. Reducing the screw speed, screw profile, feed rate or amount of preconditioning, increasing the fat, which helps lubricate the extruder barrel or a combination of these factors will compensate for this processing challenge by reducing the cook time (residence time). Residence times can be varied from 10 to 270 seconds with temperatures ranging from 80 to 200°C.[8] Because of the ingredient matrix used in pet foods, a high-temperature, short residence time (HTST) approach is used. The benefits of HTST extrusion include: 1) complete cooking, 2) destruction of microorganisms and 3) denaturing of anti-nutritional factors like trypsin inhibitor and hydrolytic enzymes that lead to rancidity.[8] Nutrient losses, however, are also incurred because of the high temperatures and shear forces. (See sidebar "Vitamin Losses During Processing and Storage.") Vitamin A and E losses of 21 to 26% and thiamin losses of 12% may occur.[9] Adding higher levels of these vitamins compensates for losses during extrusion.

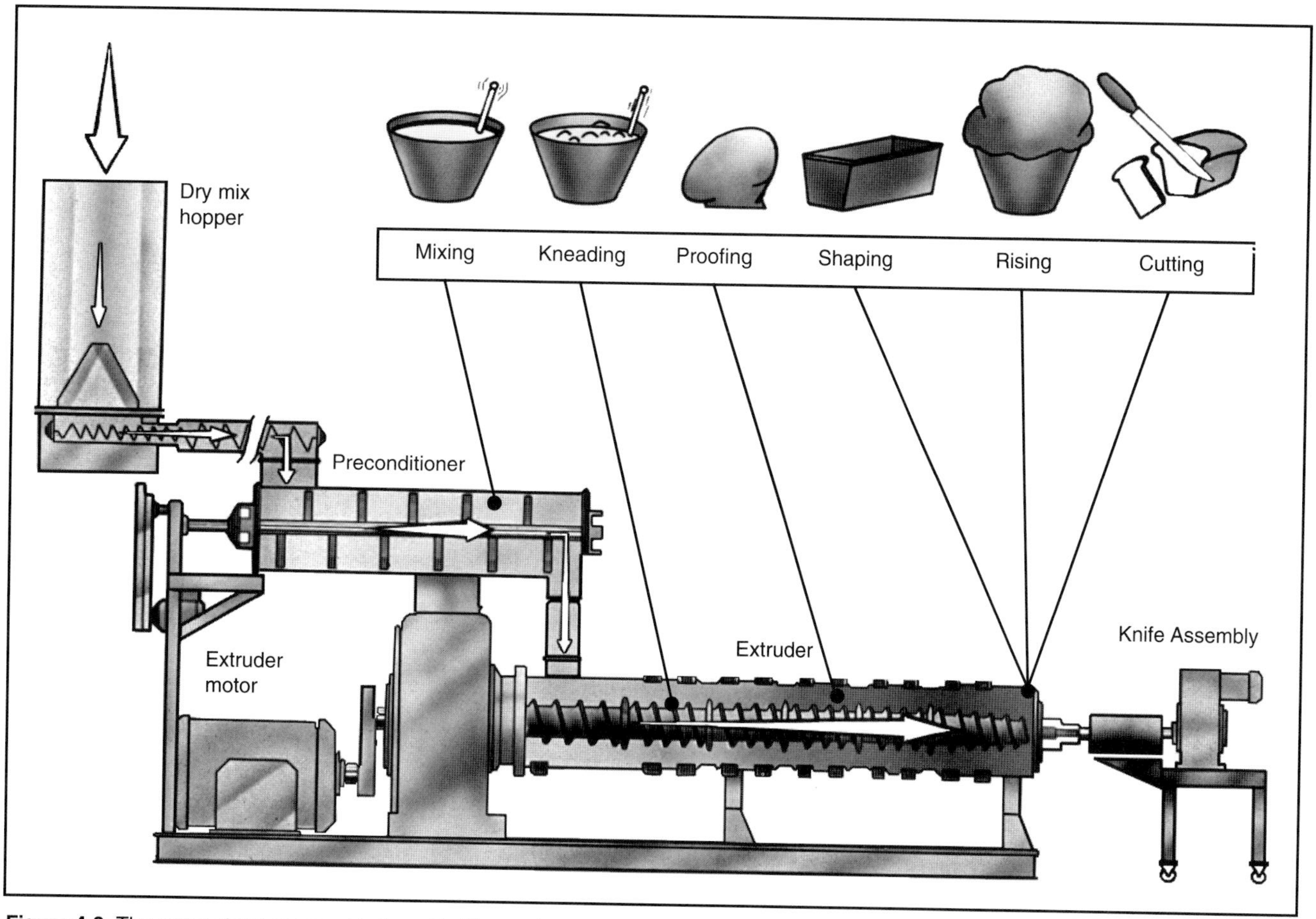

Figure 4-2. The same steps are used in bread baking and extrusion cooking: 1) mixing (preconditioner), 2) kneading (extruder barrel), 3) proofing (extruder barrel), 4) shaping (die plate), 5) rising (die plate) and cutting (rotating knives).

TWIN-SCREW EXTRUDERS

Similar to the single-screw extruder, the twin-screw extruder was borrowed from the plastics industry and introduced to the food industry in the early 1970s.[8] As their name implies, twin-screw extruders have components similar to those of single-screw extruders, except there are two screws. These screws may be either co-rotating or counter-rotating, intermeshing or non-intermeshing. The most common twin-screw extruder is the co-rotating, intermesh design (Figure 4-4).

The twin-screw design offers benefits over the single-screw extruder because its intermeshing screws mix more thoroughly, transfer more frictional energy and convey the dough forward more effectively. This allows a shorter residence time distribution (the amount of time the dough is in the extruder barrel) and more uniform cooking. Certain product formulations benefit from twin-screw extrusion. Products that contain a large percentage of internal fat (25%) can be made in the twin-screw extruder, but not in the single-screw extruder because of the lubricating effects of fat. Other products that are difficult to extrude, such as very sticky mixtures or formulas containing fresh meat, are more processable because of the increased pumping action and increased cooking ability of twin-screw extrusion.

DIE AND KNIFE

The final stage in the extrusion process occurs when the gelatinized dough-like material is forced through the openings of the die, which determines final product shape.

The die is a removable plate with one or more holes of the desired shape that is bolted to the head of the extruder barrel. Die configuration is an important piece of the process because the die contributes to the shape of the finished product (Figure 4-5), and provides the back pressure required for developing shear. The die is also the final

Figure 4-3. Extruder preconditioner used in commercial pet food production. The mixing and conveying paddles shown here initiate starch gelatinization and move the dry mix toward the extruder for cooking.

Figure 4-4. Pictures of single- (top) and twin-screw (bottom) extruders. The head of the extruder barrel has been removed showing the screw assemblies. Steam and liquid can be injected into the extruder barrel through hoses to modify the cooking process.

Figure 4-5. Various die inserts can be fitted into the plate at the end of the extruder barrel. The shape of the die will determine the shape of the dry kibble pieces. The dies shown here will produce oval, round, triangular or fish-shaped pieces.

cooking point in the extruder. The number of holes in the die, the shape of the holes and the thickness of the die all contribute to the density, texture and shape of the extrudate (the material in the extruder). Generally, several die holes will cause less expansion than a single die hole and thicker dies will produce smoother kibbles.

The extrudate is between 100 to 200ºC, contains approximately 25 to 27% moisture and is under tremendous pressure (34 to 37 atmospheres).[8] When the extrudate encounters ambient pressure and temperature at the die, moisture is flashed off, expanding the product (at least 50% greater than the die diameter) and creating the characteristic porous texture of dry pet food. A 3 to 5% moisture loss markedly cools the product and helps retain its shape.[10]

The extrudate resembles a rope as it leaves the die. A knife assembly on the face of the die is used to cut the extrudate to the desired size (Figure 4-6). The design and sharpness of the knife are critical to product appearance and size. The multi-bladed knife rotates at high speed shearing off the "rope," creating kibbles.

Drying/Cooling

The high-moisture, soft, spongy kibbles are conveyed by air to the dryer. During this conveyance, the kibbles lose another 2 to 3% moisture. The primary purpose of the dryer is to remove another 10 to 15% moisture from the kibbles. Heated air draws moisture out of the center of the kibble through the external surface where the moisture evaporates into the atmosphere. Reducing product moisture to between 8 and 10% inhibits mold and bacterial growth, thereby improving product shelf life.

The dryer is usually a long rectangular machine that contains an inlet with a swing feeder, a slow-moving conveyor belt and an exit (Figure 4-7). Dryers can be single or multiple pass, meaning that the product makes one pass through or, in the case of a double-pass dryer, the product tumbles from one level and doubles back before exiting. Various zones of the dryer can be heated to different temperatures to optimize drying. The first zones are usually heated to about 80 to 100ºC where the product is warmed and then moved into primary drying zones with temperatures of 120 to 150ºC. Finally, the kibbles are cooled to 80 to 100ºC before they exit the dryer. The typical retention time in a double-pass dryer with a cooling zone is 15 minutes for drying and seven minutes for cooling.[10]

Bed depth (height of the product on the conveyor belt), zone temperature, retention time and humidity all influence drying of pet food products. If the initial zones are too hot, the external surface of the kibble will dry too quickly sealing in the moisture, which is known as "case-hardening." As the moisture migrates through the external surface, microfissures can form that will make the kibble more fragile, leading to breakage and excess fine particles (fines) during packaging. If the product is too hot as it exits the dryer and is packaged without proper cooling, condensation will occur, creating an environment that encourages mold and bacterial growth.

Enrobing

Enrobing is the process by which coatings, either liquid or dry, are applied to the kibbles in the final step before packaging. Coatings may be applied in a rotating drum

Vitamin Losses During Processing and Storage

In a recent study conducted by a major supplier of vitamins to the human and pet food industries, investigators analyzed vitamin-fortified extruded and canned pet foods for vitamin levels. The purpose of the study was to examine the processing losses of vitamins and the recommended supplementation guidelines to offset those losses. The foods were sampled before processing, after processing and after three, six, 12 and 18 months of storage.

The results are shown in Tables 1 and 2 below.

Table 1. Vitamin losses incurred during processing and storage of canned dog and cat foods.

Vitamin	Moist cat food		Moist dog food	
	Processing*	Storage**	Processing*	Storage**
Vitamin A	0.0	0.0	10.0	0.0
Vitamin E	0.0	9.2	4.3	10.7
Vitamin B_{12}	5.7	11.3	0.0	0.0
Riboflavin	0.0	38.0	0.0	0.0
Niacin	0.0	31.7	15.1	18.3
Pantothenic acid	0.0	0.0	0.0	0.0
Choline	0.0	—	—	—
Folic acid	0.0	20.0	0.0	14.5
Thiamin	51.7	0.0	52.7	0.0
Pyridoxine	18.5	0.0	88.9	0.0
Biotin	0.0	0.0	55.4	0.0
Vitamin C	100.0	—	100.0	—
β-carotene	43.7	—	57.7	—

*Amount (%) of vitamin lost during processing.
**Additional amount (%) of vitamin lost during 18 months of storage.

Table 2. Vitamin losses incurred during processing and storage of dry dog and cat foods.

Vitamin	Dry cat food		Dry dog food	
	Processing*	Storage**	Processing*	Storage**
Vitamin A	26.3	0.0	9.5	0.0
Vitamin E	20.6	31.6	15.4	29.1
Vitamin B_{12}	0.0	38.0	0.0	34.2
Riboflavin	0.0	21.2	0.0	32.0
Niacin	3.3	20.0	0.0	33.6
Pantothenic acid	0.0	4.8	0.0	0.0
Choline	5.5	—	—	—
Folic acid	9.6	23.1	8.5	0.0
Thiamin	11.8	34.2	4.0	57.5
Pyridoxine	11.5	10.0	0.0	0.8
Biotin	0.0	0.0	0.0	0.0
Vitamin C	0.0	12.4	11.1	14.3
β-carotene	19.7	—	34.2	—

*Amount (%) of vitamin lost during processing.
**Additional amount (%) of vitamin lost during 18 months of storage.

In the high-moisture environment of moist pet foods, ascorbic acid (vitamin C) was completely unstable even when bound in the protective polyphosphate form. Typically stable vitamins (e.g., riboflavin, niacin, pantothenic acid, choline, vitamin B_{12} and biotin) had good processing resistance with the exception of biotin in moist dog foods. Heat- and moisture-labile vitamins (e.g., thiamin, folic acid and β-carotene) showed losses during the canning process. The fat-soluble vitamins benefit from research into protective coatings that make them much more resistant to processing losses. Storage losses were minimal due to the protective environment of the can.

Polyphosphate-bound ascorbic acid and the water-soluble B vitamins were more resistant during extrusion than in canning. Thiamin and vitamin B_{12} were lost during storage. The fat-soluble vitamins A and E had processing losses, but vitamin A remained stable, unlike vitamin E, through 18 months of storage.

Pet food manufacturers are aware of processing and storage losses of vitamins and overcome these predictable losses by supplementation. Principles of vitamin supplementation of pet foods include: 1) considering the lifestage of the animals to be fed, 2) understanding that vitamins from natural ingredients may be variable or unavailable, 3) meeting the animal's requirements with the supplemented level, 4) considering total levels from supplementation and natural sources to prevent toxicity, 5) considering the energy density of the product and 6) compensating for processing, storage and compounding losses.

BIBLIOGRAPHY

Frye T. Hoffmann LaRoche, Nutley, NJ. Paper presented at the Science and Technology Center, Hill's Pet Nutrition, Inc, Topeka, KS, on vitamin stability in canned and extruded pet food, 1995. Accompanied by descriptive material.

COMMERCIAL

(Figure 4-8) to which liquids (usually fat, flavor enhancers or both) are added in predetermined amounts. Fat is usually added in the enrobing step because it disrupts starch gelatinization and adversely affects expansion of the product. Flavor enhancers have their greatest effect upon

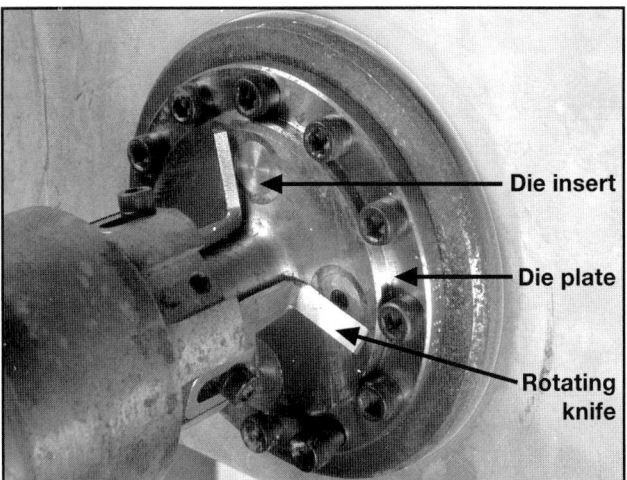

Figure 4-6. Rotating knives fit flush onto the plate at the end of the extruder barrel. The speed of rotation will determine the length of the individual food pieces.

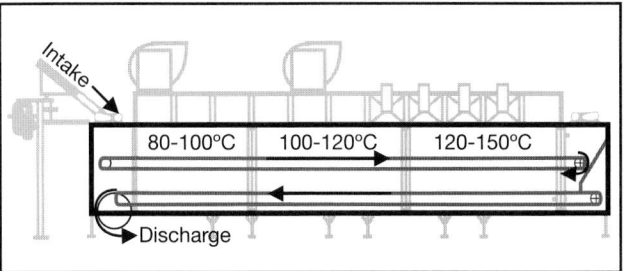

Figure 4-7. Diagram depicting pet food dryer components. Freshly extruded kibbles enter the dryer and pass through heating zones on the upper conveyor, tumble to the next conveyer, pass through the cooler zones and finally exit the dryer. (Adapted with permission, Aeroglide Corporation, Raleigh, North Carolina.)

Figure 4-8. Rotating coating drum used for applying fat and flavor enhancers to dry food. Nozzles (arrows) spray the appropriate ingredient while the product tumbles upon itself further coating each kibble.

palatability when they are applied topically. Three to four times the amount of enhancer may be needed if applied internally to achieve the same effect if applied topically. As the drum turns, the product tumbles upon itself further coating each kibble. When dry coatings are used, a fat coating is applied first to help the dry mixture adhere to the kibbles, which are then tumbled in a similar manner.

Packaging

Dry pet food packaging increases shelf life, protects the food from infestation and provides product information. Classically, the package of choice for dry pet foods is the bag, which can contain as little as 100 g of product for use as samples or up to 20 kg or more of product for sale in mass merchandising outlets and warehouses. Filling machines come in a variety of sizes and capacities to handle various package sizes and shapes. The process is usually automated and calibrated to ensure that the fill weight matches the guaranteed weight on the package label. An overage of 0.5 to 2% is not uncommon to ensure weight compliance.

An important consideration in choosing packaging is the type and amount of fat in the product to be packaged. As the fat percentage increases, protection from "grease out" must also increase. Grease out is caused by fat leaching out of the kibble through the bag, leaving grease stains on the bag surface. It is, therefore, of cosmetic concern and an indication of packaging integrity, and doesn't necessarily indicate rancidity or compromised product quality. The lamination of a polyethylene, or polypropylene, inner liner at a thickness proportional to the amount of fat, a natural paper middle liner and a clay-coated outer liner protect against grease out. Another consideration is the saturation of the fat used. Vegetable oils, because of their high degree of unsaturation, are liquid even at low temperatures and tend to migrate out of the kibble into the surrounding packaging. This process is accelerated if the kibble has rough or sharp edges that puncture the bag liner. Grease out may also occur more readily in conditions of high temperature during storage and distribution. Failure to compensate for these effects will lead to grease out and unsightly stained packages.

Dry pet food products are increasingly found in nontraditional packaging. Milk cartons, buckets and jugs are just a few examples seen in retail outlets. A consideration when using alternative packaging is the effect the material has on the flavor or odor of the food. Some plastics used in packaging materials impart "off" flavors that decrease palatability.

Principles of Semi-Moist Manufacturing

Extrusion

The pre-extrusion equipment used to manufacture semi-moist pet foods is very similar to that used in dry product manufacturing. Because of the higher moisture levels and humectants in semi-moist foods, extruders are generally configured to produce lower cooking temperatures and lower die pressures than found in dry product processing. These requirements are ideal for the twin-screw design, but single-screw extruders may be used.

Postextrusion equipment differs because the product does not go through the drying step, but rather goes through low agitation coating drums where water, humectants and acids are added, then through a cooler (refrigerated air) to set the product's structure and retain the high moisture content and spongy texture.

Mold Inhibition

Semi-moist pet foods are high in moisture (25 to 35%) and, as such, are more prone to spoilage from mold and bacteria. In addition, semi-moist foods are susceptible to moisture loss leading to loss of product integrity and texture. Semi-moist products are formulated with mold and bacterial inhibitors and humectants to retain moisture and packaged in moisture-proof barrier packaging.

The measurement of how susceptible a product is to mold growth is called a_w, or water activity. It is defined as the amount of moisture available for microbial growth and is calculated using the following formula:

$$a_w = \frac{\% \text{ Equilibrium Relative Humidity}}{100}$$

The value for a_w is a number between 0.0 and 1.0 and is obtained using a glass jar containing the product and a humidity probe. The product is allowed to equilibrate in varying levels of humidity, which are then measured and the a_w calculated. Each strain of mold or bacteria has an a_w value at which growth is no longer possible.[11] Table 4-1 describes the effect of a_w upon microbial growth.

Water activity, not moisture content, becomes more important in semi-moist pet foods. Most semi-moist pet foods have high moisture contents (>30%), but relatively low a_w values because added humectants bind free water making it unavailable for microbial growth. Early preservation techniques such as salting or adding sugar lowered the a_w value of meats and, therefore, increased the shelf life stability of those foods. Common pet food humectants include: 1) high-fructose corn syrup, 2) salt, 3) propylene glycol, 4) glycerol, 5) sorbitol and 6) other polyols. Adding large amounts of humectants results in an a_w value of around 0.70, which will inhibit most microbial growth. In the United States, propylene glycol has been removed from GRAS (generally recognized as safe) status by the Food and Drug Administration for use in cats,[12] because of its potential toxic effects. Manufacturers in the United States have responded by removing propylene glycol in favor of glycerin or polyols. To add a margin of safety, antimycotic agents (e.g., sorbate, propionate salts or both) are added in small amounts to inhibit growth of resistant organisms. In addition, acids (phosphoric, hydrochloric, etc.) may be added to lower a food's pH to maximize antimycotic effects.

Semi-Moist Packaging

Exposure to ambient air markedly increases moisture loss in semi-moist foods. About 50% loss occurs over a 24-hour period and much of that in the first four hours. Moisture loss affects product plasticity, and therefore palatability, creating a hard, crystalline structure considerably tougher than that of dry products. Barrier packaging retains moisture that is critical to maintaining shelf life.

Most feline semi-moist products are packaged in a polypropylene inner layer bound to an aluminum foil layer that inhibits diffusion of water molecules. Most man-

Table 4-1. Relationship between water activity and microbial growth.*

Water activity (a_w)	Phenomenon
0.90	Lower limit for general growth of bacteria (e.g., *Salmonella, Clostridium* and *Lactobacillus* species)
0.80	Lower limit for most enzymatic activity and growth of most fungi
0.60	Lower limit for osmophilic/xerophilic yeast and fungi
0.55	DNA becomes disordered; no growth possible

*Adapted from Bush A. Encyclopaedia of Food Science, Food Technology and Nutrition, vol. 3. London, UK: Academic Press Ltd, 1993; 1490.

ufacturers use this type of inner layer regardless of the type of outer packaging (pouch, canister, etc.). Canine products usually contain less moisture (around 25%) but contain large amounts of sugars to control the water activity. Because the a_w value and moisture are lower in these products, the packaging can be less stringent. Non-permeable polypropylene pouches without the foil membrane are often used.

Principles of Canning

Canning, as a method of food preservation, was invented by the Frenchman Nicholas Appert in 1809 in response to the French government's need for preserved foods to support its military campaigns.[13] Later work by Louis Pasteur showed the relationship between processing and the reduction of food spoilage. In the 1920s, the toxic effects of thermophilic bacteria such as *Clostridium botulinum* were documented and the importance of controlling these species with heat and pH was first understood.

Canning is a time/temperature-dependent process that can be adjusted to create different textural results with the ultimate goal being to achieve commercial sterility. Lower temperatures will require more time to attain proper core temperatures; conversely, higher temperatures require less time to achieve sterilization. Because of high process temperatures and vacuum conditions in cans, canning destroys aerobic and anaerobic bacteria, making it the best method to preserve high-moisture foods for extended periods.

Product Form

Several types of moist pet food products and various sizes and shapes of packaging materials exist. Early canned dog foods were composed primarily of ground offal and horse meat as by-products of the human food industry. These products were high in protein, fat and moisture and were similar in appearance to pâté.

"Loaf" products contain some carbohydrate sources (corn, rice, etc.) that balance the amount of protein and fat. These products are usually lower in moisture, and because of the structural properties that starch imparts, are found in finely formed loaves. Vegetable gums and other hydrocolloid thickeners are used to create a firmer texture in canned products that contain little carbohydrate.

A popular form for moist dog and cat foods is pieces of meat or fish in jelly. These products may range in form from a finely ground pâté in jelly to large chunks of meat suspended in aspic (e.g., jelly mold). This form is created by using a hygroscopic medium to create a two-phase food

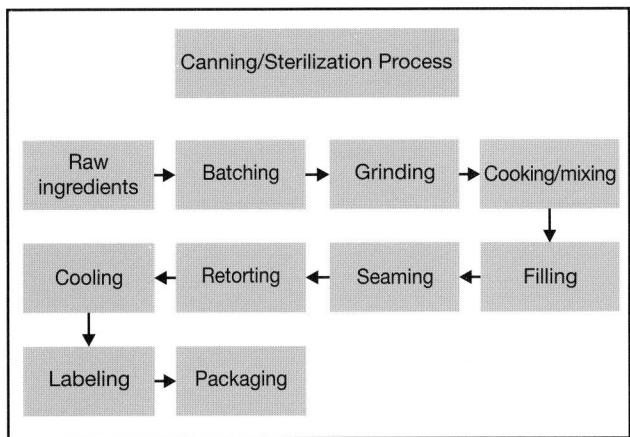

Figure 4-9. Process flow diagram for moist commercial pet food production.

Figure 4-10. As individual cans rotate, the filler/seamer fills the can and then places and seams the lid.

texture: a "piece" suspended in a medium. The viscosity of the suspension medium can vary from a semi-liquid gravy, to a jellied, savory coating to a solid, suspending jelly.

In manufacturing, the viscosity of the suspension medium is selectively regulated by using different combinations and ratios of hygroscopic sucroglycerides, starches, gums, pectins and alginates. (See Additives.) Many gums and starches are functional food "thickeners" for binding free water into semi-liquid gravies or soft jellies at room temperature. Carrageenan, carboxymethylcellulose, agar, carob, guar, acacia and xanthan gums are examples of thickeners. Pectin and alginates (seaweed derivatives) create more "solid" jellies, suspend pieces and conform to the container to form a loaf. Jellies are often golden and translucent to reveal the internally embedded pieces. Gravies are frequently opaque due to the inclusion of animal tissue meals, caramel coloring or both.

In addition to the water-binding capacity of the jellying agents, the viscosity and specific gravity of the suspension medium should approximate the density of the pieces at processing temperatures. Parity in density will help prevent separating during processing, so the pieces remain suspended.

The food pieces may be natural tissues or extruded vegetable and meat proteins. In some pet food markets, intact vegetable matter such as peas and carrots have consumer appeal. These elements can be natural or made from textured vegetable protein. Diced pieces can originate from large, flat cakes made from dough premix.

Canning Process

The canning process is generally continuous flow, highly automated and carefully controlled. Fresh and/or frozen meats are: 1) ground, 2) may or may not be mixed with grains, 3) subjected to steam and water, 4) filled into cans, 5) sealed and sterilized with a pressure cooking device, 6) cooled, 7) labeled and 8) put in cases (Figure 4-9).

MEATS/ANIMAL PROTEIN GRINDING

One of the main ingredients of any moist pet food is the animal protein component. Fresh meats and meat by-products require frequent shipments, a large refrigerated area for storage and a system of "just-in-time" manufacturing that uses the ingredients quickly to reduce waste and spoilage. Frozen meats require very large freezer storage capacity and specialized grinding equipment, but offer the manufacturer flexibility in ingredient usage.

Generally, meats, whether fresh or frozen, require grinding before canning and sterilization. In a continuous canning process using frozen ingredients, a predetermined sequence and amount of meat is fed into a machine that chips the frozen blocks of meat into smaller portions. The chipped meat then proceeds to the final grinding step where it is forced through a plate that contains many one-fourth- to three-fourth-inch openings (similar to a hammer mill). The mechanical shear grinds the frozen meats and begins the thawing process. If multiple meat sources are used, the grinding process effectively mixes them together creating a homogeneous blend. The meat mixture then proceeds to the cooker/mixer.

In a batch process, the ingredients are measured by weight, ground and placed into a cooker/mixer in one large batch. The process is repeated to achieve the desired manufacturing amount.

COOKER/MIXER

The cooker/mixer plays a critical role in the processibility, texture and flavor of the final product. In this step, the meat mixture can be blended with pre-ground or blanched grains, starches, gums, vitamin and mineral premixes and water to complete the formulation. In addition, the entire mixture is heated to specific temperatures (25 to 85°C) to gelatinize starches and begin protein denaturation, which affects the texture, flowability and flavor of the product. (See sidebar "Maillard Reactions.") The ingredients are mixed and propelled forward in the cooker/mixer by a screw that controls the speed at which the mixture travels, and therefore, the degree of cooking.

In general, high-carbohydrate moist products will require higher processing temperatures (>70°C) to fully hydrate the starch component and maintain viscosity. When the mixture does not attain appropriate viscosity, a condition known as "spin-out" occurs. As the cans are sealed the machine rotates the cans at high speeds developing centrifugal forces. If the viscosity is low, the mixture cannot "hold" ingredients like cracked corn or rice and they will migrate to the edge of the can's contents creating a product with a tough exterior and a soft interior.

Lower temperatures (<55°C) are needed to create the proper viscosity for processing formulations high in animal tissue. Excessive cooker/mixer temperature will ruin the texture of the product after sterilization.

FILLER/SEALER

The hot mixture is usually transported to a heated storage reservoir above the filler/seamer machine. The filler/seamer is a high capacity machine (300 to 600 cans/minute) that fills the cans, places a lid on each can and seams the lid (Figure 4-10). To create the vacuum necessary for commercial sterility, steam is injected over the product just before sealing. Steam effectively displaces air and after the can is sterilized and cooled, water vapor condenses and contracts, creating a relative vacuum. The steam injection step is not required if the product is hot enough to generate its own steam to displace the air in the can.

The filling/sealing process is precisely controlled to prevent potentially hazardous conditions. Underfilled cans will be underweight and subject to regulatory action. In addition, vacuum difficulties may lead to increased oxidation resulting in fat and vitamin destruction and product discoloration. Overfilled cans lack sufficient headspace to create a vacuum, thus the lid may improperly seal resulting in product spoilage and distended cans.

STERILIZATION/RETORTING

After filling and sealing is completed, the cans are sterilized in a machine called a retort. The main objectives in retorting products are to preserve the food and achieve commercial sterility. Commercial sterility can be defined as the conditions in which heat processing frees a product of microorganisms of public health significance (i.e., pathogens).[13] This is not to be confused with complete sterility in which all pathogenic and nonpathogenic microorganisms are killed. The main pathogen of concern is *Clostridium botulinum*, a rod-shaped, spore-forming, thermophilic anaerobe that produces a neuroparalytic exotoxin that causes botulism. *C. botulinum* is destroyed by temperatures above 116°C and will not grow in acidic conditions (pH <4.6). In general, process temperatures should be at least 121°C for a minimum of three minutes to kill pathogenic bacteria.

Manufacturers must document process times and temperatures for each formula produced. This time/temperature relationship can be established by process testing using cans of the formula that have thermocouples attached so that internal temperatures in all parts of the can contents can be measured. More time is needed at lower temperatures to kill the same organism. As an example, process temperatures of 121°C for three minutes are equivalent to 100°C for six hours. The relationship is established when the core temperature is greater than 116°C for the required time.

Various pressure cooking devices (retorts) are available. All retorts follow the same basic process steps, or "legs," that ensure commercial sterility: 1) bring-up leg, 2) sterilization leg and 3) cooling leg. The bring-up leg uses hot water to gradually heat the can contents to 80 to 100°C. In the sterilization leg, pressurized steam at temperatures between 116 and 129°C raise and maintain the core temperature of the can above 116°C, long enough (60 to 90 minutes) to kill all pathogenic bacteria. The bring-down leg (80 to 100°C) starts the cooling process. The cooling leg uses water at a temperature of 18 to

---

Maillard Reactions

The Maillard reactions (nonenzymatic browning reaction) between protein and reducing sugars can deteriorate the nutritional quality of foods during processing or storage by affecting the availability of some amino acids. The reaction occurs when reducing sugars, such as glucose, fructose, lactose or maltose, combine with free amino groups found on amino acids such as lysine. Heat accelerates the reaction. Digestive enzymes cannot cleave the peptide bonds adjacent to an amino acid that has a sugar attached to it. Lysine typically can be made unavailable through Maillard reactions with the reducing sugars found in most pet foods. Maillard products may also increase microbial degradation of taurine in the large intestine. Amino acid and sugar Maillard reaction products are generally not absorbed or if they are absorbed they are typically excreted in the urine and are of no nutritional value to the animal. On the other hand, controlled Maillard reactions can be used during the cooking process to produce desirable flavors, colors or aromas.

In addition to Maillard reactions, heat and alkaline pH may result in unusual cross-linking of certain amino acids and peptides that are not normally found naturally. Examples such as lysinoalanine (lysine linked with alanine), lanthionine (cysteine linked with alanine) or ornithoalanine (ornithine linked with alanine) may be formed. These compounds are not used well by animals, thus they reduce the protein quality of the food. This type of amino acid cross-linking may occur during the processing of dried meat meals, ingredients often used in pet foods. However, Maillard binding of amino acids only becomes a practical nutritional problem when the amino acid is limiting. When lysine is abundant, the protein quality is not significantly degraded.

25°C, depending on the retort used. The cans are cooled to between 38 and 49°C to allow nonmechanical drying of the outside of the can and prevent rusting. These temperatures are not hot enough to continue cooking the cans' contents.

RETORTS

Retorts have been designed to process all types of packages from baby food jars to cans that hold more than 3 kg of fruit or vegetables. Several types of retorts are used by the pet food industry, but hydrostatic and batch retorts are most common.

The hydrostatic retort is a continuous process machine that conveys the cans on carriers that are connected to a chain drive in a tower layout. The cans advance through the various legs of the process in a continuous loop transitioning from water to steam and back to water again (Figure 4-11). This type of sterilization method is called hydrostatic because the steam pressure, and therefore temperature, is controlled by water pressure in the water legs. Because the cans slowly rotate on their sides throughout the process, the gas bubble is evenly distributed on the outside surface as the cans' contents set up. This is evident by the uniform appearance of pâté and loaf-type products produced in this manner.

Batch retort sterilizers, as the name implies, are loaded, processed and cooled in a batch-type manner. These sterilizers can be configured vertically or horizontally; the vertical configuration is used most commonly in the pet food industry (Figure 4-12). Some batch retorts have three to four baskets that are filled and lowered into the retort for processing. The baskets must then be lifted out of the retort, the cans cooled and sent for labeling. The benefit to this system is that the headspace is kept constant because the cans are oriented vertically without agitation, resulting in a uniform appearance. The disadvantages are that the system is labor intensive and has a low production capacity. This system works well for test batches and pilot work, but not for production use.

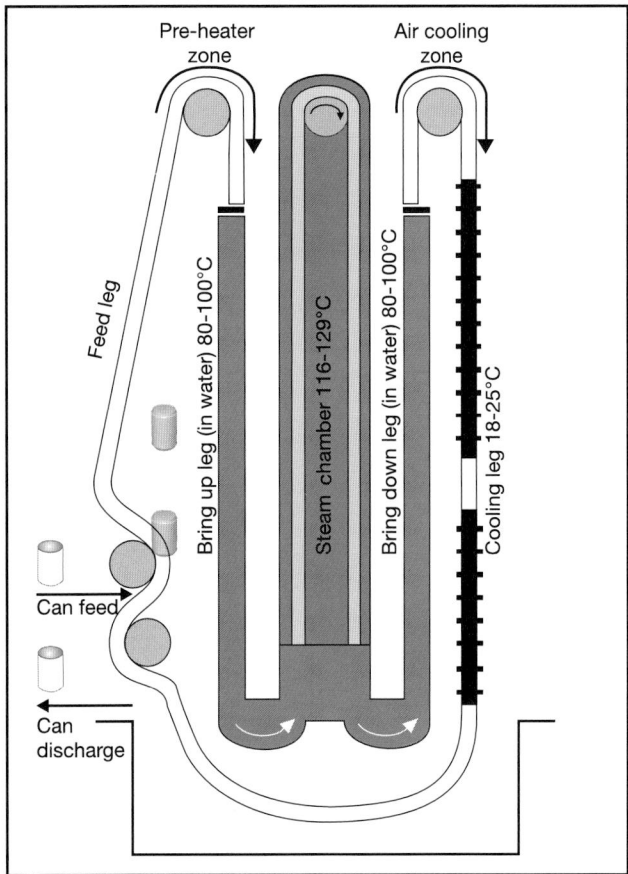

Figure 4-11. A diagram of the continuous process flow of the hydrostatic retort. Cans enter the feed leg where they are bought up to temperature, then enter the sterilization leg (steam chamber) where the product is sterilized and finally enter the bring-down leg and cooling leg where the cooling process is completed.

Table 4-2. Common grain ingredients and their carbohydrate or nitrogen-free extract (NFE) concentrations (as fed).

Grain	% NFE*
Barley	76
Corn	81
Corn flour	85
Corn starch	88
Grain sorghum	80
Oat groats	70
Rice	90
Rice bran	46
Rice flour	90
Wheat	78
Wheat flour	82
Wheat middlings	66

*NFE is the nonfiber carbohydrate fraction and is calculated as follows:
% NFE = 100% − % moisture − % crude protein − % crude fat − % crude fiber − % ash.

The automated crateless system is a newer batch retort. In this system, cans from the sealer are conveyed to a bank of vertical retorts filled with water and situated over a cooling canal filled with cold water. The first retort loads cans from the top, where they tumble to the bottom and are cushioned by water. When the first retort is filled, the conveyor moves to the next sterilizer and the process is repeated. After the retort is filled with warm water and the cans are sterilized, an unloading valve at the bottom allows the cans to tumble into the cooling canal. The cans are cooled and conveyed forward for labeling and casing. This system has four to five times the capacity of the crate retort system. Product appearance, however, may be inconsistent because the headspace bubble will settle to the top regardless of the can's orientation.

LABELING/CASING

The temperature of cans coming out of the cooling leg will be between 37 and 49°C, which causes rapid evaporation of exterior moisture. Can vacuum is determined with an electric eye that scans the tops of the cans just before labeling. If the can lid is convex, the can will be rejected automatically.

The dry cans then proceed to the labeling system, which automatically applies adhesive and the appropriate label at a rate of about 450 to 500 cans per minute. In addition, the cans are stamped with a date code that identifies the year, month, day and time of production. This information may be coded or in "open" form that is easily recognized. Reputable manufacturers will provide decoding information for those who call their toll-free numbers.

After labeling, the cans proceed to casing, which is an automated process that orients the cans, prepares the cardboard or paper case from flat stock, loads the appropriate number of cans per case and then seals the case with adhesive at a rate of about 1,000 to 1,300 cases per hour. Date code information is ink-jetted on the case for rapid identification, and the cases are loaded onto pallets for transportation.

COMMON PET FOOD INGREDIENTS

Ingredients available for use in the pet food industry range from human nonedible pet food grade by-products to human grade ingredients found in grocery stores. In the United States, ingredients are legally defined in the official handbook of the Association of American Feed Control Officials (AAFCO) and are listed on the label in order of predominance. (See Chapter 5.) This section will discuss the benefits and characteristics of ingredients available to pet food manufacturers.

Carbohydrate Ingredients

Grains are typically classified as carbohydrate ingredients. These ingredients are composed primarily of starch (>60%) with protein, fat and fiber fractions making up most of the balance. The amount of starch, as a percentage of the whole ingredient, will vary depending on the degree of milling, as in the case of whole corn vs. corn starch. Examples of carbohydrate ingredients used in pet foods are found in Table 4-2. (See sidebar "Ingredient Myths and Facts.")

Nutritional Characteristics

Grains primarily provide energy to the food, but are also a source of many different nutrients (protein, fat, fiber, minerals, vitamins) at various proportions. For example, corn contains average levels of protein, but is a good source of linoleic acid. By comparison, rice is lower in fat, phosphorus and magnesium. Barley and rice bran are higher in protein, but also higher in phosphorus. Wheat middlings are higher in protein, but also higher in fiber, and higher in nutrient variability (Figures 4-13 and 4-14). Grains differ analytically and in nutrient availability. Although corn, rice, barley and oats have nearly identical ileal and total tract carbohydrate digestibility (all >98%), whole grains have differing dry matter digestibility (rice >corn >barley >oats). Varying fiber levels between the grains account for this difference.[14]

Awareness of nutrient composition and availability differences is important when formulating foods, in order to select ingredients with nutrient compositions that agree with the overall strategy of the food being formulated. For example, if a product is being formulated to maximize energy and linoleic acid content, then corn would be the prime choice as the carbohydrate source. If the strategy is to minimize phosphorus or magnesium, rice is a good candidate (Figure 4-14). No one carbohydrate is best for every situation. Each has its own strengths and weaknesses, and combinations are often explored to achieve the desired nutrient profile.

Process Characteristics

The principal function of carbohydrates in the process of manufacturing dry pet foods is to provide structural integrity to kibbles. The starch works like a "cement" that holds kibbles together, preventing crumbling throughout the manufacturing process. It is unusual for a dry pet food to be formulated with less than 40% carbohydrate ingredients because of the minimum requirement for extrusion. Formulations designed for obesity management, however, often contain less than 40% carbohydrate and higher levels of fiber.

The choice of a carbohydrate in a moist formulation can markedly affect processing characteristics. The starch will gelatinize in moist products and combine with the denaturing protein to give the loaf structure. This structure will maintain even distribution of the formulation. However, the textural characteristics of the structure will vary widely among carbohydrates, especially if the starch is in purified form, because each reacts uniquely to cook temperature and time.

Dry Protein Ingredients

Protein ingredients are composed of higher levels of protein (>20%). Protein ingredients typically used in dry pet foods and their protein contents are listed in Table 4-3. (See sidebar "Incorporating Fresh or Frozen Meat Into Dry Extruded Pet Foods.")

Protein ingredients vary widely in the levels of protein and other nutrients they deliver to a formulation. For example, ash represents the total mineral element of the formula (the sum of calcium, phosphorus, magnesium, potassium, sodium, etc.). Ash is the material that remains after combustion or hydrolysis of the organic material. The protein-to-ash ratio is a good indicator of an ingredi-

Figure 4-12. In a batch retort sterilizer, cans are loaded, processed and cooled in baskets (batch-type manner) rather than in a continuous process as occurs in hydrostatic retorts.

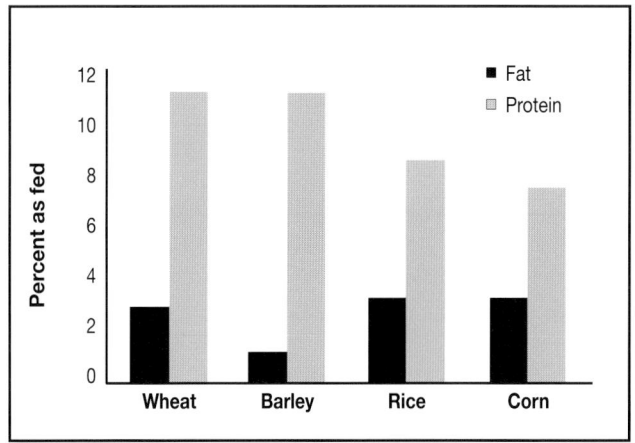

Figure 4-13. Protein and fat concentrations (% as fed) of common grains used in commercial pet foods.

Ingredient Myths and Facts

Sometimes pet foods are marketed on ingredient stories that have consumer appeal. Ingredient stories are simple and believable but sometimes mislead consumers. Animals require nutrients, not ingredients. Ingredients are the means to achieve the nutritional and palatability goals of a product. What are some of the myths and facts surrounding ingredients commonly used in pet foods?

MYTH NO. 1: Corn is a filler, is poorly digested and causes allergies.

FACT: Fillers are ingredients that serve no nutritional purpose, and corn does not fit that description. Corn is a nutritionally superior grain compared with others used in pet foods because it contains a balance of nutrients not found in other grains. Corn provides a highly available source of complex carbohydrates and substantial quantities of linoleic acid, an essential fatty acid important for healthy skin. Corn also provides essential amino acids and fiber. In a survey of veterinary dermatologists, corn was not listed among the ingredients most often suspected to cause food allergies. A review of over 200 confirmed canine cases of food allergy in the veterinary literature revealed only three were caused by corn. (See Chapter 14.) The same number was reported for rice.

MYTH NO. 2: Soybean meal causes bloat in dogs.

FACT: Bloat, or gastric dilatation/volvulus, is a condition usually seen in large, deep-chested dogs. Research has shown that gastric motility and emptying are not affected by food ingredients (moist meat-based vs. dry cereal-based food). (See Chapter 22.)

MYTH NO. 3: Corn is highly allergenic.

FACT: There have been only six confirmed cases of allergy to corn in dogs reported in the veterinary literature out of 253 total cases. (See Chapter 14.) This equates to a 2.4% incidence rate. Foods most often cited as causing canine food allergy are beef, dairy products and wheat.

MYTH NO. 4: Chicken meal is superior to poultry by-product meal.

FACT: Both chicken meal and poultry by-product meal contain quality protein that is digestible and palatable. Chicken meal, however, contains mostly rendered chicken necks and backs, which means it provides more ash per unit protein (Table 4-4) than poultry by-product meal does. This may make it less desirable for use in formulations where controlling the mineral content of the product is indicated. Poultry by-product meal is a slightly more concentrated protein source (Table 4-3).

MYTH NO. 5: By-products are of lesser quality than meat.

FACT: Pet food ingredients including muscle meat are by nature by-products. Some of the by-products used in pet foods are ingredients that are considered human grade both domestically and internationally. Examples of these are pork and beef liver, tripe and spleen. Many by-products like liver offer superior palatability over muscle meats when used in dog and cat foods.

MYTH NO. 6: There is one best fiber source.

FACT: Various fiber types can be used to provide distinct functions in pet foods. Though fiber does not serve as a major energy source for dogs or cats, it can help promote normal bowel function, maintain the health of the intestinal tract and aid in the nutritional management of certain diseases. No single fiber source or type can optimally deliver all the benefits fiber can provide in pet nutrition. Insoluble fiber is preferred in weight-loss regimens. Soluble fiber is more appropriate in the maintenance of intestinal tract health. It is important to use the fiber source or sources that achieve the nutritional goals of the product. (See Chapter 2.)

MYTH NO. 7: Cellulose fiber binds minerals and decreases the digestibility of other nutrients.

FACT: As with other fibers, dry matter digestibility decreases with increasing cellulose levels. However, research has shown that fiber type does not affect protein digestibility in dogs. In addition, purified cellulose does not decrease protein digestibility in cats. Purified cellulose is inert when it comes to mineral binding and has no effect on calcium or zinc availability in chicks or iron in dogs. More soluble fibers such as beet pulp bind calcium and zinc in chicks and iron in growing puppies. (See Chapter 2.)

---

ent's efficiency in providing protein and the ingredient's dry matter digestibility. The higher an ingredient's ash content, the lower its digestibility.

The ratios of total protein content to total ash content described in Table 4-4 and Figure 4-15 are critical to formulating dry pet foods. This is especially true for cats, which require a higher proportion of protein from animal tissue and which have higher protein requirements than dogs. A protein ingredient choice that has a low protein-to-ash ratio will make it difficult to meet a cat's protein requirement without delivering excessive levels of magnesium and phosphorus. Poultry by-product meal is readily accepted by dogs and cats. Because it contains viscera, it provides an excellent source of protein with lower mineral levels than chicken meal, which is composed primarily of rendered chicken necks and backs. Thus, poultry by-product meal is an excellent choice for feline foods to avoid excess mineral levels.

Nutritional Characteristics

Dogs are omnivorous and have lower protein requirements than cats. Therefore, formulations for dogs are more flexible and may include more vegetable proteins. Vegetable proteins typically have higher protein-to-ash ratios and contain some fiber. Soybean meal is an excellent source of the amino acids lysine and tryptophan. However, because dogs prefer animal tissues to vegetable meals, it is advantageous to add animal source proteins to the formulation. A blend of animal tissue meals and vegetable meals is appropriate and often optimal.

Wet Protein Ingredients

Wet protein ingredients are classified as fresh or frozen meats and meat by-products. These ingredients generally have moisture contents above 60%. Table 4-5 lists the typical protein ingredients used in canned pet foods. Controlling excess minerals in moist foods is easier because the protein-to-ash ratio for fresh meat ingredients is higher overall (because they contain less bone) than that of rendered meat meals used in dry pet foods.

Process Characteristics

Protein ingredients provide structural integrity to kibbles, but not nearly as much as that provided by carbohydrates. The exception to this is textured vegetable protein (TVP), which is made from wheat or soy flour. Sulfur is usually added to give the matrix more structure by increasing the disulfide bonding between protein strands. TVP absorbs moisture readily and has a texture similar to that of meat when hydrated. The meat tissues used in moist pet foods contribute greatly to the firmness and structure of the finished product. Overheating or adding strong acids will cause the structure to degenerate, affecting the finished product.

Fiber Ingredients

Fiber ingredients contain levels of crude fiber between 18 and 80%. Table 4-6 lists fiber ingredients typically used in pet foods and their fiber contents.

Nutritional Characteristics

Fiber may be classified as soluble or insoluble based on solubility in water. Soluble fiber is easily fermented in the gut by intestinal flora and provides energy and substrates for colonocyte health. (See Chapter 2.) Examples of soluble fiber include pectin, gum and hemicellulose. Beet pulp, citrus pulp and soymill run are good sources of soluble fiber. These types of fibers improve stool consistency without compromising total digestibility.

Insoluble fiber, which is found in cellulose and peanut hulls, improves stool quality (e.g., adds bulk and holds water) and modulates GI motility. Insoluble fiber is also useful in obesity management because it dilutes calories, maintains satiety and can be used at higher levels without causing flatulence. The efficiency of the fiber source is critical for formulation. For example, a product formulated for obesity management with a crude fiber content of 20% would need much greater amounts of fiber ingredients such as beet pulp to achieve the same result as cellulose (Figure 4-15).

Cellulose and peanut hulls are more efficient for diluting calories than beet pulp or soymill run. This advantage is critical when space is needed in the formula to provide protein in moist and dry products, and starch necessary for kibble integrity in dry products. As is the case for carbohydrate and protein ingredients, the choice of a fiber ingredient should be dictated by the overall formulation strategy and food purpose.

Process Characteristics

Fiber ingredients typically contribute an anti-caking effect to the flow of materials in the manufacturing process. However, they also cause high degrees of friction in the extruder and may require fat for lubrication, which may negate fiber's caloric dilution purpose.

Fat Ingredients

Fat ingredients contain more than 50% fat. Fat ingredients typically used in pet foods are animal fat (pork fat,

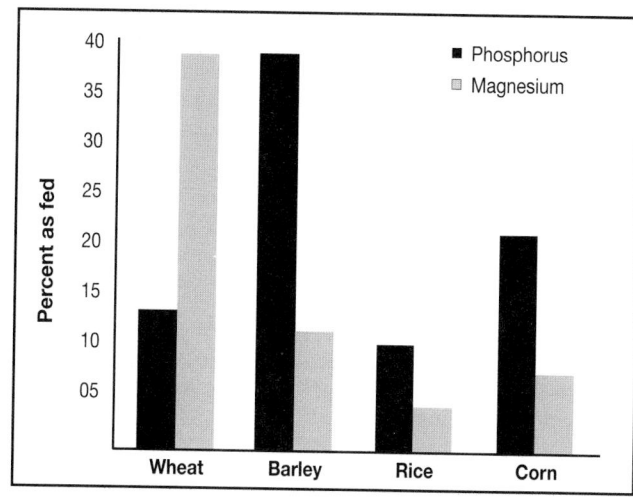

Figure 4-14. Magnesium and phosphorus concentration (% as fed) of common grains used in commercial pet foods.

Table 4-3. Dry protein sources used in commercial pet foods and their protein concentrations (as fed).

Ingredient	% Protein
Poultry by-product meal	65-70
Meat and bone meal	50-55
Chicken meal	63-67
Lamb meal	48-55
Fish meal	60-65
Soybean meal	46-50
Corn gluten meal	60-64
Rice gluten meal	40-50
Dried egg product	43-48

Table 4-4. Protein-to-ash ratios of dry protein sources used in commercial pet foods.

Ingredient	Protein:ash
Poultry by-product meal	6:1
Meat and bone meal	2:1
Chicken meal	4:1
Lamb meal	2.5:1
Fish meal	3:1
Soybean meal	10:1
Corn gluten meal	25:1
Rice gluten meal	20:1
Dried egg product	8:1

Table 4-5. Wet protein sources used in commercial pet foods and their protein concentrations (as fed).

Ingredient	% Protein
Liver (pork, beef, turkey, sheep)	17-22
Meat by-products (lungs, spleens, kidneys)	15-20
Beef (carcass)	18-22
Chicken (whole, backs, necks)	10-12
Fish (freshwater)	12-15
Fish (ocean)	20-27

Table 4-6. Common fiber ingredients used in commercial pet foods and their crude fiber concentrations (as fed).

Ingredient	% Crude fiber
Cellulose	72-78
Soymill run	32-36
Wheat bran	13-16
Beet pulp	17-20
Peanut hulls	52-58

Incorporating Fresh or Frozen Meat Into Dry Extruded Pet Foods

Until the late 1980s, the only animal source proteins used in dry commercial pet foods were dry rendered meat, chicken or poultry meals. Extrusion technology advanced during that time to allow the addition of fresh or frozen meat or poultry to dry pet foods.

A slurry composed of animal tissues, fat and water (that contains about 25 to 35% of the formula) is ground and mixed in a separate tank. It is then pumped into the preconditioner where it replaces some of the process water. The product is then extruded in the same way as when dry meat meals are used.

Because labeling regulations in the United States stipulate that ingredients must be listed in order of predominance by weight, the wet weight of the meat or poultry can be within the top three ingredients. The water in the meat (60 to 70%), however, must be dried off to make a dry product. Therefore, the actual meat or poultry ingredient, now in its dry form, would be much farther down on the label if the meat or poultry were added as a dry meat meal.

beef tallow, poultry fat) and various types of vegetable oil (soybean, sunflower, corn). Each type of fat has several different grades of quality, as measured by peroxide value and free fatty acids, which indicate rancidity. Selection of high-quality fat ensures a low oxidative potential and increases the palatability of the finished product.

Nutritional Characteristics

Fat ingredients are extremely efficient in delivering energy to a food. Fats contribute calories at 2.25 times the rate of carbohydrates or proteins. Use of fat ingredients is the most efficient method of increasing the energy density of a food to limit a pet's consumption of other nutrients. However, preventing or managing obesity in sedentary pets limits the broad application of this approach.

Process Characteristics

Fats that have low melting points can be added to the inside or sprayed on the outside of a kibble. Hard fat ingredients (tallow, grease) must be heated before they can be applied to the exterior of kibbles. Antioxidants are necessary to help prevent rancidity during prolonged heating of fats, and to extend the shelf life of dry products. Because fats are lubricants, they are extremely useful for managing product expansion and density in the extrusion process. Adding large amounts of fat, especially hard fat ingredients, to moist products without proper mixing results in fat separation.

Additives

Since 1920, legally sanctioned food additives have been used commonly in human and animal foods. Various additives are used by pet food manufacturers to generate products with visual appeal, prolonged nutritional quality, palatability and a long shelf life.

Because most commercial pet foods are designed as complete foods, nutrient enrichment with vitamins and minerals is the most important and beneficial use of pet food additives. Most ingredients with unfamiliar, chemical-sounding names are, in fact, nutrients. In general, additives other than vitamins and minerals are found least often or in smallest amounts in moist foods, and most commonly or in largest amounts in dry foods, semi-moist foods, treats and snacks.

The term "additive" is inclusive for anything imparting increased nutritional, gustatory or cosmetic appeal. Additives commonly used in prepared human and pet foods include colors, flavors, flavor enhancers, emulsifying agents, gelling substances, stabilizers, thickeners and processing aids. The terms preservative and additive are often used synonymously, but they are distinctly different. Preservatives are substances added to foods to protect or retard decay, discoloration or spoilage under normal use or storage conditions. Thus, all preservatives are additives, but not all additives serve a preservative function.

Many additives have multiple purposes in pet foods as outlined in Table 4-7. A few additive categories are described here in more detail.

Antioxidant Preservatives

See the shelf life and antioxidant sections in this chapter.

Antimicrobial Preservatives

Because semi-moist pet foods and treats have a high-moisture content and are not maintained in a sterile environment, they often contain antimicrobial preservatives. These compounds inhibit bacterial putrefaction, mold formation or both. Examples include acids, propylene glycol and propionate and sorbate salts.

Humectants

Humectants reduce water activity and prevent loss of water after processing. See the soft-moist manufacturing section in this chapter for more details.

Coloring Agents/Preservatives

Natural and synthetic colors are often added to pet food products to enhance consumer appeal. Examples of natural colors include the carotenoids. Synthetic colors used in pet foods include iron oxide; coal tar derivatives (azo dyes) such as tartrazine (Food, Drug & Cosmetic [FD&C] yellow No. 5), sunset yellow (FD&C yellow No. 6) and allura red (FD&C red dye No. 40) and nonazo dyes such as brilliant blue (FD&C blue No. 1) and indigotin (FD&C blue No. 2). An artificial color may only be used in a pet food in the United States if it is listed as safe in the United States Food and Drug Regulations (21 CFR 73 and 74). Several additives are not colors themselves but are used to prevent discoloration of products. Examples of color enhancers or preservatives are the nitrites and bisulfites.

Emulsifying Agents and Stabilizers/Thickeners

Gums (hydrocolloids), glycerin, glycerides and modified starch are used to prevent separation of ingredients and create the gravy, sauce or jelly portion of moist pet foods. These additives allow manufacture of high-moisture foods that are highly palatable to pets, but that do not have an excess of free water.

Gums are long-chain, high molecular weight polysaccharides that dissolve or disperse in water to build viscosity in or thicken products. Gums also are used for secondary effects that include stabilization of emulsions, suspension of particulates, inhibition of syneresis (release of water from fabricated foods) and formation of films or gels. Gums frequently used in pet foods include seaweed extracts such as alginates (brown seaweed) and carrageenan (red seaweed), seed gums such a guar gum (ground endosperm of guar plants), microbial gums such as xanthan gum (bacteria originally isolated from the rutabaga plant cultured on carbohydrate media) and chemically modified plant materials such as sodium carboxymethylcellulose (cellulose chemically modified to become water soluble). Modified celluloses and vegetable gums are frequently sprayed on the surface of commercial dry foods with digests. Water mixed with these dry foods creates a gravy.

Miscellaneous Additives

Polyphosphates are frequently used as additives in baked treats and moist pet foods. These additives serve as dough conditioners and help to improve texture, retain natural moisture and protein in meat ingredients, reduce oxidation and allow better color development.

Extracts of *Yucca schidigera* are marketed in pet foods as a means of reducing fecal odor. Yucca extracts, in higher concentrations, reduce atmospheric ammonia in livestock and poultry confinement units. Saponins or other active compounds in the extract appear to reduce levels of free ammonia by binding ammonia or converting ammonia to other products. Some yucca extracts may also inhibit urease enzymes. Whether binding or preventing free ammonia is an effective way of reducing pet fecal odor has not been proved. Yucca extract is not officially approved for odor reduction use in pet food, although it is approved as a flavoring agent for pet and human foods.

Palatability Enhancers

A great deal of work has been done by pet food companies in the area of palatability enhancement. In general, dogs like fats, sugars, meat ingredients and digests, which are animal tissues that have been chemically or enzymatically altered. The digestion process from which digests are made releases amino acids, such as lysine, and dipeptide combinations that enhance palatability for dogs. Cats strongly prefer meat ingredients and inorganic acids such as phosphoric acid to fats and sweet ingredients such as whey and sugar. Cats also strongly prefer the amino acids cystine and glycine. Feline digests generally have a low pH, which also aids in preservation. Digests are available in dry and liquid forms to best accommodate the manufacturer's application process.

Formulating dry pet foods with wet meat ingredients combined with fat (up to about 25% of the product) also improves palatability. (See sidebar "Incorporating Fresh or Frozen Meats Into Dry Extruded Pet Foods.") In this process, a liquid mixture of meat, water and fat is pumped into the extruder raising the overall moisture, which is then driven off during the drying process. Because the wet

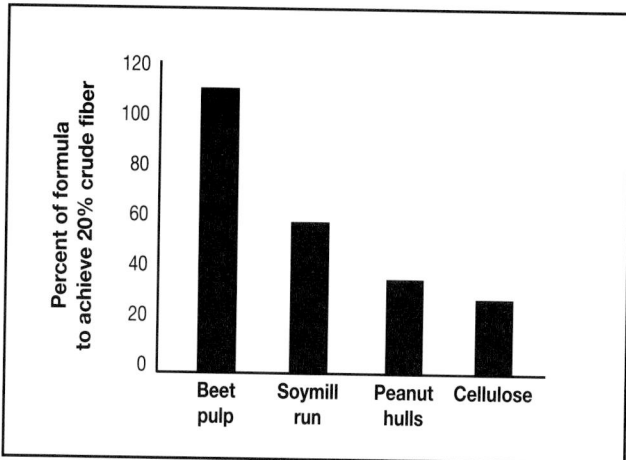

Figure 4-15. The amount (% of formula) of a particular fiber ingredient necessary to produce a product containing 20% crude fiber. Note that it is impossible to achieve 20% crude fiber in the finished food using beet pulp because the percentage exceeds 100.

meat ingredient is cooked once in the extruder, as opposed to meat meals, which are rendered first then extruded, the palatability of the finished product is enhanced.

Palatability enhancers are less effective in a canned matrix because of the high-moisture environment and deactivation from high processing temperatures. Therefore, meat selection becomes the most important factor in improving the palatability of a moist product. In addition, a higher moisture content can increase the palatability of moist foods. Table 4-7 lists some palatability enhancers commonly used in the pet food industry.

QUALITY CONTROL PROCEDURES

Because pet owners depend on people at the distribution outlet (veterinary hospital, pet store, etc.) or word of mouth (breeder, veterinarian, other pet owners) for information about a company or its products, endorsements and company reputation are direct or indirect statements about quality. Quality is a relative term meaning different things to different people.

Quality procedures for manufacture of pet foods are neither required nor regulated. Implementation of a quality program is the sole responsibility of individual pet food manufacturers. Some companies go to the expense of studying and implementing world-class manufacturing processes (benchmarking); others do very little. Some companies use high-quality human and pet food grade ingredients; others purchase the least costly ones. Some companies conduct multiple tests to evaluate the quality of raw ingredients and finished products; others do what is minimally necessary. Some companies submit to voluntary plant inspections; others avoid such evaluations.

The rest of this chapter describes quality manufacturing procedures that some pet food manufacturers follow in the continuous pursuit of product excellence. The information discussed below should give the reader examples of a quality manufacturing program employed by companies whose reputation is built upon the products and services they provide.

Table 4-7. Common pet food additives.*

Antioxidant preservatives
Ethoxyquin
Butylated hydroxyanisole (BHA)
Tertiary butylhydroquinone (BHQT)
Butylated hydroxytoluene (BHT)
Propyl gallate
Tocopherols
Rosemaric acid/rosmarequinone
Antimicrobial preservatives
Citric acid
Hydrochloric acid
Phosphoric acid
Sorbic acid
Fumaric acid
Pyroligneous acid
Propionic acid
Sodium propionate
Calcium propionate
Potassium sorbate
Sodium nitrite
Humectants
Sorbitol
Corn syrups
Sucrose/dextrose
Cane molasses
Propylene glycol
Coloring agents/preservatives
Artificial color(s)
Natural color(s)
Azo dyes (tartrazine [FD&C yellow No. 5], sunset yellow [FD&C yellow No. 6], allura red [FD&C red No. 40])
Nonazo dyes (brilliant blue [FD&C blue No. 1], indigotin [FD&C blue No. 2])
Caramel color
Sodium nitrite
Sodium erythrobate
Titanium dioxide
Iron oxide
Sodium metabisulfite
Aluminum potassium sulfate
Flavors/flavor enhancers
Digests
Artificial flavors
Natural flavors
Citrus bioflavonoids
Liver meal
Dehydrated cheese/dried cheese powder
Monosodium glutamate
Natural smoke flavor
Palatability enhancers
Digests
L-lysine
Onion powder/oil
Garlic powder/oil
Phosphoric acid
Hydrochloric acid
Sucrose, dextrose cane molasses
Spices
Acidified yeast
Whey
Meat extracts (beef, chicken, turkey)
Water (moist)
Emulsifying agents, stabilizers and thickeners
Glyceryl monostearate
Monoglycerides (of edible fats and oils)
Diglycerides (of edible fats and oils)
Glycerin
Modified starch
Gums (hydrocolloids)
　Seaweed extracts (carrageenan, alginates)
　Seed gums (guar gum)
　Microbial gums (xanthan gum)
　Chemically modified plant materials (sodium carboxymethylcellulose)
Miscellaneous
Yucca schidigera extract (flavor, odor control)
Mineral oil (reduces dust)
Sodium tripolyphosphate (dough conditioner)
Charcoal
Polyphosphates
　Sodium tripolyphosphate
　Disodium phosphate
　Tetrasodium pyrophosphate

*Adapted from Roudebush P. Pet food additives. Journal of the American Veterinary Medical Association 1993; 203: 1667-1670.

Ingredients and Process

Understanding and controlling raw ingredients and the manufacturing process are the keys to manufacturing a high-quality pet food. A good quality program to ensure raw ingredient integrity is essential. The key elements of such a program include: 1) ingredient specifications, 2) ingredient receiving and testing procedures and 3) ingredient handling procedures at the plant.

The contractual agreement with suppliers should list ingredient specifications including nutrient composition, purity requirements, key analytical criteria and shipping conditions. Receiving procedures at the manufacturing site should include analytical testing of ingredients, physical inspections and checks to ensure raw ingredients are segregated appropriately and maintained properly.

Handling procedures after receiving and initial bulk storage are designed to ensure ingredients are not damaged in any fashion. Proper conveyance mechanisms, rodent and insect control procedures and appropriate design of holding vessels to ensure first-in, first-out ingredient flow help eliminate damage and help ensure freshness. Good quality control practices include internal audits of these procedures and systems and audits by a third party, such as the American Institute of Baking.

Attention to the use of high-quality raw ingredients and high-quality processing will ensure a high-quality product. The essential element of a good quality program for the processing of pet foods is a complete understanding of each manufacturing unit's operation and its effect on the attributes of the finished product. Once these effects are understood, critical control points can be established around unit operations and quality systems set up to monitor and ensure conformance. The manufacturing process of pet foods primarily involves proper compounding of raw ingredients and then working this mixture for moist or dry extruded products. Therefore, quality programs must include: 1) calibration procedures for conveying the individual ingredients, 2) proper time and temperature measuring and 3) calibration procedures for the cooking process. For moist products, the sterilization program must be documented and recorded. Detailed records should be kept for each lot of product manufactured, clearly detailing the processing conditions. Routine, clearly documented calibration and correlation programs must be established for each process variable (i.e., weighing or scaling, temperatures, flow rates, etc.). Analytical and physical testing of finished product is another essential element of a good quality program.

Vendors

Pet foods contain numerous raw materials from many suppliers. A vendor quality control program is critical to ensuring receipt of high-quality raw ingredients.

A good quality vendor control program begins with: 1) testing methods for nutrient levels, 2) microbiologic evaluation and 3) toxicity testing. Defining these test methods ensures that multiple vendors of raw ingredients deliver against the same purchasing specification. A routine calibration and correlation program should be established to minimize method and operator variations. A vendor quality program should establish the frequency of analytical testing; however, each lot of an ingredient must be tested initially for moisture, protein and fat, at a minimum, to see if it adheres to ingredient specifications and for accurate compounding. Ingredients should also be routinely analyzed for other nutrients of concern (e.g., calcium, phosphorus, magnesium and sodium).

Beyond the testing required in a purchasing specification, further quality assurance can be attained through programs the food industry calls vendor self-certification. The objective of these programs is to shift the focus from final ingredient shipment testing to building of quality control procedures upstream in the vendors' process. For example, purchasing specifications for cereal grains would include a target value for percent moisture of the grain. Most certification programs require vendors to keep detailed records on the lots of material they purchase. The intent is to encourage vendors to define, understand and control their raw materials and processes so that they manufacture and supply ingredients that will fall within the pet food manufacturer's specifications.

Product Quality

The quality of the finished pet food product is quantified by how well the product meets the formulated nutrient content as well as other critical parameters, such as: 1) consistent appearance, 2) physical integrity, 3) package integrity, 4) adequacy of sterilization and 5) freedom from toxins and microbiologic concerns.

Sampling frequency should be established to ensure that any nonconforming product is identified and removed. This frequency depends on batch sizes, length of storage and normal ingredient variation history. Sampling every 30 minutes for moisture, protein, fat, calcium, phosphorus, sodium, potassium and magnesium to determine variation in the process is a good starting point. Samples can be analyzed either separately or as a composite sample collected over time if the manufacturing process is well-controlled.

For dry expanded pet foods, sampling should include: 1) each lot of raw ingredients received, 2) the mix of raw ingredients once compounded (weighed and mixed), 3) the product leaving the extruder, 4) the product leaving the dryer, 5) after any topical enrobing and 6) finished product in the package. For moist pet foods, samples should be taken from: 1) raw materials, 2) product in the cooker/mixer and 3) sterilized product.

Statistical Process Control

To ensure the most consistent quality of the finished product, modern factories use statistical process control in the manufacturing process. Statistical process control determines normal variation through chemical analysis of the product at various points in the process compared with nutrient specifications of the finished product. It also establishes control limits based on this variation.

Variables analyzed can be moisture, protein, fat or any other nutrient of concern for a particular product where consistency is required. Usually, two to three standard deviations from the mean represent the control limits. Adjustments to the manufacturing process are made only when finished product attributes are outside these control limits.

Analytical Tests

Finished products are analyzed to ensure conformity to formulated nutrient content and freedom from toxins and microbiologic concerns. At a minimum, a good quality program should include routine testing to determine percentages of moisture, protein, fat, ash, calcium, phosphorus, sodium, magnesium, potassium and crude fiber. Additionally, incoming raw ingredients and finished products should be tested for *Salmonella* and *Clostridium* species, aflatoxin and vomitoxin.

Each manufacturing facility should have an in-house laboratory that can run the above analyses as the product is produced. The results help operators adjust the process controls to ensure the finished product meets specifications. Faster analytical methods (e.g., near infrared) that can analyze several nutrients simultaneously with speed and accuracy help operators control the process. In addition to chemical analysis, the physical size, density and color should be part of the finished product specifications. In the case of canned pet foods, can seal, product texture and vacuum should be recorded in addition to chemical analysis results.

Shelf Life

Shelf life is the amount of time a product maintains nutritional, microbial, physical and organoleptic (sensory) integrity. The main cause of diminished shelf life in dry products is oxidation. Fat, either bound in the ingredient matrix or applied to the surface of dry products is subject to the second law of thermodynamics, which states that a system follows an irreversible cascade toward entropy, or disorder. The double bonds of polyunsaturated fatty acids are particularly susceptible to attack by oxygen molecules to form fatty acid radicals and peroxide by-products. This process is initiated by oxygen and catalyzed by iron, copper, light and warm temperatures to create a series of chemical reactions called auto-oxidation.[15-17] Unless checked, auto-oxidation will decrease palatability and destroy fat and fat-soluble vitamins. Oxidation does not occur in an environment lacking oxygen (e.g., moist pet food); therefore, moist products have a longer shelf life.

There are no recognized industry standards for shelf life, but 12 to 18 months for dry pet foods, nine to 12 months for semi-moist pet foods and 24 months for moist pet foods are reasonable estimates. Dry pet foods preserved with natural antioxidants may have a shelf life markedly shorter than 12 to 18 months because these antioxidants are not as effective as synthetic antioxidants. Shelf-life information for products should be available from manufacturers.

Table 4-8. Standard accelerated stability tests and their conditions.*

Test	Conditions	Comments
Ambient storage	Room temperature Atmospheric pressure	Too slow
Light	Room temperature Atmospheric pressure	Different mechanism
Metal catalysts	Room temperature Atmospheric pressure	More decomposition
Weight-gain method	30-80°C Atmospheric pressure	Endpoint questionable
Schaal oven	60-70°C Atmospheric pressure	Fewest problems
Oxygen uptake	80-100°C Atmospheric pressure	Different mechanism
Oxygen bomb	99°C 65-115 psi O_2	Different mechanism
Active oxygen (AOM)	98°C Air bubbling	Different mechanism
Rancimat	100-140°C	Endpoint questionable

*Frankel EN. Trends in Food Science & Technology 1993; 4: 220-225.

Antioxidants

Antioxidants are a class of compounds that function as one or more of the following: 1) electron donors, 2) oxygen scavengers, 3) free radical scavengers or 4) hydrogen donors.[16,18] Table 4-7 lists common antioxidants used in pet foods. Antioxidants can be synthetic or natural, used in combination with other antioxidants or alone. They also gain synergism with mineral chelators (e.g., citric and ascorbic acid), and emulsifiers (e.g., lecithin, propyl gallate) and have vastly different potencies depending on the matrix being modified and the antioxidant used. Antioxidants bind with free radicals breaking the cascade of auto-oxidation. Synthetic antioxidants (e.g., ethoxyquin and butylated hydroxyanisole [BHA]) are much more effective than the same quantities of natural antioxidants, such as mixed tocopherols or ascorbic acid. Synthetic antioxidants better resist processing losses and are effective longer, thereby extending shelf life.

Shelf-Life Determination

Shelf life in the pet food industry is usually determined through chemical analysis of oxidation products and by sensory evaluation (palatability testing and olfaction). Some of the chemical methods used for oxidation analysis include oxygen uptake, oxygen bomb, Schaal oven technique, active oxygen method and the Rancimat test (Table 4-8).

The methods used must be compatible with the types of fat in the food because different fats will give different results when similar analytical methods are used. In addition, most tests for oxidation rely on high temperatures (80 to 140°C), catalysts or oxygen exposure to simulate the oxidation process. These accelerated methods may produce different results than lower temperature, long-term storage tests because the process of oxidation changes dramatically at temperatures above 100°C, but at lower temperatures the results are less confounded.[19] Many of these tests, however, still have practical value to estimate the antioxidant potential of a given product because they can be conducted rapidly and produce results that correlate reasonably well with ambient storage conditions.

Although there is no standard format for shelf-life evaluation, Gross and colleagues incorporated peroxide value analysis and palatability trials in their assessment of different antioxidant systems in dog foods.[20] Their design used accelerated storage (16 weeks at 48.8 ± 2.2°C) and ambient storage (12 months at 22.2 ± 1.2°C) methodologies. Peroxide values and proximate analyses were determined monthly, and feeding trials were conducted initially and after 16 weeks of accelerated storage and after five months and 12 months of ambient storage. This method of shelf-life determination was sensitive enough to detect oxidation products (rancidity) through both chemical means and reduced palatability scores.

Nutrient Stability

The oxidation cascade not only creates rancidity with its objectionable odors and flavors, but also destroys the functionality of nutrients. Pet foods contain fat, which provides essential fatty acids and the fat-soluble vitamins A, D, E and sometimes K. These compounds can be markedly reduced by oxidation, possibly leading to a food with vitamin deficiencies. A robust antioxidant system is required to protect these essential nutrients.

REFERENCES

1. Maxwell JC. Maxwell Report. Petfood Industry 1996; 38(4): 4-8.
2. Enterline WR. Production of extruded pet foods. Petfood Industry 1986; 28(4): 26-30.
3. Marsh F. An overview of the international pet food market. In: Proceedings. Annual General Meeting of FEDIAF, 1994: 3.
4. Marsh F. Global awareness: Trends affecting pet food manufacturers. Petfood Industry 1994; 36(4): 4-9.
5. Rokey GJ. Pet food and fish food extrusion. In: Frame ND, ed. The Technology of Extrusion Cooking. London, UK: Blackie Academic & Professional, 1995; 144-189.
6. Harnby N. Mixing of powders. In: Macrae R, Robinson RK, Sadler MJ, eds. Encyclopaedia of Food Science Food Technology and Nutrition, vol. 3, London, UK: Academic Press, Ltd, 1993; 3137-3142.
7. Johnson I. Extrusion cooking. In: Macrae R, Robinson RK, Sadler MJ, eds. Encyclopaedia of Food Science Food Technology and Nutrition, vol. 3, London, UK: Academic Press, Ltd, 1993; 1700-1709.
8. Dziezak JD. Single- and twin-screw extruders in food processing. Food Technology, April 1989: 164-174.
9. Frye T. Hoffmann LaRoche, Nutley, NJ. Paper presented at the Science and Technology Center, Hill's Pet Nutrition, Inc, Topeka, KS, on vitamin stability in canned and extruded pet food, 1995. Accompanied by descriptive material.
10. Colonna P, Tayeb J, Mercier C. Extrusion cooking of starch and starchy products. In: Mercier C, Linko P, Harper JM, eds. Extrusion Cooking. St. Paul, MN: American Association of Starch Chemists, 1989; 247-319.
11. Bush A. Drying. In: Macrae R, Robinson RK, Sadler MJ, eds. Encyclopaedia of Food Science Food Technology and Nutrition, vol. 3, London, UK: Academic Press Ltd, 1993; 1490.
12. Christopher MM, Perman V, Eaton JW. Contribution of propylene glycol-induced Heinz body formation to anemia in cats. Journal of the American Veterinary Medical Association 1989; 194: 1045-1056.
13. Lopez A. A Complete Course in Canning and Related Processes, 12th ed. Baltimore, MD: The Canning Trade Inc, 1987.
14. Walker JA., Harmon DL, Gross KL, et al. Evaluation of nutrient utilization in the canine using the ileal cannulation technique. Journal of Nutrition 1994; 124: 2672S-2676S.
15. Robey W. Preventing the negative effects of nutrient oxidation on animal nutrition and performance. In: Novus International, Inc. Nutrition Update 1994, vol. 4(2).
16. Pappas AM. Antioxidants—Which ones are best for your petfood products? Petfood Industry 1991; 33(3): 8-16.
17. Halliwell B. Free radicals and antioxidants: A personal view. Nutrition Reviews 1994; 52: 253-265.
18. Hilton JW. Antioxidants: Function, types and necessity of inclusion in pet foods. Canadian Veterinary Journal 1989; 30: 682-684.
19. Frankel EN. In search of better methods to evaluate natural antioxidants and oxidative stability in food lipids. Trends in Food Science & Technology 1993; 4: 220-225.
20. Gross KL, Bollinger R, Thawnghmung P, et al. Effect of three different preservative systems on the stability of extruded dog food subjected to ambient and high temperature storage. Journal of Nutrition 1994; 124: 2638S-2642S.

CHAPTER 5

Pet Food Labels

Philip Roudebush

David A. Dzanis

Jacques Debraekeleer

R. Glenn Brown

"Tell me what you eat and I will tell you what you are."
Anthelme Brillat-Savarin, 1825

INTRODUCTION

The pet food label is the primary means by which specific product information is communicated between a manufacturer or distributor and consumers, veterinarians and regulatory officials. Commercial pet foods differ from human food products in that the final consumer, the animal, is not the purchaser. Thus there are two different "customers" with regards to safety, nutritional balance and palatability. Pet food label information is not directed to the final consumer, but to the owner or veterinarian who decides what the animal will be fed.

Implementation of the Nutrition Labeling and Education Act of 1994 in the United States has led to increased consumer awareness of the contents and effects of various human foods. Consumer interest in human food label information will lead to increased awareness of information available on pet food labels. Reading and interpreting pet food labels is one way veterinarians and pet owners obtain information about a pet food; however, labels do not provide information about digestibility and biological value. Contacting the manufacturer or nutrition experts for additional information is the best way to compare the quality of pet foods.

The Label as a Legal Document

The pet food label is more than an attractive package cover designed to sell the product; the pet food label is also a legal document. A number of agencies and organizations regulate the production, marketing and sales of commercial

pet foods in different countries. Each agency or organization has different responsibilities with varying degrees of authority (Table 5-1). Some of these agencies and organizations regulate the information found on pet food labels whereas others influence the regulatory process.

Pet foods are regulated at their point of sale. As an example, pet food manufactured in the United States for sale outside the United States must meet the labeling requirements established by the country in which the food is sold. Conversely, pet foods manufactured outside the United States must conform to Food and Drug Administration (FDA), Association of American Feed Control Officials (AAFCO) and state pet food labeling requirements when sold in the United States.

PET FOOD LABELS IN THE UNITED STATES

Regulation in the United States

AAFCO

Early regulators recognized the need for uniform and consistent regulation of animal feeds by forming AAFCO in 1909. AAFCO members include animal feed control officials from states and territories within the United States and Canada. Liaisons for AAFCO committees and investigators include representatives from pet food manufacturers and organizations such as the American Animal

KEY WORDS & TERMS—PET FOOD LABELS*

Ash	Designator	Ministries of Agriculture
Association of American Feed Control Officials (AAFCO)	Dietetic pet food	National Research Council (NRC)
	European Commission	Net weight
Brand name	European Economic Community (EEC)	Nutrition adequacy statement
Burst	European Union (EU)	Nutrition claim
Canadian Veterinary Medical Association (CVMA)	Fédération Européenne de l'Industrie des Aliments pour Aminaux Familiers (FEDIAF)	Pet Food Institute (PFI)
		Principal display panel
Canine Nutrition Expert (CNE) Subcommittee		Product family
	Feline Nutrition Expert (FNE) Subcommittee	Product identity
Center for Veterinary Medicine (CVM)		Product vignette
Confédération des Industries Agro-Alimentaires de l' UE (CIAA)	Flag	Statement of calorie content
	Food and Drug Administration (FDA)	Statutory statement
Crude fat	Guaranteed analysis	Universal product code (UPC)
Crude fiber	Information panel	United States Department of Agriculture (USDA)
Crude protein	Ingredient statement	
CVMA Pet Food Certification Program	Lead product	

Key words and terms are defined in the Glossary.

KEY POINTS—PET FOOD LABELS

1. The pet food label is more than an attractive package cover designed to sell the product; the pet food label is also a legal document.
2. In the United States, AAFCO is the official source of information on pet food labeling, ingredient definitions, official terms and standardized feed testing methodology.
3. In the United States, health claims on pet food labels or in literature accompanying the product are subject to regulation by the FDA.
4. In the United States, pet food labels that refer to NRC nutritional profiles are considered to be mislabeled. The NRC recommendations are still used by some pet food manufacturers in countries other than the United States.
5. In Canada, the CVMA Pet Food Certification Program establishes nutrient standards, lifestage feeding protocols and digestibility feeding protocols for dogs and cats.
6. Percentage rules for ingredients are important to remember when interpreting the descriptors used in the product name.
7. The CVMA Pet Food Certification Program has more extensive pet food labeling requirements than does the Canadian government.
8. In the United States, each ingredient of a pet food must be listed in the ingredient statement in descending order of its predominance by weight.
9. In Europe, three groups of additives must be declared on pet food labels when they are added to a product: preservatives, antioxidants and colorants.
10. Percentages listed in the guaranteed analysis are a general indication of the tolerances for these nutrients in the food and do not reflect the exact amounts of these nutrients.
11. Although crude fiber is used to report the fiber content of commercial pet foods, it usually underestimates the true level of fiber in the product.
12. Subtle differences in moisture content of canned and other moist products can markedly affect dry matter content and therefore the economics of using a given pet food.
13. In Europe, copper and vitamins A, D and E must be declared on the label if they have been added to the product.
14. AAFCO regulations allow two basic methods to substantiate claims: the formulation/analysis method and the feeding trial (protocol) method.
15. The feeding trial method is the preferred method of substantiating a nutritional adequacy claim because it documents how an animal performs when fed a specific food.
16. In Europe, label claims and declarations related to dietetic pet foods are strictly regulated, and statements must be written as prescribed by the directives.
17. In Europe, energy declarations are forbidden on all pet food labels except for those products specifically designed and marketed for management of obesity and convalescence.

Hospital Association, American Veterinary Medical Association, Canadian Veterinary Medical Association and the Pet Food Institute (PFI).

AAFCO provides a forum for local, state and federal feed regulatory officials to discuss and develop uniform and equitable laws, regulations and policies. AAFCO addressed the need for information about pet nutrition and pet food regulations by forming a permanent Pet Food Committee. The Pet Food Committee has solidified the AAFCO Official Pet Food Regulations, which have been adopted by approximately one-half of the states. Today, individual members look to AAFCO for guidance when establishing and revising state laws and regulations.

In addition, AAFCO remains the recognized information source for pet food labeling, ingredient definitions, official terms and standardized feed testing methodology. Recent changes in the Official Pet Food Regulations have included caloric content statement guidelines and definition of the pet

Table 5-1. Major governing agencies and organizations for commercial pet food manufacturers.

Agency	Key functions
Association of American Feed Control Officials (AAFCO)	Sets nutrient standards for substantiation of claims and provides model regulations for the states
U.S. Food and Drug Administration (FDA)	Specifies some label requirements, regulates health claims and ensures food safety
U.S. Department of Agriculture (USDA)	Regulates some pet food ingredients and inspects animal research facilities
State Department of Agriculture (or similar agency)	Adopts and enforces animal food regulations
National Research Council (NRC)	Evaluates and compiles nutrition research and makes nutrient recommendations
Pet Food Institute (PFI)	Trade organization representing major pet food manufacturers in the United States
Canadian Veterinary Medical Association (CVMA)	Administers voluntary product certification in Canada
European Commission	The main legislative body in the European Union responsible for creating new directives and regulations
European Council of Ministers	Gives final approval for directives and regulations Creates the basic laws
National Government (Ministry of Agriculture)	Implements European legislation, controls its application and houses national experts
European Federation of the Pet Food Industry (FEDIAF = Fédération Européenne de l'Industrie des Aliments pour Aminaux Familiers)	The trade organization representing major pet food manufacturers in Europe
Confederation of the Food and Drink Industries of the EU (CIAA = Confédération des Industries Agro-Alimentaires de l' UE)	The trade organization representing human food manufacturers in Europe Works closely with FEDIAF on matters of mutual interest

food descriptive terms "light," "lean" and "reduced calorie." The Pet Food Committee has also developed new criteria for the official definition of product "families" whose lead member has been tested via the AAFCO feeding trial protocol.

Many pet owners recognize the need to feed their animals nutritionally balanced pet foods. As a consequence, consumers usually purchase pet foods that are labeled "complete and balanced." One means of ensuring nutritional adequacy of a food requires that the food be formulated so essential nutrients meet recommended levels. Nutrient minimums before the early 1990s were based on the recommendations of the National Research Council (NRC). In 1990 and 1991 AAFCO established the Canine Nutrition Expert (CNE) and Feline Nutrition Expert (FNE) subcommittees to establish updated practical profiles based on commonly used ingredients. The CNE and FNE subcommittee reports formed the basis for new dog and cat food nutrient profiles to be used as standards for the formulation of dog and cat foods.[1] The AAFCO nutrient profiles differ from previous NRC recommendations. The most recent NRC levels were based on data using purified foods and the assumption of 100% availability. Further, NRC recommendations included only one profile for all lifestages. Two separate AAFCO profiles exist for each species: one for growth and reproduction, and one for adult maintenance. Lower amounts of some nutrients were thus established for adult dogs and cats, eliminating unnecessary excesses. In addition, maximum levels were established for some nutrients in dog foods, including calcium, phosphorus, magnesium, fat-soluble vitamins and many trace minerals. Maximum methionine, zinc and vit-

amin A and D levels were established for cat foods. The AAFCO nutrient profiles have replaced NRC recommendations as the basis for the substantiation of label claims.

AAFCO also publishes minimum feeding protocols for dog and cat foods.[1] These are minimum testing protocols used by manufacturers for substantiating the nutritional adequacy of pet foods via feeding trials and determining metabolizable energy of dog and cat foods.

Food and Drug Administration

Under the Federal Food, Drug and Cosmetic Act, the FDA has broad responsibilities, including authority over pet foods. Today, the Center for Veterinary Medicine (CVM), in FDA, regulates pet foods in cooperation with the individual states. FDA is responsible for: 1) establishing certain animal food labeling regulations, 2) specifying certain permitted ingredients such as drugs and additives, 3) enforcing regulations on chemical and microbiologic contamination and 4) describing acceptable manufacturing procedures. Feed control officials within each state inspect facilities and enforce these regulations. Health claims on pet food labels or literature accompanying the product are subject to regulation by CVM. A health claim is defined as the assertion or implication that consumption of a food will treat, prevent or otherwise affect a disease or condition.[2] (See sidebar "FDA Perspective: Pet Food 'Drug' Claims.")

United States Department of Agriculture

The United States Department of Agriculture (USDA) is responsible for ensuring that pet foods are labeled so they are

FDA Perspective:
Pet Food "Drug" Claims

Under FDA law, the legal definitions for "food" and "drug" become intertwined when a food label bears a claim that consumption of the product will treat, prevent or otherwise affect a disease or condition. In effect, such a claim establishes an intent to offer the product as a drug (i.e., it makes a "drug claim"). This legal distinction is critical in terms of FDA requirements. Wherein a new animal drug must be approved by FDA through demonstration of safety and efficacy by controlled studies, a food is not subject to the same criteria. Therefore, when a pet food bears a drug claim, it could be deemed an adulterated drug under the law and be subject to regulatory action.

Pet food labels usually contain claims regarding product benefits. There is often a fine distinction between an inappropriate "drug claim" and a claim that may be informally sanctioned or that is tolerable puffery. Claims relating an essential nutrient to its physiologic effect on the body may be allowed, but any connotation beyond its normal function is less tolerable. For example, a label may say "taurine is needed for your cat's vision" or "calcium helps build strong bones," but cannot say "taurine prevents blindness" or "calcium corrects bone problems."

That said, FDA recognizes that there is an integral relationship between nutrition and disease. Thus, it has considered this fact in its policies in order to allow for meaningful health-related information on pet food to reach the veterinarian and consumer without violating the intent of the law.

David A. Dzanis, DVM, PhD, Diplomate ACVN
Center for Veterinary Medicine
United States Food and Drug Administration

mals. Numerous subcommittees have assisted in developing the series *Nutrient Requirements of Domestic Animals*. The most current NRC recommendations for normal dogs and cats were published in 1985 and 1986, respectively.[4,5] Before the development and acceptance of AAFCO's Dog and Cat Food Nutrient Profiles, the NRC publications on nutrient requirements for normal dogs and cats were the recognized authority for substantiation of label claims on commercial pet foods. The AAFCO Dog and Cat Food Nutrient Profiles have replaced the NRC recommendations as the standard to be used by pet food manufacturers in the United States for formulating foods for normal dogs and cats.

The NRC does not regulate the pet food industry and has requested that its recommendations not be used to substantiate nutritional adequacy of pet foods. Pet food labels in the United States that make reference to NRC nutritional profiles are considered to be mislabeled. The NRC recommendations are still used by some pet food manufacturers in countries other than the United States and reference to NRC is still found on some pet food labels. Revisions of the NRC's *Nutrient Requirements of Dogs* and *Nutrient Requirements of Cats* will continue to be important sources of research information on small animal nutrition.

Pet Food Institute

The PFI was organized in 1958 as the national trade association of dog and cat food manufacturers in the United States. Active members of PFI produce 95% of the total dog and cat food tonnage in the United States.[6] Affiliate members of PFI include the leading suppliers of equipment, ingredients, packaging and services to the United States pet food industry.

PFI works closely with veterinarians, humane groups and local animal control officers to sponsor public affairs and owner education programs that encourage responsible dog and cat ownership. It also represents the industry before legislative and regulatory bodies at the federal and state levels. In the past 20 years, PFI has sponsored research on amino acid requirements of dogs and cats, as well as research on the benefits of pet ownership and the beneficial role of pets in society.

Individual States

Each individual state is responsible for adopting and enforcing pet food regulations. Many, but not all, states have adopted pet food regulations that follow the model bill and model regulations established by AAFCO. Pet food regulation and enforcement in most states is administered by the State Department of Agriculture, Regulatory Protection Division or State Chemist.

Label Design

A pet food label is divided into two main parts: 1) the principal display panel and 2) the information panel (Figure 5-1). The principal display panel is defined by FDA as "the part of a label that is most likely to be displayed, presented, shown or examined under customary conditions of display for retail sale."[7] The principal display panel is the primary means of attracting the consumer's attention to a product and should immediately communicate the product identity. The information panel is defined as "that part of the label immediately contiguous and to the right of the principal display panel"[7] and usually contains important information

not mistaken for human foods. The USDA inspects animal ingredients used in pet foods to ensure proper handling and to guarantee that such ingredients are not used in human foods. The USDA also inspects and regulates animal research facilities. All animal research facilities owned and operated in the United States by pet food companies must fulfill USDA requirements for: 1) record keeping, 2) physical structure, housing and care of animals, 3) food and water quality and 4) sanitation. Research facilities are subject to unannounced inspections by USDA officials at least once a year.

National Research Council

The NRC is a private, nonprofit organization that evaluates and compiles research conducted by others. The NRC functions as the working arm of the National Academy of Sciences, the National Academy of Engineers and the Institute of Medicine.[3] The National Academy of Sciences was created in 1863 to advise the United States federal government about scientific and technological matters.[3] The NRC was created in 1916 in response to the increased need for scientific and technical services during World War I.[3] The NRC is not part of the United States government, is not an enforcement agency and is not a basic research organization with laboratories of its own.

The NRC includes a Board of Agriculture with a Committee on Animal Nutrition. One of the major activities of the Committee on Animal Nutrition has been the development of nutrient requirement standards for domestic ani-

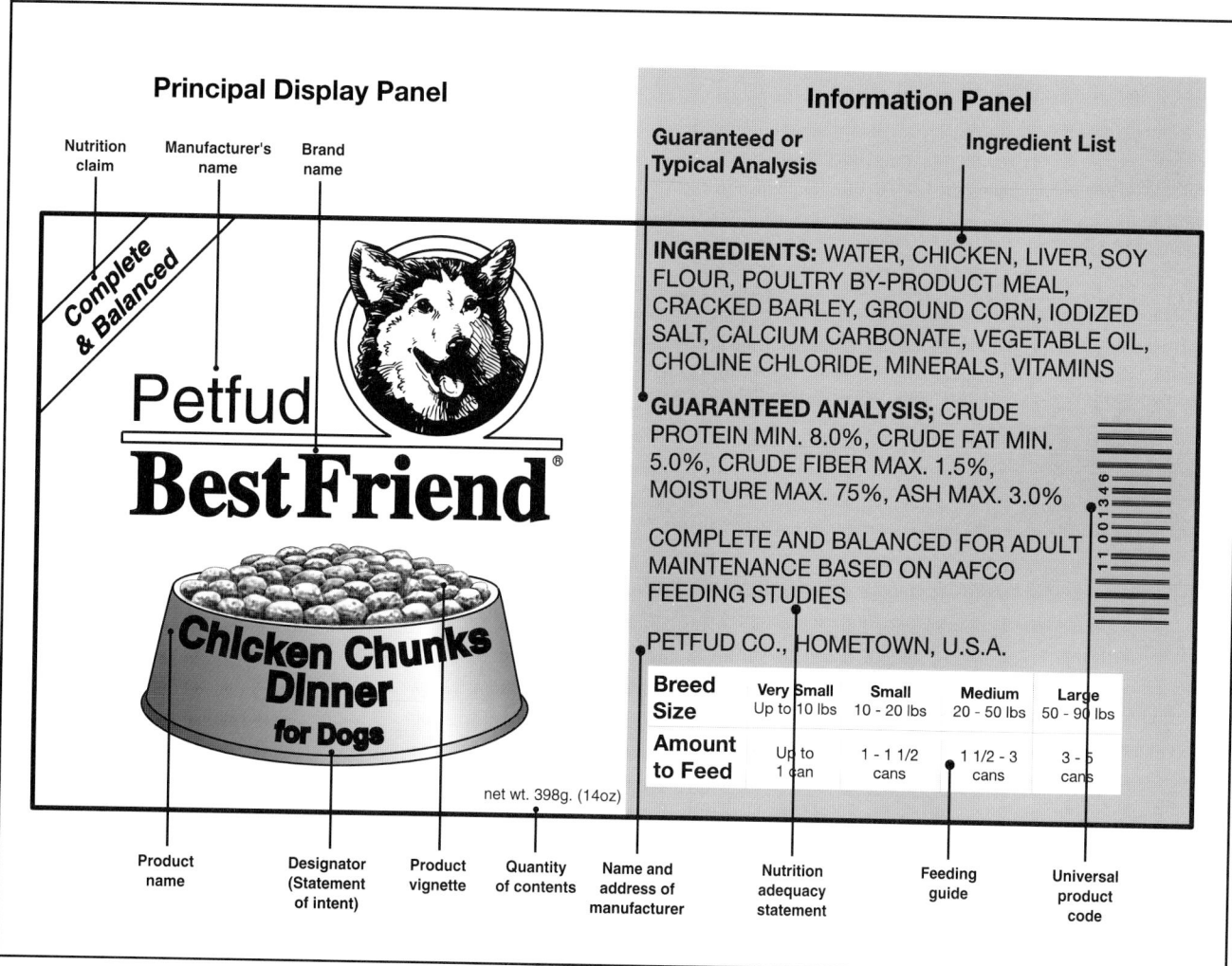

Figure 5-1. Typical pet food label with all elements.

about the product. In the United States and some other countries, several items are required by law to be included on the principal display panel and information panel (Table 5-2). The following discussion will focus on the major features found on these two portions of the pet food label.

Principal Display Panel

PRODUCT IDENTITY

The product identity is the primary means by which a specific pet food is identified by consumers. In the United States, the product identity must legally include a product name but may also include a manufacturer's name, a brand name or both. The brand name is the name by which pet food products of a given company are identified and usually conveys the overall image of the product. The product name provides information about the individual identity of the particular product within the brand. The manufacturer or distributor is not required to include its name as part of the product identity on the principal display panel, but must include its name and address on the label.

Initial assessment of pet foods is best determined by looking at the product name on the principal display panel. The product name is usually descriptive of the food and in the United States is subject to AAFCO regulations about composition of ingredients. Percentage rules are important; beef

ingredients will be used as an example (Figure 5-2): 1) the term "Beef" in a product name requires that beef ingredients be at least 70% of the total product (stated another way, beef must be 95% or more of the total weight of all ingredients exclusive of water used in processing), 2) the term "Beef dinner," "Beef platter," "Beef entree" or any similar designation requires that beef ingredients be at least 10% of the total product (stated another way, beef must be at least 25% but not more than 95% of the total weight of all ingredients exclusive of water used in processing),

Table 5-2. Key elements found on pet food labels in the United States and Canada.

Principal display panel	Information panel
Product identity	Ingredient statement*
Manufacturer's name	Guaranteed analysis*
Brand name	Nutritional adequacy statement*
Product name*	(Product description)*
Designator*	Feeding guidelines*
(Statement of intent)*	Statement of calorie content
Net weight*	Manufacturer or distributor*
Product vignette	Universal product code
Nutrition claim	Batch information
Bursts and flags	Freshness date

*Elements required on pet food labels in the United States, on labels certified by the CVMA Program and in some other countries.

Figure 5-2. Examples of pet food descriptor terms.

3) the term "with Beef" is intended to highlight minor ingredients and this example requires that beef ingredients be at least 3% of the total product and 4) the term "Beef flavor" only requires that beef is "recognizable by the pet."[1] The beef flavor designation usually indicates that beef is less than 3% of the total product. An ingredient that gives the characterizing flavor (e.g., beef digest, beef by-products) can be used instead of the actual named flavor, beef. In fact, some ingredients may be less than 1% of the total product and still appear in the product name as a flavor. This type of regulation is also found in human foods where the product names cranberry juice, cranberry juice cocktail and cranberry drink indicate different levels of actual juice in the product.

Percentage rules also apply to product names and moisture content of foods. In the United States, the maximum moisture content in all pet foods should not exceed 78%. However, pet foods can have moisture contents higher than 78% if they consist of stew, gravy, broth, juice or a milk replacer which is so labeled. High-moisture pet foods in cans or tins will have a product name with the terms "in sauce," "in aspic," "in gravy" or some similar designation.

DESIGNATOR

The words "dog food" or "cat food" or some similar terminology is called the Designator or Statement of Intent and must appear conspicuously on the principal display panel of pet foods sold in the United States. These terms clearly identify the animal for which the product is intended and that the product is not for human consumption.

NET WEIGHT

FDA regulations state that the principal display panel shall bear a declaration of the net quantity of contents.[7] The term net weight is used most often and must be displayed in conspicuous and easily legible print. The regulation of net weight descriptions is complex. Net weight descriptions must be placed on the principal display panel within the bottom 30% of the panel in lines generally parallel to the base of the package.

PRODUCT VIGNETTE

The term product vignette refers to a vignette, graphic or pictorial representation of a product on a pet food label. This representation should not misrepresent the contents of the package. This means that a picture or other depiction of the product or ingredients on the label should not look better than the actual product or ingredients.

NUTRITION CLAIM

Nutrition statements appearing on the principal display panel are usually brief. Examples include the terms "complete and nutritious," "100% nutritious," "100% complete nutrition" or some similar designation. Nutrition claims such as these on the principal display panel must be substantiated by a nutritional adequacy statement on the information panel. Manufacturers can substantiate these nutrition claims by meeting the appropriate AAFCO nutrient profile or successfully completing a protocol feeding trial. Nutrition claims substantiation is discussed in more detail below. (See sidebar "FDA Perspective: 'Health' and 'Healthy' Claims.")

BURSTS AND FLAGS

Bursts and flags (Figure 5-3) are areas of the principal display panel that are designed to highlight information or provide specific information with visual impact. Table 5-3 lists the type of information often included in bursts and flags. New products, formula or ingredient changes and improvements in taste are most often highlighted. The time allowed for a burst or flag to be on the label varies with the type of information. "New" or "New & Improved" can only appear on the label for six months, whereas a comparison such as "Preferred 4 to 1 over the leading national brand" can remain on the label for one year, unless resubstantiated.

Information Panel

INGREDIENT STATEMENT

Pet foods sold in the United States must list each ingredient of the food in the ingredient statement. Ingredients are listed in descending order by their predominance by weight according to the product's formula. AAFCO has established the name and definition of a wide variety of ingredients. The ingredient names must conform to the AAFCO name (e.g., poultry by-product meal, corn gluten meal, powdered cellulose) or should be identified by the common or usual name (e.g., beef, lamb, chicken). Brand or trade names cannot be used in the ingredient statement and no reference to quality or grade of ingredients can be made. Collective terms (e.g., "animal protein products"), allowed for use on livestock and poultry feed labels, are not allowed on pet food labels in the United States (Table 5-4).

The list of ingredients may be helpful, although it has some shortcomings that limit its usefulness for evaluating pet foods. The nutritive value of ingredients cannot be identified from the ingredient statement. A consumer must rely on the reputation or word of the manufacturer to assess the nutritive value and safety of the ingredients appearing on the list. A serious limitation of the ingredient statement is that terms such as "meat by-products" are difficult to evaluate. The nutritive value of various meat by-products varies widely. As an example, meat by-products such as liver, kidney and lungs have excellent nutritive value whereas other meat by-products such as udder, bone and connective tissue have poor nutrient availability.

Manufacturers can also misrepresent the ingredient content of pet foods. A pet food that lists several different forms of the same ingredient separately (e.g., wheat germ meal, wheat middlings, wheat bran, wheat flour) make wheat-based ingredients appear to be a lower portion of the food than is the fact. Because ingredients are listed in descending order by weight, this also allows dry ingredients to appear lower on the list than ingredients that are naturally high in moisture.

This basic principle is commonly used in moist meat-type dog foods where textured vegetable protein (TVP) is a major portion of the product. The ingredient list may look like this for a food named a "beef dinner": Water sufficient for pro-

---

FDA Perspective: "Health" and "Healthy" Claims

FDA has promulgated regulations on the proper use of the terms "health" and "healthy" for human food products. The use of these terms is limited to those products that meet certain nutritional criteria (levels of salt, fat, etc.). The only nutrient criteria applicable to pet foods are the AAFCO profiles and feeding trial protocols. Thus, a food substantiated to be "complete" or "balanced" may also be suitable for description as "healthy."

Use of the terms "health" and "healthy" in a context other than nutritional adequacy may be misleading. For example, a claim that a product is healthy because it is "all-natural," does not contain certain ingredients, etc., may be misleading. Also, claims for a product to be "healthier" (vs. "healthy") begs a comparison and may imply medical benefit. In general, any claim promising "improvement" or "results" may be misleading.

David A. Dzanis, DVM, PhD, Diplomate ACVN
Center for Veterinary Medicine
United States Food and Drug Administration

---

cessing, chicken, meat by-products, beef, soy flour, food starch. . . . In this kind of food, water is typically combined with soy flour to produce TVP. The TVP makes up a predominant portion of the food, but soy flour appears lower on the ingredient statement because it is a "dry" ingredient whereas other components of the food are added "wet." The consumer thinks he or she is purchasing a meat-based moist food (e.g., beef dinner) when the predominant ingredient is soy flour.

This same principle is used in dry pet foods where "fresh" meats are highlighted. The ingredient list may look like this for a lamb and rice dog food that claims to provide "real lamb meat": lamb, brewers rice, ground yellow corn, corn gluten meal, oat groats, poultry by-product meal, beef tallow. . . . Lamb appears first on the ingredient list because its moisture content is higher than that of the other dry ingredients. The predominant portion of the food contains a mixture of grains (rice, corn, oats) rather than "real meat."

Pet food additives such as vitamins, minerals, antioxidant preservatives, antimicrobial preservatives, humec-

---

Table 5-3. Examples of words used on bursts and flags on pet food labels.

New
New formula
New recipe
New flavor
New & improved
Pleasant aroma
New taste
New pâté style
Great new taste
More delicious taste
Great taste
Freshness guaranteed
Soy free
No artificial colors and flavors
Even fewer calories
5 Lbs more
Taste preferred over leading dog biscuit
Taste preferred 4 to 1 over leading national brand

Figure 5-3. One label with a flag and one label with a burst.

tants, coloring agents, flavors, palatability enhancers and emulsifying agents that are added by the manufacturer must be listed in the ingredient statement. Pet food additives must conform to the requirements of the applicable regulations in the United States Code of Federal Regulations, as food additives (21 CFR 573) or as ingredients generally recognized as safe (GRAS) (21 CFR 582). Some additives are listed only in the sections for human direct food additives or for GRAS substances, but are allowed in pet foods by informal review.

GUARANTEED ANALYSIS

In the United States, pet food manufacturers are required to include minimum percentages for crude protein and crude fat and maximum percentages for crude fiber and moisture (Table 5-5). Guarantees for other nutrients may follow moisture, but a nutrient need not be listed unless its presence is highlighted elsewhere on the label (e.g., "contains taurine," "calcium enriched"). The sliding scale method of listing guarantees as percentage ranges (e.g., 15 to 18%) is not allowed. It is important to recognize that these percentages generally indicate the "worst case" levels for these nutrients in the food and do not reflect the exact or typical amounts of these nutrients. This differs from pet food labels in Europe where "typical" percentages are used.

The term crude protein refers to a specific analytical procedure that estimates protein content by measuring nitrogen. Crude protein is an index of protein quantity but does not indicate protein quality (amino acid profile) or digestibility. (See Chapter 2.)

Crude fat refers to a specific analytical procedure that estimates the lipid content of a food obtained through extraction of fat from the food with ether. In addition to lipids, this procedure also isolates certain organic acids, oils, pigments, alcohols and fat-soluble vitamins. Because fats have more than twice the energy density of protein and carbohydrates, crude fat can be used to estimate the energy density of the food. If the moisture and crude fiber content of two foods are somewhat similar, the food with the higher crude fat guarantee will usually have the higher energy density.

Crude fiber represents the organic residue that remains after plant material has been treated with dilute acid and alkali solutions. It is determined by a specific analytical procedure that was originally developed for the wood pulp industry and then applied to animal foods. Although crude fiber is used to report the fiber content of commercial pet foods, it usually underestimates the true level of fiber in the product. Crude fiber is an estimate of the indigestible portion of the food for dogs and cats. (See Chapter 2.) The crude fiber method typically recovers a large percentage of cellulose and lignin in a sample, and a variable percentage of hemicellulose and even ash.

Moisture is determined by drying a sample of the product to a constant weight. The drying procedure measures water in the product as a whole, but does not distinguish between added water and water in the ingredients. Subtle differences in moisture content of moist products can result in marked differences in dry matter content and therefore the economics of feeding a given pet food. Remember, the dry matter content of the food contains all of the nutrients except water. For example, compare the dry matter content of three different moist cat foods, 1) Food A contains 72% moisture, 2) Food B contains 78% moisture and 3) Food C contains 82% moisture.

Food A	100 – 72% water = 28% dry matter
Food B	100 – 78% water = 22% dry matter
Food C	100 – 82% water = 18% dry matter

28 – 22/22 x 100 = 27% more dry matter in Food A (72% moisture) vs. Food B (78% moisture)

28 – 18/18 x 100 = 55% more dry matter in Food A (72% moisture) vs. Food C (82% moisture)

Therefore, what appears to be a small difference in water content of a food produces a marked difference in dry matter content. Guarantees are usually expressed on an "As Is" or "As Fed" basis. It is important to remember to convert these guarantees to a dry matter basis when comparing foods with differing moisture content (e.g., moist vs. dry foods).

Table 5-4. Ingredient statement from the same dry dog food as it would appear on pet food labels in different countries.

United States
Ingredients: Ground Corn, Chicken Meal, Soybean Meal, Animal Fat (preserved with BHA, propyl gallate, and citric acid), Dried Egg Product, Brewers Rice, Vegetable Oil, Iodized Salt, Choline Chloride, Calcium Carbonate, Ferrous Sulfate, Zinc Oxide, Manganous Oxide, Cobalt Carbonate, Copper Sulfate, Sodium Selenite, Vitamin A Supplement, D-Activated Animal Sterol, Vitamin E Supplement, Thiamin, Niacin, Calcium Pantothenate, Pyridoxine Hydrochloride, Riboflavin, Folic Acid, Biotin, Vitamin B_{12} Supplement.

Canada
Ingredients: Grain Products, Poultry Products, Soybean Meal, Stabilized Poultry and/or Animal Fat, Vitamins and Minerals.

CVMA-Certified Product
Ingredients: Ground Corn, Chicken Meal, Soybean Meal, Animal Fat, Dried Whole Egg, Brewers Rice, Vegetable Oil, Iodized Salt, Plus All Necessary Vitamins and Minerals.

Europe*
Ingredients: Cereals, Meat and Animal Derivatives, Vegetable Protein Extracts, Oils and Fats, Eggs and Egg Derivatives, Minerals.

*Antioxidants, preservatives, vitamins and coloring agents are not listed under ingredients because they are considered additives and are declared elsewhere on the label. Ingredients can also be listed individually.

Although a maximum ash guarantee is not required in the United States, many pet food manufacturers include one on the labels of their foods. In the United States, "low ash" claims are not allowed because "ash" per se is of no true significance. "Low magnesium" claims on cat food labels are allowed if the food meets certain FDA criteria. In such cases, a magnesium guarantee is required. To be labeled as a "low magnesium" food, the product must contain less than 0.12% magnesium, on a dry matter basis, and 25 mg per 100 kcal metabolizable energy. Actual analytical values must show that the product consistently meets these levels. The estimation of magnesium content based on calculation from the guaranteed analyses must meet these criteria as well. The only exception occurs when the label bears an AAFCO calorie content statement that is higher than would be estimated from the guaranteed analysis.

Ash consists of all noncombustible materials in the food, usually salt and other minerals. A high-ash content in dry and semi-moist foods generally indicates a high magnesium content. However, the ash content of moist cat foods usually correlates poorly with the magnesium content. Excessive magnesium intake may be one risk factor for feline struvite urolithiasis. (See Chapter 20.)

NUTRITIONAL ADEQUACY STATEMENT

Since 1984, regulations in the United States have required that all pet food labels, with the exception of products clearly labeled as treats and snacks, contain a statement and validation of nutritional adequacy (product description). When a claim of "complete and balanced," "100% nutritious" or some similar designation is used, manufacturers must indicate the method and lifestage that was used to substantiate this claim (Table 5-6).

AAFCO regulations allow two basic methods to substantiate claims.[1] The formulation method requires that the manufacturer formulate the food to meet the AAFCO Dog Food Nutrient Profiles or Cat Food Nutrient Profiles. The feeding trial (protocol) method requires that the manufacturer perform an AAFCO-protocol feeding trial using the food as the sole source of nutrition.

AAFCO nutrient profiles are published for two categories: 1) growth and reproduction and 2) adult maintenance.[1] The formulation method allows the manufacturer to substantiate a "complete and balanced" claim by calculating the nutrient content of a food using standard nutrient information about ingredients. Table 5-6 lists some of the wording that connotes this type of claim. The formulation method is less expensive and time-consuming, but has been criticized because it does not account for acceptability of the food or nutrient availability. A report in 1991 documented that some commercial pet foods that made "complete and balanced" claims by formulation methods alone did not provide adequate growth of normal animals because of poor availability of nutrients in the food.[8]

The feeding trial (protocol) method is the preferred method of substantiating a claim. Feeding tests can result in a nutritional adequacy claim for one or more of the following categories: 1) gestation and lactation, 2) growth, 3) maintenance and 4) complete for all lifestages. AAFCO has published minimum testing protocols for adult maintenance, growth and gestation/lactation. (See Appendix J.) A food that successfully completes a sequential growth and gestation/lactation trial can make a claim for all lifestages. The required terminology for labels of pet foods that have

passed these tests is as follows: "Animal feeding tests using AAFCO procedures substantiate that (brand) provides complete and balanced nutrition for (lifestage)." The inclusion of the term "feeding test," "AAFCO feeding studies" or "AAFCO feeding protocols" in a nutritional adequacy statement supports the idea that the food has successfully completed a minimum feeding protocol (Table 5-6). The same statement can also be used on product family members found to be "nutritionally similar" to the tested product.

AAFCO feeding trials are minimum protocols. As an example, the adult maintenance protocol uses eight animals that are fed the food as the sole source of nutrition for six months. The animals are examined by a veterinarian at the beginning of the study and at the end of 26 weeks to look for clinical signs of nutritional deficiency or excess. Body weight is recorded weekly and minimal laboratory evaluations (total erythrocyte count, hemoglobin, packed cell volume, serum alkaline phosphatase, serum albumin and whole blood taurine in cats) are performed. This type of protocol will usually detect nutrient deficiencies but might not detect some nutrient excesses that may be harmful when fed over a longer period. In this respect, the AAFCO profiles are better because maximum levels of some nutrients are also established. Growth protocols include feeding the food for a minimum of 10 weeks.

Pet foods that are clearly labeled as snacks or treats may make a nutritional adequacy claim but are not required to do so. Pet foods that do not meet AAFCO requirements by either of the standard methods will have a nutritional statement as follows: "this product is intended for inter-

Table 5-5. Guaranteed or typical analysis from the same dry cat food as it would appear on pet food labels in different countries.

United States

Guaranteed analysis

Crude protein	Minimum	30.0%
Crude fat	Minimum	18.0%
Crude fiber	Maximum	2.0%
Moisture	Maximum	10.0%

Canada

Guaranteed analysis

Protein	30.0%
Fat	18.0%
Moisture	10.0%

CVMA-Certified Food in Canada

Guaranteed analysis

Crude protein	Minimum	30.0%
Crude fat	Minimum	18.0%
Crude fibre	Maximum	2.0%
Moisture	Maximum	10.0%
Ash	Maximum	5.0%

Europe

Typical analysis (%)

Crude protein	31.3
Crude oils & fats	21.3
Crude fibre	2.0
Crude ash	4.7
Moisture	7.5

Additives (per kg)

Vitamin A	17,100 IU
Vitamin D_3	1,710 IU
Vitamin E	290 mg
Copper (copper chloride)	21 mg
Contains EU permitted antioxidant	
Contains EU permitted colorant	

Table 5-6. How to interpret label claims of nutritional adequacy.*

Claim 1: "Good Things Dog Food is formulated to meet the AAFCO (Association of American Feed Control Officials) dog food nutrient profile for maintenance of adult dogs."

Interpretation: This food has been formulated to meet the nutrient levels in the AAFCO Dog Food Nutrient Profile for adult maintenance. This product does not meet the nutrient profile for growth/lactation and has probably not undergone AAFCO feeding tests.

Claim 2: "Good Things Cat Food meets the nutrient requirements established by the AAFCO Nutrient Profile for all stages of a cat's life."

Interpretation: This food has been formulated to meet the nutrient levels in the AAFCO Cat Food Nutrient Profile for growth/reproduction and adult maintenance. This product has probably not undergone AAFCO feeding tests.

Claim 3: "Animal feeding tests using the AAFCO procedures substantiate that Good Things Dog Food provides complete and balanced nutrition for the growth of puppies and maintenance of adult dogs."

Interpretation: This food has successfully completed an AAFCO minimum protocol feeding trial for growing puppies (10 weeks of feeding) or is a family member of a tested product.

Claim 4: "Good Things Cat Food provides complete and balanced nutrition for kittens and adult reproducing queens as substantiated by feeding tests performed in accordance with procedures established by the Association of American Feed Control Officials (AAFCO)."

Interpretation: This cat food (or a family member) has undergone AAFCO minimum protocol feeding studies for gestation/lactation and growth. This food would be nutritionally adequate for adult cats but has not undergone an adult maintenance feeding trial and is not recommended by this manufacturer for long-term maintenance of adult cats.

Claim 5: "Complete and balanced nutrition for adult maintenance based on AAFCO protocol feeding studies conducted at the Good Things Nutrition Center."

Interpretation: This food (or a family member) has undergone AAFCO minimum protocol feeding studies for adult maintenance only and has not been tested for gestation/lactation or growth.

Claim 6: "Complete and balanced nutrition for all lifestages of the dog, substantiated by testing performed in accordance with feeding protocols established by AAFCO."

Interpretation: This dog food (or a family member) has undergone AAFCO minimum protocol feeding trials for gestation/lactation and growth.

Claim 7: "Good Things Dog Food meets or exceeds the requirements of the National Academy of Sciences (USA) for the complete nutrition of your dog or puppy."

Interpretation: This food has been formulated to meet or exceed the nutrient levels established for growth and adult maintenance by the National Research Council (NRC) in the United States. This product has probably not undergone feeding tests. This nutrition statement would be illegal in the United States because the NRC nutrient profiles have been replaced by AAFCO Dog Food Nutrient Profiles. However, references to NRC are still made on pet foods sold in countries other than the United States.

Claim 8: "Meets or exceeds the nutritional levels established by the National Research Council specifications for all stages of a cat's life."

Interpretation: This cat food has been formulated to meet or exceed the nutrient levels established for growth, gestation/lactation and adult maintenance by the National Research Council (NRC) in the United States. This product has probably not undergone feeding tests. This nutrition statement would be illegal in the United States because the NRC nutrient profiles have been replaced by AAFCO Cat Food Nutrient Profiles. However, references to NRC are still made on pet foods sold in countries other than the United States.

Claim 9: "Good Things for Dogs: CVMA Certified; Certified by the Canadian Veterinary Medical Association to meet its nutritional standards on the basis of comprehensive feeding trials, chemical analysis and ongoing monitoring."

Interpretation: This dog food meets or exceeds the standards established by the CVMA Pet Food Certification Program for adult maintenance. The food meets or exceeds the CVMA standards for nutrient content, digestibility and labeling requirements. Nutrient digestibility is the only feeding test performed once the product is initially certified.

*NOTE: Claims 2, 4, 5 and 6 appear on pet food labels in the United States market, but Claim 3 is the preferred wording for products that have passed an AAFCO protocol feeding trial and Claim 1 is the preferred wording for products that meet the profiles.

mittent or supplemental feeding only."

Veterinary therapeutic/wellness foods are those products that are intended for use by, or under the supervision or direction of, a veterinarian. These foods may contain the nutritional statement "use only as directed by your veterinarian." In addition to this statement, the food must include a supplemental feeding statement or the appropriate lifestage AAFCO claim. The absence of a feeding test claim on the label does not necessarily mean a product has not passed feeding tests.

FEEDING GUIDELINES

In the United States, dog and cat foods labeled as complete and balanced for any or all lifestages must list feeding directions on the product label. These directions must be expressed in common terms and must appear prominently on the label. Feeding directions should, at a minimum, state "Feed (weight/unit of product) per (weight unit) of dog (or cat)" and frequency of feeding. These feeding statements are general guidelines at best. Because of individual variation, many animals will require more or less food than that recommended on the label to maintain optimal body condition and health.

STATEMENT OF CALORIE CONTENT

The label of a dog or cat food in the United States may bear a statement of calorie content provided the statement is separate from the Guaranteed Analysis and appears under the heading "Calorie Content." The statement is based on kilocalories of metabolizable energy (ME) on an as fed basis and must be expressed as kilocalories per kilogram (kcal/kg) of product. The statement may also be expressed as kilocalories per familiar household measure (e.g., kcal/cup, kcal/can).

GENERAL INFORMATION

In the United States, the name and address of the manufacturer, distributor or dealer must be found on the label, usually on the information panel. The phrases "Distributed by. . . ." or "Manufactured for. . . ." or "Imported by. . . ." indicate that the pet food has been manufactured by a company other than the one selling the product. This is a common practice with private label brand pet foods. The manufacturer in this case is called a co-packer. Regulations often require that if the product is manufactured in a country other than where it is sold, the manufacturer's information is accompanied by "Product of (country of origin)."

Although not a legal requirement, most manufacturers include the universal product code (UPC) or bar code on the label. Other information such as batch numbers and date of manufacture, is also, frequently found on pet food containers or labels. This information is important to know when communicating with a manufacturer about product in a specific container. Some manufacturers will use a freshness date such as "Best before (date)" or list other guarantee policies.

PET FOOD LABELS IN CANADA

Regulation in Canada

Canadian Government

The Canadian government has few pet food labeling regulations. Three basic mandatory statements must appear in English and French languages on a pet food label for food sold in Canada: 1) product identity, 2) product net quantity (metric units first) and 3) the manufacturer's or dealer's name and address.[9] A manufacturer or dealer may choose to include more information but the information must only conform to "truth in labeling."[10]

Canadian Veterinary Medical Association Pet Food Certification

The Canadian Veterinary Medical Association (CVMA) Pet Food Certification Program was established in 1976 as a voluntary, third-party, quality assurance program for pet foods sold in Canada. The CVMA Program establishes nutrient standards, lifestage feeding protocols and digestibility feeding protocols for dogs and cats.[9,10] Similar to PFI and NRC, the CVMA is not a regulatory agency but provides a method of voluntary enforcement of certain standards for pet foods. Involvement in the CVMA Pet Food Certification Program is not mandatory.

The mission of the CVMA Pet Food Certification Program is:

> "To improve the health and well-being of pets by: 1) providing a nutritional standard for pet foods for manufacturers to meet in order to satisfy the nutritional requirements of a normal pet throughout its life, 2) certifying pet foods that meet the CVMA nutritional standards and monitoring continuously those foods to ensure that they continue to meet the standards of composition, digestibility and palatability, 3) providing the consumer with a quality assurance program and a means of identifying a nutritionally sound pet food in the marketplace, 4) ensuring the CVMA Seal of Certification becomes synonymous in the Canadian

public's mind with quality and integrity by assuring that all advertising statements are fairly presented and can be supported by the advertiser, 5) helping pet owners understand the importance of proper nutrition in preventive health care and 6) encouraging the funding of small animal nutrition research."[9]

All CVMA-certified pet foods are allowed to display the CVMA Seal of Certification on their labels for products sold in Canada. Because of AAFCO restrictions, pet food containers sold in the United States cannot display the CVMA Seal.

Principal Display Panels

Principal display panels on Canadian pet food containers may vary. The Canadian government requires that product identity and net quantity (net weight) be listed on all principal display panels of pet foods sold in Canada. Other elements of the principal display panel described under United States regulations may appear on the container depending on several factors.

The CVMA Pet Food Certification Program requires more extensive labeling requirements than does the Canadian government.[10] The CVMA Program labeling requirements include product identity, designator and net quantity, which are usually found on the principal display panel.[10] Nutritional claims can be stated but must be substantiated. Product names can contain ingredients (Beef stew, Beef flavor, etc.) as described earlier for United States' labels and follow roughly the same percentage rules. Pet foods that meet the requirements can display the CVMA Seal of Certification on the principal display panel (Figure 5-4).[9] Requirements dictate the maximum size of the logo for different sizes of containers.[9]

Commercial pet foods produced in the United States for sale in Canada will usually contain the elements of the principal display panel legally required in the United States; namely, 1) a product name, 2) designator and 3) net weight. Pet foods produced in Canada that are not CVMA certified often do not conform to the stricter labeling requirements of the United States or CVMA Program. Other elements of the principal display panel such as the manufacturer's name, brand name, product vignette and bursts/flags are also found on Canadian labels.

Information Panels

Ingredient Statements

Ingredient statements on pet food containers in Canada also vary. Canadian government regulations do not require an ingredient statement. The CVMA Program states that ingredients should be listed on the label in decreasing order of concentration in the product. Pet foods produced in the United States and sold in Canada will usually meet the United States regulations for ingredient lists. Pet foods produced in Canada that are not CVMA certified often do not conform to the stricter labeling requirements of the United States or CVMA Program (Table 5-4).

Guaranteed Analysis

The Canadian government does not require guarantees on pet food labels. Pet foods certified by the CVMA Program must include guarantees similar to those required for pet food labels in the United States. Ash maximums (not more than 6% dry matter) are required for cat foods certified by the CVMA Program, and magnesium maximums (not more than 0.1% dry matter) are required for cat foods that make a "low ash" claim.

Nutritional Adequacy Statements

The Canadian government does not have requirements for substantiation of nutritional claims on pet food labels. The CVMA Pet Food Certification Program has published nutrient standards and protocols for digestibility feeding trials for dogs and cats.[9] Nutrient, digestibility, feeding protocols and feeding guideline standards have also been published for "special foods" including light (lite) foods, calorie-reduced foods, geriatric foods, growth foods, gestation/lactation foods and low-ash, low-magnesium cat foods. Feeding trials are incorporated into the standards for geriatric foods (three-month period) and growth foods (weaning to six months). Products that meet these standards can display the CVMA Seal of Certification and use the following words as a nutritional statement: "This product meets nutritional standards established by the Canadian Veterinary Medical Association (CVMA)." In addition to the CVMA certification logo, products certified as special foods may carry language to the effect that: "This product is formulated to provide (claim for level of nutrients)" or "This product meets the CVMA standard for a (type of special food)."

Some products in Canada will reference the NRC for complete and balanced nutrition claims, although this reference is no longer legal in the United States. Based on published NRC nutrient standards, these claims refer to the formulation/analysis method. Table 5-6 includes nutritional claims that appear on pet foods sold in Canada.

Other Items on Information Panels

In Canada, pet foods certified by the CVMA must provide feeding instructions on the label if they are sold as light, calorie-reduced or geriatric foods. Pet foods certified by the CVMA Program as light, calorie-reduced or geriatric foods have energy density (kcal per gram of dry matter gross energy) standards, but caloric density is not required on the label. No other feeding guideline requirements exist for pet foods sold in Canada.

■ PET FOOD LABELS IN EUROPE

Regulation in Europe

The regulations about pet food labeling for Europe, as discussed in this chapter, apply primarily to the European Union (EU). Legislation controlling pet food labels originates in EU institutions and is then implemented into national law. Outside the EU, individual countries have different structures and rules.

Figure 5-4. The CVMA seal.

European Commission

The European Commission is the main legislative body within the EU and is independent from the council of ministers and from the different member states.[11] The commission is subdivided into 24 Directorate Generals (DGs), each of whom deals with specific matters. The pet food industry and labeling issues are largely regulated by two DGs: DG III-Industry and DG VI-Agriculture.

In most cases, the various DGs of the European Commission prepare an initial text for adoption as a Commission Proposal. During this preparation phase, national experts, the industry, consumers and other interest groups and outside professionals may be consulted.

Two kinds of legislative pieces can come forth; a directive or a regulation. A directive must be implemented into national law within a period stipulated in the directive. The national law can be more restrictive than the European directive but must always be within the scope and spirit of the directive. A regulation must be adopted by national law without changes and is applicable almost immediately after publication. The directives for feeding stuffs contain strict provisions and stipulate definitions for ingredients, for methods of sampling and analysis and for types and maximum levels of permitted additives.

National Authorities

Once a piece of legislation is published in the Official European Journal, the national government must implement it immediately (regulation) or, in the case of a directive, translate the legislation into national law within the specified time.[11] The individual countries through their Ministries of Agriculture are responsible for controlling the application of the law by checking labels and taking samples for analysis. National experts, who work closely with the European Commission on legislation, reside under the Ministries of Agriculture of the different member states.

Fédération Européenne de l'Industrie des Aliments pour Aminaux Familiers

Founded in 1970, Fédération Européenne de l'Industrie des Aliments pour Aminaux Familiers (FEDIAF) represents the pet food industry in Europe and unites the national professional organizations of 16 countries, whether they belong to the EU or not (Table 5-7).[12,13] FEDIAF represents more than 500 companies responsible for producing more than 90% of European pet food. The national organizations represent manufacturers, packers and importers of prepared pet food, including foods for dogs, cats, birds and other pets.

FEDIAF's main role is to represent the European pet food industry in all external forums.[12,13] FEDIAF cooperates with the European authorities to implement pet food laws designed to ensure the manufacture and distribution of healthy, balanced and quality products. New legislation is translated by FEDIAF into labeling guidelines, which in some countries is then implemented into a "Code of Practice" for the members.

Through the nutrition working party, FEDIAF publishes nutrition guidelines as a policy paper for members. To develop these guidelines the group uses NRC recommendations, AAFCO guidelines and studies published by internationally recognized nutritionists, veterinarians and other researchers. These guidelines are updated yearly.

Through their national organizations, FEDIAF also collaborates with local and national authorities to make pet owners more aware of their responsibilities toward their pets and society.

Confédération des Industries Agro-Alimentaires de l' UE

The Confédération des Industries Agro-Alimentaires de l' UE (CIAA), also known as the Confederation of the Food and Drink Industries, is analogous to FEDIAF for human foodstuffs. Both federations work closely together because of common interests and because they are regulated by the same legislation. Advertising, claims and environmental matters are regulated for human and animal foods by the same law.

Label Design

Pet food labels in Europe are divided into a Principal Display Panel and the Statutory Statement, although the distinction is less stringent than that for pet food labels in the United States.[14] Statutory statements are regulated by the council directive on the marketing of feeding stuffs (79/373/EEC, April 1979). This directive was updated by council directive 90/44/EEC, which has been in force since January 1992.[15] The pet food industry is also protected by human food legislation (e.g., laws that list the level of undesirable substances and relate to environmental matters and advertising).

Principal Display Panel

As in the United States, this part of the label gives information about product identity, shows graphics and pictures, includes marketing claims to promote the product and contains descriptions of meat types and other information that companies may choose to convey outside of the statutory statements.

No specific rules apply to the principal display panel other than general legislation concerning misleading claims that applies to all advertising. Labels should not mislead the purchaser; the label must not suggest that the product possesses properties that it does not have, nor should the label imply that the product is special when similar properties are found in other products.

In the absence of specific legislation and to protect the consumer against unsubstantiated claims, a policy for claiming meat and flavor varieties has been proposed within the FEDIAF (Table 5-8). These guidelines serve an advisory role and are still under discussion. Although they are not official law with force of application, in some countries (e.g., France) the authorities use those guidelines to judge labels for misleading claims. Directive 90/44/EEC allows pet food manufacturers to claim a low or high level of a specific ingredient on the condition that the percentage is specified and that the claim reflects an essential aspect of that particular food.[15]

Table 5-7. National member organizations of FEDIAF.

Austria: ÖHTV	Italy: ASSALZOO
Belgium: BKVH/CPAF	Netherlands: VKH
Denmark: FAD	Norway: Dyrematgruppen
Finland: Joint Committee	Portugal: ALIAN
France: FACCO	Spain: ANFAAC
Germany: IVH	Sweden: DLF
Greece: GPFMA	Switzerland: VHN
Ireland: PFMAI	United Kingdom: PFMA

Table 5-8. Product descriptors used in Europe.

Claim/description	Level of the named ingredient
With beef flavor Beef flavor	Greater than 0 but less than 4% of the named flavor should be present
With rabbit Contains rabbit	At least 4% of the named species should be present
High in chicken With extra chicken Extra chicken	At least 14% of the named species should be present
Beef variety Beef dinner Beef recipe Beef menu Beef with cereal	At least 26% of the named species should be present
Brand name rabbit	All contents are of the named origin with no other ingredients present except gravy, jelly, sauce, permitted additives and nutrient supplements

A pet food label must not claim that the product will prevent, treat or cure disease. The label should clearly differentiate between pet foods and foods for human consumption. In the case of moist food, the words "Animal Food" must be written on the can lid in the language(s) of the country.

Statutory Statement

GENERAL

The mandatory and optional declarations are encapsulated in what is called "The Statutory Statement" (United Kingdom) or "Cadre Réservé" (France).[14,16] In addition to being visible, legible and indelible, the statutory statement must be separate from all other information on the label (Table 5-9).

Some of this information may be outside the statutory statement, but the statutory statement must indicate where to find the information. Such information as the "best before" date, net weight and the name and address of the company responsible for the product are often found elsewhere on the label.

A pet food label must indicate whether the food is a complete or a complementary pet food (in other words, whether the food can satisfy all nutritional demands without an additional ration [complete] or whether it must be fed with another product [complementary]). For complementary foods, the other food or supplement should be stated.[17] The description "complete" or "complementary" must be considered in relation to the intended purpose of the food or to the particular lifestage for which it is defined (e.g., adult, growth or all lifestages).

The species or category of animals must be stated with the indication complete or complementary (e.g., Brand X is a complete food for adult dogs). This statement of intent is often communicated on the principal display panel, but is repeated in the statutory statement.

INGREDIENT LIST

In Europe, ingredients are declared by the individual name or grouped under various categories (Table 5-4).

Table 5-9. Information found in the statutory statements of European pet food labels.

Complete/complementary food
Species/category
Instructions for use
Ingredient list
Typical analysis
Additives
Expiration date and reference to manufacturing date
Address of person (company) responsible for the accuracy
  of declarations
Net weight and/or volume
Reference (batch) number

Table 5-10. Common ingredient categories found on European pet food labels.

Meat and animal derivatives
All fleshy parts of slaughtered warm-blooded land animals, fresh or preserved by appropriate treatment, and all products and derivatives of the processing of the carcass

Milk and milk derivatives
All milk products, fresh or preserved by appropriate treatment, and derivatives from the processing thereof

Egg and egg derivatives
All egg products, fresh or preserved by appropriate treatment, and derivatives from the processing thereof

Oils and fats
All animal and vegetable oils and fats

Yeasts
All yeasts, the cells of which have been killed and dried

Fish and fish derivatives
Fish or parts of fish, fresh or preserved by appropriate treatment, and derivatives from the processing thereof

Cereals
All types of cereals, regardless of their presentation, or made from the starchy endosperm

Vegetables
All types of vegetables and legumes, fresh or preserved by appropriate treatment

Derivatives of vegetable origin
Derivatives resulting from the treatment of vegetable products in particular cereals, vegetables, legumes and oil seeds

Vegetable protein extracts
All products of vegetable origin in which the proteins have been concentrated by an adequate process to contain at least 50% crude protein, as related to the dry matter, and which may be restructured or textured

Minerals
All inorganic substances suitable for animal feed

Various sugars
All types of sugars

These categories are designed to provide consumers with some indication of the source of raw materials used, while allowing the manufacturer some flexibility in the selection of the ingredients within a specific category.[17] These categories are well-defined and names and descriptions are officially published (Table 5-10). Ingredients should be listed in descending order by weight of each individual ingredient or category.

Vitamins are considered additives and are not listed under ingredients. Water does not have to be declared as an ingredient even if added during processing.

TYPICAL ANALYSIS

Contrary to pet food labels in the United States, where minimum and maximum guarantees are stated, the EU regulations dictate that the typical analysis must be declared for: 1) crude protein, 2) crude fat, 3) crude fiber and 4) ash (Table 5-5). Moisture must be declared if it exceeds 14%. Typical analysis (percentage) is the average of the nutrient level calculated from several samples and should correspond with the target level of each nutrient for which precise limits of variation are defined.

The typical analysis gives the percentages found in the actual food. Declaration of nutrients such as calcium, phosphorus, sodium, potassium and magnesium is optional. Energy declaration is forbidden in the EU except for some veterinary dietetic pet foods. Other nutrients must be declared if a manufacturer wants to draw attention to them by saying a food is "high in" or "low in" a particular nutrient.

ADDITIVES

Five types of substances are commonly declared as additives: 1) vitamins, 2) copper, 3) preservatives, 4) antioxidants and 5) coloring agents (Table 5-5).

Vitamins A, D and E must be declared when added by the manufacturer. The added amount should be declared although some countries ask the manufacturer to declare the total amount of the vitamins found in the food. Vitamins are declared in IU or in milligrams per kilogram (mg/kg) of food.

Pet foods are regulated by the same legislation that regulates livestock feed. Although clear exceptions are made for companion animal foods, situations arise where an unusual nutrient must be declared. This is the case for copper because sheep are much more sensitive to copper toxicity. If a copper salt is added to a pet food, the name of the salt and the total copper content must be declared.

If a container has a net weight of up to 10 kg, the manufacturer can use the following statements: "contains European Economic Community (EEC) permitted antioxidant(s)," "contains EEC permitted preservative(s)" or "contains EEC permitted colorant(s)." However, if a container has a net weight of more than 10 kg, the name of the additive must be stated in the following way: "with antioxidant X," "with preservative Y," or "preserved with Y" and "with colorant Z" or "colored with Z." Only those additives are declared that have been added during production of the food. Additives (e.g., preservatives or antioxidants) added during rendering in order to preserve raw materials (such as meat or fish meals) do not have to be declared on the label.

Maximum permitted levels of additives are strictly regulated. Additives are only permitted after a dossier is accepted by the European authorities that documents efficacy and safety.

BEST BEFORE DATE

The Best before Date is stated as day, month, year. The date itself can be indicated outside of the statutory statement in a place where it may be more convenient for printing on the container (e.g., the can lid or top of the bag). In this case the statement "Best before . . ." must appear within the statutory statement with instructions of where to find the date.

FEEDING INSTRUCTIONS

Feeding instructions are compulsory on European pet food labels but are not as strictly regulated as in the United States. The manufacturer will usually list the weight of the food to feed per body weight of the animal.

NET WEIGHT

The "net weight" declaration is regulated by packaged goods regulations. The "e" often seen after the net weight is not specific for pet foods, but indicates that the net weight is an average. Strict rules regulate the limits of variation permitted under or above the declared net weight statement to ensure that the consumer receives the full amount purchased. The net weight declaration is often mentioned on the front of the label but some countries require that the statutory statement declare where the net weight can be found.

OTHER DECLARATIONS

Regulations now incorporate the batch number into the obligatory declarations for pet foods. The name and address of the company responsible for the product must also appear.

Dietetic Pet Foods in Europe

In July 1995, labeling of dietetic pet foods for dogs and cats became strictly regulated. Definitions and scope of the legislation are published in council directive 93/74/EC, whereas three commission directives (94/39/EC, 95/9/EC, and 95/10/EC) give the applications.[18-21] As a consequence, a number of new statements have recently appeared on the labels of dietetic pet foods. The commission directives publish lists (Table 5-11) with the permitted indications for dietetic foods ("Particular Nutritional Purposes"), the characteristics of the corresponding foods and specific label declarations (Table 5-12). The objective of the legislation is to prevent unsubstantiated and misleading claims on pet food labels.

The term "dietetic pet food," and its official translations, is the only term to be used to indicate that a product falls under this legislation. The new label declarations apply without prejudice to the marketing directive and other provisions regulating nonveterinary medical pet foods.

The legislation considers most indications for nutritional management as "temporary situations" making it mandatory to publish a defined length of use on the labels. This period of time has been determined by the commission and its experts, and does not always reflect the manufacturer's recommendations.

Energy declaration is not permitted on pet food labels other than dietetic foods marketed for obesity and convalescence. The energy density is a calculated value expressed in megajoules per kilogram (MJ/kg) of product.

New nutritional purposes may be accepted when new products are marketed and the manufacturer has introduced a dossier showing sufficient data to support the claims.

Table 5-11. Indications permitted for dietetic pet foods in Europe.

Support of renal function in case of chronic renal insufficiency
Dissolution of struvite uroliths
Reduction of struvite urolith recurrence
Reduction of oxalate urolith formation
Reduction of urate urolith formation
Reduction of cystine urolith formation
Reduction of ingredient and nutrient intolerances
Reduction of acute intestinal absorptive disorders
Compensation for maldigestion (including exocrine pancreatic insufficiency)
Support of heart function in case of chronic cardiac insufficiency
Regulation of glucose supply (diabetes mellitus)
Support of liver function in case of chronic liver insufficiency
Regulation of lipid metabolism in case of hyperlipidemia
Reduction of copper in the liver
Support of skin function in case of dermatosis and excessive loss of hair
Reduction of excessive body weight

Table 5-12. Information that must appear on labels of dietetic pet foods in Europe.

Particular nutritional purpose (See Table 5-11)
Essential nutritional characteristics
Species or category of animals
Labeling declarations
Recommended length of time for use
Other provisions

REFERENCES

1. Association of American Feed Control Officials. Official Publication 1998.
2. Dzanis DA. Regulation of health claims for pet foods. Veterinary Clinical Nutrition 1994; 1: 5-11.
3. Phillips T. Meet the NRC. Pet Veterinarian 1992; 2: 10-12.
4. National Research Council. Nutrient Requirements of Dogs. Washington, DC: National Academy Press, 1985.
5. National Research Council. Nutrient Requirements of Cats. Washington, DC: National Academy Press, 1986.
6. Pet Food Institute–Fact Sheet 1994. Veterinary Clinical Nutrition 1994; 1: 30-38.
7. Food and Drug Administration. 21 CFR Chapter 1, Part 501.
8. Huber TL, Laflamme DP, Medleau L, et al. Comparison of procedures for assessing adequacy of dog foods. Journal of the American Veterinary Medical Association 1991; 199: 731-734.
9. Canadian Veterinary Medical Association. Pet food certification program. CVMA: Ottawa, Ontario, 1989.
10. Allard C. Labeling and advertising pet foods. Canadian Veterinary Journal 1988; 29: 403-404.
11. Borchardt K-D. Het ABC van het gemeenschapsrecht. Serie Europese Documentatie-Bureau voor officiële publikaties der Europese Gemeenschappen-Luxemburg, 1994.
12. FEDIAF–Information brochure. Brussels, Belgium, 1993.
13. PFMA. Profile 1993. The Pet Food Manufacturers Association: London, England.
14. The Feeding Stuffs Regulations 1991. Statutory Instruments 1991, No. 2840 Agriculture, HMSO: London, England.
15. Council directive 90/44/ECC. Official Journal of the European Communities 31.11990, No. L 27/35-44.
16. FACCO. Code des règlements et bonnes pratiques dans le commerce des aliments pour animaux familiers. Paris, France.
17. Burger IH. Reading a petfood label. Journal of Small Animal Practice 1993; 34: 189-191.
18. Council directive 93/74/EC of 13.9.1993. Official Journal of the European Communities 22.9.1993, No. L 237/23-27.
19. Commission directive 94/39/EC of 25.7.1994. Official Journal of the European Communities 10.8.1994, No. L207/20-29.
20. Commission directive 95/9/EC of 7.4.1995. Official Journal of the European Communities 22.4.1995, No. L91/35-38.
21. Commission directive 95/10/EC of 7.4.1995. Official Journal of the European Communities 1995, No. L91/39-40.

CHAPTER 6

Making Pet Foods at Home

Rebecca L. Remillard

Bernard-Marie Paragon

Stephen W. Crane

Jacques Debraekeleer

Christopher S. Cowell

"Teach thy tongue to say 'I don't know' and thou shall progress."
Anonymous

INTRODUCTION

Clients are increasingly interested in their own nutrition and that of their pets. Feeding commercially prepared pet foods offers several advantages over feeding homemade foods, including convenience, cost and consistency. Most commercial foods are easier to use, less expensive and provide better nutritional balance. Nevertheless, many owners prefer to prepare homemade foods. In doing so, they feel less guilty, and have the impression of preparing a "real meal" that is "more natural" and "more traditional."[1]

According to pet owners, veterinarians are the best source of pet health care;[2] advice about good nutrition is a reasonable extension of this role. Therefore, veterinarians and their health care teams must also be able to provide good advice about home-cooked pet foods to clients who want this option. The first part of this chapter gives practitioners more insight into the reasons why some pet owners prefer homemade foods, and covers some pet owner concerns about commercially prepared foods. The second part gives practical recommendations for assessing homemade foods. The sidebars and tables describe ingredients and methods for formulating homemade foods.

CLINICAL IMPORTANCE

Nearly all dogs and cats in the United States consume table food at some time in their lives.[3] Many dogs fed commercial foods "exclusively" have learned about the availability of table scraps after a meal, garbage on trash day and food from children and generous neighbors. The vast majority of dogs and cats in the United States, however, receive 90% or more of their calories from complete and balanced commer-

cially prepared foods.[4] In one survey, 20% of pet owners answered that they feed their pet candy or table foods every day.[5] The occasional feeding of table foods should not be of concern for healthy pets unless the food composes more than 10% of the daily dry matter intake.[6] However, for various reasons, some clients want to feed their pets a homemade food exclusively. In the United States, these clients are probably more prevalent in urban areas. Some veterinarians who practice holistic medicine strongly recommend that their clients feed only a home-prepared food.

Europe has a much more diverse pattern of homemade pet food use (Table 6-1). In the United Kingdom and the more Anglo-American oriented northern European countries, pet owners provide a high proportion of calories as commercially produced pet foods. In countries with a long-standing tradition of gourmet cooking, such as France, Italy, Spain and Belgium, many pets receive a portion of the family meal as the cultural norm. In 1987, about 13% of the dog and cat owners in France fed table foods exclusively to their dog or cat, and another 15% purchased traditional food for home cooking.[7] In 1987, about 62% of French dog owners and 79% of cat owners professed to use commercially prepared pet foods regularly.[8] However, this does not mean pet owners feed commercially prepared pet foods "exclusively." One survey estimated that commercially prepared dog foods only covered about 27% of the dogs' caloric needs.[8] In the same period, pet owners spent about one-third of their pet food budget for commercially prepared pet foods and two-thirds for homemade foods.[9]

In Europe, moist pet foods often are considered a meat source (protein source), rather than a complete pet food. Consequently, some pet food companies have developed a concept that is intermediate between homemade and commercially prepared foods. They have developed moist foods, high in protein and fat. To balance the food, the feeding guide recommends supplementation with a specif-

KEY WORDS & TERMS—MAKING PET FOODS AT HOME*

Additive	Contaminant	Preservative
Antioxidant	Natural foods	Vegan
Balance	Organic foods	Vegetarian

Key words and terms are defined in the Glossary.

KEY POINTS—MAKING PET FOODS AT HOME

1. Veterinarians should evaluate homemade recipes as a service to their clients.
2. Owners who request information about natural or organic foods must first clearly define their concerns before veterinarians can effectively recommend specific products or foods.
3. Clients often do not understand the information on pet food labels and generally do not like what they see in ingredient lists.
4. Veterinarians should ask pet owners to identify which ingredients on a pet food label are bothersome and then provide them with the legal definition of the ingredients and identify the nutrients provided by the ingredients.
5. Some clients simply want to cook for their pets.
6. Pet owners may begin feeding a young or sick dog or cat from the table only to realize later the pet will not eat commercially prepared foods.
7. Specific types or forms of dietary management that some pets require are not available commercially.
8. Most published homemade recipes for dog and cat foods have been crudely balanced using computer assimilation of average food nutrient contents. The palatability, digestibility and safety of these recipes have not been adequately tested.

9. The most common errors in making homemade foods occur when pet owners make their own food substitutions and omit ingredients because of personal preferences. Omitting the vitamin-mineral supplement is another common error.
10. Veterinarians presented with a healthy adult dog or cat that is fed a homemade food can grossly evaluate the recipe using "quick check" guidelines.
11. Homemade foods can be grossly evaluated by noting the patient's body weight, body condition and activity level and considering the results of laboratory tests and physical examination of the eyes and skin.
12. The best recommendation to clients who feed homemade foods is to bring their pets in for regular veterinary checkups (two or three visits each year).
13. When owners want to cook for their pets, it is better to provide them with a well-designed homemade recipe, rather than having them use their own or a breeder's well-intentioned formulation, which often has deficiencies and excesses.
14. Explaining the different aspects of preparing and feeding homemade foods will prevent some common problems and increase client compliance.

ic amount of rice or pasta. A cereal-based mixer is often sold as an alternative to rice and pasta. These modules contain carbohydrate and fiber ingredients that are often fortified with calcium, vitamins and trace minerals. When proper mixing ratios are used, the meal provides adequate mineral balance and appropriate protein-to-energy ratios. This may not be the case, however, when the mixer is combined with fresh meat instead of the complementary moist food. Combining, mixing, cooking and serving the modular components fulfills the owner's expectation of "proper" feeding.

RATIONALE FOR CHOOSING HOMEMADE FOODS

When a client wants to prepare pet foods at home, it is important for veterinarians to understand the client's reasons and motivation. (See sidebar "Common Reasons Pet Owners Want to Feed a Homemade Food.") In many cases it is possible to address their concerns and to recommend an appropriate commercial food. In one survey, at least 25% of pet owners said they would be influenced to purchase a specific brand of pet food based on a recommendation by their veterinarian.[5] However, when owners

strongly prefer to cook for their pet, it is better to provide them with a well-designed homemade recipe, rather than allow them to prepare food according to their own or a breeder's well-intentioned formulation that may have deficiencies and excesses.[10]

Appeal of "Natural" and "Organic" Foods

Independent health food stores in the United States sold $25 million of "natural" pet foods in 1990; whereas total annual sales of natural pet foods in the United States were approximately $130 million.[11] These sales figures may well represent the value some pet owners place on "natural" labeled foods. The Food and Drug Administration (FDA) in the United States has no legal definition for the terms natural and organic as they relate to food products.[12] The Association of American Feed Control Officials (AAFCO) initially suggested the definition for natural as "of or pertaining to a product wholly comprising ingredients completely devoid of artificial or manmade substances including but not limited to synthetic flavors, colors, preservatives, vitamins, minerals or other additives, whether added directly to the product or incidentally as a component of another ingredient."[13] Currently, AAFCO is allowing the use of the term natural or a similar designa-

Table 6-1. Dog and cat populations in selected European countries and the estimated percentage of calories provided by homemade food.

	Cats		Dogs	
	Number animals (millions)	Calories from homemade foods (%)	Number animals (millions)	Calories from homemade foods (%)
France*	8.1	50	7.7	60
Germany**	6.0	30	5.0	70
Italy***	7.0	75	6.1	90
United Kingdom**	6.6	10	7.2	50
Total Europe***	42.0	45	36.0	70

*FACCO/SOFRES 1997.
**PetFood Industry 1992; March/April: 62.
***Paragon BM. Personal communication. October 1996.

tion on a pet food label provided all ingredients and components of ingredients other than vitamins and minerals are not chemically synthesized or altered. For vitamins and minerals, a disclaimer should then be juxtaposed with the term natural or similar designation.[14]

The terms "natural" and "organic" may mean different things to different people. Some pet owners define natural as not containing any synthetic ingredient or additive. Others refer to organic foods implying that they do not contain ingredients from animals treated with hormones, or cereals or crops produced with synthetic pesticides and fertilizers. Some clients believe that fresh, wild-grown, uncooked whole foods have a "life energy." To these clients, only natural or organic ingredients can supply proper nutrition for themselves and their pets. Because definitions of natural and organic are left to the pet owner's interpretation, it is helpful to more specifically ascertain the concerns of the client before recommending any food, whether it be homemade or commercially produced. Veterinarians and their staffs should not hesitate to contact pet food manufacturers to obtain more detailed information about ingredients and product processing.

It is interesting to note that while natural pet foods have been very successfully received in the United States during the past two decades, the concept of natural pet foods has not made a real impact in Europe.[15] Although demand for "organically grown produce" for human consumption has grown phenomenally in Europe, only limited demand exists for "organic pet foods."[15] Perhaps potential users of natural and organic labeled pet foods in Europe continue to feed homemade foods, because for many of them the term natural means no physical or chemical conservation other than refrigeration.

Appeal of Vegetarian and Vegan Foods

Pet owners who want to feed a vegetarian food to their dog or cat may assume they must prepare the food at home. Commercially prepared vegetarian foods exist for dogs, and can be well-balanced using egg and milk products. Vegan foods (no animal products) should be carefully checked because they may be deficient in arginine, lysine, methionine, tryptophan, taurine, iron, calcium, zinc, vitamin A and some B vitamins.[16,17] People should be discouraged from preparing vegetarian or vegan foods at home for cats, because cats are strict carnivores. Without adequate supplementation, cats fed vegetarian and vegan diets are at high risk for taurine, arginine, tryptophan, lysine and vitamin A deficiency.

Concerns about Additives, Preservatives and Contaminants

Additives

In one survey that studied consumer understanding of the word "natural," most respondents mentioned freedom from various types of additives.[18] In consumer surveys, additives are always high on the list of food items that consumers feel may damage their health, or be a sufficient rea-

> ## Common Reasons Pet Owners and Veterinarians Want to Use a Homemade Food
>
> 1. They wish to use ingredients that are fresh, wild-grown, organic or natural.
> 2. They wish to avoid additives that are present in some commercial pet foods.
> 3. They wish to avoid contaminants thought to be present in prepared foods.
> 4. They are concerned that the ingredient list is an indecipherable list of chemicals.
> 5. They fear an ingredient in a commercial food, such as a "by-product."
> 6. They wish to maintain adequate food intake in a finicky pet through exceptional palatability.
> 7. They desire to personally cook for the pet.
> 8. The pet is addicted to table foods or a single grocery item.
> 9. They wish to feed major quantities of an ingredient not found in commercial pet foods.
> 10. They hope to construct a nutritional profile for dietary management of a disease for which no commercial food is available.
> 11. They hope to restrict the allergens/causative substances during an elimination trial or for long-term feeding of animals with adverse reactions to food.
> 12. They wish to support a sick or terminally ill animal through home cooking and hand feeding.
> 13. They wish to provide food variety as a defense against malnutrition, or because of the popular idea that pets need variety.
> 14. They wish to lower feeding costs by using significant quantities of table food and leftovers.
> 15. They wish to feed a pet according to human nutritional guidelines (e.g., low fat, low cholesterol).

HOMEMADE

son not to buy a food.[18] However, when ranking the known risks of food hazards in people, the relative risk of food-borne disease (microbial contamination) is highest, about 100,000 times the risk associated with additives.[18]

Because food technology and additives are a difficult and confusing matter for nonexperts, additives often evoke emotional responses from the misinformed.[19] In addition, the issue is not always presented correctly; consumer associations and some so-called experts often accuse additives of causing all kinds of disorders in pets. Advertising occasionally abuses the negative image of synthetic additives to promote "natural" or "additive-free" products. However, evidence linking a particular food or food constituent with a particular disease is often circumstantial and great care must be exercised in assessing its significance.[20] Veterinarians do not always have the answers when owners are alarmed by nutrition gossip, but should become more knowledgeable about pet food additives so they can accurately address client concerns.

Additives (e.g., flavorings, colorings, binders and emulsifiers) in pet foods are the same or very similar to those approved for use in human foods. In the United States, no additive may be legally used in foods unless and until the FDA has been convinced that the additive is safe at the intended level of use in the intended food using thorough scientific evidence. The FDA usually requires at least two-year feeding tests in two species of animals to reveal short- and long-term effects. Additives currently used in human and pet foods are generally regarded as safe (GRAS; 21 CFR 582) and must be removed from human and pet foods if there is an indication of harmful effects.[21] For example, propylene glycol has been removed from the GRAS list for cats.

Clients who want to avoid "additives" as a generic group are often not well-informed about the types of pet food additives and the possible negative consequences of not adding these compounds to foods. Veterinarians should explain the positive aspects of additives to give clients a sufficient comfort level to feed a commercial product instead of a homemade food. (See Chapter 4.)

In general, additives provide three benefits: 1) organoleptic—to provide structure, texture and color, 2) technologic—to serve as binding and gelling agents and 3) nutritional—to serve as vitamins and antioxidants. Clients interested in additive-free products must first specifically identify which additive (intentional vs. unintentional) they wish to avoid. Some commercially available products do not contain artificial colors, flavors and synthetic preservatives. Once a pet owner's specific concerns have been identified and discussed, perhaps an acceptable commercially prepared complete and balanced product can be located.

Preservatives

Consumer research has identified several factors that pet owners associate with natural pet food including freedom from artificial preservatives.[19] Veterinarians and their health care teams should become knowledgeable about pet food preservatives so they can accurately address client concerns. A preservative may be defined as "any substance that is capable of inhibiting or retarding the growth of microorganisms or of masking the evidence of such deterioration."[20] Protection against microbial attack may be achieved by several methods: chemical treatment (semi-moist and some dry foods), dehydration (dry foods), heat (moist and dry foods), irradiation or storage at a low temperature. Preservatives are very important to prevent molding or bacterial deterioration of semi-moist foods. Many preservatives are organic acids and their salts, such as sorbates, and are the same as those used in many human foods and dressings.

ANTIOXIDANTS

Antioxidants function to stabilize fats and fat-soluble vitamins against oxidation. There are two types of antioxidants: natural and synthetic.[22]

Natural Antioxidants

Natural antioxidants used most often are tocopherols, ascorbic acid (vitamin C) and rosemary. Tocopherols are often referred to as vitamin E. Although vitamin E (alpha-tocopherol) is the biologically active form in the body, it does not effectively stabilize the fats in food. The gamma- and delta-tocopherols exert the best antioxidant activity in food, but have very low vitamin E activity. Thus, the term "Preserved with vitamin E" is technically inaccurate, but it is commonly used to assuage client concerns. Instead, the label should indicate whether gamma- or delta-tocopherol was added.

Ascorbic acid and its salts and esters are most effective when combined with other antioxidants. Salts (L-calcium ascorbate) and esters (ascorbyl-5,6-diacetate) of ascorbic acid are synthesized compounds, but may be perceived as acceptable natural alternatives to a "more chemical sounding" antioxidant.

Rosemary has been investigated for use in pet foods. Although always considered a natural antioxidant, rosemary is not used in its original form, but as a refined extract in order to avoid influence on taste and odor.[23]

Synthetic Antioxidants

The more commonly used synthetic antioxidants are butylated hydroxytoluene (BHT), butylated hydroxyanisole (BHA) and ethoxyquin. BHT and BHA have been used in human foods since 1954 and are most effective when combined. Ethoxyquin has been approved for use in animal feeds and pet foods in the United States for more than 30 years. All three antioxidants are considered safe at their recommended levels in the United States and Europe.[24-27]

Synthetic antioxidants are more effective than natural antioxidants and better withstand the heat, pressure and moisture during food processing. In doing so, they also preserve the fat-soluble vitamins A, D and E for activity in the body. Clients should be aware that most canned foods do not contain antioxidants, and that many commercially prepared dry pet foods use vitamin antioxidants. Awareness of these facts may help clients choose a more appropriate commercially prepared food.

Contaminants

Some clients are concerned about compounds that may be present unintentionally or accidentally in pet foods (pesticides, drug residues and heavy metals). Even micro amounts (ppm or ppb) in a food are often intensely feared. Unintentional contaminants can be found occasionally in food products, although manufacturers make every effort to eliminate, or at least minimize, these residues. (See Chapter 7.) Analyses of pet foods have shown that contamination of pet foods with pesticides, polychlorinated biphenyls (PCBs) and heavy metals is not significant.[28]

Clients may elect to feed a homemade food to avoid all types of contaminants. However, ingredients in homemade foods may also contain contaminants. Therefore, making a food at home does not ensure against unintentional contaminants. For example, mercury may be found in fish-based products, but the same concern is real for pets fed fresh fish.[28,29]

Inability to Understand Pet Food Labels

The ingredient list on a pet food label often uses language unfamiliar to most pet owners; however, each term has a specific definition. Pet owners can easily be confused by terms such as meat, meat meal, meat and bone meal and meat by-products. (See sidebar "AAFCO Definitions for Meat Ingredients Commonly Used in Commercial Pet Foods.")

Further, pet owners may be alarmed about what they read in the popular press about pet food manufacturing.[30-32] Consequently, pet owners often assume the worst possible composition for these ingredients.[13,33] Veterinarians should encourage pet owners to identify confusing ingredient terms and then provide them with legal definitions.[24] For example, a pet owner who has read that meat by-products include hair and fecal material,[30-32] should be informed of the correct AAFCO definition.[24]

Some pet owners may still find meat by-products objectionable after learning the AAFCO definition. However, they may be comfortable with the definition of meat as an ingredient and feed a commercially prepared product containing meat instead of a homemade food.

Some pet owners consider the last half of the ingredient list to be nothing more than a list of chemicals and cannot identify the nutrients provided by synthetic sources. Veterinarians should ask pet owners to identify bothersome ingredient terms and then explain to them which essential nutrients are provided by those ingredients. As examples, calcium carbonate provides calcium, zinc oxide provides zinc and sodium selenite provides sodium and selenium. Some vitamin examples are: thiamin mononitrate provides vitamin B_1, calcium pantothenate provides pantothenic acid and D-activated animal sterol provides vitamin D_3. Pet owners may have fewer objections to feeding commercially made products after biochemical names have been translated into more commonly recognized vitamins and minerals.

Other points of concern include whether the ingredients are available to the pet (i.e., whether the animal is able to digest and absorb the nutrients they contain). In the United States, the pet owner's attention should be directed to the AAFCO statement required on every product that claims to be complete and balanced. (See Chapter 5.) The AAFCO statement provides valuable information (i.e., the testing procedures used and the lifestage for which the food has been substantiated). If the complete and balanced claim was not substantiated by feeding tests for the specific lifestage of the pet (i.e., growth, maintenance, reproduction), then another more appropriate product should be recommended.

Desire to Cook for the Pet

"My dog eats what I eat" is an expression often heard from people who prefer to cook for their pet. Preparing elaborate meals at home gives the owner the feeling of

---

AAFCO Definitions for Meat Ingredients Commonly Used in Commercial Pet Foods*

MEAT

Meat is the clean flesh derived from slaughtered mammals and is limited to that part of the striate muscle which is skeletal or that which is found in the tongue, in the diaphragm, in the heart, or in the esophagus; with or without the accompanying and overlying fat and the portions of the skin, sinew, nerve and blood vessels which normally accompany the flesh. It shall be suitable for use in animal foods (IFN 5-00-394).

MEAT BY-PRODUCTS

Meat by-products are the non-rendered, clean parts, other than meat, derived from slaughtered mammals. It includes, but is not limited to lungs, spleen, kidneys, brain, livers, blood, bone, partially defatted low temperature fatty tissue and stomachs and intestines freed of their contents. It does not include hair, horns, teeth and hooves. It shall be suitable for use in animal food (IFN 5-00-395).

MEAT MEAL

Meat meal is the rendered product from mammalian tissues, exclusive of any added blood, hair, hoof, horn, hide trimmings, manure, stomach and rumen contents except in such amounts as may occur unavoidably in good processing practices. It shall not contain added extraneous materials not provided for by this definition. The calcium level shall not exceed the actual phosphorus level by more than 2.2 times. It shall not contain more than 12% pepsin indigestible residue, and not more than 9% of the crude protein in the product shall be pepsin indigestible (IFN 5-00-385).

MEAT AND BONE MEAL

Meat and bone meal is the rendered product from mammal tissues, including bone, exclusive of any added blood, hair, hoof, horn, hide trimmings, manure, stomach and rumen contents except in such amounts as may occur unavoidably in good processing practices. It shall not contain added extraneous materials not provided for by this definition. It shall contain a minimum of 4.0% phosphorus, and the calcium level shall not be more than 2.2 times the actual phosphorus level. It shall not contain more than 12% pepsin indigestible residue, and not more than 9% of the crude protein in the product shall be pepsin indigestible (IFN 5-00-388).

*Association of American Feed Control Officials, Official Publication, 1998; 187-188. Definitions may be different for European products.

HOMEMADE PET FOODS

"being involved" and is an integral part of the human-animal bond. This may be particularly important for elderly, solitary persons who benefit from feeling responsible for somebody and are motivated to remain active. Other people choose to cook simply because they feel guilty, as if they don't care enough. The latter circumstance is a minor concern in the United States, but is more important in countries such as France.[5,7]

Quite often, the pet that receives home-cooked meals is a geriatric animal with a diminishing appetite, body weight and condition due to a slowly progressive disease (chronic renal failure, hepatic disease, cancer). Meal preparation and hand-feeding allow the owner to participate in the pet's supportive care. Formulating a simple homemade recipe that is approximately balanced for the animal with a chronic, progressive fatal disease is a reasonable, compassionate gesture on the part of veterinarians.

Table Foods Have Become a Bad Habit

Pet owners may begin feeding a young or sick dog or cat from the table only to realize later that the pet will not eat commercially prepared food. Therefore, table food is 100% of the animal's daily intake. There are several methods of weaning pets off one particular food and onto another. However, if the animal is persistent, the owner is reluctant to make a change or both circumstances are true, formulating a diet of table foods commonly used in the household may be the only way to ensure the pet receives balanced nutrition. In addition, these animals may have become very selective eaters. In such cases, the veterinarian should inform the owner to thoroughly mix all ingredients of the homemade food to ensure balanced nutrient intake.

A Veterinary Therapeutic Food is Unavailable or Unacceptable

Specific types or forms of nutritional management required by the pet are not always available commercially, or one pet food may not address a patient's multiple med-

Table 6-2. A balanced generic homemade formula for healthy adult dogs that meets AAFCO allowances.

Dog food (daily formulation for an 18-kg dog)

Ingredients	Grams	%
Carbohydrate, cooked*	240	58
Meat, cooked**	120	29
Fat***	10	2
Fiber†	30	7
Bone meal††	4.0	
Potassium chloride†††	1.0	

*Examples include rice, cornmeal, oatmeal, potato, pasta and various infant cereals.
**Examples include all typical meats, poultry, fish and liver.
***Chicken fat, beef fat, vegetable oil or fish oil.
†Prepared high-fiber cereals (All Bran, Fiber One) or vegetables (raw or cooked).
††Dicalcium phosphate can be used in place of bone meal.
†††Readily available as a salt substitute in grocery stores.
Human adult vitamin-mineral tablet (9 g/tablet, give 1 tablet/day).

Nutrient content (% DMB)

Protein	21
Fat	20
Crude fiber	6.5
Calcium	0.66
Phosphorus	0.59
Magnesium	0.1
Sodium	0.2
Potassium	0.6
kcal (as fed)	820

Directions: Bake or microwave meat component and cook starch component separately. Grind or finely chop meat if necessary. Pulverize the bone meal or dicalcium phosphate. Mix with all other components except the vitamin-mineral supplement. Mix well and serve immediately or cover and refrigerate. Feed the vitamin-mineral supplement with the meal; give as a pill or pulverize and thoroughly mix with food before feeding.

ical problems. Some patients' medical problems may require apparently contradictory dietary management. For example, a patient with little or no pancreatic tissue may require: 1) a highly digestible food because of a deficiency in digestive enzymes but also 2) a food with moderate-fiber levels to help manage diabetes mellitus.

A veterinary therapeutic food may be commercially available for a patient with a particular medical problem, but the product may be unacceptable to the patient or owner. Most commercial veterinary therapeutic foods are not available in a variety of flavors, and the ingredient formulation is usually fixed. If the one flavor or formulation is unacceptable, the patient may not consume adequate quantities of the food to support body weight and condition. A homemade food composed of ingredients the patient finds palatable and has consumed readily in the past and that is formulated with an appropriate nutrient profile can be offered to the client (Tables 6-2 to 6-8).

Dietary Elimination Trials

The prevalence of adverse reactions to food (including food intolerances and food allergies) has been roughly estimated at 1% of all hospital cases, or 10 to 20% of cases with allergic dermatoses presented to specialists.[34,35] Although adverse reactions to food are a small segment of practice, there is strong evidence that they do occur in pets. Homemade foods may be fed to companion animals as a diagnostic or therapeutic measure in cases in which adverse food reactions are suspected. Veterinarians should investigate possible food reactions in cases where gastrointestinal or dermatologic signs do not fully resolve with standard therapy. (See Chapter 14.)

A dietary history is required to identify ingredients that must be eliminated from the patient's food; however, examining pet food labels rarely ensures that a particular protein is not in the product. For example, the words meat and liver do not specify the species of origin (e.g., cattle, swine, sheep or goats). In Europe, most pet food labels do not list individual ingredients, which makes the dietary history even less accurate. Thus, some sources of protein (and species) cannot be adequately identified from the ingredient list, and so cannot be effectively eliminated from the food. Veterinarians should not hesitate to contact pet food manufacturers for more detailed information.

The recommended protocol for demonstrating a food allergy requires feeding a food composed of protein ingredients not previously fed to the pet. All protein and carbohydrate sources in a novel food must be changed (i.e., the meat and grain sources). Lamb, venison, rabbit and duck and potato are relatively novel meat and carbohydrate sources in North America. All other possible dietary sources of protein and carbohydrate should be discontinued including treats, snacks, table foods, vitamin-mineral supplements and chewable medications. Patients not successfully managed with a commercially prepared novel food are often fed a homemade food for four to eight weeks. Homemade foods may have an advantage because they can be better tailored to the patient's specific needs, but many have been shown to be deficient in essential nutrients.[36]

Homemade foods used in dietary elimination trials can easily be supplemented with calcium, vitamins and microminerals. Most veterinary and children's vitamin-mineral supplements and chewable/flavored medications contain proteins not derived from novel sources. Adult vitamin-mineral supplements without additives are available from health food stores and pharmacies. Any supplement should be added individually to the homemade food on a trial basis (i.e., one per week) because it may contain an item to which the pet is allergic or intolerant.

COMMON PROBLEMS WITH HOMEMADE FOODS

It is possible to achieve the same nutrient balance with a homemade food as with a commercially prepared food. However, this largely depends on the accuracy and competence of the veterinarian or animal nutritionist formulating the food, and on the compliance and discipline of the owner. Unfortunately, some homemade recipes are flawed even when followed exactly and consistently. In one survey, 90% of the homemade elimination foods prescribed by 116 veterinarians in North America were not nutritionally adequate for adult canine or feline maintenance.[36] Unlike most commercial foods, many printed homemade recipes are not complete or balanced to fulfill animal requirements.[36-38] Few of the numerous published homemade food recipes for dogs and cats have been tested to document performance over sustained periods.[10,39] Additionally, making homemade foods requires knowledge, motivation, additional financial resources and careful, consistent attention to recipe detail to ensure a consistent, balanced intake of nutrients.

Very few pet food products sold in the United States are designed to be mixed with another food at home. Some prepared meatless products are available, but the manufacturer clearly instructs the pet owner to feed the food for a limited time or to add a protein source when feeding the product long-term. In North America, homemade foods are more likely to be made "from scratch" than from modules, as in Europe.

Formulations for homemade foods should not be assumed to be complete or balanced for any canine or feline lifestage until sufficiently tested (feeding tests, nutrient analysis, etc.). Most recipes have been crudely balanced using the average nutrient content of specific foods and computer assimilation. The palatability, digestibility and safety of these recipes have not been adequately or scientifically tested.[10,30-32] Even formulations that are initially complete and balanced put pets at risk when pet owners make their own food substitutions, omit ingredients because of personal preferences or convenience or make preparation errors. Therefore, veterinarians and their health care teams should encourage regular dietary histories and patient monitoring for pets that belong to clients who feed homemade foods.

Common Nutrient Problems in Homemade Foods

It is difficult to characterize homemade foods designed by owners because each food and patient is unique However, many formulations contain excessive protein, but are deficient in calories, calcium, vitamins and microminerals. Commonly used meat and carbohydrate sources contain more phosphorus than calcium; therefore,

Table 6-3. A balanced generic homemade formula for healthy adult cats that meets AAFCO allowances.

Cat food (daily formulation for a 4.5-kg cat)

Ingredients	Grams	%
Carbohydrate, cooked*	60	50
Meat, cooked**	40	34
Fat***	10	8
Bone meal†	1.2	
Salts (NaCl/KCl††)	1.0	
Taurine	0.5	

*Examples include rice, cornmeal, oatmeal, potato, pasta and various infant cereals.
**Examples include all typical meats, poultry, fish and liver.
***Chicken fat, beef fat, vegetable oil or fish oil.
†Dicalcium phosphate can be used in place of bone meal.
††Readily available as a lite salt in grocery stores.
Human adult vitamin-mineral tablet (9 g/tablet, give 0.5 tablet/day).

Nutrient content (% DMB)

Protein	31
Fat	28
Crude fiber	2.0
Calcium	0.69
Phosphorus	0.58
Magnesium	0.1
Sodium	0.4
Potassium	0.75
kcal (as fed)	250

Directions: Bake or microwave meat component and cook starch component. Grind or finely chop meat if necessary. Pulverize the bone meal and mix with other components except the vitamin-mineral supplement. Mix well and serve immediately or cover and refrigerate. Feed the vitamin-mineral supplement with the meal; give as a pill or pulverize and mix in food before feeding.

Table 6-4. Balanced reduced-protein/low-phosphorus homemade formulas for adult dogs and cats.*,**

Daily food as fed formulation for an 18-kg dog

Ingredients	Grams	Nutrient analysis (DM)††	
Rice, white, cooked***	237	Dry matter (%)	41.0
Beef, regular, cooked†	78	Energy (kcal/100 g)	445
Egg, large, boiled	20	Protein (%)	21.1
Bread, white	50	Fat (%)	13.7
Oil, vegetable	3	Linoleic acid (%)	1.8
Calcium carbonate	1.5	Crude fiber (%)	1.4
Salt, iodized	0.5	Calcium (%)	0.43
Total	390	Phosphorus (%)	0.22
		Potassium (%)	0.26
		Sodium (%)	0.33
		Magnesium (%)	0.091

Daily food as fed formulation for a 4.5-kg cat

Ingredients	Grams	Nutrient analysis (DM)††	
Liver, chicken, cooked	21	Dry matter (%)	37.8
Rice, white, cooked***	98	Energy (kcal/100 g)	458
Chicken, white, cooked	21	Protein (%)	24.4
Oil, vegetable	7	Fat (%)	17.5
Calcium carbonate	0.7	Linoleic acid (%)	7.9
Salt, iodized	0.5	Crude fiber (%)	0.85
Salt, substitute (KCl)	0.5	Calcium (%)	0.54
Total	149	Phosphorus (%)	0.29
		Potassium (%)	0.66
		Sodium (%)	0.42
		Magnesium (%)	0.09

*Also feed one human adult vitamin-mineral tablet daily to dogs and one-half tablet to cats to ensure all vitamins and trace minerals are included. Cats should be given one-half to one taurine tablet (500 mg/tablet) daily.
**ESHA Research. Diet Analysis Software. Food Processor Plus, version 5.03, 1990 Salem, OR. Agricultural Software Consultants, Inc. Mixit 2+, version 3.0, 1991, Kingsville, TX.
***May substitute rice baby cereal and flavor either selection with meat broth during cooking.
†Retain the fat.
††Nutrients of concern are italicized.

Table 6-5. Balanced low-fat homemade formulas for adult dogs and cats.*,**

Daily food as fed formulation for an 18-kg dog			
Ingredients	Grams	Nutrient analysis (DM)††	
Chicken, white meat	65	Dry matter (%)	36.5
Egg, large, boiled	81	*Energy (kcal/100 g)*	398
Rice, white, cooked***	325	Protein (%)	22.6
Cereal, All Bran	26	*Fat (%)*	8.0
Calcium carbonate	2	Linoleic acid (%)	1.1
Salt, iodized	1	*Fiber (%)*	5.8
Salt substitute (KCl)	1	Calcium (%)	0.50
Total	501	Phosphorus (%)	0.37
		Potassium (%)	0.63
		Sodium (%)	0.45
		Magnesium (%)	0.14

Daily food as fed formulation for a 4.5-kg cat			
Ingredients	Grams	Nutrient analysis (DM)††	
Liver, chicken, cooked	125	Dry matter (%)	33.8
Rice, white, cooked***	46	*Energy (kcal/100 g)*	420
Cereal, All Bran	8	Protein (%)	52.7
Calcium carbonate	1.2	*Fat (%)*	11.4
Salt, iodized	0.3	Linoleic acid (%)	1.2
Salt, substitute (KCl)	0.3	*Fiber (%)*	5.2
Total	180	Calcium (%)	0.85
		Phosphorus (%)	0.77
		Potassium (%)	0.67
		Sodium (%)	0.44
		Magnesium (%)	0.11

*Also feed one human adult vitamin-mineral tablet daily to dogs and one-half tablet to cats to ensure all vitamins and trace minerals are included. Cats should be given one-half to one taurine tablet (500 mg/tablet) daily.
**ESHA Research. Diet Analysis Software. Food Processor Plus, version 5.03, 1990 Salem, OR. Agricultural Software Consultants, Inc. Mixit 2+, version 3.0, 1991, Kingsville, TX.
***May substitute rice baby cereal and flavor either selection with meat broth during cooking.
†Nutrients of concern are italicized.

Table 6-6. Balanced low-sodium and low-mineral homemade formulas for adult dogs and cats.*,**

Daily food as fed formulation for an 18-kg dog			
Ingredients	Grams	Nutrient analysis (DM)††	
Beef, regular cooked***	94	Dry matter (%)	38.7
Rice, white, cooked†	330	Energy (kcal/100 g)	431
Cereal, All Bran	9.0	Protein (%)	20.8
Oil, vegetable	2.0	Fat (%)	12.4
Calcium carbonate	2.0	Linoleic acid (%)	1.0
Salt, substitute (KCl)	1.0	Fiber (%)	2.9
Total	438	*Calcium (%)*	0.49
		Phosphorus (%)	0.26
		Potassium (%)	0.59
		Sodium (%)	0.12
		Magnesium (%)	0.11

Daily food as fed formulation for a 4.5-kg cat			
Ingredients	Grams	Nutrient analysis (DM)††	
Beef, lean, cooked***	67	Dry matter (%)	37.9
Rice, white, cooked†	67	Energy (kcal/100 g)	500
Calcium carbonate	0.7	Protein (%)	36.4
Salt, iodized	0.1	Fat (%)	21.5
Salt, substitute (KCl)	0.1	Linoleic acid (%)	0.73
Total	135	Fiber (%)	0.65
		Calcium (%)	0.55
		Phosphorus (%)	0.28
		Potassium (%)	0.54
		Sodium (%)	0.17
		Magnesium (%)	0.073

*Also feed one human adult vitamin-mineral tablet daily to dogs and one-half tablet to cats to ensure all vitamins and trace minerals are included. Cats should be given one-half to one taurine tablet (500 mg/tablet) daily.
**ESHA Research. Diet Analysis Software. Food Processor Plus, version 5.03, 1990 Salem, OR. Agricultural Software Consultants, Inc. Mixit 2+, version 3.0, 1991, Kingsville, TX.
***Retain the fat.
†May substitute rice baby cereal and flavor either selection with meat broth during cooking.
††Nutrients of concern are italicized.

homemade foods may have inverse calcium to phosphorus ratios as high as 1:10. Most homemade foods for dogs contain excessive quantities of meat, often far exceeding the animal's protein and phosphorus requirements.

Feline foods designed by clients are commonly deficient in fat and energy density or contain an unpalatable fat source (vegetable oil). Homemade foods are rarely balanced for microminerals and vitamins because veterinary vitamin-mineral supplements are not complete nor are the nutrients well-balanced within the product. In the United States, no one supplement can be added to homemade foods to adequately meet all the mineral and vitamin requirements of cats and dogs.

Common Ingredient Problems in Homemade Foods

People are taught that eating a variety of foods is nutritionally sound. Clients often extend this principle to their pet's nutrition. As an example, owners who purchase commercial pet foods may not be brand-loyal and often change brands "just in case" one brand is really not complete and balanced. Other pet owners will feed both moist and dry versions of complete and balanced products (of the same or different brands) "just in case there's something in one that's not in the other." Pet owners perceive that feeding a variety of foods is their best defense against malnutrition. Many times pet owners feed a variety of foods because they perceive the pet enjoys the frequent dietary changes.

Likewise, some owners feel a homemade food better meets their pet's nutritional requirements because they use a variety of ingredients. Nutritionally, this may or may not be accurate depending on ingredient substitutions. Inappropriate substitutions are a common error made by owners who design homemade pet foods.

Some owners choose the meat and carbohydrate ingredients for the pet's food based on their own preferences, product availability or affordability. Other pets are fed a variety of "leftover" ingredients such as fat trimmings, bones, vegetable skins, crusts and condiments. Pet food composed of table "leftovers" rarely represents the owner's food and is not complete and balanced for the pet.

On the other hand, some owners mistakenly feed their pet according to current and popular human nutritional guidelines such as avoiding fat, cholesterol and sodium. Such practices do not lead to consumption of a complete and balanced food for the pet. Many owners who make their pet's food according to published canine or feline recipes, over time, make their own ingredient substitutions that may or may not be correct. Foods made at home, therefore, are typically designed from a variety of table foods, and generally have no consistent ingredient composition. Inconsistency is the rule.

The second most common error made by pet owners who cook for their pets is to eliminate the vitamin-mineral supplement because of its inconvenience, expense or a failure to understand its importance. Foods made from recipes that were once crudely balanced become grossly unbalanced when owners eliminate supplements. Regular veterinary checkups are necessary to monitor the patient's progress and response to the food and to monitor the owner's level of compliance.

Some owners and breeders encourage the use of uncooked meat, liver and eggs in their homemade pet food recipes. This practice can be dangerous because uncooked animal ingredients can harbor pathogenic bacteria that normally would be killed during cooking. (See Chapter 7.)

RECOMMENDING HOMEMADE FOODS

Veterinarians should be willing to assess an existing recipe, offer nutritionally adequate recipes (Tables 6-2 and 6-3) or make appropriate formula substitutions for the client (Tables 6-4 to 6-8). These services are of value to some clients. The sidebar "Sources for Accurate Formulation of Homemade Foods" provides additional information.

Assessing Recipes

Veterinarians encounter a wide variety of pet food recipes from breeders and the popular press. Improving the ingredients in the recipe is not a simple task. It requires knowledge and good formulation skills, and an up-to-date database of locally available ingredients. The ingredients should be selected on the basis of nutrient content, tolerance, availability and cost. Information about the nutrient composition of commonly available homemade ingredients can be obtained from readily available sources; however, the information is usually presented in an obscure format such as amounts of "nutrient per serving" on an as fed basis.[40-42] Information in human food tables is not readily converted to common forms used to compare pet food formulations (e.g., percent as fed or dry matter basis). A simpler method to correct an inadequate homemade formulation is to adjust the proportions or change the ingredients in the recipe. Homemade formulations can be checked for nutritional adequacy and adjusted using the "quick check" guidelines below.

1. Do Five Food Groups Appear in the Recipe?

- A carbohydrate/fiber source from a cooked cereal grain.
- A protein source, preferably of animal origin, or if more than one protein source is used, one source should be of animal origin.
- A fat source.
- A source of minerals, particularly calcium.
- A multivitamin and trace mineral source.

2. Is the Carbohydrate Source a Cooked Cereal and Present in a Higher or Equal Quantity than the Meat Source?

The carbohydrate to protein ratio should be at least 1:1 to 2:1 for cat foods and 2:1 to 3:1 for dog foods. Carbohydrate sources for dog and cat foods are used for energy and are usually a cereal such as cooked corn, rice, wheat, potato or barley. These carbohydrate sources have similar caloric contributions, but some carbohydrate sources also contribute a significant amount of protein, fiber and fat (Table 6-9). A specific carbohydrate may be chosen based on specific changes in the patient's protein, fat and fiber requirements. For example, soybean may be substituted for corn if more protein is needed, or peas may be substituted if more fiber is needed.

Table 6-7. A balanced low-protein/low-purine homemade formula for adult dogs.*,**

Daily food as fed formulation for an 18-kg dog	
Ingredients	Grams
Rice, white, cooked	431
Egg, large, boiled	49
Oil, vegetable	27
Calcium carbonate	1.2
Salt, substitute (KCl)	1.2
Total	509

Food dry matter analysis***	
Nutrient	
Dry matter (%)	29.5
Energy (kcal/100 g)	483
Protein (%)	9.8
Fat (%)	21.8
Fiber (%)	2.2
Calcium (%)	0.38
Phosphorus (%)	0.1

*Also feed one human adult vitamin-mineral tablet daily.
**ESHA Research. Diet Analysis Software. Food Processor Plus, version 5.03, 1990 Salem, OR. Agricultural Software Consultants, Inc. Mixit 2+, version 3.0, 1991, Kingsville, TX.
***Nutrients of concern are italicized.

Table 6-8. A balanced low-residue homemade formula for adult dogs.*,**

Food as fed formulation for an 18-kg dog	
Ingredients	Grams
Rice, white, cooked	232
Cottage cheese	232
Egg, large, boiled	116
Oil, vegetable	2.0
Salt, substitute (KCl)	1.0
Calcium carbonate	1.0
Total	585

Daily food dry matter analysis***	
Nutrient	
Dry matter (%)	27.7
Energy (kcal/100 g)	450
Protein (%)	30.4
Fat (%)	15.6
Fiber (%)	0.71
Calcium (%)	0.42
Phosphorus (%)	0.39

*Also feed one human adult vitamin-mineral tablet daily.
**ESHA Research. Diet Analysis Software. Food Processor Plus, version 5.03, 1990 Salem, OR. Agricultural Software Consultants, Inc. Mixit 2+, version 3.0, 1991, Kingsville, TX.
***Nutrients of concern are italicized.

3. What is the Type and Quantity of the Primary Protein Source?

The overall protein quality in a homemade food can be improved by substituting an animal-source protein for a vegetable-source protein. Skeletal muscle protein from different animal species has very similar amino acid profiles. The protein content of various mammalian and avian skeletal muscle tissues is generally equivalent on a water-free basis. Thus, there is no great advantage to feeding one meat source over another. Any cooked animal protein source should provide the majority of a dog's or cat's essential amino acids.

The final food should contain 25 to 30% cooked meat for dogs, (one part meat to one or two parts carbohydrate, respectively) and 35 to 50% cooked meat for cats (one part meat to one to two parts carbohydrate).

Providing some liver in the meat portion is recommended once a week or no more than half of the meat portion on a regular basis. Liver corrects most potential amino acid deficiencies in homemade foods for dogs and cats. Liver not only improves the amino acid profile over that provided by vegetable and skeletal meat sources, but also contributes essential fatty acids, cholesterol, energy, vitamins and microminerals. If a pet owner requests an ovo-lacto vegetarian food, eggs are the best ingredient. If a vegan food is requested, soybeans provide the next best, but incomplete, amino acid profile.

4. Is the Primary Protein Source Lean or Fatty?

The fat content of different cuts of meat varies. When the specified protein source is "lean," an additional animal, vegetable or fish fat source should compose at least 2% of the formula weight for dogs, and 5% of the formula for cats to ensure adequate energy density and essential fatty acids. If a homemade food lacks sufficient caloric density (fat), the addition of cooked beef or chicken fat, poultry skins, vegetable or fish oils (tuna, mackerel, sardine) can markedly increase the caloric density without adding other nutrients. Changing the cut of meat can also markedly increase the fat content of a food. (See sidebar "Affect of Meat Substitutions on Fat and Energy Levels in Homemade Recipes.")

5. Is a Source of Calcium and Other Minerals Provided?

A homemade food is almost never spontaneously balanced in minerals; an absolute calcium deficiency is common. Unfortunately, pet owners erroneously assume cottage cheese, cheese or milk added in small quantities to homemade pet foods provides adequate calcium. Most foods require a specific calcium supplement. When the protein fraction equals or is greater than the carbohydrate fraction, usually only calcium carbonate is added to the food (0.5 g/4.5-kg cat/day and at least 2.0 g/15-kg dog/day). Calcium carbonate, containing 40% calcium and <1% phosphorus, is available in various size tablets from most pharmacies, health food and grocery stores.

Calcium and phosphorus supplementation may be necessary when the protein fraction is less than the carbohydrate fraction. Steamed bone meal, dicalcium phosphate and certain proprietary mineral supplements contain approximately 27% calcium and 16% phosphorus (about 2:1) and microminerals. These supplements, fed at the same dose as calcium carbonate, usually correct the calcium and phosphorus content.

6. Is a Source of Vitamins and Other Nutrients Provided?

Supplements providing vitamins, microminerals, fatty acids and specific nutrients of concern for cats and dogs can be obtained, but they may be cumbersome to feed and greatly

---

Effect of Meat Substitutions on Fat and Energy Levels in Homemade Recipes

The fat content of the animal protein source in homemade pet food recipes can markedly affect the energy density of the food. In general, animal protein sources such as fish, beef, turkey, chicken and mutton or lamb have similar protein and amino acid contents (Table 1). As a result, they can usually be substituted for one another on an as fed basis in most typical homemade food recipes. On the other hand, the fat content and therefore energy density can increase markedly depending on whether the cut of meat is regular (typical), lean or extra lean (Table 2). See Table 6-10 for more information about ingredient substitutions.

Table 1. Protein and energy content of interchangeable protein sources for a homemade cat food recipe (as fed).

Nutrient (% DMB)	Lean beef	Chicken	Tuna
Protein	28	28	29
kcal ME/g, as fed	4.5	4.4	4.4
kJ ME/g, as fed	18.7	18.5	18.2

Table 2. Fat and energy density of ground beef (30 g) with varying fat levels (as fed).

Nutrient	Extra lean (>90% lean)	Lean (>80% lean)	Regular (<80% lean)
Protein (g)	7	7	7
Fat (g)	3	5	8
Energy (kcal)	55	73	100
Energy (kJ)	230	305	418

BIBLIOGRAPHY
Nelson JK, Moxness KE, Jensen MD, et al. Appendices. In: Mayo Clinic Diet Manual: A Handbook of Nutrition Practices, 7th ed. St. Louis, MO: Mosby-Year Book, Inc, 1994.

Table 6-9. Nutrient profiles of cooked grains and vegetables for homemade foods.

Cereal	Calories (kcal/100 g DM)	Total carbohydrate (% DMB)	Sugar* (% DMB)	Protein (% DMB)	Dietary fiber (% DMB)	Fat (% DMB)
Corn	352	81	12.2	9.0	6.1	4.3
Chickpeas	412	68	3.0	22.0	12.3	6.5
Barley	388	85	2.0	10.6	20	3.2
Peas	383	72	19.5	24.6	25.9	2.0
Potato	374	87	2.0	7.4	6.5	<1.0
Rice, brown	411	85	1.5	9.6	6.3	3.3
Rice, white	406	87	<1.0	8.4	1.6	<1.0
Rice, instant	408	88	1.4	8.6	3.3	<1.0
Soybean	467	27	8.1	44.9	17.0	24.3
Wheat (pasta)	422	80	<1.0	16.7	6.5	3.2

*Readily available sugars (e.g., mono- and disaccharides).

raise the cost of the food. An adult over-the-counter vitamin-mineral tablet that contains no more than 200% of the recommended daily allowances for people works well for both dogs and cats at one-half to one tablet per day. One tablet per day of a human adult product will not oversupplement pets with calcium, phosphorus, magnesium, vitamins A, D and E, iron, copper, zinc, iodine and selenium, according to AAFCO maximum allowances for canine and feline foods.[24] In general, veterinary supplements contribute between 0 and 300% of the vitamin-mineral requirements of dogs and cats.

Specific nutrients of concern for cats—such as arginine, arachidonic acid, L-carnitine and choline—can be purchased as individual nutrient products. However, levels in homemade cat foods are usually adequate when a combination of animal proteins is used. Cats fed a homemade formula exclusively should receive 200 to 500 mg taurine daily, depending on the calculated taurine content of the food. Iodized salt should be used whenever salt is added to the food. It is difficult to meet the iodine requirement without using the iodized form (400 µg of iodine/6 g [1 tsp] sodium chloride).

Making Ingredient Substitutions or Formulating Recipes

When formulating a homemade recipe, proportions of carbohydrate, protein, fat and fiber must be maintained. Table 6-10 suggests starch, meat, fat and fiber ingredient substitutions and their relative nutrient values. When substituting one ingredient for another, determine the relative nutrient value of the old ingredient and that of the replacement ingredient. If the old recipe recommended 75 g of rice, and the owner would like to use pumpkin instead of rice, 200 g of pumpkin will be needed to supply the same amount (15 g) of carbohydrate as 75 g of rice (Table 6-10).

Several methods can be used to formulate homemade foods. Veterinary nutritionists in North America commonly use nutrition software programs such as those listed in Chapter 1. (See sidebar "Computerized Food Evaluation/Balancing Programs," page 13.) Most practicing veterinarians in North America either contact a veterinary nutritionist directly or use one of these software programs. A third method is to hand calculate the formulation using these steps: 1) determine the ingredients to be used from each food category (Table 6-10) and 2) determine the appropriate amount of each ingredient that will supply the needed amount of nutrient for the dog or cat. (See sidebar "Formulating a Homemade Food.") Each ingredient supplies more than just one nutrient (e.g., rice supplies carbohydrates and some protein). However, this simplified method of formulating a homemade food minimizes nutrient deficiencies by providing overlapping sources of nutrients.

Additional Instructions

Specific instructions for preparation, storage and feeding of homemade foods should be given to pet owners. Explaining the importance of a balanced food and providing practical recommendations about how to mix and cook the food will increase compliance. Some owners may even prefer a commercially prepared food when they realize what is involved in preparing a balanced homemade recipe.

Some owners and breeders encourage the use of uncooked meat and eggs in their homemade pet food

Sources for Accurate Formulation of Homemade Foods

The following references provide information about food sources for homemade formulas in different countries.

Instituto di Tecnica e Propaganda Agraria. Per una sana alimentazione italiana. Le basi scientifiche. Editor: Leone Barozzi. La campagna di valorizzazione MAF. L'informazione Roma, Italy, 1987.

Holland B, Welch AA, Unwin ID, et al. McCance and Widdowson's The Composition of Foods, 5th ed. Cambridge, UK: The Royal Society of Chemistry and Ministry of Agriculture, Fisheries and Food, 1991.

Meyer H, Heckötter E. Futterwerttabellen für Hunde und Katzen, 2nd ed. Hannover, Germany: Schlütersche Verlagsanstalt und Druckerei-GmbH & Co, 1986.

Watt BK, Merrill AL. Composition of foods. In: Agricultural Handbook No. 8. Washington, DC: Consumer and Food Economics Institute, Agricultural Research Service, USDA, 1975; Table 1: 6-66.

Pennington JAT. Bowes and Church's Food Values of Portions Commonly Used, 16th ed. Philadelphia, PA: JB Lippincott Co, 1994.

Randoin L, Le Gallic P, Dupuis Y, et al. Tables de Composition des Aliments, 6th ed. Malakoff, France.: Editions Jacques Lanore, 1990.

Table Belge de Composition des Aliments. Brussels, Belgium: a.s.b.l. NUBEL, 1992.

HOMEMADE PET FOODS

recipes. Pet owners should be informed that uncooked meat and eggs can harbor pathogenic bacteria that are normally killed during cooking. (See Chapter 7.) Animal ingredients (meat and eggs) should be cooked for at least 10 minutes at 82°C (180°F). Vegetable ingredients should be washed or rinsed and cooked if increased digestibility is desired. Owners can make homemade foods that lack preservatives and antioxidants in three- to seven-day batches but must refrigerate the food in airtight containers between meals (0 to 4°C [32 to 40°F]). Larger quantities of food can be frozen (-20°C [<0°F]). Because homemade foods are relatively high in moisture and lack a preservative system, they are highly susceptible to bacterial and fungal growth when left at room temperatures for more than a few hours. Pet owners who feed homemade foods must also check the food daily for color and odor changes that may indicate spoilage or deterioration. Clients should be advised of these food safety issues when feeding homemade foods. (See Chapter 7.)

Pet owners should be encouraged to use a dietary gram scale to weigh ingredients until they become familiar with the approximate volumes of each food. Ingredient compositions are published in different ways. For example, some recipes specify cooked rice, whereas others specify rice to be weighed as purchased. Formulation must take this variability into account, and the owner should be informed about it.

Cooking is necessary to improve the digestibility of starch in carbohydrate sources.[43,44] Cooking also destroys anti-nutrient factors that may be present (e.g., anti-trypsin in soybeans, thiaminase in some fish). However, carbohydrate and animal protein sources should be cooked separately. Carbohydrate sources need a longer cooking time to increase starch digestibility, due to swelling and gelatinizing of starch granules. Meat and liver, on the other hand, should not be overcooked to avoid protein denaturation. Cooking vegetables may increase starch digestibility, but does not decrease the value of vegetables as a source of fiber. Longer cooking times, however, may increase vitamin losses.[45]

Table 6-10. Ingredient substitution lists.

Ingredients	Major nutrient	18-kg dog	4.5-kg cat
Starch, cooked	Carbohydrate	60 g	12 g
Meat, cooked	Protein	28 g	9 g
Fat	Fat	10 g	10 g
Fiber	Dietary fiber	10 g (max)	5 g (max)

Starch: These foods in these amounts yield 15 g carbohydrate with 3 g protein, trace fat and 80 kcal

Bread	25 g	Breadsticks, raisin, rye, whole wheat, white
	30 g	Bagel, English muffins, buns, rolls, pita, tortilla
Cereal	20 g	Ready to eat cereals
	25 g	Bran cereals, shredded wheat
	30 g	Bran flakes, Chex
	100 g	Cooked cereals and grits
Grains	20 g	Cornmeal, flour, cornstarch, popcorn, tapioca
	75 g	Rice
	100 g	Barley, pasta
Vegetables	50 g	Baked beans, sweet potato
	75 g	Beans, peas, lentils, plantain
	80 g	Corn
	100 g	Corn on the cob, lima beans, green peas, potato, yam
	150 g	Squash, parsnips
	200 g	Pumpkin

Protein: Should be weighed after cooking and after bone, skin and excess fat have been removed
Low fat: These foods in these amounts yield 7 g protein with 3 g fat and 55 kcal

Beef	30 g	Baby beef, chipped beef, flank tenderloin, plate ribs, round (bottom, top), all rump cuts, lean spareribs, tripe, ground beef (>90% lean) and USDA good and choice
Pork	30 g	Leg, tenderloin, ham, Canadian bacon
Veal	30 g	Leg, loin, rib, shank, shoulder
Poultry	30 g	Chicken or turkey meat without skin
	90 g	Egg whites
Wild game	30 g	Venison, rabbit, squirrel, pheasant, goose without skin
Fish	30 g	Any fresh or frozen, tuna or mackerel canned in water
Seafood	30 g	Clams, crab, lobster
	90 g	Oysters
	50 g	Scallops
	60 g	Shrimp
Dairy	30 g	Cottage cheese
	45 g	Cheeses (low fat 3 g or less/oz)
Mixed meats	30 g	Low-fat luncheon meats with 3 g fat or less /oz, >90% lean

Medium fat: These foods in these amounts yield 7 g protein with 5 g fat and 73 kcal

Beef	30 g	Ground beef (>80% lean), corned beef, rib eye
Lamb	30 g	Leg, rib, sirloin, loin, shank, shoulder
Pork	30 g	Loin, shoulder arm and blade, butt
Veal	30 g	Cutlet
Poultry	30 g	Chicken or turkey meat with skin, duck and goose well-drained of fat
	50 g	Egg whole
Organ meats	30 g	Liver, kidney, heart, sweetbreads
Fish	30 g	Tuna, salmon canned in oil, drained
Dairy	30 g	Cheese: mozzarella, ricotta, farmer
Mixed meats	30 g	Low-fat luncheon meats with 3-5 g fat/oz, 85-90% lean
Vegetable	120 g	Tofu

High fat: These foods in these amounts yield 7 g protein with 8 g fat and 100 kcal

Beef	30 g	Ground beef (<80% lean), brisket, chuck, ribs, USDA prime
Lamb	30 g	Breast, ground
Pork	30 g	Spareribs, back ribs, ground, country style and deviled ham, sausage
Veal	30 g	Breast
Dairy	30 g	Cheese spreads, all regular American, blue, cheddar, Monterey, Swiss
Mixed meats	30 g	Cold cuts, sausages
	45 g	Frankfurter
Vegetable	30 g	Peanut butter

Fats: These foods in these amounts yield 5 g fat with 45 kcal

Polyunsaturated	5 g	Soft tub margarine, oil (safflower, corn, sunflower, cottonseed, sesame)
	15 g	Diet margarine with safflower, corn, sunflower oil
Monounsaturated	5 g	Margarine with soybean, cottonseed, partially hydrogenated oils, peanut oil, olive oil
Saturated	5 g	Chicken fat, beef fat, bacon fat, lard, butter, shortening
	15 g	Heavy cream, cream cheese
	30 g	Sour cream, nondairy substitutes, gravy
	45 g	Light cream, half & half

Fiber: Grams of dietary fiber per 100 g of these foods

High (5 g or more)	Beans (white, red, lima, black, broad, soy)
Medium (2-4 g)	Bamboo shoots, carrots, peas, string beans, bean sprouts, chickpea, pinto beans, summer squash, broccoli, cauliflower, pumpkin, turnips, cabbage, kidney beans, spinach, watercress
Low (0-2 g)	Asparagus, cucumber, lettuce, zucchini, alfalfa sprouts, eggplant, mushrooms, celery, green pepper, tomatoes

Formulating a Homemade Food

Bernard-Marie Paragon
National Veterinary School of Alfort
Maisons-Alfort, France

Jacques Debraekeleer
Hill's Science and Technology Center
Etten-Leur, The Netherlands

NUTRIENT SOURCES

Ingredients should be selected on the basis of nutrient content, tolerance, availability and cost. They can be classified into five nutrient groups.

1. Protein sources
Animal protein: muscle or organ meat (e.g., heart), organs (e.g., liver, kidneys), fish, milk, egg whites
Vegetable protein: soybean meal, beans, peas

2. Fat sources
Oils (soybean oil, corn oil, canola oil), high-fat meat or fish sources, egg yolk, chicken skin

3. Carbohydrate and fiber sources
Carbohydrate sources: rice, corn, wheat flour
Fiber sources: wheat bran, cellulose powder, psyllium, carrots, etc.

4. Macromineral sources

5. Trace element and vitamin sources

THE SIX-STEP FORMULATION METHOD

Formulating a homemade food should follow a step-by-step approach, starting with the allowances for energy and protein. A "six-step formulation method" designs a specific recipe for a particular patient or group of patients. This approach is more time-consuming and requires better knowledge than using a generic recipe.

1. Calculate the Nutrient Requirements of the Animal
Calculate the energy and protein requirements first. Determine the nutrients of concern for the physiologic stage or disease and calculate the amounts needed.

Energy Requirements
For cats, energy requirements can be calculated per kg body weight. Because of the wide range of canine body weights, daily energy requirements of dogs do not correlate well with body weight. Metabolic weight ($BW_{kg}^{0.75}$) or body surface area correlates better than body weights. Specific correction factors can be used to adapt the energy requirements more precisely to each individual. These factors take into account breed-specific differences, age, gender, temperament, activity, physiologic stage and illness. (See Appendix D.)

Whatever method is used to calculate the energy requirements of dogs or cats, the recommendation is only a starting point. This is particularly true for homemade foods, because the fat content (energy density) of the food may differ each time ingredients are purchased. In addition, the energy density of homemade foods is less accurately determined. Therefore, owners should weigh the animal regularly. If the animal tends to lose or gain weight, food intake and/or the recipe should be adapted. Body weight and body condition score should be routinely recorded at all veterinary appointments.

Protein Requirements
When formulating a homemade food for an individual animal, the protein requirement cannot be determined on a dry matter basis, but must be calculated based on daily intake. The dry matter content can be used later in the formulation process to assess the final recipe. Protein intake is determined in the same way as energy (i.e., as g protein/$BW_{kg}^{0.75}$). For example, a young adult dog may need 6 g crude protein/$BW_{kg}^{0.75}$. (See Chapter 9.)

Because allowances for energy and protein are determined in the same way, a protein-to-energy ratio can also be used. This ratio varies with lifestage and disease condition, and is higher in cats than in dogs (Table 1). Using the appropriate protein-to-energy ratio may save some steps during the formulation process. As for many other nutrients, the range for optimal protein intake narrows in case of disease or high performance. For a dog with chronic renal disease, for example, the range narrows to about 3 to 3.5 g/$BW_{kg}^{0.75}$ (about 3 g/100 kcal [7.17 g/MJ]) and the protein quality must be increased.

Cereal proteins (rice, corn) are low in tryptophan, lysine and methionine. Therefore, a mixture of protein sources with complementary amino acid profiles should be offered to ensure that all essential amino acids are provided. Cereal or vegetable protein should be combined with animal protein sources. The overall protein quality can be improved by increasing the ratio of animal to vegetable protein. For a dog with renal disease, for example, protein from egg, liver and cottage cheese (or curd) should deliver a larger part of the total protein. Red meat, heart and fish are also good sources.

Skeletal muscle from different mammals and poultry has a similar protein content (15 to 23% protein, as is), and there is little variation in the amino acid profile of skeletal muscle from different species. Meat from the most common fish sources also falls within the same range. Thus, protein sources can be interchanged according to preference and availability or if an animal becomes intolerant to one source. Animal protein (including muscle meat, heart, liver or kidneys) should provide the majority of a dog's or cat's essential amino acids. In most cases, they should constitute about 30 to 40% of the final food for healthy adult dogs and 50 to 60% for adult cats. As a rule of thumb, during formulation, the ratio of cereals and vegetables to animal protein sources should be between 1:1 and 3:1 for maintenance of adult dogs. This ratio should be between 1:1 and 1:2 for adult cats. The ratios may change in foods for other lifestages or in foods for diseased animals.

Adding some liver or egg to the recipe improves the amino acid balance. In recipes for cats, liver may improve palatability and the amino acid profile. Liver also provides essential fatty acids, cholesterol, energy, vitamins and microminerals. The addition of fresh beef liver (1 g/kg body weight/day) is beneficial during gestation.

Table 1. Crude protein-to-energy ratios for different lifestages.

Lifestage	Dogs g/100 kcal	Dogs g/MJ	Cats g/100 kcal	Cats g/MJ
Adult maintenance	4.5-6.5	10.5-15.5	6.0-8.0	14.3-19.1
Growth	6.0-8.5	14.3-20.3	8.0-10.0	19.0-24.0
Pregnancy	5.0-6.5	12.0-15.5	7.5-9.0	18.0-21.5
Lactation	5.0-6.5	12.0-15.5	8.0-10.0	19.0-24.0
Older	4.5-5.5	10.8-13.0	6.0-7.0	14.3-16.7
Diseases				
Obesity	7.0-11.0	16.7-26.3	9.0-12.0	21.5-28.5
Chronic renal disease	3.0-3.5	7.2-8.5	4.5-5.5	10.8-13.0

Continued on next page.

Continued from previous page.

2. Add a Fat Source

The amount of fat depends on the source used and the caloric requirements of the animal. In most cases, the fat source should supply between 5 and 15% of the total energy requirement. The fat source is chosen according to the animal's function and/or disease condition. Linoleic acid is available in vegetable oils such as soybean or corn oil. Cats need some animal fat to supply arachidonic acid. Medium- to high-fat meat supplies this requirement. Substituting fish that is high in fat (e.g., salmon or tuna) for lean meat provides a good source of n-3 fatty acids. Canola oil provides less than half of the linoleic acid in soybean oil, but contains about 10% n-3 fatty acids, with an n-6 to n-3 ratio of about 2.2:1. To improve palatability, part of the fat or oil can be added during cooking.

3. Add a Carbohydrate and Fiber Source to Supply the Remaining Energy

The energy density of the food must be calculated to ensure adequate energy density, and to maintain the correct nutrient-to-energy ratio. To do so, each g of protein and carbohydrate can be multiplied by 3.5 kcal (14.64 kJ) and each g of fat by 8.5 kcal (35.56 kJ).

4. Accommodate the Nutrients of Concern

Calculating the nutrient content as % dry matter and checking the nutrient-to-energy ratios are useful at this point to double-check the nutrient balance of the recipe. It is very important to check the nutrients of concern for the particular lifestage or disease. In some cases, it may be necessary to substitute one protein source for another. For example, when the animal is overweight, replace part of the meat with beans, which contain less fat and more fiber. Likewise, diabetic dogs should receive less fat and more complex carbohydrate.

5. Add Minerals and Vitamins

All homemade foods should be supplemented with an additional source of minerals. However, most mineral mixes sold for animals are not designed to correct calcium and phosphorus deficiencies. In many cases, the calcium-phosphorus ratio in mineral mixes is not high enough to correct the imbalances of a homemade recipe. Therefore, a single supplement can seldom adequately correct mineral deficiencies in homemade foods. It is necessary to provide a source of calcium (e.g., calcium carbonate) or of calcium and phosphorus (dicalcium phosphate) in addition to a mixture of trace elements and vitamins. Depending on the composition of the base recipe, and the requirements of the animal, calcium carbonate, dicalcium phosphate or a mixture of the two can be added. Calcium carbonate is the supplement of choice if the base diet already contains sufficient phosphorus, or if the animal has chronic renal failure. In addition, calcium carbonate has some buffering capacity, which may help prevent acidosis in patients with renal disease.

Liver is a good source of vitamin A and trace elements. Liver, kidneys and egg yolk are rich iron sources. Adding a small amount of yeast adds B vitamins, lysine and other essential amino acids.

Supplements that provide vitamins, microminerals, fatty acids and specific nutrients of concern for cats can be obtained in tablet form. But they may be cumbersome to feed and add greatly to the expense of the food. An adult over-the-counter vitamin-mineral tablet that contains no more than 200% of the recommended daily allowances for people works well for both dogs and cats at one-half to one tablet per day. Based on AAFCO maximum allowances, these dosages will not oversupplement pets with calcium, phosphorus, magnesium, vitamins A and D and trace elements.

The easiest way to correctly supplement a homemade food is to add a powdered veterinary mineral-vitamin supplement that is locally available from veterinary wholesalers or pharmacies. With powders, owners can avoid the cumbersome daily administration of tablets and the dosage is more accurate. However, powders may affect the palatability of the food.

6. Make a Final Assessment of the Recipe

Is the protein-to-energy ratio within the proper range for the animal? Is the biological value high enough in a restricted protein food? Is the final energy density adapted to the indication of the food ? Are the nutrients of concern (key nutritional factors) at the correct level for the animal's disease or lifestage? Is the nutrient-to-energy ratio appropriate?

Does a recipe for cats contain the specific nutrients in adequate amounts, whether they are supplemented or present through the chosen ingredients? Of particular concern are taurine, vitamin A and potassium. Taurine is present in muscle meat, heart and kidneys or can be added as a powder. Vitamin A must be given in the active form; liver is a good source. A potassium source (e.g., chloride, citrate or gluconate) may have to be added to the food.

EXAMPLE USING THE SIX-STEP METHOD

The following recipe is for maintenance of a five-year-old, 10-kg miniature dachshund. The dog is a household pet and has a body condition score of 3/5. The metabolic weight ($BW_{kg}^{0.75}$) of a 10-kg dog is 5.62.

1. Energy Requirement

The daily energy requirement (DER) is about 1.6 x RER: 115 kcal ME/$BW_{kg}^{0.75}$ (481 kJ ME/$BW_{kg}^{0.75}$) = 647 kcal (2,705 kJ). This will be the target for formulation (Table 2).

Table 2. Nutrient supplied by the major ingredients.

Source	Amount	Energy*	DM	Protein	Fat	NFE	CF	Ca	P	Na
Lean meat	140	157.5	36.4	28.0	7.0	0.0	0.0	0.004	0.23	0.07
Corn oil	5	45.0	5.0	0.0	5.2	0.0	0.0	0.000	0.00	0.00
Carrots	100	29.0	8.8	0.6	0.5	6.4	0.8	0.030	0.03	0.04
Cooked rice**	381	415.5	104.4	7.6	0.4	91.8	0.4	0.140	0.28	1.07
Total	**626**	**647.0**	**154.6**	**36.2**	**13.1**	**98.2**	**1.2**	**0.174**	**0.54**	**1.18**
Target		647	150-200	29-42				0.7-1.0	0.6-0.8	0.25-0.5

*Energy in kcal. To convert to kJ, multiply by 4.184.
**Many parboiled and instant rice available for home cooking already contains a fair to high amount of salt, which may raise the sodium level in the recipe to very high levels.
Key: DM = dry matter, NFE = nitrogen-free extract (carbohydrate), CF = crude fiber, Ca = calcium, P = phosphorus, Na = sodium.

Continued on next page.

Continued from previous page.

Table 3. Calculating the daily energy requirement (DER) that carbohydrates need to supply.

DER =		**647 kcal**	**2,705 kJ**
Energy from meat	140 g x 1.125 kcal =	157.5 kcal	659.0 kJ
Energy from vegetable oil	5 g x 9 kcal =	45.0 kcal	188.3 kJ
Energy from carrots	100 g x 0.29 kcal =	29.0 kcal	121.3 kJ
Energy subtotal		231.5 kcal	968.6 kJ
Energy needed from carbohydrate	647 − 231.5 =	415.5 kcal	1,737.4 kJ

Cooked whole rice is used as the carbohydrate source. Cooked rice contains about 1.09 kcal/g (4.56 kJ/g). (See Appendix T.) The amount to add: 415.5 ÷ 1.09 kcal/g (1,737.4 kJ ÷ 4.56 kJ/g) = 381 g of cooked rice to supply sufficient energy for this 10-kg dog.

2. Protein Requirement

An adult dog needs about 6 g (4.7 to 7.5) crude protein/$BW_{kg}^{0.75}$ or a protein-to-energy ratio of about 4.5 to 6.5 g crude protein per 100 kcal ME (11 to 15 g/MJ ME). Therefore, this dachshund needs 5.62 x 6 = 33.75 g crude protein per day (range from 26.5 to 42 g crude protein per day). Start with about 35 g crude protein per day. Lean beef provides about 20% protein and about 112.5 kcal/100 g (471 kJ/100 g). If meat provides 80% of the protein, then 35 x 0.8 = 28 g protein. Therefore, about 140 g of lean beef meat is required ([28 ÷ 20] x 100). (Table 2.)

3. Fat Source

For an adult 10-kg dog, at least 7% of the energy should come from fat: 647 x 7 ÷ 100 = 45.3 kcal (2,705 x 7 ÷100 = 189.5 kJ). If vegetable oil is the fat source, we need 45.3 ÷ 9 kcal (189.5 ÷ 37.66 kJ) = 5 g of oil. (Table 2.)

4. Carbohydrate and Fiber Sources

Add 100 g carrots to provide fiber (0.8% crude fiber, 0.29 kcal/g or 1.2 kJ/g). Carbohydrate needs to supply the remaining energy (Table 3).

5. Minerals and Vitamins

The calcium and phosphorus levels are deficient when using only the ingredients listed in Table 2. One g of calcium carbonate provides 0.36 g calcium and may contain traces of phosphorus. One g of dicalcium phosphate contains 0.23 g calcium and 0.19 g phosphorus.

Phosphorus

At least 0.6 g phosphorus is desired. The current ingredients provide 0.54 g phosphorus (Table 2); a minimum of 0.6 (0.54 + 0.06) g phosphorus must be added. A total of 0.32 g of dicalcium phosphate supplies this amount of phosphorus; 0.5 g dicalcium phosphate will deliver 0.115 g calcium and 0.095 g phosphorus.

Table 4. Final recipe analysis.

Nutrient	As fed (%)	Dry matter (%)
Protein	5.8	23.2
Fat	2.1	8.4
NFE	15.7	62.9
Crude fiber	0.2	0.77
Calcium	0.11	0.45
Phosphorus	0.10	0.41
Sodium	0.19	0.76
PER (g/100 kcal ME)	5.6	
kcal ME/100 g	103	414
kJ ME/100 g	431	1,732

Key: NFE = nitrogen-free extract (carbohydrate), PER = protein energy ratio.

Calcium

At this point, 0.174 g calcium are provided by the ingredients in Table 2 and 0.115 g from dicalcium phosphate for a total of 0.289 g calcium. At least 0.7 g calcium is desired; therefore, 0.41 g calcium (0.7 - 0.289) must be added. This can be provided by 1.14 g calcium carbonate (0.41 ÷ 0.36 = 1.14 g calcium carbonate).

A mixture of trace elements and vitamins should be added to the food. About 0.5 g is generally enough.

6. A Final Check

The final recipe delivers 647 kcal in 627.6 g. Table 4 gives the analysis.

BIBLIOGRAPHY

Meyer H, Schüneman C. Grunddaten zur Rationsgestaltung bei Hund und Katze. Der Praktischer Tierarzt 1986; 67: 35-38.

Kronfeld DS. Therapeutic diets for dogs and cats including a simple system of recipes. Tijdschrift voor Diergeneeskunde 1986; 111(S1): 37S-41S.

Gesellschaft für Ernährungsphysiologie Empfehlungen für die Versorgung mit Protein. In: Ausschuß für Bedarfsnormen der Gesellschaft für Ernährungsphysiologie Energie- und Nährstoffbedarf Nr. 5 Hunde. Frankfurt, Germany: DLG Verlag, 1989; 45-55.

Meyer H, Heckötter E. Taurin- und Arachidonsauregehalt in ausgewahlten Futtermitteln für Katzen. In: Futterwerttabellen für Hunde and Katzen, 2nd ed. Hannover, Germany: Schlütersche Verlagsanstalt und Druckerei-GmbH and Co, 1986; 31.

Meyer H, ed. Praktische Fütterung. In Ernährung des Hundes, 2nd ed. Stuttgart, Germany: Eugen Ulmer, 1990; 162-223.

Beare-Rogers JL. Some aspects of omega-3 fatty acids from different foods. In: Galli CL, Simopoulos AP, eds. Dietary ω 3 and ω 6 Fatty Acids: Biological Effects and Nutritional Essentiality. New York, NY: Plenum Press, 1989; 21-31.

Kronfeld DS. Optimal regimens based on recipes for cooking in home or on proprietary pet foods. In: Anderson RS, ed. Nutrition and Behaviour in Dogs and Cats. Oxford, UK: Pergamon, 1984; 43-53.

Donoghue S, Kronfeld DS. Home-made diets. In: Wills JM, Simpson KW, eds. The Waltham Book of Clinical Nutrition of the Dog & Cat. London, UK: Pergamon, 1994; 445-449.

After cooking, all ingredients should be thoroughly mixed (in a blender) to prevent the animal from picking out single food items. An unbalanced intake of nutrients may occur if ingredients of a nutritionally balanced homemade food are allowed to separate and the animal does not consume the entire mixture. Be sure the owner understands the dietary formulation only approximates the recommended nutrient intake of the pet at a given weight for a certain number of days.

Owners should be warned that although vitamins and minerals are present in only small quantities, they are very important and are not optional. Vitamin-mineral supplements should not be cooked or heated or stored with the food. Vitamins may be destroyed by heat or oxidation. The vitamin-mineral supplement should be kept separate from the food, and administered just before, during or after a meal to ensure proper dosing. Overall digestibility and availability of vitamin-mineral supplements are improved when using USP labeled products and these nutrients are present in the small intestine with a meal composed of proteins, fats and carbohydrates.

The food should be warmed to just below body temperature before feeding. Clients should be advised to carefully check for "hot spots" that could burn a pet's mouth after food has been rewarmed in a microwave oven. Wetting the food may improve palatability. Moisture content of homemade foods is approximately 70%, which is more similar to that of moist than dry food. Animals that favor dry forms may reject homemade foods.

When stored too long, the food mixture may separate and dry out, becoming less palatable. Therefore, it is best not to prepare large amounts of food that cannot be eaten in a few days. Mixing the food before warming will improve palatability.

When choosing the ingredients for specific foods, keep in mind that some ingredients are acceptable for one species, but may markedly decrease the palatability for another. For example, dogs like sugar but cats do not. When formulating a food for a patient with diabetes mellitus or colitis, for example, beans and peas may be a suitable carbohydrate and protein source for a dog. But increasing the amount of these ingredients may make a food unacceptable to cats.

Vegetable and meat sources may be substituted for similar ingredients in a recipe (Table 6-10). Feeding a variety of foods decreases the risk that a particular nutrient might be below requirements long enough to cause clinical signs of deficiency. Clients should receive a list of possible substitutes, and be informed that inappropriate substitutions may jeopardize nutritional balance.

If the patient has a history of food rejection or gastrointestinal upset with food changes, advise the client to feed the homemade food without supplements for a week or so, and then add the supplements one at a time (one per week) to avoid the problem or better identify the source of the problem.

In practices where homemade foods are regularly recommended, the staff should have experience preparing the recipes to become familiar with the preparation of homemade foods. Further, it is worthwhile and may be cost effective to send the most commonly recommended formulas to a food analytical laboratory to confirm the calculated analysis. (See Appendix U.) In the United States, AAFCO provides valuable guidelines for minimum and maximum nutrient allowances within which a food for healthy dogs and cats should be formulated if no feeding tests are done. These guidelines may be a useful target for formulating homemade foods as well. (See Appendix J.)

PATIENT ASSESSMENT AND MONITORING

Patients that eat homemade foods should be brought in for regular veterinary examinations (two to three visits per year). Because the nutritional profile of homemade foods is quite variable, a nutritional review is recommended at least twice a year. If a dog or cat eats a homemade food exclusively for more than six months, the veterinarian should ask the client to record and submit a three- to five-day food history so that the nutrient profile and ingredient substitutions can be re-evaluated.

The effectiveness of a food can be grossly evaluated by noting the patient's body weight, body condition and activity level. Laboratory data such as albumin level, red blood cell number and size and hemoglobin concentration are gross estimations of the animal's nutritional status and can be used with other clinical observations to evaluate homemade foods.

More specifically, the skin and hair should be examined closely and an ophthalmic examination, including evaluation of the lens and retina, should be performed. These tissues are more sensitive than others to nutritional status.[46-49] Stool quality should also be assessed.

Veterinarians should always: 1) offer to have a homemade recipe evaluated by a nutritionist and 2) recommend the feeding of a consistent complete and balanced commercial product as often as possible. This is especially true if the pet has a medical condition for which dietary management depends on the highest level of diet consistency and quality assurance.

REFERENCES

1. Wolter R. Modalités pratiques d'une alimentation rationelle: Rations ménagères. In: Diététique du Chien et du Chat. Paris, France: Masson SA, 1988; 21-25.
2. Practice Health: Module 1 Introduction. Hill's Pet Nutrition, Inc, Topeka, KS, 1993: 4.
3. Pet Food Institute. NPD Group, Inc. March 6, 1997.
4. Lund EM, Armstrong PJ, Kolar L, et al. Distribution of disease and diet type in a natural population of geriatric dogs and cats from private veterinary practice. In: Proceedings. Symposium on Health and Nutrition of Geriatric Cats and Dogs. Orlando, FL, 1996: 56.
5. AAHA's Fourth Annual Pet Survey Looks at the Human Animal Bond. Trends Magazine May/April 1995: 30-31.
6. Lewis LD, Morris ML Jr, Hand MS. Pet foods. In: Small Animal Clinical Nutrition III. Topeka, KS: Mark Morris Associates, 1987; Chapter 2.
7. Pibot P. Aliment Industriel: Aliment ménager Vers un compromis? Recueil de Médecine Vétérinaire 1989; 165: 537-545.
8. Bonnavaud P. Le marché des aliments industriels pour chiens. Recueil de Médecine Vétérinaire 1989; 165: 525-526.
9. Kieffer J-P. Le vétérinaire praticien et la diététique canine en France. Recueil de Médecine Vétérinaire 1989; 165: 549-554.
10. Donoghue S, Kronfeld DS. Home-made diets. In: Wills JM, Simpson KW, eds. The Waltham Book of Clinical Nutrition of the Dog & Cat. London, UK: Pergamon, 1994; 445-449.
11. Phillips T. Natural pet foods. Pet Veterinarian 1991; May/June: 4-8.
12. American Institute for Cancer Research Newsletter. Washington, DC: American Institute for Cancer Research, Winter 1990; 26: 4-5.
13. Phillips T. What is "natural?" Pet Veterinarian 1990; Sept/Oct: 46.
14. Pet Food Institute Memorandum. March 20, 1997.
15. Marsh FO. An overview of the international pet food market. Presentation to the Annual General Meeting of FEDIAF. Arcachon, France. June 10, 1994.
16. Dwyer JT. Nutritional consequences of vegetarianism. Annual Reviews of Nutrition 1991; 11: 61-91.
17. McDonald P, Edwards RA, Greenhalgh JFD, et al. Evaluation of foods–Protein. In: Animal Nutrition, 5th ed. Harlow (Essex), UK: Longman Scientific and Technical, 1995.
18. Miller M. Consumers' perceptions of food safety. In: Aruoma OI, Halliwell B, eds. Free Radicals and Food Additives. London, UK: Taylor and Francis, 1991; 1-15.
19. Potter NN. Food additives, wholesomeness, and consumer protection. In: Food Science, 4th ed. Westport, CT: AVI Publishing Co, 1986; 638-653.
20. Aruoma OI, Malliwell B. Free Radicals and Food Additivies. London, UK: Taylor & Francis, 1991; ix-xiv.
21. Roudebush P. Pet food additives. Journal of the American Veterinary Medical Association 1993; 203: 1667-1670.
22. Hilton JW. Antioxidants: Function, types and necessity of inclusion in pet foods. Canadian Veterinary Journal 1989; 30: 682-684.
23. Löliger J. The use of antioxidants in foods. In: Aruoma OI, Halliwell B, eds. Free Radicals and Food Additives. London, UK: Taylor and Francis, 1991; 121-150.

24. Association of American Feed Control Officials. Official Publication, 1998.

25. Dzanis DA. Safety of ethoxyquin in dog foods. Journal of Nutrition 1991; 121: S163-S164.

26. Council Directive 70/524/EEC. Official Journal of the European Community. December 14, 1970; L270/1-7.

27. Council Directive 91/248/EEC. Official Journal of the European Community. May 18, 1991; L124/1-6.

28. Mumma RO, Rashid KA, Shane BS, et al. Toxic and protective constituents in pet foods. American Journal of Veterinary Research 1986; 47: 1633-1637.

29. Ferrando R. Historique et perspectives actuelles de l'alimentation du chien–ses répercussions. Recueil de Médecine Vétérinaire 1989; 165: 513-521.

30. Stein D. Optimal nutrition. In: Natural Healing for Dogs and Cats. Freedom, CA: The Crossing Press, 1993; 49-83.

31. Pitcairn RH, Pitcairn SH. Natural Health for Dogs and Cats. Emmaus, PA: Rodale Press Inc, 1995; 22-79.

32. Martin A. Food Pet's Die For. Troutdale, OR: New Sage Press, 1997.

33. Remillard RL. What's for dinner? Family Dog Care 1994; 1(1): 4-10.

34. Brown CM, Armstrong PJ, Globus H. Nutritional management of food allergy in dogs and cats. Compendium on Continuing Education for the Practicing Veterinarian 1995; 17: 637-658.

35. Carlotti DN, Remy I, Prost C. Food allergy in dogs and cats. A review of 43 cases. Veterinary Dermatology 1990; 1: 55-62.

36. Roudebush P, Cowell CS. Results of a hypoallergenic diet survey of veterinarians in North America with a nutritional evaluation of home-made diet prescriptions. Veterinary Dermatology 1992; 3: 23-28.

37. Kallfez FA. Home made foods for cats. Cat Fancy 1996; January: 24-25.

38. Donoghue S, Szanto J, Kronfeld DS. Hypervitaminosis A in a dog: An example of hospital dietetics. In: Proceedings. Waltham International Symposium–Nutrition, Malnutrition and Dietetics in the Dog and Cat, Hanover, Germany, 1987: 94-95.

39. Kelly NC, Willis J. Food type and evaluation. In: Manual of Companion Animal Nutrition and Feeding. British Small Animal Veterinary Association, 1996; 22-42.

40. Watt BK, Merrill AL. Composition of foods. In: Agricultural Handbook No. 8. Washington, DC: Consumer and Food Economics Institute, Agricultural Research Service, USDA, 1975; Table 1: 6-66.

41. Carper J. The Brand Name Nutrition Counter. New York, NY: Bantam Books, 1975.

42. Pennington JAT. Bowes and Church's Food Values of Portions Commonly Used, 16th ed. Philadelphia, PA: JB Lippincott Co, 1994.

43. Walker JA, Harmon DL, Gross KL, et al. Evaluation of nutrient utilization in the canine using the ileal cannulation technique. Journal of Nutrition 1994; 124: 2672S-2676S.

44. Wolter R. Rations pratiques: A. Les rations ménagères. In: L'alimentation du Chien et du Chat. Maisons-Alfort, France: Les Editions du Point Vétérinaire, 1982; 101-108.

45. Meyer H. Futtermittelkunde. In: Ernährung des Hundes, 2nd ed. Stuttgart, Germany: Verlag Eugen Ulmer, 1990; 126-161.

46. Remillard RL, Pickett JP, Thatcher CT, et al. Comparison of kittens fed queen's milk with those fed milk replacers. American Journal Veterinary Research 1993; 54: 901-907.

47. Glaze MB, Blanchard GL. Nutritional cataracts in a Samoyed litter. Journal of the American Animal Hospital Association 1983; 19: 951-954.

48. Sousa CA, Stannard AA, Ihrke PJ, et al. Dermatosis associated with feeding a generic dog food: 13 cases (1981-1982). Journal of the American Veterinary Medical Association 1988; 192: 676-680.

49. Harvey RG. Skin diseases. In: Wills JM, Simpson KW eds. The Waltham Book of Clinical Nutrition of the Dog & Cat. London, UK: Pergamon, 1994; 425-444.

HOMEMADE PET FOODS

CASE 6-1

Lethargy and Vomiting in Three Cats

Rebecca L. Remillard, PhD, DVM
Diplomate ACVN
Angell Memorial Animal Hospital
Boston, Massachusetts, USA

Assess the Animals

Three cats were examined for lethargy and occasional vomiting. Two cats were at their optimal body weight and condition (weight = 4.5 kg, body condition score = 3/5); one cat weighed 5.5 kg and had a body condition of 4/5. All three cats were icteric, had elevated hepatic enzyme levels and were diagnosed as having hepatic lipidosis.

Assess the Food(s) and Feeding Method

The owners read about pet food manufacturing in a popular cat publication and decided they no longer wanted to feed a commercially produced food to their three cats. They discarded all pet food products in the house, chose a recipe suggested in the text that suited them and began feeding the homemade food exclusively for two weeks. Two cats reluctantly ate a little food almost every day, whereas one cat refused to eat for two weeks.

Questions

1. How should the veterinarian advise these clients about making food changes in the future?
2. These owners did not want to feed a commercially produced cat food because they were convinced the ingredients used were making their cats subclinically but progressively ill. What food recommendations should be made for the cats?

Answers and Discussion

1. When making food changes for cats, a gradual transition schedule that decreases the old food and increases the proportion of new food is highly recommended. (See Chapter 1.) Generally, cats should eat daily and should not go more than three days without eating a sufficient quantity of food to meet their resting energy requirement. Hepatic lipidosis can occur in normal and overweight cats. The condition occurs more commonly when cats are completely anorectic, but can also occur in cats that have been partially anorectic for weeks to months.

2. Because the owners are convinced they should feed a homemade food, they should be offered a nutritionally adequate generic recipe or should be referred to a nutritionist who could formulate a recipe that takes into consideration their particular concerns.

Progress Notes

The three cats were fed a complete and balanced liquid feline formula for three days (30 ml every three hours) by nasogastric tube. Moist kitten food was offered ad libitum. Two cats began eating on Days 4 and 5 and were discharged. The third cat progressively deteriorated and was euthanatized on Day 5.

CASE 6-2

Weight Loss in an Older Cat

Rebecca L. Remillard, PhD, DVM
Diplomate ACVN
Angell Memorial Animal Hospital
Boston, Massachusetts, USA

Assess the Animal

The owner of a 17-year-old, neutered female domestic shorthair cat with chronic renal failure requested a recipe so she could cook at home for her cat. The owner thought the cat's poor appetite would improve if the cat were fed a food that contained chicken, the cat's favorite ingredient. She asked the veterinarian to review a homemade recipe she obtained from a friend who is a cat breeder. The cat weighed 3.2 kg and had a body condition score of 2/5.

Assess the Food(s) and Feeding Method

The recipe was as follows:

Meat (chicken, white)	25 g	25%
Rice or pasta	55 g	55%
Vitamin-mineral supplement	13 g	13%
Brewer's yeast	5 g	5%
Spirulina (blue green algae)	2 g	2%

Question

1. Using the quick check guidelines for homemade foods, what suggestions should be made about nutrients, ingredient levels and food preparation?

Answer and Discussion

1. The meat source should constitute at least 30% of the as fed homemade food and contain more fat. The recipe as presented contains virtually no fat. This cat is underweight and has a less than optimal body condition score; it needs a more calorically dense food. If the cat distinctly prefers white meat then approximately 10 to 20 g of fat is necessary. Chicken skin, beef fat or vegetable/fish oils may be used to constitute at least 10% of the as fed weight.

The food needs a calcium source, such as 0.3 g of calcium carbonate per day. Review the vitamin-mineral supplement label to ensure the supplement contains trace minerals (copper, zinc, manganese, iron, iodine, selenium), B vitamins, vitamin A and taurine. Encourage the owner to use a dietary gram scale to weigh and blend all ingredients to prevent the cat from picking out the chicken, but administer the vitamin-mineral supplement with the meal. The revised recipe would be as follows:

Meat (chicken, white)	35 g	31%
Rice or pasta	60 g	52%
Fat (chicken skin)	15 g	13%
Vitamin-mineral supplement	4 g	3%
Calcium carbonate	0.3 g	0.25%

The client was advised to feed chicken liver once a week in place of the chicken meat. The vitamin-mineral supplement recommended was one-half of an adult vitamin-mineral tablet. Brewer's yeast adds magnesium, B vitamins, microminerals and fiber; however, nutritional yeast is fortified and has a better nutritional profile of B vitamins and microminerals. The Spirulina is of questionable nutritional value, but probably causes no harm.

CASE 6-3

Understanding Pet Food Labels

Rebecca L. Remillard, PhD, DVM
Diplomate ACVN
Angell Memorial Animal Hospital
Boston, Massachusetts, USA

Assess the Animal

A dog owner recently went to a local kennel club meeting and heard that synthetic preservatives in pet foods should be avoided. She was especially concerned about a preservative with a long name that begins with an "e." Because she does not know which pet foods in the grocery store contain the compound, she would rather just make her dog's food at home. She asked her veterinarian to review the ingredient list and specifically asks if the ingredient called "ethylenediamine dihydroiodide" is the preservative she should avoid.

Questions

1. What is ethylenediamine dihydroiodide?
2. Where or how can this information be found?
3. What should be the recommendation to the dog owner?

Answers and Discussion

1. Ethylenediamine dihydroiodide is a source of iodine in pet foods in the United States. It is not the preservative ethoxyquin.
2. The AAFCO manual readily provides this information. Alternatively, the pet food company could be contacted directly.
3. The owner need not be concerned about feeding ethoxyquin; however, if she wishes to avoid this preservative, she could choose a commercial pet food product preserved with other antioxidants (e.g., a natural preservative). A commercially prepared complete and balanced pet food is preferable to a homemade food.

Bibliography

Association of American Feed Control Officials. Official Publication, 1998.

CASE 6-4

Back Pain and Weakness in a Springer Spaniel

Rebecca L. Remillard, PhD, DVM
Diplomate ACVN
Angell Memorial Animal Hospital
Boston, Massachusetts, USA

Assess the Animal

A 13-month-old female English springer spaniel was examined for chronic small bowel diarrhea of seven months' duration. The dog weighed 5.5 kg and had a body condition score of 2/5.

Assess the Food(s) and Feeding Plan

The owner was unwilling to feed any commercially produced dog food because "he had tried them all and none of them ever worked." According to the client, the dog does well and had normal stools when fed a homemade food containing only one part boiled white chicken and two parts instant rice. The pet owner would like for the veterinarian to balance this food.

The veterinarian gives the client the following recipe:

Chicken, dark meat with skin	80 g	24%
White rice, cooked	250 g	74%
Calcium carbonate	0.6 g	0.2%
Vitamin-mineral supplement	8 g	2%
Salt (NaCl), iodized	0.4 g	0.1%

The owner was also given a printed complete set of instructions and cautions.

Reassessment

Six months later the dog presents with severe back pain, rear leg weakness, inappetence, depression and lethargy. The dog ate the homemade food exclusively for six months and has had very few episodes of diarrhea. The dog's serum calcium concentration was 8.9 mg/dl (reference range = 9 to 11 mg/dl). The dog's serum albumin concentration was normal.

Questions

1. What additional information would be important to obtain about feeding the homemade food?
2. What is the most likely food-related problem given the clinical signs of generalized muscle weakness and lethargy?
3. What common omission do clients who feed a homemade food often make?

Answers and Discussion

1. The recipe should be checked item by item to ascertain whether the owner is following the recipe and then the instructions for mixing and feeding the food should be reviewed with the client.
2. Long-term feeding of a calcium-deficient food can result in marked muscle weakness, lethargy and osteoporosis.
3. Omitting the vitamin-mineral supplementation is a common error made by owners who feed a homemade food.

Progress Notes

After reviewing the food formulation with the owner, he admitted that he had not been giving calcium carbonate supplementation because it was inconvenient to give the dog one (0.5 g calcium carbonate) tablet per day. Ten percent calcium gluconate solution was administered intravenously at 15 mg/kg slowly over one hour. Within hours the dog's attitude improved and the dog was able to stand. The dog was apparently difficult to medicate, so liquid or powdered supplements mixed in the food were suggested.

HOMEMADE PET FOODS

CHAPTER 7

Food Safety

E. Phillip Miller
James S. Cullor

"Do not eat any detestable thing . . . Do not eat anything you find already dead."
Deuteronomy 14: 3, 21

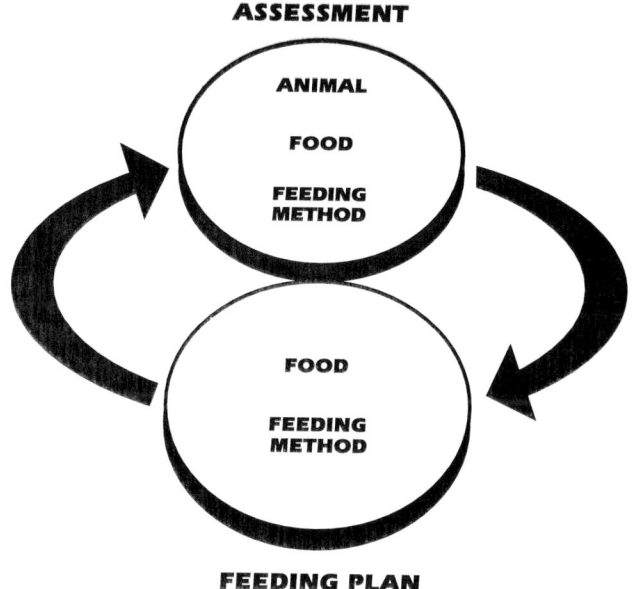

ASSESSMENT

ANIMAL
FOOD
FEEDING METHOD

FOOD
FEEDING METHOD

FEEDING PLAN

Note: The reader is referred to Chapter 1 for a detailed discussion of the iterative process of clinical nutrition.

INTRODUCTION

Each year more than 24 million Americans are affected by foodborne illnesses such as salmonellosis, botulism and staphylococcal food poisoning.[1] Luckily, the typically affected person often improves in 24 hours and has little more than an upset stomach. Likewise domesticated pets can become ill from ingesting contaminated food. Most animal feedstuffs including spoiled foods such as garbage and carrion are rich in the nutrients needed to support rapid microbial colonization.[2] This phenomenon occurs quickly because most bacteria have the ability to double their number every 30 minutes under favorable moisture and temperature conditions.

Microbes of all shapes and sizes are everywhere in our environment. Foods can be contaminated at any stage of production of the food, starting in the field and ending with storage in the home. The time between the harvesting of pet food ingredients, food handling and preparation in the home and consumption of the final product provides multiple opportunities for microbial populations to proliferate. Microbial growth can result in either food spoilage or risk of foodborne illness. The current methods of food processing and preservation simply forestall the final outcome: spoilage. The earlier in the food production cycle the contamination occurs, the more widespread the outbreak.

Foodborne diseases (Figure 7-1) can be divided into two types: 1) food infections (usually bacterial) and 2) food intoxication (microbial toxicoses).[1] Food infections such as salmonellosis and salmon disease (*Neorickettsia helminthoe-*

KEY WORDS & TERMS—FOOD SAFETY*

AAFCO	Chronic	Pesticide
Action level	Contaminate	ppb
Acute	Endotoxin	ppm
Advisory level	Enterotoxin	Saprophytic
Aerobic	Exotoxin	Spore
Anaerobic	Exposure	Tolerance
Bacillus	Heat labile	Toxin
Carrion	Microbe	Virulence

Key words and terms are defined in the Glossary.

KEY POINTS—FOOD SAFETY

1. Safety issues affect human and pet foods.
2. Drugs are the most common cause of poisonings in dogs and cats.
3. The prevalence of foodborne illness in pets is low, but clients often blame the food for acute gastrointestinal disturbances.
4. Processing methods and quality assurance programs of federally regulated pet foods limit the potential for companion animal foodborne disease.
5. Animals that roam freely and those fed raw meat or uncooked foods are at greatest risk of foodborne illness.
6. Foodborne illness in dogs and cats can be caused by bacterial infection, bacterial toxins, mycotoxins, chemicals, metals and other contaminants.
7. An extensive and accurate history is essential to the pursuit of an accurate diagnosis in foodborne illnesses.
8. Foods can be assessed by a variety of microbiologic and analytical methods.
9. Making a diagnosis of foodborne illness based solely on the successful isolation of a pathogenic bacterial species from a sample of pet food is risky.
10. An accurate final diagnosis of foodborne illness must be based on a strong correlation among the history, accessibility to the causative agent, clinical signs, clinical laboratory results, pathology and results from assays of the food and other specimens.
11. Common food hygiene methods can alleviate the majority of foodborne illnesses in dogs and cats.

ca) result from the ingestion of infectious microbial cells that invade the host's tissues and after an appropriate incubation period produce the disease. Because it takes time for these cells to replicate to pathogenic numbers, clinical disease in food infections does not become evident until at least 12 to 24 hours after ingestion.

Food poisonings, or more specifically "food intoxications," do not depend on the ingestion of viable cells, but result from the ingestion of a food that already contains a microbial toxin. Because cell replication is not required, the signs of food poisoning appear rapidly, sometimes less than one hour after ingestion. The term "food poisoning" is often incorrectly used as a synonym for foodborne illness.

CLINICAL IMPORTANCE

When a pet exhibits signs of gastrointestinal disease, the owner often concludes that food must be the culprit. In the past, when pets relied on table foods, carrion, garbage and improperly cooked pet foods for sustenance, this would have been a reasonable conclusion.[3,4] Today, foodborne disease in household pets is rare.[5] The 1990 annual report of the American Association of Poison Control Centers (AAPCC) indicated that of the 41,854 dog and cat poisoning cases reported, foodborne illnesses accounted for only 1.7% of the total (Table 7-1).[6] However, foodborne illness is still a common disease in the United States racing greyhound industry.[7]

The low incidence in domestic pets can be attributed to two primary changes in the way that they are fed. First, most pets in developed countries depend totally on commercial pet foods to meet their nutritional needs. More than 90% of the pet owners in the United States purchase commercial pet foods for their pets.[8] Although these figures are lower for the United Kingdom and Europe, the majority of pet owners in those geographic regions also feed commercial pet foods.[9]

Second, present day commercial pet foods are much safer than in the past. Modern pet foods are not composed of a

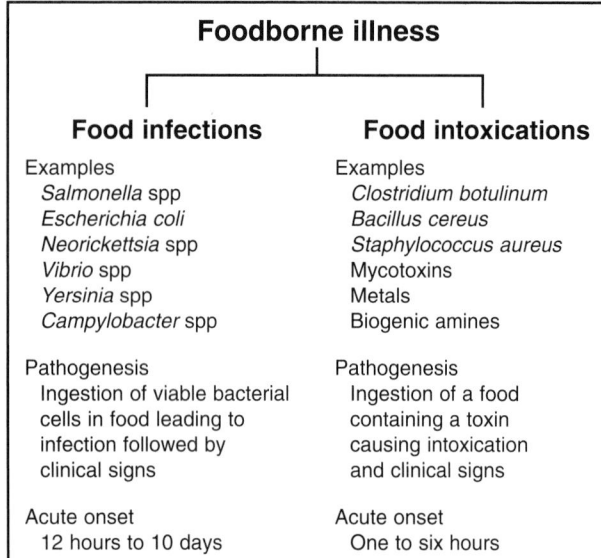

Figure 7-1. Classification of foodborne illnesses.

single ingredient but are formulated from multiple ingredients including grains, meats, meat by-products, vegetables, eggs, dairy products, fish and other added nutrients. The use of many and varied ingredients tends to dilute any contamination that might occur in a particular commodity or ingredient. Commercial pet food manufacturers commonly use manufacturing techniques such as extrusion and retorting to produce heat levels sufficient to destroy many pathogens and heat-labile toxins.[10,11] Improved packaging materials and a better knowledge of proper warehousing also help to protect raw materials and finished products from moist conditions and possible contamination during storage. Furthermore, manufacturers use sensitive analytical techniques to verify that ingredients and final products are high quality and free of contaminants. The value of these efforts is supported by a study in which researchers analyzed 35 dog and 17 cat foods and found that most were remarkably free of toxic contaminants.[12]

In addition to manufacturing quality control and storage improvements, pet foods and individual pet food ingredients are regulated by several governmental agencies to ensure safety. In the United States, foods and ingredients that are shipped across state or international boundaries are regulated by the Food and Drug Administration (FDA) under the authority of the Federal Food, Drug and Cosmetic Act (FFDCA).[13-15] Section 402 of the FFDCA states that foods, including pet foods, shall be considered adulterated when they contain an added substance that may render the food injurious to health. Section 406 of the FFDCA empowers the Secretary of Health and Human Services to promulgate regulations and tolerances that limit the quantity of contaminants, such as mycotoxins. Additionally, sections 501, 505 and 512 of the FFDCA authorize the FDA control over the use of veterinary drugs. As part of the drug approval process, the conditions of drug use in animal feeds can be set by the FDA. The use levels established for veterinary drugs prevent excessive drug residues in meat, milk and other by-products from food-producing animals that may be used as ingredients in pet foods. The FDA and the Association of American Feed Control Officials (AAFCO) publish annually the approved animal drug levels in feeds along with the species for which the drug is approved.[16,17]

Instead of a tolerance, the FDA may choose to issue either an action or an advisory level for some unnatural additives. Both are considered maximum allowable levels, but an action level is generally supported by more definitive safety data than is an advisory level. A tolerance is a codified legal regulation whereas action and advisory levels constitute nonbinding FDA guidelines that the agency uses in exercising its enforcement discretion. Therefore, some circumstances may elicit enforcement action at levels below an action or advisory level whereas others may not even though an action or advisory level has been exceeded.

Tolerances for pesticides are not set by the FDA but instead fall under the jurisdiction of the United States Environmental Protection Agency (EPA) under the authority of the FFDCA and the Federal Insecticide, Fungicide and Rodenticide Act (FIFRA).[18] The EPA establishes and publishes pesticide tolerances for the various plant and animal commodities in 40 CFR 180. These tolerances are developed by combining the results of field trials and laboratory animal toxicity testing.[19] The United States Department of Agriculture (USDA) and FDA are then jointly responsible for enforcing the pesticide tolerances.

Table 7-1. Causes of poisonings in dogs and cats.*

Substance	Percentage of total cases
Drugs	25.0
Insecticides	19.6
Plants	12.1
Miscellaneous/unknown	8.9
Rodenticides	8.4
Cleaning products	5.9
Cosmetics	2.9
Hydrocarbons	2.9
Foreign bodies	2.8
Chemicals	2.7
Fertilizers	2.2
Food	1.7
Herbicides	1.6
Paints	1.6
Bites/stings	1.2
Heavy metals	0.5

*Hornfeldt CS, Murphy MJ. 1990 Report of the American Association of Poison Control Centers: Poisonings in Animals. Journal of the American Veterinary Medical Association 1992; 200: 1077-1080.

For contaminants not covered by a tolerance, an action level or advisory level, the limit remains theoretically at zero. However, present day analytical methods have become so sensitive that minuscule amounts can be detected. Fortunately, the FDA has discretionary power when a contaminant is detected at a low level not considered to be a safety concern.

In Europe, the regulation of intentional additives (e.g., vitamins and minerals) and unintentional additives (e.g., pesticides, drug residues and metals) falls under the authority of the European Union (EU).[20] Control measures are implemented on a national basis and can be stricter but never more permissive than the EU legislation.[20] Non-EU foreign countries regulate pet food safety with a variety of internal regulations and policies.

Most regulatory agencies, both domestic and international, use monitoring programs to maintain surveillance over pet food products. Specifically, in the United States, the FDA monitors pet food and individual pet food ingredients for pesticides, mycotoxins and heavy metals as part of its Feed Contaminants Program.[14]

Intrastate pet foods are under less federal scrutiny, with primary regulation left to state and local officials. This relationship has created concern that unsuitable food components, most notably mycotoxin-contaminated grains, may be used inadvertently.[21] In addition, such products are often pelleted instead of extruded; therefore, processing temperatures may not be sufficient to kill bacteria and inactivate heat-labile toxins. Both factors tend to increase the risk of foodborne disease in locally produced foods.

The risk of litigation also encourages pet food manufacturers to be diligent in maintaining high product quality standards. Under tort claims law, all products offered for sale to the public contain an implied warranty.[22] The law specifically provides "that a person who sells a product in a defective condition unreasonably dangerous to the user or consumer or his property is liable for the physical harm the product causes . . ." News programs frequently report large verdicts against manufacturers of human food products because of the harm allegedly caused by their products.[23] Animal feed and pet food manufacturers have also been caught up in this trend. Procedural breakdowns or oversights during production or storage can have a catastrophic effect on profits or even company viability. Mycotoxin litigation alone has cost the pet food industry an estimated $7 million since 1990.[24] More recently, a case involving an alleged vomitoxin-contaminated pet food may cost the company as much as $20 million in addition to a severely damaged reputation.[25] Such experiences have made it necessary for manufacturers to devote extensive resources to documenting product quality.

The use of home-prepared pet foods also has clinical relevance to foodborne disease. Many breeders and individuals in the dog racing industry have their own special food formulas. Raw meat may make up 50 to 75% of the food consumed by racing greyhounds in the United States.[26] These foods are a common source of foodborne illness because uncooked meat may contain large numbers of bacterial cells and the foods are mass produced without proper hygiene or adequate cooking.

Some health-conscious pet owners forgo commercial foods and prepare foods for their pets daily. These owners are frequently fastidious and very careful about preparing and storing their pets' food, but they must truly be committed to the long-term maintenance of proper hygiene and preparation methods. If breeders and pet owners use high-quality ingredients that are stored properly, heat foods to temperatures sufficient to destroy pathogens and prepare amounts that are readily consumed by their pet, the potential for foodborne illness is reduced. Otherwise, the best method to lessen the risk of foodborne illness is to feed the pet a high-quality commercial pet food.

■ ASSESSMENT

Assess the Animal

The most important goal in dealing with a case of suspected foodborne illness is to obtain an accurate diagnosis. However, this may be difficult because many factors, including the pet owner, can mislead the veterinarian. One must adhere stubbornly to the principles of a proper toxicologic investigation, including the careful evaluation of information supplied by: 1) the history, 2) clinical signs, 3) postmortem findings, 4) chemical analyses and 5) laboratory animal tests.[27] For live patients, an accurate diagnosis will aid in the initiation of specific treatments and preventive measures. The veterinarian should also use preliminary information and clinical signs to guide the history-taking process.

History

Although an adequate history is important in all clinical cases, it is especially important when foodborne illness is suspected because some of the critical facts in the case may be lacking. For example, it may not be possible to obtain a sample of garbage or a carrion source. The history-taking process is also complicated by pet owners who often express the opinion that food is to blame. In such cases, veterinarians must be methodical if they are to reach an unbiased and accurate diagnosis.

The natural starting place is the discussion with the pet owner. First, ascertain when and what clinical signs first appeared. From here, veterinarians can annotate the sequence and relevant facts about the events that tran-

spired before the patient's presentation. Aspects of the history that seem vague or incomplete should be probed further. Facts that seem unrelated should be noted for later consideration. For example, it is important to know what day the neighborhood trash is left out for pickup, especially if it was the day before the illness occurred. The recent application of a pesticide to the premises or yard coupled with signs typical of pesticide toxicity would be important, particularly if the pesticide was applied by the pet owner instead of a professional exterminator. These examples lend credence to the fact that one cannot achieve an adequate history by allowing the pet owner to simply describe the events that preceded the illness. Instead, it is imperative that the veterinarian take the initiative to tactfully probe and query the pet owner for every key piece of information. Most pet owners feel that such facts are irrelevant, whereas others may refuse to admit that their pet would scavenge garbage cans. Still others may even give incorrect information to conceal their own negligence. All family members should be included in these discussions if possible. This is a good time to request that the pet owner bring the food in its container to the hospital for testing. As will be discussed later in the chapter, it is important that the entire food container be brought, not just a sample selected by the pet owner.

Exposure to other toxicants in the pet's environment, such as pesticides or cleaning chemicals, is a distinct possibility and should be thoroughly investigated. The AAPCC report noted that drugs and household products are responsible for 71% of canine and feline poisonings.[6] This report also showed that 89% of pet poisonings are from sources within the home and its immediate surroundings. Most, if not all, homes contain pesticides and other toxic chemicals. If pets are allowed to roam freely outdoors, the scope of investigation must be expanded. Free-roaming animals have access to trash and garbage, pesticides, toxic chemicals and spoiled foods. Pets on farms and ranches have an increased exposure to pesticides and agricultural chemicals. They also have the freedom to ingest animal feeds for other species that may contain toxic feed additives such as ionophores and organic arsenicals.

Contamination of a commercial pet food will usually produce an epizootic of sick pets within a wide geographic area, as exemplified by a recent event in Europe. A popular brand of cat food was inadvertently contaminated with the food animal drug salinomycin, causing paralysis and death in several hundred cats.[28] Therefore, knowledge of this principle can be used in the diagnostic process. If other animals in the same household are eating food from the same bag or container and remain asymptomatic, then implication of the food is diminished and other possible causes should be investigated. If commercial pet foods are purchased from a veterinarian, then that person would have firsthand knowledge of other animals consuming the same lot or batch of food. If other patients are asymptomatic, then the commercial food may again be discounted as the causative agent.

However, even if it appears that the commercial food has been exonerated, one should not end the investigation here because the commercial food could still be involved if the pet owner has compromised the product's integrity by improper storage or usage. The veterinarian should contact the manufacturer to determine if similar cases have been reported. Company technical personnel can also help the differential diagnosis process by supplying key information about product testing, additional areas of investigation and beneficial laboratory tests.

Physical Examination

The physical examination of patients suspected to have a foodborne illness should be thorough, just as for other diseases. Although signs of gastrointestinal disease may be obvious, one should also be alert for other clinical signs such as cutaneous lesions or signs that might signify central nervous system or hepatic disease (Table 7-2). If possible, samples of vomitus and feces should be obtained for laboratory testing. Veterinarians should also use their own olfactory senses. Many toxicities impart unique odors to the patient. For example, fishy breath emanating from a dog known to be consuming a cereal-based dry dog food would be noteworthy. Likewise, a pesticide odor on a cat's coat would be a significant observation. Again, one cannot overemphasize the investigative prowess that must be exercised in foodborne illness cases.

The second important reason for conducting a routine physical examination is to evaluate the need for symptomatic treatment. Patients may have signs such as dehydration, seizures or high fever that require symptomatic or supportive treatment before a final diagnosis is made. This determination is best made during the physical examination. If emergency treatment is warranted, consultation with a local veterinary school, state veterinary diagnostic laboratory, hospital poison center or the American Society for Prevention of Cruelty to Animals (ASPCA) National Animal Poison Center (800-548-2423) may prove helpful.

Clinical Laboratory Testing

Clinical laboratory testing should be performed routinely in all suspected foodborne illness cases. Many such illnesses are short-lived so hematologic and serum biochemistry values may be within normal limits. However, clinical biochemistry values would be invaluable in establishing the diagnosis and prognosis in serious illnesses such as the mycotoxicoses.

Vomitus, feces and urine should be collected, labeled, frozen and tested for bacteria, viruses, biotoxins, metals, pesticides or chemicals as deemed appropriate by discussions between the veterinarian and testing laboratory personnel. The collection and analysis of a urine sample is also important because many toxic compounds are concentrated in urine. In fatal cases, organ tissue samples, bile, urine, stomach and intestinal contents should be collected during the postmortem examination.

Risk Factors

Individual factors such as age, species and state of health influence susceptibility to foodborne illness. Young and old animals are most susceptible. Debilitated or immunocompromised animals are more prone to foodborne illness. Dogs are at higher risk than cats because they are more likely to forage spoiled foods (e.g., trash, garbage and carrion); cats tend to be more discerning and fastidious in their eating habits. The AAPCC reported that dogs account for 75% of all animal poisonings.[6] Historically, the risk of foodborne illnesses in pets is increased during warm weather, hunting seasons and two holidays: Thanksgiving and Christmas.[2]

Table 7-2. Clinical signs of various foodborne illnesses.

Clinical signs	Agents causing the foodborne illness
Vomiting/diarrhea	*S. aureus*, *Salmonella* spp, *Neorickettsia* spp, *E. coli*, *B. cereus*, *Yersinia* spp, *Campylobacter* spp, biogenic amines, aflatoxins, vomitoxin, cyclopiazonic acid, lead, arsenic, zinc, cadmium
Liver disorders, jaundice	Aflatoxins, fumonisins, lead, arsenic, rubratoxin, *Yersinia* spp
Blood disorders, e.g., anemia, hemorrhages	Aflatoxins, *Neorickettsia* spp, lead, onions, garlic, rubratoxin, cyclopiazonic acid, mycotoxins
CNS/nervous disturbances	*C. botulinum*, fumonisins, penitrem A, lead, arsenic, mercury, chocolate
Kidney pathology	Ochratoxin, cyclopiazonic acid, *E. coli*, lead, arsenic, mercury, cadmium, chocolate
Skin lesions	*E. coli*, garlic, arsenic, cyclopiazonic acid

The most important factors to consider in establishing risk are the food source and the environment. Knowledge of these factors will help quantify the patient's exposure to other sources of toxicants and microbial agents. If the pet owner feeds a commercial pet food, follows label directions and follows proper storage recommendations, the likelihood of foodborne illness is low. However, if the same pet is allowed to roam freely outdoors, then the risk of exposure to foodborne disease agents is increased greatly. Home-prepared foods are more risky if the owners do not follow proper preparation and storage procedures discussed later in this chapter. Animals fed foods containing large amounts of uncooked meat and offal are at much greater risk. In general, the risk of contracting foodborne illness from various food sources increases as follows (from least to greatest risk): federally regulated canned pet foods <federally regulated dry pet foods <federally regulated semi-moist pet foods <individual homemade fresh foods <locally prepared commercial dry pet foods <mass-produced kennel foods <free access to garbage, trash and carrion.

The risk of contracting a foodborne agent from any of these food sources can be markedly increased by improper storage of the food. All of the effort that goes into selection of raw ingredients, product manufacturing, choice of food or home preparation is wasted if the pet owner fails to properly store the food. Proper storage depends on control of three factors: 1) temperature, 2) moisture and 3) availability of oxygen.[1] If these factors are controlled, commercial canned products will have a shelf life of well over a year and dry foods of at least six months. Therefore, risk is also influenced by proper food storage.

Etiopathogenesis

The bacteria of major concern as potential causes of foodborne illnesses in people include: *Clostridium perfringens*, *Clostridium botulinum*, *Staphylococcus aureus*, *Bacillus cereus*, *Salmonella* species, *Listeria* species, *Yersinia* species, *Aeromonas* species, *Campylobacter jejuni*, *Escherichia coli*, *Vibrio* species, *Enterococcus faecalis*, *Enterobacter cloacae* and *Klebsiella ozaenae*.[29,30] These organisms also have the potential to cause disease in pets. However, as stated previously, the prevalence of foodborne disease is low in dogs and cats. The following discussion involves the etiopathogenesis of bacteria and other agents that can cause foodborne disease in pets.

MYCOTOXINS

Estimates suggest that one-quarter of the world's annual food crop is affected by the mold metabolites called mycotoxins.[31] They can be highly toxic and are produced by a wide variety of saprophytic and pathologic fungi.[32] Toxic syndromes range from mild gastrointestinal discomfort and vomiting to an acute fulminating episode with death. Long-term, low-level exposure can produce vague signs such as chronic organ damage (e.g., hepatic cirrhosis), immunosuppression and decreased production or performance. Although cereal grains are most commonly associated with mycotoxins, a wide variety of foodstuffs including cheeses, nuts, forages, fruits and even beer can be contaminated.[32]

Mycotoxin production occurs in the field and during harvesting, processing, transport and storage. Stressors such as drought and insect damage predispose crops to infestation and mycotoxin production. Warm ambient temperatures and high humidity also favor mycotoxin production. Some degree of mycotoxin production is unavoidable. Mycotoxin content may be controlled through identification, quantification and regulation. The genera of the three major mycotoxin-producing fungi are *Aspergillus*, *Fusarium* and *Penicillium*.

Aflatoxins

Aflatoxin, a mycotoxin produced by *Aspergillus* species, can produce varying degrees of toxicity in birds and mammals. Corn, peanuts, cottonseed and grains are potential sources of aflatoxins in pet foods. Dogs and cats are among the species most sensitive to the effects of aflatoxin, with LD_{50} values ranging from 0.5 to 1.0 mg/kg.[33,34]

The onset and severity of the clinical syndrome depend on the dose and duration of exposure. In 1955, the canine disease known as hepatitis X was successfully reproduced by feeding dogs a brand of dog food previously incriminated in cases of the same disease.[35,36] Later, researchers discovered that the identical disease syndrome could be elicited in dogs fed purified aflatoxin B_1.[37] Most recently, cases of canine aflatoxicosis resulting from contaminated food have been reported in South America and Africa.[2,38]

The principal target organ in all species is the liver. Clinical signs, such as anorexia, severe gastrointestinal disturbances, jaundice and hemorrhage, with a corresponding increase in hepatic enzyme activities and a decrease in serum protein values, are typical.[33,34,39] The most frequently observed hepatic lesions are centrilobular necrosis, fibrosis and bile duct proliferation. Intravascular coagulation can also be a complication of chronic aflatoxicosis.[40]

Today, manufacturers and governmental regulatory agencies strive to minimize exposures to aflatoxins by using low-level detection methods. Aflatoxins are heat stable and not destroyed by boiling, autoclaving or food manufacturing methods. The FDA has established an action level of 20 ppb for total aflatoxins in pet food.[41] Therefore, prevention strategies involve identification of raw materials with unacceptable levels (>20 ppb), maintenance of proper storage conditions and assay of final feeds.

Vomitoxin

Vomitoxin, chemically known as deoxynivalenol (DON), is a mycotoxin produced by members of the genus *Fusarium*.[32] Vomitoxin can be found in any grain but most commonly affects wheat and barley. Like most other mycotoxins, it is heat stable. Dogs and swine are the species most susceptible to the effects of vomitoxin, and they are affected at relatively low concentrations. Clinical signs include feed refusal, vomiting and diarrhea.

In 1993, the FDA advisory level for DON in grains and grain by-products used in pet foods was 5 ppm with the added recommendation that these ingredients not exceed 40% of the food (i.e., 2 ppm DON in the complete pet food).[42] However, feed refusal in dogs has been reported in levels approaching 2 ppm.[43] Therefore, a more practical maximum level is 1 ppm. In 1995, vomitoxin levels in winter wheat were reportedly as high as 32 ppm. One major pet food company recalled 16,000 tons of product due to DON contamination at a cost of about $20 million.[25]

Fumonisins

The fumonisins are a group of recently described mycotoxins produced by *Fusarium moniliforme*, a common field fungus found in grains, beans and fruit.[44,45] Although *F. moniliforme* reportedly infects 80 to 100% of all corn harvested in the United States, little information is available about the toxicity of the fumonisins in dogs and cats. However, these potent mycotoxins cause leukoencephalomalacia in horses and liver disease in a number of other species. Fumonisin-contaminated pet foods have not been a problem to date.

Other Mycotoxins

Although canine and feline toxicity data for many of the other foodborne mycotoxins are scant in the scientific literature, the toxic effects of penitrem A, rubratoxin B, ochratoxin A and cyclopiazonic acid (CPA) have been described and documented.[46-50]

BACTERIA AND RICKETTSIA

Salmonella species

Salmonellae are gram-negative, aerobic bacilli that are normally present in the intestinal tracts of many mammals, birds and reptiles. Healthy adult dogs and cats are fairly resistant to the pathogenic effects of the salmonellae but serve as important sources of infection for people and weak, debilitated animals. It has been estimated that 36% of healthy dogs and 17% of healthy cats harbor these organisms in their gastrointestinal tracts.[51,52]

The most common route of exposure is through the ingestion of fecal-contaminated food and water. The presence of salmonellae in food or water indicates inadequate hygiene and improper cooking. Racing greyhounds are frequently infected when they consume foods largely composed of contaminated raw meat and offal from rendering plants. Researchers who sampled and cultured raw meat used in greyhound foods found that 45% of the meat samples were contaminated with salmonellae. *S. typhimurium* was the most commonly isolated serotype.[26] When raw meat containing large numbers of cells is ingested by racing greyhounds, a clinical enteritis syndrome termed "kennel sickness" or "blowout" results.[7]

Salmonellae produce their pathologic effects by production of a heat-labile endotoxin. Clinical syndromes can be divided into gastroenteritis, bacteremia/toxemia and organ localization. Infections can usually be treated successfully with a combination of appropriate antibacterial drugs and supportive treatment. Persistent carriers are common and can be a source of human exposure. Proper cooking of foods and boiling of water will kill the vegetative bacterial cells and inactivate the endotoxin.

Clostridium botulinum

Botulism is caused by the heat-labile toxin of the gram-positive, anaerobic, spore-forming bacterium *Clostridium botulinum*. These saprophytic bacilli are commonly found in soil and as contaminants in raw meat, carrion and vegetables. They are not considered dangerous to man or animals unless allowed to grow under anaerobic conditions in uncooked meats, improperly canned foods and the carcasses of dead animals. Under anaerobic conditions, *C. botulinum* produces the most potent biotoxin known.[53] This powerful exotoxin blocks the release of the neurotransmitter acetylcholine. Dogs are less susceptible to the effects of the toxin than people, but naturally occurring botulism has occurred in dogs.[51,54,55] There have been no documented occurrences in cats.

Clinical signs can occur as early as 12 hours or as late as five to six days after the exotoxin is ingested. The primary clinical sign is a generalized paralysis that starts in the posterior limbs and progresses to quadriplegia.

Primary care consists of supportive treatment. Spontaneous recovery will occur provided the dose of toxin ingested was insufficient to severely affect vital functions such as respiration. Prevention can be achieved by heating foods before consumption to either 80°C (176°F) for 30 minutes or 100°C (212°F) for 10 minutes.[1] These heating protocols are sufficient to destroy the heat-labile toxin of *C. botulinum*; however, any bacterial spores present will survive this treatment.

Staphylococcus aureus

The staphylococci are ubiquitous and are common inhabitants of the skin and mucous membranes of man and other animals.[56] *S. aureus* is the most common cause of foodborne illness in people. The typical gastrointestinal signs result from a potent *S. aureus* enterotoxin. Although *S. aureus* organisms are easily killed by heat, their enterotoxin can withstand typical cooking temperatures and even the canning process.[57] The ingestion of about 25 µg of enterotoxin will produce nausea and vomiting within two to four hours in people. Spontaneous recovery occurs in 24 to 48 hours. Dogs and cats are reported to be tolerant to staphylococcal enterotoxin and have remained asymptomatic after administration of oral doses as high as 100 µg/kg body weight.[58,a]

Neorickettsia species

Two rickettsiae, *Neorickettsia helminthoeca* and *N. elokominica*, cause a serious systemic infection in dogs known as salmon poisoning.[59,60] The disease is transmitted by the ingestion of raw salmon, which contains the vector, a fluke named *Nanophyetus salmincola*. The fluke matures in five to seven days and then attaches to the intestinal mucosa of the host animal. The rickettsiae leave the fluke, invade the intestinal mucosa and enter the bloodstream to produce an acute systemic infection.

Clinical signs include vomiting, hemorrhagic diarrhea, high fever, dehydration and peripheral lymphadenopathy. Tetracycline therapy is the treatment of choice. Supportive treatment with parenteral fluids is also indicated. The anthelmintic preferred for elimination of the fluke is fenbendazole. If timely treatment is not instituted, mortality can reach 50 to 90%.[61]

Escherichia coli

Escherichia coli is a well-known pathogen of people. However, the role of *E. coli* as a pathogen of dogs and cats has been unclear.[61,62] Recently, *E. coli*, strain O157:H7 has been involved in a number of outbreaks of foodborne illnesses stemming from improperly cooked meat purchased from fast-food restaurants.[29] The same strain has been incriminated in an unusual clinical syndrome in racing greyhounds termed "Alabama rot" or "Greenetrack disease."[63] This disease is characterized by erythema, ulceration of the extremities and renal glomerular pathology.[7,63,64] No particular treatment has proved effective, but many animals will recover with symptomatic treatment and good nursing care.

Bacillus cereus

Bacillus cereus causes vomiting and diarrhea in people, but it is not thought to pose a significant danger for foodborne illness in animals.[65] At room temperature, *B. cereus* flourishes, producing a potent endotoxin. The organism is a ubiquitous, spore-forming aerobic saprophyte found in soil, grains, cereal products and other foods.[66] As an example, it is commonly found in uncooked rice.[1] *B. cereus* has been found as a common isolate in samples of dry pet food.[b] It has also been isolated from food packaging paper and materials.[67]

The standard heat used to manufacture pet foods is not likely to destroy the spores of this organism. However, the number of organisms isolated from pet food samples (<10^5 cells/g of food) is unlikely to cause foodborne disease in pets unless the food is exposed to moisture and heat conditions conducive to bacterial proliferation.[66,68,69] Therefore, pet owners should be warned not to add water to dry pet foods and leave them exposed to high ambient temperatures for prolonged periods.

BIOGENIC AMINES

"Cadaveric alkaloids" isolated from putrefied bodies have been known to forensic toxicologists for more than 100 years.[70] Modern chemistry has now established that these decomposition products are not alkaloids but instead are "biogenic amines." They are produced when bacteria decarboxylate amino acids in animal tissue. Examples of biogenic amines include histamine, putrescine and cadaverine.

Detection of histamine in the tissues of fish indicates decomposition or spoilage. Normal commercially canned fish contain histamine levels less than 5 to 6 ppm.[71] As the level of histamine approaches 20 ppm, spoilage becomes organoleptically and physically evident.

Excessive levels of histamine (around 500 ppm) in the flesh of spoiled fish in combination with the toxin called saurine are thought to be involved in the pathogenesis of a human foodborne illness called "scombroid fish poisoning."[71-73] This common seafood-related illness is named for its association with the consumption of scombroid fishes, such as tuna, wahoo, mackerel and sardines, although other fishes and cheese have also been implicated.[73,74] The disease produces clinical signs of an allergic nature, i.e., flushing, sweating, nausea, diarrhea, rash, dizziness, facial swelling, respiratory distress and occasionally vasodilatory shock, but the disease is rarely fatal.[73,74] The FDA has recognized histamine's role in scombroid poisoning by setting an action level maximum of 500 ppm histamine in canned fish.[71]

Histamine and other biogenic amines such as putrescine and cadaverine have also been detected in pet foods. Their presence has been attributed to the use of poultry, fish and meat by-products as raw ingredients. The levels of histamine in pet foods reported in each of two different studies ranged from 3.8 to 88.8 ppm and 16 to 65.5 ppm, respectively.[75,76] Dogs and cats are tolerant to much higher levels of histamine (2,500 ppm), but research is needed to determine whether certain hypersensitive animals may be at risk.[77]

METALS

The metals are probably the oldest toxic agents known to man.[78] They are unique in that they are never destroyed nor created, just redistributed in the environment. Food is the most common source of metal toxicity in people and other animals. Pets frequently serve as sentinels for human exposure. Pet foods can become contaminated in several ways. First, metals tend to accumulate in plant and animal matter creating the possibility of toxic levels in food ingredients. Foods can also become contaminated during commercial manufacturing and home preparation by the inadvertent addition of metal shavings, grease, oils and other chemicals. Acidic foods can leach paint, soldered joints or plating agents from the food container. Young animals may ingest lead by chewing on painted wood, linoleum, metal toys, golf balls, roofing materials, drapery weights and ornaments.[27]

Most foodborne metal toxicities in dogs and cats involve lead, zinc, cadmium and arsenic. These agents cause a variety of clinical syndromes depending on age, dose ingested and length of exposure. The specifics of metal toxicities are well-described in several veterinary toxicology textbooks and are beyond the scope of this chapter.

The tendency of metals to accumulate in plants and animals has ramifications for the manufacture of commercial pet foods. Several studies have been conducted to quantify such accumulations. In one study, researchers analyzed 28 brands of commercial dog food and seven brands of cat food and found that average levels of lead, arsenic and cadmium were 1.26, 0.37 and 0.22 ppm, respectively.[79] A later study of 35 dog foods and 13 cat foods found the average levels of lead, cadmium and zinc were 0.88, 0.80 and 122.0 ppm, respectively.[12] These studies confirm that nontoxic levels of metals may be present in some pet foods; however, their presence at these levels would not support a diagnosis of metal toxicity. Instead, a definite diagnosis must be based upon finding toxic levels in the food that correspond to elevated levels in the patient's tissues, such as blood, liver and kidney.

OTHER SOURCES

Many people supplement their own food with vitamins, herbal remedies and other items purchased at health food stores. Well-meaning pet owners likewise think that what is good for them is also good for their pets. Unfortunately, this practice fails to take into account species and dose differences. Cats, in particular, may be adversely affected by medications considered safe for people. Certainly the toxicity of vitamins A and D is well-documented. It is also known that many herbal remedies will cause adverse effects in people and animals.[80] Therefore, the safety of other "natural" supplements such as aloe, ginseng root, eucalyptus, ginger and oil of wintergreen has yet to be established for dogs and cats. As the investigation of the clinical case proceeds, the veterinarian should inquire of the owner how and why the animal's food is being supplemented with these substances.

Owners may also supplement a pet's food with onions or garlic. Onions derive part of their flavor from n-propyl disulfide, which is toxic to the erythrocytes of several species.[81] In 1990, a new phenolic compound was extracted from onions that also increased methemoglobin concentrations and caused the formation of Heinz bodies in canine erythrocytes.[82]

Onions may injure the lipid membranes of erythrocytes and irreversibly denature hemoglobin.[81] These changes result in formation of Heinz bodies, hemolytic anemia and hemoglobinuria. Cattle are most susceptible but dogs are also susceptible.[81] Heinz body anemia has occurred in dogs consuming relatively small amounts (5 to 10 g of onions/kg body weight) of raw, cooked or dehydrated onions.[83-85] In one study, consumption of approximately 30 g of raw onions/kg body weight for three consecutive days produced severe anemia, erythrocyte Heinz bodies and hemoglobinuria in all dogs fed onions.[84] One animal developed severe icterus and died on Day 5.

Cats are prone to developing erythrocyte Heinz bodies after exposure to many chemicals in the food.[81,86,87] Likewise, Heinz body anemia has occurred in cats following the consumption of onions.[88]

Garlic (*Allium sativum*) is also a member of the onion family. Chronic exposure to garlic and garlic extracts caused anemia, contact dermatitis and asthmatic attacks in dogs.[80]

Pets today are often fed "people" food. One delicacy that has potential to cause toxicity is chocolate. Chocolate products contain variable amounts of theobromine, a potent cardiovascular and central nervous system stimulant.[89] Although pet owners might believe that chocolate is innocuous, one poison center documented six cases of chocolate poisoning in dogs during a single year.[90] Signs such as vomiting, diarrhea, panting, nervousness, excitement, tremors, tachycardia, cardiac dysrhythmias, coma, convulsions and sudden death may appear in four to 15 hours after ingestion.[90-93] Renal damage may occur in severe cases.

The toxic dose of theobromine has been reported to be greater than 200 mg/kg body weight.[90] However, a springer spaniel died after ingestion of 2 lb of milk chocolate, corresponding to a dose of only 92 mg of theobromine/kg body weight.[91] Based on this case, consumption of one typical 1.55-oz. milk chocolate bar (93 mg theobromine)/kg body weight could produce clinical signs and possibly death.[92] Unsweetened baking chocolate also contains high levels of theobromine (450 mg/oz.) and has been implicated in cases of toxicity.[92] Finally, dogs have also been poisoned by ingesting cocoa powder (1 to 3% theobromine).[93]

Theobromine is eliminated very slowly in dogs.[91] This metabolic peculiarity prolongs the clinical syndrome and increases the risk of toxicity from repeated ingestion of small doses of theobromine. Because there is no available antidote for theobromine toxicity, symptomatic treatments such as administration of emetics, activated charcoal, tranquilizers, sedatives and lidocaine should be used in clinical cases of chocolate toxicity.

ASSESS THE FOOD(S) AND FEEDING METHOD

If a diagnosis of foodborne illness seems feasible, then the pet owner should be questioned extensively about the animal's food. First, the veterinarian should identify all possible food sources (including commercial foods, home-prepared foods and table scraps) and determine the feeding amounts and the availability of unintentional food sources. Common questions about commercial foods should include: 1) brand name, 2) manufacturer, 3) lot or date code, 4) form of food (i.e., dry, semi-moist, moist), 5) feeding method (i.e., meal fed, free choice), 6) the length of time the pet has been consuming the brand of food, 7) the length of time the pet has been fed from the present container of food (i.e., bag or can), 8) whether water is mixed with the food, 9) how long the food is left in the food bowl, 10) the ambient temperature at feeding and 11) the method of storing the food.

Questions about home-prepared foods should include: 1) the source of ingredients, 2) storage methods for the ingredients and the food, 3) method of preparation, 4) preparation temperatures, 5) method of measuring temperatures and 6) feeding method. Any recent change in either the food ingredients or preparation methods should be investigated further.

The amount of food consumed should be compared with the calculated amount typically consumed by an animal of similar size. If the amount consumed is markedly less than the calculated amount, it could mean that the animal doesn't like the food and may be foraging other food sources or garbage. Decreased intake may also indicate feed refusal typical of vomitoxin contamination.

Sampling Procedures

Most veterinary diagnostic laboratories can perform the tests necessary to facilitate a diagnosis of foodborne illness. A list of publicly funded and private laboratories is included as Appendix U. Many investigative tests and techniques are available to the diagnostic laboratory to help assess the case. In fact, the number is so overwhelming that only a few can be used on a particular sample. It is essential that the veterinarian discuss the likely diagnoses with laboratory personnel before test initiation to ensure the tests most critical to a correct diagnosis are performed. Veterinarians also need to determine the laboratory's preferred specimens and method of specimen preservation.

Sample/specimen collection should follow the rules of physical evidence even if the possibility of litigation seems remote or nonexistent to ensure results are admissible in court if circumstances change. The admissibility of this information in a trial depends on whether: 1) all specimens and/or samples were properly identified, 2) the "chain of custody" (Table 7-3) is documented by a specific and detailed description of all events and changes of possession starting at the time of collection, through transportation and transferal to final sample analysis at the laboratory and 3) the evidence is relevant to the case.[94] Therefore, it is also important to inform laboratory personnel if there is any possibility of litigation.

The best sources of samples for assessment of the food for possible etiologic agents are: 1) the actual food source, 2) food ingredients (homemade foods), 3) stomach contents, 4) intestinal contents and 5) feces. The following procedures and methods relate primarily to assessment of the food but also could be used to evaluate any previously described specimens (e.g., urine, blood, tissues, etc.).

The pet owner should bring the entire container of food or containers of food ingredient(s) to the veterinarian so that the collection of samples follows aseptic technique and the rules of evidence collection.[94,95] Sample collection

Table 7-3. Procedures for the collection, transfer and preservation of physical evidence.*

1. Collect, package and identify all samples according to the procedures listed in Table 7-4.
2. Maintain a record of every person who had custody of any sample(s) or other evidence from the time that it was collected until presented in court ("chain of custody") by keeping a written log or diary of all relevant facts and sample transfers.
3. Write notes documenting the time, place, description and circumstances of all samples collected in the log. Describe in detail how the samples were identified (numbered), processed, packaged, stored and shipped.
4. If possible, photograph any apparent pathologic lesions, mold growth, foreign matter in the food, etc. Number the photographs consecutively and describe each photograph in the written notes.
5. Write notes about all telephone conversations related to the case in the log, including the date, time and content of the conversation.
6. Date all new entries in the log and have the person writing in the log initial the entry.
7. Retain and store all relevant product labels in a safe place.
8. Use a shipping method that expedites delivery of the samples to the laboratory. Keep copies of all shipping records. Hand carry the samples to the laboratory if possible. Obtain written proof of delivery (a receipt).

*Grau JJ. Criminal and Civil Investigation Handbook, 2nd ed., New York, NY: McGraw-Hill, Inc., 1993.

Table 7-4. Sampling procedures for foodborne illnesses.

1. Collect samples for toxicologic and microbiologic studies as separate samples and label them accordingly.
2. Collect several samples from the same source, e.g., different areas of the food bag, stool specimen.
3. Treat samples as though they were being prepared for a legal case by following the rules of evidence.
4. Collect duplicate samples or split samples so that one sample can be retained by the veterinarian and the other submitted to the laboratory.
5. Collect samples for microbiologic testing aseptically using sterile gloves, instruments and containers.
6. Use water-tight sample containers, preferably with screw-type lids.
7. Label all sample containers with an accurate and complete description of the contents, e.g., submitter's name, client's name, date and time collected, product name, etc. Submit other sample information and any supporting descriptions with the samples.

techniques are described in detail in Table 7-4. Label all sample containers as space allows with a sample number and a description of the contents, submitter's name, pet owner's name, date, product label information and lot number. Supporting information and descriptions that cannot be written on the sample label because of space constraints should be numbered identically to the sample and submitted with the sample.[27,95,96]

Detection Methods

Bacterial Isolation and Identification

Pet food ingredients, like most other foods, contain a diverse microbial flora. Therefore, there is no single growth medium that will satisfy the requirements of all organisms that may be present in a sample. The veterinarian should discuss likely pathogens with laboratory personnel so that the best methods, enrichment techniques and selective media can be used.[96,97]

Most laboratories will use a variety of direct examination and culture techniques to attempt a successful identification.[97] First, smears of the specimens collected by either the veterinarian or laboratory personnel will be stained and examined. Then growth and colony characteristics of bacterial isolates will be determined using a variety of media. The presence or absence of certain bacterial biochemical characteristics and atmospheric growth conditions will also be explored. Finally, a variety of other tests and techniques will be used to facilitate the identification process (e.g., API 20E strips and Staph-Trac).[c]

Analytical Chemistry

Metal assays are usually performed using some type of atomic spectroscopy, e.g., atomic absorption spectroscopy and inductively coupled plasma emission spectroscopy.[96] Organic compounds such as pesticides and solvents are usually detected by chromatography, e.g., gas chromatography, high-pressure liquid chromatography, thin-layer chromatography. After a compound has been identified preliminarily by chromatography, results are often confirmed using mass spectrometry.

Mycotoxins can be detected by chromatography methods, radioimmunoassay (RIA) and enzyme-linked immunosorbent assay (ELISA).[97] The staphylococcal enterotoxins can be identified using ELISA, RIA, serologic, precipitin and gel diffusion techniques.[58] ELISA can also be used to detect the exotoxins and endotoxins of other bacterial species. The *C. botulinum* exotoxins can be identified by serum neutralization using commercially available antisera followed by assay in laboratory animals.[97]

Significant Pathogen Levels in Food

Commercial foods are not sterile and may contain species of organisms associated with foodborne illnesses in people. However, the infective dose of each foodborne pathogen can vary greatly depending on the food substrate, the immunologic status of the host and the resistance of the normal intestinal flora.[30]

The same factors apply to foodborne illness in animals with the exception that the animal species can also influence the infective or toxic dose. Therefore, the relationship between microbial populations and the quality of foods can only be estimated and must be viewed with caution especially when one considers that most sampling and microbial counting procedures possess inherent inaccuracies. Also, many organisms have fastidious growth and unique colonization requirements (i.e., medium, temperature and atmosphere). Although laboratory personnel will try various permutations, it is not always possible to find the correct combination given the limitations of sample size. In addition, the specimen may contain a microorganism that produces antimicrobial peptides that inhibit the growth of other species. Finally, the various counting procedures will also kill some of the bacteria present in the sample.

The scientific literature contains few data establishing the relative risk of foodborne illness and the microbial content of pet foods. Measuring the microbial content of pet foods is difficult but interpreting the results with respect to wholesomeness or food safety is even more difficult because risk quantification also depends on other factors such as storage conditions. However, measurement of microbial populations may yield valuable information when used to compare one sample of a pet food with another sample of the same product. For example, it would be valuable to know whether bacterial numbers had increased dramatically while the food was in the pet's bowl. This information helps establish the level of hygiene and timeliness of the pet's feeding schedule. In summary, the presence of an organism in a food does not alone establish the diagnosis but must be considered as one piece of the diagnostic "puzzle."

Control and Prevention

Methods for control and prevention of foodborne illness in pets apply to commercial (after purchase) and home-prepared foods. Foodborne illnesses in pet foods can best be prevented by following the practices described in Table 7-5.

Food storage is an important preventive measure. Proper storage depends on control of: 1) temperature, 2) moisture and 3) availability of oxygen. First, high temperatures markedly decrease the shelf life of both canned and dry foods, especially when temperatures exceed 20°C (68°F).[1,98] Therefore, all commercial pet foods should be stored in the 4.4 to 15.6°C (40 to 60°F) temperature range. Fresh, home-prepared foods should be refrigerated at –1.6 to 15.5°C (29 to 60°F) before feeding. (Most household refrigerators hold foods at 4.4 to 7.2°C [40 to 45°F].) The length of time that a food can be kept refrigerated depends on its type and age. Fresh meats, fish and poultry can be kept for two to 10 days whereas fruits and vegetables will remain wholesome for weeks when refrigerated.

Moist products are sealed and therefore not affected by moisture or air; control of these factors applies only to storage of bulk dry commercial foods. Spoilage bacteria require at least 30% moisture for growth whereas molds require 5 to 15%. Dry pet foods have a moisture content in the range of 6 to 9%. Therefore, dry commercial pet foods will have a satisfactory shelf life if stored in a cool dry place with the top of the bag or container closed. These

Table 7-5. Prevention of foodborne illness in animals.

1. Select only wholesome pet foods or pet food ingredients.
  For home-prepared foods, use raw ingredients that meet human food grade standards.
  Discard all foods with an abnormal color, composition, odor or moldy appearance.
  Discard foods from bulging or leaking cans.
2. Control food contamination.
  Use stainless steel utensils, feeding bowls, etc. whenever possible.
  Keep food preparation areas, cooking utensils and food bowls spotlessly clean. Wash and disinfect bowls and utensils daily.
  Store dry commercial foods in a cool, dry environment, free from insects and rodents.
  Empty the feeding bowl of moist or moistened foods not consumed within two to four hours if the ambient temperature is above 10°C (50°F).
  Clean, wash and disinfect food utensils and food bowls after each feeding.
  If feeding ad libitum, check food daily for mold and spoilage.
3. Control microorganisms in food using physical means.
  Cook all home-prepared foods at 82°C (180°F) for at least 10 minutes.
  Verify cooking temperatures with a cooking thermometer and internal meat temperatures with a meat thermometer.
  Validate thermometer accuracy periodically with boiling water.
  Cover all perishable foods and opened cans of pet food and store in the refrigerator at 4°C (40°F) when not being prepared, cooked or consumed.
4. Control the pet's access to unintentional foods.

precautions limit the availability of moisture and air needed for oxidative chemical degradation and microbial growth. Placing the food in a canister or other closed container will extend the shelf life by further reducing the availability of moisture and oxygen. This method of storage has the added advantage of preventing rodent and insect damage.

REASSESSMENT

The type and duration of therapy will be dictated by the diagnosis and the physical condition of the patient. Therapy typically will consist of supportive, symptomatic treatment because most foodborne illnesses are self-limiting. With illnesses such as metal poisoning or mycotoxicoses that produce characteristic blood or biochemical changes, those specific parameters should be monitored routinely for evidence of recovery. In those cases where the patient does not recover, veterinarians should first reassess the patient to ascertain whether exposure to the foodborne agent has been truly discontinued. If so, then an inaccurate diagnosis or other pathologic factors may have complicated the case. Continued monitoring of laboratory parameters is warranted. Animals that recover only to suffer another bout of foodborne illness at a later date are obviously being exposed to unsafe foods. Therefore, the veterinarian should counsel the pet owner to prevent further recurrences (Table 7-5).

ENDNOTES & REFERENCES

ENDNOTES

a. Miller EP. Unpublished data. September 1996.
b. Cullor JS. Unpublished data. May 1995.
c. Analytab Products, Inc, Plainview, NY, USA.

REFERENCES

1. Ensminger AH, Ensminger ME, Konlande JE, et al. The Concise Encyclopedia of Foods and Nutrition. Boca Raton, FL: CRC Press Inc, 1995.
2. Coppock RW, Mostrom MS. Intoxication due to contaminated garbage, food, and water. In: Kirk RW, ed. Current Veterinary Therapy IX. Philadelphia, PA: WB Saunders Co, 1986; 221-225.
3. Galton MM, Harless M, Hardy AV. Salmonella isolations from dehydrated dog meals. Journal of the American Veterinary Medical Association 1955; 126: 57-58.
4. Thornton H. The public health danger of unsterilized pet foods. Veterinary Record 1972; 91: 430-432.
5. Dillion R. Bacterial enteritis. In: Kirk RW, ed. Current Veterinary Therapy IX. Philadelphia, PA: WB Saunders Co, 1986; 872-885.
6. Hornfeldt CS, Murphy MJ. 1990 Report of the American Association of Poison Control Centers: Poisonings in animals. Journal of the American Veterinary Medical Association 1992; 200: 1077-1080.
7. Fenwick B. Food safety for the canine athlete and their owners. In: Proceedings. North American Veterinary Conference. Orlando, FL, 1996; 486-488.
8. Lund EM, Armstrong PJ, Kolar L, et al. Distribution of disease and diet type in a natural population of geriatric dogs and cats from private veterinary practice. In: Proceedings. Symposium on Health and Nutrition of Geriatric Cats and Dogs. Orlando, FL, 1996; 56.
9. Pet Food Manufacturers Association, Profile 1993. London, UK. 1994.
10. Dziezak JD. Single- and twin-screw extruders in food processing. Food Technology 1989; 43: 164-174.
11. Lopez A. A Complete Course in Canning and Related Processes. Book 1-Basic Information on Canning, 12th ed. Baltimore, MD: The Canning Trade Inc., 1987.
12. Mumma RO, Rashid KA, Shane BS, et al. Toxic and protective constituents in pet foods. American Journal of Veterinary Research 1986; 47: 1633-1637.
13. Superintendent of Documents. Federal Food, Drug and Cosmetic Act, as Amended. Washington, DC: US Government Printing Office, 1993.
14. Van Houweling CD, Bixler WB, McDowell JR. Role of the Food and Drug Administration concerning chemical contaminants in animal feeds. Journal of the American Veterinary Medical Association 1977; 171: 1153-1156.
15. Price WD, Lovell RA, McChesney DG. Naturally occurring toxins in feedstuffs: Center for Veterinary Medicine Perspective. Journal of Animal Science 1993; 71: 2556-2562.
16. Superintendent of Documents. Food and Drugs. 21 CFR Parts 500-599. Washington, DC: US Government Printing Office, 1995.
17. Association of American Feed Control Officials. Official Publication. 1998.
18. Superintendent of Documents. Protection of Environment. 40 CFR Parts 150-189. Washington, DC: US Government Printing Office, 1995.
19. National Research Council. Pesticides in the Diets of Infants and Children. Washington, DC: National Academy Press, 1993.
20. Ministry of Agriculture, Fisheries and Food. The Feeding Stuffs Regulations. London, UK: HMSO Publications, 1995.
21. Nicholson SS. Mycotoxicosis. In: Kirk RW, ed. Current Veterinary Therapy IX. Philadelphia, PA: WB Saunders Co, 1986; 225-226.
22. The American Law Institute. Section 402A. Strict liability. In: Restatement of the Law, Second, Torts 2d. vol. 2, St Paul, MN: American Law Institute Publishers, 1965.
23. Taylor SE. Legal aspects of mycotoxins. In: Proceedings. Mycotoxin Litigation/Regulation Conference. St. Louis, MO, 1996.
24. McCoy J. Courting liability. In: Proceedings. Mycotoxin Litigation/ Regulation Conference. St. Louis, MO, 1996.
25. Industry News. Petfood Industry 1995; 37: 37-38.
26. Chengappa MM, Staats J, Oberst RD, et al. Prevalence of Salmonella in raw meat used in diets of racing greyhounds. Journal of Veterinary Diagnostic Investigators 1993; 5: 372-377.
27. Osweiler GD, Carson TL, Buck WB, et al. Clinical and Diagnostic Veterinary Toxicology, 4th ed. Dubuque, IA: Kendall/Hunt Publishing Co, 1985.
28. Spillers Petfoods. Official Press Release. Stationsweg, Netherlands, 1996.
29. Potter ME. The changing face of foodborne disease. Journal of the American Veterinary Medical Association 1992; 201: 250-253.
30. Council for Agricultural Science and Technology. Foodborne pathogens: Risks and consequences. Task Force Report No. 122, Ames, IA, 1994.
31. Mannon J, Johnson E. Fungi down on the farm. New Scientist 1985; 105: 12-16.
32. Council for Agricultural Science and Technology. Mycotoxins, economic and health risks. Task Force Report No. 116, Ames, IA, 1989.
33. Newberne PM, Butler WH. Acute and chronic effects of aflatoxin on the liver of domestic and laboratory animals. A review. Cancer Research 1969; 29: 236-250.
34. Edds GT. Acute aflatoxicosis: A review. Journal of the American Veterinary Medical Association 1973; 162: 301-308.
35. Seibold HR, Bailey WS. An epizootic of hepatitis in the dog. Journal of the American Veterinary Medical Association 1952; 121: 201-206.
36. Newberne JW, Bailey WS, Seibold HR. Notes on a recent outbreak and experimental reproduction of hepatitis X in dogs. Journal of the American Veterinary Medical Association 1955; 127: 59-62.
37. Newberne PM, Russo MR, Wogan GN. Acute toxicity of aflatoxin B_1 in the dog. Veterinary Pathology 1966; 3: 331-340.
38. Hagiwara MK, Kogika MM, Malucelli BE. Disseminated intravascular coagulation in dogs with aflatoxicosis. Journal of Small Animal Practice 1990; 31: 239-243.
39. Neal GE. Inhibition of rat liver RNA. Synthesis by aflatoxin B_1. Nature 1973; 244: 432-435.
40. Green CE. Disseminated intravascular coagulation complicating aflatoxicosis in dogs. Cornell Veterinarian 1977; 67: 29-49.
41. Office of Enforcement, Division of Compliance Policy. Action levels for aflatoxins in animal feeds. FDA Compliance Policy Guide 7126.33, Rockville, MD: Food and Drug Administration, 1994.
42. Chesemore RG, Associate Commissioner for Regulatory Affairs, Food and Drug Administration. Updated advisory levels for DON (vomitoxin) in human food and animal feed. Letter to State Agricultural Directors, September 16, 1993.
43. Maune C. Vomitoxin troubles. Is your mycotoxin control program good enough? Petfood Industry 1995; 37: 4-10.

44. Gelderblom WCA, Jaskiewicz K, Marasas WFO, et al. Fumonisins—Novel mycotoxins with cancer-promoting activity produced by *Fusarium moniliforme*. Applied Environmental Microbiology 1988; 54: 1806-1811.

45. Haschek WM, Haliburton JC. *Fusarium moniliforme* and zear-alenone toxicoses in domestic animals: A review. In: Richard JL, Thurston JR, eds. Diagnosis of Mycotoxicoses. Boston, MA: Martinus Nijhoff Publishers, 1986; 213-235.

46. Arp LH, Richard JL. Intoxication of dogs with the mycotoxin penitrem A. Journal of the American Veterinary Medical Association 1979; 175: 565-566.

47. Hayes AW, Presley DB, Neville JA. Acute toxicity of penitrem A in dogs. Toxicology and Applied Pharmacology 1976; 35: 311-320.

48. Hayes AW, Williams WL. Acute toxicity of aflatoxin B$_1$ and rubratoxin B in dogs. Journal of Environmental Pathology and Toxicology 1977; 1: 59-70.

49. Szczech GM, Carlton WW, Tuite J. Ochratoxicosis in beagle dogs. I. Clinical and clinicopathological features. Veterinary Pathology 1973; 10: 135-154.

50. Nuehring LP, Rowland GN, Harrison LR, et al. Cyclopiazonic acid mycotoxicosis in the dog. American Journal of Veterinary Research 1985; 46: 1670-1676.

51. Green CE. Bacterial disease. In: Ettinger SJ, Feldman EC, eds. Textbook of Veterinary Internal Medicine, 4th ed. Philadelphia, PA: WB Saunders Co, 1995; 367-375.

52. Morse EV, Duncan MA. Canine salmonellosis: Prevalence, epizootiology, signs and public health significance. Journal of the American Veterinary Medical Association 1975; 167: 817-820.

53. Klaassen CD, Eaton DL. Principles of toxicology. In: Amdur MO, Doull J, Klaassen CD, eds. Casarett and Doull's Toxicology. The Basic Science of Poisons, 4th ed. New York, NY: McGraw-Hill Inc, 1993; 13.

54. Barsanti JA. Botulism. In: Green CE, ed. Clinical Microbiology and Infectious Diseases of the Dog and Cat. Philadelphia, PA: WB Saunders Co, 1984; 599-607.

55. Barsanti JA, Walser M, Hatheway CL, et al. Type C botulism in American foxhounds. Journal of the American Veterinary Medical Association 1978; 172: 809-813.

56. Jawetz E, Melnick JL, Adelberg EA. Review of Medical Microbiology, 14th ed. Los Altos, CA: Lange Medical Publications, 1980.

57. Tatini SR. Thermal stability of enterotoxins in food. Journal of Milk and Food Technology 1976; 39: 432-438.

58. Freer JH, Arbuthnott JP. Toxins of *Staphylococcus aureus*. In: Dorner R, Drews J, eds. Pharmacology of Bacterial Toxins. Oxford, UK: Pergamon Press Ltd., 1986; 571-633.

59. Breitschwerdt EB. The rickettsioses. In: Ettinger SJ, Feldman EC, eds. Textbook of Veterinary Internal Medicine, 4th ed. Philadelphia, PA: WB Saunders Co, 1995; 377-383.

60. Gorham JR, Foreyt WJ. Salmon poisoning disease. In: Green CE, ed. Clinical Microbiology and Infectious Diseases of the Dog and Cat. Philadelphia, PA: WB Saunders Co, 1984; 538-544.

61. Burrows CF, Batt RM, Sherding RG. Diseases of the small bowel. In: Ettinger SJ, Feldman EC, eds. Textbook of Veterinary Internal Medicine, 4th ed. Philadelphia, PA: WB Saunders Co, 1995; 1169-1232.

62. Olson P, Hedhammar A, Faris A, et al. Enterotoxigenic *Escherichia coli* (ETEC) and *Klebsiella pneumoniae* isolated from dogs with diarrhoea. Veterinary Microbiology 1985; 10: 577-589.

63. Fenwick B, Hertzke D, Cowan L. Alabama rot: Almost the complete story. In: Proceedings. Eleventh Annual International Canine Sports Medicine Symposium. Orlando, FL, 1995: 15-21.

64. Hertzke DM, Cowan LA, Schoning P, et al. Natural disease, glomerular ultrastructural lesions of idiopathic cutaneous and renal glomerular vasculopathy of greyhounds. Veterinary Pathology 1995; 32: 451-459.

65. Turnbull PCB, Kramer JM. *Bacillus*. In: Balows A, Hausler WJ, Herrmann KL, et al, eds. Manual of Clinical Microbiology, 5th ed. Washington, DC: American Society for Microbiology, 1991; 296-303.

66. van Netten P, Kramer JM. Media for the detection and enumeration of *Bacillus cereus* in foods: A review. International Journal of Food Microbiology 1992; 17: 85-99.

67. Vaisanen OM, Mentu J, Salkinoja-Salnen MS. Bacteria in food packaging paper and board. Journal of Food Microbiology 1992; 71: 130-133.

68. Claus D, Berkeley RCW. Genus *Bacillus*. In: Sneath PHA, Mair NS, Sharpe ME, Holt JG, eds. Bergey's Manual of Systematic Bacteriology. Baltimore, MD: Williams and Wilkins, 1986; 1105-1139.

69. Drobniewsk FA. *Bacillus cereus* and related species. Clinical Microbiology Reviews 1993; 6: 324-328.

70. Blanke RV, Poklis A. Analytical/forensic toxicology. In: Amdur MO, Doull J, Klaassen CD, eds. Casarett and Doull's Toxicology. The Basic Science of Poisons, 4th ed. New York, NY: McGraw-Hill Inc, 1993; 905-923.

71. Dykstra G (Food and Drug Administration). Decomposition and Histamine—Raw, frozen tuna and mahi-mahi; canned tuna; and related species; revised compliance policy guide; availability. Federal Register 1995; 60: 39754-39756.

72. Russell FE, Dart RC. Toxic effects of animal toxins. In: Amdur MO, Doull J, Klaassen CD, eds. Casarett and Doull's Toxicology. The Basic Science of Poisons, 4th ed. New York, NY: McGraw-Hill Inc, 1993; 753-803.

73. Morrow JD, Margolies GR, Rowland J, et al. Evidence that histamine is the causative toxin of scombroid-fish poisoning. New England Journal of Medicine 1991; 324: 716-720.

74. Taylor SL. Histamine food poisoning: Toxicology and clinical aspects. Critical Reviews in Toxicology 1986; 17: 91-128.

75. Guilford WG, Roudebush P, Roger QR. The histamine content of commercial pet foods. New Zealand Veterinary Journal 1994; 42: 201-204.

76. Guraya HS, Koehler PE. Histamine in cat foods: Survey and comparisons of methodologies. Veterinary and Human Toxicology 1991; 33: 124-128.

77. Blonz ER, Olcott HS. Effects of orally ingested histamine and/or commercially canned spoiled skipjack tuna on pigs, cats, dogs and rabbits. Comparative Biochemistry and Physiology 1978; 61C: 161-163.

78. Goyer RA. Toxic effects of metals. In: Amdur MO, Doull J, Klaassen CD, eds. Casarett and Doull's Toxicology. The Basic Science of Poisons, 4th ed. New York, NY: McGraw-Hill Inc, 1993; 623-680.

79. Edwards WC, McCoy CP, Coldiron VS. Lead, arsenic and cadmium levels in commercial pet foods. Veterinary Medicine/Small Animal Clinician 1979; 74: 1609-1611.

80. Poppenga RH. Risks associated with herbal remedies. In: Bonagura JD, ed. Current Veterinary Therapy XII. Philadelphia, PA: WB Saunders Co, 1995; 222-226.

81. Jain NC. Essentials of Veterinary Hematology. Philadelphia, PA: Lea & Febiger, 1993.

82. Miyata D. Isolation of a new phenolic compound from the onion (*Allium Cepa L. Onion*) and its oxidative effect on erythrocytes. Japanese Journal of Veterinary Research 1990; 38: 65.

83. Harvey JW, Rackear D. Experimental onion-induced hemolytic anemia in dogs. Veterinary Pathology 1985; 22: 387-392.

84. Ogawa E, Shinoki T, Akahori F, et al. Effect of onion ingestion on anti-oxidizing agents in dog erythrocytes. Japanese Journal of Veterinary Science 1986; 48: 685-691.

85. Lewis LD, Morris ML Jr., Hand MS. Pet foods. In: Small Animal Clinical Nutrition III. Topeka, KS: Mark Morris Associates, 1987; 2-2—2-13.

86. Hickman MA, Rogers QR, Morris JG. Effect of diet on Heinz body formation in kittens. American Journal of Veterinary Research 1990; 50: 475-478.

87. Christopher MM, Perman V, Eaton JW. Contribution of propylene glycol-induced Heinz body formation to anemia in cats. Journal of the American Veterinary Medical Association 1989; 194: 1045-1056.

88. Kobayashi K. Onion poisoning in the cat. Feline Practice 1981; 11: 22-27.

89. Clark ML, Harvey DG, Humpreys DJ. Poisonous plants. In: Veterinary Toxicology, 2nd ed. London, UK: Bailliere Tindall, 1981; 255.

90. Hornfeldt CS. Chocolate toxicity in dogs. Modern Veterinary Practice 1987; 68: 552-554.

91. Gauberg A, Blumenthal HP. Chocolate poisoning in the dog. Journal of the American Animal Hospital Association 1983; 19: 246-248.

92. Hooser SB. Chocolate poisoning in dogs—Dogs and chocolate! Topics, University of Illinois 1984; 9: 73-74.

93. Sutton RH. Cocoa poisoning in a dog. Veterinary Record 1981; 109: 563-565.

94. Grau JJ. Criminal and Civil Investigation Handbook, 2nd ed. New York, NY: McGraw-Hill Inc, 1993.

95. Edwards WC. Companion animal forensic toxicology. In: Kirk RW, ed. Current Veterinary Therapy X. Philadelphia, PA: WB Saunders Co, 1989; 114-115.

96. Galey FD. Effective use of an analytical laboratory for toxicology problems. In: Kirk RW, Bonagura JD, eds. Current Veterinary Therapy XI. Philadelphia, PA: WB Saunders Co, 1992; 168-172.

97. Quinn PJ, Carter ME, Markey BK, et al. Clinical Veterinary Microbiology. London, UK: Wolfe Publishing, 1994.

98. Containers. In: National Canners Association Research Laboratories. Laboratory Manual for Food Canners and Processors. Westport, CT: AVI Publishing Company, Inc., 1968; 436-437.

CASE 7-1

Ulcerative Dermatitis in a Greyhound

Laine Cowan, DVM
Diplomate ACVIM (Internal Medicine)
College of Veterinary Medicine
Kansas State University
Manhattan, Kansas, USA

Assess the Animal

A two-year-old female greyhound that had been in training at a racetrack in Arkansas was examined for depression, swelling of the distal limbs and feet and skin ulceration. Other dogs from the same racing kennel had been affected with similar problems in the past.

Results of physical examination included depression, vomiting, subcutaneous edema involving both rear limbs, primarily distal to the stifle and skin lesions. The skin lesions were focal, reddened areas that became dark red or black on the surface after a few hours. Several small ulcers were present on the distal extremities (Figure 1) and a large, well-demarcated ulcer was present on the left medial thigh (Figure 2). A large area of bruising and ecchymoses was evident on the ventral abdomen.

Clinical pathologic abnormalities included leukocytosis with neutrophilia, thrombocytopenia (29,000 platelets/μl; reference range = 200,000 to 500,000/μl), and severe azotemia (urea nitrogen = 240 mg/dl [10 to 20 mg/dl]; serum creatinine = 5.6 mg/dl [0.6 to 1.2 mg/dl]).

Assess the Food(s) and Feeding Method

All dogs in the kennel were fed a mixture of raw ground beef, dry commercial dog food and a powdered vitamin-mineral supplement. The beef was obtained from a commercial vendor in frozen packages and thawed before it was mixed with the dry food and supplement. The dogs were fed a portion of this mixture once daily.

Questions

1. What foodborne illnesses might be responsible for the clinical signs in this patient?
2. What specific diagnostic tests should be performed to investigate causes of foodborne illness in this patient?
3. What measures should be instituted to prevent outbreaks of foodborne illness in this kennel?

Answers and Discussion

1. Outbreaks of *Salmonella* enteritis ("kennel sickness," "blowout") and systemic salmonellosis are common among greyhounds in kennels. The clinical signs are usually mild to severe diarrhea that typically resolves in a few days. Occasional systemic infections occur with high morbidity rates, especially in puppies and young dogs. Racing greyhounds contract salmonellosis primarily by eating contaminated raw meat. Other foodborne bacterial diseases that result in gastrointestinal or systemic signs include campylobacteriosis, shigellosis and listeriosis.

A syndrome of cutaneous multifocal ulceration, often accompanied by limb edema or acute renal fail-

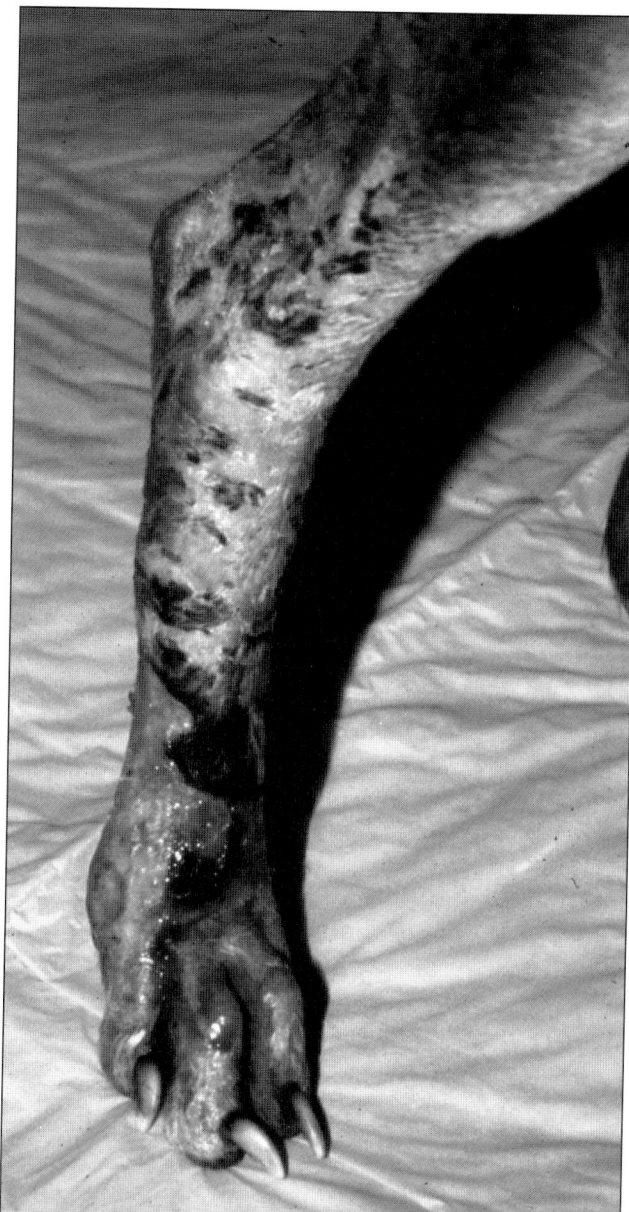

Figure 1. Right distal limb of a two-year-old female greyhound. Note the numerous small, well-demarcated ulcers.

ure, has been recognized in young, adult greyhound dogs. The syndrome has been referred to as "Alabama rot" and described as idiopathic cutaneous and renal glomerular vasculopathy. Reports of this syndrome have been limited to the greyhound breed. Clinical signs include acute erythema and edema progressing rapidly to well-demarcated cutaneous ulcers of the distal extremities, especially the hind limbs. Some dogs develop acute renal failure, which is usually fatal. Significant microscopic lesions are limited to the skin and kidney. Cutaneous lesions are characterized by vascular necrosis of arterioles, with ischemic necrosis and ulceration of the epidermis. Renal lesions are predominantly glomerular, including thrombi in glomerular capillaries and glomerular endothelial necrosis.

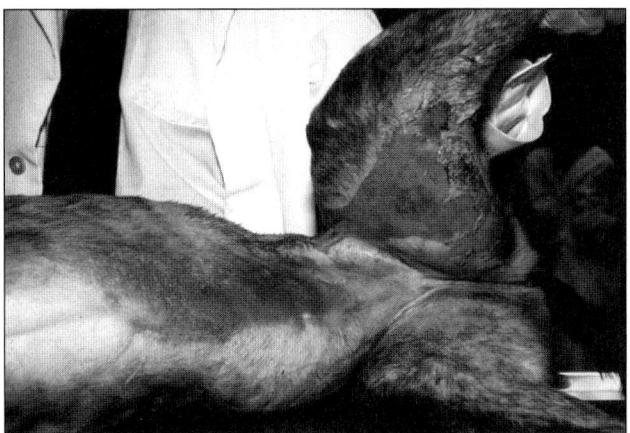

Figure 2. View of the ventral abdomen and left medial thigh of the same dog. Note the extensive contusions on the ventral abdomen and large, well-demarcated ulcer involving a large portion of the medial thigh.

This syndrome in greyhound dogs resembles hemolytic uremic syndrome in people and edema disease in swine, which are thought to involve a shiga-like toxin binding to and damaging vascular endothelium. Platelet aggregation contributes to thrombosis. Shiga-like toxins can be produced by a variety of bacteria, but *Escherichia coli* strain O157:H7 is incriminated most often. Because most racing greyhounds are fed raw meat, there is the potential for them to be exposed to shiga-like toxin-producing *E. coli*.

2. Bacterial organisms can be recovered by culturing the raw meat and commercial dry food and the patient's feces and blood. Large numbers of toxin-producing *E. coli* have been found in meat samples fed to greyhounds and in fecal samples from clinical cases.

3. The occurrence of disease related to contaminated meat is closely related to how the meat is handled on the farm or track before feeding. Preventive measures should include proper cooking and storage of meat whenever possible. Of primary importance is the temperature of the meat once it has thawed. When large blocks of frozen meat are thawed at room temperature, the outermost surface of the meat can reach unacceptably high temperatures before the center has thawed. Thawing meat slowly at refrigerator temperatures or in a camp cooler will markedly reduce surface bacterial growth.

Many foodborne pathogens persist in the environment for extended periods. In some cases, the occurrence of food poisoning is associated with inadequate hygiene and failure to isolate dogs with diarrhea that are shedding large numbers of organisms. All facilities and equipment should be frequently cleaned with soap and then disinfected with bleach or phenolic compounds.

Progress Notes

The dog was treated with intravenous fluids, parenteral antibiotics and whirlpool baths in dilute povidone-iodine solution. Cimetidine and antiemetics were given to help control vomiting. Despite these efforts, the dog died 48 hours later of acute renal failure.

Necropsy findings included slightly pale, swollen kidneys with prominent, congested glomeruli and capsular petechiae. Mural edema of the stomach and black tarry colonic contents were also evident. Microscopic renal lesions included glomerular thrombotic microangiopathy; hyalin thrombi were present in glomerular capillaries and afferent arterioles. Glomerular capillary walls were thickened.

Bibliography

Chengappa MM, Staats J, Oberst RD, et al. Prevalence of *Salmonella* in raw meat used in diets of racing greyhounds. Journal of Veterinary Diagnostic Investigation 1993; 5: 372-377.

Cowan LA, Hertzke DM, Fenwick BW, et al. Clinical and clinicopathologic abnormalities in greyhounds with cutaneous and renal glomerular vasculopathy; 18 cases (1992-1994). Journal of the American Veterinary Medical Association 1997; 210: 789-793.

Fenwick B, Hertzke D, Cowan L. Alabama rot: Almost the complete story. In: Proceedings. Eleventh Annual International Canine Sports Medicine Symposium. Orlando, FL, 1995: 15-21.

Hertzke DM, Cowan LA, Schoning P, et al. Glomerular ultrastructural lesions of idiopathic cutaneous and renal glomerulopathy of greyhounds. Veterinary Pathology 1995; 32: 451-459.

CASE 7-2

Food Poisoning in Two Dogs

Lawrence H. Arp, DVM, PhD
Diplomate ACVP
Nutley, New Jersey, USA

Assess the Animals

A three-month-old male Australian shepherd dog was examined for severe muscle tremors, polypnea, hyperkinesia and ataxia, with intermittent opisthotonos and generalized seizures. The dog was anesthetized with sodium pentobarbital to control motor activity. Intravenous fluids were administered. After recovery from anesthesia, the dog was still atactic but less hyperkinetic.

On the same day, a one-year-old male Irish setter from the same neighborhood was admitted for treatment of muscle tremors and clonic seizures. The dog vomited 30 minutes before clinical signs were observed. It was treated in a similar manner to the first dog. Both dogs were clinically normal 12 hours later except for slight incoordination.

Assess the Food(s) and Feeding Methods

The owner of the first dog reported finding a partly eaten package of moldy cream cheese in his yard. The cream cheese had been purchased about one month earlier, had been partially used and then refrigerated until it was found covered with mold. The owner had thrown it out the previous day. Both dogs had access to the cream cheese but were not seen eating it. The cream cheese was covered with a dark blue-green fungal mat. Both dogs were of normal weight for their age and had normal body condition scores (3/5). No other nutritional history was available.

Questions

1. What potential foodborne diseases might cause the clinical signs in these dogs?
2. What diagnostic tests could be performed to confirm a foodborne illness?

Answers and Discussion

1. Penitrem A and aflatoxin, two potent mycotoxins, are produced by members of the genera *Penicillium* and *Aspergillus*, respectively. These fungi are isolated most frequently from refrigerators and moldy foodstuffs in the home. These fungal genera also may be isolated from stored feeds and cereal grains that may eventually enter the pet food chain.

   Penitrem A causes acute muscle tremors, seizures and prostration in several animal species. The severity of clinical and pathologic features is dose dependent. Mildly affected dogs have transitory muscle tremors and ataxia lasting two to four hours, whereas larger doses may cause seizures and death. Normal neurologic function progressively returns after one or two days in animals that recover. Visceral petechiae, hepatic necrosis and hyperthermia may occur in dogs with mycotoxicosis.

   Ingestion or topical exposure to a variety of other compounds may also cause neurologic signs. Examples include various insecticides (pyrethrins, pyrethroids, organophosphates, carbamates), methyl-xanthines (chocolate), metaldehyde, various ornamental plants (Chinaberry, English ivy, jimson weed, tulip, yellow iris), illicit drugs (marijuana, cocaine, amphetamines), strychnine and lead.

2. The moldy cream cheese could be sent to a laboratory for identification of fungal elements and further toxicologic testing. Establishing a diagnosis of plant or illicit drug poisoning is difficult without specific evidence of ingestion. Whole blood cholinesterase activity will be depressed in organophosphate and carbamate toxicosis.

Feeding Plan

Because both dogs recovered rapidly there was no need to change the foods or the feeding plans. The owners were instructed to limit access to spoiled food by proper disposal.

Progress Notes

Examination of the moldy cream cheese by light microscopy revealed fungal elements typical of the genus *Penicillium*. The organism was later identified as *P. crustaceum*, a common contaminant of refrigerated foodstuffs. *P. crustaceum* produces large quantities of penitrem A at 4°C.

Three mice were given a moldy cheese emulsion by mouth and developed hyperkinesia, irritability, generalized muscle tremors and tonic-clonic seizures within two hours. Penitrem A was identified by thin-layer chromatography from a sample of the moldy cream cheese; therefore, this mycotoxin was considered the cause of the clinical signs in both dogs.

Bibliography

Arp LH, Richard JL. Intoxication of dogs with the mycotoxin penitrem A. Journal of the American Veterinary Medical Association 1979; 175: 565-566.

CASE 7-3

Vomiting and Diarrhea in a Puppy

James S. Cullor, DVM, PhD
School of Veterinary Medicine
University of California, Davis
Davis, California, USA

Assess the Animal

A nine-week-old male German shepherd puppy was examined for evaluation of vomiting and diarrhea. There had been no problems until six days earlier when the puppy's feces became liquid and bowel movements more frequent. Several hours after the diarrhea was first noticed, the puppy vomited twice. The vomitus contained undigested food, but no evidence of foreign material, blood or parasites. The dog was confined to the house or a fenced outdoor enclosure. The puppy was vaccinated a week before the clinical problems began. When examined the puppy was mildly lethargic, about 5% dehydrated, but otherwise healthy.

Assess the Food(s) and Feeding Method

The dog was fed a commercial dry grocery brand food formulated for puppies. Fresh water and the dry food were offered ad libitum. The food had been purchased from a large retail outlet one week before the onset of clinical signs. The puppy was eating the dry food with no obvious problems.

Three days before the onset of clinical signs, the owner began mixing the dry food with water. The moistened food remained at room temperature or outside where temperatures reached 32.2°C (90°F) for several days. The puppy became ill several hours after eating most of the moistened food.

Questions

1. What potential foodborne illnesses could be causing the clinical signs in this dog?
2. What techniques could be used to diagnose whether foodborne illness is causing the vomiting and diarrhea in this patient?

Answers and Discussion

1. A variety of foodborne illnesses can cause vomiting and diarrhea. These include contamination of food with bacterial organisms or their toxins (*Staphylococcus aureus*, *Salmonella* spp, *Neorickettsia* spp, *Escherichia coli*, *Bacillus cereus*, *Yersinia* spp, *Campylobacter* spp), biogenic amines, aflatoxins, vomitoxin and heavy metals (lead, arsenic, zinc, cadmium). The fact that the dry food was moistened with water and left at high ambient temperatures makes bacterial proliferation a likely cause of clinical signs.
2. Most veterinary diagnostic laboratories can perform the tests necessary to facilitate a diagnosis of foodborne ill-

ness. A list of laboratories is found in Appendix U. It is important to determine the laboratory's preferred specimens and method of specimen preservation. General sampling procedures are outlined in Table 7-4. Bacterial isolation techniques can often be performed on the food, vomitus and feces. Heavy metal, pesticide, biogenic amine and toxin assays can be performed on food, serum, feces and other biological samples.

Progress Notes

There was no history that the puppy had access to illicit drugs, heavy metals, pesticides, toxic ornamental plants and garbage. Results of a hemogram were normal, which made a diagnosis of viral enteritis unlikely. Three samples from the dry commercial puppy food and three from the moistened food were cultured and grown aerobically. Feces were also cultured daily over the next three days. Cultures revealed 1×10^2 colony forming units (cfu) of *Bacillus cereus*/g dry food and 1×10^7 cfu of *B. cereus*/g moistened food. These results confirmed that bacteria had proliferated after the food was moistened and left at warm to hot ambient temperatures. *B. cereus* was also cultured once from diarrheic feces. No other bacterial pathogens were recovered from the food or feces.

Therapy Including Feeding Plan

The puppy was treated with subcutaneous fluids and was fed a complete, balanced homemade food consisting of boiled lean ground beef and rice, offered in small, frequent meals. The puppy's feces gradually became firmer. After two days of therapy with the homemade food, the original commercial dry puppy food was offered, without added moisture. The puppy was feeling well, eating normal amounts of food and had normal stools by Day 7 after the onset of clinical signs. The pet owner was advised to not add water to dry pet foods and leave them exposed to ambient temperatures for more than a few hours.

A tentative diagnosis of *B. cereus* enterotoxemia was made. *B. cereus* is known to cause vomiting and diarrhea in people; however, it is not thought to pose a significant danger for foodborne illness in animals. *B. cereus* flourishes at room temperature, and certain isolates possess the genetic capability to produce a potent enterotoxin. The organism is a ubiquitous, spore-forming aerobic saprophyte found in soil, grains, cereal grain products and other foods. As an example, it is commonly found in uncooked rice. *B. cereus* has been found as a common isolate in samples of dry pet food. It has also been isolated from food packaging paper and materials.

The standard heat treatments used in pet food manufacturing are not likely to kill the spores of this organism. However, the number of organisms isolated from the pet food ($<10^5$ cells/g of food) is unlikely to cause foodborne disease in pets unless the food is exposed to moisture and heat conditions conducive to bacterial proliferation.

Bibliography

Turnbull PCB, Kramer JM. *Bacillus*. In: Balows A, Hausler WJ, Herrmann KL, et al, eds. Manual of Clinical Microbiology, 5th ed. Washington, DC: American Society for Microbiology, 1991: 296-303.

Vaisanen OM, Mentu J, Salkinoja-Salnen MS. Bacteria in food packaging paper and board. Journal of Food Microbiology 1992; 71: 130-133.

Claus D, Berkeley RCW. Genus *Bacillus*. In: Sneath PHA, Mair NS, Sharpe ME, et al, eds. Bergey's Manual of Systematic Bacteriology. Baltimore, MD: Williams and Wilkins, 1986; 1105-1139.

Drobniewsk FA. *Bacillus cereus* and related species. Clinical Microbiology Reviews 1993; 6: 324-328.

Nutritional Management of Normal Pets

CHAPTER 8

Health Maintenance Programs for Dogs and Cats

Philip Roudebush

Richard T. Goldston

"To ward off disease or recover health, men as a rule find it easier to depend on healers than to attempt the more difficult task of living wisely."
Rene Dubos

INTRODUCTION

In 1989, the Pew National Veterinary Education Program issued its report titled *Future Directions for Veterinary Medicine*.[1] The report identified three major emerging trends that will change the role of companion animal veterinarians in the United States. First, increasing competition is prompting practitioners to become more responsive to the expectations of pet owners and more aware of the importance of effective practice management. Second, veterinarians are placing a greater emphasis on maintaining the health of pets, as opposed to simply treating disease. Third, there is an increasing need for the veterinary profession to provide a wider range of health care services. The Pew Report suggests that first and foremost, the focus of the veterinary medical profession must change from managing disease to maintaining health.

People's interest in their own health care, including proper nutrition and exercise, is being carried over to their pets. The public increasingly looks to veterinarians for advice and services that relate to maintaining pet health. With a solid foundation in the fundamentals of maintaining health, veterinarians will: 1) improve the overall quality of practice, 2) help pets live a longer, more enjoyable life, 3) increase client satisfaction and 4) improve the economic well-being of the practice.

Health maintenance, disease prevention, risk factor management and wellness are terms used to describe concepts and programs that attempt to promote health, or wellness, in an individual or group. The health maintenance concept contrasts with the traditional veterinary perspective, which focuses on diagnosing, curing or managing individual diseases.

The goals of health maintenance programs are to: 1) identify health risk factors and reduce or eliminate them and 2) detect disease early. Health maintenance involves all aspects of a pet's health, including such factors as genetics, environment, history and age, oral care and nutrition. Historical information about individual pets, physical examination findings and extended laboratory databases are essential elements of a health maintenance program. This chapter will explore the concepts of risk factor management, health maintenance or wellness programs, important components of such programs and the role of appropriate life-stage nutrition. Sections in this chapter are heavily cross-referenced to other chapters where more information about nutrition can be found.

RISK FACTOR MANAGEMENT

Detection and management of health risk factors are intrinsic to health maintenance. In human medicine, a physician may see a patient with the following characteristics: middle-aged, black, male, construction worker, chain smoker, family history of heart disease, 20% overweight and high serum cholesterol level. In addition, the patient typically eats meals high in salt and fat. This patient's history, diet, environment, physical condition and blood parameters are all risk factors that must be managed to provide reasonable and expected health care.

Risk factor management has been readily accepted in human medicine, but must be extended to dogs and cats as well. For example, a veterinarian may see a patient with the following characteristics: 10-year-old, intact female dachshund, 30% overweight, lives in a high-rise apartment and

KEY WORDS & TERMS—HEALTH MAINTENANCE PROGRAMS*

Acute pyotraumatic dermatitis	Geriatrics	Open registries
Aging	Gonadectomy	Risk factor management
Behavior	Health maintenance	Risk factors
Body condition score	Malnutrition	Socialization
Canine behavior profiles	Morbidity	Species-specific behaviors
Closed registries	Mortality	Systems review
Congenital defects	National Companion Animal Study	Wellness
Developmental orthopedic disease	Nutrition counseling	World Health Organization
Future Directions for Veterinary Medicine	Nutritional risk factors	

Key words and terms are defined in the Glossary.

KEY POINTS—HEALTH MAINTENANCE PROGRAMS

1. Vaccinations and parasite control are traditional health maintenance services offered by veterinarians. Other health maintenance services veterinarians and their health care teams can provide include pet selection advice, prophylactic dentistry, neutering and many counseling services.
2. Veterinarians should take the initiative and discuss all applicable health maintenance services with clients; don't wait for them to ask. Some clients will never address the subject and the opportunity to provide optimal care for their pets will be missed.
3. Behavioral problems are a leading cause of euthanasia and pet abandonment. In many cases, behavioral problems could have been prevented through advice and counseling by veterinarians.
4. Neutering positively affects behavior and prevents tumors of reproductive tissues. It also prevents unwanted pets. Clients should be given this information early in the development of a health maintenance program.
5. Neutering profoundly affects metabolism; neutered animals are at risk for development of obesity unless caloric intake is reduced.
6. Preventing tooth loss from periodontal disease should

be a vital part of health maintenance services. Regular professional care and home oral care are topics pet owners will understand.
7. Clients should be counseled about appropriate grooming for their pets. Poorly groomed coats are risk factors for external parasites and dermatologic problems such as acute pyotraumatic dermatitis.
8. Optimal nutrition during all stages of life is an important part of any health maintenance program. Nutrition counseling is a service clients expect.
9. Aging is not a disease, but the rate of aging may be influenced by many factors, including genetics, environment and nutrition.
10. Aging affects all body systems; therefore, multiple problems often arise in older pets. A thorough systems review will help define problems, rank problems by priority and establish diagnostic and therapeutic plans.
11. Manufactured pet foods contain more-than-adequate levels of all essential nutrients needed by normal cats and dogs, including protein, phosphorus and salt. Geriatric pets may benefit from foods that avoid excess levels of these nutrients.

has a heart murmur due to valvular heart disease. Each of these risk factors should be addressed to maintain the pet's health. Physicians have been telling their patients about risk factors for years—these patients are pet owners. Thus, clients are receptive to health maintenance programs and risk factor management for their pets.

Preliminary data from the National Companion Animal Study identified the prevalence of diseases in dogs and cats presented to private North American veterinary practices.[2] The preliminary data from more than 69,000 dogs and cats are summarized in Table 8-1. Many of the diseases identified in the study are associated with risk factors and can be managed through comprehensive health maintenance programs.

Nutritional risk factors have recently been identified for people. Two examples are excessive saturated fat intake as a risk factor for cardiovascular disease and excessive sodium chloride intake as a risk factor for hypertension. Nutritional risk factors may also occur in pets (Table 8-2). Examples include excess phosphorus intake as a risk factor for progression of subclinical renal disease (See Chapter

19.) and excessive energy and calcium intake as risk factors for developmental orthopedic disease in large- and giant-breed puppies. (See Chapter 17.)

There are two complementary approaches to reducing risk factors in the pet population: 1) the population-based approach is aimed at the general pet population and 2) the high-risk or individual-based approach is aimed at individuals with defined risk profiles. An effective prevention strategy should be aimed at the general pet population and, where knowledge permits, complemented with recommendations for individual patients at high risk.

PUTTING THE CONCEPT INTO ACTION

Vaccinations and internal and external parasite control are traditional health maintenance services offered by veterinarians. But many other services, from advising clients about pet

Table 8-1. Disease prevalence by age for dogs and cats examined in North American veterinary practices.*

Dogs

0 to 7 Years (n = 24,165)	**7 to 10 Years (n = 6,699)**	**10 to 25 Years (n = 8,692)**
Healthy (32.4%)	Healthy (15.0%)	Oral disease (13.6%)
Oral disease (5.8%)	Oral disease (13.7%)	Healthy (6.9%)
Otitis externa (5.8%)	Otitis externa (5.8%)	Nuclear sclerosis (3.1%)
Dermatopathy (3.6%)	Dermatopathy (3.2%)	Arthritis (3.0%)
Lameness (1.3%)	Tumor (2.0%)	Tumor (2.8%)
Roundworms (1.2%)	Lipoma (1.9%)	Otitis externa (2.7%)
Conjunctivitis (1.2%)	Conjunctivitis (1.2%)	Cardiac murmur (2.4%)
Fleas (1.1%)	Arthritis (1.2%)	Lipoma (2.3%)
Laceration (1.0%)	Anal sac disease (1.2%)	Cataract (2.2%)
Anal sac disease (1.0%)	Lameness (1.1%)	Dermatopathy (1.5%)

Cats

0 to 7 Years (n = 9,148)	**7 to 10 Years (n = 1,795)**	**10 to 25 Years (n = 2,981)**
Healthy (34.2%)	Oral disease (20.1%)	Oral disease (19.5%)
Oral disease (9.9%)	Healthy (18.9%)	Healthy (11.9%)
Ear mites (4.4%)	Cat bite abscess (2.5%)	Chronic renal failure (2.4%)
Fleas (2.7%)	Dermatopathy (2.3%)	Weight loss (2.0%)
Cat bite abscess (2.6%)	Obesity (1.6%)	Cardiac murmur (1.8%)
Upper respiratory infection (2.2%)	Fleas (1.5%)	Hyperthyroidism (1.8%)
Tapeworms (2.0%)	Animal bites (1.5%)	Tumor (1.7%)
Conjunctivitis (1.7%)	Ear mites (1.4%)	Diabetes mellitus (1.4%)
Roundworms (1.4%)	Upper respiratory infection (1.3%)	Cat bite abscess (1.4%)
Dermatopathy (1.3%)	Vomiting (1.3%)	Vomiting (1.3%)

*Preliminary data, 1995 National Companion Animal Study, Center for Companion Animal Health, University of Minnesota, St. Paul, MN and Mark Morris Institute, Topeka, KS.

selection to providing prophylactic oral care, are important to an effective health maintenance program. The services provided in a health maintenance program for dogs and cats will vary tremendously depending on the use of the animal (e.g., house pet vs. athlete vs. show animal), the environment in which the animal resides (e.g., strictly indoors vs. mostly outdoors) and the animal's age (Tables 8-3 to 8-6).

Helping Clients Choose a Pet

Veterinarians are sometimes consulted by prospective pet owners and clients about the proper animal for their lifestyle and perceived needs. On the surface, advice about pet selection may not seem important to a health maintenance program. However, many pets are abandoned, euthanatized, taken to humane shelters or returned to the pet store, breeder or original owner because the pet's behavior was considered inappropriate. Behavioral problems not only contribute to owner dissatisfaction but often adversely affect the health of pets.

Different breeds have different behavioral characteristics.[3] It is worth the effort to find a breed with characteristics that suit an owner's environment, lifestyle and preferences. Researchers have developed canine behavior profiles for 56 popular breeds.[4] The book *The Perfect Puppy: How to Choose Your Dog Based on Its Behavior* by Benjamin and Lynette Hart is based on this research and is an excellent resource for veterinarians, their health care teams and prospective dog owners.[5] Resources are also available that address acquiring a cat.[6] In addition to advising individual clients, veterinarians should also create hospital and community education programs for pet selection.

Screening for Congenital Defects

Congenital defects are caused by hereditary factors, environmental factors or their interaction. Within species, factors such as breed, body system, level of nutrition and geo-

Table 8-2. Examples of potential nutritional risk factors for dogs and cats.

Nutrient	Disease
Excessive fat and energy intake	Developmental orthopedic disease
	Obesity
Excessive calcium intake	Developmental orthopedic disease
Excessive phosphorus intake	Progression of renal disease
Excessive sodium chloride intake	Progression of renal disease
	Hypertension
Excessive protein intake	Progression of renal disease
Excessive magnesium intake	Feline struvite urolithiasis

Table 8-3. Summary of a neonatal health maintenance program.

1. Ensure a clean, quiet environment with a controlled temperature.
2. Closely observe newborns during the first week of life when mortality is highest.
3. Weigh newborns at birth and daily thereafter to ensure proper nutrition, growth and development.
4. Administer pyrantel pamoate to puppies every two weeks starting at two weeks of age.
5. Monitor for infestation from fleas and other external parasites.
6. Ensure optimal nutrition for lactating bitches and queens. (See Chapters 9 and 11.)

graphic location modify the total number of congenital defects and the frequency of individual defects. The frequency of individual defects varies among breeds. Further, purebred dogs express genetic defects more frequently than do mixed-breed dogs. Congenital defects are estimated to affect 0.5 to 1.0% of all puppies and 1.0 to 1.5% of all kittens born.[7] In one study the overall rate of congenital defects was 15.1% for purebred puppies on arrival at a pet store.[8]

The range of congenital defects is wide; the most commonly identified defects involve the central nervous, ocular, muscular, skeletal, gastrointestinal (dental) and cardiovascular systems. Patellar luxations, eyelid abnormalities, cryptorchidism, hernias and faciodental malformations were most commonly observed in purebred puppies

Table 8-4. Summary of a pediatric/juvenile health maintenance program.

Offer a prepurchase consultation for pet selection.

At the first office visit (usually at six to eight weeks):
1. Perform a thorough physical examination, record the pet's weight and body condition score.
2. Check for external parasites and initiate appropriate control.
3. Perform a fecal examination or continue the neonatal anthelmintic program.
4. In endemic areas, initiate a heartworm preventive program.
5. Vaccinate with appropriate products.
6. Discuss the pet's behavior and socialization with the owner.
7. Discuss specific breed characteristics.
8. Discuss routine grooming procedures.
9. Discuss nutrition. Ideally, puppies and kittens should be fed the proper amount of a food designed for growth. The food should not be supplemented. (See Chapters 9 and 11.)
10. Large- and giant-breed puppies are at risk for developmental orthopedic disease. The risks of overnutrition should be specifically discussed with the client. (See Chapter 17.)
11. Counsel client to manipulate the mouth to accustom the puppy or kitten to toothbrushing later on.

At the second office visit (usually at 10 to 12 weeks):
1. Perform a thorough physical examination, record the patient's weight and body condition score.
2. Check for external parasites and initiate appropriate control.
3. Perform a fecal examination or continue the anthelmintic program.
4. Adjust the heartworm preventive dosage.
5. Vaccinate with appropriate products.
6. Discuss behavior and socialization with the client. Recommend basic obedience training for all puppies and refer the client to a reputable obedience school.
7. Discuss the pet's grooming.
8. Discuss nutrition with the client. Adjust food dosages according to growth, body weight and body condition score. (See Chapters 9 and 11.)
9. Counsel client to manipulate the mouth to accustom the puppy or kitten to toothbrushing later on.

At the third office visit (usually at 14 to 16 weeks):
1. Perform a thorough physical examination, record the patient's weight and body condition score.
2. Check for external parasites and initiate appropriate control.
3. Perform a fecal examination or continue the anthelmintic program.
4. Adjust the heartworm preventive dosage.
5. Vaccinate with appropriate products.
6. Discuss the pet's behavior; have the owner demonstrate how the dog responds to the sit command. Recommend basic obedience training and refer the client to a reputable obedience school.
7. Discuss the pet's grooming.
8. Discuss nutrition with the client. Adjust food dosages according to growth, body weight and body condition score. (See Chapters 9 and 11.)
9. Counsel client to manipulate the mouth to accustom the puppy or kitten to toothbrushing later on.
10. Discuss recommendations for neutering.

At the fourth office visit (usually 20 to 22 weeks):
1. Vaccinate the puppy against parvovirus.
2. Discuss socialization, grooming, neutering and nutrition if these were not covered during a previous visit.
3. Adjust the heartworm preventive dosage.

at a pet store.[8] Guides to congenital defects of dogs and cats are available.[9-11]

Examination of neonatal and juvenile/pediatric patients should focus on detection of congenital defects. Studies have estimated that 15% of all congenital defects in dogs involve the eyes[12] and 40% of all canine ocular problems are congenital.[13] These findings suggest that routine screening of young animals for congenital defects should focus on detecting ocular problems.

Genetic Screening

Large-scale genetic screening programs in combination with selective breeding practices are effective means of eliminating or reducing the prevalence of certain inherited diseases. Health maintenance programs should include screening protocols for these diseases. The level of individual screening will be determined by the animal's use. A breeding animal will usually be screened for genetic disorders more vigorously than an animal used as a pet or for performance. A catalog of known and suspected genetic disorders of dogs and cats, organized by breed, is available.[14]

Examples of routine screening protocols involve the musculoskeletal and ocular systems. Hip dysplasia results from the interaction of hereditary, environmental and nutritional factors.[15,16] Routine screening protocols include radiographic procedures to detect coxofemoral joint changes in young adult dogs. Closed registries exist in many countries to certify individual animals as free of radiographic evidence of hip dysplasia. Newer techniques allow the screening of dogs for passive coxofemoral joint laxity at an earlier age.[17] Increased passive hip laxity and overnutrition are risk factors for development of hip dysplasia.[16,18]

Distichiasis, cataracts, progressive retinal atrophy and congenital ectasia (collie-eye anomaly) are examples of ocular problems that can be identified by specific ophthalmic screening techniques.[12-14] A thorough ophthalmic examination including evaluation of the fundus should be a routine health maintenance procedure.

Recent advances in genetic screening include molecular genetic approaches using DNA markers[7] and open disease registry. An open genetic disease registry is a databank of genetic history for any breed of animal and for specific genetic diseases.[19] In an open registry, owners, breeders, veterinarians and scientists can trace the genetic history of any particular animal once that animal and close relatives have been registered.[19] In general, data in the open registry are available to people who need support and information that will lead to a reduction of genetic diseases in a kennel, cattery or breed. A closed registry, on the other hand, provides only phenotypic information.

Behavioral Counseling

Behavior is an inseparable blend of inherited (species specific) and learned components. Behaviors most closely tied to the survival of the species tend to be inherited. Still, the expression of these behaviors can be shaped by learning. Most behavioral problems are not due to abnormal behavior, but to normal species-specific behaviors that are incompatible with human behavior. Cats being cats and dogs being dogs, rather than furry little people, come with their own set of species-specific behaviors that are just waiting to inconvenience owners. In many cases, behavioral problems could have been prevented or treated with advice and counseling by the veterinarian. A number of references are available that specifically address normal and abnormal behavior of dogs and cats (Table 8-7).

Taking the Environment into Account

The environment in which the pet resides will profoundly influence the health of the animal. Pets housed strictly indoors are less susceptible to environmental extremes such as weather, attack from other animals or people, motor vehicle accidents and other forms of trauma. Animals that roam or are housed outdoors are at increased risk for traumatic and weather-related injuries. Trauma is a serious health hazard; 13% of all patients seen at two large hospitals were treated for injuries. Thirty-five percent of these patients had injuries that were considered severe and 9% of these patients sustained fatal injuries.[20] Three-fourths of trauma to dogs and cats fall into one of three categories: 1) motor vehicle accidents, 2) animal interactions and 3) injuries from unknown causes.[20] Exposure to motor vehicles and interaction with other animals are two major risk factors, whether the animal lives in an urban, suburban or rural environment.

The environment is also a risk factor for certain diseases. As an example, actinic (solar) dermatitis occurs commonly on white, light or damaged skin (e.g., depigmented or scarred areas) that is not sufficiently covered by hair. The duration and intensity of exposure to sunlight determine the rapidity of onset and severity of reaction. Canine nasal solar dermatitis, feline solar dermatitis involving the ears, eyelids, nose and lips and canine solar dermatitis of the trunk and extremities are the most common forms of actinic disease.

Vaccinating Against Disease

Routine vaccinations have been the part of pet health maintenance programs that have received the most attention from veterinarians in the past. Vaccines used in dogs protect against distemper, adenovirus, infectious hepatitis, parainfluenza, leptospirosis, parvovirus, rabies, coronavirus-induced diarrhea, bordetellosis and Lyme borreliosis. Vaccines used in cats protect against herpesvirus (viral rhinotracheitis), calicivirus, parvovirus (panleukopenia), rabies, chlamydiosis, feline leukemia virus, feline infectious peritonitis and dermatophytosis. Factors that influence the choice of vaccines include local disease incidence, cost, efficacy, exposure to other animals and perceived risk.

Annual revaccination is encouraged after an initial vaccination series is completed in juvenile animals. Rabies vaccination protocols vary with the vaccine used and local laws. Veterinarians should remind clients that vaccination does not always equal immunization and a small percentage of dogs and cats will not be protected by these procedures. Compendiums of currently marketed canine and feline vaccines are available.[21]

Parasite Control

External parasites of major concern to pets and their owners include fleas, ticks and ear mites. These parasitic infestations are so common that client education brochures should be developed to help clients understand parasite life cycles and parasite control programs. Environmental treatment is the key to flea control, yet many veterinarians spend little

Table 8-5. Summary of an adult health maintenance program.

1. Perform an annual physical examination, record the pet's weight and body condition score.
2. Initiate screening protocols for congenital/hereditary diseases.
3. Tell the client how the animal's environment affects its health.
4. Discuss recommendations for neutering if the pet was not neutered during the juvenile period.
5. Vaccinate with appropriate products.
6. Check for external parasites and initiate appropriate control.
7. Perform a fecal examination and initiate appropriate therapy for internal parasites.
8. In endemic areas, perform a test for heartworm infection and continue preventive therapy.
9. For all dogs older than five years, perform a urinalysis on a fresh urine specimen collected after an all-night fast.
10. Evaluate grooming procedures.
11. Discuss oral health procedures and examine the pet's mouth.
12. Discuss any behavioral problems that have arisen since adolescence.
13. Monitor the pet's feeding program, paying particular attention to maintenance requirements (See Chapters 9 and 11.) and proper feeding to prevent obesity (See Chapter 13.), especially in certain breeds and neutered animals.

Table 8-6. Summary of a geriatric health maintenance program.

1. Perform a thorough systems review (including a thorough history and complete physical examination) every six months once the animal has reached geriatric age. (See the "Systems Review in Aging Pets" section.)
2. Record the pet's body weight and body condition score.
3. Continue vaccination, parasite control, grooming and oral health care outlined in the adult health maintenance program.
4. Perform an extended laboratory database including a complete blood count, serum biochemistry profile and urinalysis. Other laboratory tests should be performed, as deemed necessary, based on the systems review.
5. Take thoracic radiographs and perform an echocardiogram if a cardiac murmur is detected or if there is a history of cough or an abnormal respiratory pattern.
6. Perform a complete ophthalmic evaluation including a fundic examination.
7. Monitor the pet's feeding program and emphasize the dietary management of obesity (See Chapter 13.), chronic progressive renal disease (See Chapter 19.), heart failure (See Chapter 18.) and constipation (See Chapter 22.).
8. Discuss behavior problems, inappropriate urination and senility.

time discussing this treatment with pet owners. Reviews of parasiticide therapy and products are available.[22-24] Company literature explains the mechanism of action, efficacy and safety of newer products.

In heartworm endemic areas, prevention programs should be started when animals are young and continued in adult pets. Adult animals should be examined annually for evidence of heartworm infection regardless of whether they are receiving preventive medication. An annual fecal examination is recommended to screen the pet for intestinal parasites. Intermediate host control (e.g., flea control) should be emphasized to clients when cestodes are recognized as a problem.

Neutering

One of the major decisions an owner has to make that may affect a pet's health and longevity is whether to neuter

Table 8-7. Reference books about pet selection and canine and feline behavior.

1. American Veterinary Medical Association. The Veterinarian's Way of Selecting a Proper Pet.
2. American Veterinary Medical Association. Your Role in Pet Selection.
3. Beaver BV. The Veterinarian's Encyclopedia of Animal Behavior. Ames, IA: Iowa State University Press, 1994.
4. Campbell WE. Behavior Problems in Dogs, 2nd ed. St. Louis, MO: CV Mosby Co, 1992.
5. Clark RD. Medical, Genetic and Behavioral Aspects of Purebred Cats. Fairway, KS: Forum Publications, 1992.
6. Hart BL, Hart LA. Canine and Feline Behavioral Therapy. Philadelphia, PA: Lea & Febiger, 1985.
7. Hart BL, Hart LA. The Perfect Puppy–How to Choose Your Dog by its Behavior. New York, NY: WH Freeman, 1988.
8. Milani MM. The Body Language and Emotion of Dogs. New York, NY: WM Morrow, 1986.
9. Houpt KA. Animal Behavior for Veterinarians and Animal Scientists, 3rd ed. Ames, IA: Iowa State University Press, 1998.
10. O'Farrell V. Manual of Canine Behavior, 2nd ed. Gloucestershire, UK: BSAVA, 1992.
11. O'Farrell V, Neville P. Manual of Feline Behavior. Glouchestershire, UK: BSAVA, 1995.
12. Overall K. Clinical Behavioral Medicine for Small Animals. St. Louis, MO: CV Mosby Co, 1997.
13. Randolph E. How to Help Your Puppy Grow Up to be a Wonderful Dog. New York, NY: Macmillan, 1987.
14. Schwartz S. Canine and Feline Behavior Problems: Instructions for Veterinary Clients, 2nd ed. St. Louis, MO: CV Mosby Co, 1997.
15. Vollmer PJ. How to Raise the Best Dog You'll Ever Have! Escondido, CA: Super Puppy Press, 1992.
16. Wright M, Walters S. The Book of the Cat. New York, NY: Summit Books, 1980.

Table 8-8. Mean age at death for dogs and cats older than one year.*

	Cats (years)	Dogs (years)
Intact males	4.1	7.5
Neutered males	6.5	9.9
Intact females	5.2	6.8
Neutered females	8.7	8.8

*Adapted from Bronson RT. American Journal of Veterinary Research 1981; 42: 1606-1608. Bronson RT. American Journal of Veterinary Research 1982; 43: 2057-2059.

the pet. The influence of neutering on behavioral characteristics, longevity and specific diseases has been reviewed.[25] This information should be shared with clients and routine neutering advised for the vast majority of pets.

Behavioral characteristics most influenced by neutering include roaming, feline urine spraying, canine urine marking and intermale aggression.[25-29] Pet owners should be informed that neutered pets live longer. The mean age at death of male and female cats older than one year was significantly higher in neutered cats than in intact cats.[30] Mean age at death was also higher in neutered vs. intact dogs, but to a lesser extent than in cats.[31] The data from these two studies are summarized in Table 8-8.

Neutering pets at an early age will prevent the occurrence of virtually all tumors of the reproductive tissues, with the notable exceptions of canine prostatic adenocarcinoma and feline mammary cancer. Protecting animals from benign and malignant tumors of the reproductive tissues, which account for 15 to 29% of all reported tumor types, is a welcome option.[32]

Testicular tumors are the second most common neoplasm affecting male dogs.[32] Testicular neoplasms represent 5 to 15% of tumors recorded in male dogs, but are exceedingly rare in male cats. Dogs with undescended testes are approximately 13 times more likely than normal dogs to develop testicular tumors, specifically Sertoli cell tumors and seminomas.[32] Intact male dogs are also at risk for perineal hernias, prostatic disease and sexually transmitted diseases such as transmissible venereal tumors and brucellosis.[25]

Mammary gland tumors are the most common tumors in female dogs. Malignant mammary tumors are by far the leading form of cancer in dogs.[32] Ovariectomy performed before the first estrus virtually eliminates the risk of mammary tumor development in dogs. When ovariectomy is delayed past the first estrus, however, the risk of mammary tumor development increases, until it levels off at 2.5 years.

Neutering profoundly alters the metabolism of dogs and cats. Recent studies suggest that neutering causes decreases in resting metabolic rate and daily energy requirement.[33,34] Thus, neutered animals are frequently at risk for obesity. Strategies should be implemented to reduce the overall caloric intake from the caloric intake before neutering.

Neutering is advocated and performed at much earlier ages (six to 14 weeks) than in the past.[35] The effects of early neutering on behavioral, skeletal and physical development have been assessed.[35,36] Early neutering does not appear to affect the growth rate of puppies, but does extend the growth period.[36] Gonadectomy at seven weeks of age in cats has no different effect on resting energy requirement or on development of obesity vs. gonadectomy at seven months.[33] Early neutering may change other nutritional requirements of growing puppies and kittens but this has not been studied.

Oral Care

Periodontal disease is the primary cause of early tooth loss in dogs and cats. Researchers have found periodontitis in more than 80% of dogs six years of age and older[37] and in 57.5% of cats studied.[38] This disease is often an incidental finding during the physical examination and may not be considered clinically important until the disease has led to extreme tooth mobility or tooth loss. Periodontal disease of this degree is generally found in older pets, leading to the erroneous conclusion that it is a geriatric condition. Gingivitis, a reversible form of periodontal disease, develops at one to two years of age and progresses to periodontitis (an irreversible change) by four to six years of age.[39] Preliminary data from the National Companion Animal Study showed that oral disease was the most commonly recognized disease in all age categories of dogs and cats (Table 8-1). Malocclusion of teeth is a risk factor for earlier and more severe periodontitis.

Regular oral care in young adults will prevent irreversible damage. This care should consist of regular dental prophylaxes by the veterinarian and home care. Oral health and disease are discussed in detail in Chapter 16. Veterinarians should be prepared to give advice about minor orthodontic procedures available for pets. It is generally considered inappropriate to offer orthodontics to breeding animals.

Grooming

Although it is true that the skin and coat reflect general health, many vigorous, normal pets have unkempt coats. The most important factor in causing an unkempt coat in an otherwise healthy pet is the coat type. A short coat retains reasonable condition with minimal care whereas some longer coat types require frequent grooming to remain in good condition. Unkempt, poorly groomed coats are risk factors for external parasites and dermatologic problems such as acute pyotraumatic dermatitis (hot spots).

Normal grooming procedures for the individual's coat type should be discussed with the pet owner as part of a health maintenance program for young dogs and cats. Grooming procedures will vary because of the variety of coat types among breeds. Clients should be told to spend a few minutes each day grooming their pets rather than several hours sporadically.

Proper training can make a world of difference in the ease of grooming, including nail trimming. Good behavior during grooming and nail trimming is most easily established during the socialization phase. (See Table 8-7.) Most properly trained pets thoroughly enjoy being groomed.

Prospective pet owners should consider grooming problems before purchasing a pet. If time and expense are likely to be problems, one should not choose a pet from a long-haired or wiry- or woolly-coated breed, but instead should select a short-coated, easy-to-groom animal. A summary of the grooming needs of five typical coat types is available.[40]

Extended Databases

Laboratory and other diagnostic tests can help identify health risk factors and early evidence of disease. In general, the following guidelines can be used when deciding which laboratory and other diagnostic tests should be used in a health maintenance program.[41]

- The tests should be accurate and simple.
- The disease the proposed test seeks to uncover should have an asymptomatic period.
- The suspected disease should cause notable morbidity and mortality, or have significant zoonotic potential.
- The suspected disease should be sufficiently common to justify the cost of the test.
- Early treatment of the suspected disease should provide a better outcome than would treatment after the onset of clinical signs.
- An effective treatment for the suspected disease should be available.

Based on these criteria, the most common extended database should include a fecal examination, tests for heartworm and feline leukemia virus infection, urinalysis and fundic examination.

In geriatric patients, the extended database should include a complete blood count and serum biochemistry profile. Thoracic radiographs and echocardiograms are included if a cardiac murmur is detected or if there is a history of cough or abnormal respiratory pattern in older pets. Other laboratory tests should be performed as deemed necessary based on the physical examination and systems review.

Nutrition Counseling

The importance of nutrition in a complete preventive health care program for people is well-documented. In 1968, a World Health Organization study found a correlation between nutrition, disease occurrence and immunity.[42] Infections were more likely to be fatal in persons with clinical or subclinical nutrient deficiencies. Malnutrition and infection were found to be synergistic. When they occur concurrently, the effects are worse than the sum of the effects of each occurring separately.[43] Protein and energy deficiency will consistently suppress cell-mediated and humoral immunity.[43] Excesses of certain nutrients will also compromise immune responsiveness[44] and may contribute to or promote certain diseases.[45] This finding reinforces the concept that optimal nutrition during all stages of life is an important part of any health maintenance program.

Health maintenance programs for people focus on a few nutrients that are risk factors for certain common illnesses. These nutrients are sometimes referred to as "nutrients of concern" or "key nutritional factors." (See Chapter 1.) The concept assumes that most nutrients in a typical diet are reasonably balanced and that imbalances, particularly moderate excesses, are not a significant health hazard. This idea allows health professionals to focus attention on a few nutrients or nutritional factors that are associated with common diseases For people, two well-known examples are avoiding saturated fat to reduce the risk for coronary artery disease and certain types of cancer.

An association between nutrients and certain common illnesses also exists for dogs and cats. This concept of "ignoring" most nutrients and focusing on a few key nutrients (See Chapter 1.) is even more appropriate for dogs and cats because most pets are fed commercially prepared food that usually meets minimum allowances for all nutrients. But as with people in affluent societies, malnutrition as a result of nutrient excess is more common than malnutrition from nutrient deficiencies.

Chapter 9 (Normal Dogs) and Chapter 11 (Normal Cats) cover nutrients of concern for health maintenance of dogs and cats at various lifestages.

Feeding for Optimal Growth

Dogs and cats that are overfed during growth may be at risk for obesity. (See Chapter 13.) Puppies and kittens that develop large numbers of adipocytes (fat cells) during growth may be predisposed to obesity as adults. Puppies and kittens should receive a body condition score (BCS) as part of their routine health maintenance examinations. (See Chapter 1 for the BCS protocol.) Clients should also be encouraged to assess body condition biweekly during rapid growth. Optimal growth can be defined as regular and sustained growth while maintaining a BCS of 3/5. Minor deviations above and below a BCS of 3/5 do not warrant significant concern.

AVOIDING EXCESS ENERGY

Large- and giant-breed puppies are at risk for developmental orthopedic disease when undergoing rapid growth.[15,16] (See Chapter 17.) Optimal skeletal development is more likely to occur if growth is slowed. These puppies should not be fed ad libitum. Fat and energy intake should be limited by restricting the total amount of food the puppy eats each day and using a food that does not contain excessive levels of energy (recommend 3.2 to 3.8 kcal [13.4 to 15.9 kJ] ME/g dry matter).

AVOIDING EXCESS CALCIUM

Excessive calcium intake is also a risk factor for developmental orthopedic disease. Large- and giant-breed puppies should receive a food without excessive levels of calcium (recommend 0.9 to 1.2% calcium in the dry matter). Dietary supplements that contain calcium should be avoided. A detailed discussion of the influence of nutrition on musculoskeletal development is found in Chapter 17.

Feeding Adult Animals

AVOIDING OBESITY

Obesity is the most significant clinical problem associated with malnutrition in adult dogs and cats. Preliminary data from the National Companion Animal Study indicate that about 25% of dogs and cats are overweight or obese.[2] Risk factors for obesity include middle age, female gender, neutered reproductive status, certain breeds, feeding foods and treats high in caloric density and lack of exercise. See Chapter 13 for problems associated with obesity. To prevent obesity, a food moderately restricted in energy density is recommended for inactive, obesity-prone adult dogs and cats. A high-fiber, low-fat food is low in caloric density, prolongs eating time and induces satiety. See Chapter 13 for examples of these types of foods. For some canine breeds or in some situations (e.g., neutered dogs and cats), it may be advisable to recommend this type of food shortly after the animal reaches skeletal maturity. Obesity prevention is an important goal in feeding adult dogs and cats, and should be aggressively pursued in dogs and cats with multiple risk factors.

Although food dosages can be estimated, energy requirements vary tremendously among individual dogs and cats. The amount of food that adult dogs and cats need varies within the general population by as much as twofold to threefold. Therefore, a calculated food dosage should only be considered an estimate or starting point. Food quantities should be adjusted based on assessment of body condition by the pet owner and veterinarian. (See Chapter 1.)

AVOIDING RENAL DISEASE

Renal disease is a significant cause of nonaccidental death in dogs and cats. Research in dogs and cats with advanced renal disease has shown that decreasing the level of dietary phosphorus slows progression and reduces the severity of renal disease, thereby lengthening the pet's life. Limiting excess phosphorus throughout an animal's adult life may reduce progression of renal disease in its earlier stages when diagnosis is difficult. Avoiding excess dietary protein, sodium and chloride throughout adulthood may also slow progression of renal disease. (See Chapter 19.)

AVOIDING PERIODONTAL DISEASE

Periodontal disease and associated problems, such as oral malodor, are the most common diseases of adult dogs and cats. A combination of veterinary care (routine dental examination and cleaning) and home care (brushing and dietary cleansing) are essential to maintaining oral health. Appropriate treats and chews are most commonly used for dietary cleansing. Specific dental foods are also available that significantly reduce the accumulation of dental plaque, stain and calculus, improve oral malodor and reduce gingivitis. (See Chapter 16.)

Feeding Reproducing Females

Malnourishment, before and during gestation, may be an important contributory factor to the 20 to 30% mortality rate of neonatal puppies and kittens. The demands of gestation and particularly lactation drastically alter a female's nutritional requirements.

A health maintenance program should encourage optimal prebreeding nutrition and care. Before breeding, evaluate the bitch and queen using the following steps:
- Conduct a thorough physical examination.
- Check and treat the patient for external and internal parasites.
- Vaccinate the patient for appropriate diseases.
- Weigh the patient and evaluate body condition. If necessary, alter the amount and type of food the animal is being fed to optimize body weight and body condition (BCS of 3/5) when bred.
- Determine hematocrit, hemoglobin and plasma protein concentrations. Values markedly below normal indicate a poor nutritional state or the presence of disease. These problems should be corrected before breeding.

Feeding a growth/lactation food is most important during the last three to four weeks of gestation. Body condition scoring is the best method to assess whether the amount of food should be adjusted. The most common errors during gestation are overfeeding and excessive supplementation. Supplementation is not routinely needed.

Lactation is one of the most nutritionally demanding periods in the life of a bitch or a queen. It is particularly important that an appropriate growth/lactation food be fed. Throughout lactation, the female should be fed enough food to maintain optimal body weight. This amount will vary with the stage of lactation and the size of the litter, but it should be about one and one-half to three times as much as the amount fed for adult maintenance. (See Chapters 9 and 11.) Free-choice feeding during lactation should be encouraged. The most common error during lactation is underfeeding. A readily accessible source of water is also important.

Feeding Stressed Animals

Ambient temperature extremes, racing, hunting, working livestock, police and sentry duty, guiding the blind and touring on the show circuit are physical and psychological stresses that may increase a dog's requirement for energy and other nutrients. Palatable, nutritionally dense and highly digestible foods are desirable for dogs undergoing these stresses. Significantly better endurance occurs when dogs are fed highly digestible, high-energy foods (stress/performance foods).[46]

Hard-working hunting dogs should be fed a stress/performance food beginning one to three weeks before conditioning. These dogs should then be conditioned for at least three weeks before hunting. Well-conditioned dogs can be fed once daily after hunting. Water should be offered several times throughout the day. See Chapter 10 for more details about feeding athletic dogs.

Feeding Older Pets

DEFINITIONS

Geriatrics (from Greek *geras*, old age, and *iatrike*, surgery, medicine) is the branch of medicine that pertains to problems peculiar to old age. Aging has been defined as a complex biologic process resulting in progressive reduction of an individual's ability to maintain homeostasis during internal physiologic and external environmental stresses, thereby increasing the individual's vulnerability to disease, and eventually causing death.[47] Aging is not a disease itself. The rate of aging may be influenced by many factors, including genetics, environment and nutrition.

In one survey, diplomates of the American Board of Veterinary Practitioners and the American Colleges of Veterinary Internal Medicine, Veterinary Surgeons and Veterinary Pathologists were asked at what age they considered dogs and cats to be geriatric or most likely to manifest problems associated with aging.[47] The ages varied according to species and size of the animal:

- Small dogs (less than 20 lb)   11.5 ± 1.9 years
- Medium dogs (21 to 50 lb)   10.2 ± 1.6 years
- Large dogs (51 to 90 lb)   8.9 ± 1.4 years
- Giant dogs (greater than 90 lb)   7.5 ± 1.3 years
- Cats   11.9 ± 1.9 years

Preliminary data from the National Companion Animal Study show that 20% of dogs and cats examined at private practices in North America are middle-aged (four to seven years of age) and 30% are older than seven years.[2] Because aging affects all body systems, there is a high likelihood of multiple problems in older pets. A thorough systems review, which should include a complete history, physical examination and extended laboratory database is important. This review enables veterinarians to define problems accurately, rank the problems according to priority and establish complete diagnostic and therapeutic plans. The following discussion will give a brief overview of geriatric problems by body systems. It is not meant to be all inclusive, but merely to illustrate the scope of common geriatric problems.

SYSTEMS REVIEW IN AGING PETS

Endocrine System

Endocrinopathies are common in middle-aged and older pets.[32] Hyperadrenocorticism usually occurs in dogs older than six years, with the median incidence in seven- to nine-year-old dogs. Adrenocortical tumors are most common in geriatric dogs (median age 10 to 11 years).

Hypothyroidism occurs most commonly in middle-aged to old, medium- to large-breed dogs within the age range of four to 10 years. Hyperthyroidism is exclusively a problem in geriatric cats (median age 12 to 13 years). (See Chapter 24.)

Cardiovascular System

Cardiovascular disease is common in geriatric animals and frequently leads to clinical problems. About one-fourth of all heart disease in dogs occurs between the ages of nine and 12 years, with one-third occurring in dogs 13 years of age and older.[48] Chronic degenerative valvular disease is the most common cardiovascular lesion causing heart failure in old dogs.

Hypertension occurs most commonly in older pets secondary to chronic renal disease and endocrinopathies. Patients with heart disease, congestive heart failure or hypertension may benefit from avoiding excess dietary sodium and chloride. (See Chapter 18.)

Musculoskeletal System

Owners commonly complain of lameness, stiffness and paresis in their geriatric pets. The astute veterinarian must differentiate musculoskeletal disorders from other diseases that contribute to musculoskeletal problems. Degenerative joint disease is the most common disorder of the musculoskeletal system. Prevention or treatment of obesity is an important goal in patients with degenerative joint disease. (See Chapter 13.) Nutritional modification may attenuate the inflammatory process in some patients with osteoarthritis. (See Chapter 26.)

Gastrointestinal System

Periodontal disease is probably the most common disease in pets over two years of age. Periodontitis, which is irreversible, is the most common form of periodontal disease in geriatric pets. Oral health care programs should be started early to acclimate pets to oral manipulation and to minimize or prevent dental problems seen in geriatric patients. Cats are susceptible to certain oral diseases that occur less often in dogs. Among these are generalized stomatitis, resorptive lesions of the teeth and certain viral diseases that affect the mouth and tongue.

Constipation is common in older pets. It may be caused by foods, drugs, neuromuscular disease, metabolic disease, pelvic and perineal pain, obstruction of the colon, rectum, or anus and other miscellaneous factors.[32] Pancreatitis is also a gastrointestinal disease that occurs more commonly in middle-aged and older dogs. Constipation and large bowel disease are examples of gastrointestinal disorders that may respond to increased levels of dietary fiber. (See Chapter 22.)

Integumentary System

The incidence (the number of new cases of a disease diagnosed in one year and expressed as cases per 100,000 of the population at risk) of canine and feline skin neoplasia is about 728 and 84, respectively.[49,50] The median ages of dogs and cats with cutaneous neoplasms are 10.5 and 12 years, respectively.[49,50] In dogs, there are about one-half as many malignant skin neoplasms as benign neoplasms. However, in cats, there are about three times as many malignant neoplasms as benign skin tumors. The most common skin neoplasms of dogs are, in approximate descending order, lipoma, mast cell tumor, sebaceous gland hyperplasia and adenoma and papilloma.[40] In cats, the approximate order is basal cell tumor, squamous cell carcinoma, fibrosarcoma and mast cell tumor.[40]

Urinary System

Renal failure, with an average age at onset of seven years, is reportedly the second leading cause of nonaccidental death in dogs.[51] Other urinary problems that are primarily seen in middle-aged and geriatric dogs are urinary incontinence and bladder neoplasms. Urinary tract infections are uncommon in young cats; however, they become a significant cause of urinary tract disease in cats 10 years of age and older.[52] Approximately two-thirds of older cats with bacterial urinary tract disease have concurrent renal failure that may indicate the presence of pyelonephritis.[52]

Kidneys of geriatric animals and people are smaller and lighter than those of younger individuals, have fewer glomeruli, have a decreased tubular size and weight and have increased mesangium and fibrosis.[53] These structural changes are associated with decreased: 1) renal blood flow, 2) glomerular filtration, 3) urine concentrating ability and 4) ability to maintain sodium, water and acid-base homeostasis. Decreased concentrations of renin, aldosterone and activated vitamin D have also been found.[53] Because renal failure is primarily a disease of older animals, standard recommendations for the conservative management of renal failure were formulated with this in mind and can usually be followed when treating geriatric animals. The nutritional management of patients with chronic renal failure should include a food that avoids excesses of dietary phosphorus, protein and sodium chloride.[53,54]

Reproductive System

Reproductive disorders are common in middle-aged and older dogs and cats. Prostate disease is most common in dogs older than five years, with an average age at occurrence of 9.3 years.[55] Prostatic cancer is seen primarily in dogs older than 10 years.[55]

Geriatric females also develop reproductive disorders. Pyometra has a mean age of occurrence of 7.2 and 7.8 years in dogs and cats, respectively.[56,57] Use of progestational compounds is a risk factor for development of pyometra at an earlier age. The most common tumor in female dogs is of mammary gland origin. The approximate median age of dogs with mammary tumors is 10 to 11 years.[32] Mammary tumors occur in dogs two to 20 years old, but their occurrence in bitches less than five years old is uncommon.

Respiratory System

Chronic obstructive pulmonary disease covers a complex of respiratory system disorders that result in: 1) abnormal respiration, 2) reduction in the size of large and small airways and 3) clinical signs of cough and dyspnea. Tracheal and bronchial collapse, chronic bronchitis and chronic valvular heart disease cause the "little old coughing dog" syndrome that is commonly observed in geriatric practice.

Obesity may complicate chronic respiratory disease seen in older dogs. Weight-reduction programs to achieve an ideal body weight may help individual dogs with chronic cough. Experimentally, salt intake appears to influence bronchial hyperreactivity; low-salt foods have a favorable effect in some people with asthma.[58] Avoiding excess dietary sodium chloride in dogs and cats with chronic bronchial disease may be helpful.

Central Nervous System

Diseases of the central nervous system that occur predominantly in middle-aged and older dogs include degenerative myelopathy and intervertebral disk disease. Degenerative myelopathy is seen mostly in German shepherd dogs older than five years, whereas disk disease is seen in older dogs belonging to chondrodystrophoid breeds.

Special Senses

The probability of vision loss increases with age. This probability rises dramatically in 12- and 13-year-old dogs because of age-related cataract formation. Further, dogs with pre-existing ophthalmic disorders such as hereditary cataracts, retinal degenerative diseases, glaucoma and opacifying keratopathies are now living longer than ever before. Thus, it is common for an owner of an elderly pet to have to cope with general age-related medical problems and vision loss. In some cases, owners may not be aware of vision loss in their aged pet until the animal's environment is changed.

Many owners of blind, aged pets also complain of concomitant hearing loss. One author believes that hearing loss often precedes the vision loss, but the hearing loss is not appreciated until vision loss is combined with it.[59]

FEEDING RECOMMENDATIONS

Manufactured pet foods contain more than adequate levels of all the essential nutrients needed by normal dogs and cats. In fact, dogs and cats fed commercial rations are consuming anywhere from: 1) three to five times their daily protein requirement, 2) three times the daily calcium and phosphorus requirements, 3) two to five times the minimum requirements of vitamins and 4) 10 times the daily requirement of sodium chloride.[45] The geriatric pet, may benefit from a food that avoids excess levels of phosphorus, protein, calcium, sodium and chloride. Chapters 9 and 11 discuss lifestage nutrition for dogs and cats, including geriatric pets.

▮ REFERENCES

1. Pritchard WR. Future Directions for Veterinary Medicine. Durham, NC: Pew National Veterinary Education Program, 1989.
2. Lund EM, Armstrong PJ, Kolar L, et al. Companion animal top ten: Disease prevalence in private practice. In: Proceedings. Fourteenth Annual Veterinary Medical Forum, American College of Veterinary Internal Medicine, San Antonio, TX 1996: 131.
3. Hart BL, Hart LA. Behavioral profiles of dog breeds. Journal of the American Veterinary Medical Association 1985; 186: 1175-1180.
4. Hart BL, Hart LA. Selecting pet dogs based on the basis of cluster analysis of breed behavioral profiles and gender. Journal of the American Veterinary Medical Association 1985; 186: 1181-1185.
5. Hart BL, Hart LA. The Perfect Puppy: How to Choose Your Dog by its Behavior. New York, NY: WH Freeman, 1988.
6. Wright M, Walters S. The Book of the Cat. New York, NY: Summit Books, 1980.
7. Leipold HW, Troyer D. Chromosomal and genetic disorders. In: Ettinger SJ, Feldman EC, eds. Textbook of Veterinary Internal Medicine, 4th ed. Philadelphia, PA: WB Saunders Co, 1995; 223-226.
8. Ruble RP, Hird DW. Congenital abnormalities in immature dogs from a pet store: 253 cases (1987-88). Journal of the American Veterinary Medical Association 1993; 202: 633-636.
9. Hoskins JD. Congenital defects of the cat. In: Ettinger SJ, Feldman EC, eds. Textbook of Veterinary Internal Medicine, 4th ed. Philadelphia, PA: WB Saunders Co, 1995; 2106-2114.
10. Hoskins JD. Congenital defects of the dog. In: Ettinger SJ, Feldman EC, eds. Textbook of Veterinary Internal Medicine, 4th ed. Philadelphia, PA: WB Saunders Co, 1995; 2115-2129.
11. Clark RD, Stainer JR. Medical and Genetic Aspects of Purebred Dogs. Fairway, KS: Forum Publications, 1994.
12. Priester WA. Congenital ocular defects in cattle, horses, cats, and dogs. Journal of the American Veterinary Medical Association 1972; 160: 1504-1511.
13. Barnett KD. Comparative aspects of canine hereditary eye disease. Advances in Veterinary Science and Comparative Medicine 1976; 20: 39-67.
14. Merton DA. Selective breeding in the dog and cat, Part II: Known and suspected genetic diseases. Compendium on Continuing Education for the Practicing Veterinarian 1982; 4: 332-360.
15. Richardson DC. Developmental orthopedics: Nutritional influences in the dog. In: Ettinger SJ, Feldman EC, eds. Textbook of Veterinary Internal Medicine, 4th ed. Philadelphia, PA: WB Saunders Co, 1995; 252-258.
16. Richardson DC. The role of nutrition in canine hip dysplasia. Veterinary Clinics of North America: Small Animal Practice 1992; 22: 529-540.
17. Smith GK, Biery DN, Gregor TP. New concepts of coxofemoral joint stability and the development of a clinical stress-radiographic method for quantitating hip joint laxity in the dog. Journal of the American Veterinary Medical Association 1990; 196: 59-70.
18. Smith GK, Popovitch CA, Gregor TP, et al. Evaluation of risk factors for degenerative joint disease associated with hip dysplasia. Journal of the American Veterinary Medical Association 1995; 206: 642-647.
19. Poulos PW. Genetic disease control–The next frontier. Institute for Genetic Disease Control in Animals, PO Box 222, Davis, CA 95617.
20. Kolata J. Trauma in dogs and cats: An overview. Veterinary Clinics of North America: Small Animal Practice 1980; 10: 512-522.
21. Compendium of Veterinary Products. Port Huron, MI: North American Compendiums Inc, 1995-1996.
22. MacDonald JM, Miller TA. Parasiticide therapy in small animal dermatology. In: Kirk RW, ed. Current Veterinary Therapy IX. Philadelphia, PA: WB Saunders Co, 1986; 571-590.
23. Flea and tick product guide. Veterinary Technician 1994; 15: 229-242.

24. MacDonald JM. Flea control: An overview of treatment concepts for North America. Veterinary Dermatology 1995; 6: 121-129.

25. Johnston SD. Questions and answers on the effects of surgically neutering dogs and cats. Journal of the American Veterinary Medical Association 1991; 198: 1206-1214.

26. Beaver BV. Veterinary Aspects of Feline Behavior. St Louis, MO: CV Mosby Co, 1980.

27. Hart BL, Barrett RE. Effects of castration on fighting, roaming and urine spraying in adult male cats. Journal of the American Veterinary Medical Association 1973; 163: 290-292.

28. Hart BL, Cooper L. Factors relating to urine spraying and fighting in prepubertally gonadectomized cats. Journal of the American Veterinary Medical Association 1984; 184: 1255-1258.

29. Hopkins SG, Schubert TA, Hart BL. Castration of adult male dogs: Effects on roaming, aggression, urine marking, and mounting. Journal of the American Veterinary Medical Association 1976; 168: 1108-1110.

30. Bronson RT. Age at death of necropsied intact and neutered cats. American Journal of Veterinary Research 1981; 42: 1606-1608.

31. Bronson RT. Variation in age at death of dogs of different sexes and breeds. American Journal of Veterinary Research 1982; 43: 2057-2059.

32. Ettinger SJ, Feldman EC, eds. Textbook of Veterinary Internal Medicine, 4th ed. Philadelphia, PA: WB Saunders Co, 1995.

33. Root MV, Johnston SD, Olson PN. Effect of prepuberal and postpuberal gonadectomy on heat production measured by indirect calorimetry in male and female domestic cats. American Journal of Veterinary Research 1996; 57: 371-374.

34. Flynn MF, Hardie EM, Armstrong PJ. Effect of ovariohysterectomy on maintenance energy requirements in cats. Journal of the American Veterinary Medical Association 1996; 209: 1572-1581.

35. Salmeri KR, Olson PN, Bloomberg MS. Elective gonadectomy in dogs: A review. Journal of the American Veterinary Medical Association 1991; 198: 1183-1192.

36. Salmeri KR, Bloomberg MS, Scruggs SL, et al. Gonadectomy in immature dogs: Effects on skeletal, physical and behavioral development. Journal of the American Veterinary Medical Association 1991; 198: 1193-1203.

37. Hamp SE, Olsson SE, Farso-Madsen K, et al. A macroscopic and radiologic investigation of dental diseases of the dog. Veterinary Radiology 1984; 25: 86-92.

38. Von Schlup D. Epidemiologische und Morphologische Utersuchumgen am Katzengebi. Kleinterpraxis 1982; 27: 87-94.

39. Grove TK. Periodontal disease. Compendium on Continuing Education for the Practicing Veterinarian 1982; 4: 564-570.

40. Scott DW, Miller WH, Griffin CE. Small Animal Dermatology, 5th ed. Philadelphia, PA: WB Saunders Co, 1995.

41. Markham RW. Preventive health care for pets 5 and older. In: How to implement a geriatric program (monograph). Hill's Pet Nutrition Inc, Topeka, KS, 1991.

42. Schrimshaw NS, Tayler CE, Gordon JE. Interaction of nutrition and infection (monograph 57). Geneva, Switzerland: World Health Organization, 1968.

43. Sheffy BE. Nutrition, infection and immunity. Compendium on Continuing Education for the Practicing Veterinarian 1985; 7: 990-997.

44. Sheffy BE, Williams AJ. Nutrition and the immune response. Journal of the American Veterinary Medical Association 1982; 180: 1073-1076.

45. Kallfelz FA, Dzanis DA. Overnutrition: An epidemic problem in pet animal practice? Veterinary Clinics of North America: Small Animal Practice 1989; 19: 433-446.

46. Downey RL, Kronfeld DS, Banta CA. Diet of beagles affects stamina. Journal of the American Animal Hospital Association 1980; 16: 273-277.

47. Goldston RT. Geriatrics and gerontology. Veterinary Clinics of North America: Small Animal Practice 1989; 19: ix-x.

48. Miller MS, Tilley LP, Smith FWK. Cardiopulmonary disease in the geriatric dog and cat. Veterinary Clinics of North America: Small Animal Practice 1989; 19: 87-102.

49. Moulton JE. Tumors in Domestic Animals, 2nd ed. Berkeley, CA: University of California Press, 1978.

50. Theilen GH, Madewell BR. Veterinary Cancer Medicine, 2nd ed. Philadelphia, PA: Lea & Febiger, 1987.

51. Cowgill LD, Spangler WL. Renal insufficiency in geriatric dogs. Veterinary Clinics of North America: Small Animal Practice 1981; 11: 727-748.

52. Bartges JW. Lower urinary tract disease in geriatric cats. In: Proceedings. Fifteenth Annual Veterinary Medical Forum. American College of Veterinary Internal Medicine, Lake Buena Vista, FL, 1997: 322-324.

53. Allen TA, Roudebush P. Canine geriatric nephrology. Compendium on Continuing Education for the Practicing Veterinarian 1990; 12: 909-917.

54. Polzin DJ, Osborne CA, Adams LD, et al. Dietary management of canine and feline chronic renal failure. Veterinary Clinics of North America: Small Animal Practice 1989; 19: 539-560.

55. Hornbuckle WE, MacCoy DM, Allan GS, et al. Prostatic disease in the dog. Cornell Veterinarian 1978; 68: 284-305.

56. Fidler IJ, Brodey RS, Howson AE, et al. Relationship of estrous irregularity, pseudopregnancy and pregnancy to canine pyometra. Journal of the American Veterinary Medical Association 1966; 149: 1043-1046.

57. Kenney KJ, Matthiesen DT, Brown NO, et al. Pyometra in cats: 183 cases (1979-1984). Journal of the American Veterinary Medical Association 1987; 191: 1130-1132.

58. Medici TC, Schmid AZ, Macki M, et al. Are asthmatics salt-sensitive? Chest 1993; 104: 1138-1143.

59. Fischer CA. Geriatric ophthalmology. Veterinary Clinics of North America: Small Animal Practice 1989; 19: 103-123.

HEALTH MAINTENANCE

Normal Dogs

Jacques Debraekeleer
Kathy L. Gross
Steven C. Zicker

"In ancient times, lack of food gave languishing bodies to death.
Now, on the contrary, it is abundance that buries them."
T. Lucretius "Coro De Rerum Natura" 55 B.C.

ASSESSMENT

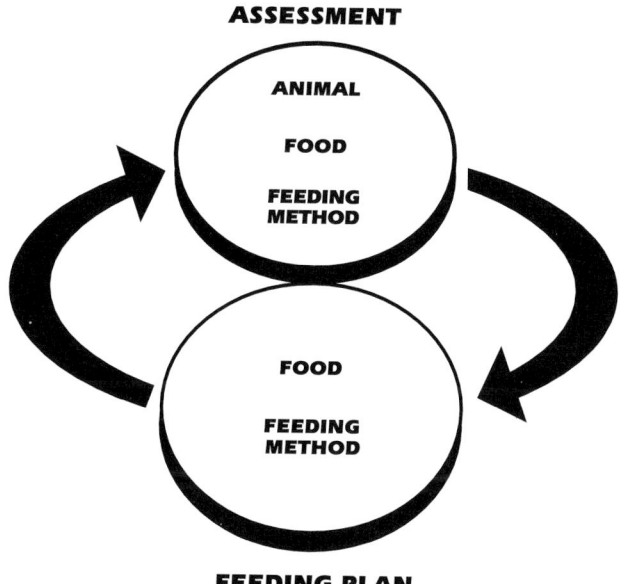

FEEDING PLAN

Note: The reader is referred to Chapter 1 for a detailed discussion of the iterative process of clinical nutrition.

CLINICAL IMPORTANCE

Much has changed in our perception and usage of dogs since the early part of the 20th century. Our society has moved from an agrarian phase into a postindustrial phase with a concomitant shift of the human population into urban settings. Dogs have, by necessity, made the shift to urban living along with us and in doing so we have discovered the remarkable adaptability and versatility of this species.

Dogs have found a job for themselves in virtually every niche of society. Dogs have been useful in law enforcement, as nursing home companions, in the military, in drug enforcement, as paraplegic assistants and in search and rescue. The human-animal bond has become a commonly taught subject in veterinary schools, which testifies to the importance of animals, including dogs, for our mental and physical well-being. The emphasis on dogs as valued members of society (See sidebar "People Treat Their Pets Like Family Members.") has driven the development of canine nutrition towards the same goals we strive for in human nutrition: long life, high quality life and enhanced performance.

Demographics

Globally, pet ownership has increased, possibly due to reduced human birth rates, changing family structure and aging populations.[1] Dog ownership is most prevalent in nations such as Australia, France and the United States of America (Table 9-1).[2] Breed popularity may vary from year to year and from region to region; however, some breeds always appear to be more desired than others (Table 9-2).[3] In addition to increased dog populations, the groups of people

KEY WORDS & TERMS—NORMAL DOGS*

Carnivore	Giant-breed dogs	Metabolizable protein
Colostrum	Growing dogs	Neonatal period
Digestibility	Herbivore	Omnivore
Digestible energy	Hunger	Partial orphan rearing
Digestible protein	Lactation	Pica
Eating behavior	Large-breed dogs	Satiety
Feeding behavior	Lifestage nutrition	Thermoneutral zone
Feeding method	Mature milk	Thermoregulation
Geriatric dogs	Metabolic weight	Weaning
Gestation	Metabolizable energy	

*Key words and terms are defined in the Glossary.

KEY POINTS—NORMAL DOGS

1. Dogs are omnivores. They are opportunistic eaters and have developed anatomic and physiologic characteristics that permit digestion and usage of a varied diet.
2. Lifestage nutrition is the practice of feeding animals foods designed to meet their optimal nutritional needs at a specific age or physiologic state (e.g., maintenance, reproduction or growth). The concept of lifestage nutrition recognizes that feeding either below or above an optimal nutrient range can negatively affect biologic performance or health.
3. Nearly all commercial dog foods meet or exceed the minimum nutrient requirements of dogs. However, certain nutrients may be outside the desired range for optimal health or risk factor reduction.
4. The general type and level of activity (e.g., house pet, confined to kennel, working dog, etc.) and neuter status should be noted because these factors are important determinants of energy requirements.
5. Obesity occurs twice as often in neutered dogs as in reproductively intact dogs.
6. Dogs kept outside in cold weather may need 10 to 90% more energy than during optimal weather conditions.
7. In general, dogs self-regulate water intake according to physiologic need. Requirements may be met by allowing free access to a source of potable water.
8. Domestic canids are the most diverse mammalian species in terms of body weight and size. Therefore, energy requirements are more closely related to metabolic weight ($BW_{kg}^{0.75}$) than body weight.
9. The overall goals of feeding adult dogs are to optimize quality and longevity of life and minimize disease.
10. Oral disease is the most common health problem of adult dogs. Foods formulated to decrease the accumulation of dental substrates (i.e., plaque, calculus) and help control gingivitis and malodor are an important part of an oral home-care program for adult dogs.
11. The objectives of a good reproductive feeding program are to optimize conception, number of puppies per litter, ability of the bitch to deliver and viability of prenatal and neonatal puppies.
12. Adequately fed bitches gain about 15 to 25% above their pre-breeding weight before whelping.
13. Energy requirements for gestation peak at about 30% above adult maintenance for bitches with smaller litters, whereas energy needs for bitches with larger litters can increase by 50 to 60%.
14. Feeding a carbohydrate-free food to pregnant bitches may result in weight loss and decreased food intake, increase the risk of stillbirths and reduce birth weight and survival.
15. During lactation, nutrient requirements are directly related to milk production, which in turn depends primarily on the number of suckling puppies. A bitch's nutrient requirements during lactation are greater than at any other adult lifestage and may be equal to or greater than for growth.
16. Although often overlooked, water is the first nutrient needed for lactation; water is needed in large quantities to produce milk.
17. Most lactating bitches should be fed free choice.
18. Hypoglycemia, hypothermia and dehydration are by far the most common nutrition-related conditions seen in neonates. Orphan puppies are at a much higher risk for developing these conditions than nursing puppies, especially when deprived of colostrum.
19. Puppies should be encouraged to start eating solid food as soon as possible. This practice will reduce reliance on the bitch, reduce the nutritional burden on the bitch, help overcome iron deficiency in the puppies and make complete weaning less stressful.
20. The ultimate goal of a feeding plan for puppies is to create a healthy adult. The specific objectives are to optimize growth and minimize obesity and developmental orthopedic disease.
21. A puppy should receive 3.0 x resting energy requirement (RER) until it reaches about 50% of its adult body weight. Thereafter, energy intake should be reduced progressively to 2.0 to 2.5 x RER until approximately 80% of adult size is reached; at that point 1.8 to 2.0 x RER will suffice.

most likely to spend money on pet food will have increased by nearly 50% from 1990 to 2000.[4] This has not gone unnoticed in the free market; sales of commercial pet food products in grocery and specialty pet food categories have increased dramatically over the past 10 years.[a] This highly competitive market and increased demand, coupled with the importance of nutrition to the health and performance of dogs, make it necessary for practicing veterinarians to

KEY NUTRITIONAL FACTORS—NORMAL DOGS

Table 9-7 lists key nutritional factors for adult dogs at maintenance (young to middle age, obese prone and older).

Table 9-13 lists key nutritional factors for reproduction (gestation and lactation).

Table 9-19 lists key nutritional factors for growing dogs.

FEEDING PLAN SUMMARY FOR NORMAL DOGS

Adult dogs

1. Body condition and other assessment criteria will determine the daily energy requirement (DER). Remember, DER calculations should be used as guidelines, starting points and estimates for individual animals and not as absolute requirements.

   Neutered adult = 1.6 x resting energy requirement (RER)

   Intact adult = 1.8 x RER

   Obese-prone adult = 1.2 to 1.4 x RER

   Working adult = 2.0 to 8.0 x RER (See Chapter 10.)

2. Select a food or foods with the following energy density.

   Ideal body condition = 3.5 to 4.5 kcal (14.6 to 18.8 kJ) metabolizable energy (ME)/g dry matter

   Obese prone = 3.0 to 3.5 kcal (12.5 to 14.6 kJ) ME/g dry matter

3. Select a food or foods with levels of key nutritional factors listed in Table 9-7.
4. Determine quantity of food based on DER calculations.
5. Determine preferred feeding method (Table 9-8).
6. Monitor body weight, body condition and general health.

Reproducing dogs

1. Body condition and other assessment criteria will determine the DER. Remember, DER calculations should be used as guidelines, starting points and estimates for individual animals and not as absolute requirements.

   Gestation = 1.8 to 2.0 x RER for first four weeks, then 2.2 to 3.5 x RER for last five weeks

   Lactation = 4.0 to 8.0 x RER (peak lactation: 1.9 x RER + 25% per puppy)

2. Select a food or foods with the following energy density.

   Gestation = 3.5 to 4.5 kcal (14.6 to 18.8 kJ) ME/g dry matter

   Lactation = 4.0 to 5.0 kcal (16.7 to 20.9 kJ) ME/g dry matter

   = 3.5 to 4.5 kcal (14.6 to 18.8 kJ) ME/g dry matter for bitches with fewer than four puppies

3. Select a food or foods with levels of key nutritional factors listed in Table 9-13.
4. Select a food or foods with above average digestibility (Table 9-11).
5. In general, free-choice feeding is the preferred feeding method.
6. Monitor body weight, body condition and general health.

Growing dogs

1. Estimate adult body weight and size, which will determine key nutritional factors.
2. Determine the DER. Remember, DER calculations should be used as guidelines, starting points and estimates for individual animals and not as absolute requirements.

   Weaning to 50% of adult body weight (four to five months of age) = 3.0 x RER

   Four to five months of age to 80% of adult weight = 2.0 to 2.5 x RER

   When 80% of adult body weight is reached = 1.8 to 2.0 x RER

   See Table 9-20 for more information about calculating DER.

3. Select a food or foods with the following energy density.

   Adult body weight <25 kg = 3.5 to 4.5 kcal (14.6 to 18.8 kJ) ME/g dry matter

   Adult body weight >25 kg = 3.25 to 3.75 kcal (13.6 to 15.7 kJ) ME/g dry matter

4. Select a food or foods with levels of key nutritional factors listed in Table 9-19.
5. Select a food or foods with above average digestibility (Table 9-11).
6. In general, free-choice feeding should be avoided; use a meal-restricted (preferred) or time-restricted feeding method.
7. Monitor body weight, body condition and general health.

NORMAL DOGS

People Treat Their Pets Like Family Members

A majority of American households (57%) currently have dogs, cats or both pets in residence, but virtually everyone—more than nine in 10—considers his or her pet a member of the family. Here's some other interesting facts about pet ownership.

1. Americans spend about $5 billion on holiday presents for their furry friends.
2. 63% of dog owners and 58% of cat owners surveyed said they give their pets presents at Christmas.
3. 40% of dog owners and 37% of cat owners hang Christmas stockings for their pets.
4. 36% of dog owners give their pets presents on their birthday, as do 20% of cat owners.
5. About one-fourth of dog owners (27%) and cat owners (23%) sign their pet's name on greeting cards or notes.
6. 64% of surveyed pet owners said they include news about their pet, and 36% include a photograph in their holiday cards.
7. About 27% of pet owners claim to have taken their pet to a professional photographer to have a picture taken with family, Santa Claus or the Easter bunny.
8. About one-third (37%) of dog owners and a similar proportion of cat owners (31%) have their pet's picture prominently displayed in their homes, and 14 and 10%, respectively, display it at their place of work.
9. About 10% of dog and cat owners carry their pet's picture in their wallet or purse.
10. In about 20% of households containing a dog or cat, the owner leaves the TV, radio or stereo on when the animal is left alone, presumably so it won't become lonely.
11. 16% of dog owners and 14% of cat owners claim to have bought a car or home with a pet in mind.
12. In 70% of feline households, cats are allowed to lie on the furniture. In 40% of canine households, dogs are allowed to do so.
13. In 65% of cat-owning households, cats are permitted to sleep at night on some family member's bed vs. 39% of dogs.
14. 45% of pet owners set up a special bed for their pet in the house.
15. In 75% of the nation's dog-owning households, the dog is treated to rides in the family car vs. 38% of households with cats.
16. In one-third (34%) of households surveyed, the dog goes along on family vacations, whereas only 11% of respondents take the cat along.
17. 25% of pet owners surveyed said they blow dry their pet's hair after a bath.
18. When a pet dies, 58% of pet owners bury the pet on their property.
19. Almost half of the pet owners surveyed admit they sometimes talk to their pet. And 80% of those people stated that on those occasions, the animal seemed to respond by means of sounds, facial expressions or body language.

BIBLIOGRAPHY

American Humane Association Fact Sheet. American Humane Association, National Resource Center, 63 Inverness Dr. E., Englewood, CO.

understand not just the basics, but some of the subtleties of canine nutrition in order to make knowledgeable recommendations to clients about optimal feeding programs.

Diversity Within the Species

The modern domestic canine species encompasses a vast number of breeds each with its own genetic idiosyncrasies.[5] The variety of dog breeds has arisen out of selection efforts by people to produce animals with specific traits that may enhance performance, show or behavioral characteristics (Table 9-3). The result is a species that displays a wide variety of morphology; head shape, size, coat characteristics (color, length, etc.) and musculoskeletal structure. By selecting for these traits, we have probably unknowingly selected for variations in metabolism and nutrient usage as has been evidenced in other species. Our knowledge about breed variation in metabolism and nutrient requirements is limited. However, there is a good body of information and research about metabolism and nutrition of this diverse species. A common unifying theme in canids is that they are omnivores.

■ DOGS AS OMNIVORES

The word carnivore can be used to indicate either a taxonomic classification or a type of feeding behavior. The order Carnivora is quite diverse (Table 9-4) and consists of 12 families containing more than 260 species. Omnivorous and carnivorous feeding behaviors are most common among members of the order Carnivora; however, the order also includes species that are herbivores (e.g., pandas).[6-8]

Eating Behavior

Several researchers have examined the eating habits of wolves (*Canis lupus*), the nearest ancestors of our domestic dogs, and close relatives such as coyotes (*Canis latrans*). Both are opportunistic predators and scavengers, hunting and eating what is available regionally.[9] Coyotes eat carrion and hunt rodents, other small mammals, birds, amphibians and other species.[9,10] In addition, they have been reported to consume

Table 9-1. Comparisons of dog and human populations in selected countries.*

Country	Human population (millions)	Dogs/100 people
Australia	17.4	18
Canada	25.9	12
Japan	122.1	6
USA	252.1	21
Europe (average)	–	11
Belgium/Luxembourg	10.4	13
Denmark	5.1	13
France	56.3	18
Germany	79.3	6
Ireland	3.5	14
Italy	57.9	9
The Netherlands	14.9	9
Portugal	10.4	13
Spain	39.0	10
United Kingdom	57.4	13

*Adapted from Marsh FO. Global awareness trends affecting petfood manufacturers. Petfood Industry 1994; 36 (July/August): 4-10.

droppings of herbivorous prey; domestic dogs also will readily consume herbivore feces.[11] Regional ungulates such as buffalo, deer, elk, moose, wildebeest, antelope and zebra are the natural prey of wolves.[9,10] Viscera are considered the choicest part; therefore, partially digested vegetable material is a normal part of the wolf's diet.[12] Both coyotes and wolves also eat plant matter such as fruits, berries, persimmons, mushrooms and melons.[9,10,13] Similarly, dogs are opportunistic eaters and have developed anatomic and physiologic characteristics that permit digestion and usage of a varied diet.

Anatomy and Physiology

Oral Cavity

The oral cavity functions to decrease the physical size of food for introduction into the rest of the alimentary tract. Decreasing the physical size of food creates particles small enough to pass through the esophagus and increases the surface area of the food, which enhances enzymatic digestion in the stomach and small intestine. Dogs have cutting canine teeth for ripping and tearing and molar teeth with large occlusal tables for crushing, which are associated teleologically with the capacity to use plant material (Figure 9-1).[8] Dogs may fix large pieces of food with their paws in order to tear off small pieces with their cutting canine teeth, after which the food particle is advanced to the back of the oral cavity where it may be crushed by the molar teeth and mixed with saliva before being swallowed.[14]

Stomach

Wild canids typically eat large meals, usually infrequently, due to intermittent food availability. Dogs may consume their daily energy requirement (DER) in one or two large meals, ingested rapidly.[15] This eating pattern means that the stomach must be able to expand markedly. On average, a medium-sized, adult domestic dog has the

Table 9-2. Ten most popular dog breeds registered by the American Kennel Club in 1996 and 1986.*

Breed	1996 Rank	1996 Number	1986 Rank	1986 Number
Labrador retriever	1	149,505	3	77,371
Rottweiler	2	89,867	15	28,257
German shepherd dog	3	79,076	5	55,958
Golden retriever	4	68,993	4	59,057
Beagle	5	56,946	7	39,849
Poodle	6	56,803	2	85,500
Dachshund	7	48,426	9	35,537
Cocker spaniel	8	45,305	1	98,330
Yorkshire terrier	9	40,216	12	32,485
Pomeranian	10	39,712	16	25,056

*Adapted from U.S. Pet Ownership & Demographics Sourcebook. Schaumburg, IL: Center for Information Management, American Veterinary Medical Association, 1997; 32-35.

Table 9-3. Examples of various functions dogs perform in society.

Assisting hearing or physically impaired persons
Entertainment
Guiding blind persons
Herding
Hunting
Military and law enforcement
Pets
Racing (sprint or endurance)
Rescue operations
Show and breeding
Social interactions

Table 9-4. Taxonomy and natural feeding behavior of the order Carnivora.*

Family	Canidae	Ursidae	Procyonidae	Ailuropodidae	Mustelidae	Viverridae
Feeding behavior	Omnivores	Omnivores Carnivores	Omnivores	Herbivores	Carnivores Omnivores	Omnivores
No. of species	35	7	13	2	63	35
Examples	Dogs Jackals Coyotes Foxes Wolves	Bears	Racoons Coatis Kinkajou Olingos	Pandas	Weasels Polecats Mink Ferrets Martens Wolverine Badgers Skunks Otters	Genets Civets Linsangs

Family	Herpestidae	Hyaenidae	Felidae	Otariidae	Odobenidae	Phocidae
Feeding behavior	Carnivores Omnivores	Carnivores	Carnivores	Carnivores	Carnivores	Carnivores
No. of species	37	4	36	14	1	19
Examples	Mongooses Meerkats	Hyenas	Leopards Pumas Cats Ocelots Serval Jaguars Lynxes Bobcats Lions Tigers Cheetahs	Eared seals Sea lions	Walrus	Earless seals

*Adapted from Corbet GB, Hill JE. A World List of Mammalian Species. New York, NY: Facts on File Publications, 1986; 105-121. Nowak RM, Paradiso JL. Walker's Mammals of the World, 4th ed. Baltimore, MD: The Johns Hopkins University Press, 1983. Ridgway SH, Harrison RJ. Handbook of Marine Mammals. New York, NY: Academic Press Inc, 1981.

NORMAL DOGS

Figure 9-1. Maxillary dentition and palate of a dog (left). Mandibular dentition and sublingual mucosa of the same dog (right). These photographs demonstrate tooth anatomy associated with an omnivorous eating behavior. The cuspid (canine) teeth are long and cutting and are used for capturing and puncturing prey. The maxillary and mandibular premolar teeth interdigitate and provide a shearing action. The carnassial teeth (upper fourth premolar and lower first molar) have broad occlusal surfaces and are used for grinding and chewing. (Adapted with permission from Harvey CE, Emily PP. Function, formation, and anatomy of oral structures in carnivores. Small Animal Dentistry. St. Louis, MO: Mosby-Year Book Inc, 1993.)

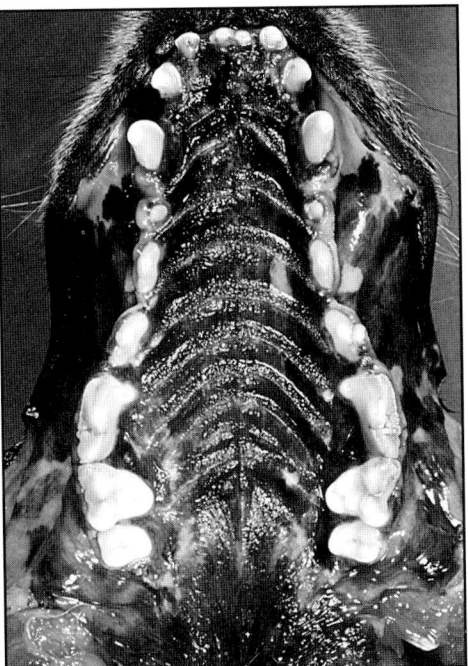 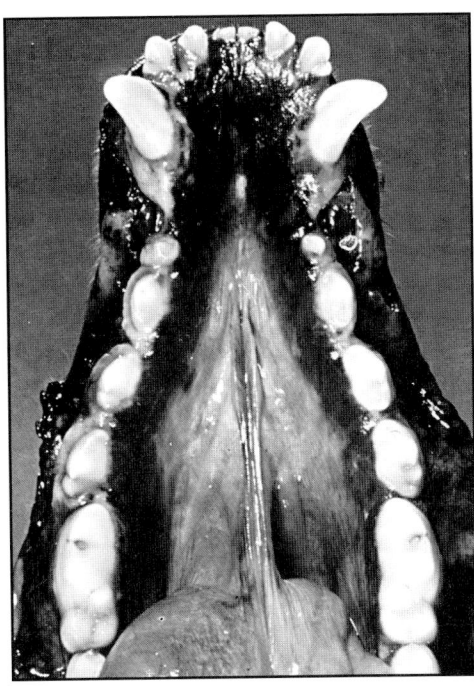

capacity to ingest 30 to 35 g of dry matter (DM) per kg body weight per day.[16,17] However, the canine stomach can adjust, within limits, to accommodate the amount of food ingested and can hold 1 to 9 liters depending on breed.[18]

Small and Large Intestine

The characteristics of the canine small intestine are consistent with those of animals that digest an omnivorous diet.[8] The small intestine composes approximately 23% of the total gastrointestinal (GI) volume of dogs[15] vs. 15% for cats.[19] The ratio of GI tract length to total body length is 6:1 for dogs, 4:1 for cats, 10:1 for rabbits and as high as 20:1 for some herbivores.[8,14,19] This anatomic rela-

tionship is consistent with ingestion of an omnivorous diet with intermediate digestibility (i.e., between low digestible herbaceous forages and highly digestible animal flesh). Dogs digest starch efficiently via pancreatic enzymes and mucosal disaccharidases.

Nutrient Requirements and Metabolism

Much can be learned about an animal's nutritional requirements simply by analyzing its natural food source. True carnivores are limited to what is available from prey tissues such as skeletal muscle and liver to provide energy and nutrients, including protein, taurine, arginine, arachidonic acid and niacin. Consequently, carnivorous

Table 9-5. Comparison between the recommended daily allowances of selected nutrients for a 10-kg dog and the nutrient content of meat (beef).*

Nutrient	RDA 10-kg dog	per 100 g	Regular ground beef Amount meeting the DER of a 10-kg dog 482 g	% of RDA	Adequacy
Metabolizable energy (kcal)	650	135	650	100	J
Moisture (ml)	650	60	289	44	na
Protein (g)	24	17	82	341	L
Fat (g)	≥8	20	96	1,204	L
Calcium (mg)	1,000	10	48	5	L
Phosphorus (mg)	750	200	963	128	K
Ca/P ratio	1:1-2:1	1:20	1:20	na	L
Sodium (mg)	250-500	70	337	100	J
Potassium (mg)	550	325	1,565	285	L
Magnesium (mg)	150	25	120	80	K
Iron (mg)	14	3.25	16	112	J
Copper (mg)	1	0.05	0.2	24	L
Zinc (mg)	10	1.5	7	70	L
Iodine (mg)	0.15	0.003	0.014	10	L

Key: RDA = recommended daily allowance, DER = daily energy requirement, na = not applicable, J = meets the optimal recommendations, K = does not meet the optimal recommendations but is neither deficient nor excessive, L = deficient or excessive.
*Adapted from Gesellschaft für Ernährungsphysiologie Ausschuß für Bedarfsnormen. Energie-und Nährstoffbedarf Nr. 5 Hunde. Frankfurt, Germany: DLG Verlag, 1989. Meyer H, Heckötter E. Futterwerttabellen für Hunde und Katzen. Hannover, Germany: Schlütersche Verlaganstalt und Druckerei, 1986. National Research Council. Nutrient Requirements of Dogs. Washington, DC: National Academy Press, 1985. Randoin L, Le Gallic P, Dupuis Y, et al. Tables de composition des aliments. Institut Scientifique d'Hygiène Alimentaire, 6th ed. Malakoff, France: LT Editions J. Lanore,1990. Watt BK, Merrill AL. Composition of Foods-Raw, Processed, Prepared. Agriculture Handbook No 8. Washington, DC: Agricultural Research Service, USDA, 1975.

animals (e.g., cats) developed more efficient pathways to use these nutrients, and have lost the ability or have a decreased ability to synthesize them from precursors. (See Chapter 11.) Being omnivorous and receiving a varied diet of plant and animal tissue, dogs maintained or improved the ability to synthesize nutrients from precursors. These differences lend more evidence to early evolutionary divergence[20] and further support the premise that dogs are omnivores.

Table 9-5 compares the recommendations for daily nutrient intake of adult dogs to the nutrient content of meat (ground beef). This comparison confirms that an all-meat food would not be balanced for dogs. Specific aspects of nutritional requirements of dogs are discussed in subsequent sections of this chapter and in Chapter 2.

LIFESTAGE NUTRITION

Lifestage nutrition is the practice of feeding animals foods designed to meet their optimal nutritional needs at a specific age or physiologic state (e.g., maintenance, reproduction, growth or senior). The concept of lifestage nutrition recognizes that feeding either below or above an optimal nutrient concentration can negatively affect biologic performance or health. (See Chapter 2, Figure 2-2.) This concept differs markedly from feeding a single product for "all lifestages" (all-purpose foods) whereby nutrients are added at levels to meet the highest potential need (usually growth and reproduction). Adult animals at maintenance are always provided nutrients well in excess of their biologic needs when fed all-purpose foods. Because the goals in nutrition are to feed for optimal health, performance and longevity, feeding foods designed to more closely meet individual needs is preferred. This philosophy is key to lifestage nutrition and preventive medicine. In addition to providing advice about animals' basic nutritional requirements, veterinarians should assess and minimize the nutrition-related health risks at each lifestage. For maximal benefit, risk assessment and prevention plans should begin well before the onset of disease.

The value of lifestage feeding is enhanced if risk factor management is incorporated into the feeding practice. In many instances, when the nutritional needs associated with a dog's age and physiologic state are combined with the nutritional goals of disease risk factor reduction, a more narrow, but optimal, range of nutrient recommendations results. Nearly all commercial dog foods meet or exceed the minimum nutrient requirements of dogs. However, certain nutrients may still be outside the desired range for optimal health or risk factor reduction. For dogs fed commercial foods, these nutrients require particular consideration and, thus, are referred to as nutrients of concern. As mentioned in Chapter 1, specific food factors such as digestibility and texture can also affect health and disease risk. Together, nutrients of concern and specific food factors are called key nutritional factors. In the following sections, the key nutritional factors for different lifestages of healthy dogs will be discussed, including those associated with reducing the risk of specific diseases and those involved with optimizing performance during different physiologic states. Dogs eating homemade foods are more at risk for developing nutrient deficiencies (e.g., too little calcium) and excesses (e.g.,

too much phosphorus); therefore, dogs fed homemade foods have a broader list of key nutritional factors than dogs fed commercial foods. (See Chapter 6.)

This chapter first covers feeding adult dogs, followed by reproducing dogs and then growing dogs. The adult dog section is divided into two parts: young to middle-aged dogs and older (senior) dogs. This chapter begins with feeding adult dogs because most dogs are adults, and the nutrient needs of adult dogs serve as a good basis for comparison of nutrient needs for other lifestages. Also, most of the general information about feeding dogs is presented in the adult dog section and is not repeated in the other sections of this chapter. Chapter 10 covers recommendations for feeding adult dogs for optimal physical performance.

YOUNG TO MIDDLE-AGED ADULT DOGS

Depending on breed, young to middle-aged dogs are those that are full grown (about 12 months old) and not over five to seven years old. Dogs are often considered older when they reach half their life expectancy.[21] The goals of nutritional management are to maximize longevity and quality of life (disease prevention). The most important health concerns that may benefit from proper nutritional management in this age group include dental disease, obesity and kidney disease. Also, many owners are concerned about outward appearances; thus, a "healthy coat" may be an additional goal.

Assessment

Assess the Animal

Animal assessment should be a structured process that includes: 1) obtaining an accurate and detailed history, 2) reviewing the medical record, 3) conducting a physical examination and 4) evaluating results of laboratory and other diagnostic tests. During assessment, the feeding goals should be established, risk factors for nutrition-related diseases considered and key nutritional factors identified.

HISTORY AND PHYSICAL EXAMINATION

For normal, healthy adult dogs, there is usually little need to obtain detailed nutritional information and the time available to obtain a dietary history and conduct a physical examination is often limited. A minimum dietary database for all canine patients should include: 1) the type of food fed to the dog (homemade, commercial, dry, moist, semi-moist, etc.), 2) recipes if homemade food represents the majority of the diet, 3) brand names of commercial foods, if known, 4) names of supplements, treats and snacks and 5) method of feeding (free choice, meal feeding, etc.). An extended dietary data base would include: 6) quantities fed, 7) recent changes in food type, intake and preferences, 8) access to food for other pets or livestock, 9) who in the family buys food for the pet, 10) who in the family feeds the pet and 11) appetite changes with estimates of magnitude and duration. The general type and level of activity (e.g., house pet, confined to kennel, working dog, etc.) and neuter status should be noted because these factors are important determinants of energy requirements. The dietary history should be expanded if

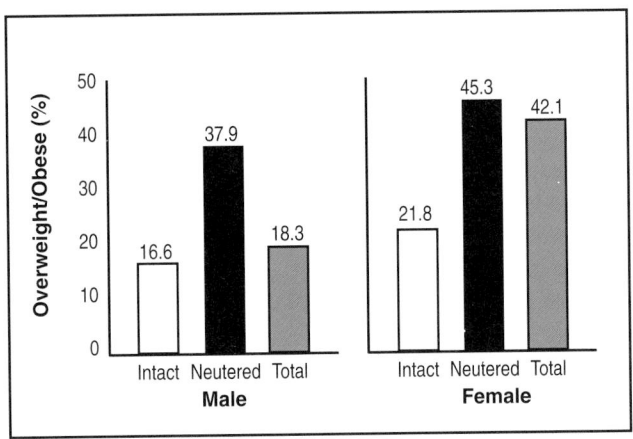

Figure 9-2. Percentage of overweight and obese dogs in intact, neutered and total female (3,828) and male (4,109) populations. (Adapted from Edney ATB, Smith PM. Study of obesity in dogs visiting veterinary practices in the United Kingdom. Veterinary Record 1986; 118: 391-396.)

Table 9-6. Influence of age on daily energy requirements of dogs.*

| Age (years) | Typical DER ranges** | | |
	kcal ME/BW$_{kg}^{0.75}$	kJ ME/BW$_{kg}^{0.75}$	x RER
1-2	120-140	500-585	1.7-2.0
3-7	100-130	420-550	1.4-1.9
>7	80-120	335-500	1.1-1.7

Key: DER = daily energy requirement, ME = metabolizable energy, RER = resting energy requirement, kcal = kilocalories, kJ = kilojoules.
*See Appendix C.
**The energy requirements indicated in this table are only starting points and should be adapted for individual dogs.

nutrition-related problems such as obesity are identified in the initial evaluation of the patient.

Body weight, body condition score (BCS) (See Chapter 1.), oral health and overall appearance of the skin and coat of all adult dogs should be assessed and recorded in the medical record. These parameters are general indicators of nutritional adequacy. An otherwise healthy young to middle-aged adult dog with normal body weight, skin and coat and BCS (3/5) and no evidence of significant dental disease is unlikely to need further nutritional assessment.

Gender and Neuter Status

No controlled studies have been performed to delineate differences in nutritional requirements of intact male vs. intact female dogs. It may be presumed that, like other mammals, intact females require less caloric intake than intact males. If this assumption is true it is probably because of gender-related differences in lean body mass. Lean body mass accounts for nearly all of an animal's resting energy requirement (RER).[22] Women require fewer calories than men because of a lower relative amount of lean body mass than men.[23] One study showed that female dogs had an average of 16% more body fat than male dogs,[24] and surveys found a much higher prevalence of overweight and obese female than male dogs (Figure 9-2).[25,26] These findings suggest that intact female dogs may need fewer calories than intact males.

Obesity occurs twice as often in neutered dogs than in reproductively intact dogs (Figure 9-2).[25] Very little is known, however, about the pathophysiology of this phenomenon. Neutering does not appear to have a marked impact on the resting energy expenditure of female dogs;[27] however, it may significantly increase food intake.[28] The increased food intake in neutered bitches is thought to be a consequence of a reduction of appetite-suppressing estrogen activity.[28,29] A decrease in physical activity is also assumed to occur in many dogs after neutering and may play a more important role in male dogs because of a decrease in roaming.[30,31] The daily energy intake should be limited to prevent rapid weight gain in neutered dogs; 1.6 x RER is a good starting point. For some breeds and individual dogs, it may be necessary to lower intake of neutered dogs to 1.2 to 1.4 x RER. (See Chapters 1 and 2.)

Breed

The breed classification should be determined in the initial assessment. Different breeds may be at risk for specific diseases or metabolic alterations that require nutritional management. As an example, certain canine breeds appear to be predisposed to obesity. (See Chapter 13.) In addition, DER differences have been delineated among different breeds, possibly because of differences in lean body mass, temperament and activity level. As examples, Newfoundland dogs have energy requirements about 15% less than average,[32] whereas Great Danes and Dalmatians may have energy requirements up to 16% higher than average.[32-35] Careful attention to specific local lineage and personal clinical impressions of breed differences may prove useful in food recommendations.

Activity Level

Activity significantly influences the energy requirements of individual dogs and should be taken into account when estimating energy requirements. For example, standing requires 40% more energy than lying down.[36] DER may range from RER for sedentary dogs to almost 15 x RER for endurance athletes under extreme conditions.[37] A consistently higher level of physical activity probably would result in a relative increase in lean body mass, which would result in an increase in energy usage, even at rest.[22] However, because the activity of individual dogs often cannot be defined precisely, feeding recommendations should initially be conservative to avoid overfeeding and the risk of obesity. Food intake should be adapted as needed to maintain optimal body weight. Chapter 10 presents more information about the influence of specific nutrients on athletic performance. (See sidebar "Special Nutritional Considerations for Stressed Dogs.")

Sedentary Animals

Estimations for DER include enough energy to support spontaneous activity, such as eating, sleeping, going outside and up to three hours of play and exercise per day. However, many dogs are relatively inactive, particularly those in urban areas. Approximately 19% of owners never play with their dogs and 22% take their dogs out for exercise fewer than three hours per week.[38]

Active and Sporting Dogs

Dogs and horses are often regarded as the elite athletes of domesticated mammals.[39] Greyhounds are sprint athletes and can reach average speeds of 56 to 60 km/hour (35 to 37.5 miles/hour) over typical race distances.[40] Sled dogs are endurance athletes and can maintain a trot of about 16 km/hour (10 miles/hour) for 10 to 14 hours per day for several consecutive days.[41] Energy requirements of dogs performing work between the two extremes of sedentary dogs and sled dogs need to be tailored to the individual. (See Chapter 10.)

Age

Age-related changes occur between the onset of adulthood and five to seven years of age. The prevalence of dental disease, obesity and kidney disease will generally increase over this time span. (See Chapters 13, 16 and 19). Apart from reproduction and imposed activity during work or sport, age may be the single most important factor influencing DER of most adult dogs (Table 9-6).[42]

Environment

The influence of the environment should not be neglected when evaluating energy and nutrient requirements. Temperature, humidity, type of housing, stress level and the

---

Special Nutritional Considerations for Stressed Dogs

STRESS

Police dogs, sentry dogs and other working dogs may refuse to eat, lose weight, develop diarrhea or become reluctant to work without obvious reason. Physiologically induced weight loss is most common in sentry dogs, in which a combination of stress, weather extremes and activity may result in loss of up to 10% of body weight during a six-hour tour of duty. Stress stimulates release of cortisol and induces a discharge of catecholamines. Besides stimulating alertness, catecholamines may depress food intake in stressed animals by activating the β-adrenergic and dopaminergic receptors in the lateral hypothalamus. This is obvious in highly stressed sentry dogs that may be reluctant to eat the volume of food they need to meet energy requirements. Dogs in various stressful situations demonstrate the same behavior. Some show dogs and racing greyhounds eat sparingly when the owner/handler prepares to depart to a show or a competition. A decrease in food intake, a slight increase in energy requirement and the catabolic effect of cortisol justify feeding a food with increased fat content (at least about 15% dry matter [DM]) and a protein level of about 25% DM. This recommendation does not compensate for energy spent for activity in addition to the stress (e.g., long-distance performances in which fat must be further increased to meet additional energy requirements).

Changing environments such as boarding or hospitalization may influence food intake due to stress. Dogs may develop diarrhea or refuse to eat when boarded. Practitioners commonly see dogs that refuse to eat in the hospital, but readily eat at home.

EFFECTS OF THE SHOW CIRCUIT

The success of a show dog is determined by genetics, general health, socialization, training and nutrition. Therefore, the preparation of a show dog starts with the correct choice of the parents, sound breeding practices and correct raising of puppies. Good nutrition allows for optimal expression of inherited qualities of a dog. Nutrition of a show dog involves feeding for correct development of skeleton and dentition, and maintenance of long-term health. More specific to show dogs are the nutritional needs for optimal condition of skin and coat, and the support of stress.

Preparation for the show may require particular attention. Skin health and correct color, length and glossiness of the hair are important for adult show dogs. The first requirement for a shiny coat is good overall health and nutrition throughout the year. See Chapter 15 for more information about nutritional effects on skin and coat.

Some show dogs may be finicky eaters, so they may need to be fed a more concentrated, palatable food, containing 25 to 30% DM protein and ≥15% DM fat. During a show, dogs don't spend much energy for physical activity; the primary increase is probably due to stress. In general a food that supports the health of skin and coat will provide all the nutrients needed to counteract stress.

EFFECTS OF MULTI-DOG HOUSEHOLDS

Individually housed dogs with limited exercise may have daily energy requirements (DER) as low as 90 to 95 kcal (375 to 400 kJ) metabolizable energy (ME) /BW$_{kg}^{0.75}$, or 1.3 x resting energy requirement (RER). When housed in kennels with other dogs in situations where much mutual interaction occurs, DER may increase to 130 to 140 kcal (545 to 585 kJ) ME/BW$_{kg}^{0.75}$, or 1.9 to 2.0 x RER or more.

In the United States, 46% of dog-owning families have more than one dog and many families own more than one species. Some dogs may increase their interest in food when a new pet is introduced to a household, whereas others refuse to eat for a day or two. Jealousy may arise over food, bones or toys, or over space in the bed. Dogs may defend their food bowl and raise the hair on their crest, withers and back or growl. Free-choice feeding may have a quieting effect in kennels or multiple-dog households, and less dominant dogs may have a better chance to get their share of the food provided. In some cases, dogs need to be fed in separate places. However, those situations are often created by the owner's intervention in the pecking order.

BIBLIOGRAPHY

American Animal Hospital Association. Fourth Annual Pet Survey. Trends Magazine April/May 1995; 30-31.

Ganong WF. Central regulation of visceral function. In: Review of Medical Physiology, 17th ed. Norwalk, CT: Appleton & Lange, 1995; 210-232.

Ganong WF. The autonomic nervous system. In: Review of Medical Physiology, 17th ed. Norwalk, CT: Appleton & Lange, 1995; 203-209.

Gesellschaft für Ernährungsphysiologie. Grunddaten für die Berechnung des Energie- und Nährstoffbedarfs. In: Ausschuß für Bedarfsnormen der Gesellschaft für Ernährungs-Physiologie Energie-Nährstoffbedarf/Energy and Nutrient Requirements, No. 5 Hunde/Dogs, Frankfurt/Main, Germany: DLG Verlag, 1989; 9-31.

Houpt KA. Feeding and drinking behavior problems. Veterinary Clinics of North America: Small Animal Practice 1991; 21: 281-298.

Knol BW, Dieleman SJ, Bevers MM, et al. Novelty stress in male dogs: The responses of plasma luteinizing hormone, testosterone and cortisol. European Society of Veterinary Internal Medicine Newsletter 1994; 4: 17.

Knol BW, Dieleman SJ, Bevers MM, et al. Social stress in dominant and subordinate male dogs: The responses of plasma luteinizing hormone, testosterone and cortisol. European Society of Veterinary Internal Medicine Newsletter 1994; 4: 18.

McNamara JH. Nutrition for working dogs under stress. Veterinary Medicine/Small Animal Clinician 1972; 67: 614-623.

Meyer H. Energie und Nährstoffe-Stoffwechsel und Bedarf. In: Ernährung des Hundes, 2nd ed. Stuttgart, Germany: E Ulmer Verlag, 1990; 67-125.

Meyer H, Stadtfeld G. Investigations on the body and organ structure of dogs. In: Anderson RS, ed. Nutrition of the Dog and Cat. Oxford, UK: Pergamon Press, 1980; 15-30.

Zentek J, Dämmrich K, Meyer H. Untersuchungen zum Cu-Mangel beim wachsenden Hund. Zentralblatt für Veterinär Medizin A (Journal of Veterinary Medicine A) 1991; 38: 561-570.

Zentek J. Ernährungsbedingte Hauterkrankungen-Bedeutung von Spurenelementen und Vitaminen. Kleintierpraxis 1991; 37: 157-162.

degree of acclimatization should be considered with respect to breed and lifestage nutrient requirements of animals. (See sidebar "Special Nutritional Considerations for Stressed Dogs.") Animal factors including insulative characteristics of skin and coat (i.e., subcutaneous fat, hair length and coat density) and differences in stature, behavior and activity interact and affect DER.

When kept outside in cold weather, dogs may need 10 to 90% more energy than during optimal weather conditions.[36,43] Heat losses are minimal at a temperature called the lower critical temperature.[44] This is the environmental temperature at which dogs reach their minimum metabolic rate. It is breed specific and is lower when the thermic insulation (i.e., coat density and length) is greater.[34,36,45-47] The lower critical temperature is estimated at 15 to 20°C (59 to 68°F) for longhaired breeds, 20 to 25°C (68 to 77°F) for shorthaired breeds and may be as low as 10 to 15°C (50 to 59°F) for arctic breeds.[35,45-47]

Only a small amount of energy is expended to dissipate heat at temperatures above the thermoneutral zone; however, increased amounts of water are required. (See sidebar "Nutrients Used for Body Cooling.")

Housing conditions may influence energy and water requirements by modifying the immediate environment. Many housing options are possible; however, any shelter with temperatures closer to the thermoneutral zone will decrease energy requirements in cold environments and water requirements in hot environments (i.e., protection from wind chill, excess sun, etc.). Conversely, shelters that move dogs further away from the thermoneutral zone will have the opposite effects (e.g., closed spaces in hot humid conditions, damp shady shelters in cold weather). The number of dogs in a shelter may also affect the adequacy of the housing; increased numbers of dogs will increase the temperature in the local environment.[44,46]

LABORATORY AND OTHER CLINICAL INFORMATION

Healthy young to middle-aged adult dogs require few laboratory and other diagnostic tests as part of routine assessment. The most common extended database includes a fecal examination for intestinal parasites, tests for heartworm infection and fundic examination. (See Chapter 8.) For dogs older than five years, a urinalysis performed on a fresh urine specimen collected after an all-night fast is added. A complete blood count, serum biochemistry profile and urinalysis should be obtained for ill adult dogs and those with suspected abnormal nutrition.

KEY NUTRITIONAL FACTORS

Table 9-7 summarizes key nutritional factors for young to middle-aged adult dogs. The following section describes these key nutritional factors in more detail.

Water

Water accounts for approximately 56% of an adult dog's body weight (73% of lean body mass).[48] The body has a limited capacity to store water, and although healthy dogs can replenish a water deficit of up to 8% of body weight in a few minutes,[49] water deprivation will result in death more quickly than withholding any other nutrient.[50] Therefore, it can be argued that water is the most important nutrient of all.

Total water intake (i.e., drinking and water from food) is influenced by several factors such as environment, physiologic state, activity, disease processes and composition of the food. Total water intake increases almost linearly with increasing salt levels in food.[49,51] Switching from a moist to a dry food and vice versa markedly affects the amount of water taken with the food; however, dogs compensate well for this difference by changing the quantity of water they drink, thus keeping their total daily water intake constant.[51] In general, dogs self-regulate water intake according to physiologic need. Requirements may be met by allowing free access to a source of potable water.[50] Healthy adult dogs need roughly the equivalent of the energy

---

Nutrients Used for Body Cooling

When ambient temperature exceeds a dog's thermoneutral zone, water and energy are used for heat loss. The ability of dogs (and people) to withstand extremely high ambient temperatures is well-demonstrated by a study conducted in 1775 by Blagden. It was reported that Blagden, and a dog in a basket (to protect its feet from being burned), entered a room kept at a 126°C (259°F) and remained there for 45 minutes. A steak he took with him was cooked; however, he and the dog were unaffected.

Bodies cool by radiation, conduction, convection and vaporization of water. As the ambient temperature increases, the conditions for heat loss by radiation, conduction and convection become increasingly unfavorable. When the ambient temperature exceeds the dog's body temperature, the dog's entire metabolic heat production and the heat received from the environment by conduction, convection and radiation must be removed by evaporation of water to maintain normal body temperature.

Vaporization of water can occur via insensible perspiration, respiration, panting and sweating. Dogs have few sweat glands and thus must pant to evaporate additional water for cooling. Panting is facilitated by the elastic properties of the thorax and respiratory system. Depending on the size of the dog, the respiratory apparatus oscillates to a natural frequency (the resonant frequency of the chest is proportional to the square root of the body mass). The amount of cooling is regulated by the duration of panting. If not for resonant elasticity, the increased muscular effort of breathing would generate more heat than the total heat that could be dissipated by panting. As a result of these elastic properties, however, panting requires only a small amount of energy.

The amount of heat lost via vaporization of water is approximately 580 kcal (2,426 kJ)/kg water. In hot desertlike conditions, in which the heat gained from the environment can be 10 times the metabolic heat production, the water required for cooling a 15-kg dog may equal 2.5% of its body mass per hour. At this rate, if uncompensated for evaporative water loss, a dog could experience a 10% reduction of its total body water within 2.5 hours. Thus, from a nutritional perspective, dogs in hot environments may have a significant increase in water requirement with only a small increase in energy needs to maintain normal body temperature.

BIBLIOGRAPHY

Blaxter K. Energy exchanges by radiation, convection, conduction and evaporation. In: Energy Metabolism in Animals and Man. Cambridge, UK: Cambridge University Press, 1989; 86-119.

Schmidt-Nielsen K. Temperature regulation. In: Animal Physiology: Adaptation and Environment. New York, NY: Cambridge University Press, 1990; 240-295.

Table 9-7. Key nutritional factors for adult dogs at maintenance.

Factors	Recommended levels in food (DM)		
	Young to middle age	Obese prone	Older
Energy density (kcal ME/g)*	3.5-4.5	3.0-3.5	3.0-4.0
Energy density (kJ ME/g)*	14.6-18.8	12.5-14.6	12.5-16.7
Crude protein (%)	15-30	15-30	15-23
Crude fat (%)	10-20	7-12	7-15
Crude fiber (%)**	≤5	≥5	≥2.0
Calcium (%)	0.5-1.0	0.5-1.0	0.5-1.0
Phosphorus (%)	0.4-0.9	0.4-0.9	0.25-0.75
Ca/P ratio	1:1-2:1	1:1-2:1	1:1-2:1
Sodium (%)	0.2-0.4	0.2-0.4	0.15-0.35
Chloride (%)	0.3-0.6	0.3-0.6	0.3-0.5

Key: DM = dry matter, kcal = kilocalories, kJ = kilojoules, ME = metabolizable energy.
*If the caloric density of the food is different, the nutrient content in the dry matter must be adapted accordingly. (See Chapter 1.)
**Crude fiber measurements underestimate total dietary fiber levels in food. See text below.

requirement in kcal metabolizoble energy (ME)/day, expressed in ml/day.[52] During warm weather, enough water must be available to compensate for evaporation by panting.[49] (See sidebar "Nutrients Used for Body Cooling.")

Energy

Domestic canids are the most diverse mammalian species in body weight and size. Therefore, energy requirements are not correlated with kg body weight in a linear way, but are more closely related to metabolic weight ($BW_{kg}^{0.75}$).[53,54] Recommendations for daily energy intake of adult, non-athletic, non-reproducing dogs have varied from 85 kcal (355 kJ) $ME/BW_{kg}^{0.75}$ to more than 220 kcal (920 kJ) ME per kg body weight to the three-fourths power.[34,55,56] This range may confuse dog owners, but it is not surprising considering that the DER of a particular dog is markedly influenced by breed, neuter status, age, daily activity, environmental temperature and insulative characteristics of the integument.[32,33,35,36,45,54,57,58,62] Graphically, the DER for a population of dogs results in a bell-shaped curve; therefore, the energy intake of individual dogs may vary by about 50% above or below the average requirements, even within the same age group. (See Figure 1-4.) The RER, however, is not markedly influenced by these factors, and is similar for all dogs, independent of breed or age. RER is approximately 70 kcal (293 kJ) per kg body weight to the three-fourths power.[54,59] (See Chapter 1.)

Because DER is the sum of RER plus all the above influences, it is better to use RER as the basis for calculating energy requirements of adult dogs and to assign different multipliers to account for differences in activity, age and environmental influences. When assigning multipliers to RER, it is important to account for neuter status because this variable can be an important factor in determining DER of household dogs. Neutered animals may have a lower DER than intact counterparts. Recent surveys have shown that the prevalence of obesity increases progressively to peak in middle-aged dogs.[60,61] Thus, prevention of obesity should be an important goal of feeding programs for young adult dogs. It is by far more beneficial to an animal to set up an appropriate weight-maintenance program than to treat obesity. (See Chapter 13.)

Three groups of adult dogs can be distinguished based on DER: 1) young adults one to two years old, 2) middle-aged dogs (three to seven years old) and 3) older dogs (more than seven years old) (Table 9-6).[32,33,42,62] The differences in DER probably reflect an age-related decrease in activity and lean body mass. A good starting point for estimating the DER of a neutered adult dog would be 1.6 x RER (115 kcal [480 kJ] $ME/BW_{kg}^{0.75}$). Most household dogs between two and seven years old would probably have a DER between 1.4 to 1.9 x RER (100 to 130 kcal [420 to 550 kJ] $ME/BW_{kg}^{0.75}$) with the higher number being used in the lower age group and the lower end being applied to the higher age group (Table 9-6). Alternatively, Table 1-7 may be used to assign different multipliers of RER that may be used as estimates of DER variation in this age group. All initial estimates of energy needs must subsequently be evaluated by body condition assessment and adjusted as needed for individual dogs.

Sedentary dogs may have a DER that approaches their RER. Sedentary dogs fed caloric intakes recommended for maintenance (1.6 x RER) will be overfed and are likely to become overweight. Based on Männer's and Heusner's work, a recommendation of 1.2 to 1.3 x RER (85 to 90 kcal [355 to 375 kJ] $ME/BW_{kg}^{0.75}$/day) seems to be a good starting point for feeding sedentary dogs.[35,45,55,56] It has been estimated that sled dogs may require more than 10,000 kcal/day (41.8 MJ/day) (up to 15 x RER) to maintain body weight under racing conditions.[37]

Table 9-7 lists recommended energy density levels for foods intended for young to middle-aged adult dogs. The levels of dietary fat and fiber are important determinants of a food's energy density. Fat provides more than twice as much energy on a weight basis than carbohydrate or protein. High-fat foods have increased energy density; conversely, low-fat foods have decreased energy density. Fiber is a poor source of energy for dogs; thus, as the fiber content of foods increases, energy density decreases. Dietary fiber reduces the energy density of the food and helps promote satiety. (See Chapters 2 and 13.) Inclusion of fiber in foods may therefore help maintain ideal body weight in dogs fed free choice. In pet foods, fiber is listed as crude fiber, which is an imprecise measure because most soluble fiber is omitted. A better measure would be total dietary fiber; however, regulations only permit declaration of crude fiber because no method for determination of total dietary fiber is yet officially recognized for pet foods. It is difficult to determine the optimal concentration of crude fiber in a complete food for dogs; however, up to 5% DM seems to be adequate. Obese-prone dogs may benefit from 10 to 15% crude fiber on a dry matter basis (DMB). Foods that are both low in fat and high in fiber tend to have the lowest energy density and are recommended for obese-prone dogs. Table 9-7 lists recommended levels of dietary fat and fiber. (See Chapter 13.)

Phosphorus and Calcium

Minimum requirements for calcium and phosphorus for adult dogs are not very different from those established for other mammals. Commercial foods contain adequate and sometimes excessive amounts of calcium and phosphorus and, therefore, should not be supplemented. However, calcium is often deficient and phosphorus may be excessive in homemade foods, especially when most of the diet comes from meat and leftovers from the table (Table 9-5). Existing commercial multiple vitamin-mineral mixes (powders, tablets, etc.) are seldom designed to correct imbalances encountered in homemade foods. When formulating homemade foods, it is better to add mineral sources such as calcium carbonate and/or dicalcium phosphate salt, which are available from drug stores and pharmacies, to correct calcium-phosphorus imbalances. (See Chapter 6.)

Based on endogenous losses, a daily intake of 100 mg calcium/kg body weight and 75 mg phosphorus/kg body weight is adequate.[63] At an energy density of 3.5 kcal (14.6 kJ)/g DM this corresponds to an average dry matter content of about 0.5 to 0.8% calcium and 0.4 to 0.6% phosphorus. Table 9-7 lists recommended levels of phosphorus and calcium for foods intended for young to middle-aged adult dogs and with energy density varying from 3.5 to 4.5 kcal/g. The calcium-phosphorus ratio in dog foods should not be less than 1:1.[53,54]

The above mentioned levels are adequate but not excessive; even a daily intake of 20 to 30% less is still sufficient.[63] Therefore, it is unnecessary to feed foods with higher levels of phosphorus, or to supplement commercial foods with calcium-phosphorus supplements. Moreover, higher levels are even contraindicated for a substantial part of the dog population; up to 25% of the young adult dog population may already be affected by subclinical kidney disease.[64-66] One clinical study revealed that 22.4% of all dogs over five years of age examined at a European veterinary teaching hospital for a variety of reasons had abnormally elevated kidney function tests.[67] Excess dietary phosphorus can accelerate progression of chronic renal disease,[68] whereas phosphorus restriction may slow the progression of chronic renal disease and improve long-term survival.[68-70] It is therefore prudent to feed foods that are adequate but not excessive in phosphorus. (See Chapter 19 for more information about mechanisms of excess dietary phosphorus in the progression of kidney disease.)

Protein

The amount of protein in commercial foods for healthy dogs varies widely (15 to 60% DM). (See Appendix L.) After the amino acid requirements are met for an individual animal, addition of more protein provides no known benefit. This fact often runs contrary to popular belief that more protein is better. Also, the addition of extra protein in commercial dog foods sometimes marketed as necessary for carnivores misrepresents the fact that dogs are omnivores. Excess dietary protein, above the amino acid requirement, is not stored as protein, but rather is deaminated by the liver. Subsequently, the kidneys excrete the by-products of protein catabolism and the remaining keto acid analogues are used for energy or stored as fat.

The subject of whether excess dietary protein contributes to the progression of subclinical kidney disease has yet to be resolved. (See Chapter 19.) Studies in people suggest that protein restriction may help slow progression of kidney disease.[71,72] Aside from any potential aggravating effects excess dietary protein may have on subclinical kidney disease, note that foods high in protein are often also high in phosphorus. As mentioned above, excess dietary phosphorus has been shown to accelerate the progression of kidney disease in dogs.

Minimum protein requirements for healthy adult dogs eating high-quality protein have been determined using nitrogen balance and endogenous nitrogen excretion. A more reliable estimate based on endogenous nitrogen excretion equates to a minimum requirement of 1.7 g metabolizable protein/$BW_{kg}^{0.75}$ for an ideal protein.[54,73,74] When protein of average quality is used (biologic value of about 70), the minimum requirements are increased to 2.1 to 2.5 g digestible protein per kg body weight to the three-fourths power.[75]

The minimum crude protein content of food depends on digestibility and quality. For example, if the digestibility of an average quality protein is 75%, then about 12% DM crude protein is adequate. Foods containing less than 12% DM crude protein must be of higher biologic value. Biologic value becomes less important for healthy adult dogs if foods contain crude protein levels greater than 12%. A daily protein intake for adult maintenance of 4.3 to 5.0 g digestible protein/$BW_{kg}^{0.75}$ (biologic value = 70) or 4.0 to 6.5 g digestible protein/100 kcal ME is recommended.[75] Table 9-7 lists recommended levels of crude protein for foods for young to middle-aged adult dogs.

Sodium and Chloride

Essential hypertension is not considered a common problem in dogs; therefore, higher intakes of dietary sodium and chloride have not been considered harmful in young, healthy dogs.[76,77] However, one study suggested that up to 10% of apparently healthy dogs may have high blood pressure.[78]

High sodium and chloride intake is contraindicated in dogs with certain diseases that may have a hypertensive component such as obesity, renal disease and some endocrinopathies.[79-83] Uncontrolled high blood pressure may lead to kidney, brain, eye, heart and cardiovascular damage.[80,82] Dietary sodium chloride restriction is the first step in and an important part of antihypertensive therapy.[80,82,83]

It is prudent to meet but not greatly exceed sodium and chloride requirements when selecting foods for adult dogs. The best estimate for a minimum requirement of sodium is about 4 mg/kg body weight/day.[84] In general, 25 to 50 mg/kg body weight/day[63] is recommended for adult maintenance; these levels are six to 12 times more than the minimum. A content of 0.15 to 0.4% DM sodium will provide this recommended intake level. Sodium levels in commercial foods for adult dogs range from 0.11 to 2.2% DM and are higher in moist foods than in dry foods. (See Appendix L.) In the absence of studies establishing chloride requirements in dogs, a value 1.5 times the sodium requirement is recommended. Table 9-7 lists recommended levels of sodium and chloride in foods intended for young to middle-aged adult dogs.

Fat and Essential Fatty Acids

Fats are an excellent source of energy, but the real requirement for fat is to supply essential fatty acids (EFAs). In addition, fat serves as a carrier for the absorption of fat-soluble vitamins (A, D, E and K). Linoleic acid and α-linolenic acid are considered essential because dogs lack the enzymes to synthesize them.[85] Linoleic acid (18:22n-6) is the parent fatty acid of the n-6 series, and α-linolenic acid of the n-3 series. EFAs have structural functions in cell membranes and are precursors of eicosanoids such as prostaglandins, thromboxanes and leukotrienes.[54,86] Linoleic acid deficiency results in two primary skin defects: hyperproliferation and increased permeability to water.[87] The epidermal water barrier consists of lamellae of lipids (sphingolipids) in the stratum corneum of the epidermis. Linoleic acid is incorporated into the ceramide-portion of sphingolipids, where it provides the specific characteristics needed for barrier function.[87] In addition, linoleic acid plays a role in fertility.[86] Ensuring an adequate intake of EFAs is key to maintaining normal skin and coat.

Whether n-3 fatty acids are essential is less certain because of the inability of n-3 fatty acids to support all of the physiologic functions that are supported by n-6 fatty acids.[86] Nevertheless, a source of dietary n-3 fatty acids is often recommended.[85] N-3 fatty acids are abundant in membrane lipids, especially in retinal and neural tissues. N-3 fatty acids may moderate excessively vigorous actions of n-6-derived eicosanoids.[86] (See Chapter 26.)

The minimum amount of fat in foods for normal, healthy adult dogs is at least 5% DMB, with at least 1% of the food as linoleic acid (DMB).[54] A source of dietary n-3 fatty acids is also recommended. Increasing the amount of fat in foods increases palatability and EFA levels; however, energy content also increases. Table 9-7 lists recommended levels of fat for foods intended for young to middle-aged adult dogs. Note that lower levels of dietary fat are recommended for obese-prone adult dogs.

OTHER NUTRITIONAL FACTORS

Food Texture
Periodontal disease is the most common health problem of adult dogs[88] and may predispose affected animals to systemic complications.[89] Periodontal disease can be prevented in many animals with routine veterinary care and frequent plaque control at home. Feeding recommendations for oral health commonly include feeding a dry pet food.[90] However, typical dry dog foods contribute little dental cleansing and the general statement that dry foods provide significant oral cleansing should be regarded with skepticism. Research has demonstrated that a maintenance dog food with specific textural properties and processing techniques can significantly decrease plaque and calculus accumulation and maintain gingival health. (See Chapter 16.)

Assess the Food(s)

After the nutritional status of the dog has been assessed and the key nutritional factors and their target levels determined, the adequacy of the food is assessed. The three most useful components when assessing foods for normal adult dogs are to: 1) ensure that the food has been tested or fed to dogs, 2) determine the food's dry matter nutrient content (especially for the key nutritional factors) and 3) compare the food's key nutritional factors with the recommended levels (Table 9-7).

Whether or not commercial foods for healthy pets have been animal tested can usually be determined from the nutritional adequacy statement on the product's label. (See Chapter 5.) Few, if any, homemade recipes have been animal tested according to prescribed feeding protocols. Commercial pet foods that have undergone Association of American Feed Control Official's (AAFCO) prescribed or other feeding tests provide reasonable assurance of nutrient availability and sufficient palatability to ensure acceptability (i.e., food intake sufficient to meet nutrient needs). However, even controlled animal testing is not infallible. Passing such tests does not ensure the food will be effective in preventing long-term nutritional/health problems. Likewise, problems with a specific food may go undetected in the feeding trial if the prevalence rate of the problem is less than 15%.[b] Thus, in addition to having passed feeding tests, the food should be evaluated to ensure that key nutritional factors are at levels appropriate for promoting long-term health and optimal performance for the intended lifestage.

Appendices L and M provide partial nutrient profiles for selected commercial foods and treats sold in the United States, Canada and Europe. In most instances, these profiles provide the necessary information about a food's or treat's nutrient content. The manufacturer should be contacted if the food or treat in question cannot be found in the appendices. Manufacturers' addresses and toll-free phone numbers are listed on pet food labels.

Comparing a food's nutrient content with the animal's nutrient needs will help identify any significant nutritional imbalances in the food being fed. This comparison is fundamental to determining whether or not to feed a different food.

The energy density of a food is an important aspect to consider when assessing foods. For example, if each of two foods contain 20% protein (DMB) but one food has an energy density of 4.5 kcal ME/g DM and the other 3.5 kcal ME/g DM, the former will provide about 25% less protein on a daily basis than the latter. This comparison, however, is not valid for foods intended for obese or obese-prone dogs and foods for active, sporting dogs. Fat is the most important contributor to a food's energy density, conversely fiber decreases a food's energy density.[91,92] Foods with a low fat content and a high fiber level tend to have the lowest energy density.

Commercial treats, snacks and table food should also be included in the food assessment step because they are part of the total food intake of an animal and, if misused, may create an imbalance in an otherwise balanced feeding plan. Excessive feeding of treats and snacks may markedly affect the cumulative nutritional profile. (See sidebar "Impact of Treats on Daily Nutrient Intake.") The impact of snacks on daily nutrient intake depends on two factors: 1) the nutrient profile of the snack and 2) the number provided daily. Thus, if snacks are fed, it is prudent to recommend those that best match the nutritional profile recommended for a particular lifestage.

Assess the Feeding Method

It may not always be necessary to change the feeding method when managing healthy adult dogs in optimal body condition. However, a thorough evaluation includes verification that an appropriate feeding method is being used. In addition, future risk factors such as obesity should be considered when evaluating the current method. Current feeding methods should have been obtained when the history was taken.

The objective of this part of the assessment process is to establish how much food has been fed and how it has been offered (i.e., when, where, by whom and how often). An important determinant of food intake in domestic dogs is the owner and family situation because these factors usually control the amounts and types of food fed.[93-96] Studies show that owners typically feed their dogs one (26 to 77% of owners) to two (19 to 50% of owners) meals per day.[38,94,97] In general, pet owners often overestimate needs and feed too much.[93] Domestic dogs may eat several small meals each day when fed a commercial dry food free choice yet maintain an

Impact of Treats on Daily Nutrient Intake

From 60 to 86% of dog owners regularly give their pets commercial treats. If table foods are included, 90% or more of dogs receive treats, snacks and biscuits as a supplement to their regular food. People like to give treats and snacks for emotional reasons, to change their pet's behavior or to improve and maintain oral health. Because several daily treats will have a marked effect on a dog's cumulative nutritional intake, specific questions about treats should be asked when taking the dietary history. Specific recommendations about treats should be provided when prescribing a food regimen for diseased or healthy dogs. This information is critical when managing specific problems such as developmental orthopedic disease in growing large-breed dogs, adverse reactions to food, obesity, urolithiasis, diabetes mellitus, heart failure and renal disease.

The impact of snacks on a dog's daily nutrient intake depends on two factors: 1) the nutrient profile of the treat and 2) the number of treats provided daily. It is best to recommend a treat that matches the nutritional profile preferred for a given lifestage or disease. Snacks provide energy; a handful of dog snacks, for example, can easily be equivalent to 40% of a small dog's daily energy requirement (DER) or 10% of a large-breed dog's DER. Therefore, the owner must compensate for the additional energy by feeding less of the dog's usual food. This recommendation is especially important for dogs in which a small snack can have a marked impact (i.e., toy- and small-breed dogs). Appendix M provides nutritional profiles of selected popular treats sold in North America and Europe, as well as profiles of table foods commonly used as snacks.

The following two examples confirm the impact of treats on daily nutrient intake in dogs.

A six-year-old, neutered male miniature pinscher weighing 4.5 kg is fed two commercial biscuit treats per day, in addition to its regular food. Each biscuit provides 15 kcal (62.8 kJ), so the dog receives a total of 30 kcal (125.5 kJ) per day from the treats. The dog's DER is about 330 kcal (1,381 kJ). Therefore, the treats provide almost 10% of the dog's DER. If the dog's DER is being met with the regular food, then the treats may contribute to long-term excess energy intake and obesity.

A five-month-old, 20-kg, female German shepherd dog is given a commercial treat marketed as a snack with "real marrow bone." Calcium is not declared on the guaranteed or typical analysis of the treat label. The owner gives the dog 10 of these treats each day as part of a training program. This number of treats is within the feeding guidelines on the label. However, analysis shows that each treat contains 426 mg of calcium. Consuming 10 treats daily increases the dog's daily calcium intake by more than 80% compared with consuming a commercial food formulated for large-breed puppies. This feeding practice increases the risk of developmental orthopedic disease. (See Chapter 17.) To facilitate learning, dogs do not need to receive edible reinforcers every time and the pieces can be very small. If praise is paired with treats, praise alone will rapidly become sufficient reinforcement for the desired behavior.

BIBLIOGRAPHY

Campbell WE. Effects of training, feeding regimens, isolation, and physical environment on canine behavior. Modern Veterinary Practice 1986; 29: 239-241.

Earle KE. Calculations of energy requirements of dogs, cats and small psittacine birds. Journal of Small Animal Practice 1993; 34: 163-173.

Slater MR, Robinson LE, Zoran D, et al. Diet and exercise patterns in pet dogs. Journal of the American Veterinary Medical Association 1995; 207: 186-190.

Spreat S, Rogers-Spreat S. Learning principles. Veterinary Clinics of North America: Small Animal Practice 1982; 12: 593-606.

Voith VL. Attachment of people to companion animals. Veterinary Clinics of North America: Small Animal Practice 1985; 15: 289-295.

ideal body weight.[94] However, dogs fed a highly palatable, energy-dense food free choice may maintain body weight at a higher set point indicating a tendency toward obesity.[96]

Dogs are usually fed either free choice or in a restricted (time restricted or food restricted) fashion. Each method has advantages and disadvantages. Although free-choice feeding is most popular, it can lead to the most problems. Meal-restricted feeding is less popular and more time-consuming; however, it is more precise in delivering the required amount of food (Table 9-8). See Chapter 1 for an in-depth discussion of feeding methods.

Nutrient requirements of animals are met by a combination of nutrient levels in food and amounts fed. Even if a food has an appropriate nutrient profile, significant malnutrition may result if excess or insufficient amounts are consumed. If the animal in question has a normal BCS (3/5), the amount being fed is probably appropriate. The amount fed can be estimated either by calculation (See Chapter 1.) or by referring to feeding guides on product labels. Calculated estimates and feeding guides represent population averages and may need to be adjusted for individual dogs.

Table 9-8. Advantages and disadvantages of various feeding methods for dogs.

Feeding methods	Advantages	Disadvantages
Free-choice feeding	Less labor intensive Less knowledge required Quieting effect in a kennel Less dominant animals have a better chance to get their share	Less control over food intake Predisposes to obesity Less monitoring of individual changes in food intake
Meal-restricted feeding	Better control of food dose Early detection of altered appetite Better control of body weight	Intermediate labor intensive Most knowledge required for food dose calculation
Time-restricted feeding	Intermediate control of food dose Some monitoring of appetite possible	Inaccurate control of food intake Risk of obesity similar to free choice Most labor intensive

Alternative Eating Behaviors

RESPONSE TO FOOD VARIETY

Dogs may display preferences for specific types of foods according to taste and texture. However, the notion that dogs need a variety of flavors or taste in their meals is incorrect and may be detrimental in some instances. Dogs prefer novel foods or flavors to familiar foods; therefore, feeding a variety of novel foods free choice may lead to overeating and obesity. Dogs may correct for excessive energy intake by decreasing or refusing food intake the next day(s). Reduction of food intake to maintain weight following engorgement may erroneously be interpreted as a dislike of the current food instead of an autoregulatory mechanism to achieve the previous set-point weight.

GARBAGE EATING

Garbage eating is probably normal behavior. Many dogs prefer food in an advanced stage of decomposition. However, garbage eating is oftentimes unhealthy. Ingestion of garbage may cause brief, mild gastroenteritis or more serious intoxication. (See Chapter 7.) Because the etiology is complex and may involve bacterial toxins, mycotoxins and by-products from putrefaction or decomposition, the clinical signs vary widely from vomiting, diarrhea, abdominal pain, weakness, incoordination and dyspnea, to shock, coma and death. Scavenging dogs may eat less of their regular meal; therefore, garbage eating may be mistaken for anorexia at home.

Spraying garbage bags with a dog repellent usually will not stop the problem. Preventing access to garbage is the obvious best solution.

GRASS EATING

Owners often ask why dogs eat grass. Plant and grass eating is normal behavior. Herbivores are the natural prey for wolves and most other canids. The viscera of prey is often eaten first and contains partially digested vegetable material. Because dogs' ancestors and close relatives in the wild regularly ingest plant material, some investigators have suggested that domestic dogs must also eat grass. Probably the better explanation is that, to date, no one knows for sure why dogs eat plants or grass, but they may simply like the way plants taste or prefer the texture.

BEGGING FOR FOOD

Begging for food may be fun when dogs sit up or perform other tricks; however, the behavior can become annoying when whining, barking, persistent nudging and scratching take over. Begging for food was one of the most common complaints raised in a study involving more than 1,400 owners and was perceived as a problem in one-third of the dogs. In addition, begging may encourage owners to feed more of the dog's regular food. Begging tends to increase with age and may indicate that most owners don't realize that they reinforce begging by continuing to offer tidbits to their begging pet. All between-meal treats reinforce begging. Also, the fact that begging for food is directly proportional to the number of people in the family may be related to an increase in the number of tidbits fed.

Treatment consists of ignoring behaviors such as begging, barking and whining. Owners should be prepared for a prolonged period of such behaviors before begging subsides completely. Intermittent reinforcement of begging when these behaviors become too much can be more powerful than continuous rewarding, even though the owner may have refused to provide snacks in the interim. It may also help to keep the dog out of the kitchen and dining areas when preparing and eating food and to feed the dog before or after the family has eaten.

PICA

Pica is defined as perverted appetite with craving for and ingestion of non-food items. The etiology of true pica is unknown. Suggested causes include mineral deficiencies, permanent anxiety and psychological disturbances. A few cases of pica have been noted in relation to zinc intoxication and hepatic encephalopathy. Pica is common in dogs with exocrine pancreatic insufficiency, probably as a manifestation of polyphagia, and perhaps as a consequence of some specific nutritional deficiency. Sometimes, coprophagy and garbage eating are mistakenly considered forms of pica.

Pica can be treated with aversion therapy, by offering a counter attraction at the moment the dog begins to eat foreign material and by punishment if there is no response. Outdoors, the dog should be kept on a leash or even muzzled. Most treatments for pica are unrewarding. Physically preventing the animal from engaging in pica is sometimes the only solution.

COPROPHAGY

Coprophagy is defined as eating feces and may involve consumption of the animal's own stools or the feces of other animals. Coprophagy is probably widespread among pet dogs and is probably more disturbing to owners than it is harmful to dogs. Bitches normally eat the feces of their puppies during the first three weeks of lactation. In rural areas and in the free-living state, the ingestion of large-animal feces by dogs is also considered normal behavior. In many cases, however, coprophagy is a behavioral problem and the etiology is unknown. Coprophagy can also be related to certain diseases.

Continued on next page.

Finally, owners are often concerned about alternative eating behaviors displayed by their dogs. In fact, these behaviors may be more offensive to the owner than detrimental to the dog. Alternative eating behaviors may be of nutritional or non-nutritional origin, and some may be indicators of underlying disease. (See sidebar "Alternative Eating Behaviors.")

Feeding Plan

When done properly, assessment of the animal, the food and the feeding method should provide all the information necessary to develop a feeding plan. In some instances, the plan currently in effect may not need to be changed. In other cases, major changes may need to be made in foods and feeding methods. In either case it is necessary to reassess the animal at regular intervals as indicated in the specific lifestage sections below.

Select a Food(s)

A new food should be selected if significant differences are seen between the recommended nutrient levels and those in the food currently fed. The new food should provide the key nutritional factors in amounts listed in Table 9-7. Appendices L and M list nutrient levels of a number of readily available commercial dog foods and treats, or manufacturers can be contacted directly for the same information. Foods selected should also have passed AAFCO or similar feeding trials for adult dogs. As mentioned, this information is usually found on the pet food label.

Continued from previous page.

Table 1 lists behavioral and metabolic disorders that may be associated with coprophagy. The danger for transmission of parasitic diseases is probably the most important health reason for managing coprophagy; however, the associated halitosis is of primary concern to owners. The dog's motivation must be reduced in order to correct coprophagy. Several measures have been proposed.

Punishment may deter the animal's behavior, but may violate the confidence between owner and pet. Punishment may also aggravate the coprophagic behavior. Thus, a good balance has to be found. Walking the dog on a leash and keeping it away from feces after the dog defecates is helpful.

Repulsive substances can be used to create aversion for feces. Many different products have been recommended including spices (e.g., pepper, sambal, hot pepper sauce), quinine, strong perfumes and specific products such as cythioate, meat tenderizers and For-Bid.[a] Adding repulsive substances to feces can be time-consuming and has questionable efficacy.

Food changes to deter coprophagy have been recommended; however, most of these recommendations lack substantiation. Using foods with increased fiber levels has been reported to help. Free-choice feeding has also been recommended, whereas a strict schedule of two meals per day and avoiding all tidbits or table foods have worked for others.

ENDNOTE
a. Alpar Laboratories Inc., La Grange, IL, USA.

BIBLIOGRAPHY

Beaver BV. Grass eating by carnivores. Veterinary Medicine/Small Animal Clinician 1981; 69: 968-969.

Bradshaw JWS. Sensory and experiential factors in the design of foods for domestic dogs and cats. Proceedings of the Nutrition Society 1991; 50: 99-106.

Campbell WE. Effects of training, feeding regimens, isolation, and physical environment on canine behavior. Modern Veterinary Practice 1986; 29: 239-241.

Campbell WE. Problem behavior in dogs: The stool eating dog. Modern Veterinary Practice 1975; 18: 574-575.

Campbell WE. The effects of social environment on canine behavior. Modern Veterinary Practice 1986; 29: 113-115.

Campbell WE. The prevalence of behavioral problems in American dogs. Modern Veterinary Practice 1986; 29: 28-31.

Cloche D. Coprofagie bij honden-Panel reacties-Coprofagie. Tijdschrift voor Diergeneeskunde 1991; 116: 1257-1258.

Houpt KA, Coren B, Hintz HF, et al. Effects of sex and reproductive status on sucrose preference, food intake, and body weight of dogs. Journal of the American Veterinary Medical Association 1979; 174: 1083-1085.

Houpt KA. Feeding and drinking behavior problems. Veterinary Clinics of North America: Small Animal Practice 1991; 21: 281-298.

Houpt KA. Ingestive behavior problems of dogs and cats. Veterinary Clinics of North America: Small Animal Practice 1982; 12: 683-692.

Knol BW. Coprofagie bij honden-Panel reacties-Coprofagie. Tijdschrift voor Diergeneeskunde 1991; 116: 1256.

Lohse CL. Preference of dogs for various meats. Journal of the American Animal Hospital Association 1974; 10: 187-192.

McCuistion WR. Coprophagy: A quest for digestive enzymes. Veterinary Medicine/Small Animal Clinician 1966; 61: 445-447.

McKeown DB, Luescher UA, Halip J. Stereotypies in companion animals and obsessive-compulsive disorders. In: Behavioral Problems in Small Animals. Purina Specialty Review. Pro-Visions, 1992; 30-35.

Meyer H. Praktische Fütterung. In: Ernährung des Hundes, 2nd ed. Stuttgart, Germany: Verlag Eugen Ulmer, 1990; 162-223.

Mugford RA. The influence of nutrition on canine behaviour. Journal of Small Animal Practice 1987; 24: 1046-1055.

Mugford RA, Thorne C. Comparative studies of meal patterns in pet and laboratory housed dogs and cats. In: Anderson RS, ed. Nutrition of the Dog and Cat. Oxford, UK: Pergamon Press, 1980; 3-14.

Nicholson SS. Toxicology. In: Ettinger SJ, Feldman EC, eds. Textbook of Veterinary Internal Medicine, 4th ed. Philadelphia, PA: WB Saunders Co, 1995; 312-326.

Rabot R. Abnormal food ingestive behaviour in dogs and cats. Friskies Veterinary International 1993; 5(4): 17-22.

Soave O, Brand CD. Coprophagia in animals: A review. Cornell Veterinarian 1991; 81: 357-364.

Spreat S, Rogers-Spreat S. Learning principles. Veterinary Clinics of North America: Small Animal Practice 1982; 12: 593-606.

Voith VL. Feeding behaviours. In: Wills JM, Simpson KW, eds. The Waltham Book of Clinical Nutrition of the Dog & Cat. Oxford, UK: Pergamon Press, 1994; 119-129.

Table 1. Factors associated with coprophagy.

Behavior
Strong dominance or extreme submissive attitude towards the owner
Reaction to punishment during house training
To attract the owner's attention
Confinement in a kennel leading to stress or competitive behavior
Confinement leading to boredom with all exploratory effort focused on feces
Young animals with a natural interest in feces
Gastrointestinal disorders
Malassimilation
Parasitic infections
Polyphagia due to diabetes mellitus or Cushing's syndrome
Food
Poorly digestible food
Overfeeding

Determine a Feeding Method

The method of feeding may not need to be revised if it appears adequate. Free-choice feeding is popular and will suffice for healthy dogs unless obesity is an issue. If so, the specific amount of food should be limited. An understanding of the other pets in the home, which family member is responsible for selecting and purchasing the dog's food and who feeds the dog regularly are helpful to evaluate the feasibility of new dietary recommendations and will increase compliance, if a food or feeding method change is necessary.

Most healthy adult dogs adapt well to new food(s). However, it is good practice to allow for a transition period to avoid digestive upsets. This is particularly true when switching from lower fat foods to higher fat foods or when changing forms of food (e.g., changing from dry to moist food). New food(s) should be increased and old food decreased in progressive amounts over a three- to seven-day period until the changeover is completed.[98] (See Chapter 1.)

Dogs may eat an insufficient amount or completely refuse new food(s). Investigation of food refusal may reveal problems with owner compliance rather than a finicky appetite. The following guidelines may be useful when a food change must be made: 1) Explain clearly to the owners why a change in food is necessary or preferable. 2) Justify your recommendation to the owners (i.e., food profile vs. specific needs of the dog). 3) As a general rule, start with one or two meals per day, always presented at the same time. Uneaten food should be removed after 15 to 20 minutes. 4) Don't give treats or table foods between meals for the first few days. If a small snack is given, it should be given immediately (i.e., within seconds) after the new food is eaten. Most dogs will accept the new food within a few days.

Reassessment

Owners should be encouraged to weigh their dog every month or so, and should be trained to observe their dog and adapt the food intake according to its needs. Dogs whose nutrition is well-managed are alert, have an ideal BCS (3/5) with a stable, normal body weight and a healthy coat. Stools should be firm, well-formed and medium to dark brown.

Reassessment by a veterinarian should take place regularly. Healthy dogs should be reassessed every six to 12 months. Because few if any homemade recipes have been tested according to prescribed feeding protocols, dogs should be reassessed more frequently if homemade food is a significant part of their caloric intake. Reassessment should take place immediately if clinical signs arise indicating that the current feeding regimen is inappropriate, or if the needs of the dog change (e.g., reproduction or change in activity).

If expected results are not obtained, the owner should also be questioned in detail about compliance with the feeding regimen or the possibility that the dog has access to other food sources.

■ OLDER DOGS

A major dimension of aging is an increase in vulnerability.[99,100] Aging in itself is not a disease; however, the likelihood of morbidity increases with age because normal changes set the stage for individual animals to become more vulnerable to diseases.[100] The influence of nutrition on vulnerability to chronic or acute disease is difficult to evaluate, and has not been explored thoroughly in dogs. In people and companion animals, nutrition may be one of the more important aspects of geriatric care because delay or elimination of the two or three leading causes of death

Table 9-9. Percent survival rates of older dogs.*

Age	10 years	15 years
Small-breed dogs	38%	7.0%
Large-breed dogs	13%	0.1%

*Deeb BJ, Wolf NS. Studying longevity and morbidity in giant and small breed dogs. Veterinary Medicine 1994; 89 (Suppl. 7): 702-713.

would profoundly affect life expectancy.[101] In dogs, the three leading non-accidental causes of death are cancer, kidney disease and heart disease.[102-105] Moreover, older animals seldom suffer from a single disease and one problem may markedly influence the course of another.[106]

The overall goals of feeding older adult dogs are similar to those for feeding young and middle-aged adult dogs: optimize quality and longevity of life and minimize disease. To understand the specific nutritional needs of older animals, it is necessary to know the major effects of aging on the dog's body systems. (See sidebar "The Older Dog.") Aging is characterized by progressive and irreversible change,[107] and its rate and manifestations are determined by intrinsic and extrinsic factors, one of which is nutrition. Because aging is progressive, the point in time at which a food change should be made is arbitrary, and in a way philosophical. Dogs often are considered older or likely to start having diseases associated with aging between seven and one-half and 13.5 years.[108] Smaller dogs tend to live longer than large dogs (Table 9-9). The life expectancy of smaller dogs may be more than 20 years. Because dogs are often considered older when they reach half of their life expectancy,[21] a food change should be considered around the age of five years for large- and giant-breed dogs and around seven years for small dogs.[109] At these ages, dogs may gradually start to gain weight and develop age-related physical and behavioral changes.[60,109] However, veterinarians should not accept the tenant that poor health and old age are synonymous.[108] There is a real opportunity to improve the quality and possibly the length of life of older dogs through proper nutritional management.

The Older Dog

Aging is the progressive changes that occur after maturity in various organs and lead to decreased ability of an organism to meet the demands of the environment. This definition underscores two primary aspects of aging. First, aging occurs "after maturity." Although nutrition in young animals will have an affect on longevity and health, changes occurring during growth should not be considered aging. Second, aging results in a "decreased ability to meet the demands of the environment." Although young organisms adapt easily to fluctuations in nutrient intake and quality, older animals may no longer be able to cope with excesses, borderline deficiencies or changes in nutrient intake and quality. Therefore, foods for older dogs should meet allowances more rigorously and consistently.

An important feature of aging is that, compared with a group of younger adults, the older dog population has a "large variation in health status" between individuals. Older animals, therefore, must be evaluated individually rather than as a group and their nutritional needs determined accordingly.

BIBLIOGRAPHY

Armstrong PJ, Lund EM. Changes in body composition and energy balance with aging. In: Proceedings. Symposium on Health and Nutrition of Geriatric Cats and Dogs, Orlando, FL, January 1996: 11-15.

Greeley EH, Kealy RD, Ballam JM, et al. The influence of age on the canine immune system (abstract 4366). Federation of American Societies for Experimental Biology Journal 1994; 8: A753.

Guilford WG. Aging and the gastrointestinal system. In: Proceedings. Symposium on Health and Nutrition of Geriatric Cats and Dogs, Orlando, FL, January 1996: 17-20.

Hayflick L. How and Why We Age. New York, NY: Ballantine Books, 1994; 43-49.

Sheffy BE, Williams AJ, Zimmer JF, et al. Nutrition and metabolism of the geriatric dog. Cornell Veterinarian 1985; 75: 324-347.

Twedt DC. Gastrointestinal motility disorders of geriatric patients. In: Geriatric Medicine. Purina Specialty Review. Pro-Visions, 1993; 11-21.

Wolter R. Alimentation du chien âgé. In: Diététique du chien et du chat. Paris, France: Masson S.A., 1988; 71-74.

Nutritional Antioxidants in Canine Foods

The immune system produces highly potent substances including cytokines and oxidant molecules (i.e., hydrogen peroxide, free radicals, hypochlorous acid) to destroy invading organisms and restore damaged tissues. Oxidants enhance interleukin-1, interleukin-8 and tumor necrosis factor production in response to inflammatory stimuli. However, oxidants and cytokines can damage healthy tissue. Excessive or inappropriate production of these substances may be associated with: 1) mortality and morbidity after infection, trauma, allergic responses, exposure to environmental pollutants, excess exposure to sunlight and other radiation sources, cancer and other inflammatory diseases and 2) aging and senile changes in a variety of tissues (e.g., senile cataracts).

Sophisticated antioxidant defenses directly and indirectly protect the host against the damaging influence of cytokines and oxidants. The nature and extent of antioxidant defenses are influenced by dietary intake of certain nutrients and other nutritional factors. These include copper, zinc, selenium, vitamin E, vitamin C, methionine, taurine, cysteine and certain carotenoids (e.g., β-carotene, α-carotene, zeaxanthin, lutein).

People who consume a diet high in vegetables and fruits have a lower risk of certain cancers. Antioxidant vitamins, which are present in vegetables and fruits, have been associated with a diminished risk of human cancers at various anatomic sites. However, randomized, controlled clinical trials to test the efficacy of antioxidant vitamins (specifically β-carotene and vitamins C and E) in preventing certain cancers in people have been disappointing. Other dietary factors may be more important in reducing the risk of cancer associated with a diet high in vegetables and fruits. These dietary factors include certain carotenoids (e.g., lycopenes), flavonoids, flavanols/flavones, isoflavones, anthocyanidins, catechins, phenolic acids and monoterpenes.

A number of commercial pet foods claim to be fortified with selected antioxidant vitamins. These pet foods are often designed for older dogs ("senior" foods) and their manufacturers often claim such foods aid proper function of the immune system and promote "clear vision." It is not known how the antioxidant vitamin levels in these foods compare with those in regular commercial pet foods. If antioxidant and anticancer nutrients or food factors do benefit dogs, then it would be better if they were provided for the entire life of the animal, not just during the older years. Supplementation with these compounds is probably not harmful, but more studies are needed to document if increased levels of antioxidant vitamins and other anticancer food factors will benefit dogs.

BIBLIOGRAPHY

Blumberg JB. Vitamins. In: Forse RA, ed. Diet, Nutrition and Immunity. Boca Raton, FL: CRC Press, Inc, 1994; 237-246.

Greenburg ER, Baron JA, Tosteson TD, et al. A clinical trial of antioxidant vitamins to prevent colorectal adenoma. New England Journal of Medicine 1994; 331: 141-147.

Grimble RF. Nutritional antioxidants and the modulation of inflammation: Theory and practice. New Horizons 1994; 2: 175-185.

Halliwell B. Antioxidants and human diseases–A general introduction. Nutrition Reviews 1997; 55: S44-S52.

Langseth L. Oxidants, Antioxidants and Disease Prevention (monograph). Washington, DC: International Life Sciences Institute, 1995.

Meydani SN, Ansari AA, eds. Conference on nutrition and immunity. Nutrition Reviews 1998; 56: S1-S183.

Robertson JM, Donner AP, Trevithick JR. A possible role for vitamins C and E in cataract prevention. American Journal of Clinical Nutrition 1991; 53: 346S-351S.

Varman SD. Scientific basis for medical therapy of cataracts by antioxidants. American Journal of Clinical Nutrition 1991; 53: 335S-345S.

Assessment

Assess the Animal

HISTORY AND PHYSICAL EXAMINATION

A thorough history should be taken and a physical examination performed to identify potential areas of nutritional concern. All of the considerations previously discussed for young to middle-aged adult dogs (i.e., breed, gender and health status) should be considered when developing key nutritional factors for older dogs. Special attention should be directed to physiologic changes associated with aging and diseases that are more prevalent in older animals such as renal disease, cancer, degenerative joint disease, cardiac disease, endocrine disorders, periodontal disease and obesity.[88,110-112] It is important to carefully monitor food intake and body condition in older dogs because these parameters may be indicators of underlying disease processes.

LABORATORY AND OTHER CLINICAL INFORMATION

Laboratory analyses become more important in health screening of dogs older than five years. (See Chapter 8.) All older dogs should be screened for renal disease and hypertension. Chronic renal disease is best diagnosed with a urinalysis (i.e., urine specific gravity, urine protein, urine sediment examination) and a serum biochemistry profile, including urea nitrogen, creatinine, electrolyte, calcium and phosphorus measurements.[113] Additional blood parameters should be evaluated based on historical and physical examination findings. In general, indirect blood pressure measurements obtained routinely during hospital visits are reasonable estimates of a dog's true blood pressure.[78] However, uncooperative, anxious dogs may have elevated blood pressure values in the hospital setting that do not reflect normal values.[114] Fundic examination may also detect changes associated with hypertension and other systemic diseases.[114] Thoracic radiographs and echocardiography should be performed if a cardiac murmur is detected or if there is a history of coughing or an abnormal respiratory pattern.

KEY NUTRITIONAL FACTORS

Veterinarians should appreciate the diversity in health status of older dogs and adapt care and nutrition to the specific needs of each geriatric animal.[103,115,116] Table 9-7 summarizes key nutritional factors for older adult dogs. The following section describes these key nutritional factors in more detail. (See sidebar "Nutritional Antioxidants in Canine Foods.")

Water

Older dogs are more prone to dehydration due to possible osmoregulatory disturbances, medications (diuretics) and chronic renal disease, with compromised urine concentrating ability. Therefore, continuous access to a fresh, clean water supply is very important for older dogs and water intake should be closely monitored.

Energy

With increasing age, lean body mass decreases, subcutaneous fat increases, basal metabolic rate gradually declines and body temperature may decrease. Older dogs become slower and less active, and their thyroid function may be impaired.[60,62,103,106,117,118] All these changes result in a 12 to 13% decrease in DER by around seven years of age (Table 9-6).[33] For older dogs, a daily energy intake of 1.4 x RER (100 kcal [418 kJ] ME/$BW_{kg}^{0.75}$) is a good starting point.[119] This amount should be modified if a dog tends to lose or gain weight when fed at the recommended level.

Very old dogs are often underweight and may have inadequate energy intake.[60,61,120] Underweight, very elderly people increase body weight when a food of higher caloric density is provided.[121] Thus, it may be appropriate to feed a more energy-dense food to very old dogs. Because of the potential for older dogs to have different energy needs, energy densities in foods recommended for this age group may vary from 3.0 to 4.0 kcal (12.6 to 16.7 kJ)/g DM (Table 9-7).

Phosphorus and Calcium

Some degree of clinical or subclinical renal disease is often present in older dogs; as many as 25% of all dogs may be affected.[64-67,122-124] Excessive phosphorus intake should therefore be avoided.[70] Researchers have observed that dogs with advanced renal disease had slowed progression and reduced severity of renal disease when phosphorus levels in foods were decreased, thereby improving survival time.[68-70,125] Foods with 0.25 to 0.75% DM phosphorus are recommended for older dogs (Table 9-7).

Osteoporosis occurs frequently in older people but is not a clinical problem in older dogs.[126] This finding is probably due, in part, to lifetime feeding of calcium-replete commercial foods to most dogs. There should be little concern about calcium deficiency in older dogs unless unbalanced homemade foods are fed. Foods with 0.5 to 1.0% DM calcium (providing 75 to 150 mg calcium/BW_{kg}) are recommended for older dogs. The calcium-phosphorus ratio should not be less than 1:1 (Table 9-7).

Protein

Recommendations for protein intake in older dogs are controversial, which parallels the debate in people.[127] The decrease in lean body mass, seen with age, together with alterations in protein synthesis and turnover have been the basis for the argument that protein intake in older dogs should be higher than for younger adults.[21,116,128] In contrast, other investigators have recommended reduced protein intake because of the increased prevalence of renal pathology in dogs older than five years of age.[67,129]

As with all lifestages, healthy older dogs should receive enough protein and energy to avoid protein-energy malnutrition. However, sufficient protein can be provided by improving protein quality, rather than increasing its intake.[118,119,130] In addition, data suggest that mild protein-energy undernutrition in older people plays a role in immunosenescence; however, supplementation with calories returned helper T cells and suppressor cells to values seen in younger people.[131] Serum protein concentrations, lymphocyte counts and muscle protein-to-DNA ratios have

indicated that a food with 18% DM protein is adequate to maintain immunocompetence in older dogs.[132] These findings confirmed earlier observations that foods with 16 to 20% DM protein are sufficient to maintain nitrogen balance and protein stores in older dogs.[128] In addition, alterations in protein metabolism and plasma protein concentrations seen in healthy elderly people are unrelated to daily protein intake, suggesting that other factors play a role.[133]

High protein intake has not been shown to contribute to the development of kidney disease in healthy animals. However, after kidney function is impaired, protein may play a role in progression of renal disease. In a four-year study with uninephrectomized healthy dogs, investigators recognized no difference in kidney function between dogs receiving a food with 34% DM protein and a food with 18% DM protein.[132] However, histologic examination revealed an increase in mesangial matrix scores and fibrosis in the high-protein group.[132] Mesangial proliferation has been described in glomerulonephritis and chronic interstitial nephritis in dogs[134,135] and may indicate more rapid renal impairment at a higher protein intake.[132] Moderately reduced protein intake during early stages of canine renal disease improved general condition.[67] In conclusion, commercial foods containing 15 to 23% DM protein will provide sufficient protein for healthy older dogs (Table 9-7).

Sodium and Chloride

There is no nutritional need for higher levels of sodium and chloride found in some commercial dog foods, especially considering the increased prevalence of heart disease and renal disease in older dogs.[136,137] High sodium chloride intake may be harmful in diseases that have a hypertensive component. Secondary hypertension is associated with obesity and chronic renal disease, which are frequently seen in older dogs.[79-83] Young, healthy dogs are able to excrete excess dietary sodium whereas older dogs with heart disease have decreased ability for eliminating excess dietary sodium. (See Chapter 18.) Although there is no need for sodium and chloride restriction in healthy, older dogs, there is no reason to give more than the recommended 25 to 50 mg sodium/kg body weight.[63] Some foods recommended for older dogs provide more than 160 mg sodium/kg body weight.

Minimum sodium and chloride requirements in older dogs are probably not different from those of younger adults, which are estimated around 4 mg sodium/kg body weight.[84] The recommended sodium levels for adult dogs (25 to 50 mg sodium/kg body weight) are still six to 12 times higher than the minimum requirement. Foods with 0.2 to 0.35% DM sodium provide recommended levels (Table 9-7). Although the chloride requirement of dogs has not been established, a chloride level 1.5 times the sodium requirement is a reasonable recommendation.

Fat

A relatively low fat intake helps prevent obesity in healthy older dogs. However, some dogs may need different foods at seven years of age than they will at 13 years of age. Very old dogs may have a tendency to lose weight.[60,61] For these dogs, increasing the fat content of the food increases energy intake, improves palatability, and improves protein efficiency.[54,74]

Research in people has indicated that increased energy intake can correct immunosenescence that is due to mild protein-energy malnutrition.[131] The general condition of elderly people improved significantly by increasing the energy density of the food.[121] Thus, a good balance should be maintained between preventing obesity and providing sufficient caloric intake.

In general, fat levels between 7 and 15% DM are recommended for most older dogs (Table 9-7). The fat level should be selected as needed to meet the desired energy density to achieve ideal body weight and condition (BCS 3/5). EFA requirements should also be met as outlined for young to middle-aged adult dogs.

OTHER NUTRITIONAL FACTORS

Fiber

Older dogs are prone to develop constipation,[138] which may justify increased fiber intake. In addition, fiber added to foods for obese-prone older dogs dilutes calories. Fiber also decreases postprandial glycemic effects in older diabetic dogs.[139] Very old dogs that tend to lose weight, however, should be offered a food with increased caloric density. Table 9-7 lists recommended levels of crude fiber for foods intended for older dogs.

Food Texture

Oral disease is the most common health problem in older dogs. Both veterinary and home care are important in the treatment and prevention of periodontal disease. Foods designed to reduce the accumulation of dental substrates (i.e., plaque, calculus) and help control gingivitis and malodor are an important part of an oral home-care program for older dogs. (See Chapter 16.)

Assess the Food(s) and Feeding Method

Assessment of the food(s) and feeding method for older dogs is similar to those procedures outlined for young and middle-aged dogs. Compare the current food's nutrient levels with key nutritional factors and nutrient requirements established during animal assessment, identify gaps between key nutritional factor levels and current intake and decide whether changes in the food are required.

It may not always be necessary to change the feeding method when managing healthy older dogs. However, a thorough evaluation includes verification that an appropriate feeding method is being used.

Feeding Plan

Older dogs are more prone to obesity, degenerative joint disease, cardiac disease, renal disease and metabolic aberrations. They also are usually less active than younger dogs. The feeding plan should be based on potential risk factors and information attained in the assessment. Because of the larger variation in health among older dogs, more attention should be paid to individual needs. Nutritional surveillance is more important for older dogs than for young and middle-aged dogs; therefore, the number of veterinary assessments per year should be increased. Goals remain the same as stated in the introduction; however, each animal must be evaluated individually.

Select a Food(s)

It may not be necessary to change the food that is currently fed. However, a new food should be selected if gaps are determined under the food assessment phase. This is accomplished by choosing a food that provides the appropriate key nutritional factors and amounts listed in Table 9-7. Appendices L and M list nutrient levels for a number of readily available commercial dog foods and treats.

Alternatively, pet food manufacturers can be contacted directly for information. Foods selected should also have passed AAFCO or similar feeding trials for adult dogs. This information may be found on the pet food label.

Determine a Feeding Method

The method of feeding should be monitored more closely in older than in younger dogs. Free-choice feeding should not be used for obese or overweight animals, but this method may be preferred for thinner, very old animals to allow increased food intake. It is very important to measure food intake of older dogs, and this measurement may be more accurate when the dog is meal fed. Measures to stimulate food intake may be necessary for some very old dogs. Most older adult dogs adapt well to new food(s), but some animals may have difficulty. It is always good practice to allow for a transition period to avoid digestive upsets. This is particularly true when switching from lower to higher fat foods. New food(s) should be increased and old food decreased in progressive amounts over a three- to seven-day period until the changeover is completed.[98] (See Chapter 1.)

Reassessment

Nutritional status for healthy older dogs should be assessed at least every six to 12 months. Immediate reassessment should take place if clinical signs arise that indicate the current regimen is inappropriate or if the needs of the dog change due to altered use.

▌ REPRODUCING DOGS

The objectives of a good reproductive feeding program are to optimize conception, number of puppies per litter, the ability of the bitch to deliver and viability of prenatal and neonatal puppies.[140] Appropriate feeding and management will increase the likelihood of successful reproductive performance, whereas improper nutrition can negatively affect reproductive performance in bitches (Table 9-10).

Females undergo the greatest extremes in nutrient requirements when the entire reproductive cycle is considered. Estrus, pregnancy and lactation are each associated with specific nutrient concerns that must be addressed. The concerns change with the intrinsic physiologic alterations and may be influenced by environmental and other extrinsic factors. Males also need adequate nutrition to achieve optimal performance and conception rates.

Many people who have experience breeding dogs and raising puppies frequently have very strong opinions about nutritional programs. Veterinarians should have a good understanding of an appropriate and practical nutrition program for reproduction and the neonatal period.

Estrus and Mating

Assessment

ASSESS THE ANIMAL

Optimal nutrition of reproducing animals should precede mating and conception.[141] As a rule, only healthy dogs in a good nutritional state (BCS 3/5) should be used for

Table 9-10. Effects of improper nutrition on reproductive performance and health in bitches.*

Factors	Reproductive and health consequences
Underfeeding	Small litter size
	Low birth weight
	Increased neonatal morbidity and mortality
	Decreased milk yield
	Decreased immunity and decreased response to vaccination
	Decreased fertility later
	Hair loss and weight loss in bitches
Obesity	Decreased ovulation
	Decreased fertility
	Silent heat
	Prolonged interestrous interval
	Anestrus
	Smaller litters
Malnutrition*	
Protein deficiency	Low birth weight
	Increased neonatal morbidity and mortality
	Decreased neonatal immunity
Carbohydrate-free food	Low birth weight
	Increased neonatal morbidity and mortality
	Increased numbers of stillbirths
Zinc deficiency	Fetal resorption
	Smaller litters
Iron deficiency	Decreased immunity and response to vaccination
Pyridoxine and biotin deficiency	Decreased immunity and response to vaccination
Hypervitaminosis A	Congenital abnormalities
	Smaller litters
Hypervitaminosis D	Soft-tissue calcification

*Malnutrition is not common when balanced commercial foods are fed, but may occur if homemade foods are not properly formulated.

breeding because effects of malnutrition before breeding are often unnoticed until puppies are born (Table 9-10). A BCS of 2/5 may be acceptable for a house pet only bred for an exceptional occasion.[142] Obese bitches may have a lower ovulation rate, smaller litter size and insufficient milk production.[117] Obesity may also cause silent heat, prolonged interestrous intervals and anestrus. Therefore, to optimize fertility, overweight bitches should lose weight before breeding.[140] A good history and general physical examination should precede breeding to document and correct problems that may interfere with successful breeding.

Key Nutritional Factors

Compared with adult maintenance, there are no special nutritional requirements for bitches during estrus.[140] Like breeding females, most sires do not have special nutritional needs beyond adult maintenance requirements and do well when fed foods for young to middle-aged adult dogs. However, intact males and females may require more energy than their neutered counterparts to maintain ideal body condition (BCS 3/5).

ASSESS THE FOOD(S) AND FEEDING METHOD

Females

For females, it has been recommended to increase food intake by 5 to 10% above maintenance levels at the time of proestrus, and to reduce the amount back to maintenance levels after mating; a practice known as flushing.[141] The purpose of flushing is to optimize conception and litter size. However, flushing is unnecessary for a bitch in good body condition.[143] Because no specific nutritional differences exist for this particular lifestage, food(s) and feeding methods recommended for young to middle-aged adults are adequate during estrus.

If a bitch is underfed before breeding and in poor body condition (BCS <2/5), it may be prudent to postpone mating and bring the bitch into good body condition for the next breeding. If breeding cannot be postponed, the bitch should be fed a well-balanced, energy-dense food (at least 4.0 kcal/g [16.7 kJ/g]), in sufficient quantities to improve body condition throughout gestation.[117] The digestibility of the nutrients in the food should be above average to achieve this goal (Table 9-11), and it should contain a minimum of 25% DM crude protein and 15% DM fat.

Bitches tend to have a depressed appetite during estrus; therefore, a decrease in food intake of about 17% can be expected during peak estrus.[28,144] Occasional vomiting may occur in bitches due to hormonal changes, nervousness, travel and environmental changes associated with mating. To reduce these problems, it may be better to feed small meals or not to feed the bitch at all, immediately before or after mating.[144]

Table 9-11. Apparent digestibility of nutrients in typical commercial pet foods.*

Nutrient	Average digestibility (%)**	Above average digestibility (%)***
Protein	80	≥85
Fat	90	≥95
Carbohydrate (NFE)	85	≥90

Key: NFE = nitrogen-free extract.
*Apparent digestibility of a nutrient is the difference between the amount ingested with the food and the amount excreted in the feces, divided by the amount ingested and multiplied by 100.
**Adapted from National Research Council. Nutrient Requirements of Dogs. Washington, DC: National Academy Press, 1985.
***Above average digestibility is defined as 5% or more above the average nutrient digestibility in pet foods. During certain physiologic states (e.g., intense exercise, late gestation, lactation and early growth), the food digestibility should be above average.

Table 9-12. Distribution of the accretion of the bitch's body weight (BW) at the end of gestation.*

Tissues	% of pre-breeding BW
Fetal mass	12
Placenta	3
Growth of uterus, mammary tissue and amniotic fluid	3
Extragenital accretion of tissue and extracellular water	7
Total accretion	25

*Adapted from Meyer H. Praktische Fütterung. In: Ernährung des Hundes, 2nd ed. Stuttgart, Germany: E Ulmer Verlag, 1990; 162-223. Gesellschaft für Ernährungsphysiologie. Grunddaten für die Berechnung des Energie- und Nährstoffbedarfs. Ausschuß für Bedarfsnormen der Gesellschaft für Ernährungsphysiologie Energie- Nährstoffbedarf/Energy and Nutrient Requirements, No. 5 Hunde/Dogs. Frankfurt/Main, Germany: DLG Verlag, 1989; 9-31.

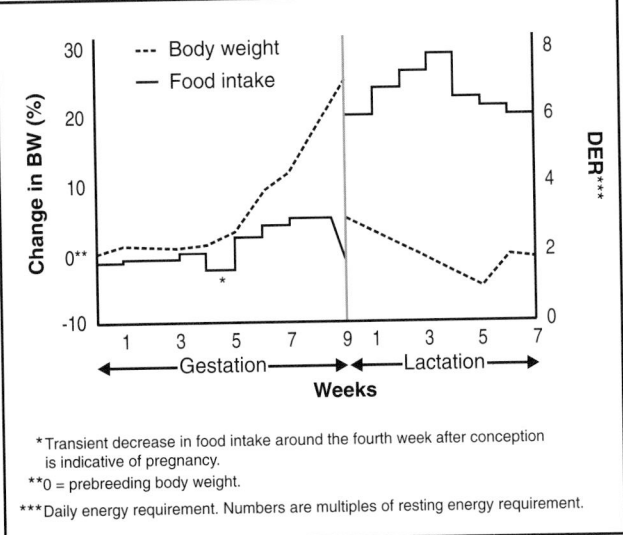

*Transient decrease in food intake around the fourth week after conception is indicative of pregnancy.
**0 = prebreeding body weight.
***Daily energy requirement. Numbers are multiples of resting energy requirement.

Figure 9-3. Typical changes in body weight and food intake of a bitch during gestation and lactation. A bitch only weighs 5 to 10% above pre-breeding weight after parturition, and should not lose more than 5% of its body weight during the first month of lactation. Food intake may drop precipitously during the last days of gestation.

Males

Some males in heavy service may have decreased food consumption and lose weight. If weight loss is a problem in reproducing males, the amount of food provided should be increased or a more energy-dense food should be fed to help maintain condition, provided other causes of weight loss have been ruled out.

Feeding Plan

Follow the guidelines discussed above for young to middle-aged adult dogs.

Reassessment

Animals should be reassessed before every estrous cycle in which a pregnancy is planned. Breeders should be encouraged to present reproducing bitches for a checkup at least a month before the upcoming estrus. Problems detected by the assessment still may be corrected before breeding. See the young to middle-aged adult dog section above for methods of assessment.

Pregnancy

Assessment

ASSESS THE ANIMAL

Gestation in dogs averages 63 days and is typically divided into 21-day trimesters. Assessment includes a detailed dietary history, a physical examination and pertinent clinical laboratory analyses. During the physical examination, particular attention should be given to body weight, body condition and vaginal discharges. Ultrasound of the abdomen provides useful additional information. Adequately fed bitches gain about 15 to 25% above their pre-breeding weight before whelping (Table 9-12 and Figure 9-3).[117,145,146] After birth, bitches should weigh about 5 to 10% more than their pre-breeding weight. This weight gain corresponds with development of mammary tissue, extracellular water and some gain in extragenital tissue.[117,145-147] Retention of more than 10% above pre-breeding weight may adversely affect whelping. Further, dogs do not need to maintain a body fat reserve to provide energy for the subsequent lactation because they can increase their food intake during lactation.[117,140]

Laboratory analyses should include a complete blood count, serum protein, glucose, calcium, phosphorus and potassium concentrations and culture of vaginal discharges, if present. During pregnancy, red blood cell counts, hematocrit values and red cell volume may decrease because of plasma volume expansion, and may reach their lowest level during the second week of lactation.[148-150] In most bitches, serum albumin and calcium concentrations also decrease during gestation.[150,151] Urea nitrogen concentrations may be below the normal range just before parturition; however, this finding should not be alarming, because levels return to normal during the first weeks of lactation.[150]

Malnutrition, whether due to inadequate or excessive intake of nutrients, may affect pregnancy and lactation (Table 9-10). Fertilized eggs may die at an early stage resulting in embryo loss. Alternatively, fetuses may develop incorrectly, die and be resorbed, expelled before term (abortion) or carried to full term (stillbirth).[152] Embryo loss and in utero resorption are manifested by smaller litter size. Malnutrition during pregnancy is also a cause of low birth weight puppies that are particularly prone to hypoglycemia, sepsis, pneumonia and hemorrhage and have reduced survival.[147,153,154]

Obesity at the end of pregnancy may increase dystocia, prolong labor and therefore predispose the puppies to hypoxia and hypoglycemia. Studies in people indicate that obesity in pregnant women is the most important factor predisposing women to preterm parturition and increases perinatal mortality sixfold.[155] Obesity in pregnant women increases the risk of congenital central nervous system defects (e.g., neural tube defects) and low birth weight infants.[155] Rats that were obese during gestation and lactation had inadequate milk production and were unable to maintain their litters. Surviving pups were significantly smaller than normal. These findings occurred irrespective of whether rats were underfed or overfed during lactation.[156]

Key Nutritional Factors

Table 9-13 summarizes key nutritional factors for pregnant dogs. The following section describes these key nutritional factors in more detail.

Table 9-13. Key nutritional factors for reproduction.

Factors	Recommended levels in food (DM)	
	Gestation/lactation*	Lactation**
Energy density (kcal ME/g)***	3.5-4.5	4.0-5.0
Energy density (kJ ME/g)***	14.6-18.8	16.7-20.9
Crude protein (%)	22-32	25-35
Crude fat (%)	10-25	≥18
Soluble carbohydrate (%)	≥23	≥23
Crude fiber (%)	≤5	≤5
Calcium (%)	0.75-1.5	1.0-1.7
Phosphorus (%)	0.6-1.3	0.7-1.3
Ca/P ratio	1:1-1.5:1	1:1-2:1
Sodium (%)	0.35-0.60	0.35-0.6
Chloride (%)	0.50-0.90	0.50-0.9
Digestibility	Above average (Table 9-11)	Above average (Table 9-11)

Key: DM = dry matter, kcal = kilocalories, kJ = kilojoules.
*Gestation for all bitches and for lactation of bitches with four or fewer puppies.
**Lactation for bitches with litters of more than four puppies. Some giant-breed bitches may need this type of food during gestation in order to maintain body weight, particularly during late pregnancy.
***If the caloric density of the food is different, the nutrient content in the dry matter must be adapted accordingly.

Energy

Only 2% of total fetal mass is developed at 35 days of pregnancy and 5.5% at 40 days (Figure 9-4). Therefore, during the first two-thirds of gestation, energy requirements are not different from those of adult maintenance.[57,157] After Day 40, fetal tissue grows exponentially;[57,146] energy intake correspondingly increases markedly during Week 5 and peaks between Weeks 6 and 8 of gestation.[117,157,158] Energy requirements for gestation peak at about 30% above adult maintenance for bitches with smaller litters, whereas energy needs for bitches with larger litters can increase by 50 to 60% (Table 9-14).[117,158,159]

Energy needs are highest during the last week of gestation; however, food intake is limited by abdominal fill (i.e., gravid uterus). Giant breeds may have difficulty ingesting enough food and maintaining body weight even before the last week of gestation.[34] Food intake may decrease precipitously just before whelping with some bitches becoming completely anorectic.[158,159] Enough energy should be provided to bitches during the earlier weeks of gestation, otherwise bitches may be underweight during mid and late gestation and have difficulty maintaining body condition and milk production after whelping.[144] During the last few weeks of gestation, the food should be high in energy density (4.0 kcal/g [16.7 kJ/g]) to provide adequate energy, especially for large-breed bitches.

Protein

Protein requirement increases from 40 to 70% above maintenance during late gestation,[75,146,159] and follows the increase in energy requirement. Thus, foods for dogs in late gestation should also have increased levels of protein to meet nutrient requirements with a limited dry matter intake. The increased protein requirement can be met by providing about 7 g of digestible protein/$BW_{kg}^{0.75}$ (an increase of 30 to 50% vs. recommendations for young adults).[75,159] The food should contain about 4 g digestible protein/100 kcal ME (about 10 g of digestible protein/MJ).[75,160] A food containing 20 to 25% DM crude protein and 4.0 kcal/g DM (16.7 kJ/g) provides this level of protein. The quality of the protein should also be higher to improve vigor of newborn puppies and minimize neonatal mortality.[157] Table 9-13 lists recommendations for protein levels in foods for pregnant bitches. Protein deficiency during pregnancy may decrease birth weight, increase

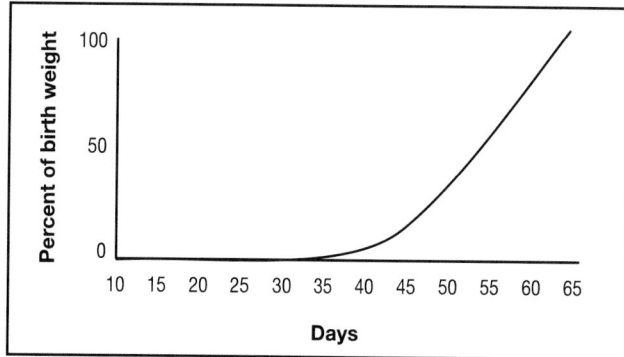

Figure 9-4. The development of fetal mass during pregnancy in beagle dogs. Only 2% of total fetal mass is developed at 35 days of pregnancy and 5.5% at 40 days. After Day 40, fetal tissue growth becomes exponential. (Adapted from Gesellschaft für Ernährungsphysiologie. Empfehlungen für die Versorgung mit Energie. Ausschuß für Bedarfsnormen der Gesellschaft für Ernährungsphysiologie Energie- und Nährstoffbedarf/Energy and Nutrient Requirements, No. 5 Hunde/Dogs. Frankfurt/Main, Germany: DLG Verlag, 1989; 32-44. Leibetseder J. Ernährung der Zuchthündin und der Junghunde. Der Praktischer Tierarzt 1989; 70: 12-20.)

Table 9-14. Practical recommendations for food intake during gestation.*

Week of gestation	Total DER	
	kcal ME/day**	kJ ME/day**
1-4	DER***	DER***
5	DER + 18 kcal ME/kg BW	DER + 75 kJ ME/kg BW
6-8	DER + 36 kcal ME/kg BW	DER + 150 kJ ME/kg BW
9	DER + 18 kcal ME/kg BW	DER + 75 kJ ME/kg BW

Key: DER = daily energy requirement, kcal = kilocalories, kJ = kilojoules, ME = metabolizable energy, BW = body weight.
*Adapted from Gesellschaft für Ernährungsphysiologie. Empfehlungen für die Versorgung mit Energie. Ausschuß für Bedarfsnormen der Gesellschaft für Ernährungsphysiologie Energie- und Nährstoffbedarf/Energy and Nutrient Requirements, No. 5 Hunde/Dogs. Frankfurt/Main, Germany: DLG Verlag, 1989; 32-44.
**Energy requirements during gestation are the sum of the energy needed for normal adult maintenance of a non-pregnant dog plus what is needed for accretion of fetal and maternal tissue. Because accretion of fetal and maternal tissue is minimal during the first 35 days of gestation, the increase in energy requirement only becomes significant from Week 6 on. However, it is better to increase the food intake progressively during Week 5. This allows the bitch to build reserves for the last week of gestation, during which food intake is compromised by abdominal fill.
***During gestation DER is estimated 1.9 x RER (DER = 132 kcal ME/$BW_{kg}^{0.75}$ or 550 kJ ME/ $BW_{kg}^{0.75}$).

NORMAL DOGS

Periparturient Hypoglycemia

Clinical hypoglycemia (i.e., glucose values <45 mg/dl or 2.5 mmol/l) occurs infrequently in bitches, but when it develops it is usually observed during the last two to three weeks of gestation. Neurologic signs of hypoglycemia predominate, and differentiation from eclampsia is not always easy. Elevated levels of serum ketones (mainly β-hydroxybutyrate) are characteristic in bitches with clinical disease; however, ketonemia may be missed when strips or tablets containing nitroprusside are used to detect ketones. Nitroprusside primarily detects acetone and acetoacetate.

Risk factors that may predispose bitches to this syndrome include: 1) poor body condition during pregnancy, 2) malnutrition and 3) feeding a high-fat, carbohydrate-free food. If a carbohydrate-free food is fed, gluconeogenic precursors such as protein should be increased by at least 50% when energy requirements are moderate and may have to be doubled if the energy requirement of the dam is high.

Treatment of clinical hypoglycemia during pregnancy should consist of intravenous administration of a bolus of 20 to 50% glucose solution, which can be followed by intravenous infusion of a 5% glucose solution at a rate of 2 ml/kg body weight/hour. During or soon after the infusion, a palatable food should be provided that has adequate soluble carbohydrate, protein and calories (Table 9-13) and has above average digestibility (Table 9-11).

BIBLIOGRAPHY

Edwards CM, Bedford CJ, Miller RI, et al. Ketonaemia in three pregnant bitches. Australian Veterinary Practitioner 1994; 24: 122-124.

Jackson RF, Bruss ML, Growney PJ, et al. Hypoglycemia-ketonemia in a pregnant bitch. Journal of the American Veterinary Medical Association 1980; 177: 1123-1127.

Kienzle E, Meyer H, Lohrie H. Einfluß kohlenhydratfreier Rationen mit unterschiedlichen Protein/Energierelationen auf foetale Entwicklung und Vitalität von Welpen sowie die Milchzusammensetzung von Hündinnen. Fortschritte in der Tierphysiologie und Tierernährung (Beihefte zur Zeitschrift für Tierphysiologie, Tierernährung und Futtermittelkunde). (Advances in Animal Physiology and Animal Nutrition [Supplement to Journal of Animal Physiology and Animal Nutrition]) 1985; Suppl. No 16: 73-99.

Kienzle E, Meyer H. The effects of carbohydrate-free diets containing different levels of protein on reproduction in the bitch. In: Burger IH, Rivers JPW, eds. Nutrition of the Dog and Cat. Cambridge, UK: Cambridge University Press, 1989; 243-257.

Meyer H. Praktische Fütterung. In: Ernährung des Hundes, 2nd ed. Stuttgart, Germany: E Ulmer Verlag, 1990; 162-223.

Moore AH, Wotton PR. Preparturient hypoglycaemia in two bitches. Veterinary Record 1993; 133: 396-397.

Romsos DR, Palmer HJ, Muiruri KL, et al. Influence of a low carbohydrate diet on performance of pregnant and lactating dogs. Journal of Nutrition 1981; 111: 678-689.

Eclampsia

Bitches are at the highest risk for developing eclampsia (puerperal tetany) during Weeks 3 and 4 of lactation (peak lactation), when calcium losses via secretion in milk are highest. The number of nursing puppies is the most important stimulus for milk production, so it is not surprising that eclampsia is commonly seen in bitches nursing large litters. Typically, affected bitches are primipara, less than four years old, in Weeks 2 to 4 of lactation and are toy-breed dogs. Occasionally, bitches may be affected at or just before whelping. Investigators have suggested that toy breeds may be more predisposed to developing eclampsia than large breeds because toy breeds tend to receive more meat-based homemade foods, which are low in calcium.

Although most bitches with eclampsia are hypocalcemic, some may be normocalcemic. Some bitches with hypocalcemia, on the other hand, may not exhibit clinical signs. This finding may indicate that factors other than calcemia determine whether tetany manifests clinically or not. Magnesium levels have been measured in bitches with eclampsia and were normal.

Hypocalcemia leads to increased neuromuscular irritability resulting in restlessness and whining, stiffness of gait, ataxia and tonic-clonic convulsions. Neuromuscular irritability is directly proportional to:

$$\frac{[Na^+] \times [K^+]}{[Ca^{++}] \times [Mg^{++}] \times [H^+]}$$

Intravenous infusion of 10% calcium gluconate administered to effect (1 to 2 mg calcium/kg body weight) results in rapid clinical improvement. To lessen the risk of relapse, calcium may be injected subcutaneously or intramuscularly in addition to the immediate intravenous infusion. Subcutaneous injections, however, may cause skin necrosis and should be administered only when other routes are inaccessible. If possible, puppies should be separated from the bitch for the first 24 hours of treatment. If tetany recurs during the same lactation, the puppies should be weaned and fed a milk replacer. Administration of corticosteroids is contraindicated because they may further decrease plasma calcium levels.

Prevention of eclampsia starts during pregnancy by feeding a balanced food without excess calcium and with a balanced calcium-phosphorus ratio. Foods with a calcium-phosphorus ratio close to 1:1 have been recommended during pregnancy. Vitamin D therapy (10,000 to 25,000 IU daily) during the last week of gestation has been proposed, just as cows are treated to prevent postparturient paresis. This approach may not be valid for bitches because eclampsia and the highest calcium losses do not occur immediately after whelping.

BIBLIOGRAPHY

Austad R, Bjerkas E. Eclampsia in the bitch. Journal of Small Animal Practice 1976; 17: 793-798.

Drazner FH. Parathyroid glands and calcium metabolism. Small Animal Endocrinology. New York, NY: Churchill Livingstone, 1987; 121-160.

Goff JP, Horst RL, Reinhardt TA. The pathophysiology and prevention of milk fever. Veterinary Medicine 1987; 82: 943-950.

Mayer P. Die Eklampsie beim Fleischfresser. Wiener Tierärztliche Monatschrift 1968; 55: 592-594.

Meuten DJ, Armstrong PJ. Parathyroid disease and calcium metabolism. In: Ettinger SJ, ed. Textbook of Veterinary Internal Medicine, 3rd ed. Philadelphia, PA: WB Saunders Co, 1989; 1610-1631.

Meyer H, Dammers C, Kienzle E. Körperzusammensetzung neugeborener Welpen und Nährstoffbedarf trägender Hündinnen. Fortschritte in der Tierphysiologie und Tierernährung (Advances in Animal Physiology and Animal Nutrition) 1985; Suppl. No. 16: 7-25.

Smith FO. Postpartum diseases. Veterinary Clinics of North America: Small Animal Practice 1986; 16: 521-524.

Wikström B. Eklampsi hos tik. Svensk Vet tidskrift 1974; 26: 34-35.

mortality during the first 48 hours of life and decrease immunocompetence of offspring (Table 9-10).[157]

Fat

Increasing fat levels in foods improves digestibility and provides energy, which in turn improves nitrogen retention.[74] Although adult maintenance-type foods are appropriate for the first two-thirds of pregnancy, a food with a target energy density of approximately 4.0 kcal (16.7 kJ) ME/g is recommended for the last third of gestation. This is usually achieved by feeding a food containing 10 to 25% DM fat. The target level may need to be altered depending on litter size, body condition of the bitch, food intake of the bitch and other extraneous factors as discussed previously. Giant-breed bitches may need a high-energy food throughout gestation.

Carbohydrate

Feeding a carbohydrate-free food to pregnant bitches may result in weight loss, decreased food intake, reduced birth weight and neonatal survival of the puppies and may increase the risk of stillbirth (Table 9-10).[158,161,162] Because more than 50% of the energy for fetal development is supplied by glucose,[158] bitches have a high metabolic requirement for glucose during the last weeks of gestation. Feeding a carbohydrate-free food to pregnant bitches increases the risk of hypoglycemia and ketosis during late pregnancy, and lactose concentration in the milk may decrease by 40% during peak lactation.[158,161,162] (See sidebar "Periparturient Hypoglycemia.")

Providing approximately 20% of the energy from carbohydrate is sufficient to prevent the negative side effects of a carbohydrate-free diet.[161,162] If no carbohydrate is given, protein intake must almost be doubled; the food must provide at least 12 to 13 g digestible protein per kg body weight to the three-fourths power.[75,161,162] In a study in which a food that had about 50% DM protein was fed, no problems with hypoglycemia or ketosis resulted and puppies were born healthy.[163] However, these protein levels are very high and may cause soft, foul-smelling stools.[164] Table 9-13 provides recommendations for minimum DM carbohydrate levels.

Calcium and Phosphorus

During the last 35 days of gestation, requirements for calcium and phosphorus roughly increase by 60% because of rapid skeletal growth of the fetuses.[63,159] As occurs with some dairy cows, excessive intake of calcium during pregnancy may decrease activity of the parathyroid glands and predispose the bitch to eclampsia during lactation.[165,166] Therefore, it has been recommended to feed a food during pregnancy that avoids large excesses of calcium (0.75 to 1.5% DM) and has a calcium-phosphorus ratio of 1.1 to 1.5:1 (Table 9-13). (See sidebar "Eclampsia.")

Digestibility

Although not a nutrient, this food characteristic is important in late gestation. Apparent digestibility is the difference between the amount of food ingested and that excreted in feces. During late gestation, the ability to ingest adequate amounts of food may exceed food intake capacity, especially if the food is poorly digestible. Therefore, it is important to assess digestibility and recommend foods with above average digestibility for these states. Above average digestibility is defined as more than 5% above average values (Table 9-11).

Other Nutritional Factors

Hematocrit, hemoglobin and plasma iron values often decrease in bitches near the end of gestation.[159] Iron requirements are particularly high during the last week of gestation, when large quantities are stored in the liver of the fetuses, and mobilized from the bitch's body for colostrum.[159] Colostrum is very rich in iron. However, iron concentrations are low in mature milk. Therefore, neonates must have an iron reserve to overcome the initial three-week nursing period, when milk is the only source of food.[159] Latent iron deficiency may impair neutrophil phagocytic function and cell-mediated immunity, increasing susceptibility to infections.[167] During periods when requirements for tissue synthesis are greater than normal (e.g., pregnancy, lactation and growth), animals are particularly susceptible to zinc deprivation. Most commercial foods provide adequate zinc. However, if zinc deficiency does occur during pregnancy, it may lead to fetal resorption or fewer, less viable offspring.[168]

ASSESS THE FOOD(S)

Food assessment includes a comparison of the current food's levels of key nutritional factors with those recommended in Table 9-13. Appendices L and M list levels of key nutritional factors for selected foods and treats. In some cases, it may be necessary to contact the manufacturer for this information. The recommended food should also have passed a feeding test to prove it will support gestation (i.e., AAFCO or equivalent). This information should be available on the product label. The food assessment step determines the appropriateness of the current food. As discussed above, gestation is a unique situation in which nutritional requirements increase markedly over a relatively short period of time. It is very important to provide the correct food.

ASSESS THE FEEDING METHOD

The feeding method for pregnant dogs may need to be altered, especially in late gestation. Evaluation of current feeding methods with foreknowledge of the demands of gestation will allow for development of an appropriate feeding plan.

One or two meals per day will suffice for most bitches during the first half of pregnancy. At least two meals per day should be provided in the last half of pregnancy.[117] Giant breeds may need to be fed free choice.[34] Bitches pregnant with a large litter may also need to be fed free choice because of abdominal fill. Restriction of food during gestation may lead to smaller litter size, lower birth weights and may compromise the subsequent lactation.[169]

During the third or fourth week of gestation, bitches commonly experience a decrease in appetite that may result in up to a 30% reduction in food intake.[129,144,170] This decrease may be due to the effect of embryo implantation, which starts around 20 days of pregnancy (Figure 9-3).[170]

The bitch is usually fed the same amount of energy as an intact adult dog (approximately 1.8 x RER) during the first two-thirds of gestation. This amount is increased to approximately 3.0 x RER during the last three weeks of gestation. Energy intake may need to be increased further to maintain normal body condition in some dogs, especially larger breeds.

Feeding Plan

Information gleaned from the assessment step (i.e., animal, food and feeding method) sets the stage for developing the feeding plan; specifically which foods to feed and which feeding methods to use in providing the food.

NORMAL DOGS

SELECT A FOOD(S)

In general, foods for non-reproducing adult dogs should suffice for the first four weeks of gestation,[57] then the dog should receive a food for growth/reproduction. As mentioned, giant-breed dogs may need a growth/reproduction-type food throughout gestation.

A different food should be selected if the current food does not provide the recommended levels of key nutritional factors as determined by the food assessment step (Table 9-13). Appendix L lists some appropriate foods. The manufacturer should be contacted for information if a food is considered that is not listed in Appendix L. Choose a food that most closely fits the recommendations. The food should have successfully passed AAFCO (or a comparable regulatory agency) feeding tests.

DETERMINE A FEEDING METHOD

Because overfeeding during gestation may have similar side effects as underfeeding, small- and medium-sized bitches should be meal fed. Large- and giant-breed dogs may be fed free choice from Week 5 on. Some giant-breed dogs may have difficulty maintaining weight and should be fed free choice throughout gestation.[34] Follow the recommendations described in the feeding methods assessment step. Also, if changing foods, gradually transition the bitch to the new food over several days as described in Chapter 1.

Reassessment

There are two occasions during pregnancy when owners should present a bitch for assessment by a veterinarian. The first time is to confirm pregnancy with ultrasonography between 17 to 20 days after breeding, or by palpation between 25 to 36 days after breeding.[149,171] A thorough physical examination should be conducted at the first visit. The owner should be encouraged to present the bitch again one week before parturition, or earlier if an abnormality is found during the first checkup. In addition to another physical examination, the following parameters should be assessed at the second checkup: a complete blood count and serum glucose, calcium and total protein concentrations.

Lactation

Successful lactation depends on body condition before breeding, and adequate nutrition throughout gestation and lactation. During lactation, nutrient requirements are directly related to milk production, which in turn depends primarily on the number of suckling puppies. A bitch's nutrient requirement during lactation is greater than at any other adult lifestage and equal to or higher, in some cases, than for growth. The superior ability of bitches to produce milk is illustrated by the following examples. A German shepherd bitch, with six puppies, may produce about 1.7 liters of milk/day during the third and fourth week of lactation.[172] Beagles with five to seven puppies are able to produce an average of 964 ml of milk/day (7.6% of body weight) at three weeks postpartum, and 1,054 ml/day (8.3% of body weight) at four weeks.[173] In contrast, a woman produces about 750 ml/day during a three-month lactation.[23] Peak milk production of bitches equates to that of dairy cows, which produce about 7.3% of body weight during peak lactation (exceptional cows can peak at 11% or higher).[174] In addition, bitch's milk contains more than twice the protein and fat of cow's milk (Table 9-15) and more protein than goat's milk. (See Appendix K.) A more nutrient-dense milk is necessary to support the more rapid growth rate (as a percent of birth weight) of puppies vs. that of calves (Table 9-16).

Assessment

ASSESS THE ANIMAL

A physical examination and anamnesis should be performed as described earlier. After parturition, a bitch should weigh 5 to 10% above its pre-breeding body weight (Table 9-12 and Figure 9-3).[117,145,146,169] Unlike cats, bitches do not need to maintain a body fat reserve to provide energy for lactation.[117,140]

During the first week of lactation, milk production is approximately 2.7% of body weight independent of the

Table 9-15. Nutrient comparison between bitch's milk and cow's milk.*

Nutrients	Canine milk (% as fed)	Bovine milk (% as fed)
Total protein	7.5	3.3
Arginine	0.42	0.13
Isoleucine	0.38	0.21
Leucine	0.98	0.36
Lysine	0.37	0.27
Valine	0.46	0.18
Total fat	9.5	3.5
Linoleic acid (C18:2)	11.7	2.5
Lactose	3.4	5.0
Gross energy (kcal/100 g)	146	74

*Meyer H, Kienzle E, Dammers C. Milchmenge und Milchzusammensetzung bei und Hündin sowie Futteraufnahme und Gewichtsenwicklung ante und post partum. Fortschritte in der Tierphysiologie und Tierernährung (Advances in Animal Physiology and Animal Nutrition) 1985; Suppl. No. 16: 51-72.
Swaisgood HE. Protein and amino acid composition of bovine milk. In: Jensen RG, ed. Handbook of Milk Composition. San Diego, CA: Academic Press Inc, 1995; 464-468.
See Appendix K for nutrient comparisons for different species and for comparisons with milk replacers.

Table 9-16. Composition of mammals' milk as related to growth rate of the young mammal.*

Species	Days required to double birth weight	Protein (%)	Calcium (%)	Phosphorus (%)
Man	180	1.6	0.03	0.014
Horse	60	2.0	0.10	0.07
Cow	47	3.3	0.12	0.10
Goat	22	2.9	na	na
Sheep	15	4.1	0.19	0.10
Pig	14	6.0	0.21	0.15
Cat	9.5	7.5	0.18	0.16
Dog	9	7.5	0.24	0.18
Rabbit	6	11.5	0.61	0.38

*As fed basis. See Appendix K for details. na = not available.

bitch's size.[150] Thereafter, milk production steadily increases and peaks during the third and fourth week of lactation.[150,157,172]

After the first two to five days of lactation, the composition of the milk is stable and the bitch's nutrient requirements are primarily determined by the quantity of milk produced.[150,172,173,175] During peak lactation, the quantity of milk produced depends primarily on the number of nursing puppies.[150,157] The puppies' intake of solid food begins to increase around the fifth week, after which milk production progressively declines.[145] Therefore, the stage of lactation and the number of nursing puppies primarily determine the bitch's protein and energy requirements for lactation.

Urea nitrogen levels may be decreased just before parturition; however, values normalize during the first few weeks of lactation. Serum total protein concentrations should be within the normal physiologic range (6.0 to 6.5 g/dl) and remain stable during lactation.[150] A decrease in total protein may indicate undernutrition. Serum calcium concentrations may temporarily decrease during Weeks 3 and 4 of lactation, whereas inorganic phosphorus concentrations should be normal or slightly increased.[150]

Key Nutritional Factors
Water
Although often overlooked, water is the first nutrient needed for lactation. Water is needed in large quantities to produce milk and also aids in thermoregulation. Water requirements in ml are roughly equal to energy requirements in kcal. A 35-kg bitch nursing a large litter may require 5 to 6 l/day at peak lactation. Therefore, it is critical that clean, fresh water be available at all times during lactation.

Digestibility
Nutrients in food should be highly available due to the considerable nutritional demands associated with lactation. Therefore, foods with above average digestibility are recommended for lactating bitches (Table 9-11).

Energy
After whelping, the bitch's energy requirement steadily increases and peaks between three and five weeks[146,157] at a level two to four times higher than the DER for non-lactating adults.[140,144,150] The energy requirement returns to adult maintenance levels about eight weeks after whelping.[157] Bitches are capable of increasing food intake during lactation;[17,150] however, the energy density of the food is usually the limiting factor for meeting DER of lactating dogs.[129] If foods with low energy density are fed (<3.5 kcal [14.6 kJ]/g), the bitch may not be physically able to consume enough food and may lose weight, have decreased milk production and display signs of severe exhaustion.[150] These signs are most pronounced in giant-breed dogs with large litters.[34] Therefore, it is better to feed such bitches foods providing more than 4 kcal ME (16.7 kJ)/g DM.

Energy requirements for lactating bitches can be subdivided into energy for maintenance and energy used for milk production. The DER, without allotment for milk production, may be slightly higher than that for average adults because of stress and increased activity associated with caring for puppies. The DER, without allotment for milk production, has been estimated to be 143 kcal (600 kJ) digestible energy per kg body weight to the three-fourths power.[150] This is equivalent to 132 kcal (550 kJ) ME/$BW_{kg}^{0.75}$ or about 1.9 x RER.

Table 9-17. Calculation of milk production in the bitch.*

TP (liters) = (BW_{kg} x k) + [(n–4) x (0.1 x BW_{kg})]

Peak milk production (Weeks 3 to 4) = TP x 0.04.

Example = 30-kg bitch with 8 puppies
TP = (30 x 2) + [(8–4) x (0.1 x 30)]
  = 60 + (4 x 3) = 72 liters milk
Peak milk production (Weeks 3 to 4) = 72 x 0.04
  = 2.9 liters/day

Key: TP = total milk production through Day 45 of lactation,
n = number of puppies,
k = 1.6 for bitches ≤8 kg BW, 1.8 for bitches >8 to <25 kg BW and 2.0 for bitches ≥25 kg BW,
BW = bitch's body weight.
*Grandjean D, Paragon B-M, Grandjean R. Rationnement alimentaire et prévention chez le chien 1. Le Point Vétérinaire 1986; 18: 519-524.

Energy used for milk production can be estimated from multiplication of the following factors: 1) gross energy of the milk determined as 1.46 kcal (6.1 kJ)/g,[150,173,175] 2) efficiency of 70 to 85% for converting maternal energy into milk energy[23,140,150] and 3) the quantity of milk produced daily. Using these values, a bitch requires 170 to 190 kcal (710 to 800 kJ) ME to produce 100 g of milk. Milk production is related to demand for milk, which is directly related to litter size and stage of lactation. Bitches with large litters will produce more milk than those with small litters and more milk is produced in mid-lactation than during late lactation. After five weeks of lactation, puppies begin eating more solid food and the number of puppies becomes less of a determinant. See Table 9-17 for a method for calculating milk production.

By combining the DER, without allotment for milk production, with the energy required for milk production, the total daily energy needed during lactation can be expressed as:

132 kcal ME per $BW_{kg}^{0.75}$ + (1.7 kcal x ml of milk/day).

In other words, during peak lactation, about 220 kcal (920 kJ) ME/kg litter weight are needed in addition to maintenance energy requirements.[129,140] As a rule of thumb, lactating bitches need 132 kcal ME/$BW_{kg}^{0.75}$ or about 1.9 x RER for maintenance; this amount should be increased 25% for each puppy. Because this is a rough estimate, body condition of bitches should be evaluated and adjustments made to feeding amounts as necessary to maintain an ideal body condition (BCS 3/5). Foods for lactation should provide between 4.0 to 5.0 kcal ME (16.7 to 20.9 kJ)/g DM (Table 9-13).[146,150,176]

Protein
The requirement for protein increases more than the requirement for energy during lactation.[150] Therefore, the protein-energy ratio must be higher in foods for lactation than in foods for adult maintenance. Ratios of 4.8 to 6.8 g digestible protein/100 kcal ME (10.5 to 15 g/MJ DE) have been recommended.[146,150,160] This recommendation corresponds to about 19 to 27% DM digestible protein of an energy-dense food (4.0 kcal [16.7 kJ] ME/g). Generally, it is recommended to feed a food containing at least 25% or more crude protein (Table 9-13)[54,177] from mixed sources with increased digestibility (Table 9-11) and sufficient energy density. (See above.) For homemade foods, the daily protein intake can be calculated on the basis of about 20 g digestible protein per kg body weight to the three-fourths power.[150]

Fat

Fat provides EFAs and energy and enhances fat-soluble vitamin absorption. The minimum level of fat in foods intended for lactating bitches (four or fewer puppies) is 10% DMB. However, an increase in fat intake results in better food efficiency during lactation.[178] Increasing concentrations of fat will also increase the caloric density of foods and help meet the high energy requirements of bitches during lactation. An increase in fat should be balanced by increasing other nutrients proportionally to match energy density (Table 9-13).

The type of dietary fat fed in conjunction with the fatty acid profiles of endogenous fat deposits may affect the fatty acid composition of milk. However, there is not sufficient information currently available to make recommendations for specific fatty acid profiles in foods for lactating bitches. Daily requirements for linoleic acid during lactation are estimated at 500 mg/kg body weight.[117] Milk fat and fatty acid composition are highly variable components of milk. Fat in bitch's milk contains a high percentage of unsaturated fatty acids and is rich in linoleic acid compared with cow's milk (Table 9-15). A recent study showed that increasing the fat content in the food from 12 to 20% DM might increase the fat content in the milk by 30%.[179] Because puppies are born with a very low energy reserve,[48,159] sufficient energy should always be available via the milk.

Carbohydrate

When lactating bitches are fed foods without soluble carbohydrates, the lactose level in the milk may decrease to about 2% vs. the normal range of 3 to 3.5%.[158,161] In one study, increasing the soluble carbohydrate level in the food corrected low lactose levels; however, the same effect was not achieved by increasing protein levels.[161] Therefore, these and other investigators recommended that foods for lactation provide at least 10 to 20% of the energy intake in the form of soluble carbohydrate to support normal lactose production.[146,161] See Table 9-13 for DM soluble carbohydrate recommendations.

Calcium and Phosphorus

Mineral requirements during lactation are determined by mineral excretion in milk[180] and thus by the number of nursing puppies. A definite increase in calcium content is seen over the course of lactation; however, the calcium-phosphorus ratio is consistently maintained around 1.3:1.[150] This is reflected by the fact that even without clinical eclampsia, plasma calcium levels tend to decrease during the third and fourth week of lactation.[159] Bitches need two to five times more calcium during peak lactation than for adult maintenance.[180,181] (See sidebar "Eclampsia.") Depending on the number of puppies, bitches need 250 to 500 mg calcium and 175 to 335 mg of phosphorus/kg body weight per day.[63] Leibetseder recommended that a food for lactation contain at least 0.8 to 1.1% calcium and 0.6 to 0.8% phosphorus;[146] however, reducing these needs by 10 to 20% will not necessarily lead to disturbances in milk mineral content. Table 9-13 lists practical recommendations for dietary calcium and phosphorus levels.[180] Calcium supplementation is necessary when homemade foods are provided, but not advised when balanced commercial foods are fed.

Other Nutritional Factors

Requirements for most trace elements depend on litter size. Iron requirements increase only slightly during lactation when compared with adult maintenance requirements because mature milk is relatively low in iron.[182] Colostrum is very rich in iron; however, levels decrease within 48 hours.[159] Requirements for copper (17 to 20 mg/kg DM), on the other hand, increase more than for energy.[182]

ASSESS THE FOOD(S)

Lactation represents an extreme test of a food's nutritional adequacy, because no other lifestage requires such a marked increase in energy density and nutrient content.[129] The nutrient demands are directly related to the dam's ability to produce milk. Food assessment includes a comparison of the current food's levels of key nutritional factors with those recommended in Table 9-13. Appendices L and M list levels of key nutritional factors for selected foods and treats. Alternatively, the manufacturer can be contacted for this information. Pet food labels usally lack information about soluble carbohydrate content, digestibility and energy density. The recommended food should also have passed an AAFCO or similar feeding test to prove it will support lactation. This information should be available on the product label. The food assessment step determines the appropriateness of the current food. Because nutritional requirements for lactation increase markedly over a relatively short period of time, it is very important to provide the correct food.

Homemade foods with rice and meat as the main ingredients may not provide enough EFAs for lactation, and may need to be supplemented with vegetable oil.[183]

ASSESS THE FEEDING METHOD

A lactating bitch's nutrient needs are met by a combination of the nutrient levels in the food and the amount fed. Even if the food has an appropriate nutrient profile, significant undernutrition may result if the bitch is fed an insufficient amount. If the bitch maintains normal body condition (BCS 3/5) and the puppies are growing at a normal rate, then the amount being fed is probably appropriate. The amount to feed can be estimated either by calculation (See Chapter 1.) or by referring to feeding guides on product labels. As a rough estimate, bitches should ingest their DER + 25% of DER for each nursing puppy. During peak lactation, a bitch's energy needs may be three to four times greater than its requirements for adult maintenance. The amount fed during lactation is usually offered either three times per day or free choice.

Feeding Plan

SELECT A FOOD(S)

A more appropriate food should be selected if food assessment indicates inadequacies or if lactation performance is suboptimal. Lactating bitches are best fed commercial foods. Dry foods are more nutrient dense, as fed, and have higher levels of carbohydrates than moist foods. These foods may benefit bitches experiencing weight loss or spending little time eating. Conversely, moist foods are often higher in fat and provide additional water to support lactation. The added water also improves palatability so bitches may be more likely to eat. Because both food types have advantages, many breeders choose to feed both forms during reproduction. Appendix L lists several commercial foods appropriate for lactation. Select a food that has passed an AAFCO or a similar feeding trial for lactation and provides levels of key nutritional factors listed in Table 9-13.

DETERMINE A FEEDING METHOD

In practice, it is best to feed bitches free choice during lactation,[129] except when the bitch has only one puppy and may have a tendency to gain weight. Free-choice feeding is especially important for lactating bitches with more than four puppies.[150] Some bitches are nervous throughout lactation and free-choice feeding will allow them to eat on their schedule. Meal-fed lactating bitches should receive at least three meals per day.[129,146] Puppies may begin to eat the bitch's food at three weeks of age; therefore, it is important to allow them access to the food.

Reassessment

Owners should carefully observe the bitch and the litter. Although experienced breeders usually are good observers, they still should be reminded to look for signs of impending problems. Owners should consult their veterinarian if the bitch's food intake decreases or an abnormal vaginal discharge develops. Other signs that should prompt veterinary care include hypersalivation, muscle contractions, seizures and/or weakness. Poor quality maternal care is another reason for owners to consult their veterinarian. Rectal temperature and mammary gland health should be evaluated regularly.[149]

Body weight gain by puppies during early lactation provides an indication of milk production by the bitch (quantity and quality) and milk intake by puppies. Failure to gain weight for more than one day or continuous vocalization may indicate that the quantity or quality of milk production is insufficient due to mastitis, agalactia or inadequate nutrition.

Body condition scoring is an important tool to assess nutritional adequacy. Breeders can easily be taught how to assess and score body condition. A bitch should not lose more than 5% of body weight during the first month of lactation, and optimal body weight should again be reached within a month after lactation ceases.[140,184] BCS should be maintained around 3/5 throughout lactation, otherwise adjustments should be made in the food or feeding method, assuming other potential causes of weight loss are ruled out.

The bitch should receive a veterinary checkup around the third or fourth week of lactation. This evaluation should include a physical examination with special attention given to mammary glands and body condition.

■ WEANING

Weaning is a gradual process with two phases. The first phase begins when the puppies begin eating solid food between three and four weeks of age. This phase should be encouraged, especially if the bitch has a large litter. In addition, nursing is an important stimulus for milk production. Therefore, milk production will progressively decline as the puppies' intake of solid food increases, making complete weaning (second phase) less stressful. However, some bitches may continue to produce large quantities of milk and are at risk for development of mammary congestion at the time the puppies are completely separated from the bitch. The feeding schedule in Table 9-18 may be helpful, particularly in cases of early weaning (around the fifth week of age).

Restricting food intake a day or two before weaning reduces nutrients available for milk production, thereby reducing mammary gland engorgement. Leaving one or two

Table 9-18. Recommended feeding schedule for reducing mammary congestion in bitches during weaning of puppies.*

Day of weaning	No food
First day after weaning	One-fourth of DER for adult maintenance (e.g., 0.5 x RER)
Second day after weaning	One-half of DER for adult maintenance (e.g., RER)
Third day after weaning	Three-fourths of DER for adult maintenance (e.g., 1.4 x RER)

Key: DER = daily energy requirement, RER = resting energy requirement.
*Meyer H. Praktische Fütterung. In: Ernährung des Hundes, 2nd ed. Stuttgart, Germany: E Ulmer Verlag, 1990; 162-223.

puppies to nurse will not alleviate mammary gland engorgement in bitches that are still producing a large amount of milk at weaning. This practice continues to stimulate milk production, and therefore prolongs the problem. When it is decided to completely separate the puppies from the mother, all puppies should be taken away at once.

■ GROWING DOGS

Compared with the young of other species, newborn puppies are relatively immature at birth. For example, their skeletons have a low degree of mineralization.[24,159] Large-breed puppies are more premature than small-breed puppies, which may be one of the reasons why they are more susceptible to malnutrition and developmental orthopedic diseases during the rapid growth phase.

Growing dogs progress through three critical phases in the first 12 months of life, during which nutrition is essential for survival and healthy development.

- A nursing period during which the transition is made from in utero nutrition to postpartum nutrition. This period is largely influenced by the nutrition of the bitch during gestation and early lactation.
- A weaning period, which is very stressful due to changes in food and environment. The transition from bitch's milk to solid food for further growth must therefore be handled properly.
- A postweaning period that occurs from two to 12 months of age and is a critical time for skeletal and other development. Proper feeding during this period is especially critical for large- and giant-breed puppies because nutrition has proved to be the most important non-genetic factor for healthy bone development.

Growing Dogs: Nursing Period

Before weaning, mortality may be as high as 10 to 30%, with two-thirds of the deaths occurring during the first week of life.[185,186] Nutrition during gestation and early lactation, behavior and health of the bitch and good neonatal care are factors critical to successful transition from fetal life to the nursing period. (See Appendix E.)

Assessment

ASSESS THE ANIMAL

History

When raising puppies, owners should be encouraged to maintain a logbook that may provide important informa-

Puppy Behavior from Birth to 12 Weeks of Age

Three phases of puppy behavior are described during the first 12 weeks of life:

- Neonatal period: From whelping to when the eyes open at about 13 days of age.
- Transition period: From when the eyes open to three weeks of age.
- Socialization period: From three weeks of age to weaning.

NEONATAL PERIOD

A newborn puppy has basically two activities: sleeping and nursing. Puppies quickly learn to find the bitch's teats when the bitch lies down for nursing. Nursing should be vigorous and active, and after nursing, the puppy's abdomen should be enlarged. Following nursing, puppies usually return to sleep. Neonates spend more than 80% of their time sleeping. However, a healthy puppy never sleeps deeply and quietly. Involuntary muscle contractions such as jerks and twitches (especially of the facial muscles) and irregular respiration are common. This pattern of activity is called "activated sleep" and should not be mistaken for shivering, a reflex that is not operant until about seven days of age. A puppy sleeping without these movements may be ill and should be observed closely. Puppies start crying when hungry or away from the litter; however, healthy puppies will stop crying soon and sleep again, even without nursing. Weak puppies may also have an enlarged abdomen but are restless and continue to vocalize. Such vocalizing is a constant high-pitched crying and is different from the crying of healthy puppies when they are hungry.

TRANSITION PERIOD

Puppies become more responsive to their environment as they become older. They no longer cry consistently when hungry or separated from littermates, but will cry when placed in an unfamiliar environment, even if warm and fed. Puppies begin to respond to visual stimuli when their eyes open. Puppies first start to play fight, clumsily pawing and mouthing at one another during this period. Tail wagging also occurs.

The first teeth may begin to erupt during the third week of life. Puppies lose the need for perineal stimulation to eliminate. Sucking on objects other than the bitch's nipples progressively decreases. By the end of the transition period puppies begin to lap liquids. A gruel or milk replacer should be presented in a bowl or saucer at this time; ground meat or thick gruels can be hand fed.

SOCIALIZATION PERIOD

Once the pup can see and hear, it begins more active social interactions with its dam, littermates and people. Social bonds are formed and social hierarchies are begun. The critical period for socialization lasts until about 12 weeks, and exposure to both people and other dogs is essential. Puppies achieve the full-grown dog form of locomotion, although they are still clumsy and have little endurance. Play fighting among puppies becomes a predominant behavior during this period. Eruption of deciduous teeth is complete by the first half of this period. The puppies no longer eliminate reflexively when the perineum is stimulated and they leave the nest box to do so. During the socialization period, puppies develop the ability to lap liquids well and they are able to eat solid foods. The dam becomes less tolerant to nursing.

BIBLIOGRAPHY

Björck G. Care and feeding of the puppy in the postnatal and weaning period. In: Anderson RS, ed. Proceedings. First Nordic Symposium on Small Animal Veterinary Medicine, Oslo, Norway, Sept. 15-18, 1982. Oxford, UK: Pergamon Press, 1984; 25-33.

Meyer H, Dammers C, Kienzle E. Körperzusammensetzung neugeborener Welpen und Nährstoffbedarf trägender Hündinnen. Fortschritte in der Tierphysiologie und Tierernährung (Advances in Animal Physiology and Animal Nutrition) 1985; Suppl. No. 16: 7-25.

O'Brien D. Neurological examination and development of the neonatal dog. Seminars in Veterinary Medicine and Surgery: Small Animal 1994; 9: 62-67.

tion about the health and nutritional status of the puppies and dam. Owners should record birth weights and then body weights of the puppies every one to two days for the first four weeks of life. Changes in behavior and other indicators of health such as opening of eyes, eruption of teeth, consistency of feces and food intake should also be recorded. Puppies should be marked (e.g., with a colored collar, nail polish, etc.) to facilitate easy recognition.

Physical Examination

The goal of a physical examination is to assess indicators of impaired health that may reveal serious metabolic perturbations such as hypoglycemia, hypothermia and dehydration. Special attention should be paid to assessment of puppy behavior, (See sidebar "Puppy Behavior from Birth to 12 Weeks of Age.") environmental conditions and hygiene. These parameters are important markers/risk factors for potential health problems. However, because puppies depend completely on the bitch's milk during the neonatal period, assessment must always include a thorough evaluation of the health and maternal behavior of the bitch.

The three most important areas of evaluation of nursing puppies are assessment of body weight (especially with respect to temporal changes), body temperature and other physical parameters.

Body Weight

Low birth weight is highly correlated to neonatal mortality. Low birth weight puppies are particularly prone to hypoglycemia and sepsis, and are less likely to survive without special care. Nursing puppies should be weighed daily or every other day on a gram scale. Monitoring the puppies' weight is a good way to evaluate the quality and quantity of milk the bitch is producing as well as the milk intake and health status of the puppies. (See sidebar "Body Weight Gain in Puppies.") Puppies should neither lose weight nor fail to gain weight for more than one day. Weight loss or failure to gain in an individual puppy or the entire litter may indicate disease in the puppies or bitch, inadequate milk production or inability to suckle. It is essential to evaluate puppies' growth rate in relation to changes in behavior such as crying, restlessness and continuous vocalization.

Body Temperature

When handling the puppy, the clinician should determine whether the puppy is warm. Neonates show a certain degree of poikilothermy during the first two weeks of life,[153] and have an extremely low level of body fat.[187] Therefore, it is vital for newborn puppies to eat and be kept in a warm environment. During the first week, the immediate environment of the puppies should be kept between 29 and 32°C (84 to 90°F). This means that the temperature in the

Body Weight Gain in Puppies

Birth weight of puppies is the single most important measure of their chances of survival, and reflects, among other factors, the adequacy of the bitch's nutrition during pregnancy. The evolution of a puppy's body weight gives useful information about food intake and general health. Body weight should be recorded within 24 hours after birth, and then daily or every other day for the first four weeks of life, using an accurate gram scale.

BIRTH WEIGHT

Due to variation in breed size, an exact optimal birth weight is difficult to estimate for individual puppies. Body weight at birth correlates primarily with the weight of the mother; birth weights range from 1% for some large and giant breeds to about 6.5% in Chihuahuas. Interestingly, investigators found a consistent ratio between the weight of the total litter and the body weight of the dam. Birth weight of the entire litter averages about 12 to 14% of adult body weight. The ratio can be slightly smaller in large breeds. Given the number of puppies and the ratio of litter to adult body weight, the birth weight of individual puppies can be evaluated in relation to the expected number of puppies per litter.

BODY WEIGHT GAIN

Daily weight gain averages about 5% of the puppy's current body weight during the first four weeks after birth. The absolute daily weight gain is lowest during the first week of life; however, the relative increase is largest (average 7.7% of body weight), and can reach 10% of body weight (Table 1). In the first 48 hours, the increase in body weight is not related to the puppy's body weight, because healthy smaller puppies eat relatively more in an effort to replete body reserves.

The puppy's body weight often doubles by eight to 10 days after birth and it may triple by the third week. Although the relative weight gain gradually decreases, weight gain in g/day varies little from the second to the fourth week of life.

Daily gain can vary markedly. Although puppies should be weighed every day or every other day, a more precise evaluation should be based on the average weekly weight gain.

Between one and two months of age, daily weight gain may average 3 g/kg adult body weight, and between 2 and 4 g/kg adult body weight until five months of age. These numbers may be used to help assess growth rates. However, dogs do not grow linearly; the growth curve has a sigmoid shape, with a fast exponential growth component first followed by slower growth. The exact timing of these phases differs from breed to breed. As a rule, small- and medium-sized dogs (up to 25 kg) reach about 50% of their adult weight around four months of age, whereas dogs with adult weights above 25 kg reach the 50% point at about five months of age. (See Appendix F.)

BIBLIOGRAPHY

Björck G. Care and feeding of the puppy in the postnatal and weaning period. In: Anderson RS, ed. Proceedings. First Nordic Symposium on Small Animal Veterinary Medicine, Oslo, Norway, September 15-18, 1982. Oxford, UK: Pergamon Press, 1984; 25-33.

Fuhrer L, Grandjean D. Modélisation mathématique de la croissance du chiot–Application à l'élaboration d'un plan de rationnement informatisé. Recueil de Médecine Vétérinaire 1986; 162: 1217-1222.

Gesellschaft für Ernährungsphysiologie. Grunddaten für die Berechnung des Energie- und Nährstoffbedarfs. In: Ausschuß für Bedarfsnormen der Gesellschaft für Ernährungs-Physiologie Energie-Nährstoffbedarf/Energy and Nutrient Requirements, No. 5 Hunde/Dogs. Frankfurt/Main, Germany: DLG Verlag, 1989; 9-31.

Grandjean D, Paragon B-M, Grandjean R. Rationnement alimentaire et prévention chez le chien 1. Le Point Vétérinaire 1986; 18: 519-524.

Jean-Blain C. Allaitement et sevrage du chiot. Revue de Médecine Vétérinaire 1973; 124: 1255-1268.

Kaiser G. Die Reproduktionsleistung der Haushunde in ihrere Beziehung zur Körpergröße und zum Gewicht der Rassen III. Teil Zeitschrift Tierzüchtg und Züchtgsbiologie 1971; 88: 316-340.

Kienzle E, Landes E. Aufzucht verwaister Jungtiere Teil II: Herstellung von Milchaustauschern und praktische Durchführung der mutterlosen Aufzucht. Kleintierpraxis 1995; 40: 687-700.

Kienzle E, Meyer H, Dammers C, et al. Milchaufnahme, Gewichtentwicklung, Milchverdaulichkeit, sowie Energie- und Nährstoffretention bei Saugwelpen. Fortschritte in der Tierphysiologie und Tierernährung (Advances in Animal Physiology and Animal Nutrition) 1985; Suppl. No. 16: 27-50.

Lawler DF. Care and diseases of neonatal puppies and kittens. In: Bonagura JD, ed. Current Veterinary Therapy XII. Philadelphia, PA: WB Saunders Co, 1995; 37-40.

Meyer H, Dammers C, Kienzle E. Körperzusammensetzung neugeborener Welpen und Nährstoffbedarf trägender Hündinnen. Fortschritte in der Tierphysiologie und Tierernährung (Advances in Animal Physiology and Animal Nutrition) 1985; Suppl. No. 16: 7-25.

Mundt H-C, Thomée A, Meyer H. Zur Energie- und Eiweißversorgung von Saugwelpen über die Muttermilch. Kleintierpraxis 1981; 26: 353-360.

Table 1. Average daily weight gain of puppies.*

Week	% of current body weight
1	8 (5-10)
2	6
3	4
4	3.5

*Adapted from Kienzle E, Meyer H, Dammers C, et al. Milchaufnahme, Gewichtentwicklung, Milchverdaulichkeit, sowie Energie- und Nährstoffretention bei Saugwelpen. Fortschritte in der Tierphysiologie und Tierernährung (Advances in Animal Physiology and Animal Nutrition) 1985; Suppl. No. 16: 27-50. Mundt H-C, Thomée A, Meyer H. Zur Energie- und Eiweißversorgung von Saugwelpen über die Muttermilch. Kleintierpraxis 1981; 26: 353-360.

room with the bitch and its litter should be maintained between 24 and 27°C (75 to 81°F). (See Appendix E.) Marginal hypothermia can often be detected by palpation of the lower limbs. (See sidebar "Hypoglycemia, Hypothermia and Dehydration in Neonates.")

The behavior of the bitch may give some indication as to whether a puppy is hypothermic or ill. A bitch may start pushing a puppy away and neglect its cries when the puppy's skin temperature drops below a certain level.[153]

Other Physical Parameters

When evaluating neonates, the clinician should hold each puppy to assess alertness, muscle tone and response to handling. The clinician should also assess the puppy's strength. Attentive and experienced breeders often are good observers and make these evaluations routinely. Gastric fullness should be evaluated, and the owner asked if the puppies are nursing. Hungry puppies will start crying; however, healthy puppies will soon stop crying and sleep, even without nursing. (See sidebar "Puppy Behavior from Birth to 12 Weeks of Age.") Small and weak puppies may appear to nurse and develop abdominal fullness, yet fail to thrive. Weak puppies may also have an enlarged abdomen but are often restless and continue vocalizing, which should alert the owner. This distention may result

Hypoglycemia, Hypothermia and Dehydration in Neonates

Before weaning, mortality of puppies can be as high as 10 to 30%, with 65% of the deaths occurring during the first week of life. Healthy puppies sleep and nurse; when a puppy continues to vocalize it is probably ill, malnourished, cold or dehydrated.

The syndrome of hypoglycemia, hypothermia and dehydration is by far the most common nutrition-related condition seen in neonates. Orphan puppies are at a much higher risk than nursing puppies, especially when deprived of colostrum.

Low fat stores and the degree of poikilothermy make puppies very dependent on effective nursing and optimal environmental temperature during the first two weeks of life. The first three days of life, however, are the most critical. Rectal temperatures of newborn puppies may decrease up to 4 to 5°C (7 to 8°F) immediately after birth. Further, healthy puppies may lose about 0.5 g of body weight every 30 minutes that they sleep without being fed.

When food intake is inadequate or when the environmental temperature is too low, newborn puppies rapidly deplete glycogen and fat stores and soon chill and become hypoglycemic, weak and dehydrated. Etiology includes inadequate milk production by the bitch (qualitative or quantitative), and all the causes of anorexia and reasons why a puppy refuses or is unable to nurse, including early maternal rejection, prematurity and low birth weight.

Infections, parasites and other illnesses lead to anorexia and may cause hypoglycemia, dehydration and hypothermia. Diarrhea rapidly causes dehydration in young puppies.

Hypoxia is an important cause of anorexia and hypoglycemia. Hypoxia may result from dystocia, prolonged birth or trauma caused by the bitch. Neonates have significantly lower blood glucose levels during the first day of life when their dam did not eat during the last days of pregnancy.

Hypoglycemia, hypothermia and dehydration are interrelated; one can cause or worsen the others, starting a vicious cycle (Figure 1).

HYPOTHERMIA

Once a puppy's rectal temperature drops below 34.5°C (94°F) the puppy becomes less active and nurses ineffectually, bowel movements stop and digestion no longer occurs. When a puppy's skin feels cold, the dam will push the puppy away and ignore its cries. The puppy then becomes hypoglycemic and is too weak to nurse, initiating a vicious cycle from which the puppy will not survive without help. Tissue hypoxia and metabolic acidosis may reach profound proportions. Once the body temperature reaches the critical level of 32°C (90°F), hypothermia becomes severe and the puppy lies motionless, with a very slow respiratory rate and an occasional air hunger response. It has been reported that healthy newborn puppies can survive up to 12 hours of deep hypothermia and recover if warmed slowly. In practice, however, hypothermic puppies can be rescued only when the problem is detected early and treated correctly.

Hypothermia that develops in puppies kept at the correct environmental temperature may indicate insufficient milk intake by the puppy due to disease or weakness, inability to reach the bitch's nipples, insufficient milk production and/or inadequate maternal behavior and poor milk quality or quantity due to insufficient nutrition of the dam, disease of the dam and/or inherited factors.

Orphan puppies are at greater risk because they are more sensitive to suboptimal temperatures without the dam. In addition, the milk replacer formula or feeding schedule may be inadequate.

HYPOGLYCEMIA

Fetuses receive continuous infusion of glucose from the placenta, so they do not depend on their own gluconeogenesis. Because they have very low fat and glycogen reserves at birth, canine neonates may develop hypoglycemia after only 12 hours of fasting. In contrast, adult dogs can undergo weeks of starvation without developing hypoglycemia. During starvation, gluconeogenesis becomes the sole means of glucose homeostasis. The neonate's small muscle mass, decreased use of free fatty acids as an alternate energy source and a possible lack of gluconeogenic enzymes limit the neonate's capacity to maintain normal glucose levels. Transient hypoglycemia is sometimes seen in toy-breed puppies between two and three months of age; however, transient hypoglycemia is different from this syndrome.

DEHYDRATION

Dehydration is characterized by wrinkled skin and dry, sticky mucous membranes, which may appear deep pink or red.

Continued on next page.

---

from aerophagia;[144] however, more often it is caused by malnutrition or illness of the bitch or puppy. Weak puppies cannot reach the bitch's nipples and stimulate milk release by kneading the mammary glands with their forelimbs.

Key Nutritional Factors
Colostrum and Milk

The liquid secretions from the mammary glands during the first few days postwhelping are known as colostrum. The composition of the milk changes rapidly to become normal or "mature" milk between 24 hours after parturition and the end of the first week of lactation. Colostrum transfers immunoglobulins, provides a concentrated source of energy and selected nutrients and produces a laxative effect.

The immune system of neonatal puppies is immature, which is offset by passive transfer of immunoglobulins from the bitch across the placenta and in the colostrum.[188,189] Investigators estimate that puppies receive only 5 to 10% of IgG from transplacental transfer; therefore, they depend primarily on immunity derived from the intake of colostrum.[189]

Colostrum contains about twice as much protein as mature milk, the difference being made up entirely by globulin proteins.[150,172] Colostrum is particularly rich in IgG as opposed to mature milk, which is richer in IgA.[188]

Colostrum has a very different composition than mature milk. Due to its high dry matter content, colostrum is somewhat sticky and viscous,[150] which makes nursing more difficult, especially for weaker puppies. Dry matter content of colostrum decreases within 12 to 24 hours after whelping, primarily reflecting a decrease in protein.

The lactose concentration of colostrum is very low compared with that of mature milk (i.e., 1.0 vs. 3.4%).[150] Levels of calcium, phosphorus and magnesium are very high in colostrum and decrease after two to three days to levels that are lower than in the subsequent mature milk.[150]

Just after whelping, colostrum contains high levels of iron, copper and zinc, which decrease to the levels in mature milk within 48 hours postpartum.[150] Colostrum is particularly high in vitamin A;[159,190] colostrum levels increase the liver reserve of vitamin A in puppies by 25% within a week.[159]

Continued from previous page.

TREATMENT

The three treatment goals for hypoglycemia, hypothermia and dehydration are to: 1) achieve optimal core body temperature, 2) maintain glucose within physiologically normal levels and 3) achieve adequate hydration status.

Chilled puppies should receive a mixture of equal amounts of physiologic saline solution (or lactated Ringer's solution) and a 5% glucose solution by subcutaneous injection before rewarming. Glucose is necessary to meet the sudden increase in energy requirements during warming.

Hypothermic puppies should first be warmed to 34.5°C (94°F), a temperature that allows digestive enzymes to become active again. If they are not warmed before being fed, hypothermic puppies will develop diarrhea, resulting in further dehydration and hypothermia, because of non-functioning digestive enzymes.

Hypothermic puppies should be warmed slowly and progressively over one to three hours to prevent oxygen and energy requirements of tissues from increasing faster than the puppy can supply. Aggressive, rapid warming can compromise vascular integrity and aggravate fluid loss and dehydration, resulting in hyperthermia, hypovolemia, shock and death. Slow warming is best accomplished by using body heat. A simple method such as placing a chilled puppy in an inside pocket of a loose-fitting garment will result in slow warming and gentle massage. Warm water (36.5°C [98°F]) or a warm-water heating blanket is a good alternative. If a closed incubator is used, humidity should be around 60%. Because their normal body temperature is lower than that of adult dogs, newborn puppies should not be warmed to adult body temperature, but to about 36 to 36.7°C (97 to 98°F). Hypothermic animals are susceptible to infections, so administration of antibiotics may be life-saving.

Dehydration should not be treated orally in markedly hypothermic puppies because of their depressed GI motility. Parenteral fluid solutions, warmed to body temperature, can be given subcutaneously, at the dose of 1 ml/30 g body weight, and repeated as needed. After body temperature is restored, oral solutions can be administered by stomach tube. Nursing should recommence as soon as possible, although hand rearing will be necessary if the bitch is incapable of feeding the puppies.

Tube feeding with an appropriate milk replacer, parenteral fluid administration and other supportive therapy should be implemented at once each time a young puppy becomes weak and before hypothermia and dehydration are a problem. (See Appendix E.)

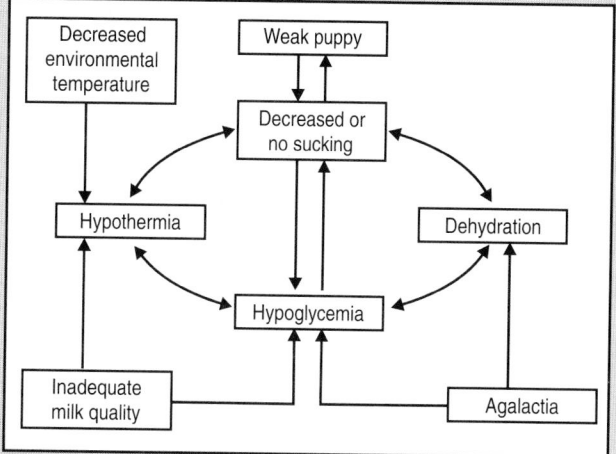

Figure 1. The figure shows how hypothermia, hypoglycemia and dehydration interrelate, creating a cycle that often results in neonatal death.

BIBLIOGRAPHY

Greco DS. The physical examination. In: Hoskins JD, ed. Veterinary Pediatrics–Dogs and Cats from Birth to Six Months. Philadelphia, PA: WB Saunders Co, 1990; 1-7.

Hoskins JD, ed. Nutrition and nutritional disorders. Veterinary Pediatrics–Dogs and Cats from Birth to Six Months. Philadelphia, PA: WB Saunders Co, 1990; 473-486.

Kienzle E, Landes E. Aufzucht verwaister Jungtiere Teil II: Herstellung von Milchaustauschern und praktische Durchführung der mutterlosen Aufzucht. Kleintierpraxis 1995; 40: 687-700.

Kienzle E, Meyer H, Dammers C, et al. Milchaufnahme, Gewichtentwicklung, Milchverdaulichkeit, sowie Energie- und Nährstoffretention bei Saugwelpen. Fortschritte in der Tierphysiologie und Tierernährung (Advances in Animal Physiology and Animal Nutrition) 1985; Suppl. 16: 27-50.

Kliegman RM, Miettinen EL, Adam PAJ. Substrate-turnover interrelationships in fasting neonatal dogs. American Journal of Physiology 1980; 239: E287-E293.

Lawler DF. Canine and feline periparturient problems. In: Small Animal Reproduction and Pediatrics. Purina Specialty Review. Pro-Visions, 1991; 21-51.

Lawler DF, Evans RH. Nutritional and environmental considerations in neonatal medicine. In: Kirk RW, ed. Current Veterinary Therapy X. Philadelphia, PA: WB Saunders Co, 1989; 1325-1333.

Wallace MS, Davidson AP. Abnormalities in pregnancy, parturition and the periparturient period. In: Ettinger SJ, Feldman EC, eds. Textbook of Veterinary Internal Medicine, 4th ed. Philadelphia, PA: WB Saunders Co, 1995; 1614-1624.

NORMAL DOGS

Milk is a complete food for neonates. The composition of milk (i.e., water, protein, fat, lactose, minerals and vitamins) is designed to support the normal growth rate of neonates. Milk from different species of mammals contains the same components but in different proportions. One reason for the difference in milk composition may be the relative growth rates of each species.[191] The faster the rate of growth, the more concentrated the milk nutrients to support growth (Table 9-16). Canine milk is higher in energy, protein and minerals than bovine milk. (See Appendix K.) The composition of milk does not change significantly over the course of the lactation.[145]

Energy

Data available from two studies show that bitch's milk is extremely digestible.[175,192] The energy intake of suckling puppies can be expressed in terms of gross energy (GE) because the energy digestibility is greater than 95%. The high digestibility of milk maximizes its usage and helps puppies survive the critical first weeks. Bitch's milk is high in energy and provides about 146 kcal GE (610 kJ)/100 g of milk.

Total milk intake per puppy is lowest during the first week of life. However, expressed per kg body weight, puppies' milk intake is highest during the first week and decreases progressively.[192] Daily intake averages about 239 kcal (1 MJ)/kg body weight/day during the first four weeks of life. Averages, however, may vary from as high as 287 kcal GE (1.2 MJ)/kg body weight during the first week of life to as low as 190 kcal GE (0.8 MJ)/kg body weight by Week 4.[173,175,192]

Energy requirements of puppies are the sum of energy needed for maintenance and the requirements for growth. Because puppies sleep more than 80% of their time, and huddle together in a warm whelping box, they are able to decrease their energy requirements for maintenance to a level that approaches RER (70 kcal/BW$_{kg}^{0.75}$) during the first week of life.[175] Therefore, all additional ingested energy can be used to grow and build body reserves. Puppies born with a lower body weight will ingest an amount of milk similar to that of their larger littermates during the first 48 hours of life to replete body reserves.[173,192]

Water

Normal puppies need 130 to 220 ml of water/kg body weight/day.[193,194]

Protein

Protein digestibility of bitch's milk is very high (up to 99%), and nitrogen retention is about 90% during the first week.[175] Compared with cow's milk, bitch's milk contains about twice as much protein per 100 ml (7.5 vs. 3.3%) (Table 9-16). Bitch's milk also provides high levels of arginine, lysine and branched-chain amino acids.[150,195] This nutrient profile is important when assessing and formulating milk replacers, and reflects the enormous anabolic activity of puppies at this young age. Protein requirements will be met if puppies ingest adequate amounts of energy as bitch's milk. (See Appendix K.)

Fat

Body fat is approximately 1.5% of total body mass at birth, which is very low when compared with the 22% body fat of non-obese adult dogs.[48,187] Puppies increase body fat during the first month of lactation; accretion of body fat is about 50% of total weight gain.[192] Body fat increases to about 10% of body weight by two weeks of age[24] and to 17% after one month.[192] The dam's milk, therefore, must contain enough energy (fat) to support development of these reserves. Milk fat and fatty acid composition are two of the most variable components of milk. The fat content and fat quality of milk depend on the food the bitch receives during lactation.[179] Bitch's milk should contain 9 g or more fat/100 g of milk.

Carbohydrate

Lactose is the primary carbohydrate in milk. Lactose levels in bitch's milk vary between 3.0 and 3.5%, which are about 30% lower than those in cow's milk. (See Appendix K.) Although the lactose content of milk varies widely among animal species, it is very consistent and maintained within narrow limits within a species. Lactose and minerals in milk are the primary contributors to osmolarity. Any increase or decrease in lactose content is offset by changes in the content of the other soluble components.[191]

Lactose is a disaccharide that is readily absorbed after digestion into its constituent monosaccharides. Lactose is unique in that its glucose and galactose molecules are linked with a β-1,4 bond instead of the α-1,4 linkage commonly found in other soluble glucose polymers.[196,197] This makes lactose a less suitable substrate for microbes that may infect the mammary gland or the neonate's GI tract. Further, large amounts of lactose may favor the colonization of the intestine by more beneficial microflora, which compete with and exclude many potential pathogens.[197] To avoid diarrhea, lactose should be the main source of carbohydrate during the first weeks of life. The activity of pancreatic amylases is insignificant at four weeks of age and is still very low at eight weeks, whereas intestinal lactase activity is high until about four months of age.[198,199]

Calcium and Phosphorus

Calcium levels are very high in colostrum; however, after two to three days, levels decrease to less than those found in subsequent mature milk.[150] An increase in calcium content is seen over the course of lactation; however, the calcium-phosphorus ratio is consistently maintained around 1.3:1.[150] Calcium and phosphorus levels in milk are not inherently different among different canine breeds. Canine milk is sufficiently rich in calcium, and levels could be regarded as recommendations for daily intake by growing puppies, despite the fact that calcification of the skeleton does not keep pace with the increase in body size until after weaning.[145,200]

Iron

Iron deficiency may occur if insufficient stores are accumulated during the last week of pregnancy, or if excessive blood loss occurs due to severe hookworm infection or severe flea infestation. During the first three to four weeks of life, body iron stores and hematocrit and hemoglobin values decrease below levels at birth. The decrease is more pronounced in fast-growing, large-breed puppies.[182]

Milk is a poor source of iron and puppy requirements are usually higher than intake.[192] Iron reserves increase again when puppies receive additional food at weaning, and body iron stores normalize around four months of age.[192] Therefore, puppies should receive additional food as soon as possible (around three weeks of age).

ASSESS THE FOOD(S)

Because direct assessment of milk quality is difficult, indirect parameters should be evaluated. Such parameters in puppies include weakness, enlarged abdomens, abnormal behaviors such as restlessness and continuous vocalization and failure to grow. Presence of these signs after illness is ruled out may indicate insufficient milk production and/or deficient milk quality.

Milk intake can be roughly estimated by weighing puppies before and after they nurse. The ratio of weight gain to milk intake may give some indication of milk quality. However, weight gains reportedly range from about 1 g/2 g of milk intake to 1 g/almost 5 g of milk intake during the first weeks of life.[173,175,201] This wide range results primarily from differences in ability to estimate milk intake. Also, an underweight bitch (BCS 1/5 or 2/5) may be at risk for producing inadequate or poor quality milk. Therefore, the bitch's food should also be assessed.

ASSESS THE FEEDING METHOD

Puppies should be encouraged to nurse as often as possible during the first week of life (eight to 12 times per day); after Week 1, they should be encouraged to nurse at least three to four times per day. Inexperienced bitches should be carefully observed to ensure that all puppies receive sufficient amounts of colostrum within 24 hours of birth, when they are still able to absorb intact proteins such as immunoglobulins. This involvement may include positioning the puppies on the bitch's nipples at feeding time or encouraging a nervous bitch to lay quietly as the puppies nurse. Handling the dam and puppies facilitates monitoring the progress of the litter.

Competition in large litters may prevent smaller, weaker puppies from nursing and predispose them to dehydration and hypoglycemia. Partial orphan rearing of the entire litter should be done in these cases. Partial orphan rearing allows the puppies to stay with the dam in their normal environment and permits proper socialization. Dividing the litter into two groups of equal number and size of puppies facilitates partial orphan rearing. One group is allowed to nurse the bitch, while the other group is given a milk replacer. The groups are exchanged three to four times per day. The group separated from the bitch should be fed before the puppies are returned to the bitch. Thus, these puppies will be full and less likely to nurse the bitch.[202] Supplementing all puppies with milk replacer is better than complete orphan feeding a few puppies. (See Appendix E for details about complete orphan feeding.)

Feeding Plan

Because nursing puppies depend completely on the bitch's milk, the feeding method used for the bitch should be evaluated and adapted if necessary. Most lactating bitches should be fed free choice. (See above.)

Puppies that fail to thrive when receiving bitch's milk should be fed immediately via partial or total orphan feeding techniques to avoid the risk of hypoglycemia, hypothermia and dehydration. (See Appendix E.)

Reassessment

Nursing puppies should be reassessed daily. Puppy body weights should be obtained at birth, daily or every other day for the first four weeks and then weekly. Adequacy of the bitch's milk production can be assessed by growth rate of the puppies, puppy contentment and mammary gland distention. To determine whether an individual mammary gland is producing milk, gently express milk from the nipple while the bitch is relaxed. Most breeders are experienced enough to do this without help. Less experienced owners may need to be taught how to do this; weekly veterinary checkups during the first month may be helpful.

Growing Dogs: Weaning Period

Puppies should be encouraged to start eating solid food as soon as possible. This practice will reduce reliance on the bitch, reduce the nutritional burden on the bitch, help overcome iron deficiency in the puppies and make complete weaning less stressful. Most puppies will start eating solid food between three and four weeks of age, the time when deciduous teeth begin to erupt. Oftentimes, during play, puppies will come in contact with the bitch's food and progressively start eating small amounts.

Puppies can be offered gruel to stimulate food intake at three weeks of age. Gruels can be made by blending a moist growth/reproduction-type food with an equal volume of warm water. Alternatively, dry food can be ground and mixed one part with three parts of warm water (volume basis). Puppies should be encouraged to lap the gruel by touching their lips to the food or the owner can place a finger tip in the gruel and then into the puppies' mouth. The gruel should be very digestible, and contain at least 450 kcal [1,880 kJ] ME/100 g DM, and 25 to 30% highly digestible protein.[146] Puppies are very prone to vomiting and diarrhea during this period. If GI disturbances occur, gruel can be made from a highly digestible moist food intended for dietary management of diarrhea with a minimum of about 25% DM protein. (See Chapter 22.)

As the puppies' interest in solid food increases, the water content of the gruel can be reduced progressively. Puppies should be eating sufficient quantities of solid food at five weeks of age because the bitch's milk production will probably start declining.

From three weeks of age on, puppies can be separated from their mother for short periods of time. The time away from the dam can be progressively increased to about four hours a day by around six weeks of age.[170] Weaning should be effectively completed between six and seven weeks of age and puppies can be removed from the dam.[170] After weaning, the puppies should be fed the same food to minimize stress and the risk of diarrhea.

Growing Dogs: Postweaning to Adulthood

The ultimate goal of a feeding plan for puppies is to create a healthy adult. The specific objectives of the puppy-feeding plan are to optimize growth and minimize obesity and developmental orthopedic disease. Growth is a complex process involving interactions between genetics, nutrition and other environmental influences. Nutrition plays a role in the health and development of growing dogs and directly affects the immune system,[203] body composition,[204,205] growth rate[204] and skeletal development.[206-208] Important health issues can arise if puppies are not properly fed during this period.

Assessment

ASSESS THE ANIMAL

Puppies should be assessed for risk factors before weaning so recommendations for appropriate nutrition can be implemented. As always, a thorough history and physical evaluation are required. Special attention should be paid to large- and giant-breed puppies (See Chapter 17.) and breeds and genders at risk for obesity. (See Chapter 13.) In addition to breed and gender risks, growth rates and BCS provide valuable information about nutritional risks.

Besides being breed dependent, growth rates of young dogs are dependent on the nutrient density of food and the amount of food fed.[204] Puppies should be fed to grow at an average rather than at a maximum rate for their breed. Growing animals reach a similar adult weight whether growth rate is rapid or slow. Feeding for maximum growth increases the risk of skeletal deformities[207,208] and has been shown to decrease longevity in other species.[209]

Appendix F lists body weights of various breeds of puppies at different ages. Despite the variability between breeds and individual dogs, these values can be used as an approximate guide to evaluate growth rates. If the body weight of a dog is markedly less than the listed values, the animal may be undernourished. Puppies weighing markedly more than the values in Appendix F are likely to be overfed, growing too fast and at risk for obesity and/or skeletal disease. As a rule of thumb, small- and medium-sized dogs (adult weights up to 25 kg) reach about 50% of their adult weight around four months of age and dogs with adult weights greater than 25 kg at about five months of age. All puppies should have their body condition evaluated and reassessed every two weeks to allow for adjustments in amounts fed and growth rates. (See Chapter 1.)

Key Nutritional Factors

The requirements for all nutrients increase during growth compared with requirements for adult dogs. However, energy and calcium levels are of special concern; energy for small- and medium-breed puppies (for obesity

Table 9-19. Key nutritional factors for growing dogs.

Factors	Recommended levels in food (DM)	
	Adult BW <25 kg*	Adult BW >25 kg**
Energy density (kcal ME/g)	3.5-4.5	3.2-3.8
Energy density (kJ ME/g)	14.6-18.8	13.6-15.7
Crude protein (%)	22-32	20-32
Crude fat (%)	10-25	8-12
Calcium (%)	0.7-1.7	0.7-1.2
Phosphorus (%)	0.6-1.3	0.6-1.1
Ca/P ratio	1:1-1.8:1	1:1-1.5:1
Digestibility	See Table 9-11	See Table 9-11

Key: DM = dry matter, BW = body weight, kcal = kilocalories, kJ = kilojoules, ME = metabolizable energy.
*For dogs with an adult BW of less than 25 kg. These dogs can be fed the same food as recommended for gestation/lactation. Balanced commercial foods may match the profile for gestation/lactation of most bitches and growth of puppies whose adult weight does not exceed 25 kg.
**For large- and giant-breed dogs (adult BW of more than 25 kg).

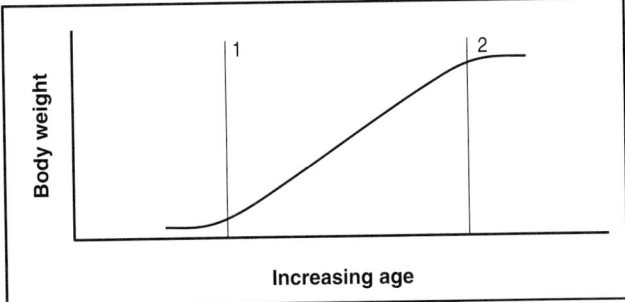

Figure 9-5. Typical sigmoidal growth curve of puppies. Growing puppies have two energy needs: the energy needed for maintenance, and the energy required for the accretion of body tissue. During the first weeks after weaning, when body weight is relatively small and growth rate exponential, puppies use about 50% of the energy for maintenance and 50% for growth. Gradually the growth curve reaches a plateau. As body weight increases, the share of energy needed for maintenance increases progressively, whereas the part for growth becomes less important. The starting (line 1) and endpoint (line 2) of exponential growth can shift depending on the breed and individual variation. (Adapted from Fuhrer L, Grandjean D. Modélisation mathématique de la croissance du chiot–Application à l'élaboration d'un plan de rationnement informatisé. Recueil de Médecine Vétérinaire 1986; 162: 1217-1222. Gesellschaft für Ernährungsphysiologie. Grunddaten für die Berechnung des Energie und Nährstoffbedarfs. Ausschuß für Bedarfsnormen Energie- und Nährstoffbedarf/Energy and Nutrient Requirements, No. 5 Hunde/Dogs. Frankfurt/Main, Germany: DLG Verlag, 1989; 9-31. Sheffy BE. Nutrition and nutritional disorders. Veterinary Clinics of North America: Small Animal Practice 1978; 8: 7-29.)

prevention) and energy and calcium for large- and giant-breed puppies (for skeletal health). In addition, the method of feeding is important especially in larger breeds.

Table 9-19 summarizes key nutritional factors for growing dogs. The following sections describe these key nutritional factors in more detail.

Energy

As previously discussed, energy requirements of growing puppies consist of energy needed for maintenance and energy required for growth. During the first weeks after weaning when body weight is relatively small and the growth rate is high, puppies use about 50% of their total energy intake for maintenance and 50% for growth.[57,141,210] Gradually, the growth curves reach a plateau, as puppies become young adults (Figure 9-5). The proportion of energy needed for maintenance increases progressively, whereas the part for growth becomes less important. Energy needed for growth decreases to about 8 to 10% of the total energy requirement when puppies reach 80% or more of adult body weight. Because of the shift in energy usage, total food intake of a typical German shepherd puppy (adult body weight 35 kg) may no longer increase after about four months of age. (See Appendix F.)

A puppy should receive 3 x RER until it reaches about 50% of its adult body weight (Table 9-20). Thereafter, energy intake should be about 2.5 x RER and can be reduced progressively to 2 x RER. When approximately 80% of adult size is reached, 1.8 to 2 x RER will suffice. Figure 9-6 depicts differences in energy requirements for different sized puppies at different ages. Great Dane puppies may have energy requirements 25% higher than those of other breeds. Young Great Dane puppies may not grow when daily energy intake is less than 175 kcal (735 kJ) ME per kg body weight to the three-fourths power (2.5 x RER).[204,211] However, this finding should not be extrapolated to other giant-breed puppies.[32] Appendix F provides a complete guide for daily energy intake during growth; values in Appendix F can be used as an initial feeding guideline. Body condition scoring should be used to adapt this information to individual dogs.

Management of obesity should start at weaning. Excessive food intake during growth may contribute to overweight and obese body conditions.[208] Obesity increases load and stress on immature bones and may contribute to skeletal disorders. In people, overfeeding during childhood results in an increased number of fat cells (hyperplastic obesity) at young adolescence, which may predispose to overt obesity later in life.[212] Whether this is also true in dogs has not been determined. Moderate dietary restriction during the postweaning growth period markedly increases longevity in rats, without retarding adult size.[209,213-215] However, feeding a food that has a low energy density and less than average digestibility leads to intake of large quantities of the food, which can overload the GI tract resulting in vomiting and diarrhea. Together, these factors make for a prudent argument to monitor energy intake at an early age.

Protein

Protein requirements of growing dogs differ quantitatively and qualitatively from those of adults. An important difference is that arginine is an essential amino acid for puppies, whereas it is only conditionally essential for adult dogs.[216] Quantitatively, protein requirements are highest around weaning, and decrease progressively.[117,217,218] In one study, beagle puppies needed a food with a minimum of 15% DM protein of high biologic value and 90% digestibility immediately after weaning to achieve optimal growth.[217] Only 11.7% DM of the same protein was needed at three months of age. These levels correspond to about 10 to 14 g of protein/$BW_{kg}^{0.75}$, or about 2.9 g/100 kcal ME (6.93 g/MJ).[54] Protein requirements for growing dogs follow a pattern similar to energy requirements. Thus, the same nutrient profile is appropriate throughout this phase of growth (postweaning to adulthood). The relatively higher requirements for protein immediately after weaning are compensated for by the higher total food intake to meet energy needs.[117]

Moreover, most foods for growing dogs contain more protein than is required just after weaning. When average-quality protein sources are used, foods containing 18%

DM digestible protein and 3.5 kcal/100 g DM, will support optimal growth from weaning to adulthood.[160,218] This corresponds to 22% crude protein of high quality and 80% digestibility.[160]

Earlier work suggested that excessive protein intake might play a role in the development of skeletal deformities in giant-breed dogs.[207] It has now been proved that foods containing 23 to 31% crude protein (6.4 to 8.8 g/100 kcal ME) do not have any deleterious effect on skeletal development and they support optimal growth, provided calcium and energy levels are appropriate.[219,220]

Fat

Growing dogs have an estimated daily requirement for EFAs (linoleic acid) of about 250 mg/kg body weight,[183] which can be provided by a food containing between 5 to 10% fat (DMB).[117] The fat source must be carefully chosen when low-fat foods (<10% DM fat) are fed so that sufficient amounts of linoleic acid are provided.

Fat contributes greatly to the energy density of a food and excessive energy intake can affect endochondral bone formation in large- and giant-breed dogs.[204,207,208] The fat content of foods for large- and giant-breed puppies should be controlled to decrease the likelihood of excessive energy intake. This can be achieved by feeding foods with a target energy density of 3.5 kcal (14.6 kJ) ME/g (range 3.2 to 3.8 kcal ME/g [13.4 to 15.9 kJ]).[221] Table 9-19 lists optimal ranges of key nutritional factors in foods for puppies of different breed sizes.

Calcium and Phosphorus

Although growing dogs need more calcium and phosphorus than adult dogs, the minimum requirements are relatively low. Puppies have been successfully raised on foods containing 0.37 to 0.6% DM calcium and 0.33% DM phosphorus.[222,223] Intestinal absorption of calcium can vary from almost 0 to 90%,[206,220] and phosphorus absorption can increase to almost 80% to adapt to intake.[63,222] In general, calcium absorption is dependent on requirements and calcium intake.[16] Calcium homeostatic mechanisms may be less precise in young puppies. In puppies between two and six months of age, intestinal absorption of calcium never decreases below approximately 40%, even if they receive high levels of calcium in foods.[206,207,220,222] Retention of calcium, therefore, increases when young dogs receive high levels of calcium, either in the food or as a supplement.[206,220] Absorption of calcium gradually becomes more regulated after puppies are about 10 months old.[207]

Foods for large- and giant-breed puppies should contain 0.7 to 1.2% DM calcium, and the food should provide about 3.5 kcal (14.6 kJ) ME/g DM. Foods with a calcium content of 1.1% DM provide more calcium to puppies just after weaning than if bitch's milk were fed exclusively.[224] Because small dogs are less sensitive to slightly overfeeding or underfeeding with calcium,[220] the level of calcium in foods for smaller breed puppies can range from 0.7 to 1.7% DM, without risk. The phosphorus intake is less critical than the calcium intake, provided the minimum requirements of 0.35% DM are met, and the calcium-phosphorus ratio is between 1:1 and 1.8:1.[222,223]

Digestibility

Puppies fed foods low in energy density and digestibility need to eat large quantities of food, increasing the risk of flatulence, vomiting, diarrhea and the development of a "pot-bellied" appearance. Therefore, foods recommended for puppies should be more digestible than average (Table 9-11).

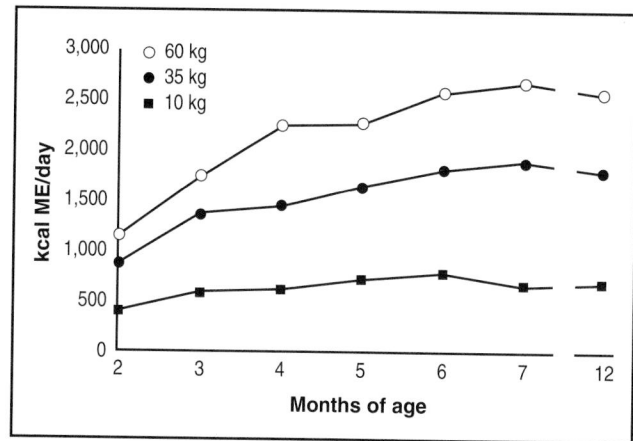

Figure 9-6. Recommendations for energy intake of growing puppies. Examples of puppies with an expected adult body weight of 10, 35 and 60 kg. (See Appendix F.) (Adapted from Gesellschaft für Ernährungsphysiologie. Grunddaten für die Berechnung des Energie und Nährstoffbedarfs. In: Ausschuß für Bedarfsnormen Energie- und Nährstoffbedarf/Energy and Nutrient Requirements, No. 5 Hunde/Dogs. Frankfurt/Main, Germany: DLG Verlag, 1989; 9-31. Gesellschaft für Ernährungsphysiologie. Empfehlungen für die Versorgung mit Energie. In: Ausschuß für Bedarfsnormen Energie- und Nährstoffbedarf/Energy and Nutrient Requirements, No. 5 Hunde/Dogs. Frankfurt/Main, Germany: DLG Verlag, 1989; 32-44.)

Other Nutritional Factors

No specific recommendations for carbohydrate levels are available for growing dogs. It has been suggested that foods contain about 20% carbohydrate until puppies are four months of age to ensure optimal health.[224] In one study, feeding young puppies a food high in protein and fat without carbohydrate resulted in lethargy, poor appetite, diarrhea and mortality, which was attributed to fatty liver syndrome.[224] However, another study failed to confirm these results.[225] Body fat is higher when puppies are fed a very high-fat, low-carbohydrate food during growth.[225]

Zinc requirements on a body weight basis are highest during the first two months of life; however, zinc requirements on a per unit of energy basis are highest between four to six months of age. Puppies are most sensitive to deficiency during this latter period; therefore, foods for growing dogs should contain zinc levels that meet the requirements between four to six months of age.[182] Excessive calcium and phosphorus intake should be avoided to ensure the availability of zinc.[182]

Most commercial pet foods should contain adequate levels of copper unless the availability is low (e.g., when sources such as copper oxide are used).[226] Puppies with copper deficiency may have loss of hair pigmentation, with graying of black and dark brown hair.[227,228] Hyperextension of the distal phalanges and splayed toes on the front feet and normochromic, normocytic anemia may develop in more extreme cases.[227,228] The recommendation for copper intake in growing puppies is between 0.25 and 0.5 mg/kg body weight.[182]

ASSESS THE FOOD(S)

The choice of an appropriate food can decrease the risks associated with rapid growth, especially for large- and giant-breed puppies. Therefore, a prerequisite for developing a feeding plan includes comparing the nutrient

Table 9-20. Recommendations for energy intake of growing dogs.

Time frame	x RER	kcal/BW$_{kg}^{0.75}$	kJ/BW$_{kg}^{0.75}$
Weaning to 50% of adult BW*	3	210	880
50 to 80% of adult BW	2.5	175	735
≥80% of adult BW	1.8-2.0	125-140	525-585

Key: RER = resting energy requirement, kcal = kilocalories,
kJ = kilojoules, BW = body weight.
*Great Dane puppies may need 20% more energy during the first two months
after weaning = 250 kcal or 1,050 kJ/BW$_{kg}^{0.75}$. (References 47 and 204).
Adapted from Gesellschaft für Ernährungsphysiologie Grunddaten für
die Berechnung des Energie- und Nährstoffbedarfs. Ausschuß für
Bedarfsnormen Energie- und Nährstoffbedarf Nr. 5 Hunde. Frankfurt/Main,
Germany: DLG Verlag, 1989; 9-31. Gesellschaft für Ernährungs
physiologie Empfehlungen für die Versorgung mit Energie. Ausschuß für
Bedarfsnormen. Energie- und Nährstoffbedarf Nr. 5 Hunde. Frankfurt/Main,
Germany: DLG Verlag, 1989; 32-44.

profile of the current food(s) with the levels of key nutritional factors listed in Table 9-19.

Puppies of small- to medium-sized breeds may continue to receive the same food as the bitch received during lactation. These puppies were probably transitioned to this food during weaning. Large- and giant-breed puppies should be fed a food that contains less energy and calcium to decrease the risk of developmental orthopedic disease. (See Chapter 17.) If possible, such foods should be fed during early weaning. The greatest influence of nutrition on the incidence of phenotypic hip dysplasia was seen when energy was restricted very early in life.[229]

Appendices L and M list levels of key nutritional factors in selected commercial foods and treats. Alternatively, pet food manufacturers can be contacted directly for this information. The guaranteed or typical analysis on pet food labels is of limited usefulness and will not contain information about digestibility. The product label indicates whether the food has successfully completed an AAFCO or similar feeding trial for growth. (See Chapter 5.) This information is important because foods with similar label declarations can have markedly different nutrient availabilities and growth performance.[230,231] Information about digestibility and energy density should be obtained from the manufacturer; digestibility must be sufficiently high to avoid GI problems.

Growing dogs should not receive vitamin-mineral supplements when fed complete, balanced commercial food(s). Supplements may be justified to balance homemade foods. Because it is very difficult for breeders to exactly balance a homemade food, large- and giant-breed puppies should only receive a commercially prepared food specifically designed for such breeds.

The calcium and energy content of treats (See Appendix M.) should be similar to that recommended for the food (Table 9-19). If not, the number of treats should be limited. Treats increase energy intake and given in large numbers may almost double a puppy's calcium intake. (See sidebar "Impact of Treats on Daily Nutrient Intake.")

ASSESS THE FEEDING METHOD

Assessment of feeding methods is critical to successful management of growing puppies, especially those of large and giant breeds. Free-choice and time-restricted feeding should be avoided during periods of rapid growth.

Free-choice feeding may increase body fat, predispose the dog to obesity and induce skeletal deformities at a young age.[221] Breeders who want to maximize growth and skeletal development of large- and giant-breed puppies must be taught that overfeeding predisposes these animals to developmental orthopedic disease. Weight gain and body condition should be monitored closely if free-choice feeding is used.

It has been recommended in the past to feed a puppy all it can eat in 20 minutes, twice daily.[129] However, recent work has shown that puppies fed using this method had increased body weight, more body fat and increased bone mineral accretion than puppies receiving the same food free choice.[205]

During the period of rapid growth, it is best for puppies to receive a specific amount of food. This amount can be fed in two to four meals per day. The energy recommendations in this section (Table 9-20) coupled with food dosage calculations (See Chapter 1.) or the feeding guidelines listed in Appendix F can be used as starting points.

Feeding Plan

SELECT A FOOD(S)

The food assessment phase will determine whether or not it is necessary to change foods. If a change is indicated, it is best to select a food that has passed an AAFCO or similar feeding trial for growth. Even so, because AAFCO feeding trials only last 10 weeks, they probably will not expose problems related to excess calcium and energy consumption, especially in large- and giant-breed puppies. Therefore, foods selected for growth should have key nutrients in the ranges provided in Table 9-19. See Appendix L for levels of key nutritional factors in selected commercial foods, or contact the manufacturer.

DETERMINE A FEEDING METHOD

Free-choice feeding is not generally recommended for puppies unless they are extremely thin (BCS 1/5) or have difficulty maintaining adequate body weight. Meal-restricted feeding is appropriate for most puppies to allow better control of body weight and growth rate. Table 9-8 outlines advantages and disadvantages of these feeding methods. Chapter 17 outlines more specific techniques to minimize nutritional risk factors for developmental orthopedic disease in rapidly growing, large- and giant-breed puppies.

Reassessment

Owners should weigh growing puppies every week and record body weights and food intake (including snacks and treats). Veterinarians can provide owners with expected body weights at different ages based on Appendix F to allow better assessment of body weight and food intake. Owners should be taught body condition scoring techniques and informed about early clinical signs of developmental orthopedic disease. Veterinarians should reassess puppies at the time of routine vaccinations and more frequently if any indication of under- or overnutrition is detected at that time. Reassessment should include body weight and body condition assessment, food assessment and determination of correct food dosage.

ENDNOTES & REFERENCES

ENDNOTES

a. Ekedahl D, Pet Food Institute, Chicago, IL. Personal communication. November 1997.

b. Lowry S, Hill's Science and Technology Center, Topeka, KS, Personal communication. August 1996.

REFERENCES

1. Anonymous. Family ties. Petfood Industry 1997; 39 (March/April): 62.

2. Marsh FO. Global awareness–Trends affecting petfood manufacturers. Petfood Industry 1994; 36: 4-10.

3. Center for Information Management. Dogs registered by the American Kennel Club 1986, 1992, and 1996. In: U.S. Pet Ownership & Demographics Sourcebook. Schaumburg, IL: American Veterinary Medical Association, 1997; 32-35.

4. Phillips T. Good News–Demographic shifts should benefit the petfood industry. Petfood Industry 1991; 33: 24-33.

5. Fogle B. Breed-related behavior in dogs: The practicing vet's view. In: Proceedings. WSAVA, BSAVA & FECAVA World Congress. Birmingham, UK, 1997: 73.

6. Corbet GB, Hill JE. A World List of Mammalian Species. New York, NY: Facts on File Publications, 1986; 105-121.

7. Morris JG, Rogers QR. Nutritional implications of some metabolic anomalies of the cat. In: Proceedings. Fiftieth American Animal Hospital Association Annual Meeting, San Antonio, TX, 1983: 325-331.

8. Morris JG, Rogers QR. Comparative aspects of nutrition and metabolism of dogs and cats. In: Burger IH, Rivers JPW, eds. Nutrition of the Dog and Cat. Cambridge, UK: Cambridge University Press, 1989; 35-66.

9. Sheldon JW. Genus Canis. In: Wild Dogs: The Natural History of the Nondomestic Canidae. San Diego, CA: Academic Press Inc, 1992; 23-61.

10. Landry SM, Van Kruiningen HJ. Food habits of feral carnivores: A review of stomach content analysis. Journal of the American Animal Hospital Association 1979; 15: 775-782.

11. Lewis LD, Morris ML Jr, Hand MS. Cats–Feeding and care. In: Small Animal Clinical Nutrition III. Topeka, KS: Mark Morris Associates, 1987; 4-1–4-12.

12. Beaver BV. Grass eating by carnivores. Veterinary Medicine/Small Animal Clinician 1981; 76: 968-969.

13. Röhrs M. Die Domestikation von Wolf und Wildkatze Parallelen und Unterschiede. In: Meyer H, Kienzle E, eds. Ernährung, Fehlernährung und Diätetik bei Hund und Katze. Proceedings International Symposium, Hannover, Germany, September 3-4, 1987: 5-12.

14. Meyer H. Bau und Funktion des Verdauungskanals. In: Ernährung des Hundes, 2nd ed. Stuttgart, Germany: E Ulmer Verlag, 1990; 27-49.

15. Ruckebusch Y, Phaneuf L-Ph, Dunlop R. Feeding behavior. In: Physiology of Small and Large Animals. Philadelphia, PA: BC Decker Inc, 1991; 209-219.

16. Meyer H. Verdauung und Absorption. In: Ernährung des Hundes, 2nd ed. Stuttgart, Germany: E Ulmer Verlag, 1990; 50-62.

17. Meyer H, Mundt H-C, Thomée A. Untersuchungen über den Einfluß der Fütterungsfrequenz auf Futteraufnahme und Verdaulichkeit bei wachsenden und adulten Hunden. Kleintierpraxis 1980; 25: 267-274.

18. Schummer A, Nickel R. Rumpfdarm der Fleischfresser. In: Nickel R, Schummer A, Seiferle E, eds. Lehrbuch der Anatomie der Haustiere Band II–Eingeweide. Berlin, Germany: P Parey, 1960; 120-136.

19. Wolter R. Particularités digestives des carnivores et conséquences. In: L'alimentation du Chien et du Chat. Maisons-Alfort, France: Les Éditions du Point Vétérinaire, 1982; 23-36.

20. Martin LD. Fossil history of the terrestrial carnivore. In: Gittleman JL, ed. Carnivore Behavior, Ecology and Evolution. Ithaca, NY: Cornell University Press, 1989; 536-568.

21. Grandjean D, Paragon B-M. Alimentation du chien âgé. Le Point Vétérinaire 1990; 22: 243-254.

22. Blaxter K. Body composition and metabolism. In: Energy Metabolism in Animals and Man. Cambridge, UK: Cambridge University Press, 1989; 137-139.

23. Pellett PL. Food energy requirements in humans. American Journal of Clinical Nutrition 1990; 51: 711-722.

24. Meyer H, Stadtfeld G. Investigations on the body and organ structure of dogs. In: Anderson RS, ed. Nutrition of the Dog and Cat. Oxford, UK: Pergamon Press, 1980; 15-30.

25. Edney ATB, Smith PM. Study of obesity in dogs visiting veterinary practices in the United Kingdom. Veterinary Record 1986; 118: 391-396.

26. Mason E. Obesity in pet dogs. Veterinary Record 1970; 86: 612-616.

27. Anantharaman-Barr G. The effect of ovariohysterectomy on energy metabolism in dogs (research abstract). Friskies Veterinary International 1990; 2: 19-20.

28. Houpt KA, Coren B, Hintz HF, et al. Effects of sex and reproductive status on sucrose preference, food intake, and body weight of dogs. Journal of the American Veterinary Medical Association 1979; 174: 1083-1085.

29. O'Farrell V, Peachey E. Behavioural effects of ovariohysterectomy on bitches. Journal of Small Animal Practice 1990; 31: 595-598.

30. Hopkins SG, Schubert TA, Hart BL. Castration of adult male dogs: Effects on roaming, aggression, urine marking and mounting. Journal of the American Veterinary Medical Association 1976; 168: 1108-1110.

31. Lewis LD. Obesity in the dog. Journal of the American Animal Hospital Association 1978; 14: 402-409.

32. Rainbird AL, Kienzle E. Untersuchungen zum Energiebedarf des Hundes in Abhängigkeit von Rassezugehörigkeit und Alter. Kleintierpraxis 1990; 35: 149-158.

33. Kienzle E, Rainbird A. Maintenance energy requirement of dogs: What is the correct value for the calculation of metabolic body weight in dogs? Journal of Nutrition 1991; 121: S39-S40.

34. Zentek J, Meyer H. Energieaufnahme adulter Deutscher Doggen. Berliner und Münchener Tierärztliche Wochenschrift 1992; 105: 325-327.

35. Männer K. Energy requirement for maintenance of adult dogs of different breeds (abstract). In: Abstract Book. Waltham International Symposium on the Nutrition of Small Companion Animals, University of California, Davis, September 4-8, 1990: 14.

36. Meyer H. Energiebedarf. In: Ernährung des Hundes. Stuttgart, Germany: E Ulmer Verlag, 1983; 97-110.

37. Hinchcliff KW, Reinhart GA, Burr JR, et al. Metabolizable energy intake and sustained energy expenditure of Alaskan sled dogs during heavy exertion in the cold. American Journal of Veterinary Research 1997; 58: 1457-1462.

38. Slater MR, Robinson LE, Zoran D, et al. Diet and exercise patterns in pet dogs. Journal of the American Veterinary Medical Association 1995; 207: 186-190.

39. Rose RJ, Bloomberg MS. Responses to sprint exercise in the greyhound: Effects on haematology, serum biochemistry and muscle metabolites. Research in Veterinary Science 1989; 47: 212-218.

40. Tompkins B, Heasman P. Appendix B Greyhound racing tracks. In: All About the Racing Greyhound, 1st ed. London, UK: Pelham Books, 1988; 127-139.

41. Grandjean D, Paragon B-M. Nutrition of racing and working dogs. Part I. Energy metabolism of dogs. Compendium on Continuing Education for the Practicing Veterinarian 1992; 14: 1608-1615.

42. Finke MD. Energy requirements of adult female beagles. Journal of Nutrition 1994; 124: 2604S-2608S.

43. Durrer JL, Hannon JP. Seasonal variations in caloric intake of dogs living in an arctic environment. American Journal of Physiology 1962; 202: 375-378.

44. Blaxter K. Metabolic effects of the physical environment. In: Energy Metabolism in Animals and Man. Cambridge, UK: Cambridge University Press, 1989; 180-218.

45. Männer K. Energy requirement for maintenance of adult dogs. Journal of Nutrition 1991; 121: S37-S38.

46. Kleiber M. Animal temperature regulation. In: The Fire of Life. Huntington, NY: RE Krieger Publishing Co, 1975; 150-178.

47. Meyer H. Energie. In: Ernährung des Hundes. Stuttgart, Germany: E Ulmer Verlag, 1990; 67-78.

48. Stadtfeld G. Untersuchungen über die Körperzusammensetzung des Hundes. Inaugural-Dissertation (Thesis), Hannover, Germany, 1978.

49. Anderson RS. Water balance in the dog and cat. Journal of Small Animal Practice 1982; 23: 588-598.

50. National Research Council. Water. In: Nutrient Requirements of Dogs. Washington, DC: National Academy Press, 1985; 39.

51. Burger IH, Anderson RS, Holme DW. Nutritional factors affecting water balance in the dog and cat. In: Anderson RS, ed. Nutrition of the Dog and Cat. Oxford, UK: Pergamon Press, 1980; 145-156.

NORMAL DOGS

52. Lewis LD, Morris ML Jr, Hand MS. Nutrients. In: Small Animal Clinical Nutrition III. Topeka, KS: Mark Morris Associates, 1987; 1-1-1-25.

53. Meyer H. Grunddaten zur Rationsgestaltung bei Hund und Katze. Der Praktischer Tierarzt 1986; 67: 35-39.

54. National Research Council. Nutrient requirements and signs of deficiency. In: Nutrient Requirements of Dogs. Washington, DC: National Academy Press, 1985; 2-38.

55. Männer K, Bronsch K, Wagner W. Energiewechselmessungen bei Beaglehunden im Erhaltungsstoffwechsel und während der Laktation. In: Proceedings. Ernährung, Fehlernährung und Diätetik bei Hund und Katze International Symposium, Hannover, Germany, September 3-4, 1987: 77-83.

56. Heusner AA. Body mass, maintenance and basal metabolism in dogs. Journal of Nutrition 1991; 12: S8-S17.

57. Gesellschaft für Ernährungsphysiologie. Empfehlungen für die Versorgung mit Energie. In: Ausschuß für Bedarfsnormen der Gesellschaft für Ernährungsphysiologie Energie- Nährstoffbedarf/Energy and Nutrient Requirements, No. 5 Hunde/Dogs. Frankfurt/Main, Germany: DLG Verlag, 1989; 32-44.

58. Burger IH. Energy needs of companion animals: Matching food intakes to requirements throughout the life cycle. Journal of Nutrition 1994; 124: 2584S-2593S.

59. Kleiber M. Body size and metabolic rate. In: The Fire of Life. Huntington, NY: RE Krieger Publishing Co, 1975; 179-222.

60. Armstrong PJ, Lund EM. Changes in body composition and energy balance with aging. Veterinary Clinical Nutrition 1996; 3: 11-15.

61. Kronfeld DS, Donoghue S, Glickman LT. Body condition and energy intakes of dogs in a referral teaching hospital. Journal of Nutrition 1991; 121: S157-S158.

62. Finke MD. Evaluation of the energy requirements of adult kennel dogs. Journal of Nutrition 1991; 121: S22-S28.

63. Gesellschaft für Ernährungsphysiologie. Empfehlungen für die Versorgung mit Mengenelementen. In: Ausschuß für Bedarfsnormen der Gesellschaft für Ernährungsphysiologie Energie- und Nährstoffbedarf/Energy and Nutrient Requirements, No. 5 Hunde/Dogs. Frankfurt/Main, Germany: DLG Verlag, 1989; 56-72.

64. Oehlert S, Oehlert H. Untersuchungen über die Häufigkeit der Nierenerkrankungen in einer normalen Hundepopulation– Zwingerhunde. Kleintierpraxis 1976; 21: 16-21.

65. Rouse BT, Lewis RJ. Canine glomerulonephritis: Prevalence in dogs submitted at random for euthanasia. Canadian Journal of Comparative Medicine 1975; 39: 365-370.

66. Shirota K, Takahashi R, Fujiwara K, et al. Canine interstitial nephritis with special reference to glomerular lesions and filariasis. Japanese Journal of Veterinary Science 1979; 41: 119-129.

67. Leibetseder J, Neufeld K. Diätempfehlungen für Hunde mit chronischer Niereninsuffizienz. In: Proceedings. XVI World Small Animal Veterinary Association World Congress, Vienna, Austria, October 2-10, 1991: 302-305.

68. Brown SA, Crowell WA, Barsanti JA, et al. Beneficial effects of dietary mineral restriction in dogs with marked reduction of functional renal mass. Journal of the American Society of Nephrology 1991; 1: 1169-1179.

69. Brown SA, Crowell WA, Barsanti JA, et al. Beneficial effects of dietary mineral restriction in dogs with marked reduction of functional renal mass. Journal of the American Society of Nephrology 1991; 1: 1169-1179.

70. Finco DR, Brown SA, Crowell WA, et al. Effects of phosphorus/calcium-restricted and phosphorus/calcium-replete 32% protein diets in dogs with chronic renal failure. American Journal of Veterinary Research 1992; 53: 157-163.

71. Mitch WE, Klahr S, eds. Handbook of Nutrition of the Kidney, 3rd ed. Philadelphia, PA: Lippincott-Raven, 1998.

72. National Kidney Foundation. In: Greenburg A, ed. Primer on Kidney Diseases, 2nd ed. San Diego, Ca: Academic Press Inc, 1998.

73. Kendall PT, Blaza SE, Holme DW. Assessment of endogenous nitrogen output in adult dogs of contrasting size using a protein-free diet. Journal of Nutrition 1982; 112: 1281-1286.

74. Schaeffer MC, Rogers QR, Morris JG. Protein in the nutrition of dogs and cats. In: Burger IH, Rivers JPW, eds. Nutrition of the Dog and Cat. Cambridge, UK: Cambridge University Press, 1989; 159-205.

75. Gesellschaft für Ernährungsphysiologie. Empfehlungen für die Versorgung mit Protein. In: Ausschuß für Bedarfsnormen der Gesellschaft für Ernährungsphysiologie Energie- und Nährstoffbedarf/ Energy and Nutrient Requirements, No. 5 Hunde/Dogs. Frankfurt/ Main, Germany: DLG Verlag, 1989; 45-55.

76. Bodey AR, Michell AR. Epidemiological study of blood pressure in domestic dogs. Journal of Small Animal Practice 1996; 37: 116-125.

77. Bovée KC. Variance of blood pressure response to oral sodium intake in hypertensive dogs (abstract). Journal of Veterinary Internal Medicine 1990; 4: 126.

78. Remillard RL, Ross JN, Eddy JB. Variance of indirect blood pressure measurements and prevalence of hypertension in clinically normal dogs. American Journal of Veterinary Research 1991; 52: 561-565.

79. Anderson LJ, Fisher EW. The blood pressure in canine interstitial nephritis. Research in Veterinary Science 1968; 9: 304-313.

80. Cowgill LD, Kallet AJ. Systemic hypertension. In: Kirk RW, ed. Current Veterinary Therapy IX. Philadelphia, PA: WB Saunders Co, 1986; 360-364.

81. Rocchini AP, Moorehead CP, Wentz E, et al. Obesity-induced hypertension in the dog. Hypertension 1987; 9 (Suppl. III): 64-68.

82. Littman MP. Chronic spontaneous systemic hypertension in dogs and cats. In: Proceedings. Eighth Veterinary Medical Forum, American College of Veterinary Internal Medicine, Washington, DC, May 1990: 209-212.

83. Ross LA. Endocrine hypertension. In: Kirk RW, Bonagura JD, eds. Current Veterinary Therapy XI. Philadelphia, PA: WB Saunders Co, 1992; 309-313.

84. Morris ML Jr, Patton RL, Teeter SM. Low sodium diet in heart disease: How low is low? Veterinary Medicine/Small Animal Clinician 1976; 71: 1225-1227.

85. Watkins BA. Role of essential fatty acids in health and nutrition. In: Proceedings. Roche Technical Symposium. Pet Food Institute Annual Industry Meeting, Chicago, IL, November 18, 1997: 33-43.

86. Lands WEM. Biosynthesis of prostaglandins. Annual Review of Nutrition 1991; 11: 41-60.

87. Ziboh VA, Miller CC. Essential fatty acids and polyunsaturated fatty acids: Significance in cutaneous biology. Annual Review of Nutrition 1990; 10: 433-450.

88. Harvey CE, Shofer FS, Laster L. Association of age and body weight with periodontal disease in North American dogs. Journal of Veterinary Dentistry 1994; 11: 94-105.

89. DeBowes LJ, Mosier D, Logan EI. Association of periodontal disease and histologic lesions in multiple organs from 45 dogs. Journal of Veterinary Dentistry 1996; 13: 57-60.

90. Golden AL, Stoller N, Harvey CE. A survey of oral and dental diseases in dogs anesthetized at a veterinary hospital. Journal of the American Animal Hospital Association 1982; 18: 891-899.

91. Kendall PT, Holme DW, Smith PhM. Methods of prediction of the digestible energy content of dog foods from gross energy value, proximate analysis, and digestive nutrient content. Journal of Science of Food and Agriculture 1982; 33: 823-831.

92. Opitz B. Untersuchungen zur Energiebewertung von Futtermitteln für Hund und Katze. Inaugural-Dissertation (Thesis). Veterinary Faculty, München, Germany, 1996.

93. Rabot R. Abnormal food ingestive behaviour in dogs and cats. Friskies Veterinary International 1993; 5: 17-22.

94. Mugford RA, Thorne C. Comparative studies of meal patterns in pet and laboratory housed dogs and cats. In: Anderson RS, ed. Nutrition of the Dog and Cat. Oxford, UK: Pergamon Press 1980; 3-14.

95. Houpt KA, Smith SL. Taste preferences and their relation to obesity in dogs and cats. Canadian Veterinary Journal 1981; 22: 77-81.

96. Houpt KA. Feeding and drinking behavior problems. Veterinary Clinics of North America: Small Animal Practice 1991; 2: 281-298.

97. Campbell WE. Effects of training, feeding regimens, isolation, and physical environment on canine behavior. Modern Veterinary Practice 1986; 29: 239-241.

98. Nott HMR, Rigby SR, Johnson JV, et al. Adaptation to a diet by cats and dogs: Implications for protocol design (abstract). Proceedings of the Nutrition Society 1993; 52: 296A.

99. Mosier JE. Effect of aging on body systems of the dog. Veterinary Clinics of North America: Small Animal Practice 1989; 19: 1-12.

100. Hayflick L. Aging is not a disease. In: How and Why We Age. New York, NY: Ballantine Books, 1994; 43-49.

101. Hayflick L. How exercise, nutrition, and weight affect longevity. In: How and Why We Age. New York, NY: Ballantine Books, 1994; 277-295.

102. Bronson RT. Variation of age at death of dogs of different sexes and breeds. American Journal of Veterinary Research 1982; 43: 2057-2059.

103. MacDougall DF, Barker J. An approach to canine geriatrics. British Veterinary Journal 1984; 140: 115-123.

104. Morris Animal Foundation. Animal health survey. Denver, CO: 1991.

105. Morris Animal Foundation. Animal health survey. Denver, CO: 1998.

106. Mosier JE. Caring for the aging dog in today's practice. Veterinary Medicine 1990; 85: 460-471.

107. Mosier JE. How aging affects body systems in the dog. In: Proceedings. Symposium on Clinical Conditions in the Older Cat and Dog, London, UK, June 15, 1988: 7-14

108. Goldston RT. Preface. Veterinary Clinics of North America: Small Animal Practice 1989; 19: ix-x.

109. Markham RW, Hodgkins EM. Geriatric nutrition. Veterinary Clinics of North America: Small Animal Practice 1989; 19: 165-185.

110. Alexander JW, Wood LL. Aging and the joints. Compendium on Continuing Education for the Practicing Veterinarian 1984; 6: 1074-1079.

111. Hoskins JD. Health care program. In: Goldston RT, Hoskins JD, eds. Geriatrics & Gerontology of the Cat and Dog. Philadelphia, PA: WB Saunders Co, 1995; 11-14.

112. Goldston RT. Introduction and overview of geriatrics. In: Goldston RT, Hoskins JD, eds. Geriatrics & Gerontology of the Cat and Dog. Philadelphia, PA: WB Saunders Co, 1995; 1-9.

113. DiBartola SP. Clinical approach and laboratory evaluation of renal disease. In: Ettinger SJ, Feldman EC, eds. Textbook of Veterinary Internal Medicine, 4th ed. Philadelphia, PA: WB Saunders Co, 1995; 1706-1719.

114. Littman MP, Drobatz KJ. Hypertensive and hypotensive disorders. In: Ettinger SJ, Feldman EC, eds. Textbook of Veterinary Internal Medicine, 4th ed. Philadelphia, PA: WB Saunders Co, 1995; 93-100.

115. Knapp WA Jr. Nutritional management of the aged dog. Veterinary Medicine/Small Animal Clinician 1964; 59: 914-917.

116. Kronfeld DS. Geriatric diets for dogs. Compendium on Continuing Education for the Practicing Veterinarian 1983; 5: 136-144.

117. Meyer H. Praktische Fütterung. In: Ernährung des Hundes, 2nd ed. Stuttgart, Germany: E Ulmer Verlag, 1990; 162-223.

118. Sheffy BE, Williams AJ, Zimmer JF, et al. Nutrition and metabolism of the geriatric dog. Cornell Veterinarian 1985; 75: 324-347.

119. Leibetseder J. Ernährung des älteren Hundes. Wiener Tierärztliche Monatschrift 1989; 76: 268-270.

120. Donoghue S, Khoo L, Glickman LT, et al. Body condition and diet of relatively healthy older dogs. Journal of Nutrition 1991; 121: S58-S59.

121. Olin AÖ, Österberg P, Hädell K, et al. Energy-enriched hospital food to improve energy intake in elderly patients. Journal of Parenteral and Enteral Nutrition 1996; 20: 93-97.

122. Bloom F, ed. Interstitial nephritis–Incidence. In: Pathology of the Dog and Cat. Evanston, IL: American Veterinary Publications, Inc, 1954; 89.

123. Crowell WA, Finco DR. Frequency of pyelitis, pyelonephritis, renal perivasculitis and renal infarction in dogs. American Journal of Veterinary Research 1975; 36: 111-114.

124. Müller-Peddinghaus R, Trautwein G. Spontaneous glomerulonephritis in dogs II. Correlation of glomerulonephritis with age, chronic interstitial nephritis and extrarenal lesions. Veterinary Pathology 1977; 14: 121-127.

125. Lopez-Hilker S, Dusso AS, Rapp NS, et al. Phosphorus restriction reverses hyperparathyroidism in uremia independent of changes in calcium and calcitriol. American Journal of Physiology 1990; 259: F432-F437.

126. Weigel J, Alexander JW. Aging and the musculoskeletal system. Veterinary Clinics of North America: Small Animal Practice 1981; 11: 749-764.

127. Pellet PL. Protein requirements in humans. American Journal of Clinical Nutrition 1990; 51: 723-737.

128. Wannemacher RW Jr, McCoy JR. Determination of optimal dietary protein requirements of young and old dogs. Journal of Nutrition 1966; 88: 67-74.

129. Lewis LD, Morris ML Jr, Hand MS. Dogs–Feeding and care. In: Small Animal Clinical Nutrition III. Topeka, KS: Mark Morris Associates, 1987; 3-1–3-32.

130. Mundt H. Die Ernährung älterer Hunde. Der Praktischer Tierarzt 1989; 7: 26-30.

131. Morley JE. Nutritional modulation of behavior and immunocompetence. Nutrition Reviews 1994; 52: S6-S8.

132. Finco DR, Brown SA, Crowell WA, et al. Effect of aging and dietary protein intake on uninephrectomized geriatric dogs. American Journal Veterinary Research 1994; 55: 1282-1290.

133. Munro HN, Suter PM, Russell RM. Nutritional requirements of the elderly. In: Annual Reviews of Nutrition, vol 7. Palo Alto, CA: Annual Reviews Inc, 1987; 23-49.

134. Müller-Peddinghaus R, Trautwein G. Spontaneous glomerulonephritis in dogs I. Classification and immunopathology. Veterinary Pathology 1977; 14: 1-13.

135. Spencer AJ, Wright NG. Glomerular lesions in chronic interstitial nephritis in the dog: Histological and ultrastructural features. Journal of Comparative Pathology 1981; 91: 393-408.

136. Detweiler DK, Patterson DF. The prevalence and type of cardiovascular disease in dogs. Annals of New York Academy of Sciences 1965; 127: 481-516.

137. Whitney JC. Observations on the effect of age on the severity of heart valve lesions in the dog. Journal of Small Animal Practice 1974; 15: 511-522.

138. Twedt DC. Gastrointestinal motility disorders of geriatric patients. In: Geriatric Medicine. Purina Specialty Review. Pro-Visions 1993; 11-21.

139. Nelson RW. The role of fiber in managing diabetes mellitus. Veterinary Medicine 1989; 84: 1156-1160.

140. Grandjean D, Paragon B-M, Grandjean R. Rationnement alimentaire et prévention chez le chien 1. Le Point Vétérinaire 1986; 18: 519-524.

141. Sheffy BE. Nutrition and nutritional disorders. Veterinary Clinics of North America: Small Animal Practice 1978; 8: 7-29.

142. Donoghue S. Nutritional recommendations for reproductive performance. In: Kirk RW, Bonagura JD, eds. Current Veterinary Therapy XI. Philadelphia, PA: WB Saunders Co, 1992; 971-980.

143. Nguyen P, Dumon H. Les besoins nutritifs du chien. Revue de Médecine Vétérinaire 1988; 139: 1027-1043.

144. Bebiak DM, Lawler DF, Reutzel LF. Nutrition and management of the dog. Veterinary Clinics of North America: Small Animal Practice 1987; 17: 505-533.

145. Gesellschaft für Ernährungsphysiologie. Grunddaten für die Berechnung des Energie- und Nährstoffbedarfs. In: Ausschuß für Bedarfsnormen der Gesellschaft für Ernährungs-physiologie Energie-Nährstoffbedarf/Energy and Nutrient Requirements, No. 5 Hunde/Dogs. Frankfurt/Main, Germany: DLG Verlag, 1989; 9-31.

146. Leibetseder J. Ernährung der Zuchthündin und der Junghunde. Der Praktischer Tierarzt 1989; 70: 12-20.

147. Mosier JE. Introduction to canine pediatrics. Veterinary Clinics of North America: Small Animal Practice 1978; 8: 3-5.

148. Concannon PW, McCann JP, Temple M. Biology and endocrinology of ovulation, pregnancy and parturition in the dog. Journal of Reproduction and Fertility 1989; 39 (Suppl.): 3-25.

149. Wallace MS, Davidson AP. Abnormalities in pregnancy, parturition and the periparturient period. In: Ettinger SJ, Feldman EC, eds. Textbook of Veterinary Internal Medicine, 4th ed. Philadelphia, PA: WB Saunders Co, 1995; 1614-1624.

150. Meyer H, Kienzle E, Dammers C. Milchmenge und Milchzusammensetzung bei und Hündin sowie Futteraufnahme und Gewichtsenwicklung ante und post partum. Fortschritte in der Tierphysiologie und Tierernährung (Advances in Animal Physiology and Animal Nutrition) 1985; Suppl. No. 16: 51-72.

151. Kaneko JJ, ed. Serum proteins and the dysproteinemias. In: Clinical Biochemistry of Domestic Animals, 4th ed. San Diego, CA: Academic Press Inc, 1989; 142-165.

152. McDonald P, Edwards RA, Greenhalgh JFD, et al. Feeding standards for reproduction. In: Animal Nutrition, 5th ed. Harlow (Essex), UK: Longman Scientific & Technical, 1995; 353-371.

153. Mosier JE. The puppy from birth to six weeks. Veterinary Clinics of North America: Small Animal Practice 1978; 8: 79-100.

154. Schroeder GE, Smith GA. Food intake and growth of German shepherd puppies. Journal of Small Animal Practice 1994; 35: 587-591.

155. Prentice A, Goldberg G. Maternal obesity increases congenital malformations. Nutrition Reviews 1996; 54: 146-152.

156. Rasmussen KM. The influence of maternal nutrition on lactation. Annual Reviews of Nutrition 1992; 12: 103-117.

157. Ontko JA, Phillips PH. Reproduction and lactation studies with bitches fed semipurified diets. Journal of Nutrition 1958; 65: 211-218.

158. Romsos DR, Palmer HJ, Muiruri KL, et al. Influence of a low carbohydrate diet on performance of pregnant and lactating dogs. Journal of Nutrition 1981; 111: 678-689.

159. Meyer H, Dammers C, Kienzle E. Körperzusammensetzung neugeborener Welpen und Nährstoffbedarf trägender Hündinnen. Fortschritte in der Tierphysiologie und Tierernährung (Advances in Animal Physiology and Animal Nutrition) 1985; Suppl. No. 16: 7-25.

160. Meyer H, Heckötter E. II. Empfehlungen zur Versorgung des Hundes mit Energie und Nährstoffen. In: Meyer H, ed. Futterwerttabellen für Hunde und Katzen. Hannover, Germany: Schlütersche Verlaganstalt, 1986; 9-12.

161. Kienzle E, Meyer H, Lohrie H. Einfluß kohlenhydratfreier Rationen mit unterschiedlichen Protein/Energierelationen auf foetale Entwicklung und Vitalität von Welpen sowie die Milchzusammensetzung von Hündinnen. Fortschritte in der Tierphysiologie und Tierernährung (Advances in Animal Physiology and Animal Nutrition) 1985; Suppl. No. 16: 73-99.

162. Kienzle E, Meyer H. The effects of carbohydrate-free diets containing different levels of protein on reproduction in the bitch. In: Burger IH, Rivers JPW, eds. Nutrition of the Dog and Cat. Cambridge, UK: Cambridge University Press, 1989; 243-257.

163. Blaza SE, Booles D, Burger IH. Is carbohydrate essential for pregnancy and lactation in dogs? In: Burger IH, Rivers JPW, eds. Nutrition of the Dog and Cat. Cambridge, UK: Cambridge University Press, 1989; 229-242.

164. Paquin J. Observations sur le comportement de chiens Beagle alimentés avec différents taux de protéines pendant trente mois. Thèse pour le Doctorat Vétérinaire, Ecole Nationale Vétérinaire d'Alfort, (France) 1979; 55.

165. Smith FO. Postpartum diseases. Veterinary Clinics of North America: Small Animal Practice 1986; 16: 521-524.

166. Drazner FH, ed. Parathyroid glands and calcium metabolism. In: Small Animal Endocrinology. New York, NY: Churchill Livingstone, 1987; 121-160.

167. Bhaskaram L. Immunology of iron-deficient subjects. In: Chandra RK, ed. Nutrition and Immunology. New York, NY: AR Liss Inc, 1988; 149-168.

168. Fletcher MP, Gershwin ME, Keen CL, et al. Trace element deficiencies and immune responsiveness in human and animal models. In: Chandra RK, ed. Nutrition and Immunology. New York, NY: AR Liss Inc, 1988; 215-239.

169. Mosier JE. Nutritional recommendations for gestation and lactation in the dog. Veterinary Clinics of North America: Small Animal Practice 1977; 7: 683-692.

170. Schroeder GE, Smith GA. Bodyweight and feed intake of German shepherd bitches during pregnancy and lactation. Journal of Small Animal Practice 1995; 36: 7-10.

171. Yeager AE, Concannon PW. Ultrasonography of the reproductive tract of the female dog and cat. In: Bonagura JD, ed. Current Veterinary Therapy XII. Philadelphia, PA: WB Saunders Co, 1995; 1040-1052.

172. Rüsse I. Die Laktation der Hündin. Zentralblatt für Veterinär Medizin 1961; 8: 252-281.

173. Oftedal OT. Lactation in the dog: Milk composition and intake by puppies. Journal of Nutrition 1984; 114: 803-812.

174. Rothbauer DL. Milk production and health in dairy cattle: Homeostasis, homeorrhesis, and nutrient flow. Veterinary Medicine 1994; 89: 1157-1162.

175. Mundt H-C, Thomée A, Meyer H. Zur Energie- und Eiweißversorgung von Saugwelpen über die Muttermilch. Kleintierpraxis 1981; 26: 353-360.

176. Grandjean D, Paragon B-M, Grandjean R. Rationnement alimentaire et prévention chez le chien 2. Le Point Vétérinaire 1987; 19: 171-177.

177. Kronfeld DS. Nature and use of commercial dog foods. Journal of the American Veterinary Medical Association 1975; 166: 487-493.

178. Siedler AJ, Schweigert BS. Effect of the level of animal fat in the diet on the maintenance, reproduction and lactation performance of dogs. Journal of Nutrition 1954; 53: 187-194.

179. Gross KL. Effect of diet on composition of milk from dogs (abstract). In: Abstract Book. Waltham Symposium on the Nutrition of Companion Animals, Adelaide, Australia, September 23-25, 1993: 29.

180. Meyer H. Mineralstoffwechsel und Mineralstoffbedarf bei Hündinnen und Saugwelpen (Mineral metabolism and requirements in bitches and suckling pups). In: Anderson RS, ed. Proceedings. First Nordic Symposium on Small Animal Veterinary Medicine, Oslo, Norway September 15-18, 1982. Oxford, UK: Pergamon Press 1982; 13-24.

181. Meyer H. Mineralstoffe: Mengenelemente. In: Ernährung des Hundes. Stuttgart, Germany: E Ulmer Verlag, 1990; 89-100.

182. Gesellschaft für Ernährungsphysiologie. Empfehlungen für die Versorgung mit Spurenelementen. In: Ausschuß für Bedarfsnormen der Gesellschaft für Ernährungsphysiologie Energie- und Nährstoffbedarf/Energy and Nutrient Requirements, No. 5 Hunde/Dogs. Frankfurt/Main, Germany: DLG Verlag, 1989; 73-85.

183. Meyer H. Sonstige essentielle bzw. semi-essentielle Stoffe. In: Ernährung des Hundes. Stuttgart, Germany: E Ulmer Verlag, 1990; 120-122.

184. Wolter R. Rationement pratique-2. Reproduction. In: L'alimentation du Chien et du Chat. Maisons-Alfort, France: Les Éditions du Point Vétérinaire, 1982; 129-143.

185. Pibot P, Jean-Blain C. Allaitement artificiel et sevrage du chiot. Recueil de Médecine Vétérinaire 1989; 165: 567-575.

186. Lawler DF, Evans RH. Nutritional and environmental considerations in neonatal medicine. In: Kirk RW, ed. Current Veterinary Therapy X. Philadelphia, PA: WB Saunders Co, 1989; 1325-1333.

187. Rauchfuss R. Untersuchungen über die Körperzusammensetzung neugeborener Hundewelpen unterschiedlich großer Rassen. Inaugural-Dissertation (Thesis). Hannover, Germany, 1978.

188. Banks KL. Changes in the immune response related to age. Veterinary Clinics of North America: Small Animal Practice 1981; 11: 683-688.

189. Tizard IR, ed. Immunity in the fetus and newborn. In: Veterinary Immunology–An Introduction, 4th ed. Philadelphia, PA: WB Saunders Co, 1992; 248-260.

190. Ferrando R, Fourlon C, Lemuet-Maisonneuve J. Les réserves hépatiques en vitamine A du chien. Recueil de Médecine Vétérinaire 1975; 151: 288-291.

191. Johnson AH. The composition of milk. In: Webb BH, Johnson AH, Alford JA, eds. Fundamentals of Dairy Chemistry. Westport, CT: AVI Publishing Co, 1974; 1-57.

192. Kienzle E, Meyer H, Dammers C, et al. Milchaufnahme, Gewichtentwicklung, Milchverdaulichkeit, sowie Energie- und Nährstoffretention bei Saugwelpen. Fortschritte in der Tierphysiologie und Tierernährung (Advances in Animal Physiology and Animal Nutrition) 1985; Suppl. No. 16: 27-50.

193. Lawler DF. Canine and feline periparturient problems. In: Small Animal Reproduction and Pediatrics. Purina Specialty Review. Pro-Visions, 1991; 21-51.

194. Mosier JE. Causes and treatment of neonatal deaths. In: Kirk RW, ed. Current Veterinary Therapy VI. Philadelphia, PA: WB Saunders Co, 1977; 44-49.

195. Swaisgood HE. Protein and amino acid composition of bovine milk. In: Jensen RG, ed. Handbook of Milk Composition. San Diego, CA: Academic Press Inc, 1995; 464-468.

196. Stryer L, ed. Sucrose, lactose and maltose are the common disaccharides. In: Biochemistry, 3rd ed. New York, NY: WH Freeman and Co, 1988; 339-341.

197. Newburg DS, Neubauer SH. Carbohydrates in milks: Analysis, quantities, and significance. In: Jensen RG, ed. Handbook of Milk Composition. San Diego, CA: Academic Press Inc, 1995; 273-349.

198. Kienzle E. Enzymaktivität in Pankreas, Darmwand und Chymus des Hundes in Abhängigkeit von Alter und Futterart. Zeitschrift für Tierphysiologie, Tierernährung und Futtermittelkunde 1988; 60: 276-288.

199. Meyer H. Laktosefütterung bei Fleischfressern (Lactose intake of carnivores). Wiener Tierärztliche Monatschrift 1992; 79: 236-241.

200. Baines FM. Milk substitutes and the hand rearing of puppies and kittens. Journal of Small Animal Practice 1981; 22: 555-578.

201. Jean-Blain C. Allaitement et sevrage du chiot. Revue de Médecine Vétérinaire 1973; 124: 1255-1268.

202. Björck G. Care and feeding of the puppy in the postnatal and weaning period. In: Anderson RS, ed. Proceedings. First Nordic Symposium on Small Animal Veterinary Medicine, Oslo, Norway, September 15-18, 1982. Oxford, UK: Pergamon Press, 1984; 25-33.

203. Sheffy BE. Nutrition, infection and immunity. Compendium on Continuing Education for the Practicing Veterinarian 1985; 7: 990-997.

204. Meyer H, Zentek J. Über den Einfluß einer unterschiedlichen Energieversorgung wachsender Doggen auf Körpermasse und Skelettentwicklung 1. Mitteilung: Körpermasseentwicklung und Energiebedarf. Journal of Veterinary Medicine A 1992; 39: 130-141.

205. Toll PW, Richardson DC, Jewell DE, et al. The effect of feeding method on growth and body composition in young puppies (abstract). In: Abstract Book. Waltham Symposium on the Nutrition of Companion Animals, Adelaide, Australia, September 23-25, 1993: 33.

206. Hazewinkel HAW. Influences of different calcium intakes on calcium metabolism and skeletal development in young Great Danes. Doctorate Thesis. Faculty of Veterinary Medicine University, Utrecht, The Netherlands, May 30, 1985.

207. Hedhammar Å, Wu F-M, Krook L, et al. Overnutrition and skeletal disease: An experimental study in growing Great Dane dogs. Cornell Veterinarian 1974; 64: 9-160.

208. Kealy RD, Olsson SE, Monti KL, et al. Effects of limited food consumption on the incidence of hip dysplasia in growing dogs. Journal of the American Veterinary Medical Association 1992; 201: 857-863.

209. Chipalkatti S, De AK, Aiyar AS. Effect of diet restriction on some biochemical parameters related to aging in mice. Journal of Nutrition 1983; 113: 944-950.

210. Fuhrer L, Grandjean D. Modélisation mathématique de la croissance du chiot–Application à l'élaboration d'un plan de rationnement informatisé. Recueil de Médecine Vétérinaire 1986; 162: 1217-1222.

211. Meyer H, Zentek J. Energy requirements of growing Great Danes. Journal of Nutrition 1991; 121: S35-S36.

212. Knittle JL, Timmers K, Ginsberg-Fellner F, et al. The growth of adipose tissue in children and adolescents. Cross-sectional and longitudinal studies of adipose cell number and size. Journal of Clinical Investigation 1979; 63: 239-246.

213. Nolen GA. Effects of various restricted dietary regimens on the growth, health, and longevity of albino rats. Journal of Nutrition 1972; 102: 1477-1493.

214. Ross MH, Bras G. Influence of protein under- and overnutrition in spontaneous turnover prevalence in the rat and length of life. Journal of Nutrition 1973; 103: 944-963.

215. Ross MH. Length of life and caloric intake. American Journal of Clinical Nutrition 1972; 25: 834-838.

216. Young HH, Milner JA, Corbin JE. Arginine requirements in immature dogs. Journal of Nutrition 1978; 108: 203-210.

217. Burns RA, Lefaivre MH, Miller JA. Effects of dietary protein quantity and quality on the growth of dogs and rats. Journal of Nutrition 1982; 112: 1843-1853.

218. Case LP, Czarnecki-Maulden GL. Protein requirements of growing pups fed practical dry-type diets containing mixed-protein sources. American Journal of Veterinary Research 1990; 51: 808-812.

219. Nap RC, Hazewinkel HAW, Voorhout G, et al. Growth and skeletal development in Great Dane pups fed different levels of protein intake. Journal of Nutrition 1991; 121: S107-S113.

220. Nap RC. Nutritional influences on growth and skeletal development in the dog. Doctorate Thesis. Faculty Veterinary Medicine University of Utrecht, The Netherlands, June 16, 1993.

221. Toll PW, Richardson DC, Wedekind KJ, et al. A preliminary report on the effect of breed, gender and nutrition on growth of large breed puppies. Journal of the American Veterinary Medical Association (In press).

222. Jenkins KJ, Phillips PH. The mineral requirements of the dog. I. Phosphorus requirement and availability. Journal of Nutrition 1960; 70: 235-240.

223. Jenkins KJ, Phillips PH. The mineral requirements of the dog. II. The relation of calcium, phosphorus and fat levels to minimal calcium and phosphorus requirements. Journal of Nutrition 1960; 70: 241-246.

224. Resnick S. Effect of age on survivability of pups eating a carbohydrate-free diet. Journal of the American Veterinary Medical Association 1978; 172: 145-148.

225. Romsos DR, Belo PS, Bennink MR, et al. Effects of dietary carbohydrate, fat and protein on growth, body composition and blood metabolite levels in the dog. Journal of Nutrition 1976; 106: 1452-1464.

226. Aoyagi S, Baker DH. Bioavailability of copper in analytical-grade and feed-grade inorganic copper sources when fed to provide copper at levels below the chick's requirement. Poultry Science 1993; 72: 1075-1083.

227. Zentek J. Ernährungsbedingte Hauterkrankungen–Bedeutung von Spurenelementen und Vitaminen. Kleintierpraxis 1991; 37: 157-162.

228. Zentek J, Dämmrich K, Meyer H. Untersuchungen zum Cu-Mangel beim wachsenden Hund. Zentralblatt für Veterinär Medizin A (Journal of Veterinary Medicine A) 1991; 38: 561-570.

229. Lust G, Geary JC, Sheffy BE. Development of hip dysplasia in dogs. American Journal of Veterinary Research 1973; 34: 87-91.

230. Huber TL, Wilson RC, McGarity SA. Variation in digestibility of dry dog foods with identical label guaranteed analysis. Journal of the American Animal Hospital Association 1986; 22: 571-575.

231. Huber TL, Laflamme DP, Medleau L, et al. Comparison of procedures for assessing adequacy of dog foods. Journal of the American Veterinary Medical Association 1991; 199: 731-734.

CASE 9-1

Weight Loss in a Lactating Great Dane Bitch

Jacques Debraekeleer, DVM
Hill's Science and Technology Center
Etten Leur, The Netherlands

Kathy L. Gross, PhD
Hill's Science and Technology Center
Topeka, Kansas, USA

Assess the Animal

A five-year-old Great Dane bitch was examined for weight loss. The dog was in its fourth week of lactation and was nursing 11 puppies. Although most of the puppies grew according to breed expectations, three had slightly lower body weights. Delivery had been uneventful.

Physical examination revealed an underweight dog (body condition score 2/5) with no vaginal discharge or other abnormalities. The bitch currently weighed 59 kg but weighed 65 kg before the pregnancy. The mammary glands were well-developed with no signs of inflammation.

A complete blood count and serum biochemistry profile were performed. Serum albumin (2.5 g/dl, normal 2.4 to 3.5 g/dl) and serum calcium (9.0 mg/dl, normal 9 to 11.8 mg/dl) concentrations were low normal. The other biochemical parameters were within normal ranges. The hemoglobin concentration (11.8 g/dl, normal 12 to 18 g/dl), packed cell volume (32%, normal 37 to 55%) and total erythrocyte count (5.13 million/µl, normal 5.5 to 8.5 million/µl) were slightly below normal.

Assess the Food(s) and Feeding Method

The owners reported that the bitch's appetite was voracious. The dog was fed twice daily; early in the morning before the owners went to work and in the evening when they returned home. The bitch received a commercial grocery brand dry food that the owners had fed for several years. The owners were feeding 15 cups (90 g/cup) twice daily; they commented that this seemed like a large amount of food. One cup of low-fat (2%) milk was poured over the food at each meal.

The manufacturer was contacted and provided the following information about the dry matter nutrient content of the food: crude protein 19.6%, crude fat 11.4%, carbohydrate (nitrogen-free extract [NFE]) 58.0%, crude fiber 3.45%, ash 7.6%, calcium 1.65%, phosphorus 1.23% and sodium 0.48%. The energy density was 3.4 kcal metabolizable energy (ME) (15.5 kJ)/g of food, as fed.

Questions

1. How should this patient's laboratory results be interpreted?
2. What are the key nutritional factors for a lactating bitch with a large litter?
3. What are the caloric requirements of the patient?
4. What feeding method should be recommended for this dog?
5. What other management techniques should be used with this bitch and its puppies?

Answers and Discussion

1. Normal pregnancy and lactation can affect canine hematologic values. Mild decreases in hemoglobin concentration, packed cell volume and total erythrocyte count occur during late gestation and lactation. These values should return to normal within several weeks after lactation ceases. Profound changes in hematologic values in pregnant and lactating bitches signal serious malnutrition and/or concurrent disease. The low normal serum albumin and calcium concentrations in this Great Dane bitch are not of immediate concern but may indicate marginal protein and calcium intake. Serum albumin has a long half-life in dogs (approximately eight days); therefore, serum albumin concentrations may not reflect changes over the last one to two weeks. Bitches with large litters secrete large quantities of calcium into the milk during peak lactation (Weeks 3 and 4 of lactation). Thus, serum calcium concentrations may be low normal to mildly decreased.
2. Key nutritional factors for lactating bitches include water, energy, protein, carbohydrate, fat, calcium, phosphorus and food digestibility. Water is needed in large quantities to produce milk. A 60-kg bitch nursing a large litter may require 10 to 11 liters of water per day during peak lactation. Energy requirements steadily increase after whelping and peak between three and five weeks at levels two to four times higher than the daily energy requirement (DER) of non-lactating adult dogs. Foods for lactating large-breed dogs should provide at least 18% fat (dry matter basis [DMB]) and 4.0 to 5.0 kcal ME (16.7 to 21 kJ)/g dry matter. During lactation, the requirements for calcium and protein increase more rapidly than the energy requirements. Generally, foods containing 25 to 35% crude protein (DMB) and 1.0 to 1.6% calcium (DMB) are adequate. Lactose concentrations in milk decrease when lactating bitches are fed foods without soluble carbohydrates. Food should provide at least 10 to 20% of energy intake in the form of carbohydrate to support normal milk lactose production. Because of the considerable nutritional demands associated with lactation, nutrients in the food should be highly available. Foods with above average digestibility are recommended for lactating dogs (Table 9-11).
3. Energy requirements for lactating dogs can be subdivided into energy for maintenance and energy used for milk production. The DER, without allotment for milk production, may be slightly higher than that for average adult dogs because of stress and increased activity associated with caring for puppies. The maintenance portion of the DER for lactating dogs has been estimated to be approximately 1.9 x resting energy requirement (RER). As a rough estimate, at peak lactation the bitch will need an additional 25% of this amount for each puppy. This amount should be adjusted based on body weight changes and body condition assessment. For this bitch, energy for maintenance at ideal body weight would be approximately 1.9 x RER (65 kg body weight) = 3,000 kcal (12.6 MJ). Energy for peak milk production (11 puppies) would be an additional 8,250 kcal (34.7 MJ). The total DER = 11,250 kcal (47.3 MJ). The bitch was currently being fed approximately 9,180 kcal (38.6 MJ) from the food plus 240 kcal (1 MJ) from the supplemental milk for a total of 9,420 kcal (39.6 MJ) per day. The estimated daily deficit is 1,830 kcal (7.7 MJ) vs. the calculated DER.
4. In general, lactating dogs should be offered food free choice. Meal feeding several times a day may be sufficient for smaller dogs or dogs with small litters.
5. The puppies should be introduced to food as soon as possible. A warm gruel prepared from moist or blended dry commercial foods formulated for canine growth should be used and can be offered several times daily to the puppies. This feeding plan will relieve the physical and nutritional stress on the bitch and begin the transition to solid food for the puppies.

Progress Notes

The bitch's food was changed to a commercial, dry specialty brand product (Science Diet Canine Growth[a]) that was higher in energy density (3.94 kcal [16.48 kJ]/g as fed) than the current food. This food also had appropriate levels of other key nutritional factors. The food and fresh, clean water were offered free choice and the milk was discontinued. Approximately 24 cups of the growth/lactation food would provide the estimated DER for peak lactation. The owners were also instructed to prepare a warm gruel for the puppies using the moist formulation of the product several times daily.

Three weeks later the owners returned with the bitch and six puppies that had not yet been sold. The puppies had been completely weaned the previous week and were now eating the dry growth formula for large-breed puppies. The bitch weighed 63.5 kg and appeared normal. The owners were encouraged to slowly change the bitch's food back to the original dry food for adult maintenance over the next week. The DER was estimated to be 1.8 x RER at an ideal weight of 65 kg, which equals 2,850 kcal (12 MJ) or nine to 10 cups of food per day.

Endnote

a. Hill's Pet Nutrition, Inc., Topeka, KS, USA.

Bibliography

Gesellschaft für Ernährungsphysiologie. Empfehlungen für die Versorgung mit Mengenelementen. In: Ausschuß für Bedarfsnormen der Gesellschaft für Ernährungsphysiologie Energie- und Nährstoffbedarf/Energy and Nutrient Requirements, No. 5 Hunde/Dogs. Frankfurt/Main, Germany: DLG Verlag, 1989; 56-72.

Kaneko JJ. Appendices. In: Clinical Biochemistry of Domestic Animals, 4th ed. San Diego, CA: Academic Press Inc, 1989; 877-901.

■ CASE 9-2

Feeding an Older Miniature Pinscher

Jacques Debraekeleer, DVM
Hill's Science and Technology Center
Etten Leur, The Netherlands

Kathy L. Gross, PhD
Hill's Science and Technology Center
Topeka, Kansas, USA

Assess the Animal

An eight-year-old intact male miniature pinscher was examined as part of a routine health maintenance program. The owners saw a magazine article recently promoting preventive health programs for older animals. They realized that their dog was aging but had not noticed any specific problems.

The dog weighed 4.5 kg and had an optimal body condition score (BCS 3/5). Physical examination was normal except for a slightly enlarged prostate gland, mild periodontal disease and a grade II/VI holosystolic cardiac murmur loudest over the mitral heart valve. Results of a complete blood count, serum biochemistry profile, urinalysis and ocular fundic examination were normal. Thoracic radiographs were normal with no evidence of cardiomegaly or pulmonary disease.

Assess the Food(s) and Feeding Method

The dog was fed several different kinds of commercial moist grocery brand dog foods and commercial jerky-type dog treats. Ice cream was also fed regularly. The owners were somewhat concerned because the dog did not seem to be eating as much as it did previously.

Questions

1. What are the key nutritional factors that should be considered in this patient?
2. Outline a feeding plan (foods and feeding method) for this dog.
3. How should the owner's concern about the reduction in appetite be addressed?

Answers and Discussion

1. Key nutritional factors for older dogs include water, energy, phosphorus, calcium, protein, sodium, chloride, fat and food texture. Chronic progressive renal disease is a leading cause of morbidity and mortality in older dogs. However, classic diagnostic tests such as the serum biochemistry profile and urinalysis that were performed for this dog will not detect renal disease until it is advanced. Although not definitively proven, older dogs with subclinical renal disease may benefit from foods that avoid excess levels of phosphorus, protein, sodium and chloride. Clean water should also be available at all times. In general, fat levels between 7 and 15% dry matter (DM) are recommended for most older dogs. Fat levels and energy density of the food should be adjusted based on the body condition of the animal. Obese-prone older dogs may benefit from lower fat, less energy-dense foods whereas very old dogs (13 years and older) often lose weight and need higher fat, more energy-dense foods. Increased levels of dietary fiber may be important for obese-prone older dogs and older dogs with constipation. Oral disease is the most common health problem in older dogs; more than two-thirds of older dogs suffer from significant periodontal disease. Both veterinary care and home care are important in treatment and prevention of periodontal disease. Foods formulated to decrease the accumulation of dental substrates (i.e., plaque, calculus) and help control gingivitis and malodor are an important part of the oral home-care program for older dogs.

2. Commercial moist grocery brand dog foods may contain excessive levels of phosphorus, fat, energy, protein, sodium and chloride. (See Appendix L.) Jerky-type commercial treats also contain excessive levels of protein, fat, sodium and chloride. (See Appendix M.) Older healthy dogs may benefit from commercial foods for senior or geriatric dogs and treats that contain lower yet adequate levels of these nutrients. (See Appendices L and M.) Excessive levels of dietary sodium and chloride should also be avoided in older dogs with evidence of cardiac disease. Ice cream should also be discontinued as a regular treat or offered in smaller amounts. Moist foods do not provide textural characteristics that prevent the accumulation of dental substrates. Dental foods formulated to improve oral health are available and would be appropriate for this dog. (See Chapter 16.) The dog's body condition suggests that the current caloric intake is appropriate and should be maintained if a new food is chosen. The estimated daily energy requirement (DER) should be 1.6 to 1.8 x resting energy requirement (RER) (330 to 370 kcal, 1,390 to 1,550 kJ). The feeding method will be dictated somewhat by whether a moist, dry, semi-moist or homemade food is fed. Moist and homemade foods should be fed once or twice daily as discrete meals, whereas dry or semi-

moist food may be fed free choice and left out for pro-longed periods.

3. The optimal BCS suggests that the dog is eating an appropriate amount of food. There may be several rea-sons why the owners expressed concern about the amount of moist food eaten by the dog. The moist foods currently fed are probably high in fat and energy dense; as little as one-half to two-thirds of a standard 400- to 450-g can will meet this dog's DER. The addi-tion of jerky-type treats and ice cream would also decrease the amount of food the dog needed. Older dogs may not be as active as they were earlier in life, which decreases their energy requirements. Periodontal disease was recognized during the physical examina-tion and significant oral pain will discourage eating in some animals. Finally, an underlying disease may be contributing to partial anorexia despite the normal

diagnostic results. All these factors should be explained to the owners and they should be encouraged to mon-itor food intake and body condition closely.

Progress Notes

The food was changed to a commercial moist specialty brand food formulated for older dogs (Science Diet Canine Senior[a]). The dog was fed three-fourths of a large can per day. The commercial jerky-type treats and ice cream were discon-tinued and replaced with a dry treat formulated for senior dogs (Science Diet Canine Senior Treats[a]). The dog was given two of these treats per day. A thorough oral examination including dental prophylaxis and polishing was recommended.

Endnote

a. Hill's Pet Nutrition, Inc., Topeka, KS, USA.

CASE 9-3

Initial Health Care for a Welsh Corgi Puppy

Jacques Debraekeleer, DVM
Hill's Science and Technology Center
Etten Leur, The Netherlands

Kathy L. Gross, PhD
Hill's Science and Technology Center
Topeka, Kansas, USA

Assess the Animal

A 10-week-old, female Welsh corgi puppy was exam-ined as part of a routine health maintenance program. The owners had recently purchased the puppy from a local breeder and had never owned a dog before. They were interested in vaccinations and any other information about caring for puppies. They had had the puppy for two days and indicated that everything appeared normal.

Physical examination revealed an alert and active puppy with no obvious problems. The puppy weighed 6.5 kg and had normal body condition (body condition score [BCS] 3/5). The estimated adult weight was about 17 kg. Results of a fecal flotation test were negative for intestinal parasites. Routine vaccinations were given.

Assess the Food(s) and Feeding Method

The breeder provided a small amount of an unknown dry food in a plastic bag. The owners had offered small amounts of this food three times per day, and the puppy ate the food very well. They were also given a bottle of chewable vitamin-mineral tablets by the breeder and instructed to give the puppy one tablet per day.

Questions

1. What are the key nutritional factors to consider in developing a feeding plan for this puppy?
2. Outline a specific feeding plan for this patient includ-ing an appropriate food and feeding method.

3. Should the owners continue to provide the chewable vitamin-mineral supplement?
4. Besides nutrition, what other health care topics for puppies should be discussed with these owners?

Answers and Discussion

1. Key nutritional factors for growing dogs include energy, protein, fat, calcium, phosphorus, carbohydrate and digestibility. Energy is required to support rapid accre-tion of new tissue; however, excessive energy intake increases the risk of obesity and developmental ortho-pedic disease. The energy density of food for puppies should be 3.5 to 4.5 kcal (14.6 to 18.8 kJ) metaboliz-able energy (ME)/g dry matter (DM). Fat makes the greatest contribution to the energy density of food and should be 10 to 20% DM in growth-type foods. Puppies also have higher protein requirements than adult dogs to support tissue growth. Protein levels of 22 to 32% DM are recommended for puppies. Adequate calcium is important in foods for growing dogs to support skeletal development. Known calcium deficiency is rarely a concern in growing dogs fed commercial foods, but it may be a problem for dogs fed homemade foods. (See Chapter 6.) Excess calcium intake is a risk factor for developmental orthopedic disease (See Chapter 17.) and may occur in growing dogs eating some commer-cial foods and/or receiving mineral supplements. Calcium levels of 0.7 to 1.7% DM are generally recom-mended for growing dogs. Phosphorus is less critical than calcium provided minimum requirements of 0.35% DM are met and the calcium-phosphorus ratio is between 1:1 and 1.8:1. No specific recommendations for dietary carbohydrate are available for growing dogs; however, puppies appear to do better if growth-type foods contain more than 20% complex carbohydrate DM. Gastrointestinal (GI) distention ("pot-bellied" appearance) and GI disturbances (i.e., flatulence, vom-iting, diarrhea) are less common in puppies fed highly digestible foods (Table 9-11).

2. A food specifically formulated for growing dogs that addresses the key nutritional factors described above

should be recommended. A number of commercial products listed in Appendix L meet these objectives. Homemade foods can also be fed to growing dogs; however, recipes should be used that contain adequate protein, fat, calcium, vitamins and trace minerals to support growth.

Feeding methods for growing dogs include free-choice (ad libitum) feeding, time-limited feeding and food-limited (meal-limited) feeding. Free-choice feeding is relatively effortless and may reduce abnormal behavior such as barking at feeding time. In addition, frequent trips to the food bowl may help reduce boredom and coprophagy, and timid or unthrifty dogs experience less competition when eating. Disadvantages of free-choice feeding include food wastage, only dry or semi-moist forms of pet food can be fed and competition or boredom may stimulate overeating. The most serious disadvantage in young growing dogs is increased risk for obesity and developmental orthopedic disease due to overconsumption of even a properly balanced food.

Time-limited feeding is a method in which dogs are allowed free access to food for a defined period, usually 10 to 15 minutes, once or twice daily. This feeding method may result in less overall food consumption when compared with puppies fed free choice. Time-limited feeding may also help in disciplining and house training young puppies. The owner interacts with the puppy during this time and is able to observe its general condition and behavior, which may lead to earlier detection of problems. A routine of feeding a puppy and then taking it outdoors can reinforce house training by taking advantage of the gastrocolic reflex. Advocates of this feeding method suggest that when some dogs fed in this manner reach adulthood they may voluntarily limit their feeding to once or twice a day and thus avoid overeating. However, recent research has shown that some dogs may eat as much in 15 minutes as when fed free choice. In this study, dogs fed by a time-limited method had higher weight gain, more body fat and increased bone mineral accretion than dogs receiving the same food free choice. This method is also less convenient for the owner than free-choice feeding.

Food-limited feeding requires feeding a measured amount of food based on the puppy's calculated daily energy requirement (DER) or as recommended by the manufacturer, divided into two or three meals per day. This is the method of choice for feeding puppies at risk for obesity and developmental orthopedic disease because it limits food intake to maintain optimal growth rate and body condition. This method is also less con-venient and more time-consuming than free-choice feeding because food amounts must be increased as growth occurs. Appendix F can be used as a starting point for recommendations for daily energy intake.

3. Routine vitamin-mineral supplementation is not necessary for healthy puppies eating balanced commercial growth foods. Supplementation is important if homemade foods are used.

4. In addition to vaccination, intestinal parasite control and nutritional counseling, the following health maintenance procedures should be discussed with puppy owners: 1) external parasites and appropriate control programs, 2) heartworm preventive programs, in endemic areas, 3) the pet's behavior and socialization, 4) specific breed characteristics, 5) routine grooming procedures, 6) basic obedience training and reputable obedience schools, 7) recommendations for neutering, 8) house training and 9) manipulation of the mouth to accustom the puppy to toothbrushing later on. All of these topics should be discussed with these clients, especially because they are novice dog owners. (See Chapter 8.)

Progress Notes

All of the health maintenance procedures mentioned above were discussed with the owners by the veterinarian or veterinary technician. A commercial specialty brand dry food formulated for canine growth (Science Diet Canine Growth[a]) was recommended. The quantity of food to be fed was based on the feeding instructions on the pet food bag. This amount was divided into three equal daily meals. The owners were instructed to discontinue the vitamin-mineral supplement and were given an instruction sheet that outlined how to assess the body condition of puppies. The food amount was to be adjusted as the puppy grew according to the feeding guidelines on the bag. The owners were asked to weigh and assign a BCS for the puppy every other week and adjust the food amount as needed to maintain an optimal body condition. The body weight and body condition would also be assessed by the veterinary technician during subsequent office visits when the puppy was 14 to 16 and 20 to 22 weeks of age.

Endnote

a. Hill's Pet Nutrition, Inc., Topeka, KS, USA.

Bibliography

Toll PW, Richardson DC, Jewell DE, et al. The effect of feeding method on growth and body composition in young puppies (abstract). In: Abstract Book. Waltham Symposium on the Nutrition of Companion Animals. Adelaide, Australia, September 23-25, 1993: 33.

CASE 9-4

Feeding a Young Basset Hound after an Ovariohysterectomy

Philip Roudebush, DVM
Diplomate ACVIM (Internal Medicine)
Hill's Science and Technology Center
Topeka, Kansas, USA

Assess the Animal

A 12-month-old female basset hound was admitted for an ovariohysterectomy. The owners had observed no problems since purchasing the dog from a pet store eight months before. Physical examination revealed a normal 20-kg dog (body condition score [BCS] 3/5) except for excessive accumulation of waxy debris in both ears. Results of preanesthetic blood work were normal.

The ovariohysterectomy was performed with no complications. The owners returned to pick up the dog the next day.

Assess the Food(s) and Feeding Method

The dog was fed a commercial specialty brand growth formula (Science Diet Lamb Meal & Rice Formula Canine Growth[a]) that the owners purchased from the pet store where they obtained the dog. The owners had been following the feeding directions on the pet food label. They were currently feeding one can of the growth formula in the morning (520 kcal, 2.18 MJ) and two cups (200 g) of the dry formulation of the same brand in the evening (780 kcal, 3.26 MJ). The dog's appetite had been good. The owners also gave the dog two commercial treats each day (Science Diet Canine Growth Treats[a]) (19 kcal [79 kJ] per treat).

Questions

1. What are the key nutritional factors to consider in developing a feeding plan for this young neutered adult dog?
2. What response should be given when the owners ask whether the ovariohysterectomy will change the feeding recommendations for their dog?
3. Outline a specific feeding plan for this patient including appropriate food(s) and feeding method.

Answers and Discussion

1. Key nutritional factors for young to middle-aged adult dogs include water, energy, phosphorus, calcium, protein, sodium, chloride, fat and essential fatty acids and food texture. In general, water requirements are met by allowing free access to a source of potable water. Energy and fat are important because prevention of obesity is an important goal of feeding adult dogs. Phosphorus, calcium, sodium and chloride requirements should be met but not greatly exceeded. Essential fatty acids are important for maintenance of normal skin and coat, a primary concern of many dog owners. Food texture is important in controlling periodontal disease, the most common health problem of adult dogs.
2. Gonadectomy increases the risk of obesity in dogs. Neutered female dogs are about twice as likely as intact female dogs to be overweight. A similar trend occurs in castrated male dogs. Gonadectomy predisposes dogs to weight gain and eventual obesity for several reasons. Daily energy requirement (DER) may decrease because of metabolic changes associated with gonadectomy. Further, studies have demonstrated that neutered female dogs eat more food and gain more weight than sham-operated females fed identical food. Thus, removal of the metabolic effects of estrogens and androgens by gonadectomy may lead to increased food consumption when at the same time the animal's energy requirement is lower due to decreased metabolic rate and physical activity. These are important considerations when creating a feeding plan for young neutered adult dogs.
3. Basset hounds are predisposed to obesity. (See Chapter 13.) Gonadectomy and the breed predisposition to obesity make obesity prevention a primary goal in developing a feeding plan for this patient. This dog has also reached adulthood; therefore, the levels of nutri-

ents found in growth-type formulas are unnecessary.

The food should be changed from a growth formula to an adult maintenance formula. In general, adult maintenance formulas of the same brand contain less energy, fat, phosphorus, calcium, sodium and chloride than growth formulas. These lower levels of nutrients exceed the minimum nutrient requirements of adult dogs while avoiding the higher nutrient levels found in growth or all-purpose type formulas. This dog's optimal BCS suggests that it is eating an appropriate amount of food. However, gonadectomy and other metabolic changes associated with maturity will probably decrease the DER. The estimated DER would be 1.4 to 1.6 x resting energy requirement (RER) (940 to 1,070 kcal, 3.93 to 4.48 MJ). The dog is currently consuming 1,300 kcal (5.44 MJ) or 2 x RER. The feeding method will be dictated somewhat by whether moist, dry, semi-moist or homemade foods are fed. The owners are currently meal feeding a combination of moist and dry foods; this feeding method can be continued with the new food(s).

Progress Notes

The dog was discharged to the owners' care with instructions to limit exercise for several days, examine the suture line daily for signs of swelling or inflammation and return for suture removal in 10 to 14 days. The owners were shown how to clean the ears and an otic cleaning solution was dispensed.

The owners were interested in continuing to feed a combination of moist and dry food. They were instructed to purchase the same brand adult maintenance food (Science Diet Lamb Meal & Rice Formula Canine Maintenance[a]) and gradually mix the new food with the old food until the moist and dry growth formulas were completely gone. A combination of the adult maintenance food consisting of one large (418 g) can of moist food in the morning (420 kcal, 1.76 MJ) and 1 2/3 cups (165 grams) of dry food in the evening (610 kcal, 2.59 MJ) would provide approximately 1.6 x RER for the dog's current weight of 20 kg. Two treats per day were also continued; however, the owners were encouraged to use the adult maintenance formula of the same treat (18 kcal [75 kJ] per treat).

Prevention of obesity was emphasized to the owners because of the risk factors discussed earlier. They were given an instruction sheet that outlined how to score the dog's body condition and encouraged them to weigh the dog monthly. They were instructed to call the practice if the dog appeared to be gaining weight or if the dog's BCS increased. Periodontal disease, veterinary oral care and routine home oral care were also discussed. (See Chapter 16.)

Endnote

a. Hill's Pet Nutrition, Inc., Topeka, KS, USA.

Bibliography

Anantharaman-Barr G. The effect of ovariohysterectomy on energy metabolism in dogs (research abstract). Friskies Veterinary International 1990; 2: 19-20.

CHAPTER 10

The Canine Athlete

Philip W. Toll

Arleigh J. Reynolds

". . . a cowdog is something special. You might say we're the elite. We have to be stronger, braver, and tougher than any brand of dog in the world. It's a special calling, . . . it ain't for the common run of mutts."

Hank The Cowdog, Head of Ranch Security

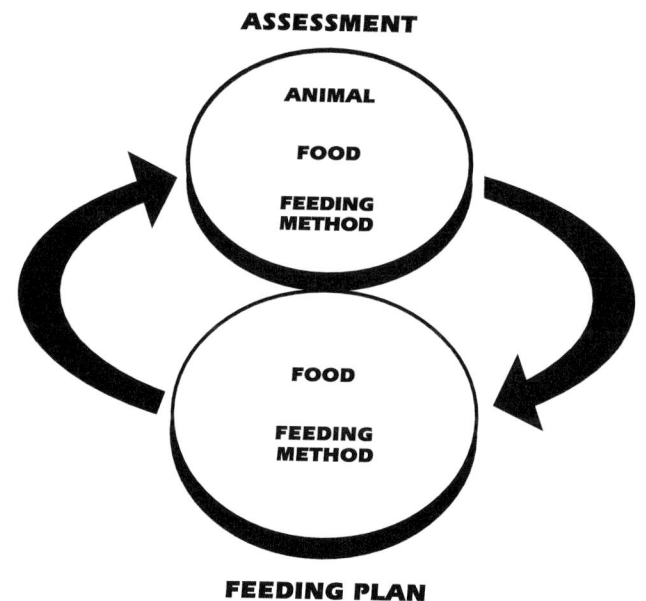

ASSESSMENT

ANIMAL

FOOD

FEEDING METHOD

FOOD

FEEDING METHOD

FEEDING PLAN

Note: The reader is referred to Chapter 1 for a detailed discussion of the iterative process of clinical nutrition.

CANINE ATHLETE

INTRODUCTION

Athletic performance depends on genetics, training and nutrition. All three must be optimal for maximal performance. A deficiency in any one of these factors limits performance; therefore, each factor must be assessed in light of the type of exercise done by the individual.

Genetics

The genetic characteristics of the dog must be appropriate for the type of exercise it does. Mental, physical and metabolic characteristics all play a role; however, many of these attributes are difficult to assess. The dog's desire to perform is crucial. For example, if a racing greyhound has no desire to chase the lure or a sheep dog has no desire to herd, other genetic characteristics, training and nutrition become irrelevant. This generalization assumes that the lack of desire is not due to injury, illness, improper training or malnutrition. Physical characteristics such as conformation, orthopedic disease, heart size and muscle fiber type set the limits for athletic performance. Maximal performance for an individual dog is achieved through appropriate training and nutrition. Although proper training and nutrition can greatly enhance performance, they cannot overcome genetic limitations.

Training

Assessment of training should assure that the intensity, duration and frequency of training match the desired level of performance. Many canine athletes are poorly trained. This is especially true for intermittent athletes such as

KEY WORDS & TERMS—THE CANINE ATHLETE*

Anaerobic threshold	Intensity	$\dot{V}O_2$
Carbohydrate threshold	Intermediate exercise	$\dot{V}O_2$ max
Duration	Power	Work
Endurance exercise	Protein calories	Workload
Exercise	Sprint exercise	
Frequency	Training	

Key words and terms are defined in the Glossary.

KEY POINTS—THE CANINE ATHLETE

1. The hallmark of exercise is increased metabolism. Providing the right amount of energy from the right sources is central to feeding canine athletes.
2. Nutrition cannot overcome deficits in genetics and training; however, matching nutrition to exercise type (i.e., intensity, duration and frequency) allows a canine athlete to perform to its genetic potential and level of training.
3. Glucose can be metabolized to regenerate ATP by anaerobic and aerobic pathways. Anaerobic metabolism of glucose (glycolysis) results in very rapid ATP production or high-metabolic power, but only yields two ATP per molecule of glucose. Aerobic metabolism, the complete oxidation of glucose to CO_2 and water, regenerates ATP less rapidly, but results in 36 ATP per molecule of glucose (higher yield).
4. Because total body glucose stores (glycogen) are relatively small (1 to 2% of body weight), aerobic metabolism of glucose cannot sustain exercise for extended periods of time. Fatty acids are the primary energy sources for prolonged exercise.
5. Amino acids are not usually a primary energy source for exercise. Oxidation of amino acids may contribute up to 5 to 15% of the energy used during exercise, depending on the intensity and duration of the task.
6. Fat provides approximately 8.5 kcal (36 kJ) of metabolizable energy per g of dry matter or more than twice the amount provided by protein and carbohydrate. The only means of significantly increasing the energy density of a food is to increase its fat concentration.
7. A 30-kg dog expends about 30 kcal to cover 1 km on a flat surface, regardless of how fast it walks or runs.
8. Functionally, exercise can be divided into three types based on intensity and duration: 1) sprint—high-intensity activities that can be sustained less than two minutes, 2) intermediate—activities lasting a few minutes to a few hours and 3) endurance—activities that last many hours.
9. The preferred source of energy depends mostly on intensity. Sprinters, even though they work at a very high intensity, have relatively low energy requirements because the duration of their events is so short and frequency is usually only a few times each week. Generally, 1.6 to 2 x resting energy requirement is adequate for most sprint athletes.
10. Intensity, duration and frequency of exercise are variable for intermediate athletes; therefore, the energy requirement is highly variable. The daily energy requirement for these athletes ranges from 2 to 5 x resting energy requirement. Foods with a higher fat content are typically fed to provide adequate dietary energy density.
11. Endurance athletes require more than 5 x resting energy requirement. Foods that are very high in fat are required for activities of long duration.
12. Enhanced digestibility increases the maximum possible delivery of nutrients to tissues. Total dry matter digestibility of any food for canine athletes should be greater than 80%.
13. Timing of feeding in relation to exercise is important. Meals should be fed more than four hours before exercise. Feeding less then two hours after exercise may help maximize muscle glycogen. Small amounts of food may be fed during exercise.
14. Repeated or continual body condition assessment is clearly the best clinical measure of energy balance. However, some very fit athletes will have a body condition score less than 3/5. Because fat in excess of what is needed for energy reserves during racing adds weight and may affect performance, many sight hounds and some sled dogs are kept very lean (body condition score 1/5 to 2/5).
15. Animals require some time to adapt to the new food whenever a dietary change is made. GI adjustments usually occur in a few days provided the transition to the new food is gradual. Metabolic changes may take six to eight weeks. Training and dietary change should occur six weeks before exercise season (e.g., hunting season).

hunting dogs that spend much of the year in a run or small yard but are expected to hunt for many hours at the onset of hunting season.

Exercise training is simply the consistent performance of some type of exercise over an extended period of time. Although genetics dictate the structural and metabolic characteristics of an individual dog, training can alter some of these characteristics and enhance performance.

Exercise training means subjecting a dog to a workload of sufficient intensity, duration and frequency to produce a measurable adaptation of the systems being trained. The types of adaptations produced by training are specific; that is, physiologic changes occur that favor the type of activity performed. To improve aerobic power, exercise intensity should be greater than 50% of maximum oxygen consumption ($\dot{V}O_2$ max) for sedentary individuals. As the level of training or fitness improves, intensity and duration must be increased to produce further improvement. The general principle is that intensity and duration must be increased until a level of overload is reached for the sys-

KEY NUTRITIONAL FACTORS—THE CANINE ATHLETE

Factors	Sprint athletes	Intermediate athletes (low/moderate duration and frequency)	Intermediate athletes (high duration and frequency)	Endurance athletes
Energy density	Use food with 3.5 to 4.0 kcal ME/g DM	Use food with 4.0 to 5.0 kcal ME/g DM	Use food with 4.5 to 5.5 kcal ME/g DM	Use food with >6.0 kcal ME/g DM
Fat	Use food with 8 to 10% fat DM or 20 to 24% of calories from fat	Use food with 15 to 30% fat DM or 30 to 55% of calories from fat	Use food with 25 to 40% fat DM or 45 to 65% of calories from fat	Use food with >50% fat DM or >75% of calories from fat
Soluble carbohydrate (nitrogen-free extract)	Use food with 55 to 65% NFE DM or 50 to 60% of calories from NFE	Use food with 30 to 55% NFE DM or 20 to 50% of calories from NFE	Use food with 30 to 35% NFE DM or 15 to 30% of calories from NFE	Use food with <15% NFE DM or <10% of calories from NFE
Protein	Use food with 22 to 28% protein DM or 20 to 25% of calories from protein	Use food with 22 to 32% protein DM or 20 to 25% of calories from protein	Use food with 22 to 30% protein DM or 18 to 25% of calories from protein	Use food with 28 to 34% protein DM or 18 to 22% of calories from protein
Digestibility	DM digestibility >80%	DM digestibility >80%	DM digestibility >80%	DM digestibility >80%
Water	Unlimited access except just before a race	Unlimited access	Unlimited access	Unlimited access

tems being trained to induce adaptation. Further, training adaptations are specific to the type of exercise performed.

Examples of training-induced changes include increased bone mass, muscle hypertrophy, increased mitochondrial density in muscle and plasma volume expansion. All of these changes support enhanced performance. Muscle hypertrophy is a well-known phenomenon. Muscle size and strength increase with use. Changes in content of various muscle enzymes and numbers of mitochondria can occur depending on the type of activity performed. Bone, ligaments and tendons also hypertrophy in response to increasing stresses but at a slower rate than muscle.

Cardiovascular function increases to meet increased needs of muscle for substrates and waste removal. Plasma volume expansion is a well-known result of chronic exercise training that supports increased cardiac output.[1,2] Heart rates of trained animals are lower for a given workload because of greater cardiovascular efficiency. Training also influences the type and amount of substrate that can be used to support exercise.

Nutrition

Nutrition cannot overcome deficits in genetics and training. However, matching nutrition to exercise type (i.e., intensity, duration and frequency) allows a canine athlete to perform to its genetic potential and level of training. The goal of feeding canine athletes is to provide appropriate nutrition for health and optimal performance. As with feeding any animal, it is important that the food type, amount and feeding method be matched to the animal's needs. This chapter discusses exercise physiology, how to assess canine athletes and their needs, how to meet these needs through the feeding plan and how to monitor how well the needs are met.

CLINICAL IMPORTANCE

Canids represent one of the most diverse mammalian species. The wide range of athletic ability and types of

canine athletes comes as no surprise in light of this diversity. At one extreme is the racing greyhound, which is capable of sprinting a quarter mile in less than 26 seconds and reaching maximum speeds in excess of 35 mph (60 km/hr). At the other extreme is the sled dog, which is capable of running vast distances, day after day, in arctic conditions. In between these extremes is a plethora of different kinds of working, hunting and sporting dogs that participate in a wide range of athletic activities (Table 10-1).

The American Kennel Club lists 24 sporting breeds, 16 herding breeds and 20 breeds of working dogs; however, it is difficult to quantify how many of these dogs actually participate in athletic events.[3] Eighty different breeds of hounds are found worldwide and all these breeds were originally hunting dogs. In addition, there exist 13 sight

CANINE ATHLETE

Table 10-1. Canine athletic activities listed by exercise type.

Exercise type	Activity
Sprint	Racing (greyhounds, whippets)
	Coursing (sight hounds)
	Weight pulling
Intermediate	Hunting (game birds, rabbits)
	Field trials
	Pursuit (raccoon, coyote, fox, deer, wild boar)
	Tracking
	Frisbee trials
	Agility
	Service work (guide dogs, assistance dogs)
	Police work
	Guarding
	Military
	Border patrol, customs
	Drug detection
	Search and rescue
	Livestock management (cattle, sheep, hogs)
	Exercise with people (running, bicycling)
Endurance	Sled pulling (racing, expedition)

hound breeds, 49 herding or shepherd dogs and 31 recognized terrier breeds.[4-6] Using a different classification system, another author lists 91 hounds, 43 working breeds, 44 herding dogs, 49 gun dogs and 31 terriers.[4]

Working dogs are employed by many government agencies including those involved in national defense, customs service and border patrol. Additionally, in the United States, more than 28,000 dogs work for state and local law enforcement agencies. Numbers of active sporting dogs are difficult to document. In the United States, survey results from one publisher estimate that readers of their hunting magazines own more than 700,000 active hunting dogs.[a] These same readers spend 150 to 200 hours per year training their dogs and 40 days per year hunting in the field with their dogs. In 1994, the United Kingdom and Ireland had 450 packs of hounds that were actively hunting. Of these 450 packs, 250 hunted foxes, 150 hunted hare and 50 were used for deer or mink hunting, drag hunt or clean boot.[7] In France, hounds are still very popular for hunting deer, roe and wild boar in what is called the vénérie (pack hunting). The vénérie in France still counts about 12,000 to 13,000 dogs, divided over fewer than 10 breeds.[7]

In the United States, the National Greyhound Association registers about 35,000 greyhound puppies annually and estimates that more than 40,000 dogs are racing or preparing to race at the country's 40 dog tracks.[b]

Because canine athletes participate in a wide variety of working and sporting activities, and the level of participation varies from full-time athlete to intermittent activity, it is difficult to assess how much of the canine population participates in athletic events. It is clear, however, that large numbers of dogs participate in these activities.

EXERCISE PHYSIOLOGY

Exercise requires increased function of several organ systems and energy metabolism pathways. Dramatic changes take place within dogs to support exercise and as a result of exercise. Certainly, nutritional needs are affected by exercise. An understanding of exercise physiology is fundamental to assessing and developing a feeding plan for canine athletes.

The following review of exercise physiology relates particularly to nutrition of canine athletes. This discussion includes: 1) a review of muscle metabolism that outlines the energy needs of working muscles, substrate requirements and the by-products of energy metabolism, 2) exercise type and intensity, which determine the preferred metabolic substrates and therefore the nutrient profile, 3) some of the physiologic changes that occur during exercise and how they may affect nutrient needs and 4) the energy cost of running, which dictates dietary energy needs. All of these factors are important to nutritional assessment of canine athletes and form the basis for a good feeding plan.

Muscle Metabolism

Muscle Fiber Types

Muscles are not homogeneous. They are composed of fibers with different contractile and metabolic characteristics. Muscle fibers are classified into two groups based on contractile properties and histochemical staining: Type I or slow twitch and Type II or fast twitch (Table 10-2). Type I fibers have high oxidative capacity and endurance. These fibers are smaller than Type II fibers and have high capillary density and high numbers of mitochondria. They are low in glycolytic ability and low in staining for myofibrillar ATPase, an enzyme associated with fast contraction and relaxation. Conversely, Type II fibers are high in myofibrillar ATPase, larger, contain more glycolytic enzymes and have greater strength. Type II fibers can be further subdivided into Type IIa and Type IIb. Contraction characteristics are similar for Type IIa and Type IIb fibers, but Type IIa fibers have greater oxidative capacity than Type IIb fibers.

The fiber composition varies between muscles and between individuals. High-power athletes such as racing greyhounds have a higher proportion of Type II fibers, whereas endurance athletes have a higher proportion of

Table 10-2. Skeletal muscle fiber types.

Property	Slow twitch fibers	Fast twitch fibers	
	Type I	Type IIa	Type IIb
Fiber size	Small	Large	Large
Contractile speed	Low	High	High
Endurance	High	Medium	Low
Capillary density	High	Medium	Low
Myoglobin content	High	Medium	Low
Glycogenolytic enzyme activity	Low	High	High
Mitochondrial enzyme activity	High	Medium	Low
Myofibrillar ATPase activity	Low	High	High

Table 10-3. Percent fast twitch fibers (Type II) by selected canine breeds.*

Muscle	Greyhound	Crossbred	Foxhound
Triceps (long head)	94.2	77.2	64.9
Vastus lateralis	96.6	61.4	80.7
Biceps femoris	88.6	67.2	63.0
Semitendinosus	98.9	85.3	69.6

*Adapted from Guy PS, Snow DH. Skeletal muscle fibre composition in the dog and its relationship to athletic ability. Research in Veterinary Science 1981; 31: 244-248.

Table 10-4. Metabolism, use and storage sites of metabolic fuels.

Fuel	Metabolism	Use	Storage sites
ATP	Anaerobic	Primary fuel for synthetic processes, ion pumps and muscle contraction	Muscle cells (concentration is low and highly regulated)
Cr-P	Anaerobic	Regenerate ATP	Muscle cells (low concentration)
Glucose	Anaerobic (glycolysis) and aerobic (TCA cycle)	Rapidly available energy source	Muscle and liver glycogen (1 to 2% of body weight)
Fatty acids	Aerobic (beta oxidation and TCA cycle)	Long-lasting energy source	Adipose tissue (2 to 20% of body weight)
Amino acids	Aerobic (TCA cycle)	Small contribution to energy (may contribute up to 5 to 15%)	Structural proteins

Key: ATP = adenosine triphosphate, Cr-P = creatine phosphate, TCA = tricarboxylic acid.

Type I fibers (Table 10-3). Because the work performed by most intermediate athletes resembles that done by endurance athletes, but is of shorter duration, the muscle fiber-type profile of intermediate athletes should resemble that of endurance athletes more than that of sprint athletes. Muscle fiber type is a function of genetics and dictates the type of exercise for which an individual is best suited. However, some modification is possible through training. Endurance training increases the number and volume of mitochondria and increases capillary density in all fiber types.[8] In other words, the distribution between Type IIa and IIb can change in response to training.

Muscle Energetics

Exercise requires the transfer of chemical energy into physical work. Chemical energy stored in high-energy phosphate bonds of adenosine triphosphate (ATP) is the sole source of energy for muscle contraction. ATP is cleaved to ADP during contraction. The amount of ATP used is proportional to the amount of work performed (Fenn effect). ATP is vital not only for the events of contraction (See sidebar "The Events of Muscle Contraction."), but also for relaxation and maintenance of important ion gradients. Normal excitability of nerve and muscle is due to an electrochemical gradient maintained by the sodium-potassium pump at the expense of ATP. The calcium pump uses ATP to maintain a low concentration of calcium in the muscle cell in the relaxed state. An estimated one-third of the basal energy requirement is used to maintain electrolyte concentration gradients across cellular membranes.[9,10]

Although ATP is the high-energy compound that cells use as fuel to perform work, the energy required for exercise can ultimately come from a variety of sources. Because the concentration of ATP in muscle cells is relatively low in comparison to the cell's need during exercise, ATP must be replenished from other fuel sources. These metabolic fuels are stored in muscle (endogenous) and at other body sites (exogenous). The metabolism of these fuels occurs either with oxygen (aerobic) or without oxygen (anaerobic). The anaerobic pathways (i.e., the creatine phosphate shuttle and glycolysis) occur in the cytoplasm, whereas the aerobic pathways (i.e., complete oxidation of glucose, fatty acids and amino acids) take place in mitochondria. Figure 10-1 shows an overview of these pathways. The proportion of each pathway used is determined by the duration and intensity of the task performed and by the conditioning and nutritional status of the animal.[9,11-15] Table 10-4 lists metabolic fuels, their uses and storage sites.

The concentration of ATP is tightly regulated, although it is rapidly consumed during exercise.[9,11,16,17] Resting muscle cells have only enough ATP to fuel muscle contraction for a few seconds. If work continues beyond this point, ATP must be regenerated from other metabolic fuels at a rate comparable to that at which it is being consumed.[9,11,12,17,18] Creatine phosphate (Cr-P) is an endogenously stored fuel that muscles can rapidly convert to ATP. The Cr-P shuttle permits the maximum rate of ATP synthesis possible; however, this pathway can only support maximal efforts for five to 15 seconds (Figure 10-2) because muscle Cr-P stores are very limited.[12,18,19]

Glucose is a versatile metabolic fuel that is stored endogenously as muscle glycogen and exogenously as

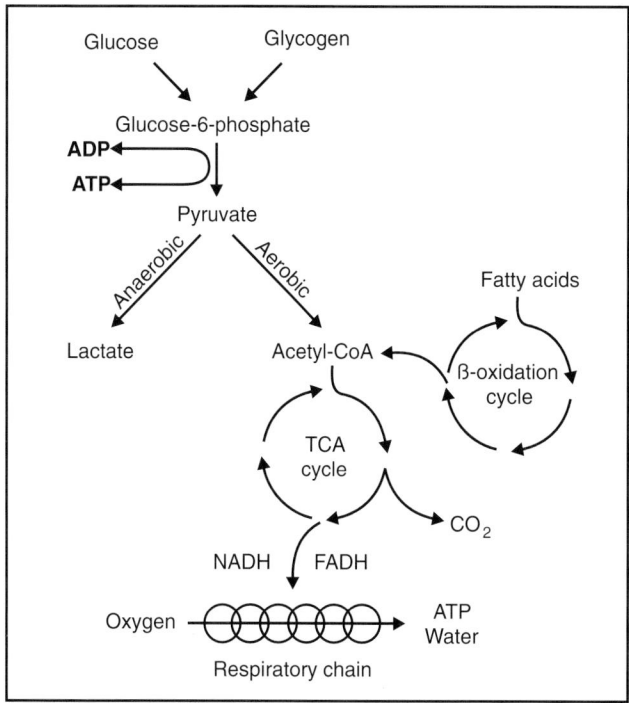

Figure 10-1. Summary of major energy-generating pathways used during exercise. Key: ADP = adenosine diphosphate, ATP = adenosine triphosphate, TCA = tricarboxylic acid, NADH = reduced form of nicotinamide dinucleotide, FADH = reduced form of flavin-adenine dinucleotide.

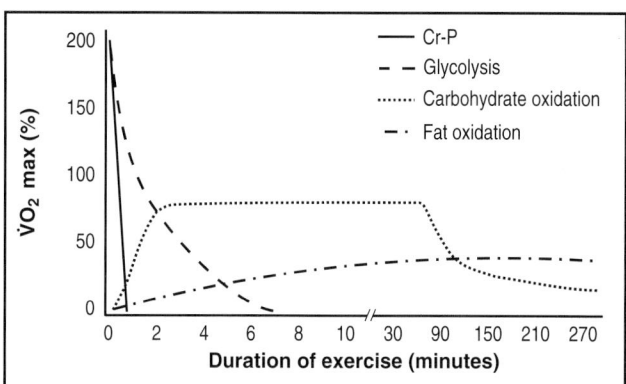

Figure 10-2. Relative contributions of the four energy-generating pathways, depending on exercise intensity and duration. Key: Cr-P = creatine phosphate.

glycogen in the liver and to a much smaller extent as free glucose in the blood. Glucose can be metabolized to regenerate ATP by both anaerobic and aerobic pathways. Anaerobic metabolism of glucose (glycolysis) results in very rapid ATP production (Figure 10-2) or high metabolic power (See sidebar "Metabolic Power and Yield."), but only yields two ATP per molecule of glucose. Aerobic metabolism, the complete oxidation of glucose to CO_2 and water, regenerates ATP less rapidly (See sidebar "Metabolic Power and Yield."), but results in a much greater yield (36 ATP per molecule of glucose). Because total body glucose stores (glycogen) are relatively small (1 to 2% of body weight), even aerobic metabolism of glucose cannot sustain exercise for extended periods of time. Fatty acids are stored in ample supply in adipose tissue and within muscle. They are the primary energy source for long-lasting

The Events of Muscle Contraction

Muscle contraction occurs when a muscle fiber is excited by a nerve resulting in a muscle action potential (loss of the normal -90 millivolt resting membrane potential). The action potential travels throughout the muscle fiber causing calcium to be released into the cytoplasm from the sarcoplasmic reticulum. This flood of calcium around the contractile proteins elicits a conformational change that allows the contractile proteins (actin and myosin) to bind together (Figure 1). This attachment allows the energy stored in the "pre-cocked" head of the myosin filament to be discharged in a "power stroke" that causes muscle shortening. The two filaments are released when ATP binds to the myosin active site. The head of the myosin filament is re-cocked when this ATP molecule is cleaved. When the calcium concentration remains high, the head of the myosin filament binds to another site on the actin filament and the sequence is repeated. This sequence of events continues until either minimum fiber length (maximum shortening) or maximum load is exceeded. Relaxation occurs when the calcium concentration drops to pre-contraction levels because of the action of the calcium pump.

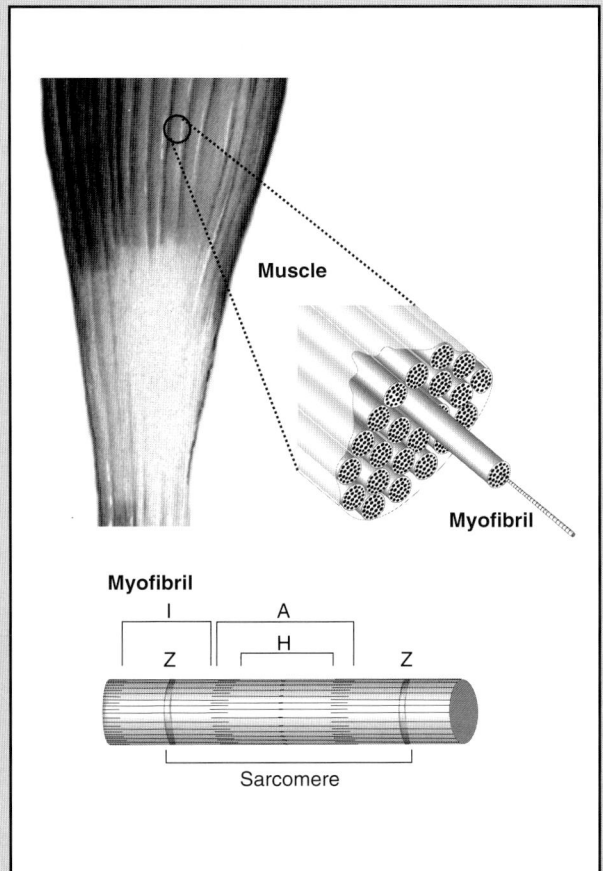

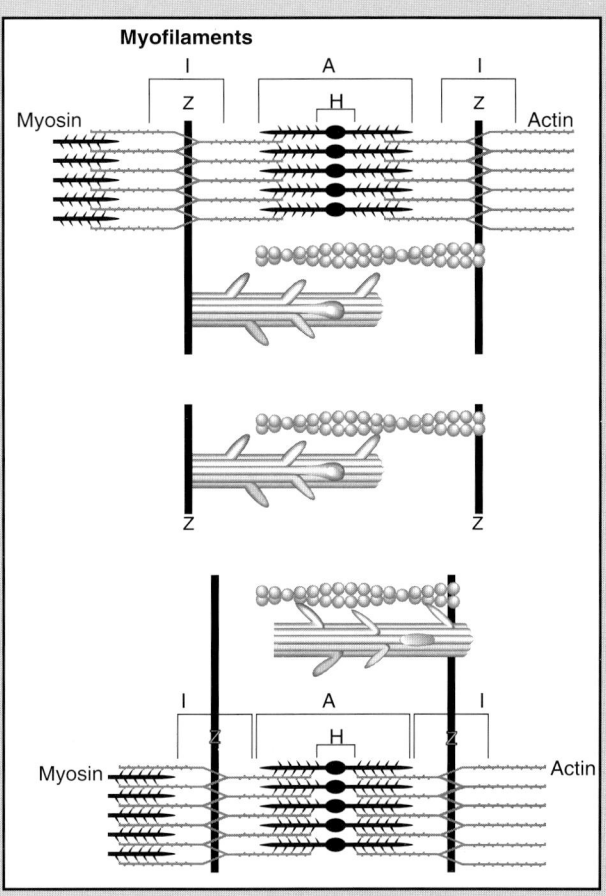

Figure 1. Components of striated muscle cells. Each striated muscle cell or fiber contains hundreds to thousands of myofibrils. Each myofibril contains a series of interlocking myofilaments (i.e., actin and myosin filaments). The **H band** is the center of the myosin filaments, the **A band** is the entire length of the myosin filaments, the **Z disk or plate** is the center and attachment site of the actin filaments, the **I band** encompasses the entire length of the actin filaments except for the portions that overlap the myosin filaments. The compartments between the Z plates are called **sarcomeres**. During contraction, the Z plates are pulled towards one another as the degree of overlap of thick and thin filaments increases; I band and H bands shorten. Maximum contraction is attained when the ends of the thick filaments butt against Z plates.

exercise. Although small amounts of fatty acids are stored in muscle, this source may contribute up to 60% of the fatty acids oxidized during the first two to three hours of exercise.[20]

Amino acids are usually not a primary energy source for exercise. Oxidation of amino acids may contribute up to 5 to 15% of the energy used during exercise, depending on the intensity and duration of the task.[21-23] Most of this energy comes from the oxidation of the branched-chain amino acids leucine, isoleucine and valine.[24,25] Most amino acids

are structural or functional components of proteins and the size of the labile amino acid pool is very small, making amino acids a less significant fuel source for exercise in most circumstances.

The proportion of energy substrates and metabolic pathways used during exercise depends on the intensity and duration of the exercise. As exercise intensity increases, the power output and the rate of energy metabolism must also increase. As exercise duration increases, total substrate availability and energy yield become more important. (See sidebar "Metabolic Power and Yield.") High-power activities (e.g., sprinting) rely heavily on anaerobic metabolism, whereas more prolonged activities require the higher energy yield provided by oxidation of glucose and fatty acids. As the duration of exercise increases, oxidation of fatty acids becomes more important (Figure 10-2).

By-Products of Muscular Work

Heat is the primary by-product of muscle contraction; 75 to 80% of the energy used during muscular work is converted to heat. A 10-fold increase in metabolism results in a 10-fold increase in heat production. Unless the animal is working in a very cold environment, this heat is a by-product that must be removed. In dogs, the respiratory tract is responsible for dissipating most of this heat. During very intense exercise or exercise in hot environmental temperatures, heat production exceeds the ability of the respiratory tract to lose heat, causing the body temperature to increase. The body temperature of racing greyhounds may increase more than $1°C$ ($1.8°F$) as the result of a 30-second race. Because evaporative heat loss is the primary way dogs dissipate heat, ensuring adequate hydration is crucial for maintenance of normal body temperature.

Metabolic acid is another by-product of energy metabolism that must be eliminated during and after exercise. Aerobic metabolism generates ATP by combustion of carbohydrates and fats to CO_2 and water. Lactate is the endpoint of anaerobic metabolism. Either way, acid is produced that must be eliminated in some way for exercise to continue. Muscle enzyme activity is highly pH sensitive. Therefore, if energy metabolism and muscle contraction are to proceed optimally, muscle pH must be tightly regulated. Intracellular buffers can blunt some of the acute effects of increased concentrations of CO_2 and lactate. However, elimination of organic acids from muscle cells is the primary strategy for avoiding deleterious decreases in muscle pH. Because it is a weak electrolyte, CO_2 has less effect on pH than lactate (a strong electrolyte) and is handled differently by the body.

Assuming no other primary acid-base changes, CO_2 and bicarbonate (HCO_3^-) increase in parallel because of the following relationship:

$$CO_2 + H_2O \leftrightarrow HCO_3^- + H^+$$

The CO_2 load produced during exercise can be eliminated via two routes: 1) respiratory loss of CO_2 (acute) and 2) renal excretion of HCO_3^- (long-term). The ability of the kidneys to respond acutely may be impaired because of decreased plasma volume and renal blood flow during exercise. The respiratory system responds very quickly by increasing ventilation to excrete excess CO_2 (and excess heat). Aerobic exercise generally does not produce large acid-base changes, because the respiratory system can excrete CO_2 as fast as it is produced.

The acid-base consequences of anaerobic metabolism are more severe and less easily dealt with by the body. Lactate is a strong organic acid and does not participate in any dissociation equilibria. This means that lactate has greater effect on pH than CO_2 and its acid-base effects must be ameliorated by other compensatory changes until it is metabolized. Lactate is oxidized for energy by muscle or converted back to glucose in the liver (Cori cycle).

Metabolic Power and Yield

Metabolic power is the speed with which energy substrates can be converted to ATP, whereas metabolic yield is the amount of ATP that can be made from energy substrates. High-intensity exercise (e.g., sprinting) requires rapid mobilization of stored energy for a very short time; therefore, metabolic power is very important. Because duration of exercise is very short for sprinters, metabolic yield is less important. Conversely, endurance activities are longer in duration and lower in intensity. For these activities, the rapidity with which ATP is made from substrates (power) is less important than the amount of ATP made (yield). Tables 1 and 2 show maximum power and yield from various substrates using aerobic and anaerobic pathways.

Clinically, canine sprint athletes rely heavily on anaerobic metabolism of carbohydrates whereas canine endurance athletes rely more on oxidation of fats.

CLINICAL EXAMPLE

Compare a 30-kg racing greyhound with a 30-kg sled dog. Assume the racing greyhound runs an 800-meter race in about 48 seconds. The total energy needed for the race is about 24 kcal, whereas the energy use rate or metabolic power is about 30 kcal per minute (an increase of more than 25 times resting). Total daily energy requirement (DER) is about 1,600 kcal. In contrast, consider a sled dog that runs 80 km pulling a sled (its share is about 15 kg) for five hours. The sled dog needs about 3,600 additional kcal for the event and uses them at a rate of 12 kcal per minute. Total DER is about 5,000 kcal (more than 5 x resting energy requirement). To convert to kJ, multiply kcal x 4.184.

BIBLIOGRAPHY

Hochachka PW. Design of energy metabolism. In: Prosser CL, ed. Environmental and Metabolic Animal Physiology, 4th ed. New York, NY: Wiley-Liss Inc, 1991; 325-352.

Table 1. Estimated maximum metabolic power output for human skeletal muscle using different substrates and metabolic profiles.*

Process	Metabolic power output (µmole of ATP/g of muscle/minute)
Aerobic metabolism	
Fatty acid oxidation	20.4
Glycogen oxidation	30
Anaerobic metabolism	
Glycogen glycolysis	60
Creatine phosphate and ATP hydrolysis	96-360

*Adapted from Hochachka PW. Design of energy metabolism. In: Prosser CL, ed. Environmental and Metabolic Animal Physiology, 4th ed. New York, NY: Wiley-Liss, 1991; 332.

Table 2. Energy yield using different substrates and metabolic pathways.*

Process	Energy yield (moles of ATP/moles of substrate)
Aerobic metabolism	
Triglyceride oxidation (glycerol + 3 palmitate)	403
Fatty acid oxidation (palmitate)	129
Glycogen oxidation	38
Glucose oxidation	36
Proline oxidation	21
Lactate oxidation	18
Anaerobic metabolism	
Glycolysis (glycogen)	3
Glycolysis (glucose)	2
Creatine phosphate hydrolysis	1

*Adapted from Hochachka PW. Design of energy metabolism. In: Prosser CL, ed. Environmental and Metabolic Animal Physiology, 4th ed. New York, NY: Wiley-Liss, 1991; 327-329.

Exercise Intensity and Duration

Energy and other nutrient requirements for canine athletes are determined by the intensity and duration of exercise. Exercise intensity can be described in a variety of ways depending on body weight and type of activity. Exercise intensity is a measure of work done per unit time. For dogs, the type of work done is usually running and the amount of work done depends on body weight, distance traveled and change in elevation. The amount of work done is directly proportional to the amount of energy used. Therefore, energy use describes work done.

For example, a 30-kg dog expends about 30 kcal to cover 1 km on a flat surface, regardless of how fast it walks or runs (minor differences may occur due to differences in efficiency of various gaits for running at a specific speed). Running speed (distance/time) is a measure of exercise intensity (work/time) or power (energy/time). A direct relationship exists between running speed (km/hr) and energy use rate (kcal/hr or kJ/hr) for an individual of a given size. However, individuals of different sizes expend different amounts of energy to run the same speed, making running speed a poor measure for comparison of workload between individuals of different sizes.

Exercise physiologists have traditionally used oxygen consumption ($\dot{V}O_2$) as a measure of workload. Oxygen is only used by the body for combustion of substrates to produce energy. Each liter of oxygen consumed represents an energy expenditure of about 4.8 kcal or 20.1 kJ. Therefore, the $\dot{V}O_2$ indicates the rate of energy use, at least at submaximal exercise levels. At very high workloads, exercise intensity can be increased without a further increase in $\dot{V}O_2$ (Figure 10-3). The workload at which this occurs is called maximal oxygen consumption ($\dot{V}O_2$ max).

Exercise intensity is frequently expressed as a percentage of $\dot{V}O_2$ max in order to compare different types of activities for individuals of different size within a species and between species. Exercise intensity dictates the severity and types of physiologic changes associated with exercise, including substrate use, metabolic pathways and waste production. Low-intensity exercise is up to 30% of $\dot{V}O_2$ max and is completely aerobic, using mostly fatty acids. Exercise intensities from 30 to 50% of $\dot{V}O_2$ max (moderate intensity) are still completely aerobic, but carbohydrates become an important energy substrate (carbo-

hydrate threshold). At high-intensity exercise (75 to 100% of $\dot{V}O_2$ max) anaerobic metabolism becomes important and lactate begins to accumulate in the blood. The anaerobic threshold is the workload at which lactate concentration in the blood increases to 4 mmol/l or more.[26] When working at exercise intensities at or above the anaerobic threshold, lactate in the blood begins to accumulate at an exponential rate, potentially limiting the duration of the exercise. Workloads above $\dot{V}O_2$ max are called either maximal or supramaximal, are highly dependent on anaerobic metabolism and result in large increases in blood lactate concentrations.

Exercise intensity dictates metabolic pathways and substrate use. High-intensity activities (sprinting) depend on anaerobic metabolism of carbohydrate (glucose and glycogen), which is supported by high-carbohydrate foods. The severe acidemia produced by high-intensity activities underscores the need for adequate electrolyte and water intake. Endurance events that take place at low to moderate intensity for long periods are completely aerobic and rely mostly on oxidation of fatty acids. Thus, as exercise duration increases, the fat fraction of the food becomes more important to supply energy needs. Intermediate exercise (as performed by most canine athletes) is usually of low to moderate intensity, but may include some short periods of high-intensity work. Both fats and carbohydrates are important fuel sources in intermediate exercise.

Physiologic Changes Due to Exercise

The hallmark of exercise is increased metabolism. Many organ systems increase their activity, some by several-fold, whereas some systems decrease their function. The systemic changes that occur during exercise seem to be driven by the muscles' need for substrates and removal of metabolic waste. Working muscle metabolizes substrates (mostly fatty acids and glucose) to release energy stored in chemical bonds for contraction. The products of muscle metabolism are contraction, heat, CO_2, NH_3/NH_4^+, water, and in some cases, lactate.

Muscle metabolism can increase more than 20-fold in dogs, depending on the intensity of the exercise. Likewise, cardiac output increases proportionally with the workload. Both stroke volume and heart rate increase. Blood is the transport medium that carries oxygen and other substrates to the working muscle and removes by-products such as heat, CO_2 and lactate. Increased function of the respiratory system (both increased rate and depth) supplies oxygen and disposes of CO_2. Dogs and other mammals with contractile spleens can increase effective circulating blood volume and hematocrit by expelling red blood cells from the spleen before or during exercise. For example, racing greyhounds increase blood volume as much as 24% and hematocrit as much as 29% before racing, even in the face of a 10% shift of plasma volume to other fluid compartments.[27] (See sidebar "Acute Physiologic Changes in Racing Greyhounds.")

Plasma volume decreases during exercise because of hydrostatic and osmotic forces. Increases in blood pressure during exercise cause a shift of fluid from the intravascular space to the interstitial compartment.[28] Muscle activity tends to increase intracellular osmotic pressure, encouraging fluid movement from the interstitial to the intracellular spaces.[10] The kidneys conserve plasma volume losses dur-

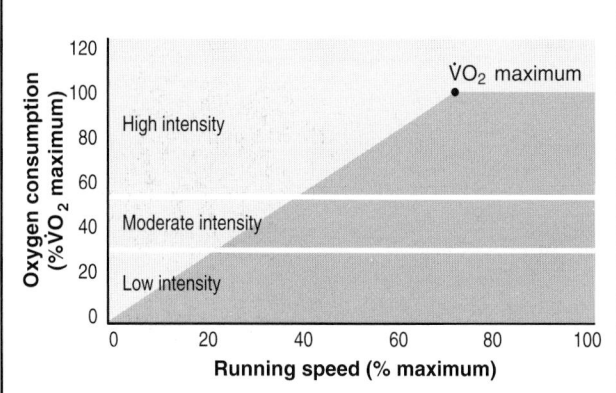

Figure 10-3. Relationship between energy consumption ($\dot{V}O_2$) and running speed (workload). $\dot{V}O_2$ max is the point at which $\dot{V}O_2$ no longer increases with increasing workload.

ing exercise. Decreases in plasma volume that decrease central venous pressure cause renal vasoconstriction and diminish glomerular filtration rate (GFR).[10,29] Decreasing GFR will normally decrease urine output and thus diminish plasma volume losses. Increases in plasma osmotic concentration that occur during prolonged exercise also stimulate secretion of antidiuretic hormone (ADH), which conserves plasma volume by stimulating production of a more concentrated urine.[10,29]

Exercise affects plasma volume and composition. Loss of fluid to the intracellular compartment increases the concentrations of plasma proteins, electrolytes and all other solutes in the extravascular compartment. Other primary plasma changes that are needed to support increased muscle activity are a direct result of that activity. Glucose concentration may increase or decrease depending on the intensity and duration of exercise. The concentration of free fatty acids increases during prolonged exercise. At very high workloads, the partial pressure of oxygen may fall dramatically. Acidemia is also common with maximum intensity exercise because of anaerobic metabolism and accumulation of lactate in the blood.

The important points from the above discussion are: 1) exercise increases metabolism and therefore increases the need for energy, 2) cardiovascular function increases and fluid shifts/losses occur during exercise—adequate water intake is important to support these needs and 3) transient changes also occur in the composition of blood that can influence the interpretation of results from blood samples drawn soon after exercise.

Energy Cost of Running

The energy cost of running depends on body size and distance traveled. Table 10-5 shows the caloric cost of running 1 km for dogs of various sizes. This table also illustrates an important principle about the mass-specific caloric cost of running as size changes. As body size increases, the efficiency of running increases (i.e., larger animals use fewer kcal/kg to run the same distance). By using the data in Table 10-5, it is possible to estimate the energy requirement for a dog of a known size to run a given distance. (See Case 10-2.) The sidebar "The Energy Cost of Running" discusses this concept in greater detail.

■ ASSESSMENT

Assess the Animal

History

In addition to the normal historical information that is usually obtained about a patient, the following information should be gathered from owners of canine athletes: environmental/housing data, medications, dietary history and exercise type, amount, frequency and performance. Detailed information should be gathered about how the animal is housed, including: indoors or outdoors, size and type of housing, opportunity for spontaneous exercise, type of surfaces, number of animals housed together and access to food and water. All medications used should be recorded, including drugs used to suppress estrus and drugs used to enhance performance.

Acute Physiologic Changes in Racing Greyhounds

Because racing greyhounds exercise at a very high intensity, they exhibit very dramatic physical and biochemical changes during and after racing. Packed cell volume (PCV) may increase to 68%, jugular venous pH values may decrease to 6.95 and plasma lactate concentrations may increase to 32 mEq/l (normal 1 to 2 mEq/l). Hyperventilation after a race can result in jugular venous pCO_2 values as low as 14 torr (normal = 40 torr) and rectal temperatures can increase more than 1°C (1.8°F) during a 30-second race. After the race, plasma sodium concentrations may reach 171 mEq/l (an 18 mEq/l increase from rest) and potassium concentrations may increase to 7.8 mEq/l (normal = 4 mEq/l). Plasma protein concentrations also increase after racing, implying a fluid shift out of the plasma compartment.

A study examined the effect of excitement before racing on these variables and quantified the effects of fluid shift on plasma volume, blood volume and PCV before and after racing. Arterial blood samples were obtained at rest, just before and five minutes after a 704-m race to quantify changes in hematologic variables, plasma electrolyte and protein concentrations, osmolality and acid-base variables. Changes in plasma volume were estimated from the change in plasma protein concentration. Immediately before the race, plasma volume decreased by 10% from rest and total circulating red blood cell (RBC) volume increased by 60% attributable to increased RBC numbers rather than size. Increases in blood volume (BV) by 24% and PCV by 29% also were detected before the race. Five minutes after the race, plasma volume was 21% below the resting value and total circulating RBC volume had increased 73% above the resting value, resulting in a 40% increase in PCV. Contraction of the spleen appeared responsible for the increased PCV and BV before the race and maintenance of BV after the race.

Plasma chloride concentration was the same before and after the race, meaning the plasma chloride content decreased by the same fraction (22%) as did the plasma volume, indicating Cl^- loss from the plasma. Plasma Na^+ content decreased by a smaller fraction (13%), causing Na^+ concentration to increase from 151 mEq/l at rest to 167 mEq/l after the race. Assuming that Na^+ concentration was the same throughout the extracellular fluid, water likely moved into the intracellular compartment. As a consequence of these changes, the inorganic strong ion difference in plasma increased by about 16 mEq/l, which tended to minimize the acid-base disturbance induced by the 33 mEq/l increase in lactate concentration.

These results indicate that the physiologic changes taking effect during strenuous sprint exercise in racing greyhounds enhance blood volume and aid in acid-base homeostasis, both of which are adaptive for this type of exercise.

BIBLIOGRAPHY
Dobson GP, Parkhouse WS, Weber JM, et al. Metabolic changes in skeletal muscle and blood of greyhounds during 800-m track sprint. American Journal of Physiology 1988; 255: R513-R519.

Ilkiw JE, Davis PE, Church DB. Hematologic, biochemical, blood-gas, and acid base values in greyhounds before and after exercise. American Journal of Veterinary Research 1989; 59: 583-586.

Pieschl RL, Toll PW, Leith DE, et al. Acid-base changes in the running greyhound: Contributing variables. Journal of Applied Physiology 1992; 73: 2297-2304.

Rose RJ, Bloomberg MS. Response to sprint exercise in the greyhound: Effects on hematology, serum biochemistry, and muscle metabolites. Research in Veterinary Science 1989; 47: 212-218.

Snow DH, Harris RC, Stuttard E. Changes in haematology and plasma biochemistry during maximal exercise in greyhounds. Veterinary Record 1988; 123: 487-489.

Toll PW, Pieschl RL, Gaethgens P, et al. Fluid, electrolyte, and packed cell volume shift in the racing greyhound. American Journal of Veterinary Research 1995; 56: 227-232.

The dietary history should include all foods and supplements used. The amount fed, nutrient profile and timing of feeding in relation to exercise should be noted. The amount eaten should also be assessed (i.e., does the dog have a normal appetite and is it actually consuming a reasonable amount?). In some cases, the composition of the overall diet (food plus supplements) may be complex and individual meals may vary in composition. It is also important to ascertain the duration of a particular feeding plan. Abrupt or frequent changes in food or feeding method may affect performance.

EXERCISE TYPE

Functionally, exercise can be divided into three types (Table 10-1) based on intensity and duration: 1) sprint—

The Energy Cost of Running

Daily energy requirement (DER) for canine athletes is highly variable and is directly related to the amount of work done in a day. Work for canine athletes is usually running. A racing greyhound that usually only runs a fraction of a mile in a race has a DER very similar to that of a house pet (1.6 to 1.8 x resting energy requirement [RER]). At the other extreme is the sled dog that runs many miles a day pulling a load and has a very high DER (up to 11 x RER). Understanding the energy cost of running and being able to quantify it in kilocalories is central to the correct feeding of canine athletes.

The following discussion and calculations are based on experimental data and on running on a flat surface. However, these data show good agreement with data from food consumption records. These calculations are essential for assessing feeding methods (food dose) and making feeding recommendations for canine athletes.

RUNNING

Running is the predominant type of work done by canine athletes. Force generation in the muscle is transmitted through the skeleton to move the dog's mass through a distance. The physics and biomechanics of running are complicated and are described elsewhere (McMahon). The rate of energy use (power) is proportional to running speed. However, the amount of energy used to cover a given distance is independent of velocity. For running on a flat surface, energy use is a function of body size and distance. Taylor and colleagues described the effect of size on the energy cost of running for a variety of mammals. They developed an equation relating $\dot{V}O_2$ to velocity and body weight. The following equation, which was derived from Taylor et al's equation, relates the energy cost of running to body weight and distance, assuming an energy yield of 4.8 kcal (20.1 kJ)/l of oxygen consumed.

$$ERR = 1.77d \times BW^{-0.40} + 1.25BW^{-0.25}$$

Where ERR is the energy requirement for running in kcal/kg, d is distance in km, and BW is body weight in kg. Larger animals have a biomechanical advantage resulting in greater efficiency of running and lower mass specific cost of running (kcal/kg) for a given distance. The negative exponents in the equation make calculations difficult. Therefore, Table 10-5 summarizes the caloric cost of running for dogs of various sizes.

RUNNING WITH WEIGHTS

The caloric cost of running with weights is the sum of the cost of running without added weight and the incremental cost of carrying that weight. When carrying added weight, $\dot{V}O_2$ increases the same percentage as gross weight. In other words, the percentage increase in the cost of running is equal to the percentage increase in gross weight. This is not the same as simply increasing the dog's size. Efficiency of running changes with body size whereas simply adding weight increases workload without affecting efficiency (increased gross weight with no change in body size). The total cost of running (ERR$_{tot}$) is calculated by adding the cost of running (ERR) and the incremental cost of running with added weight (ERR$_{incr}$). The incremental cost of running is the product of ERR and the percent increase in gross weight.

$$ERR_{incr} = ERR \times \% \text{ increase in gross weight}$$
$$ERR_{tot} = ERR + ERR_{incr} \text{ or}$$
$$ERR_{tot} = ERR \times \text{gross weight} \div \text{body weight}$$

Clinical Example

What is the caloric requirement of 30-kg dog carrying a 3-kg pack on a 15-mile (25-km) hike with its owner? The energy requirement of running for a 30-kg dog is 30 kcal/km (Table 10-5) or 750 kcal for 25 km. The incremental energy required for carrying the 3-kg pack is 750 kcal x 3 kg ÷ 30 kg or 75 kcal. The total energy required for exercise is 750 kcal + 75 kcal or 825 kcal. The DER for an average dog this size is 1.6 x RER or 1,435 kcal/day. With the added activity of carrying extra weight, the DER becomes 2,260 kcal/day (2.5 x RER). To convert to kJ, multiply kcal x 4.184.

PULLING WEIGHT

The kinematics of running and center of mass seem to be unaffected with added weight, at least up to 30% of body weight (i.e., the biomechanics do not change with added weight). This finding is unlikely to be true for dogs pulling weight such as sleds. However, it seems reasonable to assume that the cost of pulling a weight on a flat surface is similar to that of carrying the same weight. When applied to sled dogs, the calculations used above agree well with food record data. The incremental cost of running for a sled dog is based on the fraction of sled weight pulled by that dog.

Clinical Example

What is the caloric requirement for a 25-kg racing sled dog that runs 167 km (100 miles) per day pulling a sled and driver with a combined weight of 180 kg in a team of 12 dogs? The cost of running (ERR) for this 25-kg dog is 4,342 kcal, based on an efficiency of a 25-kg dog of 26 kcal/km (Table 10-5) and a distance of 167 km. Assuming all dogs pull equally, the weight pulled by this dog is 15 kg (total sled weight ÷ number of dogs) or 60% of the dog's body weight. The incremental cost of running (ERR$_{incr}$) is 60% of ERR or 2,605 kcal. The total cost of running (ERR$_{tot}$) for this dog is 6,947 kcal. Note that RER for a 25-kg dog is 783 kcal (3.28 MJ). The energy needed for exercise in this dog is almost nine times RER. The DER for this dog is 10 times RER, assuming no additional energy is needed for thermogenesis. To convert to kJ, multiply kcal x 4.184.

BIBLIOGRAPHY

McMahon TA. Muscles, Reflexes, and Locomotion. Princeton, NJ: Princeton University Press, 1984.

Schmidt-Nielsen K. Scaling: Why is Animal Size so Important. New York, NY: Cambridge University Press, 1984.

Taylor CR, Schmidt-Nielsen K, Raab JL. Scaling of energetic cost of running to body size in mammals. American Journal of Physiology 1970; 219: 1104-1107.

high-intensity activities that can be sustained less than two minutes, 2) intermediate—activities lasting a few minutes to a few hours and 3) endurance—activities that last many hours. These definitions are arbitrary and vague, but are useful for assessing and developing feeding plans.

Most canine sprinters are sight hounds. Racing greyhounds are the most notable example. Metabolically, weight-pull dogs also fit into this category. Some racing sled dogs that participate in shorter, high-speed events are referred to as "sprinters." However, they fit better in the intermediate or endurance categories from a metabolic and nutritional standpoint because their events may last several hours.

Most canine athletes participate in intermediate exercise activities. Most of these activities are of low to moderate intensity and last only a few hours. Intensity and duration of exercise vary widely within this category. For example, most guide dogs work at a low level of physical exertion for variable lengths of time throughout the day, whereas a search and rescue dog may work at a much higher level for many consecutive hours. Dogs that work at a relatively high intensity level for an extended time, such as sled dogs, have much greater metabolic requirements and are true endurance athletes.

Exercise amount can be quantified as hours per day or week. Frequency is how often the animal exercises: daily, weekly, weekends only or seasonally. Many hunting dogs only work hard on weekends during hunting season, whereas some livestock dogs may work several hours daily. Canine athletes should be categorized as either "full-time" or "part-time" athletes.

ENVIRONMENTAL INFLUENCES ON EXERCISE

Ambient temperature, psychological stress and geography are environmental factors that may influence nutritional needs of canine athletes. Of these, ambient temperature exerts the greatest effect. Hot temperatures result in increased work and water loss (i.e., to excrete metabolic heat and maintain body temperature homeostasis). High humidity impairs evaporative cooling thus adding to the work of heat excretion. Cold temperatures without exercise increase the energy requirement for thermogenesis. For working dogs, cold environmental temperatures aid in heat dissipation during exercise. Excitement or stress associated with some activities increases body temperature and respiration, leading to greater requirements for energy, water and perhaps electrolytes. Stress may also negatively affect food intake. Geographic factors such as high elevation, changing elevation (running up and down hills) and the presence of sand or tall grass underfoot can increase workload.

Physical Examination

During the physical examination, the veterinarian should evaluate the dog's general health, musculoskeletal soundness, hydration, cardiopulmonary function and body condition. A complete physical examination is crucial because disease affecting any body system can impair performance. For example, severe periodontal disease can cause sufficient pain to affect food intake, thus causing a retriever to retrieve poorly or a greyhound to run poorly. Likewise any injury or deterioration of the musculoskeletal system affects performance. All major muscle groups

Table 10-5. Caloric cost of running 1 km for dogs of varying size.

Body weight (kg)	Cost of running (kcal) 1 km/kg body weight*	Cost of running 1 km (kcal)**
5	1.77	9
10	1.41	14
15	1.23	19
20	1.13	23
25	1.05	26
30	0.99	30
35	0.94	33
40	0.90	36
45	0.87	39
50	0.84	42
70	0.76	53

*Formula: $Energy_{(kcal)}/BW_{(kg)} = 1.77 \times distance_{(km)} \times BW_{(kg)}^{-0.4} + 1.25 \times BW_{(kg)}^{-0.25}$
**To convert to kJ, multiply kcal x 4.184.

and joints should be palpated and moved through a complete range of motion during the routine physical examination of canine athletes.

Cardiopulmonary function is best assessed during routine physical examination by thorough auscultation of the heart and lung fields in a quiet environment. Energy balance can be evaluated by body condition scoring. The body condition score (BCS) is an indication of fat mass. If dietary energy intake is less than energy needs, fat mass declines and BCS decreases. Conversely, if intake exceeds requirement, fat mass and BCS increase. Chapter 1 describes body condition scoring in detail. A BCS of 3/5 is normal for most pets and for many canine athletes. However, a much leaner body composition is desirable for some canine athletes (e.g., racing greyhounds and sled dogs). Even small excesses of body fat may represent an unnecessary handicap for racing dogs.

The ability of any athlete to excel at a given event depends on that athlete's physical and metabolic characteristics, level of training and drive or desire. Some dogs are not well suited to some activities. Greyhounds make poor sled dogs and sled dogs make poor retrievers. Assessing how well an individual is suited to a particular type of exercise is partly common sense and partly experience; the fine points may take years of careful observation.

It is possible, however, to make some generalizations about characteristics that favor athletic performance. Sprinters tend to be very lean and fine-boned. A study comparing racing greyhounds to other breeds of dogs noted that as a percent of total body mass, greyhounds have more muscle (58% of body mass), the same amount of bone and less fat than other breeds.[30] Maximal muscle mass with no extra weight in the form of fat or excess bone are obvious advantages for a sprinter. Endurance athletes may require more body fat to meet energy needs during long trips.

Laboratory and Other Clinical Information

Laboratory tests are not usually required for the routine assessment of healthy canine athletes. However, when performing laboratory tests, a few factors should be kept in mind. Exercise can cause transient changes in blood and serum parameters. Concentrations of blood-borne substrates such as glucose and fatty acids may increase or decrease in relation to exercise. Total protein and electrolyte concentrations may increase simply due to fluid shift. As discussed above, contraction of the spleen and fluid shifts cause dramatic increases in packed cell volume. Lactate may accumulate in the plasma and blood pH may decrease with very high workloads.

These changes are related to the normal physiology of exercise and may be present to variable degrees up to two hours following exercise. Persistence of these changes may indicate a problem and should be investigated further. Small, persistent increases in concentration of the muscle isoenzyme of creatine phosphokinase (CPK) may occur in response to continuous exercise training. However, grossly elevated values indicate major muscle injury or rhabdomyolysis.

Key Nutritional Factors

The Key Nutritional Factors table summarizes the key nutritional factors for athletic dogs. The following section describes these key nutritional factors in more detail.

ENERGY

Providing the right amount of energy from the right sources is central to feeding canine athletes. Providing the correct amount of energy is partly controlled by the amount fed and feeding method, whereas nutrient profile affects the maximum possible caloric consumption. Additionally, the preferred source of energy (fat vs. carbohydrate) depends on exercise type. Energy for exercise comes from three nutrients: fat, carbohydrate and protein. Fats and carbohydrates are the primary energy substrates for exercise. Fat is the preferred substrate for longer duration exercise, whereas sprinters depend more on carbohydrate. Under most conditions, the energy contribution of protein during exercise is small.[23]

Energy required for exercise depends on the intensity, duration and frequency of exercise. The amount of energy required for exercise depends on total work done (intensity x duration x frequency). The preferred source of energy depends mostly on intensity. Sprinters, even though they work at a very high intensity, have relatively low energy requirements because the duration of their events is so short and frequency is usually only a few times each week. Generally, 1.6 to 2 x resting energy requirement (RER) is adequate for most sprint athletes (note the daily energy requirement [DER] for the average pet dog is 1.6 x RER).

For activities of very short duration and high intensity, the energy substrate source is the main determinant of the nutrient profile. Foods for sprint athletes should be high in carbohydrate and lower in fat, with a resulting energy density lower than that of many dog foods. Intensity, duration and frequency of exercise are variable for intermediate athletes; therefore, the energy requirement is highly variable. DER for these athletes ranges from 2 to 5 x RER. Foods with a higher fat content are typically fed to provide adequate dietary energy density. Endurance athletes require more than 5 x RER. For activities of long duration, providing adequate energy is a major determinant in the choice of a nutrient profile for exercising dogs. Foods that are very high in fat are required.

FAT

Fat provides approximately 8.5 kcal (36 kJ) of metabolizable energy per g of dry matter or more than twice the amount provided by protein and carbohydrate. Because of

these differences in caloric density, the only practical means of significantly increasing the energy density of a food is to increase its fat concentration. Reasonable increases in fat also increase palatability. Energy density and palatability make dietary fat levels an important consideration in the formulation of foods for canine athletes.

Ingesting adequate kilocalories to meet daily energy expenditure is often a serious problem for working dogs. In extreme cases, sled dogs in long-distance races expend from 6,000 to 10,000 kcal/day (25 to 42 MJ/day), in which case dry matter intake becomes a performance-limiting factor. Because the total daily dry matter intake is limited to about 3.5% of body weight,[c] the energy density of a ration should be maximized. Under these circumstances, each nonessential gram of protein and carbohydrate ingested potentially robs the dog of 5 kcal (21 kJ). The calorie deficit is paid through mobilization of body fat stores. Over-reliance on these depots may lead to catabolism of more functionally crucial energy sources, such as muscle and plasma proteins. In addition to its role as an energy store, adipose tissue also functions as an insulator. Excessive adipose depletion may increase a dog's cost of maintaining its body temperature, especially at rest in cold environments.

Even under the less severe conditions of intermediate exercise, increased dietary fat levels provide needed kilocalories and other valuable benefits. Fatigue and dehydration may decrease appetite. Increasing dietary fat concentration increases energy intake and encourages stressed dogs to ingest more food because the higher fat content improves palatability.

Feeding high levels of fat may also positively affect endurance. Training may elevate the carbohydrate threshold, thus increasing the proportion of energy supplied by free fatty acid (FFA) oxidation at all but the highest intensities of exercise. Increasing dietary fat concentration may augment this process by enhancing FFA availability.[13,14,31] Working dogs fed high-fat foods have higher circulating levels of FFA at rest and respond to exercise stimuli by releasing more FFA than those fed isocaloric amounts of a high-carbohydrate food.[13,14,21] This difference in FFA availability may be related to the decreased resting plasma concentration of insulin in animals fed high-fat foods, and the induction of key lipolytic enzymes.

The effect of food on insulin levels has also been demonstrated in well-trained human athletes.[32-36] People eating high-fat foods had significantly lower resting insulin concentrations than those eating high-carbohydrate foods.[37] Insulin decreases the release of FFA from peripheral adipose stores through its inhibitory effects on the activity of hormone-sensitive lipase. Dogs rely more heavily on FFA for energy generation at all exercise intensities than people do; therefore, the effect of food on resting insulin levels is a matter of even greater concern for canine athletes.[38] Increased dietary fat (from 25 to 65% of kilocalories) has been shown to increase $\dot{V}O_2$ max and the maximal rate of fat oxidation by 20 to 30% in well-trained dogs.[39] These increases were associated with a 25 to 30% increase in mitochondrial volume, possibly accounting for the increased oxidative capacity. Protein and total caloric intake were identical between the groups.

The relationship between fat intake and canine endurance is well established. Downey and colleagues[40] found that the time to exhaustion for well-conditioned beagles running on a treadmill was directly related to energy density, digestibility and digestible fat intake (Table 10-6). Practical applications of this concept are evident in the performance rations currently fed to many successful canine athletes. As the duration of the event performed by the athlete increases, so should the dietary fat intake.

Dogs can tolerate high levels of dietary fat if fat is gradually introduced and an adequate intake of non-fat nutrients is maintained. Steatorrhea and a decrease in food palatability are indicators that a ration has exceeded an animal's fat tolerance. Under conditions of extreme training, sled dogs may ingest up to 60% of their kilocalories as fat. During ultra-endurance events, such as the Iditarod or the Yukon Quest, fat intake may compose 80% of the kilocalories ingested.[d] This "super fat loading" should be attempted only during the most strenuous periods of such events, when it is difficult or impossible for canine athletes to ingest as many kilocalories as they are expending.

Anemia has been associated with impaired performance in dog teams fed very high-fat foods (i.e., 80% kilocalories from fat) for prolonged periods (i.e., weeks to months).[41] However, during several long expeditions (including the trans-Antarctica expedition of 1991), Will Steger observed no decrement of performance when dogs were fed food containing 80% fat kilocalories and 17% protein kilocalories.[e] Other factors such as environment, training and dietary intake of non-fat nutrients may play a role in the development of anemia.

The type of fat used must also be considered in the formulation of a performance ration. Essential fatty acids should make up at least 2% of the dry matter of a ration. (See Chapter 2.) The remainder of the fat may come from any of a number of plant or animal sources. Many greyhound and sled dog trainers believe that dogs run "hotter" when fed saturated rather than unsaturated fatty acids. No objective evidence supports this theory. Because dogs do not share the same risk for developing atherosclerosis as people, there is less reason to limit their intake of saturated fatty acids.

Alternatively, large intakes of unsaturated fatty acids may increase the risk of membrane lipid peroxidation,[42,43] which can severely damage cell membrane function with potentially disastrous implications for working dogs. Relative to their sedentary colleagues, dogs participating in endurance events are at particular risk for developing peroxidative membrane damage because they consume more fat and metabolize more oxygen per unit body weight per day. The risk of lipid peroxidation may be reduced by feeding only well-stabilized (preserved) unsaturated fatty acids. Increasing vitamin E and selenium intake to bolster cellular antioxidant capacity has also been recommended.[44]

Unsaturated fatty acids are an important component in a well-balanced food. They are largely responsible for membrane fluidity, a property critical to the function of all cell membranes. Unsaturated fatty acids are also required for biosynthesis of many regulatory molecules and maintenance of epidermal integrity. Indeed, all essential fatty acids are unsaturated. In weighing the biologic significance of unsaturated fatty acids with the possible health risks associated with their overconsumption, balanced amounts of saturated and unsaturated fatty acids may be the best solution.

Certain fatty acids are purported to have ergogenic effects. The n-3 family of fatty acids contained in fish oils has been reported to enhance oxygen uptake.[45] The results

Table 10-6. Effect of nutrient profile on stamina.*

Nutrient (DMB)	Food A	Food B	Food C
Energy (kcal/g)	4.7	5.9	6.0
Fat (%)	12.8	28.3	33.1
Protein (%)	22.9	48.7	30.5
Performance			
Time (minutes)	103.7	136.1	137.6
Distance (miles)	15.5	20.4	20.6

Key: DMB = dry matter basis.
  Food A - Grocery brand dry food.
  Food B - Grocery brand moist food.
  Food C - Specialty brand dry food.
*Downey RL, Kronfeld DS, Banta CA. Diet of beagles affects stamina. Journal of the American Animal Hospital Association 1980; 6: 273-277.

reported in this study lacked statistical significance, prompting the need for further investigations. Medium-chain triglyceride (MCT) supplementation reportedly enhances performance.[46,47] These intermediate length (eight to 12 carbon) fatty acids do not rely on carnitine for transport across the inner mitochondrial membrane. Because they bypass this rate-limiting step in fatty acid oxidation, some investigators have theorized that increasing the dietary MCT level may increase the maximal rate of fatty acid oxidation. A study of the effects of MCT supplementation failed to demonstrate an increase in oxygen consumption or FFA oxidation in human athletes.[45] Further research to determine the consequences of MCT supplementation in working dogs is needed.

Sprint exercise is almost entirely dependent on carbohydrate; therefore, the fat requirement for sprinters is not different than that for other dogs. Total fat content should be 8 to 10% of dry matter or 20 to 24% of kilocalories. Dietary fat needs for intermediate athletes are directly proportional to the amount of work done. Part-time athletes during off season should be fed as other dogs. (See Chapter 9.) Dietary fat content should be increased as the amount of work increases—15 to 30% dry matter (30 to 55% fat kilocalories) for moderate amounts of work and 25 to 40% dry matter (45 to 65% fat kilocalories) for large amounts of work. Endurance athletes require very high levels of dietary fat to meet their energy needs, in excess of 50% dry matter and 75% fat kilocalories. The Key Nutritional Factors table summarizes recommendations for fat and other nutrients by exercise type.

CARBOHYDRATE

Provided sufficient gluconeogenic precursors are available, dogs have no dietary requirement for carbohydrates except during gestation and neonatal development. (See Chapter 9.) Dogs are quite capable of maintaining normal blood glucose and tissue glycogen levels when fed carbohydrate-free foods.[14,15] Compared with people, dogs are less likely to develop ketosis during long periods of exercise or starvation.[14,48] Despite these facts, dogs have great ability to use carbohydrate.

Canine athletes requiring less than twice maintenance levels of energy may derive a significant portion of their kilocalories from carbohydrate sources. This is an advantage for high-power athletes, such as racing greyhounds, that are highly dependent on anaerobic metabolism. Because carbohydrates contain only about 3.5 kcal (15 kJ) metabolizable energy/g, they cannot be used to increase the energy density of a food. This limitation is an important consideration for endurance athletes that have difficulty ingesting a sufficient volume of food to meet caloric requirements.

Racing greyhounds are highly dependent on carbohydrate stored in the muscle as glycogen because they must mobilize energy quickly to run a race. Studies have shown that greyhounds use significant amounts of glycogen during a race; up to 70% of available glycogen in some muscles for an 800-meter race.[49,50] Further, evidence suggests that the rate of glycogen use (and, therefore, energy production) depends on the concentration of glycogen in muscle.[51] It is logical, therefore, to hypothesize that increasing muscle glycogen will enhance sprint performance. Muscle glycogen content can be increased through a combination of dietary and training protocol changes in some animals (rats, people,[52] horses[53]); these techniques have been used as a means of improving endurance performance.[52,54] The possible benefits of increased muscle glycogen on sprint exercise performance of dogs have not been established. It is also unclear if continuous feeding of high-carbohydrate food(s) to dogs will increase muscle glycogen. For sled dogs, it may be more advantageous to promote glycogen sparing by feeding a high-fat food than increasing pre-exercise glycogen concentrations via ingestion of a high-carbohydrate food. Reynolds and colleagues demonstrated an increase in the amount of muscle glycogen stored and a greater rate of glycogen use in sled dogs fed a high-carbohydrate food (65% of kilocalories).[38] When isocaloric amounts of a high-fat food were fed, glycogen was used at a much slower rate, promoting better endurance at all submaximal exercise intensities. In sled dogs, carbohydrate sparing appears to be a more successful strategy than carbohydrate loading.

Two studies have reported the effect of different fat and carbohydrate levels on race time in greyhounds.[55,56] Both studies used seven adult racing greyhounds in a crossover design and used race time in a 5/16-mile (502-m) race as the measure of performance. Investigators in the first study used two foods similar in composition except for fat and carbohydrate content.[55] The high-carbohydrate food contained 16% dry matter fat (34% of kilocalories) and 52% dry matter carbohydrate (44% of kilocalories), whereas the low-carbohydrate food contained 56% fat (80% of kilocalories) and 8% carbohydrate (5% of kilocalories). No significant difference in race times between the two food groups was detected for the first four weekly measurements. At the end of the fifth week, the dogs fed the high-carbohydrate food ran faster (33.08 sec ± 0.05) than when they were fed the low-carbohydrate food (33.34 sec ± 0.05). The results were statistically significant (p <0.05). In this study, dogs performed better when fed a high-carbohydrate/low-fat food than they did when fed a high-fat/low-carbohydrate food. The delay before differences occurred may indicate that some time may be required to adapt to a new food before performance is affected.

The second study compared results of feeding a "high-fat" food (38.2% energy from fat, 23% energy from protein, 38.8% energy from carbohydrate) with those of feeding a "moderate-fat" food (27.6% energy from fat, 20.4% energy from protein, 52.1% energy from carbohydrate).[56] Dogs were fed each food for eight weeks. Race times were faster when the dogs were fed the high-fat food than when they were fed the medium-fat food (32.9 ± 0.7 vs. 33.1 ± 0.6 sec at α = 0.1, β = 0.2).

Neither of these studies evaluated a truly high-carbohydrate level (60 to 70% of dietary kilocalories) as is now recommended for glycogen loading in people.[57] Further, although the results of these two studies are mixed, physiologic principles suggest that carbohydrate supplementation should benefit racing greyhounds.

Even endurance athletes may benefit from a low level of dietary carbohydrate. Studies involving sled dogs fed 0 or 17% of their kilocalories as carbohydrate showed that dogs were more susceptible to developing "stress" diarrhea when fed foods devoid of carbohydrate.[58] There are other advantages associated with feeding carbohydrates to sprint athletes. Because these dogs derive more of their energy for exercise from glucose/glycogen, glycogen depletion may play a role in the onset of fatigue for athletes working at or above their anaerobic threshold.[18,24,59-61]

Carbohydrate availability to working muscles is a limiting factor for prolonged exercise in people and other species. This finding has led to development of strategies for carbohydrate loading or glycogen supercompensation. The classic method (Åstrand method) uses a combination of exhaustive exercise and low-carbohydrate foods (≤ 10% kilocalories from carbohydrate) to deplete muscle glycogen. Glycogen depletion is followed by consumption of high-carbohydrate foods (80 to 90% kilocalories from carbohydrate) and little activity. This method has been shown to dramatically increase muscle glycogen in people.[62] An alternative carbohydrate-loading method (Sherman/Costill method) simply requires consumption of 60 to 70% of kilocalories from carbohydrate consistently over time. In people, this method has achieved results similar to those achieved by the classic method.[62]

Glycogen loading is probably not as beneficial for canine endurance athletes as continuous feeding of high-fat levels. However, high-power athletes (e.g., racing greyhounds) should benefit from glycogen loading. Because racing greyhounds do not have dramatically increased energy needs and cannot use fatty acids effectively during a race lasting less than 60 seconds, there is no benefit to feeding high levels of fat. Additionally, glycogen stores are rapidly mobilized during racing. In one study, greyhounds running an 800-m race in 48 seconds mobilized 50 to 70% of their glycogen stores in specific running muscles.[49]

Studies in people have shown that feeding moderate amounts of carbohydrate (2 g glucose/kg body weight) during a brief postexercise time window permits very rapid rates of glycogen resynthesis.[57,59,63] This period lasts about 30 minutes postexercise.[58] Glucose administered during this window permits up to four times the rate of glycogen resynthesis supported by the same amount of glucose administered after this two-hour window. The form of the glucose (i.e., polymer or simple sugar) does not seem to affect the rate of glycogen repletion.[59] Severely hypertonic solutions should be avoided to prevent excessive osmotic movement of fluid into the gut, which may lead to cramping and gastrointestinal distress.[12,64] This strategy for glycogen repletion is effective in human athletes and recent research indicates that it is also effective in dogs.[38]

The carbohydrates used in foods for canine athletes should be highly digestible to limit fecal bulk. Excessive amounts of undigested carbohydrates reaching the colon may increase water loss via the stool, increase colonic gas production and increase overall fecal bulk. These changes in fecal consistency have been proposed to increase an athlete's risk of developing "stress diarrhea," further increasing fecal water losses.[58] Bulky stools have also been associated with rectal bleeding during exercise-induced colonic evacuation.[58] Excessive fecal bulk is also extra weight that must be carried by the athlete. One study estimated that 150 g of extra stool generated by a racing sled dog was equal to a 7-kg handicap for a thoroughbred horse.[13]

Metabolic power or a high rate of ATP generation is required for sprint performance. Consequently, anaerobic metabolism of glucose and glycogen is the dominant energy generation pathway. High-carbohydrate foods should be fed to maximize muscle glycogen. Dietary carbohydrates should compose 50 to 70% of total kilocalories to maximize muscle glycogen levels (based on research done with people).

The dietary carbohydrate recommendation for intermediate athletes is highly variable, depending on the intensity and duration of work. Dogs that perform relatively long bouts of low to moderate intensity work require more dietary energy (higher fat) and relatively low-carbohydrate levels (as low as 15% of kilocalories). Dogs that perform short bursts of higher intensity work should be fed more carbohydrate, up to 50% of kilocalories.

Endurance athletes require very little carbohydrate. Endurance rations should contain less than 15% of kilocalories from carbohydrate to achieve the energy density required for the amount of work done by these dogs. Some carbohydrate and/or soluble fiber should be included in the ration to avoid loose stools. The Key Nutritional Factors table summarizes carbohydrate recommendations for canine athletes by exercise type.

PROTEIN

Dietary protein is used to fulfill structural, biochemical and, to a lesser extent, energy requirements. Work increases the requirement for protein. The magnitude of this increase and the best strategy for meeting it are subjects of much debate in canine performance nutrition.

The work-induced elevation in protein requirement is most pronounced when the intensity and/or duration of exercise performed is rapidly increased above an animal's present level of conditioning. These circumstances are encountered at the onset of a training program, when the duration or intensity of training bouts is increased and especially during performances.[22,23] The increase in protein demand is due to combined increases in the rates of tissue protein synthesis and catabolism.

Several anabolic processes contribute to the exercise-induced increment in protein requirement. Protein demand is elevated due to an increase in the synthesis of structural and functional proteins. Training induces synthesis of many enzymes and transport proteins in each of the energy-generating pathways.[11,12,65,66] Blood volume also expands during aerobic training.[11,12,22,23] Such expansion necessitates an increase in plasma protein synthesis to maintain oncotic and osmotic balance between the plasma and the interstitial fluids.[10] The increase in hematocrit sometimes observed during endurance conditioning programs may reflect an increase in tissue protein synthesis.[11-13] Anaerobic training regimens may also induce muscle hypertrophy.[23] Amino acids are used in the formation of new muscle tissue and in the repair of damage that may occur to muscle and connective tissue during intensive conditioning programs.

In addition to enhancing the rate of tissue protein synthesis, exercise increases the rate of amino acid catabolism. Amino acids may provide between 5 and 15% of the energy used during exercise, depending on the intensity and duration of the task.[21-23] Most of this energy comes from the oxidation of branched-chain amino acids.[24,25] All three amino acids belonging to this group (leucine, isoleucine, valine) are "essential" and thus cannot be synthesized from other amino acids in sufficient quantities to meet requirements. The branched-chain amino acids lost through exercise must be replaced through dietary intake.

The proportion of energy supplied by amino acids may be even greater in underfed athletes and those participating in ultra-endurance events in which there is a high risk for depletion of endogenous carbohydrate stores.[22,24] In these instances, gluconeogenesis becomes the major pathway for maintaining blood glucose levels.[22,24] Because amino acids are the predominant substrate used by the gluconeogenic pathway, their rate of catabolism is increased whenever this pathway is accelerated.[23,67]

This concept raises an important point: it is disadvantageous for an athlete to rely heavily on endogenous sources of protein for energy. There are no known labile stores of protein in the canine body. All protein sources serve a structural or functional purpose.[67] Interestingly, skeletal muscle is readily mobilized. Over-use of this source would have an obvious negative impact on performance. Because the small pool of circulating amino acids is insufficient to meet the amino acid requirements of the anabolic and catabolic processes described above, dietary protein intake must supply the deficit if nitrogen balance is to be maintained.[22]

For endurance athletes, there may also be some disadvantages inherent in exploiting dietary protein sources for energy. Protein has only about 3.5 kcal (15 kJ) metabolizable energy/g dry matter. The energy density of a ration thus cannot be increased by increasing the proportion of protein in the formulation. The energy density of the food is one of the major determinants of endurance capacity when working dogs have difficulty ingesting as many kilocalories as they expend.[40]

Excessive protein intake may predispose an animal to increased amino acid catabolism because dietary amino acids are not stored in labile protein depots, but are deaminated.[23] The resulting ketoacids are either oxidized for energy directly or converted into fatty acids and/or glucose and then stored as adipose tissue or glycogen. The urea produced from amino acid breakdown is excreted from the body in urine. In healthy animals, the amount of water lost increases with increases in urea production.

An optimal food for canine athletes should contain enough high-quality protein to meet the dog's anabolic requirements and enough non-protein energy nutrients to meet its energy requirements. Such a food encourages the use of ingested protein in synthetic rather than energy-generating processes. As non-protein caloric intake increases, less dietary protein is used for energy and more is available for use in anabolic processes. Energy requirements should be met by fat and carbohydrate, leaving the majority of amino acids available for synthetic purposes. During long-duration exercise, DER may increase several-fold whereas protein requirement increases only a few percent. To meet the energy needs of hard-working dogs, either more food must be consumed (increasing both energy and protein intake equally) or a higher energy, lower protein food must be fed (increasing energy intake more than protein intake). Providing sufficient dietary kilocalories by increasing fat content should limit the use of amino acids for energy production. Increased caloric requirements are better met from dietary fat, leaving amino acids available for synthetic purposes. Because the protein requirement is actually a requirement for available amino acids, the digestibility and essential amino acid content of ingested protein will also determine how efficiently amino acids are incorporated into tissue proteins.

Research attempts with define the optimal dietary protein intake for working dogs have been inconclusive. Several field studies performed on racing sled dogs in the 1970s and early 1980s found that well-conditioned dogs fed a high-fat, high-protein food maintained higher packed cell volumes and serum albumin concentrations than those fed a relatively high-carbohydrate, low-protein food.[14,58,68] The investigators concluded that the high-fat, high-protein food may offer a performance advantage by maintaining better blood volume and oxygen carrying capacity than the other foods tested. These investigators recommended that 30 to 40% of kilocalories of a performance ration should come from protein.

A recent study examined the effects of feeding isocaloric foods (4.5 kcal [19 kJ] metabolizable energy/g) containing 16, 24, 32 and 40% of their energy as protein on performance and biochemical parameters.[69] During training and racing, dogs fed only 16% protein kilocalories suffered significantly more injuries and had a significant decline in $\dot{V}O_2$ max when compared with age-, gender- and ability-matched sled dogs fed 24, 32 or 40% protein kilocalories. Additionally in people, long-duration exercise leading to glycogen depletion increases protein requirement more than weight lifting. There were no noticeable differences in performance between the dogs fed 24, 32 or 40% protein kilocalories, although the dogs fed 40% protein kilocalories maintained a significantly higher packed cell volume and total plasma volume. This study indicated that 16% protein kilocalories may be insufficient to meet the needs of extremely hard-working dogs and that such animals should ingest a minimum of 24% of their kilocalories as protein.

The protein requirement for exercise is only mildly increased (5 to 15%) regardless of exercise type. Protein is used for muscle hypertrophy and muscle maintenance/repair and the branched-chain amino acids can contribute to energy production. Dietary protein should be at least 24% of kilocalories. Because the energy requirement of some endurance athletes is so high (up to 10 or 11 x RER), it may not be feasible to feed even this level of protein and provide adequate kilocalories. Protein kilocalories at 16% should be viewed as an absolute minimum. Note that for endurance exercise, energy requirement increases many fold (up to 11-fold), whereas protein requirements increase much less (5 to 15%). For a given food, as intake increases to meet energy requirements, protein intake increases proportionally. Because of the disparity between the increase in need for energy and protein for exercise, as total dietary energy requirement increases, the percent protein kilocalories of the food may decrease. The Key Nutritional Factors table summarizes protein recommendations by exercise type.

DIGESTIBILITY

Dry matter digestibility of food is important to canine athletes for two reasons. First, exercise may be limited by a dog's ability to obtain sufficient amounts of nutrients (usually energy). Enhanced digestibility increases the maximum possible delivery of nutrients to tissues. Second, lower digestibility means greater fecal bulk, and therefore a greater handicap. Although increased animal size results in greater running efficiency, increased fecal weight creates a greater energetic cost of running with no benefit. Total dry matter digestibility of any food for canine athletes should exceed 80%.[40,70]

WATER

Water is arguably the most essential of all nutrients. It is the solvent for nearly all biologic solutes and a transport medium for nutrients, wastes and heat. It also absorbs physical shock and lubricates various internal and external surfaces of the body. Approximately two-thirds of the body's weight is composed of water.[10,29,71] Total body water is divided into four major compartments. Approximately 62 to 64% of water is located within cells, 22% within interstitial spaces and 7% within the intravascular space in plasma.[47,63] The remaining 7% is present as transcellular fluids such as vitreous and aqueous humor, cerebral spinal fluid, joint fluid and digestive secretions.[10,29] Fluid balance between compartments is directed by osmotic, oncotic and hydrostatic pressures as well as the permeability characteristics of individual membranes. Total body water balance is maintained by dietary water intake and metabolic water production (10 to 16 ml/100 kcal and 3 to 4 ml/g glycogen)[10,29] on one hand and evaporative, urinary and fecal losses on the other.

The fluid content of individual tissues and compartments changes with the onset of muscular activity. Cardiac output, partially a function of plasma volume, increases during exercise to meet the muscle's heightened demand for nutrient delivery and waste removal. The increase in blood flow also helps dissipate the heat produced by working muscles. Only about 20 to 30% of the energy consumed within muscle cells during exercise produces work; the remaining 70 to 80% is converted into heat. This is about the same efficiency as a gasoline automobile engine.[72] This heat must be dissipated to prevent performance impairments and perhaps life-threatening increases in body temperature.[10,73,74]

During prolonged periods of exercise in warm and humid environments, heat dissipation leads to a decrease in total body water and plasma volume. Approximately 60% of the heat dissipated during exercise is lost through fluid evaporation from the upper respiratory tract.[75] Exercise in very cold, dry environments also increases evaporative fluid losses. Significant fluid loss during exercise may impair performance. Even mild dehydration can limit exercise performance.[70] Several studies indicate that hydration status is the single most important determinant of endurance capacity.[13,40,76]

There is currently much debate over the best strategy to maintain fluid and electrolyte balance in working dogs. Under most exercise situations, these athletes lose more water than electrolytes, causing a decrease in plasma volume and an increase in plasma osmolality. Efforts to return electrolyte values to normal should thus concentrate on water replacement. Ideally, clean fresh water should be available at all times. There are occasions when such accommodations cannot be made due to the nature of the athletic event or the environmental conditions. Under these conditions, water should be offered at least three

Vitamins, Minerals and Exercise

Although vitamins and minerals are obviously important for exercise, it is unclear if exercise alters the requirements for these nutrients. Additionally, some vitamins and minerals are believed to be beneficial as ergogenic aids. Unfortunately, little well-controlled research has been conducted in this area and current results are conflicting.

Exercise-induced increases in demand have been suggested for nearly all of the B-complex vitamins. Many of these compounds are used as cofactors in key enzymes of energy-generating pathways; others function in tissue synthesis and repair initiated by exercise. Likewise, the demand for vitamin C has been postulated to increase due to its role in carnitine and collagen synthesis and its antioxidant functions. Exercise may also hasten the excretion of water-soluble vitamins because exercise increases total body water turnover. Five to 10 times maintenance levels of the water-soluble vitamins have been safely fed to working dogs

High consumption of polyunsaturated fatty acids (PUFA) and increased oxygen metabolism may also increase an athlete's risk of peroxidative membrane damage. Such damage may induce myodystrophy and decrease endurance. Vitamin E intakes of one to five times maintenance have been recommended for prophylaxis. Other authors have recommended supplementation of vitamins C and β-carotene to prevent peroxidative damage. At present, there is no evidence to indicate that exercise increases dietary requirements for vitamins D and K.

Metabolic acidosis induced by lactic acidosis associated with strenuous work may increase excretion of calcium, magnesium and potassium. Foods containing low levels of magnesium (but at levels above the minimum AAFCO allowance) resulted in clinical signs of magnesium deficiency in greyhound dogs. These signs were alleviated when foods containing magnesium at 0.12% of the dry matter were fed.

Canine athletes fed high-fat foods or those whose food is supplemented with meat (as is common with greyhounds and sled dogs) may require additional calcium. The high level of fat in performance foods enhances the formation of insoluble calcium soaps, thus rendering a portion of the ingested calcium unavailable. Additionally, red meat is rich in phosphorus and nearly devoid of calcium. Meat supplementation may thus require calcium supplementation to maintain a normal calcium content and calcium-phosphorus ratio in the diet. Dietary calcium levels of 1.2 to 2.0% of a food's dry matter have been successfully fed to working dogs. Very high-fat foods with lower calcium concentrations may be deficient in available calcium. Excessive calcium supplementation may also predispose a dog to zinc deficiency by inhibiting absorption of this nutrient. (See Chapter 15.)

The requirement for iron is also thought to increase with exercise. Commercial performance foods and foods supplemented with substantial quantities of red meat should easily meet this increased demand. In such instances, iron supplementation is contraindicated because it may lead to irritation of the lower GI tract and predispose the canine athlete to developing bloody diarrhea.

Large doses of vitamins and minerals individually or in combination have not been demonstrated to increase the physical capabilities of human or canine athletes. Dietary intake of these nutrients should be aimed at meeting increased physiologic requirements rather than attempting to produce an unproved pharmacologic enhancement of performance.

Several considerations must be weighed in determining the optimal vitamin and mineral content of a performance food. One must estimate the availability and the tolerance levels of these nutrients as well as possible nutrient interactions. For example, iron and zinc must be present in proper proportions; an excess of one may lead to a relative deficiency of the other because they share a common mechanism of absorption. Similarly, a disproportionate supplementation of one fat-soluble vitamin may inhibit absorption of the others. The concentrations and types of energy-producing nutrients in the food can also influence vitamin and mineral requirements. As mentioned, PUFA intake can alter the demand for vitamin E and selenium.

Although dogs have no known dietary vitamin C and carnitine requirement, some workers argue that canine athletes may be unable to synthesize adequate quantities of these nutrients to meet the metabolic demands of extremely hard work. Studies with human athletes have shown little or no performance benefit from supplementation of these nutrients. It is also unclear whether requirements for vitamins and minerals increase in proportion to caloric intake or whether they approach an asymptote. Further research is needed to resolve these issues.

Those wishing to supplement with vitamins and minerals are advised to do so carefully. Such supplementation should only be undertaken with a knowledge of nutrient availability, interactions and tolerance levels because dietary overcompensation of these nutrients may be as detrimental to performance as dietary deficiencies.

BIBLIOGRAPHY

Bucci LR. Nutritional and Ergogenic Aids. Boca Raton, FL: CRC Press, 1989.

Comar CL, Bronner F. Mineral Metabolism: An Advanced Treatise. New York, NY: Academic Press, 1964.

Donoghue S, Kronfeld DS, Banta CA. A possible vitamin C requirement in racing sled dogs fed a high fat diet. In: Meyer H, Kienzle E, eds. Nutrition, Malnutrition and Diet in Dogs and Cats. Hannover, Germany: Tieraztliche Hochschule, 1988; 110-114.

Eichner ER. Men of iron (hematochromatosis). Sports Medicine Digest 1990; 2: 5-6.

Grandjean D, Paragon B-M. Alimentation du chien de traineau: 1. Bases physiologiques et metaboliques. Recueil de Médecine Vétérinaire 1986; 162: 1167-1180.

Grandjean D, Paragon B-M. Alimentation du chien de traineau. Recueil de Médecine Vétérinaire 1987; 163: 7-14.

Haynes EM. Trace minerals and exercise. In: Wolinsky I, Hickson JF, eds. Nutrition in Exercise and Sport, 2nd ed. Boca Raton, FL: CRC Press, 1994; 223-243.

Kagan VE, Spirichev VB, Serbinova EA, et al. The significance of vitamin E and free radicals in physical exercise. In: Wolinsky I, Hickson JF, eds. Nutrition in Exercise and Sport, 2nd ed. Boca Raton, FL: CRC Press, 1994; 185-213.

Keith RE. Vitamins and physical activity. In: Wolinsky I, Hickson JF, eds. Nutrition in Exercise and Sport, 2nd ed. Boca Raton, FL: CRC Press, 1994; 159-183.

Kronfeld DS. Vitamin and mineral supplementation for dogs and cats: A monograph on micronutrients. Santa Barbara, CA: Veterinary Practice Publishing Co, 1989.

Rose BD. Clinical Physiology of Acid-Base and Electrolyte Disorders, 2nd ed. New York, NY: McGraw-Hill Book Co, 1984.

Williams MH. Beyond Training: How Athletes Enhance Performance Legally and Illegally. Champaign, IL: Leisure Press, 1989.

Williams MH. Nutritional Aspects of Human Physical and Athletic Performance, 2nd ed. Springfield, IL: Charles C Thomas, 1985.

Wolinsky I, Hickson JF, Arnaud SB. Bone and calcium in physical activity and sport. In: Wolinsky I, Hickson JF, eds. Nutrition in Exercise and Sport, 2nd ed. Boca Raton, FL: CRC Press, 1994; 215-222.

Wolinsky I, Driskell JA. Sports Medicine: Vitamins and Trace Elements. Boca Raton, FL: CRC Press, 1997.

Wolter R. Feeding the sporting dog. Fairbanks, AK: Kobuk International, 1985.

CANINE ATH: FTF

Electrolytes and Exercise

Electrolytes are integral components of nearly all chemical reactions and transmembrane transport systems. About one-third of basal energy requirement is expended to maintain electrolyte concentration gradients across cellular membranes. The narrow range within which these concentrations are regulated and the high cost of achieving this regulation is evidence of their biologic significance. The electrolytes sodium, potassium and chloride are involved in control of fluid balance, maintenance of normal muscle and nerve excitability and control of acid-base status.

The electrolytes (primarily sodium) play a major role in regulation of total body water. Hyperosmolality stimulates thirst and causes the kidneys to conserve water. In cases of electrolyte depletion, aldosterone may reduce renal losses by stimulating tubular reabsorption of sodium and water. Sodium depletion occurs commonly in horses, people and other mammals that sweat; however, exercise-related loss of sodium may also be significant in canine athletes. The amount of sodium lost via saliva in exercising dogs depends on salivary flow rate. As salivary flow increases, the osmotic concentration of the initially hypotonic saliva increases; saliva approaches isotonicity with plasma at maximum flow rates. Warm or humid conditions that elicit increased salivary flow rates during exercise may also significantly increase sodium, bicarbonate and chloride losses.

Abnormal electrolyte concentrations impair physical performance by altering membrane potentials across muscle and nerve cells, and altering the functions of catalytic and contractile proteins. These changes hinder performance by diminishing the rate of energy and force generation. They also interfere with heat dissipation, which is particularly impaired by increases in plasma osmolarity.

Either water or an electrolyte solution may be used to maintain or replace fluid-electrolyte losses during and after exercise. Electrolyte solutions, while popular, are of limited value for most dogs eating a balanced food. Additionally, there is much debate about the proper concentration of these solutions. Hypertonic and even isotonic solutions administered orally may not return postexercise plasma osmolarity to normal. These solutions may encourage water transfer into epithelial cells if they are more hypertonic than the fluid of the interstitial spaces. Such fluids may lead to GI cramping, vomiting and diarrhea and thus exacerbate dehydration. Anecdotally, even isotonic solutions administered before exercise have been associated with snow "dipping" or ingesting snow during sled dog races. This phenomenon may be caused by the effect of the electrolyte solution on plasma osmolarity and thus thirst. Snow dipping is considered unde-

sirable in racing dogs because it disturbs the rhythm and speed of the team.

Proponents of electrolyte supplementation note that in proper concentrations, such solutions increase fluid palatability and the rate of fluid absorption from the gut. Some argue these solutions may help maintain plasma volume during exercise and may aid in its restoration in the postexercise period. Because diarrhea is a common disorder among working dogs, the use of electrolyte replacement solutions may play a role in the clinical management of these cases.

Clearly, more research is needed before recommendations can be given about the administration of electrolyte solutions to canine athletes before, during and after exercise. Under nearly all conditions, it is more important to replace water losses. Under conditions where electrolyte administration is deemed beneficial, it is safer to err on the side of hypotonic rather than hypertonic oral supplementation.

BIBLIOGRAPHY
Blaxter K. Energy Metabolism in Animals and Man. New York, NY: Cambridge University Press, 1989.

Champaigne C, Champaigne-Wright R. Fairbanks, AK, USA. Personal communication, October 1994.

Harrison MH, Edwards RJ, Leitch DR. Effect of exercise and thermal stress on plasma volume. Journal of Applied Physiology 1975; 39: 925-931.

Houpt TR. Water, electrolytes, and acid base balance. In: Duke's Physiology of Domestic Animals, 10th ed. Ithaca, NY: Cornell University Press, 1984; 486-506.

Kozlowski S, Brezenska Z, Kruk B, et al. Hyperthermia as a factor limiting performance; Temperature effect on muscle metabolism. Journal of Applied Physiology 1985; 59: 766-773.

Kruk B, Kaciuba-Uscilko H, Nazar K, et al. Hypothalamic, rectal, and muscle temperatures in exercising dogs; Effect of cooling. Journal of Applied Physiology 1985; 58: 1444-1448.

Pivarnik JM. Water and electrolyte balance during rest and exercise. In: Wolinsky I, Hickson JF, eds. Nutrition in Exercise and Sport, 2nd ed. Boca Raton, FL: CRC Press, 1994; 245-263.

Puhl SM, Buskirk ER. Nutrient beverages for exercise and sport. In: Wolinsky I, Hickson JF, eds. Nutrition in Exercise and Sport, 2nd ed. Boca Raton, FL: CRC Press, 1994; 264-294.

Williams MH. Nutritional Aspects of Human Physical and Athletic Performance, 2nd ed. Springfield, IL: Charles C Thomas, 1985.

Young DR, Mosher R, Erve P, et al. Temperature and heat exchange during treadmill running in dogs. Journal of Applied Physiology 1959; 14: 839-843.

Young DR, Price R, Elder NE, et al. Energy and electrolyte metabolism and adrenal responses during work in dogs. Journal of Applied Physiology 1962; 17: 669-674.

times a day and more often if possible. Water intake can be encouraged by "baiting" the water with a flavor enhancer such as meat juice.

OTHER NUTRITIONAL FACTORS

Vitamins, minerals and electrolytes play important roles in maintaining homeostasis and chemical reactions during exercise. (See sidebars "Vitamins, Minerals and Exercise" and "Electrolytes and Exercise.") However, they are of secondary concern when feeding canine athletes and are found in adequate amounts in most commercial foods. Likewise, the acid-base composition of the food and base-loading may also affect performance (See sidebar "Acid-Base Balance and Exercise."); however, these effects are

poorly understood in canine athletes. Because exercise increases metabolic rate and the opportunity for free radical formation, it is important to ensure adequate intake of antioxidant nutrients. Evidence that canine athletes have an increased need for these nutrients is inconclusive.

Assess the Food(s)

Although the working dog's needs can be met via many different dietary approaches, all foods for canine athletes (performance foods) should share a few important characteristics. First, the food should be calorically dense so that canine athletes can consume enough food to meet their energy requirements. Second, the food must be acceptable and highly digestible. Dry matter digestibility should exceed 80%.[40,70] High digestibility reduces fecal bulk and fecal water loss and may decrease the risk of developing stress diarrhea.[29,40] Finally, the food should be practical. Factors such as the cost of the food, the form of the food, the environment in which the food is stored and fed and the number of dogs being fed are all important considerations. What is practical for a single hunting dog at home may not be practical for a team of sled dogs hundreds of miles from civilization or racing greyhounds at a track.

Because the greatest nutritional demand of exercise is for energy, foods for canine athletes must provide sufficient kilocalories from the right sources. Energy density is usually enhanced by increasing the fat content of the food. The appropriate fat content is dictated by energy need and exercise intensity. Dogs participating in short-duration, maximal exercise may benefit from lower-fat, higher-carbohydrate foods.

Assessment of the food includes: 1) physical evaluation of the food, 2) evaluation of the product label for commercial foods and 3) evaluation of the food's nutritional content relative to the animal's needs (key nutritional factors). (See Chapter 1.)

Canine athletes are fed a wide variety of foods and supplements. When assessing the overall ration, it is important to assess all foods and supplements fed. The nutrient profile of the total daily ration should be evaluated for the key nutritional factors based on the type and amount of exercise performed by each dog. (See the Key Nutritional Factors table.)

Most intermediate athletes are fed commercial foods, whereas many sprint and endurance athletes are fed homemade foods or more commonly a mixture of commercial food and other ingredients. The use of supplements is prevalent with canine athletes of all types.

Commercial Foods

Appendix L lists the nutrients of concern for many commercial dog foods and Table 10-7 lists selected commercial foods formulated for active dogs and canine athletes. For those commercial foods not found in Appendix L or Table 10-7, minimum fat and protein levels are listed in the guaranteed or typical analysis on the pet food label. (See Chapter 1 for limitations of this information.) Some products list a customer service telephone number on their label, which is another source of this information. Caloric density may also be listed on the label but usually must be obtained from the manufacturer or estimated from the guaranteed analysis. (See Chapter 1.) The carbohydrate (nitrogen free extract [NFE]) content is estimated from the guaranteed analysis if a value is assumed for ash content (100% – % moisture – % fat – % protein – % fiber – 5% ash). (See Figure 2-3.) Digestibility information is usually only available from the manufacturer.

Homemade Foods

Homemade foods can be very complicated mixtures of many ingredients. Chapter 6 discusses assessment of homemade foods in detail. Fortunately, most homemade rations for canine athletes use a commercial dry dog food as a base. Many racing greyhound rations contain dry dog food mixed with either raw or cooked meat, water, vitamin and mineral supplements and a variety of other ingredi-

---

Acid-Base Balance and Exercise

Muscle contraction produces metabolic acid (CO_2 and/or lactate), which decreases the intracellular pH of muscles. Changes in intracellular pH can affect the function of muscle enzymes responsible for ATP generation and contraction. The mechanisms that act to blunt the detrimental effects of acid production within muscles include: 1) intracellular buffering and 2) removal of acids by the bloodstream.

In equine athletes, two approaches have been used to help counteract exercise-induced acidosis to improve athletic performance. The first is to base-load the horse via stomach tube several hours before exercise. Sodium bicarbonate in water is the base used most often. This solution is frequently called a "milkshake" due to its milky white appearance. This approach can effectively alter resting acid-base status, but hasn't been proven to alter performance. The second approach is to alter the ionic composition of food to change the acid-base status of the animal. Investigators have been able to alter resting acid-base status by altering the dietary cation-anion balance of the food, but again it is unclear if this alteration affects performance. Alteration of acid-base status by dietary or supplementation means has not been investigated extensively in dogs; however, the basic principles investigated in horses should apply to dogs.

BIBLIOGRAPHY

Autran de Morais HS. A nontraditional approach to acid-base disorders. In: DiBartola ST, ed. Fluid Therapy in Small Animal Practice, Philadelphia, PA: WB Saunders Co, 1992.

Ferrante PL, Menninger JH, Spencer PA, et al. Metabolic response of horses to a high soluble carbohydrate diet: Effects of low-intensity submaximal exercise and sodium bicarbonate supplementation. American Journal of Veterinary Research 1992; 53: 321-325.

Greenhaff PL, Gleeson M, Maughan RJ. The effects of dietary manipulation on blood acid-base status and the performance of high intensity exercise. European Journal of Applied Physiology 1987; 56: 331-337.

Harkins JD, Kamerling SG. Effects of induced alkalosis on performance in Thoroughbreds during a 1,600-m race. Equine Veterinary Journal 1992; 24: 94-98.

Rose RJ, Lloyd DR. Sodium bicarbonate: More than just a "milkshake"? Equine Veterinary Journal 1992; 24: 75-76.

Stutz WA, Topliff DR, Freeman DW, et al. Effect of dietary cation-anion balance on blood parameters in exercising horses. Equine Veterinary Science 1992; 12: 169-171.

CANINE ATHLETE

---

ents. Likewise, many sled dog mushers mix animal fat or both meat and fat with dry dog food and other ingredients. If the commercial dry food constitutes 50 to 75% of the mixture on a weight basis and most of the added ingredients are wet ingredients or fat, it is unlikely that vitamin and mineral deficiencies will occur.

Because many elite canine athletes (racing greyhounds and sled dogs) are fed homemade foods containing meat and animal by-products of variable quality, the safety of these foods should always be evaluated. Some raw meat sources contain abundant bacteria and bacterial toxins. (See Case 7-1.) These materials may pose a health hazard for the people that care for these animals and for the athletes themselves. Chapter 7 discusses food safety in detail.

Assess the Feeding Method

Performance can be influenced by the composition of the food and how it is fed. It is possible to feed the right food in the wrong way and vice versa. Items to be assessed should include amount fed, frequency of feeding, timing of meals in relation to exercise, access to water and the use of supplements. If the animal is in appropriate body condition and hydration status, it is likely that the amount of food and water consumed is appropriate.

Amount to Feed

An increase in energy requirement is the hallmark of exercise. The wide variation in the intensity and duration of exercise and therefore energy requirement of different types of canine athletes emphasizes the need for food dose calculations. The basics of energy requirement and food dose calculation are covered in detail in Chapter 1.

DER is the product of RER and a factor that accounts for normal activity. For the average neutered adult dog, DER is 1.6 x RER. DER for exercising dogs has a wide range of values from 1.8 x RER to 11 x RER, depending on the intensity and duration of exercise. As discussed earlier, the caloric cost of running is determined by the size of the animal (BW), weight carried or pulled and distance traveled.

Energy is also used to maintain body temperature. Extreme arctic and tropical temperatures will both increase a dog's RER.[70,75] Dogs working in cold climates may require less energy than the sum of those determined for work and for thermoregulation because exercise generates significant quantities of heat. RER for non-working dogs in hot environments increases only marginally as a result of increased work of the respiratory muscles (panting) (See sidebar "Nutrients Used for Body Cooling," Chapter 9.) Working dogs already have increased respiratory rate, thus, additional energy for thermoregulation during exercise in hot climates should be negligible. Total DER is the sum of the needs for rest (RER), exercise (EER) and thermoregulation (ET) (DER for canine athletes = RER + EER + ET).

Most working dogs expending fewer kilocalories than 3 x RER can adequately fulfill their energy needs by eating a commercial food formulated for performance (Table 10-

7). These foods are acceptable, complete and convenient in most situations. Athletes working in extremely warm or extremely cold environments or those working for several hours a day for several days in a row may expend more calories than 3 x RER. Dry matter intake is limited to about 3.5% of body weight under most physiologic conditions.[c] This quantity of a performance food (30% protein, 20% fat, 40% carbohydrate DMB, >80% DM digestibility) provides a maximum of 5 x RER for a 25-kg dog.

Because true endurance athletes have a DER greater than 5 x RER, providing sufficient dietary energy becomes the focus of feeding these athletes. Long-distance sled dog drivers frequently encounter situations in which their 25- to 30-kg dogs require 6,000 to 10,000 kcal/day (25 to 42 MJ/day) (7 to 11 x RER). Under these extreme circumstances, dogs are fed 1,500 to 2,500 kcal (6 to 11 MJ) of a dry commercial food in an attempt to fulfill protein, carbohydrate, vitamin and mineral requirements. Energy intake is then maximized by fulfilling the rest of the dog's dry matter intake with fat or fatty meat. Strategies that maximize fat intake have been successfully used in virtually all of the recent Iditarod, Quest and Alpirod victories and in sled dog expeditions to both poles.[d-g] These extremely high-fat foods, which derive up to 80% of their kilocalories from lipid sources, should be fed only to dogs previously acclimated to high-fat intake (i.e., 30 to 60% fat kilocalories), through feeding and training. Also, there may be a limited amount of time that dogs can be maintained on such a food or at such a level of stress.

Another strategy used by sled dog mushers is to feed their dogs so they begin a long-distance race with 1.36 to 2.3 kg of extra adipose tissue. This gives the dogs a reserve to draw upon when caloric intake cannot meet energy expenditure. The additional insulation may also help dogs reduce heat loss during rest periods.

Feeding to Maintain Proper Body Condition

Food-dose calculations are based on average energy needs for a population of animals and therefore will not be accurate for all animals in various circumstances. Variation in individual metabolic rate, environmental temperature and exercise affect energy requirement and food dose. Repeated

Table 10-7. Levels of key nutrients in selected commercial foods used for active and athletic dogs.*

	kcal (ME/g)	Protein (%)	Fat (%)	NFE (%)	Digestibility (%)
Diamond Professional Dog Food, dry	4.50	33.2	22.3	33.1	na
Dr. Ballard Great Performance, dry	4.50	34.1	26.0	31.3	na
Eagle Pack Kennel Pack, dry	3.94	28.1	16.3	44.7	na
Eagle Pack Power Pack, dry	4.20	32.8	21.7	34.2	na
Hill's Science Diet Canine Active/Performance, moist	4.97	30.1	25.8	36.9	86
Hill's Science Diet Canine Active/Performance, dry	4.52	30.5	27.0	35.0	85
Iams Eukanuba Premium Performance, dry	4.83	34.0	23.0	35.1	na
Nutro's Natural Choice Plus, dry	4.17	32.2	20.0	38.4	na
Pedigree Chum Advance Formula Activity Plus, dry	4.28	34.8	21.7	32.1	na
Purina Hi Pro, dry	4.08	30.2	11.8	49.7	83
Purina Pro Plan Performance, dry	4.71	34.1	21.6	36.9	84
Royal Canin HE30, dry	4.44	32.6	17.4	36.4	na
Royal Canin ST35, dry	4.48	38.0	27.2	21.2	na
Wafcol Energy Plus, dry	3.82	26.7	10.7	49.2	na

*This list represents products with the largest market share and for which published information is available. Manufacturers' published values or analyses performed in June 1996; expressed on % dry matter .
To convert to kJ, multiply kcal x 4.184.
na = information not published by manufacturer.

or continual body condition assessment is clearly the best clinical measure of energy balance. Body condition scoring is primarily a measure of body fat. Increasing body fat indicates positive energy balance; therefore, food dosage should be decreased. If body fat falls below optimal, energy balance is negative and food dosage should be increased to ensure adequate energy for maximal performance. One method of body condition scoring is presented in Chapter 1. A BCS of 2/5 or 3/5 is normal for most canine athletes. Because fat in excess of what is needed for energy reserves during racing adds weight and may affect performance, many sight hounds and some sled dogs are kept very lean (BCS 1 to 2/5).

Most racing greyhounds normally have a BCS of 1/5. Being very lean may be an important physical characteristic for maximal sprint performance. Excess body fat adds weight, which is unnecessary, especially in light of the greyhound's very limited ability to use fat as an energy source for sprinting.

When to Feed

It is not enough to feed the right amount of the right food; it must be fed at the right times. To gain maximum benefit from a specific food, meals must be fed at the right time in relation to exercise and ample time must be allowed for metabolism to adapt to a new food type when changing foods.

After the amount to feed has been determined, an appropriate feeding schedule should be used. The temporal relationship between food intake and exercise greatly affects nutrient use. In one study, dogs fed within six hours of exercise developed a higher working body temperature than those fed 17 hours before exercise.[21] The elevated body temperatures in dogs fed closest to the onset of exercise may have been caused by the heat released by the digestive process (specific dynamic action of food), and by vasodilatation of the splanchnic vessels. Such shunting may decrease cutaneous circulation and thus diminish heat dissipation. In performing the same task, dogs fed within six hours of exercise used more glucose and less fat than postabsorptive dogs.[21,76,77] This alteration in substrate use may be caused by higher circulating insulin levels in the more recently fed dogs.[18] Because insulin tends to decrease free fatty acid mobilization from peripheral adipose depots, feeding too close to exercise may impair endurance by encouraging use and thus depletion of limited carbohydrate (glycogen) stores.[18]

The importance of the temporal relationship between feeding and exercise is seen in the poorly documented syndrome known as hunting dog hypoglycemia. The exact etiology of this syndrome is unknown. It is often associated with hyperactive, under-conditioned hunting dogs. Elevated ambient temperature has also been implicated as a risk factor.[70] Dogs experiencing this syndrome begin working normally and then develop signs of weakness and tremors that may progress to seizures and even death. Their purported inability to maintain normoglycemia has been attributed to inadequate glycogen mobilization (due to a lack of a glycogen debranching enzyme), excessive rates of glycogen mobilization or a combination of the two.[70] Feeding these dogs several hours (≥4) before the onset of exercise may help decrease insulin levels at the onset of exercise. Exercise also dampens the insulin response to ingested carbohydrate.[18] Providing exogenous carbohydrate via small amounts of food offered at the onset of and periodically during exercise may aid blood glucose homeostasis in these dogs.[70]

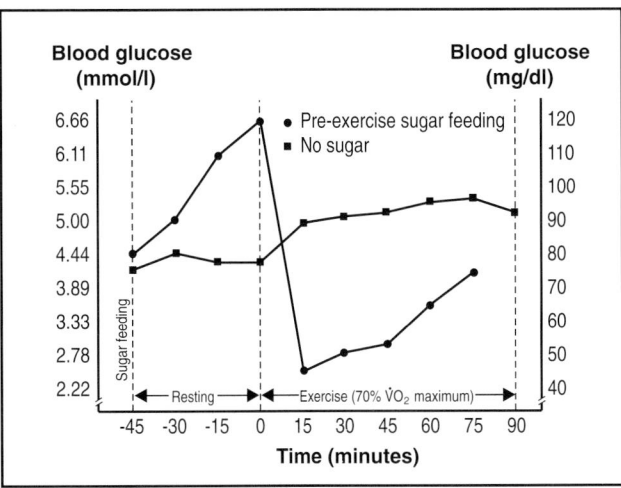

Figure 10-4. Differences in blood glucose concentrations between people exercising on a bicycle ergometer following administration of glucose drink or placebo (Adapted from Costill DL, Miller JM. Nutrition for endurance sport: Carbohydrate and fluid balance. International Journal of Sports Medicine 1980; 1: 2-14.).

Figure 10-4 shows blood glucose results from a study that examined the effect of feeding time on blood glucose concentration during exercise in people riding a stationary bicycle.[78] One group was given a drink containing glucose 45 minutes before the onset of exercise, whereas the other group received a placebo drink. Blood glucose levels remained constant in the non-fed group, whereas people ingesting the glucose drink had a normal postprandial increase in blood glucose followed by a severe drop at the onset of exercise.

Feeding long before exercise (more than four hours) may also aid endurance by allowing the dog to evacuate its bowels before it begins work. This decreases the weight carried by the dog and may decrease its risk of developing stress diarrhea. Although the cause of loose stools postexercise has not been determined, some researchers have attributed it to the presence of stool in the colon at the onset of exercise.[g]

As with pre-exercise feedings, the timing of postexercise meals also influences nutrient use. Glycogen synthesis postexercise occurs much more rapidly in human athletes given exogenous substrates within 30 minutes to two hours postexercise. Feeding within this time frame may aid repletion of glycogen stores in athletes who must perform strenuous exercise on several consecutive days.

The practical application of the above information is: 1) feed more than four hours before exercise, 2) feed within two hours after exercise and 3) small amounts of food may be fed during exercise. Feeding must be done during exercise or during short breaks. Feeding a hunting dog that has hypoglycemic tendencies at the beginning of a 45-minute lunch break may contribute to exercise-induced hypoglycemia (Figure 10-4).

Because large volumes of urine represent additional weight and a possible time handicap for racing dogs, many handlers will not water an animal closer than two hours before a competition. The dog is then confined for one and one-half to two hours after drinking and will usually empty its bladder upon being released from the cage. Water should be offered as soon as is practicably possible after exercise. Cooler fluids seem to be absorbed most

Table 10-8. Feeding plan summary for canine athletes.

Sprint athletes
1. Feed a highly digestible, high-carbohydrate, low-fat, moderate-protein food. (See Key Nutritional Factors table.)
2. Feed the right amount of food (DER = 1.6 to 2 x RER).
3. Check body condition frequently to assess energy balance and food dose.
4. Time meals and snacks correctly. Provide food or snack >four hours before racing; offer high-carbohydrate snack within 30 minutes after racing to enhance glycogen repletion.
5. Allow free access to water except just before racing.
6. Monitor hydration status frequently.

Intermediate athletes (working)
1. Feed a highly digestible, moderate-carbohydrate, moderate- to high-fat, moderate-protein food. The energy density of the food should be high enough to allow consumption of DER. (See Key Nutritional Factors table.)
2. Feed the right amount of food. The food dose will be highly variable depending on duration and frequency of exercise (DER = 2 to 5 x RER) and should be calculated after assessing the amount of exercise performed.
3. Check body condition frequently to assess energy balance and food dose.
4. Time meals and snacks correctly. Feed after exercise or >four hours before exercise. Snacks should be given during exercise or at the end of breaks <15 minutes before resuming exercise.
5. Allow free access to water.
6. Monitor hydration status frequently.

Intermediate athletes (training)
1. Feed the same as for work (see above).
2. Allow adequate time to adapt to new food (>six weeks) before seasonal work.
3. Begin training and new food at least six weeks before seasonal work begins.
4. Allow free access to water.

Intermediate athletes (idle)
1. Feed as typical adult dog. (See Chapter 9.)
2. Feed a performance food (smaller amount) or typical adult maintenance food as needed to maintain optimal body condition.
3. Allow free access to water.

Endurance athletes
1. Feed a highly digestible, high-fat, low-carbohydrate, moderate-protein food. The energy density of the food should be high enough to allow consumption of DER. (See Key Nutritional Factors table.)
2. Feed the right amount of food. The food dose will be highly variable depending on duration and frequency of exercise (DER = 5 to 11 x RER) and should be calculated after assessing amount of exercise performed.
3. Check body condition frequently to assess energy balance and food dose.
4. Time meals and snacks correctly. Feed after exercise or >four hours before exercise. If snacks are used they should be given during or after exercise.
5. Allow free access to water.
6. Monitor hydration status frequently.

rapidly.[62] Canine athletes may become significantly dehydrated after prolonged exercise and under relatively warm or humid conditions. Attempts should not be made to replace the entire fluid deficit orally or at once. Gradual oral replacement can be supplemented with subcutaneous (or in severe cases intravenous) isotonic solutions. Body temperature should be monitored because dehydrated animals are less capable of regulating this parameter.[79]

Food Adaptation

Animals require some time to adapt to a new food whenever a dietary change is made. When dramatic changes in proportion of fat and carbohydrate are made, GI and metabolic adaptations occur. The GI adjustments usually happen in a few days provided the transition to the new food is gradual. The metabolic changes generally take more time. Muscle glycogen responds to feeding a high-carbohydrate food in a few days to a few weeks.[80] Changes in muscle enzymes and oxidative capacity occur in response to high-fat rations in six to eight weeks. Allowing appropriate time for these adaptations to occur is especially important for seasonal athletes that may be fed a high-fat performance food only part of the year and a maintenance food the remainder of the year.[31] Both training and dietary change should occur six weeks before exercise season (e.g., hunting season).

▌ DETERMINE A FEEDING PLAN

The feeding plan (Table 10-8) should be formulated based on realistic and quantifiable nutritional objectives after the animal, food and feeding method have been assessed. The feeding plan guides the selection of food(s) and feeding method.

Select a Food(s)

Comparing the nutritional content of the current food to the key nutritional factors for the canine athlete allows decisions to be made about the adequacy of the food for that individual. If the current food is appropriate (key nutritional factors in balance with the athlete's needs) then that food can continue to be fed. If discrepancies exist between the key nutritional factors for the animal and the content of the food, the food should be changed or "balanced" to meet the athlete's needs. Table 10-7 lists commercial foods that are often fed to active dogs and canine athletes.

Determine a Feeding Method

As discussed above (See Assess The Feeding Method.), several aspects of the feeding method are important to canine athletic performance. These include the amount fed, timing of feeding in relation to exercise and food adaptation. All of these factors should be matched to the individual athlete and the type of exercise performed (intensity, duration, frequency, season). If the current feeding method matches the individual's needs based on the assessment, no changes are necessary. Changes should be made if the assessment reveals gaps in the feeding method.

The amount of a new food to feed a canine athlete can be estimated several ways. Feeding guidelines from the manufacturer and those on pet food labels are seldom correct for canine athletes. Energy needs and food doses usually must be calculated. If the amount of the previous food was correct (i.e., appropriate body condition was maintained) and the metabolizable energy of the food is known, simply feed the same amount of the new food to supply the same metabolizable energy. If this method isn't feasible, the food dose should be calculated based on the animal's needs as shown above. (See Assess the Feeding Method.) In all cases, the animal should be assessed frequently and adjustments should be made to maintain correct body condition.

Timing of feeding and timing of food changes are important for canine athletes. (See Assess the Feeding Method.) Timing of feeding in relation to exercise influences hormonal status, substrate availability and performance. When changing foods, adequate time must be allowed for the animal to adapt to the new food type to take full advantage of its nutrient profile.

REASSESSMENT

After the feeding plan has been implemented, the animal should be monitored to evaluate the appropriateness of the feeding plan. This process is identical to the original assessment of the animal. Frequent physical examinations are important for early detection of injuries or illnesses. Daily monitoring of food consumption is an early indicator of problems. Frequent evaluation of stool quality may indicate how well the animal is tolerating the food. Weekly measurements of body condition and body weight allow assessment of energy balance (i.e., whether food intake matches energy expenditure). Appropriate body condition is also important for optimal performance. Excess fat represents an unneeded handicap, whereas excessively lean animals may not have sufficient energy stores.

Hydration status should be monitored frequently. Water plays a vital role in supporting cardiovascular function, transport of metabolic substrates and wastes and thermoregulation. Respiratory water losses can be large, particularly during lengthy exercise or under hot or cold environmental conditions.

Ultimately, athletic performance is the best means of monitoring the feeding plan for canine athletes.

ACKNOWLEDGMENT

The authors and editors thank Dr. David Kronfeld, Pembroke, VA, USA, for his review and suggested revisions to this chapter.

ENDNOTES & REFERENCES

ENDNOTES

a. Publisher. Gun Dog Magazine, Stover Publishing Co, Des Moines, IA, USA. Personal communication. Summer 1997.

b. National Greyhound Association. Abilene, KS, USA. Personal communication. Summer 1996.

c. Burrows C. University of Florida, Gainesville, FL, USA. Personal communication. Summer 1991.

d. Runyan J. Fairbanks, AK, USA. Alaska Dog Racing Association Annual Meeting. Personal communication. October 1994.

e. Steger W. International Arctic Project, Minneapolis, MN, USA. Personal communication. Summer 1994.

f. Champaigne C, Champaigne-Wright R. Fairbanks, AK, USA. Personal communication. October 1994.

g. Kronfeld D. University of Pennsylvania, Philadelphia, PA, USA. Personal communication. Spring 1991.

REFERENCES

1. McKeever KH, Schurg WA, Convertino VA. Exercise training-induced hypervolemia in greyhounds: Role of water intake and renal mechanisms. American Journal of Physiology 1985; 248: R422-R425.

2. Convertino VA, Greenleaf JE, Bernauer EM. Role of thermal and exercise factors in the mechanisms of hypervolemia. Journal of Applied Physiology 1980; 48: 657-664.

3. American Kennel Club. Breed Standards. New York, NY: American Kennel Club, Inc.

4. Palmer J. Breed groups. In: The Illustrated Encyclopedia of Dog Breeds. Edison, NJ: The Wellfleet Press, 1994; 16-19.

5. van Lier ALC. Brakken–Overzicht van de Rassen. In: Handboek Kynologie. Zaventem, Belgium: Bohn-Stafleu-Van Loghum, 1995; 8502-1–8502-13.

6. van Leeuwen FX. Terriërs–Groepsbeschrijving. In: Handboek Kynologie. Zaventem, Belgium: Bohn-Stafleu-Van Loghum, 1995; 8701-1–8701-7.

7. Popelier T. In: Handboek Kynologie. Zaventem, Belgium: Bohn-Stafleu-Van Loghum, 1995; 8505-1–8505-13, 8506-1–8506-15.

8. Åstrand PO. Textbook of Work Physiology. New York, NY: McGraw-Hill Inc, 1986; 350.

9. Blaxter K. Energy Metabolism in Animals and Man. New York, NY: Cambridge University Press, 1989; 149-151.

10. Pivarnik JM. Water and electrolyte balance during rest and exercise. In: Wolinsky I, Hickson JF, eds. Nutrition in Exercise and Sport, 2nd ed. Boca Raton, FL: CRC Press, 1994; 245-283.

11. Nadel ER. Adaptations to aerobic training. American Scientist 1985; 73: 334-343.

12. Williams MH. Nutritional Aspects of Human Physical and Athletic Performance, 2nd ed. Springfield, IL: Charles C Thomas, 1985; 21-23.

13. Kronfeld DS, Downey RL. Nutritional strategies for stamina in dogs and horses. In: Proceedings. Nutrition Society of Australia, 1981: 21-29.

14. Kronfeld DS, Hammel EP, Ramberg CF, et al. Hematological and metabolic responses to training in racing sled dogs fed diets containing medium, low, or zero carbohydrate. American Journal of Clinical Nutrition 1977; 30: 419-430.

15. Hammel EP, Kronfeld DS, Ganjam VK, et al. Metabolic responses to exhaustive exercise in racing sled dogs fed diets containing medium, low, or zero carbohydrate. American Journal of Clinical Nutrition 1977; 30: 409-418.

16. Stryer L. Biochemistry, 3rd ed. New York, NY: WH Freeman and Co, 1988; 316-320.

17. Rusko H, Luhtanen P, Rahkila P, et al. Muscle metabolism, blood lactate, and oxygen uptake in steady state aerobic and anaerobic exercise. European Journal of Applied Physiology 1986; 55: 181-186.

18. Pate TD, Brunn JC. The fundamentals of carbohydrate metabolism. In: Hickson JF, Wolinsky I, eds. Nutrition in Exercise and Sport, 1st ed. Boca Raton, FL: CRC Press, 1989; 37-49.

19. Newsholme EA. Application of principles of metabolic control to the problem of metabolic limitations in sprinting, middle-distance, and marathon running. International Journal of Sports Medicine 1986; 7: 66-70.

20. Weber JM, Brichon G, Roberts T, et al. Oxidative substrate pathways and symorphysis II. Relative roles of circulatory and intramuscular sources. In: Proceedings. Thirty-Second Congress of IUPS, Glasgow, Scotland; 1993.

21. Young DR, Price R, Elder NE, et al. Energy and electrolyte metabolism and adrenal responses during work in dogs. Journal of Applied Physiology 1962; 17: 669-674.

22. Zackin MJ. Protein requirements for athletes. Sports Medicine Digest 1990; 12: 1-3.

23. Hickson JF, Wolinsky I. Human protein intake and metabolism in exercise and sport. In: Hickson JF, Wolinsky I, eds. Nutrition in Exercise and Sport, 1st ed. Boca Raton, FL: CRC Press, 1989; 5-35.

CANINE ATHLETE

24. Miller GD, Massaro EJ. Carbohydrate in ultra-endurance performance. In: Hickson JF, Wolinsky I, eds. Nutrition in Exercise and Sport, 1st ed. Boca Raton, FL: CRC Press, 1989; 51-62.

25. Blomstrand E, Celsing F, Newsholme EA. Changes in plasma concentrations of aromatic and branched-chain amino acids during sustained exercise in man and their possible role in fatigue. Acta Physiologica Scandinavica 1988; 133: 115-121.

26. Hollman W. Historical remarks on the development of the aerobic-anaerobic threshold up to 1966. International Journal of Sports Medicine 1985; 6: 109-116.

27. Toll PW, Pieschl RL, Gaethgens P, et al. Fluid, electrolyte, and packed cell volume shift in the racing greyhound. American Journal of Veterinary Research 1995; 56: 227-232.

28. Harrison MH, Edwards RJ, Leitch DR. Effect of exercise and thermal stress on plasma volume. Journal of Applied Physiology 1975; 39: 925-931.

29. Houpt TR. Water, electrolytes, and acid base balance. In: Duke's Physiology of Domestic Animals, 10th ed. Ithaca, NY: Cornell University Press, 1984; 486-506.

30. Gunn HM. The proportions of muscle, bone and fat in two different types of dogs. Research in Veterinary Science 1978; 24: 277-282.

31. Reynolds AJ, Fuhrer L, Dunlap HL, et al. Lipid metabolite responses to diet and training in sled dogs. Journal of Nutrition 1994; 124: 2754S-2759S.

32. Gleeson M, Maughan RJ, Greenhaff PL. Comparison of the effects of pre-exercise feeding of glucose, glycerol and a placebo on endurance and fuel homeostasis in man. European Journal of Applied Physiology 1986; 55: 645-653.

33. Martin B, Robinsin S, Robertshaw D. Influence of diet on leg uptake of glucose during heavy exercise. American Journal of Clinical Nutrition 1978; 31: 62-67.

34. Coyle EF, Cogan AR, Hemmert MK, et al. Substrate usage during prolonged exercise following a pre-exercise meal. Journal of Applied Physiology 1985; 59: 429-433.

35. Yoshida T. Effect of dietary modifications on anaerobic threshold. Sports Medicine 1986; 3: 4-9.

36. Brouns F, Saris WHM, Beckers E, et al. Metabolic changes induced by exhaustive cycling and diet manipulation. International Journal of Sports Medicine 1989; 10: S49-S62.

37. Maughan RJ, Greenhaff PL, Gleeson M, et al. The effect of dietary carbohydrate intake on the metabolic response to prolonged walking on consecutive days. European Journal of Applied Physiology 1987; 56: 583-591.

38. Reynolds AJ, Carey DP, Reinhart GA, et al. Effect of postexercise carbohydrate supplementation on muscle glycogen repletion in trained sled dogs. American Journal of Veterinary Research 1997; 58: 1252-1256.

39. Reynolds AJ, Hoppeler H, Reinhart GA, et al. Sled dog endurance: A result of high fat diet on selective breeding. Federation of American Societies for Experimental Biology Journal 1995; 9: A996.

40. Downey RL, Kronfeld DS, Banta CA. Diet of beagles affects stamina. Journal of the American Animal Hospital Association 1980; 6: 273-277.

41. Reynolds AJ. Nutritional considerations for racing sled dogs. In: Proceedings. Fourth Annual International Sled Dog Veterinary Medical Association Symposium, Nashua, NH, September 19-21, 1997: 33-51.

42. Nutrient Requirements of Dogs. Washington, DC: National Academy Press, 1985.

43. Van Vleet JF. Current knowledge of selenium-vitamin E deficiency in domestic animals. Journal of the American Veterinary Medical Association 1980; 176: 321-325.

44. Kronfeld DS. Vitamin and mineral supplementation for dogs and cats: A monograph on micronutrients. Santa Barbara, CA: Veterinary Practice Publishing Co, 1989; 33-102.

45. Brilla LR, Landerholm TE. Effect of fish oil supplementation and exercise on serum lipids and aerobic fitness. Journal of Sports Medicine and Physical Fitness 1990; 30: 173-180.

46. Grandjean D, Paragon B-M. Alimentation du chien de traineau. Recueil de Médecine Vétérinaire 1987; 163: 7-14.

47. Wolter R. Feeding the Sporting Dog. Fairbanks, AK: Kobuk International, 1985.

48. Crandall LA. A comparison of ketosis in man and the dog. Journal of Biological Chemistry 1941; 138: 123.

49. Dobson GP, Parkhouse WS, Weber JM, et al. Metabolic changes in skeletal muscle and blood of greyhounds during 800-m track sprint. American Journal of Physiology 1988; 255: R513-R519.

50. Rose RJ, Bloomberg MS. Response to sprint exercise in the greyhound: Effects on hematology, serum biochemistry, and muscle metabolites. Research in Veterinary Science 1989; 47: 212-218.

51. Richter EA, Glabo H. High glycogen levels enhance glycogen breakdown in isolated contracting muscle. Journal of Applied Physiology 1986; 61: 827-831.

52. Conlee RK. Muscle glycogen and exercise endurance: A twenty-year perspective. Exercise and Sports Science Review 1987; 15: 1-28.

53. Oldham SL, Potter GD, Evans JW, et al. Storage and mobilization of muscle glycogen in race horses fed a control and high-fat diet. In: Proceedings. Eleventh Equine Nutrition and Physiology Symposium, Stillwater, OK, 1989; 57-61.

54. Bergstrom J, Hermansen L, Hultman E, et al. Diet muscle glycogen and physical performance. Acta Physiologica Scandinavica 1967; 71: 140-150.

55. Toll PW, Pieschl RL, Hand MS. The effect of dietary fat and carbohydrate on sprint performance in racing greyhound dogs. In: Proceedings. The Eighth International Racing Greyhound Symposium, Orlando, FL, 1992: 1-3.

56. Hill RC, Bloomberg MS, Legrand-Defretin V, et al. Energy, dietary fat and performance in greyhounds (abstract). Journal of Veterinary Internal Medicine 1996; 10: 170.

57. Goodyear LJ, Hirshman MF, King PA, et al. Skeletal muscle plasma membrane glucose transport and glucose transporters after exercise. Journal of Applied Physiology 1990; 68: 193-198.

58. Kronfeld DS. Diet and performance in racing sled dogs. Journal of the American Veterinary Medical Association 1973; 162: 470-474.

59. Keizer HA, Kuipers H, vanKranenberg G, et al. Influence of liquid and solid meals on muscle glycogen resynthesis, plasma fuel, hormone response, and maximal working capacity. International Journal of Sports Medicine 1986; 8: 99-104.

60. Issekutz B Jr. Effects of glucose infusion on hepatic and muscle glycogenolysis in exercising dogs. American Journal of Physiology 1981; 240: E451-E457.

61. Burke LM, Read KSD. A study of carbohydrate loading techniques used by marathon runners. Canadian Journal of Sports Sciences 1987; 12: 6-10.

62. Bucci LR. Nutrients as Ergogenic Aids for Sports and Exercise. Boca Raton, FL: CRC Press, 1993; 9-13.

63. Ivy JL, Katz AL, Cutter CL, et al. Muscle glycogen synthesis after exercise: Effect of time on carbohydrate ingestion. Journal of Applied Physiology 1988; 64: 1480-1485.

64. Buskirk ER, Puhl S. Nutritional beverages: Exercise and sport. In: Hickson JF, Wolinsky I, eds. Nutrition in Exercise and Sport, 1st ed. Boca Raton, FL: CRC Press, 1989; 201-232.

65. Costill DL, Fink WJ, Getchell WH, et al. Lipid metabolism in skeletal muscle of endurance trained males and females. Journal of Applied Physiology 1979; 47: 787-791.

66. Costill DL, Coyle EF, Fink WF, et al. Adaptations in skeletal muscle following strength training. Journal of Applied Physiology 1979; 46: 96-99.

67. Cahill GF, Marliss EB, Akoi TT. Fat and Nitrogen Metabolism in Fasting Man. New York, NY: Academic Press, 1970; 181-185.

68. Adkins TO, Kronfeld DS. Diet of racing sled dogs affects erythrocyte depression by stress. Canadian Veterinary Journal 1982; 23: 250-263.

69. Reynolds AJ, Reinhart GA, Carey DP, et al. Protein intake during training affects biochemical and performance parameters in sled dogs. American Journal of Veterinary Research (in press).

70. Lewis LD, Morris ML Jr, Hand MS. Small Animal Clinical Nutrition III. Topeka, KS: Mark Morris Associates, 1989; 3-25–3-28.

71. Swenson MJ. Physiological properties and chemical constituents of blood. In: Swenson MJ, ed. Duke's Physiology of Domestic Animals. 10th ed. Ithaca, NY: Cornell University Press, 1984, 15-40.

72. Serway RA. Physics for Scientists and Engineers, with Modern Physics, 3rd ed. Philadelphia, PA: Saunders College Publishing, 1990; 589.

73. Kozlowski S, Brzezinska Z, Kruk B, et al. Exercise hyperthermia as a factor limiting performance; Temperature effect on muscle metabolism. Journal of Applied Physiology 1985; 59: 766-773.

74. Kruk B, Kaciuba-Uscilko H, Nazar K, et al. Hypothalamic, rectal, and muscle temperatures in exercising dogs; Effect of cooling. Journal of Applied Physiology 1985; 58: 1444-1448.

75. Young DR, Mosher R, Erve P, et al. Temperature and heat exchange during treadmill running in dogs. Journal of Applied Physiology 1959; 14: 839-843.

76. Young DR, Iacovino A, Erve P, et al. Effect of time after feeding and carbohydrate or water supplementation on work in dogs. Journal of Applied Physiology 1959; 14: 1013-1017.

77. Young DR. Effect of food deprivation on treadmill running in dogs. Journal of Applied Physiology 1959; 14: 1018-1022.

78. Costill DL, Miller JM. Nutrition for endurance sport: Carbohydrate and fluid balance. International Journal of Sports Medicine 1980; 1: 2-14.

79. Greenleaf JE, Kolzowski S, Nazar K, et al. Ion-osmotic hyperthermia during exercise in dogs. American Journal of Physiology 1976; 230: 74-79.

80. Reynolds AJ, Fuhrer L, Dunlap HL, et al. Effect of diet and training on muscle glycogen storage and utilization in sled dogs. Journal of Applied Physiology 1995; 79: 1601-1607.

■ CASE 10-1

Poor Performance in Racing Greyhounds

Philip W. Toll, DVM, MS
Hill's Science and Technology Center
Topeka, Kansas, USA

Assess the Animals

A litter of 14-month-old greyhound dogs (four males, two females) was examined for poor performance. The dogs are owned by a rural mail carrier who recently started a small greyhound farm. This litter of dogs is currently in training and they should begin racing within 60 days. The dogs are being schooled by racing 3/16 mile twice a week at a local training track; however, their performance is not up to the owner's expectations.

The physical examination of all dogs was normal except for a profound overbite (brachygnathia) in two males and one female. All dogs had body condition scores (BCS) of 1/5 and weighed approximately 30 kg each. Fecal examination (composite sample) was negative for parasites. Results of complete blood counts and serum biochemistry profiles from samples obtained from two of the dogs were normal.

Assess the Food(s) and Feeding Method

The dogs are fed individually once daily. They receive a ration composed of the following:
2 cups dry puppy food
1 lb raw meat (90% lean)
1 tbs bone meal
1 tbs dry vitamin supplement
1 cup milk
A trainer at a neighboring greyhound farm suggested feeding more meat and adding one-fourth cup vinegar to the ration.

Questions

1. What are the key nutritional factors and dietary recommendations for sprint athletes?
2. What additional information is necessary to fully assess the food and feeding method for these dogs?
3. What recommendations should be made about the food recipe for these dogs?
4. What is an appropriate feeding method?

Answers and Discussion

1. The key nutritional factors for sprint athletes include energy density, fat, soluble carbohydrate, protein, water and food digestibility. The ideal food or ration for sprint athletes should have an energy density between 3.5 to 4.0 kcal (15 to 17 kJ) ME/g dry matter (DM) and contain these levels of nutrients: fat 8 to 10% DM, soluble carbohydrate (nitrogen-free extract, NFE) 55 to 65% DM, protein 22 to 28% DM and DM digestibility greater than 80%. Water should be available at all times except just before a race.

2. Further assessment should include the following: 1) Nutrient levels in the final ration are needed. Table 1 estimates the key nutrient levels for the current ration. 2) Amount of food fed to each dog and the timing of feeding in relationship to exercise (training). 3) Food safety issues must be addressed for animals that are fed a homemade ration containing raw meat. Greyhounds are frequently fed raw meat that may contain large numbers of bacteria and toxins. Information is needed about how the meat is stored, thawed and handled.

3. The current ration is a typical food for racing greyhounds. The recommendation from the other trainer to increase the meat fraction will increase the protein and fat content of the ration. Although most greyhound trainers believe that meat is essential for optimal performance, the protein and fat content of this

Table 1. Nutrient levels in the current ration for greyhounds during training.

	Dry puppy food (as fed)	Meat (as fed)	Milk (as fed)	Total ration (as fed)	Total ration (DMB)
Moisture (%)	8	68	87	58.3	0
Energy (kcal/g)*	3.95	1.79	0.65	1.87	4.44
Protein (%)	27	21	3.5	17.9	42.8
Fat (%)	18	10	3.5	10.2	24.6
NFE (%)	39	0	4.9	10.9	26
Amount (g)	226	454	244	924	na

Key: DMB = dry matter basis, NFE = nitrogen-free extract (soluble carbohydrate), na = not applicable.
*To calculate kJ, multiply kcal x 4.184.

Table 2. Nutrient levels in the recommended ration for greyhounds during training.

	Dry adult food (as fed)	Meat (as fed)	Milk (as fed)	Total ration (as fed)	Total ration (DMB)
Moisture (%)	8	68	87	48.6	0
Energy (kcal/g)*	3.4	1.79	0.65	1.72	3.37
Protein (%)	23	21	3.5	16.6	32.2
Fat (%)	14	10	3.5	9.7	18.9
NFE (%)	49	0	4.9	22	42.8
Amount (g)	340	227	244	811	na

Key: DMB = dry matter basis, NFE = nitrogen-free extract (soluble carbohydrate), na = not applicable.
*To calculate kJ, multiply kcal x 4.184.

recipe is already more than adequate. The appropriate recommendation is to increase the carbohydrate content of the ration by increasing the amount of a balanced commercial dry dog food in the ration. This food should be a commercial dry food formulated for adult dogs (lower in fat and protein and higher in carbohydrate than the puppy food). Vitamin and micronutrient deficiencies are unlikely to occur if a balanced commercial dry food makes up at least 50% of the recipe on an as fed weight basis. Cooking raw meat is recommended for homemade dog foods although many greyhound trainers believe that raw meat is vital for optimal performance. Therefore, efforts should focus on meat quality, storage, handling and sanitation. (See Chapter 7 and Case 7-1.) Food storage and preparation should emphasize sanitation and minimize the opportunity for bacterial growth in the food mixture. Meat should be kept frozen until near the time of use and be cooked to kill bacteria and decrease quantities of heat-labile toxins. Greyhound trainers often use and recommend a wide variety of unusual dietary supplements. However, most of these supplements are unnecessary and no data exist to support their use. Because greyhounds produce large amounts of metabolic acid when racing, adding an acid such as vinegar to the ration is inappropriate.

4. Meals should be fed more than four hours before training or racing. Water should be available at all times except just before racing. Food dose should be

adjusted to maintain proper body condition (usually 1 or 2/5 for racing greyhounds).

Progress Notes

The recipe was changed to the following:
3 cups dry adult food
0.5 lb meat
1 cup milk
1 Tbs vitamin supplement
The recommendations decreased the protein and fat levels and increased the soluble carbohydrate levels of the ration while not markedly changing the overall feeding regimen. Nutritionally speaking, this was not an ideal ration, but rather a compromise between the need to improve the nutrient profile, while maintaining the owner's desire to continue feeding raw meat. Table 2 lists the key nutrient levels. The owner was pleased with these suggestions and they were implemented as part of the training program.

Bibliography

Hill RC, Butterwick R. New developments in the nutrition of racing greyhounds. In: Proceedings. Fourteenth International Sports Medicine Symposium, Orlando, FL, 1998: 12-14.

Toll PW. Racing greyhound nutrition: Metabolic considerations. In: Proceedings. Eighth International Racing Greyhound Symposium, Orlando, FL, 1992: 19-21.

CASE 10-2

Weight Loss in a Cattle Dog

Philip W. Toll, DVM, MS
Hill's Science and Technology Center
Topeka, Kansas, USA

Assess the Animal

A 14-month-old, intact male Australian cattle dog cross that weighed 20 kg was examined for weight loss. The dog was owned by a cowboy who worked on a 10,000-acre ranch in the western United States. According to the owner, the dog had always been thin but had recently lost weight and was having trouble keeping up with its owner as he checked cattle on horseback. The owner estimated that the daily ride was about 15 to 20 miles. The dog had been kicked by horses several times in the past and was treated for rattlesnake envenomation three months earlier.

There were no apparent long-term health effects from these problems.

The results of a physical examination were unremarkable except for one testicle in the scrotum and a body condition score (BCS) of 1/5. Ideal body weight was estimated to be 25 kg. Fecal examination and heartworm test results were negative. Complete blood count, serum biochemistry profile and urinalysis results were normal.

Assess the Food(s) and Feeding Method

The dog was fed a generic, "high-protein" dry dog food produced at a local feed mill. The food was offered free choice, but the dog usually ate in the morning and evening. The guaranteed analysis on the food bag was as follows: Crude protein, not less than 32%; Crude fat, not less than 11%; Crude fiber, not more than 4%; Moisture, not more than 12%; Calcium, not less than 1.2%;

Phosphorus, not less than 0.9%. The ingredient list was as follows: corn, corn gluten meal, rice, meat and bone meal, soybean meal, animal fat, wheat, vitamins and minerals. The nutritional adequacy statement read "provides complete and balanced nutrition for adult dogs as established by the AAFCO Dog Food Nutrient Profiles."

Questions

1. What additional dietary history would be important to obtain for this patient?
2. Outline an appropriate feeding plan (food and feeding method) for this dog, assuming there are no underlying metabolic or medical problems contributing to the weight loss.
3. What client education is appropriate about the feeding plan?

Answers and Discussion

1. The normal physical examination and normal laboratory database in an otherwise healthy young dog rules out many causes of chronic weight loss. The weight loss could be due to insufficient food intake in the face of strenuous exercise. The actual amount of food that is being offered free choice and the actual amount being consumed by the dog should be documented. This result can be compared with the daily energy requirement (DER) calculated in Answer 2 below.
2. The food for this dog should provide the nutrient levels outlined for intermediate athletic dogs (high duration and frequency) in the Key Nutritional Factors table. In general, the food should have moderate protein and carbohydrate levels, high-fat levels, high energy density and above average digestibility as defined in these tables.

   The estimated DER should include energy for maintenance of young, intact adult dogs (1.8 x resting energy requirement [RER]) plus energy for additional running. RER at an ideal weight of 25 kg = 820 kcal x 1.8 = 1,476 kcal/day (3.4 MJ x 1.8 = 6.2 MJ) for adult maintenance activities. Energy required for a 25-kg dog running 20 miles (33 km)/day = 33 km x 30 kcal/km = 990 kcal/day (4.1 MJ). (See Table 10-5.) The added energy cost of running increases the DER to 2,460 kcal (10.3 MJ) (3 x RER).

   The amount of food to achieve the estimated DER should be divided into two to three meals.

3. The owner should be told that hard work dramatically increases the requirement for calories. By comparison, the need for protein and other nutrients increases only slightly with increasing workload. The idea that athletic dogs require markedly more protein than nonworking dogs is not accurate. The energy density of the current food is probably less than 3.5 kcal metabolizable energy (ME)/g dry matter, which will not provide enough kilocalories in the amount of food the dog normally consumes. Using a food with higher fat levels will ensure a higher energy density. A food with 25 to 30% fat on a dry matter basis (DMB) is recommended. The current food has 12 to 13% fat DMB (estimated from the guaranteed analysis).

   The food should also have above average digestibility to ensure that the energy and nutrients are readily available to the dog. The nutritional adequacy statement shows that the food has not undergone feeding trials, which suggests that the digestibility of the food is unknown.

   Routine body condition scoring is the best way to assess whether the appropriate food is being fed in the correct amounts. A food with a higher fat content and higher energy density should be fed free choice until the dog achieves an ideal body condition (BCS 3/5). Then the amount should be adjusted to maintain that weight and body condition.

Progress Notes

The dog was eating 5 cups of the current food per day, which was estimated to provide 1,700 kcal/day (7.1 MJ/day). This caloric intake was clearly inadequate to provide the estimated DER with the added cost of running. The food was changed to a dry commercial specialty brand food (Science Diet Canine Active[a]) with 30.5% DM protein, 26.2% DM fat, 4.4 kcal ME/g DM and dry matter digestibility exceeding 85%. The new food was gradually exchanged for the old food over several days. The new food was offered free choice until a BCS of 3/5 was achieved, and the daily amount was then stabilized at 2,500 kcal (10.5 MJ) (5 cups) when the dog was working cattle. The amount was decreased to approximately 1,500 kcal (6.3 MJ) (3 cups) on days the dog was not working.

Endnote

a. Hill's Pet Nutrition, Inc., Topeka, KS, USA. This product is also marketed as Science Plan Canine Performance.

CASE 10-3

Poor Performance in a Hunting Dog

Philip W. Toll, DVM, MS
Hill's Science and Technology Center
Topeka, Kansas, USA

Assess the Animal

A five-year-old neutered female golden retriever was examined for collapsing during a game bird hunting trip. The dog was a sedentary house pet for most of the year, but was used as a retriever for game bird hunting each fall. The dog's general health had always been good but its retrieving ability was considered only fair. The dog had received routine heartworm preventive medication since it was a puppy.

On the opening day of hunting season, the dog was fed at 5:30 a.m., loaded in the truck about 6:00 a.m. and began hunting at 7:00 a.m. The dog worked hard through the morning and covered about 10 miles. The weather was unseasonably warm (23.8°C; 75°F) for the fall season in the upper Great Plains region of the United States. The hunters and dog took a lunch break from 11:00 a.m. to noon. The dog was given 1 cup of food and water at 11:00 a.m. and snacked on a small bag of potato chips around 11:30 a.m. The dog rested peacefully until noon when hunting resumed. Half an hour after hunting resumed, the dog began to falter, became ataxic and then collapsed. The dog never appeared to lose consciousness or develop seizures.

The dog was carried back to the truck and taken immediately to a veterinary hospital. During the trip to the hospital the dog seemed to improve. The physical examination was normal. The dog weighed 30 kg and had a body condition score of 3/5. Heart rate and heart sounds were normal with no pulse deficits. Hydration status was normal. A packed cell volume and serum glucose concentration were normal and a heartworm test was negative.

Assess the Food(s) and Feeding Method

The dog was fed a commercial private label brand dry food formulated for adult dogs. The owners fed the dog one meal daily (1,500 kcal [6.3 MJ]; 4.5 cups) at 7:00 a.m. before they went to work. The dog received several biscuit treats in the evening and occasionally leftover food from family meals.

Questions

1. What are possible causes of the dog's collapse during the hunting trip?
2. What education should be provided to the owner about management of the dog?
3. What food should be recommended for this dog during the hunting season?
4. What feeding methods should be used during the hunting season?

Answers and Discussion

1. Causes of sudden collapse of a healthy-appearing dog while hunting include hyperthermia, dehydration, hypoglycemia, heartworm disease, cardiac dysrhythmia and/or muscle cramping. Heartworm disease is unlikely based on the history of a good preventive medication program and negative heartworm test. A cardiac dysrhythmia may have occurred in the field and spontaneously resolved during travel to the veterinarian. Dehydration is unlikely because the dog received water during the lunch break and no clinical evidence of dehydration was found. Hyperthermia may have occurred due to excessive work in a warm environment, but the dog's rectal temperature was not elevated at the hospital. Transient hypoglycemia may have occurred. (See Figure 10-4.) Muscle cramping

may accompany electrolyte abnormalities, dehydration and poor training and conditioning.

2. The dog was poorly trained and went from a sedentary house pet to working dog very abruptly. Physical training should begin about six weeks before hunting season for part-time athletes such as this dog. One hour of brisk walking each day is a good starting point. The dog should work for several hours at an intensity level similar to what is expected in the field during the last two weeks of training.
3. A performance-type food (See Table 10-7.) should be recommended if the dog will be used frequently for long periods of time during the hunting season. Performance foods are usually higher in fat, the preferred muscle fuel for longer lasting exercise. Additionally, higher fat levels increase a food's energy density, which is needed for additional work in the field. A 30-kg dog traveling 10 miles requires 480 kcal (2.0 MJ). The food should be changed well before hunting season (preferably six weeks before) to allow for metabolic adaptation. Adaptation allows a dog to take full advantage of the higher dietary fat content.
4. Timing of feeding is also important. Working dogs should be fed four or more hours before exercise to allow some time for food assimilation and for blood glucose and insulin concentrations to return to normal. (See Figure 10-4.) Snacks during exercise are helpful. However, they should be spaced throughout the day and each snack should compose no more than 10% of the normal daily food amount. Feeding at the end of a break will cause less blood glucose disturbance.

Progress Notes

The food was changed to a commercial specialty brand dry food that was higher in fat, energy density and digestibility (Science Diet Canine Active[a]) than the previous food. The owner reported that the dog performed well through the rest of the hunting season with no further collapsing episodes. In addition to the change in feeding plan, the dog now runs four to five miles several times weekly with the owner's daughter.

Endnote

a. Hill's Pet Nutrition, Inc., Topeka, KS, USA. This product is also marketed as Science Plan Canine Performance.

▮ CASE 10-4

Diarrhea in a Team of Sled Dogs

Arleigh J. Reynolds, DVM, PhD
Diplomate ACVN
Cornell University
Ithaca, New York, USA

Assess the Animals

A team of Alaskan husky-type dogs was examined for recurrent bouts of hemorrhagic diarrhea during exercise. The owner was a neophyte musher from upstate New York and noted that the dogs were eating well and eager to

work. However, they would defecate loose feces during and immediately after each training run. Sometimes the feces were flecked with bright red blood. At other times during the day, the feces were of normal consistency without blood. At the time they were examined, the dogs were running four 10-mile training sessions each week.

Physical examination revealed a group of bright, alert, well-hydrated dogs averaging 20 kg body weight. Muscle tone and mass were slightly greater than is usual for sedentary dogs. Their body condition score (BCS) was 2/5. Their overall condition was judged to be normal for this breed at this stage of training. The only abnormality noted on physical examination was mild brown staining of the hair on the ventral aspects of the tail and caudal aspects of both hindlimbs.

The results from fecal smears and flotation tests for parasite ova, blood and abnormal bacteria were negative. Manual rectal palpation results, hematocrit and total solids measurement were normal.

Assess the Food(s) and Feeding Method

The owner was feeding a dry commercial dog food with the following guaranteed analysis: Crude protein, not less than 26%; Crude fat, not less than 12%; Crude fiber, not more than 9%; Moisture, not more than 10%; Ash, not more than 8%. The dogs did quite well on this food during the summer and early fall training. By November, with the cold, wet climate and increased training mileage, the owner was feeding twice the volume of food he fed during the summer. Each 20-kg dog was receiving 800 g of food per day to maintain body weight. The dogs were fed half that amount in the morning (8:00 a.m.) and half in the evening (8:00 p.m.). The training runs usually occurred around noon.

Questions

1. What is the most likely cause of the diarrhea observed in these dogs?
2. What characteristics of the food and feeding method might have contributed to the diarrhea?
3. What recommendations should be made to the owner to prevent this problem from continuing?

Answers and Discussion

1. The observation that the dogs had normal feces except during and immediately after running suggests that stress or physiologic diarrhea is the most likely diagnosis. This problem is usually observed when exercise takes place while feces remain in the lower gastrointestinal tract.
2. The food is relatively low in fat and energy density for a performance ration; therefore, a large volume of food must be fed to meet the increased energy requirements associated with intense training and cold environmental temperatures. Feeding a large volume of food and feeding close to the time of exercise increases the fecal volume present during exercise. One theory is that the constant concussion between feces and colonic mucosa, termed "cecal slap," may irritate the colonic mucosa and alter colonic motility, thereby inducing diarrhea during and immediately after exercise.
3. The musher should switch to a commercial food with higher fat content and higher energy density so that a smaller volume can be fed. (See Tables 10-6 and 10-7.) For sled dogs exercising once a day, a single meal given within two hours after exercise will give maximal time for ingesta to pass completely through the gastrointestinal tract before the next exercise session.

Progress Notes

The dogs' food was changed to commercial performance ration (Eukanuba Original[a]) containing 32% protein and 20% fat (as fed). Each day, the dogs were fed approximately 500 g of the commercial food and 2 oz of a fat supplement (poultry fat, beef tallow or corn oil) within two hours postexercise. Within two weeks, the problem had resolved in all dogs and defecation during performance was nearly eliminated.

Endnote

a. The Iams Co., Dayton, OH, USA.

CHAPTER 11

Normal Cats

Claudia A. Kirk
Jacques Debraekeleer
P. Jane Armstrong

"So first, your memory I'll jog, and say: a cat is not a dog."
T.S. Eliot

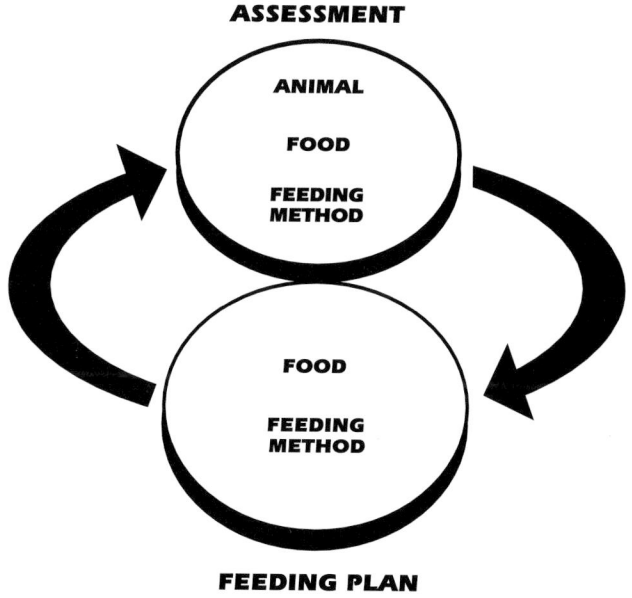

ASSESSMENT

ANIMAL

FOOD

FEEDING METHOD

FOOD

FEEDING METHOD

FEEDING PLAN

Note: The reader is referred to Chapter 1 for a detailed discussion of the iterative process of clinical nutrition.

INTRODUCTION

Cats are thought to have been domesticated between 1600 and 1500 BC. They were considered sacred by the early Egyptians and valued for their natural hunting and predatory behavior, which helped control rodent populations. Little consideration for the nutritional needs of cats was required during the early days of domestication. As domestic cats evolved from mouse catcher to household companion, the need to understand their unique nutritional requirements also increased. Today, it is well accepted that proper nutrition and care throughout life maximizes health, longevity and quality of life. Providing proper guidance about the nutritional management of cats requires an understanding of: 1) the basic principles of nutrition as discussed in Chapter 2, 2) the foods and nutrients commonly fed to cats, 3) how to assess nutrient availability and quality of various foodstuffs and foods, 4) foods and feeding practices that may negatively affect health and 5) the unique nutritional needs and feeding behavior of cats throughout the life cycle, which is the focus of this chapter.

Despite the long history of domestication, a detailed knowledge of the nutritional requirements of cats has emerged relatively recently and is still evolving.

Demographics

In 1997, cats were the most popular pets in the United States, totaling approximately 70 million, which represents a 3.1% increase in population over 1996.[1] More than one-third of the households in the United States owned

NORMAL CATS

KEY WORDS & TERMS—NORMAL CATS*

Arachidonic acid	Gestation	Neonatal period
Arginine	Glucokinase	Queen
Carnivore	Growing cats	Senior cats
Colostrum	Hexokinase	Taurine
Digestibility	Lactation	Tomcat
Eating behavior	Lifestage nutrition	Urea cycle
Feeding behavior	Mature milk	Urinary pH
Feeding method	Metabolic weight	Weaning
Geriatric cats	Metabolizable energy	

*Key words and terms are defined in the Glossary.

KEY POINTS—NORMAL CATS

1. It is well accepted that proper nutrition and care throughout life maximizes health, longevity and quality of life.
2. Cats are the most popular pets in the United States, totaling approximately 70 million.
3. Cats and other members of the superfamily *Feloidea* are strict or true carnivores.
4. Cats prefer foods offered at body temperature (38.5°C [101.5°F]) and poorly accept or reject foods served at temperature extremes.
5. Cats have very low liver glucokinase activity and, therefore, a limited ability to metabolize large amounts of simple carbohydrates.
6. Protein metabolism is unique in cats and is manifested by an unusually high maintenance requirement for protein as compared to dogs.
7. In cats, dietary taurine is essential and clinical disease results if insufficient amounts are present in food. Determination of sufficient taurine supplementation requires animal testing.
8. Unlike dogs, cats cannot synthesize arachidonic acid (20:4n6) from linoleic acid (18:2n6) and, therefore, require a dietary source of arachidonic acid. Arachidonic acid is available from animal tissues.
9. Cats typically reach adulthood between 10 to 12 months of age.
10. Neutering reduces the daily energy requirement of adult cats by 24 to 33% compared to that of intact cats.
11. Sedentary, inactive, caged and older cats often have energy requirements very near or even below the average resting energy requirement of the average young adult.
12. Cats do not fully adjust water intake to the dry matter content of the food and, therefore, have reduced total water intake when fed dry foods.
13. The potassium requirement of cats varies with the dietary protein concentration, the effect of the food on urinary pH, renal function and, possibly, with age.
14. Food ingredients and feeding methods contribute to the urinary pH produced by cats.
15. Food texture influences oral health and the palatability and acceptability of foods for cats.
16. Cats are often considered as being senior at seven to eight years of age and geriatric or very old beginning at 10 to 12 years of age.
17. Older cats frequently have clinical or subclinical renal disease that can impair their ability to compensate for altered acid-base status resulting from metabolic and dietary influences.
18. The objectives of a good feeding program for feline reproduction are to optimize: 1) the health and body condition of the queen throughout the various reproductive periods, 2) reproductive performance and 3) kitten health and development through the weaning period.
19. Continuous weight gain by the kittens is the best indicator of the queen's lactation performance. Neonatal kittens should gain, on average, between 10 to 15 g daily. Gains less than 7 g/day are inadequate.
20. Although a true carbohydrate requirement for cats has not been demonstrated, carbohydrates apparently protect against weight loss in queens during lactation, which can diminish lactation performance.
21. Most domestic shorthair kittens are weaned by six weeks of age, whereas purebred kittens are usually weaned around eight to nine weeks of age. Later weaning allows more time for kitten growth and immune system maturation, which may help reduce kitten mortality in the postweaning period.
22. Colostrum provides water, other nutrients, growth factors, digestive enzymes and maternal immunoglobulins, all of which are critical to survival of neonatal kittens.
23. Weaned kittens appear to be fairly insensitive to inverse calcium-phosphorus ratios (e.g., kittens have been fed foods with ratios as low as 0.38:1 with no deleterious effects).
24. The ultimate goal of feeding kittens is to ensure a healthy adult. The specific objectives, however, are to optimize growth, minimize risk factors for disease and achieve optimal health.
25. Treats are unnecessary but may be fed in small quantities (i.e., less than 10% of the daily intake). Milk is commonly offered to kittens as a treat. Amounts offered should be limited because intestinal lactase levels decline shortly after weaning.

cats with an average of 2.19 cats per cat-owning household. In 1996, the ratio of male to female cats was roughly equal and nearly 80% of pet cats were neutered (Table 11-1).[a] Although most cats in the United States are nonpedigreed, the Cat Fanciers Association registered 39 different breeds in 1996. The number of pedigreed cats regis-

KEY NUTRITIONAL FACTORS—NORMAL CATS

Table 11-8 lists key nutritional factors for adult cats at maintenance.

Table 11-12 lists key nutritional factors for reproducing cats (mating, gestation, lactation).

Table 11-13 lists energy requirements of pregnant queens.

Table 11-14 lists daily energy requirements of lactating queens over the lactation period.

Table 11-17 lists key nutritional factors for growing kittens.

FEEDING PLAN SUMMARY FOR NORMAL CATS

Adult cats

1. Body condition and other assessment criteria will determine the daily energy requirement (DER). DER is calculated by multiplying resting energy requirement (RER) by an appropriate factor. Remember, DER calculations should be used as guidelines, starting points and estimates for individual animals and not as absolute requirements.

   Neutered adult = 1.2 to 1.4 x RER

   Intact adult = 1.4 to 1.6 x RER

   Obese-prone adult = 1.0 x RER

   Senior adult (seven to 11 years) = 1.1 to 1.4 x RER

   Very old adult (≥12 years) = 1.1 to 1.6 x RER

2. Select a food with an appropriate energy density.

   Young to middle-aged adult = 4.0 to 5.0 kcal (17 to 21 kJ) metabolizable energy (ME)/g dry matter

   Obese-prone adult = 3.3 to 3.8 kcal (13.8 to 15.9 kJ) ME/g dry matter

   Senior adult = 3.5 to 4.5 kcal (14.6 to 18.8 kJ) ME/g dry matter

   Very old adult = 4.0 to 4.5 kcal (17 to 18.8 kJ) ME/g dry matter

3. Select a food with levels of key nutritional factors and desired urinary pH values listed in Table 11-8.

4. Determine quantity of food based on DER calculation (DER ÷ food energy density).

5. Determine preferred feeding method (Table 11-9).

6. Monitor body condition, body weight and general health.

Reproducing cats

1. Body condition and other assessment criteria will determine the DER. Remember, DER calculations should be used as guidelines, starting points and estimates for individual animals and not as absolute requirements. See Tables 11-13 and 11-14 for detailed DER information.

   Breeding male = 1.4 to 1.6 x RER

   Breeding female = 1.6 x RER

   Gestation = 1.6 to 2.0 x RER

   Lactation = 2.0 to 6.0 x RER

2. Select a food with an appropriate energy density.

   Breeding male and female = 4.5 to 5.0 kcal (18.8 to 21 kJ) ME/g dry matter

   Gestation = 4.0 to 5.0 kcal (17 to 21 kJ) ME/g dry matter

   Lactation = 4.0 to 5.0 kcal (17 to 21 kJ) ME/g dry matter

3. Select a food with levels of key nutritional factors, high digestibility and desired urinary pH values listed in Table 11-12 (gestation and lactation) or Table 11-8 (breeding males).

4. Determine quantity of food based on DER calculation (DER ÷ food energy density) or provide food free choice.

5. Determine an appropriate feeding method (Table 11-9). Free choice is the preferred method of feeding gestating/lactating queens.

6. Monitor body condition, body weight, general health, reproductive performance and kitten growth rates.

Growing cats

1. Age, body condition and other assessment criteria will determine the DER. Remember, DER calculations are only guidelines, starting points and estimates for individual animals and do not represent absolute requirements.

   Neonatal and postweaning kittens: See Table 11-16 for details about calculating DER for growing kittens

2. Select a food with an appropriate energy density.

   Postweaning to adult = 4.0 to 5.0 kcal (17 to 21 kJ) ME/g dry matter

3. Select a food with above average digestibility (>85%).

4. Select a food with levels of key nutritional factors and desired urinary pH values listed in Table 11-17. Remember urinary pH values are lower in kittens compared to those of adult cats and highly acidified foods should be avoided.

5. Determine quantity of food based on DER calculation (DER ÷ food energy density) or provide food free choice.

6. Determine preferred feeding method. In general, free-choice feeding is preferred for kittens less than five months of age (Table 11-9).

7. Monitor body condition, weight gain and general health.

Table 11-1. Age and gender distribution of cats in the United States (1996).*

Gender	Status	% of population
	Male	9.7
	Neutered male	41.2
	Female	11.7
	Spayed female	34.4
Age (years)	0-1	25.7
	1-4	27
	4-7	17.6
	7-10	12
	10-15	13.4
	15+	4.4

*Adapted from Lund EM, Armstrong PJ, Kolar L, et al. National Companion Animal Study (Preliminary results). In: Proceedings. Hill's Symposium on Geriatric Health and Nutrition, Orlando, Fl, 1996: 56.

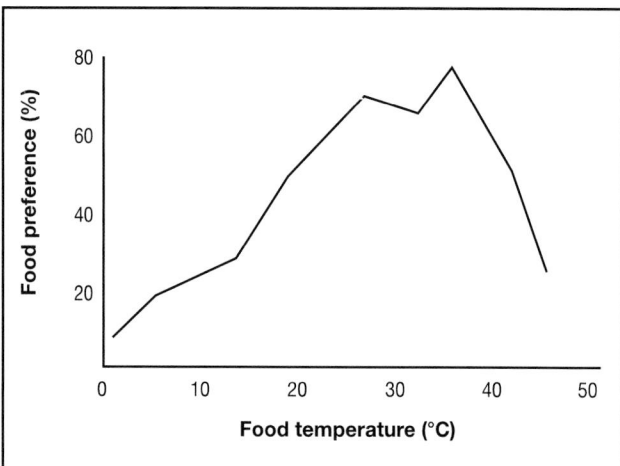

Figure 11-1. Influence of food temperature on food preference in cats (mean food preference demonstrated by 23 cats fed moist food at various temperatures vs. the same food at 20°C [68°F]). Note how preference increases for food served at body temperature but decreases when food is served at temperature extremes. (Adapted from Sohail MA. The ingestive behavior of the domestic cat–A review. Nutritional Abstracts and Reviews Series B 1983; 53: 177-186.)

tered totaled 68,948 representing a decline over previous years. The five most represented breeds were Persian, Maine coon, Siamese, Abyssinian and exotic; these five accounted for 79.1% of the pedigreed cats.[2]

Cats traditionally make up a smaller proportion of the pets seen by veterinarians, compared with dogs, but that proportion is increasing. Now, nearly 68% of cat owners regularly use veterinary services. In 1996, cats visited veterinary clinics once per year compared with 0.79 visits per year in 1987.[2] In 1996, cat owners spent nearly $4 billion toward the health and well-being of their cats. Cat food sales followed the upward trend in cat ownership and health care with almost $4.3 billion of sales in the United States in 1997.[1] The largest growth occurred in dry cat foods and treats, whereas sales of semi-moist products decreased.

The percentage of cats that are six years and older increased from 28.5 to 37.4% of the cat population during the past 10 years (Table 11-1). Cats apparently are living longer because of increased care and proper nutrition. An understanding of proper nutrition for cats begins with the fact that cats are not small dogs; cats are carnivores.

CATS AS CARNIVORES

Taxonomically, cats and dogs are members of the order Carnivora and are therefore classified as carnivores. (See Table 9-4.) However, from a dietary perspective, dogs are omnivores (See Chapter 9.) and cats and other members of the superfamily *Feloidea* are strict or true carnivores. The difference in food usage is evident from the unique anatomic, physiologic, metabolic and behavioral adaptations of cats to a strictly carnivorous diet.

Behavior

Domestic cats share several feeding behaviors with their wild counterparts. Unlike most mammals, cats do not display a regular daily rhythmicity in sleep-wake cycles, activity, feeding and drinking. Cats typically eat 10 to 20 small meals throughout the day and night.[3,4] This eating pattern probably reflects the evolutionary relationship of cats and their prey. With the exception of African lions, cats are solitary hunters. Small rodents (e.g., voles and mice) make up 40% or more of the feral domestic cat diet; however, young rabbits and hares may compose a large portion of prey.[5] A variety of other prey (e.g., birds, reptiles, frogs and insects) are also taken, but in smaller amounts. The average mouse provides approximately 30 kcal (125 kJ)[6] or an estimated 8% of a feral cat's daily energy requirement (DER). Thus, repeated cycles of hunting throughout the day and night are required to provide sufficient food for an average cat. Additionally, repeated cycles of hunting have evolved into normal feeding behavior for house cats.

The predatory drive is so strong in cats that they will stop eating to make a kill.[7] This strategy allows for multiple kills, which optimizes food availability. Unfortunately, this behavior and others may frustrate owners who confuse predatory behavior with hunger. (See sidebar "Eating Behaviors.") Many owners reason that a fed cat will not hunt and are disappointed when their housecat kills song birds. Supplemental feeding may reduce hunting time, but otherwise does not alter hunting behavior.[8]

Cats are very sensitive to the physical form, odor and taste of foods. Cats consume their prey beginning at the head. This head-first consumption is dictated by the direction of hair on the prey. Thus, oral tactile sensation is important to normal feeding behavior in cats and should be considered when feeding novel foods. Cats prefer solid, moist foods typical of flesh.[9] Cats poorly accept food with powdery, sticky and very greasy textures.[9,10]

Cats find certain flavors very attractive, which seems to reflect the nutritional characteristics of their natural foods. Cats prefer the tastes of various animal products including fat, protein hydrolysates (digests), meat extracts and certain free amino acids abundant in muscle tissue (i.e., alanine, proline, lysine and histidine). Unlike dogs and other omnivores, cats are not attracted to the taste of sugars and are averse to flavors derived from plant products (e.g., glutamic acid and medium-chain triglycerides).[4] A great deal of variation in preference is apparent in the cat population; owners often report that cats have an appetite for cantaloupe, pumpkin, bananas or celery. The flavor and texture preferences of individual cats are often influenced by early experience. Cats accustomed to a specific texture or type of food (i.e., moist, dry, semi-moist) may refuse foods

Eating Behaviors

Although there are such things as aberrant eating behaviors, many of the behaviors observed are actually normal behaviors that owners happen to find objectionable.

COPROPHAGIA

Coprophagia, or consumption of excreta, is normal behavior in queens with kittens less than 30 days of age. The queen stimulates the kittens' urogenital reflexes and elimination by grooming the kittens' perineum. Then, the queen consumes the products of elimination. This process is important as an aid to elimination in young kittens. In addition, coprophagia maintains sanitation and reduces odors in the nest box. Thus, coprophagia has important survival value in wild or feral cats by reducing factors that could attract predators to the nest site. It is very uncommon for cats to continue coprophagia after the kittens are weaned.

CANNIBALISM/INFANTICIDE

Cannibalism or infanticide is often normal behavior in male and female cats. Queens typically cannibalize aborted, dead and weak kittens. This behavior may serve to reduce the spread of disease to healthy kittens, conserve maternal resources and optimize survival of the most fit kittens and help keep the nest box clean. In addition, the queen derives nutritional benefits from consuming dead kittens. Occasionally, queens will kill an apparently healthy litter. Environmental factors that cause kittens to mimic early signs of illness (e.g., inactivity, hyperthermia or hypothermia) may trigger infanticide and cannibalism. Maternal stress, malnourishment and hormonal insufficiency may contribute to unexplained cannibalism as well. Maternal experience or parity does not appear to play a role.

Tomcats may indiscriminately kill unrelated kittens. This behavior usually occurs when a strange male enters a new territory and encounters a lactating queen and kittens. A queen rapidly returns to estrus after the loss of its kittens. Thus, infanticide optimizes a male's genetic potential, in that it now has an opportunity to sire subsequent litters. Infanticide is an uncommon behavior by resident male cats.

The health status, dietary management and husbandry practices should be reviewed in queens or catteries experiencing persistent problems with cannibalism. Males should not have access to young kittens to reduce the chance of infanticide. Although resident male cats rarely pose a problem, it is prudent to err on the side of safety.

PLANT AND GRASS EATING

Plant and grass eating is a natural behavior of cats. A variety of explanations have been advanced for grass eating. Because grass is not digested within the cat's gastrointestinal (GI) tract, it acts as a local irritant and sometimes stimulates vomiting. Thus, grass eating may serve as a purgative to eliminate hair or other indigestible material. However, many cats readily eat grass but do not vomit. Other explanations for the behavior include a response to nutritional deficiencies, boredom or a taste preference. Despite a wealth of theories, scientific support is lacking and the cause remains unknown.

RESPONSE TO CATNIP

The smell or ingestion of catnip (*Nepeta cataria*) can invoke wild behavior for five to 15 minutes after exposure. Cats may become refractory for an hour or more after cessation of the initial response. The active ingredient, cis-transnepetalactone, is thought to act as a hallucinogen although stimulation of neurologic centers associated with estrous behaviors has also been suggested. Cats may respond to catnip by head rubbing and shaking, salivating, gazing, skin twitches, rolling and animated leaping. Only 50 to 70% of cats exhibit a behavioral response, which may have a genetic basis. Prolonged exposure may lead to a chronic state of partial unawareness.

WOOL CHEWING

A commonly reported behavioral abnormality in cats is wool chewing. The behavior first appears near puberty when cats begin to lick, suck, chew or eat wool or other clothing articles. Although the cause is poorly understood, nutritional deficiencies are unlikely. Affected cats may be seeking the odor of lanolin or human sweat or the behavior may be a manifestation of prolonged nursing. Siamese, Siamese-cross and Burmese cats are primarily affected. Therefore, a strong genetic link is probable. Wool chewing is managed by limiting access to attractive items and through behavior modification. Feeding a high-fiber food or providing a continuous supply of dry food reduces fabric eating in some cats.

PROLONGED NURSING

Prolonged nursing may occur in kittens that strive to satisfy a desire for non-nutritional sucking. Non-nutritional sucking normally subsides near weaning. Kittens may develop nursing vices when they are deprived of normal nursing behavior because they were orphaned, prematurely weaned or required bottle feeding. Within the litter, kittens will often nurse tails, ears, skin folds and/or the genitalia of their littermates. After a kitten is separated from its litter, it may transfer sucking vices to people, stuffed toys, clothing or other pets.

ANOREXIA

Although a few days of inappetence is not particularly detrimental to an otherwise healthy cat, prolonged inanition results in malnutrition, reduced immune function and increased risk for hepatic lipidosis. Anorexia may be caused by stress, unacceptable foods or concurrent disease. Most commonly, cats presented to veterinarians for anorexia have a concurrent disease. Cats may endure prolonged starvation rather than eat a poorly palatable food. Therefore, advising owners that a cat will "eat when it gets hungry enough" can have deadly results.

A thorough history is useful in differentiating potential causes of anorexia. To determine if poor food acceptance is the cause, offer a small selection of highly palatable foods along with the typical food. Because improperly stored foods may develop off flavors, bacterial contamination or fungal growth, confirm that the product is fresh and wholesome. Environmental or emotional factors reported to result in stress-mediated anorexia include hospitalization, boarding, travel, introduction of new people or pets to the household, loss of a companion, overcrowding, high temperatures and excessive handling. Stress-mediated anorexia is usually diagnosed from the history and by ruling out other diseases. Providing a quiet secluded area will often allow a cat to relax sufficiently enough to begin eating. Often, increasing the food's palatability will improve food intake. Food palatability can be enhanced by warming, adding water or choosing foods high in animal protein and fat. If cats are highly stressed or appropriate feeding sites are unavailable, mild tranquilizers or appetite stimulants (e.g., diazepam, oxazepam or cyproheptadine) may be beneficial. (See Chapter 12.) Force feeding may stimulate taste receptors and appetite in some cats. Other cats find the process so stressful that any benefit is far outweighed by the additional stress.

Continued on next page.

Continued from previous page.

FIXED-FOOD PREFERENCES

The food type fed by the owner during a kitten's first six months influences the pattern of food preferences throughout life. Although uncommon, kittens exposed to a very limited number of foods may develop a food fixation, refusing to eat anything but a single food. Adult cats fed highly palatable, single-item foods have been reported to develop fixed-food preferences as well.

Cats with food fixations can be particularly troublesome if dietary modifications are necessary. Cats with strong food preferences should be transitioned to the new food over a prolonged period. Convert to the desired food by replacing 10 to 20% of the old food with an equal amount of the new food on Day 1, then gradually increase the ratio of new to old over the next 14 days. A more gradual transition may be required if food intake drops below 70% of maintenance levels. Cats should be monitored to ensure they are not selecting the preferred food from the food dish and that food intake remains adequate. Food fixations can be avoided by feeding cats a complex ration-type commercial food and not feeding single-item foods.

LEARNED TASTE AVERSIONS

Cats may develop learned aversions to certain foods when feeding is paired with a negative GI experience. The negative experience can be physical, emotional or physiologic. Typically, aversions occur when cats are fed before an episode of nausea or vomiting. Foods that were readily consumed before a negative incident will be avoided subsequently. Clinically, aversions may develop when GI upset is induced by various diseases, drugs or treatments protocols. Foods with high salience (i.e., strong odors or high protein levels) are more likely to become aversive and should not be fed within 24 hours of anticipated GI upsets. Aversions have been documented to last up to 40 days in cats. Learned aversions are considered an adaptive response. By avoiding foods that previously caused gastric distress, cats will avoid eating foods likely to be spoiled or tainted. Learned aversions have also been suggested to reduce repeated

bouts of food allergy. Although this response may occur when feeding single-food items, it does not appear to be of particular benefit to cats fed commercial foods.

POLYPHAGIA

Excessive food consumption can be mediated by various diseases, drugs and psychological stresses. Rarely, polyphagia (hyperphagia) may occur with CNS disease, particularly with lesions of the ventromedial hypothalamus. Presence of weight loss or gain is of key diagnostic importance. Polyphagia with weight loss is almost always associated with an underlying disease process or simple underfeeding. Caloric intake should always be calculated because underfeeding can result in a ravenous appetite that may be misinterpreted as abnormal. Nutritional management of polyphagia requires an accurate diagnosis because treatment is aimed at the primary disease.

BIBLIOGRAPHY

Beaver BV, ed. Feline ingestive behavior. Feline Behavior: A Guide for Veterinarians. Philadelphia, PA: WB Saunders Co, 1992.

Beaver BV. Grass eating by carnivores. Veterinary Medicine 1987; 76: 968-969.

Hart BL, Hart LA. Canine and Feline Behavioral Therapy. Philadelphia, PA: Lea & Febiger, 1985.

Hart BL, Pedersen NC. Behavior. In: Pedersen NC, ed. Feline Husbandry: Diseases and Management in the Multiple-Cat Environment. Goleta, CA: American Veterinary Publications, 1991; 289-323.

Kuo ZY. The Dynamics of Behavior, "An Epigenetic View." New York, NY: Random House, 1967.

Mugford RA. External influences on the feeding of carnivores. In: Dare MR, Maller O, eds. The Chemical Senses and Nutrition. New York, NY: Academic Press Inc, 1977; 25-50.

Nelson RW. Disorders of metabolism. In: Nelson RW, Couto CG, eds. Essentials of Small Animal Internal Medicine. St. Louis, MO: Mosby-Year Book, 1992; 611-612.

Neville PF, Bradshaw JWS. Fabric eating in cats. Veterinary Practice Staff 1994; 6: 26-29.

Rozin P, Kalat JW. Specific hungers and poison avoidance as adaptive specializations of learning. Psychological Reviews 1971; 78: 459-486.

with different texture. This becomes an important consideration when feeding cats novel diets.

Despite the cat's reputation as a finicky eater, many cats will choose a new food over a currently fed food. Thus, cats are considered to be neophilic. The reverse is true in new or stressful situations in which cats tend to refuse novel foods (i.e., neophobic). These features of cat feeding behavior should be considered when feeding hospitalized cats, but are often overlooked as a cause of food refusal.

Even the feeding behaviors of cats in the wild reflect their preference for animal tissues. When ingesting prey, wild cats avoid consuming plant materials contained in the entrails. African lions have been observed to first empty the ingesta from the entrails by expressing the contents with their tongue.[11] This behavior contrasts with that of a pack of wild dogs or wolves eating similar game. Wolves often first consume the viscera of prey.[12] Herbivores are common prey; therefore, the gastrointestinal (GI) contents are generally of plant origin. Thus, a certain amount of plant material is included in the diet of animals ingesting entrails.

Food temperature also influences food acceptance by cats (Figure 11-1). Cats do not readily accept food served at temperature extremes, whereas foods offered near body

temperature (38.5°C [101.5°F]) are most preferred. This preference is logical considering that in the wild a cat's diet is freshly killed prey, having near normal body temperature at the time of consumption.

Anatomy and Physiology

Sensory Structures

Cat eyes are well adapted to hunting. Their visual acuity is greater than that of dogs because of their larger optic cortex. A cat's ears are upright, face forward and have 20 associated muscles to provide the fine control needed to precisely locate sound. Cats also respond to high-pitched sounds, which represent the range of sound frequencies emitted by typical prey.[13] Finally, the highly sensitive facial whiskers and tactile hairs are thought to help cats hunt in dim light and to protect their eyes.

Limbs

The retractable claws of cats are a unique adaptation to hunting. The sharp tips of the claws with their hook-like curve and needle features are ideal for capturing and

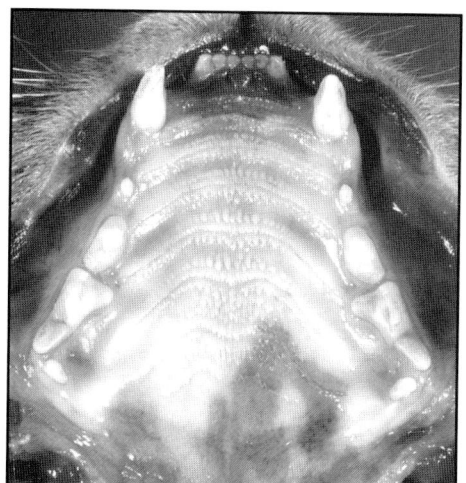 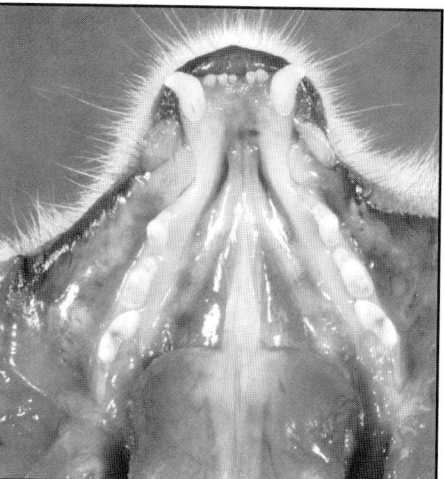

Figure 11-2. Maxillary dentition and hard palate of a cat (Left). Mandibular dentition and sublingual mucosa of the same cat (Right). These photographs demonstrate tooth anatomy associated with a carnivorous eating behavior. The canine teeth are slightly curved and taper to a pointed tip suitable for grasping and puncturing prey. The premolar and molar teeth are conical and sharply pointed, making them suitable for shearing and tearing flesh. There are no grinding (flat, table) surfaces present. (Adapted with permission from Harvey CE, Emily PP, eds. Function, formation, and anatomy of oral structures in carnivores. In: Small Animal Dentistry. St. Louis, MO: Mosby-Year Book, 1993.)

securing prey, yet they are easily retracted so they do not make noise when cats stalk prey. In contrast, the claws of dogs play only a secondary role in capturing prey.

Oral Cavity

Cats and dogs have the same number of incisor, prominent canine and carnassial teeth (i.e., the enlarged upper premolar and lower molar teeth specialized for shearing flesh). However, cats have fewer premolar and molar teeth, and they do not possess fissured crowns, which are a hallmark of omnivorous animals (Figure 11-2). The jaws of cats have limited lateromedial and craniocaudal movement, thereby limiting grinding ability. The scissors-like action of the carnassial teeth is ideal for delivering the cervical bite used to transect the spinal cord and immobilize or kill prey.

Cats lack salivary amylase used to initiate digestion of dietary starches. This adaptation reflects the nutritional composition of the typical prey (i.e., small starch content).

Stomach

Because cats in the wild evolved to eat small frequent meals, the stomach is less important as a storage reservoir compared with the stomach of dogs. Thus, the stomach of domestic cats is simpler than that of dogs (i.e., relatively smaller with a smaller glandular fundus).

Small and Large Intestine

Intestinal length, as determined by the ratio of intestine to body length, is markedly shorter in cats than in omnivores and herbivores (Table 11-2). To some extent, a greater villus height improves the absorptive surface area. Overall, the absorptive capacity is estimated to be 10% less than that of dogs.[14,15] Therefore, dogs can more efficiently use a variety of foods, some of which may require more digestion than animal tissues.

The sugar transport system of the small intestines of cats is not adaptive to varying levels of dietary carbohydrate.[16] Cats do not waste energy or protein by turning over carriers or enzyme systems of little value because free sugars and complex carbohydrates would normally make up a negligible percentage of their food (Table 11-3). This lack of adaptability has been noted in other strict carnivores, such as rap-

Table 11-2. Comparison of small intestinal length to body length in selected species.

Species	Ratio
Cat	4:1
Dog	6:1
Rabbit	10:1
Pig	14:1

Table 11-3. Comparison between AAFCO nutrient allowances for adult feline maintenance and selected nutrients in raw meat (beef) and rat carcasses.

Nutrients*	AAFCO allowance**	Raw beef***	Rat carcass†
Moisture (%)	–	60	63.6
Protein (%)	26	42.5	55
Fat (%)	9	50	38.1
Linoleic acid (%)	0.5	–	9.1
Carbohydrate (%)	–	–	1.2
Fiber (%)	–	–	0.55
Ash (%)	–	–	5.22
Calculated ME (kcal/g)	–	3.4	5.7
Calcium (%)	0.6	0.03	1.15
Phosphorus (%)	0.5	0.5	0.98
Potassium (%)	0.6	0.81	0.79
Magnesium (%)	0.04	0.06	0.08
Sodium (%)	0.2	0.18	0.25
Zinc (mg/kg)	75	37.5	71.4
Copper (mg/kg)	5	1.25	12.4
Iron (mg/kg)	80	81.2	288
Vitamin A (IU/kg)	5,000	–	84,800
Vitamin E (IU/kg)	30	–	33
Thiamin (mg/kg)	5	–	5.8
Riboflavin (mg/kg)	4	–	10.7
Niacin (mg/kg)	60	–	156.6
Folic acid (mg/kg)	0.8	–	2.8
Pantothenic acid (mg/kg)	5.0	–	54.9
Pyridoxine (mg/kg)	4.0	–	5.2
Vitamin B_{12} (µg/kg)	20	–	22.5
Choline (mg/kg)	2,400	–	3,242
Taurine (ppm) (canned)	2,000	–	–
Taurine (ppm) (extruded)	1,000	–	–

Key: ME = metabolizable energy. To convert from kcal to kJ multiply kcal by 4.184.
*All nutrients expressed on a dry matter basis except moisture.
**Association of American Feed Control Officials, Official Publication, 1998.
***Adapted from Watt BK, Merrill AL. Composition of Foods: Raw, Processed, Prepared. Agriculture Handbook No. 8. Washington, DC: Agricultural Research Service, USDA, 1975.
†Fresh entire rat carcasses. Adapted from Vondruska JF. The effect of a rat carcass diet on the urinary pH of the cat. Companion Animal Practice 1987; 1 (August): 5-9.

Carbohydrate Usage by Strict Carnivores

Cats have evolved to a carnivorous diet that is high in protein and low in carbohydrates. Several adaptations are evident when comparing carbohydrate metabolism of this strict carnivore with that of more omnivorous species.

GLUCOKINASE

The feline liver has several unique features that are evident in energy metabolism. In omnivores, both hexokinase and glucokinase are responsible for phosphorylation of glucose to glucose-6-phosphate in the pathway of glucose oxidation. The glucokinase system operates only when the liver receives a large load of glucose from the portal vein, whereas hexokinase is active even at very low concentrations of glucose. Thus, it should be no surprise that cats have minimal liver glucokinase activity. Low glucokinase activity, though practical in a species consuming little carbohydrate, limits the cat's ability to metabolize large glucose loads.

FRUCTOKINASE

Feline liver apparently lacks fructokinase. This finding is compatible with the observations by Kienzle that cats consuming high-sucrose diets (>25%) have significant fructosuria. The fact that cats, unlike many mammals, have no taste preference for sucrose further supports evolution to a diet devoid of simple carbohydrates.

GLUCONEOGENESIS

Because cats naturally eat high-protein, low-carbohydrate foods, continuous activity of amino acid catabolic enzymes provides a continuous source of carbon skeletons for glucose or energy production and nitrogen for synthesis of dispensable amino acids and other nitrogenous compounds. This constant degradation of amino acids results in continuous shuttling of amino acids through either gluconeogenic enzymes or energy-producing pathways such as the tricarboxylic acid (TCA) cycle. Gluconeogenic enzymes convert glucogenic amino acids, lactic acid, propionic acid and glycerol to glucose and, thereby, sustain blood glucose concentration. However, continuous protein catabolism limits the cat's ability to conserve protein, leading to an obligate nitrogen loss and a higher dietary protein requirement than omnivores.

Because cats have adapted to diets low in carbohydrate, gluconeogenesis is maximal during food absorption compared with the postabsorptive phase in omnivores. Dietary amino acids are potent secretogogues of insulin in cats; consequently, gluconeogenic activity is important in maintaining blood glucose levels in the face of high insulin concentrations and low intakes of dietary carbohydrate. After energy, amino acid, nitrogen and glucose needs have been met, surplus protein (in the form of amino acids) is metabolized for energy or stored as fat. In view of the limited capacity to store protein within the body, this is an important means of energy conservation during protein surplus.

INTESTINAL ADAPTATION

Within the intestine, several physiologic mechanisms responsible for digestion and uptake of starches and sugars have adapted to low carbohydrate intake by cats. Amylase, which initiates starch and sugar digestion in the oral cavity, is missing from cat saliva. Intestinal amylase appears to be derived exclusively from the pancreas and adapts minimally to changing dietary carbohydrate intakes. Pancreatic amylase levels in cats are only 5% of those found in dogs, and levels within the feline intestine are approximately 10% of canine values. The sugar transporter in the feline intestine is also nonadaptive to changes in dietary carbohydrate levels, unlike that of omnivores. Additionally, disaccharidase activity (i.e., the brush border enzymes responsible for sugar digestion) is nonadaptive and only 40% of the activity in dogs. This lack of adaptability is evolutionary sensible. Cats neither waste energy nor nitrogen by turning over enzyme systems of little value because free sugars and carbohydrates make up a negligible percentage of the wild-type diet (Table 11-3). Other carnivorous species besides cats (e.g., trout) also lack adaptability; however, omnivores are highly adaptable.

These findings do not, however, imply cats cannot use dietary carbohydrates. Despite apparent disadvantages in carbohydrate metabolism, cats efficiently use carbohydrates (similar to how swine use this nutrient). Sugar digestibility is generally greater than 94% with a few exceptions. Lactose digestion declines precipitously in most kittens after seven weeks of age. This is due to the decline in intestinal lactase activity that occurs in most mammals. Most adult cats can consume lactose at about 1.3 g/kg body weight/day without deleterious effects (i.e., diarrhea, gas, bloating, etc.) although certain individuals have greater tolerance. Nursing kittens rely on lactose for about 20% of their daily energy needs. Starch intakes up to 4 g/kg body weight/day (approximately 20% of the energy intake) have been suggested as an upper limit for adult cats. Nevertheless, dry foods containing 40% or more dietary carbohydrates with an average digestibility of 85% are well tolerated by cats. Although no requirement for dietary carbohydrates has been demonstrated for adult cats, carbohydrates are a good source of energy and appear necessary for adequate lactation in queens.

BIBLIOGRAPHY

Ballard FJ. Glucose utilization in the mammalian liver. Comparative Biochemistry and Physiology 1965; 14: 437-443.

Buddington RK, Diamond J. Ontogenetic development of nutrient transporters in cat intestine. American Journal of Physiology 1992; 263: G605-G616.

Curry DL, Morris JG, Rogers QR, et al. Dynamics of insulin and glucagon secretion by the isolated perfused cat pancreas. Comparative Biochemistry and Physiology. Part A 1982; 72: 333-338.

Kendall PT, Holme DW, Smith PM. Comparative evaluation of net digestive and absorptive efficiency in dogs and cats fed a variety of contrasting diet types. Journal of Small Animal Practice 1982; 23: 577-587.

Kienzle E. Blood sugar levels and renal sugar excretion after the intake of high carbohydrate diets in cats. Journal of Nutrition 1994; 124: 2563S-2567S.

Kienzle E. Carbohydrate metabolism of the cat 1. Activity of amylase in the gastrointestinal tract of the cat. Journal of Animal Physiology and Animal Nutrition 1993; 69: 92-101.

Kienzle E. Carbohydrate metabolism of the cat 2. Digestion of starch. Journal of Animal Physiology and Animal Nutrition 1993; 69: 102-114.

Kienzle E. Carbohydrate metabolism of the cat 3. Digestion of sugars. Journal of Animal Physiology and Animal Nutrition 1993; 69: 203-210.

Kienzle E. Carbohydrate metabolism of the cat 4. Activity of maltase, isomaltase, sucrase and lactase in the gastrointestinal tract in relation to age and diet. Journal of Animal Physiology and Animal Nutrition 1993; 70: 89-96.

MacDonald ML, Rogers QR, Morris JG. Nutrition of the domestic cat, a mammalian carnivore. Annual Review of Nutrition 1984; 4: 521-562.

McGeachin RL, Akin JR. Amylase levels in the tissues and body fluids of the domestic cat (*Felis catus*). Comparative Biochemistry and Physiology 1979; 63B: 437-439.

Morris JG, Rogers QR. Metabolic basis for some of the nutritional peculiarities of the cat. Journal of Small Animal Practice 1982; 23: 599-613.

Morris JG, Trudell J, Pencovic T. Carbohydrate digestion by the domestic cat (*Felis catus*). British Journal of Nutrition 1977; 37: 365-373.

National Research Council. Nutrient Requirements of Cats. Washington, DC: National Academy Press, 1986.

Piechota TR, Rogers QR, Morris JG. Nitrogen requirements of cats during gestation and lactation. Nutrition Research 1995; 15: 1535-1546.

tors and coldwater fish. (See sidebar "Carbohydrate Usage by Strict Carnivores.") In contrast, sugar transport systems are highly adaptive in omnivores. Also, cats have low activities of intestinal disaccharidases (i.e., sucrase, maltase and isomaltase).[17] This reflects adaptation to a food limited in simple sugars and carbohydrates. In cats, pancreatic amylase production is about 5% of that in dogs.[18,19] Pancreatic enzyme production is relatively nonadaptive in cats, as would be expected in a species unaccustomed to significant changes in dietary carbohydrate levels.

Certain amino acid transporters in the small intestines of cats are highly adaptable, particularly the transporter responsible for arginine uptake. This finding underscores the importance of the amount of protein and the specific amino acids in foods for cats. Unlike omnivores, cats are unable to synthesize significant quantities of ornithine or citrulline within the intestine. Both are precursors to arginine synthesis. This inability results in the absolute requirement for arginine in foods for cats, which is discussed below.

Cats have a vestigial cecum and short colon. These anatomic features limit the cat's capability to use poorly digestible starches and fiber by microbial fermentation in the large bowel.[15]

Nutrient Requirements and Metabolism

The evolution of cats as strict carnivores has resulted in notable nutritional and metabolic adaptations. Although these adaptations have resulted in nutritional requirements peculiar to cats, the basic physiologic and metabolic systems are relatively similar among all mammals. Nevertheless, adaptations to foods composed strictly of animal tissues obligates cats to be "meat eaters."

Energy Metabolism

The liver of most animals has two active enzyme systems for converting glucose to glucose-6-phosphate: hexokinase and glucokinase. This conversion is necessary before glucose can be used by the liver. The glucokinase system operates only when the liver receives a large amount of glucose from the portal vein. Because the natural diet of cats is primarily animal not plant tissue, it contains only small amounts of soluble carbohydrate. Therefore, when cats consume natural diets, the portal system delivers very little absorbed glucose to the liver. Thus, cats have very low liver glucokinase activity and a limited ability to metabolize large amounts of simple carbohydrates. Omnivores (e.g., people, dogs and rats) have higher hepatic glucokinase activity.[4] (See sidebar "Carbohydrate Usage by Strict Carnivores.")

Kittens naturally ingest soluble carbohydrates (i.e., lactose or milk sugar) before weaning; however, as adults they must rely primarily on gluconeogenesis from glucogenic amino acids (ketoacids), lactic acid and glycerol for maintenance of blood glucose concentration. In omnivores, maximal gluconeogenesis occurs in the postabsorptive state when the direct contribution of dietary glucose is absent. In cats, gluconeogenesis is maximal in the absorptive phase immediately after a meal.

Table 11-4. Comparison of dietary protein requirements during maintenance and growth in selected mammals.

Classifications	Species	Growth (%)*	Maintenance (%)*	G:M ratio**
Omnivore***	Dog	12	4	3
Omnivore***	Rat	12	4.2	2.9
Carnivore†	Cat	24	14	1.7
Carnivore***	Cat	29	19	1.5
Carnivore†	Mink	31	20	1.6
Carnivore†	Fox	24	16	1.5

*Percent of diet (dry matter basis).
**G:M ratio = ratio of growth to maintenance requirements.
***Ideal protein (i.e., meets all known essential amino acid requirements).
Adapted from MacDonald ML, Rogers QR, Morris JG. Nutrition of the domestic cat, a mammalian carnivore. Annual Review in Nutrition 1984; 4: 521-562.
†NRC requirements. Adapted from National Research Council. Nutrient Requirements of Cats. Washington, DC: National Academy Press, 1986.

Table 11-5. Comparison of minimal protein and amino acid requirements for growth in kittens and puppies.*

Nutrients	Kittens		Puppies	
	g/100 kcal	% DM**	g/100 kcal	% DM**
Crude protein	5.1	24	4.5	21
EAA	1.5	7.0	1.5	7.0
Amino acids				
Arginine***	0.21	1.0	0.16	0.8
Histidine	0.06	0.3	0.05	0.26
Isoleucine	0.13	0.6	0.12	0.55
Leucine	0.26	1.2	0.20	96
Lysine	0.17	0.8	0.20	1.0
Methionine (met + cys)	0.08 (1.6)	0.4 (0.75)	0.09 (0.15)	0.41 (0.72)
Phenylalanine (phe + tyr)	0.11 (0.21)	0.5 (1.0)	0.13 (0.26)	0.6 (1.2)
Threonine	0.15	0.7	0.14	0.64
Tryptophan	0.03	0.15	0.04	0.19
Valine	0.13	0.6	0.15	0.69
Taurine† (extruded)	0.02	0.1	–	–
Taurine† (canned)	0.04	0.2	–	–

Key: EAA = essential amino acids.
*Adapted from Rogers QR, Morris JG. Optimizing protein and amino acid nutrition for cats and dogs. In: Proceedings. Roche Technical Symposium and 1997 Petfood Institute Conference and Trade Show, Chicago, IL: 19-32.
**Based on a dietary energy content of 4.7 kcal/g dry matter.
***Arginine requirement increases in kittens with increased dietary protein; approximately 2 g/kg (9.2%) should be added for each 10% increase in crude protein above the minimum allowance (24%).
†From AAFCO recommended allowances in commercial foods.

Urea Cycle Adaptation

Urea cycle enzymes are nonadaptive in cats, whereas in omnivores (e.g., dogs) the activity of these enzymes changes in response to changing dietary protein levels. Although this lack of adaptation results in reduced nitrogen conservation in cats, it allows for highly efficient detoxification of nitrogenous wastes from protein catabolism. After a period of fasting or reduced protein intake, omnivores, unlike cats, require a period of dietary adaptation to accommodate a high nitrogen load. This lack of urea cycle enzyme adaptability in cats does not mean the cycle is unregulated in this species. During fasting or reduced protein intake, urea cycle intermediates become depleted and the cycle slows. As intermediates are replenished with a protein meal, the cycle continues at an efficient rate.

The urea cycle provides a "clean-up function" during protein metabolism; that is, it disposes of nitrogen wastes via urea synthesis. Omnivores and herbivores are able to increase or decrease urea enzyme activity in response to dietary nitrogen levels, thereby avoiding elevations in blood ammonia and conserving nitrogen as needed. Urea cycle enzymes in the liver of cats are nonadaptive and always "turned on." One key control mechanism of urea cycle activity in cats is the mediation of urea synthesis by the availability of the cycle intermediate ornithine (arginine is the dietary source). When ornithine levels decline, the cycle slows. After cats consume a protein-containing meal, cycle intermediates are replenished and urea synthesis immediately resumes. This type of regulation provides an immediate response to ingested proteins. Sudden increases in the nitrogen load in animals that rely on enzyme adaptation

for regulation may overwhelm the urea cycle resulting in hyperammonemia. Though cats are somewhat protected from this effect, they can develop hyperammonemia if fed arginine-deficient foods. (See Arginine requirements.)

Ultimately, the above metabolic peculiarities impair the cat's ability to conserve nitrogen when dietary protein is limited. Because of the reliably high intake of dietary protein from the natural diet, there was little evolutionary drive toward adaptive metabolic enzyme systems. This shift to constitutive enzyme activity conserves energy by eliminating the cost of enzyme synthesis and degradation. In the natural state, cats realize an advantage from these metabolic differences.

BIBLIOGRAPHY

Costello MJ, Morris JG, Rogers QR. Effect of dietary arginine level on urinary orotate and citrate excretion in growing kittens. Journal of Nutrition 1980; 110: 1204-1208.

Devlin TM, ed. Amino acid metabolism 1: General pathways. In: Textbook of Biochemistry with Clinical Correlations, 2nd ed. New York, NY: John Wiley & Sons, 1986; 443-451.

Morris JG, Rogers QR. Arginine: An essential amino acid for the cat. Journal of Nutrition 1978; 108: 1944-1953.

Morris JG, Rogers QR. Metabolic basis for some of the nutritional peculiarities of the cat. Journal of Small Animal Practice 1982; 23: 599-613.

Rogers QR, Morris JG, Freedland RA. Lack of hepatic enzyme adaptation to low and high levels of dietary protein in the adult cat. Enzyme 1977; 22: 348-356.

Protein Metabolism

Protein metabolism is unique in cats and is manifested by an unusually high maintenance requirement for protein as compared with canine requirements (Table 11-4). The protein requirement for growth in kittens is only 50% higher than that of puppies, whereas the protein requirement for feline maintenance is twice that of adult dogs. The higher protein requirement of cats is not due to an exceptionally high requirement for any specific amino acid (Table 11-5); instead, it is caused by a high activity of hepatic enzymes (i.e., transaminases and deaminases) that remove amino groups from amino acids so the resulting ketoacids can be used for energy or glucose production, as discussed above. Unlike omnivores (e.g., dogs) and herbivores, cats cannot decrease the activity of these enzymes when fed low-protein foods. The cat's strict adherence to a diet of animal tissue likely resulted in a lack of evolutionary pressure to accommodate lower protein diets. As a result, hepatic enzyme systems are constantly active; therefore, a fixed amount of dietary protein is always catabolized for energy.[4] The gluconeogenic enzymes in the liver of cats appear to be continuously active, unlike the situation in most other species, including dogs.[4] In addition, an alternate hepatic gluconeogenic pathway common in flesh-eating animals is active in cats.[20] This pathway uses serine as a glucose precursor. Serine is a nonessential amino acid found in large amounts in muscle, milk and egg. Cats also have a special need for four amino acids: arginine, taurine and methionine and cystine.

ARGININE

Arginine deficiency in cats causes one of the most dramatic responses of any nutrient deficiency. (See sidebar "Urea Cycle Adaptation.") Feeding foods devoid of arginine may result in hyperammonemia in less than one hour. Affected cats exhibit severe signs of ammonia toxicity and may die within two to five hours.[4] As mentioned above, cats cannot synthesize sufficient ornithine or citrulline for conversion to arginine, which is needed for the urea cycle. After a cat eats an arginine-deficient meal, the highly active protein catabolic enzymes in its liver produce ammonia. Without arginine, the urea cycle cannot convert ammonia to urea and ammonia toxicity occurs.[4] Because the natural diet of cats consists of animal tissue high in protein (including arginine), cats have apparently lost a flexibility in protein metabolism seen in other animal species (e.g., dogs) that eat foods with a more varied protein content. However, arginine deficiency is rare and has only been reported to occur in cats fed experimental foods specifically formulated to be arginine deficient or certain casein-based enteral products.[21]

TAURINE

Taurine is a β-amino sulfonic acid, abundant in the natural food of cats. In cats, dietary taurine is essential and clinical disease results if insufficient amounts are present. Many species can use glycine or taurine to conjugate bile acids into bile salts before they are secreted into bile. Cats can only conjugate bile acids with taurine. The loss of taurine in bile coupled with a low rate of taurine synthesis contributes to the obligatory taurine requirement of cats. (See sidebar "Taurine.")

Taurine

As a β-amino acid, taurine is neither incorporated into proteins nor degraded by mammalian tissues. However, taurine has important functions in virtually all body systems. In addition to its importance in normal bile salt function, taurine is essential for normal retinal, cardiac, neurologic, reproductive, immune and platelet function. Taurine is needed for normal fetal development and may function as an antioxidant, osmolyte and neuromodulator. Most animal tissues, particularly muscle, viscera and brain, contain high levels of taurine; plants contain none. Taurine is essential in foods for cats because of two factors.

- The feline liver has a limited capacity to synthesize taurine. The rate-limiting enzymes responsible for conversion of methionine and cysteine to taurine (i.e., cysteine dioxygenase and cysteine sulfinic acid decarboxylase) are minimally active.
- Cats have an obligate loss of taurine via the enterohepatic circulation of bile acids. Taurine is important in the conjugation and secretion of bile acids. Many animals conserve taurine by switching to glycine conjugation when dietary taurine becomes scarce. Feline hepatic enzymes do not use glycine, but conjugate bile acids mostly to taurine. Most bile salts secreted into the intestinal lumen are returned to the liver after intestinal uptake. However, once deconjugated, taurine is available for intestinal uptake, fecal excretion or degradation by intestinal microbes. Microbial degradation appears to account for deconjugation and substantial wasting of free taurine. This process also results in an obligate taurine loss.

The requirement for taurine is influenced by dietary factors and the metabolic needs of the cat. The protein source, commercial processing, sulfur-containing amino acid content and dietary fiber levels alter taurine requirements. In general, taurine is abundant in animal tissues and absent in plants; thus, homemade vegetarian diets and cereal-based dog foods have long been known to cause taurine deficiency when fed to cats. However, in 1987, taurine deficiency was reported to occur in cats fed commercial foods containing the National Research Council recommended levels of taurine (400 mg taurine/kg food). This finding underscored the food-dependent nature of the taurine requirement and prompted an increase in taurine recommendations by AAFCO to 1,000 mg/kg and 2,000 mg/kg (ppm) food in commercial dry and moist foods, respectively. However, taurine levels of 2,500 ppm are often recommended for moist products. Taurine adequacy is best established through feeding trials.

Because taurine functions throughout the body, signs of deficiency have been demonstrated in virtually all body systems. Three syndromes of taurine deficiency in cats have been well established: 1) feline central retinal degeneration (FCRD), 2) reproductive failure and impaired fetal development and 3) feline dilated cardiomyopathy (DCM). Hearing loss, platelet hyperaggregation and impaired immune function have also been demonstrated although specific clinical disorders have not been recognized.

CLINICAL SIGNS

Clinical signs of taurine deficiency occur only after prolonged periods of depletion (i.e., five months to two years). Typically in non-reproducing adults, taurine deficiency may manifest as FCRD, DCM or both, with only about 40% of taurine-deficient cats exhibiting clinical signs.[a,b]

Clinical signs of FCRD are inapparent until significant visual impairment has occurred. Then, owners may notice their cat bumping into objects or "miscalculating" jumps. Early disease may be detected during ophthalmic examination. Changes in retinal function can be demonstrated by electroretinograms before retinal lesions appear. The development of FCRD apparently requires three or more months of taurine depletion. Initially, lesions appear as dark granular focal defects in the area centralis, slightly temporal to the optic disk. As degeneration progresses, the lesion becomes hyperreflective and extends in a band across the tapetum. Complete blindness ensues with full degeneration of the retina and attenuation of retinal vessels. Structural changes within the retina are permanent. Therefore, a diagnosis of FCRD does not reflect the current taurine status of a cat, but indicates a period of prolonged taurine deficiency has occurred.

Cats with DCM may be clinically normal or present acutely with signs of heart failure. Clinical signs may include lethargy, anorexia and dyspnea. Physical findings may include pleural effusion, pulmonary edema, gallop heart rhythms, systolic murmurs and ventricular dysrhythmias. Cats in severe heart failure are hypothermic, have pale mucous membranes, poor pulse quality and are often too weak to stand. Only about one-third of cats with DCM have concurrent FCRD. DCM is confirmed by echocardiography. Findings most often include dilatation of the left atrium and ventricle and decreased left ventricle contractility.

REPRODUCTION AND FETAL DEVELOPMENT

Reproduction and fetal development are severely impaired in taurine-deficient queens. Conception and implantation appear normal; however, fetal death is frequently observed near 25 days of gestation, followed by abortion or resorption. In a group of taurine-deficient queens, only 38% of 33 matings resulted in term deliveries, with an average of 2.1 live births.

Developmental abnormalities reported to occur in kittens born to taurine-deficient queens include poor survival, cerebellar dysgenesis, abnormal hind-limb development and thoracic kyphosis, which appears as a dorsoventral flattening of the thoracic cavity. Severe hydrocephalus and anencephaly may be present in aborted fetuses. Surviving kittens are often small and weak. Growth is depressed up to 40% in the immediate postnatal period.

DIAGNOSIS

The diagnosis of taurine deficiency is based on clinical signs and low plasma and whole blood taurine concentrations. Care must be used when evaluating plasma taurine concentrations because levels may be altered by sample handling errors and feeding. Fasting may reduce plasma taurine concentrations, whereas poor handling may allow taurine contamination from platelets and white blood cells. Although plasma taurine concentrations reflect the labile taurine pool, whole blood taurine concentrations better reflect tissue taurine status. Normal plasma taurine levels in cats may vary up to fivefold (50 to 250 ηmol/ml). Plasma taurine values less than 40 ηmol/ml may suggest taurine deficiency. Cats with clinical signs of deficiency typically have plasma taurine values less than 10 ηmol/ml. Therefore, taurine deficiency is best evaluated using whole blood taurine concentrations. Whole blood taurine levels are normally greater than 300 ηmol/ml, and values less than 160 ηmol/ml are considered deficient, whereas values less than 50 ηmol/ml are common. Samples should be collected and submitted according to protocols recommended by the individual clinical laboratory. Care should be used when collecting blood and plasma for taurine analysis. Falsely elevated plasma taurine levels may result from even small amounts of clotting, hemolysis or inclusion of platelets and white cells in the plasma sample.

PATHOPHYSIOLOGY

A central uniform mechanism of taurine action has not been determined, and may not exist. FCRD represents a dis-

Continued on next page.

Continued from previous page.

ruption and loss of the photoreceptor outer segment. Within the retina, taurine may stabilize cell membranes, possibly acting as an antioxidant. In DCM, taurine is thought to regulate myocardial calcium flux through ionic channels, thereby regulating myocardial contractility and/or mitochondrial energy production. Taurine may act as a neuromodulator or neurotransmitter in fetal development. Finally, taurine appears to influence reproduction at the level of the uterus and placenta by unknown mechanisms.

TREATMENT

Cats with taurine deficiency should be supplemented with 250 to 500 mg of taurine twice daily to rapidly replete tissue stores. Cats with DCM may show clinical improvement within one to three weeks, whereas FCRD and developmental defects are irreversible.

PREVENTION

The taurine requirement of cats depends on diet composition. Poor-quality protein, Maillard reaction products or other factors that enhance bacterial overgrowth in the intestinal tract may increase the requirement two- to sixfold. Cats require approximately 50 mg of available taurine per day, which can be supplied by high-quality animal tissues or as a crystalline amino acid supplement. Commercial foods are typically supplemented with taurine in addition to the taurine provided naturally by the ingredients. Animal feeding trials are essential to ensure dietary taurine adequacy.

ENDNOTES

a. Pion PD. University of California, Davis, USA. Personal communication. 1994.
b. Rogers QR. University of California, Davis, USA. Personal communication. 1990.

BIBLIOGRAPHY

Backus RC, Morris JG, Kim SW, et al. Dietary taurine needs of cats vary with dietary protein quality and concentration. Veterinary Clinical Nutrition 1998; 5: 18-22.

Dieter JA, Stewart DR, Haggart MA, et al. Pregnancy failure in cats associated with long-term dietary taurine insufficiency. Journal of Reproduction and Fertility 1993; 47 (Suppl.): 457-463.

Hayes KC, Carey RE, Schmidt SY. Retinal degeneration associated with taurine deficiency in the cat. Science 1975; 188: 949-951.

Hayes KC, Trautwein EA. Taurine deficiency syndrome in cats. Veterinary Clinics of North America: Small Animal Practice 1989; 19: 403-413.

Huxtable RJ. Physiological actions of taurine. Physiological Reviews 1992; 72: 101-163.

Kirk CA, Rogers QR, Morris JG. Relationship of dietary taurine to reproductive efficiency in the queen. International Symposium on Amino Acids, Vienna, Austria, August 1995.

Morris JG, Rogers QR, Pacioretty LM. Taurine: An essential nutrient for cats. Journal of Small Animal Practice 1990; 31: 502-509.

Morris JG, Rogers QR. The metabolic basis for the taurine requirement of cats. Advances in Experimental Medicine and Biology 1992; 315: 33-44.

National Research Council. Nutrient Requirements of Cats. Washington, DC: National Academy Press, 1986.

Pion PD, Kittleson MD, Rogers QR, et al. Myocardial failure in cats associated with low plasma taurine: A reversible cardiomyopathy. Science 1987; 237: 764-768.

Sisson DD, Thomas WP. Myocardial diseases. In: Ettinger SJ, Feldman EC, eds. Textbook of Veterinary Internal Medicine, 4th ed. Philadelphia, PA: WB Saunders Co, 1995; 1014-1016.

Sturman JA. Dietary taurine and feline reproduction and development. Journal of Nutrition 1991; 121: S166-S170.

Sturman JA, Gargano AD, Messing JM, et al. Feline maternal taurine deficiency: Effect on mother and offspring. Journal of Nutrition 1986; 116: 655-657.

Felinine

Felinine is a branched-chain, sulfur-containing amino acid synthesized from cystine. Felinine levels are high in the urine of adult male cats but lower in female cats and kittens. The metabolism and function of felinine is largely unknown but the amino acid is possibly used for territorial marking. Felinine is excreted in the urine and may account for up to 20% of the sulfur amino acid requirement supplied by cystine.

BIBLIOGRAPHY

Hendriks WH, Moughan PJ, Tarttelin MF, et al. Felinine: A urinary amino acid of *Felidae*. Comparative Biochemistry and Physiology. Part B, Biochemistry and Molecular Biology 1995; 112: 581-588.

Hendriks WH, Tarttelin MF, Moughan PJ. Twenty-four hour felinine (corrected) excretion patterns in entire and castrated cats. Physiology and Behavior 1995; 58: 467-469.

MacDonald ML, Rogers QR, Morris JG. Nutrition of the domestic cat, a mammalian carnivore. Annual Review of Nutrition 1984; 4: 521-562.

Tarttelin MF, Hendriks WH, Moughan PJ. Relationship between plasma testosterone and urinary felinine in the growing kitten. Physiology and Behavior 1998; 65: 83-87.

METHIONINE AND CYSTINE

The sulfur-containing amino acids methionine and cystine are required in higher amounts by cats than most other species especially during growth. Methionine and cystine are considered together because cystine can replace up to half of the methionine requirement of cats.[9] Although these amino acids are present in high amounts in animal flesh, methionine tends to be the first limiting amino acid in many food ingredients. Nutritional deficiencies are possible, especially in cats fed home-prepared or vegetable-based foods. Clinical signs of methionine deficiency include poor growth and a crusting dermatitis at the mucocutaneous junctions of the mouth and nose. Approximately 19% of a food must be composed of animal protein to meet the methionine requirement of kittens.[4] Foods high in plant proteins require additional methionine, which can be supplied as DL-methionine, a crystalline form of the amino acid.

There have been numerous, but unproved explanations for the high methionine and cystine requirement of cats. Methionine needs may be increased because of an increased S-adenosyl methionine requirement, cysteine synthesis, taurine synthesis or because of a high rate of methionine catabolism. Additional cystine may be required for the synthesis of hair and the amino acid felinine. Felinine excretion rates of 95 mg/day have been recorded in intact male cats and may significantly increase the daily sulfur amino acid requirement.[22] (See sidebar "Felinine.")

Fat Metabolism

Cats have the ability to digest and use high levels of dietary fat (as is present in animal tissue). Cats have a special need for arachidonic acid (20:4n6) because they cannot synthesize it from linoleic acid (18:2n6) as can dogs.[4,23] The basis for this additional requirement is the low hepatic delta-6 desaturase activity in cats.[24] Delta-6 desaturase is the rate-limiting factor in the conversion of linoleic acid to γ-linolenic acid, which is further elongated and desaturated to form arachidonic acid. Arachidonic acid is abundant in animal tissues, particularly in organ meats and neural tissues. Thus, the dietary requirement for arachidonic acid has little consequence if cats consume animal tissues. Plants, on the other hand, do not contain arachidonic acid. Therefore, foods composed predominantly of plant-based ingredients may not meet the arachidonic acid requirement of cats. Domestic cats are not the only carnivores that lack the ability to convert linoleic to arachidonic acid. African lions, turbots (a carnivorous fish) and even mosquitoes have the same inability to synthesize arachidonic acid. This metabolic peculiarity appears to be correlated with the strict carnivorous behavior of certain species, regardless of their position on the phylogenetic tree.[4]

Vitamin Metabolism

The vitamin needs of cats differ from those of dogs in several ways. Cats do not convert tryptophan to niacin.[25] Although, cats posses all the enzymes needed for niacin synthesis, the high activity of enzymes in the catabolic pathway (picolinic carboxylase) prevents niacin synthesis.[26] As a result, the niacin requirement of cats is four times higher than that of dogs.[9,27] Animal tissue is high in niacin.

The prosthetic group of all transaminases is pyridoxine (vitamin B_6).[28] As discussed, flesh-eaters (e.g., cats) derive considerable energy from dietary protein. Cats have high transaminase activity. Therefore, it is logical to expect that their pyridoxine turnover and requirement would be higher than that of omnivores. The pyridoxine requirement of cats is about four times higher than that of dogs.[9,27]

Vitamin A occurs naturally only in animal tissue. Vitamin A precursors (e.g., β-carotene) are synthesized by plants. Omnivorous and herbivorous animals can convert β-carotene to vitamin A; cats cannot because they lack intestinal dioxygenase that cleaves β-carotene to retinol. In addition, cats have insufficient 7-dehydrocholesterol in the skin to meet the metabolic need for vitamin D photosynthesis; therefore, they require a dietary source of vitamin D.[29-31] Vitamin D is relatively abundant in animal liver; therefore, the need for dermal production is minimal and 7-dehydrocholesterol is rapidly metabolized by alternate pathways. Vitamin D is fairly ubiquitous in animal fats and primary vitamin D deficiency has been identified only in cats fed experimental diets.

Water

Water needs of cats also differ from those of dogs, not because of feline feeding behaviors (i.e., carnivorous vs. omnivorous) but because of their ancestors' adaptation to environmental extremes. Domestic cats are thought to

have descended from the African wildcat (*Felis silvestris libyca*), a desert dweller. Several unique features of water balance in cats may be explained by adaptation to a dry environment. The stimulus for thirst appears to be less sensitive in cats than in dogs. Cats are able to survive on less water than dogs and may ignore minor levels of dehydration, up to 4% of body weight.[32] Cats compensate for reduced water intake, in part, by forming a highly concentrated urine. Unfortunately, this strong concentrating ability coupled with a weak thirst drive may result in a highly saturated urine, increasing the risk of crystalluria or urolithiasis, both components of the feline lower urinary tract disease (FLUTD) complex.

Cats consume 1.5 to 2 ml of water/g of dry matter (DM). This 2:1 ratio of water to dry matter is similar to that of typical prey. This ratio represents approximately 0.5 ml water/kcal metabolizable energy (ME) intake. Practical recommendations for water provision are somewhat higher at 1 ml water/kcal ME.

Much can be learned about an animal's nutritional requirements simply by analyzing its natural food. None of the so-called metabolic "peculiarities" of cats are really peculiar. They are what one would expect in a true carnivore.

LIFESTAGE NUTRITION

Lifestage nutrition is the practice of feeding foods designed to meet an animal's optimal nutritional needs at a specific age or physiologic state (e.g., maintenance, reproduction or growth). The concept of lifestage nutrition recognizes that feeding either below or above an optimal nutrient concentration can negatively affect biologic performance or health. (See Figure 2-2.) This concept differs markedly from feeding a single product for all lifestages (i.e., all-purpose foods), whereby nutrients are added at levels to meet the highest potential need (i.e., usually growth and reproduction). The goal in nutrition is to feed for optimal health, performance and longevity, thus feeding foods optimized toward individual needs is preferred. This philosophy is key to lifestage nutrition and preventive medicine. In addition to meeting the basic nutritional requirements of an animal, the nutrition-related health risks at each lifestage should be assessed and minimized. For maximum benefit, risk assessment and prevention plans should begin well before the onset of disease.

The value of lifestage feeding is greater if risk factor management is also incorporated into the feeding practice. A more narrow but optimal range of nutrient recommendations often emerges when age and physiologic needs are reviewed in conjunction with reducing nutritional risk factors. Nearly all commercial cat foods meet or exceed the minimum nutrient requirements of cats. However, certain nutrients may still be outside of the desired nutrient range for optimal health or risk factor reduction. For cats fed commercial foods, these nutrients require particular consideration and, thus, are referred to as nutrients of concern. Specific food factors (e.g., digestibility, texture and effect on urinary pH) can also affect health and risk of disease. (See Chapter 1.) Together, nutrients of concern and specific food factors are called key nutritional factors. The key nutritional factors for different lifestages of healthy cats will be discussed in the following sections, including those associated

Alternative Foods, Food Fads and Feeding Faux Pas

TREATS

An estimated 41 to 60% of cats are regularly fed table foods. In one survey, most treats consisted of human food items, although commercial treats were provided to 34% of the cats receiving treats.[a] Feeding treats allows more social interaction with the owner, increases diet variety and provides additional caloric intake. Some commercial treats claim dental benefits either by mechanical cleansing or through use of an active ingredient. However, providing treats for cats is unnecessary and may negatively affect a well-balanced food when fed in excess. Although several commercial treats are nutritionally adequate and fit well into a nutritional plan, many others are not. Table food tends to be highly palatable, calorically dense and nutritionally incomplete. Because most commercial cat foods contain vitamins and minerals well above the nutritional needs of cats, table foods and treats fed at less than 10% of the total daily intake should be safe. This recommendation is based on the premise that the extra nutrients in the commercial food can overcome deficiencies at this level of diet supplementation. To date, no reports have documented this level of safety. Adverse effects of providing table foods, scraps and treats are not limited to the nutritional adequacy of the diet. Chapter 7 presents a detailed description of food safety; therefore, those aspects of feeding treats will not be covered here. Overnutrition and food toxicity are of particular concern. Providing high-calorie treats can contribute to obesity. Treats high in certain nutrients can promote nutrient excesses alone or in combination with commercial foods. For example, liver or cod liver oil can markedly increase vitamin A intake, potentially to a toxic level. Because significant health consequences may result from inappropriately feeding treats, veterinarians should pay particular attention to the quality and quantity of treats being fed to their patients and offer appropriate nutritional advice.

MILK

One of the most common human foods offered to cats is milk. Milk is highly palatable and small quantities are well tolerated by most healthy cats. However, after weaning, intestinal lactase activity declines. Undigested lactose is subject to bacterial fermentation and promotes osmotic diarrhea. Feeding large quantities of milk may overwhelm digestive capacity resulting in diarrhea, flatulence or gastrointestinal (GI) distress. Although commercial lactase supplements may alleviate signs of lactose intolerance, lactose avoidance is more prudent.

NUTRITIONAL SUPPLEMENTS

Although many supplements are legitimate sources of essential nutrients, others represent food fads that reflect current trends in human nutrition. Poor-quality foods are rarely "fixed" by adding a supplement. Changing to a higher quality food is a more appropriate recommendation and often less costly.

Calcium

Breeders sometimes supplement calcium during pregnancy, lactation or growth. Additional calcium is rarely necessary and may lead to nutritional excess or nutrient imbalances in cats fed complete and balanced commercial feline products. Cats with eclampsia and those fed a homemade food typically require calcium supplementation.

Chromium

Chromium has been called a "glucose tolerance factor" for its role in normal glucose homeostasis and insulin action in experimental animals. Chromium supplementation promotes lean tissue accretion in growing livestock. Thus, health food stores now stock chromium as an "anti-diabetic" nutrient and "fat-burner" for people. Little information exists about the effect of chromium supplementation in cats. Some caution may be warranted given excess chromium has been associated with chromosomal damage.

Brewer's Yeast/Thiamin

Brewer's yeast and thiamin have been promoted as coat conditioners and flea preventives for dogs and cats. Although brewer's yeast is a good source of B vitamins, particularly thiamin, research has not proven its efficacy as a flea repellent.

Vitamin C

Vitamin C is synthesized by the liver of cats and is not a required nutrient. Nevertheless, vitamin C has been advocated for use in cats as a "natural" urinary acidifier, an antioxidant and as an anti-viral agent. Doses from 250 to 2,000 mg are commonly advocated. The benefit of supplemental vitamin C has not been documented. Ascorbic acid will promote acidic urine, but must be given three to four times daily to achieve adequate acidification. Detrimental effects have been reported to occur in people, dogs, ferrets and laboratory animals fed megadoses of vitamin C. Because vitamin C is metabolized to oxalate, supplementation should be strictly avoided in cats prone to calcium oxalate crystalluria.

RAW MEATS

Raw meats are commonly fed to cats by breeders and owners. Raw muscle and organ meats are highly palatable, digestible and generally nutritious when supplemented with appropriate vitamins and minerals. Cooking destroys some nutrients and increases the availability of others. A benefit to feeding raw meat to cats has not been documented, and the disadvantages far outweigh any advantages. Raw meat, even when "flash frozen," may contain harmful bacteria (e.g., *Salmonella* spp and *Escherichia coli*) and parasites (e.g., *Toxoplasma gondii*). Unless supplemented with vitamins and minerals, raw meat is nutritionally incomplete and can lead to nutritional secondary hyperparathyroidism or iodine deficiency. Meat mixes composed of large percentages of organ meats may provide excessive levels of vitamin A. Finally, cats fed raw meat diets sometimes develop fixed-food preferences, making subsequent food changes difficult.

FEEDING BONES

Bones are a concentrated source of calcium, phosphorus and magnesium. Steamed bone meal is a very good choice for supplying calcium to homemade or all-meat diets. However, feeding whole bones to cats should be discouraged. Bones with jagged or sharp points are often to blame for oral trauma and become esophageal foreign bodies. Bone feeding is also associated with colitis and constipation in small animals. Bones used as a nutritional supplement should be thoroughly cooked and ground into fine particles.

VEGETARIAN DIETS

Although the nutritional needs of cats are best met by a carnivorous diet, vegetarian diets can be designed to provide adequate nutrition. Vegetarian formulas are commercially available and several commercial supplements are available to provide nutrients normally missing, inadequate or poorly available in plant-based diets. Several nutrients in vegetarian formulations require special attention.

Protein

Plants are typically low in protein relative to the dietary needs of cats. Additionally, the quality of protein, in many cases, is much poorer than protein from animal sources. Concentrated sources of plant protein available to supplement feline foods include isolated soybean protein and corn gluten meal. Care must be taken to feed

Continued on next page.

Continued from previous page.

sufficient protein to meet the overall nitrogen needs and the minimum requirements of available individual amino acids.

Amino Acids

Taurine is not present in plant ingredients. Therefore, cats fed plant-based foods require taurine supplementation. Chemically synthesized sources of taurine are available from pharmacies and health food stores. Similarly, carnitine, a vitamin-like amino acid, is synthesized only by animal tissues. Although dietary carnitine is not required by healthy cats, some authors suggest a dietary source may be conditionally essential during growth. Synthetic supplements are available. The common limiting amino acids in plants are methionine, lysine and tryptophan. Diets must be closely evaluated to ensure the availability of sufficient quantities of these amino acids. Plant proteins contain large amounts of glutamate. Cats may poorly tolerate high-glutamate foods.

Vitamins

Because cats cannot use β-carotene, pre-formed vitamin A must be supplied in the food. Also, many vitamin A supplements contain vitamin D. All sources of vitamin D should be considered to avoid excess. Vegetarian diets also require supplementation with vitamin B_{12}, which is not supplied by plant ingredients. Vitamin B_{12}-enriched yeast and synthetic supplements are commercially available. Finally, the niacin content of vegetarian diets should be closely evaluated. Although niacin is present in high amounts in many plant ingredients, the availability is often poor and additional supplementation may be required.

Minerals

Providing adequate calcium is a concern in any homemade food. A variety of calcium supplements are available from health food stores and pharmacies. Many plant ingredients contain components (e.g., fibers or phytates) that severely compromise the availability of certain trace elements. The availability of iron, zinc and copper is of particular concern in high-phytate and high-fiber foods. (See Chapter 2.) These minerals should be provided as a highly available source.

Fat

Of the nutrients required by the cat, arachidonic acid is the one not commercially available. To provide arachidonate directly, cats must be given animal fat or tissue as a nutritional source. However, cats can convert γ-linolenate (18:3n6) to arachidonate (20:4n6) via delta 5-desaturase. γ-linolenate is available from plant oils (e.g., borage and evening primrose oils). Prolonged feeding and reproductive trials using γ-linolenate have not been reported; thus, the suitability of these oils as long-term arachidonate supplements is unknown. Because cats fed foods high in polyunsaturated fatty acids (PUFA) may develop steatitis, vegetarian foods and other foods containing PUFA using large quantities of plant oils should be protected with added vitamin E.

DOG FOOD

Most dog foods are nutritionally inadequate for the maintenance, growth and reproduction of cats. Nutrients most likely to be deficient are protein, taurine, niacin, vitamin B_6, methionine and choline. Clinical signs of deficiency depend on which nutrients are deficient and to what degree. In addition, dog foods do not address dietary acidification or magnesium content appropriate for reducing risk for struvite crystal formation. Therefore, cats fed foods designed for dogs are likely to consume a high-magnesium, alkalinizing food and increase their risk for struvite urolith formation.

FOOD TOXINS

Food toxicities are relatively infrequent in cats. Most notable is hemolytic anemia caused by onion toxicity. Certain

disulfides found in onions promote oxidative damage to cat hemoglobin, resulting in Heinz body production and red cell removal. The toxic compound appears to be highly stable, because it remains active in cooked onion-based broth and onion powder. Hemolytic anemia has been described in a cat fed commercial baby food containing onion powder. Onion toxicity was not proved but the anemia resolved with a diet change. Subsequent studies have demonstrated toxic effects at levels of 2.5% dry matter. Therefore, it is prudent to avoid feeding food or seasonings containing onion powder or onions.

Theobromine

Theobromine is a toxic methylxanthine found in chocolate. The clinical signs of toxicity include vomiting, diarrhea, vascular collapse and death. The oral LD_{50} of theobromine is 200 mg/kg body weight. Approximately 40 to 50 g of cocoa would need to be consumed to provide this dose of theobromine, which is undoubtedly why clinical reports of chocolate toxicoses in cats are rare.

Histamine

Histamine is a primary amine arising from the decarboxylation of histidine. Histamine toxicosis has been reported to occur in cats after ingestion of certain species of spoiled fish. Affected cats developed salivation, vomiting and diarrhea about 30 minutes after eating uncooked anchovies. Myosis, lacrimation, tachypnea and tachycardia were evident upon physical examination. A survey detailing the histamine content of North American cat foods found foods were well below the 500 μg/g (wet/weight) level considered hazardous in people. Thus, histamine toxicosis is most likely to occur in cats fed improperly handled fish that has undergone spoilage.

Propylene Glycol

Propylene glycol is a preservative and humectant previously added to semi-moist foods. Several studies have reported Heinz body formation and decreased red blood cell survival in cats consuming foods preserved with propylene glycol. Since the early 1990s manufacturers have discontinued the use of propylene glycol in cat foods, eliminating it as a concern.

ENDNOTE

a. Kirk CA. Unpublished data. 1992.

BIBLIOGRAPHY

Czarnecki-Maulden GL. Nutritional fads: Facts behind the myths. Companion Animal Practice 1988: 45-51.

Guilford WG, Roudebush P, Rogers QR. The histamine content of commercial pet foods. New Zealand Veterinary Journal 1994; 42: 201-224.

Kaplan AJ. Onion powder in baby food may induce anemia in cats (Letter to the editor). Journal of the American Veterinary Medical Association 1995; 207: 1405.

Kirk CA, Ling GV, Franti CE, et al. Evaluation of factors associated with development of calcium oxalate urolithiasis in cats. Journal of the American Veterinary Medical Association 1995; 207: 1429-1434.

Kobayashi K. Onion poisoning in the cat. Feline Practice 1981; 11: 22.

MacDonald ML, Rogers QR, Morris JG. Nutrition of the domestic cat, a mammalian carnivore. Annual Review of Nutrition 1984; 4: 521-562.

Odle J. Betaine and carnitine. Feed management 1996; 47: 25-27.

Pitcairn RH, Pitcairn SH. In: Dr. Pitcairn's Complete Guide to Natural Health for Dogs & Cats. Emmaus, PA: Rodale Press, 1982.

Robertson JE, Christopher MM, Rogers QR. Heinz body formation in cats fed baby food containing onion powder. Journal of the American Veterinary Medical Association 1998; 212: 1260-1266.

Scarlett JM, Donoghue S, Saidla J, et al. Overweight cats: Prevalence and risk factors. International Journal of Obesity 1994; 18: S22-S28.

Stearns DM, Wise JP, Patierno SR, et al. Chromium (III) picolinate produces chromosome damage in Chinese hamster ovary cells. Federation of American Societies for Experimental Biology Journal 1995; 9: 1643-1649.

with reducing the risk of specific diseases and those involved with optimizing performance during different physiologic states. Cats eating homemade foods are at greater risk for nutrient deficiencies (e.g., calcium) and excesses (e.g., phosphorus) than those eating commercial foods. Therefore, these cats have a broader list of key nutritional factors, which are discussed in Chapter 6 and in the sidebar "Alternative Foods, Food Fads and Feeding Faux Pas."

In sequence, this chapter covers feeding adult cats, reproducing cats and growing kittens. The adult cat section is divided into young to middle-aged cats and older (senior) cats. The chapter begins with feeding adult cats because most pet cats are adults and the nutrient needs of adults serve as a good basis for comparing nutrient needs for reproduction, lactation and growth. Also, note that

Table 11-6. Factors to consider during nutritional assessment.

Signalment
Activity level
Age
Breed
Disease status
Environment
Gender
Reproductive status
Use

Dietary history
Adverse food reactions
Amount eaten
Amount offered
Appetite (interest)
Brand fed
Feeding method
Feeding schedule
Food aversions
Food storage
Nutritional losses
Previous foods
Supplements
Treats
Type
Water availability

Weight history
Current weight
Ideal weight
Percent weight change
Rate of change
Usual weight

Physical examination
Body condition
Bone structure
Coat condition
Eyes
Hydration
Muscle mass
Oral health
Skin condition
Strength/activity

Diagnostic studies
Albumin
Creatine kinase
Hematocrit
Hemoglobin
Lymphocyte count
Potassium
Prothrombin time
Serum urea nitrogen
Sodium

most of the general information about feeding cats is included in the adult cat section and is not repeated in the other sections of this chapter.

YOUNG TO MIDDLE-AGED ADULT CATS

Cats generally reach adulthood between 10 to 12 months of age and commonly live 20 or more years. The span of time from 12 months to death represents the adult life of cats. However, cats near seven years of age may be considered older, or senior, because of the increasing prevalence of age-related diseases and onset of mild behavioral, physical and metabolic changes related to aging. In this chapter, adult maintenance refers to the needs of nonreproducing cats one to seven years of age. Nutrition for cats older than seven years will be discussed later in the next section. (See Older Cats.)

Nutritional recommendations for young to middle-aged adult cats provide for basal nutrient requirements with additional allowances for prehension, consumption and digestion of food, average physical activity and modest thermoregulation. They do not account for strenuous activity, extremes in ambient temperature and humidity, reproduction and growth. Optimal nutritional requirements for adult cats tend to be the most broadly defined of any lifestage. This is due, in part, because young to middle-aged adult cats have the greatest ability to tolerate or compensate for metabolic and physiologic perturbations. The goals of feeding adult cats are to maximize health, longevity and quality of life.

Assessment

Assess the Animal

Animal assessment encompasses the complete evaluation of the animal, its environment and risk factors for disease (Table 11-6). (See Chapter 1.) A systematic evaluation of each cat's signalment, history and physical examination should be performed before making nutritional recommendations. The purpose of first assessing the animal is to establish feeding goals, recognize risk factors for nutrition-related diseases and identify key nutritional factors for individual cats.

HISTORY AND PHYSICAL EXAMINATION

When evaluating a cat's nutritional status, the history should be taken and a physical examination performed and both assessed in relation to the signalment. Key features include the age, gender, activity and environment of the cat. Differences in these factors influence energy requirements and risks for certain diseases. The initial dietary history for healthy adult cats should establish the brand, type and amount of foods fed regularly, including treats, table foods and nutritional supplements. The feeding method and appetite should be noted as well as any recent changes in body weight and stool quality. The extent of the evaluation depends on the preliminary findings. A more detailed dietary history may be required if significant abnormalities are uncovered during the history or physical examination (e.g., anorexia, unexplained weight loss, poor diet, etc.). A detailed dietary history should evaluate the factors listed in Table 11-6.

Table 11-7. Common nutrition-related disorders in cats.

Disorders	Nutrients	Feeding errors	Chapters*
Obesity	Calorie excess	High-fat foods or excessive food portions	Chapter 13
Hepatic lipidosis	Incomplete understanding	Fasting or low food intake in obese cats	Chapter 23
		Protein deficiency	
		Methionine and choline deficiency	
Pansteatitis	Vitamin E deficiency	High-PUFA foods with insufficient vitamin E (red meat tuna)	Chapter 2
Nutritional secondary hyperparathyroidism	Calcium deficiency with or without phosphorus excess	All-meat foods with no mineral supplementation	Chapter 6
Hypokalemic nephropathy/ myopathy	Potassium deficiency	Low-potassium foods with urinary acidification	Chapter 19
Feline central retinal degeneration	Taurine deficiency	Vegetarian foods, dog foods, moist foods without supplemental taurine	Chapter 11
Dilated cardiomyopathy			
Reproductive failure			
Thiamin deficiency	Thiamin deficiency	Heat-processed foods without added thiamin	Chapter 2
Internal bleeding	Vitamin K deficiency	Fish-based moist foods without added vitamin K	Chapter 2
Hyperammonemia	Arginine deficiency	High-casein foods without supplemental arginine	-
Deforming cervical spondylosis	Vitamin A excess	Large intake of animal liver	Chapter 2
Hypervitaminosis A		Vitamin A nutritional supplements (cod liver oil)	
Lower urinary tract disease (struvite related)	Low water intake	Dry foods	Chapter 21
	Alkaline urinary pH	Alkaline urinary pH	
	Magnesium excess	High-magnesium food ingredients	
Lower urinary tract disease (calcium oxalate related)	Low water intake		
	Acidic urinary pH (possibly)	Dry foods	Chapter 21
		Acidic urinary pH	

Key: PUFA = polyunsaturated fatty acids.
*Cases at the end of the respective chapters illustrate common clinical conditions, including nutrient deficiency and excess diseases.

If the dietary history is perceived to be incomplete, it may prove useful to have owners continue to feed and medicate their pet as usual and record amounts, types and brands of all foods and supplements given for one to two weeks. Such dietary records help better define nutrient intake, nutritional problems and errors in feeding management.

A thorough physical examination should include a systematic evaluation of each body system by observation and palpation and auscultation where possible. Special attention should be given to the oral cavity, hydration status, skin and coat condition, body weight and body condition score (BCS). (See Chapter 1.) Careful observation is needed to assess lean body mass, muscle tone and body composition. Apparent loss of lean body mass may indicate recent weight loss, nutritional deficiency or disease, even in obese cats. Several nutritional deficiencies and toxicities have classic physical manifestations in cats (Table 11-7) that may be detected during the physical examination. (See Chapter 2.) Any physical abnormalities should be correlated to the signalment and history to pinpoint issues that require further exploration.

Gender

Evaluation of gender involves identification of the cat's sex and neuter status. Small differences in growth rate, body composition and energy intake between male and female cats have been reported.[9,33] The differences in energy intake appear to be due to gender-related differences in lean body mass.[33,34] In addition, risk factors for certain diseases vary by gender. However, these differences are less than the individual variation between animals and rarely warrant a gender-specific nutritional plan. Exceptions include reproducing cats and cats that have been neutered.

Neutering reduces the DER of adult cats by 24 to 33% compared with the DER of intact cats.[35,36] The decrease in

DER does not appear to be influenced by age at neutering.[35] The reduction in energy requirement is most likely attributable to a reduction in basal metabolic rate because obvious changes in behavior and activity were not observed after neutering.[36]

The mechanisms behind the reduction in basal metabolism after neutering are unknown but may include a potential reduction in lean body mass after removal of reproductive hormones,[35] or changes in thermogenic activity within the liver.[36] Because a reduction in DER without a reduction in food intake leads to obesity, nutritional counseling should be provided to owners who present cats for neutering. Although most cats are apparently able to adjust food intake to meet the reduced energy requirement after neutering, feeding low-fat foods reduces the risk for obesity in neutered cats.[37] Kittens neutered at less than six months of age should be fed foods designed for growth until they reach skeletal maturity between eight and 10 months of age. Many foods designed for growing kittens are energy dense; therefore, portion control and regular monitoring of body condition is advised.

Activity Level

Activity level is one of the key determinants of DER. By nature, cats do not participate in heavy work or endurance-type activities, thus the variation in energy requirement between active and sedentary cats is small compared with that in dogs. Nevertheless, twofold differences in energy requirement have been observed between active and sedentary cats.[38,39] Therefore, food intake should be adjusted according to activity level to maintain optimal body condition (BCS 3/5).

Sedentary, inactive, caged and older cats often have energy requirements very near or even below the average resting energy requirement (RER) (0.8 to 1.2 x RER) or 40 to 60 kcal/kg body weight/day (167 to 251 kJ/kg body weight/day).[36,38] This should be a consideration for cats that are hospitalized or boarded. A reduction in food intake is expected in normally active cats that are subsequently confined. These cats may become overweight if food intake is not adjusted accordingly. A normal decline in food intake should not be confused with inappetence due to stress or disease.

Cats with unlimited activity may have energy needs 10 to 15% above normal.[40] Very active or "high strung" cats may expend markedly more energy than other cats. For example, the energy requirement of Abyssinian cats has been reported as 79 kcal/kg body weight/day (330 kJ/kg body weight/day), or 1.6 x RER, which is 30% greater than that required for average adult house cats.[39]

Age

Aging in healthy animals is associated with metabolic changes that affect nutritional recommendations at different lifestages. Overlaid on these changes are the concerns of age-associated diseases, which also affect nutritional recommendations. Young to middle-aged cats may have specific nutrient concerns especially with respect to weight control, lower urinary tract health, dental health and subclinical kidney disease.[a]

Environment

DER for cats may be markedly altered when ambient temperatures deviate significantly from a thermoneutral environment. Behavioral responses usually compensate for minor deviations in temperature with little effect on a cat's water or energy needs. However, temperatures low enough to cause shivering (5 to 8°C [41 to 46.4°F]) can increase the resting caloric requirement from two to five times normal.[41,42] Cats kept in very hot environments (>38°C [>100.4°F]) may initially reduce food intake by 15 to 40%; however, as respiratory rate and grooming behavior increase and panting begins, the requirement for calories and water increases. Water is critically important to prevent heat stress in hot environments. Cats pant and wet their coats with saliva to maximize evaporative water loss and cooling. Cats that are dehydrated have a 50% reduction in their ability to use evaporative water loss for thermoregulation.[43] Significant elevations of core body temperature may occur with loss of evaporative cooling. Owners should be advised to monitor body condition and adjust feeding protocols as needed to meet these changing demands.

Cats thrive when humidity is low and temperatures are warm.[44] National Institutes of Health and United States Department of Agriculture guidelines for feline housing recommend humidity values between 30 to 70%, room temperatures between 18 to 29°C (64.4 to 84.2°F) and 10 to 15 room exchanges/hour (ventilation).[45,46] However, no studies document a health benefit using these requirements. More practical recommendation are temperatures between 10 to 29.5°C (50 to 85°F) and humidity levels between 10 to 50%.[47] Energy requirements change very little within these environmental conditions.

There is little information about the influence of housing type on the nutritional management of cats. Cats housed outdoors have less protection from the environment snd temperature fluctuations and are presumably more active than indoor cats. Thus, the optimal food and feeding methods may be different for outdoor cats than for cats housed indoors.

In general, cats confined indoors are less active and have a lower DER than outdoor cats. Most indoor cats have "run of the house" and are still able to maintain a moderate activity level. However, some indoor housing includes confinement to small areas (e.g., caging in hospitals, kennels, animal shelters or catteries). Activity is markedly limited in these conditions as reflected by lower energy requirements. (See Activity Level.) In addition to the influence of housing on activity and thermoregulation, the psychological stressors associated with an indoor environment (e.g., noise, children, multiple cats, etc.) can negatively affect feeding behavior and food intake.

Multi-cat environments refer to individual households with two or more cats; however, the definition also includes catteries, shelters and research institutions. Cats are solitary animals; therefore, multi-cat environments can lead to social and psychological stress, particularly if there is overcrowding. Households with more than five cats appear to be at increased risk.[49] Common problems associated with multi-cat households include changes in food intake, behavioral problems and infectious diseases. The combination of chronic stress, overcrowding, poor ventilation and inadequate nutrition makes infectious diseases very difficult to control. Unsanitary litter boxes can result in elevated environmental ammonia concentrations that impair health.[47] Other challenges associated with feeding cats in a multi-cat environment include difficulty in monitoring food and water intake, ensuring all cats have unfettered access to food and providing specialized foods to individual cats. Obtaining accurate dietary histories and achieving good dietary compliance for cats from multi-cat households can be challenging for veterinarians and owners. However, modification of feeding and management practices can alleviate many problems.

Modifying the environment to include multi-level resting areas, visual barriers and quiet hiding spots where cats can retreat from unwanted social interactions and avoid certain household activities helps reduce the overall stress level in the population. Multiple feeding stations and individual feed pans, particularly if placed at different levels, allow timid and low-status cats to eat alone or away from dominant cats. These practices also benefit dominant cats by reducing tension and allowing time for dominant cats to eat quietly instead of defending food or constantly harassing cats of lower social status.

Cats that are under stress may develop diminished appetites or complete anorexia. However, overeating and resultant weight gain are reported consequences of stress in some cats.[49] Short-term bouts of anorexia (i.e., one to five days) have little overall effect on otherwise healthy adult cats, although metabolic changes are evident by the third day of fasting.[50,51] A prolonged reduction in food intake in healthy cats or short-term food deprivation in sick cats can lead to malnourishment and increased risk of hepatic lipidosis.

Breed

Although different breeds of cats may have varying nutritional requirements, the variation is less pronounced than that of dog breeds. Certain breeds of cats (e.g., Abyssinians) are noted for their lively and rambunctious disposition, whereas others (e.g., Persians or ragdolls) tend to be quiet and tranquil.[52] Thus, disposition affects energy requirements among breeds. Other nutritional variances may be elucidated with continued research into specific requirements of different cat breeds.

LABORATORY AND OTHER CLINICAL INFORMATION

Laboratory analyses may help develop a complete picture of nutritional status. Results should always be interpreted in relation to the physical examination and historical findings. Complete blood counts, serum biochemistry analyses, fecal analyses and urinalyses may prove useful in assessing nutritional status, depending on the physiologic state, specific nutrient of interest and disease process present. Special diagnostic tests (e.g., plasma aminograms, clotting profiles, urinary clearance ratios and hormone assays) may help assess specific disease processes. Ancillary diagnostic procedures include ultrasonography, radiography and tissue biopsy as dictated by physical and laboratory analyses. Fecal analysis for intestinal parasites and testing for feline leukemia virus (FeLV) and feline immunodeficiency virus (FIV) should be routine for healthy adult cats.

KEY NUTRITIONAL FACTORS

Table 11-8 summarizes key nutritional factors for young to middle-aged adult cats. The following section describes these key nutritional factors in more detail.

Water

Although water is the most important nutrient for cats, a finite water requirement has been not established because: 1) cats adjust water intake to the dry matter content of the diet, 2) cats conserve total body water by forming highly concentrated urine and 3) the water requirement of cats varies with physiologic and environmental conditions. In general, it is recommended that cats drink 1 ml water/kcal ME requirement. In practice, adult cats should have unlimited access to potable water. Increased water intake is thought to be useful for managing urolithiasis by reducing the urinary concentration of urolith-forming minerals. Feeding moist foods (vs. dry foods) increases water intake and urine volume in most cats.[53] Unlike dogs, cats do not fully compensate for differences in food moisture content by altering free water intake. When allowed free access to water, the total water intake of cats eating dry food was only half that of cats eating moist food.[54,55]

Energy

The DER of average young to middle-aged adult cats is generally between 60 to 80 kcal/kg body weight/day (251 to 335 kJ/kg body weight/day) or approximately 1.2 to 1.6 x RER, where RER in kcal = $70(BW_{kg})^{0.75}$ or RER in kJ = $293(BW_{kg})^{0.75}$. Caloric requirements for neutered or inactive cats are calculated using the lower end of the range (1.2 x RER), whereas the upper end of the range (1.4 to 1.6 x RER) is used for active sexually intact cats. Most neutered house cats require between 1.2 to 1.4 x RER. Despite the relative uniformity of size within the domestic cat population, there are size-associated differences in energy requirements. Smaller cats consume more calories per kg body weight than larger cats.[38,39]

Determination of DER for a population of cats results in a bell-shaped curve. (See Figure 1-4.) Individual cats may have energy requirements that vary by up to 50% or more above or below the average requirement. This range is not surprising considering that the DER of a particular cat is influenced by differences in lean body mass, activity, environmental temperature and genetic traits. Thus, it is

Table 11-8. Key nutritional factors for adult cats at maintenance.

Factors	Recommended food levels*		
	Young to middle aged	Obese prone	Older
Energy density (kcal ME/g)	4.0-5.0	3.3-3.8	3.5-4.5
Energy density (kJ ME/g)	16.7-20.9	13.8-15.9	14.6-18.8
Protein (%)	30-45	30-45	30-45
Fat (%)	10-30	8-17	10-25
Crude fiber (%)	<5	5-15	<10
Calcium (%)	0.5-1.0	0.5-1.0	0.6-1.0
Phosphorus (%)	0.5-0.8	0.5-0.9	0.5-0.7
Ca/P ratio	0.9:1-1.5:1	0.9:1-1.5:1	0.9:1-1.5:1
Sodium (%)	0.2-0.6	0.2-0.6	0.2-0.5
Potassium (%)	0.6-1.0	0.6-1.0	0.6-1.0
Magnesium (%)	0.04-0.1	0.04-0.1	0.05-0.1
Chloride (%)	>0.3	>0.3	>0.3
Average urinary pH	6.2-6.5	6.2-6.5	6.2-6.6

*Dry matter basis. Concentrations presume an energy density of 4.0 kcal/g. Levels should be corrected for foods with higher energy densities. Adjustment is unnecessary for foods with lower energy densities.

important to remember that calculated energy requirements are only estimates for individual cats. The true caloric requirement for an individual cat is the amount of food that will maintain an ideal body condition (BCS 3/5) and stable weight.

Controlling energy intake is important in managing and preventing obesity. Approximately 25% of pet cats in the United States are overweight. The prevalence is highest in middle-aged cats (seven to eight years); nearly 50% of this age group are overweight or obese (BCS 4/5 or 5/5).[37,a] Obesity increases the risk of death in middle-aged cats 2.7 times above that of lean cats,[56] thus preventing obesity has important consequences for long-term health. (See Chapter 13.) Risk factors associated with obesity include: 1) middle age, 2) neuter status, 3) low activity and 4) high-fat, high-calorie foods.[37] Some cats that are inactive, confined or obese prone may require markedly fewer calories than predicted by equations to determine DER (i.e., 1.0 x RER or 39 to 66 kcal/kg body weight/day or 163 to 276 kJ/kg body weight/day).[38] Obese cats may require as few as 0.8 x RER or 44 to 54 kcal/kg ideal body weight (184 to 226 kJ/kg ideal body weight/day) to achieve an average weight loss of 1% of body weight per week.[57]

Food digestibility and energy density may influence the risk for FLUTD. Energy-dense foods reduce overall dry matter intake. Lower dry matter intake decreases stool volume, which subsequently reduces fecal water loss. Both features are beneficial in reducing total magnesium intake and increasing urine volume. Controlled food intake should be used when feeding high-calorie foods. Excessive intake of calorically dense foods (e.g., with free-choice feeding) can induce obesity, also a risk factor for urolithiasis. See Table 11-8 for recommended levels of fat, fiber and energy density of foods for cats at risk for obesity.

Protein

The protein requirements of adult cats have generally been established using experimental foods containing essential amino acids at or above the minimum requirement for growth. From these studies, the National Research Council (NRC)[9] suggested the minimum protein requirement for adult cats is 14% (dry matter basis [DMB]), or 12% protein calories.[4] Commercial foods prepared from natural ingredients and processed may have lower protein digestibility than the experimental foods used to establish

NORMAL CATS

these minimums. To provide a margin of safety and account for differences in protein quality, the Association of American Feed Control Officials (AAFCO) has suggested a minimum dietary protein level of 26% DM for adult maintenance.[58] Protein and amino acid requirements vary with the energy content of a food. The minimum protein allowance suggested by AAFCO is based on foods containing 4.0 kcal/g (16.7 kJ/g) DM and should be corrected in foods with energy densities greater than 4.5 kcal/g (18.8 kJ/g). (See Chapter 1 for the correction method.)

Meeting the minimum protein needs of cats is critical because they have minimal capacity to adapt to low levels of dietary protein. However, protein in excess of the requirement is rapidly catabolized and used to provide energy and maintain blood glucose levels. Any excess energy will be stored as fat. Therefore, there appears to be little benefit to feeding large excesses of protein to cats. Conversely, dietary protein excess may increase proteinuria and the progression of subclinical renal disease.[59-61] Similar to findings in people and dogs, the role of protein and the progression of renal disease in cats is controversial. Nevertheless, avoiding excess dietary protein in cat foods may be beneficial, whereas feeding excess protein simply provides extra energy.

Although cats can be fed vegetable-based foods, most protein in the food should be derived from animal tissues. The amino acid profile of most animal tissues better reflects the nutritional requirements of cats. Moist products usually list animal-based ingredients within the first two ingredients (excluding water), whereas dry products usually list animal-based ingredients in the first three ingredients. The recommended protein allowance for normal adult cats is 30 to 45% of the dry matter (Table 11-8).

Taurine

Taurine is a key nutrient for all feline lifestages. Although the requirement varies somewhat throughout the lifestage, variations due to nutritional factors are far greater than those related to age. Although taurine deficiency is no longer common in adult cats, awareness of the nutritional factors that affect taurine availability is important. Sporadic cases of taurine depletion continue to be diagnosed. Therefore, dietary taurine concentrations should be evaluated in cats with signs of deficiency or disease. (See sidebar "Taurine.")

Fats and Essential Fatty Acids

Cats use dietary fat for energy and essential fatty acids and to facilitate absorption of fat-soluble vitamins. A minimum requirement for fat has not been established for cats although foods containing less than 5% DM fat have been fed successfully to hyperlipidemic cats.[b] Signs of essential fatty acid deficiency in cats include fatty degeneration of the liver, kidneys and adrenal glands. Scaly skin, mild hyperkeratosis and hair loss have also been noted. Linoleic acid and α-linolenic acid are essential for normal membrane structure and function, including growth, lipid transport, maintenance of the epidermal permeability barrier and normal skin and coat.[62] Arachidonic acid, on the other hand, is important for functions that rely on eicosanoid synthesis. In cats, deficiency of arachidonic acid is associated with impaired platelet aggregation, inflammatory skin lesions and reproductive failure in queens.[63,64] Male cats are capable of converting linoleic acid to arachidonic acid within the testes, resulting in normal spermatogenesis.[64]

Fatty acids of the n-3 series (linolenic acid, 18:3n-3) are probably required in the diet of all animals.[65] Studies indicate n-3 fatty acids are essential for normal neural development in neonates.[66] Cats would normally consume n-3 fatty acids when eating the neural tissues of their prey. A minimum requirement has not been defined for most mammals, including cats. The role of n-3 fatty acids in companion animal medicine has focused mostly on their pharmacologic-like properties and ability to modulate the immune response and inflammation. (See Chapter 26.) Although these effects may benefit some animals, untoward effects are possible. Cats appear particularly susceptible to the deleterious effects of lipid oxidation. Foods high in polyunsaturated fatty acids have been associated with the development of feline pansteatitis when not adequately supplemented with vitamin E.[67-69] In one study, cats developed increased bleeding times and decreased platelet function when fed foods supplemented with high levels of n-3 fatty acids.[70] However, no adverse effects were found in similar studies.[71,72] The current understanding of n-3 fatty acid metabolism in cats is limited, thus n-3 fatty acid supplementation should be used judiciously.

Fat levels above 9.0% DM are recommended for most cats. When both fatty acids are present, linoleic acid is required at 0.5% of the food and arachidonic acid at 0.02% of the food, or 5% and 0.04% of the dietary energy as linoleic acid and arachidonic acid, respectively.[4,9] Fat enhances the palatability of food; cats prefer foods with levels near 25% DM vs. foods at 10 or 50% DM.[10]

High-fat foods have been associated with an increased incidence of obesity in cats.[37] Most cats do well on foods with 10 to 30% fat. However, cats prone to obesity should be fed foods with lower levels of dietary fat (8 to 17% DM) (Table 11-8).

Fiber

Although cats do not require dietary fiber, small amounts in commercial foods enhance stool quality and promote normal GI function. The natural foods of cats typically contain less than 1% dietary fiber although much higher levels are well tolerated.[73,74] Fiber concentrations less than 5% DM are recommended for normal adult cats. Obese-prone cats may benefit from foods that contain up to 15% crude fiber (DM) (Table 11-8). (See Chapter 13.) Fiber supplementation may benefit cats with frequent hairballs, but its effects for this problem have not been well studied. Clinical evidence and field trials have demonstrated a reduction in the frequency of hairball vomiting with fiber supplementation.[c]

Calcium and Phosphorus

Deficiencies of calcium and phosphorus are uncommon in cats fed commercial foods. Most cases of calcium deficiency have occurred in cats eating only unsupplemented meats, in which the calcium concentration is excessively low and the phosphorus concentration excessively high. Phosphorus excess appears to be of greater concern for adult cats fed commercial foods, especially as related to lower urinary tract and renal disease. (See Chapters 19 and 21.) The calcium requirement for growing kittens is 0.5% (DM) of the diet.[75] Adult needs are typically less than those for growth. Calcium and phosphorus requirements of adult cats have recently been determined.[76] The minimum calcium requirement was reported as 132 mg/MJ (60 mg/100 kcal or 0.25% DM at an energy density of 4.5 kcal/g). The minimum phosphorus requirement was 143 mg/MJ (55 mg/100 kcal or 0.27% DM at an energy density of 4.5 kcal/g). Both values are nearly half the AAFCO minimum allowance (i.e., 0.6% DM for calcium and 0.5% DM for phosphorus).[58] Typical commercial foods contain calcium and phosphorus levels well in excess of these guidelines. (See Appendix L.)

Daily calcium intakes of 200 to 400 mg per day meet the needs of adult cats when fed foods with a calcium-phosphorus ratio of 0.9:1 to 1.1:1.[77] Although foods with much broader ratios of calcium to phosphorus have been fed successfully, ratios near 1:1 calcium to phosphorus optimize the availability of phosphorus.[78] When the calcium-phosphorus ratio is increased to 2:1, phosphorus availability declines by 41%. Calcium-phosphorus ratios between 0.9:1 to 1.5:1 appear optimal for most feline foods.

Dietary phosphorus is a key nutrient in the management of two common feline diseases: struvite-mediated FLUTD and renal disease. The mineral constituents of struvite are magnesium, ammonium and phosphate. Although the primary objectives for preventing FLUTD due to struvite precipitates are to reduce urinary pH and, to a lesser extent, restrict dietary magnesium, limiting dietary phosphorus may be beneficial. (See Chapter 21.) The kidneys excrete excess dietary phosphorus to maintain phosphorus balance. The risk of clinically apparent struvite crystalluria and urolithiasis appears highest in adult cats from two to five years of age. Controlling phosphorus intake in combination with appropriate reductions in dietary magnesium concentrations and urinary pH reduces the risk of struvite-associated FLUTD in cats of this age group.

In one survey among pet owners, renal disease was the second most common cause of non-accidental death in cats; its prevalence increases with age.[79] Excess dietary phosphorus is not considered a cause of renal damage but accelerates the progression of renal disease toward failure and death.[80] High levels of dietary phosphorus (1.2 to 1.8% DM) lower creatinine clearance values and possibly reduce renal function in young, healthy cats.[81] Phosphorus reduction is advised in the early nutritional management of renal disease in cats to decrease the renal excretory workload and avoid phosphorus retention. (See Chapter 19 for a discussion of the pathophysiology of phosphorus retention in renal disease.) Cats with renal insufficiency are often not diagnosed until three-fourths or more of kidney function has been lost and older cats have an increased prevalence of kidney disease. Generalized phosphorus reduction may slow progression of renal disease in cats with subclinical or undiagnosed disease. Dietary phosphorus may be reduced as low as 0.3% DM in cats with overt renal disease, otherwise levels of 0.5 to 0.7 % are recommended (Table 11-8). (See Chapter 19.)

Sodium and Chloride

The long-term effects of high sodium or salt intake by cats have not been studied. In people, limiting sodium intake to levels that meet the requirement without significant excess reduces the risk of hypertension and is considered important to long-term health.[82] This same nutritional practice has been advocated for cats. In a study involving feline hypertension, nearly 50% of hypertensive cats fed a low-sodium food had a significant reduction in blood pressure.[83] This response is similar to that seen in people in that not all people are "salt-sensitive." In cats, hypertension is commonly associated with renal failure, hyperthyroidism, cardiac disease and possibly obesity.[84,85] High blood pressure has been associated with significant end-organ damage in

hypertensive cats. Blindness, retinal hemorrhage, stroke, cardiac dilatation and murmurs and renal damage were common findings among the cats studied.[83] Avoiding excess sodium chloride seems prudent because: 1) hypertension has significant deleterious health effects, 2) diagnostics to detect hypertension are not commonly performed and 3) the medical conditions associated with hypertension are common in cats. Chloride has been implicated more recently as a major determinant in the development of hypertension in salt-sensitive people. The interaction of sodium with chloride appears to cause the greatest increase in blood pressure compared with sodium combined with other anions.[86] The minimum chloride requirement is not known for cats, but the NRC recommended concentration (i.e., 0.19% DM) appears sufficient.[9]

In addition to exacerbating hypertensive disorders, high dietary sodium is reported to enhance urinary calcium excretion.[87] Whether excess dietary sodium plays a role in the development of calcium oxalate urolithiasis in cats is unknown. However, the negative effects of high sodium intake outweigh the benefits; therefore, sodium excess, particularly in the form of sodium chloride, should be avoided.

The minimum sodium requirement for adult cats is estimated at 9.2 mg/kg body weight/day or approximately 0.08% DM;[9,88] however, the optimal sodium content of cat foods has not been established. The average sodium content of prey is relatively low (e.g., approximately 0.25% DM in whole rat carcasses).[73] Short-term studies have shown adult cats tolerate a wide range of dietary sodium intakes (i.e., 0.04 to 2.0%).[4,9,54] Dietary salt (sodium chloride) added at concentrations of 4% DM or greater will markedly enhance water intake and increase urine volume when fed to cats.[54] However, the long-term consequences of feeding such high levels of sodium chloride are unknown. Sodium concentrations from 0.2 to 0.5% DM will satisfy the needs of healthy adult cats without providing excessive levels (Table 11-8).

Potassium

The potassium requirement of cats varies with the dietary protein concentration and the effect of the food on urinary pH. High-protein foods and foods that result in an acidic urinary pH increase the potassium requirement of cats.[89-93] Previously recommended levels of 0.4% DM[9] resulted in hypokalemia in adult cats and kittens when combined with dietary acidification. Dietary potassium levels in foods for normal adult cats should be greater than 0.5% DM and ideally between 0.6 to 1.0% DM to prevent hypokalemia (Table 11-8). Increased potassium losses occur in cats with certain metabolic abnormalities (e.g., renal insufficiency, renal tubular acidosis, diabetes mellitus and enteritis). Potassium supplementation may be necessary to maintain normal potassium balance in cats with these conditions.

Magnesium

Magnesium is an essential nutrient, but is also a major constituent of struvite crystals (magnesium ammonium phosphate). Struvite precipitation in the urinary tract contributes significantly to the development of FLUTD. Struvite-mediated FLUTD has declined following the industry-wide reduction of dietary magnesium and inclusion of acidifying ingredients in commercial cat foods.[94] To reduce the risk of FLUTD due to struvite, dietary magnesium concentrations should be less than 20 mg/100 kcal of food (or less than 0.10% DM) in conjunction with a reduced urinary pH (i.e., average pH values <6.5 pH units). These levels are similar to those found in the natural food of cats.

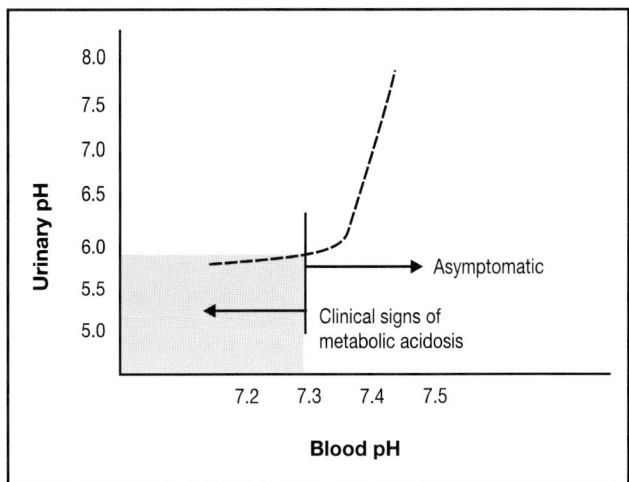

Figure 11-3. Correlation between urinary and blood pH in cats. Many cats develop metabolic acidosis when urinary pH is consistently less than 6.0. (Adapted from Allen TA, Bartges JW, Cowgill LD, et al. Colloquium on urology. Feline Practice 1997; 25: 32.)

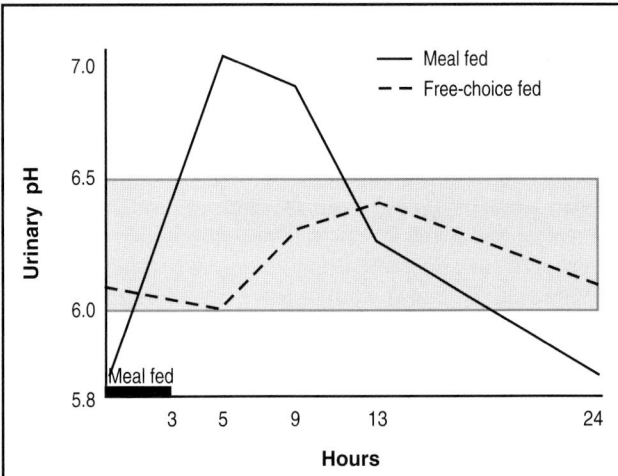

Figure 11-4. Effect of feeding method on urinary pH in cats. Note the significant increase in urinary pH after a single meal (meal fed). This effect is termed "postprandial alkaline tide." Food provided free choice modulates urinary pH by dampening the postprandial alkaline tide that occurs three to six hours following ingestion of larger meals. The shaded area represents the acceptable urinary pH range for adult cats. (Adapted from Taton GF, Hamar D, Lewis LD. Evaluation of ammonium chloride as a urinary acidifier in the cat. Journal of the American Veterinary Medical Association 1984; 184:

Magnesium concentrations of 0.08% DM were measured in whole rat carcasses.[73] The minimum magnesium requirement for adult cats is 4.1 mg/100 kcal (9.7 mg/MJ or 0.016% DM).[76] Excessive magnesium restriction may be associated with the increasing prevalence of calcium oxalate uroliths in cats.[95] Therefore, excessive restriction of magnesium (i.e., less than 0.04% DM) is not recommended (Table 11-8).

Urinary pH

Food ingredients and feeding methods contribute to the urinary pH produced by cats. The risk of struvite precipitation and FLUTD is greatly reduced at urinary pH values less than 6.5.[96] Many cats develop metabolic acidosis when the urinary pH is less than 6.0 (Figure 11-3).[92] Metabolic acidosis may promote bone demineralization,

urinary calcium and potassium loss[90,91] and increase the risk of calcium oxalate urolithiasis.[95,97] Free-choice food intake modulates urinary pH by dampening the postprandial alkaline tide that occurs three to six hours following larger meals. Meal feeding promotes a much greater alkaline tide and higher average urinary pH (Figure 11-4). Commercial foods commonly balance dietary cations and anions to achieve the appropriate urinary pH. Animal proteins, corn gluten meal, certain mineral salts, methionine and phosphoric acid are common ingredients that reduce urinary pH when added to feline foods.[98]

Foods that produce average urinary pH values of 6.2 to 6.5 when fed free choice reduce the risk of struvite-mediated FLUTD and avoid metabolic acidosis in most adult cats. The normal urinary pH of cats eating mice and rats is 6.2 to 6.4.[98] Thus, 6.2 to 6.4 is the "normal acidic urinary pH" of cats fed a wild-type food and the recommended range for healthy adult cats (Table 11-8).

Texture

Food texture influences oral health. (See Chapter 16.) Dental calculus and periodontal disease are the most prevalent diseases in cats one year and older.[a] Dry foods specifically designed to promote oral health are beneficial in reducing accumulation of dental plaque and calculus and reducing the severity of gingivitis. Generally, dry foods result in less plaque and calculus accumulation in cats than do moist and semi-moist foods.[99,100]

Recently, very hard foods have been implicated as a potential factor in the etiology of feline odontoclastic resorptive lesions (i.e., neck lesions).[d] Chronic tooth trauma may result in abfraction (fractures) of the enamel at the gum line. This trauma alone or together with poor oral hygiene may initiate odontoclastic resorptive lesions in cats. Although a direct association has yet to be demonstrated, it seems prudent to avoid very hard foods (e.g., bones) when possible, especially in cats with dental disease.

Food texture also influences the palatability and acceptability of foods for cats. A sudden change in texture may result in reduced food intake or food refusal. Cats accustomed to eating only dry foods may refuse moist foods and vice versa. Recognizing the preferred food texture from the dietary history will help identify textural change as a cause of inappetence.

Assess the Food(s)

After the nutritional status of the cat has been assessed and the key nutritional factors and their target levels have been determined, the adequacy of the food being fed can be assessed. The three steps to food assessment include: 1) ensuring the food has undergone feeding trials with cats, 2) determining the food's dry matter nutrient content (especially for the key nutritional factors) and 3) comparing the food's key nutritional factors with the recommended levels (Table 11-8).

In the United States, commercial foods that have been animal tested will usually have a nutritional adequacy statement on the label. (See Chapter 5.) Few if any homemade recipes have been animal tested according to prescribed feeding protocols. Commercial cat foods that have passed AAFCO-prescribed or other feeding tests provide reasonable assurance of nutrient availability and sufficient palatability to ensure that food intake will be sufficient to meet nutrient needs. However, even controlled animal testing is not infallible. Passing such tests does not ensure the food will be effective in preventing long-term nutrition and health problems. Therefore, in addition to having passed feeding tests, the food should be evaluated to ensure that the key nutritional factors are at levels appropriate for promoting long-term health.

Appendices L and M provide partial nutrient profiles for selected commercial foods and treats sold in the United States, Canada and Europe. The manufacturer should be contacted if the food in question cannot be found in these tables. Manufacturers' addresses and toll-free customer service numbers are listed on pet food labels. If the manufacturer cannot provide the necessary information, consider switching to a food for which this information is available.

Comparing a food's nutrient content with the cat's nutrient needs (Table 11-8) will help identify any significant nutritional imbalances in the food being fed. This comparison is fundamental to deciding whether or not to feed a different food.

Treats are either human foods (table foods) or commercial treats and are offered to cats for a variety of reasons. Excessive feeding of treats, however, can markedly affect the cumulative nutritional profile. Therefore, it is important to assess the impact of treats with respect to the dietary needs of an individual cat. The impact of treats on daily nutrient intake depends on three factors: 1) the nutrient profile of the treat, 2) the number of treats provided daily and 3) the nutrient composition of the cat's regular food. Meeting nutrient requirements is not the primary goal of feeding treats; therefore, many commercial treats are not complete and balanced. Appendix M lists common commercially available treats and their nutrient content. Similarly, most table foods are nutritionally incomplete and unbalanced and may contain high levels of fat, minerals or protein. If snacks are fed, it is simplest to recommend those that best match the nutritional profile recommended for a particular lifestage. Otherwise, the nutritional composition of the treat and food must be combined and assessed as the entire diet.

Assess the Feeding Method

The veterinarian should evaluate the feeding method, feeding frequency and the amount of food offered. It is also useful to know how the food is prepared (e.g., heated, water added, etc.) and by whom and where the cat is fed.

This information may help explain any apparent discrepancies between the dietary history and the physical findings and help identify risk factors associated with various feeding methods. It may not always be necessary to change the feeding method when managing healthy cats. However, a thorough evaluation includes verification that an appropriate feeding method is being used. (See Chapter 1.)

No single feeding method is optimal for all cats. The preferred method of feeding an individual cat is often determined by non-nutritional factors (i.e., food type, owner preference, owner schedule and feeding environment). Nutritional considerations for selecting an appropriate feeding regimen include the cat's body condition, health status/disease risk factors and the food's energy density and palatability.

Two methods are typically used to feed cats: 1) free choice in which the food is continuously available and the cat eats as much as it wants whenever it wants and 2) meal feeding in which a discrete amount of food is offered one or more times per day. Many owners use a combination of free-choice and meal-feeding methods. Typically, dry food is available throughout the day and supplemented with one or more meals of moist food. Free-choice or combination feeding accommodates the normal feeding behavior of cats by allowing the animal to eat several small meals spaced irregularly throughout the day and night.[3] Each feeding method has advantages and disadvantages that should be considered when making feeding recommendations (Table 11-9). The major disadvantages to combination feeding is the inability to accurately monitor and control food intake.

The amount fed is important because nutrient requirements are met by a combination of nutrient levels in the food and the amount of food fed. Even if a food has an appropriate profile of key nutritional factors, significant malnutrition could result from feeding excessive or insufficient amounts. The amount fed is appropriate if the cat has an optimal BCS (3/5) (See Chapter 1.) and body weight is stable. The amount fed can be estimated by calculation (See Chapter 1.) or by referring to feeding guides on product labels or product information. These guides, however, usually represent population averages and thus may not be optimal for individual cats.

Domestic cats display a variety of feeding behaviors that may have nutritional or non-nutritional bases. (See sidebar "Eating Behaviors.") Some of these behaviors are

Table 11-9. Advantages and disadvantages of various feeding methods for cats.

Methods	Advantages	Disadvantages	Food types
Free choice	Convenient Ensures adequate food availability Mimics natural feeding behavior Dampens postprandial alkaline tide (lower mean urinary pH)	Overconsumption leads to weight gain or obesity Difficult to monitor appetite and food intake Moist food may spoil Less owner contact	Dry Semi moist
Meal fed*	Enhances human-animal bond Facilitates monitoring of appetite and food intake Enhanced control of food intake	Enhanced postprandial alkaline tide (higher mean urinary pH) Large meals may result in vomiting Less convenient Three or more meals for pregnant or nursing queens, kittens or debilitated cats	Dry Semi moist Moist
Combination**	Enhances human-animal bond (vs. free choice) Variable effect on urinary pH	Poor monitoring of appetite and food intake Poor control of food intake Less convenient than free choice Variable effect on urinary pH	Dry Semi moist Moist

*One or more individual feedings per day, one to two hour availability per feeding.
**Dry foods available free choice, moist foods meal fed one or more times daily.

worrisome to owners and considered abnormal, when in fact they are normal. Other behaviors may indicate an underlying disease.

Determine a Feeding Plan

The aforementioned assessment of the cat, current food and feeding method should provide the necessary information to develop a feeding plan. Sometimes, the assessment steps determine that the current plan is optimal and no changes are necessary. However, changes in food, feeding method or both will need to be made if results of the assessment indicate that the food or feeding method is inappropriate. In either case, the cat should be reassessed regularly.

Select a Food(s)

It is not necessary to change foods if the food currently fed supplies the correct amounts of the key nutritional factors and the food has been test fed to cats at similar lifestages. However, a new food should be selected if discrepancies were determined during the food assessment phase. The new food should provide levels of the key nutritional factors listed in Table 11-8. Appendices L and M list nutrient levels for selected, readily available commercial cat foods and treats. The same information can be obtained directly from the manufacturer. Be sure to confirm that the new food is complete and balanced by verifying it has passed animal feeding tests.

Determine a Feeding Method

The method of feeding may not need to be revised if it appears adequate. Adult cats may be meal fed, free-choice fed or fed using a combination of methods. The method of choice largely depends on the food form, the ability of the cat to regulate food intake and owner preference. Most obese-prone cats should be fed a measured quantity of food; however, some cats can be fed low-calorie foods free

choice. Most cats tolerate once daily feeding with no problems; however, meal feeding at least twice daily is preferred. Cats should be allowed one to two hours to complete a measured meal; many cats will return for several small feedings before finishing the entire offering. Food should be available at all times for underweight cats to encourage sufficient food intake. In general, clean drinking water should be continuously available.

Cats are not typically bothered by food changes and food variety stimulates increased food intake.[6] Unfortunately, in a few cats, rapid changes in the food or feeding method can cause GI upsets or food refusal. Transitioning to a new food over four to seven days may be required to avoid food intolerances. To change to a new food, replace 25% of the old food with the new food on Day 1 and continue this incremental change daily until the change is complete on Day 4. A slower transition may be required for cats that have been historically sensitive to dietary changes, those with GI diseases and when the new food differs markedly from the old (e.g., low fat vs. high fat or raw meat vs. dry food).

Food and water bowls should be cleaned regularly with warm soapy water and rinsed well. Pans used for moist foods need daily cleaning, whereas dry food feeders should be cleaned at least weekly. Many cats prefer shallow dishes, especially "flat-faced" breeds such as Persians. Contamination of the chin and face with food particles can exacerbate feline acne. Using shallow pans and regular pan cleaning can help reduce the severity of the problem.

Reassessment

Cats provided proper nutritional management are healthy and alert, have ideal body condition and stable weight and have a clean, glossy coat. The owner should evaluate body condition every two to four weeks. In addition, owners should monitor daily food and water intake and observe the cat's interest in its food and its appetite. Stools should be evaluated regularly because changes in frequency or character may signify nutritional problems or disease. Normal stools should be firm, well-formed and medium to dark brown. Any abnormalities should be investigated. The veterinarian should also conduct a nutritional assessment as part of the annual physical examination and vaccination visit.

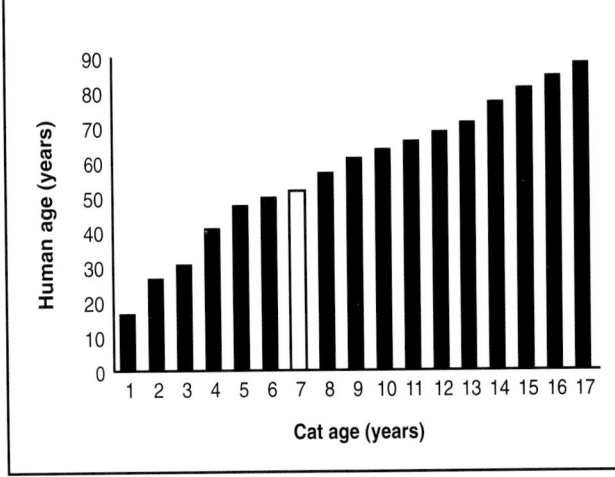

Figure 11-5. Comparison of age in cats and people. Age seven in cats (white bar) roughly corresponds to the age at which people are considered senior (51 years), whereas 12-year-old cats correspond to very old or geriatric people (69+ years). (Adapted from Reichenbach T. Comparison of age in cats and humans. Feline Practice 1987; 17: 28-30. Hayflick L. How and Why We Age. New York, NY: Ballantine Books, 1994.)

◼ OLDER CATS

For nutritional purposes, cats are often considered as being senior at seven to eight years of age and geriatric or very old beginning at 10 to 12 years of age.[101,102] There is an increasing prevalence of age-related diseases around seven years of age coupled with the gradual onset of behavioral, physical and metabolic changes related to aging.[103,a] Interestingly, age seven in cats roughly corresponds to the age at which people are considered senior (51 years), whereas 12-year-old cats correspond to very old or geriatric people (i.e., 69 years) (Figure 11-5).[101,104] Outwardly, a seven-year-old cat may not appear old, but changes in nutritional management and preventive care are important to reduce risk factors for common age-associated diseases, maintain good health and maximize longevity. It is important to remember the aging process is influenced by genetics, nutrition and environment. Further, an animal's chronologic age may not accurately reflect the animal's physiologic age (e.g., an eight-year-old cat with kidney disease and poor nutritional status is likely to be "physiologically older" than a healthy 11-year-old cat).

The minimum nutrient requirements of older cats are probably similar to those of young and middle-aged adult cats. The few studies evaluating the effect of aging on the nutritional needs of cats have shown minimal changes in nutrient requirements. Therefore, nutritional recommendations for older cats are based on risk factor management, extension of learning from other species and prudence. However, it is important to recognize the only nutritional modification known to slow aging and increase the life span is caloric restriction. Reducing caloric intake by 20 to 30% of normal while meeting essential nutrient needs reduces the aging process, cancer, renal disease and immune-mediated diseases in the animal models tested to date.[105] This level of caloric restriction is difficult to achieve in the long term and has not been incorporated into mainstream nutritional advice.

Older cats become less active and have reduced lean body mass. Together, these changes reduce the basal metabolic rate. Additionally, changes occur in virtually all body systems. Age-associated changes in physiologic function include reduced digestive function, immune response, glucose tolerance, renal function, smell, taste perception and numerous other changes (Table 11-10).[106-107] Not all cats develop all age-associated changes nor will the changes that develop necessarily occur in any predictable sequence. Aging cats become less adaptable and have reduced physiologic reserve to withstand perturbations in their health and environment, including changes in their food. Different rates of aging occur among older cats, thus there is greater diversity in individual animal needs than at any other lifestage. Individualization of nutritional management becomes even more important because of the poor adaptability of older cats. The goals for the nutritional management of older cats are:

- Maintenance of optimal nutrition (i.e., maintenance of ideal body condition and weight, adequate intake of a nutritious food and good hydration)

Table 11-10. Common physiologic changes and diseases associated with aging in cats.*

Body systems/functions	Age-related changes	Associated conditions and diseases
Metabolism	Decreased thirst sensitivity	Dehydration
	Decreased thermoregulation	Hypothermia or hyperthermia
	Decreased immunocompetence	Susceptibility to infections, disease and cancer
	Decreased rate of drug metabolism	Drug intolerance
	Increased sleep	Irritability
	Decreased activity and metabolic rate	Loss of body mass, reduced BMR and obesity
Special senses	Decreased olfaction	Reduced food intake and weight loss
	Decreased taste perception	Reduced food intake and weight loss
	Decreased hearing	
	Decreased visual acuity	
Oral cavity	Decreased salivary secretion	Increased oral disease
	Increased tooth loss, dental calculus	Painful or difficult prehension
		Reduced food intake and weight loss
	Increased periodontal disease	Susceptibility to sepsis and end-organ damage
Gastrointestinal	Decreased liver function	Reduced nutrient assimilation
	Increased cellular infiltrates	
	Decreased digestive function	Reduced nutrient digestibility
	Decreased colonic motility	Constipation
	Decreased pancreatic function	Reduced nutrient digestibility
Endocrine	Decreased pancreatic function	Glucose intolerance and diabetes mellitus
	Decreased adrenal function	Reduced ability to respond to stress
	Alterations in thyroid structure and function	Hyperthyroidism
Integumentary	Loss of elasticity, dry, thin coat, hyperplasia of sebaceous glands with decreased sebum and increased waxy secretions	Dermatitis
		Intradermal cysts
		Dry, flaky coat
Urinary	Decreased total renal function	Chronic renal failure
		Hypokalemia
	Alterations in acid excretion	Decreased acid-base regulation
		Metabolic acidosis
Reproductive	Testicular tumors and atrophy, mammary gland nodules	Reproductive gland neoplasia
		Reproductive failure
	Irregular estrous cycles	Pyometra
	Decreased conception rates	
	Cystic endometrial hyperplasia	
Musculoskeletal	Decreased lean mass and tone	Decreased BMR, weakness, decreased activity
	Decreased bone mass	
	Degenerative joint changes	Osteoarthritis, spondylosis
Cardiovascular	Decreased cardiac output, increased peripheral resistance, hypertension	Cardiomyopathy, valvular regurgitation
		Hypertension and end-organ damage
	Valvular thickening	
Respiratory	Reduced vital capacity and compliance	Chronic respiratory disease
	Increased respiratory rate and residual air capacity	
Nervous	Alterations in neurotransmitter levels	Senility
	Progressive decline in cellularity of nervous tissues	Decline in special senses
	Decreased reactivity to stimuli and cognition decline	Behavioral changes

Key: BMR = basal metabolic rate.
*As in any biologic system there is much individual variation. An individual aging animal may have few to many of these changes. Also, the age at which changes occur, and their severity, is quite variable.

- Risk factor management (i.e., minimization of associated disease risks)
- Disease management (i.e., amelioration of clinical signs of common diseases, slowing progression of certain chronic diseases)
- Improvement in the quality and longevity of life.

This section describes how to assess older cats and meet their nutritional needs.

Assessment

Assess the Animal

HISTORY AND PHYSICAL EXAMINATION

A complete history should be taken and physical examination performed, as described for young to middle-aged adult cats. Of particular interest are physiologic changes associated with aging and age-related diseases. Note any changes in appetite, food or water intake, activity, oral health and body condition. Abnormalities in these parameters are often early indicators of underlying disease. Oral disease is the most prevalent disease in older cats; however, weight loss, renal disease, cardiac disorders, diabetes mellitus and hyperthyroidism are frequently diagnosed in this age category. Kidney disease may affect nearly 30% of older cats and is a major cause of feline death.[79,109] Physical evaluation of renal size, shape and firmness may uncover kidney abnormalities, whereas thoracic auscultation may expose cardiac disease. Hyperthyroidism may be detected by palpating enlarged thyroid glands or may be suspected based on the history and other physical findings. A fundic examination may help detect hypertension, which is often secondary to renal, cardiac or thyroid disease in older cats. Retinal hemorrhage was a common finding in a group of older hypertensive cats.[83]

LABORATORY AND OTHER CLINICAL INFORMATION

Specific abnormalities in the physical and historical examination should be pursued further using appropriate

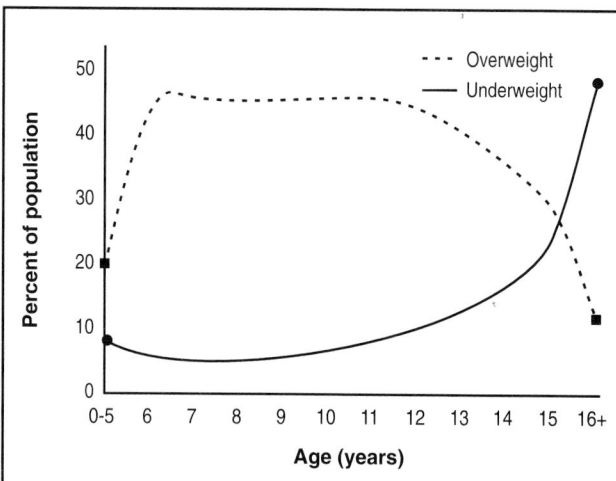

Figure 11-6. Proportion of overweight (body condition score [BCS] 4/5 or 5/5) and underweight (BCS 1/5 or 2/5) cats. Note that middle-aged and older cats are commonly overweight (six to 12 years old), whereas very old or geriatric cats (over 12 years old) are at greater risk of being underweight. (Adapted from Armstrong PJ, Lund EM. Changes in body composition and energy balance with aging. Veterinary Clinical Nutrition 1996; 3: 83-96.)

diagnostic procedures. A geriatric-type blood panel to screen for common age-associated diseases should be performed annually. The minimum database should include a complete blood count, urine specific gravity and sediment examination and a serum biochemistry profile. The biochemistry panel should include measurements of albumin, globulin, urea nitrogen, creatinine, glucose, alkaline phosphatase, alanine aminotransferase, calcium, potassium, phosphorus, sodium, chloride and bicarbonate. Serum total thyroxine (T_4) concentrations should be assessed if clinical or biochemical abnormalities suggest hyperthyroidism. FeLV and FIV testing should be current and repeated if potential exposure has occurred or suspicious clinical signs are present. Specialized diagnostics may be indicated by the physical or biochemical findings (e.g., electrocardiography, ultrasonography, radiography, blood pressure monitoring).

KEY NUTRITIONAL FACTORS

The nutrient requirements of older cats are unlikely to be significantly different from those of young to middle-aged adult cats. However, the recommended range of nutrient allowances can be optimized to support changes in physiologic function and reduce risk factors for common age-related diseases. Table 11-8 summarizes key nutritional factors for older adult cats.

Water

Water is an often overlooked but critical nutrient in the health of older cats. Aging impairs thirst sensitivity, which is already low in cats compared with other species.[4,107] In addition, the decline in renal function observed in many older cats may increase water losses due to impaired urine concentrating ability. Together, these characteristics predispose older cats to dehydration. Chronic dehydration can impair normal metabolic processes and exacerbate subclinical disease. In addition, dehydration reduces the cat's ability to thermoregulate. Water intake in healthy cats without increased losses is 200 to 250 ml per day.[110] This intake comes from a combination of free water, metabolic water and water contained in food. The water content of food may be increased by changing to a moist food or adding water to the food (moist or dry). Offering low-salt broth, meat juices or "pet drinks" has been advocated as a means to enhance water consumption; however, the long-term effectiveness of this strategy is unknown. Clean fresh water should be continuously available and readily accessible to further encourage increased water intake.

Energy

Well-controlled studies to determine the energy needs of older cats have not been conducted. Reductions in lean body mass, basal metabolic rate and physical activity are factors that decrease energy requirements as animals age.[105,111] In many species, the decline in lean body mass is counterbalanced by an increase in total body fat such that obesity becomes more prevalent with age.[103,105] However, studies reveal the prevalence of obesity plateaus and then declines in cats after seven years of age, whereas the prevalence of underweight conditions increases dramatically after 11 years of age (Figure 11-6).[37,103] This observation may be explained by the high occurrence of disease in this age group, reduced food intake due to impaired appetite or sensory function, an age-related decline in food digestion or assimilation or a combination of these factors. Although the prevalence of obesity declines after seven years, a significant proportion of older cats remain overweight (Figure 11-6). Both obesity and cachexia significantly increase the risk of mortality in cats over eight years of age, with obese cats nearly three times as likely to die as cats of optimal weight.[56] Therefore, it is critical to recommend foods and feeding methods that will achieve optimal weight and body condition in individual older cats.

In a study of healthy cats, energy intake (ME) declined slightly until approximately 10 years of age. However, a sharp increase in food intake was observed in very old cats (12 years and older).[111] A 10% reduction in fat digestibility was responsible for a similar reduction in total food digestibility in these very old cats. The digestibility of dietary fat declined significantly with age, whereas protein and carbohydrate digestibility remained stable. Thus, reduced fat digestibility in very old cats was offset by increased food intake, as a result digestible energy intake was not different between age groups.[106] From these studies, it is not clear if changes in the metabolic rate of older cats are compensated for by a reduction in fat digestion, or if older cats simply compensate for impaired digestion by consuming more food. The latter seems more likely based on observations that weight loss is more prevalent than obesity in very old cats. A decline in pancreatic enzyme secretion is a common physiologic change associated with aging in many species and could be expected to reduce digestibility of dietary fat. In addition, hepatic changes seen in older cats may influence nutrient assimilation.[103] Based on these studies, the energy density of foods formulated for senior cats should be between 3.5 to 4.5 kcal/g (14.6 to 18.8 kJ/g) DMB. Very old cats should be fed energy-dense foods (4.0 to 4.5 kcal/g [16.7 to 18.8 kJ/g] DMB) and caloric intake should not be restricted, except to prevent or treat obesity.

Reasonable estimates of caloric needs in senior cats are 1.1 to 1.4 x RER (55 to 70 kcal/kg body weight [230 to 293 kJ/kg body weight]), with very old cats needing up to 1.6 x RER (80 kcal/kg body weight [344 kJ/kg body weight]).[111] Obese cats can be managed with standard weight-control programs appropriate for adult maintenance. (See Chapter 13.)

Protein

Dietary protein should not be restricted in apparently healthy older cats. Adequate protein and energy intake are needed to sustain lean body mass, protein synthesis and immune function in aging cats. Although controversial, the protein needs of older animals may be somewhat greater than those of young to middle-aged adults.[112,113] In people, the recommended daily allowance of protein for the elderly is increased by 25% above that for adult maintenance. The equivalent increase in minimum protein requirement for cats is approximately to 18% DM protein or 15% protein calories using ideal proteins. The recommended protein allowance for healthy older cats fed commercial foods is 30% of the diet dry matter when the variable digestibility and protein quality of natural food ingredients are considered. An additional benefit to maintaining moderate protein concentrations in foods for older cats is the palatability-enhancing effect of animal proteins. Enhanced palatability resulting from animal proteins may conceivably improve food intake and weight maintenance in very old cats. However, the long-term effects of feeding foods with high dietary protein levels to healthy cats are still largely unknown. High-protein foods have been implicated in the progression of renal failure.[114] Protein restriction in

foods for older cats has been advocated because of the high prevalence of renal disease in this age group[111] and the knowledge that renal failure is rarely diagnosed until at least three-fourths of renal function is lost. The potential benefits of this restriction include a delay in age-related renal impairment and slowed progression of subclinical renal disease. In one study, investigators examining the effect of protein-calorie restriction in cats following five-sixths nephrectomy observed a reduction in proteinuria and glomerular injury in cats fed reduced-protein foods (27.6% DM) compared with high-protein foods (51.7% DM).[59] A secondary finding was an increased occurrence of hypokalemia in cats fed the high-protein food.[115] However, a subsequent study demonstrated no change in renal pathology following protein restriction and a slight benefit (i.e., reduced cellular infiltrates and tubular lesions) to caloric restriction (i.e., 56 kcal/kg body weight [low-calorie group] vs. 75 kcal/kg body weight [high-calorie group]).[116] Unfortunately, these studies may not be directly comparable because the dietary protein sources were markedly different. Thus, there is no consensus about the role of protein reduction in slowing progression of feline renal disease.

Healthy older cats should receive sufficient protein to adequately meet protein needs and avoid protein-calorie malnutrition. Any additional protein needs of older cats can be fulfilled by improving protein quality without increasing protein intake. Until further research defines an optimal range of dietary protein for older cats, moderate levels of dietary protein (30 to 45%) are recommended (Table 11-8).

Fat

Although weight loss is prevalent in very old cats, obesity still affects a large portion of the older cat population (Figure 11-6).[103] Certain diseases associated with obesity are also common in older cats (e.g., diabetes mellitus, hypertension and heart disease). In addition, the risk of death increases nearly threefold in older obese cats (i.e., eight to 12 years).[56,107,117] Moderate to low levels of fat are indicated to reduce the risk of obesity.[37,118] However, very old cats need energy-dense foods and ample levels of essential fatty acids. Essential fatty acids (i.e., linoleic, arachidonic and possibly linolenic acid) help maintain normal skin and coat condition. As animals age, they tend to lose skin elasticity, develop epidermal and follicular atrophy and have reduced sebum secretion.[107] Marked reduction in dietary fat (i.e., calorie-restricted or "light" foods) is not ideal for older cats unless they are obese prone. Fat should be highly digestible in foods intended for older cats. As discussed above, fat digestion declines as cats age, which may account for the weight decline noted in very old cats.[111] Dietary fat improves the palatability of food and contributes significantly to the energy density. Therefore, maintaining moderate fat concentrations improves food and caloric intake in older cats and enhances absorption of fat-soluble vitamins.[10] Table 11-8 lists recommendations for the fat content in foods for older cats. Foods with lower fat levels are recommended for obese-prone cats, and foods with higher fat levels should be fed to thin cats (BCS <3/5) and cats with poor appetites. Essential fatty acids should be provided at levels at or above those recommended for young to middle-aged adults.

Fiber

Fiber facilitates GI health by a variety of mechanisms. (See Chapters 2 and 22.) Dietary fiber promotes normal intestinal motility and provides fuel for colonocytes via volatile fatty acids resulting from fermentation by colonic

NORMAL CATS

Table 11-11. Most common causes of mortality in cats.*

Cause of death	Proportion of deaths (%)
Cancer	35
Kidney disease	24.9
Heart disease	10.7
Diabetes mellitus	7.6
Feline infectious peritonitis	5.9

*Morris Animal Foundation. Animal health survey: Top five causes of death as reported by owners. Denver, CO. 1998.

microbes. These effects can be attained by feeding small amounts (i.e., <5%) of soluble and insoluble fiber. Promoting intestinal motility may benefit older cats with constipation.[107] Constipation is common in older animals because of a combination of factors, including reduced water intake, limited activity and reduced colonic motility. Although fiber should not be the sole factor in managing constipation, it is beneficial when provided regularly. Dietary fiber also is beneficial in the management of obesity, diabetes mellitus and hyperlipidemia.[118-121] (See Chapters 13 and 24.)

High levels of dietary fiber (>10%) reduce food dry matter digestibility and dilute caloric density. Very old cats appear to need energy-dense foods; therefore, high levels of dietary fiber are not recommended except to manage obesity and fiber-responsive diseases (i.e., diabetes mellitus, colitis and constipation).

Calcium and Phosphorus

After skeletal growth is complete, the nutritional requirement for calcium and phosphorus declines to levels needed by adult cats and is thought to remain relatively constant for life. Unlike the situation in people, osteoporosis is not commonly diagnosed in very old cats. Nevertheless, the bone mass of adult cats remains stable until seven years of age and then declines.[33] The reason for the decline has not been characterized but is presumably related to the loss in lean and total body mass that occurs with aging. With loss of body mass, less bone mass is required for structural support. Alternatively, bone loss resulting from buffering chronic elevations of metabolic acids cannot be ruled out. Older cats have been reported to maintain a greater metabolic acid load and a significantly lower urinary pH compared with young adult cats.[122,123] Interestingly, a lower urinary pH (i.e., higher metabolic acid load) is also a risk factor for development of calcium oxalate urolithiasis, which is most prevalent in older cats.[95,97] Older cats should receive foods with moderate levels of available dietary calcium (Table 11-8) to help maintain bone mass and possibly reduce the risk of calcium oxalate urolithiasis.

In contrast to the moderate calcium needs during aging, reduction of dietary phosphorus is commonly recommended in foods designed for older cats. The recommendation is predicated on the fact that nearly 30% of older cats may have kidney disease.[109] Further, in a survey of pet owners, kidney disease was the second leading cause of nonaccidental death in cats (Table 11-11).[79] As discussed in the section on feeding young and middle-aged cats, renal insufficiency is rarely diagnosed until significant loss of renal function has occurred. Thus, a large proportion of older cats have subclinical renal damage and may benefit from reduced dietary phosphorus. It is commonly accepted that phosphorus restriction slows the progression of renal disease in cats. (See Chapter 19.) Phosphorus reduction helps decrease: 1) the renal excretory workload, 2) phosphorus retention, 3) renal secondary hyperparathyroidism and 4) the subsequent renal mineralization in cats with chronic renal insufficiency.[80,114] Therefore, phosphorus levels should be reduced from levels typically found in commercial foods (See Appendix L.) in the early nutritional management of renal disease in dogs and cats.[60] Slowing progression of early renal disease in affected older cats should extend longevity. Phosphorus may be reduced to as low as 0.3% of the food (DM) for cats with overt renal disease, otherwise the general population of older cats should be fed foods containing 0.5 to 0.7% DM phosphorus. Table 11-8 lists recommended levels of calcium and phosphorus for foods intended for older cats. Although adult cats appear to be remarkably tolerant to perturbations in dietary calcium-phosphorus ratios,[124] a ratio between 0.9:1 to 1.1:1 maximizes availability[77] and ratios between 0.9:1 to 1.5:1 are recommended.

Potassium

The potassium requirement for older cats is thought to be greater than that for young to middle-aged cats. This impression has come from anecdotal reports of low serum potassium levels and improved attitude, appetite, muscle strength and renal function following oral potassium supplementation in older cats. However, the potassium requirement of healthy older cats has not been determined and an increased need remains speculative. Nevertheless, factors common in older cats that support the need for increased dietary potassium include: 1) kaliuresis as a result of kidney disease, high dietary protein or high metabolic and/or dietary acid load, 2) reduced food intake and 3) increased intestinal loss. Older cats with normal appetite and renal function probably do not benefit significantly from increased dietary potassium levels. However, hypokalemia can cause signs ranging from mild lethargy to marked polymyopathy or nephropathy. Thus, increasing dietary potassium to support moderate losses may benefit some older cats. Levels as low as 0.3% resulted in hypokalemia when provided in high-protein or acidified foods.[93] Dietary potassium levels for older cats should be at least 0.6% of the diet dry matter (Table 11-8).

Magnesium

Increased losses of magnesium, similar to those seen with potassium, may affect magnesium balance in older cats. Hypomagnesemia has also been associated with refractory hypokalemia, particularly in cats with diabetes mellitus.[125] The benefit of limiting dietary magnesium in cats is a reduced risk of struvite-mediated lower urinary tract disease. However, the risk of struvite-mediated disease is low in older cats (Figure 11-7).[126] Further, foods containing very low levels of magnesium have been associated with the development of calcium oxalate uroliths in an epidemiologic survey of cats[95] and deficiency is known to increase urolith formation in rats.[127] Therefore, magnesium should be provided at moderate levels (Table 11-8) and severe magnesium restriction should be avoided (less than 0.04% DM).

Sodium and Chloride

Avoiding excessive sodium intake to reduce risk factors appears even more important in older cats than in young to middle-aged cats. Although the sodium and chloride requirements of older cats are not likely to be different from those of young to middle-aged adults, the prevalence of chronic diseases associated with hypertension (e.g., renal disease, hyperthyroidism, cardiac disease) increases with age. The exact prevalence of secondary hypertension in the feline population is unknown, but it appears highest in older cats. In one study, systolic arterial pressures were significantly higher in older cats than in middle-aged or younger cats.[128] Further, hypertension affects 60 to 65% of cats with renal disease and 23% of cats with hyperthyroidism.[61,85,129] Chronic hypertension results in end-organ damage and progression of renal and cardiac disease; therefore, control of risk factors for salt-sensitive individuals is desirable. Unfortunately, accurate monitoring of blood pressure in all feline patients is uncommon and hypertension is rarely diagnosed until clinical signs are evident. Therefore, nutritional needs for sodium and chloride should be met, but excesses should be avoided.

Regulation of acid-base homeostasis and normal plasma osmolality depends, in part, on adequate sodium and chloride intake. Deficiencies of sodium and chloride can have deleterious effects in older cats; therefore, over-restriction should be avoided. The minimum dietary requirement of sodium for adult cats is 0.08% DM.[9,88] AAFCO recommends an intake of 0.2% of the diet dry matter, or 2.5 times the minimum requirement.[58] Some commercial moist foods exceed 1.0% dietary sodium (DM) or 12.5 times the requirement. (See Appendix L.) Sodium intake at this level is markedly above that needed for optimal health. Chloride is now recognized as a co-determinant in salt-sensitive hypertension, thus control of dietary excess is equally important.[86,130] Unfortunately, little information is available about the chloride requirement of cats. An intake of 0.2 to 0.6% DM sodium is recommended to ensure sodium adequacy and simultaneously avoid excess in older cats (Table 11-8). Minimum chloride levels of 0.19% are suggested; however, more typically, chloride values are approximately 1.5 times the concentration of sodium.

Urinary pH

Older cats frequently have clinical or subclinical renal disease that can impair their ability to compensate for acid-base alterations resulting from metabolic or dietary influences. In a study in which cats were fed a food with higher urinary acidifying potential (pH 6.39 vs. pH 6.6 in the control food), older cats lost more weight, had lower red cell counts and had greater systemic acid loads than younger cats.[131] This observation, combined with the reduced risk of struvite urolithiasis, increased risk of calcium oxalate urolithiasis and high frequency of kidney disease in older cats, supports the idea that foods fed to older cats should have a lower urine acidifying potential (i.e., higher published urinary pH averages) than foods for young and middle-aged adults. A safe range of *measured* urinary pH values in older cats is still between 6.2 to 6.5.

The acidifying potential of commercial foods is not typically tested for in older cats, despite the fact that older cats generate a significantly lower urinary pH than younger cats fed the same foods.[123] To achieve a normal urinary pH, the acidifying potential of foods for older cats should be lower than that of foods for young to middle-aged cats. Published urinary pH averages should be greater for foods for older cats than for foods for young to middle-aged adults, unless the foods have been specifically tested in old (senior) or very old cats and found to be safe. Providing food with less acidifying potential helps avoid metabolic acidosis and its complications in older cats.[95,97]

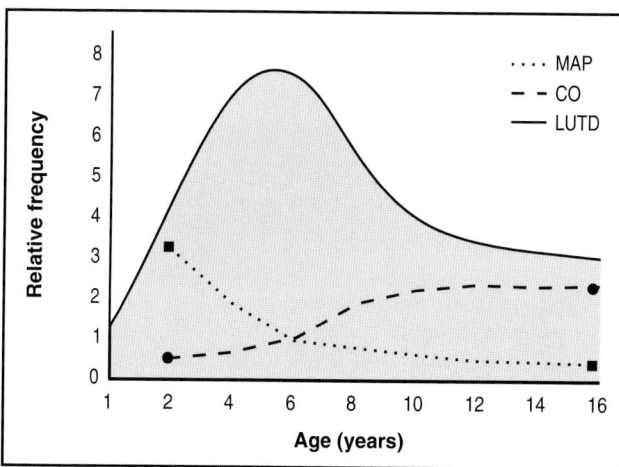

Figure 11-7. Relative frequency of feline lower urinary tract disease (LUTD), struvite (magnesium ammonium phosphate, MAP) urolithiasis and calcium oxalate (CO) urolithiasis in various age cats. Note that LUTD is most common in adult cats, struvite urolithiasis is most common in adult cats less than six years old and calcium oxalate urolithiasis is most common in cats over six years old. (Adapted from Bartges JW. Lower urinary tract disease in older cats: What's common, what's not. Veterinary Clinical Nutrition 1996; 3: 57-62. Thumchai R, Lulich JP, Osborne CA, et al. Epizootiologic evaluation of urolithiasis in cats: 3498 cases (1982-1992). Journal of the American Veterinary Medical Association 1996; 208: 547-551.)

Palatability and Digestibility

Reduced smell or taste, the presence of oral disease or metabolic disturbances, the use of medications or a combination of factors can impair appetite and food intake in older cats (Table 11-10). Foods for very old cats should be highly palatable and highly digestible to lessen concerns about weight loss and inadequate food intake.

Texture

Oral disease is the most common disease of older cats.[a] Age-related changes include an increased prevalence of dental calculus, periodontal disease, loss of teeth and oral neoplasia.[132] Cats with poor oral health have more difficulty eating, and pathologic lesions may act as a portal for bacteria into the body. In addition, decreased salivary secretions and immune function may exacerbate oral infection and disease.[133] Food texture can play an important role in the well-being of older cats. As in young to middle-aged adult cats, the texture of dry foods fed to older cats may result in less calculus and plaque accumulation than if moist foods are fed.[99,100] Dry foods designed with dental cleansing benefits improve oral health by reducing accumulation of dental substrates (i.e., plaque and calculus) and reducing the severity of gingivitis.[99,134] (See Chapter 16.) Conversely, hard dry foods may cause oral pain if fed to cats with gingivitis or periodontitis. Dry foods with softer texture, semi-moist foods or moist foods may be easier to chew. The optimal texture depends on the oral health and food texture preference of individual older cats.

Assess The Food(s) and Feeding Method

After assessing the cat and identifying key nutritional factors, the food(s) and feeding methods should be assessed as described for young and middle-aged cats. Foods currently being fed should be evaluated as discussed previously. (See Chapter 1.)

- Ensure feeding tests have been conducted (i.e., review package label for statement).
- Compare the nutrient content of the current food with the cat's nutrient needs and the key nutritional factors. (See Table 11-8 and Appendix L.)
- Identify discrepancies between the key nutritional factors and the food currently fed.

It may not always be necessary to change the food and feeding method when managing healthy geriatric cats. However, a thorough evaluation includes verification that an appropriate food and feeding method are being used. Older cats should be re-evaluated at each examination because nutrition and health needs change with disease status, risk factors and overall health.

Determine a Feeding Plan

Older cats are more prone to weight loss, cardiac disease, renal disease and metabolic aberrations and usually have a decreased activity level than younger cats. The feeding plan should be based on the information obtained in the assessment as well as detected risk factors. Nutritional surveillance and therefore the number of contacts per year should be increased for older cats. Although goals remain the same as those listed in the introduction, each animal should be evaluated individually.

Select a Food(s)

Several nutrients are of particular interest because of their role in the management of health risks or age-related disease or because older cats poorly tolerate and adapt to wider variations in nutrient concentrations. The nutrient profile of the current food should be compared with the appropriate key nutritional factors to determine if the food is satisfactory.

A different food should be selected if discrepancies are found between the recommended levels of key nutritional factors and those in the current food (Table 11-8). Appendix L lists nutrient levels for several readily available commercial cat foods, or the product manufacturer can be contacted for the same information. Foods that have passed AAFCO or similar feeding trials for adult cats are recommended.

An important goal when managing the nutrition of older cats is to ensure proper food intake. There is little need to change the form of food a cat eats well simply because of age. In fact, some cats will refuse to eat a new form or texture of food. However, cats with poor intake may benefit from changing food forms if the new food is more palatable and easier to chew.

Determine a Feeding Method

As mentioned above, healthy senior cats may be fed free choice, meal fed or fed by a combination of methods. Obese cats should be offered measured amounts of food. The measured quantity may be fed in meals or dispensed at one time to allow continuous access throughout the day. Underweight cats should be allowed to eat free choice. Only dry and semi-moist foods may be fed free choice and these foods are typically less palatable than moist foods. Older cats may have reduced olfaction and taste perception; therefore, it may be preferable to feed moist and warm foods to encourage food intake. Providing dry foods for free-choice consumption and moist foods in several meals throughout the day may optimize food intake. Adding broth or canned meat juices to dry foods may enhance food and water intake in geriatric cats.

Although most cats do not experience digestive upsets with typical food changes, a gradual transition to a new food may benefit older cats. Progressively exchanging the new food for the usual food over four to seven days will minimize untoward effects and food refusal.

Reassessment

Veterinarians should examine and conduct a nutritional assessment of geriatric cats regularly. The frequency of monitoring depends on the overall health of the cat and the presence or absence of chronic diseases. Annual veterinary examinations are usually recommended for older cats, whereas biannual check-ups are recommended for very old cats.[102]

The owner should evaluate body condition every two to four weeks. Although lean body mass tends to decline as cats reach extreme geriatric age (older than 16 years), significant loss of muscle mass or body weight warrants immediate evaluation by a veterinarian. Owners should also monitor daily food and water intake and stools and urination. Any persistent change, whether increased or decreased, should prompt the veterinarian to assess the cat and perform diagnostics as indicated.

Dental disease is the most frequent diagnosis made in geriatric cats.[a] Therefore, a dental health program should be part of every older cat's preventive health care plan. (See Chapter 16.)

■ REPRODUCING CATS

Domestic cats generally reach puberty by six to nine months of age. However, the best age for breeding is between one and one-half to seven years of age.[135] Before 10 to 12 months of age, queens are still growing and must meet nutritional demands for their own growth as well as for their kittens, if pregnant. Queens older than seven years should not be bred due to reproductive complications, irregular estrous cycles and reduced litter size.[135] The reproductive stage of the queen can be divided into four periods: 1) estrus and mating, 2) gestation, 3) lactation and 4) weaning. Reproducing cats have significantly altered nutritional needs compared with maintenance requirements, especially during late pregnancy and lactation. During reproduction, energy requirements increase and the minimum requirements for certain nutrients exceed even those required for growth.

The objectives of a good feeding program for reproduction are to optimize: 1) the health and body condition of the queen throughout the various reproductive periods, 2) reproductive performance and 3) kitten health and development through the weaning period. Key indicators of optimal reproduction are ease of conception, a low rate of fetal and neonatal death, normal parturition, maximum litter size, adequate lactation and an optimal rate of growth of healthy kittens. Providing adequate nutrition throughout reproduction has long-range health implications for the offspring. Immune function is impaired for life in animals born to nutritionally deficient dams.[136] Meeting the nutritional needs of reproducing queens is critical to successful conception, delivery and weaning of healthy kittens.

Lactation begins at parturition and lasts six to 12 weeks depending on breed, kitten growth rates and management practices. Most kittens are sufficiently mature at eight weeks of age to maintain adequate food intake for optimal development. Purebred kittens are typically weaned later than domestic shorthair kittens. Lactation is the most demanding stage of reproduction. The queen must maintain its own nutritional needs and provide nutritionally complete, energy-dense milk to support the needs of growing kittens. Consequently, queens should enter lactation with sufficient energy stores to support needs above those supplied by daily food intake. Poor lactation performance is common without these reserves. Thus, successful lactation depends on appropriate nutritional management during the pre-breeding period, gestation and lactation.

Assessment

Assess the Animal

ESTRUS AND MATING

Optimal nutrition of reproducing cats should precede mating and conception, and ideally start when the animal is a kitten. Female cats are seasonally polyestrous. Repeated estrous cycles occur throughout the breeding season, which typically occurs from January through September in the northern hemisphere. Light duration and intensity are major determinants for the estrous period. Therefore, artificial lighting and latitude variation alter the breeding period for individual cats. Estrus in the queen is characterized by vocalizing, rolling, rubbing and treading; these behaviors culminate in acceptance of the male. Behavioral estrus averages seven to nine days (range one to 21). Cats are induced ovulators (i.e., coital contact is typically required for a luteinizing hormone surge and ovulation).

Queens should have a current vaccination history and be treated for internal and external parasites before breeding. A history and physical examination should precede breeding to assess problems that may interfere with conception, parturition and lactation. Queens should be at ideal body weight at mating (BCS 3/5). Small variations in body condition can be corrected during pregnancy; however, breeding should be delayed in cats that are significantly under- or overweight (BCS <2/5 or >4/5). Both obesity and undernourishment can be detrimental to reproduction. Malnourished queens may fail to conceive, abort or bear small underweight kittens. Malnourished cats may have a markedly reduced lactation. Lactating queens normally lose weight, but their body weight should return to normal before the next breeding. Obese cats are reported to have a greater incidence of dystocia.[137] Historical or physical evidence of a narrow pelvic canal, whether due to trauma, genetics or nutritional deficiency warrants careful assessment. Mammary tissue and teat development should be evaluated. Although congenital defects (e.g., multiple teats or teat malformation) rarely prevent queens from raising normal-sized litters, selection of such genetics is questionable. Only cats in excellent health should be considered for breeding.

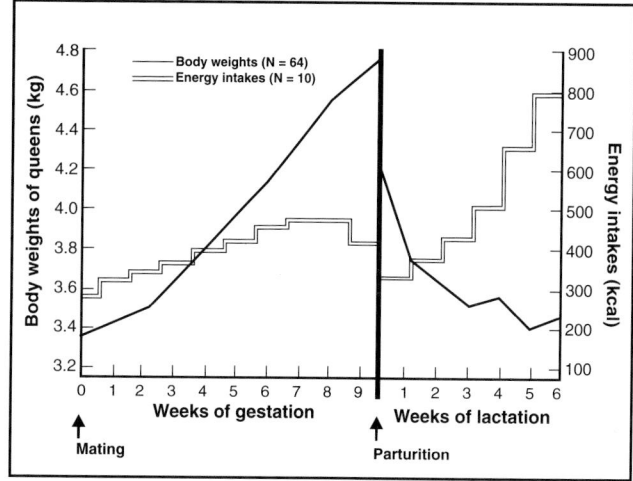

Figure 11-8. Body weight and energy intake during gestation and lactation in queens. Unlike bitches, which have a dramatic increase in energy intake and body weight during the last trimester, queens have a regular linear increase in both body weight and energy intake throughout gestation. Mobilized stores of body fat provide needed energy during lactation, which accounts for weight loss during this period. Food intake parallels lactation and peaks during the sixth to seventh week. (Adapted from Loveridge GG. Body weight changes and energy intake of cats during gestation and lactation. Animal Technology 1985; 37: 7-15.)

Tomcats should also be healthy and in optimal body condition (3/5); however, abnormalities associated with moderate deviations from ideal (BCS 2/5 to 4/5) have not been reported. In addition to a standard physical examination, the penis, prepuce and testes should be evaluated for anatomic defects. Previous reproductive performance including a weight history should be reviewed. The level of activity required during the breeding period should be ascertained. Single matings result in minimal changes in energy needs, whereas multiple matings may require an increase in the amount of food fed or an adjustment in feeding method, based on body condition.

PREGNANCY

The first assessment step is to diagnose pregnancy. Abdominal palpation is the most commonly used procedure to diagnose pregnancy in cats. The fetal vesicles can be reliably palpated from 14 to 25 days of gestation.[135] An enlarged uterus is palpable from Day 25 to parturition. Ultrasound can detect pregnancy as early Day 11 of gestation and fetal heartbeats are typically heard at 22 days.[138] Radiographic diagnosis requires calcification of the fetal skeleton and is most reliable after Day 45 of gestation. Gestation usually lasts 63 to 65 days (range 58 to 70 days) in queens, thus radiography is not useful for early pregnancy diagnosis but is most useful for determining litter size. In addition to the diagnosis of pregnancy, an assessment should include a dietary history, physical examination and any indicated laboratory analyses. Evaluations of body condition, weight gain and food intake are most important. Minimal diagnostics are usually required if the pelvic structures and mammary glands were evaluated and parasite, FeLV/FIV and vaccination status were determined before breeding.

One of the early indicators of successful breeding and conception is a steady gain in body weight. Weight gain increases linearly from conception to parturition in queens (Figure 11-8). This pattern is different from that of most other species, which experience small increases in body weight until the last third of gestation when weight gain and energy intake greatly increase. Weight gain in early pregnancy is not associated with significant growth of reproductive tissues or conceptuses but appears to be stored in energy depots (presumably as fat) to support lactation.[139] Mean weight gain during gestation is approximately 40% of the pre-mating weight (900 to 1,200 g for a litter of average size) and has been described by the equation:[139]

Weight gain (g) = 888.9 + (106.5)n
(where n = number of neonates)

At parturition, only 40% of the weight gained by queens during gestation will be lost,[139] whereas bitches should return to pre-breeding weight.[140] The remaining 60% of prepartum weight gain will be used during lactation to sustain milk production. Poor nutrition may lead to failure to conceive, fetal death, fetal malformations and underweight kittens. Queens underweight at parturition may subsequently experience poor lactation performance and inability to maintain body condition. As mentioned above, poor maternal nutrition may impair the kittens' immunocompetence for life.

Overnutrition or obesity (BCS 5/5) has an equally negative effect on pregnancy outcome. Stillbirths, dystocia and cesarean sections occur more frequently in obese queens than in cats at ideal body condition.[137,141] Ensuring the queen is at ideal weight (BCS 3/5) before breeding is preferable to limiting food intake during gestation. Therefore, good nutritional management is important to optimal reproductive performance.

If queens are listless or have a poor appetite, the physical examination should closely evaluate uterine size and shape and any vaginal discharges. Laboratory evaluation should include a complete blood count and measurement of serum concentrations of glucose, calcium, protein, urea nitrogen, creatinine, phosphorus and potassium. The abdomen and uterus should be evaluated by ultrasound to evaluate fetal viability or when pyometra is suspected.

LACTATION

Unless difficulties arise during parturition or lactation, most queens will not be examined by a veterinarian. Thus, pre-lactation counseling of the breeder or owner is important because most of the assessment will be performed without veterinary supervision. The queen and kittens should be weighed within 24 hours after parturition. The queen should weigh 700 to 900 g above the pre-breeding weight and each kitten should weigh approximately 100 g. The queen should be evaluated for vaginal discharges, body temperature and maternal behavioral characteristics. A dark reddish vaginal discharge is normal. Bright red discharges indicate hemorrhage, whereas foul-smelling, greenish, gray or brown discharges may indicate a retained fetus, retained placenta or infection. The queen's appetite, which is reduced 24 to 48 hours before parturition, should return to normal or to an increased level within 24 hours of parturition.[142] All kittens should nurse soon after parturition and within the first six to eight hours to ensure transfer of colostral antibodies. Neonatal kittens may not absorb immunoglobulins after 12 hours postpartum. This window of absorption is much shorter in kittens than in puppies and livestock.[143]

Milk production should begin at parturition. Colostrum is produced during the first 24 to 72 hours of lactation. Milk yield depends on litter size and stage of lactation, with peak lactation occurring at three to four weeks. Investigators measured average milk yields of 1 to 3% of the queen's body weight/day during Week 1.[144] Yields increased to 1.3 to 5.9% of the queen's body weight/day at peak lactation then declined slightly until weaning. Although mammary glands should be closely evaluated to ensure health and ready access for the kittens, expressing milk from each gland does not ensure adequate milk production. Continuous weight gain by the kittens is the best indicator of the queen's lactation performance. Neonatal kittens should gain between 10 to 15 g daily. Gains less than 7 g/day are inadequate.[142]

If health problems arise during lactation or kitten growth rates are suboptimal, the queen and litter should be immediately evaluated by a veterinarian. A complete physical evaluation, anamnesis and review of the reproduction records and the nutritional plan should be performed. A minimum database should be collected on the queen including a complete blood count, urinalysis and serum biochemistry analysis including electrolytes. Ancillary tests should be done as indicated.

KEY NUTRITIONAL FACTORS

There are few studies establishing the minimum nutritional requirements for reproducing queens and breeding male cats. Most nutrient recommendations are extrapolated from growth studies, results from other species and clinical experience. Although most foods appropriate for growing kittens are deemed adequate for female reproduction, complete and balanced foods specifically designed to support gestation/lactation should be fed. Table 11-12 summarizes key nutritional factors for reproducing cats. The following section describes these key nutritional factors in more detail. Energy requirements during estrus and mating are increased above normal lifestyle requirements for adult cats; other nutrient levels are presumed to be similar to those for intact cats.

Water
Water is important for normal reproduction. Expansion of extracellular fluid compartments and maternal and fetal tissues during pregnancy increases the need for water. Water is particularly important for milk production during lactation. Water needs for lactating queens vary according to maintenance needs, type of food (moist vs. dry) and the rate of milk production. Although specific levels of water intake have not been established, reproducing queens should be provided with ample potable water at all times. Some queens are reluctant to leave the nest box during the first few days after parturition. Water intake should be encouraged by placing water very near the enclosure to allow easy access. Feeding moist foods or adding water to food can improve water intake.

Energy
Energy Requirements During Estrus and Mating
The energy requirements of queens during mating do not appear to be significantly different from those of young to middle-aged adults. However, during behavioral estrus, queens typically reduce food intake and body weight may decline. Food intake and body weight rebound upon cessation of estrus. A nutrient-dense (4.5 to 5.0 kcal/g food [18.8 to 20.9 kJ/g food]), palatable food is appropriate to ensure optimal body condition at conception. Intact female cats typically require more calories than neutered house cats. The DER for sexually intact cats is 1.4 to 1.6 x RER.

Breeding male cats that are used infrequently or in small catteries have energy requirements similar to those of intact young to middle-aged cats (1.4 to 1.6 x RER). Tomcats that are used extensively for breeding may have difficulty maintaining proper body condition due to increased energy expenditure or, more often, reduced food intake. The stress of travel, new environments, social interactions and preoccupation with breeding may contribute to inappetence. These tomcats should be managed similarly to cats that are very active or under stress. Energy-dense (4.5 to 5.0 kcal/g food [18.8 to 20.9 kJ/g food]), highly digestible foods (>85%) with above average palatability should help these cats maintain ideal body condition (BCS 3/5) and activity.

Energy Requirements During Pregnancy

One of the most important changes in nutrient requirements of gestating cats is an increase in energy requirement. Although many essential nutrients are required at increased levels during gestation, dietary energy is often the most limiting "nutrient."

As mentioned previously, energy intake and weight gain increase linearly from conception to parturition in queens (Figure 11-8). However, food intake normally fluctuates slightly throughout gestation. There are two common times when food intake and weight decline. Reduced food intake occurs approximately two weeks after mating and is thought to occur in association with fetal implantation at about Day 15 postconception.[135] Energy intake increases then peaks between six to seven weeks of gestation. The second decline in food intake occurs during the last week of gestation. These transient declines in food intake and weight do not appear harmful. However, poor food intake over the course of gestation may impair weight gain, the subsequent lactation and kitten health. The recommended energy allowance for gestation is 25 to 50% above maintenance levels or approximately 90 to 110 kcal/kg body weight/day (376 to 460 kJ/kg body weight/day), although total caloric intake may increase as much as 70% above maintenance.[9,139] The increased need for energy can be met by providing 1.6 x RER at breeding with a gradual increase to 2 x RER at parturition (Table 11-13). Energy requirements sometimes exceed the recommended energy allowance due to individual cat variation and increased energy needs of queens with large litters. Therefore, free-choice feeding allows queens to adjust food intake as needed to meet the energy requirement for gestation.

Feeding energy-dense foods (ME = 4.0 to 5.0 kcal/g DM [16.74 to 20.9 kJ/g DM]) helps meet the energy needs of pregnant queens, especially during late gestation when the gravid uterus reduces stomach capacity.

Table 11-12. Key nutritional factors for reproducing cats.*

| Factors | Recommended food levels | | |
	Mating	Gestation	Lactation
Energy density (kcal ME/g)	4.5-5.0	4.0-5.0	4.0-5.0
Energy density (kJ ME/g)	19-21	17-21	17-21
Protein (%)	30-45	35-50	35-50
Fat (%)	10-30	18-35	18-35
Carbohydrate (%)	–	10	10
Crude fiber (%)	<5	<5	<5
Calcium (%)	0.6-1.0	1.0-1.6	1.0-1.6
Phosphorus (%)	0.5-1.0	0.8-1.4	0.8-1.4
Ca/P ratio	1:1-1:1.5	1:1-1:1.5:1	1:1-1:1.5:1
Sodium (%)	0.2-0.6	0.3-0.6	0.3-0.6
Chloride (%)	≥0.3	≥0.45	≥0.45
Potassium (%)	0.6-1.0	0.6-1.2	0.6-1.2
Magnesium (%)	0.04-0.1	0.08-0.15	0.08-0.15
Copper (ppm)	≥5	≥15	≥5
Taurine (ppm) (dry kibble)	1,000	1,000	1,000
Taurine (ppm) (moist)	2,500	2,500	2,500
Average urinary pH	6.2-6.5	6.2-6.5	6.2-6.5

*Dry matter basis. Concentrations presume an energy density of 4.0 kcal/g. Levels should be corrected for foods with higher energy densities. Adjustment is unnecessary for foods with lower energy densities.

Energy Requirements During Lactation

Lactation is the most energy-demanding stage of a cat's life. Peak milk production typically occurs at three to four weeks of lactation and, theoretically, peak energy demand should occur concurrently. However, actual peak energy demand occurs at six to seven weeks postpartum when energy requirements may exceed 250 kcal/kg body weight/day (1.05 MJ/kg body weight/day) or 2 to 6 x RER (Table 11-14). Observed energy intakes during lactation increase from 90 kcal/kg body weight/day (376 kJ/kg body weight/day) at parturition to 270 kcal/kg body weight/day (1.13 MJ/kg body weight/day) at Week 7.[145] The discrepancy in the timing of peak lactation and peak energy demand is due to combined food consumption by kittens and the queen. Kittens begin eating the queen's food in increasing amounts from three weeks of age until weaning. Therefore, the above estimates of energy requirement for the lactating queen include energy consumed by the queen and its kittens (Figure 11-9). When energy intake was measured for the queen alone, the energy requirement at Week 6 of lactation was 229 kcal/kg body weight/day (962 kJ/kg body weight/day).[146] Within large litters, up to 50% of the total energy was consumed by kittens, increasing the total energy consumption (i.e., kittens and queens) to as high as 306 kcal/kg body weight/day (1.28 MJ/kg body weight/day). Even with these large increases in energy intake, queens will continue to lose weight during lactation and return to pre-mating weight by weaning. Queens that lose excessive weight are prone to lactation fail-

Table 11-13. Energy requirements of pregnant queens.*

| Body weights | | kcal ME per day | | kJ ME per day | |
kg	lb	At 90 kcal/kg BW	At 100 kcal/kg BW	At 375 kJ/kg BW	At 420 kJ/kg BW
2	4.4	180	200	750	840
3	6.6	270	300	1,125	1,260
4	8.8	360	400	1,500	1,680
5	11.0	450	500	1,875	2,100
6	13.2	540	600	2,250	2,520
7	15.4	630	700	2,625	2,940
8	17.6	720	800	3,000	3,360

Key: ME = metabolizable energy, BW = body weight.
*Adapted from National Research Council. Nutrient Requirements of Cats. Washington, DC: National Academy Press, 1986.

Table 11-14. Daily energy requirements of lactating queens over the lactation period.*

Weeks of lactation	Daily energy requirements		
	Factor x RER	kcal/kg BW**	kJ/kg BW
1	2.3	115	481
2	2.5	125	523
3	3.0	150	628
4	3.5	175	732
5	4.0	200	837
6	5.0	250	1,046

Key: RER = resting energy requirement, $70(BW_{kg})^{0.75}$ or $30\ BW_{kg} + 70$.
*Based on average queen at parturition (3.8 kg) nursing four to five kittens. These values represent average energy requirements for lactating queens. Individual animal variation and litter size may alter total daily energy needs. (See Appendix G.)
**Adapted from National Research Council. Nutrient Requirements of Cats. Washington, DC: National Academy Press, 1986.

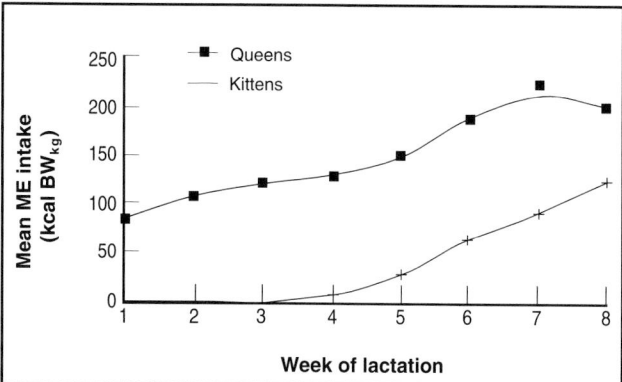

Figure 11-9. Food energy intake during lactation of queens and their kittens. Kittens begin eating the queen's food in increasing amounts from about four weeks of age until weaning. Energy intake peaks for queens at seven weeks and then decreases as kittens consume a larger percentage of their energy from food rather than milk. (Adapted from Munday HS, Earle KE. The energy requirements of the queen during lactation and kittens from birth to 12 weeks. Journal of Nutrition 1991; 121: S43-S44.)

ure. Table 11-14 is a guide to estimate the energy requirements of lactating queens. However, it is preferable to feed lactating queens free choice because the wide variation in energy needs makes accurate prediction difficult.

The high energy demands during lactation require a marked increase in total food intake. Feeding an energy-dense food (4.0 to 5.0 kcal ME/g DM, [16.74 to 20.9 kJ ME/g]) helps meet these demands without overwhelming gastric capacity.

If kittens are encouraged to eat a solid food beginning at three weeks of age, the energy demands placed on the lactating queen will decline as kittens increasingly obtain nutrition from solid food. Maintenance energy levels are sufficient for queens at ideal body condition after the kittens are weaned. Queens that have lost excess body weight during lactation should be provided additional food to restore ideal body condition (BCS 3/5).

Protein
Protein synthesis in the queen is greatly increased during gestation. In addition, protein quality and quantity are important to provide essential amino acids for growth and development of the fetuses. In gestating queens fed energy-dense (4.8 kcal/g [20 kJ/g]) purified foods, protein levels of 20% DM sustained adequate gestation. However,

30% DM dietary protein resulted in near optimal weight gain in queens during gestation and kittens during lactation.[147] Considering the varying nutrient availability in typical pet food ingredients compared with purified foods, protein levels at or above 35% DM are recommended for gestating queens (Table 11-12). Animal-based proteins are preferred as the major contributor to dietary protein because they generally have greater digestibility and more desirable amino-acid profiles for cats. Protein deficiency during pregnancy may result in lower birth weights, higher neonatal mortality and impaired immunocompetency in the kittens.[136] In addition, feeding queens protein-restricted foods during late gestation and lactation results in delayed home orientation (i.e., ability of kittens to orient to and return to the nest), aberrant locomotor development and decreased emotional responsiveness in the kittens.[148]

During lactation, queens increase protein synthesis to supply milk with protein concentrations suitable for growth (i.e., approximately 36% DM milk protein). Milk protein output for a 4-kg cat nursing a large litter may reach 19 g crude protein/day.[144] Thus, it is not surprising that protein needs during lactation exceed even gestational requirements. Providing 25% DM crude protein to lactating queens results in satisfactory reproductive performance.[147] However, near optimal performance is achieved with foods containing 30% DM crude protein. Queens fed foods with 30% protein lose less body weight than those fed foods with protein levels of 20 or 25% DM. Additionally, food intake and kitten growth rates are higher at dietary protein levels of 30% DM.[147] Because of variations in food digestibility and ingredient quality and the goal to promote optimal reproductive performance, the recommended crude protein allowance for lactation is at least 35% DM (Table 11-12). The protein source in commercial foods should be highly digestible and have high biologic value. Animal-based proteins should provide the major source of amino acids and protein for lactating queens.

Inadequate protein concentrations result in poor lactation and kitten growth. Queens fed foods containing 20% DM protein had lower hematocrit values at Week 6 of lactation compared with queens fed foods with higher protein levels.[147]

Taurine
Taurine is required for normal reproduction and fetal development. (See sidebar "Taurine.") Taurine deficiency in gestating queens may result in fetal death near the 25th day of gestation, abortions throughout gestation, fetal deformities and delayed growth and development.[149] However, the taurine requirement for gestation is similar to that at other lifestages (i.e., a minimum of 0.1% DM taurine in dry foods and 0.20% DM in moist foods).[58,150]

Fats and Essential Fatty Acids
High-energy foods are beneficial because of the increased energy demand during gestation. Fat delivers 2.25 times the number of calories as the same amount of protein or carbohydrate; therefore, fat represents an important source of calories. In studies comparing the effect of two different foods on reproductive performance, a food containing 21% DM fat resulted in improved kitten birth weights, survival and growth compared with a food containing 12% DM fat.[e] In a similar study, increasing dietary fat from 15 to 27% of

the food dry matter: 1) increased the number of kittens per litter, 2) decreased kitten mortality from more than 20 to 9% and 3) improved reproductive efficiency in queens from 1.4 to 2.3 litters/year.[151] For optimal reproductive performance, foods for gestating queens should contain at least 18% DM fat, although foods with lower levels of fat have been successfully fed during gestation.

As previously mentioned, linoleic and arachidonic acid and possibly α-linolenic acid are required in foods for cats. Signs of linoleic acid deficiency in cats are similar to those in other animals. (See Chapter 15.) However, the long-term deficiency of dietary arachidonic acid also results in reproductive failure. Queens with an arachidonic-acid deficiency appear unable to bear live kittens.[64] In contrast to queens, male cats do not appear to require arachidonic acid for reproduction. Spermatogenesis remains normal in males with an arachidonic-acid deficiency possibly because testes convert linoleic acid to arachidonic acid. Arachidonic acid at 0.04% of the dietary energy supports normal reproduction in queens. However, lower levels have been used when interference from n-3 fatty acids is avoided.[64] Current AAFCO allowances for linoleic and arachidonic acid are appropriate for gestating cats.[58] (See Appendix J.)

As in gestation, the high energy demands of lactation are best met by feeding energy-dense foods. Moderate- to high-fat foods enhance lactation performance in queens. As previously mentioned, queens have improved reproductive performance when switched from lower fat foods (12 to 15% DM) to moderately high-fat foods (21 to 27% DM).[151,e] Kitten survival and growth rate and reproductive efficiency of queens are improved if queens are fed higher fat foods throughout lactation. For optimal reproductive performance, foods for lactating queens should contain between 18 and 35% fat (Table 11-12).

In addition to meeting the essential fatty acid needs of lactation and aiding in absorption of fat-soluble vitamins, higher levels of fat in foods for lactation increase the food's energy density. Thus, smaller amounts of food can be consumed to meet the queen's energy demands. Other nutrients in the food should be balanced to the higher energy content of energy-dense foods (>4.5 kcal/g DM [18.8 kJ/g DM]).

Minimum essential fatty acid requirements for lactation do not appear to differ significantly from those of gestation. However, a dietary source of docosahexaenoic acid (DHA, 22:6n-3) is required for normal development of retinal function in nursing kittens.[66] Milk concentrations of DHA parallel dietary intake. Therefore, DHA should be included in foods fed to lactating queens. Common ingredients such as fish and poultry meal represent a source of DHA in the diet of queens.

Calcium and Phosphorus

Calcium and phosphorus are required at levels greater than maintenance to support fetal skeletal development and lactation. Recommended dietary calcium levels are 1.0 to 1.6% DM while maintaining a normal calcium-phosphorus ratio (1:1 to 1.5:1). These levels are typically found in commercial cat foods; therefore, supplementation is rarely indicated except for homemade foods.

Although eclampsia is uncommon in cats, it does occur pre- and postparturiently. In cows, high dietary calcium intake during gestation is a risk factor for postparturient eclampsia and a similar mechanism has been proposed for

---

Eclampsia in the Queen

Eclampsia, or periparturient hypocalcemia, is uncommon in cats. Clinical signs are the result of severe hypocalcemia with or without other biochemical abnormalities (e.g., hypoglycemia). The predisposing factors may include improper perinatal nutrition, inappropriate calcium supplementation and heavy lactation demands. Whereas dogs typically present within the first four weeks of lactation, cats are more commonly presented during the last three weeks of pregnancy. Clinical signs include depression, weakness, tachypnea and mild muscle tremors. Additional signs may include vomiting, anorexia, hypothermia, flaccid paralysis, hyperexcitability and other signs of malaise.

The pathophysiology of periparturient hypocalcemia in cats is not well understood. Excessive prenatal calcium intake has been implicated by some. High intake of calcium may down-regulate parathyroid gland secretion and impair normal mobilization of calcium from skeletal stores. As demand for calcium increases during late gestation and lactation, calcium homeostasis is no longer able to maintain critical serum levels. Although high calcium intake is an accepted cause of periparturient tetany in cattle, it remains speculative as the cause of the disease in dogs and cats.

Treatment is aimed at immediate correction of hypocalcemia with intravenous infusion of 10% calcium gluconate (1.0 to 1.5 ml/kg body weight over 10 to 30 minutes) given to effect. Dextrose may be administered by intravenous bolus (50% solution) or by intravenous infusion (5% dextrose in saline solution) to correct hypoglycemia. After acute signs are corrected, oral supplementation of calcium carbonate (10 to 30 mg/kg body weight every eight hours) is begun and continued throughout gestation and lactation. In contrast to dogs, it is rarely necessary to wean kittens early. Recurrence of periparturient tetany has not be reported to occur in cats.

BIBLIOGRAPHY

Fascetti AJ, Hickman MA. Preparturient hypocalcemia in the cat: 4 cases. Journal of the American Veterinary Medical Association 1999; (In press).

Wallace MS, Davidson AP. Abnormalities in pregnancy, parturition, and the periparturient period. In: Ettinger SJ, Feldman EC, eds. Textbook of Veterinary Internal Medicine, 4th ed. Philadelphia, PA: WB Saunders Co, 1995; 1614-1623.

---

eclampsia in dogs and cats. However, a relationship to dietary factors has not been identified in cats and the pathophysiology of the disorder remains obscure. Queens with a history of eclampsia may benefit from calcium supplementation during subsequent lactations; however, the efficacy of this treatment in preventing recurrence has not been reported. Occasionally, pregnant queens may develop hypocalcemia, hypoglycemia or both one to two weeks before parturition. Initially, affected queens should be treated with intravenous calcium and glucose solutions, followed by oral calcium supplements throughout the remainder of gestation. After treatment, gestation proceeds normally and calcium supplementation is not typically required during lactation. (See sidebar "Eclampsia in the Queen.")

Carbohydrate

Although a true carbohydrate requirement for cats has not been demonstrated, carbohydrates apparently protect against weight loss in queens during lactation.[147] Carbohydrates spare protein necessary to sustain blood glucose concentrations in queens and provide a substrate for lactose during milk production. Even with an abundant supply of dietary protein, providing some dietary carbohydrate improves lactation performance.[147] Observations that dry foods generally outperform moist rations can be explained by the increased carbohydrate content of dry foods. Until further studies define optimal levels of carbohydrates for lactation, at least 10% DM carbohydrate should be included in foods for lactating queens.

OTHER NUTRITIONAL FACTORS

Magnesium

Magnesium should not be overly restricted in foods for reproducing female cats. Foods intended for prevention of struvite urolithiasis often have magnesium levels less than AAFCO recommendations for growth and reproduction (0.08% DMB).[58] Dietary magnesium levels of 0.08 to 0.15% DM are recommended in foods for reproducing female cats.

Copper

Copper is required for normal iron metabolism and as an enzyme cofactor in several key metabolic pathways, including those responsible for myelin, melanin and connective tissue production. Copper requirements for growth and reproduction are thought to be approximately 5 mg/kg food.[152] However, copper deficiency has been reported to occur in queens fed a food containing 15 mg copper/kg food, supplied, in part, by copper oxide.[153] Copper from copper oxide is poorly available. The combination of poorly available copper from the diet and competition from high levels of dietary zinc, iron, calcium and phytate significantly impair copper availability. Clinical signs of copper deficiency in one group of cats included fetal death and abortions, achromotrichia, arthrogryposis, fusion of digits, craniofacial deformities and cerebral dysgenesis.[f] For this reason, copper levels of 15 mg/kg food (DM) from an available source have been recommended for queens eating dry foods. A previous report of experimental copper deficiency cited histochemical defects of the aorta.[152] Hematologic abnormalities are not a typical feature of copper deficiency in cats, as in other species. Supplemental copper in feline foods should be highly available. Copper sulfate and copper chelates appear to be good dietary sources.

Digestibility

Foods with dry matter digestibility greater than 85% are better suited than less digestible foods for pregnant cats because: 1) nutrient needs increase as pregnancy progresses and 2) increased abdominal fullness as the pregnancy progresses may impair the queen's ability to ingest adequate amounts of nutrients, especially if the food is poorly digestible.

Dry matter digestibility and availability of foods intended for lactation should also be above average because of the high nutritional demands of lactation. Apparent dry matter digestibility of 85% or greater is desirable. By comparison, the digestibility of fresh meat (uncooked) is 96%.[15]

Urinary pH

Highly acidified foods should be avoided during gestation because metabolic acidosis may impair bone mineralization in adult cats and kittens, which can be especially detrimental to developing fetuses.[90-92,154,155] Anecdotal reports have implicated certain highly acidified semi-moist foods in poor reproductive performance in queens.[g] Foods designed to produce average urinary pH values between 6.2 to 6.5 appear to be safe.[94]

Assess the Food(s)

Assessment of the food and the individual animal allows for development of an appropriate feeding plan. The following general steps should be followed: 1) Compare the current food's nutrient profile with the nutrient recommendations for reproduction (Table 11-12). Appendices L and M list the key nutritional factors in selected commercial foods and treats. The same information can be obtained from the pet food manufacturer. 2) Identify discrepancies between the key nutritional factors and the cat's current intake. 3) Ensure the food is appropriate for reproduction based on AAFCO-type feeding trials.

The nutritional adequacy statement on the pet food label should indicate if the food is complete and balanced for reproduction, gestation and lactation, or all lifestages. The statement of nutritional adequacy should also be based on animal feeding trials. Lactation is the most nutritionally demanding lifestage for cats; therefore, the manufacturer must prove the food's nutrients are available through successful animal feeding. After it has been established that the minimum standards have been met, the food's nutrient levels should be compared with the key nutritional factors for lactation (Table 11-12). Any discrepancies between target levels and the levels in the food are then noted. Particular attention should be devoted to the protein source, food digestibility and energy density. Foods with an energy density in the upper range should be chosen (4.7 to 5.0 kcal ME/g DM [19.7 to 20.9 kJ ME/g DM]) for queens with large litters and those with marginal weight gain during pregnancy. Queens with small litters and those prone to obesity may benefit from foods with a lower caloric density (4.0 to 4.5 kcal ME/g DM [16.74 to 18.8 kJ ME/g DM]) to avoid excessive weight gain and obesity.

Food assessment during lactation also includes assessment of lactation performance. Evaluation of kitten growth rate and queen weight loss can point to nutritional inadequacies. Nursing kittens should gain approximately 100 g/week or 10 to 15 g/day. Weight gains less than 7 g/day require immediate evaluation of the food, the queen and the kittens. Queens normally lose weight during lactation and return to within 2% of their pre-breeding body weight by weaning (Figure 11-8). Weight loss is related to litter size. The weight loss of queens from Week 0 to 3 can be approximated by the following equation:[139]

Total queen's body weight loss (g) = 339.2 + (58.8)n
(where n = number of kittens).

If either the queen's rate of loss or the kittens' growth rate is inadequate, the food and feeding method should be carefully reviewed. If inadequacies exist, a more appropriate food should be selected. Supplements should not be given to improve lactation performance. Supplements, unless carefully balanced to the nutrients in the food, can unbalance a food or impair availability of other nutrients.

Assess the Feeding Method

It may be necessary to alter the feeding method when managing reproducing cats, especially in late-term pregnancy, when a queen is carrying a very large litter and during lactation. Evaluation of current feeding methods with foreknowledge of reproductive demands will allow for development of a rational feeding plan.

Free-choice feeding is the preferred method for reproducing female cats. Meal size and therefore caloric intake may be limited as the uterus and fetal mass occupy much of the abdominal cavity and limit gastric capacity. The queen's energy needs may increase fourfold over maintenance requirements during peak lactation. Providing food free choice allows reproducing female cats to consume sufficient calories in multiple small feedings. Cats may also be fed multiple meals (three to four/day) using the recommended allowances in Table 11-13. However, food intake should not be limited unless obesity becomes a problem. Table 11-14 lists estimates of average food intake during lactation.

Obese queens (i.e., those with heavy fat accumulations over the ribs and bony prominences) should be fed controlled amounts of food during gestation; however, they should not be fed to reduce weight. Obesity reportedly increases the risk of dystocia and kitten mortality; therefore, careful weight management before breeding and monitoring during gestation is important.[137]

Clean water should be available at all times. Food and water should be placed within easy reach for the queen. Food should be placed directly in or very near the box during the first few days after parturition, when many queens refuse to leave the nest box. Some authors have advocated removing the kittens from the nest box for 30 to 60 minutes at a time to encourage queens to eat.[142] This recommendation is effective for some queens, but makes others so frantic it becomes counterproductive. Other methods to improve food intake include adding water or moist food to dry food to enhance palatability and increase water intake.

Determine a Feeding Plan

The feeding plan should be tailored to each animal and its specific nutritional requirements. In general, recommendations are based on information from populations of animals at similar lifestages. However, the feeding plan should be tailored to meet the needs of the individual cat based on unique variations in genetics, environment, litter size and health status.

Select a Food(s)

Queens should be fed a food appropriate for gestation and lactation at or before mating. This recommendation is generally accomplished by: 1) selecting a food that has been proved suitable for reproduction by animal feeding trials (i.e., see the product's label) and 2) choosing a food that provides recommended levels of key nutritional factors (Table 11-12). Although, nutritional demands are greatest in the last one-half to one-third of pregnancy, conception rate and in utero fetal viability are markedly impaired in queens fed foods with marginal nutrient content and availability at breeding and early gestation. Changing to a new food more suitable for gestation and lactation before conception avoids any reduction in food intake or GI upsets during the critical time of conception and implantation, improves any marginal nutrient stores and typically increases energy intake.

The food form selected for reproducing female cats

bears consideration. Semi-moist products should be selected cautiously because many produce urinary pH values below desired levels. Dry foods are more nutrient dense as fed and have higher carbohydrate levels than moist foods. Dry foods may benefit queens undergoing rapid weight loss and those spending little time eating. Conversely, moist foods often have higher fat levels and provide additional water to support lactation. The added water also improves palatability; therefore, queens may spend more time eating. Dry and moist food types each have advantages; therefore, many breeders choose to feed both forms during reproduction.

Intact male cats in heavy service and those stressed during breeding should be fed foods with high energy density (4.5 to 5.0 kcal/g DM [18.8 to 20.9 kJ/g DM]). Otherwise, foods appropriate for young to middle-aged cats are adequate (Table 11-8). Male cats used in harem-breeding programs are typically fed the same foods as the queens. Although the vitamin and mineral levels of these foods are typically well in excess of the male cat's needs, the high energy density may be beneficial.

Determine a Feeding Method

The practice of flushing, that is, increasing food intake by 5 to 15% at proestrus through breeding, has been not been evaluated in cats. Even if it were proved to be of value, it would be difficult to apply flushing to cats because proestrus is rarely observed in this species (i.e., cats are induced ovulators).

Free-choice feeding is preferred for most queens during reproduction. Overweight or obese-prone queens should be fed measured portions adequate for weight maintenance. If both dry and moist foods are fed, it may be desirable to feed dry foods free choice and provide multiple meals of moist foods. Obese-prone cats should be fed three to four meals per day in controlled portions. Kittens should be allowed access to the queen's food, which they typically begin eating at three weeks of age. Kittens may need to be fed away from the queen if the queen is fed portion-controlled amounts of food.

Some queens with strong maternal instincts are reluctant to leave the nest box. When this occurs, food and water should be in the immediate vicinity of the nest box. Use care when placing water bowls near neonates to avoid accidental drowning. If food intake does not improve, the kittens may be removed from the queen for short periods three to four times a day.

Reassessment

Male and female cats should be reassessed before every reproductive cycle. Females should have returned to optimal body weight and condition (BCS 3/5) before the next breeding. Oral health should be optimal and vaccinations and parasite control should be completed before the next reproductive cycle. The last reproductive performance should be evaluated and compared with previous performance and the cattery average. If performance was suboptimal, a detailed review of genetic selection, husbandry and nutritional management should be completed to identify deficiencies. Modifications can be then be incorporated to improve subsequent reproductive outcomes.

Monitoring the queen during gestation should include weekly assessment of food intake and body weight. Body condition scoring is particularly important in assessing weight gain during gestation. Inadequate nutrition and poor weight gain may be overlooked if total body weight and the queen's expanding abdomen are the only criteria used to monitor weight gain. If underfed, the queen may continue to gain weight as the kittens grow, but fail to develop the energy reserves needed for lactation. Body condition scoring during gestation should ignore the abdominal component of the scoring process and allow for slight increases in body fat. (See Figure 1-2.) When assigning body condition scores to pregnant queens, the areas of focus include muscle mass and fat covering the ribs and bony prominences. Body weight and food intake should change gradually in a pattern similar to that depicted in Figure 11-8. The queen and each kitten should be thoroughly evaluated at parturition. Average weight loss at parturition is 6 to 14% (254 to 638 g) of the prepartum weight, depending on litter size.[145] The remaining 700 to 850 g of gain will be used to sustain normal lactation. Evaluation of gestational performance should include: 1) the queen's weight record, 2) litter size, 3) kitten birth weights, 4) kitten growth rates, 5) kitten vigor, 6) mortality rates and 7) congenital defects. Although stools may normally vary from soft to firm during reproduction, stool quality should be monitored. Constipation and diarrhea are always considered abnormal and should be evaluated and treated as needed.

Reassessment of lactating queens is similar to that of pregnant queens. Most observations will be made by the owner/breeder. The queen should be regularly evaluated for vaginal discharge, mammary gland engorgement or mastitis and matted abdominal hair that interferes with nursing. Body weight and condition should be evaluated after parturition and weekly thereafter. Kittens should exhibit steady weight gain, have good muscle tone and suckle vigorously. Young kittens are quiet between feedings. Kittens are often restless and cry excessively if milk production is inadequate. Gastric distention is not a good indicator of adequate nursing. Aerophagia can give the appearance of gastric fullness in kittens, despite inadequate milk intake.

Kitten mortality reportedly varies from 9 to 63% depending on the source of cats and the cattery.[44] Breeders should compare reproductive performance of each queen to the cattery standard. Several genetic, husbandry and nutritional factors may cause high kitten mortality. If kitten death or cannibalism rates are high, all three areas should be investigated thoroughly.

WEANING

Weaning is usually a gradual process that begins with the queen avoiding the kittens and kittens eating increasing amounts of solid food. This phase begins when kittens are three to four weeks old and is complete at six to 10 weeks of age. At three to four weeks of age, kittens begin to eat solid foods although approximately 95% of their caloric intake is still provided by the queen's milk.[146] By five to six weeks of age, kittens eat nearly 30% of their caloric requirement as solid food and the remainder as milk. A progressive intake of solid food continues until the kittens are completely independent of the queen. Most

domestic shorthair kittens are weaned by six weeks of age, whereas purebred kittens are usually weaned around eight to nine weeks of age. Later weaning allows more time for kitten growth and immune system maturation, which may help reduce kitten mortality in the postweaning period.

The weaning process may be initiated by the gradual refusal of the queen to allow the kittens to nurse or by the breeder who separates the kittens from the queen. During weaning, many queens will reduce food intake and milk production gradually. Regardless, the queen's energy requirement will decrease from lactation to maintenance levels after weaning is complete.

Restricting the food of queens that are abruptly removed from the kittens and those that are heavy milk producers a day or two before weaning reduces energy available for milk production, thereby minimizing mammary gland engorgement. A commonly used weaning schedule follows: kittens and food are withheld from the queen the day before weaning. The kittens are returned at the end of the day and allowed to nurse. The following day, the kittens are removed and the queen is given one-fourth of its ration. Food amounts are then gradually increased over the next three days to pre-breeding levels.

Weaning can be a stressful event in the kitten's life. Transition to independent feeding, greater environmental exposure and waning maternal antibodies result in reduced immune defense. These factors contribute to increased morbidity and mortality in the postweaning period.[44] Proper nutrition and careful husbandry can reduce these rates markedly.

Recommended nutrient allowances for weanling kittens are similar to those for older growing kittens. Energy requirements for weanling kittens are between 200 to 250 kcal/kg body weight (837 to 1,046 kJ/kg body weight).[9,156] The stomach volume of kittens is small; therefore, feeding energy-dense foods helps meet the higher energy needs of weanling kittens without exceeding gastric capacity. Kittens from queens with lower body weights reportedly have limited growth. Milk production is thought to be compromised in underweight queens.[156] Once weaned, however, smaller kittens compensate by increasing food intake and growth rate until they attain their expected size.

At the onset of weaning, kittens should be offered moist foods or dry foods moistened with water or milk replacer. The food should be moistened until it forms a soft but not liquid gruel. Kittens at this stage lap at food but do not prehend food. By six to eight weeks of age, most kittens have learned to eat solid, unmoistened foods; therefore, a gruel is no longer necessary. The food should be highly digestible (i.e., apparent dry matter >80% and protein digestibility >85%), and complete and balanced for growth and reproduction. Semi-moist foods that promote a highly acidic urinary pH should not be fed as the sole food source for growing kittens. High levels of dietary acid may lead to metabolic acidosis and impaired bone mineralization. Limited amounts of semi-moist treats are acceptable.

The weaning process will be less stressful if kittens are initially offered the same food that will be fed after weaning. Not only will kittens readily recognize this diet as food, but GI upsets associated with food transitions will be avoided. Water should be accessible to kittens when they are about three weeks old.

Kittens should have water and food available at all times in addition to free access to the queen. Food and water should be easily accessible and offered in broad shallow pans. Food should be replenished three to four times daily. High-moisture foods begin to spoil and harbor high levels of bacteria when left at room temperature for prolonged periods. Ideally, food should be warmed to about 38°C (100°F) or at least brought to room temperature. Kittens first eat by accident, as they step into food and then ingest it during grooming. This process can be hastened by smearing small quantities of food around the kittens' mouth.

Monitoring consists of daily evaluation of physical appearance, activity, stool quality and food intake. Normal kittens should be weighed and their body condition assessed weekly; they should continue to grow at approximately 100 g/week. Gender differences in growth rate are now evident; female kittens are normally smaller than males (Figure 11-10). Kittens should demonstrate increasing activity and social and exploratory behavior. After a meal, the kittens' abdomen should be well-rounded but not overly distended. Crying in neonates and older kittens usually indicates discomfort (e.g., cold, hunger, pain, disease or isolation).

The queen still consumes the kittens' feces to keep the nest box clean early during this phase. At about four weeks, the kittens begin to defecate outside the nest box and stools can be readily monitored. Kittens eating solid foods should have soft-formed stools, whereas those eating predominantly milk will have pasty yellow to light brown stools. It is vital during this phase to practice good cattery husbandry and monitor kittens closely for disease. Weaning is a stressful event and outbreaks of diarrhea and disease are very common. Growth rate is universally impaired in sick and malnourished kittens.

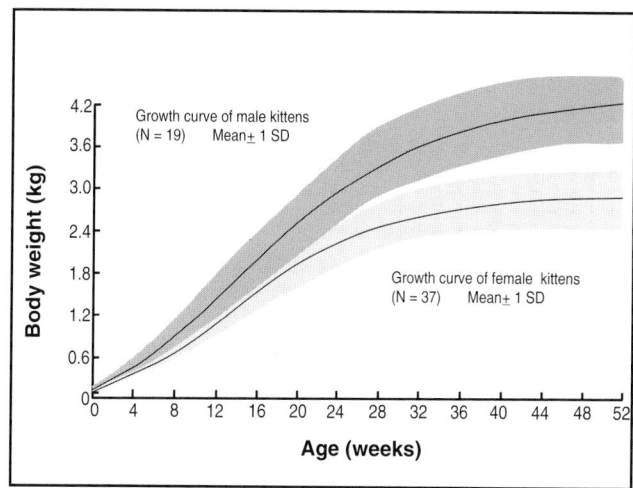

Figure 11-10. Growth curve for female and male kittens. Note after four weeks of age there are significant gender differences in growth rates; female kittens grow at a slower rate and are normally smaller than males. (Adapted from National Research Council. Nutrient Requirements of Cats. Washington, DC: National Academy Press, 1986; 2.)

■ GROWING KITTENS

Kittens usually depend on the queen to provide food during the neonatal or nursing period (discussed first below). Specific information about raising orphan kittens and using milk replacers is found in Appendices E and K. The transition from queen's milk to solid food (weaning period) was discussed above. Feeding kittens from two to 12 months of age is discussed below, after the section on kittens in the neonatal period.

Growing Kittens: Neonatal Period

Proper nutrition of the queen during gestation and lactation, the behavior and health of the queen and good neonatal care are important to achieving a successful transition from fetal life to the nursing period.

Assessment

ASSESS THE ANIMAL

History

Persons who raise kittens (i.e., orphaned, fostered and normal) should be encouraged to keep log books of all data that may provide information about the health and nutritional status of kittens and the reproductive performance of the queen. Records should include food intake, body weight, body temperature and stool characteristics, especially during the first two weeks postpartum. Changes in kitten behavior, activity and other indicators of normal development (e.g., opening of eyes, eruption of teeth and coat quality) may prove useful as well. In some instances, it may be helpful to mark kittens (e.g., with nail polish or nontoxic dyes) to differentiate individual kittens.

It is particularly important that good records be maintained for orphaned and foster kittens. Orphaned kittens are hand-raised kittens, whereas foster kittens are those raised by a queen other than their mother. Successful management of these kittens depends on the quick recognition and correction of health and management problems. Parameters such as weight gain, daily food intake, stool characteristics and kitten vigor (i.e., muscle tone, activity and alertness) should be recorded. Kittens should be observed for suckling activity in addition to the above parameters. Orphaned kittens should have consistent weight gains similar to those of suckling kittens (Figure 11-10).[157] Queens should also be monitored for signs of impending cannibalism (e.g., extreme nervousness, aggressiveness toward the kitten and kitten rejection). Unfortunately, cannibalism often occurs without warning. In addition, housing and environmental hygiene should also be evaluated. Improper housing and hygiene are important risk factors for poor kitten development and impaired health.

Physical Examination

The goals of the neonatal physical examination are to: 1) establish baseline data for future reference, 2) assess overall health and development of the kittens and 3) detect abnormalities that may impair normal development and health. During the physical examination, particular attention should be given to kitten behavior, body weight, body temperature and oral cavity health. In addition, the umbilicus of each kitten should be closely evaluated. Normally, the queen will cut the umbilicus leaving approximately one and one-half inches. On occasion, queens will remove excessive cord resulting in an umbilicus flush with the abdomen or an open hernia (Figure 11-11). Careful wound management and antibiotic therapy are often required to prevent omphalitis and/or septicemia. Umbilical cords left too long may wrap around the kitten's legs or paws cutting off circulation to the affected limb.

Kitten Behavior

Normal kittens are vigorous and have good muscle tone. They should nurse immediately or soon after parturition and have a strong sucking reflex. Well-fed kittens should have a distended abdomen and are quiet after feeding. Kittens that are hungry, cold, hot or in discomfort will cry continuously and should be closely monitored. Nursing behavior and milk intake should be carefully observed because some kittens develop rounded abdomens as a result of aerophagia. Kittens may have difficulty nursing queens of longhaired breeds due to hair accumulation or matting around the nipples. In these cases, abdominal hair can be clipped to allow kittens easy access to the queen's nipples. Care should be taken not to damage nipples during this process.

The behavioral response of kittens to the litter and queen is also important. Poor maternal-kitten interaction may result in cannibalism or neglect. Kittens depend on

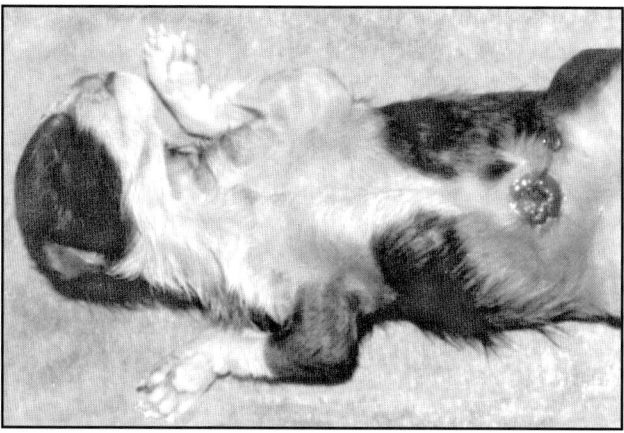

Figure 11-11. A neonatal kitten with an open umbilical hernia following excessive umbilical cord removal by the queen after birth.

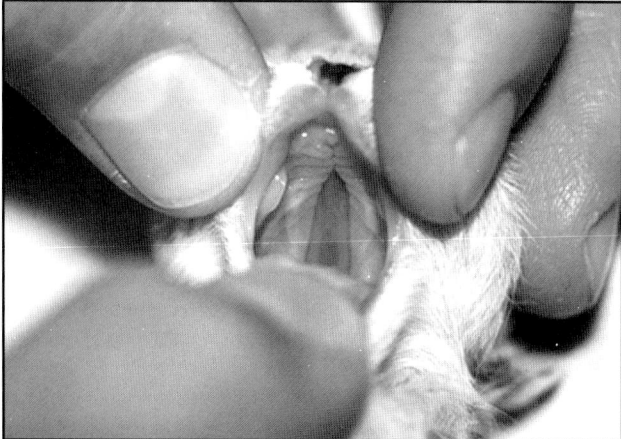

Figure 11-12. Cleft palate in a neonatal kitten. This is a common birth defect in kittens and may be associated with malnutrition of the queen during gestation. Nutrients commonly associated with a cleft palate include deficiencies of zinc and copper, as well as, vitamin A toxicosis during gestation.

the queen for food, antibodies, warmth and hygiene; therefore, serious metabolic alterations (e.g., hypoglycemia, hypothermia, dehydration and malnutrition), infectious disease and death are common sequelae to abnormal behavior and maternal neglect.

Body Weight

Monitoring initial and subsequent body weight is a good way to evaluate milk intake and health status of nursing and orphaned kittens. Healthy nursing kittens should be weighed at birth and weekly thereafter using a gram scale. Daily weighing is important to evaluate the queen's milk production and to help assess sick, weak and underweight kittens. Weight loss or slow weight gain in individuals or entire litters may indicate one or more of the following: 1) disease in kittens or the queen, 2) inability of kittens to suckle or 3) inadequate milk production.

Birth weights are normally between 85 to 120 g with mean weights of approximately 100 g. Kittens weighing less than 75 g have very high mortality rates and require extra care and monitoring if they are to survive. Low birth weight kittens should be weighed every 24 to 48 hours for the first one to three weeks of life to ensure proper weight gain. Kittens gain an average of 100 g/week for the first six months of life. Minimally, they should gain 7 g/day.[142]

Body Temperature

Kittens regulate body temperature poorly during the first four weeks of life. Normal body temperature is approximately 36.0°C (96.8°F) at birth and increases to 37.5°C (100.0°F) by one week of age.[142] Extreme environmental conditions or abandonment by the queen may lead to hypothermia, which may quickly result in circulatory failure and death.

Normally the queen maintains the temperature and humidity in the nest box. Without the queen, kittens can quickly become hypothermic. Artificial heat should provide age-optimal environmental temperatures. (See Appendix E.) It is best to set heat sources to establish heat gradation in the nest box. This allows kittens to move away from the heat source as needed to avoid hyperthermia. Hyperthermia can be as detrimental as hypothermia; hyperthermic kittens can rapidly become dehydrated. Maintaining humidity near 50% helps reduce water loss in kittens and maintains the moisture and health of mucous membranes.

Oral Cavity

Examination of the oral cavity should include careful evaluation of the mucous membranes and hard palate. The mucous membranes should be light pink and moist. Cleft palates are relatively common defects in kittens (Figure 11-12). Vitamin A toxicity and trace mineral deficiencies (i.e., copper and zinc) during gestation have been associated with the development of cleft palates in kittens. However, in most cases, a cause is not identified. Most kittens with a cleft palate are unable to nurse effectively. Affected kittens must either be tube fed until the time of surgical correction or spontaneous closure, or they should be humanely euthanatized.

Laboratory Evaluation

Laboratory tests should be performed as needed to assess any abnormalities noted during the physical examination. Particular attention should be given to hydration status and serum glucose and electrolyte concentrations. When evaluating laboratory data in kittens, age-appropriate reference values should be used because concentra-

Table 11-15. Nutrient comparison among queen's colostrum, queen's milk and milk of selected species.

Nutrients	Queen's colostrum*	Queen's milk*	Bitch's milk**	Cow's milk***	Goat's milk***
Moisture (g/100 g)	–	79	77.3	87.7	87.0
Dry matter (g/100 g)	–	21	22.7	12.3	13
Crude protein (g/100 g)	8.3	7.5	7.5	3.3	3.6
Arginine (mg/100 g)	357	347	420	119	119
Taurine (mg/100 g)	26	27	–	0.13	–
Methionine (mg/100 g)	202	188	–	82	80
Crude fat (g/100 g)	9.3	8.5	9.5	3.6	4.1
Lactose (g/100 g)	3.0	4.0	3.3	4.7	4.0
Minerals					
Calcium (mg/100 g)	46	180	240	119	133
Phosphorus (mg/100 g)	114	162	180	93	111
Potassium (mg/100 g)	–	103	120	150	204
Magnesium (mg/100 g)	11	9	11	14	14
Copper (mg/100 g)	0.04	0.11	0.33	–	–
Iron (mg/100 g)	0.19	0.35	0.70	0.05	0.05
ME (kcal/100 g)	130	121	146	64	69
ME (kJ/100 g)	544	506	610	268	288

See Appendix K for nutrient comparisons for different species and for comparisons with milk replacers.
*Adkins Y, Zicker SC, Lepine A, et al. Changes in nutrient and protein composition of cat milk during lactation. American Journal of Veterinary Research 1997; 58: 370-375. Zottman B, Dobenecker B, Kienzle E, et al. Investigations on milk composition and milk yield in queens (abstract). In: Proceedings. The Waltham International Symposium, Orlando, FL, 1997.
**Meyer H, Kienzle E, Dammers C. Milchmenge und Milchzusammensetzung bei und Hündin sowie Futteraufnahme und Gewichtsenwicklung ante und post partum.Fortschritte in der Tierphysiologie und tierernährung (Advances in Animal Physiology and Animal Nutrition) 1985; Suppl. No. 16: 51-72.
***From Pennington JA. Food Values of Portions Commonly Used. New York, NY: Harper Collins, 1989.

tions of certain analytes (e.g., phosphorus, hematocrit, serum proteins) vary markedly from adult values.[158]

Key Nutritional Factors
Colostrum and Milk
Colostrum is milk provided by the queen during the first 24 to 72 hours after parturition. Colostrum provides nutrients, water, growth factors, digestive enzymes and maternal immunoglobulins, all of which are critical to survival of neonatal kittens. Colostrum differs from mature milk in water and nutrient composition (Table 11-15). The dry matter content of colostrum is high, which accounts for its sticky concentrated appearance compared with mature milk. The dry matter concentration declines as water content increases from Day 1 to 3 of lactation.[159] Lactose concentrations are low in colostrum (29.9 g/l or 23 mg/kcal) and increase as milk matures. Protein and lipid levels decline markedly from Day 1 to 3; however, this decline likely reflects the initial change in water content because nutrient levels rebound after Day 3 and increase slightly over the course of lactation. Like protein and lipid levels, the calculated gross energy of colostrum is high on Day 1 of lactation (1,300 kcal/l or 5.44 MJ/l) and falls significantly by Day 3. However, the energy content then increases throughout lactation (Table 11-15). Changes in mineral content also vary with time. Calcium and phosphorus concentrations increase up to Day 14, whereas iron, copper and magnesium concentrations decline. Early studies reported very low calcium concentrations and calcium-phosphorus ratios of 0.5:1 in queen's milk. These values likely represent colostral milk (calcium-phosphorus ratio = 0.4:1).[160] Recent studies of queen's milk report calcium-phosphorus ratios between 0.8:1 to 1:1 on Day 7; ratios reach 1.2:1 by late lactation.[144,159] The variation in nutrient content with time probably explains the discrepancy in milk composition published by different investigators. Different values probably represent milk from different stages of lactation.

In addition to providing complete nutrition for nursing kittens, queen's milk also supplies non-nutritive factors that enhance food digestion, neonatal development and immune protection. The immunoglobulin concentration of cat colostrum and mature milk may not be significantly different as they are in most species.[143] More studies are needed to further evaluate this difference; a decline in immunoglobulin concentrations and an increased casein-whey ratio with time contradict this finding.[159] Regardless, kittens acquire passive systemic and local immunity from consuming either colostrum or mature milk.[143] Kittens should receive colostrum within the first 12 hours of life to obtain adequate systemic immunity; after 16 hours, passive immunoglobulin transfer does not occur in kittens.[143] During this time, kittens absorb intact immunoglobulins across the intestine. Failure to ingest colostrum or queen's milk during this absorptive window leaves kittens immunologically compromised and susceptible to infections and sepsis. Passive transfer of systemic immunity is particularly important to orphaned and hand-raised kittens that are fed only milk replacers. Consumption of queen's milk provides local concentrations of immunoglobulins within the GI tract and helps prevent invasion of microorganisms into the bloodstream (passive local immunity). Local immunity persists as long as kittens receive queen's milk. Both systemic and local immunity are important in maintaining kitten health until maturation of the kittens' immune system.

Mature milk is a complete food for nursing kittens. Water, protein, fat, lactose, minerals and vitamins are provided in amounts sufficient for normal growth and development. As mentioned previously, mature milk from a queen may sustain high immunoglobulin levels similar to those provided by colostrum. Continued nursing provides high immunoglobulin levels for passive local immunity. Thus, the major feature differentiating mature queen's milk from colostrum is the nutrient content (Table 11-15). As lactation progresses, milk energy, protein, lactose, calcium and phosphorus levels increase whereas copper, iron and magnesium concentrations decrease.[159] The amino acid profiles of colostrum and mature milk also differ.

Table 11-16. Daily energy requirements of growing kittens.

Age (months)	kcal/kg BW/day	kJ/kg BW/day
Birth	250	1,045
1	240	1,005
2	210	880
3	200	840
4*	175	730
5	145	610
6**	135	565
7	120	500
8	110	460
9***	100	420
10	95	400
11	90	375
12	85	355

Key: BW = body weight, RER = resting energy requirement = 70 x $(BW_{kg})^{0.75}$.
*Up to 50% of adult BW (at about four months of age) or 3.0 x RER.
**Between 50 and 70% of adult BW (around six months of age) or 2.5 x RER.
***Between 70 and 100% of adult BW (around nine to 12 months of age) or 2 x RER. See Appendices C and F.

Notable features include the relatively high concentrations of arginine and taurine in queen's milk, which likely reflect the unique metabolism of cats.

The nutrient requirements of nursing kittens have not been well studied. Although the nutrient profile of queen's milk is thought to provide optimal nutrition, faster growth rates are typically observed in kittens fed milk replacers.[157] Nevertheless, nutrient recommendations for neonates are based on the composition of queen's milk (Table 11-15) and growth studies in weaned kittens. Despite discrepancies in published nutrient values, queen's milk varies markedly from milk of other species. (See Appendix K.) Consequently, milk from other species is not suitable for nursing kittens. Replacement formulas with a nutrient profile similar to that of mature milk should be used for orphans and supplemental feedings. For nutrients in which the concentration in mature milk is unknown, values recommended by AAFCO for growth should suffice.[58]

Energy

Queen's milk typically meets the energy requirements of nursing kittens. Estimated caloric intake is approximately 200 kcal/kg body weight (837 kJ/kg body weight) for kittens up to four weeks of age, and 250 kcal/kg body weight (1,046 kJ/kg body weight) for kittens over four weeks of age (Table 11-16). By six weeks of age, male kittens are significantly heavier than female kittens and consume a proportionately larger quantity of food. As a rule, milk contains from 0.85 to 1.6 kcal/ml (3.6 to 6.7 kJ/ml) and milk replacers contain approximately 1 kcal/ml (4.2 kJ/ml) as fed. (See Appendix K.)

Water

Kittens contain 78.8% body water at one week of age.[161] Total body water decreases to 70.1% at weaning. By comparison, adult cats are composed of only 61.7% water.[161] Thus, the water intake of kittens is relatively high. A normal kitten needs about 155 to 230 ml water/kg body weight/day (i.e., 4.4 to 6.5 ml water/oz.).

Protein

The minimum protein requirement of nursing kittens has not been established. However, it is assumed to be comparable to that of weanling kittens, which is approximately 18 to 20% DM.[162] These requirements were established using purified diets and may not accurately reflect the needs of kittens fed commercial foods made from typical ingredi-

ents. The AAFCO recommendation of 30% DM appears adequate;[58] however, the protein content of queen's milk ranges from 33 to 44% DM.[159,160]

Taurine

Taurine is important for normal growth and development of kittens. Fortunately, dietary taurine is more available in kittens than adult cats,[163] presumably because of reduced bacterial destruction in the GI tract. Normal plasma taurine concentrations were maintained in 12- and 18-week-old kittens fed taurine at 150 to 197 mg/kg body weight/day.[163] Queen's milk supplies about 300 mg taurine/liter.[9,159] Queens fed low-taurine foods have significantly lower milk taurine levels, which may impair normal growth and development.[h] Milk taurine concentrations are influenced by dietary taurine intake, thus it is not surprising that cow's milk is a poor source of taurine (i.e., only 1.3 mg/l).[9] Therefore, homemade milk replacers based on cow's milk should be supplemented with taurine.

Fat

Milk fat is an important source of energy and essential fatty acids for nursing kittens. The composition of the queen's diet can significantly influence milk fat quantity and quality, which translates into fat composition of the offspring.[164] The fat content of queen's milk increases throughout lactation. Average fat concentrations of 28% DM or 86 g/l appear typical.[144,159,160] Queen's milk provides the essential fatty acids linoleic and arachidonic acid at 5.8 and 0.5% DM, respectively.[144] Docosahexaenoic acid is also essential for normal retinal development and function in kittens.[66] Milk concentrations of DHA reflect the dietary intake of the queen.

Carbohydrate

No carbohydrate requirements have been established for nursing and growing kittens. However, the lactose concentration of queen's milk ranges from 14 to 26% DM. Intestinal lactase activity declines to adult levels very soon after weaning.[18] Overfeeding cow's milk causes diarrhea, bloating and abdominal discomfort in kittens due to bacterial metabolism of undigested lactose in the large intestine. Owners who wish to offer cow's milk should be advised to limit the quantities given and to discontinue feeding cow's milk if intolerance occurs.

Calcium and Phosphorus

Calcium concentrations are low in colostrum (0.22% DM) and increase significantly to approximately 1% DM by mid to late lactation.[159] Thus, requirements appear limited early on and increase with bone mineralization and growth. Milk phosphorus concentrations do not vary to the same extent. Thus, calcium-phosphorus ratios change from 0.4:1 on Day 1 of lactation to approximately 1.2:1 at one week and remain as such throughout lactation.

Trace Minerals

Queen's milk contains iron, copper and zinc concentrations markedly higher than those in human and bovine milk but similar to those in canine milk. Copper and iron levels tend to gradually decline throughout lactation, whereas zinc concentrations remains constant. Thus, mineral deficiencies are rarely reported to occur in nursing kittens fed queen's milk. However, milk replacers made from cow's milk should be supplemented to levels typically found in queen's milk (Table 11-15) to avoid deficiency.

ASSESS THE FOOD(S)

Foods should be liquid until kittens are three to four weeks old, then semi-solid to solid foods may be introduced. Foods may consist of queen's milk, commercial milk replacers and homemade milk replacers (including supplemented human enteral formulas). See Appendix K for more information about milk and milk replacers.

Queen's milk is considered ideal, providing all essential nutrients, antibodies, enzymes and hormones. Commercial milk replacers and homemade replacer recipes may mimic the essential nutrient content of queen's milk but lack its other beneficial properties.

The quality of queen's milk and milk replacers is difficult to assess without analysis. Indirect measurement of kitten growth is probably the most practical method of assessment. In addition, the queen's food should be assessed if the queen is losing excessive weight. A thin queen (BCS 1/5 to 2/5) may not produce enough milk or may produce poor-quality milk. If milk analysis is required, a sample can be collected by manually expressing milk from the queen after preventing the kittens from nursing for a short time. Parenteral oxytocin (5 IU/queen) facilitates milk collection. Small samples (1 to 3 ml) are easily collected during normal lactation and should be frozen until analysis. Commercial laboratories do not routinely analyze such small milk samples; therefore, an appropriate research facility should be contacted for specific information about sample size and preservation and shipping instructions.

ASSESS THE FEEDING METHOD

It may be necessary to alter the feeding method when managing neonatal kittens, especially if they are hand reared. Evaluation of current feeding methods with foreknowledge of growth demands will allow for development of a rational feeding plan.

Nursing kittens should be allowed free access to the queen. Kittens should be observed to ensure they have received colostrum by 12 hours after birth. Most neonatal kittens require feeding every two to four hours during the first week of life then every four to six hours until weaning. Weak kittens may need to be placed on the queen and held steady to facilitate nursing. Chilled kittens will not suckle and have reduced GI function. Thus, it is imperative to adequately warm weak kittens before they are fed. Hypoglycemia and hypothermia may occur simultaneously in neonates and have similar clinical signs. If kittens fail to respond to warming, a dilute glucose solution (2.5% glucose) may be given orally. This should be repeated until kittens are able to initiate a strong sucking reflex. Orphaned kittens and those too weak to nurse may be fed with a stomach tube, pet nurser or small syringe. (See Appendix E.) At three to five weeks of age, kittens begin to eat semi-solid foods and enter the transition period from nursing to weaning.

Determine a Feeding Plan

Nursing kittens should be allowed to suckle the queen as the preferred feeding method. Nursing kittens depend completely on queen's milk; therefore, the feeding plan for the queen should be evaluated and modified if necessary. (See Reproducing Cats.)

Kittens should receive colostrum within the first 12 hours after birth. After this time, immunoglobulins are no longer absorbed from the GI tract[143] and passive transfer will not occur. If colostrum is unavailable, milk collected from queens at any stage of lactation may be substituted. Antibody levels in non-colostral milk appear to adequately transfer passive immunity to kittens.[143] Alternatively, sterile

serum may be given to kittens subcutaneously if milk is unavailable.[47] After the first 24 hours, kittens should be fed queen's milk or a complete and balanced milk replacer.

If circumstances require alternate feeding methods, the next best option is to attempt to foster kittens to a surrogate queen. Finally, feeding by bottle, syringe or stomach tube may be required. The method of choice largely depends on the age, vitality and adequacy of the suckling reflex of the kitten and the handler's expertise. (See Appendix E.)

Reassessment

Kittens should be reassessed daily. Body weights should be obtained at birth then once weekly, if no complications are present. Poor weight gain or failure to thrive should prompt the breeder/owner to seek an immediate evaluation by a veterinarian.

Adequacy of the queen's milk production can be assessed by the growth rate of the kittens, kitten contentment and, to some extent, the degree of mammary gland distention. Expressing milk from a queen's nipples demonstrates the functionality of individual mammary glands, but does not indicate adequate milk production.

Growing Kittens: Postweaning to Adulthood

The postweaning growth period includes kittens from about eight weeks of age until adulthood (i.e., 10 to 12 months). The nutritional needs of growing kittens include maintenance needs similar to those of adult cats and energy and substrates necessary for rapid tissue accretion (Figure 11-13). Growth rate slows if nutritional deficiencies exist. Thus, nutritional requirements are easiest to determine in growing animals using growth rates as a nutritional marker. The nutritional needs of postweaning, growing kittens are best understood by comparing them with the needs during other lifestages. Nevertheless, the optimal nutrient levels for growth may not represent the optimal levels for other physiologic functions (e.g., immune function). Further research may redefine nutrient requirements of growing kittens as physiologic parameters other than growth are studied. The ultimate goal of feeding

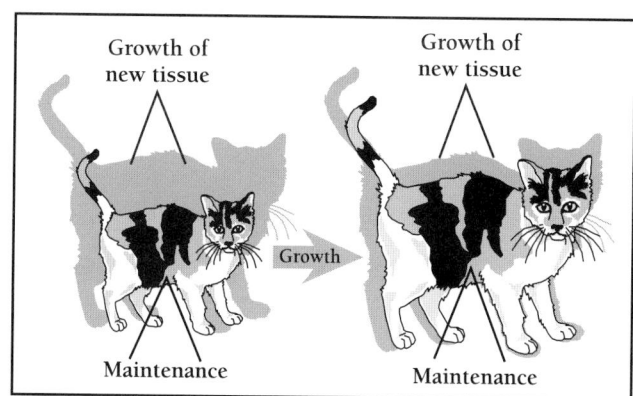

Figure 11-13. Representation of nutritional requirements of kittens. The nutritional needs of growing cats include maintenance requirements similar to those of adult cats (depicted here as the body of the cat) plus nutrients necessary for rapid tissue accretion (shaded area). The proportion of nutrient intake needed for maintenance vs. tissue accretion changes throughout growth as depicted here.

Table 11-17. Key nutritional factors for growing kittens.*

Factors	Recommended food levels**
Energy density (kcal ME/g)	4.0-5.0
Energy density (kJ ME/g)	17-21
Protein (%)	35-50
Fat (%)	18-35
Carbohydrate (%)	10
Crude fiber (%)	<5
Calcium (%)	0.8-1.6
Phosphorus (%)	0.6-1.4
Ca/P ratio	1:1-1.5:1
Sodium (%)	0.3-0.6
Chloride (%)	≥0.45
Potassium (%)	0.6-1.2
Magnesium (%)	0.08-0.15
Taurine (ppm) (extruded)	1,000
Taurine (ppm) (moist)	2,500
Average urinary pH***	6.2-6.5

*Concentrations presume an energy density of 4.0 kcal/g. Levels should be corrected for foods with higher energy densities. Adjustment is unnecessary for foods with lower energy densities.
**Dry matter basis.
***As determined in growing kittens.

kittens is to ensure a healthy adult. The specific objectives, however, are to optimize growth, minimize risk factors for disease and achieve optimal health.

Assessment

ASSESS THE ANIMAL

History and Physical Examination

The general health and risk factors should be determined for every kitten early in the growing phase. A thorough history and physical examination, including determination of body weight and body condition, are generally sufficient. Ideally, a veterinarian should assess the kitten at weaning and monthly thereafter until the kitten is four months old. This schedule coincides with typical vaccination protocols for young kittens. The veterinary health care team should educate the owner about nutrition, weight management, neutering and dental care during these examinations. The owner can then evaluate body condition, stool and appetite weekly or biweekly.

Kittens should continue to grow at approximately 100 g/week until about 20 weeks of age. At 20 weeks, males typically gain 20 g/day whereas females gain 11 g/day.[9] Growth rate slows as kittens approach 80% of adult size at 30 weeks and reach adult body weight at Week 40 (10 months) (Figure 11-10). Most cats will achieve skeletal maturity at 10 months of age although some growth plates have yet to close. Additional weight gain may occur after 12 months of age and represents a phase of maturation and muscle development.

There is no evidence that the age at neutering alters rate of growth. Investigators evaluating early neutering found kittens neutered at 12 weeks of age reached similar size as adults neutered at the more typical ages of six to nine months.[35] Unfortunately, energy requirements decline with neutering and the risk for obesity increases.[35-37] Neutering, however, is not the only risk factor for obesity. Practitioners have noted an alarming increase in the number of young cats with marked abdominal fat accumulation before neutering. An indoor lifestyle, high-fat foods, overfeeding and certain feeding practices (e.g., free-choice feeding) are additional risk factors for obesity.[37] Obesity

should be prevented at an early age because it significantly affects the health and longevity of cats.[56] Therefore, the risks for obesity should be determined as part of each cat's health evaluation at each veterinary visit.

Key Nutritional Factors

Many of the key nutritional factors were discussed in the Neonatal Kittens section above and are outlined in Tables 11-16 and 11-17. Key nutritional factors as they relate to postweaning, growing kittens are reviewed here.

Energy

Growing kittens have high energy requirements to meet the needs of a rapid growth rate, thermoregulation and maintenance. Kittens may grow at rates from 14 to 30 g/day during the rapid growth phase. Although ensuring optimal growth is desired, excessive energy intake may lead to obesity. Ten-week-old kittens have a DER of approximately 200 kcal/kg body weight (837 kJ/kg body weight), which declines to adult levels (80 kcal/kg body weight [335 kJ/kg body weight]) at 10 months of age. After 10 months, age-related changes in energy requirement have not been observed.[35] Neutering reduces energy requirements by 24 to 33% regardless of the age at neutering.[35,36] After neutering, limiting food intake or decreasing dietary energy may be required to prevent excessive weight gain. The energy density of the food fed to rapidly growing kittens should be between 4.0 to 5.0 kcal ME/g (16.7 to 20.9 kJ ME/g) (Table 11-17). A higher energy density allows smaller volumes of food intake to satisfy caloric needs. However, foods with energy densities at the lower end of this range should be fed to neutered kittens and those with a BCS of 4/5 or greater. The prevalence of obesity increases dramatically after one year of age. Apparently, overnutrition is becoming of greater concern than undernutrition in growing kittens.

Protein

The protein requirements of kittens reflect their essential amino acid requirements and minimal nitrogen needs. Protein also provides sulfur-containing amino acids, which are required in greater amounts in kittens than in other species.[4] Protein requirements are high at weaning then decrease gradually to adult levels. Kittens fed purified foods meeting all essential amino acids at or above the requirement have minimum protein needs of 20% DM, or approximately 17% protein calories in food containing 4.7 kcal ME/g (19.7 kJ ME/g) or (5.3 g/100 kcal).[4,162] As mentioned, protein biologic value and amino acid digestibility in practical cat foods are typically lower than in purified foods.[9] AAFCO recommends a minimum crude protein level of 30% DM or 26% protein calories (7.5 g/100 kcal).[58] This level of crude protein resulted in maximum growth rates of approximately 30 g body weight/day in kittens fed purified foods.[165] To provide sufficient sulfur-containing amino acids without additional supplementation, at least 19% of the food must come from animal protein.[4] Table 11-17 lists crude protein recommendations in practical foods for growing kittens.

Appendix J summarizes the essential amino acid requirements for kittens. However, feeding a food using the ratio of essential amino acids listed in Appendix J at high crude protein levels results in weight loss.[166] Apparently, methionine and arginine are toxic when their concentration markedly exceeds 2.25 times the NRC requirement. Conversely, high-protein foods (56% DM) must contain arginine at 1.5 times the requirement to maintain normal urea cycle function.[166]

Fat

As kittens grow, body composition changes dramatically. Body fat composes only 5.5% of body weight in eight-week-old kittens and increases to 14.6% of body weight by 18 weeks.[167] Dietary fat serves three primary functions in growing kittens: 1) it supplies essential fatty acids, 2) it acts as a carrier for fat-soluble vitamins and 3) it provides a concentrated source of energy in the food. However, excessive fat and caloric intake may predispose young kittens to obesity. In another study, kittens had 24.3% body fat by six months of age, which is the upper end of body fat for ideal body condition.[167]

Kittens tolerate wide levels of dietary fat (1 to 64% DM).[9] Fat digestibility is typically greater than 90% for high-fat foods. Kittens, like adults, require linoleic and arachidonic acid, and they also require fatty acids of the n-3 series (DHA, 20:6n-3). Studies indicate n-3 fatty acids are essential for normal neural development in kittens.[66] Although true fat requirements are much lower, AAFCO recommendations for growth are 9.0, 0.5 and 0.02% for total fat, linoleic acid and arachidonic acid, respectively.[58] These levels will sustain adequate growth; however, optimal growth rates are achieved with higher fat intake. When kittens are offered foods with differing levels of fat, they select foods with a fat content of 25% DM.[10] Unless excessive growth or weight gain is evident, feeding foods with 18 to 35% fat is preferred to enhance palatability, meet essential fatty acid needs and maintain the energy density of the food above 4.5 kcal ME/g (18.8 kJ ME/g). Overweight and neutered kittens may require foods with dietary fat levels well below these to achieve ideal body condition (BCS 3/5). The minimum requirement for linolenic acid has not been established.

Calcium and Phosphorus

Weaned kittens appear to be fairly insensitive to inverse calcium-phosphorus ratios (e.g., kittens have been fed foods with ratios as low as 0.38:1 with no deleterious effects).[75] The minimum requirement for dietary calcium in growing kittens is approximately 5 g/kg food (0.5% DM).[75] Thus, AAFCO minimum allowances for calcium (0.8% DM) and phosphorus (0.6% DM) are appropriate for nursing, weanling and postweaning kittens.[9,58] The AAFCO calcium allowance is higher than the established minimum requirement to compensate for foods with poor calcium availability. Unlike the situation with puppies, calcium excess in kittens is not associated with developmental orthopedic disease. However, very high concentrations of calcium significantly reduce magnesium availability.[168] Dietary calcium concentrations of 2% resulted in a nearly twofold increase in the magnesium requirement of growing kittens. Providing calcium in amounts sufficient to meet the needs of growing kittens and avoid impairing the availability of other nutrients is the basis for the levels recommended in Table 11-17.

Calcium deficiency coupled with phosphorus excess is most commonly observed in kittens fed unsupplemented all-meat diets. Nutritional secondary hyperparathyroidism results in osteitis fibrosa and is manifested by limping, pain and reluctance to move. Kittens fed such foods should immediately be fed a commercial food that meets the recommended minimum requirements with a calcium-phosphorus ratio of 1.2:1 to 2:1. Additional supplementation of calcium is not recommended and may lead to hypercalcemia as a result of serum parathyroid hormone (PTH) excess.

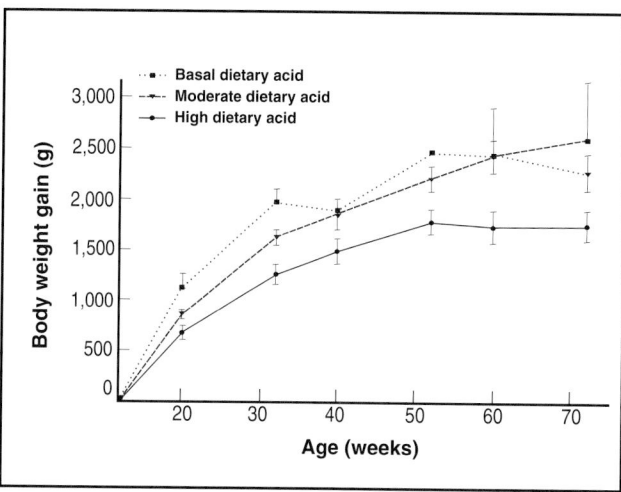

Figure 11-14. Effect of dietary acid load on body weight gain in kittens. Kittens fed highly acidifying foods grow more slowly and plateau at lower body weights than kittens fed more basic foods. (Adapted from Buffington CA, Rogers QR, Morris JG. Effects of age and food deprivation on urine pH of cats. Veterinary Clinical Nutrition 1994; 1: 12-17.)

Potassium

The potassium requirement of kittens is highly dependent on the protein content of the food and the effect of the food on acid-base balance.[89] Urinary potassium loss is markedly increased when kittens are fed high-protein, acidified foods. To avoid syndromes associated with hypokalemia, postweaning kittens should not be fed highly acidifying foods and potassium allowances should be at least 0.6% of the dry matter intake. Chloride levels of 0.1% DM also cause hypokalemia despite adequate potassium levels.[88] Some foods intended for lifestage feeding target urinary pH levels more appropriate for adult cats. These foods should be carefully assessed to ensure potassium is provided at appropriate levels (Table 11-17).

Other Nutritional Factors

Urinary pH

The urinary pH of growing kittens is lower than that of adults fed similar foods. Presumably, the lower pH is caused by hydrogen ions released during bone formation, which are excreted into the urine. This increased response to dietary acidification continues until kittens are about 12 months old (Figure 11-14).[169] Kittens fed highly acidifying foods (e.g., free-choice fed, urinary pH at or below 6.0) grow more slowly and plateau at lower body weights than kittens fed more basic foods. In addition to contributing to slow growth rates, feeding highly acidified foods results in poor bone mineralization in growing kittens.[154] To reduce the risk of acidification on bone mineralization and growth, kittens should not be fed foods that produce urinary pH values less than 6.2 when fed free choice. Because growing kittens have a reduced risk for developing struvite-mediated lower urinary tract disease,[126] an upper maximum for urinary pH is poorly defined. A maximum urinary pH of 6.5 will reduce the risk of struvite precipitates in cats at risk for lower urinary tract disease and avoid overacidification.

Digestibility

The food should be palatable with apparent dry matter digestibility greater than 80% and protein digestibility greater than 85%. The small stomach capacity of young kittens and relatively high energy demands limit food intake capacity. Providing highly digestible foods maximizes usage of the nutrients consumed.

Carbohydrates

Carbohydrates are not required in the food of growing kittens as long as an adequate supply of glucogenic amino acids is available. Nevertheless, cats can readily digest starch in cereal grains (i.e., >95% digestible). Excessive feeding of poorly digestible carbohydrates may result in bloating, gas and diarrhea. These signs are often observed in kittens offered large quantities of cow's milk after weaning. The combination of high lactose levels with waning intestinal lactase levels results in carbohydrate overload.

ASSESS THE FOOD(S)

A more appropriate food should be selected if the food currently being fed has markedly different levels of key nutritional factors than those recommended in Table 11-17. It is better to change to a food formulated specifically for kittens than to try balancing an inappropriate food. A food that is complete and balanced as demonstrated by AAFCO or similar animal feeding trials should be fed to kittens until they reach adulthood (10 to 12 months).

Unmoistened dry foods and moist foods are appropriate for weaned kittens. Dry foods are more energy dense per volume of food, which benefits small kittens needing increased numbers of calories. Moist foods tend to be more palatable and thus encourage food intake. Semimoist foods that excessively acidify the urine (i.e., <6.0 pH units) should be avoided until skeletal growth is completed. Identification of health risks such as obesity or overacidification necessitates a scrupulous review of foods provided for growth. Appendix L lists nutrient information for selected foods. The manufacturer should be contacted for additional information. Alternatively, laboratories can analyze food samples. (See Appendix U.) This approach is usually necessary to obtain information about homemade foods.

Treats are unnecessary but may be fed in small quantities (i.e., <10% of the daily intake). Milk is commonly offered to kittens as a treat. Amounts offered should be limited because intestinal lactase levels decline shortly after weaning.[66] Appendix M lists nutritional profiles of common treats.

ASSESS THE FEEDING METHOD

Several feeding methods are appropriate for growing kittens. However, the method should be tailored to the individual animal's needs, the type of food being offered and the owner's preference (Table 11-9). Free-choice feeding is often preferred because it reduces the risk of underfeeding and reduces the marked gastric distention that sometimes accompanies rapid meal feeding in young kittens. The feeding frequency should be three to four times daily for meal-fed kittens less than six months old. This frequency ensures sufficient food intake to meet the high nutritional demands without encouraging engorgement. By six months of age, most kittens will tolerate twice daily feeding.

If kittens are thriving on their current regimen, alterations in the feeding method are unnecessary. A more appropriate feeding method should be considered for kittens with poor growth rates and those with excess weight gain and obesity. Free-choice feeding methods should be used for underweight and slow-growing kittens. Providing unlimited food for free-choice intake is inappropriate for overweight and obese kittens. A defined food quantity should be measured then offered as meals or fed free choice until gone. Neutering increases the risk for obesity; therefore, free-choice feeding of high-fat foods to neutered kittens should be done very cautiously. Table 11-16 outlines the recommended daily ME intake for growing kittens.

To determine the amount to feed, the DER may be calculated based on the age-appropriate energy requirements listed in Table 11-16, divided by the caloric content of the food. The caloric content of many foods is not readily available; therefore, feeding guides on food labels and the manufacturers' literature are useful starting places. After an initial food amount is chosen, weight gain and body condition can be evaluated to tailor the feeding amounts to individual cats. Young postweaning kittens should be evaluated weekly. Biweekly evaluations are appropriate after kittens are about four months old. Owners can easily evaluate body weight and condition, and their findings should be confirmed by the veterinarian during vaccination and wellness visits.

Determine a Feeding Plan

Assessment of the kitten, the current food and the feeding method should provide the necessary information to develop a feeding plan. If it is concluded that the food or feeding method is not appropriate, then changes in the food, feeding method or both will need to be made. Often the assessment steps will determine that the current plan is optimal and no changes are necessary.

SELECT A FOOD(S)

A more appropriate food should be selected if the current food does not adequately address the key nutritional factors listed in Table 11-17. Appendix L lists the key nutritional factors in selected commercial foods. Or, the manufacturer can be contacted for additional information and for foods not listed in Appendix L. Of key importance, foods for kittens should have undergone feeding trials appropriate for growth. Foods labeled for all lifestages, for growth and reproduction or for growth are appropriate for kittens if the label claim is supported by animal feeding tests.

SELECT A FEEDING METHOD

As described previously, all types of feeding methods are appropriate for kittens. The method should be tailored to the individual animal's needs, the food type and the owner's preference. Free-choice feeding is preferred for kittens younger than five months. Fresh water should be provided daily and be available at all times. Young kittens should be fed in shallow pans to facilitate access to food. Food should be offered at room temperature; however, moist foods should not be left out for prolonged periods to reduce spoilage.

Reassessment

After weaning, kittens should be weighed once a month until they are four to five months old. Weighing is usually performed at the time of vaccinations or veterinary examinations. The growth rate varies from ideal by gender, breed and nutritional status; however, it can be evaluated using Figure 11-10 as a guide. Owners should continue to monitor daily food and water consumption to ensure normal appetite. Determination of total intake is necessary only if inappetence, illness or poor growth rate is evident. Body condition scoring every one to two weeks is a better means to assess growth and adequacy of food intake. Results of body condition assessment allow owners to monitor kitten growth and adjust food offerings as needed to maintain ideal body condition (BCS 3/5). Kittens provided proper nutrition are healthy and alert and have ideal body condition, steady weight gain and a clean, glossy coat. Normal stools are firm, well formed and medium to dark brown. The veterinarian should conduct a nutritional assessment at each visit, or approximately monthly from six to 16 weeks of age, and then annually. Instructions for nutritional modifications and dental care can be given at that time.

■ SUMMARY

The nutritional peculiarities of cats are easily understood if one considers the consistency of the natural diet to which cats evolved. Failure to feed nutritionally complete and balance foods appropriate for the age, activity and use of the cat can impair health and vitality. To ensure the best possible nutrition for cats and to alleviate problems caused by feeding errors:

- Feed a good-quality food proven nutritionally adequate for cats.
- Choose a food for which nutritional adequacy was established through animal feeding trials.
- Select a food formulated for the purpose for which it is being fed.
- Provide continuous access to fresh clean water.
- Limit treats to 10% or less of the daily intake.
- Provide supplements only when medically indicated.
- Regularly monitor the cat's body condition, appetite and food intake.
- Adjust food offerings to maintain ideal body condition (BCS 3/5).

"Again I must remind you that
A Dog's a Dog, A CAT'S A CAT."
T.S. Eliot

■ ENDNOTES AND REFERENCES

ENDNOTES

a. Lund EM, College of Veterinary Medicine, University of Minnesota, St. Paul, USA. Personal communication. 1996. National Companion Animal Survey: Preliminary Data.

b. Kirk CA. Unpublished data. 1990.

c. Hill's Pet Nutrition, Inc., Topeka, KS, USA. Data on file.

d. Lyons K, Mesa Veterinary Hospital, Mesa, AZ, USA. Personal communication. 1997.

e. Lewis LD, Mark Morris Associates, Topeka, KS, USA. Unpublished data. 1987.

f. Kirk CA. Unpublished data. 1994.

g. Buffington CA, The Ohio State University, Columbus. Personal communication. 1994.

h. Kirk CA. Unpublished data. 1994.

REFERENCES

1. Maxwell JC Jr. Maxwell Report. Petfood Industry 1998; 40(7): 40-47.
2. Center for Information Management. U.S. Pet Ownership and Demographics Sourcebook. Schaumburg, IL: American Veterinary Medical Association, 1997.
3. Kane E, Rogers QR, Morris JG, et al. Feeding behavior of the cat fed laboratory and commercial diets. Nutrition Research 1981; 1: 499-507.
4. MacDonald ML, Rogers QR, Morris JG. Nutrition of the domestic cat, a mammalian carnivore. Annual Review of Nutrition 1984; 4: 521-562.
5. Fitzgerald BM. Diets of domestic cats and their impact on prey population. In: Turner DC, Bateson P, eds. The Domestic Cat: The Biology of its Behaviour. Cambridge, UK: Cambridge University Press, 1988; 123-150.
6. Mugford RA. External influences on the feeding of carnivores. In: Dare MR, Maller O, eds. The Chemical Senses and Nutrition. New York, NY: Academic Press Inc, 1977; 25-50.
7. Adamec RE. The interaction of hunger and preying in the domestic cat (*Felis catus*): An adaptive hierarchy? Behavioural Biology 1976; 18: 263-272.
8. Turner DC, Meister O. Hunting behaviour of the domestic cat. In: Turner DC, Bateson P, eds. The Domestic Cat: The Biology of its Behaviour. Cambridge, UK: Cambridge University Press, 1988; 111-122.
9. National Research Council. Nutrient Requirements of Cats. Washington, DC: National Academy Press, 1986.
10. Kane E, Morris JG, Rogers QR. Acceptability and digestibility by adult cats of diets made with various sources and levels of fat. Journal of Animal Science 1981; 53: 1516-1523.
11. Leyhausen P. Cat Behavior: The Predatory and Social Behavior of Domestic and Wild Cats. New York, NY: Garland Press, 1979; 6-53.
12. Mech DL. The Wolf: The Ecology and Behavior of an Endangered Species. Garden City, NY: Natural History Press, 1970; 181-192.
13. Tabor R. The Wild Life of the Domestic Cat. London, UK: Arrow Books, 1983.
14. Kendall PT, Holme DW, Smith PhM. Comparative evaluation of net digesta and absorptive efficiency in dogs and cats fed a variety of contrasting diet types. Journal of Small Animal Practice 1982; 23: 577-587.
15. Morris JG, Rogers QR. Comparative aspects of nutrition and metabolism of dogs and cats. In: Burger IH, Rivers JPW, eds. Nutrition of the Dog and Cat. Cambridge, UK: Cambridge University Press, 1989; 35-66.
16. Buddington RK, Diamond J. Ontogenetic development of nutrient transporters in cat intestine. American Journal of Physiology 1992; 263: G605-G616.
17. Kienzle E. Carbohydrate metabolism of the cat 4. Activity of maltase, isomaltase, sucrase and lactase in the gastrointestinal tract in relation to age and diet. Journal of Animal Physiology and Animal Nutrition 1993; 70: 89-96.
18. Kienzle E. Activity of carbohydrate-cleaving enzymes in cats as a function of age and feeding. In: Edney ATB, ed. Nutrition, Malnutrition and Dietetics in the Dog and Cat. Proceedings of an International Symposium. Hannover, Germany, September 1987: 19-22.
19. Kienzle E. Carbohydrate metabolism of the cat 1. Activity of amylase in the gastrointestinal tract of the cat. Journal of Animal Physiology and Animal Nutrition 1993; 69: 92-101.
20. Beliveau GP, Freedland RA. Metabolism of serine, glycine and threonine in isolated cat hepatocytes. Comparative Biochemistry and Physiology 1982; 71B: 13-18.
21. Diehl KJ, Wheeler SJ. Evaluation of three enteral feeding formulas in cats (abstract). In: Proceedings. Tenth Annual Veterinary Medical Forum, American College of Veterinary Internal Medicine, San Diego, CA, 1992: 813.
22. Hendriks WH, Moughan PJ, Tarttelin MF, et al. Felinine: A urinary amino acid of Felidae. Comparative Biochemistry and Physiology. Part B, Biochemistry and Molecular Biology 1995; 112: 581-588.

NORMAL CATS

23. MacDonald ML, Anderson FC, Rogers QR, et al. Essential fatty acid requirements of cats: Pathology of essential fatty acid deficiency. American Journal of Veterinary Research 1984; 45: 1310-1317.

24. Sinclair AJ, McLean JG, Monger EA. Metabolism of linoleic acid in the cat. Lipids 1979; 14: 932-936.

25. DaSilva AC, Fried R, deAngelis RC. The domestic cat as a laboratory animal for experimental nutrition studies. III Niacin requirement and tryptophan metabolism. Journal of Nutrition 1952; 46: 399-409.

26. Morris JG, Rogers QR. Nutritional implications of some metabolic anomalies of the cat. In: Proceedings. Fiftieth Annual Meeting, American Animal Hospital Association, San Antonio, TX, 1983: 325-331.

27. National Research Council. Nutrient Requirements of Dogs. Washington, DC: National Academy Press, 1985.

28. Stryer L. Amino acid degradation and the urea cycle. In: Biochemistry. San Francisco, CA: WH Freeman and Co, 1975; 407-429.

29. How KL, Hazewinkel HAW, Mol JA. Dietary vitamin D dependence of the cat and dog due to inadequate cutaneous synthesis of vitamin D. General and Comparative Endocrinology 1994; 96: 12-18.

30. How KL, Hazewinkel HAW, Mol JA. Photosynthesis of vitamin D_3 in cats. Veterinary Record 1994; 134: 384.

31. Morris JG. Vitamin D synthesis by kittens. Veterinary Clinical Nutrition 1996; 3: 88-92.

32. Anderson RS. Water balance in the dog and cat. Journal of Small Animal Practice 1982; 23: 588-598.

33. Jewell DE, Kirk CA, Berryhill SA, et al. The effect of age on body composition in dogs and cats. In: Proceedings. Symposium on Health and Nutrition of Geriatric Cats and Dogs, Orlando, FL, January 1996: 52.

34. Klausen B, Toubro S, Astrup A. Age and sex effects on energy expenditure. American Journal of Clinical Nutrition 1997; 65: 895-907.

35. Root MV. Early spay and neuter in the cat: Effect on development of obesity and metabolic rate. Veterinary Clinical Nutrition 1995; 2: 132-134.

36. Flynn MF, Hardie EM, Armstrong PJ. Effect of ovariohysterectomy on maintenance energy requirement in cats. Journal of the American Veterinary Medical Association 1996; 209: 1572-1581.

37. Scarlett JM, Donoghue S, Saidla J, et al. Overweight cats: Prevalence and risk factors. International Journal of Obesity 1994; 18: S22-S28.

38. Earle KE, Smith PM. Digestible energy requirements of adult cats at maintenance. Journal of Nutrition 1991; 121: S45-S46.

39. Finke MD, Lutschaunig MT. Energy requirements of adult Abyssinian cats. Veterinary Clinical Nutrition 1995; 2: 64.

40. Miller SA, Allison JB. The dietary nitrogen requirements of the cat. Journal of Nutrition 1958; 64: 493.

41. Hensel H, Banet M. Adaptive changes in cats after long-term exposure to various temperatures. Journal of Applied Physiology 1982; 52: 1008-1012.

42. Precht H, Christophersen J, Hensel H, eds. Temperature and Life. Berlin, West Germany: Springer-Verlag, 1973; 503-761.

43. Doris PA, Baker MA. Effects of dehydration on thermoregulation in cats exposed to high ambient temperatures. Journal of Applied Physiology 1981; 51: 46-54.

44. Pedersen NC, ed. Common infectious diseases of multiple-cat environments. In: Feline Husbandry: Diseases and Management in the Multiple-Cat Environment. Goleta, CA: American Veterinary Publications, 1991; 163-288.

45. National Institutes of Health Guide Supplement for Grants and Contracts 14(8). Bethesda, MD: United States Government Printing Office, 1985; 527-567.

46. Animal and Plant Health Inspection Service, United States Department of Agriculture. Housing Facilities, General. Bethesda, MD: United States Government Printing Office, 1985; 528-559.

47. Pederson NC, Wastlhuber J. Cattery design and management. In: Pedersen NC, ed. Feline Husbandry: Diseases and Management in the Multiple-Cat Environment. Goleta, CA: American Veterinary Publications, 1991; 393-438.

48. Hart BL, Pedersen NC. Behavior. In: Pedersen NC, ed. Feline Husbandry: Diseases and Management in the Multiple-Cat Environment. Goleta, CA: American Veterinary Publications, 1991; 289-323.

49. Beaver BV, ed. Feline ingestive behavior. In: Feline Behavior: A Guide for Veterinarians. Philadelphia, PA: WB Saunders Co, 1992; 171-202.

50. Biourge VC, Groff JM, Munn RJ, et al. Experimental induction of hepatic lipidosis in cats. American Journal of Veterinary Research 1994; 55: 1291-1302.

51. Pazak HE. The response of lipid metabolism and transport to a short term fast in cats: Application to idiopathic feline hepatic lipidosis. PhD Thesis. University of Georgia, Athens, 1997.

52. Pugnetti G. Longhair breeds and shorthair breeds. In: Siegal M, ed. Simon and Schuster's Guide to Cats. New York, NY: Simon and Schuster, 1983; 128-241.

53. Gaskell CJ. The role of fluid in the feline urological syndrome. In: Burger IH, Rivers JPW, eds. Nutrition of the Dog and Cat. Cambridge, UK: Cambridge University Press, 1989; 353-356.

54. Burger IH, Anderson RS, Holme DW. Nutritional factors affecting water balance in the dog and cat. In: Anderson RS, ed. Nutrition of the Dog and Cat. Oxford, UK: Pergamon Press, 1980; 145-156.

55. Seefeldt SL, Chapman TE. Body water content and turnover in cats fed dry and canned rations. American Journal of Veterinary Research 1979; 40: 183-185.

56. Scarlett JM, Donoghue S. Health effects of obesity in cats (abstract). In: Proceedings. The Waltham International Symposium, Orlando, FL, May 1997: 90.

57. LaFlamme DP, Jackson JR. Weight loss protocols for overweight cats (abstract). Veterinary Clinical Nutrition 1995; 2: 143.

58. Association of American Feed Control Officials. Official Publication. 1999.

59. Adams LG, Polzin DJ, Osborne CA, et al. Influence of dietary protein/calorie intake on renal morphology and function in cats with 5/6 nephrectomy. Laboratory Investigation 1994; 70: 347-357.

60. Brown SA, Crowell WA, Brown CA, et al. Pathophysiology and management of progressive renal disease. Veterinary Journal 1997; 154: 93-109.

61. Ross LA. Hypertension and chronic renal failure. Seminars in Veterinary Medicine: Small Animal 1992; 7: 221-226.

62. MacDonald ML, Anderson FC, Rogers QR, et al. Essential fatty acid requirements of cats: Pathology of essential fatty acid deficiency. American Journal of Veterinary Research 1984; 45: 1310-1317.

63. MacDonald ML, Rogers QR, Morris JG. Effects of dietary arachidonate deficiency on the aggregation of cat platelets. Comparative Biochemistry and Physiology. Part C 1984; 78: 123-126.

64. MacDonald ML, Rogers QR, Morris JG, et al. Effects of linoleate and arachidonate deficiencies on reproduction and spermatogenesis in the cat. Journal of Nutrition 1984; 114: 719-726.

65. Watkins BA. Role of essential fatty acids in health and nutrition. In: Proceedings. Roche Technical Symposium. Pet Food Institute, Annual Industry Meeting, Chicago, IL, November 1997: 33-43.

66. Pawlosky RJ, Denkins Y, Ward G, et al. Retinal and brain accretion of long-chain polyunsaturated fatty acids in developing felines: The effects of corn oil-based maternal diets. American Journal of Clinical Nutrition 1997, 65: 465-472.

67. Gershoff SN, Norkin SA. Vitamin E deficiency in cats. Journal of Nutrition 1962; 77: 303-308.

68. Cordy DR. Experimental production of steatitis (yellow fat disease) in kittens fed a commercial canned food and prevention of the condition by vitamin E. Cornell Veterinarian 1954; 44: 310-318.

69. Coffin DL, Holzworth J. "Yellow fat" in two laboratory cats: Acid-fast pigmentation associated with a fish-base ration. Cornell Veterinarian 1954; 44: 63-71.

70. Saker KE, Eddy A, Thatcher CD, et al. Manipulation of dietary (n-6) and (n-3) fatty acids alters platelet function in cats (abstract). Journal of Nutrition 1998; 128: 2654S.

71. Lechowski R, Sawosz E, Klucinski W. The effect of the addition of oil preparation with increased content of n-3 fatty acids on serum lipid profile and clinical condition of cats with miliary dermatitis. Zentralbl Veterinarmed A 1998; 45: 417-424.

72. Bright JM, Sullivan PS, Melton SL, et al. The effects of n-3 fatty acid supplementation on bleeding time, plasma fatty acid composition, and in vitro platelet aggregation in cats. Journal of Veterinary Internal Medicine 1994; 8: 247-252.

73. Vondruska JF. The effect of a rat carcass diet on the urinary pH of the cat. Companion Animal Practice 1987; August: 5-9.

74. Dimski DS, Buffington CA. Dietary fiber in small animal therapeutics. Journal of the American Veterinary Medical Association 1991; 199: 1142-1146.

75. Morris JG, Earle KE. Vitamin D and calcium requirements of kittens. Veterinary Clinical Nutrition 1996; 3: 93-96.

76. Pastoor FJH. Interactions of dietary minerals in the cat. PhD Thesis. University of Utrecht, Utrecht, The Netherlands, November 1993.

77. Scott PP, Scott MG. Nutritive requirements for Carnivora. In: Husbandry of Laboratory Animals. London, UK: Academic Press Inc, 1967; 163-186.

78. Kienzle E, Thielen C, Pessinger C. Investigations on phosphorus requirements of adult cats (abstract). Journal of Nutrition 1998; 128: 2598S.

79. Morris Animal Foundation. Animal health survey. Denver, CO, 1998.

80. Ross LA, Finco DR, Crowell WA. Effect of dietary phosphorus restriction on the kidneys of cats with reduced renal mass. American Journal of Veterinary Research 1982; 43: 1023-1026.

81. Pastoor FJH, Van'T Klooster ATh, Mathot JNJJ, et al. Increasing phosphorus intake reduces urinary concentrations of magnesium and calcium in adult ovariectomized cats fed purified diets. Journal of Nutrition 1995; 125: 1334-1341.

82. Stamler J. Adverse effects of habitual high dietary salt on health and longevity. Perspectives in Applied Nutrition 1995; 3: 116-120.

83. Littman MP. Spontaneous systemic hypertension in 24 cats. Journal of Veterinary Internal Medicine 1994; 8: 79-86.

84. Cowgill LD, Kallet AJ. Systemic hypertension. In Kirk RW, ed. Current Veterinary Therapy IX. Philadelphia, PA: WB Saunders Co, 1986; 360-364.

85. Kobayashi DL, Peterson ME, Graves TK, et al. Hypertension in cats with chronic renal failure or hyperthyroidism. Journal of Veterinary Internal Medicine 1990; 4: 58-62.

86. Kurtz TW, Al-Bander HA, Morris RC Jr, et al. "Salt-sensitive" essential hypertension in men. Is the sodium ion alone important? New England Journal of Medicine 1987; 317: 1043-1048.

87. Osborne CA, Lulich JP, Bartges JW, et al. Feline metabolic uroliths: Risk factor management. In: Kirk RW, Bonagura JD, eds. Current Veterinary Therapy XI. Philadelphia, PA: WB Saunders Co, 1992; 905-908.

88. Yu S, Morris JG. Hypokalemia in kittens induced by a chlorine-deficient diet (abstract). Federation of American Societies for Experimental Biology Journal 1998; A1277.

89. Hills DL, Morris JG, Rogers QR. Potassium requirement of kittens as affected by dietary protein. Journal of Nutrition 1982; 112: 216-222.

90. Ching SV, Fettman MJ, Hamar DW, et al. The effect of chronic dietary acidification using ammonium chloride on acid-base and mineral metabolism in the adult cat. Journal of Nutrition 1989; 119: 902-915.

91. Ching SV, Norrdin RW, Fettman MJ, et al. Trabecular bone remodeling and bone mineral density in the adult cat during chronic dietary acidification with ammonium chloride. Journal of Bone Mineral Research 1990; 5: 547-556.

92. Dow SW, Fettman MJ, Smith KR, et al. Effects of dietary acidification and potassium depletion on acid-base balance, mineral metabolism and renal function in adult cats. Journal of Nutrition 1990; 120: 569-578.

93. DiBartola SP, Buffington CA, Chew DJ, et al. Development of chronic renal disease in cats fed a commercial diet. Journal of the American Veterinary Medical Association 1993; 202: 744-751.

94. Allen TA, Bartges JW, Cowgill LD, et al. Colloquium on urology. Feline Practice 1997; 25: 1-32.

95. Thumchai R, Lulich JP, Osborne CA, et al. Epizootiologic evaluation of urolithiasis in cats: 3,498 cases (1982-1992). Journal of the American Veterinary Medical Association 1996; 208: 547-551.

96. Buffington CA. Nutrition and nutritional disorders. In: Pedersen NC, ed. Feline Husbandry: Diseases and Management in the Multiple-Cat Environment. Goleta, CA: American Veterinary Publications, 1991; 325-356.

97. Kirk CA, Ling GV, Franti CE, et al. Evaluation of factors associated with development of calcium oxalate urolithiasis in cats. Journal of the American Veterinary Medical Association 1995; 207: 1429-1434.

98. Hand MS, Allen TA, Armstrong PJ. Feline nutrition: Taurine, urinary pH and potassium. Veterinary Medicine Report 1988; 1: 27-41.

99. Logan EI. Oral cleansing by dietary means: Feline methodology and study results. In: Proceedings. Companion Animal Oral Health Conference, Lawrence, KS, 1996: 31-34.

100. Studer E, Stapley RB. The role of dry foods in maintaining healthy teeth and gums in the cat. Veterinary Medicine/Small Animal Clinician 1973; 68: 1124-1126.

101. Reichenbach T. Comparison of age in cats and humans. Feline Practice 1987; 17: 28-30.

102. Wolf A, Denoff D, Schaer M, et al. The geriatric cat, Part 1. Feline Practice 1996; 24: 8-12.

103. Armstrong PJ, Lund EM. Changes in body composition and energy balance with aging. Veterinary Clinical Nutrition 1996; 3: 83-96.

104. Hayflick L. How and Why We Age. New York, NY: Ballantine Books, 1994.

105. Sheffy BE, Williams AJ. Nutrition and the aging animal. Veterinary Clinics of North America: Small Animal Practice 1981; 11: 669-675.

106. Harper J. The energy requirements of senior cats. Waltham Focus 1996; 6: 32.

107. Markham RW, Hodgkins EM. Geriatric nutrition. Veterinary Clinics of North America: Small Animal Practice 1989; 19: 165-185.

108. Cowan LA, Kirk CA, McVey S, et al. Immune status in old vs young adult cats (abstract). In: Proceedings. Sixteenth Annual Veterinary Medical Forum, American College of Veterinary Internal Medicine, San Diego, CA, 1998: 734.

109. Lulich JP, Osborne CA, O'Brien TD, et al. Feline renal failure: Questions, answers, questions. Compendium on Continuing Education for the Practicing Veterinarian 1992; 14: 127-153.

110. Burger IH, Smith PM. Effects of diet on the urine characteristics of the cat. In: Nutrition, Malnutrition and Dietetics in the Dog and Cat: Proceedings of an International Symposium. Hannover, Germany, September 1987: 71-72.

111. Taylor EJ, Adams C, Nevile R. Some nutritional aspects of aging in dogs and cats. Proceedings of the Nutrition Society 1995; 54: 645-656.

112. Wannemacher RW Jr, McCoy JR. Determination of optimal dietary protein requirements of young and old dogs. Journal of Nutrition 1966; 88: 66-74.

113. Carter WJ. Macronutrient requirements for elderly persons. In: Chernoff R, ed. Geriatric Nutrition. Gaithersburg, MD: Aspen Publishers Inc, 1991; 11-24.

114. Polzin DJ, Osborne CA, Lulich JP. Diet therapy guidelines for cats with chronic renal failure. Veterinary Clinics of North America: Small Animal Practice 1996; 26: 1269-1275.

115. Adams LG, Polzin DJ, Osborne CA, et al. Effects of dietary protein and calorie restriction in clinically normal cats and in cats with surgically induced chronic renal failure. American Journal of Veterinary Research 1993; 54: 1653-1662.

116. Finco DR, Brown SA, Brown CA, et al. Protein and calorie effects on progression of induced chronic renal failure in cats. American Journal of Veterinary Research 1998; 59: 575-582.

117. Kirk CA, Toll PW. Obesity treatment: Reasons for failure, the blueprint for success. In: Proceedings. Fourteenth Annual Veterinary Medical Forum, American College of Veterinary Internal Medicine, San Antonio, TX, 1996: 74-76.

118. Hand MS, Armstrong PJ, Allen TA. Obesity: Occurrence, treatment and prevention. Veterinary Clinics of North America: Small Animal Practice 1989; 19: 447-474.

119. Nelson RW, Lewis LD. Nutritional management of diabetes mellitus. Seminars in Veterinary Medicine and Surgery: Small Animal 1990; 5: 178-186.

120. Nelson RW, Scott-Moncrief C, DeVries S, et al. Dietary insoluble fiber and glycemic control of diabetic cats (abstract). Journal of Veterinary Internal Medicine 1994; 8: 165.

121. Bauer JE. Diet-induced alterations of lipoprotein metabolism. Journal of the American Veterinary Medical Association 1992; 201: 1691-1694.

122. Lawler DF, Ballam JM. Responses of older cats to degree of dietary acidification (abstract). Veterinary Clinical Nutrition 1996; 3: 29.

123. Smith BHE, Moodie SJ, Wensley S, et al. Differences in urinary pH and relative supersaturation values between senior and young adult cats (abstract). In: Proceedings. Fifteenth Annual Veterinary Medical Forum, American College of Veterinary Internal Medicine, Lake Buena Vista, FL, 1997: 674.

124. Kealy RD, Lawler DF, Ballam JM. Dietary calcium:phosphorus ratios for adult cats (abstract). Veterinary Clinical Nutrition 1996; 3: 28.

125. Dhupa N. Magnesium therapy. In: Bonagura JD, ed. Current Veterinary Therapy XII. Philadelphia, PA: WB Saunders Co, 1995; 132-133.

126. Bartges JW. Lower urinary tract disease in older cats: What's common, what's not. Veterinary Clinical Nutrition 1996; 3: 57-62.

127. Su CJ, Shevock PN, Khan SR, et al. Effect of magnesium on calcium oxalate urolithiasis. Journal of Urology 1991; 145: 1092-1095.

128. Lawler DF, Keltner DG, Binns S, et al. Age-related differences in feline blood pressure (abstract). Veterinary Clinical Nutrition 1996; 3: 29.

129. Stiles J, Polzin DJ, Bistner SI. The prevalence of retinopathy in cats with systemic hypertension and chronic renal failure or hyperthyroidism. Journal of the American Animal Hospital Association 1994; 30: 564-572.

130. Kotchen TA, Welch WJ, Lorenz JN, et al. Renal tubular chloride and renin release. Journal of Laboratory Clinical Medicine 1987; 110: 533-539.

131. Lawler DF, Ballam JM. Age-based feline metabolic responses to an acidified diet (abstract). Veterinary Clinical Nutrition 1995; 2: 144-145.

132. Guilford WG. Aging and the gastrointestinal tract. In: Proceedings. Symposium on Health and Nutrition of Geriatric Cats and Dogs, January 1996, Orlando, FL: 17-20.

133. Hefferren JJ, Boyce E, Bresnahan J. Aging and oral health. Veterinary Clinical Nutrition 1996; 3: 97-101.

134. Logan EI, Boyce EN, Berg M, et al. Effects of dietary form on plaque and calculus accumulation and gingival health in cats: Methodology and results. In: Proceedings. Fifth World Veterinary Dental Congress, Birmingham, UK, April 1997: 28.

135. Feldman EC, Nelson RW, eds. Feline reproduction. In: Canine and Feline Endocrinology and Reproduction, 2nd ed. Philadelphia, PA: WB Saunders Co, 1996; 741-768.

136. Burkholder WJ, Swecker WS Jr. Nutritional influences on immunity. Seminars in Veterinary Medicine and Surgery: Small Animal 1990; 5: 154-166.

137. Lawler DF, Monti KL. Morbidity and mortality in neonatal kittens. American Journal of Veterinary Research 1984; 45: 1455-1459.

138. Davidson AP, Nyland TG, Tsutsui T. Pregnancy diagnosis with ultrasound in the domestic cat. Veterinary Radiology 1986; 27: 109-114.

139. Loveridge GG, Rivers JPW. Bodyweight changes and energy intakes of cats during pregnancy and lactation. In: Burger IH, Rivers JPW, eds. Nutrition of the Dog and Cat. Cambridge, UK: Cambridge University Press, 1989; 113-132.

140. Feldman EC, Nelson RW, eds. Breeding, pregnancy, and parturition. In: Canine and Feline Endocrinology and Reproduction, 2nd ed. Philadelphia, PA: WB Saunders Co, 1996; 547-571.

141. Bilkei G. Effect of the nutrition status on parturition in the cat. Berliner und Munchener Tierarztliche Wochenschrift 1990; 103: 49-51.

142. Lawler DF, Bebiak DM. Nutrition and management of reproduction in the cat. Veterinary Clinics of North America: Small Animal Practice 1986; 16: 495-519.

143. Casal ML, Jezyk PF, Giger U. Transfer of colostral antibodies from queens to their kittens. American Journal of Veterinary Research 1996; 57: 1653-1658.

144. Dobenecker B, Zottman B, Kienzle E, et al. Investigations on milk composition and milk yield in queens (abstract). Journal of Nutrition 1998; 128: 2618S.

145. Loveridge GG. Bodyweight changes and energy intake of cats during gestation and lactation. Animal Technology 1985; 37: 7-15.

146. Munday HS, Earle KE. The energy requirements of the queen during lactation and kittens from birth to 12 weeks. Journal of Nutrition 1991; 121: S43-S44.

147. Piechota TR, Rogers QR, Morris JG. Nitrogen requirements of cats during gestation and lactation. Nutrition Research 1995; 15: 1535-1546.

148. Gallo PV, Werboff J, Knox K. Development of home orientation in offspring of protein-restricted cats. Developmental Psychobiology 1984; 17: 437-449.

149. Sturman JA. Dietary taurine and feline reproduction and development. Journal of Nutrition 1991; 121: S166-S170.

150. Kirk CA, Rogers QR, Morris JG. Relationship of dietary taurine to reproductive efficiency in the queen. International Symposium on Amino Acids, Vienna, Austria, August 1995.

151. Olovson SG. Diet and breeding performance in cats. Laboratory Animals 1986; 20: 221-230.

152. Doong G, Keen DL, Rogers QR, et al. Selected features of copper metabolism in the cat. Journal of Nutrition 1983; 113: 1963-1971.

153. Morris JG, Rogers QR. Assessment of the nutritional adequacy of pet foods through the life cycle. Journal of Nutrition 1994; 124: 2520S-2534S.

154. Buffington CA. Effects of diet on the feline struvite urolithiasis syndrome. PhD Thesis. University of California, Davis, 1988.

155. Hardardottir H, Lahiri T, Egan JF. Renal tubular acidosis in pregnancy: Case report and literature review. Journal of Maternal and Fetal Medicine 1997; 6: 16-20.

156. Loveridge GG. Factors affecting kitten growth. In: Edney ATB, ed. Nutrition, Malnutrition and Dietetics in the Dog and Cat. Proceedings of an International Symposium. Hannover, Germany, September 1987: 6-61.

157. Remillard RL, Pickett JP, Thatcher CD, et al. Comparison of kittens fed queen's milk with those fed milk replacers. American Journal of Veterinary Research 1993; 54: 901-907.

158. Hoskins JD. Clinical evaluation of the kitten from birth to eight weeks of age. Compendium on Continuing Education for the Practicing Veterinarian 1990; 12: 1215-1225.

159. Adkins Y, Zicker SC, Lepine A, et al. Changes in nutrient and protein composition of cat milk during lactation. American Journal of Veterinary Research 1997; 58: 370-375.

160. Baines FM. Milk substitutes and the hand rearing of orphan puppies and kittens. Journal of Small Animal Practice 1981; 22: 555-578.

161. Halle I. Nutrition of the cat. Journal of Veterinary Nutrition. 1992; 1: 17-30.

162. Smalley KA, Rogers QR, Morris JG, et al. The nitrogen requirement of the weanling kitten. British Journal of Nutrition 1985; 53: 501-512.

163. Earle KE, Smith PM. The taurine requirement of the kitten fed canned food. Journal of Nutrition 1994; 124: 2552S-2554S.

164. Pawlosky RJ, Salem N. Is dietary arachidonic acid necessary for feline reproduction? Journal of Nutrition 1996; 126: 1081S-1085S.

165. Rogers QR, Strieker MJ, Morris JG. Effect of quantity and pattern of dietary amino acids on amino acid requirements of the dog and cat. In: Edney ATB, ed. Nutrition, Malnutrition and Dietetics in the Dog and Cat. Proceedings of an International Symposium. Hannover, Germany, September 1987: 52-56.

166. Rogers QR, Taylor TP, Morris JG. Optimizing dietary amino acid patterns at various levels of crude protein for the cat (abstract). Journal of Nutrition 1998; 128: 2577S.

167. Munday HS, Earle KE, Anderson P. Changes in the body composition of the domestic shorthaired cat during growth and development. Journal of Nutrition 1994; 124: 2622S-2623S.

168. Howard KA, Rogers QR, Morris JG. Magnesium requirement of kittens is increased by high dietary calcium (abstract). Journal of Nutrition 1998; 128: 2601S.

169. Buffington CA, Rogers QR, Morris JG. Effects of age and food deprivation on urine pH of cats. Veterinary Clinical Nutrition 1994; 1: 12-17.

CASE 11-1

Elective Surgery in a Young Siamese Cat

Claudia A. Kirk, DVM, PhD
Diplomate ACVN and ACVIM (Internal Medicine)
Hill's Science and Technology Center
Topeka, Kansas, USA

Assess the Animal

An 11-month-old female Siamese cat was presented for routine ovariohysterectomy. The owner obtained the cat from a friend as a young kitten. The cat had been healthy except for one episode of upper respiratory infection, flea infestation and tapeworm infection. The cat lived with the owner in an apartment and rarely went outdoors.

Physical examination revealed a normal young adult cat. Body weight was 3.2 kg with ideal body condition (body condition score [BCS] 3/5). A packed cell volume (normal), feline leukemia virus test (negative) and fecal flotation test (negative) were performed before surgery. The ovariohysterectomy was completed uneventfully and the cat was released to the owner's care the next day.

Assess the Food(s) and Feeding Method

The cat was fed a dry commercial grocery brand food formulated for growing kittens (Purina Kitten Chow Dairy Flavor[a]) and several varieties of moist commercial grocery brand foods. The dry food was available free choice and a small portion of moist food was fed each evening when the owner returned from work. Tuna flavor cat treats were also offered daily. Dairy products were fed intermittently; the cat was allowed to lick bowls used for cereal and ice cream.

Questions

1. When should the owner stop feeding kitten food?
2. Will the ovariohysterectomy change the nutrient requirements for this young cat?
3. What are the key nutritional factors for a cat entering adulthood?
4. Outline an appropriate feeding plan.

Answers and Discussion

1. An 11-month-old cat has reached its adult size and is finishing the maturation process. Foods specifically formulated for growing cats are usually fed until approximately one year of age. At that time, the food can be slowly changed to one formulated for young to middle-aged adult cats.
2. Neutering markedly alters a cat's metabolism. Changes occur within three months of neutering and include decreased resting energy requirement (RER) (basal metabolic rate; approximate decline 27 to 33%) and less ability to regulate food intake. These changes make gonadectomy a risk factor for obesity. Neutered cats are more likely to become overweight than are intact cats of either gender. Therefore, neutered cats should be fed less energy than intact cats to reduce the risk for obesity. (See Table 1-7.)
3. Key nutritional factors for young to middle-aged adult cats include water, energy, protein, taurine, fat and essential fatty acids, minerals (calcium, phosphorus, sodium, chloride, potassium, magnesium), urinary pH and food texture. Table 11-8 lists recommended levels of key nutrients. Foods that produce average urinary pH values of 6.2 to 6.5 when fed free choice reduce the risk of struvite urolithiasis and avoid metabolic acidosis in most adult cats. Food texture influences oral health. Dental disease is the most prevalent disease in cats one year old and older. Dry foods specifically designed to promote oral health are beneficial in reducing plaque and calculus accumulation and controlling gingivitis.

4. A food specifically formulated for adult cats should be chosen based on appropriate levels of key nutritional factors. A commercial dry adult cat food or a combination of dry and moist adult cat foods can be used. The forms of food chosen will dictate the feeding method used; meal feeding rather than free-choice feeding helps control obesity. The owner should be informed that neutering may markedly decrease the energy requirements of the cat. An estimated daily energy requirement (DER) can be calculated as a target for the owner. The DER of average young to middle-aged adult cats is approximately 1.4 x RER (70 kcal/kg body weight/day [293 kJ/kg body weight/day]). Caloric requirements for neutered or inactive cats may be less than this amount, whereas active intact cats may require a higher intake of energy. Treats should be eliminated or used sparingly. Body weight and condition should be monitored by the owner every two to three months to determine if DER should be adjusted. Free-choice access to potable water is important.

Progress Notes

The veterinary technician discussed the metabolic and behavioral changes that result from ovariohysterectomy with the owner when the cat was discharged. Dry and moist formulations of a commercial food formulated for adult cats (Science Diet Feline Maintenance[b]) were sent home with the owner. The owner was instructed to mix the dry adult food with the remaining growth food. The moist adult food was dispensed to replace the other moist foods after they were fed. The estimated DER was 1.4 x RER = 230 kcal (962 kJ). This DER would be met by offering one-fourth cup dry food in the morning and giving two-thirds of a 5.5-oz. can of food in the evening. The owner was given a body condition scoring chart for cats, and she indicated her willingness to evaluate the cat regularly.

Endnotes

a. Ralston Purina Co., St. Louis, MO, USA.
b. Hill's Pet Nutrition, Inc., Topeka, KS, USA.

Bibliography

Buffington CA, Rogers QR, Morris JG. Effects of age and food deprivation on urine pH of cats. Veterinary Clinical Nutrition 1994; 1: 12-17.

Flynn MF, Hardie EM, Armstrong PJ. Effect of ovariohysterectomy on maintenance energy requirement in cats. Journal of the American Veterinary Medical Association 1996; 209: 1572-1581.

Munday HS, Earle KE, Anderson P. Changes in the body composition of the domestic shorthaired cat during growth and development. Journal of Nutrition 1994; 124: 2622S-2623S.

National Research Council. Nutrient Requirements of Cats. Washington, DC: National Academy Press, 1986.

Root MV. Early spay and neuter in the cat: Effect on development of obesity and metabolic rate. Veterinary Clinical Nutrition 1995; 2: 132-134.

Scarlett JM, Donoghue S, Saidla J, et al. Overweight cats: Prevalence and risk factors. International Journal of Obesity 1994; 18: S22-S28.

CASE 11-2

Weight Loss in an Older Cat

Claudia A. Kirk, DVM, PhD
Diplomate ACVN and ACVIM (Internal Medicine)
Hill's Science and Technology Center
Topeka, Kansas, USA

Assess the Animal

A 14-year-old neutered male domestic shorthair cat was examined as part of a routine geriatric health maintenance program. The owner reported no major illnesses except for one episode of urethral obstruction four years earlier. The diagnosis at that time was bacterial cystitis. The cat spends most of its time sleeping on the couch interspersed by brief forays into a pasture to catch voles, field mice and crickets. The owner mentioned that the cat seemed to be losing weight although its appetite had not changed.

Physical examination revealed a bright, alert, 3.5-kg cat with slight loss of body fat and muscle (body condition score [BCS] 2/5). The cat weighed 4.4 kg and had a BCS of 4/5 when last examined 18 months earlier. Oral examination revealed moderate dental disease with several missing teeth and odontoclastic resorptive lesions involving the left upper 4th premolar and both 1st molar teeth. The lesions on the upper 4th premolar were so severe that the crown had fractured leaving a small portion of the tooth root exposed. Moderately severe gingivitis was present. No other abnormalities were noted.

The hospital at which this cat was seen had a geriatric health maintenance program for cats that included a complete blood count, serum biochemistry profile, urinalysis, fecal flotation test, thoracic radiographs, thyroxine (T_4) measurement, ocular fundic examination and tests for feline leukemia and feline immunodeficiency virus infection. Results of the complete blood count, fundic examination, T_4 measurement, thoracic radiographs and urinalysis were normal. The fecal flotation test and tests for viral infection were also negative. The serum biochemistry profile was normal except for a slightly elevated serum urea nitrogen concentration (28 mg/dl, normal 10 to 25 mg/dl) and slightly decreased serum potassium concentration (3.5 mEq/l, normal 3.7 to 5.2 mEq/l). The urinalysis was normal; the urinary pH was 6.0 and the urine specific gravity was 1.030.

Assess the Food(s) and Feeding Method

The cat ate commercial dry and canned specialty brand foods (Science Diet Feline Maintenance[a]). The dry food was offered free choice, and a variety of canned products (beef formula, seafood formula or turkey formula) were offered once daily. The owner was unsure how much dry food was consumed daily. The bowl was filled with dry food as needed. The cat also caught one to two voles or mice per week and ate only the head, leaving the body on the porch.

Water was available at all times. The cat often drank from the faucet when allowed.

Questions

1. Has the geriatric assessment found any reason for the cat's weight loss?

2. What key nutritional factors are important for this geriatric patient?
3. Outline a treatment and feeding plan [food(s) and feeding method] for this cat.
4. How should this patient be monitored?

Answers and Discussion

1. The only abnormalities noted on the geriatric assessment are dental disease and laboratory results consistent with possible early chronic renal disease. The extensive dental disease may contribute to weight loss if food intake is reduced because of oral pain. Renal insufficiency would not be expected to cause weight loss at this time. Hyperthyroidism is a common cause of weight loss in older cats (See Chapter 24.), but is less likely in this patient because no cervical mass was found and the serum T_4 concentration was normal. However, hyperthyroidism may occur in cats without these abnormal findings. Repeating the resting T_4 concentration test or performing a T_3 suppression test should be considered for this patient. Many older cats have reduced lean body mass due to: 1) the high occurrence of disease in this age group, 2) reduced food intake because of impaired appetite or sensory function and 3) an age-related decline in food assimilation.

2. Key nutritional factors in older cats include water, energy, protein, fat, minerals (phosphorus, calcium, magnesium, potassium, sodium, chloride), urinary pH, palatability, digestibility and food texture. Water intake is important in older cats because chronic renal disease is very common in this age group. Fat and energy intake are also important in older cats that are susceptible to weight loss. Cats over 12 years of age should be fed energy-dense foods (4.0 to 4.5 kcal ME/g dry matter [16.7 to 18.8 kJ ME/g]) and caloric intake should not be restricted, except as necessary to treat or prevent obesity. Excessive dietary phosphorus, protein, sodium and chloride should be avoided to help control progression of renal disease and hypertension. Hypokalemia is a potential complication of chronic renal disease and has also been reported to occur in older cats. Therefore, potassium-replete foods should be used. The reduced risk of struvite urolithiasis, increased risk of calcium oxalate urolithiasis and decline in renal function observed in older cats support the use of foods with a lower urine acidifying potential (higher published urinary pH values) compared with foods for young to middle-aged cats. Because weight loss and inadequate food intake are concerns for many very old cats, their foods should be highly palatable and digestible to ensure optimal intake and nutrient usage. The optimal food texture for older cats depends on the individual's oral health and food texture preference.

3. The cat should be anesthetized for a thorough dental examination and appropriate treatment (i.e., cleaning, extractions, etc.). Commercial foods formulated for older cats are appropriate for this patient. Many of these products have appropriate nutrient levels as discussed above. Specific nutrient levels for many products for older cats can be found in Appendix L. Many

cats and their owners favor the use of dry and moist foods. The use of more than one form of food and the current feeding method are appropriate and can be continued. An estimated daily energy requirement (DER) should be calculated and the owner encouraged to monitor whether the cat is eating enough food to meet this requirement.

4. Monitoring should include an oral examination and complete physical examination every six months, including a complete blood count, serum biochemistry profile and urinalysis to assess renal function and measurement of potassium and resting T_4 concentrations. Feeding a veterinary therapeutic food formulated for cats with renal failure may be indicated if renal function deteriorates. Adding a potassium supplement is necessary if serum potassium concentrations remain low.

Progress Notes

An oral antibiotic (clindamycin[b]) was dispensed for administration at home for one week before anesthesia was planned for dental examination and treatment. Tooth scaling, polishing and extractions were performed and the cat recovered uneventfully. The antibiotic was continued for another week. The food was changed to a formula for older cats (Science Diet Feline Senior[a]). The DER was estimated to be 1.2 to 1.4 x resting energy requirement (RER) for an ideal body weight of 4.0 kg (230 to 270 kcal [962 to 1,130 kJ]). This energy requirement would be met by feeding one 5.5-oz. can (165 kcal [690 kJ]) and one-fourth to one-third cup dry food per day. The owner agreed to monitor the cat's daily food intake and to weigh the cat weekly. An appointment was made to assess the cat again in six months.

Endnotes

a. Hill's Pet Nutrition, Inc., Topeka, KS, USA.
b. Antirobe. The Upjohn Company (Animal Health Division), Kalamazoo, MI, USA.

Bibliography

Armstrong PJ, Lund EM. Changes in body composition and energy balance with aging. Veterinary Clinical Nutrition 1996; 3: 83-96.

Bartges JW. Lower urinary tract disease in older cats: What's common, what's not. Veterinary Clinical Nutrition 1996; 3:57-62.

Bodey AR, Sansom J. Epidemiological study of blood pressure in domestic cats. Journal of Small Animal Practice 1998; 39: 567-573.

Graves TK, Peterson ME. Diagnostic tests for feline hyperthyroidism. Veterinary Clinics of North America: Small Animal Practice 1994; 24: 567-576.

Hefferren JJ, Boyce E, Bresnahan J. Aging and oral health. Veterinary Clinical Nutrition 1996; 3: 97-100.

Markham RW, Hodgkins EM. Geriatric nutrition. Veterinary Clinics of North America: Small Animal Practice 1989; 19: 165-185.

Phillips SL, Polzin DJ. Clinical disorders of potassium homeostasis. Hyperkalemia and hypokalemia. Veterinary Clinics of North America: Small Animal Practice 1998; 28: 545-564

Polzin DJ, Osborne CA, Lulich JP. Diet therapy guidelines for cats with chronic renal failure. Veterinary Clinics of North America: Small Animal Practice 1996; 26: 1269-1275.

Richards JR, Rodan I, Beekman GK, et al. Panel Report on Feline Senior Care. American Association of Feline Practitioners/Academy of Feline Medicine, Albuquerque, NM, 1998.

Wolf A, Denoff D, Schaer M, et al. The geriatric cat, Part 1. Feline Practice 1996; 24(3): 8-12.

Wolf A, Denoff D, Schaer M, et al. The geriatric cat, Part 2. Feline Practice 1996; 24(4): 13-17.

Wolf A, Denoff D, Schaer M, et al. The geriatric cat, Part 3. Feline Practice 1996; 24(5): 5-9.

CASE 11-3

Alopecia in a Pregnant Cat

Claudia A. Kirk, DVM, PhD
Diplomate ACVN and ACVIM (Internal Medicine)
Hill's Science and Technology Center
Topeka, Kansas, USA

Assess the Animal

A five-year-old intact female domestic longhair cat was examined for hair loss. The alopecia was generalized and patchy with no evidence of pruritus, excoriations, crusts or primary lesions (e.g., papules or pustules). There was no evidence of flea or other external parasite infestation. The coat was dull, dry and unkempt. The cat appeared thin (body condition score [BCS] 2/5) and weighed 3.0 kg. The remainder of the physical examination was normal.

The queen had delivered five kittens four weeks earlier. The kittens were apparently healthy but had become restless and cried constantly during the previous five days. The kittens had attempted to nurse, but the owner did not know if they were actually obtaining milk. The owner also commented that the kittens had not grown during the past week. The queen's mammary glands did not appear adequately distended for the stage of lactation.

Multiple skin scrapings and a tape preparation were negative for ectoparasites. The hairs appeared somewhat brittle and were easily epilated. Results of a packed cell volume (PCV) were slightly below normal (28%, normal 30 to 52%).

Assess the Food(s) and Feeding Method

The cat was fed a commercial private label dry cat food purchased from a local farm and feed store. The nutritional adequacy statement on the bag indicated that the product "meets the nutritional levels established by the AAFCO nutrient profiles for all stages of a cat's life." A cup of dry food mixed with chicken broth was offered twice daily.

Questions

1. What is the most likely cause of this patient's alopecia?
2. Is there a connection between the alopecia and restless, crying kittens?
3. Are there any other diagnostic tests that should be performed?
4. Outline a more appropriate feeding plan for this queen.

Answers and Discussion

1. The integument is a metabolically active organ that is affected by the nutritional status of the animal. Protein and energy are required for development of new hair and skin. Developing hair requires sulfur-containing and other amino acids. Therefore, the animal's food should provide optimal protein quantity, quality (i.e., appropriate levels of essential amino acids) and digestibility for normal skin and hair. Animals have increased protein and energy requirements during growth, gestation, lactation and illness. Abnormal skin and hair will often be noted if nutritionally inadequate foods are fed during these stages and conditions. Telogen defluxion is usually recognized as hair loss associated with a stressful event (e.g., pregnancy, severe illness, surgery) that causes the abrupt, premature cessation of growth of many anagen hair follicles and the synchronization of these hair follicles in catagen, then in telogen. Short-term deficiency of protein, energy or other nutrients during growth, gestation, lactation and illness may cause telogen defluxion if appropriate dietary changes are not instituted. Bitches and queens in late gestation and lactation and growing puppies and kittens are at risk unless they are fed nutritionally balanced, highly digestible foods that meet their increased nutritional requirements.

2. Excessive crying, restless behavior and poor weight gain of kittens are clinical signs associated with lactation failure in queens. Lactation failure can result from inadequate intake of energy and protein to support proper lactation and can thus be linked to the same cause of telogen defluxion.

3. A complete blood count and serum biochemistry profile should be considered to rule out systemic disease as the cause of alopecia and lactation failure. Plucking hairs from the skin and examining them microscopically is termed trichography. This technique is helpful in diagnosing a number of conditions affecting the skin and coat including nutritional diseases. Estimating the ratio of anagen to telogen hair bulbs can be useful. (See Chapter 15.) All the hair of normal animals should not be in telogen. A diagnosis of telogen defluxion or follicular arrest is suggested when all the hair is in telogen. Inappropriate numbers of telogen hairs (e.g., mostly telogen hairs during the summer when the ratio should be approximately 50:50) suggest a diagnosis of nutritional, endocrine or metabolic disease. In people, the ratio of telogen to anagen hair increases with prolonged protein deficiency. Unfortunately, well-established normal values are not available for trichograms, which somewhat limits their usefulness in veterinary medicine. The use of site-, age-, breed- and climate-matched controls, if possible, may increase the usefulness of this diagnostic technique.

4. The commercial dry food fed currently does not appear adequate to support normal lactation, body condition or coat quality in this lactating queen. A commercial food specifically formulated for feline growth and lactation should be recommended. The label of the new product should indicate that the food has undergone AAFCO or similar feeding trials in gestating and lactating cats. This documentation ensures that the nutrient levels and availability are adequate to support normal lactation. The food and water should be offered free choice. If a dry food is chosen, chicken broth or moist foods can also be offered to encourage food intake by the queen.

Progress Notes

The results of a complete blood count and serum biochemistry profile were normal. Plucked hairs had bulbs that exhibited changes consistent with only telogen hairs. (See Chapter 15.) The food was changed to a commercial dry specialty brand food specifically formulated for feline growth and reproduction (Science Diet Feline Growth[a]). The dry food and water were offered free choice. The queen's daily energy requirement (DER) was estimated to be 4 to 6 x resting energy requirement (RER) for an ideal weight of 3.5 kg (DER = 700 to 1,000 kcal [2.9 to 4.2 MJ]). Approximately one-fourth of the estimated DER (200 kcal [837 kJ]) was offered as dry food mixed with a highly palatable, gravy-style flavor enhancer (Science Diet Canine & Feline Mixit[a]). This combination of dry food with gravy mixer was offered twice daily in addition to dry food offered free choice.

The kittens were allowed to remain with the queen but were offered a supplemental gruel made from equal parts commercial milk replacer (KMR Liquid[b]) and moist Science Diet Feline Growth four times per day. The queen and kittens were separated during these feedings. The kittens readily consumed the food mixture. The amount of milk replacer was gradually decreased over the following week until the kittens were eating moist food three times daily without milk replacer. The kittens also consumed increasing amounts of the dry growth formula that was available for the queen. The kittens' crying and excess activity declined with supplemental feeding. The kittens were weaned at six weeks of age when they all weighed at least 500 g.

The owner reported that the queen ate both the dry food and dry food mixed with flavor enhancer very well. The cat gained a small amount of weight during the next month, seemed to produce more milk and stopped losing hair. The queen was fed the growth food for six weeks after the kittens were weaned to improve its body condition and coat. At that point, the food was changed to a similar brand food for adult maintenance.

Endnotes

a. Hill's Pet Nutrition, Inc., Topeka, KS, USA.
b. Pet-Ag Inc., Elgin, IL, USA.

Bibliography

Hoskins JD. Clinical evaluation of the kitten: From birth to eight weeks of age. Compendium on Continuing Education for the Practicing Veterinarian 1990; 12: 1215-1225.

Lawler DF, Bebiak DM. Nutrition and management of reproduction in the cat. Veterinary Clinics of North America: Small Animal Practice 1986; 16: 495-519.

Morris JG, Rogers QR. Assessment of the nutritional adequacy of pet foods through the life cycle. Journal of Nutrition 1994; 124: 2520S-2534S.

National Research Council. Nutrient Requirements of Cats. Washington, DC: National Academy Press, 1986.

Piechota TR, Rogers QR, Morris JG. Nitrogen requirements of cats during gestation and lactation. Nutrition Research 1995; 15: 1535-1546.

Scott DW, Miller WH, Griffin CE. Small Animal Dermatology, 5th ed. Philadelphia, PA: WB Saunders Co, 1995.

CASE 11-4

Dyspnea in a Cat

Claudia A. Kirk, DVM, PhD
Diplomate ACVN and ACVIM (Internal Medicine)
Hill's Science and Technology Center
Topeka, Kansas, USA

Assess the Animals

A three-year-old intact female domestic shorthair cat was examined for acute onset of lethargy, vomiting and dyspnea. The cat had queened four weeks earlier. Two small kittens were dead at birth and one kitten lived. This kitten was presented with the queen.

Physical examination revealed a recumbent, weak cat. Mucous membranes were pale with prolonged capillary refill time. The pulse was weak and the rate was greater than 200 beats/minute. Respiratory rate was elevated (65 breaths/min.) and breathing was labored. Heart sounds were muffled and hepatomegaly was noted during abdominal palpation.

Thoracentesis was performed immediately; 100 ml of clear, pale yellow fluid was removed from the left hemithorax and 75 ml of similar fluid from the right hemithorax. The cat appeared more comfortable and relaxed as its labored breathing improved. Laboratory analysis of the fluid was consistent with a modified transudate. Following thoracentesis, the queen's body weight was 3 kg. The cat's body condition score (BCS) was 2/5.

Thoracic radiographs revealed cardiomegaly and pleural effusion. No intrathoracic mass lesions were noted.

The kitten was active although small and underweight for its age. A prominent thoracic kyphosis was evident, but the kitten was otherwise normal.

Assess the Food(s) and Feeding Method

The owner was a strict vegan vegetarian and incorporated her beliefs into the feeding plans for her pets. The cat was fed a strict vegetarian diet twice daily. The food consisted of rice, soy, lentil, safflower oil and fresh vegetables with no added supplements.

Questions

1. What is the most likely diagnosis for this cat?
2. What other assessment steps (diagnostic tests) should be used to confirm the diagnosis?
3. What other nutritional abnormalities might arise in this cat from the described feeding practices?
4. Outline an appropriate feeding plan for this cat, including foods and feeding method.

Answers and Discussion

1. Dilated cardiomyopathy secondary to dietary taurine deficiency is consistent with the dietary history and clinical signs of cardiomegaly and congestive heart failure. Taurine is found in appreciable amounts only in animal tissues, and taurine deficiency is a well-recognized cause of dilated cardiomyopathy and systolic cardiac failure in cats. Taurine is an essential dietary nutrient for cats because cats cannot synthesize sufficient quantities of taurine to meet metabolic needs. Further, cats have obligate losses of taurine via conjugated bile salts.

Reproductive failure in queens with kitten loss, poor kitten growth and abnormal kitten development have also been reported to occur with taurine deficiency.

2. Additional tests such as electrocardiography, a complete blood count, serum biochemistry profile and urinalysis are indicated for complete assessment of the patient. An ultrasonic examination of the heart will confirm that the cardiomegaly is due to dilatation with impaired contractility rather than other forms of cardiac disease (e.g., hypertrophic cardiomyopathy). A retinal examination may indicate central retinal degeneration attributable to taurine deficiency. However, these lesions are permanent and are unreliable indicators of current taurine status. Plasma taurine concentrations can be measured and reflect short-term taurine status. Plasma taurine levels may be depressed by fasting or elevated by improper sample handling. Whole blood taurine concentrations can also be measured and are more reliable indicators of long-term taurine status.

3. Vitamin A deficiency. Plants contain β-carotene rather than preformed vitamin A. Cats cannot use β-carotene.

Arachidonic acid deficiency. Arachidonic acid is found primarily in animal tissues (although specific algae produce supplemental arachidonic acid). Cats lack delta-6-desaturase activity required to make arachidonate from linoleic acid.

Vitamin B_{12} deficiency. Vitamin B_{12} is not found in plants.

Niacin deficiency. Cats require a dietary source of niacin because of their inability to make niacin from tryptophan. Niacin is poorly available from cereal grains and would be deficient in this cat's diet.

Calcium/phosphate. Plant material is often deficient in calcium and the phosphate may be bound and unavailable. This cat's diet would likely be deficient without supplementation with a specific source of calcium and phosphorus.

Protein and energy. Protein and energy requirements are increased in late gestation and lactation. The soy, lentil and vegetable oil may provide enough energy and protein if the cat eats sufficient quantities of these ingredients. However, palatability and acceptability of such a diet would usually be suboptimal.

4. This cat should be fed a commercial cat food or a homemade food that is balanced. (See Chapter 6.) Commercial foods that have passed AAFCO feeding trials are proven to maintain adequate whole blood taurine concentrations. Balanced vegetarian foods can be formulated for adult, non-reproducing cats but usually require supplementation with several essential amino acids (i.e., taurine, lysine, methionine, arginine, tryptophan), essential fatty acids, macrominerals, trace minerals and vitamins. Regardless of the food, taurine supplementation (250 to 500 mg, b.i.d.) should be used in conjunction with the dietary change until the cardiomyopathy and clinical signs have resolved. Assisted feeding may be indicated if the cat is too ill to eat spontaneously. (See Chapter 12 and Appendix V.) The food(s) should be warmed and offered several times daily to improve acceptability.

Progress Notes

The queen was hospitalized for treatment and the kitten was weaned immediately. Medical management of the cardiomyopathy included cage rest, furosemide and captopril. Taurine supplementation was started at 500 mg per os twice daily. Client education about the nutritional needs of cats resulted in the owner's willingness to change the diet to a commercial meat-based food. The queen was offered a commercial moist veterinary therapeutic food (Prescription Diet Feline p/d[a]) designed for use as a recuperative formula. This particular food is lower in sodium and chloride than most other recovery foods. The food was fed free choice.

Food intake was measured daily to ensure caloric needs were being met voluntarily. The queen's resting energy requirement (RER) was calculated at an estimated ideal weight of 3.5 kg or 179 kcal/day (749 kJ/day). Because the queen was inactive (cage rest), under metabolic stress, underweight and a non-reproducing intact female, the energy factor for maintenance was estimated at 1.4. Thus, the daily energy requirement (DER) was estimated to be 1.4 x 179 or 251 kcal/day (1,050 kJ/day). Voluntary food intake was measured at one-half of a 14.25-oz. can of food daily or approximately 280 kcal/day (1,172 kJ/day).

The cat was released to the owner after five days and subsequent examinations documented progressive improvement in clinical signs and cardiac contractility. The cat weighed 3.6 kg one year later, cardiac function had returned to normal and all medications had been discontinued. The queen was subsequently neutered and fed a moist food suitable for adult cats.

The kitten was initially offered a gruel made from commercial milk replacer (KMR Liquid[b]) mixed with the same moist formula offered to the queen (Prescription Diet Feline p/d). This food provided sufficient taurine for growth; additional taurine supplementation is not required because the developmental defects resulting from taurine deficiency are irreversible. The food mixture was offered free choice and was readily eaten. The milk replacer was progressively discontinued over the next 10 days. The kitten's growth rate increased markedly. However, the kitten continued to be small for its age and the moderate thoracic kyphosis did not improve.

Endnotes

a. Hill's Pet Nutrition, Inc., Topeka, KS, USA.
b. Pet-Ag Inc., Elgin, IL, USA.

Bibliography

Baker DH, Czarnecki-Maulden GL. Comparative nutrition of cats and dogs. Annual Review of Nutrition 1991; 11: 239-263.

Hayes KC, Trautwein EA. Taurine deficiency syndrome in cats. Veterinary Clinics of North America: Small Animal Practice 1989; 19: 403-413.

Leon A, Bain SA, Levick WR. Hypokalemic episodic polymyopathy in cats fed a vegetarian diet. Australian Veterinary Journal 1992; 69: 249-254.

MacDonald ML, Rogers QR, Morris JG. Nutrition of the domestic cat, a mammalian carnivore. Annual Review of Nutrition 1984; 4: 521-562.

Morris JG, Rogers QR, Pacioretty LM. Taurine: An essential nutrient for cats. Journal of Small Animal Practice 1990; 31: 502-509.

Pion PD, Kittleson MD, Rogers QR, et al. Myocardial failure in cats associated with low plasma taurine: A reversible cardiomyopathy. Science 1987; 237: 764-768.

Sturman JA. Dietary taurine and feline reproduction and development. Journal of Nutrition 1991; 121: S166-S170.

■ CASE 11-5

Lumbar Pain in a Young Cat

M. Anne Hickman, DVM, PhD
Diplomate ACVN
Pfizer, Inc.
Groton, Connecticut, USA

Claudia A. Kirk, DVM, PhD
Diplomate ACVN and ACVIM (Internal Medicine)
Hill's Science and Technology Center
Topeka, Kansas, USA

Assess the Animal

An eight-month-old castrated male domestic shorthair cat was examined for hind-limb stiffness, lethargy and a soft tissue mass in the lumbar region. The cat suffered a twisting fall one month earlier. It was subsequently stiff and lethargic and had some lumbar pain. An examination at that time revealed no significant findings. Treatment included restriction of exercise, antibiotics (cefadroxil) and oral glucocorticoids (dexamethasone). No improvement occurred over the next month; therefore, the cat was presented for a second opinion.

Physical examination revealed a 3.2-kg cat with good body condition (body condition score [BCS] 3/5). The cat was stiff in the rear legs, had an arched back and soft tissue swelling in the thoracolumbar region that was very sensitive to palpation. Neurologic evaluation was unremarkable. No other abnormalities were noted.

Results of a complete blood count were normal except for moderate Heinz body formation on red blood cells. Serum biochemistry analyses were within normal limits. Urinalysis results were normal. Radiographs of the spine revealed diffuse osteopenia, increased opacity over the caudal aspect of L_1 and a mild subluxation between L_1 and L_2. Ultrasonographic examination of the lumbar region and abdomen was unremarkable.

Assess the Food(s) and Feeding Method

The cat was fed a diet consisting of ground sirloin and beef and veal baby foods. These foods were offered in several meals throughout the day.

Questions

1. What is the approximate calcium-phosphorus ratio of this diet?
2. What is the tentative diagnosis for this patient?
3. What caused the Heinz body formation in this cat?
4. Outline a feeding plan, including an appropriate food and feeding method.

Answers and Discussion

1. This cat's diet consists of all-meat ingredients (beef and veal). In general, meat is relatively high in phosphorus and low in calcium, which gives an inverse calcium-phosphorus ratio, approximately 1:20.

2. A diagnosis of secondary nutritional hyperparathyroidism is likely based on the dietary history and generalized skeletal osteopenia. The clinical signs of thoracolumbar swelling and pain are probably related to a compression fracture of L_1 and L_1-L_2 subluxation that occurred during the fall. The osteopenia probably contributed to the injury.

3. Heinz body formation is caused by oxidative denaturation of hemoglobin in erythrocytes. In cats, the unusual metabolism and unique hemoglobin structure of erythrocytes increase their sensitivity to oxidant injury. Heinz bodies usually appear within 24 hours of exposure of erythrocytes to an intoxicant. Affected erythrocytes undergo hemolysis or are removed within several days. Mild to severe anemia may result. Causes of Heinz body formation include ingestion of onions, acetaminophen, phenacetin, phenazopyridine, methylene blue, D,L-methionine, propylene glycol, benzocaine, zinc toxicosis, excessive vitamin K_3, diabetes mellitus and other systemic diseases. Onion powder used in human baby foods has been implicated in excessive Heinz body formation in cats. This is the most likely cause in this patient because it was regularly fed two different baby foods.

4. The diet should be changed to a balanced commercial or homemade cat food. Homemade food recipes should have an obvious source of calcium such as dicalcium phosphate, bone meal or calcium carbonate. Changing the cat's food from an all-meat diet to a balanced food may be difficult. The new food should be introduced gradually over several weeks. If necessary, a nutritionist can be contacted to formulate a homemade food to include the cooked sirloin the cat is currently eating. If food refusal becomes a major problem, hand feeding or assisted feeding with a feeding tube may be necessary. Caloric requirements should be calculated to reflect a young cat that will probably be confined with limited opportunities for exercise.

Progress Notes

Cerebrospinal fluid was collected and analyzed to rule out central nervous system infection as a cause of back pain. Results were normal. Blood samples were collected to measure parathyroid hormone (PTH) concentrations. PTH concentrations were elevated, confirming a diagnosis of hyperparathyroidism.

A balanced commercial moist cat food formulated for growing cats was chosen (Science Diet Feline Growth[a]). The cat's daily energy requirement (DER) was estimated to be 1.4 x resting energy requirement (RER) because the cat was still maturing and would be strictly confined. DER for a 3.2-kg cat = 166 kcal (695 kJ) x 1.4 = 232 kcal (971 kJ) or one-half of a 5.5-oz. can twice daily. This food was mixed in increasing portions with cooked ground sirloin for several weeks. Within three weeks, the cat was eating only the commercial moist food. The food was warmed to body temperature in a microwave oven and offered in several meals throughout the day to encourage acceptance.

Exercise was severely restricted. The owners were instructed to confine the cat to a small kennel or small room to prevent jumping. The owners were also advised that the cat should be reassessed monthly. The reassessment should include a dietary history, physical examination and radiographs to monitor bone density. By 12 months of age, the cat's bone density should return to normal and the cat can then be fed a commercial or homemade food that meets adult maintenance requirements. At that time, the DER also could be increased to reflect normal activity levels.

Endnote

a. Hill's Pet Nutrition, Inc., Topeka, KS, USA.

Bibliography

Cook JL, Gross MM. What is you diagnosis? Generalized loss of cortical bone density and a displaced compression fracture of 10th thoracic vertebra. Journal of the American Veterinary Medical Association 1996; 208: 1019-1020.

Johnson KA, Watson ADJ, Page RL. Skeletal diseases. In: Ettinger SJ, Feldman EC, eds. Textbook of Veterinary Internal Medicine, 4th ed. Philadelphia, PA: WB Saunders Co, 1995; 2077-2103.

Kaplan AJ. Onion powder in baby food may induce anemia in cats (Letter to the editor). Journal of the American Veterinary Medical Association 1995; 207: 1405.

Morris JG, Earle KE. Vitamin D and calcium requirements of kittens. Veterinary Clinical Nutrition 1996; 3: 93-96.

Robertson JE, Christopher MM, Rogers QR. Heinz body formation in cats fed baby food containing onion powder. Journal of the American Veterinary Medical Association 1998; 212: 1260-1266.

SECTION IV

Nutritional Management of Clinical Patients

Assisted Feeding in Hospitalized Patients: Enteral and Parenteral Nutrition

Rebecca L. Remillard

P. Jane Armstrong

Deborah J. Davenport

"When the facts change, I change my mind. What do you do?"
John Maynard Kane

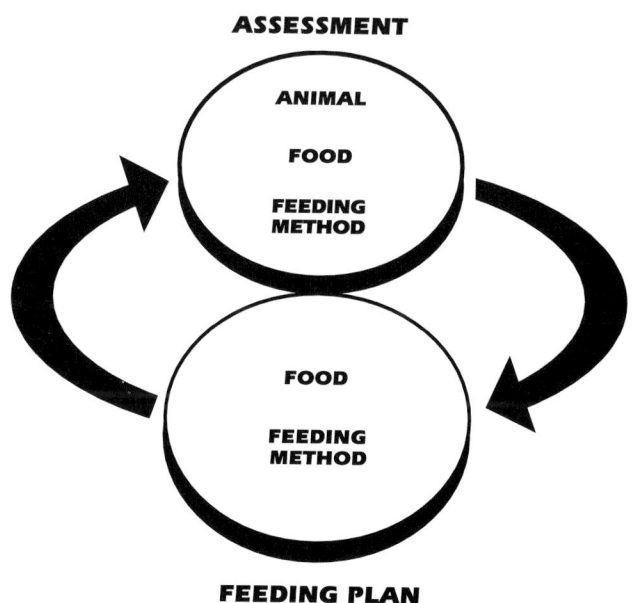

ASSESSMENT

ANIMAL

FOOD

FEEDING METHOD

FOOD

FEEDING METHOD

FEEDING PLAN

Note: The reader is referred to Chapter 1 for a detailed discussion of the iterative process of clinical nutrition.

CLINICAL IMPORTANCE

Patients of any age or lifestage may become malnourished from inadequate nutrient intake. By most estimates, many hospitalized people and companion animals do not receive adequate nutrition. Malnutrition is any disorder with inadequate or unbalanced nutrition that is associated with either nutritional deficiencies or excessive nutrient intakes. Hospitalized veterinary patients are more commonly malnourished due to a decreased total food intake. The major consequences of malnutrition in all patients, but more prominently in sick or injured patients, are decreased immunocompetence, decreased tissue synthesis and repair and altered intermediary drug metabolism.

Immunocompetence

The reciprocal relationship between nutrition and immunity has been recognized for centuries. A malnourished person or animal is more susceptible to infections and a septic patient is more likely to be anorectic, which results in malnutrition. Nutrient imbalances suppress immune function, which increases the risk of disease; conversely, certain diseases alter some nutrient requirements.[1-3] Decreased protein-calorie intake is the most common cause of secondary immunodeficiency in people. Progressively poorer responses have been noted in several aspects of the immune system with malnutrition including significantly impaired cell-mediated responses, secretory IgA production, phagocytosis, complement function, antibody affinity and cytokine production.[4-9] Studies have shown that protein

KEY WORDS & TERMS—ASSISTED FEEDING*

Acute disease	Intermediary metabolism	Partial anorexia
Anorexia	Km	Partial parenteral nutrition
Cachexia	Labile proteins	Peripheral proteins
Central proteins	Liquid diets	Polymeric liquid food
Chronic disease	Metabolism	Postprandial
Colloid solution	Modular liquid food	Preprandial
Complete anorexia	Monomeric liquid food	Respiratory quotient
Crystalloid solution	Osmolality	Total nutrient admixture (TNA)
Elemental liquid food	Osmolarity	Total parenteral nutrition
Enteral feeding	Parenteral	Undernutrition

*Key words and terms are defined in the Glossary.

KEY POINTS—ASSISTED FEEDING

1. The major consequences of malnutrition in all patients are decreased immunocompetence, decreased tissue synthesis and repair and altered intermediary drug metabolism.
2. A nutritional assessment includes a patient history, a physical examination with special attention given to certain risk factors, body condition scoring and laboratory tests.
3. Patients with a history of nausea, vomiting and diarrhea are at increased risk for malnutrition because nutritional intake has been less than optimal for some time before admission.
4. Animals use body carbohydrate, fat and protein stores to maintain blood glucose concentrations throughout the course of food deprivation, trying to maintain vital functions for as long as possible. The proportion of each stored component used varies over the course of food deprivation.
5. The adaptation from the fed to the fasting state is one in which fuel usage by the animal shifts from primarily a mixture of fuels to one in which the primary fuels are glycerol and fatty acids.
6. An understanding of the metabolic changes that occur during simple starvation is essential to understanding the underlying metabolic alterations present during anorexia with concurrent illness.

7. Major electrolyte and acid-base abnormalities and blood glucose levels should be corrected or near normal before instituting either enteral or parenteral nutritional support.
8. A practical goal is to begin nutritional support within 24 hours of the injury or illness.
9. Patients with a suspected or documented food intake less than their calculated daily resting energy requirement (RER) for more than three days are candidates for assisted feeding.
10. Hospitalized patients should be fed at their calculated RER, realizing their actual energy requirement is likely to change over the course of the disease process through recovery.
11. Nutritional support by an enteral, parenteral or a combination method should initially deliver sufficient calories and protein to meet the patient's RER at its current weight, adjusted for body condition. To begin feeding patients at RER is a rational and safe estimate that decreases the probability of metabolic complications.
12. To minimize the metabolic complications of refeeding, the refeeding formula should contain a complete balance of nutrients. However, it should have a carbohydrate, fat and protein profile similar to that which the liver is estimated to be using from body stores.

deficiencies that limit amino acid and nucleotide substrates for cell proliferation result in reduced numbers of circulating T lymphocytes, helper and suppressor cells.[10-13] Conversely, numbers of T_4 helper cells and T_8 cytotoxic suppressor cells in malnourished people return to normal quickly with refeeding.[10,14,15] Malnutrition also decreases immune function of existing cells through reduced complement secretions, less effective macrophage function and decreased killer cell activity.[10,16-18] Cytokine production and release are independently impaired in protein-calorie malnutrition and in several micronutrient deficiencies.[19,20] Single-nutrient deficiencies of zinc, iron, pyridoxine, vitamin A, copper and selenium impair the immune system.[21]

Immunoglobulins and circulating antibodies are maintained at relatively low levels during malnutrition, but are highly responsive to appropriate refeeding stimuli. For example, investigators measured serum globulin concentrations in 12 healthy beagles before and 24 hours after small bowel resection. All dogs were fed via gastrostomy tube immediately after surgery. Six dogs received a monomeric food whereas the other six were fed an electrolyte solution. Dogs fed the monomeric food synthesized more than twice the amount of globulin (12 g) than those dogs fed the electrolyte solution (5.3 g) 24 hours postoperatively.[22] In summary, the immune system is dependent upon and responsive to adequate nutrition.

Tissue Synthesis and Repair

Tissue synthesis and wound healing are a function of local and whole body nutritional status.[23] Locally, amino acids and carbohydrates are needed for collagen and ground substance synthesis. Fibroblasts require energy to synthesize the RNA, DNA and ATP necessary for protein anabolism. Migration of fibroblasts and epithelial and endothelial cells also requires energy.

KEY NUTRITIONAL FACTORS—ASSISTED FEEDING

Factors	Associated conditions	Enteral recommendations	Parenteral recommendations
Water	Dehydration	Correct dehydration with parenteral fluid therapy before starting assisted feeding.	Recalculate or increase intravenous fluid rate if dehydration persists or occurs.
	Edema		Recalculate or decrease intravenous fluid rate if edema occurs.
Electrolytes	Cardiac dysrhythmias Muscle weakness Hypo- or hyperkalemia Hypo- or hyperphosphatemia	Correct electrolyte abnormalities with fluid therapy before starting enteral feeding. Use food that contains macrominerals.	Correct electrolyte abnormalities with fluid therapy before starting parenteral feeding.
Energy	Weight loss Depressed attitude and lethargy	If the patient is not eating at least resting energy requirement (RER) per os, provide nutritional support by assisted-feeding techniques to meet this requirement. By the fifth day of food deprivation or longer, patients should receive the majority (60 to 90%) of their calculated RER as lipid. If using a liquid or blended food, select a product that provides 1.0 to 2.0 kcal/ml (1.0 to 2.0 kcal/g) as fed.	Provide at least RER each day with parenteral feeding. By the fifth day of food deprivation or longer, patients should receive the majority (60 to 90%) of their calculated RER as lipid.
Protein	Weight loss Muscle wasting Decreased serum protein levels Depressed immune response Poor wound healing	Provide essential and conditionally essential (arginine, glutamine) amino acids. Dogs: Use a food that provides at least 4 to 6 g protein/100 kcal. Cats: Use a food that provides at least 6 to 8 g protein/100 kcal.	Dogs: Use a solution that provides at least 2 to 3 g protein/100 kcal. Cats: Use a solution that provides at least 3 to 4 g protein/100 kcal.
B-complex vitamins	Poor energy metabolism Anorexia	Use a food that is fortified with B-complex vitamins.	Add B-complex vitamins to parenteral feeding solutions.

At distant sites, the liver has energy and protein needs specifically for synthesis of fibronectin, complement and glucose. The bone marrow requires nutrients for production of platelets, leukocytes and monocytes. Transportation of these necessary components and oxygen to wound sites requires the muscular activities of respiration and cardiac work. Tissue trauma and healing alter the normal continuous cycle of protein turnover (synthesis and degradation) in the body. In a rat model, the rates of protein synthesis and degradation were both increased after trauma.[24] Other protein turnover studies in perioperatively fed people indicate a 91% increase in protein synthesis with only a 10% increase in protein degradation.[25] Conversely, perioperatively fasted people had only a 50% increase in protein synthesis with a 79% increase in protein degradation.[26] Therefore, proper nutrition for local tissue synthesis and wound healing depends on adequate whole body nutrition.

Intermediary Drug Metabolism

It has been known for many years that cellular activities are dependent upon and regulated by the coordinated actions of peptides, lipids, vitamins and minerals as substrates, enzymes, coenzymes and cofactors of intermediary metabolism. Therefore, all nutrients are essential for the maintenance of normal cellular structure and function.[27] Nutrient deprivation alters the normal metabolic synergy responsible for ion gradients, membrane potentials, production of high-energy phosphate compounds and antioxidant defenses. Enteral and parenteral nutritional support with products containing little or no lipid decreases hepatic cytochrome P-450 concentration and activity, which significantly decreases specific drug clearances.[28,29] Protein-calorie deficiencies may result in decreased: 1) hepatic biotransformation of certain antibiotics, 2) concentrations of serum proteins that bind and transport drugs throughout the body and 3) renal blood flow, which decreases the rate of drug elimination and increases the possibility of drug overdose.[30] Therefore, protein-calorie malnutrition may alter the normal or expected metabolism of certain drugs, which may increase or decrease their therapeutic effect even when given at recommended dosages.[31-34] (See Chapter 27.) Animals receiving sufficient calories and protein are expected to have better or near expected drug distribution, metabolism and elimination than animals with protein-calorie malnutrition.

Malnutrition in people, even imprecisely defined, is associated with prolonged ventilatory dependence and increased complication rates with longer hospital stays and higher costs.[35,36] Similarly in veterinary patients, malnutrition is thought to increase morbidity and mortality. In summary, diseased and debilitated patients require nutrients daily to maintain optimal immune function, tissue synthesis and repair and metabolic reactions.

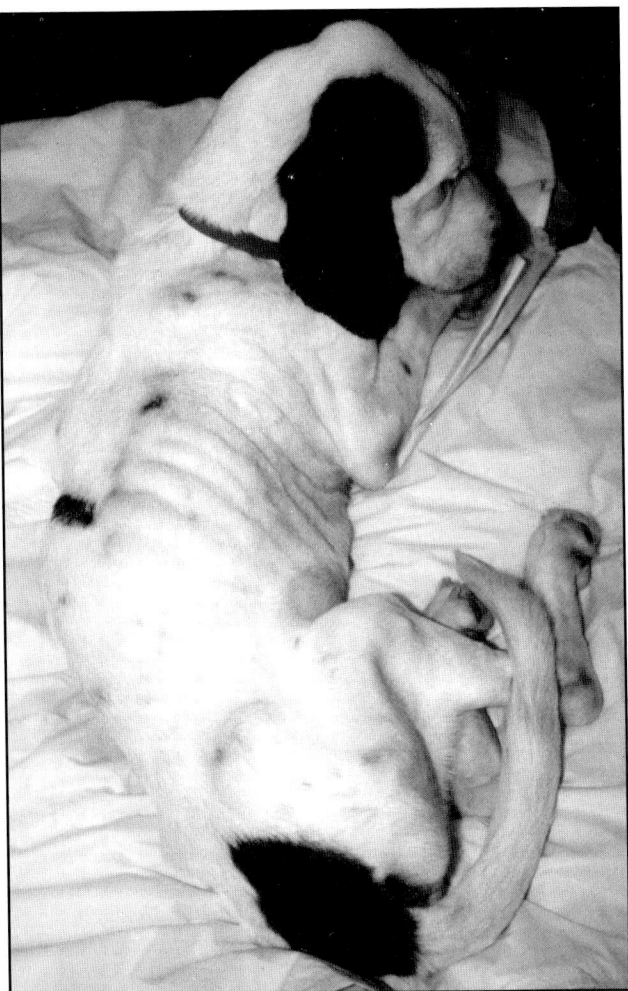

Figure 12-1. This dog experienced four months of starvation because its owner was unable to care for it due to a chronic terminal illness. Table 12-1 presents laboratory data from this animal.

Table 12-1. Laboratory data of a dog after four months of starvation.

Tests	Results	Reference ranges
Complete blood cell count*		
RBC (x 10⁶/mm³)	2.73	4.62-8.3
HGB (g/dl)	6.5	11.6-20.6
HCT (%)	18.2	33.1-66.4
Reticulocyte (%)	0.0	0-3
WBC (x 10³/mm³)	3.4	4.8-16.2
Fibrinogen (mg/dl)	430	88-380
Serum biochemistry profile**		
Glucose (mg/dl)	172	65-110
AST (U/l)	79	9-43
ALT (U/l)	75	14-50
Alkaline phosphatase (U/l)	230	5-125
Total protein (g/dl)	4.0	4.6-7.0
Albumin (g/dl)	2.1	2.6-4.2
Calcium (mg/dl)	8.5	8.9-11.1
Phosphorus (mg/dl)	2.9	3.0-5.9
BUN (mg/dl)	28	7.0-25.0
Creatinine (mg/dl)	0.2	0.6-1.6
Urinalysis		
Specific gravity	1.052	1.015-1.045
pH	7.0	6.0-7.5
Ketones	Trace	—

Key: HGB = hemoglobin, HCT = hematocrit, AST = aspartate aminotransferase, ALT = alanine aminotransferase, BUN = blood urea nitrogen.
*MCV, MCH, MCHC, platelet numbers, WBC differential, blood lead and coagulation profile were normal.
**Serum K, Mg, Na, Cl and total bilirubin concentrations were normal.

ASSESSMENT

Assess the Animal

Malnutrition can be recognized in patients through use of a nutritional assessment protocol. Nutritional assessment helps identify those patients that require assisted feeding to avoid or reduce nutrient deficiencies and the associated complications. Although inadequate nutrient intake may complicate many disorders, anorexia has been traditionally viewed as a secondary problem that will improve when the primary disease problem has resolved (i.e., "They'll eat when they feel better."). Conversely, it is better to be proactive and recognize the value of administering nutrients to veterinary patients and realize that "they'll feel better when they eat."

Diseased and debilitated patients (hospitalized or not) need to be assessed frequently, regardless of their age or lifestage. Assessment uses a number of parameters taken together to give an overall impression of whether a patient is experiencing malnutrition and requires specific nutritional intervention. Useful parameters to be assessed have been identified in large populations of people; however, no such parameters have been specifically formulated for dogs and cats.[37] A veterinary nutritional assessment protocol should include history, physical examination with special attention given to certain risk factors, body condition assessment (body condition score [BCS]) and laboratory tests.[38] Weight and dietary history, physical examination and body condition are relatively easy parameters to obtain. However, specific laboratory and immunologic tests that correlate well with nutritional status have not been identified. To date, very few clinical studies have been performed in veterinary patient populations to determine which parameters are applicable and their accuracy in determining nutritional status and predicting outcome.[39]

History and Physical Examination

All patients should receive a physical examination including an accurate determination of body weight and an estimate of body condition. Weight changes must be viewed as a proportion or percentage of "normal, usual or optimal" weight within a certain time period as opposed to absolute changes in units (e.g., g or kg lost). Weight loss of more than 10% within a week is clinically significant and warrants further assessment. As a point of reference, a weight change of 10 to 15% within several days is most likely a hydration problem and should be corrected first with medical or fluid management. Pets on a designated weight-loss program can safely lose 1 to 4%, more typically 1 to 2%, of their body weight per week.[40] (See Chapter 13.) A 10% (5 kg) weight loss within seven days for a 50-kg dog is easily recognized as significant, but a similar weight loss within seven days for a 5-kg cat (i.e., 0.5 kg) is not easily recognized. This weight loss should be considered as serious as the same percentage weight loss in the dog. It is more difficult to accurately determine a 0.5-kg weight change than a 5-kg change; therefore, cats should be weighed on a scale that has an increased sensitivity between 0 and 15 kg.

Body weight is an objective measurement, whereas body condition is a more subjective evaluation of the patient's tissue composition relative to its weight (i.e., fat, muscle

Future Laboratory Tests for Nutritional Assessment

DELAYED-TYPE HYPERSENSITIVITY TESTING

The delayed-type hypersensitivity (DTH) skin test has been promoted as an inexpensive and simple bedside preoperative test for people with sepsis-related mortality risk, again relating the close tie between immunocompetence and patient outcome. Patients who did not have an appropriate skin reaction to a multi-antigen intradermal injection had a sepsis rate of 34% and a mortality rate of 38% vs. a 7% sepsis rate and 3% mortality rate for patients who reacted to the test injection. Several diseases and drugs, however, may alter the specificity of this test as an indicator of malnutrition.

Delayed-type intradermal hypersensitivity testing is not currently used in dogs and cats; however, some preliminary work in cats has shown promise. Cats known to be infected with the feline leukemia virus and feline immunodeficiency virus had a DTH response less than that of normal cats. In another study, healthy cats receiving no food had a significantly reduced response to an intradermal injection of feline rhinotracheitis-calicivirus-panleukopenia antigens on Day 4 vs. when they received food daily.[a]

LYMPHOCYTE FUNCTION TESTING

Other promising indicators of nutritional status for dogs and cats, just now being developed, are specific immune function tests. A battery of immune function tests has been developed for use in cats, including: 1) immunophenotyping to identify relationships between immunosuppressor and helper cells, 2) measuring membrane calcium flux to evaluate membrane function, 3) immunophenotyping to identify cells expressing major histocompatibility class II surface antigen, 4) measuring phagocytic capabilities of monocytes and 5) assessing neutrophil activation. Preliminary data indicate there are differences in these lymphocyte function tests among normal-fed, normal-fasted and ill anorectic cats.[b]

ACUTE-PHASE PROTEIN TESTING

Laboratory tests available in other species, but not yet fully investigated as parameters of nutritional assessment in dogs and cats include serum prealbumin, transferrin, retinol-binding protein, fibronectin and cholesterol concentrations and total ironbinding capacity. A group of down-regulated proteins (prealbumin, transferrin, fibronectin and retinol-binding protein) and up-regulated proteins (ceruloplasmin, α-1-antitrypsin, α-1-acid glycoprotein and C-reactive protein) may prove useful in nutritional assessment. These proteins have relatively short half-lives (two hours to 10 days) in people, and so have been suggested as indicators of the patient's energy and protein status. The half-lives of these proteins are unknown in cats and dogs but are assumed to be relatively short and related to the nutritional status of the animal.

GENE EXPRESSION TESTING

Gene expression of metabolic enzymes and hormones in the fed vs. fasted state can be differentiated. The means by which food affects genetic activity probably differs among responding organs but also depends on the duration of the fast and the composition of the refeeding food. Many nutritional studies using animals have demonstrated the expression of enzymatic genes using a three-day fast followed by refeeding specific dietary formulations. For example, this starvation-refeeding paradigm has demonstrated that fasting causes adaptive increases in the concentrations of many hepatic and renal enzymes that convert amino acids to precursors of glucose and fatty acids. Conversely, feeding a carbohydrate diet decreases the activity of those enzymes involved in gluconeogenesis and amino acid catabolism. Fasting and refeeding alter the structure of chromatin in regions near the structural genes involved in metabolic regulation. The alterations in chromatin also depend on the amount of carbohydrate, protein and fat in the refeeding food. The method of refeeding has also been shown to affect transcriptional regulation of certain genes. In the future, it should be possible to more accurately assess the metabolic state (i.e., nutritional status) of animal patients by measuring the activities of specific enzymes, cell receptors and gene signaling pathways and then to administer an appropriate refeeding formulation.

ENDNOTES

a. Saker KE, Virginia-Maryland Regional College of Veterinary Medicine, Blacksburg, VA, USA. Unpublished data. October 1997.

b. Saker KE, Remillard RL, Virginia-Maryland Regional College of Veterinary Medicine, Blacksburg, VA, USA, and Angell Memorial Animal Hospital, Boston, MA, USA. Unpublished data. January 1997.

BIBLIOGRAPHY

Castro EC. Nutrient effects on DNA and chromatin structure. Annual Review of Nutrition 1987; 7: 407-421.

Chan DKC, Hargrove JL. Effects of dietary protein on gene expression. In: Berdanier CD, Hargrove JL, eds. Nutrition and Gene Expression. Boca Raton, FL: CRC Press Inc, 1993; 353-375.

Charney P. Nutrition assessment in the 1990s: Where are we now? Nutrition in Clinical Practice 1995; 10: 131-139.

Hauptman JG, Feldman BF, O'Neill SL, et al. A turbidimetric method for fibronectin assay in the dog. American Journal of Veterinary Research 1988; 49: 1935-1936.

Heymsfield SB, Tighe A, Wang ZM. Nutritional assessment by anthropometric and biochemical methods. In: Shils ME, Olson JA, Shike M, eds. Modern Nutrition in Health and Disease, 8th ed. Philadelphia, PA: Lea & Febiger, 1994; 839.

Jeejeebhoy KN. How should we monitor nutritional support: Structure or function? New Horizons 1994; 2: 131-138.

Lupo L, Pannarale O, Altomare D, et al. Reliability of clinical judgment in evaluation of the nutritional status of surgical patients. British Journal of Surgery 1993; 80: 1553-1556.

Morimoto T, Tsujinaka T, Ogawa A, et al. Effects of cyclic and continuous parenteral nutrition on albumin gene transcription in rat liver. American Journal of Clinical Nutrition 1997; 65: 994-999.Tellado-Rodriquez J, Christou NV. Clinical assessment of host defense. Surgical Infections 1988; 68: 41-55.

Ogawa H, Fujioka M, Su Y, et al. Nutritional regulation and tissue-specific expression of the serine dehydratase gene in rats. Journal of Biological Chemistry 1991; 266: 20412-20417.

Otto CM, Brown CA, Lindl PA, et al. Delayed hypersensitivity testing as a clinical measure of cell-mediated immunity in the cat. Veterinary Immunology and Immunopathology 1993; 38: 91-102.

Spiekerman AM. Proteins used in nutritional assessment. Clinics in Laboratory Medicine 1993; 13: 353-369.

ASSISTED FEEDING

and bone). (See Chapter 1.) A BCS adds valuable information to the breed and body weight data. Fat stores indicate previous energy intake (i.e., decreasing fat stores indicate low energy intake and vice versa). Muscle wasting implies protein intake has been insufficient because skeletal muscle mass supports hepatic protein synthesis when dietary intake is inadequate. In one human study, using three independent clinicians' nutritional assessment of the same 64 patients, there was a 77% agreement among clinicians, and their clinical judgment of nutritional risk correlated well with objective data such as albumin, transferrin and cholesterol concentrations and weight loss history.[41]

Survival rates of people have been directly correlated with available muscle mass. Loss of more than 25 to 30%

Regulation of Food Intake

Appetite is the desire for food and is often used synonymously with hunger. Satiety is the opposite of hunger and means that hunger has been satisfied. The body is normally in a state of hunger, which is intermittently relieved by eating. Hunger and satiety centers are found in the brain. The lateral hypothalamus contains the hunger center. Stimulation of this area causes an animal to eat voraciously. The ventromedial hypothalamus contains the satiety center. Stimulation of this area causes complete satiety. Many neuroendocrine and metabolic factors affect these centers and therefore control appetite (Figure 1).

In addition, the special senses of taste and smell are involved in the regulation of food intake. Taste is mediated through taste buds and free nerve endings. Cells that compose the taste buds are constantly being renewed by dividing epithelial cells surrounding the taste buds. Taste buds are located on the tongue, soft palate, pharynx, larynx, epiglottis, cranial esophagus and even on the lips and cheeks of some species. Gustatory information received from taste buds is projected by cranial nerves to several areas of the brain including the lateral hypothalamus. Olfaction occurs via axons of bipolar neurons that course through the small holes of the cribriform plate of the ethmoid bone and form connections in the olfactory bulb. As with taste, there are olfactory projections to the hypothalamus.

BIBLIOGRAPHY

Schiffman SS. Taste and smell in disease (first of two parts). New England Journal of Medicine 1983; 308: 1275-1279.

Schiffman SS. Taste and smell in disease (second of two parts). New England Journal of Medicine 1983; 308: 1337-1343.

Strubbe JH. Regulation of food intake. In: Westerterp-Plantenga MS, Fredrix EWHM, Steffens AB, eds. Food Intake and Energy Expenditure. Boca Raton, FL: CRC Press Inc, 1994; 141-154.

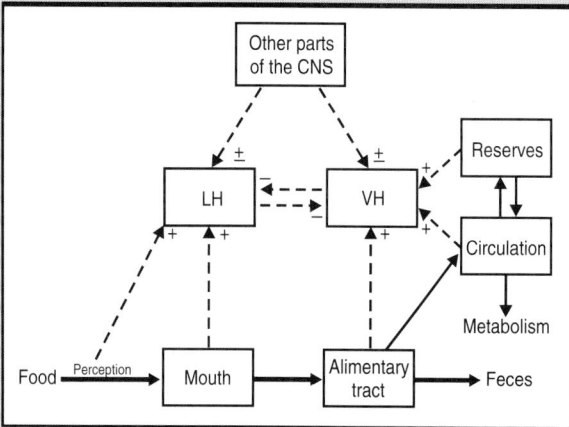

Figure 1. Simplified model depicting the control of feeding behavior. (Adapted from Strubbe JH. Regulation of food intake. In: Westerterp-Plantenga MS, Fredrix EWHM, Steffens AB, eds. Food Intake and Energy Expenditure. Boca Raton, FL: CRC Press Inc, 1994; 141-154.) Key: CNS = central nervous system, LH = lateral hypothalamus, VH = ventromedial hypothalamus.

---

of body protein compromises the immune system and muscle strength, and death results from infection, pulmonary failure or both.[42] Decreased muscle mass may occur before serum protein levels drop below normal in chronic states because overall muscle wasting is less life threatening than decreased serum protein concentrations. Muscle atrophy due to protein malnutrition occurs bilaterally and should involve several muscle groups. Bedridden patients can develop muscle atrophy due to decreased use just as astronauts develop muscle atrophy of anti-gravity muscles because muscle size depends on exercise and gravity.[43,44] Selected muscle groups may be atrophied in animals that have limited use of a limb. Therefore, lack of activity should be considered when evaluating the muscles of a patient, particularly one that is partially paralyzed or has a long-term illness.

Laboratory Data and Other Clinical Information

The changes in most laboratory data due to malnutrition are indistinguishable from those occurring in some disease processes; however, malnutrition should be considered when examining the animal and reviewing the data (Figure 12-1 and Table 12-1). Red blood cell number, hemoglobin content, urea nitrogen, potassium, albumin and total protein concentrations, total white blood cell count (WBC) and lymphocyte count are useful in nutritional assessment of adequately hydrated patients. Red blood cells, hemoglobin, albumin and total protein have moderately long half-lives of one to eight weeks and are an indication of the energy and protein status of the animal over the preceding weeks to months. In one study, dogs fed a protein-deficient food (4% protein dry matter basis [DMB]) with adequate caloric intake (19% fat DMB) had below normal serum albumin and total protein levels but normal globulin concentrations after four weeks.[45] Several studies in people have demonstrated that a low serum albumin value correlates with complications during recovery; however, the sensitivity of albumin as a single variable is only 10%.[46]

Decreased serum protein levels may occur in more acute states of inadequate protein intake relative to a large protein loss (e.g., protein-losing enteropathies, open abdomen). In starving people and other animals, the loss of muscle mass decreases the body's protein reserves and, together with a slower rate of protein turnover in the remaining muscle, decreases the body's ability to synthesize proteins in response to metabolic needs.[47-49] Such patients are poor surgical candidates because the body's protein reserves (muscle mass) have been catabolized to maintain the higher priority protein pools. If surgery can be safely postponed, several days of preoperative nutritional support in such patients is advisable. There is evidence to suggest that only one to three days of adequate energy and protein intake is required to up-regulate hepatic and muscle anabolic enzymes.[50,51]

Serum potassium and urea nitrogen concentrations can also be lower in anorectic animals because these variables are largely affected by food intake on a day-to-day basis. Urea nitrogen, however, tends to increase in end-stage starvation because muscle is catabolized for energy when fat stores are depleted. Serum creatine kinase levels have also been evaluated as a possible marker in feline malnutrition and refeeding.[52] Creatine kinase concentrations, however,

Table 12-2. Disorders and drugs that affect taste and smell in people.*

Disorders

Adrenocortical insufficiency	Hepatic cirrhosis
Allergic rhinitis	Hypertension
Bronchial asthma	Hypothyroidism
Burn	Influenza-like infections
Cancer	Nasal polyposis
Chronic renal failure	Niacin deficiency
Cobalamin deficiency	Radiation therapy
Cushing's syndrome	Sinusitis
Diabetes mellitus	Viral hepatitis (acute)
Head trauma	Zinc deficiency

Drugs

Drug classification	Examples
Amebicides	Metronidazole
Antiepileptic drugs	Phenytoin
Anesthetics (local)	Benzocaine, procaine hydrochloride, tetracaine hydrochloride
Antihistamines	Chlorpheniramine maleate
Antimicrobial agents	Amphotericin B, ampicillin, cephalosporins, chloramphenicol, gentamicin, griseofulvin, kanamycin, lincomycin, neomycin, nitrofurantoin, sulfonamides, streptomycin, tetracyclines
Antineoplastic agents	Doxorubicin, methotrexate, vincristine sulfate
Antirheumatic, analgesic, antipyretic, antiinflammatory, immunosuppressive agents	Allopurinol, azathioprine, colchicine, levamisole, D-penicillamine, phenylbutazone
Antithyroid agents	Propylthiouracil, thiouracil
Diuretics and antihypertensive agents	Captopril, furosemide, thiazides
Opiates	Codeine, morphine
Sympathomimetic drugs	Amphetamines, ephedrine
Others	Digitalis glycosides, estrogens, iron sorbitex, oral antidiabetic agents, vitamin D

*Adapted from Schiffman SS. Taste and smell in disease (first of two parts). New England Journal of Medicine 1983: 308. 1275-1279. Schiffman SS. Taste and smell in disease (second of two parts). New England Journal of Medicine 1983; 308: 1337-1343.

will also increase and decrease in many disease states.[53,54] Several different types of tests that may lead to better nutritional assessment are currently under investigation. (See sidebar "Future Laboratory Tests for Nutritional Assessment.")

Risk Factors

PHYSIOLOGIC STATE

The physiologic status of the patient should be noted. This is relatively simple but rarely noted in the medical record. Knowing the gender, reproductive status, age and activity level of a patient aids in the nutritional evaluation. For example, a neutered bitch at less than optimal weight and body condition (BCS 2/5) is clearly very different from one currently lactating for eight puppies. Dietary recommendations should reflect the obvious difference in energy requirement. Reproductive status (intact vs. neutered) alters metabolic rate and energy needs in animals.[55,56] The metabolic processes of growth, gestation and lactation do not necessarily cease when an animal becomes acutely ill. Several days of inadequate energy intake may be necessary before the hormonal milieu for growth, gestation or lactation is down regulated. Environmental temperature is usually a minor risk factor because most hospitalized dogs and cats are kept in normothermic environments.

HISTORY OF MALNUTRITION

Animals fed homemade food, table food, vegetarian or single-item foods are at greater risk for developing subclinical nutritional imbalances and warrant further nutritional assessment. Foods designed, formulated or prepared by owners are rarely nutritionally complete, balanced or consistent. (See Chapter 6.) These patients may not only have protein-calorie malnutrition, but are more likely to have several vitamin and mineral imbalances concurrently (e.g., calcium and microminal deficiencies and/or subclinical vitamin A and D toxicoses).

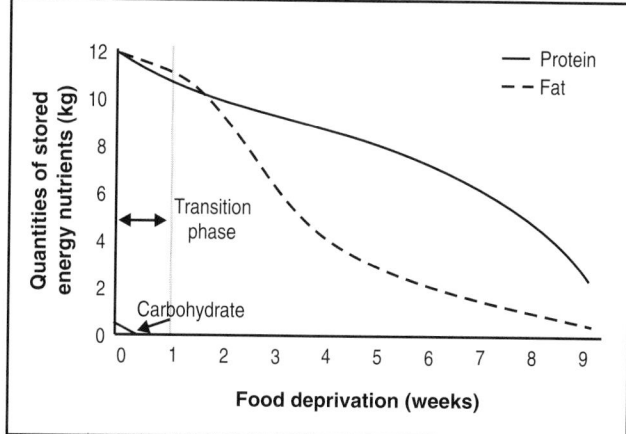

Figure 12-2. Disappearance of nutrient stores during starvation. (Adapted from Lewis LD, Morris ML Jr, Hand MS. Anorexia. In: Small Animal Clinical Nutrition III. Topeka, KS: Mark Morris Associates, 1987; 5-6.)

Patients with a history of nausea, vomiting and diarrhea are at increased risk of malnutrition because nutritional intake probably has been less than optimal before admission. Nutrient intake may be voluntarily decreased with nausea, whereas nutrient digestion and absorption can be compromised by vomiting and diarrhea. Such clinical signs are also associated with additional losses of body protein.

Anorexia, Cachexia and Accommodation

Normally satiety occurs after an animal's caloric needs have been met. Anorexia is the loss of desire for food before caloric needs have been satisfied. (See sidebar "Regulation of Food Intake.") Anorexia may be partial or complete. The anorexia is complete if an animal consumes no food for a period beyond that considered normal. The anorexia is partial if the animal consumes some food but less than that considered a normal daily intake.

The flavor of food results from chemical stimulation of the taste buds and free nerve endings in the nose, mouth and throat. "Taste" disorders often result from abnormalities in olfaction. Disorders of taste or smell can impair appetite and occur because of:

- Old age. The number of taste buds declines with age. Olfaction is usually the first sensory system to show an age effect.
- Damage to neural connections due to surgery or traumatic head injury. Accidental blows to the head can shear the fine olfactory nerves that pass through the cribriform plate and are a common cause of anosmia (inability to smell) in people.
- Impaired renewal of taste buds and olfactory epithelium. Decreased chemosensory cell turnover is consistent with the decreased cell renewal that has been reported to occur in the small intestinal epithelium as a result of food deprivation, radiation therapy, uremia, vitamin B_{12} deficiency and therapy with methotrexate. Many endocrine factors also depress cell proliferation. These factors and many conditions and drugs (Table 12-2) probably impair regeneration and function of taste buds and olfactory cells in the same manner that they impair regeneration of intestinal epithelium. The turnover time of taste bud and olfactory cells is about 10 days. Therefore, a return to normal taste function after mitosis is interrupted requires at least 10 days and usually longer.
- Modification of receptor cells as a result of a chronic change in local environment (e.g., an alteration in saliva or the fluids bathing the olfactory mucosa) due to drugs or metabolic agents such as urea.

Numerous medical problems including organic disease, inflammation, trauma and neoplasia can cause anorexia. In addition, pain, fear and other components of emotional stress inhibit the desire for food.[57] If anorexia persists, nutritional depletion occurs. Nutritional depletion may also result from facial or oral injuries, or obstruction or dysfunction of the gastrointestinal (GI) tract, liver or pancreas so that the animal is incapable of ingesting, chewing, swallowing, digesting or absorbing food. In general, animals not eating for more than 48 hours or those consuming less than 50% of normal intake for more than three days should be of concern and noted as having a form of anorexia. Cats and dogs with a history of complete anorexia for three or more days or animals with a history of partial anorexia for several weeks warrant further nutritional assessment.

Cachexia is a state of general illness, malnutrition and profound disability. Investigators and nutritionists have recognized for nearly 50 years that cachexia and a resultant low BCS are associated with increased risk of complications in people.[58] Loss of peripheral (skeletal) and central (visceral) proteins can have adverse anatomic and functional consequences in food-deprived animals. These adverse effects include anemia, reduced heart muscle mass and function, decreased pulmonary mechanical function and diminished respiratory drive, altered intestinal morphology and mildly impaired absorptive abilities.[59-61] Cachexia may affect dogs and cats with long-standing cardiac disease, renal disease or cancer. (See Chapters 18, 19 and 25, respectively.) A state of metabolic "accommodation" that prolongs survival has been recognized in people with chronic diseases. A similar state of metabolic accommodation probably occurs in dogs and cats.

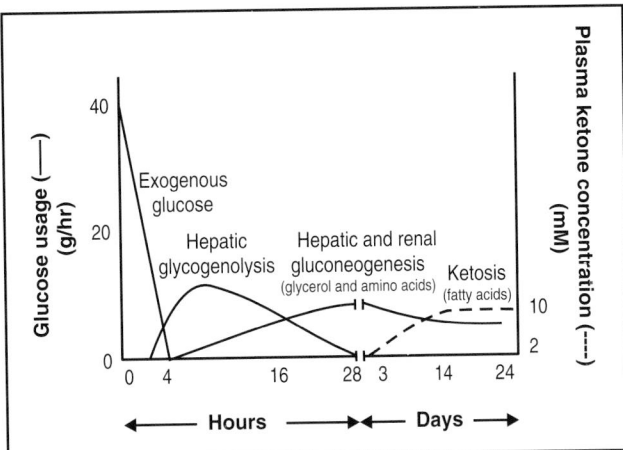

Figure 12-3. Graph of glucose usage and source during starvation. (Adapted from Engelking LR, Anwer MS. Liver and biliary tract. In: Anderson NV, Sherding RG, Merritt AM, et al, eds. Veterinary Gastroenterology, 2nd ed. Philadelphia, PA: Lea & Febiger, 1992; 211-274.)

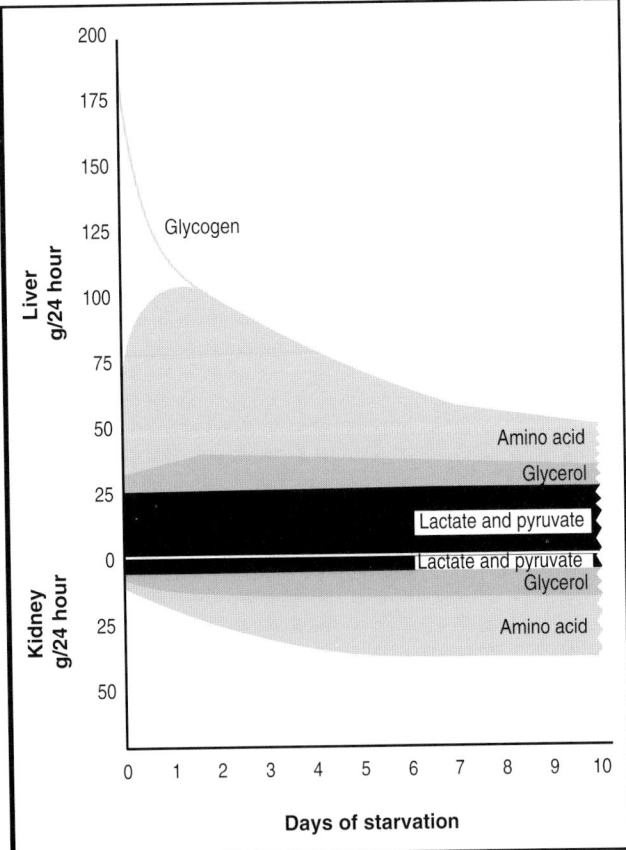

Figure 12-4. Graph of glucose production and source by the liver and kidneys. (Adapted from Owen OE, Felig P, Morgan AP, et al. Liver and kidney metabolism during starvation. Journal of Clinical Investigation 1969; 48: 574-583.)

Accommodation occurs when the energy equilibrium is re-established at a constant but lower food intake and lean-tissue wasting is arrested before protein deficiency becomes fatal. Accommodation in people is successful when: 1) total lean-tissue depletion is less than that considered critical, 2) weight is low but stable and 3) albumin levels and total peripheral WBC counts are normal with an intact delayed cutaneous hypersensitivity response.[62,63]

Accommodation with the exception of an intact delayed cutaneous hypersensitivity response, accurately describes the condition of some chronically ill animals (i.e., those with chronic renal, hepatic or cardiac insufficiency). Some chronically ill, cachectic cats and dogs may be maintained at a less than optimal body weight and condition for some time, even though important organ function deficits are apparent. In these cases, metabolic rate has been down regulated and protein turnover has been altered to establish a fragile homeostasis. This homeostasis can be maintained until a new stress supervenes. Affected animals very often do not survive additional stresses such as trauma, surgery, infection or tumors, as might a previously healthy animal.

METABOLIC CHANGES THROUGH DAYS OF FOOD DEPRIVATION

Simple Starvation

The metabolic changes that occur in mammals as days of food deprivation continue in the absence of disease are known and are often referred to as simple starvation. The time course of these metabolic changes should be the basis by which hospitalized patients are fed. In the immediate postprandial period, exogenous dietary nutrients are first used to meet immediate metabolic needs, sparing endogenous fuels. The second priority is to replenish glycogen reserves in the liver, fat and muscle, and to replace proteins catabolized since the last meal. The third priority is to convert any excess energy consumed as carbohydrate, fat or protein into triacylglycerides and to store that energy as fat in adipose tissue, muscle and liver. In the fed state when blood glucose concentrations are high, the liver traps glucose by phosphorylation with glucokinase, thus becoming a net importer of glucose. Glucokinase is an inducible hepatic enzyme with a high Km (180 mg/dl), which means high blood glucose concentrations, with the help of insulin, support maximal enzyme activity.[64]

Priorities are reversed in food deprivation and, under the influence of endocrine changes, energy is drawn from endogenous stores. Animals use different proportions of stored body carbohydrate, fat and protein to maintain blood glucose concentrations throughout the course of starvation to maintain vital functions as long as possible (Figure 12-2). The adaptation from the fed to starved state is one in which fuel usage by the animal shifts from primarily a mixture of fuels, to one in which the primary fuel is fatty acids. Carbohydrate metabolism is profoundly altered during the first week of starvation. An understanding of these metabolic changes, which occur primarily in the liver, during simple starvation is essential to understanding the underlying metabolic alterations present during anorexia, illness and cachexia.

As blood glucose levels fall below 120 mg/dl in simple, uncomplicated starvation, glucokinase in mammalian liver cells becomes less active, and the liver becomes a net exporter of glucose to maintain blood glucose concentrations (Figure 12-3). Omnivores (e.g., dogs) maintain blood glucose levels during the first two days of food deprivation through glycogenolysis and gluconeogenesis. The glycogenolysis will begin intraprandially but cease at the next meal. After four to five hours of fasting, however, the liver will begin to export glucose from the breakdown of glycogen stores to maintain blood glucose concentrations. Glycogenolysis maintains blood glucose levels for only another 12 to 28 hours. Thereafter, gluconeogenesis must maintain blood glucose concentrations because hepatic glycogen stores will have been depleted.[65] Carnivores (e.g., cats) maintain blood glucose levels via gluconeogenesis beginning intraprandially because hepatic glycogen stores are minimal. Hepatic glycogen storage in carnivores is relatively small compared with that in omnivores, in part because of lower glycogen synthase and glucokinase concentrations (Table 12-3).

Gluconeogenesis by the liver and kidneys using glycerol, lactate and glucogenic amino acids is initiated by glucagon but later maintained by glucocorticoids as blood glucose levels decrease (Figure 12-4). Adipose tissue supplies glycerol for glucose production and fatty acids for oxidation to supply energy, whereas muscle catabolism releases glucogenic amino acids, lactic acid and pyruvate for glucose production by the liver.[66] Hexokinase, which is present in all mammalian cells, has a low Km (1 mg/dl) and does not require the action of insulin. Therefore, extrahepatic tissues can trap glucose intracellularly even at very low blood glucose levels.[64] By the third day of food deprivation in all mammals, there is a reduction in metabolic rate that continues for several weeks to slow fat and muscle catabolism in an effort to survive long-term starvation. Food deprivation in normal animals causes a decrease in blood glucose levels, which results in lower serum levels of insulin. The conversion of thyroxine (T_4) to triiodothyronine (T_3) is responsive to insulin; therefore, as insulin levels decline, conversion to T_3 declines.[67] Triiodothyronine levels decrease within 24 hours of fasting and may be 40 to 50% less than levels in fed animals within three days.[68] Thus, animals receiving less than their daily energy requirement (DER), regardless of the circumstances (e.g., food deprivation or anorexia), have a decreased metabolic rate to conserve body functions until appropriate caloric intake resumes.

In addition to these changes in gluconeogenesis, the liver releases ketone bodies from fatty acids as an alternate fuel for non-glucose-dependent tissues within the first few days of food deprivation. The liver produces ketone bodies by partial oxidation of long-chain fatty acids, which originate from triacylglycerol stored in adipose tissue. Ketone bodies are essential to maintaining an energy supply to all tissues because the distribution of fatty acids (ketone precursors) is limited. Fatty acids have a limited distribution because they are water insoluble and must be carried in blood bound to albumin. This insolubility severely limits the serum concentration of fatty acids and their rate of diffusion into cells. Thus, fatty acids are restricted from serving directly as an alternate energy source for vital organs such as the brain.

The advantages of converting fatty acids to ketone bodies are threefold: ketones are water soluble, do not require albumin for transport and can provide a lipid fuel to cells at a much higher blood and interstitial fluid concentration. In mammals, serum ketone concentrations can reach 2 to 3 mM within a few days of starvation, with levels increasing to 7 to 8 mM after one week, which is greater

Table 12-3. Relative hepatic enzyme concentrations.

Enzymes	Dogs	Cats
Glycogen synthase	13*	1*
Glucokinase	55	5
Hexokinase	1.2	1

*Relative activity levels.

than the normal glucose concentration of 5 mM.[64] The increase in levels of blood ketones causes enzymatic changes in peripheral tissues and in the brain to promote ketone use and decrease glucose demand, which then conserves body protein. These changes effectively spare glucose for the non-adaptive, glucose-dependent tissues (i.e., erythrocytes and renal medullary cells).

Ketosis in food deprivation is an appropriate physiologic response and may not lead to severe ketoacidosis except in diabetic dogs and cats. Thus, ketone bodies serve as a readily diffusible lipid fuel for muscles, kidney cortex, peripheral nerves and the brain during periods of starvation. Ketone body production is usually maintained until adipose tissue is depleted.

By Day 5 of food deprivation in all mammals, endocrine changes have mandated a metabolic shift from exogenous fuel usage in the fed state to endogenous fatty acid and ketone body usage. Blood glucose concentrations decrease, thus insulin levels decrease, which allows lipolysis. Measurement of the respiratory quotient (RQ) gives a relative indication of the substrate(s) undergoing catabolism. An RQ of 0.7 indicates fat catabolism, 0.8 indicates protein catabolism and 1.0 indicates carbohydrate is the primary fuel. In studies, the RQ of well-fed resting dogs was 0.94, indicating high carbohydrate use, whereas the RQ values of the same dogs measured after five to 15 days of starvation was 0.8, indicating less carbohydrate use and increased fat and/or protein catabolism.[69] Therefore, fat from adipose tissue becomes an important fuel for the body in starvation after three to five days.[70]

Muscles also begin using ketone bodies for energy, sparing glucose. Muscles catabolize branched-chain amino acids, export the nitrogen in combination with pyruvate as alanine, and to a lesser extent as glutamine. These amino acids are deaminated and transaminated for hepatic protein synthesis and their ketoacid analogs are used for hepatic and renal glucose synthesis.[71] Fatty acid oxidation partially spares oxidation of amino acids for energy, which helps maintain muscle protein stores throughout starvation until the end stages.[72] Overall, blood glucose levels are maintained within the normal range throughout starvation for the non-adaptive, glucose-dependent tissues.

As described, animals use different proportions of stored body carbohydrate, fat and protein to maintain blood glucose levels and for other vital functions at different times throughout the first week of food deprivation. A patient's dietary history will indicate the number of "no food" days. Matching the number of no food days with the pattern of fuel use (i.e., adaptation from using a mixture of fuels to primarily using fat) throughout the course of food deprivation is important in selecting the first refeeding formula. Animals deprived of food are in a state of catabolism, which can often be reversed by refeeding, if body protein losses have not exceeded 25 to 30%. To minimize the metabolic complications of refeeding, the refeeding formula should contain a complete balance of nutrients, and should have a carbohydrate, fat and protein profile similar to that which the liver has become adapted, or is estimated to be using from body stores.

Disease State

Diseased patients have similar metabolic changes as patients in simple starvation (i.e., insulin resistance with decreased glucose use and increased proteolysis and lipolysis). These metabolic and physiologic alterations are mediated by general neuroendocrine responses and local mediators common to stressful stimuli. The specific hormonal and subsequent physiologic changes that occur in a stressed patient are unique to that disease condition, the time course of the disease and other complicating diseases or conditions. Hormonal and tissue substrate changes have best been characterized in disease conditions with a known acute onset such as trauma or infection.[73] The response has been described as having an acute (ebb) phase and then an adaptive (flow) phase.[74] The acute and adaptive phases can vary in duration and intensity depending on the specifics of the condition. The response to infection is qualitatively similar to that occurring with trauma except that the response to trauma is usually limited in time, whereas the response to infection will continue until the infection has been eliminated.

The acute phase generally occurs within the first 24 to 72 hours and is associated with catabolism. The response is similar to simple starvation except that the response is driven by a milieu of neuroendocrine and locally activated mediators rather than decreased triiodothyronine concentrations. Simultaneous sympathetic nervous system stimulation and release of catecholamines, cortisol, adrenocorticoids, glucagon, growth hormones and antidiuretic hormones induce metabolic and physiologic responses:
- Suppression of insulin release.
- Hyperglycemia from glycogenolysis and gluconeogenesis, which provides an energy source for the "flight or fight" response.
- Increased proteolysis and net protein catabolism from albumin and skeletal muscle sources to supply glucogenic amino acids for glucose production.
- Increased lipolysis to provide fatty acids and glycerol for energy and glucose production.
- Increased rate and depth of respiration, and increased cardiac work to deliver oxygen, remove carbon dioxide and supply blood components to muscles and wound sites.

During an infection, a toxic response results from the invasive organisms and resorption of necrotic tissue. Lysosomal enzymes and specific chemical mediators are released including histamine, kinins, prostaglandins and serotonin. These substances amplify the previously mentioned responses to trauma. Fever, induced by interleukin-1, increases energy expenditure 10 to 13% per degree Celsius increase in body temperature. Cytokine release also increases degradation of muscle protein and stimulates production of hepatic acute-phase proteins. Endotoxins released from dead gram-negative bacteria trigger coagulation cascades and profoundly affect carbohydrate metabolism.

In the acute phase, glucose is the preferred fuel; however, muscles are insulin resistant and hyperglycemia is maintained for net hepatic and immune tissue anabolism. As in starvation, these metabolic changes benefit the animal.[75] Hyperglycemia ensures an energy source in the face of hypotension or poorly perfused organs. Tissue sequestration of minerals and trace elements (e.g., iron) slows bacterial growth. General feelings of malaise and anorexia signal the animal to reduce activity levels of skeletal muscle and the GI tract to conserve energy for essential tissue maintenance and repair.

The catabolic phase will continue until the neuroendocrine stimuli and cytokine mediators are removed. During severe head trauma, multiple trauma, burns and sepsis, weight and lean-tissue loss are rapid and unremitting in the absence of feeding. Providing maintenance or even supraphysiologic quantities of nutrients to patients with these injuries and conditions will not reverse the ongoing catabolism, and may not achieve nitrogen balance.[76] The goal in providing nutrition to these catabolic patients is to feed the catabolism with exogenous sources of protein and fat. Feeding spares endogenous protein, which is critical because loss of 25 to 30% body protein stores has been associated with reduced heart muscle mass and function, decreased pulmonary function and diminished respiratory drive, compromised immune function and, therefore, increased mortality.[42]

There is a definite turning point in which clinicians note a subjective improvement in their patients. This noted improvement is associated with the adaptive phase in which net anabolism occurs. The adaptive phase is characterized by increased metabolic rate, nitrogen gain and normal body temperature and may last for several days, weeks or years.[75] The convalescent anabolic phase rebuilds damaged and catabolized lean tissue, and therefore, requires exogenous energy and protein sources. Investigators have measured the RQ in resting postoperative and severely traumatized dogs at 0.76, indicating that fat was the preferred energy fuel.[77]

Cats have very low glucokinase activity and cannot effectively transport glucose given in high intravenous concentrations into hepatic cells (Table 12-3). This phenomenon is probably one of many metabolic reasons why hyperglycemia is often seen in cats as a refeeding complication, but rarely in dogs. Therefore, in the adaptive or recovery phase of disease, fat is well-used by dogs and cats as the primary fuel. The recovery phase is different for each patient, which underscores the need for continuous monitoring.

Metabolic changes occur in animals with cancer.[78] Neoplastic tissues can be very aggressive and compete with the host for energy and nitrogen-supplying nutrients. Some tumors use glucose anaerobically and therefore are metabolically inefficient, placing a disproportionate energy burden on the host and in the process generating increased amounts of lactic acid. (See Chapter 25.) Hormonal and substrate changes over time are not well characterized for dogs and cats with chronic diseases with an insidious onset such as renal, hepatic or cardiac failure.

Key Nutritional Factors

Association of American Feed Control Officials (AAFCO) allowances are appropriate when initially estimating average nutrient requirements of dogs and cats to be fed enterally. Most foods used in assisted feeding have nutrient digestibilities greater than those of typical pet foods.[79] When estimating nutrient intakes for animals receiving parenteral nutri-

tion, the National Research Council (NRC) recommendations are probably better estimates. NRC recommendations were determined using synthetic diets, which better approximate 100% availability.[80,81]

Nutrient requirements for critically ill patients are more often expressed on an energy basis rather than on a DMB. (See Chapter 1.) This designation is primarily an extension of the units used in actual clinical metabolic trials. In addition, nutrient profiles of oral liquid products and parenteral solutions used in nutritional support/recovery are more commonly expressed on an energy basis rather than a DMB.

FLUID AND ELECTROLYTE THERAPY

Initial support often involves management of fluid, electrolyte and acid-base disorders. The water requirements of normal healthy animals approximate their DER (i.e., 1 kcal [4.2kJ] = 1 ml of water). Fresh, clean water should be available to patients at all times, unless the patient requires a period of nothing per os. Most patients in an intensive care unit have venous catheters in place and are receiving crystalloid fluid therapy. These patients may have fluid restrictions or conversely may require diuresis. In these cases, the water or fluid administered will not be equal to the patient's DER. Daily maintenance fluid requirements are approximately 60 ml/kg body weight/day.

The patient's fluid and electrolyte balance (sodium, potassium, calcium, magnesium and phosphorus) should be within near normal limits before assisted feeding is begun. Nutritional support should not be initiated until the patient is hemodynamically stable because administering enteral or parenteral nutrition may further compromise the patient. Nutritional support should not be initiated as a "last ditch" effort in unstable patients. Major electrolyte disorders, acid-base abnormalities and blood glucose levels should be corrected before instituting enteral or parenteral nutritional support. It is also desirable to correct severe tachycardia, hypotension, colloid and volume deficits before starting assisted feeding.[82] A practical goal is to begin nutritional assessment and support within 24 hours of the injury, illness or presentation.[83,84]

ENERGY

Knowing the patient's approximate caloric requirement is important because feeding more of any food than is necessary may cause metabolic complications. Overfeeding patients is possible through a feeding tube or with parenteral nutritional support. In people and several different animal models, excessive carbohydrate intake has been associated with hyperglycemia, hypercarbia, fatty liver, increased ventilatory drive and failure to wean from a ventilator.[85,86] Excessive fat administration has been associated with hyperlipidemia, hypoxia, increased rate of infection and higher postoperative mortality.[87-89]

The proportion of fat, carbohydrate and protein in foods fed to hospitalized patients should be similar to that which the liver is estimated to be using from body stores. Caloric density is important in both enteral and parenteral feedings when volume is limited. Enterally fed patients can be volume restricted due to gastric or intestinal sensitivities. Parenterally fed patients can be fluid restricted due to cardiorespiratory diseases and functional disabilities. In general, most dogs and cats tolerate the volume of food or solutions that meet the patients' resting energy requirement (RER).

Patients with disease have metabolic rates and energy requirements that are less than those of comparable normal healthy individuals. In malnutrition, without disease or injury, decreased triiodothyronine concentrations decrease the metabolic rate in an effort to conserve body functions. However, with an ongoing disease process or traumatic

injury, the neuroendocrine responses to stress increase the metabolic rate above that found in simple starvation. Respiration calorimetry measurements of more than 3,000 people with a wide variety of diseases, specifically excluding hyperthyroidism, showed that 90% of the patients had energy requirements from 15% above to 15% below RER.[90] The energy expenditure in people with trauma peaks in three to four days and then subsides by Days 7 to 10 unless complicated by sepsis.[91] Energy expenditure of people with other disease conditions probably follows a similar pattern; however, varying requirements above RER may occur over time.

In all probability, hospitalized veterinary patients are very similar to ill people and have metabolic rates very near their RER. (See sidebar "Current Feeding Trends in Hospitalized People.") Results of a few preliminary respiration calorimetry measurements in dogs with specific disease conditions suggested that most had requirements near RER.[77,92,93] Estimating the RER of hospitalized patients can be relatively simple using the equation RER = $70(BW_{kg})$ to the three-fourths power. (See Chapter 2.) Most hospitalized veterinary patients should be fed at their calculated RER, realizing their actual energy requirement is likely to change over the course of the disease process and recovery. In human surgical patients, there was relatively little additional benefit to increasing intake after half of the caloric requirement of patients had been achieved.[94] Therefore, initially feeding patients at RER, or slightly greater than 50% of RER if 100% is not possible, is a rational and safe recommendation that decreases the probability of metabolic complications. Regular nutritional assessment of the patient is strongly recommended to adjust initial feeding rates.

There are exceptions when the caloric requirement will be greater than RER. Particular cases have energy requirements 1.3 to 2.1 x RER as determined by bedside respiration calorimetry in people.[91,95] For example, according to indirect respiration calorimetry, people with severe closed-head and brain injury have energy requirements 40 to 60% above their calculated RER.[96] Brain injury apparently increases oxygen consumption and acute-phase protein synthesis, which increases patients' caloric and protein requirements significantly above RER. Energy requirements of twice RER appear to be the upper limit in the most severe head injuries. Energy expenditure may be 30 to 50% above RER in patients with multisystem trauma.[91] Severely burned patients also have energy and protein requirements 80 to 100% above RER, relative to the extent of skin damage and surface area exposed.[91,97] The body loses heat, moisture and protein through wounds with little or no epithelial covering. The patient's actual metabolic rate and resultant energy requirement are related to the degree of trauma, disease and/or complications and can only be approximated in a clinical setting.

PROTEIN

Protein in the body is always in a flux between synthesis and breakdown. Protein synthesis requires that amino acids be present within cells at the correct time and ratio so that a protein may be constructed successfully. Protein degradation involves the release of amino acids, and if the amino acid is deaminated, the ketoacid analog is converted to glucose or fat and the amino group enters the hepatic urea cycle and is ultimately excreted in the urine. Under most circumstances, about 15% of the RER comes from the oxidation of amino acids.[98,99] (See sidebar "Adjusting for Protein Calories.") Providing a protein source to ani-

---

Current Feeding Trends in Hospitalized People

In recent years, there has been a clear trend to feed patients less than previously prescribed. The current recommendation is to feed hospitalized patients at approximately 80% of their energy requirement during illness, which is most likely the resting energy requirement (RER) for most patients. The Harris-Benedict equation estimates RER in people and has been used widely in the United States for predicting the energy requirements of hospitalized patients. Nutritional support teams in major hospitals currently begin feeding their patients at or near their RER and then adjust the food accordingly based on routine nutritional assessments.

Most hospitalized people receive energy intakes between 25 and 35 kcal/kg (105 to 146 kJ/kg) body weight/day. The age and gender of the patient do not appear to directly affect the energy requirement of people, but rather energy expenditure depends on body size, body composition and activity, which varies with age and gender. The average, well-nourished, 70-kg person has a seven- to 10-day energy and protein reserve. However, if the catabolic response to injury continues beyond that time, the cumulative losses increase the risk of morbidity and mortality. Therefore, in severely injured persons whose injury response will certainly extend beyond seven days, assisted feeding is started once the patient is hemodynamically stable. For less severe injuries, the five-day rule applies (i.e., if the patient has not resumed eating by Day 5, assisted feeding is instituted).

BIBLIOGRAPHY

Daley BJ, Bistrian BR. Nutritional assessment. In: Zaloga GP, ed. Nutrition in Critical Care. St. Louis, MO: Mosby, 1994; 9-33.

DeBiasse MA, Wilmore DW. What is optimal nutritional support? New Horizons 1994; 2: 122-130.

Donaldson-Andersen J, Fitzsimmons L. Metabolic requirements of the critically ill, mechanically ventilated trauma patient: Measured versus predicted energy expenditure. Nutrition in Clinical Practice 1998; 13: 25-31.

Forse RA. Nutrition in critical care. In: Blackburn GL, Bothe A, Bistrian BR, eds. In: Proceedings. Malnutrition in the Hospitalized Patient, New England Deaconess Hospital and Harvard Medical School, Boston, MA, May 5, 1995.

Klausen B, Toubro S, Astrup A. Age and sex effects on energy expenditure. American Journal of Clinical Nutrition 1997; 65: 895-907.

McMahon MM. Nutritional assessment of the hospitalized patient. In: Blackburn GL, Bothe A, Bistrian BR, eds. In: Proceedings. Hyperalimentation: A Practical Approach, New England Deaconess Hospital and Harvard Medical School, Boston, MA, Sept 15, 1993.

Pellett PL. Food energy requirements in humans. American Journal of Nutrition 1990; 51: 711-722.

Tellado-Rodriquez J, Christou NV. Clinical assessment of host defense. Surgical Infections 1988; 68: 41-55.

Woolfson AMI. Amino acids–Their role as an energy source. Proceedings of the Nutrition Society 1983; 42: 489-495.

mals in catabolic states spares endogenous skeletal muscle protein and supplies essential amino acids and amino groups for acute-phase proteins and the immune response. Excessive dietary protein should be avoided in patients with liver or kidney disease. (See Chapters 19 and 23.) However, increased dietary protein seems to be handled well by canine and feline critical care patients and replaces dietary carbohydrate, which is not well tolerated. (See sidebar "Disease-Specific Nutritional Support.")

Protein administration should complement nonprotein calories because amino acids will be oxidized for energy when total energy need has not been met first. Sufficient calories must be available from fat and/or glucose before amino acids will be used for tissue synthesis and repair.[100-102] Excessive protein feeding requires energy expenditure to rid the body of excess nitrogen, which may or may not be handled well in particular patients by the liver (urea cycle) and kidneys and can result in hyperammonemia with accompanying clinical signs of encephalopathy. Conversely, insufficient protein has been linked to low albumin concentrations, poor immune response, impaired healing and increased risk of wound dehiscence and muscle wasting. The most efficient use of protein in people occurs when 2 to 6 g protein/100 kcal are administered.[103] Due to a lack of evidence to the contrary, most veterinary species are also assumed to have protein-calorie requirements within this range.

In formulating nutritional support, it is prudent to first provide for total caloric needs with fat and carbohydrate, and then meet the protein requirement with protein. It is important to remember that if sufficient calories are supplied to patients as either fat or carbohydrate, then most of the protein will be used for protein synthesis and not burned for energy. A starting point of 4 to 6 g protein/100 kcal enterally[79] and 2 to 3 g protein/100 kcal parenterally[104,105] can be used for most dogs that do not have an extraordinary protein loss and that can excrete protein waste products. Higher ranges (6 to 8 g/100 kcal enterally[79] and 3 to 4 g/100 kcal parenterally) are a more reasonable estimate for cats because of their constant state of gluconeogenesis and higher protein requirement. Protein intake can then be adjusted based on the patient's needs and ability to handle the initial protein recommendation (e.g., decreasing serum albumin concentration or encephalopathic signs).

B VITAMINS

B-complex vitamins (i.e., folic acid, thiamin, riboflavin, niacin, pantothenic acid, pyridoxine and B_{12}) are essential for hepatic metabolism of glucose, fat and protein. These are coenzymes for the tricarboxylic acid (TCA) cycle, ATP production and red blood cell metabolism. B vitamins are required in small amounts relative to other nutrients, but they are required daily and are necessary for efficient energy metabolism. B vitamins should be added to the fluids of all animals that are not eating but receiving fluid therapy. B vitamins are easily and inexpensively replaced and should be included in all forms of assisted feeding. Most pet foods contain adequate amounts of these nutrients, so deficiency should not be of concern if the patient is eating enough food to meet its RER.

MICROMINERALS

Zinc, copper, manganese, chromium and selenium are vital cofactors for optimal hepatic and peripheral metabo-

Adjusting for Protein Calories

Calculating and adjusting for protein calories is of minor consequence when feeding at resting energy requirement (RER). If one assumes that part of the caloric intake is to be supplied by protein, then that fraction of protein intake to be burned (i.e., used for energy) vs. that which is used for protein synthesis must be estimated because the same amino acid cannot do both. Theoretically, if protein were supplied at 4 g/100 kcal to the patient but all of it was oxidized for energy with none going to synthesis, the protein could only account for 14% (4 g x 3.5 kcal/g) of the total caloric intake at best.

The most conservative and simplest method is to first provide the entire caloric need with fat and carbohydrate, and then meet the protein requirement entirely with amino acids, and not bother to estimate the fraction of the protein that may be catabolized vs. anabolized. This method will not shortchange either the caloric or protein requirement because the fraction of amino acids actually burned for energy will provide only a small amount (<15%) of additional calories. Essential amino acids provided by food are most efficiently used in protein synthesis and should not be burned for energy, if at all possible.

Disease-Specific Nutritional Support

Enteral-feeding products have been designed for human patients who have specific medical conditions that may require nutrient modification. Disease-specific enteral products are available for human patients with renal failure, hepatic failure, respiratory failure and glucose intolerance.

Moist veterinary therapeutic foods are available with nutrient profiles that assist in the management of different disease conditions in dogs and cats. These moist foods can be blended with water and strained to produce slurries or gruels that are administered through medium- and large-bore feeding tubes (i.e., 14 Fr. or larger). Examples of patients that may benefit from these blended therapeutic formulas include those with renal failure, hepatic failure, diabetes mellitus, hyperlipidemia and heart failure.

Blended pet food is prepared by blending 400 g of moist food with 1.5 to 2.5 cups of water at high speed for one minute and then straining the mixture once through a kitchen strainer (approximately 1-mm mesh). Appropriate moist foods are listed in the respective disease chapters.

ASSISTED FEEDING

lism of energy substrates. Microminerals are important cofactors (metalloenzymes) and participate in tissue repair and albumin synthesis; therefore, they should be included in all food forms used for assisted feeding. Most pet foods contain adequate amounts of these nutrients, thus deficiency should not be of concern if the patient is eating enough food to meet its RER.

Refeeding Syndrome

Refeeding syndrome in people is characterized by generalized muscle weakness, tetany, myocardial dysfunction, dysrhythmias, seizures, excessive sodium and water retention, hemolytic anemia and death due to cardiac or respiratory failure. A similar syndrome occurs rarely in veterinary patients. When it does occur, it is most often seen in patients receiving parenteral nutrition (PN) and most commonly presents as hypokalemia or hypophosphatemia. Significant electrolyte shifts occur from extracellular to intracellular compartments as energy and amino acids are reintroduced. This electrolyte shift will occur regardless of the route of administration (i.e., enteral or parenteral). Often serum ion levels are deceptively normal in anorectic patients before refeeding begins (Table 12-1). However, when calories are reintroduced, particularly from carbohydrate, potassium and phosphate shift intracellularly with glucose resulting in hypokalemia and hypophosphatemia.

Potassium moves into cells with refeeding because glucose stimulates insulin release, which in turn stimulates the Na-K ATPase pump and glycogen synthesis, which requires 0.33 mEq potassium/g of glycogen. Phosphate moves into cells with refeeding to support the increased production of phosphorylated intermediary compounds of energy metabolism. Severe hypophosphatemia, hemolytic anemia and death have occurred in cats within 12 to 72 hours of refeeding with either an apparently normal or phosphorus-deficient diet. The refeeding formula should contain at least the Association of American Feed Control Officials recommended minimum allowance of 0.5% phosphorus (dry matter basis).

In people, hypomagnesemia is another common electrolyte complication that must be corrected. Hypomagnesemia increases urinary excretion of potassium, exacerbates hypokalemia and causes hypocalcemia, which is refractory to supplementation until the hypomagnesemia is corrected. Little information is available about magnesium status in hospitalized dogs and cats; however, serum magnesium levels should probably be monitored in veterinary patients with abnormal serum electrolytes.

RECOMMENDATIONS FOR AVOIDING COMPLICATIONS OF THE REFEEDING SYNDROME

1. Anticipate the potential for the problem and refeed with formulations known to contain adequate potassium, phosphate and magnesium levels.
2. Use initial nutritional refeeding rates that do not exceed the patient's resting energy requirement (RER) and 2 to 6 g protein/100 kcal. These rates can be increased as needed over subsequent days. Consider refeeding a high-fat, low-carbohydrate formula to patients that have not eaten for five days or more.
3. Monitor serum potassium, phosphate and magnesium levels as needed. Once a day is sufficient for most cases.
4. Supply water-soluble vitamins free choice, particularly thiamin, to facilitate energy metabolism.
5. Monitor patients daily for signs of fluid overload and congestive heart failure.

BIBLIOGRAPHY

Davenport DJ. Tube feeding: Managing complications of enteral feeding. In: Proceedings. International Veterinary Emergency and Critical Care Society, San Antonio, TX, 1996: 297-302.

Forrester SD, Moreland KJ. Hypophosphatemia. Journal of Veterinary Internal Medicine 1989; 3: 149-159.

Hamaoui E, Kodsi R. Complications of enteral feeding and their prevention. In: Rombeau JL, Rolandelli RH, eds. Clinical Nutrition; Enteral and Tube Feeding, 3rd ed. Philadelphia, PA: WB Saunders Co, 1997; 554-574.

Justin RB, Hohenhaus AE. Hypophosphatemia associated with enteral alimentation in cats. Journal of Veterinary Internal Medicine 1995; 9: 228-233.

Martin LG, Van Pelt DR, Wingfield WE. Magnesium and the critically ill patient. In: Bonagura JD, ed. Current Veterinary Therapy XII. Philadelphia, PA: WB Saunders Co, 1995; 128-131.

Oh MS. Water, electrolyte and acid-base balance. In: Shils ME, Olson JA, Shike M, eds. Modern Nutrition in Health and Disease. Philadelphia, PA: Lea & Febiger, 1994; 128.

Solomon SM, Kirby DF. The refeeding syndrome: A review. Journal of Parenteral and Enteral Nutrition 1990; 14: 90-97.

OTHER FACTORS

Fat-Soluble Vitamins and Macrominerals

Hospitalized patients rarely need fat-soluble vitamins, non-electrolytes and minerals. Most patients have fat and hepatic stores of the fat-soluble vitamins sufficient to meet metabolic needs for months to years. However, administering fat-soluble vitamins should be considered in cases of prolonged malnutrition in which the patient is severely underweight with little to no fat stores (i.e., BCS 1/5). Macrominerals (i.e., calcium, phosphorus, magnesium, sodium and potassium) are rarely needed by patients above that required to obtain and maintain serum electrolyte levels. Whole body stores of these minerals are usually not the problem. However, correct distribution between the intracellular and extracellular fluid space can be a problem and imbalances should be corrected before assisted feeding is begun. (See sidebar "Refeeding Syndrome.") Sodium, potassium and magnesium levels may become a concern in patients experiencing excessive urinary loss of those minerals due to intensive diuretic therapy.

Palatability

Many patients have poor appetites in the hospital for numerous reasons. Therefore, highly palatable foods should be offered whenever possible. In general, foods that are moist (i.e., dry matter [DM] >30%), warmed to room temperature with higher percentages of fat and protein are more palatable than dry, cold foods with very low levels of fat and protein. A dietary history should also clarify the type of foods (i.e., moist, dry, homemade) the patient normally consumes. Many cats and small dogs prefer one form of food (e.g., moist vs. dry) over the other; therefore, food acceptance in the hospital can be improved by offering the same form fed at home. Owners are usually willing to bring in the pet's own food in order to improve food intake during hospitalization.

N-3 Fatty Acids, Nucleotides and Amino Acids

The roles of n-3 fatty acids, dietary nucleotides and the amino acids arginine and glutamine have become the subject of much research in people and laboratory animals. For more information, see sidebars "Arginine and n-3 Fatty Acids," "Dietary Nucleotides" and "Glutamine" and Chapter 25.

Arginine and n-3 Fatty Acids

Inadequate nutritional support can suppress the immune response, cause organ dysfunction, impair wound healing, result in muscle wasting and weakness, increase the incidence of acquired infections and increase mortality. As an example, a 50% decrease in jejunal mucosal mass and thickness normally occurs after burn injuries when no enteral feedings are given for 24 hours. Early feeding prevents this mucosal atrophy. In addition, specific nutrients affect immunocompetence. Some nutrients/food factors act directly on the lymphoid system and immune cell function, thereby altering host immune response to pathogens. As an example, arginine- and fish oil-enriched diets are associated with significant reduction in wound infection and length of hospital stay in human burn patients. Other examples include glutamine and dietary nucleotides. (See sidebars "Glutamine" and "Dietary Nucleotides.")

ARGININE

Arginine is essential to the traumatized host. It has a marked immunopreserving effect in the face of immunosuppression induced by protein malnutrition and cancer. In postsurgical patients, arginine supplementation enhances T-lymphocyte response and augments T-helper cell numbers, with a rapid return to normal T-cell function postoperatively compared with findings in control patients. These data taken together suggest that arginine supplementation may increase or preserve function in high-risk surgical patients and theoretically enhance the host's capacity to resist infection. Arginine enrichment stimulates the immune system, improves wound healing and decreases morbidity and mortality in burn patients. A feeding regimen with arginine as 9% of the protein source has been suggested and tested in burn patients. Those receiving the arginine-enriched diet had a significant reduction in the incidence of wound infection and shorter hospital stays. As a nutrient substrate, arginine was nontoxic and may benefit surgical patients who are at increased risk of infection. The optimal arginine intake for people is not known, so selection of enteral diets based solely on arginine content is not recommended.

Numerous studies in a variety of animal models demonstrated the efficacy of arginine-supplemented foods in reducing the catabolic response to major trauma, sepsis and injury and in improving the immune response after a variety of adverse stimuli. For example, a diet containing arginine as 2% of the total nonprotein calories significantly increased animal survival after 30% surface burns. Further, in animal studies, exogenous arginine supplementation consistently improved nitrogen retention, protein turnover and wound healing. Arginine augments cellular immunity, as evidenced by enhanced skin allograft rejection in normal mice, and it improves delayed hypersensitivity responses.

Arginine has been recognized as an essential amino acid in dogs and cats for more than a decade. Therefore, most pet foods meeting Association of American Feed Control Officials (AAFCO) nutrient concentrations should contain at least 146 mg arginine/100 kcal for adult dogs and 250 mg arginine/100 kcal for adult cats (approximately 80 to 200 mg/kg body weight). Arginine content of human enteral products is variable but usually stated on the label. Human enteral products must contain at least adequate amounts of arginine if used for more than a few days in dogs or cats.

N-3 FATTY ACIDS

Mechanisms by which dietary fats alter humoral and cellular immune responses have been of interest over the past two decades. The effect of dietary fat on the immune system depends on which fat is fed and what specific aspects of the immune system are evaluated. Dietary fats are thought to affect the immune system by three mechanisms: 1) altered eicosanoid synthesis, 2) changes in cell membranes that affect membrane-associated protein and receptor function and 3) changes in intracellular nonesterified fatty acid pools (NEFA) that affect cytokine production. Generally, n-3 (omega-3) fatty acids produce less inflammatory cytokines, whereas n-6 fatty acids produce more pro-inflammatory cytokines.

Available evidence unequivocally indicates that eicosanoids and lipoxygenase products, when produced in excess (e.g., trauma, injury, postoperative states), are generally immunosuppressive. The capacity of tissues and white blood cells to produce prostaglandins and lipoxygenase products is largely determined by the amount of arachidonic acid present, which is mostly determined by dietary linoleic acid. A significant reduction in n-6 polyunsaturated fatty acids (PUFA) appears prudent in the diet of immunocompromised, traumatized, postoperative or infected patients. The inclusion of n-3 PUFA in such diets would seem to be beneficial in decreasing eicosanoid production. Recent findings suggest that marked improvement can be made in foods by adjusting the n-6 and n-3 components to ensure optimal immune function.

There is some clinical evidence that dietary n-3 fatty acids have been beneficial in managing severe inflammatory and autoimmune disorders in rodents and people. The n-3 PUFA are metabolized to the 3-series prostaglandins and 5-series leukotrienes. These less inflammatory substances alter immune function and may improve survival in patients in which the inflammatory process threatens to cause irreversible damage, as in septic shock or endotoxemia. N-3 PUFA shift the response away from intense inflammation. In other studies, fish oil protected guinea pigs from endotoxic shock and lactic acidosis, providing them with a survival advantage.

NEFA in tissues has been effectively altered within hours of oral dosing with n-3 fatty acids. In pigs, plasma phospholipid profiles differed significantly within eight days (measurements were not taken before eight days). Intestinal mucosa and plasma had an altered fatty acid profile within four weeks, whereas an alteration in the fatty acid profile of skin has taken more than six weeks and possibly as long as 12 weeks of supplementation. In dogs, however, investigators found plasma fatty acid profile changes within two weeks after the onset of n-3 dietary supplementation. Thus, there may not be enough time for dietary n-3 fatty acid therapy to affect an acute inflammatory process, depending on the affected tissue unless the fatty acids were incorporated into the animal's diet before the onset of disease. The dietary dose that favors a less inflammatory cascade during a disease process has not yet been determined in any species.

N-3 PUFA, once incorporated into the plasma membrane, affects monocyte function by altering membrane fluidity and second messenger function, and by diminishing production of dienoic prostaglandins. These changes may be responsible for alterations in such cell functions as macrophage phagocytosis, production of interleukin-1 and production of superoxides.

On the other hand, chronically suppressing an immune response by feeding n-3 fatty acids should be done cautiously and is not warranted in disease states in which a fully competent immune system is essential for survival and recovery. Some studies in mice suggest that dietary n-3 fatty acids com-

Continued on next page.

Continued from previous page.

promise the animal's resistance in an infectious disease state. However, these mice were prefed (two to four weeks) extremely high levels of n-3 fatty acids (40% of calories as fish oil). As with many other nutrients, excessive levels of n-3 fatty acids can be detrimental.

BENEFITS OF ENTERAL FOODS CONTAINING ARGININE, N-3 FATTY ACIDS AND NUCLEOTIDES FED TO CRITICALLY ILL PATIENTS

Two recent studies investigated the effects of a human enteral product enriched with arginine, n-3 fatty acids and dietary nucleotides (Impact[a]). In one study, researchers investigated the effects of this enriched enteral product on immune parameters of patients undergoing major abdominal surgery. In general, patients receiving the enriched product had enhanced immunocompetence and fewer infectious complications than patients in other groups. In the other study, a subset of patients with sepsis who were fed the enriched enteral product (Impact) had shorter hospital stays and a major reduction in the frequency of acquired infections vs. other groups.

ENDNOTE
a. Sandoz Nutrition, Minneapolis, MN, USA.

BIBLIOGRAPHY
Arginine Sources

Bohles H, Segerer H, Fekl W. Improved nitrogen retention during L-carnitine-supplemented total parenteral nutrition. Journal of Parenteral and Enteral Nutrition 1984; 8: 9-13.

Bower RH, Cerra FB, Bershadsky B, et al. Early enteral feeding of a formula (Impact) supplemented with arginine, nucleotides, and fish oil in intensive care unit patients: Results of a multicenter, prospective, randomized, clinical trial. Critical Care Medicine 1995; 23: 436-449.

Chyun JH, Griminger P. Improvement of nitrogen retention by arginine and glycine supplementation and its relation to collagen synthesis in traumatized mature and aged rats. Journal of Nutrition 1984; 114: 1697-1704.

Daly JM, Reynolds J, Sigal RK, et al. Effect of dietary protein and amino acids on immune function. Critical Care Medicine 1990; 18: S86.

Daly JM, Reynolds J, Thom A, et al. Immune and metabolic effects of arginine in the surgical patient. Annals of Surgery 1988; 208: 512-522.

Goffschlich MM, Jenkins M, Warden GD, et al. Differential effects of three dietary regimens on selected outcome variables in burn patients. Journal of Parenteral and Enteral Nutrition 1990; 14: 225-236.

Gottschlich MM, Shronts EP, Hutchins AM. Defined formula diets. In: Rombeau JL, Rolandelli RH, eds. Clinical Nutrition; Enteral and Tube Feeding, 3rd ed. Philadelphia, PA: WB Saunders Co, 1997; 207-239.

Hall JB, Schmidt GA, Wood LDH, et al, eds. Principles of Critical Care, 2nd ed. New York, NY: McGraw-Hill, 1998.

Ireton-Jones CS, Baxter CR. Nutrition for adult burn patients: A review. Nutrition in Clinical Practice 1990; 6: 3-7.

Kirk SJ, Barbul A. Role of arginine in trauma, sepsis and immunity. Journal of Parenteral and Enteral Nutrition 1990; 14: 226S-229S.

Schilling J, Vranjes N, Fierz W, et al. Clinical outcome and immunology of postoperative arginine, ω-3 fatty acids, and nucleotide-enriched enteral feeding; A randomized prospective comparison with standard enteral and low calorie/low fat IV solutions. Nutrition 1996; 12: 423-429.

n-3 Fatty Acid Sources

Bloch KJ, Ho B, Xu LL, et al. Effect of fish-fat or beef-fat supplemented diet on immune complex-induced enteropathy in the rat. Prostaglandins 1989; 38: 385-396.

Campbell KD, Dorn GP. Effects of oral sunflower oil and olive oil on serum and cutaneous fatty acids concentrations in dogs. Research in Veterinary Science 1992; 53: 172-178.

Chang HR, Dulloo AG, Vladonianu IR, et al. Fish oil decreases natural resistance of mice to infection with *Salmonella typhimurium*. Metabolism 1992; 41: 1-2.

Dinarello CA. An overview of the pathophysiology of cytokines. In: Dinarello CA, Kluger MJ, Powanda MC, et al, eds. The Physiological and Pathological Effects of Cytokines. New York, NY: Wiley-Liss, 1990; 1-6.

Dunn CJ. Cytokines as mediators of chronic inflammatory disease. In: Kimball ES, ed. Cytokines and Inflammation. Boca Raton, FL: CRC Press Inc, 1991; 1-33.

Fernandes G, Venkatraman JT, Fernandes A, et al. Effect of ω-3 fatty acid diet therapy on autoimmune disease with and without caloric restriction. In: Artemis P, Simopoulos AP, Kifer RR, et al, eds. Proceedings. International Conference on Health Effects of Omega-3 Polyunsaturated Fatty Acids in Seafoods. World Review of Nutrition and Dietetics, vol. 66. New York, NY: Karga, 1991.

Fritsche KL, McGuire SO. The adverse effects of an in vivo inflammatory challenge on the vitamin E status of rats is accentuated by fish oil feeding. Journal of Nutritional Biochemistry 1996; 7: 623-631.

Fritsche KL, Shahbazian LM, Feng C, et al. Dietary fish oil reduces survival and impairs bacterial clearance in C3H/Hen mice challenged with *Listeria monocytogenes*. Clinical Science 1997; 92: 95-101.

Geusens P, Wouters C, Nijs J, et al. Long-term effect of omega-3 fatty acid supplementation in active rheumatoid arthritis. Arthritis and Rheumatism 1994; 37: 824-829.

Kinsella JE, Lokesh B. Dietary lipids, eicosanoids, and the immune system. Critical Care Medicine 1990; 18: S94-S111.

Lands WEM, Kulmacz RJ. The regulation of the biosynthesis of prostaglandins and leukotrienes. Progress in Lipid Research 1986; 25: 105-109.

Lands WEM. Biochemistry and physiology of n-3 fatty acids. Federation of American Societies for Experimental Biology Journal 1992; 6: 2530-2536.

Lee TH, Hoover RL, Williams JD, et al. Effect of dietary enrichment with eicosapentaenoic and docosahexaenoic acids on in vitro neutrophil and monocyte leukotriene generation and neutrophil function. New England Journal of Medicine 1985; 312: 1217-1224.

Lorenz R, Weber PC, Szimnau P, et al. Supplementation with n-3 fatty acids from fish oil in chronic inflammatory bowel disease–A randomized, placebo-controlled, double-blinded, crossover trial. Journal of Internal Medicine 1989; 731 (Suppl.): 225-232.

Murray MJ, Svingen BA, Holman RT, et al. Effects of a fish oil diet on pigs' cardiopulmonary response to bacteremia. Journal of Parenteral and Enteral Nutrition 1991; 15: 152-158.

Peck MD, Alexander JW, Ogle CK, et al. The effect of dietary fatty acids on response to *Pseudomonas* infection in burned mice. Journal of Trauma 1990; 30: 445-452.

Remillard RL. Omega 3 fatty acids in canine and feline diets: A clinical success or failure? Journal of Veterinary Clinical Nutrition 1998; 5: 6-11.

Vilaseca J, Salas A, Guarner F, et al. Dietary fish oil reduces progression of chronic inflammatory lesions in a rat model of granulomatous colitis. Gut 1990; 31: 539-544.

Von Schacky C, Fischer S, Weber PC. Long-term effects of dietary marine ω-3 fatty acids upon plasma and cellular lipids, platelet function and eicosanoid formation in humans. Journal of Clinical Investigation 1985; 76: 1626-1631.

Dietary Nucleotides

Nucleotides are precursors of DNA and RNA, but they also participate in a number of metabolic reactions fundamental to cellular activity. Dietary nucleotides appear to be important for maintenance of normal cellular immunity and are vital to maintain host defenses against bacterial and fungal pathogens. Dietary nucleotides appear essential to the normal maturation of lymphocytes.

In vitro mixed lymphocyte culture response and mitogen stimulation are suppressed in animals supported on a casein-based laboratory food. Such foods are nucleotide free. Mice maintained on nucleotide-free diets are much more susceptible to lethal infections caused by *Candida albicans* and *Staphylococcus aureus* than are nucleotide-fed mice. Macrophage bactericidal activity is depressed in nucleotide-free mice. Animals fed a nucleotide-free diet for six weeks had significant immunosuppression as demonstrated by enhanced cardiac allografts and diminished ability to survive a fungal challenge. These findings are significant because all commercially available parenteral and nearly all enteral human products are devoid of nucleotides. Pet foods that use meats and cereal grains as ingredients should provide adequate levels of dietary nucleotides. Dietary nucleotides are a vital component of regimens to maintain or restore immune function and host defense.

BIBLIOGRAPHY

Bower RH, Cerra FB, Bershadsky B, et al. Early enteral feeding of a formula (Impact) supplemented with arginine, nucleotides, and fish oil in intensive care unit patients: Results of a multicenter, prospective, randomized, clinical trial. Critical Care Medicine 1995; 23: 436-449.

Hall JB, Schmidt GA, Wood LDH, et al, eds. Principles of Critical Care, 2nd ed. New York, NY: McGraw-Hill, 1998.

Schilling J, Vranjes N, Fierz W, et al. Clinical outcome and immunology of postoperative arginine, ω-3 fatty acids, and nucleotide-enriched enteral feeding; A randomized prospective comparison with standard enteral and low calorie/low fat IV solutions. Nutrition 1996; 12: 423-429.

Assess The Food(s) and Feeding Method

Ideally, all hospitalized patients should consume at least enough balanced food to meet their daily RER and sufficient fluid to meet their water requirement. Requirements for all other nutrients need not be calculated when the food contains non-energy nutrients properly balanced to the caloric density of the product. When the patient consumes the proper amount of a balanced food, all other nutrient needs have been met, unless known losses of particular nutrients occur (e.g., protein and electrolytes). When it becomes certain the patient is not eating enough food to meet at least RER, then assisted feeding should be instituted and the feeding plan revised.

Evaluating the diet of a pet with medical problems is more involved and requires more frequent and detailed attention than when dealing with a healthy pet. Case reviews may occur several times daily and should include a food-intake assessment. Feeding orders of hospitalized patients should be clear and complete. Properly written hospital feeding orders identify a specific food product with the amount, frequency and the route of intake specified, if not per os (Table 12-4). In a multi-center study of 276 hospitalized dogs, fewer than 20% of approximately 1,000 written feeding orders were complete and accurate.[106]

Recording the food intake of hospitalized patients is essential to determining whether or not assisted feeding is necessary. In addition to having complete feeding orders, the medical record should also contain the time of day and amount of food actually consumed by the patient. Consumption can be simply recorded as some percentage of the food offered (e.g., 0%, 50%, 100%). If feeding orders are properly written and food consumption is recorded, it will be apparent after 24 hours of hospitalization whether or not the patient is consuming sufficient food to meet its RER, and whether assisted feeding is necessary. In the aforementioned study of 276 hospitalized dogs, a positive-energy balance (>95% RER) was achieved in only 27% of 821 dog days recorded, whereas a negative-energy balance (<95% RER) was observed on the majority (73%) of the dog days. The primary reasons for the 601 negative-energy balance dog days were: 1) dogs refused to eat any or all of the food offered (43%) and 2) nil per os (NPO) was ordered by the attending veterinarian (34%).[106] Currently, many hospitalized dogs do not consume their RER primarily because they refuse to eat the food offered to them.

Table 12-4. Examples of hospital feeding orders.

1. Offer 2 cans of product XX every 6 hr PO.
2. Give 100 ml of product YY gruel every 6 hr via PEG tube.
3. Administer 300 ml of parenteral solution IV every 8 hr.

Sometimes the feeding orders should contain special conditions, such as:

4. Begin feeding liquid product ZZ at 10 ml/hr via NG tube. D/C (discontinue) all feeding if vomiting begins.
5. Administer 300 ml of parenteral solution IV every 8 hr. Check urine glucose and decrease rate to 150 ml every 8 hr if urine is positive. Recheck serum K daily and increase to 40 mEq/l if below normal.
6. Give 30 ml of product YY gruel every 6 hr via PEG tube. Increase meal volume fed by 10 ml every 24 hr. Decrease volume by 50% if vomiting begins.

FEEDING PLAN

Devising a feeding plan for hospitalized patients requires complete knowledge of the case and the plan often needs to be individually tailored because of each case's unique circumstances. Nutritional plans require an understanding of the patient's metabolic state relative to changes in metabolism resulting from ongoing food deprivation (Figure 12-3). Refeeding patients in the early phase vs. refeeding in the later phases of food deprivation dictates the proportion of fat and carbohydrate in the refeeding formula. For example, the refeeding formula for a patient that has not eaten in seven days or more should contain predominantly fat as the energy fuel, as opposed to higher levels of carbohydrate (e.g., glucose).

ASSISTED FEEDING

Glutamine

Glutamine is an amino acid that plays an important role in many cellular processes. Recent studies suggest that glutamine concentrations in whole blood and skeletal muscle decrease markedly following injury and other catabolic states, thus making it "conditionally" essential. Glutamine is consumed by replicating cells such as fibroblasts, lymphocytes and intestinal epithelial cells. These cells have high glutaminase activity and low levels of intracellular glutamine. These findings may be important for patients with large wounds or inflammation associated with infection. Intravenous glutamine supplementation provided to protein-depleted rats resulted in increased villous height, increased small-bowel mucosal weight and enhanced DNA activity. The visceral glutamine requirement may be even greater during critical illness, when glutamine metabolism by the small intestine is increased. Provision of exogenous glutamine to stressed patients might better support the metabolic requirements of the small intestine and possibly decrease the rate of systemic protein catabolism. There is now considerable evidence that glutamine is important in stimulating immune function, possibly through an effect on gut-associated lymphoid tissue or through stimulation of macrophage function. Glutamine is the preferred fuel for rapidly dividing tissues such as white blood cells and intestinal mucosa.

Historically glutamine has been considered a nonessential amino acid in dogs and cats. Intestinal uptake of glutamine increases with surgery or trauma, most likely because glutamine is the preferred fuel for enterocytes. At least 80% of the published data in animals demonstrate a positive effect with glutamine-enriched feedings. Feeding a glutamine-enriched enteral diet has positive effects on: 1) protein metabolism, 2) intestinal and pancreatic repair and regeneration, 3) nutrient absorption, 4) gut-barrier function, 5) systemic and intestinal immune function and 6) animal survival. The optimal concentration of glutamine for different disease states is still under study. It is presently unclear whether glutamine must be in the free form to be beneficial or if the protein-bound form is also beneficial in maintaining gut integrity. Most enteral diets contain some protein-bound glutamine, but the glutamine concentration of these products must be estimated. Some enteral product have added free glutamine. The glutamine content of these products is often stated on the label.

Glutamine is now thought to be a conditionally essential amino acid and probably need only be administered during early periods of physiologic stress to stimulate DNA synthesis and increase mucosal mass. For example, rats undergoing abdominal radiation and fed glutamine orally for the following eight days had significantly increased jejunal villous number and height, and an increased number of mitoses per crypt, whereas non-irradiated control rats, fed the same glutamine diet, had no significant increase in mucosal cell activity. Similarly, dogs had an increased intestinal requirement for glutamine during the immediate postoperative phase (less than seven days), but uptake rates returned to normal later during the recovery phase (after 10 days).

In short-term (one-week) rat models, adding glutamine to nutritional intravenous solutions reduced some aspects of disuse intestinal atrophy and enhanced intestinal immune function. In other studies of adult rats fed parenterally, glutamine administered intravenously for six to seven days improved intestinal weight, DNA content, villous height and sucrase and lactase activities. Intravenous glutamine is expensive and should probably be limited to short-term use (one week) just before oral refeeding.

Researchers in the Netherlands investigated the effect of glutamine-supplemented enteral nutrition on infectious morbidity in patients with multiple trauma. In these studies of patients fed for five days or more, those given the glutamine-supplemented feeding had significantly less pneumonia, bacteremia and sepsis than patients given the control feeding.

BIBILOGRAPHY

Grant W, Snyder PJ. Use of L-glutamine in total parenteral nutrition. Journal of Surgical Research 1988; 44: 506-513.

Hall JB, Schmidt GA, Wood LDH, et al, eds. Principles of Critical Care, 2nd ed. New York, NY: McGraw-Hill, 1998.

Houdijik APJ, Rijnsburger ER, Jansen J, et al. Randomized trial of glutamine-enriched enteral nutrition on infectious morbidity in patients with multiple trauma. Lancet 1998; 352: 772-776.

Klimberg VS, Salloum RM, Kasper M, et al. Oral glutamine accelerates healing of the small intestine and improves outcome after whole abdominal radiation. Archives of Surgery 1990; 125: 1040-1045.

Lacey JM, Wilmore DW. Is glutamine a conditionally essential amino acid? Nutrition Reviews 1989; 97: 1033-1042.

Negro F, Cerra FB. Nutritional monitoring in the ICU: Rational and practical application. Critical Care Clinics 1988; 4: 34-47.

O'Dwyer ST, Smith RJ, Hwang TL, et al. Maintenance of small bowel mucosa with glutamine-enriched parenteral nutrition. Journal of Parenteral and Enteral Nutrition 1989; 13: 579-585.

Remillard RL, Guerino F, Dudgeon DL, et al. Intravenous glutamine or limited enteral feedings in piglets: Amelioration of 0small intestinal disuse atrophy. Journal of Nutrition 1998; 128 (Suppl.): 2723S-2726S.

Scott TE, Moellman JR. Intravenous glutamine fails to improve gut morphology after radiation injury. Journal of Parenteral and Enteral Nutrition 1992; 16: 440-444.

Souba WW, Klimberg VS, Plumley DA, et al. The role of glutamine in maintaining a healthy gut and supporting the metabolic response to injury and infection. Journal of Surgical Research 1990; 48: 383-391.

Souba WW, Roughneen PT, Goldwater DL, et al. Postoperative alterations in interorgan glutamine exchange in enterectomized dogs. Journal of Surgical Research 1987; 42: 117-125.

Souba WW. The gut as a nitrogen-processing organ in the metabolic response to critical illness. Nutritional Support Services 1988; 8: 15-22.

Vanderhoof JA, Blackwood DJ, Mohammadpour H, et al. Effects of oral supplementation of glutamine on small intestinal mucosal mass following resection. Journal of the American College of Nutrition 1992; 11: 223-227.

Ziegler TR, Young LS. Therapeutic effects of specific nutrients. In: Rombeau JL, Rolandelli RH, eds. Clinical Nutrition; Enteral and Tube Feeding, 3rd ed. Philadelphia, PA: WB Saunders Co, 1997; 112-137.

Pre-existing condition(s) requiring specific nutritional modifications (e.g., renal insufficiency) or dietary modifications (e.g., adverse reactions to foods) must be understood and incorporated into the new feeding plan for the patient. For example, a cat just diagnosed as having colitis with a history of chronic renal insufficiency will require a feeding plan compatible with both diseases.

Prior knowledge that a patient requires other medical and surgical procedures should also be taken into account when formulating an assisted-feeding plan. For example, feeding tubes can easily be placed at the end of a procedure requiring anesthesia or tranquilization. Nutritional plans should also consider the treatment plan and owners' expectations. Some nutritional plans can only be

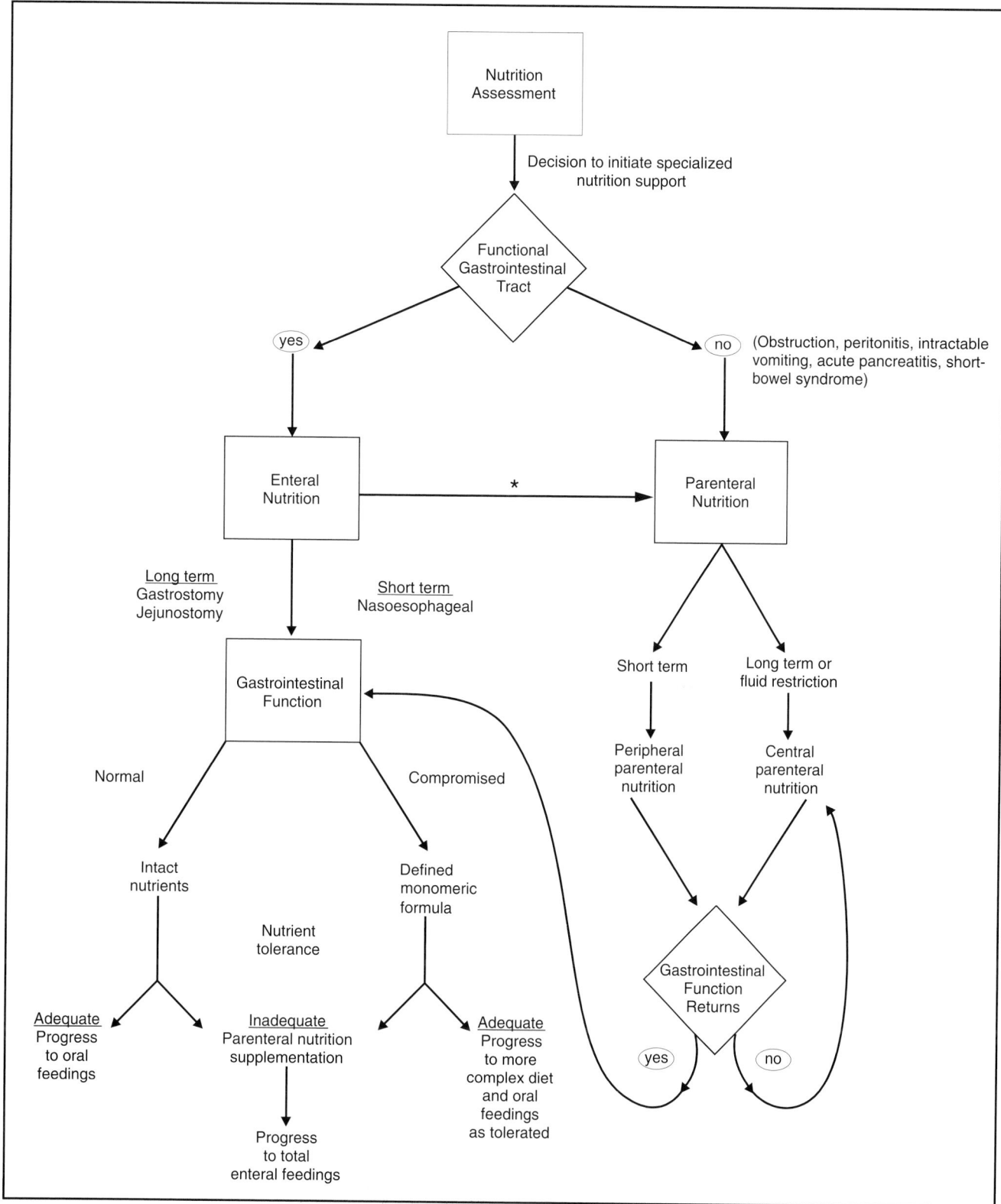

Figure 12-5. Clinical decision making algorithm for selecting the route of nutritional support. (Adapted from Hudak CM, Gallo BM, Gonce-Morton P, eds. Patient management: Gastrointestinal system. Critical Care Nursing, 7th ed. Philadelphia, PA: Lippincott, 1998; 771.)
*Nasoesophageal tube not tolerated or anesthesia not possible.

implemented while the patient is in the hospital, whereas others can be implemented at home by the owner. A feeding tube may be placed differently depending on whether it will be used by trained personnel in the hospital or by owners at home.

Patient and Feeding Method Selection

Any patient with a suspected or documented food intake below the calculated daily RER for more than three days is a good candidate for assisted feeding. Nutritional support should initially deliver sufficient amounts of a nutritionally balanced food to provide enough calories and protein to meet the RER of the patient at its current weight when the BCS is 3/5 or less. RER is primarily determined by total weight of metabolically active tissues such as skeletal and smooth muscle and visceral organs. BCS is primarily a measure of body fat stores. RER and BCS taken together are used to initially estimate the patient's daily caloric requirement. Animals with a BCS of 4/5 or 5/5 generally have the same muscle and organ mass as those with a BCS of 3/5; however, these animals have increased fat stores, which does not increase RER. It may be prudent, therefore, to calculate RER on an estimate of optimal weight in overweight patients to prevent overfeeding. (See Chapter 13.) After several days, the food intake may be increased as warranted on a case-by-case basis.

There are only two methods by which nutrients can be supplied to the body: enterally and parenterally (Figure 12-5). Enteral feeding provides adequate nutrition simply and cost effectively whether done orally or by feeding tube. Enteral feeding is preferred to parenteral feeding in most clinical cases because using the GI tract is less expensive, stimulates the immune system and avoids most metabolic complications. However, nutrients must be administered parenterally when the small intestine is not functioning adequately or accessible to meet at least the patient's nutrient requirements enterally. The two methods are not mutually exclusive; supplementing what the patient consumes voluntarily with a parenteral caloric and protein infusion is possible in most veterinary practices. Therefore, overall patient assessment, paying particular attention to GI function, is essential when deciding how assisted feeding should be provided.

Parenteral nutrition (PN) is valuable in meeting a patient's daily resting energy and amino acid requirements. However, patient selection is very important to the successful use of PN support. Patients with small intestinal impairment that is unlikely to be resolved within the next three days are candidates for PN support. PN can be used initially to meet energy and amino acid requirements for cases in which enteral access cannot be safely acquired for several days. Depending on patient size, it may not be cost effective to use PN as the only method of assisted feeding for less than a three-day course. There is a substantial startup cost to compounding (preparing) the parenteral solution. The procedure becomes cost-effective when the cost is spread over several days or more than one animal.

There is some evidence that between 48 to 72 hours are required to reverse a catabolic state and begin measurable anabolism.[50,51] Thus, proper patient selection mandates that the patient be hospitalized for at least three days because instituting PN for only one or two days is of questionable cost benefit. However, when PN is done in conjunction with some enteral intake, a course shorter than three days may be cost-effective and of great nutritional benefit. PN support should not begin until the patient is hemodynamically stable and electrolyte and acid-base abnormalities, severe tachycardia, hypotension and volume deficits have been corrected (Table 12-5).

There are many published lists of disease situations and case examples when PN could or should be instituted. The number and type of veterinary patients that would benefit from PN is greatly expanded, however, if the goal in assisted feeding is to deliver the patient's energy and amino acid needs daily by any means.[104,107] Parenteral administration of nutrients has value in patients with inflammatory (small and large) bowel disease, parvoviral enteritis and other causes of impaired GI motility, peritonitis, pancreatitis, intestinal lymphosarcoma and short-bowel syndrome (extensive small bowel resection). Neurologic patients and those that are comatose or receiving large doses of pain-control medications that cause lateral recumbency with questionable swallowing reflexes and/or risk of aspiration when oral or tube feedings are attempted also benefit from PN. PN has been used successfully in complicated cases of feline hepatic lipidosis, in animals with facial fractures, pneumonia, lung lobe torsion or contusion and diaphragmatic hernias, and in other patients that are high anesthetic risks.

PN can be administered until patients are more stable and can tolerate placement of a feeding tube. Septic and anemic patients and those with severe upper respiratory infections that cause persistently poor appetites may benefit from PN. Sometimes PN support may be as simple as augmenting oral intake with intravenous lipids to meet RER. Any patient with a poor appetite that also has large heat and/or protein losses (e.g., continuous-suction chest or abdominal drains, large areas of skin loss due to burns, degloving injuries) benefit from PN in addition to any voluntary oral food intake.

The goal of assisted feeding is to provide adequate nutrition to meet the patient's RER. The logistics of that

Table 12-5. Patient criteria for administration of parenteral nutrition.

1. The patient is hemodynamically stable and major electrolyte and acid-base abnormalities, severe tachycardia, hypotension and volume deficits have been corrected.
2. Actual or anticipated food intake is less than calculated resting energy requirement for more than three days.
3. Concurrent small intestinal disorder is known or suspected to be present, or a safe enteral nutritional access cannot be established.
4. The patient is expected to be hospitalized for at least the next three days.

Table 12-6. Pharmacologic appetite stimulants.*

Pharmaceutical agents	Effects
Cyproheptadine	Antihistamine and antiserotonin effects. Dose cats at: a) 2-4 mg per cat per os once or twice daily, b) 2 mg per cat every 12 hr. May take up to 24 hr for a response. Give at this dosage for one week and then taper.
Diazepam	Short-lived appetite stimulant with sedative properties. Dose in cats varies: a) 0.05-0.15 mg/kg IV once daily to every other day or 1 mg per os once daily, b) 0.05-0.4 mg/kg IV, IM or per os. Eating may begin within a few seconds after IV administration. Have food readily available.
Oxazepam	Short-lived appetite stimulant with sedative properties. Dose cats at 2 mg per cat (total dose) every 12 hr.
Prednisolone	Dose glucocorticoids at 0.25-0.5 mg/kg per os every day, every other day or intermittently as needed in dogs.

*Adapted from Plumb DC. Veterinary Drug Handbook, 3rd ed. White Bear, MN: Pharma Veterinary Publishing, 1999.

support should be determined on a case-by-case basis. The guidelines presented here are to help establish a foundation. But never underestimate the need for attentiveness, initiative and ingenuity in meeting the patient's nutritional needs, because no two cases are alike.

Enteral-Assisted Feeding

Enteral-assisted feeding is providing nutrients to the patient using some portion of the GI tract. Patients that cannot or will not eat but that can digest and absorb nutrients from the small intestine should receive enteral-assisted feeding. Feeding via the GI tract can be the simplest, fastest, easiest, safest, least expensive and most physiologic method of feeding patients.

Methods of Enteral Delivery

There are several methods of enteral feeding, but the first attempt usually should be oral feeding. Placing a bolus of food in the proximal portion of the mouth may stimulate the swallowing reflex and, if the patient offers no resistance, is a plausible method as long as the patient receives enough food to meet its RER. Syringe feeding a liquid product is also possible. For dogs, the syringe tip is placed between the molar teeth and cheek with the head held in a normal or lowered position; for cats, the syringe tip is placed between the four canine teeth (Figure 12-6). The patient may choose to swallow the liquid or allow it to flow out of the mouth by gravity. Some patients refuse to swallow boluses of food; therefore, forced feeding may increase the risk of food aspiration. Oral feeding should be discontinued if the patient does not swallow food voluntarily. Appetite stimulants may be used to induce food consumption in some patients; however, voluntary food intake rarely continues and the animal's RER is often not met (Table 12-6).

Orogastric tubes require placement at each feeding but may provide a useful option for one or two days of feeding. (See Appendix V.) Neonates appear to tolerate multiple daily oral tube feedings better than adults. A red rubber or polyvinyl chloride tube (8 to 24 Fr.)[a] may be used with the tip placed in the caudal esophagus or stomach. An indwelling feeding tube is the method of choice if enteral-assisted feeding is necessary for more than two days.

After an indwelling feeding tube has been placed, feeding is easier and less stressful on the patient than forced feeding or placing an orogastric tube. Nasoesophageal, pharyngostomy, esophagostomy, gastrostomy or enterostomy are potential placement sites. (See Appendix V.) Tubes should be placed in the most proximal functioning portion of the GI tract possible via the least invasive method, and whenever possible, the stomach should be used.

NASOESOPHAGEAL TUBES

Nasoesophageal tubes are generally used for three to seven days, but are occasionally used longer (weeks). Polyurethane tubes (6 to 8 Fr., 90 to 100 cm) with or without a tungsten-weighted tip[b] and silicone[c] feeding tubes (3.5 to 10 Fr., 20 to 105 cm) may be placed in the caudal esophagus or stomach. The preferred placement of all tubes originating cranial to the stomach is in the caudal esophagus to minimize gastric reflux and subsequent esophagitis. An 8-Fr. tube will pass through the nasal cavity of most dogs. A 5-Fr. tube is more comfortable in cats. Either orogastric or nasoesophageal feedings may be used in anorectic patients that do not have nasal, oral or

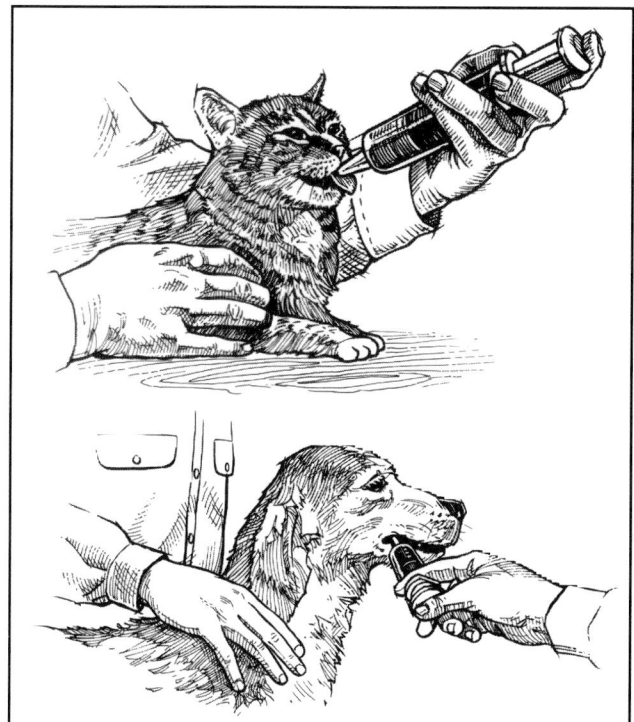

Figure 12-6. Syringe-feeding techniques for cats and dogs.

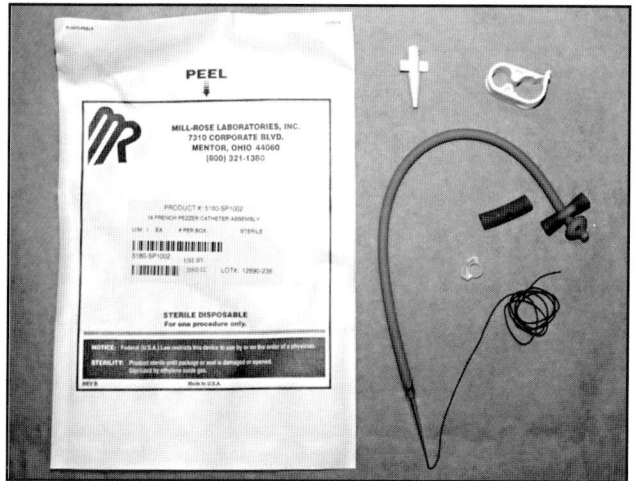

Figure 12-7. Commercial gastrostomy kit for enteral feeding (Pezzer Catheter. Mill Ross Labs, Mentor, OH, USA).

pharyngeal disease or trauma. Anesthesia or tranquilization is not necessary to place an orogastric or nasoesophageal tube. Therefore, these tubes provide enteral access to patients considered anesthetic risks. These tubes are most often used in the hospital, although nasoesophageal tubes can be used at home by conscientious owners. See Appendix V for a description of tube placement.

PHARYNGOSTOMY/ESOPHAGOSTOMY/ GASTROSTOMY TUBES

Pharyngostomy or esophagostomy tubes (8 to 16 Fr.) may be placed in patients with disease or trauma to the nasal or oral cavity. The tip of the tube is placed in the caudal esophagus and the tube can be used for long-term (weeks to months) in-hospital or home feedings.

For patients in which the pharynx and esophagus must be bypassed, gastrostomy tubes (mushroom-tipped, 16 to

Table 12-7. Selected commercial products used for enteral feeding of veterinary patients.*

	Form	Energy (kcal/ml or g)	Osmolality (mOsm/kg)	Protein (g/100 kcal)	Fat (kcal %)	CHO (kcal %)	Fatty acid ratio (n-6:n-3)	Arginine (mg/100 kcal)	Glutamine (mg/100 kcal)	Carnitine (mg/100 kcal)	Tube feeding (Fr.)
Abbott CliniCare Canine	L	1	230	5.5	55	25	6.4:1	249	550	na	5/8**
Abbott CliniCare Feline	L	1	235	8.6	45	25	6.4:1	350	720	na	5/8**
Abbott CliniCare RF Feline	L	1	165	5.6	57	21	6.4:1	350	600	na	5/8**
Hill's Prescription Diet Canine/Feline a/d	MH	1.3	na	8.8	53	12	2.2:1	372	1,180	1.15	18***
Iams Eukanuba Maximum-Calorie/Canine & Feline	MH	2.1	na	7.4	66	5	8.3:1	417	na	na	18***
Purina CNM CV-Formula	M	1.4	na	8.7	50	18	na	na	na	na	na
Select Care Canine Development Formula	M	0.9	na	8	30	42	10.3:1	na	na	na	na
Select Care Feline Development Formula	M	1	na	10.4	54	10	5.3:1	na	na	na	na
Waltham/Pedigree Concentration Diet/Canine	M	1.4	na	11.4	48	23	na	na	na	na	na
Waltham/Whiskas Concentration Diet/Feline	M	1.2	na	11	64	3	na	na	na	na	na
Waltham/Pedigree Concentration Instant Diet/Canine	L	1.5	na	14.3	37	25	na	na	na	na	5/8**
Waltham/Whiskas Concentration Instant Diet/Feline	L	1.3	na	11	48	15	na	na	na	na	5/8**

Key: L = liquid, M = moist, MH = moist homogenized, FA = fatty acid, CHO = soluble carbohydrate, na = information not available or not applicable.
*These products meet or exceed AAFCO nutrient profiles for intended species.
**5/8 French is the smallest tube size using a feeding pump/catheter-tip syringe and comfortable pressure.
***18 French is the smallest tube size using a catheter-tip syringe and comfortable pressure.

Table 12-8. Selected commercial human products used for enteral feeding of veterinary patients.*

	Energy (kcal/ml)	Osmolality (mOsm/kg)	Protein (g/100 kcal)	Fat (kcal %)	CHO (kcal %)	Arginine (mg/100 kcal)	Glutamine (mg/100 kcal)	Carnitine (mg/100 kcal)	Comments	Tube feeding (Fr.)
Polymeric liquid products										
Ensure HN (Ross Laboratories)	1.1	470	4.2	30	53	163	452	0	No MCTs	5/8**
Impact (Sandoz Nutrition)	1	375	5.6	25	53	na	350	na	27% MCTs; menhaden fish oil	8***
Jevity (Ross Laboratories)	1.1	310	4.2	29	54	146	484	11	20% MCTs; soluble (soy) fiber	8***
Osmolite HN (Ross Laboratories)	1.1	300	4.2	29	54	155	436	11	19% MCTs	5/8**
Pulmocare (Ross Laboratories)	1.5	475	4.2	55	28	220	333	10	20% MCTs	8**
Sustacal (Mead Johnson)	1	650	6.1	21	55	220	1,280	na	No MCTs	8***
Monomeric liquid products										
Peptamen (CliniTec Nutrition)	1	260	4.4	33	51	118	730	na	70% MCTs	5/8**
Perative (Ross Laboratories)	1.3	385	5.2	25	55	1,130	415	10	40% MCTs	5/8**
Vital HN (Ross Laboratories)	1	500	4.1	9	74	200	210	0	32% MCTs	5/8**
Vivonex (Sandoz Nutrition)	1	630	2.1	2	83	292	491	na	No MCTs	5/8**

Key: MCT = medium-chain triglycerides, CHO = soluble carbohydrate, na = information not available.
*Note: Veterinary enteral products should be routinely used rather than the commercial human enteral products listed in this table. Veterinary products are complete and balanced for the intended species, which might not be the case for human products. Polymeric and monomeric products listed in this table are appropriate for short-term or emergency use in dogs and cats.
**5/8 French is the smallest red rubber tube size using a pump; 8 French is the smallest sideport red rubber tube using a 35-ml Luer-tip syringe and comfortable pressure.
***8 French is the smallest sideport red rubber tube size using a pump or a 35-ml Luer-tip syringe and comfortable pressure.

Table 12-9. Selected dry commercial veterinary products used for feeding hospitalized veterinary patients.

	Energy (kcal/g)	Protein (g/100 kcal)	Protein (kcal %)	Fat (kcal %)	CHO (kcal %)	FA ratio (n-6:n-3)	Arginine (mg/100 kcal)
Canine products							
Hill's Prescription Diet Canine a/d	4.5	7.9	30	47	23	7.6:1	438
Iams Eukanuba Maximum-Calorie/Canine	4.7	7.8	31	54	15	5.1:1	na
Select Care Canine Development Formula	3.6	6.6	23	34	43	7.0:1	na
Feline products							
Iams Eukanuba Maximum-Calorie/Feline	4.9	8.2	31	54	15	4.9:1	na
Select Care Feline Development Formula	4	8.1	28	47	25	5.2:1	na

Key: CHO = soluble carbohydrate, FA = fatty acid, na = information not available.

22 Fr.)[d] (Figure 12-7) can be placed either intraoperatively or percutaneously using an endoscope or a gastrostomy tube introduction device.[e,108] Gastrostomy tubes are also recommended for long-term feeding (weeks to months) if needed, and have generally replaced pharyngostomy tubes, even when the esophagus is normal. Gastrostomy tubes are convenient and safe for in-hospital and at-home feedings. See Appendix V for descriptions of tube placement.

Any tube that has been placed into the esophagus or stomach allows bolus or meal-type feeding schedules because the stomach acts as a food reservoir. The exception to this rule is the patient that cannot tolerate bolus feeding to the stomach without vomiting. Such patients benefit from a slow, continuous drip administration (by pump or gravity flow) of food to the stomach. Most veterinary patients receive bolus feedings of enteral nutritional support via nasoesophageal or gastrostomy feeding tubes.

JEJUNOSTOMY TUBES

Jejunostomy tubes (J-tubes, 5 to 8 Fr.) are placed within the small intestine, ideally at the time of exploratory celiotomy, to bypass the proximal GI tract.[109] Jejunostomy tubes may also be placed by mini-laporatomy.[f] Another method of jejunostomy tube placement is to thread a small feeding tube through a larger esophagostomy, pharyngostomy or gastrostomy feeding tube and place the tip of the smaller tube in the jejunum. A feeding tube with a tungsten-weighted tip may be threaded through the pylorus into the jejunum using an endoscope or during a surgical procedure with the cranial end exiting through a larger tube in the stomach, pharynx or esophagus.[110] There is risk, however, that even a weighted-tip tube will be returned to the stomach by reverse peristalsis.[f] Ideally, food should be administered through jejunostomy tubes at a slow, continuous drip delivered by a pump. Some patients, however, will tolerate frequent small-bolus feedings. See Appendix V for descriptions of tube placement.

Selecting an Enteral Food

Food selection depends on tube size and location within the GI tract, the availability and cost of products and the experience of the clinician. Commercial foods available for enteral use in veterinary patients can be divided into two major types: 1) liquid or modular products and 2) blended pet foods. Nasal and jejunostomy tubes usually have a small diameter (<8 Fr.), which requires use of liquid foods. Orogastric, pharyngostomy, esophagostomy and gastrostomy tubes have large diameters (>8 Fr.) and are suitable for blended pet foods. Tables 12-7 and 12-8 list commercial foods available for enteral use. Table 12-9 lists selected dry commercial foods marketed for recovery of critically ill patients. These foods may be used when patients are able to eat sufficiently on their own; alternatively, the patient may be fed the food it was accustomed to eating before the injury or illness. The latter approach reduces the number of food changes that ultimately will need to be made.

LIQUID FOODS AND MODULES

In general, human liquid foods cost more than veterinary liquid products. Most human liquid foods are adequate for adult dogs but are too low in protein for cats, puppies and adult dogs with increased protein losses (e.g., protein-losing enteropathies, drains). Human liquid enteral products may not contain adequate concentrations of protein, taurine, arginine and arachidonic acid for long-term feeding of cats, but are satisfactory for fewer than seven days.

Liquid foods are of two basic types: 1) elemental or monomeric and 2) polymeric. Foods said to be "elemental" are not truly elemental, but contain nutrients in small hydrolyzed absorbable forms and are best described as monomeric. The proteins are usually present as free amino acids, small dipeptides or tripeptides or larger hydrolyzed protein fractions. The fat source is often an oil of mixed (medium- and long-chain) fatty acids and the carbohydrate sources are mono-, di- and trisaccharides. There are several liquid foods on the human medical market that are positioned as monomeric or hydrolyzed diets and are suitable when initially refeeding dogs and cats. These monomeric products are homogenized liquids that can be fed through any feeding tube including a J-tube. Monomeric foods are indicated in disease conditions such as inflammatory bowel disease, lymphangiectasia, refeeding parvoviral enteritis and pancreatitis cases and any other condition in which a patient's digestive capabilities are questionable (Table 12-9).

Polymeric products contain mixtures of more complex nutrients. Protein is supplied in the form of large peptides (e.g., casein or whey). Carbohydrates are usually supplied as corn starch or syrup, and fats are provided by medium-chain triglycerides (MCT) or vegetable oil. These foods require normal digestive processes and are appropriate for most veterinary clinical situations, especially when a small tube (<8 Fr.) has been placed and particular nutrient profiles are needed (e.g., low sodium, high protein, soluble fiber) (Table 12-9).

One of the leading liquid veterinary foods[g] is a polymeric form that meets the current AAFCO nutrient allowances for adult dogs and cats. This product is a homogenized liquid containing 1 kcal/ml (4.2 kJ/ml) and

Table 12-10. Modules for augmenting foods.

Products	Key features
ProMod (Ross Laboratories)	23.6 g protein/100 kcal, 18.2 g glutamine/100 g powder, 1.48 kcal/ml reconstituted
Arginine (various)	Available OTC as 500-mg capsules in most pharmacies and health food stores
Taurine (various)	Available OTC as 250-mg and 500-mg tablets in most pharmacies and health food stores
Glutamine (various)	Available as powder from chemical catalogs and most pharmacies and health food stores
Carnitine (various)	Available OTC as capsules and powder from chemical catalogs and in most pharmacies and health food stores
Medium-chain triglyceride oil (Mead Johnson)	Fractionated coconut oil, 8.3 kcal/ml
Corn syrup (various)	Mostly maltose, 2.9 kcal/ml
Psyllium fiber (Metamucil Regular, Searle)	Available OTC as a powder containing 17% crude protein, 53% total dietary fiber, 44% soluble fiber
Psyllium fiber (FiberAll Regular, Rydelle Labs)	Available OTC as a powder containing 8% crude protein, 85% total dietary fiber, 72% soluble fiber
Pectin (various)	Available OTC as a powder containing <1% crude protein and ~90% soluble fiber

Key: OTC = over the counter.

is usually accepted better than human liquid products containing MCT oil. This liquid food is the best option currently available in North America when small-diameter nasogastric and jejunostomy feeding tubes have been placed, or when continuous drip feedings are necessary. Historically, these polymeric foods have caused diarrhea in cats after 24 hours of feeding. However, the manufacturer recently reformulated the product to reduce the incidence of diarrhea. The number of osmotically active particles was decreased by replacing a small-chain maltodextrin source with a larger-chain maltodextrin, and the caseinate source no longer contains lactose, thereby eliminating a lactase degradation process.

Several liquid milk replacer products are available; however, these products are not appropriate to feed to adult dogs and cats. They typically contain lactose, have high osmolarity, are lower in caloric density and do not meet AAFCO nutrient allowances for adult animals.

Module products are concentrated powdered or liquid forms of nutrients and are primarily supplemental (Table 12-10). These products may be added to a liquid product to increase the concentration of a specific nutrient. There are protein, fat and carbohydrate modules (e.g., casein powder, vegetable oil or corn syrup). For example, a protein modular product may be added to a human liquid product for an animal with high protein requirements. Soluble fiber can be added to these foods using psyllium husk fiber or pectin; however, these fibers may block the small side ports in 8-Fr. and smaller tubes.

BLENDED PET FOODS

Blended pet foods refer to commercial products nutritionally complete and balanced according to AAFCO allowances for dogs and cats. These products can easily be blended with a liquid to make a consistency that flows through a feeding tube. Some products have a blended texture, a high water content and very small particle size, whereas others are products that must be blenderized with water and may have to be strained to remove particulate matter.

The best recommendation when using the blended pet food method is to use a product that has been tested in feeding trials and is proven to be balanced and complete for dogs or cats. These products are more readily available, better tolerated and less expensive than the human liquid foods. These pet food products contain essential amino acids and essential micronutrients properly balanced to the caloric density of the food. Fewer medical complications (e.g., diarrhea) are likely to result. However, blended products are more likely to plug the feeding tube if the tube is not properly flushed after feeding. Patients may later consume the pet food orally, eliminating a diet change when the patient's appetite returns and the tube has been removed. These products are appropriate for patients in catabolic states that are using fat and protein substrates from body stores. When using small-diameter (<8 Fr.) feeding tubes, it will be necessary to dilute the pet food with water, which dilutes the caloric density. Blenderized moist veterinary therapeutic foods may have a place in assisted feeding of patients with specific disease conditions. (See sidebar "Disease-Specific Nutritional Support.")

HUMAN BABY FOODS

Veterinarians have fed human baby foods packed in jars because some canine and feline patients voluntarily eat these products. In general, the meat and/or egg baby foods are high in protein (30 to 70% DM) and fat (20 to 60% DM), which compares favorably with blended pet food products. However, baby foods are more costly, contain only one or two food types (protein, protein/grain) and do not contain a balanced mixture of other essential nutrients (amino acids, vitamins and minerals). For example, these products contain only 10% of the calcium required by dogs and cats, and therefore have a large inverse calcium-phosphorus ratio. Some products contain onion powder, which has resulted in Heinz body formation in cats.[111] These products will flow through 8-Fr. or larger feeding tubes and may be used on a very limited, short-term basis when an appropriate pet food is unavailable. The human and veterinary liquid products have a better nutritional profile than do the human baby food products.

Enteral Feeding Schedule

The feeding schedule is often determined by the patient's ability to tolerate food and the logistics of feeding. Feeding an amount equal to the patient's RER during the first 24 hours of food re-introduction, if physically tolerated, is recommended. Initially feeding one-third of RER and then increasing the amount by one-third every 24 hours is a more cautious approach to initial feeding, but isn't always necessary. Foods should be warmed to room temperature, but not higher than body temperature before feeding.

Food boluses must be infused slowly (over approximately one minute) to allow gastric expansion. Daily food dosage should be divided into several meals according to the expected stomach capacity. Capacities for cats and dogs are 5 to 10 ml/kg body weight during initial food re-introduction. Maximum capacities as high as 45 to 90 ml/kg body weight have been measured in cats and dogs when fully re-alimented. Most often, meeting the patient's RER can be done in volumes far less than these maximums. Salivating, gulping, retching and even vomiting may occur when too much food has been infused or when the infusion rate is too fast.

Research in people has demonstrated that the stomach does not "shrink" during a prolonged fast, but rather the stretch receptors are more sensitive and stimulated by a smaller volume when refeeding occurs.[112] Feeding should be stopped at the first sign of retching or salivating, the meal size reduced by 50% for 24 hours and then increased by 25% gradually. Foods provided via J-tubes must be infused slowly and often in either very small quantities or by a slow gravity drip or enteral pump with an hourly rate equal to RER/24 hours because the jejunum is volume sensitive.

Each meal must be followed by a water flush to clear the feeding tube of food residue. When the patient is volume sensitive, it is important to know the minimum volume required to flush the tube. The patient's daily fluid requirement must also be met and additional tap water may be administered through the feeding tube to meet that requirement. Liquid oral medications may also be administered easily through feeding tubes. Plugged feeding tubes can be cleared by filling the tube with water or a nonalcoholic carbonated beverage and allowing time for the food plug to dissolve. In general, endport tubes are easier to maintain than sideport tubes because food tends to become trapped in the blind end of sideport tubes. All tubes except orogastric and nasoesophageal tubes require standard every-other-day bandage care.

Parenteral-Assisted Feeding

Nomenclature

The term "parenteral" indicates administration of nutrients in a manner other than through the GI tract. Parenteral could therefore be administration by intravenous, intramuscular, subcutaneous, intraosseous or intraperitoneal routes, but not via the alimentary canal. PN has been further characterized in human medicine as total or partial (relative to meeting all nutrient requirements), central or peripheral (relative to venous access). A common misnomer associated with PN, originally from the human literature, is the term "hyperalimentation." This incorrectly implies the administration of nutrients via the GI tract in excess of need. Use of the term "parenteral nutrition" is encouraged, and used throughout this text because it simply and correctly identifies a general method of administering nutrients to a patient.

Another common misnomer is total parenteral nutrition (TPN). In veterinary medicine, parenteral nutrition is not total because there isn't a need to worry about meeting all essential amino and fatty acids, fat- and water-soluble vitamins and macro, trace and ultra-trace element requirements as there is in people. In veterinary medicine, clini-

cians attempt to meet the patient's estimated RER and most (but not all) of the patient's requirements for essential amino and fatty acids, and supply some water-soluble vitamins and selected macro and trace elements.

There are several valid reasons why partial parenteral nutrition, rather than TPN, is used in veterinary medicine. The foremost reason is the comparatively short period parenteral nutrition is administered to animals (three to 14 days for animals vs. weeks to years in people). In people, long-term feeding implies 10 days and longer. The shorter time frame of assisted feeding of pets allows omission of less immediately essential nutrients (e.g., fat-soluble vitamins). Until there is a demand by pet owners for a longer period of support (weeks to months), parenteral nutrition support in animals will be composed of only the most immediately essential nutrients (i.e., electrolytes, energy and amino acids).

The second reason for partial parenteral nutrition is that only some of the nutrients are readily available in water-soluble form. Adding all available nutrients to a PN solution requires multiple single nutrient additions of specially prepared water-insoluble products. Such nutrients are cost prohibitive and difficult to justify on a short-term basis. As more nutrient compounds are added to the solution, the risk of incompatibility increases and chances for an insoluble precipitate forming are greater. PN solutions currently used in veterinary medicine contain only the less expensive essential nutrients. PN solutions are therefore limited by necessity, pharmacokinetics, cost and exact nutritional knowledge.

Parenteral Products

Compounding a PN solution is beyond the scope of most veterinary practices; however, most veterinary practices can administer parenteral nutrition to patients. Individual PN solutions of dextrose, lipid and amino acids can be combined as a "three-in-one" solution, also called a total nutrient admixture (TNA). TNA in veterinary medicine refers to a one-fluid bag containing a sufficient mixture of parenteral solutions to meet a particular patient's fluid, energy, amino acid, electrolyte and B-vitamin needs for a 24-hour period. This is a very convenient method requiring only one bag, one infusion pump and one administration set. Almost any infusion pump can be used. The formulation is designed specifically for the patient based on the current RER, daily fluid and electrolyte requirements, approximate protein need and ability to handle dextrose vs. lipid.

The TNA solution should be calculated to first meet the patient's RER and protein needs with water-soluble vitamins and trace minerals (if available) added. Second, the total fluid volume is adjusted with standard crystalloid solution (e.g., lactated Ringer's solution, Plasmalyte A) to meet the patient's daily fluid requirement. Then electrolytes are adjusted, if necessary (Table 12-11). Alternatively, the additional crystalloid fluids with added potassium may be administered via a separate intravenous line piggybacked into the same catheter.

ENERGY SOLUTIONS

A TNA solution should supply sufficient energy to meet, but not exceed, the patient's daily RER. It is becoming increasingly evident that the negative consequences of PN administration (i.e., metabolic complications) are due to administer-

Table 12-11. Standard total nutrient admixture (TNA) formulations.

PART A. CALCULATION WORKSHEET

Patient data needed
1. Current body weight in kg
2. Calculate resting energy requirement (RER) as kcal/day
3. Expected fluid volume in ml/kg/day
4. Calories from fat as a percent
5. Protein-calorie ratio as g/100 kcal RER
6. Potassium concentration as mEq/l

Parenteral solution formula

1. Determine volume of fat and dextrose needed daily
Calculate RER calories from fat
Calculate volume of 20% lipid needed
Calculate RER calories from dextrose
Calculate volume of 50% dextrose needed
2. Determine volume of amino acid solution needed daily
Calculate g of protein needed
Calculate volume of 8.5% amino acid needed
3. Determine volume of B vitamins and trace minerals needed daily
Calculate B vitamins needed
Calculate trace minerals needed
Daily parenteral nutrition formula

4. Determine volume of crystalloid solution needed to meet daily fluid requirement
Daily fluid volume requested
Volume required is daily total – PN total
5. Determine phosphorus supplementation
Phosphorus from amino acids
Desired final phosphorus concentration in the TNA
6. Determine potassium supplementation
K⁺ from lactated Ringer's solution
K⁺ from amino acid solution
Total K⁺ in TNA solution
Desired final K⁺ concentration in TNA
KCl (2.0 mEq/ml) required

Feline example
4.1 kg
200 kcal/day
70 ml/kg
80%
4 g/100 kcal RER
30 mEq/l

200 x 0.80 = 160 kcal
160 kcal ÷ 2 kcal/ml = **80 ml/day**
200-160 = 40 kcal
40 kcal ÷ 1.7 kcal/ml = **24 ml/day**

RER x 4 g/100 kcal = 8 g protein/day
8 g ÷ 0.085 g/ml = **95 ml/day**

RER x 1 ml/100 kcal = **2 ml/day**
RER x 1 ml/100 kcal = **2 ml/day**

80 ml of 20% lipid emulsion
24 ml of 50% dextrose
95 ml of 8.5% amino acid with electrolytes
2 ml of vitamin-B complex
2 ml of trace elements
Total = 203 ml

4.1 kg x 70 ml/kg = 287 ml/day
287 – 204 = 83 ml

95 x 30 mM/l = 2.9 mM
= 10 mM/l x 287= 2.9 mM (no phosphorus is needed)

83 ml x 4 mEq/l = 0.3 mEq
95 ml x 60 mEq/l = 5.7 mEq
0.3 mEq + 5.7 mEq = 6.0 mEq
30 mEq/l x 287 ml = 8.6 mEq
8.6 mEq – 6.0 mEq = 2.6 mEq ÷ 2.0 = 1.3 ml

PART B. FELINE FORMULA EXAMPLE

Animal data
Body weight
RER
Calories from fat
Calories from glucose
Protein-calorie ratio
Fluid volume
Potassium concentration
Parenteral solution
50% dextrose
20% lipid emulsion
8.5% amino acids with electrolytes
Potassium chloride
Vitamin-B complex
Trace elements
Lactated Ringer's solution
Total fluid volume

4.1 kg
200 kcal/day
80%
20%
4 g/100 kcal (adequate for most cats)
70 ml/kg (maintenance fluid volume)
30 mEq/l

24 ml providing 40 kcal
80 ml providing 160 kcal
95 ml providing 8 g of amino acids
1.3 ml
2 ml
2 ml
83 ml
288 ml

This final solution is a 500-ml bag containing 200 kcal (80% from fat), adequate nitrogen, major B vitamins with the following electrolyte profile
Sodium
Potassium
Magnesium
Phosphorus
Chloride
Calcium
Zinc
Copper
Manganese
Chromium
Final osmolarity
Approximate cost = $100 for a three-day supply

61.6 mEq/l
29.5 mEq/l
3.3 mEq/l
9.8 mM/l
55.4 mEq/l
0.8 mEq/l
2 mg
1 mg
0.2 mg
8 mg
755 mOsm/l

(Continued on next page.)

Table 12-11. Standard total nutrient admixture (TNA) formulations. (*Continued from previous page.*)

PART C. CANINE FORMULA EXAMPLE
Animal data

Body weight	14 kg
RER	507 kcal/day
Calories from fat	90%
Calories from glucose	10%
Protein-calorie ratio	3 g/100 kcal (adequate for most dogs)
Fluid volume	70 ml/kg (maintenance fluid volume requested)
Potassium concentration	20 mEq/l

Parenteral solution

50% dextrose	30 ml providing 51 kcal
20% lipid emulsion	227 ml providing 454 kcal
8.5% amino acids with electrolytes	178 ml providing 15 g of amino acids
Potassium phosphate	1.4 ml
Vitamin-B complex	5 ml
Trace elements	5 ml
Plasmalyte A	516 ml
Total fluid volume	1,014 ml

This final solution is a 1-liter bag containing 507 kcal (90% from fat), adequate nitrogen, major B vitamins with the following electrolyte profile

Sodium	88.0 mEq/l
Potassium	20.3 mEq/l
Magnesium	3.5 mEq/l
Phosphorus	9.9 mM/l
Chloride	65.5 mEq/l
Calcium	0 mEq/l
Zinc	5 mg
Copper	2 mg
Chromium	20 mg
Manganese	0.5 mg
Final osmolarity	528 mOsm/l
Approximate cost = $130 for a three-day supply	

ing energy in excess of patient expenditure.[85-87,113,114] Initially in people, PN solutions containing dextrose and "liberal" amounts of protein were administered at rates providing 3,000 to 5,000 kcal/day (12.55 to 20.92 MJ) to a 70-kg person.[115] This "hyperalimentation" actually increased catabolism by exceeding the patients' endogenous usage of energy and produced multiple adverse metabolic effects. There has been a more recent move toward feeding people at RER instead of RER times a disease factor.[116-118] Currently, patients are given 1,000 to 2,400 kcal (4.2 to 10 MJ) with 75 to 100 g of protein per day and, as a result, metabolic complications are observed less frequently.[99] Energy is routinely provided to veterinary patients receiving PN as a combination of dextrose and lipid. Several companies manufacture dextrose and lipid products of various strengths and attributes (Table 12-12). The vast majority of TNA solutions formulated for veterinary patients use 50% dextrose and 20% lipid. Dextrose solutions range from 2.5 to 70% glucose, which is usually derived from hydrolyzed corn starch. Osmolarity ranges from 126 to 3,530 mOsm/l and is directly proportional to the glucose concentration.[119] Dextrose solutions are maintained in the pH range of 3.5 to 5.5 and are sterilized by autoclave to prolong shelf life at room temperature.

Lipid (10, 20 or 30%) products (Table 12-12), reintroduced in the 1970s, contain emulsified fat particles (0.5 μm) of soybean oil and/or safflower oil, glycerin and linoleic and linolenic acids. Earlier formulations made with cottonseed oil were taken off the market in 1965 because they caused severe adverse reactions in people. Lipid emulsions are maintained in a pH range of 6.0 to 8.9 and have an osmolarity range of 260 to 310 mOsm/l, which effectively decreases the final osmolarity of the

TNA.[119] Today, dextrose and lipids are readily available and both are strongly recommended as sources of energy in a TNA solution.

Dextrose-Fat Ratio

When PN is begun, most patients have not consumed their daily RER for at least three days, and are more likely even further along in the course of food deprivation (Day 5 or more). The proportion of glucose to lipid in the PN solution should mirror the current metabolic condition of the liver. Fewer metabolic complications will arise if the glucose-lipid ratio in the PN solution is well tolerated by the liver.

PN is rarely instituted during the early phases of food deprivation (less than three days of anorexia); however, if PN is indicated, canine patients should tolerate a moderate percentage of their calculated RER as dextrose. For example, dogs in this early phase of food deprivation maintain blood glucose levels by glycogenolysis and therefore should receive 60 to 90% of the RER as dextrose. However, feline patients in the early phases of food deprivation maintain blood glucose levels by lipolysis and gluconeogenesis, and should receive 60 to 90% of their RER from lipid.

By Day 5 of food deprivation or longer, in the authors' opinion, patients should receive the majority (60 to 90%) of their calculated RER as lipid because the liver is using glycerol from endogenous fat for gluconeogenesis. Giving high doses of glucose at a time when the animal's natural response is to minimize glucose usage is unlikely to result in optimal glucose use. This is the most likely cause of the hyperglycemia commonly reported as a complication in people and veterinary patients. There is evidence to suggest the proportion of calories needed from fat increases

ASSISTED FEEDING

Table 12-12. Nutritional comparison of parenteral products.

Products	Caloric density (kcal/ml)	Osmolarity (mOsm/l)	Amino acids (g/100 ml)	Fat (g/100 ml)	Carbohydrate (g/100 ml)	Electrolytes	Comments
Amino acids 8.5% without electrolytes (Abbott, Baxter)	na	785-860	8.5	0	0	Few	Contains all essential amino acids except taurine, nitrogen 1.3 g/100 ml, pH 5.3-6.5, available in 500- and 1,000-ml sizes.
Amino acids 8.5% with electrolytes (Abbott, Baxter)	na	1,160	8.5	0	0	Yes	Contains all essential amino acids except taurine, nitrogen 1.3 g/100 ml, pH 5.3-6.5, electrolytes Na, K, Mg, Cl, PO_4, available in 500- and 1,000-ml sizes.
ProcalAmine (McGaw)	0.25	735	3	0	3	Yes	Contains 3% glycerol and 3% amino acids, nitrogen 4.6 g/1,000 ml, pH 6.5-7.0, electrolytes Na, K, Mg, Cl, PO_4, available in 500- and 1,000-ml sizes. Contains 13 nonprotein kcal/ml and 22.5 g amino acids/100 nonprotein kcal as is. Mix 775 ml ProcalAmine with 300 ml 20% lipid to get 1,075 ml of a 3.2 g protein/100 nonprotein kcal solution.
Lipid 10% (Abbott, Baxter)	1.1	268	0	10	0	No	Contains soybean and/or safflower oil, glycerin, linoleic and linolenic acids, egg yolk as phospholipid emulsifier, pH 6.0-8.9, available in 50-, 100-, 250- and 500-ml sizes.
Lipid 20% (Abbott, Baxter)	2	268	0	20	0	No	Contains soybean and/or safflower oil, glycerin, linoleic and linolenic acids, egg yolk as phospholipid emulsifier, pH 6.0-8.9, available in 50-, 100-, 250- and 500-ml sizes.
Dextrose 2.5-70% (various)	0.09-2.4	126-3,535	0	0	2.5-70	No	Contains hydrolyzed corn starch, pH 3.5-5.5, available in 50- and 500-ml sizes.

Key: na = not available.

markedly (>60%) in starving and diseased states. For example, in an acute sepsis model, rats given a fat-free glucose solution parenterally had increased and extensive mobilization of endogenous fat. Control, nonseptic rats had no mobilization of endogenous fat when a high glucose solution was given.[103] A measured shift in the preferred fuel occurred from glucose to endogenous fat in these septic animals. Several studies in people demonstrated that fat is well oxidized in the septic state, and as the sepsis worsens the amount of fat oxidized increases and the glucose oxidative capacity decreases.[120] Dogs with a septic abdomen receiving PN with both glucose and lipid maintained nitrogen balance better than dogs receiving glucose-only PN solutions.[121]

There is a consensus, based on a variety of parameters, that the optimal caloric source is a mixture of glucose and fat; however, the precise ratio is unknown.[103] The reasoning is that a mixed fuel source should decrease the possibility of fat deposition in the liver when any metabolic pathway that handles either fat or glucose becomes overloaded. Studies have shown that serum glucose, lactate, pyruvate, free fatty acid, triacylglyceride and insulin concentrations were more stable and more closely approximated the normal postabsorptive state in people when all three substrates were administered (i.e., simultaneous fat infusion with glucose and amino acids), as opposed to fat-free PN solutions.[122] The old recommendation that fat

Complications of Fat Administration

LIVER PATHOLOGY

Administering parenteral total nutrient admixture (TNA) solutions to human adults and infants for long periods (weeks to months) has been reported to cause steatosis, intrahepatic cholestasis, periportal inflammation and even cirrhosis. Fatty infiltration of the liver is the earliest and most common change noted. This undesirable relationship between long-term parenteral feeding and hepatic changes is thought to be multifactorial, but is not yet well understood. These complications are not specific to parenteral nutrition or lipid emulsions. Lipid additions are now encouraged, even in patients with hepatic disease, because replacing a portion of the glucose with lipid ameliorates some hepatic pathology. Choline is not routinely included in TNA solutions but is a conditionally essential nutrient in people. Studies have correlated choline deficiency and hepatic steatosis in people receiving total parenteral nutrition (TPN). Investigators studying TPN-fed rats reported reversal of hepatic complications with both oral and intravenous choline administration. Today, it is extremely rare for a veterinary patient to receive a parenteral nutrition solution for more than two or three weeks; therefore, hepatic complications from prolonged parenteral nutrition administration are unlikely, though choline is an essential nutrient in dogs and cats.

COAGULOPATHIES AND THROMBOCYTOPENIA

Lipid infusions have been reported to cause fat overload syndrome in people and, in the past, were associated with hyperlipidemia, hemolytic anemia, coagulopathies, thrombocytopenia and respiratory impairment with liver and renal dysfunction. Most adverse reports were associated with the use of a cottonseed oil emulsion, which was withdrawn from the market in the 1960s. Only isolated cases have been reported to occur with the soybean or safflower oil emulsions used today, and no cases have been associated with the relatively limited use of medium-chain triglyceride (MCT) emulsions. Thrombocytopenia has been reported as a rare complication of soybean oil emulsions and is now considered an idiosyncratic reaction. In vitro, lipids have been shown to have a limited effect on shortening prothrombin times, but this effect may be due to the phospholipids or vitamin K in emulsions. Reduced aggregation of platelets has also been produced in vitro and at high triglyceride concentrations. It is important to emphasize that slow continuous infusion of lipids has little or no effect on platelet number, aggregation or bleeding time. Fat infusion rates for people have been recommended at 0.10 to 0.15 g/kg body weight/hour. Infusing veterinary patients with parenteral nutrition solutions containing 80 to 90% of nonprotein calories as fat over a 24-hour period is usually within these guidelines.

ALTERED IMMUNE FUNCTION

Lipid infusions have also been associated with altered and impaired immune function. Major controversies exist about the role lipid emulsions play in affecting reticuloendothelial cells and eicosanoid, cytokine and complement synthesis. Many of these effects have not been observed with slow infusion of pure soybean oil or during rapid infusion of MCT emulsions. One review of many studies concluded there was no evidence supporting the opinion that lipid infusions detrimentally alter immune function.

BIBLIOGRAPHY

Carpentier YA, Gossum AV, Dubois DY, et al. Lipid metabolism in parenteral nutrition. In: Rombeau JL, Caldwell MD, eds. Clinical Nutrition; Parenteral Nutrition, 2nd ed. Philadelphia, PA: WB Saunders Co, 1993; 35-74.

Carter AL, Frenkel R. The relationship of choline and carnitine in the choline deficient rat. Journal of Nutrition 1978; 108: 1748-1754.

Freund HR. Abnormalities of liver function and hepatic damage associated with total parenteral nutrition. Nutrition 1991; 7: 1-6.

Herson VC, Block C, Eisenfield L, et al. Effects of intravenous fat infusion on neonatal neutrophil and platelet function. Journal of Parenteral and Enteral Nutrition 1989; 13: 620-622.

Jensen GL, Mascioli ES, Seidner DL, et al. Parenteral infusion of long- and medium-chain triglycerides and reticuloendothelial system function in man. Journal of Parenteral and Enteral Nutrition 1990; 14: 467-471.

Miles JM. Intravenous fat emulsions in nutritional support. Current Opinion in Gastroenterology 1991; 7: 306-311.

Nussbaum MS, Fischer JE. Pathogenesis of hepatic steatosis during total parenteral nutrition. Surgery Annual 1991; 23: 1-11.

Nussbaum MS, Li S, Bower RH, et al. Lipid additions to total parenteral nutrition prevent hepatic steatosis in rats by lowering the portal venous insulin/glucagon ratio. Journal of Parenteral and Enteral Nutrition 1992; 16: 106-109.

Palmblad J. Intravenous lipid emulsions and host defense—A critical review. Clinical Nutrition 1991; 10: 303-308.

Remillard RL, Thatcher CD. Parenteral nutritional support in the small animal patient. Veterinary Clinics of North America: Small Animal Practice 1989; 19: 1287-1306.

Shronts EP. Essential nature of choline with implications for total parenteral nutrition (abstract). Nutrition in Clinical Practice 1998; 13: 43.

should not compose more than 4 g/kg body weight/day or 60% of the calories has been perpetuated many times for reasons that are not apparent.[h] Over the last decade, the recommended proportion of calories from fat supplied to burn victims has progressively increased from 5 to 15 to 50%. Further, higher proportions of fat calories (75 to 80%) have been recommended in other disease states.[123-125]

The negative effects of high-fat infusions have centered around reports of liver pathology, coagulopathies, thrombocytopenia, altered immune function, atherosclerosis and the overall unknown effect of synthetic chylomicrons on blood vessels when administered to people for more than 10 days. These adverse effects occurred in people and other animals during high infusion rates in which lipids were provided in excess of energy need.[126-129] In addition, some of the products used in these studies are no longer available. (See sidebar "Complications of Fat Administration.")

To date, there appears to be little in the veterinary literature documenting why lipids could not or should not provide more than 60% of a dog's or cat's RER. In fact, when central venous access is limited and the patient requires fluid therapy at or below maintenance rates, administering a lipid emulsion via peripheral access (providing 100% of the caloric intake as fat) is not only possible but well tolerated. Though the use of high-fat solutions (60 to 90%) is contrary to all published recommendations, one author (RLR) has used solutions with these fat and glucose percentages in more than 500 dogs and cats receiving PN during a five-year period.[i] PN may be successfully adminis-

Table 12-13. Advantages to administering a high-fat total nutrient admixture (TNA) solution.

1. The liver is metabolically geared for lipolysis and preferentially uses fat as a source of calories. Therefore, supplying a high-fat solution accommodates that profile, spares endogenous fat stores and does not raise insulin levels.*
2. The osmolarity of the fat solution is 260 mOsm/l and can be administered by peripheral catheter alone. Fat included in a TNA solution decreases the final osmolarity:

80% calories from 50% dextrose and 20% calories from 20% lipid	= 862 mOsm/l**
20% calories from 50% dextrose and 80% calories from 20% lipid	= 535 mOsm/l**
5% dextrose and lactated Ringer's solution	= 525 mOsm/l
Blood or plasma	= ~300 mOsm/l

3. The pH of the final TNA solution that includes fat is closer to 7.0 than solutions of dextrose and amino acids excluding fat, thus imposing less of an acid load.
4. Patients with compromised pulmonary function are prone to developing respiratory acidosis when given high dextrose solutions. High-fat solutions produce less carbon dioxide to be expelled than high dextrose solutions.***

*Stein TP. Protein metabolism and parenteral nutrition. In: Rombeau JL, Caldwell MD, eds. Clinical Nutrition; Parenteral Nutrition, 1st ed. Philadelphia, PA: WB Saunders Co, 1986; 100-134.
**These osmolarity examples are based on a total fluid volume of 70 ml/kg body weight, 3 g protein/100 kcal RER and 30 mEq K+/liter.
***Askanazi J, Nordenstrom J, Rosenbaum SH, et al. Nutrition for the patient with respiratory failure: Glucose vs. fat. Anesthesiology 1981; 54: 373-377.

tered to ferrets and rabbits using the same overall guidelines. No unusual metabolic or hematologic complications have been associated with these infusions (Table 12-13).

Most patients receiving high-fat solutions do not develop hyperglycemia, based on regular urine glucose checks, as was common in previous reports.[113,114] Glycemia is better controlled in cases of diabetes mellitus, pancreatitis and septicemia with a TNA solution that provides most of the calories as fat. A TNA solution with 80% fat calories will contain 1 to 3% dextrose. Intravenous infusion of lipid emulsion routinely causes a transient increase in plasma triglyceride levels. However, this should not be considered a true hyperlipidemia because most patients can clear these chylomicron-size lipid particles within 30 minutes. The half-life of chylomicrons from the diet or intravenous infusion of soybean oil and safflower oil emulsions in the plasma of dogs ranged from seven to 16 minutes.[130,131] Therefore, it is sometimes necessary to shut off the TNA infusion pump 20 to 30 minutes before blood is drawn if hyperlipidemia is a problem. Fat from the TNA solution interferes with certain serum biochemistry tests. (See Chapter 24.)

The PN guidelines for people state that the role of intravenous artificial lipid emulsions in influencing the course of pancreatitis is not defined, despite the well-documented relationship between pancreatitis and elevated endogenous circulating triglyceride levels in people with genetic and secondary hyperlipidemias.[132] Lipid emulsions are safely used in hyperlipidemic people when serum triglyceride concentrations remain below 400 mg/dl or serum levels are less than 250 mg/dl four hours after infusion.[132] Dogs and cats at risk for developing hypertriglyceridemia (e.g., those with pancreatitis) have received a high-fat TNA at their RER with no additional problems.[1] The exact consequences of persistent hypertriglyceridemia that result when veterinary patients are given artificial lipid emulsions for several days are unknown.

PROTEIN SOLUTIONS

Patients must receive a source of essential and nonessential amino acids. Solutions are available containing 3.5 to 15% amino acids. These solutions are maintained in the pH range of 5.3 to 6.5, have an osmolarity between 300 and 1,400 mOsm/l and may also contain various combinations of electrolytes and/or dextrose.[119] Modified formulas are available with disproportionate concentrations of branched-chained vs. aromatic amino acids, particularly designed for patients with renal or liver failure or multiple trauma. These special formulas have not been widely used in veterinary medicine. The most commonly used product in veterinary medicine is the conventional 8.5% amino acid solution either with or without electrolytes (Table 12-12). Most amino acid solutions contain all the essential amino acids for dogs and cats, except taurine. However, some specialized pediatric amino acid products contain taurine.

Protein should be provided to the patient within a ratio of 1 to 6 g/100 kcal of nonprotein energy provided. Adult dogs do well on 2 to 3 g/100 kcal, whereas, adult cats do well on 3 to 4 g/100 kcal. Ferrets do well receiving protein intakes similar to those for cats (4 to 5 g protein/100 kcal), whereas rabbits do well with lower protein intakes (1 to 2 g protein/100 kcal). The lower protein-calorie ratios are recommended in patients with renal or hepatic insufficiency. The higher protein intakes are recommended with increased protein needs (e.g., albumin losses, chest-tube drains). The exact protein intake for each patient cannot be determined prospectively. It is therefore important to use the levels recommended here as guidelines only. A reasonable estimate of a patient's protein need should be made, the patient's response to that particular protein intake should be monitored and the intake should be adjusted accordingly. Patients are rarely azotemic due to PN administration when amino acids are provided within these protein-energy ratios and a product that provides mostly essential amino acids is used.

There are some combination amino acid/glycerin products available that provide amino acids and an energy source in a fixed ratio (Table 12-12). Some of these combinations are provided as a two-compartment bag with dextrose and amino acid solutions separated by a breakable divider. Most of these prepackaged dextrose/amino-acid mixes contain very high protein-calorie ratios and do not contain fat.

ELECTROLYTE SOLUTIONS

The more common electrolyte abnormalities associated with PN occur with the major intracellular cation potassium and the anion phosphorus. Potassium and phosphorus rapidly move intracellularly with refeeding by either enteral or parenteral methods or by the administration of glucose or insulin.[133] Potassium moves intracellularly with the correction of acidosis and in response to insulin release. A TNA solution composed of 8.5% amino acids with electrolytes and lactated Ringer's solution contains approximately 12 mEq potassium/l, which is not adequate to maintain normal serum potassium levels. Potassium can be added to the PN solution using either a 2 mEq/ml potassium chloride solution or a 4.4 mEq/ml potassium phosphate solution.

If the patient is normokalemic when PN is initiated, 20 to 30 mEq potassium/l will usually maintain normokalemia. However, if the patient is hypokalemic when PN is started, 40 or more mEq potassium/l will be required. If the patient is hyperkalemic when PN is to be initiated, no additional potassium is recommended, but serum potassium concentrations should be monitored daily. Crystalloid solutions containing potassium and administered via a second intravenous line are a convenient method of regulating serum potassium levels in difficult cases.

Phosphorus moves intracellularly with refeeding because of increased production of high-energy phosphate compounds.[134] Animals receiving PN rarely become hypophosphatemic. Sufficient quantities of phosphorus (5 to 10 mM/l) appear to be available in the TNA from lipids (15 mM/l) and amino acid/electrolyte (30 mM/l) solutions. However, adding a potassium phosphate solution containing 4.4 mEq potassium and 3 mM phosphorus/ml will increase the potassium and phosphorus content of the TNA. The phosphorus content of TNA for people is generally recommended at 10 to 20 mM/l. In cases of hyperphosphatemia, the quantity of amino acids, electrolytes and fat must be reduced to lower TNA phosphate concentrations in the TNA. Alternatively, an amino acid solution without electrolytes and potassium chloride can be used.

VITAMIN SOLUTIONS

Very few veterinary patients receiving PN require fat-soluble vitamins unless there is a history of prolonged weight loss, inappetence and decreased fat absorption (diarrhea/steatorrhea). Dogs and cats usually have sufficient body stores of vitamins A, D, E and K to last several months. Fat-soluble vitamin supplementation is warranted in cases of long-term fat malabsorption (months). One-time administration of 1 ml of a vitamin A, D and E product,[j] divided into two intramuscular sites, is simple, cost-effective and supplies fat-soluble vitamins for about three months. Vitamin K_1 injections (3 to 5 mg/cat, b.i.d., subcutaneously) reportedly improve abnormal coagulation times in cases of severe idiopathic hepatic lipidosis.[135,136]

Water-soluble vitamins, however, must be supplied daily by either the enteral or parenteral route. Most veterinary vitamin B-complex products do not contain all 11 B-complex vitamins, because some B vitamins are not compatible (e.g., folic acid is incompatible with riboflavin in the same solution). Folic acid, therefore, must be administered separately if needed. Based on the NRC daily vitamin recommendations for healthy dogs and cats and given the vitamin concentrations available in most solutions,[k] the recommended dose of 1 ml of B vitamins per 100 kcal exceeds daily B-vitamin requirements by several-fold, except for B_{12}. Most previously healthy pets and people, however, have sufficient hepatic stores of B_{12}.

Some clinicians administer vitamin C to ill dogs and cats, particularly those with chronic liver disease, as a precautionary measure, although there is no documented

Table 12-14. Drug incompatibility with B-complex vitamins.*

Known incompatible	Suspected incompatible
2-PAM (pralidoxime chloride)	4-methylpyrazole
Aminophylline	Adriamycin
Asparaginase	Carboplatin
Bicarbonate	Cisplatin
Calcium versonate	Dobutamine
Cefazolin	Dopamine
Diazepam	Fentanyl
Digoxin (injectable)	Propranolol
Mannitol	
Nitroprusside	
Penicillin G	
Quinidine	

*Plumb DC. Veterinary Drug Handbook, 3rd ed. White Bear, MN: Pharma Veterinary Publishing, 1999.

need or recommended dose to date. (See Chapter 23.) The vitamin C recommendation in people receiving TNA is 200 to 225 mg/day.[137] Assuming the dose for people is based on an average 70-kg person, the comparable dog or cat dose of vitamin C would be 4 to 5 mg/kg body weight. Because vitamins C and B are water soluble, except for B_{12}, exceeding an animal's actual requirement is usually not a problem.

Some B vitamins are light labile and most B-vitamin preparations should be kept in a light-resistant bottle and stored between 15 to 30°C (59 to 86°F). Riboflavin, perhaps the most light-labile B vitamin, still has 50% of its original activity after exposure to indoor fluorescent lighting for eight hours.[138] Given the NRC recommended dose of riboflavin and the concentration of riboflavin in the TNA at 1 ml B vitamins/100 kcal, the patient would receive the daily recommended amount of riboflavin well within the first two hours of TNA therapy. Thus, covering the intravenous fluid bag to protect B vitamins is probably unnecessary. Also, the addition of lipid increases the opacity of the final solution, reduces light penetration and precludes having to cover the PN solution from light.[138] In summary, adding B vitamins is a low-cost (pennies per day), effective means of improving energy metabolism. However, B vitamins are incompatible with some drugs commonly administered to veterinary patients by continuous intravenous infusion (Table 12-14).

TRACE-ELEMENT SOLUTIONS

Trace-element requirements have not been determined for catabolic veterinary patients and dosing recommendations for zinc and copper in PN solutions are still evolving. In studies, dogs receiving a zinc-free PN solution had serum levels 50% of normal after one week; therefore, some zinc supplementation is recommended.[139] Supplementing PN solutions with at least 0.1 to 0.2 mg zinc/100 kcal has been suggested.[140,141] Piglets receiving PN for four weeks with a solution containing 5 mg zinc and 0.3 mg copper/100 kcal had toxic zinc but normal copper hepatic concentrations and evidence of pancreatic necrosis associated with zinc toxicosis. Piglets receiving a similar PN protocol with 1.2 mg zinc and 0.3 mg copper/100 kcal had normal hepatic zinc and copper concentrations and no pancreatic pathology.[142] Based on the published evidence, the NRC daily zinc and copper recommendations for dogs and cats and one author's (RLR) experience, PN solutions may contain 1 mg zinc and 0.5 mg copper/100 kcal. These elements can be added to the PN solution most economically (pennies per

Table 12-15. Drugs compatible with total nutrient admixtures (TNA).*

Aminophylline
Ampicillin
Cefazolin
Chloramphenicol
Cimetidine
Clindamycin
Digoxin
Diphenhydramine
Dopamine
Erythromycin
Furosemide
Gentamicin
Heparin
Insulin (regular)
Lidocaine
Metoclopramide
Penicillin G
Phytonadione
Ranitidine
Ticarcillin

*Dickerson RN, Brown RO, White KG. Parenteral nutrition solutions. In: Rombeau JL, Caldwell MD, eds. Clinical Nutrition; Parenteral Nutrition, 2nd ed. Philadelphia, PA: WB Saunders Co, 1993; 310-333.

day) using a multiple trace-element[i] combination available in multiple-dose vials. Approximately 1 ml of the trace-element solution should be added per 100 kcal daily.[143]

Drug Additions

Although it is very convenient to administer drugs intravenously with the PN solution, *extreme caution must be taken before any medications are added to the TNA.* Drug and TNA solution compatibility studies are ongoing, and there are published lists of drugs known to be compatible and safe.[144] Table 12-15 lists the drugs of most interest to veterinarians that can be incorporated into a three-in-one mixture. The *Handbook on Injectable Drugs* is updated and published every two years and is a good source for current information about drug compatibility with PN solutions.[145] After a medication has been added to the day's PN solution, a decision to discontinue that medication can be costly, because a new bag of PN solution must be compounded. Therefore, use of a second peripheral catheter or a double-lumen central catheter may be preferable to adding drugs to PN solutions.

Compounding

PN solutions can be obtained from several sources. Some human hospitals and independent pharmaceutical companies will compound TNA solutions for veterinarians. A prescription must be written indicating the volume or final concentration of each nutrient (fat, dextrose, amino acids and each electrolyte), and the person preparing the TNA is likely to refer to the solution as "TPN." Some veterinary schools, large referral practices and private veterinary hospitals maintain parenteral solution compounders and supplies for their own use and will compound and sell TNA bags directly to practitioners. Several bags of PN solution (up to 10 days' worth) can be sent by overnight mail services directly to the practice. This is often the safest, most convenient and economical method of obtaining an all-in-one PN solution for the occasional patient in most practices.

TNA solutions can be compounded by one of three basic methods: 1) syringe, 2) gravity flow or 3) computerized flow.[104] Several variants of each method exist but will not be discussed here. All-in-one PN or TNA supplies can be purchased from the same sources that provide the PN solutions. The least desirable method uses a 35- or 60-ml syringe to transfer each nutrient solution (dextrose, amino acid and lipid) into a sterile, empty fluid bag. This method is the most time-consuming and carries the greatest risk of contamination because of the multiple transfers required. Transfers are ideally done under a laminar flow hood.

The second method uses a closed-circuit fluid system in which the all-in-one bag comes with a pre-attached three-lead transfer set. Each lead, with a vented filter spike, is inserted directly into the individual nutrient solutions (dextrose, amino acid and lipid), and the nutrients are transferred directly into the all-in-one bag by gravity flow. This method is faster and safer than the syringe method, but transfer of exact quantities is not possible. This method may be most economical when few patients require PN. Both syringe and gravity feed methods usually leave partially unused bottles of dextrose, fat and amino acids.

The third and best method, used by most human hospitals and some large referral veterinary hospitals, employs a high-speed, closed-circuit fluid compounder that pumps three or four solutions (dextrose, amino acid, lipid and fluid) directly into one TNA bag within 60 seconds. Each solution is accurately transferred to within 1 ml. The method has a mean error of less than 2% (Figure 12-8). Multiple bags of TNA for several patients can be efficiently made at one time using partial bottles of dextrose, fat and amino acids. Making TNA bags with a compounder is safe, fast, accurate and efficient. Veterinary technicians can routinely accomplish this task.[146] A computerized compounder has been used in one author's (RLR) practice to formulate more than 1,500 TNA bags over a five-year period. To date there have been no confirmed or suspected cases of microbial contamination during formulation.[m] All-in-one or TNA solutions can be refrigerated for at least seven and possibly up to 14 days. (See sidebar "Complications of Total Nutrient Admixture Solutions.")

Administration

PN solutions can be delivered to patients by a central, peripheral, intraosseous or intraperitoneal catheter. PN solutions with an osmolarity greater than 600 mOsm/l should be administered into a central vein to avoid thrombophlebitis. Solutions less than 600 mOsm/l may be administered via a peripheral vein.

PERIPHERAL VEIN INFUSION

There is an increased interest in human medicine in administering PN via peripheral veins because of the increased risk and additional expense of placing central venous catheters and the introduction of catheter materials that reduce the incidence of peripheral vein thrombophlebitis.[147-149] PN solutions with osmolarities ranging from 600 to 1,250 mOsm/l are administered peripherally to people for short periods (three days).[150-153] Phlebitis is the principal complication, usually occurring within the first 72 hours in 26 to 48% of human patients.[154] In another study, phlebitis was significantly increased in patients receiving TNA solutions containing amino acids, potassium or antibiotics, and in all people receiving solutions with osmolarity values greater than 600 mOsm/l.[155] There are no published clinical reports in which TNA solutions were administered peripherally to dogs or cats. However, calories can easily be administered peripherally to dogs and cats using a TNA of 400 to 600 mOsm/l or an isomolar 20% lipid solution piggybacked with standard fluid therapy at volumes sufficient to meet RER.[n]

TNA solutions can be administered to dogs and cats through peripherally inserted central lines. Cats, compared with most dogs, are smaller, have higher protein requirements and sometimes have restrictive fluid allowances. Therefore, for cats (more than for dogs), the final osmolarity of the PN solution will be between 600 and 800 mOsm/l and the solution should be administered into a large vein. Placing a 10- to 20-cm polyurethane[o] or silicone[p] catheter (with a break-away needle) into the medial saphenous vein at the level of the tarsus and advancing the catheter up the vein places the tip of the catheter into the caudal vena cava of the cat. A similar, but longer (20- to 30-cm) polyurethane or silicone catheter, placed in the lateral saphenous vein, is more useful in dogs weighing less than 20 kg. For long-term applications (more than three days), silicone and polyurethane remain the only acceptable catheter materials, and they need not be removed at a predetermined time.

CENTRAL VEIN INFUSION

A single- or multiple-lumen polyurethane or silicone elastomer catheter can be placed by a percutaneous procedure (or rarely a cut-down procedure) in the external jugular vein of most dogs and cats. Placing a jugular catheter in ferrets usually involves a cut-down procedure. The tip of the catheter should be located in the cranial vena cava or right atrium. Catheters made of silicone elastomer and polyurethane are softer and less irritating, though more expensive, than the polytetrafluoroethylene (Teflon) catheters often used for fluid administration in veterinary patients. Silicone and polyurethane are likely to result in fewer mechanical and septic complications and are less thrombogenic. Again, for long-term applications (more than three days), silicone and polyurethane are the only acceptable catheter materials.

Central catheters are changed as indicated by particular problems (e.g., infection, subcutaneous migration, thrombosis) and not at predetermined intervals.[104] Multiple-lumen catheters allow multipurpose venous access for administering incompatible fluid/drug therapies or different fluids at different rates. Although use of central catheters has not been adequately evaluated in veterinary patients, their use for PN administration in people is associated with an increase in septic complications.[156] No known or suspected cases of sepsis have been encountered in canine patients receiving PN via dual-lumen jugular catheters in one author's (PJA) practice.[q] Many sources advocate that the central catheter must be "dedicated" to PN administration, and should not be used for blood sampling, medication or blood product administration or central venous pressure monitoring. However, when venous access is limited, the PN catheter may be used for blood sampling and administering medications if adequately flushed before and after the interruption in PN administration. It is imperative, as with any catheter, that excellent aseptic handling techniques be used during these line interruptions.

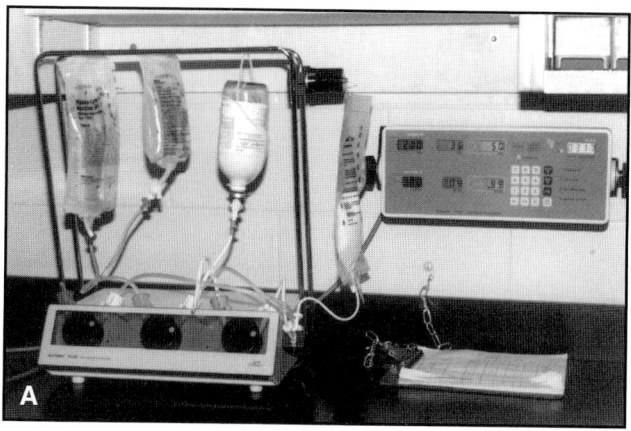

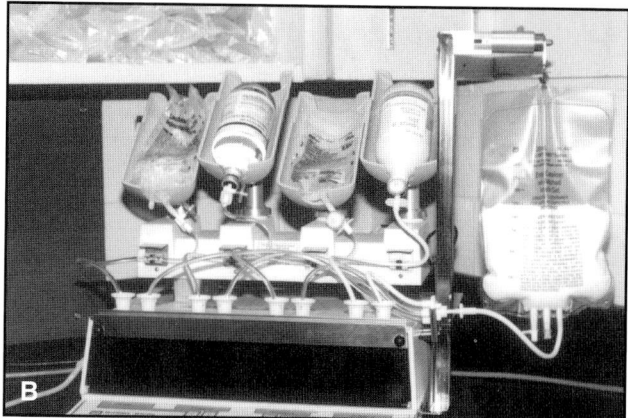

Figure 12-8. A three-station (A) and four-station (B) total nutrient admixture compounder.

OTHER ROUTES OF PN INFUSION

Nutritional solutions have been infused by intraosseous and intraperitoneal routes in several laboratory species, people (adults and children) and dogs. A solution containing electrolytes, amino acids, dextrose and vitamins has been successfully infused intraosseously in dogs.[157] There are no known literature citations referring to intraosseous infusion of lipid. However, a TNA solution (850 mOsm/l) has been successfully infused intraperitoneally for more than 20 days in 19 normal dogs and in 12 normal dogs that had undergone intestinal resection.[158,159] Intraperitoneal infusion of a 10% lipid solution into three-month-old beagles demonstrated that fat was quantitatively absorbed from the peritoneal cavity over a four-hour period.[160]

CATHETER COMPLICATIONS

TNA solutions should be administered at room temperature. Also, it is prudent not to extend the delivery of any one bag more than 24 hours. The most clinically significant problem in administering TNA solutions involves the catheter, including loss of access, thrombophlebitis and infection. Loss of venous access is due to catheter kinking, catheter tip migration or blockage. In these instances, the catheter should be removed and a second catheter placed in another vein.

Thrombophlebitis

Thrombophlebitis is a response of the vein intima to the unique combination of the infusate, the catheter mate-

Complications of Total Nutrient Admixture Solutions

The diverse composition of total nutrient admixture (TNA) solutions increases the risk of physiochemical incompatibilities. The most likely problem is deterioration of the lipid emulsion within the TNA in which individual fat particles collide forming larger particles creating a potentially dangerous intravenous mixture. TNA solutions containing 10 or 20% lipid have an osmolarity of about 300 mOsm/l, a pH of 7.0 and are stable when stored as directed at room temperature. The 4- to 5-μm lipid particles are stabilized by an egg-yolk phospholipid emulsifier, giving the surface a negative charge to maintain a repulsive electrostatic force between particles. Fat breakdown in individual bottles of lipids rarely occurs.

In a TNA, however, fat particles can aggregate and larger particles will migrate to the surface of the solution, creating a whiter band at the top of the TNA solution. This process is called "creaming." It can be easily reversed by gently mixing the TNA solution, and is of no danger to the patient. However, when the negative surface charge is neutralized, the emulsion destabilizes irreversibly and, with repeated collisions between fat particles, the emulsion completely destabilizes. This irreversible process of coalescence results in two immiscible phases of oil and water. Coalescence is associated with a dark yellow color, either in a line across the top portion of the TNA or as large yellow globules throughout the TNA solution. B-vitamin additions to a TNA solution give the solution a light but uniform yellow color, and should not be confused with coalescence. Bags with evidence of coalescence should not be administered to patients because the larger particles can become fat emboli that will plug 5-μm pulmonary capillaries.

Adding divalent cations (e.g., calcium or magnesium) to the TNA solution is not advisable because the positive charge can destabilize the negatively charged surface of fat, break the emulsion and cause coalescence. The addition of solutions that reduce the final solution pH to near or below 5 will also cause the emulsion to breakdown. Individual dextrose solutions are kept at a pH of 5 to minimize microbial growth, whereas amino acid solutions are buffered and have a pH of 6. When mixing a TNA solution, it is important to add the lipid last when there is a large volume of fluid with a higher pH already in the parenteral nutrition bag.

BIBLIOGRAPHY

Atik M. Hemodynamic changes following infusion of intravenous fat emulsions. International Journal of Pharmaceutics 1978; 1: 141-150.

Driscoll DF, Baptista RJ, Bistrian BR, et al. Practical considerations regarding the use of total nutrient admixtures. American Journal of Hospital Pharmacy 1986; 43: 416-419.

Driscoll DF, Bhargava HN, Li L, et al. Physicochemical stability of total nutrient admixtures. American Journal of Health-System Pharmacy 1995; 52: 623-634.

Leveen HH, Giordano P, Spletzer J. The mechanism of removal of intravenous fat. Its relationship to toxicity. Archives of Surgery 1961; 83: 311-321.

rial and placement and the ratio of catheter to vessel size. Intravenous catheters reduce blood flow and frequently induce thrombophlebitis within 72 hours; therefore, they are routinely changed every three days. The catheter material is thought to be the single most important factor in the severity of infusion thrombophlebitis.[161,162] Investigators have concluded that three characteristics of the catheter material contribute to thrombosis: 1) roughness, 2) stiffness and 3) platelet adhesion.[163]

Teflon[r] intravenous catheters are commonly used in veterinary medicine, and can be used routinely as short-term (two to three days) peripheral catheters. These catheters are easy to insert, are inexpensive and result in relatively low rates of phlebitis.[164] Recently, Vialon, a poly-etherurethane hydromer,[s] has become available. Catheters made of this material are easier to insert, have lower rates of phlebitis and are less thrombogenic than Teflon catheters.[165] In research comparing peripheral catheters in people at 72 hours, Vialon catheters resulted in significantly fewer (24%) cases of phlebitis than did Teflon catheters (40%).[162]

More recently, investigators have conducted several studies comparing PN administration to people using Teflon, Silastic (silicone) and polyurethane peripheral catheters. In one study, chemical phlebitis occurred in 17% of patients with silicone catheters vs. 91% of those with Teflon catheters.[166] In another study in which a 650 mOsm/l PN solution was administered, peripheral silicone catheters were determined to be safe, durable and well tolerated with a lower incidence of thrombophlebitis (10%) relative to Teflon catheters (48%).[167] However, in a third study silicone catheters induced a higher incidence of phlebitis (36%) than did those made from polyurethane (6%).[163] In summary, the list of catheter materials in order of increasing thrombogenicity is: Vialon (lowest), polyurethane, silicone and Teflon (highest).[168,169] In a review of approximately 25 canine cases administered heparin-free PN solutions of 600 mOsm/l or less using a 2.5-cm Vialon peripheral catheter revealed thrombophlebitis in about 15% of the cases within 24 to 48 hours.[1]

In people, the incidence of thrombophlebitis can also be reduced by adding low-dose heparin (0.5 to 1 U/ml), hydrocortisone (10 mg/l) or both compounds to the PN solution.[170-172] This heparin dose prolongs peripheral catheter patency by reducing phlebitis at the catheter tip, but does not affect normal hemostatic systems in most patients. A low incidence of thrombophlebitis has been reported to occur in dogs and cats in which 1 U sodium heparin was added per ml of TNA administered by central catheter. This dose will not affect coagulation function in animals with normal hemostatic systems.[114] There have been no comparative veterinary studies to document whether heparin or hydrocortisone reduces phlebitis due to peripheral catheters.

Infection

Infectious complications with intravenous infusions have been recognized for more than 40 years and are now primarily associated with substandard catheter care. Most catheter-related septicemias are due to microbial invasion at the catheter wound, either during or after insertion.[173,174] Hospitals that use iodine solutions to disinfect the skin and emphasize catheter site asepsis have significantly lower rates of positive catheter cultures and septicemias.[175] Catheters for PN administration must be placed using meticulous aseptic technique. The catheter bandage and administration sets should be changed at least every other day, if not daily. When the bandage is changed, the venipuncture site should be cleaned with an iodine solution and examined for redness, edema or swelling. A topical antibiotic ointment (e.g., povidone iodine) that contains antifungal properties should be applied at the catheter-skin junction. When redness, edema or swelling is noticed, the catheter should be removed and cultured and the site should be kept clean and hot packed, if necessary, to reduce swelling. Appropriate antibiotics should be given if the catheter or TNA solution is shown to be contaminated by culture and antimicrobial sensitivity testing.

Second, thrombi at the catheter tip may be seeded hematogenously with organisms from urinary tract infections, abscesses, pneumonia or other infected sites. Bacterial translocation from the GI tract may also occur. In a prospective study of 200 consecutive human patients receiving PN, 75% of the catheters removed because of septicemia were determined, retrospectively, not to have been the cause of the infection.[176] Other infected sites were subsequently identified in most of these patients.

Infusion of contaminated fluid is a third source of infection. However, contamination in this manner is unlikely to occur when the TNA is compounded in a closed-circuit fluid system. For many years TNA solutions were thought to favor microbial growth; however, current TNA solutions using crystalline amino acids do not. Earlier statements and cautions were based on information determined using a dextrose and protein hydrolysate solution, which is now unavailable.[177] Protein hydrolysate products contained peptides or ammonia that bacteria used for growth. The crystalline amino acid products now used in TNA solutions do not contain peptides or ammonia, are hypertonic and acidic, thus prohibiting bacterial growth.[178,179]

There is conflicting evidence about whether bacteria grow slowly or at all in currently recommended TNA solutions.[180,181] Fungi can still proliferate in admixtures, though refrigeration at 4°C suppresses all microbial growth. Lipid emulsions alone, on the other hand, support gram-positive and gram-negative bacterial growth or fungal growth if contaminated. The Centers for Disease Control has recommended that lipid emulsions be administered for no longer than 12 hours, except in TNA systems, which can be administered over a 24-hour period.[182] In summary, infection associated with TNA administration is a rare complication. It is most often attributed to substandard catheter care or, less likely, contamination of TNA solutions during manipulation of the fluid lines.

Combined Enteral and Parenteral Feeding

In human medicine, there has been renewed interest in using tube feeding in combination with parenteral nutrition.[183,184] Prolonged fasting (more than three days) results in enterocyte deterioration and decreased GI immunity.[185] A possible source of infection with parenteral administration is translocation of enteric bacteria due to a compromised intestinal mucosal barrier. A combination of enteral and parenteral administration has been suggested because enteral infusion of small quantities of a liquid diet has helped prevent intestinal mucosal deterioration during parenteral nutrition in piglets (2 ml/kg body weight b.i.d.), human infants (4 to 5 ml/kg body weight/hour) and adults (0.7 ml/kg body weight/hour).[186-189] In addition, intestinal adaptations after disease and intestinal hypertrophy after surgery require the presence of intraluminal nutrients. Food intake promotes intestinal hyperplasia and brush border enzyme activity.[190] Therefore, most recent recommendations encourage some enteral feeding to patients receiving parenteral nutritional support, if possible. Feeding both the small bowel and the patient is important.[75]

▌ REASSESSMENT

Regular reassessment is a critical step in successful nutritional management of hospitalized patients, regardless of whether the enteral route, the parenteral route or both routes are used. Malnutrition in the form of insufficient nutrient intake to support tissue metabolism undermines appropriate medical and/or surgical therapeutic management of a case. The authors believe that malnutrition is far more common in veterinary patients than is currently recognized. Patients resting in a cage have been mistakenly assumed to require little or no nutrition when, in fact, the nutrient costs of tissue repair, immunocompetence and drug metabolism are significant. Therefore, reassessment of nutritional status is important whether the animal remains in the hospital or recovers at home.

Monitoring Parameters

Food intake or administration of nutritional support for hospitalized patients should be reviewed at least daily. Body weight should be recorded daily. Body condition should be noted; however, an animal's BCS is unlikely to change during the course of a hospital stay. Laboratory assessments specifically for patients receiving nutritional support are generally not necessary beyond those tests already routinely performed for critically ill patients. The most common alterations that occur in laboratory parameters associated with nutrient administration are decreases in serum potassium and phosphate levels, increases in serum glucose concentrations and triglyceridemia (Table 12-16). (See sidebar "Refeeding Syndrome.") Even apparently stable patients might develop metabolic complications as a result of ongoing disease processes or from undiagnosed subclinical disease states. However, most patients show subjective improvement in attitude within 36 hours of refeeding.[11]

Most parameters used to assess the nutritional status of patients will not change as a result of assisted feeding during the course of hospitalization. Laboratory parameters (e.g., albumin and total protein concentrations, RBC count and hemoglobin content) are unlikely to change in less than two weeks. Perhaps laboratory parameters that change during a hospital stay as a result of assisted feeding may be detected when acute-phase proteins with half-lives between two and 12 hours can be measured reliably in dogs and cats. The patient's body weight and condition and some laboratory parameters (albumin and total protein concentrations) should improve over the course of weeks.[191]

Changing Foods

Parenterally fed patients should be fed enterally as soon as possible, but may continue to receive PN as enteral intake increases to meet RER. The food offered enterally

Table 12-16. Metabolic complications of parenteral-nutrition (PN) administration, treatment and potential patient considerations.

Complications are listed in descending order of likely occurrence and treatments are listed from immediate to longer term solutions. To minimize complications, patients should be hemodynamically stable and any electrolyte and acid-base abnormalities, severe tachycardia, hypotension and volume deficits should be corrected before starting PN.

Complications	Treatments	Patient considerations

Hyperglycemia	Stop infusion, recheck in two to four hours, decrease PN infusion by 50% until normal, then increase infusion rate slowly
	Subcutaneous insulin therapy
	Change caloric sources:
	  Increase lipid fraction of calories
	  Decrease glucose fraction of calories
		Glucose intolerance

Hypokalemia	Add KCl or KPO_4 to PN bag
	Correct serum Mg as needed
	Change caloric sources:
	  Increase lipid fraction of calories
	  Decrease glucose fraction of calories
		GI or renal losses
		Drug therapies that increase urinary excretion
		Insulin therapy

Hypophosphatemia	Add $NaPO_4$ or KPO_4 to PN bag	Diabetic ketoacidosis

Hyperlipidemia	Stop infusion, recheck in two to four hours, decrease PN infusion by 50% until normal, then increase infusion rate slowly
	Change caloric sources:
	  Decrease lipid fraction of calories
	  Increase glucose fraction of calories
		Decreased lipid clearance

Phlebitis	Change catheter and infusion site
	Lower PN osmolality:
	  Increase lipid fraction of calories
	  Decrease glucose fraction of calories
	Add heparin to PN bag
		Properly hydrated
		Endogenous site of infection

Hyperkalemia	Change PN bag and decrease K^+	Acidosis, renal failure, sepsis Drug therapies that decrease urinary excretion
Hyperammonemia	Decrease PN infusion by 50% until normal Change PN bag, decrease amino acid concentration Use branched-chain amino acid sources	Liver dysfunction, GI bleeding
Hypomagnesemia	Add $MgSO_3$ to PN bag	GI or renal losses Drug therapies that increase urinary excretion

Hypoglycemia	Piggyback 50% dextrose drip until normal
	Change caloric sources:
	  Decrease lipid fraction of calories
	  Increase glucose fraction of calories
		Sepsis
		Insulin therapy
		Insulinoma

Infected catheter site	Change catheter and infusion site Culture catheter and PN solution Give antibiotics based on culture and antimicrobial sensitivity tests Hot pack site	Substandard catheter care Endogenous site of infection Properly hydrated

may be a fixed-formula therapeutic food intended as the food to be fed to the patient at home because of an ongoing disease condition. When the patient has a decreased appetite, a highly palatable, fixed-formula food may be offered initially to stimulate oral consumption. This food may then be mixed in gradually decreasing proportions with the food intended to be fed on a long-term basis. (See Chapter 1.) Vomiting and diarrhea are the most common problems seen when refeeding patients orally. Foods should be introduced in amounts equal to RER in small frequent meals, and the amounts increased if well tolerated over the course of several days.

Sometimes the patient only needs a specific therapeutic formula for a short time and then may be changed back to its regular food. Changing from a therapeutic formula to an over-the-counter brand may also be done according to the short schedule in Table 1-10. Should a problem such as vomiting, diarrhea or food refusal occur, the last successful food mixture should be offered for several more days before proceeding. Most pets undergo dietary changes with few or no detectable GI disturbances.

ENDNOTES & REFERENCES

ENDNOTES

a. Sovereign Feeding Tube. Sherwood Medical, St. Louis, MO, USA.

b. Kangaroo Enteral Feeding Tube. Sherwood Medical, St. Louis, MO, USA. KeoFeed II Feeding Tube. IVAC Corp., San Diego, CA, USA.

c. Feeding Tube. Cook Veterinary Products, Bloomington, IN, USA.

d. Pezzer Catheter. Mill Ross Labs, Mentor, OH, USA.

e. Gastrostomy Tube Introduction Set. Cook Veterinary Products, Bloomington, IN, USA.

f. Armstrong PJ, University of Minnesota, St. Paul, MN, USA. Unpublished data. 1997.

g. CliniCare. Abbott Laboratories, North Chicago, IL, USA.

h. Prescribing information for Intralipid Intravenous Fat Emulsion, 1981. Cutter Laboratories, Berkeley, CA, USA.

i. Remillard RL, Angell Memorial Animal Hospital, Boston, MA, USA. Unpublished data. January 1998.

j. Vital E-A+D containing 100 IU of D and 300 IU of alpha-tocopherol per ml. Schering-Plough Animal Health Corp., Kenilworth, NJ, USA.

k. B-Vitamin Complex containing 50 mg thiamin, 2 mg riboflavin, 100 mg niacin, 2 mg pyridoxine, 10 mg pantothenic acid, 0.4 µg B_{12} per ml. Butler Co., Columbus, OH, USA.

l. MTE-4 contains 1.7 mg zinc, 0.42 mg copper, 0.37 mg manganese and 6 µg chromium per ml containing the preservative benzyl alcohol. Abbott Laboratories, Chicago, IL, USA.

m. Remillard RL, Angell Memorial Animal Hospital, Boston, MA, USA. Unpublished data. January 1999.

n. Remillard RL, Angell Memorial Animal Hospital, Boston, MA, USA. Unpublished data. October 1997.

o. L-Cath (16 and 18 ga.). Luther Medical Products, Inc., Santa Ana, CA, USA. Central venous (20 to 16 ga.) catheters. Cook Veterinary Products, Bloomington, IL, USA.

p. Silicone (20 to 16 ga.) catheters (50 to 60 cm) can be cut to appropriate lengths. Cook Critical Care, Bloomington, IL, USA.

q. Armstrong PJ, University of Minnesota, St. Paul, MN, USA. Unpublished data. January 1998.

r. Jelco (24 ga., 5 cm). Critikon, Tampa, FL, USA.

s. Instye (24 to 18 ga., 5 cm). Becton-Dickinson, Sandy, UT, USA.

t. Remillard RL, Angell Memorial Animal Hospital, Boston, MA, USA. Unpublished data. May 1997.

u. Remillard RL, Armstrong PJ, Guilford WG. Personal clinical experience.

REFERENCES

1. Semba RD, Meydani SN, Kramer TR, et al. Micronutrient influences on immune response. Conference on Nutrition and Immunity as Part of the International Conference Series on Nutrition and Health Promotion. International Life Sciences Institute. Atlanta, GA, May 5-7, 1997: 9-18.

2. Burkholder WJ, Swecker WS. Nutritional influences on immunity. Seminars in Veterinary Medicine and Surgery: Small Animal 1990; 5: 154-166.

3. Fischer JE, Glory ME. Protein depletion and immunity in the hospitalized patient. In: Wrought RA, Heymsfield S, eds. Nutritional Assessment. Boston, MA: Blackwell Scientific, 1984; 111-129.

4. Chandra RK, ed. Nutritional regulation of immunity: An introduction. In: Nutrition and Immunology. New York, NY: Alan R Liss Inc, 1988; 1-8.

5. Chandra RK. Immunodeficiency in undernutrition and overnutrition. Nutrition Reviews 1981; 39: 225-231.

6. Shikora SA, Blackburn GL, Forse RA. Nutrition and immunology: Clinician's approach. In: Forse RA, ed. Diet, Nutrition and Immunity. Boca Raton, FL: CRC Press Inc, 1994; 9-21.

7. Chandra RK. Protein-energy malnutrition and immunological responses. Journal of Nutrition 1992; 122: 597-600.

8. Chandra RK. Immunocompetence is a sensitive and functional barometer of nutritional status. Acta Paediatric Scandinavica 1991; 374 (Suppl.): 129-132.

9. Redmond HP, Leon P, Lieberman MD, et al. Impaired macrophage function in severe protein-energy malnutrition. Archives of Surgery 1991; 126: 192-196.

10. Kahan BD. Nutrition and host defense mechanisms. Surgical Clinics of North America 1981; 61: 557-570.

11. Kulkarni AD, Fanslow WC, Drath DB, et al. Influence of dietary nucleotide restriction on bacterial sepsis and phagocytic cell function in mice. Archives of Surgery 1986; 121: 169-172.

12. Ortiz R, Betancourt M. Cell proliferation in bone marrow cells of severely malnourished animals. Journal of Nutrition 1984; 114: 472-476.

13. Chandra RK, Kumari S. Nutrition and immunity: An overview. Journal of Nutrition 1994; 124: 1433S-1435S.

14. Chandra RK, Gupta S, Singh H. Inducer and suppressor T-cell subsets in protein-energy malnutrition. Analysis by monoclonal antibodies. Nutrition Research 1982: 2; 223-232.

15. Chandra RK. Numerical and functional deficiency in T helper cells in protein-energy malnutrition. Clinical and Experimental Immunology 1983; 51: 126-132.

16. Sirisinha S, Suskind RM, Edelman R. Secretory and serum IgA in children with protein-calories malnutrition. Pediatrics 1975; 55: 166-170.

17. Keusch CT, Urrutia JJ, Fernandez R, et al. Humoral and cellular aspects of intracellular bacteria killing in Guatemalan children with protein-calories malnutrition. In: Suskind RE, ed. Malnutrition and the Immune Response. New York, NY: Raven, 1977; 245.

18. Saxena QB, Saxena RK, Alder WH. Effect of protein calorie malnutrition on the levels of natural and inducible cytotoxic activities in mouse spleen cells. Immunology 1984; 51: 727-733.

19. Meydani SN. Dietary modulation of cytokine production and biological functions. Nutrition Reviews 1990; 48: 361-369.

20. Grimble RF. Nutrition and cytokine action. Nutrition Research Reviews 1990; 3: 193-210.

21. Chandra RK. Nutrition and immunoregulation. Significance for host resistance to tumors and infectious diseases in humans and rodents. Journal of Nutrition 1992; 122: 754-757.

22. Moss G. Immediately postoperative full nutrition and sepsis resistance: Immune globulin synthesis (abstract). Journal of Parenteral and Enteral Nutrition 1978; 1: 36.

23. Crane SW. Nutritional aspects of wound healing. Seminars in Veterinary Medicine and Surgery: Small Animal 1989; 4: 263-267.

24. Stein TP, Oram-Smith JC, Wallace HW, et al. The effect of trauma on protein synthesis. Journal of Surgical Research 1976; 21: 201-203.

25. Kien CL, Young VR, Rohrbaugh DK, et al. Increased rates of whole body protein synthesis and breakdown in children recovering from burns. Annals of Surgery 1978; 187: 383-391.

26. Birkham RH, Long CL, Fitkins D, et al. Effects of major skeletal trauma on whole body protein turnover in man measured by L-[1,^{14}C]-leucine. Surgery 1980; 88: 294-300.

27. Parke DV. Nutritional requirements for detoxication of environmental chemicals. Food Additives and Contaminants 1991; 8: 381-396.

28. Knodell RG. Effects of formula composition on hepatic and intestinal drug metabolism during enteral nutrition. Journal of Parenteral and Enteral Nutrition 1990; 14: 34-38.

29. Raftogianis RB, Franklin MR, Galinsky RE. The depression of hepatic drug conjugation reactions in rats after lipid-free total parenteral nutrition administered via the portal vein. Journal of Parenteral and Enteral Nutrition 1995; 19: 303-309.

30. Walter-Sack I, Klotz U. Influence of diet and nutritional status on drug metabolism. Clinical Pharmacokinetics 1996; 31: 47-64.

31. Pelissier MA, Darmon N, Desjeux JF. Effects of protein deficiency on lipid peroxidation in the small intestine and liver of rats. Food Chemistry and Toxicology 1993; 1: 59-62.

32. Varma DR. Protein deficiency and drug interactions. Drug Development Research 1981; 1: 183-198.

33. Anderson KE. Influences of diet and nutrition on clinical pharmacokinetics. Clinical Pharmacokinetics 1988; 14: 325-346.

34. Krishnaswamy K. Drug metabolism and pharmacokinetics in malnourished children. Clinical Pharmacokinetics 1989; 17 (Suppl.): 68-88.

35. Remillard RL, Martin RA. Nutritional support in the surgical patient. Seminars in Veterinary Medicine and Surgery: Small Animal 1990; 5: 197-207.

36. Meguid MM, Mughal MM, Meguid V, et al. Risk-benefit analysis of malnutrition and perioperative nutritional support: A review. Nutrition International 1987; 3: 25-34.

37. Buzby GP, Mullen JL. Nutritional assessment. In: Rombeau JL, Caldwell MD, eds. Clinical Nutrition; Enteral and Tube Feeding. Philadelphia, PA: WB Saunders Co, 1984; 127-147.

38. Buffington CA. Nutritional support of critically ill patients, Why bother? In: Proceedings. International Veterinary Emergency and Critical Care Society, San Antonio, TX, 1994: 323-326.

39. Michel K. Prognostic value of clinical nutritional assessment in canine patients. Journal of Veterinary Emergency and Critical Care 1993; 3: 96-104.

40. Laflamme DP. Body condition scoring and weight maintenance. In: Proceedings. North American Veterinary Conference, Orlando, FL, 1993: 290-291.

41. Lupo L, Pannarale O, Altomare D, et al. Reliability of clinical judgment in evaluation of the nutritional status of surgical patients. British Journal of Surgery 1993; 80: 1553-1556.

42. Matthews DE, Fong Y. Amino acid and protein metabolism. In: Rombeau JL, Caldwell MD, eds. Clinical Nutrition; Parenteral Nutrition, 2nd ed. Philadelphia, PA: WB Saunders Co, 1993; 75-112.

43. Shonheyder F, Heilskov NCS, Oleson K. Isotopic studies on the mechanism of negative nitrogen balance produced by immobilization. Scandinavian Journal of Clinical and Laboratory Investigations 1954; 6: 178-188.

44. Lane HW, LeBlanc AD, Putcha L, et al. Nutrition and human physiological adaptations to space flight. American Journal of Clinical Nutrition 1993; 58: 583-588.

45. Davenport DJ, Mostardi RA, Richardson DC, et al. Protein-deficient diet alters serum alkaline phosphatase, bile acids, proteins and urea nitrogen in dogs. Journal of Nutrition 1994; 124: 2677S-2679S.

46. Anderson CF, Moxness K, Meister J, et al. The sensitivity and specificity of nutrition-related variables in relationship to the duration of hospital stay and the rate of complications. Mayo Clinic Proceedings 1984; 59: 477-483.

47. Millward DJ. Protein deficiency, starvation and protein metabolism. Proceedings of the Nutrition Society 1979; 38: 77-88.

48. Munro HN, Chalmers MF. Fracture metabolism at different levels of protein intake. British Journal of Experimental Pathology 1945; 26: 396-404.

49. Tomkins AM, Garlick PJ, Schofield WN, et al. The combined effects of infection and malnutrition on protein metabolism. Clinical Science 1983; 65: 313-324.

50. Zeiderman MR, King RFGJ, Young GA, et al. Metabolic changes in human liver associated with pre-operative intravenous nutrition. Clinical Science 1989; 77: 343-349.

51. Wernerman J, von der Decken A, Vinnars E. Polyribosome concentration in human skeletal muscle after starvation and parenteral or enteral refeeding. Metabolism 1986; 35: 447-451.

52. Fascetti AJ, Mauldin GE, Mauldin GN. Correlation between serum creatine kinase activities and anorexia in cats. Journal of Veterinary Internal Medicine 1997; 11: 9-13.

53. Kitagawa H, Kano M, Sasaki Y, et al. Serum creatine kinase in dogs with dirofilariasis. Journal of Veterinary Medical Science 1991; 53: 569-575.

54. Antonas KN. Nutrition status and the laboratory (letter). Nutrition 1994; 10: 88-89.

55. Root M, Johnston SD, Olson PN. The effect of prepuberal and post-puberal gonadectomy on heat production measured by indirect calorimetry in male and female domestic cats. American Journal of Veterinary Research 1996; 57: 371-374.

56. Flynn MF, Hardie EM, Armstrong PJ. Effect of ovariohysterectomy on maintenance energy requirements in cats. Journal of the American Veterinary Medical Association 1996; 209: 1572-1581.

57. Schiffman SS. Taste and smell in disease. New England Journal of Medicine 1983; 308: 1337-1343.

58. Windsor JA. Underweight patients and the risks of major surgery. World Journal of Surgery 1993; 17: 165-172.

59. Grant JP. Clinical impact of protein malnutrition on organ mass and function. In: Blackburn GL, Grant JP, Young VR, eds. Amino Acids: Metabolism and Medical Applications. Boston, MA: John Wright, 1983; 347-358.

60. Biden TJ, Taylor KW. Effects of ketone bodies on insulin release and islet-cell metabolism in the rat. Biochemical Journal 1983; 212: 371-377.

61. Heymsfield SB, Hoff RD, Gray TF, et al. Heart diseases. In: Kinney JM, Jeejeebhoy KN, Hill GL, et al, eds. Nutrition and Metabolism in Patient Care. Philadelphia, PA: WB Saunders Co, 1988; 477-509.

62. Bistrian BR. Nutritional assessment of the hospitalized patient: A practical approach. In: Wright RA, Heymsfield S, eds. Nutritional Assessment. Boston, MA: Blackwell Scientific, 1984; 183-205.

63. Hoffer LJ. Starvation. In: Shils ME, Olson JA, Shike M, eds. Modern Nutrition in Health and Disease, 8th ed. Philadelphia, PA: Lea & Febiger, 1994; 927-949.

64. Engelking LR, Anwer MS. Liver and biliary tract. In: Anderson NV, ed. Veterinary Gastroenterology, 2nd ed. Philadelphia, PA: Lea & Febiger, 1992; 211-274.

65. Cahill GF, Owen OE. Starvation and survival. Transactions of the American Climatological and Clinical Association 1968; 79: 13-20.

66. Welborn MB, Moldawer LL. Glucose metabolism. In: Rombeau JL, Rolandelli RH, eds. Clinical Nutrition; Enteral and Tube Feeding, 3rd ed. Philadelphia, PA: WB Saunders Co, 1997; 61-80.

67. Gavin LA, Moeller M. The mechanism of recovery of hepatic T4-5'deiodinase during glucose refeeding: Role of glucagon and insulin. Metabolism 1983; 32: 543-551.

68. Vagenakis AG, Burger A, Portnay GI, et al. Diversion of peripheral thyroxine metabolism from activating to inactivating pathways during complete fasting. Journal of Clinical Endocrinology and Metabolism 1975; 41: 191-194.

69. Himwich HE, Rose MI. The respiratory quotient of exercising muscle (abstract). American Journal of Physiology 1927; 81: 485-486.

70. Owen OE, Felig P, Morgan AP, et al. Liver and kidney metabolism during prolonged starvation. Journal of Clinical Investigation 1969; 48: 574-583.

71. Felig P, Owen OE, Wahren J, et al. Amino acid metabolism during prolonged starvation. Journal of Clinical Investigation 1969; 48: 584-594.

72. Fulks RM, Li F, Goldberg A. Effects of insulin, glucose and amino acids on protein turnover in rat diaphragm. Journal of Biological Chemistry 1975; 250: 290-298.

73. Cuthbertson DP. The metabolic response to injury and its nutritional implications: Retrospect and prospect. Journal of Parenteral and Enteral Nutrition 1979; 3: 108-129.

74. Popp MB, Brennan MF. Metabolic response to trauma and infection. In: Fischer JE, ed. Surgical Nutrition. Boston, MA: Little, Brown and Co, 1983; 479-513.

75. Daley BJ, Bistrian BR. Nutritional assessment. In: Zaloga GP, ed. Nutrition in Critical Care. St. Louis, MO: Mosby, 1994; 9-33.

76. Streat SJ, Beddoe AH, Hill GL. Aggressive nutritional support does not prevent protein loss despite fat gain in septic intensive care patients. Journal of Trauma 1987; 27: 262-266.

77. Walton RS, Wingfield WE, Ogilvie GK, et al. Energy expenditure in 104 postoperative and traumatically injured dogs with indirect calorimetry. Journal of Veterinary Emergency and Critical Care 1996; 6: 71-79.

78. Copeland EM, Dudrick SJ, Daley JM, et al. Nutritional changes in neoplasia. In: Fischer JE, ed. Surgical Nutrition. Boston, MA: Little, Brown and Co, 1983; 515-534.

79. Association of American Feed Control Officials. Official Publication, 1999.

80. National Research Council. Nutrient Requirements of Dogs. Washington, DC: National Academy Press, 1985; 44.

81. National Research Council. Nutrient Requirements of Cats. Washington, DC: National Academy Press, 1986; 42.

82. Minard G, Kudsk KA. Is early feeding beneficial? How early is early? New Horizons 1994; 2: 156-163.

83. Burkholder WJ. Metabolic rates and nutrient requirements of sick dogs and cats. Journal of the American Veterinary Medical Association 1995; 206: 614-618.

84. Devey JJ, Crowe DT, Kirby R, et al. Postsurgical nutritional support (letter). Journal of the American Veterinary Medical Association 1995; 206: 1673-1675.

85. Deitel M, Williams VP, Rice TW. Nutrition and the patient requiring mechanical ventilatory support. Journal of the American College of Nutrition 1983; 2: 25-32.

86. Pilbeam SP, Head A, Grossman GD, et al. Undernutrition and the respiratory system. Respiratory Therapy 1983; Part 1 Sept/Oct: 65-69 and Part 2 Nov/Dec: 72-78.

87. Chang S, Silvis SE. Fatty liver produced by hyperalimentation of rats. American Journal of Gastroenterology 1974; 62: 410-418.

88. Lowry SF, Brennan MF. Abnormal liver function during parenteral nutrition: Relation to infusion excess. Journal of Surgical Research 1979; 26: 300-307.

89. Hirai Y, Sanada Y, Fujiwara T, et al. High calorie infusion-induced hepatic impairments in infants. Journal of Parenteral and Enteral Nutrition 1979; 3: 146-150.

90. Boothby WM, Sandiford I. Basal metabolism. Physiological Reviews 1924; 4: 69-161.

91. Moore FA, Moore EE. Trauma. In: Zaloga GP, ed. Nutrition in Critical Care. St. Louis, MO: Mosby, 1994; 571-586.

92. Ogilvie GK, Walters LM, Salman MD, et al. Resting energy expenditure in dogs with nonhematopoietic malignancies before and after excision of tumors. American Journal of Veterinary Research 1996; 57: 1463-1467.

93. Ogilvie GK, Salman MD, Kesel ML, et al. Effect of anesthesia and surgery on energy expenditure determined by indirect calorimetry in dogs with malignant and nonmalignant conditions. American Journal of Veterinary Research 1996; 57: 1321-1326.

94. Elwyn DH, Kinney JM, Askanazi J. Energy expenditure in surgical patients. Surgical Clinics of North America 1981; 61: 545-546.

95. Mann S, Westenskow DR, Houtchens BA. Measured and predicted caloric expenditure in the acutely ill. Critical Care Medicine 1985; 13: 173-177.

96. Ott L, Young B, Phillips R, et al. Brain injury and nutrition. Nutrition in Clinical Practice 1990; 5: 68-73.

97. Wilmore DW, Long JM, Mason AD, et al. Catecholamines: Mediator of the hypermetabolic response to thermal injury. Annals of Surgery 1974; 180: 653-666.

98. Kinney JM, ed. Energy metabolism: Heat, fuel and life. In: Nutrition and Metabolism in Patient Care. Philadelphia, PA: WB Saunders Co, 1988; 3-34.

99. Woolfson AMI. Amino acids–Their role as an energy source. Proceedings of the Nutrition Society 1983; 42: 489-495.

100. Mallet JO. Calculating parenteral feedings: A programmed instruction. Journal of the American Dietetic Association 1984; 84: 1312-1320.

101. Porta EA, Hartroft WS. Protein deficiency and liver injury. American Journal of Nutrition 1970; 23: 447-461.

102. Truswell AS, Hanson JDL, Watson CE, et al. Relation of serum lipids and lipoproteins to fatty liver in Kwashiorkor. American Journal of Nutrition 1969; 22: 568-576.

103. Stein TP. Protein metabolism and parenteral nutrition. In: Rombeau JL, Caldwell MD, eds. Clinical Nutrition; Parenteral Nutrition, 1st ed. Philadelphia, PA: WB Saunders Co, 1986; 100-134.

104. Remillard RL, Thatcher CD. Parenteral nutritional support in the small animal patient. Veterinary Clinics of North America: Small Animal Practice 1989; 19: 1287-1306.

105. Dudrick SJ, Wilmore DW, Vars HM, et al. Long-term total parenteral nutrition with growth, development and positive nitrogen balance. Surgery 1968; 64: 134-142.

106. Remillard RL, Darden D, Michel K, et al. Caloric intake of hospitalized patients (abstract). Journal of Veterinary Clinical Nutrition 1998; (Suppl.): 70.

107. Lippert AC, Buffington CA. Parenteral nutrition. In: DiBartola SP, ed. Fluid Therapy in Small Animal Practice. Philadelphia, PA: WB Saunders Co, 1992; 384-418.

108. Clary EM, Hardie EM, Fischer W, et al. Nonendoscopic antegrade percutaneous gastrostomy: The effect of preplacement gastric insufflation on tube position and intra-abdominal anatomy. Journal of Veterinary Internal Medicine 1996; 10: 15-20.

109. Orton EC. Enteral hyperalimentation administered via needle catheter-jejunostoma as an adjunct to cranial abdominal surgery in dogs and cats. Journal of the American Veterinary Medical Association 1986; 188: 1406-1411.

110. Crowe DT. Methods of enteral feeding in the seriously ill or injured patient: Part I and Part II. Journal of Veterinary Emergency and Critical Care 1986; 3: 1-17.

111. Robertson JE, Christopher MM, Rogers QR. Heinz body formation in cats fed baby food with onion powder (abstract). In: Proceedings. Fifteenth Annual Veterinary Medical Forum, American College of Veterinary Internal Medicine, Lake Buena Vista, FL, 1997: 678.

112. Geliebter A, Schachter S, Lohmann-Walter C, et al. Reduced stomach capacity in obese subjects after dieting. American Journal of Clinical Nutrition 1996; 63: 170-173.

113. The Veterans Affairs Total Parenteral Nutrition Cooperative Study Group. Perioperative total parenteral nutrition in surgical patients. New England Journal of Medicine 1991; 325: 525-532.

114. Lippert AC, Fulton RB, Parr A. A retrospective study of the use of total parenteral nutrition in dogs and cats. Journal of Veterinary Internal Medicine 1993; 7: 52-64.

115. Solomon SM, Kirby DF. The refeeding syndrome: A review. Journal of Parenteral and Enteral Nutrition 1990; 14: 90-97.

116. McMahon MM. Nutritional assessment of the hospitalized patient. In: Blackburn GL, Bothe A, Bistrian BR, eds. In: Proceedings. Hyperalimentation: A Practical Approach. New England Deaconess Hospital and Harvard Medical School, Boston, MA, Sept 15, 1993.

117. Forse RA. Nutrition in critical care. In: Blackburn GL, Bothe A, Bistrian BR, eds. In: Proceedings. Malnutrition in the Hospitalized Patient. New England Deaconess Hospital and Harvard Medical School, Boston, MA, May 5, 1995.

118. DeBiasse MA, Wilmore DW. What is optimal nutritional support? New Horizons 1994; 2: 122-130.

119. American Hospital Formulary Service. Drug Information 1997. American Society of Health-System Pharmacists.

120. Stoner HB, Little RA, Frayn KN, et al. The effect of sepsis on the oxidation of carbohydrate and fat. British Journal of Surgery 1983; 70: 32-35.

121. Iriyama K, Nishiwaki H, Kusaka N, et al. Nitrogen sparing effect of lipid emulsions in septic dogs. Japanese Journal of Surgery 1985; 15: 321-323.

122. MacFie J, Courtney DF, Brennan TG. Continuous versus intermittent infusion of fat emulsions during total parenteral nutrition: Clinical trial. Nutrition 1991; 7: 99-103.

123. Nordenstrom J, Askanazi J, Elwyn DH, et al. Nitrogen balance during total parenteral nutrition. Annals of Surgery 1983; 197: 27-33.

124. Chiarelli A, Siliprandi L. Burns. In: Zaloga GP, ed. Nutrition in Critical Care. St. Louis, MO: Mosby, 1994; 587-597.

125. Deitel M, Kaminsky MV. Total parenteral nutrition by peripheral vein: The lipid system. Canadian Medical Association Journal 1974; 111: 152-154.

126. Klein S, Miles JM. Metabolic effects of long-chain and medium-chain triglyceride emulsions in humans (editorial). Journal of Parenteral and Enteral Nutrition 1994; 18: 396.

127. Mashima Y. Effect of calorie overload on puppy livers during parenteral nutrition. Journal of Parenteral and Enteral Nutrition 1979; 3: 139-145.

128. Meguid MM, Akahoshi MP, Jeffers S, et al. Amelioration of metabolic complications of conventional total parenteral nutrition. Archives of Surgery 1984; 119: 1294-1298.

129. Adamkin DH, Gelke KN, Andrews BF. Fat emulsions and hypertriglyceridemia. Journal of Parenteral and Enteral Nutrition 1984; 8: 563-567.

130. Edgren B, Meng HC. The removal of dietary chylomicrons and artificial fat emulsions from the circulation of rats and dogs. Acta Physiologica Scandinavica 1962; 56: 237-243.

131. Kesterson J. Acute intravenous clearance study of 10% and 20% safflower oil emulsions and 10% and 20% Intralipid in dogs. Abbott Laboratories, Chicago, IL. Study No. T77-527. 1978.

132. ASPEN Board of Directors. Guidelines for the use of parenteral and enteral nutrition in adult and pediatric patients. Journal of Parenteral and Enteral Nutrition 1993; 17 (Suppl.): 16SA.

133. Forrester SD, Moreland KJ. Hypophosphatemia: Causes and clinical consequences. Journal of Veterinary Internal Medicine 1989; 3: 149-159.

134. Hardy RM, Adams LG. Hypophosphatemia. In: Kirk RW, ed. Current Veterinary Therapy X. Philadelphia, PA: WB Saunders Co, 1989; 43-47.

135. Center SA. Hepatic lipidosis, glucocorticoid hepatopathy, vascular hepatopathy, storage disorders, amyloidosis and iron toxicity. In: Guilford WG, Center SA, Strombeck DR, et al, eds. Strombeck's Small Animal Gastroenterology, 3rd ed. Philadelphia, PA: WB Saunders Co, 1996; 766-801.

136. Center SA. Pathophysiology, laboratory diagnosis, and diseases of the liver. In: Ettinger SJ, Feldman EC, eds. Textbook of Veterinary Internal Medicine, 4th ed. Philadelphia, PA: WB Saunders Co, 1995; 1261-1419.

137. Demetriou AA, Jones LK. Vitamins. In: Rombeau JL, Caldwell MD, eds. Clinical Nutrition; Parenteral Nutrition, 2nd ed. Philadelphia, PA: WB Saunders Co, 1993; 184-202.

138. Smith JL, Canhan JE, Wells PA. Effect of phototherapy light, sodium bisulfite, and pH on vitamin stability in total parenteral nutrition admixtures. Journal of Parenteral and Enteral Nutrition 1988; 12: 394-402.

139. Iriyama K, Mori T, Takenaka T, et al. Effect of serum zinc level on amount of collagen hydroxyproline in the healing gut during total parenteral nutrition: An experimental study. Journal of Parenteral and Enteral Nutrition 1982; 6: 416-420.

140. Buffington CAT. Nutritional management of critical care patients. In: Campfield WW, ed. Fourteenth Proceedings of the Kal Kan Waltham Symposium: Emergency Medicine and Critical Care Medicine. Vernon, CA: Kal Kan Foods, 1991: 133-139.

141. Hill RC. Critical care nutrition. In: Wills JM, Simpson KW, eds. The Waltham Book of Clinical Nutrition of the Dog & Cat. Tarrytown, NY: Pergamon, 1994; 39-61.

142. Gabrielson K, Remillard RL, Huso DL. Zinc toxicity with pancreatic necrosis in parenterally fed piglets. Veterinary Pathology 1996; 33: 692-696.

143. Jeejeebhoy KN. Trace element requirements in parenteral nutrition. Report of the Second Ross Conference on Medical Research. Nutritional Assessment–Present Status, Future Directions and Prospects. Columbus, OH, 1981: 76-77.

ASSISTED
FEEDING

144. Trissel LA, Gilbert DL, Martinez JF, et al. Compatibility of medications with 3-in-1 parenteral nutrition admixtures. Journal of Parenteral and Enteral Nutrition 1999; 23: 67-74.

145. Trissel LA. Handbook on Injectable Drugs, 9th ed. Bethesda, MD: American Society of Hospital Pharmacists, 1996.

146. McClendon RR. Clinical evaluation of the IV formulator for fabricating TPN solutions. American Journal of Intravenous Therapy and Clinical Nutrition 1981; 8: 17-20.

147. Payne-James JJ, Khawaja HT. First choice for total parenteral nutrition: The peripheral route. Journal of Parenteral and Enteral Nutrition 1993; 17: 468-478.

148. Everitt NJ, McMahon MJ. Peripheral intravenous nutrition. Nutrition 1994; 10: 49-57.

149. Kohlhardt SR, Smith RC, Wright CR. Peripheral versus central intravenous nutrition: Comparison of two delivery systems. British Journal of Surgery 1994; 81: 66-70.

150. Matsusue S, Nishimura S, Koizumi S, et al. Preventive effect of simultaneously infused lipid emulsions against thrombophlebitis during postoperative peripheral parenteral nutrition. Surgery Today 1995; 25: 667-671.

151. Daly JM, Masser E, Hansen L, et al. Peripheral vein infusion of dextrose/amino acid solutions ± 20% fat emulsion. Journal of Parenteral and Enteral Nutrition 1985; 9: 296-299.

152. Isaacs JW, Millikan WJ, Stackhouse J, et al. Parenteral nutrition of adults with a 900 milliosmolar solution via peripheral veins. American Journal of Clinical Nutrition 1977; 30: 552-559.

153. Maden M, Alexander DJ, McMahon MJ. Influence of catheter type on occurrence of thrombophlebitis during peripheral intravenous nutrition. Lancet 1992; 339: 101-103.

154. Bayer-Berger M, Chiolero R, Freeman J. Incidence of phlebitis in peripheral parenteral nutrition: Effect of the different nutrient solutions. Clinical Nutrition 1989; 8: 181-186.

155. Gazitua R, Wilson K, Bistrian BR, et al. Factors determining peripheral vein tolerance to amino acid infusions. Archives of Surgery 1979; 114: 897-900.

156. McCarthy MC, Shives JK, Robinson RJ, et al. Prospective evaluation of single and triple lumen catheters in total parenteral nutrition. Journal of Parenteral and Enteral Nutrition 1987; 11: 259-262.

157. Otto CM, Kaufman GM, Crowe DT. Intraosseous infusion of fluids and therapeutics. Compendium on Continuing Education for the Practicing Veterinarian 1989; 11: 421-430.

158. Moran JM, Limon M, Mehedero G, et al. Long term peritoneal nutrition in dogs: Metabolic and histopathological results. Nutrition 1989; 5: 89-93.

159. Garcia-Gamito FJ, Moran JM, Mehedero G, et al. Long term peritoneal nutrition in dogs, both normal and after intestinal resection. International Surgery 1991; 76: 235-240.

160. Klein MD, Coran AG, Drongowski RA, et al. The quantitative transperitoneal absorption of a fat emulsion: Implications for intraperitoneal nutrition. Journal of Pediatric Surgery 1983; 18: 724-731.

161. Gaukroger PB, Roberts JO, Manners TA. Infusion thrombophlebitis: A prospective comparison of 645 Vialon and Teflon cannulae in anaesthetic and postoperative use. Anaesthesia and Intensive Care 1988; 16: 265-271.

162. McKee JM, Shell JA, Warren TA, et al. Complications of intravenous therapy: A randomized prospective study–Vialon vs. Teflon. Journal of Intravenous Nursing 1989; 12: 288-295.

163. Linder LE, Curelaru I, Gustavsson B, et al. Material thrombogenicity in central venous catheterizations: A comparison between soft antebrachial catheters of silicone elastomer and polyurethane. Journal of Parenteral and Enteral Nutrition 1984; 8: 399-406.

164. Hershey DO, Tomford JW, McLaren CE, et al. The natural history of intravenous catheter associated phlebitis. Archives of Internal Medicine 1984; 144: 1373-1375.

165. Myles PS, Buckland MR, Burnett WJ. Single versus double occlusive dressing technique to minimize infusion thrombophlebitis: Vialon and Teflon cannulae reassessed. Anaesthesia and Intensive Care 1991; 19: 525-529.

166. Kohlhardt SR, Smith RC, Wright CR, et al. Fine-bore peripheral catheters versus central venous catheters for delivery of intravenous nutrition. Nutrition 1992; 8: 412-417.

167. Reynolds JV, Walsh K, Ruigrok J, et al. Randomized comparison of sil-

icone versus Teflon cannulas for peripheral intravenous nutrition. Annals of the Royal College of Surgeons of England 1995; 75: 447-449.

168. Borow M, Crowley JG. Evaluation of central venous catheter thrombogenicity. Acta Anaesthesiologica Scandinavica 1985; 81 (Suppl.): 59-64.

169. di Costanzo J, Sastre B, Choux R, et al. Mechanism of thrombogenesis during total parenteral nutrition: Role of catheter composition. Journal of Parenteral and Enteral Nutrition 1988; 12: 190-194.

170. Imperial J, Bistrian BR, Bothe A, et al. Limitation of central vein thrombosis in total parenteral nutrition by continuous infusion of low-dose heparin. Journal of the American College of Nutrition 1983; 2: 63-73.

171. Roongpisuthipong C, Puchaiwatananon O, Songchitsomboon S, et al. Hydrocortisone, heparin and peripheral intravenous infusion. Nutrition 1994; 10: 211-213.

172. Alpan G, Eyal F, Springer C, et al. Heparinization of alimentation solutions administered through peripheral veins in premature infants: A controlled study. Pediatrics 1984; 74: 375-378.

173. Bozzetti F. Central venous catheter sepsis. Surgery, Gynecology and Obstetrics 1985; 161: 293-301.

174. Maki DG, Weise CE, Sarafin HW. A semiquantitative culture method for identifying intravenous catheter-related infection. New England Journal of Medicine 1977; 296: 1305-1309.

175. Maki DG, Goldmann DA, Rhame FS. Infection control in intravenous therapy. Annals of Internal Medicine 1973; 79: 867-887.

176. Ryan JA, Abel RM, Abbott WM, et al. Catheter complications in total parenteral nutrition: A prospective study of 200 consecutive patients. New England Journal of Medicine 1974; 290: 757-761.

177. Herruzo-Bareara R, Garcia-Caballero J, Vera-Cortes L, et al. Growth of microorganisms in parenteral nutrition solutions. American Journal of Hospital Pharmacy 1984; 41: 1178-1180.

178. Goldmann DA, Martin WT, Worthington JW. Growth of bacteria and fungi in total parenteral nutrition solutions. American Journal of Surgery 1971; 126: 314-318.

179. Wilkinson WR, Flores LL, Pagones JN. Growth of microorganisms in parenteral nutritional fluids. Drug Intelligence and Clinical Pharmacy 1973; 7: 226-231.

180. Schecekelhoff DJ, Mirtallo MJ, Ayers LW, et al. Growth of bacteria and fungi in total nutrient admixtures. American Journal of Hospital Pharmacy 1986; 43: 73-77.

181. Rowe CE, Fukuyama TT, Martinoff JT. Growth of microorganisms in total nutrient admixtures. Drug Intelligence and Clinical Pharmacy 1987; 21: 633-638.

182. Simmons BP, Hotton TM, Wong ES, et al. CDC guidelines for prevention of intravascular infections. Infection Control 1982; 3: 52-67.

183. Adams S, Dellinger EP, Wurtz MJ, et al. Enteral versus parenteral nutritional support following laparotomy for trauma: A randomized prospective trial. Journal of Trauma 1986; 26: 882-891.

184. Moore EE, Jones TN. Benefits of immediate jejunostomy feeding after major abdominal trauma–A prospective randomized study. Journal of Trauma 1986; 26: 874-881.

185. Alverdy J, Chi HS, Sheldon GE. The effect of parenteral nutrition on gastrointestinal immunity. Annals of Surgery 1985; 202: 681-684.

186. Remillard RL, Guerino F, Dudgeon DL, et al. Effects of intravenous glutamine and limited enteral feedings in piglets: Amelioration of small intestinal disuse atrophy. Journal of Nutrition 1998; 128: 2723S-2726S.

187. Remillard RL, Dudgeon DL, Yardley J. Atrophied small intestinal responses to oral feedings of milk (abstract). Journal of Nutrition 1998; 128: 2727S-2729S.

188. Andrassy RJ, Mahour GH, Harrison MR, et al. The role of early postoperative feeding in the pediatric surgical patient. Journal of Pediatric Surgeon 1979; 14: 381-385.

189. Andrassy RJ, Dubois T, Page CP, et al. Early postoperative nutritional enhancement utilizing enteral branched-chain amino acids by way of a needle catheter jejunostomy. American Journal of Surgery 1985; 150: 730-734.

190. Hermann-Zaidius MG. Malabsorption in adults: Etiology, evaluation and management. Journal of the American Dietetic Association 1986; 86: 1171-1178.

191. McAdams P, DeChicco RS, Matarese LE, et al. Biochemical assessment and monitoring of nutritional status. In: Latifi R, Dudrick SJ, eds. Current Surgical Nutrition. Austin, TX: RG Landes, Chapman & Hall, 1996; 1-31.

■ CASE 12-1

Inappropriate Hospital Feeding Plan

Rebecca L. Remillard, PhD, DVM
Diplomate ACVN
Angell Memorial Animal Hospital
Boston, Massachusetts, USA

Assess the Animal

A three-year-old castrated male boxer was referred to the orthopedic surgery service for examination of its rear legs. The dog had been hit by a garbage truck the day before and was stabilized by the referring veterinarian. The dog was bright and alert on admission but was experiencing pain and unwilling to walk on its hind quarters. The dog's rear legs had been trapped under the garbage truck's tires immediately after being hit. Severe shearing and degloving-type injuries to both hind feet were present from the tarsus distally. Some metatarsal bones and phalanges were missing from both hind limbs; however, no fractures were detected radiographically. The initial plan was to hospitalize the dog in a regular ward for the next 10 to 12 days for daily wet-to-dry bandage changes and wound débridement. Before the accident the dog was healthy, weighed 21 kg and had a body condition score (BCS) of 3/5.

The dog was anesthetized daily for wound assessment, débridement and rebandaging. On Day 7 of hospitalization, the anesthesiologist requested a nutritional consult because the patient had been steadily losing weight and body condition as indicated by the daily recorded body weights for drug-dose calculations. Nutritional assessment noted the patient weighed 18 kg. The dog had lost 3 kg (14% of body weight) within one week of hospitalization and now had a BCS of 2/5. Serum biochemistry data were within normal limits except for an albumin concentration of 2.1 g/dl (normal 2.6 to 4.2 g/dl).

Assess the Food(s) and Feeding Method

Before the accident the dog consumed Purina Dog Chow[a] free choice. The dog had been hospitalized in a regular ward with a twice a day feeding schedule. The clinician indicated no special dietary considerations for this dog; therefore, the dog was to be fed the standard hospital food for its species and lifestage (Science Diet Canine Maintenance[b]) twice daily. The amount fed was to be determined by the ward attendant according to a product feeding guide (one and one-fourth cans/meal). However, when the medical record for this dog was examined, it became clear that the regular ward feeding times of 8:00 a.m. and 3:00 p.m. always coincided with clinician's orders of NPO (nil per os). The dog was fasted every morning to allow anesthesia in the early afternoon, and the dog was always subsequently held off food until it fully recovered from anesthesia, which generally occurred around 5:00 p.m. Without special arrangements, there was no ward attendant available after 3:00 p.m. for feeding.

Questions

1. What was the dog's daily energy requirement (DER) upon entry to the hospital? If the dog had not been fasted, was the standard hospital feeding protocol appropriate to maintain optimal body weight?

2. What evidence is there that the standard hospital food and feeding schedule used in the ward were inappropriate for the patient? More specifically, which component of the standard hospital orders (food and/or feeding method) was insufficient for this case? Why?

3. What are the major nutrients of concern for this underweight patient?

4. What are appropriate feeding orders for this dog during the remainder of its hospital stay?

Answers and Discussion

1. The estimated DER for this 21-kg dog (BCS of 3/5) upon entry was 1,099 kcal (4.6 MJ). Resting energy requirement (RER) = $(21)^{0.75}$ x 70 = 687 kcal. DER = 1.6 x 687 = 1,099 kcal/day. Science Diet Canine Maintenance contains 437 kcal/can (1.83 MJ/can). Therefore, two and one-half cans per day = 1,093 kcal/day (3.66 MJ/day) should have been sufficient to maintain body weight and condition in this patient. Thus, the standard hospital feeding protocol should have been sufficient for this patient had the clinician not ordered NPO daily.

2. The anesthesia record clearly demonstrated a history of weight loss. When the dog was first admitted to the hospital, one and one-fourth cans of Science Diet Canine Maintenance twice daily should have been appropriate. However, the regular ward feeding times (feeding method) were not appropriate for this case given the dog's fasting schedule for anesthesia.

3. The primary nutritional goal for this patient is to increase its energy and protein intake because of the decreased eating time and increased heat and protein losses from large wound areas. The best product would be a highly palatable, complete and balanced food that is high in protein and fat and nutrient dense. The estimated RER for this 18-kg dog is 612 kcal/day (2.56 MJ). RER = $(18)^{0.75}$ x 70 = 612 kcal.

4. Science Diet Feline Maintenance[b] contains 454 kcal/14.25-oz can (1.90 MJ/can) and was also readily available in the regular ward. Therefore, feeding orders were specifically written for a member of the nursing staff to offer the dog, after adequate recovery from daily anesthesia (around 6:00 p.m.), one and one-third 14.25-oz cans of Science Diet Feline Maintenance and a second can and one-third at midnight for the remainder of the dog's hospital stay. Food intake and appetite were to be recorded daily.

This product was chosen because a relatively small volume of food could be fed during the evening hours and still meet the dog's nutritional requirements. Further, the feeding schedule should allow the dog to have an empty stomach by mid-morning the next day for anesthesia and another bandage change. If the dog had not lost weight, feeding two cans of Science Diet Canine Maintenance twice throughout the evening hours probably would have been adequate. However, a more calorically dense food was chosen to enhance weight gain before the dog was discharged from the hospital.

Progress Notes

The new hospital feeding plan was instituted immediately. The dog maintained a good appetite, consumed the two and two-thirds cans readily during the late evening hours, but did not gain weight before leaving the hospital five days later. The dog did not develop any gastrointestinal problems such as diarrhea when the food was changed, nor did vomiting occur when the dog was anesthetized. Adequate weight gain would require more than 1,100 kcal (4.6 MJ) per day (DER at 21 kg) for several weeks. Therefore, the owner was instructed to feed a dry canine growth food (Science Diet Canine Growth[b]) (four cups/day divided into two meals [1,450 kcal/day, 6.07 MJ/day]) until the dog regained normal body weight and condition at 21 kg. After body weight and condition were achieved, the owner was instructed to feed three cups of the dog's previous food for maintenance.

Bandage changes were rescheduled every third day and the dog was weighed at each recheck. One month later, the dog weighed 22 kg, had a BCS of 3/5, was eating its regular food and reportedly had 80 to 90% use of its hind legs.

Endnotes

a. Ralston Purina Co., St. Louis, MO, USA.
b. Hill's Pet Nutrition, Inc., Topeka, KS, USA.

Bibliography

Moore FA, Moore EE. Trauma. In: Zaloga GP, ed. Nutrition in Critical Care. St. Louis, MO: Mosby, 1994; 571-586.

■ CASE 12-2

Weight Loss in a Cat

Philip Roudebush, DVM
Diplomate ACVIM (Internal Medicine)
Hill's Science and Technology Center
Topeka, Kansas, USA

Assess the Animal

An adult female cat of unknown age was examined for lethargy and weakness. The cat was found the day before as a stray animal; therefore, no additional history or information was available. Physical examination revealed a depressed, febrile (rectal temperature 41.5°C [106°F]), dehydrated (estimated 5 to 7%) cat with a large fluctuant abscess on the right forelimb. The cat weighed 3 kg and had a body condition score (BCS) of 2/5. No other abnormalities were noted except for a dull, unkempt coat.

The cat was anesthetized to lance, drain and débride the abscess site. Subcutaneous fluids (200 ml of lactated Ringer's solution) were administered to treat the dehydration and amoxicillin (Amoxi-Inject[a]) was injected intramuscularly.

The cat was much more alert the next morning with a mild fever (39°C [102.2°F]). The abscess was flushed with an antimicrobial solution and the amoxicillin was changed to an oral preparation (Amoxi-Tabs[a]). Subcutaneous fluids were changed from lactated Ringer's solution to 150 ml 5% dextrose in water (D-5-W).

Assess the Food(s) and Feeding Method

The dietary history was unknown. The cat was offered moist and dry adult maintenance foods on the second day of hospitalization, but ate very little. The cat was then offered a small-animal dietary supplement (Nutri-Cal[b]) and readily consumed the product. The amount recommended on the package label was 3 tsp/10 lb body weight once a day. The guaranteed analysis of the supplement was as follows: crude protein 1.5% minimum, crude fat 34.5% minimum, crude fiber 3.7% maximum, moisture 14% maximum. The supplement also contained minerals and vitamins. The energy content was listed as 30 kcal/tsp (125.5 kJ/tsp).

Questions

1. How do the levels of key nutritional factors in this product compare with an optimal nutrient profile for recovery from infection, weight loss and stress in this patient?

2. Will the subcutaneous dextrose solution and recommended amounts of dietary supplement meet the daily energy requirement (DER) for this cat?

3. Outline another feeding plan for this patient.

Answers and Discussion

1. The dietary supplement provides dry matter nutrient levels as follows: protein 1.7%, fat 40%, crude fiber 4.3% and carbohydrate 45 to 50% (estimated). The amount of protein is clearly inadequate to meet the patient's metabolic needs for tissue repair and synthesis, weight gain and immune function to combat the local and systemic bacterial infection. The fat and energy content are adequate to meet the DER, provided an appropriate amount is fed. The dietary supplement contains vitamins that are important metabolic cofactors.

2. The estimated DER for this cat in the hospital would approximate its resting energy requirement (RER). The RER at the cat's current body weight of 3 kg is approximately 160 kcal (670 kJ). This could be increased to 200 kcal (837 kJ) for an ideal body weight of 4 kg. Dextrose solutions routinely used for parenteral fluid therapy, generally D-5-W, are good sources of water but poor sources of energy. The energy provided by the 150 ml of D-5-W administered to this cat is only 30 to 35 kcal (125 to 146 kJ). The dietary supplement fed at the recommended amount (2 tsp/day) contributes another 60 kcal (251 kJ). Thus, the energy content of these combined sources provides only about 50% of the RER for this patient.

3. Assisted feeding is recommended because the cat is not eating its estimated RER. However, appropriate fluid therapy, wound management and systemic antibiotics should result in rapid recovery if no other medical problems exist. Dose syringe or hand feeding an appropriate blended recovery or moist adult maintenance food should successfully meet the short-term nutritional requirements of this patient until it feels better. Syringe or hand feeding is often not successful for longer term feeding because of time constraints with the hospital staff or pet owner and intransigence of the patient. Placement of a nasoesophageal tube and use of an appropriate liquid recovery food (nutrient profile appropriate for cats) would also be prudent. More aggressive feeding techniques are probably not warranted at this time.

Progress Notes

The oral amoxicillin was continued. The food was changed to a higher protein blended recovery food (Prescription Diet Canine/Feline a/d[c]) that was offered through a dose syringe. The estimated RER (160 kcal [670 kJ]) was divided into four equal feedings (30 ml each). By the fourth day of hospitalization, the cat was feeling much better and eating enough of the blended food to meet its RER. The cat was discharged for further care at home. A moist adult maintenance food was offered twice daily and a dry adult maintenance food was available free choice. The cat reached its optimal body weight of 4 kg within 10 days and was given to another family.

Endnotes

a. Pfizer Animal Health, Exton, PA, USA.
b. EVSCO Pharmaceuticals, Buena, NJ, USA.
c. Hill's Pet Nutrition, Inc., Topeka, KS, USA.

CASE 12-3

Gastric Tube Feeding in a Cat

Stephen D. Gilson, DVM
Diplomate ACVS
Sonora Veterinary Surgery and Oncology
Scottsdale, Arizona, USA

Assess the Animal

A two-year-old castrated male Persian cat was examined for evaluation and treatment of suspected septic peritonitis secondary to dehiscence of an intestinal anastomosis. Eight days before, the cat had been diagnosed with an intestinal intussusception. A jejunal resection (6 cm) and anastomosis had been performed. After surgery, the cat remained depressed, weak and was intermittently febrile with rectal temperatures spiking at 41.6°C (107°F).

When examined, the cat was thin (body weight 3.5 kg, body condition score 2/5), febrile (41.2°C [106.2°F]), depressed and showed signs of circulatory shock. Ten ml of purulent fluid were recovered by abdominocentesis. Microscopically, the effusion contained 99% degenerative neutrophils. Bacteria were present in large numbers.

Assess the Food(s) and Feeding Method

The owners reported that the cat was normally fed a commercial grocery brand dry food free choice and was a hearty eater before the intussusception occurred. Except for a small meal three days after surgery, the cat had not eaten for nine days.

Questions

1. What is an appropriate treatment plan for this patient?
2. What are the key nutritional factors to consider in this anorectic cat with sepsis?
3. What feeding techniques should be considered to support this patient?

Answers and Discussion

1. Septic shock should be managed very aggressively, and management should precede surgical exploration of the abdomen. Intravenous fluid therapy helps maintain cardiac output and prevents further decline in cardiopulmonary function. Vasoactive drugs may also be needed to maintain cardiac output. Electrolyte imbalances and hypoglycemia are common in patients with peritonitis and should be corrected in addition to providing intravenous fluids. Standard shock therapy with corticosteroids and bicarbonate is usually indicated. To combat sepsis, antimicrobial therapy should be started while awaiting the results of specific culture and antimicrobial sensitivity testing from samples obtained by prior centesis of the peritoneal cavity. After the patient has been stabilized, exploratory surgery is indicated to drain and lavage the abdomen, find the cause of the sepsis (probably dehiscence of the previous anastomosis) and repair the defect. Aggressive nutritional support is also indicated in an underweight, septic patient recovering from major surgery. Nutritional support will help reverse the catabolic process associated with sepsis, improve the immune response and optimize healing.

2. Key nutritional factors in this patient include energy, fat and protein. Providing protein and other nutrients in an energy-dense formula will aid in sparing lean-body mass and maintain host defenses. Palatability is another key factor in anorectic patients; foods with high concentrations of protein, fat and water are usually palatable.

3. Intestinal function should be normal unless a large portion of the intestinal tract is removed during the second surgery. Therefore, assisted feeding using enteral techniques is recommended for this patient during the postoperative period. Nasoesophageal tube feeding is a short-term option (five to 10 days), does not require sedation or general anesthesia, takes less than 10 minutes to complete and is less expensive than placing other tubes. Nasoesophageal tubes could also be used if the patient is unable to tolerate anesthesia or if surgery had to be postponed. Enteral tube placement (i.e., esophagostomy, pharyngostomy or gastrostomy tubes) during surgery would be easy, convenient and allow enteral feeding to begin early in the recovery period. A gastrostomy tube would be large enough to handle a variety of commercial foods specifically formulated for cats. The daily energy requirement (DER) in the hospital should be equal to at least resting energy requirement (RER) at the patient's current weight. The amount of food provided daily should be divided into multiple small meals. Assisted feeding should be continued until the cat is eating at least 50% of DER voluntarily for two to three days.

Progress Notes

The cat was initially treated for septic shock. An exploratory celiotomy was performed after the cat's physiologic parameters stabilized. A small dehiscence at the anastomosis site and severe secondary generalized peritonitis were found. A partial omentectomy was performed, the affected portion of small intestine was resected and healthy bowel was anastomosed. A mushroom-tipped, 18-Fr. Pezzer gastrostomy tube was placed intraoperatively and the abdomen was copiously lavaged and sutured closed routinely.

The cat's RER was calculated to be 180 kcal/day (753 kJ/day) at its current weight of 3.5 kg (RER = 70[3.5]$^{0.75}$). Feeding was begun via the gastrostomy tube six hours postsurgery. A commercial moist homogenized recovery formula (Prescription Diet Canine/Feline a/d[a]) was chosen because it is complete and balanced for cats and can be administered through a gastrostomy tube. The food was made into a gruel by blending two 5.5-oz. cans with 50 ml water. The total volume was approximately 300 ml of liquid gruel that contained 300 kcal (1.26 MJ) metabolizable energy. The feeding protocol for the first 24 hours of hospitalization included six 30-ml feedings of the gruel (i.e., every four hours). The gruel was given through the gastrostomy tube over three to five minutes while the cat was monitored for signs of intolerance (i.e., nausea, discomfort and vomiting). Although no signs of intolerance were noted, the appropriate strategy to follow should they occur is to discontinue feeding and attempt to feed the patient again 60 minutes later. Ten ml of water were flushed through the tube at the end of each bolus feeding. The cat's maintenance fluid requirement was approximately 210 ml/day (60 ml/kg body weight/day). The gruel provided approximately 180 ml of fluid plus six 10-ml water

flushes through the gastrostomy tube per day provided 240 ml of fluid per day, which adequately maintained hydration.

The feeding protocol was modified to five 35-ml feedings of the same gruel during Day 2 of hospitalization. On Day 3, the feeding protocol was modified to four 45-ml feedings of the same gruel (i.e., every six hours). No problems with intolerance were noted. Fresh food (dry recovery formula cat food) and water were offered and the cat's voluntary food intake was monitored. Gastrostomy tube feedings were continued for eight days, but were gradually reduced as the cat voluntarily ate more dry food. The gastrostomy tube was removed 14 days after surgery, the cat's regular food was reintroduced gradually over several days and the cat made an uneventful recovery.

Endnote

a. Hill's Pet Nutrition, Inc., Topeka, KS, USA.

Bibliography

Gilson SD. Nutritional assessment and feeding of the anorectic acute care patient. In: Enteral Nutrition: Its Performance in Recovery (monograph). Topeka, KS: Hill's Pet Nutrition, Inc., 1992; 15-27.

Davenport DJ. Enteral and parenteral nutritional support. In: Ettinger SJ, Feldman EC, eds. Textbook of Veterinary Internal Medicine, 4th ed. Philadelphia, PA: WB Saunders Co, 1995; 244-252.

Abood SK, Mauterer JV, McLoughlin MA, et al. Nutritional support of hospitalized patients. In: Slatter DJ, ed. Textbook of Small Animal Surgery, 2nd ed. Philadelphia, PA: WB Saunders Co, 1993; 63-83.

■ CASE 12-4

Jejunostomy-Tube Feeding in a Dog

Korin F. Saker, MS, DVM, PhD
Virginia-Maryland Regional College
   of Veterinary Medicine
Blacksburg, Virginia, USA

Assess the Animal

An 11-year-old neutered male cocker spaniel was presented with a six-month history of recurrent episodes of regurgitation upon eating solid food. The dog was able to drink and eat moist food blended with water, but ingestion of dry food or solid moist food consistently resulted in regurgitation. Three years earlier, the patient had been diagnosed with an esophageal stricture and secondary megaesophagus, which had been successfully managed with esophageal dilatation, medications (sucralfate[a], cimetidine[b], metoclopramide[c]), a sequence of dietary changes (See below.) and elevated feeding for two and one-half years. At that time, a small (1 cm in diameter) gastric mass was detected. The owner elected to monitor the mass via endoscopy every three to four months rather than to have it resected.

On physical examination, the dog was alert with a normal temperature, pulse and respiratory rate. Results of serum biochemistry analysis, complete blood count and urinalysis were normal. Although mild right-heart enlargement was noted on thoracic radiographs, the pul-

monary parenchyma was normal and no esophageal abnormalities were detected. The dog weighed 8.6 kg and had a body condition score of 2/5 but had lost 3 kg over the last six months. An endoscopic examination revealed pyloric hypertrophy and a marked enlargement of the previously noted gastric mass. An exploratory celiotomy was performed during which two separate gastroesophageal masses were removed. Biopsy specimens were obtained from the pylorus. The histologic diagnosis of the gastric masses was leiomyoma; however, the pylorus was histologically normal. A 5-Fr. jejunostomy tube was placed intraoperatively.

Assess the Food(s) and Feeding Method

After the initial esophageal dilatation procedure, chronic regurgitation in this patient was initially managed using a moist slurry made from 454 g of Prescription Diet Canine i/d[d] blenderized with 340-ml water and fed in an elevated position. The dog was transitioned from the slurry to moist food, then water-soaked kibbles and finally to small dry kibbles (Iams Mini-Chunks[e], 1 to 1.5 cups/day). Neither regurgitation nor vomiting had been observed for 2.5 years postesophageal dilatation.

Jejunostomy-tube feeding was initiated 12 hours postoperatively using a polymeric canine liquid food (Canine CliniCare[f]) supplying 1.0 kcal/ml (4.2 kJ/ml) with a nutrient profile of 27.2% protein, 30.8% fat, 33.4% carbohydrate and 4.8% ash on a dry matter basis. This food was delivered via an enteral pump system for a continuous rate infusion. In addition, fluid therapy was maintained through a peripheral venous catheter.

Questions

1. After the esophageal dilatation, chronic regurgitation was initially managed in this patient using a highly digestible moist slurry fed in an elevated position. Discuss how the feeding schedule, form and nutrient composition of the dog's food facilitated gastric emptying during this time.

2. A polymeric liquid food supplying 1 kcal/ml (4.2 kJ/ml) with an osmolality of 230 mOsm/kg was administered through the jejunostomy tube. Calculate the dog's resting energy requirement (RER) and maintenance fluid requirement. Write the feeding orders for the continuous rate infusion of a liquid enteral food and concurrent crystalloid intravenous fluid administration to meet the patient's fluid requirement and RER.

3. Potential complications of enteral feeding include vomiting, abdominal discomfort and diarrhea. Discuss how the general characteristics, administration and infusion rate of polymeric foods reduced these complications.

Answers and Discussion

1. In general, smaller meals have a faster rate of gastric emptying than larger meals. Increasing the moisture content of foods increases the rate of gastric emptying suggesting that a moist food will leave the stomach faster than dry kibble. Increasing the fat content of the food slows gastric emptying. Therefore, feeding this dog small meals of a highly digestible, moderate-fat, low-fiber moist product facilitated gastric emptying when the dog was initially presented three years ago. An elevated feeding position is indicated in the dietary management of megaesophagus to allow gravitational forces to enhance passage of food into the stomach.

2. The RER of this patient was 352 kcal/day (1,473 kJ/day) (RER = $70[BW_{kg}]^{0.75}$ or $[8.6]^{0.75}$ x 70). The caloric density of the liquid diet was 1 kcal/ml (4.2 kJ/ml). To meet the daily RER, the patient must be fed 352 ml of the food every 24 hours. On Day 1, 176 ml or 50% of RER were delivered at a continuous infusion rate of 7 ml/hour. This amount supplied approximately 170 ml of the patient's daily water requirement. The volume of liquid food was increased to supply 100% of RER on Day 2 using an infusion rate of 14 ml/hour, which supplied 352 ml of the daily water requirement. Because the maintenance fluid requirement for this patient was 516 ml/day (516 ml = 8.6 kg x 60 ml/kg body weight/day), the infusion of crystalloid intravenous fluid was reduced to 340 ml/day and 180 ml/day on Days 1 and 2 of jejunostomy-tube feeding, respectively.

3. The digestion process begins in the oral cavity as the particle size of the meal is reduced through mastication and salivary enzyme secretions. As the meal reaches the gastrointestinal tract, gastric and pancreatic secretions further breakdown dietary protein and carbohydrate to dipeptides and tripeptides and monosaccharides and disaccharides, respectively. Bile salts, phospholipids and cholesterol from the gallbladder and liver solubilize dietary fat within the intestine. Water moves into the duodenum diluting the chyme and reducing the osmolarity from 1,200 to 1,500 mOsm/l to 300 to 350 mOsm/l. Peristalsis and segmentation in the duodenum deliver small volumes of an isosmolar, water-soluble chyme to the jejunum for further digestion and absorption. The isosmolar polymeric food administered to this patient was composed of small peptides, saccharides and emulsified long-chain triacylglycerides. Continuous infusion of small volumes of liquid food (14 ml/hour [0.23 ml/min.]) mimicked normal physiology of the jejunum, fostering nutrient absorption and lessening the likelihood of abdominal cramping and diarrhea.

Progress Notes

Jejunostomy-tube feeding was continued for four days postoperatively. On Day 2, the dog was offered and drank small amounts of water. On Day 3, 1 tablespoon of a moderate-fat, low-fiber moist food (Prescription Diet Canine i/d) was offered every four hours. No vomiting occurred. The jejunostomy-tube infusion rate was reduced by 50% on Day 4 as the dog ate increasing amounts of the moist food. Tube feeding was discontinued and the tube removed on Day 5 postoperatively. The dog was maintained on two-thirds of a 15-oz can of Prescription Diet Canine i/d (supplying 362 kcal/day [1,515 kJ/day]), divided between four meals per day until it was discharged on Day 7. The owners were instructed to feed one can (544 kcal/day [2,276 kJ/day]) of food, divided equally between three daily meals to exceed the dog's daily energy requirement (DER) of 492 kcal/day (2,058 kJ/day) (DER = 1.4 x $70[8.6]^{0.75}$). When the patient returned for suture removal 14 days later, the owners reported that regurgitation had not occurred and the patient had gained 0.8 kg. The owners were encouraged to continue feeding the moist food until the dog had ideal body condition.

Endnotes

a. Carafate. Marion Merrell Dow, Kansas City, MO, USA.
b. Tagamet. SmithKline Beecham, Philadelphia, PA, USA.
c. Reglan. A.H. Robins Co., Richmond, VA, USA.
d. Hill's Pet Nutrition, Inc., Topeka, KS, USA.
e. The Iams Co., Dayton, OH, USA.
f. Abbott Laboratories, North Chicago, IL, USA.

ASSISTED FEEDING

Bibliography

Abood SK, Mauterer JV, Melouglinin MA, et al. Nutritional support of hospitalized patients. In: Slatter DJ, ed. Textbook of Small Animal Surgery, 2nd ed. Philadelphia, PA: WB Saunders Co, 1993; 63-83.

Guilford WG, Strombeck DR. Chronic gastric diseases. In: Guilford WG, Center S, Strombeck DR, et al, eds. Strombeck's Small Animal Gastroenterology. Philadelphia, PA: WB Saunders Co, 1996; 275-302.

Khoury TL, Borlase BC, Forse RA, et al. Early enteral feeding: A safe technique in critically ill patients. In: Borlase BC, Bell SJ, Blackburn GL, et al, eds. Enteral Nutrition. New York, NY: Chapman & Hall, Inc, 1994; 142-151.

CASE 12-5

Peripheral Parenteral Nutrition in a Dog

Korinn Saker, MS, DVM, PhD
Virginia-Maryland Regional College
    of Veterinary Medicine
Blacksburg, Virginia, USA

Assess the Animal

A six-year-old intact male mixed-breed dog weighing 29.5 kg with a body condition score (BCS) of 3/5 was presented for evaluation of suspected sepsis following a severe neck wound. A large open wound on the right side of the dog's neck was first noticed five days earlier. The local veterinarian flushed and closed the wound and initiated antibiotic therapy (enrofloxacin[a], amoxicillin[b] and a single dose of cephalexin[c]). The dog's clinical condition continued to deteriorate; therefore, the dog was referred for further evaluation.

On physical examination, the dog was depressed and laterally recumbent. The wound on the right side of the dog's neck extended from the dorsal margin of the ear pinna to the ventral midline. There was a necrotic odor originating from the wound. A fluid-filled pocket ventral to the wound was incised, releasing a large volume of purulent material. Specimens were collected for bacteriologic studies. Removal of skin sutures revealed a large wound extending deep into the tissues on the left side of the neck. The trachea, jugular vein and several nerves were visible at the wound margins, along with large amounts of green necrotic tissue. Skin surrounding the wound was indurated and necrotic. The dog's right ear was swollen and edematous with a creamy exudate originating from wounds on the medial aspect. Crackles could be auscultated in the right caudal lung field and the patient was mildly dyspneic.

Laboratory abnormalities included neutrophilia with a left shift, thrombocytopenia, decreased total protein (5.2 g/dl [normal 5.5 to 7.4 g/dl]) and albumin (2.3 g/dl [normal 2.8 to 3.6 g/dl]) values, lymphopenia, elevated bilirubin (5.0 mg/dl [normal 0.1 to 0.5 mg/dl]) concentration and increased alanine aminotransferase (367 U/l [normal 13 to 100 U/l]) and alkaline phosphatase (2,954 [normal 20 to 167 U/l]) activities.

After initial presentation to the teaching hospital, the dog was sedated twice daily for aggressive wound management and bandage care with wet-to-dry bandages. Aerobic and anaerobic wound cultures grew *Pseudomonas aeruginosa*, *Eubacterium aureofaciens*, *Bacteroides bivius* and *Clostridium perfringens*. The patient regurgitated white foam numerous times during the first three days of hospitalization and showed evidence of dysphagia.

Assess the Food(s) and Feeding Method

The dog had not eaten during the five days before presentation and was not offered food for the first three days of hospitalization while undergoing wound exploration and débridement and diagnostic cultures, radiography, bronchoscopy and esophagoscopy. Although nutritional support was not offered, a physiologic replacement fluid (lactated Ringer's solution) containing 20 mEq of potassium chloride/l was administered in the first 12 hours to replace an estimated fluid deficit of 10%. Fluids were reduced to maintenance rates thereafter.

Questions

1. What techniques and parameters could be used to assess the nutritional status of this patient?
2. Which nutrients would be beneficial in enhancing tissue repair and immunocompetence?
3. When and by what method should nutritional support be initiated?

Answers and Discussion

1. At the present time, nutritional assessment is limited to the veterinary version of anthropometric measures (i.e., body weight and condition), routine laboratory tests (e.g., total protein and albumin levels, lymphocyte counts) and clinical examination. Weight loss of more than 10% in sick or injured patients is considered a guideline for implementing nutritional support. Albumin has a half-life of eight days in normal dogs, thus it may remain within the normal range during short-term (one week) nutritional deprivation. The albumin concentration will decrease as the period of anorexia and lack of nutritional support is prolonged. The lymphocyte count also is altered in a relatively short period (days) as a result of nutrient deprivation. However, both hypoalbuminemia and lymphopenia can result from non-nutritionally related causes.

2. The patient's immune system was not responding optimally because of the infection and sepsis related to the neck injury. As a result of eight days of nutritional deprivation, the patient's body was now metabolizing fat and protein stores for energy and tissue repair. The labile protein pool (free amino acids) was becoming depleted and visceral and muscle protein was mobilized, which will result in atrophy and wasting in prolonged states of food deprivation in the face of accelerated catabolism.

   Immune cells and damaged muscle tissue benefit from dietary protein and fat. Research has shown that protein-energy malnutrition (PEM) results in immune system dysfunction. PEM increases the risk of mortality from infection, because it compromises innate and adaptive barriers to disease challenges. Specific alterations include: 1) a decreased marrow pool of neutrophils, 2) depressed neutrophil and monocyte phagocytic activity, 3) depressed antigen-presenting capacity of macrophages, 4) atrophy of lymphoid organs, 5) alterations in critical CD4 and CD8 cell subsets, 6) increased adhesion of organisms to mucosal epithelia and 7) alterations in regulation of inflammatory mediators. Micronutrients such as zinc, copper, iron, selenium and vitamins A, E and C should also be supplied because they are integral components in enzyme systems that promote antioxidant activity, antibody formation, cell activation and proliferation and protein synthesis.

3. Nutritional support should be instituted immediately. The twice daily wound débridement and bandage

changes with sedation limit the time this patient is alert enough to assimilate oral nutrients. Additionally, this patient has a history of regurgitation and dysphagia since being admitted to the teaching hospital. In light of these factors, as well as the physical inaccessibility to the neck region because of the wound and bandages, this patient is an excellent candidate for peripheral parenteral feeding. The peripheral route of intravenous feeding can supply 100% of resting energy requirement (RER), amino acids plus maintenance electrolytes, minerals, vitamins and trace elements.

The intravenous admixture should be formulated as a high-fat, low-carbohydrate solution to mirror the patient's current metabolic profile. A total admixture containing 3 g protein/100 kcal with 80 to 90% fat calories and 10 to 20% dextrose calories plus maintenance fluid therapy will ensure an osmolarity less than 600 mOsm/l and that the admixture can be administered peripherally. This high-fat admixture will also reduce the incidence of hyperglycemia and hyperinsulinemia, and improve nitrogen balance, which is particularly important in this case because of the patient's extensive tissue necrosis. A high-fat diet has also been recommended in cases with pulmonary compromise as observed in this patient. Metabolism of fat calories produces less carbon dioxide for excretion than carbohydrate metabolism. Feeding fat decreases the pulmonary work to excrete carbon dioxide and thereby reduces ventilatory work.

This nutrient admixture administered through a peripheral access should be done using a silicone or polyurethane catheter. Sodium heparin can be added to the admixture (0.5 to 1 U/ml of total admixture) to prevent formation of fibrin clots around the catheter tip when it is placed in a small vessel. To promote or maintain gastrointestinal health, the patient should also be fed small amounts of a high-protein, high-fat liquid or moist food per os as soon as clinically possible. The oral food should be enriched with glutamine, arginine and n-3 fatty acids to enhance enterocyte proliferation and immune cell function.

Progress Notes

The patient received peripheral parenteral feeding (Table 1) for eight days during which time the frequency of wound débridement and bandage changes was decreased to once daily. The patient's food assimilation and swallowing reflex improved so that the patient was able to eat a food with high protein, fat and moisture con-

Table 1. Peripheral parenteral TNA for one day.*

Nutrients/fluids	Quantities (ml)
50% dextrose	52
20% lipid emulsion	400
8.5% amino acids (with electrolytes)	312
Potassium phosphate (4.4 mEq K, 3 mM P/ml)	4.9
Potassium chloride (2 mEq/ml)	7.5
Vitamin-B complex**	9
Trace elements***	9
Lactated Ringer's solution	1,252

*RER ([29.5]$^{0.75}$ x 70) = 886 kcal ME/day (3.7 MJ). Calories from lipid = 90%. Calories from dextrose = 10%. Protein-calorie ratio = 3 g/100 kcal. [K] = 29.6 mEq/l. [P] = 11.8 mM/l. Osmolarity = 486 mOsm/l.
**B-vitamin complex contains 50 mg thiamin, 2 mg riboflavin, 100 mg niacin, 2 mg pyridoxine, 10 mg pantothenic acid and 0.4 µg B$_{12}$ per ml. Butler Co., Columbus, OH, USA.
***MTE-4 contains 1.7 mg zinc, 0.42 mg copper, 0.37 mg manganese and 6 µg chromium per ml containing the preservative benzyl alcohol. Abbott Laboratories, Chicago, IL, USA.

tent (Prescription Diet Canine/Feline a/d^d gruel and then Prescription Diet Canine p/d^d meatballs) to meet its RER. Just before the patient was discharged, its laboratory values were normal except for mild hypoalbuminemia (2.4 g/dl). The patient was discharged with antibiotic therapy and instructions to the owners for daily wound care. The dog returned for weekly evaluations. Tissue healing was marked but not complete four weeks after hospitalization. The owners were advised to feed 4.5 cups of a moderately high-protein, calorie-dense food (Science Diet Canine Growth^d dry) to meet the dog's daily energy requirement (DER) of 1,595 kcal (DER = 1.8 x RER) (6.67 MJ) until tissue healing was complete.

Endnotes

a. Baytril. Bayer Animal Health, Shawnee, KS, USA.
b. Amoxi-Tabs. Pfizer Animal Health, Exton, PA, USA.
c. Cephalexin. Teva Pharm, Sellersville, PA, USA.
d. Hill's Pet Nutrition, Inc., Topeka, KS, USA.

Bibliography

Nelson KM, Long CL. Physiological basis for nutrition in sepsis. In: Schneider PD, Bell S, eds. Selected Reviews in Nutrition Support. Silver Spring, MD: Aspen Publications, 1993; 142-151.

Neuvonen PT, Salvo M. Effects of short term starvation on the immune response. Nutrition Research 1984; 4: 771-776.

Zaloga G, Ackerman MH. A review of disease-specific formulas. American Association of Critical-Care Nurses: Clinical Issues 1994; 421-435.

Codina LM. Peripheral parenteral nutrition. In: Shikora SA, Blackburn GL, eds. Nutrition Support: Theory and Therapeutics. New York, NY: Chapman & Hall, 1997; 169-176.

ASSISTED FEEDING

CASE 12-6

Central Parenteral Nutrition in a Cat

Kathryn E. Michel, DVM, MS
Diplomate ACVN
School of Veterinary Medicine
University of Pennsylvania
Philadelphia, Pennsylvania, USA

Assess the Animal

A 10-year-old spayed female domestic shorthair cat presented to the emergency service with a three-week history of poor appetite and weight loss. The chief complaint was facial swelling (especially around the nose) and nasal discoloration. The cat's problems were originally associated with an episode of pollakiuria and inappropriate urination, which resolved with antibiotic therapy (sulfadimethoxine^a). About two weeks before presentation, the cat became lethargic and

Table 1. Central parenteral TNA for one day.*

Nutrients/fluids	Quantities (ml)
50% dextrose	38
20% lipid emulsion	48
8.5% amino acids (without electrolytes)	113
Potassium phosphate (4.4 mEq K, 3 mM P/ml)	1.4
Potassium chloride (2 mEq/ml)	1.4
Vitamin-B complex**	1
Trace elements***	0.1

*RER ($[3.0]^{0.75}$ x 70) = 160 kcal ME/day (670 kJ/day). Calories from lipid = 60%. Calories from dextrose = 40%. Protein-calorie ratio = 6 g/100 kcal. [K] = 29.7 mEq/l. [P] = 11.8 mM/l. Osmolarity = 1,188 mOsm/l.
**B-vitamin complex contains 50 mg thiamin, 2 mg riboflavin, 100 mg niacin, 2 mg pyridoxine, 10 mg pantothenic acid and 0.4 µg B_{12} per ml. Butler Co., Columbus, OH, USA.
***MTE-4 contains 1.7 mg zinc, 0.42 mg copper, 0.37 mg manganese and 6 µg chromium per ml containing the preservative benzyl alcohol. Abbott Laboratories, Chicago, IL, USA.

tachypneic and its appetite deteriorated further. The owners noticed at this time that the cat's normally pink nose had become discolored. They initially observed a small bloody spot on the bridge of the nose overlying bluish skin. Over the course of a week the nose became progressively swollen and the skin blackened. The cat developed mild epistaxis.

On physical examination, the patient was depressed, moderately dehydrated (8 to 10%) and hypothermic (36.7°C [98.2°F]). The cat weighed 3 kg and its body condition was considered cachectic (body condition score [BCS] of 1/5). Mucous membranes were pale and slightly tacky. Ecchymoses and petechiae were present on the sclera, pinnae and gingiva. Harsh lung sounds were auscultated bilaterally. Swelling and discoloration were noted on the nose, upper lip and tail.

Initial laboratory work included a serum biochemistry analysis, a complete blood count (CBC), a coagulation profile, activated clotting time (ACT) and blood typing. The cat had previously tested negative for feline leukemia virus and feline immunodeficiency virus. Results of the serum biochemistry profile were within normal limits. Abnormalities on the CBC included a hematocrit of 11% (normal 27 to 45%), hemoglobin of 3.5 g/dl (normal 8 to 15 g/dl) and an inflammatory leukogram with a left shift. The cat had a platelet count of 88,000/µl (normal 175,000 to 425,000/µl) and a corrected reticulocyte count of 8.28% (normal 1 to 10%). The coagulation profile was within normal limits, although the ACT was abnormal and the blood never completely clotted. Thoracic radiographs revealed an alveolar pattern in the cranioventral lung fields and overall increased density in the caudodorsal lung fields. Active inflammation and hemorrhage were noted on the tracheal wash. Biopsy specimens were submitted from the nose and upper lip. A cardiac consult revealed no evidence of primary heart disease and an occult heartworm test was negative.

The problem list included cachexia, anemia, neutrophilia, thrombocytopenia and alveolar disease. The differential diagnosis included thromboembolic disease, pneumonia and cold agglutinin disease. Microscopic thrombi consistent with cold agglutinin disease were found on biopsy specimens. Cold agglutinin disease was confirmed by a positive Coomb's test at 7°C.

Assess the Food(s) and Feeding Method

The cat showed no interest in food even though a variety of foods were offered and efforts were made to coax it

to eat. The cat had been fed a commercial grocery brand dry cat food (Purina Cat Chow[b]) free choice for several years. It would accept only a small amount of food when given by syringe. The necrotic condition of the cat's nose probably affected its ability to smell food and that in combination with dyspnea and anemia caused the lack of appetite. The cat's poor body condition, the severity of its illness and the likelihood of a prolonged clinical course prompted a more aggressive approach for providing nutrition to this patient.

Initial therapy included a maintenance infusion (65 ml/kg body weight/day) of 0.9% NaCl with 20 mEq K/l, antibiotic therapy (enrofloxacin[c] and ampicillin[d]) and a transfusion with whole blood and fresh frozen plasma. The cat was admitted to the intensive care unit (ICU) where it was placed in an oxygen cage with orders to keep it warm. The cat was started on cyproheptadine[e] (2 mg per os, t.i.d.) with orders to offer a variety of warmed foods and to coax it to eat. A central venous polyurethane catheter was placed in the left femoral vein and a parenteral nutrition (PN) admixture containing 50% dextrose, 20% lipid emulsion, 8.5% amino acid solution without electrolytes, potassium phosphate, potassium chloride, trace elements and injectable B complex was begun (Table 1). The PN solution was delivered at a rate of 5 ml/hour for the first 24 hours to deliver two-thirds of the calculated resting energy requirement (RER). On subsequent days, it was delivered at a rate of 7 ml/hour (56 ml/kg body weight/day) to deliver 100% of the RER ($[3.0]^{0.75}$ x 70 = 160 kcal/day, 670 kJ). The peripheral catheter infusion rate of NaCl solution was reduced to 9 ml/kg body weight/day to accommodate the central PN infusion and meet the cat's daily maintenance fluid requirement.

Questions

1. Discuss which other feeding routes might have been considered to support this patient and why they may have been rejected in favor of centrally administered PN.
2. Were any micronutrients absent from the PN formulation that might be important for erythropoiesis?
3. What types of metabolic complications should be anticipated in a critically ill patient receiving PN?

Answers and Discussion

1. A number of enteral feeding routes and PN infusion via peripheral venous access were considered for this patient. The nasoesophageal route was rejected for several reasons. The most obvious reason was the condition of the patient's nares, which were partially obstructed due to necrosis. Also, there was the concern of provoking epistaxis in a thrombocytopenic and severely anemic patient as the tube was advanced through the nose. Finally, there was the issue of blocking the nares in an animal already experiencing difficulty breathing through its nose. All other routes of enteral feeding (i.e., esophagostomy, pharyngostomy, gastrostomy and enterostomy) require heavy sedation or general anesthesia with varying degrees of surgical intervention. The cat's compromised pulmonary function and thrombocytopenia were considered contraindications for these procedures. (There was a missed opportunity later on in this case to place a less

invasive type of enteral feeding tube [e.g., an esophagostomy tube]. On Day 10 of hospitalization the cat was anesthetized for a bronchioalveolar lavage and a bone marrow aspirate). Central infusion of PN was selected instead of peripheral infusion because there was a concern of fluid overload, given the extent of alveolar disease in this patient. Therefore, a more concentrated, smaller volume admixture was conservatively infused via a central vein rather than peripherally.

2. Two micronutrients important for red blood cell production, and which are associated with anemia when deficient, were omitted from the PN admixture because of noncompatibility issues. The first was iron. Parenteral iron solutions are not approved for mixing with any vehicle including PN admixtures and are therefore commonly given separately by intramuscular or intravenous routes. However, the concern that this patient would become iron deficient was minor because the cat had received multiple red blood cell transfusions during the course of hospitalization.

The other missing nutrient was folic acid. Folic acid is omitted from standard veterinary parenteral B-complex formulations because of noncompatibility and stability issues. Some human parenteral vitamin formulations contain folic acid; however, at the time this case presented, there was a severe shortage of these products and their use in a veterinary patient could not be justified. Although omission of folic acid from this cat's nutritional support was not optimal, the extent of folic acid deficiency may have been limited due to ongoing efforts to feed the cat per os throughout the time it received PN.

3. Common metabolic complications associated with PN include hyperglycemia, lipemia and electrolyte disturbances. Hyperglycemia and lipemia were not noted at any time during PN infusion in this patient, probably due in part to the conservative estimate of its caloric requirements and because the cat received only 40% of its nonprotein calories as dextrose. Serum potassium, sodium, chloride and ionized calcium levels were monitored daily. Serum phosphorus and magnesium levels were monitored two or three times per week.

Progress Notes

The patient continued to require oxygen therapy. The thrombocytopenia resolved, but the anemia persisted with a poor regenerative response. *Pasteurella multocida* was cultured from a tracheal wash but it was unclear whether this isolate was the cause of the alveolar disease or a contaminant. The cat's appetite was poor despite continued efforts to coax the cat to eat. The cyproheptadine was discontinued after four days. On Day 4 of PN, a low serum magnesium concentration was detected and corrected with an infusion of magnesium sulfate at a rate of 1 mg/kg body weight/day via the peripheral catheter. The serum magnesium level returned to normal within 24 hours and the magnesium sulfate infusion was discontinued. Mild hypokalemia also occurred and was corrected by increasing the admixture potassium concentration to 30 mEq/l. Low serum phosphorus levels were not detected in this patient.

On Day 7, the cat was still receiving most of its nutrition parenterally. Therefore, injections of fat-soluble vitamins were given (1,000 IU vitamin A, 100 IU vitamin D, 3 IU vitamin E intramuscularly and 7.5 mg vitamin K subcuta-

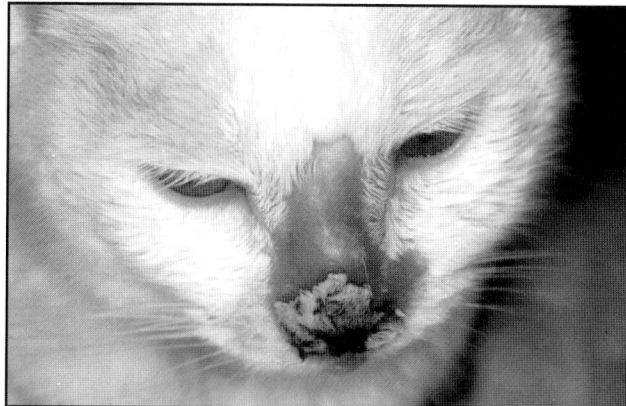

Figure 1. A 10-year-old domestic shorthair cat with cold agglutinin disease on Day 19 of hospitalization.

neously). On Day 10, the cat was anesthetized for bronchoscopy, an ultrasound-guided fine-needle lung aspirate and a bone marrow aspirate. There were no abnormalities found on the bone marrow aspirate or grossly at bronchoscopy. Cultures of the bronchoalveolar lavage revealed different organisms from the tracheal wash; however, the pulmonary disease seemed to be improving. The decision was made to start immunosuppressive therapy (prednisolone acetate 1 mg/kg, subcutaneously, b.i.d.) because the cat's red blood cells were still agglutinating.

The patient started to improve, and by Day 13 no longer required oxygen therapy. The necrotic tissue on the cat's nose had begun to scab over. By Day 19 (Figure 1), the Coomb's test was negative at 4°C (39.2°F), the nares became clear of scabs and the cat's appetite returned. The patient started to eat a maintenance dry cat food (Science Diet Feline Maintenance[f]) voluntarily with an excellent appetite and consumed sufficient quantities of food to exceed its RER. On Day 20, central venous access was lost, but because the cat was eating well, there was no concern about continuing PN. On Day 22, the necrotic portion of the cat's tail was removed using local ring-block anesthesia. The patient continued to improve and was discharged from the hospital on Day 25. At the time of discharge, the cat weighed 3.2 kg and had a hematocrit of 19%. The cat continued to do well at home. At two weeks after discharge it weighed 3.4 kg, was still thin (BCS 2/5) but no longer cachectic and had a hematocrit of 22% with a corrected reticulocyte count of 6.2%. One year later on a routine annual examination, the cat weighed 4.1 kg (BCS 3/5), had a normal PCV with no reticulocytes and was reportedly doing very well.

Endnotes

a. Albon. Pfizer Animal Health, Exton, PA, USA.

b. Ralston Purina Co., St. Louis, MO, USA.

c. Baytril. Bayer Animal Health, Shawnee, KS, USA.

d. Amoxi-Tabs. Pfizer Animal Health, Exton, PA, USA.

e. Periactin. Merck and Company, Inc., Rahway, NJ, USA.

f. Hill's Pet Nutrition, Inc., Topeka, KS, USA.

Bibliography

Godfrey DR, Anderson RM. Cold agglutinin disease in a cat. Journal of Small Animal Practice 1994; 35: 267-270.

Lippert AC, Fulton RB, Parr AM. A retrospective study of the use of total parenteral nutrition in dogs and cats. Journal of Veterinary Internal Medicine 1993; 7: 52-64.

CHAPTER 13

Obesity

William J. Burkholder
Philip W. Toll

"Overweight is tempting fate."
Anonymous

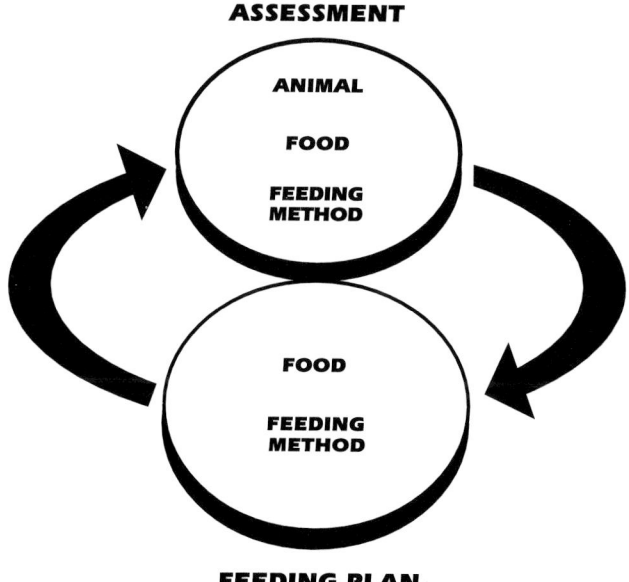

ASSESSMENT

ANIMAL

FOOD

FEEDING METHOD

FOOD

FEEDING METHOD

FEEDING PLAN

Note: The reader is referred to Chapter 1 for a detailed discussion of the iterative process of clinical nutrition.

CLINICAL IMPORTANCE

Overconsumption of calories resulting in excess body fat is believed to be the most prevalent form of malnutrition in pets of westernized societies. Cross-sectional epidemiologic surveys attempting to quantify body condition of dogs evaluated by veterinarians have estimated the prevalence of overweight and obese dogs to be 24 to 30%.[1-4] In the largest survey from Great Britain, researchers collected data on 8,268 dogs from 11 veterinary practices; results indicated 24% of the dogs were overweight or grossly obese.[4] Results from a large survey done in the United States indicated 25% of 23,000 dogs from 60 private veterinary practices were overweight or obese.[1] Researchers also estimated that 25% of 2,000 to 10,000 cats presented to veterinarians were overweight or obese.[1,5] Thus, the most extensive surveys estimate that approximately one-fourth of the dogs and cats presented to small animal practitioners in westernized societies are overweight to grossly obese.[1,4,5]

Deciding when a given animal is in optimal, overweight or obese body condition has clinical relevance because obesity may adversely affect an animal's health. By definition, obesity is the accumulation of an excessive quantity of fat. Body weight increases as fat accumulates; thus, having excessive body fat and being overweight are related. However, body weight can increase from the accumulation of any tissue or fluid. Muscle hypertrophy in athletic individuals and fluid retention due to ascites are two examples of increased body weight unrelated to obesity. The majority of overweight dogs and cats, however, are overweight from excess body fat.

OBESITY

KEY WORDS & TERMS—OBESITY*

Body condition score (BCS)	Fat	Percent body fat (%BF)
Body weight	Fiber	Relative body weight (RBW)
Caloric density	Lean body mass	Resting energy requirement (RER)
Daily energy requirement (DER)	Morphometry	Satiety
Dietary history	Obesity	Thermic effect of food (TEF)
Exercise energy requirement (EER)	Overweight	

Key words and terms are defined in the Glossary.

KEY POINTS—OBESITY

1. Twenty-five percent of the dogs and cats seen by veterinarians are overweight or obese.
2. Excessive weight is an associative cause or exacerbating factor for specific orthopedic, endocrine, cardiovascular and neoplastic diseases in dogs and cats, and complicates therapeutic and diagnostic procedures by making pets less tolerant or resilient to metabolic stress.
3. Genetics (breed), neutering, decreased physical activity, age and consumption of more calorically dense foods can predispose a cat or dog to obesity.
4. Body condition scoring, relative body weight and morphometry (tape measurements) are practical methods for assessing body condition and the extent to which pets are over or under their optimal weight.
5. Complete weight-reduction programs are composed of three equally important plans: a feeding plan, an exercise plan and a recheck plan.
6. Neglecting or omitting one or two of the three plans listed in Number 5 seriously compromises the chance for successful weight loss.
7. Multiple equations have been purported to be the best estimate for caloric restriction to produce weight loss. A quantitative feeding record (dietary history) is essential to assess whether any of these equations results in caloric estimates that will allow the pet to lose weight.
8. Daily energy requirements correlate with the amount of lean body mass (lean tissues and organs). Excess weight requires very little energy to maintain.
9. Simply feeding less of a food that is not calorie restricted is unlikely to produce weight loss without creating deficiencies in protein, vitamins, minerals and energy in pets that truly need to lose weight.
10. Commercial foods that are truly calorie restricted contain 3,100 kcal (12.97 MJ) or less per kg of food as fed for dogs and 3,250 kcal (13.60 MJ) or less per kg of food as fed for cats.
11. Both the fat content and the total calories delivered by the pet's daily foods are important in determining whether the pet gains, loses or maintains body weight.
12. Owners must measure exactly the amount of food they feed the pet for weight reduction and maintenance of reduced body weight.
13. Some types of treat foods can be used in weight-reduction programs but the calories from treats must be included in the total daily calories prescribed for weight reduction.
14. Initially the amount of exercise prescribed for an overweight pet to lose weight is whatever amount of walking or increased activity the animal can comfortably perform.
15. The goal for exercise is 20 to 60 minutes of leash walking per day or its equivalent.
16. Swimming is an excellent alternative for exercising orthopedic patients if facilities are available to the owner.
17. Rechecks to determine the amount and rate of weight loss should occur every two weeks initially, every four to six weeks after weight loss is steady and every one to two weeks when food is being changed or increased to maintain reduced body weight.
18. Experience suggests that most pets require eight to 12 months to go from a relative weight of 120 to 100%.
19. Successful weight reduction is likely to improve the clinical benefits from surgical and pharmacologic treatments and is often required to achieve maximal benefits from these treatments.

Body weight relative to an animal's optimal weight has been used as a defining criterion for obesity because body weight is easier to measure than body fat. People are defined as mildly obese when actual body weight exceeds optimal body weight by 15 to 30%.[6,7] Similar definitions have been proposed for dogs and cats.[8,9] The authors choose to subdivide overweight dogs and cats into three categories: 1) those animals 1 to 9% above optimal weight are simply above optimal, 2) those 10 to 19% above optimal are considered overweight and 3) those 20% above optimal are considered obese.

Fat mass expressed as a percentage of body weight can also be used to define obesity. People are considered obese when percent body fat (%BF) exceeds 20 to 30% of total weight.[6,7] Body composition studies of dogs and cats indicate that animals judged to be in optimal body condition have 15 to 20% body fat.[10-13]

Health Risks of Obesity

Excessive deposition of body fat has detrimental effects on health and longevity. In people, these detrimental effects begin, and thus obesity has been defined, when body fat exceeds 20 to 30% of body weight.[6,14] Obesity has also been demonstrated to have detrimental effects on the health of dogs and cats. Grossly obese dogs have an increased prevalence of traumatic and degenerative orthopedic disorders.[4] Obese dogs have an increased prevalence of cardiovascular disease in the form of congestive heart failure.[4] Increases in blood pressure have been documented to occur in dogs under experimental conditions immediately after increases in body weight, but the long-term response of blood pressure from weight gain and its clinical significance in cats and dogs remain to be deter-

KEY NUTRITIONAL FACTORS—OBESITY

Factors	Dietary recommendations
Energy	Calorie-restricted dog foods should contain <3.4 kcal (14.23 kJ) ME/g dry matter for weight loss Calorie-restricted cat foods should contain <3.6 kcal (15.06 kJ) ME/g dry matter for weight loss Weight loss in dogs: 1.0 to 1.2 x RER for optimal weight Weight loss in cats: 0.8 to 1.0 x RER for optimal weight See Figure 13-5 for more information about setting calories for weight loss
Fat	Dogs: calorie-restricted foods should contain 5 to 12% fat (dry matter basis) for weight loss and prevention of weight gain in obese-prone dogs Cats: calorie-restricted foods should contain 7 to 14% fat (dry matter basis) for weight loss and prevention of weight gain in obese-prone cats
Fiber	Weight loss: 12 to 30% crude fiber (dry matter basis) may be helpful, indicated and required Prevention of weight gain: 6 to 30% crude fiber (dry matter basis) may be helpful, indicated and required
Protein	Dogs: foods for weight loss should contain >25% crude protein (dry matter basis) to help prevent loss of lean body tissues Cats: foods for weight loss should contain >35% crude protein (dry matter basis) to help prevent loss of lean body tissues

mined.[15-17] Obesity has been reported to predispose dogs and cats to diabetes mellitus or exacerbate this illness.[18-22] Obesity is a predisposing factor to idiopathic hepatic lipidosis in cats that become anorectic.[23,24] Overweight dogs have an increased risk of developing transitional cell carcinoma of the bladder.[25] A less well-documented effect of obesity in dogs and cats is an increased risk for anesthetic complications, a belief held by many veterinary practitioners.[26] Decreased heat tolerance and stamina are also purported consequences of obesity in dogs and cats.[27,28] Other health problems purported to be associated with or exacerbated by obesity include dyspnea, dystocia, dermatologic problems and decreases in immune functions, although the association between obesity and these clinical effects is less than definitively documented.[17,29,30]

Table 13-1 lists abnormalities thought to be associated with or exacerbated by excess body weight. Obesity can be a clinical sign accompanying the endocrinopathies listed in Table 13-1. Hyperadrenocorticism, hypothyroidism and diabetes mellitus are the endocrinopathies most amenable to treatment. Obesity is caused by the physiologic alterations resulting from hyperadrenocorticism and hypothyroidism. Although hypothyroidism is commonly thought of in association with obesity in dogs, hypothyroidism is not a common cause of obesity. The prevalence of hypothyroidism in dogs is only 1%.[31] No more than one-fourth of hypothyroid dogs are obese, whereas the prevalence of obesity in dogs is 25%.[31] Obesity may either cause or occasionally result from diabetes mellitus. In either case, weight loss in an obese diabetic will improve the chances for better regulation of blood glucose concentrations and perhaps decrease or eliminate the need for insulin administration to achieve glycemic control. (See Chapter 24.)

Animals with insulinomas may or may not present with obesity and their condition can at best be palliated for some period before they succumb to the disease. The recommendation for feeding insulinoma patients foods increased in fat and protein to minimize stimulation of insulin secretion is diametrically opposed to recommendations for weight loss. Thus, weight loss is unlikely to be achieved in an overweight insulinoma patient before the terminal stages of the disease.

Treatment of the remaining endocrinopathies in Table 13-1 is often unrewarding. They are listed for completeness and reference, and should be considered after the more common

diagnoses are excluded and when patients do not lose weight with even the most severe caloric restriction. A veterinarian presented with an obese patient should use historical information as well as physical examination and clinical pathologic findings to include or exclude the possibility of a systemic problem causing or contributing to the obesity.

ASSESSMENT

Assess the Animal

Determining whether a cat or dog is overweight, of optimal weight or underweight would not seem to be a very challenging task. However, in the clinical setting, the sub-

Table 13-1. Diseases associated with or exacerbated by obesity.*

Metabolic alterations
Hyperlipidemia
Insulin resistance
Glucose intolerance
Hepatic lipidosis (cats)
Anesthetic complications

Endocrinopathies
Hyperadrenocorticism
Hypothyroidism
Diabetes mellitus
Insulinoma
Pituitary chromophobe adenoma
Hypopituitarism
Hypothalamic lesions

Functional alterations
Joint stress/musculoskeletal pain
Dyspnea
Hypertension
Dystocia
Exercise intolerance
Heat intolerance
Decreased immune function

Other diseases
Degenerative joint and orthopedic disease
Cardiovascular disease
Transitional cell carcinoma (bladder)

*Adapted from References 3, 15 to 28.

OBESITY

Table 13-2. Relationships between actual, optimal and relative weight, anticipated body condition score (BCS) and percent body fat (%BF).

	Relative weight				
	0.8 or 80%	0.9 or 90%	1.0 or 100%	1.1 or 110%	1.20 or 120%
Ideal weight (kg)			Actual body weight (kg)		
1	0.8	0.9	1.0	1.1	1.2
2	1.6	1.8	2.0	2.2	2.4
3	2.4	2.7	3.0	3.3	3.6
4	3.2	3.6	4.0	4.4	4.8
5	4.0	4.5	5.0	5.5	6.0
10	8.0	9.0	10.0	11.0	12.0
15	12.0	13.5	15.0	16.5	18.0
20	16.0	18.0	20.0	22.0	24.0
25	20.0	22.5	25.0	27.5	30.0
30	24.0	27.0	30.0	33.0	36.0
35	28.0	31.5	35.0	38.5	42.0
40	32.0	36.0	40.0	44.0	48.0
45	36.0	40.5	45.0	49.5	54.0
50	40.0	45.0	50.0	55.0	60.0
55	44.0	49.5	55.0	60.5	66.0
60	48.0	54.0	60.0	66.0	72.0
65	52.0	58.5	65.0	71.5	78.0
70	56.0	63.0	70.0	77.0	84.0
75	60.0	67.5	75.0	82.5	90.0
80	64.0	72.0	80.0	88.0	96.0
			Anticipated BCS		
	1	2	3	4	5
			Anticipated %BF		
	<5	5 to 15	16 to 25	26 to 35	>35

jectivity inherent in such a determination makes irrefutable, objective measurement challenging. The subjectivity results from variation in body conformation across breeds, variation of frame size within breeds, especially for dogs, as well as the veterinarian's and owner's bias for what is an ideal body weight and conformation for the pet. There is not an ideal, definitive method for deciding whether a dog or cat is in a thin, optimal or obese body condition. In reality, there is a continuum from emaciation to morbid obesity, making absolute definitions and divisions somewhat academic and arbitrary. A variety of methods are available for body composition measurement in research settings: 1) magnetic resonance imaging (MRI), 2) computed tomography (CT), 3) neutron activation, 4) hydrodensitometry, 5) total body water by isotope dilution, 6) total body potassium, 7) ultrasound, 8) bioelectrical impedance and 9) dual energy x-ray absorptiometry (DEXA).[32-34] Unfortunately, these methods are not practical for use in veterinary hospitals.

Clinically, it is useful to assess body condition of cats and dogs as objectively as possible. The ability to assess body condition is necessary to determine when a dog or cat is likely to benefit from weight loss, and to substantiate a diagnosis of obesity to pet owners and convince them that their pet needs to lose weight. Additionally, quantifying excess body weight and determining ideal body weight are essential to a weight-loss program. Several clinical methods can be used to differentiate between optimal, overweight and obese body conditions. Relative body weight (RBW), body condition score (BCS) and morphometric analysis are all tools that can be used to substantiate a diagnosis of obesity.

Relative Body Weight

RBW is simply an animal's current weight divided by its estimated optimal weight. Animals that are at their optimal weight have an RBW of 1.00 or 100%. Animals weighing less than optimal have an RBW less than 1 and animals weighing more than optimal have an RBW greater than 1. The values of 1.10 and 1.20 have been suggested as division points for placing people,[14] and by extrapolation dogs and cats, into overweight and obese categories, respectively.

Other values have been suggested as division points for deciding when a cat or dog is overweight vs. obese. Some authors conservatively suggest obesity begins when an animal is 15% above its optimal weight (RBW of 1.15).[35] More liberal estimates suggest obesity does not have clinical relevance until the animal is 40% above its optimal weight (RBW of 1.40).[17] Much epidemiologic data are still needed to definitively define overweight vs. obese conditions for dogs and cats based on increased health risks. The authors have arbitrarily chosen to use the relative weight of 120% as the division and definition for obesity until such time as data allow a definitive division point to be established. Table 13-2 lists absolute weights corresponding to RBWs from 0.80 and 1.20 for animals that should optimally weigh from 1 to 80 kg.

Although the method of RBW is easy to apply, there are two potential problems with its use. First, care must be used when establishing an individual animal's optimal body weight, because body condition indicated by relative weight can change markedly simply by changing the value used for optimal weight. Second, strict interpretation of the clinical significance between a change in RBW of 1 or even 5% is not possible or justifiable. Thus, it cannot be concluded that dogs or cats with RBWs of 1.19 do not need to lose weight to avoid potential consequences of obesity, but those with RBWs of 1.20 do. Rather, RBW is like driving above the posted speed limit. The greater the actual speed relative to the posted speed limit, and the longer the excess speed is maintained, the more likely it is that the driver will get a speeding ticket. Similarly, the more animals exceed optimal weight, and the longer they exceed it, the more likely they are to suffer some detrimental effect from being overweight or obese, and the more likely they are to benefit from weight loss.[14]

Deciding on an optimal weight can be problematic for the veterinarian and the pet owner, especially if the two disagree. An individual dog's or cat's optimal weight can be estimated from several sources. The best estimate is a recorded mature adult weight at a time when the pet's body condition was simultaneously assessed as optimal. Weight at the time the dog or cat reached adult age is often a good indicator of the optimal weight if body condition assessments are unavailable. However, weight at maturity may not automatically be optimal if the animal was underfed or overfed during growth. For most dogs and cats, maturity occurs around 12 months of age. Giant-breed dogs, however, may require up to 18 months to reach mature adult weight. Average weights determined by the American Kennel Club for individual breeds and gender may be used if there is no record of an animal's past weight(s). (See Appendix H.) However, optimal weights among individual dogs of a given breed may vary 25% or more, as indicated by the range of optimal weights listed for different breeds in Appendix H. For example, the average optimal weight for Labrador retrievers implies that any 30.7-kg Labrador retriever is in optimal body condition. A Labrador retriever weighing 30.7 kg that really should weigh 25 kg will have an RBW of 1.00, if 30.7 kg is arbitrarily selected as the optimal weight for this dog instead of using its appropriate optimal weight of 25 kg, which gives an RBW of 1.23. Thus, frame size of the individual becomes important for selecting or determining optimal weight from published averages.

Establishing absolute weights to indicate obesity for cats is somewhat easier than for dogs. Most domestic cats have an optimal body weight in the range of 3.2 to 4.5 kg. Some cats may weigh up to 5.5 kg without being overweight. However, any domestic cat weighing more than 6.4 kg is likely to be obese unless it has an exceptionally large skeletal frame. These ranges are similar to average body weights of 4.8 and 6.5 kg for optimal and overweight, respectively, as determined in a recent assessment of prevalence and risk factors for obesity in cats.[5] (See Appendix I.)

An alternate way of assessing an animal's degree of obesity is to derive some estimate of its %BF. As mentioned, there are multiple methods that vary widely in cost, sophistication and precision for estimating %BF in people.[32-34] Body condition scoring and morphometric measures are two techniques of assessing %BF that can be used in veterinary practice because they are inexpensive and noninvasive.

Body Condition Scoring

The BCS is a subjective assessment of an animal's body fat, and to a lesser extent protein stores, that takes into account the animal's frame size independent of its weight. Scoring systems using defined criteria help make the process more objective, but cannot remove all subjectivity involved in assigning a score to a given animal. Different scoring systems for dogs and cats contain from three to nine categories for body condition and have been assessed to different extents for precision, accuracy and repeatability.[1,2,4,5,8,11-13,36]

Chapter 1 presents a 5-point body condition scoring system in detail. Systems with either five or nine categories are used most commonly. A 5-point system scored

to the nearest half score and a 9-point system scored to the nearest whole score each have nine total scores for body condition. A 5-point system scored to the nearest half score subdivides into three categories each for insufficient, optimal and excess body conditions, with a score of 3.0 falling in the middle of the optimal range.

In general, dogs and cats in optimal body condition have: 1) normal body contours and silhouettes, 2) bony prominences that can be readily palpated but not seen or felt above skin surfaces and 3) intra-abdominal fat insufficient to obscure or interfere with abdominal palpation. The most critical division points in a 5-point system are between the scores of 2.0 vs. 2.5 and 3.5 vs. 4.0, because assignment of a BCS less than 2.5 or greater than 3.5 suggests action should be taken to return the animal's BCS to the optimal range. Certainly, action should be taken to restore optimal weight and body condition for dogs and cats with a BCS of 1.0, 1.5, 4.5 or 5.0.

In addition to body weight, the BCS should always be recorded in the hospital record whenever an animal is examined by a veterinarian. Body weight alone does not indicate how appropriate the weight is for an individual animal. A Labrador retriever weighing 30 kg or a domestic shorthair cat weighing 4 kg may be underweight, at optimal weight or overweight. The BCS puts body weight in perspective for what individual dogs and cats ought to weigh.

Table 13-2 shows the anticipated relationship between BCS and RBW. Although similar to RBW, body condition scoring uses physical attributes rather than fixed quantities to assess when body condition, and thus weight, is optimal for an individual animal. Body condition scoring like other physical examination techniques is a learned art. Within the range of defined criteria, the scorer still must learn by experience what visual and palpable characteristics correspond with a given BCS. Standardization of scores between observers scoring a given animal can be problematic. What one scorer feels to be an excessive amount of fat covering the ribs, another scorer may assess as being an appropriate amount. However, once learned, body condition scoring has been demonstrated to be a reliable indicator for determining the proportion of body fat or body composition.[11,36-38]

Body condition can be formally defined as the ratio of fat to nonfat tissues in the body and thus can be used to estimate %BF.[39] If 15 to 25% body fat is accepted as optimal for dogs and cats, then an animal with a BCS of 3.0 out of 5.0 (3/5) should have about 20% body fat. Research to critically assess the capability of BCS to predict body composition suggests that %BF changes by 10% for each change in condition score on a 5-point scale.[11] For example, as BCS increases from 3 to 5, the corresponding body fat increases from 20 to 40%. Therefore, a BCS of 4.0 correlates with an average of 30% body fat, which is similar to the critical %BF for assessing when people are at risk for ill effects from being overweight. Most studies critically assessing the precision of BCS against some criterion measure of body fat indicate that %BF is estimated with a standard deviation of ± 4 to 5%.[11,13,36-38]

One misconception that could arise about body condition scoring is the implication that some maximum amount of body fat corresponds to the maximum BCS. Body condition scores have a maximum upper number assigned to the fattest animals used to define the scoring criteria, which consequently is associated with the mean

Table 13-3. Equations for converting morphometric measurements into estimates of percent body fat (%BF).

Dogs*

Males %BF = –1.4(HS[cm]) + 0.77(PC[cm]) + 4
Females %BF = –1.7(HS[cm]) + 0.93(PC[cm]) + 5
Either gender %BF = $\dfrac{-0.0034(\text{HS}_{[cm]})^2 + 0.0027(\text{PC}_{[cm]})^2 - 1.9}{\text{BW}_{(kg)}}$

Cats**

%BF = –0.02($L^2_{[cm]}$/BW$_{[kg]}$) – 4.12(RF$_{[cm]}$) + 1.48(PC$_{[cm]}$) – 1.16(CTC$_{[cm]}$) + 92.93

%BF = $\dfrac{0.04(\text{PC}_{[cm]}) - 0.0004(L^2_{[cm]}/\text{BW}_{[kg]}) - 0.08(\text{RF}_{[cm]}) + 1.11}{\text{BW}_{(kg)}}$

Key: %BF = percent body fat, HS = length of right rear limb from the calcanean tuber to the mid-patellar ligament (hock to stifle), PC = pelvic circumference, L = body length from nose to sacrococcygeal junction, RF = length of right forelimb from shoulder to carpus, CTC = cranial thoracic circumference, BW = body weight.

*Adapted from Reference 13.
**Adapted from Reference 10.

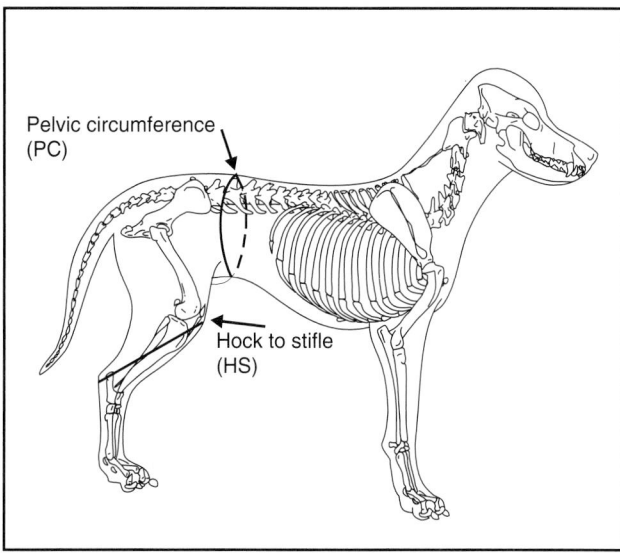

Figure 13-1. Anatomic sites for measurement of zoometric variables for dogs.

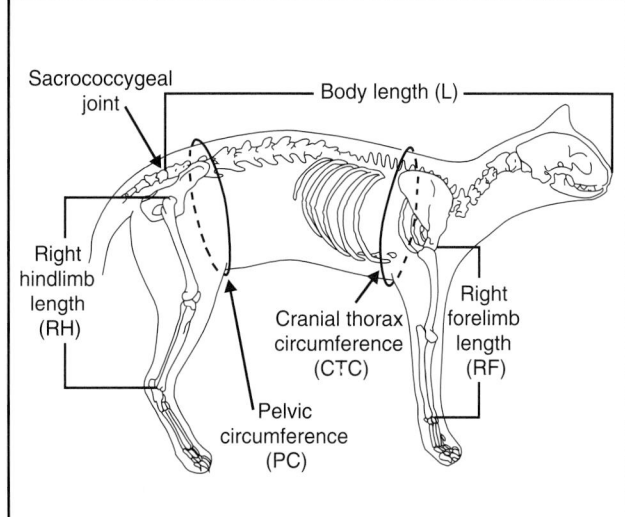

Figure 13-2. Anatomic sites for measurement of zoometric variables of cat cadavers. (Adapted with permission from Stanton CA, Hamar DW, Johnson DE, et al. American Journal of Veterinary Research 1992; 53: 251-257.)

%BF of those animals. However, the maximum amount of body fat compatible with life is not definitively known, is very likely more than 40% and certainly more than the average %BF of all dogs or cats with a BCS of 5/5. The correct interpretation for %BF based on assigning a maximum BCS should be that the animal is at least 40% body fat ± 5%.

Morphometric Measurements

Body fat can also be estimated from morphometric measures. Morphometry simply means the measurement of form. Morphometric analysis is routinely used in people to estimate body composition and %BF from measurement of various anatomic circumferences and lengths.[40-43] The success for measurements made in specific locations to estimate overall body composition depends on whether the measurements are correlated to composition throughout the body. Fat is deposited in slightly different regions of the body in cats compared to dogs. Cats store most of their fat subcutaneously along their ventral abdomen, in their faces and intra-abdominally. Dogs deposit significant amounts of fat subcutaneously in thoracic, lumbar and coccygeal areas as well as intra-abdominally.

Regardless of differences in fat deposition between the two species, the dimension of the body that changes most with increasing weight is the pelvic circumference.[10,13] Two studies have demonstrated pelvic circumference to be proportional to the amount of fat in dogs and cats.[10,13] These studies also indicate morphometry can be used to estimate %BF (Table 13-3). A measuring tape (graduated in centimeters) and a cooperative patient are required to make the needed measurements.

One to three other measurements described in Table 13-3 are needed to estimate body composition, along with the pelvic circumference. These additional measurements account for frame size or are correlated to lean body mass. Studies that developed the equations for estimating body fat from morphometry indicate the estimates are accurate to ± 2 to 4 %BF.[10,13]

Morphometry, like RBW and BCS, must be used cautiously in diagnosing obesity from %BF. Anyone can measure the pelvic and thoracic circumferences of dogs and cats to determine progressive weight loss and changing body composition. However, measurements must be made carefully and the animals to which the equations are applied must be selected judiciously if the estimated %BF is to be appropriate, realistic and accurate. To obtain an accurate estimate of %BF, it is critical to make the measurements in the exact anatomic location with the animal in the same position as the animals in the original study groups (Figures 13-1 and 13-2). Circumferences must be measured without excessive pressure or slack on the tape. The tape should be pulled tight until the animal's coat is just compressed against its skin.

A dog should stand squarely, looking straight forward with its head in normal carriage. Cats were anesthetized and measured in lateral recumbency in the original study. Thus, routine application of these measurements is somewhat difficult in cats. To avoid anesthesia for the sake of taking morphometric measurements to estimate body fat in client-owned cats, measurements can be taken with the cat in a standing position similar to that used for dogs. However, this modification compromises the accuracy and standard error of the estimate, making the estimate useful only as a relative means of assessing changes in body composition over time.

The range in body weights and %BF in the original study groups used to derive the morphometric equations should also be kept in mind when applying regression equations from morphometric studies to pet animals. Dogs used to derive the equations in Table 13-3 ranged from 7.3 to 34.5 kg and 1 to 33% body fat. Cats used to derive the equations in Table 13-3 ranged from 1.98 to 4.95 kg and from 7 to 25% body fat. Dogs and cats exist with body weights and %BF outside the limits covered in the studies. Technically, regression equations should not be used when the individual exceeds the maximum or minimum extent of the range used to derive the regression equations. Although the regression lines from both studies appear linear, their performance outside of the data range has not been critically assessed. Furthermore, cats are fairly standard in conformation and relative body proportions across all breeds, but dogs are not. Regression equations derived from dogs of retriever proportions are very unlikely to accurately reflect the body composition of brachycephalic or dolichocephalic breeds. Thus, application of the equations in Table 13-3 to brachycephalic or dolichocephalic breeds will cause spurious results at best. Caution is advised against overinterpretation of the results when regressions are extrapolated past the data range of derivation.

Summary of Animal Assessment

An integrated approach is recommended using at least RBW and BCS to evaluate or diagnose the degree of excess body fat in client-owned pets, despite the limitations and imperfections of each method. Multiple estimates provide checks against wrong initial impressions and inaccurate conclusions drawn using one particular method. Body condition scoring is probably the single most useful of the three methods. Body condition scoring can be used to demonstrate to the owner what contours are absent that otherwise should be present and what bony prominences should be easily felt but are not readily palpable. To some extent the BCS identifies candidates for weight loss; dogs and cats with scores of 4.5/5 or 5/5 are such candidates.

After body condition scoring, RBW can be used as an indicator for the need to lose weight. Often the issue of RBW is approached when determinations are made for daily calories to feed, especially if the calculation is based on optimal body weight. Finally, an estimate of %BF from morphometric measures can be used to check or modify the %BF suggested by the BCS and the category of overweight vs. obese suggested by the BCS and RBW. Animals with RBWs around 1.20 should also have a %BF greater than or equal to 30% if a diagnosis is unclear for overweight vs. obese body condition. Table 13-2 summarizes the expected relationships between BCS, RBW and %BF for animals whose optimal weights range from 1 to 80 kg.

Other Procedures for Diagnosing Obesity

Radiographic or sonographic images can often help an owner appreciate the degree of excess fat deposited subcutaneously or intra-abdominally, particularly when viewed next to radiographs or sonograms of similar size animals that are in optimal body condition (Figures 13-3 and 13-4). However, radiographs should not be taken solely for diagnosing obesity.

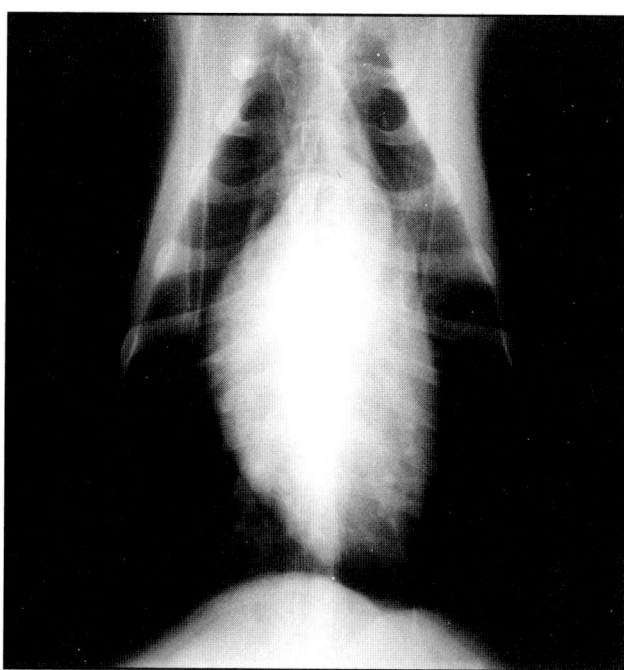

Figures 13-3A and 13-3B. Ventrodorsal radiographs of a normal dog (BCS 3/5, above) and an obese dog (BCS 5/5, below). Compare the body wall thickness of the two dogs.

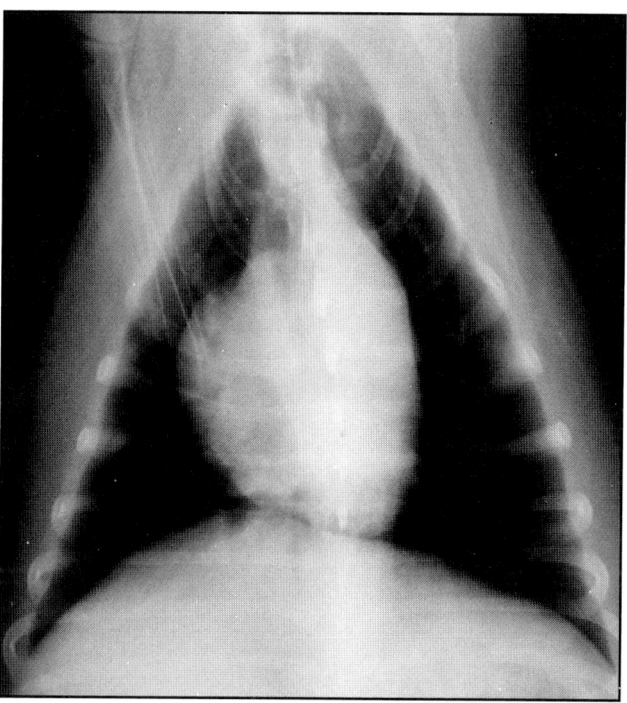

Risk Factors for Obesity

Obesity develops when animals are in positive energy balance for an extended period of time. This occurs when energy intake increases, energy expenditure decreases or both happen. Under most circumstances, homeostatic mechanisms control energy intake and maintain body composition at or near some "set point." Several risk factors contribute to positive energy balance and/or affect the body's compositional set point. Genetics, gender, age, physical activity and caloric composition of foods have been demonstrated as risk factors for positive energy balance, weight gain and obesity. These risk factors must be understood if obesity is to be prevented or treated effectively.

GENETICS

Researchers have found that obesity in people has a large propensity for being heritable.[44,45] Genetics are likely to determine the concentration and activity of various metabolic regulators, their receptors and, thus, metabolic efficiency.[46-49] Clearly, some breeds are more likely to be overweight when compared with others. Breed prevalence within a geographic area will influence the prevalence of obesity in specific breeds. Labrador retrievers, Cairn terriers, cocker spaniels, long-haired dachshunds, Shetland sheepdogs, basset hounds, cavalier King Charles spaniels and beagles have a greater prevalence of obesity than other breeds.[2,4] In contrast to dogs, cats of mixed breeding are more likely to be obese than are purebred cats.[5] These findings suggest that genetics influence metabolic set points for energy requirements and the tendency for weight gain or loss in dogs and cats.

GENDER AND GONADECTOMY

Gonadectomy increases the risk of obesity in dogs and cats. Neutered cats are more likely to be overweight than

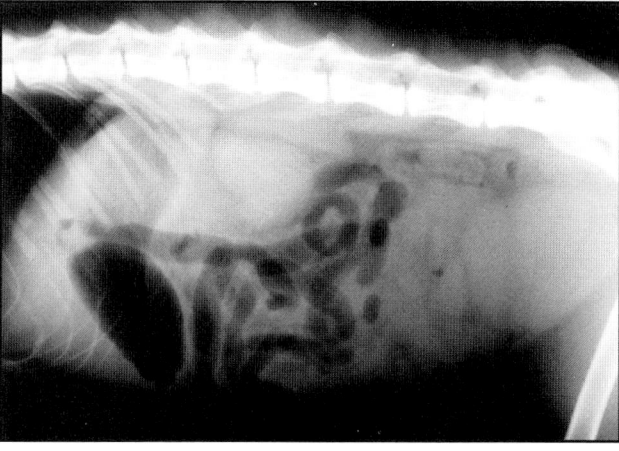

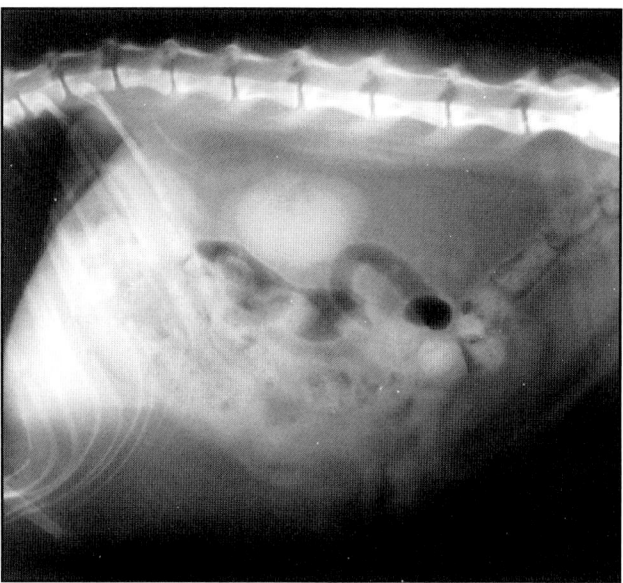

Figures 13-4A and 13-4B. Lateral abdominal radiographs of a normal cat (BCS 3/5, above) and an obese cat (BCS 5/5, below). Note the enlarged abdomen and ventral fat deposition in the obese cat.

are intact cats of either gender.[5,50,51] Neutered female dogs are about twice as likely to be overweight than are intact female dogs.[4] A similar trend occurs in castrated male dogs.[4] Gonadectomy predisposes dogs and cats to weight gain and eventual obesity for several reasons. Gonadectomized cats had resting metabolic rates 20 to 25% below those of intact cats of similar age, as measured by indirect calorimetry.[52] In practical terms, this finding indicates that neutered cats require only 75 to 80% of the food required by intact animals to maintain optimal body weight. These measurements confirm the previously suspected decrease in metabolic rate caused by the loss of estrogens and androgens from gonadectomy. This reduction in resting metabolic rate appears to be in addition to any decrease in physical activity that might occur from decreased roaming and sexual behavior.[53,54]

Furthermore, estrogens suppress appetite in several species of animals.[55] Studies have demonstrated that neutered female beagles and cats will eat more food and gain more weight than sham-operated females fed an identical food.[51,56] Thus, removal of the metabolic effects of estrogens and androgens by gonadectomy may lead to increased food consumption, when at the same time the animal's energy requirement is lower because of its decreased metabolic rate and physical activity.

AGE

Age has been correlated with prevalence of excess body weight in dogs and cats in several studies.[1,2,5,57,58] Very few animals younger than two years of age are classified as overweight. After two years of age the prevalence of overweight dogs and cats increases and reaches a maximum at around six to eight years of age. Studies show a plateau or slight decrease in prevalence of overweight dogs and cats until about 12 years of age when the prevalence tends to decrease markedly in most cross-sectional studies.[1,5,57,58] These observations have bearing on two theories concerning obesity and aging. First, one theory suggests that aging causes a decrease in energy requirement as a result of concomitant loss of lean body tissue and that obesity will result if energy intake does not also decrease. Except for the study by Mason,[2] the data from other cross-sectional studies do not appear to support this theory on initial examination.[1,5,57,58] Rather, it seems that as dogs and cats age past 10 to 12 years, they become thinner and even have a tendency to be in less than optimal body condition.[1,5,58]

However, an alternate hypothesis suggests that overweight dogs and cats die sooner and do not reach ages attained by thinner animals because excess weight is detrimental to overall health.[1] Caloric consumption has been inversely related to life span of rodents.[59-61] This effect is unconfirmed in dogs and cats and demonstrates the need for longitudinal epidemiologic studies of dogs and cats that differ in body condition to determine if life spans of obese pets are shorter.

ACTIVITY

Activity or exercise can contribute markedly to daily energy expenditure. Thus, it is not surprising that animals with decreased activity or restricted opportunities for exercise are at greater risk for becoming overweight.[5]

FOOD AND FEEDING

One study found no difference in types of food given to overweight pets compared with foods given to animals in optimal body condition.[4] Other studies have demonstrated an increased risk for being overweight when certain categories of foods are fed.[2,5] All of the associated foods, whether commercial or home prepared, could be considered calorically dense, although caloric density per se was not the variable tested for increased risk of being overweight.

Feeding very palatable foods free choice to dogs and cats may encourage consumption that exceeds requirements. Likewise, excessive use of treats or substitution of food for other types of interaction between the owner and pet may also encourage excess consumption of food.

Energy Requirements

Daily consumption of calories must exceed daily energy expenditure for a sustained period in order for overweight or obese body conditions to develop. An understanding of the components that contribute to the daily energy requirement (DER) is useful to appreciate why animals of similar body weight and frame size can have different caloric requirements independent of genetics or neuter status. An understanding of the components that contribute to DER is also important to understanding the rationale behind recommendations and alterations made to correct obesity.

The DER to maintain body weight of an animal can be subdivided into: 1) resting energy requirement (RER), 2) exercise energy requirement (EER), 3) thermic effect of food (TEF) and 4) adaptive thermogenesis (AT). RER correlates closely with lean body mass in people, and accounts for 60 to 80% of the total DER for adult maintenance.[62-64] The RER represents energy used to maintain normal physiologic functions at rest in a thermoneutral environment several hours after eating.[63] These physiologic functions are performed by lean tissues with very little energy required to maintain adipose tissue.

EER is the energy expended for muscular activity. The contribution of EER to DER is determined by the animal's body weight plus the time and intensity of muscular activity. Certainly, animals that are less active or have little opportunity to exercise expend less energy compared with active animals of similar size. The EER can account for 10 to 20% of total daily energy expended by nonathletic people.[62]

TEF is the obligatory cost of digesting and absorbing food. TEF constitutes approximately 10% of total expenditure and is affected by food composition and the number of meals eaten per day.[62,63] The obligatory cost associated with digesting and absorbing each meal is the reason weight-reduction programs recommend multiple small meals per day rather than one or two large meals. RER, EER and TEF make up the majority of DER; thus, these are the components that can be manipulated to affect the amount and rate of weight loss.

AT makes up the smallest proportion of the DER for most pets. AT is the energy expended to regulate body temperature during exposure to ambient temperatures below or above the thermoneutral zone or during transient periods of excess caloric consumption.

Imbalances favoring caloric intake relative to caloric expenditure (positive energy balance) can occur several different ways. Gonadectomy may suddenly make the number of calories fed before surgery excessive for the animal's subsequent rate of metabolism. Determining amounts to feed

based on manufacturer recommendations may also lead to excessive caloric intake. This results not because manufacturers make inappropriate or self-serving recommendations, but rather because manufacturers base recommendations on ranges and average caloric requirements for a given body weight. Recommendations often list a minimum and maximum amount of food to feed within a given range of body weights (e.g., two to four cups for a 5.9- to 11.4-kg dog). The maximum amount can be one and one-half to four times the minimum amount listed for a given range of body weights. Excess caloric intake can occur if the pet owner interprets that a smaller dog should be fed the larger amount.

When manufacturers recommend only one amount of food for a specific body weight, the amount is generally based on the average caloric requirement for that body weight. However, averages are population means and energy requirements vary widely around the population mean for any specified body weight. A recommended amount of food to supply the average caloric requirement for a 10-kg dog will be inappropriate for a 10-kg dog that requires only 60 to 80% of the average because of lower metabolic rate (decreased RER) or less activity (lower EER).

Intake of calories can become excessive if changes occur in a pet's lifestyle or daily routine that markedly reduce activity without reducing calories. Such changes include moving to smaller dwellings, musculoskeletal injuries and diseases that require persistent long-term use of central nervous system depressants or corticosteroids. Finally, caloric requirements will decrease as some animals age. Certainly, requirements for a given weight are less for maintenance of adults than for growing individuals of similar weight. Some older animals may also require slightly less energy than younger adults as a result of reduced activity and possibly a reduction in amount of lean body mass as a normal consequence of aging.

Assess the Food(s)

A pet's body weight and condition are determined by the nutrient composition of the food and the amount of food eaten daily. An accurate, complete history of the types and amounts of all foods eaten by the pet is necessary for making feeding recommendations in general, but especially for weight loss. Besides total quantity of food and calories, some consideration should be given to which nutrients (protein, fat and soluble carbohydrate) supply what proportion of the calories. The proportion of these nutrients in a food determines the food's caloric density and to some extent the acceptability of the food for reducing or maintaining body weight and condition of the pet. The Key Nutritional Factors table lists guidelines and ranges for energy, fat and protein content in foods suitable for producing weight loss or maintaining weight in dogs and cats that have lost weight or are predisposed to being overweight. Reasons for these ranges in nutrient content for weight loss or control are discussed in detail below.

Food Amount

A quantitative food record is an essential diagnostic step in developing a weight-loss program. To be quantitative, the food record must include amounts of all foods and account for all calories the patient consumes. Caloric content of commercial pet foods and treats can either be obtained from manufacturers or calculated. (See Chapter 1.) Appendices L

Regulatory Definitions for Descriptive Terms Indicating Restricted Calories or Fat

The 1997 Official Publication of the Association of American Feed Control Officials (AAFCO) contained Regulation PF8 Descriptive Terms that defined limits and labeled requirements for the calorie and fat content of foods using descriptive terms such as "light," "lite," "low calorie," "less," "reduced calorie," "low fat," "reduced fat" and "lean." These definitions were implemented in the United States in January 1998.

The definitions for the descriptive terms are summarized below.

"Light," "Lite" and "Lean"

	Dry foods (<20% moisture)	Semi-moist foods (20 to 65% moisture)	Moist foods (>65% moisture)
		Dogs	
Light	3,100 kcal ME/kg food	2,500 kcal ME/kg food	900 kcal ME/kg food
Lean	9% fat as fed	7% fat as fed	4% fat as fed
		Cats	
Light	3,250 kcal ME/kg food	2,650 kcal ME/kg food	950 kcal ME/kg food
Lean	10% fat as fed	8% fat as fed	5% fat as fed

"Less" or "Reduced Calories"

For dog or cat food labels bearing a claim of "less calories," "reduced calories" or similar words, the percentage of reduction and the product of comparison should be explicitly stated on the label. The product label should also bear a calorie content statement and feeding directions should reflect a reduction in calories compared with feeding directions for the product of comparison. Comparisons between products in different categories of moisture content are considered misleading.

"Less" or "Reduced Fat"

For dog or cat food labels bearing the claims of "less fat," "reduced fat" or similar words, the percentage of reduction and the product of comparison should be explicitly stated on the label. The product label should also bear a maximum crude fat guarantee immediately after the minimum crude fat guarantee in the mandatory guaranteed analysis information. Comparisons between products in different categories of moisture content are considered misleading.

BIBLIOGRAPHY
Association of American Feed Control Officials. Official Publication 1997; 119-120.

---

and M list caloric content for many other foods and treats. Most packaged human foods include caloric content on the label. The cases at the end of this chapter demonstrate the utility of a quantitative food record for determining appropriate amounts of food for achieving weight loss.

A quantitative food record helps determine how efficiently an animal uses calories and how easy it will be to return the animal to optimal weight. The food record can be indispensable for determining how severe caloric restriction will need to be to produce weight loss, both in total calories and in product selection. Equations to estimate energy requirements for cats or dogs often produce erroneous results because of wide variation between individual animals. In practice, individual animals are encountered that need precisely the same, markedly fewer and, occasionally, markedly more calories than the calculations suggest. Caloric restriction may be insufficient to produce weight loss or may even produce weight gain in some animals if calculations for caloric restriction are applied without taking into account the calories being eaten to maintain the animal's current weight.

Food Type

Decreasing the caloric density of the food fed to overweight pets is the primary strategy for producing weight loss. Pet foods marketed as restricted in calories can vary widely in caloric content, proportion of nutrients contributing calories, fiber and digestibility. Table 13-4 lists selected veterinary therapeutic and commercial pet foods marketed specifically for loss or control of body weight. Regulatory definitions for the terms light, lean, reduced calorie and reduced fat have been implemented in the United States. (See sidebar "Regulatory Definitions for Descriptive Terms Indicating Restricted Calories or Fat.") A rough guideline from the authors' experience is that the caloric content of dog foods for weight loss and control should be no more than 3.4 kcal (14.23 kJ) metabolizable energy (ME)/g on a dry matter basis (3,400 kcal [14.23 MJ] ME/kg DMB). For cat foods, the caloric content should be less than 3.6 kcal (15.06 kJ) ME/g DMB (3,600 kcal [15.06 MJ] ME/kg DMB) to produce weight loss in cats that are obese and resistant to losing weight (Table 13-4).

Pet food manufacturers decrease the caloric density of foods by reducing fat and simultaneously increasing the fiber, air or moisture content of the food. Pet owners facing the challenge of getting their pet to lose weight often ask whether feeding less of the pet's current food would produce weight loss rather than having to switch to a calorie-restricted food. This approach is usually unsuccessful for three reasons.

First, most calorically dense pet foods contain more fat than do calorie-restricted foods. Fat has about 2.25 times

Table 13-4. Levels of key nutrients in selected commercial foods marketed for caloric restriction and weight loss.

	kcal/kg (DM*)	MJ/kg (DM)	% kcal or kJ from fat**	Fat (% DM)	Crude fiber (% DM)	Protein (% DM)
Dry canine products						
Hill's Prescription Diet Canine r/d	2,966	12.4	24.0	8.4	23.5	24.8
Hill's Prescription Diet Canine w/d	3,216	13.5	23.0	8.8	16.8	16.7
Hill's Science Diet Canine Maintenance Light	3,293	13.8	23.0	9.0	14.8	18.6
Iams Eukanuba Reduced Fat Formula	4,306	18.0	23.0	10.0	4.4	21.1
Iams Eukanuba Restricted-Calorie	4,053	17.0	15.0	6.6	1.9	19.2
Iams Less Active	4,281	17.9	28.0	12.5	5.6	22.2
Leo Specific Finess CRD	3,633	15.2	14.6	5.6	8.9	24.4
Medi-Cal Canine Fibre Formula	3,078	12.9	na	10.1	15.8	24.3
Medi-Cal Canine Weight Control/Geriatric	3,434	14.4	na	8.3	5.9	19.6
Purina CNM OM-Formula	2,783	11.6	17.7	6.0	15.2	22.8
Purina Fit & Trim	3,100	13.0	17.4	7.4	10.8	15.3
Purina O.N.E. Reduced Calorie Formula	3,623	15.2	20.4	8.9	3.1	18.2
Purina Pro Plan Reduced Calorie Formula	3,638	15.2	24.1	9.7	2.7	15.9
Quaker Cycle Lite	3,217	13.5	24.3	10.1	4.8	18.7
Select Care Canine Hifactor Formula	3,278	13.7	28.0	10.8	14.7	25.7
Waltham/Pedigree Calorie Control/Low Calorie	3,500	14.6	22.7	8.9	1.8	32.2
Moist canine products						
Hill's Prescription Diet Canine r/d	3,000	12.6	24.0	8.3	21.2	25.3
Hill's Prescription Diet Canine w/d	3,114	13.0	31.0	12.5	12.2	16.1
Hill's Science Diet Canine Maintenance Light	3,540	14.8	22.0	9.6	10.5	18.8
Iams Less Active (Beef & Liver Formula)	5,416	23.1	40.0	20.5	4.5	40.9
Leo Specific Finess CRW (foil pack)	3,511	14.7	23.0	8.9	17.7	31.6
Medi-Cal Canine Fibre Formula	3,309	13.8	na	7.9	15.9	24.7
Medi-Cal Canine Weight Control	na	na	na	12.3	6.1	21.8
Purina CNM OM-Formula	2,478	10.4	28.1	8.4	19.2	44.1
Quaker Cycle Lite	3,904	16.3	41.6	18.7	8.4	31.9
Select Care Canine Hifactor Formula	3,077	12.9	25.0	9.0	15.0	24.8
Waltham/Pedigree Calorie Control/Low Calorie	3,662	15.4	36.5	16.9	2.1	52.8
Dry feline products						
Hill's Prescription Diet Feline r/d	3,277	13.7	24.0	9.1	14.6	37.4
Hill's Prescription Diet Feline w/d	3,531	14.8	23.0	9.3	7.9	38.8
Hill's Science Diet Feline Maintenance Light	3,523	14.7	22.0	9.0	8.5	40.8
Iams Eukanuba Restricted-Calorie	4,352	18.2	23.0	10.3	2.1	36.3
Iams Less Active Formula	4,437	18.6	29.0	13.6	3.3	31.1
Leo Specific Finess FRD	3,290	13.8	na	7.2	18.7	36.4
Medi-Cal Feline Fibre Control	2,813	11.8	na	13.8	7.3	34.1
Medi-Cal Feline Weight Control	3,831	16.0	na	12.3	3.8	34.4
Purina CNM OM-Formula	3,034	12.7	26.9	7.7	11.5	37.0
Purina Pro Plan Cat Reduced Calorie Formula	4,118	17.2	23.4	9.4	2.5	34.8
Select Care Feline Hifactor Formula	3,778	15.8	29.0	12.9	5.0	38.2
Select Care Feline Weight Formula	3,800	15.9	27.0	12.2	3.6	36.2
Whiskas Feline Calorie Control	3,389	14.2	na	8.9	4.4	46.7
Moist feline products						
Hill's Prescription Diet Feline r/d	3,236	13.5	24.0	9.1	17.3	36.0
Hill's Prescription Diet Feline w/d	3,327	15.6	38.0	16.6	12.3	41.1
Hill's Science Diet Feline Maintenance Light	3,550	14.9	29.0	12.1	9.2	45.0
Leo Specific Finess FRW (foil pack)	3,458	14.5	25.8	9.3	18.7	42.1
Medi-Cal Feline Fibre Formula	3,391	14.2	na	14.4	8.6	40.2
Medi-Cal Feline Weight Control	3,873	16.2	na	17.7	5.5	40.2
Select Care Feline Hifactor Formula	3,857	16.1	36.0	16.1	7.2	34.1
Waltham/Whiskas Feline Calorie Control/Low Calorie	3,904	16.3	50.0	24.0	2.1	50.0

Key: na = information not published by manufacturer.
*From manufacturers' published information or calculated from manufacturers' published as fed values.
**From manufacturers' published information or calculated using energy factors of 4 kcal/g for nitrogen-free extract and crude protein and 9 kcal/g for crude fat.

the calories of an equivalent weight of carbohydrate or protein. In addition, fat is a very efficiently digested and metabolized source of energy. In one study, overweight dogs fed restricted calories from a food containing more fat lost less body weight and body fat than did overweight dogs fed equivalent calories from a food containing less fat.[65] The TEF from absorption of fat has been found to be less than the TEF from absorption of carbohydrate or protein in obese people.[66] Studies in people have also determined that fat stored in the body comes primarily from dietary fat, whereas TEF is more closely correlated with carbohydrate intake.[62] Thus, a food with more calories

supplied from fat will tend to support retention of body weight and body fat even when total calories consumed are reduced.

Second, digestibility of a food (i.e., the amount eaten that is digested and absorbed) is inversely proportional to the total amount of food eaten. When less of a calorically dense food is fed, the proportion digested and thus the proportion of total energy extracted from the food will increase slightly. This is a secondary contributor to the caloric efficiency that occurs when less of a calorically dense food is fed. However, the amount of energy derived from the food is slightly greater than expected based on

Does Dietary Fiber Affect Satiety?

Dennis E. Jewell and Philip W. Toll
Hill's Science and Technology Center, Topeka, Kansas, USA

Satiety is difficult to measure in dogs and cats, but a sense of "fullness" can be inferred by a decrease in food-seeking activities and reduced consumption of foods when meals are offered. The amount of dietary fiber can influence food consumption and food-seeking activities, and therefore, energy intake.

In a two-phase study, investigators randomly assigned 30 beagle dogs to one of two groups. In the first phase, one group was offered a 45-minute meal consisting of a low-fiber commercial dog food[a] (<2% crude fiber, dry matter basis [DMB]) and the other group a medium-fiber commercial dog food[b] (12% crude fiber, DMB). After 14 days the groups were fed the opposite food for two more weeks (28 days total). A second 45-minute meal (called an intruded meal) was offered on Days 7, 14, 21 and 28.

The same crossover design was used in Phase 2; however, two different foods were fed. The first commercial dog food contained low fiber[c] (<2% crude fiber, DMB); the second commercial dog food contained high-fiber levels[d] (21% crude fiber, DMB).

Dogs fed the medium-fiber[b] (12% crude fiber, Phase 1) and high-fiber[d] (21% crude fiber, Phase 2) commercial foods consumed less energy in their daily meals (Figures 1 and 2) and in the intruded meals (Figures 3 and 4). Dogs in the high-fiber group also consumed less dry matter during the intruded meal (Figure 4).

Increasing fiber in canine foods decreased voluntary food intake, a measure of satiety. Commercial foods containing 12 and 21% crude fiber on a DMB increased satiety and voluntary reduction of energy consumption, compared to commercial foods containing less than 2% crude fiber on a DMB.

The study shows that low levels of dietary fiber (<2%, DMB) apparently do not sufficiently affect satiety to influence daily caloric intake, whereas medium- to high-fiber levels (>12%, DMB) can influence daily caloric intake and the desire to eat unexpected snacks or meals.

ENDNOTES

a. Eukanuba Light. The Iams Co., Dayton, OH, USA.
b. Science Diet Canine Maintenance Light. Hill's Pet Nutrition, Inc., Topeka, KS, USA.
c. Eukanuba Restricted-Calorie Formula. The Iams Co., Dayton, OH, USA.
d. Prescription Diet Canine r/d. Hill's Pet Nutrition, Inc., Topeka, KS, USA.

BIBLIOGRAPHY

Jewell DE, Toll PW. Effects of fiber on food intake in dogs. Veterinary Clinical Nutrition 1996; 3: 115-118.

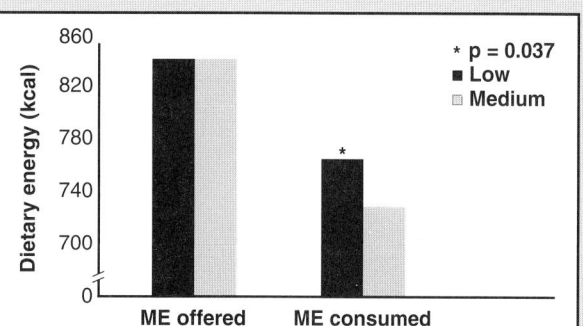

Figure 1. Phase 1: The effect of foods containing 1.5 or 12% fiber on daily energy intake. Dogs eating the low-fiber food consumed significantly more metabolizable energy (ME).

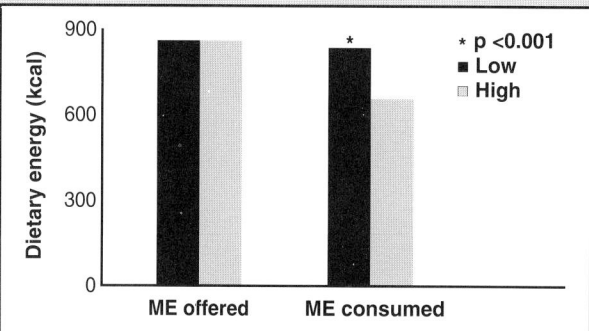

Figure 2. Phase 2: The effect of foods containing 1.5 or 21% fiber on daily energy intake. Dogs eating the low-fiber food consumed significantly more metabolizable energy (ME).

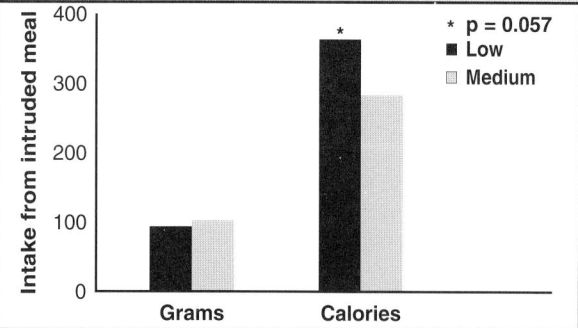

Figure 3. Phase 1: The effect of foods containing 1.5 or 12% fiber on intruded food intake. Dogs eating the low-fiber food consumed significantly more calories (ME).

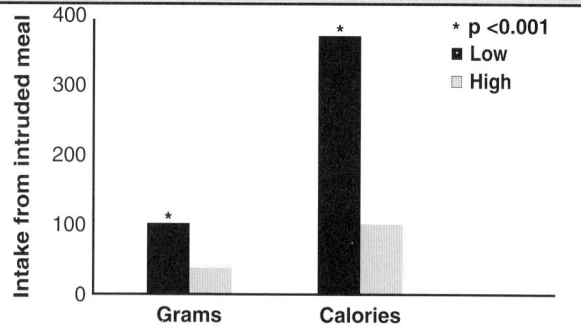

Figure 4. Phase 2: The effect of foods containing 1.5 or 21% fiber on intruded food intake. Dogs eating the low-fiber food consumed significantly more dry matter and calories (ME).

calculations using the reported energy density of the food and the amount eaten.

Third, all nutrients are reduced when amounts of a calorically dense food are decreased to restrict calories. A food for weight loss ideally should be replete in all nutrients except energy so that protein, essential fatty acids, vitamins and minerals are present in amounts sufficient to support normal physiologic processes and retention of lean body tissue. Most pet foods are balanced for all other nutrients based on the energy content of the food and the expected intake required to support a given body weight. A deficiency in energy and other nutrients will occur if the amount of a maintenance food is markedly decreased to produce weight loss. Calorie-restricted foods generally have proportional increases in protein, vitamins and minerals to avert or minimize the creation of other nutrient deficiencies when fewer total calories are fed. The goal of a reducing food should be to restrict only energy, not other nutrients.

In addition to decreasing fat content to decrease caloric density, increasing the air in dry extruded foods, water in moist formulas and indigestible fiber in either moist or dry products can further dilute calories per volume of food on an as fed basis. The primary reason for diluting calories by one of these methods is to allow the animal to eat a larger volume of food without consuming additional calories. This is an attempt to accomplish two things. First, feeding larger volumes of food attempts to avert perceptions by some owners that the pet is being fed too little. Second, volume is increased in an effort to maximize the effect of bulk fill in the gastrointestinal tract for satiety (i.e., the transient postprandial interruption in hunger sensations and food-seeking activity of animals). Unfortunately, the result is often less than adequate. Despite feeding more food, the degree and duration of satiety produced is insufficient to prevent total uninterest in food between meals. The owner interprets the animal's lack of satiety as hunger or starvation.

Gastrointestinal fill is only one of many factors that contribute to satiety and its associated behaviors. Induction of satiety depends on the cumulative effect from an integrated cascade of physical, chemical, hormonal and neural events in the gastrointestinal tract and central nervous system.[67-69] Events in the gastrointestinal and nervous systems are linked via vagal nerve impulses and small peptide hormones such as cholecystokinin and bombesin. Satiety is also influenced by the nutrient composition of the food, the amount of hepatic glycogen and the amount of fat stored in adipocytes.[68-71] Thus, caloric dilution by itself does not produce satiety in some animals.

Use of Fiber in Foods for Weight Reduction

There is some debate regarding the use of calorie-diluting agents in foods intended for weight management. Potential calorie-diluting agents are dietary fiber, dietary water and air added to dry foods. Water and air are quickly removed from the gastrointestinal tract and contribute only transiently to gastrointestinal fill. However, dietary fiber, besides diluting calories, offers several biologic and nutritional effects worthy of consideration.

Theoretically, dietary fiber helps produce weight loss by diluting calories, increasing satiety and limiting food consumption as a result of more bulk being present in the gastrointestinal tract.[72] Fiber may also help produce weight loss by decreasing the availability of calories by interfering with the digestion and absorption of fat, protein and soluble carbohydrate.[72] Many of the effects of dietary fiber depend on the specific type, form and amount of fiber used.

Studies suggest that increased levels of dietary fiber contribute to satiety via prolonged distention of the gastrointestinal tract. Fiber types affect duration of gastric and intestinal distention differently. Insoluble fibers have little effect on gastric emptying, whereas soluble fibers slow gastric emptying.[72-74] Although both soluble and insoluble fibers slow intestinal transit, insoluble fiber (purified cellulose) produces the greater effect.[75] Thus, even though the type of fiber affects the two segments of the gastrointestinal tract differently, total transit time through the entire gastrointestinal tract is increased and is approximately the same for soluble and insoluble fibers.

Actual documentation of increased satiety from dietary fiber is difficult to prove in people and more so in other animals, because satiety is a subjective feeling of fullness and a lack of desire to eat. Indirect evidence for satiety can be obtained from animals by measuring decreases in food consumption and food-seeking activities. In people, increased intake of dietary fiber decreases food intake for variable periods lasting up to eight hours.[76-78] Studies in dogs have produced variable results. Some studies in dogs showed no effect on caloric intake when foods containing 12 to 14% of dry matter as soluble or insoluble fibers were fed.[79,80] In one study, foods containing either 2.2 or 15.6% fiber did not produce any measurable difference in satiety.[81] However, the dogs in this study were fed quantities of food supplying only 40% of calories for adult maintenance, and this degree of caloric restriction may have overshadowed any effect of fiber between the two groups.[81] In another study, dogs offered maintenance calories from food containing 21% insoluble fiber consumed significantly less food and calories than when offered equivalent calories from foods containing less fiber.[82] These same dogs also ate less food when subsequent meals were offered 30 to 45 minutes after consuming the high-fiber food, indicating a satiety effect.[82] (See sidebar "Does Dietary Fiber Affect Satiety?")

Another factor regarding the value of dietary fiber in weight-management foods is fiber decreases the apparent digestibility of energy-providing nutrients in the food by 2 to 8%.[72,74,80,83,84] Fiber decreases pancreatic enzyme activity in vitro and pancreatic lipase secretion in vivo.[85,86] Fiber also increases the fecal excretion of bile acids and fat.[73] It is well-documented that some dietary fibers slow the absorption rate of carbohydrate and fat, but the total quantity absorbed during the entire period of digestion is not significantly less than the quantity absorbed from fiber-free foods.[74,87,88] The apparent digestibility of dietary protein is decreased by increased dietary fiber when fecal nitrogen is measured.[74,80,83,84] However, it is unclear whether the increased fecal nitrogen is from dietary protein that would normally be digested and absorbed, or whether the nitrogen is from increased numbers of bacteria, endogenous loss of mucosal cells or a component of the fiber itself. The effect of dietary fiber on mineral availability depends on the specific fiber(s) and mineral(s). In general, insoluble fibers such as cellulose are less likely to reduce mineral availability than are soluble fibers. (See Chapter 2.)

Dietary fiber increases the amount of fecal material and frequency of defecation.[73,80] Dogs fed soluble fiber produced more feces than dogs fed similar amounts of predominantly insoluble fiber.[79] There is some evidence that beet pulp and pectin are not tolerated well by dogs when fed in amounts greater than 10 and 13% dry matter, respectively.[80,88] Pet owners should be informed that the quantity of feces the animal produces will probably increase when their cats and dogs are fed foods containing more than 10% dry matter from fiber. Excessive flatus can also be an unwelcome side effect of feeding high-fiber foods. Fiber solubility roughly equates with fiber fermentability. (See Chapter 2.) Increased amounts of highly fermentable fiber in a food are more likely to result in flatulence.

Taken together, all of these study results support the use of dietary fiber in foods intended for weight loss and weight maintenance. Table 13-4 shows that the crude fiber content of selected commercial products marketed as reduced-calorie or weight-loss products can be similar to the crude fiber content of non-calorie-restricted pet foods (<5% of dry matter), mildly increased (5 to 10% of dry matter), moderately increased (10 to 15% of dry matter) or greatly increased (15 to 30% of dry matter). For the reasons noted above, most commercial calorie-restricted foods with increased fiber contain primarily insoluble fiber.

Assess the Feeding Method

Consideration must be given to how the owner feeds the pet. Feeding foods free choice may work for individual cats and dogs that can self-regulate their daily intake of food to match their DER. However, free-choice feeding rarely works for weight loss or for maintenance of reduced body weight even with the most calorie-restricted foods. The owner's quantitative description of how much pet food, treats, table food and consumable chew toys are provided for the dog or cat must be assessed. "Bowls," "cups" and "handfuls" reported by owners come in all sizes; thus, the amount of food and calories these objects contain varies as well. The veterinary nutritionist's "cup" is a standard 8-oz. volume measure. The amount of dry dog or cat food reportedly fed by owners needs to be converted to this standard or some other usable quantity (i.e., weight) for determining calories, if the food record is to be quantitative. Treats, consumable chew toys and table food can supply significant calories, especially if the owner is unaware of their caloric content or how many the animal eats daily.

Whether the pet has access to any other sources of food also needs to be determined. Other sources include other pets' food in multi-pet households. Having multiple people feeding the pet can result in multiple sources of food, particularly if different people have different opinions about the body condition of the pet. The previous two situations can condemn a weight-reduction program to failure before it ever begins if the owner cannot, or will not, feed the overweight pet separately and keep the overweight pet from eating other pets' food. Dogs and cats that roam unsupervised also have the opportunity to eat at other locations besides their own food bowls.

■ FEEDING PLAN

Weight-Reduction Programs and Plans

A successful weight-reduction program is a multi-step process that requires pet owner commitment, a feeding plan, an exercise plan, pet owner communication and patient monitoring.

Pet Owner Commitment

The first step, and the foundation for weight loss, is for everyone involved in feeding the pet to recognize, accept and understand the reason why the pet should lose weight, and to make a commitment to accomplish that goal. Weight loss will not occur unless the pet owners recognize the problem and are willing to take corrective steps.

Several methods and techniques can be used to help owners recognize and accept that their pet is overweight and not just "stocky." Some of these techniques have already been discussed. Past body weights and BCS in the patient's medical record can be used along with RBW to show an owner how excessive present body weight relates to the animal's frame size and optimal body weight. References to breed standards for adults in optimal weight can be used if no records of the patient's body weight are available. The owner can be shown and made to feel where bony structures on the patient should be readily palpable but are not, and where body contours of the patient differ from optimal. The BCS or morphometric measures can be used to estimate %BF for additional body composition information. Estimates of %BF should be interpreted for the owner in relation to ranges of %BF found in animals of optimal body condition (15 to 25%), with obesity being defined as greater than 30% body fat.

If thoracic or abdominal radiographs have been taken, a side-by-side comparison with similar radiographic views from an animal of similar size at optimal body weight can quite effectively demonstrate to the owner the excess subcutaneous or intra-abdominal fat on the pet (Figures 13-3 and 13-4). Practitioners should consider keeping a reference set of radiographs for cats and dogs in optimal body condition for this specific purpose. Also, a side-by-side comparison of the overweight animal and one of the same breed and frame size in optimal body condition can serve the same purpose if an animal of optimal weight is available.

After the owners recognize and accept that the pet is overweight, the next step is for them to commit to a weight-loss program. There are several strategies to help owners make this commitment. Owners can be informed about documented problems associated with obesity and how returning the animal to optimal weight will reduce the risk of one or more of these problems. The risks can be quantified economically for animals likely to suffer orthopedic or metabolic problems because of their degree of obesity. The average hospitalization bill for repair of a ruptured cranial cruciate ligament was $575 for 10 overweight dogs from May 1995 to May 1996 at Texas A & M University.[a] Costs for calorie-restricted food and rechecks for these patients for 10 months of weight reduction was $374 to $525, depending on the size of the dog. The cost of diagnosing and treating cats with uncomplicated hepatic lipidosis during the same period was $500 to $600.[a] The cost of food and monitoring during a 12-month period of weight loss was $225. Often a strong motivating factor for commitment is to improve or palliate a problem caused or exacerbated by obesity. Weight loss in these cases becomes part of the overall therapeutic plan and can be crucial for realizing clinical improvement and benefit from other treatments.

One-time fees (where the pet owner pays for the entire weight-loss program for a certain period) have been suggested as being useful to gain and retain commitment. One-time fees may help retain commitment, but they may also shift the responsibility for accomplishing weight loss from the pet owner to the veterinarian. The core motivation for achieving weight loss should be the owner's desire to improve the quality of the pet's life and avoid paying money to correct problems in the future. The

Starvation for Weight Loss

Starvation cannot be used to produce weight loss in cats because of the risk of inducing hepatic lipidosis. Starvation can be used to produce weight loss in dogs, but starvation has several disadvantages. First, more lean body mass is lost during starvation as a result of the protein deficiency that is created.

Second, starvation requires that the dog be hospitalized and given only water plus a vitamin-mineral supplement formulated to meet the dog's daily requirements. There are few supplements that provide 100% of canine minimum daily requirements for all fat-soluble vitamins, water-soluble vitamins and macro- and microminerals. Thus, a deficiency of one or more of these nutrients is possible unless exemplary research and formulation are undertaken to ensure the adequacy of all 23 noncalorie nutrients.

Third, owner participation in the weight-loss program is eliminated because of the hospitalization that is necessary to closely monitor the patient and ensure no calories are consumed. This eliminates the opportunity for pet owners to change the way they feed and exercise their dog. Thus, owners are unaware and unappreciative of the feeding and exercise regimens required to maintain the dog at its reduced weight. Unawareness and lack of owner participation make it more likely that weight will be regained after the dog is discharged to the owner.

Fourth, some people consider starvation to be inhumane. Starvation is currently considered an unacceptable method of therapy for weight reduction in people. Starvation should rarely be considered an option for producing weight loss in dogs and then only in cases of morbid obesity that require immediate weight reduction to maximize the dog's chances of survival.

BIBLIOGRAPHY
Fisler JS, Drenick EJ. Starvation and semistarvation diets in the management of obesity. Annual Review of Nutrition 1987; 7: 465-484.

owner should not be trying to derive benefit from money already spent.

Veterinarians have fulfilled their responsibilities if they have presented pet owners with the reasons and options for weight loss, whether or not the owners decide to pursue that course of therapy. Ultimately, the pet is the property of the owner to do with as he or she sees fit. Because most dogs and cats are kept for pleasure, owners have the right to decide whether they derive more pleasure from feeding the pet than from gaining improvements in the pet's health as a result of weight loss. If the pet owner commits to weight loss for the pet, the veterinarian's responsibility is to use knowledge of the physiology and nutrition involved with weight loss to prescribe a program with the best chance of succeeding. The veterinarian also has the responsibility to adjust the initial plan based on monitoring of the patient's progress and to reinforce the owner's commitment during the difficult periods that almost always occur when less weight is lost than was expected. Ideally, pet owners are responsible for the daily tasks that will produce weight loss, because then they will modify the way they feed and exercise the pet.

Reports and position statements addressing obesity in people indicate the combination of reduced-calorie foods, regular exercise and behavior modification has the greatest chance of achieving and maintaining weight loss.[64,69,89-91] Formulation of a program for achieving weight reduction consists of: 1) setting a goal for the amount of weight to lose, 2) setting an amount for daily caloric intake, 3) selecting a specific food and feeding method, 4) selecting a specific amount of exercise, 5) monitoring the progress of weight loss, 6) adjusting calories, food and exercise as necessary and 7) stabilizing caloric intake of the animal at its reduced weight to ensure that weight is not regained.

Select a Food(s)

Formulating a dietary plan involves 1) setting the amount of calories the animal is allowed daily, 2) selecting and specifying the food(s) and amount(s) to supply daily calories and 3) selecting the way the food is to be fed. Development of an appropriate dietary plan must include calculation of the current caloric intake (DER for obese weight), determination of the animal's ideal body weight, calculation of a food dose (DER for weight loss) and adjustments to the plan based on monitoring.

Calculation of Caloric Intake

A detailed quantitative food record or feeding history completed by the owner is the only way of estimating the DER for maintaining a given body weight of an individual animal. It is crucial to know the number of calories required to maintain a pet's obese weight in order to specify the amount of food that will produce calorie-restricted weight loss. Although some obese patients may actually have "average" caloric requirements and simply overeat, many have caloric requirements that are below average. The only way to differentiate between the two is to compare the individual's current intake with the expected average DER for the present body weight. For the food record to be useful, all calories consumed must be accounted for as discussed in the food assessment section.

Determination of Ideal Body Weight

Determination of ideal body weight is important to set a goal for weight loss and provide one reference point for calculating amounts of food for caloric restriction. Because adipose tissue requires very little energy for maintenance, lean body mass primarily determines DER. Therefore, a given animal will have similar DER in ideal and obese body conditions (assuming similar lean body mass). Using ideal weight for energy requirement calculations will usually avoid overestimation of DER. Ideal weight is determined using the methods described above. Table 13-2 lists ideal weight in comparison to current weight and BCS.

Food Dose Calculation

If triglycerides were the only tissue component lost during weight reduction, then simply starving dogs, but not cats, would be an acceptable option for weight loss from a physiologic perspective. There are several disadvantages, however, to using starvation for weight reduction in dogs. (See sidebar "Starvation for Weight Loss.") Unfortunately, when body weight is lost under the best of circumstances, 10 to 25% of the loss comes from lean tissues.[92,93] Loss of lean body mass ultimately decreases an animal's RER and the number of calories required for DER, unless the level of activity is increased to that associated with athletic training. Therefore, the underlying objective in setting the number of daily calories for weight loss is to restrict calories enough to produce weight loss, but still provide enough calories, protein, vitamins and minerals to prevent or minimize nutrient deficiencies and loss of lean body tissue.

Multiple recommendations, equations and methods have been published for determining caloric restriction appropriate for producing weight loss. The situation is similar to the multiple recommendations and equations for calculating RER and DER. The range in caloric restriction given by the various equations or methods for estimating calories appropriate for producing weight loss is evidence that no single method or equation is appropriate for all dogs and cats. Most calculations are based on the animal's estimated optimal body weight, but some are based on present obese weight. Equations based on optimal weight tend to be more restrictive than equations using obese weight. Also, the starting point for estimating calories appropriate for producing weight loss can either be DER for optimal or obese weights or RER for optimal weight. Ultimately, however, the practitioner is faced with the challenge of restricting caloric intake enough to produce results that maintain owner interest and satisfaction without being so severely restrictive that more lean body mass is lost than absolutely necessary.

As discussed above, maintenance of adipose tissue requires relatively little energy, so most calories consumed are used to maintain lean body tissues and physiologic functions. Therefore, if lean body mass is similar at ideal and obese body conditions, the energy required to maintain each body condition should also be similar. This is one reason why standard energy calculations may overestimate energy requirements for most obese patients. Daily caloric intake must be less than calories needed to maintain lean body tissues in order to use adipose tissue to supply energy to meet DER. For dogs, the authors recommend using 1.0 to 1.2 x RER (50 to 60% of DER) for optimal weight as an initial calculated estimate of calories required to produce appropriate weight loss. Theoretically this level of restriction will make caloric intake nearly equal to the calories required to support lean body mass at optimal weight. Energy for exercise and digestion of food must subsequently be supplied by catabolizing fat stores.

Recommendations for caloric restriction to produce weight loss in cats range from 50 to 80% of maintenance calories for optimal weight. Restricting calories for maintenance of optimal weight of a cat by more than 70% effectively makes caloric intake less than RER because DER for cats is only 1.2 to 1.4 x RER. RER represents a theoretical minimum for daily energy consumption. Restrictions to less than RER might seem problematic especially in overweight cats in which severe caloric restriction has been demonstrated to produce hepatic lipidosis.[24] However, experimental and clinical trials using caloric restrictions between 59 and 80% of RER produced acceptable rates of weight loss in overweight cats with no biochemical evidence of hepatic lipidosis.[94]

The number of calories estimated for weight loss needs to be compared with the number of calories currently being consumed as indicated in the feeding record. This comparison is necessary to ensure the calculated caloric restriction is less than what the animal is currently eating. More severe caloric restriction will be required than calculations suggest if calories calculated to produce weight loss are greater than or equal to calories being consumed to maintain the animal's excess body weight. In such cases, caloric restriction markedly less than the calculated RER may be required to achieve weight loss. Initially 80% of present consumption is a reasonable starting point if an animal is maintaining excess weight on fewer calories than 1.2 x RER for optimal weight. Figure 13-5 is an algorithm for setting caloric restriction to produce weight loss by comparing and reconciling caloric estimates from calculations and the feeding history.

Ideally treats, snacks and human foods should be eliminated from reducing diets for dogs and cats to maximize the chances for successful weight loss. A portion of the total daily calories for weight loss can be reserved for treats if the owner must feed treats or snacks. Treats should be low-calorie foods such as the dry form of the reducing food, popcorn popped without butter, low-fat, low-starch vegetables or low-fat commercial treats. The calories supplied by the treats must be accounted for within the total calories allowed in the feeding plan.

Determine a Feeding Method

Pet owners must quantitatively account for the foods they feed their pets. As little as one-fourth cup of a calorie-restricted food per day can be the difference between achieving or not achieving weight loss. Similarly, treats can be the difference between achieving or not achieving weight loss, if they are not accounted for within the total allowed calories or their specified number is exceeded. If the owner must feed treats, the number can be controlled by placing a specific quantity of treats containing the number of calories reserved for treats in a "treat container" each day. No additional treats are allowed for that day after the treat container is empty. In multi-pet households, the obese pet must be fed separately to prevent access to other pets' food.

Dogs and cats on weight-reduction programs should be fed multiple small meals during the day rather than a single large meal in order to take advantage of the obligatory energy cost for digesting and absorbing food. The optimal number of meals for maximizing caloric expenditure from thermic effect of food has not been determined. However, the total daily food should be divided into at least two portions fed eight to 12 hours apart. Most pet owners can feed two meals per day without disruption of their schedules. Clients who can conveniently feed three or more meals per day should do so.

Meal sizes should be in portions that are practical to measure (i.e., to the nearest one-fourth cup or can). If the daily amount of food does not divide evenly into portions that are readily measurable, some meals will contain less and others more food. The meals containing more food should be fed when the owner will be with the pet for the longest time between meals. The pet should be kept out of the kitchen and dining areas during preparation and consumption of family meals. These practices can help reduce

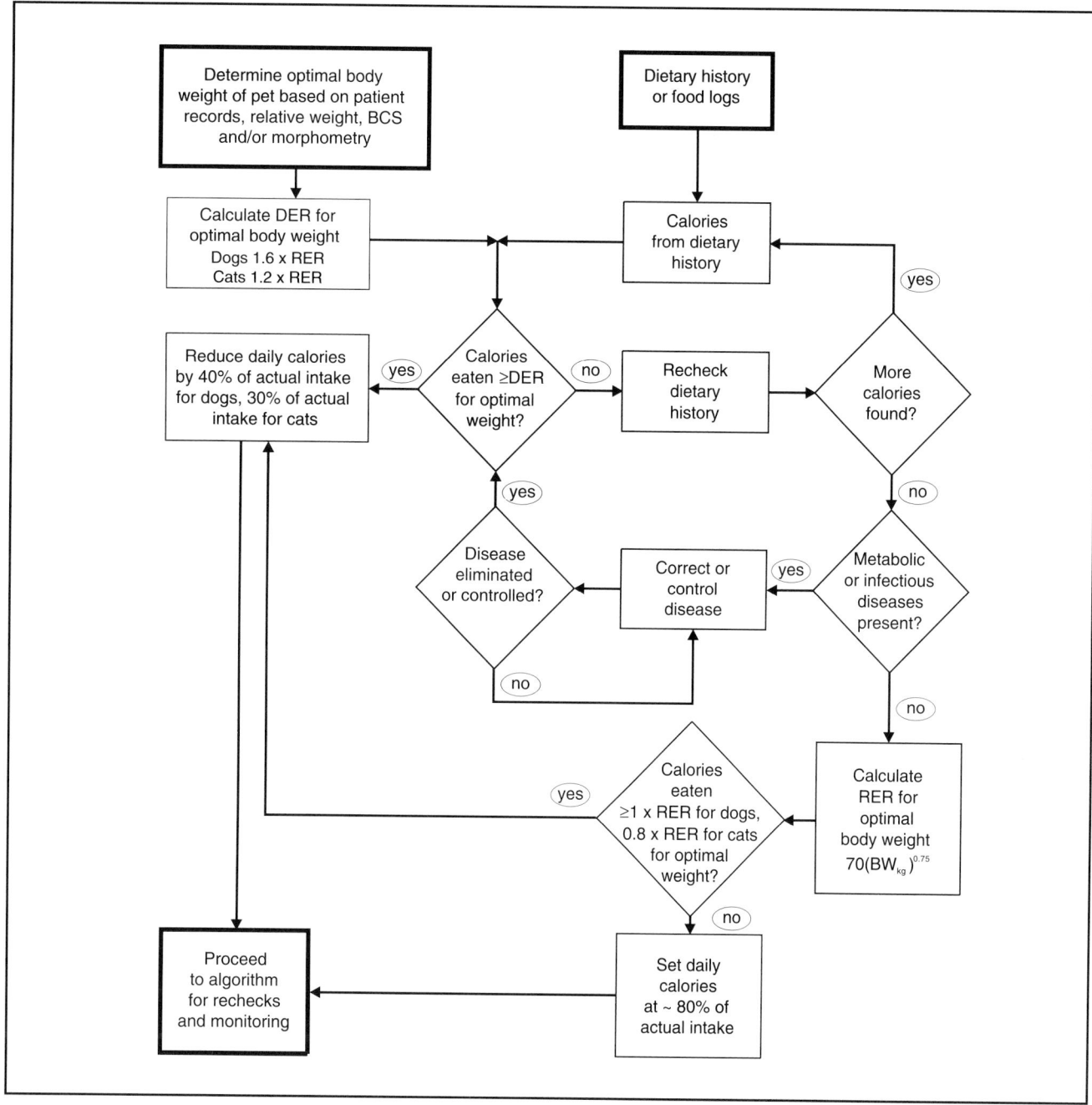

Figure 13-5. Algorithm for determining calories for weight loss.

Exercise

Exercise is the only practical means of increasing energy expenditure to create or widen a deficit between energy consumed and energy expended for patients fed calorie-restricted foods. The metabolic rate of people undergoing weight reduction decreases more than expected after corrections have been made for decreased thermogenic effects of food due to decreased intakes and decreased RER due to loss of lean body mass.[95-97] The only way to successfully sustain or increase overall energy expenditure during weight reduction is to increase the amount of physical activity. Exercise may also benefit obese patients by reducing the

the pet's begging and the owner's urge to give the pet additional food or treats.

loss of lean body mass and maintaining or improving RER.[98,99] In some cases, pets fail to lose weight unless exercise is part of the weight-reduction plan, regardless of the severity of caloric restriction.

The optimal amount of exercise for dogs and cats fed calorie-restricted foods has not been determined. Two brisk 20-minute walks per day have been recommended as beneficial for dogs fed reducing foods.[9] Up to an hour of walking has been reported to be practical and enjoyable for some owners and pets.[100] Exercise should be implemented gradually, starting with amounts the patient can comfortably tolerate, especially if orthopedic, cardiovascular or pulmonary disease is also present. It is more important that the animal increase its activity by some amount each day even if it initially is able to walk only out the door to the sidewalk and

Canine and Feline Obesity
Clinical Nutrition Support Service
Texas Veterinary Medical Center
Texas A&M University

Obesity is the most common nutritional problem in dogs and cats. Obesity is defined as a body weight that is greater than 20% above optimal body weight. For example, a dog that has an optimal body weight of 20 pounds. is considered obese if his or her body weight exceeds 24 pounds. The most common cause of obesity is an excessive intake of calories. A weight-reduction program has been designed to improve your pet's quality of life. An optimal body weight, a specific diet and amount have been determined for your pet and a specific amount of daily activity has been recommended.

To successfully manage a weight reduction plan for your pet, you should:
1. Feed the balanced, low-calorie diet as prescribed.
2. Feed your pet alone, away from other pets.
3. Not feed table scraps, treats, snacks or other rewards.
4. Exercise your pet as prescribed.
5. Weigh your pet regularly and record body weights on the chart below.
6. Not handle, prepare or eat food in the presence of your pet.
7. Have your pet checked on a regular basis by your veterinarian to monitor the progress of the weight-loss program.

Weight-reduction program

Date _____

Patient _____   Record number _____

Clinician _____   Nutritionist _____

Present weight _____   Estimated optimal weight _____

Diet: Food   Amount/meal[a]   Meals/day

_____   _____   _____

_____   _____   _____

_____   _____   _____

Exercise:

_____

_____

Weigh your pet every_____weeks, and record the weight on the chart below. Estimated minimum time to reach optimal weight if all instructions are followed:_____ months.

[a]"cup" is a standard 8-ounce volume measuring cup.

Weight reduction chart
for
_____

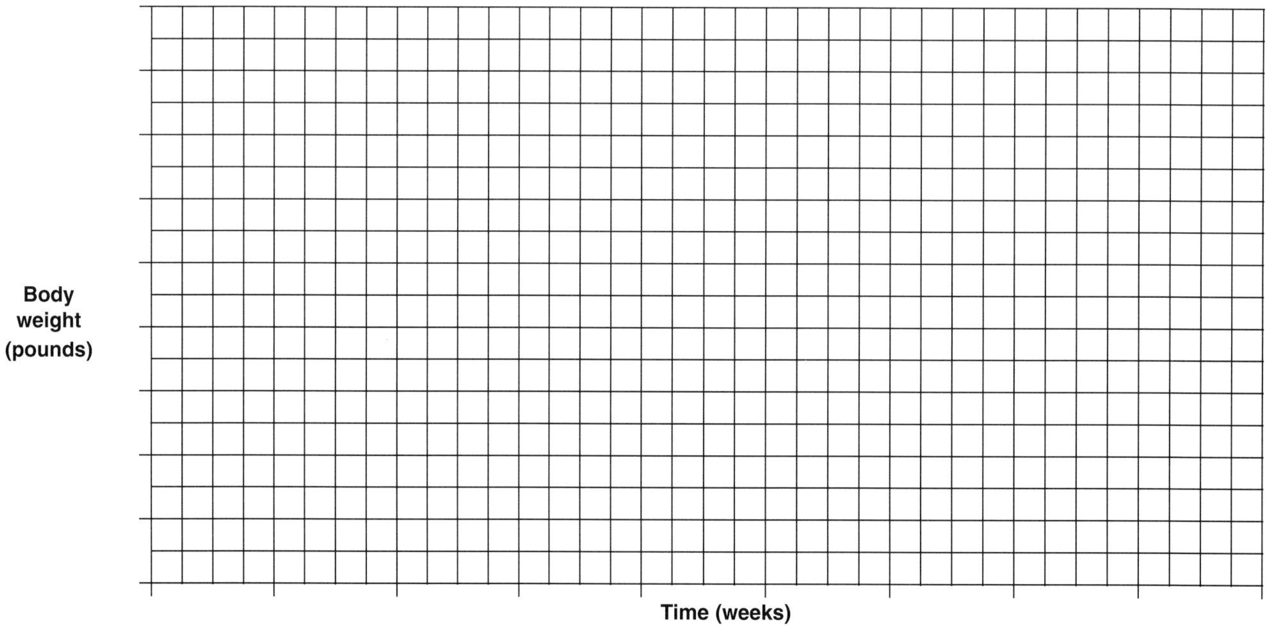

Body weight (pounds)

Time (weeks)

Figure 13-6. Canine and feline obesity fact and monitoring sheet.

back inside. The goal should be to work up to 20 minutes of uninterrupted walking if the animal cannot do this initially. Exercise may need to be omitted initially for patients recovering from orthopedic surgery because walking may exacerbate joint pain. Swimming is an alternative to walking that sometimes works for orthopedic patients if facilities are available to the owner. Because swimming requires more calories per minute than walking, the same number of calories can be expended in less time.[101]

Some creativity is often required to increase the activity of an overweight cat. Although cats are not typically trained to walk on a leash, they can be if the owner is patient and persistent. Sometimes a cat will walk back home on a leash if an exceptionally dedicated owner is willing to carry the cat on the out-bound half of the walk. Less extraordinary ways of increasing a cat's daily activity are to engage the cat in supervised play with string, balls, laser "mice,"other toys or other pets.

Pet Owner Communication

The typical pet owner who has a 15- to 30-minute appointment with a veterinarian can easily be overwhelmed by even a small portion of the information presented in this chapter. Provided the pet owner has agreed to implement a weight-loss plan, the specific recommendations for feeding, exercising and rechecking the animal need to be provided in a clear, concise, written format. Several pet food companies have brochures available that briefly explain obesity, its consequences and provide space to write in individual instructions for feeding, exercise and recheck appointments. These forms usually have a space to document progress on a graph or to record weights on specific dates. Several computer software programs will also generate forms incorporating recommendations and progress updates for a particular pet and owner. A practice may also elect to design and distribute its own printed or computer-generated material for this purpose. Information for a weight-reduction program should be clear, concise and should fit on both sides of an 8.5- x 11-in. sheet of paper. Figure 13-6 is an example of such a form developed and used by the Clinical Nutrition Service at the Virginia-Maryland Regional College of Veterinary Medicine and the Clinical Nutrition Support Service at the Texas A & M Veterinary Medical Teaching Hospital.

◼ REASSESSMENT

Regular monitoring of patient weight loss is important to ensure the prescribed program is effective and to motivate the owner. Simply telling a pet's owner to feed a certain quantity of a calorie-restricted food and increase the pet's activity is unlikely to produce weight loss for several reasons. Office rechecks or weigh-ins to monitor patient progress throughout weight loss are an integral component of a weight-reduction program, equal in importance to diet and exercise. There are three critical times during a weight-reduction program when rechecks can prevent the program from failing. These are at the very beginning, the very end and anytime in between when weight loss slows or stops. Figure 13-7 is an algorithm for monitoring progression of weight loss and making decisions to keep weight loss progressing toward the optimal weight.

Rechecks are used to accomplish several things necessary to ensure success of the weight-loss program.

First, rechecks reinforce the importance of weight loss for the pet and the veterinary practice's commitment to helping the pet owner get the animal to lose weight. Rechecks also reinforce the owner's commitment to get the animal to lose weight. Rechecks become a moment of truth for both pet owner and veterinarian. Rechecks give pet owners an opportunity to see the results of their efforts or to see the impact of inadvertently or purposefully feeding extra calories or not ensuring that the pet performed the specified amount of exercise since the last recheck. Rechecks allow the veterinary health care team to adjust the caloric intake, feeding plan and exercise recommendations to get or keep weight loss proceeding at a reasonable rate. The opportunity to make these adjustments is an extremely important iterative step in a weight-loss program. The initial considerations and calculations for caloric restriction and the feeding plan, no matter how carefully or scientifically made, are only an educated guess at what the caloric restriction and food should be for a safe and reasonable rate of weight loss for an individual animal. The success and appropriateness of this educated guess are ultimately determined by changes in the body weight measured on scales, the BCS and the morphometric circumferences measured with a tape.

Pet owners need reinforcement in the form of compliments and encouragement when overweight animals lose weight. Pet owners are likely to be experiencing one or more consequences as a result of changing what and how they feed their pet. The dog or cat is often manifesting some behavior that the owner interprets as hunger. Some pet owners will still feel they are depriving their pet of needed food or affection despite having made a commitment to getting the pet to lose weight. The pet owner's resistance against acquiescing to the pet's behavior and the urge to feed the pet more food should be acknowledged and reinforced.

Reinforcement and encouragement are certainly required when weight remains the same or increases from one recheck to the next. Lack of progress can occur for any number of reasons, but, regardless of the cause, it is discouraging to the pet owner. The reason for lack of progress needs to be determined and explained. Sometimes the animal is actually losing weight and it is simply not detected, either because the scale is not sensitive enough or the gastrointestinal or urinary tract has above average contents at the time of the weighing. If this is the case, the weight is likely to be decreased at the next recheck. Progress will be stopped by consumption of additional food, either because the animal had unlimited access to food while unsupervised or the owners fed more treats or snacks than allowed. Insufficient exercise will also decrease or stop weight loss. In any of these cases, pet owners need to understand and accept that the observed results were produced by these actions, and efforts should be redoubled to make the animal and the owners adhere to the feeding and exercise plan.

Finally, the amount of caloric restriction may be insufficient to accomplish weight loss for an individual animal despite what any calculation would suggest and despite 100% compliance by the owner. Problems with caloric restriction can occur initially or after some period of weight loss, perhaps because of a decreasing metabolic rate from the weight loss. If monitoring and counseling in the form of rechecks are not being done, these problems

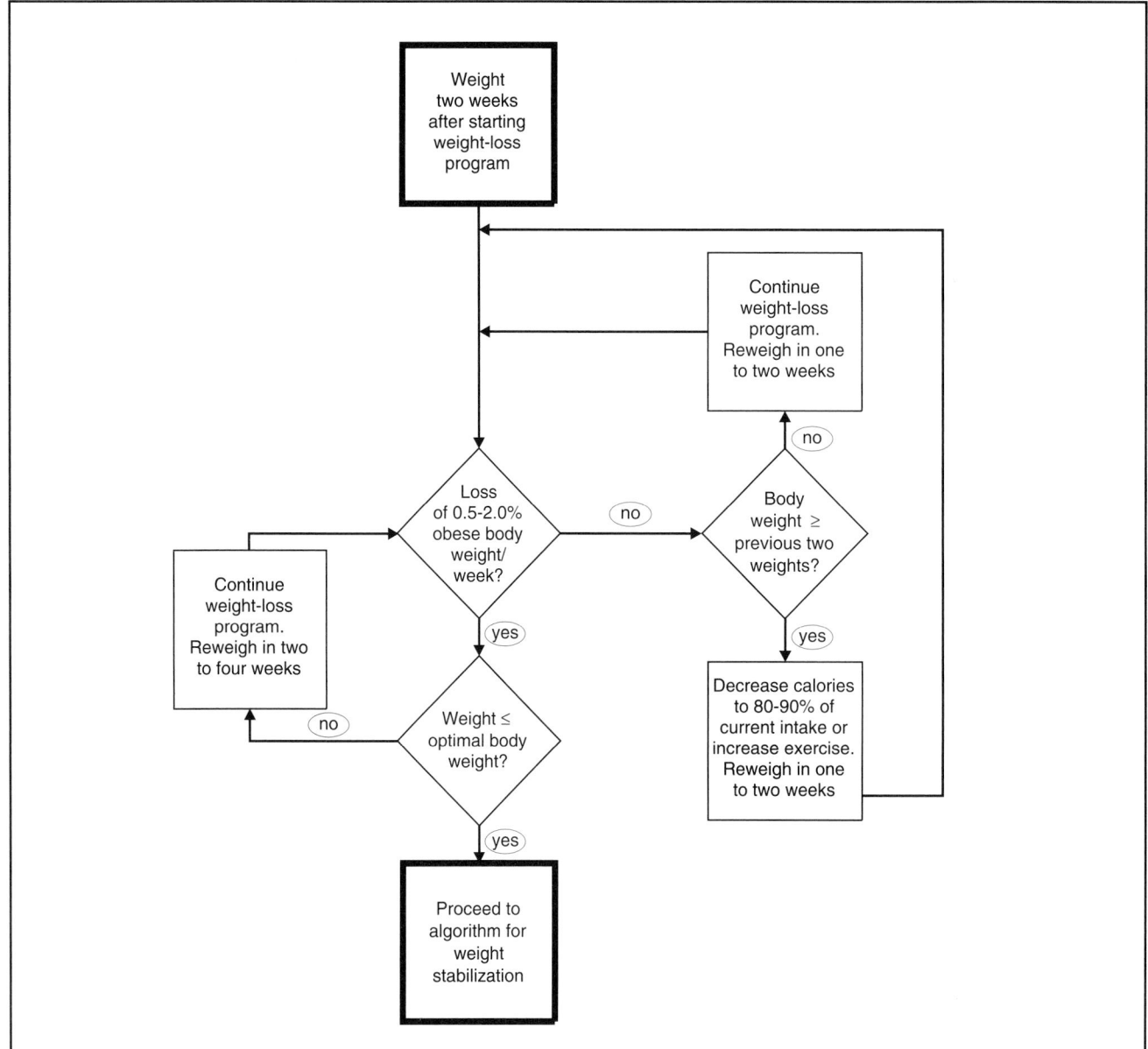

Figure 13-7. Algorithm for decision making and patient monitoring during weight loss.

will not be detected until the animal is seen some time in the future weighing the same or more than when the weight-loss program was started. The opportunity to promote weight loss in such animals will probably be lost because the pet owner will conclude that switching the food and tolerating undesirable behaviors did not produce results and was not worth the trouble or expense involved.

The best reinforcement and encouragement come initially from seeing the pet's body weight decrease, and later from seeing the return of normal body contours and resolution of clinical signs (e.g., better exercise tolerance, reduced lameness or decreased insulin doses). Often weight loss is imperceptible to the owner and requires objective documentation with scales or tapes. Change in body weight is the ultimate criterion for judging success or failure of the weight-loss program. However, if the period of time between rechecks is short, or the rate of weight loss is particularly slow, progress based on body weight alone may not be readily apparent.

When dogs and cats lose or gain weight, the body dimension that changes most is the abdominal or pelvic circumference. The thoracic circumference will also change somewhat, but the magnitude will not be as great nor the change as readily measurable as in the pelvic region. If progress is slow, sometimes the pelvic circumference will decrease between rechecks when body weight remains constant or vice versa. The decrease in circumference indicates progress and does not need to be converted into a decrease in body fat to be interpreted. In fact, progression of weight loss could be tracked by simply measuring pelvic and thoracic circumferences at each recheck and periodically reevaluating the BCS of the pet. These methods of assessing weight loss should be considered in settings such as house-call practices where veterinarians may not have scales capable of measuring the change in a pet's body weight.

Rechecks should be continued after the pet attains its optimal or target weight. Simply feeding the animal its previous food, even at reduced amounts, may lead to weight

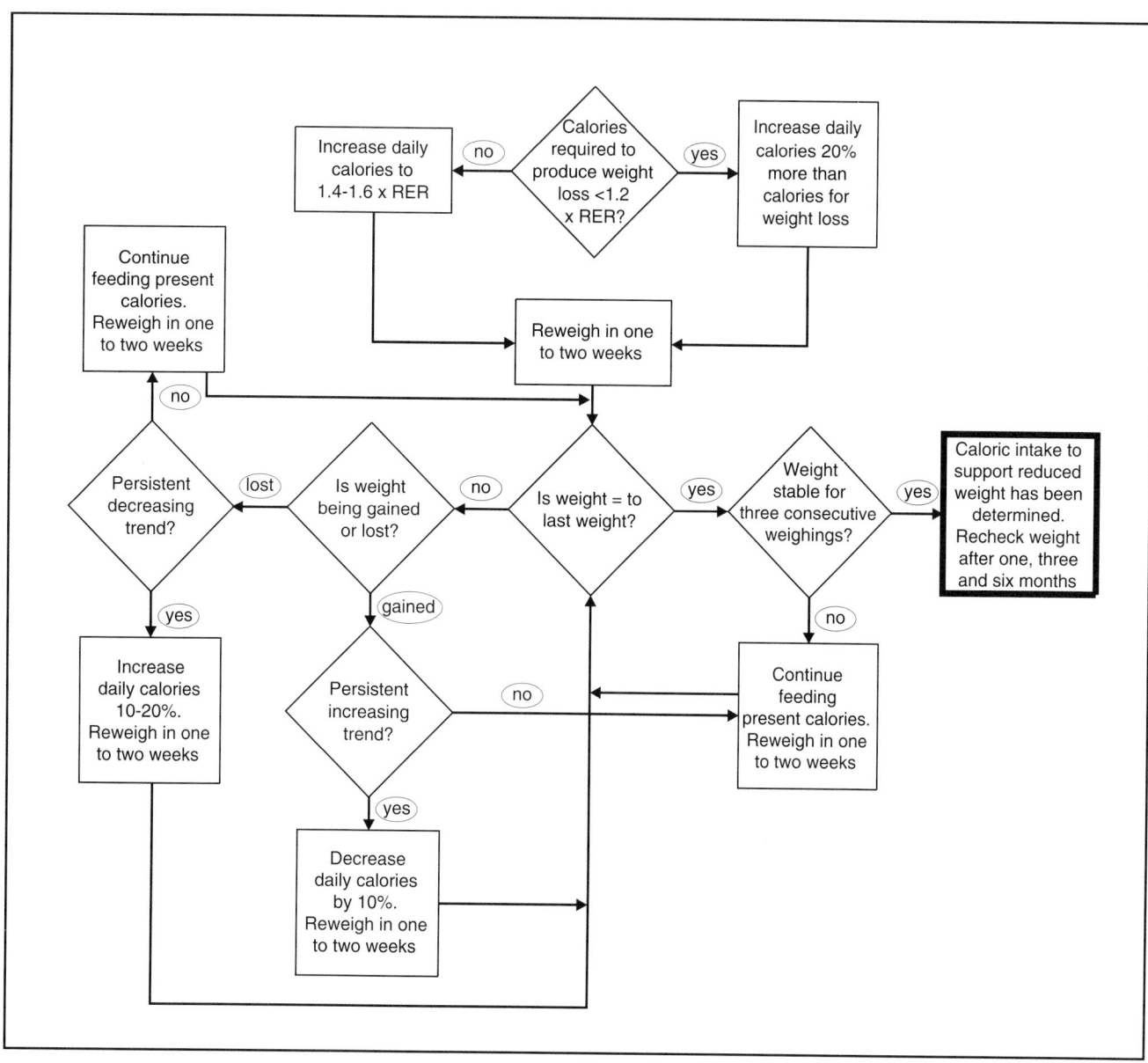

Figure 13-8. Algorithm for stabilizing body weight after weight loss.

gain, negating the effort required to produce weight loss and the resulting benefits. Recommendations for the specific food and calories required to maintain reduced body weight need to be individualized for each patient. The number of calories needed to maintain the reduced weight can be gauged from how many calories the pet ate to maintain its obese weight compared with standard estimates for that weight. The required calories can range from somewhat less than the estimated RER to the largest estimates for the DER. Animals that are under caloric restriction but are losing weight slower than expected probably will require fewer calories than the calculated DER for reduced weight. Animals that remain overweight when fed fewer calories than the calculated DER and need severe caloric restriction to produce slow weight loss are very likely to maintain that weight on calories close to estimates for RER of the reduced weight. These animals are likely to require reduced-calorie, reduced-fat foods for the long term. Animals in this last group need careful supervision to prevent weight from being regained. Figure 13-8 is an algorithm for determining the

amount of food needed to stabilize and maintain reduced body weight after a pet has reached its target weight.

Rechecks should be scheduled to allow enough time for detectable progress, but not so much time that the pet owner becomes dismayed at the lack of progress when problems are finally detected. Shorter intervals between rechecks are needed at the beginning and end of a weight-reduction program when the caloric content and amounts of food are changed. At the minimum, a week will be required before any progress can be detected. Generally two weeks is a safe and reasonable interval for most animals. Cats and some small dogs may take three weeks to lose enough weight for scales to measure the loss. At the most, no more than four weeks should pass before the animal is rechecked. However, four weeks may be too long for some animals if changes need to be made to the feeding or exercise plans.

Three body weights are usually required to establish a trend and rate for changes in weight. Thus, a determination that initial caloric restriction is insufficient to produce weight loss can be made sooner with a two-week recheck interval than with a four-week interval, saving at least two and perhaps six weeks, during which the animal is not losing weight. Intervals between rechecks can be increased to every four to six weeks after weight loss is documented to occur at a steady rate acceptable to the pet owner and veterinary health care team. If the animal fails to lose weight during a four- to six-week interval with no apparent explanation (i.e., more calories or less exercise) then the rechecks need to be more frequent to determine if weight loss has stopped and to assess the degree of caloric restriction needed for weight loss to recur.

More frequent rechecks are needed when the animal reaches its target weight and calories are increased to maintain that weight. Rechecks should occur every one to two weeks to assess the appropriateness of caloric intake in conjunction with continued exercise. During this stage of the weight-loss program, no more than two weeks should elapse between weighings because consumption of too little or too much food has undesirable consequences.

The authors prefer to focus on acceptable rates of weight loss instead of calculating a specific number of days that pet owners view as the time it will take to complete the weight-loss program. It can be disheartening to pet owners and harmful to the veterinarian's credibility if a single specific time is projected for returning the animal to optimal weight and then, as in most cases, it actually takes more time. However, the minimum and maximum acceptable times for a cat or dog to complete a weight-loss program can be calculated. (See sidebar "Calculating Time for Weight Loss and its Use in Monitoring Patients.")

Studies in people indicate that loss of more than 2% of body weight per week is unhealthy.[102,103] A greater proportion of lean body tissue is lost when more than 2% of body weight is lost per week. This ultimately reduces the RER and works against the goal of maintaining the greatest metabolic rate possible in a weight-reduced animal. A 2% loss of initial body weight per week is a reasonable estimate of the maximum acceptable rate of weight loss. However,

Calculating Time for Weight Loss and its Use in Monitoring Patients

The loss of 2% of initial body weight per week can be used as the maximum desired rate of weight loss in typical obese patients and a loss of 0.5% of initial body weight per week can be used as the minimum desired rate of weight loss. These two weight-loss rates can be used to calculate the minimum and maximum time expected for a dog or cat to reach its ideal or target body weight. The following case will demonstrate a simple method for determining this time interval and show its use in monitoring response to therapy in an obese cat.

METHOD
Obese weight – desired weight = A (kg)
Obese weight x 2% = B (kg/week)
A ÷ B = C (number of weeks necessary for weight loss at 2% rate)
C x 4 = D (number of weeks necessary for weight loss at 0.5% rate)
Desired weight loss should occur within these two time frames.

CASE

Assess the Animal

A three-year-old neutered female spayed domestic shorthair cat weighing 5.9 kg is presented for annual vaccinations. The owner had recently acquired the cat from her parents and was concerned that the cat was overweight compared with a cat owned by her roommate. All physical examination findings were normal except for obesity. Results of a complete blood count, serum biochemistry profile and urinalysis were normal.

The cat's body condition was assessed as 4.5/5. Optimal body weight was estimated to be 4.5 kg; therefore, the cat's initial weight was 31% above optimal (RBW = 1.31)

Assess the Food and Feeding Method

The cat was fed one-half cup of a dry specialty brand cat food and 3 oz. of various brands and flavors of moist cat foods once daily. The cat consumed at least 400 kcal (1,674 kJ) of metabolizable energy (ME) daily.

Feeding Plan

The resting energy requirement (RER) at the estimated optimal body weight was calculated as follows: RER optimal weight = 70(4.5)$^{0.75}$ = 218 kcal ME (912 kJ). Daily energy requirement would be approximately 1.4 x RER or 305 kcal

ME (1,276 kJ). The daily caloric intake was much higher than the estimated daily energy requirement.

The initial caloric restriction was set at RER calculated for optimal body weight. The owner was also instructed to increase the cat's activity as much as possible. The food was changed to commercial products containing less fat and more fiber. The owner was asked to return every two weeks for the first two months to monitor progress.

Calculations for Weight Loss

Obese weight   = 5.9 kg
Desired weight   = 4.5 kg
Desired weight loss   = 1.4 kg

5.9 x 2% = 0.12 kg/week
1.4 kg ÷ 0.12 = 12 weeks at 2% rate
12 weeks x 4 = 48 weeks at 0.5% rate

Reassess

The accompanying figure shows the weight loss that occurred with this feeding plan and exercise. The actual body weight loss for this cat falls nicely within the calculated minimum and maximum rates. The feeding plan was changed at 22 weeks to stabilize the body weight at 4.5 kg.

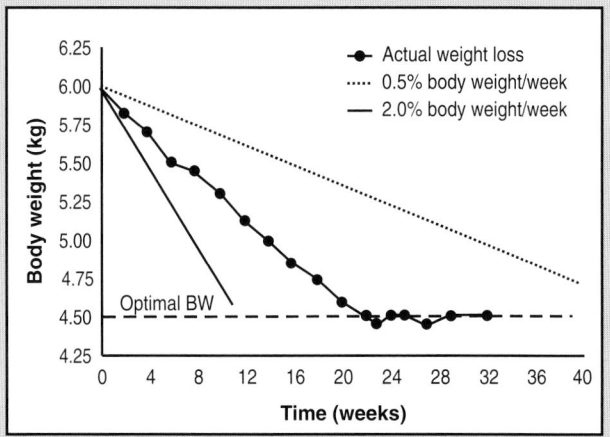

the impact of losing more than 2% of the initial body weight per week on the proportion of fat vs. lean tissue loss and on the metabolic rate has not been reported from weight-loss studies using dogs or cats. Very few animals fed reduced-calorie foods by the methods discussed above will lose more than 2% of their initial body weight per week.

At the other extreme, a rate of at least 0.5% of the initial body weight per week is needed to maintain owner interest and complete the weight-reduction program in a reasonable period. Realistically, eight to 12 months will be required to complete weight-reduction of most dogs and cats that are truly obese and that have metabolic rates slower than predicted by standard equations. See the sidebar "Other Treatment Modalities" for a discussion of other methods used to treat morbid obesity in people.

▇ OBESITY PREVENTION

The battle to correct excess body weight is better prevented than fought. Successful prevention of obesity requires risk factor assessment, body composition evaluation and appropriate feeding recommendations. Pets that have increased risk or are beginning to increase body fat above optimal amounts should be fed fewer calories. Calculated DER is about 1.6 x RER for most dogs and 1.2 x RER for most cats. Obesity-prone pets should be fed about 15% fewer calories (or 1.4 x RER for dogs and 1.0 x RER for cats). These are guidelines or starting points. Individual energy requirements can vary markedly from average estimates. Food amounts and feeding methods need to be evaluated and adjusted on an individual basis to maintain optimal body condition.

Growing animals that are overweight or obese have a greater risk of becoming overweight or obese adults.[104] Pet owners who present new puppies and kittens for vaccinations should be counseled on how to feed their pets to prevent excessive rates of growth and weight gain. No single feeding method and type of food will work for all pets and exceptions can be found to refute any standard recommendation. Body condition and rate of growth are the ultimate criteria for determining whether the type of food, amount of food and feeding method are appropriate for a given individual. Pet owners should be told the characteristics of optimal body condition and shown how to assess

---

Other Treatment Modalities

Several pharmacologic compounds have been used along with food and exercise to treat obesity in people. Most of these drugs have side effects in dogs and cats that prevent their use. The authors are unaware of any drug for weight loss in cats or dogs that has been fully evaluated for efficacy and safety.

DHEA

Dehydroepiandrosterone (DHEA) is an endogenous steroid produced by adrenal and gonadal tissue. A precursor of androgens and estrogens, DHEA has been used to induce weight loss in obese laboratory rodents without reductions in food consumption. An initial study using DHEA administered orally to spontaneously obese dogs produced weight loss in 13 of 19 dogs with no restriction in food or calories. The average rate of weight loss during the three months of treatment was 0.75% of body weight per week in the dogs that lost weight. Preliminary results of a placebo-controlled trial in which DHEA or the placebo was given along with a calorie-restricted food showed that DHEA produced greater rates and amounts of weight loss. However, final confirmation of dose, efficacy and safety during long-term use has not been published.

Surgery

Various surgical procedures and devices have been used to treat morbidly obese people who failed to lose weight using conventional methods of food, exercise and behavior modification. The procedures limit the quantity of food contained in the gastrointestinal tract or the ability of the gastrointestinal tract to digest and absorb nutrients. Perioperative mortality ranges from 0.5 to 1.3% of patients undergoing the various surgeries. Postoperative metabolic complications occur in 10 to 70% of patients, especially in patients who have surgical procedures to bypass portions of their small intestine. Complications that occur within days to months of surgery include vomiting, diarrhea due to malabsorption or gastrointestinal dumping, overt protein-energy deficiency and subtle to overt vitamin-mineral deficiencies. In addition to micronutrient deficiencies, long-term complications include anemia, liver failure, autoimmune arthritis, peripheral neuropathy, nephrocalcinosis from calcium oxalate deposition, decreased formation and mineralization of bone and dermatopathies. These patients must undergo long-term monitoring for systemic disease and the adequacy of vitamin and mineral intake and absorption. Such monitoring is more intensive and extensive than what is presently done for most veterinary patients that undergo surgical procedures or have chronic diseases. Also, people who are candidates for surgical treatment of obesity usually have relative weights greater than 200%. Most obese dogs and cats have relative weights of 120 to 200%. Gastrointestinal surgery for correcting obesity in dogs or cats probably is not a practical therapeutic modality considering the cost of surgery and the subsequent monitoring and treatments required to avert nutritional and metabolic complications. The authors know of no veterinary referral centers that use this method to treat obesity in pets, and do not recommend it based on the expected cost of surgery and monitoring as well as the probability of secondary complications.

BIBLIOGRAPHY

Cleary MP, Shepherd A, Jenks B. Effect of dehydroepiandrosterone on growth in lean and obese Zucker rats. Journal of Nutrition 1984; 114: 1242-1251.

Cleary MP, Zisk JF. Anti-obesity effect of two different levels of dehydroepiandrosterone in lean and middle-aged Zucker rats. International Journal of Obesity 1986; 10: 193-204.

Halverson JD. Metabolic risk of obesity surgery and long-term follow-up. American Journal of Clinical Nutrition 1992; 55: 602S-605S.

Kurzman ID, MacEwen EG, Haffa ALM. Reduction in body weight and cholesterol in spontaneously obese dogs by dehydroepiandrosterone. International Journal of Obesity 1990; 14: 95-104.

MacEwen EG, Kurzman ID. Obesity in the dog: Role of the adrenal steroid dehydroepiandrosterone (DHEA). Journal of Nutrition 1991; 121: S51-S55.

O'Leary JP. Gastrointestinal malabsorptive procedures. American Journal of Clinical Nutrition 1992; 55: 567S-570S.

Tagliaferro AR, Davis JR, Truchon S, et al. Effects of dehydroepiandrosterone acetate on metabolism, body weight and composition of male and female rats. Journal of Nutrition 1986; 116: 1977-1983.

OBESITY

the body condition of their pets. Owners can also be given target weights for age based on reasonable guidelines for appropriate rates of growth for the breed of dog. (See Appendix F.) Several different feeding methods and foods can be used to successfully grow and maintain a cat or dog if the owner can assess the body condition and keep track of growth.

When pets are presented for gonadectomy, their owners should also be counseled that the amount of food given to cats and dogs that have been neutered will probably need to be reduced to maintain optimal body condition. Body condition should also be closely monitored in animals with orthopedic or physiologic conditions that decrease their physical activity or metabolic rate.

SUMMARY

Successful completion of a weight-reduction program can be one of the most challenging treatments attempted by small-animal practitioners. Successful weight-reduction programs are much more complex than simply telling an owner to feed the pet less food or switch to a calorie-restricted food. Successful weight-reduction programs are composed of three key plans or prescriptions for feeding, exercise and rechecking progress. All three components are of equal importance for accomplishing weight loss. An analogy can be made between a weight-reduction program and a three-legged stool. Each of the legs on the stool represents one component of the weight-reduction program. As long as the stool has three legs it will be stable on most surfaces. If one leg is removed, great effort must be exerted by someone trying to stand on the stool to keep it stable. If two legs are removed the probability of standing upright on the remaining leg is very small. Prescriptions for weight reduction that neglect rechecks and exercise are almost certain to fail, just as the stool is likely to fall if one or two of its legs are removed.

The tools for weight reduction might appear archaic as medical technology becomes more sophisticated. In many cases, however, the low-tech solution is crucial for achieving the desired clinical improvement and deriving the full benefit from more technologically sophisticated and costly treatments or for avoiding those treatments altogether. The frustrations of owners and veterinary health care teams struggling to help lethargic, limping, dyspneic or diabetic pets lose weight are reduced or alleviated when the pet becomes more active, walks with normal gait, is able to breathe normally or requires less or no insulin.

ENDNOTE & REFERENCES

ENDNOTE
a. Burkholder WJ. Unpublished data. June 1996.

REFERENCES
1. Armstrong PJ, Lund EM. Changes in body composition and energy balance with aging. Veterinary Clinical Nutrition 1996; 3: 83-87.
2. Mason E. Obesity in pet dogs. Veterinary Record 1970; 86: 612-616.
3. Meyer H, Drochner W, Weidenhaupt C. Ein beitrag zum vorkommen und der behandluny der adipositas des hundes. Deutsche Tierarztliche Wochenschrift 1978; 85: 133-136.
4. Edney ATB, Smith PM. Study of obesity in dogs visiting veterinary practices in the United Kingdom. Veterinary Record 1986; 118: 391-396.
5. Scarlett JM, Donoghue S, Saidla J, et al. Overweight cats: Prevalence and risk factors. International Journal of Obesity 1994; 18 (Suppl. 1): S22-S28.
6. National Institutes of Health Consensus Development Panel on the Health Implications of Obesity. Health implications of obesity: National Institutes of Health consensus development conference statement. Annals of Internal Medicine 1985; 103: 147-151.
7. Owen OE. Obesity. In: Kinney JM, Jeejeebhoy KN, Hill GL, et al, eds. Nutrition and Metabolism in Patient Care. Philadelphia, PA: WB Saunders Co, 1988; 167-192.
8. Joshua JO. The obese dog and some clinical repercussions. Journal of Small Animal Practice 1970; 11: 601-606.
9. Lewis LD, Morris ML Jr, Hand MS. Obesity. In: Small Animal Clinical Nutrition III. Topeka, KS: Mark Morris Associates, 1987; 6-1-6-39.
10. Stanton CA, Hamar DW, Johnson DE, et al. Bioelectrical impedance and zoometry for body composition analysis in domestic cats. American Journal of Veterinary Research 1992; 53: 251-257.
11. Laflamme DP, Kealy RD, Schmidt DA. Estimation of body fat by body condition score (abstract). In: Proceedings. Twelfth Annual Veterinary Medical Forum, American College of Veterinary Internal Medicine. San Francisco, CA, 1994: 985.
12. Laflamme DP, Schmidt DA, Deshmukh A. Correlation of body fat in cats using body condition score or DEXA (abstract). In: Proceedings. Thirteenth Annual Veterinary Medical Forum, American College of Veterinary Internal Medicine, Lake Buena Vista, FL, 1995: 1029.
13. Burkholder WJ. Body Composition of Dogs Determined by Carcass Composition Analysis, Deuterium Oxide Dilution, Subjective and Objective Morphometry and Bioelectrical Impedance (PhD Dissertation). Blacksburg, VA: Virginia Polytechnic Institute and State University, 1994; 357.
14. Lew EA, Garfinkel L. Variations in mortality by weight among 750,000 men and women. Journal of Chronic Diseases 1979; 32: 563-576.
15. Rocchini AP, Moorehead CP, Wentz E, et al. Obesity-induced hypertension in the dog. Hypertension 1987; 9 (Suppl. III): 64-67.
16. Rocchini AP, Moorehead CP, DeRemer S, et al. Pathogenesis of weight-related changes in blood pressure in dogs. Hypertension 1989; 13: 922-928.
17. Buffington CA. Management of obesity–The clinical nutritionist's experience. International Journal of Obesity 1994; 18 (Suppl. 1): S29-S35.
18. Mattheeuws D, Rottiers R, Kaneko JJ, et al. Diabetes mellitus in dogs: Relationship of obesity to glucose tolerance and insulin response. American Journal of Veterinary Research 1984; 45: 98-103.
19. Mattheeuws D, Rottiers R, Baeyens D, et al. Glucose tolerance and insulin response in obese dogs. Journal of the American Animal Hospital Association 1984; 20: 287-293.
20. Nelson RW, Himsel CA, Feldman EC, et al. Glucose tolerance and insulin response in normal-weight and obese cats. American Journal of Veterinary Research 1990; 51: 1357-1361.
21. Nelson RW. Feline diabetes mellitus. In: Proceedings. Eighth Annual Veterinary Medical Forum, American College of Veterinary Internal Medicine, Washington, DC, 1990: 189-192.
22. Panciera DL, Thomas CB, Eicker SW, et al. Epizootiologic patterns of diabetes mellitus in cats: 333 cases (1980-1986). Journal of the American Veterinary Medical Association 1990; 197: 1504-1508.
23. Armstrong PJ. Feline hepatic lipidosis. In: Proceedings. Seventh Annual Veterinary Medical Forum, American College of Veterinary Internal Medicine, San Diego, CA, 1989: 335-337.
24. Biourge VC, Groff JM, Munn RJ, et al. Experimental induction of hepatic lipidosis in cats. American Journal of Veterinary Research 1994; 55: 1291-1302.
25. Glickman LT, Schofer FS, McKee LJ, et al. Epidemiologic study of insecticide exposure, obesity, and risk of bladder cancer in household dogs. Journal of Toxicology and Environmental Health 1989; 28: 407-414.
26. Clutton RE. The medical implications of canine obesity and their relevance to anesthesia. British Veterinary Journal 1988; 144: 21-28.
27. Anderson GL, Lewis LD. Obesity. In: Kirk RW, ed. Current Veterinary Therapy VII. Philadelphia, PA: WB Saunders Co, 1980; 1034-1039.
28. Edney ATB. Management of obesity in the dog. Veterinary Medicine/Small Animal Clinician 1974; 69: 46-49.
29. Newberne PM. Overnutrition and resistance of dogs to distemper virus. Federation Proceedings 1966; 25: 1701-1710.
30. Williams GD, Newberne PM. Decreased resistance to *Salmonella* infection in obese dogs (abstract 2107). Federation Proceedings 1971; 30: 572.
31. Chastain CB, Panciera DL. Hypothyroid diseases. In: Ettinger SJ, Feldman EC, eds. Textbook of Veterinary Internal Medicine, 4th ed. Philadelphia, PA: WB Saunders Co, 1995; 1487-1501.

32. Brodie DA. Techniques of measurement of body composition. Part I. Sports Medicine 1988; 5: 11-40.

33. Brodie DA. Techniques of measurement of body composition. Part II. Sports Medicine 1988; 5: 74-98.

34. Lukaski HC. Methods for the assessment of human body composition: Traditional and new. American Journal of Clinical Nutrition 1987; 46: 537-556.

35. Hand MS, Armstrong PJ, Allen TA. Obesity: Occurrence, treatment, and prevention. Veterinary Clinics of North America: Small Animal Practice 1989; 19: 447-474.

36. Laflamme DP. Body condition scoring and weight maintenance. In: Proceedings. North American Veterinary Conference, Orlando, FL, 1993: 290-291.

37. Graham JF, Clark AJ, Spiker SA. The repeatability and accuracy of condition scoring beef cattle. Proceedings of the Australian Society of Animal Production 1982; 15: 684.

38. Croxton D, Stollard RJ. Use of body condition scoring as a management aid in dairy and beef herds. Animal Production 1976; 22: 146-147.

39. Murray JA. Meat production. Journal of Agricultural Science 1919; 9: 174-181.

40. Houmard JA, Wheeler WS, McCammon MR, et al. An evaluation of waist to hip ratio measurement methods in relation to lipid and carbohydrate metabolism in men. International Journal of Obesity 1991; 15: 181-188.

41. Weltman A, Seip RL, Tran ZV. Practical assessment of body composition in adult obese males. Human Biology 1987; 59: 523-535.

42. Weltman A, Levine S, Seip RL, et al. Accurate assessment of body composition in obese females. American Journal of Clinical Nutrition 1988; 48: 1179-1183.

43. Davis PO, Dotson CO, Curtis AV. A simplified technique for the determination of per cent body fat in adult males. Journal of Sports Medicine and Physical Fitness 1985; 25: 255-261.

44. Stunkard AJ, Sorensen TIA, Hanis C, et al. An adoption study of human obesity. New England Journal of Medicine 1986; 314: 193-198.

45. Stunkard AJ, Harris JR, Pedersen NL, et al. The body mass index of twins who have been reared apart. New England Journal of Medicine 1990; 322: 1483-1487.

46. Bogardus C, Lillioja S, Ravussin E, et al. Familial dependence on the resting metabolic rate. New England Journal of Medicine 1986; 315: 96-100.

47. Campfield LA, Smith FJ, Guisez Y, et al. Recombinant mouse ob protein: Evidence for a peripheral signal linking adiposity and central neural networks. Science 1995; 269: 546-549.

48. Halaas JL, Gajiwala KS, Maffei M, et al. Weight-reducing effects of the plasma protein encoded by the obese gene. Science 1995; 269: 543-546.

49. Pelleymounter MA, Cullen MJ, Baker MB, et al. Effects of the obese gene product on body weight regulation in ob/ob mice. Science 1995; 269: 540-543.

50. Root MV, Johnston SD. The effect of early spay-neuter in the development of feline obesity. Veterinary Forum 1995; 12(11): 38-43.

51. Flynn MF, Hardie EM, Armstrong PJ. Effect of ovariohysterectomy on maintenance energy requirement in cats. Journal of the American Veterinary Medical Association 1996; 209: 1572-1581.

52. Root MV, Johnston SD, Olson PN. Effect of prepuberal and postpuberal gonadectomy on heat production measured by indirect calorimetry in male and female domestic cats. American Journal of Veterinary Research 1996; 57: 371-374.

53. Hart BL, Barrett RE. Effects of castration on fighting, roaming, and urine spraying in adult male cats. Journal of the American Veterinary Medical Association 1973; 163: 290-292.

54. Hopkins GS, Schubert TA, Hart BL. Castration of adult male dogs: Effects on roaming, aggression, urine marking, and mounting. Journal of the American Veterinary Medical Association 1976; 168: 1108-1110.

55. Czaja JA, Goy RW. Ovarian hormones and food intake in female guinea pigs and rhesus monkeys. Hormones and Behavior 1975; 6: 329-349.

56. Houpt KA, Coren B, Hintz HF, et al. Effect of sex and reproductive status on sucrose preference, food intake, and body weight of dogs. Journal of the American Veterinary Medical Association 1979; 174: 1083-1085.

57. Sloth C. Practical management of obesity in dogs and cats. Journal of Small Animal Practice 1992; 33: 178-182.

58. Kronfeld DS, Donoghue S, Glickman LT. Body condition and energy intakes of dogs in a referral teaching hospital. Journal of Nutrition 1991; 121: S157-S158.

59. Masoro EJ. Nutrition as a modulator of the aging process. The Physiologist 1984; 27: 98-101.

60. Masoro EJ. Minireview: Food restriction in rodents: An evaluation of its role in the study of aging. Journal of Gerontology 1988; 43: B59-B64.

61. Masoro EJ. Retardation of aging processes by nutritional means. Annals of the New York Academy of Sciences 1992; 673: 29-35.

62. Danforth E Jr. Diet and obesity. American Journal of Clinical Nutrition 1985; 41: 1132-1145.

63. Horton ES. Introduction: An overview of the assessment and regulation of energy balance in humans. American Journal of Clinical Nutrition 1983; 38: 972-977.

64. Wilson WA. Southwestern internal medicine conference: Treatment of obesity. American Journal of Medical Science 1990; 299: 62-68.

65. Borne AT, Wolfsheimer KJ, Truett AA, et al. Differential metabolic effects of energy restriction in dogs using diets varying in fat and fiber content. Obesity Research 1996; 4: 337-345.

66. Swaminathan R, King RFGJ, Holmfield J, et al. Thermic effect of feeding carbohydrate, fat, protein, and mixed meal in lean and obese subjects. American Journal of Clinical Nutrition 1985; 42: 177-181.

67. Powers MA, Pappas TN. Physiologic approaches to the control of obesity. Annals of Surgery 1989; 209: 255-260.

68. Rolls BJ. Carbohydrates, fats and satiety. American Journal of Clinical Nutrition 1995; 61 (Suppl.): 960S-967S.

69. Vasselli JR, Cleary MP, Van Itallie TB. Modern concepts of obesity. Nutrition Reviews 1983; 41: 361-373.

70. Van Itallie TB, Kissileff HR. The physiologic control of energy intake: An economical perspective. American Journal of Clinical Nutrition 1983; 38: 978-988.

71. Leibel RL, Rosenbaum M, Hirsch J. Changes in energy expenditure resulting from altered body weight. New England Journal of Medicine 1995; 332: 621-628.

72. Levine AS, Billington CJ. Dietary fiber: Does it affect food intake and body weight? In: Fernstrom JD, Miller GD, eds. Appetite and Body Weight Regulation, Sugar, Fat, and Macronutrient Substitutes. Boca Raton, FL: CRC Press, 1994; 191-200.

73. Vahouny GV. Effects of dietary fiber on digestion and absorption. In: Johnson LR, ed. Physiology of the Gastrointestinal Tract, 2nd ed. New York, NY: Raven Press, 1987; 1623-1648.

74. de Haan V, Istasse L, Jakovljevic S, et al. Effects of cellulose, pectin and guar gum on gastric emptying, digestibility and absorption in resting dogs (abstract). Proceedings of the Nutrition Society, 1990; 49: 146A.

75. Bueno L, Praddaude F, Fioramonti J, et al. Effect of dietary fiber on gastrointestinal motility and jejunal transit time in dogs. Gastroenterology 1981; 80: 701-707.

76. Burley VJ, Leeds AR, Blundell JE. The effect of high and low-fibre breakfasts on hunger, satiety and food intake in a subsequent meal. International Journal of Obesity 1987; 11 (Suppl. 1): 87-93.

77. Delargy HJ, Burley VJ, O'Sullivan KR, et al. The effects of fibre in the breakfast upon short-term appetite control: A comparison of soluble and insoluble fibre. Proceedings of the Nutrition Society 1993; 52: 381A.

78. Stevens J, Levitsky DA, VanSoest PJ, et al. Effect of psyllium gum and wheat bran on spontaneous energy intake. American Journal of Clinical Nutrition 1987; 46: 812-817.

79. Fahey GC Jr, Merchen NR, Corbin JE, et al. Dietary fiber for dogs: II. Iso-total dietary fiber (TDF) additions of divergent fiber sources to dog diets and their effects on nutrient intake, digestibility, metabolizable energy and digesta mean retention time. Journal of Animal Science 1990; 68: 4229-4235.

80. Fahey GC Jr, Merchen NR, Corbin JE, et al. Dietary fiber for dogs: I. Effects of graded levels of dietary beet pulp on nutrient intake, digestibility, metabolizable energy and digesta mean retention time. Journal of Animal Science 1990; 68: 4221-4228.

81. Butterwick RF, Markwell PJ, Thorne CJ. Effect of level and source of dietary fiber on food intake in the dog. Journal of Nutrition 1994; 124: 2695S-2700S.

82. Jewell DE, Toll PW. Effect of fiber on food intake in dogs. Veterinary Clinical Nutrition 1996; 3: 115-118.

83. Kelsay JL, Behall KM, Prather ES. Effect of fiber from fruits and vegetables on metabolic responses of human subjects. I. Bowel transit time, number of defecations, fecal weight, urinary excretions of energy and nitrogen and apparent digestibilities of energy, nitrogen, and fat. American Journal of Clinical Nutrition 1978; 31: 1149-1153.

84. Farrell DJ, Girle L, Arthur J. Effects of dietary fibre on the apparent digestibility of major food components and on blood lipids in men. Australian Journal of Experimental Biology and Medical Science 1978; 56: 469-479.

85. Isaksson G, Lundquist I, Ihse I. Effect of dietary fiber on pancreatic enzyme activity in vitro. Gastroenterology 1982; 82: 918-924.

86. Stock-Damge C, Bouchet P, Dentinger A, et al. Effect of dietary fiber supplementation on the secretory function of the exocrine pancreas in the dog. American Journal of Clinical Nutrition 1983; 38: 843-848.

87. Edwards CA. The physiological effects of dietary fiber. In: Kritchevsky D, Bonfield C, eds. Dietary Fiber in Health & Disease. St. Paul, MN: Eagan Press, 1992; 58-71.

88. Nelson RW, Ihle SL, Lewis LD, et al. Effect of dietary fiber supplementation on glycemic control in dogs with alloxan-induced diabetes mellitus. American Journal of Veterinary Research 1991; 52: 2060-2066.

89. Leaf DA. Overweight: Assessment and management issues. American Family Physician 1990; 42: 653-660.

90. Caterson ID. Management strategies for weight control. Eating, exercise, and behavior. Drugs 1990; 39 (Suppl. 3): 20-32.

91. Council on Scientific Affairs. Treatment of obesity in adults. Journal of the American Medical Association 1988; 260: 2547-2551.

92. Burgess NS. Effect of a very-low-calorie diet on body composition and resting metabolic rate in obese men and women. Journal of the American Dietetic Association 1991; 91: 430-434.

93. Butterwick RF, Markwell PJ. Changes in the body composition of cats during weight reduction by controlled dietary energy restriction. Veterinary Record 1996; 138: 354-357.

94. Markwell PJ, Butterwick RF, Watson DG, et al. Considerations in safe weight reduction in cats and clinical experience with an aggressive weight loss regime. In: Proceedings. North American Veterinary Conference. Orlando, FL, 1996: 322-324.

95. de Boer JO, van Es AJH, Roovers LCA, et al. Adaptation of energy metabolism of overweight women to low-energy intake, studied with whole-body calorimeters. American Journal of Clinical Nutrition 1986; 44: 585-595.

96. Elliot DL, Goldberg L, Kuehl KS, et al. Sustained depression of the resting metabolic rate after massive weight loss. American Journal of Clinical Nutrition 1989; 49: 93-96.

97. Ravussin E, Burnand B, Schultz Y, et al. Energy expenditure before and during energy restriction in obese patients. American Journal of Clinical Nutrition 1985; 41: 753-759.

98. Pavlou KN, Steffee WP, Learman RH, et al. Effects of dieting and exercise on lean body mass, oxygen uptake, and strength. Medicine and Science in Sports and Exercise 1985; 17: 466-471.

99. Frey-Hewitt B, Vranizan KM, Dreon DM, et al. The effect of weight loss by dieting or exercise on resting metabolic rate in overweight men. International Journal of Obesity 1990; 14: 327-334.

100. Wolfsheimer KJ. Obesity in dogs. Compendium on Continuing Education for the Practicing Veterinarian 1994; 16: 981-998.

101. McArdle WD, Katch FI, Katch VL. Appendix 3: Selected examples for energy expenditure in household, recreational and sports activities. In: Essentials of Exercise Physiology. Philadelphia, PA: Lea & Febiger, 1994; 544-545.

102. Weinsier RL, Wadden TA, Ritenbaugh C, et al. Recommended therapeutic guidelines for professional weight control programs. American Journal of Clinical Nutrition 1984; 40: 865-872.

103. Weinsier RL, Wilson LJ, Lee J. Medically safe rate of weight loss for the treatment of obesity: A guideline based on risk of gallstone formation. American Journal of Medicine 1995; 98: 115-117.

104. Glickman LT, Sonnenschein EG, Glickman NT, et al. Pattern of diet and obesity in female adult pet dogs. Veterinary Clinical Nutrition 1995; 2: 6-13.

CASE 13-1

Respiratory Distress in an Obese Miniature Poodle

William J. Burkholder, DVM, PhD
Diplomate ACVN
College of Veterinary Medicine
Texas A & M University
College Station, Texas, USA

Assess the Animal

A four-year-old intact male miniature poodle weighing 17.3 kg was admitted for coughing, dyspnea, cyanosis and exercise intolerance. Physical examination findings were normal except for obesity. Results of a complete blood count, serum biochemistry profile, urinalysis, thoracic radiographs and fluoroscopic examination of the trachea were normal. Bronchoscopy revealed no abnormalities. Cultures of tracheal and bronchial washings were negative

for growth of pathogenic organisms. Lung scintigraphy showed no pulmonary vascular deficits.

Body condition score was 5/5. Morphometric measures estimated 47% of the dog's weight was fat. Optimal body weight was estimated to be 9.1 kg, making the patient's initial body weight 90% above optimal.

Assess the Food(s) and Feeding Method

Table 1 lists the dietary history.

Questions

1. Estimate the amount of energy consumed by this patient each day.
2. Calculate the daily energy requirement (DER) for this patient at its estimated optimal body weight and compare this number with the energy estimate in Question 1.
3. Outline a feeding, exercise and monitoring plan for weight reduction for this dog.

Answers and Discussion

1. The energy consumed by the dog each day is at least 1,247 kcal (5,219 kJ). This is estimated from the moist food (one can, 556 kcal/can [2,326 kJ/can]), dry food (one cup, 327 kcal/cup [1,368 kJ/cup]), commercial treats (five treats, 20 kcal/treat [84 kJ/treat]) and ice cream (one cup, 264 kcal/cup [1,105 kJ/cup]). The daily caloric consumption was probably higher because the dog also ate various meats from the owner's meals.
2. The resting energy requirement (RER) at the estimat-

Table 1. Foods and feeding method assessment of an obese miniature poodle with respiratory distress.

Foods	Feeding method
Science Diet Canine Maintenance, moist[a]	One can, once daily
Science Diet Canine Maintenance, dry[a]	One cup, once daily
Milk-Bone treats (small)[b]	Five, daily
Ice cream	One cup, once daily
Various meats from owner's meals	Once or twice daily

Table 2. Feeding plan for weight reduction.

Foods	Feeding method	kcal(kJ)
Prescription Diet Canine r/d, moist[a]	Three-fourths can, once daily	150(628)
Science Diet Canine Maintenance Light, dry[a]	One cup, once daily	221(925)
Milk-Bone treats (small)	Two treats, daily	40(167)
Total = 411 kcal/day (1,720 kJ)		

Table 3. Feeding plan to stabilize reduced body weight.

Foods	Feeding method	kcal(kJ)
Science Diet Canine Maintenance, moist[a]	One-half can, once daily	278(1,163)
Science Diet Canine Maintenance, dry	One cup, once daily	327(1,368)
Milk-Bone treats (small)	Four treats, daily	80(335)
Total = 685 kcal/day (2,866 kJ)		

ed optimal body weight is calculated as follows: RER optimal weight = $70(9.1)^{0.75}$ = 367 kcal (1,535 kJ). DER would be approximately 1.4 to 1.6 x RER or 514 to 587 kcal (2,151 to 2,456 kJ). The daily caloric intake estimated in Question 1 is much higher than the estimated DER (about double).

3. The initial caloric restriction was set at an amount slightly above RER calculated for optimal body weight. The owners were instructed to feed no ice cream, meat or other table foods. The commercial treats were continued but fewer were given per day. The food was changed to a commercial product containing less fat and more crude fiber. Caloric restriction was accomplished using the specific foods and feeding methods listed in Table 2.

The owners were also instructed to walk the dog on a leash daily. Initially they were to walk only as far as the dog could tolerate without becoming dyspneic. The walks were gradually increased to 20 to 30 minutes per walk, once or twice a day. The owners were asked to return every two weeks for the first couple of months to weigh the dog and monitor the progress.

Progress Notes

Figure 1 shows the weight loss that occurred with this feeding plan and exercise. The coughing and dyspnea gradually resolved after the dog lost approximately 2 kg. The owners noticed a dramatic increase in the dog's activity after three months. The food was changed on Week 34 of the weight-reduction program to the foods and feeding meth-

ods listed in Table 3. Body weight stabilized (Figure 1) and the dog remained free of respiratory signs and distress.

Animals that are obese because of gross overfeeding are the patients most likely to achieve expected rates of weight loss when owners comply with caloric restriction.

Endnotes

a. Hill's Pet Nutrition, Inc., Topeka, KS, USA.
b. Nabisco, East Hanover, NJ, USA.

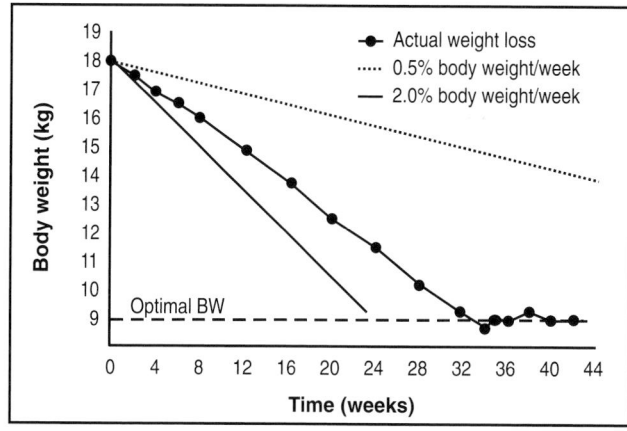

Figure 1. Progression of body weight loss compared with the minimum (loss of 0.5% of initial body weight/week) and maximum (loss of 2% of initial body weight/week) rates of weight loss.

■ CASE 13-2

An Overweight Cat

William J. Burkholder, DVM, PhD
Diplomate ACVN
College of Veterinary Medicine
Texas A & M University
College Station, Texas, USA

Assess the Animal

An eight-year-old neutered male domestic longhair cat weighing 6.6 kg was diagnosed with asymmetric hypertro-

phy of the interventricular septum via echocardiography. No abnormalities were noted on physical examination except for excessive body weight. Complete blood count, serum biochemistry profile and urinalysis results were normal.

The cat's body condition was assessed as 4.5/5. Optimal body weight was estimated to be 5.5 kg, making the initial body weight 20% above optimal.

Assess the Food(s) and Feeding Method

The cat was fed a commercial food that was lower in fat and higher in crude fiber than regular commercial cat foods (Science Diet Feline Maintenance Light;[a] one-third cup, twice daily).

Questions

1. Estimate the amount of energy consumed by this patient each day.
2. Calculate the daily energy requirement (DER) for this patient at its estimated optimal body weight and compare this number with the assessment in Question 1.
3. Outline a feeding and monitoring plan for weight reduction for this cat.

Answers and Discussion

1. The energy consumed by the cat each day was approximately 168 kcal (703 kJ). This is estimated from the

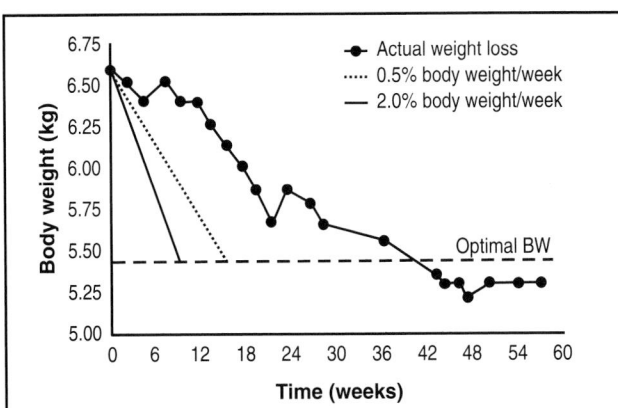

Figure 1. Progression of body weight loss compared with minimum and maximum rates of weight loss.

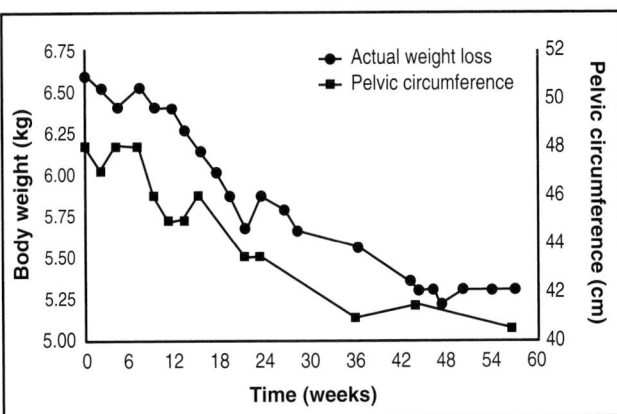

Figure 2. Comparison of body weight loss and decrease in pelvic circumference during the weight-reduction program.

dry food (two-thirds cup, 248 kcal/cup[1,038 kJ]).

2. The resting energy requirement (RER) at the estimated optimal body weight is calculated as follows: RER optimal weight = $70(5.5)^{0.75}$ = 250 kcal (1,046 kJ). DER at optimal body weight would be approximately 1.2 x RER or 300 kcal (1,255 kJ). The daily caloric intake estimated in Question 1 is actually lower than the RER for optimal body weight.

3. The cat was switched to a commercial dry feline food that had a slightly higher fiber content but approximately the same fat content and caloric density as the current food (Prescription Diet Feline w/d;[a] one-third cup twice daily, 165 kcal/day [690 kJ]). This food supplied only 66% of the calories estimated for RER at the optimal body weight. The owner was also instructed to increase the cat's activity as much as possible. The owner was asked to return every two weeks for the first couple of months to weigh the cat and monitor the progress.

Progress Notes

Figure 1 shows the weight loss that occurred with this feeding plan and exercise. Note that the initial weight loss stopped by Week 13. At that time, the food was reduced to one-fourth cup, twice daily, which supplied 123 kcal (515 kJ) or 49% of RER at optimal body weight. The two times when body weight increased were associated with the cat being fed by other people because the owner was out of town for several weeks. These lapses emphasize the need to have everyone understand the need for adhering to and measuring out the prescribed amounts of food. The cat's owner understood the need for strict adherence to the feeding schedule, but those who fed the cat in the owner's absence did not. Some decrease in exercise level may also have occurred in the owner's absence.

Figure 2 compares weight loss with measurements of the cat's pelvic circumference. This shows how the pelvic circumference can be used along with body weight to track relative progression of weight loss.

Weight was stabilized at 5.3 kg by returning the cat to the original food and increasing daily caloric intake to 165 kcal (690 kJ). This was done in two steps. On Week 43, the food was changed to Science Diet Feline Maintenance Light;[a] one-fourth cup was fed in the morning and one-third cup in the evening. This feeding plan provided 144 kcal (602 kJ) per day. Weight loss slowed but body weight still tended to decrease. On Week 47, the food was increased to one-third cup twice daily and body weight stabilized.

Endnote

a. Hill's Pet Nutrition, Inc., Topeka, KS, USA.

CASE 13-3

Lameness in an Obese Labrador Retriever

William J. Burkholder, DVM, PhD
Diplomate ACVN
College of Veterinary Medicine
Texas A & M University
College Station, Texas, USA

Assess the Animal

A nine-year-old neutered female Labrador retriever weighing 41.8 kg was admitted six months after repair of a ruptured left anterior cruciate ligament. The dog was still limping on its left rear leg. Radiographs of the stifle showed evidence of mild osteoarthrosis. Orthopedic examination of the stifle for stability and range of motion was normal. No other abnormalities were found on physical examination. Results of a complete blood count, serum biochemistry profile, urinalysis and serum T_3 and T_4 concentrations were normal.

The dog's body condition was assessed as 4.5/5. Optimal body weight was estimated to be 34 kg, making the initial body weight 23% above optimal. Morphometric measures estimated 35% of the dog's body weight was fat.

Assess the Food(s) and Feeding Method

Caloric restriction had been initiated after surgery in an attempt to promote weight loss. Table 1 lists the assessment of the foods and feeding management. No weight loss had occurred in the last three to four months.

Questions

1. What are some risk factors for obesity that can be identified from the animal assessment?
2. Estimate the amount of energy consumed by this patient each day.
3. Calculate the daily energy requirement (DER) for this patient at its estimated optimal body weight and compare this number with the assessment in Question 2.
4. Outline a feeding, exercise and monitoring plan for weight reduction for this dog.

Answers and Discussion

1. Risk factors for obesity in this patient include age (middle-aged dogs are more prone to obesity than younger animals), gender (female dogs are at higher risk than male dogs), reproductive status (neutered dogs are at more risk than intact animals), breed (Labrador retrievers are considered an obesity-prone breed) and exercise level (the dog had been sedentary since the knee surgery). Obesity may have contributed to the anterior cruciate rupture and restricted exercise since surgery may have contributed to persistent obesity despite recent caloric restriction.
2. The energy consumed by the dog each day was approximately 920 kcal (3,849 kJ). This is estimated from the moist food (two cans, 250 kcal/can [1,046 kJ/can]), dry food (two cups, 200 kcal/cup [837 kJ/cup]) and commercial treats (one treat, 20 kcal/treat [84 kJ/treat]).
3. The resting energy requirement (RER) at the estimated optimal body weight is calculated as follows: RER

optimal weight = $70(34)^{0.75}$ = 988 kcal (4,134 kJ). DER at optimal body weight would be approximately 1.4 to 1.6 x RER or 1,383 to 1,581 kcal (5,786 to 6,615 kJ). The daily caloric intake estimated in Question 2 is actually lower than RER for optimal body weight.

4. Because the current intake of 920 kcal (3,849 kJ) was slightly less than RER for an optimal weight of 34 kg, this level of caloric restriction was not initially changed. Because the dog had been minimally active since the knee surgery, 20 to 60 minutes of persistent leash walking per day was initiated. The owners were instructed to work up gradually to whatever amount of walking the dog could do comfortably without soreness. The owners were asked to return every two weeks for the first couple of months to weigh the dog and monitor progress.

Table 1. Foods and feeding method assessment of an obese Labrador retriever with lameness.

Foods	Feeding method
Prescription Diet Canine r/d, moist[a]	One can, twice daily
Prescription Diet Canine r/d, dry[a]	One cup, twice daily
Milk-Bone treats (small)[b]	One treat, once daily

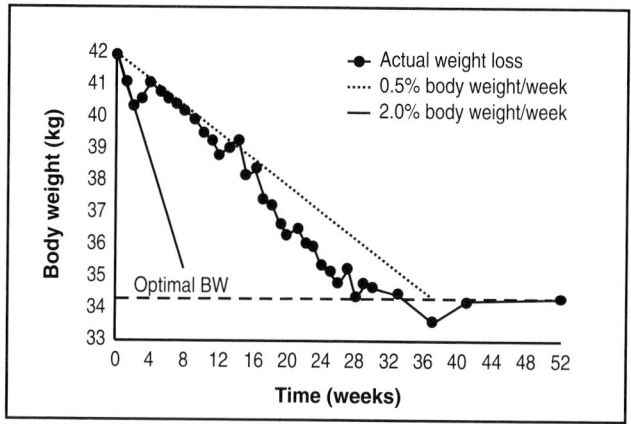

Figure 1. Progression of body weight loss compared with minimum and maximum rates of weight loss.

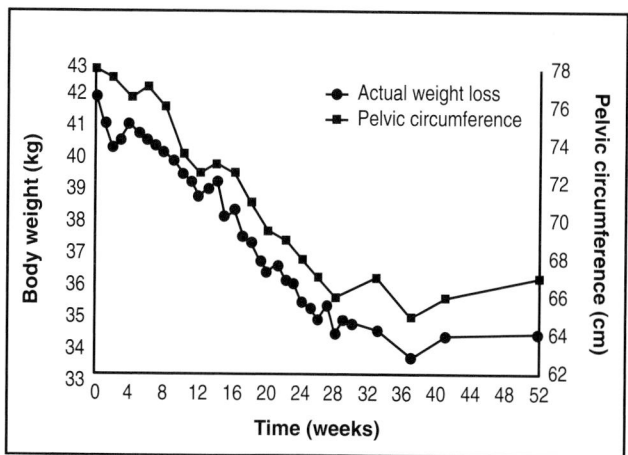

Figure 2. Comparison of body weight loss and pelvic circumference during the weight-reduction program.

Table 2. Feeding plan for further weight reduction.

Foods	Feeding method	kcal(kJ)
Prescription Diet Canine r/d, moist[a]	One-half can, morning	125(523)
Prescription Diet Canine r/d, dry	One and one-half cups, twice daily	600(2,510)
Total = 725 kcal/day (3,033 kJ)		

Table 3. Feeding plan to stabilize reduced body weight.

Foods	Feeding method	kcal(kJ)
Prescription Diet Canine r/d, moist[a]	One-half can, twice daily	250(1,046)
Prescription Diet Canine r/d, dry	One and two-thirds cups, twice daily	668(2,795)
Total = 918 kcal/day (3,841 kJ)		

Progress Notes

Figure 1 shows the weight loss that occurred with this feeding and exercise plan. Loss of almost 2% of starting weight (the maximum acceptable rate of weight loss) was achieved during the first two weeks by the addition of exercise. Unfortunately, weight was actually gained during Weeks 3 and 4, which greatly discouraged the owners. The owners were counseled to persist with the leash walking and the daily caloric intake was decreased to 725 kcal/day (3,033 kJ) (approximately 80% of calories indicated by the dietary assessment) using the foods and feeding methods listed in Table 2.

After approximately 3 kg had been lost by Week 10, the dog ceased to limp and had a normal gait thereafter. The owners were unable to walk the dog during Weeks 12 to 14 and some weight gain occurred. Weight loss continued when leash walks were resumed. This finding demonstrates the importance of exercise as a component of daily energy expenditure, especially during weight reduction of calorically efficient animals.

Figure 2 compares weight loss with measurements of the dog's pelvic circumference. This shows how the pelvic circumference can be used with body weight to track relative progression of weight loss.

Calories were increased on Week 28 to maintain a body weight of 34 kg (Table 3). This dog maintained the reduced weight on the same number of calories as it used to maintain the obese weight. This indirectly supports the assertion that adipose tissue requires very few calories to maintain its mass.

Endnotes

a. Hill's Pet Nutrition, Inc., Topeka, KS, USA.
b. Nabisco, East Hanover, NJ, USA.

CHAPTER 14

Adverse Reactions to Food

Philip Roudebush

W. Grant Guilford

Kevin J. Shanley

"For this changed concept of reactivity, I propose the term allergy. 'Allos' implies deviation from the original state, from the behavior of the normal individual . . ."
Von Pirquet 1906

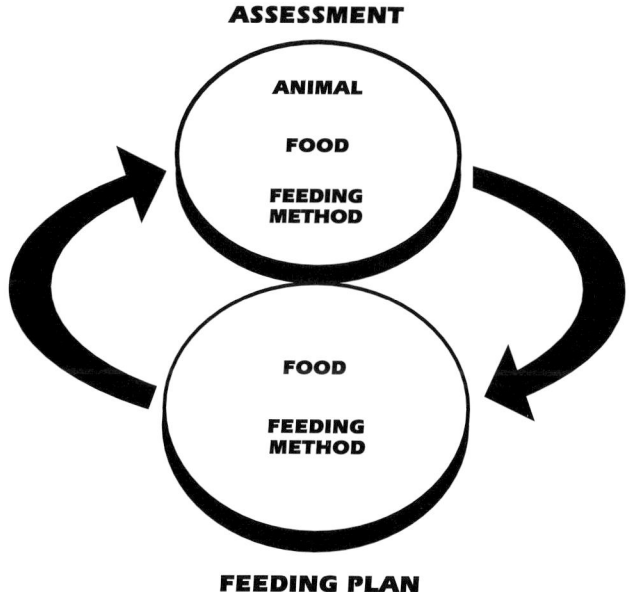

ASSESSMENT

ANIMAL

FOOD

FEEDING METHOD

FOOD

FEEDING METHOD

FEEDING PLAN

Note: The reader is referred to Chapter 1 for a detailed discussion of the iterative process of clinical nutrition.

INTRODUCTION

An adverse reaction to food is an abnormal response to an ingested food or food additive. Adverse reactions to food are composed of a variety of subclassifications based on pathomechanisms (Figure 14-1).[1,2] The terms and definitions in the glossary (See Glossary for definitions of key words and terms.) are recommended by the American Academy of Allergy and Immunology.[1,2] The terms food allergy and food hypersensitivity should be reserved for those adverse reactions to food that have an immunologic basis. Food intolerance refers to a large category of adverse food reactions due to nonimmunologic mechanisms. Traditionally, the terms food hypersensitivity and food allergy have been used to describe all adverse reactions to food in dogs and cats, including reactions that were truly food intolerances. The newer terminology is used throughout this chapter and should be used to describe adverse food reactions in veterinary patients.

CLINICAL IMPORTANCE

In view of the number of diverse foods that are routinely ingested by animals, it is not surprising that adverse reactions develop. The fact that food-related reactions appear relatively infrequently is testimony to the effectiveness of the gastrointestinal (GI) mucosal barrier and oral tolerance. Adverse reactions to food were reported in dogs and cats as early as 1920 and have been blamed for a vari-

KEY WORDS & TERMS—ADVERSE REACTIONS TO FOOD*

Adverse reaction to food	Food idiosyncrasy	Metabolic food reaction
Atopy	Food intolerance	Oral tolerance
Dietary indiscretion	Food poisoning (food toxicosis)	Pharmacologic food reaction
Food allergy (food hypersensitivity)	GALT (gut-associated lymphoid tissue)	Vasoactive amines
Food anaphylaxis	Glycoprotein	

*Key words and terms are defined in the Glossary.

KEY POINTS—ADVERSE REACTIONS TO FOOD

1. Food allergy is thought to make up 10 to 20% of allergic skin disease in dogs and cats.
2. Most of the reported adverse food reactions that cause dermatoses have been termed food allergy or food hypersensitivity, but usually no specific tests have been done to confirm the immunologic basis for the clinical disease.
3. An adverse reaction to food is an abnormal response to an ingested food or food additive that may have either an immunologic or nonimmunologic basis.
4. Although food additives are frequently incriminated as causing problems in dogs and cats, few data exist to confirm this perception.
5. Up to one-third of adverse food reactions that cause dermatologic manifestations occur in dogs less than one year of age.
6. Adverse food reactions should always be suspected in dogs with pruritic, bilateral otitis externa even if accompanied by secondary bacterial or yeast infection.
7. Adverse food reactions may cause self-inflicted alopecia (psychogenic alopecia, neurodermatitis), eosinophilic plaques and indolent ulcers of the lip in some cats.
8. Every level of the gastrointestinal tract can be damaged by food allergies resulting in vomiting, small bowel diarrhea and/or large bowel diarrhea.
9. The defense against hypersensitivity to food antigens includes an effective mucosal barrier and oral tolerance generated by the gut-associated lymphoid tissue.
10. The gut is one of the largest immune organs in the body.
11. The most common food allergens in dogs and cats with dermatologic disease include beef, dairy products, fish and wheat.
12. The pathogenesis of gluten intolerance in dogs is unknown.
13. The highest levels of histamine are found in moist fish-based cat foods and those cat foods containing fish solubles.
14. Diarrhea, bloating and abdominal discomfort are relatively common in dogs and cats experiencing a metabolic adverse food reaction associated with lactose intolerance.
15. Owners should keep a daily diary during elimination trials to document the types of food ingested and associated clinical signs.
16. Many of the homemade foods recommended for the initial management of dogs and cats with a suspected food allergy are nutritionally inadequate.
17. Recipes for complete and balanced homemade foods are available and should always be used when these foods are used in elimination trials.
18. Only a few commercial foods marketed for patients with adverse food reactions have undergone the scrutiny of clinical trials.

ety of clinical syndromes usually involving the skin and GI tract.

Carefully controlled prevalence studies of adverse food reactions in dogs and cats have not been performed. The major problem with establishing prevalence is that adverse food reactions mimic other diseases, especially pruritic dermatoses, and they often coexist with other allergic conditions. Veterinary dermatologists suggest that adverse food reactions account for 1 to 6% of all dermatoses in general practice and that food allergy constitutes 10 to 20% of allergic responses in dogs and cats.[3,4] Several investigators have suggested that adverse food reactions are relatively more common in cats than in dogs.[3,4] Food allergy is probably the third most common hypersensitivity skin disease in dogs and cats after arthropod (flea) hypersensitivity and atopy.[3,4] Adverse food reactions can cause a wide variety of cutaneous lesions and should be considered in any pruritic dog or cat. Most of the reported adverse food reactions causing dermatoses have been termed food allergy or food hypersensitivity, although no specific tests were performed to confirm an immunologic basis for the clinical signs.

The true prevalence of adverse food reactions in people is unknown. Although the public perceives the prevalence of food allergic reactions to be quite high, many authorities suggest that the "true prevalence" of food allergy is less than 1% of the human population.[5] Unfortunately, few data exist to support these claims. Each of the carefully controlled human prevalence studies has revealed that the vast majority of food allergic reactions occur in the first year of life and that "perceived" food allergy is much more common than "true" food allergy. However, true food allergy may occur in up to 8% of human infants less than three years of age.[5]

Plasmacytic-lymphocytic enteritis and eosinophilic enteritis are the most common forms of inflammatory bowel disease identified in dogs and cats, and are the most common cause of chronic vomiting and diarrhea in these two species.[6] Plasmacytic-lymphocytic and eosinophilic intestinal infiltrates may be associated with many conditions, but no obvious cause can be identified in most cases.[6] Food sensitivity seems to be involved in some cases.[7,8] Clinical response to a modification in the feeding plan suggests that hypersensitivity to food antigens plays a role in

KEY NUTRITIONAL FACTORS—ADVERSE REACTIONS TO FOOD

Factors	Associated conditions	Dietary recommendations
Dogs		
Protein	Nonseasonal pruritic dermatitis Pruritic bilateral otitis externa Recurrent bacterial pyoderma Angioedema Atopy Flea-allergy dermatitis Vomiting Small bowel diarrhea Colitis	Limit dietary protein to one or two sources Use protein sources to which the dog has not been exposed previously Avoid excess levels of dietary protein (dermatologic cases only) Protein 16 to 20% (dry matter basis) Use a food with protein digestibility >87% or one containing a protein hydrolysate Use a food that is nutritionally balanced for dogs Avoid foods that contain wheat, barley or rye (dogs with diarrhea)
Vasoactive amines	Same as above	Avoid foods that contain certain fish ingredients (tuna, mackerel)
Food additives	Same as above Erythema multiforme	Use a food that is free of or has reduced numbers of food additives
Cats		

Protein	Severe, generalized pruritus
	Miliary dermatitis
	Pruritus with self trauma
	Self-inflicted alopecia
	Eosinophilic plaque
	Angioedema, urticaria or
	  conjunctivitis
	Indolent ulcer of lip
	Vomiting
	Small bowel diarrhea
	Colitis
		Limit dietary protein to one or two sources
		Use protein sources to which the cat has not been exposed previously
		Avoid excess levels of dietary protein (dermatologic cases only)
		    Protein 30 to 45% (dry matter basis)
		Use a food with protein digestibility >87% or one containing a protein hydrolysate
		Use a food that is nutritionally balanced for cats

Vasoactive amines	Same as above	Avoid foods that contain certain fish ingredients (tuna, mackerel)
Food additives	Same as above Erythema multiforme	Use a food that is free of or has reduced numbers of food additives

dogs with chronic idiopathic or plasmacytic-lymphocytic colitis.[9-11] It is not known if chronic colitis or other forms of inflammatory disease of the small bowel are a direct manifestation of an adverse food reaction or if modifying the feeding plan is merely palliative in some animals.

In people, food additives have been blamed for such diverse problems as nausea, vomiting, diarrhea, abdominal pain and cramping, headache, asthma provocation, chronic urticaria or angioedema, nonspecific rash, allergic vascular purpura, atopic dermatitis and behavioral disorders in children.[12-15] The self-diagnosis of food additive intolerance has become commonplace, but it is unclear how often perceptions mesh with reality. Food additives, preservatives and dyes are frequently mentioned by veterinarians as ingredients that may be associated with adverse food reactions, specifically dermatologic and GI signs due to food allergy.[16] Although additives are frequently incriminated as causing problems in dogs and cats, few data confirm this perception.[17]

ASSESSMENT

Assess the Animal

Nutritional History

The authors of two series of dermatologic cases due to adverse food reactions could not relate the onset of clinical signs with recent food changes.[18,19] This finding suggests that dogs and cats may develop food allergy after prolonged exposure to one brand, type or form of food. In contrast, adverse reactions due to food intolerance may

occur after a single exposure to a food ingredient because immune amplification is not necessary.

The nutritional history of the patient should be reviewed carefully for ingredients thought to be commonly associated with adverse food reactions. The nutritional history should include a complete list of the foods used in the pet's regular feeding plan or as treats including: 1) specific commercial foods, 2) commercial snacks or treats, 3) supplements, 4) chewable medications, 5) chew toys, 6) human foods and 7) access to other sources of food. As an example, a dog might be given a dry commercial food as its main source of nutrition, but may also be given rawhide chews, commercial dog biscuits and leftover foods from human meals, and it may have access to commercial food fed to cats in the household. It is often helpful to have the pet owner keep a diary for several weeks documenting the types of food and other items the pet ingests daily. Nutritional assessment is described in more detail later in this chapter.

History and Physical Examination

DERMATOLOGIC RESPONSES TO ADVERSE FOOD REACTIONS IN DOGS

Reports of adverse food reactions in dogs with cutaneous disease did not document a gender predisposition and ages ranged from four months to 14 years.[3,4,18-28] Up to one-third of canine cases, however, may occur in dogs less than one year of age.[25,26] Because many adverse food reactions occur in young dogs, the index of suspicion for food allergy may rise above that for atopic disease when pruritic dermatoses occur in dogs less than six months old.[4] Most investigators have not found a breed predilection, whereas others have

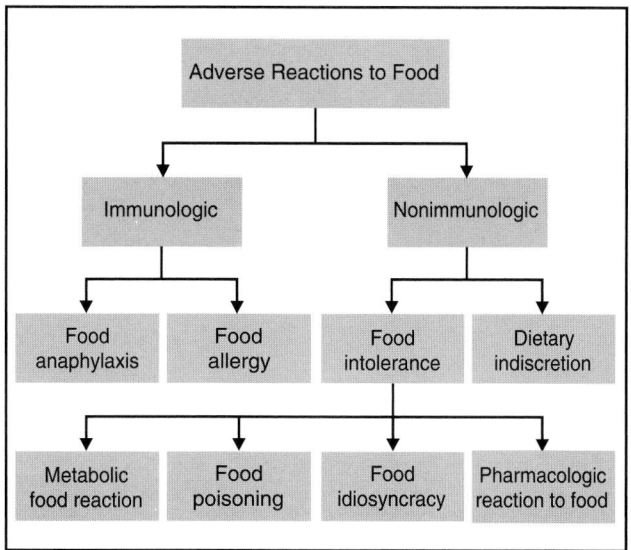

Figure 14-1. Classification of adverse reactions to food.

found that cocker spaniels, springer spaniels, Labrador retrievers, collies, miniature schnauzers, Chinese Shar-Pei, West Highland white terriers, wheaten terriers, boxers, dachshunds, Dalmatians, Lhasa apsos, German shepherd dogs and golden retrievers are at increased risk.[4,25,26]

Adverse food reactions in dogs typically occur as non-seasonal pruritic dermatitis, occasionally accompanied by GI signs.[3,4,18-28] The pruritus varies in severity. Lesion distribution is often indistinguishable from that seen with atopy; feet, face, axillae, perineal region, inguinal region, rump and ears are often affected.[3,4,18-26] One-fourth of dogs with adverse food reactions have lesions only in the region of the ears.[25] This finding suggests that adverse food reactions should always be suspected in dogs with pruritic, bilateral otitis externa, even if accompanied by secondary bacterial or *Malassezia* infections.[3,4]

Adverse food reactions in dogs produce no set of pathognomonic cutaneous signs. A variety of primary and secondary skin lesions occur and include: 1) papules, 2) erythroderma, 3) excoriations, 4) hyperpigmentation, 5) epidermal collarettes, 6) pododermatitis, 7) seborrhea sicca and 8) otitis externa. Adverse food reactions often mimic other common canine skin disorders including pyoderma, pruritic seborrheic dermatoses, folliculitis and ectoparasitism.[3,4] Twenty to 30% or more of dogs with suspected adverse food reactions may have concurrent allergic disease, such as flea-allergic dermatitis or atopy.[19,23,25] Some dogs present with only recurrent bacterial pyoderma, with or without pruritus, wherein all clinical signs resolve temporarily with antibiotic therapy.[4,21,26]

Food anaphylaxis is an acute reaction to food or food additives with systemic consequences. The most common clinical manifestation in dogs occurs in localized form referred to as angioedema or facioconjunctival edema.[4,29] Angioedema is typically manifested by large edematous swellings of the lips, face, eyelids, ears, conjunctiva and/or tongue, with or without pruritus.[4,29] Angioedema is evoked by the same types of substances that induce systemic anaphylaxis.[29] Most veterinary practitioners attribute angioedema solely to insect envenomation (biting or stinging insects) but a number of other common causes

include food, drugs, vaccines, infections, atopy and blood transfusions.[4] Urticarial reactions (hives) are characterized by localized or generalized wheals, which may or may not be pruritic.[4,29] They usually occur within minutes of allergen exposure and generally subside after one to two hours.

One of the authors (PR) has seen angioedema of the tongue, palate and throat repeatedly in the same dogs after indiscreet ingestion of mushrooms, domestic flowers or other plants. This presentation resembles the oral allergy syndrome in people, which is a form of contact urticaria confined almost exclusively to the oropharynx.[5] Symptoms in people include rapid onset of pruritus and angioedema of the lips, tongue, palate and throat. Symptoms usually resolve rapidly. This syndrome is most commonly associated with the ingestion of various fresh fruits and vegetables. People with allergic rhinitis associated with certain airborne pollens (especially birch or ragweed pollens) are most frequently afflicted with this syndrome.

DERMATOLOGIC RESPONSES TO ADVERSE FOOD REACTIONS IN CATS

Gender predisposition has not been documented in adverse food reactions in cats and ages have ranged from six months to 12 years.[22,30-34] In one study, almost half of the cats developed the disease by two years of age.[31] Siamese or Siamese cross cats may be at increased risk because they accounted for nearly one-third of cases in two studies.[22,31]

Dermatologic signs include several different clinical reaction patterns such as: 1) severe, generalized pruritus without lesions, 2) miliary dermatitis, 3) pruritus with self trauma centered around the head, neck and ears, 4) traumatic alopecia, 5) moist dermatitis and 6) scaling dermatoses.[3,4,22,30-34] In one study, angioedema, urticaria or conjunctivitis occurred in one-third of cats with adverse food reactions.[31] Adverse reactions to food may also cause self-inflicted alopecia (i.e., psychogenic alopecia, neurodermatitis), eosinophilic plaques and indolent ulcers of the lips in some cats.[3,4,33] Concurrent flea-allergy dermatitis or atopy may occur in up to 30% of cats with suspected adverse food reactions.[22,31]

Moderate to marked peripheral lymphadomegaly is found in up to one-third of cats with dermatologic manifestations of food allergy.[4] Absolute peripheral eosinophilia occurs in 20 to 50% of feline cases.[4,30,34]

GI RESPONSES TO ADVERSE FOOD REACTIONS IN DOGS AND CATS

Gender predilections have not been established for GI disease resulting from adverse reactions to foods.[18,19] Similarly, there are no well-documented breed predispositions to GI food allergy, but Chinese Shar-Pei and German shepherd dogs are commonly affected. Furthermore, gluten-sensitive enteropathy has been well documented in Irish setter dogs.[35] A wide age range of patients can be affected, including dogs and cats as young as weaning age.

Every level of the GI tract can be damaged by food allergies. In dogs, cats and people, clinical signs usually relate to gastric and small bowel dysfunction, but colitis can also occur.[36,37] Vomiting and diarrhea are prominent features. The diarrhea can be profuse and watery, mucoid or hemorrhagic.[37,38] Intermittent abdominal pain is occasionally seen. Concurrent cutaneous signs may be seen. GI disturbances occur in 10 to 15% of dogs and cats with cutaneous manifestations of food sensitivity.[3,4] In experimentally induced food hypersensitivity, the most common clinical signs are diarrhea, an increase in the number of bowel movements and occasional vomiting.[35,39] One veterinary dermatologist has observed that pruritic dogs with more than three bowel movements per day are more likely to have an adverse reaction to food as part of the reason for their dermatoses.[4,27]

There are at least five subacute to chronic GI conditions thought to involve food allergy in people: 1) food protein-induced enterocolitis, 2) food-induced colitis syndrome, 3) food-induced malabsorption syndrome, 4) gluten-sensitive enteropathy and 5) allergic eosinophilic gastroenteritis.[40,41] All of these conditions can occur in dogs and cats. The role of food allergy in canine and feline inflammatory bowel disease (IBD) is unknown. Hypersensitivity to food is probably involved in the pathogenesis of this syndrome; at least some affected animals could be more appropriately diagnosed as suffering from food protein-induced enterocolitis. In one case, a dog with IBD was tested for the presence of fecal and serum antibodies against a variety of food and parasitic antigens, but the search was unrewarding.[42]

Currently, 10% of dogs with IBD diagnosed by one of the authors (WGG) have positive gastroscopic food sensitivity tests (GFST) to food antigens. (See sidebar "Gastroscopic Food Sensitivity Testing.") Positive GFST results to foods used in the treatment of the disease are often detected during follow-up endoscopic studies. This finding strongly implies that food allergy is involved in the perpetuation of IBD but that it may not be the primary cause. That is, inflammation of the mucosa predisposes animals to the development of acquired food allergies. Therefore, a change in food antigens may temporarily reduce the immune-mediated mucosal inflammatory response. The longevity of this amelioration is questionable, however, because most of the so-called "hypoallergenic" foods commonly used in veterinary medicine contain intact proteins that are hypoallergenic primarily by virtue of their novelty to the host's immune system. The duration of protein novelty to the gut-associated lymphoid tissue (GALT) is likely to be very limited if the antigen is fed to an animal with a highly porous mucosal barrier. The subclassification of IBD in which hypersensitivity to food antigens is most likely to play a causal role is eosinophilic enterocolitis.

Irritable bowel syndrome is a disease of dogs characterized by chronic recurrent abdominal pain and large bowel diarrhea. Feeding changes will often alleviate the signs of irritable bowel disease, implying that food sensitivity plays a role in this syndrome. In the experience of one of the authors (WGG), avoiding gas-producing foods (e.g., homemade vegetable-based foods) or foods with a high-fat content is particularly advantageous in the management of dogs with irritable bowel syndrome. In affected dogs, the adverse reactions to these nutrients are most likely due to a food intolerance rather than a food allergy.

Risk Factors

Risk factors for adverse food reactions in animals are poorly documented but may include: 1) certain foods or food ingredients, 2) poorly digestible proteins, 3) any disease that increases intestinal mucosal permeability (e.g., viral enteritis), 4) selective IgA deficiency, 5) certain breeds, 6) age (less than one year old) and 7) concurrent allergic disease.

Gastroscopic Food Sensitivity Testing

Gastroscopic food sensitivity testing (GFST) is a diagnostic technique in which food extracts (5,000 to 15,000 protein nitrogen units/ml) are dripped onto the gastric mucosa by means of the operating channel of an endoscope. The site is then observed for two to three minutes. Mucosal swelling suggests an immediate sensitivity to the food extract tested. Erythema, blanching, edema and petechiation at the mucosal site also suggest the test subject is hypersensitive to the food, and the food, therefore, should not be used as part of the sensitive patient's diet. Sampling of the mucosal site with subsequent measuring of histamine levels, other mediator levels or mast cell degranulation can be used to determine whether the response was immune mediated. Although the diagnostic accuracy of GFST isn't known, research is currently underway in a number of species including dogs and cats to determine its clinical utility.

BIBLIOGRAPHY

Guilford WG, Strombeck DR, Robers G, et al. Development of gastroscopic food sensitivity testing in dogs. Journal of Veterinary Internal Medicine 1994; 8: 414-422.

Guilford WG. Adverse reactions to food. In: Guilford WG, Center SA, Strombeck DR, et al, eds. Strombeck's Small Animal Gastroenterology, 3rd ed. Philadelphia, PA: WB Saunders Co, 1996; 443.

Table 14-1. Gastrointestinal barriers to ingested food antigens.

Physiologic barriers
Break down ingested antigens
  Gastric acid and pepsin
  Pancreatic enzymes
  Intestinal enzymes
  Intestinal epithelial cell lysozyme activity
Block penetration of ingested antigens
  Unstirred water layer
  Intestinal mucous coat (glycocalyx)
  Intestinal microvillous membrane composition
  Intestinal peristalsis
Immunologic barriers
Block penetration of ingested antigens
  Antigen-specific secretory IgA in gut lumen
Clear antigens penetrating GI barrier
  Monocyte-macrophage system
  Serum antigen-specific IgA and IgG

Etiopathogenesis

NORMAL MUCOSAL BARRIER AND ORAL TOLERANCE

Ingested food represents the greatest foreign antigenic load confronting the immune system. The defense against hypersensitivity to food antigens includes an effective mucosal barrier and oral tolerance generated by the cellular immune system of the GALT.[2,5,43,44]

An important adaptation of the GI tract is the development of a mucosal barrier that prevents the overwhelming uptake of food antigens.[5,43,44] Efficient functioning of the mucosal barrier excludes the majority of ingested antigens, thus minimizing antigen exposure to GALT. The concept of a mucosal barrier includes effective digestion, the mucous layer, intact and functioning epithelial cells and immunoglobulin A (Table 14-1 and Figure 14-2).

Complete digestion of food protein results in free amino acids and small peptides that are poor antigens. An incom-

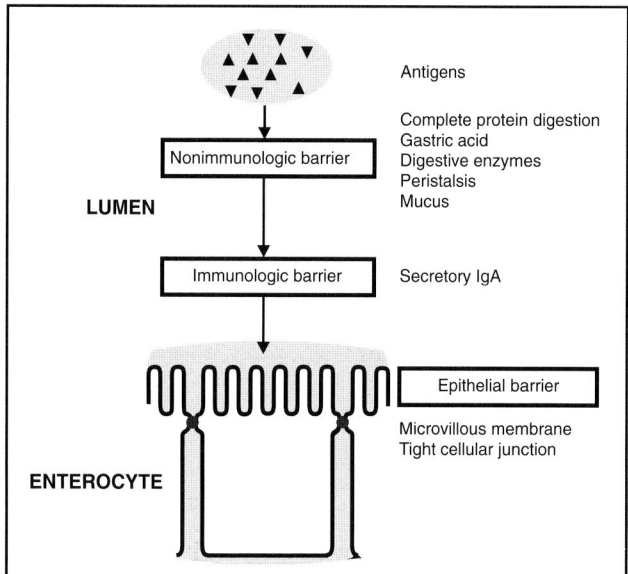

Figure 14-2. Diagrammatic representation of barriers to antigen penetration of the intestinal mucosa. Antigens are prevented from entering the mucosa by nonimmunologic and immunologic mechanisms and the physical structure of the epithelium. (Adapted from Iyngkaren N, Abidin Z. Intolerance to food proteins. In: Lifshitz F, ed. Pediatric Nutrition. New York, NY: Dekker, 1981; 453.)

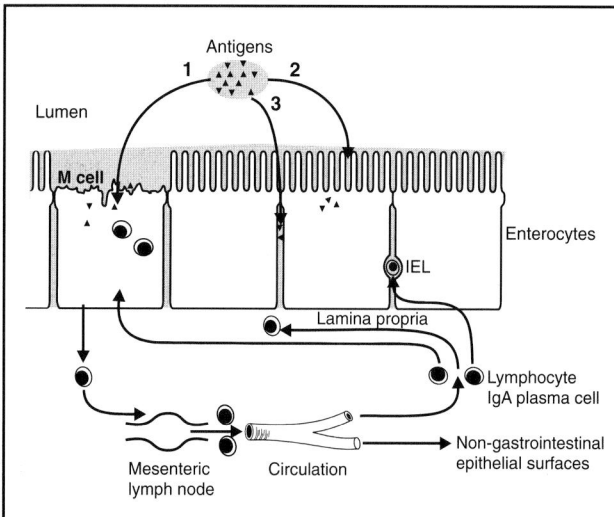

Figure 14-3. Diagrammatic representation of the gut-associated lymphoid tissue (GALT) and the mucosal immune cycle. GALT is composed of Peyer's patches, lamina propria, lymphocytes and plasma cells, intraepithelial lymphocytes (IEL) and mesenteric lymph nodes. Food antigens are absorbed via specialized M cells (1) or enterocytes (2,3). These antigens stimulate lymphocytes, which migrate by way of the intestinal lymphatics to mesenteric lymph nodes, ultimately reaching the systemic circulation via the thoracic duct. Specific immune-primed lymphocytes cycle back to GALT or are deposited at other mucosal surfaces. (Adapted from Patrick MK, Gall DG. Protein intolerance and immunocyte and enterocyte interaction. Pediatric Clinics of North America 1988; 35: 17-34.)

pletely digested food protein has the potential to incite an allergic response because of residual antigenic proteins and large polypeptides. The composition of the mucous coat overlying the intestinal surface contributes to the defense against antigen attachment and penetration. Mucus contains carbohydrate moieties that may act as receptor inhibitors, thereby interfering with attachment of antigens to the intestinal microvillous surface.[5,43,44] A direct association between intestinal cell membrane protein/phospholipid ratios and antigen uptake has been demonstrated in some species. Changes in cell membrane composition and function occur early in life, but how these changes affect food antigen uptake is unknown. IgA is the major immunologic component of the mucosal barrier because it is present in high concentrations in intestinal secretions. IgA may complex with food antigens in the intestinal lumen or within the mucous coat, thereby preventing their transport.

Despite these defense mechanisms, the mucosal barrier is not completely impervious to macromolecules; food proteins cross the intact intestinal mucosa in small but significant amounts. Antigens that enter and pass through the lamina propria are removed by the mononuclear-macrophage (reticuloendothelial) system of the liver and mesenteric lymph nodes.

The intestine, traditionally viewed as an organ of digestion and absorption of nutrients, maintains an indispensable immunologic function.[43,44] The gut is probably one of the largest immune organs in the body. GALT is composed of four distinct lymphoid compartments: 1) aggregates of lymphoid follicles throughout the intestinal mucosa, 2) lymphocytes and plasma cells scattered throughout the lamina propria, 3) intraepithelial lymphocytes interdigitated between enterocytes and 4) mesenteric lymph nodes (Figure 14-3).[5]

Although GALT must mount a rapid and potent response against potentially harmful foreign substances and pathogenic organisms, it also must remain unresponsive to enormous quantities of food antigens. Absorbed food antigens are presented to the GALT in such a manner that a potent gut-associated, cell-mediated suppressive response to that antigen develops (Figure 14-4). This suppressor response is the basis of oral tolerance. Conversely, an allergic response may result if the antigen encounters a defective suppressor arm of GALT or escapes into the systemic circulation. The concept of "immune exclusion" of food antigens is important because systemic lymphoid tissue responds by active immunoreactivity, which could lead to allergic clinical signs rather than immune suppression (tolerance).

IMMUNOLOGIC REACTIONS TO FOOD

Food Allergens

The specific food allergens or ingredients that cause problems in animals have been poorly documented (Table 14-2). In general, the major food allergens that have been identified in people are water-soluble glycoproteins that have molecular weights ranging from 10,000 to 60,000 daltons and are stable to treatment with heat, acid and proteases.[5] Other physiochemical properties that account for their unique allergenicity are poorly understood.

The most common food allergens in children are found in chicken egg, peanut, cow's milk, fish, soy and wheat.[5,45-47] In human adults, various fruits, tree nuts, peanut, fish, seafood (mollusks, crustaceans) and cow's milk are confirmed most often as causing food allergy.[5,45-47] Discussion of the specific protein fractions and allergens in these foods that are thought to cause problems are reviewed elsewhere.[5,45]

A survey of veterinarians in North America incriminated food preservatives and dyes, wheat, beef, chicken egg, corn, poultry, soy and dairy products as commonly causing dermatologic signs of food allergy in dogs.[16] It is interesting to compare these clinical perceptions with documented case studies in the literature. Ten different studies, representing 253 dogs, described cutaneous lesions associated with adverse reactions to specific foods or ingredients.[7,18,22-24,26,27,48-50] In these studies, adverse reactions to beef, dairy products or wheat accounted for more than 65% of all the reported cases.[7,18,22-24,26,27,48-50] Adverse reactions to chicken, chicken egg, lamb or soy accounted for approximately 25% of the reported canine cases.[7,18,22-24,26,27,48-50]

Food allergens incriminated in North American cats with dermatologic disease include fish, beef, chicken/poultry, dairy products, preservatives and dyes.[16] Eight different studies or case reports, representing 45 cats, described cutaneous lesions associated with adverse reactions to specific foods or ingredients.[18,22,30,32,51-54] In these studies, adverse reactions to beef, dairy products or fish accounted for more than 89% of all the reported cases in cats.[18,22,30,32,51-54]

Human allergy reference books often contain phylogenetic tables of animal and vegetable foods, so food-allergic persons can avoid other closely related foods. In clinical practice, human patients often report cross-reactivity among various fish and crustaceans, but less cross-reactivity within vegetable food groups. Results of oral food challenges in children demonstrate that clinically important cross-reactivity to legumes (peanut, soybean, green bean, lima bean, peas, lentils) is very rare.[55] Wheat, rye and barley cross react in allergic people, but oat allergens appear to cross react only weakly.[56] Cross-reactivity between milk proteins from cows, goats and sheep has been noted. In children, chicken egg has also been shown to cross react with egg proteins of other birds.[5] Certain allergens are apparently common to both foods and pollens. Common allergens have been reported in ragweed pollen, melon, and banana and mugwort pollen and celery and birch pollen and apple.[45] Cross-reactivity among food allergens has only been briefly investigated in pet animals.[48]

Pathophysiologic Mechanisms

Abnormalities in the GI defense mechanisms may predispose patients to food allergies.[2] Predisposing factors for food allergy include: 1) mucosal barrier failure (poorly digestible proteins, incomplete protein digestion, increased intestinal mucosal permeability, age-related changes in microvillous cell membrane composition, inflammatory-induced changes in mucus composition) and 2) defective immunoregulation (decreased IgA secretion, deranged cell-mediated responses of GALT, monocyte-macrophage system dysfunction) (Figure 14-4). Which of these pathomechanisms are important predisposing factors in dogs and cats awaits further investigation. Selected IgA deficiency may be common in dogs with chronic dermatopathies and enteropathies, and may occur in some allergic cats.

The most extensively studied and best-defined food-allergic reactions in people and laboratory animals involve IgE-mediated responses that result in clinical signs of immediate hypersensitivity (within minutes to hours).[5] IgE-activated mast cells also may release a variety of cytokines that mediate a late-phase response (within several hours to days). With

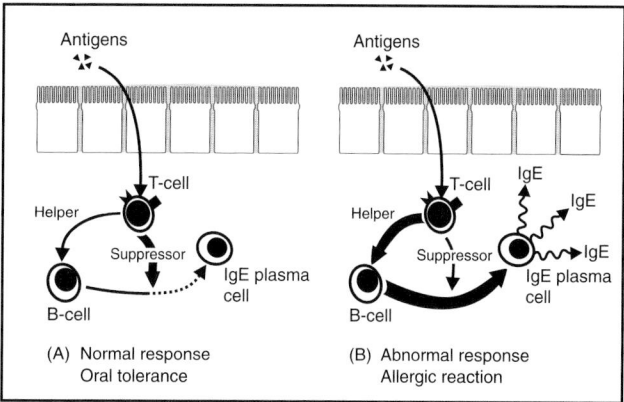

Figure 14-4. Diagrammatic representation of food antigen absorption under different conditions. With a normal response (A), T-cell suppressor activity occurs and contributes to oral tolerance. In (B), an abnormal immune response contributes to production of excess IgE and may result in allergic disease. (Adapted from Walker WA. Pathophysiology of intestinal uptake and absorption of antigens in food allergy. Annals of Allergy 1987; 59: 7-16.)

Table 14-2. Ingredients commonly associated with adverse food reactions.*

Dogs		Cats	
Beef	} 68% reported cases	Beef	} 89% reported cases
Dairy products		Dairy products	
Wheat		Fish	
Lamb	} 25% reported cases		
Chicken egg		Chicken/poultry**	
Chicken		Food additives**	
Soy			
Corn**			
Food additives**			

*Data from cases reported in North America, Europe, Australia and New Zealand. Common food allergens may differ in other geographic locations.
**These pet food ingredients are commonly incriminated as causing adverse food reactions but are rarely reported in the literature.

repeated ingestion of a food allergen, mononuclear cells are stimulated to secrete histamine-releasing factor, a cytokine that interacts with IgE bound to the surface of basophils and mast cells and increases their releasability.[57] This in vitro phenomenon has been associated with increased cutaneous reactivity in children with atopic dermatitis.[57]

Studies have been unable to detect food antigen-specific IgE in dogs with known adverse food reactions.[49,58] Either the dogs in these studies did not have IgE-mediated disease or the test methods were unable to detect antigen-specific IgE.[49,58] Type II (cytotoxic reactions), Type III (immune complex) and Type IV (cell-mediated) hypersensitivity reactions have been implicated in food-allergic disorders in people and other animals, but their involvement in food allergy has not been clearly established.[3-5]

Gluten (Gliadin) Enteropathy

Gluten-induced enteropathy (celiac disease) is an important chronic inflammatory disease of the small intestine of people. The prevalence of gluten intolerance in dogs and cats is unknown. Recent work has conclusively demonstrated that an analogous disorder affects the Irish setter dog,[35] and clinical experience suggests that other breeds may also be affected.

Flour from cereal grains contains various proteins including: 1) water-soluble albumins, 2) saline-soluble globulins, 3) ethanol-soluble prolamins and 4) acid- or alkali-soluble glutelin.[45] Prolamins of wheat, rye and barley have marked sequence homology, but not the prolamins of rice and corn, which do not exacerbate the disorder.[59] The prolamin and the glutelin proteins of wheat are gliadin and glutenin. Gliadin is a glutamine- and proline-rich polypeptide with a molecular weight of 15,000 daltons. Gliadin is composed of four major electrophoretic fractions, the most toxic of which in people appears to be alpha-gliadin.[59] "Gluten" is a crude mixture of gliadin and glutenin. These peptides are normally digested by pancreatic enzymes in the intestinal lumen and intracellular enzymes of the mucosal brush border. Completely hydrolyzed gliadin is nontoxic.

The cause of gluten sensitivity is unknown. Studies involving gluten-intolerant Irish setters have demonstrated that increased mucosal permeability predates development of the disease.[60] The pathogenesis of gluten-sensitive enteropathy has been debated for many years, but researchers now think gluten sensitivity in people is probably mediated by the immune system. Knowledge of the complete sequence of immunologic events is far from complete, but it appears the immune damage is not mediated by IgE. Instead, evidence suggests that delayed hypersensitivity to gluten is responsible.[61] Gliadin-activated macrophages may possibly recruit lamina propria lymphocytes resulting in a delayed hypersensitivity response and various inflammatory changes such as infiltration of inflammatory cells, mast cell degranulation, production of eicosanoids, increased microvascular permeability and complement activation.[61,62] In gluten-sensitive dogs, the lymphocyte density of the mucosal intraepithelium is increased and serum total IgA levels are elevated.[63]

In contrast to findings in people, anti-gliadin antibody (IgG) levels are lower in affected dogs than in age-matched control dogs. In addition, serum immune complex levels are not elevated in dogs whereas they are frequently elevated in people.[63] These findings do not support a role for a systemic immune response in the pathogenesis of canine gluten-sensitive enteropathy but do not rule out a mucosal delayed hypersensitivity response.

NONIMMUNOLOGIC REACTIONS TO FOOD

Nonimmunologic, abnormal physiologic reactions to food include food intolerance and dietary indiscretion (Figure 14-1). Like the terms food allergy and food hypersensitivity, the term food intolerance has been applied inappropriately to any and all adverse reactions to food. Food intolerance mimics food allergy except that it can occur on the first exposure to a food or food additive, because nonimmunologic mechanisms are involved. The incidence of food intolerance vs. food hypersensitivity or food allergy is unknown.

Food Poisoning

Food poisoning or food toxicosis is an adverse effect caused by the direct action of a food or food additive on the host. Examples of food poisoning (See Chapter 7.) include ingestion of: 1) nutrient excesses (vitamin A or vitamin D toxicosis), 2) food contaminated with microorganisms or their toxic metabolites (e.g., scavenging putrefied material, vomitoxin), 3) specific foods (onions, chocolate) or 4) toxic food preservatives (benzoic acid or propylene glycol in cats).

Food poisoning is a frequent cause of GI disease in dogs and cats. In addition to ingestion of pathogenic microorganisms or their toxins, food poisoning can result from the ingestion of plant-derived toxins or irritants. For example, high levels of oxalates and anthraquinone glycosides contained in rhubarb, spinach and beets can lead to a corrosive gastroenteritis, and large quantities of spices such as peppers can cause abdominal discomfort in people.

Reactions to Food Additives

Idiosyncratic adverse reactions to food additives often occur in people.[12-15] Food additives frequently incriminated in human adverse reactions include sulfites, monosodium glutamate, tartrazine and other azo or nonazo dyes, benzoates, parabens and spices.[12-15] Few of the adverse reactions to food additives appear to involve an immunologic mechanism, although IgE-mediated reactions may occur.[12-15] Confirmed reactions to food additives are best described as food intolerances or food idiosyncrasies because clinical signs resulting from their ingestion are thought to be nonimmunologically mediated. Examples are reactions to azo dyes, nonazo dyes and antioxidants that can directly cause histamine release from leukocytes of clinically normal people.[64]

Although food additives are frequently incriminated as causing problems in dogs and cats, few data confirm this perception.[16,17] Propylene glycol has been documented to cause hematologic abnormalities in cats and subsequently has been eliminated from cat foods sold in the United States and some other countries.[65,66] Disulfides found in onions (e.g., onion powder, onion-based broth and baby foods containing onion) promote oxidative damage to hemoglobin in canine and feline red blood cells.[67] The result is Heinz body production and red cell destruction. Ethoxyquin, a synthetic antioxidant, has received considerable consumer and media attention. Ethoxyquin has been blamed for widespread infertility, neonatal illness and death, skin and coat problems, immune disorders, dysfunction of the thyroid, pancreas and liver and behavioral disorders in purebred dogs. To date, the United States Food and Drug Administration has found no scientific or medical evidence that ethoxyquin used at approved levels is injurious to human or animal health.[68]

Some veterinary dermatologists have incriminated food colorants and other food additives as causes of erythema multiforme and other "drug-like" skin eruptions.[69,a] Erythema multiforme is a cutaneous reaction pattern of multifactorial etiology seen uncommonly in dogs and rarely in cats. Lesions include erythematous macules and papules that spread to produce annular target and arciform lesions.[3,4] The oral and nasal mucosa, pinnae, axillae and groin areas are commonly involved.[3,4] Most documented cases of erythema multiforme in dogs and cats are associated with drug hypersensitivity; neoplasia and infection are less common causes. Food additives have been suspected in some cases but their role has been poorly documented.[69,a] Further studies are needed to document the occurrence of adverse reactions to pet food additives and the responsible pathomechanisms.

Reactions to Vasoactive Amines in Food

Another cause of food intolerance is pharmacologic reactions to substances found in food. Vasoactive or biogenic amines such as histamine cause clinical signs in people when present in excessive levels in food.[70,71] Scombroid fish such as tuna, mackerel, skipjack and bonito that spoil before consumption are a frequent cause of histamine toxicosis in people.[70,71] Clinical signs usually include diarrhea, flushing, sweating, nausea, vomiting, urticaria, facial swelling and erythroderma.

The role of histamine and other vasoactive amines in food intolerance in animals is unknown. Adverse reactions to ingested scombroid fish have been observed in cats and dogs.[72] Recent surveys to detect histamine in pet foods found the highest levels of histamine in moist fish-based cat foods and those cat foods containing fish solubles.[72,73] Vasoactive amines such as cadaverine may also exacerbate adverse reactions to spoiled fish by inhibiting histamine metabolism.[70,74] Tyramine, spermine, spermidine, phenethylamine, putrescine and cadaverine are other vasoactive amines found in pet foods.[b] Vasoactive or biogenic amines may not be present in levels high enough to cause clinical signs, but could lower the threshold levels for allergens in individual dogs and cats. Idiosyncratic intolerances to small quantities of histamine have been reported to occur in people and animals.[72]

Carbohydrate Intolerance

Adult hypolactasia, infantile lactase deficiency, congenital lactose intolerance and congenital glucose-galactose malabsorption are disorders of carbohydrate intolerance in people.[75] Fewer conditions are associated with recognized carbohydrate intolerance in dogs and cats. However, neonatal death following episodes of diarrhea are common and the same spectrum of metabolic disorders resulting in carbohydrate intolerance in people may occur in dogs and cats.[2,75]

The diarrhea, bloating and abdominal discomfort that occur when animals with lactose intolerance ingest milk are relatively common metabolic adverse reactions in dogs and cats.[76,77] Puppies and kittens normally have adequate levels of intestinal lactase to permit digestion of lactose in the dam's milk. In many subjects, brush border disaccharidase activity decreases after weaning to a fraction of the activity found in young animals. Osmotic diarrhea will often occur when excessive levels of lactose are consumed. Puppies, kittens or adult animals may develop diarrhea when given cow's or goat's milk because these milk sources contain more lactose than either bitch's or queen's milk. (See Appendix K.) One study showed that adult dogs were able to use up to 1 g of lactose/kg body weight/day,[78] an amount equivalent to 20 to 22 ml/kg of cow's or goat's milk. Greater amounts increased intestinal lactose and lactic acid concentrations, fecal water content and frequency of defecation.

Intolerance to disaccharides commonly occurs secondary to enteritis or rapid food changes. Loss of intestinal brush border disaccharidase activity contributes to the diarrhea associated with enteritis. Inadequate intestinal disaccharidase activity is also one of the factors responsible for diarrhea subsequent to rapid food changes. Several days are required for intestinal disaccharidase activity to adapt to changes in food carbohydrate sources.

Dietary Indiscretion

Dietary indiscretions such as gluttony, pica and garbage ingestion usually cause GI signs and can be suspected based on the environmental and nutritional history. The clinical signs may be caused by ingestion of excessive fat, bacterial or fungal toxins, vasoactive amines or indigestible materials such as bone, plastic, wood and aluminum foil.

Key Nutritional Factors

Because most food allergens are thought to be glycoproteins, protein in food is the nutrient of most concern in patients with suspected adverse food reactions. The number of different proteins in the food, amount of protein, digestibility of the protein and whether the patient has been exposed previously to the protein are all important factors. Pet food additives such as antimicrobial preservatives, colorants, antioxidant preservatives and emulsifying agents may cause either food intolerance or food allergy.

■ ASSESS THE FOOD(S) AND FEEDING METHOD

Ingredient statements on commercial pet food labels in the United States are sources of information for identifying all the food ingredients that might cause adverse reactions. An individual animal may develop an adverse reaction to virtually any pet food ingredient. However, particular attention should be directed at those ingredients that contain protein and food additives. Unfortunately, pet food labeling requirements in other countries are not as stringent and ingredient statement information is often incomplete. (See Chapter 5.) When the ingredient statement is incomplete, the manufacturer or distributor should be contacted for detailed ingredient information.

Commercial pet foods also contain a large number of ingredients that differ from typical foods for human consumption and may be unfamiliar to veterinarians, veterinary health care team members and animal owners. These ingredients are often by-products of human food preparation. Examples of such ingredients are poultry by-product meal and meat and bone meal, which are frequently used as animal protein sources in dry pet foods. Poultry by-product meal is the ground, rendered, clean parts of the carcass such as necks, feet, undeveloped eggs and viscera, exclusive of feathers.[79] Meat and bone meal is the rendered product from slaughtered mammalian tissues, including bone, but exclusive of any added hair, blood, hoof, horn, hide trimmings, stomach and rumen contents, except in amounts as may occur during processing.[79] In North America, meat and bone meal usually represents beef, pork or both tissues. Whether ingredients such as poultry by-product meal and meat and bone meal contain potential allergens analogous to those found in chicken, beef and pork skeletal tissue is not known. Chicken for human consumption, chicken used in moist pet foods and poultry by-product meal used in dry pet foods may each contain unique allergens.

In addition to questioning the pet owner about the regular food eaten by the animal, the nutritional assessment should ask about other items the pet may have ingested that contain protein or food additives. Examples include commercial snacks and treats, chew toys, human foods routinely fed to the pet and access to other sources of food (e.g., a dog with access to cat food in the same household). Supplements such as chewable vitamin tablets, chewable medications and fatty acid capsules, liquids and powders may also contain allergenic proteins or additives. It is often helpful to have the pet owner keep a diary for several weeks to document what types of food, supplements and other items are ingested daily by the animal.

Although pet food additives are frequently incriminated as causing food allergy or food intolerance, there have been no published case reports to date of an adverse food reaction in dogs or cats specifically caused by a pet food additive.[69,a] Additives are found least often in moist pet foods and most commonly in semi-moist foods, treats, snacks and dry foods. Many moist commercial pet foods are free of additives. Two of the most frequently incriminated additives in human foods, benzoates and tartrazine, are rarely found in commercial pet foods. However, other additives that have been documented to cause problems in people are found in pet foods (Table 14-3). These include azo dyes, nonazo dyes, sodium bisulfite, sodium glutamate, sodium nitrate, butylated hydroxyanisole (BHA), spices, sodium alginate, guar gum and propylene glycol.[17]

Nutritional assessment should also evaluate foods or pet food ingredients for excessive levels of vasoactive or biogenic amines such as histamine. As mentioned above, the highest levels of histamine occur in moist fish-based cat foods and cat foods containing fish solubles.[72,73] Human foods that may contain excessive levels of vasoactive or biogenic amines include tomato, avocado, cheese, liver, processed meats such as sausage and certain fish.

It may not always be necessary to change the feeding method when managing a patient with an adverse food reaction, but a thorough assessment includes verification that an appropriate feeding method is being used. Items to consider include feeding route, amount fed, how the food is offered, access to other food and who feeds the animal. All of this information should have been gathered when the history of the animal was obtained. If the animal has a normal body condition score (3/5), the amount of food it was fed previously (energy basis) was probably appropriate.

Table 14-3. Pet food additives that may cause adverse reactions.*

Antioxidant preservatives
    Butylated hydroxyanisole (BHA)
    Butylated hydroxytoluene (BHT)
Antimicrobial preservatives
    Sodium nitrite
Humectants
    Propylene glycol
Coloring agents/preservatives
    Azo dyes
        Tartrazine (FD&C No. 5)
        Sunset yellow (FD&C No. 6)
        Allura red (FD&C No. 40)
    Nonazo dyes
        Brilliant blue (FD&C No. 1)
        Indigotin (FD&C No. 2)
Flavors/flavor enhancers
    Monosodium glutamate
    Spices
Emulsifying agents, stabilizers, thickeners
    Seaweed extracts (carrageenan, alginates)
    Seed gums (guar gum)

*This list includes food additives that cause adverse reactions in people and that are found in pet foods. These additives are frequently incriminated as causing adverse food reactions in animals, but there are no well-documented case reports to substantiate this perception.

Table 14-4. Characteristics of an ideal elimination food.

Limited number of protein sources
Novel protein sources
Avoids excess levels of dietary protein
High-protein digestibility (greater than 87%) or contains a protein
    hydrolysate
Free of food additives
Free of excessive levels of vasoactive amines
Nutritionally adequate for the intended species, age and lifestyle
    of the animal

FEEDING PLAN

The Ideal Elimination Food

Dietary elimination trials are the main diagnostic method used in dogs and cats with suspected adverse food reactions. At the present time, intradermal skin testing, radioallergosorbent tests (RASTs) and enzyme-linked immunosorbent assays (ELISAs) for food hypersensitivity are considered unreliable in animals with dermatologic disease.[5,23,24]

The ideal elimination food should: 1) include a reduced number of novel, highly digestible protein sources or contain a protein hydrolysate, 2) avoid protein excesses, 3) avoid additives and vasoactive amines and 4) be nutritionally adequate for the animal's lifestage and condition (Table 14-4). Ingredients in an ideal elimination food should provide a limited number of novel protein sources; preferably one to two different types of protein to which the animal has not been previously exposed. This recommendation often includes a commercial or homemade food with one animal protein source and one vegetable protein source. Excess protein levels should be avoided to reduce the amount of potential allergens to which the dermatologic patient is exposed. A higher protein level may be necessary to counteract protein losses from the GI tract or impaired absorption in patients with hypoproteinemia and weight loss associated with severe GI disease.

Protein digestibility is also an important factor when assessing an elimination food. Complete digestion of food protein results in free amino acids and small peptides that are poor antigens.[45] Thus, an incompletely digested food protein has the potential to incite an allergic response because of residual antigenic proteins and large polypeptides. Protein digestibility has been documented for some commercial pet foods marketed as hypoallergenic or elimination foods.[80] A protein digestibility exceeding 87% is recommended for such foods. An alternate strategy is to use a food containing protein hydrolysate(s). Protein hydrolysates have molecular weights below levels that commonly elicit an allergic response.

Although specific pet food additives have not been documented to cause adverse food reactions, food additives generally should be avoided in elimination foods. The ideal elimination food should avoid ingredients such as certain kinds of fish that are known to contain higher levels of vasoactive amines than do other pet food ingredients.[72,73]

Finally, although elimination trials are only performed for several weeks to months, the food used in the trial should be nutritionally complete and balanced for the intended species, age and lifestyle of the animal. Elimination trials are often performed with young animals in which nutritionally inadequate foods are more likely to result in nutritional disease.

Homemade Elimination Foods

Results of a survey of veterinarians in the American Academy of Veterinary Dermatology (AAVD) showed homemade foods were recommended most often as the initial test food for dogs and cats with suspected food allergy.[16] Homemade test foods usually include a single protein source or a combination of a single protein source and a single carbohydrate source. Ingredients recommended most often for homemade feline foods include lamb baby food, lamb, rice and rabbit. Ingredients recommended most often for homemade canine foods include lamb, rice, potato, fish, rabbit, venison and tofu.

Most of the homemade foods recommended in the AAVD survey for initial management of dogs and cats with suspected food allergy were nutritionally inadequate for growth or adult maintenance.[16] Most homemade foods fail to meet nutritional requirements because they are made from a minimum of ingredients. In general, homemade foods lack a source of calcium, essential fatty acids, certain vitamins and other micronutrients and contain excessive levels of protein, which are contraindicated in food allergy cases.

Feeding nutritionally inadequate homemade foods to young dogs and cats for more than three weeks may result in nutritional disease. Clinical signs of anorexia and poor growth occur in puppies within 10 to 20 days of feeding a thiamin-deficient food.[81] Anorexia and emesis also appear within one to two weeks of feeding a thiamin-deficient food

to cats.[82] Many previously recommended homemade elimination foods have a severe inverse calcium-to-phosphorus ratio of 1:10. Foods with severe mineral imbalances can cause skeletal disease in young dogs within four weeks[83,84] and should not be fed for longer than three weeks.[85]

Complete and balanced homemade food recipes are available in this book (See Chapter 6.) and in other references.[85-91] Nonflavored vitamin and mineral supplements are not perceived as causes of adverse food reactions. Additive-free supplements that do not contain animal or vegetable proteins are unlikely to be sources of ingested allergens. Intolerance to calcium supplements in atopic children has been reported but is rare.[92] Homemade rations should also contain a source of essential fatty acids, such as vegetable oil. Vegetable oils are not a routine source of ingested allergens; studies show that

Table 14-5. Selected commercial products marketed or recommended as elimination foods.

	Protein sources*
Moist canine products	
Hill's Prescription Diet Canine d/d Lamb & Rice	rice, lamb, lamb liver
Hill's Prescription Diet Canine d/d Whitefish & Rice	whitefish, rice
Hill's Prescription Diet Canine s/d	egg, pork liver
Hill's Prescription Diet Canine u/d	chicken, egg, rice, pork liver
Iams Eukanuba Response Formula	catfish, herring meal, potato, beet pulp
IVD Limited Ingredient Duck & Potato	potato, duck, duck by-products
IVD Limited Ingredient Lamb & Potato	potato, lamb, lamb by-products, lamb liver
IVD Limited Ingredient Rabbit & Potato	potato, rabbit, rabbit by-products
IVD Limited Ingredient Venison & Potato	potato, venison, venison by-products
Leo Specific Dermil CDW (foil pack)	mutton, rice
Lick Your Chops Lamb & Rice Diet	lamb, lamb liver, rice, quinoa, flax, kelp
Waltham/Pedigree Selected Protein Diet-Chicken & Rice	chicken by-products, chicken, rice, natural flavors
Waltham/Pedigree Selected Protein Diet-Lamb & Rice	lamb by-products, lamb, rice, natural flavors
Waltham/Pedigree Selected Protein Diet-Venison	venison, venison by-products, rice, natural flavors
Wysong Canine Anergen	lamb, lamb liver, brown rice, flax, yeast
Dry canine products	
Hill's Prescription Diet Canine d/d Rice & Duck	rice, duck by-products, rice protein concentrate
Hill's Prescription Diet Canine d/d Rice & Egg	rice, egg
Hill's Prescription Diet Canine d/d Rice & Salmon	rice, salmon, rice protein concentrate
Hill's Prescription Diet Canine u/d	rice, egg, whey
Iams Eukanuba Response Formula	potato, herring meal, catfish, beet pulp, fish digest
IVD Limited Ingredient Duck & Potato	potato, duck meal, duck, duck digest
IVD Limited Ingredient Lamb & Potato	potato, lamb, lamb meal, lamb digest
IVD Limited Ingredient Venison & Potato	potato, venison, venison meal, venison liver
Leo Specific Dermil CDD	egg, rice
Medi-Cal Canine Hypoallergenic Formula	oat flour, duck meal, oat bran, yeast, potato protein, duck digest
Nature's Recipe Non-Meat Kibble	rice, soy, barley, carrots
Purina CNM HA-Formula	modified soy protein, corn starch
Purina CNM LA-Formula	rice, salmon meal, trout, canola meal, yeast
Waltham/Pedigree Selected Protein Diet-Rice & Catfish	rice, catfish meal, rice gluten, catfish, natural flavor
Waltham/Pedigree Selected Protein Diet-Chicken & Rice	chicken by-products, chicken, rice, natural flavors
Waltham/Pedigree Selected Protein Diet-Capelin & Tapioca	tapioca, capelin
Wysong Canine Anergen	lamb meal, chicken, brown rice, flax, quinoa, yeast, kelp
Moist feline products	
Hill's Prescription Diet Feline c/d	beef lungs, pork liver, corn, glandular meal
Hill's Prescription Diet Feline d/d	lamb lungs, lamb liver, rice
Iams Eukanuba Response Formula LB	lamb liver, lamb tripe, barley, lamb meal, beet pulp
IVD Limited Ingredient Lamb & Potato	lamb, lamb by-products, lamb liver, potato
IVD Limited Ingredient Rabbit & Potato	rabbit, rabbit by-products, potato
IVD Limited Ingredient Venison & Potato	venison, venison by-products, venison liver, potato
Lick Your Chops Lamb & Rice Diet	lamb, lamb liver, brown rice, kelp
Waltham/Whiskas Selected Protein Diet with Venison & Rice	venison, venison by-products, rice, natural flavors
Waltham/Whiskas Selected Protein Diet-Chicken & Rice	chicken, rice
Wysong Feline Anergen	lamb, lamb liver, brown rice, kelp, quinoa
Dry feline products	
Hill's Prescription Diet Feline c/d	rice, poultry meal, corn, glandular meal
IVD Limited Ingredient Duck & Potato	potato, duck, duck meal, duck digest
IVD Limited Ingredient Lamb & Potato	potato, lamb, lamb meal, lamb digest
IVD Limited Ingredient Venison & Potato	potato, venison, venison meal, venison liver, venison digest
Medi-Cal Feline Hypoallergenic/Gastro Formula	oat flour, duck meal, potato protein, duck digest, yeast, oat bran
Waltham/Whiskas Selected Protein Diet - Capelin & Tapioca	tapioca, capelin
Wysong Feline Anergen	poultry, poultry meal, rice, oats, lamb meal, liver digest, flax, kelp, yeast

*Sources obtained from ingredient list on information panel of package or manufacturer's technical information.

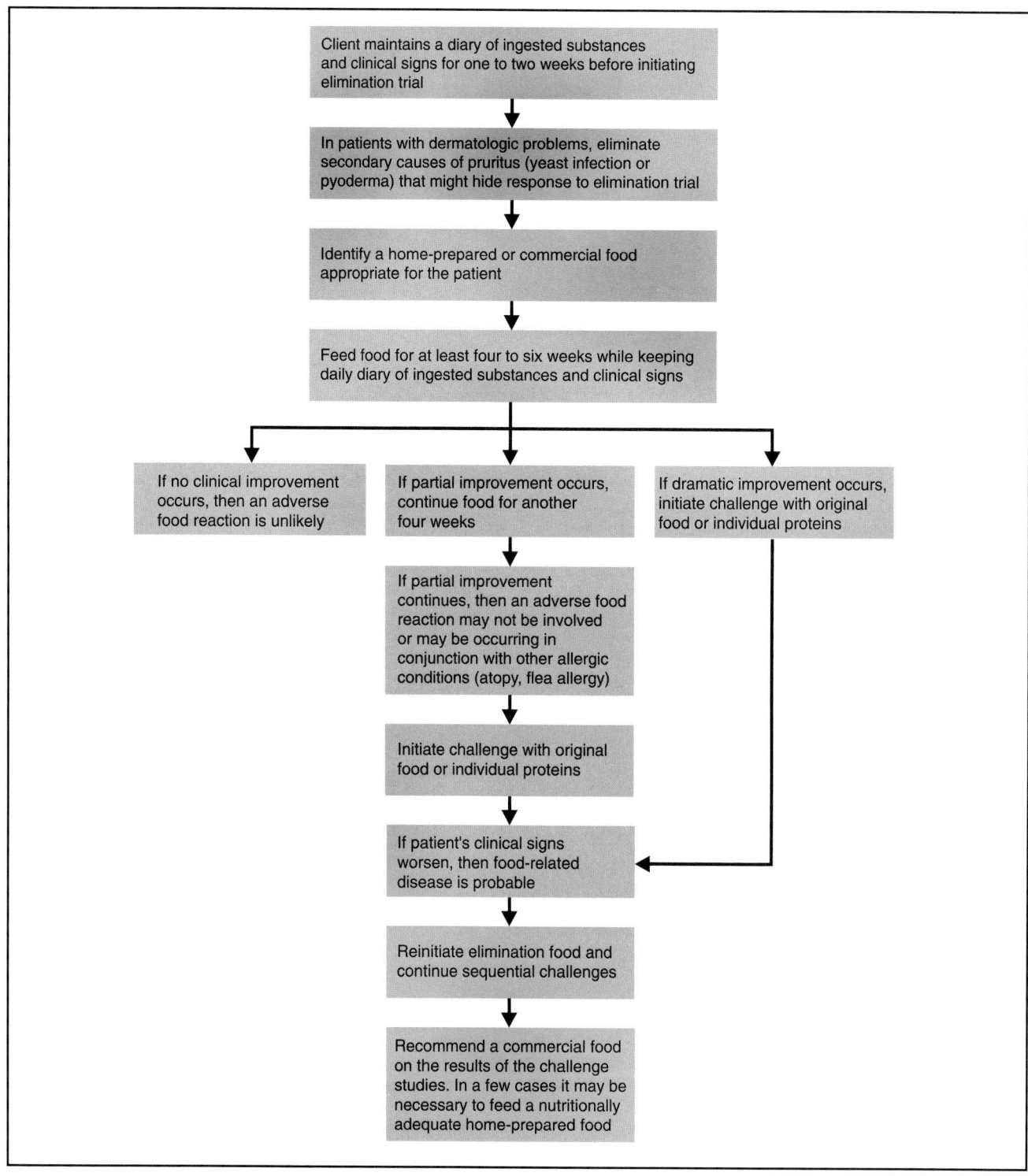

Figure 14-5. Protocol for elimination-challenge trials for the diagnosis of adverse reactions to food.

people allergic to peanuts and soybeans can safely ingest peanut oil or soybean oil.[93-96] Homemade food recipes should provide an optimal amount of protein and foods for cats should be supplemented with taurine.

Commercial Elimination Foods

A variety of foods with limited and different protein sources are manufactured by several companies (Table 14-5). These commercial products are attractive because they are convenient, often contain novel protein sources and are nutritionally complete and balanced for either dogs or cats. (See sidebar "FDA Perspective: 'Hypoallergenic' Claims.") Protein digestibility among these products varies markedly.[76] Further, few of these commercial foods have been adequately tested in dogs and cats with known adverse food reactions; only a few commercial foods have undergone the scrutiny of clinical trials using patients with dermatologic or GI disease.[8,9,11,23,25,27,28,33,54] In published clinical trials, two-thirds to three-fourths of patients with suspected adverse food reactions showed significant improvement in clinical signs when fed commercial elimination-type foods.

Performing an Elimination Trial in Patients with Dermatologic Disease

Before an elimination trial is initiated, the client should feed the dog or cat its usual food for seven to 14 days. During this time the client should record the type and amount of food ingested, any other ingested food items, such as table foods, treats and snacks, and the occurrence and character of adverse reactions (Figure 14-5). The patient is then fed a controlled elimination food for four to 12 weeks. In addition to the feeding change, no other substances should be ingested including treats, flavored vitamin supplements, chewable medications, fatty acid supplements and chew toys. During the elimination trial, the client should document daily the type and amount of food ingested and the occurrence and character of adverse reactions (Figure 14-6). A daily food diary helps document progression of clinical signs during the elimination trial and whether a strict elimination trial was performed in the home environment. The diary will often reveal different findings than those offered to the clinician by the client during the recheck examination.

A tentative diagnosis of an adverse food reaction in dermatologic patients is made if the level of pruritus markedly decreases. This improvement may be gradual and may take four to 12 weeks to become evident.

A diagnosis of an adverse food reaction is confirmed if clinical signs reappear within 10 to 14 days after the animal's former food and other ingested substances are offered as a challenge. Reinstituting the elimination food should resolve the clinical signs induced by the food challenge. Food challenges can be performed in an "open," "single-blind" or "double-blind" manner. In an open food challenge, both the client and veterinarian are aware that a specific food or previous food is being fed. In a single-blind food challenge, only the client is unaware of what food is being given. In a double-blind food challenge, both the client and veterinarian are unaware of whether a specific food is being given. Double-blind, placebo-controlled food challenges are considered to be the "gold standard" for the diagnosis of adverse food reactions in people.[5,96] Only half the human patients thought to be allergic to a food react to the food when they are challenged in controlled, blinded conditions.[96] Unfortunately, all reports and most food challenge recommendations in the veterinary literature have been open challenges. Open challenges will continue as the most practical method of establishing tentative diagnoses of adverse food reaction in dogs and cats, but are subject to false interpretation by clients and veterinarians.

Provocation involves introducing single ingredients until as many positive reactions as possible can be documented. Clients and veterinarians are often reluctant to pursue challenge and provocation once clinical signs have improved or been eliminated. Provocation may also be difficult to perform in many dogs and cats because commercial pet foods contain large numbers of ingredients and feeding the same ingredients often cannot be duplicated in challenge studies. As an example, use of chicken meat in a provocative food challenge may not duplicate the types or levels of antigens found in poultry by-product meal.

Elimination trials are often difficult to interpret because of concurrent allergic skin disease. In several studies, at least 20 to 30% of dogs and cats with adverse food reactions had con-

FDA Perspective: "Hypoallergenic" Claims

Elimination diets for the diagnosis and management of food allergies in pets have been on the market for years. Traditionally, lamb and rice were used in the elimination diet. There is nothing special or unique about these ingredients in terms of allergenicity, and prolonged exposure to these ingredients could also induce an allergic condition. However, they were historically novel sources of protein, because they were not commonly used in commercial dog foods. As such, a pre-existing allergy would be unlikely.

In recent years, a plethora of products containing lamb and rice entered the consumer market. Many of these products were labeled as "hypoallergenic," or otherwise espoused the benefits of lamb and rice in the treatment and prevention of food allergies. Such claims were made even for products that contained other sources of protein that would disqualify them as effective elimination diets. This new marketing niche was detrimental in two respects. The true nature and the incidence of food allergies were clearly overemphasized and misrepresented. Also, the novelty of lamb and rice was diminished, so the usefulness of these ingredients as elimination diets was markedly decreased.

The FDA does not object to the use of lamb or rice in pet foods. Foods that contain these ingredients in sufficient quantities to meet AAFCO labeling criteria may make claims to the presence of these ingredients. However, any claim to be "hypoallergenic," or any other expressed or implied claim relating ingredients with benefits beyond normal nutritive value is a drug claim.

David A. Dzanis, DVM, PhD, Diplomate ACVN
Center for Veterinary Medicine
United States Food and Drug Administration

current hypersensitivities.[21,22,25,27,28,31] These patients may only partially respond to an elimination trial. Flea-allergy dermatitis and atopy are the most common canine and feline allergies and should be eliminated through other diagnostic testing.

Performing an Elimination Trial in Patients with GI Disease

Elimination-challenge trial designs for patients with GI disease are similar to those for patients with dermatologic problems. However, shorter elimination periods are usually satisfactory (two to four weeks). In chronic relapsing conditions, the elimination period chosen must be greater than the usual symptom-free period of the patient to allow reliable assessment of how food sensitivity contributes to the patient's signs.

As with skin disease, the degree of clinical improvement during the elimination trial will be 100% only if food sensitivity is the sole cause of the patient's problems. For instance, resolution of allergies acquired as a *result* of GI disease will not eliminate the clinical signs due to the primary GI disease process. Recrudescence of GI signs after challenge of a food-sensitive patient with the responsible allergen will usually occur within the first three days, but may take as long as seven days, particularly if the responsible allergen was removed from the food for longer than one month.[18]

ADVERSE REACTIONS

Diary for Dietary Elimination Trial

Day	Date	Food Offered	Food Consumed	Other Items Ingested*	Clinical Signs (Scale 0-5 and Comments)**	Feces (Scale 1-5 and Comments)***	Other Observations
1							
2							
3							
4							
5							
6							
7							
8							
9							
10							
11							
12							
13							
14							
15							
16							
17							
18							
19							
20							
21							
22							
23							
24							
25							
26							
27							
28							
29							
30							

Figure 14-6. Example of a diary that can be maintained at home by clients during a food elimination trial.

31				
32				
33				
34				
35				
36				
37				
38				
39				
40				
41				
42				
43				
44				
45				
46				
47				
48				
49				
50				
51				
52				
53				
54				
55				
56				
57				
58				
59				
60				

***Other Items Ingested**
List rawhide chews, vitamin supplements, chewable medications, treats or snacks, fatty acid supplements, table foods, fresh food or access to other food sources (e.g., dog eating cat food or cat eating an animal it has captured outdoors).

****Clinical Signs**
0 = no clinical signs
5 = severe clinical signs
Itching (scratching, rubbing face, chewing, licking, head shaking); hair loss; skin lesions (scabs, scales, bleeding, red skin, pimples)

*****Feces**
1 = liquid feces that have lost all form
2 = soft-liquid feces with no form
3 = soft feces that form a pile
4 = mixture of soft and firm feces with a cylindrical shape
5 = firm feces with cylindrical shape
Presence of mucus or fresh blood; number of daily bowel movements

◼ REASSESSMENT

For most adverse food reactions, avoiding the offending foods or food additives is the most effective treatment. How selective or meticulous an avoidance diet must be depends on the individual animal's sensitivity. Some dogs and cats may suffer adverse reactions to even trace quantities of an offending food or food additive, whereas others may have a higher tolerance level. Concurrent allergies will influence the threshold level of clinical signs in some animals. Symptomatic therapy for pruritic animals may also include corticosteroids and antihistamines. Corticosteroids along with feeding changes are often used in cats with inflammatory bowel disease.

One-third of people fed a strict avoidance food for one to two years have tolerated the reintroduction of food allergens.[97] This finding suggests that strict avoidance of food allergens may allow some dogs and cats to tolerate exposure to the same food allergens later in life.

Both homemade and commercial foods can be used for long-term maintenance of patients with suspected food allergy. Homemade recipes for long-term maintenance must be nutritionally adequate. An attempt should always be made to find an acceptable commercial food that will increase owner compliance with the feeding change and ensure a nutritionally adequate ration.

◼ ENDNOTES & REFERENCES

ENDNOTES

a. Mason KW. Queensland, Australia. Personal communication. 1994.
b. Roudebush P. Unpublished data. May 1992.

REFERENCES

1. Anderson JA. The establishment of common language concerning adverse reactions to foods and food additives. Journal of Allergy and Clinical Immunology 1986; 78: 140-144.
2. Strombeck DR, Guilford WG. Small Animal Gastroenterology, 2nd ed. Davis, CA: Stonegate Publishing, 1991; 344-356.
3. MacDonald JM. Food allergy. In: Griffin CE, Kwochka KW, MacDonald JM, eds. Current Veterinary Dermatology. St Louis, MO: Mosby-Year Book Inc, 1993; 121-132.
4. Scott DW, Miller WH, Griffin CE. Small Animal Dermatology, 5th ed. Philadelphia, PA: WB Saunders Co, 1995.
5. Sampson HA. Adverse reactions to foods. In: Middleton E, Reed CE, Ellis EF, et al, eds. Allergy: Principles and Practice. St Louis, MO: Mosby-Year Book Inc, 1993; 1661-1686.
6. Burrows CF, Batt RM, Sherding RG. Diseases of the small intestine. In: Ettinger SJ, Feldman EC, eds. Textbook of Veterinary Internal Medicine, 4th ed. Philadelphia, PA: WB Saunders Co, 1995; 1220-1223.
7. Elwood CM, Rutgers HC, Batt RM. Gastroscopic food sensitivity testing in 17 dogs. Journal of Small Animal Practice 1994; 35: 199-203.
8. Rutgers HC, Batt RM, Hall EJ, et al. Intestinal permeability testing in dogs with diet-responsive intestinal disease. Journal of Small Animal Practice 1995; 36: 295-301.
9. Simpson JW, Maskell IE, Markwell PJ. Use of a restricted antigen diet in the management of idiopathic canine colitis. Journal of Small Animal Practice 1994; 35: 233-238.
10. Leib MS, Hay WH, Roth L. Plasmacytic-lymphocytic colitis in dogs. In: Kirk RW, ed. Current Veterinary Therapy X. Philadelphia, PA: WB Saunders Co, 1989; 939-944.
11. Nelson RW, Stookey LJ, Kazacos E. Nutritional management of idiopathic chronic colitis in the dog. Journal of Veterinary Internal Medicine 1988; 2: 133-137.
12. Hannuksela M, Haahtela T. Hypersensitivity reactions to food additives. Allergy 1987; 42: 561-575.
13. Simon RA, Stevenson DD. Adverse reactions to food and drug additives. In: Middleton E, Reed CE, Ellis EF, et al, eds. Allergy: Principles and Practice. St Louis, MO: Mosby-Year Book Inc, 1993; 1687-1704.
14. Metcalfe DD, Sampson HA, Simon RA, eds. In: Food Allergy: Adverse Reactions to Foods and Food Additives. Boston, MA: Blackwell Scientific, 1991.

15. Fuglsang G, Madsen C, Halken S, et al. Adverse reactions to food additives in children with atopic symptoms. Allergy 1994; 49: 31-37.
16. Roudebush P, Cowell CS. Results of a hypoallergenic diet survey of veterinarians in North America with a nutritional evaluation of homemade diet prescriptions. Veterinary Dermatology 1992; 3: 23-28.
17. Roudebush P. Pet food additives. Journal of the American Veterinary Medical Association 1993; 203: 1667-1670.
18. Walton GS. Skin responses in the dog and cat to ingested allergens. Veterinary Record 1967; 81: 709-713.
19. Baker E. Food allergy. Veterinary Clinics of North America: Small Animal Practice 1974; 4: 79-89.
20. August JR. Dietary hypersensitivity in dogs: Cutaneous manifestations, diagnosis and management. Compendium on Continuing Education for the Practicing Veterinarian 1985; 7: 469-477.
21. White SD. Food hypersensitivity in 30 dogs. Journal of the American Veterinary Medical Association 1986; 188: 695-698.
22. Carlotti DN, Remy I, Prost C. Food allergy in dogs and cats. A review and report of 43 cases. Veterinary Dermatology 1990; 1: 55-62.
23. Jeffers JG, Shanley KJ, Meyer EK. Diagnostic testing of dogs for food hypersensitivity. Journal of the American Veterinary Medical Association 1991; 189: 245-250.
24. Kunkle G, Horner S. Validity of skin testing for diagnosis of food allergy in dogs. Journal of the American Veterinary Medical Association 1992; 200: 677-680.
25. Rosser EJ. Diagnosis of food allergy in dogs. Journal of the American Veterinary Medical Association 1993; 203: 259-262.
26. Harvey RG. Food allergy and dietary intolerance in dogs: A report of 25 cases. Journal of Small Animal Practice 1993; 34: 175-179.
27. Paterson S. Food hypersensitivity in 20 dogs with skin and gastrointestinal signs. Journal of Small Animal Practice 1995; 36: 529-534.
28. Roudebush P, Schick RO. Evaluation of a commercial canned lamb and rice diet for the management of adverse reactions to food in dogs. Veterinary Dermatology 1995; 5: 63-67.
29. Thompson JP. Immunologic diseases. In: Ettinger SJ, Feldman EC, eds. Textbook of Veterinary Internal Medicine, 4th ed. Philadelphia, PA: WB Saunders Co, 1995; 2004-2005.
30. White SD, Sequoia D. Food hypersensitivity in cats: 14 cases (1982-1987). Journal of the American Veterinary Medical Association 1989; 194: 692-695.
31. Rosser EJ. Food allergy in the cat: A prospective study of 13 cats. In: Ihrke PJ, Mason IS, White SD, eds. Advances in Veterinary Dermatology, vol 2. New York, NY: Pergamon Press, 1993; 33-39.
32. Guaguere E. Food intolerance in cats with cutaneous manifestations: A review of 17 cases. European Journal of Companion Animal Practice 1995; 5: 27-35.
33. Roudebush P, McKeever PJ. Evaluation of a commercial canned lamb and rice diet for the management of cutaneous adverse reactions to foods in cats. Veterinary Dermatology 1993; 4: 1-4.
34. Medleau L, Latimer KS, Duncan JR. Food hypersensitivity in a cat. Journal of the American Veterinary Medical Association 1986; 189: 692-693.
35. Batt RM, Carter MW, McLean L. Morphological and biochemical studies of a naturally occurring enteropathy in the Irish setter dog: A comparison with coeliac disease in man. Research in Veterinary Science 1984; 37: 339-346.
36. Heyman MB. Food sensitivity and eosinophilic gastroenteropathies. In: Sleisinger MH, Fordtran JS, eds. Gastrointestinal Disease, 4th ed. Philadelphia, PA: WB Saunders Co, 1989; 1113-1134.
37. Guilford WG, Badcoe LM. Development of a model of food allergy in the dog. Journal of Veterinary Internal Medicine 1992; 6: 128.
38. Baker E. Food allergy. In: Small Animal Allergy: A Practical Guide. Philadelphia, PA: Lea & Febiger, 1990; 94-118.
39. Frick OL. Pathogenesis of chronic allergic reactions using the atopic dog as a model. In: Proceedings. Annual Meeting of the Academy of Veterinary Allergy, Scottsdale, AZ, 1991: 7-10.
40. Sampson HA. Immunologic mechanisms in adverse reactions to foods. Immunology and Allergy Clinics of North America 1991; 11: 701-716.
41. Proujansky R, Winter HS, Walker WA. Gastrointestinal syndromes associated with food sensitivity. Advances in Pediatrics 1988; 35: 219-238.
42. Hayden DW, Van Kruiningen HJ. Lymphocytic-plasmacytic enteritis in German shepherd dogs. Journal of the American Animal Hospital Association 1982; 18: 89-96.
43. Walker WA. Pathophysiology of intestinal uptake and absorption of antigens in food allergy. Annals of Allergy 1987; 59: 7-16.
44. Murphy MS, Walker WA. Antigen absorption. In: Metcalfe DD, Sampson HA, Simon RA, eds. Food Allergy: Adverse Reactions to Foods and Food Additives. Boston, MA: Blackwell Scientific, 1991; 52-66.
45. Yunginger JW. Food antigens. In: Metcalfe DD, Sampson HA, Simon

RA, eds. Food Allergy: Adverse Reactions to Foods and Food Additives. Boston, MA: Blackwell Scientific, 1991; 36-51.

46. Sampson HA. Eczema and food hypersensitivity. In: Metcalfe DD, Sampson HA, Simon RA, eds. Food Allergy: Adverse Reactions to Foods and Food Additives. Boston, MA: Blackwell Scientific, 1991; 114-128.

47. Sampson HA. The role of food allergy and mediator release in atopic dermatitis. Journal of Allergy and Clinical Immunology 1988; 81: 635-645.

48. Jeffers JG, Meyer EK, Sosis EJ. Responses of dogs with food allergies to single-ingredient dietary provocation. Journal of the American Veterinary Medical Association 1991; 189: 245-250.

49. Mueller RS, Tsohalis J. Evaluation of serum allergen-specific IgE for the diagnosis of food adverse reactions in the dog. Veterinary Dermatology 1998; 9: 167-171.

50. Nichols PR, Beale KM, Morris DO. A retrospective study of canine and feline cutaneous vasculitis (abstract). In: Proceedings. Annual Members Meeting AAVD & ACVD, San Antonio, Texas, 1998: 27-28.

51. Walton GS, Parish WE, Coombs RAA. Spontaneous allergic dermatitis and enteritis in a cat. Veterinary Record 1968; 83: 35-41.

52. Stogdale L, Bomzon L, Bland van den Berg P. Food allergy in cats. Journal of the American Animal Hospital Association 1982; 18: 188-194.

53. Reedy LM. Food hypersensitivity to lamb in a cat. Journal of the American Veterinary Medical Association 1994; 204: 1039-1040.

54. Guilford WG, Jones BR, Harte JG, et al. Prevalence of food sensitivity in cats with chronic vomiting, diarrhea or pruritus (abstract). Journal of Veterinary Internal Medicine 1996; 10: 156.

55. Bernhisel-Broadbent J, Sampson HA. Cross-allergenicity in the legume botanical family in children with food hypersensitivity. Journal of Allergy and Clinical Immunology 1989; 83: 435-440.

56. Varjonen E, Savolainen J, Mattila L, et al. IgE-binding components of wheat, rye, barley and oats recognized by immunoblotting analysis with sera from adult atopic dermatitis patients. Clinical and Experimental Allergy 1994; 22: 481-489.

57. Sampson HA, Broadbent KR, Bernhisel-Broadbent J. Spontaneous release of histamine from basophils and histamine-releasing factor in patients with atopic dermatitis and food hypersensitivity. New England Journal of Medicine 1989; 321: 228-232.

58. Hillier A, Kunkle G. Inability to demonstrate food antigen-specific IgE antibodies in the serum of food allergic dogs using the PK and oral PK tests. In: Proceedings. Annual Members Meeting AAVD & ACVD, Charleston, SC, 1994: 28-29.

59. Kasadra DD, Bernardin JE, Nimmo CC. Wheat proteins. In: Pomeranz Y, ed. Advances in Cereal Science and Technology, vol. 1. St Paul, MN: American Association of Cereal Chemists, 1976; 158-236.

60. Hall EJ, Batt RM. Enhanced permeability to ^{51}Cr-EDTA in canine small intestinal disease. Journal of the American Veterinary Medical Association 1990; 196: 91-95.

61. Marsh MN. Gluten, major histocompatibility complex, and the small intestine. Gastroenterology 1992; 102: 330-354.

62. Loft DE, Marsh MN, Sandle GI, et al. Studies of intestinal lymphoid tissue. XII. Epithelial lymphocyte and mucosal responses to rectal gluten challenge in celiac sprue. Gastroenterology 1989; 97: 29-37.

63. Hall EJ, Carter SD, Barnes A, et al. Immune responses to dietary antigens in gluten-sensitive enteropathy of Irish setters. Research in Veterinary Science 1992; 53: 293-299.

64. Murdoch RD, Lessof MH, Pollock I, et al. Effects of food additives on leukocyte histamine release in normal and urticaria subjects. Journal of the Royal College of Physicians 1987; 21: 251-256.

65. Hickman MA, Rogers QR, Morris JG. Effect of diet on Heinz body formation in kittens. American Journal of Veterinary Research 1990; 50: 475-478.

66. Weiss DJ, McClay CB, Christopher MM, et al. Effects of propylene glycol-containing diets on acetaminophen-induced methemoglobinemia in cats. Journal of the American Veterinary Medical Association 1990; 196: 1816-1819.

67. Robertson JE, Christopher MM, Rogers QR. Heinz body formation in cats fed baby food containing onion powder. Journal of the American Veterinary Medical Association 1998; 212: 1260-1266.

68. Dzanis DA. Safety of ethoxyquin in dog foods. Journal of Nutrition 1991; 121: S163-S164.

69. Affolter VK, Shaw SE. Cutaneous drug eruptions. In: Ihrke PJ, Mason IS, White SD, eds. Advances in Veterinary Dermatology, vol. 2. New York, NY: Pergamon Press, 1993; 450.

70. Taylor SL. Histamine food poisoning: Toxicology and clinical aspects. CRC Critical Reviews of Toxicology 1986; 17: 91-128.

71. Morrow JD, Margolies GR, Rowland J, et al. Evidence that histamine is the causative toxin of scombroid-fish poisoning. New England Journal of Medicine 1991; 324: 716-720.

72. Guilford WG, Roudebush P, Rogers QR. The histamine content of commercial pet foods. New Zealand Veterinary Journal 1994; 42: 201-204.

73. Guraya HS, Koehler PE. Histamine in cat foods: Survey and comparison of methodologies. Veterinary and Human Toxicology 1991; 33: 124-128.

74. Bjeldanes LF, Schutz DE, Morris MM. On the aetiology of scombroid poisoning: Cadaverine potentiation of histamine toxicity in the guinea pig. Food and Cosmetic Toxicology 1978; 16: 157-159.

75. Halliwell REW. Comparative aspects of food intolerance. Veterinary Medicine 1992; 87: 893-899.

76. Hill FWG, Kelley DF. Naturally occurring intestinal malabsorption in the dog. American Journal of Digestive Diseases 1974; 19: 649-665.

77. Mundt HC, Meyer H. Pathogenesis of lactose-induced diarrhea and its prevention by enzymatic-splitting of lactose. In: Burger IH, Rivers JPW, eds. Nutrition of the Dog and Cat. New York, NY: Cambridge University Press, 1989; 267-274.

78. Meyer H, Kienzle E, Hannes M, et al. Nutrition in dogs with hydrolyzed milk. Kleintierpraxis 1984; 29: 301-308.

79. Association of American Feed Control Officials. Official Manual, 1999.

80. Roudebush P, Gross KL, Lowry SR. Protein characteristics of commercial canine and feline hypoallergenic diets. Veterinary Dermatology 1995; 5: 69-74.

81. National Research Council. Nutrient Requirements of Dogs. Washington, DC: National Academy of Sciences, 1985.

82. National Research Council. Nutrient Requirements of Cats. Washington, DC: National Academy of Sciences, 1986.

83. Goddard KM, Williams GD, Newberne PM, et al. Comparison of all-meat, semi-moist, and dry-type dog foods as diets in growing beagles. Journal of the American Veterinary Medical Association 1970; 157: 1233-1236.

84. Morris ML, Teeter SM, Collins DR. The effects of the exclusive feeding of an all-meat dog food. Journal of the American Veterinary Medical Association 1971; 158: 477-488.

85. Codner EC, Thatcher CD. The role of nutrition in the management of dermatoses. Seminars in Veterinary Medicine and Surgery 1990; 5: 167-177.

86. Lewis LD, Morris ML Jr, Hand MS. Small Animal Clinical Nutrition III. Topeka, KS: Mark Morris Associates, 1987; A3-1–A3-3.

87. Remillard RL, Thatcher CD. Dietary and nutritional management of gastrointestinal diseases. Veterinary Clinics of North America: Small Animal Practice 1989; 19: 809.

88. Meyer H. Ernahung des hundes. Stuttgart, Germany: Eugen Ulmer & Co, 1990.

89. Roudebush P. Nutritional management of the allergic patient. In: August JR, ed. Seminars in Feline Internal Medicine, 2nd ed. Philadelphia, PA: WB Saunders Co, 1994; 201-208.

90. Brown CM, Armstrong PJ, Globus H. Nutritional management of food allergy in dogs and cats. Compendium on Continuing Education for the Practicing Veterinarian 1995; 17: 637-658.

91. Strombeck DR, ed. Home-Prepared Dog and Cat Diets: The Healthful Alternative. Ames, Iowa: Iowa State University Press, 1999.

92. Devlin J, David TJ. Intolerance to oral and intravenous calcium supplements in atopic eczema. Journal of the Royal Society of Medicine 1990; 83: 497-498.

93. Taylor SL, Busse WW, Sachs MI, et al. Peanut oil is not allergenic to peanut-sensitive individuals. Journal of Allergy and Clinical Immunology 1981; 68: 372-375.

94. Nordlee JA, Taylor SL, Jones RT, et al. Allergenicity of various peanut products as determined by RAST inhibition. Journal of Allergy and Clinical Immunology 1981; 68: 376-382.

95. Bush RK, Taylor SL, Nordlee JA, et al. Soybean oil is not allergenic to soybean-sensitive individuals. Journal of Allergy and Clinical Immunology 1985; 76: 242-245.

96. Bock SA. Oral challenge procedures. In: Metcalfe DD, Sampson HA, Simon RA, eds. Food Allergy: Adverse Reactions to Foods and Food Additives. Boston, MA: Blackwell Scientific, 1991; 81-95.

97. Pastorello EA, Stocchi L, Pravetonni V, et al. Role of the elimination diet in adults with food allergy. Journal of Allergy and Clinical Immunology 1989; 84: 475-483.

CASE 14-1

Pruritic Dermatitis in a Domestic Shorthair Cat

Philip Roudebush, DVM
Diplomate ACVIM (Internal Medicine)
Hill's Science and Technology Center
Topeka, Kansas, USA

Assess the Animal

A five-year-old neutered female domestic shorthair cat was referred for severe pruritus with self trauma. The owner reported that intense pruritus had been evident for several weeks and that antihistamines given by another veterinarian had been only partially effective in decreasing the itching. The owner took systemic corticosteroids herself several years ago and developed severe side effects. Because of her experience, she was very reluctant to give corticosteroids to her cat. The owner was very upset about the intense pruritus and apologized for her cat's appearance.

The medical history was unremarkable except for intermittent bouts of lower urinary tract disease that had been treated with antibiotics and a veterinary therapeutic food. The cat spent almost all of its time indoors; no other animals were in the home.

Physical examination revealed excoriations and evidence of self trauma around the face, neck, ventral abdomen and posterior aspects of the forelimbs (Figures 1-3). No other abnormalities were noted. There was no evidence of flea infestation. The cat weighed 3.2 kg and had a body condition score of 3/5.

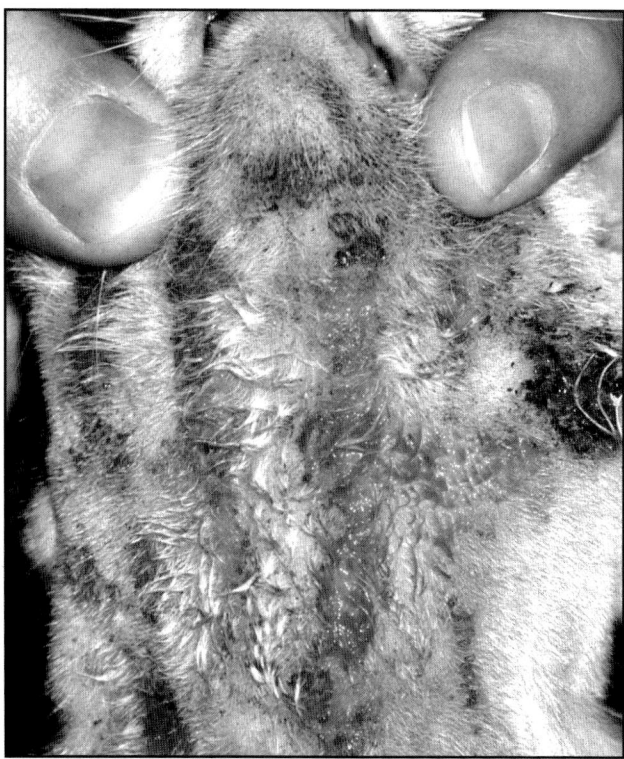

Figure 1. The ventral neck of a five-year-old female domestic shorthair cat showing evidence of severe pruritus with self trauma.[a]

Assess the Food(s) and Feeding Method

The cat was currently fed a dry veterinary therapeutic food (Prescription Diet Feline c/d[b]) and various commercial moist cat foods from the grocery store. The dry food was available free choice and small amounts of the moist foods were offered each day.

Questions

1. What are the major rule outs (differential diagnoses) for this cat's generalized pruritus?
2. If an adverse reaction to food is suspected as a cause of this cat's problem, then an elimination trial would be appropriate. What criteria should be used to select a food for the elimination trial?
3. Describe the feeding method and reassessment plan for this patient.
4. How will the history of lower urinary tract disease influence the feeding plan for this patient?

Answers and Discussion

1. The major rule outs for pruritic dermatitis in cats include:

   Dermatophytosis. Feline dermatophytosis most often appears as one or more irregular or annular areas of alopecia on the head, pinnae or paws. The alopecia may be severe and widespread, accompanied by little evidence of inflammation. Some cats have a more inflammatory reaction with pruritus and widespread papulocrustous dermatitis. Dermatophytosis is more common in young cats.

   Otodectic mange. Otodectes cynotis (ear mite) is a nonburrowing, psoroptid mite that lives on the surface of the skin. Lesions are usually restricted to the ear canal (otitis externa) but mites are commonly found on other areas of the body, especially on the neck, rump and tail. These ectopic mites often cause no disease but some animals have a pruritic dermatitis that may resemble flea-bite hypersensitivity, atopy or food allergy.

   Adverse reaction to food (food allergy or food intolerance). The intense pruritus in this patient with traumatic alopecia centered around the head, neck and ears is one of the more common clinical manifestations of adverse food reactions in cats. Other dermatologic signs of adverse food reactions in cats include severe, generalized pruritus without significant lesions, miliary dermatitis, moist dermatitis and scaling dermatoses. Angioedema, urticaria and conjunctivitis may occur in up to one-third of cats with adverse food reactions. Concurrent flea-allergy dermatitis and atopy also commonly occur in these patients.

   Arthropod hypersensitivity. Flea-bite hypersensitivity (flea-allergy dermatitis) is the most common feline hypersensitivity disease in areas where fleas are present, causing a variety of clinical syndromes all characterized by pruritus. No age, breed or gender predilections have been reported in cats. Papulocrustous eruptions are the most typical lesions, although alopecia, excoriations, crusts and scales may also be found. The presence of fleas, flea dirt, flea eggs or infection with the tapeworm *Dipylidium caninum* all provide circumstantial evidence of flea allergy. Recent bathing or grooming may, however, remove all evidence of fleas. In this case, there was no history of flea exposure and no evidence of fleas on the cat.

Atopy. Feline atopy is caused by an exaggerated or inappropriate response of the affected cat to environmental allergens. It is considered the second most common hypersensitivity in cats after flea-allergy dermatitis. The most common clinical signs are noninflammatory alopecia, eosinophilic granuloma complex lesions, miliary dermatitis and pruritus of the face or pinnae. The clinical signs in this patient are compatible with those of feline atopy although concurrent flea-bite hypersensitivity and adverse food reactions may also occur.

Irritant contact dermatitis. Contact dermatitis is an inflammatory skin reaction caused by direct contact with an offending substance. Primary irritant contact dermatitis causes cutaneous inflammation in cats without any previous exposure or sensitization. Potential causative agents include soaps (shampoos), detergents, disinfectants, weed and insecticidal (flea) sprays, insecticidal dips, fertilizers and carpet cleaners. There was no history of exposure to these types of agents.

Papulocrustous dermatitis (miliary dermatitis). Miliary dermatitis is a clinical reaction pattern commonly seen in cats with dermatologic disease. The differential diagnosis of widespread papulocrustous dermatitis in cats includes hypersensitivity reactions (flea bite, atopy, food, drug), ectoparasitisms, dermatophytosis and, rarely, nutritional imbalances (fatty acid deficiency). Miliary dermatitis should not be considered a diagnosis itself but should prompt a thorough evaluation of the patient for an underlying causative disease. Widespread papulocrustous eruptions were not found on this cat.

2. The ideal elimination food for feline patients with dermatologic disease should: 1) have limited number of protein sources, 2) have protein sources to which the animal has not been previously exposed (novel protein sources), 3) avoid excess levels of protein, 4) have high protein digestibility (greater than 87% or contain a protein hydrolysate), 5) be free of food additives, 6) avoid excessive levels of biogenic amines such as histamine, putrescine, cadaverine, etc. and 7) be nutritionally adequate for the adult cat. See Table 14-5 for a list of selected commercial cat foods that meet many of these criteria.

3. Before an elimination trial is initiated, the client should be instructed to feed the cat its usual food for seven to 14 days. During this time the client should record the type and amount of food ingested, any other ingested food items such as table scraps, treats or snacks and the occurrence and character of adverse reactions. The patient should then be fed a controlled elimination food for four to 12 weeks. No other substances such as treats, flavored vitamin supplements, fatty acid supplements or toys should be offered. During the elimination trial, the client should document daily the type and amount of food ingested, and the occurrence and character of adverse reactions. (See Figure 14-6.) This daily diary is important in documenting the progression of clinical signs during the elimination trial and will help determine whether a strict elimination trial was performed in the home environment. The diary will often document different

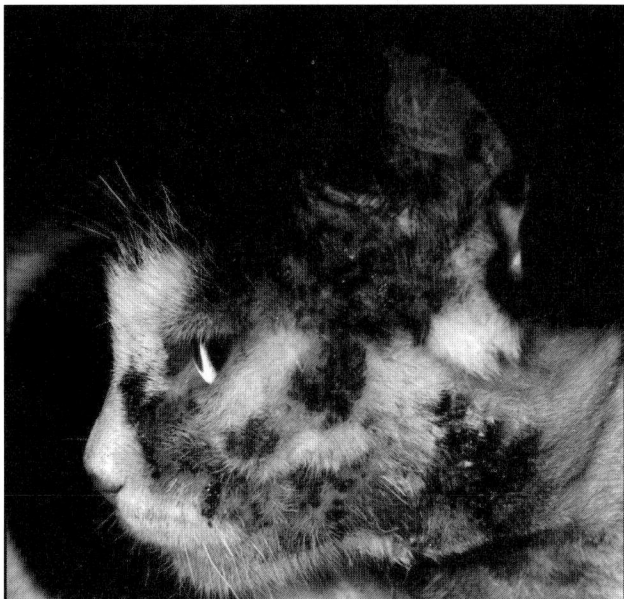

Figures 2. The head and face of the same cat with evidence of intense pruritus and self trauma.[a]

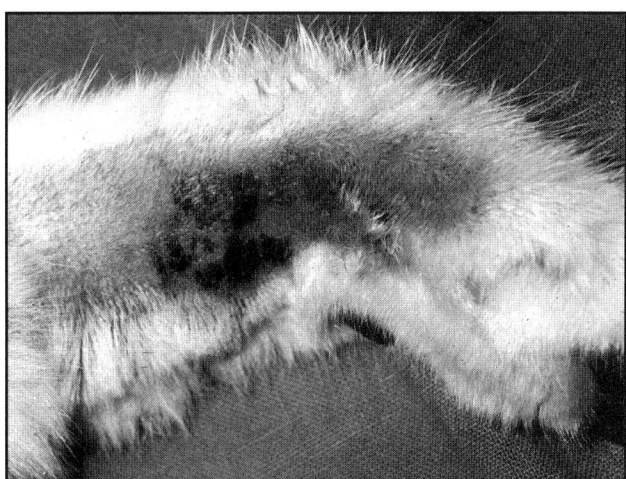

Figure 3. The antebrachium showing where excessive licking has resulted in erythroderma and hair loss.[a]

findings than those described by the client during the recheck examination.

A tentative diagnosis of an adverse food reaction is made if the level of pruritus markedly decreases. Improvement may take four to 12 weeks to become evident.

4. Further questioning revealed that this cat had previous problems with struvite urinary precipitates. The struvite precipitates had been well controlled by the veterinary therapeutic food. Struvite precipitates are prevented by offering a food that avoids excess magnesium and produces a normal acidic urine. (See Chapter 21.) Therefore, commercial or homemade elimination foods used in this patient should also avoid excess magnesium (<0.1% dry matter magnesium) and produce a normal acidic urine (urinary pH 6.2 to 6.4). The urinary pH can be checked periodically as part of the reassessment.

Progress Notes

Diagnostic evaluation included multiple skin scrapings (negative), cytologic evaluation of ear swabs (negative), Wood's lamp examination (negative), fungal culture (negative), fecal flotation (negative), complete blood count (normal) and a feline leukemia virus test (negative). A skin biopsy specimen was obtained from an area where excoriations and other evidence of self trauma were minimal. Dermatohistopathologic results were compatible with a diagnosis of allergic dermatosis. Intradermal skin testing revealed a few positive reactions to house dust mite antigen and several different mold antigens. The cat was treated with an anthelmintic twice at three-week intervals.

Food and Feeding Method

The cat was fed a homemade lamb-based food for four weeks. The food dosage was calculated to maintain current body weight and optimum body condition.

Reassessment

The cat improved slightly after being fed the homemade food for four weeks. Severe pruritus with self trauma occurred when the previous dry veterinary therapeutic food and one of the moist grocery store foods were fed. The owner refused further testing to establish exactly which ingredients in these foods were causing the problem. Nutritional therapy with a commercial canned lamb and rice food (Prescription Diet Feline d/d;[b] 0.5 can per day) was begun and the cat again responded partially.

A tentative diagnosis of concurrent atopy and adverse food reaction (probably food allergy) was made based on the positive skin test results and partial response to a dietary elimination trial. Concurrent allergies are reported to occur in up to 20% of cats with adverse reactions to food. The commercial lamb and rice food was continued at the same dosage and an antihistamine (chlorpheniramine) was used to manage periods of intermittent pruritus.

Endnotes

a. Adapted with permission from Roudebush P. Nutritional management of the allergic patient. August JR, ed. Consultations in Feline Internal Medicine, 2nd ed. Philadelphia, PA: WB Saunders Co, 1994; 201-208.

b. Hill's Pet Nutrition Inc., Topeka, KS, USA.

Bibliography

White SD, Sequoia D. Food hypersensitivity in cats: 14 cases (1982-1987). Journal of the American Veterinary Medical Association 1989; 194: 692-695.

Rosser EJ: Food allergy in the cat: A prospective study of 13 cats. In: Ihrke PJ, Mason IS, White SD, eds. Advances in Veterinary Dermatology, vol. 2. New York, NY: Pergamon Press, 1993; 33-39.

Guaguere E. Food intolerance in cats with cutaneous manifestations: A review of 17 cases. European Journal of Companion Animal Practice 1995; 5: 27-35.

Roudebush P, McKeever PJ. Evaluation of a commercial canned lamb and rice diet for the management of cutaneous adverse reactions to foods in cats. Veterinary Dermatology 1993; 4: 1-4.

CASE 14-2

Allergic Dermatitis in a German Shepherd Dog

Kevin J. Shanley, DVM
Diplomate ACVD
West Chester, Pennsylvania, USA

Assess the Animal

A seven-year-old neutered male German shepherd dog weighing 37 kg (body condition score of 3/5) was admitted with the primary complaint of moderate to severe pruritus during the previous two years. The pruritus began on the face and feet, and progressed to involve the axillae, ears and abdomen. The pruritus was nonseasonal, but worsened slightly in the summer when it also involved the dorsal lumbosacral area.

The dog spent most of its time indoors but also had access to a fenced yard for several hours a day. The other household pet, a cat, had no dermatologic disease or pruritus. None of the people associated with the dog had pruritus or dermatologic disease. The dog had three episodes of bilateral ear infections the previous year that were treated with unknown topical medications that resolved the problem.

Prior treatment with injectable and oral glucocorticoids provided marked relief but not complete remission of the pruritus. The pruritus returned within a few days of discontinuing the corticosteroid therapy. Oral antihistamines (diphenhydramine and hydroxyzine) and various medicated shampoos and topical sprays provided little benefit.

Dermatologic examination revealed marked traumatic and complete alopecia with hyperpigmentation and erythema involving the periocular areas, inner pinnae, axillae, feet and ventral abdomen (Figures 1-3). Small numbers of papules were found on the ventral abdomen. Excoriations were present in the axillae and periocular areas.

Assess the Food(s) and Feeding Method

The dog was fed a variety of commercial dry foods; the client changed brands frequently. The dry food was fed free choice. Other food sources included occasional table food, commercial canine biscuit treats, rawhide chews and flavored heartworm preventive medication, which was given monthly for nine months of the year.

Questions

1. What are the primary diseases in the differential diagnosis of this patient? What secondary diseases may be present?
2. Describe a food(s) and feeding method for this patient.
3. How might the dog's otitis externa correlate with the other evidence of dermatologic disease?

Answers and Discussion

1. The primary diseases in the differential diagnosis include:

Atopy. Most atopic patients have pruritus and clinical disease at six months to three years of age. A seasonal history also suggests atopy. This dog's dermatologic problems began at five years of age and the pruritus is nonseasonal, which is still compatible with atopy. Atopy is more common than food allergy but less common than flea allergy.

Adverse reaction to food (food allergy or food intolerance). The typical age at onset of food allergy is unclear. A recent report described an age predilection of several months to three years of age whereas previous reports did not find an age predilection. The pruritus associated with food allergy is nonseasonal and a variety of clinical presentations and distribution of lesions may be seen. The response to corticosteroid therapy is variable. Food allergy is not as common as flea allergy or atopy.

Flea-allergy dermatitis. Flea allergy usually begins at three to seven years of age and has a marked predilection for the dorsal lumbosacral area, the ventral abdomen and legs. This dog is the correct age for development of flea-allergy dermatitis, but the distribution of lesions on the face, feet and ears is not likely without more prominent disease on the dorsal lumbosacrum. The increased pruritus and involvement of the dorsal lumbosacrum in the summer suggests that flea allergy may be adding to the pruritus seasonally.

Scabies. Infestation with *Sarcoptes scabiei* is often difficult to prove. Pruritus is usually severe and nonseasonal. No age, breed or gender predilection is present. The pinnal margins, periocular areas, elbows, hocks and ventrum are usually involved. Contagion or zoonosis is present in approximately 30% of the cases. Skin scrapings are positive in 25% of affected dogs. Response to therapy may be the only way to diagnose many cases.

Dermatophytosis. The dermatologic lesions typically seen with dermatophyte infections include many of those seen in this patient. Although no strong breed or gender predilection exists, young animals are affected most often. Pruritus is variable. The distribution of lesions is quite variable but usually is not bilaterally symmetric as seen in this patient.

The secondary diseases in the differential diagnosis include:

Superficial pyoderma (bacterial folliculitis). Superficial pyoderma is a secondary infection seen with many pruritic skin diseases, including food allergy and food intolerance. *Staphylococcus intermedius* is the most common causal bacteria in dogs. Typical lesions include follicular papules, pustules, complete alopecia, epidermal collarettes, erythema and focal circular postinflammatory hyperpigmention. Oral antibiotic therapy should clear the lesions and pruritus associated with the pyoderma.

Malassezia dermatitis. Pruritus associated with *Malassezia* infection is common. *Malassezia* species proliferate in moist, hyperplastic apposed skin surfaces, particularly lip folds, nasal folds, interdigital areas, axillae, ventral abdominal skin, ear canals and the ventral neck. Underlying allergies, including adverse reactions to food, are common diseases that predispose animals to yeast infection. Topical and oral therapy may be necessary to correct the yeast infec-

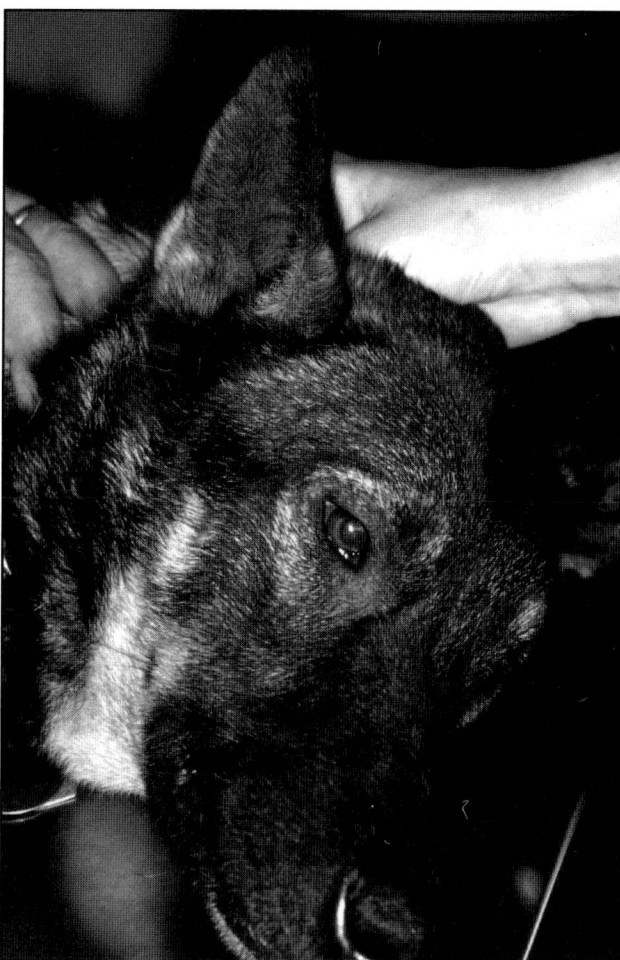

Figure 1. View of the lateral face and right pinna of a seven-year-old male German shepherd dog with periocular alopecia, hyperpigmentation, erythema and mild excoriations. The inner pinnal surface was hyperpigmented, erythematous and alopecic.

tion and will also control any pruritus associated with the *Malassezia* infection.

2. An appropriate food for an elimination trial would include limited numbers of ingredients, particularly protein and carbohydrate sources. The protein and carbohydrate sources should be novel (not ingredients that the animal has been exposed to previously). The food should avoid excessive levels of protein, should have high digestibility or contain a protein hydrolysate, and should be free of food additives and excessive levels of biogenic amines. See Table 14-5 for a list of selected commercial dog foods that meet many of these criteria.

The elimination food should be gradually introduced over several days as the current food is discontinued. The pet owner should feed only the elimination food for up to three months. For this patient, the table food, biscuit snacks, rawhide chews and flavored heartworm medication should also be discontinued. A nonchewable heartworm medication can be used. The client should keep a daily diary to record the clinical progress and degree of pruritus, as well as any other foods, table scraps, treats or snacks given in addition to the elimination food. (See Figure 14-6.)

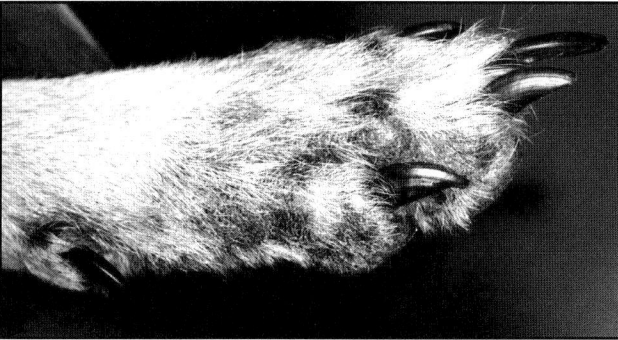

Figure 2. View of the left front foot showing traumatic alopecia with hyperpigmentation and focal excoriations.

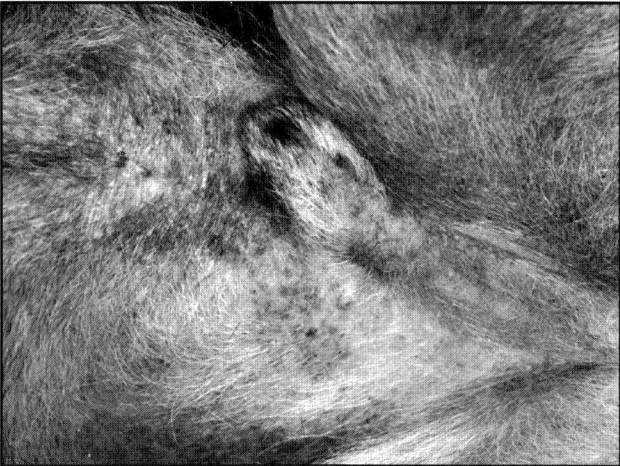

Figure 3. The ventral abdomen and medial thighs showing mild alopecia, hyperpigmentation, erythema and papules.

The client should be instructed to watch for a marked (at least 50%) decrease in the pruritus. Periodic re-examination by the veterinarian will help monitor the patient's progress and help reinforce the feeding restrictions.

3. Otitis externa is a frequent clinical presentation with atopy and adverse food reactions. One study found that many dogs with adverse food reactions presented with only ear problems and no other dermatologic disease. Food allergy and food intolerance should always be suspected in dogs with chronic or recurrent otitis externa. Although otitis externa is usually bilateral, some patients may present with unilateral otitis.

Diagnosis of otitis externa is best accomplished with otoscopic examination and impression smears of aural exudate. Underlying allergies often predispose the animal to otic bacterial and yeast infections.

Progress Notes

Flea combing revealed no fleas or flea dirt; skin scrapings were also negative. Impression smears of the affected areas revealed few cocci or neutrophils. No *Malassezia* species were present. Intradermal allergy testing revealed no reactions to any of the inhaled allergens that were tested.

Food and Feeding Method

A commercial dry food composed of lamb meal and rice was initiated and fed exclusively for six weeks. The food dosage was calculated to maintain the dog's current body weight and optimal body condition.

Reassessment

The pruritus decreased dramatically over several days. After minimal pruritus was noted for one week, one of the previously fed dog foods was given for seven days. By the third day, there was a significant return of the pruritus at all of the previously affected sites. The elimination food was reinitiated and the pruritus resolved in 10 days.

After the pruritus decreased, individual food ingredients were added to the elimination food for up to seven days each. These challenge ingredients were derived from the list of foods and ingredients that had been fed previously. The ingredients included beef, chicken, corn, wheat, eggs and milk. Marked pruritus occurred when beef was fed and moderate pruritus when corn was fed. The final diagnosis was an adverse reaction (food allergy or food intolerance) to beef, corn and possibly other ingredients that were not tested. The commercial food used in the elimination trial was continued because it was complete and balanced for maintenance of adult dogs.

Bibliography

White SD. Food hypersensitivity in 30 dogs. Journal of the American Veterinary Medical Association 1986; 188: 695-698.

Carlotti DN, Remy I, Prost C. Food allergy in dogs and cats. A review and report of 43 cases. Veterinary Dermatology 1990; 1: 55-62.

Jeffers JG, Shanley KJ, Meyer EK. Diagnostic testing of dogs for food hypersensitivity. Journal of the American Veterinary Medical Association 1991; 189: 245-250.

Rosser EJ. Diagnosis of food allergy in dogs. Journal of the American Veterinary Medical Association 1993; 203: 259-262.

Harvey RG. Food allergy and dietary intolerance in dogs: A report of 25 cases. Journal of Small Animal Practice 1993; 34: 175-179.

CASE 14-3

Protein-Losing Enteropathy in a Dog

W. Grant Guilford, BVSc, BPhil, PhD, FACVSc
Diplomate ACVIM (Internal Medicine)
School of Veterinary Medicine
Massey University, New Zealand

Assess the Animal

An eight-year-old, male English setter was referred with the primary complaints of diarrhea and weight loss of six months' duration. The diarrhea had been continuous over this period but varied in severity. The feces were very liquid, increased in volume and pale yellow. No fecal blood or mucus had been seen. The dog defecated four to five times per day. The weight loss was classified as moderately severe by the owner. There had been no vomiting. The dog's appetite and demeanor remained normal. Past treatments included a variety of antibiotics and gut protectants to which there had been no response. Physical examination revealed a thin (body condition score of 2/5), bright and alert dog that weighed 27 kg. The remainder of the physical examination was normal.

The problems identified were chronic small bowel diarrhea with associated weight loss. Diagnostic procedures included fecal flotations, fecal culture, serum trypsin-like immunoreactivity, complete blood count, serum biochemistry profile, gastroduodenoscopy, endoscopic pinch biopsy of the stomach and duodenum, quantitative bacterial culture of the small intestine and rectal mucosal biopsy.

The most significant laboratory abnormality was panhypoproteinemia (albumin 1.51 g/dl [reference range = 2.2 to 3.5 g/dl]; globulin 2.39 g/dl [reference range = 2.2 to 4.5 g/dl]). Endoscopy findings included mildly increased duodenal mucosal granularity and friability. Results of histopathologic examination of gastric biopsy specimens showed a very mild lymphocytic gastritis; duodenal and rectal histopathologic results included mild to moderate plasmacytic-lymphocytic enteritis and colitis. Results of quantitative bacterial culture of the small intestine were normal. The tentative diagnosis was mild inflammatory bowel disease and protein-losing enteropathy.

Assess the Food(s) and Feeding Method

The dog's food(s) before and during the diarrheic episode were a variety of moist and dry commercial dog foods fed free choice. The dog's water intake was increased but there had been no polyuria.

Questions

1. What are the key nutritional factors to consider in this patient?
2. Calculate the energy requirements for this patient.

Answers and Discussion

1. The ideal food for dogs with chronic small bowel-type diarrhea should: 1) be highly digestible, 2) be free of gluten (gliadin), 3) have a limited number of protein sources to which the dog has not been recently exposed (novel proteins), 4) be isoosmolar and 5) avoid excess fat and lactose.

   Protein requirements increase in patients with protein-losing enteropathy because of excessive protein loss. Excess fat should be avoided during gastrointestinal dysfunction because malabsorbed fatty acids and bile acids cause secretory diarrhea.

2. The patient's resting energy requirement (RER) calculated at the current weight (27 kg) would be approximately 880 kcal/day (3,682 kJ/day), but that would increase to 1,000 kcal/day (4,184 kJ/day) for the patient's ideal body weight of 30 kg. To calculate this dog's daily energy requirement to achieve optimal body

condition, the factor used to multiply times the RER must be greater than that used in calculations for normal mature dogs. The dog's daily energy requirement would be 1,600 to 2,000 kcal (6,694 to 8,368 kJ). The body condition score should be monitored closely.

Therapy Including Feeding Plan

The dog was initially treated with prednisone for five weeks (60 mg twice daily for 14 days; then 40 mg once daily for 14 days; then 20 mg once daily for one week) but the feeding plan was not modified. At five weeks, the dog was re-examined. Its body weight remained constant despite an improved appetite. The diarrhea had improved to a "cow pat" consistency. Albumin (2.58 g/dl) and globulin (2.91 g/dl) concentrations had improved markedly. When the dog was re-examined endoscopically, scattered shallow erosions were visible in the gastric antrum; these were attributed to the prednisone therapy. Histopathologic examination of biopsy specimens taken from the small intestine during endoscopy showed that the prednisone therapy had had little effect. The histologic diagnosis remained mild to moderate plasmacytic-lymphocytic enterocolitis.

After the dog was discharged after the five-week recheck, the owner was instructed to prepare a homemade food of chicken and rice with added vitamins and minerals. Food dosage was calculated to achieve optimal body condition. Within three days of this food change, the dog's stools became firm and remained normal thereafter. Nine months later, the dog's body weight had improved to 31 kg and the body condition score was 3/5. Serum albumin and globulin levels were 2.71 g/dl and 4.21 g/dl.

Further Discussion

This case suggests that protein-losing enteropathy can accompany food sensitivity. Protein exudation into the bowel has been demonstrated during gastrointestinal type I hypersensitivity responses in laboratory animals and may occur in clinical patients.

The lack of complete response to prednisone emphasizes that corticosteroids often will not control the clinical signs of food-sensitive patients without concurrent feeding of a suitable hypoallergenic food. This case also illustrates how closely food sensitivity can mimic the clinical and histologic findings of idiopathic inflammatory bowel disease.

Bibliography

Guilford WG. Adverse reactions to food: A gastrointestinal perspective. Compendium on Continuing Education for the Practicing Veterinarian 1994; 16: 957-969.

Patrick MK, Gall DG. Protein intolerance and immunocyte and enterocyte interaction. Pediatric Clinics of North America 1988; 35: 17-34.

CHAPTER 15

Skin and Hair Disorders

Philip Roudebush

Candace A. Sousa

Dawn E. Logas

"Dermatoses affecting various species of animals are more commonly associated with malnutrition than they are with . . . a good state of nutrition."
F Kral and BJ Novak. Veterinary Dermatology, 1953

ASSESSMENT

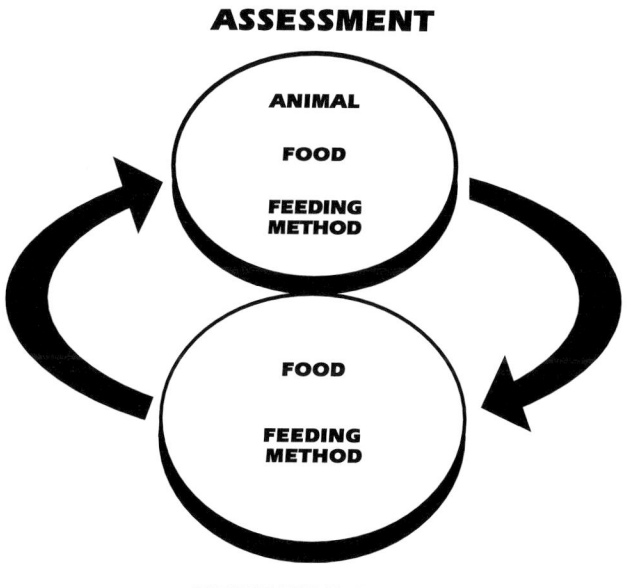

FEEDING PLAN

Note: The reader is referred to Chapter 1 for a detailed discussion of the iterative process of clinical nutrition.

CLINICAL IMPORTANCE

Very little information is available concerning the demographics of canine and feline skin and hair disorders. Surveys and textbooks suggest that skin disorders are the most common reason for patient visits to the veterinarian's office.[1] Surveys also indicate that 15 to 25% of all small animal practice activity is involved with the diagnosis and treatment of problems with the skin and coat.[1]

The most commonly diagnosed canine skin disorders are: 1) allergy (flea-bite hypersensitivity, atopy), 2) cutaneous neoplasms, 3) bacterial pyoderma, 4) seborrhea, 5) parasitic dermatoses, 6) adverse reactions to food (food hypersensitivity or food intolerance), 7) immune-mediated dermatoses and 8) endocrine dermatoses.[2,3] The most common feline skin disorders are: 1) abscesses, 2) parasitic dermatoses, 3) allergy (flea-bite hypersensitivity, atopy), 4) miliary dermatitis, 5) eosinophilic granuloma complex, 6) fungal infections, 7) adverse reactions to food, 8) psychogenic dermatoses, 9) seborrheic conditions, 10) neoplastic tumors and 11) immune-mediated dermatoses.[3,4]

Clearly, skin and hair disorders are an important part of small animal practice; bacterial infections, ectoparasitisms, allergies, fungal infections and neoplasia are common problems. Aside from adverse reactions to food, nutritional skin diseases in pets fed nutritionally adequate commercial pet food appear to be very uncommon. However, the skin and coat can be affected by many nutritional factors (See Key Nutritional Factors—Skin and Hair Disorders.), and many pet owners are anxious to improve the quality and appearance of their animal's coat. This emphasizes the importance

KEY WORDS & TERMS—SKIN AND HAIR DISORDERS*

Achromotrichia	Fatty acid	Phytin/phytate/phytic acid
Alopecia	Hair cycle	Protein-calorie malnutrition
Anagen	Hyperkeratosis	Retinoid-responsive dermatoses
Anagen defluxion	Hyperplasia	Retinoids
Atopy	Keratin	Scale
Catagen	Keratinization	Telogen
Crust	Melanin	Telogen defluxion
Dermis	Nutrient-responsive dermatoses	Trichography/trichogram
EFA-responsive dermatoses	Orthokeratosis	Vitamin E-responsive dermatoses
Epidermis	Parakeratosis	Xerosis
Essential fatty acids (EFA)	Paronychia	Zinc-responsive dermatoses

*Key words and terms are defined in the Glossary.

KEY POINTS—SKIN AND HAIR DISORDERS

1. Pet owners often want to improve the quality and appearance of their animal's coat.
2. Most skin and coat changes due to nutritional deficiencies occur in young growing animals or adult females during gestation and lactation.
3. The cutaneous changes associated with nutritional abnormalities are often indistinguishable from other more common skin diseases.
4. Examining the bulb and shaft of plucked hairs microscopically is helpful in diagnosing some nutritional diseases.
5. Skin biopsy should be performed within three weeks for any dermatosis that does not respond to initial management with a food change or nutritional supplementation.
6. Analysis of the chemical composition of hair is not a routinely used diagnostic technique.
7. Telogen defluxion is usually recognized as hair loss associated with a stressful event.
8. Dogs with severe primary seborrhea may have increased nutrient requirements.
9. Metabolic epidermal necrosis can be associated with hypoaminoacidemia.
10. Clinical signs resembling those caused by an essential fatty acid deficiency can also be induced by a deficiency in other nutrients.
11. Copper availability varies widely among plant and animal feed ingredients.
12. Zinc and essential fatty acid metabolism interact and are closely linked.
13. Retinoic acid influences the skin by binding to and activating a specific set of cell nuclear receptors.
14. It is unlikely for vitamin A, vitamin E or B-complex vitamin deficiencies to occur in dogs and cats eating typical commercial pet foods.
15. Zinc-responsive skin lesions have been frequently described in rapidly growing puppies.
16. Zinc-responsive cutaneous disease is usually confirmed by characteristic dermatohistopathologic changes, such as marked parakeratotic hyperkeratosis.
17. Essential fatty acid supplementation can influence transepidermal water loss.
18. Cutaneous disease due to nutrient deficiency will usually respond rapidly and dramatically to appropriate nutritional change or supplementation.

of understanding the nutritional factors that affect normal skin and hair and the nutritional factors that should be investigated in animals with skin disorders. This chapter discusses the nutritional factors that affect skin and hair, except for adverse reactions to food (food allergy and food intolerance), which are specifically addressed in Chapter 14, and nutritional modification of inflammatory skin disease, which is addressed in Chapter 26.

ASSESSMENT

Assess the Animal

History

The signalment (species, breed, age, gender, reproductive status, hair color) is an important part of the historical information that should be obtained for patients with

dermatologic problems and especially those with possible nutritional disorders (Table 15-1). Both dogs and cats develop nutritionally related skin and hair disorders, although certain conditions such as zinc-responsive dermatoses are best characterized in dogs.

The age of the animal is important; most skin and coat changes due to nutritional deficiencies occur in young growing animals or adult females during gestation and lactation. The requirement for most nutrients is highest during growth and lactation, which accounts for the increase in nutritionally related skin and hair problems seen during these lifestages. As an example, a biotin-deficient food will cause dermatitis, alopecia, dull fur and achromotrichia when fed to young growing kittens but will not cause similar clinical signs when fed to nonlactating adult cats.[5] There are many other examples of nutritional skin diseases that occur during periods of increased nutritional demand but do not occur during the normal adult lifestage. This age-related phenomenon is complicated by the fact that congenital defects of the integument and cer-

KEY NUTRITIONAL FACTORS—SKIN AND HAIR DISORDERS

Factors	Associated conditions	Nutritional recommendations

Protein and energy	Keratinization abnormalities
	Loss of normal hair color
	Secondary bacterial or yeast infection
	Impaired wound healing
	Decubital ulcers
	Telogen defluxion
	Anagen defluxion
		Avoid protein and energy deficiency
		  Adult maintenance
		    Dog: Protein = 25 to 30% (dry matter basis)
		            Fat = 10 to 15% (dry matter basis)
		    Cat: Protein = 30 to 45% (dry matter basis)
		            Fat = 15 to 25% (dry matter basis)
		  Growth/lactation
		    Dog: Protein = 30 to 35% (dry matter basis)
		            Fat = 15 to 30% (dry matter basis)
		    Cat: Protein = 35 to 50% (dry matter basis)
		            Fat = 20 to 35% (dry matter basis)
		Use food with dry matter digestibility >80%

Essential fatty acids	Excessive scales (seborrhea sicca)
	Alopecia
	Dry, dull coat
	Lack of normal hair growth
	Erythroderma
	Interdigital exudation
		Avoid fatty acid deficiency
		    Dog: Linoleic acid >1.0% (dry matter basis)
		    Cat: Linoleic acid >0.5% (dry matter basis)
		Some dogs and cats respond to levels in excess of those listed above
		Provide adequate levels and availability of zinc, B-complex vitamins and vitamin E

Zinc	Alopecia
	Skin ulceration
	Dermatitis
	Paronychia
	Foot pad disease
	Slow hair growth
	Buccal margin ulceration
	Hyperkeratotic plaques
	Secondary bacterial or yeast infection
		Avoid zinc deficiency
		    Dog: 100 to 200 mg/kg food (dry matter basis)
		    Cat: 50 to 150 mg/kg food (dry matter basis)
		Avoid excess calcium
		  Higher levels of zinc should be present in foods with calcium >1.5%
		    (dry matter basis)
		Avoid excess copper (copper < 200 mg/kg food; dry matter basis)
		Avoid essential fatty acid deficiency (see above)
		Zinc supplementation (Do not give with food)
		  Zinc sulfate 10 mg/kg body weight/day per os
		                   10 to 15 mg/kg body weight/week IV
		  Zinc methionine 2 mg/kg body weight/day

Copper	Loss of normal color
	Dull or rough hair coat
	Reduced density of hair
	Alopecia
		Avoid copper deficiency
		    Dog: >5 to 10 mg/kg food (dry matter basis)
		    Cat: >15 mg/kg food (dry matter basis)
		Avoid excess zinc (zinc <1,000 mg/kg food; dry matter basis)
		Avoid ingredients that have low copper availability
		  Copper oxide
		  Liver from simple-stomached mammals
		Avoid excess calcium
		  Higher levels of copper should be present in foods with calcium >1.5%
		    (dry matter basis)

Vitamin A	Seborrheic skin disease
	  (mainly cocker spaniel breed)
	Keratinization disorders
	Chin acne
	Nasodigital hyperkeratosis
	Ear margin seborrhea/dermatosis
	Callus
	Actinic keratosis
	Cutaneous neoplasms
	Schnauzer comedo syndrome
	Sebaceous adenitis
	Lamellar ichthyosis
		Treatment with retinoids: See Table 15-4 for details
		
		Vitamin A alcohol
		  625 to 1,000 U/kg body weight, q24h, per os
		  10,000 U q24h, per os cocker spaniel, miniature schnauzer
		  50,000 U q24h, per os Labrador retriever
		Tretinoin
		  Apply topically q12 to 24h
		Isotretinoin
		  1 to 3 mg/kg body weight, q24h, per os
		Etretinate
		  0.75 to 1.0 mg/kg body weight, q24h, per os

Vitamin E	Discoid lupus erythematosus Systemic lupus erythematosus Pemphigus erythematosus Sterile panniculitis Acanthosis nigricans Dermatomyositis Ear margin vasculitis	Treatment with vitamin E Dog: 200 to 800 IU twice daily, per os

tain parasitic, fungal and bacterial infections of the skin are also more common in dogs and cats younger than six months. Gender and reproductive status affect the prevalence of certain skin problems, but they are not usual risk factors in nutritional skin disorders, unless the increased nutritional demands of pregnancy or lactation are present.

The clinician should obtain a complete medical history in all cases. Specific details of the dermatologic history are found in other references.[1] The nutritional history should focus on the adequacy of the specific food for the animal's

Table 15-1. Breed predilection for non-neoplastic skin diseases often managed by food changes or supplementation.*

Breed	Disease
Airedale terrier	Atopy
Akita	Sebaceous adenitis
Basenji	Atopy
Basset hound	Atopy
Beagle	Atopy
Boston terrier	Atopy
Boxer	Atopy
	Adverse reactions to food
Bull terrier	Atopy
	Acrodermatitis
	Zinc-responsive dermatosis
Chesapeake Bay retriever	Atopy
Dalmatian	Atopy
English bulldog	Atopy
German shepherd dog	Atopy
	Adverse reactions to food
	Seborrhea, primary
Golden retriever	Atopy
Gordon setter	Atopy
Irish setter	Atopy
	Seborrhea, primary
Labrador retriever	Atopy
	Adverse reactions to food
	Seborrhea, primary
Lhasa apso	Atopy
Malamute	Zinc-responsive dermatosis
Old English sheepdog	Atopy
Poodle, standard	Sebaceous adenitis
Pug	Atopy
Schnauzer, miniature	Atopy
Shar Pei	Atopy
	Adverse reactions to food
Shih Tzu	Atopy
Siberian husky	Zinc-responsive dermatosis
Spaniels	Atopy (American cocker)
	Adverse reactions to food
	Seborrhea, primary
Terriers	Atopy
Vizsla	Sebaceous adenitis

*Atopy is often managed with fatty acid supplementation, sebaceous adenitis and primary seborrhea with retinoid supplementation, zinc-responsive dermatosis with zinc supplementation and adverse reactions to food with dietary changes. Specific nutrient deficiencies are usually not breed-specific.

lifestage, and types and dosages of nutritional supplements. The veterinarian or a veterinary nutritionist should evaluate home-prepared foods for nutritional adequacy (See Chapter 6.) because nutrient deficiencies or imbalances are more likely to occur in animals eating homemade vs. commercial foods. Excessive nutrient levels in food can cause skin disease due to direct toxicosis or interaction with other nutrients in the food.

Physical Examination

A comprehensive physical examination that evaluates all body systems should be performed on patients with skin or hair disease. Internal disease is often manifested as skin and coat disease, and this diagnostic possibility should not be overlooked by concentrating on the integumentary changes alone.

The skin can be affected by many nutritional factors, but usually responds in a limited number of ways. The cutaneous changes associated with nutritional abnormalities are often indistinguishable from those caused by other more common skin diseases. (See sidebar "The Skin in Pictures.") Changes that raise the suspicion for nutritional abnormalities include: 1) a sparse, dry, dull and brittle coat with hairs

that epilate easily, 2) slow hair growth or slow regrowth from areas that have been clipped, 3) abnormal scale accumulation (seborrhea sicca), 4) loss of hair, erythema or crusting in areas of friction or stretch such as the distal extremities, 5) decubital ulcers and poor wound healing and 6) loss of normal hair color. Primary lesions such as papules and pustules rarely occur with nutritional abnormalities, but can occur with bacterial pyoderma secondary to nutritional, allergic or other underlying problems.

Laboratory and Other Clinical Information

Routine laboratory evaluations including a complete blood count, serum biochemistry profile, urinalysis and thyroid panel are rarely helpful in evaluating nutritional skin disease. However, these tests can be used to rule out internal or metabolic diseases as causes of cutaneous problems.

Routine laboratory procedures for patients with dermatologic problems include skin scrapings for parasites, hair examination, cytologic examination of tissue or fluids, fungal culture, bacterial culture and biopsy for dermatohistopathologic examination. Of these procedures, hair examination and dermatohistopathology are most helpful for evaluation of potential nutritional problems.

HAIR EXAMINATION

Plucking hairs from the skin and examining them microscopically is termed trichography. This technique helps diagnose a number of conditions including nutritional diseases. Trichography is performed by grasping a small number of hairs with the fingertips or hemostats, pulling them completely, laying them on a microscope slide, adding mineral oil and examining them with the low-power objective of the microscope.

The hair bulbs are examined first. Hairs do not grow continuously but rather in cycles. Each cycle consists of a growing period (anagen), during which the follicle is actively growing hair, a transitional period (catagen) and a resting period (telogen), during which the hair is retained in the follicle as a dead or club hair that is subsequently lost.[1] Anagen hair bulbs are rounded, smooth, shiny, glistening, often pigmented and soft, so the root may bend. In some cases, the end of the anagen bulb is tightly attached to the dermal papilla and when plucked the hair appears squared at the tip with a slight flair; likened to a "pant's leg." Telogen bulbs are club- or spear-shaped, rough-surfaced, nonpigmented and generally straight. Normal adult animals have a mixture of anagen and telogen hairs, the ratio of which varies with the season and other factors. Estimation of the ratio of anagen to telogen hair bulbs can be useful. All the hair of normal animals should not be in telogen; this finding suggests a diagnosis of telogen defluxion or follicular arrest. Inappropriate numbers of telogen hairs (e.g., mostly telogen hairs during the summer when the ratio should be about 50:50) suggest a diagnosis of nutritional, endocrine or metabolic disease.[1] In people, the ratio of telogen to anagen hair increases with prolonged protein deficiency.[6] Unfortunately, well-established normal trichogram values are not available in veterinary medicine, limiting their usefulness. The use of site, age, breed and climate matched controls, if possible, may increase the usefulness of this diagnostic technique.

Examination of the hair shaft follows bulbar examination. A normal hair shaft is uniform in diameter and tapers gently to the tip. The hairs may be straight or twisted depending on the coat type of the animal. All hairs should have a clearly discernible cuticle, and a sharply demarcated cortex and medulla. Hair pigmentation depends on the coat color and breed of animal. Hairs that are inappropriately curled, misshapen and malformed suggest an underlying nutritional or metabolic disease.[1] When unusual pigmentation is observed, external sources (salivary staining, chemicals, topical medications), nutritional disorders, color dilution/color mutant disorders and endocrine disorders should be considered.[1]

Hairs with a normal shaft that are suddenly and cleanly broken indicate external trauma from licking, scratching or grooming. Breakage of hairs with abnormal shafts suggests nutritional disorders, dermatophytosis or congenitohereditary disorders such as color dilution alopecia. Morphologic changes in the hair bulb and hair diameter are sensitive indicators of overall protein status. Hair bulb atrophy, constriction and hair depigmentation may be seen in people after as little as two weeks of protein deprivation.[6] Protein deprivation may not produce changes as rapidly in dog and cat hair because the hair in these species spends more time in telogen and less time in anagen.

BIOPSY AND DERMATOHISTOPATHOLOGY

The following are general guidelines for when a skin biopsy should be performed: 1) all obviously neoplastic or suspected neoplastic lesions, 2) all persistent ulcerations, 3) any case involving a major disease that is most readily diagnosed by biopsy (e.g., immune-mediated skin disease), 4) a dermatosis that is unresponsive to conventional therapy, 5) any unusual or serious dermatosis and 6) vesicular dermatitis. Some nutritional skin diseases, such as zinc-responsive dermatosis, have clearly delineated histopathologic lesions that are easily recognized during microscopic examination of a skin biopsy specimen. In general, skin biopsy should be performed within three weeks for any dermatosis that does not respond to appropriate therapy. This includes those dermatoses that do not respond to initial management with a food change or supplementation.

CHEMICAL COMPOSITION OF HAIR

Some investigators and clinicians have advocated the use of chemical analysis of hair as a useful diagnostic technique. Hair is a complex tissue consisting of several morphologic components (epicuticle, exocuticle, endocuticle, medulla); each component has a different chemical composition. Chemical composition of hair is influenced by genetic factors, nutrition, environmental effects and cosmetic treatment.[7-9] These complex factors and the expense of analysis make it unlikely that chemical composition of hair will be routinely used as a diagnostic technique.

Hair, depending on its moisture content, consists of 65 to 95% protein. The remaining constituents are water, lipids, pigment and trace elements. The amount of moisture in hair plays a critical role in its physical and cosmetic properties. Moisture of hair often depends on relative humidity; as relative humidity increases from 29 to 70%, the approximate moisture content of hair increases from 6 to 14%.[7]

Hair consists of surface (external) lipid and internal lipid. In addition, part of the internal lipid is free lipid and part is structural lipid of the cell membrane complex. Skin surface lipids of cats and dogs contain more sterol esters, free cholesterol esters and diester waxes, but fewer triglyc-

erides, monoglycerides, free fatty acids, monoester waxes and squalene than do skin surface lipids of people.[1] It has been suggested that the skin surface lipids of cats and dogs are mainly of epidermal origin, whereas those of people are mainly of sebaceous gland origin.[1]

Hair generally has very low mineral content (less than 1%), and it is difficult to determine whether this inorganic matter is derived from extraneous sources or whether it arises during fiber synthesis. Hair length and pigmentation intensity have been reported to affect concentrations of zinc and other macro and trace elements in canine hair.[8,9] Zinc and copper concentrations in hair from normal cats have also been documented.[10]

Risk Factors for Nutritionally Related Skin Disease

Genotype, lifestage, food type and food supplementation are risk factors for nutritionally related skin disease. Breed predilection determines the prevalence of some skin disorders. Tables of common skin diseases categorized by breed are readily available (Table 15-1). In general, more than 30 dog breeds are at increased risk for skin diseases.[11] The nutrient-sensitive skin diseases such as zinc-responsive dermatoses and retinoid-responsive dermatoses often occur in specific breeds. As an example, one form of zinc-responsive dermatosis is frequently seen in arctic-type dog breeds such as malamutes and Siberian husky dogs.

As mentioned before, nutrient deficiencies that cause skin disease are more likely to occur during growth, gestation, lactation and illness when nutritional requirements are highest.

Some dry commercial generic, private label brand and grocery pet foods have lower fat content, lower nutrient digestibility and higher mineral content than other grocery and specialty brands. Low amounts of fat and poor-quality fat are risk factors for essential fatty acid deficiency; poor nutrient digestibility contributes to protein-energy malnutrition, especially during growth and lactation; and high levels of minerals such as calcium inhibit the absorption of nutrients such as zinc, which are essential for normal, healthy skin.

An animal that obtains most of its nutrients from home-prepared foods is at risk for several nutritional problems. (See Chapter 6.) In general, homemade foods lack adequate calcium, essential fatty acids, certain vitamins and other micronutrients.[12] Homemade foods should include: 1) a calcium source such as bone meal, oyster shell or dicalcium phosphate, 2) a source of essential fatty acids such as corn oil, safflower oil or some other vegetable oil and 3) a multivitamin-trace mineral supplement. Also, homemade cat foods should be supplemented with taurine.

The final risk factor for nutritionally related skin disease is oversupplementation with naturally occurring foods or commercial supplements. Vitamin A toxicosis is associated with excessive use of liver as a supplement. High levels of minerals such as calcium in commercial supplements can interfere with absorption of essential trace elements such as zinc.

The Skin as a Metabolic Organ

The skin is the largest organ of the body and the anatomic and physiologic barrier between the animal and its environment. The skin protects against water loss and physical, chemical and microbiologic injury while its sensory components perceive heat, cold, pain, touch, pruritus and pressure.[1] In addition, the skin is contiguous with several internal organs and may reflect internal pathologic processes. The subcutis, skin and hair of a newborn puppy represent 24% of its body weight, which decreases in some breeds to only 12 to 14% of mature body weight.[13]

The skin and coat significantly influence nutrient requirements. The ability of an animal's coat to regulate body temperature and energy requirements in cold environments correlates closely with hair length, thickness, density and with the medullation of individual hair fibers. In general, coats composed of long, fine, poorly medullated fibers are the most efficient for thermal insulation at low environmental temperatures and thus help modulate energy requirements. The skin also influences water requirements by minimizing transepidermal moisture loss. Loss of this normal barrier function as a result of fatty acid deficiency can increase an animal's water requirement, which is clinically manifested as polydipsia.[14-16]

The hair cycle, and thus the coat, is influenced by the general state of health, genetics, photoperiod, ambient temperature, hormones, nutrition and poorly understood intrinsic factors.[1,17]

Hair growth rate varies by breed, season, body region and length of hair. Canine and feline hair is replaced in a mosaic pattern because neighboring hair follicles are in different stages of the hair cycle at any one time. Hair replacement occurs predominantly in response to photoperiod, and to a lesser extent, to ambient temperature. In temperate latitudes, hair follicle activity, and thus hair growth rate, is maximal in summer and minimal in winter.[1,17]

Dog breeds can be classified as having high, moderate and low weights of hair. Long-haired breeds with relatively large body surface areas per body weight, such as Pomeranians, have the largest relative amount of hair. Estimates indicate that as much as 30% of protein in food is needed to maintain daily hair growth in small breeds with long coats.[8,9] On the other hand, larger dogs with short coats may use less than 10% of food protein to maintain daily hair growth.[8,9] Whether dogs of similar body surface areas have different requirements for protein and other nutrients based solely on their type of coat is unknown, but of possible clinical significance. For example, there may be differences in nutrient requirements during peak hair growth for a Pomeranian vs. a Chihuahua or an Old English sheepdog vs. a German shorthaired pointer based on coat type alone.

The epidermis has a renewable cell population. Keratinocytes migrate from the mitotically active pool in the basal layer of the epidermis, through the spinous layer and granular layer, and finally into the superficial stratum corneum, followed by normal exfoliation. The normal canine epidermis has a very slowly renewing cell population. Only 1.5% of epidermal basal cells undergo DNA replication at any point in time.[18-20] In dogs, it takes approximately 22 days for cells to migrate from the basal layer to, but not through, the stratum corneum.

The upper external root sheath of the hair follicle and sebaceous gland have essentially the same cell kinetic growth characteristics as the surface epidermis.[18-20] Conversely, the root matrix of anagen hairs is one of the most rapidly renewing cell populations of the body.[19] In actively growing hair, up to 24% of cells are undergoing DNA replication.

Key Nutritional Factors

PROTEIN AND ENERGY

As mentioned previously, the integument is a metabolically active organ that is affected by the nutritional status of the animal. Protein and energy are required for the development of new hair and skin. Developing hair requires sulfur-containing and other amino acids. Therefore, for normal skin and hair, it is important for the animal's food to provide optimal protein quantity, quality (appropriate levels of essential amino acids) and digestibility. Animals have increased protein and energy requirements during growth, gestation, lactation and illness. Abnormal skin and hair will often be noted if nutritionally inadequate foods are fed during these stages.[21,22] Optimal nutrient profiles for various lifestages of dogs and cats are listed in Chapters 9 and 11.

Foods inadequate in protein and energy can cause keratinization abnormalities, depigmentation of hair and changes in epidermal and sebaceous lipids. The skin loses its protective barrier function in animals with protein-energy malnutrition and becomes more susceptible to secondary bacterial or yeast infection. Impaired wound healing and decubital ulcers are also sequelae to protein-energy malnutrition. Protein-deficient animals have patchy alopecia and coats that are dry, dull and brittle.

Telogen defluxion is usually recognized as hair loss associated with a stressful event (e.g., pregnancy, severe illness, surgery) that causes the abrupt, premature cessation of growth of many anagen hair follicles and the synchronization of these hair follicles in catagen, then in telogen.[1,23] Short-term increased requirements of energy, protein and other nutrients during growth, gestation, lactation and illness may cause telogen defluxion if appropriate nutritional changes are not instituted. Bitches and queens in late gestation and lactation, and growing puppies and kittens are at risk unless they are fed nutritionally balanced, highly digestible foods that meet their increased nutritional requirements.

Anagen defluxion is a sudden loss of hair due to an unusual event (e.g., antimitotic drugs, infectious disease, metabolic disease) that interferes with anagen, resulting in abnormalities of hair follicles and shafts. Animals suffering from the stress of illness, injury and surgery often require increased amounts of energy, protein, specific amino acids and other nutrients. Animals with severe illness that do not receive adequate nutritional support are at risk for telogen defluxion, anagen defluxion or other coat abnormalities.

Dogs with severe primary seborrhea may have increased protein and other nutrient requirements. The calculated epidermal cell renewal time is approximately seven to eight days for dogs with primary seborrhea.[24,25] The hyperproliferative nature of the skin of dogs with primary seborrhea, with at least a threefold increase in epidermal cell renewal, may change the nutrient requirements of these dogs. However, no studies to date have evaluated the specific nutrient requirements of dogs with severe primary seborrhea vs. age- and breed-matched controls. Some authors suggest that primary seborrhea worsens markedly in dogs with nutritional inadequacies.[1] Dogs with severe deep pyoderma secondary to generalized demodicosis or other underlying diseases may have increased nutrient requirements above those found in the normal adult animal.

Metabolic Epidermal Necrosis

Metabolic epidermal necrosis is a rare cutaneous disease that in most cases is a marker for a serious underlying metabolic disorder. In dogs, this syndrome has findings similar to those of necrolytic migratory erythema of people and has also been termed hepatocutaneous syndrome or superficial necrolytic dermatitis. Clinical features include crusting acral dermatopathy with erosions around the mouth, eyes, legs, feet and genitalia.[1,26] Hyperkeratosis, ulceration of foot pads or both conditions are also prominent. The cutaneous syndrome is often associated with hepatic cirrhosis, other hepatopathies, diabetes mellitus, hyperadrenocorticism, and rarely, glucagon-secreting pancreatic tumors. Metabolic changes often include carbohydrate intolerance and hypoaminoacidemia.

Specific treatment is aimed at correcting the underlying metabolic disease. Unfortunately, most cases are associated with irreversible chronic liver disease and hepatic cirrhosis. (See Chapter 23.) Symptomatic treatment includes antimicrobials for secondary infections, insulin therapy as needed for diabetes mellitus, hydrotherapy to help remove crusts and lessen pruritus and glucocorticoids. Treatment of hypoaminoacidemia may reverse the skin lesions. Anecdotal reports suggest that foods for repletion/recovery containing moderate protein levels (Prescription Diet Canine/Feline a/d[a]), zinc, egg yolks or intravenous administration of crystalline amino acid solutions will reverse the skin lesions in some patients.[b,c]

ESSENTIAL FATTY ACIDS

Functions in the Skin

The essential fatty acids (EFA) are polyunsaturated fatty acids derived from and including the parent EFA, cis-linoleic acid and alpha-linolenic acid. Figure 15-1 summarizes the metabolic pathway of the EFA. The skin of adult mice, guinea pigs and presumably other animals lacks delta-6-desaturase and delta-5-desaturase activity.[27] Thus, the epidermis depends on food to supply EFA or the continuous formation of gamma-linolenic acid, arachidonic acid and eicosapentaenoic acid by the liver, with subsequent transportation to the skin by the blood.[27-29]

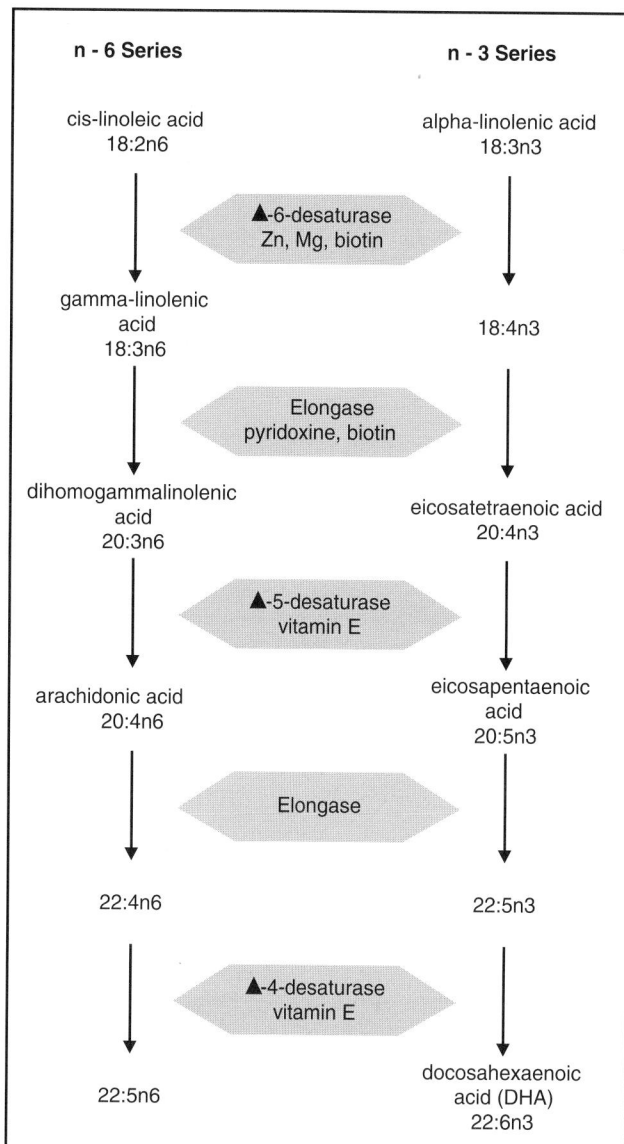

Figure 15-1. Diagram of metabolic pathways for essential fatty acids.

In the skin, EFA are principally found in phospholipids, and so have an accepted structural function in the lipoproteins of cell membranes. The high degree of unsaturation of EFA bestows fluidity to these structures at physiologic temperatures, allowing conformational changes to occur.[30] One of the most important skin-related functions of EFA is the incorporation of linoleic acid into the ceramides of the lipid portion of the epidermal cornified envelope. This envelope serves an essential barrier function to prevent loss of water and other nutrients. EFA are a source of energy for the skin and serve as precursors to a variety of potent, short-lived molecules including prostaglandins, leukotrienes and their metabolites.

Essential Fatty Acid Deficiency

When mammals are deprived of fats, they develop characteristic signs of deficiency. The existence of EFA was first recognized when rats deprived of fat had poor weight gain, increased water intake, necrosis of the tail and scaly skin.[14,15] The skin scaliness was exacerbated by low ambient humidity or restricted access to water. The increased water intake was later linked to increased transepidermal water loss.[16] When newly weaned rats were fed foods devoid of EFA, linoleic acid and arachidonic acid levels in the skin rapidly declined.[16] After five weeks, these acids were virtually absent from the skin, weight loss and increased water intake ensued and scaly skin developed. After 10 weeks, the rate of transepidermal water loss began to increase rapidly to values about 10 times those of normal rats. Growth stunting caused by EFA deficiency is predominantly due to the increase in thermogenesis required to counter heat loss from accelerated transepidermal water evaporation.[31]

Cutaneous changes have been described in fatty acid deficiency in dogs[32] and cats.[33,34] These cutaneous abnormalities include scaliness (seborrhea sicca), matting of hair, loss of skin elasticity, alopecia, a dry and dull coat, erythroderma, hyperkeratosis, epidermal peeling, interdigital exudation, otitis externa and lack of hair regrowth following plucking. These changes are associated with epidermal and dermal metabolic effects leading to: 1) increased transepidermal water loss, 2) increased epidermal cell turnover, 3) sebaceous gland hypertrophy, 4) increased sebum viscosity, 5) poor wound healing, 6) increased susceptibility to infection and 7) weakening of cutaneous capillaries.

Dogs with cutaneous abnormalities due to low-fat foods have lower levels of fatty acids in serum, skin, liver, kidneys and heart muscle than do animals with healthy skin.[32] Cats fed an EFA-deficient food developed moderate seborrhea sicca and mild hair loss after six months.[34] Severe seborrhea sicca with large scales developed in EFA-deficient cats when the environmental relative humidity decreased from approximately 75 to 55%.[34] Hair loss is extensive and stroking causes clumps of hair to fall out.

Clinical signs resembling those caused by experimental EFA deficiency can also be induced by deficiency of other nutrients, particularly zinc,[35] vitamin E[36] and pyridoxine.[37] EFA intake influences the requirement of these nutrients. In rodents, clinical signs of zinc deficiency can be largely prevented by EFA supplementation.[38]

Fatty acid deficiency is rapidly reversible if EFA are introduced orally, parenterally or topically. Various abnormal cutaneous parameters of dogs[32] and cats[33,34] are restored within a few days by linoleic acid supplementation. Supplementation with EFA will increase fatty acid levels in serum of dogs[39,40] and cats,[34] and in the skin of both normal and seborrheic dogs.[39,40]

Use of Fatty Acids for Seborrhea

Fats and fatty acids have been recommended for many years as supplements to improve the sheen and luster of hair. In the past, animal and vegetable sources of fat were recommended to improve coat quality.

Campbell and others showed that dogs with seborrhea have abnormally low cutaneous levels of linoleic acid and increased cutaneous levels of oleic acid.[39] These low cutaneous levels are found despite normal food and serum fatty acid concentrations. Following supplementation for 30 days with a vegetable oil high in linoleic acid (sunflower oil), the cutaneous fatty acid concentrations return to near normal and clinical signs of seborrhea improved. This study suggests that clinical signs of seborrhea in dogs may be partly attributable to a localized deficiency of linoleic acid, elevated levels of arachidonic acid in the skin or both. However, White found no significant differences in the serum and skin fatty acid profiles of normal and a small number of seborrheic dogs.[41]

Seborrhea sicca is also associated with increased transepidermal water loss, which can be reversed with cutaneous administration of vegetable oils rich in linoleic acid.[42] Transepidermal water loss can also be decreased by supplementing the food with alpha-linolenic acid.[40] Further studies will be needed to determine the effects of supplementation of food with other fatty acids and to determine the optimal dose of fatty acid supplements for patients with seborrhea.

MINERALS

Minerals in the food interact with one another (Figure 15-2) and this interaction must be kept in mind when assessing integumentary problems that might be associated with certain homemade foods, commercial foods or nutritional supplements. Skin manifestations of mineral imbalances are seen most commonly with primary (nutritional inadequacy) or secondary (nutrient interaction) deficiencies of copper and zinc.

Copper

Copper is an essential trace element of all plant and animal cells.[43] Copper is involved in various biologic functions, primarily as a component of storage and transport proteins and cuproenzymes. Cuproenzymes are required for maturation of all connective tissue and are required to cross-link aldehydes in collagen and elastin.[43] Cuproenzymes also catalyze the conversion of carotene to retinal, the formation of keratin from prekeratin and the biosynthesis of melanin from L-tyrosine.

Cutaneous manifestations of copper deficiency include achromotrichia or loss of normal hair coloration, reduced density or lack of hair and a dull or rough coat. Pigmented hair on the head and face loses its normal color, develops a "washed out" appearance and becomes gray.[44-46] This change may extend to the entire body.[21,45] In dogs and cats with cutaneous manifestations of copper deficiency, copper concentrations are significantly reduced in plasma, hair, liver, kidney and heart muscle.[44-46] Copper deficiency is seen most commonly in young puppies and kittens.

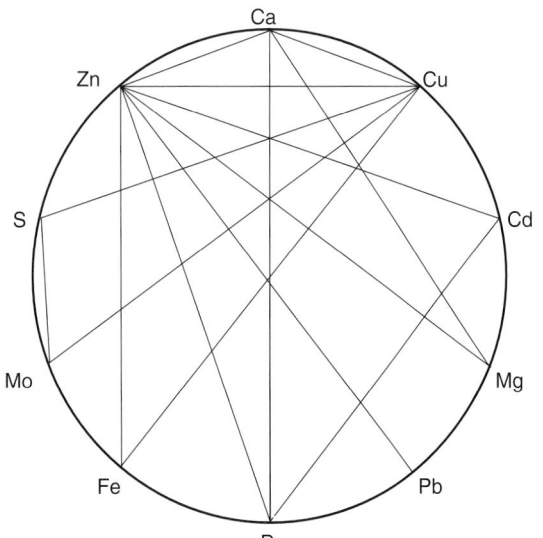

Figure 15-2. Diagram of clinically important mineral interactions in patients with cutaneous disease.

Dogs and cats can develop copper deficiency due to: 1) a lack of copper in food, 2) poor availability of copper in food or 3) an excess of competing minerals. Zinc, in particular, can adversely affect copper homeostasis. Zinc is thought to inhibit copper absorption by its action on intestinal metallothioneins, which sequester copper in the intestinal epithelial cells and make copper unavailable for use elsewhere in the body.[47] The greater the intake of zinc and the lower the intake of copper (absolute or relative), the greater the potential for copper sequestration and ultimately, copper deficiency. Studies involving people and foals have shown increased nutritional copper requirements as the amount of zinc in the food increases.[47,48]

Copper availability varies widely among feed ingredients.[49] Copper availability is relatively high in poultry by-product meal, avian liver (chicken and turkey) and ruminant liver (beef and sheep); copper from soybean meal and corn gluten meal is moderately available; copper from monogastric mammalian liver (pork and rat) and copper oxide is poorly available.[45,49-51] Risk factors for copper deficiency in dogs and cats include: 1) rapid growth, 2) unsupplemented homemade foods, 3) commercial or homemade foods supplemented with copper oxide and 4) homemade or commercial foods supplemented with excessive levels of zinc, calcium or iron.

Zinc

Zinc Deficiency

Zinc is an important cofactor of numerous metalloenzymes and modulator of many critical biologic functions. Investigation of zinc nutrition in dogs and cats began 70 years ago[52] and has culminated with a plethora of reports over the past 15 years linking zinc deficiency to many dermatoses.

Zinc deficiency in animals is well documented through experiments with rats, mice, swine, sheep, calves, ducks, chickens, dogs and cats. After feeding a calcium-supplemented, zinc-deficient, corn-soy food to dogs, Robertson and Burns reported decreases in plasma zinc concentrations, a dull and rough coat and skin lesions on the abdomen and hindlimbs.[53] Sanecki and colleagues fed a corn-soy, zinc-deficient food to young puppies and documented the progressive development of cutaneous lesions.[54] Puppies developed alopecia, skin ulceration, dermatitis, parakeratotic hyperkeratosis, follicular hyperkeratosis and generalized acanthosis similar to lesions described in other animals with zinc deficiency.[54] These changes were prominent in areas of contact and trauma (footpads), areas of stretch (skin over joints), areas of friction (axillae, groin), distal extremities and tail, mucocutaneous junctions and ear canals. The feet were severely affected with paronychia and fissured, cracked and focally eroded footpads. The cutaneous lesions were completely reversible within six weeks of adding zinc to the food.

Banta also reported that dogs fed a zinc-deficient food developed skin lesions, which improved dramatically within 72 hours of adding zinc to the food.[55] Kane and colleagues described poor coats characterized by hair thinning, slow hair growth, scaliness and buccal margin ulcerations in kittens fed a zinc-deficient food.[56]

Studies in rodents have demonstrated the close linkage of zinc and EFA metabolism.[38,57,58] Zinc deficiency accelerates development of clinical signs of EFA deficiency; conversely, clinical signs of zinc deficiency can be largely reversed by supplementing with EFA. Several of the man-

Table 15-2. Classification scheme for zinc-related cutaneous disorders in dogs.

Previous classification schemes
  Dry juvenile pyoderma
  Syndrome I (Siberian husky, malamute, other breeds)
  Syndrome II (growing dogs)
  Generic dog food syndrome
  Acrodermatitis of bull terriers
Proposed classification
  Nutritional abnormalities
    Primary zinc deficiency
    Secondary zinc deficiency
    Essential fatty acid deficiency
  Animal abnormalities
    Acrodermatitis of bull terriers
    Zinc malabsorption (Siberian husky, malamute)

ifestations of zinc deficiency are mediated by a relative state of EFA deficiency attributed, in part, to reduced delta-6-desaturase enzyme activity.[38,57,58] Zinc deficiency may impair the absorption of EFA and vice versa.[58] Low zinc intake during pregnancy prevents the normal accumulation of long-chain fatty acids and differentially depletes maternal whole-body stores of linoleic and alpha-linolenic acids.[59] This finding suggests that low zinc intake during pregnancy and lactation may be a risk factor for fatty acid deficiency. It is unknown whether similar interactions of zinc and EFA also occur in dogs and cats.

Zinc-Related Dermatoses

Over the past 20 years, a variety of cutaneous diseases in dogs have been described that are thought to be primary or secondary zinc deficiency, or that respond to zinc supplementation. The classification of these skin diseases is confusing and often overlaps (Table 15-2). Baker, Anderson and others reported a crusted dermatosis in young short-haired dog breeds termed dry juvenile pyoderma or juvenile hyperkeratosis.[60,61] Many cases were not caused by primary bacterial infection and often resolved spontaneously at sexual maturity. In retrospect, these case reports most likely represent the first clinical descriptions of cutaneous disease caused by zinc deficiency in young dogs. Kunkle proposed a classification scheme in 1980 for zinc-responsive dermatoses that included two syndromes.[62] Syndrome I included Siberian husky and malamute dogs, which usually developed lesions in early adulthood and responded to zinc supplementation. Syndrome II included rapidly growing puppies that developed lesions due to zinc deficiency and responded to food change, zinc supplementation or both. Several years later, Sousa and colleagues described a generic dog food syndrome in adult dogs and rapidly growing puppies consuming a poor-quality food.[63] These animals had lesions consistent with zinc deficiency and responded to a food change. At this same time, acrodermatitis was described in bull terriers and linked to abnormal zinc absorption and metabolism.[64,65]

In all these syndromes, the dermatoses are clearly associated with zinc deficiency and possibly a deficiency or abnormal metabolism of other nutrients. A more practical classification scheme for zinc-related cutaneous changes in dogs includes clinical syndromes due to nutritional abnormalities (primary or secondary zinc deficiency) or animal abnormalities of zinc metabolism (Table 15-2).

Zinc-Related Dermatoses Associated with Nutritional Abnormalities. Zinc-responsive cutaneous lesions have been frequently described in rapidly growing puppies and

Table 15-3. Risk factors for zinc-related skin disease in dogs.

Certain breeds
  Siberian husky
  Malamute
  Bull terrier
  Great Dane
  Labrador retriever
  Other rapidly growing large and giant breeds
Food
  High mineral levels (calcium, phosphorus, magnesium)
  High phytate levels (high levels of cereal ingredients)
  Low essential fatty acid levels
Dietary supplements
  Calcium and/or other mineral supplements
  Cottage cheese or other dairy products
Small intestinal disease
  Viral enteritis
  Malassimilation (malabsorption, maldigestion)

less frequently in adult dogs. Many breeds may be affected, but Great Danes, Doberman pinschers, German shepherd dogs, German shorthaired pointers, beagles, standard poodles, Rhodesian ridgebacks and Labrador retrievers are reportedly affected more often.[1,35,46,62,63,66-70] Lesions somewhat resemble those of experimental zinc deficiency in puppies and include erythroderma, alopecia and hyperkeratotic plaques (exudative crusts) on the face, head, distal extremities and mucocutaneous junctions.[1,69] Thickened, fissured footpads are also frequently seen. Severely affected animals have systemic signs of lymphadomegaly, poor growth, fever, depression and anorexia. Microscopic examination of skin biopsy specimens shows hyperplastic superficial perivascular dermatitis with diffuse parakeratotic hyperkeratosis.

Risk factors for development of zinc-responsive cutaneous disease are listed in Table 15-3. Foods with high mineral levels (calcium, phosphorus, magnesium), poor digestibility, high levels of phytate and/or low levels of total fat and EFA are significant risk factors, especially when fed to puppies during the rapid growth phase. As shown in Figure 15-2, zinc absorption is influenced by levels of other minerals in the food. Foods high in calcium, phosphorus and magnesium adversely affect absorption of zinc. Excessive use of mineral supplements containing calcium in large- and giant-breed puppies is common and can inhibit zinc absorption.

Phytin, phytate and phytic acid are different forms of organic phosphorus, presumably inositol hexaphosphate, found in plant proteins. Foods high in cereal ingredients often have excessive levels of phytate that complex with and prevent normal absorption of zinc. Phytate and calcium also interact to affect zinc absorption.[71] The relative effect of phytate on zinc absorption increases with the calcium level in the food. Thus, foods high in phytate and calcium have an even greater negative impact on zinc absorption.

Low-cost commercial generic or private label brand dry pet foods are often low in total fat and EFA because fat is an expensive ingredient. Zinc and EFA metabolism interact and foods with marginal concentrations of zinc and EFA may be more likely to cause clinical disease.

Viral enteritis and prolonged diarrhea adversely affect zinc absorption in swine and similar changes may occur in other animals.[72]

Zinc Deficiency Associated with Metabolic Abnormalities. Lesions attributed to zinc deficiency develop early

in adulthood in Siberian huskies, malamutes and bull terriers and progress at a variable rate.[1] Skin lesions develop in these breeds despite consumption of well-balanced foods containing adequate levels of zinc. Lesions include erythroderma, alopecia, crusting, scaling and suppuration involving the head, extremities and mucocutaneous junctions. The footpads may become hyperkeratotic. Secondary *Malassezia* and bacterial infections are common. Some malamute and Siberian husky dogs have a decreased capability for zinc absorption.[73,74] Bull terriers that are siblings of those with acrodermatitis may also be affected and probably have abnormal zinc absorption and metabolism.[1] These animals probably require zinc supplementation for life to maintain normal tissue zinc concentrations and avert clinical disease.

Acrodermatitis is an inherited, autosomal recessive metabolic disease reported to occur in bull terriers in the United States, Canada and the United Kingdom.[64,65,75,76] The syndrome develops shortly after birth and is associated with defects in zinc absorption and metabolism. The condition has been termed lethal acrodermatitis because homozygously affected dogs rarely live beyond 18 months of age.

Cutaneous and systemic clinical signs resemble those of severe zinc deficiency and include growth retardation, gastrointestinal disease, chronic bacterial infections and progressive, erythematous, exfoliative, papular to pustular dermatitis of the distal extremities and skin surrounding the mucocutaneous junctions.[64,65,75,76] Surface crusts usually contain numerous bacteria and yeast organisms.[75] Owners complain that their dogs have difficulty eating and are affected by skin disease, poor growth and large, splayed, painful feet.[76] Ulcerated and thick, crusted lesions are prominent on the muzzle and ears. Abnormal keratinization of the footpads, severe nail dystrophy and paronychia are also common. Histopathologic examination of skin reveals massive parakeratotic hyperkeratosis.

Mundell showed that two affected dogs had significantly lower plasma zinc concentrations, lower zinc and copper concentrations in the kidneys and liver and lower zinc absorption when compared with age-matched control dogs.[65] Serum zinc concentrations may also be normal.[75,76] Supplementation with oral or intravenous zinc fails to ameliorate clinical signs. Treatment with systemic antimicrobials, especially for secondary superficial yeast infections, may result in marked improvement, although systemic and cutaneous infections recur. Some apparently normal littermates may develop a zinc-responsive dermatitis.[1]

Diagnosis and Management of Zinc-Responsive Skin Disease

Diagnosis of zinc-responsive cutaneous disease is based on the history, physical examination and results of skin biopsy evaluation. Hyperplastic superficial perivascular dermatitis with marked diffuse and follicular parakeratotic hyperkeratosis is suggestive of zinc deficiency.[69] In general, zinc concentrations in serum, leukocytes and hair are not a good indicator of zinc status in dogs.[46,68,77,78] Serum zinc concentration is affected by age, seasonal variation and many diseases.[79,80] Logas and colleagues found no significant difference in serum zinc concentrations between normal dogs, dogs that were ill without skin disease, dogs with allergic skin disease and dogs with other dermatoses.[78]

Treatment generally includes changing to a food that avoids excess minerals and contains adequate amounts of zinc and EFA. This type of change will usually result in rapid improvement in puppies and some adult dogs. Zinc supplementation will be necessary in those breeds in which decreased ability to absorb zinc is suspected. Oral supplementation with zinc sulfate (10 mg/kg body weight/day) or zinc methionine (2 mg/kg body weight/day) is adequate in most cases. Zinc absorption is maximal if supplements are given between rather than with meals. Supplemental zinc from zinc amino acid chelates may be more available to dogs than are inorganic zinc sources.[81] Some dogs, especially Siberian huskies, do not respond to oral zinc supplementation. Intravenous injection of sterile zinc sulfate solutions at dosages of 10 to 15 mg/kg body weight has been effective in these dogs.[74] Weekly injections for at least four weeks are necessary to resolve the lesions, and maintenance injections every one to six months may be necessary to prevent relapses.

Existing skin lesions can be improved by hydrating the crusts with wet dressings, applying petrolatum or petrolatum-based topical agents or whole-body warm water soakings. Dogs with evidence of superficial pyoderma or *Malassezia* infections should be treated with appropriate antimicrobials. Some authors also recommend low doses of oral, short-acting glucocorticoids.[82]

VITAMINS

Vitamin A

Retinol, retinal and retinoic acid are three natural compounds that have vitamin A activity in mammals. Food sources include retinyl esters (vitamin A palmitate) in animal tissues and carotenoids (β-carotene) in vegetables. These sources are assimilated and ultimately stored as retinyl palmitate in the liver. Cats require preformed vitamin A because they lack the ability to effectively convert β-carotene to vitamin A.[83]

The general functions of vitamin A include growth promotion, differentiation and maintenance of epithelial tissue and maintenance of normal reproductive and visual functions. Retinoic acid affects differentiation and proliferation of epithelial cells by binding to and activating a specific set of cell nuclear receptors.[84,85] In particular, the skin has a specific nuclear receptor for retinoic acid.[85] The mechanism of action of retinoic acid is similar to that of steroid hormones and thyroxine, and involves activation of specific genes. Retinoic acid and thyroid hormone actually control overlapping gene networks, regulating growth and differentiation through nuclear receptors that can modify rates of gene transcription.

Retinoic acid influences epidermal differentiation and directly affects keratinization by action of retinoic acid receptors on regulatory sites in keratin genes. Retinoic acid may also influence hair growth through activity at the hair bulb.

Vitamin A deficiency in dogs was among the first of the vitamin deficiencies to be studied experimentally.[86] Skin lesions and focal atrophy of the skin have been reported with experimental vitamin A deficiency in dogs and cats, although it is seldom encountered clinically.[83,86] Some of the earliest work with vitamin A showed that puppies had heavier, more lustrous coats when foods were supplemented with vitamin A.[87] It is unlikely that vitamin A deficiency would occur in dogs and cats eating typical commercial pet foods because these foods contain several times the minimum daily requirement of vitamin A.[88]

Table 15-4. Indications and dosages for retinoids in primary keratinization disorders.

Vitamin A alcohol (retinol)
Subset of seborrheic skin disease, primarily in cocker spaniels
Dosage: 625 to 1,000 IU/kg q24h per os
10,000 IU q24h per os in cocker spaniels and miniature schnauzers
50,000 IU q24h per os in Labrador retrievers

Tretinoin (all-trans retinoic acid)
Chin acne of dogs and cats
Nasodigital hyperkeratosis
Ear margin seborrhea/dermatosis
Dosage: Apply topically q12 to 24h to control; then decrease frequency for maintenance

Isotretinoin (13-cis retinoic acid)
Schnauzer comedo syndrome
Sebaceous adenitis
Lamellar ichthyosis
Dosage: 1 to 3 mg/kg q24h per os for control; then try to decrease to alternate-day therapy

Etretinate (analogue of retinoic acid ethyl ester)
Idiopathic seborrhea, especially of cocker spaniels
Sebaceous adenitis
Lamellar ichthyosis
Actinic keratosis
Dosage: 0.75 to 1.0 mg/kg q24h per os for control; then try to decrease to alternate-day therapy

Retinoid-Responsive Dermatoses

The term "retinoids" refers to the entire group of naturally occurring and synthetic vitamin A derivatives. These therapeutic agents should be reserved for cases in which there are clinical and histopathologic abnormalities most consistent with primary keratinization disorders of the surface and/or follicular epithelium or abnormalities of the sebaceous glands.[89,90] Other causes of clinical scaling (ectoparasitism, allergies, infections, endocrinopathies) should first be eliminated through other diagnostic testing.

A vitamin A-responsive dermatosis has been described primarily in cocker spaniels but it has also been recognized in a Labrador retriever and a miniature schnauzer.[1,90] The condition is characterized by adult-onset, medically refractory seborrheic skin disease with marked follicular plugging and hyperkeratotic plaques, primarily on the ventral and lateral thorax and abdomen.[1,90] A ceruminous otitis externa and unthrifty appearing coat are often present. The clinical lesions are characterized histologically by marked follicular orthokeratotic hyperkeratosis. Improvement is noted within three to four weeks of starting oral vitamin A alcohol (retinol) with complete remission by eight to 10 weeks.[1,90] It is important to remember that this syndrome represents only a small subset of seborrheic disease in cocker spaniels. However, it is logical to try a four- to eight-week course of vitamin A in dogs with ventral hyperkeratotic plaques that do not respond well to other therapy.[90]

In the last 20 years, many synthetic retinoids have been developed to offer better therapeutic response and less toxicity than naturally occurring vitamin A compounds. The most widely available and commonly used synthetic retinoids include tretinoin, isotretinoin and etretinate.

Tretinoin is effective topically as therapy for localized follicular and epidermal keratinization disorders such as chin acne, nasodigital hyperkeratosis, calluses and ear margin seborrhea/dermatosis.[1,89,90] Isotretinoin and etretinate are given orally and may be useful to manage primary idiopathic seborrhea in cocker spaniels, keratinization dis-

Table 15-5. Optimal food nutrient profiles for patients with skin and hair disorders.*

Physiologic state	Protein (%)	Fat (%)	Zinc (mg/kg)	Copper (mg/kg)	Total EFA** (%)	Dry matter digestibility (% as fed)
Adult maintenance						
Dog	25-30	10-15	100-200	5-10	>3.0	>80
Cat	30-45	15-25	50-150	15-30	>1.5	>80
Growth/lactation						
Dog	30-45	15-30	100-200	5-10	>3.0	>80
Cat	35-50	20-35	50-150	15-30	>1.5	>80

*All nutrients expressed on a dry matter basis.
**Total essential fatty acids (EFA) = total n-6 and n-3 families of fatty acids.

orders in other breeds, schnauzer comedo syndrome, sebaceous adenitis, lamellar ichthyosis, actinic keratosis (solar-induced precancerous lesions) and various cutaneous neoplastic disorders (squamous cell carcinoma, cutaneous T-cell lymphoma, multiple keratocanthomas).

Dosages commonly recommended by veterinary dermatologists are outlined in Table 15-4. Side effects that occur commonly with retinoids include conjunctivitis, decreased tear production, arthralgia/mylagia, moderate to marked elevations in serum triglyceride levels, elevations in liver enzyme activity and teratogenic effects.

Vitamin E

Vitamin E activity is represented by eight isomeric forms of tocopherol with α-tocopherol being most important biologically. Vitamin E quenches free radicals in polyunsaturated fatty acids (PUFA) of membrane phospholipids. The nutritional requirement of vitamin E is closely related to concentration of PUFA.

Naturally occurring vitamin E deficiency has only been reported to occur in cats. Steatitis occurs when sources of highly unsaturated fatty acids, such as red meat tuna, are fed to cats without adequate vitamin E. Clinical signs and laboratory findings include anorexia, fever, hyperesthesia, hemolytic anemia, leukocytosis and firm subcutaneous nodules. Diagnosis is confirmed by microscopic examination of biopsy specimens from adipose tissue. Typical lesions are firm, yellow to orange-brown fat with lobular panniculitis and ceroid within lipocytes, macrophages and giant cells. Treatment includes a change of food to a complete and balanced ration, supplemental vitamin E (25 to 75 mg/kg body weight/day), corticosteroids and supportive care. Appendix A lists factors for converting mg/kg to IU.

Naturally occurring vitamin E deficiency has not been reported to occur in dogs, but experimentally induced vitamin E deficiency does produce skin lesions.[36] Initial lesions consist of a keratinization defect (seborrhea sicca), followed by a greasy and inflammatory stage (erythroderma and seborrhea oleosa) and secondary bacterial pyoderma. The dermatosis rapidly responds to vitamin E supplementation. All lesions respond within eight to 10 weeks. It is unlikely that vitamin E deficiency would occur in dogs and cats that eat typical commercial pet foods because such foods contain three to five times the minimum daily requirement of vitamin E.[88]

Vitamin E-Responsive Dermatoses

A number of inflammatory dermatoses in animals have been treated with oral vitamin E, including discoid lupus erythematosus, systemic lupus erythematosus, pemphigus erythematosus, sterile panniculitis, acanthosis nigricans, dermatomyositis and ear margin vasculitis. Vitamin E is often used in conjunction with systemic glucocorticoids, topical steroids and other immunosuppressive agents.

Large doses of vitamin E may stabilize cell and lysomal membranes against damage induced by free radicals and peroxides, modulate arachidonic acid and prostaglandin metabolism, inhibit proteolytic enzymes, enhance phagocytic activity and enhance humoral and cellular immunity.

Vitamin E appears to have limited value as an antipruritic agent. One uncontrolled study in allergic dogs that received vitamin E failed to document a reduction in pruritus.[91] A well-controlled study in adult people with atopic dermatitis also failed to demonstrate improvement with vitamin E or selenium supplementation.[92]

The oral dosage of vitamin E for inflammatory dermatoses is 200 to 800 IU twice daily.[1,93] This dose is 20 to 100 times the daily requirement for a 10-kg dog. Anecdotal reports suggest that topical vitamin E may help resolve discoid lupus erythematosus lesions.[93]

B-Complex Vitamins

Experimental deficiencies of biotin, riboflavin, niacin and pyridoxine cause cutaneous lesions in dogs and cats.[83,86] The most common clinical signs include anorexia, weight loss, diarrhea, alopecia and dry, flaky seborrhea. Clinical lesions are more likely to occur in young, growing animals than in adults.[5]

Several B-complex vitamins act as cofactors in EFA metabolism. Both linoleic acid desaturation and gamma-linolenic acid elongation may be impaired in pyridoxine deficiency.[37] EFA may have a sparing effect on the cutaneous lesions caused by B-complex vitamin deficiency and vice versa.[37]

It is unlikely that B-complex vitamin deficiency would occur in dogs and cats that eat typical commercial pet foods, because most foods contain several times the minimum daily requirement of these vitamins. B-complex deficiency could occur in animals eating unusual homemade foods that are not supplemented with vitamins.

Assess the Food(s)

Nutrients of concern for skin and hair include protein, EFAs, zinc, copper and various fat-soluble and water-soluble vitamins. (See Key Nutritional Factors—Skin and Hair Disorders.) The food should include optimal levels of these nutrients, and the nutrients should be available to the animal. Digestibility and assimilation of nutrients are especially important during periods of increased nutrient demand such as growth, gestation and lactation. Use of maintenance-type foods (which are lower in protein, fat, minerals, vitamins and digestibility than growth/lactation or foods for repletion/recovery) may be a risk factor for nutritional skin disease during these lifestages. Table 15-5 outlines optimal levels of key nutrients for skin and hair disorders. Levels of these nutrients in specific foods can be obtained by contacting the manufacturer or distributor of the food. (Selected foods are listed in Appendix L.)

A detailed assessment of nutritional supplements is also important. Vitamin supplements are rarely indicated except in those nutrient-sensitive disorders that respond to high levels of vitamin A or vitamin E. Excessive use of mineral supplements can interfere with assimilation of zinc and copper.

Assess the Feeding Method

It may not always be necessary to change the feeding method when managing a patient with skin or hair disease, but a thorough assessment includes verification that an appropriate feeding method is being used. Items to consider include feeding route, amount fed, how the food is offered, access to other food and who feeds the animal. All of this information should have been gathered when the history of the animal was obtained. If the animal has a normal body condition score (3/5), the amount of food it was fed previously (energy basis) was probably appropriate.

FEEDING PLAN

Select a Food(s)

In general, an animal's food(s) should be changed if one of the following skin or coat conditions develops:
- Loss of normal hair color, especially lightening or graying of normally pigmented hair,
- Brittle and easily broken hair,
- Generalized scaling, crusting, alopecia or loss of normal hair sheen for which no underlying skin disorder can be identified through routine diagnostic evaluation,
- Poor wound healing or decubital ulcers,
- Severe, generalized inflammatory skin disease such as deep pyoderma or immune-mediated skin disease,
- Hyperproliferative skin disorder such as primary seborrhea,
- Abnormal hair growth or failure of hair to regrow where clipped or lost.

In these situations, the food should be changed to one with increased levels of protein, EFA, zinc and copper and with increased digestibility.

Nutrition supplements can be used in conjunction with the food change or can be added to the original food. Changing to a food appropriate for the animal's lifestage will usually reverse cutaneous signs associated with a nutrient deficiency (Table 15-5). Supplementation alone will not usually improve a poor-quality food. Supplementation with fatty acids, zinc, retinoids and vitamin E usually exceeds levels used to meet nutrient requirements. In these cases, nutrient supplements are being used as therapeutic agents.

Determine a Feeding Method

The method of feeding is often not altered in the nutritional management of skin and hair disease. If a new food is fed, the amount to feed can be determined from the product label or other supporting materials. The food dosage may need to be changed if the caloric density of the new food differs from that of the previous food. The food dosage is usually divided into two or more meals per day.

The food dosage and feeding method should be altered if the animal's body weight and condition are not optimal.

For clinical nutrition to be effective, there needs to be good compliance. Enabling compliance includes limiting access to other foods and knowing who feeds the animal. If the animal comes from a household with multiple pets, it should be determined whether the pet with skin disease has access to the other pets' food.

REASSESSMENT

Cutaneous disease due to a nutrient deficiency will usually respond rapidly and dramatically to appropriate nutritional change or supplementation. Patients will usually improve within a few days to a couple weeks. Nutrient-sensitive disorders usually respond to supplements more slowly, over several weeks to several months. Once a nutritional change or supplementation has been started, the patient should be examined monthly for significant changes in skin lesions and hair quality. Trichograms can be repeated in those patients that have abnormal hair quality or hair growth.

ENDNOTES & REFERENCES

ENDNOTES
a. Hill's Pet Nutrition, Inc., Topeka, KS, USA.
b. Byrne K. University of Illinois, Urbana, IL, USA. Personal communication. 1995.
c. Power HT. What's up about the hepatocutaneous syndrome? Derm Dialogue, Winter 1999: 13-14.

REFERENCES
1. Scott DW, Miller WH, Griffin CE. Small Animal Dermatology, 5th ed. Philadelphia, PA: WB Saunders Co, 1995.
2. Sischo WM, Ihrke PJ, Franti CE. Regional distribution of 10 common skin diseases in dogs. Journal of the American Veterinary Medical Association 1989; 195: 752-756.
3. Scott DW, Paradis M. A survey of canine and feline skin disorders seen in a university practice. Canadian Veterinary Journal 1990; 31: 830-835.
4. Nesbitt GH. Incidence of feline skin disease: A survey. In: Proceedings. Annual Members Meeting AAVD & ACVD, Las Vegas, NV, 1982.
5. Pastoor FJH, Van Herck H, Van't Klooster ATh, et al. Biotin deficiency in cats as induced by feeding a purified diet containing egg white. Journal of Nutrition 1991; 121: S73-S74.
6. Bradfield RB, Bailey MA, Margen S. Morphologic changes in human scalp hair roots during protein deprivation. Science 1967; 157: 438-439.
7. Robbins CR. In: Chemical and Physical Behavior of Human Hair, 2nd ed. New York, NY: Springer-Verlag, 1988.
8. Stafforst C. Untersuchungen uber gewicht, wachstum und zusammensetzung des hundehaarkleides (Investigation of weight, growth and composition of dog hair). Diss Med Vet, (thesis), Hanover, Germany, 1982.
9. Mundt HC, Stafforst C. Production and composition of dog hair. In: Edney ATB, ed. Nutrition, Malnutrition and Dietetics in the Dog and Cat. British Veterinary Association, 1987; 62-65.
10. van den Broek AHM, Stafford WL, Keay G. Zinc and copper concentrations in the plasma and hair of normal cats. Veterinary Record 1992; 131: 512-513.
11. Ihrke PJ, Franti CE. Breed as a risk factor associated with skin diseases in dogs seen in northern California. California Veterinarian 1985; 39(5): 13-16.
12. Roudebush P, Cowell CS. A survey of hypoallergenic diet recommendations by North American veterinarians and analysis of homemade diet prescriptions. Veterinary Dermatology 1992; 3: 23-28.
13. Miller ME, Christensen GC, Evans HE. Anatomy of the Dog. Philadelphia, PA: WB Saunders Co, 1964; 875.

14. Burr GO, Burr MM. A new deficiency disease produced by the rigid exclusion of fat from the diet. Journal of Biological Chemistry 1929; 82: 345-367.

15. Burr GO, Burr MM. On the nature and role of fatty acids essential in nutrition. Journal of Biological Chemistry 1930; 86: 587-621.

16. Basnayake V, Sinclair HM. The effect of deficiency of essential fatty acids upon the skin. In: Popyak G, LeBreton E, eds. Biochemical Problems of Lipids. London, UK: Butterworth, 1956; 476.

17. Scott DW. The biology of hair and its distribution. In: vonTschnarner C, Halliwell REW, eds. Advances in Veterinary Dermatology, vol. 1, Philadelphia, PA: Bailliere Tindall, 1990; 3-33.

18. Kwochka KW, Rademakers AM. Cell proliferation kinetics of epidermis, hair follicles, and sebaceous glands of beagles and cocker spaniels with healthy skin. American Journal of Veterinary Research 1989; 50: 587-591.

19. Kwochka KW. Cell proliferation kinetics in the hair root matrix of dogs with healthy skin and dogs with idiopathic seborrhea. American Journal of Veterinary Research 1990; 51: 1570-1573.

20. Kwochka KW. In vivo and in vitro examination of cell proliferation kinetics in the normal and seborrheic canine epidermis. In: Proceedings. Annual Members Meeting AAVD & ACVD, Scottsdale, AZ, 1991: 46.

21. Ralston Purina Company. Technical Bulletin GP 7829B-8403, 1987.

22. Huber TL, Laflamme DP, Medleau L, et al. Comparison of procedures for assessing adequacy of dog foods. Journal of the American Veterinary Medical Association 1991; 199: 731-734.

23. Harvey RG. Skin disease. In: Wills JM, Simpson KW, eds. The Waltham Book of Clinical Nutrition of the Dog & Cat. New York, NY, Pergamon, 1994; 425-444.

24. Kwochka KW, Rademakers AM. Cell proliferation kinetics of epidermis, hair follicles, and sebaceous glands of cocker spaniels with idiopathic seborrhea. American Journal of Veterinary Research 1990; 50: 1918-1922.

25. Baker BB, Maibach HI. Epidermal cell renewal in seborrheic skin of dogs. American Journal of Veterinary Research 1987; 48: 726-728.

26. Angarano DW. Metabolic epidermal necrosis. In: Griffin CE, Kwochka KW, MacDonald JM, eds. Current Veterinary Dermatology. St Louis, MO: Mosby-Year Book Inc, 1993; 302-305.

27. Chapkin RS, Ziboh VA, McCullough JL. Dietary influences of evening primrose and fish oil on the skin of EFA-deficient guinea pigs. Journal of Nutrition 1987; 117: 1360-1370.

28. Horrobin DF. Essential fatty acids in clinical dermatology. Journal of the American Academy of Dermatology 1989; 20: 1045.

29. Campbell KL. Fatty acid supplementation and skin disease. Veterinary Clinics of North America: Small Animal Practice 1990; 20: 1475-1486.

30. Prottey C. Essential fatty acids and the skin. British Journal of Dermatology 1976; 94: 579-587.

31. Phinney SD, Clarke SD, Odin RS, et al. Thermogenesis secondary to transdermal water loss causes growth retardation in essential fatty acid-deficient rats. Metabolism 1993; 42: 1022-1026.

32. Hansen AE, Weise HF. Fat in the diet in relation to nutrition of the dog. I. Characteristic appearance and changes of animals fed diets with and without fat. Texas Report of Biological Medicine 1951; 9: 491-515.

33. Frankel TL, Rivers JPW. The nutritional and metabolic impact of gamma-linolenic acid on cats deprived of animal lipid. British Journal of Nutrition 1978; 39: 227-231.

34. MacDonald ML, Anderson BC, Rogers QR, et al. Essential fatty acid requirements of cats: Pathology of essential fatty acid deficiency. American Journal of Veterinary Research 1984; 45: 1310-1317.

35. Ohlen B, Scott DW. Zinc responsive dermatitis in puppies. Canine Practice 1986; 13: 6-10.

36. Scott DW, Sheffey BE. Dermatosis in dogs caused by vitamin E deficiency. Companion Animal Practice 1987; 1: 11-19.

37. Cunnane SC, Manku MS, Horrobin DF. Accumulation of linoleic and gamma-linolenic acids in tissue lipids of pyridoxine-deficient rats. Journal of Nutrition 1984; 114: 1754-1761.

38. Cunnane SC, Horrobin DF. Parenteral linoleic and gamma-linolenic acids ameliorate the gross effects of zinc deficiency. Proceedings of the Society of Experimental Biology and Medicine 1980; 164: 583-588.

39. Campbell KL, Uhland CF, Dorn GP. Effects of oral sunflower oil on serum and cutaneous fatty acid concentration profiles in seborrheic dogs. Veterinary Dermatology 1992; 3: 29-35.

40. Campbell KL, Roudebush P. Effects of four diets on serum and cutaneous fatty acids, transepidermal water losses, skin surface lipids, hydration and condition of the skin and haircoat of dogs (abstract). In: Proceedings. Annual Members Meeting AAVD & ACVD, Santa Fe, NM, 1995: 80-81.

41. White PD. Evaluation of serum and cutaneous essential fatty acid profiles in normal, atopic, and seborrheic dogs (abstract). In: Proceedings. Annual Members Meeting AAVD & ACVD, San Francisco, CA, 1990: 37-38.

42. Campbell KL, Kirkwood AR. Topical application of sunflower oil reduces transepidermal water loss in dogs with seborrhea sicca. In: Ihrke PJ, Mason IS, White SD, eds. Advances in Veterinary Dermatology, vol. 2. New York, NY: Pergamon Press, 1993; 157-162.

43. Brewer NR. Comparative metabolism of copper. Journal of the American Veterinary Medical Association 1987; 190: 654-658.

44. Zentek J, Meyer H. Investigations on copper deficiency in growing dogs. Journal of Nutrition 1991; 121: S83-S84.

45. Morris JG, Rogers QR. Copper oxide is an ineffective source of copper in queen diets. In: Proceedings. Pet Food Forum, Chicago, IL, 1995: 107-108.

46. van den Broek AHM, Thoday KL. Skin diseases in dogs associated with zinc deficiency: A report of 5 cases. Journal of Small Animal Practice 1986; 27: 313-323.

47. Fosmire GJ. Zinc toxicity. American Journal of Clinical Nutrition 1990; 51: 225-227.

48. Bridges CH, Moffitt PG. Influence of variable content of dietary zinc on copper metabolism of weanling foals. American Journal of Veterinary Research 1990; 51: 275-280.

49. Aoyagi S, Baker DH, Wedekind KL. Estimates of copper bioavailability from liver of different animal species and from feed ingredients derived from plants and animals. Poultry Science 1993; 72: 1746-1755.

50. Aoyagi S, Baker DH. Bioavailability of copper in analytical-grade and feed-grade inorganic copper sources when fed to provide copper at levels below the chick's requirements. Poultry Science 1993; 72: 1075-1083.

51. Czarnecki-Maulden GL, Rudnick RC, Chausow DG. Copper availability and requirement in the dog: Comparison of copper oxide and copper sulfate (abstract). Federation of American Societies for Experimental Biology Journal 1993; 7: A306.

52. Drinker KR, Thompson PK, Marsh M. An investigation of the effect of long-continual ingestion of zinc in the form of zinc oxide in cats and dogs, together with observations upon the excretion and storage of zinc. American Journal of Physiology 1927; 80: 31-64.

53. Robertson BT, Burns MJ. Zinc metabolism and zinc-deficiency syndrome in the dog. American Journal of Veterinary Research 1963; 24: 997-1002.

54. Sanecki RK, Corbin RE, Forbes RM. Tissue changes in dogs fed a zinc-deficient ration. American Journal of Veterinary Research 1982; 43: 1642-1646.

55. Banta CA. The role of zinc in canine and feline nutrition. In: Burger IH, Rivers JPW, eds. Nutrition of the Dog and Cat. New York, NY: Cambridge University Press, 1989; 317-327.

56. Kane E, Morris JG, Rogers QR, et al. Zinc deficiency in the cat. Journal of Nutrition 1981; 111: 488-495.

57. Cunnane SC. Differential regulation of essential fatty acid metabolism to the prostaglandins: Possible basis for the interaction of zinc and copper in biological systems. Progress in Lipid Research 1982; 21: 73-90.

58. Huang YS, Cunnane SC, Horrobin DF, et al. Most biological effects of zinc deficiency corrected by γ-linolenic acid but not by linoleic acid. Atherosclerosis 1982; 41: 193-207.

59. Cunnane SC, Yang J, Chen ZY. Low zinc intake increases apparent oxidation of linoleic and alpha-linolenic acids in the pregnant rat. Canadian Journal of Physiology and Pharmacology 1993; 71: 205-210.

60. Baker BB. Canine pyoderma. In: Kirk RW, ed. Current Veterinary Therapy V. Philadelphia, PA: WB Saunders Co, 1974; 418-421.

61. Anderson RK. A crusted skin disease resembling dry juvenile pyoderma: A case report. Journal of the American Animal Hospital Association 1977; 13: 701-703.

62. Kunkle GA. Zinc responsive dermatosis in dogs. In: Kirk RW, ed. Current Veterinary Therapy VII. Philadelphia, PA: WB Saunders Co, 1980; 472-476.

63. Sousa CA, Stannard AA, Ihrke PJ, et al. Dermatosis associated with feeding generic dog food: 13 cases (1981-1982). Journal of the American Veterinary Medical Association 1988; 192: 676-680.

64. Jezyk PF, Haskins ME, Mackay-Smith MA, et al. Lethal acrodermatitis in bull terriers. Journal of the American Veterinary Medical Association 1986; 188: 833-839.

65. Mundell AC. Mineral analysis in bull terriers with lethal acrodermatitis (abstract). In: Proceedings. Annual Members Meeting AAVD & ACVD, Washington, DC, 1988: 22.

66. Fadok VA. Zinc responsive dermatosis in a Great Dane: A case report. Journal of the American Animal Hospital Association 1982; 18: 409-414.

67. Wright RP. Identification of zinc-responsive dermatosis. Veterinary Medicine 1985; 80(8): 37-40.

68. Wolf AM. Zinc-responsive dermatosis in a Rhodesian Ridgeback. Veterinary Medicine 1987; 82: 908-912.

69. Gross TL, Ihrke PJ, Walder EJ. Veterinary Dermatopathology. St Louis, MO: Mosby-Year Book Inc, 1992; 102-108.

70. Degryse AD, Fransen J, van Cutsem J, et al. Recurrent zinc-responsive dermatosis in a Siberian husky. Journal of Small Animal Practice 1987; 28: 721-726.

71. Forbes RM, Parker HM, Erdman JW. Effects of dietary phytate, calcium and magnesium levels on zinc bioavailability to rats. Journal of Nutrition 1984; 114: 1421-1425.

72. Whiteneck DL, Whitehair CK, Miller ER. Influence of enteric infection on zinc utilization and clinical signs and lesions of zinc deficiency in young swine. American Journal of Veterinary Research 1978; 39: 1447-1454.

73. Brown RG, Hoag GN, Smart ME, et al. Alaskan malamute chondrodysplasia. V. Decreased gut zinc absorption. Growth 1978; 42: 1-6.

74. Willemse T. Zinc-related cutaneous disorders of dogs. In: Kirk RW, Bonagura JD, eds. Current Veterinary Therapy XI. Philadelphia, PA: WB Saunders Co, 1992; 532-534.

75. Smits B, Croft DL, Abrams-Ogg ACG. Lethal acrodermatitis in bull terriers: A problem of defective zinc metabolism. Veterinary Dermatology 1991; 2: 91-95.

76. McEwan NA. Confirmation and investigation of lethal acrodermatitis of bull terriers in Britain. In: Ihrke PJ, Mason IS, White SD, eds. Advances in Veterinary Dermatology, vol. 2. New York, NY: Pergamon Press, 1993; 151-156.

77. van den Broek AHM, Stafford WL, Keay G. Diagnostic value of zinc concentrations in serum leucocytes and hair of dogs with zinc-responsive dermatosis. Research in Veterinary Science 1988; 44: 41-44.

78. Logas D, Kunkle GA, McDowell L. Comparison of serum zinc levels in healthy, systemically ill and dermatologically diseased dogs. Veterinary Dermatology 1993; 4: 61-64.

79. Fisher GL. Effects of disease on serum copper and zinc values in the beagle. American Journal of Veterinary Research 1977; 39: 935-940.

80. Keene CL, Lonnerdal B, Fisher GL. Seasonal variation and effects of age on serum copper and zinc values in the dog. American Journal of Veterinary Research 1981; 42: 342-350.

81. Lowe JA, Wiseman J, Cole DJA. Zinc source influences zinc retention in hair and hair growth in the dog. Journal of Nutrition 1994; 124: 257S-276S.

82. Kwochka KW. Primary keratinization disorders of dogs. In: Griffin CE, Kwochka KW, MacDonald JM, eds. Current Veterinary Dermatology. St Louis, MO: Mosby-Year Book Inc, 1993; 180-182.

83. National Academy of Sciences. Nutrient Requirements of Cats. Washington, DC: National Academy Press, 1986.

84. Wolf G. Recent progress in vitamin A research: Nuclear retinoic acid receptors and their interaction with gene elements. Journal of Nutritional Biochemistry 1990; 1: 284-289.

85. Blumenberg M, Connolly DM, Freedberg IM. Regulation of keratin gene expression: The role of the nuclear receptors for retinoic acid, thyroid hormone and vitamin D3. Journal of Investigative Dermatology 1992; 98: 42S-49S.

86. National Academy of Sciences. Nutrient Requirements of Dogs. Washington, DC: National Academy Press, 1985.

87. Bradfield D, Smith MC. The ability of the dog to utilize vitamin A from plant and animal sources. American Journal of Physiology 1938; 124: 168-173.

88. Kallfelz FA, Dzanis DA. Overnutrition: An epidemic problem in pet animal practice? Veterinary Clinics of North America: Small Animal Practice 1989; 19: 433-446.

89. Power HT, Ihrke PJ. Synthetic retinoids in veterinary dermatology. Veterinary Clinics of North America: Small Animal Practice 1990; 20: 1525-1539.

90. Kwochka KW. Retinoids and vitamin A therapy. In: Griffin CE, Kwochka KW, MacDonald JM, eds. Current Veterinary Dermatology. St Louis, MO: Mosby-Year Book Inc, 1993; 203-210.

91. Miller WH. Nonsteroidal anti-inflammatory agents in the management of canine and feline pruritus. In: Kirk RW, ed. Current Veterinary Therapy X. Philadelphia, PA: WB Saunders Co, 1989; 566-569.

92. Farris GM, Perkins PJ, Lloyd B, et al. The effect on atopic dermatitis of supplementation with selenium and vitamin E. Acta Dermato-Venereologica, Supplementum Stockholm 1989; 69: 359-362.

93. Rosenkrantz WR. Discoid lupus erythematosus. In: Griffin CE, Kwochka KW, MacDonald JM, eds. Current Veterinary Dermatology. St Louis, MO: Mosby-Year Book Inc, 1993; 149-153.

CASE 15-1

Seborrheic Dermatitis in a Cocker Spaniel

Dawn Logas, DVM
Diplomate ACVD
College of Veterinary Medicine
University of Florida
Gainesville, Florida, USA

Assess the Animal

A four-year-old spayed female cocker spaniel had a two-year history of seborrhea. The dog had previously been treated with antibiotics, steroids and topical antiseborrheic shampoos with minimal improvement. The dog weighed 10 kg and had a body condition score of 3/5.

The only abnormalities noted on physical examination were an odoriferous generalized dermatosis and bilateral otitis externa. The dermatosis was characterized by erythematous and hyperpigmented hyperkeratotic plaques in which the hairs were coated with keratinaceous casts that formed "fronds" (Figure 1). Multiple papules and pustules were noted on the ventrum and dorsum. Both ear canals were mildly erythematous and swollen with a thick, yellow waxy discharge.

Figure 1. Hyperpigmented, hyperkeratotic plaques with fronding on the ventrum of a four-year-old cocker spaniel.

Skin scrapings for parasites and fungal culture for dermatophytes were negative. Tape preparations of the skin revealed many cocci. Ear cytology revealed numerous yeast organisms. A culture specimen from a pustule grew moderate numbers of *Staphylococcus intermedius* colonies that were sensitive to all antibiotics except penicillin,

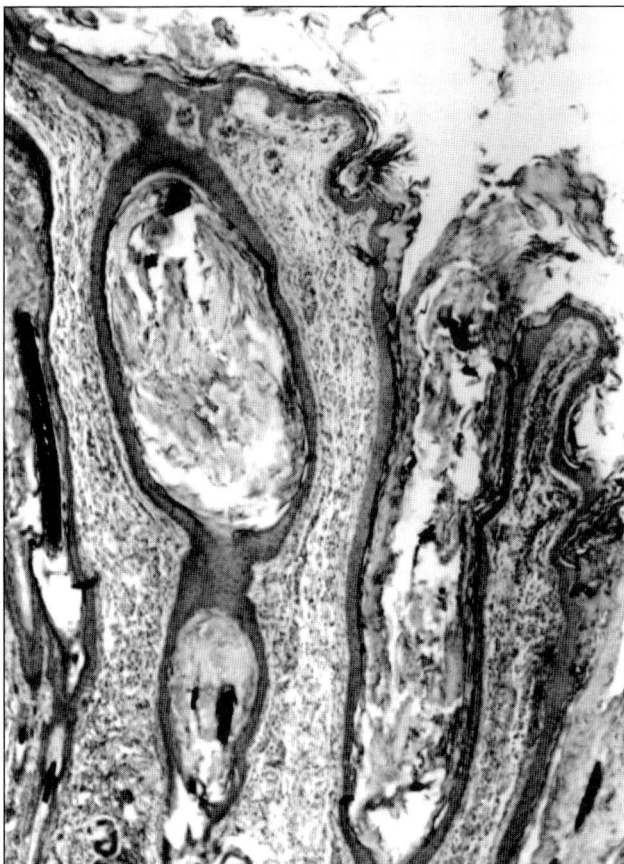

Figure 2. Skin biopsy specimen from a seborrheic cocker spaniel. The epidermis is mildly hyperplastic and hyperkeratotic. There is severe follicular hyperkeratosis and dilatation. (Magnification 10X.)

amoxicillin and tetracycline. Histopathologically the hyperkeratotic plaques were characterized by marked follicular hyperkeratosis with distended follicular ostia, orthokeratotic hyperkeratosis of the epidermis and irregular epidermal hyperplasia (Figure 2).

Assess the Food(s) and Feeding Method

For the past three years the dog had eaten a commercial specialty brand dry dog food supplemented with table foods.

Therapy Including Feeding Plan

The tentative diagnosis was vitamin A-responsive dermatosis with superficial pyoderma and yeast otitis. Treatment was initiated with 10,000 IU of vitamin A orally along with the dog's original food. The patient was also given an appropriate antibiotic for the pyoderma and a topical antifungal for the yeast otitis.

Questions

1. Why is vitamin A essential for normal epidermal function?
2. Why is this condition referred to as vitamin A-responsive dermatosis?
3. What are possible mechanisms by which vitamin A might correct the keratinization defect of this dermatosis?
4. How long must vitamin A be given to this dog and what potential side effects of vitamin A therapy might be expected?

Answers and Discussion

1. Vitamin A appears essential in the control of epidermal differentiation from basal cells to corneocytes. This is best illustrated by comparing the dermatologic signs of vitamin A deficiency with the signs associated with vitamin A excess. Mucous membrane epithelium is normally composed of nonkeratinizing cells. In vitamin A deficiency, nonkeratinizing mucous membrane cells are replaced by keratinizing cells and cells that normally keratinize in the skin become hyperkeratotic. The opposite response occurs when vitamin A is given in excess; mucous or ciliated squamous cells replace cells that normally keratinize.
2. Serum vitamin A levels have been normal in all of the reported cases of vitamin A-responsive dermatosis. This finding suggests that systemic vitamin A deficiency is an unlikely cause of the dermatosis. These cases also fail to show other clinical signs associated with vitamin A deficiency such as retinal degeneration, hind leg weakness and keratinization of mucous membranes. Improvement is noted within three to four weeks of starting oral vitamin A alcohol (retinol) supplementation, with complete remission by eight to 10 weeks. The specific cause of the dermatosis is unknown but may represent a local or functional deficiency of vitamin A.
3. Vitamin A may be able to correct this dermatosis via antikeratinization effects. Vitamin A normalizes the proliferation of keratinocytes and decreases the epidermal hyperproliferation. Vitamin A also alters the expression of certain structural genes that are important in epidermal differentiation and cornification. Examples include the suppression of transglutaminase, which is important in cell envelope formation, and the alteration of keratins to K19 and K13, which are normally not found in adult skin but are in fetal skin. Finally, vitamin A induces growth factors and the expression of growth factor receptors that also suppress epidermal differentiation.
4. These dogs usually must be given vitamin A for life. Discontinuing vitamin A supplementation usually results in recrudescence of dermatologic signs. Dogs generally tolerate vitamin A therapy quite well with minor side effects. Vitamin A should be used with caution in breeding animals because it may be teratogenic.

Progress Notes

The dog has done very well as long as vitamin A supplementation has been maintained. Cutaneous lesions reappeared when vitamin A supplementation was discontinued.

Bibliography

Ihrke PJ, Goldschmidt MH. Vitamin A-responsive dermatosis in the dog. Journal of the American Veterinary Medical Association 1983; 182: 687-690.

Kwochka KW. Retinoids and vitamin A therapy. In: Griffin CE, Kwochka KW, MacDonald JM, eds. Current Veterinary Dermatology. St Louis, MO: Mosby-Year Book Inc, 1993; 203-210.

Parker W, Yager-Johnson JA, Hardy MH. Vitamin A-responsive seborrheic dermatosis in the dog: A case report. Journal of the American Animal Hospital Association 1983; 19: 548-554.

Scott DW. Vitamin A-responsive dermatosis in the cocker spaniel. Journal of the American Animal Hospital Association 1986; 22: 125-129.

CASE 15-2

Recurrent Pyoderma in a Chesapeake Bay Retriever

Dawn Logas, DVM
Diplomate ACVD
College of Veterinary Medicine
University of Florida
Gainesville, Florida, USA

Assess the Animal

A two-year-old intact male Chesapeake Bay retriever was presented with a 12-month history of recurrent bacterial pyoderma and seborrhea sicca. The dog had previously been treated with two- to three-week courses of various antibiotics at appropriate doses. Response to therapy was partial; papules and pustules would resolve but epidermal flakes and dry brittle hair persisted. All dermatologic signs including papules and pustules would return within weeks after antibiotic therapy was discontinued. Historically, the dog had no other problems.

The dog was slightly underweight (body condition score 2/5), normothermic, alert and well-hydrated. Mucous membranes were pink and capillary refill time was 1.5 seconds. Lymph node size, chest auscultation and abdominal palpation were all within normal limits. No abnormalities were noted on ocular or musculoskeletal examination. Both ears had a slight accumulation of yellow waxy exudate but were not inflamed. The coat was thin, dry and lacked sheen. The dermatosis was generalized, sparing only the head and feet. It consisted of large white flakes, papules, pustules, epidermal collarettes and crusts. The dog was only mildly to moderately pruritic; the pruritus historically abated with antibiotic therapy.

Skin scrapings for parasites and fungal culture for dermatophytes were negative. Tape preparation of the skin revealed moderate numbers of cocci bacteria. *Staphylococcus intermedius* was cultured from a pustule. Thyroid profile results were within normal limits.

Assess the Food(s) and Feeding Method

The dog was fed a grocery store brand dry puppy food until 10 months of age at which time the client switched to a generic dry adult dog food. The owner would often purchase whatever generic dog food was on sale.

Therapy Including Feeding Plan

The dog was diagnosed as having a recurrent pyoderma possibly secondary to malnutrition associated with consumption of generic dog food. The pyoderma was treated for six consecutive weeks with an appropriate antibiotic. The food was changed to a grocery brand dry adult dog food supplemented with one tablespoon of corn oil for 12 weeks.

Questions

1. Which major nutrients are essential for normal epidermal function and how might dermatoses due to malnutrition occur in patients eating generic pet foods?
2. How might consumption of generic food have contributed to the dog's recurrent pyoderma?
3. Could nutritional deficiencies account for the dermatologic signs (other than the pyoderma) observed in this dog?

Answers and Discussion

1. Nutrients of special concern for maintaining normal skin and hair include protein, essential fatty acids (EFA), copper, zinc and certain vitamins. A previous report summarized the dermatologic signs that occurred in 13 dogs fed generic pet foods. Generic pet foods are marketed based on low daily cost of feeding. The low cost of the food is usually achieved by using ingredients that often have low total digestibility, low nutrient availability, high mineral content and low quantities of fat and EFA. Food with high mineral levels (calcium, phosphorus, magnesium), poor digestibility, high levels of phytate and/or low levels of total fat and EFA is a significant risk factor for zinc-responsive cutaneous disease. See the section of this chapter that discusses the dermatologic signs associated with fatty acid and zinc deficiency.

2. Malnutrition resulting from consumption of generic dog food may have contributed to the recurrent pyoderma in this dog. Decreases in zinc and EFA can lead to changes in the microenvironment of the stratum corneum, which allow pathogenic bacteria to colonize the surface of skin. Once colonized, the skin may also be less able to control the infection because decreases in zinc, protein and EFA may diminish normal humoral and cellular immunity. Zinc deficiency impairs macrophage phagocytosis, diminishes chemotaxis and leads to lymphopenia. Decreased levels of EFA, which are normally converted to potent inflammatory mediators called eicosanoids, lead to decreases in chemotaxis, margination and killing ability of leukocytes, particularly neutrophils. Inadequate protein intake, particularly of essential amino acids, can alter the immune response.

3. EFA and zinc deficiency could account for the dry dull coat, fine scale and hyperkeratotic crusts. EFA are necessary for the formation of lamellar granules, which contain much of the epidermal lipids in dogs. These lipids are essential for the formation of the transepidermal water barrier. Without these lipids, the stratum corneum water loss increases and fine scales are formed. EFA are also necessary for the formation of normal sebaceous gland lipids. The sebaceous lipids are important for coating hairs and giving them their sheen.

Zinc is necessary for normal keratinization. Although the exact mechanisms of zinc's effect on keratinization are unknown, they may be related to the many zinc metalloenzymes, which are found in the epidermis and are essential for epidermal cell differentiation. Therefore, zinc deficiency could lead to the hyperkeratotic crusts noted in this case.

Progress Notes

After six weeks of therapy there was no evidence of bacterial pyoderma or dry flakes. The patient's coat was much softer, shinier and fuller. Eight months after discontinuing antibiotic therapy, the dog's coat and skin remained normal with no recurrence of the pyoderma.

Bibliography

Sousa CA, Stannard AA, Ihrke PJ, et al. Dermatosis associated with feeding generic dog food: 13 cases (1981-1983). Journal of the American Veterinary Medical Association 1988; 192: 676-680.

CASE 15-3

Crusting Dermatitis in a Bull Terrier

Candace A. Sousa, DVM
Diplomate ABVP and ACVD
Animal Dermatology Clinic
Sacramento, California, USA

Assess the Animal

A four-year-old spayed female bull terrier was examined for severe skin crusting. The crusting had been present since the dog was five months old and had progressively worsened. Previous diagnostic tests included multiple skin scrapings for parasites (negative), a fungal culture (negative) and failure of a clinical response to several empirical therapies (antibiotics, shampoos).

Physical examination demonstrated a mature bitch that was well-fleshed but smaller than breed standards (11.7 kg, body condition score 3/5). There were no abnormal physical findings other than those related to the integument. The coat was dull and brittle. Cream-colored patches of thick, tightly-adherent crusts were present above each eye, within the inner pinnae (Figure 1) and overlying the elbows and hocks. All of the footpads were thickened and cracked with "feathers" of adherent keratin extruding from the edges (Figures 2).

Results of a complete blood count, serum biochemistry profile and urinalysis were normal. Histopathology of skin biopsy specimens revealed marked parakeratotic hyperkeratosis. Neutrophils infiltrated the superficial dermis with some exocytosis, spongiosis and scattered individual dyskeratotic keratinocytes in the epidermis.

Assess the Food(s) and Feeding Method

The dog had been fed a dry commercial food formulated for puppies for the first 10 months of life and several different dry dog foods formulated for adult maintenance during the next three years.

Therapy Including Feeding Plan

Based on the age at onset, breed, diagnostic results and a lack of response to various therapies, a tentative diagnosis of acrodermatitis of bull terriers was made.

Questions

1. What nutritional therapy should be advocated for this dog?
2. What other information should the owner be given regarding this disease and the prognosis for the dog?

Answers and Discussion

1. Acrodermatitis develops in bull terriers shortly after birth and is associated with defects in zinc absorption and metabolism. Cutaneous and systemic clinical signs resemble severe zinc deficiency with growth retardation, gastrointestinal disease, chronic bacterial infections and progressive, erythematous, exfoliative, papular to pustular dermatitis of the distal extremities and skin surrounding the mucocutaneous junctions. Surface crusts usually contain numerous bacteria and yeast organisms.

Supplementation of the food with oral or intravenous zinc usually fails to ameliorate clinical signs. Treatment with systemic antimicrobials, especially for secondary superficial yeast infections, may result in marked improvement, although systemic and cutaneous infections recur. This dog was treated with a zinc methio-

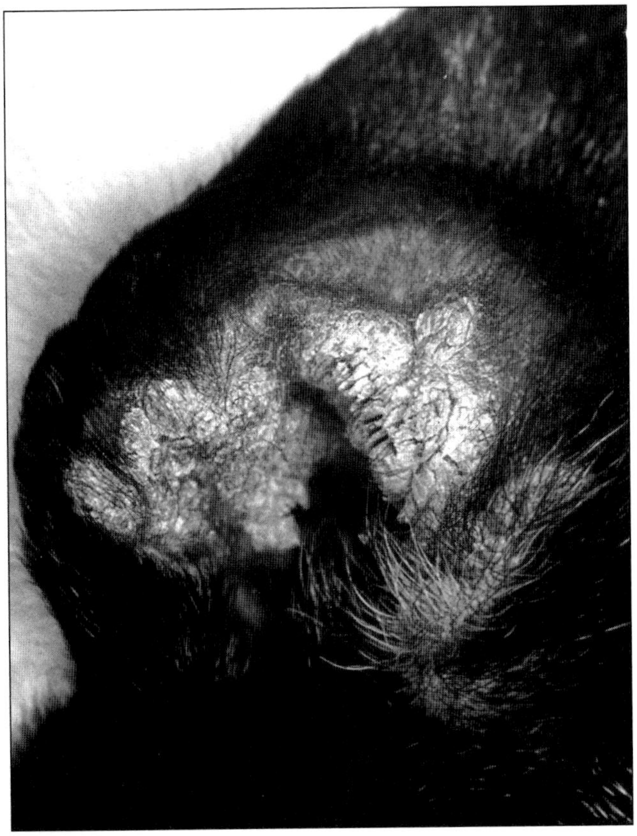

Figure 1. A four-year-old bull terrier with thick crusts in the inner pinna at the ear canal entrance.

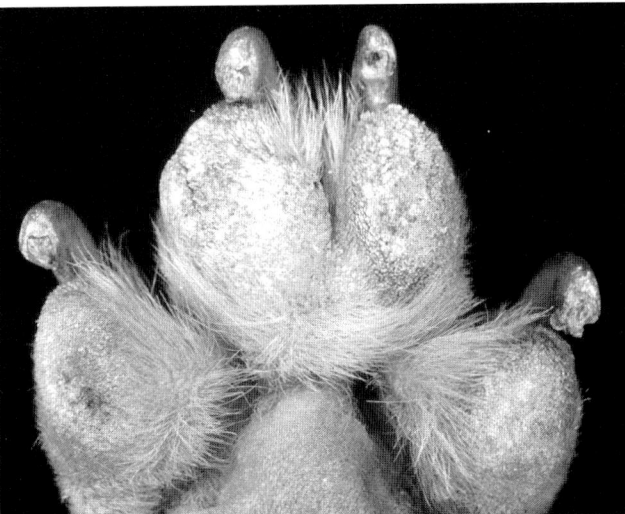

Figure 2. The same dog with hyperkeratosis of the foot pads.

nine supplement (50 mg once daily) and oral cephalexin (250 mg b.i.d.) for secondary pyoderma.

2. Acrodermatitis is an inherited, autosomal recessive metabolic disease reported to occur in bull terriers in the United States, Canada and the United Kingdom. This bitch had already been spayed but further breeding of this dog's parents should be discouraged. The condition has been termed lethal acrodermatitis because homozygously affected dogs rarely live beyond 18 months of age. Some of the apparently normal littermates may develop zinc-responsive dermatitis. Owners of affected dogs usually complain that their pets have skin disease, stunting, difficulty with eating and large, splayed, painful feet. Ulcerated and thick, crusted lesions are prominent on the muzzle and ears. Abnormal keratinization of the footpads, severe nail dystrophy and paronychia are also common. Prognosis is guarded to poor for severely affected dogs.

Progress Notes

After eight weeks of therapy, the crusting shown in the pictures had decreased about 30%. At that point, the dog was lost to any further evaluation.

Bibliography

Jezyk PF, Haskins ME, Mackay-Smith MA, et al. Lethal acrodermatitis in bull terriers. Journal of the American Veterinary Medical Association 1986; 188: 833-839.

McEwan NA. Confirmation and investigation of lethal acrodermatitis of bull terriers in Britain. In: Ihrke PJ, Mason IS, White SD, eds. Advances in Veterinary Dermatology, vol. 2. New York, NY: Pergamon Press, 1993; 151-156.

Mundell AC. Mineral analysis in bull terriers with lethal acrodermatitis (abstract). In: Proceedings. Annual Members Meeting AAVD & ACVD, Washington, DC, 1988: 22.

Smits B, Croft DL, Abrams-Ogg ACG. Lethal acrodermatitis in bull terriers: A problem of defective zinc metabolism. Veterinary Dermatology 1991; 2: 91-95.

CASE 15-4

Crusting Dermatosis in a Siberian Husky Crossbred Dog

Candace A. Sousa, DVM
Diplomate ABVP and ACVD
Animal Dermatology Clinic
Sacramento, California, USA

Assess the Animal

A four-month-old male Siberian husky cross breed dog weighing 18 kg was presented for evaluation of an eight-week history of variable but persistent crusting. The lesions were first noticed above the eyes and around the mouth, but now extended to the chin and neck. A fungal culture was negative for dermatophytes. Therapy with topical agents, cephalexin and griseofulvin resulted in no clinical improvement. No history was available for either the parents or related dogs.

Physical examination revealed a bright, active and alert puppy with a body condition score of 3/5 (ideal). The only abnormalities noted were limited to the skin. Thick, tightly adherent white crusts were noted above both eyes. The outer ear pinnae were alopecic and crusty. Scattered, white, tightly adherent crusts 1 to 3 cm in diameter were found around the lip margins (Figure 1) and ventral neck.

Histopathology of multiple skin biopsy specimens demonstrated severe irregular acanthosis accompanied by prominent parakeratosis and marked serocellular crusting. The parakeratosis extended into the superficial hair follicles. A mixed inflammatory infiltrate, which included lymphocytes, macrophages, neutrophils, plasma cells and scattered eosinophils, was found beneath the acanthotic and multifocally spongiotic epidermis.

Assess the Food(s) and Feeding Method

After the owners obtained the dog from a private home at nine weeks of age, they had fed it a combination of commercial moist and dry foods formulated for puppies.

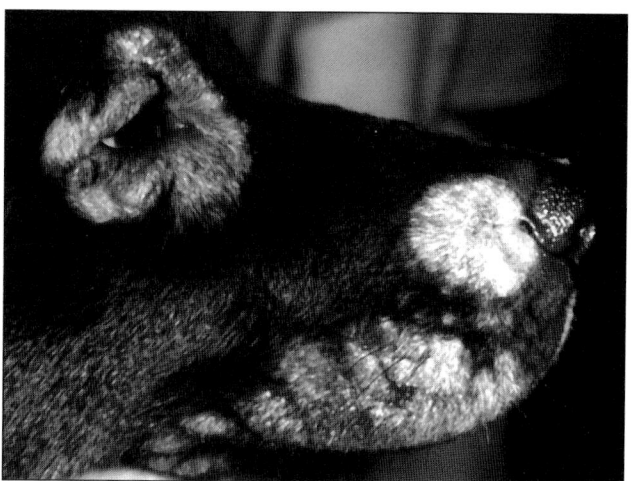

Figure 1. A four-month-old male Siberian husky cross with marked alopecia, lichenification and crusting of the periocular and perioral skin.

Questions

1. Given the signalment and clinical signs, what diseases should be considered?
2. What are the risk factors for development of zinc-responsive cutaneous disease in dogs?
3. What are the best methods to diagnose zinc-related cutaneous disease in animals?
4. Outline an appropriate feeding plan for this puppy.

Answers and Discussion

1. The list of differential diagnoses for this dog should include demodicosis, dermatophytosis, bacterial pyoderma, primary keratinization defect (e.g., ichthyosis), nutritional dermatosis (vitamin A-responsive or zinc-responsive dermatosis) and autoimmune skin disease (e.g., pemphigus foliaceus, pemphigus erythematosus and lupus erythematosus). The histopathologic changes were most compatible with a zinc-responsive dermatosis and secondary pyoderma.

2. Risk factors for zinc-responsive skin disease in dogs include breed, high mineral or phytate levels in the food, low essential fatty acid levels, supplementation with calcium or other minerals and small intestinal disease resulting in malabsorption or maldigestion. Breeds in which zinc-responsive disease has been reported to occur include Siberian huskies, malamutes, bull terriers, Great Danes, Labrador retrievers and other rapidly growing large- and giant-breed dogs.

3. Diagnosis of zinc-responsive cutaneous disease is based on the history, physical examination and skin biopsy results. Hyperplastic superficial perivascular dermatitis with marked diffuse and follicular parakeratotic hyperkeratosis is suggestive of zinc deficiency. In general, concentrations of zinc in serum, leukocytes and hair are not good indicators of zinc status in dogs.

4. The tentative diagnosis was zinc-responsive dermatosis, which is often seen in Siberian husky dogs. Treatment generally includes changing to a food that avoids excess minerals and contains adequate amounts of zinc and essential fatty acids. Zinc supplementation will be necessary in those breeds in which decreased ability to absorb zinc is suspected. Siberian huskies are one such breed.

Progress Notes

Initial therapy consisted of feeding the moist food supplemented with 50 mg of zinc given orally once daily. Within two months, the lesions disappeared and the dog's coat had returned to normal. When the dog was 10 months old, the owner discontinued the zinc supplement and lesions began to return. Based on this finding, the dog will probably need zinc supplementation for the remainder of its life. Some Siberian huskies do not respond to oral zinc supplementation; however, intravenous injections of zinc sulfate solutions may be effective in these animals.

Bibliography

Brown RG, Hoag GN, Smart ME, et al. Alaskan malamute chondrodysplasia. V. Decreased gut zinc absorption. Growth 1978; 42: 1-6.

Degryse AD, Fransen J, van Cutsem J, et al. Recurrent zinc-responsive dermatosis in a Siberian husky. Journal of Small Animal Practice 1987; 28: 721-726.

Gross TL, Ihrke PJ, Walder EJ. Veterinary Dermatopathology. St Louis, MO: Mosby-Year Book Inc, 1992; 102-108.

Scott DW, Miller WH, Griffin CE. Small Animal Dermatology, 5th ed. Philadelphia, PA: WB Saunders Co, 1995; 897-899.

Willemse T. Zinc-related cutaneous disorders of dogs. In: Kirk RW, Bonagura JD, eds. Current Veterinary Therapy XI. Philadelphia, PA: WB Saunders Co, 1992; 532-534.

CHAPTER 16

Dental Disease

Ellen I. Logan

Robert B. Wiggs

Karl Zetner

John J. Hefferren

"Dirty teeth . . . foul the whole system, just as a dirty entrance to a field soils the whole field."

Henry Gray, 1934

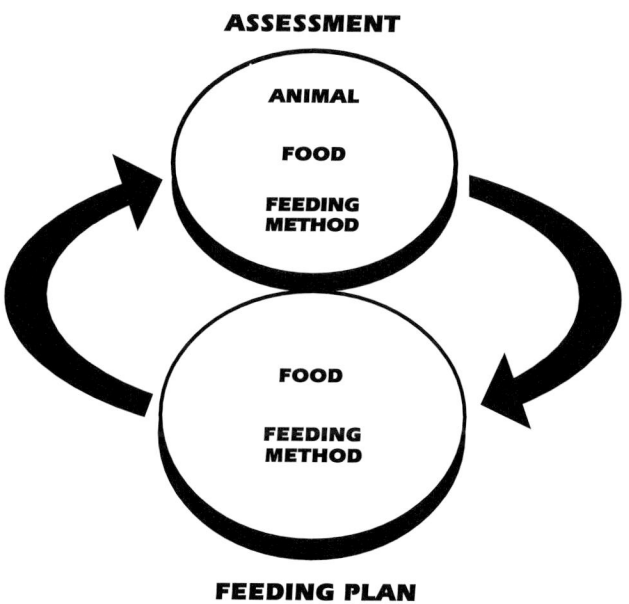

ASSESSMENT

ANIMAL

FOOD

FEEDING METHOD

FOOD

FEEDING METHOD

FEEDING PLAN

Note: The reader is referred to Chapter 1 for a detailed discussion of the iterative process of clinical nutrition.

INTRODUCTION

Veterinary dentistry is a relatively new specialty. Before 1970, dental work was often restricted to scalings and extractions. Veterinary curricula did not routinely include small animal dentistry beyond teaching basic tooth structure and dental formulas. Because diseases affecting the oral cavity are common in dogs and cats, dentistry will play an increasingly important role in veterinary practice.

Primary oral diseases can be subdivided into conditions affecting the tooth, the periodontium or other oral tissues (Table 16-1). Diseases that affect tooth structure may result in lesions of the periodontal apparatus, oral mucosa or both. Diseases affecting the periodontium may result in exfoliation of the tooth. Additionally, primary diseases of other organs may cause oral lesions and are important considerations in formulating differential diagnoses.

The goals of promoting oral health and nutritional management of oral disease in dogs and cats are to: 1) control plaque, the cause of periodontal disease, 2) assess the level of plaque control necessary to prevent gingivitis in each patient, 3) determine each pet owner's ability to control substrate accumulation and select methods most likely to ensure compliance, 4) feed a food with an appropriate texture and nutritional profile and 5) recognize that oral health may affect systemic health; therefore, a healthy oral cavity may affect longevity and quality of life.

Dental Anatomy

The oral cavity serves a variety of functions. It is the entrance to the gastrointestinal and the respiratory tracts. Salivary fluids bathe the oral cavity and assist in mastication and deglutition. These fluids possess antimicrobial

KEY WORDS & TERMS—DENTAL DISEASE*

Abrasion	Diphyodont	Oral malodor (halitosis)
Acquired pellicle	Facial	Palatal
Alveolar process	Furcation	Periodontal disease
Apical	Gingiva	Periodontal ligament
Attrition	Gingival margin	Periodontitis
Brachycephalic	Gingival recession	Periodontium
Buccal	Gingival sulcus	Plaque
Calculus (tartar)	Gingivitis	Resorptive lesion
Caries	Kibble	Stain
Cervical	Labial	Stomatitis
Coronal	Lingual	Subgingival
Crevicular	Malocclusion	Supragingival
Dental substrate	Materia alba	

*Key words and terms are defined in the Glossary.

KEY POINTS—DENTAL DISEASE

1. Dogs and cats are diphyodont, erupting two sets of teeth, deciduous and permanent.
2. The dental formula for adult dogs is 2(I3/3, C1/1, P4/4, M2/3); for adult cats 2(I3/3, C1/1, P3/2, M1/1).
3. The majority of dogs and cats enter adulthood with healthy mouths.
4. Periodontal disease is the most common disease of adult dogs and cats.
5. Odontoclastic resorptive lesions are the most common disease affecting the tooth structure of adult cats.
6. Enamel caries occurs infrequently in dogs and cats.
7. A complete physical examination should include extraoral and intraoral examinations.
8. A definitive oral examination is best achieved with the patient anesthetized.
9. Accurate charting is essential to monitor oral health over the life span of the patient.
10. Tooth-accumulated materials include pellicle, plaque, calculus, stain and materia alba.
11. Plaque is the primary cause of periodontal disease and is the key substrate that must be controlled in order to control the occurrence and severity of periodontal disease.
12. Species, breed, age, immunocompetence, food characteristics and chewing behavior are risk factors associated with oral and dental diseases.
13. Periodontal disease typically refers to gingivitis and periodontitis. Gingivitis is reversible; periodontitis is irreversible.
14. Periodontal disease is episodic, with periods of active tissue destruction followed by periods of inactivity and healing. Not all teeth are affected at the same rate nor to the same degree.
15. Oral disease may compromise systemic health. Orally initiated bacteremia may infect other organs such as the heart, lungs and kidneys.
16. Nutrient composition and the form of a food (texture) can affect oral health.
17. A variety of dental claims are used in marketing dental foods and treats. Many product manufacturers make cosmetic and structure-function claims with little or no supportive data.
18. Oral health is a function of professional therapy and effective home care to control plaque accumulation.

properties that help protect oral tissues from bacterial invasion. Evaporation of salivary fluids aids in heat loss. The teeth and the tongue are important in eating, grooming, defense and behavior.

The teeth of dogs and cats serve specific functions. The incisor teeth are used for grasping and nibbling. The canine teeth are used for capturing and puncturing prey. The premolar and molar teeth are used for shearing, grinding and chewing. The carnassial teeth, designated as the upper fourth premolar and the lower first molar, are the teeth primarily used for chewing.[1]

Although the teeth of dogs and cats vary in size, shape and function, the components and structure of all teeth are similar (Figure 16-1). A normal, mature tooth has a crown and one to three roots. The junction of the crown and the root is termed the cementoenamel junction (CEJ). The crown is the portion of the tooth above the CEJ and is covered by dense, smooth enamel. Enamel is primarily inorganic hydroxyapatite crystal and is very hard and not easily damaged. Enamel is fully formed before eruption.

Inflammation and trauma, however, may affect enamel during formation.

The root or roots are the portion of the tooth below the CEJ and serve to anchor the tooth in the alveolar bone as well as provide the neurovascular port (apical delta). The root is covered by a thin layer of cementum, a calcified structure in which the periodontal fibers are embedded.

The dentin underlies the enamel and the cementum. Dentin is primarily collagen and inorganic hydroxyapatite. There are three types of dentin: primary, secondary and tertiary. Primary dentin is present during formation of deciduous and permanent teeth. As the animal ages, primary dentin is replaced continuously by secondary dentin. Tertiary dentin is laid down as a reparative substance; a response by odontoblasts to trauma or excessive wear. The internal layer of the tooth, the pulp cavity, contains blood and lymphatic vessels, nerves and odontoblasts supported in a connective tissue matrix.

The tooth is supported and protected by the periodontal apparatus, which consists of the gingiva, periodontal ligament, cementum and alveolar bone.[2] The gingiva is an exten-

KEY NUTRITIONAL FACTORS—DENTAL DISEASE

Nutritional factors	Associated conditions	Dietary recommendations

Protein	Plaque accumulation
	Periodontitis
	Dystrophic periodontium changes
	(protein deficiency)
		Avoid protein deficiency or excess
		  Adult maintenance
		    Dogs: 16 to 25% protein (dry matter basis)
		    Cats: 30 to 40% protein (dry matter basis)
		  Growth/lactation
		    Dogs: 30 to 35% protein (dry matter basis)
		    Cats: 35 to 50% protein (dry matter basis)
		Use food with dry matter digestibility >80%

Calcium/phosphorus	Calcium deficiency
	  Nutritional secondary hyper-
	  parathyroidism
	  Significant loss of alveolar bone
	Calcium and/or phosphorus excess
	  Promotes calculus formation
		Avoid calcium deficiency
		  Ensure homemade food recipes contain a source of calcium
		Ensure food has proper calcium levels
		  Adult maintenance (dogs and cats)
		    0.5 to 1.0% calcium (dry matter basis)
		    0.4 to 0.9% phosphorus (dry matter basis)
		  Growth/lactation (dogs and cats)
		    1.0 to 1.5% calcium (dry matter basis)
		    0.8 to 1.3% phosphorus (dry matter basis)

Food texture	Plaque and calculus accumulation	Provide food that promotes chewing and mechanical cleansing
		  of teeth
		    Dogs: Prescription Diet Canine t/d
		    Cats: Prescription Diet Feline t/d
		Add dental treat (with proven efficacy) without changing the food(s)
		Add new toy (appropriate for individual) without changing the
		  food(s)
		Add toothbrushing or other type of oral hygiene

sion of the oral mucosa and consists of keratinized epithelial tissue that attaches to the alveolar process and extends to the neck of the tooth. The gingivae are divided into the attached gingiva and the free gingiva. Normal attached gingiva extends from the mucogingival line to the CEJ. Normal free gingiva surrounds the neck of the tooth without attachment. The coronal edge of the free gingiva is termed the marginal gingiva. The space between the free gingiva and the tooth surface is the gingival sulcus or crevice.[3]

The periodontal ligament is composed of collagenous connective tissue fibers that attach the teeth to the alveolar bone. The periodontal ligament acts as a cushion, allowing slight movement of the tooth during mastication to prevent trauma to the tooth from occlusal and root-to-alveolar bone contact.

Thin, dense alveolar bone lines the tooth socket (lamina dura) and surrounds the root, providing attachment for the periodontal ligament and passage of blood and lymphatic vessels. Alveolar bone is surrounded and supported by trabecular and compact bone, which varies in thickness depending on the anatomic location. The alveolar process is a relatively active tissue that responds by resorption and remodeling to external forces and systemic influences.[4]

Dental Formulas

Dental formulas designate the number and types of teeth present. Dogs and cats are diphyodont, erupting deciduous and permanent teeth. Deciduous teeth begin erupting around three weeks of age in dogs and cats (Table 16-2). Eruption times may be influenced by breed, environment, nutrition, hormones and season. A dental formula represents the number of teeth in a hemijaw designated by maxilla/mandible. The total number of teeth is calculated by multiplying the number of teeth in each hemijaw by two.

Puppies have 28 teeth and adult dogs 42 teeth. Normal dental formulas for dogs are:[5]

> Deciduous: 2(I3/3, C1/1, P3/3)
> Permanent: 2(I3/3, C1/1, P4/4, M2/3)

Kittens have 26 teeth and adult cats 30 teeth. Normal dental formulas for cats are:[6]

> Deciduous: 2(I3/3, C1/1, P3/2)
> Permanent: 2(I3/3, C1/1, P3/2, M1/1)

Dental formulas represent the teeth that should normally be present in all dogs and cats. Anatomically, the maxillary first premolars and the mandibular first and second premolars are absent in cats. Thus, feline premolars are identified as the maxillary second, third and fourth, and the mandibular third and fourth.[7] Individual dogs and cats may have abnormal numbers of teeth. Oligodontia and supernumerary teeth occur commonly in dogs and less frequently in cats. Missing teeth may predispose the animal to soft tissue trauma from occluding teeth and may reduce the effect of oral cleansing, particularly in the carnassial area. Extra teeth may lead to overcrowding. There should never be more than one tooth occupying the same anatomic space.

Table 16-1. Conditions affecting the oral cavity.

Conditions primarily affecting teeth	Conditions primarily affecting the periodontium/oral mucosa
Abrasion	Gingivitis
Attrition	Periodontitis
Erosion	Gingival hyperplasia
Intrinsic staining	Periapical abscess
Odontoclastic resorption	Gingivostomatitis
Fracture	Neoplasia
Pulpitis	Chemical or thermal burns
	Ulcers

Positioning

Tooth surfaces are identified based on the structure they face. Facial refers to tooth surfaces that contact the lips and cheeks. Facial surfaces are commonly subdivided into labial for the incisor and canine teeth, and buccal for the premolar and molar teeth (Figure 16-2). The inside surface of maxillary teeth is termed the palatal surface; the inside surface of mandibular teeth is lingual. Mesial and distal are commonly used to identify the surface most rostral and caudal, respectively.[8] Correct and consistent usage of proper terminology is important for accurate lesion description and for proper charting during oral examination.

Occlusion

Dental occlusion refers to the position of each tooth and its relation to all other teeth. The normal occlusal pattern of dogs and cats is classified as a scissors bite (Figure 16-3): 1) the maxillary incisor teeth slightly overlap the mandibular incisor teeth, 2) the mandibular canine tooth falls between the maxillary third incisor tooth and canine tooth without touching either tooth and 3) the maxillary premolar teeth interdigitate with and close distal to the mandibular premolar teeth.

Table 16-2. Age when teeth erupt in dogs and cats (weeks).

| | Deciduous teeth | | Permanent teeth | |
	Dogs	Cats	Dogs	Cats
Incisors	4-6	3-4	12-16	11-16
Canines	3-5	3-4	16-24	12-20
Premolars	5-12	5-6	16-24	16-24
Molars	–	–	20-28	16-20

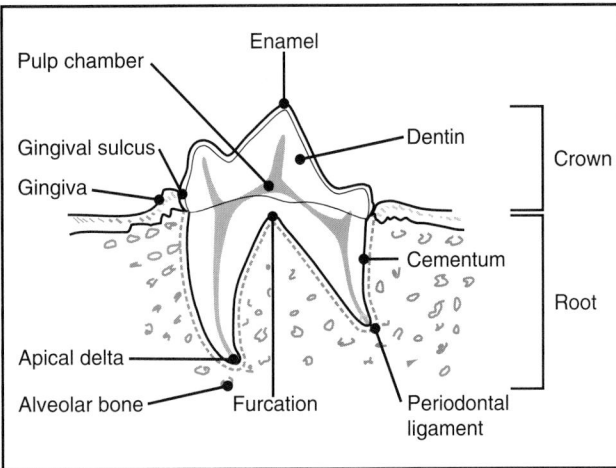

Figure 16-1. Normal tooth and periodontal anatomy.

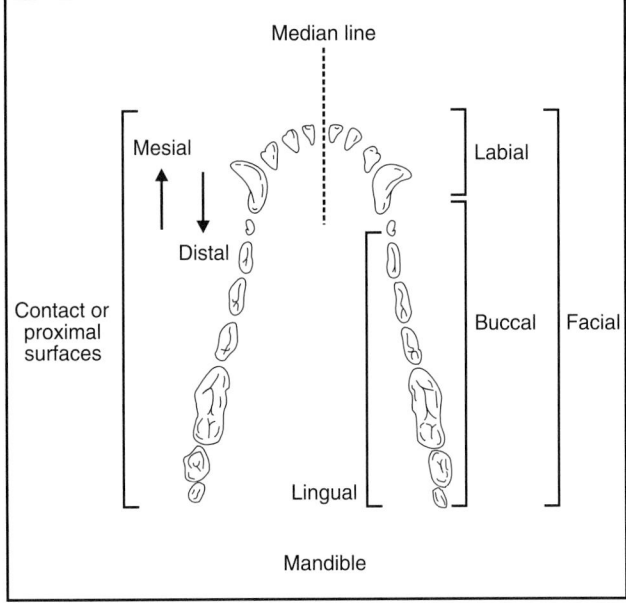

Figure 16-2. Directional nomenclature used to describe anatomic position of tooth surfaces. (Adapted from Wiggs RB. Canine oral anatomy and physiology. Compendium on Continuing Education for the Practicing Veterinarian 1989; 11: 1476.)

█ CLINICAL IMPORTANCE

Prevalence of Periodontal Disease

Periodontal disease is the most common disease of adult dogs and cats. As early as 1899, Eugene Talbot described "interstitial gingivitis or so-called pyorrhoea alveolaris" found in dogs at necropsy.[9] In 1939, Wright stated that "the incidence of disease of the teeth in the dog is so high that dental surgery occupies a prominent place in the work of the veterinarian engaged in small-animal practice. The most common affection necessitating surgical interference is paradontal disease."[10]

Periodontal disease has been observed in dogs and cats of varying breed, gender and age. Surveys from several countries report prevalence rates of periodontal disease that range from 60 to more than 80% of dogs and cats examined.[11-24]

Preliminary data from the National Companion Animal Study representing 54 veterinary practices across the United States suggest that oral disease was the most frequent diagnosis in all age categories of 39,556 dogs and 13,924 cats (Tables 16-3 and 16-4).[a]

Odontoclastic Resorptive Lesions

Resorptive lesions are defined as noncarious defects of enamel, cementum and dentin, and have been commonly referred to as neck or cervical line lesions because they occur most often in the cervical or neck region of the tooth at the CEJ.[25] Van Wessum reported that resorptive lesions are common in domestic cats, affecting more than 50% of cats examined.[26] Odontoclastic resorptive lesions occur infrequently in dogs.[27]

Dental Caries

Dental caries is decay of the tooth structure. Dental caries occurs infrequently in dogs.[28] Researchers conducting a survey from the School of Veterinary Medicine, University of Pennsylvania, Philadelphia, reported carious lesions in two of 63 dogs examined.[20] A report from Sweden indicated that 71 of 200 dogs were affected with carious lesions.[29] Caries occurs rarely in cats. Early reports often confused carious lesions with odontoclastic resorptive lesions.

Inflammatory and Immune-Mediated Diseases

Several oral conditions have an inflammatory or immune-mediated component different from the typical inflammatory-mediated response seen in periodontal disease.[30] Although the specific etiology of many of these conditions remains unknown, many are associated with oral bacteria and concurrent periodontal disease.

Ulcerative stomatitis occurs in dogs in which the mucosal surfaces contact plaque-covered teeth. Immune-mediated ulcerative gingivostomatitis has been reported to occur in Maltese dogs with minimal periodontal disease and has been reported to occur in other dogs with varying degrees of periodontal disease.[31] A condition reported as lympho-cytic- plasmacytic stomatitis occurs frequently in cats and is often refractory to treatment. Cats with this condition often exhibit severe oral pain and anorexia.[32]

Malocclusion

Malocclusion is any occlusal abnormality and may affect individual teeth, groups or quadrants of teeth or the entire dental arch. Domesticated dogs and cats have been selectively bred for specific head types that result in a variety of malocclusions (Figures 16-4 and 16-5). Occlusal abnormalities affect the relationship of the teeth to each other, and to other oral structures including the periodontium, palates, tongue, oral mucosa and lips. Potential ramifications include: 1) a compromise in oral function, 2) self-induced oral trauma and 3) an increased risk of incidence and severity of plaque-associated dental diseases.[33]

Attrition and Abrasion

Dental attrition is abnormal wear of tooth surfaces due to contact with occluding teeth during mastication. Attrition may result from excessive chewing on inappropriate materials such as rocks or other hard objects.[34] The incisor teeth, particularly in dogs, may show marked wear due to excessive chewing behaviors, as well as excessive

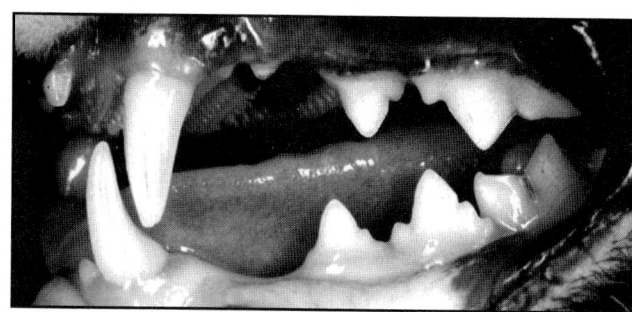

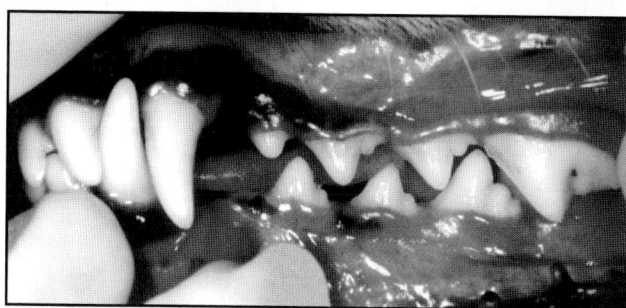

Figure 16-3. Normal occlusal pattern of adult cats (top) and dogs (bottom). The maxillary incisors overlap the mandibular incisors, which rest near the cingulum (enamel shelf on the palatal surface of the maxillary incisors). The mandibular canine teeth are positioned midway between the maxillary third incisors and the canine teeth. The premolar teeth interdigitate with the maxillary fourth premolar closing over the facial cusp of the mandibular first molar.

grooming associated with dermatologic conditions such as flea-bite dermatitis.

Abrasion is abnormal wear of tooth surfaces due to application of an external force, such as excessive toothbrushing or inappropriate use of power instruments.

Table 16-3. Top 10 canine diagnoses by age category.*

0 to 7 years (n = 24,165)	7 to 10 years (n = 6,699)	10 to 25 years (n = 8,692)
Healthy (32.4%)	Healthy (15.0%)	Oral disease (13.6%)
Oral disease (5.8%)	Oral disease (13.7%)	Healthy (6.9%)
Otitis externa (5.8%)	Otitis externa (5.8%)	Nuclear sclerosis (3.1%)
Dermatopathy (3.6%)	Dermatopathy (3.2%)	Arthritis (3.0%)
Lameness (1.3%)	Tumor (2.0%)	Tumor (2.8%)
Roundworms (1.2%)	Lipoma (1.9%)	Otitis externa (2.7%)
Conjunctivitis (1.2%)	Conjunctivitis (1.2%)	Cardiac murmur (2.4%)
Fleas (1.1%)	Arthritis (1.2%)	Lipoma (2.3%)
Laceration (1.0%)	Anal sac disease (1.2%)	Cataract (2.2%)
Anal sac disease (1.0%)	Lameness (1.1%)	Dermatopathy (1.5%)

*Preliminary data. 1995 National Companion Animal Study. Center for Companion Animal Health, University of Minnesota, St. Paul and Mark Morris Institute, Topeka, KS.

Table 16-4. Top 10 feline diagnoses by age category.*

0 to 7 years (n = 9,148)	7 to 10 years (n = 1,795)	10 to 25 years (n = 2,981)
Healthy (34.2%)	Oral disease (20.1%)	Oral disease (19.5%)
Oral disease (9.9%)	Healthy (18.9%)	Healthy (11.9%)
Ear mites (4.4%)	Cat bite abscess (2.5%)	Chronic renal failure (2.4%)
Fleas (2.7%)	Dermatopathy (2.3%)	Weight loss (2.0%)
Cat bite abscess (2.6%)	Obesity (1.6%)	Cardiac murmur (1.8%)
Upper respiratory infection (2.2%)	Fleas (1.5%)	Hyperthyroidism (1.8%)
Tapeworms (2.0%)	Animal bites (1.5%)	Tumor (1.7%)
Conjunctivitis (1.7%)	Ear mites (1.4%)	Diabetes mellitus (1.4%)
Roundworms (1.4%)	Upper respiratory infection (1.3%)	Cat bite abscess (1.4%)
Dermatopathy (1.3%)	Vomiting (1.3%)	Vomiting (1.3%)

*Preliminary data. 1995 National Companion Animal Study. Center for Companion Animal Health, University of Minnesota, St. Paul and Mark Morris Institute, Topeka, KS.

Figure 16-4A. Brachycephalic dog with a short, broad facial profile.

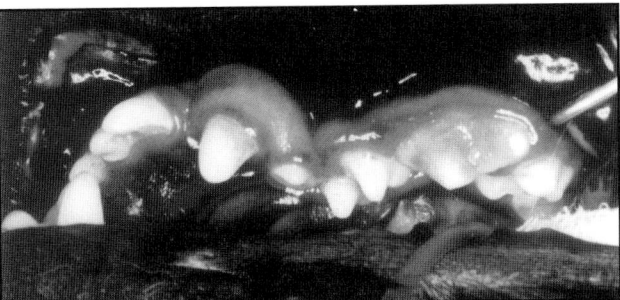

Figure 16-4B. Overcrowding and rotation of teeth typically present in brachycephalic breeds.

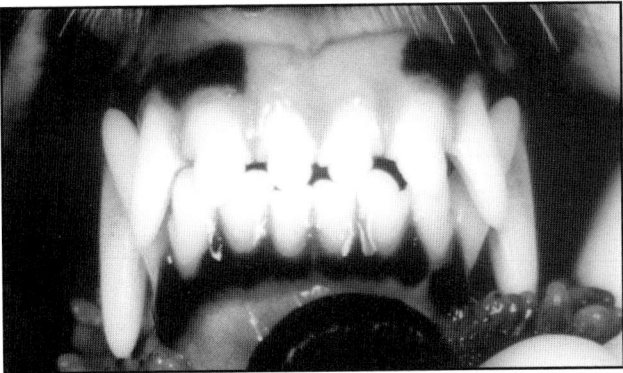

Figure 16-5A. Normal incisor occlusion. The maxillary incisors slightly overlap the mandibular incisors.

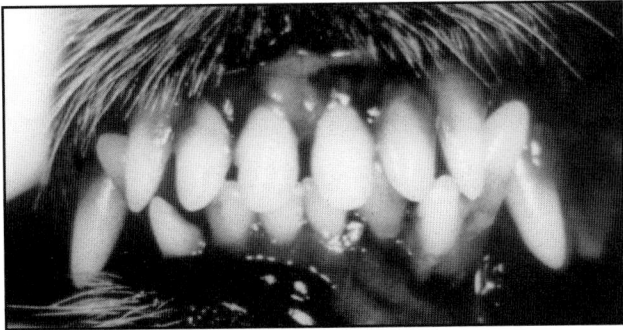

Figure 16-5B. Abnormal incisor occlusion often seen in many small-breed dogs. The incisor teeth are crowded and malpositioned. The mandibular canine teeth are displaced lingually and the maxillary canine teeth flare laterally (facially).

Excessive wear is not immediately pathologic as long as the wear rate does not exceed the rate of reparative dentin formation. However, rapid wear can lead to pulpal exposure and infection as well as compromised tooth strength, predisposing the tooth to fracture.

Excessive wear was not associated with increased prevalence of periodontal disease in a survey of 63 dogs.[20] Research has indicated that occlusal trauma in the absence of periodontal disease can damage the periodontal ligament and affect periodontal health. Occlusal trauma can exacerbate periodontal disease.[35]

ASSESSMENT

Assess the Animal

History

A complete history is important to diagnosis and treatment planning and is an integral tool to development of a complete health maintenance program for pets. An adequate health history must include: 1) information about previous medical and surgical procedures, 2) current preventive measures such as vaccination status and heartworm medication administration, 3) the pet's general environment, including confinement, 4) other household pets and 5) who in the household is responsible for primary care.

Inquiries specific to nutrition and oral care should include past and present information about: 1) oral hygiene, 2) chewing behavior, 3) access to dental treats and toys, 4) access to rocks and other materials that may cause occlusal trauma, 5) presence of any signs that may be related to oral dysfunction, 6) eating behavior and 7) foods eaten, with special attention given to texture and other factors. (See Key Nutritional Factors—Dental Disease.)

Physical Examination

INITIAL ORAL EXAMINATION

Examination of the skull and the oral cavity should be a regular part of every physical examination. An extraoral examination should be done before opening the mouth to inspect the skull and facial areas for any abnormalities, such as muscle atrophy, swelling, draining tracts and ocular or nasal discharge. Extraoral examination should also include inspection for facial symmetry, palpation of the temporomandibular joints, regional lymph nodes and salivary glands and thorough inspection of the skin and lips. Extraoral abnormalities related to oral dysfunction may include mucopurulent discharge from the eyes or nostrils, soft or hard swellings, crepitus, salivation and an inability to open or close the mouth.[36-39]

After the extraoral examination, the lips should be gently parted or retracted to allow inspection of the oral mucosa. Animals experiencing severe oral pain may not tolerate even a cursory oral examination without sedation. The facial surfaces of the teeth and gingivae should be examined for substrate accumulation (i.e., plaque, calculus and stain [See Etiopathogenesis.]), inflammation, trauma and capillary refill time. Tooth position and occlusion should be evaluated. The lingual surfaces of the teeth and gingivae should be inspected, as well as the palates, tongue (ventral and dorsal), frenulum, oropharyngeal area and tonsils.

COMPREHENSIVE ORAL EXAMINATION

A definitive oral examination must be done with the patient heavily sedated or anesthetized, and is often done immediately before periodontal therapy. The general examination should be used as a starting point in client communication with the understanding that the definitive oral examination may uncover other lesions that require treatment.

The examination should begin with a thorough inspection of all oral tissues. An overall assessment of oral health should consider the amount and location of substrate accumulation. Substrate location and accumulation provide valuable information about the frequency and effectiveness of oral hygiene.[40] Common substrate and periodontal indices used to measure oral health have been described.[41,42]

The remainder of the periodontal indices (e.g., probe depth, attachment loss, furcation exposure and tooth mobility) are usually charted after prophylaxis or periodontal therapy to ensure accurate assessment after removal of subgingival debris that may impede measurement. Each tooth and its associated periodontium should be evaluated using a dental explorer-probe to examine the tooth for defects, lesions or both. The same instrument should be used to evaluate periodontal health by measuring the extent of gingival inflammation, attachment loss and alveolar bone loss. Any abnormalities in tooth or periodontal structures should be noted on the dental chart. Detailed dental charting allows for disease assessment and provides a record for future reference. The results should become part of the patient's permanent health record.

Radiographic Examination

Oral radiography may be indicated to identify lesions that cannot be detected visually or manually, and to determine the extent of pathology. Root fractures, periapical abscesses, alveolar bone loss, acute resorptive lesions and anatomic anomalies are lesions that are difficult to assess without radiography. Additionally, oral radiographs are useful in selecting a definitive treatment plan and assessing the outcome of a dental procedure. Oral radiographic techniques have been well described elsewhere.[43]

Laboratory Studies

A complete blood count, serum biochemistry profile, bacterial culture, virus isolation, cytologic examination and biopsy may add useful information. Other diagnostic tests such as urinalyses and cardiac examinations may be indicated, particularly in animals with suspected renal or cardiac disease. Such animals may be compromised by bacteremia associated with dental manipulations.

Risk Factors

The primary etiologic agent associated with periodontal disease is bacterial plaque and bacterial by-products.[44-48] Bacterial plaque is also directly involved in the pathogenesis of enamel caries, and may be a contributing factor in the development and progression of odontoclastic resorptive and other oral inflammatory lesions. Any factor that enhances bacterial accumulation or affects the resistance of the periodontium may influence the disease process. Specific risk factors that contribute to the severity and progression of dental diseases include: 1) species, 2) breed, 3) age, 4) immunocompetence, 5) nutrition and food characteristics, 6) chewing behavior and 7) systemic health.[49]

SPECIES

Periodontal disease occurs frequently in dogs and cats. Other dental diseases appear to be more species dependent. Inflammation of the gingival tissues and oral mucosa (ulcerative stomatitis, pharyngitis-gingivostomatitis complex) occurs as a separate entity from periodontal disease in dogs and cats.[30] Odontoclastic resorptive lesions occur more frequently in cats but have been reported to occur in dogs.[27] Attrition is observed more commonly in dogs. Enamel caries occurs infrequently in dogs and cats.

BREED

Breed plays a major role in the development of dental disease. Small, toy and brachycephalic breeds are prone to malocclusive disorders including overcrowding and rotation of teeth, retained deciduous teeth and supernumerary teeth (Figures 16-4 and 16-5). Occlusal abnormalities provide plaque retentive areas and increase the difficulty of oral hygiene procedures. Brachycephalic breeds are also predisposed to mouth breathing, which tends to dry and irritate oral tissues.[50] Periodontal disease, resorptive lesions and gingivostomatitis have been reported to occur with relatively greater frequency in purebred cats, particularly Asian breeds such as Siamese and Abyssinians.[26] Ulcerative stomatitis has been documented in family clusters of Maltese dogs.[30]

AGE

Several surveys have reported that older animals have a greater frequency and an increased severity of dental disease. Harvey and colleagues reported results of a detailed survey of owners of 1,350 dogs in which calculus deposition, gingival inflammation, tooth mobility, furcation exposure, attachment loss and missing teeth all increased significantly with increasing age.[51] In an evaluation of 4,776 cats aged seven to 25 years and 8,692 dogs aged 10 to 25 years, oral disease was the most frequent diagnosis reported.[a]

It has long been reported that periodontal disease in people increases in severity with increasing age. However, recent data suggest that the severity of disease may represent a lifetime disease accumulation and not necessarily be an age-specific condition.[52-54] It is not surprising that geriatric animals with little history of oral hygiene or veterinary oral care demonstrate an increased prevalence and severity of periodontal disease.

IMMUNOCOMPETENCE

The host immune response protects against systemic infection from periodontal pathogens. An overexaggerated immune response can cause severe local periodontal destruction. An inadequate immune response may predispose the animal to opportunistic or overwhelming systemic infection.[55]

NUTRITION AND FOOD CHARACTERISTICS

The dramatic difference in food form represented by commercial dog and cat foods as compared with the natural prey of wild canids and felids is often implicated as a significant cause of the degree of periodontal disease diagnosed in domestic dogs and cats.[11,56,57] Colyer examined 1,157 wild canid skulls and reported that periodontal disease as suggested by alveolar bone destruction was present in only 2% of specimens.[56] The subject of how well specific commercial food types promote oral health is discussed below. (See sidebar "Do Commercial Cat Foods Cause Odontoclastic Resorptive Lesions?")

CHEWING BEHAVIOR

Chewing behavior can adversely affect dental and oral health. Chewing on hard materials such as rocks, hard bones, fences and inappropriate chew toys may affect dental health by causing attrition, fractures, avulsions and gingival lacerations, with the potential to infect exposed pulpal tissue and exacerbate periodontal disease.[58] Additionally, electrical or chemical burns from appliance cords and household chemicals can damage teeth and other oral tissues.[59]

"Cage-biter syndrome" is an abnormal abrasion of teeth, particularly canine teeth, caused by repeated biting of the bars of a kennel or fence.[60] Common sequelae are tooth fractures due to weakened enamel, dentin or both. Tooth substance is lost primarily at the distal aspect of affected teeth. Aggression, boredom, frustration and social behavior are the primary reasons for cage biting in guard dogs (e.g., military, police). Cage biting can be averted by covering kennels with steel or aluminum plates, reducing the diameter of the netting and decreasing the fence mobility; the swaying movement of the cage often triggers biting activity.

Etiopathogenesis

TOOTH-ACCUMULATED MATERIALS

Several materials accumulate on tooth surfaces and participate in the pathophysiology of dental and periodontal disease. These substances are commonly referred to as tooth-accumulated materials or dental substrates and are categorized as: 1) acquired enamel pellicle, 2) microbial plaque, 3) materia alba/debris, 4) calculus and 5) stain. These substrates accumulate in a dynamic continuum, initiated by the adsorption of salivary constituents onto tooth surfaces.[61,62]

Saliva is a critical oral fluid primarily recognized for its digestive functions. However, saliva also bathes the oral cavity with a fluid rich in proteins, glycoproteins, electrolytes and lipids that provides an initial protective barrier to pathogenic invasion. In people, diminished salivary function (xerostomia) is associated with increased prevalence of caries and periodontal disease, mucosal irritation, difficulties in chewing and swallowing and impaired taste. Saliva initiates film formation on all oral surfaces.[63]

Enamel Pellicle

Enamel pellicle is a thin film or cuticle. Early enamel pellicle is composed of proteins and glycoproteins deposited from saliva and gingival crevicular fluid. A clean enamel surface has readily accessible phosphate groups that are hypothesized to combine with calcium ions from saliva and bridge with negatively charged groups on salivary and crevicular fluid components.[64] Early enamel pellicle protects and lubricates.

As pellicle ages, existing constituents are modified and additional salivary, crevicular and bacterial components are incorporated. Enamel pellicle and its components provide a framework for initial bacterial colonization and also function in the maturation of dental plaque.[63,65]

Dental Plaque

Pellicle deposition and subsequent bacterial colonization occur almost immediately after a dental prophylaxis. Studies have demonstrated that within minutes after polishing, approximately one million organisms are deposited per mm^2 of enamel surface.[66] Aggregates of bacteria combine with salivary glycoproteins, extracellular polysaccharides and occasionally epithelial and inflammatory cells to form a soft adherent plaque that covers tooth surfaces. Dental plaque is not easily removed by normal tongue actions, water drinking or forced water spray, but can be affected by mechanical and chemical means.

Do Commercial Cat Foods Cause Odontoclastic Resorptive Lesions?

An area of recent concern has been the increased prevalence of odontoclastic resorptive lesions, primarily in cats. The etiology of these lesions is unknown. Examination of skulls dating pre-1900s revealed a low prevalence of these lesions. Commercial pet foods have been suggested as a causative factor in the prevalence of resorptive lesions in cats. These pet foods were suspected because of the common practice of applying an acid coating to dry cat foods (e.g., feline digest) to enhance palatability, and the possibility that hard dry cat foods cause microfractures that predispose the tooth to infection and initiate the inflammatory cascade leading to odontoclastic activation.

Human studies have demonstrated that consumption of a food or beverage with an acidic pH contributes to erosive lesions. Additionally, chronic vomiting/regurgitation has been associated with these lesions because vomitus is acidic.

Zetner and Steurer investigated the tooth surface pH of three groups of cats: 1) 18 cats with resorptive lesions, 2) 14 cats with chronic oral inflammatory disease and 3) 22 cats with no oral lesions. Cats with resorptive lesions had lower pH values than the other groups. In the same study, the researchers measured tooth surface pH after cats consumed either a commercial moist food or a commercial acid-coated dry food. Results demonstrated that although the tooth surface pH was more acidic in cats that consumed the dry food, consumption of the dry food did not contribute to the pathogenesis of resorptive lesions. In other long-term studies to determine the effects of dry cat food on tooth and periodontal health, researchers found no correlation between the consumption of acid-coated food and increased prevalence of periodontal disease and resorptive lesions.

BIBLIOGRAPHY

Anderson JG, Harvey CE, Flax B. Clinical and radiographic evaluation of external odontoclastic resorptive lesions in cats (abstract). Journal of Veterinary Internal Medicine 1993; 7: 134.

Harvey CE, Anderson JG, Miller BR. Longitudinal study of periodontal health in cats. In: Proceedings. European Veterinary Dental Society, Brussels, Belgium, 1995.

Harvey CE. Dental diseases in cat skulls acquired before 1960. In: Proceedings. Veterinary Dental Forum, American Veterinary Dental College and Academy of Veterinary Dentistry, Las Vegas, NV, 1990: 41-44.

Harvey CE. Epidemiology of periodontal conditions in dogs and cats (abstract). In: Proceedings. Sixth Annual Veterinary Dental Forum, American Veterinary Dental College and Academy of Veterinary Dentistry, Las Vegas, NV, 1992: 45-46.

Robinson HBG, Miller AS. Diseases of the teeth and supporting structures. In: Thomas ME, ed. Colby, Kerr and Robinson's Color Atlas of Oral Pathology, 4th ed. Philadelphia, PA: JB Lippincott Co, 1983: 54-56.

Zetner K, Steurer I. The influence of dry food on the development of feline neck lesions. Journal of Veterinary Dentistry 1992; 9: 4-6.

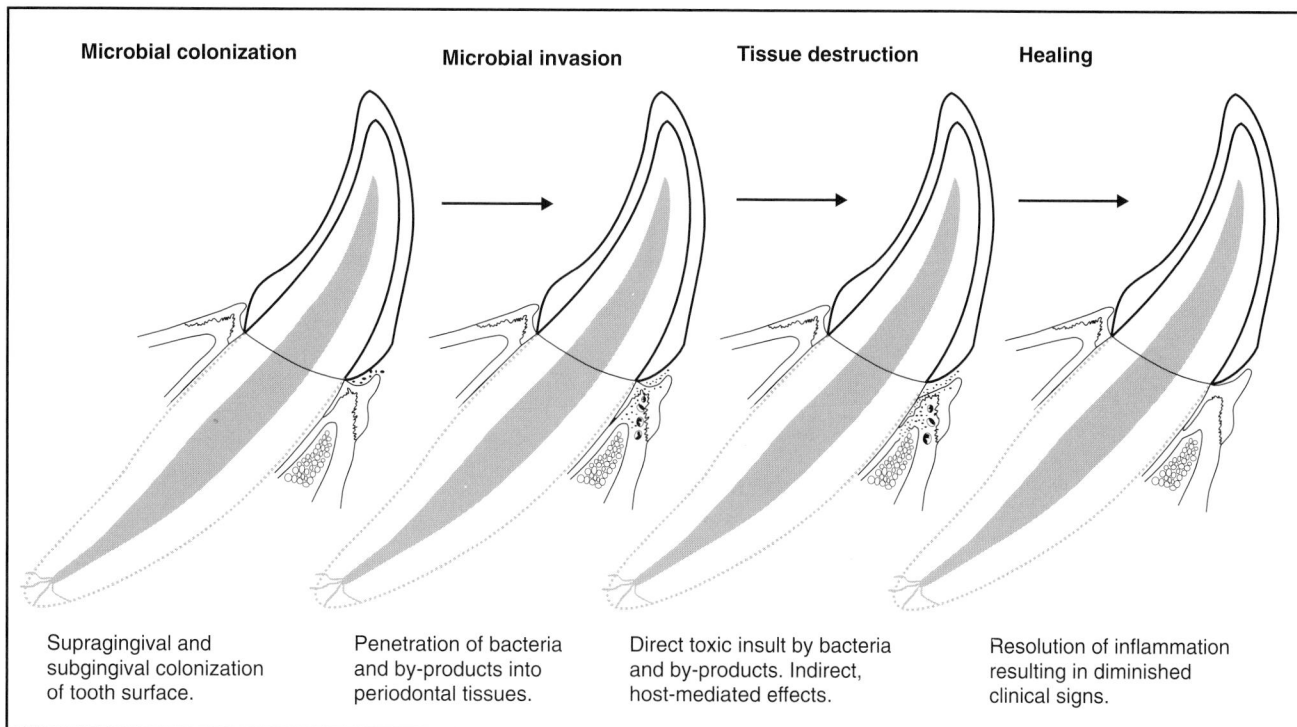

Microbial colonization	Microbial invasion	Tissue destruction	Healing
Supragingival and subgingival colonization of tooth surface.	Penetration of bacteria and by-products into periodontal tissues.	Direct toxic insult by bacteria and by-products. Indirect, host-mediated effects.	Resolution of inflammation resulting in diminished clinical signs.

Figure 16-6. Host-bacterial interactions in the pathogenesis of periodontal disease. Periodontal disease is cyclic with bursts of tissue destruction followed by periods of healing and relative quiescence. Four stages in the pathogenesis of periodontal disease have been proposed: 1) Microbial colonization. Salivary pellicle is deposited on the enamel surface and is soon colonized by oral bacteria that multiply forming plaque. 2) Microbial invasion. Plaque bacteria and their by-products invade the gingival tissues and initiate a host inflammatory response. 3) Tissue destruction. Direct toxic effects of bacteria and their by-products and indirect host-mediated toxic responses lead to destruction of periodontal tissue. 4) Healing. Periods of disease remission are characterized by a reduction in the inflammatory response and gingival healing. (Adapted from Genco RJ, Goldman HM, Cohen WD, eds. Contemporary Periodontics. St Louis, MO: CV Mosby Co, 1990; 189.)

Dental plaque has a specific composition and structure that changes with time. Supragingival dental plaque forms above and along the free gingival margin; subgingival dental plaque is formed entirely within the gingival sulcus. Growth and maturation of supragingival plaque are necessary for subsequent colonization of subgingival surfaces by dental plaque.[67] Supragingival and subgingival plaque are distinct compositional masses that influence the inflammatory reaction of gingival tissues. Studies in people have demonstrated an organized progression of microbial colonization and growth that leads to the development of mature pathogenic dental plaque.[66]

Canine and feline studies characterizing the microbial composition of supragingival and subgingival plaque have been reported. Supragingival plaque in dogs with clinically healthy gingivae is primarily composed of gram-positive aerobic organisms. As plaque matures, the bacterial composition shifts to a predominately gram-negative anaerobic flora.[68-79] The inflammation and destruction that accompanies periodontal disease results from the direct action of bacteria and their by-products on periodontal tissues as well as the indirect activation of the host immune response.[80] Thus, bacterial plaque is the most important substrate in the development of periodontal disease.

Materia Alba and Other Oral Debris

Materia alba is a soft mixture of salivary proteins, bacteria, desquamated epithelial cells and leukocyte fragments. Materia alba and dental plaque are two distinct materials. Materia alba does not have the organized bacterial struc-

ture or the adherence properties of dental plaque;[62] it can generally be washed off with a forced water spray. The role of materia alba in the etiopathogenesis of plaque accumulation and periodontal disease remains unclear.

Other debris commonly observed in the oral cavity of dogs and to some extent in cats include food, impacted hair and miscellaneous foreign materials acquired through chewing behaviors. Food debris retained in the mouth after eating can usually be removed by the action of the oral musculature and saliva.

Dogs and cats fed soft, sticky foods, particularly those breeds compromised by occlusal abnormalities, may retain more food debris. No reports directly correlate retention of food debris with increased plaque accumulation and peri-

Table 16-5. Stages of periodontal disease.

Stage 1	**Gingivitis** Inflammatory changes affect the gingivae only
Stage 2	**Mild periodontal disease** Gingival inflammation with early destructive changes affect the periodontium (<25% attachment loss)
Stage 3	**Moderate periodontal disease** Gingival inflammation with progressive destruction of the periodontium (25 to 50% attachment loss)
Stage 4	**Severe periodontal disease** Gingival inflammation with severe destruction of the periodontium (>50% attachment loss)

Table 16-6. Clinical signs associated with periodontal disease.

Halitosis	Red, swollen or bleeding gingivae
Anorexia	Tooth mobility
Difficulty eating	Ulcerations on gingivae or oral mucosa
Ptyalism	Substrate accumulation (plaque, calculus,
Head shaking	stain)
Behavioral changes	

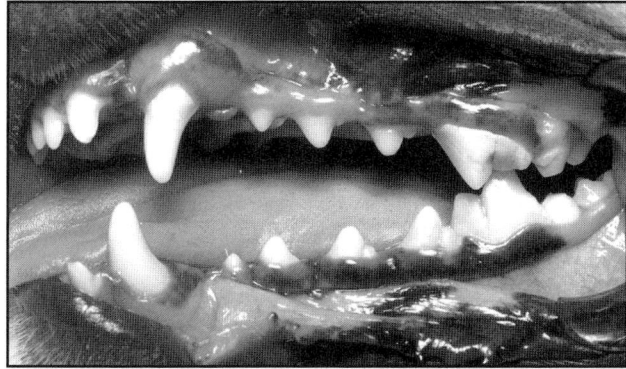

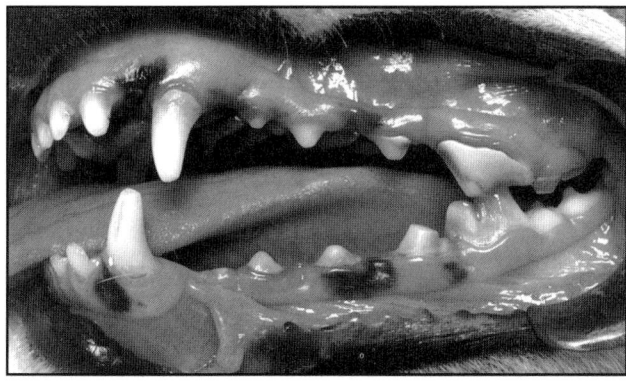

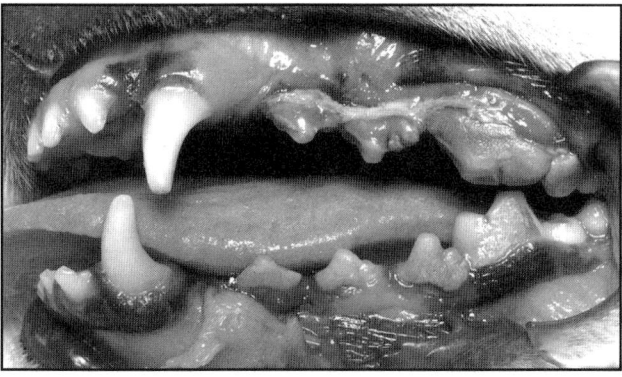

Figure 16-7. Photographic representations of mild, moderate and severe periodontal disease in dogs. (Top) Mild periodontal disease. Some accumulation of plaque and calculus is evident on the tooth crowns. There is slight gingival recession around the maxillary canine tooth and the gingival margins are slightly rounded, particularly around the caudal premolar teeth. (Middle) Heavy plaque and calculus accumulation is evident on most teeth. Accumulations are abundant on the maxillary fourth premolar and first molar. A distinct margin of gingival inflammation is present around the maxillary fourth premolar. Inflammatory changes including swelling, reddening and recession are evident around most teeth. (Bottom) Gross plaque and calculus accumulation is present on the premolar and molar teeth. Distinct marginal gingivitis with severe gingival recession and periodontal tissue loss is present. Impaction of hair and foreign material occurs commonly at sites of severe tissue destruction.

odontal disease in dogs and cats. Egelberg reported that neither the frequency of feeding nor bypassing the oral cavity by tube feeding affected the accumulation of plaque and the development of gingivitis in a group of six mongrel dogs with medium to large body size.[81] The effect of food retention in small and brachycephalic breeds is unknown. Retained or impacted debris may act as a nidus for plaque accumulation and exacerbate gingival inflammation. The role of food type and texture in oral health and disease is discussed below.

Dental Calculus

Dental calculus is mineralized plaque. Calculus is a hard substrate formed by the interactions of salivary and crevicular calcium and phosphate salts with existing plaque. Dental calculus is observed frequently in dogs and cats.[23,51,82,83] Calculus accumulates supragingivally and subgingivally; calculus deposits thicken with time. Undisturbed calculus is always covered by vital dental plaque. Aged calculus may chip or break off with mastication; however, a film of plaque remains that is rapidly mineralized. Calculus provides a roughened surface to enhance plaque attachment and accumulation and chronically irritates gingival tissues.[84-86]

Dental Stain

Acquired dental stain (extrinsic stain) is initially stained pellicle that becomes part of the mineralized, layered laminate of pellicle, plaque and calculus. Dental stain occurs frequently in dogs.[87] Various nutritional, chemical and bacterial factors affect the presence and intensity of stain. Although nonpathogenic, dental stain is of aesthetic concern to pet owners and may signal teeth abnormalities.

Enamel staining (intrinsic stain) occurs due to trauma or antibiotic administration during development or before tooth eruption. Erupted teeth may also be injured with resulting discoloration due to hemorrhage into the dentinal tubules. Enamel staining varies in intensity and distribution of discoloration and is distinguished from acquired stain by its irreversible nature.[34]

PATHOPHYSIOLOGIC BASIS OF CLINICAL SIGNS

Periodontal Disease

Plaque accumulation along the gingival margin induces inflammation in adjacent gingival tissues.[88,89] Without plaque removal or control, gingivitis progresses in severity, and local changes occur allowing subsequent bacterial colonization of subgingival sites. Inflammatory mediators damage the integrity of the gingival margin and sulcular epithelium, allowing infiltration of bacteria that release factors that interfere with normal host cell function or contribute to destruction or lysis of cells or cellular components. The immune response of the host attempts to localize the invasion to the periodontal tissues; the result may be further destruction of local tissues due to cytokines released from inflammatory cells.

Periodontal disease is episodic with periods of active tissue destruction followed by periods of inactivity and healing (Figure 16-6). Additionally, not all teeth are affected at the same rate nor to the same degree. Periodontal disease begins with gingivitis and progresses through increased destruction of the periodontal apparatus, resulting in tooth mobility and eventual tooth loss. Generally, a stage classification system is used, beginning with a healthy periodontium and ending with tooth exfoliation (Table 16-5 and Figure 16-7).[90]

Periodontal disease is often a silent process that progresses without detection. Even in cases of severe disease, dogs and cats may not demonstrate obvious discomfort. One signal often noticed by pet owners is oral malodor,[91] but even then pet owners may not link bad breath to periodontal disease. Oral disease is a primary cause of offensive breath odor, but other metabolic processes may be involved.[92-95] Simone and colleagues reported a positive correlation between periodontal disease and malodor in beagles.[96]

Other signs of periodontal disease include: 1) accumulation of dental substrates on tooth surfaces, 2) gingival redness, 3) swelling and bleeding of the gingival margin, 4) gingival recession, 5) periodontal pocket formation, 6) accumulation of purulent material in the gingival sulcus or periodontal pocket and 7) tissue destruction with loss of attachment, furcation exposure and tooth mobility (Table 16-6).

Systemic Complications of Periodontal Disease

Periodontal disease may predispose affected animals to systemic complications. In people, periodontal disease has been: 1) identified as a risk factor for heart disease, 2) implicated in pulmonary infection and cerebral infarction and, most recently, 3) positively correlated with low birth weight.[97-103]

Numerous reports speculate on the association between chronic periodontal disease and conditions affecting the heart valves and pulmonary airways of dogs.[104-107] DeBowes and colleagues found a positive correlation between the severity of periodontal disease and histopathologic changes in the kidneys, myocardium and liver.[108]

Periodontal infections allow bacterial migration into lymphatic and blood vessels, resulting in bacteremia.[109,110] The host defenses of normal healthy animals can effectively clear transient bacteremia; however, blood-borne bacteria may colonize distant sites in animals with impaired immune function or organ compromise.[111]

Odontoclastic Resorptive Lesions

The specific etiology of other diseases affecting the oral cavity of dogs and cats remains unclear. Odontoclastic resorptive lesions occur commonly in cats and have been reported to occur in dogs. Some type of noxious stimulus may elicit a physiologic change in the dental pulp leading to vasodilatation, release of inflammatory mediators and stimulation of odontoclast activity.[25]

Odontoclastic resorptive lesions present initially as shallow defects typically located at the CEJ. Early lesions are concavities that do not involve the pulpal tissue. Odontoclasts line the lesions. Moderate and advanced lesions are characterized by progressive destruction of crown and root with eventual involvement of the pulp cavity. These lesions are typically observed as external lesions, but may occur internally or apically.[112] Odontoclastic resorptive lesions are often detected in cats with concurrent periodontal disease, stomatitis or both.[113]

Stomatitis

Stomatitis occurs in dogs and cats.[114] The condition in cats is often referred to as lymphocytic-plasmacytic stomatitis because of the histologic appearance of the lesions. Inflammation may be limited to specific areas, such as the gingival margin, pharyngeal area or the glossopalatine arches, or may be more generalized, resulting in extensive stomatitis. The specific etiology is unknown, but several bacterial and viral factors may be involved. An excessive

host immune response may also be involved.[115] Zetner and colleagues were able to demonstrate by means of antigen-specific monoclonal antibodies that elevated IgE levels against various ingredients of food may occur in the sera of cats with chronic gingivitis/periodontitis.[116] Specific elevated IgE levels were found against cereal grains and different types of meat. These findings support clinical evidence that adverse reactions against ingredients of the food (food hypersensitivity) may occur in cats with chronic inflammatory oral disease. Changing the food (e.g., to a hypoallergenic type) may lessen the painful gingivitis/periodontitis response. Cats often have severe oral pain, ptyalism, dysphagia, anorexia and depression. Affected tissues appear bright red, swollen or proliferative, ulcerative and may be very friable.

Stomatitis in dogs usually results from direct contact of oral mucosa with plaque-laden teeth. These lesions are characteristically round, well-demarcated ulcerations that may coalesce in severe cases. Affected dogs generally have periodontal disease, halitosis, ptyalism, anorexia and behavioral changes associated with oral pain and discomfort such as lethargy and withdrawal.

Key Nutritional Factors

Food texture and composition can directly affect the oral environment through: 1) maintenance of tissue integrity, 2) metabolism of plaque bacteria, 3) stimulation of salivary flow and 4) contact with tooth and oral surfaces. Nutritional factors have the potential to affect all of the various oral tissues during development, maturation and maintenance. (See Key Nutritional Factors—Dental Disease.) Mature enamel is a static tissue, but nutrition may affect its growth and maturation. The periodontal apparatus surrounds, protects and supports the teeth. Any negative influences affecting these structures may progress to tooth mobility and exfoliation. Oral mucosa has a high turnover rate; adequate nutrition is necessary to maintain tissue integrity.

Although the effects of malnutrition are well recognized in the development and maturation of oral tissues (e.g., increases host susceptibility, contributes to progression and severity of oral diseases), there has been little published on the effect of specific nutrients on oral disease.

The effect of specific nutrient deficiencies and excesses on tissue integrity, microbial populations and plaque and calculus accumulation demands further research. Specific nutrients that have been investigated, at least in part, include water, protein, carbohydrates (soluble and insoluble), minerals and vitamins. Most commercial foods provide adequate levels of nutrients to prevent deficiency diseases provided the food meets levels recommended by the Association of American Feed Control Officials (AAFCO) and adequate amounts are fed to meet daily energy requirements.[117,118]

WATER

Water is a critical nutrient. Fresh, palatable water should be available at all times. Food is a source of water for dogs and cats; the moisture content of a pet food dictates its form. Food form can directly influence plaque and calculus accumulation as will be discussed later.

PROTEIN

Protein deficiencies cause degenerative changes in the periodontium, specifically the gingivae, periodontal liga-

Home Care

Oral health is achieved through a combination of professional therapy and home care. Dental home care refers to the procedures clients use to control plaque in their pets. Client education and communication are necessary to determine the commitment and capability of pet owners to provide adequate plaque control necessary for maintenance of oral health or a successful therapeutic outcome. It is a disservice to clients and their pets to provide extensive periodontal therapy without adequate home care instruction. Similarly, clients must understand that home care is just one part of maintaining the health of their pets. Routine examinations to assess oral condition will determine the recall time necessary for professional prophylaxis and appropriate periodontal therapy.

Dental home care begins with educating clients about the pathophysiology of periodontal disease and discussing the degree of plaque control appropriate to control gingivitis and therefore to maintain the oral health of their pets. Many clients have not been exposed to the need for oral care for their pets and, therefore, they underestimate the importance of controlling plaque. Additionally, clients may perceive that feeding a typical dry pet food or biscuit is adequate plaque control.[a]

COMPLIANCE

The level of owner compliance determines the method of periodontal therapy and the home care recommendations. Miller and Harvey reported that with proper home care education and provision of effective tools, 53% of clients were still brushing their dogs' teeth several times a week six months or more after periodontal treatment. Unfortunately, as the authors discuss, 47% of clients were not satisfactorily compliant. This study demonstrates the need for recall visits and home care reinstruction and remotivation.

Some clients may be willing to provide home care, but the pet may not be compliant. It may take consistent training and handling over time to accustom a pet to an oral hygiene routine. Clients should be instructed in techniques to condition their pets to accept oral manipulations and applications of oral hygiene tools and materials. Clients should also be made aware of the potential for harm to themselves and their pets. Pet owners may be bitten or scratched trying to manipulate the oral cavity. Additionally, clients may inadvertently damage their pets' health through excessive restraint or inappropriate use of oral hygiene aids. It may be necessary for some pets to be brought to the clinic for routine plaque control by a veterinary health care team member, although this may be inconvenient for some clients.

HOME CARE PRODUCTS

A variety of products are available for dental home care. Mechanical means of plaque control include brushing or rubbing the teeth with a toothbrush or other applicator to physically disrupt plaque accumulation. Some dentifrices and powders may offer mechanical action through the use of abrasives. Foods with appropriate nutrient levels and texture can also mechanically control plaque. Chemical products available for plaque control include antimicrobials and enzymatic agents.

HOW TO BEGIN

With consistent behavior modification and positive reinforcement, most pets will learn to tolerate oral manipulations and application of oral hygiene. The training should begin with the animal and the owner in a relaxed and comfortable atmosphere. Initially, the owner should simply handle the pet's head and mouth, stroking and lifting the lips. When the animal is accustomed to oral manipulations, the owner can proceed to rubbing the teeth and gingivae with gauze, finger cots, a sponge or cotton-tipped applicators. A pet toothbrush may be introduced after these procedures are accepted. The caudal premolar and molar areas should be cleaned cautiously to avoid injury to the owner and the pet. Lingual manipulations should be done only on very compliant pets.

HOW TO BRUSH A PET'S TEETH

The advantages of toothbrushing include its effectiveness and affordability. Disadvantages can include difficulty of application and the potential for oral trauma. There are several types of pet toothbrushes available. The softness of the bristles and the design of the handle and head make these very desirable for use in pets. It is important to fit the head size and shape to the pet's mouth to allow for safe and effective oral cleansing.

The brush stroke routinely recommended is a modified Bass technique, in which the bristles are placed at a 45° angle to the gingiva and gentle circular strokes are made beginning at the gingival sulcus and continuing coronally. The mechanical action of the brush is adequate to control plaque if used correctly and routinely. Use of flavored dentifrices, gels or powders may increase palatability and acceptability to the pet. Addition of abrasives or chemicals to dentifrices may compensate somewhat for inadequate brushing technique. Finger cots, gauze applicators and oral swabs are alternatives to the toothbrush and may be better tolerated by smaller pets and pets in the early phases of oral hygiene training.

FLUORIDE'S ROLE

The importance of fluoride in the prevention of dental caries in people is well recognized. In veterinary dentistry, fluoride is commonly used to decrease tooth sensitivity and inhibit plaque production. Some chemical agents incorporate fluoride as a plaque inhibitor. Because of the potential for toxicity, fluoride should be used cautiously and only under professional supervision.

COMPLIANCE FAILURE

Even with client education and good pet compliance, some owners are not able to provide routine and effective plaque control. Compliance failure may be due to: 1) lack of skill, 2) lack of perceived benefit, 3) unpleasantness of procedure, 4) lack of noticeable impact and 5) lifestyle constraints. Emphasizing the benefits, including improved oral and systemic health, less breath odor, cost effectiveness and strengthening of the owner-pet bond, may increase compliance. Long-term success depends on the degree of plaque control the client is capable of providing between professional visits.

Veterinarians should combine their knowledge of a pet's oral condition and degree of periodontal therapy with an understanding of the level of owner and pet compliance when recommending home care.

ENDNOTE
a. Laurie D. Hill's Pet Nutrition, Inc., Topeka, KS, Personal communication. August 1994.

BIBLIOGRAPHY
Aller SA. Basic prophylaxis and home care. Compendium on Continuing Education for the Practicing Veterinarian 1989; 11: 1447-1457.

Eisner ER. Helping clients care for their pets' teeth at home. Veterinary Medicine 1989; 84: 1070-1074.

Lyon KF. Dental home care. Pet Focus 1990; 2: 40-43.

Miller BR, Harvey CE. Compliance with oral hygiene recommendations following periodontal treatment in client-owned dogs. Journal of Veterinary Dentistry 1994; 11: 18-19.

Touger-Decker R. Nutrition in dental health. In: Mahan LK, Escott-Stump S, eds. Food, Nutrition, and Diet Therapy, 9th ed. Philadelphia, PA: WB Saunders Co, 1996; 581-593.

Woodhall IR. Preventing periodontal disease. In: Genco RJ, Goldman HM, Cohen DW, eds. Contemporary Periodontics. St. Louis, MO: CV Mosby Co, 1990; 361-370.

ment and alveolar bone in laboratory animals.[119] In 1962, Ruben investigated the effects of a soft consistency, protein-deficient food on the periodontium of 22 dogs over a one-year period. Results included inflammatory and dystrophic changes in the gingivae, periodontal ligament and alveolar bone. However, the study did not quantitate the individual effects of food consistency and protein content.[120] Protein deficiency, however, occurs rarely in dogs and cats and is not a practical consideration as a typical cause of periodontal disease in these species. The effects of protein excess are unknown; however, protein and its components provide nutrients for oral bacteria, which may contribute to increased substrate accumulation.

CARBOHYDRATES

The role of soluble carbohydrates (sugars) in the development of dental caries has been well documented in people and rodents.[121] Dental caries, however, occurs infrequently in dogs and cats. One study demonstrated that dogs do not develop carious lesions even after long periods of consuming carbohydrate-rich foods.[122] Carlsson and Egelberg reported that the addition of sucrose to a soft food resulted in no difference in plaque accumulation and gingival inflammation in a group of 12 mongrel dogs.[123] Human studies have demonstrated that larger amounts of plaque were formed when sucrose was the primary sugar consumed.[124,125] Commercial and homemade pet foods typically contain large quantities of soluble carbohydrates, usually in the form of starch.

Fiber-containing foods have long been viewed as "nature's toothbrush." Investigators have theorized that fibrous foods: 1) exercise the gums, 2) promote gingival keratinization and 3) clean the teeth. Fiber in foods, especially as it relates to texture, has been shown to affect plaque and calculus accumulation and gingival health in dogs and cats and will be discussed below.[57,126,127]

CALCIUM AND PHOSPHORUS

Foods deficient in calcium and excessive in phosphorus may lead to secondary nutritional hyperparathyroidism and significant loss of alveolar bone.[128,129] Experiments in dogs have demonstrated resorption of alveolar bone following consumption of a low-calcium-high-phosphorus food.[130]

Krook and colleagues have proposed that periodontal disease results from a nutritional deficiency of calcium, an excess of phosphorus or both.[131,132] Svanberg and colleagues reported that nutritional secondary hyperparathyroidism occurred in a group of beagles fed a food deficient in calcium. The food did not have any effect on the initiation or rate of progression of periodontal disease when compared with findings in a control group fed a nutritionally adequate food.[133] Although secondary nutritional hyperparathyroidism may contribute to bone loss and thus affect the progression of periodontal disease, there is little evidence to support the theory that it is the primary cause. Calcium deficiency is essentially unheard of in dogs and cats that consume commercial pet foods that contain calcium levels that meet AAFCO allowances.

A more realistic concern is the excessive levels of calcium and phosphorus present in many commercial pet foods. High levels of phosphate and calcium are calculogenic in rats.[134] In people, the plaque deposits of heavy calculus formers contain significantly higher levels of calcium and phosphorus compared with deposits of slow calculus

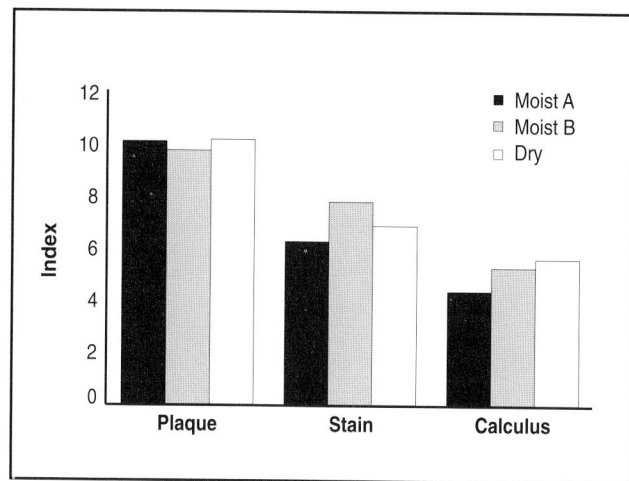

Figure 16-8. Comparison of plaque, stain and calculus accumulation in dogs fed a specialty brand moist food (Moist A), a grocery brand moist food (Moist B) and a grocery brand dry food. There is no significant difference in substrate accumulation among dogs fed the three foods. Moist foods do not always promote increased plaque and calculus formation in comparison to dry foods.

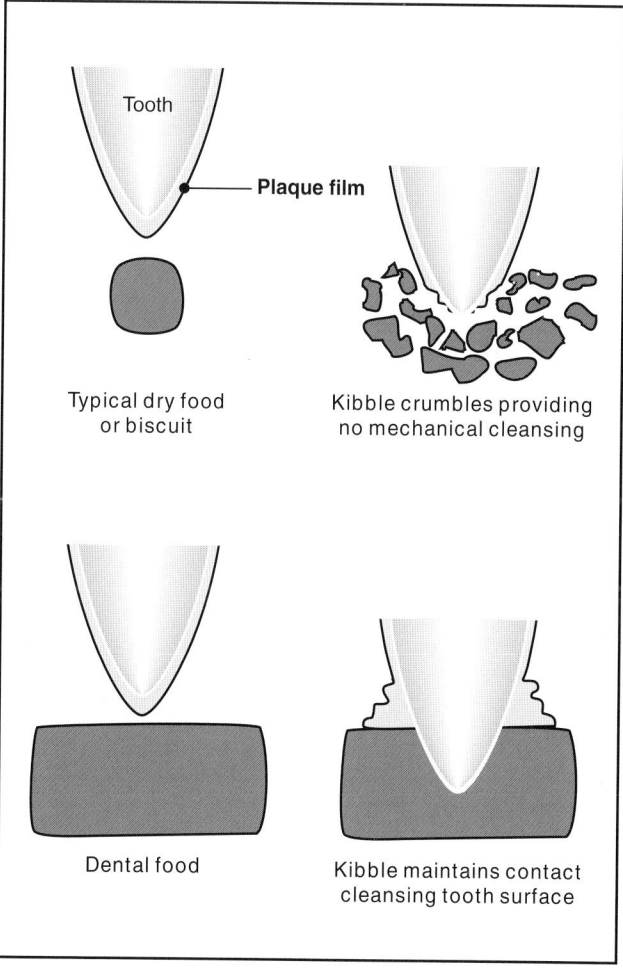

Figure 16-9. This illustration depicts the mechanical cleansing properties of commercial dog and cat foods. The top illustration demonstrates what happens when a dog or cat chews a typical dry food. The kibble crumbles providing little to no mechanical cleansing. The bottom illustration demonstrates what happens when a dog or cat chews a dental food. The kibble stays together, maintaining contact with the tooth surface and providing mechanical cleansing.

Table 16-7. Dental benefits of selected commercial foods and treats.

Products*	Recommended feeding method**	Prot.	Fat	Fiber (% dry matter)	Cal.	Phos.	Manufacturer's claim**	Comments
Dog foods								
Hill's Prescription Diet Canine t/d (Original Bites and Small Bites)	Feed as adult maintenance food	16.7	15.8	11.6	0.56	0.42	Reduces the accumulation of plaque, stain and calculus on the teeth of adult dogs. Reduces oral malodor. Maintains gingival health.	Published research supports efficacy claims for control of plaque, stain, calculus, malodor and gingivitis. VOHC Seal of Acceptance
Dog treats or snacks								
Friskies Cheew-eez Treats (Rawhide chew)	Give at least two treats daily	89.0	2.4	0.6	na	na	Helps fight tartar and gives cleaner, healthier teeth. 50% less tartar than dogs fed dry food alone.	Published research supports claims for supra-gingival calculus control compared to feeding dry food or plain biscuits when fed two to three times/day.
Heinz Tartar Check (Hexametaphosphate-coated biscuit)	Give two biscuits each day	14.0	8.8	2.7	0.84	0.36	Reduces tartar buildup by 45%. Cleans teeth and freshens breath.	Published data support hexametaphosphate as a calculus-control agent.
Iams Original Formula (Small biscuit)	Feed as a treat; not more than two biscuits per cup of dry food	28.3	7.1	3.3	1.30	0.98	Promotes clean teeth, fresh breath, and healthy gums.	No published data.
Nabisco Milk-Bone Biscuit	Feed five biscuits (small) twice a day	23.6	6.8	3.0	1.51	1.14	Fights tartar buildup above the gum line. Helps remove plaque.	No published data.
Nutro Tartar Control Dog Biscuit	Feed two to three biscuits throughout the day	29.2	9.0	3.4	1.12	1.12	They scrub away tartar buildup to help keep teeth and gums healthy.	No published data.
Pedigree Dentabone/Rask	Offer as a chewing snack	26.0	5.5	0.1	1.71	0.76	Reduces tartar and plaque buildup.	Published research supports efficacy claims when fed daily.
Pedigree Maxi Biscuit	Feed two to three biscuits daily	14.0	7.4	1.4	3.60	1.02	Promotes cleaner teeth and reduces plaque buildup.	No published data.
President's Choice All-Natural Biscuit	No specific feeding recommendations	26.7	6.8	2.5	1.36	1.09	Helps keep teeth and gums healthy. Helps prevent tartar buildup.	No published data.
VRx C.E.T. Chews (Enzymatic Beefhide Chew)	Feed at least one chew on those days when toothbrushing does not occur	na	na	na	na	na	When combined with brushing they can be an effective method of removing plaque and food debris on a daily basis.	No published data.
Waltham Formula Tartar Chew	Feed daily as a treat; not suitable for dogs under 5 kg	14.3	2.6	0.1	na	na	Clinically proven to reduce tartar and plaque buildup.	No published data.
Cat foods								
Friskies Dental Diet	Feed as adult maintenance food	32.0	11.0	5.3	1.79	1.53	Helps maintain dental health. Reduces plaque and tartar buildup by 25% vs. leading brands.	VOHC Seal of Acceptance.
Hill's Prescription Diet Feline t/d	Feed as adult maintenance food	34.8	16.5	9.2	1.01	0.76	Reduces the accumulation of plaque, stain and calculus on the teeth of adult cats. Maintains gingival health.	Published research supports efficacy claims for control of plaque, stain, calculus and gingivitis. VOHC Seal of Acceptance.
Cat treats or snacks								
Pounce Tartar Control (Dry cat treat)	Feed 10 to 26 pieces per day (approximately 12.5% of daily food intake)	33.1	12.3	2.0	1.33	1.20	Reduces tartar buildup and helps maintain the overall health of the teeth.	No published data.
Whisker Lickins Tartar Control (Dry cat treat)	Feed as a daily snack to your cat	35.0	11.2	4.5	1.24	1.16	Helps reduce tartar buildup and maintain overall health of the teeth. It's our crunchy texture that scrapes away the plaque and tartar on your cat's teeth.	No published data.
VRx C.E.T. Forte Chews	Feed one chew on days tooth brushing does not occur	na	na	na	na	na	Uniquely formulated to provide abrasive cleansing action. Specially treated with an antibacterial enzyme system to help maintain oral health.	One clinical trial indicated a reduction in plaque and calculus accumulation when cats ate one treat/day.

Key: VOHC = Veterinary Oral Health Council, na = information not available.
*This list represents products with the largest market share and for which published information is available.
**Obtained from product label or packaging.

formers. Further research in the role of dietary calcium and phosphorus is warranted; however, the role these minerals have in calculus formation should be kept in mind when recommending a food as part of an oral care regimen.

VITAMINS

Vitamins that have been studied in relation to periodontal disease include A, B, C and D. Deficiencies in vitamin A have been reported to cause marginal gingivitis, gingival hypoplasia and resorption of alveolar bone.[135] Vitamin B-complex (including folic acid, niacin, pantothenic acid and riboflavin) deficiencies have been associated with gingival inflammation, epithelial necrosis and resorption of alveolar bone.[136] Vitamin C plays a key role in collagen synthesis. Deficiencies in ascorbic acid in people have been reported to adversely affect periodontal tissues.[137] Vitamin D helps regulate serum calcium concentrations. Deficiencies of vitamin D affect calcium homeostasis and reportedly affect the gingivae, periodontal ligament and alveolar bone.[129] Almost all commercial pet foods contain adequate levels of these vitamins.

Assess the Food(s)

Foods influence the growth and maturation of oral microflora. Thus, they affect substrate accumulation and periodontal health, by direct nutrient availability from food/particle retention, as well as by systemic absorption and distribution of nutrients through serum, and salivary and crevicular fluids. Therefore, it would be prudent to assess nutrient composition, particularly protein, carbohydrates, calcium and phosphorus, when evaluating a food as a component of an oral care regimen. (See Key Nutritional Factors—Dental Disease.)

A dental food should provide optimal nutritional balance for dogs and cats and be orally and systemically safe. The specific key nutritional factors mentioned above should be evaluated. Optimal nutrient balance is critical to tissue integrity and should not be overlooked when assessing an appropriate dental food.

Assessment of the food for dogs and cats to preserve oral health or to help manage periodontal disease includes two components: 1) ensuring the food meets AAFCO recommendations for the age/use of the pet evaluated, without providing excess nutrients that might cause imbalances or might contribute to substrate formation (See Key Nutritional Factors—Dental Disease.) and 2) determining whether the client's plaque control protocol effectively prevents gingivitis.

Puppies and kittens are born edentulous. However, the nutrition they receive from the bitch or queen can affect oral development. The bitch or queen should receive an appropriate growth/lactation food during lactation to ensure adequate milk production and to meet ongoing needs. The deciduous teeth will begin to erupt at about three weeks of age. Most puppies and kittens can be given access to soft food at this age. Full deciduous dentition should be present in puppies by 12 weeks of age and in kittens by six weeks of age. The permanent tooth bud will already be formed, so it is essential to dental health that puppies and kittens receive appropriate nutrition during the early weeks of development. This is also the ideal time to train a pet to accept oral hygiene. Handling the mouth, introducing a brushing device and applying oral hygiene products should be part of puppy and kitten socialization.

Most dogs and cats enter adulthood with healthy mouths. In many cases, periodontal disease can be prevented with appropriate plaque control. The level of plaque control necessary to maintain oral health must be assessed for each individual animal. Frequent plaque removal (daily, if possible) is widely recommended in the veterinary dental literature. Brushing, when done correctly and conscientiously, is a very effective method for achieving the level of plaque control necessary to control gingivitis. (See sidebar "Home Care.")

If the pet owner is able to provide effective plaque control through toothbrushing, then the form of the food and other methods of plaque control may be of less concern.[48,138,139] Realistically, however, compliance with toothbrushing may be a problem for many pet owners. Some animals may require aggressive plaque control combined with frequent professional care to maintain optimal oral health.

Plaque is the key substrate that must be controlled in order to control periodontal disease. This section reviews: 1) various methods of plaque control available to veterinarians and pet owners, 2) research that supports or dispels the dental benefit claims made by manufacturers of treats, foods

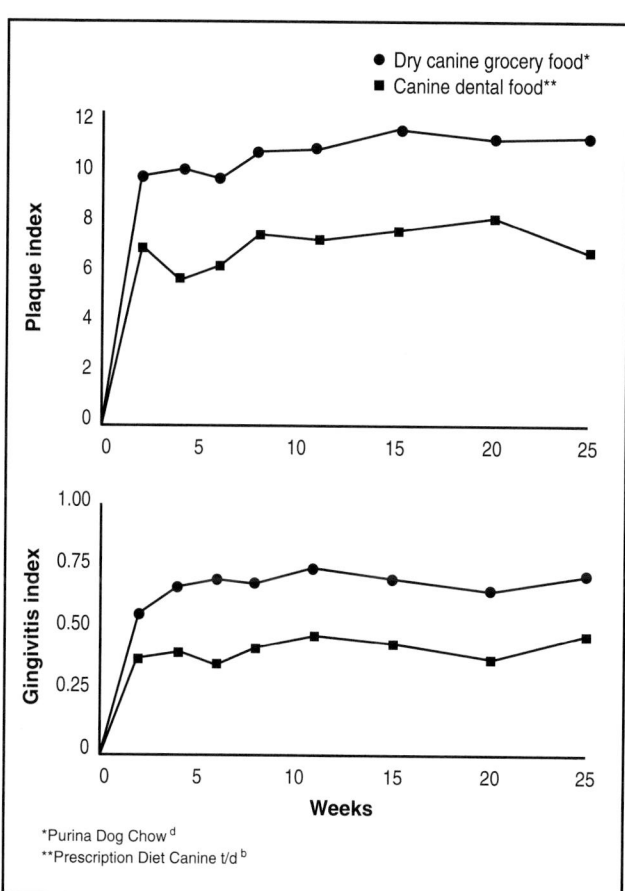

*Purina Dog Chow [d]
**Prescription Diet Canine t/d [b]

Figure 16-10. The effects of commercial dog foods on plaque accumulation and gingival health in dogs. These graphs compare plaque accumulation and gingival inflammation in dogs fed two different foods for six months. Each group of dogs began the study with a plaque index of zero and clinically healthy gingivae. At all time points, the dogs consuming the test food (Prescription Diet Canine t/d) had significantly lower scores for plaque accumulation and gingival inflammation than the dogs consuming the control food (Purina Dog Chow).

and other products and 3) research that proves the effectiveness of textural fiber as a means of controlling accumulation of plaque and improving gingivitis when used in maintenance foods for adult cats and dogs (Table 16-7).

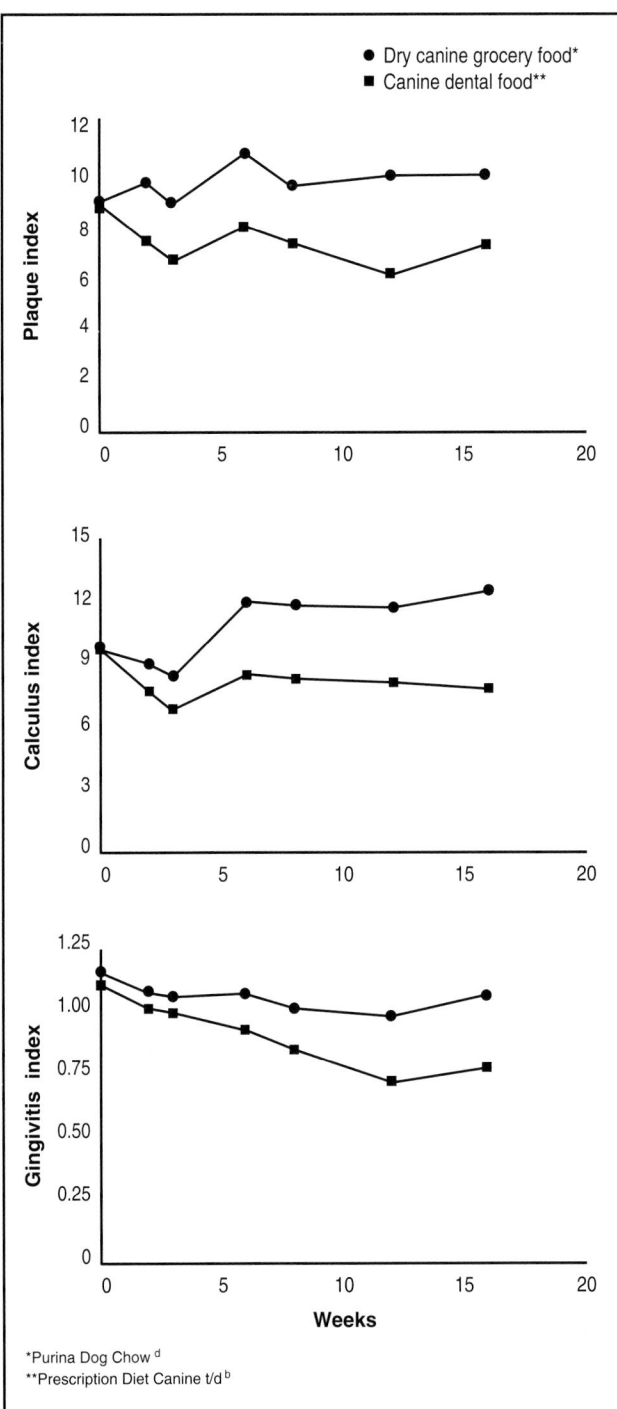

*Purina Dog Chow [d]
**Prescription Diet Canine t/d [b]

Figure 16-11. The effects of commercial dog foods on existing plaque, calculus and gingivitis in dogs. Each group of dogs entered the study with similar amounts of plaque, calculus and gingivitis. Dogs were fed either a control food (Purina Dog Chow) or a test food (Prescription Diet Canine t/d). Plaque, calculus and gingivitis were evaluated over a four-month period. Dogs eating the test food demonstrated a highly significant reduction in plaque, calculus and gingival inflammation whereas dogs eating the control food had a significant increase in plaque, a highly significant increase in calculus and no significant change in gingivitis.

Food Forms: Facts and Fallacies

The physical consistency of foods has been reported to affect oral health of dogs and cats; feeding recommendations for oral health commonly include feeding a dry pet food. Hard food purportedly increases mastication, which aids oral health by exercising the gums, increasing keratinization of the gingivae and reducing accumulation of plaque and calculus.[140]

NATURAL DIETS

Early literature reported that the natural diets of wild canids and felids had a plaque-retardant effect and that wild canids and felids were not afflicted with the generalized form of periodontal disease seen in domesticated pets.[141] Pet food commercialization is often implicated as a contributing factor to the increased prevalence and severity of periodontal disease in domestic dogs and cats.[142] (See sidebar "Do Commercial Cat Foods Cause Odontoclastic Resorptive Lesions?") Natural diets for wild canids and felids probably depend on geographic location, environmental season and hunting capabilities of individual animals. However, historically a natural diet refers to small rodents/mammals that would typically fall prey to wolves, coyotes, etc. Colyer specifically refers to "flesh that the animals must rend with their teeth."[141] Wild canids in particular probably eat fruits and vegetables and an array of tissues including blood, intestines plus contents, muscle, cartilage, bone marrow and bones.

Despite these assertions, there are no published data that compare controlled populations of domestic dogs or cats consuming a natural diet with those consuming a commercial food. In addition, even if it were possible to make such comparisons, confounding variables might include dramatic changes in food form (moist, semi-moist, dry and evolving pet owner preferences) through development of commercial pet foods, specific nutrient variation and selective breeding, which has resulted in dramatic differences in body size and head types of dogs and cats.

There are emerging reports on the oral condition of small populations of dogs and cats consuming a natural diet. Robinson examined 67 English foxhounds, one to nine years of age, that were routinely fed raw carcasses consisting of the bony skeleton, muscle and associated tissues. Oral examinations of the pack revealed that all dogs had varying signs of periodontal disease as well as a high prevalence of tooth fractures.[143] Clark and Cameron examined 45 small feral cats from an Australian national park and reported conditions including calculus deposits, periodontal disease, fractured teeth, attrition and odontoclastic resorptive lesions.[144] Examination of gastrointestinal contents of these cats revealed the presence of a natural diet including small mammals, birds, lizards and insects. These findings cast skepticism on the long-held view that a natural diet prevents development of oral disease, particularly periodontal disease, in dogs and cats.

DENTAL BENEFITS OF SOFT VS. HARD FOODS

Numerous studies have reported that dogs and cats fed soft foods have increased accumulations of plaque and calculus and a higher prevalence or severity of periodontal disease when compared with animals fed hard foods. These studies are difficult to compare because different methods were used to assess substrate accumulation and gingival health, and different populations of animals were studied.

Many of the studies traditionally cited to substantiate claims that dry foods reduce accumulation of plaque and calculus are old reports that used small numbers of animals, had varying evaluation methods and did not report data analysis.[145-148]

Although consumption of soft foods may promote plaque accumulation, the general belief that dry foods provide significant oral cleansing should be regarded with skepticism. A moist food may perform similarly to a typical dry food in affecting plaque, stain and calculus accumulation (Figure 16-8).[126] In a large epidemiologic survey, dogs consuming dry food alone did not consistently demonstrate improved periodontal health when compared with dogs eating moist foods.[149]

Foods with Textural Characteristics

Typical dry dog and cat foods contribute little dental cleansing. As a tooth penetrates a kibble or treat the initial contact causes the food to shatter and crumble with contact only at the coronal tip of the tooth surface (Figure 16-9). To provide effective mechanical cleansing, a food should promote chewing and maintain contact with the tooth surface (Figure 16-9).

The general statement that dry foods promote oral health may be better stated that foods with enhanced textural characteristics promote oral health. Two maintenance pet foods[b,c] are available that provide significant oral cleansing compared with commercial dry, moist or snack foods. Numerous studies have demonstrated that these foods provide significant plaque, calculus and stain control in dogs and cats.[127,150-154] A six-month study investigating the effects of food on plaque accumulation and gingival inflammation in 40 adult mongrel dogs reported that dogs fed the test food (Prescription Diet Canine t/d[b]) had 39% less plaque accumulation and 36% less gingival inflammation than dogs fed the control food (Purina Dog Chow[d]) (Figure 16-10). These studies used a clean-tooth model in which plaque, calculus and stain were evaluated at a specified time following a dental prophylaxis. (See Product Claims below.)

One study reported that feeding Canine t/d to beagles with existing plaque, calculus and gingivitis resulted in a significant decrease in mean plaque and calculus indices after two weeks and in the gingival index after six weeks (Figure 16-11). Beagles eating the control food (Purina Dog Chow) had a significant increase in plaque and calculus accumulation and no change in gingival inflammation over the 16-week test period.[155]

Combining an increased fiber content with a size and shape pattern (texture) that promotes chewing and maximizes contact with teeth is critical to obtaining a dental benefit. A typical dry food does not possess the textural characteristics for adequate dental cleansing. Simply enlarging the kibble or varying the shape of the product is likewise inadequate. In the absence of effective plaque control through other measures or in cases demanding adjunctive plaque control, mechanical control of plaque and calculus accumulation daily with a maintenance dental food is reasonable. Given the prevalence of periodontal disease in dogs and cats, and the need for effective home care products that improve owner compliance, it is likely dental benefit technology will be added to more foods in the future.

Other Methods of Substrate Control: Facts and Fallacies

TREATS

Many treats that claim a wide variety of dental benefits are available to pet owners. Rawhide strips have been reported to control calculus accumulation, provided the dog actively chews the strips daily.[156] Two rawhide chews each day are typically recommended.[e] Compacted rawhide treats in the shape of balls and bones can cause tooth fractures if chewed aggressively or if used as "catch" toys. Flat rawhide chews coated with an enzymatic system[f] are also available, but there are no published data demonstrating that these are any more effective than plain rawhide strips (Table 16-7).

A treat made of rice and whey and formed into a bone shape[g] to promote chewing activity has been reported to reduce accumulation of plaque and calculus in small dogs over a four-week period.[157] The disadvantages of these products may include pet acceptance, potential for gastrointestinal side effects, cost of the recommended feeding dosage and nutritional influences such as caloric excess and nutrient imbalances.[158]

BISCUITS

Plain baked biscuits, although long thought of as "dental" treats, provide little additional plaque and calculus reduction when compared with the feeding of dry dog food alone (Figure 16-12 and Table 16-7). Additionally, there are feline treats that make a tartar control claim;[h,i] however, two studies have failed to demonstrate an effect on plaque and calculus accumulation compared with feeding dry or moist foods

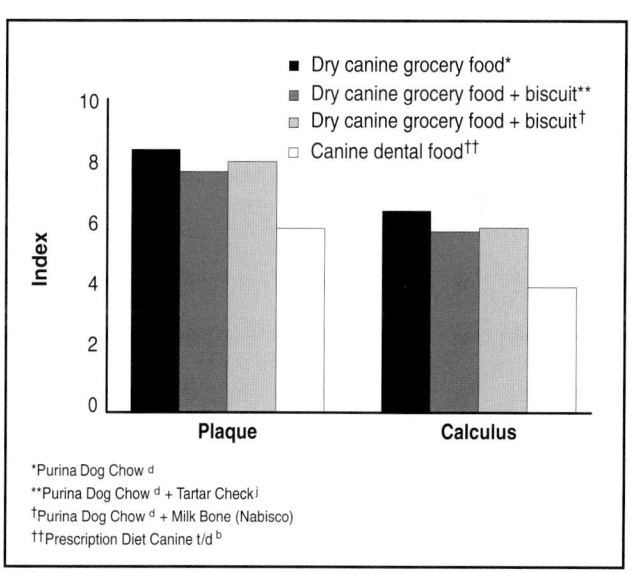

*Purina Dog Chow [d]
**Purina Dog Chow [d] + Tartar Check[i]
[†]Purina Dog Chow [d] + Milk Bone (Nabisco)
[††]Prescription Diet Canine t/d [b]

Figure 16-12. The effects of four different food regimens on plaque and calculus accumulation in dogs. Forty mongrel dogs were fed one of four food regimens: 1) Control (Purina Dog Chow), 2) Control plus two hexametaphosphate-coated biscuits/day (Tartar Check), 3) Control plus seven medium or four large (based on manufacturer's feeding directions) plain biscuits/day (Milk-Bone) or 4) Prescription Diet Canine t/d. There was no significant difference in plaque or calculus accumulation in dogs fed either Purina Dog Chow or Purina Dog Chow plus Milk-Bone or Tartar Check biscuits. Dogs fed Prescription Diet Canine t/d had significantly less accumulation of plaque and calculus than dogs fed either Purina Dog Chow or Purina Dog Chow plus Milk-Bone or Tartar Check biscuits.

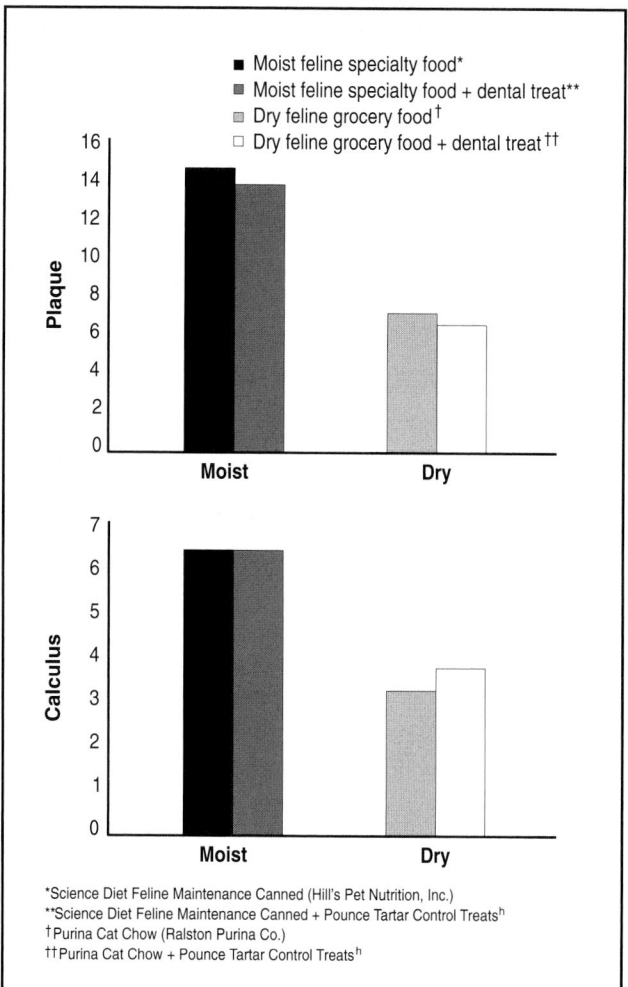

Figure 16-13. The effects of "dental" treats in cats fed commercial dry or moist foods. The top graph illustrates plaque accumulation in cats fed either a moist or dry cat food or the same food plus dental treats. The bottom graph illustrates calculus accumulation in cats fed either a moist cat food or the same food plus dental treats. There was no significant difference in plaque or calculus accumulation with the addition of dental treats to either a dry or a moist cat food.

alone.[154,159] Figure 16-13 describes the effect of dental treats on plaque and calculus accumulation in cats fed dry and moist foods with and without supplemental treats.

The addition of hexametaphosphate (HMP) to the surface of baked biscuits[j] significantly reduced calculus accumulation in beagles over a four-week period compared with a regimen of plain baked biscuits and dry food alone.[160,161] One three-week study, however, demonstrated no significant differences in plaque and calculus accumulation in dogs fed dry food, dry food plus baked biscuits or dry food plus HMP-coated biscuits.[k]

CHEW TOYS

The last category of products that claim an oral benefit for dogs are chew toys (Figure 16-14). Many varieties are available with claims ranging from "flosses teeth" to "reduces harmful plaque;" however, few data in the literature substantiate these claims. One report claimed less calculus accumulation in 14 of 20 client-owned dogs when dogs were allowed access to a urethane chewing device[l] for one month.[162] Anecdotal reports of

oral trauma (e.g., gingival lacerations and tooth fractures) resulting from aggressive chewing of some dental toys can also be found in the veterinary dental literature.

PRODUCT CLAIMS

Not surprisingly, it can be very confusing for veterinarians, and particularly for pet owners, to discern which products provide a significant dental benefit and thus warrant use as oral hygiene agents. The Center for Veterinary Medicine of the Food and Drug Administration (CVM-FDA) monitors and regulates dental health claims in the United States. (See sidebar "Guidelines for Tartar Control Claims.") Cosmetic claims are not objectionable and structure-function claims are not stringently regulated, thus the wide availability of products that make some type of plaque or calculus claim with little or no research to document their effectiveness. Phrases such as "cleans teeth, freshens breath" are commonplace on commercial treats packages. Because "crunchy" foods provide little dental benefit, the purported ability of these types of foods to provide any significant level of oral hygiene is a misrepresentation to pet owners (Table 16-7).

The need for standardized and scientifically sound methods by which to measure substrate accumulation in dogs and cats and evaluate product efficacy has been recognized by the veterinary dental community. The participants of the 1994 International Symposium on Veterinary Oral Care adopted a set of guidelines that provided minimum criteria by which to conduct dental studies in dogs and measure accumulation of plaque, calculus and stain.[42,163] Evaluation of substrate accumulations are based on a clean-tooth model (i.e., this type of model measures accumulation of plaque, calculus or stain following a dental prophylaxis). Pellicle, plaque and calculus are deposited continuously, and all layers can be affected by stain. The advantage of the clean-tooth model is that all study participants start with a substrate accumulation index of zero. This allows for accurate and repeatable measurement of substrate accumulation. Studies can be done to investigate the effects of various treatments on existing substrate accumulations, but the repeatability of results in such studies is low.

The clean-tooth model for measuring plaque, calculus and stain accumulation in dogs has been published and used by other investigators and partly incorporated into the guidelines for study design recommended by the Veterinary Oral Health Council.[164] (See sidebar "Veterinary Oral Health Council: A System for Recognizing Effective Dental Products.") These clean-tooth methodologies provide specific criteria by which to measure substrate accumulation, including tooth divisions, aids to enhance substrate visualization, anesthetic techniques amenable to repetitive research design and tooth subsets to be evaluated. The initial methodology recommendation incorporated 22 teeth, including bilaterally the maxillary third incisor, canine and all four premolars, and the mandibular canine, second, third and fourth premolar and the first molar. Since the adoption of those criteria, the maxillary first molar has been added to the subset of evaluated teeth.[152]

In addition, a six-month study was conducted to investigate the correlation of results obtained in a relatively short-term model to a more clinically relevant time frame of six months. Data from a six-month study of 40 dogs (19 beagles, 21 mongrels) demonstrated that the relationships between treatment groups evident from the first evaluations continued throughout the entire study, and that indications of product efficacy obtained at one to four weeks can be expected to be valid through a six-month period (Figure 16-15).[127] Similar methods have been proposed for cats.[150,154]

Products that increase chewing time and salivation and that maintain contact with the tooth surface have the potential to provide an oral health benefit through reduced accumulation of plaque and calculus. It is the veterinarian's responsibility to be aware of dental claims made by manufacturers and recommend oral hygiene aids that are safe and effective for clients' pets. (See sidebars "Guidelines for Tartar Control Claims" and "FDA Perspective—Dental Claims.")

Assess the Feeding Method

Changing the feeding method in the management of dental disease may not always be necessary, but verifying that an appropriate feeding method is being used is part of a thorough assessment. Items to consider in the management of oral disease include the feeding route, amount of food fed, how the food is offered (including its form), the pet's access to other foods or chewing materials, who feeds the animal and oral hygiene methods.

All of this information should have been gathered when the history of the animal was obtained. If the animal has a normal body condition score (3/5), it is likely that the amount fed previously (energy basis) was appropriate. For each animal, the feeding method should consider the condition of the oral cavity and the ability of the pet owner to provide oral hygiene.

■ FEEDING PLAN

Select a Food(s)

Oral disease should be treated with appropriate professional therapy. However, aftercare, or continued dental hygiene provided by the pet owner, will determine the overall success of professional therapy. Many pets can resume their normal nutritional regimen immediately after receiving professional care, provided the client has been instructed in appropriate plaque control procedures. (See sidebar "Home Care.") If the client isn't physically able to brush the pet's teeth often enough to control gingivitis or if the pet's temperament precludes such procedures, then nutritional recommendations should include feeding dental foods[b,c] with textural characteristics sufficient to control plaque, calculus and gingivitis daily.

A regimen of soft food may be recommended after invasive or advanced procedures during the initial healing phase. Chemical plaque control should be provided in these instances until mechanical plaque control can be resumed.

Determine a Feeding Method

The method of feeding is often not altered in the nutritional management of oral disease. If a new food is fed, the amount to feed can be determined from the product label or other supporting materials. The food dosage may need to be changed if the caloric density of the new food differs from that of the previous food. The food dosage and feeding method should be altered if the animal's body weight and condition are not optimal.

Good compliance is necessary for effective clinical nutrition. Enabling compliance includes limiting access to other foods and knowing who feeds the animal. Oral hygiene compliance can be improved by communicating the need for and the methods of effective plaque control. The feeding method can directly affect the health of the oral cavity.

Figure 16-14. Manufacturers of many toys and devices make dental claims. Some of these claims include, "removes/reduces tartar, massages gums and flosses teeth." In most cases, no scientific studies substantiate these claims and pet owners can easily be misled. There is clinical evidence, however, that suggests gum lacerations and fractured teeth may result from inappropriate use of toys and devices, including failure to match toy size to pet size, use of hard toys, particularly with puppies and toy use with pets that chew aggressively.

Guidelines for Tartar Control Claims

The AAFCO Pet Food Committee supports and recommends the following guidelines as developed by the Center for Veterinary Medicine (CVM) of the United States Food and Drug Administration for dental health claims with respect to rawhides, biscuits and other food products:

1. Foods bearing claims to cleanse, freshen or whiten teeth by virtue of their abrasive or mechanical action are not objectionable.
2. Foods bearing claims for plaque or tartar reduction or prevention or control of breath odor may be misbranded. However, if these claims are made only with respect to the products' abrasive action, enforcement would be a low priority. Thus CVM is exercising discretion by not objecting to these types of claims at this time.
3. Foods bearing expressed or implied drug claims to prevent or treat dental disease (e.g., gingivitis, gum problems, tooth loss) are not permissible unless they are the subject of approved New Animal Drug Applications.
4. Food ingredients that are not GRAS (generally recognized as safe) for the intended purpose of affecting the teeth or gums may be unapproved food additives or unapproved drugs, depending on the nature of the claim.

BIBLIOGRAPHY
Association of American Feed Control Officials. Official Publication, 1997.

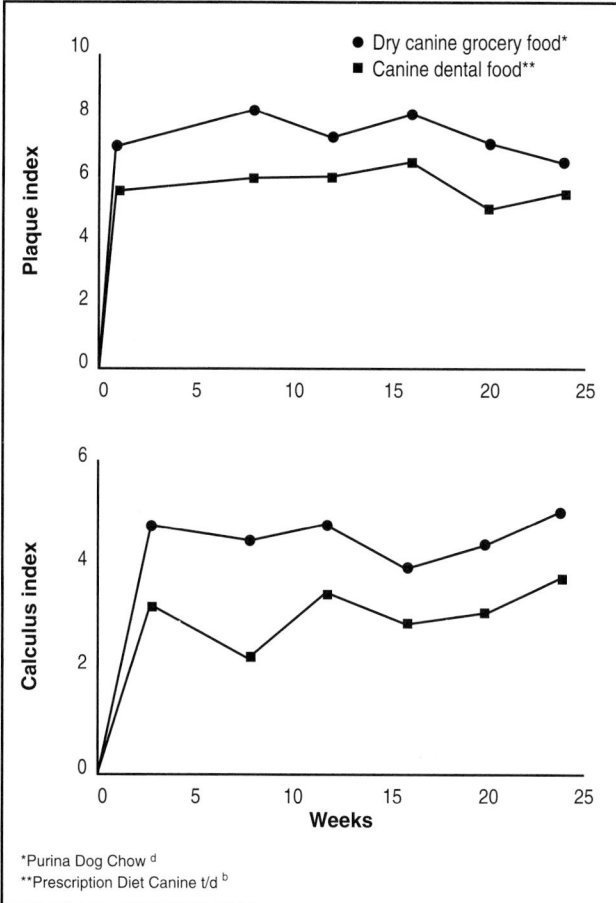

*Purina Dog Chow ᵈ
**Prescription Diet Canine t/d ᵇ

Figure 16-15. The effects of two different foods on plaque and calculus accumulation in dogs. This study evaluated and compared treatment differences using a three-week clean tooth model (Day 0 = dental prophylaxis, Day 7 = plaque evaluation, Day 21 = calculus evaluation) and extended the time period to six months. Dogs fed the test food (Prescription Diet Canine t/d) had significantly less accumulation of plaque and calculus than dogs fed the control food (Purina Dog Chow) at all time points. The differences detected between groups in the three-week model continued throughout the six-month time period.

▮ REASSESSMENT

The degree of monitoring required will depend on the: 1) degree of oral pathology, 2) level of periodontal therapy and 3) ability of the owner to provide routine oral hygiene. An annual oral examination and professional prophylaxis should be adequate for adult dogs and cats with good oral health and normal occlusion. As the severity of oral disease increases, the degree of periodontal therapy required to treat the condition will increase as well. An increased level of oral hygiene will be necessary to prevent disease progression for advanced stages of periodontal disease (i.e., worse than gingivitis).

Initially, patients should be rechecked weekly to monitor healing and oral hygiene. If both are satisfactory, the time between recalls can increase to three-month intervals. If the animal has severe pathology affecting plaque retention or if the owner is unable to provide effective plaque control, the time between periodontal therapy will need to be adjusted to maintain oral health. These recommendations are initial guidelines. Veterinarians must decide appropriate recall for each case, depending on the degree of oral pathology, periodontal therapy and owner compliance.

Veterinary Oral Health Council: A System for Recognizing Effective Veterinary Dental Products

The Veterinary Oral Health Council (VOHC) was established in 1997 after 10 years of open meetings, which included representatives from the American Veterinary Dental College (AVDC), Academy of Veterinary Dentistry, American Veterinary Dental Society, American Veterinary Medical Association, American Animal Hospital Association, United States Food and Drug Administration, private practice and industry. The purpose of the VOHC is to provide an independent, objective and credible means of recognizing veterinary dental products that effectively control accumulation of plaque and/or calculus (tartar). The VOHC system is similar to the American Dental Association (ADA) Seal of Acceptance system.

The VOHC consists of a director and eight board members including diplomates of the AVDC and other scientists active in the field of dental research. The VOHC does not conduct efficacy testing; the council reviews results of tests performed in accordance with approved protocols set by the VOHC. The first canine and feline dental products to receive the VOHC Seal of Acceptance were Prescription Diet Canine t/d and Feline t/d, respectively.

FDA Perspective: Dental Claims

Pet food label claims to treat or prevent gingivitis or periodontal disease are drug claims under the law and should not appear on pet food labels. Plaque or tartar control claims may also be implied drug claims, as they directly relate to dental disease. FDA has exercised some regulatory discretion with respect to plaque and tartar claims for products that achieve their effects by mechanical actions. However, products that contain chemical ingredients, such as pyrophosphates or enzymes, are of more concern. An ingredient that is not generally recognized as safe (GRAS) and is not the subject of an approved food additive petition for its intended use may be an unapproved food additive. A food additive, which is defined as a substance that is not GRAS and that may become a component or otherwise affect the characteristics of a food, must be shown to be safe and functional for its intended use before it may be legally marketed. Therefore, even without drug claims, pet food products containing unapproved food additives may be subject to regulatory actions. Products containing substances for plaque or tartar control that are approved or GRAS for other uses may be tolerated in the product, provided they are added in accordance to their allowed use and no specific reference to the ingredients as a control agent is made.

*David A. Dzanis, DVM, PhD, Diplomate ACVN
Center for Veterinary Medicine
United States Food and Drug Administration*

■ ENDNOTES & REFERENCES

ENDNOTES

a. Lund E. University of Minnesota, St. Paul. National Companion Animal Study. Personal communication. February 1996.

b. Prescription Diet Canine t/d. Hill's Pet Nutrition, Inc., Topeka, KS, USA.

c. Prescription Diet Feline t/d. Hill's Pet Nutrition, Inc., Topeka, KS, USA.

d. Purina Dog Chow. Ralston Purina Co., St. Louis, MO, USA.

e. Friskies Chew-eez. Friskies PetCare Products, Glendale, CA, USA.

f. C.E.T. Chews. VRx Products, Harbor City, CA, USA.

g. Pedigree Chum Rask or Dentabone. Kal Kan Foods, Vernon, CA, USA.

h. Pounce Tartar Control Treats. Quaker Oats, Chicago, IL, USA.

i. Whisker Lickin's Tartar Control Treats. Ralston Purina Co., St. Louis, MO, USA.

j. Tartar Check. Heinz Pet Products, Newport, KY, USA.

k. Logan EI. Unpublished data. December 1996.

l. Nylabone. Nylabone Products, Neptune, NJ, USA.

REFERENCES

1. Harvey CE, ed. Function and formation of the oral cavity. In: Veterinary Dentistry. Philadelphia, PA: WB Saunders Co, 1985; 5-22.

2. Grove TK. Periodontal disease. In: Harvey CE, ed. Veterinary Dentistry. Philadelphia, PA: WB Saunders Co, 1985; 59-78.

3. Löe H, Listgarten MA, Terranova VP. The gingiva. In: Genco RJ, Goldman HM, Cohen DW, eds. Contemporary Periodontics. St. Louis, MO: CV Mosby Co, 1990; 3-32.

4. Terranova VP, Goldman HM, Listgarten MA. The periodontal attachment apparatus. In: Genco RJ, Goldman HM, Cohen DW, eds. Contemporary Periodontics. St. Louis, MO: CV Mosby Co, 1990; 33-54.

5. Page RC, Schroeder HE. Periodontitis in other mammalian animals. In: Page RC, ed. Periodontitis in Man and Other Animals. Switzerland: S. Karger AG, 1982; 127-158.

6. Orsini P, Hennet P. Anatomy of the mouth and teeth of the cat. Veterinary Clinics of North America: Small Animal Practice 1992; 22: 1265-1277.

7. Colyer F. Variation in number, size and shape. In: Miles AEW, Grigson C, eds. Variations and Diseases of the Teeth of Animals. New York, NY: Cambridge University Press, 1990; 62-64.

8. Wiggs RB. Basic anatomy and oral examination. In: Proceedings. Twelfth Annual Frank W. Jordan Seminar, Manhattan, KS, 1992: 2-4.

9. Talbot E. Interstitial gingivitis or so-called pyorrhoea alveolaris. Philadelphia, PA: SS White Dental Manufacturing, 1899.

10. Wright JG. Some observations on dental disease in the dog. Veterinary Record 1939; 51: 409-422.

11. Gray H. Pyorrhoea in the dog. Veterinary Record 1923; 10: 167-169.

12. Bell AF. Dental disease in the dog. Journal of Small Animal Practice 1965; 6: 421-428.

13. Rosenberg HM, Rehfeld CE, Emmering TE. A method for the epidemiologic assessment of periodontal health-disease state in a beagle hound colony. Journal of Periodontology 1966; 37: 208-213.

14. Saxe SR, Greene JC, Bohann HM, et al. Oral debris, calculus and periodontal disease in the beagle dog. Periodontics 1967; 5: 217-225.

15. Gad T. Periodontal disease in dogs. Journal of Periodontal Research 1968; 3: 268-272.

16. Hamp SV, Viklands P, Farso-Madsen K, et al. Prevalence of periodontal disease in dogs (abstract). Journal of Dental Research 1975; SIA: 19.

17. Hamp SV, Lindberg R. Histopathology of spontaneous periodontitis in dogs. Journal of Periodontal Research 1971; 6: 266-277.

18. Sorensen WP, Löe H, Ramfjord SP. Periodontal disease in the beagle dog. Journal of Periodontal Research 1980; 15: 380-389.

19. Page RC, Schroeder HE. Spontaneous chronic periodontitis in adult dogs. Journal of Periodontology 1979; 52: 60-73.

20. Golden AL, Stoller N, Harvey CE. A survey of oral and dental diseases in dogs anesthetized at a veterinary hospital. Journal of the American Animal Hospital Association 1982; 18: 891-899.

21. Reichart PA, Dürr UM, Triadan H, et al. Periodontal disease in the domestic cat. Journal of Periodontal Research 1984; 19: 67-75.

22. Isogai H, Isogai E, Okamoto H, et al. Epidemiological study on periodontal diseases and some other dental disorders in dogs. Japanese Journal of Veterinary Science 1989; 51: 1151-1162.

23. Harvey CE. Epidemiology of periodontal conditions in dogs and cats (abstract). In: Proceedings. Sixth Annual Veterinary Dental Forum, American Veterinary Dental College and Academy of Veterinary Dentistry, Las Vegas, NV, 1992: 45-46.

24. Hoffman TH, Gaengler P. Epidemiology of periodontal disease in poodles. Journal of Small Animal Practice 1996; 37: 309-316.

25. Okuda A, Harvey CE. Etiopathogenesis of feline dental resorptive lesions. Veterinary Clinics of North America: Small Animal Practice 1992; 22: 1385-1404.

26. Van Wessum R, Harvey CE, Hennet P. Feline dental resorptive lesions. Prevalence patterns. Veterinary Clinics of North America: Small Animal Practice 1992; 22: 1405-1416.

27. Harvey CE. Dental resorptive lesions in dogs. In: Proceedings. American Veterinary Dental Society, Seattle, WA, 1993: 11-12.

28. Gardner AF, Darke BH, Keary GT. Dental caries in domesticated dogs. Journal of the American Veterinary Medical Association 1962; 140: 433-436.

29. Meyer R, Suter G. Epidemiologische und morphologische untersuchunger aur hundergebiss. Schwiez Arch Tierheil 1976; 118: 307-317.

30. Harvey CE, Emily PP. Oral inflammatory and immune-mediated diseases. In: Ladig D, ed. Small Animal Dentistry, St. Louis, MO: Mosby-Year Book, Inc, 1993; 145-155.

31. Harvey CE, ed. Oral medicine. In: Veterinary Dentistry. Philadelphia, PA: WB Saunders Co, 1989; 34-58.

32. Pedersen NC. Inflammatory oral cavity diseases of the cat. Veterinary Clinics of North America: Small Animal Practice 1992; 22: 1323-1345.

33. Harvey CE, Emily PP. Occlusion, occlusive abnormalities, and orthodontic treatment. In: Ladig D, ed. Small Animal Dentistry. St. Louis, MO: Mosby-Year Book Inc, 1993; 266-273.

34. Robinson HBG, Miller AS. Diseases of the teeth and supporting structures. In: Thomas ME, ed. Colby, Kerr and Robinson's Color Atlas of Oral Pathology, 4th ed. Philadelphia, PA: JB Lippincott Co, 1983; 54-56.

35. Lindhe J, Svanberg GK. Influence of trauma from occlusion on progression of experimental periodontitis in the beagle dog. Journal of Clinical Periodontology. 1974; 1: 3-14.

36. Marretta SM. The common and uncommon clinical presentations and treatment of periodontal disease in the dog and cat. In: Murtaugh R, ed. Seminars in Veterinary Medicine and Surgery: Small Animal 1987; 2: 230-240.

37. Kapatkin AS, Marretta SM, Patnaik AK, et al. Mandibular swellings in cats: Prospective study of 24 cats. Journal of the American Animal Hospital Association 1991; 27: 575-580.

38. Marretta SM. Chronic rhinitis and dental disease. Veterinary Clinics of North America: Small Animal Practice 1992; 22: 1101-1117.

39. Ramsey DT, Marretta SM, Hamor RE, et al. Ophthalmic manifestations and complications of dental disease in dogs and cats. Journal of the American Animal Hospital Association 1996; 32: 215-224.

40. Woodall IR. Achieving patient cooperation. In: Genco RJ, Goldman HM, Cohen DW, eds. Contemporary Periodontics. St. Louis, MO: CV Mosby Co, 1990; 520-524.

41. Logan EI, Boyce EN, Taylor G. Scoring techniques for assessment of periodontal disease in dogs and cats. In: Proceedings. Sixth Annual Veterinary Dental Forum, American Veterinary Dental College and Academy of Veterinary Dentistry, Las Vegas, NV, 1992: 49-53.

42. Logan EI, Boyce EN. Oral health assessment in dogs: Parameters and methods. Journal of Veterinary Dentistry 1994; 11: 58-63.

43. Wiggs RB, Lobprise HB, eds. Dental and oral radiology. In: Veterinary Dentistry: Principles and Practice. Philadelphia, PA: Lippincott-Raven, 1997; 140-166.

44. Löe H, Theilade E, Jensen SE. Experimental gingivitis in man. Journal of Periodontology 1965; 36: 177-187.

45. Theilade E, Wright WH, Jensen SE, et al. Experimental gingivitis in man. II. A longitudinal clinical and bacteriological investigation. Journal of Periodontal Research 1966; 1: 1-13.

46. Socransky SS. Relationship of bacteria to the etiology of periodontal disease. Journal of Dental Research 1979; 49: 203-222.

47. Lindhe J, Hamp SE, Löe H. Experimental periodontitis in the beagle dog. Journal of Periodontal Research 1973; 8: 1-10.

48. Lindhe J, Rylander H. Experimental gingivitis in young dogs. Scandinavian Journal of Dental Research 1975; 83: 314-326.

49. Wiggs RB. Periodontal disease and its multifactorial cause. In: Proceedings. Japanese Dental Society, Tokyo, Japan, 1995.

50. West-Hyde L, Floyd M. Dentistry. In: Ettinger SJ, Feldman EC, eds. Textbook of Veterinary Internal Medicine, 4th ed. Philadelphia, PA: WB Saunders Co, 1995; 1097-1124.

51. Harvey CE, Shofer FS, Laster L. Association of age and body weight with periodontal disease in North American dogs. Journal of Veterinary Dentistry 1994; 11: 94-105.

52. Page RC. Periodontal diseases in the elderly: A critical evaluation of current information. Gerodontology 1984; 3: 63-70.

53. Van der Velden U. Effect of age on the periodontium. Journal of the

American Dental Association 1984; 11: 281-294.

54. Johnson BD, Mulligan K, Kiyak HA, et al. Aging or disease? Periodontal changes and treatment considerations in the older dental patient. Gerodontology 1989; 8: 109-118.

55. Genco RJ. Host responses in periodontal diseases: Current concepts. Journal of Periodontology 1992; 63: 338-355.

56. Colyer F. Periodontal disease. In: Miles AEW, Grigson C, eds. Colyer's Variations and Diseases of the Teeth of Animals, revised ed. Cambridge, UK: Cambridge University Press, 1990; 543-550.

57. Watson ADJ. Diet and periodontal disease in dogs and cats. Australian Veterinary Journal 1994; 71: 313-318.

58. Wiggs RB. Home care/client education. In: Proceedings. Veterinary Dentistry Today, Twelfth Annual Frank W. Jordan Seminar, Manhattan, KS, 1995: 13.

59. Kolata RJ, Burrows CF. The clinical features of injury by chewing electrical cords in dogs and cats. Journal of the American Animal Hospital Association 1981; 17: 219-222.

60. Steurer I. Vergleich verschiedener behandlungsmethoden und vorschläge zue prophylaxe des kafigbeissersyndromes des hundes. Thesis. Veterinary Medicine, University Wein, 1990.

61. Fedi PF. Etiology of periodontal disease. In: Fedi PF, ed. The Periodontic Syllabus. Philadelphia, PA: Lea & Febiger, 1985; 13-18.

62. Schwartz RS, Massler M, Le Beau LJ. Gingival reactions to different types of tooth accumulation. Journal of Periodontology 1971; 42: 144-151.

63. Scannapieco FA, Levine MJ. Saliva and dental pellicles. In: Genco RJ, Goldman HM, Cohen DW, eds. Contemporary Periodontics. St. Louis, MO: CV Mosby Co, 1990; 117-125.

64. Brecx M. Influence of optimal and excluded oral hygiene on early formation of dental plaque on plastic films: A quantitative and descriptive light and electron microscopic study. Journal of Clinical Periodontology 1980; 7: 361-373.

65. Rolla G. Pellicle formation. In: Lazzari EP, ed. Handbook of Experimental Aspects of Oral Biochemistry. Boca Raton, FL: CRC Press, 1983; 245-250.

66. Lindhe J, ed. Pathogenesis of plaque-associated periodontal disease. In: Textbook of Clinical Periodontology, 2nd ed. Copenhagen, Denmark: WB Saunders Co, 1989; 189.

67. Kornman KS. The role of supragingival plaque in the prevention and treatment of periodontal diseases. A review of current concepts. Journal of Periodontal Research 1986; 21 (Suppl.): 5-22.

68. Courant PR, Saxe SR, Nash L, et al. Sulcular bacteria in the beagle dog. Periodontics 1968; 6: 250-253.

69. Soames JV, Davis RM. The distribution of spirochetes in the gingival crevice of a beagle dog. Journal of Small Animal Practice 1974; 25: 2230-2232.

70. Wunder JA, Briner WW, Calkins GP. Identification of the cultivable bacteria in dental plaque from the beagle dog. Journal of Dental Research 1976; 55: 1097-1102.

71. Syed SA, Svanberg M, Svanberg G. The predominant cultivable dental plaque flora of beagle dogs with gingivitis. Journal of Periodontal Research 1980; 15: 123-136.

72. Syed SA, Svanberg M, Svanberg G. The predominant cultivable dental plaque flora of beagle dogs with periodontitis. Journal of Periodontal Research 1981; 16: 45-56.

73. Svanberg G, Syed SA, Scott BW. Differences between gingivitis and periodontitis associated microbial flora in the beagle dog. Journal of Periodontal Research 1982; 17: 1-11.

74. Isogai E, Isogai H, Miura H, et al. Oral flora of mongrel and beagle dogs with periodontal disease. Japanese Journal of Veterinary Science 1988; 51: 110-118.

75. Mallonee DH, Harvey CE, Venner M, et al. Bacteriology of periodontal disease in the cat. Archives of Oral Biology 1988; 33: 677-683.

76. Hennet PR, Harvey CE. Aerobes in periodontal disease in the dog: A review. Journal of Veterinary Dentistry 1991; 8(1): 9-11.

77. Hennet PR, Harvey CE. Anaerobes in periodontal disease in the dog: A review. Journal of Veterinary Dentistry 1991; 8(2): 18-21.

78. Hennet PR, Harvey CE. Spirochetes in periodontal disease in the dog: A review. Journal of Veterinary Dentistry 1991; 8(3): 16-17.

79. Boyce EN, Ching RJW, Logan EI, et al. Occurrence of gram-negative black-pigmented anaerobes in subgingival plaque during the development of canine periodontal disease. Clinical Infectious Diseases 1995; 20 (Suppl. 2): S317-S319.

80. Genco RJ. Pathogenesis and host responses in periodontal disease. In: Genco RJ, Goldman HM, Cohen DW, eds. Contemporary Periodontics. St. Louis, MO: CV Mosby Co, 1990; 184-193.

81. Egelberg J. Local effect of diet on plaque formation and development of gingivitis in dogs. III. Effect of frequency of meal and tube feeding. Odontologisk Revy 1965; 16: 50-60.

82. Richardson RL. Effect of administering antibiotics, removing the major salivary glands, and toothbrushing on dental calculi formation in the cat. Archives of Oral Biology 1965; 10: 245-253.

83. Coignoul F, Cheville N. Calcified microbial plaque. Dental calculus of dogs. American Journal of Pathology 1984; 19: 499-501.

84. Lindhe J, ed. Dental plaque and dental calculus. In: Textbook of Clinical Periodontology, 2nd ed. Copenhagen, Denmark: WB Saunders Co, 1989; 92-128.

85. Mandel ID. Dental calculus (calcified dental plaque). In: Genco RJ, Goldman HM, Cohen DW, eds. Contemporary Periodontics. St. Louis, MO: CV Mosby Co, 1990: 135-146.

86. Schroeder HE. Epidemiology, physiology and clinical significance of dental calculus. In: Formation and Inhibition of Dental Calculus. Berne, Switzerland: Hans Huber, 1969; 10-35.

87. Schemehorn BR, MacDonald JL, Stookey GK. The use of the beagle dog as a dental stain model. Journal of Dental Research 1982; 61: 1028-1030.

88. Grove TK. Periodontal disease. Compendium on Continuing Education for the Practicing Veterinarian 1982; 4: 564-570.

89. Genco RJ. Pathogenesis of periodontal disease: New concepts. Journal of the Canadian Dental Association 1984; 59: 391-395.

90. Wiggs RB, Lobprise HB, eds. Periodontology. In: Veterinary Dentistry: Principles and Practice. Philadelphia, PA: Lippincott-Raven, 1997; 186-231.

91. Hennet PR, Delille B, Davot JL. Oral malodor in dogs: Measurement using a sulfide monitor. Journal of Veterinary Dentistry 1995; 12: 101-103.

92. Tonzetich J. Production and origin of oral malodor: A review of mechanism and methods of analysis. Journal of Periodontology 1977; 48: 13-20.

93. Tonzetich J. Oral malodour: An indicator of health status and oral cleanliness. International Dental Journal 1978; 28: 309-319.

94. Preti G, Clark L, Cowart BJ, et al. Non-oral etiologies of oral malodor and altered chemosensation. Journal of Periodontology 1992; 63: 790-796.

95. Chen S, Zieve L, Mahadevan V. Mercaptans and dimethyl sulfide in the breath of patients with cirrhosis of the liver. Journal of Laboratory and Clinical Medicine 1970; 75: 628-635.

96. Simone AJ, Logan EI, Livgren R, et al. Oral malodor in beagles: Association with indicators of periodontal disease. Journal of Clinical Dentistry 1997; 8: 163-168.

97. Syrjanen J. Vascular diseases and oral infections. Journal of Clinical Periodontology 1990; 17: 497-500.

98. Petrone JA. Mediastinal abscess and pneumonia of dental origin. Journal of the New Jersey Dental Association 1992; 63(4): 19-23.

99. Matsuura H. Systemic complications and their management during dental treatment. International Dental Journal 1989; 39: 113-121.

100. Wahl MJ, Wahl PT. Prevention of infective endocarditis: An update for clinicians. Oral Medicine 1993; 24: 171-175.

101. DeStefano F, Anda RF, Kahn HS, et al. Dental disease and risk of coronary heart disease and mortality. British Medical Journal 1993; 306: 688-691.

102. Loesche WJ. Periodontal disease as a risk factor for heart disease. Compendium on Continuing Education in Dentistry 1994; 15: 976-992.

103. Offenbacher S, Katz V, Fertik G, et al. Periodontal infection as a possible risk factor for preterm low birth weight. Journal of Periodontology 1996; 67: 1103-1113.

104. Hamlin RL. Identifying the cardiovascular and pulmonary diseases that affect old dogs. Veterinary Medicine 1990; 85: 483-487.

105. Prueter JC, Sherding RG. Canine chronic bronchitis. Veterinary Clinics of North America: Small Animal Practice 1985; 15: 1085-1096.

106. Calvert CA, Dow SW. Cardiovascular infections. In: Greene CE, ed. Infectious Diseases of the Dog and Cat. Philadelphia, PA: WB Saunders Co, 1990; 97-110.

107. Bonagura JD. Cardiopulmonary disorders in the geriatric dog. Veterinary Clinics of North America: Small Animal Practice 1981; 11: 705-726.

108. DeBowes LJ, Mosier D, Logan EI, et al. Association of periodontal disease and histologic lesions in multiple organs from 45 dogs. Journal of Veterinary Dentistry 1996; 13: 57-60.

109. Harari J, Besser TE, Gustafson SB, et al. Bacterial isolates from blood cultures of dogs undergoing dentistry. Veterinary Surgery 1993; 22: 27-30.

110. Harari J, Gustafson SB, Meinkoth K. Dental bacteremia in cats. Feline Practice 1991; 19(4): 27-29.

111. Calvert CA, Green CE. Bacteremias in dogs: Diagnosis, treatment and prognosis. Compendium on Continuing Education for the Practicing Veterinarian 1986; 8: 179-186.

112. Wiggs RB, Lobprise HB, eds. Domestic feline oral and dental disease. In: Veterinary Dentistry: Principles and Practice. Philadelphia, PA: Lippincott-Raven, 1997; 482-517.

113. Eisner E. Chronic subgingival tooth erosion in cats. Veterinary Medicine 1989; 84: 378-387.

114. Smith MM. Oral and salivary gland disorders. In: Ettinger SJ, Feldman EC, eds. Textbook of Veterinary Internal Medicine, 4th ed. Philadelphia, PA: WB Saunders Co, 1995; 1084-1096.

115. Williams CA, Aller MS. Gingivitis/stomatitis in cats. Veterinary Clinics of North America: Small Animal Practice 1992; 22: 1361-1383.

116. Zetner K, Bigler B, Kolbl S, et al. Die bedeutung von IgE im serum von katzen mit chronischer gingivitis/parodontitis 1996: Der Praktische Tierarzt 3/1996.

117. Association of American Feed Control Officials. Official Publication 1997.

118. Dzanis DA. The AAFCO dog and cat food nutrient profiles. In: Bonagura JD, ed. Current Veterinary Therapy XII. Philadelphia, PA: WB Saunders Co, 1995; 1418-1421.

119. Chawla TN, Glickman I. Protein deprivation and the periodontal structures of the albino rat. Oral Surgery, Oral Medicine, Oral Pathology 1951; 4: 578-602.

120. Ruben MP, McCoy J, Person P, et al. Effects of soft dietary consistency and protein deprivation on the periodontium of the dog. Oral Surgery, Oral Medicine, Oral Pathology 1962; 15: 1061-1070.

121. DePaola D, Faine MP, Vogel RI. Nutrition in relation to dental medicine. In: Shils ME, Olson JA, Shike M, eds., Modern Nutrition in Health and Disease, 8th ed. Philadelphia, PA: Lea & Febiger, 1994; 1007-1028.

122. Lewis TM. Resistance of dogs to dental caries: A two-year study. Journal of Dental Research 1965; 44: 1354-1357.

123. Carlsson J, Egelberg J. Local effect of diet on plaque formation and development of gingivitis in dogs. II. Effect of high carbohydrate versus high protein-fat diets. Odontologisk Revy 1965; 16: 42-49.

124. Carlsson J, Egelberg J. Effect of diet on early plaque formation in man. Odontologisk Revy 1965; 16: 112-125.

125. Makinen KK, Scheinin A. Turku sugar studies VII; Principal biochemical findings on whole saliva and plaque. Acta Odontology Scandinavia 1975; 33: 129-171.

126. Boyce EN, Logan EI. Oral health assessment in dogs: Study design and results. Journal of Veterinary Dentistry 1994; 11: 64-74.

127. Logan EI. Oral cleansing by dietary means: Results of six-month studies. In: Proceedings. Companion Animal Oral Health Conference, Lawrence, KS, 1996: 11-15.

128. Bawden JW, Anderson JJB, Garner SC. Calcium and phosphorus nutrition in health and disease: Dental tissues. In: Wolinsky I, Hickson JF, eds. Modern Nutrition. Boca Raton, FL: CRC Press, 1995; 119-126.

129. Becks H, Weber M. The influence of diet on the bone system with special reference to the alveolar process and labyrinthine capsule. Journal of the American Dental Association 1931; 18: 197-264.

130. Henrikson PA. Periodontal disease and calcium deficiency. An experimental study in the dog. Acta Odontologica Scandinavia 1968; 26 (Suppl. 50): 1-132.

131. Krook L, Lutwak L, Whalen JP, et al. Human periodontal disease. Morphology and response to calcium therapy. Cornell Veterinarian 1972; 62: 32-53.

132. Krook L, Whalen JP, Less GV, et al. Human periodontal disease and osteoporosis. Cornell Veterinarian 1972; 62: 371-381.

133. Svanberg G, Lindhe J, Hugoson A, et al. Effect of nutritional hyperparathyroidism on experimental periodontitis in the dog. Scandinavian Journal of Dental Research 1973; 81: 155-162.

134. Navia JM. Experimental oral calculus. In: Navia JM, ed. Animal Models in Dental Research. University, AL: University of Alabama Press, 1977; 298-311.

135. King JD. Abnormalities in the gingival and subgingival tissues due to diets deficient in vitamin A and carotene. British Dental Journal 1940; 68: 349-360.

136. Becks H, Wainwright WW, Morgan AF. Comparative study of oral changes in dogs due to deficiencies of pantothenic acid, nicotinic acid and an unknown of the B vitamin complex. American Journal of Orthodontology and Oral Surgery 1943; 29: 183-207.

137. Ismail AI. Relation between ascorbic acid intake and periodontal disease in the United States. Journal of the American Dental Association 1983; 107: 927-931.

138. Tromp JA, van Rijn LJ, Jansen J. Experimental gingivitis and frequency of toothbrushing in the beagle dog model: Clinical findings. Journal of Clinical Periodontology 1986; 12: 190-194.

139. Tromp JA, Jansen J, Pilot T. Gingival health and frequency of toothbrushing in the beagle dog model: Clinical findings. Journal of Clinical Periodontology 1986; 13: 164-168.

140. O'Rourke JT. The relation of the physical character of the diet to the health of the periodontal tissues. American Journal of Orthodontology 1947; 33: 687-700.

141. Colyer F. Dental disease in animals. British Dental Journal 1947; 82: 31-35.

142. Harvey CE, Emily PP. Periodontal disease. In: Ladig D, ed. Small Animal Dentistry. St. Louis, MO: Mosby-Year Book Inc, 1993; 89-144.

143. Robinson JGA, Gorrel C. The oral status of a pack of foxhounds fed a 'natural' diet. In: Proceedings. World Veterinary Dental Congress, Birmingham, England, 1997: 35-37.

144. Clark DE, Cameron A. Dental conditions in feral Australian cats. In: Proceedings. World Veterinary Dental Congress, Birmingham, England, 1997: 27.

145. Burwasser P, Hill TJ. The effect of hard and soft diets on the gingival tissues of dogs. Journal of Dental Research 1939; 18: 389-393.

146. Egelberg J. Local effect of diet on plaque formation and development of gingivitis in dogs. I. Effect of hard and soft diets. Odontologisk Revy 1965; 16: 31-41.

147. Krasse B, Brill N. Effect of consistency of diet on bacteria in gingival pockets in dogs. Odontologisk Revy 1960; 11: 152-165.

148. Studer E, Stapley RB. The role of dry foods in maintaining healthy teeth and gums in the cat. Veterinary Medicine/Small Animal Clinician 1973; 1124-1126.

149. Harvey CE, Shofer FS, Laster L. Correlation of diet, other chewing activities and periodontal disease in North American client-owned dogs. Journal of Veterinary Dentistry 1996; 13: 101-105.

150. Boyce EN. Feline experimental models for control of periodontal disease. Veterinary Clinics of North America: Small Animal Practice 1992; 22: 1309-1321.

151. Jensen L, Logan EI, Finney O, et al. Reduction in accumulation of plaque, stain and calculus in dogs by dietary means. Journal of Veterinary Dentistry 1995; 12: 161-163.

152. Logan EI, Finney O, Irvine G, et al. Dietary influences on gingivitis in the dog. In: Proceedings. Fourth World Veterinary Dental Congress, Philadelphia, PA, 1995: 101-102.

153. Finney O. Dental research and product development: A project manager's perspective. In: Proceedings. Companion Animal Oral Health Conference, Lawrence, KS, 1996: 17-22.

154. Logan EI. Oral cleansing by dietary means: Feline methodology and study results. In: Proceedings. Companion Animal Oral Health Conference, Lawrence, KS, 1996: 31-34.

155. Finney O, Logan EI, Simone AJ, et al. Effects of diet on existing plaque, calculus and gingivitis in dogs. In: Proceedings. Tenth Annual Veterinary Dental Forum, Houston, TX, 1996: 143-146.

156. Lage A, Lausen N, Tracy R, et al. Effect of chewing rawhide and cereal biscuit on removal of dental calculus in dogs. Journal of the American Veterinary Medical Association 1990; 197: 213-219.

157. Gorrel C, Rawlings JM. The role of a 'dental hygiene chew' in maintaining periodontal health in dogs. Journal of Veterinary Dentistry 1996; 13: 31-34.

158. Crane S. Chewing on the nature of tasty pet treats. Veterinary Forum 1990: 46-48.

159. Logan EI, Boyce EN, Berg M, et al. Effects of dietary form on plaque and calculus and gingival health in cats—Methodology and results. In: Proceedings. World Veterinary Dental Congress, Birmingham, England, 1997: 28-32.

160. Stookey GK, Warrick JM, Miller LL. Sodium hexametaphosphate reduces calculus formation in dogs. American Journal of Veterinary Research 1995; 56: 913-918.

161. Stookey GK, Warrick JM, Miller LL, et al. Hexametaphosphate-coated snack biscuits significantly reduces calculus formation in dogs. Journal of Veterinary Dentistry 1996; 13: 27-30.

162. Duke A. How a chewing device affects calculus build-up in dogs. Veterinary Medicine 1989; 84: 1110-1114.

163. Guidelines for measurement of supragingival plaque and calculus in canine clinical studies. Consensus statement of participants of the International Symposium on Veterinary Oral Care. Journal of Veterinary Dentistry 1994; 11: 80.

164. Harvey CE. Establishment of a veterinary oral health center proposed to AVMA. Journal of Veterinary Dentistry 1995; 12: 115-117.

CASE 16-1

Oral Foreign Body in a Doberman Pinscher

Robert B. Wiggs, DVM
Diplomate AVDC
Coit Road Animal Hospital
Dallas, Texas, USA

Assess the Animal

A five-year-old, 30-kg, male Doberman pinscher was presented for removal of a large beef knuckle bone that was lodged in its mouth. The dog was excited, salivating profusely and difficult to handle. The bone was lodged caudal to the canine teeth between the dental arcades and was holding the dog's mouth open to the point of causing strain upon the jaws. Attempts to remove the bone from the awake patient were unsuccessful. The dog's excited condition and the obstructing bone made a complete physical and oral examination impossible before sedation. After the dog was sedated, it was possible to gradually extricate the bone foreign body without causing further damage to the teeth or oral tissues (Figures 1A and 1B). The dog was intubated and anesthetized to allow a comprehensive oral examination.

The jaw had a full range of movement and no crepitation was detected over the temporomandibular joints. A laceration about 7 mm long and of moderate depth was found ventrally on the right side of the tongue in the proximity of the distal premolars. This laceration probably occurred as a result of the tongue pressing against the lower premolars.

The right carnassial teeth (maxillary fourth premolar and mandibular first molar) had Class VI/VI, cusp-type slab fractures. A slab of tooth was lost from the buccal side of the maxillary fourth premolar (Figure 2) and from the lingual side of the mandibular first molar. These tooth surfaces are commonly affected by this type of injury. Both fractures involved the pulp chamber; the exposed sites were dark and open. The pulp of these teeth was nonvital. Calculus accumulation and gingivitis were present on both arcades.

Assess the Food(s) and Feeding Method

The owner had been feeding the dog various dry commercial dog foods sometimes mixed with water or moist foods. When the dog was examined and vaccinated by the referring veterinarian approximately seven months earlier, the owner had been informed that the teeth were in generally good shape but there was slight calculus accumulation. The veterinarian had recommended a dental prophylaxis, which the owner declined. Shortly thereafter, the owner had begun feeding bones to the dog at the suggestion of a friend who said that bones could clean the teeth. All bones had been cooked before they were given to the dog. This was the first time the dog had received a large knuckle bone.

Questions

1. What are the treatment options for the two fractured teeth?
2. What safety concerns are associated with feeding bones to dogs?
3. What recommendations should be made concerning the dog's food?
4. When should a dog's teeth be cleaned?

Answers and Discussion

1. There are typically six options for treating fractured teeth: 1) leave them as they are, 2) smooth the fractured edges and seal the dentinal tubules, 3) place a restoration, 4) perform a pulp capping, 5) perform a root canal or 6) extraction. Small enamel chips of vital teeth may be left as is; however, the jagged edges of these teeth should be smoothed. In this case, the pulp was exposed; therefore, leaving the teeth untreated could lead to abscessation or more likely to a chronic active granuloma at the root apex or tip. Chronic shedding of bacteria into the bloodstream may gradually damage organs such as the heart, kidneys and liver. It would be medically unsound to leave these

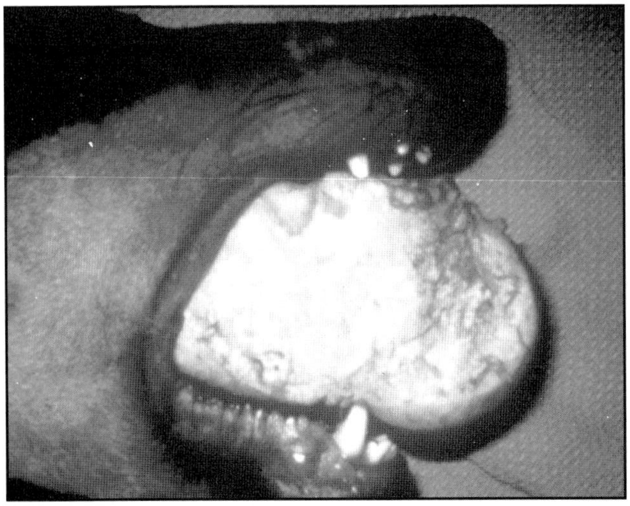

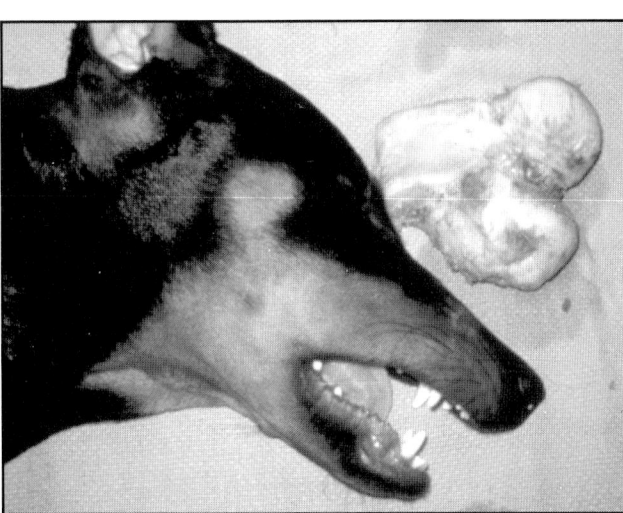

Figure 1A. A large bone lodged in the oral cavity of a Doberman pinscher.

Figure 1B. The same patient after the bone was removed. Note the size of the bone in relation to the patient's head and mouth.

teeth untreated. The most common repair technique for fractures of vital teeth that extend into the dentin is to smooth the fracture edges and seal the dentinal tubules with a dentinal bonding agent and possibly apply a restorative agent. This technique is also used in association with a pulp capping or root canal procedure. For this patient, this treatment would be appropriate only if done in conjunction with an endodontic procedure. Restoratives, such as a metal, composite, glass, porcelain or porcelain fused to a metal crown or inlay, are also used to repair fractures of vital teeth that extend into the dentin. These are also used in association with a pulp capping or endodontic procedure. Treatment with a restorative would be appropriate for this dog only in conjunction with an endodontic procedure. Pulp capping procedures are used for repair of fractured teeth with pulp exposure in which the pulp is still vital or alive. Successful pulp capping procedures inconsistently maintain the vitality of the tooth. At least 20% of the procedures fail even when performed under optimal circumstances. The severity of the trauma, amount of contamination, elapsed exposure time and degree of pulp exposure all play a crucial role in the success of pulp capping procedures. In this case, the teeth have Class VI/VI fractures and the pulp is nonvital, so a pulp capping procedure would be inappropriate.

Root canal or complete endodontic procedures are used when fractured teeth have pulp cavity exposure and the pulp is either in a state of irreversible pulpitis or already nonvital. A root canal procedure is an option for this patient. The determining factors for selecting this treatment include the extent of damage to the tooth crown, the state of the external root structure, the condition of the pulp cavity, the status of the periodontal tissues and the ability of the owner to eliminate or nullify causative agents. If these conditions are all favorable, this procedure plus some form of restoration would be the treatment of choice to maintain the function of the carnassial teeth.

The above procedures require advanced training and dental equipment. Extraction (exodontia) is a treatment option for damaged teeth, teeth affected by severe periodontal disease, highly mobile teeth that cannot be stabilized and teeth with root fractures. The type of extraction process is determined by the tooth type and location, number of roots, status of surrounding periodontal tissues and supporting bone and indications of root abnormalities (i.e., dilacerated, ankylosed, etc.). Extraction is a reasonable alternative for veterinarians who lack the training or equipment to perform the treatments discussed above.

2. Some pet owners believe that feeding cooked bones to domesticated pets helps control calculus accumulation. However, there are no reliable, published studies showing dental benefits derived from bone chewing. This practice has gradually fallen into disfavor among many veterinarians because bone consumption often results in health problems such as fractured teeth, bone lodgments, constipation, intestinal or rectal blockages and esophageal, gastric and intestinal perforations.

Recently, some veterinarians have again begun recommending the feeding of bones. However, the recommendation is to feed raw bones with meat

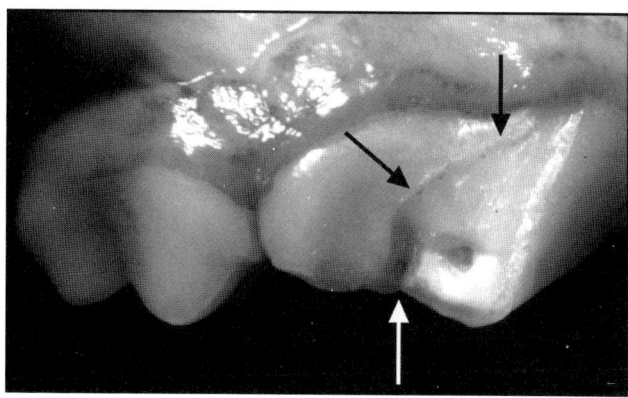

Figure 2. Slab fracture (dark arrows) of the maxillary fourth premolar with an exposed pulp chamber (white arrow).

attached, sometimes designated "raw and meaty bones." Current theory proposes that uncooked bones are not as hard as cooked bones and do not fracture teeth or cause other problems associated with cooked bones. However, anecdotal reports suggest the health concerns presented with cooked bones also occur commonly with raw, meaty bones. Feeding raw, whole chicken or chicken parts has been suggested as providing dental benefits without the risk of dental fractures because chicken bones are smaller. However, feeding raw meats, particularly chicken, raises food safety concerns. (See Chapter 7.) The safety and efficacy of feeding bones, regardless of type, remain undetermined. Veterinarians should be cautious about recommending bones for dental benefits.

3. There is little reliable scientific information about the dental benefits of most commercial dog and cat foods or about the dental benefits of one food compared with those of another. In general, dry foods have been accepted as causing less calculus and plaque accumulation than moist foods, even though controversies and inconsistencies exist in the literature. A commercial canine veterinary therapeutic food, Prescription Diet Canine t/dª has valid data documenting effective dietary cleansing. Research has demonstrated this food influences the control or reduction of plaque, calculus, stain and gingivitis. Canine t/d would be an appropriate food for this dog.

4. Teeth cleaning and professional dental prophylaxis are not always synonymous. The term prophylaxis means to prevent disease, whereas the teeth cleaning means to prevent or treat disease. Teeth should be cleaned when calculus accumulations occur, or when stomatitis and periodontal disease develop. The professional dental prophylaxis, if taken literally, must be performed at intervals needed to prevent stomatitis or periodontal disease from developing. There are no definitive time intervals for the veterinary professional dental prophylaxis. The veterinarian must combine information about the animal's health status, oral and tooth pathology, degree of successful home care, foods offered to the pet and the pet's chewing behavior to customize a professional dental prophylaxis program. A reasonable starting point is every six to 12 months for large-breed dogs.

Progress Notes

The tongue laceration was sutured and a comprehensive oral examination was completed at the initial visit. The clinical findings and treatment options were discussed with the owner. Three days after the original incident, a root canal procedure was performed on the dog's two fractured carnassial teeth and the tooth crowns were prepared for restoration. A dental prophylaxis was also performed at that time. About two weeks later the crowns were cemented, seated and adjusted. Initial owner instructions included restricting the dog's access to all bones and excessively hard chew toys. After endodontic treatment and crown preparation, the dog was fed a soft food to avoid injury to the prepared teeth. Following crown placement the dog was fed Prescription Diet Canine t/d.

The tongue had healed well when examined at the time of crown placement. When the dog was re-examined six months after the incident, no calculus accumulation was present and the gingivitis had resolved. The dog's general condition was very good. Its current weight was 31 kg with a body condition score of 3/5.

Endnote

a. Hill's Pet Nutrition, Inc., Topeka, KS, USA.

Bibliography

Wiggs RB, Lobprise HB, eds. Basic endodontic therapy. In: Veterinary Dentistry: Principles and Practice. Philadelphia, PA: Lippincott-Raven, 1997; 280-324.

Holmstrom SE, Frost P, Gammon RL. Veterinary Dentistry Techniques for the Small Animal Practitioner. Philadelphia, PA: WB Saunders Co, 1992; 207-266.

Shipp AD, Farhenkrug P. Practitioners' Guide to Veterinary Dentistry. Beverly Hill's, CA: Dr. Shipp's Lab, 1992; 77-94.

Emily PP. Problems associated with diagnosis and treatment of endodontic disease. Problems in Veterinary Medicine: Dentistry 1990; 2: 152-182.

Gorrell C, Robinson J. Endodontics in small carnivores. In: Crossley DA, Penman S, eds. Manual of Small Animal Dentistry, 2nd. ed. London, UK: British Small Animal Veterinary Association, 1995; 168-192.

Emily P, Penman S. Endodontics. In: Handbook of Small Animal Dentistry. New York, NY: Pergamon Press, 1990: 65-80.

■ CASE 16-2

Inappetence in a Cat

Robert B. Wiggs, DVM
Diplomate AVDC
Coit Road Animal Hospital
Dallas, Texas, USA

Assess the Animal

A three-year-old, 3.4-kg, neutered female domestic shorthair cat (body condition score 3/5) was referred for inappetence, salivation, periodic gagging and resistance to oral examination. The condition began suddenly two days earlier. The cat's abdomen was painful when palpated. Cervical lymph nodes and the thyroid glands were normal, although the animal resented palpation of the lower neck region. Eyes and ears were normal.

The cat's resistance to the oral examination limited the initial assessment. Moderate calculus accumulation and gingivitis were noted, however. A raised, uninflamed mass of gingival tissue was present where the crown of the lower left third premolar should have been located. Due to the cat's agitation, the teeth and their associated sulci could not be examined with a dental explorer/probe. The lips, alveolar mucosa, dorsal surface of the tongue and hard and soft palate appeared normal. Examination of the ventral tongue base revealed a string foreign body.

Following sedation, the string was found to extend across the base and caudally around the lateral sides of the tongue into the pharyngeal region. The two leaders of the string extended into the esophagus. The tongue was lifted and the string grasped with Brown Adson thumb forceps and gently pulled rostrally out of the mouth with no resistance. The string appeared to be a cotton-like material, 32 cm long. Endoscopic and radiographic examination of the esophagus and stomach were recommended.

The cat was intubated and anesthetized with isoflurane. Radiography showed the left mandibular gingival mass cov-

ered the roots of the lower third molar and that the majority of the crown was absent. The mass appeared to be a Stage V feline dental resorptive lesion (Table 1). Other findings included moderate calculus accumulation and mild gingivitis.

A professional dental prophylaxis was performed and the cat was given antibiotics for 10 days.

Assess the Food(s) and Feeding Method

The cat was fed a variety of moist foods purchased from grocery outlets.

Questions

1. What are the safety concerns of string-type chew toys?
2. What should be done concerning the gingival mass?
3. What recommendations should be made concerning the cat's food?

Answers and Discussion

1. The foreign body was similar to material from one of the cat's toys. When purchased, the toy was a ball made from loops of a cotton-like string, which purportedly would help clean and floss the teeth when the cat chewed on the toy. The toy came with a package of roughly ground dried catnip with instructions to sprinkle the catnip on the toy to entice the cat to play with and chew on it. The owners said that it was one of the cat's favorite toys, especially when the catnip was applied. String, thread and pieces of fabric commonly cause problems when ingested by cats. Apparently, the type, diameter and length of fiber and the proportional length of fiber to cat size all play an important role in whether these fibers cause problems or pass through the gastrointestinal tract. No studies concerning these factors have been published. Short lengths of a multi-stranded, absorbable material would

seem most appropriate, but more research is needed to determine safety requirements. Some string and rope chew toys are promoted for their "flossing effect." However, no research documents these claims. Additionally, some packages instruct the owner to use the toys in a tug-of-war with the pet to attain the flossing action. Strings tangled around teeth can avulse or fracture teeth. Therefore, these types of chew toys for dogs and cats should be recommended with extreme care, particularly for animals with moderate to advanced periodontal disease and mobile teeth. Clients who use string and rope-type chew toys should be encouraged to supervise their use and dispose of them at the first sign of unraveling or fraying.

2. The gingival mass was a Stage V feline resorptive lesion (Table 1). There are three options for these lesions: 1) restoration of the tooth, 2) extraction of the tooth and 3) no treatment (leave the lesion as it is). Restorations, usually with glass ionomers, are generally used in repair of Stage I and, to a limited degree, Stage II lesions. Success of restoration for Stage II lesions is generally poor, but is an option the client should be given. Stage II to IV lesions can be extremely painful and should be treated. Careful extraction of tooth roots should be considered in Stage V lesions if inflammation is present in the gingival area overlying the retained roots. If inflammation is not present and the lesion is not painful or sensitive to the patient, the roots may be left in place. Often the roots will completely resorb with no further problems. In this case, there was no inflammation associated with the mass and no treatment was performed.

3. There are currently two commercially available cat foods that provide effective dietary cleansing through

Table 1. Staging feline odontoclastic resorptive lesions.

Stage I	Lesion extends into cementum or enamel only
Stage II	Lesion extends into the dentin
Stage III	Lesion extends into the pulp cavity
Stage IV	Extensive structural damage to tooth, root or both
Stage V	Root retention with complete loss of crown

mechanical reduction of plaque and calculus accumulation (Prescription Diet Feline t/d[a] and Friskies Dental Diet[b]).

Progress Notes

Fiberoptic and radiographic examination of the esophagus and stomach revealed no abnormalities. The cat's food was changed to Prescription Diet Feline t/d. The cat was re-examined three weeks after the initial presentation. The gingival mass appeared unchanged to slightly smaller with no inflammation. The cat was eating well and no calculus accumulation was present.

Endnotes

a. Hill's Pet Nutrition, Inc., Topeka, KS, USA.
b. Friskies Pet Care Co., Glendale, CA, USA.

Bibliography

Wiggs RB, Lobprise HB, eds. Domestic feline oral and dental disease. In: Veterinary Dentistry: Principles and Practice. Philadelphia, PA: Lippincott-Raven, 1997; 482-517.

Wiggs RB, Lobprise HB. Dental disease. In: Norsworthy GD, ed. Feline Practice. Philadelphia, PA: JB Lippincott Co, 1993; 290-304.

Harvey CE, Emily PP. Atlas of oral pathology of the dog and cat. In: Small Animal Dentistry. St. Louis, MO: Mosby-Year Book, Inc., 1993; 48-56.

■ CASE 16-3

Periodontal Disease in a Geriatric Miniature Schnauzer

Robert B. Wiggs, DVM
Diplomate AVDC
Coit Road Animal Hospital
Dallas, Texas, USA

Assess the Animal

A 12-year-old, 10-kg male miniature schnauzer was examined for severe halitosis and reluctance to eat dry food. Physical examination revealed a grade 1/6 heart murmur and a body condition score of 3/5. Abnormal oral findings included moderate accumulations of plaque and calculus on both dental arcades, gingivitis, furcation exposure and attachment loss, most prominent around the mandibular caudal premolar and molar teeth.

After the initial oral examination, the dog was given enrofloxacin (Baytril[a]) to control infection while further evaluations were performed. Results of a complete blood count were normal. Results of a serum biochemistry profile were normal except for mild azotemia (BUN = 42 mg/dl, normal = 10 to 25). A cardiac evaluation indicated mild valvular endocardiosis.

Assess the Food(s) and Feeding Method

The owner had been feeding various commercial dry and moist grocery brand dog foods. Approximately six months earlier the dog became reluctant to eat dry foods and was currently eating only moist foods.

Questions

1. At what age should periodontal therapy be discontinued due to anesthetic risks?
2. When are antibiotics appropriate in periodontal therapy?
3. What medications may have adverse oral effects, particularly in geriatric dogs?
4. Is maintenance of alveolar bone under the tooth (alveolar ridge) a concern when extracting permanent teeth?
5. Outline an appropriate feeding plan for this geriatric patient.

Answers and Discussion

1. Many owners and veterinarians are reluctant to anesthetize geriatric animals for periodontal procedures. There is no specific age, however, when an animal cannot be anesthetized. An appropriate preanesthetic assessment should be made in all cases to identify potential risks and

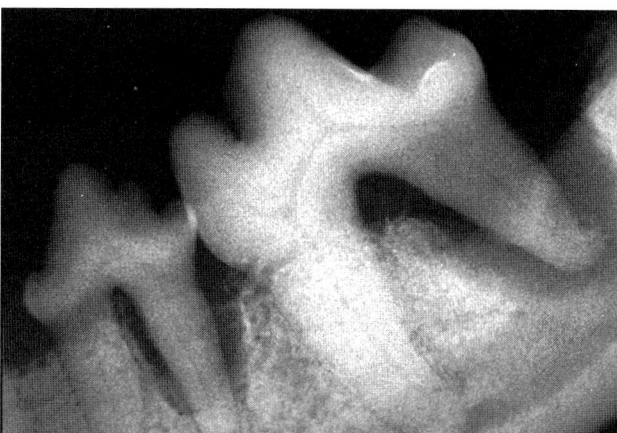

Figure 1. Radiographic evaluation indicating severe alveolar bone loss around the distal roots of the mandibular fourth premolar and first molar.

define an appropriate anesthetic regimen. Placing an intravenous catheter and administering fluids during periodontal procedures reduces the risk of anesthetic complications. Periodontal disease is associated with bacterial infection. The potential for systemic disease due to chronic showering of the bloodstream with oral bacteria may pose a greater risk to the animal than the anesthesia required for appropriate periodontal therapy.

2. Antibiotics may be used before, during or after dental procedures. Each period has specific justification. Antibiotics used before dental procedures help control the existing periodontal infection, thereby decreasing inflammation, which allows for more accurate clinical assessment and helps when making therapeutic choices. Antibiotics used during dental procedures are generally administered to protect the body from infection resulting from bacteremia. Healthy immunocompetent animals clear this bacteremia within 20 minutes. However, animals with organ pathology or a compromised immune system may be predisposed to sequential infection. Antibiotics given after dental procedures are generally prescribed to prevent oral reinfection during the healing stages.

3. Many medications can affect oral physiology, particularly salivary flow. Saliva is rich in proteins, glycoproteins, electrolytes and lipids and provides a protective barrier to oral tissues. Reduced salivary flow is associated with an increased prevalence of caries, periodontal disease and oral irritation in people. Animals receiving medications that alter the oral environment may need additional professional or home care to maintain oral health. Examples of such drugs include narcotic analgesics, anticonvulsants, antihistamines, antiarrhythmics, antineoplastics, antiemetics, diuretics and tranquilizers.

4. Alveolar ridge maintenance is a concern, particularly if the mandibular incisor, canine or carnassial teeth are extracted. Atrophy of the alveolar ridge and mandibular weakening are common following extraction of these teeth, and may result in future pathologic or iatrogenic fractures. Packing extraction sites with osseopromotive material may reduce and in some cases prevent alveolar ridge atrophy.

5. Because aging affects all body systems, there is a high likelihood of multiple problems in older pets. A thorough systems review, which should include a complete history, physical examination and extended laboratory database, is important in older pets. (See Chapter 8.) This review enables the veterinarian to define problems accurately, prioritize the problems and establish appropriate diagnostic, therapeutic and feeding plans. Chronic valvular heart disease (endocardiosis) and renal failure are common causes of morbidity and mortality in older dogs. Because these conditions are so common, geriatric dogs may benefit from a food that avoids excess levels of phosphorus, protein, sodium and chloride. (See Chapters 18 and 19.) Other nutrient levels and the feeding method may need to be adjusted based on body condition of the patient and results of the comprehensive systems review.

This dog has clinical and laboratory evidence of dental disease, chronic valvular heart disease and renal disease. Accordingly, it may benefit from a food that avoids excess levels of phosphorus, protein, sodium and chloride. In addition, oral care at home should be initiated to prevent accumulation of dental subtrates and further periodontal disease. A food of dental treat that enhances mechanical cleansing or teeth would be appropriate.

Prescription Diet Canine t/d[b] is a dry veterinary therapeutic food formulated to reduce accumulation of plaque and calculus and reduce gingivitis. This food is most effective when fed as the sole maintenance food for adult dogs. However, some animals with dental disease should receive food(s) with different nutrient profiles because of concurrent disease.

Progress Notes

The dog was given a vasodilator (isosorbide dinitrate) and a canned veterinary therapeutic food that avoids excess phosphorus, protein, sodium and chloride (Prescription Diet Canine k/d[b]).

Therapeutic options for the oral problems were discussed with the owner and the decision was made to proceed with periodontal therapy. The dog was anesthetized with isoflurane (administered via mask and intubation), and supragingival scaling followed by root planing and subgingival curettage was performed. Severe periodontal disease was present (Table 16-5) around the left mandibular fourth premolar and first molar teeth. Advanced bone loss was noted around the distal roots (Figure 1); a mobility index of 3/3 (severe mobility) was present. Both teeth were extracted by crown sectioning and elevation. The alveolar sockets were curetted and bony spicules were smoothed. An osseopromotive bioactive material (Bioglass[c]) was placed into the sockets to aid in alveolar ridge maintenance. The extraction sites were closed with sutures and the remaining teeth were polished. Oral clindamycin (Antirobe[d]), an oral ascorbic acid/zinc gluconate rinse (Maxiguard[e]) and the canned veterinary therapeutic food (Prescription Diet Canine k/d) were prescribed for two weeks.

After two weeks, the dog was re-examined. The extraction sites were healing well and the owner commented that the dog was more active than it had been for many months. The dog was fed the dry form of the same renal food (Prescription Diet Canine k/d) and the owner was instructed to provide daily oral care through toothbrushing and feeding four kibbles/day of Prescription Diet Canine t/d. The combined foods were calculated to deliver approximately 500 kcal/day (2.1 MJ/day).

Endnotes

a. Bayer Animal Health, Shawnee, KS, USA.
b. Hill's Pet Nutrition, Inc., Topeka, KS, USA.
c. Nutramax Laboratories, Inc., Baltimore, MD, USA.
d. Upjohn Veterinary Products, Kalamazoo, MI, USA.
e. Addison Laboratories, Fayette, MO, USA.

Bibliography

Wiggs RB, Lobprise HB, eds. Periodontology. In: Veterinary Dentistry: Principles and Practice. Philadelphia, PA: Lippincott-Raven, 1997; 186-231.

Marretta SM. Oropharynx. In: Birchard SJ, Sherding RG, eds. Manual of Small Animal Practice. Philadelphia, PA: WB Saunders Co, 1994; 607-629.

Edgar WM, O'Mullane DM, eds. Factors influencing salivary flow rate and composition. In: Saliva and Dental Health. British Dental Association, 1990.

CASE 16-4

Periodontal Disease in a Miniature Poodle

Karl Zetner, DVM
Veterinaermedizinische Universitaet Wien
Vienna, Austria

Assess the Animal

A six-year-old miniature poodle was examined for severe halitosis and decreased food intake. The poodle weighed 8 kg and had a body condition score of 3/5. Oral examination revealed generalized gingivitis/periodontitis with heavy accumulations of plaque and calculus. The area of most interest, however, was the area between the lower canine tooth and the lower third incisor. Recession of the gingivae led to partial exposure of the tooth roots with abundant accumulation of materia alba, plaque, calculus, food and hair (Figure 1). After dental prophylaxis (Figure 2), this area was clean but prone to rapid accumulation of plaque, calculus and other materials. The rapid accumulation of dental substrates occurred because the distal enamel projection of the third incisor hindered nat-ural oral self-cleansing mechanisms and the owner's efforts to brush the dog's teeth.

Assess the Food(s) and Feeding Method

The dog was fed a commercial moist grocery brand food once daily.

Questions

1. What techniques can be used to enhance the normal self-cleansing mechanisms in the mouth of this patient?
2. Following routine dental prophylaxis and teeth cleaning, what steps can the owner take at home to help maintain the oral health of this dog?

Answers and Discussion

1. The prominent projection of the third incisor can be removed to improve the mouth's self-cleaning (i.e., saliva, tongue and lip movements).

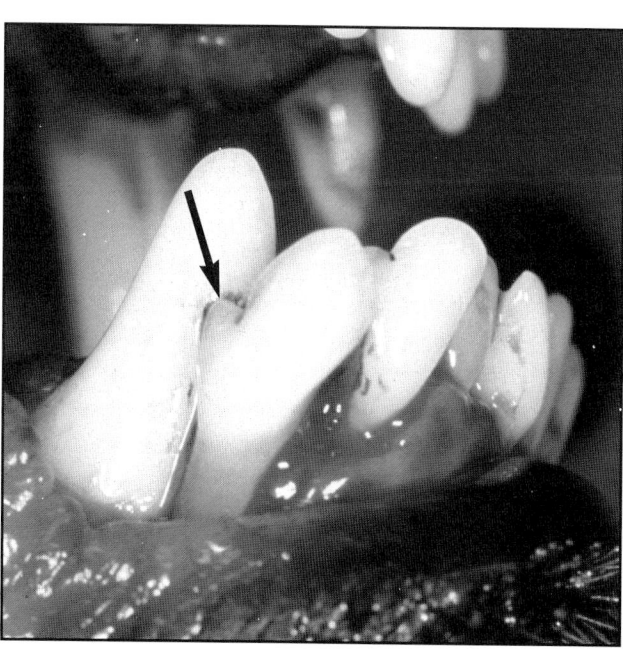

Figure 2. Same site as Figure 1 following periodontal therapy. This area will be prone to rapid reaccummulation of plaque, calculus and other oral debris due to the malpositioning of the teeth and the distal enamel projection of the third incisor (arrow).

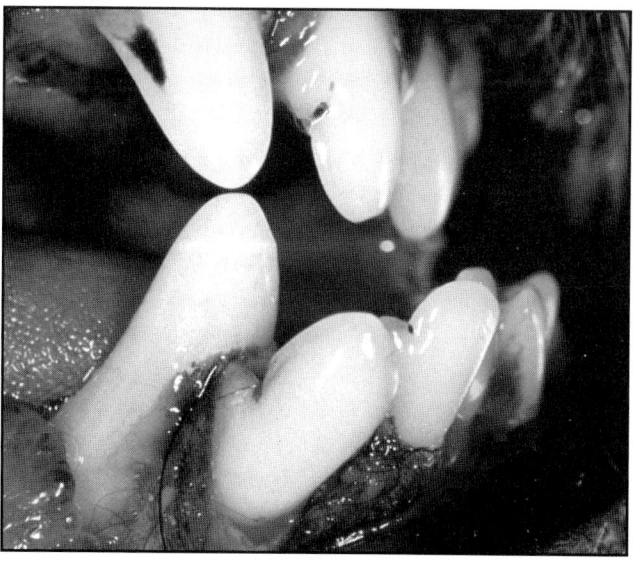

Figure 1. Malposition of the mandibular canine and third incisor. There is abundant accumulation of materia alba, plaque, calculus, food debris and hair.

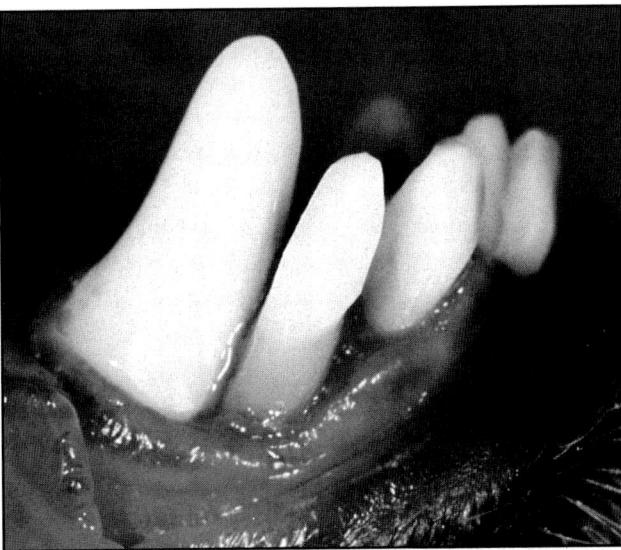

Figure 3. Same site as Figure 1 following removal of the distal enamel projection of the third incisor. This technique enhances the self-cleansing mechanism of the oral cavity as well as home oral hygiene provided by the pet owner.

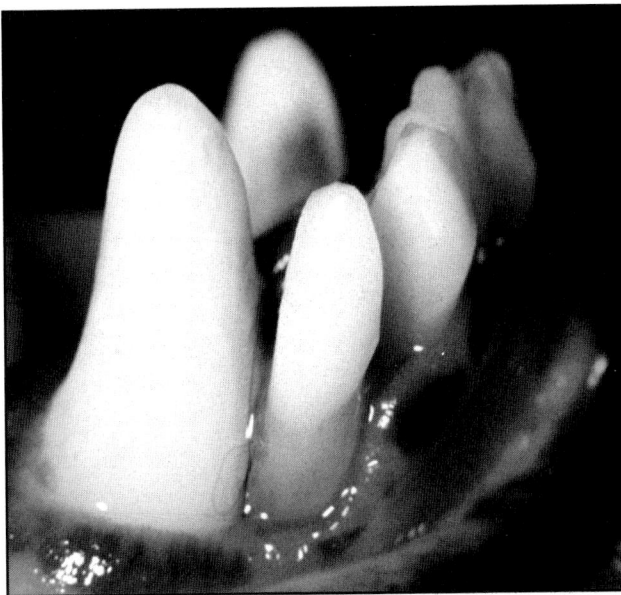

Figure 4. Same site as Figure 1 one year following initial treatment.

2. A food with a soft texture should be fed for the first two weeks after extensive periodontal treatment to enhance healing of the gingival and periodontal tissues. Home care should be delayed for several weeks if oral surgical procedures (gingivoplasty, gingivectomy, flap operations) are performed. Antibiotic therapy (clindamycin, amoxicillin/clavulanic acid) is also indicated.

After the initial healing period, regular oral home care is recommended to reduce accumulation and maturation of plaque and calculus. A comprehensive oral home care program should include a combination of mechanical and/or chemical cleaning methods. Mechanical methods include toothbrushing and dietary cleansing with Prescription Diet Canine t/d[a] or rawhide chews. Chemical methods include use of topical antimicrobials (chlorhexidine, zinc chloride) or calcium chelators (pyrophosphate, hexametaphosphate). Most of the biscuits and other treats purported to have dental benefits do not provide any additional benefits above those obtained from feeding regular dry dog foods.

Progress Notes

The prominent projection on the third incisor was removed and the surface of the tooth polished (Figure 3). During the first two weeks after periodontal treatment, the dog was fed a high-moisture canned grocery brand food (Pedigree PAL[b]) to avoid disturbing the healing phase of the gingivae and other periodontal tissues. The owner was instructed in proper home care techniques including toothbrushing and application of long-acting chlorhexidine gel. After the initial two weeks, the food was changed to a semi-moist grocery brand food (Pedigree Frolic[b]). The benefit of odontoplasty in combination with good oral home care is demonstrated in Figure 4, which shows the patient one year later.

Endnotes

a. Hill's Pet Nutrition, Inc., Topeka, KS, USA.
b. Master Foods Austria, Bruck/Leitha, Austria.

Bibliography

Emily P, Tholen M. Periodontal therapy. In: Bojrab MJ, Tholen M, eds. Small Animal Oral Medicine and Surgery, Philadelphia, PA: Lea & Febiger, 1990; 143-145.

CHAPTER 17

Developmental Orthopedic Disease of Dogs

Daniel C. Richardson
Jürgen Zentek
Herman A. W. Hazewinkel
Philip W. Toll
Steven C. Zicker

"The beginning is the most important part of the work."
Plato

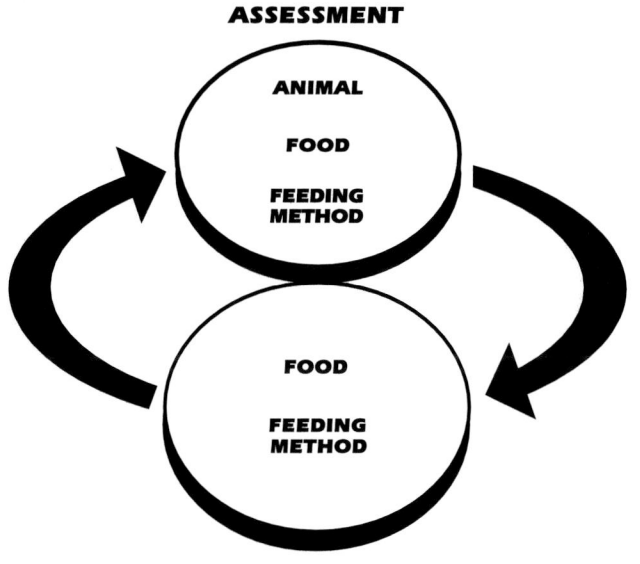

ASSESSMENT

FEEDING PLAN

The Dance of the Solids

The Polymers, those giant Molecules
Like Starch and Polyoxymethylene,
Flesh out, as protein serfs and plastic fools,
This Kingdom with Life's Stuff. Our time has seen
The synthesis of Polyisoprene
And many cross-linked Helixes unknown
To Robert Hooke; but each primordial Bean
Knew Cellulose by heart. Nature alone
Of Collagen and Apatite compounded Bone.

John Updike

Note: The reader is referred to Chapter 1 for a detailed discussion of the iterative process of clinical nutrition.

CLINICAL IMPORTANCE

The prevalence of musculoskeletal disorders for all dogs at multicenter referral practices has been reported to be approximately one in four, with 70% of these disorders involving the appendicular skeleton.[1] Further, the prevalence of musculoskeletal problems in dogs less than one year old in all breeds is about 22%, with 20% possibly having a nutrition-related etiology.[a] Developmental orthopedic disease (DOD) includes a diverse group of musculoskeletal disorders that occur in growing animals (most commonly fast-growing, large- and giant-breed dogs) and that are sometimes related to nutrition. Canine hip dysplasia (CHD) and osteochondrosis make up the overwhelming majority of the musculoskeletal problems with a possible nutrition-related etiology.[a]

KEY WORDS & TERMS—DEVELOPMENTAL ORTHOPEDIC DISEASE*

Bone remodeling	Developmental orthopedic disease	Overnutrition
Calcitonin	Hypercalcitoninism	Parathyroid hormone (PTH)
Canine hip dysplasia	Hyperparathyroidism	Rickets
Chondrocyte	Osteochondritis dissecans (OCD)	
Degenerative joint disease	Osteochondrosis	

*Key words and terms are defined in the Glossary.

KEY POINTS—DEVELOPMENTAL ORTHOPEDIC DISEASE

1. Developmental orthopedic disease (DOD) includes a diverse group of musculoskeletal disorders that occur in growing animals.
2. Canine hip dysplasia and osteochondrosis make up the overwhelming majority of musculoskeletal problems with a possible nutrition-related etiology.
3. Breed and familial history are important predisposing factors for DOD.
4. Bone contains 99% of the calcium in the body and functions physiologically as a structural material and as an ion reservoir.
5. The most critical period for development of DOD occurs during the growth phase, before epiphyseal closure.
6. Specific factors that are currently thought to increase the risk of DOD in young dogs include: 1) belonging to a large or giant breed, 2) free-choice feeding, 3) feeding high-energy foods and 4) excessive calcium intake from food, treats and supplements.
7. The biochemical stress induced by rapid weight gain during growth has been cited as an etiology of DOD.
8. Hypercalcitoninism associated with excessive intake of calcium may be a contributing factor to DOD in dogs.
9. Excessive dietary intakes of calcium and energy, together with rapid growth, appear to predispose puppies to hip dysplasia and osteochondrosis.
10. The goal of feeding programs for large- and giant-breed puppies should be to achieve moderate energy restriction.
11. In general, a good starting point is to feed puppies three times resting energy requirement (RER) from weaning to four months of age, followed by two times RER until about one year of age.
12. In the face of adequate levels of calcium in the food, the absolute level of calcium, rather than an imbalance in the calcium-phosphorus ratio, influences skeletal development.
13. Protein excess has not been shown to negatively affect skeletal development in growing dogs.
14. Meal-limited feeding is the recommended feeding method for rapidly growing dogs.
15. In general, free-choice feeding is contraindicated in puppies at risk for DOD until they have reached skeletal maturity.
16. Clients who use the free-choice feeding method for growing dogs should be advised that it is especially important to feed a food with an energy density less than 3.8 kcal/g (15.9 kJ/g) (less than 12% fat on a dry matter basis) to decrease the risk of excess energy intake.
17. Vitamin and/or mineral supplements, especially those containing calcium, phosphorus, vitamin D and vitamin A, should not be routinely given to growing dogs eating commercial foods. They may be indicated for growing dogs eating homemade foods.
18. Rapidly growing, large- and giant-breed dogs have a very steep growth curve and their food requirements can change dramatically in a short time. These puppies should be weighed, their body condition evaluated and their daily feeding amount adjusted at least

Canine Hip Dysplasia

CHD is the most frequently encountered orthopedic disease in veterinary medicine with heritability and a potential nutrition-related etiology.[1] CHD is an abnormal development, or growth, of the hip joint (Figure 17-1) manifested by varying degrees of laxity of surrounding soft tissues, instability of the joint and malformation of the femoral head and acetabulum with osteoarthrosis.[2] The actual number of cases of CHD is estimated to be in the millions worldwide.[3]

Osteochondrosis

Osteochondrosis is widespread among people and young, rapidly growing, warm-blooded domesticated species. Generally, osteochondrosis is a disruption in endochondral ossification that results in a focal lesion.[4] Osteochondrosis occurs in the physis and/or epiphysis of growth cartilage, and may be considered a generalized or systemic disease.

Clinical signs of osteochondrosis are related to the severity and location of disease.

When osteochondrosis affects physeal cartilage, it may cause growth abnormalities in long bones such as angular limb deformities. Osteochondrosis of articular epiphyseal cartilage commonly occurs in the shoulder (proximal humerus, Figure 17-2), stifle (distal femur), hock (talus) and elbow (distal humerus). Acute inflammatory joint disease (or degenerative joint disease) may ensue subsequent to development of osteochondrosis when the cartilage surface is disrupted and subchondral bone is exposed to synovial fluid. Inflammatory mediators and cartilage fragments are released into the joint (osteochondritis dissecans), which perpetuates the cycle of degenerative joint disease.[5] Other disease processes such as spondylolisthesis, intra-articular fracture, complete or partial epiphysiolysis and deformed joint surfaces have been associated with osteochondrosis but their etiology is still undetermined.

KEY NUTRITIONAL FACTORS—DEVELOPMENTAL ORTHOPEDIC DISEASE

Factors	Associated conditions	Dietary recommendations

Energy	Canine hip dysplasia
	Osteochondrosis
	Obesity
		Initially, calculate energy intake as follows:
		  0 to 4 months of age = 3 x resting energy requirement
		  4 to 12 months of age = 2 x resting energy requirement
		Use a food with metabolizable energy of 3.2 to 3.8 kcal/g DM (13.4 to 15.9 kJ/g DM)

Fat	See above	Feed a food that does not exceed 12% fat (DMB), especially if feeding free choice
Calcium	Canine hip dysplasia Osteochondrosis	Feed a food with 0.7 to 1.2% calcium (DMB)
Supplements	See above	None recommended if a commercial food is fed

ASSESSMENT

Assess the Animal

History and Physical Examination

Breed and familial history are important predisposing factors for DOD. For mixed-breed dogs, it is useful to know the breed of the stud and bitch as well as historical wellness of offspring. If possible, it may be helpful to gather information pertaining to skeletal abnormalities of previous litters from the same bitch and stud.

Food intake and history should be evaluated as described in Chapter 1. Any treats and supplements fed to the patient should be scrutinized closely, paying special attention to the calcium and energy intake. It is critical to calculate, or closely estimate, metabolizable energy (ME) and calcium intake in order to provide rational advice for feeding growing large- and giant-breed dogs.

Dogs should be weighed during the initial visit and all subsequent visits to help monitor their growth rate. A body condition score (BCS) should be determined and recorded at each visit. (See Chapter 1.) Attention to abnormal changes in weight or BCS will help in assessing and managing growing dogs. In some cases, graphs of body weight and BCS may prove useful in recognizing variances from desired goals.

Before a physical examination is conducted, historical information should be gathered about the degree, if any, of perceived lameness, the affected limb(s), duration of lameness and any peculiarities regarding the lameness. Following historical evaluation, the animal should be observed at rest for any gross conformational abnormalities. Next, the animal should be observed in motion to ascertain the degree of lameness and location of involvement.[6]

If a locomotor defect is confirmed, the etiology should be determined. To determine the cause, the examination should include: 1) palpation of limbs for asymmetry, swelling, heat and sensitivity, 2) deep palpation of long bones, 3) flexion/extension of joints to determine range of motion, crepitation, instability and sensitivity and 4) neurologic evaluation. Even after a thorough physical examination, the exact cause of the lameness may remain undetermined.

Radiography

Radiographs should be taken to further define the clinical diagnosis. Radiographic identification of lesions aids

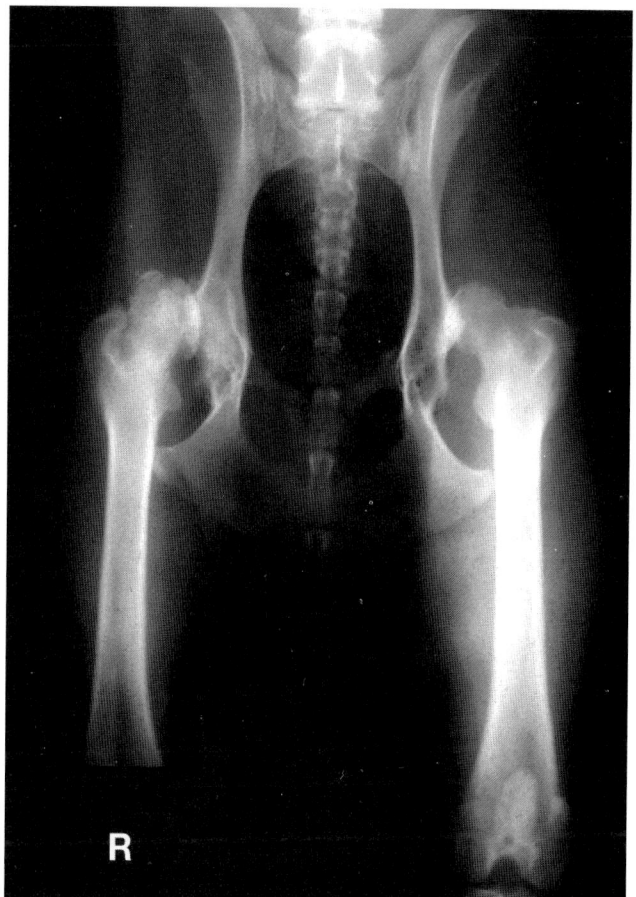

Figure 17-1. Progression of joint disease in a dog with rear-limb lameness due to severe bilateral hip dysplasia. This ventrodorsal radiograph shows degenerative joint disease in both coxofemoral joints. The right hip has advanced osteophyte formation on the femoral neck. The right acetabular cup and femoral head have remodeled to form a pseudoarthrosis. The left femoral neck also has osteophyte formation and the hip is luxated craniodorsally.

in confirming the disease. However, inability to identify lesions by survey radiography does not always negate the presence of disease.[4,7] (See sidebar "Use of DEXA to Assess the Skeleton.")

Laboratory Information

Diagnostic tests to detect other diseases that may result in skeletal abnormalities should be considered when appro-

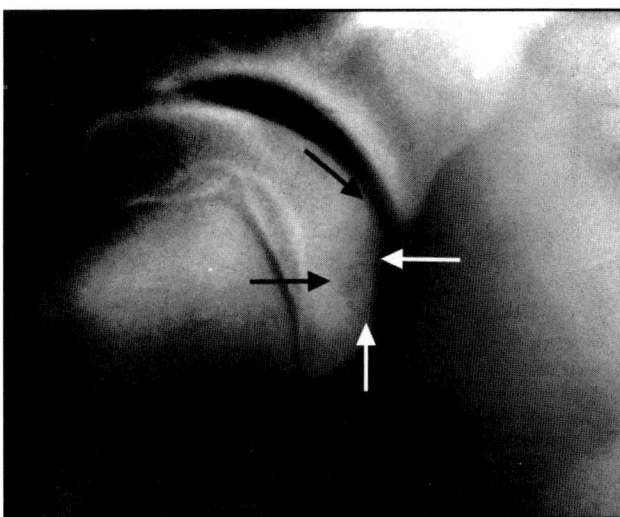

Figure 17-2A. Radiograph of the proximal humerus of a nine-month-old male Labrador retriever examined for forelimb lameness. The radiolucent area (arrows) indicates disrupted endochondral ossification and subchondral bone necrosis associated with osteochondrosis.

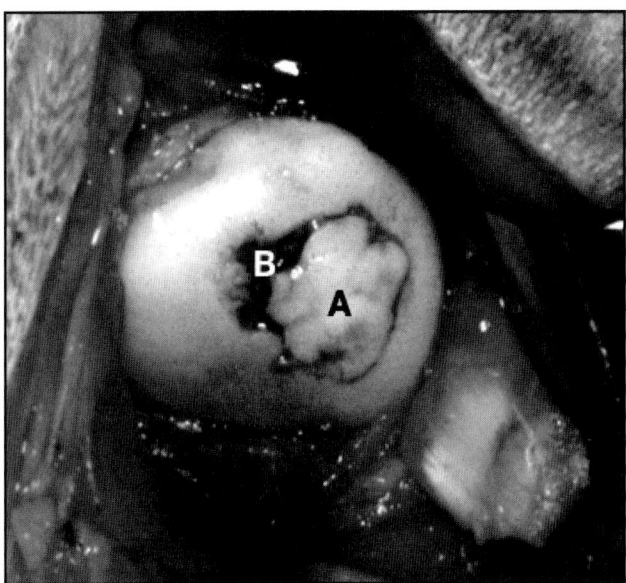

Figure 17-2B. Intraoperative view of an osteochondritis dissecans lesion in the articular epiphyseal cartilage of the proximal cartilage of the same dog. Note the cartilage flap (A) and exposed subchondral bone (B) where a portion of the cartilage flap is missing.

priate. Confounding diseases such as osteomyelitis, septic emboli and mycotic infection should be considered. DOD is usually typified by a lack of abnormal laboratory findings.[8,9]

Uncomplicated cases of DOD rarely have altered complete blood counts. Severe elevations or decreases in white blood cell counts usually indicate other disease processes. If anemia is present, classifying the type may give insight to other causes for select skeletal disorders (e.g., copper deficiency).[10,11]

On occasion, serum concentrations of calcium and phosphorus may be elevated or decreased during the genesis of DOD. However, absence of calcium or phosphorus perturbations does not rule out a diagnosis of DOD. Conversely, many other disease processes may result in altered calcium or phosphorus homeostasis, which indicates abnormal values are not pathognomonic for a diagnosis of DOD.[9]

Increased bone remodeling may result in increased serum alkaline phosphatase activity. This parameter is already high in young, growing animals and may not be a very sensitive indicator of ongoing metabolic bone disease. Other enzymatic activities in serum are not very useful for diagnosis of DOD. Biochemical markers of human metabolic bone disease such as type I collagen propeptides, tartrate-resistant acid phosphatase and osteocalcin may prove useful in the future for veterinary diagnostics.[12,b]

Urinalysis results are usually within normal limits for animals with DOD. Advanced techniques, including measurement of calcium and phosphorus partial clearance ratios, may add insight about calcium and phosphorus nutrition, but repeated measurements may be needed for accurate interpretation. Evaluation of other mineral partial clearances may give some insight into dietary excesses or deficiencies. Analysis of urine for markers of bone turnover such as hydroxylysine glycosides, free pyridinolines or pyridinoline cross-links of collagen may prove useful in the future.[13]

MEASURING AND INTERPRETING SPECIFIC LABORATORY TESTS

Parathyroid Hormone

Interpretation of serum parathyroid hormone (PTH) concentrations from other species has proven that evaluation must be made in conjunction with presenting signs and other biochemical tests such as concentrations of ionized calcium and 1,25-dihydroxyvitamin D_3 (Table 17-1). PTH values may be increased, decreased or normal in DOD depending on the etiology. Increased PTH concentrations may be observed in association with renal disease, vitamin D deficiency and states in which insufficient calcium is present in foods. Decreased PTH concentrations may be observed when excess calcium or vitamin D is present in foods, and in other metabolic diseases.

PTH concentration is most accurately measured by a "two-site" immunoassay. This assay eliminates interference by mid-region or terminal fragments that are abundant in animal serum. Single time-point evaluations of PTH may not prove useful in determining the etiology of DOD. Repeated evaluations may yield more useable information, but are probably not cost effective.

Calcitonin

Calcitonin, a peptide hormone, is released primarily from C-cells of the thyroid gland in response to sudden increased concentrations of ionized calcium in serum. Calcitonin may also be released in response to other stimuli such as gastrin secretion stimulated by food intake.[14] Calcitonin is measured by radioimmunoassay.[15] The test is not commercially available and rational interpretation requires multiple sample evaluations. If calcitonin levels are evaluated to investigate the etiology of DOD, results should be compared to normal values for the laboratory and interpreted in conjunction with results of other tests (e.g., PTH, ionized calcium and vitamin D_3 analyses).

Vitamin D

Vitamin D_3 may be required in foods for dogs because endogenous synthesis may be limited.[16,17] Because commercial foods contain added vitamin D_3, and in light of potentially limited endogenous synthesis, measurement of vita-

Table 17-1. Parathyroid hormone (PTH), ionized calcium and 1,25-dihydroxyvitamin D_3 concentrations in different physiologic/disease states.*

States	PTH	Ionized calcium	1,25-dihydroxyvitamin D_3
Primary hyperparathyroidism	High	High	Normal/high
Lymphosarcoma	Low	High	Low
Chronic renal failure	High	Low/normal	Normal/low
Apocrine gland tumors of the anal sacs	Low	High	Low
Hypervitaminosis D	Low	High	Normal/high
High calcium intake	Low	High	Normal/low
Hypoparathyroidism	Low	Low	Low

*Adapted from Feldman EC, Nelson RW, eds. Canine and Feline Endocrinology and Reproduction, 2nd ed. Philadelphia, PA: WB Saunders Co, 1996; 455-493. Hazewinkel HAW. In: Bojrab MJ, ed. Disease Mechanisms in Small Animal Surgery, 2nd ed. Philadelphia, PA: Lea & Febiger, 1993; 1119-1128. Chastain CB, Ganjam VK, eds. Clinical Endocrinology of Companion Animals. Philadelphia, PA: Lea & Febiger, 1986; 192-217.

min D_3 in serum may reflect dietary changes rather than specific disease states. 25-hydroxyvitamin D_3 is produced in the liver from vitamin D_3 and is a good indicator of general vitamin D_3 deficiency or excess. Another useful indicator of vitamin D_3 status is measurement of the most biologically active metabolite of vitamin D_3, 1,25-dihydroxyvitamin D_3, which is produced in the kidneys via the 1-α-hydroxylase enzyme. The concentration of 1,25-dihydroxyvitamin D_3 in serum is not a good indicator of vitamin D_3 toxicity; however, it is a more sensitive indicator of deficiency than serum concentrations of 25-hydroxyvitamin D_3.

All metabolites of vitamin D_3 in serum may be measured by high-pressure liquid chromatography. Concentrations should be compared with reference values from laboratories performing the analysis, preferably derived from healthy dogs fed similar foods.[18] A multitude of factors affect production of 1,25-dihydroxyvitamin D_3 and laboratory results should be interpreted in conjunction with other physical and biochemical findings (Table 17-2). Generally, high concentrations of 1,25-dihydroxyvitamin D_3 indicate low availability of calcium to animals, normal concentrations indicate adequate calcium availability and low concentrations may indicate vitamin D_3 deficiency.

Calcium

Bone contains 99% of the calcium in the body with the majority in the form of hydroxyapatite crystals (Table 17-3, see sidebar "Calcium Deposition in Bone"). Bone functions physiologically as a structural material and an ion reservoir. When bone acts as an ion reservoir, it is in equilibrium with serum ionized calcium and under tight homeostatic control.

Calcium homeostasis is maintained by the sum of physiochemical and calciotropic hormonal processes. Calcium in blood is in equilibrium between the ionized state (45 to 50%), a protein-bound state (40 to 45%) and a complexed or chelated state (5 to 10%). In general, the concentration of ionized calcium is approximately 45 to 50% of the total concentration of calcium in serum over a wide range of total calcium concentrations. The concentration of ionized calcium is the most important determinant of calciotropic homeostatic regulation initiated by the parathyroid gland and the C-cells of the thyroid gland. Sudden increases in ionized calcium concentrations stimulate release of calcitonin from the thyroid gland, whereas decreases in concentrations of ionized calcium stimulate release of PTH from the parathyroid gland. The total concentration of calcium in serum is affected by the interplay of the homeostatic mechanisms involving influx (gastrointestinal [GI] absorption and bone resorption), efflux (GI and renal loss) and skeletal mineralization of the less labile bone pool as outlined below.

Table 17-2. Factors affecting activity of 25-hydroxyvitamin D_3 renal 1-α-hydroxylase.*

Factors	Changes
Increased parathyroid hormone	Increase
Decreased parathyroid hormone	Decrease
Increased 1,25-dihydroxyvitamin D_3	Decrease
Increased ionized calcium	Decrease
Decreased ionized calcium	Increase
Increased phosphate (serum)	Decrease
Increased calcitonin	Increase/decrease/no effect
Sex steroids	Increase
Pregnancy	Increase
Insulin	Increase
Insulin-like growth factor-1	Increase
Prolactin	Increase/no effect
Acidosis	Decrease
Alkalosis	Increase
Increasing age	Decrease

*Adapted from Tenenhouse HS. In: Simmons DJ, ed. Nutrition and Bone Development. New York, NY: Oxford University Press, 1990; 164-201.

Table 17-3. Composition of bone.

Bone is composed of a mineral phase, a non-mineral (organic) phase and a cellular phase
Mineral phase
 99% of body calcium
 85% of body phosphorus
 40-60% of body sodium and magnesium
 Ca/P ratio 1.67:1 on a molar basis. Ratio is 2.15:1 on a weight basis (hydroxyapatite crystals = $[Ca_{10}(PO_4)_6(OH)_2]$)
Organic phase
 Type I collagen (90% of bone protein)
 Noncollagenous protein (cell attachment proteins, proteoglycans, gamma carboxylated gla proteins, growth-related proteins)
Cellular phase
 Osteoclasts
 Osteoblasts
 Osteocytes

When concentrations of ionized calcium are below the normal range:
1. PTH secretion is stimulated, which in turn stimulates conversion of 25-hydroxyvitamin D_3 to the biologically more potent 1,25-dihydroxyvitamin D_3 in the kidneys.
2. 1,25-dihydroxyvitamin D_3 stimulates calcium uptake in the gut via receptor-mediated mechanisms.
3. 1,25-dihydroxyvitamin D_3, in conjunction with PTH, stimulates bone resorption and calcium reabsorption in the kidneys.
4. PTH induces phosphaturia.

When concentrations of ionized calcium are above the normal range:

1. Calcitonin secretion is stimulated, PTH secretion is suppressed and 1,25-dihydroxyvitamin D_3 production is not stimulated. Instead, the kidneys produce 24,25-dihydroxyvitamin D_3, which is generally considered biologically inactive.
2. Gut absorption and bone resorption of calcium are not stimulated.
3. Calcitonin decreases osteoclastic activity.
4. Renal calcium excretion is increased.

The equilibrium between the protein-bound and ionized fraction of calcium is affected by a variety of physiologic conditions. Alterations of serum proteins usually do not affect the equilibrium of bound to ionized calcium, but the total calcium may be increased or decreased. Alterations in albumin or total serum protein concentrations should be corrected before calcium values are evaluated.[19]

Albumin correction:

Corrected total calcium (mg/dl) =
Total calcium (mg/dl) – albumin (g/dl) + 3.5

Total serum protein correction:

Corrected total calcium (mg/dl) –
(0.4 x total protein [g/dl]) + 3.3

The percent of total calcium bound to protein may be roughly estimated using differential binding affinities of albumin and globulin.[20]

% protein-bound calcium =
8 x albumin (g/dl) + 2 x globulin (g/dl) + 3

Acidosis shifts the equilibrium toward ionized calcium and is not accounted for by the above equation. Other physiologic perturbations, such as alkalosis, chloride ion concentration and phosphate ion concentration may also affect the equilibrium and are not accounted for by the above equation. Accurate determination of ionized calcium is best performed using ion selective electrodes.

Risk Factors

The genesis of DOD is presumed to be a multifactorial process. It appears that management (environmental), genetic and nutritional interactions have significant influence in young, growing animals. The most critical period for development of DOD is during the growth phase, before epiphyseal closure (Figure 17-3). Specific factors that are currently thought to increase the risk of DOD in young dogs include: 1) belonging to a large or giant breed (genetics), 2) free-choice feeding (management/genetic), 3) feeding of high-energy foods (nutrition) and 4) excessive intake of calcium from food, treats and supplements (nutrition) (Table 17-4).[15,21-32] Nutritional intervention had minimal impact on the frequency of DOD before the above risk factors were identified. Foods specifically formulated for large- and giant-breed growing dogs at risk for DOD will hopefully change this trend.

Etiopathogenesis

A variety of mechanisms are plausible in considering the pathogenesis of DOD. No one specific etiology is considered ultimately responsible for all observed clinical manifestations of DOD. Historically, feeding dogs imbalanced foods, especially those deficient in calcium, phosphorus or vitamin D_3, was the main risk factor predisposing them to skeletal diseases such as secondary hyperparathyroidism with subsequent development of osteodystrophia fibrosa.[21] Dietary deficiencies are rare in young, growing dogs fed commercial growth foods because most foods are formulated to meet or exceed allowances for specific nutrients.[33] Two popular, current theories for the pathogenesis of some types of DOD are discussed in the following sections. Specific nutrients are addressed in the Key Nutritional Factors section.

THEORY 1: ENERGY/GROWTH/ BIOMECHANICAL STRESS

The musculoskeletal system changes constantly throughout life with the most rapid changes occurring during the first few months (Figure 17-4).[23,26,34-43] The skeletal system apparently is most susceptible to physical, nutritional and metabolic insults during the first 12 months of life because of heightened metabolic activity. Large- and giant-breed dogs are most susceptible to DOD, presumably because of their genetic propensity for rapid growth.[21,44]

Present knowledge about energy intake effects on bone growth gives rise to an hypothesis for the etiopathogenesis of growth disorders associated with overfeeding of energy to young, large- and giant-breed dogs. High energy intake directly affects growth velocity via nutrient supply and indirectly through changes in concentrations of growth hormone, insulin-like growth factor 1 (IGF-1), triiodothy-

---

Use of DEXA to Assess the Skeleton

The ability to make repeated, accurate assessments of body composition is crucial to the investigation of many key nutritional issues of cats and dogs. In a research setting, dual energy x-ray absorptiometry (DEXA) allows the body to be viewed as three compartments: bone mineral, fat tissue and lean tissue. The ability to evaluate changes in these three compartments independently greatly benefits the study of growth, obesity and geriatrics.

DEXA uses x-rays of two different energy levels (70 and 140 kVp) to distinguish the nature and amount of each tissue in the part of the body being scanned. The x-ray source below the table and the detector above the table move in concert to measure the amount of radiation passing through the subject. Because x-rays of different energy levels are impeded differently by bone mineral, fat and lean tissue, it is possible to calculate the quantity of each tissue in each area scanned.

The accuracy of DEXA in companion animals has not been widely studied, but preliminary data indicate a good correlation ($r^2 > 0.9$) between values obtained from DEXA and chemical analysis.

BIBLIOGRAPHY

Toll PW, Anderson DE, Berryhill SA, et al. The effect of storage of excised bone on measurement of bone mineral using dual energy x-ray absorptiometry (DEXA). Journal of Bone Mineral Research 1994; 9 (Suppl.): S185.

Toll PW, Berryhill SA, Jewell DE. Usefulness of dual energy x-ray absorptiometry (DEXA) for body composition assessment in nutritional studies of dogs. Waltham Symposium on the Nutrition of Companion Animals, Adelaide, Australia, 1993.

Wedekind K, Toll PW, Richardson DC, et al. Validation of dual energy x-ray absorptiometry as a quantitative measure of body composition in small subjects (abstract). Journal of Bone Mineral Research 1992; 7 (Suppl. 1): S256.

ronine (T$_3$), thyroxine (T$_4$) and insulin.[45-48] Dysregulation of these endocrine factors, whether attributable to nutrition, feeding management or genetics, during this critical period of skeletal growth may be responsible for producing an environment in which DOD develops.

Growth hormone and IGF-1 stimulate chondrocyte proliferation and differentiation.[49-55] Growth hormone release in non-canids is influenced primarily by energy intake but may also be affected by food protein content, specific amino acids or peptides, exercise and environmental factors.[9,45,51,56] IGF-1 is released systemically primarily from the liver but also locally from chondrocytes in response to growth hormone stimulus. Little is known about dietary influences on growth hormone secretion in dogs; however, young Labrador retrievers had a temporal decrease in concentrations of growth hormone from weaning to 14 weeks of age, followed by an increase in the prepubertal period.[41] IGF-1 was found in significantly higher concentrations in growing dogs fed free choice compared with animals on restricted feed allowance,[45] whereas dietary protein intake only weakly influenced IGF-1 levels.[57]

Free-choice feeding of dogs is also accompanied by higher circulating concentrations of T$_3$ and T$_4$ compared with levels in food-restricted controls, reflecting a general stimulation of metabolic processes.[45] Thyroid hormones are not only general stimuli for metabolic processes, including increasing the rate of bone formation and resorption, but are also important for capillary penetration of degenerating cartilage cells and the final stage of endochondral bone formation.[51] In conjunction with the food-hormone relationships summarized here, additional endocrine or autocrine factors are involved in cartilage and bone metabolism;[51] unfortunately, relevant data for growing dogs are not available. The result of these hormonal influences is enhanced mitotic activity of proliferative cartilage cells, which may enlarge the width of the inherently mechanically unstable zone of chondrocyte growth.

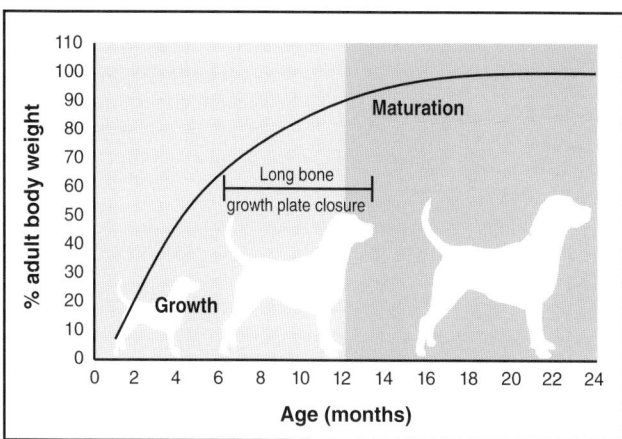

Figure 17-3. Growth phase vs. long bone physeal closure in dogs. Note that weight gain still occurs under the maturation phase although growth plate closure is complete. This is attributable to bone remodeling and acquisition of adult body mass.

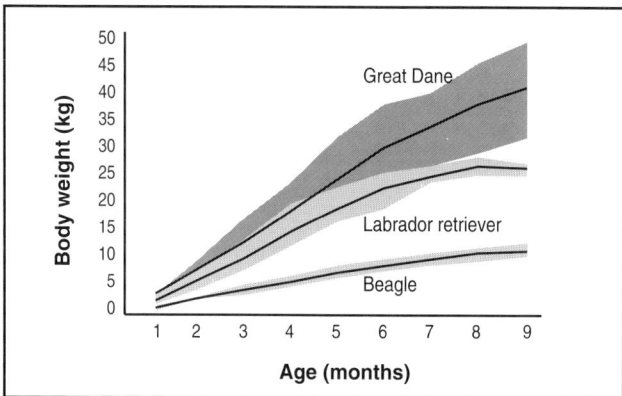

Figure 17-4. Growth curves (weight vs. age) for Great Dane, Labrador retriever and beagle dogs. Note that rapid growth occurs during the first few months in all breeds, but is prolonged in giant-breed dogs such as Great Danes.

Table 17-4. Summary of reports delineating risk factors for developmental orthopedic disease in dogs.

Diseases	Key points	Interpretation	Risk factors	Reference numbers
CHD	Rapid weight gain German shepherd dogs First 60 days of age	Rapid weight gain increased risk of CHD Dysplastic parents increased risk	Breed Rapid weight gain	29
CHD	Pups born by cesarean section- hand reared Vaginally born pups, pair-fed bitch milk at 70% free choice	Free-choice feeding resulted in increased weight gain and increased occurrence of CHD	Free-choice feeding Rapid weight gain	26
CHD	Labrador retrievers Rapid growth rate	Early fusion of triradiate growth plate in acetabulum	Breed Rapid weight gain	27
CHD	Weight gain > breed standards	Increased occurrence of CHD	Rapid weight gain	24
CHD	Restricted feeding Labrador retrievers	Restricted feeding decreased occurrence of CHD	Breed Rapid weight gain	25
OC	Epidemiologic study	Labrador retrievers, Great Danes, Newfoundlands, rottweilers at greatest risk All large breeds at increased risk	Breed Gender Anatomic location	30,31
OC	Epidemiologic study	Males at higher risk of OCD in shoulder	Gender Calcium content Well water	22,30,31
OC	Great Danes Rapid growth Overnutrition	Rapid growth increased occurrence of DOD	Breed Rapid growth	21,23,28
OC	Great Danes Excess calcium	Excessive calcium intake increased occurrence of DOD	Breed Excessive calcium	15
DOD	Large breeds Rapid growth	Excessive energy intake increased occurrence of DOD	Breed Rapid growth High energy density food	32

Key: CHD = canine hip dysplasia, DOD = developmental orthopedic disease, OC = osteochondrosis.

Calcium Deposition in Bone

The actual physical mechanism of calcium deposition in bone is controversial. Evidence suggests the following:
- Calcium and phosphorus exist in metastable equilibrium in solution.
- A nucleation molecule initiates precipitation of solid calcium in collagen.
- Calcium is deposited initially as poorly crystalline type B (carbonate) apatite.
- Initial crystals have brushite properties but as they mature they become more hydroxyapatite in nature.
- Initial nucleation sites are within collagen fibrils.

- Nucleation sites are independent of each other (multicentric).
- Nucleation initiating molecules may include: phosphoproteins, proteolipids and complex acidic phospholipids.
- Proteoglycans may inhibit or promote calcification centers.

BIBLIOGRAPHY
Glimcher MJ. The nature of the mineral composition of bone and the mechanism of calcification. In: Avioli LV, Krane SM, eds. Metabolic Bone Disease and Clinically Related Disorders, 2nd ed. Philadelphia, PA: WB Saunders Co, 1990; 42-68.

Histologic examinations have revealed articular cartilage is less well supported by solid bone plates in rapidly growing dogs, compared with smaller breeds or to littermates fed restricted amounts after weaning.[21] The epiphyseal spongiosa of giant-breed dogs is inherently less dense and therefore assumed to be weaker than the spongiosa in small breeds, a tendency that may be exaggerated by overnutrition. Free-choice feeding may lead to a mismatch between bone growth and body growth, resulting in a lower ratio of long bone diaphyseal shaft cross-sectional area to body weight and also a less dense epiphyseal spongiosa.

The biomechanical stress induced by rapid weight gain during growth as discussed above has been cited as an etiology for DOD. It is unknown whether small focal cartilaginous lesions occur first and are then exacerbated by biomechanical stress,[21,58] or if biomechanical stress first induces cartilaginous lesions.[15,23] In either case, immature skeletons may be damaged by increased static forces (weight load) and dynamic forces (muscle pull), especial-

ly in large- and giant-breed dogs. These dysregulations of nutrient supply, bone formation and endocrine regulation may interfere with skeletal maturation, thus increasing the risk for DOD in young animals (Figure 17-5).

THEORY 2: EXCESS CALCIUM AND HYPERCALCITONINISM

A contrasting theory to the preceding theory about high energy intake and rapid growth rate stems from the observation that the rate of DOD is increased in dogs with high calcium intakes.[22,31,59,60] Young Great Danes fed a food high in energy and minerals free choice,[23] or high in calcium alone,[15] developed osteochondrosis lesions with overt clinical signs of disease (Figure 17-6). These lesions appeared at both weight-bearing sites and sites where weight bearing was of no influence, such as the growth plates of ribs.

Feeding high-calcium foods to growing small-breed dogs results in histologic lesions but no clinical manifestations of DOD.[61] Large-breed dogs raised on food with a high calcium content or high calcium and phosphorus content had disturbed endochondral ossification,[62,63] retained cartilaginous cores in the distal radius and ulna[59,60] and delayed skeletal maturation and growth of bone length.[60] Calcium intake, therefore, seems to be a significant determining factor in DOD. This may occur either directly by calcium competing with other minerals or indirectly by stimulating hormonal effects (PTH or calcitonin) or acid-base balance (See sidebar "Dietary Cation-Anion Balance."). Accordingly, hypercalcitoninism may be a contributing factor to DOD in dogs.[15,23] Dogs ingesting excessive amounts of calcium for a prolonged period exhibited hyperplastic C-cells in their thyroid glands.[63,64] These same dogs had clinical and radiographic evidence of DOD when compared with controls.[15,63,64]

Calcitonin is released into blood, where it has a half-life of a few minutes, and reduces concentrations of calcium and phosphorus.[8,64]

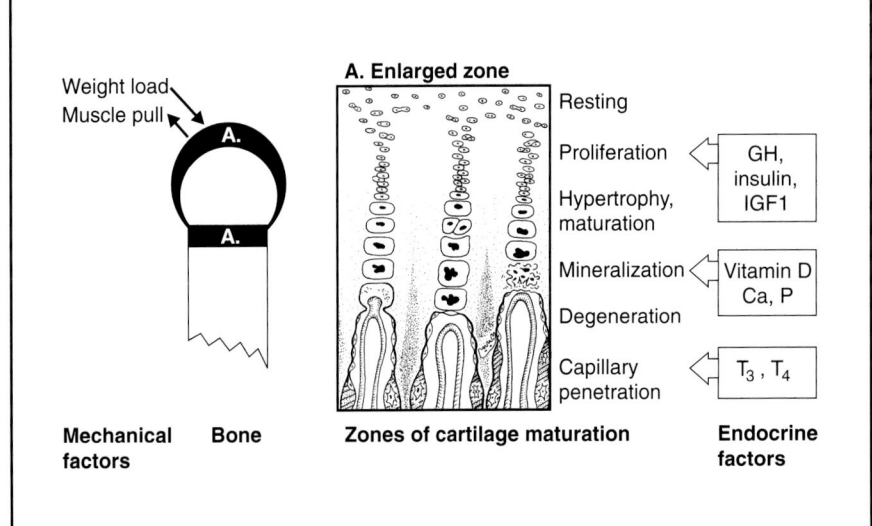

Figure 17-5. Biomechanical and endocrinologic influences on the growing skeleton are depicted. Biomechanically, immature skeletons can be damaged by excessive static (weight load) and dynamic (muscle pull) forces. Note the various zones of cartilage maturation (resting zone, proliferation, hypertrophy and maturation, mineralization, degeneration, capillary penetration) where hormonal influences are thought to occur.

Extrapolation of calcitonin action in other species indicates that increased osteoblastic activity and decreased osteoclastic activity are responsible for shifts in plasma concentrations of calcium and phosphorus, which in turn may affect production of 1,25-dihydroxyvitamin D_3 (Table 17-2).[65] It has been proposed that the physiologic action of calcitonin on bone turnover (decreased skeletal remodeling) and endochondral ossification are inciting causes of DOD in dogs.

Key Nutritional Factors

Nutrients must be provided in appropriate amounts and balances for optimal bone development. Excesses of calcium and energy, together with rapid growth, appear to predispose dogs to certain musculoskeletal disorders such as osteochondrosis and CHD.[23,44] However, severe excesses, deficits and imbalances of any nutrient may affect bone development.

ENERGY/FAT

Energy intake, which depends on a variety of physiologic factors, is the main nutritional factor that determines growth intensity, as long as other nutrients are supplied in adequate and balanced amounts. The risk of DOD appears to be increased in large- and giant-breed dogs fed well-balanced, highly palatable, energy-dense foods, free choice as discussed previously.[21,23,25,28,66-68] The detrimental influence of high energy intake on skeletal development during growth has been demonstrated in dogs[23,25,69,70] and other

animal species (e.g., turkeys, pigs).[71-73] Lesions appear in physeal or articular epiphyseal cartilages as disturbances of endochondral ossification.[21]

Fat must be considered when assessing the energy density of foods. As the fat content of foods rises, the energy density also increases unless fiber is substituted for other metabolizable nutrients (Table 17-5). Dogs grow slower and have less fat deposition when they are fed a low energy density food free choice (3.16 kcal [13.22 kJ]/g ME, 8.0% fat dry matter basis [DMB]) compared with a high

Table 17-5. Effect of increasing fat content, above the AAFCO minimum for growth (8% DMB), on ME content of dog food (DMB). Assume a 10% ash and 22% protein content, with no fiber added. Use modified Atwater values of 3.5 kcal [14.45 kJ]/g for protein and nitrogen-free extract (NFE, soluble carbohydrate DMB), and 8.5 kcal [35.56 kJ]/g for fat (DMB).

Fat (%)	NFE (%)	ME/g	% increase in ME/g
8	60	3.55	0.0
12	56	3.75	5.6
20	48	4.15	16.9
24	44	4.35	22.5
32	36	4.75	33.8
36	32	4.95	39.4
40	28	5.15	45.1
44	24	5.35	50.7
50	18	5.65	59.2

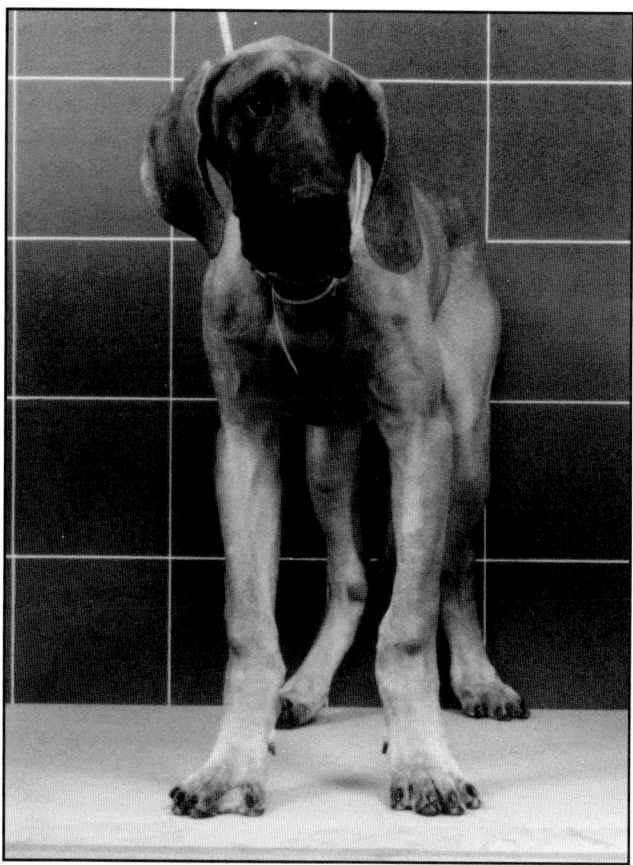 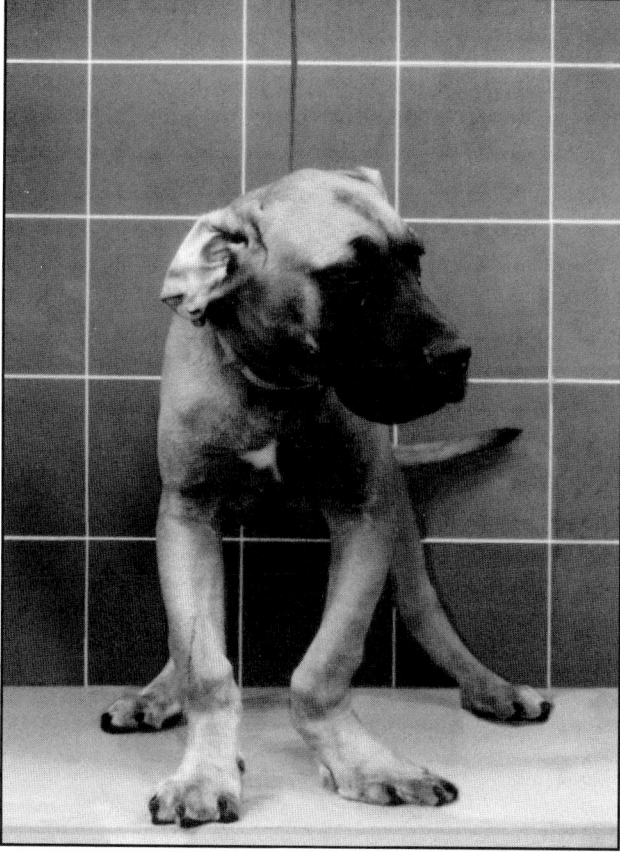

Figure 17-6. Littermate Great Dane puppies fed two different levels of dietary calcium. The puppy on the left was fed a growth food containing 1.1% calcium (DMB). The puppy on the right was fed a similar growth food containing 3.3% calcium (DMB). Note the poor growth and angular limb deformities in the puppy consuming excess calcium.

energy density food (3.98 kcal [16.65 kJ]/g ME, 23.9% fat DMB)[c] (Figure 17-7). This finding indicates that growing dogs may receive better satiety signals from low energy density foods than high energy density foods and thus may avoid overconsumption of energy.

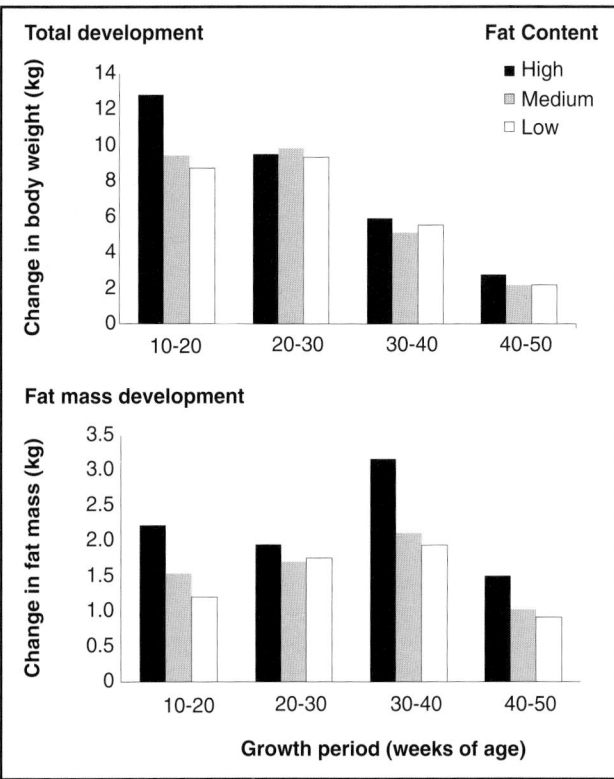

Figure 17-7. Effect of feeding high (3.98 kcal [16.65 kJ]/g; fat = 23.9% DMB), medium (3.5 kcal [14.64 kJ]/g; fat = 10.8% DMB), and low (3.16 kcal [13.22 kJ]/g; fat = 8.0% DMB) energy density foods free choice on body weight and fat mass development in 30 growing large-breed dogs. Note excess fat deposition at 30 to 40 weeks of age compared with total body weight at the same period. (Toll PW, Richardson DC. Unpublished data. 1996.)

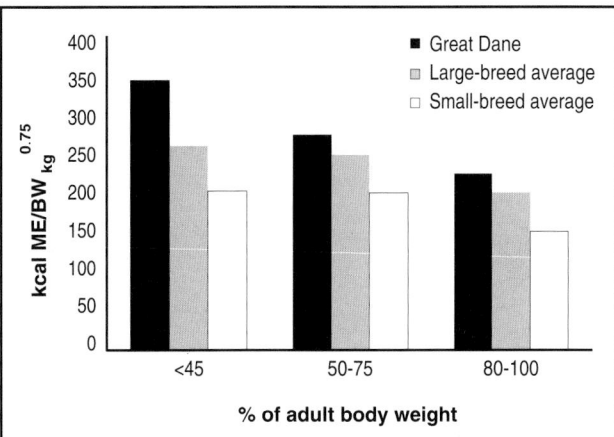

Figure 17-8. Average free-choice energy intake of Great Dane, large-breed and small-breed dogs in kcal ME/$BW_{kg}^{0.75}$ as a percent of adult body weight. Note that energy intake reaches a maximum, as related to body weight, in the second to fourth month of life (<45% adult body weight). Great Danes appear to have higher energy requirements for growth than other large-breed dogs. (Data from References 23, 28, 43, 67, 113 and 114.)

Because an increased growth rate is a risk factor for fast-growing, large- and giant-breed dogs, it follows that increased fat content (>12% DMB), or increased ME/g of dry matter of foods, must be considered risk factors. However, some fat in the food is important for absorption of fat-soluble vitamins and for palatability. Concentrations of essential nutrients may need to be increased in order to meet nutritional requirements when the energy density of foods is altered.

In addition to overall fat content, lipid metabolism may play a role in DOD. Metabolism of lipid in bone is thought to be under the same regulatory controls as in other tissues.[74] Lipid content of mineralized tissues ranges from 1.7% of dry weight for cartilage to 0.2% for bone and dentin. Although specific studies on long bone growth have not been performed, interesting results have been obtained in studies of dentin formation. Essential fatty acid deficiency leads to abnormal calculus deposition, loosened teeth and poor gingival color in rats. Other lipids may play equally important roles in several metabolic aspects of tissue calcification:

1. Phospholipids form matrix vesicles that may be important in new calcification sites.
2. Calcium-acidic phospholipid phosphate complexes may signal nucleation and apatite formation under appropriate conditions.
3. Proteolipids may help initiate apatite formation and calcification.
4. Prostaglandins may influence calcium resorption similar to PTH, and affect collagen synthesis.
5. Inositol phospholipids may mediate calcium transport in and out of cell organelles via second messenger systems.
6. Glycolipids are important constituents of most cell membranes and are found in high concentrations in epiphyseal cartilage. Their specific function is not understood.
7. Phosphatidylserine may act as an ionophore to mediate calcium translocation.

Although no specific studies have been performed in growing dogs to assess the effect of n-3 or n-6 fatty acids on musculoskeletal growth, some recent studies in other species may prove important. Rats fed foods high in lard (animal fat) compared with those fed foods high in linolenic acid (vegetable fat) had increased weight gain and depressed T_3 concentrations.[75] Chicks fed four different lipid sources had the highest bone formation rate when fed butter and corn oil as the dietary fat.[76] Dietary lipids modulate bone prostaglandin E and IGF-1 production, and bone formation rate in chicks. Alteration of dietary n-6 and n-3 fatty acid concentrations alters eicosanoid production in dogs and may help in managing osteoarthritis. (See Chapter 26.)

It is difficult to determine the appropriate daily energy requirement (DER) for growing dogs because few well-controlled studies have been conducted. Energy intake reaches a maximum, as related to body weight, in the second to fourth month of life (<45% adult body weight) (Figure 17-8). Breed differences in DER during growth seem to occur, but it is difficult to give specific recommendations because of the lack of data. In general, a good starting point is to feed dogs three times the resting energy requirement (RER) from weaning to four months of age, followed by two times the RER until about one year of age. The body condition of dogs should be evaluated every two weeks and the food dose adjusted as necessary (Table 17-6). It is usually best to keep the energy content of a growth food for larger breed puppies below 3.8 kcal [15.9 kJ]/g, which approximates 12% fat on a DMB, especially if fed free choice.

CALCIUM

The amount of true calcium absorption in dogs ranges from 25 to 90% depending on the amount of intake and the age of the animal.[9,77] Calcium is absorbed via three modalities: 1) active absorption, 2) facilitated absorption and 3) passive diffusion. Passive diffusion is especially important in young individuals. Active absorption is most important in the proximal GI tract. Passive diffusion and facilitated absorption, however, are important in the distal GI tract, primarily because of prolonged transit time and increased calcium concentration through that section. Vitamin D_3 metabolites, especially 1,25-dihydroxyvitamin D_3, are the most important hormonal regulators of GI calcium absorption.[78] Renal handling of calcium is modulated by PTH, vitamin D_3 and dietary cation-anion balance (See sidebar "Dietary Cation-Anion Balance."), whereas calcitonin does not play a significant role in this aspect in dogs.

In the face of adequate levels of calcium in the food, the absolute level of calcium, rather than an imbalance in the calcium-phosphorus ratio, influences skeletal development.[15,77] (See sidebars "Dangers of Feeding Puppies Adult Maintenance Foods to Decrease Energy Intake" and "Dangers of Feeding Calcium Supplements to Dogs.") In one study, the prevalence of DOD was significantly increased in young, giant-breed dogs fed a food containing excess calcium (3.3% DMB) with either normal phosphorus (0.9% DMB) or high phosphorus (3% DMB, to maintain a normal calcium-phosphorus ratio).[77] These puppies apparently were unable to protect themselves against the negative effects of long-term calcium excess.[15] Further, long-term calcium intake increases the frequency and severity of osteochondrosis.[9] Because the previously discussed studies have demonstrated the safety and adequacy

Dietary Cation-Anion Balance

Alteration of dietary cation-anion balance (DCAB) has been reported to influence skeletal development in several species. The DCAB of a food can be described, most simply, by the equation ([Na] + [K] − [Cl]mEq)/100 g dry matter. As the DCAB increases, the net physiologic effect is alkalinization. Conversely, as it decreases an acidification effect is observed and calcium excretion in urine is increased. Acidification will be buffered by carbonate liberated from bone by increased osteoclasia, thus increasing osteoporosis in adult and bone remodeling in young animals. The mechanism for these effects on skeletal development is unclear. In addition, regulation of body acid-base balance, calcium homeostasis and osmolality of the synovial fluid compartment may be influenced.

The role of electrolyte balance in canine nutrition appears to be most relevant to preventing canine hip dysplasia (CHD). Investigators have associated the DCAB with the radiographic changes of subluxation in the coxofemoral joints in several canine breeds. A food with a DCAB ([Na] + [K] − [Cl]) <23 mEq/100 g dry matter fed to large-breed puppies was associated with less severe femoral head subluxation, on average, when the puppies reached six months of age. The slowed progression of subluxation was also observed in dogs fed a food with a reduced DCAB from 33 to 45 weeks of age. Hip joint laxity was determined using Norberg hip scores computed from radiographs. Significant correlation between radiographic findings (e.g., Norberg hip scores) and progression of CHD, either radiographic or clinical, was not proved. The authors proposed the balance of anions and cations in the food (specifically Na, K, Cl) influenced the electrolytes and osmolality in joint fluid. The joint fluid of dysplastic dogs has higher osmolality and is increased in volume when compared with that of disease-free hips from dogs of the same breed. The changes in osmolality and fluid volume could be a result rather than a cause of CHD. These studies suggest an association between DCAB and joint laxity without proving a mechanism of action. Most commercial growth foods encompass a very small range of DCAB and probably do not vary greatly in risk.

In commercial dog foods, the relation between cations and anions is 22 to 46 mEq/100 g dry matter. The balance of only the electrolytes Na, K, Cl, calculated as equivalents, will be between 15 to 42 mEq/100 g dry matter. Feeding dogs foods with a dietary anion gap of 8 mEq/100 g dry matter lowered the severity of subluxation of the femoral head in growing dogs of different breeds. Increasing this relation to 41 mEq/100 g food was accompanied by a higher degree of subluxation as determined by the Norberg angle on radiography. Because the knowledge and experimental databases are very small in dogs, mineral salts should not be added in large amounts to nutritionally balanced foods. Problems may arise not only from the addition of anions, but also from increasing the amounts of cations. Further research is needed in this field but it seems prudent to avoid excessive acidifying foods or acidifying agents in growing puppies.

BIBLIOGRAPHY

Abu Damir HD, Scott N, Loveridge W, et al. The effect of feeding diets containing either NaHCO$_3$ or NH$_4$Cl on indices of bone formation and resorption and on mineral balance in the lamb. Experimental Physiology 1991; 76: 725-732.

Kealy RD, Lawler DF, Monti KL, et al. Effects of dietary electrolyte balance on subluxation of the femoral head in growing dogs. American Journal of Veterinary Research 1993; 54: 555-562.

Mongin P. Recent advances in dietary anion-cation balance: Applications in poultry. Proceedings of the Nutrition Society 1981; 40: 285-294.

Patience JF. The physiological basis of electrolytes in animal nutrition. In: Haresign W, Cole DJA, eds. Recent Advances in Animal Nutrition. London, UK: Butterworths, 1989; 223-228.

Poulos PW, Reiland S, Elwinger K, et al. Skeletal lesions in the broiler, with special reference to dyschondroplasia (osteochondrosis). Acta Radiologica Suppl. (Stockholm) 1978; 358: 197-227.

Van der Wal PG, Hemminga H, Goedegebuure SA, et al. The effect of replacement of 0.30% sodium chloride by 0.43% sodium bicarbonate in rations of fattening pigs on leg weakness, osteochondrosis and growth. Veterinary Quarterly 1994; 8: 136-144.

of 1.1% calcium (DMB), the authors recommend that growth foods for at-risk puppies should contain calcium levels between 0.7 and 1.2% with no supplementation (Figure 17-6).[32]

Table 17-6. Worksheet for calculating the initial feeding plan for large- and giant-breed dogs.

I. Weigh (determine weight in kg)  WEIGH

II. Feed (determine daily energy requirement [DER]) FEED

   A. Caloric requirement formulas
   Linear method
   RER $= 30(BW_{kg}) + 70 =$ initial estimate in kcal*
   DER $=$ RER x 3.0 (two to four months of age)
   $=$ RER x 2.0 (four to 12 months of age)
   $=$ RER x 1.8 (intact adult)
   $=$ RER x 1.6 (neutered adult)

   Exponential method
   RER $= 70(BW_{kg})^{0.75} =$ initial estimate in kcal*
   DER $=$ RER x 3.0 (2 to 4 months of age)
   $=$ RER x 2.0 (4 to 12 months of age)
   $=$ RER x 1.8 (intact adult)
   $=$ RER x 1.6 (neutered adult)
   B. Convert kcal to cups or grams
   Contact manufacturer to obtain energy density

III. Evaluate (reassess every two weeks)  EVALUATE
   A. Weigh
   B. Body condition score (BCS)
   C. Clinical judgment

IV. Adjust (as needed) ADJUST
   A. If BCS >3/5, decrease intake by 10%
   B. If BCS <2/5, increase intake by 10%

*Key: RER = resting energy requirement. To determine kJ, multiply kcal by 4.184.

Dangers of Feeding Puppies Adult Maintenance Foods to Decrease Energy Intake

Often puppies are switched from growth to adult maintenance-type foods under the pretense it will help avoid calcium excess and skeletal disease. However, because some maintenance foods have much lower energy density than most growth foods, the puppy must consume more dry matter volume to meet its energy requirement. If the calcium levels are similar (DMB) between the two foods, the puppy may actually consume more calcium when fed the maintenance food.

This point is exemplified in the case of switching a 15-week-old, 15-kg, male rottweiler puppy from a growth food containing, on an as fed basis, 4.0 kcal (16.74 kJ)/g ME and 1.35% calcium (1.5% on a DMB) to a maintenance food containing the same amount of calcium but at a lower energy density (3.2 kcal [13.4 kJ]/g). The puppy would require approximately 1,600 kcal/day (6.69 MJ). To meet this energy need, the puppy would consume approximately 400 g of the growth food (containing 5.4 g of calcium) vs. 500 g of the maintenance food (containing approximately 6.7 g of calcium).

OTHER NUTRITIONAL FACTORS

Digestibility

Although not a nutrient, digestibility is a nutritional factor that becomes important in certain physiologic states such as growth. Apparent digestibility is the difference between the amount of food ingested and that excreted in feces. During the growth period, the ability to ingest and absorb adequate amounts of various nutrients depends on food intake capacity and the quality of ingredients. It is especially important to consider quality of ingredients when trying to limit energy intake for at-risk dogs. The goal of energy restriction is not to provide low-quality foods that are poorly digestible, but to provide high-quality foods in a low energy density package that will promote appropriate growth. It is important to assess digestibility and recommend foods with above average digestibility for growth. Above average digestibility is suggested at levels more than 5% above the average values defined by AAFCO (See Table 9-11.)[79]

Other Minerals

Phosphorus

Excessive as well as inadequate phosphorus intake may affect calcium homeostasis and thus bone development. Chronic, inadequate phosphorus intake, to a lesser degree than calcium depletion, may stimulate 1,25-dihydroxyvitamin D_3 synthesis (Table 17-2), which stimulates calcium and phosphorus resorption from bone and absorption in the gut.[80] Mobilization of calcium and phosphorus decreases PTH secretion, increases the renal threshold for phosphorus and eliminates excess calcium in the urine. The result is an increase in serum phosphorus concentration while maintaining serum calcium levels.[81]

Conversely, excessive phosphorus intake with inadequate calcium intake may result in nutritional secondary hyperparathyroidism. The excess phosphorus in food reduces the ionized calcium concentration in serum via mass action equilibrium, thus resulting in hypersecretion of PTH. The end result is a decreased renal threshold for phosphorus and excessive osteoclasia and pathologic fractures of growing bone.

The level of phosphorus recommended must be considered in conjunction with calcium recommendations. The calcium-phosphorus ratio should be maintained at 1.1:1 to 2:1; however, 1.1:1 is preferred. The absolute amount of calcium in the food is more important than the calcium-phosphorus ratio in young growing dogs.[59,77] Great Dane puppies raised on food with a calcium to phosphorus ratio of 1.1:1 but with an excessive absolute amount of calcium (3.3% calcium:3.0% phosphorus DMB) developed more severe signs of DOD than did control dogs (1.1% calcium:1.0% phosphorus DMB) or dogs raised on low-calcium food (0.55% calcium:0.9% phosphorus DMB). The last group (e.g., those fed the lowest calcium level) developed pathologic fractures due to hyperparathyroidism as described above. When calcium intake is set at 0.7 to 1.2% of the food, as recommended previously for large breeds at risk for DOD, the phosphorus content of the food should be 0.6 to 1.1% of the dry matter.[82]

Copper

Copper plays an important role in the metabolism of collagen and elastin. The copper-dependent lysyl oxidase is specific for connective tissue and functions biologically to catalyze the oxidative deamination of the ε-amino groups of lysine and hydroxylysine to form allysyl or hydroxyallysyl residues.[83,84] This step forms intermolecular cross links between collagen fibrils, and is therefore essential for stabilization of connective tissues.[85]

In several animal species and in people, copper deficiency induces severe skeletal disease.[86] Dietary copper levels less than 1 mg/kg dry matter were related to severe growth deformities, fractures, wide "knotty" epiphyses and especially severe hyperextension of the limb axis in growing dogs.[87] In young beagles, clinical signs of copper deficiency were less severe than those previously listed, but hyperextension of the forelegs was a characteristic feature.[10] Feeding a low-copper food (1.2 mg/kg dry matter) vs. a normal copper food (14.1 mg/kg dry matter) resulted in depletion of plasma (1.4 vs. 9.7 μmol/l) and liver copper stores (19 vs. 246 mg copper/kg dry matter). Secondary copper deficiency resulted in osteoporotic lesions in growing Great Dane puppies, which could be attributed to impaired osteoblastic function.[88] These dogs were fed an experimental food containing high concentrations of molybdate, which strongly impaired copper absorption and induced secondary copper deficiency.

The overall prevalence of primary copper deficiency (i.e., a dietary deficiency) should not be overestimated. Most common ingredients are rich in copper; however, some homemade, unsupplemented foods (made of rice, dairy products, fat, starch) may contain low or suboptimal copper concentrations. Under certain circumstances, these foods may contribute to the development of skeletal disease, even if copper levels are higher than in deficient experimental foods. A suboptimal copper supply could evoke negative effects especially if combined with high growth intensity or other dietary imbalances (e.g., calcium, zinc or carbohydrates). The possibility that large dogs are more susceptible to a low dietary copper intake cannot be excluded.[d] Impaired copper absorption may also occur with high dietary calcium or zinc levels; the latter induces copper binding metallothionein in the gut mucosa.[89] High amounts of poorly digestible carbohydrates or foods that are rich in dietary fiber may also reduce copper absorption.[90]

The recommendation for copper in canine growth foods has been 7.3 ppm,[79] but, to achieve a safety margin for at-risk dogs, a minimum level of 10 ppm is encouraged. Most commercial canine growth foods deliver copper in a range from 10 to 20 mg/kg dry matter to meet this minimum recommendation.

Zinc

Zinc is an essential trace element that is widely distributed in the body. It serves as an important coenzyme in numerous biochemical processes. The zinc concentration in newborn puppies is about 22 mg/kg body weight and concentrations increase to 120 mg/kg in tissues formed during the growth phase.[91] Inadequate zinc supply, especially in growing animals, will lead to severe clinical signs within days, resulting mainly in growth depression, skin defects, impaired immune function and growth disorders of the skeleton. These disorders may be linked to the role of zinc as a cofactor in enzymes that are important for connective tissue metabolism. A low activity of alkaline phosphatase (<300 IU/l) is a good indicator of a low zinc status (e.g., deficient zinc intake) in growing animals and young dogs.[d,92] There are no reports that excessive zinc intake is detrimental to skeletal development in dogs, but excess

---

Dangers of Feeding Calcium Supplements to Dogs

Feeding dogs treats that contain calcium or providing calcium supplements further increases daily calcium intake. Two level teaspoons of a typical calcium supplement (calcium carbonate) added to the growth food of a 15-week-old, 15-kg, rottweiler puppy would more than double its daily calcium intake. This calcium intake is well beyond levels shown to increase the risk for DOD. A review article best summed up the need for calcium supplements: "Because virtually all dog foods contain more calcium than is needed to meet the requirement, the use of a calcium supplement certainly is unnecessary. Now that the deleterious effects of excess dietary calcium have been delineated, we can say that the feeding of calcium supplements not only is unnecessary, but, in fact, contraindicated!"

BIBLIOGRAPHY
Kallfelz FA, Dzanis DA. Overnutrition: An epidemic problem in pet animal practice. Veterinary Clinics of North America: Small Animal Practice 1989; 19: 433-446.

---

zinc may be presumed to be toxic at higher levels, as observed in other species.

The essentiality of zinc for skeletal development is unequivocal; reports are available for many species describing severe growth disorders induced by zinc deficiency.[93] Zinc deficiency in dogs is of practical importance mainly with regard to skin diseases.[11] (See Chapter 15.) Skeletal abnormalities have been described in Alaskan malamutes with an inborn error in zinc metabolism[94,95] and skeletal malformation in bull terriers with lethal acrodermatitis enteropathica, a genetically determined defect of zinc metabolism.[96] Experimental zinc deficiency in beagles leads to a significant decrease of zinc concentrations in the skeleton[d] especially in metaphyseal bone, which represents newly formed tissue. It is not known to what extent a marginal zinc intake, due to either subnormal dietary zinc concentrations or high concentrations of interacting substances (e.g., phytic acid, calcium, copper, low digestible carbohydrates),[90] contributes to DOD. Foods for growing dogs should contain enough zinc to compensate for negative interactions with other dietary ingredients, especially if the originally balanced food is "improved" by dog owners who add large amounts of calcium carbonate or other calcium salts. Canine growth foods should contain 120 to 130 mg/kg dry matter zinc. Most commercial canine growth foods contain 200 to 300 mg/kg dry matter zinc to ensure this minimum recommendation is met.

Iodine

Iodine is essential for function of the thyroid glands.[97] The amino acid tyrosine is iodinated and, in subsequent metabolic steps, thyroxine and the biologically more active form triiodothyronine are formed. Both hormones, but particularly triiodothyronine, influence normal degeneration of growing cartilage, penetration of capillaries and mineralization of newly formed bone. Thyroid hormones stimulate formation and resorption of bone, which results in remodeling of the skeleton.[98] Boxers with congenital hypothyroidism were found to have shortened limb bones and severe disturbances of the ossification and mineralization process, problems that were alleviated by L-thyroxine supplementation.[99]

Low dietary iodine induces dysfunction of the thyroid glands. Goiter (enlarged thyroid glands) develops with extreme deficiency. In some regions of the world, goiter still occurs in dogs because they are fed unbalanced, homemade rations.[100] Stunted limb development, hyperplasia of the thyroid glands, myxedema with no loss of hair typically occur in young pups born to bitches that were iodine deficient during pregnancy. Most commercial foods meet the AAFCO-recommended iodine level of 1.5 mg/kg dry matter.[79]

Manganese

Manganese acts as a coenzyme in glycosyl transferases in the metabolism of the ground substance in cartilage. In different species, experimental dietary deficiency leads to disproportionate shortened and thickened long bones, defective skull development and otoliths in the inner ear.[101] Currently, no reports describing manganese deficiency in dogs exist. Less than 5% of dietary manganese is absorbed in the canine intestinal tract and the process seems to be strictly regulated.[90] The dietary requirement of manganese for dogs appears to be lower than that of most other species (1.4 mg/1,000 kcal [0.33 mg/MJ] ME).[11,67] Most commercial foods meet or exceed the recommended allowance of 5 mg/kg dry matter.[79]

Protein

Protein is required for a variety of structural and functional molecules to achieve proper growth. The minimum adequate level of dietary protein depends on digestibility, amino acid composition, proper ratios among the essential amino acids, energy density of the food and amino acid availability from protein sources. The dietary protein requirements of healthy growing dogs decrease as they approach adulthood.[32]

Protein excess has not been shown to negatively affect health or skeletal development during growth of Great Dane puppies when compared with isoenergetically fed controls.[102] Protein deficiency may affect the general health of developing puppies, decrease plasma growth hormone levels and reduce skeletal growth.[11,103] In Great Dane puppies, a protein level of 14.6% (DMB) with 13% of the dietary energy derived from protein resulted in significant decreases in body weight and plasma albumin and urea concentrations with no increased frequency of osteochondrosis.[102,104] A growth food with average energy density should contain 22 to 32% protein (DMB) of high biologic value.[82]

Vitamins
Vitamin D

Metabolites of vitamin D_3 act in concert with other hormones to regulate calcium metabolism and therefore skeletal development in dogs. Vitamin D_3 metabolites aid in calcium and phosphorus absorption from the gut and influence bone cell activity.[105] Dogs may require vitamin D in food sources from plants (vitamin D_2) or animals (vitamin D_3).[17]

Clinical cases of vitamin D_3 deficiency (rickets) are extremely rare in animals fed commercial foods.[33] A diagnosis of vitamin D_3 deficiency can be made by measuring the circulating levels of vitamin D_3 metabolites. Increased growth plate width and thin bone cortices are not associated with low-calcium, high-phosphorus foods, but are strong indicators of rickets.[105]

Excess vitamin D can cause hypercalcemia, hyperphosphatemia, anorexia, polydipsia, polyuria, vomiting, muscle weakness, generalized soft tissue mineralization and lameness. In growing dogs, supplementation with excess vitamin D can markedly disturb normal skeletal development because of increased calcium and phosphorus absorption.[32,105] Minimum recommendations have been suggested to be 500 IU vitamin D/kg of dry matter (143 IU/1,000 kcal [34.2 IU/MJ] ME)[33,79,82] Commercial pet foods contain from two to 10 times the minimum amount recommended by AAFCO.[33]

Vitamin A

Vitamin A is an essential factor in bone metabolism, especially osteoclastic activity.[106] Deficiency or excess may lead to severe metabolic bone disease in growing dogs.[11] Concentrations of vitamin A in canine serum range from 1,800 to 18,000 IU/l.[107]

Hypervitaminosis A may result in anorexia, decreased weight gain, hyperesthesia, narrowing of long bone epiphyseal cartilage, ankylosis, new bone formation without osteolysis and thin bone cortices.[8] High doses of vitamin A given to pregnant bitches may result in cleft palates in puppies.[108] Adult beagles fed at maintenance levels for 26 weeks demonstrated a very high tolerance to 200,000 IU of vitamin A/kg body weight with no detrimental effects on selected parameters.[109]

Hypovitaminosis A results in a variety of clinical signs including anorexia, weight loss, ataxia, xerophthalmia, metaplasia of bronchiolar epithelium, conjunctivitis and increased susceptibility to infection. In addition, faulty bone remodeling may constrict nerves passing through bone foramina resulting in neural degeneration.

The recommended concentration of vitamin A in dog foods is 5,000 IU/kg dry matter (1,429 IU/1,000 kcal [342 IU/MJ] ME).[11,79] Most commercial dog foods are supplemented well above the minimum requirement for vitamin A. In the rare case of suspected vitamin A toxicosis, foods low in vitamin A should be fed until signs diminish.[110]

Vitamin C

L-ascorbic acid (vitamin C) is integral to hydroxylation of proline and lysine during biosynthesis of collagen, of which type I collagen is the most widely distributed in connective tissue (primarily in bone and ligaments). Foods devoid of vitamin C and fed to puppies for 147 to 154 days neither affected growth nor caused skeletal lesions.[82] Dogs supplemented with vitamin C had transiently elevated plasma vitamin C concentrations; however, long-term supplementation did not increase concentrations much above normal.[11] Excess vitamin C supplementation is generally considered to have little or no effect on the skeleton but may enhance calcium absorption in some cases, thus increasing the risk for DOD.[111] The relationship between vitamin C and DOD in dogs is unproved; therefore, and supplementation is not recommended.[112] There are no known dietary requirements for vitamin C in dogs.[82]

Assess the Food(s)

The food should consist of a commercial food, or well-balanced homemade food, specific for the unique nutrient requirements of fast-growing, large- and giant-breed dogs. Recommended nutrient intake in fast-growing, large- and giant-breed dogs is similar to that of other breeds (See Chapter 9.), except for more stringent restrictions for fat, energy and calcium intake. (See Key Nutritional Factors—

Developmental Orthopedic Disease.) Several commercial foods are available that have been formulated for fast-growing, large- and giant-breed dogs (Table 17-7). Large-breed growth formulations have marked differences in key nutrients (e.g., calcium and energy density) considered risk factors for skeletal disease in large- and giant-breed puppies. The energy density of a food depends on the components that make up the food. In general, as the fat content of a food increases, the energy density increases (Table 17-5). The higher the energy content, the more likely dogs are to consume excess energy unless they are fed in a food-restricted manner. In addition, other nutrients may be under-consumed, if the formulation is not adjusted to compensate for the increased energy content.

Assess the Feeding Method

Assessment of the feeding methods requires owner knowledge of current feeding practices, which includes the amount being fed. If owners do not know how much food their puppies are consuming, they should measure how much is being ingested under the current feeding regimen for several days. This information will help when making recommendations for future feeding plans. Both the nutrient profile of a food and how it is fed are risk factors for DOD.

The aim of feeding programs for large- and giant-breed puppies is to achieve moderate energy restriction. This energy restriction may be as high as 10 to 25% of free-choice intake of higher energy density foods.[23,25,28,42] This recommendation does not mean starving a dog or feeding it a weight-control food formulated for obese adult dogs. If healthy growing dogs eat to satiety, foods formulated for weight control may result in insufficient mineral, protein or

vitamin intake. Rather, these puppies should be fed correct dietary allowances to satisfy physiologic needs for optimal skeletal growth in conjunction with moderate energy restriction.[28,67,69,70,79] Slow growth during the first year does not deleteriously affect final adult body size (Figure 17-9).

Figure 17-8 illustrates data averaged from weaning to 45% of adult body weight (approximately two to four months of age) for several breeds with free-choice energy intakes. These average intakes may be used as a crude guideline for determining energy requirements in growing puppies of different breeds.

The average ME intake for Great Dane puppies ranged from 311 kcal (1,300 kJ)/(BW$_{kg}$)$^{0.75}$ at weaning to 263 kcal (1,100 kJ)/(BW$_{kg}$)$^{0.75}$ at six months of age. These values are approximately 20% higher than for other large breeds and are consistent with reports of higher requirements for Great Dane puppies.[43,67,113,114] Marked restriction of ME (191 kcal[800 kJ]/BW$_{kg}$]$^{0.75}$) for Great Dane puppies may lead to unacceptable body composition.[113]

There are three basic methods of feeding growing dogs: 1) free choice (ad libitum), 2) time limited or 3) food limited. In any feeding regimen an initial estimate of the amount to be fed is required. Table 17-6 provides formulas for estimating initial food intake for at-risk breeds. It may be necessary to contact the food manufacturer to obtain the energy density of a particular food.

Free-Choice Feeding

Free-choice feeding is relatively effortless and may reduce abnormal behavior such as barking at feeding time. In addition, frequent trips to the food bowl may help reduce boredom and timid or unthrifty animals experience less compe-

Table 17-7. Recommended levels of key nutrients for dogs at risk for developmental orthopedic disease vs. levels in selected commercial dog foods.*

	Calcium (%)	Phosphorus (%)	Energy (kcal ME/g)	Fat (%)	Protein (%)
Recommended levels	0.7-1.2	0.6-1.1	3.2-3.8	8-12	22-32
AAFCO nutrient profile	1.0-2.5	0.8-1.6	3.5-4.0	8.0 min.	22.0 min.
Specific-purpose growth foods					
Bench & Field Puppy Plus, dry	3.1	1.8	3.7	13.5	31.5
Blue Seal Gentry, dry	2.5	1.4	3.9	23.8	33.9
Hill's Prescription Diet Canine p/d, dry	1.7	1.2	4.2	22.7	29.4
Hill's Prescription Diet Canine p/d Large Breed, dry	0.9	0.7	3.2	9.2	29.4
Hill's Science Diet Canine Growth, dry	1.4	1.2	3.9	19.2	29.3
Hill's Science Diet Large Breed Canine Growth, dry	1.0	0.8	3.5	10.6	29.7
Hill's Science Diet Lamb Meal & Rice Canine Growth, dry	1.7	1.2	4.5	19.9	29.1
Iams Eukanuba Large Breed Puppy, dry	1.0	0.8	4.1	17.2	28.8
Iams Eukanuba Medium Breed Puppy, dry	1.4	1.1	4.1	23.9	36.2
Iams Eukanuba Natural Lamb & Rice Puppy, dry	1.3	1.0	4.3	17.3	29.9
Iams Natural Lamb Meal & Rice for Puppies, dry	1.9	1.5	4.1	16.3	29.3
Iams Puppy, dry	1.4	1.0	4.3	19.9	32.1
NutroMax Puppy, dry	1.7	1.4	4.3	20.3	32.6
Nutro Natural Choice Puppy, dry	1.6	1.4	3.6	14.0	29.1
Purina Pro Plan Growth, dry	1.4	1.0	4.2	19.5	31.8
Purina Puppy Chow, dry	1.4	1.0	3.8	12.5	30.9
Select Balance Puppy, dry	1.3	1.1	3.8	19.0	30.4
Solid Gold, dry	3.4	1.9	3.7	10.1	31.1
All-purpose foods					
Alpo Chunky with Liver, moist	2.2	1.5	4.4	25.7	50.4
Mighty Dog Beef, moist	4.5	2.5	5.2	40.7	41.5
Pedigree Chopped Combo, moist	4.1	2.4	5.1	38.0	40.3
Pedigree Mealtime Rice & Vegetables, dry	1.8	1.2	3.7	11.5	23.2
Pedigree with Chunky Chicken, moist	2.8	1.7	5.3	43.3	38.1
Purina Dog Chow, dry	1.6	1.0	3.7	10.3	24.9

*Nutrients are expressed on dry matter basis except energy, which is expressed on an as fed basis. To convert to kJ, multiply kcal x 4.184.

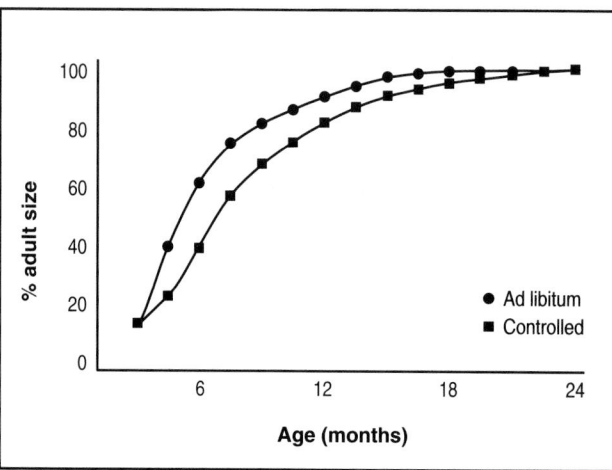

Figure 17-9. Comparison of growth curves of large-breed dogs fed free choice vs. those in a food-restricted feeding regimen.

tition when eating. Coprophagy may be decreased and frequent small meals may result in a more constant blood level of nutrients and hormones. Disadvantages of free-choice feeding include food wastage, only dry or semi-moist forms of pet food can be fed and competition or boredom may stimulate overeating. The most serious disadvantage in young growing dogs is increased risk of DOD because of overconsumption by large- and giant-breed puppies.[23,25,42,44] It is especially important to recommend a food with an energy density less than 3.8 kcal/g (15.9 kJ) (less than 12% fat DMB) to decrease the risk of excess energy intake when dog owners use this feeding method.

Time-Restricted Meal Feeding

Time-limited feeding is a method in which dogs are allowed free access to food for a defined period, usually 10 to 15 minutes, once or twice daily. Some investigators have proposed that puppies fed in this way consume less food because they have a smaller stomach volume than adults. The energy requirement of young animals may be two to three times that of adult dogs of the same weight, but the stomach volume may be smaller on a per body weight basis.

Investigators who advocate this feeding method suggest that puppies have slightly reduced growth rates, but achieve similar adult size and lean body mass when compared with puppies fed free choice.[115] Other studies have shown that feeding 15 minutes twice a day did not reduce food intake between free-choice and time-restricted groups.[116] Again, it is important in this type of feeding program to recommend foods with a lower energy density (less than 12% fat DMB) to decrease the risk of overconsumption.

Time-limited feeding may also help in disciplining and housetraining young puppies. The owner interacts with the puppy during this time and is able to observe its general condition and behavior, which may lead to earlier detection of health problems. A routine of feeding a puppy and then taking it outdoors can enforce housetraining by taking advantage of the gastrocolic reflex. Advocates of this feeding method suggest that when some dogs fed in this manner reach adulthood they may voluntarily limit their feeding to once or twice a day and thus avoid overeating.

Food-Restricted Meal Feeding

The method of choice for feeding puppies at risk for DOD is limiting food intake to maintain optimal growth rate and body condition. Food-limited feeding requires feeding a measured amount of food based on the dog's calculated DER (Table 17-6), or as recommended by the manufacturer, divided into two or three meals per day. Energy requirement is most easily calculated by using RER as a base to build on. RER can be calculated using either of the following equations:

$$RER (kcal/day) = 70(BW_{kg})^{0.75} \text{ or}$$
$$RER (kcal/day) = 30(BW_{kg}) + 70$$

The kilocalories (kcal) can be converted to kilojoules (kJ) by multiplying kcal by 4.184. As a starting point use 3 x RER for the first four months of life and 2 x RER from four months of age to 80% of expected mature weight (about 10 to 12 months for most breeds). Most large- and giant-breed dogs will continue to have increases in body weight and muscle mass after 12 months, but the growth rate is reduced and most if not all growth plates are closed. At 12 months, these puppies can be fed as adults (1.6 x RER for neutered dogs and 1.8 x RER for intact dogs).

■ FEEDING PLAN

Prevention of DOD

1. Determine if the dog is at risk for DOD. (As are all large- and giant-breed dogs.)
2. If the dog is at risk, control the nutrients of concern through food composition (Table 17-7) and feeding method. (See above.)
3. Do not add vitamin or mineral supplements to balanced foods, particularly calcium, phosphorus, vitamin D and vitamin A. If a nutritionally adequate growth food is being fed, supplementation is contraindicated.
4. Determine the dog's BCS every two weeks. (See Chapter 1.) Dogs should have a BCS of 2/5 to 3/5.

Treatment of Affected Dogs

1. If possible, determine if a nutritional imbalance is causing the skeletal disease observed. The feeding history, clinical signs, radiographic changes and laboratory values may be helpful.
2. To correct either deficiencies or excesses, recommend the pet owner feed a nutritionally adequate growth food designed for large-breed puppies. (See Key Nutritional Factors—Developmental Orthopedic Disease.)
3. If a well-balanced growth food is being fed and skeletal diseases occur, reduce food intake up to 25%.
4. Do not give vitamin or mineral supplements to dogs eating commercial foods, particularly calcium, phosphorus, vitamin D and vitamin A. If a nutritionally adequate commercial growth food is being fed, supplementation is contraindicated.
5. Provide appropriate treatment for specific problems, such as pathologic fractures.

Remember, dietary recommendations are inferred from limited group/breed observations and applied to individual animals. All feeding programs need to be tailored to individual animal and client situations. Initial dietary recommendations are a generalized starting point for veterinary/client interactions. Dietary adequacy must be assessed by monitoring the BCS, which necessitates veterinarian-client interaction at regular intervals.

Select a Food(s)

In general, dry foods are more economical and less energy dense than moist foods. Considering most DOD occurs in large- and giant-breed dogs, the usual type of food selected is a dry formulation. However, moist foods may be fed as long as special attention is paid to key nutritional factors.

Foods for growth should at the very least have passed an AAFCO or similar feeding trial specific for that lifestage. However, feeding trials do not ensure adequacy or safety for every breed. When dealing with dogs at risk for DOD, veterinarians should focus special attention on the energy density and calcium content of the food and the feeding method. (See Key Nutritional Factors—Developmental Orthopedic Disease.)

Determine a Feeding Method

In general, free-choice feeding is contraindicated in at-risk dogs until they have reached skeletal maturity (about 12 months of age or at least 80 to 90% of adult weight). If time-limited feeding is used, five- to 10-minute feeding periods may be required to decrease food intake in some puppies (three times per day for the first month after weaning, then twice per day). In some cases, the feeding periods may need to be even shorter.

Food-limited feeding is the recommended feeding method for rapidly growing puppies. Energy intake should be restricted up to 25% less than free-choice intake, if the puppy is fed high energy density foods (>3.8 kcal/g [15.9 kJ]). A rough starting point for energy intake is 3 x RER from weaning to four months of age for fast-growing, large- and giant-breed dogs. Great Dane puppies are the exception to this recommendation. They may require 20% more ME per metabolic body weight than other dogs. After the daily caloric requirement has been calculated, divide this number by the energy density of the food (kcal or) to determine the number of cups or cans to feed per day. Remember, these calculations and the manufacturer recommendations are only starting points.

■ REASSESSMENT

Regular clinical evaluation of growing puppies and adjustments in the food offered are crucial. Rapidly growing, large- and giant-breed dogs have a very steep growth curve and their intake requirements can change dramatically over short periods. These puppies should be weighed, their body condition evaluated and their daily feeding amount adjusted at least once every two weeks (Figure 17-10 and Table 17-6). This evaluation can be performed in the hospital by the veterinarian or veterinary health care team, or owners can be taught to perform this evaluation at home.

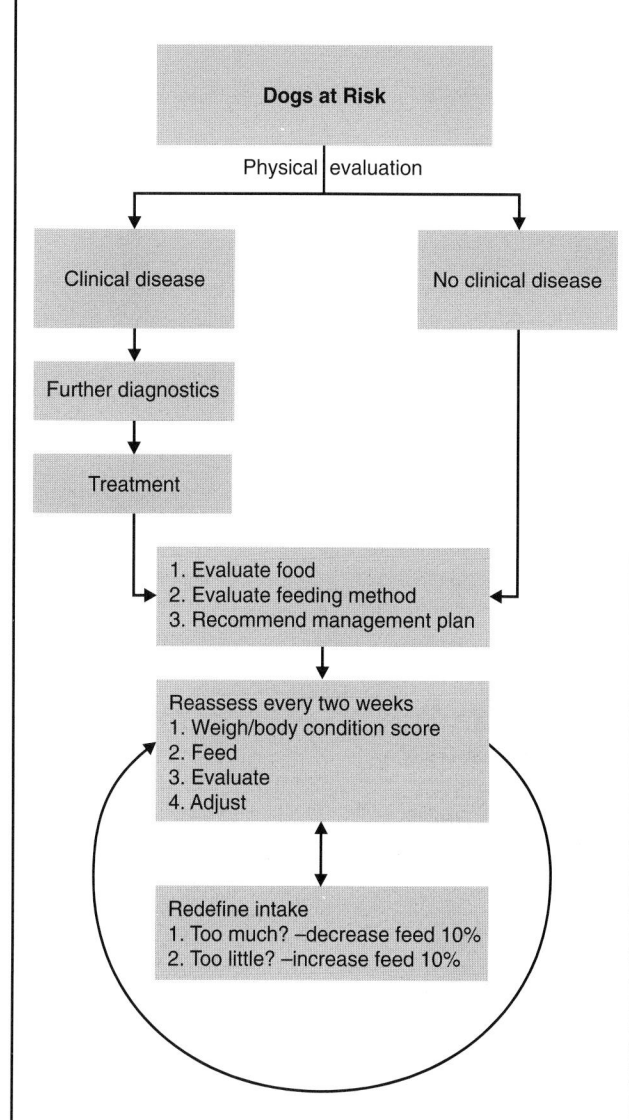

Figure 17-10. Flowchart for assessing dogs at risk for developmental orthopedic disease.

■ SUMMARY

Skeletal disease can be influenced during growth by feeding technique and nutrient profile. However, nutritional management alone will not completely control DOD because there is an hereditary component (i.e., CHD and osteochondrosis can develop in genetically affected animals raised on balanced foods). In addition, the occurrence and clinical signs of DOD can be aggravated when forced exercise or environment are not adapted to the vulnerability of the young skeleton. Dietary deficiencies are of minimal concern in this age of commercial foods specifically prepared for young, growing dogs; the major potential for harm results from excess consumption of energy and calcium.

A balanced food fed at an appropriate quantity will help to optimize the conditions of skeletal development and decrease the risk of DOD. After DOD has been manifested, nutritional management becomes a minor component of treatment unless obesity is a contributing factor.

ENDNOTES & REFERENCES

ENDNOTES

a. Breuer GJ. Purdue University, West Lafayette, IN, USA. Unpublished data. 1997.

b. Schoenmakers I, Hackeng WHL. Utrecht University, The Netherlands. Unpublished data. 1997.

c. Toll PW, Richardson DC. Unpublished data, 1996.

d. Zentek J. Unpublished data, 1996.

REFERENCES

1. Johnson JA, Austin C, Breuer GJ. Incidence of canine appendicular musculoskeletal disorders in 16 veterinary teaching hospitals from 1980-1989. Journal of Veterinary Comparative Orthopedics and Traumatology 1994; 7: 56-69.

2. Brinker WO, Piermattei DL, Flo GL, eds. Diagnosis and treatment of orthopedic conditions of the hindlimb. In: Handbook of Small Animal Orthopedics and Fracture Treatment, 2nd ed. Philadelphia, PA: WB Saunders Co, 1990; 341-470.

3. Corley EA, Hogan PM. Trends in hip dysplasia control: Analysis of radiographs submitted to the Orthopedic Foundation for Animals 1974 to 1984. Journal of the American Veterinary Medical Association 1985; 187: 805-809.

4. Brinker WO, Piermattei DL, Flo GL, eds. Osteochondrosis. In: Handbook of Small Animal Orthopedics and Fracture Treatment, 2nd ed. Philadelphia, PA: WB Saunders Co, 1990; 305-311.

5. Hill MA, Ruth GR, Hilley HD, et al. Dyschondroplasias, including osteochondrosis, of boars between 25 and 169 days of age: Histologic changes. American Journal of Veterinary Research 1984; 45: 903-926.

6. Brinker WO, Piermattei DL, Flo GL. Physical examination for lameness. In: Handbook of Small Animal Orthopedics and Fracture Treatment, 2nd ed. Philadelphia, PA: WB Saunders Co, 1990; 267-277.

7. Henry GA. Radiographic development of canine hip dysplasia. Veterinary Clinics of North America: Small Animal Practice 1992; 22: 559-578.

8. Hazewinkel HAW. Skeletal disease. In: Wills JM, Simpson KW, eds. The Waltham Book of Clinical Nutrition of the Dog & Cat. Tarrytown, NY: Pergamon, 1994; 395-423.

9. Nap RC, Hazewinkel HAW. Growth and skeletal development in the dog in relation to nutrition: A review. Veterinary Quarterly 1994; 16: 50-59.

10. Zentek J, Daemmrich K, Meyer H. Untersuchungen zum Cu-Mangel beim Wachsenden Hund. Journal of Veterinary Medicine A 1991; 38: 561-570.

11. National Research Council. Nutrient Requirements of Dogs. Washington, DC: National Academy of Sciences, 1985.

12. Robey PG, Termine JD. Biochemical markers of metabolic bone disease. In: Avioli LV, Krane SM, eds. Metabolic Bone Disease and Clinically Related Disorders, 2nd ed. Philadelphia, PA: WB Saunders Co, 1990; 244-263.

13. Eyre DR. Biochemical markers of bone turnover. In: Favus MJ, ed. Primer on Metabolic Bone Diseases and Disorders of Mineral Metabolism, 3rd ed. Philadelphia, PA: Lippincott-Raven, 1996; 114-119.

14. Azria M. The calcitonins. In: Physiology and Pharmacology. Basel, Switzerland: S Karger AG, 1989; 1-152.

15. Hazewinkel HAW, Goedgebuure SA, Poulos PW, et al. Influences of chronic calcium excess on the skeletal development of growing Great Danes. Journal of the American Animal Hospital Association 1985; 21: 377-391.

16. Hazewinkel HAW, How KL, Bosch R, et al. Ungenugende photosythese von Vitamin D bei Hunden. In: Meyer H, Kienzle E, eds. Ernahrung, Fehlernahrung und Diaetetik bei Hund und Katze. Hanover, Germany: Dobler Druck, Alfeld, Germany, 1987; 125-129.

17. How KL, Hazewinkel HAW, Mol JA. Dietary vitamin D dependence of cats and dogs due to inadequate cutaneous synthesis of vitamin D. General and Comparative Endocrinology 1994; 96: 12-18.

18. Tenenhouse HS. The vitamin D endocrine system. In: Simmons DJ, ed. Nutrition and Bone Development. New York, NY: Oxford University Press, 1990; 164-201.

19. Feldman EC, Nelson RW, eds. Hypercalcemia and primary hyperparathyroidism. In: Canine and Feline Endocrinology and Reproduction, 2nd ed. Philadelphia, PA: WB Saunders Co, 1996; 455-493.

20. Arnaud CD, Kolb FO. The calciotropic hormones and metabolic bone disease. In: Greenspan FS, ed. Basic and Clinical Endocrinology. Los Altos, CA: Lange Medical Publications, 1991; 247.

21. Daemmrich K. Relationship between nutrition and bone growth in large and giant dogs. Journal of Nutrition 1991; 121: S114-S121.

22. Dobenencker B, Kienzle E, Matis U. Mal- and overnutrition in puppies with and without clinical disorders of skeletal development (abstract). In: Proceedings. European Society of Veterinary and Comparative Nutrition, Munich, Germany, 1997; 25.

23. Hedhammar A, Wu F, Krook L, et al. Overnutrition and skeletal disease. An experimental study in growing Great Dane dogs. Cornell Veterinarian 1974; 64 (Suppl. 5): 1-160.

24. Kasstrom J. Nutrition, weight gain and development of hip dysplasia. Acta Radiologica Supp. (Stockholm) 1975; 344: 135-179.

25. Kealy RD, Olsson SE, Monti KL, et al. Effects of limited food consumption on the incidence of hip dysplasia in growing dogs. Journal of the American Veterinary Medical Association 1992; 210: 857-863.

26. Lust G, Geary JC, Sheffy BE. Development of hip dysplasia in dogs. American Journal of Veterinary Research 1973; 34: 87-91.

27. Lust G, Rendano VT, Summers BA. Canine hip dysplasia: Concepts and diagnosis. Journal of the American Veterinary Medical Association 1985; 187: 638-640.

28. Meyer H, Zentek J. Über den Einfluß einer unterschiedlichen Energieversorgung wachsender Doggen auf Körpermasse und Skelettentwicklung. Journal of Veterinary Medicine A 1992; 39: 130-141.

29. Riser WH, Cohen D, Linquist S, et al. Influence of early rapid growth and weight gain on hip dysplasia in the German Shepherd dog. Journal of the American Veterinary Medical Association 1964; 145: 661-668.

30. Slater MR, Scarlett JM, Kaderly RE, et al. Breed, gender, and age risk factors for canine osteochondritis dissecans. Journal of Veterinary Comparative Orthopedics and Traumatology 1991; 4: 100-106.

31. Slater MR, Scarlett JM, Donoghue S, et al. Diet and exercise as potential risk factors for osteochondritis dissecans in dogs. American Journal of Veterinary Research 1992; 53: 2119-2124.

32. Richardson DC, Toll PW. Relationship of nutrition to developmental skeletal disease in young dogs. Veterinary Clinical Nutrition 1997; 4: 6-13.

33. Kallfelz FA, Dzanis DA. Overnutrition: An epidemic problem in pet animal practice. Veterinary Clinics of North America: Small Animal Practice 1989; 19: 433-446.

34. Alexander JE, Moore MP, Wood LLH. Comparative growth studies in Labrador retrievers fed 5 commercial calorie-dense diets. Modern Veterinary Practice 1988; 69: 144-148.

35. Allard RL, Douglass GM, Kerr WW. The effect of breed and sex on dog growth. Companion Animal Practice 1988; 2: 15-19.

36. Booles D, Burger IH, Whyte AL, et al. Effect of two levels of zinc intake on growth and trace element status in Labrador puppies. Journal of Nutrition 1991; 121: S79-S80.

37. Booles D, Poore DW, Legrand-Defretin V, et al. Body composition of male and female Labrador retriever puppies at 20 weeks of age. Journal of Nutrition 1994; 124: S2624-S2625.

38. Meyer H, Zentek J. Untersuchungen zum Wachstum verschiedener Hunderassen in Abhängigkeit von der Fütterung. Proc. 35. Jahrestagung, Deutsche Veterinärmedizinische Gesellschaft, Fachgruppe Kleintierkrankheiten, Gießen (FRG); 1989; 39-50.

39. Romsos DR, Belo PS, Bennink MR, et al. Effects of dietary carbohydrate, fat and protein on growth, body composition and blood metabolite levels in the dog. Journal of Nutrition 1976; 106: 1452-1464.

40. Sheng HP, Huggins RA. Growth of the beagle: Changes in chemical composition. Growth 1971; 35: 369-376.

41. Chakraborty PK, Stewart AP, Seager SW. Relationship of growth and serum growth hormone concentration in the prepubertal bitch. Laboratory Animal Science 1983; 33: 51-55.

42. Lavelle RB. The effects of overfeeding of a balanced complete commercial diet to a group of growing Great Danes. In: Burger IH, Rivers JW, eds. Nutrition of the Dog and Cat. Cambridge, UK: Cambridge University Press, 1989; 303-315.

43. Rainbird A, Kienzle E. Untersuchungen zum Energiebedarf des Hundes in Abhängigkeit von Rassezugehörigkeit und Alter. Kleintierpraxis 1990; 35: 149-158.

44. Meyer H, Zentek J. Energy requirements of growing Great Danes. Journal of Nutrition 1991; 121: S35-S36.

45. Blum JW, Zentek J, Meyer H. Untersuchungen einer unterschiedlichen Energieversorgung auf die Wachstumsintensität und Skelettentwicklung bei wachsenden Doggen. 2. Mitteilung: Einfluß auf den insulinähnlichen Wachstumsfaktor I und die Schilddrüsenhormone. Journal of Veterinary Medicine A 1992; 39: 568-574.

46. Danforth E, Burger AG. The impact of nutrition on thyroid hormone physiology and action. Annual Review of Nutrition 1989; 9: 201-227.

47. Eigenmann JE, DeBruijne JJ, Froesch ER. Insulin-like-growth-factor I and growth hormone in canine starvation. Acta Endocrinologica (Kbh.) 1985; 108: 161-166.

48. Nap RC. Nutritional influences on growth and skeletal development in the dog. Thesis. Proefschrift, Rijksuniversiteit Utrecht,1993.

49. Daughaday WH, Hall K, Salmon WD, et al. Somatomedin: Proposed designation for sulfation factor. Nature 1972; 235: 107.

50. Froesch ER, Schmid C, Schwander J, et al. Actions of insulin-like growth factors. Annual Review of Physiology 1985; 47: 443-467.

51. Glade MJ. The control of cartilage growth in osteochondrosis: A review. Equine Veterinary Science 1984; 6: 1175-1187.

52. Harris WH, Heaney RP. Skeletal renewal and metabolic disease. New England Journal of Medicine 1969; 280: 193-202.

53. Hochberg Z, Maor G, Lewinson D, et al. The direct effects of growth hormone on chondrogenesis and osteogenesis. In: Heap RB, Prosser CG, Lamming GE, eds. Biotechnology in Growth Regulation. London, UK: Butterworths, 1989; 123-128.

54. Isaksson OGP, Jansson JO, Gause IAM. Growth hormone stimulates longitudinal bone growth directly. Science 1982; 216: 1237-1239.

55. Isaksson OGP, Lindahl A, Nilsson A, et al. Mechanisms of the stimulatory effect of growth hormone on longitudinal bone growth. Endocrinological Reviews 1987; 8: 426-434.

56. Eigenmann JE. Wachstumshormon und insulinähnlicher Wachstumsfaktor beim Hund: Klinische und experimentelle Untersuchungen. Schweizer Archiv für Tierheilkunde 1986; 128: 57-78.

57. Nap RC, Mol JA, Hazewinkel HAW. Age-related plasma concentrations of growth hormone (GH) and insulin-like growth factor 1 (IGF-1) in Great Dane pups fed different dietary levels of protein. Domestic Animal Endocrinology 1993; 10: 237-247.

58. Carlson CS, Meuten DJ, Richardson DC. Ischemic necrosis of cartilage in spontaneous and experimental lesions of osteochondrosis. Journal of Orthopaedic Research 1991; 9: 317-329.

59. Schoenmakers I, Hazewinkel HAW, Voorhut G, et al. Calcium and phosphorous absorption and retention in Great Danes raised on foods with different calcium and phosphorous contents (abstract). European Society of Veterinary Comparative Nutrition 1997; 24.

60. Voorhout A, Hazewinkel HAW. A radiographic study on the development of the antebrachium in Great Dane pups on different calcium intakes. Veterinary Radiology 1987; 28: 152-157

61. Nap RC, Hazewinkel HAW, Voorhout G, et al. Growth and skeletal development in miniature poodles fed different levels of calcium. In: Nap RC, ed. Nutritional Influences on Growth and Skeletal Development in the Dog. Thesis. Proefschrift, Utrecht, 1993; 75-93.

62. Nunez EA, Hedhammar A, Wu FM, et al. Ultrastructure of the thyroid C cells and the parathyroid cells in growing dogs on a high calcium diet. Laboratory Investigation 1974; 31: 96-108.

63. Goedegebuure SA, Hazewinkel HAW. Morphological findings in young dogs chronically fed a diet containing excess calcium. Veterinary Pathology 1986; 23: 594-605.

64. Martin TJ, Moseley JM. Calcitonin. In: Avioli LV, Krane SM, eds. Metabolic Bone Disease and Clinically Related Disorders. Philadelphia, PA: WB Saunders Co, 1990; 131-154.

65. Weisbrode SE, Capen CC. The ultrastructural effects of parathyroid-hormone, calcitonin, and vitamin D on bone. In: Bonucci E, Motta PM, eds. Ultrastructure of Skeletal Tissues. Bone and Cartilage in Health and Disease. Dordrecht, The Netherlands: Academic Publishing, 1990; 253-269.

66. Hoefling B. Untersuchungen über die Aufzuchtintensität von Junghunden unter besonderer Berücksichtigung der Skelettentwicklung. Thesis. Hanover, Germany, 1989.

67. Meyer H. In: Ernährung des Hundes, 2nd ed. Stuttgart, Germany: Auflage. Eugen Ulmer, 1990.

68. Richardson DC. The role of nutrition in canine hip dysplasia. Veterinary Clinics of North America: Small Animal Practice 1992; 22: 529-540.

69. Zentek J, Meyer H, Daemmrich K. Untersuchungen einer Unterschiedlichen Energieversorgung auf die Wachstumsintensität und Skelettentwicklung bei Wachsenden Doggen. 3. Mitteilung: Klinisches Bild und chemische Skelettuntersuchungen. Journal of Veterinary Medicine A 1995c; 42: 69-80.

70. Daemmrich K, Zentek J, Meyer H. Untersuchungen einer Unterschiedlichen Energieversorgung auf die Wachstumsintensität und Skelettentwicklung bei Wachsenden Doggen. 4. Mitteilung: Pathologisch-Anatomische Untersuchungen.

71. Hester PY, Krueger KK, Jackson M. The effect of restrictive and compensatory growth on the incidence of leg abnormalities and performance of commercial male turkeys. Poultry Science 1990; 69: 1731-1742.

72. Carlson CS, Hilley HD, Meuten DJ, et al. Effect of reduced growth rate on the prevalence and severity of osteochondrosis in gilts. American Journal of Veterinary Research 1988; 49: 396-402.

73. Nakano T, Aherne FX. The pathogenesis of osteochondrosis—A hypothesis. Medical Hypotheses 1994; 43: 1-5.

74. Gilder H, Boskey AL. Dietary lipids and the calcifying tissue. In: Simmons DJ, ed. Nutrition and Bone Development. New York, NY: Oxford University Press, 1990; 244-265.

75. Takeuchi H, Matsuo T, Tokuyama K, et al. Serum triiodothyronine concentration and $Na^+ K^+$ -ATPase activity in liver and skeletal muscle are influenced by dietary fat type in rats. Journal of Nutrition 1995; 125: 2364-2369.

76. Watkins BA, Shen C-L, McMurty JP, et al. Dietary lipids modulate bone prostaglandin E_2 production, insulin-like growth factor-I concentration and formation rate in chicks. Journal of Nutrition 1997; 127: 1084-1091.

77. Hazewinkel HAW, Vandenbrom WE, Van't Klooster AT, et al. Calcium metabolism in Great Dane dogs fed diets with various calcium and phosphorous levels. Journal of Nutrition 1991; 121: S99-S106.

78. Birge SJ, Avioli LV. Pathophysiology of calcium and phosphate disorders. In: Avioli LV, Krane SM, eds. Metabolic Bone Disease and Clinically Related Disorders. Philadelphia, PA: WB Saunders Co, 1990; 196-221.

79. Association of American Feed Control Officials. Official Publication, 1998.

80. Tanaka Y, DeLuca HF. The control of 25-hydroxyvitamin D metabolism by inorganic phosphorous. Archives of Biochemistry and Biophysiology 1977; 154: 566-574.

81. Broadus AE. Mineral balance and homeostasis. In: Favus MJ, ed. Primer on the Metabolic Bone Diseases and Disorders of Mineral Metabolism. Philadelphia, PA: Lippincott-Raven, 1996; 57-63.

82. Dzanis DA. The AAFCO dog and cat nutrient profiles. In: Bonagura JD, ed. Current Veterinary Therapy XII. Philadelphia, PA: WB Saunders Co, 1995; 1418-1421.

83. Harris ED, Rayton JK, Balthrop JE, et al. Copper and the synthesis of elastin and collagen. In: Ciba Foundation Symposium 79, Biological Roles of Copper. Amsterdam: Excerpta Medica, 1980; 163-182.

84. Siegel RC. Lysyl oxidase. International Review of Connective Tissue Research 1979; 8: 73-118.

85. Eyre DR, Paz MA, Gallop PM. Cross-linking in collagen and elastin. Annual Review of Biochemistry 1984; 53: 717-748.

86. Danks DM. Copper deficiency in humans. In: Ciba Foundation Symposium 79, Biological Roles of Copper. Amsterdam: Excerpta Medica, 1980; 209-225.

87. Baxter JH, Van Wyk JJ. A bone disorder associated with copper deficiency. I. Gross morphological, roentgenological, and chemical observations. Bulletin of the Johns Hopkins Hospital 1953; 93: 1-13.

88. Read RA, Kent GN, Price RI. Inhibition of osteoblastic function in the osteoporosis of copper deficiency in dogs. Journal of Veterinary Comparative Orthopedics and Traumatology 1989; 1: 25-40.

89. Brewer GJ, Dick RD, Schall W, et al. Use of zinc acetate to treat copper toxicosis in dogs. Journal of the American Veterinary Medical Association 1992; 201: 564-568.

90. Zentek J. Beobachtungen zur scheinbaren Verdaulichkeit von Kupfer, Zink, Eisen und Mangan beim Hund. Deutsche Tierärztliche Wochenschrift 1995; 108: 310-315.

91. Gesellschaft für Ernährungsphysiologie: Energie- und Nährstoffbedarf. Nr. 5, Hunde. Frankfurt, Germany: DLG Verlag, 1989.

92. Kirchgessner M. Experimentelle Ergebnisse aus der ernährungsphysiologischen und metabolischen Spurenelementforschung. Übersichten zur Tierernährung 1987; 15: 153-192.

93. Hambidge KM, Casey CE, Krebs NF. Zinc. In: Mertz W, ed. Trace Elements in Human and Animal Nutrition. Orlando, FL: Academic Press, 1986; 1-137.

94. Smart ME, Fletch S. A hereditary growth defect in purebred Alaskan malamutes. Canadian Veterinary Journal 1971; 12: 31-32.

95. Brown RC, Hoag GN, Smart ME, et al. Alaskan malamute chondrodysplasia. V. Decreased gut zinc absorption. Growth 1978; 42: 1-6.

96. Jezyk PF, Haskins ME, MacKay-Smith WE, et al. Lethal acrodermatitis in bull terriers. Journal of the American Veterinary Medical Association 1986; 188: 833-839.

97. Belshaw BE, Cooper TB, Becker DV. The iodine requirement and influence of iodine on iodine metabolism and thyroid function in the adult beagle. Endocrinology 1975; 96: 1280-1291.

98. High WB, Capen CC, Black HE. Effect of thyroxine on cortical bone remodeling in adult dogs. A histomorphometric study. American Journal of Pathology 1981; 102: 438-446.

99. Saunders HM, Jezyk PF. The radiographic appearance of canine congenital hypothyroidism: Skeletal changes with delayed treatment. Veterinary Radiology 1991; 32: 171-177.

100. Kienzle E, Hall DK. Inappropriate feeding: The importance of a balanced diet. In: Wills JM, Simpson KW, eds. The Waltham Book of Clinical Nutrition of the Dog & Cat. Tarrytown, NY: Pergamon, 1994; 1-14.

101. Hurley LS, Keen CL. Manganese. In: Mertz W, ed. Trace Elements in Human and Animal Nutrition. Orlando, FL: Academic Press, 1986; 185-223.

102. Nap RC, Hazewinkel HAW, Voorhout G, et al. The influence of the dietary protein content on growth in giant breed dogs. Journal of Veterinary Comparative Orthopedics and Traumatology 1993; 6: 1-8.

103. Gessert CF, Phillips PH. Protein in the nutrition of the growing dog. Journal of Nutrition 1956; 58: 415-421.

104. Nap RC, Hazewinkel HAW, Voorhout G, et al. Growth and skeletal development in Great Dane pups fed different levels of protein intake. Journal of Nutrition 1991; 121: S107-S113.

105. Hazewinkel HAW. Nutrition in orthopedics. In: Bojrab MJ, ed. Disease Mechanisms in Small Animal Surgery, 2nd ed. Philadelphia, PA: Lea & Febiger, 1993; 1119-1128.

106. Hayes KC. On the pathophysiology of vitamin A deficiency. Nutrition Reviews 1971; 29: 3-6.

107. Keane KW, Nakamura FI, Morris ML. Vitamin A plasma levels of dogs. North American Veterinarian 1947; 28: 587.

108. Wiersig DO, Swenson MJ. Teratogenicity of vitamin A in the canine. Federal Proceedings 1967; 26: 486.

109. Goldy GG, Burr JR, Longardner CN, et al. Effects of measured doses of vitamin A fed to healthy beagle dogs for 26 weeks. Veterinary Clinical Nutrition 1996; 3: 42-49.

110. Donoghue S, Szanto J, Kronfeld DS. Hypervitaminosis A in a dog: An example of hospital dietetics. In: Proceedings. Nutrition, Malnutrition, and Dietetics in the Dog and Cat, Hanover, Germany, 1987: 94-96.

111. Teare JA, Krook L, Kallfelz FA, et al. Ascorbic acid deficiency and hypertrophic osteodystrophy in the dog: A rebuttal. Cornell Veterinarian 1979; 69: 384-401.

112. Richardson DC. Developmental orthopedics: Nutritional influences in the dog. In: Ettinger SJ, Feldman EC, eds. Textbook of Veterinary Internal Medicine, 4th ed. Philadelphia, PA: WB Saunders Co, 1995; 252-257.

113. Zentek J, Meyer H. Energieaufnahme adulter Deutscher Doggen. Berliner und Münchener Tierärztliche Wochenschrift 1992; 105: 325-327.

114. Zentek J, Daemmrich K, Meyer H. Zur Pathogenese fütterungsbedingter Skeletterkrankungen bei Junghunden großwüchsiger Rassen. Kleintierpraxis 1995; 40: 469-482.

115. Alexander JE, Wood LLH. Growth studies in Labrador retrievers fed a caloric dense diet: Time-restricted versus free choice feeding. Canine Practice 1987; 14: 41-47.

116. Toll PW, Richardson DC, Jewell DE, et al. The effect of feeding method on growth and body composition in young puppies (abstract). In: Proceedings. Waltham Symposium on the Nutrition of Companion Animals, Adelaide, Australia, 1993: 33.

■ CASE 17-1

Lameness in a Labrador Retriever

H.A.W. Hazewinkel, DVM, PhD
Diplomate ECVS
School of Veterinary Medicine
University of Utrecht
Utrecht, The Netherlands

Assess the Animal

A four-year-old female Labrador retriever was examined for difficulty in rising (standing up) and walking, especially the first few minutes of a walk. These problems were worse after the animal had been out for a long walk or played with other dogs, as often happened on weekends. The current exercise program included three 15- to 30-minute walks per day, free exercise in the yard between walks and two 60-minute walks in the woods on weekends.

Physical examination was unremarkable except for moderate obesity (body weight 45 kg, body condition score [BCS] 4/5) and abnormalities identified in the musculoskeletal system. The range of motion of both hip joints was diminished, crepitation was palpated and the dog reacted painfully when the hips were extended. Neither hindlimb could be abducted normally in the sagittal plane when the dog was in dorsal recumbency. A thorough examination of limbs and lumbosacral area revealed no other abnormalities.

Radiographs of the coxofemoral joints confirmed a diagnosis of severe osteoarthritis due to hip dysplasia (Figure 1).

Assess the Food(s) and Feeding Method

The dog was fed four cups (1,500 kcal [6.28 MJ]) of a commercial dry dog food and table foods. The dry food was fed once daily. The table foods were leftovers from the childrens' food; the amount varied daily. The owners indicated the dog gained most of its weight after an ovariohysterectomy two years earlier and during the summer holidays when the dog spent a month with the owners' parents who lived in an apartment for retired people. The food intake during that month was unknown.

Questions

1. What feeding plan should be implemented to improve the condition of this patient?

2. What non-nutritional management practices can be used to reduce the biomechanical stress on the hip joints of this patient?

Answers and Discussion

1. The biomechanical stress induced by rapid weight gain during growth has been cited as a popular etiology for development of canine developmental orthopedic disease (DOD). It is unknown, and somewhat contested, whether skeletal lesions occur first and are then exacerbated by biomechanical stress, or if biomechanical stress first induces cartilaginous lesions. In either case, increased static forces (excessive weight load) or dynamic forces (excessive muscle pull) may damage immature skeletons.

   In older overweight dogs with established osteoarthritis, biomechanical stress can be diminished with weight reduction. Weight reduction should be continued until very little subcutaneous fat is evident (BCS 2/5). Weight-reduction programs are discussed in more detail in Chapter 13.

   Dietary fatty acid changes may provide anti-inflammatory benefits that result in clinical improvement in some dogs with osteoarthritis. Fatty acid levels in the diet can be manipulated by changing the food or adding a supplement. A detailed discussion of the role of dietary fatty acids in patients with arthritis is found in Chapter 26.

2. Biomechanical stress on the hip joints can also be reduced through alterations in the exercise protocol for the dog. Exercise is an important component of weight-loss and weight-control programs but must be carefully managed in patients with arthritis. Swimming is an excellent form of exercise that builds cardiovascular endurance and hastens weight loss without overloading the joints. Short, frequent walks on a leash should also be encouraged to prevent overloading of the joints, rather than long walks or unsupervised exercise. Nonsteroidal antiinflammatory drugs can be prescribed as needed for joint pain and lameness.

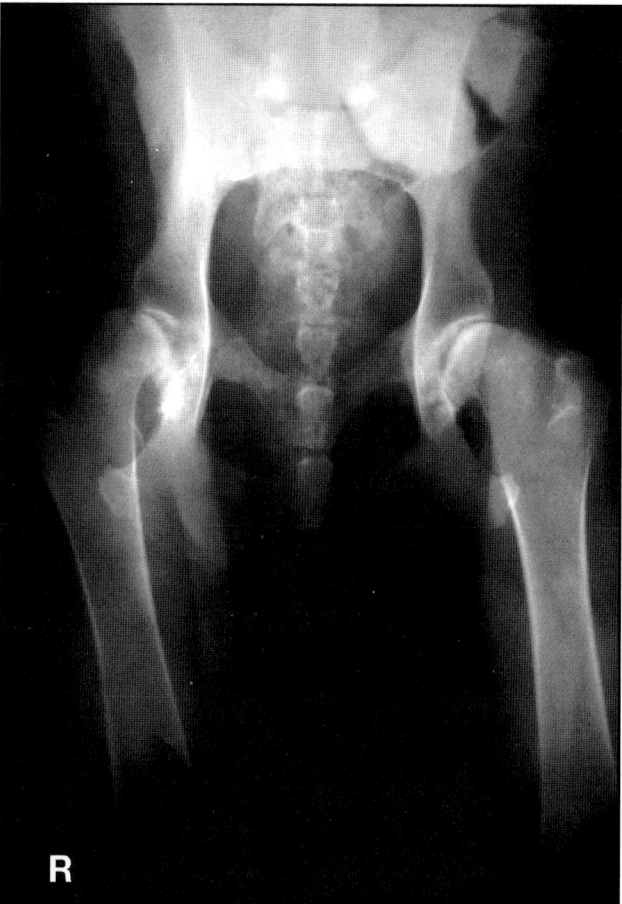

Figure 1. Ventrodorsal radiograph of a four-year-old Labrador retriever with bilateral hip dysplasia. Degenerative joint disease is evident in both coxofemoral joints. Note that the femoral heads have remodeling changes, the acetabuli are shallow and subchondral sclerosis and osteophyte formation are present in the femoral and acetabular components of the joint.

Progress Notes

A weight-reduction program was outlined for the owners. All table scraps were eliminated and the owners chose to feed a reduced quantity of the dog's current food (two cups [750 kcal, 3.14 MJ] per day divided into two equal feedings). The owners were advised to take the dog for daily swims or as often as possible. In addition, the owners walked the dog on a leash several times daily for approximately 20 minutes or for shorter periods when they recognized the dog was having difficulty rising. The target weight loss was 1% of body weight per week. The owners were instructed to return to the clinic every two weeks for body weight recordings and reinforcement of the program.

The target weight of 35 kg was reached in four months with this controlled exercise and feeding plan. The owners reported the dog was "happier" and could more easily accompany them on long walks. Few signs of lameness were present after the dog reached optimal body weight. The exercise and feeding plans were changed to maintain the dog's weight at 35 kg.

CASE 17-2

Feeding a Golden Retriever Puppy

Daniel C. Richardson, DVM
Diplomate ACVS
Hill's Science and Technology Center
Topeka, Kansas, USA

Assess the Animal

A 10-week-old male golden retriever puppy was presented for examination and routine health maintenance procedures. The owner had purchased the puppy from a breeder in a neighboring state. The dog was to be used as a family pet and for occasional hunting. The puppy was housed indoors and in an outdoor fenced enclosure.

Physical examination revealed a normal 6.7-kg puppy with a body condition score (BCS) of 3/5. Results of a fecal flotation test were negative. The puppy was vaccinated with an appropriate product and heartworm preventive medication was dispensed. Routine grooming procedures and socialization were discussed with the owner.

Assess the Food(s) and Feeding Method

The breeder had given the owner a bag of a commercial dry specialty brand food (NutroMax Puppy[a]) specifically formulated for growing dogs. The owner brought the bag of food with him to the veterinary clinic. The guaranteed analysis was: crude protein, 28% minimum; crude fat, 17% minimum; crude fiber, 4% maximum; moisture, 10% maximum and ash, 8% maximum (8.9% DMB). The breeder had instructed the owner to offer as much of this food as the dog would eat each day.

The owner was also given a dietary supplement, which was to be added to the food each day. The supplement powder was to be sprinkled over the food (1.5 scoops/day) or moistened to make a broth. The supplement's guaranteed analysis was: crude protein, not less than 42%; crude fat, not less than 19%; crude fiber, not more than 1% and moisture, not more than 4%.

Questions

1. What key nutritional factors are important to consider for this puppy?
2. What additional information is important to obtain about the food and supplement that have been recommended for this puppy?
3. Outline an appropriate feeding plan (foods and feeding method) and monitoring plan for this patient.

Answers and Discussion

1. The key nutritional factors for growing, large- and giant-breed puppies at risk for developmental orthopedic disease (DOD) include energy, fat and calcium. Excessive intake of energy (fat is the primary contributor to energy intake) during growth directly affects growth velocity, contributes to rapid weight gain and may contribute to endocrine dysregulation. Abnormalities of nutrient supply, bone formation and endocrine regulation may interfere with skeletal maturation, thus increasing the risk for DOD in young animals.

   Dogs that ingest excessive amounts of calcium for prolonged periods may develop hypercalcitoninism. The physiologic action of calcitonin on bone turnover (decreased skeletal remodeling) has been proposed as an inciting cause of DOD in dogs.

   Adequate dietary protein is necessary for growth; however, excessive protein intake is not considered a risk factor for canine DOD.
2. The food should be assessed for energy density and specific levels of fat, calcium, phosphorus and protein. These nutrient levels should then be compared with those levels known to be optimal for growth and

development of large- and giant-breed puppies. (See Key Nutritional Factors—Developmental Orthopedic Disease.) Most of this information is not found on the guaranteed analysis of the package label. The information should be obtained by contacting the manufacturer, reading manufacturers' technical information or consulting other published information. (See Appendix L.) A food for growing dogs should also have passed an Association of American Feed Control Officials (AAFCO) or similar feeding trial. Similar information should be obtained for the supplement.
3. The feeding and monitoring plan should include these steps:
   - Weigh the patient.
   - Estimate the caloric requirement (daily energy requirement [DER] = 3 x resting energy requirement [RER]).
   - Choose a food with metabolizable energy of 3.2 to 3.8 kcal/g (13.4 to 15.9 kJ/g), not more than 12% dry matter fat, 0.7 to 1.2% dry matter calcium and 22 to 32% dry matter protein.
   - Feed the calculated amount of food (energy basis) divided into two to three feedings per day.
   - Reassess the patient every two weeks by weighing it and evaluating its body condition (dogs should have a BCS of 2/5 to 3/5).
   - Adjust the amount of food offered if the BCS is greater than 3/5 or less than 2/5.

Progress Notes

The manufacturers of the food and supplement were contacted. The food had the following nutrient profile (DMB): fat = 20.3%, calcium = 1.67%, energy density = 4.4 kcal/g (18.4 kJ). All other nutrient levels exceeded minimum recommendations established by AAFCO for growing dogs. The supplement had the following nutrient profile (DMB): fat = 19%, calcium = 3.3%. The supplement also contained essential amino acids, essential fatty acids, vitamins and other minerals.

The combination of the food, supplement and free-choice feeding method probably provided excessive amounts of energy and calcium for optimal growth. The food was changed to another commercial dry specialty brand food (Science Diet Large Breed Canine Growth[b]), which is specifically formulated to reduce nutritional risk factors for DOD in dogs. This food contains 1% dry matter calcium, 10.6% dry matter fat, and has an energy density of 3.4 kcal/g (14.23 kJ/g). The DER was estimated (3 x RER = 800 kcal/day [3.35 MJ]) and the owner was asked to discontinue free-choice feeding and begin meal feeding (DER divided into two or three meals per day). The owner was shown how to assign a BCS, asked to record the weight and BCS of his puppy every two weeks and to adjust the amount of food to maintain a BCS of 2/5 to 3/5. The weight and BCS were also recorded in the medical record at 10, 20 and 30 weeks of age when the puppy returned for further vaccinations and other health maintenance procedures. The supplement was discontinued. The owner was also encouraged to maintain a regular exercise and obedience program with the puppy.

Table 1 shows growth data for the puppy during the next 12 months. When the dog was 12 months old, its food was changed to a commercial dry specialty brand

Table 1. Body weights and body condition scores (BCS) for a golden retriever puppy at 10-week intervals.

Age (weeks)	Weight (kg)	BCS (1-5)
10	6.7	3
20	16.3	3
30	24.0	3
40	28.2	3
50	28.8	3

food for adult dogs (Science Diet Canine Maintenance[b]). At two years of age, there was no radiographic evidence of hip dysplasia and no clinical problems associated with the musculoskeletal system.

Endnotes

a. Nutro Products Inc., City of Industry, CA, USA.
b. Hill's Pet Nutrition, Inc., Topeka, KS, USA.

Bibliography

Richardson DC. Developmental orthopedics: Nutritional influences in the dog. In: Ettinger SJ, Feldman EC, eds. Textbook of Veterinary Internal Medicine, 4th ed. Philadelphia, PA: WB Saunders Co, 1995; 252-258.

CASE 17-3

Forelimb Lameness in a Great Dane Puppy

Jürgen Zentek, Dr med vet
Department of Animal Nutrition
Tierarztliche Hochschule
Hanover, Germany

Assess the Animal

An eight-month-old, male Great Dane puppy was examined for a stiff gait at the outset of walking and right forelimb lameness after taking a long walk. The dog was otherwise healthy but slightly overweight (body weight 48 kg, body condition score [BCS] 4/5). The owner reported that the dog was one of the largest of the litter and that it grew very fast from four to six months of age.

Physical examination was normal except for the musculoskeletal system. Palpation of the scapular region revealed bilateral muscle atrophy that was more pronounced on the right side. Passive movement of all the digits, carpi and elbow joints allowed full range of motion with no pain. Deep palpation of the radius, ulna and humerus did not elicit pain. Movement of both shoulder joints caused slight crepitation and elicited a painful response, especially with hyperflexion of the joint.

Radiographs of the shoulder joints were obtained (Figure 1).

Assess the Food(s) and Feeding Method

The puppy was initially fed a commercial dry food formulated for growth (protein = 29%, fat = 18%, calcium = 1.6%, phosphorus = 1.2%, all values listed on a dry matter basis) ad libitum. Because the puppy was "such a good eater," the owner supplemented the food occasionally with meat and table foods. When the puppy was 14 weeks old, the owner switched foods because the puppy developed abnormal locomotion, which members of the owner's dog club attributed to excessive protein intake. The new food was a commercial dry product formulated for adult maintenance (protein = 20%, fat = 13.3%, calcium = 1.7%, all values listed on a dry matter basis). The new food was offered free choice because of the puppy's "good appetite."

Questions

1. What is the tentative diagnosis and how does this condition cause the clinical signs in this dog?
2. How should this patient be managed?
3. Outline an appropriate feeding plan for this dog.

Answers and Discussion

1. Great Danes and other large- and giant-breed dogs are prone to osteochondrosis in the shoulder joints, espe-

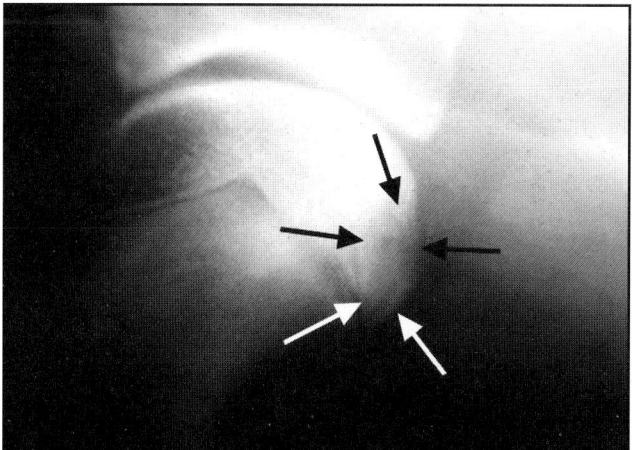

Figure 1. Radiograph of the proximal humerus of an eight-month-old male Great Dane examined for forelimb lameness. The radiolucent area (arrows) is associated with disrupted endochondral ossification (osteochondrosis).

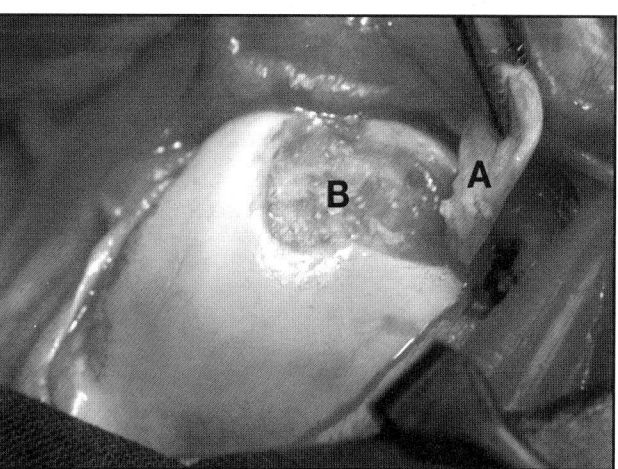

Figure 2. Intraoperative view of an osteochondritis dissecans lesion in the articular epiphyseal cartilage of the proximal cartilage of the same dog. Note the cartilage flap (A) and exposed subchondral bone (B) where a portion of the cartilage flap is missing.

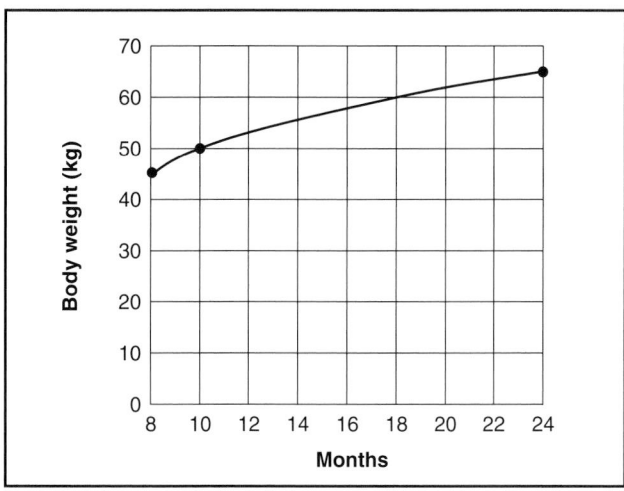

Figure 3. Growth curve recommended for an overweight eight-month-old Great Dane puppy with osteochondrosis.

cially when excessive energy and calcium are consumed during the period of rapid growth (two to six months of age). Osteochondrosis is a disturbance in endochondral ossification that can result in localized separation of articular cartilage and subchondral bone, and may lead to splitting of cartilage fragments into the joint, i.e., osteochondritis dissecans (OCD). Osteochondrosis is not painful; OCD causes osteoarthritis and inflammation of subchondral bone, which is painful. A diagnosis of OCD is very likely in this case based on the clinical (painful shoulder joints) and radiologic findings (indentation in the caudal humeral head).

Because flexion and extension of both shoulder joints is painful with OCD, dogs will shift their body weight to the rear limbs, resulting in abnormal locomotion. Dogs with OCD of the shoulder joints also appear stiff because of the limited range of joint motion and have variable degrees of lameness.

2. Surgical treatment is indicated for most cases of shoulder joint OCD when lameness is present and persisting, and when manipulation of the joint is painful. The loose cartilage flap is removed and the flap bed curetted until the subchondral bone bleeds. Granulation tissue and, ultimately, fibrocartilage fill the curetted defect in the articular surface. The joint is thoroughly irrigated and any floating "joint mice" or bony ossicles attached to the joint capsule are removed. Recovery is predictable with appropriate surgical treatment. Osteochondrosis and OCD of the shoulder joint will cause secondary osteoarthritis, possibly causing clinical problems in later years, although osteoarthritis of the shoulder joint is usually well tolerated by dogs.

3. Altering the feeding plan may have no beneficial effects on osteochondrosis or OCD at this stage of the disease process. Excess energy and calcium intake should be avoided during the rapid growth phase between two and six months of age. (See Figure 17-3.) This puppy is slightly overweight; therefore, feeding to maintain a BCS of 2/5 can reduce biomechanical stress on the shoulder joints. Appropriate body condition is especially important considering 60 to 65% of the body weight is normally carried by the forelimbs of walking dogs. Daily energy requirement (DER) should be estimated for the ideal weight at the current age. The owner should discontinue free-choice feeding the puppy and begin meal feeding (DER divided into two or three meals per day). The owner should be shown how to assess body condition, and should record the weight and BCS of his puppy every two weeks. He should adjust the amount of food as necessary to obtain a BCS of 2/5.

Decreasing energy intake by decreasing food intake (meal feeding) and switching to a food with a lower fat level should effectively slow this puppy's growth rate. Adequate dietary protein is necessary for growth; however, excessive protein intake is not considered a risk factor for canine DOD.

Progress Notes

An arthrotomy was performed on the right shoulder and confirmed a diagnosis of OCD (Figure 2). The cartilage flap was removed and the lesion curetted. Examination six weeks later revealed normal locomotion. A decision was made not to perform surgery on the left shoulder.

Because the puppy weighed more than the upper limit for its age, a feeding plan was implemented to slow growth for the next few months. The dog's mature body weight was estimated to be 65 kg, based on knowledge of adult body weights of its parents. The puppy should attain this target body weight at 18 to 24 months of age and have a BCS of not more than 3/5. The owner was given a recommended growth curve (Figure 3), taught body condition scoring techniques and given a new feeding plan.

The food was changed to a commercial dry food with 4.14 kcal (17.29 kJ)/g, 25% protein, 12% fat and 1.1% calcium, all values reported on a dry matter basis. No other foods or supplements were fed. The initial DER was estimated to be 1.6 x resting energy requirement at the current body weight or 2,484 kcal (10.37 MJ). It was emphasized to the owner that this was only a starting point and that he would need to monitor body weight and BCS carefully, and compare body weights with values on the recommended growth curve. Food intake should be increased 10 to 15% if poor body condition occurred.

Bibliography

Zentek J, Daemmrich K, Meyer H. Zur Pathogenese futterungsbedingter Skeletterkrankungen bei Junghunden grobwuchsiger Rassen. Kleintierpraxis 1995; 40: 469-482.

CHAPTER 18

Cardiovascular Disease

Philip Roudebush

Bruce W. Keene

H. Leland Mizelle

"The sacredness and dignity of salt! This mineral is like unto the four elements—earth, air, fire and water. So universal, so necessary to life, it is the fifth element."
Jean de Marcounille, 1594

ASSESSMENT

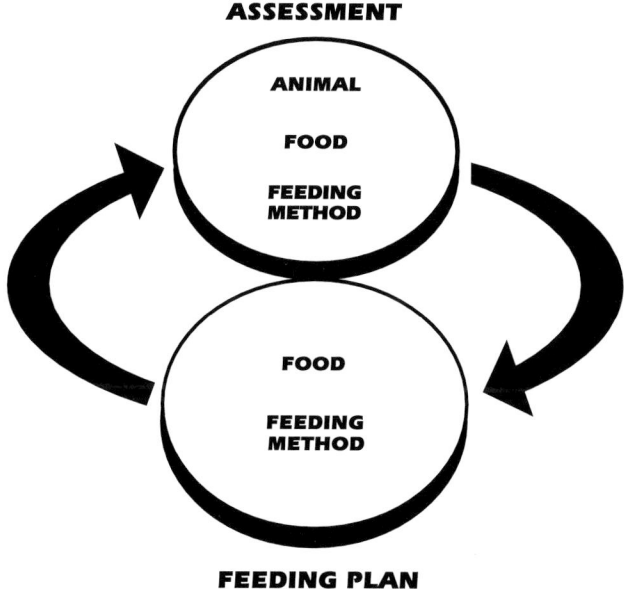

FEEDING PLAN

Note: The reader is referred to Chapter 1 for a detailed discussion of the iterative process of clinical nutrition.

CLINICAL IMPORTANCE

Cardiovascular disease and congestive heart failure (CHF) are common conditions in dogs and cats. The types and prevalence of heart disease in dogs in the United States were characterized more than 30 years ago in a survey of 5,000 dogs at the University of Pennsylvania.[1] Eleven percent of dogs had reliable signs of heart disease and another 9% had possible heart disease. Congenital heart disease has been recognized in 0.56 to 0.85% of dogs and 0.2% of cats.[1-3]

According to Buchanan, the overall prevalence of heart disease appears to be similar today, but comparable epidemiologic data for acquired heart disease in the United States are not available.[3] A clinical review in Italy found heart disease in 11% of 7,148 dogs.[4] One informal survey identified heart problems as the third leading cause of nonaccidental death of dogs.[5]

Chronic mitral valvular disease (endocardiosis) is the most common acquired cardiac abnormality in dogs, affecting more than one-third of those over 10 years of age.[3,6] The tricuspid valve is also frequently involved (approximately 30% of cases) but disease is less severe. Chronic valvular disease occurs with relatively greater frequency in small dogs, especially poodles, miniature schnauzers, Chihuahuas, cocker spaniels, fox terriers, Boston terriers, dachshunds, Pekingese, miniature pinschers and whippets.[6,7] Mitral valvular disease has been identified in more than 50% of cavalier King Charles spaniels in the United Kingdom, Sweden and the United States.[8,9] Acquired valvular disease in cats is rare.

Since 1987, dilated (congestive) cardiomyopathy in cats has decreased markedly following the discovery that

KEY WORDS & TERMS—CARDIOVASCULAR DISEASE*

Afterload	Cardiac cachexia	Hypertension
Aldosterone	Cardiac glycosides	Hypotension
Angiotensin	Cardiac output	Natriuresis
Angiotensin converting enzyme	Carnitine	Preload
(ACE)	Congestive heart failure	Renin
Arginine vasopressin (AVP)	Cor pulmonale	Taurine
Atrial natriuretic peptide/factor	Endocardiosis	Tumor necrosis factor (TNF)
(ANP/ANF)	Heart disease	Uremia
Azotemia	Heart failure	

Key words and terms are defined in the Glossary.

KEY POINTS—CARDIOVASCULAR DISEASE

1. Chronic mitral valvular disease (endocardiosis) is the most common acquired cardiac abnormality of dogs.
2. Obesity and pulmonary diseases are the most important conditions leading to a false-positive diagnosis of heart failure.
3. A new heart failure classification scheme has been developed for veterinary patients.
4. Blood pressure measurements obtained during routine hospital visits are reasonable estimates of a dog's true blood pressure.
5. Whole blood taurine concentration is a more reliable index of taurine status in cats than is plasma taurine concentration.
6. Increased concentrations of renin, aldosterone, norepinephrine and atrial natriuretic peptide occur in dogs with spontaneous heart failure.
7. Both sympathetic nervous stimulation and parasympathetic nervous withdrawal occur in patients with advanced heart disease and failure.
8. Increased levels of atrial natriuretic peptide help counteract blood volume expansion and tissue edema in CHF.
9. Obesity is a disease of blood volume expansion.
10. Elevated circulating levels of tumor necrosis factor and interleukin-1 may contribute to cardiac cachexia.
11. The mechanism of heart failure in taurine-deficient cats and dogs is poorly understood.
12. Carnitine is a critical component of enzymes that transport fatty acids into mitochondria of myocytes.
13. Chloride may be as important as sodium in the pathogenesis of CHF and some forms of hypertension.
14. Levels of sodium found in foods for cardiac patients exceed the AAFCO minimum allowance for normal cats and dogs.
15. Moist commercial dog and cat foods contain the highest average levels of sodium chloride.
16. Many sodium chloride-restricted foods have comparable or better palatability than commercial grocery or specialty brand pet foods.
17. The cost of L-carnitine supplementation in large-breed dogs may be prohibitive for some clients.
18. Hyperkalemia and renal insufficiency are potential complications of using ACE inhibitors and certain foods in patients with cardiovascular disease.
19. Serum electrolyte and magnesium concentrations and renal function should be monitored in cardiovascular patients every one to two weeks after nutritional therapy and drug therapy are initiated.

taurine deficiency was the principal cause,[10,11] and the subsequent supplementation of most commercial feline foods with taurine. One study documented that the prevalence of dilated cardiomyopathy as a cause of myocardial failure in cats decreased from 28% in 1986 to only 6% in 1989, whereas the occurrence of hypertrophic cardiomyopathy did not change.[12] Hypertrophic and restrictive cardiomyopathy are now the most common causes of myocardial failure in cats.

Various types of myocardial disease that were not recognized 30 years ago are now seen commonly in dogs.[3] Large-breed dogs, especially males, are predisposed to dilated cardiomyopathy. Doberman pinscher dogs are particularly susceptible. Hypertrophic cardiomyopathy occurs rarely in dogs.

Pulmonary vascular disease with secondary cor pulmonale is most commonly associated with *Dirofilaria immitis* infection (heartworm disease). The prevalence of this disease is high in endemic areas and in those dogs that do not routinely receive preventive medication. Pulmonary hypertension unrelated to heartworm disease appears to be uncommon, but the frequency of diagnosis has increased because of heightened awareness about the condition.[13] Pulmonary thromboembolism is most commonly associated with renal disease, hyperadrenocorticism, corticosteroid therapy, neoplasia, nephrotic syndrome, pancreatitis and immune-mediated hemolytic anemia. Primary systemic vascular disease is uncommon, but atherosclerosis and aortic or coronary thrombosis are occasionally recognized, particularly in dogs with hypothyroidism and elevated serum cholesterol concentrations. Secondary aortic thromboembolism in cats may occur with any of the forms of cardiomyopathy and is the most frequently acquired feline vascular abnormality.

Hypertension in dogs and cats appears to be more common than studies indicated 30 years ago.[3] Because blood pressure is not yet routinely measured, the prevalence of systemic hypertension in dogs and cats is still unknown. Spontaneous essential hypertension occurs in dogs, but hypertension most commonly develops secondary to chronic renal disease in both dogs and cats, hyperadrenocorticism in dogs and hyperthyroidism in cats.[14]

KEY NUTRITIONAL FACTORS—CARDIOVASCULAR DISEASE

Factors	Associated conditions	Nutritional recommendations
Sodium, chloride	Sodium, chloride and fluid retention Systemic hypertension Congestive heart failure	Avoid excess sodium chloride Restrict sodium to 0.07 to 0.25% dry matter in dogs and 0.3% dry matter in cats. Chloride levels are typically 1.5 times sodium levels.
Potassium	Hypokalemia; associated with use of loop or thiazide diuretics especially in patients receiving low potassium levels in food; associated with chronic renal failure in cats; may predispose to cardiac dysrhythmias and taurine deficiency	Oral potassium supplementation (3-5 mEq or mmol/kg body weight/day) Change to a food with a higher potassium concentration
	Hyperkalemia; associated with use of ACE inhibitors and/or potassium-sparing diuretics, especially in patients fed high dietary potassium or those with an acute uremic crisis	Withdraw potassium supplements Switch from potassium-sparing diuretic to a loop or thiazide diuretic Change to a food with a lower potassium concentration
Magnesium	Hypomagnesemia; associated with use of diuretics, especially in patients receiving low dietary magnesium; may predispose to cardiac dysrhythmias	Oral magnesium supplementation 20 to 40 mg/kg body weight/day per os (magnesium oxide) Change to a food with a higher magnesium concentration
Energy	Cachexia associated with protein-energy malnutrition and altered metabolism.	Ensure adequate energy intake
	Obesity associated with neurohumoral activation, hypertension and/or blood volume expansion	Treatment: reduce body fat while maintaining lean body mass Prevention: caloric restriction if animal is at risk
Phosphorus	Hyperphosphatemia; associated with chronic renal failure	Avoid excess phosphorus Restrict phosphorus to 0.2 to 0.3% dry matter in dogs and 0.5% in cats Consider use of phosphate binders

Taurine	Cat: dilated cardiomyopathy associated with taurine deficiency	Prevention: provide adequate taurine
		    1,000 to 2,000 mg/kg dry weight (dry extruded food)
		    2,000 to 3,000 mg/kg dry weight (moist food)
		Treatment: 250- to 500-mg taurine daily per os
		    Use veterinary therapeutic food (cardiac food) containing increased levels of taurine

	Dog: dilated cardiomyopathy in American cocker spaniels	Treatment: 500-mg taurine twice daily per os Use veterinary therapeutic food (cardiac food) containing increased levels of taurine
Carnitine	Dog: dilated cardiomyopathy	Treatment: 50- to 100-mg L-carnitine/kg body weight three times daily per os

The most frequently encountered problems associated with cardiovascular disease that require nutritional modification are fluid retention states associated with chronic CHF, primary or secondary hypertension, obesity, cachexia and myocardial diseases related to a specific nutrient deficiency (taurine- and carnitine-associated cardiomyopathy and electrolyte disorders that potentiate cardiac dysrhythmias).

ASSESSMENT

Assess the Animal

History and Physical Examination

Heart failure is a condition characterized by inadequate cardiac output and insufficient delivery of nutrients relative to tissue metabolic needs. Heart failure is not a specific disease, but a clinical syndrome caused by a variety of structural and functional disorders of the heart or great vessels. Clinical manifestations of heart failure are due to reduced cardiac output (weakness, exercise intolerance, syncope), pulmonary congestion (dyspnea,

orthopnea, cough, abnormal breath sounds with crackles and wheezes), systemic fluid retention (jugular venous distention, hepatomegaly, ascites, pleural effusion) or a combination of these conditions.

In general, the clinical manifestations of heart failure are similar irrespective of the underlying cause, although the onset may vary. Occasionally, for example, heart failure may occur abruptly and lead to acute pulmonary edema with ruptured chorda tendineae. Diagnosis of this fulminant form of heart failure is based on the history and overt, acute clinical signs. In many instances, however, heart failure becomes evident gradually; a long period of mild clinical signs that worsen precedes its diagnosis. Most of the clinical signs used as the basis for diagnosing chronic heart failure occur in other conditions.

Validity of a clinical diagnosis of heart failure in human patients was studied in a primary health care setting.[15] One-third of human patients who were initially diagnosed with heart failure were subsequently found to have other conditions that caused their clinical problems. Obesity and pulmonary diseases were the most important conditions leading to false-positive diagnosis of heart failure in this population of human patients. Obesity and chronic bronchitis often occur in dogs and cats with heart disease and cause clinical manifestations similar to those of heart fail

Table 18-1. Functional classes of heart failure.*

Class I. The asymptomatic patient
Heart disease is detectable (cardiac murmur, dysrhythmia), but the patient is not overtly affected and does not demonstrate clinical signs of heart failure.
a. Heart disease is detectable but no signs of compensation are evident, such as volume or pressure overload ventricular hypertrophy.
b. Heart disease is detectable in conjunction with radiographic or echocardiographic evidence of compensation, such as volume or pressure overload ventricular hypertrophy.

Class II. Mild to moderate heart failure
Clinical signs of heart failure are evident at rest or with mild exercise and adversely affect the quality of life. Typical clinical signs include exercise intolerance, cough, tachypnea, mild respiratory distress and mild to moderate ascites. Hypoperfusion at rest is generally not present.

Class III. Advanced heart failure
Clinical signs of CHF are immediately evident. These clinical signs include respiratory distress (dyspnea), marked ascites, profound exercise intolerance and hypoperfusion at rest. In the most severe cases, the patient is moribund and suffers from cardiogenic shock.

*Adapted from International Small Animal Cardiac Health Council. In: Recommendations for the Diagnosis of Heart Disease and the Treatment of Heart Failure in Small Animals. Academy of Veterinary Cardiology, 1994.

ure, thereby complicating the diagnosis. As an example, a small-breed dog may be admitted with moderate obesity, cough, tachypnea, exercise intolerance, abnormal breath sounds with crackles and a holosystolic murmur loudest over the mitral valve. It is important that this patient be evaluated thoroughly to determine whether the cause of the clinical signs is: 1) chronic bronchitis, 2) early heart failure, 3) obesity or 4) a combination of these conditions.

Human patients with heart disease and failure are categorized according to a functional scheme based on the signs and symptoms evident at rest and during exercise (New York Heart Association functional classes). This scheme often does not apply to veterinary patients with heart failure. Members of the International Small Animal Cardiac Health Council have developed a new classification scheme that is more applicable to veterinary patients (Table 18-1).[16] This classification system is based on anatomic diagnosis and the severity of clinical signs at rest.

Although hypertensive dogs and cats may present at any age, most often they are middle-aged to geriatric (mean age: dogs nine years; cats 15 years).[14] The strength of the peripheral pulses does not help detect systemic hypertension; absolute blood pressure numbers need to be determined. Retinal hemorrhages and detachments are common end-organ changes in patients with moderate to severe hypertension. These ocular signs are often the first evidence of cardiovascular disease, which suggests that a fundic examination should be included in the routine evaluation of all dogs and cats. Other clinical signs are related to the underlying disease that causes systemic hypertension.

Body condition is the most important assessment of the nutritional status of animals with cardiovascular disease. As will be discussed later, obesity causes cardiovascular changes that can complicate cardiovascular diseases. Treatment of the underlying cardiovascular disease may not be successful without first managing obesity. Cachexia is a syndrome of severe wasting seen clinically in a variety of diseases, especially chronic heart failure, cancer and acquired immunodeficiency syndrome. Cachexia is an additional risk factor in people with heart failure; loss of

lean body mass is a negative predictor of survival.[17] Systems for accurately assessing and scoring body condition are available for dogs and cats. (See Chapter 1.) The body condition of dogs and cats with cardiovascular disease should be followed closely as part of reassessment.

Laboratory and Other Clinical Information

MEASUREMENT OF SYSTEMIC BLOOD PRESSURE

Hypertension is often defined as that blood pressure two standard deviations above the mean for the population.[14] Most investigators agree that the systemic systolic/diastolic blood pressure in awake, untrained dogs and cats normally should not exceed 180/100 millimeters of mercury (mm Hg), with values up to 200/110 mm Hg considered borderline or mild hypertension.[14]

Direct blood pressure measurement is obtained by inserting a needle or catheter into an artery. The needle or catheter is connected to a pressure transducer and the result displayed on an oscilloscope/recording device. Anxiety and pain may falsely elevate the blood pressure of awake, restrained or uncooperative animals when measured by direct techniques.

Indirect blood pressure measurement is noninvasive and obtained with a cuff constricting a peripheral artery (leg or tail). An ultrasonic, oscillometric or photoplethysmographic transducer distal to the cuff is used to detect blood flow or arterial wall motion.[18] Blood pressure values obtained by direct and indirect methods generally correlate well, but indirect methods may produce values less than those obtained simultaneously by direct methods. In general, blood pressure measurements obtained routinely during hospital visits are reasonable estimates of a dog's true blood pressure.[19] Uncooperative, anxious animals may have elevated blood pressure measurements in the hospital setting that do not reflect normal values. A recent review of blood pressure measurements describes these techniques.[18]

SCREENING FOR CONCOMITANT DISEASE

Cardiovascular disease is frequently associated with or exacerbates underlying chronic renal disease in dogs and cats. All patients with cardiovascular disease should be screened for concomitant renal disease. This is best accomplished with a urinalysis and a serum biochemistry profile, which includes urea nitrogen, creatinine, electrolyte, calcium and phosphorus concentrations.

Hyperthyroidism in cats is a risk factor for secondary hypertrophic cardiomyopathy and systemic hypertension. Older cats with evidence of cardiovascular disease should be screened for hyperthyroidism. (See Chapter 24.)

MEASURING AND INTERPRETING TISSUE NUTRIENTS AND HORMONES

Electrolytes and Magnesium

Serum electrolyte and magnesium concentrations are important factors to assess in patients with cardiovascular disease. Abnormalities in electrolyte and magnesium homeostasis can cause cardiac dysrhythmias, decreased myocardial contractility and profound muscle weakness. Electrolyte and magnesium abnormalities can also potentiate adverse effects from cardiac glycosides and other cardiac drugs. Unfortunately, the precise diagnosis of potassium and magnesium depletion can be difficult to make because these are primarily intracellular constituents. Normal serum potassium and magnesium concentrations can occur in the presence of total body depletion of these elements; therefore, serum potassium and magnesium concentrations do not always reflect total body stores.

Taurine

Plasma and whole blood taurine concentrations are routinely measured to evaluate the taurine status of cats and dogs. Most early experimental and clinical studies used plasma taurine concentration to define taurine status. Values for plasma taurine of less than 20 to 30 nmol/ml (µmol/l) have been associated with deficiency in clinical studies involving client-owned cats[10,20] and dogs.[21]

Studies involving laboratory cats have shown that plasma, but not whole blood taurine concentrations are affected by meals and food deprivation.[22,23] Therefore, whole blood taurine concentration is a more reliable index of taurine status in cats. In general, the whole blood taurine pool is remarkably stable and declines only during prolonged depletion, whereas plasma taurine concentrations fluctuate acutely depending on availability in food. Cats with whole blood taurine concentrations consistently less than 150 nmol/ml should be considered taurine deficient.[11,23] Whole blood taurine concentrations have also been adopted by the Association of American Feed Control Officials (AAFCO) as part of its feeding protocols for cats. To successfully complete an AAFCO feeding protocol, no individual cat, kitten or queen can have a whole blood taurine concentration less than 200 nmol/ml.[24]

Assessment of urinary taurine excretion has also been advocated as an alternative to measuring plasma or whole blood taurine concentrations.[25] Urinary taurine excretion may provide vital information in the experimental setting for proper formulation of feline foods, but this assessment is probably not a practical technique for use with client-owned cats.

In North America, several laboratories routinely perform plasma and whole blood taurine assays. These laboratories are most easily accessed through regional veterinary reference laboratories that perform routine diagnostic services.

Carnitine

Many investigators have reported blood and tissue carnitine concentrations in animals. The lowest levels are usually found in serum; in contrast, heart and skeletal muscle contain very high levels of carnitine, which underscores its importance in these tissues. Normal canine and feline values are similar for total, free and esterified carnitine concentrations in plasma based on measurements from a small number of healthy animals fed a standard dry commercial food (Table 18-2).[26-29] Total carnitine concentrations in plasma are influenced by intake of carnitine in the food. Plasma concentrations will be elevated in animals that eat foods high in carnitine (e.g., raw meat or moist foods high in skeletal muscle content). To measure carnitine concentration, approximately 1 ml of heparinized plasma should be immediately separated, frozen and submitted to an appropriate laboratory.[a]

Carnitine concentrations are also routinely measured in cardiac muscle, skeletal muscle and liver.[26-29] Cardiac tissue is obtained by using a modified transvenous endomyocardial biopsy technique.[30] Skeletal muscle and liver tissue are obtained using standard biopsy techniques. Tissue specimens are blotted dry, immediately frozen in liquid nitrogen and stored at –70°C until the carnitine concentration

Table 18-2. Normal plasma carnitine concentrations of healthy dogs and cats eating commercial dry pet foods.*

Plasma carnitine (µmol/l)	Dog	Cat
Total	12-40	9-35
Free	9-36	7-30
Esters	<7	<8

*Adapted from Jacobs G, et al. American Journal of Veterinary Research 1990; 51: 1345-1348. Keene BW. In: Kirk RW, Bonagura JD, eds. Current Veterinary Therapy XI. Philadelphia, PA: WB Saunders Co, 1992; 780-783.

is measured at an appropriate laboratory.[a] Tissues for carnitine assay should not be placed in formalin. Dogs with confirmed lipid storage myopathy can have tissue carnitine assays performed at a nominal charge as part of an ongoing investigation.[29,b]

Blood Constituents Associated with Neurohumoral Activation

It is well established that activity of several neurohumoral systems is increased in many patients with chronic CHF. Elevated levels of renin, angiotensin, aldosterone and arginine vasopressin (AVP; antidiuretic hormone) occur in experimental canine models of CHF.[31-36] Increased concentrations of renin, aldosterone, norepinephrine and atrial natriuretic peptide or atrial natriuretic factor (ANP or ANF) occur in dogs with spontaneous heart disease and failure.[37-43] Aldosterone, norepinephrine and ANP concentrations also increase with the severity of heart failure.[37,38,42] Aldosterone concentrations may offer some prognostic information about the severity of heart failure.[37] Similar information is not available for cats with experimental or spontaneous heart failure.

Norepinephrine, angiotensin, ANP and AVP analyses are only available through research laboratories. Plasma renin activity and aldosterone measurements are available through several reference laboratories.

Risk Factors

Risk factors for causing or complicating cardiovascular disease include breed, obesity, renal disease, drug therapy, endocrinopathies and heartworm infection. Breed is the most important risk factor for cardiovascular disease in dogs. A number of breeds are at increased risk for several different congenital cardiovascular malformations, including patent ductus arteriosus, portacaval shunts, aortic stenosis, pulmonic stenosis, ventricular septal defects, tricuspid dysplasia, and persistent aortic arch and related vascular abnormalities. Estimated relative risks (odds ratios) are listed elsewhere by breed for many of these congenital abnormalities.[3] Chronic valvular heart disease occurs with relatively greater frequency in small dogs, whereas large dogs, especially males, are predisposed to dilated cardiomyopathy. Certain canine breeds also have characteristic cardiac dysrhythmias that may occur with or without significant cardiomegaly or signs of CHF. Finally, an increased risk of pericardial effusion is noted in golden retrievers, Labrador retrievers, German shepherd dogs, German shorthaired pointers and Akitas.[3]

Obesity occurs frequently in dogs and cats with cardiovascular disease. Obesity not only produces clinical signs that mimic those of early heart failure (i.e., exercise intolerance, tachypnea, weakness), but also causes cardiovascular changes that can exacerbate underlying cardiovascular disease.

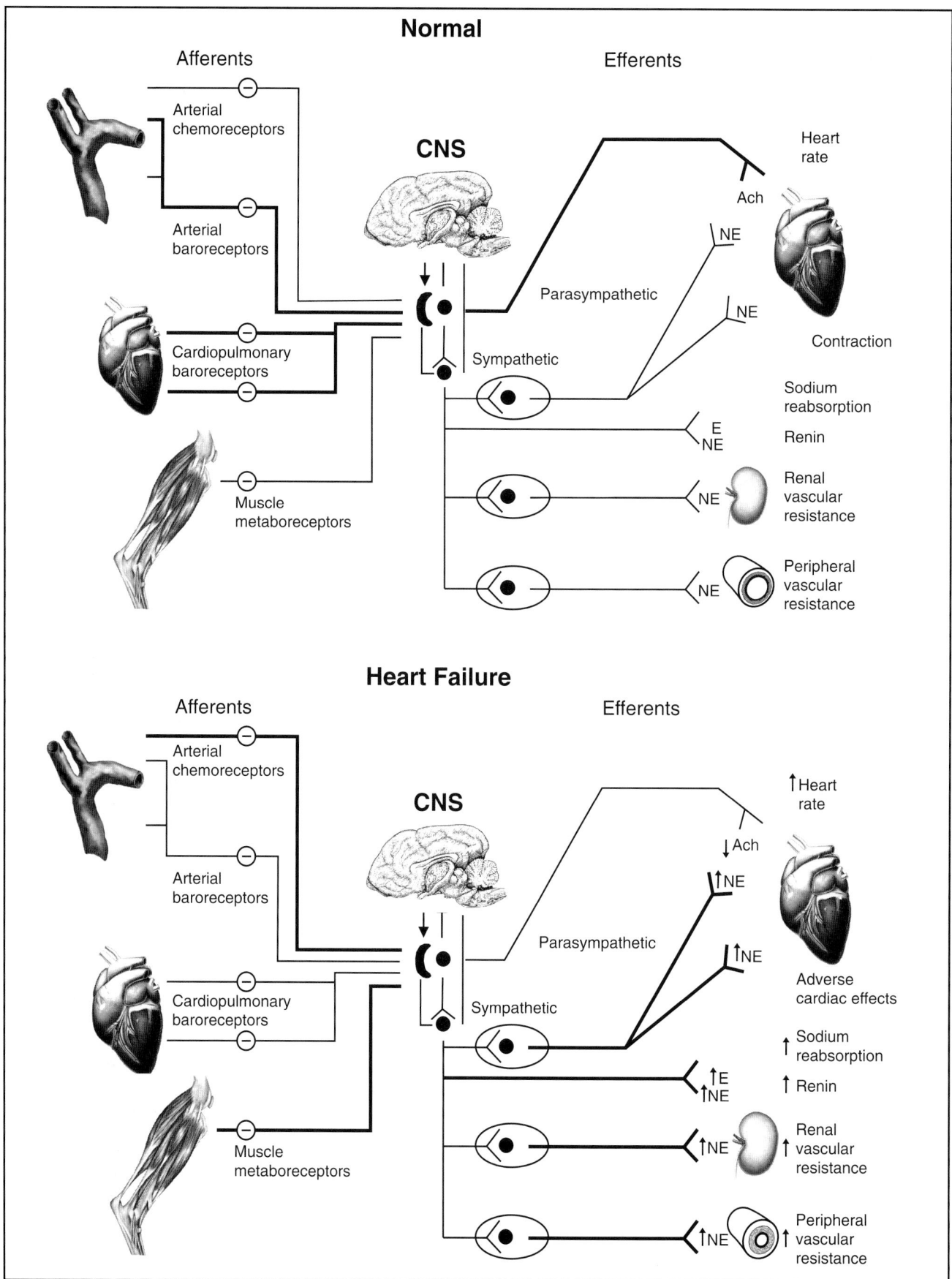

Figure 18-1. Mechanisms for generalized sympathetic activation and parasympathetic withdrawal in heart failure. Normally (top figure), inhibitory input from arterial and cardiopulmonary receptors is high and heart rate is controlled by parasympathetic input (heavy lines). With progressing heart failure (bottom figure), sympathetic activity increases with resulting increases in vascular resistance, heart rate and adverse cardiac effects (heavy lines). Key: Ach = acetylcholine, E = epinephrine, NE = norepinephrine, CNS = central nervous system. (Adapted from Floras JS. Journal of the American College of Cardiology 1993; 22 [Suppl. A]: 72A-84A.)

Chronic progressive renal disease and failure often occur in dogs and cats with cardiovascular disease, especially in older patients. Cardiac disease often exacerbates underlying renal disease because a large proportion of the cardiac output is normally destined for the kidneys. Renal disease influences the types and dosages of medications that are used to treat patients with cardiovascular disease. Chronic renal disease is also a risk factor for secondary hypertension in dogs and cats.

Therapy for CHF often includes: 1) diuretics and salt restriction to reduce preload and venous congestion, 2) cardiac glycosides to increase contractility and control supraventricular dysrhythmias and 3) vasodilators to reduce venous congestion, preload and afterload. Dehydration, systemic hypotension, renal insufficiency, electrolyte abnormalities and acid-base disturbances are all potential complications of combined pharmacologic and nutritional therapy for patients with CHF.

Hyperthyroidism is a risk factor for both hypertrophic cardiomyopathy and secondary hypertension in older cats. Hyperadrenocorticism is a risk factor for pulmonary thromboembolism. Heartworm infection is a risk factor for pulmonary vascular disease, cor pulmonale, right-sided CHF and pulmonary thromboembolism.

Etiopathogenesis

COMPENSATORY MECHANISMS IN HEART FAILURE

The first priority of the cardiovascular system is to provide oxygen and nutrients to critical organs such as the brain, kidneys and heart. The next priority is to supply nutrients to all other tissues; a final priority is to maintain normal venous pressure. In heart failure, these cardiovascular priorities are lost in reverse order. The body will sacrifice normal venous pressure to provide nutrients to tissues. Increased venous pressure values above normal often result in clinical signs of CHF. The first and second cardiovascular priorities are maintained through compensatory responses from several neurohumoral mechanisms (Table 18-3), including the sympathetic nervous system, AVP secretion and the renin-angiotensin-aldosterone (RAA) system.[44-46] In some animals, these compensatory changes ultimately result in: 1) sodium and water retention, 2) expanded extracellular fluid volume, 3) increased venous filling pressure and 4) clinical signs of cough, dyspnea, orthopnea, tachypnea, hepatomegaly and ascites.

Sympathetic Nervous System

The entire myocardium and peripheral vascular system are supplied with sympathetic nerve terminals. When cardiac output falls, the sympathetic nervous system coordinates increases in heart rate, strength of cardiac contraction and selective peripheral vascular vasoconstriction to restore hemodynamic equilibrium. Increased sympathetic discharge causes: 1) vasoconstriction of arterial resistance vessels with increased cardiac afterload, 2) increased renal neural traffic, which stimulates renin release and thus activation of the RAA system, 3) direct stimulation of renal sodium and water reabsorption and 4) splanchnic venoconstriction with central translocation of blood volume and increased cardiac preload (Figure 18-1). Sympathetic stimulation also causes the nonosmotic release of AVP. Diminished circulatory perfusion of arterial baroreceptors appears to activate simultaneously the three major vaso-

Table 18-3. Compensatory mechanisms in heart failure.

Autonomic nervous system
  Heart
    Increased heart rate
    Increased myocardial contractile stimulation
  Peripheral circulation
    Arterial vasoconstriction (increased afterload)
    Venous vasoconstriction (increased preload)
Kidney (renin-angiotensin-aldosterone)
  Arterial vasoconstriction (increased afterload)
  Venous vasoconstriction (increased preload)
  Sodium, chloride and water retention (increased preload and afterload)
  Increased myocardial contractile stimulation
Endothelin 1 (increased preload and afterload)
Arginine vasopressin (increased preload and afterload)
Atrial natriuretic peptide (decreased afterload)
Prostaglandins
Frank-Starling law of the heart
  Increased end-diastolic fiber length, volume and pressure (increased preload)
Hypertrophy
Peripheral oxygen delivery
  Redistribution of cardiac output
  Altered oxygen-hemoglobin dissociation
  Increased oxygen extraction by tissues
Anaerobic metabolism

constrictor systems: 1) the sympathetic nervous system, 2) the RAA system and 3) the nonosmotic release of AVP.

Generalized neurohumoral excitation occurs with impaired parasympathetic control of heart rate.[47] The pathophysiologic implications of parasympathetic withdrawal in patients with heart failure have not been fully investigated.

Excessive sympathetic drive to the periphery can exacerbate the hemodynamic derangements of heart failure by increasing preload and afterload. Sympathetic activation occurs in dogs with spontaneous heart failure.[38] Compared with clinically normal dogs, dogs with heart failure due to chronic mitral valvular disease or dilated cardiomyopathy have increased plasma norepinephrine concentrations that correlate positively with the clinical severity of disease.[38] Dogs with the most severe degree of heart failure have mean norepinephrine concentrations significantly greater than those of dogs with all other functional classes of heart failure.

Renal-Adrenal-Pituitary Interactions

In normal hearts and in those affected with mild disease, sympathoadrenal stimulation is the primary mechanism for adjusting to transient increases in workload.[44] However, as cardiovascular disease progresses, it imposes chronic, sustained changes in hemodynamics that require more stable, long-term adaptations. In this regard, the kidney plays a pivotal role in expanding blood volume and facilitating ventricular filling (increased preload).

Blood volume expansion results from renal conservation of sodium, chloride and water brought about by a combination of intrarenal hemodynamic alterations and neurohumoral stimulation. A decrease in cardiac output and blood pressure decreases renal perfusion pressure, which triggers renin release from the adjacent juxtaglomerular cells. Renin release is also stimulated by a decrease in the amount of sodium and chloride delivered to the distal renal tubules and by direct adrenergic stimulation of the juxtaglomerular cells. (See Sympathetic Nervous System above.) Renin acts on the circulating substrate angiotensinogen to produce angiotensin I. This relatively inactive decapeptide

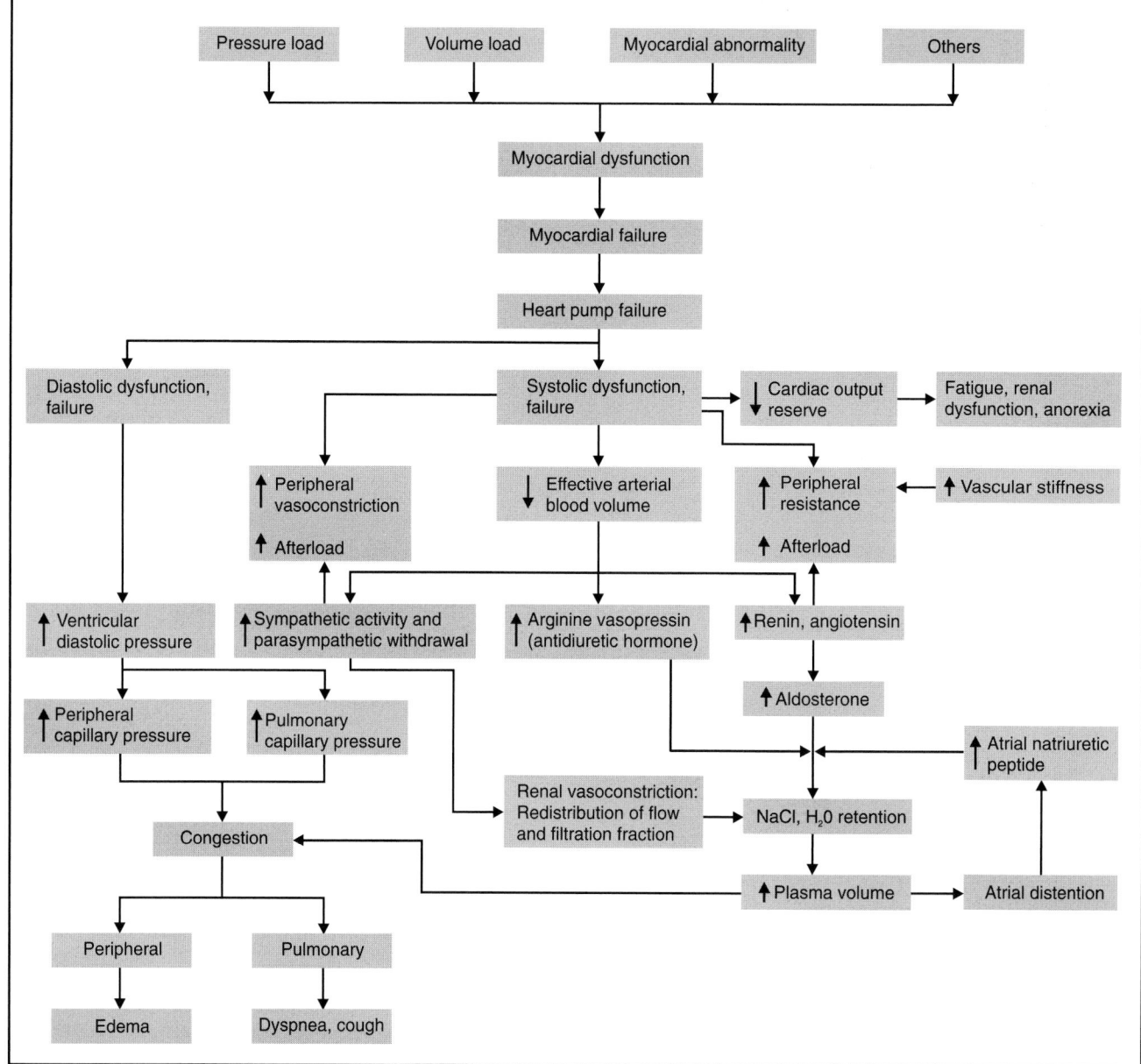

Figure 18-2. Schema of the sequence of events in heart failure. An increased load or myocardial abnormality leads to myocardial failure and eventually to heart failure. This results in increased sympathetic activity, increased levels of renin-angiotensin-aldosterone, pulmonary and peripheral congestion and edema and decreased cardiac output reserve. (Adapted from Schlant RC, Sonnenblick EH. Pathophysiology of heart failure. In: Schlant RC, Alexander RW, eds. The Heart, 8th ed. New York, NY: McGraw-Hill, 1994; 525.)

is converted by a peptidase enzyme, angiotensin converting enzyme (ACE), to the octapeptide angiotensin II.

Angiotensin II counters a decline in effective arterial blood volume by serving as a potent constrictor of both veins and arteries, and as a regulator of sodium-potassium homeostasis. Venoconstriction facilitates the return of blood to the heart and increases cardiac preload. Arteriolar vasoconstriction helps maintain systemic blood pressure. Angiotensin II also plays an important role in maintaining blood pressure and volume by stimulating secretion of aldosterone from the adrenal cortex. Aldosterone promotes reabsorption of sodium and chloride, and thus water, from the distal renal tubules and collecting ducts. The effects of aldosterone on sodium excretion may be less important than the direct intrarenal actions of angiotensin II. Studies in dogs support the theory that the intrarenal

action of angiotensin II itself increases sodium and water retention.[48] Angiotensin II also stimulates thirst, which facilitates expansion of blood and interstitial fluid volume. Blood levels of aldosterone tend to parallel those of renin and angiotensin II.[32] If effective blood volume is restored, the stimulus for RAA secretion is withdrawn. However, if cardiovascular disease is severe, these hormones continue to stimulate the kidneys and tissue edema ensues or worsens (Figures 18-2 and 18-3).

In addition to the RAA system, a locally active paracrine renin-angiotensin system may exist in a number of tissues, particularly those associated with cardiovascular homeostasis.[49,50] ACE activity, renin substrate and renin-like enzymatic activity have been found in a number of sites including vascular, cardiac, renal, brain and adrenal tissues. Tissue renin-angiotensin activity may con-

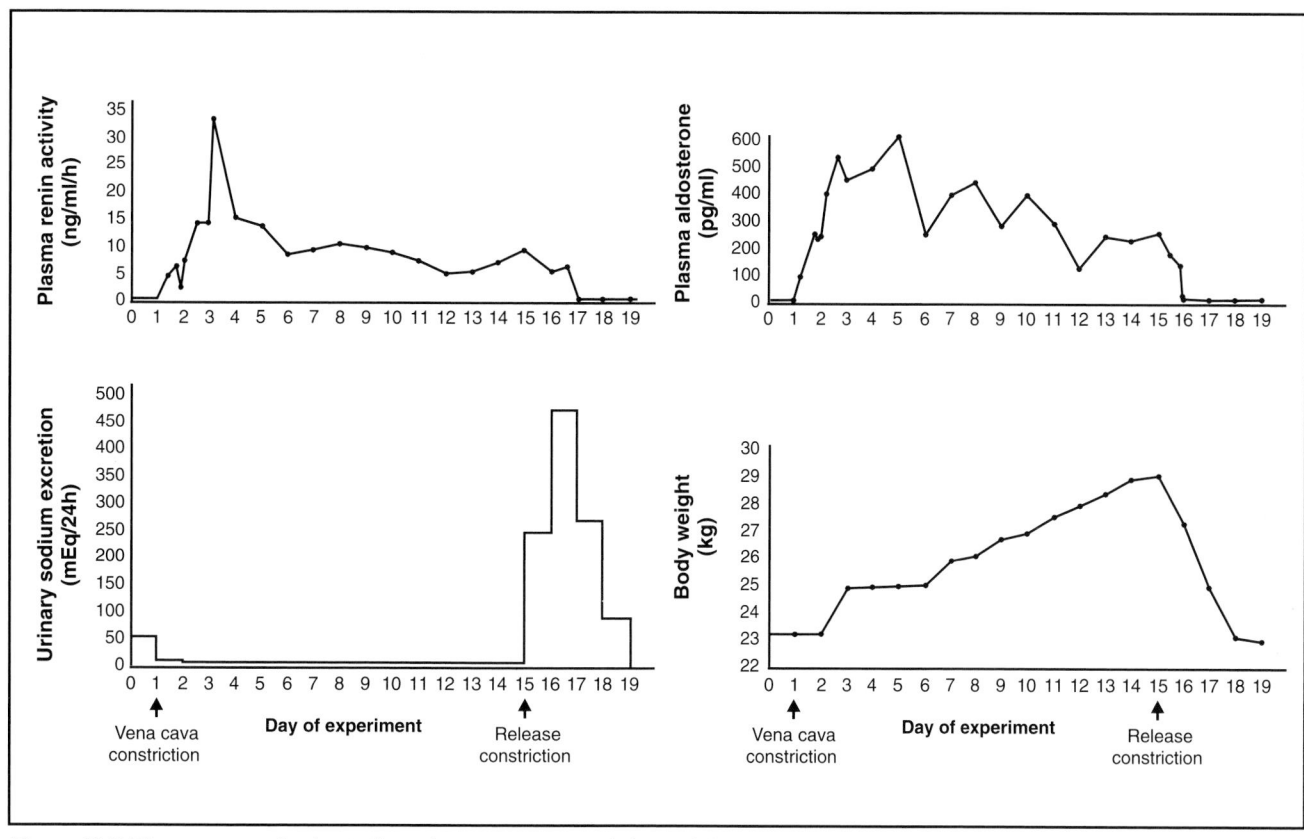

Figure 18-3. The response of a dog to thoracic vena cava constriction and the development of moderate to severe CHF. The first arrow indicates when vena cava constriction was applied. Note the persistent elevation in plasma renin activity (PRA) and plasma aldosterone (PA) concentration with a subsequent decrease in urinary sodium excretion and increase in body weight. The second arrow denotes when vena cava constriction was released. Note the rapid decrease in PRA and PA concentration with marked excretion of excess sodium in the urine and decrease in body weight. (Adapted from Watkins L, et al. Journal of Clinical Investigation 1976; 57: 1606-1617.)

tribute to the pathophysiology of heart failure, but this is a topic of considerable debate.[48] Further studies are needed to elucidate the role of extrarenal renin in the development and progression of heart failure.

AVP is secreted by the posterior lobe of the pituitary gland in response to nonosmotic stimuli. (See Sympathetic Nervous System above.) AVP is a potent vasoconstrictor and increases thirst and permeability of cortical and medullary collecting tubules, which allows reabsorption of free water. AVP secretion does not play a major role in the pathogenesis of edema. However, inappropriate AVP secretion probably plays a role in the pathogenesis of the hyponatremia associated with CHF.

Elevated levels of renin, angiotensin, aldosterone and AVP occur in experimental models of CHF in dogs (Table 18-4).[31-36] Plasma renin activity and aldosterone concentrations are also increased in dogs with spontaneous heart disease and failure.[37,41,43] As disease in human patients progresses from early asymptomatic (heart disease but no heart failure) or mildly symptomatic left ventricular dysfunction to symptomatic heart failure, neuroendocrine mechanisms are progressively activated.[51] The point at which significant neuroendocrine activation occurs in dogs and cats with spontaneous heart disease and failure has not been well documented.

Cardiorenal Interactions

The volume expansion induced by activation of the RAA system is helpful to a point, after which deleterious clinical signs of pulmonary and peripheral edema begin to develop. ANP, primarily of atrial origin, counteracts these effects. An increase in transmural pressure (atrial distention or stretch) causes release of ANP, which triggers natriuresis and vasodilatation. ANP acts directly on the kidneys to: 1) cause diuresis through increased sodium and chloride excretion, 2) promote vasodilatation and 3) suppress aldosterone secretion and plasma renin activity. The last effect is presumably a result of the increase in sodium and chloride delivery to the distal tubule and macula densa.

Table 18-4. Cardiac and humoral data from an experimental model of congestive heart failure in dogs.*

Parameter	Day			
	0	**5**	**14**	**20**
PAP (mm Hg)	13	25	32	13
PRA (ng/ml/h)	4	10	17	4
Ang II (pg/ml)	35	60	200	30
Aldo (pg/ml)	5	15	32	5
AVP (pg/ml)	10	10	25	8
POsm (mOsm/kg)	303	301	296	310
CO (l/min)	3.5	–	1.6	3.5

Key: PAP = pulmonary artery pressure
PRA = plasma renin activity
Ang II = angiotensin II
Aldo = aldosterone
AVP = arginine vasopressin
POsm = plasma osmolality
CO = cardiac output

*Values are means from six dogs that underwent rapid ventricular pacing for 14 days and developed CHF. Note the increased concentrations of renin, angiotensin II, aldosterone and arginine vasopressin during heart failure (Days 5 and 14), which subsequently returned to normal when pacing was stopped and heart failure resolved (Day 20). Adapted from Riegger AJG, Liebau G. Clinical Science 1982; 62: 465-469.

Table 18-5. Cardiovascular and neurohumoral adaptations that occur during the transition from lean to obese body condition.

Increased perfusion requirements of expanding adipose tissue
Elevated cardiac output
Abnormal left ventricular function
Variable blood pressure response (normotensive to hypertensive)
Increased retention of sodium and water by the kidney with subsequent increase in plasma volume
Increased plasma aldosterone and norepinephrine concentrations
Increased left atrial pressure
Increased heart rate
Exercise intolerance

Table 18-6. Comparison of cardiovascular and neurohumoral data from a group of obese adolescent people (Group A), a group of age-matched nonobese individuals (Group B) and a subset of Group A that lost more than 1 kg of body weight (Group C).*

Parameter	Obese (A)	Nonobese (B)	Weight loss (C)
No. subjects	60	18	36
Body fat (%)	44	22	38
BP (mm Hg)	92	75	82
CO (l/min)	11.9	7.6	9.5
PV (ml)	3,896	2,665	3,158
Plasma insulin (10^{-2} IU/l)	26	9	16
Plasma Aldo (pmol/l)	332	200	241
Plasma NE (nmol/l)	2.8	1.6	1.5
PRA (ng/l/sec)	0.36	0.50	–

Key: BP = blood pressure
CO = cardiac output
PV = plasma volume
Aldo = aldosterone
NE = norepinephrine
PRA = plasma renin activity

*Note that the obese group (A) had higher blood volume, blood pressure and neurohumoral activation than the control group (B). These values moved toward normal after weight loss was achieved (C). Adapted from Rocchini AP, et al. New England Journal of Medicine 1989; 321: 580-585.

Studies have demonstrated a significant natriuretic and diuretic response using physiologic levels of ANP in normal dogs and dogs with experimental heart failure.[32,52,53] The renin-inhibiting effects of ANP may be dependent on the degree of activation of the RAA system.[54]

Although ANP is unable to normalize hemodynamics and natriuresis, it appears to provide an important modulating effect on the pathogenesis of CHF. Elevated ANP concentrations occur in dogs with spontaneous heart failure; further, ANP concentration increases with increasing severity of heart failure.[39,40,42]

CHF-Associated Hyponatremia

Although the precise pathogenesis of CHF-associated hyponatremia remains controversial, the important factors can be divided into two categories.[55] First, the increase in plasma angiotensin II concentration promotes thirst resulting in greater water intake. Second, renal diluting ability is impaired because the delivery of glomerular filtrate to the distal renal tubule is decreased (resulting from a reduced glomerular filtration rate and enhanced reabsorption proximally) and the plasma levels of AVP are increased. Both of these abnormalities might be mediated in part by angiotensin II. The osmotically inappropriate increase in plasma AVP concentration may be caused by a downward resetting of the osmostat because of a reduction in the effective blood volume.[55] Aggressive use of diuretics may also contribute to the pathogenesis of hyponatremia in some animals.

CHF-associated hyponatremia is an important marker of poor prognosis in people with heart failure; it is seen almost exclusively in decompensated patients.[56] People with heart failure and hyponatremia seem to have decreased renal blood flow, higher serum urea nitrogen concentrations, lower blood pressure and higher plasma renin activity.[55,56] Anecdotal reports also suggest that hyponatremic animals in CHF have a poorer prognosis.

OBESITY

Obesity has profound cardiovascular consequences. From a cardiovascular perspective, obesity is a disease of blood volume expansion with: 1) elevated cardiac output, 2) increased plasma and extracellular fluid volume, 3) increased neurohumoral activation, 4) reduced urinary sodium and water excretion, 5) increased heart rate, 6) abnormal systolic and diastolic ventricular function, 7) exercise intolerance and 8) variable blood pressure response (Table 18-5).[57,58]

Obese people have increased plasma volume, cardiac output and plasma insulin, aldosterone and norepinephrine concentrations when compared with age-matched nonobese individuals (Table 18-6).[59] These changes occur whether the individuals eat high- or low-salt foods. Increases in blood pressure, heart rate, cardiac output, left atrial pressure and extracellular fluid volume also occur in dogs with experimentally induced obesity.[60,61] Blood pressure always increases with increasing weight in dogs, regardless of the initial blood pressure.

The tendency toward blood volume expansion and neurohumoral activation in obese animals parallels the compensatory changes that often occur in animals with cardiac disease. Obesity, therefore, may have profound adverse effects in animals with concomitant cardiovascular disease.

Body weight and blood pressure correlate strongly in people. Hypertension occurs more often in obese individuals than in nonobese individuals.[57] The increase in blood pressure may be due to the combined effects of hyperinsulinemia, hyperaldosteronemia and increased sympathetic nervous system activity that characteristically occurs in obesity.[59] Hyperinsulinemia and blood pressure elevation also occur in dogs that have become rapidly obese.[62] Hyperinsulinemia markedly reduces urinary sodium excretion (antinatriuresis) with resultant sodium and water retention,[63-65] possibly contributing to blood pressure changes. However, hyperinsulinemia for up to 28 days at levels comparable to those found in obese hypertensive people does not elevate mean arterial pressure in dogs with reduced renal mass even when sodium intake is high.[63] This finding suggests that chronic hyperinsulinemia per se cannot account for obesity-associated hypertension. Further studies are needed to elucidate the pathophysiology of blood pressure responses and hypertension in obese animals.

CACHEXIA

Cachexia is a syndrome of weight loss (unintentional loss of more than 10% body weight), lean tissue wasting and anorexia seen clinically in a variety of diseases, including chronic heart failure. The loss of lean body mass seen in cachexia is caused by a mismatch between food intake and nutritional requirements, resulting in negative nitrogen and energy balances.[17] These imbalances may be due to inadequate intake, excessive losses or altered metabolism (Figure 18-4).

In patients with heart failure, anorexia may be due to the heart failure itself (dyspnea, fatigue), concomitant dis-

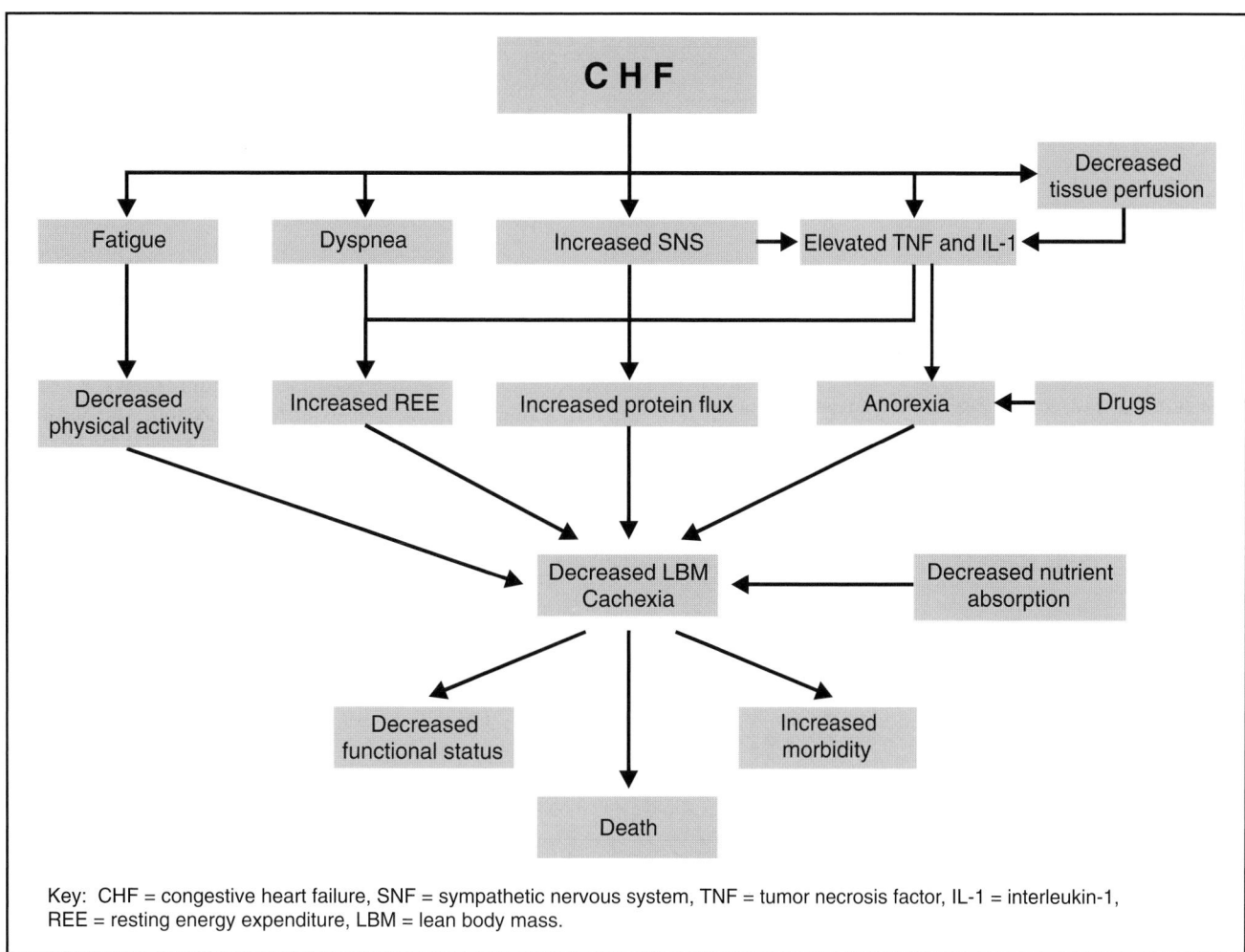

Figure 18-4. The cascade of factors in CHF that contributes to loss of lean body mass and cardiac cachexia. (Adapted from Freeman LM, Roubenoff R. Nutrition Reviews 1994; 52: 340-347.)

ease (nausea associated with renal failure), use of drugs that cause nausea (cardiac glycosides, ACE inhibitors) or sudden nutritional changes. However, the rate of loss of lean body mass with cardiac cachexia exceeds that attributable to anorexia alone. With simple starvation, most weight loss is loss of fat mass, whereas lean tissue is relatively spared, at least early on. Cachexia involves depletion of lean body mass. Physical inactivity may also contribute to loss of lean body mass because exercise is routinely restricted in patients with moderate to severe heart failure.

Altered metabolism appears to play a role in the pathogenesis of cachexia (Figure 18-4). Resting energy expenditure is elevated in some people with heart failure,[66] and may be caused by increased ventilatory effort, sympathetic nervous system activity and concentrations of certain cytokines, specifically tumor necrosis factor (TNF, cachectin) and interleukin-1 (IL-1). Elevated serum TNF concentrations occur in people, dogs and cats with CHF.[67-69] Both TNF and IL-1 cause cachexia by suppressing food intake and altering metabolism.[70-74] TNF suppresses the expression of several genes that encode for essential lipogenic enzymes, including lipoprotein lipase, and promotes the breakdown of adipose tissue and skeletal muscle.[70-74] TNF may also change the normal metabolic adaptation that accompanies caloric restriction and thus contribute to the nutritional imbalances observed in cachectic patients.[71]

As heart failure worsens, tissue perfusion and renal blood flow decline progressively. The kidneys release renin and prostaglandins, particularly prostaglandin E_2, into the circulation in response to decreased renal blood flow. Prostaglandin E_2 stimulates production of TNF from monocytes in vitro.[67] Further studies are needed to confirm whether this pathogenic mechanism occurs in animals with cardiac cachexia and to explore the interaction of TNF with IL-1 and other cytokines.

RELATIONSHIP OF TAURINE DEFICIENCY TO MYOCARDIAL DISEASE

Taurine is an essential amino acid in cats. Cats have a limited ability to synthesize taurine from cysteine and methionine because their tissues contain low concentrations of cysteine dioxygenase and cysteine sulfinate acid decarboxylase, key enzymes in the synthesis of taurine. Cats must also use taurine exclusively for conjugation of bile acids, which contributes to an obligatory loss of taurine. The decreased ability to synthesize taurine and the continuous obligatory losses predispose cats to taurine deficiency when they eat foods with low taurine concentrations.

Pion and colleagues first reported the association of feline dilated cardiomyopathy with low plasma concentrations of taurine in 1987.[10] This observation was subsequently confirmed by large studies in North America and Europe.[20] Treatment with oral taurine supplements signifi-

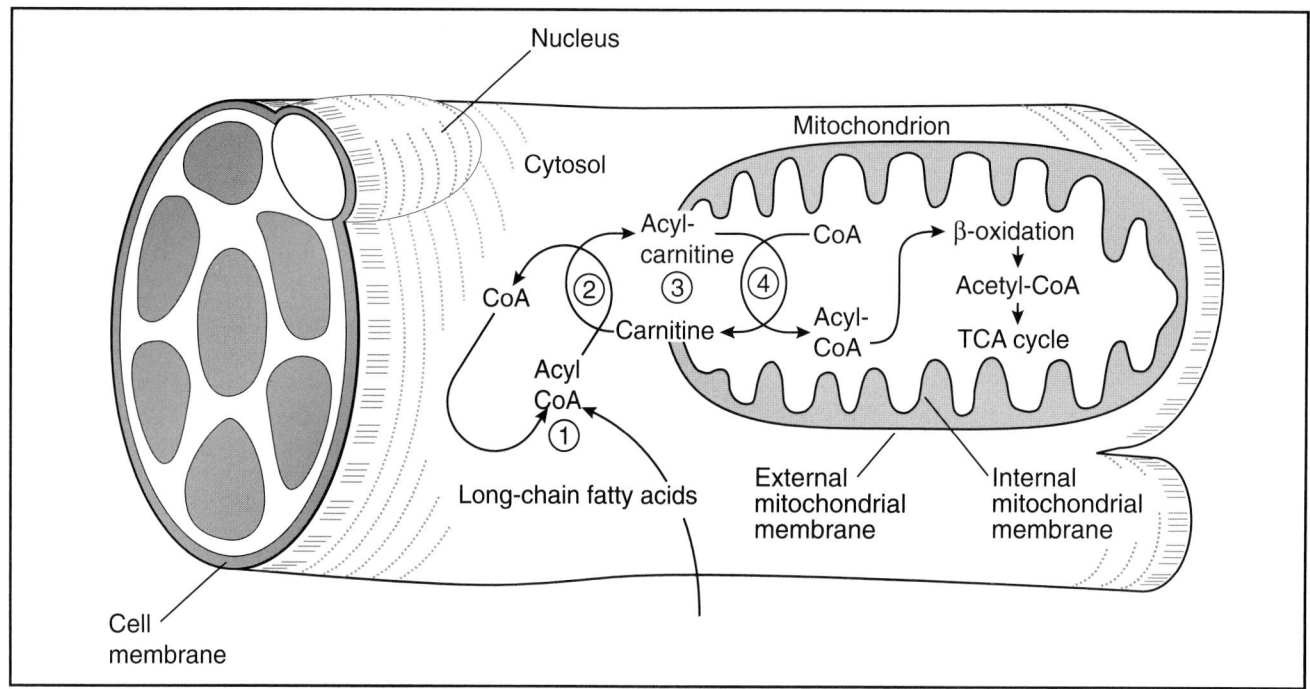

Figure 18-5. Carnitine is essential for aerobic mitochondrial energy production and assists in the transit of energy (ATP) into the cytoplasm, where it provides the fuel for cellular functions. After entry into the cell, fatty acids are activated to form acyl-CoA (1). The acyl-CoA can then be transported into the mitochondrion as acyl-carnitine (2) via a carnitine-dependent shuttle (3). Acyl-carnitine then undergoes beta-oxidation to acetyl-CoA on the inner mitochondrial membrane (4) for entry into the TCA cycle and production of ATP. Secondarily, carnitine is involved in processes that prevent accumulation of toxic metabolites inside the mitochondrion. (Adapted from Neu H. Kleintierpraxis; 40: 197-220.)

cantly improved clinical signs, restored myocardial function and improved survival of cats with dilated cardiomyopathy. Since 1987, supplementation of most commercial cat foods with taurine has resulted in a marked decline in the number of feline dilated cardiomyopathy cases. Several controlled experiments support the clinical studies. Myocardial taurine concentrations are reduced and left ventricular dilatation and myocardial dysfunction occur in cats fed foods low in taurine.[75-77] However, idiopathic dilated cardiomyopathy is occasionally diagnosed in cats that show no evidence of taurine deficiency, and the condition does not improve with taurine supplementation.[20] Dilated cardiomyopathy has also been associated with plasma taurine deficiency and low myocardial taurine concentrations in captive foxes[78] and a small number of dogs.[21,79,80]

The mechanism of heart failure in taurine-deficient cats and dogs is poorly understood. Taurine has been suggested to function in osmoregulation, calcium modulation and inactivation of free radicals.[80] Other unidentified factors may be involved in the development of myocardial failure in animals with taurine deficiency. Many cats fed taurine-deficient foods for prolonged periods fail to develop clinical myocardial dysfunction. Dilated cardiomyopathy and heart failure may result from an inciting or contributing factor or factors in combination with taurine deficiency.[77]

Several studies have demonstrated an association between taurine and potassium balance in cats.[81] Inadequate potassium intake may be sufficient to induce significant taurine depletion and cardiovascular disease in healthy cats.[81] Female cats with dilated cardiomyopathy have significantly lower plasma taurine concentrations than do similarly affected male cats.[82] This finding suggests that male cats are more prone to developing taurine-

dependent dilated cardiomyopathy than are female cats, or they are more prone to developing clinical signs associated with cardiac decompensation at higher plasma taurine concentrations.[82]

RELATIONSHIP OF CARNITINE DEFICIENCY TO MYOCARDIAL DISEASE

L-carnitine is a small, water-soluble, vitamin-like quaternary amine found in high concentrations in mammalian heart and skeletal muscle. In dogs, L-carnitine is synthesized from the amino acids lysine and methionine, primarily in the liver. A poorly understood transport mechanism concentrates L-carnitine in cardiac and skeletal myocytes.

Although the heart uses various metabolic substrates to maintain the constant energy supply needed to sustain effective contraction and relaxation, it is well established that long-chain fatty acids are quantitatively the most important. Carnitine is a critical component of the mitochondrial membrane enzymes that transport activated fatty acids in the form of acyl-carnitine esters across the mitochondrial membranes to the matrix, where beta-oxidation and subsequent high-energy phosphate generation occur (Figure 18-5). In addition to its role in fatty acid transport, free carnitine serves as a mitochondrial detoxifying agent by accepting (or "scavenging") acyl groups and other potentially toxic metabolites and transporting them out of the mitochondria as carnitine esters.[80]

A subset of dogs with dilated cardiomyopathy apparently suffers from myopathic carnitine deficiency and may respond to carnitine supplementation.[28,80] Plasma carnitine deficiency appears to be a specific but insensitive marker for myocardial carnitine deficiency in dogs with dilated cardiomyopathy;[28,80] unfortunately, dogs with myocardial carnitine deficiency do not always have low plasma carnitine concentrations. Most dogs in which myocardial carnitine deficiency has been associated with dilated cardiomyopathy fall into the classification of myopathic carnitine deficiency (i.e., decreased myocardial carnitine concentrations in the presence of normal or elevated plasma carnitine concentrations). Many of these dogs may suffer from a membrane transport defect that prevents adequate amounts of carnitine from moving into the myocardium from the plasma at plasma carnitine concentrations found in dogs fed most commercial foods. Systemic carnitine deficiency (decreased plasma and myocardial carnitine concentrations) accounts for approximately 20% of the cases.

HYPERTENSION

Regulation of systemic blood pressure involves complex relationships between central and peripheral nervous, renal, endocrine and vascular systems.[14] Most people with hypertension have essential hypertension, which means their hypertension occurs without a discernible organic cause (primary or idiopathic hypertension). Hypertension secondary to an obvious underlying cause is more common in dogs and cats.

The kidneys ultimately provide long-term control of blood pressure because they are able to excrete sodium and water.[83] This control is accomplished by manipulating the determinants of systemic blood pressure: cardiac output and total peripheral resistance (BP = CO x TPR). Cardiac output is related to heart rate and stroke volume (CO = HR x SV). Diseases associated with hypertension that increase heart rate include: 1) hyperthyroidism, 2) anemia, 3) hyperviscosity, 4) polycythemia and 5) pheochromocytoma. Increased stroke volume may occur during hypervolemic states, but is usually due to increased retention of sodium, chloride and water. Renal failure, hyperadrenocorticism and hyperaldosteronism may cause increased total body sodium, chloride and water.

Activation of the RAA pathway may elevate blood pressure by increasing stroke volume and total peripheral resistance. Angiotensin II is a potent vasoconstrictor, and angiotensin II and aldosterone stimulate renal sodium and chloride retention. Increased arteriolar tone, sensitivity to circulating vasopressors and levels of circulating catecholamines and decreased arteriolar elasticity may also increase total peripheral resistance.

Common causes of secondary hypertension include: 1) chronic progressive renal disease in dogs and cats (glomerulonephritis, amyloidosis, chronic interstitial nephritis, pyelonephritis, polycystic renal disease), 2) hyperadrenocorticism in dogs and 3) hyperthyroidism in cats. The "target organs" or end-organs or systems that appear most sensitive to increased blood pressure include the eyes, kidneys, cardiovascular system and cerebrovascular system.[14] Clinical signs related to end-organ damage are usually the reason an animal with hypertension is brought to a veterinarian for examination.

PLEURAL EFFUSION

Hydrostatic and oncotic forces (Starling's forces) are balanced within the pleurae and pleural space. Hydrostatic and oncotic pressures within the systemic circulation, pulmonary circulation and intrapleural space favor transudation of pleural fluid from the parietal pleura (pleura covering the inner chest wall) into the pleural space with subsequent absorption of the fluid into the visceral pleura's

vasculature.[84] The result is a continuous flow of fluid through the pleural space. This delicate balance can be disrupted by any disorder that alters oncotic pressure, systemic or pulmonary capillary pressure, lymphatic compliance, capillary permeability or effective pleural surface area.

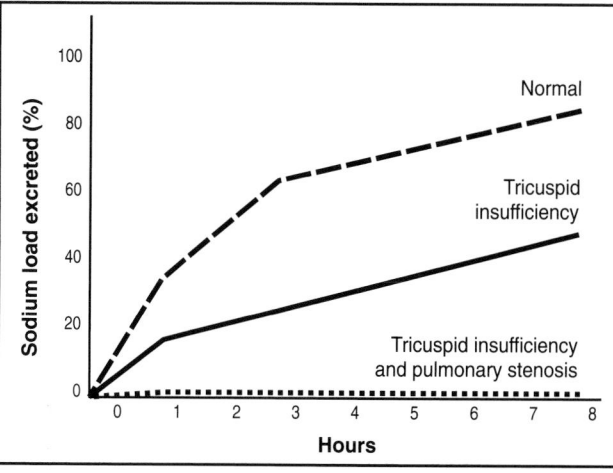

Figure 18-6. The cumulative excretion of sodium after a sodium load in a normal dog (top curve), the same dog with tricuspid insufficiency (middle curve) and the same dog with combined tricuspid insufficiency and pulmonary stenosis with the development of CHF (bottom curve). The inability of the dog to excrete excess sodium is the result of compensatory mechanisms that occur with advanced heart disease. (Adapted from Barger AC, et al. American Journal of Physiology 1955; 180: 249-260.)

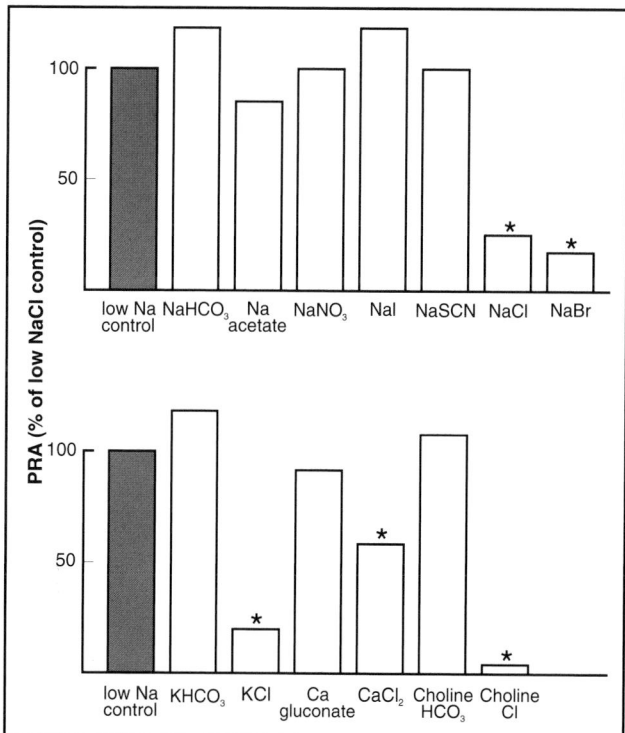

Figure 18-7. Effect of nutritional loading with different sodium and chloride salts on plasma renin activity (PRA) in sodium chloride-deprived rats. Bars marked with * are significantly different (p<0.05) compared with the low-sodium control. These data suggest that chloride is an important determinant of renin secretion by the kidneys. (Adapted from Kotchen TA, et al. Journal of Laboratory Clinical Medicine 1987; 110: 533-539.)

Table 18-7. Sodium content of selected foods.*

Food	Amounts	Sodium (mg)
Bread, cereals and potatoes		
Recommended		
Potato	1 (medium)	<5
Polished rice	1/2 cup	1-10
Macaroni	1 cup	1-10
Puffed wheat	1 oz	1-10
Spaghetti	1 cup	1-10
Not recommended		
Bread	1 slice	200
Pretzel	1	275
Potato chips	1 oz	300
Corn chips	1 oz	230
Margarine and oil		
Recommended		
Unsalted margarine	1 tsp	0-1
Vegetable shortening	1 tbs	0-1
Not recommended		
Mayonnaise	1 tbs	60-90
Dairy products		
Not recommended		
Milk (regular and skim)	1 cup	122
Cream cheese	1 1/2 oz	100-120
Cottage cheese	3 oz	200-300
American cheese	1 oz	200-300
Butter	1 tsp	50
Meats, poultry, fish		
Recommended		
Beef (fresh)	3 1/2 oz	50
Pork (fresh)	3 1/2 oz	62
Lamb (fresh)	3 1/2 oz	84
Chicken (no skin)		
Light meat	3 1/2 oz	64
Dark meat	3 1/2 oz	86
Turkey (no skin)		
Light meat	3 1/2 oz	82
Dark meat	3 1/2 oz	98
Not recommended		
Egg	1	70
Bacon	2 slices	385
Ham (processed)	3 oz	940
Frankfurter	1	560
Tuna (canned)	1 can	320
Vegetables (fresh or dietetic canned)		
Recommended		
Green beans	1/2 cup	<5
Peas	1/2 cup	<5
Green pepper	1/4 cup	<5
Tomato	1	<5
Lettuce	1/4 cup	<5
Corn	1/2 cup	<5
Cucumber	1/2 cup	<5
Not recommended		
Most canned vegetables	1/2 cup	190-450
Fruits		
Most fresh and canned fruits are low in sodium and are permitted		
Other food items		
Not recommended		
Pizza, cheese	1 slice	650
Macaroni with cheese	1 cup	1,000
Peanut butter	1 tbs	81
Dessert		
Recommended		
Sherbet	1/2 cup	15-25
Gelatins	1/2 cup	60-85
Ice cream	1/2 cup	60-85
Puddings	1/2 cup	100-200
Cookies	1	35-100

*Adapted from Morris ML Jr, Ettinger SJ. In: Ettinger SJ, Feldman EC, eds. Textbook of Veterinary Internal Medicine, 4th ed. Philadelphia, PA: WB Saunders Co, 1995; 237.

Biventricular CHF with systemic and pulmonary venous hypertension is a primary cause of pleural effusion. However, other causes of pleural effusion can masquerade as heart failure and may occur in patients with known heart disease, especially older dogs and cats. Other common causes of pleural effusion include diseases that increase capillary permeability and alter the normal flow and absorption of pleural fluid (e.g., primary intrathoracic or metastatic malignancy, pleural space infection, traumatic diaphragmatic hernia with incarceration of abdominal viscera).

Chylothorax is the accumulation of intestinal lymph (chyle) in the pleural space. This milky fluid has a high concentration of chylomicrons and triglycerides (the triglyceride concentration usually exceeds 100 mg/dl) and is low in cholesterol (the triglyceride-cholesterol ratio is greater than 1).[85] The etiology of chylothorax is poorly understood, but has been associated with: 1) traumatic leakage, 2) diaphragmatic hernia, 3) lymphosarcoma, 4) cranial mediastinal masses, 5) pulmonary neoplasia, 6) dirofilariasis, 7) congenital abnormalities of the thoracic duct and 8) CHF. Experimental and clinical evidence suggests that cranial mediastinal lymphangiectasia in cats is produced by either a functional or mechanical obstruction to thoracic duct flow. Obstruction of blood flow to the heart via the cranial vena cava, increased lymph flow from biventricular heart failure, elevated central venous pressure and direct duct obstruction may also contribute to lymphangectasia and chyle accumulation in the pleural space.[86]

Removal of large volumes of chyle via thoracentesis or chest drains may cause dehydration, electrolyte imbalances and protein-calorie malnutrition. A balance must be established between adequately evacuating the pleural space to prevent respiratory distress and meeting the animal's nutritional, fluid and electrolyte needs.

Key Nutritional Factors

Because CHF is associated with retention of sodium, chloride and water, these nutrients are of primary importance in patients with cardiovascular disease. Within a few hours of ingesting high levels of sodium, normal dogs and cats easily excrete the excess in their urine. Early in the course of cardiac disease, animals may lose this ability to excrete excess sodium because of compensatory mechanisms described earlier. In one experimental model, creation of valvular insufficiency in a dog reduced the excretion of excess sodium by almost 50% (Figure 18-6).[87] As heart disease worsens and CHF ensues, the ability to excrete excess sodium is severely depressed (Figure 18-6).

In the past, retention of sodium was primarily implicated in the pathogenesis of CHF and some forms of hypertension. A number of studies have examined the interaction of sodium with other ions, including chloride. The full expression of sodium chloride-sensitive hypertension in people depends on the concomitant administration of both sodium and chloride.[88-90] In experimental models of sodium chloride-sensitive hypertension in rodents and in clinical studies with small numbers of hypertensive people, blood pressure or volume was not increased by a high sodium intake provided with anions other than chloride, and high chloride intake without sodium affected blood pressure less than the intake of sodium chloride (Figure 18-7).[88,89,91] The failure of nonchloride sodium salts to produce hypertension or hypervolemia may be related to their failure to expand plasma volume; renin release occurs in response to renal tubular chloride concentration.[89-92] Chloride may also act as a direct renal vasoconstrictor.[89] These findings suggest that both sodium and chloride are nutrients of concern in patients with hypertension and heart disease.

Potassium and magnesium are nutrients of concern in patients with cardiovascular disease. Abnormalities in their homeostasis can: 1) cause cardiac dysrhythmias, 2) decrease myocardial contractility, 3) produce profound muscle weakness and 4) potentiate adverse effects from cardiac glycosides and other cardiac drugs. Nutrients that contribute to energy intake are important to consider in patients with either obesity or cachexia. Phosphorus and protein are nutrients of concern in patients with concurrent chronic renal disease. (See Chapter 19.) Taurine and carnitine are of importance in dogs and cats with myocardial failure. The Key Nutritional Factors—Cardiovascular Disease table summarizes nutrients of concern in cardiovascular disease.

Assess the Food(s)

The food(s) for animals with cardiovascular disease should be evaluated for all the key nutritional factors mentioned above. The protein and fat content of the food can be estimated from the information provided by the guaranteed or typical analysis on the commercial pet food label. (See Chapter 5.) Some commercial pet food labels may also include information about the energy density of the food, although this information is not required and is prohibited in some countries. Levels of sodium, chloride, potassium, magnesium and phosphorus are not required on the guaranteed or typical analysis of pet food labels and are usually not listed. Levels of these nutrients must be obtained by contacting the manufacturer or consulting published product information. (See Appendix L.) Levels of protein, sodium, chloride, potassium, magnesium and phosphorus in commercial pet foods intended for normal animals usually greatly exceed the minimum requirements for these nutrients.

In general, most commercial cat foods should have taurine added as an ingredient. Taurine is naturally high in many species of fish; therefore, fish-based moist cat foods often provide adequate levels of taurine without supplementation. For pet foods sold in the United States, taurine must appear in the ingredient list of foods if it is added by a pet food manufacturer. Taurine may appear on labels of foods sold in other countries. Cat foods that have passed an AAFCO protocol feeding trial (See Chapter 5.) can be assumed to maintain adequate tissue taurine stores. Information about carnitine levels in pet foods is not widely available.

Nutrient sources other than commercial pet foods should be investigated. Water quality varies considerably, even within the same community. Water can be a significant source of sodium, chloride and other minerals. Veterinarians should be familiar with the mineral levels in their local water supply. Water samples can be submitted to state or other government laboratories for analysis, municipal water companies can be contacted or private companies that market water conditioning systems can be asked about mineral levels in local water supplies.

Other sources of nutrients include commercial treats and snacks for pets, and human foods offered as snacks or part of the pet's food. Commercial pet treats (See Appendix M.) and processed human foods are often high in sodium (Table 18-7), phosphorus and other minerals.

The caloric intake should be determined for patients with obesity or cachexia. A diary maintained by the client

Table 18-8. Classification of commercial pet foods by sodium content.*

Category	Dog food Average sodium content (% dry matter basis)
High-sodium foods	
Grocery moist foods (14)	1.13
Moderate-sodium foods	
Grocery dry foods (17)	0.41
Specialty dry foods (19)	0.41
Specialty moist foods (9)	0.40
Low-sodium foods	
Geriatric/senior foods (8)	0.20
Renal foods (8)	0.22
Very low-sodium foods	
Cardiac foods (5)	0.10
AAFCO minimum allowance	**0.06**

Category	Cat food Average sodium content (% dry matter basis)
High-sodium foods	
Grocery moist foods (17)	1.09
Moderate-sodium foods	
Grocery dry foods (12)	0.43
Specialty dry foods (9)	0.38
Specialty moist foods (11)	0.34
Low-sodium foods	
Renal foods (5)	0.25
Cardiac foods (3)	0.28
AAFCO minimum allowance	**0.20**

*Sodium contents are based on published or analytical values obtained for the leading products in the United States based on market share. The number in parentheses is the number of products used to determine the average value for each product category. Grocery foods are those pet foods usually purchased in grocery or mass merchandising outlets. Specialty and geriatric/senior foods are usually purchased in pet stores, veterinary hospitals or mass merchandising outlets. Renal and cardiac foods are veterinary therapeutic foods purchased in veterinary hospitals.

is helpful in documenting what types and quantities of foods and supplements are being offered and eaten by the animal. This caloric intake can be compared with the number of calories that are usually needed to maintain ideal body weight and condition in that animal.

Assess the Feeding Method

It may not always be necessary to change the feeding method when managing a patient with cardiovascular disease, but a thorough assessment includes verification that an appropriate feeding method is being used. Items to consider include feeding route, amount fed, how the food is offered, access to other food and who feeds the animal. All of this information should have been gathered when the history of the animal was obtained. If the animal has a normal body condition score (3/5), the amount of food it was fed previously (energy basis) was probably appropriate.

FEEDING PLAN

Select a Food(s)

Avoiding Excess Sodium Chloride

Table 18-8 classifies commercial dog foods by sodium content. This classification assumes that most of the foods in these categories have an energy density of 3.5 to 4.5 kcal

Table 18-9. Levels of key nutrients in selected commercial foods used in patients with cardiovascular disease.*

	Protein	Fat	Sodium	Chloride	Potassium	Magnesium	Phosphorus
Moist canine products							
Hill's Prescription Diet Canine g/d	18.9	10.7	0.22	0.84	0.78	0.07	0.41
Hill's Prescription Diet Canine h/d	17.3	28.8	0.10	0.32	0.83	0.13	0.54
Hill's Prescription Diet Canine k/d	14.9	26.2	0.22	0.45	0.36	0.15	0.18
Hill's Prescription Diet Canine w/d	16.1	12.5	0.31	0.80	0.62	0.07	0.50
Leo Specific Cardil CHW	17.0	27.2	0.10	na	1.05	0.07	0.61
Purina CNM Canine CV-Formula	17.8	31.9	0.12	1.27	1.21	0.06	0.40
Purina CNM Canine NF-Formula	16.5	27.4	0.24	0.43	0.72	0.08	0.30
Select Care Canine Modified Formula	16.8	21.8	0.24	na	0.96	0.07	0.35
Waltham/Pedigree Low Sodium Diet	26.3	38.0	0.10	na	0.83	0.10	0.67
Dry canine products							
Hill's Prescription Diet Canine g/d	17.2	10.0	0.17	0.53	0.61	0.05	0.40
Hill's Prescription Diet Canine h/d	17.2	20.1	0.07	0.33	0.74	0.12	0.62
Hill's Prescription Diet Canine k/d	14.6	19.0	0.22	0.59	0.65	0.09	0.25
Hill's Prescription Diet Canine w/d	16.7	8.8	0.21	0.58	0.79	0.10	0.48
Purina CNM Canine NF-Formula	15.9	15.7	0.22	0.57	0.86	0.07	0.29
Select Care Canine Modified Formula	14.4	19.7	0.28	na	0.88	0.09	0.34
Moist feline products							
Hill's Prescription Diet Feline g/d	35.1	19.4	0.29	0.57	0.74	0.08	0.54
Hill's Prescription Diet Feline h/d	43.4	26.7	0.31	0.75	0.89	0.07	0.68
Hill's Prescription Diet Feline k/d	29.5	26.7	0.32	0.55	1.05	0.04	0.39
Purina CNM Feline CV-Formula	42.5	26.8	0.20	1.09	1.33	0.07	0.92
Select Care Feline Modified Formula	35.0	53.0	0.23	na	1.07	0.06	0.49
Dry feline products							
Hill's Prescription Diet Feline g/d	33.4	18.9	0.34	0.68	0.75	0.05	0.55
Hill's Prescription Diet Feline k/d	28.2	22.3	0.25	0.50	0.76	0.04	0.46
Purina CNM Feline NF-Formula	30.8	12.9	0.20	0.64	0.88	0.10	0.41
Select Care Feline Modified Formula	28.3	22.1	0.27	na	0.92	0.07	0.92

Key: na = information not published by manufacturer
*This list represents products with the largest market share and for which published information is available.
Manufacturers' published values; expressed as % dry matter.

(14.7 to 18.9 kJ) metabolizable energy per gram dry matter. Grocery (foods from grocery and mass merchandising outlets) moist dog foods have the highest average sodium content, with levels 19 times higher than the AAFCO minimum sodium allowance for adult maintenance. Grocery dry dog foods and specialty foods have moderate sodium levels that are six to seven times the AAFCO minimum allowance. Low sodium intake can be achieved with most foods specifically formulated for geriatric dogs and veterinary therapeutic foods formulated for dogs and cats with renal disease. Veterinary therapeutic foods formulated for dogs with cardiovascular disease provide the lowest sodium levels. The levels of sodium in foods for dogs with cardiovascular disease still exceed the AAFCO minimum allowance.[24,91]

Although there is currently little or no evidence that proves foods low in sodium chloride delay disease progression in the initial stages of heart disease in dogs, a prudent recommendation is to begin avoiding excess sodium chloride early in the disease process. At the first sign of heart disease without cardiac dilatation (Class Ia), foods in the moderate- to low-sodium category should be introduced. Early intervention may help the patient accept foods when more restricted sodium chloride levels are necessary later, and reminds the owners to remain vigilant for signs of disease progression. Further, avoiding excess sodium chloride early in heart disease has not been shown to be harmful.

When cardiac dilatation becomes evident on radiographs or echocardiograms (Class Ib), then foods in the low sodium chloride category are appropriate. Cardiac dilatation implies abnormal sodium chloride handling and

intravascular volume expansion, and it is a prelude to congestion. The presence of moderate to severe cardiac dilatation, congestion or both conditions (Class II or III) indicates that foods low to very low in sodium chloride are appropriate. Many veterinary cardiologists prescribe foods in the low sodium chloride category when ACE inhibitors are used, especially when used in combination with diuretics. Nutrient profiles of selected veterinary therapeutic foods commonly used for patients with cardiovascular disease are listed in Table 18-9.

Avoiding excess sodium chloride may also be important in patients with some forms of chronic respiratory disease such as chronic bronchitis or asthma. Both epidemiologic and experimental evidence in people suggest that high sodium chloride intake may increase airway responsiveness and exacerbate clinical signs associated with asthma.[94-97] When people with asthma are subjected to salt loading, clinical signs worsen, lung function deteriorates and the need for anti-asthmatic drugs increases.[97] A serum-borne factor in human patients with airway hyperresponsiveness stimulates increased sodium influx into cells.[98] Reduced sodium levels in food also result in increased levels of vasoactive intestinal peptide (VIP) in the plasma and lung; VIP acts as a bronchodilator.[99] Although similar canine and feline studies have not been completed, low-salt foods may be helpful in conjunction with other forms of therapy in animals with chronic bronchitis or asthma-like clinical signs.

Table 18-8 also classifies commercial cat foods by sodium content. Avoiding excess sodium chloride in cats is more difficult than in dogs because cat foods contain more sodium chloride than do dog foods. Ingredients used to meet the higher protein requirement of cats also contain moderate to high levels of sodium chloride and thus increase the sodium chloride content of cat food.

Table 18-10 outlines the daily sodium intake of a 15-kg dog and a 4-kg cat given specific brands of food from different sodium categories. Normal animals are able to eliminate the excess levels of sodium found in many commercial foods, but patients with heart disease and failure have an impaired ability to handle these sodium levels.

Water, commercial treats and snacks and human foods offered as snacks are also sources of sodium, chloride and other minerals. Distilled water or water with less than 150 ppm sodium is recommended for patients with advanced heart disease and failure.[93,100] Some commercial snacks or treats and processed human foods are often high in sodium chloride and should also be avoided (Table 18-7).[101] Commercial rawhide chews do not contain excessive levels of sodium.[101]

Palatability of Low-Salt Foods

The question often arises whether sodium chloride enhances palatability of foods for dogs and cats. Sodium chloride and other inorganic salts stimulate specific taste chemosensory neural groups in dogs and cats.[102] This finding suggests that dogs and cats can indeed taste sodium chloride and other inorganic salts. These "taste" groups are also stimulated by simple sugars in dogs and specific amino acids in dogs and cats.[102] Standard palatability testing indicated that dogs preferred the taste of a moist food as the level of sodium chloride was increased, whereas increasing levels of salt in a dry food had no effect on palatability of the food.[c] Palatability enhancers added topically to dry pet foods probably mask any taste effects of sodium chloride or other salts. Many foods with reduced sodium chloride levels for use in patients with cardiovascular disease have comparable or better palatability than grocery or specialty brand pet foods (Table 18-11).

Occasionally, it is difficult to get a patient to accept a change to a lower salt commercial food. This can occur because of: 1) advanced illness associated with heart failure, 2) established feeding habits of older patients and their owners, 3) anorexia associated with concurrent renal failure and some cardiac drugs and 4) the "all or nothing" approach to feeding, rather than slowly changing to the new food. Changing the eating habits of most dogs is relatively easy, but changing the feeding habits and preconceptions (e.g., low-salt food is always unpalatable) of some pet owners and veterinarians is often much more difficult. Results of feeding studies using hospitalized dogs have shown that most dogs will readily accept a food that is very low in sodium chloride by the third day.[100] For individual dogs, these foods can be made more palatable by warming the food or adding flavor enhancers (low-sodium soup or tomato sauce; sweeteners

Table 18-10. Daily sodium intake for a dog and a cat eating various foods.

Daily sodium consumption for a 15-kg dog eating 935 kcal/day

Food	Sodium intake (mg/day)
Grocery moist food*	2,845
Grocery dry food**	1,144
Specialty dry food***	655
Geriatric dry food†	438
Renal moist food††	468
Cardiac dry food†††	152
Cardiac dry food + 1 slice bread	370
Renal moist food + 30 g cheese	700

   * Alpo Prime Cuts Gourmet Dinner
  ** Purina Dog Chow
 *** Hill's Science Diet Canine Maintenance
   † Hill's Prescription Diet Canine g/d
  †† Purina CNM Canine NF-Formula
 ††† Hill's Prescription Diet Canine h/d

Daily sodium consumption for a 4-kg cat eating 270 kcal/day

Food	Sodium intake (mg/day)
Grocery moist food‡	952
Grocery dry food‡‡	371
Specialty dry food‡‡‡	189
Renal dry food§	135
Cardiac moist food§§	135
Renal dry food + ½ can tuna	295

   ‡ Whiskas Choice Cuts with Beef & Chicken
  ‡‡ Purina Meow Mix
 ‡‡‡ Hill's Science Diet Feline Maintenance
   § Purina CNM Feline NF-Formula
  §§ Hill's Prescription Diet Feline h/d

such as honey or syrup). Use of foods that are very low in sodium chloride in advanced heart disease and failure will be much easier if the dog has already been fed a food in the low-sodium category (Table 18-8).

A common mistake is to insist that an owner feed only a salt-restricted food even if caloric intake is inadequate. Although avoiding excess sodium chloride is important in CHF patients, offering only a salt-restricted food should not be imposed to the detriment of overall nutrient intake. Changing to a different commercial food or homemade food may be a more beneficial solution in some patients. Appetite may be cyclical in patients with advanced heart failure, both in respect to overall appetite and food preferences. A dedicated owner is often required and a trial and error approach must be used with different foods and feeding methods.

Ensuring Optimal Intake of Potassium, Magnesium and Phosphorus

Electrolyte abnormalities, including hypokalemia, hyperkalemia and hypomagnesemia, are potential complications of drug therapy in patients with cardiovascular disease. Patients receiving diuretic therapy should receive adequate amounts of potassium and magnesium. Patients treated with ACE inhibitors may be predisposed to mild

Table 18-11. Comparison of feeding very low-sodium foods vs. commercial foods with higher sodium levels.*

Food A	Food B	Preferring Food A (%)	Preferring Food B (%)	Number of animals
Prescription Diet Canine h/d, dry	Purina Dog Chow	95	5	60
Prescription Diet Canine h/d, dry	Iams Chunks	60	40	60
Prescription Diet Canine h/d, dry	Pedigree Chum Original	95	5	60
Prescription Diet Canine h/d, canned	Ken-L-Ration Original with Chicken and Beef	100	0	60

*Tests performed between December 1995 and March 1996 by one of the authors (PR).

Table 18-12. Taurine concentrations (mg/kg dry weight) in selected commercial pet foods and natural food sources.

Commercial pet food	
AAFCO minimum allowance, extruded cat food	1,000
AAFCO minimum allowance, canned cat food	2,000
Hill's Prescription Diet Canine h/d, dry	1,200
Hill's Prescription Diet Canine h/d, moist	2,200
Hill's Prescription Diet Feline h/d, moist	3,800
Purina CNM Feline CV-Formula	3,100
Natural sources	
Mouse carcass	7,000
Tuna, canned	2,500
Beef muscle, uncooked	1,200
Lamb muscle, uncooked	1,600
Pork muscle, uncooked	1,600
Chicken muscle, uncooked	1,100
Cod fish, uncooked	1,000

hyperkalemia; so their food should not contain excess levels of potassium. Chronic renal disease is often a concomitant disease of patients with cardiovascular disorders. Patients with chronic renal disease should be fed foods without excess levels of phosphorus. (See Chapter 19.)

Protein and Energy Intake

Obesity causes profound changes that can complicate cardiovascular disorders. Obese patients should undergo management with a calorie-restricted food and client education should focus on the importance of the pet achieving an ideal body weight and condition. (See Chapter 13.) The veterinary health care team should emphasize the potentially damaging effects of obesity in patients with heart disease to clients to enlist their active participation in a successful weight-management program.

The protein requirements of patients with cardiac cachexia have not been investigated and it is unknown how the metabolic changes associated with cachexia affect overall nutrient requirements. Many patients with cachexia have concomitant disease, such as chronic renal failure, which affects nutrient requirements. Profound anorexia enhances protein-energy malnutrition in animals with cachexia. Animals with cachexia should be encouraged to eat a complete and balanced food that contains adequate calories and high-quality protein.

The cytokines TNF and IL-1 have been implicated as pathogenic mediators in cardiac cachexia. Fish oil, which is high in omega-3 (n-3) fatty acids, alters cytokine production. Preliminary results suggest that fish-oil-mediated alterations in cytokine production may benefit dogs with CHF.[103] Circulating TNF and IL-1 concentrations decreased significantly in a group of dogs with CHF secondary to idiopathic dilated cardiomyopathy when they were treated with fish oil supplements. Dogs receiving fish oil tended to be judged as less cachectic when compared with those in the placebo group. Ventricular function also improved significantly in the group treated with fish oil when compared with dogs receiving a placebo. These findings suggest that heart failure patients with cachexia may benefit from the alterations of cytokine production brought about by omega-3 fatty acid supplementation or other methods.

Taurine Supplementation

Cats and dogs with myocardial failure may benefit from taurine supplementation to their regular food or use of foods that already contain high levels of taurine. Animals with documented taurine deficiency are more likely to respond favorably to taurine supplementation. In dogs, the association between taurine deficiency and dilated cardiomyopathy is strongest in American cocker spaniels and golden retrievers.[21,79,80,104] Cats should receive 250- to 500-mg taurine per os daily,[11] whereas dogs should receive 500- to 1,000-mg taurine per os three times daily.[80] Some foods formulated for nutritional management of cardiovascular disease already contain high levels of taurine (e.g., Prescription Diet Feline h/d and Canine h/d[d]). Animals eating these foods usually do not need additional taurine supplementation. Table 18-12 lists levels of taurine found in various types of foods.

Taurine supplementation of feline foods can be discontinued within 12 to 16 weeks if: 1) clinical signs of heart failure have resolved, 2) echocardiographic values are near normal and 3) the cat will eat a food known to support normal whole blood taurine concentrations. The length of time needed for taurine supplementation of canine foods is currently unknown.

Carnitine Supplementation

The recommended oral dosage for dogs with myocardial carnitine deficiency is 50 to 100 mg L-carnitine/kg body weight three times daily.[28] Dogs weighing 25 to 40 kg are most often affected and should receive 2 g of L-carnitine mixed with food three times daily. This high oral dosage will elevate plasma carnitine concentration 10 to 20 times above usual pretreatment values.[105] These high plasma carnitine levels will usually, but not always, raise myocardial carnitine concentrations into the normal range. The cost of this level of L-carnitine supplementation is approximately $100 to $200 (U.S.) per month for a large-breed dog. Carnitine is usually available in human health food stores.

Dogs that respond dramatically to carnitine therapy do so in a reasonably predictable manner. Owners often report generalized improvement in clinical signs within one to four weeks and echocardiographic improvement is noted after eight to 12 weeks of supplementation. Improvement may continue for about six to eight months, at which time patients often reach a plateau and though they appear clinically normal they have depressed ventricular function as determined by echocardiography.[28]

Feeding Plans for Patients with Chylothorax

Depending on the chronicity of the disease, amount of pleural effusion and prior treatment attempts, dogs and cats with chylothorax may be emaciated and dehydrated. The goal of medical management is to support the metabolic and nutritional needs of the patient until the effusion spontaneously resolves, specific therapy for an underlying disease is instituted (e.g., chemotherapy, radiation therapy or both for a mediastinal mass; surgical correction of diaphragmatic hernia) or the patient's thoracic duct is ligated.

Dehydration and electrolyte abnormalities should be corrected before initiating nutritional support. Serious hyponatremia and hyperkalemia occur in dogs with chylothorax and should be corrected, especially if anesthesia is planned for placement of a thoracic tube or exploratory thoracotomy.[106] Parenteral nutrition is a proven way to reduce the quantity of lymph flow through the thoracic duct in human patients with chylothorax and can be used in feline and canine patients. (See Chapter 12.) No clinical trials to evaluate the efficacy of parenteral nutrition in animals with chylothorax have been reported.

In the past, feeding a low-fat homemade or commercial food supplemented with medium-chain triglycerides was recommended for patients with chylothorax because it was thought to minimize thoracic duct flow. Recent information has challenged this concept and shown that thoracic duct flow may not be altered significantly by nutritional changes in dogs.[107] Until more information is available, the primary management goals for chylothorax should be to meet the overall nutritional needs of the patient rather than focusing on nutritional changes designed to reduce chyle production. In most patients, medical and nutritional management are usually temporary means to support the patient until surgery.[108,109] Fewer than 20% of cats with idiopathic chylothorax respond to long-term medical and nutritional management alone.[109]

Determine a Feeding Method

The method of feeding is often not altered in the nutritional management of cardiovascular disease. If a new food is fed, the amount to feed can be determined from the product label or other supporting materials. The food dosage may need to be changed if the caloric density of the new food differs from that of the previous food. The food dosage is usually divided into two or more meals per day. The food dosage and feeding method should be altered if the animal's body weight and condition are not optimal.

For clinical nutrition to be effective, there needs to be good compliance. Enabling compliance includes limiting access to other foods and knowing who feeds the animal. If the animal comes from a household with multiple pets, it should be determined whether the pet with cardiovascular disease has access to the other pets' food. Access to other food (table food, other pets' food, etc.) may contribute to cardiovascular disease and thus should be denied. (See Chapter 1.)

▎REASSESSMENT

Nutrient-Drug Interactions

Most patients with cardiovascular disease in which nutritional management is used also receive drug therapy. In the past, drug-drug interactions received considerable attention but few investigators evaluated or discussed how nutrient levels might affect drug availability and pharmacokinetics and vice versa. (See Chapter 27.) Because many cardiovascular patients are treated with a combination of veterinary therapeutic foods and drugs, potential food-drug or nutrient-drug interactions are important.

Diuretics

Diuretics continue to be a pharmacologic mainstay of acute therapy for heart failure. Sodium restriction, ACE inhibition, venodilating drugs and diuretics represent the major available methods for preload reduction.

Sodium chloride restriction is a key component of CHF treatment even with the use of diuretics. Well-controlled studies have demonstrated that loop diuretics such as

furosemide given once a day fail to achieve a negative sodium balance in people with high sodium intake.[110] Although there is an impressive natriuresis for several hours after furosemide administration, a compensatory increase in sodium reabsorption in the next 24 hours exactly matches the earlier losses.[110] Thus, it is essential to limit sodium intake to ensure negative sodium balance. Balance studies with normal people have demonstrated that significant negative sodium balance can be predictably obtained with loop diuretics if sodium intake is limited to 20 mEq/day (roughly equivalent to 460 mg sodium or 1.2 g sodium chloride per day).[111] This level of sodium restriction in people is equivalent to that achieved with use of foods formulated for patients with cardiovascular disease. (See "Cardiac foods" [Table 18-8].)

Blood volume contraction and circulatory impairment are potential complications of aggressive diuretic therapy. These complications can exacerbate pre-existing renal disease, alter excretion of drugs dependent on renal elimination and reduce cardiac output by reducing cardiac filling pressures.[112] Reduced levels of sodium in the food have been implicated, but have not been proven to contribute to volume depletion from excessive diuresis.[112] Fractional excretion of sodium in the urine actually decreases in normal dogs fed a sodium-restricted food.[113] The influence of diuretics on sodium and chloride balance in dogs with heart disease and failure fed sodium- and chloride-restricted foods has not been evaluated.

Furosemide contributes to hypokalemia and hypomagnesemia because of increased urinary loss of potassium and magnesium.[112] The role of magnesium and potassium in the development of cardiac dysrhythmias has not received attention beyond the recognition that digitalis toxicosis appears to be much more dysrhythmogenic in hypomagnesemic and hypokalemic patients.[114] Hypomagnesemia may potentiate cardiac dysrhythmias caused by catecholamine release and is also associated with increased vascular reactivity.[115]

Conflicting reports have been published about the serum electrolyte and magnesium concentrations of dogs with CHF. A study of 113 dogs with CHF identified only four dogs with hypomagnesemia.[114] Three of the four hypomagnesemic dogs received combined therapy with a commercial sodium-restricted veterinary therapeutic food, furosemide and either hydralazine or enalapril. In another study, furosemide-treated dogs with heart failure had significantly lower serum magnesium and potassium values than did age-matched healthy controls.[116] A third study showed no significant differences in serum magnesium concentrations between clinically normal dogs, dogs with heart failure before any treatment, heart-failure dogs treated only with furosemide and heart-failure dogs treated with furosemide and digoxin.[117] The feeding history was not included in the last two studies so specific food-diuretic interactions could not be interpreted. Normal dogs treated with a commercial sodium-restricted veterinary therapeutic food and furosemide for four weeks had no significant change in serum potassium concentrations.[118]

Several studies have shown that the RAA system is not activated in human patients with moderate heart failure in the absence of diuretic therapy.[45,119] The major increase in plasma renin activity and plasma aldosterone concentration occurs with the introduction of diuretic drugs into the treatment regimen rather than as a result of the disease process itself. Furosemide apparently stimulates renin release by inhibiting chloride transport in the ascending limb of the loop of Henle, even if blood volume contraction is prevented.[91] Treatment of normal geriatric dogs with moderate doses of furosemide profoundly stimulates the RAA system, irrespective of the sodium level in the food.[120] Use of furosemide with either hydralazine or enalapril also stimulates the RAA system in dogs with heart failure due to acquired mitral valve regurgitation.[121]

Although diuretics will remain important first-line drugs for management of acute cardiogenic pulmonary edema, findings in people suggest that diuretics continue to stimulate the RAA system and may play a pivotal role in the progressive self-perpetuating cycle of heart failure.[45] Veterinary cardiologists are now questioning the use of diuretic monotherapy early in the management of symptomatic heart failure.[122] Diuretics should be reserved for managing more advanced heart failure in patients already receiving sodium-chloride-restricted foods, ACE inhibitors, digoxin or combination therapy. Feeding patients foods without excess sodium chloride may allow lower dosages of diuretics to be used for control of the clinical signs of CHF.

The sodium, chloride, potassium and magnesium levels in commercial pet foods and veterinary therapeutic foods for dogs and cats with cardiovascular disease and heart failure vary tremendously (Tables 18-8 and 18-9). The levels of minerals in the food should be considered when using concurrent diuretic therapy.

Long-term furosemide therapy may be associated with clinically significant thiamin deficiency, due to excessive urinary loss of thiamin, and may contribute to impaired cardiac performance in patients with CHF.[123] Animals receiving long-term diuretic therapy should be given supplements containing thiamin and other water-soluble vitamins or be fed a commercial food with increased concentrations of these vitamins. Veterinary therapeutic foods for patients with cardiac and renal disease are often formulated with higher levels of water-soluble vitamins to offset excessive urinary losses.

ACE Inhibitors

Captopril, enalapril and lisinopril, all ACE inhibitors, have emerged as drugs of choice for treating many dogs and cats with CHF. Inhibition of angiotensin II results in vascular dilatation and decreased circulating plasma aldosterone concentrations. Angiotensin II and aldosterone play important roles in the maintenance of vascular volume and potassium balance. Both increase the reabsorption of sodium and chloride, and aldosterone promotes the excretion of potassium.

The use of ACE inhibitors in human patients with severe renal insufficiency or in patients given potassium supplements may increase the risk for hyperkalemia.[124-126] In a study, more than half the dogs with CHF developed mild serum potassium elevations when treated with a commercial sodium-restricted veterinary therapeutic food, furosemide and captopril.[118] Another study confirmed that heart-failure dogs treated with furosemide, digoxin and an ACE inhibitor had significantly higher mean serum potassium concentrations when compared with clinically normal dogs, dogs with heart failure before any treatment, heart-failure dogs treated only with furosemide and heart-failure dogs treated with furosemide and digoxin.[117] Mild elevations in serum potassium concentrations have also been observed in dogs treated with enalapril.[127] In another study, serum potassium concentration decreased in a subset of heart-failure dogs treated with ACE inhibitors and furosemide, although the specific feeding history was not reported.[116]

When mild hyperkalemia occurs in people with heart failure, reducing oral potassium intake and discontinuing potassium-sparing diuretics is recommended.[126] Although clinically significant hyperkalemia (serum potassium ≥6.5 mEq/l) is uncommon, the use of ACE inhibitors in dogs with CHF or renal insufficiency fed commercial or veterinary therapeutic foods with high potassium content may increase the risk for hyperkalemia.[118]

Functional renal insufficiency occurs in up to one-third of human patients with severe CHF treated with sodium chloride restriction, ACE inhibitors and diuretics.[128] This decline in renal function has been attributed to loss of angiotensin II-mediated systemic and intrarenal vasoconstrictor effects, which maintain renal perfusion pressure and glomerular filtration rate in low-output heart failure. Functional renal insufficiency appears to be alleviated in human patients when efforts are made to replenish total body stores of sodium by reducing the diuretic dosage and liberalizing sodium intake.[128] Renal insufficiency is a potential complication of ACE inhibitor therapy in dogs with CHF, but the role of sodium restriction is unknown.[118,129,130] Four of 10 heart-failure dogs treated with captopril, furosemide and a sodium-restricted veterinary therapeutic food developed azotemia during the first five weeks of treatment; one of these dogs developed clinical signs of uremia.[118] Two of the dogs that developed severe azotemia had isosthenuria on the initial urinalysis, which suggested some degree of pre-existing renal insufficiency. Azotemia is a more frequent complication when canine heart failure is treated with furosemide and enalapril rather than with furosemide alone.[130]

Drug-induced azotemia in heart-failure patients is treated by reducing the ACE inhibitor dose (usually by half), reducing the diuretic dose (usually by half), increasing the sodium intake to the next level (Table 18-8) or using a combination of these tactics.

Cardiac Glycosides

Cardiac glycosides have been used for more than two centuries and are still widely prescribed to manage cardiac disorders in dogs and cats. Appropriate use of cardiac glycosides is based on an appreciation of the nutritional factors that influence the pharmacokinetic properties of these drugs.

Absorption of the cardiac glycosides is influenced by the formulation of the drug and its administration in relation to meals. (See Chapter 27.) Because administering digoxin or digitoxin with food may result in up to a 50% reduction in serum concentrations, these drugs are best given between meals.[131] The body condition of the animal can also influence the pharmacokinetics of these drugs. Digoxin is minimally distributed in adipose tissue; the dosage of the drug should be based on lean body weight even for obese patients. Digitoxin is more lipid soluble than digoxin; so its dosage need not be adjusted for overweight animals.

The dosage of digoxin for cats is influenced by concurrent drug and nutritional therapy. The digoxin dose should be reduced by one-third if the cat is receiving concomitant furosemide, aspirin and a sodium-restricted veterinary therapeutic food.[132]

Metabolic derangements associated with increased risk of digoxin toxicosis include hypokalemia, hypomagnesemia, hypercalcemia, renal insufficiency, hypothyroidism and obesity.[131] Serum electrolyte and magnesium concentrations should be measured and corrections made before starting cardiac glycoside therapy.

Management of Hyponatremia

The correction of hyponatremia associated with CHF has been evaluated in people but not in domestic animals. The combined administration of an ACE inhibitor and furosemide (but usually not of either agent alone) usually reverses CHF-associated hyponatremia in people, at least in part.[55] The reversal of hyponatremia probably results from the combined effects of the ACE inhibitor (i.e., decreased thirst, decreased proximal tubular reabsorption of sodium chloride, interference with the hydro-osmotic effect of AVP) and the loop diuretic (i.e., increased distal delivery of glomerular filtrate, reduction in urine osmolality) acting to offset the pathophysiologic factors that impair excretion of water.[55,133] Studies are needed to determine whether similar measures are effective in reversing CHF-associated hyponatremia in animals.

Overall Reassessment Strategy

In general, the survival of patients with heart failure is related to the degree of myocardial failure, whereas their clinical signs are related more to CHF and its compensatory mechanisms. The overall objectives of treatment for chronic heart failure, as for almost any cardiovascular disease, are threefold: 1) prevention (prevent myocardial damage, prevent recurrence of heart failure), 2) relief of clinical signs (eliminate edema and fluid retention, increase exercise capacity, reduce fatigue and respiratory compromise) and 3) improvement of prognosis (reduce mortality).

Dogs and cats with suspected cardiovascular disease should undergo a routine serum biochemistry profile and urinalysis before any nutritional or drug therapy is initiated. Dogs and cats with heart failure and evidence of pre-existing renal disease, including isosthenuria, may be at increased risk for developing azotemia during combined food-drug therapy. There are no universal recommendations for controlling: levels of sodium, chloride and potassium; fluid intake; ACE inhibition and diuretic administration for animals with cardiovascular disease. Rather, each patient must be monitored frequently (weekly for the first four to six weeks). Reassessment should include: 1) measurement of body weight, 2) assessment of body condition, 3) determination of serum electrolyte and magnesium concentrations and 4) evaluation of renal function.

■ ENDNOTES & REFERENCES

ENDNOTES

a. Metabolic Analysis Lab, Inc., 1202 Ann Street, Madison, WI 53713, USA.

b. Shelton GD. Director, Comparative Neuromuscular Laboratory, School of Medicine, University of California-San Diego, LaJolla, CA 92093-0614, USA.

c. Roudebush P. Unpublished data. June 1995.

d. Prescription Diet Feline h/d, Prescription Diet Canine h/d; Hill's Pet Nutrition Inc., Topeka, KS, USA.

REFERENCES

1. Detweiler DK, Patterson DF. Prevalence and types of cardiovascular disease in dogs. Annals of the New York Academy of Sciences 1965; 127: 481-516.

2. Harpster NK, Zook BC. The cardiovascular system. In: Holzworth J, ed. Diseases of the Cat: Medicine and Surgery. Philadelphia, PA: WB Saunders Co, 1987; 820-933.

3. Buchanan JW. Causes and prevalence of cardiovascular disease. In: Kirk RW, Bonagura JD, eds. Current Veterinary Therapy XI. Philadelphia, PA: WB Saunders Co, 1992; 647-655.

4. Fioretti M, Delli Carri E. Epidemiological survey of dilatative cardiomyopathy in dogs. Veterinaria 1988; 2: 81-90.

5. Morris Animal Foundation. Animal health survey. Denver, CO, 1991.

6. Buchanan JW. Chronic valvular disease (endocardiosis) in dogs. Advances in Veterinary Science and Comparative Medicine 1977; 21: 75-106.

7. Thrusfield MV, Aitken CGG, Darke PGG. Observations on breed and sex in relation to canine heart valve incompetence. Journal of Small Animal Practice 1985; 26: 709-717.

8. Darke PGG. Mitral valve disease in cavalier King Charles spaniels. In: Bonagura JD, ed. Current Veterinary Therapy XII. Philadelphia, PA: WB Saunders Co, 1995; 837-841.

9. Beardrow AW, Buchanan JW. Chronic valve disease in cavalier King Charles spaniels: 95 cases (1987-1991). Journal of the American Veterinary Medical Association 1993; 203: 1023-1029.

10. Pion PD, Kittleson MD, Rogers QR. Myocardial failure in cats associated with low plasma taurine: A reversible cardiomyopathy. Science 1987; 237: 764-768.

11. Pion PD, Kittleson MD, Rogers QR. Cardiomyopathy in the cat and its relationship to taurine deficiency. In: Kirk RW, ed. Current Veterinary Therapy X. Philadelphia, PA: WB Saunders Co, 1989; 251-262.

12. Skiles ML, Pion PD, Hird DW, et al. Epidemiologic evaluation of taurine deficiency and dilated cardiomyopathy in cats (abstract). Journal of Veterinary Internal Medicine 1990; 4: 117.

13. Johnson LR, Hamlin RL. Recognition and treatment of pulmonary hypertension. In: Bonagura JD, ed. Current Veterinary Therapy XII. Philadelphia, PA: WB Saunders Co, 1995; 887-892.

14. Littman MP, Drobatz KJ. Hypertensive and hypotensive disorders. In: Ettinger SJ, Feldman EC, eds. Textbook of Veterinary Internal Medicine, 4th ed. Philadelphia, PA: WB Saunders Co, 1995; 93-97.

15. Remes J, Miettinen H, Reunanen A, et al. Validity of clinical diagnosis of heart failure in primary health care. European Heart Journal 1991; 12: 315-321.

16. International Small Animal Cardiac Health Council. Functional classes of heart failure. In: Recommendations for the Diagnosis of Heart Disease and the Treatment of Heart Failure in Small Animals. Academy of Veterinary Cardiology, 1994; 5.

17. Freeman LM, Roubenoff R. The nutrition implications of cardiac cachexia. Nutrition Reviews 1994; 52: 340-347.

18. Hansen B. Blood pressure measurement. In: Bonagura JD, ed. Current Veterinary Therapy XII. Philadelphia, PA: WB Saunders Co, 1995; 110-112.

19. Remillard RL, Ross JN, Eddy JB. Variance of indirect blood pressure measurements and prevalence of hypertension in clinically normal dogs. American Journal of Veterinary Research 1991; 52: 561-565.

20. Sisson DD, Knight DH, Helinski C, et al. Plasma taurine concentrations and M-mode echocardiographic measures in healthy cats and in cats with dilated cardiomyopathy. Journal of Veterinary Internal Medicine 1991; 5: 232-238.

21. Kramer GA, Kittleson MD, Fox PR, et al. Plasma taurine concentration in normal dogs and in dogs with heart disease. Journal of Veterinary Internal Medicine 1995; 9: 253-258.

22. Trautwein EA, Hayes KC. Gender and dietary amino acid supplementation influence the plasma and whole blood taurine status of taurine-depleted cats (expanded abstract). Journal of Nutrition 1991; 121: S173-S174.

23. Pion PD, Lewis J, Greene K, et al. Effect of meal-feeding and food deprivation on plasma and whole blood taurine concentrations in cats (expanded abstract). Journal of Nutrition 1991; 121: S177-S178.

24. Association of American Feed Control Officials. Official Publication, 1998.

25. Glass EN, Odle J, Baker DH. Urinary taurine excretion as a function of taurine intake in adult cats. Journal of Nutrition 1992; 122: 1135-1142.

26. Jacobs G, Keene BW, Cornelius LM, et al. Plasma, tissue and urine carnitine concentrations in healthy adult cats and kittens. American Journal of Veterinary Research 1990; 51: 1345-1348.

27. Jacobs G, Cornelius LM, Keene BW, et al. Comparison of plasma, liver, and skeletal muscle carnitine concentrations in cats with idiopathic hepatic lipidosis and in healthy cats. American Journal of Veterinary Research 1990; 51: 1349-1351.

28. Keene BW. L-carnitine deficiency in canine dilated cardiomyopathy. In: Kirk RW, Bonagura JD, eds. Current Veterinary Therapy XI. Philadelphia, PA: WB Saunders Co, 1992; 780-783.

29. Shelton GD. Canine lipid storage myopathies. In: Bonagura JD, ed. Current Veterinary Therapy XII. Philadelphia, PA: WB Saunders Co, 1995; 1161-1163.

30. Keene BW, Kittleson MD, Atkins CE, et al. Modified transvenous endomyocardial biopsy technique in dogs. American Journal of Veterinary Research 1990; 51: 1769-1772.

31. Watkins L, Burton JA, Haber E, et al. The renin-angiotensin-aldosterone system in congestive heart failure in conscious dogs. Journal of Clinical Investigation 1976; 57: 1606-1617.

32. Riegger AJG, Liebau G. The renin-angiotensin-aldosterone system, antidiuretic hormone and sympathetic nerve activity in an experimental model of congestive heart failure in the dog. Clinical Science 1982; 62: 465-469.

33. Riegger AJG, Elsner D, Kromer EP, et al. Atrial natriuretic peptide in congestive heart failure in the dog: Plasma levels, cyclic guanosine monophosphate, ultrastructure of atrial myoendocrine cells, and hemodynamic, hormonal and renal effects. Circulation 1988; 77: 398-406.

34. Maher E, Cernacek P, Levy M. Heterogeneous renal responses to atrial natriuretic factor I. Chronic caval dogs. American Journal of Physiology 1989; 257: R1057-R1067.

35. Villarreal D, Freeman RH, Brands MW. ANF and postprandial control of sodium excretion in dogs with compensated heart failure. American Journal of Physiology 1990; 258: R232-R239.

36. Himura Y, Chang-Seng L, Naoaki I, et al. Short-term effects of naloxone on hemodynamics and baroreflex function in conscious dogs with pacing-induced congestive heart failure. Journal of the American College of Cardiology 1994; 23: 194-200.

37. Knowlen GG, Kittleson MD, Nachreiner RF, et al. Comparison of plasma aldosterone concentration among clinical status groups of dogs with chronic heart failure. Journal of the American Veterinary Medical Association 1983; 183: 991-996.

38. Ware WA, Lund DD, Subieta AR, et al. Sympathetic activation in dogs with congestive heart failure caused by chronic mitral valve disease and dilated cardiomyopathy. Journal of the American Veterinary Medical Association 1990; 197: 1475-1481.

39. Takemura N, Koyama H, Sako T, et al. Atrial natriuretic peptide in the dog with mitral regurgitation. Research in Veterinary Science 1991; 50: 86-88.

40. Vollmar AM, Reusch C, Kraft W, et al. Atrial natriuretic peptide concentration in dogs with congestive heart failure, chronic renal failure, and hyperadrenocorticism. American Journal of Veterinary Research 1991; 52: 1831-1834.

41. Buoro IBJ, Atwell RB, Tummy T. Plasma levels of renin and aldosterone in right-sided congestive heart failure due to canine dirofilariasis. Canine Practice 1992; 17: 21-24.

42. Haggstrom J, Hansson K, Karlberg BE, et al. Plasma concentration of atrial natriuretic peptide in relation to severity of mitral regurgitation in cavalier King Charles spaniels. American Journal of Veterinary Research 1994; 55: 698-703.

43. Pederson HD, Koch J, Poulsen K, et al. Activation of the renin-angiotensin system in dogs with asymptomatic and mildly symptomatic mitral valvular insufficiency. Journal of Veterinary Internal Medicine 1995; 9: 328-331.

44. Schlant RC, Sonnenblick EH. Pathophysiology of heart failure. In: Schlant RC, Alexander RW, eds. The Heart, 8th ed. New York, NY: McGraw-Hill, 1994; 515-555.

45. Kubo SH. Neurohormonal activity in congestive heart failure. Critical Care Medicine 1990; 18: S39-S44.

46. Knight DH. Pathophysiology of heart failure and clinical evaluation of cardiac function. In: Ettinger SJ, Feldman EC, eds. Textbook of Veterinary Internal Medicine, 4th ed. Philadelphia, PA: WB Saunders Co, 1995; 851-855.

47. Floras JS. Clinical aspects of sympathetic activation and parasympathetic withdrawal in heart failure. Journal of the American College of Cardiology 1993; 22 (Suppl. A): 72A-84A.

48. Hall JE, Brands MW. The renin-angiotensin-aldosterone systems. In: Seldin DW, Giebisch G, eds. The Kidney: Physiology and Pathophysiology, 2nd ed. New York, NY: Raven Press, 1992; 1455-1504.

49. MacFadyen RJ. Role of the circulating and tissue-based renin-angiotensin system in the development of heart failure: Implications for therapy. Cardiology 1993; 83: 38-48.

50. Straeter-Knowlen IM, Hankes GH, Dillon AR, et al. Left ventricular compensation in experimental mitral regurgitation causes right ventricular compression and superfunction: Role of the local renin angiotensin system (abstract). Journal of Veterinary Internal Medicine 1995; 9: 201.

51. Francis GS, Benedict C, Johnstone DE, et al. Comparison of neuroendocrine activation in patients with left ventricular dysfunction with and without congestive heart failure. Circulation 1990; 82: 1724-1729.

52. Scriven TA, Burnett JC. Effects of synthetic atrial natriuretic peptide on renal function and renin release in acute experimental heart failure. Circulation 1985; 72: 892-897.

53. Zimmerman RS, Schirger JA, Edwards BS, et al. Cardio-renal-endocrine dynamics during stepwise infusion of physiologic and pharmacologic concentrations of atrial natriuretic factor in the dog. Circulatory Research 1987; 61: 63-69.

54. Kivlighn SD, Lowmeier TE, Yang HM, et al. Chronic effects of a physiologic dose of ANP on arterial pressure and renin release. American Journal of Physiology 1990; 258: H1491-H1497.

55. Oster JR, Preston RA, Materson BJ. Fluid and electrolyte disorders in congestive heart failure. Seminars in Nephrology 1994; 14: 485-505.

56. Lee WH, Packer M. Prognostic importance of serum sodium concentration and its modification by converting-enzyme inhibition in patients with severe chronic heart failure. Circulation 1986; 73: 257-267.

57. Alexander JK. The heart and obesity. In: Hurst JW, ed. The Heart, 6th ed. New York, NY: McGraw-Hill, 1986; 1452-1458.

58. Crandall DL, DiGirolamo M. Hemodynamic and metabolic correlates in adipose tissue: Pathophysiologic considerations. Federation of American Societies for Experimental Biology Journal 1990; 4: 1441-1447.

59. Rocchini AP, Key J, Bondie D, et al. The effect of weight loss on the sensitivity of blood pressure to sodium in obese adolescents. New England Journal of Medicine 1989; 321: 580-585.

60. Hall JE, Brands MW, Dixon WN, et al. Obesity-induced hypertension: Renal function and systemic hemodynamics. Hypertension 1993; 22: 292-299.

61. Mizelle HL, Edwards TC, Montani JP. Abnormal cardiovascular responses to exercise during the development of obesity in dogs. American Journal of Hypertension 1994; 7: 374-378.

62. Rocchini AP, Moorehead C, Wentz E, et al. Obesity-induced hypertension in the dog. Hypertension 1987; 9 (Suppl. III): III64-III68.

63. Hall JE, Coleman TG, Mizelle HL, et al. Chronic hyperinsulinemia and blood pressure regulation. American Journal of Physiology 1990; 258: F722-F731.

64. Hall JE, Brands MW, Kivlighn SD, et al. Chronic hyperinsulinemia and blood pressure: Interaction with catecholamines? Hypertension 1990; 15: 519-527.

65. Brands MW, Mizelle HL, Gaillard CA, et al. The hemodynamic response to chronic hyperinsulinemia in conscious dogs. American Journal of Hypertension 1991; 4: 164-168.

66. Riley M, Elbron JS, McKane WR, et al. Resting energy expenditure in chronic cardiac failure. Clinical Sciences 1991; 80: 633-639.

67. Levine B, Kalman J, Mayer L, et al. Elevated circulating levels of tumor necrosis factor in chronic heart failure. New England Journal of Medicine 1990; 323: 236-241.

68. Freeman LM, Rush JE, Brown DJ, et al. Elevated concentration of tumor necrosis factor in dogs with congestive heart failure (abstract). Journal of Veterinary Internal Medicine 1994; 8: 146.

69. Meurs KM, Miller MW, Fox PR, et al. Serum tumor necrosis factor concentration in cats with congestive heart failure (abstract). Journal of Veterinary Internal Medicine 1995; 9: 200.

70. Le J, Vilcek J. Tumor necrosis factor and interleukin 1: Cytokines with multiple overlapping biological activities. Laboratory Investigation 1987; 56: 234-248.

71. Oliff A. The role of tumor necrosis factor (cachectin) in cachexia. Cell 1988; 554: 141-142.

72. Tracey KJ, Wei H, Manogue KR, et al. Cachectin/tumor necrosis factor induces cachexia, anemia and inflammation. Journal of Experimental Medicine 1988; 167: 1211-1227.

73. Tracey KJ, Lowry SF, Cerami A. Cachectin: A hormone that triggers acute shock and chronic cachexia. Journal of Infectious Diseases 1988; 157: 413-420.

74. Schollmeier K. Immunologic and pathophysiologic role of tumor necrosis factor. American Journal of Respiratory and Cell Molecular Biology 1990; 3: 11-12.

75. Pion PD, Kittleson MD, Thomas WP, et al. Clinical findings in cats with dilated cardiomyopathy and relationship of findings to taurine deficiency. Journal of the American Veterinary Medical Association 1992; 201: 267-274.

76. Pion PD, Kittleson MD, Thomas WP, et al. Response of cats with dilated cardiomyopathy to taurine supplementation. Journal of the American Veterinary Medical Association 1992; 201: 275-284.

77. Fox PR, Sturman JA. Myocardial taurine concentrations in cats with cardiac disease and in healthy cats fed taurine-modified diets. American Journal of Veterinary Research 1992; 53: 237-241.

78. Moise NS, Pacioretty LM, Kallfelz FA, et al. Dietary taurine deficiency and dilated cardiomyopathy in the fox. American Heart Journal 1991; 121: 541-547.

79. Kittleson MD, Keene BW, Pion PD, et al. Results of the Multicenter Spaniel Trial (MUST): Taurine- and carnitine-responsive dilated cardiomyopathy in American Cocker spaniels with decreased plasma taurine concentration. Journal of Veterinary Internal Medicine 1997; 11: 204-211.

80. Pion PD, Sanderson SL, Kittleson MD. The effectiveness of taurine and levocarnitine in dogs with heart disease. Veterinary Clinics of North America: Small Animal Practice 1998; 28: 1495-1514.

81. Dow SW, Fettman MJ, Smith KR, et al. Taurine depletion and cardiovascular disease in adult cats fed a potassium-depleted acidified diet. American Journal of Veterinary Research 1992; 553: 402-405.

82. Fox PR, Trautwein EA, Hayes KC, et al. Comparison of taurine, α-tocopherol, retinol, selenium, and total triglycerides and cholesterol concentrations in cats with cardiac disease and in healthy cats. American Journal of Veterinary Research 1994; 54: 563-569.

83. Guyton AC. The relationship of cardiac output and arterial pressure control. Circulation 1981; 64: 1079-1088.

84. Bauer T, Woodfield JA. Mediastinal, pleural and extrapleural diseases. In: Ettinger SJ, Feldman EC, eds. Textbook of Veterinary Internal Medicine, 4th ed. Philadelphia, PA: WB Saunders Co, 1995; 817-829.

85. Fossum TW, Jacobs RM, Birchard SJ. Evaluation of cholesterol and triglyceride concentrations in differentiating chylous and nonchylous pleural effusions in dogs and cats. Journal of the American Veterinary Medical Association 1986; 188: 49-51.

86. Smeak DD, Kerpsack SJ. Management of feline chylothorax. In: Bonagura JD, ed. Current Veterinary Therapy XII. Philadelphia, PA: WB Saunders Co, 1995; 921-927.

87. Barger AC, Ross RS, Price HL. Reduced sodium excretion in dogs with mild valvular lesions of the heart and in dogs with congestive failure. American Journal of Physiology 1955; 180: 249-260.

88. Kurtz TW, Al-Bander HA, Morris RC. "Salt-sensitive" essential hypertension in men. New England Journal of Medicine 1987; 317: 1043-1048.

89. Boegehold MA, Kotchen TA. Relative contributions of dietary Na$^+$ and Cl$^-$ to salt-sensitive hypertension. Hypertension 1989; 14: 579-583.

90. Luft FC, Zemel MB, Sowers JA, et al. Sodium bicarbonate and sodium chloride: Effects on blood pressure and electrolyte homeostasis in normal and hypertensive men. Journal of Hypertension 1990; 8: 663-670.

91. Kotchen TA, Luke RG, Ott CE, et al. Effect of chloride on renin and blood pressure responses to sodium chloride. Annals of Internal Medicine 1981; 98: 817-822.

92. Kotchen TA, Welch WJ, Lorenz JN, et al. Renal tubular chloride and renin release. Journal of Laboratory Clinical Medicine 1987; 110: 533-539.

93. Morris ML Jr, Patton RL, Teeter SM. Low sodium diet in heart disease: How low is low? Veterinary Medicine/Small Animal Clinician 1976; 71: 1225-1227.

94. Burney PGJ. A diet rich in sodium may potentiate asthma: Epidemiological evidence for a new hypothesis. Chest 1987; 91: 143S-148S.

95. Burney PGJ, Neild JE, Twort CHC, et al. Effect of changing dietary sodium on the airway response to histamine. Thorax 1989; 44: 36-41.

96. Carey OJ, Lock CR, Cookson JB. Effect of alterations of dietary sodium on the severity of asthma in men. Thorax 1993; 48: 714-718.

97. Medici TC, Schmid AZ, Hacki M, et al. Are asthmatics salt sensitive? A preliminary controlled study. Chest 1993; 104: 1138-1143.

98. Tribe RM, Barton JR, Poston L, et al. Dietary sodium intake, airway responsiveness, and cellular sodium transport. American Journal of Respiratory and Critical Care Medicine 1994; 149: 1426-1433.

99. Ye VFC, Duggan KA. The effect of dietary sodium on the concentration of vasoactive intestinal peptide in plasma and lung. Chest 1995; 108: 535-538.

100. Ross JN. Heart failure. In: Lewis LD, Morris ML Jr, Hand MS, eds. Small Animal Clinical Nutrition III. Topeka, KS: Mark Morris Associates, 1987; 11-1–11-38.

101. Morris ML Jr, Ettinger SJ. Dietary modifications in cardiac disease. In: Ettinger SJ, Feldman EC, eds. Textbook of Veterinary Internal Medicine, 4th ed. Philadelphia, PA: WB Saunders Co, 1995; 233-238.

102. Boudreau JC, White TD. Flavor chemistry of carnivore taste systems. In: Bullard RW, ed. Flavor Chemistry of Animal Foods (ACS Symposium Series 67). Washington, DC: American Chemical Society, 1978; 102-128.

103. Freeman LM, Rush JE, Brown DJ, et al. The use of fish oil in dogs with congestive heart failure (abstract). Journal of Veterinary Internal Medicine 1995; 9: 203.

104. Kittleson MD, Pion PD, DeLillis LA, et al. Dilated cardiomyopathy in American cocker spaniels–Taurine deficiency and preliminary results of response to supplementation (abstract). In: Proceedings. Ninth Veterinary Medical Forum, American College of Veterinary Internal Medicine, New Orleans, LA 1991: 878.

105. Keene BW, Panciera DP, Atkins CE, et al. Myocardial L-carnitine deficiency in a family of dogs with dilated cardiomyopathy. Journal of the American Veterinary Medical Association 1991; 198: 647-650.

106. Willard MD, Fossum TW, Torrance A, et al. Hyponatremia and hyperkalemia associated with idiopathic or experimentally induced chylothorax in four dogs. Journal of the American Veterinary Medical Association 1991; 199: 353-358.

107. Sikkema DA, McLoughlin MA, Birchard SJ, et al. Effect of dietary fat on thoracic duct lymph volume and composition in dogs (abstract). Journal of Veterinary Internal Medicine 1993; 7: 119.

108. Birchard SJ, Smeak DD, Fossum TW. Results of thoracic duct ligation in dogs with chylothorax. Journal of the American Veterinary Medical Association 1988; 193: 68-71.

109. Fossum TW, Forrester SD, Swenson CL, et al. Chylothorax in cats: 37 cases (1969-1989). Journal of the American Veterinary Medical Association 1991; 198: 672-678.

110. Wilcox CS, Mitch WE, Kelly RA, et al. Response of the kidney to furosemide. I. Effects of salt intake and renal compensation. Journal of Laboratory Clinical Medicine 1983; 102: 450-458.

111. Kokko JP. Use of diuretics in specific circumstances. In: Schlant RC, Alexander RW, eds. The Heart, 8th ed. New York, NY: McGraw-Hill, 1994; 603-605.

112. Fox PR. Current uses and hazards of diuretic therapy. In: Kirk RW, Bonagura JD, eds. Current Veterinary Therapy XI. Philadelphia, PA: WB Saunders Co, 1992; 668-676.

113. Navar LG, Jirakulsomchok D, Bell PD, et al. Influence of converting enzyme inhibition on renal hemodynamics and glomerular dynamics in sodium-restricted dogs. Hypertension 1982; 4: 58-68.

114. Edwards NJ. Magnesium and heart failure. In: Proceedings. Ninth Annual Veterinary Medical Forum, American College of Veterinary Internal Medicine, New Orleans, LA 1991: 679-680.

115. Bean BL, Varghese PJ. Role of dietary magnesium deficiency in the pressor and arrhythmogenic response to epinephrine in the intact dog. American Heart Journal 1994; 127: 96-102.

116. Cobb M, Michell AR. Plasma electrolyte concentrations in dogs receiving diuretic therapy for cardiac failure. Journal of Small Animal Practice 1991; 33: 526-529.

117. O'Keefe D, Sisson DD. Serum electrolytes in dogs with congestive heart failure (abstract). Journal of Veterinary Internal Medicine 1993; 7: 118.

118. Roudebush P, Allen TA, Kuehn NF, et al. The effect of combined therapy with captopril, furosemide and a sodium restricted diet on serum electrolyte concentrations and renal function in normal dogs and dogs with congestive heart failure. Journal of Veterinary Internal Medicine 1994; 8: 337-342.

119. Bayliss J, Norell M, Canepa-Anson R, et al. Untreated heart failure: Clinical and neuroendocrine effects of introducing diuretics. British Heart Journal 1987; 57: 17-22.

120. Roudebush P, Allen TA. Effect of dietary sodium and furosemide on hematological, biochemical and endocrine parameters in normal geriatric dogs (abstract). Journal of Veterinary Internal Medicine 1996; 10: 171.

121. Haggstrom J, Hansson K, Karlberg BE, et al. Effects of long-term treatment with enalapril or hydralazine on the renin-angiotensin-aldosterone system and fluid balance in dogs with naturally acquired mitral valve regurgitation. American Journal of Veterinary Research 1996; 57: 1645-1652.

122. Keene BW, Rush JE. Therapy of heart failure. In: Ettinger SJ, Feldman EC, eds. Textbook of Veterinary Internal Medicine, 4th ed. Philadelphia, PA: WB Saunders Co, 1995; 878-881.

123. Seligman H, Halkin H, Rauchfleisch S, et al. Thiamine deficiency in patients with congestive heart failure receiving long-term furosemide therapy: A pilot study. American Journal of Medicine 1991; 91: 151-155.

124. Warren SE, O'Connor DT. Hyperkalemia resulting from captopril administration. Journal of the American Medical Association 1980; 244: 2551-2552.

125. Dzau VJ, Colucci WS, Williams GH, et al. Sustained effectiveness of converting enzyme inhibitors in patients with severe congestive heart failure. New England Journal of Medicine 1980; 302: 1373-1379.

126. Rotmensch HH, Vlasses PH, Ferguson RK. Angiotensin converting enzyme inhibitors. Medical Clinics of North America 1988; 72: 399-424.

127. COVE Study Group. Controlled clinical evaluation of enalapril in dogs with heart failure: Results of the cooperative veterinary enalapril study group. Journal of Veterinary Internal Medicine 1995; 9: 243-252.

128. Parker M, Lee WH, Medina N, et al. Functional renal insufficiency during long-term therapy with captopril and enalapril in severe chronic heart failure. Annals of Internal Medicine 1987; 106: 346-354.

129. Longhofer SL, Ericsson GF, Cifelli A, et al. Renal function in heart failure dogs receiving furosemide and enalapril maleate (abstract). Journal of Veterinary Internal Medicine 1993; 7: 123.

130. DeLillis LA, Kittleson MD. Current uses and hazards of vasodilator therapy in heart failure. In: Kirk RW, Bonagura JD, eds. Current Veterinary Therapy XI. Philadelphia, PA: WB Saunders Co, 1992; 700-708.

131. Snyder PS, Atkins CE. Current uses and hazards of the digitalis glycosides. In: Kirk RW, Bonagura JD, eds. Current Veterinary Therapy XI. Philadelphia, PA: WB Saunders Co, 1992; 689-693.

132. Atkins CE, Snyder PS, Keene BW. Effect of aspirin, furosemide, and commercial low salt diet on digoxin pharmacokinetic properties in clinically normal cats. Journal of the American Veterinary Medical Association 1988; 193: 1264-1268.

133. Packer M, Medina N, Yushak M. Correction of dilutional hyponatremia in severe chronic heart failure by converting-enzyme inhibition. Annals of Internal Medicine 1984; 100: 782-789.

CASE 18-1

Congestive Heart Failure in a Beagle Crossbred Dog

Bruce W. Keene, DVM
Diplomate ACVIM (Cardiology)
College of Veterinary Medicine
North Carolina State University
Raleigh, North Carolina, USA

Assess the Animal

An 11-year-old, neutered female beagle crossbred dog weighing 10 kg was admitted to the hospital with a three-month history of weight loss and reduced appetite. The dog had been short of breath for the past 24 hours and would not lie down the previous night. The dog had been examined by a veterinarian two months earlier for coughing and exercise intolerance. At that time a tentative diagnosis of tracheobronchitis was made and the dog was treated with a trimethoprim-sulfadiazine combination for seven days and a sustained-release theophylline compound for three weeks. Clinical signs improved some during the first week of therapy.

The dog's vaccinations were current. Yearly heartworm antigen tests were negative for the past five years. The patient received ivermectin monthly for heartworm prevention, and except for intermittent flea problems and mild periodontal disease, had been exceptionally healthy its entire life.

On presentation, the dog's rectal temperature was 38.9°C (102.1°F), the pulse 160/min. and the respiratory rate 70/min. The dog appeared alert and anxious, with rapid, labored breathing. Mucous membranes were pale pink and the capillary refill time was slightly slow. A modest amount of periodontal disease and dental calculus were noted.

The bronchovesicular sounds were louder than normal and end-inspiratory crackles were heard diffusely over the lung fields bilaterally, accompanied by some expiratory wheezes. The precordial impulse was normally located and the arterial pulses were rapid but regular. A 3/6 holosystolic (regurgitant quality) murmur heard best at the left cardiac apex and radiating somewhat to the heart base was auscultated. A softer, regurgitant quality systolic murmur was

audible at the right hemithorax. The jugular veins were modestly distended and a systolic jugular venous pulse was present. The abdomen was nonpainful. The liver was descended about 2 cm below the costal arch. Body condition score was 2/5. The rest of the physical examination was unremarkable.

Results of the initial laboratory tests included: complete blood count (normal), urinalysis (urine specific gravity = 1.022 [reference range = 1.001 to 1.070]; dipstick and sediment examination were normal) and serum biochemistry profile (normal, except for a mild elevation in serum creatinine concentration). Generalized cardiomegaly with especially prominent left atrial and left ventricular enlargement was evident radiographically. Pulmonary venous distention and air bronchograms typical of cardiogenic pulmonary edema were also visualized (Figures 1A and 1B).

The clinical diagnosis was congestive heart failure (CHF) secondary to chronic valvular heart disease (endocardiosis) and mitral/tricuspid regurgitation.

Assess the Food(s) and Feeding Method

The dog was fed a mixture of commercial moist and dry dog food, with 10 to 20% of the intake from lean meat and vegetable table foods.

Questions

1. What are nutrients of concern and general nutritional recommendations for patients with cardiac disease and CHF?
2. What are the potential interactions between pharmacologic and nutritional prescriptions that might be made for this patient?
3. What is the patient's daily energy requirement (DER)?

Answers and Discussion

1. General nutritional recommendations for patients with cardiac disease and CHF include: avoid excess sodium and chloride; ensure adequate magnesium intake; ensure adequate potassium intake, if using diuretics; avoid excess potassium intake, if using

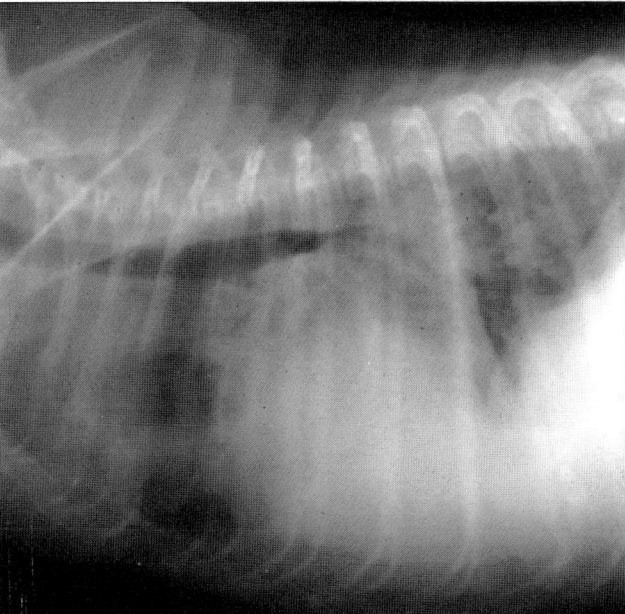

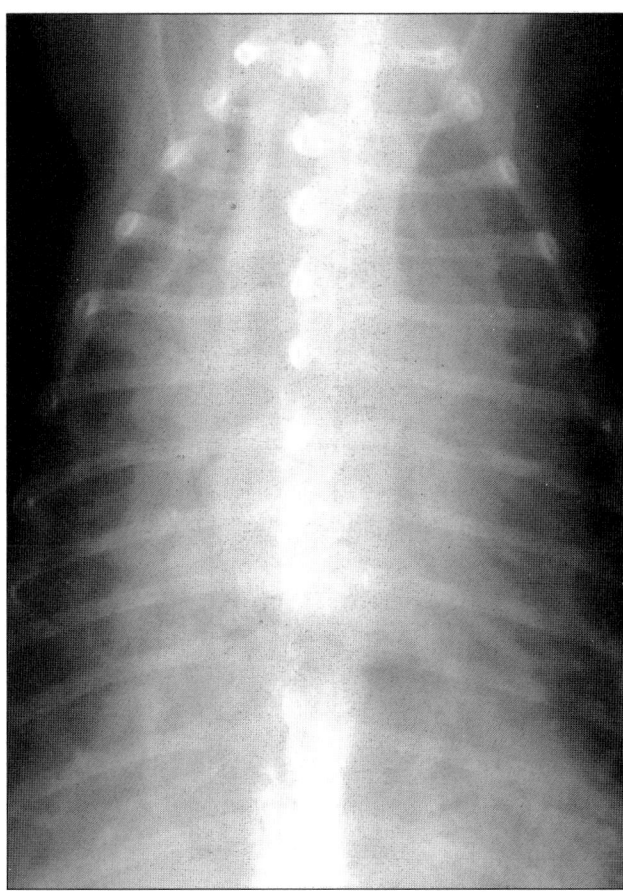

Figures 1A (above) and 1B (right). Lateral and ventrodorsal thoracic radiographs taken on the day of admission to the hospital. Generalized cardiomegaly with prominent left atrial and ventricular enlargement is present. Pulmonary venous distention and air bronchograms typical of cardiogenic pulmonary edema are also visualized.

angiotensin converting enzyme (ACE) inhibitor drugs; ensure adequate energy and protein intake; avoid excess phosphorus and protein intake, especially when renal disease is present; and provide additional taurine and carnitine, if myocardial failure is present.

2. Most patients with advanced heart disease and failure are treated with a combination of nutritional management and drug therapy. The interaction between drugs and nutrient levels in foods used in cardiovascular patients is an important consideration.

Furosemide may contribute to hypokalemia and hypomagnesemia (especially in animals with anorexia) by increasing urinary loss of potassium and magnesium. Hypokalemia and hypomagnesemia may potentiate cardiac dysrhythmias. Patients receiving diuretic therapy should be encouraged to eat a food that provides moderate, but not excessive, intake of these nutrients (0.10 to 0.15% magnesium on a dry matter basis; 0.6 to 0.9% potassium on a dry matter basis).

Mild elevations in serum potassium concentrations have been noted in some dogs treated with ACE inhibitors such as captopril and enalapril. Although clinically significant hyperkalemia (serum potassium >6.5 mEq/l) is uncommon, the use of ACE inhibitors in dogs with CHF or renal insufficiency fed commercial or veterinary therapeutic foods with high potassium content may increase the risk for hyperkalemia.

Hypotension and renal insufficiency are two common complications of ACE inhibitor therapy. When these complications occur, the dosage of the ACE inhibitor drug is often reduced. An alternative method is to replete total body sodium concentrations by reducing the dosage of diuretic and increasing the daily sodium intake of the animal. This may be successful in reversing hypotension or renal insufficiency without having to change the ACE inhibitor drug dosage.

3. This patient's calculated resting energy requirement (RER), based on a body weight of 10 kg, is approximately 370 kcal/day (1,548 kJ/day). However, the RER is probably higher because of the patient's increased heart and respiratory rates. Calculation of RER based on an estimated ideal body weight of 12 kg can be used and would result in an RER of 430 kcal/day (1,799 kJ/day). The dog's DER would be 520 to 600 kcal/day (2,176 to 2,510 kJ/day). Frequent monitoring of body condition is important so that appropriate adjustments to energy intake can be made.

Therapy Including Feeding Plan

The patient was treated initially with a diuretic (furosemide, 3 mg/kg body weight subcutaneously) and nitroglycerine (5 mg/24-hr transdermal patch), and was placed in an oxygen-enriched environment. Within four hours, breathing was less labored and oxygen supplementation was discontinued. A second dose of furosemide (2 mg/kg body weight orally) was administered and water was offered free choice. The dog spent a quiet night.

The next day, an electrocardiogram confirmed the presence of a sinus rhythm with evidence of left atrial and ventricular enlargement. An echocardiogram disclosed thickened mitral and tricuspid valve leaflets typical of endocardiosis (Figure 2). Also, severe mitral and tricuspid regurgitation was seen on color flow Doppler. Enalapril was initiated (0.5 mg/kg body weight per os, twice daily), furosemide was continued (1 mg/kg body weight per os, twice daily), and digoxin was begun (0.006 mg/kg body weight per os, twice daily).

The dog was fed one can of Prescription Diet Canine k/d[a] (570 kcal/can; 2,384 kJ/can) per day and discharged from the hospital. The owners were instructed to return with the dog in five days for further evaluation.

Progress Notes

During the recheck examination, the owners reported that the dog was doing well. The body weight remained stable at 10 kg, the serum digoxin concentration was 1.4 ng/ml (therapeutic range = 1.0 to 2.0 ng/ml) and serum electrolyte, urea nitrogen and creatinine concentrations were within normal ranges. Rechecks were scheduled at three-month intervals, or sooner if clinical problems arose. The owners were instructed to adjust the furosemide dosage as needed to keep the dog comfortable, within a range of 0.5 to 2.0 mg/kg body weight once to twice daily.

The dog remained well for about eight months, when it was admitted to the hospital for evaluation of mild dyspnea. The owners reported that they had been gradually increasing the furosemide dosage, which was now consistently at 2 mg/kg body weight per os, twice daily. Several house guests had fed the dog pretzels and potato chips several hours before presentation. Auscultation revealed some end-inspiratory crackles over the lung fields. An additional dose of 2 mg/kg body weight of furosemide was administered subcutaneously. Serum urea nitrogen, creatinine and electrolyte concentrations were within normal limits. The serum digoxin concentration was 1.2 ng/ml.

The food was changed to moist Prescription Diet Canine h/d[a] (583 kcal/can; 2,439 kJ/can), which is lower in sodium than the food fed previously. Three days later, the owners reported that the dog was feeling well. Its serum biochemistry values continued to be normal.

Approximately 10 months later, another episode of severe pulmonary edema occurred that was not associated with any known nutritional indiscretion. This condition was unresponsive to 12 hours of intensive preload and afterload reducing therapy (increasing doses of furosemide, the arterial dilator hydralazine and nitroglycerine). The dog was euthanatized at an emergency clinic at the owner's request. Postmortem examination revealed a

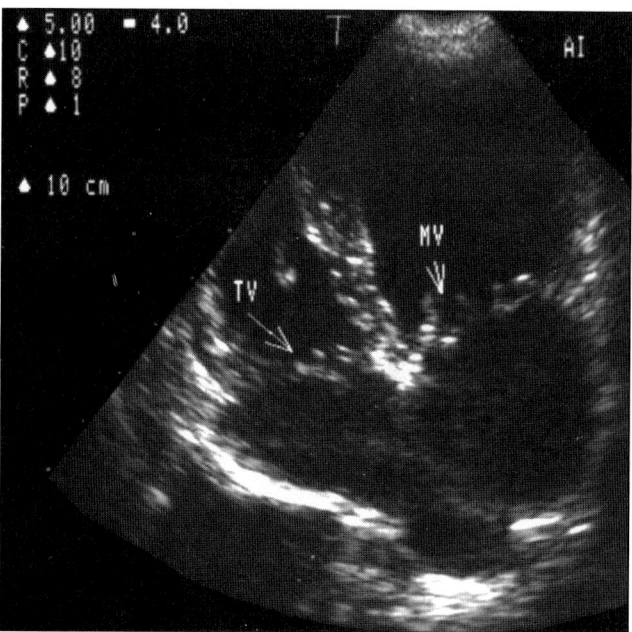

Figure 2. An echocardiogram obtained on the second day of hospitalization shows thickened mitral (MV) and tricuspid (TV) valve leaflets typical of endocardiosis.

ruptured primary chorda tendinea to be the cause of the dramatically worsened mitral regurgitation and unresponsive pulmonary edema.

Endnote

a. Hill's Pet Nutrition Inc., Topeka, KS, USA.

Bibliography

Roudebush P, Allen TA, Kuehn NF, et al. The effect of combined therapy with captopril, furosemide and a sodium restricted diet on serum electrolyte concentrations and renal function in normal dogs and dogs with congestive heart failure. Journal of Veterinary Internal Medicine 1994; 8: 337-342.

Keene BW, Rush JE. Therapy of heart failure. In: Ettinger SJ, Feldman EC, eds. Textbook of Veterinary Internal Medicine, 4th ed. Philadelphia, PA: WB Saunders Co, 1995; 878-881.

■ CASE 18-2

Dilated Cardiomyopathy in an American Cocker Spaniel Dog

Bruce W. Keene, DVM
Diplomate ACVIM (Cardiology)
College of Veterinary Medicine
North Carolina State University
Raleigh, North Carolina, USA

Assess the Animal

A nine-year-old, male black American cocker spaniel dog was examined for dyspnea and lethargy that began two days after a routine elective surgical procedure (removal of a subcutaneous mass). The dog was thin (body condition score 2/5) and weighed 12 kg. Vaccinations were current and the dog received heartworm preventive medication. The dog had not had any major health problems in the past.

The heart rate was 180 beats/min. and regular, the respiratory rate 76 breaths/min. and the rectal temperature 39.9°C (103.8°F). The mucous membranes were dusky pink, with slow capillary refill. A soft (1/6 to 2/6) holosystolic murmur was heard best at the left cardiac apex, accompanied by a diastolic gallop sound (felt to be S3). The lung sounds were loud with some inspiratory crackles heard bilaterally. Otitis externa was noted bilaterally. An incision behind the right shoulder oozed slightly on palpation.

Thoracic radiographs revealed generalized, severe cardiomegaly with alveolar pulmonary edema (Figures 1A and 1B). An echocardiogram revealed a left ventricular diameter of 5.68 cm in diastole (extremely dilated), with only an 8% shortening fraction (normal = 30 to 45%), but no major structural lesions were found on any valves (Figure 2). The echocardiographic findings were consistent with a diagnosis of dilated cardiomyopathy.

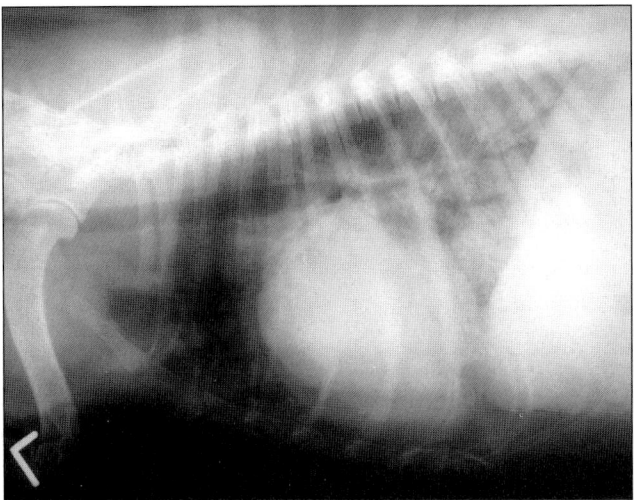

Figures 1A (above) and 1B (right). Lateral and ventrodorsal radiographs taken at the time of admission. Generalized cardiomegaly and pulmonary edema consistent with CHF are present.

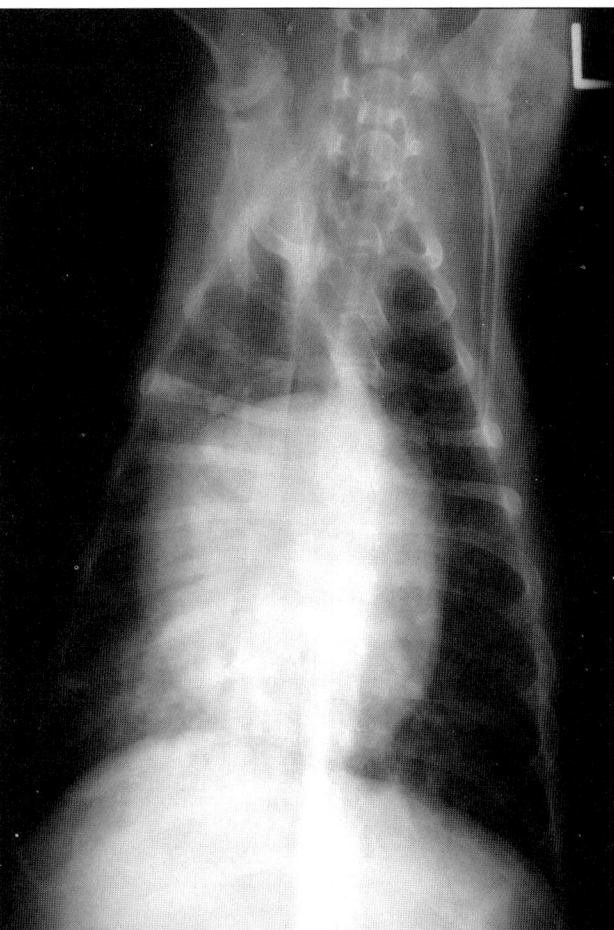

Results of an arterial blood gas analysis revealed hypoxemia and hyperventilation (PaO_2 = 71 mm Hg [reference range = 92.1 ± 5.6], pH = 7.4 [7.4], $PaCO_2$ = 30.8 mm Hg [36.8 ± 3.0]). Results of a complete blood count included normal red cell indices (PCV = 39%[reference range = 38 to 57]), with an elevated leukocyte count (23,900/µl [reference range = 6.1 to 17.4]) consisting of a neutrophilia with a left shift (2,868 bands/µl [reference range = 0 to 300]). The platelet count was normal. Results of a serum biochemistry profile (including albumin, creatinine, urea nitrogen, electrolytes and liver enzymes) were within normal limits. Urinalysis disclosed an inactive sediment with a urine specific gravity of 1.024 (reference range = 1.001 to 1.070). The taurine concentration in a sample of whole blood was decreased (28.6 µmol/l; normal = 40.0 to 120.0), as was the plasma concentration of L-carnitine (plasma free carnitine 4.2 µmol/l; normal = 8.0 to 36.0).

Assess the Food(s) and Feeding Method

The dog was fed a variety of dry commercial dog foods, free choice.

Questions

1. What is the feeding plan for this patient?
2. Should this dog be given nutritional supplementation?

Answers and Discussion

1. General nutritional recommendations for patients with cardiac disease and congestive heart failure (CHF) include the following: avoid excess sodium and chloride; ensure adequate magnesium intake; ensure adequate potassium intake, if using diuretics; avoid excess potassium intake, if using angiotensin converting enzyme (ACE) inhibitor drugs; ensure adequate energy and protein intake; avoid excess phosphorus and protein intake, especially with evidence of concurrent renal disease; and provide additional taurine and carnitine, if myocardial failure is

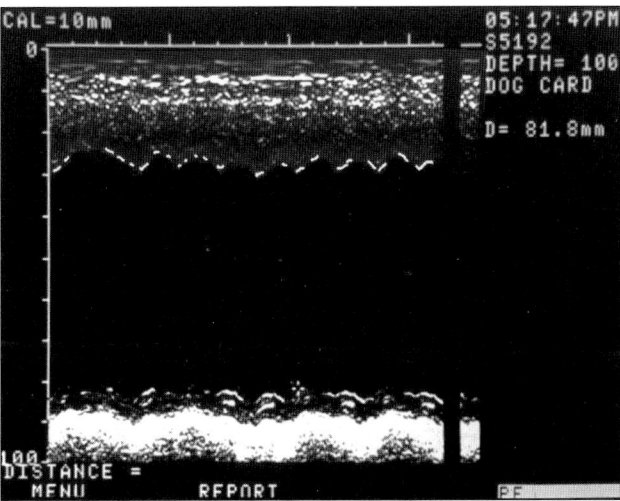

Figure 2. M-mode echocardiography reveals a marked increase in ventricular volume due to myocardial failure.

present. This patient's calculated resting energy requirement (RER), based on the current body weight of 12 kg, is approximately 430 kcal/day (1,806 kJ/day). However, the RER is probably higher because of the patient's increased heart and respiratory rates. The dog's daily energy requirement (DER) would be 600 to 700 kcal/day (2,510 to 2,928 kJ/day). Frequent monitoring of body condition helps guide appropriate adjustments to this energy calculation.

2. Because of the suspected association of carnitine and taurine deficiency with dilated cardiomyopathy in American cocker spaniel dogs, supplementation with L-carnitine (1 g per os, three times daily) and taurine (500 mg per os, twice daily) was also begun. In this case, the whole blood taurine and plasma carnitine concentrations were depressed, justifying use of these supplements. In many cases of L-carnitine deficiency, the plasma carnitine concentration is "normal" (for dogs fed commercial dry foods), although endomyocardial biopsy may disclose myocardial carnitine deficiency. The relationship between blood and myocardial taurine concentrations is less well defined, but it seems prudent to supplement the food of American cocker spaniels with both taurine and L-carnitine.

Therapy Including Feeding Plan

Therapy was initiated with furosemide (2 mg/kg body weight subcutaneously, twice daily), enalapril (0.5 mg/kg body weight per os, twice daily), digoxin (0.006 mg/kg body weight per os, twice daily) and nitroglycerine (0.2 mg/hr transdermal patch, applied for the initial 12 hours of hospitalization). After culture of the surgical wound, a first-generation cephalosporin was given orally. The dog was maintained in an oxygen-enriched environment (40% oxygen) and its respiratory rate was monitored hourly.

A commercial veterinary therapeutic food designed for patients with cardiovascular disease (Prescription Diet Canine h/d[a]) was initially offered free choice, but was refused by the dog. A different commercial veterinary therapeutic food (Prescription Diet Canine k/d[a]) was offered two days later when the azotemia was beginning to resolve; this food was readily accepted. Canine k/d avoids excess sodium, chloride, phosphorus, potassium and protein found in regular commercial dog foods. (See Table 18-9.)

Progress Notes

The next day, the dog weighed 0.5 kg less, was afebrile, depressed and refused food, but was breathing much easier. Oxygen supplementation and nitroglycerine were discontinued. A serum biochemistry profile revealed that the serum urea nitrogen and creatinine concentrations had risen dramatically. An intravenous catheter was placed and maintenance fluid therapy was initiated with a relatively low-sodium physiologic electrolyte solution. Digoxin was withheld for 24 hours, and furosemide and enalapril were discontinued for 12 hours. Dobutamine (2.5 µg/kg body weight/min., increased to 5 µg/kg body weight/min. four hours later) was begun by continuous intravenous infusion to improve cardiac and renal function. An electrocardiogram was monitored continuously during dobutamine therapy for ventricular ectopic activity or other tachyarrhythmias.

The dog was much brighter and more active the following day. The serum urea nitrogen and creatinine concentrations had decreased. Fluid therapy and enalapril were continued, and the dobutamine drip was tapered over 12 hours. That evening, furosemide and enalapril were administered. The serum urea nitrogen and creatinine concentrations were normal the next day. The dog was now drinking and ate the veterinary therapeutic food that was offered (Prescription Diet Canine k/d, one can). Fluid therapy was discontinued and digoxin (0.006 mg/kg body weight per os, twice daily), enalapril (0.5 mg/kg

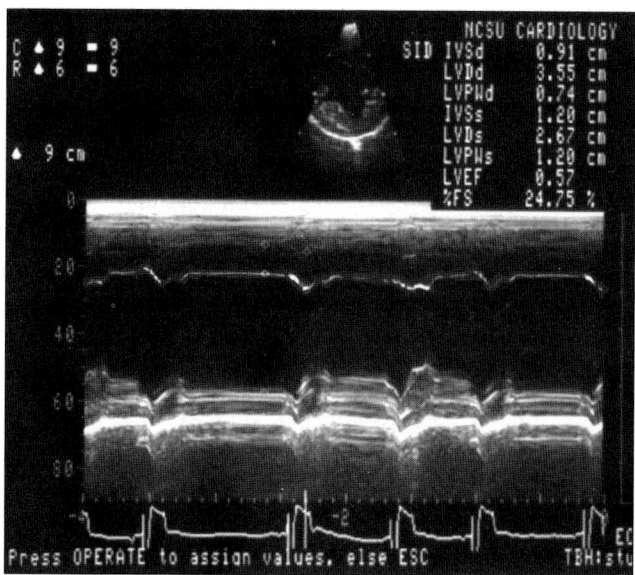

Figure 3. M-mode echocardiography one year after the initial admission for heart failure reveals normal left ventricular volume and function.

body weight per os, twice daily) and furosemide (1 mg/kg body weight per os, twice daily) were administered.

The dog improved and was able to go home four days after entering the hospital. Five days later, the owner reported that the patient was feeling better than it had in months. One and one-third cans of the veterinary therapeutic food were fed to meet the increased DER expected in the home environment. Three months postadmission, an echocardiogram and chest radiographs showed some improvement in fractional shortening, and complete resolution of pulmonary edema and pulmonary venous distention. Results of a serum biochemistry profile were normal. Furosemide was discontinued at that time. Body weight was now 13.2 kg. Digoxin, enalapril, Canine k/d and taurine and carnitine supplementation were continued. Canine k/d was fed in the same amount.

One year after the initial admission, an echocardiogram (Figure 3) disclosed remarkable reduction in left ventricular size and improved left ventricular systolic function (left ventricular diastolic diameter 3.55 cm; left ventricular shortening fraction 24.75%). Thoracic radiographs revealed no cardiomegaly or pulmonary edema (Figures 4A and 4B). The owner had discontinued digoxin and enalapril approximately 10 months after the first admission (he had gone out of town and not started therapy again when he returned), although he continued to feed Canine k/d and administer the taurine and carnitine supplements. The dog weighed 13.6 kg and had a body condition score of 3/5. The dog did well for three additional years, maintaining its improved ventricular function.

Four years after the initial diagnosis, the dog developed ascites. The heart and lungs were unchanged and the central venous pressure was normal. Ultrasonographic evaluation of the abdomen revealed a mass originating in the left adrenal gland, with intravascular invasion and extension into the right adrenal gland and obstruction of the caudal vena cava. Body weight was 10.5 kg with cachexia (body condition score of 1/5). A pheochromocytoma was diagnosed at postmortem examination.

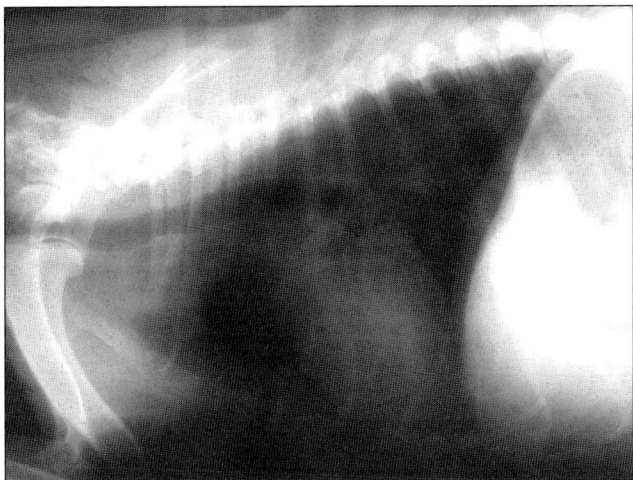

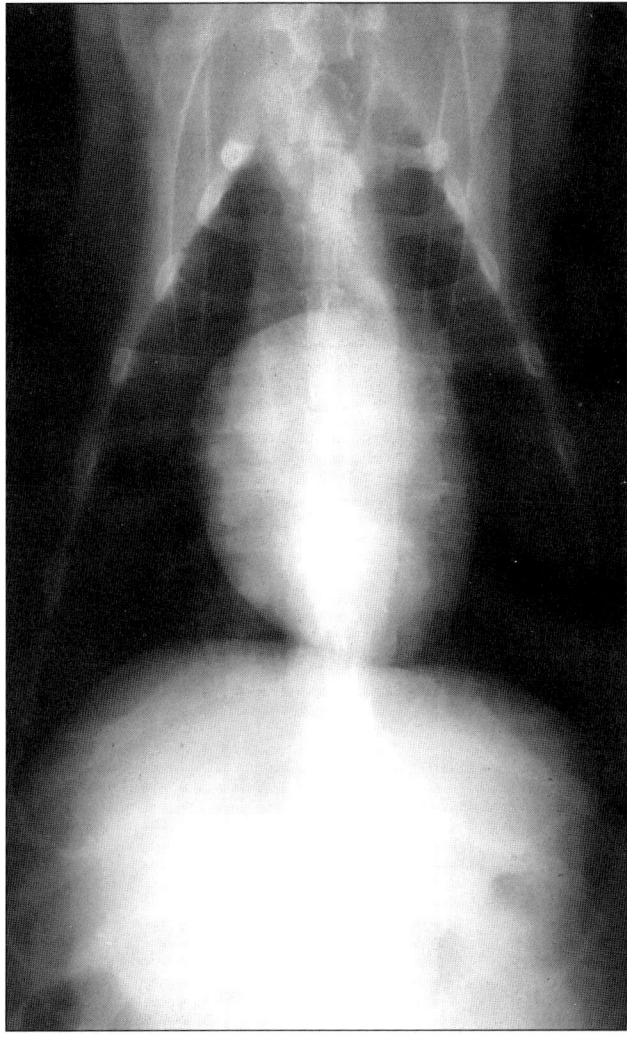

Figures 4A (above) and 4B (right). Lateral and ventrodorsal radiographs taken one year after the initial admission for heart failure reveal normal cardiac size and no evidence of pulmonary edema.

Endnote

a. Hill's Pet Nutrition Inc., Topeka, KS, USA.

Bibliography

Keene BW. L-carnitine deficiency in canine dilated cardiomyopathy. In: Kirk RW, Bonagura JD, eds. Current Veterinary Therapy XI. Philadelphia, PA: WB Saunders Co, 1992; 780-783.

Kittleson MD, Keene BW, Pion PD, et al. Results of the Multicenter Spaniel Trial (MUST): Taurine- and carnitine-responsive dilated cardiomyopathy in American Cocker spaniels with decreased plasma taurine concentration. Journal of Veterinary Internal Medicine 1997; 11: 204-211.

Kramer GA, Kittleson MD, Fox PR, et al. Plasma taurine concentrations in normal dogs and dogs with heart disease. Journal of Veterinary Internal Medicine 1995; 9: 252-258.

CASE 18-3

Systemic Hypertension in a Domestic Shorthair Cat

Lisa Freeman, DVM, PhD
Diplomate ACVN
School of Veterinary Medicine
Tufts University
North Grafton, Massachusetts, USA

Assess the Animal

A 17-year-old, castrated male domestic shorthair cat was examined for hyphema and apparent vision loss. The cat appeared disoriented for several days and the owner noticed blood in the cat's left eye on the day of admission.

One year before this admission, the cat had been diagnosed with chronic renal failure on the basis of mild azotemia (serum urea nitrogen = 43 mg/dl [reference range = 14 to 28]; serum creatinine = 2.4 mg/dl [<2.0]); and a urine specific gravity of 1.016 (1.002 to 1.080). Nutritional therapy for chronic renal failure was implemented, and clinical and laboratory parameters were monitored frequently. The cat's condition remained stable. No other medical problems were recognized during the past year. Vaccinations were current.

When examined, the cat had a rectal temperature of 38.4°C (101.2°F), heart rate of 220 beats/min. and respiratory rate of 28 breaths/min. The cat's current body weight was 4.5 kg (body condition score 2/5). The cat's normal body weight was 5.2 kg. A 2/6 systolic murmur was auscultated over the left sternal border. Both kidneys were decreased in size on palpation. The thyroid glands were not palpable.

An ocular examination revealed bilateral retinal detachment, with moderate hyphema and vitreal hemorrhages in the left eye (Figure 1). Blood pressure, measured by Doppler technique, was 300/220 mm Hg. An echocardiogram demonstrated mild left atrial enlargement and moderate hypertrophy of the left ventricle with symmetric thickening of the left ventricular free wall and interventricular septum (Figures 2A and 2B).

Results of a complete blood count and serum biochemistry profile included mild nonregenerative anemia and mild azotemia. The T_4 concentration was within normal limits (1.9 µg/dl [reference range = 1.0 to 3.8]).

The clinical problems included weight loss, systemic hypertension with secondary cardiac hypertrophy, bilateral retinal detachment with vitreal hemorrhage and chronic renal failure.

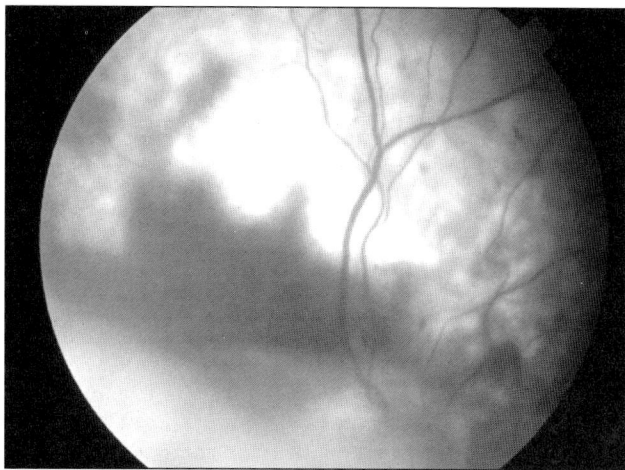

Figure 1. Retinal detachment and vitreal hemorrhages observed in the left eye of a 17-year-old cat.

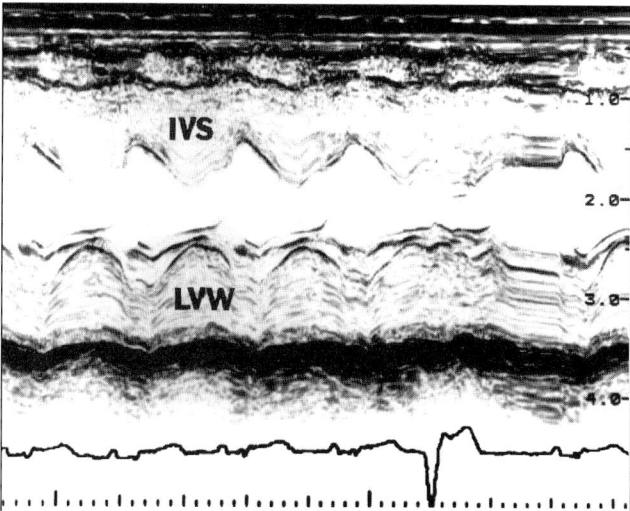

Figure 2B. M-mode echocardiogram of the left ventricle demonstrating symmetric hypertrophy of the left ventricular free wall (LVW) and interventricular septum (IVS). One ventricular premature depolarization is noted on the electrocardiogram at the bottom.

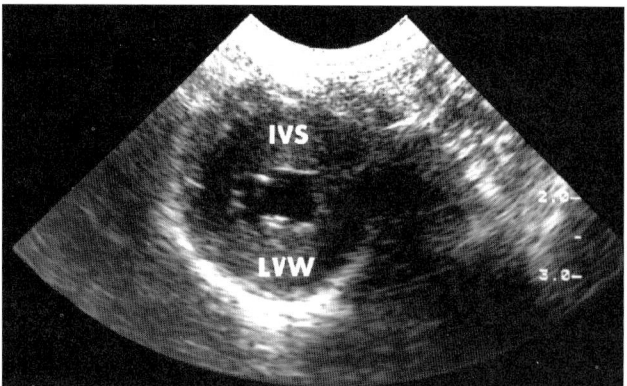

Figure 2A. Two-dimensional echocardiogram showing a short-axis view of the left ventricle and demonstrating symmetric hypertrophy of the left ventricular free wall (LVW) and interventricular septum (IVS).

Assess the Food(s) and Feeding Method

Treatment for chronic renal failure consisted of free choice feeding of a dry veterinary therapeutic food that avoids excess levels of protein, phosphorus and sodium (Prescription Diet Feline k/d[a]).

Questions

1. What are the energy requirements for this patient?
2. Which nutrients are of special concern for this patient and at what levels should they be fed?
3. Assuming that the patient is not anorectic, what techniques can be used for restoring optimal body weight?

Answers and Discussion

1. This patient's resting energy requirement (RER), based on usual body weight, is approximately 226 kcal/day (946 kJ/day). The daily energy requirement (DER) would, therefore, be approximately 316 kcal/day (1,322 kJ/day).
2. The nutrients of special concern are sodium, chloride, potassium, magnesium, phosphorus and protein.

Sodium and chloride. Retention of sodium and chloride has been implicated in the pathogenesis of some forms of hypertension in people. The full expression of sodium chloride-sensitive hypertension in people depends on the concomitant administration of both sodium and chloride. It is currently unknown whether retention of sodium and chloride is an important part of the pathogenesis of systemic hypertension in dogs and cats with renal failure. However, a prudent recommendation would be to feed an adult feline maintenance food or veterinary therapeutic food (a renal or cardiac food) that avoids excess levels of sodium and chloride (0.20 to 0.30% dry matter).

Potassium. Cats with chronic renal disease are at risk for hypokalemia, in part due to excessive urinary loss of potassium and chronic metabolic acidosis. (See Chapter 19.) The link between potassium and blood pressure has been the subject of growing interest in people. Although higher potassium intake in people is generally associated with lower blood pressure, potassium's antihypertensive effect appears to be mediated by nutrient interactions. Potassium supplementation reverses hypertension in several experimental models, including both sodium chloride-sensitive and non-sodium chloride-sensitive varieties of experimental hypertension. Although administration of potassium reduces blood pressure in some people, not all studies have revealed a beneficial effect. A prudent recommendation would be to avoid hypokalemia by using a food with moderate potassium levels (0.80 to 1.0% dry matter) and reduced acid load. A veterinary therapeutic food designed for feline renal failure meets these nutritional goals.

Magnesium. Only a few well-designed trials have examined the effects of supplemental magnesium on blood pressure in people with essential hypertension. The results of these trials have been inconsistent. Current recommendations would be to provide a food with moderate magnesium levels (0.10 to 0.15% dry matter) for hypertensive animals.

Phosphorus and protein. Avoiding excess phosphorus and protein in patients with chronic renal failure may slow progression of the disease and help alleviate clinical signs associated with azotemia, uremia and hyperparathyroidism. (See Chapter 19.)

3. Weight loss is a potential problem in patients with chronic renal disease. Because this patient has lost 0.7 kg, restoration of usual body weight and condition and prevention of further weight loss is recommended. Simple means of improving appetite include:
   - Treat any underlying problems (dental disease, dehydration, hypokalemia, anemia).
   - Replace part or all of the dry food with moist food, to be fed in small frequent meals.
   - Warm the food to body temperature.
   - Have the owner weigh and measure portions and keep a record of actual food intake.

   Anemia secondary to erythropoietin deficiency is an invariable consequence of chronic renal failure in dogs and cats. Recombinant human erythropoietin produces a rapid and effective erythroid proliferative response in most dogs and cats with naturally occurring renal failure. Improvements in appetite, energy and weight gain and increased alertness are seen in most patients treated with recombinant human erythropoietin. The improvements in well-being facilitate the concurrent nutritional management and often bolster owner satisfaction and commitment to therapy.

Therapy Including Feeding Plan

The patient was started on amlodipine (0.625 mg per os, once daily) and topical ocular corticosteroids. A moist veterinary therapeutic food that avoids excess protein, phosphorus, sodium and chloride (Prescription Diet Feline k/d;[a] one-eighth can twice daily) was offered in addition to ad libitum feeding of the dry renal food.

Progress Notes

Two weeks later, the cat's weight was 4.8 kg. Systemic blood pressure, measured by Doppler technique, was 250/140 mm Hg. Enalapril (2.5 mg per os, once daily) was added to the treatment regimen. A serum biochemistry profile performed two weeks after the initiation of enalapril therapy showed no change in the serum urea nitrogen, creatinine or potassium concentrations. The patient's blood pressure was eventually reduced to 150/110 mm Hg due to combined amlodipine and enalapril therapy. The cat had areas of retinal reattachment and regained vision in the right eye, but blindness persisted in the left eye. Feeding the dry food free choice and a moist food twice daily helped maintain body weight between 4.8 and 5.1 kg. The patient died acutely 23 months after its initial admission.

Endnote

a. Hill's Pet Nutrition Inc., Topeka, KS, USA.

Bibliography

Reusser ME, McCarron DA. Micronutrient effects on blood pressure regulation. Nutrition Reviews 1994; 52: 367-375.

Kobayashi DL, Peterson ME, Graves TK, et al. Hypertension in cats with chronic renal failure or hyperthyroidism. Journal of Veterinary Internal Medicine 1990; 4: 58-62.

Osborne CA, Lulich JP, Sanderson SL, et al. Treatment of uremic anorexia. In: Bonagura JD, ed. Current Veterinary Therapy XII. Philadelphia, PA: WB Saunders Co, 1995; 966-971.

Littman MP. Update: Treatment of hypertension in dogs and cats. In: Kirk RW, Bonagura JD, eds. Current Veterinary Therapy XI. Philadelphia, PA: WB Saunders Co, 1992; 838-841.

Cowgill LD. CVT update: Use of recombinant human erythropoietin. In: Bonagura JD, ed. Current Veterinary Therapy XII. Philadelphia, PA: WB Saunders Co, 1995; 961-963.

CASE 18-4

Cachexia in a Labrador Retriever Crossbred Dog

Lisa Freeman, DVM, PhD
Diplomate ACVN
School of Veterinary Medicine
Tufts University
North Grafton, Massachusetts, USA

Assess the Animal

A nine-year-old, castrated male Labrador retriever crossbred dog was examined for exercise intolerance and coughing of one week's duration. The dog had become less active during the preceding three months and now tires after a 15-minute walk, but the owners attributed this loss of endurance to advancing age. Coughing, especially at night, developed in the last several days. Vaccinations were current and the patient received heartworm preventive medication monthly.

On physical examination, the dog weighed 23 kg (body condition score 2/5) and had visible muscle wasting over the temporal, gluteal, scapular and lumbar regions (Figure 1). Rectal temperature was 38.6°C (101.4°F), heart rate was 160 beats/min. and respiratory rate was 32 breaths/min. No murmur was auscultated, but femoral pulses were weak and jugular pulses were present.

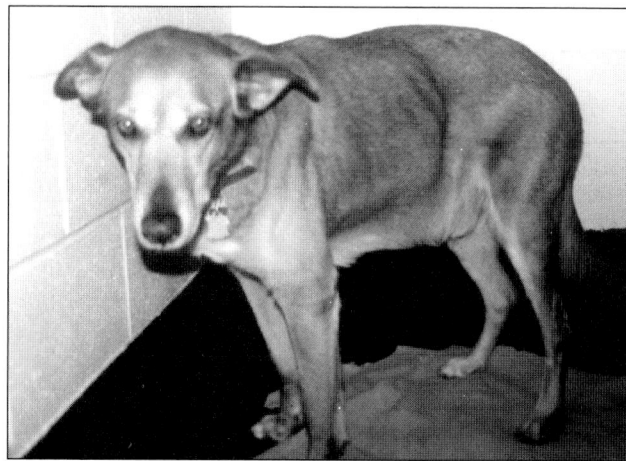

Figure 1. A nine-year-old, castrated male Labrador retriever crossbred dog at the time of initial presentation. Note the prominent muscle wasting observed in the temporal, gluteal, lumbar and scapular areas.

An electrocardiogram revealed sinus tachycardia with rare ventricular premature depolarizations (Figure 2). Thoracic radiographs revealed generalized cardiomegaly with mild pulmonary edema (Figures 3A and 3B). The echocardiogram

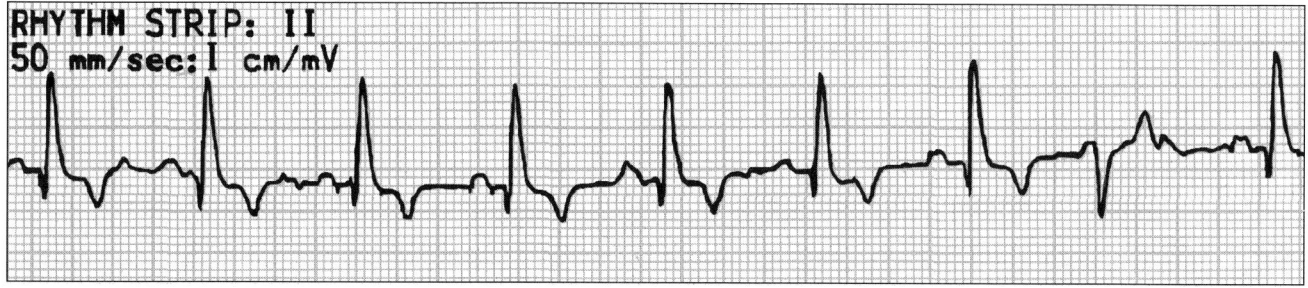

Figure 2. Lead II electrocardiogram (50 mm/sec, 1 cm/mV) showing sinus tachycardia with one ventricular premature depolarization.

Table 1. Systolic function in a Labrador retriever crossbred dog.

	Patient*	Reference*
Left ventricular internal dimension (diastole)	5.36	4.10-4.60
Left ventricular internal dimension (systole)	4.96	2.70-3.20
Left ventricular free wall (diastole)	0.62	0.68-0.82
Left ventricular free wall (systole)	0.83	1.00-1.30
Interventricular septum (diastole)	0.51	0.77-0.95
Interventricular septum (systole)	0.77	1.16-1.42
Left atrium	2.88	1.90-2.30
Aorta	2.41	2.20-2.50
Fractional shortening (%)	6	28-40

*All values are expressed in cm unless otherwise specified.

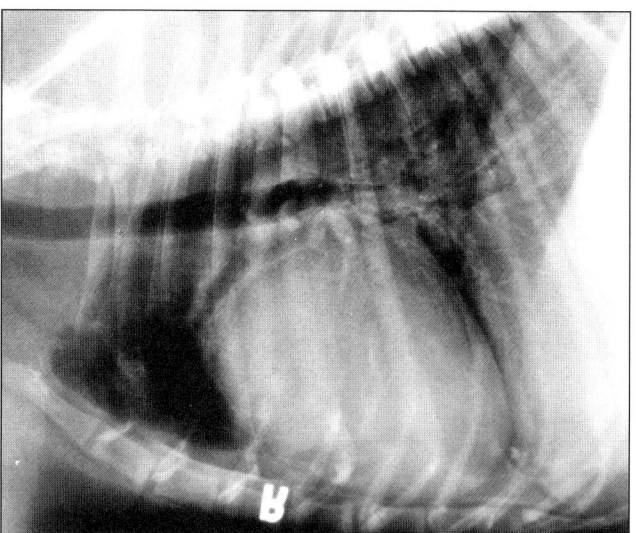

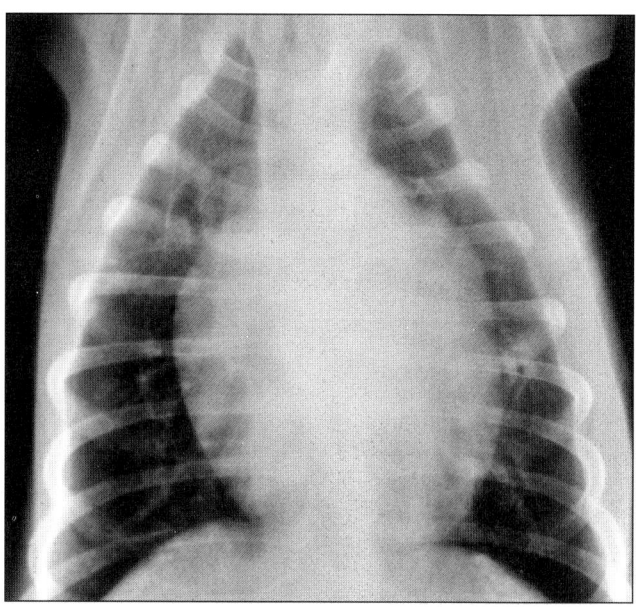

Figures 3A (above) and 3B (below). Right lateral and dorsoventral thoracic radiographs demonstrating generalized cardiomegaly and mild pulmonary edema.

demonstrated left ventricular and left atrial enlargement (Figures 4A and 4B), with severely depressed systolic function (Table 1). Results of a serum biochemistry profile were within normal limits.

The clinical problem list included idiopathic dilated cardiomyopathy, congestive heart failure (CHF) and cardiac cachexia.

Assess the Food(s) and Feeding Method

The dog was fed a commercial dry, low-fat, moderate-fiber food (Prescription Diet Canine w/d[a]) for management of inflammatory bowel disease, which had been diagnosed previously. The patient was eating approximately the same amount of food as in the past and its body weight had not changed over the past six months, although the dog was now somewhat pickier about the foods it would eat.

Questions

1. What are the energy requirements for this patient?
2. What nutrients are of special concern for dogs with CHF?
3. Should body weight be used to assess body condition in dogs with CHF?
4. What are the factors contributing to weight loss in this patient and how can they be managed?

Answers and Discussion

1. This patient's calculated resting energy requirement (RER), based on a body weight of 23 kg, is approxi-
mately 760 kcal/day (3,180 kJ/day). However, the RER is probably higher because of the patient's increased heart and respiratory rates. The ideal body weight for similar mature crossbred dogs is usually 25 to 34 kg. Calculation of RER based on ideal body weight would result in an increased RER value. The dog's total daily energy require-

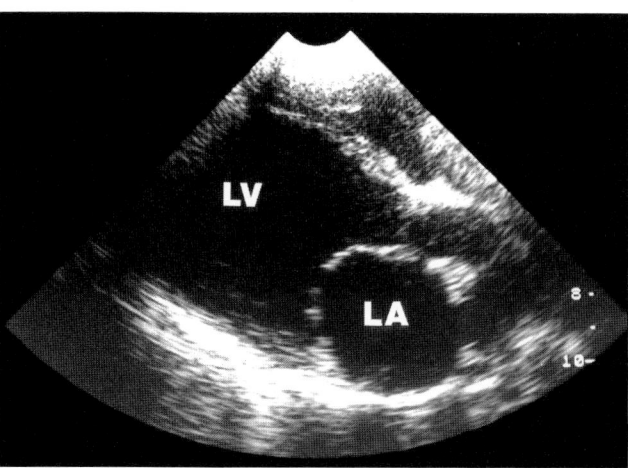

Figure 4A. Two-dimensional echocardiogram showing a long-axis view of the left ventricle (LA = left atrium; LV = left ventricle).

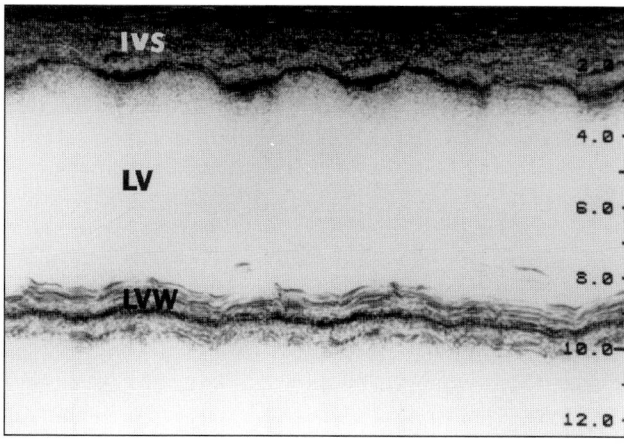

Figure 4B. M-mode echocardiogram demonstrating severely depressed systolic function (fractional shortening = 6%) (IVS = interventricular septum, LV = left ventricle, LVW = left ventricular free wall).

ment (DER) would be 1,300 to 1,500 kcal/day (5,439 to 6,276 kJ/day). Frequent monitoring of body condition score is important because it guides adjustments to DER.

2. Nutrients of special concern in dogs with CHF are sodium, chloride, potassium and magnesium.

Sodium and chloride. Because CHF is associated with retention of sodium, chloride and water, these nutrients are of primary importance in patients with cardiovascular disease. Moderate to severe cardiac dilatation and evidence of congestion (pulmonary edema) indicate the need for food that avoids excess sodium and chloride. A number of different commercial foods are available that meet this objective. (See Table 18-9.)

Water, commercial pet treats and snacks and human foods offered as snacks are also sources of sodium and chloride. Distilled water or water with less than 150 ppm sodium is recommended for patients with advanced heart disease and failure. Some commercial snacks and treats (See Appendix M.) and processed human foods (See Table 18-7.) are often high in sodium and chloride and should also be avoided.

Potassium and magnesium. Electrolyte abnormalities, including hypokalemia, hyperkalemia and hypomagnesemia, are potential complications of drug therapy in patients with cardiovascular disease. Patients receiving diuretic therapy should receive adequate amounts of potassium and magnesium in their food. Patients receiving angiotensin converting enzyme (ACE) inhibitors may be predisposed to mild hyperkalemia and their food should avoid excess levels of potassium.

3. Fluid accumulation, a hallmark of CHF, can dramatically alter the body weight of a dog. Therefore, a dog that has lost significant amounts of lean body mass may have no changes in body weight because of pulmonary edema, pleural effusion or ascites. Assessing body condition in conjunction with body weight is important in these patients. Muscle wasting is usually first noted in the lumbar, gluteal, scapular and temporal areas. Even dogs that do not have the classic appearance of cardiac cachexia are likely to lose lean body mass.

4. Cachexia is a syndrome of weight loss, lean tissue wasting and anorexia seen in many animals with chronic heart failure. The loss of lean body mass seen in cachexia is caused by a mismatch between nutri-

tional intake and requirements, resulting in negative nitrogen and energy balances. These imbalances may be due to inadequate intake, excessive losses or altered metabolism. Prevalence of malnutrition has been estimated to be as high as 68% in human patients with heart failure. Total body malnutrition has been defined clinically in people as body weight less than 80% of the ideal value, marked muscle wasting, body fat less than 15% or a combination of factors. More sophisticated screening methods for malnutrition in people with CHF have shown that malnutrition is more prevalent than recognized with traditional clinical parameters such as body weight. This suggests that animals with chronic heart failure are at risk for malnutrition in the absence of overt signs of cachexia.

In patients with heart failure, anorexia is common and may be due to the heart failure (dyspnea, fatigue), concomitant disease (nausea associated with renal failure), use of drugs that cause nausea (cardiac glycosides) or sudden nutritional changes. However, the loss of lean body mass with cardiac cachexia exceeds that attributable to anorexia alone. In simple starvation, most of the weight loss is fat mass, whereas lean tissue is relatively spared. Cachexia depletes lean body mass. The cytokines tumor necrosis factor and interleukin-1 appear to play a role in the pathogenesis of this syndrome. Physical inactivity may also contribute to lean body mass loss because exercise restriction is routinely recommended for patients with moderate to severe heart failure.

Management efforts in underweight cardiac patients should include the following:
• If possible, avoid drug-induced anorexia.
• Have the owner weigh and measure portions and keep a record of actual food intake, and compare that intake to energy calculations.
• Feed small meals frequently.
• Add moist food if the dog is eating primarily a dry food.
• Warm the food to body temperature.
• Add honey, cane syrup or other low-salt flavor enhancers to the food.
• Use a homemade food if the animal normally eats a commercial pet food.

• Add fish oil to the food.

Fish oil, which is high in omega-3 (n-3) fatty acids, alters cytokine production. Preliminary study results suggest that alteration of cytokine production through omega-3 fatty acid supplementation or other methods may benefit dogs with heart failure and cachexia.

Therapy Including Feeding Plan

Enalapril (20 mg per os, once daily), digoxin (0.125 mg per os, twice daily) and furosemide (50 mg per os, once daily) were initiated. A gradual change to a commercial dry veterinary therapeutic food formulated for patients with cardiac disease (Prescription Diet Canine h/d,[a] two cups twice daily) was recommended.

Progress Notes

Two weeks later, the dog was neither coughing nor dyspneic. Its appetite was good and body weight 22.5 kg. The clients felt the dog had improved dramatically in terms of exercise tolerance and appetite. No pulmonary edema was detected on thoracic radiographs and ascites was not apparent. Results of a serum biochemistry profile were within normal limits and the serum digoxin level was within the therapeutic range (1.2 ng/ml, therapeutic range = 0.8 to 2.0). No medication adjustments were made.

Six months after the initial diagnosis of dilated cardiomyopathy, the dog was examined for recurrence of coughing and anorexia. At this time, atrial fibrillation was present, along with severe pulmonary edema and mild pleural effusion. Body weight was 22.4 kg. Echocardiographic measurements were similar to those taken previously except that the left atrium was larger. The dog was hospitalized for three days for stabilization and was discharged with prescriptions for furosemide, enalapril, digoxin, diltiazem and spironolactone/hydrochlorothiazide. Even after stabilization, the patient's appetite continued to be poor; only half of its DER was met with the quantities of commercial dry food eaten. At this point, the owners were instructed to feed one-half can of a similar veterinary therapeutic food (Prescription Diet Canine h/d), in addition to two cups of dry food per day.

Over the next three months the dog's weight decreased to 22.0 kg. At this time, the dog's appetite again waned. The serum digoxin level was within the therapeutic range (1.3 ng/ml) and a renal profile was within normal limits. Warming the food and adding garlic powder, honey or low-sodium bouillon did not improve the dog's appetite, so the owners were instructed to experiment with a variety of human foods and found that the dog liked chicken and rice. A balanced homemade food containing chicken, rice, calcium phosphate and a vitamin/mineral supplement was formulated. (See Chapter 6.) This food was fed exclusively in appropriate quantities to meet caloric requirements until the dog was euthanatized 11 months after the initial diagnosis because of refractory CHF.

Endnote

a. Hill's Pet Nutrition Inc., Topeka, KS, USA.

CHAPTER 19

Renal Disease

Timothy A. Allen
David J. Polzin
Larry G. Adams

"As to science itself, it can only grow."
Galileo, 1632

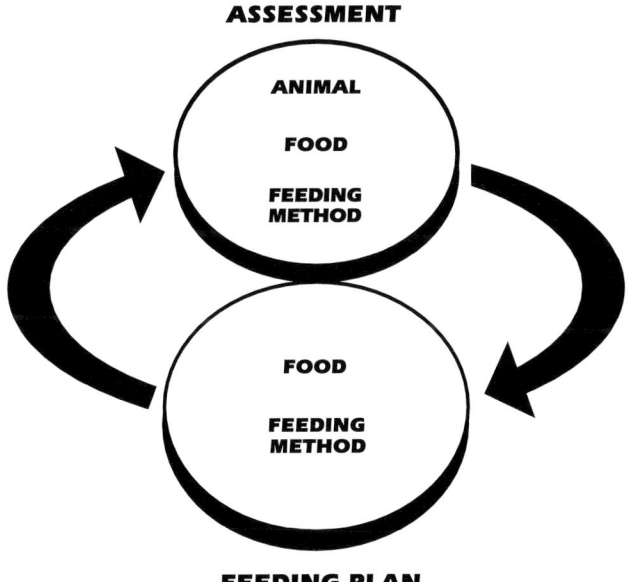

ASSESSMENT

ANIMAL

FOOD

FEEDING
METHOD

FOOD

FEEDING
METHOD

FEEDING PLAN

Note: The reader is referred to Chapter 1 for a detailed discussion of the iterative process of clinical nutrition.

INTRODUCTION

Chronic renal disease appears to be a progressive condition composed of four phases: 1) loss of renal reserve, 2) renal insufficiency, 3) azotemia and 4) uremia (Figure 19-1). Clinical signs are not obvious during the first two phases; therefore, detection is difficult. Renal function is markedly reduced in the azotemic phase, but clinical signs are often mild and go undetected. The final, uremic phase is characterized by overt clinical signs. The goal of this chapter is to provide pathophysiologic concepts and practical nutritional management recommendations for cats and dogs with chronic renal disease.

Nutritional management of patients with chronic renal disease includes measures to reduce signs of uremia and to slow progression to the uremic phase. There is little controversy regarding nutritional management of chronic renal failure (CRF) when overt signs are present. However, there is controversy regarding the impact of nutritional management on slowing progression. Thus, in a sense, the question is not whether to use nutritional management but when to initiate nutritional management. Because detection of chronic renal disease in its early phases is difficult and there appears to be no harm in avoiding nutrient excess during earlier phases, nutritional management should be instituted as soon as renal dysfunction is demonstrated. Verified loss of urine concentrating ability or significant renal proteinuria, even in the absence of azotemia, reflects marked renal damage and signals the need for nutritional management.

KEY WORDS & TERMS—RENAL DISEASE*

Acute renal failure	Glomerular capillary hypertension	Renal disease
Azotemia	Glomerular hyperfiltration	Renal insufficiency
Chronic interstitial nephritis	Glomerulopathy	Renal osteodystrophy
Chronic progressive renal failure	Hypertension (systemic)	Renal secondary hyperparathyroidism
Chronic renal failure	Metabolic acidosis	Uremia
Congenital renal disease	Nephrocalcinosis	Uremic syndrome
Familial nephropathy	Proteinuria	

*Key words and terms are defined in the Glossary.

KEY POINTS—RENAL DISEASE

1. Mortality from kidney disease in dogs is greater than mortality in people from accidents, lung cancer, breast cancer or acquired immunodeficiency syndrome.
2. Chronic renal disease is a progressive condition composed of four phases: 1) loss of renal reserve, 2) renal insufficiency, 3) azotemia and 4) uremia. Clinical signs are not obvious during the first two phases; therefore, detection is difficult.
3. Chronic renal failure (CRF) occurs in dogs and cats of all ages; however, it is often a disease of older animals.
4. Risk factors for renal disease include breed/family, infections, drug therapy, advancing age, hypertension, ischemia and diabetes mellitus.
5. In a retrospective clinical series of cats with CRF, polydipsia and polyuria were observed in only 40% of patients.
6. The most commonly evaluated kidney function is glomerular filtration rate.
7. Proteinuria is the hallmark of altered membrane permselectivity.
8. The kidneys produce erythropoietin, calcitriol and renin; degrade and eliminate parathyroid hormone (PTH), thyroid hormone, insulin and thyrotropic hormone and respond to atrial natriuretic peptide, aldosterone, antidiuretic hormone, PTH and growth hormone.
9. Possible mechanisms for progressive renal injury include glomerular capillary hypertension, glomerular hyperfiltration, increased renal ammoniagenesis, increased renal oxygen consumption, secondary renal hyperparathyroidism and compensatory renal growth (hypertrophy). Sequelae of CRF (e.g., hypertension, metabolic acidosis and tubulointerstitial injury) may also contribute to progression.
10. Dietary lipids can influence progression of CRF by affecting: 1) renal hemodynamics, 2) platelet aggregation, 3) lipid peroxidation, 4) systemic blood pressure, 5) proliferation of glomerular mesangial cells and 6) plasma lipid concentration.
11. Dietary therapy is the mainstay of conservative medical management of canine and feline CRF. Dietary management prevents or mitigates the clinical signs of uremia, minimizes signs of mineral and electrolyte imbalance and may slow progression of CRF.
12. Avoiding excess dietary phosphorus reduces renal pathology in cats and improves survival of dogs with experimentally induced renal failure.
13. Cats with renal failure appear to be particularly predisposed to disorders in potassium homeostasis.
14. Metabolic acidosis is commonly associated with CRF in dogs and cats and contributes to loss of lean muscle mass.
15. Calcitriol plays an important role in the pathogenesis of secondary renal hyperparathyroidism.
16. Although it has not been clearly established at what point during progressive renal insufficiency protein restriction should be initiated, it seems logical to feed a food with reduced protein levels when renal dysfunction is documented (i.e., persistent renal proteinuria, loss of urine concentrating ability or azotemia).
17. The keys to prevention and treatment of renal secondary hyperparathyroidism and renal osteodystrophy are: 1) avoiding excess dietary phosphorus, 2) using phosphate binders and 3) providing supplemental calcium.
18. Avoiding excess dietary sodium chloride may help control hypertension associated with CRF.
19. Vitamin D therapy can be considered if the combination of avoiding excess dietary phosphorus intake and using phosphate-binder therapy does not control hyperphosphatemia.
20. Dogs and cats with protein-losing glomerulonephropathy should initially be fed reduced-protein foods designed for patients with renal failure. Patients should be monitored at two- to four-week intervals to determine the optimal quantity of dietary protein.

CLINICAL IMPORTANCE

Overall Estimated Prevalence of Renal Disease in Dogs and Cats

Mortality data for dogs are sparse. However, in a retrospective study Bronson found that 2% of dogs died from chronic nephritis, 2% from pyelonephritis and 1% from glomerulonephritis.[1] Thus, the overall mortality from kidney diseases was 5%. With the exception of cancer, kidney disease was the most common cause of death in this study.

Mortality from kidney disease in dogs is greater than mortality in people from accidents, lung cancer, breast cancer or acquired immunodeficiency syndrome (AIDS) (Table 19-1). Mortality is the total number of deaths from a given disease in a population during a specific interval of time. According to Heart and Stroke Facts, 2,220,190 deaths

KEY NUTRITIONAL FACTORS—RENAL DISEASE

Factors	Associated conditions	Dietary recommendations
Water	Dehydration Electrolyte imbalances Blood volume contraction Renal hypoperfusion	Offer water free choice at all times Parenteral fluid therapy if dehydration, blood volume contraction or renal hypoperfusion are clinically significant
Phosphorus	Hyperphosphatemia Hyperparathyroidism Nephrocalcinosis	Avoid excess dietary phosphorus Restrict phosphorus to 0.15 to 0.3% dry matter in dogs and 0.04 to 0.60% dry matter in cats

Protein	Uremia
	Metabolic acidosis
	Glomerular capillary hypertension
	Glomerular hyperfiltration
	Proteinuria
	Hypoproteinemia (protein-losing
	   nephropathy)
		Avoid excess dietary protein
		Restrict protein to ≤15% dry matter in dogs and ≤30% dry matter
		   in cats

Sodium and chloride	Systemic hypertension Increased renal oxygen consumption	Avoid excess dietary sodium Restrict sodium to less than 0.25% dry matter in dogs and less than 0.35% dry matter in cats
Acid load	Renal ammoniagenesis Tubulointerstitial changes	Avoid excess dietary acid
Energy	Cachexia	Ensure adequate energy intake in the form of non-protein calories
Potassium	Hypokalemia (especially cats) Hyperkalemia	Provide oral potassium supplementation (3 to 5 mEq or mmol/kg body weight/day) Change to a food with a higher potassium concentration Discontinue potassium supplementation Switch from potassium-sparing diuretics to loop or thiazide diuretics Change to a food with a lower potassium concentration

occurred in the United States in 1992.[2] Cardiovascular disease claimed 925,079 lives, cancer 521,100, stroke 143,640, accidents 86,300 and AIDS 33,600.

Dogs frequently develop kidney problems with advancing age. Although exact statistics are lacking, several pieces of evidence suggest that kidney problems are more common than is frequently realized. For example, in a survey of 1,600 pet dogs over five years of age examined at a European veterinary college for a variety of reasons, approximately 20% had abnormally elevated kidney function tests.[3]

The incidence of azotemia was 18.47% in a closed colony of aging beagle dogs studied at the University of California, Davis. Uremia was the direct cause of death or was severe enough to warrant euthanasia in eight of the 157 (5.1%) dogs. The onset of azotemia in this group occurred at an average of 11.34 years of age and progressed to death or euthanasia over an average of approximately two years (range 0 to 3.2 years).[4]

The prevalence of renal failure in cats of all ages examined at the University of Minnesota Veterinary Teaching Hospital, St. Paul, from 1980 to 1990 was 3.05%.[5] The prevalence of renal failure was highest in cats older than 15 years; nearly one-third of cats older than 15 years presented in renal failure. Data from the University of Minnesota and the Veterinary Medical Data Base, Purdue University, West Lafayette, IN, suggest the prevalence of renal failure in cats is increasing. The apparent increase in prevalence of renal failure may be due to cats living longer, more older cats being evaluated by veterinarians and increased awareness of renal failure by veterinarians.

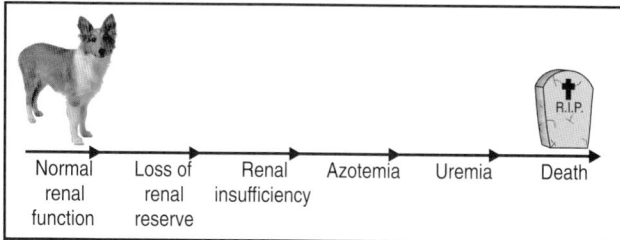

Figure 19-1. Stages of chronic progressive renal disease. The critical amount of renal damage required to initiate relentless self-progression is unknown. Many experts recommend treatment at the earliest stage renal dysfunction is verified (renal insufficiency), whereas others recommend treatment be postponed until uremia is present.

Table 19-1. Relative mortality due to renal disease in dogs compared with that from common human diseases.*

Diseases	Mortality (%)
Cardiovascular	42.5
Cancer	23.5
Stroke	6.6
Kidney disease (dogs)	**5**
Accidents	3.9
Lung cancer	2.4
Breast cancer	2
AIDS	1.5

*Mortality data are for people unless marked otherwise.

In an Internet survey of causes of death in dogs, veterinarians reported the proportional morbidity rate for renal failure was 5%. Only neoplasia (all types) had a higher proportional morbidity rate (15.6%).[6] In a 1991 survey of readers of Companion Animal News, the Morris Animal Foundation learned that of 325 cats lost by survey respondents, 94 succumbed to kidney disease.[7] By comparison, 39 of the 325 died of feline leukemia and 45 more died due to other causes.

Another important aspect of kidney disease in aging animals is the insidious nature of progressive renal deterioration. Eleven older dogs were carefully evaluated with routine kidney function tests in one study. Although none of the dogs initially had abnormal kidney test results, 10 of the 11 dogs died of kidney failure within 2.5 years.[8]

Relationship Between Age and Renal Failure

Chronic renal failure occurs in dogs and cats of all ages, but it is frequently a disease of older animals. In a survey of 170 canine and 36 feline CRF patients, the mean age at diagnosis was 7.0 years for dogs and 7.4 years for cats.[9] Analysis of data contributed to the Veterinary Medical Data Base from 1980 to 1990, indicated that 37% of cats with renal failure were less than 10 years old, 31% of cats were between 10 and 15 years old and 32% of cats were older than 15 years.[5] In 1990, the prevalence of renal failure was 16 cases/1,000 cats of all ages examined; in cats 10 years old or older 77/1,000; and in cats older than 15 years the prevalence increased to 153/1,000.[5]

A similar relationship between aging and the prevalence of renal failure occurs in dogs. The prevalence of renal failure was reported to be nine cases/1,000 dogs of all ages examined; in dogs between seven and 10 years old 12.5/1,000; in dogs between 10 and 15 years old 24/1,000; and in dogs over 15 years 57/1,000.[9]

Familial Nephropathies in Dogs and Cats

Familial renal disease resulting in CRF has been documented or suspected to occur in a number of breeds (e.g., Abyssinian cats and Lhasa apso dogs) (See Risk Factors–Breed/Family).[10] Familial nephropathies should be suspected when renal disease is diagnosed in related animals and there is no apparent underlying cause. Familial nephropathies lead to renal disease in related animals at a higher frequency than expected based on the overall prevalence estimates. The age at presentation of cats and dogs with familial nephropathies is often less than that of pets presenting with CRF.

Acquired Renal Disease

A substantial, but as yet undetermined, proportion of end-stage renal disease in dogs and cats may be due to drug-induced nephrotoxicity. Drugs that may cause nephrotoxicity include antimicrobials (aminoglycosides and tetracycline), antifungals (amphotericin B), analgesics (ibuprofen and phenylbutazone), cardiovascular drugs (captopril), immunosuppressive agents (penicillamine) and chemotherapeutic drugs (cisplatin).[11]

Geriatric patients may be at greater risk for drug-induced nephrotoxicity because of a decline in renal function associated with aging and use of multiple drugs with nephrotoxic potential. Drug absorption, distribution, biotransformation and excretion may also be altered in geriatric patients because of altered gastrointestinal (GI) function, reduced muscle mass, increased body fat and decreased renal function. Age-associated changes in pharmacokinetics may increase the risk of nephrotoxicity.

Hyperthyroidism and CRF commonly occur in older cats. Azotemia and renal failure can develop following treatment of hyperthyroidism in cats.[12,13] Renal function declines regardless of treatment (i.e., radioactive iodine [^{131}I], methimazole or bilateral surgical thyroidectomy). Glomerular filtration rate (GFR) and renal plasma flow are increased in hyperthyroid cats because of thyroid hormone-mediated increased cardiac output and intrarenal vasodilatation.[12,13] Treatment for hyperthyroidism decreases cardiac output and GFR, which may unmask concurrent renal disease. The increase in serum creatinine concentration observed after treatment may be due to a decrease in GFR or weight gain and increased muscle mass or a combination of these effects.[12,13]

Acute Renal Failure

Acute renal failure (ARF) refers to the sudden inability of the kidneys to regulate water and solute balance with rapid deterioration of renal function resulting in azotemia. This definition applies whether urine output is decreased, normal or increased. Normal urine output is 1 to 2

Table 19-2. Classification scheme for acute renal failure.

Prerenal azotemia
  Hypotension (shock, heart failure)
  Hemorrhage
  Severe volume contraction (severe gastroenteritis)
Renal acute renal failure
  Ischemia
    Prolonged prerenal conditions
    Sepsis
    Thromboemboli of renal vessels
  Nephrotoxic injury
    Pharmacologic agents
    Ethylene glycol
    Organic solvents
    Heavy metals
    Pesticides
    Leptospirosis
    Miscellaneous agents (snake venom)
Postrenal
  Obstruction
    Neoplasia
    Urolithiasis
  Rupture
    Bladder
    Ureter
    Urethra

Table 19-3. Historical questions for owners of pets that are suspected of having renal dysfunction.

1. Age?
2. Breed? Family history of renal disease?
3. Duration of the present illness?
4. Previous illness, injury, anesthesia, surgery or drug administration?
5. History of renal disease? Previous laboratory evaluation of renal function?
6. Exposure to toxins?
7. Polyuria or polydipsia?
8. Urination: Frequency? Urinary incontinence? Change in color, odor or volume? "Accidents" in the house?
9. General signs potentially referable to renal failure: Anorexia? Vomiting? Diarrhea? Weight loss? Are these signs increasing, decreasing or unchanged?

ml/hour/kg body weight and oliguria is characterized by a urine output less than 0.25 ml/hour/kg body weight. Oliguric ARF is the form most commonly recognized. ARF is generally not detected until hours or days after its onset. Most cases of ARF in hospitalized animals are multifactorial; affected patients frequently are receiving nephrotoxic drugs and suffer from dehydration, hypotension and malnutrition. The renal damage associated with ARF may be reversible or irreversible. Irreversible damage may lead to rapid death or slowly progressive renal damage unrelated to the initial insult. Table 19-2 outlines a classification scheme for ARF.

ASSESSMENT

Assess the Animal

History

Table 19-3 lists the historical information important to obtain in patients with suspected renal disease or failure. Historical findings in patients with ARF usually include sudden onset of anorexia, listlessness, vomiting (with or without hemorrhage), diarrhea (with or without hemorrhage), ataxia, halitosis, seizures, known toxin exposure, recent medical or surgical conditions and oliguria/anuria or polyuria. Historical findings in patients with CRF usually include polyuria/polydipsia (less frequent in cats than dogs), anorexia, lethargy, vomiting, weight loss, nocturia, constipation, diarrhea, acute blindness (because of hypertension) and seizures or coma (late). Cats may also have ptyalism and muscle weakness with cervical ventroflexion (hypokalemic myopathy).

In a retrospective clinical series of cats with renal failure, polyuria and polydipsia were observed in only 40% of affected cats.[5] In this series, the diagnostic criteria for the renal failure group were concurrent azotemia (i.e., serum creatinine concentration >1.9 mg/dl and/or serum urea nitrogen concentration >30 mg/dl) and lack of appropriate urine concentrating ability (i.e., urine specific gravity <1.035). Vomiting was observed in 52% of affected cats and diarrhea in just 3%. Inappropriate urination was observed in fewer than 10% of the cats.

DIFFERENTIATING PRERENAL AZOTEMIA AND ARF FROM CRF

It is extremely important to diagnose and differentiate ARF from prerenal azotemia and CRF. Prerenal azotemia is rapidly corrected when dehydration is corrected. The medical history can provide useful information. A history of polyuria and/or polydipsia or laboratory evidence of progressive decline in renal function suggests CRF. A careful medical history may reveal causes of ARF (e.g., ingestion of a nephrotoxin such as ethylene glycol). Laboratory findings may also help in differentiating these conditions. The presence of mild to moderate normochromic, normocytic nonregenerative anemia suggests CRF. Reduced renal size may aid in the differentiation of ARF from CRF. Small, irregular kidneys detected by palpation or ultrasonic/radiographic imaging suggests CRF. Renal images less than 2.5 to 3.5 times the length of the second lumbar vertebra are consistent with CRF. However, certain chronic renal diseases produce enlarged kidneys (e.g., lymphosarcoma). Urine sediment examination may be helpful. If calcium oxalate crystals are present, ethylene glycol-induced ARF should be considered.

Most veterinary nephrologists define renal failure as loss of sufficient functional mass (i.e., generally more than 75% loss) to impair homeostasis. Renal azotemia, rather than pre- or postrenal azotemia, is diagnosed based on concurrent impaired urine concentrating ability.

Recently, carbamylated hemoglobin concentration has been shown to be a method for differentiating ARF from CRF.[14] Carbamylated hemoglobin is formed when a nonenzymatic, post-transcriptional reaction occurs between breakdown products of urea and hemoglobin. In simple terms, carbamylated hemoglobin represents the time-averaged blood urea nitrogen concentration over the life of a red blood cell. Thus, carbamylated hemoglobin is analogous to glycosylated (glycated) hemoglobin.

Physical Examination

Physical examination of a patient suspected to have renal failure should include the factors listed in Table 19-4. Dehydration (70%) and an underweight body condition (58%) were the most common abnormal physical examination findings in a clinical series of feline renal failure patients.[5] An abnormally large kidney was detected by palpation in 25% of cases and an abnormally small kidney in 16% of cases in this series. Gingivitis, halitosis and oral ulcers were only occasionally reported.

Firm swellings in the nasomaxillary region and extending to frontal sites may be present in young dogs with end-stage renal disease. Firm swelling along the maxillary and mandibular gingival surfaces may also be present. These changes are due to renal osteodystrophy.

The most common presenting complaint in dogs with hypertension is blindness caused by retinal hemorrhage and detachment. Stiles and colleagues noted that 15 of 23 cats (65%) with CRF had indirect blood pressure measurements consistent with systemic hypertension.[15] Twelve of the 15 cats (80%) with hypertension associated with CRF had active hypertensive retinopathy. The retinal lesions observed included increased tortuosity of arteries, retinal edema and focal detachments.

Table 19-4. Elements of the physical examination that should be emphasized in patients with suspected renal failure.

1. Temperature, pulse, heart and respiratory rate
2. Assessment of hydration status
3. Body weight and body condition score
4. Oral examination: Mucosal ulcers? Pallor? Necrosis or discoloration of tongue?
5. Cardiovascular system: Abnormal heart sounds? Increased tortuosity of superficial veins? Systemic blood pressure (direct or indirect measurement) abnormalities? Pulse rate and character?
6. Kidneys: Both palpable? Size? Shape? Position? Surface contours? Pain? Bilaterally symmetrical?
7. Urinary bladder: Size? Position? Shape? Pain? Thickness of wall? Intraluminal masses? Grating sensation?
8. Genitourinary tract (urethra, prostate, penis, prepuce, vulva): Shape? Position? Pain? Discharge?
9. Fundus: Retinal detachment? Hemorrhage? Increased tortuosity of arteries? Retinal edema? Lipemia retinalis?
10. Skeleton: Rubber jaw?
11. Cervical region: Thyroid masses (cats)?

RENAL DISEASE

Table 19-5. Minimum diagnostic database for patients with suspected renal disease.

1. Urinalysis, including microscopic examination of the urine sediment
2. Serum biochemistry profile
3. Automated cell count, differential white cell count, if indicated
4. Urine culture, especially if bacteriuria, pyuria or hematuria is present
5. Abdominal radiography
6. Blood pressure measurement
7. Renal ultrasonography
8. Urine protein-creatinine ratio, if significant proteinuria is evident by dipstick analysis
9. Intravenous urography, if indicated
10. Renal biopsy, if indicated

Laboratory and Other Clinical Data

Clinically, disorders of one of five major categories of renal function are recognized: 1) glomerular filtration, 2) membrane permselectivity, 3) urine concentration, 4) tubular resorption and 5) endocrine function. Functionally, renal diseases can be generalized or specific and involve only one function (e.g., tubular resorption in Fanconi syndrome). Each major function can be evaluated diagnostically.[16] Table 19-5 lists the minimum diagnostic database for most patients with suspected renal disease.

GLOMERULAR FILTRATION

The most commonly evaluated kidney function is GFR. Under steady state conditions, serum concentrations of urea nitrogen and creatinine are the time-honored means of indirectly estimating GFR. These tests are useful for detecting large decreases in GFR (75% or greater), but lack sensitivity for detecting smaller decreases. Serum urea nitrogen and creatinine values are affected by nonrenal factors; this fact contributes to the broad ranges for normal values.

Urea is produced in the liver from ammonia derived from the ornithine cycle, which catabolizes amino acids. The catabolized amino acids come from exogenous (dietary) and endogenous proteins. Urea is distributed throughout intracellular and extracellular water and is freely diffusible. The kidneys excrete urea by glomerular filtration and serum urea nitrogen concentrations are inversely proportional to GFR. Because urea is passively reabsorbed in the tubules, especially at reduced tubular flow rates, urea clearance is not an accurate measure of GFR when dehydration and blood volume depletion are present.

In dogs, serum urea nitrogen concentration increases slightly within eight hours of feeding. The increase is greatest with moist foods.[17] Clinical conditions that can increase serum urea concentration include GI hemorrhage, fever and starvation. Drugs that increase tissue catabolism (e.g., glucocorticoids) can also increase serum urea concentration. Severe liver disease (e.g., portosystemic vascular shunts) or feeding a low-protein food can decrease serum urea nitrogen concentrations.

Creatinine is produced by the nonenzymatic breakdown of muscle phosphocreatine. During steady states, daily production of creatinine is constant and is related to muscle mass. Serum creatinine concentration is less influenced by feeding than serum urea nitrogen concentration. Breed and body size also influence serum creatinine concentration.[18] In advanced renal failure, serum creatinine

levels may not increase in proportion to the decrease in GFR because of a reduction in muscle mass.

The relationship between serum urea nitrogen or serum creatinine concentration and GFR is graphically represented by a rectangular hyperbola. The slope of the curve is small when GFR is slightly or moderately decreased and large when GFR is severely decreased. Thus, very large changes in GFR early in the natural history of chronic renal disease cause only small changes in serum urea nitrogen and creatinine concentrations. These small changes may not exceed the upper limit of the laboratory reference range and thus may go unrecognized. Late in the course of renal disease, small decreases in GFR cause large increases in serum urea nitrogen and serum creatinine concentrations.

Measurement of GFR is very useful in identifying early, nonazotemic renal disease (e.g., assessing renal function in breeds known to have familial renal disease, calculating the dose of a drug cleared by glomerular filtration and monitoring response to treatment). Urinary clearance of infused inulin is the classic reference method for assessing glomerular filtration. This method requires collection of multiple, timed blood and urine samples and a constant infusion of inulin. Timed urine collections require use of metabolism cages and urinary catheters. Placing a urinary catheter can be difficult, time-consuming, traumatic to the patient and predispose the patient to urinary tract infection.

Several methods of measuring GFR have been studied in dogs and cats. These methods are based on one or more improvements over the classic inulin clearance method. The purported advantages include: 1) ease of measurement, and the presence of more readily available clearance markers, 2) single injection vs. continuous intravenous infusion and 3) plasma disappearance rather than clearance, thereby eliminating the requirement of timed urine collection.[19]

Sodium sulfanilate and creatinine have been used as exogenous markers to estimate GFR. Endogenous creatinine clearance underestimates GFR because noncreatinine chromogens are present in plasma. When endogenous creatinine clearance and inulin clearance were compared, endogenous creatinine clearance was significantly lower than simultaneously measured radiolabeled inulin clearance. Exogenous administration of creatinine reduces this potential problem by reducing the proportion of noncreatinine chromogens in plasma. A newer creatinine-specific enzymatic analytical method eliminates the problem.[20] However, in cats exogenous creatinine clearance does not accurately measure GFR.[21]

Factors other than GFR can affect creatinine clearance and serum creatinine concentration.[22] In people, protein intake influences creatinine secretion and excretion.[23] Creatinine secretion in human patients is also influenced by antihypertensive therapy and the type of renal disease.

A variety of other methods have been used experimentally to measure GFR in dogs and cats; however, these techniques are not currently used for routine assessment of clinical patients. Examples of these procedures include renal clearance or plasma disappearance of radiolabeled solutes (e.g., ³H-inulin and ¹²⁵I-iothalamate), plasma clearance of intravenously injected, nonradioactive substances (e.g., inulin, iohexol, iopromide, creatinine) and nuclear scintigraphy of the kidney after intravenous administration of a radiolabeled substance.[20,24,25]

MEMBRANE PERMSELECTIVITY

Proteinuria is the hallmark of altered membrane permselectivity. In glomerulopathies, the permselective properties of the glomerular capillary wall are altered and increased amounts of protein are present in urine. Glomerulopathies are the most common cause of severe (heavy) proteinuria. Glomerulopathies can be primary (e.g., renal amyloidosis or idiopathic membranous nephropathy) or secondary to systemic diseases (e.g., lupus erythematosus).

Proteinuria is defined as excretion of greater than normal amounts of protein in the urine and is classically expressed in terms of 24-hour urinary protein excretion. Normal protein loss in cats of both genders is ≤29 mg/kg body weight/24 hours. Normal protein loss in dogs is <10 mg/kg body weight/24 hours.[26] Proteinuria is commonly observed in dogs and cats. Potential causes of proteinuria include hemorrhage or inflammation within the urinary tract, tubular resorptive defects, "overflow" proteinuria and altered glomerular permselectivity. The clinical significance of proteinuria depends on the severity and persistence. In the absence of hyperproteinemia and hematuria or urinary tract inflammation, persistent proteinuria usually indicates renal disease and more severe proteinuria is generally associated with glomerular disease. The magnitude of proteinuria does not predict the reversibility of the underlying disease. Serial quantitative evaluation of proteinuria is necessary for prognosis and assessment of response to therapy.

Clinicians should confirm the persistence and attempt to localize the source of proteinuria before performing invasive and expensive diagnostic tests such as renal biopsy. The significance of proteinuria should always be interpreted in the context of other laboratory and clinical findings (e.g., microscopic urine sediment examination).

Timed urine collections and quantitative protein analytical methods are necessary to assess the severity of proteinuria. Unfortunately, 24-hour urine collections and quantitative protein analytical methods are impractical for routine screening purposes. Qualitative estimates performed on random urine samples are used for screening. Qualitative tests are very sensitive, but they are influenced by urine concentration.

Qualitative techniques include dipstick methods and precipitation techniques such as sulfosalicylic acid. Urine concentration (refractive index, specific gravity) should be considered when interpreting the results of these qualitative techniques.[27] The most commonly used qualitative test is the citrate-buffered tetrabromphenol colorimetric dipstick test. The test depends on the ability of proteins, especially albumin, to alter the color reaction in paper impregnated with a pH-sensitive dye, tetrabromphenol blue. The test pad is buffered so that color changes reflect changes in protein concentration. False-positive reactions can occur with the dipstick test. Strongly alkaline urine and urine contaminated with quaternary ammonium compounds can give positive reactions in the absence of marked proteinuria. Although the sensitivity of the dipstick test is good, the precision is low. Observer variation is a documented and unavoidable source of error with dipstick tests. Another qualitative test is based on the precipitation of protein by sulfosalicylic acid. The technique is sensitive to all proteins, but is more cumbersome to perform than the dipstick test. In a retrospective series of cases of feline renal failure, 63% of cats were positive (1+ to 4+ dipstick method) for proteinuria.[5]

Extremely concentrated or grossly hematuric urine samples can give positive test results with the dipstick method and the sulfosalicylic acid method. If a qualitative test is 1+ or greater in the absence of gross hematuria, the finding should be verified by testing a second urine sample in several days. If subsequent qualitative tests indicate proteinuria, a semiquantitative or quantitative test for proteinuria should be performed.

In patients with stable renal function, the urinary protein-creatinine (UPC) ratio is a semiquantitative method for assessing proteinuria.[28] The UPC ratio is calculated by dividing the protein concentration by the creatinine concentration. Urinary protein is measured by a quantitative analytical technique rather than by dipstick. Because the urinary excretion of creatinine and protein is presumed constant in the presence of stable GFR, the UPC ratio in a single urine sample can be used to estimate the urinary protein loss. The time and method of urine sample collection do not appear to be critical. The UPC ratio eliminates the potentially confounding effect of urine concentration on the interpretation of the urinary protein concentration. A UPC ratio less than 0.5 was found in the majority of nonproteinuric dogs studied.[29-31] A UPC ratio greater than 1.0 corresponds to proteinuria in excess of 20 mg/kg body weight/24 hours and is generally considered abnormal. The significance of a UPC ratio between 0.5 and 1.0 is unknown. Dogs with chronic interstitial nephritis have variable but mild glomerular involvement, correspondingly the UPC ratio falls between values for normal dogs and dogs with glomerulopathies.[31]

The UPC ratio in healthy, normal cats correlates well with 24-hour urinary protein loss. The upper limit of the reference range for UPC ratios in cats is 0.[32,33] The 24-hour urinary protein loss is greater in normal male than in female cats. This difference may be attributable to secretions of the secondary sex glands in male cats. Dietary protein intake significantly affected UPC values in normal cats and cats with surgically induced CRF.[33] Consequently, dietary protein levels should be considered when interpreting UPC values.

No single quantitative technique has been adopted by clinical laboratories; a number of methods are used widely. Protein in urine is measured by turbidimetry, dye binding or formation of a colored reactant. Turbidimetry methods commonly involve trichloroacetic acid (TCA) or sulfosalicylic acid (SAS). The dye binding methods include Coomassie brilliant blue and Ponceau-S. The biuret and Folin-Lowry reactions form color. The choice of a laboratory standard solution is important in measuring urinary protein concentration because urinary protein is a mixture of many different proteins. The standard laboratory solution should contain albumin and globulins and should not be used when measuring protein in other body fluids besides urine.

URINE CONCENTRATION

Disorders of urine concentrating ability generally involve abnormalities in the secretion or response to antidiuretic hormone (ADH). Loss of concentrating ability can be one of the earliest indicators of severe renal dysfunction. In CRF, the interstitial osmolality gradient is decreased because of osmotic diuresis per nephron. The resultant decrease in responsiveness to ADH leads to excretion of urine of relatively fixed osmolality or specific gravity (i.e., isosthenuria).

The normal total solute concentration for urine is 50 to 2,500 mmol/kg body weight in dogs and 50 to more than 3,000 mmol/kg body weight in cats. The concentration of solute in urine is most accurately determined by measuring urine vapor pressure with an osmometer. However, estimation of urine concentration from urine specific gravity or refractive index is adequate for routine clinical purposes. Specific gravity is the density of urine relative to water and is measured by buoyancy of the urinometer. The physiologic range for urine specific gravity is 1.001 to 1.070 in dogs and 1.001 to 1.080 in cats. Because of the wide physiologic range of urine concentration, measurements of urine concentration must be interpreted in the context of the clinical setting (e.g., hydration status, concurrent disease, medications, etc.). After 5% dehydration, urine osmolality ranges from 1,787 to 2,791 mmol/kg body weight in dogs[34] and 1,581 to 2,984 mmol/kg body weight in cats.[35]

The refractive index of a solution is related to its density. The major advantage of a refractometer over a urinometer is that only a drop of urine is required for analysis. In principle, heavy solutes (e.g., proteins) can distort this relationship because they increase specific gravity, but do not significantly affect osmolality.

Reagent pads for assessing urine concentration are available on some dipsticks. The reagent pad is impregnated with a pH indicator dye and polyelectrolytes with acid groups that dissociate in the presence of other ions. Thus, the color of the pad is influenced by the concentration of ions in urine. These pads underestimate urine concentration in the presence of high concentrations of nonionic substances (e.g., urea and glucose) or if the urinary pH is greater than 6.5. Consequently, these reagent pads should be considered a screening method only for assessing urine concentration in dogs and cats.

In a retrospective series of clinical cases of feline renal failure, 37% of cats had urine specific gravities between 1.008 to 1.012 and 60% between 1.013 and 1.034.[5] In an experimental study of surgically induced renal failure in cats (i.e., cats underwent renal vessel ligation and contralateral nephrectomy), urine specific gravity tended to be higher. The mean urine specific gravity in a group of cats fed a 27.6% protein food was 1.050 ± 0.015 and 1.038 ± 0.013 in a group fed a 51.7% protein food.[33]

TUBULAR REABSORPTION

Water and many solutes are reabsorbed from the tubular lumen into the peritubular interstitial fluid and ultimately the blood. Generally speaking, tubular reabsorption conserves substances that are essential for normal function (e.g., electrolytes, water, glucose and amino acids). Alterations in the renal handling of solutes may indicate renal dysfunction. Tubular reabsorption dysfunction may be generalized or limited to one or more tubular transport processes. Clinical syndromes are defined by the particular transport process involved. These syndromes include diverse disorders such as nephrogenic diabetes insipidus, renal tubular acidosis, renal glycosuria and aminoaciduria.

An example of aminoaciduria is cystinuria in Newfoundland dogs. The molecular defect is a mutation in the transport protein gene in this autosomal recessive disorder. Cystinuria can be detected in dogs with routine urinalysis and nitroprusside spot tests. Hexagonal crystals may be observed microscopically in urine samples with pH values less than 7. Crystals can be precipitated in alkaline samples by adding a few drops of acid to the urine specimen to decrease the pH below 7. The cyanide nitroprusside spot test identifies disulfide groups. This test can be performed on fresh urine samples or on samples in which urine is allowed to dry on filter paper. Quantitation of urinary amino acid concentrations confirms a renal defect. In affected dogs, lysine, ornithine, arginine and cystine concentrations are increased compared with values in phenotypically normal dogs. Renal clearance studies demonstrate that affected dogs fail to reabsorb cystine and dibasic amino acids.

ENDOCRINE FUNCTION

The kidneys produce, modify or degrade and respond to hormones. Hormones produced or modified by the kidneys include erythropoietin, calcitriol and renin. Changes in hormone production may lead to anemia, renal osteodystrophy and hypertension. The kidneys degrade and eliminate hormones, including parathyroid hormone (PTH), thyroid hormone, insulin and thyrotropic hormone. The hormones the kidneys respond to include atrial natriuretic peptide, aldosterone, ADH, PTH and growth hormone.

Renal endocrine function can be evaluated by directly measuring the plasma concentration of the hormone or by indirectly assessing the action of that hormone. For example, erythropoietin levels can be measured in plasma or the action of erythropoietin can be assessed by measuring hemoglobin, hematocrit or red blood cell numbers. A commercial enzyme-linked immunosorbent assay (ELISA) for erythropoietin has been validated for dogs and cats.[36] The ELISA kit uses a murine monoclonal antibody against human erythropoietin that cross reacts with canine and feline erythropoietin.

Diagnosis of hyperparathyroidism is based on increased plasma concentrations of intact PTH. Intact serum PTH levels are best measured by two-site immunoradiometric assay (IRMA) or N-terminal radioimmunoassay.[37] Intact molecule assays have been validated for dogs and cats. Mid-region and C-terminal radioimmunoassays measure both intact PTH and C-terminal PTH, which is less useful clinically.

Persistent hyperphosphatemia in patients with renal dysfunction generally indicates hyperparathyroidism. Under normal conditions, phosphate in the body is present primarily as hydroxyapatite in bone. Approximately 10% of total body phosphate occurs intracellularly in soft tissues. Phosphate is the major intracellular anion and exists in organic (i.e., nucleic acids, phospholipids, adenosine triphosphate) and inorganic forms. The kidneys are the major regulators of serum phosphorus concentrations. Renal excretion of phosphate is determined by GFR and the maximum tubular reabsorption rate. PTH regulates the maximum tubular reabsorption rate.

Serum phosphorus is measured as inorganic orthophosphate.[38] Phosphate is usually expressed as elemental phosphorus. Conversion factors are as follows: 3.1 mg phosphorus/dl = 1 mmol/l phosphorus or 1 mmol/l phosphate.[39] Approximately 80% of serum inorganic phosphate is present as the dibasic form (HPO_4^{2-}) with the balance primarily in the monobasic form ($H_2PO_4^-$). Thus, the average valence is -1.8 and 1 mmol/l phosphate is equivalent to 1.8 mEq/l phosphate. Hemolysis of red cells with subsequent release of intracellular phosphate will artificially increase serum phosphate levels. Feeding foods with high levels of carbohydrates can decrease serum phosphate levels as phosphate shifts intracellularly due to increased phosphorylated intermediates associated with glycolysis.[37] Foods with high meat content may increase serum phosphate concentrations because of high phosphate levels.[37] Serum phosphate levels may be increased in younger dogs because growth hormone influences renal tubular reabsorption of phosphate.[40]

ULTRASONOGRAPHY/RADIOGRAPHY

The urinary tract is imaged to assess function and structure and to localize disease. Ultrasonography and radiography are complementary imaging modalities.[41] Renal function can be assessed qualitatively by performing excretory urography. In survey radiographs, renal size can be assessed by comparing the length of the kidneys with the length of the second lumbar vertebral body. In a retrospective series of cases of feline renal failure, 33% of cats had small kidneys, 40% had normal sized kidneys and 27% had larger than normal kidneys as determined by imaging procedures.[5] Polycystic kidney disease and lymphosarcoma were the most common causes of renomegaly in cats. Feline renal cystic disease can be diagnosed ultrasonographically with a high level of confidence, although care should be taken to differentiate extensive cystic disease from severe hydronephrosis.[42]

Ultrasonography can provide information about intrarenal architecture when reduced renal function makes excretory urography impractical.[42,43] Ultrasonography can also provide images of the kidneys when abdominal effusion or loss of abdominal fat reduces radiographic contrast. Ultrasonographic patterns are not specific for histologic lesions; however, it is possible to differentiate solid lesions from fluid-filled lesions and to assess distribution patterns.

Radiography is also useful in the diagnosis of renal osteodystrophy. In young dogs with advanced chronic renal disease, radiographs of the skull reveal generalized osteopenia, irregular mineralization and dense soft-tissue swelling of the mandibles, maxillae and zygomatic arches. The most striking radiographic finding is demineralization of lamina dura dentes. Radiographs of long bones reveal normal-looking cortices with a coarse trabecular pattern involving the metaphyseal and epiphyseal regions, suggesting demineralization. Spontaneous fractures may be evident. The radiographic diagnosis, fibrous osteodystrophy, is applied to this constellation of findings.

MEASUREMENT OF BLOOD PRESSURE

Blood pressure is normally markedly variable. This normal variability is compounded by variation due to the anxiety associated with measuring blood pressure in awake pets in a clinic or hospital setting.[44,45] About 10% of healthy dogs[45] and 50 to 93% of dogs with CRF are hypertensive.[46] Approximately 65% of cats with renal insufficiency are hypertensive.[47] Despite difficulties measuring blood pressure and confusion regarding diagnostic criteria, hypertension is a significant problem because of its apparent prevalence and associated end-organ damage (e.g., retinal hemorrhage and left ventricular hypertrophy).[48-50]

In a study comparing direct arterial measurements and indirect methods in anesthetized normal cats, Doppler and photoplethysmographic devices had the highest overall accuracy, as assessed by mean error values of less than 10 mm Hg. The oscillometric device was least accurate with mean error values varying from 10 to 22 mm Hg.[51]

Haberman and colleagues compared direct blood pressure measurements using a radiotelemetric system with indirect measurements in conscious, unrestrained dogs and cats.[52] These investigators found that indirect measurements vary markedly and recommended Doppler measurement in awake cats and oscillometric measurement in awake dogs. In awake cats, at least three determinations are recommended from two sites when the cat is calm and not moving. In awake dogs, at least three determinations are recommended when the dog is calm and still.

Risk Factors

The presence of risk factors associated with kidney disease should increase the index of suspicion of renal disease. If risk factors are noted, additional laboratory tests may be warranted to rule in or rule out renal disease.

BREED/FAMILY

The term familial nephropathy is used when renal disease occurs in related animals with a higher frequency than would be expected by chance. In some familial nephropathies, the kidneys are seemingly normal at birth; however, because of an inborn metabolic defect, progressive structural and functional deterioration develops in the first few years of life. The term hereditary nephropathy is reserved for conditions in which an inherited basis has been documented by pedigree analysis or test breedings. Juvenile kidney disease increases suspicion of a familial nephropathy; however, juvenile kidney disease may be due to nongenetic causes. The specific term juvenile nephropathy has been used to describe disorganized nephrogenesis including renal failure in young dogs. The term renal dysplasia describes abnormal differentiation of the kidneys. Specific histologic findings in renal dysplasia include fetal glomeruli, atypical tubular epithelia and persistent mesenchyme. Renal dysplasia may or may not be inherited.

Familial nephropathy has been reported to occur in cocker spaniels, Norwegian elkhounds, Lhasa apsos, Shih Tzus, Doberman pinschers, standard poodles, soft-coated wheaten terriers, bull terriers, Samoyeds, Bernese mountain dogs, rottweilers, beagles, golden retrievers and chow chows.[10] Commonly observed clinical signs include lethargy, anorexia, vomiting and weight loss or failure to gain weight. Common laboratory changes include normocytic, normochromic anemia, hypoalbuminemia, azotemia, hypercholesterolemia, proteinuria and inappropriately low urine specific gravity values.

Hereditary nephropathy has been reported to occur in Samoyeds, English cocker spaniels and bull terriers. Affected male Samoyed dogs with x-linked hereditary nephritis have splitting of glomerular basement membranes and develop renal failure within the first year of life. The underlying inborn error is a defect in the formation of Type IV collagen. Carrier females with x-linked nephritis have isolated splitting of glomerular basement membranes; however, renal failure is not observed until later in life.[53] In English cocker spaniels, the defect is probably transmitted as an autosomal recessive trait and proteinuria is the initial finding. Affected dogs typically die of renal failure between six and 24 months of age. Light microscopic renal lesions are mild and nonspecific; however, distinctive electron microscopy changes are observed in the glomerular basement membrane.[54] The defect in bull terriers appears to be an autosomal dominant disorder.[55] The rate of progression in bull terriers is quite variable with dogs dying of renal failure from a few months to 10 years of age. Hematuria is observed in many affected bull terriers.

Two distinct familial nephropathies have been reported to occur in soft-coated wheaten terriers. One nephropathy is a form of renal dysplasia.[56] Kidneys from affected dogs are small, irregular and fibrous. Glomeruli are small and hypercellular with increased numbers of fetal glomeruli. The second form of nephropathy in soft-coated wheaten terriers is characterized by a protein-losing enteropathy and nephropathy syndrome. Although a genetic basis for this syndrome has not been proved, dogs become symptomatic between two to five years of age. Membranoproliferative glomerulonephritis, glomerulosclerosis or both are present microscopically.

Renal amyloidosis has been recognized in a family of beagles. Histologic findings included moderate to severe glomerular amyloidosis with inconsistent mild medullary interstitial amyloidosis.[57] Renal amyloidosis has also been recognized as a familial nephropathy affecting young Abyssinian cats. In affected cats, amyloid is deposited preferentially in the medullary interstitium, with relative sparing of the glomeruli. By comparison, renal amyloidosis in dogs primarily involves glomeruli with resultant severe proteinuria.[10,58]

Juvenile nephropathy has been reported to occur in a litter of Alaskan malamutes and in golden retrievers. Both males and females were affected. The lesions included moderate to severe interstitial fibrosis and mild to moderate lymphoplasmacytic interstitial inflammation. Mild to moderate tubular dilatation and atrophy were also present. Cystic glomerular atrophy and periglomerular fibrosis were prominent findings in most dogs.[59]

Renal failure was recognized more than twice as often in Maine coon, Abyssinian, Siamese, Russian blue and Burmese feline breeds.[5]

INFECTIONS

In children, urinary tract infections associated with an anatomic or functional abnormality can cause renal damage. Chronic pyelonephritis is a cause of hypertension in children.[60] In adult human beings, there is little evidence that urinary tract infection beginning as an adult leads to progressive chronic renal injury. It is possible that urinary tract infection superimposed on other processes can accelerate the rate of renal injury. Consequently, whenever urinary tract infection is diagnosed, prompt treatment with renal-sparing antimicrobials is indicated.

A recent review of naturally acquired leptospirosis in dogs revealed that ARF is the most common presentation. *Leptospira pomona* and *L. grippotyphosa* were the serovars associated with renal injury.[61]

DRUG THERAPY

A substantial, but as yet undetermined proportion of renal disease in dogs and cats may be due to drug-induced nephrotoxicity. Drugs that can cause nephrotoxicity include antimicrobials (e.g., aminoglycosides, sulfonamides and tetracycline), antifungals (e.g., amphotericin B), anesthetics (e.g., methoxyflurane and enflurane), analgesics (e.g., aspirin, acetaminophen, ibuprofen and phenylbutazone), cardiovascular drugs (e.g., captopril), immunosuppressive agents (e.g., penicillamine) and chemotherapeutic drugs (e.g., cisplatin, methotrexate and daunorubicin).[11]

ADVANCING AGE

Dogs frequently develop renal dysfunction with advancing age. Although thorough surveys of aging animals are not available, there is some evidence to suggest that kidney problems are more common in older dogs than is commonly realized. In one survey, approximately 20% of 1,600 pet dogs over five years of age had abnormally elevated kidney function tests.[3] In an Internet survey of causes of death in dogs, the peak age for death attributed to renal failure was 15 years.[6]

CRF occurs in dogs and cats of all ages, but it is frequently a disease of older animals. (See Overall Estimated Prevalence of Renal Disease in Dogs and Cats above.)

Geriatric patients may be at greater risk of drug-induced nephrotoxicity because of a decline in renal function associated with aging and use of multiple drugs with nephrotoxic potential. Age-associated changes in pharmacokinetics may increase the risk of nephrotoxicity. Drug absorption, distribution, biotransformation and excretion may be altered in geriatric patients because of altered GI function, reduced muscle mass, increased body fat and decreased renal function.

As mentioned above, hyperthyroidism and CRF commonly occur in older cats. (See Acquired Renal Disease above.) Hyperthyroidism may also more directly contribute to the development of chronic renal disease in older cats. Systemic hypertension is present in most cats with hyperthyroidism.[12,13] The normal protective role of autoregulation may be lost in hyperthyroidism because of increased cardiac output and intrarenal vasodilatation. If systemic hypertension is transmitted to glomeruli undamped, intraglomerular hypertension and glomerular hyperfiltration will result. These factors have been associated with progressive renal damage in other species.[12,13]

ISCHEMIA

Ischemic events that could lead to renal damage include: 1) shock (i.e., septic, hypotensive, hemorrhagic and hypovolemic), 2) decreased cardiac output (i.e., congestive heart failure and severe dysrhythmias), 3) hypotension due to anesthesia or blood loss, 4) renal vessel thrombosis, 5) disseminated intravascular coagulation and 6) decreased renal prostaglandin formation.

DIABETES MELLITUS

In people, diabetic nephropathy is the single most frequent cause of end-stage renal disease.[62] It has been well-demonstrated that diabetes mellitus produces renal microvascular disease. Late diabetic nephropathy is characterized by mesangial expansion and glomerular basement membrane thickening. However, the specific diabetes-related factor that causes microvascular disease is unknown. A number of factors have been incriminated as the instigator of glomerular injury. These factors include nonenzymatic glycosylation, renal hypertrophy, hormonal changes (e.g., increased levels of growth hormone), hyperperfusion and hyperfiltration.

Diabetic nephropathy is not frequently recognized in dogs and cats. The lower prevalence of diabetic nephropathy in pets compared with people may reflect the much shorter survival of animals with diabetes mellitus. Histologic changes in diabetic nephropathy are distinctive. The first functional changes with insulin-dependent diabetes mellitus in people are an increase in albumin excretion and an elevated GFR.

Etiopathogenesis

Several etiopathogenic mechanisms may be involved in naturally occurring renal disease (Table 19-6). The specific mechanisms for progressive renal injury are unknown. Possible mechanisms include a variety of compensatory or adaptive responses. Examples include glomerular capillary hypertension, glomerular hyperfiltration, increased renal ammoniagenesis, increased renal oxygen consumption, secondary renal hyperparathyroidism and compensatory renal growth (hypertrophy). In addition, sequelae of CRF (e.g., hypertension, metabolic acidosis and tubulointerstitial injury) may contribute to progression. Changes in lipid metabolism, coagulation and normal renal aging may also contribute to progression.

Some of these mechanisms are initially adaptive when renal function declines, but they may ultimately lead to progressive renal injury (Figure 19-2). These etiopathogenic mechanisms are not mutually exclusive and in some instances may act synergistically.

The so-called remnant kidney model is characterized by progressive azotemia, proteinuria, arterial hypertension and eventually death due to renal failure. Relentless progression to end-stage renal failure occurs in rats when a critical mass of functioning nephrons is lost. Progression occurs when approximately three-fourths of the functional renal mass is destroyed by infarction or resection. In human patients, progression from renal insufficiency to renal failure has been reported regardless of the inciting renal injury and whether the inciting cause is present or not.[63] There is some controversy as to whether progressive renal injury occurs in dogs. In experimental studies in dogs, reduction of renal mass resulted in glomerular changes and proteinuria.[64] The severity of these changes appeared to be correlated with the amount of renal tissue ablated. Two other experimental studies involving dogs did not show a progressive decline in renal function.[65,66] It is possible that progression was not observed because the extent of the induced renal injury was not sufficient to alter glomerular hypertension or renal autoregulation. Progression was noted, however, in a group of untreated dogs with naturally occurring renal disease.[8]

GLOMERULAR CAPILLARY HYPERTENSION AND GLOMERULAR HYPERFILTRATION

In a normal kidney, single-nephron GFR (SNGFR) and single-nephron plasma flow are submaximal under basal conditions. Reduction of nephron mass leads to hypertrophy of the residual nephrons with increases in filtration and perfusion of surviving nephrons.[67] SNGFR increases are accompanied by glomerular hyperfiltration and intraglomerular hemodynamic changes, which increase flux of plasma proteins through the mesangium. These proteins stimulate mesangial cell proliferation and matrix production and eventually lead to glomerulosclerosis (Figure 19-3). Glomerular capillary hypertension is the critical intraglomerular hemodynamic factor responsible for promoting glomerular injury. Although these compensatory increases in SNGFR and renal plasma flow initially help to maintain body homeostasis, eventually these hemodynamic changes contribute to progressive renal damage. Dietary protein restriction has been shown to prevent these hemodynamic changes and to preserve normal glomerular structure in rats.[68]

Table 19-6. Etiopathogenic mechanisms that may be involved in renal failure.

1. Glomerular capillary hypertension and glomerular hyperfiltration
2. Increased renal ammoniagenesis
3. Increased renal oxygen consumption
4. Phosphorus retention and hyperparathyroidism
5. Compensatory renal growth
6. Hypertension
7. Metabolic acidosis
8. Tubulointerstitial changes
9. Altered lipid metabolism
10. Effects of renal aging
11. Amyloidosis
12. Acute renal failure
13. Inadequate urinary concentration

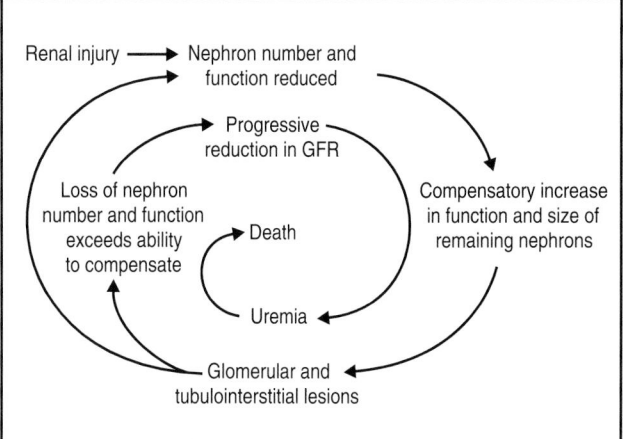

Figure 19-2. Vicious cycle of relentless progression of chronic renal disease. After a critical amount of damage has occurred, compensatory mechanisms, which are initially beneficial, are activated and ultimately contribute to progressive injury. The amount of damage required to trigger progression probably varies from species to species and from individual to individual. (Adapted from Churchill J, Polzin DJ, Osborne CA, et al. The influence of dietary protein intake on progression of chronic renal failure in dogs. Seminars in Veterinary Medicine and Surgery: Small Animal 1992; 7: 246.)

As renal disease develops, the afferent renal arterioles dilate, causing glomerular hypertension, which distends the capillaries. The resultant mesangial stretch stimulates the accumulation of collagen[69] and progressive loss of function (Figure 19-4). High pressure distends capillary lumens in perfused rat glomeruli. Mesangial cells are stretched because of their relationship to capillaries and their attachment to the glomerular basement membrane. When mesangial cells in culture are stretched and relaxed repeatedly, stretch-induced release of transforming growth factor b mediates the production of collagen.[70]

RENAL AMMONIAGENESIS

Renal ammonia production allows net acid excretion and thus is essential for acid-base homeostasis. Adaptive changes in ammoniagenesis occur as functional renal mass is decreased. Although total ammonia production is reduced, ammonia production per surviving nephron is increased several-fold. Ammonia activates the third component of complement, C_3. Supplementation with bicarbonate reduces C_3 and C_{5b-9} (i.e., membrane attack complex) levels.[71] Bicarbonate administration also reduces cor-

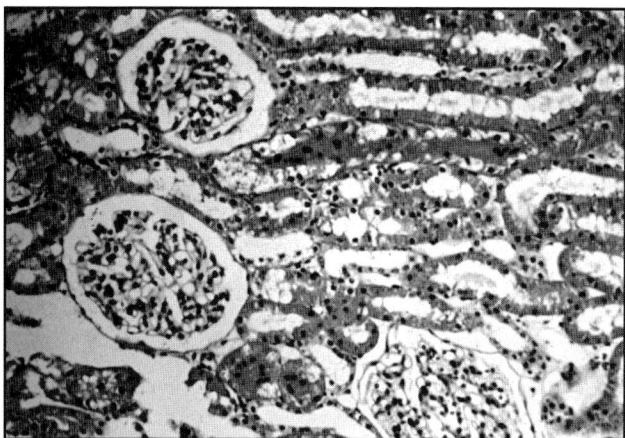

Figure 19-3. Microscopic view of early stages of renal disease. (Above) Photomicrograph (hematoxylin-eosin stain) showing normal glomeruli, tubules and interstitium. (Below) Early chronic progressive renal disease. Photomicrograph (hematoxylin-eosin stain) showing increased mesangial matrix, increased glomerular cellularity and increased interstitial infiltrates.

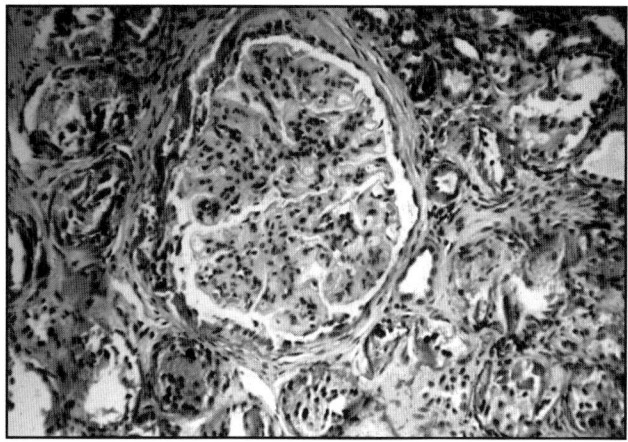

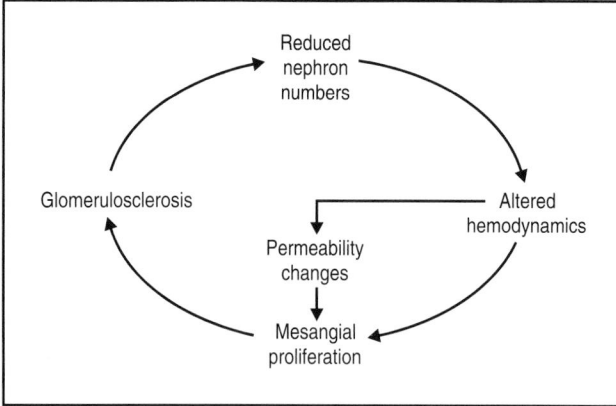

Figure 19-4. Schematic showing the progressive effect of glomerular capillary hypertension.

tical levels of ammonia, decreases proteinuria, reduces structural damage and improves tubular function.

Activation of the alternate complement cascade leads to renal injury by several mechanisms. Activated C_3 is a potent stimulus for the release of reactive oxygen species and peroxidase from leukocytes. An activated component of the alternate complement pathway is a vasoactive chemoattractant. Another activated component causes cell

lysis at high doses and the release of cytokines, prostanoids and reactive oxygen species at lower doses. Lower doses also stimulate collagen synthesis. Production of C_3 by tubular epithelial cells is upregulated by cytokines. This provides a positive feedback loop for tubulointerstitial injury.

The interaction of ammonia and complement in the etiopathogenesis of tubulointerstitial disease has also been demonstrated in studies of hypokalemic nephropathy in rats.[71] Chronic potassium depletion stimulates ammonia synthesis. Potassium deficiency influences ammonia synthesis at the same site as chronic metabolic acidosis.

Extensive interstitial fibrosis is a naturally occurring feature of canine end-stage kidney disease. The tubulointerstitial damage may be due, at least in part, to the self-perpetuating cycle of tubular functional impairment, compensatory changes in ammoniagenesis and further damage due to activation of the alternate complement pathway. Dietary protein restriction and alkali supplementation both reduce tubular hyperfunction by decreasing the renal acid load and decreasing renal ammoniagenesis.

INCREASED RENAL OXYGEN CONSUMPTION

The kidney has a very high rate of oxygen consumption, the majority of which is expended reabsorbing sodium. With renal damage, surviving nephrons increase sodium reabsorption and correspondingly oxygen consumption. Hypoxia of the renal medulla can predispose a patient to acute and chronic renal injury.[72] The renal medulla conserves body water by concentrating urine up to four times the osmolality of plasma. The medulla concentrates urine by means of the countercurrent system of blood vessels and tubules that actively absorb sodium. The major determinant of medullary oxygen demand is the rate of active absorption in the medullary thick ascending loop.

Increased rates of oxygen consumption have been incriminated in progressive renal injury because interventions that decrease progression (e.g., dietary protein and phosphate restriction) concomitantly decrease renal oxygen consumption. Increased renal oxidative metabolism has been linked to increased renal ammoniagenesis and increased generation of reactive oxygen species (e.g., hydrogen peroxide).

Reactive oxygen species, generated by increased oxygen consumption, have been incriminated in progressive injury.[73] In rats with remnant kidneys, increased oxygen consumption associated with increased dietary protein is accompanied by increased urinary clearance of oxidative products.[74] The role of reactive oxygen species in progressive renal injury has also been evaluated in studies using vitamin E and selenium-deficient diets.[74] Vitamin E is a major scavenger of reactive oxygen species in lipid bilayers, and selenium is required for glutathione peroxidase activity. Glutathione peroxidase is the enzyme that degrades hydrogen peroxide. Deficiency of vitamin E or selenium favors hydrogen peroxide accumulation and associated oxidative effects. Specifically, antioxidant deficiency decreases GFR, increases proteinuria and increases tubulointerstitial injury. Reactive oxidative species may also induce expression of collagen gene activity and contribute to renal fibrosis.

A variety of mechanisms regulate medullary oxygen homeostasis. These include medullary vasodilators such as nitric oxide, prostaglandin E_2, adenosine, dopamine and urodilatin and vasoconstrictors such as endothelin, angiotensin II and vasopressin. Tubuloglomerular feedback controls glomerular filtration and, indirectly, medullary oxygen demand. Reduced reabsorption of sodium activates signals that constrict the glomerulus, reducing glomerular filtration and subsequent delivery and reabsorption of sodium from the tubule. A related reaction is shifting of the corticomedullary blood flow to the medulla when renal blood flow is reduced.

In CRF, increased fibrosis in the kidneys may result from intrarenal hypoxia due to increased oxygen consumption by surviving nephrons. Hypoxia causes release of cytokines that stimulate the intrarenal production of collagen.

Because the work of concentrating urine predisposes a patient to medullary hypoxic injury, reducing the need for concentration of urine may prevent medullary injury. Reducing transport activity protects medullary tubules from hypoxic injury. Dehydration, salt and volume depletion and renal hypoperfusion stimulate urine concentration. Avoiding dehydration and sodium depletion reduce the work of urine concentration and stimulate intrarenal protective mechanisms, such as prostaglandin and dopamine production.

PHOSPHORUS RETENTION AND HYPER-PARATHYROIDISM

Phosphorus retention and secondary hyperparathyroidism have been incriminated as causes of progressive renal injury.[75,76] PTH administration causes interstitial nephritis and calcium deposition in the kidney; human patients with primary hyperparathyroidism and hypercalcemia develop renal dysfunction.[77]

Phosphorus plays a critical role in the synthesis of adenosine triphosphate, cell membrane integrity, energy metabolism, acid-base balance and oxygen delivery to tissues. Carbohydrate intolerance is common in people with CRF. Carbohydrate intolerance is due to peripheral resistance to the action of insulin and to inappropriate insulin release. Hyperparathyroidism impairs the ability of the pancreas to secrete insulin, but does not affect the peripheral resistance to the action of insulin. Prevention or correction of hyperparathyroidism tends to normalize associated glucose intolerance.

Secondary hyperparathyroidism is an inevitable consequence of CRF (Figure 19-5). The pathogenesis is complex (Figure 19-6); however, there is evidence that decreased circulating levels of vitamin D disrupt the feedback loop that normally inhibits PTH synthesis. Decreased renal synthesis of vitamin D results from inhibition of 25-hydroxyvitamin D 1-α-hydroxylase activity by hyperphosphatemia and decreased renal parenchyma.

Resistance to the calcemic action of PTH and decreased sensitivity of parathyroid cells to hypercalcemia contribute to the development of secondary hyperparathyroidism in CRF. Metabolic acidosis can increase PTH levels independent of changes in ionized calcium or calcitriol concentrations.[78] Low calcitriol levels, phosphorus retention and down-regulation of bone cell PTH receptors are the primary reasons for resistance to the calcemic action of PTH. Although controversy exists regarding the mechanism by which phosphorus retention produces secondary hyperparathyroidism, it is clear that secondary hyperparathyroidism can be prevented if hyperphosphatemia can be avoided.

Phosphorus modulates renal 1-α-hydroxylase activity.[79] Phosphorus retention decreases ionized calcium concentration, which stimulates PTH secretion. Renal parenchymal damage and high levels of intracellular phosphate inhibit

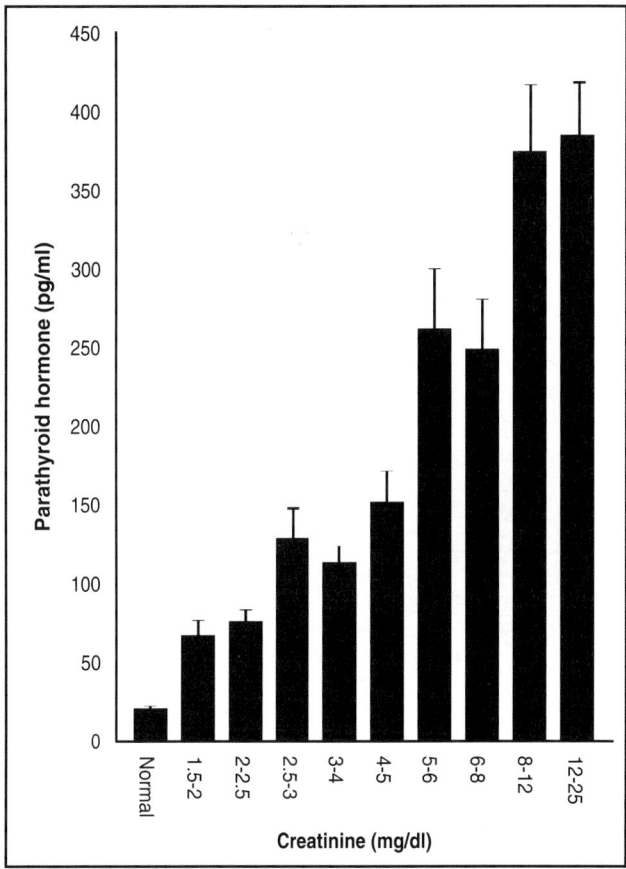

Figure 19-5. Relationship of serum parathyroid hormone concentrations to serum creatinine concentrations in 35 normal dogs and 333 dogs with uremia. (Adapted from Nagode LA, Chew DJ. Nephrocalcinosis caused by hyperparathyroidism in progression of renal failure: Treatment with calcitriol. Seminars in Veterinary Medicine and Surgery: Small Animal 1992; 7: 206.)

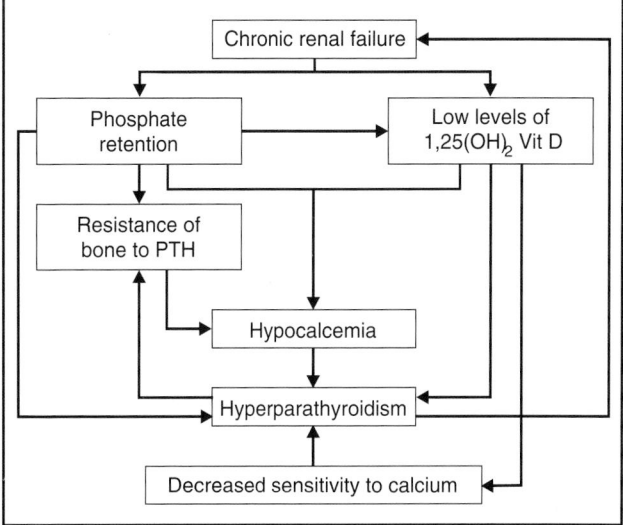

Figure 19-6. The pathogenesis of secondary renal hyperparathyroidism. Key: PTH = parathyroid hormone, 1,25(OH)$_2$ Vit D = 1,25-dihydroxycholecalciferol.

the synthesis of 1,25-dihydroxycholecalciferol (calcitriol). Low levels of calcitriol, in turn, impair intestinal absorption of calcium, which worsens hypocalcemia. Because calcitriol normally inhibits PTH secretion, reduced levels of calcitriol increase PTH secretion and PTH secretion becomes less sensitive to inhibition by calcium. Consequently, secondary renal hyperparathyroidism can occur in the absence of hyperphosphatemia and hypocalcemia.

At the same time hyperphosphatemia and hyperparathyroidism occur, metabolic acidosis decreases citrate production and increases citrate reabsorption, reducing citrate concentrations in the proximal tubule. The decreased citrate and increased phosphorus in tubular fluid increase the likelihood of calcium phosphate precipitation in the tubule. Increased PTH levels elevate cytosolic free calcium. Increased cytosolic calcium with increased transcellular calcium and phosphorus fluxes and decreased citrate availability increase the possibility of calcium-induced cellular damage.

Renal osteodystrophy, the term used to describe the skeletal and mineral homeostasis problems associated with end-stage renal disease, is a multifactorial problem resulting in bone remodeling. The bone lesions that accompany CRF involve one or more of a variety of changes that include: 1) osteitis fibrosa, 2) osteomalacia, 3) osteosclerosis and 4) osteopenia. Osteomalacia is recognized by widening of the osteoid seam, which is evidence of decreased mineral deposition. Osteosclerosis and osteopenia refer to variations in the amount of osteodystrophic bone.

Secondary hyperparathyroidism and deficiency of calcitriol are major contributors to renal osteodystrophy. Various cytokines (e.g., interleukin-1, tumor necrosis factor α, interleukin-6 and interleukin-11) and their receptors are involved in bone remodeling and exhibit increased activity with end-stage renal disease. Renal osteodystrophy is classified as osteitis fibrosa, osteomalacia, or mixed or adynamic disease based on histologic features. PTH decreases the production of proteins associated with bone formation (e.g., Type I collagen and bone matrix proteins) by mature osteoblasts. Osteoclasts are attracted and activated by matrix-dissolution products produced by the actions of PTH. PTH also stimulates the release of locally acting cytokines.

Dietary phosphorus reduction in proportion to reduction in GFR prevents and reverses pre-existing renal hyperparathyroidism.[80] More recent studies have shown that reduction of dietary phosphorus improves secondary hyperparathyroidism by a mechanism independent of levels of calcitriol or ionized serum calcium.[81]

COMPENSATORY RENAL GROWTH

In response to decreases in renal function, surviving nephrons undergo compensatory growth (i.e., residual glomeruli and tubules increase in size). This hypertrophic response, in the long-term, is deleterious and leads to progressive glomerular sclerosis and end-stage renal failure.[82] Strategies that suppress renal growth including dietary protein and salt restriction reduce renal injury.

Glomerular growth may be damaging even when glomerular pressure is unchanged due to increased wall tension.[82] According to the Law of Laplace, wall tension = transmural pressure x radius. Thus, increased wall tension occurs with glomerular growth. This same mechanism has been proposed for tubulointerstitial injury. Altered urine flow may lead to altered tubular structure and subsequent tubular damage because of increased wall tension.

HYPERTENSION

In dogs and cats, hypertension is usually secondary to other diseases. Diseases associated with systemic hypertension in dogs and cats include renal failure, obesity, hyperadrenocorticism, hyperthyroidism, pheochromocytoma and diabetes mellitus.[46,83,84] Renal failure appears to be the disease most commonly associated with systemic hypertension. The majority of dogs and cats with renal failure have systemic hypertension.[46,47] When considering hypertension in renal disease, it is important to note that renal disease causes hypertension and hypertension can cause renal disease. Systemic hypertension can damage a number of other end organs, including the eyes and the cardiovascular system.[48,85]

High blood pressure has been linked to kidney failure for a long time. But recently, it has been proved that even slight increases in blood pressure increase the risk of kidney failure.[85] In fact, a small increase (i.e., 16 mm Hg systolic and 11 mm Hg diastolic) in blood pressure can double the risk of kidney failure in men later in life. Mild

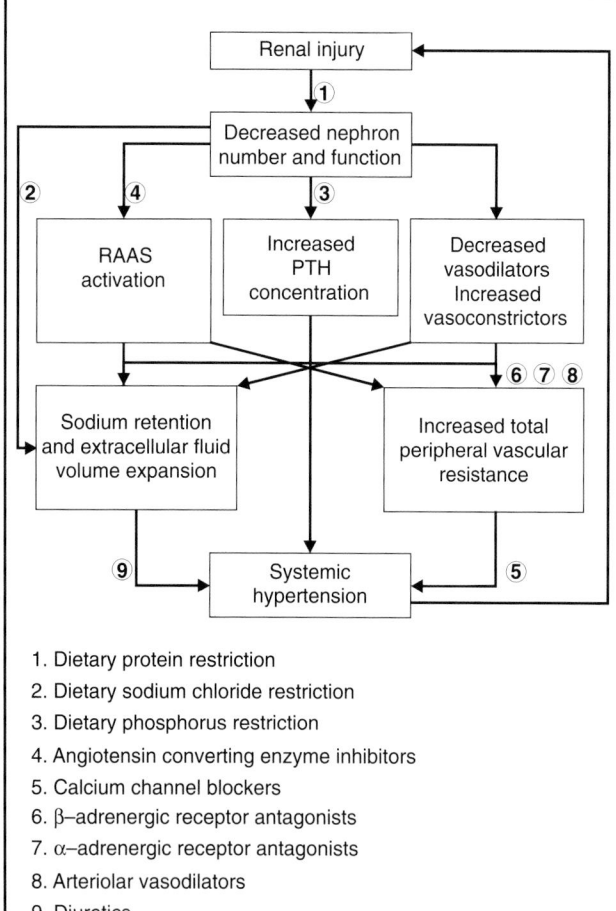

1. Dietary protein restriction
2. Dietary sodium chloride restriction
3. Dietary phosphorus restriction
4. Angiotensin converting enzyme inhibitors
5. Calcium channel blockers
6. β–adrenergic receptor antagonists
7. α–adrenergic receptor antagonists
8. Arteriolar vasodilators
9. Diuretics

Figure 19-7. Proposed mechanisms and effects of nutritional management and pharmacologic agents on systemic hypertension and renal injury. Key: RAAS = renin-angiotensin-aldosterone system. (Adapted from Bartges JW, Willis AM, Polzin DJ. Hypertension and renal disease. Veterinary Clinics of North America: Small Animal Practice 1996; 26: 1334.)

Mechanisms Causing Loss of Lean Muscle Mass in Renal Disease

Loss of lean body mass is common in human and veterinary patients with acute and chronic renal failure (CRF). The mechanisms causing this loss are only beginning to be understood. Potential mechanisms include inadequate dietary protein intake, altered response to restricted protein intake, metabolic acidosis and activation of cytokines by chronic inflammation. Uremic patients seem unable to activate the critical metabolic responses that maintain protein balance when dietary protein is limited. Negative nitrogen balance and loss of lean body mass will occur if uremia prevents suppression of essential amino acid or protein degradation when dietary protein intake is reduced by anorexia.

Metabolic acidosis, a common complication of uremia, stimulates the degradation of branched-chain amino acids and proteins and blocks the ability of the patient to respond appropriately to lower protein intake. The specific mechanisms involve increased activity of branched-chain ketoacid dehydrogenase and the ubiquitin-proteasome proteolytic pathway.

Several kinds of evidence indicate that acidosis causes loss of lean body mass: 1) human CRF patients treated with sodium bicarbonate have improved nitrogen balance, 2) metabolic acidosis blocks the ability of human CRF patients to adapt to a low-protein diet, 3) acidosis-stimulated breakdown of muscle protein can be linked to glucocorticoids in CRF patients (i.e., increased muscle protein breakdown was seen in human subjects with lower serum bicarbonate concentrations; muscle protein breakdown also was directly correlated with serum cortisol concentration), 4) feeding ammonium chloride to induce acidosis in normal adult people not only causes negative nitrogen balance but also inhibits albumin synthesis and 5) acidosis in normal adult people or human patients with CRF stimulates whole-body protein degradation.

Besides acidosis, cytokines activate the ubiquitin-proteasome proteolytic pathway and cytokine release occurs with chronic inflammation. These potential mechanisms for loss of muscle mass emphasize the importance of controlling metabolic acidosis, infection and other stressors in patients with chronic renal failure.

BIBLIOGRAPHY

Ballmer PE, McNurlan MA, Hulter HN, et al. Chronic metabolic acidosis decreases albumin synthesis and induces negative nitrogen balance in humans. Journal of Clinical Investigation 1995; 95: 39-45.

Mitch WE. Mechanisms causing loss of lean body mass in kidney disease. American Journal of Clinical Nutrition 1998; 67: 359-366.

Mitch WE, Goldberg AL. Mechanisms of muscle wasting: The role of the ubiquitin-proteasome system. New England Journal of Medicine 1996; 335: 1897-1905.

Papadoyannakis HJ, Stefanidis CJ, McGeown M. The effect of correction of metabolic acidosis on nitrogen and protein balance of patients with chronic renal failure. American Journal of Clinical Nutrition 1984; 40: 623-627.

Reaich D, Channon SM, Scrimgeour CM, et al. Ammonium chloride-induced acidosis increases protein breakdown and amino acid oxidation in humans. American Journal of Physiology 1992; 263: E735-E739.

Reaich D, Channon SM, Scrimgeour CM, et al. Correction of acidosis in humans with CRF decreases protein degradation and amino acid oxidation. American Journal of Physiology 1993; 265: E230-E235.

Williams B, Hattersley J, Layward E, et al. Metabolic acidosis and skeletal muscle adaptation to low protein diets in chronic uremia. Kidney International 1991; 40: 779-786.

increases in blood pressure tripled the risk of kidney failure and severe high blood pressure increased the risk of kidney failure 11 times. These findings were independent of age, smoking, blood cholesterol levels, presence of diabetes and heart attacks.

The authors of a recent epidemiologic survey of blood pressure in dogs found that dogs with renal disease have average systolic and diastolic pressure clearly above normal; however, they characterized the increases as modest compared with other conditions associated with hypertension.[44] As noted above, even slight increases in blood pressure increase the risk of renal failure.

Impaired autoregulation has been demonstrated to occur in dogs with ischemic ARF and reduced renal mass. In normal dogs, the renal autoregulatory mechanism limits the effect of systemic blood pressure changes on renal blood flow and GFR. This protection is achieved by adjusting preglomerular resistance so that renal hemodynamics remain stable between mean systemic arterial blood pressures of 70 to 150 mm Hg. Dogs with severe reductions in functional mass have impaired renal autoregulation with excursions in renal arterial pressure. Impaired autoregulation may lead to renal injury during systemic hypertensive episodes and contribute to a progressive decline in kidney function.[86] Figure 19-7 outlines proposed mechanisms for arterial hypertension in CRF.

METABOLIC ACIDOSIS

Because renal ammonia production increases acid excretion, metabolic acidosis is associated with increased ammoniagenesis. As noted above, renal ammoniagenesis has been incriminated in progressive renal injury. CRF is associated with progressive loss of lean body mass and bone disease. The pathophysiology of these changes is complex; however, chronic metabolic acidosis plays a pivotal role in the pathophysiology of protein catabolism and renal osteodystrophy.

Metabolic acidosis rather than uremia per se is an important stimulus for net protein catabolism. Metabolic acidosis contributes to negative nitrogen balance, decreased muscle protein and loss of lean body mass by several mechanisms. Protein catabolism provides a source of glutamine, which is a substrate for renal ammoniagenesis. The kidney converts glutamine to ammonia. Ammonia is a key urinary buffer, absorbing hydrogen ions.

Another mechanism for protein catabolism in CRF is activation of proteolytic pathways by metabolic acidosis. Acidosis increases protein degradation by a glucocorticoid-dependent mechanism, which increases the amount and activity of branched-chain ketoacid dehydrogenase. Even mild metabolic acidosis enhances branched-chain amino acid catabolism. Acidosis stimulates proteolysis in muscle by inducing the transcription of genes encoding for enzymes participating in the ATP-dependent cytosolic ubiquitin-proteasome proteolytic pathway. (See sidebar "Mechanisms Causing Loss of Lean Muscle Mass in Renal Disease.")

Inadequately controlled metabolic acidosis contributes to renal osteodystrophy. Deleterious effects of metabolic acidosis include increased sensitivity of bone to PTH and inhibition of vitamin D_3-1-α-hydroxylation.[87]

The kidneys eliminate the body's metabolic and dietary acid load. Because of the unceasing production of acid, normal animals are in constant jeopardy of metabolic acidosis. The kidneys prevent the development of acidosis by reabsorbing filtered bicarbonate, by excreting the daily acid load and by simultaneously resynthesizing bicarbonate lost buffering metabolic acids. The kidneys can increase the amount of net acid excretion in urine and generate bicarbonate in response to exogenous acid loads. The kidneys respond to exogenous acid loads by excreting hydrogen ions in the form of titratable acid and ammonium ions (NH_4^+). Ammonia exists in two forms in aqueous solution: the nonionized NH_3 and the monovalent cation NH_4^+. The nonionized form is lipid-soluble and readily traverses cell membranes in the direction determined by concentration gradients. At the pH of renal tubular fluid, hydrogen ions (H^+) avidly combine with NH_3 to form NH_4^+. The ionized form, unlike NH_3, is not lipid-soluble; consequently, the NH_4^+ is trapped within the tubular lumen and is excreted in the form of neutral salts (e.g., NH_4Cl).

Proximal bicarbonate reabsorption is affected primarily by neutral Na^+/H^+ exchange, which is driven by the lumen-to-cell sodium gradient. Hydrogen ions secreted into the lumen of the proximal convoluted tubules combine with filtered bicarbonate to form carbonic acid. Carbonic acid, catalyzed by membrane-bound carbonic anhydrase, is broken down to CO_2. At equilibrium, dissolved CO_2 equilibrates with the gas phase in contact with the liquid phase (i.e., the respiratory gas in the pulmonary alveoli). Dissolved CO_2 diffuses into the cell and combines with hydroxyl ions. Newly formed HCO_3^- and reabsorbed sodium are added to the blood in the process. The net result is the excretion of H^+ and the replenishment of HCO_3^-.

Cats may respond to metabolic acidosis differently than other species. The authors of one report concluded that cats do not appear to increase production of ammonia from glutamine during metabolic acidosis.[88] However, another report showed that cats increase urine ammonium ion excretion in response to an acid load.[89]

The normal response of the kidneys to an acid load is to excrete a strongly acidic, bicarbonate-free urine. In normal subjects, the total capacity to excrete hydrogen ions by renal tubular cells is only partially used (i.e., a secretory reserve exists). This reserve is saturated in patients with renal failure. Acidosis can result from failure to reabsorb filtered bicarbonate or failure to acidify the urine.

Human patients with azotemic acidosis with stable bicarbonate levels excrete less acid than they produce metabolically.[90] Because this positive acid balance occurs despite constant bicarbonate levels, an extrarenal nonbicarbonate buffer must neutralize endogenous acid. Bone serves this function in the acidosis of CRF. Balance studies have shown that positive acid balance is accompanied by a comparable degree of negative calcium balance.[91] Retained acid is neutralized by calcium carbonate in bone, thus protecting serum bicarbonate levels. Therefore, acidosis contributes to renal osteodystrophy and abnormal phosphate homeostasis and calcium phosphorus precipitates may play a role in progressive renal injury.

TUBULOINTERSTITIAL CHANGES

Tubulointerstitial changes are a constant feature in CRF, irrespective of the cause or initial structure involved.[92] Unlike glomerular injury, the extent of tubulointerstitial injury correlates with the decline in renal function. It appears that GFR is influenced to a greater degree by interstitial fibrosis than by glomerulosclerosis.[93]

Although chronic, progressive tubulointerstitial disease plays a critical role in progression of renal lesions, the basic mechanisms that generate the tubulointerstitial damage remain unclear. There appears to be a clinically silent acute phase that is characterized by inflammation and tubular cell injury. Possible mediators of tubular injury include: antibodies, reactive oxygen metabolites, obstruction, complement and lysosomal enzymes.[92] Damaged tubular cells can regenerate or die. Factors responsible for recruitment of mononuclear cells to the interstitium are important because of evidence that monocytes and macrophages play a key role in interstitial fibrosis.[94] Recruitment is probably mediated by the release of fibrosis-promoting cytokines, such as transforming growth factor-b1. Transforming growth factor-b1 appears to trigger increased matrix production by perivascular and interstitial fibroblasts. Dietary protein restriction inhibits the secretion of transforming growth factor-b1 and glomerular scarring in rats with glomerulonephritis.[95]

Interstitial fibrosis may be due in part to a failure of matrix degradation by metalloproteinases and plasmin. Decreased enzymatic breakdown of matrix is due to increased expression of enzyme inhibitors.[96]

Tubulointerstitial injury can impair renal function by a number of mechanisms including: 1) vascular effects, 2) glomerular injury, 3) interstitial and tubuloepithelial processes, 4) nephron obstruction and 5) deposition of crystals.[93] Postglomerular blood flow is decreased when the cortical interstitium expands due to fibrosis and mononuclear infiltration. Decreased blood supply also results from release of vasoactive cytokines, growth factors and reactive oxidant species produced by the interstitial infiltrate and damaged tubules. Decreased postglomerular blood flow decreases tubular blood flow and changes glomerular size and pressure. Decreased tubular blood flow may impair tubular function and glomerular size and pressure changes may lead to glomerular injury.[93] The renal interstitium is important in the regulation of renal function and tubuloglomerular feedback. The expression of certain cytoskeleton proteins can be used as an early indicator of fibrosis.

Abnormal glomerular function can incite tubulointerstitial injury.[97] Loss of glomerular permselectivity and resultant proteinuria are accompanied by tubulointerstitial damage. Increased trafficking of protein in the proximal tubules may cause cellular damage. In the proximal tubules, filtered protein is endocytosed and subsequently degraded by lysosomal action. Excessive release of lysosomal enzymes may be one of the pathways for tubular damage. Tubular damage may also be induced by plasma proteins that have escaped into the urine. Incriminated plasma proteins include lipoproteins, complement components and transferrin. The model for this mechanism is tubular damage induced by Bence Jones protein.

Complement proteins, including C_{5b-9} (membrane attack complex), are present in urine with Bence Jones protein. This finding may reflect glomerular immune-complex injury or be due to the activation of the alternate complement pathway in the brush border of tubules.

Another pathway for tubular damage is iron-dependent injury.[98] Decreased glomerular permselectivity allows transferrin to escape into the urinary space. Iron is released from transferrin as the pH decreases in the distal nephron and during lysosomal degradation of endocytosed transferrin. Released iron catalyzes the generation of hydroxyl ions and other tubule-damaging oxidants. Glomerular diseases allow red blood cells to enter the urinary space. Hemoglobin may also produce tubular damage by an iron-dependent free radical generating process.

Albumin that has passed through the glomerular barrier may also induce tubulointerstitial damage.[99] A macrophage chemotactic factor is released when albumin is metabolized by the proximal tubules. Glomerular damage may directly cause infiltration of the interstitium. The infiltrate, consisting of macrophages and T cells, originates from the hilar area of the glomerulus and spreads throughout the cortical interstitium. Because antibody was not detected in this area, researchers have suggested that leukocytes are recruited to the hilar area by cytokines or autocoids produced in the hilar region.[100] Research evidence also suggests that cytokines and growth factors produced outside the glomeruli stimulate collagen synthesis, resulting in interstitial fibrosis.[101]

Immune processes may sustain tubulointerstitial damage regardless of the inciting cause. Evidence for this view includes the presence of immunologically active mononuclear cells in the interstitium, changes in antigenicity with nonimmune injury and the role of tubules as antigen-presenting cells. Tubular handling of filtered protein and resultant lysosomal activation may injure tubules and present hidden antigens.

LIPIDS

Dietary lipids can influence the kidneys by several different mechanisms. Dietary lipids can influence progression of chronic renal disease by affecting: 1) renal hemodynamics, 2) platelet aggregation, 3) lipid peroxidation, 4) systemic blood pressure, 5) proliferation of glomerular mesangial cells and 6) plasma lipid concentration.

Dietary lipid intake can change the balance of renal eicosanoids.[102] Eicosanoids are derived from cell membrane polyunsaturated fatty acids and include prostaglandins, prostacyclin and thromboxanes. When n-3 fatty acids are included in the food, eicosapentaenoic acid and docosahexaenoic acid compete with arachidonic acid in several ways. (See Chapter 26.) Eicosapentaenoic acid and docosahexaenoic acid inhibit the synthesis of arachidonic acid from linoleic acid. They compete with arachidonic acid for incorporation into membrane phospholipids and eicosapentaenoic acid competes with arachidonic acid as the substrate for cyclooxygenase. The principal eicosanoids derived from arachidonic acid include prostaglandin E_2, prostacyclin and thromboxane A_2. In general, prostaglandin E_2 and prostacyclin are vasodilators and thromboxane A_2 is a vasoconstrictor. Prostaglandin E_2 and prostacyclin increase renal blood flow and GFR, whereas thromboxane A_2 decreases renal blood flow and GFR. Both thromboxane A_2 and prostacyclin alter platelet function; thromboxane A_2 enhances and prostacyclin inhibits platelet aggregation. The end result of increased dietary intake of n-3 fatty acids is a shift in the balance toward greater vasodilatation and less platelet aggregation. Supplementation with n-3 fatty acids may decrease platelet aggregation and reduce platelet-induced progressive glomerular injury. Dogs readily convert linole-

ic acid to arachidonic acid; however, cats have limited delta-6-desaturase activity. Therefore, the conversion of linoleic to arachidonic acid is limited in this species. The saturated fatty acids found in animal fats do not serve as precursors for eicosanoid production.

Supplementation with n-3 fatty acids possibly improves renal function because of the effect of altered eicosanoid production on lipid peroxidation. Carbon double bonds are susceptible to attack by electrophilic oxygen molecules. The oxidation of double bonds in membrane polyunsaturated fatty acids by electrophilic oxygen compounds is called lipid peroxidation. Free radical derivatives of oxygen and polyunsaturated fatty acids produce a self-generating lipid peroxidation chain reaction. Lipid peroxidation damages cell membranes and may play a role in progressive renal injury.

Abnormalities of lipid metabolism in dogs with renal disease generally include increased serum levels of total cholesterol, low-density lipoproteins and triglycerides.[103] Cats with experimentally induced renal dysfunction demonstrate hypercholesterolemia compared with normal cats. Cholesterol, triglycerides and possibly some classes of lipoproteins are cytotoxic to endothelial cells and stimulate glomerular mesangial cell proliferation and production of excess mesangial matrix.

The ratio of the urinary eicosanoids thromboxane B_2 (a stable urinary metabolite of thromboxane A_2) and prostaglandin E_2 has been used as an index of renal vascular tone in normal and CRF dogs fed foods supplemented with safflower and menhaden fish oil.[104] The oil supplement had no significant effect on the ratio. The failure to demonstrate a change in the ratio may be related to the length of the washout period (three weeks) and uncertain stability of lipid supplements in this study.

The amount and ratio of dietary polyunsaturated fatty acids can also influence platelet aggregation[105] and proliferation of glomerular mesangial cells. N-3 fatty acids inhibit endothelial production of growth factors, which resemble platelet-derived growth factor and cause abnormal cell proliferation. These actions may influence progression of renal injury. The ratio of n-6 to n-3 fatty acids has also been shown to influence systemic blood pressure and, as described above, even slight elevations in blood pressure have been shown to damage the kidney.

In a canine gentamicin-induced ARF model, n-3 fatty acid supplementation increased urinary excretion of prostaglandin E_2 and prostaglandin $F_{1\alpha}$ but was less renoprotective than pharmacologic thromboxane synthetase inhibition.[106]

EFFECTS OF RENAL AGING

The kidney is one of the most vulnerable organs to age-associated changes. Renal changes associated with aging are manifested by significant structural and functional alterations. Functional changes include decreased GFR, decreased renal blood flow, decreased urine concentrating ability and decreased ability to maintain sodium, water, endocrine and acid-base homeostasis.

Structural changes include alterations in weight, volume and histologic appearance. The weight and volume of the human kidney decreases 20 to 30% between the ages of 30 and 90 years. The number of glomeruli decrease by 30 to 50% with an increasing percentage of sclerotic and abnormal glomeruli. Glomerular mesangial volume increases by 50% and one in 10 glomeruli is sclerotic by age 80 years compared with one in 100 in the young adult. The renal tubules decrease in number, and proximal tubule volume and length decrease.[107]

Fibroconnective tissue replaces functionally active parenchyma in aging kidneys. Fibroblast-like cells in the interstitium can express certain cytoskeleton proteins, such as vimentine. Vimentine is expressed under conditions of cell injury and normal aging. Collagen modifications seem to be associated with the aging process; these changes may be due to the formation of highly reactive free radicals that cause DNA deletions and thus alter protein transcription.[74] Long-term enalapril therapy in aging mice decreases renal interstitial fibrosis.[108]

In the juxtamedullary area, afferent and efferent arterioles may fuse to form continuous units as glomeruli sclerose with advancing age. The formation of a direct channel between afferent and efferent arterioles results in arteriole recta verae, or agglomerular arterioles. Presumably, formation of these channels contributes to the maintenance of medullary blood flow as cortical perfusion decreases. This increased medullary blood flow may interfere with the capacity of the countercurrent system to generate hypertonicity. This, in conjunction with the selective loss of juxtamedullary nephrons and changes in renal tubules, may explain the decreased urine concentrating ability observed in older patients. The age-related decrease in the capacity to form concentrated urine may also have a central component (i.e., impaired release of vasopressin). Decreased concentrating ability is further compounded by the decreased thirst and water intake in response to water deprivation and thermal dehydration reported to occur in elderly men. Impaired concentrating ability and decreased thirst result in a predisposition to volume depletion in older dogs, which may lead to decreased renal blood flow and an abrupt deterioration in renal function.

Elderly people have a defect in urinary acidification that may not be apparent under normal conditions.[109] Frequently, the serum bicarbonate level is low normal or slightly depressed because of an age-related inability to excrete an acid load.

GFR and renal blood flow rate decline linearly in people after the age of 30 years. The GFR of a healthy octogenarian is only half to two-thirds that measured in young adults. Using data combined from 30 studies, Wesson demonstrated a progressive decline in renal plasma flow in human patients after the fourth decade of life.[110]

Biochemical analysis of the glomerular basement membrane in the aging human kidney demonstrates decreased sulfation of glycosaminoglycans. This change could reduce the net negative charge and result in increased permeability of the glomerular basement membrane to protein.

Endocrine status gradually changes with age. Decreased concentrations of renin, aldosterone and calcitriol have been reported to occur in people.[111] A highly significant increase in serum levels of PTH was observed in old dogs (mean of 11 years, ranging from nine to 14 years) compared with young dogs (mean of 2.5 years, ranging from one to five years).[112] Although renal function was not evaluated in this study, increased PTH concentrations may be a "marker" of decreased renal function.

In addition to the prevalence of primary renal disease increasing with advancing age, the frequency of renal failure associated with diseases such as cardiac failure, malignancy, diabetes mellitus, hypertension, urinary tract infection and urinary tract obstruction increases with increasing age. Additional risk factors for renal damage include hypotension associated with volume depletion and injudicious use of nephrotoxic drugs, especially the aminoglycoside antimicrobials.

In a study of dogs with spontaneous glomerulonephritis, the incidence of interstitial nephritis increased with increasing age. Interstitial nephritis was present in 10% of dogs less than one year old, in 60% of dogs between one and five years old and in 85% of dogs more than five years old.[113] In another study, 59% of the dogs older than four years had evidence of interstitial nephritis.[114] Glomerular lesions were noted in 43 to 78% of these dogs. Based on these reports, interstitial nephritis and glomerulosclerosis apparently are common and occur with increased frequency in aging dogs.

AMYLOIDOSIS

Amyloidosis is characterized by the deposition of proteins with β-pleated sheet configuration in a variety of tissues. In dogs, the kidneys are the most common site of deposition, but deposits can be found in the liver, spleen and other organs. The β-pleated sheet structure is responsible for the unique staining and optical characteristics of amyloid, as well as its insolubility and resistance to proteolysis in vivo.

A number of classification schemes are used to categorize amyloidosis in people, but in dogs the most common form is reactive (secondary) amyloidosis. Reactive amyloidosis is frequently idiopathic, but may be associated with chronic inflammatory, infectious or neoplastic conditions. Reactive amyloid displays green birefringence when stained with Congo red dye and viewed under polarized light. Amyloid AA fibrils, typical of reactive amyloidosis, are sensitive to permanganate oxidation. The precursor protein for reactive amyloid protein AA is the acute-phase reactant serum amyloid A protein. Cytokines released as a result of tissue injury stimulate production of this protein by the liver. Serum amyloid A protein is subsequently degraded by monocytes. Thus, amyloidosis may result from chronic tissue injury in individuals predisposed to produce amyloidogenic protein variants or those with defective protein degradation mechanisms.

Most dogs and cats with renal amyloidosis are older than five years. Beagles, collies and Walker hounds were at increased risk and German shepherd dogs and mixed-breed dogs were at decreased risk in one study.[115] Familial amyloidosis with extensive renal involvement has been described in Abyssinian cats and beagle and Chinese Shar-Pei dogs. Beagles display predominantly glomerular involvement, whereas medullary amyloidosis predominates in Chinese Shar-Pei dogs and Abyssinian cats.

ACUTE RENAL FAILURE

ARF is usually caused by an ischemic or toxic insult. Pre-renal azotemia describes a state of inadequate blood perfusion. Structurally, the kidneys are normal; therefore, changes are rapidly reversible if perfusion improves before renal cells are damaged. The renal circulation is influenced by systemic arterial blood pressure. When systemic blood pressure decreases below the limits of autoregulation, severe vasoconstriction results with redistribution of the renal blood supply away from the superficial cortex.

The pathophysiology of ischemic ARF is complex. Restoration of total renal blood flow shortly after an ischemic insult does not prevent ARF. Reduced renal blood flow and/or alterations in the distribution of renal blood flow initiate ARF, but ischemia sets off a sequence of pathophysiologic processes that, once initiated, perpetuate the tissue damage and functional defects independent of total renal blood flow.

Delivery of oxygen and other metabolic substrates to tubular cells is decreased when renal blood flow is decreased. The ATP pool is rapidly depleted and cellular transport pumps are affected (sodium/potassium and sodium/calcium ATPase). Increased intracellular concentrations of sodium result in transit of water into cells and cellular swelling. Cellular swelling occludes vascular and tubular lumens. Damage to cell membranes results in excessive influx of calcium into tubular epithelial cells, which activates phospholipases, damages mitochondria and further constricts blood vessels. Decreased energy production causes further membrane damage and formation of free radicals. Free radicals that are not scavenged contribute to further membrane and cellular damage. Leukotrienes and thromboxane A_2 are produced, which cause infiltration of inflammatory cells.

The functional integrity of the microvasculature depends on the proper balance between vasoconstrictive and vasodilatory factors.[116] Damage to the endothelium can cause local vasoconstriction due to increased production of vasoconstrictive substances (e.g., endothelium) or decreased production of vasodilatory substances (e.g., nitric oxide). These changes may be important in the local loss of autoregulation that occurs in ischemic ARF.

Not all of the cellular injury that occurs with ischemia happens during the period of ischemia. A significant amount of damage occurs after reperfusion. Reactive oxygen species have been implicated in the renal cell injury that occurs with reperfusion.[117]

Some investigators have proposed that calcium is the principal mediator of cellular injury associated with ischemia.[118] Calcium accumulates in damaged and dead cells; however, it is not known whether increased levels of calcium cause ischemic injury or are the consequence of the injury.

Blood flow to the superficial cortex and outer medulla is reduced in ARF with a resultant decrease in delivery of oxygen and nutrients to tubules in this region. Swelling of cells interferes with blood flow through the vasa recta, which worsens the ischemia. Because of the vasa recta countercurrent exchange, oxygen tension decreases with increasing distance into the medulla from the cortex. Ischemic injury occurs when a reduction in blood flow decreases the delivery of oxygen and substrates to a level inadequate to maintain cellular energy status.[119] Cellular depletion of ATP results, leading to a series of morphologic, biochemical and physiologic changes. These changes include loss of microvilli and loss of tight junction integrity. This results in a marked decrease in membrane surface area for absorption of nutrients and water, and back-leakage of filtrate from the lumen. Function of membrane proteins is also altered. For example, the absorption of glucose by the proximal cells is decreased after ischemic injury.

Ischemia damages the tubular cells. Injured tubular cells slough into the lumen, contributing to cast formation, obstructing the lumen, increasing tubular pressure and reducing SNGFR. Recent discoveries in cellular and molecular biology have shown that cell-matrix and cell-cell adhesion contribute to ARF.[120] Although a synonym for ARF is acute tubular necrosis, necrotic tubular cells are rarely seen. Instead, the tubular basement membrane is denuded or covered by only a thin layer of cytoplasm. After acute injury to the renal tubular epithelium, there is redistribution of integrin receptors and remodeling of the cellular cytoskeleton. Disordered adhesion results in exfoliation of renal tubular epithelial cells.

Phospholipid degradation contributes to ischemic injury in the kidneys. During ischemic injury, phospholipase A_2 is activated, which ultimately leads to membrane damage and elaboration of vasoactive or chemotactic factors that contribute to cell death.

In addition to its effect on renal perfusion, ischemic renal injury triggers an inflammatory response. Ischemic changes involve expression of major histocompatibility complex products, a mild interstitial infiltrate and a number of cytokines.[121]

Feeding a food containing 27% protein on a dry matter basis (DMB) before and during gentamicin administration reduced nephrotoxicosis.[122] Dietary protein levels appear to exert this renoprotective effect by influencing gentamicin pharmacokinetics. Higher levels of dietary protein change the volume distribution and decrease tubular uptake of gentamicin.[123]

Thromboxane A_2 is a powerful vasoconstrictor and produces mesangial cell contraction. Increased production of thromboxane secondary to ischemic or toxic injury is thought to be a major cause of the renal vasoconstriction associated with ARF. Dietary supplementation with n-3 fatty acids can reduce thromboxane synthesis. The mechanism for this action is the substitution of n-3 fatty acids for arachidonic acid in membrane phospholipid resulting in decreased synthesis of thromboxane A_2 by cyclooxygenase. Dietary n-3 fatty acid supplementation protects dogs from experimental ischemic renal failure. In dogs supplemented with fatty acids, GFR did not decrease and there was no increase in urinary thromboxane excretion.[124] Dietary n-3 fatty acid supplementation in dogs with gentamicin-induced nephrotoxicosis increased excretion of vasodilatory prostaglandins but was not renoprotective.[106]

URINE CONCENTRATION

A number of observations suggest that protein-induced and urine concentration-induced changes in kidney function and morphology share a common yet poorly understood mechanism.[125] The similarities between the effects of high protein intake in rats and sustained stimulation of urine concentration suggest that vasopressin plays a role in the renal response to high dietary protein levels. Vasopressin is necessary for the full manifestation of the effects of high protein intake on the kidney in rats with diabetes insipidus.[126] Protein-induced changes (e.g., altered glomerular hemodynamics, kidney weight and free water reabsorption) are very similar to changes due to chronic stimulation of urine concentration. Microscopically, protein-induced and concentration-induced changes enlarge the nephron segment most directly involved in the process of concentrating urine. ADH is required for the development of protein-induced changes in renal function and morphology. ADH levels are increased with acute and chronic protein ingestion. Concentrating solutes in the urine represents "osmotic work" for the kidneys and represents a burden for diseased kidneys. Reducing the amount of solutes to be concentrated by decreasing the dietary protein intake or by providing more water for the excretion of the same amount of solutes independently reduces the amount of osmotic work.

Key Nutritional Factors

Dietary therapy is the mainstay of conservative medical management of canine and feline CRF. Dietary management prevents or mitigates the clinical signs of uremia, minimizes signs of mineral and electrolyte imbalance and may slow progression of CRF (Figure 19-8).

WATER

Healthy animals are in water balance. Water balance occurs when the sum of water intake and metabolic water produced equals output. Water input is composed of drinking water, moisture in food and water formed during metabolism. Metabolic water is a small component in healthy animals. Water output occurs via the GI, respiratory, integumentary and urinary systems. The major organ system involved in water output, capable of regulating water relative to need, is the urinary system. If water is in excess, the kidneys excrete free water; if water is deficient, the kidneys retain water by concentrating urine.

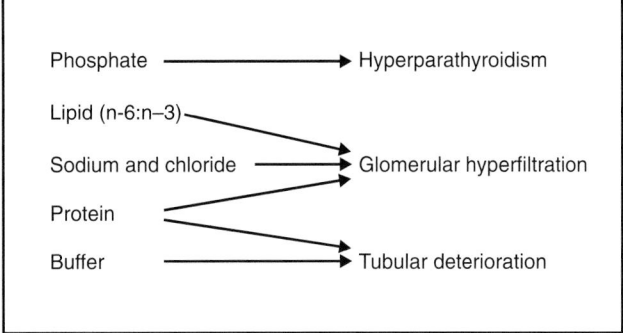

Figure 19-8. Key nutritional factors in the management of chronic renal disease and the pathophysiologic mechanisms they affect. Key: n-6:n-3 = fatty acid ratio.

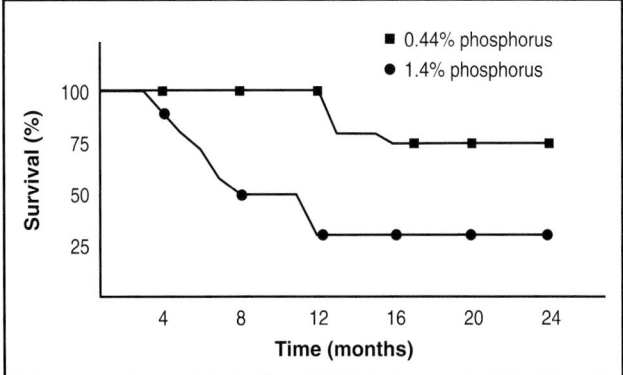

Figure 19-9. Survival of dogs with experimentally induced chronic renal disease fed low-protein foods with different levels of phosphorus. Note that survival was much improved in dogs consuming the low-phosphorus food. (Adapted from Brown SA, Crowell WA, Barsanti JA, et al. Beneficial effects of dietary mineral restriction in dogs with marked reduction of functional renal mass. Journal of the American Society of Nephrology 1991; 1: 1169-1179.)

Renal disease causes a progressive decline in urine concentrating capacity.[127] The maximum urine osmolality approaches that of plasma (300 mOsm/kg) in renal insufficiency. If total solute excretion remains normal, but the maximal achievable urine osmolality decreases, obligatory water loss will occur to eliminate the osmolar load. This obligatory water loss may lead to the development of polyuria.

Because concentrating urine predisposes an individual to renal injury, reducing the need to concentrate urine may be beneficial. Dehydration, volume depletion, renal hypoperfusion and dietary salt intake stimulate urine concentration. Avoiding dehydration and hypoperfusion reduces the work of concentrating urine and maintains intrarenal protective mechanisms such as prostaglandin and dopamine production. Reducing urinary solute transport activity may protect against renal injury. CRF patients should have unlimited access to fresh water for free-choice consumption.

PHOSPHORUS/CALCIUM

The objectives of mineral nutriture in patients with decreased renal function are to maintain plasma concentrations of phosphorus and ionized calcium within reference limits, prevent or reduce secondary hyperparathyroidism and prevent or reverse renal osteodystrophy (i.e., soft-tissue mineralization and skeletal disease).

In an experimental study in dogs, Brown and co-workers reduced kidney function by roughly 75% using surgery.[103] After a three-month stabilization period, the dogs were fed either a low-phosphorus (0.44% dry matter [DM]) food or a high-phosphorus (1.44% DM) food for 24 months. Both foods provided 18% DM protein. Survival rate in the high-phosphorus group was only 33%. In contrast, the survival rate was 75% in the low-phosphorus group (Figure 19-9). Kidney function also deteriorated at a more rapid rate in the high-phosphorus group. The mechanism for the protective effect of phosphorus restriction is unknown. Possible etiologies include reduced nephrocalcinosis, suppression of hyperparathyroidism, reduced cellular energy metabolism, amelioration of the lipoprotein abnormalities associated with uremia and altered renal hemodynamics. These mechanisms may synergistically contribute to the beneficial effects of phosphorus restriction.

Approximately a 75% reduction in kidney function was induced in dogs at the start of the study described above. This level of reduction typically corresponds to the point at which serum creatinine and urea nitrogen concentrations first exceed the upper limit of the reference range.

Brown and co-workers also found that decrements of renal function were more closely related to nephrocalcinosis and tubulointerstitial lesions than to glomerular pathology.[103] Specifically, in this study, progression and fatality were associated with interstitial fibrosis, tubular atrophy and dilatation and mineralization of cortical basement membranes, tubular epithelia and vascular and tubular lumina. The association of progression with tubulointerstitial lesions and nephrocalcinosis, however, does not necessarily establish a causal role for nephrocalcinosis.

In another study in cats with induced renal failure, high dietary phosphorus intake (1.56% DM phosphorus) for 65 to 343 days was associated with renal mineralization, fibrosis and mononuclear cell infiltration.[128] Low levels of phosphorus intake (0.42% DM phosphorus) prevented these histologic abnormalities (Figure 19-10). Progressive renal dysfunction was not detected in either the normal or restricted-phosphorus groups.

An intake of 0.15 to 0.3% DM phosphorus is recommended for most dogs with CRF and 0.4 to 0.6% DM phosphorus for most cats with CRF.

PROTEIN

One rationale for manipulation of diet in managing renal failure is the observation that many of the clinical and metabolic disturbances associated with uremia are direct results of accumulated waste products derived from the catabolism of protein. Early studies in laboratory animals showed rapid improvement when dietary protein was restricted.[129,130] Excessive dietary protein is catabolized to urea and other nitrogenous compounds normally excreted by the kidneys. Decreased renal function leads to accumulation of these compounds. Endogenous proteins will be degraded if amino acid intake is insufficient to maintain nitrogen balance. One goal of nutritional therapy is to achieve nitrogen balance and limit the accumulation of waste products by proportionally decreasing protein intake as renal function declines.

The effect of protein restriction on the progression of renal insufficiency has been vigorously debated. Nutritional factors have been shown to play a significant role in preventing deterioration of glomerular function in various experimental and clinical glomerular diseases. Recently, several reports have been published that indicate a beneficial role for protein restriction in several forms of human renal disease. Ihle and colleagues demonstrated the beneficial effects of protein restriction in slowing the rate of renal impairment in a prospective, randomized study of human patients with stable, moderate renal failure.[63] Additionally, Hostetter's group showed that dietary protein restriction improves glomerular permselectivity in human patients with proteinuric glomerular disease and in patients with chronic renal transplant rejection.[131]

Pedrini and co-workers concluded that dietary protein restriction is beneficial in human renal disease. "Our analyses show that dietary protein restriction slows the progression of both diabetic and nondiabetic renal diseases. . . We found that dietary protein restriction significantly reduced the risk of renal failure and death . . ." The authors combined a number of smaller studies using meta analysis. Inconclusive or contradictory conclusions in the individual studies were due to differences in outcome measures (i.e., rate of decline in creatinine clearance or GFR or increase in serum creatinine concentration) and insufficient sample size to detect a beneficial effect on the incidence of renal failure and death. The authors calculated that more than 1,000 patients are necessary in order to detect a 33% risk reduction by dietary protein restriction.[132]

A study involving dogs with hereditary nephritis demonstrated a beneficial response to protein restriction. Beginning at 35 days of age, one group of dogs was fed a regular food. A second group was fed a food reduced in calcium, phosphorus and protein. The onset and progression of renal failure were delayed and the severity of glomerular basement membrane splitting was reduced. The dogs fed the food with restricted nutrient levels lived 53% longer than dogs fed the regular food.[53]

Dietary protein restriction potentially limits progression of renal dysfunction in cats. In a study involving cats with surgically induced renal failure, restricting dietary

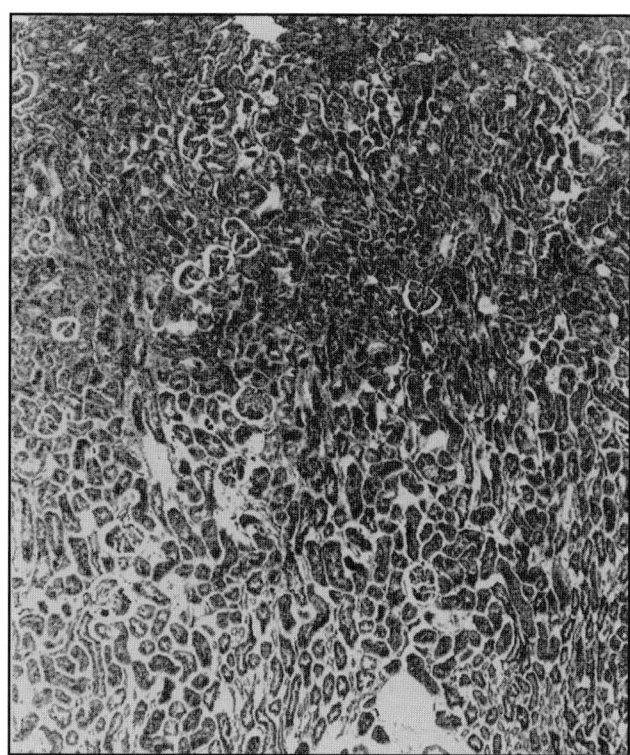

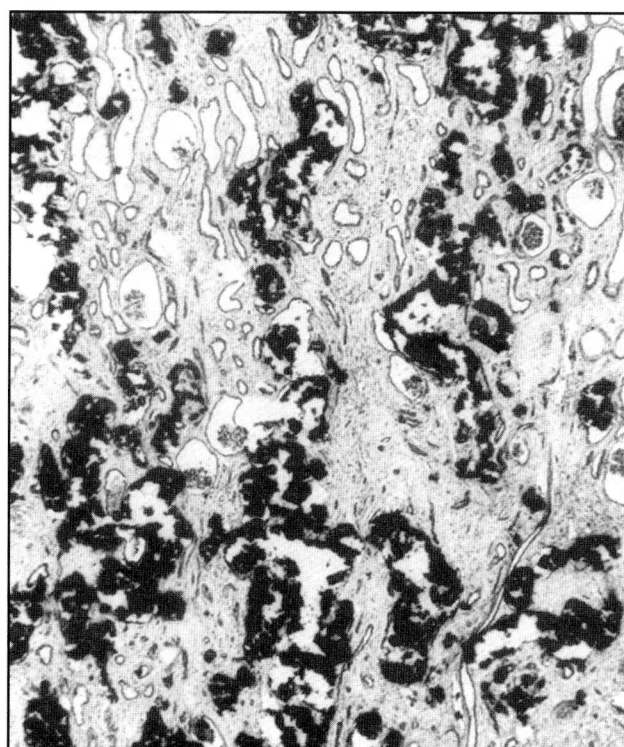

Figure 19-10. Photomicrographs of the renal cortex from cats with experimentally induced chronic renal disease. (Above) Renal tissue from a cat fed a low-phosphorus food (0.42% DM phosphorus). Mineralized foci are not seen in this kidney (hematoxylin-eosin stain). (Below) Renal tissue from a cat fed a food with normal phosphorus levels (1.56% DM phosphorus). Mineralization (black foci), fibrosis and mononuclear cell infiltrates are extensive compared with that seen on a renal photomicrograph from a cat eating the lower phosphorus food (von Kossa's stain). (Reprinted with permission from Ross LA, Finco DR, Crowell WA. Effect of dietary phosphorus restriction on the kidneys of cats with reduced renal mass. American Journal of Veterinary Research 1982; 43: 1023-1026.)

Modification of Diet in Renal Disease Human Multi-Center Trial

A large prospective, controlled, multi-center trial was sponsored by the National Institutes of Health and conducted to evaluate the effect of modification of diet in human renal disease. Patients in Study A of the Modification of Diet in Renal Disease (MDRD) trial were randomized to receive a usual or low-protein diet, whereas those in Study B were randomized to receive a low-protein or very low-protein diet supplemented with a ketoacid-amino acid supplement. The daily protein intakes were 1.3, 0.6 and 0.3 g/kg body weight/day for the usual, low- and very low-protein diets, respectively. In study patients with various forms of renal disease and baseline glomerular filtration rates (GFR) of 25 to 55 ml/minute/1.73 m^2, the GFR projected to the third year of follow-up was higher in the low-protein group compared with that in the usual protein group. Because this difference in GFR did not achieve statistical significance, it was initially concluded that the benefit of the low-protein diet was not conclusively proved. Nevertheless, there was absolutely no evidence that the low-protein diet caused harm.

The primary analysis of data from the MDRD Study concluded that the effect of a low-protein diet was inconclusive because of a nonlinear GFR decline and limited duration of follow-up. However, in a secondary analysis, 585 patients were randomly assigned to follow either a low-protein diet or a usual protein diet. Outcomes included the rate of GFR decline, incidence of renal failure, death and change in urine protein excretion. Analysis of these data provide support for the hypothesis that dietary protein restriction slows progression of moderate renal disease.

A complicating factor in the interpretation of the MDRD Study is the proportion of patients with various forms of renal disease. Two hundred of the 840 participants enrolled in the MDRD Study had autosomal dominant polycystic kidney disease (ADPKD). The rate of GFR decline in these patients was more rapid than in patients with other diagnoses. The process causing this more rapid loss of kidney function is unknown, but it has been suggested that it may be due to a form of programmed cell death known as apoptosis. Because ADPKD patients may progress by a unique mechanism that is not influenced by diet, the MDRD study may have been biased against finding a benefit of low-protein diets.

A conference was held April 4-5, 1994, to develop practical management recommendations. The conference consisted of several panels of nephrology experts from around the world. The panels reviewed literature, heard presentations on published studies and reviewed manuscripts in press from secondary analyses of the MDRD data. The conference report stated, "Several large clinical trials on the management/prevention of progressive renal disease have been published within the last year. Those studies show that the incidence of chronic renal disease can be decreased by approximately 50%, that the rate of progression of proteinuria can be decreased by a similar percentage, and that these favorable results also apply to those with advanced nephropathy. Thus, for the first time, it has been conclusively shown that chronic progressive renal disease is amenable to both prevention and treatment."

BIBLIOGRAPHY

Finco DR, Brown SA, Crowell SA, et al. Effects of dietary phosphorus and protein in dogs with chronic renal failure. American Journal of Veterinary Research 1992; 53: 2264-2271.

Klahr S, Levey AS, Beck GJ, et al. The effect of dietary protein restriction and blood pressure control on the progression of chronic renal disease. New England Journal of Medicine 1994; 330: 877-884.

Levey AS, Adler S, Caggiula AW, et al. Effects of dietary protein restriction on the progression of moderate renal disease in the modulation of diet in renal disease study. Journal of the American Society of Nephrology 1996; 7: 2616-2626.

Robertson JL, Goldschmidt M, Kronfeld DS, et al. Long-term renal responses to high dietary protein in dogs with 75% nephrectomy. Kidney International 1986; 29: 511-519.

Woo D. Apoptosis and loss of renal tissue in polycystic kidney diseases. New England Journal of Medicine 1995; 333: 18-25.

protein intake reduced glomerular and interstitial lesions in the kidneys.[33] During the 12-month study, renal function remained stable in the restricted and high protein intake groups. Because the restricted dietary protein group also consumed fewer calories, the observed benefit may have been due to caloric restriction. In a trial involving cats with naturally occurring renal disease, serum creatinine concentrations progressively increased in the group receiving high dietary protein and progressively declined in the group in which dietary protein was restricted.[133]

A large, prospective, controlled, multi-center trial was conducted to evaluate the effect of modification of diet in human renal disease. The sidebar "Modification of Diet in Renal Disease Human Multi-Center Trial" summarizes the results of this study.

A veterinary therapeutic food with 11 to 12% of calories as high biologic value protein (14.5 to 15% DM protein) is recommended for most dogs with CRF and 19 to 21% of calories as high biologic value protein (28 to 30% DM protein) for most cats with CRF. Even lower levels may be necessary for dogs with advanced CRF. The nutritional objective of feeding lower protein levels is to obviate uremic signs. Patients should be monitored for signs of protein insufficiency.

The concept of ideal protein is useful when considering biologic value.[134] As proposed by Baker and Czarnecki-Maulden, lysine is the limiting amino acid in practical foods for dogs and cats. However, experience with typical ingredients used in commercial veterinary therapeutic foods suggests that tryptophan is more frequently limiting. Therefore, based on the concept of ideal protein, foods that meet the requirement for tryptophan can be assumed to meet the requirement for all indispensable amino acids.

LIPID

Several studies have addressed the effect of fat and fatty acids on progression of renal failure.[135-137] Potential mechanisms include alterations in renal eicosanoid production and plasma lipid concentration. Dietary fat could influence progression of renal failure by changing platelet aggregation, fibrinolytic activity, immunologic responses and blood pressure.

Eicosanoids are compounds derived from polyunsaturated fatty acids within cell membranes and include prostaglandins, prostacyclin and thromboxanes. The usual precursor for eicosanoids is arachidonic acid. In dogs, arachidonic acid is derived from the polyunsaturated fatty acid, linoleic acid, which is the major constituent of plant oils. Linoleic acid is referred to as an n-6 (omega-6) fatty acid because the first carbon double bond is at the sixth carbon from the methyl group end. Cats have limited hepatic delta-6-desaturase activity and thus cannot efficiently convert linoleic to arachidonic acid. Therefore, both arachidonic and linoleic acids are considered essential in cats.

As mentioned above, the principal eicosanoids derived from arachidonic acid include prostaglandin E_2, prostacyclin and thromboxane A_2. The vasodilatory eicosanoids, prostaglandin E_2 and prostacyclin, increase renal blood flow and GFR. Thromboxane A_2 is a renal vasoconstrictor and decreases renal blood flow and GFR. Thromboxane A_2 enhances platelet aggregation and prostacyclin inhibits platelet aggregation.

Specific lipid-containing ingredients (e.g., menhaden fish oil) contain n-3 (omega-3) fatty acids that compete with arachidonic acid in the production of eicosanoids. Thus, animals fed menhaden fish oil have decreased levels of 2-series eicosanoids, which are normally derived from arachidonic acid, and increased levels of 3-series eicosanoids derived from n-3 fatty acids. The 3-series eicosanoids are less potent at inducing vasoconstriction and platelet aggregation than the 2-series eicosanoids. The saturated fatty acids found in animal fat do not serve as precursors for eicosanoid production.

Studies in nephrectomized rats have shown excessive increases in glomerular capillary pressure and filtration due to increased renal eicosanoid production. In laboratory animals, manipulation of dietary intake of n-3 and n-6 fatty acids improves renal function.[138]

Dietary fat composition alters the rate of progression of CRF in dogs following 15/16 nephrectomy (Figure 19-11).[139] A low-fat diet (<1% DM fat) was supplemented with one of three different fat sources (menhaden fish oil, beef tallow or safflower oil) to achieve a total fat concentration in the diet of 15% DMB. Dogs were assigned to dietary treatment two months following nephrectomies and followed for 20 months. Menhaden fish oil lowered plasma cholesterol and triglyceride concentrations. Compared with the beef tallow-supplemented diet, safflower oil resulted in intermediate plasma cholesterol and triglyceride concentrations. Compared with the other two groups, the group receiving the diet supplemented with safflower oil had greater glomerular enlargement and mean glomerular capillary pressure.[139] Dietary fatty acid composition appeared to alter hemodynamic responses to renal insufficiency. Final mean exogenous creatinine clearance was 1.3 ml/minute/kg body weight for the menhaden fish oil group, 0.9 ml/minute/kg body weight for the beef tallow group and 0.5 ml/minute/kg body weight for the safflower oil group. Mean UPC ratios were 0.6 in the menhaden fish oil group, 1.5 in the beef tallow group and 2.1 in the safflower oil group. Survival was similar in groups receiving menhaden oil and beef tallow; however, four of seven dogs in the safflower oil group were euthanatized.

Although the optimal dietary levels of fatty acids and fatty acid ratios for patients with CRF have not been determined, an n-6 to n-3 fatty acid ratio less than 2.5:1 seems reasonable based on available data.

ENERGY

Energy requirements of patients with renal failure are presumed to be similar to those of normal animals. Energy

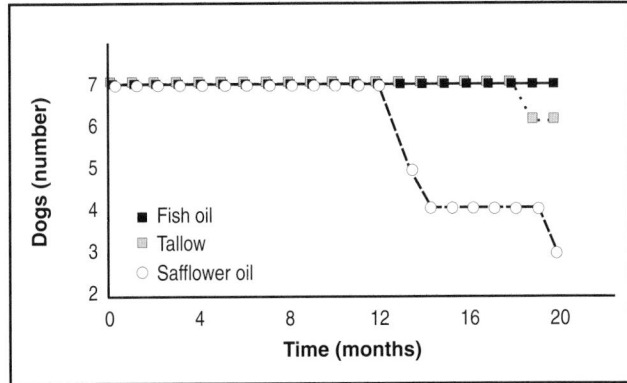

Figure 19-11. Survival of dogs with experimentally induced chronic renal disease fed foods with three different fat sources (fish oil, tallow, safflower oil). Note that survival was increased in those dogs consuming foods with either tallow or fish oil compared to safflower oil. Dietary fatty acid composition appears to affect hemodynamic adaptations to renal disease in dogs. (Adapted from Brown SA, Brown CA, Crowell WA, et al. Dietary lipid composition alters chronic course of canine renal disease (abstract). Journal of Veterinary Internal Medicine 1996; 10: 168.)

intake tends to decline as renal function declines because of progressive anorexia. Dietary protein and energy are interrelated. When considering the level of dietary protein intake, it is important to assess the adequacy of energy intake. Numerous factors (e.g., gender, environment, activity) influence the energy requirement. The starting point for estimating daily energy requirement (DER) for an individual patient is to calculate the resting energy requirement (RER) and multiple this number by a factor that varies based on the severity of chronic metabolic disease. The formula for calculating RER in kcal/day is $70 \times (BW_{kg})^{0.75}$. The recommended range for most canine patients with CRF is 1.1 to 1.6 x RER. The range for most feline patients with CRF is 1.1 to 1.4 x RER. Food dose should be adjusted to maintain optimal body weight and condition from these calculated starting points.

Patients with CRF frequently have weakness and exercise intolerance. Decreased muscle oxidative energy metabolism has been documented by means of ^{31}P nuclear magnetic resonance (NMR) spectroscopy in human renal failure patients. Possible mechanisms include decreased blood flow to muscles, anemia, defective muscle lipid or amino acid metabolism, endocrinopathies, insulin resistance and inhibition of muscle metabolism by uremic toxins. A recent study demonstrated that abnormalities of muscle energy metabolism observed in patients with CRF are due, in part, to intrinsic changes to key enzymes in the major energy-providing pathways.[140]

POTASSIUM

Normally, the majority of ingested potassium is excreted in the urine with the remainder excreted in the feces. In CRF, the proportion excreted in the feces increases.[141] Potassium excretion per nephron also increases and the amount of potassium excreted approaches and may even exceed the filtered load of potassium. In CRF, aldosterone and the rate of fluid flow in the distal nephron mediate the increased potassium secretion in the distal tubule. In general, these mechanisms maintain plasma potassium concentration within the reference limits until renal function

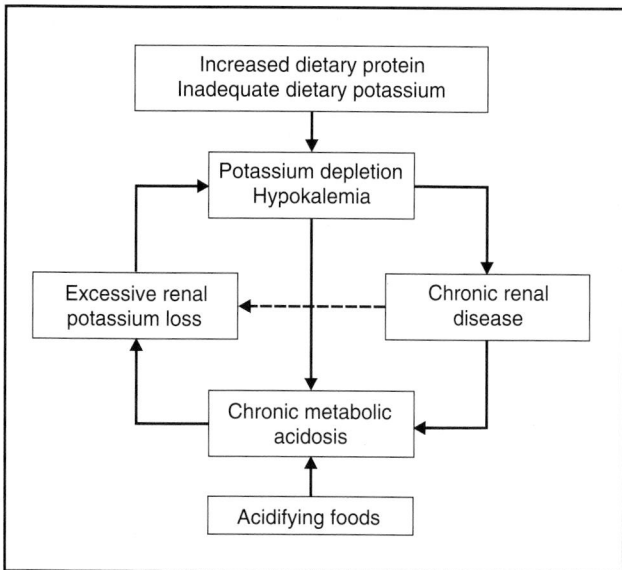

Figure 19-12. Putative relationship between dietary potassium intake, excessively acidifying foods and feline chronic renal disease.

is severely reduced. It is possible that low aldosterone and renin levels could produce hyperkalemia earlier in the course of CRF. Plasma potassium concentrations might also increase because of redistribution of potassium between intracellular and extracellular compartments as acidosis develops. Intracellular potassium leaves the cells and is replaced by hydrogen and sodium.

The secretory rate for potassium may be maximal at very low GFR to maintain homeostasis. Thus with advanced renal failure, oliguria, sudden increases in potassium intake and sudden worsening of metabolic acidosis or catabolism can produce severe hyperkalemia. Severe hyperkalemia can develop in advanced renal failure despite the fact that total body potassium might be markedly reduced.

Cats with renal failure appear to be particularly predisposed to disorders in potassium homeostasis (Figure 19-12 and Case 19-3). Decreased dietary intake due to anorexia or vomiting and increased urinary losses due to polyuria can contribute to hypokalemia in renal failure. Hypokalemia (potassium <3.5 mEq/l) occurred in 19% of cases in a clinical series of cats with renal failure.[142] Hypokalemia was moderate to severe (potassium <3.1 mEq/l) in more than half of these cases. Conversely, hyperkalemia was observed in 13% of these cats. Hyperkalemia was observed in both oliguric and polyuric renal failure.

Potassium depletion leads to functional and morphologic changes in the kidneys of dogs and cats. Functional changes include reduction in GFR and reduced urine concentrating ability. In hypokalemic rats, increased renal ammoniagenesis contributed to chronic lymphoplasmacytic tubulointerstitial nephritis.[71] Studies in cats demonstrated that potassium depletion may result from feeding acidifying foods that are high in protein and low in potassium. CRF was observed in three of nine adult cats fed a food high in protein (40% DM) and low in potassium (0.32% DM) content for two years. Lymphoplasmacytic interstitial nephritis and interstitial fibrosis were detected in these cats and in two other cats without laboratory abnormalities.[143]

The potassium requirement for cats is proportional to the protein content of the food. Using purified diets, 0.3% potassium was required for growth in kittens fed a 33% protein diet; however, 0.5% potassium was required with a 68% protein diet.[144] Acidifying foods and chronic metabolic acidosis may contribute to hypokalemia (Figure 19-12).[145]

An intake of 0.08 to 0.12 g of potassium/100 kcal metabolizable energy (ME) (0.3 to 0.5% DM potassium) is recommended for most dogs with CRF. In cats, the objective is to maintain serum potassium concentrations above 4.0 mEq/l. This is generally achieved by feeding a food that contains approximately 0.18 g of potassium/100 kcal ME (0.9% DM potassium). Oral supplementation with potassium gluconate should be considered if diet alone does not maintain serum potassium concentration above 4.0 mEq/l.

Potassium supplementation is indicated whenever hypokalemia is documented. Oral administration is safest and is the preferred route unless a critical emergency exists or if oral administration is impossible or contraindicated. Oral potassium gluconate appears to be tolerated well. The initial recommended dose for potassium gluconate is 2 to 6 mEq/cat/day, depending on the size of the cat and severity of clinical signs. The potassium gluconate dose should be adjusted based on clinical response and serial analyses of serum potassium concentration. During the initial treatment, serum potassium concentration should be checked every two to four days. Later, serum potassium level should be checked every two to four weeks. Routine potassium supplementation of all cats with renal disease, regardless of serum potassium concentration, is not recommended. Potassium supplementation did not have a significant effect on muscle potassium levels.[146]

ACID LOAD

Approximately 80% of renal failure cats in a retrospective clinical series had metabolic acidosis based on decreased levels of plasma bicarbonate and blood pH.[5] In human patients, severe acidemia due to renal failure generally does not occur until GFR is roughly less than 20% of normal.[147] Plasma bicarbonate levels are frequently decreased when GFR is above 20% of normal. Even at equivalent levels of GFR, the degree of acidosis is highly variable. Variability is due to differences in the nature of the underlying renal disease, diet, extracellular fluid volume status, potassium status and degree of respiratory compensation.

Dietary acid is derived from several sources. Sulfuric acid is formed when sulfur-containing amino acids (i.e., methionine and cysteine) are oxidized to sulfate. In general, animal-source proteins are higher in sulfur-containing amino acids than are plant-source proteins. Exogenous and endogenous proteins are equally important; foods deficient in calories that result in protein catabolism increase hydrogen ion production. Urinary urea production and total urinary hydrogen ion excretion are directly proportional.

Organic acids are produced from intermediary metabolism products formed from partial oxidation of carbohydrates, fats, proteins and nucleic acids. The organic acids generated contribute to net acid production when conjugate bases are excreted in the urine as negatively charged organic anions. If complete oxidation of organic acids occurs, the hydrogen ions are reclaimed and eliminated as water with carbon dioxide.

Phosphoric acid can be ingested in the food or it can be produced endogenously. Phosphoric acid is used in cat foods as a palatability enhancer, either separately or as a component of topically applied animal digests. Phosphoric acid can be derived from hydrolysis of phosphate esters in proteins and nucleic acids, if they are not neutralized by mineral cations (e.g., sodium, potassium and magnesium). The contribution of dietary phosphate to acid production depends on the type of protein ingested. Some proteins generate phosphoric acid, whereas others generate only neutral phosphate salts.

Hydrochloric acid is generated when positively charged cationic amino acids (e.g., lysine and arginine) are broken down into neutral products.

Mineral salts vary in their effect on urinary pH. Differences in the absorption of the cation and anion portion of the salt are important. Intestinal absorption of calcium and magnesium is relatively low; however, absorption of accompanying anions can be high and influence urinary pH. Nonmetabolizable anions (e.g., chloride, phosphate and sulfate) absorbed in excess of their accompanying cations are acidifying, whereas oxides and carbonates are alkalinizing.

The ability of the anion accompanying the proton in an acid to be reabsorbed can markedly influence the effect of the acid load. Nonreabsorbable anions enhance the kidney's ability to generate a distal tubule potential difference and augment hydrogen ion excretion. The accompanying anions of sulfuric and nitric acids are sufficiently impermeable to escape proximal reabsorption. The associated sodium is rapidly carried to distal acidification sites for electronic sodium reabsorption and electrically coupled proton secretion. The degree of acidosis induced is therefore less than that occuring with hydrochloric acid.

In general, protein metabolism is the major source of hydrogen ions. Consequently, avoiding excess dietary protein and decreasing endogenous protein catabolism for energy contribute markedly to the maintenance of acid-base balance.[148]

The plasma bicarbonate concentration should be maintained between 17 and 22 mEq/l. If the plasma bicarbonate concentration is not within this target range two to four weeks after changing to a food that avoids excess acid load, additional restriction of acid load should be considered. Finally, if dietary change alone does not achieve the targeted bicarbonate level, alkali therapy should be considered.

SODIUM/CHLORIDE

As renal function deteriorates, fractional sodium excretion increases to maintain external sodium balance and preserve extracellular fluid volume. When dietary sodium intake changes, the fractional excretion of sodium must change markedly to maintain sodium balance.[149] Patients with decreased renal function can only vary sodium excretion over a limited range, which narrows progressively as GFR declines. Thus, renal failure patients cannot tolerate excessively high or low dietary sodium intake levels. If excessive sodium is ingested, sodium retention with expansion of extracellular fluid volume can occur and produce or worsen pre-existing hypertension, fluid overload and edema. If sodium intake is inadequate, negative sodium balance develops with resultant declines in extracellular fluid volume, plasma volume and GFR.

The incidence of hypertension in dogs with renal disease has been estimated to be between 58 and 93%.[46] This wide range may be due to differences in types of renal disease, method of measurement or variable criteria for hypertension. The mechanism for hypertension in renal parenchymal disease is unknown. It has been postulated that reduced intrarenal blood flow activates the renin-angiotensin-aldosterone system, which leads to chronic expansion of the extracellular fluid and elevations in blood pressure. Other possible mechanisms include secondary renal hyperparathyroidism and reduced levels of renal vasodilators such as prostaglandins. The fact that blood pressure in dogs with renal failure decreases when a sodium-restricted food is fed supports chronic volume expansion as a causative mechanism.[46]

The kidney has a dual role in hypertension. Renal disease may cause hypertension, and the kidneys may suffer the consequences of uncontrolled hypertension. The mechanism by which hypertension damages the kidney is not completely understood.[150]

A number of recent studies have examined the interaction of dietary sodium with other ions, including chloride. The full expression of sodium chloride-sensitive hypertension in people is dependent on the concomitant administration of both sodium and chloride.[151-153] In experimental models using rodents with sodium chloride-sensitive hypertension and in clinical studies with small numbers of hypertensive people, blood pressure or blood volume was not increased by a high dietary sodium intake provided with anions other than chloride. Further, high chloride intake without sodium has less effect on blood pressure than does sodium chloride intake.[151,152,154] (See Figure 18-7.) The failure of nonchloride sodium salts to produce hypertension or hypervolemia may be related to their failure to expand plasma volume because the renal tubular signal for renin release is responsive to renal tubular chloride.[152-155] Chloride may also act as a direct renal vasoconstrictor.[152] These findings suggest that both sodium and chloride are nutrients of concern in patients with hypertension and CRF.

A sodium intake between 0.1 and 0.25% DM is recommended for most dogs with CRF. The recommended daily intake for most cats with CRF is 10 to 40 mg/kg body weight/24 hours or 0.2 to 0.35% DM.[46] Although the chloride requirement of dogs and cats has not been established, a chloride level at least 1.5 times the sodium requirement is often recommended. Some animals may have obligatory urinary sodium losses; therefore, abruptly changing these animals to a sodium-restricted food may result in dangerous contraction of the extracellular fluid volume.

Other Nutrients of Concern

ARGININE

In mammalian cells, nitric oxide is synthesized from L-arginine by nitric oxide synthases in the vascular endothelium. Nitric oxide is responsible for the vasodilator tone that is essential for regulation of blood pressure. The search for endothelium-derived relaxing factor led to the discovery of the enzyme nitric oxide synthase in the vasculature. This enzyme is calcium- and calmodulin-dependent and releases small amounts of nitric oxide in response to receptor stimulation. Activation of endothelial cells by stimuli (e.g., pulsatile flow and shear stress) seems to maintain nitric oxide-dependent vasodilator tone. The pharmacologic compounds nitroglycerin and nitroprusside act after conversion to nitric oxide.

Arginine administration prevents the development of hypertension in susceptible laboratory animals.[156] Arginine also produces a rapid decrease in blood pressure when infused into normal people and patients with essential hypertension.[157] Some of the effects of angiotensin-converting enzyme (ACE) inhibitors may be due to prolonging the effective duration of bradykinin, which stimulates release of nitric oxide. However, exact data are not available to support making a routine recommendation for arginine levels for patients with CRF. Arginine derivatives that inhibit nitric oxide synthase accumulate in plasma of patients with renal failure. Inhibition of nitric oxide synthase may contribute to hypertension in patients with renal failure.[158]

VITAMIN A

Hypervitaminosis A is a common finding in human renal failure patients. Serum creatinine concentrations correlate positively with plasma vitamin A concentrations. The major factor causing high plasma vitamin A concentrations is increased serum concentrations of retinol-binding protein in renal failure. Although hypervitaminosis A is common in people with renal failure, toxicity is rare because most of the vitamin A is bound to retinol-binding protein and is therefore inactive.[159] It is unknown whether similar changes occur in dogs or cats with renal failure. Exact data are not available to support a recommendation for vitamin A levels for patients with CRF.

VITAMIN D

Calcitriol (1,25-dihydroxyvitamin D) plays an important role in the pathogenesis of secondary renal hyperparathyroidism. Animals with severe CRF have decreased circulating levels of 1,25-dihydroxyvitamin D because of decreased synthesis by the kidney. Hyperphosphatemia and the progressive loss of renal epithelial cells inhibit conversion of 25-hydroxyvitamin D to calcitriol by renal 1-α-hydroxylase. At earlier stages of CRF, circulating levels of 1,25-dihydroxyvitamin D may be normal due to the compensatory effect of increased concentrations of PTH on renal 1-α-hydroxylase activity and tubular synthesis of 1,25-dihydroxyvitamin D.

Calcitriol is an important regulator of parathyroid chief cell function. Calcitriol acts by decreasing PTH messenger RNA expression, increasing expression of vitamin D receptors and controlling the "set point" of chief cells, which determines responsiveness to negative feedback by ionized serum calcium concentrations. Decreased circulating calcitriol levels in CRF lead to chief cell hyperplasia and increased secretion of PTH. Increased PTH levels have been suggested to play a role in the severity of clinical signs and progression of renal failure.[160]

Avoiding excess dietary phosphorus and using phosphate binders reduce the inhibitory effects of hyperphosphatemia on renal 1-α-hydroxylase activity, thereby increasing calcitriol production by tubular cells. Oral administration of very low doses of calcitriol (1.7 to 3.4 ng/kg body weight) reportedly normalizes serum PTH levels and slows progression of naturally occurring renal disease in dogs and cats.[160]

B VITAMINS

There is limited information concerning vitamin nutrition in animals with CRF. Animals with renal failure are at risk for B-vitamin deficiency because of decreased appetite, vomiting, diarrhea and polyuria. Human renal failure patients apparently are especially prone to pyridoxine and folate deficiency.[159] Thiamin and niacin deficiency may contribute to anorexia associated with renal failure. Empirical administration of vitamins seems appropriate in anorectic renal failure patients. However, care must be taken not to give excessive amounts of fat-soluble vitamins.

TRACE MINERALS

Presumably, metabolism of trace minerals is altered in CRF. For example, nutrients such as copper and zinc that are highly bound to protein may be lost with severe proteinuria. Aluminum may accumulate in renal failure patients treated with aluminum-containing phosphate binders. Aluminum toxicity can cause metabolic bone disease, encephalopathy and anemia. However, exact data are not available to support making a routine recommendation for trace mineral levels for patients with CRF.

SOLUBLE FIBER

It is well established that soluble fiber causes bacterial proliferation in the large intestine. Bacterial growth requires a source of nitrogen. Although dietary protein provides some nitrogen, blood urea is the largest and most available source of nitrogen for bacterial protein synthesis in the large intestine.[161] Urea is the major end product of protein catabolism in mammals. When blood urea diffuses into the large bowel it is broken down by bacterial ureases and used for bacterial protein synthesis. These bacterial proteins are excreted in the feces. The net effect is increased fecal urea excretion, reduced serum urea nitrogen concentration and reduced urinary urea excretion.[161-163]

It is important to differentiate excretion of acid by the kidney from urea (protein) excretion. The kidney is involved with excretion of hydrogen ions by means of nonionic diffusion (diffusion trapping). In response to acid load, the renal tubule cells synthesize NH_3 primarily from glutamine. NH_3 is non-ionized, lipid soluble and freely diffuses across the cell membrane down its concentration gradient into the tubular lumen. Because of the pK of the NH_3/NH_4^+ buffer system, hydrogen ions avidly combine with NH_3. This ionized form is not lipid soluble and thus is trapped within the tubular lumen and is then excreted in the form of neutral salts, such as ammonium chloride or ammonium sulfate.

Assess the Food(s)

The food(s) for animals with renal disease should be evaluated for all the key nutritional factors mentioned above. Levels of the nutrients of concern (i.e., phosphorus, protein, fat, fatty acids, energy, potassium, sodium and chloride) and other specific food factors (i.e., acid load) in the current food should be compared with the levels appropriate for renal failure patients. (See Key Nutritional Factors—Renal Disease table.) A new food should be selected if discrepancies exist between the recommended levels of key nutritional factors and those in the current food.

The protein and fat content of the food(s) can be estimated from the information provided by the guaranteed analysis or typical analysis on the commercial pet food label. Some commercial pet food labels also include information about energy density of the food, although this is not required and is actually prohibited in some countries. Levels of phosphorus, sodium, chloride and potassium are not required on the guaranteed or typical analysis of pet food labels and are usually not listed. Levels of these nutrients and the expected acid load that is supplied by the food must be obtained by contacting the manufacturer or consulting published product information. Levels of phosphorus, protein, sodium, chloride and potassium in commercial pet foods intended for normal animals greatly exceed minimum requirements and are often excessive for renal failure patients. (See Appendix L.)

Other sources of nutrients include commercial treats and snacks for pets and human foods offered as snacks or part of the regular diet. Commercial pet treats and processed human foods are often high in sodium, phosphorus and other minerals. (See Appendix M.)

The caloric intake should be determined for patients with obesity or cachexia. A diary maintained by the client is helpful in documenting what types and quantities of foods and supplements are being offered and eaten by the animal. This caloric intake can be compared with the number of calories usually needed to maintain ideal body weight and condition in that animal.

Assess the Feeding Method

Changing the feeding method in the management of CRF may not be necessary, especially in patients with uncomplicated renal disease or early renal failure. It is important, however, to verify that an appropriate feeding method is being used. Items to consider include access to water, amount fed, how food is offered, access to other

Table 19-7. Levels of selected nutrients in typical commercial pet foods (average analyses) and those used in patients with renal disease.*

	Protein	Fat	Phosphorus	Calcium	Sodium	Chloride	Potassium	Dietary acid load
Moist canine products								
Grocery brand foods (average 31 products)**	41.7	27.8	1.39	1.75	0.87	1.20	1.15	na
Specialty brand foods (average 40 products)**	31.8	21.9	0.92	1.19	0.52	0.85	0.88	na
Hill's Prescription Diet Canine g/d	18.9	10.8	0.42	0.62	0.24	0.84	0.78	Normal
Hill's Prescription Diet Canine k/d	14.8	26.1	0.19	0.83	0.23	0.45	0.36	Reduced
Hill's Prescription Diet Canine u/d	11.5	27.2	0.11	0.29	0.25	0.43	0.39	Reduced
Hill's Prescription Diet Canine w/d	16.1	12.6	0.50	0.67	0.31	0.82	0.60	na
Leo Specific Renil CKW	18.8	15.8	0.38	0.38	0.15	na	0.94	na
Leo Specific Uremil CUW	13.1	18.4	0.35	0.35	0.14	na	0.96	na
Medi-Cal Canine Reduced Protein	17.3	21.2	0.33	0.63	0.24	na	na	na
Purina CNM Canine NF-Formula	16.5	27.4	0.30	0.50	0.24	0.43	0.72	na
Select Care Canine Modified Formula	16.8	21.8	0.35	0.83	0.24	na	0.96	na
Waltham/Pedigree Low Protein	17.4	30.8	0.18	0.64	0.36	na	0.30	na
Waltham/Pedigree Medium Protein	27.6	33.4	0.19	0.68	0.31	na	0.77	na
Dry canine products								
Grocery brand foods (average 32 products)**	25.0	12.3	1.02	1.32	0.42	0.66	0.64	na
Specialty brand foods (average 93 products)**	28.0	16.2	1.00	1.32	0.41	0.69	0.72	na
Hill's Prescription Diet Canine g/d	18.7	10.9	0.40	0.61	0.18	0.53	0.61	Normal
Hill's Prescription Diet Canine k/d	14.6	19.0	0.24	0.80	0.22	0.59	0.65	Reduced
Hill's Prescription Diet Canine u/d	9.3	20.6	0.19	0.40	0.24	0.45	0.62	Reduced
Hill's Prescription Diet Canine w/d	16.7	8.80	0.48	0.63	0.21	0.58	0.79	na
Iams Eukanuba Kidney Formula-Early Stage	21.0	14.5	0.44	0.88	0.53	1.34	0.71	Reduced
Iams Eukanuba Kidney Formula-Advanced	15.5	15.2	0.26	0.69	0.51	1.44	0.60	Reduced
Leo Specific Renil CKD	14.7	19.6	0.33	0.43	0.14	na	0.99	na
Medi-Cal Canine Reduced Protein	14.9	19.7	0.27	0.82	0.28	na	na	na
Purina CNM Canine NF-Formula	15.9	15.7	0.29	0.76	0.22	0.57	0.86	na
Select Care Canine Modified Formula	14.4	19.7	0.34	0.82	0.28	na	0.88	na
Waltham/Pedigree Low Phosphorus Low Protein	17.8	20.0	0.18	0.60	0.26	na	0.78	na
Waltham/Pedigree Low Phosphorus Medium Protein	24.4	22.2	0.19	0.62	0.28	na	0.62	na
Moist feline products								
Grocery brand foods (average 31 products)**	51.5	25.8	1.54	1.84	0.90	1.30	1.04	na
Specialty brand foods (average 36 products)**	45.8	28.0	0.97	1.13	0.51	0.97	0.92	na
Hill's Prescription Diet Feline g/d	35.4	19.5	0.55	0.68	0.28	0.57	0.74	Normal
Hill's Prescription Diet Feline k/d	29.4	26.8	0.39	0.64	0.30	0.55	1.05	Reduced
Leo Specific Renil FUW	34.9	39.7	0.60	0.71	0.28	na	0.83	na
Medi-Cal Feline Reduced Protein	35.3	51.9	0.59	0.90	0.27	na	na	na
Purina CNM Feline NF-Formula	31.1	29.5	0.52	1.03	0.16	0.45	0.96	Normal
Select Care Modified Formula	35.0	53.0	0.49	0.71	0.23	na	1.00	na
Waltham/Whiskas Low Protein	34.5	51.0	0.39	0.79	0.33	na	0.99	na
Dry feline products								
Grocery brand foods (average 25 products)**	35.1	12.9	1.18	1.35	0.42	0.80	0.76	na
Specialty brand foods (average 43 products)**	35.3	18.9	0.95	1.11	0.46	0.69	0.69	na
Hill's Prescription Diet Feline g/d	33.4	18.9	0.55	0.51	0.34	0.68	0.75	Normal
Hill's Prescription Diet Feline k/d	28.3	22.2	0.47	0.76	0.25	0.50	0.76	Reduced
Purina CNM Feline NF-Formula	30.8	12.9	0.41	0.69	0.20	0.64	0.88	Normal
Select Care Modified Formula	28.3	22.1	0.52	0.77	0.27	na	0.92	na
Waltham/Whiskas Low Phosphorus Low Protein	26.1	22.2	0.34	0.64	0.22	na	0.89	na

Key: na = information not published by manufacturer.
*This list represents products with the largest market share and for which published information is available.
Manufacturers' published values; expressed as % dry matter.
**Averages for grocery and specialty foods were obtained from Appendix L.

Dietary Management of Protein-Losing Glomerulonephropathy

Protein-losing glomerulonephropathy is a challenging disease to manage. Many cases are diagnosed late in their course, the underlying cause often remains obscure and glomerular disease is usually progressive despite the best treatment efforts.

Although factors such as magnitude of proteinuria and development of hypoalbuminemia, thrombosis, edema, protein malnutrition and uremia influence a patient's prognosis, none of these factors alone can be used to accurately predict the reversibility of glomerular lesions. Serial evaluation of appropriate laboratory tests, including urine protein-creatinine (UPC) ratios, is a good means of reassessment. Increasing UPC ratios can indicate worsening glomerular disease, whereas declining UPC ratios are consistent with clinical improvement. Decreases in urine protein concentrations, however, may not always be associated with improved glomerular function. If accompanied by increases in serum creatinine concentrations, declining UPC ratios may reflect progressive glomerular sclerosis and obsolescence. As glomeruli become obsolescent, they no longer lose protein; however, these same glomeruli also lose their functional ability, potentially resulting in azotemia.

At one time, replacing persistent renal protein loss with equivalent quantities of dietary protein was commonly recommended for patients with glomerular disease. This recommendation seemed prudent but was not validated. The advisability of replacing persistent, severe renal protein loss has been questioned. Investigations in people and laboratory animals with protein-losing glomerulonephropathy indicate that reductions in dietary protein limit proteinuria and preserve serum albumin concentrations without impairing protein nutrition. In one study, dogs with hereditary primary glomerulopathy lived more than 50% longer when fed a reduced-protein food (13.5% dry matter [DM] protein) compared with those dogs fed a higher protein food (23% DM protein). In one of the author's (TAA) experience, reductions in dietary protein markedly reduce the magnitude of proteinuria in many dogs with protein-losing glomerulonephropathy.

Dogs and cats with protein-losing glomerulonephropathy should initially be fed reduced-protein foods designed for patients with renal failure. Patients should be monitored at two- to four-week intervals to determine the optimal quantity of dietary protein. The food with reduced levels of dietary protein should continue to be fed if the magnitude of proteinuria declines (as measured by UPC ratios) without substantial evidence of protein malnutrition (i.e., stable or increasing serum albumin and total protein concentrations, stable body weight and body condition score). If evidence of protein malnutrition develops, dietary protein intake should be gradually increased in stepwise fashion while closely monitoring the patient. Overall therapy should be monitored by assessing serum concentrations of creatinine, urea nitrogen, albumin, calcium, sodium, potassium, phosphorus, total CO_2, UPC ratios, body weight and condition, urine culture, blood pressure and fundic examination.

BIBLIOGRAPHY

Lulich JP, Osborne CA, Polzin DJ. Diagnosis and long-term management of protein-losing glomerulonephropathy: A 5-year case-based approach. Veterinary Clinics of North America: Small Animal Practice 1996; 26: 1401-1416.

Valli VEO, Baumal R, Thorner P, et al. Dietary modification reduces splitting of glomerular basement membranes and delays death due to renal failure in canine X-linked hereditary nephritis. Laboratory Investigation 1991; 65: 67-73.

FEEDING PLAN

Anorexia, vomiting and diarrhea may be prominent in patients with moderate to severe renal disease and evidence of systemic illness (uremia). These patients should receive aggressive fluid and electrolyte therapy in an attempt to ameliorate the azotemia, uremia, electrolyte abnormalities and acidosis before initiating a traditional feeding plan.

Select a Food(s)

Typical pet foods contain excessive amounts of phosphorus, protein, sodium, chloride and acid load for patients with renal failure. Table 19-7 lists nutrient profiles of selected veterinary therapeutic foods commonly used in patients with renal failure. This table also provides average nutrient levels found in other types of foods.

Avoiding Excess Dietary Protein

Although it has not been clearly established at what point during progressive renal insufficiency protein restriction should be initiated, it seems logical to feed a food with reduced protein levels when renal dysfunction is documented. In practice, documentation might consist of persistent renal proteinuria, loss of urine concentrating ability or azotemia. Protein restriction is more likely to be accepted by the patient and owner if it is initiated before the onset of more severe GI signs and anorexia.

The controversy surrounding whether protein restriction slows progression of chronic renal disease has focused primarily on the specific role of protein in the renal ablation experimental model of CRF. The debate has overlooked an important mechanism by which protein may exert its effect, details of the studies cited in the debate and the appropriateness of the renal ablation model.

In a study widely cited to support the position that protein restriction is not effective in slowing progression of renal disease, dogs in the high-protein groups, but not the low-protein groups, were supplemented with potassium citrate to correct the metabolic acidosis observed with high dietary protein intake.[164] Metabolic acidosis has been shown to contribute to renal injury by increasing renal ammoniagenesis and may increase oxygen consumption. Thus, conclusions regarding the effect of protein restriction on progression based on this study may not be valid because the study neutralized one mechanism by which protein may exert its effect.

In the same study, some dogs developed "diet-related uremia" when they were abruptly switched to the high-protein food following renal ablation.[164] Those dogs were removed from the study. In effect by eliminating uremic dogs, the investigators may have selected for study dogs "resistant" to the effects of protein.

Another question that has rarely been addressed in the debate on the effect of protein restriction on progressive renal injury is whether studies had sufficient statistical power. Before declaring that there is no treatment effect, it is useful to consider whether the group size studied was sufficient to detect an effect if one truly existed. At the conclusion of a one frequently cited study, there were four dogs evaluated in the high-protein group, three dogs in the moderate-protein group and four dogs in the low-protein group.[165] The authors of this study did not address the question of whether group sizes were adequate to support their conclusions.

Finally, in studying the role of protein in chronic renal disease most veterinary investigators have used the renal ablation model. Although this model eliminates some of the variability associated with clinical trials, renal ablation does not exactly mimic naturally occurring renal disease and all of the conclusions drawn from this model may not be applicable to clinical cases.

Although uncommon, the potential problem of protein deficiency due to prolonged dietary protein restriction should be considered. The protein status of patients should be periodically evaluated. (See Reassessment below.) The ratio of serum urea nitrogen to serum creatinine can be used to crudely assess the adequacy of protein restriction. This ratio will be increased if excess protein is being consumed. However, increased tissue catabolism and degradation of endogenous protein can also increase serum urea nitrogen levels. Inadequate energy intake, metabolic acidosis, concurrent infections and corticosteroid administration may also alter the ratio. Protein deficiency may be manifested by worsening anemia, hypoalbuminemia, loss of muscle mass or a dry, unthrifty coat. (See sidebar "Dietary Management of Protein-Losing Glomerulonephropathy.")

A common mistake is to insist that an owner feed only a protein-restricted food even if caloric intake is inadequate. Although avoiding excess dietary protein and minerals is important in renal failure patients, offering only such a food should not be imposed to the detriment of overall nutrient intake. Changing to a different commercial food or homemade food may be a more beneficial solution for some patients. Appetite may be cyclical in patients with advanced renal failure, both in respect to overall appetite and food preferences. A dedicated owner is often required and a trial and error approach must be used with different foods and feeding methods.

Control of Mineral Imbalances

The keys to prevention and treatment of renal secondary hyperparathyroidism and renal osteodystrophy are: 1) avoiding excess dietary phosphorus, 2) using phosphate binders and 3) providing supplemental calcium. Secondary renal hyperparathyroidism can be reduced by controlling hyperphosphatemia (Figure 19-13). The nutritional goal is to normalize fasting serum phosphorus concentrations. Hyperphosphatemia is controlled by limiting dietary phosphate intake and intestinal absorption of phosphate.

Reducing dietary intake alone may be sufficient to control hyperphosphatemia in mild to moderate CRF. Typical commercial dog foods contain 1 to 2% DM phosphorus. Veterinary therapeutic foods designed for canine renal failure patients contain 0.11 to 0.3% DM phosphorus. Typical commercial cat foods contain about 1 to 1.5% DM phosphorus. Veterinary therapeutic foods designed for feline renal failure patients contain approximately 0.4 to 0.6% DM phosphorus. Because protein-providing ingredients in pet foods tend to be high in minerals, avoiding excess dietary protein usually limits dietary phosphate intake. High-phosphorus human foods (e.g., milk, milk products, cheese, fish, beef liver, chocolate, nuts and legumes) should be avoided or limited.

Oral administration of phosphate binders with each meal is indicated if hyperphosphatemia persists despite feeding a food that avoids excess phosphate. Initially, serum phosphorus concentrations should be monitored every two to three weeks until levels stabilize within the laboratory reference range.

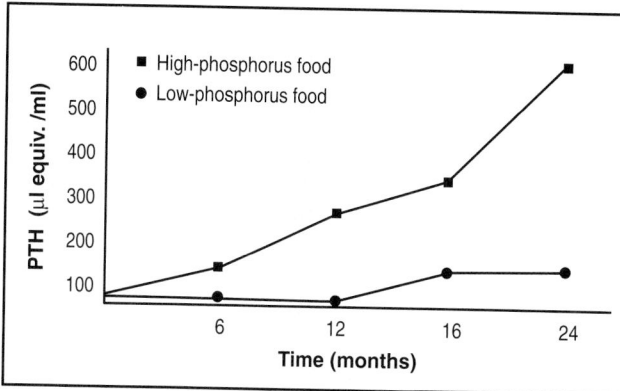

Figure 19-13. The effect of dietary phosphorus on serum parathyroid hormone (PTH) concentrations in dogs with experimentally induced renal disease. Note that consumption of higher levels of phosphorus resulted in excessive PTH secretion. High phosphorus means dogs ingested 60 to 80 mg phosphorus/kg body weight/day, Low phosphorus means dogs ingested 15 to 40 mg phosphorus/kg body weight/day. (Adapted from Rutherford WE, Bordier P, Marie P, et al. Phosphate control and 25-hydroxycholecalciferol administration in preventing experimental renal osteodystrophy in the dog. Journal of Clinical Investigation 1977; 60: 332-341.)

Serum phosphorus concentrations tend to decrease slowly at first. Administering phosphate binders without reducing dietary intake of phosphorus is ineffective. Aluminum carbonate administered at doses between 1,500 and 2,500 mg did not consistently correct hyperphosphatemia in dogs consuming foods containing more than 1% DM phosphorus.[166]

Intestinal phosphate binders prevent the absorption of ingested phosphorus and bind phosphorus contained in saliva, bile and intestinal fluid. Commonly used phosphate binders are either aluminum or calcium salts. Aluminum-containing salts include aluminum hydroxide, aluminum carbonate and aluminum oxide. Although aluminum salts have been used as phosphate binders in the past, recent studies have demonstrated the toxic effects of aluminum in human renal failure patients. Chronic administration of aluminum-containing phosphate binders has been associated with aluminum toxicity, including encephalopathies, bone disease and microcytic anemia.[167]

Calcium-containing salts include calcium citrate, calcium carbonate and calcium acetate. The calcium-containing agents may produce hypercalcemia; therefore, serum calcium concentrations should be monitored periodically. Calcium acetate is apparently the most effective calcium-containing phosphate binder and is less likely to contribute to hypercalcemia. Phosphate binders should be administered with meals to increase efficacy and obviate calcium absorption and potential hypercalcemia. Phosphate binders are available as liquids, tablets and capsules. Liquids seem to be more effective than tablets or capsules, but continued owner compliance is less likely with liquid preparations.

A starting dose of 60 to 90 mg/kg body weight/day has been recommended for calcium acetate. The dosage of phosphate-binding agents should be adjusted to maintain normal serum phosphorus concentrations. Excessive doses of phosphate-binding agents may cause hypophosphatemia. Constipation and vomiting have also been reported to occur with administration of high doses of phosphate-binding agents.[9]

Vitamin D therapy can be considered if the combination of dietary phosphorus restriction and phosphate-binder therapy does not control hyperphosphatemia. None of the vitamin D analogues should be used in the presence of hyperphosphatemia because of the risk of a high serum calcium/phosphorus product and extraskeletal calcification. Intermittent intravenous or oral calcitriol administration is considered the most effective means of suppressing PTH secretion in human renal failure patients.

Calcitriol and other vitamin D preparations (i.e., dihydrotachysterol and calcifediol) have been used in human renal failure patients to treat secondary hyperparathyroidism and to compensate for decreased endogenous production of 1,25-dihydroxycholecalciferol. These agents lessen bone pain, improve the histologic appearance of bone and suppress PTH secretion. Calcitriol is considered the most potent PTH-suppressing substance in human end-stage renal failure patients.

In mild renal failure, calcitriol deficiency results primarily from inhibition of renal 1-α-hydroxylase activity by phosphorus retention. Dietary phosphorus reduction alone or with phosphate binders increases calcitriol production in mild renal failure. Loss of renal parenchyma decreases the quantity of calcitriol that can be synthesized in more advanced renal failure. Exogenous administration of calcitriol rapidly decreases secondary renal hyperparathyroidism by: 1) binding to receptors on PTH-secreting cells and blocking PTH synthesis and secretion, 2) inhibiting PTH gene transcription, 3) lowering the calcium "set point" to allow calcium to inhibit PTH secretion and reversing parathyroid gland hyperplasia and 4) increasing absorption of calcium from the GI tract and ionized calcium levels in the blood. Despite these potential benefits, calcitriol therapy should be approached very cautiously because of the high incidence of hypercalcemia and subsequent renal damage that may result.

Compared with other vitamin D analogues, calcitriol has the advantage of not requiring renal activation. However calcitriol, like the other vitamin D preparations, can cause hypercalcemia. The recommended oral calcitriol dose for dogs and cats is 1.5 to 3.5 ng/kg body weight/day.[168] The endpoint of calcitriol therapy is normalization of PTH levels. Hypercalcemia can occur at any time during treatment; therefore, it is important to serially monitor serum calcium concentrations. Because calcitriol has a short duration of effect, discontinuation of treatment results in a rapid decline in serum calcium concentration. Calcium-containing phosphate binders are contraindicated with calcitriol treatment because of the increased risk of hypercalcemia.

Calcitriol is supplied in 0.25- and 0.50-mg capsules (Rocaltrol[a]). Doses recommended for dogs and cats are markedly less per kg body weight than the dose for people. Therefore, it is necessary to have pharmacies custom make appropriately sized capsules for dogs and cats.

Control of serum calcium concentration is another important nutritional goal. Calcium malabsorption is very common in end-stage renal disease because of deficiency of calcitriol. Maintaining serum calcium concentration at the upper end of the reference range presumably suppresses oversecretion of PTH. The "set point" for calcium suppression of PTH release shifts in uremia. A higher concentration of ionized calcium is required to suppress PTH release in secondary hyperparathyroidism.

The timing of oral calcium supplementation is important; calcium taken between meals is more a calcium supplement than a phosphate binder. Oral calcium administration is not without hazard because of the risk of GI distress and hypercalcemia. Calcium supplementation should not be initiated until the serum phosphorus level is below the upper limit of the laboratory reference range. Calcium carbonate is inexpensive, virtually tasteless and generally well-tolerated. Calcium carbonate is 40% elemental calcium, whereas calcium acetate is only 20%. Calcium carbonate and calcium lactate have an alkalinizing effect. Calcium chloride is acidifying. The recommended initial dose of calcium carbonate is 100 mg/kg body weight/day. The dose should be adjusted according to the response. The goal of therapy is to maintain the total serum calcium or ionized calcium concentration just within the upper laboratory reference limit.

Prevention/Treatment of Metabolic Acidosis

Metabolic acidosis occurs when the balance between the addition of hydrogen ions to body fluids and their excretion by the kidney is disrupted. Ingestion of dietary acids can add hydrogen ions to body fluids. Failure to excrete hydrogen ions in the required quantities can occur with decreased kidney function. In a retrospective clinical series of feline renal failure, 88% of cats reviewed were acidemic.[5] Veterinary therapeutic foods used in patients with renal failure should be formulated to reduce the dietary acid load (Table 19-7).

Determine a Feeding Method

Changing to a new food should take place gradually over several days to weeks. A gradual transition improves acceptance and decreases the likelihood of problems in those animals that cannot rapidly adjust urinary sodium levels because of their renal dysfunction. Dogs with CRF usually tolerate a dietary change over seven to 10 days, whereas cats with renal failure may need one to four weeks or longer to make a successful transition to a new food.

Occasionally, some patients may resist a change to a commercial food with reduced protein and mineral levels. This may occur because of: 1) advanced illness associated with renal failure, 2) established feeding habits of older patients and their owners, 3) anorexia associated with concurrent drug administration and 4) the "all or nothing" approach to feeding, rather than transitioning to the new food over several days to weeks. Changing the eating habits of most dogs and cats is relatively easy, but changing the feeding habits and preconceptions of some pet owners and veterinarians is often much more difficult (e.g., the idea that low-protein food is always unpalatable).

When switching to veterinary therapeutic foods, the patient should usually be maintained on a familiar form of food (e.g., moist, dry or combination). These foods can be made more palatable by warming them and adding water or flavoring agents such as tuna juice, clam juice, chicken broth, low-sodium soup, garlic, brewer's yeast or sweeteners (dogs only) such as honey or syrup.

The food dose should be changed if the energy density of the new food differs from the density of the previous food. The total daily food dose is usually divided into two or more meals per day. The food dose and method of feeding should be altered if body condition is not normal (i.e., body condition score greater or less than 3/5).

Owner compliance and pet acceptance of the food must be adequate for clinical nutrition to be effective. Knowing who feeds the patient is important for compliance, and limiting the patient's access to other foods improves acceptability. It is usually necessary to limit a patient's access to another animal's food (e.g., a dog having access to cat food). Uremic patients with anorexia and nausea should be offered small quantities of food several times per day. Feeding location and presentation are important. Timid animals should be fed in a quiet place. Cats should be fed away from loud, persistent barking. Food should be offered in wide bowls to avoid stimulation of tactile whiskers. Placing small quantities of palatable food in a patient's mouth or on its paws to stimulate licking or swallowing (i.e., hand feeding) may facilitate eating. Licking and swallowing in turn may activate neural and hormonal responses associated with normal feeding cues. Pieces of dry veterinary therapeutic foods (Table 19-7) can be offered as treats.

Food aversion is possible if a nauseated animal is force-fed or if a painful or unpleasant experience is associated with feeding. Disagreeable medications (e.g., phosphate binders) should not be mixed with veterinary therapeutic foods. Managing underlying abnormalities in fluid, electrolyte and acid-base balance will help minimize nausea and vomiting. Pharmacologic agents (e.g., cimetidine, ranitidine, metoclopramide and sucralfate) can be used to limit uremic gastritis, nausea and vomiting. Veterinary therapeutic foods intended for long-term management of renal failure should not be offered during periods of nausea and vomiting to prevent possible food aversions. Consider using an appropriate, alternative food temporarily during hospitalization for dogs and cats with uremic crises.

Recombinant human erythropoietin (r-HuEPO[b]) has been used successfully to improve clinical well-being of cats with renal failure.[169] The most consistent and conspicuous change in renal failure cats treated with r-HuEPO is an increased appetite that may precede improvement in hematocrit values and other clinical parameters. Some cats will only eat their veterinary therapeutic food readily after treatment with r-HuEPO. This finding reinforces the necessity to manage anemia as a part of the comprehensive approach to CRF management.

◼ REASSESSMENT

Hospitalized patients with renal failure should be monitored for the following abnormalities that could be acutely life-threatening: 1) severe dehydration, 2) severe metabolic acidosis, 3) severe hypokalemia or hyperkalemia and 4) severe hypocalcemia. Other abnormalities that are less likely to be life-threatening in the short term include: 1) severe azotemia, 2) severe hyperphosphatemia, 3) anemia and 4) hypercalcemia.

Potentially treatable prerenal, renal and postrenal causes may contribute to azotemia in patients with established primary renal failure. Prerenal causes include: 1) decreased renal perfusion secondary to dehydration, decreased cardiac output and severe hypoalbuminemia and 2) increased urea metabolism secondary to GI hemorrhage, severe tissue necrosis, high dietary protein intake and catabolic drugs (e.g., glucocorticoids, tetracyclines, excessive thyroid hormone supplementation and chemotherapeutic agents). Renal causes that are potentially avoidable or treatable include ARF secondary to ischemia or nephrotoxic injury, urinary tract infection, hypercalcemic nephropathy, adverse drug reactions and heat stroke. Postrenal causes that are potentially treatable include ARF secondary to urethral obstruction due to uroliths.

Frequency of reassessment depends on the stage of renal failure. Patients with azotemia should be rechecked every two to three months and uremic patients should be rechecked as often as every two to four weeks. Parameters included in the reassessment are listed in Table 19-8.

Table 19-8. Reassessment methods for patients with chronic renal failure.

Physical examination
Body weight
Body condition/muscle mass
Coat quality
Hydration status
Abdominal palpation (size and contour of kidneys, presence of ascites)
Oral examination (uremic ulcers, ammoniacal odor)
Fundic examination (retinal hemorrhage, detached retina suggests hypertension)
Blood pressure measurement

Laboratory evaluation
Urinalysis
  Microscopic sediment exam (pyuria or bacteriuria may indicate urinary tract infection)
  Urine specific gravity (crude index of tubulointerstitial function)
  Dipstick (protein evaluation is a screening test for glomerular involvement)
  pH (very crude index of acid-base status)
Serum urea nitrogen
Serum creatinine
Serum albumin
Serum electrolytes (calcium, potassium, chloride, sodium, magnesium)
Total serum carbon dioxide or venous blood gases (blood pH, bicarbonate, base excess) to evaluate acid-base status

Imaging
Abdominal radiographs (assess kidney shape and size, reference L_2 vertebra)
Intravenous urogram (assess obstruction due to nephroliths, pyelonephritis, etc.)
Ultrasound (assess kidney and prostate gland, determine presence of hydronephrosis or hydroureter)

A food that avoids excess sodium chloride is recommended for hypertensive dogs and cats. A few animals with renal dysfunction may adapt slowly to changes in dietary sodium chloride intake. Therefore, the amount of the new food with reduced sodium chloride levels should be increased gradually over several days (dogs) to weeks (cats) while the amount of the old food is decreased. In general, if blood pressure does not normalize, the next step is to administer a diuretic. However, care should be exercised not to cause dehydration, which may further decrease renal function. Antihypertensive drugs should be instituted only if it is possible to serially monitor blood pressure. Indirect methods (i.e., oscillometric and ultrasonic) are adequate for clinical assessment of blood pressure in dogs and cats. All modifications to the antihypertensive regimen should be based on measured changes in blood pressure after a minimum of 14 days. Procedures for measuring blood pressure should be consistent so that results over time can be compared and response to therapy assessed. Heart rate can be used to indicate stress-induced activation of the sympathetic nervous system. Blood pressure may be spuriously elevated due to activation of the sympathetic nervous system if the heart rate is greater than 90 beats per minute.

Nutrient-Drug Interactions

In general, catabolic drugs (e.g., glucocorticoids, tetracyclines and antineoplastic agents) should be avoided in patients with renal failure. If the animal is volume-depleted, nonsteroidal antiinflammatory agents should also be avoided. Urine acidifiers (e.g., ammonium chloride and methionine) will exacerbate metabolic acidosis. Similarly, urinary antiseptics (e.g., methenamine and nalidixic acid) should be avoided.

Aminoglycoside (Gentamicin) Toxicity

Feeding a food containing 27% DM protein to dogs before and during administration of toxic levels of gentamicin has been shown to reduce nephrotoxicosis.[122] The renoprotective effect was due to more rapid clearance of gentamicin and a larger volume of distribution in the 27% DM protein group than in the 14% or 9.4% DM protein groups. Therefore, feeding foods with moderate protein levels before and during gentamicin administration may decrease the risk of nephrotoxicity in patients without pre-existing renal dysfunction.

Erythropoietin-Iron Interaction

The dose of erythropoietin needed to achieve an adequate hematocrit response in adult people with chronic renal insufficiency may depend on the severity of secondary hyperparathyroidism and the extent of bone marrow fibrosis.[170] Repletion of iron stores is necessary for the optimal hematologic response to erythropoietin. Commercial pet foods are usually replete with iron but homemade foods may need to be supplemented. An adequate dialysis prescription is required in human patients for optimal response to exogenous erythropoietin.

Angiotensin-Converting Enzyme Inhibitors

ACE inhibitors block angiotensin II production, which results in dilatation of efferent arterioles with a subsequent decline in glomerular transcapillary pressure. In dogs with unilateral nephrectomies and experimentally induced diabetes mellitus, ACE inhibition with lisinopril reduced glomerular transcapillary hydraulic pressure, glomerular cell hypertrophy and proteinuria.[171]

Treatment of Samoyeds affected by familial x-linked nephritis with enalapril improved renal function and prolonged survival. The treated dogs survived a mean of 261 days, whereas the untreated control dogs survived 197 days.[172]

Treatment with ACE inhibitors probably decreases proteinuria and slows progression of renal disease by several mechanisms. ACE inhibitors may decrease glomerular capillary hypertension, which may be a major cause of the progressive decline in renal function observed in naturally occurring renal disease. The use of ACE inhibitors in people, rats and dogs has been associated with a decreased decline of GFR, decreased glomerular cell hypertrophy and decreased glomerulosclerosis.[173] Enalapril has been shown to prevent the loss of glomerular heparin sulfate that can occur with glomerular disease.[173] Heparin sulfate contributes to the negative charge that is a component of the permselectivity of the glomerular membrane. ACE inhibitors may also decrease proteinuria by decreasing the size of glomerular capillary cell pores. Reducing proteinuria may have a renoprotective effect. Long-term enalapril treatment in aging mice decreased renal interstitial fibrosis.[108]

ACE inhibitors should be used with caution in dogs with renal failure. These drugs can cause an abrupt decline in renal function if systemic hypotension develops or if angiotensin II is critical for the maintenance of glomerular pressures (e.g., in dogs with concurrent congestive renal failure).

Heart Failure and Renal Function

Therapy for congestive heart failure in dogs frequently includes the use of sodium chloride-restricted foods (See Chapter 18.) and diuretics to reduce preload and venous congestion and vasodilators to reduce preload, afterload and venous congestion. Renal insufficiency has been demonstrated in up to one-third of human patients with severe congestive heart failure receiving a salt-restricted diet, ACE inhibitors and furosemide. Decreased renal function, in this situation, has been attributed to loss of angiotensin II-mediated vasoconstriction, which maintains renal perfusion and glomerular filtration when cardiac output is reduced. ACE inhibition in conjunction with decreased renal function and potassium supplementation has been incriminated as a cause of hyperkalemia.[174]

Electrolyte concentrations and renal function were evaluated in normal dogs and dogs with congestive heart failure receiving captopril, furosemide and a sodium-restricted food.[175] Four of 10 dogs with congestive heart failure treated with captopril, furosemide, sodium-restricted food and digoxin became azotemic at some time during the study period. Dogs with evidence of pre-existing renal dysfunction (e.g., isosthenuria) appear to be at increased risk for developing azotemia. Dogs receiving a combination of diuretics, vasodilators, cardiac glycosides and sodium-restricted foods should be monitored carefully.

■ ENDNOTES & REFERENCES

ENDNOTES
  a. Rocaltrol. Roche Laboratories, Nutley, NJ, USA.
  b. Epogen. Amgen Inc., Thousand Oaks, CA, USA.

REFERENCES
  1. Bronson RT. Variation in age at death of dogs of different sexes and breeds. American Journal of Veterinary Research 1982; 43: 2057-2059.
  2. Anonymous. Heart and Stroke Facts: 1995 Statistical Supplement. American Heart Association, National Center, Dallas, TX; 12.
  3. Leibetseder J, Neufeld K. Dogs with chronic renal failure. In: Proceedings. World Congress, World Small Animal Veterinary Association, Vienna, Austria, 1991: 271-274.
  4. Cowgill LD, Spangler WL. Renal insufficiency in geriatric dogs. Veterinary Clinics of North America: Small Animal Practice 1983; 11: 727-748.
  5. Lulich JP, Osborne CA, O'Brien TD, et al. Feline renal failure: Questions, answers, questions. Compendium on Continuing Education for the Practicing Veterinarian 1992; 14: 127-153.
  6. Gobar GM, Case JT, Kass PH. Program for surveillance of cause of death of dogs, using the Internet to survey small animal practitioners. Journal of the American Veterinary Medical Association 1998; 213: 251-256.
  7. Morris Animal Foundation. Animal health survey. Denver, CO: 1991.
  8. Allen TA, Jaenke RS, Fettman MJ. A technique for estimating progression of chronic renal failure in the dog. Journal of the American Veterinary Medical Association 1987; 190: 866-868.
  9. Polzin DJ, Osborne CA, Bartges JW, et al. Chronic renal failure. In: Ettinger SJ, Feldman EC, eds. Textbook of Veterinary Internal Medicine, 4th ed. Philadelphia, PA: WB Saunders Co, 1995; 1734-1760.
  10. Lees GE. Congenital renal diseases. Veterinary Clinics of North America: Small Animal Practice 1996; 26: 1379-1399.
  11. Grauer GF. Prevention of acute renal failure. Veterinary Clinics of North America: Small Animal Practice 1996; 26: 1447-1459.
  12. Graves TK, Olivier NB, Nachreiner RF, et al. Changes in renal function associated with treatment of hyperthyroidism in cats. American Journal of Veterinary Research 1994; 55: 1745-1750.

13. DiBartola SP, Broome MR, Stein BS, et al. Effect of treatment of hyperthyroidism on renal function in cats. Journal of the American Veterinary Medical Association 1996; 208: 875-878.

14. Vaden SL, Gookin JL, Trogdon MM. Carbamylated hemoglobin levels in dogs with renal failure (abstract). In: Proceedings. Fourteenth Annual Veterinary Medical Forum, American College of Veterinary Internal Medicine, San Antonio, TX, 1996: 751.

15. Stiles J, Polzin DJ, Bistner SI. The prevalence of retinopathy in cats with systemic hypertension and chronic renal failure or hyperthyroidism. Journal of the American Animal Hospital Association 1994; 30: 564-572.

16. DiBartola SP. Clinical approach and laboratory evaluation of renal disease. In: Ettinger SJ, Feldman EC, eds. Textbook of Veterinary Internal Medicine, 4th ed. Philadelphia, PA: WB Saunders Co, 1995; 1706-1719.

17. Watson ADJ, Church DB, Fairburn AJ. Post-prandial changes in plasma urea and creatinine concentrations in dogs. American Journal of Veterinary Research 1981; 42: 1878-1880.

18. Gleadhill A. Analysis of breed differences in canine blood creatinine concentrations (abstract). In: Proceedings. European Society of Veterinary Internal Medicine, Cambridge, England, 1995: 58.

19. Fettman MJ, Allen TA, Wilke WL, et al. Single-injection method for evaluation of renal function with ^{14}C-inulin and ^{3}H-tetraethylammonium bromide in dogs and cats. American Journal of Veterinary Research 1985; 46: 482-485.

20. Finco DR, Tabaru H, Brown SA, et al. Endogenous creatinine clearance measurement of glomerular filtration rate in dogs. American Journal of Veterinary Research 1993; 54: 1575-1578.

21. Finco DR, Brown SA, Cooper T, et al. Creatinine clearance does not reliably measure GFR in cats. In: Proceedings. Fourteenth Annual Veterinary Medical Forum, American College of Veterinary Internal Medicine, San Antonio, TX, 1996: 750.

22. Tabaru H, Finco DR, Brown SA, et al. Influence of hydration state on renal functions of dogs. American Journal of Veterinary Research 1993; 54: 1758-1764.

23. Levey AS, Bosch JP, Coggins CH, et al. Effects of diet and antihypertensive therapy on creatinine clearance and serum creatinine concentration in the modification of diet in renal disease study. Journal of the American Society of Nephrology 1996; 7: 556-565.

24. Brown SA, Finco DR, Boudinot FD, et al. Evaluation of a single injection method, using iohexol, for estimating glomerular filtration rate in cats and dogs. American Journal of Veterinary Research 1996; 57: 105-110.

25. Rogers KS, Komkov A, Brown SA, et al. Comparison of four methods of estimating glomerular filtration in cats. American Journal of Veterinary Research 1991; 52: 961-964.

26. Biewenga WJ, Gruys E, Hendricks HJ. Urinary protein loss in the dog: Nephrological study of 29 dogs without signs of renal disease. Research in Veterinary Science 1982; 33: 366-374.

27. Finco DR. Urinary protein loss. In: Osborne CA, Finco DR, eds. Canine and Feline Nephrology and Urology. Baltimore, MD: Williams & Wilkins, 1995; 211-215.

28. Lulich JP, Osborne CA. Interpretation of urine protein-creatinine ratios in dogs with glomerular and nonglomerular disorders. Compendium on Continuing Education for the Practicing Veterinarian 1990; 12: 59-71.

29. Grauer GF, Thomas CB, Eicker SW. Estimation of quantitative proteinuria in the dog, using the protein-to-creatinine ratio from a random, voided sample. American Journal of Veterinary Research 1985; 46: 2116-2119.

30. White JV, Oliver NB, Reimann K, et al. Use of protein-to-creatinine ratio in a single urine specimen for quantitative estimation of canine proteinuria. Journal of the American Veterinary Medical Association 1984; 185: 882-885.

31. Center SA, Wilkinson E, Smith CA, et al. 24-hour urine protein/creatinine ratio in dogs with protein-losing nephropathies. Journal of the American Veterinary Medical Association 1985; 187: 820-824.

32. Monroe WE, Davenport DJ, Saunders GK. Twenty-four-hour urinary protein loss in healthy cats and the urinary protein-creatinine ratio as an estimate. American Journal of Veterinary Research 1989; 50: 1906-1909.

33. Adams L, Polzin DJ, Osborne CA, et al. Influence of dietary protein/calorie intake on renal morphology and function in cats with 5/6 nephrectomy. Laboratory Investigation 1994; 70: 347-357.

34. Hardy RM, Osborne CA. Water deprivation test in the dog: Maximal normal values. Journal of the American Veterinary Medical Association 1979; 174: 479-483.

35. Ross LA, Finco DR. Relationship of selected clinical renal function tests to glomerular filtration rate and renal blood flow in cats. American Journal of Veterinary Research 1981; 42: 1704-1710.

36. Bornmann-Hollstein A. Enzymimmunolgischeer nachweis von erytropoietin im blut von hund, datze und pferd. Thesis. Tieraztliche Hochschule. Hannover, Germany, 1993; 1-135.

37. Rosol TJ, Capen CC. Pathophysiology of calcium, phosphorus, and magnesium metabolism in animals. Veterinary Clinics of North America: Small Animal Practice 1996; 26: 1155-1184.

38. Woo J, Cannon DC. Metabolic intermediates and inorganic ions. In: Henry JB, ed. Clinical Diagnosis and Management by Laboratory Methods, 17th ed. Philadelphia, PA: WB Saunders Co, 1984; 133-164.

39. DiBartola SP, ed. Disorders in phosphorus: Hypophosphatemia and hyperphosphatemia. Fluid Therapy in Small Animal Practice. Philadelphia, PA: WB Saunders Co, 1992; 178.

40. Rosol TJ, Capen CC. Calcium-regulating hormones and diseases of abnormal mineral (calcium, phosphorus, magnesium) metabolism. In: Kaneko JJ, Harvey JW, Bruss ML, eds. Clinical Biochemistry of Domestic Animals, 5th ed. San Diego, CA: Academic Press, Inc, 1997; 647.

41. Rivers BJ, Johnston GR. Diagnostic imaging strategies in small animal nephrology. Veterinary Clinics of North America: Small Animal Practice 1996; 26: 1505-1517.

42. Walter PA, Johnston GR, Feeney DA, et al. Applications of ultrasonography in the diagnosis of parenchymal kidney disease in cats: 24 cases (1981-1986). Journal of the American Veterinary Medical Association 1988; 192: 92-98.

43. Walter PA, Feeney DA, Johnston GR, et al. Ultrasonographic evaluation of renal parenchymal disease in dogs: 32 cases (1981-1986). Journal of the American Veterinary Medical Association 1987; 191: 999-1007.

44. Bodey AR, Michell AR. Epidemiological study of blood pressure in domestic dogs. Journal of Small Animal Practice 1996; 37: 116-125.

45. Remillard RL, Ross JN, Eddy JB. Variance of indirect blood pressure measurements and prevalence of hypertension in clinically normal dogs. American Journal of Veterinary Research 1991; 52: 561-565.

46. Cowgill LD, Kallet AJ. Systemic hypertension. In: Kirk RW, ed. Current Veterinary Therapy IX. Philadelphia, PA: WB Saunders Co, 1986; 360-364.

47. Ross LA. Hypertension and chronic renal failure. Seminars in Veterinary Medicine and Surgery: Small Animal 1992; 7: 221-226.

48. Morgan RV. Systemic hypertension in four cats: Ocular and medical findings. Journal of the American Animal Hospital Association 1986; 22: 615-621.

49. Labato MA, Ross LA. Diagnosis and management of hypertension. In: August JR, ed. Consultations in Feline Medicine. Philadelphia, PA: WB Saunders Co, 1991; 301-308.

50. Littman MP. Spontaneous hypertension in 24 cats. Journal of Veterinary Internal Medicine 1994; 8: 79-86.

51. Binns SH, Sisson DD, Buoscio DA, et al. Doppler ultrasonographic, oscillometric sphygmomanometric, and photoplethysmographic techniques for noninvasive blood pressure measurement in anesthetized cats. Journal of Veterinary Internal Medicine 1995; 9: 405-414.

52. Haberman CE, Morgan J, Brown SA. Measurement of blood pressure in cats and dogs. In: Proceedings. Fourteenth Annual Veterinary Medical Forum, American College of Veterinary Internal Medicine, San Antonio, TX, 1996: 688-689.

53. Valli VEO, Baumal R, Thorner P, et al. Dietary modification reduces splitting of glomerular basement membranes and delays death due to renal failure in canine X-linked hereditary nephritis. Laboratory Investigation 1991; 65: 67-73.

54. Lees GE, Helman RG, Homco LD, et al. Early diagnosis of familial nephropathy in English cocker spaniel dogs (abstract). In: Proceedings. Thirteenth Annual Veterinary Medical Forum, American College of Veterinary Internal Medicine, Lake Buena Vista, FL, 1995: 1025.

55. Hood JC, Savige J. Bull terrier hereditary nephritis: A model for autosomal dominant Alport syndrome. Kidney International 1995; 47: 758-761.

56. Ericksen K, Grondalen J. Familial renal disease in soft-coated wheaten terriers. Journal of Small Animal Practice 1984; 25: 489-500.

57. Bowles MH, Mosier DA. Renal amyloidosis in a family of beagles. Journal of the American Veterinary Medical Association 1992; 20: 569-574.

58. Chew DJ, DiBartola SP, Boyce JT, et al. Renal amyloidosis in related Abyssinian cats. Journal of the American Veterinary Medical Association 1982; 181: 139-142.

59. deMorais HSA, DiBartola SP. Disorders of potassium: Hypokalemia and hyperkalemia. In: Proceedings. Thirteenth Annual Veterinary Medical Forum, American College of Veterinary Internal Medicine, Lake Buena Vista, FL, 1995: 620-623.

60. Jones KV. Urinary tract infection in infancy and childhood. In: Davison AM, Cameron JS, Grünfeld J-P, et al, eds. Oxford Textbook of Clinical Nephrology, 2nd ed. Oxford, UK: Oxford University Press, 1998; 1261-1276.

61. Birnbaum N, Barr SC, Center CA, et al. Naturally acquired leptospirosis in 36 dogs: Serological and clinicopathologic features. Journal of Small Animal Practice 1998; 39: 231-236.

62. Breyer J. Diabetic nephropathy. In: Greenburg A, Cheung AK, Coffman TM, et al, eds. National Kidney Foundation's Primer on Kidney Diseases, 2nd ed. San Diego, CA: Academic Press Inc, 1998; 215-220.

63. Ihle BV, Becker GJ, Whitworth JA, et al. The effect of protein restriction on the progression of renal insufficiency. New England Journal of Medicine 1989; 321: 1773-1777.

64. Bourgoignie JJ, Gavellas G, Martinez E, et al. Glomerular function and morphology after renal mass reduction in dogs. Journal of Laboratory and Clinical Medicine 1987; 109: 380-388.

65. Bovee KC. Influence of dietary protein on renal function in dogs. Journal of Nutrition 1991; 121: S128-S139.

66. Polzin DJ, Osborne CA, O'Brien TD, et al. Effect of protein intake on progression of canine chronic renal failure. In: Proceedings. Eleventh Annual Veterinary Medical Forum, American College of Veterinary Internal Medicine, Washington, DC, 1993: 93.

67. Polzin DJ, Osborne CA. Pathophysiology of renal failure and uremia. In: Osborne CA, Finco DR, eds. Canine and Feline Nephrology and Urology. Baltimore, MD: Williams & Wilkins, 1995; 335-367.

68. Brenner BM, Meter TW, Hostetter TH. Dietary protein intake and the progressive nature of kidney disease: The role of hemodynamically mediated glomerular injury in the pathogenesis of progressive glomerular sclerosis in aging, renal ablation, and intrinsic renal disease. New England Journal of Medicine 1982; 307: 652.

69. Riser BL, Cortes P, Zhao X, et al. Intraglomerular pressure and mesangial stretching stimulate extracellular matrix formation in the rat. Journal of Clinical Investigation 1992; 90: 1932-1943.

70. Cortes P, Riser BL, Zhao X, et al. Glomerular volume expansion and mesangial cell mechanical strain; Mediators of glomerular pressure injury. Kidney International 1994; 45 (Suppl.): S11-S16.

71. Nath KA, Hostetter MK, Hostetter TH. Pathophysiology of chronic tubulointerstitial disease in rats: Interactions of dietary acid load, ammonia, and complement component C3. Journal of Clinical Investigation 1985; 76: 667-675.

72. Brezia M, Rosen S. Hypoxia of the renal medulla–Its implications for disease. New England Journal of Medicine 1995; 332: 647-665.

73. Diamond JR, Bonventre JV, Karnovsky MJ. A role for oxygen free radicals in aminonucleoside nephrosis. Kidney International 1986; 29: 478-483.

74. Nath KA, Fischereder M, Hostetter TH. The role of antioxidants in progressive renal injury. Kidney International 1994; 45 (Suppl.): S111-S115.

75. Felsenfeld AJ, Llach F. Parathyroid gland function in chronic renal failure. Kidney International 1993; 43: 771-789.

76. Lumlertgul D, Burke TJ, Gillum DM, et al. Phosphate depletion arrests progression of chronic renal failure independent of protein intake. Kidney International 1986; 29: 658-666.

77. Bushinsky DA. Disorders of calcium and phosphorus homeostasis. In: Greenburg A, Cheung AK, Coffman TM, et al, eds. National Kidney Foundation's Primer on Kidney Diseases, 2nd ed. San Diego, CA: Academic Press Inc, 1998; 106-113.

78. Bichara M, Mercier O, Borensztein P, et al. Acute metabolic acidosis enhances circulating parathyroid hormone, which contributes to the renal response against acidosis in the rat. Journal of Clinical Investigation 1990; 86: 430-443.

79. Nagode LA, Chew DJ, Podell M. Benefits of calcitriol therapy and serum phosphorus control in dogs and cats with chronic renal failure: Both are essential to prevent or suppress toxic hyperparathyroidism. Veterinary Clinics of North America: Small Animal Practice 1996; 26: 1293-1330.

80. Kaplan MA, Canterbury JM, Bourgoignie JJ, et al. Reversal of hyperparathyroidism in response to dietary phosphorus restriction in uremic dogs. Kidney International 1979; 15: 43-48.

81. Lopez-Hilker S, Dusso AS, Rapp NS, et al. Phosphorus restriction reverses hyperparathyroidism in uremia independent of changes in calcium and calcitriol. American Journal of Physiology 1990; 259: F432-F437.

82. Daniels BS, Hostetter TH. Adverse effects of growth in the glomerular microcirculation. American Journal of Physiology 1990; 258: F1409-F1416.

83. Kobayashi DL, Peterson ME, Graves TK, et al. Hypertension in cats with chronic renal failure or hyperthyroidism. Journal of Veterinary Internal Medicine 1990; 4: 58-62.

84. Rocchini AP, Moorehead C, Wentz E, et al. Obesity-induced hypertension in the dog. Hypertension 1987; 9 (Suppl. III): III64-III68.

85. Klag MJ, Whelton PK, Tandall BL, et al. Blood pressure and end-stage renal disease in men. New England Journal of Medicine 1996; 334: 13-18.

86. Brown SA, Finco DR, Navar LG. Impaired renal autoregulatory ability in dogs with reduced renal mass. Journal of the American Society of Nephrology 1995; 5: 1768-1774.

87. Reddy GS, Jones G, Kook SW, et al. Inhibition of 25-hydroxyvitamin D_3-1-hydroxylase by chronic metabolic acidosis. American Journal of Physiology 1982; 243: E265-E271.

88. Lemieux GCL, Lemieux C, Duplessis S, et al. Metabolic characteristics of cat kidney: Failure to adapt to metabolic acidosis. American Journal of Physiology 1990; 259: R277-R281.

89. Rubin SI, Outerbridge C, Myers SL, et al. Urine ammonium ion excretion and urine anion gap in cats following the administration of ammonium chloride (abstract). Journal of Veterinary Internal Medicine 1995; 9: 211.

90. Bourgoignie JJ, Jacob AI, Salbman AL, et al. Water, electrolyte and acid-base abnormalities in chronic renal failure. Seminars in Nephrology 1981; 1: 91-111.

91. Bushinsky DA. The contribution of acidosis to renal osteodystrophy. Kidney International 1995; 47: 1816-1832.

92. Eddy AA. Experimental insights into the tubulointerstitial changes accompanying primary glomerular lesions. Journal of the American Society of Nephrology 1994; 5: 1273-1287.

93. Nath KA. Tubulointerstitial changes as a major determinant in the progression of renal disease. American Journal of Kidney Diseases 1992; 20: 1-17.

94. Eddy AA, McCulloch L, Liu E, et al. A relationship between proteinuria and acute tubulointerstitial disease in rats with experimental nephrotic syndrome. American Journal of Pathology 1991; 138: 1111-1123.

95. Fukui M, Nakamura T, Ebihara I, et al. Low protein diet attenuates increased gene expression of platelet-derived growth factor and transforming growth factor b in experimental glomerular sclerosis. Journal of Clinical and Laboratory Medicine 1993; 121: 224-234.

96. Davies M, Martin J, Thomas GJ, et al. Proteinases and glomerular matrix turnover. Kidney International 1992; 41: 671-678.

97. Diamond JR, Anderson S. Irreversible tubulointerstitial damage associated with chronic aminonucleoside nephrosis. American Journal of Pathology 1990; 37: 1323-1332.

98. Alfrey AC, Froment DH, Hammond WS. Role of iron in tubulointerstitial injury in nephrotoxic serum nephritis. Kidney International 1989; 36: 753-759.

99. Kees-Folts D, Schreiner GF. A lipid chemotactic factor associated with proteinuria and interstitial nephritis induced by protein overload (abstract). Journal of the American Society of Nephrology 1991; 2: 548.

100. Neilson EG, Jimenez SA, Phillips SM. Cell-mediated immunity in interstitial nephritis: III. T lymphocyte-mediated fibroblast proliferation and collagen synthesis: An immune mechanism for renal fibrogenesis. Journal of Immunology 1980; 125: 1708-1714.

101. Clemens MR, Bursa-Zanetti Z. Lipid abnormalities and peroxidation of erythrocytes in nephrotic syndrome. Nephron 1989; 53: 325-329.

102. Patrono C, Dunn MJ. The clinical significance of inhibition of renal prostaglandin synthesis. Kidney International 1987; 32: 1-15.

103. Brown SA, Crowell WA, Barsanti JA, et al. Beneficial effects of dietary mineral restriction in dogs with marked reduction in renal mass. Journal of the American Society of Nephrology 1991; 1: 1169-1179.

104. Crocker R, Bauer J, Malcik K, et al. Effects of dietary polyunsaturated fatty acids on urinary eicosanoids in chronic renal failure dogs (abstract). Journal of Veterinary Internal Medicine 1996; 10: 166.

105. Bright J, Sullivan PS, Melton SL, et al. The effect of n-3 fatty acid supplementation on bleeding time, plasma fatty acid composition and in vitro platelet aggregation in cats. Journal of Veterinary Internal Medicine 1994; 8: 247-252.

106. Grauer GF, Greco DS, Behrend EN, et al. Effects of dietary n-3 fatty acid supplementation versus thromboxane synthetase inhibition on gentamicin-induced nephrotoxicosis in healthy male dogs. American Journal of Veterinary Research 1996; 57: 948-956.

107. Brown WW, Davis BB, Spray LA. Aging and the kidney. Archives of Internal Medicine 1986; 146: 1790-1796.

108. Inserra F, Romano LA, Cavanagh de EMV, et al. Renal interstitial sclerosis in aging: Effects of enalapril and nifedipine. Journal of the American Society of Nephrology 1996; 7: 676-680.

109. Palmer BF, Levi M. Effect of aging on renal function and disease. In: Brenner BM, ed. The Kidney, 5th ed. Philadelphia, PA: WB Saunders Co, 1996; 2274-2296.

110. Wesson LG Jr. Renal hemodynamics in physiological states. In: Physiology of the Human Kidney. New York, NY: Grune and Stratton, 1969; 96-108.

111. Epstein M. Aging and the kidney. Journal of the American Society of Nephrology 1996; 7: 1106-1122.

112. Meller Y, Kestenbaum RS, Yagil R, et al. The influence of age and sex on blood levels of calcium-regulating hormones in dogs. Clinical Orthopaedics and Related Research 1984; 187: 296-298.

113. Muller-Peddinghaus R, Trautwein G. Spontaneous glomerulonephritis in dogs II. Correlation of glomerulonephritis with age, chronic interstitial nephritis and extrarenal lesions. Veterinary Pathology 1977; 14: 121-128.

114. Shirota K, Takahashi R, Fiyiuara K, et al. Canine interstitial nephritis with special reference to glomerular lesions and filariasis. Japanese Journal of Veterinary Science 1979; 41: 119-125.

115. DiBartola SP, Tarr MJ, Parker AT, et al. Clinicopathologic findings in dogs with renal amyloidosis: 59 cases (1976-1986). Journal of the American Veterinary Medical Association 1989; 195: 358-364.

116. Bonventre JV. Mechanisms of ischemic acute renal failure. Kidney International 1993; 43: 1160-1178.

117. Thadhani R, Pascual M, Bonventre JV. Acute renal failure. New England Journal of Medicine 1996; 334: 1448-1460.

118. Humes HD. Role of calcium in the pathogenesis of acute renal failure. American Journal of Physiology 1986; 250: F579-F585.

119. Fish EM, Molitoris BA. Alterations in epithelial polarity and the pathogenesis of disease states. New England Journal of Medicine 1994; 330: 1580-1588.

120. Goligorsky MS, Lieberthal W, Racusen L, et al. Integrin receptors in renal tubular epithelium: New insights into pathophysiology of acute renal failure. American Journal of Physiology 1993; 264: F1-F8.

121. Goes N, Urmson J, Ramassar V, et al. Ischemic acute tubular necrosis induces an extensive local cytokine response. Transplantation 1995; 59: 565-572.

122. Grauer GF, Behrend EN, Greco DS, et al. Effects of dietary protein conditioning on gentamicin-induced nephrotoxicosis in healthy male dogs. American Journal of Veterinary Research 1994; 55: 90-97.

123. Behrend EN, Grauer GF, Greco DS, et al. Effects of dietary protein conditioning on gentamicin pharmacokinetics in dogs. Journal of Veterinary Pharmacology and Therapeutics 1994; 17: 259-264.

124. Neumayer HH, Heinrich M, Schmissas M, et al. Amelioration of ischemic acute renal failure by dietary fish oil administration in conscious dogs. Journal of the American Society of Nephrology 1992; 3: 1312-1320.

125. Bankir L, Kriz W. Adaptation of the kidney to protein intake and to urine concentrating activity: Similar consequences in health and CRF. Kidney International 1994; 47: 7-24.

126. Bouby N, Tring-Trang-Tan M-M, Coutaud C, et al. Vasopressin is involved in renal effects of high-protein diet: Study in homozygous Brattleboro rats. American Journal of Physiology 1991; 260: F96-F100.

127. Kleeman CR, Adams DA, Maxwell MH. An evaluation of maximal water diuresis in chronic renal disease. Journal of Laboratory and Clinical Medicine 1961; 58: 169-184.

128. Ross LA, Finco DR, Crowell WA. Effect of dietary phosphorus restriction on the kidneys of cats with reduced renal mass. American Journal of Veterinary Research 1982; 43: 1023-1026.

129. Klahr S, Buerkert J, Purkerson ML. Role of dietary factors in the progression of renal disease. Kidney International 1983; 24: 579-587.

130. Brenner BM. Hemodynamically mediated glomerular injury and the progressive nature of kidney disease. Kidney International 1983; 23: 647-655.

131. Salahudeen AK, Hostetter TH, Raatz SK, et al. Low protein diet improves glomerular permselectivity in chronic rejection (abstract). In: Proceedings. 22nd Annual Meeting of the American Society of Nephrology, Washington, DC, 1989: 424A.

132. Pedrini MT, Levey AS, Lau J, et al. The effect of dietary protein restriction on the progression of diabetic and nondiabetic renal diseases: A meta analysis. Annals of Internal Medicine 1996; 124: 627-632.

133. Harte J, Markwell P, Moraillion R, et al. Dietary management of naturally occurring chronic renal failure in cats. Journal of Nutrition 1994; 124: 2660S-2662S.

134. Baker DH, Czarnecki-Maulden GL. Comparative nutrition of dogs and cats. Annual Review of Nutrition 1991; 11: 239-263.

135. Keane WF, Kasiske BL, O'Donnell MP. Hyperlipidemia and the progression of renal disease. American Journal of Clinical Nutrition 1988; 47: 157-160.

136. Down LK, Krawiec DR. Lipid abnormalities in canine chronic renal failure (abstract). In: Proceedings. Thirteenth Annual Veterinary Medical Forum, American College of Veterinary Internal Medicine, Lake Buena Vista, FL, 1995: 1027.

137. Brown SA, Brown CA, Finco DR, et al. Effects of variation in dietary fatty acid composition (abstract). In: Proceedings. Sixteenth Annual Veterinary Medical Forum, American College of Veterinary Internal Medicine, San Diego, CA, 1998: 712.

138. Scharschmidt LA, Gibbons NB, McGarry L, et al. Effects of dietary fish oil on renal insufficiency in rats with subtotal nephrectomy. Kidney International 1987; 32: 700-709.

139. Brown SA, Brown CA, Crowell WA, et al. Dietary lipid composition alters chronic course of canine renal disease (abstract). In: Proceedings. Fourteenth Annual Veterinary Medical Forum, American College of Veterinary Internal Medicine, San Antonio, TX, 1996: 750.

140. Conjard A, Ferrier B, Martin M, et al. Effects of chronic renal failure on enzymes of energy metabolism in individual human muscle fibers. American Society of Nephrology 1995; 6: 68-74.

141. Schultze RG. Recent advances in the physiology and pathophysiology of potassium excretion. Archives of Internal Medicine 1973; 131: 885-897.

142. DiBartola SP, Rutgers HC, Zach PM, et al. Clinicopathologic findings associated with chronic renal disease in cats: 74 cases (1973-1984). Journal of the American Veterinary Medical Association 1987; 190: 1198-1202.

143. DiBartola SP, Buffington CA, Chew DJ, et al. Development of chronic renal disease in cats fed a commercial diet. Journal of the American Veterinary Medical Association 1993; 202: 744-751.

144. Hills DL, Morris JG, Rogers QR. Potassium requirements of kittens as affected by dietary protein. Journal of Nutrition 1982; 112: 216-222.

145. Dow SW, Fettman MJ, Smith KR, et al. Effects of dietary acidification and potassium depletion on acid-base balance, mineral metabolism and renal function in adult cats. Journal of Nutrition 1990; 120: 569-578.

146. Theisen SK, DiBartola SP, Radin MJ, et al. Muscle potassium content and potassium gluconate supplementation in normokalemic cats with naturally occurring chronic renal failure. Journal of Veterinary Internal Medicine 1997; 11: 212-217.

147. Hamm LL, Klahr S. Alterations of acid-base balance. In Klahr S, ed. Differential Diagnosis in Renal and Electrolyte Disorders, 2nd ed. Norwalk, CT: Appleton-Century-Crofts, 1984; 231-250.

148. Relman A, Lennon EJ, Lemman J Jr. Endogenous production of fixed acid and the measurement of the net balance of acid in normal subjects. Journal of Clinical Investigation 1961; 40: 1621-1630.

149. Klahr S, Slatopolsky E. Renal regulation of sodium excretion. Archives of Internal Medicine 1973; 131: 780-791.

150. Klahr S. The kidney in hypertension–Villain and victim. New England Journal of Medicine 1989; 320: 731-733.

151. Kurtz TW, Al-Bander HA, Morris RC. Salt-sensitive essential hypertension in men. New England Journal of Medicine 1987; 317: 1043-1048.

152. Boegehold MA, Kotchen TA. Relative contributions of dietary Na^+ and Cl^- to salt-sensitive hypertension. Hypertension 1989; 14: 579-583.

153. Luft FC, Zemel MB, Sowers JA, et al. Sodium bicarbonate and sodium chloride: Effects on blood pressure and electrolyte homeostasis in normal and hypertensive men. Journal of Hypertension 1990; 8: 663-670.

154. Kotchen TA, Luke RG, Ott CE, et al. Effect of chloride on renin and blood pressure responses to sodium chloride. Annals of Internal Medicine 1981; 98: 817-822.

155. Kotchen TA, Welch WJ, Lorenz JN, et al. Renal tubular chloride and renin release. Journal of Laboratory Clinical Medicine 1987; 110: 533-539.

156. Chen PY, Sanders PW. L-arginine abrogates salt-sensitive hypertension in Dahl/Rapp rats. Journal of Clinical Investigation 1991; 88: 1559-1567.

157. Nakaki T, Hishikawa K, Suzuki H, et al. L-arginine-induced hypotension (letter). Lancet 1990; 336: 1016-1017.

158. Vallance P, Leone A, Calver A, et al. Accumulation of an endogenous inhibitor of nitric oxide synthesis in chronic renal failure. Lancet 1992; 339: 572-575.

159. Gilmour ER, Harlty GH, Goodship THJ. Trace elements and vitamins in renal disease. In: Mitch WE, Klahr S, eds. Nutrition and the Kidney, 2nd ed. Boston, MA: Little-Brown, 1993; 114-131.

160. Nagode LA, Chew DJ. Nephrocalcinosis caused by hyperparathyroidism in progression of renal failure: Treatment with calcitriol. Seminars in Veterinary Medicine and Surgery: Small Animal 1992; 7: 202-220.

161. Younes H, Garleb K, Behr S, et al. Fermentable fibers or oligosaccharides reduce urinary nitrogen excretion by increasing urea disposal in the rat cecum. Journal of Nutrition 1995; 125: 1010-1016.

162. Bliss DZ, Stein TP, Schleifer CR, et al. Supplementation with gum arabic fiber increases fecal nitrogen excretion and lowers serum urea nitrogen concentration in chronic renal failure patients consuming a low-protein diet. American Journal of Clinical Nutrition 1996; 63: 392-398.

163. Younes H, Demigne C, Behr SR, et al. Dietary fiber decreases urinary nitrogen excretion and blood urea in rats fed a low protein diet (abstract). Federation of American Societies for Experimental Biology Journal 1996; 10: A257.

164. Finco DR, Brown SA, Crowell WA, et al. Effects of dietary phosphorus and protein in dogs with chronic renal failure. American Journal of Veterinary Research 1992; 53: 2264-2271.

165. Robertson JL, Goldschmidt M, Kronfeld DS, et al. Long-term renal responses to high dietary protein in dogs with 75% nephrectomy. Kidney International 1986; 29: 511-519.

166. Finco DR, Crowell WA, Barsanti JA. Effects of three different diets on dogs with induced chronic renal failure. American Journal of Veterinary Research 1985; 46: 646-653.

167. Touam M, Martinez F, Lacour B, et al. Aluminum-induced, reversible microcytic anemia in chronic renal failure: Clinical and experimental studies. Clinical Nephrology 1983; 19: 295-298.

168. Chew D, Nagode L. Calcitriol in the treatment of chronic renal failure. In: Kirk RW, Bonagura JD, eds. Current Veterinary Therapy XI. Philadelphia, PA: WB Saunders Co, 1992; 857-860.

169. Cowgill LD, Feldman B, Levy J, et al. Efficacy of recombinant human erythropoetin (rHuEPO) in dogs and cats with renal failure (abstract). Journal of Veterinary Internal Medicine 1990; 4: 126.

170. Rao DS, Shih M-S, Mohini R. Effect of serum parathyroid hormone and bone marrow fibrosis on the response to erythropoietin in uremia. New England Journal of Medicine 1993; 328: 171-175.

171. Brown SA, Walton C, Crawford P, et al. Long-term effects of antihypertensive regimes on renal hemodynamics and proteinuria. Kidney International 1993; 43: 1210-1218.

172. Grodiecki K, Gaines M, Jacobs R, et al. ACE inhibitor treatment of chronic renal failure in a canine model of hereditary nephritis (abstract). Veterinary Pathology 1995; 32: 555.

173. Neuringer JR, Anderson S, Brenner BM. The role of systemic and intraglomerular hypertension. In: Mitch WE, Stein J, eds. The Progressive Nature of Renal Disease, 2nd ed. New York, NY: Churchill Livingstone, 1992; 1-21.

174. DiBartola SP, deMorais HAS. Disorders of potassium: Hypokalemia and hyperkalemia. In: DiBartola SP, ed. Fluid Therapy in Small Animal Practice. Philadelphia, PA: WB Saunders Co, 1992; 89-115.

175. Roudebush P, Allen TA, Kuehn NF, et al. The effect of combined therapy with captopril, furosemide, and a sodium-restricted diet on serum electrolyte concentrations and renal function in normal dogs and dogs with congestive heart failure. Journal of Veterinary Internal Medicine 1994; 8: 337-342.

CASE 19-1

Hematemesis in a Shih Tzu

Larry G. Adams, DVM, PhD
Diplomate ACVIM (Internal Medicine)
Purdue University
School of Veterinary Medicine
West Lafayette, Indiana, USA

Assess the Patient

A four-year-old intact male Shih Tzu was initially evaluated by the referring veterinarian for hematuria, anorexia and vomiting. The dog had been diagnosed with renal failure and a possible urinary tract infection. The suspected urinary tract infection had been treated with a combination of trimethoprim and sulfamethoxazole. The dog had also developed thrombocytopenia (platelet count 11 x $10^3/\mu l$ [reference range 300 to 900 x $10^3/\mu l$]) and progressive anemia in the month before referral. The trimethoprim-sulfamethoxazole combination was discontinued and the dog was treated with prednisone for thrombocytopenia and suspected immune-mediated hemolytic anemia. The current history included vomiting, hematemesis, hematochezia and decreased appetite. The dog also had a lifelong history of polydipsia and polyuria.

Physical examination revealed 5% dehydration, thin body condition (body condition score 2/5, body weight 5.9 kg), pale mucous membranes, poor coat quality, blood dripping from the penis and a small, irregular left kidney. Rectal examination revealed symmetric, nonpainful prostatomegaly and hematochezia.

Clinicopathologic abnormalities included nonregenerative anemia (hematocrit 15% [reference range 37 to 55%]), azotemia (urea nitrogen 139 mg/dl [reference range 7 to 32 mg/dl], creatinine 3.3 mg/dl [reference range 0.5 to 1.5 mg/dl]) and hyperphosphatemia (8.3 mg/dl [reference range 2.2 to 7.9 mg/dl]). Examination of the blood smear revealed acanthocytosis (1+), poikilocytosis (1+) and occasional schistocytes. Spherocytes were not present. The platelet count was within normal limits (341 x $10^3/\mu l$). Urinalysis revealed isosthenuria (specific gravity 1.012) and hematuria (too numerous to count red blood cells per high-power field).

Problems identified included chronic renal failure (CRF), nonregenerative anemia, prostatomegaly, hematemesis and hematochezia. Additional diagnostic procedures performed included fecal flotation, urine culture, bone marrow aspiration, indirect blood pressure measurement, fundic examination, abdominal radiographs and ultrasound and ultrasound-guided fine-needle aspiration of the prostate gland. The fecal flotation test was negative for intestinal parasites. Aerobic urine culture yielded no bacterial growth. Cytologic examination of the bone marrow aspirate revealed erythroid hypoplasia with adequate iron stores. Abdominal radiographs revealed prostatomegaly and small irregular kidney margins. Abdominal ultrasonography revealed that the kidneys were bilaterally hyperechoic with very thin renal cortices (3 cm width). Considering the dog's age and breed, these findings were consistent with congenital renal dysplasia. Ultrasonography of the prostate gland revealed diffuse prostatomegaly with multiple small intraprostatic cysts. Examination of the aspirates from the prostate gland revealed normal prostatic epithelial cells, numerous RBCs and small numbers of neutrophils and macrophages. The ultrasonographic and cytologic findings were consistent with benign prostatic hyperplasia with intraprostatic cyst formation. Aerobic culture of the prostatic aspirate yielded no bacterial growth. Indirect blood pressure measurements were within normal limits. The fundic examination was normal.

Assess the Food(s) and Feeding Method

The dog had been fed a commercial dry dog food before the diagnosis of renal failure by the referring veterinarian. Thereafter, the food was changed to a protein- and phosphorus-restricted veterinary therapeutic food (Prescription Diet Canine k/dᵃ); however, the dog was still vomiting and anorectic, and refused to eat the food. The owner had switched to a commercial grocery brand moist beef and liver dog food supplemented with commercial treats. The moist food was fed twice daily and treats were given multiple times throughout the day to encourage the dog to eat. The dog only ate small amounts of the moist food and some treats in the week before admission.

Questions

1. What are the most likely reasons for this dog's anemia?
2. Why was the magnitude of the increase in serum creatinine and urea nitrogen concentrations markedly different?
3. What dietary recommendations should be made to optimize management of this dog's problems?
4. What other therapies might improve patient compliance with the dietary recommendations?

Answers and Discussion

1. There were multiple reasons for this dog's anemia. Although the anemia was initially presumed to be an immune-mediated hemolytic anemia, this diagnosis was unlikely. The referring veterinarian submitted a sample to a commercial laboratory for a Coombs test, which was negative. The red blood cell morphology revealed evidence of fragmentation (which occurs with uremia) and no spherocytes. Likewise, the serum bilirubin concentration remained normal and bilirubinuria was not present. The presumption of an immune-mediated process was based on the concurrent thrombocytopenia and progressive anemia following trimethoprim-sulfamethoxazole therapy. The thrombocytopenia quickly resolved with discontinuation of trimethoprim-sulfamethoxazole therapy and treatment with prednisone. However, the anemia worsened progressively. The thrombocytopenia was likely immune-mediated secondary to trimethoprim-sulfamethoxazole therapy; however, there was no evidence of immune-mediated hemolytic anemia.

The bone marrow examination was interpreted to be consistent with a hypoproliferative anemia secondary to a relative erythropoietin deficiency. Dogs with moderate to severe CRF consistently have low erythropoietin concentrations relative to the degree of anemia. Therefore, based on the bone marrow findings and the concurrent diagnosis of CRF, it was likely that erythropoietin deficiency secondary to renal failure was responsible for a major component of the anemia.

Another contributing factor to the anemia was gastrointestinal (GI) blood loss from uremic gastritis and concurrent prednisone therapy. The dog had a history of hematemesis (both fresh blood and "coffee grounds"-like vomitus) and hematochezia. Additionally, during hospitalization the dog had marked melena. Uremic gastritis may contribute to GI bleeding, vomiting and anorexia as seen in this dog. Prednisone therapy probably contributed to some of the GI ulceration presumed to be present.

2. There are also multiple reasons for the magnitude of the different elevations in serum creatinine and urea nitrogen concentrations in this dog. Creatinine enters the blood as a result of the nonenzymatic breakdown of phosphocreatine in skeletal muscle. Therefore, the rate of entry of creatinine into the blood depends on muscle mass. The serum creatinine concentration will be lower than would be expected from the glomerular filtration rate (GFR) in a dog with decreased muscle mass. Therefore, the serum creatinine concentration was probably low in this dog relative to the serum urea nitrogen concentration, thereby overestimating the relative GFR (i.e., underestimating the severity of renal failure).

The urea nitrogen concentration was probably higher relative to the GFR in this dog. The rate of urea production is dependent on dietary protein intake, rate of production by the liver and catabolism of endogenous body protein stores. This dog was currently being fed relatively high levels of dietary protein, which would contribute to greater production of nitrogenous waste products such as urea. GI hemorrhage mimics a high-protein meal resulting in an increased rate of urea synthesis by the liver. Also, administration of corticosteroids results in catabolism of body proteins, which releases nitrogen-containing amino acids. Urea is produced when these amino acids are catabolized for energy. Therefore, the rate of urea production in this dog was probably increased from GI bleeding and catabolism induced by the prednisone therapy. The net result is that the urea nitrogen concentration was increased relative to the serum creatinine concentration and actual GFR.

Increased production of potentially toxic nitrogenous breakdown products (represented by urea) was probably making the uremic syndrome more severe in this dog.

3. This dog was classified as having moderately severe renal failure. Dogs with moderate to severe renal failure benefit from consuming foods restricted in protein and phosphorus content with adequate buffering capacity. Dietary protein restriction is important in advanced renal failure to prevent overt uremia. However, attempting to immediately feed any food to an animal with anorexia and vomiting from severe uremic gastritis is likely to fail. Therefore, our recom-

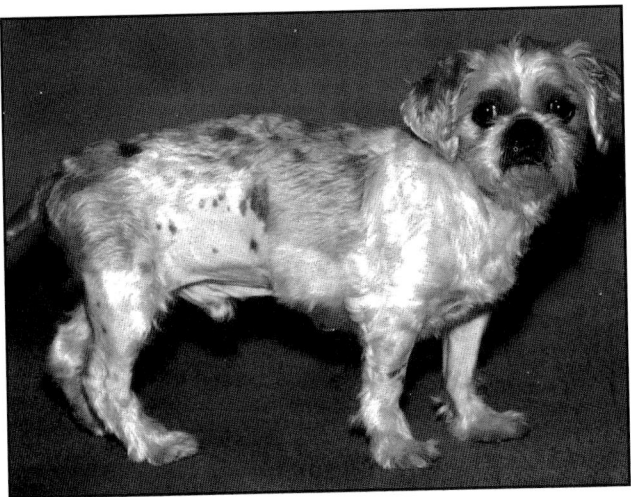

Figure 1. Postoperative picture of a four-year-old male Shih Tzu with chronic renal failure and probable uremic vasculitis involving the tail. The tail was amputated and a castration was performed.

Figure 2. A four-year-old castrated male Shih Tzu two months after therapy was instituted for chronic renal failure. The dog's coat quality had returned to normal.

mendation was to treat the uremic crisis first, then reintroduce an appropriate food after the uremic gastritis was controlled.

4. Other therapies to treat the consequences of the uremic syndrome are indicated when a dog has moderate to severe renal failure. The therapy should be aimed at controlling uremic gastritis, renal secondary hyperparathyroidism, anemia and hypertension (if present).

Uremic gastritis is thought to occur secondary to hypergastrinemia in dogs with renal failure. Therapy designed to minimize uremic gastritis and gastric and duodenal ulceration includes H_2-receptor antagonists (i.e., cimetidine, famotidine, etc.), misoprostol, omeprazole and sucralfate. Therapy designed to minimize renal secondary hyperparathyroidism includes dietary phosphorus restriction, intestinal phosphate-binding agents and potentially low-dose calcitriol therapy. The most effective method of treating the anemia of CRF is to administer recombinant human erythropoietin (r-HuEPO). Therapy with r-HuEPO is reserved for patients with moderately severe anemia (i.e., hematocrit values <20 to 25% in dogs).

Therapy Including Feeding Plan

The dog was initially treated with intravenous fluid therapy, intravenous cimetidine[b] and oral misoprostol[c] and sucralfate.[d] Food was initially withheld for 48 hours until the vomiting ceased. The dog was then offered Prescription Diet Canine k/d in four small meals per day. The amount of food was initially calculated to meet the resting energy requirement (RER) for an ideal body weight of 7.5 kg.

Progress Notes

The vomiting, hematemesis, hematochezia and melena resolved. The azotemia improved with intravenous fluid therapy; the serum urea nitrogen concentration decreased to 58 mg/dl and the serum creatinine level decreased to 2.1 mg/dl. However, the hematocrit decreased to a low of 11%. The dog was discharged after five days of hospitalization while the owners considered castration. Dietary recom-

mendations were to feed Prescription Diet Canine k/d or a homemade food with restricted levels of protein and phosphorus. Therapy was continued at home including oral cimetidine, oral aluminum hydroxide and subcutaneous injections of r-HuEPO[e] three times per week.

The dog was re-evaluated nine days after it was discharged from the hospital. The dog's attitude and appetite were much better. The dog had been chewing on its tail for two days. The distal 4 cm of the tail was dark blue to black, had several scabs and lacked pain sensation. The tail lesions were thought to be due to ischemic necrosis related to uremic vasculitis. The serum creatinine concentration was 3.1 mg/dl and the urea nitrogen concentration was 111 mg/dl. The hematocrit had improved to 19%. The dog was given intravenous fluid therapy in preparation for surgical amputation of the distal tail. Castration was also recommended to treat the benign prostatic hyperplasia with intraprostatic cysts. The serum urea nitrogen and creatinine concentrations decreased with fluid therapy and surgery was performed for tail amputation and castration (Figure 1). The dog was discharged with similar treatment recommendations to those listed above. In addition, a combination of amoxicillin and clavulanic acid[f] was administered for two weeks as a prophylactic antibiotic for the tail amputation, and low-dose calcitriol[g] therapy was initiated. Calcitriol was administered to decrease serum parathyroid hormone concentration associated with renal secondary hyperparathyroidism.

The dog did well with this combination of dietary and medical therapy for several months. The dog ate Prescription Diet Canine k/d well and gained weight (body weight 7.5 kg). The coat returned to normal quality (Figure 2). The anemia resolved and the r-HuEPO was decreased to a maintenance dose twice weekly. The azotemia was slowly progressive over the next six months. Subcutaneous fluid therapy (100 ml every other day) was added after the serum creatinine concentration exceeded 5 mg/dl. The dog died of progressive CRF 11 months after initial evaluation.

Endnotes

a. Hill's Pet Nutrition, Inc., Topeka, KS, USA.

b. Tagamet. SmithKline Beecham Pharmaceuticals, Philadelphia, PA, USA.

c. Cytotec. GD Searle & Co, Chicago, IL, USA.

d. Carafate. Marion Merrell Dow, Kansas City, MO, USA.

e. Epogen. Amgen Inc., Thousand Oaks, CA, USA.

f. Clavamox. Pfizer Animal Health, Exton, PA, USA.

g. Rocaltrol. Roche Laboratories, Nutley, NJ, USA.

Bibliography

Adams LG. Chronic renal failure. In: Tilley LP, Smith FWK, eds. The 5 Minute Veterinary Consult. Baltimore, MD: Williams & Wilkins, 1997; 1018-1019.

Chew DJ, DiBartola SP, Nagode LA, et al. Phosphorus restriction in the treatment of chronic renal failure. In: Kirk RW, Bonagura JD, eds. Current Veterinary Therapy XI. Philadelphia, PA: WB Saunders Co, 1992; 853-857.

Chew DJ, Nagode LA. Calcitriol in the treatment of chronic renal failure. In: Kirk RW, Bonagura JD, eds. Current Veterinary Therapy XI. Philadelphia, PA: WB Saunders Co, 1992; 857-860.

Polzin DJ, Osborne CA, James KM, et al. Chronic renal failure. In: Ettinger SJ, Feldman EC, eds. Textbook of Veterinary Internal Medicine, 4th ed. Philadelphia, PA: WB Saunders Co, 1995; 1734-1760.

CASE 19-2

Weight Loss in a Cat

David J. Polzin, DVM, PhD
Diplomate ACVIM (Internal Medicine)
College of Veterinary Medicine
University of Minnesota
St Paul, Minnesota, USA

Assess the Animal

A 13-year-old neutered female domestic shorthair cat was examined for weight loss of several months' duration. The owners had also noticed an increase in water intake, increased urination, decreased appetite and a few episodes of vomiting in the last month. The cat also seemed weaker than usual. Characteristics of the feces were unknown because the family dog often consumed any material deposited in the litter box. The cat usually remained indoors but did spend some time outdoors during the summer.

Physical examination revealed a very thin cat, with a body weight of 2.4 kg and a body condition score of 1/5. The medical record indicated that the cat had weighed 5 kg four years earlier. Moderate accumulation of dental calculus was noted. Abdominal palpation revealed excess accumulation of gas in the intestines and a small left kidney. The right kidney could not be palpated.

Results of a complete blood count included anemia (i.e., decreased total erythrocyte count, hemoglobin and hematocrit). Significant serum biochemistry profile findings included azotemia, hyperphosphatemia, low normal serum potassium concentration and metabolic acidosis (Table 1). Serum thyroxine (T_4) concentration was normal. Urinalysis was normal except for a urine specific gravity of 1.009. The tentative diagnosis was chronic renal failure (CRF).

Assess the Food(s) and Feeding Method

The cat was normally fed a mixture of two different commercial specialty brand dry cat foods; one was a "light" food and the other was a food formulated for older cats (senior food). The combination of dry foods was offered free choice. The owners noted that the cat was still eating but its overall appetite was decreased.

Questions

1. What are the key nutritional factors to consider in cats with CRF?
2. Prepare a treatment and feeding plan for this cat.
3. What parameters should be monitored if this patient goes home with conservative management?

Answers and Discussion

1. Key nutritional factors to consider in cats with CRF include water, phosphorus, protein, sodium, chloride, potassium, energy and dietary acid load. Adequate water intake is important to maintain hydration, blood volume and renal perfusion in an animal with polyuria. Parenteral fluids are indicated if vomiting, diarrhea, dehydration, blood volume contraction and renal hypoperfusion are clinically significant. Avoiding excess dietary phosphorus, protein and acid load will help reduce clinical signs of uremia and may slow progression of renal disease. Avoiding excess dietary sodium chloride may help control systemic hypertension, which is a common sequela to CRF in cats. Potassium is also an important nutrient because potassium depletion contributes to renal injury and may lead directly to clinical signs in some cats. (See Case 19-3.) Adequate energy intake in the form of nonprotein calories is important in this cat to promote weight gain and minimize further catabolism of lean body mass.

2. Parenteral fluid therapy is indicated to promote excretion of nitrogenous wastes and improve overall hydration status. Water should be offered in copious quantities free choice at all times. The food(s) offered to this cat should avoid excess levels of phosphorus, protein, sodium, chloride and acid load while providing

Table 1. Selected serum biochemistry values from a cat with vomiting and weight loss.

Parameters	Day 1	Day 57	Day 160	Reference values
Urea nitrogen (mg/dl)	104	78	66	10-32
Creatinine (mg/dl)	7.4	5.4	5.0	0.1-2.1
Phosphorus (mg/dl)	8.2	5.4	5.2	2.4-6.1
Potassium (mg/dl)	3.4	4.7	4.8	3.2-6.2
Total CO_2 (mmol/l)	12.8	20.0	18.5	8-21

adequate levels of potassium and high caloric density. A commercial veterinary therapeutic food or home-made food designed for renal failure should meet these nutritional goals. Because of nausea associated with uremia, the food should be offered in small, frequent meals. The daily energy requirement (DER) should be calculated to promote weight gain (i.e., 1.2 x resting energy requirement [RER] for an ideal body weight of 4.5 kg) after a normal appetite has returned. Enteral or parenteral nutritional support may be necessary if the cat is eating less than its calculated RER per day. Adjunctive medical therapy might include antiemetics and H_2-receptor antagonists for uremic gastropathy and erythropoietin therapy for the anemia and to improve the overall well-being of the patient.

3. Clinical and biochemical parameters should be monitored two to four weeks after the patient has gone home with a dietary change. A good response to conservative management includes decreased vomiting, increased appetite and activity level, weight gain, decreased serum urea nitrogen and phosphorus concentrations and increased plasma bicarbonate concentration (or total CO_2). Plasma bicarbonate concentration should be maintained between 17 and 22 mmol/l. Alkalinization therapy should be considered if the plasma bicarbonate or total CO_2 concentration remains below the recommended range. Phosphorus binders should be considered if hyperphosphatemia persists despite restricted dietary intake. Retinal examinations are important to evaluate for end-organ changes associated with systemic hypertension. The owner should be encouraged to closely monitor the cat's daily food intake to ensure that adequate energy is being consumed.

Progress Notes

The cat was stabilized with parenteral fluid therapy and started on a commercial veterinary therapeutic food that avoids excess levels of phosphorus, protein, sodium, chloride and acid load while providing adequate levels of potassium and high caloric density (Prescription Diet Feline k/d[a]). The DER was calculated at 1.2 x RER for an ideal body weight of 4.5 kg to promote weight gain. This was approximately 250 kcal (1,046 kJ) or one-half cup of dry food daily. Subcutaneous fluids (120 ml/24 hours) were continued at home.

Two months later (Day 57), the cat was examined and found to have gained weight (body weight 3.1 kg). Serum urea nitrogen, creatinine and phosphorus concentrations were decreased and serum potassium and total CO_2 concentrations were increased (Table 1). These serum biochemistry changes persisted when the cat was re-evaluated on Day 160; however, body weight was not recorded at that time. The owners reported that the cat was active, maintained a good appetite and had no evidence of vomiting when the combination of dietary therapy and subcutaneous fluids was used.

The owners did not return with the cat again until one year later. The cat was experiencing an acute uremic crisis and was euthanatized at the owners' request without further diagnostic or postmortem evaluation.

Endnote

a. Hill's Pet Nutrition, Inc., Topeka, KS, USA.

Bibliography

Krawiec DR. Managing gastrointestinal complications of uremia. Veterinary Clinics of North America: Small Animal Practice 1996; 26: 1287-1292.

Polzin DJ, James K, Osborne CA. Metabolic acidosis in renal failure: Consequences, diagnosis and treatment. In: Bonagura JD, ed. Current Veterinary Therapy XII. Philadelphia, PA: WB Saunders Co, 1995; 956-958.

Polzin DJ, Osborne CA, Lulich JP. Diet therapy guidelines for cats with chronic renal failure. Veterinary Clinics of North America: Small Animal Practice 1996; 26: 1269-1275.

CASE 19-3

Generalized Weakness in a Cat

Timothy A. Allen, DVM
Diplomate ACVIM (Internal Medicine)
Hill's Science and Technology Center
Topeka, Kansas, USA

Assess the Animal

A 13.5-year-old neutered female domestic shorthair cat was examined for lethargy, weakness and anorexia of two days' duration. The owner reported that the cat was so weak that it could not lift its head. Physical examination revealed a thin cat (body condition score [BCS] 1/5) weighing 2.2 kg. The coat was dull and unkempt. Generalized weakness, cervical ventroflexion and ataxia were noted. Small, irregular kidneys were evident during abdominal palpation. Dehydration was suspected because of tacky mucous membranes.

The cat was hospitalized and a blood sample obtained for a complete blood count and serum biochemistry profile. Urine was obtained via cystocentesis for urinalysis. The complete blood count was normal except for a low hematocrit value. Serum biochemistry profile abnormalities included azotemia, hypernatremia, hyperchloremia, hypokalemia, decreased total CO_2 and elevated total protein levels (Table 1). Urinalysis results included a urine specific gravity of 1.013, 2+ protein on the dipstick and normal sediment.

The tentative diagnosis was renal failure (i.e., elevated urea nitrogen and creatinine values with low urine specific gravity and small, irregular kidneys) with associated dehydration and blood volume contraction (i.e., tacky mucous membranes and elevated total protein, sodium and chloride concentrations), anemia (i.e., low hematocrit with dehydration), metabolic acidosis (i.e., decreased TCO_2) and hypokalemia.

Assess the Food(s) and Feeding Method

The cat was fed a mixture of commercial semi-moist and dry cat foods. These foods and water were always available.

Questions

1. What is the cause of this cat's generalized weakness and cervical ventroflexion?

Table 1. Selected serum biochemistry values from a cat with generalized weakness.

Parameters	Day 1	Day 2	Day 3	Day 4	Day 6	Day 25	Reference values
Hematocrit (%)	31	20.3	ND	ND	ND	ND	30-45
Hemoglobin (g/dl)	9.9	6.7	ND	ND	ND	ND	8-15
Total protein (g/dl)	7.9	7.1	6.1	6.3	6.5	ND	6.1-7.7
Urea nitrogen (mg/dl)	53	58	47	48	51	36	15-25
Creatinine (mg/dl)	3.0	3.1	2.0	1.9	2.1	2.3	0.8-1.8
Sodium (mmol/l)	165	167	160	158	153	152	140-157
Potassium (mmol/l)	3.0	3.4	4.2	5.5	4.6	5.2	3.8-5.3
Chloride (mmol/l)	137	134	124	122	116	118	115-128
Total CO_2 (mmol/l)	11	17	23	29	28	23	13-23

Key: ND = not done.

2. What is the likely cause of the hypokalemia?
3. Outline a treatment and feeding plan for this cat.
4. What parameters should be monitored to assess response to treatment?

Answers and Discussion

1. Potassium depletion results in morphologic and functional changes in muscle and kidney, alterations in carbohydrate metabolism and protein synthesis and disturbances in acid-base balance. Muscle weakness develops when the serum potassium concentration falls below 3.0 mEq (mmol)/l and frank rhabdomyolysis or life-threatening respiratory muscle paralysis may occur when the serum potassium concentration is less than 2.0 mEq/liter.

   Clinical signs of hypokalemic polymyopathy include appendicular muscle weakness, reluctance to walk or a stiff stilted gait with forelimb hypermetria and a broad-based hind-limb stance and apparent pain on palpation of muscles. The most dramatic myopathic finding is a characteristic cervical ventroflexion due to weakness of the extensor muscles of the neck. Similar ventroflexion has been observed in cats with thiamin deficiency and myasthenia gravis. Other neuromuscular signs may be observed in some cats, including bilateral mydriasis, disorientation, staggering and falling.

2. In retrospective studies, hypokalemia was found in 20 to 30% of cats with chronic renal failure (CRF) and chronic renal disease was the most common associated disorder in cats with hypokalemia. The hypokalemia observed in cats with CRF presumably is caused by a combination of anorexia, weight loss with muscle wasting and polyuria. A clinically distinct syndrome of polymyopathy and nephropathy characterized by hypokalemia, azotemia, impaired renal concentrating ability and lymphoplasmacytic tubulointerstitial nephritis has been documented to occur in cats fed a food low in potassium and high in acid content.

3. The initial management of cats with potassium-depletion polymyopathy and nephropathy requires diligent potassium supplementation by oral and intravenous routes. Potassium chloride is usually added to parenteral fluids for intravenous administration. Infusion of potassium-containing fluids initially may be associated with a further decrease in serum potassium concentration as a result of dilution, increased distal renal tubular flow and cellular uptake of potassium, especially if the fluid contains glucose. This complication can be minimized by selecting a fluid that does not contain glucose, administering fluids at an appropriate rate and beginning oral potassium supplementation as soon as possible.

   Potassium gluconate is recommended for oral supplementation of hypokalemic cats because potassium chloride and potassium bicarbonate are often unpalatable. The recommended initial oral dosage of potassium gluconate is 5 to 10 mEq/day divided into two or three doses. Clinical improvement is usually seen after one to three days of treatment at which time the dosage may be decreased. Supplementation of normokalemic CRF cats with potassium gluconate does not appear to be beneficial.

4. It is difficult to estimate the amount of potassium required to re-establish normal potassium balance in a given patient. Thus, the amount of potassium required must be determined by judicious supplementation and serial measurement of serum potassium concentrations during treatment and recovery. Treatment usually results in resolution of muscle weakness within one to two weeks, weight gain and an improved coat. During recovery, renal function (i.e., urea nitrogen and creatinine concentrations) and anemia (i.e., hematocrit values and red blood cell count) may stabilize and improve in some cats. Persistent CRF is managed using conservative medical and nutritional management.

Progress Notes

An intravenous catheter was inserted in the cat's jugular vein and 20 ml of lactated Ringer's solution was administered per hour during the first eight hours. After eight hours, the rate was reduced to 12 ml/hour. Sixteen mEq of potassium chloride were added to each liter of lactated Ringer's solution to produce a final potassium concentration of 20 mEq/l. During the first day of hospitalization, 4 mEq of potassium gluconate gel (Tumil-K[a]) were administered per os every 12 hours. Water was offered free choice. Body weight was measured daily using the same pediatric scale, and urine output was estimated by weighing the litter box before and after voiding.

The cat's weakness was noticeably improved by Day 2. The cat's resting energy requirement (RER) was calculated at its estimated ideal body weight of 3.5 kg (RER at 3.5 kg = 175 kcal [732 kJ]). The cat was offered small quantities of a commercial dry and moist veterinary therapeutic food formulated for cats with renal failure (Prescription Diet Feline k/d[b]). These foods were offered every three to four hours. The cat was consuming sufficient food to meet its RER by Day 4.

The azotemia, hypokalemia, acidosis and muscle strength progressively improved over the next three days (Table 1). Six days after initial hospitalization, the cat was discharged to the owner's care with instructions to continue feeding the dry therapeutic food and to administer 4 mEq potassium gluconate gel every 12 hours. The quantity of food was increased to a daily energy requirement of 1.4 x RER.

The owner reported that the cat was bright, alert, active and eating well with normal muscle strength 25 days after initial examination. Physical examination was normal except the cat was still underweight (body weight 2.8 kg, BCS 2/5) and the kidneys were still palpably small and irregular. Results of a serum biochemistry profile included mild azotemia, normal serum electrolyte concentrations and normal acid-base status (Table 1). Oral potassium gluconate was discontinued and the dry renal food was continued.

Endnotes

a. Daniels Pharmaceuticals Inc., St. Petersburg, FL, USA.
b. Hill's Pet Nutrition, Inc., Topeka, KS, USA.

Bibliography

DiBartola SP, Buffington CA, Chew DJ, et al. Development of chronic renal failure in cats fed a commercial diet. Journal of the American Veterinary Medical Association 1993; 202: 744-751.

Dow SW, LeCouteur RA, Fettman MJ, et al. Hypokalemia in cats: 186 cases (1984-1987). Journal of the American Veterinary Medical Association 1989; 194: 1604-1608.

Dow SW, LeCouteur RA, Fettman MJ, et al. Potassium depletion in cats: Hypokalemic polymyopathy. Journal of the American Veterinary Medical Association 1987; 191: 1569-1575.

Theisen SK, DiBartola SP, Radin J, et al. Muscle potassium content and potassium gluconate supplementation in normokalemic cats with naturally occurring chronic renal failure. Journal of Veterinary Internal Medicine 1997; 11: 212-217.

CHAPTER 20

Canine Urolithiasis

Carl A. Osborne

Joseph W. Bartges

Jody P. Lulich

David J. Polzin

Timothy A. Allen

"If the patient you treat is harmed more than helped,
then best leave the stones alone.
But by taking a look at the thoughts in this book,
ways to treat stones by how patients eat you'll be shown."
Carl A. Osborne, 1999

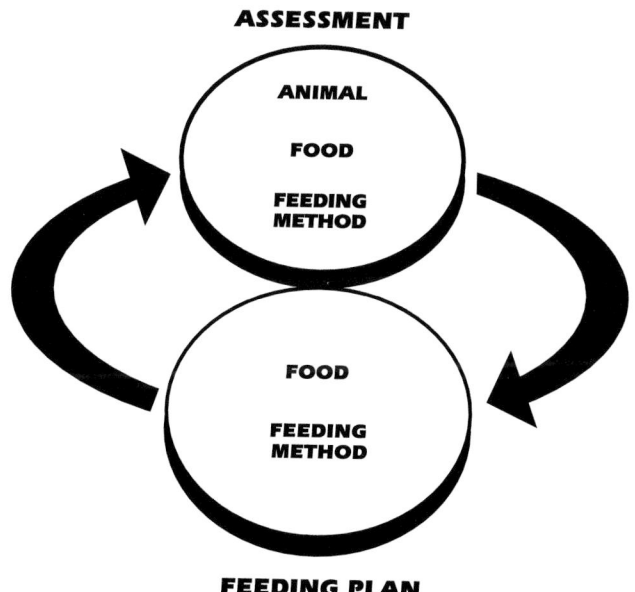

ASSESSMENT

ANIMAL

FOOD

FEEDING METHOD

FOOD

FEEDING METHOD

FEEDING PLAN

Note: The reader is referred to Chapter 1 for a detailed discussion of the iterative process of clinical nutrition.

CLINICAL IMPORTANCE

Urolithiasis is considered to be a common disorder of the urinary tract in dogs. However, the incidence (annual rate of appearance of new cases among the entire population at risk for the disease) of canine urolithiasis has not been established. Urolithiasis was diagnosed in 3,628 of 676,668 dogs (0.53%) admitted to veterinary teaching hospitals in North America between 1980 and 1993. The proportion of dogs with urolithiasis admitted to veterinary hospitals in Germany was similar.[1]

Clinical signs of urolithiasis may be the first indication of underlying systemic disorders, or defects in the structure or function of the urinary tract (Table 20-1). Uroliths may pass through various parts of the excretory pathway of the urinary tract, they may dissolve, they may become inactive or they may continue to form and grow. If uroliths associated with clinical signs are allowed to remain untreated, they may result in more serious sequelae. Uroliths frequently recur if risk factors associated with their formation are not corrected, despite urolith removal by voiding, dissolution protocols or surgery.

Urolithiasis should not be viewed as a single disease, but rather as a sequela of one or more underlying abnormalities. The fact that urolith formation is often erratic and unpredictable indicates that several interrelated complex physiologic and pathologic factors are involved. Therefore, detection of uroliths is only the beginning of the diagnostic process. Determination of urolith composition narrows etiologic possibilities. Knowledge of the patient's diet and serum and urine concentrations of calculogenic minerals, crystallization promoters, crystalliza-

KEY WORDS & TERMS—CANINE UROLITHIASIS*

Ammonium urate urolithiasis	Crystalluria	Nucleation	Urate
Calcium oxalate urolithiasis	Cystine urolithiasis	Pollakiuria	Urease
Calcium phosphate urolithiasis	Cystinuria	Purine urolithiasis	Uric acid
Calculogenic minerals	Hypercalciuria	Pyelonephritis	Urinary acidifier
Calculolytic food	Hyperoxaluria	Renolith	Urocystolith
Compound uroliths	Lamination	Saturated solution	Urohydropropulsion
Crystallization	Matrix	Silica urolithiasis	Urolith
Crystallization inhibitors	Metastable solution	Struvite urolithiasis	Urolithiasis
Crystallization promoters	Mineral	Supersaturated solution	Xanthine
	Nidus	Undersaturated solution	Xanthine oxidase inhibitor

Key words and terms are defined in the Glossary. (Also see sidebar "Urolithiasis Terms and Concepts.")

KEY POINTS—CANINE UROLITHIASIS

1. Urine is a complex solution containing a variety of substances that can inhibit or promote crystal formation and growth.
2. A dietary history should be obtained for all patients with urolithiasis with the objective of identifying risk factors that predispose the patient to specific mineral types.
3. Detection of some types of crystals (e.g., cystine and ammonium urate) in clinically asymptomatic patients, frequent detection of large aggregates of crystals (e.g., calcium oxalate or magnesium ammonium phosphate) in apparently normal individuals or detection of any form of crystals in fresh urine collected from patients with confirmed urolithiasis may be of diagnostic, prognostic and/or therapeutic importance.
4. Although there is not a direct relationship between crystalluria and urolithiasis, detection of crystals in urine is proof that the urine sample is oversaturated with crystallogenic substances.
5. Risk factors for urate lithogenesis in dogs include: 1) increased renal excretion and urine concentration of uric acid, 2) increased renal excretion, renal production or microbial urease production of ammonium ions, 3) low urinary pH and 4) presence of promoters or absence of inhibitors of urate urolith formation. Genetic factors may be important because urate uroliths are common in certain dog breeds (e.g., Dalmatians and English bulldogs).
6. Current recommendations for medical dissolution of canine ammonium urate uroliths include a combination of: 1) calculolytic foods, 2) administration of xanthine oxidase inhibitors (i.e., allopurinol), 3) alkalinization of urine, 4) eradication or control of urinary tract infections (UTIs) and 5) formation of an increased quantity of less concentrated urine.
7. The goal of dietary modification for patients with uric acid or ammonium urate uroliths is to reduce urine concentration of uric acid, ammonium ions and hydrogen ions (i.e., purine-restricted, moist, alkalinizing food).
8. Dogs with calcium oxalate urolithiasis frequently consume human food and/or commercially available treats. The high sodium content of some commercial dog treats may help explain this association because sodium consumption promotes hypercalciuria.
9. The rate of recurrence of calcium oxalate uroliths increases with the length of time that dogs are evaluated: 3% recurred after three months, 9% after six months, 36% after one year, 42% after two years and 48% after three years.
10. Surgery is the time-honored method to remove calcium oxalate uroliths from the urinary tract; however, complete surgical removal of all visible uroliths may be difficult because of their small size and irregular contour.

11. The goals of dietary prevention of calcium oxalate urolithiasis include: 1) reducing calcium concentration in urine, 2) reducing oxalic acid concentration in urine, 3) promoting high concentration and activity of inhibitors of calcium oxalate crystal growth and aggregation in urine and 4) reducing urine concentration.
12. Surgery remains the most reliable way to remove active calcium phosphate uroliths from the urinary tract. Voiding urohydropropulsion may be used to remove small urocystoliths.
13. For dogs with calcium phosphate urolithiasis, it seems reasonable to recommend trial therapy with foods lower in protein, sodium, calcium and vitamin D compared with the food consumed at the time the urolith formed.
14. Because cystinuria is an inherited defect, uroliths commonly recur after two to 12 months in young to middle-aged dogs unless prophylactic therapy has been initiated.
15. Current recommendations for dissolution of cystine uroliths encompass reducing urine concentration of cystine and increasing the solubility of cystine in urine. This may be accomplished by various combinations of: 1) dietary modification, 2) administration of thiol-containing drugs and 3) alkalinization of urine, if necessary.
16. Dietary management should result in formation of less concentrated urine without cystine crystalluria; urinary specific gravity values should be less than 1.020. Orally administered potassium citrate may be considered to alkalinize urine.
17. The most common type of mineral encountered in uroliths of dogs is magnesium ammonium phosphate hexahydrate or struvite.
18. Clinical and experimental studies of dogs have repeatedly demonstrated a close relationship between formation of struvite uroliths and UTIs caused by urease-producing bacteria.
19. The quantity of dietary protein catabolized for energy influences formation and dissolution of infection-induced struvite uroliths. Consumption of dietary protein in quantities that exceed daily protein requirements for anabolism results in increased urinary excretion of urea derived from catabolism of amino acids. Microbial hydrolysis of urea to ammonia promotes struvite urolith formation.
20. Clinical and experimental studies revealed that struvite uroliths can form within two to eight weeks after infection with urease-producing staphylococci.
21. Recommendations for medical dissolution of canine struvite uroliths include: 1) eradication or control of UTI (if present), 2) use of calculolytic foods and 3) administration

Continued on next page.

Continued from previous page.

of urease inhibitors (acetohydroxamic acid) to patients if struvite uroliths persist because of persistent UTI caused by urease-producing microbes.

22. The goal of dietary modification for patients with struvite uroliths is to reduce urine concentration of urea (the substrate of microbial urease), phosphorus and magnesium.

23. Reductions in concentrations of serum urea nitrogen may be used as one index of client and patient compliance with dietary therapy.

24. The size of uroliths being dissolved by medical means should be monitored monthly by survey radiography or ultrasonography.

25. Struvite crystals should not form in fresh uncontaminated urine if therapy has been effective in promoting formation of urine that is undersaturated with magnesium ammonium phosphate.

26. Because small uroliths may escape detection by survey radiography or ultrasonography, dietary and antimicrobial therapy should be continued for at least one month after survey radiographic or ultrasonographic documentation of urolith dissolution.

27. Eradication or control of UTIs due to urease-producing bacteria is the most important factor in preventing recurrence of most infection-induced struvite uroliths.

28. When considering dietary management, emphasis should be placed on minimizing recurrence of calcium oxalate or calcium phosphate uroliths, because these types of uroliths cannot be dissolved by medical management.

29. Effective medical protocols to induce dissolution of canine silica jackstones have not yet been developed.

KEY NUTRITIONAL FACTORS—CANINE UROLITHIASIS

Factors	Dietary recommendations
Ammonium urate and other purine uroliths (dissolution and prevention)	
Water	Water intake should be encouraged to achieve urine specific gravity <1.020
Protein	Avoid excess dietary protein
	Restrict dietary protein to 10 to 18% dry matter
Urinary pH	Feed a food that maintains an alkaline urine (urinary pH = 7.1 to 7.7)
Calcium oxalate uroliths (prevention)	
Water	Water intake should be encouraged to achieve urine specific gravity <1.020
Protein	Avoid excess dietary protein
	Restrict dietary protein to 10 to 18% dry matter
Calcium	Avoid excess dietary calcium
	Restrict dietary calcium to 0.3 to 0.6% dry matter
Sodium	Avoid excess dietary sodium
	Restrict dietary sodium to less than 0.3% dry matter
Magnesium	Avoid excess or deficient dietary magnesium (0.04 to 0.15% dry matter)
Oxalate	Avoid foods high in oxalates (See Table 20-21)
Vitamin D	Avoid excess dietary vitamin D
	Restrict dietary vitamin D to 500 to 1,500 IU/kg
	Avoid using supplements that contain vitamin D
Pyridoxine (vitamin B$_6$)	Avoid pyridoxine deficiency
	Feed a food with pyridoxine greater than 1.0 mg/kg dry matter
Ascorbic acid (vitamin C)	Avoid pet foods, supplements or human foods that contain ascorbic acid
Calcium phosphate uroliths (prevention)	
Water	Water intake should be encouraged to achieve urine specific gravity <1.020
Calcium	Avoid excess dietary calcium
	Restrict dietary calcium to 0.3 to 0.6% dry matter
Phosphorus	Avoid excess dietary phosphorus
	Restrict dietary phosphorus to less than 0.6% dry matter
Sodium	Avoid excess dietary sodium
	Restrict dietary sodium to less than 0.3% dry matter
Vitamin D	Avoid excess dietary vitamin D
	Restrict dietary vitamin D to 500 to 1,500 IU/kg
Cystine uroliths (dissolution and prevention)	
Water	Water intake should be encouraged to achieve urine specific gravity <1.020
Protein	Avoid excess dietary protein
	Restrict dietary protein to 10 to 18% dry matter
Urinary pH	Feed a food that maintains an alkaline urine (urinary pH = 7.1 to 7.7)
Struvite uroliths	
Water	Water intake should be encouraged to achieve urine specific gravity <1.020
Protein	Avoid excess dietary protein
	Dissolution: restrict dietary protein to less than 8% dry matter
	Prevention: restrict dietary protein to less than 25% dry matter
Phosphorus	Avoid excess dietary phosphorus
	Dissolution: restrict dietary phosphorus to 0.1% dry matter
	Prevention: restrict dietary phosphorus to less than 0.6% dry matter
Magnesium	Avoid excess dietary magnesium
	Dissolution: restrict dietary magnesium to 0.02% dry matter
	Prevention: restrict dietary magnesium to 0.04 to 0.1% dry matter
Urinary pH	Feed a food that maintains an acid urine
	Dissolution: urinary pH = 5.9 to 6.1
	Prevention: urinary pH = 6.2 to 6.4

Table 20-1. Clinical importance of urolithiasis.

First evidence of an underlying systemic disorder
Hypercalcemia
    Calcium oxalate uroliths
    Calcium phosphate uroliths
Cushing's syndrome
    Calcium oxalate uroliths
    Calcium phosphate uroliths
    Struvite uroliths
Defects in purine metabolism
    Portal vascular anomalies
        Ammonium urate uroliths
    Enzyme defects
        Xanthine uroliths
First evidence of an underlying urinary tract disorder
Renal tubular transport defect
    Cystinuria
        Cystine uroliths
    Renal tubular acidosis
        Calcium oxalate uroliths
        Calcium phosphate uroliths
Defect in local host defenses against urease-producing microbes
    Struvite uroliths
Foreign bodies in urinary tract
    Suture material
        Usually struvite uroliths
    Catheters
        Usually struvite uroliths
Sequelae to urolithiasis
Dysuria, pollakiuria, urge incontinence
Secondary microbial urinary tract infection
Partial or total obstruction to urine outflow
    Bacterial urinary tract infection that may progress
    Impaired renal function and postrenal azotemia
    Rupture of the outflow tract
        Uroperitoneum
        Inflammation of tissues adjacent to various portions of
          the urinary tract
Formation of inflammatory bladder polyps

tion inhibitors and their interactions aids in the diagnosis, treatment and prevention of urolithiasis. (See sidebar "Urolithiasis Terms and Concepts.")

FORMATION OF UROLITHS

Initiation and Growth of Uroliths

Urolith formation is associated with two complementary but separate phases: initiation and growth. It appears that initiating events are not the same for all types of uroliths. In addition, factors that initiate urolith formation may be different from those that allow urolith growth.

The initial step in urolith formation is formation of a crystal nidus (or crystal embryo). This initiation phase of urolith formation, called nucleation, is dependent on supersaturation of urine with calculogenic crystalloids. The degree of urine supersaturation may be influenced by the magnitude of renal excretion of crystalloids, urinary pH and/or crystallization inhibitors or promoters in urine. Noncrystalline proteinaceous matrix substances may also play a role in nucleation in some instances.

Three theories have been proposed to explain initiation of lithogenesis: 1) supersaturation-crystallization theory, 2) matrix-nucleation theory and 3) crystallization-inhibition theory.[2] Each theory emphasizes a single factor. The supersaturation-crystallization theory incriminates exces-

sive supersaturation of urine with urolith-forming crystalloids as the primary event in lithogenesis. In this hypothesis, crystal nucleation is considered to be a physiochemical process involving precipitation of crystalloids from a supersaturated solution. Urolith formation is thought to occur independently of preformed matrix or crystallization inhibitors.

The matrix-nucleation theory incriminates preformed organic matrix (thought to be a mucoprotein with calcium-binding properties) as the primary determinant in lithogenesis. This theory is based on the assumption that preformed organic matrix forms an initial nucleus that subsequently permits urolith formation by precipitation of crystalloids. The role of organic matrix in calculogenesis has not been defined with certainty; however, the similarity of the overall composition of matrix from human uroliths of various mineral composition supports this hypothesis.

The crystallization-inhibition theory proposes that reduction or absence of organic and inorganic inhibitors of crystallization is the primary determinant of calcium oxalate and calcium phosphate lithogenesis. This theory is based on the fact that several lithogenic substances in urine are maintained in solution at concentrations significantly higher than is possible in water (i.e., driving forces for crystal precipitation of normally saturated urine are minimized by crystallization inhibitors). Similarly, inhibitors are important in minimizing crystal growth and aggregation. These three theories are not mutually exclusive. In fact, supersaturation of urine with the crystal's components is a prerequisite for each theory of nucleation.

Further growth of the crystal nidus is dependent on: 1) its ability to remain in the lumen of the excretory pathway of the urinary system, 2) the degree and duration of supersaturation of urine with crystalloids identical or different from those in the nidus and 3) physical characteristics of the crystal nidus. Crystals that are compatible with other crystalloids may align themselves and grow on the surface of other crystals. This is called epitaxial growth. Epitaxy may represent a heterogeneous form of nucleation, and may account for mixed and compound uroliths. For example, in people, the structural similarities of uric acid and calcium oxalate permit urolith growth by epitaxy.[3]

Nucleation

Nucleation refers to the initial event in the formation (or precipitation) of uroliths and is characterized by the appearance of submicroscopic molecular aggregates of crystalloids. Initially, the aggregates are approximately 100 molecules in size and represent potential crystal embryos (or a nidus). Crystals represent an orderly arrangement of atoms in a periodic pattern or lattice. To become a urolith, crystal embryos must have a lattice arrangement that allows continued growth. They must also be large enough to prevent dispersion back into the dissolved phase.[4]

Nucleation has been classified as homogeneous (also called self nucleation or generalized nucleation) or heterogeneous (also called localized nucleation).[5] Homogeneous nucleation occurs spontaneously in highly supersaturated urine in the absence of foreign substances (Figure 20-1). Therefore, the nidus is composed of identical crystalloids. Heterogeneous nucleation is catalyzed by foreign material such as suture material, indwelling catheters, tissue debris, crystal embryos of different composition, etc. (Figure 20-2).

Urolithiasis Terms and Concepts

UROLITHIASIS

The urinary system is designed to dispose of waste products in soluble form. However, some waste products are sparingly soluble and occasionally precipitate out of solution to form crystals. Growth or aggregation of microscopic crystals may lead to formation of macroscopic uroliths. Urolithiasis may be conceptually defined as the formation of uroliths anywhere in the urinary tract from less soluble crystalloids of urine as a result of multiple congenital and/or acquired physiologic and pathologic processes. If such crystalloids become trapped in the urinary system, they may grow to sufficient size to cause clinical signs.

Urolithiasis should not be thought of as a single disease, but rather as a sequela of one or more underlying abnormalities. The fact that urolith formation is often erratic and unpredictable indicates that several interrelated complex physiologic and pathologic factors are involved. Therefore, detection of uroliths is only the beginning of the diagnostic process. Determination of urolith composition narrows etiologic possibilities. Knowledge of the patient's diet, and serum and urine concentrations of calculogenic minerals, crystallization promoters, crystallization inhibitors and their interactions aids in the diagnosis, treatment and prevention of urolithiasis.

UROLITHS

Uroliths are polycrystalline concretions that typically contain more than 90 to 95% organic or inorganic crystalloids, and less than 5 to 10% organic matrices (weight vs. weight ratio). They also may contain a number of minor constituents. A variety of different types of uroliths may occur in dogs (Figure 1). Uroliths are typically composed of organized crystal aggregates with a complex internal structure. Cross sections of uroliths frequently reveal nuclei and laminations, and less frequently radial striations. The urine that bathes uroliths varies in composition (and probably in degree of saturation with calculogenic crystalloids) from day to day and perhaps from hour to hour. This phenomenon is of conceptual importance in understanding the physical characteristics of uroliths.

The incidence and composition of uroliths may be influenced by a variety of factors including: 1) species, 2) breed, 3) gender, 4) age, 5) geography, 6) diet, 7) anatomic abnormalities, 8) physiologic abnormalities, 9) urinary tract infection and 10) urinary pH. Uroliths may be named according to mineral composition, location (i.e., nephroliths, ureteroliths, cystoliths, vesical calculi, urethroliths) or shape (i.e., smooth, faceted, pyramidal, laminated, mulberry, jackstone, staghorn or branched). Characteristic shapes of crystals and uroliths are influenced primarily by the internal structure of crystals and the environment in which they form. Crystals of calcium oxalate monohydrate tend to fuse, producing smoothly rounded or mamillated uroliths. Local factors that influence the size and shape of uroliths include: 1) number of uroliths present, 2) mobility or fixation of uroliths, 3) flow characteristics of urine and 4) anatomic configuration of the structure in which uroliths grow.

MINERAL

A mineral is a naturally occurring, inorganically formed substance that has a characteristic chemical composition and usually has an ordered atomic arrangement that may influence its external geometric form. Minerals commonly found in uroliths often have a chemical name and a crystal (or mineral) name. Even though a particular mineral usually predominates, the mineral composition of many uroliths may be mixed. On occasion, the center of a urolith may be composed of one type of crystalloid (e.g., silica), whereas outer layers are composed of a different crystalloid (especially struvite). Detection, treatment and prevention of the underlying causes of urolithiasis are dependent on knowledge of the composition and structure of all portions of uroliths.

MATRIX

The nondialyzable portion of uroliths that remains after crystalline components have been dissolved with mild solvents is organic matrix. Uroliths consistently contain variable quantities of organic matrix substances in addition to crystalloids. Organic matrix substances identified in human uroliths and experimentally produced in animals include matrix substance A, Tamm-Horsfall glycoprotein, uromucoid, serum albumin and alpha and gamma globulins. Of these, matrix substance A, Tamm-Horsfall glycoprotein and uromucoid appear to be quantitatively more significant than alpha and gamma globulins.

The complex of diverse mucoprotein compounds composing matrix substances may represent the skeleton of uroliths. Although the physical characteristics of uroliths suggest organized relationships between the matrix skeleton and crystalline building blocks, the role of each of these components in formation, retention and growth of uroliths is still poorly understood.

Organic matrix may affect urolith formation by one or more of several mechanisms including: 1) sites of heterogeneous nucleation, 2) templates for organizing and modifying growth of crystals 3) binding agents that cement urolith particles together and promote retention of crystals and 4) protective colloids that prevent further growth of uroliths. Organic matrix may also be composed of passive substances that have no effect on urolith formation or growth.

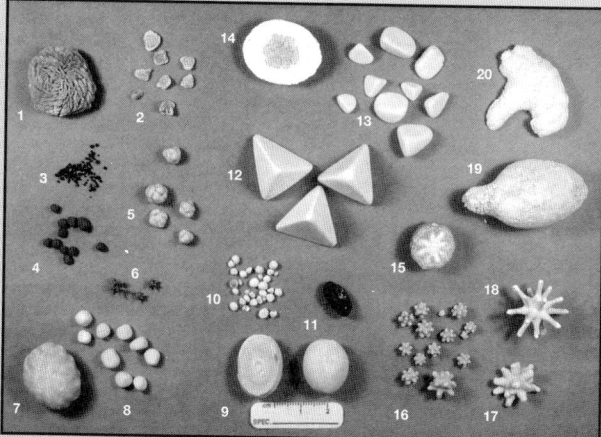

Figure 1. Different mineral types of canine uroliths illustrating common sizes, shapes and surface characteristics. 1) Calcium oxalate dihydrate; 2) Calcium oxalate dihydrate; 3) Calcium oxalate monohydrate; 4) Calcium oxalate monohydrate; 5) Calcium oxalate monohydrate; 6) Calcium oxalate dihydrate; 7) Cystine; 8) Cystine; 9) Ammonium urate (left urolith has been bisected to illustrate laminations); 10) Ammonium urate; 11) Ammonium urate; 12) Struvite; 13) Struvite; 14) Compound urolith with a nidus of calcium oxalate monohydrate surrounded by a shell of struvite and calcium carbonate apatite; 15) Compound urolith with a nidus of silica surrounded by shells containing a mixture of calcium oxalate, silica and ammonium urate; 16) Silica; 17) Silica; 18) Silica; 19) Struvite that has the shape of the urinary bladder and proximal urethra; 20) Struvite that has the shape of the renal pelvis and proximal ureter.

Continued on next page.

Continued from previous page.

NUCLEI AND LAMINATIONS

Examination of cross sections of uroliths often reveals a nucleus and adjacent peripheral laminations. Laminated uroliths may be detected by radiography. Nuclei are focal points (or cores) that differ in appearance from more peripheral portions of the urolith. Nuclei are usually but not invariably located in the center of uroliths. Nuclei may be of crystalline composition or they may be composed of foreign material, tissue debris, blood clots, bacteria, etc. The mineral composition of crystalline nuclei may be identical or different from the remainder of the urolith. Nuclei surrounded by well-defined layers (or lamellae) of solid material suggest an early phase of urolith evolution. Crystalline nuclei large enough to be detected visually, however, are far too large to represent an initial crystalline nidus for crystal nucleation in the physiochemical sense. Centrally located nuclei imply that the urolith was freely accessible to urine from all sides and that growth proceeded at a similar rate on all sides.

Laminated uroliths are common and may represent: 1) alternating bands of different mineral types, 2) periods during which urolith growth occurred without interruption or 3) alternating periods of precipitation of minerals and gel. Although a difference in appearance between two consecutive layers should prompt suspicion of differences in composition, this is not always the case.

MATRIX CONCRETIONS

By definition, a urolith must contain some minerals. However, concretions composed primarily (more than 65%) of matrix may occur. These concretions, commonly called matrix stones, often occur in the urethra of male cats and male sheep, and sometimes occur in dogs and people. They may form a cast of that portion of the excretory pathway in which they are formed (e.g., urethral plugs), implying a rapid rate of formation. In dogs, matrix concretions usually occur secondary to bacterial infections.

COMPOUND UROLITHS

Compound uroliths have one or more layers of mineral composition (e.g., struvite) different from minerals identified in the nucleus (e.g., calcium oxalate).

MIXED UROLITHS

Mixed uroliths contain more than one mineral, neither of which composes at least 70% of the urolith, but without a nucleus or well-defined laminations.

BIBLIOGRAPHY

Bovee KC, ed. Urolithiasis. In: Canine Nephrology. Media, PA: Harwal, 1984; 355-379.

Breslau NA, Pak CYC. Lack of effect of salt intake on urinary uric acid excretion. Journal of Urology 1983; 129: 531-532.

Coe FL, Flavus MJ. Nephrolithiasis. In: Brenner BM, Rector FC Jr, eds. The Kidney, 4th ed. Philadelphia, PA: WB Saunders Co, 1991; 1728-1767.

Griffith DP, Klein AS. Infection-induced urinary stones. In: Roth RA, Finlayson B, eds. Clinical Management of Urolithiasis. International Perspectives in Urology 1983; 6: 210-227.

Kimberling CV, Arnold KS. Diseases of the urinary system in sheep and goats. Veterinary Clinics of North America: Large Animal Practice 1983; 5: 637-655.

Krawiec DR, Osborne CA, Leininger JR, et al. Effect of acetohydroxamic acid on prevention of canine struvite uroliths. American Journal of Veterinary Research 1984; 45: 1276-1282.

Ling GV. Lower Urinary Tract Diseases of Dogs and Cats. St. Louis, MO: Mosby, 1995.

Osborne CA, Clinton CW. Urolithiasis: Terms and concepts. Veterinary Clinics of North America: Small Animal Practice 1986; 16: 3.

Osborne CA, Johnston GR, Polzin DJ, et al. Feline urologic syndrome: A heterogeneous phenomenon? Journal of the American Animal Hospital Association 1984; 20: 17-32.

Osborne CA, Kruger JM. Initiation and growth of uroliths. Veterinary Clinics of North America: Small Animal Practice 1984; 14: 439-454.

Osborne CA, Lulich JP, Kruger JM, et al. Feline urethral plugs: Etiology and pathophysiology. Veterinary Clinics of North America: Small Animal Practice 1996; 26: 233-253.

Osborne CA, Lulich JP, Unger LK, et al. Canine and feline urolithiasis: Relationship of etiopathogenesis to treatment and prevention. In: Osborne CA, Finco DR, eds. Canine and Feline Nephrology and Urology. Baltimore, MD: Williams & Wilkins, 1995; 798-888.

Pak CYC. Disorders of stone formation. In: Brenner BM, Rector FC Jr, eds. The Kidney, vol 2. Philadelphia, PA: WB Saunders Co, 1976.

Robertson WB, Peacock M. Risk factors in the formation of urinary stones. In: Chisholm GD, Williams DI, eds. Scientific Foundations of Urology, 2nd ed. London, UK: William Medical Books, 1982; 267-278.

Wickham JEA. The matrix of renal calculi. In: Williams DI, et al, eds. Scientific Foundations of Urology, vol 1. Chicago, IL: Year Book Medical Publishers Inc, 1976; 323-329.

Urine contains many impurities that might promote heterogeneous nucleation and initiate crystal formation at a concentration of crystalloids below the formation concentration. These substances may be thought of as facilitators or potentiators of crystallization. Any crystal type may be a potential nidus for nucleation of another crystal type. A greater degree of supersaturation (i.e., a higher formation product) is required for homogeneous nucleation than for heterogeneous nucleation. Once nucleation has occurred, however, crystal growth can occur at any degree of supersaturation (even at metastability).

Undersaturated Solutions

An undersaturated solution contains a sufficiently low concentration of a crystalloid to permit dissolution of additional quantities of the crystalloid. Urine is undersaturated when the solute concentration (or activity product) is less than the solubility of the solute in question. Formation of urine that is undersaturated with calculogenic crystalloids may permit varying degrees of urolith dissolution.

Saturated Solutions

Saturated solutions are in equilibrium with undissolved solute at a given temperature. Saturated solutions contain so much dissolved substances that no more can be dissolved at a given temperature. With respect to urine, the saturation concentration is that concentration of a crystalloid that remains unchanged when the urine is mixed with uroliths (or the solid phase) containing that crystalloid. The saturation of salts in urine is influenced by several variables including pH, ionic strength and temperature.

Supersaturated Solutions

A supersaturated solution is more saturated with a substance at a given temperature than would be normally expected. In other words, it is any concentration greater than the saturation concentration. Supersaturated urine contains a greater concentration of a crystalloid (cystine, phosphate, calcium, ammonium, etc.) than the associated solvent (water) would be predicted to be able to normally hold in solution. Supersaturation can vary in degree. Urine is metastable at lower levels of supersaturation. At higher levels of supersaturation, however, urine becomes unstable with regard to its capacity to keep crystallogenic substances in solution (Figure 20-3). Factors that increase the saturation of crystalloids in urine predispose patients to precipitation of crystals and thus urolith formation. Spontaneous precipitation will occur if the concentration of the crystalloid is greater than its formation product.

Metastable Region

The metastable region refers to the degree of supersaturation of a crystalloid that lies between the solubility product and the formation product. Metastability applies to those liquids (e.g., urine) that have the capacity to retain more of a compound in solution than would be predicted by knowledge of its true solubility in water. The term "metastable" is appropriate because it implies a condition subject to change. A metastable solution is thermodynamically unstable, but does not contain enough energy to initiate crystal formation. However, crystals already present may grow. The region of metastability varies with the type of calculogenic crystalloid. For example, in people, it has been estimated that the difference between the solubility product and the formation product of calcium oxalate in urine is a multiple of about 8.5 to 10.0.[6]

Oversaturated Solutions

An oversaturated solution is one in which the degree of supersaturation of a crystalloid is greater than the formation product (Figure 20-3). Recall that supersaturated urine exceeds the solubility product, but does not exceed the formation product. Oversaturated urine is no longer metastable. Nucleation will take place in the absence of heterogeneous factors. Crystals observed by microscopic examination of urine sediment are thought to be caused by oversaturation of urine.

Inhibitors and Promoters of Crystal Formation

Urine is a complex solution containing a variety of substances that can inhibit or promote crystal formation and growth. Inhibitors include molecules that reduce calcium oxalate and calcium phosphate supersaturation. Some inhibitors (e.g., citrate, magnesium, pyrophosphate) form soluble salts with calcium, oxalic acid or phosphoric acid, thereby reducing the quantity of these metabolites available for precipitation. Other inhibitors (e.g., nephrocalcin, uropontin, glycosaminoglycans, Tamm-Horsfall glycoprotein, other inert ions) interfere with the ability of calcium and oxalic acid to combine, thereby minimizing crystal formation and growth. Also, glycosaminoglycans act as protectors by preventing crystals from adhering to the urinary tract mucosa.

Clinical Concepts of Urine Supersaturation

Salts (crystals) are neutral compounds derived from the reversible interaction of a cation (e.g., calcium) and an

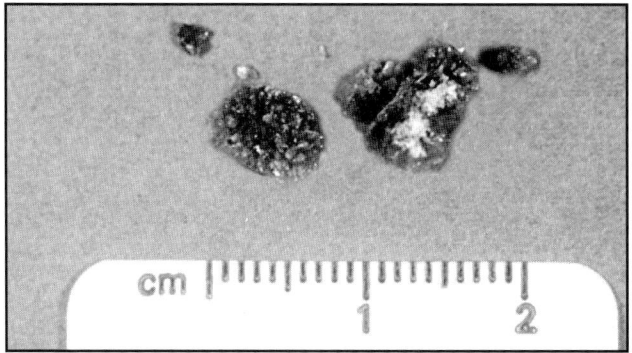

Figure 20-1. Layered urocystolith composed of 100% calcium oxalate dihydrate removed from an adult male miniature schnauzer. The difference in color of the center of the urolith vs. the outer layer is due to the large quantity of blood in the matrix of the outer layer.

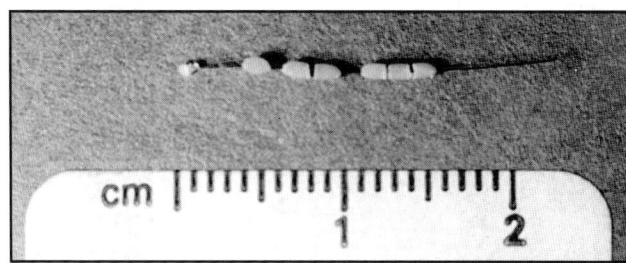

Figure 20-2. Struvite uroliths that have formed on a hairshaft.

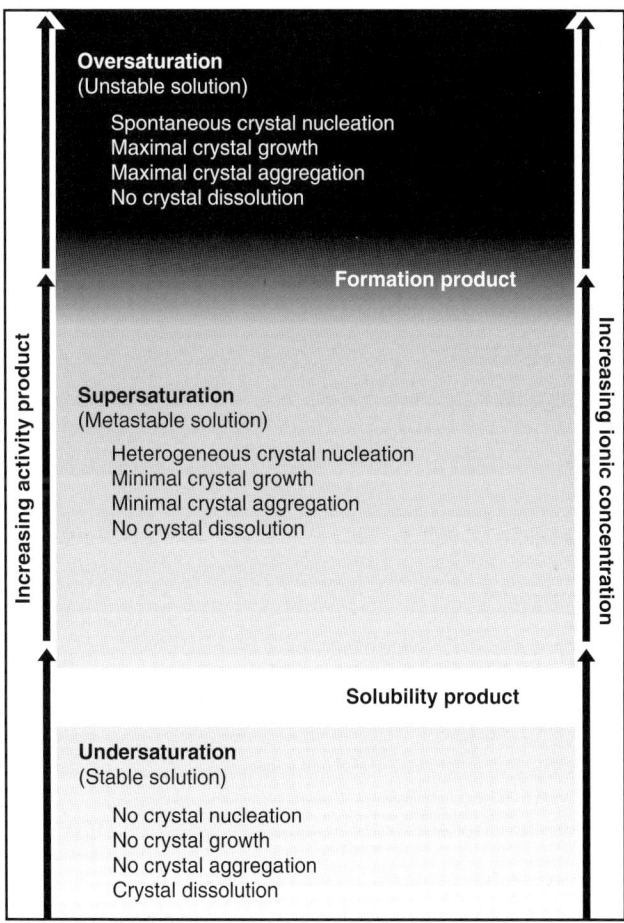

Figure 20-3. Probable events in formation of crystals in urine. A variety of factors influence the solubility of minerals in urine including concentration of lithogenic and nonlithogenic minerals, the concentration of crystallization inhibitors and crystallization promoters, urine temperature, urinary pH and urine ionic strength.

anion (e.g., oxalic acid). The ability of a salt to dissolve in solution is dependent on the concentration of its ions in solution, and its interaction with other ions and neutral molecules in the same solution. For example, the state of urine saturation for any specific crystal system is the product of urine solute concentration, pH, ionic strength, temperature and preformed chemical complexes.

To illustrate these principles, consider the example of pure water as a solution and calcium oxalate as a salt. Small amounts of calcium oxalate added to water dissolve completely because water is undersaturated with calcium and oxalic acid ions. As more calcium oxalate is added, the water's capacity to dissolve additional calcium oxalate is decreased until the solution becomes saturated. In this context, saturation of the solution with calcium and oxalic acid ions occurs when no additional calcium oxalate can be dissolved at a given pH and temperature of the solution. If additional calcium oxalate is added, it will appear as a solid.

As in water, calcium oxalate can also be dissolved in undersaturated urine. However, unlike water, urine is a complex solution containing a unique combination of ionic and nonionic molecules that may increase the solubility of calcium oxalate. Therefore, calcium oxalate added beyond the point of saturation will remain in solution. Thus, the solution becomes supersaturated with calcium and oxalic acid ions. Supersaturation is conceptually significant because the solution contains enough energy to form solids from dissolved ions (i.e., it is thermodynamically unstable). When supersaturated, the solution must "struggle" to maintain the homogeneous nature between the ions it contains. One method by which the solution returns to thermodynamic stability is by concentrating excess calcium and oxalic acid ions as solids or crystals on pre-existing surfaces or templates (e.g., other crystals or foreign material). This phenomenon is called heterogeneous nucleation. However, if the solution becomes oversaturated by addition of more calcium and oxalic acid ions, calcium oxalate crystals will form without an existing template (so-called homogeneous nucleation). After crystals have formed, available thermodynamic energy favors crystal growth whereby free ions become incorporated into the crystals. Crystal growth continues until ions in solution become depleted, allowing the solution to return to thermodynamic stability (or saturation). Crystals retained in the urinary tract may grow (the second phase of urolith formation).

Urine is a complex solution containing "inert" ions (i.e., sulfate, sodium, potassium, magnesium) unlikely to chemically bond with calcium and oxalic acid. In this way, they increase calcium oxalate solubility. The negative ions (e.g., sulfate) surround positive calcium ions, and the positive ions (e.g., sodium, potassium, magnesium) surround negative oxalic acid ions. The net effect is a decrease in attraction between calcium and oxalic acid ions. Because calcium and oxalic acid ion interaction is required for crystal formation, the solubility of calcium oxalate increases as the concentration of "inert" ions increases.

Supersaturation of urine with certain lithogenic ions is also dependent on another group of substances called "crystallization inhibitors." These include citric acid and pyrophosphates, which chelate calcium but remain dissolved in solution. Likewise, certain mucoproteins, gly-cosaminoglycans, glycoproteins (e.g., nephrocalcin) and other poorly identified substances may interact with calcium. The result is a decrease in the amount of calcium available to bind with oxalic acid (and phosphoric acid). It is of interest that these inhibitors have been found to be deficient or abnormal in some calcium oxalate urolith-forming patients.

Activity Product

The product of the chemical activities of two ionic materials is called the activity product. It is a mathematical expression used to estimate the degrees of saturation (i.e., undersaturation, supersaturation or oversaturation) of a dog's urine with calculogenic minerals (Figure 20-3). In addition to concentration of minerals, it encompasses other variables including urinary pH and ionic strength of the solution.[7] Activity product encompasses solubility product and formation product. Activity products are calculated by measuring total concentrations of major ionizable solutes in urine. For efficiency, computer programs are commonly used to aid calculation of ion concentrations and activity products.[8]

Solubility Product

The solubility product is a type of activity product reflecting the urine's ability to dissolve a known concentration of calculogenic ions at variable but known pH and temperature. It is constant for each mineral component at a given temperature and pH. Therefore, urine is saturated when the solubility product value is reached. Below this value, urine is undersaturated with calculogenic ions; above this value urine is supersaturated. When devising medical protocols to dissolve or prevent urolith formation, the goal is to achieve an activity product less than the solubility product (or a state of undersaturation) (Figure 20-3).

Formation Product

The formation product is a type of activity product reflecting the concentration of ions at which precipitation of solute (homogeneous nucleation and eventually crystal formation) occurs at a given pH and temperature. It is the upper limit of metastability. Urinary pH may affect the ionization of some urine constituents and thus their solubility. If urinary pH varies during the day, urine may be intermittently supersaturated or oversaturated. Ion activities above the formation product are associated with an unstable state of oversaturation resulting in spontaneous crystal formation and rapid crystal growth. Because this condition may be influenced by the product of several factors (including the time of incubation, a crystallizable matrix and inhibitors of nucleation) in addition to the concentration of calculogenic crystalloids, it is commonly called the formation product. In people, the formation product for calcium oxalate is approximately 8.5 to 10 times greater than its solubility product.[6] This indicates that urine, because of the addition of a variety of crystallization inhibitors, must be saturated at least eight times above the solubility product before crystals will form. In general, urine of urolith formers is more supersaturated with respect to the constituents of their uroliths than is the urine of normal subjects.

ASSESS THE ANIMAL
History and Physical Examination

The history of dogs with urolithiasis is dependent on: 1) anatomic location(s) of uroliths, 2) duration of uroliths in specific location(s), 3) physical characteristics of uroliths (size, shape, number), 4) secondary urinary tract infection (UTI) and virulence of infecting organism(s) and 5) presence of concomitant diseases in the urinary tract and other body systems. After a diagnosis of urolithiasis has been confirmed, the history and physical examination should focus on detection of any underlying illness that may predispose the dog to urolith formation.

A dietary history should also be obtained for all patients with urolithiasis, with the objective of identifying risk factors that predispose the patient to specific mineral types. Likewise, owners should be questioned about vitamin-mineral supplements, previous illnesses and medications that may predispose the patient to various types of uroliths.

Signs typical of lower urinary tract disease include dysuria, pollakiuria, hematuria, urge incontinence, paradoxical incontinence and voiding small uroliths during micturition. Signs of uremia may occur if urine flow has been obstructed for a sufficient period, or if there is extravasation of urine into the peritoneal cavity due to rupture of the excretory pathways.

Signs of upper tract disease include painless hematuria, polyuria if sufficient nephrons have impaired function and abdominal pain if there is overdistention of the renal pelvis with urine due to outflow obstruction (Table 20-2). Many patients with uroliths have no clinical signs. Absence of signs is especially common in patients with nephroliths.

If gross hematuria is present, determining when during the process of micturition it is most severe may be of value in localizing its source. If hematuria occurs throughout micturition, lesions (including uroliths) may be present in the kidneys, ureters, urinary bladder, prostate gland and/or urethra. If hematuria occurs primarily at the end of micturition, lesions of the ventral bladder wall or intermittent renal hematuria should be suspected. If hematuria occurs at the beginning or is independent of micturition, lesions in the urethra or genital tract should be suspected.

Digital palpation of the entire urethra, including evaluation by rectal examination, may reveal urethroliths or uroliths lodged in the bladder neck. A firm, nonyielding mass may be palpated in the urinary bladder if a solitary urolith is present; a grating sensation confined to the bladder may be detected if multiple uroliths are present. It may be impossible to palpate small or solitary urocystoliths if the bladder wall is contracted and/or thickened due to inflammation. Likewise, it may be impossible to palpate uroliths in a distended or overdistended bladder. In this situation, the bladder should be repalpated after urine has been eliminated by voiding, manual compression of the bladder, cystocentesis or catheterization. One should suspect urethral uroliths when urethral catheters cannot be advanced into the bladder. However, inability to advance a catheter through the urethra may also be associated with urethral strictures or space occupying lesions that partially or totally occlude the urethral lumen.

In the absence of infection or outflow obstruction, abnormalities are usually not associated with renoliths

Table 20-2. Clinical signs of uroliths that may be associated with urinary system dysfunction.

Urethroliths
Asymptomatic
Dysuria, pollakiuria and urge incontinence
Gross hematuria
Palpable urethral uroliths
Spontaneous voiding of small uroliths
Partial or complete urine outflow obstruction
    Overflow incontinence
    Anuria
    Palpation of an overdistended and painful urinary bladder
    Urinary bladder rupture, abdominal distention and
        abdominal pain
    Signs of postrenal azotemia (anorexia, depression, vomiting
        and diarrhea)
Signs associated with concurrent urocystoliths, ureteroliths
    and/or renoliths

Urocystoliths
Asymptomatic
Dysuria, pollakiuria and urge incontinence
Gross hematuria
Palpable bladder uroliths
Palpably thickened urinary bladder wall
Partial or complete urine outflow obstruction of bladder neck
    (See Urethroliths.)
Other signs associated with concurrent urethroliths, ureteroliths
    and/or renoliths

Ureteroliths
Asymptomatic
Gross hematuria
Constant abdominal pain
Unilateral or bilateral urine outflow obstruction
    Palpably enlarged kidney(s)
    Signs of postrenal azotemia (See Urethroliths.)
May have other signs associated with concurrent urethroliths,
    urocystoliths and/or renoliths

Renoliths
Asymptomatic
Gross hematuria
Constant abdominal pain
Signs of systemic illness if generalized renal infection is present
    (anorexia, depression, fever and polyuria)
Palpably enlarged kidney(s)
Signs of postrenal azotemia (See Urethroliths.)
Other signs associated with concurrent urethroliths, urocystoliths
    and/or ureteroliths

unless bilateral renoliths are associated with sufficient renal damage to cause uremia. If infection or obstruction is present, there may be pain in the area of the kidneys and/or palpable enlargement of the affected kidney(s). Concomitant bacterial pyelonephritis may be associated with polysystemic signs due to sepsis.

Diagnostic Studies

Urinalysis

Results of urinalysis are usually characterized by abnormalities typical of inflammation (pyuria, proteinuria, hematuria and increased numbers of epithelial cells), which may or may not be associated with infection. Whereas urease-producing microbes (staphylococci, *Proteus* spp, ureaplasmas) may cause infection-induced struvite uroliths to form, opportunistic bacteria that are not calculogenic (e.g., *Escherichia coli* and streptococci) may colonize the urinary tract as a result of urolith-induced alterations in local host defenses. The authors advocate quantitative urine culture of all patients with uroliths because knowledge of bacterial type is important in predicting the mineral composition of uroliths, and in selecting an appropriate antimicrobial agent for treatment.

The pH of urine obtained from patients with uroliths is variable; however, it may become persistently alkaline if secondary infection with urease-producing bacteria occurs. The significance of a single urinary pH measurement should be interpreted with appropriate caution because there are significant fluctuations throughout the day, especially with respect to the time(s), amount and types of food consumption. In general, magnesium ammonium phosphate and calcium phosphate uroliths are associated with alkaline urine, whereas ammonium urate, sodium urate, uric acid, calcium oxalate, cystine and silica uroliths are associated with acidic urine.

The advent of effective medical protocols to dissolve and prevent uroliths in dogs and cats has resulted in renewed interest in detection and interpretation of crystalluria. Evaluation of urine crystals may aid in: 1) detection of disorders predisposing animals to urolith formation, 2) estimation of the mineral composition of uroliths and 3) evaluation of the effectiveness of medical protocols initiated to dissolve or prevent uroliths.

Crystals form only in urine that is or recently has been supersaturated with crystallogenic substances. Therefore, crystalluria represents a risk factor for urolithiasis. However, detection of urine crystals is not synonymous with urolithiasis and clinical signs associated with uroliths. Nor are urine crystals irrefutable evidence of a urolith-forming tendency. For example, crystalluria that occurs in individuals with anatomically and functionally normal urinary tracts is usually harmless because the crystals are eliminated before they aggregate or grow to sufficient size to interfere with normal urinary function. In addition, crystals that form after elimination or removal of urine from the patient often are of no clinical importance. Identification of crystals that have formed in vitro does not justify therapy.

On the other hand, detection of some types of crystals (e.g., cystine and ammonium urate) in clinically asymptomatic patients, frequent detection of large aggregates of crystals (e.g., calcium oxalate or magnesium ammonium phosphate) in apparently normal individuals or detection of any form of crystals in fresh urine collected from patients with confirmed urolithiasis may be of diagnostic, prognostic and therapeutic importance. Large crystals and aggregates of crystals are more likely to be retained in the urinary tract, and therefore may be of greater clinical significance than small or single crystals.

Although there is not a direct relationship between crystalluria and urolithiasis, detection of crystals in urine is proof that the urine sample is oversaturated with crystallogenic substances. However, oversaturation may occur as a result of in vitro events in addition to or instead of in vivo events. Therefore, care must be used not to overinterpret the significance of crystalluria. In vivo variables that influence crystalluria include: 1) the concentration of crystallogenic substances in urine (which in turn is influenced by their rate of excretion and the volume of water in which they are excreted), 2) urinary pH (Table 20-3), 3) the solubility of crystallogenic substances and 4) excretion of diagnostic agents (e.g., radiopaque contrast media) and medications (e.g., sulfonamides).

In vitro variables that influence crystalluria include: 1) temperature, 2) evaporation, 3) urinary pH and 4) the technique of specimen preparation (e.g., centrifugation vs. noncentrifugation and volume of urine examined) and preservation. As mentioned above, in vitro changes that occur after urine collection may enhance formation or dissolution of crystals. Although in vitro changes may be used to enhance detection of certain types of crystals (e.g., acidification to cause precipitation of cystine), in vitro crystal formation may have no clinical relevance to in vivo formation of crystals in urine. When knowledge of in vivo urine crystal type is especially

Table 20-3. Common characteristics of selected urine crystals.

Crystal types	Appearances	Urinary pH at which crystals commonly form		
		Acidic	Neutral	Alkaline
Ammonium urate	Yellow-brown spherulites, thorn apples	+	+	+
Amorphous urates	Amorphous or spheroidal yellow-brown structures	+	±	-
Bilirubin	Reddish-brown needles or granules	+	-	-
Calcium carbonate	Large yellow-brown spheroids with radial striations, or small crystals with spheroidal or dumbbell shapes	-	±	+
Calcium oxalate dihydrate	Small colorless envelopes (octahedral form)	+	+	±
Calcium oxalate monohydrate	Small spindles "hemp seed" or dumbbells	+	+	±
Calcium phosphate	Amorphous or long thin prisms	±	+	+
Cholesterol	Flat colorless plates with corner notch	+	+	-
Cystine	Flat colorless hexagonal plates	+	+	±
Hippuric acid	Four- to six-sided colorless elongated plates or prisms with rounded corners	+	+	±
Leucine	Yellow-brown spheroids with radial and concentric laminations	+	+	-
Magnesium ammonium phosphate	Three- to six-sided colorless prisms	±	+	+
Sodium urate	Colorless or yellow-brown needles or slender prisms, sometimes in clusters or sheaves	+	±	-
Sulfa metabolites	Sheaves of needles with central or eccentric binding, sometimes fan-shaped clusters	+	±	-
Tyrosine	Fine colorless or yellow needles arranged in sheaves or rosettes	+	-	-
Uric acid	Diamond or rhombic rosettes, or oval plates, structures with pointed ends, occasionally six-sided plates	+	-	-
Xanthine	Yellow-brown amorphous, spheroidal or ovoid structures	+	±	-

Key: + = crystals commonly occur at this pH, ± = crystals may occur at this pH, but are more common at the other pH, - = crystals are uncommon at this pH.

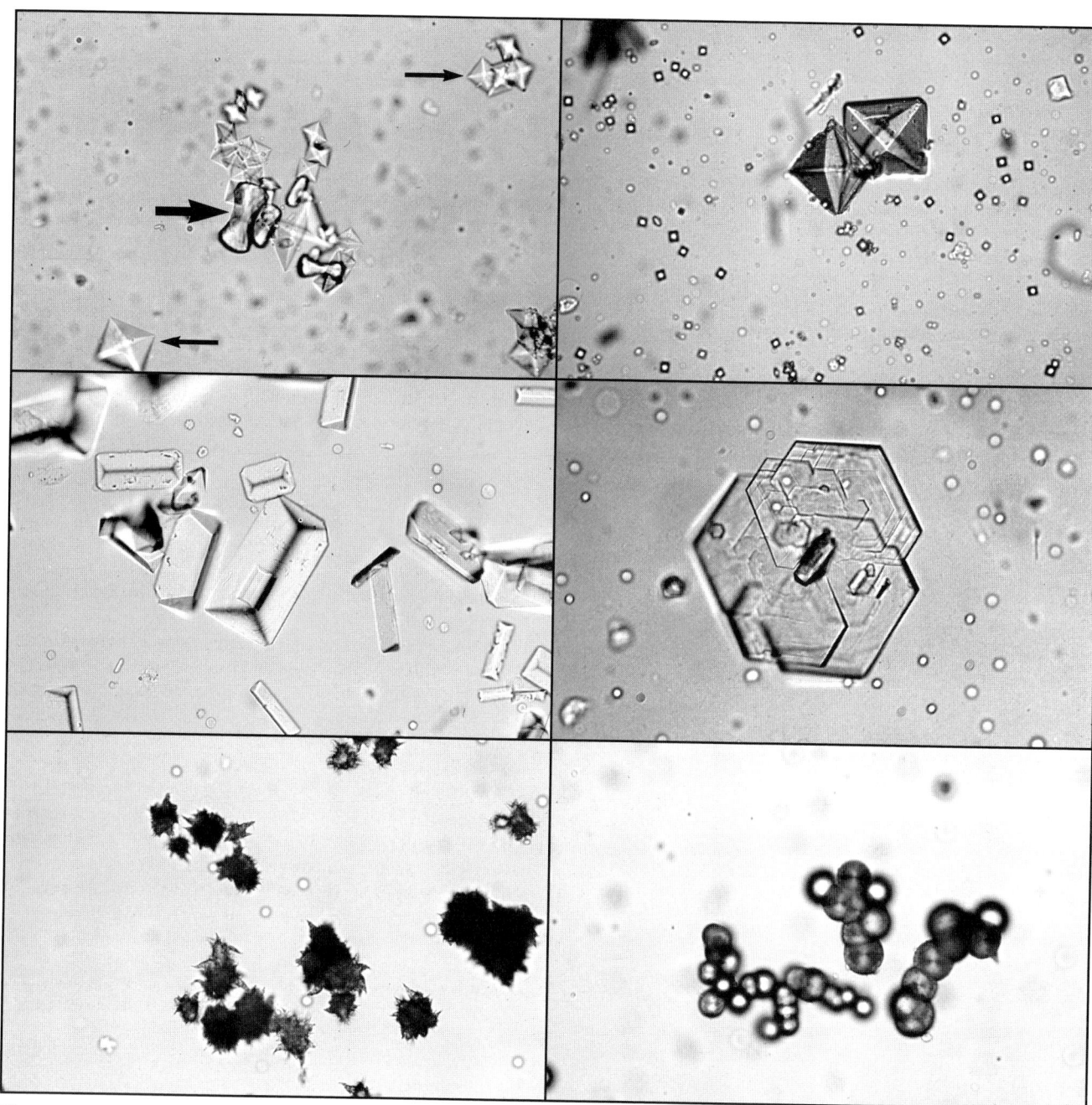

Figure 20-4. Photomicrographs of common crystals found in urine sediment. Calcium oxalate monohydrate (dumbbell form, large arrow) and calcium oxalate dihydrate (octahedral form, small arrows) (Top, Left). Calcium oxalate dihydrate; octahedral form (Top, Right). Magnesium ammonium phosphate (struvite); prisms (Middle, Left). Cystine; flat, colorless hexagonal plates (Middle, Right). Ammonium urate; thorn apple form (Bottom, Left). Amorphous xanthine; spheroids (Bottom, Right).

important, fresh, warm specimens should be serially examined. The number, size and structure of crystals should be evaluated, as well as their tendency to aggregate.

Urinary pH influences the formation and persistence of several types of crystals. Therefore, it is often useful to consider pH when interpreting crystalluria (Table 20-3). Different crystals tend to form and persist in certain urinary pH ranges, although there are exceptions. Exceptions may be related to large concentrations of crystallogenic substances in urine or recent in vivo or in vitro changes in urinary pH.

Refrigeration is an excellent method to preserve many physical, chemical and morphologic properties of urine sediment. However, refrigeration must be used with caution when evalu-

ating crystalluria from qualitative and quantitative standpoints. Although refrigeration of urine samples is likely to enhance formation of various types of crystals, this phenomenon may have no relationship to events occurring in the patient's body.

Crystalluria may also be influenced by diet, including water intake. Dietary influence on crystalluria is of diagnostic importance because urine crystal formation that occurs while patients are consuming hospital foods may be dissimilar to urine crystal formation that occurs when patients are consuming foods fed at home.

Microscopic evaluation of urine crystals should not be used as the sole criterion to predict the mineral composition of macroliths in patients with confirmed urolithiasis

Table 20-4. Advantages and disadvantages of survey radiography, double-contrast radiography and ultrasonography in assessing uroliths.

Parameters	Survey radiography	Double-contrast radiography	Ultrasonography
Assessment of urethroliths	Yes, if radiodense	Indirectly*	Poor
Assessment of radiolucent urocystoliths	Unreliable	Yes	Yes
Distinguishing blood clots from urocystoliths	No	Probably	Yes
Assessment of laminated urocystoliths	Best of the three methods	Probably	No
Assessment of other bladder disorders	Unreliable	Yes	Sometimes
Assessment of urocystolith number	Yes (>3 mm)	Yes (>1 mm)	Equipment and observer dependent
Assessment of urocystolith size	Yes (>3 mm)	Yes (>1 mm)	Equipment and observer dependent
Assessment of urocystolith density	Yes (>3 mm)	No	No
Assessment of urocystolith shape	Yes (>3 mm)	Yes (>1 mm)	No
Immediate postsurgical assessment for uroliths	Yes	Not recommended**	No (air artefacts)
Risk of air artefact in bladder	No	Yes	No
Risk of iatrogenic bacterial urinary tract infection	No	Yes	No
Exposure to ionizing radiation	Yes	Yes	No
Necessary to remove hair	No	No	Often
Authors' overall choice	**Screening**	**Investigation**	**Third choice**

*During transurethral catheterization.
**Due to risk of iatrogenic bacterial urinary tract infection.

Table 20-5. Comparison of relative densities of common uroliths detected by survey radiography.*

Mineral types	Relative atomic number**
Water	**7.7**
Urate	6.9-7.7
Struvite	9.81
Cystine	10
Silica	11.6
Calcium oxalate dihydrate	13
Calcium oxalate monohydrate	13.6
Cortical bone	**15**
Calcium phosphate	15.9

*Adapted from Feeney DA, Weichselbaum RC, Jessen CR, et al. Imaging canine urocystoliths: Detection and prediction of mineral content. Veterinary Clinics of North America: Small Animal Practice 1999; 29: 59-72.
**Effective atomic numbers (Zeff), which is the sum of different elements in the urocystolith and is related to its mass.

(Table 20-3 and Figure 20-4). Only quantitative analysis can provide definitive information about the mineral composition of the entire urolith. However, interpretation of crystalluria in light of other clinical findings often allows the clinician to tentatively identify the mineral composition of uroliths, especially their outermost layers. Subsequent reduction or elimination of crystals by therapy provides a useful index of the efficacy of medical protocols designed to dissolve or prevent uroliths.

Radiography and Ultrasonography

The primary objective of radiographic or ultrasonographic evaluation of patients suspected of having uroliths is to determine the site(s), number, density and shape of uroliths. However, the size and number of uroliths are not a reliable index of the probable efficacy of therapy. After urolithiasis has been confirmed, radiographic or ultrasonographic evaluation also aids in detection of predisposing abnormalities (Table 20-4).

The size, number, location and mineral composition of uroliths influence their radiographic and ultrasonographic appearance. Most uroliths greater than 3 mm in diameter have varying degrees of radiodensity, and therefore can be detected by survey abdominal radiography or ultra-

sonography.[9] Very small uroliths (less than 3 mm in diameter) may not be visualized by survey radiography or ultrasonography. Uroliths greater than 1 mm in diameter can usually be detected by double-contrast cystography, provided excessive contrast medium is not used.[10] Table 20-5 lists relative densities of common uroliths based on survey radiography.[10] Because of significant variation, the radiodensity of uroliths is not by itself a reliable index of mineral composition.

Uroliths greater than 3 mm in diameter are not commonly radiolucent. An exception to this generality is uroliths composed of 100% ammonium or sodium urate or uric acid. However, in the authors' experience many ammonium urate uroliths of dogs are marginally radiodense. This finding may be related to a variable quantity of phosphates and other minerals in urate uroliths of dogs.

Matrix uroliths may be radiolucent or have some radiodensity. Blood clots are radiolucent and may be mistaken for radiolucent uroliths. Radiolucent uroliths may be readily distinguished from blood clots when evaluated by two-dimensional, gray-scale ultrasonography. Uroliths are usually in the dependent portion of the bladder lumen, produce sharply marginated shadows containing few echoes and are associated with acoustic shadowing. Blood clots may be located anywhere in the bladder lumen, typically have an irregular outline and indistinct margins and are not associated with acoustic shadowing.

Uroliths that are radiodense on survey radiographs may appear to be radiolucent when evaluated by positive-contrast radiography. This finding is related to the fact that many uroliths are more radiodense than body tissue, but less radiodense than the contrast material. A diagnosis of radiolucent uroliths should be based on their radiodensity compared with soft tissues, and not their radiodensity compared with positive-contrast medium.

A urolith may be larger than that depicted by its radiodensity if only a portion of it contains radiodense minerals. This phenomenon is most likely to occur with rapidly growing struvite uroliths that contain large quantities of matrix.

Hematology and Serum Chemistry

Hemograms of dogs with uroliths are usually normal unless there is concomitant generalized infection of the kidneys or prostate gland associated with leukocytosis. Microcytosis, anemia, target cells and leukocytosis have occasionally been associated with portal vascular anomalies in dogs with and without urate uroliths.[11-14]

Serum chemistry values are usually normal in patients with infection-induced magnesium ammonium phosphate, cystine and silica uroliths unless obstruction of urine outflow or generalized renal infection leads to changes characteristic of renal failure. Although most patients with calcium oxalate and calcium phosphate uroliths are normocalcemic, some are hypercalcemic.

Calcium phosphate and sterile struvite uroliths may be associated with distal renal tubular acidosis (RTA) characterized by hyperchloremic (normal anion gap) metabolic acidosis, urinary pH values consistently greater than approximately 6 and hypokalemia.

A variety of biochemical alterations may exist in patients with urate urolithiasis. The following changes may be observed in patients with urate uroliths due to congenital or acquired hepatic disorders:[14-16] 1) decreased urea nitrogen concentrations, 2) decreased total protein and albumin concentrations, 3) abnormal bile acid concentrations, 4) increased concentrations of total bilirubin and fasting blood ammonia and 5) increased serum alanine aminotransferase and serum alkaline phosphatase enzyme activities. Dogs with portal vascular anomalies typically have reduced hepatic functional mass and altered portal blood flow evidenced by abnormally elevated bile acid concentrations, prolonged sulfobromophthalein (BSP) retention times and abnormal ammonia tolerance tests.[13-17]

Urine Chemistry

Detection of the underlying causes of specific types of urolithiasis is often linked to evaluation of the biochemical composition of urine. For best results, at least one and preferably two consecutive 24-hour urine samples should be collected because determination of fractional excretion of many metabolites in "spot" urine samples does not accurately reflect 24-hour metabolite excretion (Table 20-6).

Water consumption and hydration status must be considered when interpreting laboratory results. Decreased water consumption and dehydration are associated with several alterations, including decreased renal clearance of metabolites and increased urine specific gravity and urine solute concentrations.[18] Caution must be used in interpreting 24-hour excretion of solutes in the diagnosis and therapy of urolithiasis if hospitalized animals consume less water than in the home environment.

Urine concentrations of potentially lithogenic metabolites are also influenced by the amount and composition of food consumed, and whether urine was collected during conditions of fasting or food consumption.[19,20] Aldosterone secretion increases following food deprivation. Increased aldosterone secretion promotes renal tubular sodium reabsorption and potassium excretion. As a consequence, plasma potassium concentration decreases, urinary potassium excretion increases and urinary sodium and chloride excretion decrease.[20] Urinary calcium, magnesium and uric acid excretions are reduced during fasting. However, urinary excretion of phosphorus, oxalate and citrate are apparently unaffected by fasting.[20] In dogs, urinary ammonia, titratable acid and hydrogen ion excretion decrease and urinary pH values increase when food is withheld.[20,21] Therefore, values for 24-hour urinary solute excretion may differ when measured following food consumption vs. values obtained when food is withheld.

Consumption of food stimulates gastric secretion of hydrochloric acid. As a result, concentrations of chloride decrease and bicarbonate increase in venous blood draining the stomach. Total serum concentration of carbon dioxide increases. The resulting metabolic alkalosis is commonly called the postprandial alkaline tide. Urinary pH will increase unless acidifying substances are contained in the food. In a study of healthy beagles, eating was associated with increased urinary excretion of hydrogen ions, ammonia, sodium, potassium, calcium, magnesium and uric acid.[20]

Laboratory results may be markedly affected by changes in foods fed in a home environment vs. different foods fed in a hospital environment. For example, urinary excretion of potentially calculogenic metabolites while animals consume foods fed in the hospital may be different from those excreted by animals eating at home. To determine the influence of home-fed foods on laboratory test results, consider asking clients to bring home-fed foods for use during periods of diagnostic hospitalization.[22]

Urolith Analysis

Small uroliths in the urinary bladder or urethra are commonly voided during micturition by female dogs and occasionally by male dogs. Uroliths with a smooth surface (e.g., those composed of ammonium urate or calcium oxalate monohydrate) are more likely to pass through the urethra than uroliths with a rough surface (e.g., those composed of calcium oxalate dihydrate or silica). Commercially manufactured tropical fish nets designed for household aquariums facilitate retrieval of uroliths during voiding.[23] They are much less expensive than collection cups with wire mesh bottoms designed for people and available from medical supply houses. Urocystoliths may also be obtained by voiding urohydropropulsion (Figure 20-5). If a urolith can be detected by the unaided eye, it will usually be sufficient size for quantitative analysis.

CATHETER-ASSISTED RETRIEVAL OF UROCYSTOLITHS

Small urocystoliths may be retrieved for analysis by aspirating them through a urethral catheter into a syringe.[23,24] Urocystoliths detected by survey radiography may be too large to be removed with the aid of a urethral catheter. However, large urocystoliths are often associated with small ones that may be detected by double-contrast cystography. The diameter of uroliths retrieved is limited by the size of openings or "eyes" in the proximal portion of the catheter and by the diameter of the catheter lumen. Therefore, it is best to select the largest-diameter catheter that can be advanced into the bladder lumen without causing trauma to the urethral mucosa. Well-lubricated, soft, flexible catheters are preferable to less flexible ones. The size of openings in the proximal portion of the catheter may be enlarged with a scalpel, razor blade or scissors to facilitate retrieval of urocystoliths. However, care must be used not to weaken the catheter to the point where it

Table 20-6. Protocol for measuring 24-hour urinary excretion of various substances associated with urolithiasis.

Technique
1. To allow for food acclimation, feed the patient either the food it was consuming just before urolith formation or a standard food at home for 10 to 14 days. The authors commonly use Prescription Diet Canine k/d* as the standard food.
2. If possible, house and feed the dog in the urine collection cage for at least one day before urine collection. As dogs become acclimated to their new environment, they are more likely to consume quantities of food and water similar to that consumed in their home environment.
3. Begin each 24-hour urine collection period by removing urine from the urinary bladder by transurethral catheterization. This urine is discarded. Record the actual time that urine collection is initiated.
4. Weigh the dog.
5. Then feed the dog its food as if at home. Water should be continuously available for consumption.
6. Begin administering a broad-spectrum antibiotic that achieves high concentrations in urine to prevent catheter-induced urinary tract infection. The dosage, dosing interval and route of administration should be based on manufacturer recommendations.
7. Keep the patient in a collection cage during urine collection. When using metabolism cages designed for urine collection, catheterization of the urinary tract is unnecessary except at the end of the 24 hours. House-trained dogs may not voluntarily void in their cage. Bladder catheterization may be necessary to obtain urine from these dogs. Dogs may be catheterized as often as necessary to keep them comfortable (usually every six to eight hours).
8. Catheterize the urinary bladder at the end of 24 hours to remove all urine. Save this urine.
9. Record the exact time of collection termination.
10. Pool all urine collected during the 24-hour period in a single container and measure its volume.
11. Thoroughly mix the pooled urine before removing aliquots for analysis.

Preservation
1. Preservatives have different roles, but are often used to minimize bacterial growth, reduce chemical decomposition, solubilize constituents that might otherwise precipitate out of solution or decrease atmospheric oxidation of unstable compounds.
2. The method of preservation may vary depending on the substances being measured and the tests used to measure them. Consult the laboratory to determine the recommended method of preservation.
3. Preservatives should not be added to some specimens because of possible interference with analytical methods.
4. Refrigeration is a common method for preserving urine collected for analysis. Urine removed by intermittent catheterization can be stored in a refrigerator in clean containers with screw top lids. Containers used for continuous collection beneath metabolism cages can be surrounded by ice packs and then insulated. Refrigeration causes some minerals to precipitate out of solution.
5. Specimens can be acidified (add 10 ml of 1 N hydrochloric acid per liter to achieve a pH of 3 or less) to preserve oxalate and calcium for analysis. However, acidified urine is unsuitable for measuring uric acid because it precipitates in acidic solutions.

Storage of selected analytes in urine
1. No single preservative is ideal if multiple substances in urine are to be analyzed. To minimize degradation, the authors routinely collect urine under conditions of refrigeration. Immediately following urine collection, preservatives are added to appropriate aliquots of urine for storage until analysis.
2. Uric acid and xanthine: Aliquots of urine should be diluted (1 ml of urine with 19 ml of distilled water) to preserve uric acid and xanthine. This mixture can then be frozen.
3. Ammonia: Aliquots of urine (3 to 5 ml) may be frozen for up to 30 days.
4. Oxalate: Aliquots of urine (2 ml) are diluted with 1 N hydrochloric acid (1.66 ml) and then frozen.

Calculations
1. Calculating 24-hour urine volume
   a. Although 24-hour urine specimens are recommended to minimize the effects of short-term biologic variations in mineral excretion, collecting perfectly timed 24-hour samples may be difficult. The following formula can be used to adjust actual urine volume to a 24-hour period: 1,440 ÷ actual time interval (minutes) x urine volume (1,440 = number of minutes in 24 hours).
   b. Example: A 24-hour urine collection was started at 9:30 a.m. and ended the following day at 8:30 a.m. A total of 350 ml of urine were collected during this period. What is the 24-hour urine volume? 1,440 ÷ 1,380 x 350 = 356.2 ml.
2. Converting mmol/l to mg/dl
   a. Scientists are striving to adopt a uniform system of measurement termed the *System International d 'Unites* to standardize measurements. In this system, concentration is often expressed as moles, millimoles or micromoles of a substance per liter of fluid. Most normal values in the United States are expressed as mg/dl. The following formula can be used to convert mmol/l to mg/dl: mmol/l x atomic weight of substance ÷ 10. The atomic weights of elements can be found in the periodic tables of general chemistry books.
   b. Example: The concentration of calcium from a 24-hour urine sample was 1.35 mmol/l. Convert this value to mg/dl for comparison with normal values. The atomic weight of calcium is 40.08. 1.35 mmol/l x 40.08 ÷ 10 = 5.4 mg/dl.
3. Calculating mg/kg/24-hour or mEq/kg/24-hour excretion
   a. Excretion of metabolites is often expressed on a per kg basis to standardize excretion for dogs of different weights. The following formula can be used to standardize excretion rates: Concentration of substance x 24-hour urine volume ÷ body weight in kg. The units used to express the volume of urine and the concentration of the substance evaluated must be the same.
   b. Example: The concentration of calcium in a 24-hour urine sample was 5.4 mg/dl. A total of 356.2 ml of urine was collected. The dog weighed 10 kg. What is the daily calcium excretion on a per kg basis? First, express the volume of urine collected in the same units as the concentration of the substance measured. The 356.2 ml = 3.562 dl; therefore, 5.4 mg/dl x 3.562 dl ÷ 10 kg = 1.92 mg/kg/24 hours.

Additional considerations
1. Midpoint blood samples. Evaluation of blood during the midpoint of a 24-hour urine collection may help determine if changes in urine concentration reflect changes in serum or plasma concentration of analytes. This information can help detect underlying causes and mechanisms of abnormal mineral excretion. Likewise, evaluation of blood concentrations of some hormones (i.e., parathyroid hormone, calcitriol, etc.) may be helpful in determining the role of hormones in the regulation of mineral excretion.
2. Antimicrobials
   a. Antimicrobials are administered to prevent iatrogenic urinary tract infection during catheterization of the urinary bladder. The dosage, dosing interval and route should be based on the recommendations of the manufacturer. The authors recommend that antimicrobial administration be continued for three to five days after urine collection. This represents the time required for normal urothelial repair and replacement.

Continued on next page.

Table 20-6. *Continued from previous page.*

b. Select antimicrobials that are primarily excreted in the urine and that minimally affect urine concentrations of minerals, promoters and inhibitors associated with urolith formation. Because some antimicrobials are formulated as salts of sodium or potassium, high concentrations of sodium or potassium may be excreted in urine. The authors routinely use cephalosporins when collecting urine for amino acid evaluation (i.e., cystine urolithiasis), and ampicillin when collecting urine from dogs with calcium oxalate or urate uroliths.

3. Fasting urine collection
   a. Fasting urine collections have been evaluated to characterize the pathophysiologic mechanism of hypercalciuria in dogs with calcium oxalate uroliths. Dogs that absorb excessive amounts of calcium from their food and subsequently excrete large quantities of calcium in their urine have intestinal hypercalciuria. Hypercalciuria primarily occurs during food consumption; normal or lower quantities of urine calcium are excreted when food is withheld. In addition, dogs with intestinal hypercalciuria have normal serum concentrations of calcium and normal or low serum concentrations of parathyroid hormone. In contrast, urinary calcium excretion during fed and nonfed conditions is similar in dogs with primary hyperparathyroidism (resorptive hypercalciuria) or impaired renal tubular absorption of calcium (renal-leak hypercalciuria).
   b. Fasting urine collections are initiated immediately following collection of urine during standard feeding.

4. Urinary pH. The solubility of mineral salts is influenced by urinary pH. Determination of urinary pH from 24-hour urine samples may be helpful in understanding crystal formation, and can also be used to calculate activity products for several mineral salts commonly found in uroliths. The authors use an ion selective electrode and pH meter to accurately measure urinary pH.

5. Activity products
   a. The activity product of urine is a mathematical expression used to estimate the degree of saturation of urine with mineral salts. Activity products are calculated by measuring concentrations of major ionizable solutes in urine. For efficiency, computer programs are commonly used to aid in calculating activity products.
   b. Urine in which the activity product exceeds the solubility product is saturated for that particular mineral salt. Although crystals may not form at this degree of saturation, uroliths already present are likely to grow.
   c. Urine in which the activity product exceeds the formation product for a particular mineral salt is associated with an unstable state of oversaturation. Crystal nucleation and rapid crystal growth are likely at this urine concentration.

*Hill's Pet Nutrition, Inc., Topeka, KS, USA.

could break while being inserted into or removed from the urethra and urinary bladder.

Uroliths may be retrieved by catheter aspiration as follows (Figure 20-6). With the patient in lateral recumbency, a well-lubricated catheter should be advanced through the urethra into the bladder lumen. The tip of the catheter should be positioned so that it will not interfere with movement of the bladder wall as fluid is aspirated from the bladder lumen. If the urinary bladder is not distended with urine, it should be partially distended with physiologic (0.9%) saline solution. As a rule of thumb, a normal, empty canine or feline urinary bladder can be partially distended by injecting 3 to 4 ml of fluid per kg body weight. However, the urinary bladder should be palpated per abdomen during the time it is distended with saline solution to ensure that it is not overdistended.

The next step is crucial to successful retrieval of urocystoliths. While urine (and saline solution) is aspirated into the syringe, an assistant should vigorously and repeatedly move the patient's abdomen in an up-and-down motion. This maneuver disperses uroliths located in the dependent portion of the bladder throughout fluid in the bladder lumen. Small uroliths in the vicinity of the catheter tip may then be aspirated into the catheter along with the urine-saline mixture. It may be necessary to repeat this sequence of steps several times before a sufficient number of uroliths are retrieved. The bladder lumen should be redistended with saline solution each time. Difficulty in aspirating urine and saline solution into the syringe may be caused by poor positioning of the catheter tip or by partial occlusion of the catheter lumen with one or more uroliths. Uroliths that occlude the catheter lumen can be readily retrieved by flushing saline solution through the catheter after it has been removed from the patient.

Care must be used not to overdistend the urinary bladder with saline solution because this will increase the space in which the uroliths are suspended. Because patients with uroliths are predisposed to catheter-induced bacterial UTIs, antimicrobial therapy should be considered immediately before this procedure and for an appropriate period afterward. Proper selection, insertion and

positioning of urethral catheters minimize iatrogenic trauma to the lower urinary tract.

COLLECTION AND QUANTITATIVE ANALYSIS OF URINE CRYSTALS

If available data do not indicate the probable mineral composition of uroliths and if uroliths cannot be retrieved with the aid of a urethral catheter, consider preparing a large pellet of urine crystals by centrifugation of urine in a conical-tip

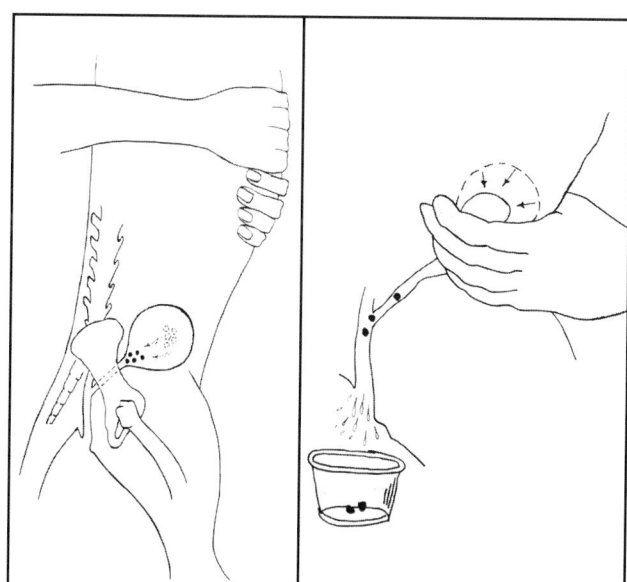

Figure 20-5. To remove urocystoliths by voiding urohydropropulsion, position the patient so that its vertebral column is approximately vertical (Left). The urinary bladder is then gently agitated to promote gravitational movement of urocystoliths into the bladder neck. To expel urocystoliths (Right), voiding is induced by applying steady digital pressure to the urinary bladder. (Adapted from Lulich JP, Osborne CA, Carlson M, et al. Nonsurgical removal of uroliths from dogs and cats by voiding urohydropropulsion. Journal of the American Veterinary Medical Association 1993; 203: 660-663.)

centrifuge tube.[9,23] The quantity of crystalline sediment available for analysis may be increased by repeatedly removing the supernatant after centrifugation, adding additional noncentrifuged urine to the tube containing sediment and again centrifuging the preparation. If the conditions that caused urolith formation are still present, evaluation of the pellet formed from crystalline sediment by quantitative methods designed for urolith analysis may provide meaningful information about the mineral composition of a patient's uroliths. However, crystals identified by this method may only reflect the outer portions of compound uroliths. Therefore, results of quantitative urine crystal analysis should be interpreted in conjunction with other pertinent clinical data.

QUANTITATIVE ANALYSIS OF UROLITHS

The location, number, size, shape, color and consistency of uroliths removed from the urinary tract should be recorded. All uroliths should be saved in a container (preferably a sterile one) and submitted for analysis. Do not give uroliths to owners before analysis. If multiple uroliths are present, one may be placed into a container of 10% buffered formalin for demineralization and microscopic examination. However, formalin should not be used to preserve uroliths for mineral analysis because formalin may alter the results. Because many uroliths contain two or more mineral components, it is important to examine representative portions. The mineral composition of crystalline nuclei may be identical or different from outer layers of uroliths (Figure 20-7). The nuclei of uroliths should be analyzed separately from outer layers because knowledge of the mineral composition of the nuclei may suggest the initiating cause of the urolith. Uroliths should not be broken before submission for analysis because the central core may be distorted or lost.

The authors do not recommend routine analysis of uroliths by qualitative methods of chemical analysis. The major disadvantage of this procedure is that only some of the chemical radicals and ions can be detected. In addition, the proportion of the different chemical constituents in the urolith cannot be quantified. In contrast to chemical methods of analysis, physical methods have proved to be far superior in identification of crystalline substances. Physical methods also permit differentiation of various subgroups of minerals (e.g., calcium oxalate monohydrate and calcium oxalate dihydrate, or uric acid, ammonium acid urate and xanthine) and allow semiquantitative determination of various mineral components. Physical methods commonly used by laboratories that specialize in quantitative urolith analysis include a combination of polarizing light microscopy, x-ray diffractometry and infrared spectroscopy.[25-27] Some laboratories also are equipped to perform elemental analysis with an energy dispersive x-ray microanalyzer or by neutron activation. On occasion, chemical methods of analysis and paper chromatography may be used to supplement information provided by physical methods. See Chapter 21 for a list of selected laboratories that perform quantitative analysis of uroliths.

UROLITH CULTURE

Bacterial culture of the interior of uroliths is indicated if: 1) urine obtained from the patient has not been previously cultured, 2) culture of urine obtained from patients suspected of having struvite uroliths yields no growth or 3) the patient has a UTI with bacteria that do not produce urease. Bacteria harbored inside uroliths are not always the same as those present in urine. Bacteria detected within uroliths probably represent those present at the time they were formed, and may serve as a source of recurrent UTI. Bacteria may remain viable within uroliths for long periods. In a pilot study, the authors were able to culture viable

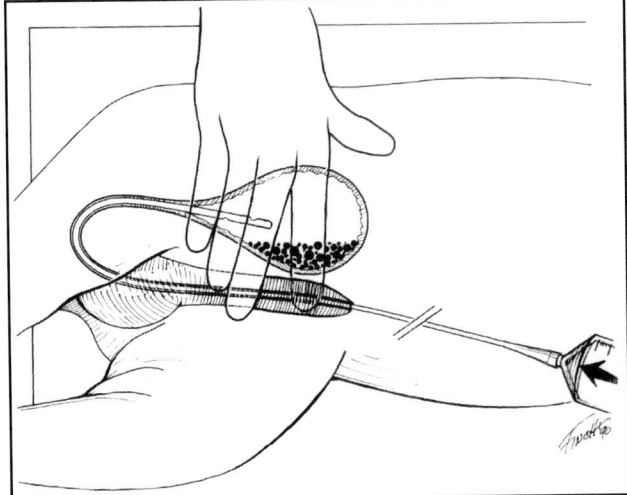

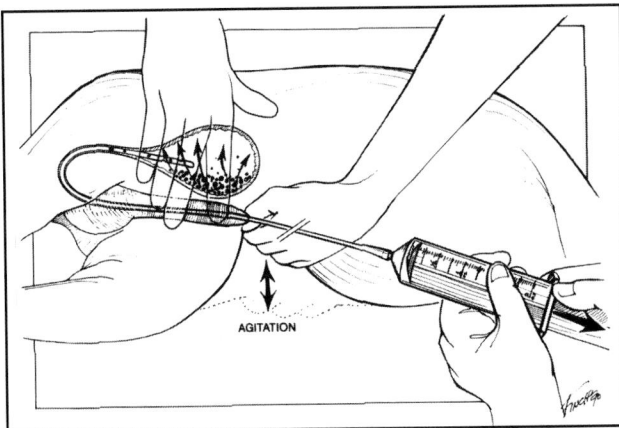

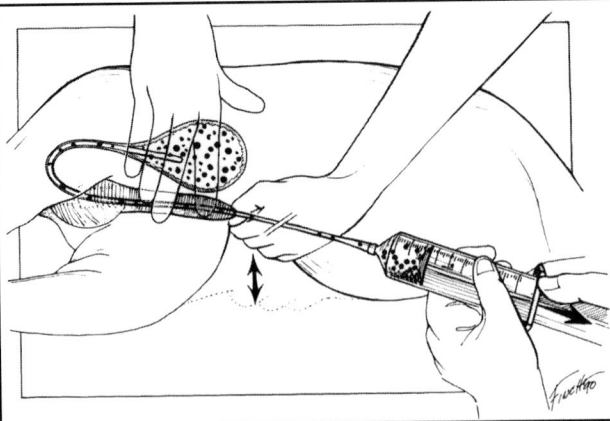

Figure 20-6. Illustration of catheter-assisted retrieval of urocystoliths. With the patient in lateral recumbency, uroliths have gravitated to the dependent portion of the urinary bladder (Top). The bladder lumen has been distended by injection of 0.9% saline solution. Vigorous movement of the abdomen in an up-and-down motion disperses uroliths throughout fluid in the bladder lumen (Middle). Aspiration of fluid from the urinary bladder during movement of the abdominal wall (Bottom) may result in movement of one or more small uroliths into the catheter and syringe. (Adapted from Lulich JP, Osborne CA. Catheter assisted retrieval of canine and feline urocystoliths. Journal of the American Veterinary Medical Association 1992; 201: 111-113.)

staphylococci from struvite uroliths removed from a miniature schnauzer up to three months following surgery. If all the uroliths have not been removed from the patient, knowledge of the type and antimicrobic susceptibility of bacteria inside uroliths that have been voided or removed may be of therapeutic significance. Procedures for culture of microbes from the inner portions of uroliths have been developed[25,28] and can be performed by most veterinary diagnostic laboratories.

GUESSTIMATION OF UROLITH COMPOSITION

Formulation of effective medical protocols for urolith dissolution is dependent on knowledge of the mineral composition of uroliths. Because a variety of different types of uroliths and nephroliths occur in dogs (Tables 20-7 and 20-8), the authors recommend a protocol that facilitates determination of the mineral composition of uroliths based on probability (Tables 20-9 and 20-10). Formulation of medical therapy based on the mineral composition of uroliths determined by this protocol is usually associated with a high degree of success in dissolving uroliths or arresting their growth.

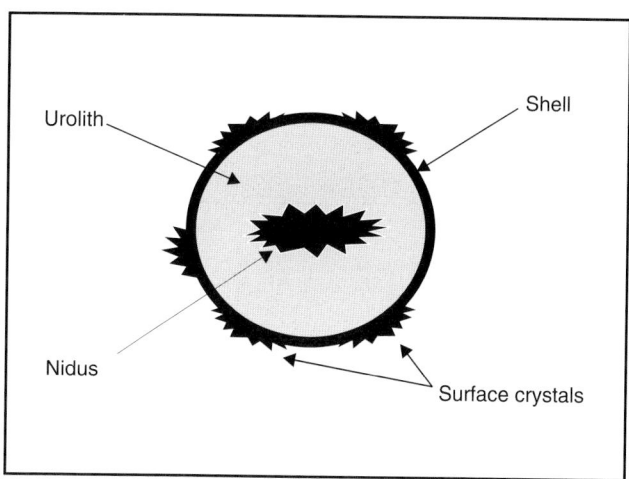

Figure 20-7. Schematic demonstrating the different components that may be observed on the cut surface of a bisected urolith. (Adapted from Osborne CA, Lulich JP, Polzin DJ, et al. Analysis of 77,000 canine uroliths: Perspectives from the Minnesota Urolith Center. Veterinary Clinics of North America: Small Animal Practice 1999; 29: 23.)

Table 20-7. Mineral composition of 77,191 canine uroliths evaluated at the Minnesota Urolith Center by quantitative methods: 1981 to 1997.

Predominant mineral type	Proportion of predominant mineral (%)	Number	Percent
Magnesium ammonium phosphate•6H$_2$O		**38,285**	**49.6**
	100	(20,469)	(26.5)
	70-99*	(17,816)	(23.1)
Magnesium hydrogen phosphate•3H$_2$O		**14**	**<0.1**
	100	(7)	(<0.1)
	70-99*	(7)	(<0.1)
Calcium oxalate		**24,267**	**31.4**
Calcium oxalate monohydrate	100	(10,236)	(13.3)
	70-99*	(6,120)	(7.9)
Calcium oxalate dihydrate	100	(2,256)	(2.9)
	70-99*	(3,026)	(3.9)
Calcium oxalate monohydrate and dihydrate	100	(2,162)	(2.8)
	70-99*	(466)	(0.6)
Calcium phosphate		**435**	**0.6**
Calcium phosphate	100	(93)	(0.1)
	70-99	(172)	(0.2)
Calcium hydrogen phosphate•2H$_2$0	100	(76)	(0.1)
	70-99	(93)	(0.1)
Tricalcium phosphate	70-99	(1)	(<0.1)
Purines		**6,144**	**8.0**
Ammonium acid urate	100	(4,479)	(5.8)
	70-99*	(782)	(1.0)
Sodium acid urate	100	(528)	(0.7)
	70-99*	(21)	(<0.1)
Sodium calcium urate	100	(194)	(0.6)
	70-99*	(45)	(0.1)
Ammonium calcium urate	70-99*	(1)	(<0.1)
Uric acid	100	(33)	(<0.1)
	70-99*	(11)	(<0.1)
Xanthine	100	(41)	(<0.1)
	70-99*	(9)	(<0.1)
Cystine		**760**	**1.0**
	100	(730)	(1.0)
	70-99*	(30)	(<0.1)
Silica		**659**	**0.9**
	100	(446)	(0.6)
	70-99*	(213)	(0.3)
Dolomite	100	1	<0.1
Mixed**		1,464	1.0
Compound***		5,113	6.6
Matrix		45	<0.1
Drug metabolite		4	<0.1

*Urolith composed of 70 to 99% of mineral type listed; no nucleus and shell detected.
**Uroliths did not contain at least 70% of mineral type listed; no nucleus or shell detected.
***Uroliths contained an identifiable nucleus and one or more surrounding layers of a different mineral type.

Table 20-8. Mineral composition of 797 canine nephroliths evaluated at the Minnesota Urolith Center by quantitative methods: 1991 to 1997.

Predominate mineral type	Proportion of predominant mineral (%)	Number	Percent
Calcium oxalate		**308**	**38.6**
Calcium oxalate monohydrate	70-100*	(248)	(31.1)
Calcium oxalate dihydrate	70-100	(38)	(4.8)
Calcium oxalate monohydrate and dihydrate	70-100	(22)	(2.8)
Calcium phosphate		**18**	**2.3**
Calcium apatite	70-100	(16)	(2.0)
Calcium hydrogen phosphate•2H$_2$O	70-100	(2)	(0.3)
Magnesium ammonium phosphate•6H$_2$O	**70-100**	**264**	**33.1**
Purines		**97**	**12.2**
Ammonium acid urate	70-100	(85)	(10.7)
Sodium acid urate	70-100	(5)	(0.6)
Sodium calcium urate	70-100	(4)	(0.5)
Xanthine	70-100	(3)	(0.3)
Silica	**70-100**	**4**	**0.5**
Mixed**		**35**	**4.4**
Compound***		**62**	**7.8**
Matrix		**6**	**0.8**

*Uroliths composed of 70% of mineral type listed; no nucleus and shell detected.
**Uroliths contained less than 70% of predominant mineral; no nucleus or shell detected.
***Uroliths contained an identifiable nucleus and one or more surrounding layers of a different mineral type.

Table 20-9. Problem-specific and therapeutic-specific database for diagnosis and management of urolithiasis.

1. Obtain appropriate history and perform physical examination, including a rectal examination of the urethra.
2. Perform complete urinalysis; save aliquots of urine for possible determination of mineral concentration.
3. Obtain quantitative urine culture and determine urease activity; test for antimicrobial susceptibility if bacterial pathogens are identified. Consider attempts to isolate ureaplasmas if urease-positive urine is bacteriologically sterile.
4. Perform a complete blood cell count.
5. Freeze an aliquot of serum collected at the time the sample was obtained for the complete blood cell count for possible determination of urea nitrogen, creatinine, calcium and/or uric acid concentrations.
6. Obtain radiographs.
   a. Take survey radiographs of the entire urinary system.
   b. Consider intravenous urography for patients with renal or ureteral uroliths.
   c. Consider intravenous urography or contrast cystography for patients with bladder uroliths.
   d. Consider contrast urethrography for patients with urethral uroliths.
   e. Ultrasonography is recommended if equipment is available.
7. Determine mineral composition of uroliths.
   a. Submit uroliths passed during micturition or retrieved during diagnostic procedures for quantitative analysis.
   b. Use results obtained from the history, physical examination, laboratory examination and radiography to determine probable mineral composition of uroliths.
8. Initiate therapy to eradicate urinary tract infection, if present.
9. Initiate therapy for urolithiasis.
   a. Initiate therapy to promote dissolution of uroliths if amenable to medical therapy.
      Formulate follow-up protocol to monitor dissolution of uroliths.
      Formulate alternative treatment options if uroliths do not dissolve or if problems such as recurrent outflow obstruction occur.
   b. Remove uroliths by voiding urohydropropulsion.
   c. Remove uroliths by nephrotomy or cystotomy.
      Obtain bladder or kidney biopsy specimens for microscopic examination during surgical procedure.
      Correct any anatomic defects, if present.
      Compare number of uroliths removed during surgery with the number identified by radiography.
      Obtain postsurgical radiographs to evaluate completeness of urolith removal.
      Submit uroliths for quantitative analysis.
10. After uroliths are surgically removed or medically dissolved, initiate therapy to prevent recurrence.
11. Formulate follow-up protocol with clients.

Principles of Urolith Treatment and Prevention

OVERVIEW

Surgery has been the time-honored method of managing all types of urolithiasis in dogs. Although surgery has been an effective method that provides immediate elimination of uroliths, it is associated with several limitations, including: 1) persistence of underlying causes and a high rate of recurrence of uroliths despite surgery, 2) patient factors that enhance adverse consequences of general anesthesia or surgery and 3) inability to remove all uroliths or fragments of uroliths during surgery. In addition, situations occasionally arise in which owners of companion animals will not consent to surgical therapy but will consider medical therapy. Medical dissolu-

tion of uroliths may be considered for these and other reasons (i.e., the urolith is asymptomatic).

Results of several experimental and clinical investigations have confirmed the efficacy of medical dissolution of canine uroliths. Despite the feasibility of dissolution of uroliths, however, this form of therapy is associated with potential hazards. Uroliths always predispose patients to urinary tract infection (UTI) and obstructive uropathy. Risks and benefits of medical vs. surgical and medical therapy must be considered for each patient.

Detailed descriptions of nonsurgical and surgical methods for re-establishing urine outflow are beyond the scope of the

Continued on next page.

Continued from previous page.

discussion but are available elsewhere. Likewise, details pertaining to surgical removal of uroliths, endoscopic and percutaneous manipulation of uroliths, chemolysis via nephrostomy, disintegration of renal and ureteral uroliths via ultrasound and shock-wave lithotripsy have been reviewed.

MEDICAL DISSOLUTION OF UROLITHS

Therapy should not be initiated before appropriate samples have been collected for diagnosis. The objectives of medical management of uroliths are to arrest further growth and to promote urolith dissolution by correcting or controlling underlying abnormalities. For therapy to be effective, it must induce undersaturation of urine with calculogenic crystalloids by: 1) increasing the solubility of crystalloids in urine, 2) increasing the volume of urine in which crystalloids are dissolved or suspended and 3) reducing the quantity of calculogenic crystalloids in urine. For example, attempts to increase the solubility of crystalloids in urine often include administration of medications designed to change urinary pH in order to create a less favorable environment for crystallization. Likewise, diuresis is commonly induced to increase the volume of urine in which crystalloids are dissolved or suspended. A dietary change is an example of a method to reduce the quantity of calculogenic crystalloids in urine.

In general, medical treatment should be formulated in stepwise fashion, with the initial goal of reducing the urine concentration of calculogenic substances. Medications that have the potential to induce a sustained alteration in body composition of metabolites, in addition to urine concentration of metabolites, should be reserved for patients with active or frequently recurrent uroliths. Caution must be used so that the side effects of treatment are not more detrimental than the effects of the uroliths.

Results of experimental and clinical studies have revealed that the size and number of uroliths do not dictate the likelihood of response to therapy. The authors have had success in dissolving uroliths that are small and large, single and multiple. However the rate of dissolution is related to size and surface area of the urolith exposed to urine. Just as one large ice cube dissolves more slowly than an equal volume of crushed ice, one large urolith will dissolve more slowly than an equal volume of many smaller uroliths. Rate of dissolution is influenced by surface area of the urolith exposed to undersaturated urine.

Difficulty in inducing complete dissolution of uroliths by creating urine that is undersaturated with the suspected calculogenic crystalloid should prompt consideration that: 1) the wrong mineral component was identified, 2) the nucleus of the urolith is of different mineral composition than outer portions and/or 3) the owner or the patient is not complying with therapy.

SURGICAL REMOVAL OF UROLITHS

Detection of uroliths is not in itself an indication for surgery. However, along with medical management, surgical intervention may have a vital role in therapy of urolithiasis. Surgical candidates include patients: 1) with urolith-induced obstruction to urine outflow that cannot be corrected by nonsurgical techniques, especially in patients with concomitant UTI, 2) with uroliths that are refractory to current methods of medical dissolution (e.g., silica, calcium oxalate and calcium phosphate uroliths), 3) with uroliths that are increasing in size or number despite medical therapy designed to inhibit their growth or cause their dissolution (especially if they are obstructing urine outflow or causing progressive deterioration in renal function), 4) with nephroliths and renal dysfunction of such a nature that the time required to induce medical dissolution is likely to be associated with more renal dysfunction than that associated with surgical procedures, 5) with anatomic defects of the urogenital tract that predispose patients to recurrent UTI and urolithiasis and are amenable to

surgical correction at the time uroliths are removed and 6) unable to respond to medical management because of poor client compliance with therapeutic recommendations.

Complete obstruction to urine outflow caused by uroliths in patients with concomitant UTI should be regarded as a surgical emergency. In this situation, rapid spread of infection and associated damage to the urinary tract, especially the kidneys, are likely to induce septicemia and peracute renal failure caused by a combination of obstruction and pyelonephritis.

Unilateral renoliths and ureteroliths that cause outflow obstruction and markedly impair function of the associated kidney should be managed by surgical intervention or (if possible) percutaneous nephropyelonephrostomy. Medical therapy designed to induce urolith dissolution over several weeks in patients with poorly draining kidneys is unlikely to be effective because the urolith(s) will not be continuously bathed with newly formed urine modified to induce litholysis. The same concept applies to urethroliths that cannot be removed by nonsurgical methods.

Surgical removal of uroliths followed by medical calculolytic protocols may be of value in some patients. Examples include patients in which uroliths or fragments of uroliths remain after surgery, and patients with crystalluria of a character and magnitude that indicate rapid recurrence is likely. Surgical incisions should be repaired using meticulous technique if protein-restricted canine calculolytic foods are used.

PREVENTION OF UROLITH RECURRENCE

Uroliths tend to recur. Prevention of recurrent uroliths, which reduces the need for medical therapy and surgery, is therefore cost effective. In general, preventive strategies are designed to eliminate or control the underlying causes of various types of uroliths. When causes cannot be identified, preventive strategies encompass efforts to minimize risk factors associated with calculogenesis. These strategies commonly include dietary modification.

BIBLIOGRAPHY

Abdullahi SU, Osborne CA, Leininger JR, et al. Evaluation of a calculolytic diet in female dogs with induced struvite urolithiasis. American Journal of Veterinary Research 1984; 45: 1508-1519.

Bartges JW, Osborne CA, Polzin DJ. Recurrent sterile struvite urocystolithiasis in three related cocker spaniels. Journal of the American Animal Hospital Association 1992; 28: 459-469.

Krawiec DR, Osborne CA, Leininger JR, et al. Effect of acetohydroxamic acid on dissolution of canine uroliths. American Journal of Veterinary Research 1984; 45: 1266-1275.

Krawiec DR, Osborne CA, Leininger JR, et al. Effect of acetohydroxamic acid on prevention of canine struvite uroliths. American Journal of Veterinary Research 1984; 45: 1276-1282.

Osborne CA, Hoppe A, O'Brien TD. Medical dissolution and prevention of cystine urolithiasis. In: Kirk RW, ed. Current Veterinary Therapy X. Philadelphia, PA: WB Saunders Co, 1989; 1189-1193.

Osborne CA, Kruger JM, Johnston GR, et al. Dissolution of canine ammonium urate uroliths. Veterinary Clinics of North America: Small Animal Practice 1986; 16: 375-388.

Osborne CA, Lulich JP, Unger LK, et al. Canine and feline urolithiasis: Relationship of etiopathogenesis to treatment and prevention. In: Osborne CA, Finco DR, eds. Canine and Feline Nephrology and Urology. Baltimore, MD: Williams & Wilkins, 1995; 798-888.

Osborne CA, Polzin DJ, Abdullahi SU, et al. Struvite urolithiasis in animals and man: Formation, detection and dissolution. Advances in Veterinary Science and Comparative Medicine 1985; 29: 1-101.

Osborne CA, Polzin DJ, Feeney DA, et al. The urinary system: Pathophysiology, diagnosis and treatment. In: Gourley IM, Vasseur PB, eds. General Small Animal Surgery. Philadelphia, PA: JB Lippincott, 1985; 479-658.

Osborne CA, Polzin DJ, Kruger JM, et al. Medical dissolution and prevention of canine struvite uroliths. In: Kirk RW, ed. Current Veterinary Therapy IX. Philadelphia, PA: WB Saunders Co, 1986; 1177-1187.

Table 20-10. Predicting mineral composition of common canine uroliths.

Mineral type	Urinary pH	Crystal appearance	Urine culture	Radiographic density	Radiographic contour	Serum abnormalities	Breed predisposition	Gender predisposition	Common ages
				Predictors					
Magnesium ammonium phosphate	Neutral to alkaline	Three- to eight-sided colorless prisms	Urease-producing bacteria (staphylococci, Proteus spp, Ureaplasma spp)	1+ to 4+ (sometimes laminated)	Smooth, round or faceted May assume shape of renal pelvis, ureter, bladder or urethra	None	Miniature schnauzer, miniature poodle, bichon frise, cocker spaniel	Female (>80%)	2 to 9 years
Calcium oxalate	Acidic to neutral	Colorless envelope or octahedral shape (dihydrate salt) Spindles or dumbbell shape (monohydrate salt)	Negative	2+ to 4+	Rough or spiculated (dihydrate salt) Small, smooth, round (monohydrate salt) Sometimes jackstone	Usually normocalcemic, occasionally hypercalcemic	Miniature schnauzer, standard schnauzer, Lhasa apso, Yorkshire terrier, miniature poodle, Shi Tzu, bichon frise	Males (>70%)	5 to 12 years
Urate	Acidic to neutral	Yellow-brown amorphous shapes (ammonium urate)	Negative	0 to 2+	Smooth (occasionally irregular) round or oval	Low serum urea nitrogen and albumin values in dogs with hepatic portosystemic shunts	Dalmatian, English bulldog, miniature schnauzer, Yorkshire terrier, Shi Tzu	Males (>90%)	1 to 5 years
Calcium phosphate	Alkaline to neutral (brushite forms in acidic urine)	Amorphous or long thin prisms	Negative	2+ to 4+	Smooth or irregular, round or faceted	Occasionally hypercalcemic	Yorkshire terrier, miniature schnauzer, Shi Tzu	Males (>55%)	<1 year, 6 to 10 years
Cystine	Acidic to neutral	Flat colorless hexagonal plates	Negative	1+ to 2+	Smooth (occasionally) irregular, round or oval	None	English bulldog, dachshund, basset hound, Newfoundland	Males (>98%)	1 to 7 years
Silica	Acidic to neutral	None observed	Negative	2+ to 3+	Round center with radial spoke-like projections (jackstone)	None	German shepherd, golden retriever, Labrador retriever, miniature schnauzer, cavalier King Charles spaniel	Males (95%)	3 to 10 years

Attempts to induce dissolution of uroliths may be hampered if the uroliths are heterogeneous in composition. This has not been a significant problem in dogs with uroliths composed primarily of magnesium ammonium phosphate with small quantities of calcium apatite because the solubility characteristics of the two minerals are similar. The authors have encountered difficulty in dissolving uroliths composed primarily of struvite with an outer shell composed primarily of calcium apatite. Difficulty will also be encountered in attempting to induce complete dissolution of a urolith with a nucleus of calcium oxalate, calcium phosphate, ammonium urate or silica and a shell of struvite because the solubility characteristics of this combination of minerals are dissimilar. These phenomena should be considered if medical therapy seems to be ineffective after initially reducing the size of uroliths. (See sidebar "Principles of Urolith Treatment and Prevention.")

AMMONIUM URATE AND OTHER PURINE UROLITHS

Prevalence and Mineral Composition

Purine uroliths (ammonium urate, sodium urate, calcium urate, uric acid and xanthine) accounted for 8% of all canine uroliths submitted to the Minnesota Urolith Center from 1981 to 1997 (Table 20-7), and 9% (1,427 of 15,259) of all canine uroliths analyzed in 1997. Purines accounted for 12% of all canine nephroliths analyzed at the Minnesota Urolith Center from 1981 to 1997 (Table 20-8). All dogs with xanthine uroliths had a history of treatment

with allopurinol. Purines composed 19% of uroliths retrieved from dogs less than 12 months old. The mean age of dogs at the time of ammonium urate urolith retrieval was 4.1 ± 2.6 years (range one month to 17 years). The mean age of dogs at the time of sodium urate and calcium urate urolith retrieval was 4.6 ± 2.6 years (range six months to 14 years). The mean age of dogs at the time of uric acid urolith retrieval was 3.2 ± 3.9 years (range one month to 12 years). The mean age at the time of xanthine urolith retrieval was 4.7 ± 2.0 years (range one and one-half to nine years). Males were affected more often than females with ammonium urate (90 vs. 10%), sodium and calcium urate (99 vs. 1%), uric acid (88 vs. 12%) and xanthine (81 vs.19%) uroliths.

Sixty-six different breeds were affected with ammonium urate uroliths including Dalmatians (61%), miniature schnauzers (7%), Yorkshire terriers (5%), Shih Tzus (4%) and English bulldogs (4%). Twelve different breeds had sodium and calcium urate uroliths; however, these uroliths were primarily encountered in Dalmatians (92%) and English bulldogs (4%). Six different breeds had uric acid uroliths; Dalmatians were affected most commonly (80%). Five different breeds had xanthine uroliths, including Dalmatians (56%) and English bulldogs (35%).

Ammonium urate (97%), sodium and calcium urate (96%), uric acid (100%) and xanthine (94%) uroliths were more commonly removed from the lower urinary tract than the upper urinary tract.

Ammonium urate, sodium and calcium urate and uric acid uroliths typically appear as multiple, small, smooth, hard, round or ovoid structures with a characteristic brown-green color (Table 20-11). However, the physical appearance of urate uroliths may vary depending on additional mineral components, quantity of matrix, site of for-

Table 20-11. Common characteristics of canine purine uroliths.

Chemical names	Formulas
Ammonium acid urate	$C_5H_3N_4O_3NH_4H_2O$
Sodium acid urate	$C_5H_3N_4O_3NaH_2O$
Uric acid	$C_5H_4N_4O_3 2H_2O$
Xanthine	$C_5H_4N_4O_2$

Variations in mineral composition
Ammonium acid urate only
Sodium acid urate only
Uric acid only
Xanthine only
Ammonium urate mixed with variable quantities of sodium urate, magnesium ammonium phosphate and/or calcium oxalate
Sodium and calcium oxalate
Xanthine and uric acid

Physical characteristics
Color: Light or dark brown, brown-green
Shape: Variable. Usually round or ovoid in urinary bladder, may assume shape of renal pelvis (funnel shaped), may assume jackstone appearance. Usually smooth, occasionally irregular or rough.
Nuclei: Nuclei and concentric laminations are common.
Density: Usually dense and brittle. Radiographically, purine uroliths have marginal radiodensity compared with soft tissue. Some may be radiolucent.
Number: Single or multiple
Location: May be located in kidneys, ureters, urinary bladder (most common) and/or urethra.
Size: Usually small (1 mm to 1 cm in diameter), occasionally large (more than 1 cm)

Prevalence
Approximately 7 to 8% of all canine uroliths. Approximately 12% of canine nephroliths.
May be recurrent

Characteristics of affected canine patients
In Dalmatians, most common in males
Mean age at diagnosis is four years (range <1 to >17 years).
Most commonly observed in Dalmatians, miniature schnauzers, Yorkshire terriers, Shih Tzus and English bulldogs.

mation and growth and other concurrent urinary tract disorders. Rarely, they form jackstones. Examination of cross sections of urate uroliths frequently reveals concentric laminations and nuclei located in the geographic center of the urolith.

Etiopathogenesis and Risk Factors

Uric acid is one of several biodegradation products of purine nucleotide metabolism (Figure 20-8). Purines are made up of three groups of compounds: 1) oxypurines (hypoxanthine, xanthine, uric acid, allantoin), 2) aminopurines (adenine, guanine) and 3) methylpurines (caffeine, theophylline, theobromine). In most dogs and cats, allantoin is the major metabolic end product,[29,30] and it is the most soluble of the purine metabolic products excreted in urine.[31,32]

Uroliths composed of uric acid (anhydrous uric acid, uric acid dihydrate, sodium urate, ammonium urate) or xanthine form because urine is oversaturated with these substances.

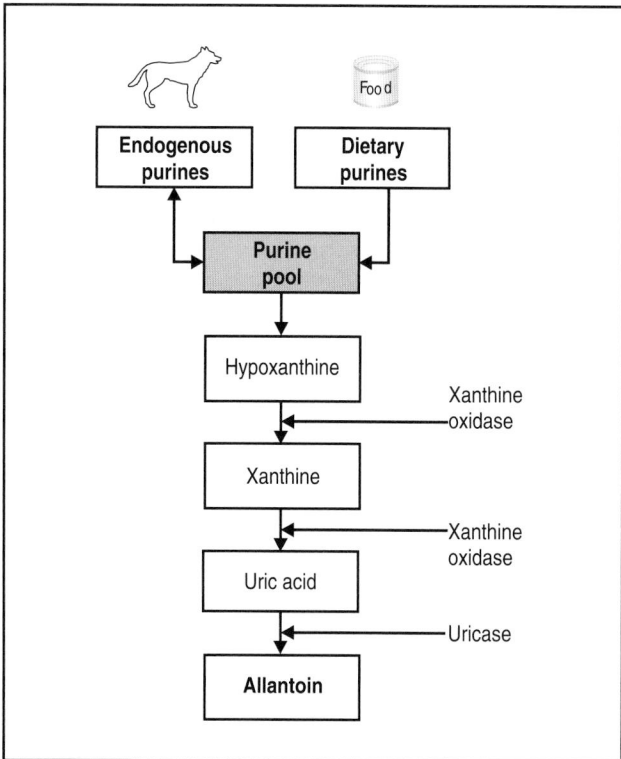

Figure 20-8. Diagram of normal canine purine degradation.

Ammonium urate (also known as ammonium acid urate and ammonium biurate) is the monobasic ammonium salt of uric acid. It is the most common naturally occurring purine urolith form observed in dogs.[9] Other naturally occurring purine uroliths include sodium urate (also known as sodium acid urate or monosodium urate), sodium calcium urate, potassium urate and uric acid dihydrate.[9,33]

Uric Acid, Sodium Urate, Ammonium Urate

Risk factors for urate lithogenesis in dogs include: 1) increased renal excretion and urine concentration of uric acid, 2) increased renal excretion, renal production or microbial urease production of ammonium ions, 3) low urinary pH and 4) presence of promoters or absence of inhibitors of urate urolith formation.[34] Genetic factors may be important because urate uroliths are common in certain breeds of dogs. For example, Dalmatian dogs have an inherent predisposition to forming urate uroliths. (See section on Dalmatian dogs.) Dietary components may promote urate urolith formation in predisposed dogs because dietary purines may be digested, absorbed, incorporated into the body's purine pool and eventually excreted in the urine (Tables 20-12 and 20-13). Thus, metabolism of dietary purines may result in oversaturation of urine with urate calculogenic substances. In studies of normal dogs, consumption of high-protein foods was associated with greater urinary uric acid excretion and increased urine saturation with uric acid, sodium urate and ammonium urate, when compared with consumption of low-protein foods.[35-37]

Xanthine

Xanthine is a product of purine metabolism and is converted to uric acid by the enzyme xanthine oxidase. Hereditary xanthinuria is a rarely recognized disorder of people characterized by a deficiency of xanthine oxidase.[38] As a consequence, abnormal quantities of xanthine are excreted in urine as a major end product of purine metabolism. Because xanthine is the least soluble of the purines naturally excreted in urine, xanthinuria may be associated with formation of uroliths.[39-41] The most common cause of xanthinuria is treatment with allopurinol. However, naturally occurring xanthinuria and xanthine urolithiasis have been reported to occur in cavalier King Charles spaniels.[42]

Dalmatian Dogs

Dalmatian dogs are predisposed to urate uroliths because their ability to oxidize uric acid to allantoin is

Table 20-12. Some potential risk factors for canine purine uroliths.

Diet	Urine	Metabolic	Drugs
High purine content (See Table 20-13.)	Hyperuricuria	Males	Urine acidifiers
Acidifying potential	Hyperammonuria	Breed	Salicylates
Low moisture content	Acidic pH	Dalmatians	Chemotherapeutic agents
Ascorbic acid?	Urine concentration	English bulldogs	(especially 6-mercaptopurine)
	Urine retention	Miniature schnauzers	
	Urease-producing microburia	Yorkshire terriers	
	Increased promoters?	Shih Tzus	
	Decreased inhibitors?	Hyperuricemia	
		Hyperammonuria	
		Hepatic dysfunction	
		Neoplasia with rapid cell destruction	

Table 20-13. Purine content of selected foods.

Foods to avoid (high purine concentration)	Foods to use sparingly (moderately high purine concentration)	Foods that can be fed (negligible purine concentration)
Anchovies	Asparagus	Breads (whole grain cereal products)
Brains	Cauliflower	Butter and fats
Clams	Fish*	Cheese
Goose	Legumes (beans and peas)	Eggs
Gravies	Lentils	Fruits and fruit juices
Heart	Meats	Gelatin
Kidney	Mushrooms	Milk
Liver	Spinach	Nuts
Mackerel		Refined cereals
Meat extracts including bouillon		Sugars
Mussels		Vegetable soups
Oysters		Cream soups
Salmon		Vegetables**
Sardines		Water
Scallops		
Shrimp		
Sweetbreads		
Tuna		
Yeast (baker's and brewer's)		

*Except those listed in the first column.
**Except those listed in the second column.

intermediate between that of people and most non-Dalmatian dogs.[43-45] People have a serum uric acid concentration of approximately 3 to 7 mg/dl, and excrete approximately 500 to 700 mg of uric acid in their urine per day.[46] Most non-Dalmatian dogs have a serum uric acid concentration of less than 0.5 mg/dl, and excrete approximately 10 to 60 mg of uric acid in their urine per day. Dalmatians have a serum uric acid concentration that is two to four times that of non-Dalmatian dogs and excrete more than 400 to 600 mg of uric acid in their urine per day.[47,48]

Studies of the fate of uric acid in Dalmatians have revealed unique hepatic and renal pathways of metabolism. Of these two metabolic sites, reciprocal allogenic renal and hepatic transplantations between Dalmatians and non-Dalmatians indicate that the hepatic mechanism is quantitatively the more significant.[49-51] The liver of Dalmatians does not completely oxidize available uric acid, even though it contains sufficient concentrations of uricase. Compared with non-Dalmatians, Dalmatians convert uric acid to allantoin at a reduced rate. It has been hypothesized that their hepatic cellular membranes are partially impermeable to uric acid.[52,53]

The proximal renal tubules of Dalmatians reabsorb less uric acid than those of non-Dalmatian dogs; a small amount is secreted by the distal tubules.[54] In non-Dalmatian dogs, 98 to 100% of the uric acid in the glomerular filtrate is reabsorbed by the proximal tubules and returned to the liver for further metabolism.[55] Uric acid in urine of non-Dalmatian dogs is thought to be secreted by the distal tubules.[56]

The definitive mechanism of urate urolith formation in Dalmatian dogs is unknown. Increased urinary excretion of uric acid is a risk factor rather than a primary cause. Urate uroliths occur more commonly in males than females; the average age of dogs when uroliths are diagnosed is 4.5 years. Although all Dalmatian dogs excrete relatively high quantities of uric acid in their urine, apparently only a small percentage form urate uroliths.[57,58] At one time, it was thought that urolith-forming Dalmatians did not excrete greater quantities of uric acid in their urine than non-urolith-forming Dalmatians. However, recent studies indicate that insensitive methods for measuring urine uric acid concentration were responsible for this erroneous conclusion. When steps are taken to ensure that urine uric acid remains in solution, differences in urine uric acid concentrations between non-urolith-forming Dalmatians and urolith-forming Dalmatians may be expected.[59,60]

Although urate uroliths commonly affect Dalmatian dogs, not all uroliths formed by Dalmatians are composed of ammonium urate. For example, of 2,020 uroliths formed by Dalmatian dogs, 93% were composed of purines (ammonium urate, sodium urate, uric acid and xanthine), 3% were of mixed composition, 1% were struvite, 1% were calcium oxalate, 2% were compound uroliths and less than 1% were cystine.[22,57]

Non-Dalmatian Dogs

Comparatively little is known about urate lithogenesis in non-Dalmatian dogs that do not have portal vascular anomalies. Many breeds of dogs have been reported to be affected with urate urolithiasis. Although urate uroliths are commonly encountered in Dalmatian dogs, approximately 30 to 60% of all canine urate uroliths analyzed by quantitative methods are found in other breeds.[61-63] English bulldogs have a significantly higher incidence of urate urolithiasis compared with other breeds.[57] Clinical evaluation of eight male English bulldogs with confirmed ammonium urate urocystoliths revealed mild elevations in serum uric acid concentration. The size of their livers was normal, as was serum concentration of hepatic enzymes, blood concentration of ammonia and BSP retention. Other non-Dalmatian breeds that appear to have a significantly higher incidence of urate urolithiasis based on quantitative urolith analyses are miniature schnauzers, Shih Tzus and Yorkshire terriers.[63]

Urate uroliths from non-Dalmatian dogs have been recognized most frequently in males. Uroliths have been detected throughout the life-span of affected dogs; however, they were most frequently detected in dogs three to six years of age.

Regardless of cause, severe hepatic dysfunction may predispose dogs to urate lithogenesis, especially ammonium urate uroliths. Our observations and evidence derived from experimental models suggest that prolonged consumption of foods with markedly restricted levels of protein may be associated with formation of urate uroliths in dogs.[34] Biochemical and histologic evaluation of these dogs suggests that long-term consumption of foods severely restricted in protein may induce hepatocellular dysfunction and concomitant hyperuricemia. Hepatic cirrhosis has also been associated with urate uroliths in dogs and other species.[14,64] However, in the authors' experience, cirrhosis, foods with severely restricted protein levels and other causes of hepatic dysfunction have been uncommon causes of ammonium urate urolithiasis. Nonetheless, their significance relative to ammonium urate lithogenesis deserves further study.

Water as an Important Nutrient in Patients with Urolithiasis

A primary goal in dietary management of canine urolithiasis, regardless of the urolith type, is to create urine that is undersaturated with calculogenic crystalloids. One method of creating undersaturated urine is to reduce urine concentration. This can be accomplished by feeding foods that are very low in protein (8 to 11% dry matter) and encouraging ingestion of water.

Generous fluid intake is recommended in the management of all types of urolithiasis affecting people. Fluid intake in people at risk for urolith formation should be distributed throughout the day to ensure a constantly high urine output. In moderate climates, people are advised to drink 250 to 300 ml of fluid per hour and to void on each occasion during the night when the person is awake. The amount of fluid that must be consumed is greater in warmer climates and for physically active people. At least half of the fluid ingested should be water.

Adding salt to food to increase thirst and urine volume may be associated with benefits and risks. The obvious benefit is an increase in urine volume; however, sodium increases calcium excretion in urine and therefore is a risk factor for calcium oxalate and calcium phosphate urolithiasis. Sodium chloride also may contribute to hypertension in salt-sensitive dogs. For these reasons, the authors do not routinely recommend use of sodium chloride to enhance urine volume.

Water and fluid intake should also be encouraged in dogs at risk for urolithiasis. Strive for a urine specific gravity value less than 1.020. The following guidelines can be used.

1. Ensure multiple bowls are available in prominent locations in the dog's environment. This may mean providing several bowls outside in a large enclosure or a bowl on each level of the house. Bowls should always be filled with clean water.
2. Add small amounts of flavoring substances (e.g., salt-free bouillon) to water sources.
3. Offer ice cubes as treats or snacks.
4. Recommend feeding moist (canned) foods because compared to dry foods, they minimize formation of concentrated urine.
5. If dry food is selected, add liberal quantities of water.

Dogs with Portal Vascular Anomalies

A high incidence of ammonium urate uroliths has been observed in dogs with portal vascular anomalies. These uroliths occur in males and females and usually have been detected before dogs reach three years of age.[14,16,34,65]

Direct communication between the portal and systemic vasculature shunts blood around the liver, resulting in severe hepatic atrophy and diminished hepatic function. Hepatic dysfunction in turn is associated with reduced hepatic conversion of uric acid to allantoin, and reduced conversion of ammonia to urea. The predisposition of dogs with portal vascular anomalies to urate urolithiasis is probably associated with concomitant hyperuricemia, hyperammonemia, hyperuricuria and hyperammonuria.[34,65] Serum uric acid concentrations in 15 dogs with portal vascular anomalies evaluated at the University of Minnesota Veterinary Teaching Hospital were increased (values ranged from 1.2 to 4.0 mg/dl).[65] Concurrent hyperuricuria, hyperammonuria, hyperuricemia and hyperammonemia were observed in an 18-month-old Bernese mountain dog with recurrent ammonium urate uroliths associated with a portal vascular anomaly.[34] This dog had a urine uric acid concentration of 42 mg/kg body weight/day and a urine ammonia concentration of 3.2 mM/kg body weight/day while the dog was fed a protein-restricted food. Hyperuricuria, hyperammonuria, hyperuricemia and hyperammonemia were observed in three miniature schnauzers with ammonium urate uroliths associated with portal vascular anomalies. In these dogs, urine uric acid concentrations were approximately 50 mg/kg body weight/day and urine ammonia concentrations were approximately 1.5 mM/kg body weight/day while the dogs consumed a growth food. When two of these dogs consumed a purine-restricted food, urine uric acid concentrations were approximately 17 mg/kg body weight/day and urine ammonia concentrations were approximately 0.6 mM/kg body weight/day.

Not all dogs with portal systemic anomalies develop concurrent ammonium urate urolithiasis. Definition and characterization of other factors responsible for promoting or inhibiting urate lithogenesis in affected dogs require further investigation.

Dietary Risk Factors

Concentrations of calculogenic substances in urine are dependent on urine volume. Because commercial dry foods are associated with production of less volume of urine compared with moist foods, consumption of dry foods may be considered a risk factor for urate urolith formation. (See Key Nutritional Factors table.) (See sidebar "Water as an Important Nutrient in Patients with Urolithiasis.")

The authors' observation has been that Dalmatian dogs consuming foods containing more than 20% protein (dry matter), and having protein sources that are high in purines and purine precursors (Table 20-13) are at increased risk for urate lithogenesis. However, purine uroliths have been reported to form in some dogs consuming lesser amounts of dietary purines; therefore, other factors are apparently involved. The range of dietary protein content associated with urate urolith formation in dogs with portal vascular anomalies is unknown. In dogs with portosystemic shunts, the degree of urine saturation with purines is probably related, at least in part, to the degree of vascular shunting in addition to the dietary protein consumption. Because urate uroliths associated with portal vascular anomalies are often diagnosed in dogs less than one year of age, it is probable that they were consuming foods with increased protein content.

Urine acidity is a risk factor for urate lithogenesis because the solubility of most purines, especially ammonium urate, is pH-dependent. Therefore, consumption of foods that promote aciduria (e.g., high-protein foods or those with other acidifying ingredients) may be a risk factor. Whether the feeding method (meal vs. free-choice feeding) is important in urate urolith formation is not known. Meal feeding may result in increased urinary uric acid excretion postprandially; however, free-choice feeding is often associated with more persistent aciduria compared with meal feeding. Overconsumption of purines or purine precursors increases the risk of urate urolith formation. Therefore, dietary purines should be restricted in animals at risk for forming purine uroliths.

Biologic Behavior

Purine uroliths have the potential to undergo spontaneous dissolution, remain active (grow) or become inactive (remain unchanged). Although spontaneous dissolution of non-urate-containing uroliths has occasionally been observed, the authors have not yet observed spontaneous dissolution of urate uroliths.

Recurrence of urate uroliths may be influenced by several factors including: 1) persistence of underlying causes, 2) incomplete removal of all uroliths from the urinary tract at the time of surgery, 3) persistence or recurrence of UTIs

with urease-producing bacteria or 4) failure to comply with therapeutic or prophylactic recommendations. Frequent recurrence of urate uroliths is not surprising considering the persistence of disorders associated with urate urolithiasis.

A relatively high incidence of recurrence following surgical removal is a unique characteristic of urate urolithiasis in Dalmatian and non-Dalmatian dogs. In several studies using qualitative methods of urolith analysis, recurrence was reported in 33 to 50% of dogs with urate uroliths.[66-68] In these dogs, uroliths generally recurred within one year after diagnosis and treatment. The authors' experience is similar. Recurrence of urate urolithiasis in non-Dalmatian dogs with portal vascular anomalies also appears to be similar.[16,65] In dogs, recurrence of urolithiasis with uroliths composed of minerals other than those present during the initial episode is uncommon. However, uroliths predominantly composed of minerals other than ammonium urate, sodium urate or uric acid may form in canine patients originally affected with urate uroliths.[30,66]

Feeding Plan and Treatment

The authors' current recommendations for medical dissolution of canine ammonium urate uroliths include a combination of: 1) calculolytic foods, 2) administration of xanthine oxidase inhibitors (i.e., allopurinol), 3) alkalinization of urine, 4) eradication or control of UTIs and 5) formation of an increased quantity of less concentrated urine.[1,39,48] There is little information concerning uric acid, sodium urate and sodium calcium urate urolithiasis in dogs; therefore, the following recommendations may be used for these types of uroliths. Recommendations have been developed for urate urolith dissolution and prevention (Table 20-14).

Table 20-14. Summary of recommendations for medical dissolution and prevention of canine ammonium acid urate uroliths.

1. Perform appropriate diagnostic studies, including complete urinalysis, quantitative urine culture and diagnostic radiography. Determine precise location, size and number of uroliths. The size and number of uroliths are not a reliable index of probable therapeutic efficacy.
2. If uroliths are available, determine their mineral composition. If unavailable, determine their composition by evaluating appropriate clinical data.
3. Consider surgical correction if uroliths obstruct urine outflow. Small urocystoliths may be removed by voiding urohydropropulsion.
4. Determine baseline pretreatment serum uric acid concentrations and (if possible) 24-hour excretion of urine uric acid.
5. Initiate therapy with a low-purine calculolytic food (Prescription Diet Canine u/d*). Other foods or supplements should not be fed to the patient. Reduction in serum urea nitrogen concentration (usually <10 mg/dl) suggests compliance with dietary recommendation.
6. Initiate therapy with allopurinol at a dosage of 30 mg/kg body weight/day divided into two equal subdoses (azotemic patients require a lesser dose). Xanthine uroliths may form if foods containing excessive purines are fed or if excessive allopurinol is given.
7. If necessary, administer sodium bicarbonate or potassium citrate orally in order to eliminate aciduria. Strive for a urinary pH of approximately 7.
8. If necessary, eradicate or control urinary tract infections with appropriate antimicrobial agents. Maintain antimicrobial therapy during and for an appropriate period after urate urolith dissolution.
9. Devise a protocol to monitor efficacy of therapy.
   a. Try to avoid diagnostic follow-up studies that require urinary tract catheterization. If they are required, give appropriate peri-catheterization antimicrobial agents to prevent iatrogenic urinary tract infection.
   b. Perform serial urinalyses. Determination of urinary pH and specific gravity and microscopic examination of sediment for urate crystals are especially important. Remember, crystals formed in urine stored at room or refrigeration temperatures may represent in vitro artifacts.
   c. Serially evaluate serum uric acid concentrations and (if possible) fractional excretion of urine uric acid.
   d. Evaluate the location(s), number, size, density and shape of uroliths at monthly intervals. Intravenous urography or ultrasonography may be used for radiolucent uroliths located in the kidneys, ureters or urinary bladder. Retrograde contrast urethrocystography may be required for radiolucent uroliths in the bladder and urethra.
   e. If necessary, perform quantitative urine cultures. They are especially important in patients that are infected before therapy and in patients that are catheterized during therapy.
10. Continue the calculolytic food, allopurinol and alkalinizing therapy for approximately one month following the disappearance of uroliths as detected by radiography.
11. Prevention. Urate uroliths are highly recurrent. Preventive therapy should be directed at minimizing urine concentrations of ammonia and uric acid. This may be achieved by feeding a food low in protein that also promotes an alkaline urine. The effectiveness of dietary management for the prevention of ammonium urate uroliths in dogs with portosystemic shunts is unknown. The long-term use of allopurinol is discouraged because of the potential for development of xanthine uroliths.

*Hill's Pet Nutrition, Inc., Topeka, KS, USA.

Table 20-15. Levels of selected nutrients in commercial products used in canine patients with urolithiasis.*

	Protein	Fat	Phosphorus	Calcium	Magnesium	Sodium	Urinary pH**
Struvite urolith dissolution							
Hill's Prescription Diet Canine s/d, moist	7.6	26.2	0.1	0.28	0.02	1.28	5.9-6.1
Struvite urolith prevention							
Hill's Prescription Diet Canine c/d, moist	22.8	23.9	0.48	0.63	0.07	0.29	6.2-6.4
Hill's Prescription Diet Canine c/d, dry	21.8	21.1	0.52	0.63	0.11	0.27	6.2-6.4
Hill's Prescription Diet Canine w/d, moist	16.5	12	0.52	0.52	0.08	0.3	6.2-6.4
Hill's Prescription Diet Canine w/d, dry	16.7	6.9	0.51	0.56	0.12	0.21	6.2-6.4
Purina CNM DCO-Formula, dry	25.3	12.4	0.93	1.22	0.13	0.34	na
Purina CNM EN-Formula, dry	25.8	11.7	0.9	1.38	0.08	0.36	na
Select Care Canine Control Formula, moist	23.8	20.4	0.71	1.08	0.08	0.29	mean 6.5
Select Care Canine Control Formula, dry	21.2	16.2	0.71	0.95	0.08	0.27	mean 6.5
Calcium oxalate urolith prevention							
Hill's Prescription Diet Canine k/d, moist	14.8	27.8	0.19	0.81	0.03	0.22	6.8-7.2
Hill's Prescription Diet Canine k/d, dry	14.6	19.5	0.29	0.85	0.06	0.19	6.8-7.2
Hill's Prescription Diet Canine u/d, moist	11.5	27.2	0.14	0.29	0.03	0.25	7.1-7.7
Hill's Prescription Diet Canine u/d, dry	9.3	20.6	0.19	0.4	0.04	0.24	7.1-7.7
Purina CNM NF-Formula, moist	16.5	27.4	0.3	0.5	0.08	0.24	na
Purina CNM NF-Formula, dry	15.9	15.7	0.29	0.76	0.07	0.22	na
Select Care Canine Modified Formula, moist	16.8	22.5	0.46	0.61	0.07	0.18	mean 7.0
Select Care Canine Modified Formula, dry	13.7	18.3	0.41	0.85	0.1	0.22	mean 7.0
Ammonium urate and other purine uroliths							
Hill's Prescription Diet Canine u/d, moist	11.5	27.2	0.14	0.29	0.03	0.25	7.1-7.7
Hill's Prescription Diet Canine u/d, dry	9.3	20.6	0.19	0.4	0.04	0.24	7.1-7.7
Purina CNM NF-Formula, dry	15.9	15.7	0.29	0.76	0.07	0.22	na
Cystine uroliths							
Hill's Prescription Diet Canine u/d, moist	11.5	27.2	0.14	0.29	0.03	0.25	7.1-7.7
Hill's Prescription Diet Canine u/d, dry	9.3	20.6	0.19	0.4	0.04	0.24	7.1-7.7
Calcium phosphate uroliths							
Hill's Prescription Diet Canine u/d, moist	11.5	27.2	0.14	0.29	0.03	0.25	7.1-7.7
Hill's Prescription Diet Canine u/d, dry	9.3	20.6	0.19	0.4	0.04	0.24	7.1-7.7

Key: na = information not published by manufacturer.
*This list represents products with the largest market share for which published information is available.
Manufacturers' published values; nutrients expressed as % dry matter.
**Protocols for measuring urinary pH may vary.

Calculolytic Foods

The goal of dietary modification for patients with uric acid or ammonium urate uroliths is to reduce urine con-centration of uric acid, ammonium ions and hydrogen ions (Tables 20-14 and 20-15). The authors use a purine-restricted, alkalinizing food that does not contain supple-mental sodium (Prescription Diet Canine u/d[a]).[35,36,70] Consumption of this food by healthy and urate urolith-forming dogs results in marked reductions in urinary uric acid and ammonia excretion.[1,35]

Xanthine Oxidase Inhibitors

Allopurinol is a synthetic isomer of hypoxanthine.[71] It rapidly binds to and inhibits the action of xanthine oxi-dase, and thereby decreases production of uric acid by inhibiting the conversion of hypoxanthine to xanthine, and xanthine to uric acid. The result is a reduction in serum and urine uric acid concentration within approxi-mately two days, and a concomitant but lesser increase in the serum concentrations of hypoxanthine and xan-thine.[56,72] Although allopurinol has a short half-life in peo-ple with normal renal function (approximately 90 min-utes), its metabolic derivative oxypurinol is also a xan-thine oxidase inhibitor and has a half-life of 12 to 16 hours.[73] In mongrel dogs and beagles, the half-life of allo-purinol is dose dependent (approximately 2.5 hours fol-lowing a 5 mg/kg body weight dose and three hours fol-lowing a 10 mg/kg body weight dose). The half-life of oxy-purinol is three to five hours.[74,75] Food does not affect availability of allopurinol; therefore, it can be adminis-tered with meals.

The dosage of allopurinol that the authors have used for dissolution of ammonium urate uroliths in dogs is 15

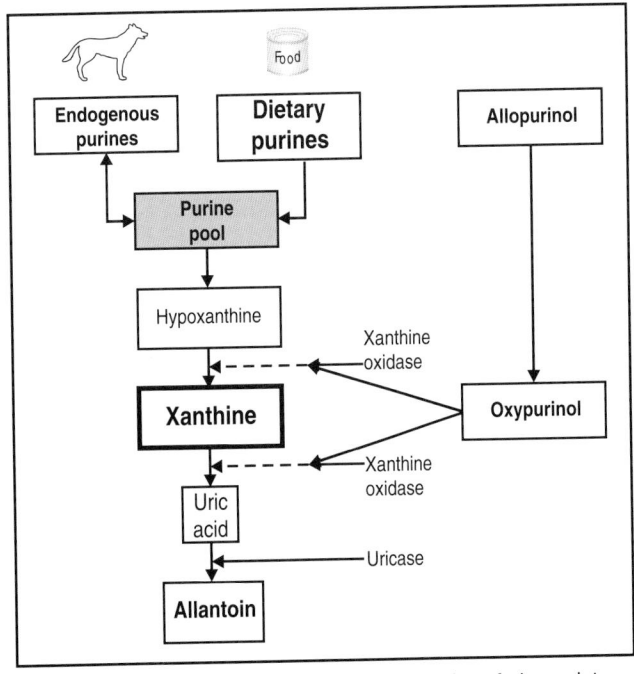

Figure 20-9. Diagram of purine degradation in dogs fed a mainte-nance food and given allopurinol.

mg/kg body weight q12h.[1,39,72] According to the manufacturer, the drug has been given to normal dogs at this dosage for one year without causing significant abnormalities.[b] The authors have given this dosage to nonazotemic, urate urolith-forming dogs for up to six months without detectable consequences. However, when owners supplemented the diet with foods containing purine precursors, a layer of xanthine formed around ammonium urate uroliths (Figures 20-9 and 20-10). Therefore, to minimize xanthine formation, allopurinol should only be administered to animals consuming purine-restricted foods (Figure 20-11).[40]

Reported adverse effects of allopurinol in people include gastrointestinal disturbances, skin rashes, leukopenia, thrombocytopenia, vasculitis and hepatitis.[76,77] There is only one report of a possible immune-mediated reaction (hemolytic anemia, trigeminal neuropathy) to allopurinol administration in a dog.[78] Because allopurinol and its metabolites are dependent on the kidneys for elimination, the dosage is commonly reduced in people with renal dysfunction. Allopurinol has been reported to cause life-threatening erythematous desquamative skin rashes, fever, hepatitis, eosinopenia and further decline in renal function when given to people with renal insufficiency.[71] Pending further studies, appropriate precautions should be used when considering use of allopurinol in dogs with primary renal failure.

Alkalinization of Urine

Because ammonium ions and hydrogen ions appear to precipitate urates in dog urine, oral administration of alkalinizing agents (e.g., sodium bicarbonate or potassium citrate) may be of value in preventing acid metabolites from increasing renal tubular production of ammonia. Under physiologic conditions associated with alkaluria, urine contains low concentrations of ammonia and ammonium ions.[79]

Dosage of urine alkalinizers should be individualized for each patient. Preliminary dosages of sodium bicarbonate vary from approximately 25 to 50 mg/kg body weight q12h depending on the status of the patient and pretreatment urinary pH values. Alternatively, potassium citrate in wax matrix tablets (Urocit-K[c]) or as a liquid (Polycitra-K[d]) (40 to 75 mg/kg body weight q12h) may be given. Because sodium may combine with uric acid to form sodium urate, potassium citrate may be preferable to sodium bicarbonate as a urine alkalinizer. Divided doses should be administered to maintain a consistently nonacidic environment in the urinary tract. The food used for urate dissolution (Prescription Diet Canine u/d) is formulated to contain potassium citrate, and its consumption typically results in alkaluria in dogs.[35,36]

The goal of treatment with urine alkalinizers or the urate calculolytic food is to maintain a urinary pH of approximately 7.0. Higher values (>7.5) should be avoided until it is determined whether or not they provide a significant risk factor for formation of calcium phosphate uroliths. Deposition of a layer of calcium phosphate crystals around existing urate uroliths may impede urolith dissolution. Owners may monitor urinary pH with pH paper or handheld "pocket" pH meters.

Eradication or Control of UTIs

Clinical studies indicate that UTIs in dogs with ammonium urate uroliths usually occur as a consequence of

altered local host defenses. These alterations may be caused by urolith-induced trauma to the urothelium, or they may occur as a consequence of catheterization or other invasive diagnostic procedures. Effort should be made to prevent, eradicate or control infections because they may cause problems of equal or greater severity as the uroliths.

Studies of ammonium urate uroliths in people have been interpreted to suggest that UTI caused by urease-producing microbes may be a causative factor.[80] In this cir-

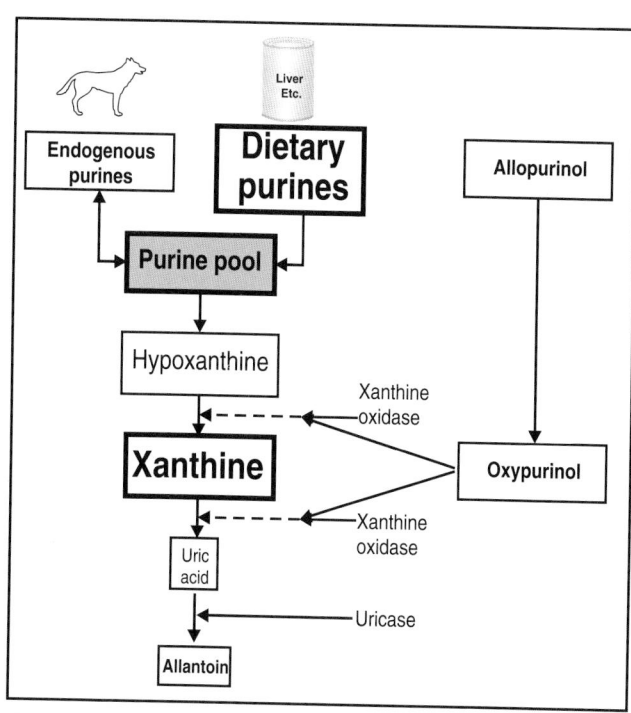

Figure 20-10. Diagram of purine metabolism in dogs that consume a purine-rich diet and are given allopurinol.

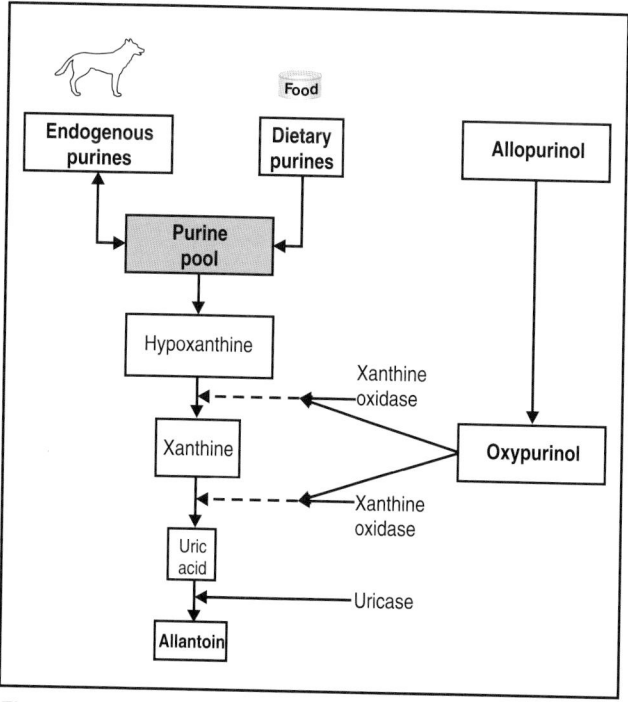

Figure 20-11. Diagram of purine metabolism in dogs that consume a purine-restricted food and are given allopurinol.

cumstance, formation of ammonium ions as a consequence of urease-mediated hydrolysis of urea may result in formation of insoluble ammonium urate crystals. If a similar phenomenon occurs in dogs, eradication or control of potent urease-producing microbes (staphylococci, *Proteus* spp and ureaplasma) would be especially important.

Appropriate antimicrobial agents selected on the basis of susceptibility or minimum inhibitory concentration tests should be used at therapeutic dosages. The fact that diuresis reduces the urine concentration of the antimicrobial agent should be considered when formulating antimicrobial dosages.

Augmenting Urine Volume

Augmenting urine volume with the goal of decreasing urine uric acid and ammonium concentrations and enhancing urine flow through the excretory pathway appears to be a logical recommendation. Because the calculolytic food used for urate urolith dissolution impairs urine concentrating capacity by decreasing renal medullary urea concentration, additional diuretic agents are unnecessary. Because excessive sodium excretion may cause hypercalciuria, excessive dietary sodium should be avoided, particularly if the urinary pH is high. This event may in turn cause calcium phosphate crystals to form. (See the Calcium Phosphate Urolithiasis section.)

It is of interest that sodium chloride given orally to normal human volunteers for 10 days did not alter urine uric acid concentration.[81] Long-term administration (up to three years) of hydrochlorothiazide to human patients with uroliths containing calcium salts resulted in increased serum and urine uric acid concentrations.[82]

Dogs Without Portal Vascular Anomalies

At the University of Minnesota, 25 dogs with ammonium urate uroliths were treated with dietary and allopurinol therapy. Complete dissolution occurred in nine dogs (36%), partial dissolution occurred in eight dogs (32%) and no dissolution occurred in eight dogs (32%). A similar dissolution protocol in seven dogs with sodium urate uroliths resulted in complete dissolution in two dogs (29%), partial dissolution in three dogs (42%) and no dissolution in two dogs (29%).[69] Inability to dissolve urate uroliths was usually associated with formation of xanthine. In some dogs with partial urolith dissolution, the remaining uroliths were completely retrieved using voiding urohydropropulsion[83] or catheter-assisted retrieval.[24] The mean time of urate urolith dissolution in 11 dogs was 3.5 months (median one month, range one to 18 months). Using the above protocol, the authors dissolved a nephrolith presumed to be composed of urate in nine months in a six-year-old, neutered female English bulldog.

Dogs with Portal Vascular Anomalies

There apparently have been few studies of the biologic behavior of ammonium urate uroliths in dogs with portal vascular anomalies. It is logical to hypothesize that elimi-

---

Use of Low-Protein Foods in Canine Patients with Urolithiasis

A commercial veterinary therapeutic food that reduces urine concentration, produces alkaline urine and avoids excess levels of dietary protein, purines, calcium and phosphorus (Prescription Diet Canine u/d[a]) is frequently recommended for management of several different canine uroliths. This commercial food has not been recommended by some individuals because the protein levels (10 to 11% dry matter) are less than the recommended dietary allowance for protein established by the Association of American Feed Control Officials (AAFCO) (minimum 18% dry matter for adult maintenance).

However, based on several criteria, Canine u/d is nutritionally adequate for maintenance of adult, non-reproducing dogs. First, moist and dry formulations of Canine u/d have successfully completed AAFCO adult maintenance feeding trials.[b] Second, in addition to a dietary allowance for protein, AAFCO has established dietary allowances for 12 essential amino acids. Although Canine u/d does not meet the dietary allowance for total protein, it does meet or exceed the dietary allowances for all essential amino acids except tryptophan. Even so, tryptophan levels in Canine u/d exceed those established as the minimum requirement. In addition, protein digestibility in Canine u/d approaches 100%, which means the essential amino acids are readily available to dogs. The final criterion is practical experience with this food. Canine u/d has been used successfully for long-term feeding of thousands of canine patients with urolithiasis.

The dry formulation of Canine u/d can be modified for growing dogs (Table 1). However, the safety and efficacy of this modified food in young dogs with urate or other uroliths is unknown. Growing dogs should be monitored closely when fed these recipes.

Table 1. Modified recipes for growing dogs based on the dry formulation of Prescription Diet Canine u/d.

Recipe A
1 cup dry Prescription Diet Canine u/d
1 tsp dicalcium phosphate
1 cup cottage cheese
Multivitamin-mineral supplement for dogs

Nutrient levels (% dry matter)	
Protein	30.5
Fat	19.5
Calcium	1.0
Phosphorus	1.0
Magnesium	0.02
Sodium	0.6
Potassium	0.5

Recipe B
1 cup dry Prescription Diet Canine u/d
3/4 tsp dicalcium phosphate
2 cooked eggs
Multivitamin-mineral supplement for dogs

Nutrient levels (% dry matter)	
Protein	17.6
Fat	27.1
Calcium	1.1
Phosphorus	1.0
Magnesium	0.02
Sodium	0.4
Potassium	0.6

ENDNOTES
a. Hill's Pet Nutrition, Inc., Topeka, KS, USA.
b. Data on file. Hill's Pet Nutrition, Inc., Topeka, KS, USA.

nation of hyperuricuria and reduction of urine ammonium concentration following surgical correction of anomalous shunts would result in spontaneous dissolution of uroliths composed primarily of ammonium urate. Appropriate clinical studies are needed to prove or disprove this hypothesis.[34] The authors have occasionally been successful in medically dissolving urate uroliths in dogs with portal vascular anomalies. In addition, the authors observed dissolution of a urolith presumed to be composed of ammonium urate in a two-year-old female miniature schnauzer with a portal vascular anomaly. The dog was consuming a veterinary therapeutic food designed for treatment of renal failure (Prescription Diet Canine k/d[a]). The mechanisms involved were presumably decreased production of ammonium ions from urea and reduced formation of uric acid from dietary protein.

Likewise, a renolith in the right renal pelvis of a seven-year-old female malamute with a portal vascular anomaly disappeared while the dog consumed Prescription Diet Canine k/d. Also, the authors observed a marked reduction of urine uric acid concentration in a three-month-old female miniature schnauzer following surgical correction of an extrahepatic portacaval shunt. Further, the authors have observed undersaturation of urine with ammonium urate and no recurrence of urolith formation in two dogs with surgically uncorrectable portal vascular anomalies and ammonium urate uroliths. The dogs were fed Prescription Diet Canine u/d for prevention of recurrence of the uroliths and for management of hepatic encephalopathy. Additional clinical studies are needed to evaluate the relative value of calculolytic foods, allopurinol and/or alkalinization of urine in dissolving ammonium urate uroliths in dogs with portal vascular anomalies. The efficacy of allopurinol may be altered in such dogs because biotransformation of this drug, which has a very short half-life, to oxypurinol, which has a longer half-life, requires adequate hepatic function.[72]

Immature Dogs with Urate Uroliths

Providing safe and effective therapy for urate uroliths in immature dogs presents a challenge. Formation of urate uroliths associated with portal vascular anomalies and their management are discussed in previous sections. Growing dogs usually consume greater quantities of pro-tein and, thus, purines than adult dogs. The safety and efficacy of calculolytic foods in young dogs with urate uroliths are unknown. Adding non-purine-containing protein to the calculolytic food may be effective; however, no studies have yet been performed to confirm this hypothesis. Also, the metabolism of allopurinol in young animals has not been evaluated. Therefore, surgical removal of large uroliths remains the option with the most predictable short-term outcome. (See sidebar "Use of Low-Protein Foods in Patients with Urolithiasis.")

Surgical and Medical Combinations

There are several situations in which a combination of surgical removal of urate uroliths followed by medical dissolution protocols might be beneficial. One involves the inability to remove all uroliths by surgery. This occasionally occurs because ammonium urate uroliths are frequently multiple and small. The fact that they may be radiolucent creates an additional problem by interfering with their radiographic detection immediately after surgery.

In some patients, immediate surgery may be required to remove uroliths obstructing the renal pelvis, ureter(s) or urethra. Initiation of medical dissolution protocols may prove advantageous if such patients have multiple uroliths in several locations, and if circumstances preclude their surgical removal at the time the obstructing urolith is removed.

Certain patients with portal vascular anomalies and urate uroliths may also benefit from a combination of surgical and medical urolith dissolution protocols. Techniques have been devised to correct some types of intrahepatic and extrahepatic shunts in dogs. However, the condition of the patient and factors related to anesthesia and surgery may preclude urolith removal at the time the anomalous portal vessels are corrected. In this situation, postsurgical medical therapy designed to dissolve uroliths should be considered. Also, some types of portal vascular anomalies are not amenable to surgical correction. If the uroliths are causing unacceptable signs of urinary tract disease, they should be surgically removed and postsurgical preventive measures should be initiated. Voiding urohydropropulsion may be used to remove small urocystoliths (Table 20-16).

Table 20-16. Voiding urohydropropulsion: A nonsurgical technique for removing small urocystoliths.

1. Perform appropriate diagnostic studies, including complete urinalysis, quantitative urine culture and diagnostic radiography. Determine the location, size, surface contour and number of urocystoliths.
2. Anesthetize the patient, if needed.
3. If the urinary bladder is not distended with urine, moderately distend it with a physiologic solution (e.g., saline, Ringer's, etc.) injected through a transurethral catheter. To prevent overdistention, palpate the bladder per abdomen during infusion. Remove the catheter.
4. Position the patient such that the vertebral spine is approximately vertical.
5. Gently agitate the urinary bladder, with the objective of promoting gravitational movement of urocystoliths into the bladder neck.
6. Induce voiding by manually expressing the urinary bladder. Use steady digital pressure rather than an intermittent squeezing motion.
7. Collect urine and uroliths in a cup. Compare urolith number and size to those detected by radiography and submit them for quantitative analysis.
8. If needed, repeat Steps 3 through 7 until the number of uroliths detected by radiography are removed or until uroliths are no longer voided.
9. Perform double-contrast cystography to ensure that no uroliths remain in the urinary bladder. Repeat voiding urohydropropulsion if small urocystoliths remain.
10. Administer prophylactic antimicrobials for three to five days, or longer if needed.
11. Monitor the patient for adverse complications (i.e., hematuria, dysuria, bacterial urinary tract infection and urethral obstruction with uroliths).
12. Formulate appropriate recommendations to minimize urolith recurrence or to manage uroliths remaining in the urinary tract on the basis of quantitative mineral analysis of voided urocystoliths.

Reassessment

In the authors' experience, ammonium urate urocystoliths have a propensity to move into the urethra of dogs. This finding may be related to their small size, round to ovoid shape and smooth surface. If small enough, they readily pass through the urethra. However, they often become lodged behind the os penis of male dogs. Owners should be informed of this likelihood and given a written summary of associated clinical findings. Urethroliths causing clinical signs may be easily returned to the bladder lumen by urohydropropulsion.[83] The physical characteristics that promote their passage into the urethra also facilitate their removal from the urethra.

When attempting medical dissolution of urate uroliths, owners must be advised to adhere strictly to feeding low-purine foods. Consumption of a high-purine diet by dogs while receiving allopurinol may result in formation of a xanthine shell around urate uroliths or formation of xanthine uroliths (Figure 20-10).[39,41,84] Xanthine uroliths may not dissolve. However, the authors have observed spontaneous dissolution of xanthine shells and underlying uroliths by discontinuing allopurinol and continuing the low-purine food.[69] Alternatively, dissolution of urate uroliths may occur as a result of a combination of feeding a low-purine food and administering allopurinol at a lower dose to dogs that previously formed xanthine shells.

Because allopurinol and its metabolites are excreted from the body primarily in urine, the drug should be used with appropriate caution in patients with renal dysfunction.[74,79] Reduction in the dosage of allopurinol is recommended for human patients with primary renal failure. Pending further studies, a similar recommendation should be applied to dogs with primary renal failure.

The size of the uroliths should be periodically monitored by survey and (if necessary) double-contrast radiography or ultrasonography (Table 20-17). It is more difficult to monitor changes in size and number if the uroliths are radiolucent. The authors believe that double-contrast cystography is superior to ultrasonography because: 1) it is minimally invasive, 2) sedation is usually not required to perform the procedure, 3) all uroliths can be visualized, including their size, shape and number and 4) uroliths may be retrieved through the catheter and submitted for quantitative analysis. Although the authors have successfully used retrograde, double-contrast urethrocystography to monitor dissolution of radiolucent urethrocystoliths without causing iatrogenic UTIs, appropriate prophylactic antibiotics should be administered around the time of urinary catheterization. Excretory urography or ultrasonography should be used to monitor dissolution or recurrence of urate nephroliths.

Urinary pH should be monitored at appropriate intervals (Table 20-17). Periodic evaluation of urine sediment for crystalluria should also be considered. Ammonium urate crystals should not form in fresh urine if therapy has been effective in promoting formation of urine that is undersaturated with ammonium ions and uric acid. Periodic evaluation of serum urea nitrogen concentration, serum uric acid concentration and (if possible) urine uric acid concentration is recommended. Reduction of serum urea nitrogen concentration below pretreatment values (usually <10 mg/dl in previously nonazotemic patients), reduction of urine specific gravity (usually <1.020) and an increase in urinary pH (usually >7.0) indicate owner and patient compliance with dietary therapy (Table 20-17). Reductions in serum and urine uric acid concentrations also indicate compliance with recommendations for dietary and allopurinol therapy.

Determination of urine urate-to-creatinine ratios in randomly collected single urine samples has been recommended to aid in diagnosis of dogs with urate uroliths and to monitor medical therapy of dogs with urate uroliths.[60,85] However, in a controlled study, spot urine urate-to-creatinine ratios correlated poorly with 24-hour urinary uric acid excretion in healthy non-urolith-forming beagles.[86] Although urine urate-to-creatinine ratios decrease significantly in dogs with urate uroliths given allopurinol,[87] they do not correlate with 24-hour urinary uric acid excretions in these dogs, nor are they useful in predicting urolith dissolution.[e] Further, urine xanthine-to-creatinine ratios in these dogs did not correlate with 24-hour urinary xanthine excretions, nor were they predictive for urate urolith dissolution or xanthine formation.[e]

There is no rigid time interval after which response to dissolution therapy is unlikely. The fact that current medical protocols are not designed to induce dissolution of urolith matrix may be a factor that influences dissolution rate. The time required to induce dissolution of nine episodes of urate urolithiasis in the authors' clinical study has ranged from four to 40 weeks (mean 14.2 weeks). Re-evaluation of the diagnosis and/or alternate methods of management should be considered if uroliths enlarge during therapy or do not begin to decrease in size after approximately eight weeks of appropriate medical therapy (Table 20-18).

If it is difficult to completely dissolve urate uroliths by creating urine that is undersaturated with uric acid and ammonium ions, consider that: 1) the wrong mineral com-

Table 20-17. Expected changes associated with medical therapy of ammonium urate uroliths.

Factors	Pre-therapy	During therapy	Prevention therapy
Polyuria	±	1+ to 3+	1+ to 3+
Pollakiuria	0 to 4+	↑ then ↓	0
Hematuria	0 to 4+	↓	0
Urine specific gravity	Variable	1.004 to 1.015	1.004 to 1.015
Urinary pH	<7.0	>7.0	>7.0
Pyuria 0 to 4+	↓	0	
Urate crystals	0 to 4+	0	Variable
Bacteriuria	0 to 4+	0	0
Bacterial culture of urine	0 to 4+	0	0
Urea nitrogen (mg/dl)	Variable	≤15	≤15
Urolith size and number	Small to large	↓	0

ponent was identified, 2) the nucleus of the urolith is of different mineral composition than the outer portions of the urolith, 3) a xanthine shell or xanthine uroliths have formed or 4) the owner or patient is not complying with therapeutic recommendations.

Prevention of Urate Urolithiasis

Dalmatian Dogs

Prophylactic therapy should be considered for urate-forming Dalmatian dogs because of the high risk for recurrent urate uroliths. As a first choice, foods that are restricted in purines and that promote formation of less concentrated alkaline urine should be considered (Table 20-15). In one study of naturally occurring ammonium urate urocystoliths in Dalmatian dogs, a low-protein nonacidifying moist food (Prescription Diet Canine u/d) reduced urolith recurrence by 50% compared with an adult moist maintenance food.[88] If dry foods are fed, water should be added with the goal of maintaining a urine specific gravity less than approximately 1.025.

If urate crystalluria or hyperuricuria persists, serial urinary pH measurements are indicated to ensure appropriate alkalinization. If necessary, urine alkalinizing agents may be added to the protocol. If difficulties persist, low doses of allopurinol (approximately 10 to 20 mg/kg body weight/day) may be given cautiously. Studies performed at the University of California, Davis and the University of Minnesota indicate that prolonged administration of high doses (30 mg/kg body weight/day) of allopurinol may result in formation of xanthine uroliths.[39,48] The risk of xanthine urolithiasis is enhanced if dietary purines are not restricted during allopurinol therapy. Therefore, appropriate caution in long-term administration of this drug is indicated. Because it is possible to induce dissolution of recurrent ammonium urate uroliths, it is unnecessary to risk the use of prophylactic protocols that may themselves cause disorders.

When considering use of foods to minimize occurrence of urolithiasis, the authors avoid an "always" or "never" approach. The final decision should be based on the overall balance of benefits to the patient and associated risks (if any).

Table 20-18. Managing urate uroliths refractory to complete dissolution.

Causes	Identification	Therapeutic goal
Client and patient factors		
Inadequate dietary compliance	Question owner Persistent urate crystalluria Urea nitrogen >10-17 mg/dl Urine specific gravity >1.010-1.020 Urinary pH <7.0-7.5 during treatment with Prescription Diet Canine u/d* (use lower values for canned food)	Emphasize need to exclusively feed dissolution food
Inadequate allopurinol administration	Question owner Count remaining pills	Emphasize need to administer allopurinol Determine if owner is capable and willing to administer medication Demonstrate a variety of methods to administer medication
Clinician factors		
Incorrect prediction of mineral type	Analysis of retrieved urolith	Alter therapy based on identification of mineral type
Excessive allopurinol administration	Xanthine urolith formation	Reduce allopurinol administration in conjunction with appropriate dietary therapy to minimize purine consumption Clinically active uroliths may require surgical removal Remove small uroliths by voiding urohydropropulsion
Disease factors		
Xanthine urolith formation	Analysis of retrieved urolith Allopurinol administration without concomitant reduction in dietary protein consumption Excessive allopurinol dose	Clinically active uroliths may require surgical removal Remove small uroliths by voiding urohydropropulsion
Inadequate hepatic function	Suspect hepatic portosystemic shunts in breeds other than Dalmatians and English bulldogs Elevated postprandial serum bile acid concentration Microhepatica	Clinically active uroliths may require surgical removal Remove small uroliths by voiding urohydropropulsion Repair vascular anomaly
Compound urolith	Radiographic density of nucleus and outer layer(s) of urolith is different Analysis of retrieved urolith	Alter therapy based on identification of a new mineral type Uroliths not causing clinical signs should be monitored for potentially adverse consequences (obstruction, urinary tract infection, etc.) Clinically active uroliths may require surgical removal Remove small uroliths by voiding urohydropropulsion

*Hill's Pet Nutrition, Inc., Topeka, KS, USA.

Non-Dalmatian Dogs

There is no published information concerning recurrence rates of urate uroliths in non-Dalmatian dogs; however, the authors have observed recurrence of urate uroliths in three of five English bulldogs. Therefore, the authors recommend that preventive measures for Dalmatian dogs also be used for non-Dalmatian dogs.

There have been few studies of the biologic behavior of ammonium urate uroliths in dogs and cats with portal vascular anomalies. It is logical to hypothesize that elimination of hyperuricuria and reduction of urine ammonium concentration following surgical correction of anomalous shunts would result in spontaneous dissolution of uroliths composed primarily of ammonium urate.

Additional clinical studies are needed to evaluate the relative value of calculolytic foods, allopurinol and/or alkalinization of urine in dissolving ammonium urate uroliths in dogs and cats with portal vascular anomalies. The likelihood of adverse side effects or further deterioration in hepatic function following administration of allo-purinol to dogs with portal vascular anomalies has not been determined. Reversible hepatitis has been reported to be an uncommon reaction to allopurinol given to people.[76,89,90] Pending further study, appropriate precautions should be taken to monitor patients for adverse reactions if allopurinol is given to dogs with portal vascular anomalies.

Because tetracycline exacerbates hepatic and renal dysfunction in dogs with experimentally produced portal vascular anomalies, it should not be used to treat UTIs in dogs with naturally occurring portal vascular anomalies.[91]

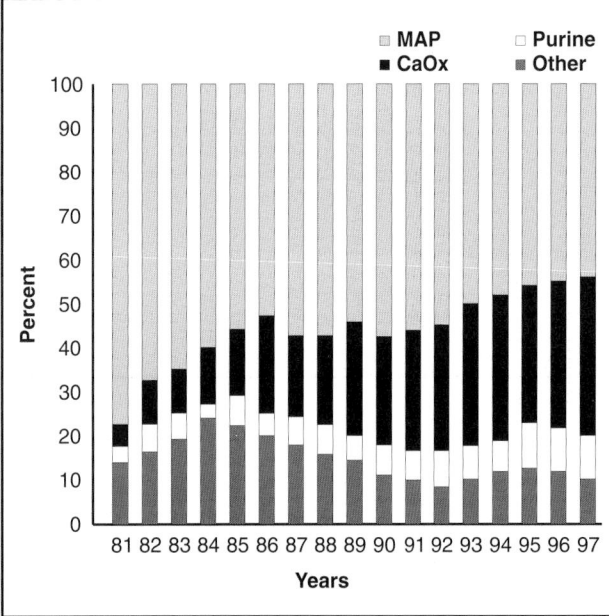

Figure 20-12. Bar graph illustrating increased occurrence of canine calcium oxalate uroliths submitted to the Minnesota Urolith Center from 1981 to 1997. Note the decline in struvite urolith submissions. MAP = magnesium ammonium phosphate, CaOx = calcium oxalate, Purine = purine uroliths, Other = all other urolith types combined. (Adapted from Osborne CA, Lulich JP, Polzin DJ, et al. Analysis of 77,000 canine uroliths: Perspectives from the Minnesota Urolith Center. Veterinary Clinics of North America: Small Animal Practice 1999; 29: 25.)

■ CALCIUM OXALATE UROLITHS

Prevalence and Mineral Composition

Calcium oxalate accounted for 31% of all canine uroliths submitted to the Minnesota Urolith Center from 1981 to 1997 (Table 20-7) and 35% (5,401 of 15,259) of all canine uroliths submitted in 1997 (Figure 20-12). Calcium oxalate accounted for 38% of all canine nephroliths analyzed at the Minnesota Urolith Center from 1981 to 1997 (Table 20-8). Calcium oxalate composed only 4% of uroliths retrieved from dogs less than 12 months old. The mean age of dogs at the time of calcium oxalate urolith retrieval was 8.5 ± 2.9 years (range one to 25 years). Males (72%) were affected more often than females (28%). One hundred and twenty different breeds were affected including miniature schnauzers (25%), mixed breeds (13%), Lhasa apsos (9%), Yorkshire terriers (8%), Shih Tzus (5%) and bichon frises (5%). Calcium oxalate uroliths were more commonly removed from the lower urinary tract (97%) than the upper urinary tract (3%).

Although different combinations of calcium oxalate salts have been identified in canine uroliths, the predominant form encountered in the authors' series has been calcium oxalate monohydrate (whewellite; Table 20-7).[92] Pure calcium oxalate monohydrate has been observed in dogs more frequently than pure calcium oxalate dihydrate (weddelite). A similar observation has been made in cats and people with calcium oxalate uroliths. When calcium oxalate salts occur in combination in human and canine uroliths, the dihydrate salt is usually found surrounding a nucleus of the monohydrate salt.[93] The significance of this observation has not yet been determined, although it has been suggested that calcium oxalate dihydrate may form initially and then be converted to calcium oxalate monohydrate.[94-97]

The importance of differentiating calcium oxalate monohydrate from calcium oxalate dihydrate in canine uroliths remains to be established. In people, it has been suggested that detection of calcium oxalate dihydrate on the outside of a urolith is indicative of recent formation, whereas detection of external layers of calcium oxalate monohydrate indicates lack of recent urolith formation.[98] If valid, this hypothesis would be of clinical significance because it would help to determine the persistence of disorders leading to calcium oxalate urolith formation and, therefore, the need for continuous therapy to minimize urolith recurrence. In one study, human patients with calcium oxalate dihydrate uroliths had more recurrences of uroliths than did patients with calcium oxalate monohydrate uroliths.[93]

Calcium oxalate monohydrate and dihydrate uroliths are typically dense and brittle; they have relatively small quantities of matrix. Pure calcium oxalate monohydrate and calcium oxalate dihydrate have different colors and shapes (Table 20-19). In people, uroliths composed of calcium oxalate monohydrate frequently assume the shape of mulberries or jackstones.[95] To date, the authors have observed only a few canine calcium oxalate jackstones.

Etiopathogenesis and Risk Factors

In order for uroliths to form, urine must be supersaturated with respect to that crystal system. Therefore, increasing the urine concentration of calcium or oxalic acid promotes calcium oxalate crystal formation.

Hypercalciuria has been documented to occur in dogs with calcium oxalate uroliths.[19] It has been argued that increases in urine oxalic acid concentration promote calcium oxalate urolith formation to a greater degree than comparable increases in urine calcium concentration.[99] Although hyperoxaluria has not been documented to occur in dogs with calcium oxalate uroliths, the relationship between the concentrations of calcium and oxalic acid within the digestive and the urinary tracts is fundamental to formation of calcium oxalate uroliths.

Dietary Risk Factors

Dietary ingredients that promote hypercalciuria or hyperoxaluria represent nutritional risk factors for calcium oxalate urolith formation (Tables 20-20 and 20-21).

Therefore, reduction of dietary calcium and oxalate appears to be a logical therapeutic goal; however, it is not necessarily a harmless maneuver. Reducing consumption of only one of these substances (i.e., calcium) may increase the availability of the other (i.e., oxalic acid) for intestinal absorption and subsequent urinary excretion. In general, reduction in dietary calcium should be accompanied by an appropriate reduction in dietary oxalate.

It has been the authors' experience that dogs with calcium oxalate urolithiasis frequently consume human food. Calcium oxalate is the most common urolith type recognized in people living in developed countries. As people feed their dogs the same dietary proportions and ingredients they feed themselves, it is logical to assume that dogs would be exposed to the same nutritional risk factors for urolith formation (Tables 20-20).

Table 20-19. Common characteristics of canine calcium oxalate uroliths.

Chemical names	Formulas	Crystal names
Calcium oxalate monohydrate	$CaC_2O_4 \cdot H_2O$	Whewellite
Calcium oxalate dihydrate	$CaC_2O_4 \cdot 2H_2O$	Weddellite

Variations in mineral composition
Calcium oxalate monohydrate only
Calcium oxalate dihydrate only
Combinations of calcium oxalate monohydrate and dihydrate
Calcium oxalate (monohydrate and/or dihydrate) mixed with variable quantities of calcium phosphate. Variable quantities of struvite or ammonium acid urate may also be present.
Calcium oxalate (monohydrate and/or dihydrate) nucleus surrounded by other minerals especially infection-induced struvite

Physical characteristics
Color: Calcium oxalate monohydrate uroliths are usually tan or brown. Calcium oxalate dihydrate uroliths are usually white or cream-colored. Surfaces may be red to black if uroliths are coated with blood.
Shape: Variable. Calcium oxalate monohydrate uroliths are usually round or elliptical and have a smooth, polished surface. On occasion they may develop a jackstone or mulberry shape. Calcium oxalate dihydrate uroliths and mixed calcium oxalate monohydrate/calcium oxalate dihydrate uroliths are usually round to ovoid and have an irregular surface caused by protrusion of sharp-edged crystals. On occasion, they may develop a jackstone shape.
Nuclei: Radial striations and concentric laminations may occur.
Density: Very dense and brittle. Survey radiographs reveal that calcium-containing uroliths are radiodense compared with soft tissue.
Number: Single or multiple
Location: May be located in renal pelves, ureters, urinary bladder (most common) and/or urethra.
Size: Sub-visual to several centimeters

Prevalence
Approximately 30% of all canine uroliths. More than 38% of canine nephroliths.
May be recurrent (more than 50% recur by three years after removal)

Characteristics of affected canine patients
More common in males (57%) than females (43%)
Mean age at diagnosis is about eight years (range <1 to >25 years)
Most commonly observed in miniature schnauzers, miniature poodles, Lhasa apsos, Yorkshire terriers, Shih Tzus and bichon frises

Table 20-20. Some potential risk factors for canine calcium oxalate uroliths.

Diet	Urine	Metabolic	Drugs
Acidifying potential	Hypercalciuria	Chronic metabolic acidosis	Urine acidifiers
High protein content	Hyperoxaluria	Males	Furosemide
High sodium content	Hypocitraturia?	Breed	Glucocorticoids
Excessive calcium content	Hypomagnesuria?	Miniature schnauzers	Sodium chloride
Excessive restriction of calcium	Hyperuricuria?	Miniature poodles	Vitamin D
Low moisture content	Increased crystal promoters	Lhasa apsos	Ascorbic acid
Excessive phosphorus restriction	Decreased crystal inhibitors	Yorkshire terriers	
Excessive magnesium content	Urine concentration	Shih Tzus	
Excessive magnesium restriction	Urine retention	Bichon frises	
Excessive vitamin D content		Older age	
Excessive vitamin C content		Hypercalcemia	
Deficient pyridoxine?		Glucocorticoid excess	
High oxalate content		Hypophosphatemia	
		Hyperoxalemia?	
		Osteolysis?	

In addition to human food consumption, the authors have also recognized an association between calcium oxalate urolithiasis and consumption of commercially available treats. The high sodium content of some commercial dog treats may help explain this association because sodium consumption promotes hypercalciuria.[100]

Table 20-21. Selected human foods to limit or avoid feeding to dogs with calcium oxalate uroliths.[*]

Food items	Moderate/high-calcium foods
Meats	Bologna (M)
	Herring (M)
	Oysters (M)
	Salmon (H)
	Sardines (H)
Vegetables	Baked beans (M)
	Broccoli (H)
	Collards (H)
	Lima beans (M)
	Spinach (M)
	Tofu (soybean curd) (M)
Milk and dairy products	Cheese (H)
	Ice cream (H)
	Milk (H)
	Yogurt (H)
Breads, grains, nuts	Brazil nuts (M)
Miscellaneous	Cocoa (M)
	Hot chocolate (M)

Food items	Moderate/high-oxalate foods
Meats	Sardines (M)
Vegetables	Asparagus (M)
	Broccoli (M)
	Carrots (M)
	Celery (H)
	Corn (M)
	Cucumber (H)
	Eggplant (H)
	Green beans (H)
	Green peppers (H)
	Lettuce (M)
	Spinach (H)
	Summer squash (H)
	Sweet potatoes (H)
	Tofu (H)
	Tomatoes (M)
Fruits	Apples (H)
	Apricots (H)
	Cherries (M)
	Most berries (H)
	Oranges (M)
	Peaches (M)
	Pears (M)
	Peel of lemon, lime or orange (H)
	Pineapple (M)
	Tangerine (H)
Breads, grains, nuts	Corn bread (M)
	Fruit cake (H)
	Grits (H)
	Peanuts (H)
	Pecans (H)
	Soybeans (H)
	Wheat germ (H)
Miscellaneous	Beer (H)
	Chocolate (H)
	Cocoa (H)
	Coffee (M)
	Tea (H)
	Tomato soup (H)
	Vegetable soup (H)

Key: M = moderate; feed in limited amounts. H = high; avoid feeding.
*Adapted from Wainer L, Resnick VA, Resnick MI. Nutritional aspects of stone disease. In: Pak CYC, ed. Renal Stone Disease, Pathogenesis, Prevention, and Treatment. Boston, MA: Martinus Nihoff Publishing, 1987; 85-120. Burroughs M. Renal diseases and disorders. In: Nelson JK, Moxness KE, Jensen MD, et al, eds. Mayo Clinic Diet Manual, 7th ed. St. Louis, MO: Mosby, 1994; 208-209.

Certain dietary excesses and deficiencies have also been recognized as potential risk factors. Excessive administration of vitamin D, sodium or magnesium promotes hypercalciuria. Excessive administration of ascorbic acid should be minimized because it is a precursor of oxalate. Although dogs with calcium oxalate uroliths have not been evaluated for pyridoxine deficiency, kittens fed pyridoxine-deficient foods exhibited hyperoxaluria.[101]

Other Risk Factors

Calcium oxalate uroliths have been recognized in many breeds of dogs. However, miniature schnauzers, Lhasa apsos, Shih Tzus, Yorkshire terriers, miniature poodles and bichon frises have been most commonly affected. Infrequently affected breeds include Boxers, English bulldogs, golden retrievers and Labrador retrievers. Approximately 70% of calcium oxalate uroliths have affected male dogs. Most were detected in adults (mean age eight to nine years).

Geographic location has been identified as a risk factor for calcium oxalate urolith formation in people living in the United States.[102] The southeastern United States (Alabama, Arkansas, Florida, Georgia, Louisiana, Mississippi, North and South Carolina, Tennessee and Virginia) has the highest rate of urolith formation. Studies evaluating geographic location as a risk factor for calcium oxalate urolith formation in dogs have apparently not been reported.

Certain clinical conditions also represent potential risk factors for calcium oxalate urolith formation. Hyperparathyroidism, hyperadrenocorticism, hypervitaminosis D, paraneoplastic hypercalcemia and furosemide administration promote hypercalciuria. Intestinal resection, hereditary hyperoxaluria and excessive ascorbic acid administration promote hyperoxaluria.

Hypercalciuria

Calcium homeostasis is principally achieved through the actions of parathyroid hormone (PTH) and 1,25-cholecalciferol (1,25-vitamin D) on the skeleton, intestine and kidneys. For example, states of low serum ionized calcium concentration result in enhanced PTH- and 1,25-vitamin D-mediated mobilization of calcium from the skeleton, absorption of calcium from the intestine and conservation of calcium by the kidneys. High serum ionized calcium concentrations suppress release of PTH and production of 1,25-vitamin D. The result is decreased skeletal mobilization and intestinal absorption of calcium and enhanced renal calcium excretion. Thus, it is apparent that hypercalciuria can result from increased renal clearance of calcium due to: 1) excessive intestinal absorption of calcium, 2) impaired renal conservation of calcium and 3) excessive skeletal mobilization of calcium.

Hypercalcemic hypercalciuria results from increased glomerular filtration of mobilized calcium, which overwhelms normal renal tubular reabsorptive mechanisms (so-called resorptive hypercalciuria because excessive bone resorption is associated with increased serum calcium concentrations). In dogs, normocalcemic hypercalciuria is thought to result from either intestinal hyperabsorption of calcium (so-called absorptive hypercalciuria), or decreased renal tubular reabsorption of calcium (so-called renal-leak hypercalciuria) (Table 20-22). Absorptive hypercalciuria is characterized by increased urinary calcium excretion, normal serum calcium concentration and normal or low

Table 20-22. Summary of distinguishing clinical manifestations for different types of hypercalciuria.

Features	Absorptive hypercalciuria	Renal-leak hypercalciuria	Resorptive hypercalciuria
Serum calcium	Normal	Normal	Increased
Serum parathyroid hormone	Decreased/normal	Increased	Increased
Serum phosphorus	Normal/increased	Normal	Decreased/increased*
Urine calcium			
Fasting	Normal	Increased	Increased
Dx food**	Increased	Increased	Increased
Urine oxalate	Normal	Normal	Normal
Urine uric acid	Normal	Normal	Normal
Bone density	Normal	Decreased	Decreased
Calcium balance (total body)	Positive	Negative	Negative

*Phosphorus is retained in serum as glomerular filtration rate declines.
**Dx food = diagnostic food used in the evaluation of normal dogs and those with calcium oxalate uroliths.

serum PTH concentration. Because absorptive hypercalciuria is dependent on dietary calcium, urinary calcium excretion during the fasting state is normal or significantly reduced when compared with urinary calcium excretion during nonfasting conditions. Mean 24-hour urinary calcium excretion in 33 normal beagles was 0.32 ± 0.2 mg/kg body weight/day during fasting and 0.51 ± 0.3 mg/kg body weight/day when dogs consumed a standard food (Prescription Diet Canine k/d).[20] By comparison, mean urinary calcium excretion in five miniature schnauzers with calcium oxalate urolithiasis and absorptive hypercalciuria was 1.0 ± 0.5 mg/kg body weight/day during fasting and 2.84 ± 0.9 mg/kg body weight/day during nonfasting urine collections.[19] A primary defect observed in people with absorptive hypercalciuria is intestinal hyperabsorption of calcium, which results in increased excretion of excess calcium in urine. In addition to enhanced glomerular filtration of absorbed dietary calcium, decreased PTH secretion results in decreased renal tubular reabsorption of filtered calcium. The same phenomenon appears to occur in dogs with absorptive hypercalciuria.

Primary intestinal abnormalities in calcium absorption, disorders of 1,25-vitamin D production and hypophosphatemia-induced hypervitaminosis D have been recognized as causes in people. A single pathogenic mechanism for absorptive hypercalciuria has not been identified in dogs evaluated by the authors. However, the authors did not observe hypophosphatemia or elevated levels of 1,25-vitamin D in five dogs with absorptive hypercalciuria.

In studies conducted by the authors, renal-leak hypercalciuria and resorptive hypercalciuria have been recognized, but less frequently than excessive intestinal absorption of calcium. The defect with renal-leak hypercalciuria is impaired tubular reabsorption of calcium. Patients with renal-leak hypercalciuria have high serum PTH concentrations. Increasing PTH secretion counters the effect of additional calcium lost in urine and maintains normal blood calcium levels. Hypercalcemia associated with calcium oxalate uroliths is the hallmark of patients with resorptive hypercalciuria. Hypercalcemia is not a characteristic of patients with excessive intestinal absorption of calcium or renal-leak hypercalciuria.

Hyperoxaluria

Intestinal hyperabsorption or accelerated synthesis of oxalic acid can result in hyperoxaluria. The majority of urine oxalic acid is derived from the endogenous metabolism of ascorbic acid, glycine, glyoxylate and tryptophan. The daily quantity of endogenously produced oxalic acid appears to vary minimally. In people, hyperoxaluria has been associated with inherited abnormalities of excessive oxalate synthesis (primary hyperoxaluria), increased consumption of foods containing high quantities of oxalic acid or oxalic acid precursors (Table 20-21), pyridoxine deficiency and disorders associated with fat absorption.[103] The authors have not observed inherited hyperoxaluria, nor hyperoxaluria associated with intestinal resection and fat malabsorption in dogs. However, increases in urinary oxalic excretion have been recognized in kittens fed pyridoxine-deficient foods.[101]

In people, approximately 10 to 20% of urine oxalic acid is absorbed from dietary ingredients. It had been observed that urinary oxalic acid excretion is inversely related to dietary intake of calcium. In the intestinal tract, oxalic acid complexes with calcium and is excreted in feces as an insoluble salt. Decreased combination of oxalic acid with calcium to form calcium oxalate results in more soluble oxalic acid available for intestinal absorption. Therefore, it is logical to assume that urolith-forming patients with intestinal hyperabsorption of calcium, or those consuming foods with inappropriately low calcium compared with oxalate, would be at risk for increased intestinal absorption of dietary oxalate, hyperoxaluria and subsequent calcium oxalate urolith formation.

Hypocitraturia

Hypocitraturia is a common physiologic disturbance in people with calcium oxalate urolithiasis. Urine citric acid has been recognized as one inhibitor of calcium oxalate urolith formation. Citrate complexes with calcium ions to form the relatively soluble salt calcium citrate, thereby reducing the quantity of calcium available to bind with oxalate.

The role of low urine citric acid concentration in the etiology of canine calcium oxalate urolithiasis is not completely resolved. Hypocitraturia has been observed in dogs with calcium oxalate uroliths; however, mechanisms responsible for decreased urinary citric acid excretion are unknown. It is known that acid-base homeostasis influences the quantity of citric acid excreted in urine.[104] In normal dogs, acidosis is associated with decreased urinary citric acid excretion, whereas alkalosis promotes urinary citric acid excretion.

Macromolecular Crystal Growth Inhibitors

In addition to urinary concentration of calculogenic minerals and other ions, large molecular weight glycoproteins in urine profoundly enhance solubility of calcium oxalate. One such protein called nephrocalcin minimizes calcium oxalate crystal growth in human urine.[105] In studies, nephrocalcin from urolith-forming patients lacked appropriate quantities of carboxyglutamic acid residues and was unable to effectively prevent crystal growth. The authors' preliminary studies of urine obtained from dogs with calcium oxalate uroliths have revealed that nephrocalcin also lacks appropriate numbers of carboxyglutamic acid residues compared with nephrocalcin isolated from normal canine urine.

Tamm-Horsfall glycoprotein and glycosaminoglycans inhibit calcium oxalate crystal aggregation. One theory suggests that these proteins block growth sites on crystals, thereby inhibiting formation of calcium oxalate uroliths.[106]

Biologic Behavior

Calcium oxalate uroliths may be voided in the urine or become lodged in any portion of the urinary tract. Uroliths that remain in the urinary tract may continue to grow or become inactive (no further growth). Not all persistent uroliths are associated with clinical signs. Most calcium oxalate uroliths are not associated with UTI. In the authors' experience, uroliths composed of the dihydrate salt of calcium oxalate are less likely to cause complete urinary obstruction because the urolith's irregular contour prevents the urolith from forming a continuous seal within the lumen of the urethra. However, if uroliths remain in the urinary tract, dysuria, UTI, partial or total urinary obstruction and polyp formation are potential sequelae. As of yet, the authors have not observed spontaneous urolith dissolution of calcium oxalate uroliths in dogs.

In a retrospective clinical survey of 438 dogs surgically treated for urolithiasis at the Animal Medical Center in New York, 111 patients had 155 known recurrences.[66] Recurrence was observed in 25% of dogs with calcium oxalate uroliths. At the University of Minnesota, results of a retrospective study indicted that the rate of recurrence of calcium oxalate uroliths increased with the length of time that dogs were evaluated: 3% recurred after three months, 9% after six months, 36% after one year, 42% after two years and 48% after three years.[107] The tendency for uroliths to recur is influenced by owner and patient compliance with therapy and persistence of factors responsible for urolith initiation at the time of urolith eradication.

Assess the Food(s)

Patients the authors have identified with calcium oxalate uroliths have consumed a variety of foods. Dogs consuming dry commercial foods may be at greater risk for urolithiasis than dogs consuming moist foods because dry foods are often associated with higher urine concentrations of calcium and oxalic acid and more concentrated urine. Likewise, foods with high protein content also contribute to hypercalciuria and hyperoxaluria.

Feeding foods designed to dissolve struvite uroliths provide some benefits, but also some risks to patients with calcium oxalic uroliths (Table 20-15 and Table 20-20). The lower protein content and potential to enhance formation of less concentrated urine help reduce calcium and oxalate concentrations in urine. Although formation of acidic urine is desirable for management of struvite uroliths, foods that promote acidic urine promote hypercalciuria and hypocitraturia. Therefore, consumption of foods that result in formation of acidic urine enhances the risk of calcium oxalate urolithiasis in susceptible dogs. Likewise, reducing dietary phosphorus may also promote hypercalciuria. If struvite uroliths have occurred in breeds of dogs commonly affected with calcium oxalate uroliths, the authors currently recommend that they be evaluated for calcium oxalate crystalluria after initiating dietary therapy to prevent struvite urolith formation. If calcium oxalate crystalluria persists, alternate methods of preventing struvite uroliths should be considered.

Feeding Plan and Treatment

Though struvite, urate and cystine uroliths dissolve when urine is no longer supersaturated with calculogenic substances, the authors have, as yet, been unable to dissolve calcium oxalate uroliths in dogs. Only physical methods are currently available for removing clinically active calcium oxalate uroliths. Surgery is the time-honored method to remove calcium oxalate uroliths from the urinary tract; however, complete surgical removal of all visible uroliths may be difficult because of their small size

---

Table 20-23. Recommendations for the management of calcium oxalate urolithiasis in dogs.

1. Obtain baseline data (postsurgical radiography, complete urinalysis, serum concentrations of calcium, urea nitrogen and creatinine) to evaluate effectiveness of surgery, renal function and calcium homeostasis.
2. If the dog is hypercalcemic, correct underlying cause.
3. If the dog is normocalcemic, consider foods with reduced calcium, oxalate, sodium and protein that do not promote formation of acidic urine. Ideally foods should contain additional water and citrate and have adequate phosphorus and magnesium. Avoid vitamins C and D. The authors commonly recommend Prescription Diet Canine u/d or Canine w/d.*
4. Reevaluate patient in two to four weeks to verify dietary compliance (urine specific gravity and pH and serum urea nitrogen concentration) and amelioration of crystalluria (urine sediment examination).
5. Consider additional potassium citrate if calcium oxalate crystals and aciduria persist.
6. Reevaluate patient in two to four weeks to verify dietary compliance (urine specific gravity and pH and serum urea nitrogen concentration) and amelioration of crystalluria (urine sediment examination). Consider vitamin B$_6$ supplementation (2 to 4 mg/kg body weight q 24 to 48 hours) if calcium oxalate crystalluria persists.
7. Again, reevaluate patient in two to four weeks to verify dietary compliance and amelioration of crystalluria. Consider administration of hydrochlorothiazide (2 mg/kg body weight q 24 to 48 hours) if calcium oxalate crystalluria persists. Adverse effects of hydrochlorothiazide administration include dehydration, hypokalemia and hypercalcemia.
8. After three to six months, reevaluate patient to verify dietary compliance and amelioration of crystalluria. Check for urolith recurrence by abdominal radiography. If no uroliths are present, continue current therapy and reevaluate in three to six months. If uroliths have recurred, consider voiding urohydropropulsion. If unsuccessful and clinical signs referable to urocystoliths are persistent, consider surgery. Continue therapy to minimize urolith growth if clinical signs are not present.

*Hill's Pet Nutrition, Inc., Topeka, KS, USA.

and irregular contour. Small urocystoliths may be aspirated through a transurethral catheter or removed by voiding urohydropropulsion (Table 20-16).[24,83] Lithotripsy provides a nonsurgical means of removing calcium oxalate uroliths from kidneys and ureters.[108] In some patients, however, calcium oxalate uroliths are clinically silent, obviating the need for intervention. For those patients in which surgery is not indicated, the clinical status of uroliths should be periodically assessed by urinalyses, renal function tests and radiography or ultrasonography.

In general, medical therapy should be implemented in stepwise fashion, with the initial goal of reducing the urine concentration of calculogenic substances (Table 20-23). Medications that have the potential to induce unwanted, sustained, detrimental alterations in the composition of metabolites should be reserved for patients with active or frequently recurring calcium oxalate uroliths. Caution should be used to ensure that side effects of treatment are not more detrimental than the effects of uroliths. The cause of hypercalcemia (e.g., primary hyperparathyroidism) should be corrected in patients with hypercalcemia and resorptive hypercalciuria. An attempt should be made to identify risk factors for urolith formation in patients with normal serum calcium concentrations (Table 20-20). Amelioration or control of the consequences of risk factors (e.g., urine oversaturation with calculogenic minerals) should minimize urolith growth and recurrence.

Select a Food(s)

The following observations emphasize the feasibility of managing canine calcium oxalate uroliths with the aid of dietary modification: 1) components of calcium oxalate uroliths are found in the ingredients of dog foods, 2) dogs with calcium oxalate uroliths may have intestinal hyperabsorption of calcium and 3) urinary pH and urine concentration can be modified by diet. The goals of dietary prevention include: 1) reducing calcium concentration in urine, 2) reducing oxalic acid concentration in urine, 3) promoting high concentration and activity of inhibitors of calcium oxalate crystal growth and aggregation in urine and 4) reducing urine concentration.

Reduction of dietary calcium appears to be a logical therapeutic goal because intestinal hyperabsorption of calcium has been identified as one mechanism promoting hypercalciuria in dogs with calcium oxalate uroliths. However, reducing consumption of calcium may increase the availability of oxalic acid for intestinal absorption and subsequent urinary excretion. As in the urinary bladder, calcium and oxalic acid in the intestinal lumen form an insoluble compound, thereby preventing the absorption of one other. This may explain why an epidemiologic study evaluating risk factors for calcium oxalate urolith formation in people unexpectedly discovered that higher calcium-containing diets were associated with reduced risk for urolith formation.[109] Therefore, reduction in dietary calcium should be accompanied by an appropriate reduction in dietary oxalic acid (Tables 20-21 and 20-24).

People with calcium oxalate uroliths are often cautioned to avoid milk and milk products because the carbohydrate component (lactose) of these products may augment intestinal absorption of calcium from any dietary source.[110] Likewise, they are often discouraged from consuming foods containing relatively high quantities of oxalate (Table 20-21). Although there is agreement that excessive consumption of calcium and oxalate should be avoided, the consensus of urologists is that it is inadvisable to restrict dietary calcium unless absorptive hypercalciuria has been documented. Even then, only moderate restriction is advocated in order to prevent negative calcium balance in the body.

Consumption of high levels of sodium may augment renal excretion of calcium. Daily urinary calcium excretion of normal dogs consuming foods with 0.8% sodium (dry weight analysis) was comparable to calcium excretion observed in dogs with calcium oxalate uroliths.[111] Therefore, moderate dietary restriction of sodium (less than 0.3% sodium dry matter basis [DMB]) is recommended for active calcium oxalate urolith formers.

Studies of laboratory animals, dogs and people suggest that dietary phosphorus should not be restricted in patients with calcium oxalate urolithiasis because reduction in dietary phosphorus is often associated with augmentation of intestinal calcium absorption and hypercalciuria.[112] If calcium oxalate urolithiasis is associated with hypophosphatemia and normal serum calcium concentra-

Table 20-24. Selected human foods with minimal calcium or oxalate content.

Food items	Low-calcium foods	Low-oxalate foods
Meats and eggs	Eggs Poultry	Beef Eggs Fish and shellfish* Lamb Pork Poultry
Vegetables		Cabbage Cauliflower Mushrooms Peas, green Radishes Potatoes, white
Milk and dairy products		Cheese* Milk* Yogurt*

Fruits		Apple
		Avocado
		Banana
		Bing cherries
		Grapefruit
		Grapes, green
		Mangos
		Melons
		  Cantaloupe
		  Casaba
		  Honeydew
		  Watermelon
		Plums, green or yellow

Breads, grains, nuts	Almonds Macaroni Pretzels Rice Spaghetti Walnuts	Bread, white Macaroni Noodles Rice Spaghetti
Miscellaneous	Popcorn	Jellies Preserves Soups with allowed ingredients

*Low in oxalate, but not low in calcium content.

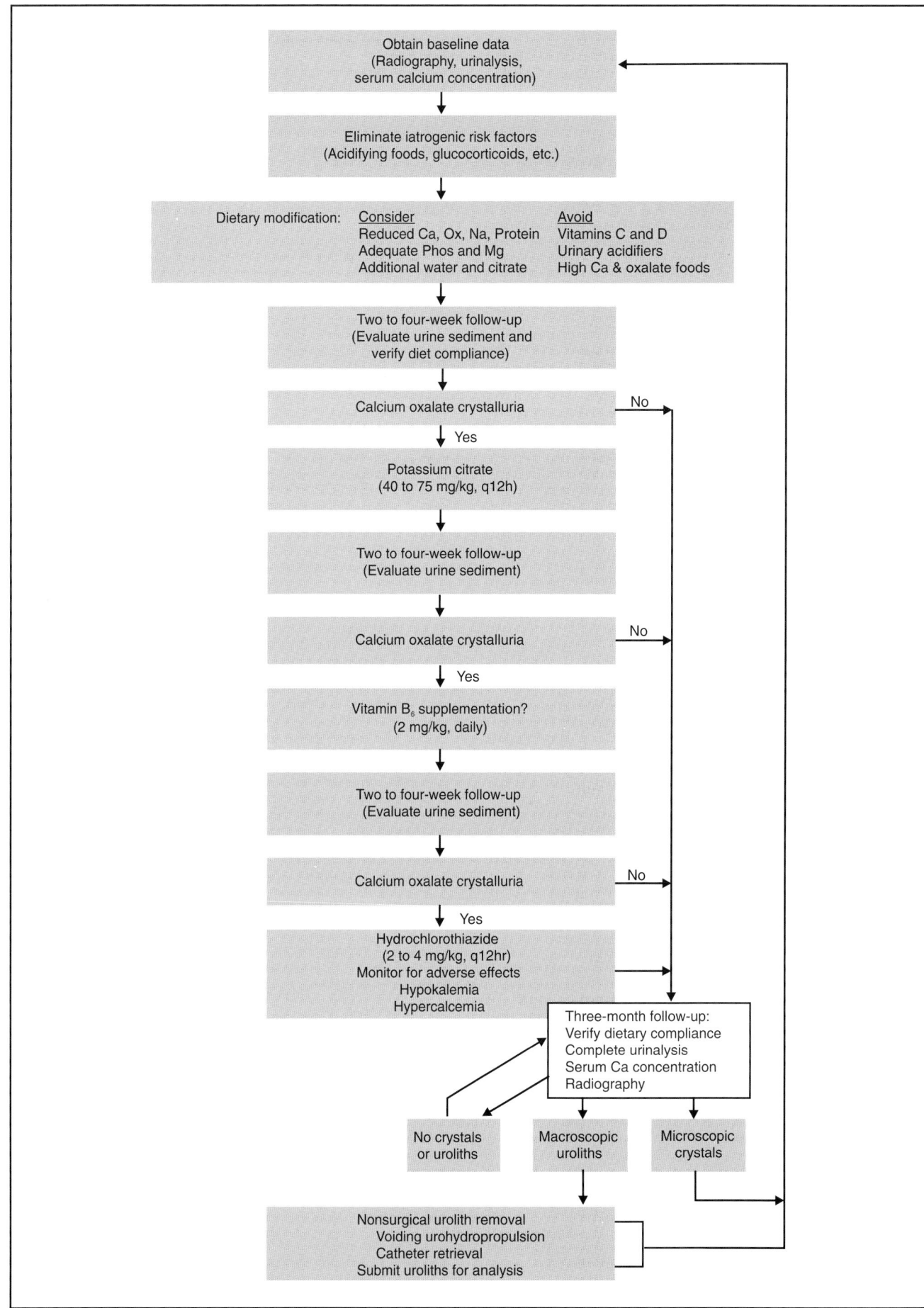

Figure 20-13. Algorithm for medical management of calcium oxalate uroliths in dogs.

tion, oral phosphorus supplementation should be considered. However, caution must be used because excessive dietary phosphorus may predispose patients to formation of calcium phosphate uroliths.

Although supplemental dietary magnesium contributes to formation of magnesium ammonium phosphate uroliths in some species (cats and ruminants), urine magnesium apparently impairs formation of calcium oxalate crystals.[113-115] Therefore, supplemental magnesium has been used in people in an attempt to minimize recurrence of calcium oxalate uroliths.[116] However, the authors observed increased urinary excretion of calcium by normal dogs given supplemental magnesium. Urinary calcium excretion was 0.5 ± 0.2 mg/kg body weight/day in six normal dogs consuming a food containing 0.03% magnesium on a DMB vs. 2.65 ± 1.7 mg/kg body weight/day when the same dogs consumed a food containing 0.38% magnesium DMB.[117] Pending further studies, the authors do not recommend dietary magnesium restriction or supplementation for treatment of canine calcium oxalate uroliths.

Ingestion of foods that contain high quantities of animal protein may contribute to calcium oxalate urolithiasis by increasing urinary calcium excretion and decreasing urinary citrate excretion.[118] Some of these consequences result from obligatory acid excretion associated with protein metabolism. The authors have observed hypercalciuria in normal dogs fed high-protein foods (40% dry weight analysis). Therefore, excessive dietary protein consumption should be avoided in dogs with active calcium oxalate urolithiasis.

A food that avoids excess protein, calcium, oxalate and sodium (Table 20-15) may be considered to minimize recurrence of active calcium oxalate uroliths in dogs. Dry foods are not generally recommended because they tend to result in formation of concentrated urine. Ideally, foods should not be restricted or supplemented with phosphorus or magnesium. Excessive levels of vitamin D (which promotes intestinal absorption of calcium) and ascorbic acid (a precursor of oxalate) should also be avoided. A deficiency of pyridoxine should be avoided because vitamin B_6 promotes endogenous production of oxalate.[119]

Vitamin B_6 (pyridoxine) increases the transamination of glyoxylate, an important precursor of oxalic acid, to glycine. Experimentally induced pyridoxine deficiency resulted in renal precipitation of calcium oxalate and hyperoxaluria in kittens.[101] Commercial foods routinely fortified with vitamin supplements would not be deficient in pyridoxine or other vitamins. A homemade food might be deficient in pyridoxine if a multivitamin supplement is not added. The ability of supplemental pyridoxine (above nutritional requirements) to reduce urinary oxalic acid excretion in dogs is unknown.

Citric Acid

Citric acid forms soluble salts with calcium thereby inhibiting calcium oxalate crystal formation.[120] Citric acid is also beneficial because it is metabolized to bicarbonate and promotes formation of alkaline urine.[121] In dogs, chronic metabolic acidosis inhibits renal tubular reabsorption of calcium, whereas metabolic alkalosis enhances tubular reabsorption of calcium.[122] Potassium citrate is preferred to sodium bicarbonate as an alkalinizing agent

Table 20-25. Expected changes associated with medical therapy to minimize recurrence of calcium oxalate uroliths.

Factors	Pre-therapy	Prevention therapy
Polyuria	±	Variable
Pollakiuria	0 to 4+	0
Hematuria	0 to 4+	0
Urine specific gravity	Variable	1.004-1.015
Urinary pH	<7.0	>7.0
Pyuria	0 to 4+	0
Calcium oxalate crystals	0 to 4+	0
Bacteriuria	0 to 4+	0
Bacterial culture of urine	0 to 4+	0
Urea nitrogen (mg/dl)	>15	<15
Urolith size and number	Small to large	0

because oral administration of sodium enhances urinary calcium excretion. If persistent aciduria or hypocitraturia is recognized in dogs (mean urinary citrate excretion of 33 normal beagles was 2.57 ± 2.31 mg/kg body weight/day), therapy with wax matrix tablets of potassium citrate (Urocit-K) should be considered. A liquid product (Polycitra-K) works well for small dogs. The authors currently recommend a dose of 40 to 75 mg/kg body weight q12h. Because Prescription Diet Canine u/d already contains adequate quantities of potassium citrate, additional potassium citrate is often not needed.

Thiazide Diuretics

Thiazide diuretics have been recommended to reduce recurrence of calcium-containing uroliths in people because of their ability to reduce urinary calcium excretion.[123] The authors have observed a beneficial reduction in urinary calcium excretion in dogs with calcium oxalate urolithiasis following administration of hydrochlorothiazide (2 to 4 mg/kg body weight q12h) for two weeks. A reduction in urinary calcium excretion was not detected following chlorothiazide administration (20 to 65 mg/kg body weight q12h) in clinically healthy beagles.[124] Thiazide diuretic administration should be accompanied by appropriate clinical and laboratory monitoring for early detection of adverse effects (dehydration, hypokalemia, hypercalcemia).

Reassessment

The goal of therapy is to prevent calcium oxalate urolith recurrence (Figure 20-13). However, this expectation may be unrealistic because the primary causes responsible for urolith formation are multifactorial and incompletely understood. With the information and techniques currently available, however, veterinarians can minimize urolith recurrence and prevent future surgical urolith removal with careful and planned monitoring and intervention.

The authors recommend that therapy be instituted in a stepwise fashion (Table 20-23). Dietary and pharmacologic management should result in formation of less concentrated urine without calcium oxalate crystalluria (Table 20-25). Strive to achieve urine specific gravity values less than 1.020. After this is achieved, a urinalysis and survey lateral abdominal radiograph should be performed every two to four months. Dietary and pharmacologic changes can be

Table 20-26. Managing highly recurrent calcium oxalate uroliths.

Causes	Identification	Therapeutic goal
Client and patient causes		
Inadequate dietary compliance	Question owner Persistent calcium oxalate crystalluria Urea nitrogen >10-15 mg/dl Urine specific gravity >1.010-1.020 Urinary pH <7.0-7.5 during treatment with Prescription Diet Canine u/d* (use lower values for the canned food)	Emphasize need to feed dissolution food exclusively
Administration of vitamin-mineral supplements	Question owner	Discontinue vitamin-mineral supplements containing calcium and vitamins C and D
Clinician factors		
Incomplete surgical removal of uroliths	Postsurgical radiography revealing uroliths Persistence of clinical signs after cystotomy or recurrence of clinical signs soon after cystotomy (within one to three months)	Uroliths not causing clinical signs should be monitored for potentially adverse consequences (obstruction, urinary tract infection, etc.) Clinically active uroliths may require surgical removal Remove small uroliths by voiding urohydropropulsion
Inappropriate food choice	Persistent calcium oxalate crystalluria	Choose foods with reduced levels of calcium, oxalate, protein and sodium that do not promote formation of acidic urine Consider adding potassium citrate if aciduria persists
Inadequate monitoring	Postsurgical radiography to verify complete urolith removal was not performed Urinalysis or urine sediment examinations were not performed within three to six months of initiation of therapy	Perform postsurgical radiography to evaluate success of surgery Perform complete urinalysis within one to three months of initiation of therapy Once stable, urinalysis should be performed every four to six months Perform survey lateral abdominal radiography every four to six months to assess recurrence
Corticosteroid administration	Corticosteroids were prescribed to manage other disease conditions	If possible, discontinue corticosteroid administration
Disease factors		
Hypercalcemia	Elevated serum calcium concentration	Identify and, if possible, eliminate underlying cause for hypercalcemia (hyperparathyroidism, neoplasia, hypervitaminosis D, etc.)
Recurrence of uroliths despite appropriate management	Lateral radiograph of abdomen	Uroliths not causing clinical signs should be monitored for potentially adverse consequences (obstruction, urinary tract infection, etc.) Clinically active uroliths may require surgical removal Remove small uroliths by voiding urohydropropulsion

*Hill's Pet Nutrition, Inc., Topeka, KS, USA.

made if crystalluria or a concentrated urine persist (Table 20-26). By following these recommendations, recurrent urocystoliths detected by radiography should be small enough to remove by voiding urohydropropulsion. After a rate of urolith recurrence has been established, the frequency of evaluation can be modified such that predicted recurrences can be diagnosed and managed accordingly.

CALCIUM PHOSPHATE UROLITHS

Prevalence and Mineral Composition

Uroliths composed predominantly of calcium phosphate have been infrequently identified in dogs and cats. However, calcium phosphate is commonly found as a minor component in naturally occurring struvite and calcium oxalate uroliths. Occasionally a shell of calcium phosphate will form around a urolith composed primarily of struvite.

At least four mineral types have been identified in calcium phosphate uroliths (Table 20-27). The most com-

mon form identified in calcium phosphate uroliths from dogs and cats is hydroxyapatite, followed by brushite. Calcium carbonate uncommonly exists as a separate compound in canine and feline uroliths as it does in equine, rabbit and guinea pig uroliths. However, in the presence of conditions associated with UTIs caused by urease-positive bacteria, carbonate radicals may be generated that associate with the complex apatite structure to form a carbonate apatite lattice. Less commonly identified crystalline forms of calcium phosphate in uroliths include whitlockite and octacalcium phosphate. More than one crystalline form of calcium phosphate may be present in a single urolith. In alkaline urine, brushite is readily transformed to apatite; it is possible that some apatite identified in uroliths originated from brushite.[125] In addition, mixtures of calcium phosphate and calcium oxalate often occur. With the exception of brushite, canine calcium phosphate uroliths do not have a characteristic shape.

Calcium phosphate accounted for 0.6% of all canine uroliths submitted to the Minnesota Urolith Center from 1981 to 1997 (Table 20-7), and 0.3% (52 of 15,259) of the uroliths submitted in 1994. Calcium phosphate accounted

Table 20-27. Common characteristics of canine calcium phosphate uroliths.

Chemical names	Formulas	Crystal names
β-tricalcium phosphate (calcium orthophosphate)	$β\text{-}Ca_2(PO_4)_2$	Whitlockite
Carbonate apatite	$Ca_{10}(PO_4CO_3OH)_6(OH)_2$	Carbonate apatite
Calcium hydrogen phosphate dihydrate	$CaHPO_4 \cdot 2H_2O$	Brushite
Calcium phosphate	$Ca_{10}(PO_4)_6(OH)_2$	Hydroxyapatite or calcium apatite

Variations in mineral composition
Calcium apatite only
Brushite only
Calcium apatite mixed with calcium oxalate
Brushite mixed with calcium oxalate
The carbonate apatite form of calcium phosphate is most commonly detected as a minor component of infection-induced struvite

Physical characteristics
Color: Calcium phosphate uroliths are usually cream or tan. Blood clots mineralized with calcium oxalate are black.
Shape: Variable. With the exception of brushite, calcium phosphate uroliths do not have a characteristic shape. Brushite uroliths are typically round and smooth.
Nuclei: Brushite uroliths are often laminated.
Density: Generally dense and brittle, sometimes chalk-like. Mineralized blood clots may be softer. All forms of calcium phosphate are radiodense compared to soft tissue.
Number: Single or multiple
Location: Kidneys, ureters, urinary bladder (most common) and/or urethra
Size: Variable, with smaller sizes more common

Prevalence
Approximately 1% of all canine uroliths. Approximately 2% of canine nephroliths.

Characteristics of affected canine patients
No gender prevalence for calcium apatite. Brushite is more common in males. Mean age at diagnosis is seven years (range <1 to >6 years).

for 2.3% of canine nephroliths analyzed at the Minnesota Urolith Center from 1981 to 1997 (Table 20-8). Calcium phosphate accounted for 3% of uroliths retrieved from dogs less than 12 months old.

Of 176 canine hydroxyapatite and carbonate apatite uroliths, 68 were composed entirely (100%) of calcium phosphate, and 62 were composed of at least 70% of these minerals. The mean age of dogs at the time of urolith retrieval was 7 ± 4 years (range one month to 16 years). Males were affected (56%) more commonly than females (44%). Forty different breeds were affected including cocker spaniels (10%), mixed breeds (20%), miniature schnauzers (10%), Yorkshire terriers (7%), Shih Tzus (6%) and springer spaniels (5%). Hydroxyapatite uroliths were more commonly removed from the lower urinary tract (81%) than the upper urinary tract (8%). The location of 11% of the hydroxyapatite uroliths was not specified.

Of 117 calcium hydrogen phosphate dihydrate uroliths, 55 were composed entirely (100%) of this mineral, and 62 were composed of at least 70% of this mineral. The mean age of dogs at the time of urolith retrieval was 7.3 ± 2.8 years (range one month to 16 years). Males were affected (83%) more commonly than females (17%). Twenty-seven breeds were affected including Yorkshire terriers (14%), Shih Tzus (11%), bichon frises (7%), Pomeranians (7%), miniature poodles (7%) and mixed breeds (14%). Brushite uroliths were more commonly retrieved from the lower urinary tract (94%) than the upper urinary tract (3%). The location of 3% of brushite uroliths was not recorded.

Etiopathogenesis and Risk Factors

Solubility of Calcium Phosphates in Urine

The solubility of calcium phosphates in urine is dependent on: 1) urinary pH, 2) urine calcium ion concentration, 3) total urine inorganic phosphate concentration, 4) urine concentration of inhibitors of calcium crystallization and 5) urine concentration of potentiators of crystallization. Factors that decrease calcium phosphate solubility predispose patients to urolith formation.

URINARY PH

Urinary pH has a profound effect on the solubility of some forms of calcium phosphate. With the exception of brushite, calcium phosphate solubility markedly decreases in alkaline urine and increases in acidic urine. Increased urinary pH increases the availability of ionic PO_4^{3-} and HPO_4^{2-}, which are available for incorporation into calcium phosphates.[126] Apatite will not crystallize from human urine unless the pH is 6.6 or greater.[127] Approximately 400 mg of calcium phosphate/l can be held in solution at a pH of 5.5, whereas only 32 mg of calcium phosphate/l will be held in solution at a pH of 7.8.[128] Therefore, people with disorders associated with persistent elevation of urinary pH (e.g., distal RTA) are predisposed to calcium phosphate urolith formation.

HYPERCALCIURIA

Hypercalciuria decreases calcium phosphate solubility and may result in oversaturation with calcium phosphate.[129] Hypercalciuria may result from excessive resorption of calcium from bone, enhanced intestinal absorption of calcium, impaired renal tubular reabsorption of calcium or combinations of these factors. Urine specimens obtained from human patients with hypercalciuria and calcium uroliths are usually supersaturated with brushite.

Controversy exists as to the relative importance of urinary pH and hypercalciuria as determinants of calcium phosphate solubility in vivo. Some investigators believe that calcium phosphate crystallization is primarily governed by changes in urinary pH; they minimize the importance of hypercalciuria.[127] However, other investigators suggest that persistent hypercalciuria tends to increase the calcium phosphate saturation of urine so that small increases in urinary pH will result in calcium phosphate crystalluria. There have been no studies on the relative effect of hypercalciuria and urinary pH on the solubility of different types of calcium phosphate in canine urine.

CRYSTALLIZATION INHIBITORS

Normally, urine contains calcium phosphate crystal inhibitors. Inhibitors prevent urolith formation by chelating urolith constituents, making them unavailable for nidus formation or crystal growth. In addition, crystallization inhibitors may alter crystalline structure to prevent crystal growth and aggregation. Inhibitors of calcium phosphate crystallization include inorganic pyrophosphates, citrate and magnesium ions.[130] These inhibitors provide 30 to 40% of the inhibitory capacity of normal human urine to calcium phosphate crystallization. The remaining 60 to 70% is provided by as yet unidentified low-molecular-weight inhibitors.

Pyrophosphates increase the upper limit of urine calcium phosphate saturation at which spontaneous precipitation occurs. Pyrophosphates also retard growth of hydroxyapatite crystals by adsorbing to their surfaces and blocking active growth sites. In addition, pyrophosphates inhibit transformation of amorphous calcium phosphate into crystalline form.[130] Citrate forms soluble complexes with calcium, thereby decreasing the availability of calcium for incorporation into crystals. Magnesium may replace calcium on the surface of growing crystals and thus block epitaxial growth.

CRYSTALLIZATION PROMOTERS

Epitaxy may promote formation of calcium phosphate uroliths. Epitaxy is the process by which crystals of one salt induce the formation of crystals of another salt. Epitaxic induction occurs between crystals having similar lattice dimensions. Calcium oxalate and monosodium urate crystals reportedly stimulate calcium phosphate precipitation.[130]

Disorders Associated with Formation of Calcium Phosphate Uroliths

Calcium phosphate uroliths may occur in patients with primary hyperparathyroidism, other hypercalcemic disorders, distal RTA and idiopathic hypercalciuria (Table 20-28). Because the prevalence of calcium phosphate uroliths in dogs is low, and because appropriate metabolic studies have rarely been performed in affected cases, the association of calcium phosphate uroliths with other canine metabolic disorders has not been as well established as it has been in people.

PRIMARY HYPERPARATHYROIDISM

Between 18 to 20% of human patients with primary hyperparathyroidism have uroliths at the time of diagnosis.[131] In one study, four of 21 dogs (20%) with primary

Table 20-28. Disorders that may predispose dogs to formation of calcium phosphate uroliths.

Primary hyperparathyroidism
Other hypercalcemic disorders
  Neoplasia
  Vitamin D intoxication
  Excess calcium intake
  Thyrotoxicosis
  Hyperadrenocorticism
  Immobilization
Distal renal tubular acidosis
Normocalcemic hypercalciuria
  Intestinal hyperabsorption
  Renal leak

hyperparathyroidism had uroliths.[132] Uroliths from patients with primary hyperparathyroidism are typically composed of calcium phosphate, calcium oxalate or a mixture of the two. Uroliths composed predominantly of calcium phosphate are more commonly identified in people and dogs with primary hyperparathyroidism; uroliths composed primarily of calcium oxalate are more commonly identified in people and dogs with normocalcemic hypercalciuria. Bladder uroliths composed primarily of calcium phosphate have been experimentally induced in dogs following injections of PTH.[133]

Factors that predispose patients with primary hyperparathyroidism to calcium phosphate urolith formation include: hypercalciuria, increased urinary pH and increased renal excretion of substances that promote spontaneous precipitation of calcium salts. Hypercalcemia results from PTH-induced bone resorption and renal tubular reabsorption of calcium. In addition, increased intestinal absorption of calcium results from PTH-stimulated conversion of 25-hydroxycholecalciferol to 1,25-dihydroxycholecalciferol.[129] Hypercalcemia results in increased glomerular filtration of calcium and hypercalciuria, which in turn enhances the likelihood of urolith formation by increasing urine saturation with brushite and calcium oxalate.[129] The urine of most hypercalciuric people with primary hyperparathyroidism is supersaturated with brushite and calcium oxalate. Hypercalciuria has been documented to occur in dogs with primary hyperparathyroidism and calcium uroliths.[133,134]

Persistent elevation in urinary pH may predispose some patients with primary hyperparathyroidism to calcium phosphate urolithiasis. Urinary pH is elevated in these patients because of impaired renal tubular reabsorption of bicarbonate.[135] This abnormality may explain, at least in part, the increased incidence of calcium phosphate uroliths in patients with primary hyperparathyroidism compared with patients with other hypercalciuric diseases.

It has been suggested that some human patients with primary hyperparathyroidism excrete a substance in their urine that facilitates calcium phosphate and calcium oxalate precipitation.[129] The specific nature of this urolithiasis-promoting factor has not been determined.

OTHER HYPERCALCEMIC DISORDERS

In addition to primary hyperparathyroidism, other hypercalcemic disorders may predispose patients to formation of calcium phosphate uroliths. Uroliths have been identified in human patients with hypervitaminosis D, neoplastic disorders, Cushing's syndrome and in some patients who are immobilized for long periods.[136] Although calcium phosphate is the most frequently identified mineral in uroliths obtained from these patients, calcium oxalate may also be present. Because the frequency of occurrence of uroliths in patients with these hypercalcemic disorders is low, it is likely that factors other than hypercalcemia are involved.

DISTAL RENAL TUBULAR ACIDOSIS

Nephrolithiasis is a common manifestation of hereditary distal RTA (type I) in people.[137] Uroliths are typically composed entirely of calcium phosphate, although calcium oxalate and struvite uroliths have also been identified.[137] Urolith formation has not been observed in patients with acquired distal or proximal RTA (type II).

Distal RTA results from functional inability of the distal nephron to establish a hydrogen ion gradient between blood and tubular fluid, regardless of the severity of acidemia. The disorder in people is characterized by inability to decrease urinary pH below 5.4, hypokalemia, hyperchloremia, hypophosphatemia, hypocalcemia, metabolic acidosis, osteomalacia, nephrocalcinosis and urolithiasis.[138]

Hypercalciuria, alkaline urine, low citrate concentration in urine and excessive urinary phosphate excretion contribute to formation of calcium phosphate uroliths observed in patients with distal RTA. Hypercalciuria and hyperphosphaturia tend to increase urine saturation with calcium phosphate. Acidosis increases calcium mobilization from bone, causing an increase in the quantity of calcium excreted in urine.[133] In addition, acidosis decreases renal tubular reabsorption of calcium, further increasing calcium excretion. Acidosis may alter renal tubular calcium transport, the response of the tubules to PTH or both.

Elevated urinary pH increases the availability of PO_4^{3-} and HPO_4^{2-}, which may be incorporated into ionic octacalcium phosphate and brushite, respectively.[126] Increased urinary pH is considered more important than hypercalciuria in predisposing patients with distal RTA to calcium phosphate urolith formation.[126]

Patients with distal RTA excrete decreased amounts of citrate in their urine. Citrate is reabsorbed more avidly in proximal convoluted tubules as a consequence of intracellular acidosis.[138] Recall that because citrate is a major chelator of calcium, decreased citrate concentration decreases calcium solubility.

In people, distal RTA sometimes occurs as an incomplete form in which urolith formation occurs without systemic acidosis. Urolithiasis may be the only clinical manifestation of this disorder.[137] The tubular defect can only be recognized by abnormal response to an ammonium chloride loading test.

NORMOCALCEMIC HYPERCALCIURIA

Normocalcemic hypercalciuria is a syndrome characterized by normal serum calcium concentration, increased urinary excretion of calcium, absence of systemic disease and increased tendency for formation of calcium phosphate or calcium oxalate uroliths. Approximately 33% of human calcium urolith formers have normocalcemic hypercalciuria.[126]

Two types of normocalcemic hypercalciuria have been recognized in dogs.[20] One type, called absorptive hypercalciuria, is associated with increased intestinal absorption of calcium. The subsequent increase in serum calcium concentration suppresses PTH secretion, resulting in decreased tubular reabsorption of calcium and hypercalciuria. Hyperabsorption of calcium from the intestinal tract may result from a primary intestinal disturbance in calcium transport. It is also possible that increased calcium absorption results from increased synthesis of 1,25-dihydroxycholecalciferol. Absorptive hypercalciuria has been divided into subtypes based on urinary calcium excretion following consumption of different levels of dietary calcium.[126]

The second type of normocalcemic hypercalciuria, termed renal-leak hypercalciuria, is thought to result from impaired ability of the proximal tubules to reabsorb filtered calcium.[20] A defect in reabsorption of magnesium may also be present. Renal calcium loss stimulates 1,25-dihydroxycholecalciferol and PTH synthesis, resulting in an increase in intestinal absorption of calcium.

Hypercalciuria is probably not the only factor involved in urolith formation in patients with normocalcemic hypercalciuria because many hypercalciuric patients do not form uroliths. Interaction of crystallization inhibitors and promoters are important contributing factors.

The diagnosis of idiopathic hypercalciuria is established by demonstrating an increase in 24-hour urinary calcium excretion and by eliminating other nonhypercalcemic, hypercalciuric disorders such as RTA. Unlike absorptive hypercalciuria, renal-leak hypercalciuria is not affected by withholding food.

MINERALIZATION OF BLOOD CLOTS

The authors have observed nephroliths, urocystoliths and urethroliths composed of blood clots mineralized with calcium phosphate on numerous occasions in dogs. Formation of highly concentrated urine in patients with gross hematuria may favor formation of mineralized blood clots. Contrary to one theory, these black-colored uroliths are not composed of bile metabolites.

Biologic Behavior

The authors have not had the opportunity to assess the long-term biologic behavior of calcium phosphate urolithiasis in dogs. However, the authors hypothesize that calcium phosphate uroliths will increase in size and number if underlying causes persist. In the authors' experience blood clots within the urinary tract that have become mineralized with calcium phosphate often remain inactive for years.

Assess the Food(s)

Dogs with calcium phosphate uroliths have consumed a variety of foods. Dogs consuming dry commercial foods may be at greater risk for urolith formation than dogs consuming moist foods because dry foods tend to be associated with formation of more concentrated urine. Foods with high protein content contribute to hypercalciuria and hyperphosphaturia.

Table 20-29. Some potential risk factors for canine calcium phosphate uroliths.

Diet	Urine	Metabolic
Alkalinizing potential	Alkaline pH	Hypercalcemia
High calcium content	Hypercalciuria	Distal renal tubular acidosis
High sodium content	High-phosphate ion concentration	
High phosphorus content?	Increased concentration of promoters	
Low-moisture content	Decreased concentration of inhibitors	
Excessive vitamin D content	Hypocitraturia	
Others?	Hypomagnesuria	
	Blood clots	
	Urine concentration	
	Urine retention	

Foods with restricted quantities of protein tend to reduce urine concentrating capacity and urinary phosphorus and calcium excretion. Foods with higher quantities of sodium or vitamin D may promote hypercalciuria (Table 20-29).

Foods with higher levels of phosphorus tend to augment hyperphosphaturia. However, excessive restriction of dietary phosphorus may enhance the availability of dietary calcium for intestinal absorption, and also enhance production of 1,25-vitamin D by the kidneys, thereby promoting hypercalciuria. Although these trends serve as guidelines, the optimal level of phosphorus for dogs with calcium phosphate urolithiasis has yet to be determined.

Most forms of calcium phosphate are least soluble in alkaline urine. Formation of calcium phosphate is enhanced because alkaline urine favors dissociation of monobasic phosphate ($H_2PO_4^-$) to dibasic phosphate (HPO_4^{2-}) and phosphate ions (PO_4^{3-}). Although formation of acidic urine may enhance the solubility of calcium phosphate (except brushite), acidosis promotes hypercalciuria and hypocitraturia.

Feeding Plan and Treatment

Surgery remains the most reliable way to remove active calcium phosphate uroliths from the urinary tract. However, the authors emphasize that surgery may be unnecessary for clinically inactive calcium phosphate uroliths. Voiding urohydropropulsion may be used to remove small urocystoliths (Table 20-16). Although calcium chelating agents have been reported to be of value in dissolving calcium phosphate uroliths in people, the feasibility of this type of therapy has not been reported in dogs and cats.

Primary Hyperparathyroidism

Patients with primary hyperparathyroidism usually require surgery.[132] Parathyroidectomy may result in dissolution of uroliths and generally prevents their recurrence. Parathyroidectomy in a dog with primary hyperparathyroidism and recurrent calcium phosphate uroliths resulted in decreased urinary calcium excretion and prevention of new urolith formation.[134]

Distal Renal Tubular Acidosis

To the authors' knowledge, medical dissolution of calcium phosphate uroliths has not been attempted in dogs with distal RTA. Foods designed to dissolve struvite uroliths would generally not be expected to promote dissolution of calcium phosphate uroliths, in part because they tend to promote acidemia and aciduria, thus potentially enhancing hypercalciuria and hypocitraturia. However, correction of hypercalciuria, hyperphosphaturia and hypocitraturia by alkalinization therapy with potassium citrate might promote dissolution of these uroliths in patients with complete or incomplete distal RTA.

Long-term alkalinization therapy appears to be beneficial in preventing calcium phosphate urolith formation in people with distal RTA.[137] Such therapy has been advocated for patients with complete or incomplete forms of distal RTA because it decreases urolith formation and nephrocalcinosis and increases urine citrate concentration. Oral administration of sodium chloride, long recommended for all forms of urolithiasis, may promote hypercalciuria and calcium phosphate urolith formation. Therefore, oral salt therapy is not recommended to promote diuresis in dogs with uroliths containing calcium salts.

Normocalcemic Hypercalciuria

Several different medical protocols have been reported to be of value in people with normocalcemic hypercalciuria.[126] Ideally, the choice of therapy should be based on the cause of idiopathic hypercalciuria. There has been little clinical experience using pharmaceutical agents in dogs with calcium phosphate uroliths. However, medications that may enhance calcium excretion such as glucocorticoids, furosemide and those containing large quantities of sodium should be avoided if possible.

DIETARY MODIFICATION

An optimal food remains a goal for the future. Until such a food becomes available, it seems reasonable to recommend trial therapy with foods lower in certain nutrient levels (i.e., foods formulated to avoid excessive protein, sodium, calcium and vitamin D may be of benefit) compared with the food consumed at the time the urolith formed (Table 20-15). Encouraging water consumption is likely to be of benefit; therefore, enhancing urine volume by feeding a moist food (and/or a protein-restricted food to reduce renal medullary urea concentration) may be helpful. Although understandably difficult in some patients, fluid intake should be encouraged throughout the day to promote a constantly high urine volume. Excessive restriction or supplementation of dietary phosphorus should probably be avoided. In people, some high-fiber foods have been shown to reduce intestinal absorption and urinary excretion of calcium.

URINE ACIDIFIERS

With the exception of brushite, calcium phosphates tend to be less soluble in alkaline urine. Acidification reduces urine concentrations of ionic phosphate (PO_4^{3-}) and hydroxyl ions (OH^-). However, whether or not patients with calcium phosphate uroliths would benefit from appropriate dosages of acidifiers is unknown. Acidification tends to enhance urinary calcium excretion and is a risk factor for calcium oxalate urolith formation. Pending further studies, the authors are unable to recommend the routine use of urine acidifiers for patients with calcium phosphate urolithiasis.

Because calcium hydrogen phosphate dihydrate (brushite) is less soluble in acidic urine, it might seem logical to promote formation of alkaline urine in patients with brushite uroliths. However, brushite may be converted to other insoluble forms of calcium phosphate in alkaline urine. Use of potassium citrate, an alkalinizing agent, might be rationalized on the basis of minimizing acidosis-induced hypercalciuria, and formation of soluble calcium citrate rather than insoluble calcium phosphate in urine. The authors emphasize that the beneficial or detrimental effects of orally administered potassium citrate to dogs and cats with calcium phosphate urolithiasis have not been carefully evaluated. Consult the section on canine calcium oxalate urolithiasis for additional therapeutic information about potassium citrate.

THIAZIDE DIURETICS

Because thiazide diuretics decrease renal calcium excretion, they may be considered to minimize renal-leak hypercalciuria. Hydrochlorothiazide may be given on a trial basis to dogs with recurrent calcium phosphate urolithiasis at a dosage of 2 to 4 mg/kg body weight q12h. Because administration of thiazide diuretics may be associated with unwanted side effects (i.e., dehydration,

Table 20-30. Summary of recommendations for management of canine calcium phosphate uroliths.

1. Surgery remains the most reliable way to remove active calcium phosphate uroliths from the urinary tract. However, the authors emphasize that surgery may be unnecessary for clinically inactive calcium phosphate uroliths. Small urocystoliths may be nonsurgically removed by voiding urohydropropulsion (Table 20-16 and Figure 20-5) or by aspiration through a urinary catheter (Figure 20-6). Medical therapy of patients with recurrent calcium phosphate uroliths should then be directed at removing or minimizing risk factors that contribute to supersaturation of urine with calcium phosphate.
2. Patients with hypercalcemia and primary hyperparathyroidism usually require surgery. Parathyroidectomy may result in dissolution of uroliths and generally prevents their recurrence.
3. Several different medical protocols have been reported to be of value in people with normocalcemic hypercalciuria. Ideally, the choice of therapy should be based on the cause of idiopathic hypercalciuria.
   a. There has been little clinical experience with the use of drugs in dogs and cats with calcium phosphate uroliths. However, medications that can enhance calcium excretion such as glucocorticoids, furosemide and those containing large quantities of sodium should be avoided if possible.
   b. Foods designed to avoid excessive protein, sodium, calcium and vitamin D may be of benefit. Excessive restriction or supplementation of dietary phosphorus should probably be avoided. Enhancing urine volume by feeding a moist food (and/or a protein-restricted food to dogs to reduce renal medullary urea concentrations) and encouraging water consumption may be of benefit. Although understandably difficult to accomplish in some patients, fluid intake should be encouraged throughout the day to promote a constantly high urine volume. In people, some high-fiber diets have been shown to reduce intestinal absorption and urinary excretion of calcium.
   c. With the exception of brushite, calcium phosphates tend to be less soluble in alkaline urine. Whether or not patients with such mineral types would benefit from appropriate dosages of urine acidifiers is unknown. Acidification tends to enhance urine calcium excretion and is a risk factor for calcium oxalate urolith formation. Pending further studies, the authors are unable to recommend the routine use of urine acidifiers for patients with calcium phosphate urolithiasis.
4. To the authors' knowledge, medical dissolution of calcium phosphate uroliths has not been attempted in dogs with distal renal tubular acidosis (RTA). Foods designed to dissolve struvite uroliths would generally not be expected to promote dissolution of calcium phosphate uroliths, in part because they may tend to promote acidemia and aciduria, thus potentially enhancing hypercalciuria and hypocitraturia. However, correction of hypercalciuria, hyperphosphaturia and hypocitraturia by alkalinization therapy with potassium citrate might promote dissolution of these uroliths in patients with complete or incomplete distal RTA. Long-term alkalinization therapy appears to be beneficial in preventing calcium phosphate urolith formation in people with distal RTA. Such therapy has been advocated for patients with complete or incomplete forms of distal RTA because it decreases urolith formation and nephrocalcinosis and increases urine citrate concentration. Oral administration of sodium chloride, long recommended for all forms of urolithiasis, may promote hypercalciuria and calcium phosphate urolith formation. Therefore, oral salt therapy is not recommended to promote diuresis in dogs with uroliths containing calcium salts.

hypercalcemia, hypokalemia and magnesium depletion), patients should be appropriately monitored during therapy. Thiazide diuretic therapy is not recommended to treat absorptive hypercalciuria because it does not correct the hyperabsorptive state and may promote positive systemic calcium balance with possible soft-tissue calcification.

OTHER AGENTS

Other drugs have been used in an attempt to minimize hypercalciuria in people.[126] Sodium cellulose phosphate, the sodium salt of the phosphoric ester of cellulose, is an ion-exchange cellulose with special affinity for divalent ions. In the gastrointestinal tract it exchanges sodium for dietary calcium, which is then eliminated in the feces. It also binds calcium secreted into the gastrointestinal tract, minimizing its reabsorption. Oral administration of orthophosphates to people with normocalcemic hypercalciuria reduces urinary excretion of calcium and increases urine crystal inhibitory activity by increasing the urine concentration of pyrophosphates.[139]

Reassessment

The likelihood of recurrence of calcium phosphate uroliths following removal is not well established. Therefore, patients should be periodically monitored by urinalysis, radiographic or ultrasonographic procedures and other hematologic and urologic laboratory tests, if indicated (Table 20-30). Small, recurrent urocystoliths may be removed by voiding urohydropropulsion or by aspiration through a urinary catheter.[24,83] Medical therapy of patients with recurring calcium phosphate uroliths should be directed at removing or minimizing risk factors that contribute to supersaturation of urine with calcium phosphate.

CYSTINE UROLITHIASIS

Prevalence and Mineral Composition

The prevalence of cystine uroliths in dogs varies with geographic location. The prevalence is 1 to 3% of the uroliths removed from dogs in the United States[61,62,140,141] and as high as 39% in some European centers.[142] Cystine accounted for 1.0% of all uroliths submitted to the Minnesota Urolith Center from 1981 to 1997 (Table 20-7) and 0.8% (118 of 15,259) uroliths submitted in 1997. Cystine accounted for 0.4% of nephroliths analyzed at the Minnesota Urolith Center from 1981 to 1997 (Table 20-8). Only 1% of uroliths retrieved from dogs less than 12 months of age were cystine.

Quantitative analysis of canine cystine uroliths has revealed that most are pure; however, a few contain ammonium urate or calcium oxalate. Ammonium urate and calcium oxalate uroliths like cystine uroliths tend to form in acidic urine. Although uncommon, secondary UTIs with urease-producing microbes may result in a nucleus of cystine surrounded by layers of struvite.

The mean age of dogs at the time of cystine urolith retrieval was 4.8 ± 2.5 years (range three months to 14 years). Males (98%) were affected more often than females (2%). Sixty-seven different breeds were affected including English bulldogs (19%), mixed breeds (12%), dachshunds (10%), basset hounds (5%) and Newfoundlands (4%). Cystine uroliths were more commonly removed from the lower (97%) than the upper urinary tract (3%). The upper and lower urinary tract of Newfoundlands may contain cystine uroliths. Although cystine uroliths are radiodense, they are typically less dense than calcium-containing and struvite uroliths. Pure cystine uroliths are usually multiple, ovoid and smooth. They are light yellow and vary from 0.5 mm to several cm in diameter.

Etiopathogenesis and Risk Factors

Cystinuria is an inborn error of metabolism characterized by abnormal transport of cystine (a nonessential sulfur-containing amino acid composed of two molecules of cysteine) and other amino acids by the renal tubules. The name cystine was coined because this substance was first identified from urine removed from the urinary bladder (or urocyst) and, therefore, was thought to have originated from the bladder.[143]

Cystine is normally present in low concentrations in plasma. Normally, circulating cystine is freely filtered at the glomerulus and most is actively reabsorbed in the proximal tubules. The solubility of cystine in urine is pH dependent. It is relatively insoluble in acidic urine, but becomes more soluble in alkaline urine.

Unlike normal dogs, some cystinuric dogs reabsorb a much smaller proportion of the amino acid from the glomerular filtrate.[47] Some may even have net cystine secretion.

The molecular mechanism of cystinuria in people has been clarified. Mutations affecting the cystine transport gene called rBAT are associated with cystinuria.[144] The exact mechanism of abnormal renal tubular transport of cystine in dogs is unknown. Plasma concentrations of cystine in affected dogs are normal, indicating faulty tubular function rather than hyperexcretion.[47,145,146] Levels of plasma methionine, a precursor of cystine, are elevated in cystinuric dogs. Some studies in people suggest that tubular reabsorption of cysteine, the immediate precursor of cystine, may be abnormal.[147] In this situation, the increase in urine cystine concentration may result from dimerization of two cysteine molecules in tubular urine.

More than 60 breeds of dogs have been encountered with cystinuria. The exact pattern of aminoaciduria is variable in dogs with cystinuria.[145,148-150] Several different populations of cystinuric dogs have been reported.[145,151] One group had cystinuria without loss of other amino acids. Another group had cystinuria and a lesser degree of lysinuria. Studies by the authors indicate that English bulldogs that form cystine uroliths have cystinuria and lysinuria. A third group had cystinuria, ornithinuria, lysinuria and arginuria. Yet another group had cystinuria, glutaminuria, threoninuria and citrullinuria.[152] The magnitude of cystinuria varies widely among cystinuric dogs, varies between serial measurements of urine from the same dog and may decline in older dogs. Some variability may be related to differences in foods consumed by cystinuric dogs and urine collections during fasting and postprandial states. The authors have observed a cystinuric dachshund with carnitinuria.[153]

Unless protein intake is severely restricted, most cystinuric dogs have no detectable abnormalities associated with amino acid loss, with the exception of cystine urolith formation. This phenomenon occurs because cystine is sparingly soluble at the usual urinary pH range of 5.5 to 7.0. Cystinuria would be a medical curiosity in most dogs if cystine were not the least soluble naturally occurring amino acid. The major causes of morbidity and mortality associated with this disorder are the sequelae of urolith formation. One exception to this generality is cystinuric

dogs with carnitinuria. Carnitinuric dogs consuming foods with reduced quantities of carnitine are predisposed to dilated cardiomyopathy.[153]

The exact mechanism of cystine urolith formation is unknown. Because not all cystinuric dogs form uroliths, cystinuria is a predisposing factor rather than a primary cause of cystine urolith formation. In one study, four of 14 dogs with a history of cystine urolith formation had urine cystine concentrations that fell within the range of that found in control dogs.[145] Many breeds of dogs have been reported to develop cystine uroliths, especially dachshunds, English bulldogs, Newfoundlands, basset hounds, Chihuahuas, silky terriers, basenjis, mastiffs, bull mastiffs, Australian cattle dogs, Australian shepherd dogs, Scottish deerhounds, Staffordshire bull terriers, Welsh corgis, miniature pinchers and bichon frises.[145,154,155]

With few exceptions, notably Newfoundlands, cystine uroliths have been reported to occur only in male dogs.[9,62,156] The authors have also observed cystine urocystoliths in a nine-month-old female Scottish terrier. Cystinuria, however, has been observed in female dogs.[47,151]

Biologic Behavior

Cystine uroliths are often not recognized in most affected dogs until after they reach maturity. The average age at detection in many breeds is approximately two to five years. This is surprising inasmuch as one might expect an earlier onset of clinical manifestations of an inherited disorder. Cystinuria and cystine uroliths have been detected in male and female Newfoundlands less than one year of age.[151]

Compared with the situation in other breeds, the severity of the tubular transport defect for cystine in Newfoundlands appears to be more severe. This provides a plausible explanation for the earlier onset of cystine urolith formation in this breed and for the involvement of the kidneys in addition to the urinary bladder in female as well as male dogs.[151]

Because cystinuria is an inherited defect, uroliths commonly recur in two to 12 months unless prophylactic therapy has been initiated. Recurrence in Newfoundlands appears to be more rapid than in other breeds.

In some older dogs, the rate of recurrence declines as a consequence of a reduction in magnitude of cystinuria. Spontaneous partial dissolution of cystine uroliths occurred in a 10-year-old neutered male dachshund adopted by one of the authors (CAO). This dachshund was eating a moist maintenance food because it would not eat foods designed to minimize some risk factors for cystine urolithiasis.

Feeding Plan and Treatment

Current recommendations for dissolution of cystine uroliths encompass reducing urine concentration of cystine and increasing the solubility of cystine in urine. This may be accomplished by various combinations of: 1) dietary modification, 2) administration of thiol-containing drugs and 3) alkalinization of urine, if necessary (Table 20-31). Small cystine urocystoliths may be removed by voiding urohydropropulsion (Table 20-16 and Figure 20-5).

Dietary Modification

Reduction of dietary protein has the potential of minimizing formation of cystine uroliths. Pilot studies per-

Table 20-31. Summary of recommendations for medical dissolution and prevention of canine cystine uroliths.

1. Perform appropriate diagnostic studies including complete urinalysis, quantitative urine culture and diagnostic radiography. Determine precise location, size and number of uroliths. The size and number of uroliths are not a reliable index of probable therapeutic efficacy.
2. If uroliths are available, determine their mineral composition. If they are unavailable, determine their composition by evaluation of appropriate clinical data.
3. Consider surgical correction if uroliths obstruct urine outflow and/or if correctable abnormalities predisposing the patient to recurrent urinary tract infection are identified by radiography or other means. Small urocystoliths may be removed by voiding urohydropropulsion (Table 20-16 and Figure 20-5).
4. Initiate therapy with a calculolytic food (Prescription Diet Canine u/d*). No other food or mineral supplements should be fed to the patient. Compliance with dietary recommendation is suggested by a reduction in urea nitrogen concentration (usually <10 mg/dl).
5. Initiate therapy with N-(2-mercaptopropionyl)-glycine (2-MPG)** at a daily dosage of approximately 30 mg/kg body weight, divided into two equal subdoses.
6. If necessary, administer potassium citrate orally to eliminate aciduria. Strive for a urinary pH of approximately 7.5.
7. If necessary, eradicate or control urinary tract infections with appropriate antimicrobial agents.
   1. Devise a protocol for follow-up therapy.
      a. Try to avoid diagnostic follow-up studies that require urinary catheterization. If they are required, give appropriate peri-catheterization antimicrobial agents to prevent iatrogenic urinary tract infection.
      b. Perform serial urinalyses. Urinary pH, specific gravity and microscopic examination of sediment for crystals are especially important. Remember, crystals formed in urine stored at room or refrigeration temperatures may represent in vitro artifacts.
      c. Perform serial radiography monthly to evaluate urolith location(s), number, size, density and shape. Intravenous urography may be used to identify radiolucent uroliths in the kidneys, ureters and urinary bladder. Antegrade contrast cystourethrography may be required for radiolucent uroliths located in the bladder and urethra.
   2. Continue calculolytic food, 2-MPG and alkalinizing therapy for approximately one month after disappearance of uroliths as detected by radiography.
   3. Prevention. Feeding a low-protein food that promotes an alkaline urine has been effective in preventing cystine urolith recurrence. If necessary, low doses of 2-MPG may also be given.

*Hill's Pet Nutrition, Inc., Topeka, KS, USA.
**Thiola, Mission Pharmacal, San Antonio, TX, USA.

formed on cystinuric dogs at the University of Minnesota revealed a 20 to 25% reduction in urinary cystine excretion when subjects consumed a moist veterinary therapeutic food (Prescription Diet Canine u/d) vs. when they received a moist canine adult maintenance food. Reducing the renal medullary urea concentration and the associated urine concentration is an important indirect effect.[157] A protein-restricted alkalinizing food without other therapy (Prescription Diet Canine u/d) had a beneficial effect in promoting reduction in cystine urocystolith size in a three-year-old male dachshund.[158]

THIOL-CONTAINING DRUGS

D-penicillamine[f] (dimethylcysteine) is a nonmetabolizable degradation product of penicillin that may combine with cysteine to form cysteine-D-penicillamine disulfide.[159] This disulfide exchange reaction is facilitated by an alkaline pH. The resulting compound has been reported to be 50 times more soluble than free cystine.[160] The cysteine-D-penicillamine complex does not react with nitroprusside as does cystine, thus providing a mechanism to titrate dosage of the drug.[159]

Although D-penicillamine is effective in reducing urine cystine concentrations, drug-related adverse events limit its use. The most commonly used dosage of D-penicillamine for dogs has been 30 mg/kg body weight/day given in two divided doses.[161] Higher dosages frequently cause vomiting and may cause other undesirable reactions. If nausea and vomiting occur with the aforementioned dosage, the drug may be mixed with food or given at mealtimes. In some instances, it may be necessary to prevent gastrointestinal disturbances by initiating therapy with low dosages and gradually increasing them until full dosage is reached.

D-penicillamine has been associated with a variety of adverse reactions in people, including immune complex glomerulonephropathy, fever, lymphadenopathy and skin hypersensitivity.[159] The authors have observed fever and lymphadenopathy in a dachshund given D-penicillamine at a dosage of 30 mg/kg body weight/day.[158] The signs subsided after withdrawal of the drug and administration of glucocorticoids. The authors prefer to use N-(2-mercaptopropionyl)-glycine (2-MPG)[g] rather than D-penicillamine to minimize such adverse drug events.

2-MPG decreases the concentration of cystine by a thiol-disulfide exchange reaction similar to that of D-penicillamine.[159,162] Studies in dogs indicate that the drug is highly effective in reducing urinary cystine concentration and has less toxicity than D-penicillamine.[162]

Oral administration of 2-MPG at a daily dosage of approximately 30 to 40 mg/kg body weight (divided in two equal doses) was effective in inducing dissolution of multiple cystine urocystoliths in nine of 17 dogs evaluated.[163,164] Dissolution required two to four months of therapy. One dog developed nonpruritic vesicular skin lesions after three months of therapy. The skin lesions healed one month after the daily dosage of 2-MPG was reduced from 30 to 25 mg/kg body weight. Thrombocytopenia, anemia and increased hepatic enzyme activity have also occurred in a few cystinuric dogs treated with 2-MPG.[163,164]

Dogs that become hypersensitive to D-penicillamine may simultaneously become hypersensitive to 2-MPG. To avoid this predicament when thiol-containing drugs are needed, the authors discourage use of D-penicillamine and encourage use of 2-MPG. Appropriate hematologic and biochemical evaluations should be performed during use of 2-MPG in dogs with a history of D-penicillamine hypersensitivity.

In the authors' experience, a combination of a calculolytic food and 2-MPG therapy is more effective than either alone. The authors induced dissolution of 18 episodes of cystine urocystoliths affecting 14 dogs using combination dietary and drug therapy.[9] The mean time required to dissolve the cystine uroliths was 78 days (range 11 to 211 days).

Alkalinization of Urine

The solubility of cystine is pH dependent. In dogs, the solubility of cystine at a urinary pH of 7.8 has been reported to be approximately double that at a urinary pH of 5.0.[165] Changes in urinary pH that remain in the acidic range have minimal effect on cystine solubility. Therefore, if cystine uroliths fail to dissolve in dogs whose urinary pH does not become sufficiently alkaline as a result of dietary therapy, a sufficient quantity of potassium citrate or sodium bicarbonate should be given orally in divided doses to sustain a urinary pH of approximately 7.5. Data derived from studies in cystinuric people suggest that dietary sodium may enhance cystinuria.[166] Therefore, potassium citrate may be preferable to sodium bicarbonate as a urine alkalinizing agent. Further studies are required to evaluate the effect of dietary sodium on urinary excretion of cystine in dogs.

It is of interest that UTI caused by urease-producing bacteria in an adult male human patient with cystine nephroliths resulted in extreme urine alkalinity and subsequent urolith dissolution.[167]

Reassessment

The goal of therapy is to promote cystine urolith dissolution. Careful and planned monitoring is necessary for consistent effectiveness (Tables 20-32 and 20-33). Dietary management should result in formation of less concentrated urine without cystine crystalluria; strive to achieve urinary specific gravity values less than 1.020. Orally administered potassium citrate may be considered if owners and patients are known to be compliant with dietary therapy and the urinary pH remains acidic. The authors recommend that a urinalysis and survey abdominal radiographs be performed about every four weeks. Reduction in serum urea nitrogen concentration provides supportive evidence that the owner is complying with dietary recommendations.

Prevention

Because cystinuria is an inherited metabolic defect, and because cystine uroliths recur in a high percentage of

Table 20-32. Expected changes associated with medical therapy of cystine uroliths.

Factors	Pre-therapy	During therapy	Prevention therapy
Polyuria	±	1+ to 3+	1+ to 3+
Pollakiuria	0 to 4+	↑ then ↓	0
Hematuria	0 to 4+	↓	0
Urine specific gravity	Variable	1.004-1.014	1.004-1.014
Urinary pH	<7.0	>7.0	>7.0
Pyuria	0 to 4+	↓	0
Cystine crystals	0 to 4+	0	Variable
Bacteriuria	0 to 4+	0	0
Bacterial culture of urine	0 to 4+	0	0
Urea nitrogen (mg/dl)	Variable	<15	≤15
Urolith size and number	Small to large	↓	0

Table 20-33. Managing cystine uroliths refractory to complete dissolution.

Causes	Identification	Therapeutic goal
Client and patient factors		
Inadequate dietary compliance	Question owner Persistent cystine crystalluria Urea nitrogen >10-17 mg/dl Urine specific gravity >1.010-1.020 Urinary pH <7.0-7.5 during treatment with Prescription Diet Canine u/d* (use lower values for the canned food)	Emphasize need to feed dissolution food exclusively
Inadequate 2-MPG** administration	Question owner Count remaining pills	Emphasize need to administer the full dose of medication Determine if owner is capable and willing to administer medication Demonstrate a variety of methods to administer medication
Clinician factors		
Incorrect prediction of mineral type	Analysis of retrieved urolith	Alter therapy based on identification of mineral type
Inadequate 2-MPG dose for degree of diuresis	No change in urolith size after two months of appropriate therapy	Increase 2-MPG dose to 20 mg/kg body weight q12hr
Disease factors		
Compound urolith	Radiographic density of nucleus and outer layer(s) of urolith is different Analysis of retrieved urolith	Alter therapy based on identification of new mineral type Uroliths not causing clinical signs should be monitored for potentially adverse consequences (obstruction, urinary tract infection, etc.) Clinically active uroliths may require surgical removal Remove small uroliths by voiding urohydropropulsion

*Hill's Pet Nutrition, Inc., Topeka, KS, USA.
**2-MPG = N-(2-mercaptopropionyl)-glycine. Thiola. Mission Pharmacal, San Antonio, TX, USA.

young to middle-aged dogs within two to 12 months after surgical removal, prophylactic therapy should be considered.[146] Dietary therapy and if necessary, urine alkalinization may be initiated with the objective of minimizing cystine crystalluria and promoting a negative cyanide-nitroprusside test result. If necessary, 2-MPG may be added to the regimen in sufficient quantities to maintain a urine concentration of cystine less than approximately 200 mg/liter. If the dosage cannot be titrated by measurement of urine cystine concentration, 2-MPG may be given at a dosage of 15 mg/kg body weight q12h. Continuous therapy of urolith-free cystinuric dogs with 2-MPG has been effective in preventing formation of cystine uroliths in studies performed in Sweden and at the University of Minnesota.[163,164,168]

STRUVITE UROLITHIASIS
Prevalence and Mineral Composition

The most common type of mineral encountered in uroliths from dogs is magnesium ammonium phosphate hexahydrate (MAP) or struvite (Figure 20-12). Struvite accounted for 50% of all canine uroliths submitted to the Minnesota Urolith Center from 1981 to 1997 (Table 20-7) and 45% (6,923 of 15,259) of all canine uroliths submitted during 1997. Struvite accounted for 33% of canine nephroliths analyzed at the Minnesota Urolith Center from 1981 to 1997 (Table 20-8).

Although urolithiasis is most commonly recognized in adult dogs, 1.6% of the canine uroliths analyzed at the Minnesota Urolith Center were obtained from dogs less than 12 months old. Quantitative analysis of these uroliths revealed that 63% were struvite, 19% were purines (ammonium and sodium urate, uric acid), 3% were calcium phosphate, 4% were calcium oxalate, 1% were cystine and 1%

were silica; 4% were of mixed mineral composition and 6% were compound uroliths (minerals in the center of uroliths were different from minerals in outer layers).

The mean age at the time of magnesium ammonium phosphate retrieval from dogs was 5.9 ± 2.9 years (range one month to 19 years). Females (84%) were affected more often than males (16%). A total of 156 different breeds were affected, including mixed breeds (25%), miniature schnauzers (13%), bichon frises (7%), miniature poodles (5%) and cocker spaniels (5%). Struvite uroliths were more commonly removed from the lower urinary tract (99%) than the upper urinary tract (1%). They form in a variety of shapes and sizes (Table 20-34).

Etiopathogenesis and Risk Factors

Infection-Induced Struvite Uroliths

SEQUENTIAL STEPS IN UROLITH FORMATION

Urine must be supersaturated with magnesium ammonium phosphate hexahydrate for struvite uroliths to form.[169] However, acidic urine from people and presumably dogs is normally undersaturated with respect to magnesium ammonium phosphate.[170,171] Normally, urine ammonium (NH_4^+) concentration increases only when acid catabolites are excreted in high concentration by the kidneys. The increase in urine concentration of ammonium in this situation represents a normal compensatory response by the renal tubular cells to secrete ammonia (NH_3) into the tubular lumen to reduce acidity by subsequent formation of ammonium.

Whereas ammonia is lipid soluble and can penetrate tubular cell walls, ammonium is lipid insoluble and cannot penetrate cell walls (so-called ion trapping). Likewise, excretion of alkaline urine under physiologic conditions is associated with reduced renal production of ammonia and,

Table 20-34. Common characteristics of canine struvite uroliths.

Chemical name	Formula	Crystal name
Magnesium ammonium phosphate hexahydrate	$MgNH_4PO_4 \cdot 6H_2O$	Struvite

Variations in mineral composition
Struvite only
Struvite mixed with lesser quantities of calcium apatite and/or ammonium acid urate
Nucleus of a different mineral surrounded by variable layers composed primarily of struvite. Small quantities of calcium apatite and/or ammonium acid urate also may be present.

Physical characteristics
Color: Struvite uroliths are usually white, cream or light brown. The surface of uroliths is commonly red because of concomitant hematuria and may be green due to bile pigments.
Shape: Variable. Solitary urocystoliths are commonly round or elliptic. Multiple urocystoliths may be any shape, but are often pyramidal. Rapidly growing uroliths with a large quantity of matrix may form a cast of the lumen (renal pelvis, ureter, bladder, urethra) in which they are formed.
Nuclei and laminations: Common in infection-induced uroliths
Density: Variable. Soft if they contain a large quantity of matrix. Dense and harder to cut if little matrix is present. A combination of hard and soft internal density may occur within the same urolith. Radiodense compared with nonskeletal tissue on survey radiographs. Degree of radiodensity is related to the quantity of matrix (inversely proportional) and other minerals, especially calcium apatite (more proportional).
Number: Single or multiple
Location: May be located in the kidney, ureter, urinary bladder and/or urethra. Most occur in the urinary bladder.
Size: Subvisual to a size limited by the capacity of the structure (kidney and urinary bladder) in which they form. Very large uroliths are often composed of struvite.

Predisposing factors
Urinary tract infections with urease-producing microbes in patients whose urine contains a large quantity of urea
Alkaline urinary pH
Unidentified factors

Characteristics of affected patients
Mean age: six years (range less than one to more than nine years). Especially common in miniature schnauzers, bichon frises, miniature poodles and cocker spaniels; however, any breed may be affected. More common in females (84%) than males (16%).

$$NH_2\text{-}\overset{\overset{\displaystyle O}{\|}}{C}\text{-}NH_2 + H_2O \xrightarrow{\text{urease}} 2NH_3 + CO_2$$

$$CO_2 + H_2O \longleftrightarrow H_2CO_3 \longleftrightarrow H^+ + HCO_3^- \longleftrightarrow CO_3^=$$

$$NH_3 + H_2O \longleftrightarrow NH_4^+ + OH^-$$

Figure 20-14. Illustration of factors leading to formation of struvite, calcium apatite and carbonate apatite as a consequence of degradation of urea by microbial urease. See text below for details.

thus, reduced quantities of ammonium ions in urine. When UTI with urease-producing microbes occurs in animals forming urine with a sufficient quantity of urea, the unique combination of concomitant elevation in the concentrations of ammonium and carbonate (CO_3^{2-}) in an alkaline environment may develop. These conditions favor formation of uroliths containing struvite [$MgNH_4PO_4\bullet6H_2O$], calcium apatite [$Ca_{10}(PO_4)_6(OH)_2$] and carbonate apatite [$Ca_{10}(PO_4CO_3OH_4)_6(OH)_2$] (Figure 20-14). The following mechanisms are involved.[169] First, urease (a metalloenzyme containing nickel) produced by bacteria or ureaplasmas hydrolyzes urea to form two molecules of ammonia and a molecule of carbon dioxide. Second, the ammonia molecules react spontaneously with water to form ammonium and hydroxyl ions (pK of NH_3 9.03), which alkalinize urine by reducing hydrogen ion concentration. The solubility of struvite and calcium apatite decreases in alkaline urine.[172] In addition to alkalinization of urine, the newly generated ammonium ions are available for formation of magnesium ammonium phosphate crystals. Third, the newly generated molecules of carbon dioxide combine with water to form carbonic acid, which in turn dissociates to form bicarbonate (pK 6.33) and hydrogen ions. In an extremely alkaline environment, bicarbonate may lose its proton to become carbonate (pK 10.1). Carbonate anions may displace phosphate anions in calcium apatite crystals to form carbonate apatite crystals. Fourth, in the progressively alkaline environment induced by microbial hydrolysis of urea, dissociation of monobasic hydrogen phosphate ($H_2PO_4^-$) results in an increased concentration of dibasic hydrogen phosphate ($H_2PO_4^{2-}$) and anionic phosphate (PO_4^{3-}). Given a constant concentration of total phosphate, a change in pH from 6.8 to 7.4 increases the PO_4^{3-} concentration by a factor of approximately 6.[173] Anionic phosphate is then available in increased quantities to combine with magnesium and ammonium to form struvite or with calcium to form calcium apatite. Fifth, ammonium ions may combine with urates to form ammonium acid urate.[80,174]

Both urea (molecular weight 60 daltons) and urease (molecular weight 483,000 daltons) are required for ammonia production, alkalinization, supersaturation and subsequent precipitation of struvite, calcium apatite and carbonate apatite crystals. The majority of urea in urine originates from dietary protein,[175] whereas the urease in vertebrates must be derived from microbes (some bacteria, some yeasts or ureaplasmas).[176-179] The high concentration of urea normally present in urine of individuals that consume dietary protein in excess of daily requirement for protein anabolism makes urine an environment well suit-

ed to support the pathogenic effects of urease-producing microbes. Because of the importance of urease in the etiopathogenesis of struvite urolithiasis in people and many other animals, the name "urease stones" has been proposed.[180] Following a parallel line of reasoning, the name "urea stones" would also be appropriate.[157]

Continued production of ammonia and perhaps other toxic reactants as a consequence of urease-induced ureolysis appears to induce an inflammatory response in the urothelium and adjacent structures.[181-183] In fact, urease production contributes to the virulence of uropathogens that produce this enzyme.[184-187] The associated increase in urine concentration of proteinaceous inflammatory products acts as a form of matrix and contributes to calculogenesis.

Another mechanism that has been hypothesized to predispose patients with UTIs to urolithiasis is a bacteria-mediated reduction in the urine concentration of citrate.[188-190] Citrate is often called a crystallization inhibitor because it can combine with cations such as calcium and magnesium to increase their solubility.[191] It has also been suggested that bacteria may produce calculogenic matrix substances.[192]

BACTERIAL UTIs

Clinical and experimental studies of dogs have repeatedly demonstrated a close relationship between formation of struvite uroliths and UTIs caused by urease-producing bacteria.[169] Bacterial UTIs have been such a common finding in dogs with struvite uroliths that they are sometimes called infection stones.[180,193]

Several in vitro observations indicate that bacterial urease-induced supersaturation of urine with magnesium ammonium phosphate is the primary (but not necessarily the only) cause of infection-induced struvite uroliths.[180,194,195] First, growth of urease-producing *Proteus* spp in urea-free urine, or in urine containing a urease inhibitor, did not cause alkalinization, supersaturation or crystallization of struvite and apatite. Second, growth of weak urease-producing bacteria (*Klebsiella* spp and *Pseudomonas* spp) and non-urease-producing bacteria (*Escherichia* spp) was not associated with alkalinization, supersaturation and subsequent precipitation of struvite and apatite crystals.

Staphylococcus and *Proteus* spp are consistent and potent urease producers and have been commonly isolated from animals and people with infection-induced struvite uroliths.[180,181,193] For reasons that are unexplained, staphylococci have been more commonly associated with struvite uroliths in dogs than *Proteus* spp, whereas *Proteus* spp are more commonly associated with struvite uroliths in people.[169,177,196-199] It appears that some strains of *Proteus mirabilis* have special affinity for the urinary tract of people.[200] In pilot studies of dogs at the University of Minnesota, the authors had better success in experimentally inducing struvite uroliths with clinical isolates of staphylococci than with *Proteus* spp. Likewise, results of experimental studies in rats were interpreted to indicate that different strains of staphylococci had different calculogenic potential.[201]

Although other organisms such as *Klebsiella* spp and *Pseudomonas* spp have potential to produce varying quantities of urease,[180] they have not been as commonly associated with initiation of struvite urolith formation in people or dogs. Likewise, *Escherichia coli* and other non-urease-producing microbes have not been linked to naturally occur-

Table 20-35. Some potential risk factors for canine infection-induced struvite uroliths.

Diet	Urine	Metabolic	Drugs
High protein content (source of urea)	Urease-positive UTI	Females	Glucocorticoid-associated bacterial UTI
Urine alkalinizing potential	High urea concentration	Breeds	
High phosphorus content	Hyperammonuria	Miniature schnauzers	
High magnesium content	High-ionic phosphorus concentration	Miniature poodles	
	High magnesium levels	Bichon frises	
	High pH	Cocker spaniels	
	Urine retention	Hyperadrenocorticism associated with bacterial UTI	
	Concentration of urine and thus calculogenic substances		

Key: UTI = urinary tract infection.

ring struvite uroliths, presumably because they infrequently produce urease.[180,202] However, it has been reported that urease activity may be transferred by bacterial plasmids.[203]

The bacterial flora of urine may change after formation of struvite uroliths in dogs as a result of staphylococcal UTI. The change in bacterial flora may be associated with damage to local host defense mechanisms by uroliths, iatrogenic infection induced by urinary catheters or administration of antimicrobial agents.

A small percentage of dogs with struvite uroliths have sterile urine. In some of these cases, however, bacteria have been isolated from the inside of uroliths. This observation indicates that bacterial infection of the urinary tract may undergo spontaneous remission after initiating urolith formation in some patients. Bacteria that become trapped within struvite uroliths may remain viable for long periods. Several studies have revealed that calculogenic bacteria harbored within uroliths are protected from the destructive effects of antimicrobial agents in urine.[131,204-207]

In contrast to struvite uroliths, bacterial infection of the urinary tract is not a consistent finding in dogs with nonstruvite uroliths (ammonium urate, calcium oxalate, cystine, silica, etc.). When infection does occur in association with these so-called metabolic uroliths, it appears to be a sequela rather than a predisposing cause of urolith formation.

UREAPLASMA UTIs

Ureaplasmas differ from all other mycoplasmas by their production of urease and, therefore, their ability to hydrolyze urea.[208,209] Urea is required for growth of these organisms.[208,209] Ureaplasmas received consideration as etiologic agents in struvite urolithiasis when struvite uroliths were rapidly produced in male rat urinary bladders by intrarenal or intravesical injection of urease-producing ureaplasmas isolated from people.[210,211]

Ureaplasma urealyticum has been isolated from struvite uroliths removed from the renal pelves of people.[172,212] However, the organism could not be isolated from renoliths composed of calcium oxalate, calcium phosphate or uric acid. The authors have repeatedly isolated large numbers of ureaplasmas from an adult female basset hound with uroliths presumed to be composed of struvite and located in the renal pelves and urinary bladder.[h] Although the urine from this dog contained urease, urease-producing bacteria could not be isolated from it.

Efforts at the University of Minnesota to isolate ureaplasmas from urine of other dogs with nonbacterial struvite uroliths have been unsuccessful. Further studies are necessary, however, because ureaplasmas are fastidious and cell associated. Factors reported to limit growth of ureaplasmas in broth cultures include pH values greater than 7.5,[208,209] osmotic activity more than 600 mOsm/kg[213] and a high ammonia concentration.[187,208]

DIET

The quantity of dietary protein catabolized for energy influences formation and dissolution of infection-induced struvite uroliths. Consumption of dietary protein in quantities that exceed daily protein requirements for anabolism results in formation of urea from catabolism of amino acids. Hyperammonuria, hypercarbonaturia and alkaluria mediated by microbial urease are dependent on the quantity of urea (the substrate of urease) in urine (Table 20-35).

Abnormal urinary excretion of minerals as a result of enhanced glomerular filtration rate, reduced tubular reabsorption or enhanced tubular secretion is not required for initiation and growth of infection-induced uroliths.

GENETICS

The high incidence of struvite urolithiasis in some breeds of dogs such as miniature schnauzers suggests a familial tendency (Table 20-35). The authors hypothesize that susceptible miniature schnauzers inherit some abnormality of local host defenses of the urinary tract that increases their susceptibility to UTIs.[214,215] Hereditary factors thought to be associated with inbreeding have been reported to increase the incidence of struvite uroliths in beagles.[216] The incidence of struvite uroliths was 10.7% in an inbred line of beagles vs. only 2.0% in an outbred line of beagles.

Sterile Struvite Uroliths

Clinical studies indicate that microbial urease is not involved in formation of struvite uroliths in some dogs.[61,157,169] Several observations suggest that dietary or metabolic factors may be involved in the genesis of sterile struvite uroliths. Pilot studies involving clinical cases of struvite uroliths in dogs at the University of Minnesota revealed a population of patients (nine of 20) whose urine was frequently alkaline but did not contain identifiable bacteria and did not contain detectable quantities of urease. Microscopic examination of demineralized, gram-stained sections of some struvite uroliths removed from dogs with bacteriologically sterile urine did not reveal gram-positive bacteria.[217,h] Whereas infection-induced struvite uroliths from people frequently contain calcium apatite or carbonate apatite, a large number of the canine sterile uroliths were 100% struvite.

The authors encountered recurrent urocystoliths apparently composed of sterile struvite in three related English cocker spaniels: a sire and two of its male offspring from different dams.[218] Episodes of struvite urocystolithiasis were associated with alkaluria, but not with bacterial UTI, urinary urease enzyme activity or RTA.

Other investigators have also observed sterile struvite urocystoliths in English cocker spaniel dogs.[219]

Although struvite is less soluble in alkaline than acidic urine, the mechanism(s) of sterile struvite urolith formation in dogs is not clear. Under physiologic conditions associated with alkaluria, urine contains low concentrations of ammonia (and thus ammonium ions).[220] Therefore, alkaline urine formed in the absence of ureolysis would not be expected to favor formation of crystals that contain ammonium ions (e.g., magnesium ammonium phosphate hexahydrate). Clinical studies of naturally occurring urolithiasis in people support this generality.[177]

Formation of persistently alkaline urine in the absence of urease-mediated ureolysis may predispose patients to formation of uroliths containing hydroxyapatite $[Ca_{10}(PO_4)_6(OH)_2]$ but not carbonate apatite. Pathologic conditions that may result in this sequence of events include distal RTA,[126] incomplete distal RTA[221] and perhaps primary hyperparathyroidism.[126,134] Because alkaline urine favors dissociation of monobasic phosphate ($H_2PO_4^-$) to dibasic phosphate (HPO_4^{2-}) and phosphate ion (PO_4^{3-}), formation of calcium phosphate is enhanced. Patients with distal RTA have impaired ability to acidify urine associated with hypercalciuria and excretion of reduced concentration of urine citrate.[126,222-224]

Biologic Behavior

Clinical and experimental studies performed at the University of Minnesota revealed that struvite uroliths can form within two to eight weeks after infection with urease-producing staphylococci.[214,215] Struvite uroliths associated with UTI caused by staphylococci or *Proteus* spp have been detected in puppies as young as five weeks of age.[225]

Spontaneous dissolution of uroliths appears to be uncommon. The authors have observed five cases (two renoliths and three cystic uroliths) of struvite urolithiasis in dogs in which uroliths underwent spontaneous dissolution.[226] Spontaneous dissolution of canine nephroliths has also been reported by others.[227] Bilateral renal uroliths were reported to exist for approximately four years in a miniature schnauzer before causing death from renal failure.[228]

Uroliths located in the urinary bladder frequently pass into the urethra. In male dogs, they commonly lodge behind the os penis, but in female dogs they are frequently voided to the exterior. Small renoliths may pass into the ureters. The rapid rates at which struvite uroliths form and the potential they have to migrate to lower portions of the urinary tract are of clinical importance. If several days have elapsed between the date of diagnostic radiography or ultrasonography and the date of surgery scheduled to remove uroliths, the number and location of uroliths should be re-evaluated by radiography.

Table 20-36. Summary of recommendations for medical dissolution of canine struvite uroliths.

1. Adult dogs with urinary tract infection
    a. Perform appropriate diagnostic studies including complete urinalysis, quantitative urine culture and diagnostic radiography. Determine precise location, size and number of uroliths. The size and number of uroliths are not a reliable index of probable therapeutic efficacy.
    b. If uroliths are available, determine their mineral composition. If unavailable, determine their composition by evaluation of appropriate clinical data.
    c. Consider surgical correction if uroliths obstruct urine outflow and/or if correctable abnormalities predisposing the patient to recurrent urinary tract infection are identified by radiography or other means. Small urocystoliths may be removed by voiding urohydropropulsion (Table 20-16 and Figure 20-5).
    d. Eradicate or control urinary tract infections with appropriate antimicrobial agents. Maintain full-dose antimicrobial therapy during and for three to four weeks after urolith dissolution.
    e. Initiate therapy with calculolytic foods. No other food or mineral supplements should be fed to the patient. Compliance with dietary recommendations is suggested by a reduction in urea nitrogen concentration (usually <10 mg/dl).
    f. Devise a protocol to monitor efficacy of therapy.
        1) Try to avoid diagnostic follow-up studies that require urinary tract catheterization. If they are required, give appropriate peri-catheterization antimicrobial agents to prevent iatrogenic urinary tract infection.
        2) Perform serial urinalyses. Determination of urinary pH and specific gravity and microscopic examination of sediment for crystals are especially important. Remember, crystals formed in urine stored at room or refrigeration temperatures may represent in vitro artifacts.
        3) Perform serial radiography monthly to evaluate urolith location(s), number, size, density and shape.
        4) If necessary, perform quantitative urine cultures. They are especially important in patients infected before therapy and in patients catheterized during therapy.
        5) Feed patients a calculolytic food for one month following disappearance of uroliths as detected by survey radiography.
        6) Consider alternative methods if uroliths increase in size during dietary management, or do not begin to decrease in size after four to eight weeks of appropriate medical management. Difficulty in inducing complete dissolution of uroliths by creating urine that is undersaturated with the suspected calculogenic crystalloids should prompt consideration that: a) the wrong mineral component was identified, b) the nucleus of the uroliths is of different mineral composition than other portions of the urolith and c) the owner or the patient is not complying with medical recommendations.
    g. Consider administration of acetohydroxamic acid (25 mg/kg body weight/day divided into two equal doses) to patients with persistent uroliths and persistent urease-producing microburia despite the use of antimicrobial agents and calculolytic foods.
2. Adult dogs with persistently sterile urine
    a. Follow the protocol described above, but do not administer antimicrobial agents or acetohydroxamic acid.
    b. Periodically culture urine specimens obtained by cystocentesis to detect secondary urinary tract infections. Initiate antimicrobial therapy if a urinary tract infection develops.
3. Immature dogs
    a. Use caution when feeding protein-restricted foods to growing dogs.
    b. Short-term therapy with calculolytic foods has been effective in dissolving struvite urocystoliths. If initiated, monitor the patient for evidence of nutritional deficiencies (especially protein malnutrition).
    c. Acetohydroxamic acid has not been evaluated in growing dogs.
    d. Small urocystoliths may be removed by voiding urohydropropulsion (Table 20-16 and Figure 20-5). Pending further studies, surgery remains the safest means of removing large uroliths from immature dogs.

Struvite uroliths have a tendency to recur after surgical removal or medical dissolution.[66,216,229] The authors have evaluated miniature schnauzers with more than seven known recurrences following surgery. However, many episodes of multiple recurrence have been associated with lack of removal of all uroliths at the time of surgery (pseudorecurrence), and poor control of recurrent UTI with urease-producing microbes. With the advent of effective therapeutic and preventive antimicrobial protocols to control recurrent or persistent UTI, the frequency of recurrent infection-induced struvite urolithiasis in dogs has declined. The authors have also observed multiple recurrences of sterile struvite uroliths in dogs, presumably because the underlying mechanisms causing their formation persisted following medical dissolution or surgical removal.

In the authors' experience, the rate of recurrence following medical dissolution of canine struvite uroliths is less frequent than that associated with surgery. In addition, time elapsed between recurrent episodes is longer following medical dissolution. The apparent higher rate of recurrence associated with surgical removal of uroliths may be associated with inability to remove all uroliths, especially those located in inaccessible sites or those that are subvisual. The tendency for uroliths to recur after surgery may also be associated with persistence of an environment that favors initiation and growth of struvite at the time of removal.

Assess the Food(s)

Infection-Induced Struvite Uroliths

Both urea and microbial urease are required for ammonia production, alkalinization, supersaturation and subsequent precipitation of struvite crystals. The majority of urea in urine originates from dietary protein,[175] whereas the urease in vertebrates must be derived from microbes (some bacteria, some yeasts or ureaplasmas).[176-179] Hyperammonuria and alkaluria mediated by microbial urease are dependent on the quantity of urea (the substrate of urease) in urine. In addition, foods high in protein are also high in phosphorus (Table 20-35). The high concentration of urea and phosphorus normally present in urine of individuals consuming dietary protein in excess of daily requirement for protein anabolism makes urine an environment well suited to support the pathogenic effects of urease-producing microbes.

Sterile Struvite Uroliths

Although not validated by experimental or clinical studies in dogs, foods high in magnesium and phosphorus would be expected to predispose susceptible dogs to sterile struvite urolith formation. In vitro studies in which magnesium ($MgSO_4$), ammonium (NH_4Cl) or phosphate ($NH_4H_2PO_4$ or NaH_2PO_4) was added to sterile human urine ranging in pH from 5.0 to 9.6 revealed that struvite crystals could be induced to form in an acidic or an alkaline environment.[230] High ammonia concentrations were not necessary for formation of struvite crystals provided the concentration of $(Mg) \times (NH_4) \times (PO_4)$ was of sufficient magnitude at a given pH. Corresponding in vivo studies in dogs have not been performed.

Feeding Plan and Treatment

The authors' current recommendations for medical dissolution of canine struvite uroliths include: 1) eradication or control of UTI (if present), 2) use of calculolytic foods (Table 20-15) and 3) administration of urease inhibitors (acetohydroxamic acid) to patients if struvite uroliths persist because of persistent UTI caused by urease-producing microbes (Table 20-36).

Infection-Induced Struvite Urocystoliths

ERADICATION OR CONTROL OF UTIs

The importance of UTIs with urease-producing bacteria in the formation of many struvite uroliths in dogs emphasizes the need to eliminate or control infection. Because of the quantity of urease produced by bacterial pathogens, it may be impossible to acidify urine with urine acidifiers administered at dosages that do not cause systemic acidosis.[231] Therefore, sterilization of urine appears to be an important objective in creating a state of struvite undersaturation that may prevent further growth of uroliths or that promotes their dissolution.

Appropriate antimicrobial agents selected on the basis of susceptibility or minimum inhibitory concentrations should be used at therapeutic dosages. The fact that diuresis reduces the urine concentration of the antimicrobial agent should be considered when formulating antimicrobial dosages.[232] Antimicrobial agents should be administered as long as uroliths can be identified by survey radiography. This recommendation is based on the fact that bacterial pathogens harbored inside uroliths may be protected from antimicrobial agents.[233] Although the urine and surface of uroliths may be sterilized following appropriate antimicrobial therapy, the original and secondary infecting organisms may remain viable below the surface of the urolith. Therefore, discontinuation of antimicrobial therapy may result in relapse of bacteriuria and infection.

Although use of antimicrobial agents alone may result in dissolution of struvite uroliths in some patients, experimental studies in rats[234] and dogs[h] and clinical studies in people[196,235,236,h] indicate that this phenomenon represents the exception rather than the rule. In one controlled experimental study performed by the authors, six dogs with struvite uroliths were given therapeutic dosages of oral ampicillin (16 mg/kg body weight/day divided into three equal subdoses) and were fed a maintenance food. Only two uroliths dissolved; the remaining four uroliths increased in size.[h] In addition to the unpredictable response to this form of therapy, the time required to induce urolith dissolution with antimicrobial agents is usually measured in multiples of months rather than in multiples of weeks.

CALCULOLYTIC FOODS

The goal of dietary modification for patients with struvite uroliths is to reduce urine concentration of urea (the substrate of urease), phosphorus and magnesium. A commercial veterinary therapeutic food (Prescription Diet Canine s/d[a]) was formulated that contained a reduced quantity of a high-quality protein and reduced quantities of phosphorus and magnesium.[175] The food was supplemented with sodium chloride to stimulate thirst and induce compensatory polyuria. Reduction of hepatic production of urea from dietary protein reduced renal medullary urea concentration and further contributed to diuresis.

The efficacy of Prescription Diet Canine s/d in inducing dissolution of infected struvite uroliths has been confirmed by controlled experimental studies in dogs. The calculolytic food was highly effective in inducing dissolution of struvite uroliths in five of six dogs despite persistent infection with urease-producing bacteria. The uroliths underwent dissolution in about 3.5 months (range eight to 20 weeks). The urolith in the remaining dog decreased to less than one-half its pretreatment size at the termination of the study, six months following initiation of dietary therapy. UTIs persisted in these dogs until the uroliths dissolved, at which time they underwent remission in three dogs. In the corresponding control group fed a maintenance food (10% protein, 0.19% phosphorus and 0.06% magnesium, as fed basis), uroliths increased by a mean of 5.5 times their pretreatment size (range three to eight times). A urolith developed in the renal pelvis of one of these dogs. UTIs persisted in control dogs throughout the six-month study.

Consumption of Prescription Diet Canine s/d by dogs with induced staphylococcal UTI and struvite uroliths was associated with a marked reduction in the serum concentration of urea nitrogen and mild reductions in the serum concentrations of magnesium, phosphorus and albumin.[175] A mild increase in the serum activity of hepatic alkaline phosphatase also was observed. These alterations in serum chemistry values were of no clinical consequence during six-month experimental studies or during clinical studies. However, they underscore the fact that Canine s/d is designed for short-term (weeks to months) dissolution therapy rather than long-term (months to years) prophylactic therapy. Appropriate reduction in concentrations of serum urea nitrogen may be used as one index of client and patient compliance with dietary therapy (Table 20-37).

The calculolytic effect of various combinations of antibiotics (ampicillin given orally at a dosage of 16 mg/kg body weight/day), acetohydroxamic acid and Prescription Diet Canine s/d were studied in dogs with staphylococcal-induced struvite uroliths.[h] After five months of therapy, four uroliths increased in size and two dissolved in six dogs given ampicillin and an adult maintenance-type food. Four of six uroliths dissolved and two decreased in size in six dogs given ampicillin and Prescription Diet Canine s/d over the same time frame. All uroliths in six dogs dissolved six weeks after initiation of therapy with a combination of Prescription Diet Canine s/d, ampicillin and acetohydroxamic acid.

Similar results were obtained when a combination of Prescription Diet Canine s/d and antimicrobial agents was given to 11 dogs with naturally occurring urease-positive UTIs and urocystoliths presumed to be composed of struvite.[157,237] The mean time required to induce urocystolith dissolution in these dogs was approximately three months (range two weeks to seven months).

UREASE INHIBITORS

Experimental and clinical studies in dogs have revealed that administration of microbial urease inhibitors in pharmacologic doses is capable of inhibiting struvite urolith growth and promoting struvite urolith dissolution. Acetohydroxamic acid given orally to dogs at a dosage of 25 mg/kg body weight (divided into two daily subdoses) reduced urease activity, struvite crystalluria and urolith growth.[182] By reducing the pathogenicity of staphylococci, acetohydroxamic acid may also result in less severe dysuria, bacteriuria, pyuria, hematuria and proteinuria.

Although higher dosages of acetohydroxamic acid may result in urolith dissolution, they are not recommended because they may cause a reversible hemolytic anemia and abnormalities in bilirubin metabolism.[182,238] Likewise, acetohydroxamic acid should not be administered to pregnant dogs because it is teratogenic.[239]

The authors have not routinely used acetohydroxamic acid in promoting dissolution of infection-induced struvite uroliths in dogs because of the efficacy of the calculolytic food and antimicrobial therapy. However, the

Table 20-37. Characteristic clinical findings before and after initiation of medical therapy to dissolve struvite uroliths in nonazotemic dogs.*

Factors	Pre-therapy	During therapy	After successful therapy**
Polyuria	±	1+ to 3+	Negative
Pollakiuria	1+ to 4+	Transient↑; subsequent ↓	Negative
Gross hematuria	0 to 4+	↓ by 5 to 10 days	Negative
Abnormal urine odor	0 to 4+	↓ by 5 to 10 days	Negative
Small uroliths voided	±	Common in females	Negative
Urine specific gravity	Variable	1.004 to 1.014	Normal
Urinary pH	≥7	Decreased (usually acidic)	Variable
Urine protein	1+ to 4+	Decreased to absent	Negative
Urine RBC	1+ to 4+	Decreased to absent	Negative
Urine WBC	1+ to 4+	Decreased to absent	Negative
Struvite crystals	0 to 4+	Usually absent	Variable
Other crystals	Variable	May persist	May persist
Bacteriuria	0 to 4+	Decreased to absent	Negative
Quantitative bacterial urine culture	0 to 4+	Decreased to absent	Negative
Serum urea nitrogen	>15 mg/dl	<10 mg/dl	Dependent on food
Serum creatinine	Normal	Normal	Normal
Serum alkaline phosphatase	Normal	↑by 2 to 5 times	Normal
Serum albumin	Normal	↓ by 0.5 to 1 g/dl	Normal
Serum phosphorus	Normal	Slight decrease	Normal
Urolith size (radiographic)	Small to large	Progressive decrease	Negative
Hemogram	Normal	Normal	Normal

*For dogs with urinary tract infection, therapy consists of a calculolytic food and antimicrobial agents. For dogs without urinary tract infection, therapy consists of a calculolytic food.
**All forms of therapy withdrawn.

authors have used acetohydroxamic acid in combination with calculolytic foods and antimicrobial agents in patients that have recalcitrant urease-producing UTIs associated with persistent struvite uroliths. Acetohydroxamic acid may be added to the therapeutic regimen if infection-induced struvite uroliths do not dissolve after an appropriate therapeutic trial with diet modification and antimicrobial agents.

Infection-Induced Struvite Nephroliths

Nephroliths and ureteroliths causing outflow obstruction and marked impairment of renal function should be managed by surgical intervention or, if possible, by percutaneous nephropyelonephrostomy, especially if associated with concomitant bacterial infection.[240] Medical therapy designed to induce urolith dissolution over several weeks is unlikely to be effective in patients with poorly functioning kidneys because uroliths must be completely surrounded by urine that is undersaturated with struvite for prolonged periods to be dissolved. Intermittent passage of urine through a partially obstructed kidney or ureter would logically preclude dissolution of struvite nephroliths or ureteroliths.

The authors have successfully induced dissolution of nephroliths presumed to be composed of infection-induced struvite in six dogs. The mean time required for dissolution was 184 days (range 67 to 300 days). Although the dogs had varying degrees of impaired capacity to concentrate urine as a result of pyelonephritis, none had primary renal azotemia at the time therapy was initiated with Prescription Diet Canine s/d and antimicrobial agents. This point is emphasized because dogs with moderate to severe primary renal failure require a greater quantity of protein for anabolism than normal. The calculolytic food used in the authors' studies could induce or aggravate protein malnutrition if given for prolonged periods to dogs with moderate azotemic primary renal failure, or other concomitant disorders associated with protein malnutrition.[241]

Sterile Struvite Uroliths

Current recommendations include use of calculolytic foods and urine acidifiers (Table 20-36). Antibiotics and urease inhibitors are not required unless secondary UTI develops.

Controlled experimental and clinical studies have confirmed the efficacy of Prescription Diet Canine s/d in inducing sterile struvite urolith dissolution.[157,242] The time required to induce dissolution of sterile struvite uroliths is usually less than that required for infection-induced struvite uroliths.

In a study of induced sterile struvite uroliths in dogs, consumption of Prescription Diet Canine s/d resulted in urolith dissolution in a mean of 3.3 weeks (range two to four weeks).[175] In a corresponding control group fed a maintenance-type food, uroliths in four dogs dissolved over a mean of 14 weeks (range two to five months). Uroliths were one-fifth of their initial size at the termination of the study in the remaining two control dogs.

When the calculolytic food was fed to nine dogs with naturally occurring sterile uroliths presumed to be composed of struvite, uroliths dissolved in a mean of six weeks (range one month to three months).[157,243,h] Management of six episodes of naturally occurring sterile struvite urocystoliths affecting two related male English cocker spaniel

dogs with Prescription Diet Canine s/d resulted in urolith dissolution in a mean of 38.5 ± 12.8 days.[218]

Preliminary studies indicate that protein restriction is not essential for dissolution of canine sterile struvite uroliths. Acidification of urine to approximately 6.0 has been effective in promoting sterile struvite urolith dissolution.[70] In this respect, they are similar to feline sterile struvite uroliths. However, dietary protein restriction has the advantage of contributing to obligatory polyuria by decreasing renal medullary urea concentration and thus enhancing the rate of sterile struvite urolith dissolution.

Struvite Uroliths in Immature Dogs

The authors have successfully dissolved struvite urocystoliths in several immature dogs (Table 20-36). One was a 12-week-old female miniature dachshund with a sterile struvite urocystolith.[243] The urocystolith was dissolved within two weeks after feeding was begun with Prescription Diet Canine s/d. Another dog was a nine-week-old, male, mixed-breed puppy with a vesicourachal diverticulum, urethral stricture, *Staphylococcus intermedius* UTI and multiple struvite urocystoliths.[244] These urocystoliths dissolved within nine days of initiation of therapy with the calculolytic food and a combination of amoxicillin and clavulanic acid. The food was discontinued on Day 10. Slight reductions in serum albumin concentration (from approximately 3.2 to 2.7 g/dl) were observed in both dogs during the two weeks of dietary therapy. Serum albumin concentrations returned to reference values soon after the puppies resumed eating a normal growth food.

The authors do not recommend feeding Prescription Diet Canine s/d to immature dogs for more than two weeks. If the food is used, the authors recommend serially monitoring body weight, body condition, serum albumin concentration and packed cell volume for evidence of protein/calorie malnutrition. Appropriate adjustments in dietary management should be made if marked reductions in these variables are observed. The urocystoliths may be removed by voiding urohydropropulsion if they have been reduced enough to pass through a distended urethra.[83]

Reassessment

Because calculolytic foods stimulate thirst and promote diuresis, the magnitude of pollakiuria in dogs with urocystoliths may increase for a variable time following initiation of dietary therapy. Pollakiuria and the abnormal urine odor caused by bacterial degradation of urea usually subside as infection is controlled and uroliths decrease in size (Table 20-37). Reduction in ammonia-induced and chemical inflammation as a result of ureolysis may also be involved in remission of these clinical signs.

The size of uroliths should be periodically monitored by survey radiography or ultrasonography. The authors recommend radiography at monthly intervals. Survey radiography or ultrasonography is usually preferred to retrograde double-contrast radiography because use of catheters during retrograde radiographic studies may result in iatrogenic UTI. Alternatively, intravenous urography may be considered.

Periodic evaluation of urine sediment for crystalluria also may be considered. Struvite crystals should not form in fresh uncontaminated urine if therapy has been effec-

tive in promoting formation of urine that is undersaturated with magnesium ammonium phosphate.

UTIs may persist despite antimicrobial therapy in patients having infection-induced struvite uroliths and consuming the calculolytic food. In most patients, however, the magnitude of bacteriuria is markedly reduced (i.e., from more than 100,000 to 100 to 1,000 bacteria/ml of urine) and the associated inflammatory response progressively subsides. Difficulty in eradicating the infection while uroliths persist may be related to persistence of viable microbes within the uroliths.[233] Diet-induced diuresis should be considered when formulating dosages of antimicrobial agents that will achieve minimum inhibitory concentrations in urine. Despite persistent bacteriuria during antimicrobial and dietary treatment of infected patients with struvite uroliths, the authors have had excellent success in inducing dissolution of uroliths. Even though the urine is not sterile, reduction in bacterial colony counts by logarithmic magnitudes (e.g., from 10^6 to 10^4 colony forming units) has a marked effect in reducing the quantity of microbial urease in urine.[245] Concomitant use of calculolytic foods, antimicrobial agents and acetohydroxamic acid is the most effective method of inducing dissolution of uroliths when UTI complications persist.

Urine collected by cystocentesis should be quantitatively cultured during therapy and five to seven days after antimicrobial therapy is discontinued. Results of urine culture may not be the same as results obtained before therapy or from cultures of the interior of uroliths. Rapid recurrence of UTI caused by the same type of organism (relapse) or a different type of bacterial pathogen (reinfection) following withdrawal of antimicrobial therapy may indicate residual uroliths within the urinary tract or other abnormalities in local host defense mechanisms that predispose the patient to UTI and subsequent urolithiasis.

Because small uroliths may escape detection by survey radiography or ultrasonography, the authors recommend that Prescription Diet Canine s/d and (if necessary) antimicrobial agents be continued for at least one month after radiographic or ultrasonographic documentation of urolith dissolution. This protocol is likely to prevent rapid recurrence of radiographically detectable uroliths and bacterial UTI after therapy is discontinued.

Alternate methods of management should be considered if uroliths increase in size during therapy or if urolith size remains unchanged after approximately eight weeks of appropriate medical therapy. Small uroliths that become lodged in the urethra of male or female dogs during therapy may be readily returned to the urinary bladder lumen by retrograde urohydropropulsion. Complete obstruction of a ureter or renal pelvis with a urolith, especially with concomitant urinary infection, is an indication for surgical intervention.

Attempts to induce dissolution of struvite uroliths may be hampered if the uroliths are heterogeneous in composition (Table 20-38). This has not been a significant problem in dogs with uroliths composed primarily of magnesium ammonium phosphate with lesser quantities of calcium apatite because the solubility characteristics of the two minerals are similar. However, the authors have encountered difficulty in dissolving uroliths composed primarily of struvite with an outer shell composed primarily of calcium apatite. Difficulty will also be encoun-

tered in attempting to induce complete dissolution of a urolith with a nucleus of calcium oxalate or silica and a shell of struvite because the solubility characteristics of these minerals are dissimilar. This phenomenon should be considered if medical therapy seems to be ineffective after initially reducing the size of a urolith.

Precautions with Calculolytic Foods

There are benefits and risks associated with feeding calculolytic foods. Not all patients are candidates for dietary medical management. Benefits and risks of such therapy should be considered and discussed with the client if the following problems coexist in dogs with struvite uroliths, or if risk factors for their development are present. During such discussions with clients, the authors avoid making "all or none" and "always or never" statements because risk factor associations are not synonymous with cause and effect relationships.

ABNORMAL FLUID RETENTION

The food (Prescription Diet Canine s/d) designed to dissolve canine struvite uroliths is restricted in protein and supplemented with sodium chloride. Both could affect fluid balance. Therefore, the food should not be routinely fed to patients with concomitant diseases associated with positive fluid balance (e.g., heart failure, nephrotic syndrome) or hypertension.

AZOTEMIC PRIMARY RENAL FAILURE

Complete obstruction of urine outflow caused by uroliths in patients with a concomitant UTI should be regarded as an emergency. In this situation, rapid spread of infection and associated damage to the urinary tract, especially the kidneys, are likely to induce septicemia and acute renal failure by a combination of obstruction and pyelonephritis. The risks and benefits associated with medical therapy to dissolve uroliths should not be considered until adequate urine flow has been restored.

Nonobstructing struvite nephroliths have been dissolved in patients with nonazotemic renal failure caused by ascending pyelonephritis.[157,242] Nevertheless, protein-restricted calculolytic foods should be used with caution in patients with azotemic primary renal failure. Such foods may induce protein malnutrition if given for prolonged periods to dogs with moderate azotemic primary renal failure.[241]

To minimize adverse drug reactions/events, adjustments in doses and maintenance intervals of drugs excreted primarily by the kidneys should be considered in patients with azotemic primary renal failure.

PATIENTS AT RISK FOR PANCREATITIS

Approximately one in 250 dogs seen in private veterinary practice is affected by pancreatitis (0.4%). There appears to be no relationship between pancreatitis and gender, but there is a significant relationship between the disease and age. The mean age of dogs with pancreatitis in private veterinary practice is eight years vs. 5.5 years for the general canine population. Breed is another strong risk factor for pancreatitis. For example, miniature schnauzers have a fivefold increase in risk for pancreatitis (i.e., about one in 50 miniature schnauzers can be expected to have pancreatitis.) Other breeds at increased risk include bichon frises, Yorkshire terriers, Chihuahuas, Jack Russell terriers, Japanese spaniels, Labrador retrievers, Maltese, and Shetland sheepdogs. (See Chapter 22.)

Table 20-38. Managing magnesium ammonium phosphate uroliths refractory to complete dissolution.

Causes	Identification	Therapeutic goal
Client and patient factors		
Inadequate dietary compliance	Question owner Persistent struvite crystalluria Urea nitrogen >8-12 mg/dl Urine specific gravity >1.010-1.015 Urinary pH is alkaline during treatment with Prescription Diet Canine s/d*	Emphasize need to feed dissolution food exclusively
Inadequate antibiotic administration	Question owner Count remaining antibiotic pills	Emphasize need to administer the full dose of antibiotics Determine if owner is capable and willing to administer medication Demonstrate a variety of methods to administer medication
Clinician factors		
Incorrect prediction of mineral type	Analysis of retrieved urolith	Alter therapy based on identification of mineral type
Inappropriate antibiotic choice	Positive urine culture with poor susceptibility for chosen antibiotic	Choose antibiotics based on susceptibility testing
Inappropriate antibiotic dose for degree of diuresis	Positive quantitative urine culture with same bacterial species and same susceptibility; number of bacteria may be lower (See text.)	Administer antibiotic at the higher recommended dose or consider a higher dose than recommended
Premature discontinuation of antibiotic	Discontinuing antibiotic before complete urolith dissolution Positive urine culture with same bacterial species and the same susceptibility (See text.)	Prescribe full antibiotic dose for the entire period of urolith dissolution
Disease factors		
Change in bacterial susceptibility	Positive urine culture with susceptibility results different from those of previous culture	Choose antibiotic based on susceptibility testing
New bacterial infection	Positive urine culture identifying new bacterial species	Choose antibiotic effective against both bacteria Avoid procedures requiring urinary tract catheterization
Compound urolith	Radiographic density of nucleus and outer layer(s) of urolith is different Analysis of retrieved urolith	Alter therapy based on identification of new mineral type Uroliths not causing clinical signs should be monitored for potentially adverse consequences (obstruction, urinary tract infection, etc.) Clinically active uroliths may require removal Remove small uroliths by voiding urohydropropulsion

*Hill's Pet Nutrition, Inc., Topeka, KS, USA.

Investigators conducting an independent epidemiologic study recently surveyed veterinarians to ascertain the health of dogs fed Prescription Diet brand pet foods.[a] This study disclosed an association between feeding Prescription Diet Canine s/d and acute pancreatitis. The risk of a dog developing pancreatitis when fed Canine s/d is comparable to that of a miniature schnauzer developing acute pancreatitis, or about one in 40 (i.e., about one in 40 dogs fed Canine s/d might develop pancreatitis).

The calculolytic food is relatively high in fat, which serves primarily as a source of calories. Because dietary fat is a risk factor for pancreatitis, the serum activity of pancreatic enzymes (amylase, lipase, trypsin-like immunoreactivity) should be monitored before initiating therapy in patients known to be at increased risk for pancreatitis. These tests should be repeated if signs of pancreatitis develop during therapy. Because abnormal increases in activity of these enzymes are not pathognomonic for pancreatitis, other relevant findings should also be considered.

The authors emphasize that female miniature schnauzers are at increased risk for infection-induced struvite uroliths and pancreatitis. Likewise, patients with hyperadrenocorticism are at increased risk for UTIs (which could include staphylococci) and pancreatitis. Although risk factors are not synonymous with cause and effect, clients should be informed of these associations and advised of how to respond to adverse events if they occur. They should be informed about adverse events that need medical attention and those that need medical attention only if they continue or are bothersome.

Prevention

Infection-Induced Struvite Uroliths

Eradication or control of UTIs due to urease-producing bacteria is the most important factor in preventing recurrence of most infection-induced struvite uroliths. If UTI persists or is recurrent, indefinite therapy is indicated with prophylactic dosages of antimicrobial agents eliminated in high concentration in urine. These may include amoxicillin, nitrofurantoin, enrofloxacin and trimethoprim-sulfadiazine; however, the final choice is best determined by the results of the most recent antimicrobial susceptibility test. In light of the effectiveness of foods in inducing dissolution of struvite uroliths, use of dietary modification (Table 20-15) to prevent recurrence of uroliths is logical and feasible. However, further studies must be performed to evaluate the long-term effects of low-protein calculolytic foods in dogs before reliable recommendations can be established. Because such foods induce polyuria, varying degrees of hypoalbuminemia and mild alterations in hepatic enzyme activities and morphology, the authors recommend long-term use of calculolytic foods with severely reduced protein levels only if patients develop frequently recurrent urolithiasis despite attempts to control infection, augment fluid intake and urine acidification.

Studies to evaluate the effectiveness of acetohydroxamic acid in the prevention of struvite urolithiasis in dogs with persistent UTI with urease-producing bacteria have been encouraging. Administration of 25 mg of acetohydroxamic acid/kg body weight/day to dogs with urinary bladder foreign bodies (zinc disks) and experimentally induced urease-positive staphylococcal UTIs has been effective in preventing formation of and minimizing the growth rate of uroliths.[183] Acetohydroxamic acid has also been reported to be effective in preventing struvite uroliths induced by ureaplasmas in rats.[h]

Studies are in progress to evaluate the preventive efficacy of acidifying foods with mild to moderately reduced levels of protein, magnesium and phosphorus (Table 20-15). Caution must be used in deciding whether or not to induce prophylactic diuresis in patients with a history of struvite uroliths induced by recurrent UTI. Although formation of less concentrated urine tends to minimize the supersaturation of urine with calculogenic crystalloids, it tends to counteract innate antimicrobial properties of urine. Experimental studies performed in rats and cats indicate that diuresis tends to minimize pyelonephritis, but enhance lower UTIs.

Sterile Struvite Uroliths

Sterile struvite uroliths have a greater tendency to recur vs. infection-induced struvite uroliths in which the UTI has been eradicated or controlled. Administration of urine acidifiers should be considered if the urinary pH of patients with sterile struvite uroliths remains alkaline despite dietary therapy. The prophylactic value of concomitant restriction of dietary phosphorus and magnesium has not yet been determined.

Uncontrollable risk factors (i.e., defective inhibitors of crystal formation and/or defective inhibitors of crystal aggregation) may be present in those situations in which dogs have documented occurrences of either calcium oxalate or calcium phosphate followed by struvite urolithiasis. If struvite urolithiasis is associated with urease-positive UTIs, appropriate therapy should be devised to eradicate the UTI and prevent its recurrence.

When considering dietary management (Table 20-15), the authors recommend that emphasis be placed on minimizing recurrence of calcium oxalate or calcium phosphate uroliths, because these types of urolith cannot be dissolved by medical management. Should struvite uroliths recur, they often can be dissolved by dietary management and antimicrobial agents, if necessary. This strategy tends to minimize the need for repeated surgical intervention.

SILICA UROLITHIASIS

Prevalence and Mineral Composition

Silica accounted for 0.9% of all canine uroliths submitted to the Minnesota Urolith Center from 1981 to 1997 (Table 20-7) and 0.5% (69 of 15,259) of uroliths submitted in 1997. Silica accounted for 0.5% of all canine nephroliths analyzed at the Minnesota Urolith Center from 1981 to 1997 (Table 20-8). Of 428 canine silica uroliths, 284 were composed entirely (100%) of silica, and 144 were composed of at least 70% of this mineral. Silica uroliths may contain varying quantities of other minerals, especially calcium oxalate. The authors have encountered only a few silica uroliths in dogs less than 12 months old.

The mean age of dogs at the time of urolith retrieval was 7.0 ± 3.1 years (range one to 17 years). Males were affected (96%) more commonly than females (4%). The authors hypothesize that female dogs void small silica uroliths before they induce clinical signs, thereby reducing the detection rate. Seventy different breeds were affected including mixed breeds (15%), golden retrievers (9%), German shepherd dogs (7%), cocker spaniels (6%), miniature schnauzers (6%) and black Labrador retrievers (5%). Silica uroliths were more commonly removed from the lower urinary tract (99%) than the upper urinary tract (1%).

In the authors' series, most silica uroliths had a jackstone configuration. The name jackstone was selected because the urolith's shape is similar to the small, six-pronged metal pieces used in the children's games of jacks. Protrusions from different uroliths vary in number (usually from 15 to 30), length (from a few mm to more than 1 cm) and diameter. Some protrusions are long and slender; whereas others are blunt, imparting a mamillary appearance to the urolith. Protrusions from individual uroliths are usually but not invariably similar in length and diameter. Canine silica jackstones are distinctly laminated. In most dogs, silica jackstones occurred in multiples with some patients having more than 30. However, a few dogs have solitary uroliths. Silica uroliths ranged in diameter from less than 1 mm to more than 3 cm. Not all uroliths composed primarily of silica had a jackstone configuration. However, all had some form of surface protrusions at more or less regular intervals, imparting a regularly uneven surface contour to the uroliths. Some silica jackstones were coated with layers of struvite, which altered their characteristic shape. In some instances, struvite completely surrounded silica jackstones.

Etiopathogenesis and Risk Factors

Naturally occurring silica jackstones were first encountered in dogs in the mid-1970s.[246] A review of the literature revealed a conspicuous absence of this type of canine urolith before that time. In the mid 1970s, silica uroliths were reported to occur only in dogs from the United States and Canada. However, in 1985, canine silica jackstones were recognized in Japan and shortly thereafter they were recognized in Europe. Calcium magnesium aluminum silicate uroliths without a jackstone configuration were identified in dogs native to Kenya in 1977.[247]

Relationship of Silica Uroliths to Diet

Although silicate minerals constitute more than 90% of the earth's crust, they occur in only very low concentrations in most animals.[248] Therefore, ingredients in pet foods derived from animal sources are an unlikely source of silica. The generally low quantities of silica in most animals may be attributable to low solubility in all but a very few naturally occurring waters. Silica solubility in water remains constant below a pH of 9. In contrast, plants contain larger quantities of silica. Grasses contain between 1 and 4% dry weight silica. Plants noted for their high silica content include rice and scouring rushes (*Equisetum* spp [horsetails]), both of which contain up to 16% silica.[249] The Canadian prairie grass *Fescuta scabrella* contains 4 to 8% silica.[250]

Several observations prompt the hypothesis that development of canine silica uroliths may be related to hyperexcretion of silica in urine after consumption of an absorbable form of silica in various foods. For example, silicic acid is readily absorbed across the intestinal wall.[251-253] Silica uroliths have occurred in several people who consumed large quantities of antacids containing magnesium trisilicate to alleviate signs of peptic ulcers.[254-258]

One possibility as to why canine silica uroliths began to be recognized in the mid 1970s is increased use of plant-derived ingredients by the pet food industry in moist and dry dog foods. Silicon is taken up by the roots of plants and deposited in cell walls as silica, soluble silicates and organic combinations. Another factor could have been the addition of fiber sources (e.g., rice hulls or soybean hulls) containing relatively large quantities of silica to pet foods designed for management of obesity.[253]

Corn gluten feed, a by-product of the wet milling and distilling process designed to separate shelled corn into various components, may be another suspect as a source of silica in some pet foods. Corn gluten feed remains after extraction of starch, gluten and germ from shelled corn. The term gluten, meaning "glue'" in Latin, refers to the sticky characteristic of substances derived from corn, wheat and other grains. Corn gluten feed contains about 40% protein and is found in some low-quality pet foods. The authors emphasize that corn gluten feed is not the same as corn gluten meal. Corn gluten meal is found in many higher quality manufactured foods because it is readily digestible and a good source of protein (approximately 60%), vitamins, minerals and energy. Corn gluten meal is an unlikely source of the silica in uroliths. Another potential source of silica in foods is microfine silica, which is used in small quantities as an anti-caking agent in the pet food manufacturing process. Although a cause and effect relationship between microfine silica and silica urolithiasis is unlikely, it seems logical to avoid giving foods containing this ingredient to dogs with recurrent silica urolithiasis.

A word of caution is in order. Studies performed in rats indicate that the type of silica compound ingested influences its absorption from the gastrointestinal tract.[259] In addition, other factors (such as pH) may be involved.[259,260] Therefore, detection of a relatively large quantity of silica in food is not itself synonymous with risk for silica urolith formation. Instead, the latter is dependent on detection of abnormal quantities of silicic acid or other silica metabolites in urine.

Biologic Behavior

The time required for naturally occurring silica uroliths to develop in susceptible dogs is unknown. Silica uroliths were induced in dogs four months after foods containing large quantities of silicic acid were fed.[261] Silica uroliths have been produced in rats within eight weeks after consumption of tetraethylorthosilicate.[255,262,263] Silicious uroliths have been observed in calves by the time they were approximately four months old.[255] Evaluation of case reports of people who developed silica uroliths while consuming silicate-containing antacids suggests that the uroliths developed over a period of years.[254,257]

Because many of the silica uroliths evaluated in the authors' series were submitted for analysis by veterinarians throughout the United States and Canada, long-term follow-up of the majority of affected dogs was not possible. However, silica uroliths have recurred in at least five dogs following surgical removal from the lower urinary tract. Struvite urocystoliths developed in at least two dogs as a consequence of infection with urease-producing staphylococci following surgical removal of silica urocystoliths. Formation of struvite uroliths in this situation is not surprising because urease-producing staphylococci are calculogenic in dogs.

Assess the Food(s)

Foods with large quantities of plant-derived ingredients are suspected to be risk factors for silica uroliths in susceptible dogs. Corn gluten feed, rice hulls and soybean hulls have been incriminated.[246]

Concentrations of calculogenic substances in urine are dependent on urine volume. Because commercial dry foods are associated with production of a lesser volume of urine vs. moist foods, consumption of dry foods may also be considered a risk factor for silica urolith formation.

Feeding Plan and Treatment

Effective medical protocols to induce dissolution of canine silica jackstones have not yet been developed. Calculolytic foods that do not contain large quantities of vegetable proteins and that induce diuresis may prevent further growth of silica uroliths. Voiding urohydropropulsion may be used to remove small urocystoliths (Table 20-16 and Figure 20-5). Surgery is the only viable alternative to remove large silica uroliths.

Because initiating and perpetuating causes of silica urolithiasis are unknown, only nonspecific measures to reduce the degree of supersaturation of urine with calculogenic substances can be recommended for prevention. At this time, the authors' recommendations include change of diet, augmentation of urine volume and possibly altering urinary pH (Table 20-39).[246,248]

Although the role of diet in the genesis of canine silica uroliths is speculative, it seems reasonable to recommend that food(s) of affected patients be changed, especially if the problem is recurrent. Even though empirical, this maneuver is unlikely to be harmful and may be helpful. Based on the assumption that the primary source of excessive silica in foods is vegetable in origin, selection of a food with reduced quantities of plant ingredients is recommended.

For dogs with recurrent silica urolithiasis, increasing the volume of urine produced by increasing water consumption will increase the volume of urine in which calculogenic substances are dissolved or suspended. Moist foods rather than dry foods should be considered. Oral administration of sodium chloride has been a favored empirical

Table 20-39. Summary of recommendations for prevention of canine silica uroliths.

1. Perform appropriate diagnostic studies including complete urinalysis, quantitative urine culture and diagnostic radiography. Determine precise location, size and number of uroliths.
2. If uroliths are available, determine their mineral composition. If unavailable, determine their composition by evaluation of appropriate clinical data.
3. Small urocystoliths may be removed by voiding urohydropropulsion (Table 20-16 and Figure 20-5). Consider surgical removal of larger uroliths causing clinical disease.
4. To prevent further growth of existing silica uroliths or to prevent recurrence of silica uroliths after surgical removal:
   a. Avoid use of foods containing large quantities of plant proteins, and especially avoid those containing soybean hulls or corn gluten feed.
   b. Enhance diuresis by adding moisture to the food.
   c. Avoid efforts to deliberately acidify urine.
5. If necessary, eradicate or control urinary tract infections with appropriate antimicrobial agents.

method to induce diuresis in dogs with uroliths. However, the authors do not recommend sodium chloride to promote diuresis in dogs that form silica uroliths because of the unpredictable but marked occurrence of calcium oxalate in silica uroliths and because orally administered sodium chloride is associated with hypercalciuria.

Silica is less soluble in acidic than alkaline water and currently available information suggests that silica is less soluble in acidic than alkaline biologic environments.[246,248] It is noteworthy that the urinary pH of eight uninfected dogs with silica uroliths was acidic to neutral at the time of diagnosis (mean 6.0, range 5.0 to 7.0).[246] Whether or not alkalinization of urine is of benefit in increasing the solubility of silica or silicates in urine is unknown. Likewise, the effects of orally administered alkalinizing agents (e.g., sodium bicarbonate) on the absorbability of silica from the gastrointestinal tract have not been evaluated. Nonetheless, it seems prudent to avoid efforts to deliberately acidify the urine of dogs with recurrent silica uroliths.

Reassessment

The goal of therapy is to prevent silica urolith recurrence. Dietary management should minimize exposure to minerals predisposing to silica uroliths and result in formation of less concentrated urine; strive to achieve urine specific gravity values less than 1.020. After this is achieved, a urinalysis and lateral abdominal radiograph should be performed every three to four months. By following these recommendations, recurrent urocystoliths detected by radiography should be small enough to remove by voiding urohydropropulsion. After a rate of urolith recurrence has been established, the frequency of evaluation can be modified such that predicted recurrences can be diagnosed and managed accordingly.

COMPOUND UROLITHS

Compound uroliths (nucleus composed of one mineral type and shells of a different mineral type) occurred in approximately 7% of the canine uroliths analyzed in the authors' series (Table 20-7). Examples include: 1) a nucleus of 100% calcium oxalate monohydrate surrounded by a shell of 80% magnesium ammonium phosphate and 20% calcium phosphate, 2) a nucleus composed of 95% magnesium ammonium phosphate and 5% calcium phosphate surrounded by a shell of 95% ammonium acid urate and 5% magnesium ammonium phosphate and 3) a nucleus composed of 95% silica and 5% calcium oxalate monohydrate surrounded by a shell of 100% calcium oxalate monohydrate.

Voiding urohydropropulsion may be used to remove small compound urocystoliths (Table 20-16 and Figure 20-5). Surgery remains the only reliable method to remove large compound uroliths.

Because risk factors that predispose patients to precipitation (nucleation) of different minerals vary, the occurrence of compound uroliths poses a unique challenge in terms of preventing recurrence. In the absence of clinical evidence to the contrary, it seems logical to recommend management protocols designed primarily to minimize recurrence of minerals composing the nucleus (rather than those in shells) of compound uroliths.[264] Follow-up studies designed to evaluate efficacy of preventive protocols should include complete urinalyses, radiography or ultrasonography and if available, evaluation of the urine concentration of calculogenic metabolites.

▮ ENDNOTES & REFERENCES

ENDNOTES

a. Hill's Pet Nutrition, Inc., Topeka, KS, USA.
b. Zyloprim. Glaxo Wellcome, Research Triangle Park, NC, USA.
c. Urocit-K. Mission Pharmacal, San Antonio, TX, USA.
d. Polycitra-K. Willen Drug Co., Baltimore, MD, USA.
e. Bartges JW. Unpublished data. 1995.
f. Cuprimine. Merck and Co., Rahway, NJ, USA.
g. Thiola. Mission Pharmacal, San Antonio, TX, USA.
h. Osborne CA, Unpublished data. 1987.

REFERENCES

1. Lulich JP, Osborne CA, Bartges JW, et al. Canine lower urinary tract disorders. In: Ettinger SJ, Feldman EC, eds. Textbook of Veterinary Internal Medicine, 4th ed. Philadelphia, PA: WB Saunders Co, 1995: 1833-1861.
2. Osborne CA, Kruger JM. Initiation and growth of uroliths. Veterinary Clinics of North America: Small Animal Practice 1984; 14: 439-454.
3. Coe FL. Treated and untreated recurrent calcium nephrolithiasis in patients with idiopathic hypercalciuria, hyperuricosuria, or no metabolic disorder. Annals of Internal Medicine 1977; 87: 404-410.
4. Pak CYC. Disorders of stone formation. In: Brenner BM, Rector FC Jr, eds. The Kidney, vol 2. Philadelphia, PA: WB Saunders Co, 1976.
5. Lyon ES, Vermeulen CW. Crystallization concepts and calculogenesis. Observations and artificial concretions. Investigative Urology 1965; 3: 309-320.
6. Coe FL. Nephrolithiasis: Pathogenesis and Treatment. Chicago, IL: Year Book Medical Publishers Inc, 1978.
7. Pak CYC, Hayashi Y, Finlayson B, et al. Estimation of the state of saturation of brushite and calcium oxalate in urine: A comparison of three methods. Journal of Laboratory and Clinical Medicine 1977; 89: 891-901.
8. Brown CM, Ackerman DK, Purich DL. EQUIL93: A tool for experimental and clinical urolithiasis. Urological Research 1994; 22: 119-126.

9. Osborne CA, Lulich JP, Unger LK, et al. Canine and feline urolithiasis: Relationship of etiopathogenesis to treatment and prevention. In: Osborne CA, Finco DR, eds. Canine and Feline Nephrology and Urology, Baltimore, MD: Williams & Wilkins, 1995; 798-888.

10. Feeney DA, Weichselbaum RC, Jessen CR, et al. Imaging canine urocystoliths: Detection and prediction of mineral content. Veterinary Clinics of North America: Small Animal Practice 1999; 29: 59-72.

11. Cornelius LM, Thrall DE, Halliwell WH, et al. Anomalous portosystemic anastomoses associated with chronic hepatic insufficiency in six young dogs. Journal of the American Veterinary Medical Association 1975; 167: 220-228.

12. Ewing GO, Suter PF, Bailey CS. Hepatic insufficiency associated with congenital anomalies of the portal vein in dogs. Journal of the American Animal Hospital Association 1974; 10: 463-476.

13. Griffiths GL, Lumsden JH, Valli VEO. Hematologic and biochemical changes in dogs with portosystemic shunts. Journal of the American Animal Hospital Association 1981; 17: 705-710.

14. Rothuizen J, van den Ingh T. Urolithiasis due to liver failure in the dog. Journal of the Netherlands Small Animal Veterinary Association 1980; 19: 9-10.

15. Barrett RE, DeLahunta A, Roenick WJ, et al. Four cases of congenital portacaval shunt in the dog. Journal of Small Animal Practice 1976; 17: 71-85.

16. Marretta SM, Pask AJ, Greene RW, et al. Urinary calculi associated with portosystemic shunts in six dogs. Journal of the American Veterinary Medical Association 1981; 178: 133-137.

17. Center SA, Baldwin BH, DeLahunta A, et al. Evaluation of serum bile acid concentrations for the diagnosis of portosystemic venous anomalies in the dog and cat. Journal of the American Veterinary Medical Association 1985; 186: 1090-1094.

18. Tabaru H, Finco DR, Brown SA, et al. Influence of hydration state on renal functions of dogs. American Journal of Veterinary Research 1993; 54: 1758-1764.

19. Lulich JP, Osborne CA, Nagode LA, et al. Evaluation of urine and serum metabolites in miniature schnauzers with calcium oxalate urolithiasis. American Journal of Veterinary Research 1991; 52: 1583-1590.

20. Lulich JP, Osborne CA, Polzin DJ, et al. Urine metabolic values in fed and nonfed clinically normal beagles. American Journal of Veterinary Research 1991; 52: 1573-1578.

21. Lemieux G, Plante GE. The effect of starvation in the normal dog including the Dalmatian coach hound. Metabolism 1968; 17: 620-630.

22. Osborne CA, Lulich JP, Bartges JW, et al. Medical dissolution and prevention of canine and feline uroliths: Diagnostic and therapeutic caveats. Veterinary Record 1990; 127: 369-373.

23. Osborne CA, Lulich JP, Unger LK. Nonsurgical retrieval of uroliths for mineral analysis. In: Kirk RW, Bonagura JD, eds. Current Veterinary Therapy XI. Philadelphia, PA: WB Saunders Co, 1992; 886-889.

24. Lulich JP, Osborne CA. Catheter-assisted retrieval of urocystoliths from dogs and cats. Journal of the American Veterinary Medical Association 1992; 201: 111-113.

25. Osborne CA, Klausner JS, Clinton CW. Analysis of canine and feline uroliths. In: Kirk RW, ed. Current Veterinary Therapy VIII. Philadelphia, PA: WB Saunders Co, 1983; 1061-1066.

26. Zinn KR, Glascock MD, Schmidt DA. Instrumental neutron-activation analysis of canine urinary calculi. American Journal of Veterinary Research 1986; 47: 2536-2538.

27. Ulrich LK, Bird K, Koehler L, et al. Urolith analysis: Submission, methods, and interpretation. Veterinary Clinics of North America: Small Animal Practice 1996; 26: 393-400.

28. Ruby AL, Ling GV. Bacterial culture of uroliths: Techniques and interpretation of results. Veterinary Clinics of North America: Small Animal Practice 1986; 16: 325-331.

29. Jackson OF, Sutor DJ. Ammonium acid urate calculus in a cat with a high uric acid excretion possibly due to a renal tubular reabsorption defect. Veterinary Record 1970; 86: 335-337.

30. Porter P. Urinary calculi in the dog: II. Urate stones and purine metabolism. Journal of Comparative Pathology 1963; 73: 121-135.

31. Loffler W, Groboner W, Zollner N. Influence of dietary protein on serum and urinary uric acid. In: Rapado A, Watts RWE, De Bruyn CHMM, eds. Purine Metabolism in Man–III: Clinical and Therapeutic Aspects. New York, NY: Plenum Press 1979; 209-213.

32. Rodwell VW. Metabolism of purine and pyrimidine nucleotides. In: Murray RK, Granner DK, Mayes PA, et al, eds. Harper's Biochemistry. Norwalk, CT: Appleton & Lange, 1988; 344-361.

33. Escolar E, Bellanato J, Medina JA. Structure and composition of canine urinary calculi. Research in Veterinary Science 1990; 49: 327-333.

34. Kruger JM, Osborne CA. Etiopathogenesis of uric acid and ammonium urate uroliths in non-Dalmatian dogs. Veterinary Clinics of North America: Small Animal Practice 1986; 16: 87-126.

35. Bartges JW, Osborne CA, Felice LJ, et al. Influence of four diets containing approximately 11% protein (dry weight) on uric acid, sodium urate, and ammonium urate urine activity product ratios of healthy beagles. American Journal of Veterinary Research 1995; 56: 60-65.

36. Bartges JW, Osborne CA, Felice LJ, et al. Diet effect on activity product ratios of uric acid, sodium urate, and ammonium urate in urine formed by healthy beagles. American Journal of Veterinary Research 1995; 56: 329-333.

37. Bartges JW, Osborne CA, Felice LJ, et al. Influence of two amounts of dietary casein on uric acid, sodium urate, and ammonium urate urinary activity product ratios of healthy beagles. American Journal of Veterinary Research 1995; 56: 893-897.

38. Holmes EWJ, Mason DHJ, Goldstein LI, et al. Xanthine oxidase deficiency: Studies of a previously unreported case. Clinical Chemistry 1974; 20: 1076-1079.

39. Bartges JW, Osborne CA, Felice LJ. Canine xanthine uroliths: Risk factor management. In: Kirk RW, Bonagura JD, eds. Current Veterinary Therapy XI. Philadelphia, PA: WB Saunders Co, 1992; 900-905.

40. Bartges JW, Osborne CA, Felice LJ, et al. Influence of allopurinol and two diets on 24-hour urinary excretions of uric acid, xanthine, and ammonia by healthy dogs. American Journal of Veterinary Research 1995; 56: 595-599.

41. Ling GV, Ruby AL, Harrold DR, et al. Xanthine-containing urinary calculi in dogs given allopurinol. Journal of the American Veterinary Medical Association 1991; 198: 1935-1940.

42. van Zuilen CD, Nickel RF, van Dijk, et al. Xanthinuria in a family of cavalier King Charles spaniels. Veterinary Quarterly 1997; 19: 172-174.

43. Duncan H, Curtiss AS. Observations on uric acid transport in man, the Dalmatian, and the non-Dalmatian dog. Henry Ford Hospital Medical Journal 1971; 19: 105-114.

44. Duncan H, Wakim KG, Ward LE. The effect of intravenous administration of uric acid on its concentration in plasma and urine of Dalmatian and non-Dalmatian dogs. Journal of Laboratory and Clinical Medicine 1961; 58: 876-883.

45. Friedman M, Byers SO. Observations concerning the causes of the excess excretion of uric acid in the Dalmatian dog. Journal of Biological Chemistry 1948; 175: 727-735.

46. Williams AW, Wilson DM. Uric acid metabolism in humans. Seminars in Nephrology 1990; 10: 9-14.

47. Bovee KC, ed. Urolithiasis. In: Canine Nephrology. Media, PA: Harwal, 1984: 355-379.

48. Ling GV. Lower Urinary Tract Diseases of Dogs and Cats. St. Louis, MO: Mosby, 1995.

49. Appleman RM, Hallenbeck GA, Shorter RG. Effect of reciprocal allogeneic renal transplantation between Dalmatian and non-Dalmatian dogs on urinary excretion of uric acid. Proceedings of the Society for Experimental Biology and Medicine 1966; 121: 1094-1097.

50. Cohn R, Cibbell DG, Laub DR, et al. Renal allotransplantation and allantoin excretion of Dalmatians. Archives of Surgery 1965; 91: 911-912.

51. Kuster G, Shorter RG, Dawson B, et al. Uric acid metabolism in Dalmatians and other dogs: Role of the liver. Archives of Internal Medicine 1972; 129: 492-496.

52. Giesecke D, Tiemeyer W. Defect of uric acid uptake in Dalmatian dog liver. Experientia 1984; 40: 145-146.

53. Harvey AM, Christensen HN. Uric acid transport system: Apparent absence in erythrocytes of the Dalmatian coach hound. Science 1964; 145: 826-827.

54. Kessler RH, Hierholzer K, Gurd RS. Localization of urate transport in the nephron of mongrel and Dalmatian dog kidney. American Journal of Physiology 1959; 197: 601-603.

CANINE
UROLITHIASIS

55. Roch-Ramel F, Peters G. Urinary excretion of uric acid in nonhuman mammalian species. In: Kelley WN, Weiner IM, eds. Handbook of Experimental Pharmacology, Uric Acid. Berlin, Germany: Springer-Verlag, 1978; 211-255.

56. Foreman JW. Renal handling of urate and other organic acids. In: Bovee KC, ed. Canine Nephrology. Media, PA: Harwal, 1984; 135-151.

57. Bartges JW, Osborne CA, Lulich JP, et al. Prevalence of cystine and urate uroliths in English bulldogs and urate uroliths in Dalmatians (1981-1992). Journal of the American Veterinary Medical Association 1993; 204: 1914-1918.

58. Case LC, Ling GV, Ruby AL, et al. Urolithiasis in Dalmatians: 275 cases (1981-1990). Journal of the American Veterinary Medical Association 1993; 203: 96-100.

59. Felice LJ, Dombrovskis D, Lafond E, et al. Determination of uric acid in canine serum and urine by high performance liquid chromatography. Veterinary Clinical Pathology 1990; 19: 86-89.

60. Schaible RH. Genetic predisposition to purine uroliths in Dalmatian dogs. Veterinary Clinics of North America: Small Animal Practice 1986; 16: 127-131.

61. Bovee KC, McGuire T. Qualitative and quantitative analysis of uroliths in dogs: Definitive determination of chemical type. Journal of the American Veterinary Medical Association 1984; 185: 983-987.

62. Ling GV, Ruby AL. Canine uroliths: Analysis of data derived from 813 specimens. Veterinary Clinics of North America: Small Animal Practice 1986; 16: 303-317.

63. Osborne CA, Sanna JJ, Unger LK, et al. Analyzing the mineral composition of uroliths from dogs, cats, horses, cattle, sheep, goats, and pigs. Veterinary Medicine 1989; 84: 750-764.

64. Ungar H, Ungar R. Further studies on the pathogenesis of urate calculi in the urinary tract of white rats. American Journal of Pathology 1952; 28: 291-301.

65. Hardy RM, Klausner JS. Urate calculi associated with portal vascular anomalies. In: Kirk RW, ed. Current Veterinary Therapy VIII. Philadelphia, PA: WB Saunders Co, 1983; 1073-1076.

66. Brown NO, Parks JL, Greene RW. Recurrence of canine urolithiasis. Journal of the American Veterinary Medical Association 1977; 170: 419-422.

67. Finco DR, Rosin E, Johnson KH. Canine urolithiasis: A review of 133 clinical and 23 necropsy cases. Journal of the American Veterinary Medical Association 1970; 157: 1225-1228.

68. Weaver AD. Canine urolithiasis: Incidence, chemical composition, and outcome of 100 cases. Journal of Small Animal Practice 1970; 11: 93-107.

69. Bartges JW, Osborne CA, Koehler LA, et al. An algorithmic approach to canine urate uroliths. In: Proceedings. Twelfth Annual Veterinary Medical Forum, American College of Veterinary Internal Medicine, San Francisco, CA, 1994: 467-468.

70. Osborne CA, Polzin DJ, Johnston GR, et al. Medical management of canine uroliths with special emphasis on dietary modifications. Companion Animal Practice 1987; 1: 72-87.

71. Hande K, Reed E, Chabner B. Allopurinol kinetics. Clinical Pharmacology and Therapeutics 1978; 23: 598-605.

72. Osborne CA, Kruger JM, Johnston GR, et al. Dissolution of canine ammonium urate uroliths. Veterinary Clinics of North America: Small Animal Practice 1986; 16: 375-388.

73. Elion GB, Kovensky A, Hitchings GH, et al. Metabolic studies of allopurinol, an inhibitor of xanthine oxidase. Biochemical Pharmacology 1966; 15: 863-880.

74. Bartges JW. Effects of modified diets and allopurinol on plasma and urine concentrations of uric acid and xanthine in healthy dogs. PhD Thesis. University of Minnesota, St. Paul, 1993.

75. Elion GB. Enzymatic and metabolic studies with allopurinol. Annals of the Rheumatic Diseases 1966; 25: 608-614.

76. Al-Kawas FH, Seeff LB, Berendson RA, et al. Allopurinol hepatotoxicity: Report of two cases and review of the literature. Annals of Internal Medicine 1981; 95: 588-590.

77. Medline A, Cohen LB, Tobe BA, et al. Liver granulomas and allopurinol. British Medical Journal 1978; 1: 1320-1321.

78. Pedroia V. Allopurinol-induced immune disorders. Canine Practice 1981; 8: 19-22.

79. Hande KR, Noone RM, Stone WJ. Severe allopurinol toxicity: Description and guidelines for prevention in patients with renal insufficiency. American Journal of Medicine 1984; 78: 47-56.

80. Garcia de la Pena E, Cifuentes Delatte L. Forms of ammonium urate presentation in urinary calculi of noninfectious and infectious origin. In: Smith LH, Robertson WG, Finlayson B, et al, eds. Urolithiasis: Clinical and Basic Research. New York, NY: Plenum Press, 1981; 935-942.

81. Breslau NA, Pak CYC. Lack of effect of salt intake on urinary uric acid excretion. Journal of Urology 1983; 129: 531-532.

82. Pak CYC, Tolentino R, Stewart A, et al. Enhancement of renal excretion of uric acid during long-term thiazide therapy. Investigative Urology 1978; 16: 191-193.

83. Lulich JP, Osborne CA, Carlson M, et al. Nonsurgical removal of urocystoliths by voiding urohydropropulsion. Journal of the American Veterinary Medical Association 1993; 203: 660-663.

84. Osborne CA, Oldroyd NO, Clinton CW. Etiopathogenesis of uncommon canine uroliths: Xanthine, carbonate, drugs, and drug metabolites. Veterinary Clinics of North America: Small Animal Practice 1986; 16: 217-225.

85. Senior DF. Medical management of urate uroliths. In: Kirk RW, ed. Current Veterinary Therapy X. Philadelphia, PA: WB Saunders Co, 1989; 1178-1181.

86. Bartges JW, Osborne CA, Felice LJ, et al. Reliability of single urine and serum samples for estimation of 24-hour urinary uric acid excretion in six healthy beagles. American Journal of Veterinary Research 1994; 55: 472-476.

87. Moentk JA, DiBartola SP, Buffington CA. Effect of allopurinol on urine urate-to-creatinine ratios in normal Dalmatians. Journal of the American Animal Hospital Association 1994; 30: 483-486.

88. Lulich JP, Osborne CA, Sanderson S, et al. Preventing urate uroliths in Dalmatians: Risk factor management. In: Proceedings. Sixteenth Annual Veterinary Medical Forum, American College of Veterinary Internal Medicine, 1998, San Diego, CA: 654-655.

89. Murrell GAC, Rapeport WG. Clinical pharmacokinetics of allopurinol. Clinical Pharmacokinetics 1986; 11: 343-353.

90. Nelson DJ, Elion GB. Metabolic studies of high doses of allopurinol in humans. In: DeBruyn CHMM, Simmonds HA, Muller M, eds. Purine Metabolism in Man-IV, Part A. New York, NY: Plenum Press, 1984; 167-170.

91. Faraj BA, Ali FM, Fulenwider JT, et al. Hepatorenal failure induced by tetracycline in dogs with portacaval shunt. Journal of Pharmacology and Experimental Therapeutics 1982; 22: 558-563.

92. Lulich JP, Osborne CA, Thumchai R, et al. Epidemiology of canine calcium oxalate uroliths: Identifying risk factors. Veterinary Clinics of North America: Small Animal Practice 1999; 29: 113-139.

93. Koide T, Itatani H, Yoshioka T, et al. Clinical manifestations of calcium oxalate monohydrate and dihydrate urolithiasis. Journal of Urology 1982; 127: 1067-1069.

94. Leusmann DB, Meyer-Jurgens UB, Kleinhans G. Scanning electron microscopy of urinary calculi: Some peculiarities. Scanning Electron Microscopy 1984; 3: 1427-1432.

95. Otnes B. Urinary stone analysis: Methods, materials and value. Scandinavian Journal of Urology and Nephrology 1983; 71(Suppl.): 7-109.

96. Schubert G, Brien G. Crystallographic investigations of urinary calcium oxalate calculi. International Journal of Urology and Nephrology 1981; 13: 249-260.

97. Tomazic BB, Nancollas GH. The dissolution of calcium oxalate kidney stones: A kinetic study. Journal of Urology 1982; 128: 205-208.

98. Berenyl M, Frang D, Legrady J. Theoretical and clinical importance of the differentiation between the two types of calcium oxalate hydrate. International Journal of Urology and Nephrology 1972; 4: 341-345.

99. Smith LH. Diet and hyperoxaluria in the syndrome of idiopathic calcium oxalate urolithiasis. American Journal of Kidney Disease 1991; 17: 370-375.

100. Lulich JP, Osborne CA, Smith CL. Canine calcium oxalate urolithiasis: Risk factor management. In: Kirk RW, Bonagura JD, eds. Current Veterinary Therapy XI. Philadelphia, PA: WB Saunders, 1992; 892-899.

101. Bai SC, Sampson DA, Morris JG, et al. Vitamin B$_6$ requirement of growing kittens. Journal of Nutrition 1989; 119: 1020-1027.

102. Mandel NS, Mandel GS. Urinary tract stone disease in the United States veteran population. I. Geographical frequency of occurrence. Journal of Urology 1989; 142: 1513-1515.

103. Williams HE, Smith LH. Primary hyperoxaluria. In: Stanbury JB, Wyngaarden JB, Fredickson DS, et al, eds. The Metabolic Basis of Inherited Disease, 5th ed. New York, NY: McGraw-Hill, 1983; 204-228.

104. Simpson DP. Citrate excretion: A window on renal metabolism. American Journal of Physiology 1983; 244: F223-F234.

105. Nakagawa Y, Abram V, Kezdy FJ, et al. Purification and characterization of the principal inhibitor of calcium oxalate monohydrate crystal growth in human urine. Journal of Biological Chemistry 1983; 258: 12594-12599.

106. Deganello S. The interaction between nephrocalcin and Tamm-Horsfall proteins with calcium oxalate dihydrate. Scanning Microscopy 1993; 7: 1111-1118.

107. Lulich JP, Perrine L, Osborne CA, et al. Postsurgical recurrence of calcium oxalate uroliths in dogs (abstract). Journal of Veterinary Internal Medicine 1992; 6: 119.

108. Adams LG, Senior DF. Electrohydraulic and extracorporeal shockwave lithotripsy. Veterinary Clinics of North America: Small Animal Practice 1999; 29: 293-302.

109. Curhan GC, Willett WC, Rimm EB, et al. A prospective study of dietary calcium and other nutrients and the risk of symptomatic kidney stones. New England Journal of Medicine 1993; 328: 833-838.

110. Leman J, Piering WF, Lennon EJ. Possible role of carbohydrate-induced calciuria in calcium oxalate kidney-stone formation. New England Journal of Medicine 1969; 280: 232-237.

111. Lulich JP. Influence of dietary sodium on urinary calcium excretion in clinically normal dogs. PhD Thesis. University of Minnesota, St. Paul, 1991; 123-133.

112. Brautbar N, Walling MW, Coburn JW. Role of dietary phosphate in the intestinal absorption of calcium and the response to vitamin D. Mineral and Electrolyte Metabolism 1979; 2: 211-212.

113. Finco DR, Barasanti JA, Crowell WA. Characterization of magnesium-induced urinary disease in the cat and comparison with feline urologic syndrome. American Journal of Veterinary Research 1985; 46: 391-400.

114. Kallfelz FA, Crosetti C, Tukenmez I. Urinary tract obstruction in calves induced by dietary management. Proceedings of the Internal Atomic Energy Agency 1986; 292: 535-546.

115. Meyer JL, Smith LH. Growth of calcium oxalate crystals. II. Inhibition by natural urinary crystal growth inhibitors. Investigative Urology 1969; 6: 412-422.

116. Melnick I, Landes RR, Hoffmann AA, et al. Magnesium therapy for recurring calcium oxalate urinary calculi. Journal of Urology 1971; 105: 119-122.

117. Lulich JP. Influence of dietary magnesium on urinary calcium excretion in clinically normal dogs. PhD Thesis. University of Minnesota, St. Paul, 1991; 141-151.

118. Breslau NA, Brinkley L, Hill KD, et al. Relationship of animal protein-rich diet to kidney stone formation and calcium metabolism. Journal of Clinical Endocrinology 1988; 140: 140-146.

119. Smith LH. Hyperoxaluric states. In: Coe FL, Favus MJ, eds. Disorders of Bone and Mineral Metabolism. New York, NY: Raven Press Ltd, 1992; 707-727.

120. Nicar MJ, Hill K, Pak CYC. Inhibition by citrate of spontaneous precipitation of calcium oxalate in vitro. Journal of Bone Mineral Research 1987; 2: 215-220.

121. Baruch SB, Burich RL, Eun CK, et al. Renal metabolism of citrate. Medical Clinics of North America 1975; 59: 569-582.

122. Sutton RA, Wong NL, Dirks J. Effects of metabolic acidosis and alkalosis on sodium and calcium transport in the dog kidney. Kidney International 1979; 15: 520-533.

123. Churchill DN, Taylor DW. Thiazides for patients with recurrent calcium stones. Journal of Urology 1985; 133: 749-751.

124. Lulich JP. Effects of chlorothiazide on urinary excretion of calcium in clinically normal dogs. PhD Thesis. University of Minnesota, St. Paul, 1991; 161-182.

125. Pak CYC, Eanes EO, Ruskin B. Spontaneous precipitation of brushite in urine: Evidence that brushite is the nidus of renal stones originating as calcium phosphate. Proceedings of the National Academy of Sciences 1971; 68: 1456-1460.

126. Coe FL, Flavus MJ. Nephrolithiasis. In: Brenner BM, Rector FC Jr, eds. The Kidney, 4th ed, Philadelphia, PA: WB Saunders Co, 1991; 1728-1767.

127. Elliot JS. Solubility and crystallization in urinary stone disease. In: Hodgkinson A, Nordin BEC, eds. Proceedings of the Renal Stone Research Symposium, London, UK: J&A Churchill Ltd, 1968; 199-207.

128. Elliot JS. Urinary calculus disease. Surgical Clinics of North America 1965; 45: 1393-1404.

129. Pak CYC. Primary hyperparathyroidism and other causes of hypercalciuria. In: Calcium Urolithiasis: Pathogenesis, Diagnosis and Management. New York, NY: Plenum Medical Books Co, 1978; 81-117.

130. Fleisch H. Inhibitors and promoters of stone formation. Kidney International 1978; 13: 361-371.

131. Nikkila MT, Saaristo JJ, Koivula TA. Clinical and biochemical features of primary hyperparathyroidism. Surgery 1989; 105: 148-153.

132. Berger B, Feldman EC. Primary hyperparathyroidism in dogs: 21 cases (1976-1986). Journal of the American Veterinary Medical Association 1987; 191: 350-356.

133. Klausner JS, Osborne CA. Calcium phosphate urolithiasis. Veterinary Clinics of North America: Small Animal Practice 1986; 16: 171-184.

134. Klausner JS, O'Leary TP, Osborne CA. Calcium urolithiasis in two dogs with parathyroid adenomas. Journal of the American Veterinary Medical Association 1987; 191: 1423-1426.

135. Rasmussen E, et al. Hormonal control of skeletal and mineral homeostasis. American Journal of Veterinary Research 1974; 56: 751-758.

136. Smith LH. Urolithiasis. In: Earley LE, Gottschalk CW, eds. Strauss and Welt's Diseases of the Kidney, 3rd ed. Boston, MA: Little, Brown & Co, 1979; 893-903.

137. Konnak JW, Kogan BA, Lau K. Renal calculi associated with incomplete renal tubular acidosis. Journal of Urology 1982; 128: 900-902.

138. DeFronzo RA, Thier SO. Inherited disorders of renal function. In: Brenner BM, Rector FC Jr, eds. The Kidney. Philadelphia, PA: WB Saunders Co, 1981; 1816-1871.

139. Pak CYC. Pathophysiology of calcium nephrolithiasis. In: Seldin DW, Giebisch G, eds. The Kidney: Physiology and Pathophysiology. New York, NY: Raven Press, 1985; 1365-1379.

140. Osborne CA, Lulich JP, Polzin DJ, et al. Analysis of 77,000 canine uroliths: Perspectives from the Minnesota Urolith Center. Veterinary Clinics of North America: Small Animal Practice 1999; 29: 17-38.

141. Osborne CA, Clinton CW, Banman LK, et al. Prevalence of canine uroliths: Minnesota Urolith Center. Veterinary Clinics of North America: Small Animal Practice 1986; 16: 27-44.

142. Hicking W, Hesse H, Gebhardt M, et al. Investigation with polarizing microscopy for the classification of urinary stones from humans and dogs. In: Smith LH, Robertson WG, Finlayson B, eds. Urolithiasis: Clinical and Basic Research. New York, NY: Plenum Press, 1981; 901-906.

143. Segal S, Thier SO. Cystinuria. In: Stanbury JB, Wyngaarden JB, Fredickson DS, eds. The Metabolic Basis for Inherited Disease, 5th ed. New York, NY: McGraw-Hill, 1983; 1774.

144. Calonge MJ, Volpini V, Bisceglia L, et al. Molecular genetics of cystinuria: Genetic heterogeneity in cystinuria: The SLC3A1 gene is linked to type I but not type III cystinuria. Proceedings of the National Academy of Sciences 1995; 92: 9667-9671.

145. Bovee KC, ed. Genetic and metabolic diseases of the kidney. In: Canine Nephrology. Media, PA: Harwal, 1984; 339-354.

146. Bovee KC. Canine cystine urolithiasis. Veterinary Clinics of North America: Small Animal Practice 1986; 16: 211-216.

147. Bartter FC, Lotz M, Thier S, et al. Cystinuria. Annals of Internal Medicine 1965; 62: 796-822.

148. Clark WT, Cuddeford D. A study of amino-acids in urine from dogs with cystine urolithiasis. Veterinary Record 1971; 88: 414-417.

149. Cornelius CE, Bishop JA, Schaffer MH. A quantitative study of amino aciduria in dachshunds with a history of cystine urolithiasis. Cornell Veterinarian 1967; 57: 177-183.

150. Crane CW, Turner AW. Amino acid patterns of urine and blood plasma in a cystinuric Labrador dog. Nature 1956; 177: 237-238.

151. Casal ML, Giger U, Bovee KC, et al. Inheritance of cystinuria and renal defect in Newfoundlands. Journal of the American Veterinary Medical Association 1995; 217: 1585-1589.

152. Hoppe A, Denneberg T, Jeppson JO, et al. Urinary excretion of amino acids in normal and cystinuric dogs. British Veterinary Journal 1993; 149: 253-268.

153. Sanderson S, Osborne CA, Ogburn PN, et al. Canine cystinuria associated with carnitinuria and carnitine deficiency (abstract). Journal of Veterinary Internal Medicine 1995; 9: 212.

154. Case LC, Ling GV, Franti CE, et al. Cystine-containing urinary calculi in dogs: 102 cases (1981-1989). Journal of the American Veterinary Medical Association 1992; 201: 129-133.

155. Wallerstrom BI, Wageburg TI, Lagergren CH. Cystine calculi in the dog: A epidemiological retrospective study. Journal of Small Animal Practice 1992; 33: 78-84.

156. Brown NO, Parks JL, Greene RW. Canine urolithiasis. Retrospective analysis of 438 cases. Journal of the American Veterinary Medical Association 1977; 170: 415-418.

157. Osborne CA, Polzin DJ, Abdullahi SU, et al. Struvite urolithiasis in animals and man: Formation, detection and dissolution. Advances in Veterinary Science and Comparative Medicine 1985; 29: 1-101.

158. Osborne CA, Polzin DJ, Lulich JP, et al. Relationship of nutritional factors to the cause, dissolution, and prevention of canine uroliths. Veterinary Clinics of North America: Small Animal Practice 1989; 19: 583-619.

159. Pahira JJ. Management of the patient with cystinuria. Urology Clinics of North America 1987; 14: 339-446.

160. Lotz M, Potts JT Jr, Bartter FC, et al. D-penicillamine therapy in cystinuria. Journal of Urology 1966; 95: 257-263.

161. Frimpter GW, Thouin P, Ewalds BH. Penicillamine in canine cystinuria. Journal of the American Veterinary Medical Association 1967; 151: 1084-1086.

162. Pak CYC, Fuller C, Sakhaee K, et al. Management of cystine nephrolithiasis with alpha-mercaptopropionyl glycine. Journal of Urology 1986; 136: 1003-1008.

163. Hoppe A, Denneberg T, Jepsson JO, et al. Canine cystinuria: An extended study on the effects of 2-mercaptopropionylglycine on cystine urolithiasis and urinary cystine excretion. British Veterinary Journal 1993; 149: 235-251.

164. Hoppe A, Denneberg T, Kagedal B. Treatment of clinically normal and cystinuric dogs with 2-mercaptopropionylglycine. American Journal of Veterinary Research 1988; 49: 923-928.

165. Treacher RJ. Urolithiasis in the dog. II Biochemical aspects. Journal of Small Animal Practice 1966; 7: 537-547.

166. Jaeger P, Portmann L, Saunders A, et al. Anticystinuric effects of glutamine and of dietary sodium restriction. New England Journal of Medicine 1986; 315: 1120-1123.

167. Gutierrez Millet V, Praga M, Miranda B. Ureolytic *Citrobacter freundii* infection of the urine as a cause of dissolution of cystine renal calculi. Journal of Urology 1985; 133: 443-446.

168. Osborne CA, Sanderson SL, Lulich JP, et al. Canine cystine urolithiasis. Veterinary Clinics of North America: Small Animal Practice 1999; 29: 193-211.

169. Osborne CA, Lulich JP, Polzin DJ, et al. Medical dissolution and prevention of canine struvite urolithiasis: Twenty years of experience. Veterinary Clinics of North America: Small Animal Practice 1999; 29: 73-111.

170. Elliot JS, Quaide WL, Sharp RF, et al. Mineralogic studies of urine: The relationship of apatite, brushite, and struvite to urinary pH. Journal of Urology 1958; 80: 269-271.

171. Elliot JS, Sharp RF, Lewis L. The solubility of struvite in urine. Journal of Urology 1959; 81: 366-368.

172. Hedelin H, Brorson JE, Grenabo L, et al. *Ureaplasma urealyticum* and renal stones. Urological Research 1984; 12: 30.

173. Burns JR, Finlayson B. Solubility product of magnesium ammonium phosphate hexahydrate at various temperatures. Journal of Urology 1982; 128: 426-428.

174. He J, Liu GD, Shen SJ. Composition and structure of infected stones. Urological Research 1984; 12: 94.

175. Abdullahi SU, Osborne CA, Leininger JR, et al. Evaluation of a calculolytic diet in female dogs with induced struvite urolithiasis. American Journal of Veterinary Research 1984; 45: 1508-1519.

176. Delluva AM, Markley K, Davies RE. The absence of gastric urease in germ-free animals. Biochemical and Biophysical Acta 1968; 151: 646-650.

177. Griffith DP, Klein AS. Infection-induced urinary stones. In: Roth RA, Finlayson B, eds. Clinical Management of Urolithiasis. International Perspectives in Urology 1983; 6: 210-227.

178. Kornberg HL, Davies RE, Wood DR. The breakdown of urea in cats not secreting gastric juice. Biochemical Journal 1954; 56: 355-363.

179. Levenson SM, Crowley LV, Horowitz RE, et al. The metabolism of carbon-labeled urea in the germ-free rat. Journal of Biological Chemistry 1959; 234: 2061-2062.

180. Griffith DP. Struvite stones. Kidney International 1978; 13: 372-378.

181. Griffith DP. Infection-induced stones. In: Coe FL, ed. Nephrolithiasis: Pathogenesis and Management. Chicago, IL: Year Book Medical Publishers Inc, 1978; 203-228.

182. Krawiec DR, Osborne CA, Leininger JR, et al. Effect of acetohydroxamic acid on dissolution of canine uroliths. American Journal of Veterinary Research 1984; 45: 1266-1275.

183. Krawiec DR, Osborne CA, Leininger JR, et al. Effect of acetohydroxamic acid on prevention of canine struvite uroliths. American Journal of Veterinary Research 1984; 45: 1276-1282.

184. Brande AI, Siemienski J. Role of bacterial urease in experimental pyelonephritis. Journal of Bacteriology 1960; 80: 171-179.

185. MacLaren DM. The significance of urease in *Proteus* pyelonephritis: A bacteriological study. Journal of Pathology and Bacteriology 1968; 96: 45-56.

186. Parsons CL, Stauffer C, Mulholland SG, et al. Effect of ammonia on bacterial adherence to bladder transitional epithelium. Journal of Urology 1984; 132: 365-366.

187. Rosenstein IJM, Hamilton-Miller JMT. Inhibitors of urease as chemotherapeutic agents. Critical Reviews in Microbiology 1984; 11: 1-12.

188. Conway NS, Maitland AI, Rennie JB. Urinary citrate in patients with renal calculi. British Journal of Urology 1949; 21: 30-38.

189. Robertson WB, Peacock M. Risk factors in the formation of urinary stones. In: Chisholm GD, Williams DI, eds. Scientific Foundations of Urology, 2nd ed. London, UK: William Medical Books, 1982; 267-278.

190. Scott WW, Huggins C, Selman BC. Metabolism of citric acid in urolithiasis. Journal of Urology 1943; 50: 202-209.

191. Schwille PO, Scholz D, Paulus M. Citrate in daily and fasting urine. Results of controls, patients and recurrent idiopathic calcium urolithiasis and primary hyperparathyroidism. Investigative Urology 1979; 16: 457-462.

192. Stegmayr B, Stegmayr B. Crystal formation induced by uropathogenic bacteria. Scandinavian Journal of Urology and Nephrology 1983; 17: 197-203.

193. Osborne CA, Klausner JS, Krawiec DR, et al. Canine struvite urolithiasis: Problems and their dissolution. Journal of the American Veterinary Medical Association 1981; 179: 239-244.

194. Griffith DP, Bragin S, Musher DM. Dissolution of struvite stones: Experimental studies in vitro. Investigative Urology 1976; 13: 351-353.

195. Griffith DP, Musher DM. Acetohydroxamic acid. Urology 1975; 5: 299-302.

196. Feit RM, Fair WR. The treatment of infection stones with penicillin. Journal of Urology 1979; 122: 592-594.

197. Krajden S, Fuksa M, Lizewski S, et al. *Proteus penneri* and urinary calculi formation. Journal of Clinical Microbiology 1984; 19: 541-542.

198. Lewis HJE, White A, Hutchinson AG, et al. The bacteriology of urine and renal calculi. Urological Research 1984; 12: 107-109.

199. Stamey TA. Pathogenesis and Treatment of Urinary Tract Infections. Baltimore, MD: Williams & Wilkins, 1980.

200. Senior BW. The special affinity of particular types of *Proteus mirabilis* for the urinary tract. Journal of Medical Microbiology 1979; 12: 1-8.

201. Vermeulen CW, Goetz R. Experimental urolithiasis. IX. Influence of infection on stone growth in rats. Journal of Urology 1954; 72: 761-769.

202. Lesher RJ, Jones WA. Urease production from clinical isolates of beta-hemolytic *Escherichia coli*. Journal of Clinical Microbiology 1978; 8: 344-345.

203. Grant RB, Penner JL, Hennessy JN, et al. Transferable urease activity in *Providencia stuartii*. Journal of Clinical Microbiology 1981; 13: 561-565.

204. Fowler JE. Bacteriology of branched renal calculi and accompanying urinary tract infection. Journal of Urology 1984; 131: 213-215.

205. Nemoy NJ, Stamey TA. Surgical, bacteriological, and biochemical management of infection stones. Journal of the American Medical Association 1971; 215: 1470-1476.

206. Rocha AH, Santos LCS. Relapse of urinary tract infection in the presence of urinary tract calculi: The role of bacteria within calculi. Journal of Medical Microbiology 1969; 2: 372-376.

207. Takeuchi H, Takayama H, Konishi T, et al. Scanning electron microscopy detects bacteria with infection stones. Journal of Urology 1984; 132: 67-69.

208. Ford DK, MacDonald J. Influence of urea on the growth of T-strain mycoplasmas. Journal of Bacteriology 1967; 93: 1509-1512.

209. Shepard MC, Lunceford CD. Occurrence of urease in T-strains of mycoplasma. Journal of Bacteriology 1967; 93: 1513-1520.

210. Friedlander AM, Braude AI. Production of bladder stones by human T-mycoplasmas. Nature 1974; 247: 67-69.

211. Lamm DL, Johnson SA, Friedlander AM, et al. Medical therapy of experimental infection stones. Urology 1977; 10: 418-421.

212. Pettersson S, Brorson JE, Grenabo L, et al. *Ureaplasma urealyticum* in infectious urinary tract stones. Lancet 1983; 1: 526-527.

213. Kenney GE, Cartwright FD. Effect of urea concentration on growth on *Ureaplasma urealyticum* (T-strain mycoplasma). Journal of Bacteriology 1977; 132: 144-150.

214. Klausner JS, Osborne CA, O'Leary TP, et al. Struvite urolithiasis in a litter of miniature schnauzer dogs. American Journal of Veterinary Research 1980; 40: 712-719.

215. Klausner JS, Osborne CA, O'Leary TP, et al. Experimental induction of struvite uroliths in miniature schnauzers and beagle dogs. Investigative Urology 1980; 18: 127-132.

216. Kasper LV, Poole CM, Norris WP. Incidence of struvite urinary calculi in two ancestral lines of beagles. Laboratory Animal Science 1978; 28: 545-550.

217. Clark WT. Staphylococcal infection of the urinary tract and its relation to urolithiasis in dogs. Veterinary Record 1974; 95: 204-206.

218. Bartges JW, Osborne CA, Polzin DJ. Recurrent sterile struvite urocystolithiasis in three related cocker spaniels. Journal of the American Animal Hospital Association 1992; 28: 459-469.

219. Lees GE, Helman RG, Homco LD, et al. Early diagnosis of familial nephropathy in English cocker spaniels. Journal of the American Animal Hospital Association 1998; 34: 189-195.

220. Tannen RL. Ammonia and acid-base homeostasis. Medical Clinics of North America 1983; 67: 781-798.

221. Backman U, Danielson BG, Felstrom B, et al. The clinical importance of renal tubular acidosis in recurrent renal stone formers. In: Smith LH, Robertson WG, Finlayson B, eds. Urolithiasis: Clinical and Basic Research. New York, NY: Plenum Press, 1981; 67-69.

222. Dedmond RE, Wrong O. The excretion of organic anion in renal tubular acidosis with particular reference of citrate. Clinical Science 1962; 22: 19-32.

223. Morrissey JF, Ochoa M, Lotspeich WD, et al. Citrate excretion in renal tubular acidosis. Annals of Internal Medicine 1963; 58: 159-166.

224. Thornhill JA. Renal tubular acidosis. In: Kirk RW, ed. Current Veterinary Therapy VII. Philadelphia, PA: WB Saunders Co, 1977; 1087-1097.

225. Hardy RM, Osborne CA, Cassidy FC. Urolithiasis in immature dogs. Veterinary Medicine/Small Animal Clinician 1972; 67: 1205-1211.

226. Klausner JS, Osborne CA. Dissolution of a struvite nephrolith in a dog. Journal of the American Veterinary Medical Association 1979; 174: 1100-1104.

227. Kirby R, Crane S, Schaer M. Dissolution of a nephrolith in a dog. Journal of the American Veterinary Medical Association 1983; 178: 827-828.

228. Pollack S, Wagner BM. Renal calculi in a dog: A four-year clinical picture. Veterinary Medicine/Small Animal Clinician 1976; 71: 1693-1696.

229. Brodey RS. Canine urolithiasis: A survey and discussion of fifty-two clinical cases. Journal of the American Veterinary Medical Association 1955; 126: 1-9.

230. Boistelle R, Abbona F, Berland Y, et al. Growth and stability of magnesium phosphate (struvite) in acidic sterile urine. Urological Research 1984; 12: 79.

231. Musher DM, Griffith DP, Tyler M, et al. Potentiation of the antibacterial effect of methenamine by acetohydroxamic acid. Antimicrobial Agents and Chemotherapy 1974; 5: 101-105.

232. Ling GV, Hirsch DC. Antimicrobial susceptibility tests for urinary tract pathogens. In: Kirk RW, ed. Current Veterinary Therapy VIII. Philadelphia, PA: WB Saunders Co, 1983; 1048-1051.

233. Nickel JC, Emtage J, Costerton JW. Ultrastructural microbial ecology of infection-induced urinary stones. Journal of Urology 1985; 133: 622-627.

234. Musher DM, Saenz C, Griffith DP. Interaction between acetohydroxamic acid and 12 antibiotics against 14 gram-negative pathogenic bacteria. Antimicrobial Agents and Chemotherapy 1974; 5: 106-110.

235. Lewis GA, Schuster GA, Cooper RA. Dissolution of renal calculi with dicloxacillin. Urology 1983; 22: 401-403.

236. Senior DF, Thomas WC, Gaskin JM, et al. Relative merit of various strategies of nonsurgical treatment of infection stones in dogs. Urological Research 1984; 12: 39.

237. Osborne CA, Abdullahi SU, Polzin DJ, et al. Current status of medical dissolution of canine and feline uroliths. In: Proceedings. Seventh Kal Kan Symposium, Vernon, CA, 1984: 52-79.

238. Kobashi K, Kumaki K, Hose J. Effect of acyl residues of hydroxamic acids on urease inhibition. Biochemical and Biophysical Acta 1971; 227: 429-441.

239. Bailie NC, Osborne CA, Leininger JR, et al. Teratogenic effect of acetohydroxamic acid in clinically normal beagles. American Journal of Veterinary Research 1986; 47: 2604-2611.

240. Ross SJ, Osborne CA, Lulich JP, et al. Canine and feline nephrolithiasis: Epidemiology, detection, and management. Veterinary Clinics of North America: Small Animal Practice 1999; 29: 231-250.

241. Polzin DJ, Osborne CA, Hayden DW, et al. Effects of modified protein diets in dogs with chronic renal failure. Journal of the American Veterinary Medical Association 1983; 183: 980-986.

242. Osborne CA, Polzin DJ, Kruger JM, et al. Medical dissolution and prevention of canine struvite uroliths. In: Kirk RW, ed. Current Veterinary Therapy IX. Philadelphia, PA: WB Saunders Co, 1986; 1177-1187.

243. Osborne CA, Polzin DJ, Kruger JM, et al. Medical dissolution of canine struvite uroliths. Veterinary Clinics of North America: Small Animal Practice 1986; 16: 349-374.

244. Lulich JP, Osborne CA, Johnston GR. Non-surgical correction of infection-induced struvite uroliths and a vesicourachal diverticulum in an immature dog. Journal of Small Animal Practice 1989; 30: 613-617.

245. Griffith DP, Osborne CA. Infection (urease) stones. Mineral and Electrolyte Metabolism 1987; 13: 278-285.

246. Osborne CA, Clinton CW, Kim KM, et al. Etiopathogenesis, clinical manifestations and management of silica urolithiasis. Veterinary Clinics of North America: Small Animal Practice 1986; 16: 185-207.

247. Brodey RS, Thomson R, Sayer P, et al. Silicate renal calculi in Kenyan dogs. Journal of Small Animal Practice 1977; 18: 523-528.

248. Osborne CA, Jacob F, Lulich JP, et al. Canine silica urolithiasis: Risk factors, detection, treatment and prevention. Veterinary Clinics of North America: Small Animal Practice 1999; 29: 213-230.

249. Salisbury FB, Ross CW. In: Plant Physiology, 3rd ed. Belmont, CA: Wadsworth Publishing Co, 1985; 540.

250. Bailey CB. Siliceous urinary calculi in calves: Prevention by addition of sodium chloride to the diet. Science 1966; 155: 696-697.

251. Ammerman CB, Fontenot JP, Fox MRS, et al. Silicon. In: Mineral Tolerance of Domestic Animals. Washington, DC: National Academy Press, 1980; 421-430.

252. Sutor DJ, Wooley SE, Jackson OF. Crystalline material from the feline bladder. Research in Veterinary Science 1970; 11: 298-299.

253. Underwood EJ. In: Trace Elements in Human and Animal Nutrition, 4th ed. New York, NY: Academic Press Inc, 1977; 398-409.

254. Farber JH, Raifer J. Silicate urolithiasis. Journal of Urology 1984; 132: 739-740.

255. Forman SA, Whiting F, Connell R. Silica urolithiasis in cattle. 3. Chemical and physical composition of uroliths. Canadian Journal of Comparative Medicine 1959; 4: 157-162.

256. Herman JR, Goldberg AS. New type of urinary calculus caused by antacid therapy. Journal of the American Veterinary Medical Association 1960; 174: 1206-1207.

257. Levison DA, Crocker PR, Banim S, et al. Silica stones in the urinary bladder. Lancet 1982; 1: 704-705.

258. Medina JA, Sanchidrian JR, Cifuentes Delatte L. Silica in urinary calculi. In: Smith LH, Robertson WG, Finlayson B, et al, eds. Urolithiasis: Clinical and Basic Research. New York, NY: Plenum Press, 1981; 923-926.

259. Yokoi H, Enomoto S. Effect of degree of polymerization of silicic acid on the gastrointestinal absorption of silicate in rats. Chemical and Pharmaceutical Bulletin (Tokyo) 1979; 27: 1733-1739.

260. Pyrah LN. Renal Calculus. New York, NY: Springer-Verlag, 1979; 95-99.

261. McCullagh KG, Elhrhard LA. Silica urolithiasis in laboratory dogs fed semisynthetic diets. Journal of the American Veterinary Medical Association 1974; 164: 712-714.

262. Emerick RJ. Chloride and phosphate as impediments to silica urinary calculi in rats fed tetraethyl orthosilicate. Journal of Nutrition 1984; 114: 733-738.

263. Emerick RJ, Kugel EE, Wallace V. Urinary excretion of silica and the production of siliceous urinary calculi in rats. American Journal of Veterinary Research 1963; 24: 610-613.

264. Lulich JP, Osborne CA. Compound uroliths: Treatment and prevention. In: Bonagura JD, ed. Current Veterinary Therapy XIII. Philadelphia, PA: WB Saunders Co, 1999; In press.

CASE 20-1

Dysuria in a German Shepherd Crossbred Dog

Carl A. Osborne, DVM, PhD
Diplomate ACVIM (Internal Medicine)
College of Veterinary Medicine
University of Minnesota
St. Paul, Minnesota, USA

Assess the Animal

A 12-year-old neutered female German shepherd crossbred dog was examined for dysuria and pollakiuria of two months' duration. Other than nonspecific dermatitis and a perianal adenoma, the dog had no previous history of illness.

Physical examination revealed an alert, active, overweight dog (body weight 27 kg, body condition score 4/5). Multiple uroliths were palpated in the urinary bladder. No other abnormalities were detected.

Results of a complete blood count and a serum biochemistry profile were normal except for a mild elevation in alkaline phosphatase activity (Tables 1 and 2). Analysis of a urine specimen collected by cystocentesis (Table 3) revealed an alkaline pH, struvite crystalluria and findings typical of inflammation (i.e., hematuria, pyuria, proteinuria). Quantitative culture of urine revealed more than 10^5 colony-forming units of urease-producing *Staphylococcus intermedius* organisms per ml of urine. The bacteria were susceptible to most antimicrobial drugs. Survey radiographs of the abdomen revealed three uroliths within the bladder lumen (Figures 1 and 2); the sizes of the kidneys and liver were normal.

Assess the Food(s) and Feeding Method

A commercial dry adult maintenance food was offered free choice and table foods were fed frequently.

Questions

1. What is the probable mineral composition of the uroliths in this dog?
2. What are the advantages and disadvantages of surgical vs. medical management of these uroliths?
3. How should therapeutic efficacy be monitored?

Table 1. Hemograms of a 12-year-old spayed female German shepherd crossbred dog with urocystoliths.

Factors**	Reference values	Day* 1	35	63	102	132	159	196	256
PCV (%)	38.5-56.7	41	40	41	39	38	38	38	40
Hb (g/dl)	13.5-19.9	15.6	15.3	15.1	15.8	15.2	14.7	15.0	16.4
WBC ($10^3/\mu l$)	4.1-13.3	16	8.9	7.3	6.2	8.9	9.4	7.4	4.7
Lymphocytes ($10^3/\mu l$)	0.3-5.1	16	26	34	23	42	34	26	46
Neutrophils ($10^3/\mu l$)	2.1-11.2	75	71	60	69	52	55	58	51
Eosinophils ($10^3/\mu l$)	0.0-1.2	1	0	2	2	3	5	9	2
Monocytes ($10^3/\mu l$)	0.0-1.2	8	3	4	6	3	4	6	1

Key: PCV = packed cell volume, Hb = hemoglobin, WBC = white blood cells.
*Therapy consisting of a calculolytic food and an antimicrobial agent was initiated on Day 5 and discontinued on Day 159.
**Platelets were estimated on a blood film and considered adequate in all specimens. Normoblasts and basophils were not observed.

Table 2. Serum biochemistry values of a 12-year-old spayed female German shepherd crossbred dog with urocystoliths.

Factors	Reference values	Day* 1	35	63	102	132	159	196	256
SUN (mg/dl)	7-28	24	4	3	3	3	3	29	40
Creatinine (mg/dl)	0.5-1.5	1.3	1.4	1.4	1.4	1.4	1.3	1.7	1.5
Calcium (mg/dl)	9.3-11.4	10.2	9.7	10.0	10.1	10.4	10.0	10.7	10.3
Phosphorus (mg/dl)	1.9-7.0	3.5	3.5	4.3	3.0	3.6	3.1	3.6	4.7
Magnesium (mg/dl)	1.5-2.7	2.3	1.9	2.0	1.8	1.7	1.8	2.1	2.1
Sodium (mEq/l)	143-150	149	147	145	147	146	144	147	148
Potassium (mEq/l)	3.2-5.6	4.6	5.0	5.5	5.6	5.1	5.3	4.8	5.2
Chloride (mEq/l)	108-125	119	119	119	118	118	118	117	115
Albumin (g/dl)	2.4-3.8	2.4	2.2	2.2	2.3	2.3	2.1	2.8	–
ALT activity (U/l)	5-62	56	46	32	26	25	28	31	35
Alk phos activity (U/l)	10-149	238	1,270	1,580	1,920	1,470	695	337	208
Total bilirubin (mg/dl)	0.1-0.6	0.1	0.1	0.2	0.2	0.1	0.2	0.1	0.1

Key: SUN = serum urea nitrogen, ALT = alanine aminotransferase, Alk phos = alkaline phosphatase.
*Therapy consisting of a calculolytic food and an antimicrobial agent was initiated on Day 5 and discontinued on Day 159.

Table 3. Urinalyses of a 12-year-old spayed female German shepherd crossbred dog with urocystoliths.*

Factors***	Day**							
	1	35	63	102	132	159	196	256
Specific gravity	1.019	1.008	1.007	1.008	1.007	1.006	1.019	1.018
pH	8.5	6.5	7.0	7.5	6.5	5.0	6.0	7.0
Protein†	4+	2+	2+	1+	1+	Trace	1+	2+
RBC††	TNTC	TNTC	TNTC	9-11	0	0	0	0
WBC††	75-85	1-2	0	1-3	0	0	0	0
Crystals†††	Struvite	Struvite	Struvite	Amorphous phosphate	0	0	0	0

Key: RBC = red blood cells, TNTC = too numerous to count, WBC = white blood cells.
*Samples collected by cystocentesis.
**Therapy consisting of a calculolytic food and an antimicrobial agent was initiated on Day 5 and discontinued on Day 159.
***Glucose, bilirubin and acetone were not detected in any specimen.
†Values represent semiquantitative evaluations based on a scale of 0 to 4; urine volume was not considered.
††Number per high power field (x450).
†††Number per low power field (x100).

Answers and Discussion

1. The most likely mineral composition of the uroliths is struvite based on: 1) urease-positive staphylococcal urinary tract infection, 2) alkaline urinary pH, 3) struvite crystalluria (no oxalate, cystine or urate crystals) and 4) presence of radiodense uroliths.

2. Although surgery may be effective, medical protocols have been developed to dissolve struvite uroliths. Surgical removal of urocystoliths has the obvious advantage of rapid correction of the disease process. Medical therapy may also be effective and includes using a commercial veterinary therapeutic food (Prescription Diet Canine s/dª) specifically formulated as a struvite calculolytic diet. Concurrent treatment of the urinary tract infection with appropriate antimicrobials is an essential part of the treatment protocol. The calculolytic food should be fed until radiographic evidence of urolith dissolution is obtained. The food is usually fed for one additional "insurance" month following dissolution because survey radiography is not sufficiently sensitive to detect small uroliths (≤3 mm).

3. Therapeutic efficacy should be monitored by monthly evaluation of clinical signs, radiographs, urinalyses and urine cultures. Clinical signs often resolve within three to five days of initiating therapy. Consumption of the calculolytic food is usually associated with polyuria, formation of less concentrated acidic urine, marked reduction in serum urea nitrogen concentration, reduction in serum magnesium concentration and an increase in serum alkaline phosphatase activity. Hematuria, pyuria and bacteriuria should resolve with dietary and appropriate antimicrobial therapy.

Progress Notes

Therapy was initiated with Canine s/d (1,150 kcal [4.8 MJ], one can fed twice daily) and ampicillin administered orally (7 mg/kg body weight q12h). Survey radiographs obtained monthly revealed progressive reduction in the size of the uroliths (Figures 3 to 6). Radiodense uroliths could not be detected by survey radiography on Day 132 (Figure 6).

Following initiation of antimicrobial therapy, bacteria could not be cultured from urine specimens obtained by cystocentesis. Urinalysis revealed acidification of urine and disappearance of pyuria and hematuria (Table 2). Consumption of the calculolytic food was associated with formation of less concentrated urine, reduction in serum urea nitrogen con-

centration, reduction in serum magnesium concentration and an increase in serum alkaline phosphatase activity (Tables 2 and 3). Results of complete blood counts were normal over the treatment period. Most laboratory parameters returned to baseline values following withdrawal of antimicrobial therapy and a return to a commercial adult maintenance-type food on Day 159 (Table 2 and 3).

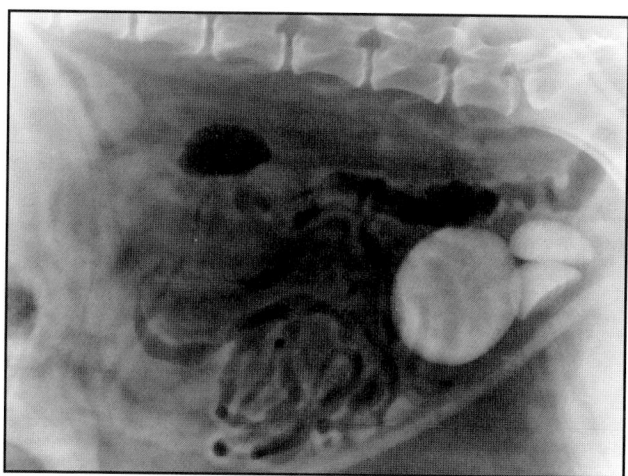

Figure 1. Survey lateral abdominal radiograph illustrating multiple radiodense uroliths in the urinary bladder of a 12-year-old spayed female German shepherd crossbred dog.

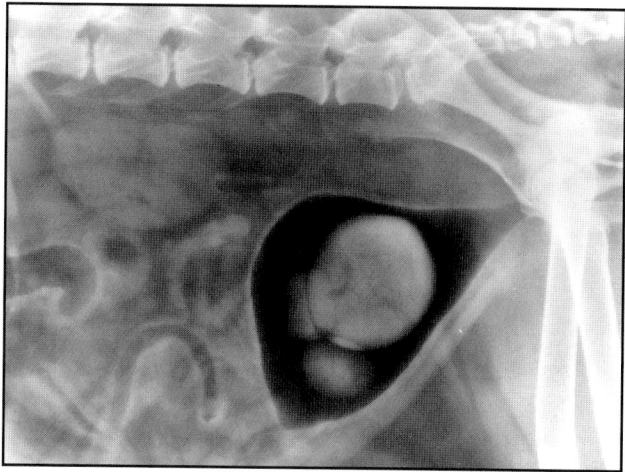

Figure 2. Pneumocystogram of the dog described in Figure 1, illustrating a diverticulum at the vertex of the urinary bladder.

Because the dog was overweight at the beginning of therapy, the owners fed a reduced amount of food to promote weight loss. The dog lost 1.6 kg during therapy.

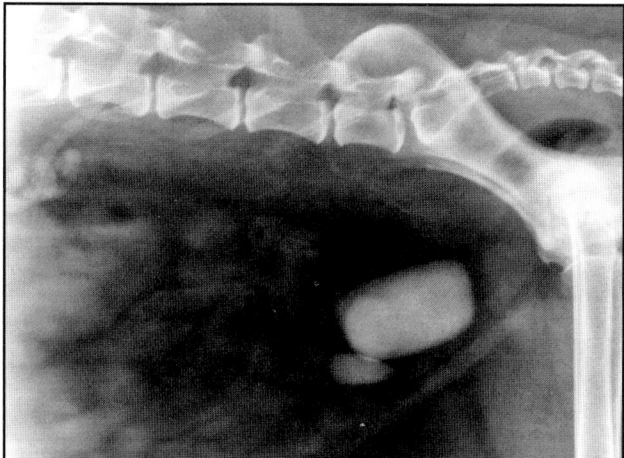

Figure 3. Survey lateral abdominal radiograph of the dog described in Figure 1. This radiograph was obtained 30 days after initiation of calculolytic therapy. (Compare this Figure with Figures 4 through 6.)

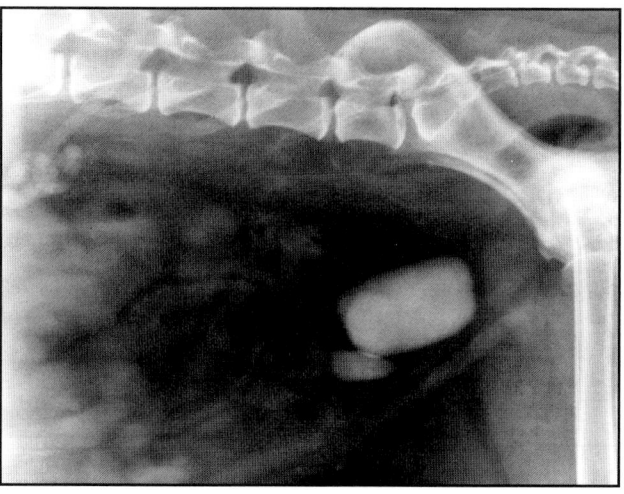

Figure 4. Survey lateral abdominal radiograph of the dog described in Figure 1. This radiograph was obtained 58 days after initiation of calculolytic therapy. (Compare this Figure with Figures 5 and 6.)

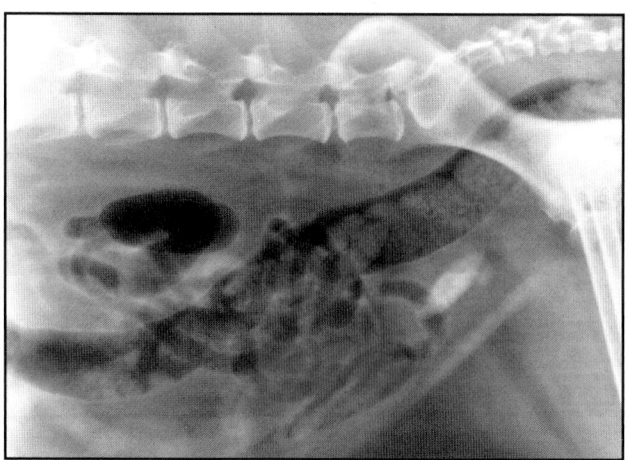

Figure 5. Survey lateral abdominal radiograph of the dog described in Figure 1. This radiograph was obtained 97 days after initiation of calculolytic therapy. (Compare this Figure with Figure 6.)

Further Discussion

This case typifies medical dissolution of larger urocystoliths. Reduction in the concentration of urea nitrogen, acidification of urine and formation of urine with a low specific gravity indicate that the owner and the dog were complying with therapy.

Sterilization of urine indicated that the proper antimicrobial agent was being given at the correct dosage and was being excreted in effective concentrations in urine. However, urine sterilization is not always achieved during medical therapy designed to induce urolith dissolution. Inability to sterilize urine during therapy may be related to: 1) release of bacteria from the urolith during dissolution, 2) induction of diuresis, which impairs the antimicrobial effects of urine, 3) induction of diuresis, which reduces the concentration of antimicrobial agent in urine and 4) reduced clearance of urea, which may impair the antimicrobial effects of urine. Despite persistence of bacteriuria during therapy, however, uroliths composed of struvite will dissolve and the associated inflammatory response will subside. Antimicrobial therapy should be continued until the uroliths completely dissolve.

Varying degrees of elevated serum alkaline phosphatase activity frequently occur in dogs fed very low-protein foods such as the veterinary therapeutic food fed to this patient. Studies in dogs indicate that the alkaline phosphatase is of hepatic origin. The greatest increases in serum alkaline phosphatase activity occur in dogs that do not consume an adequate amount of the veterinary therapeutic food. Contrary to the situation in this case, the calculolytic food should not be fed with a goal of weight reduction because this practice may contribute to negative nitrogen balance. Weight reduction should be achieved with an appropriate food after resolution of the urocystolith problem.

Endnote

a. Hill's Pet Nutrition, Inc., Topeka, KS, USA.

Bibliography

Osborne CA, Lulich JP, Bartges JW, et al. Canine and feline urolithiasis: Relationship of etiopathogenesis to treatment and prevention. In: Osborne CA, Finco DR, eds. Canine and Feline Nephrology and Urology. Baltimore, MD: Williams & Wilkins, 1995; 798-888.

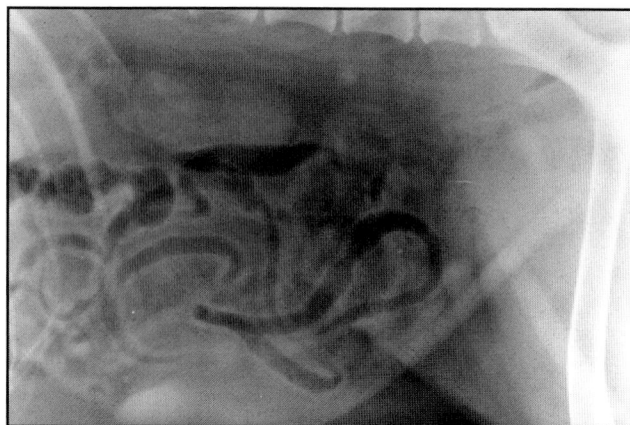

Figure 6. Survey lateral abdominal radiograph of the dog described in Figure 1. This radiograph was obtained 127 days after initiation of calculolytic therapy.

CASE 20-2

Urine Dribbling in a Yorkshire Terrier

Jody P. Lulich, DVM, PhD
Diplomate ACVIM (Internal Medicine)

Carl A. Osborne, DVM, PhD
Diplomate ACVIM (Internal Medicine)
College of Veterinary Medicine
University of Minnesota
St. Paul, Minnesota, USA

Assess the Animal

A nine-year-old, neutered male Yorkshire terrier was examined for urine dribbling and depression of two days' duration. Physical examination revealed that dog was 8 to 10% dehydrated; capillary refill time was slightly delayed. The dog voided small spurts of reddish brown urine onto the examination table when its abdomen was palpated. The physical examination was otherwise normal. Body weight was 5 kg; the dog had a normal body condition score (3/5). Survey abdominal radiographs revealed a large urinary bladder and a radiodense urolith in the urethra at the proximal end of the os penis. Several uroliths were also detected in the urinary bladder (Figure 1).

The diagnosis was urolithiasis of the lower urinary tract associated with urethral obstruction. The depression was probably a consequence of postrenal azotemia.

Assess the Food(s) and Feeding Method

The dog was fed a commercial moist adult maintenance food twice daily and various table foods.

Questions

1. What additional assessments should be performed?
2. What should be the patient's initial treatment plan?

Answers and Discussion

1. A blood sample should be submitted for biochemical analysis to evaluate the degree of azotemia and detect concurrent electrolyte abnormalities. A urinalysis and aerobic bacterial culture of the urine will help predict the mineral composition of the uroliths.
2. Replacement of the patient's fluid deficits with an appropriate fluid given intravenously is important. The urinary bladder can be evacuated by decompressive cystocentesis to enhance renal elimination of waste products. Reducing pressure in the urinary bladder also would facilitate retrograde urohydropropulsion of the urethrolith.

Further Assessment

Results of laboratory tests revealed azotemia, hyperphosphatemia and hypobicarbonatemia (Table 1). Serum alkaline phosphatase activity was also increased. Crystals were not observed by urine sediment examination and the urine culture was negative (Table 2). The urethrolith was

Table 1. Serum biochemistry values of a nine-year-old male Yorkshire terrier with radiodense urocystoliths.*

Factors	Reference values	Day 1	Day 2	Day 3
SUN (mg/dl)	7-28	186	141	16
Creatinine (mg/dl)	0.5-1.5	6.5	1.2	0.9
Calcium (mg/dl)	9.3-11.4	8.7	8.2	8.7
Phosphorus (mg/dl)	1.9-7.0	19.2	3.5	3.2
Sodium (mEq/l)	143-150	144	149	149
Potassium (mEq/l)	3.2-5.6	4.7	3.6	3.3
ALT activity (U/l)	5-62	78	ND	ND
Alk phos activity (U/l)	10-149	223	ND	ND
Total CO$_2$ (mEq/l)	17-26	14.5	ND	ND

Key: SUN = serum urea nitrogen, ALT = alanine aminotransferase, Alk phos = alkaline phosphatase, ND = not done.
*Dietary therapy was initiated on Day 14.

Table 2. Urinalyses of a nine-year-old male Yorkshire terrier with radiodense urocystoliths.*

Factors**	Day 1	Day 14***	Day 28	Day 60
Specific gravity	1.015	1.025	1.008	1.015
pH	6.0	6.5	7.5	7.5
Protein†	1+	1+	Trace	Trace
RBC††	100-150	8-12	0	1-3
WBC††	12-16	2-4	1-2	0
Crystals†††	None	None	None	None
Aerobic bacterial culture	Neg	Neg	Neg	Neg

Key: RBC = red blood cells, WBC = white blood cells, Neg = negative.
*Samples collected by cystocentesis.
**Glucose, bilirubin and acetone were not detected in any specimen.
***Dietary therapy was initiated on Day 14.
†Values represent semiquantitative evaluations based on a scale of 0 to 4; urine volume was not considered.
††Per high power field (x450).
†††Per low power field (x100).

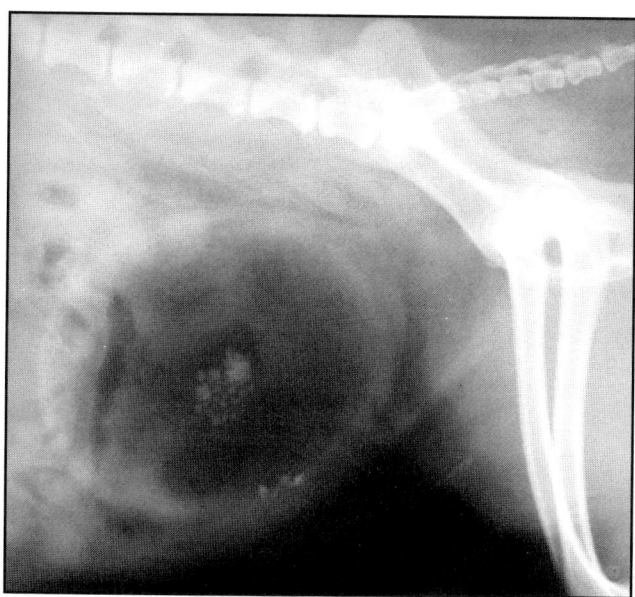

Figure 1. Survey lateral abdominal radiograph of a nine-year-old male Yorkshire terrier revealing multiple radiodense uroliths in the urinary bladder. A radiodense urolith in the urethra at the proximal end of the os penis was also noted.

Table 3. The advantages and disadvantages of medical urolith dissolution and surgical urolith removal can be accurately assessed after the mineral composition of the urolith is known or predicted. This table lists factors used to predict mineral composition of radiodense uroliths when no uroliths are available for quantitative analysis vs. clinical findings in the patient described in this case.*

Factors	MAP	CaOx	CaP	Silica	Cystine
Typical urinary pH	No	Yes	Possible	Yes	Yes
Typical crystalluria	Possible	Possible	Possible	Possible	Possible
Typical urine culture	No	Yes	Yes	Yes	Yes
Typical radiographic density	Yes	Yes	Yes	Yes	Yes
Typical radiographic contour	Yes	Yes	Yes	No	No
Typical serum biochemistry values	Yes	Yes	Possible	Yes	Yes
Typical breed	No	Yes	Yes	No	No
Typical gender	No	Yes	Yes	Yes	Yes
Typical age	No	Yes	Yes	Yes	No

Key: MAP = magnesium ammonium phosphate, CaOx = calcium oxalate, CaP = calcium phosphate.
*Characteristics of urate uroliths were not considered because they are typically radiolucent.

successfully flushed into the urinary bladder by retrograde urohydropropulsion. Prophylactic antimicrobials were administered (amoxicillin with clavulanic acid, 14 mg/kg, q12h) to prevent iatrogenic bacterial urinary tract infection associated with transurethral catheterization.

Additional Question

1. What is the most likely mineral composition of these radiodense uroliths?

Answer and Discussion

1. The advantages and disadvantages of medical urolith dissolution and surgical urolith removal can be more accurately assessed by predicting the mineral composition of uroliths. Magnesium ammonium phosphate (struvite), calcium oxalate, calcium phosphate, silica and cystine uroliths can all be radiodense (Table 3). It was surmised that this patient's uroliths were probably not composed of magnesium ammonium phosphate because of the breed and gender of the dog along with findings of aciduria and a negative bacterial culture. These findings suggested that the uroliths were not composed of struvite and therefore were not amenable to medical dissolution.

Treatment and Further Assessment

The uroliths were surgically removed following resolution of azotemia on the third day of hospitalization (Table 1). Postsurgical radiographs verified that all uroliths were removed. Quantitative analysis revealed that uroliths were composed of 100% calcium oxalate monohydrate.

Further Questions

1. Outline an appropriate feeding plan (foods and feeding method) for this dog.
2. Is reassessment important for this patient?

Answers and Discussion

1. Medical therapy to prevent urolith recurrence was initiated at the time of suture removal. Dietary recommendations included reducing calcium, oxalate, protein and sodium, providing additional water and citrate and maintaining adequate phosphorus and magnesium. A moist veterinary therapeutic food (Prescription Diet Canine u/d[a]) was chosen because its nutrient content matches this nutrient profile. Canine u/d avoids excess dietary protein, oxalate and calcium, and promotes formation of less concentrated, alkaline urine. These dietary characteristics are helpful in preventing recurrence of calcium oxalate uroliths. The food was offered in two separate meals each day (one-fourth can twice daily, total 375 kcal [1.57 MJ]). The owners were also instructed to avoid feeding the dog any human foods, commercial dog treats and vitamin-mineral supplements (especially those containing vitamins C and D and calcium).

2. Regular reassessment is important because calcium oxalate uroliths commonly recur. Results of a retrospective study on the recurrence rate of calcium oxalate uroliths in dogs indicated that the rate of recurrence increased with the length of time that dogs were evaluated: 3% recurred after three months, 9% after six months, 35% after one year, 42% after two years and 48% after three years. This dog should be examined (i.e., urinalysis, survey abdominal radiography) at regular intervals to evaluate efficacy of medical therapy and to detect uroliths while they are small enough to remove with nonsurgical techniques. This patient should also be evaluated for hyperadrenocorticism because of the increased serum alkaline phosphatase activity. Glucocorticoid administration and hyperadrenocorticism are associated with hypercalciuria and increase the risk for calcium oxalate urolith formation.

Progress Notes

Table 2 summarizes the urinalysis results following six weeks of dietary management. Canine u/d was successful in promoting less concentrated, alkaline urine in this dog. Reassessment every three to six months was recommended to the owner.

Endnote

a. Hill's Pet Nutrition Inc., Topeka, KS, USA.

Bibliography

Osborne CA, Lulich JP, Bartges JW, et al. Canine and feline urolithiasis: Relationship of etiopathogenesis to treatment and prevention. In: Osborne CA, Finco DR, eds. Canine and Feline Nephrology and Urology. Baltimore, MD: Williams & Wilkins, 1995; 798-888.

CASE 20-3

Stranguria in a Dalmatian

Joseph W. Bartges, DVM, PhD
Diplomate ACVN and ACVIM (Internal Medicine)
College of Veterinary Medicine
University of Tennessee
Knoxville, Tennessee, USA

Assess the Animal

A three-year-old, neutered male Dalmatian was referred to the University of Minnesota Veterinary Teaching Hospital for inability to urinate and straining to urinate during the past 24 hours (Figure 1). The dog had received an antibiotic (unknown type and dosage) for the past month because of bacterial folliculitis (Figure 2).

Physical examination revealed a depressed dog with patchy areas of alopecia and erythema, and a distended, tense, painful urinary bladder. The dog weighed 34.2 kg and had a normal body condition score (BCS 3/5). No other abnormalities were noted.

Blood samples were submitted for a complete blood count (Table 1) and a serum biochemistry profile (Table 2). These tests revealed leukocytosis due to mature neutrophilia and an elevated serum uric acid concentration. Survey radiographs revealed three slightly radiopaque round densities in the region of the urinary bladder (Figure 3) and multiple urethroliths. A urine sample was collected for a complete urinalysis and aerobic bacterial culture (Table 3).

An 8-Fr. urinary catheter was advanced into the urinary bladder without difficulty. The catheter and many small round, smooth, green uroliths were voided. The urinary catheter was reinserted, all of the urine removed and a double-contrast cystogram was performed (Figure 4).

Assess the Food(s) and Feeding Method

At the time of admission, the dog was being fed a dry veterinary therapeutic food (Prescription Diet Canine

Figure 1. A three-year-old, neutered male Dalmatian with dysuria and inability to void urine.

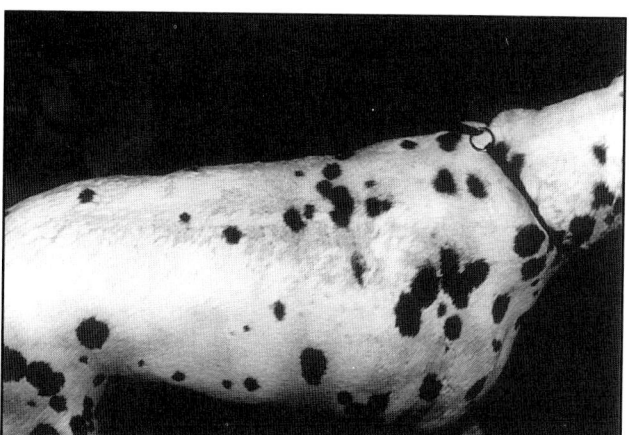

Figure 2. Photograph of the dog described in Figure 1 demonstrating patchy alopecia due to folliculitis.

Table 1. Hemograms of a three-year-old, neutered male Dalmatian with urocystoliths.

Factors	Reference values	1	25	59	88	123	157	186	214	247	275
						Day*					
Hct (%)	30-58	49.6	47.6	46.1	47.6	46.0	48.6	46.5	48.7	48.0	46.2
RBC (10⁶/µl)	5.2-8.1	6.95	6.77	6.48	6.74	6.53	6.80	6.65	6.92	6.82	6.53
Hemoglobin (g/dl)	10.2-16.9	17.3	16.7	15.9	16.5	16.1	16.0	19.1	16.9	16.9	19.8
MCV (fl)	63-72	71	70	71	71	70	71	70	70	70	71
MCH (pg)	22-25	25	25	25	35	25	24	29	24	25	30
MCHC (%)	34-37	35	35	35	35	35	33	41	35	35	43
Nucleated RBC (/µl)	–	0	0	0	1	0	1	1	1	0	0
WBC (10³/µl)	5.4-15.3	23.4	11.5	11.5	11.2	13.7	12.8	12.8	13.1	10.7	13.6
Seg. neutrophils (10³/µl)	2.75-12.85	21.18	6.56	8.34	7.49	9.86	10.6	9.02	8.06	7.92	10.0
Band neutrophils (/µl)	0-150	0	0	0	0	0	0	0	0	50	70
Metamyelocytes (/µl)	0	0	0	0	0	0	0	0	0	0	2,040
Lymphocytes (/µl)	430-5,800	820	3,050	1,440	2,220	2,400	1,400	2,600	3,770	1,870	200
Monocytes (/µl)	50-1,400	1,290	400	350	170	340	320	440	460	160	1,290
Eosinophils (/µl)	0-1,400	120	1,500	1,380	1,220	1,100	380	570	720	700	0
Basophils (/µl)	Rare	0	0	0	0	0	0	60	0	0	0
Platelets (10³/µl)	160-525	378	378	381	352	395	406	644	369	358	Normal**
Total solids (g/dl)	5.8-7.5	7.3	6.6	6.5	6.8	6.7	7.0	9.3	7.1	7.3	9.1
Comments								Lipemic			Lipemic

Key: Hct = hematocrit, RBC = red blood cells, MCV = mean corpuscular volume, MCH = mean corpuscular hemoglobin, MCHC = mean corpuscular hemoglobin concentration, WBC = white blood cells.
*Therapy consisting of a purine-restricted food and allopurinol was initiated on Day 2; allopurinol therapy was discontinued on Day 186.
**Platelets were estimated on a blood film and considered adequate.

Table 2. Serum biochemistry values of a three-year-old, neutered male Dalmatian with urocystoliths.

Factors	Reference values	Day* 1	25	59	88	123	157	186	214	247	275	924	1,268
Urea nitrogen (mg/dl)	7-26	17	9	7	7	5	6	5	4	4	3	5	4
Creatinine (mg/dl)	0.6-1.4	1.0	1.3	1.1	1.2	1.0	1.0	0.9	1.0	1.1	1.0	0.9	0.9
Alk phos activity (U/l)	3-60	53	83	66	94	142	212	258	239	335	490	854	760
ALT activity (U/l)	4-91	28	22	27	26	25	26	24	25	26	27	21	21
Total bilirubin (mg/dl)	0-0.7	0.6	0.4	0.4	0.3	0.7	0.8	1.5	0.9	0.9	1.3	0.4	0.6
Glucose (mg/dl)	79-140	136	122	123	113	127	133	113	116	125	132	129	115
Total protein (g/dl)	5.8-7.9	7.4	6.3	6.3	6.5	5.9	5.5	5.7	6.1	6.1	6.0	6.4	6.7
Albumin (g/dl)	2.6-4.0	3.8	3.3	3.2	3.3	3.1	3.3	3.4	3.1	3.3	3.3	2.6	2.7
Globulin (g/dl)	2.2-4.0	3.6	3.0	3.1	3.2	2.8	2.2	2.3	3.0	2.8	2.7	3.8	4.0
Uric acid (mg/dl)	0-0.6	1.5	0.3	0.4	0.3	0.4	0.4	0.5	0.7	2.0	1.7	0.9	0.8
CK (U/l)	36-155	394	79	70	76	57	66	90	90	57	67	50	–
Amylase activity (U/l)	220-1,400	976	779	742	997	715	805	786	851	795	963	856	912
Sodium (mEq/l)	146-156	148	150	150	140	150	151	150	150	150	151	147	148
Potassium (mEq/l)	3.8-5.1	3.6	4.5	4.0	3.6	4.4	4.4	4.0	4.3	4.0	4.3	4.5	4.5
Chloride (mEq/l)	109-122	110	114	116	112	114	111	112	113	114	111	111	110
Total CO₂ (mEq/l)	17-27	21	23	21	18	23	23	23	22	22	24	22	23
Anion gap	8-20	17	13	13	10	13	17	15	15	14	16	14	15
Osmolality (mOsm/l)	289-313	298	298	297	278	297	299	296	296	296	298	291	292
Calcium (mg/dl)	9.6-11.6	9.9	9.9	9.7	9.7	9.8	9.9	9.6	10.1	10.0	10.1	9.6	10.4
Phosphorus (mg/dl)	2.5-6.2	3.9	2.4	4.2	2.5	3.9	4.1	3.5	3.2	2.1	3.1	4.2	5.2

Key: ALT = alanine aminotransferase, Alk phos = alkaline phosphatase, CK = creatine kinase.
*Therapy consisting of a purine-restricted food and allopurinol was initiated on Day 2; allopurinol therapy was discontinued on Day 186.

Table 3. Urinalyses of a three-year-old, neutered male Dalmatian with urocystoliths.

Factors**	Day* 1	25	59	88	123	157	186	214	247	275
Method of collection	Voided	Midstream	Cysto	Cath	Cath	Cath	Cysto	Cath	Cath	Cysto
Specific gravity	1.028	1.018	1.014	1.022	1.019	1.013	1.018	1.017	1.010	1.008
pH	7.0	8.0	7.5	8.5	8.0	8.0	8.0	8.0	8.5	8.5
Protein***	1+	Trace	0	1+	1+	Trace	Trace	2+	Trace	Trace
Epithelial cells†	Rare	Few	0	Mod	0	Few	0	Few	0	Few
WBC†	0	0	0	0	0	0	0	0	0	0
RBC†	1-2	120-150	Rare	Rare	Occ	20-24	0	0	0	0
Crystals††	Many urate	Few urate	0	0	Rare urate	Rare urate	0	Few amorphous	0	0

Day* Factors**	598	654	728	924	1,046	1,254	1,268	1,580	1,640
(Continued from above)									
Method of collection	Cath	Cath	Cysto	Cysto	Cath	Cath	Cath	Cath	Cath
Specific gravity	1.012	1.013	1.006	1.006	1.010	1.006	1.008	1.005	1.011
pH	8.5	8.5	7.0	7.5	8.0	8.0	7.5	7.0	8.5
Protein***	1+	3+	Trace	0	1+	1+	1+	Trace	1+
Epithelial cells†	Mod	Mod	0	Occ	Occ	Few	Few	Rare	Rare
WBC†	0	0	0	0	0	0	0	0	0
RBC†	Rare	0-2	25-30	0	0	0	Rare	0-1	0
Crystals††	0	0	0	0	0	0	0	0	0

Key: Cysto = cystocentesis, Cath = catheterization, Mod = moderate, WBC = white blood cells, RBC = red blood cells, Occ = occasionally.
*Therapy consisting of a purine-restricted food and allopurinol was initiated on Day 2; allopurinol therapy was discontinued on Day 186.
**Glucose, bilirubin, acetone and bacteria were not detected in any specimen.
***Values represent semiquantitative evaluations based on a scale of 0 to 4; urine volume was not considered.
†Number per high power field (x450).
††Number per low power field (x100).

k/dª) that avoids excess levels of phosphorus, sodium and protein. The food was offered free choice.

Questions

1. What is the probable mineral composition of the uroliths in this dog?
2. What are the advantages and disadvantages of surgical vs. medical management of these uroliths?
3. If medical dissolution is chosen as the treatment plan, what parameters should be monitored?

Answers and Discussion

1. The most likely mineral composition of the uroliths is ammonium urate based on the physical and radi-ographic characteristics of the uroliths, the presence of ammonium urate crystalluria and the breed of dog. Dalmatians are predisposed to formation of purine uroliths, primarily ammonium urate, because of unique purine metabolism that results in greater urinary excretion and concentration of uric acid compared with most non-Dalmatian dogs.

2. Although surgery may be effective, medical protocols have been developed to dissolve ammonium urate uroliths. Surgical removal of urocystoliths has the obvious advantage of rapid correction of the disease process. Medical therapy may also be effective and includes using a low-purine commercial veterinary therapeutic food (Prescription Diet Canine u/dª) and allopurinol, a xanthine oxidase inhibitor. In a prospective controlled study

of canine ammonium urate urocystoliths, complete dissolution was achieved in approximately 40% of the cases and reduction of urolith size and/or number occurred in another 30% of cases. With medical therapy, the average time for dissolution of ammonium urate uroliths is three and one-half months; however, the median time is approximately one month. Thus, most ammonium urate uroliths dissolve in approximately one month.

3. Clinical signs often resolve within three to five days of initiating therapy. Clients should be advised that urethral obstruction may occur at any time when uroliths are present in the bladder. If urethral obstruction with uroliths recurs, the urolith(s) can be retropulsed back into the bladder. Urocystoliths (bladder stones) can be dissolved but urethroliths (urethral stones) cannot. The dog should be re-examined every four weeks by urinalysis and double-contrast cystography. With good compliance, the urine specific gravity should be reduced (<1.015), the urinary pH should be alkaline, no ammonium urate crystalluria should be detected and uroliths should be smaller and/or fewer as detected by double-contrast radiography. The serum urea nitrogen concentration should be low (<15 mg/dl) if additional blood work is performed.

Progress Notes

Uroliths retrieved on Day 1 were analyzed and found to be composed of 100% ammonium urate. Medical therapy was initiated with moist Canine u/d and allopurinol (15 mg/kg body weight, per os, q12 h). The dog's daily energy requirement was estimated to be 1,745 kcal/day (7.3 MJ) (1.5 cans twice daily). Amoxicillin-clavulanic acid (22 mg/kg, per os, q12h) was also used because of suspected superficial staphylococcal pyoderma. Twenty-five days later, the owners reported that urination was normal although an increased urine volume was noticed. Physical examination was normal and the folliculitis had resolved. The urine specific gravity and serum concentrations of urea nitrogen and uric acid were predictably decreased (Tables 2 and 3) and the urinary pH was alkaline. Double-contrast cystography revealed that the urocystoliths were approximately 50% smaller.

Thereafter, the dog was evaluated approximately every four weeks. Uroliths progressively decreased in size and number until they were no longer visible by double-contrast cystography (Day 186, Figure 5). Medical therapy was continued for an additional month at which time allopurinol was discontinued. Prophylactic therapy consisted of continuing the veterinary therapeutic food. Uroliths did not recur over the next four years (Tables 2 and 3). Superficial pyoderma recurred seasonally and was treated with appropriate antibiotics.

Further Discussion

Ammonium urate uroliths are highly recurrent, so prophylactic therapy should always be considered. Use of a food that avoids excessive levels of dietary purines and promotes formation of dilute, alkaline urine (Canine u/d) is effective in preventing recurrence of ammonium urate uroliths approximately 80% of the time. Allopurinol has been recommended for preventive therapy; however, recent studies indicate that prolonged administration of high doses of allopurinol may result in formation of xanthine uroliths. The risk of xanthine urolith formation is enhanced if dietary purines are not restricted during allopurinol administration.

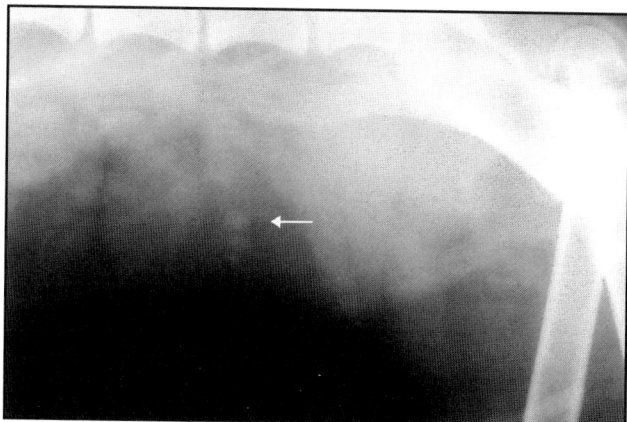

Figure 3. Survey abdominal radiograph of the dog described in Figure 1. Note the radiodense urocystoliths in the urinary bladder (arrow). Several uroliths of marginal density were also located near the os penis.

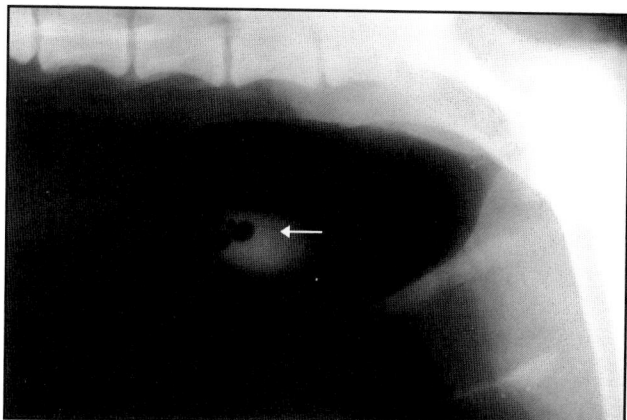

Figure 4. Double-contrast cystogram revealing four urocystoliths (arrow).

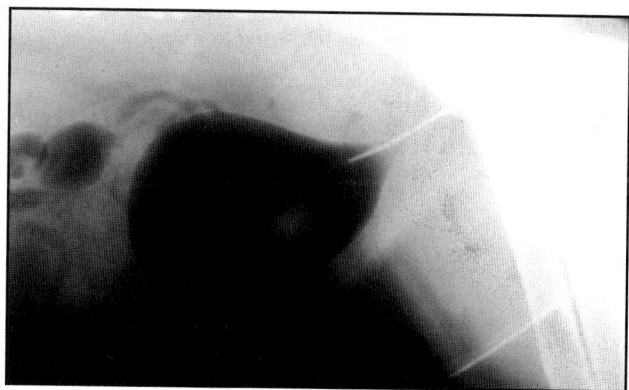

Figure 5. Double-contrast cystogram 186 days after initiating medical therapy to dissolve ammonium urate uroliths. No uroliths are detectable in the urinary bladder.

Endnote

a. Hill's Pet Nutrition Inc., Topeka, KS, USA.

Bibliography

Osborne CA, Lulich JP, Bartges JW, et al. Canine and feline urolithiasis: Relationship of etiopathogenesis to treatment and prevention. In: Osborne CA, Finco DR, eds. Canine and Feline Nephrology and Urology. Baltimore, MD: Williams & Wilkins, 1995; 798-888.

CASE 20-4

Inappropriate Urination in a Yorkshire Terrier Cross

Jody P. Lulich, DVM, PhD
Diplomate ACVIM (Internal Medicine)

Carl A. Osborne, DVM, PhD
Diplomate ACVIM (Internal Medicine)
College of Veterinary Medicine
University of Minnesota
St. Paul, Minnesota, USA

Assess the Animal

An 11-year-old, neutered female Yorkshire terrier cross weighing 5 kg was examined for inappropriate urination. The dog had been urinating in the house during the day while the owners were at work. Sometimes the urine appeared red. Physical examination was normal except for dental calculus and gingivitis. Body condition was normal (body condition score 3/5).

Table 1. Urinalyses of an 11-year-old female Yorkshire terrier crossbred dog with inappropriate urination.*

			Day		
Factors**	1	14***	28	60
Specific gravity	1.028	1.035	1.005	1.007
pH	8.0	6.0	7.0	7.5
Protein†	2+	Trace	Trace	Trace
RBC††	3-6	0	0	0
WBC††	30-40	0	0	0
Epithelial cells††	Occ	Occ	None	Few
Bacteria††	Moderate	None	None	None
Crystals†††	Struvite	None	None	Few
Aerobic bacterial culture	S. intermedius	Neg	Neg	Neg

Key: RBC = red blood cells, WBC = white blood cells, Occ = occasionally, Neg = negative.
*Samples collected by cystocentesis on Days 14, 28 and 60.
**Glucose, bilirubin and acetone were not detected in any specimen.
***Dietary therapy was initiated on Day 14.
†Values represent semiquantitative evaluations based on a scale of 0 to 4; urine volume was not considered.
††Per high power field (x450).
†††Per low power field (x100).

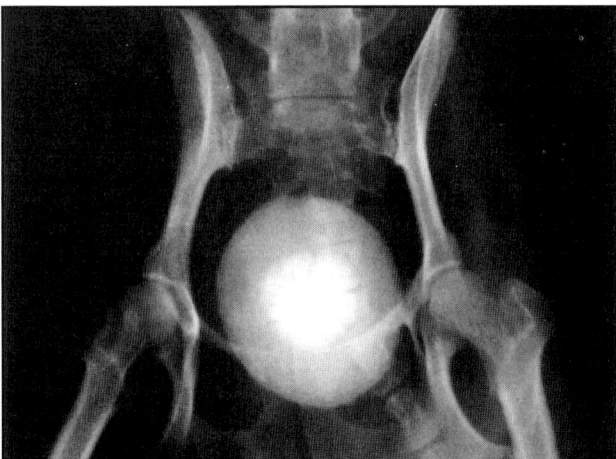

Figure 1. Survey abdominal radiograph (ventrodorsal view) showing a solitary urocystolith. Note that the urolith nidus is radiographically denser than the outer layer.

Results of urinalysis on a voided sample included alkaline urine with hematuria, proteinuria, pyuria, bacteriuria and a few struvite crystals (Table 1). A presumptive diagnosis of bacterial urinary tract infection was made. Urine collected by cystocentesis was submitted for aerobic bacterial culture. Pending culture results, the dog was given a combination of amoxicillin and clavulanic acid (14 mg/kg body weight, per os, q12h). Urine culture results identified *Staphylococcus intermedius*, which was susceptible to the prescribed antimicrobial.

One week later the dog was examined for continued hematuria and dysuria. Bacterial culture of urine was negative indicating that antimicrobial therapy was successful. Survey abdominal radiographs (Figure 1) revealed a large solitary radiodense urocystolith with a distinct central core (outside diameter = 2.9 cm, core diameter = 1.3 cm). The urolith core was more dense than the outer layer. A urinalysis was not performed.

Assess the Food(s) and Feeding Method

The dog ate a commercial moist grocery brand food supplemented with milk, turkey and chicken meat.

Questions

1. What is the probable mineral composition of this dog's urolith?
2. What are the advantages and disadvantages of surgical vs. medical management of this urolith?

Answers and Discussion

1. Based on the clinical findings, the outer portion of the urolith was probably composed of magnesium ammonium phosphate (struvite) (Table 2). Because of the difference in radiodensity, the nidus may be composed of a different mineral salt.
2. Although struvite urocystoliths are amenable to medical dissolution, surgical removal is probably the best treatment option in cases of suspected compound uroliths.

Progress Notes

Results of a serum biochemistry profile were normal. The urolith was removed surgically and antimicrobial therapy was continued for an additional two weeks. Quantitative mineral analysis of the urolith revealed that the nidus was composed of 100% calcium oxalate monohydrate and the outer layer was composed of 95% magnesium ammonium phosphate and 5% calcium phosphate carbonate.

Further Questions

1. How does a compound urolith develop?
2. How can recurrence of urolithiasis be minimized in this patient?

Answers and Discussion

1. Although the exact mechanisms responsible for calcium oxalate urolith formation are unknown, supersaturation of urine with calcium and oxalate is a prerequisite. The calcium oxalate nidus probably disrupted local defense mechanisms predisposing this patient to a staphylococcal bacterial infection of the urinary bladder. These bacteria produce the enzyme urease, leading

Table 2. The advantages and disadvantages of medical urolith dissolution and surgical urolith removal can be accurately assessed after the mineral composition of the urolith is known or predicted. This table lists factors used to predict mineral composition of radiodense uroliths when no uroliths are available for quantitative analysis vs. clinical findings in the patient described in this case.*

Factors	MAP	CaOx	CaP	Silica	Cystine
Typical urinary pH	Yes	No	Possible	No	No
Typical crystalluria	Yes	No	No	No	No
Typical urine culture	Yes	No	No	No	No
Typical radiographic density	Yes	Yes	Yes	Yes	No
Typical radiographic contour	Yes	Possible	Possible	No	No
Typical breed	No	Yes	Yes	No	No
Typical gender	Yes	No	No	No	No
Typical age	No	Yes	Yes	No	No

Key: MAP = magnesium ammonium phosphate, CaOx = calcium oxalate, CaP = calcium phosphate.
*Characteristics of urate uroliths were not considered because they are typically radiolucent.

to urine alkalinity and oversaturation with struvite. The calcium oxalate nidus served as template for struvite crystal deposition (heterogeneous nucleation).

2. Some strategies designed to prevent calcium oxalate urolith formation increase the risk for struvite urolith formation. The reverse is also true. When managing patients with compound uroliths containing both mineral salts, minimizing calcium oxalate urolith recurrence is given priority over minimizing struvite urolith formation because struvite uroliths can be medically dissolved. At present, there is no strategy to dissolve calcium oxalate uroliths.

Dietary recommendations to minimize recurrence of calcium oxalate uroliths include reducing calcium, oxalate, protein and sodium, providing additional water and citrate and maintaining adequate phosphorus and magnesium. One therapeutic goal to prevent calcium oxalate recurrence is alkalinization of urine, which minimizes calcium excretion and augments citrate excretion. Although urine alkalinization increases saturation for struvite, other factors appear to have a greater impact on struvite urolith formation in dogs. In this patient, struvite formed as a result of a urinary tract infection with bacteria that produce urease. Therefore, it is unlikely that struvite will reform without recurrence of a urease-positive urinary tract infection. Urine cultures should be evaluated periodically to detect and eradicate urinary tract infections early so that struvite uroliths do not form.

Progress Notes

A commercial veterinary therapeutic food (Prescription Diet Canine u/d[a]) was recommended (one-half can per day, 375 kcal [1.57 MJ]) and the owners were instructed to avoid feeding the dog human foods, commercial dog treats and vitamin-mineral supplements (especially those containing vitamins C and D and calcium). Urinalysis, urine culture and survey abdominal radiographs were recommended at regular intervals (i.e., every six months).

Endnote

a. Hill's Pet Nutrition Inc., Topeka, KS, USA.

Bibliography

Osborne CA, Lulich JP, Bartges JW, et al. Canine and feline urolithiasis: Relationship of etiopathogenesis to treatment and prevention. In: Osborne CA, Finco DR, eds. Canine and Feline Nephrology and Urology. Baltimore, MD: Williams & Wilkins, 1995; 798-888.

CASE 20-5

Dysuria in a Dachshund

Carl A. Osborne, DVM, PhD
Diplomate ACVIM (Internal Medicine)
College of Veterinary Medicine
University of Minnesota
St. Paul, Minnesota, USA

Assess the Animal

A four-year-old, neutered male dachshund was examined for vomiting, depression, dysuria and anuria of two days' duration. Dysuria and pollakiuria had been present for two weeks. Physical examination revealed a depressed, mildly dehydrated dog with a large urinary bladder. The dog weighed 6.5 kg and had a normal body condition score (3/5).

Survey radiographs confirmed obstructive uropathy due to multiple urethroliths with marginal radiodensity (Figure 1). Blood and urine were collected for routine diagnostic tests. The urethroliths were flushed back into the bladder lumen by urohydropropulsion after the bladder was decompressed via cystocentesis (Figure 2). Lactated Ringer's solution was given subcutaneously to correct

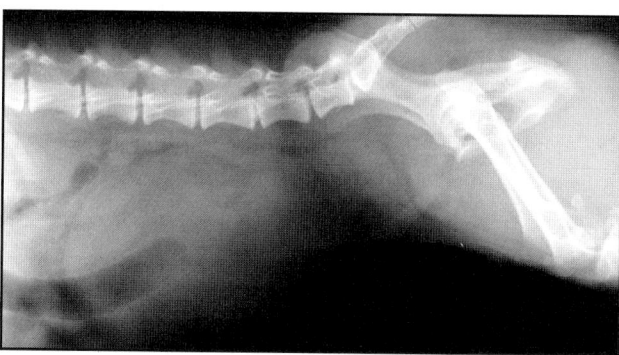

Figure 1. Survey abdominal radiograph of a four-year-old male dachshund illustrating marked distention of the urinary bladder. Two marginally radiodense urethroliths were located behind the os penis.

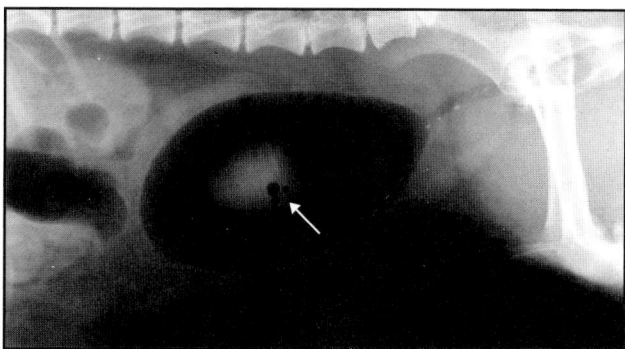

Figure 2. Double-contrast cystogram of the dog described in Figure 1. Three urocystoliths (arrow) can be seen surrounded by contrast material.

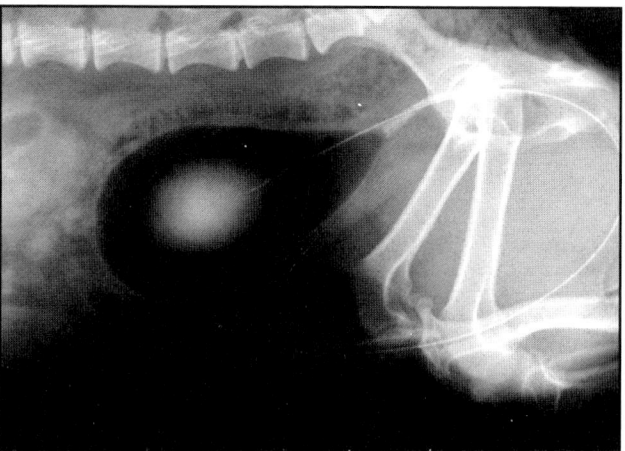

Figure 3. Double-contrast cystogram of the dog described in Figures 1 and 2 taken 40 days after initiation of therapy with 2-MPG and Canine u/d. There are no uroliths in the bladder lumen. Contrast urethrography confirmed that there were no uroliths in the urethral lumen.

the dehydration and oral amoxicillin-clavulanic acid (Clavamox[a]) was given to prevent urinary tract infection.

Results of the complete blood count were normal. The major serum biochemistry abnormalities were azotemia (urea nitrogen = 52 mg/dl, normal 4 to 26 mg/dl; creatinine = 3.1 mg/dl, normal 0.4 to 1.5 mg/dl) and hyperphosphatemia (phosphorus = 8.4 mg/dl, normal 2.9 to 6.4 mg/dl). Urinalysis results included the following: specific gravity = 1.025, pH = 6.5, hematuria, pyuria, proteinuria and numerous cystine crystals.

The diagnosis was obstructive uropathy due to urethroliths and postrenal azotemia.

Assess the Food(s) and Feeding Method

The dog was fed a commercial dry adult maintenance food free choice and received a vitamin-mineral supplement each day.

Questions

1. What is the most likely mineral composition of this dog's uroliths?
2. Outline a treatment and feeding plan for this patient.

Answers and Discussion

1. The key diagnostic findings in this dog include: 1) multiple, smooth uroliths with marginal radiodensity, 2) urinary pH = 6.5, 3) cystine crystalluria, 4) sterile urine, 5) normal serum biochemistry profile results, other than azotemia and hyperphosphatemia and 6) the dachshund breed. All these findings are most consistent with cystine uroliths.
2. Fluid therapy should be continued if azotemia persists. Urohydropropulsion can be repeated if urethral obstruction occurs again. Medical dissolution of canine cystine uroliths is accomplished by a combination of N-(2-mercaptopropionyl)-glycine (2-MPG[b]) and dietary management with a food that reduces urinary excretion of cystine, promotes formation of alkaline urine and reduces urinary concentration. Prescription Diet Canine u/d[c] meets these dietary goals. 2-MPG reduces the urine concentration of cystine by combining with cysteine to form cysteine-2-MPG, which is more soluble than cystine. In studies conducted at the University of Minnesota, mean dissolution time with this combination of therapy was 10 weeks (range two to 30 weeks). Drug-induced adverse events associated with 2-MPG are uncommon in dogs, but when they occur they include Coombs positive spherocytic anemia, thrombocytopenia and increased hepatic enzyme activity. Antibiotics should also be continued for at least 10 more days. The vitamin-mineral supplement is unnecessary and should be discontinued.

Progress Notes

The azotemia and hyperphosphatemia had resolved by the second day of hospitalization. The combination of amoxicillin and clavulanic acid was continued. The dog was released from the hospital with instructions for the owner to give 2-MPG at a dosage of 15 mg/kg body weight, per os, twice daily. The food was changed to moist Canine u/d and the vitamin-mineral supplement was discontinued. Radiographs taken 40 days after initial hospitalization showed no evidence of uroliths (Figure 3). Urinalysis results included unconcentrated, alkaline urine with amorphous crystals. The serum urea nitrogen concentration was 4 mg/dl, which confirmed that the low-protein food was being fed at home. 2-MPG was discontinued and Canine u/d was continued. Examination 75 and 232 days after initial hospitalization revealed that the urine continued to be unconcentrated and alkaline with no evidence of crystalluria. The urea nitrogen concentration remained low (5 to 6 mg/dl), which indicated that the owner was compliant with the feeding plan.

Endnotes

a. Pfizer Animal Health, Exton, PA, USA.
b. Thiola. Mission Pharmacal, San Antonio, TX, USA.
c. Hill's Pet Nutrition, Inc., Topeka, KS, USA.

Bibliography

Osborne CA, Lulich JP, Bartges JW, et al. Canine and feline urolithiasis: Relationship of etiopathogenesis to treatment and prevention. In: Osborne CA, Finco DR, eds. Canine and Feline Nephrology and Urology. Baltimore, MD: Williams & Wilkins, 1995; 798-888.

CASE 20-6

Dysuria in a Puppy

Jody P. Lulich, DVM, PhD
Diplomate ACVIM (Internal Medicine)

Carl A. Osborne, DVM, PhD
Diplomate ACVIM (Internal Medicine)
College of Veterinary Medicine
University of Minnesota
St. Paul, Minnesota, USA

Assess the Animal

A nine-week-old, male, mixed-breed puppy was examined for dysuria, anorexia, vomiting and depression of one day's duration. The history was incomplete because the owners had acquired the puppy only five days earlier. Physical examination was unremarkable except for an overdistended, painful urinary bladder. Palpation of the urinary bladder induced a micturition reflex, but the puppy was unable to void. The puppy's body weight (5 kg) and condition (body condition score 3/5) were normal.

Survey abdominal radiographs revealed multiple, radiodense uroliths in the penile urethra. Following decompression of the urinary bladder by abdominal cystocentesis, the urethroliths were returned to the urinary bladder lumen by urohydropropulsion (Figure 1). Analysis of an aliquot of urine collected by cystocentesis revealed an inflammatory response associated with bacteriuria (Table 1). Quantitative aerobic and anaerobic culture of urine revealed >10⁵ colony-forming units/ml of urease-positive *Staphylococcus intermedius*. The bacteria were susceptible to most commonly used antimicrobial agents. Results of a complete blood count were normal except for a stress-induced mature neutrophilic leukocytosis. Results of a serum biochemistry profile were unremarkable (Table 2).

A small urolith was spontaneously voided and submitted for quantitative mineral analysis one day later.

Assess the Food(s) and Feeding Method

The dog was fed a commercial dry specialty brand growth food (Science Diet Canine Growth[a]) twice daily.

Questions

1. What is the most likely urolith type in this patient?
2. What additional diagnostic tests might be important?
3. Outline an appropriate treatment and feeding plan for this puppy.

Answers and Discussion

1. The most likely urolith type in this patient is magnesium ammonium phosphate (struvite). This "guesstimate" is based on finding a urinary tract infection with a urease-producing staphylococcal bacteria and radiodense uroliths. Infection-induced struvite uroliths can form within days and may occur in dogs at any age including very young dogs.
2. Anatomic defects of the urinary tract can predispose animals to bacterial infection. Ultrasound and/or con-

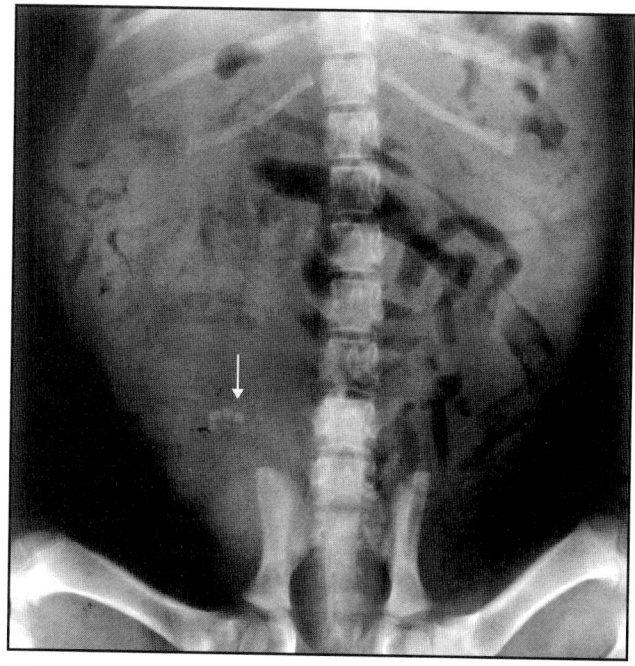

Figure 1. Ventrodorsal survey abdominal radiograph of a nine-week-old male dog with multiple radiodense urocystoliths (arrow).

Table 1. Urinalyses of an immature male, mixed-breed dog with dysuria.*

| Factors | \multicolumn{6}{c}{Day**} |
	1	10	25	39	73	226
Specific gravity	1.021	1.005	1.042	1.050	1.030	1.052
pH	6.5	5.5	6.0	6.0	7.0	6.5
Protein***	3+	Trace	1+	1+	Neg	1+
RBC†	TNTC	20-30	20-30	TNTC	0	0
WBC†	TNTC	0	2-3	20-25	0	0
Bacteria†	Many cocci	0	0	0	0	0
Crystals††	0	0	0	0	0	0
Culture	S. intermedius	Neg	Neg	Neg	Neg	Neg

Key: Neg = negative, RBC = red blood cells, TNTC = too numerous to count, WBC = white blood cells.
*Samples collected by cystocentesis.
**Dietary therapy for urinary tract infection and urolith dissolution was initiated on Day 2 and discontinued on Day 10. Antibiotic therapy for urinary tract infection was initiated on Day 2 and discontinued on Day 39.
***Values represent semiquantitative evaluations based on a scale of 0 to 4; urine volume was not considered.
†Number per high power field (x450).
††Number per low power field (x100).

Table 2. Serum biochemistry values of an immature male, mixed-breed dog with dysuria.

Factors	Reference values	Day* 1	10	25	39	73	226
SUN (mg/dl)	7-28	28	2	8	20	12	12
Creatinine (mg/dl)	0.5-1.5	1.0	0.7	0.5	0.7	0.9	1.2
Calcium (mg/dl)	9.3-11.4	9.5	11.3	11.3	11.1	11.3	11.0
Phosphorus (mg/dl)	1.9-7.0	8.9	6.7	9.3	9.5	7.6	5.1
Sodium (mEq/l)	143-150	139	148	147	151	147	148
Chloride (mEq/l)	108-125	104	114	110	113	109	111
Potassium (mEq/l)	3.2-5.6	3.9	6.8	5.2	4.8	4.6	4.4
Albumin (g/dl)	2.4-3.8	3.2	2.7	3.1	3.3	3.7	4.1
ALT activity (U/l)	5-62	32	27	58	61	55	68
Alk phos activity (U/l)	10-149	180	349	207	186	113	62
Total bilirubin (mg/dl)	0.1-0.6	0.2	0.6	0.2	0.3	0.2	0.2
Total CO_2 (mEq/l)	17-26	20.5	21.1	20.8	23.4	21.6	20.1

Key: SUN = serum urea nitrogen, ALT = alanine aminotransferase, Alk phos = alkaline phosphatase.
*Dietary therapy for urinary tract infection and urolith dissolution was initiated on Day 2 and discontinued on Day 10. Antibiotic therapy for urinary tract infection was initiated on Day 2 and discontinued on Day 39.

trast radiography should be considered to evaluate the lower urinary tract for such defects.

3. Medical or surgical protocols can be used to treat this puppy. Medical therapy designed to induce struvite urolith dissolution includes an appropriate orally administered antimicrobial agent and a food with restricted levels of protein, magnesium and phosphorus that is metabolized to produce an acidic urinary pH. Because foods formulated to aid in dissolution of struvite uroliths contain reduced quantities of protein, calcium, magnesium and phosphorus and thus are not designed to meet the long-term nutritional requirements of immature dogs, the feeding plan should be monitored closely. Monitoring serum biochemistry parameters (albumin, phosphorus, calcium, etc.) is an acceptable means of determining nutritional status in young dogs. An alternate treatment method includes a cystotomy to remove the uroliths; however, anesthesia and surgery in an immature dog are also associated with some degree of risk.

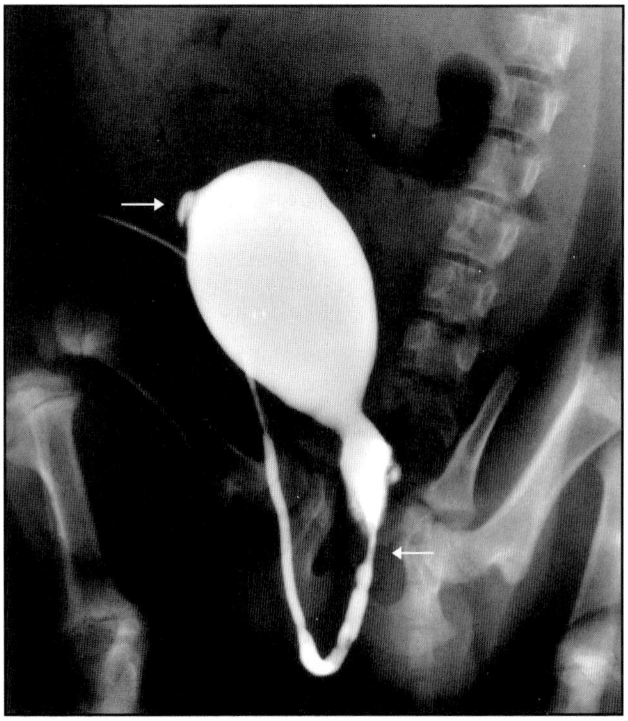

Progress Notes

Quantitative analysis of the voided urolith revealed that it was composed of 95% magnesium ammonium phosphate hexahydrate and 5% carbonate apatite. Retrograde positive-contrast urethrocystography and double-contrast cystography revealed a diverticulum located at the bladder vertex (Figures 2 and 3). The urethral lumen was also narrowed just distal to the site normally occupied by the prostate gland.

Medical therapy included a combination of amoxicillin and clavulanic acid (Clavamox[b]) given orally and feeding a food designed to aid in dissolution of struvite uroliths (Prescription Diet Canine s/d[a]). Compared with average dog foods, Canine s/d is greatly reduced in protein (7.6% dry matter [DM]), reduced in phosphorus (0.10% DM), calcium (0.28% DM) and magnesium (0.02% DM) and

Figure 2. Positive-contrast retrograde urethrocystogram of the same dog described in Figure 1. Note the vesicourachal diverticulum (top arrow) and narrowing of the proximal portion of the urethra (bottom arrow).

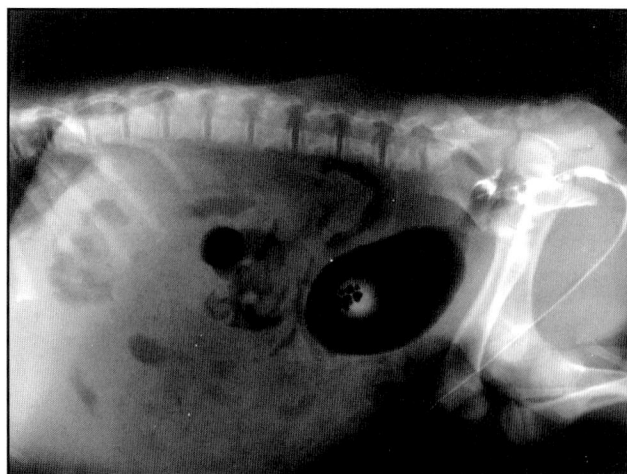

Figure 3. Double-contrast cystogram of the same dog described in Figure 1 with at least eight uroliths in the bladder lumen. Radiopaque contrast medium has refluxed into the periurethral tissue in the area of the prostate gland. The urethral lumen contains air bubbles surrounded by contrast medium.

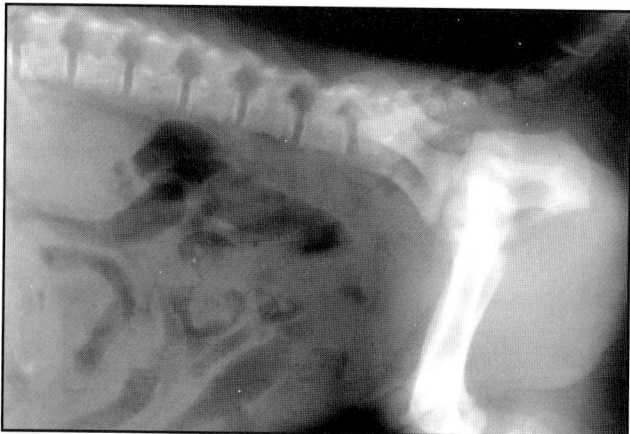

Figure 4. Survey abdominal radiograph obtained 10 days following initiation of therapy with an antibiotic and a food designed to dissolve struvite uroliths. Radiodense uroliths cannot be detected within the urinary tract.

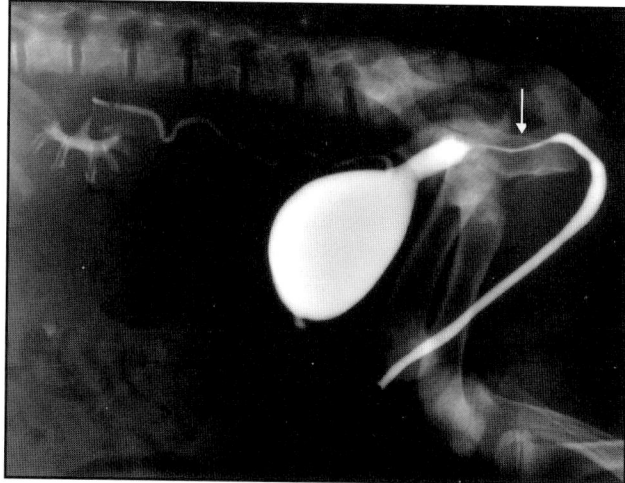

Figure 5. Positive-contrast retrograde urethrocystogram obtained 39 days following diagnosis of uroliths and a vesicourachal diverticulum. There is no evidence of a vesicourachal diverticulum, but narrowing of the lumen of the proximal urethra is still present (arrow).

produces a more acidic urine (target urinary pH = 5.9 to 6.1). The puppy was fed one-half can three times daily (700 kcal [2.93 MJ]).

Gross hematuria and dysuria progressively declined. A urine sample collected by cystocentesis 10 days later revealed acidification of the urine and marked reduction in the inflammatory response (Table 1). Formation of less concentrated urine (reduction in renal medullary urea concentration) and marked reduction in serum urea nitrogen concentration (Table 2) was attributed to the low-protein food. Aerobic culture of urine resulted in no growth. Survey abdominal radiography, positive-contrast urethrocystography and double-contrast cystography revealed no evidence of uroliths in the lower urinary tract. The vesicourachal diverticulum was still present but reduced in size (Figure 4). Serum albumin (2.7 g/dl), phosphorus (6.7 mg/dl) and urea nitrogen (2 mg/dl) concentrations had decreased from initial values (Table 2).

Because urolith dissolution was complete and because of diet-related alterations in serum phosphorus and albumin concentrations, the food was changed to a moist product designed for growing dogs (Science Diet Canine Growth), fed twice daily. The oral antimicrobial agent was continued for an additional two weeks.

Re-evaluation of the dog 25 days after the initial diagnosis revealed further reduction in the size of the vesicourachal diverticulum. The dog was forming concentrated urine, but still had microscopic hematuria (Table 1). Serum albumin and phosphorus concentrations were normal (Table 2). Antimicrobial therapy was continued.

Fourteen days later (39 days after the initial diagnosis), survey and contrast radiographs revealed no evidence of the vesicourachal diverticulum or uroliths (Figure 5). However, the urethral lumen adjacent to the prostate gland was still reduced. Nevertheless, the dog had no clinical signs of lower urinary tract disease. Although bacteria could not be cultured by aerobic techniques, urinalysis revealed an inflammatory response (Table 1).

No clinical or laboratory evidence of disease was present 73 days after the initial diagnosis (Tables 1 and 2).

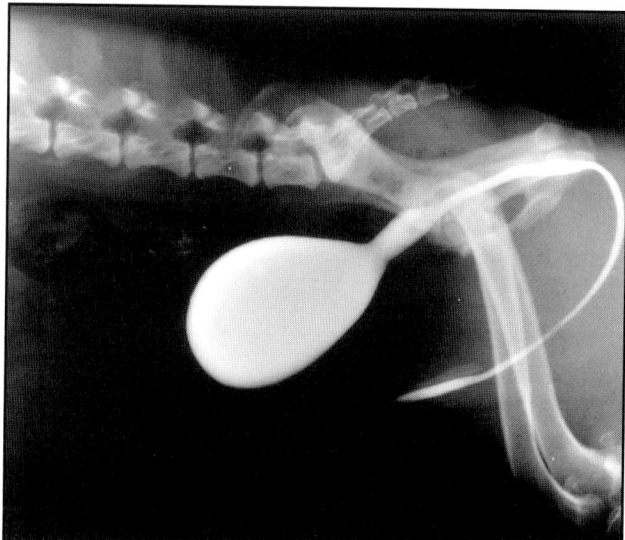

Figure 6. Positive-contrast retrograde urethrocystogram obtained 226 days following initial assessment. The lower urinary tract appears normal.

Antimicrobial therapy was discontinued. Evaluation at 10 months of age revealed a normal dog with no detectable radiographic abnormalities of the lower urinary tract (Figure 6).

Endnotes

a. Hill's Pet Nutrition, Inc., Topeka, KS, USA.

b. Pfizer Animal Health, Exton, PA, USA.

Bibliography

Osborne CA, Lulich JP, Bartges JW, et al. Canine and feline urolithiasis: Relationship of etiopathogenesis to treatment and prevention. In: Osborne CA, Finco DR, eds. Canine and Feline Nephrology and Urology. Baltimore, MD: Williams & Wilkins, 1995; 798-888.

CASE 20-7

Recurrent Urolithiasis in an English Bulldog

Carl A. Osborne, DVM, PhD
Diplomate ACVIM (Internal Medicine)
College of Veterinary Medicine
University of Minnesota
St. Paul, Minnesota, USA

Assess the Animal

A two-year-old, intact male English bulldog with normal body condition (3/5) and weight (24 kg) was evaluated for recurrent urolithiasis. The dog had voided uroliths since it was a puppy. A cystotomy was performed six months earlier to remove urocystoliths, which were not submitted for quantitative mineral analysis. Urethral obstruction occurred three months ago. Urethral patency was re-established by retrograde urohydropropulsion but the uroliths had again not been analyzed. The dog was voiding small uroliths again (Figure 1). Physical examination was normal; uroliths were not palpable in the bladder or urethra.

Results of a complete blood count and serum biochemistry profile were normal, except for a mildly elevated uric acid concentration. Analysis of a urine specimen obtained by cystocentesis revealed the following: specific gravity = 1.035, pH = 6.0, proteinuria, numerous urate crystals and no erythrocytes, leukocytes or bacteria (Table 1). Aerobic bacterial culture of an aliquot of urine was negative.

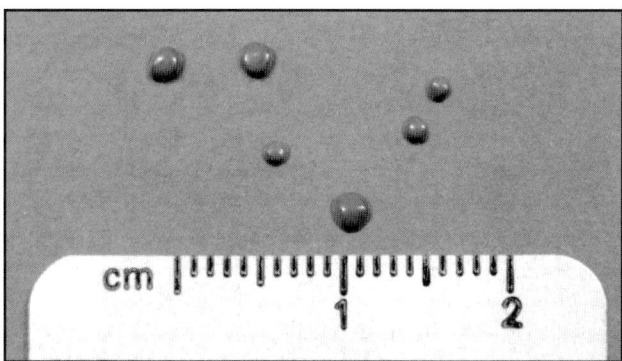

Figure 1. Photograph of ammonium urate uroliths voided by a two-year-old intact male English bulldog.

Uroliths were not detected by survey abdominal radiography (Figure 2). However, numerous small urocystoliths were detected by double-contrast cystography (Figure 3).

Assess the Food(s) and Feeding Method

The dog was fed a commercial dry grocery brand food (Purina Dog Chow[a]) free choice.

Questions

1. Based on the available information, what is the most likely mineral composition of the uroliths in this patient?
2. Outline a treatment and feeding plan for this dog.
3. How should response to therapy to monitored?

Answers and Discussion

1. The mineral composition of the uroliths in this dog is most likely ammonium acid urate based on the following: 1) multiple radiolucent uroliths, 2) urinary pH = 6.0, 3) ammonium urate crystalluria, 4) sterile urine, 5) a slight increase in serum uric acid concentration and 6) the English bulldog breed. Quantitative mineral analysis of a voided urolith would be important to confirm this diagnostic impression.
2. Dissolution of ammonium urate uroliths can be accomplished using a combination of a commercial veterinary therapeutic food (Prescription Diet Canine u/d[b]) and allopurinol (Zyloprim[c]). Secondary urinary tract infections should also be eradicated or controlled with appropriate antimicrobial therapy. Canine u/d contains low levels of dietary purines, which are the precursors of uric acid, and results in production of less concentrated, alkaline urine that enhances urate crystal solubility. Allopurinol is a xanthine oxidase inhibitor that decreases production of uric acid.
3. Therapeutic efficacy should be monitored by physical examination and serial evaluation of radiographs, urinalyses and quantitative urine cultures, if necessary. Dietary therapy and allopurinol should be continued for one month following radiographic disappearance of uroliths. Compliance with the feeding plan is indicated by a reduction in the serum urea nitrogen concentration and formation of less concentrated, alkaline urine.

Table 1. Results of selected urinalysis and serum biochemistry parameters of a two-year-old male English bulldog with recurrent urocystoliths.

Factors	Reference values	Day* 1	35	78	114
Urine specific gravity	–	1.035	1.005	1.006	1.027
Urinary pH	–	6	6	7.5	6
Hematuria	–	0	0	+	+
Pyuria	–	0	0	0	+
Crystals	–	Urate	0	0	Urate
Urine culture	–	Neg	Neg	Neg	Neg
SUN (mg/dl)	7-28	13	4	4	8
Creatinine (mg/dl)	0.5-1.5	1.1	0.7	0.7	0.9
Albumin (g/dl)	2.4-3.8	3.3	3.0	3.1	3.5

Key: 0 = absent, + = present, Neg = negative, SUN = serum urea nitrogen.
*Therapy consisting of a calculolytic food and allopurinol was initiated on Day 1 and discontinued on Day 78.

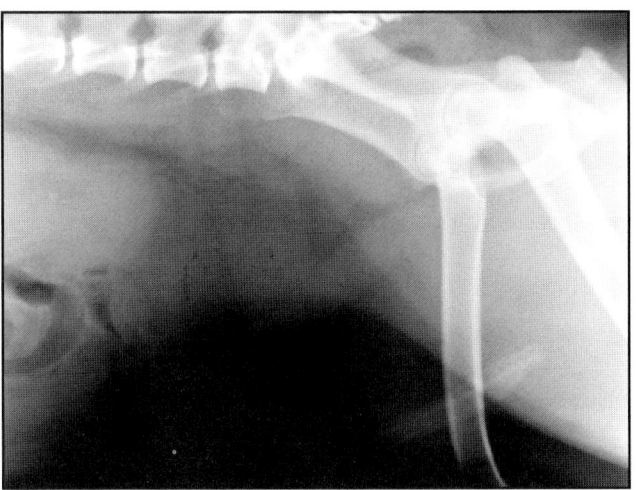

Figure 2. Survey abdominal radiograph of the same dog described in Figure 1. The dog voided small ammonium urate uroliths during micturition. Note that radiodense uroliths are not detectable in the bladder.

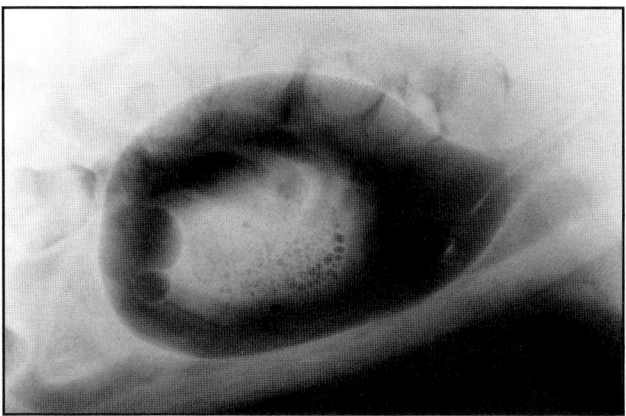

Figure 3. Double-contrast cystogram of the same dog described in Figure 1 demonstrating numerous ammonium urate urocystoliths.

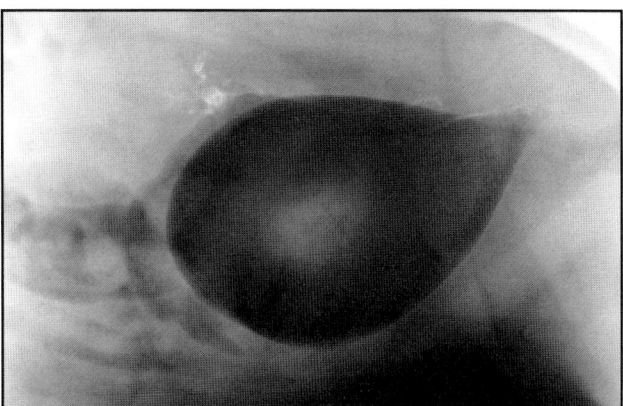

Figure 4. Double-contrast cystogram of the same dog described in Figure 1 obtained 35 days after initiating therapy. There is no evidence of urocystoliths.

Progress Notes

Quantitative analysis of a voided urolith confirmed it was composed of 100% ammonium acid urate. Combination therapy with Canine u/d moist food and allopurinol (15 mg/kg body weight, per os, twice daily) was initiated. The daily energy requirement was estimated to be approximately 1,265 kcal (5.29 MJ) (1.6 x resting energy requirement) or one can of Canine u/d twice daily. By Day 35 following initiation of therapy, there was no radiographic evidence of uroliths (Figure 4). Urinalysis revealed less concentrated urine with no evidence of crystalluria. The serum urea nitrogen concentration was decreased, which implied good compliance with the feeding plan (Table 1). The dietary and drug therapy was continued for another month. Similar clinical findings were observed (Table 1, Day 78).

The owner elected to discontinue both the dietary and drug therapy. By Day 114 after the original diagnosis, urine specific gravity was increased and pyuria and urate crystalluria were evident (Table 1). The dog was voiding uroliths again three months later. These uroliths were found to be composed of 100% ammonium acid urate. Multiple urocystoliths were confirmed by double-contrast cystography. Combination dietary and drug therapy was used again for dissolution of the uroliths. Prevention of recurrence included feeding Canine u/d moist food and using allopurinol only as necessary to help control urate crystalluria. Monitoring over the next nine months docu-

mented one episode of bacterial urinary tract infection; however, the dog had been asymptomatic and no uroliths were detected by contrast radiography.

Endnotes

a. Ralston Purina Co., St. Louis, MO, USA.
b. Hill's Pet Nutrition, Inc., Topeka, KS, USA.
c. Glaxo Welcome Inc., Research Triangle Park, NC, USA.

Bibliography

Osborne CA, Lulich JP, Bartges JW, et al. Canine and feline urolithiasis: Relationship of etiopathogenesis to treatment and prevention. In: Osborne CA, Finco DR, eds. Canine and Feline Nephrology and Urology. Baltimore, MD: Williams & Wilkins, 1995; 798-888.

CASE 20-8
Recurrent Urinary Tract Infection in a Rottweiler

Carl A. Osborne, DVM, PhD
Diplomate ACVIM (Internal Medicine)
College of Veterinary Medicine
University of Minnesota
St. Paul, Minnesota, USA

Assess the Animal

A five-year-old, 41-kg, neutered male rottweiler was examined for recurrent dysuria and pollakiuria of six months' duration, presumed to be caused by bacterial urinary tract infection. These clinical signs had been treated intermittently with a variety of orally administered antibiotics given for intervals ranging from 10 to 21 days.

Table 1. Results of selected urinalysis and serum biochemistry parameters of a five-year-old neutered male rottweiler with recurrent urinary tract infection.

Factors	Reference values	Week*							
		0	5	9	13	18	25	29	34
Urine specific gravity	–	1.015	1.007	1.007	1.007	1.015	1.008	1.022	1.015
Urinary pH	–	7	6	6	8	7	7	7.5	6
Hematuria	–	+	+	+	0	0	0	0	0
Pyuria	–	+	0	0	0	0	0	0	0
Bacteriuria	–	+	0	0	0	0	0	0	0
SUN (mg/dl)	7-28	26	5	9	5	6	6	13	11
Creatinine (mg/dl)	0.50-1.5	1.6	1.4	1.4	1.4	1.1	1.1	1.5	1.1
Magnesium (mg/dl)	1.5-2.7	2.3	1.9	1.8	2.0	1.8	1.6	1.8	2.0
Albumin (g/dl)	2.4-3.8	3.5	3.1	3.3	3.3	3.4	2.9	3.5	3.4
Alkaline phosphatase (U/l)	10-149	28	56	67	65	123	164	43	29

Key: + = present, 0 = absent, SUN = serum urea nitrogen.
*Therapy with a calculolytic food and antibiotics was initiated during Week 1 and discontinued on Week 25.

Treatment was associated with remission of dysuria and pollakiuria, but these signs recurred a short time following cessation of therapy.

The results of physical examination, including rectal palpation and body condition assessment (body condition score 3/5), were normal. Micturition was normal. Analysis of a urine sample collected by cystocentesis revealed that the urine was slightly concentrated (specific gravity 1.015), had a neutral pH and contained evidence of inflammation, most likely due to an infectious process (Table 1). Crystals were not observed. Aerobic culture of an aliquot of urine revealed significant numbers (>10^5 colony-forming units/ml) of urease-producing *Staphylococcus intermedius*, which was susceptible to many antimicrobial agents. Results of a complete blood count and serum biochemistry profile were normal (Table 1).

Problems identified on the basis of the animal assessment included bacterial urinary tract infection characterized by dysuria and pollakiuria, possible impaired urine concentrating capacity and hematuria, pyuria, proteinuria and bacteriuria.

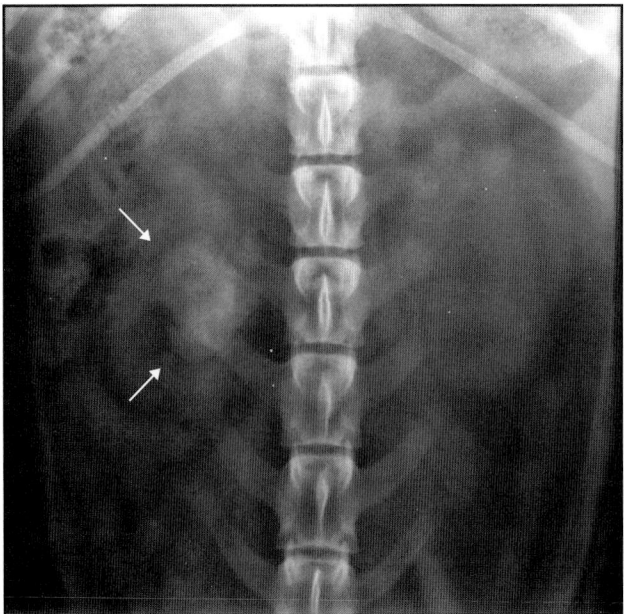

Figure 1. Survey ventrodorsal abdominal radiograph illustrating a large radiodense nephrolith (arrows) in the renal pelvis of the right kidney of a five-year-old neutered male rottweiler.

Assess the Food(s) and Feeding Method

The dog was fed a commercial dry adult maintenance food free choice and offered commercial treats/snacks several times each day.

Questions

1. What is the anatomic site or sites of the bacterial urinary tract infection?
2. Are further diagnostic tests justified for this patient?

Answers and Discussion

1. Dysuria and pollakiuria suggest involvement of the lower urinary tract but formation of urine with a specific gravity of 1.015 in absence of azotemia suggests that ascending infection may have involved the medullary portions of the kidney.
2. Additional diagnostic tests should be considered because: 1) the bacterial urinary tract infection appears to be recurrent, 2) the sites of infection and inflammation have not been confirmed and 3) the predisposing causes of infection are unknown. There is no evidence of diabetes mellitus or hyperadrenocorticism, both of which are frequently associated with recurrent bacterial urinary tract infection. Another urinalysis is indicated to assess the concentrating capacity of the kidneys. Survey and contrast abdominal radiography and/or ultrasonography will help evaluate the patient for uroliths, neoplasia and anatomic abnormalities. These imaging procedures will also assist in evaluation of the prostate gland.

Further Assessment

Results of a second urinalysis included a urine specific gravity of 1.021. Hematuria, pyuria, proteinuria and bacteriuria were still present. Survey radiography and ultrasonography of the abdomen revealed a large urolith in the pelvis of the right kidney (Figure 1 and 2). Retrograde positive-contrast urethrocystography revealed normal size, shape and position of the lower urinary tract and prostate gland. Double-contrast cystography revealed a few uroliths approximately 1 mm in diameter in the bladder. An intravenous urogram revealed no evidence of outflow obstruction in the ureters (Figure 2).

Further Questions

1. On the basis of the available data, what is the most likely mineral composition of this patient's uroliths?

2. Why were crystals not identified in the urine sediment even though the patient had multiple uroliths?
3. Outline a treatment and feeding plan for this dog.

Answers and Discussion

1. The mineral composition of the nephrolith and urocystoliths most likely is infection-induced struvite because: 1) staphylococci may cause formation of struvite uroliths, 2) very large radiodense nephroliths are usually composed of infection-induced struvite, 3) the urinary pH was not acidic and 4) crystals associated with other types of uroliths were not detected.
2. The combination of risk factors necessary for struvite crystals to form was not present at the time urine samples were collected for analysis. Consumption of food that usually results in acidic urine, administration of an antibiotic and formation of poorly concentrated urine may have reduced the likelihood of struvite crystalluria.
3. Dissolution of nephroliths presumed to be composed of infection-induced struvite can be accomplished using a combination of a commercial veterinary therapeutic food (Prescription Diet Canine s/dª) and antimicrobial therapy. In studies conducted at the University of Minnesota, the mean time required for dissolution of infection-induced nephroliths was 26 weeks (range nine to 42 weeks). Nephroliths and/or ureteroliths causing complete outflow obstruction and marked impairment of function in the associated kidney should be managed by surgical intervention. Surgical removal of uroliths has the obvious advantage of rapid correction of the mechanical components of the disease process; however, surgery cannot be relied upon to remove very small uroliths or to prevent their recurrence. Likewise, nephrectomy is always associated with destruction of nephrons, the magnitude of which is influenced by the number of renal end arteries that are transected.

Progress Notes

The owners requested medical treatment. A combination of a struvite calculolytic food and a bactericidal antimicrobial agent (amoxicillin and clavulanic acidᵇ), chosen on the basis of antimicrobial susceptibility results, was used. The daily energy requirement was estimated to be approximately 1,800 kcal (7.5 MJ) (1.4 x resting energy requirement) or 1.5 cans of Canine s/d twice daily. In order to facilitate dietary compliance, the owners were asked to restrict treats to baked slices of the moist therapeutic food. Therapeutic efficacy was monitored by physical examination and serial evaluation of survey radiographs (a ventrodorsal view is best for nephroliths and a lateral view is best for urocystoliths), urinalyses, urine cultures, serum biochemistry profiles and complete blood counts (Table 1). A reduction in the serum urea nitrogen concentration and formation of less concentrated urine indicates compliance with the feeding plan.

Survey abdominal radiographs obtained at four- to five-week intervals revealed progressive reduction in the size of the nephrolith (Figure 3). Radiodense uroliths could not be detected on Week 18 (Figure 4). After initiation of antimicrobial therapy, bacteria could not be cultured from urine samples collected by cystocentesis. Urinalysis

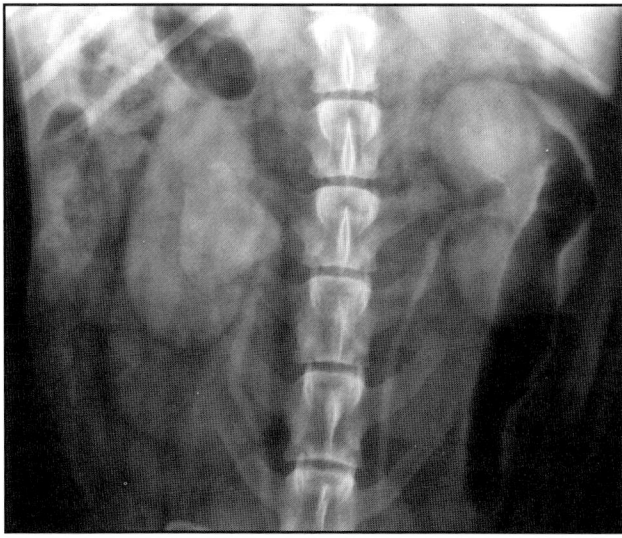

Figure 2. Intravenous urogram of the same dog described in Figure 1 showing both ureters filled with contrast material and no evidence of outflow obstruction.

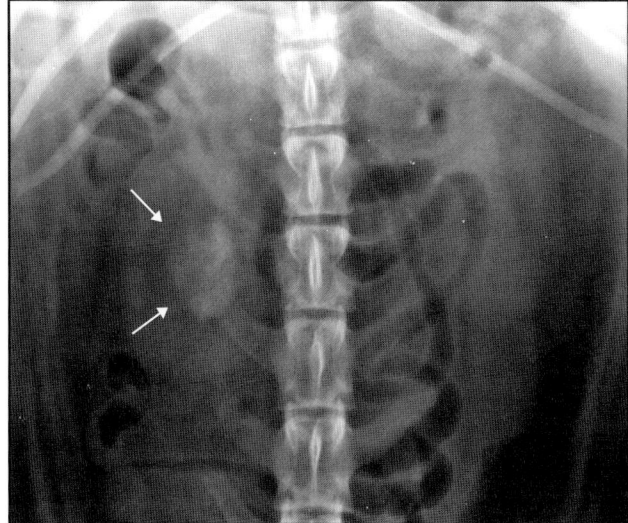

Figure 3. Survey ventrodorsal radiograph obtained five weeks after initiation of therapy with a calculolytic food and antibiotics. The nephrolith (arrows) is about 75% of its original size.

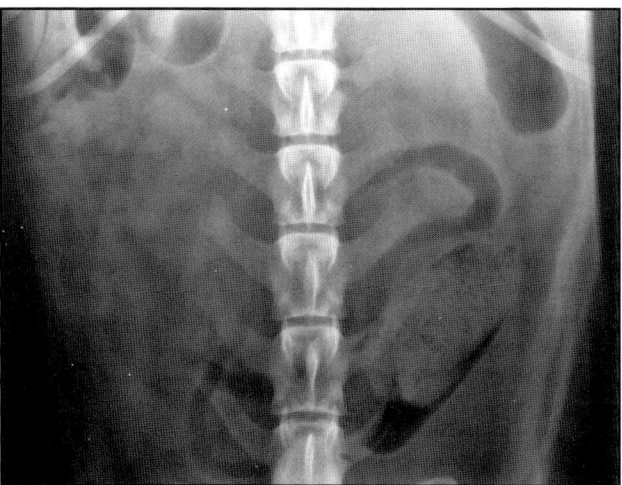

Figure 4. Survey ventrodorsal abdominal radiograph obtained 18 weeks after initiation of therapy. There is no evidence of the nephrolith in the right kidney.

revealed progressive reduction in hematuria and pyuria (Table 1).

Consumption of the calculolytic food was associated with polyuria, formation of less concentrated urine, reduction in the serum concentration of urea nitrogen and magnesium and an increase in serum alkaline phosphatase activity. Clinically significant changes were not observed in serial hemograms. Dietary and antimicrobial therapy was discontinued on Week 25. Most diagnostic parameters returned to baseline values by Weeks 29 and 34 (Table 1).

The owners indicated that the dog readily consumed the food and gained 3.5 kg during the treatment period. Decreasing the amount of food offered and consumed during the treatment period may have prevented significant weight gain.

Endnotes

a. Hill's Pet Nutrition, Inc., Topeka, KS, USA.

b. Pfizer Animal Health, Exton, PA, USA.

Bibliography

Osborne CA, Lulich JP, Bartges JW, et al. Canine and feline urolithiasis: Relationship of etiopathogenesis to treatment and prevention. In: Osborne CA, Finco DR, eds. Canine and Feline Nephrology and Urology. Baltimore, MD: Williams & Wilkins, 1995, 798-888.

CHAPTER 21

Feline Lower Urinary Tract Disease

Timothy A. Allen

John M. Kruger

"It is a common error to infer that things which are consecutive in order of time have necessarily the relations of cause and effect."
Jacob Bigelow

ASSESSMENT

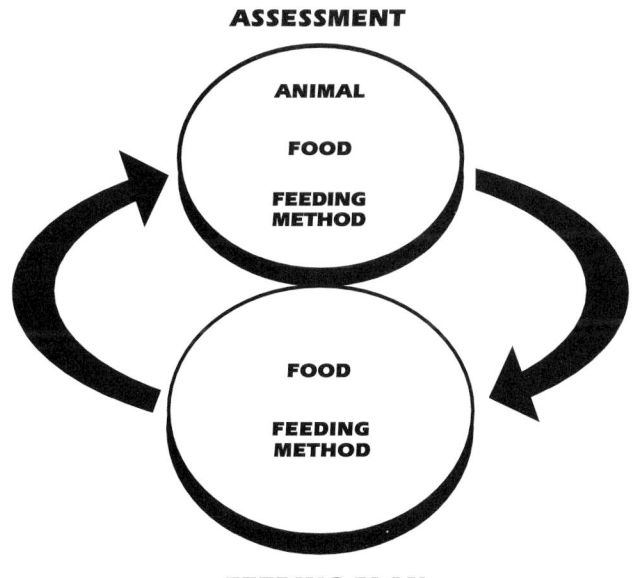

FEEDING PLAN

Note: The reader is referred to Chapter 1 for a detailed discussion of the iterative process of clinical nutrition.

CLINICAL IMPORTANCE

Urolithiasis, urinary tract infection (UTI), neoplasia, inflammation and congenital defects of the urinary tract cause signs of lower urinary tract disease. Although feline lower urinary tract disease (FLUTD) has diverse causes, this chapter will focus on struvite and calcium oxalate urolithiasis and idiopathic causes. The incidence of FLUTD is unknown. Previous estimates of the incidence in the United States and the United Kingdom have been approximately 0.85 to 1.0% per year.[1,2] These estimates were based on only the presence of clinical signs and therefore did not consider subsets of cats with specific diagnoses, such as struvite urolithiasis or idiopathic lower urinary tract disease. Clinical nutrition is an important adjunct in the management of struvite, and to a lesser extent, calcium oxalate urolithiasis. Generally, idiopathic lower urinary tract disease resolves within seven to 10 days, regardless of the feeding plan.

The frequency with which cases are seen at veterinary hospitals is the proportional morbidity rate. The proportional morbidity rate of cats with lower urinary tract disease has been reported to be as high as 10%.[3] Although the more commonly reported proportional morbidity rate is between 1 and 6%.[3,4] Proportional morbidity rates, however, are not reliable estimates of disease incidence because morbidity rates are affected by such parameters as type of veterinary practice, expertise of veterinarians and economic status of clients served by veterinary hospitals.

Another measure of the importance of a clinical problem is the degree of owner concern. In the Animal Health Survey prepared for the Morris Animal Foundation in

KEY WORDS & TERMS—FELINE LOWER URINARY TRACT DISEASE*

Activity product	Glomerulations	Proportional morbidity
Activity product ratio	Idiopathic cystitis	Urethral plugs
Analytes	Incidence	Urinary acidifier
Crystalluria	Interstitial cystitis	Urolith
Feline lower urinary tract disease	Metastable solution	Urolithiasis
(FLUTD)	Nucleation	
Feline urologic syndrome (FUS)	Prevalence	

Key words and terms are defined in the Glossary.

KEY POINTS—FELINE LOWER URINARY TRACT DISEASE

1. The clinical signs of hematuria, dysuria, pollakiuria and/or urethral obstruction are the hallmarks of feline lower urinary tract disease (FLUTD).
2. It is well established that FLUTD may result from a number of different etiologies including infection, urolithiasis, neoplasia, neurologic disorders, anatomic abnormalities and inflammatory conditions.
3. Struvite (magnesium ammonium phosphate) and calcium oxalate are the most common minerals associated with feline uroliths and urethral plugs.
4. Less common feline uroliths include those composed of ammonium acid urate, calcium phosphate, cystine and xanthine.
5. Microscopic examination of urine sediment from cats with lower urinary tract disease helps: 1) detect conditions that may predispose a cat to urolith or urethral plug formation, 2) infer mineral composition of uroliths or urethral plugs and 3) evaluate response to treatment or preventive measures.
6. Urine cultures are negative in cats with idiopathic lower urinary tract disease.
7. Urinary pH varies throughout the day due to the influence of food, time of eating, method of feeding and amount of food consumed.
8. Survey radiography or ultrasonography may not detect uroliths less than 3 mm in diameter.
9. Feline nephroliths are more commonly composed of calcium salts than struvite.
10. Because recommendations for urolith dissolution and prevention are mineral-composition specific, uroliths should be analyzed quantitatively whenever possible.
11. Uroliths consist of small amounts of matrix and macroscopic crystalline mineral concretions.
12. In its simplest form, the initiation and growth of uroliths, and perhaps urethral plugs, involves chemical precipitation of dissolved ions or molecules from a solution that is supersaturated with respect to those components.
13. Comparisons have been drawn between idiopathic FLUTD and interstitial cystitis in human beings.
14. Idiopathic cystitis in cats is probably not amenable to nutritional therapy.
15. Key nutritional factors for cats with or at risk for struvite uroliths or urethral plugs are protein, phosphorus, magnesium and urinary pH. Other food factors of interest in these patients include potassium and fat.
16. Key nutritional factors for cats at risk for calcium oxalate uroliths are protein, calcium, sodium, magnesium and urinary pH. Other food factors of interest in these patients include oxalate, vitamin D and pyridoxine.
17. Medical protocols are available for dissolution of struvite uroliths but not calcium oxalate uroliths.
18. Moist rather than dry foods can be used to increase water consumption and thus reduce the urinary concentration of crystal-forming elements.
19. A urinalysis, including urinary pH measurement and microscopic sediment examination, should be conducted at least every six months in cats at risk for urolith formation.
20. The widespread use of urinary acidifying drugs for nonobstructive lower urinary tract disease in cats is not recommended.

1998, 2,003 animal owners indicated that their top feline health concerns were urinary diseases, dentistry, cancer and feline leukemia.[5]

ASSESSMENT

Assess the Animal

History

The dietary history should include specific brand(s) of food fed, the form (dry, moist, semi-moist or a combination), method of feeding (meal fed, free choice) and whether table food, supplements and treats are offered. Access to other food should be assessed (e.g., other pets in the household that eat different foods, access to food at other households, etc.). Trends in water consumption (i.e., increased, decreased, unchanged) should be ascertained and recorded.

The pet owner should be carefully questioned about: 1) the duration of clinical signs, 2) progression of clinical signs (same, better, worse), 3) whether the episode was the patient's first or a recurrence, 4) the interval between recurrences, 5) previous treatments (medical, surgical, nutritional), including doses of pharmaceutical agents prescribed and response to therapy, 6) presence of other illnesses, injuries or trauma (current or previous), 7) presence of systemic signs (anorexia, vomiting, diarrhea,

KEY NUTRITIONAL FACTORS—FELINE LOWER URINARY TRACT DISEASE

Factors	Dietary recommendations
Struvite uroliths and urethral plugs	
Water	Promote water intake by using a moist food or other measures
Protein	Avoid excess dietary protein Dissolution and prevention: restrict dietary protein to 30 to 45% dry matter
Phosphorus	Avoid excess dietary phosphorus Dissolution: restrict dietary phosphorus to 0.5 to 0.8% dry matter Prevention: restrict dietary phosphorus to 0.5 to 0.9% dry matter
Magnesium	Avoid excess dietary magnesium Dissolution: restrict dietary magnesium to 0.04 to 0.06% dry matter Prevention: restrict dietary magnesium to 0.04 to 0.10% dry matter
Mean daily urinary pH	Use a food that maintains an acidic urine Dissolution: urinary pH = 5.9 to 6.1 Prevention: urinary pH = 6.2 to 6.4
Calcium oxalate uroliths (prevention)	
Water	Promote water intake by using a moist food or other measures
Protein	Avoid excess dietary protein Restrict dietary protein to 30 to 45% dry matter
Calcium	Avoid excess dietary calcium Restrict dietary calcium to 0.5 to 0.8% dry matter
Sodium	Avoid excess dietary sodium Restrict dietary sodium to 0.10 to 0.40% dry matter
Magnesium	Avoid excess or deficient dietary magnesium (0.04 to 0.10% dry matter)
Mean daily urinary pH	Use a food that maintains a urinary pH between 6.6 to 6.8

FLUTD

weight loss) and 8) presence of localizing signs such as licking at the prepuce or vulva and altered micturition or altered urine characteristics.

The pet owner's description of micturition is especially important. Questions should be directed to determine the presence or absence of the following parameters: 1) dysuria, 2) pollakiuria, 3) urinary incontinence, 4) micturition in unusual places, 5) hematuria and 6) uroliths or urethral plugs voided during micturition. The approximate urine volume and changes should be determined.

Pharmaceutical agents administered should be recorded as described above. Specific pharmaceutical agents may be risk factors for FLUTD. Corticosteroids and furosemide can predispose cats to hypercalcemia and hypercalciuria. Sulfadiazine-containing drugs may predispose cats to uroliths containing varying amounts of sulfadiazine. Allopurinol may predispose cats to xanthine uroliths or shells. Urinary acidifiers can cause metabolic acidosis and subsequent hypercalciuria and may predispose cats to calcium-containing uroliths.

Physical Examination

The urinary bladder should be palpated to evaluate its size, shape, surface contours, thickness of the bladder wall, pain and masses and grating within the bladder lumen. Most feline urocystoliths, however, cannot be detected by abdominal palpation. The penis and prepuce should be examined for urethral abnormalities. Rectal palpation should be performed to assess the size, position and shape of the urethra and any associated masses or pain. The kidneys should be evaluated for size, shape, surface contour and bilateral symmetry. The patient should be observed micturating, if possible (i.e., size of urine stream, dysuria, color of urine).

Laboratory and Other Clinical Information

The following diagnostic studies are often used to evaluate cats with lower urinary tract disease: 1) urinalyses, 2) quantitative urine culture(s), 3) survey abdominal radiography, 4) contrast urethrocystography if urethral plugs or uroliths are noted, 5) intravenous urography or contrast cystography if cystoliths are noted, 6) intravenous urography if ureteral or renal uroliths are noted, 7) ultrasonography of kidneys and urinary bladder, 8) complete blood cell counts, 9) serum biochemistry profiles and 10) cystoscopy (Table 21-1).

URINALYSIS

Urine sediment findings in cats with urolithiasis usually indicate inflammation (i.e., pyuria, proteinuria, hematuria and increased numbers of epithelial cells). Microscopic examination of urine sediment helps: 1) detect conditions that may predispose cats to urolith or urethral plug formation, 2) infer mineral composition of uroliths or urethral plugs (Figure 21-1) and 3) evaluate response to treatment or preventive measures.[6] Hematuria and proteinuria are typical urinalysis findings in cats with idiopathic lower urinary tract disease.

Crystals only form when urine is supersaturated with crystallogenic materials. Therefore, crystalluria is a risk factor for formation of uroliths and urethral plugs. However, crystalluria is not, in itself, pathognomonic for uroliths or urethral plugs. (See sidebar "Management of Crystalluria.") Urine crystals can be an artifact due to external factors that influence crystal formation, such as temperature, evaporation, urinary pH and method of sediment specimen preparation. Conversely, urolithiasis is possible without associated crystalluria.

Table 21-1. Summary of diagnostic plans—feline lower urinary tract disease.

Clinical findings	Rule outs	Uncomplicated minimum database	Recurrent minimum database
Hematuria with dysuria	Idiopathic disease Urolithiasis	Urinalysis Survey radiography	Bacterial urine culture Double-contrast cystography Serum biochemistry profile Ultrasonography Cystoscopy
Hematuria without dysuria	Renal hemorrhage Lower urinary tract hemorrhage Coagulopathy Catheter or cystocentesis related	Voided urinalysis Survey radiography Complete blood count Bleeding time Prothrombin time	Intravenous urography Platelet count Cystoscopy Serum biochemistry profile
Urethral obstruction	Urethral plug (matrix + crystals) Urolithiasis	Urinalysis Urine culture Survey radiography Urea nitrogen Creatinine Potassium	Urethrocystography Ultrasonography Serum biochemistry profile

Management of Crystalluria

Detection of crystalluria does not mean a cat will subsequently develop urolithiasis. Crystalluria that occurs in cats with normal anatomy and physiology of the urinary tract is usually of no clinical significance. These crystals are voided before they grow to sufficient size to interfere with urinary tract function and health.

Crystals that form after a urine specimen is collected or voided are often of no clinical importance. Temperature, evaporation and pH are in vitro variables that may cause a urine specimen to become oversaturated, leading to crystal formation. Importantly, in vitro conditions may cause crystals to dissolve or grow. Urine allowed to remain at room temperature after collection may lose carbon dioxide into the atmosphere, affecting the pH value. Bacterial contamination of urine specimens may also occur. Urease-producing bacteria (e.g., staphylococci, *Proteus* spp) alkalinize urine, possibly altering crystal composition and disrupting cellular components in urine (e.g., RBCs, WBCs). Other bacteria produce acid metabolites with similar consequences. Urine samples should be analyzed promptly (within 15 minutes) when an accurate interpretation of urine crystals is important. Serial evaluations provide more diagnostic information. Urine samples should be refrigerated if they cannot be evaluated promptly.

The diet, including water intake, may affect crystalluria. Diagnostically, this phenomenon is important if cats are fed different foods in hospital settings than at home.

Crystalluria (if present) should not be used as the sole criterion to predict the mineral type of confirmed uroliths. Only quantitative analysis of a retrieved urolith can provide that information. However, in the absence of a urolith, crystalluria can be used along with other factors such as history, age, breed, urinary pH, radiographic appearance, other urinalysis findings and biochemistry profile results to predict mineral type. Uroliths may be present without concurrent crystalluria. In this case, factors that influenced the formation and growth of crystals may be transiently absent. Factors typically responsible for this phenomenon include food changes, anorexia, increased water intake, different urinary pH values and the in vitro changes mentioned above in urine specimens that are not fresh. The crystal type may be different from the urolith type in some cases. This dichotomy exists when cats are assumed to have one urolith type, which isn't confirmed by quantitative analysis (e.g., assumed to have struvite uroliths and fed according to struvite dissolution or preventive protocols), when in reality the cat has a calcium oxalate urolith and calcium oxalate crystalluria. Finally, cats may have more than one crystal type concurrently (i.e., struvite and calcium oxalate).

Struvite crystals may occur in: 1) normal cats, 2) cats with infection-induced struvite uroliths, 3) cats with sterile struvite uroliths, 4) cats with nonstruvite uroliths, 5) cats with uroliths of mixed mineral type and 6) cats with urinary tract disease without uroliths. Calcium oxalate dihydrate crystals occur uncommonly in normal cats. Large quantities of these crystals alone or in combination with calcium oxalate monohydrate crystals in fresh urine specimens probably indicate a hypercalciuric or hyperoxaluric disorder such as ethylene glycol toxicity or calcium oxalate urolithiasis. However, calcium oxalate crystals may occur in normal cats.

Should crystalluria be treated? Cystine and ammonium urate crystalluria should always be investigated and the cause treated. Struvite and calcium oxalate crystalluria without urolithiasis in patients with no history of urolithiasis should be monitored serially. Frequent detection of large crystals and aggregates of crystals may be clinically important, especially if the cat has a history of urolith formation. In this case, preventive nutritional therapy should be implemented, and the cat should be encouraged to increase its water intake. Crystalluria can be used as a preventive index. Crystalluria should be reduced or eliminated with appropriate medical and pharmacologic therapy.

BIBLIOGRAPHY

Osborne CA, Lulich JP, Ulrich LK, et al. Feline crystalluria. Veterinary Clinics of North America: Small Animal Practice 1996; 26: 369-391.

Osborne CA, Stevens JB, Lulich JP, et al. A clinician's analysis of urinalysis. In: Osborne CA, Finco DR, eds. Canine and Feline Nephrology and Urology. Baltimore, MD: Williams & Wilkins, 1995; 188-203.

Because crystals formed after voiding are not significant, examination of sediment from fresh, warm urine specimens is recommended. Diagnostic agents (e.g., radiographic contrast agents) and drugs (e.g., sulfonamides) can produce urinary crystals. Several factors influence the number of crystals, including the volume of urine centrifuged, centrifugation speed and the volume of sediment resuspended and transferred to the microscope slide. Consequently, it is difficult to attach clinical significance to the number of crystals observed. In addition to evaluating crystal type, the sediment should be evaluated for tendencies for crystals to aggregate. Detection of large aggregates of struvite or calcium oxalate crystals is an important finding when monitoring the efficacy of preventive measures. In summary, it is important to interpret crystalluria in the context of the patient's medical history, the laboratory methods used and the complete laboratory findings.

URINE CULTURE

Infection with urease-producing staphylococci and *Proteus* spp may be associated with formation of struvite uroliths (Table 21-2). Urinary pH is persistently alkaline with UTI due to urease-producing microorganisms. Infection can also result from bacterial colonization of the urinary tract due to urolith-induced changes in host defense mechanisms. Thirty percent of feline patients with urocystoliths have positive urine cultures.[6] Although UTIs are uncommon in young cats, they become a significant cause of urinary tract disease in cats

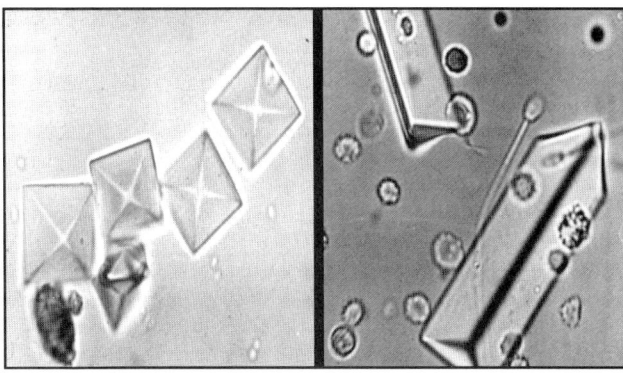

Figure 21-1. Common crystals found in urine of cats with urolithiasis. Calcium oxalate dihydrate crystals (Left) typically are colorless and have a characteristic octahedral or envelope shape. They resemble small squares whose corners are connected by intersecting diagonal lines. Magnesium ammonium phosphate (struvite) crystals (Right) typically are colorless, orthorhombic, coffin-like prisms. Struvite crystals may have square or rectangular dimensions, vary in size, may have three to six sides and often have oblique ends.

10 years of age and older.[7] Microorganisms may remain viable within uroliths. Culture of urine may be negative or yield the same or different organisms than cultures from uroliths. Urine cultures are negative in cats with idiopathic lower urinary tract disease and feline interstitial cystitis.

FLUTD

Table 21-2. Checklist of factors that suggest probable mineral composition of feline uroliths.*

Urinary pH
    Struvite and calcium apatite uroliths, usually alkaline. Sterile struvite uroliths may be observed with urinary pH values of 6.5 or higher.
    Ammonium urate uroliths, acidic to neutral.**
    Cystine uroliths, acidic.**
    Calcium oxalate, often acidic to neutral.**

Identification of crystals in uncontaminated fresh urine sediment, preferably at body temperature

Type of bacteria, if any, isolated from urine
    Urease from bacteria, especially staphylococci and less frequently *Proteus* spp, may be associated with struvite uroliths.
    Urinary tract infections often are absent in patients with calcium oxalate, cystine or ammonium urate uroliths.
    Calcium oxalate, cystine or ammonium urate uroliths may predispose to urinary tract infections. If infections are caused by urease-producing bacteria, struvite may precipitate around metabolic uroliths.

Radiographic density and physical characteristics of uroliths
    Struvite, 1+ to 4+ radiopacity, uroliths are rough or smooth, round or faceted, sometimes disk-shaped.
    Calcium oxalate, 3+ to 4+ radiopacity, uroliths are rough or smooth, usually small, occasionally jackstone shaped.
    Calcium phosphate, 4+ radiopacity, uroliths are smooth or rough, round or faceted.
    Cystine, 0 to 2+ radiopacity, uroliths are smooth, small.
    Ammonium urate/uric acid, 0 to 2+ radiopacity, uroliths are smooth, occasionally irregular.

Serum biochemistry evaluation
    Hypercalcemia may be associated with calcium-containing uroliths.
    Hyperuricemia may be associated with uric acid or urate uroliths.
    Hyperchloremia, hypokalemia and acidemia may be associated with distal renal tubular acidosis and calcium phosphate or struvite uroliths.

Urine chemistry evaluation
    Patient should be consuming a standard diagnostic food or the food consumed when uroliths formed.
    Excessive quantities of one or more minerals contained in the urolith are expected. The concentration of crystallization inhibitors may be decreased.

Breed of cat and history of uroliths in patient's ancestors or littermates

Drugs
    Corticosteroids and furosemide predispose to hypercalciuria.
    Allopurinol predisposes to xanthine uroliths.
    Drugs containing sulfadiazine predispose to formation of uroliths containing varying quantities of sulfadiazine.

Quantitative analysis of uroliths voided during micturition or collected via catheter technique

*Adapted from Osborne CA, Kruger JM, Lulich JP, et al. Disorders of the feline lower urinary tract. In: Osborne CA, Finco DR, eds. Canine and Feline Nephrology and Urology. Baltimore, MD: Williams & Wilkins, 1995; 651.
**Concomitant infection with urease-producing microbes may result in formation of alkaline urine.

URINARY PH

Urinary pH influences formation of several crystal types. Although there are exceptions, certain crystal types tend to form and persist at certain urinary pH ranges (Table 21-2). In general, struvite uroliths are associated with an alkaline urinary pH and calcium oxalate uroliths are associated with an acidic urinary pH.

Urinary pH is not directly regulated, but rather it varies indirectly in response to homeostatically directed changes. In general, renal tubular hydrogen ion secretion influences urinary pH; however, the direct connection is complicated by the quantity of buffer in urine. A number of hormones are responsible for regulation of renal hydrogen ion secretion. In the proximal tubule, α-adrenergic catecholamines increase the rate of hydrogen ion secretion by regulation of Na-H antiporter activity.

Urinary pH can be measured with pH meters or indicator paper. Recently, relatively inexpensive microprocessor-based, pocket-sized pH meters have become available (pH Testr 1 Oakton Model 35624-00[a]). These instruments provide accurate measurements in the hospital and can be dispensed for in-home use by clients.

In laboratories, pH meters with glass electrodes and reference electrodes are used to make pH measurements. The glass electrode is composed of a thin-walled bulb of special hydrogen ion permeable glass surrounding a KCl solution in acetic acid or buffers and a standard electrode. The pH meter does not provide an absolute measure of hydrogen ion concentration and the electrode must be periodically calibrated against buffers of known pH. The hydro-

gen ion concentration of a solution is expressed as pH, which is defined as the logarithm of the reciprocal of the hydrogen ion concentration. Because the logarithm of a reciprocal equals the negative logarithm of a number, pH can also be defined as the negative logarithm of the hydrogen ion concentration. The whole number exponent is the characteristic and the decimal fraction exponent is the mantissa. When the hydrogen ion concentration of a solution is quantitatively expressed, the value for a normal solution of strong acid approaches 1; the value for a normal solution of a strong alkali is 1×10^{-14}. It is convenient, therefore, to express hydrogen ion concentration using logarithmic notation, with the mantissa rounded off to one or two decimal places.

Most multi-test reagent strips and test tapes use indicator paper impregnated with two indicator dyes: methyl red and bromthymol blue. The typical pH range is roughly from 5.0 (orange) to 9.0 (blue). According to most manufacturers, pH values measured with indicator paper are only accurate to within 0.5 pH units. Indicator squares on reagent strips should be compared with the manufacturer's color standards only in well-illuminated areas.

Urinary pH varies throughout the day due to the influence of food, time of eating, method of feeding and amount of food consumed. Consequently, it is difficult to interpret a single urinary pH value, especially if time of eating and food are unknown. Further, it has been reported that simply putting a cat in a carrier and traveling to a veterinary hospital can increase urinary pH.[8]

RADIOGRAPHY

The rationale for radiography is to confirm the diagnosis of urolithiasis. Radiography can determine the size, shape, location and number of uroliths. Survey radiography or ultrasonography may fail to detect small uroliths (i.e., less than 3 mm in diameter).[9] Uroliths greater than 1 mm in diameter can usually be detected with double-contrast cystography, if care is taken not to infuse too much contrast medium.

The relative radiodensity of uroliths can be used to make a rough guess of mineral composition (Table 21-2). Calcium oxalate and struvite uroliths are usually radiodense. Radiographic shape, contour and size can also be used as an inexact predictor of mineral composition. Struvite uroliths can be smooth or rough, round or faceted. Calcium oxalate dihydrate uroliths are usually small, rough and round to oval. Calcium oxalate monohydrate uroliths are usually small, smooth and round. Occasionally, calcium oxalate monohydrate uroliths have a jackstone appearance. The size and number of urocystoliths does not predict whether medical dissolution will be successful.

Feline nephroliths are more commonly composed of calcium salts than struvite. Only approximately 5% of nephroliths are struvite. Nephroliths must be differentiated from dystrophic or metastatic calcification of renal parenchyma, calcified mesenteric lymph nodes and ingesta or medications in the intestinal tract.

ULTRASONOGRAPHY

The use of ultrasonography for evaluation of lower urinary tract disease in cats is limited because of the size and superficial location of the urinary bladder and the location of much of the urethra within the bony pelvis. The bladder should be catheterized and distended with fluid and examined with a high-frequency 7.5-mHz transducer with

---

Table 21-3. Urolith analysis laboratories in the United States.

Corning Clinical Laboratories
2320 Schuetz Road
St. Louis, MO 63146-3417

Heterogeneous Equilibria LTD
John Riter Jr., PhD
2507 South Kearney Street
Denver, CO 80222

Lab Corporation of America
PO Box 2230
Burlington, NC 27215

Laboratory for Stone Research
81 Wyman Street
PO Box 129
Newton, MA 02168

Louis Herring & Co.
PO Box 2191
Orlando, FL 32802

Minnesota Urolith Center
c/o Carl A. Osborne, DVM, PhD
Department of Small Animal Clinical Sciences
College of Veterinary Medicine
University of Minnesota
1352 Boyd Avenue
St. Paul, MN 55108

Urinary Stone Analysis Laboratory
Department of Medicine
Room 3106 MSI-A
School of Veterinary Medicine
Davis, CA 95616

Urolithiasis Laboratory
PO Box 25375
Houston, TX 77265-5375

a built-in or interposed standoff for optimal sonographic evaluation.[10] Without some form of standoff, the urinary bladder may be outside the focal zone of many transducers. Studies comparing the sensitivity and specificity of contrast radiography and ultrasonography for detection and characterization of uroliths are currently underway.

SERUM BIOCHEMISTRY PROFILE

Serum biochemistry profiles are useful in cases of recurrent FLUTD (Table 21-2). Approximately one-third of cats with calcium oxalate uroliths are hypercalcemic. In evaluating cats with concurrent calcium oxalate uroliths and hypercalcemia, the veterinarian should rule out potential causes of persistent hypercalcemia such as hyperparathyroidism, malignancy-associated hypercalcemia and hypervitaminosis D. Presumably, persistent hypercalcemia increases the risk of forming calcium-containing uroliths by increasing the excretion of calcium in urine. It is also possible that the processes involved with formation of calcium-containing uroliths and hypercalcemia are unrelated.

Acidemia, as evidenced by decreased total carbon dioxide, is also common in patients with calcium oxalate uroliths. Metabolic acidosis may contribute to calcium urolith formation. Normal serum concentrations do not rule out increased urinary concentrations of calculogenic substances. Increased serum concentrations of calculogenic substances (e.g., calcium) may provide clues about the underlying etiology of uroliths. Automated chemistry methods used to assay uric acid in human serum can be misleading in cats.

UROLITH ANALYSIS

Because recommendations for urolith dissolution and prevention are mineral composition specific, it is important to analyze uroliths whenever possible. In addition to surgical removal, several less invasive techniques for obtaining uroliths should always be considered. These methods include retrieval with a urinary catheter, voiding urohydropropulsion and voiding into an empty or plastic bead-filled litter box.[11]

Uroliths can be analyzed qualitatively or quantitatively. Qualitative analysis uses spot tests to identify radicals and ions; however, these tests do not reveal the proportion of mineral types and do not detect certain mineral crystals such as silica and drug crystals such as sulfadiazine. Qualitative tests lack specificity and sensitivity for analyzing canine uroliths.[9,12,13] Investigators at the Minnesota Urolith Center examined 223 uroliths by qualitative and quantitative methods.[14] Qualitative methods yielded false-negative results in 38.1% of the uroliths and false-positive results in 6.7%; the two methods agreed in only 43.1% of the analyses. Uroliths, therefore, should be analyzed quantitatively (Table 21-3).

Quantitative analysis methods include optical crystallography, x-ray diffraction and infrared spectroscopy. In optical crystallography, crystalline material is removed from representative areas of the urolith using a dissecting microscope. The optical characteristics of the crystalline material (e.g., refractive index and birefringence) are then determined by polarizing microscopy and compared with known standards to determine mineral composition. Methods such as infrared spectroscopy are used if results of optical crystallography are inconclusive.

Different minerals may be deposited in layers or mixed throughout the urolith. Although one mineral type pre-

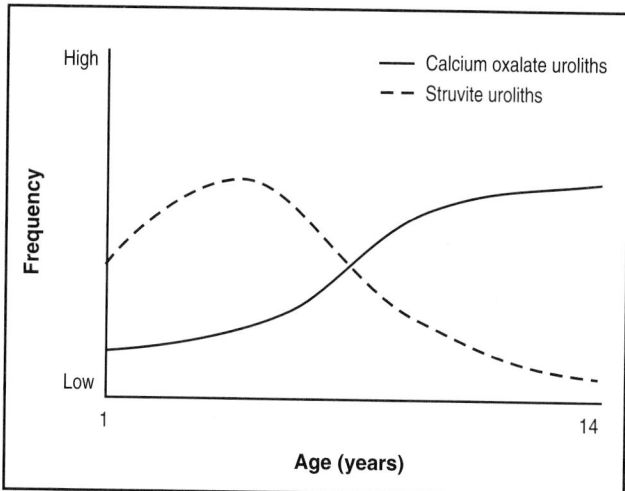

Figure 21-2. The relationship between urolith type and age in cats. Note that struvite urolithiasis occurs more frequently in young cats, whereas calcium oxalate urolithiasis occurs more frequently in older cats.

Table 21-4. Some risk factors reported to occur in cats with lower urinary tract disease.*

Factors	Comments
Age	Uncommon in cats younger than one year. Most common between ages one and 10 years, with peak between two and six years.
Gender	Urethral obstruction occurs most commonly in males. Males and females have a similar risk for nonobstructive forms of the disease.
Neuter status	Increased risk of disease in neutered males and females, regardless of age at neutering.
Food	Consumption of an increased proportion of dry food in the daily ration is associated with increased risk of disease.
Feeding frequency	Increased frequency of feeding is associated with an increased risk of disease, regardless of food.
Excessive weight	Obesity is associated with increased risk of disease.
Water consumption	Decreased daily water consumption is associated with increased risk of disease.
Sedentary lifestyle	Inactive cats are at increased risk for disease.
Spring or winter season	Seasonal variation has been implicated as a risk factor by some investigators, but not by others.
Indoor lifestyle	Cats using indoor litter boxes for micturition and defecation have increased risk for disease.

*Adapted from Osborne CA, Kruger JM, Lulich JP, et al. Disorders of the feline lower urinary tract. In: Osborne CA, Finco DR, eds. Canine and Feline Nephrology and Urology. Baltimore, MD: Williams & Wilkins, 1995; 628.

dominates, the composition of uroliths is frequently mixed. Thus, sampling and reporting results from different parts of the urolith become important when considering urolith dissolution and prevention. The following terms are sometimes used: the *nidus* is where growth apparently started, it is not necessarily the geometric center of the urolith. *Shells* are one or more complete outer layers of the urolith. *Surface crystals* refer to an incom-

FLUTD

plete, outermost layer. Grossly visible layers do not always mean different mineral composition. The layers represent different phases of deposition and may be composed of the same or different minerals.

URINE CHEMISTRY

Measuring levels of key analytes in urine can be helpful in rare clinical cases and as a research method to assess predisposition to urolith formation. The preferred method of measuring the urinary excretion of analytes is 24-hour urine collections. Urinary concentration of calculogenic substances or calculated fractional excretions from spot urine samples are unreliable due to diurnal variation. Because the concentration of calculogenic materials may be influenced by food, the food fed during the 24-hour urine collection should be a standardized test food or the food fed when the urolith(s) formed. The concentration of calculogenic substances also varies in the fasted and postprandial state. Laboratory methods used to assay calculogenic substances should be validated for use in cat urine. Uric acid and ammonium urate may precipitate in refrigerated samples during storage, resulting in falsely lowered levels.

Risk Factors

A review of data from the Veterinary Medical Data Base, Purdue University, West Lafayette, IN, collected between 1980 and 1990 revealed that lower urinary tract disease is more prevalent in cats one to 10 years of age than in cats less than one year of age or more than 10 years of age.[15] The mineral type of urocystoliths and urethroliths in immature cats is usually struvite, associated with infection with urease-producing microorganisms. In general, metabolic uroliths (e.g., calcium oxalate) are rarely observed in immature cats (Figure 21-2).

Table 21-5. Summary of causes of lower urinary tract disease in cats.*

Uroliths
  Struvite
  Calcium oxalate
  Calcium phosphate
  Ammonium urate
  Uric acid
  Cystine
  Xanthine
  Matrix
Urethral plugs
  Struvite crystals only
  Matrix only
  Matrix and struvite crystals
  Matrix and other crystals
Infections
  Bacterial
  Fungal
  Parasitic
  Viral?
  Others?
Other causes
  Interstitial cystitis
  Anatomic abnormalities
  Neoplastic
  Neurogenic
  Traumatic
  Iatrogenic

*Adapted from Osborne CA, Kruger JM, Lulich JP. Feline lower urinary tract disorders: Definition of terms and concepts. Veterinary Clinics of North America: Small Animal Practice 1996; 26: 169-179.

Potential risk factors for formation of sterile struvite uroliths include mineral and moisture content and energy density of the food, method of feeding, urine concentration and retention of urine (Table 21-4).[16,17]

Burmese, Persian and Himalayan breeds are at increased risk for developing calcium oxalate uroliths, but at reduced risk for developing struvite uroliths.[18] Nutritional risk factors associated with calcium oxalate urolith formation in cats include urinary acidifiers, acidifying foods, limited food variety, free-choice feeding and dry foods. By far, the strongest association in one epidemiologic study was urinary acidifiers.[19] The risk of calcium oxalate urolith formation increases with age. Nephroliths are more likely to be composed of calcium oxalate than struvite.

Calcium oxalate nephroliths occur more frequently in people with a family history of nephrolith formation. In addition to genetics, there are several possible explanations for the increased risk. For example, people with a family history of calcium oxalate nephroliths are more likely to share similar environmental risk factors, such as diet and geographic region. In this cohort study, when diet and region were controlled, family history remained a significant association.[20]

Etiopathogenesis

The clinical signs of hematuria, dysuria, pollakiuria and/or urethral obstruction are the hallmarks of FLUTD. It is well established that these signs may result from a number of different etiologies affecting the lower urinary tract (Table 21-5). These etiologies include infection (i.e., bacterial, *Ureaplasma* spp, *Mycoplasma* spp, viral, fungal and parasitic), urolithiasis, neoplasia, neurologic disorders, inflammatory conditions and anatomic abnormalities (i.e., congenital or acquired).[6] The causes of FLUTD may act alone or in combination. The appropriate descriptive term should be applied if a specific cause has been identified. If clinical signs are present and a specific cause is not identified after appropriate evaluation, the preferred term is idiopathic FLUTD.

Between January 1980 and June 1993, 221,477 cats were examined at 23 veterinary colleges and findings recorded in the Veterinary Medical Data Base, Purdue University.[21] Of these 221,477 cats, 15,349 (6.9%) were diagnosed with some type of lower urinary tract disease. Within this category, the five most common recorded diagnoses were feline urologic syndrome (34.3%), cystitis (29.8%), urethral obstruction (21.9%), urethral uroliths (7.6%) and urocystoliths (4.7%). Other less common diagnoses included urinary incontinence, bacterial cystitis, urethral stricture, urinary bladder diverticula and neoplasia.[21]

The real prevalence of the various etiologies of FLUTD is unknown and difficult to discern from a retrospective analysis of a large multi-center database. The largest and most detailed prospective, clinical series characterizing FLUTD was performed from 1982 to 1985 at the University of Minnesota.[22] Table 21-6 presents updated data from that study. Three groups of untreated cats were selected for this series: unobstructed female cats with hematuria, dysuria or both; unobstructed male cats with hematuria, dysuria or both; and male cats with urethral obstruction. Uroliths were detected in 23% (32 of 141) of cats in this study. The majority of the uroliths were struvite. An additional 21% (30 of 141) had urethral plugs. Struvite was the most commonly identified mineral component in these plugs. Struvite crystalluria was also more common in cats with urethral plugs than in cats with other causes of FLUTD and in control cats. Thus, it can be argued that struvite urinary precipitates were involved in roughly 44% of the cases in this series. Seventy-seven (55%) of these cases were diagnosed with idiopathic FLUTD by exclusion of known causes of hematuria, dysuria and urethral obstruction. Table 21-7 presents data from a more recent study involving 109 cats presented for signs of nonobstructive lower urinary tract disease. In this series, an etiologic diagnosis was made in 27% (29/109) of the cases; uroliths were detected in 15% (16/109) of the cases. Based on radiographic or cystoscopic signs of inflammation, 64% (70/109) of the cats in this study had a diagnosis of idiopathic cystitis.[23]

URETHRAL PLUGS

Urethral plugs are typically white or tan unless blood clots are present. Plugs are often cylindrical but sometimes are shapeless (Figure 21-3). Because plugs contain large amounts of matrix, they tend to be soft, compressible and friable. The diameter of cylindrical plugs approximates the diameter of the urethra and their length varies from a few mm to several centimeters. Plugs can be single or multiple.

Urethral plugs and urethral uroliths are physically different and may be due to different pathogenic mechanisms. Urethral plugs are typically composed of large amounts (>50%) of matrix mixed with smaller amounts of crystalline minerals (Table 21-8). However, on occasion, plugs can be composed almost completely of matrix, blood cells, inflammatory cells and sloughed tissue.

Matrix is the nondialysable portion of uroliths and urethral plugs that remains after mild solvents have dissolved crystalline components. It has been hypothesized that matrix provides the "glue" for urolith and plug formation.[24] Specific matrix substances identified in people include matrix substance A, Tamm-Horsfall mucoprotein (uromucoid), albumin and globulins. The exact composition of feline urethral plug matrix is unknown. It is possible that a major component of matrix is Tamm-Horsfall mucoprotein based on the observation that the urinary concentration of Tamm-Horsfall mucoprotein is increased in cats with lower urinary tract disease.[25] Tamm-Horsfall mucoprotein may be a local host defense against bacterial and viral urinary tract infections.

It has been hypothesized that formation of matrix-crystalline urethral plugs requires two simultaneous but unrelated events (Figure 21-4).[26] One event is the formation of matrix that might be due to bacterial or viral UTI or some other inflammatory process (e.g., feline idiopathic cystitis). The other event is the formation of crystalline precipitates. If matrix forms without concomitant crystals, the noncrystalline gel is voided; however, nonobstructive dysuria and hematuria result. In the presence of crystals, a more rigid plug forms that may obstruct the urethra. The mineral composition of crystals can serve as the basis for preventive efforts. This process has been compared with the formation of renal casts in renal tubular lumina. Urinary mucoprotein provides a gel that traps intact cells (cellular casts) or disintegrating cellular elements (granular casts). A more trivial analogy is the creation of fruit gelatin (Figure 21-5). The gelatin (matrix) traps pieces of fruit (crystals) as it forms.

Table 21-6. Type of disorders in 143 cats with hematuria and dysuria.*

Disorders	No. cats	Percent
Idiopathic conditions	77	53.8
Urethral plugs	32	22.4
Uroliths	30	21.0
Uroliths and bacterial UTIs	2	1.4
Bacterial UTIs	2	1.4
Total	143	100.0

Key: UTI = urinary tract infection.
*Adapted from Osborne CA, Polzin DJ, Kruger JM, et al. Relationship of nutritional factors to the cause, dissolution, and prevention of feline uroliths and urethral plugs. Veterinary Clinics of North America: Small Animal Practice 1989; 19: 562.

Table 21-7. Diagnosis by gender of 109 cats with signs of nonobstructive lower urinary tract disease (1993-1995).*

Diagnoses	Male	Female
Idiopathic cystitis	40	30
Anatomic defect	6	6
Behavioral abnormality	4	6
Struvite urolith	6	2
Calcium oxalate urolith	6	1
Neoplasia**	0	2
Unidentified urolith***	0	1
Urinary tract infection	0	1

*Buffington CAT, Chew DJ, Kendall MS, et al. Clinical evaluation of cats with nonobstructive lower urinary tract disease. Journal of the American Veterinary Medical Association 1997; 210: 45-50.
**One cat also had a struvite urolith.
***This cat also had an anatomic defect.

Table 21-8. Mineral composition of 1,050 feline urethral plugs analyzed by quantitative methods.*

Predominant mineral types	Percent
Struvite	76
Matrix	16
Mixed	3.6
Calcium phosphate	2.1
Calcium oxalates	1.4
Ammonium acid urate	0.6

*Adapted from Osborne CA, Kruger JM, Lulich JP. Feline lower urinary tract disorders: Definition of terms and concepts. Veterinary Clinics of North America: Small Animal Practice 1996; 26: 175.

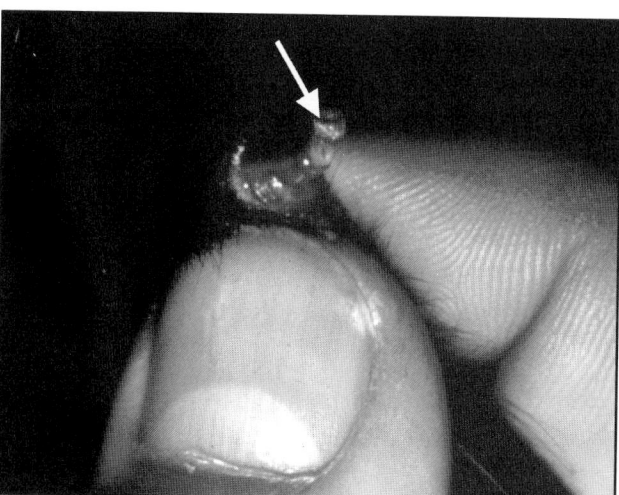

Figure 21-3. A urethral plug (arrow) is seen extruding from the tip of the penis in a cat with urethral obstruction. Urethral plugs are usually soft, compressible, friable and composed of large amounts of matrix mixed with smaller amounts of crystalline minerals.

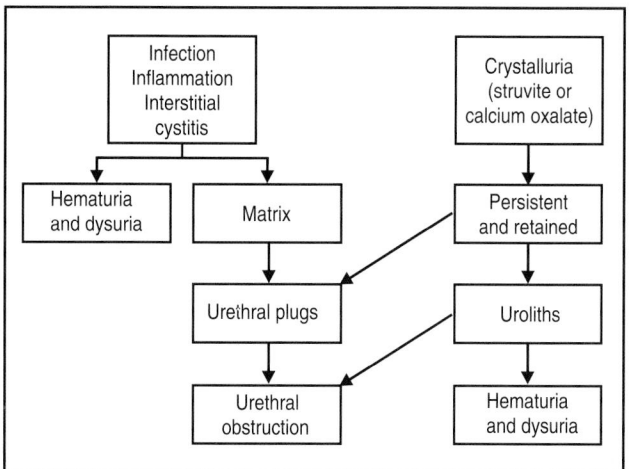

Figure 21-4. Unifying concept for feline lower urinary tract disease. Infection or inflammation (e.g., idiopathic cystitis) results in clinical signs of lower urinary tract disease and production of excess matrix. Persistent crystalluria can combine with matrix to form urethral plugs or contribute to urolith formation and typical clinical signs. (Adapted from Osborne CA, Kruger JM, Lulich JP. Feline lower urinary tract disorders: Definition of terms and concepts. Veterinary Clinics of North America: Small Animal Practice 1996; 76: 169-179.

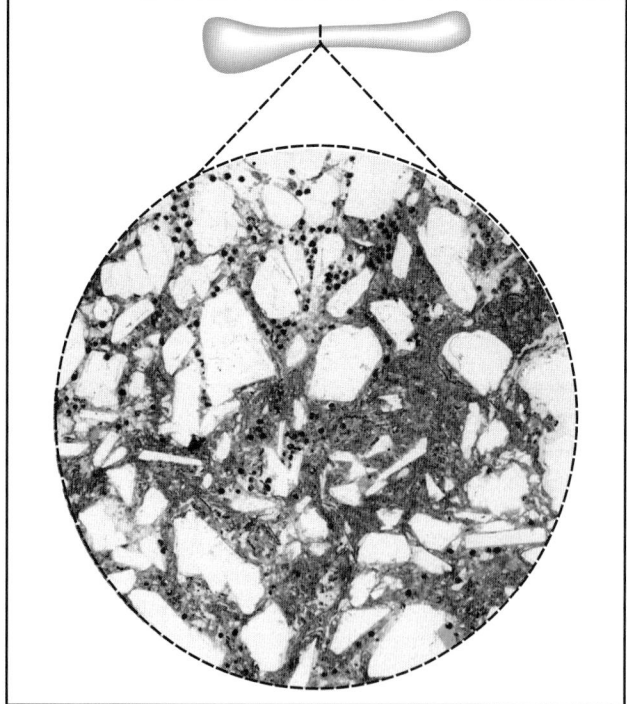

Figure 21-5. A cross-section of a matrix-crystalline urethral plug. Note the spaces previously occupied by struvite crystals are surrounded by matrix containing amorphous material, cellular debris and small numbers of inflammatory cells. This phenomenon is analogous to a gelatin salad that contains various fruits or vegetables (i.e., crystals, cells, cellular material) embedded in a gelatin matrix.

This so-called unifying hypothesis of causes is also consistent with the observation of viral particles and bacteria incorporated in matrix-crystalline plugs.

UROLITHS

Uroliths consist of small amounts of matrix and macroscopic crystalline mineral concretions. Urolithiasis is a multifaceted process that begins with the formation of microcrystals in urine and ends with the formation of mature uroliths somewhere in the urinary tract. The most common urolith mineral types found in cats are struvite (magnesium ammonium phosphate) (Figures 21-6 and 21-7) and calcium oxalate (Figure 21-8). Usually one mineral type predominates, but the composition may be mixed. Different mineral types may be dispersed throughout the urolith or may be organized into separate, discrete bands or layers.

The numbers in Table 21-9 represent cumulative totals over several years. The cumulative numbers tend to mask an apparent trend that was first recognized in the late 1980s. The proportion of struvite uroliths submitted to specialized urolith analysis laboratories has decreased and the proportion of calcium oxalate uroliths has increased. Although the prevalence of calcium oxalate uroliths submitted for analysis appears to be increasing, several relevant questions remain unanswered: 1) How has the apparent aging feline population affected the relative frequency of different urolith types? 2) Is the apparent increase in calcium oxalate uroliths relative because fewer struvite uroliths are being submitted for analysis due to the availability of struvite dissolution protocols? 3) Are veterinarians better at diagnosing calcium oxalate uroliths? 4) Why has the prevalence of calcium oxalate uroliths also increased in cats, dogs and people?

Formation of Uroliths

The initiation and growth of crystals involves chemical precipitation of dissolved ions or molecules from urine that has become supersaturated with these components. To understand this from a physiochemical point of view, it is useful to describe how the degree of supersaturation or undersaturation of urine influences the probability that a crystal will form or dissolve.

In its simplest form, the initiation and growth of uroliths, and perhaps urethral plugs, involves chemical precipitation of dissolved ions or molecules from a solution that has become supersaturated with respect to those components (Figure 21-9). From a physiochemical perspective, the degree of saturation or undersaturation of urine influences the probability that precipitates will form, or if already present, dissolve. Relatively simple diagrams depict the states of saturation of any solution (Figures 21-10 and 21-11). These diagrams provide the framework for understanding the concept of how nutritional management influences the probability of urolith formation or dissolution. Units and numerical values are not included in these diagrams because they differ for each of the urolith components; however, the general features apply to all crystalline materials. A more detailed description of this process is found in Chapter 20.

The solubility product is the concentration product at which dissolved and crystalline components are in equilibrium with each other at a given set of conditions. At concentrations below the solubility product (undersaturation zone) it is impossible for crystals to form under any circumstances. Crystals added to such a solution would dissolve. Crystals would grow if added to a solution with a concentration greater than the solubility product. The formation product is the concentration at which crystals will begin to precipitate at a significant rate in the absence of preformed crystalline material.

The solubility product is constant for a pure crystalline material. The formation product is much more difficult to demonstrate experimentally. Thus, this area is illustrated by a shaded band rather than a line (Figure 21-11). Strictly speaking the ionic activities, not concentrations, of the species govern the solubility principles described here. Ionic activities are influenced by the presence of other ions in solution (ionic strength) and by the presence of other species that form complex ions, thereby reducing their "free" concentrations in solution.

The metastable zone is of most interest from a clinical perspective (Figure 21-11). In this concentration range: 1) crystal growth will occur, 2) crystal aggregation will occur and 3) inhibitors will impede or prevent crystallization. This so-called metastable (unstable) region corresponds to the urinary concentration of crystal-forming substances found in normal people and many urolith-forming human patients. Risk factor reduction and nutritional interventions may be most beneficial with urine in this region. A precarious balance exists between crystal formation and inhibition in the metastable zone. Anatomic defects within the urinary tract that allow for stasis of metastable urine will lead to formation and growth of crystals. Urine containing microscopic impurities will facilitate crystal formation and growth. This process is called heterogeneous nucleation. Crystal formation is much less likely in urine without impurities (homogeneous solution).

See sidebar "Relative Supersaturation vs. Activity Product Ratios" for discussion of laboratory techniques used to measure these changes in urine.

Struvite Uroliths

Struvite uroliths form as a result of supersaturation of urine with magnesium ammonium phosphate. This supersaturation can occur in the presence of infection with a urease-producing organism. However, approximately 70% of struvite uroliths in cats form in sterile urine.[27] Urinary magnesium levels are related to dietary intake (Figure 21-12).[28,29] (See sidebar "Urinary pH, Ammonium and Anionic Phosphate.")

Calcium Oxalate Uroliths

As noted above, the prevalence of feline calcium oxalate uroliths is apparently increasing. In people, the composition of uroliths has also changed. Before industrialization, uroliths were predominantly composed of struvite and uric acid. During the past several decades in the United States, the incidence of calcium-containing renal uroliths in people has steadily increased. Currently, roughly 60 to 80% of human uroliths are composed of calcium oxalate.

The occurrence of calcium oxalate uroliths in people is strongly correlated with consumption of animal protein, sodium and refined carbohydrates.[30] Additional risk factors that predispose people to calcium urolith formation are familial history (genetics), gender (males are affected more than females), low urine volume and urine biochemical abnormalities such as hyperoxaluria, hypercalciuria, hyperuricuria and hypocitraturia. Urinary oxalate is an important biochemical risk factor in idiopathic calcium oxalate urolith formation; increased levels of urinary oxalate can be demonstrated in human nephrolith patients.[31]

Urinary oxalate is a more important determinant of calcium oxalate supersaturation than calcium because small increases in oxalate excretion profoundly influence the activity product ratio. Oxalate is a metabolic by-product of glycine usage and forms a number of complexes and salts in solution. Oxalic acid, a relatively strong organic acid, is a simple two-carbon dicarboxylic acid. The calcium salt is

relatively insoluble and pH does not influence solubility over the physiologic range.

Some investigators think the metabolic pool of oxalate in people is derived from intestinal absorption and endogenous production. Little is known about endogenous oxalate metabolism in cats. In people, 5 to 15% of urinary oxalate is from the diet; the remaining 85 to 95% is produced endogenously. Oxalate is poorly absorbed from the intestinal tract. Uptake from human diets has been esti-

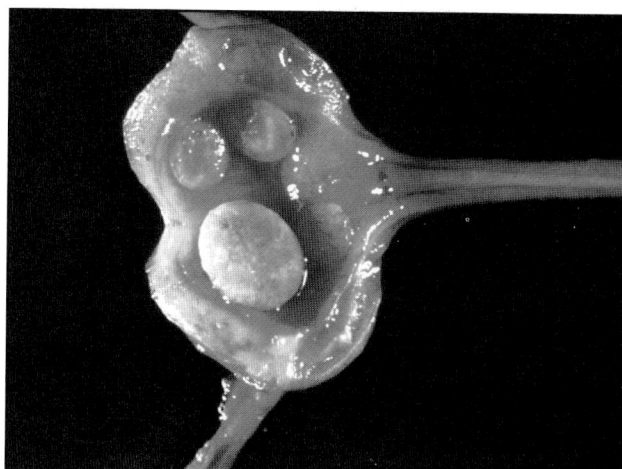

Figure 21-6. Bladder from a cat with struvite urolithiasis. Note the thickened bladder wall and several struvite uroliths within the urinary bladder lumen.

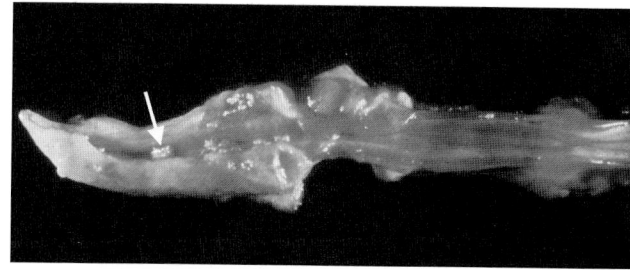

Figure 21-7. Penis and urethra from a cat with urethral obstruction. Note the small struvite urolith (arrow) in the penile urethra. Uroliths consist of small amounts of matrix and macroscopic crystalline mineral concretions. They are less common causes of urethral obstruction in male cats than urethral plugs. (See Figure 21-3.)

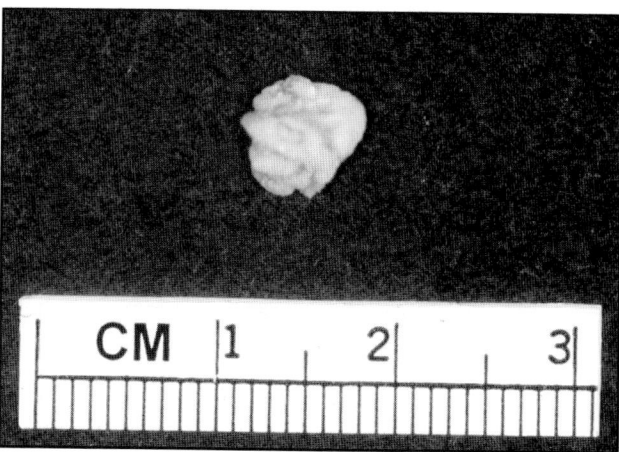

Figure 21-8. Calcium oxalate dihydrate urolith removed from the bladder of a cat with hematuria and dysuria.

Table 21-9. Mineral composition of 9,481 feline uroliths analyzed by quantitative methods.*

Predominant mineral types	Percent
Struvite	48
Calcium oxalates	40
Ammonium acid urate	6.1
Mixed/compound	3.6
Matrix	1.4
Calcium phosphate	0.8
Cystine	0.3
Xanthine	0.1

*Adapted from Osborne CA, Kruger JM, Lulich JP. Feline lower urinary tract disorders: Definition of terms and concepts. Veterinary Clinics of North America: Small Animal Practice 1996; 26: 173.

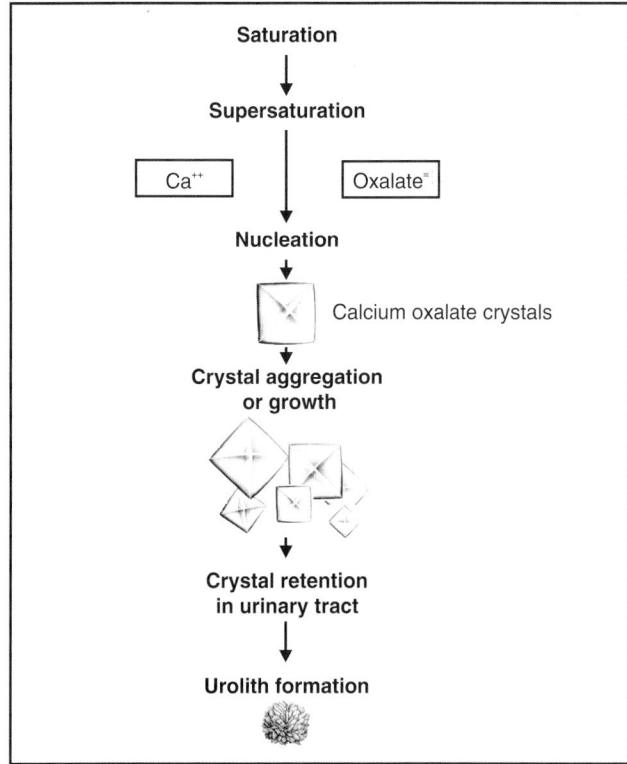

Figure 21-9. Supersaturation of urine with urolith-forming constituents (e.g., calcium, oxalate) results in crystal growth, aggregation and ultimately urolith formation, if the components are retained in the urinary tract. (Adapted from Bartges JW, Osborne CA, Lulich JP, et al. Methods for evaluating treatment of uroliths. Veterinary Clinics of North America: Small Animal Practice 1999; 29: 46.)

mated to be between 2 and 7%.[32] The uptake of oxalate from the gut seems to depend on whether oxalate is administered separately or as part of a complex food. When radiolabeled oxalate was administered as a single dose to normal people, 10 to 30% was recovered from the urine.[33]

Oxalate is absorbed throughout the large and small bowel by facilitated diffusion using an anion exchange mechanism.[34] The calcium salt of oxalate is just as insoluble in the luminal content of the intestinal tract as in other complex solutions. Consequently, dietary calcium is an important determinant of oxalate availability and thus absorption. Because of analytical problems, no data are available about the oxalate content of pet food ingredients and finished pet foods.

Colorimetric, isotope dilution and enzymatic techniques are available for analyzing oxalate. Sample extrac-

tion and purification is the most difficult part of the analysis. Because the oxalate content of food is typically low and the net intestinal absorption of oxalate is poor, hyperoxaluria due to excessive intake is rare in human patients. Human foods relatively high in oxalate include rhubarb, spinach, peanuts, pecans, wheat germ, peppers, beets, okra, strawberries, chocolate and tea.[35] Cats are unlikely to eat excessive amounts of these foods.

The major metabolic sources of oxalate are ascorbic acid and glyoxylate. In people, metabolism of ascorbic acid accounts for 30 to 40% of total daily oxalate production and excretion. Under normal circumstances, the pathways for metabolism of ascorbic acid to oxalate are saturated. Thus, a reasonable increase in dietary intake does not increase urinary oxalate excretion. Megadoses of ascorbic acid increase oxalate production and excretion; however, the clinical significance of this increase is unknown.[36]

The oxidation of glyoxylate accounts for the remainder of daily oxalate production. Lactic dehydrogenase seems to be the most important enzyme in the conversion of glyoxylate to oxalate. A large part of the metabolic pool of glyoxylate is transaminated to glycine by the enzyme alanine glyoxylate aminotransferase, which requires pyridoxine as a cofactor.[37] Pyridoxine deficiency has been reported to lead to increased oxalate production and urinary excretion in cats.[38,39] Documented cases of clinical pyridoxine deficiency, however, are extremely rare. Pharmacologic doses of pyridoxine are empirically recommended to drive the transamination reaction in the direction of glycine and thus decrease the conversion of glyoxylate to oxalate. Primary hyperoxaluria due to reduced levels of hepatic D-glycerate dehydrogenase has been recognized in a family of cats.[40]

Urinary excretion is the primary route of oxalate elimination from the extracellular pool. Circulating oxalate is freely filtered by the glomeruli and there is net tubular secretion of oxalate. In rats, the proximal tubule is the main site of tubular excretion. Secretion in the proximal tubules does not occur by means of the classic organic acid mechanism that transports para-aminohippuric acid.[41]

In human patients, hyperoxaluria often is present in malabsorptive states.[42] This secondary hyperoxaluria has been called enteric or absorptive. Enteric hyperoxaluria is the most common form of hyperoxaluria in people with calcium oxalate uroliths. Hyperoxaluria and predisposition to calcium oxalate uroliths are recognized in a variety of gastrointestinal (GI) conditions, including regional enteritis, blind loop syndrome and ileal resection. Hyperoxaluria is also observed in chronic pancreatic and biliary tract diseases. The underlying mechanism is increased intestinal absorption of oxalate. The extent of intestinal absorption of oxalate correlates with the degree of fat malabsorption and severity of steatorrhea. The major site of oxalate absorption is the colon.

Three theories have been advanced to explain increased colonic absorption of oxalate by patients with enteric hyperoxaluria. In one theory (i.e., solubility theory), unabsorbed fatty acids bind calcium within the luminal contents, thus making more free oxalate available for passive absorption. In the second theory (i.e., permeability theory), unabsorbed fatty acids and bile acids irritate the colonic mucosa and the irritated mucosa becomes more permeable to oxalate. In the third theory (oxalate-degrading microflora theory), changes in the intestinal microflo-

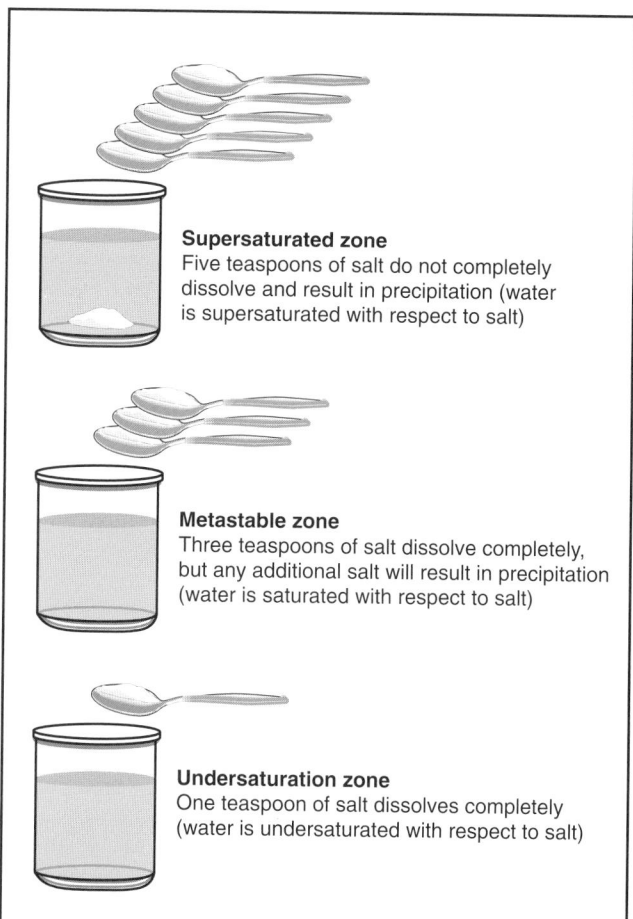

Figure 21-10. Schematic depicting how increasing amounts of table salt dissolved in water result in undersaturated, metastable and supersaturated solutions. Similar phenomena occur with mineral salts in urine. (Adapted from Bartges JW, Osborne CA, Lulich JP, et al. Methods for evaluating treatment of uroliths. Veterinary Clinics of North America: Small Animal Practice 1999; 29: 47.)

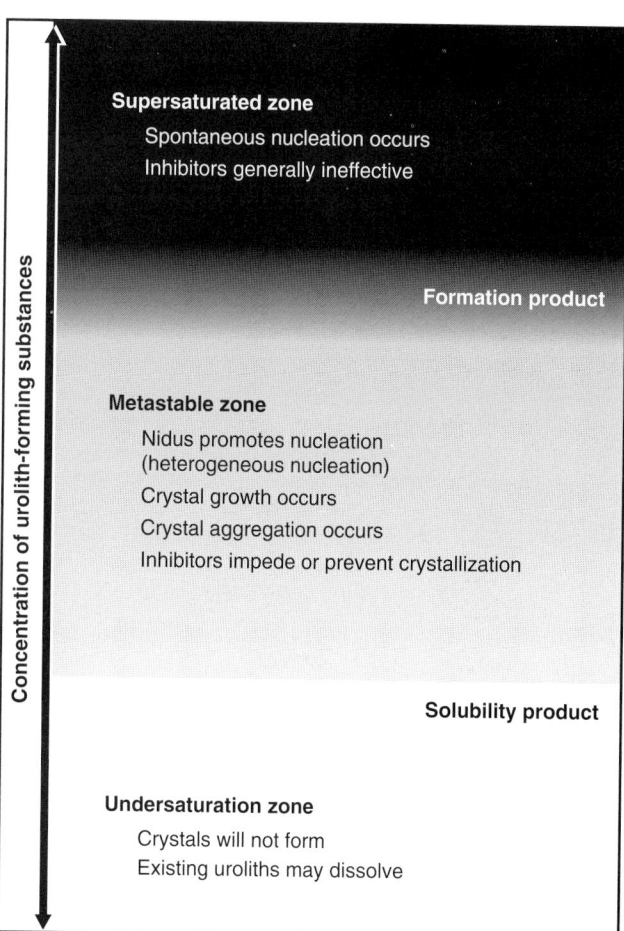

Figure 21-11. Increasing concentrations of urolith-forming substances result in metastable and supersaturated urine. Crystal growth and aggregation may occur in the metastable zone. Presence of a nidus promotes nucleation (heterogeneous nucleation) and subsequent crystal formation. Inhibitors in the metastable zone may impede or prevent crystallization. Spontaneous nucleation occurs when concentrations of urolith-forming substances increase to the point of supersaturation. At this point, inhibitors of crystal formation are generally ineffective.

ra reduce the number of oxalate-degrading bacteria in the gut, thereby increasing the amount of oxalate available for absorption.

The pathogenesis of calcium oxalate uroliths in patients with enteric hyperoxaluria is multifactorial. Hyperoxaluria is just one of several urolith risk factors in patients with GI disease. Additional risk factors include decreased urine volume, hypocitraturia, hypomagnesuria and decreased urinary levels of pyrophosphate.[43]

Most human patients with calcium oxalate uroliths excrete increased amounts of calcium and/or oxalate. Hypercalciuria is more common and is seen in approximately 50% of human patients. Three terms have been applied to the concepts proposed to explain the pathogenesis of hypercalciuria in people: 1) absorptive hypercalciuria, 2) renal hypercalciuria and 3) resorptive hypercalciuria.[44]

The primary abnormality in absorptive hypercalciuria is increased intestinal calcium absorption. The increased calcium absorption results in high normal levels of serum calcium with a reciprocal decrease in parathyroid hormone (PTH) levels. In some people, this condition occurs secondary to increased production or sensitivity to vitamin D metabolites. Intestinal absorption of magnesium is normal and oxalate absorption is increased.

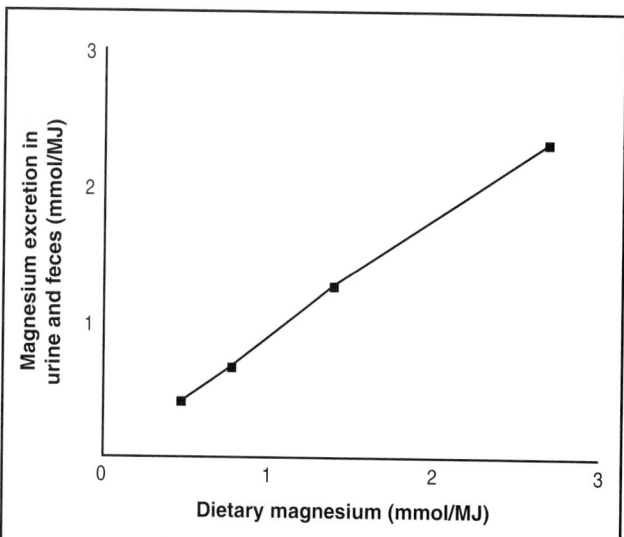

Figure 21-12. Relationship between dietary magnesium and magnesium excretion in urine and feces of cats. Note the direct linear relationship between dietary magnesium and magnesium excretion. (Adapted from Pastoor FJH. Interactions of dietary minerals in the cat. PhD Thesis, University of Utrecht, The Netherlands, 1993; 75.)

Relative Supersaturation vs. Activity Product Ratios

Analytical data indicate that urine is often supersaturated with respect to most common urolith components. Thus, the question is not why a specific animal formed a urolith, but rather why doesn't every animal form uroliths? Inhibitors in urine probably explain the less than predicted prevalence. Because we don't know how to manipulate or change

inhibitors, the current therapeutic strategy is to reduce risk factors by decreasing the degree of supersaturation. One way to express urinary saturation is to determine the relative supersaturation (RSS) of a urolith type such as calcium oxalate or struvite. RSS is determined by measuring the concentration of a number of urinary analytes, including sodium, calcium, oxalate, magnesium, and potassium. The concentrations of these analytes are entered into a computer program that calculates the saturation of the urolith elements compared with a standard human urine sample. RSS has limitations because it is highly dependent on urine volume and involves comparison with standard values for human urine.

A better technique for predicting the likelihood of crystal formation is the activity product ratio (APR) (Figure 1). The APR for calcium oxalate is the mathematical product of the activity of calcium and the activity of oxalate. Activity is different than simple concentration of the substance of interest in an aqueous solution. Activity refers to the ionic activity, which is influenced by the concentration of the substance of interest, other substances in urine and factors such as pH and temperature. Like RSS, APR involves measurement of a number of analytes in urine such as sodium, potassium, calcium, oxalate and magnesium. Values are also entered into a computer program. But unlike RSS, the APR technique requires incubation of seed crystals such as calcium oxalate in an aliquot of urine. After incubation, the urinary analytes are measured again and the postincubation activity product is determined. Dividing the pre-incubation activity product by the postincubation activity product yields the APR. An APR less than 1 indicates that crystals dissolved during incubation. The APR provides a better indication of risk of crystal formation than RSS because APR considers the influence of unmeasured inhibitors and promoters and is not unduly influenced by urine volume. APRs can be used to quantitatively evaluate the influence of nutrients, complete foods and drugs on the risk of crystal formation.

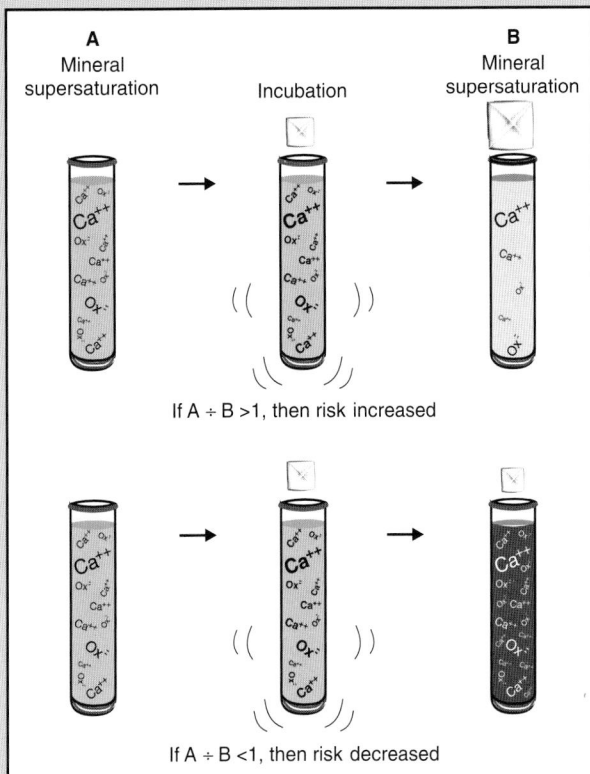

Figure 1. Schematic depicting how activity product ratios (APRs) are calculated. Urine from a cat is analyzed for pertinent minerals (Tube A) and is then incubated with a seed crystal. After incubation, the urine is analyzed for the same mineral constituents (Tube B). The risk of urolith formation increases with an APR greater than 1. This means the seed crystal has grown and the urine is supersaturated and/or contains inadequate concentrations of crystal inhibitors. The risk of urolith formation decreases with an APR less than 1. This means the seed crystal became smaller during the incubation process and the urine is undersaturated or contains adequate concentrations of crystal inhibitors.

BIBLIOGRAPHY

Bartges JW, Osborne CA, Felice LJ, et al. Diet effect on activity product ratios of uric acid, sodium urate, and ammonium urate in urine formed by healthy beagles. American Journal of Veterinary Research 1995; 56: 329-333.

Bartges JW, Osborne CA, Felice LJ, et al. Influence of four diets containing approximately 11% protein (dry weight) on uric acid, sodium urate, and ammonium urate urine activity product ratios of healthy beagles. American Journal of Veterinary Research 1995; 56: 60-65.

Werness PG, Brown CM, Smith LH, et al. Equil 2: A basic computer program for the calculation of urinary saturation. Journal of Urology 1985; 134: 1242-1244.

In renal hypercalciuria, the underlying problem is a primary renal calcium leak. The resultant decrease in serum calcium concentration stimulates PTH production. This in turn leads to increased hydroxylation of 25-hydroxyvitamin D to 1,25-dihydroxyvitamin D in the kidney, which stimulates increased calcium absorption in the intestine. In some patients, renal calcium leak occurs secondary to excessive sodium intake.

Resorptive hypercalciuria is the equivalent of mild hyperparathyroidism. Hypercalciuria occurs due to increased PTH-dependent bone resorption and increased calcium absorption from the gut. The large filtered load of calcium overwhelms the increased renal tubular reabsorption of calcium mediated by PTH.

Low concentrations of urinary citrate are common in human patients with calcium oxalate uroliths.[45] Prior administration of citrate should decrease the risk of calcium oxalate uroliths. The physiochemical effects of potassium citrate administration are increased urinary citrate excretion and urinary alkalinization. The increase in urinary citrate levels inhibits crystallization of calcium oxalate by binding calcium. At higher pH values, more phosphate and citrate ions become dissociated, increasing the complexation of calcium. The resulting reduction in ionized calcium concentration decreases the urinary saturation of this urolith component. The increase in urinary pH also increases the dissociation of uric acid, reducing the concentration of undissociated uric acid and the prob-

Urinary pH, Ammonium and Anionic Phosphate

The normal urinary concentration of total phosphate ions is high and not subject to great variation by dietary manipulation. Although complexes are formed between phosphate ions and calcium and magnesium ions, these complexes do not markedly decrease the free phosphate ion concentration. The urinary variable that has the greatest impact on trivalent phosphate ion concentration is urinary pH. Urinary pH influences formation of struvite precipitates because it influences the amount of total urinary phosphorus present as the free trivalent phosphate ion. The concentration of the free trivalent ion is dependent upon the position of the acid-base equilibria of the two principal phosphate species that exist in the normal urinary pH range: HPO_4^{2-} and $H_2PO_4^-$. As urinary pH increases, the concentration of free trivalent ions increases as the monobasic and dibasic phosphates are deprotonated.

$$H_2PO_4^- = HPO_4^{2-} + H^+$$
$$HPO_4^{2-} = PO_4^{3-} + H^+$$

According to the above equations, an increase in hydrogen ion concentration will shift both equilibria to the left, resulting in lower concentrations of free trivalent phosphate (PO_4^{3-}). Decreasing urinary pH from 8.5 to 5.5, the approximate physiologic range for cats, results in a 14-thousandfold decrease in free trivalent ion concentration, with no change in total urinary phosphate.

Urinary pH also influences the concentration of ammonium ions. Ammonia generated by urease enzymes provides necessary ions that react with available hydrogen ions as follows to increase urinary pH:

$$NH_3 + H^+ = NH_4^+$$

Reduction in urinary pH from the upper to the lower end of the physiologic range changes the ratio of NH_4^+ to NH_3 from 3.4:1 to 3,400:1. Thus, foods that produce an acidic urine increase urinary ammonium concentration. However, because the effect on free trivalent phosphate ion concentration is greater, the net effect of urine acidification is a reduction in the likelihood of struvite precipitate formation.

BIBLIOGRAPHY

Buffington CA, Rogers QR, Morris JG. Effect of diet on struvite activity product in feline urine. American Journal of Veterinary Research 1990; 51: 2026-2030.

Rogers QR, Morris JG. The effect of diet on feline struvite urolithiasis syndrome. In: Proceedings. Purina Faculty Symposium, St. Louis, MO, June 1987: 1-9.

FLUTD

Citrate

Experimental studies have shown that citrate is an inhibitor of calcium oxalate crystallization, and hypocitraturia is common in human patients with calcium-containing uroliths. Citrate inhibits calcium oxalate crystal formation by promoting formation of alkaline urine and by forming complexes with calcium (Figure 1). When citrate complexes with calcium, ionic calcium concentration and urine saturation with calcium oxalate are reduced. In various studies, hypocitraturia is reported to occur in 19 to 63% of human patients with calcium oxalate urolithiasis. The frequency of hypocitraturia in cats with calcium oxalate urolithiasis is unknown.

Citrate is a key component in the citric acid cycle and thus is an important energy source and found ubiquitously in the body. Only a small amount of the total citrate in the body is excreted in the urine.

Changes in acid-base status influence renal handling of citrate. Metabolic acidosis virtually eliminates urinary citrate excretion by promoting citrate oxidation. Acidosis favors the influx of citrate into renal mitochondria and inhibits efflux of citrate from mitochondria. Tubular and peritubular citrate uptake increases when cytosolic citrate concentration decreases. Increased reabsorption of citrate reduces urinary citrate excretion. The citrate in urine is the small quantity that escapes reabsorption. In metabolic alkalosis, urinary citrate increases because mitochondrial uptake and thus oxidation of citrate is reduced, cytosolic citrate concentration increases, reabsorption decreases and urinary excretion of citrate increases.

Potassium citrate is preferred as a urinary alkalinizing agent over sodium bicarbonate because oral administration of sodium increases urinary calcium excretion. Generally, the liquid product Polycitra-K[a] is recommended at a dose of 100 to 150 mg/kg body weight/day divided two or three times per day.

ENDNOTE

a. Mission Pharmacal, San Antonio, TX, USA.

BIBLIOGRAPHY

Lulich JP, Osborne CA, Felice L, et al. Managing calcium oxalate urolithiasis. In: Proceedings. Eleventh Annual Veterinary Medical Forum, American College of Veterinary Internal Medicine, Washington, DC, 1993: 374 -377.

Pak CYC. Hypocitraturic calcium nephrolithiasis. In: Resnick MI, Pak CYC, eds. Urolithiasis: A Medical and Surgical Reference. Philadelphia, PA: WB Saunders Co, 1990; 92-93.

Simpson DP. Citrate excretion: A window on renal metabolism. American Journal of Physiology 1983; 244: F223-F234.

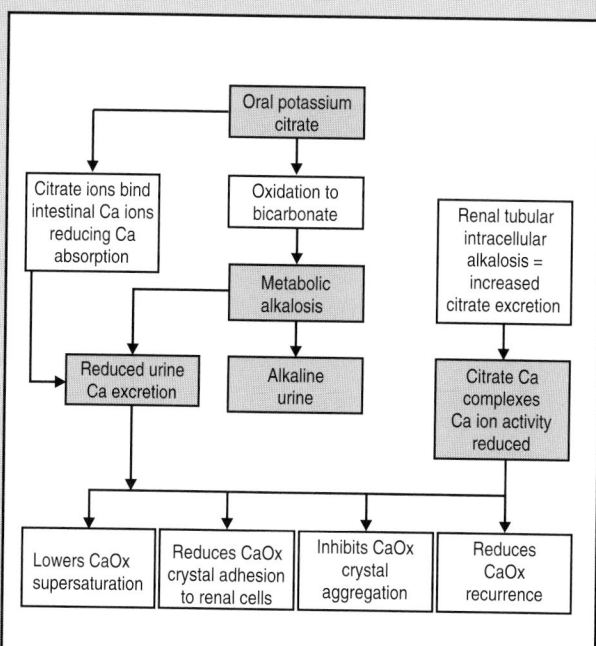

Figure 1. Schematic depicting the role of citrate in promoting formation of alkaline urine and preventing calcium oxalate urolith formation.

ability of uric acid urolith formation. Citrate prevents heterogeneous nucleation of calcium oxalate by monosodium urate. Long-term treatment of human patients with potassium citrate produces a sustained reduction in the urinary saturation of calcium oxalate. When used as a pharmacologic agent, the recommended dose of potassium citrate is 100 to 150 mg/kg body weight, divided into two or three daily doses.

Citric acid, in the form of citrate, is the most abundant organic acid found in urine. In people and cats, dietary citrate appears to have little effect on urinary citrate.[46] This finding also appears to be true in cats. Kienzle and Maiwald fed up to 100 mg citric acid/kg body weight to cats and found practically no effect on urine citrate concentrations.[47] In people, citrate circulates in blood at a concentration of 1 to 6 mg/dl, almost exclusively as the citrate ion. Ionic citrate is freely filtered by glomeruli and some is reabsorbed in the proximal tubules. (See sidebar "Citrate.")

Table 21-10. Crystal inhibitors found in urine.

Small molecules
  Citrate
  Pyrophosphate
Macromolecules
  Nephrocalcin
  Crystal matrix protein
  Tamm-Horsfall protein (inhibitor or promoter)
  Osteopontin (uropontin)

Nephrocalcin

Nephrocalcin is an anionic, glycosylated, phosphorylated protein with a monomeric molecular weight of approximately 14,000 daltons. Nephrocalcin contains residues of γ-carboxyglutamic acid. Although the complete amino acid sequence is not yet known, nephrocalcin apparently contains a large number of acidic amino acid residues. Immunohistochemical data indicate that nephrocalcin is found in the proximal tubules and the thick ascending limb of the loop of Henle. Although the mechanisms of how nephrocalcin is regulated are unknown, pregnant women who become hypercalciuric have increased urinary levels of nephrocalcin.

Nephrocalcin inhibits growth of calcium oxalate crystals in metastable supersaturated solutions of calcium oxalate in vitro, and increasing amounts of nephrocalcin progressively slow crystal growth. Crystal growth is inhibited in vitro at concentrations similar to those reported to occur in urine. Nephrocalcin does not chelate calcium in solution but rather binds to crystal surfaces thereby inhibiting crystal growth.

BIBLIOGRAPHY

Nakagawa Y, Abrams V, Parks JH, et al. Urine glycoprotein crystal growth inhibitors, evidence for a molecular abnormality in calcium oxalate nephrolithiasis. Journal of Clinical Investigation 1985; 76: 1455-1462.

Nakagawa Y, Ahmed M, Hall SL, et al. Isolation from human calcium oxalate renal stones of nephrocalcin, a glycoprotein inhibitor of calcium oxalate growth: Evidence that nephrocalcin from patients with calcium oxalate nephrolithiasis is deficient in γ-carboxyglutamic acid. Journal of Clinical Investigation 1987; 79: 1782-1787.

Acid-base status influences citrate excretion. Metabolic alkalosis induces a rapid and marked increase in urinary citrate excretion. This increase appears to be due to inhibition of citrate metabolism in renal tubular cells. Conversely, metabolic acidosis is associated with decreased urinary citrate excretion and increased citrate metabolism by renal tubular cells. The influence of acid-base status on citrate excretion may by mediated by pH gradients across mitochondrial membranes and mitochondrial uptake and oxidation of citrate. Potassium depletion produces intracellular metabolic acidosis in the renal cortex, resulting in hypocitraturia.[48]

Magnesium is a potent inhibitor of calcium oxalate crystallization in vitro and calcium oxalate urolith formation in experimental models.[49] Low excretion of magnesium in urine has been suggested as a possible risk factor for development of calcium-containing uroliths. In studies, magnesium deficiency in rats promoted nephrocalcinosis and nephrolithiasis. Magnesium deficiency causes increased urinary excretion of phosphate. Magnesium administration effectively prevented renal deposition of calcium oxalate in pyridoxine-deficient and hyperoxaluric rats. Magnesium presumably increases urinary pH and urinary excretion of citrate. This effect of magnesium depends on which specific salt is used (e.g., magnesium oxide has an alkalinizing effect, whereas magnesium sulfate has an acidifying effect).

Inhibitors

Urine contains substances that modify and inhibit nucleation, growth and aggregation of crystals (Table 21-10). These substances include small molecules such as citrate and pyrophosphate and macromolecules, such as mucoproteins, glycoproteins, glycosaminoglycans and proteoglycans. Inhibitors of crystal growth have been isolated from urine. These inhibitors include nephrocalcin, osteopontin (uropontin) and crystal matrix protein. Abnormalities in structure and/or function of these proteins have been detected in human patients with recurrent uroliths. Studies of urinary inhibitors are complicated because there is no universally accepted model system for quantifying inhibition and it is difficult to create in vitro systems that mimic in vivo conditions.

Recently, research interest has shifted from crystal growth to other stages in urolith formation. Nephrocalcin can inhibit crystal nucleation and both nephrocalcin and Tamm-Horsfall mucoprotein inhibit crystal aggregation.[50,51] Nephrocalcin and Tamm-Horsfall mucoprotein from recurrent urolith formers are less active in preventing aggregation, and under specific conditions, Tamm-Horsfall mucoprotein may promote formation of crystal aggregates. (See sidebar "Nephrocalcin.")

Some recurrent urolith formers may have defective inhibitory substances (Table 21-10). For example, some highly recurrent calcium urolith formers excrete Tamm-Horsfall mucoprotein, which compared with normal Tamm-Horsfall mucoprotein, self-aggregates at low pH and high sodium concentrations and is less effective at inhibiting calcium oxalate monohydrate aggregation.[51]

The urine of most human beings is continuously saturated with calcium oxalate, yet only 4% of the human population will form calcium oxalate uroliths during their lifetime. This underscores the importance of nucleation, crystal growth and crystal aggregation in urine. Patients with a history of urolithiasis should particularly avoid saturation conditions that favor specific urolith types.

Table 21-11. Comparison of human and feline interstitial cystitis.

Features	Feline interstitial cystitis	Human interstitial cystitis
Age/gender	Young/male and female	Middle-age/female predominantly
Signs	Episodic hematuria Dysuria Pollakiuria Urethral obstruction Self-limiting	Chronic persistent pain Increased urgency
Urinalysis findings	Hematuria Decreased glycosaminoglycan Proteinuria Increased numbers of mast cells	Hematuria (occasionally) Decreased glycosaminoglycan Increased numbers of mast cells
Urine bacterial culture	Sterile	Sterile
Cystoscopy findings	Glomerulations	Glomerulations Hunner ulcers Decreased capacity
Biopsy findings	Hemorrhage Ulcerations Round cell infiltrates Increased numbers of mast cells Granulation/fibrosis	Hemorrhage Ulcerations Round cell infiltrates Granulation tissue Vasculitis Increased numbers of mast cells

BACTERIAL INFECTION

Although bacterial UTIs are a common cause of lower urinary tract disease in dogs, bacterial UTIs were present in only four of 143 cases (2.8%) in a prospective clinical series of FLUTD (obstructed and unobstructed), with no history of previous catheterization or urethrostomy.[52] Prior instrumentation or surgery of the urinary tract markedly increases the likelihood of UTI.

Perineal urethrostomies are associated with significant postoperative sequelae, including urethral strictures, bacterial UTI and struvite urolithiasis. These postoperative sequelae can produce clinical signs associated with lower urinary tract disease. In a prospective clinical study of 30 male cats with intraluminal urethral obstruction, investigators randomly assigned cats to receive one of three treatments: nutritional management with a struvite calculolytic food, perineal urethrostomy or both surgery and nutritional management. Episodes of bacterial UTI were documented in 17% of the group managed by surgery alone, and 10% of the group managed by nutrition and surgery. None of the cats managed by nutrition alone had any episodes of UTI. Three of the infected cats from the urethrostomy-only group subsequently developed urocystoliths.[53]

Several factors associated with perineal urethrostomies have been incriminated as risk factors for bacterial UTI. These include decreased length of the urethra postsurgery, loss of normal penile urethral mucosal defense mechanisms, transurethral catheterization, wider external urethral orifices, impaired function of the striated urethralis muscle and decreased intraluminal pressure. Some cats have decreased postprostatic urethral pressure and decreased activity of the striated muscle sphincter after perineal urethrostomy as determined by urethral pressure profiles and electromyographic changes.[54] These changes were linked to extensive tissue dissection and damage to the pudendal nerve during surgery.

A modified surgical procedure, designed to preserve function of the striated urethral sphincter, was evaluated in a group of healthy neutered male cats and a group of cats with recurrent or persistent urethral obstruction. All cats had normal urethral pressure profiles and elec-

tromyographic results postoperatively. Twenty-two percent of the cats with persistent or recurrent urethral obstruction had bacterial UTIs vs. none of the normal cats. These findings suggest that decreased urethral pressure does not predispose cats to ascending UTI.[55]

Vesicourachal diverticula were reported in one of every four cats with dysuria, hematuria and/or urethral obstruction.[56] Vesicourachal diverticula can be congenital or acquired. Because diverticula alter the normal flow of urine, in theory, they may predispose patients to UTI, infection-related urolithiasis and formation of urinary precipitates. It has been suggested that acquired diverticula occur as a result of increased intraluminal pressure due to urethral obstruction or hyperactivity of the detrusor muscle associated with inflammation. Spontaneous resolution of diverticula has been observed in cats.[56,57]

INTERSTITIAL CYSTITIS

Comparisons have been drawn between idiopathic FLUTD and interstitial cystitis in human beings (Table 21-11).[23,58-60] Investigators have proposed that cats with idiopathic FLUTD, in fact, have interstitial cystitis (See sidebar "Human Interstitial Cystitis.") The comparisons are based on clinical signs and diagnostic features. All of the National Institutes of Health (NIH) criteria (i.e., history, laboratory evaluation, cystoscopy and cystometrics) for interstitial cystitis in human patients have been applied to cats.[61] Affected cats and people present as adults with signs/symptoms of variable severity that are influenced by stress. Spontaneous remissions occur in both cats and people. The dominant clinical signs include increased frequency of urination, urgency and pain. The diagnosis is based on signs, absence of urinary tract infection and exclusion of other potential causes of lower urinary tract disease. According to NIH criteria, the diagnosis in people also requires cystoscopic lesions, either glomerulations or a Hunner ulcer. Glomerulations are submucosal petechial hemorrhages. A Hunner ulcer is a small patch of brownish-red mucosa, surrounded by a network of radiating vessels.

Veterinary investigators report that lesions indistinguishable from glomerulations are commonly observed during cystoscopic examination of cats with lower urinary tract disease.[62] In addition to glomerulations, increased vascularity and

Human Interstitial Cystitis

The term interstitial cystitis is used in human patients, predominantly women, with lower urinary tract symptoms when other more objective and common causes have been ruled out. A specific set of inclusion and exclusion criteria was established for human interstitial cystitis research studies at two workshops sponsored by the Division of Kidney, Urologic, and Hematologic Diseases of the National Institute of Diabetes and Digestive and Kidney Diseases. According to these criteria, in order to receive a diagnosis of interstitial cystitis, a patient must have either glomerulations or a classic Hunner ulcer on cystoscopic examination and either bladder pain or urgency. Hunner or Fenwick-Hunner ulcers are small patches of brownish-red mucosa, surrounded by a network of radiating blood vessels. The lesions may heal superficially and can be difficult to detect.

The exclusion criteria for human patients include: 1) specific cystometrographic findings such as an awake bladder capacity greater than 350 ml, 2) duration of symptoms less than nine months, 3) absence of nocturia, 4) response to antimicrobials, antiseptics, anticholinergics or antispasmodics, 5) frequency of urination while awake of fewer than eight times per day, 6) diagnosis of bacterial cystitis or prostatitis within three months and 7) presence of uroliths, urethral diverticula or neoplasia of the genitourinary tract. A cystometrogram is a recording of pressure dynamics within the urinary bladder during filling, storage and voiding. Pressure measurements are made via a urinary catheter placed transurethrally or perabdominally. Infusions are made via the same catheter.

An epidemiologic survey of 374 human patients was conducted to determine the natural history of interstitial cystitis using the Division of Kidney, Urologic, and Hematologic Diseases inclusion and exclusion criteria. Approximately 71% of patients reported one or more risk factors from a group of immunopathologic abnormalities that included sensitivity or allergic reaction to medication, rheumatoid arthritis, sinusitis, food allergy, hay fever or asthma. Sixty-four percent had one or more risk factors from a group of findings that included hysterectomy, abdominal cramping, irritable bowel syndrome or spastic colon. Overall, hematuria was present in 20.1% of respondents. A high proportion of patients reported psychological symptoms or problems with everyday activities.

Although the etiology of interstitial cystitis in people is unknown, investigators have suggested that an abnormal permeability of the bladder epithelium or a primary defect in the glycosaminoglycan layer may be at fault. A defect in these layers may allow urine to irritate the epithelium and cause inflammation. Patients with interstitial cystitis reportedly excrete abnormally low amounts of glycosaminoglycans. This reduction in urinary concentration has been attributed to increased binding of glycosaminoglycan to the bladder epithelium. Putative successful treatment of interstitial cystitis with sodium pentosanpolysulfate has been cited as support for this theory. Sodium pentosanpolysulfate reinforces the glycosaminoglycan layer of the bladder.

Some investigators have suggested that immunohistochemical staining for Tamm-Horsfall mucoprotein in the bladder epithelium may be a marker for interstitial cystitis. Using immunoperoxidase staining for Tamm-Horsfall, other workers were not able to confirm the presence of Tamm-Horsfall mucoprotein within the epithelium.

BIBLIOGRAPHY

Buffington CAT, Blaisdell JL, Binns SP, et al. Decreased urine glycosaminoglycan excretion in cats with interstitial cystitis. Journal of Urology 1996; 155: 1801-1804.

Buffington CAT, Chew DJ, DiBartola SP. Interstitial cystitis in cats. Veterinary Clinics of North America: Small Animal Practice 1996; 26: 317-326.

Buffington CAT, Chew DJ, Hubler M, et al. Does interstitial cystitis occur in cats? In: Bonagura JD, ed. Current Veterinary Therapy XII. Philadelphia, PA: WB Saunders Co, 1995; 1009-1011.

Buffington CAT, Chew DJ, Kendall MS, et al. Clinical evaluation of cats with non-obstructive lower urinary tract disease: 109 cases (1993-1995). Journal of the American Veterinary Medical Association 1997; 210: 45-50.

Chew DJ, Buffington CAT, Kendall MS, et al. Amitriptyline treatment for severe recurrent idiopathic cystitis in cats. Journal of the American Veterinary Medical Association 1998; 213: 1282-1286.

Elbadawi A. Interstitial cystitis: A critique of current concepts with a new proposal for pathologic diagnosis and prognosis. Urology 1997; 49 (Suppl. 5A): 14-40.

Fowler JE Jr, Lynes WL, Lau JLT, et al. Interstitial cystitis is associated with intraurothelial Tamm-Horsfall protein. Journal of Urology 1988; 140: 1385-1389.

Koziol JA, Clark DC, Gittes RF, et al. The natural history of interstitial cystitis: A survey of 374 patients. Journal of Urology 1993; 149: 465-469.

Stone AR, Vogelsang P, Miller CH, et al. Tamm-Horsfall protein as a marker in interstitial cystitis. Journal of Urology 1992; 148: 1406-1408.

Striker GE. Special Communication: KUH Notes. Journal of Urology 1989; 142: 139.

denuding of the superficial layer overlying the epithelium with crystal adherence to the exposed epithelium is observed in some human patients during periods of active signs and during remission of signs. In interstitial cystitis, examination of bladder biopsy specimens stained with hematoxylin and eosin is unrewarding. Approximately 30 to 50% of interstitial cystitis cases have increased numbers of mast cells in the bladder wall and/or urine when special stains are used.[59] The presence of mast cells is not specific for interstitial cystitis in human beings. Preliminary findings of increased numbers of mast cells in the bladder and increased histamine concentration in the cystoscopy effluent following overdistention in some affected cats has been reported.[63] It has been theorized that mast cells release substances that mediate the signs observed. Maximal fluid distention to pressures of 80 cm of water during cystoscopy has been described in cats.[58]

Decreased glycosaminoglycan levels in cats with idiopathic lower urinary tract disease have been reported.[58] Bladder permeability to drugs was evaluated in five normal cats and five cats with feline interstitial cystitis. The study revealed a significantly higher permeability to salicylate in cats with interstitial cystitis. Symptomatic cats had a twofold higher availability and absorption rate.

A final argument for reclassifying idiopathic FLUTD as interstitial cystitis is based on the purported role of neurogenic inflammation in the pathophysiology of interstitial cystitis.[64] One investigator proposes that increased density of sensory afferent neurons in the bladder may play a significant role in interstitial cystitis.[60] Sensory afferent neurons are small fibers that transmit pain signals to the central nervous system and release neuropeptides locally, such as substance P (i.e., axon reflex). Tentatively, sensory afferent neuron

---

Less Common Urolith Types

The most common urolith mineral types found in cats are struvite (magnesium ammonium phosphate) and calcium oxalate. Less common mineral types include ammonium acid urate, uric acid, xanthine, calcium phosphate and cystine (Table 21-9 and Table 1). In general, metabolic uroliths (e.g., ammonium urate and cystine) are rarely observed in immature cats. Ammonium urate uroliths in cats with portosystemic shunts are an important exception to this generalization about metabolic uroliths.

Likewise, these mineral types make up a small percentage of the mineral in feline urethral plugs (Table 21-8). However, detection of certain crystals (e.g., cystine and ammonium urate), even in patients without clinical signs, suggests an important underlying metabolic defect.

In general, ammonium urate and cystine uroliths are associated with an acidic urinary pH. Cystine and ammonium urate uroliths are less dense than struvite and calcium-containing uroliths. Cystine uroliths are small, smooth and round to oval. Ammonium urate and uric acid uroliths are smooth, but occasionally irregular and round to oval (Table 21-2).

Renal tubular acidosis is a risk factor for development of calcium phosphate uroliths in people. When the kidneys have reduced ability to decrease urinary pH, the resultant higher urinary pH increases the proportion of phosphate in the divalent and trivalent forms, which combine with calcium. This results in urine supersaturated with calcium phosphate and formation of calcium phosphate crystals. Further, if the kidney's ability to excrete acid is severely reduced, blood pH will also be reduced. Acidosis decreases the concentration of urinary citrate and increases urinary calcium levels. Distal tubular acidosis should be considered when a cat with acidosis has a urinary pH greater than 6 and renal function is otherwise normal.

Persistent alkaline urine not attributable to more common causes, such as infection with urease-producing bacteria (e.g., *Staphylococcus intermedius*), can be due to distal tubular acidosis. This condition, however, is extremely rare in cats. In other species, distal tubular acidosis has been associated with drugs (e.g., acetazolamide) and diseases (e.g., hepatic cirrhosis, myeloma, nephrotic syndrome and systemic lupus erythematosus) or it may be idiopathic.

BIBLIOGRAPHY

DiBartola SP, Chew DJ, Horton ML. Cystinuria in a cat. Journal of the American Veterinary Medical Association 1991; 198: 102-104.

Halperin ML, Goldstein MB, Stinebaugh BJ, et al. Renal tubular acidosis. In: Clinical Disorders of Fluid and Electrolyte Metabolism, 4th ed. New York, NY: McGraw-Hill, 1987; 675-684.

Osborne CA, Kruger JM, Lulich JP, et al. Disorders of the feline lower urinary tract. In: Osborne CA, Finco DR, eds. Canine and Feline Nephrology and Urology. Baltimore, MD: Williams & Wilkins, 1995; 625-680.

Table 1. Key nutritional factors—uncommon feline urolith types.

Nutritional factors	Dietary recommendations
Calcium phosphate uroliths (prevention)	
Water	Promote water intake by using a moist food or other measures
Calcium	Avoid excess dietary calcium
	Restrict dietary calcium to 0.6 to 0.8% dry matter
Phosphorus	Avoid excess dietary phosphorus
	Restrict dietary phosphorus to <0.8% dry matter
Sodium	Avoid excess dietary sodium
	Restrict dietary sodium to <0.30% dry matter
Vitamin D	Avoid excess dietary vitamin D
	Restrict dietary vitamin D to <5,000 IU/kg food
Purine uroliths (prevention)	
Water	Promote water intake by using a moist food or other measures
Protein	Avoid excess dietary protein
	Use protein sources with low purine content (i.e., those with few cell nuclei), such as milk and egg. Avoid proteins with many cell nuclei such as brain, liver and yeast.
	Restrict dietary protein to 28 to 30% dry matter
Urinary pH	Use a food that helps maintain a more alkaline urine (6.6 to 6.8)

---

involvement has been demonstrated in cats with idiopathic FLUTD by demonstrating substance P in the effluent of cats following distention of the bladder with water.

The tricyclic antidepressant drug amitriptyline has been recommended for treatment of interstitial cystitis in cats.[60] In addition to modifying behavior, amitriptyline is reported to have analgesic properties. Amitriptyline (10 mg by mouth daily) was evaluated in 15 cats with severe recurrent interstitial cystitis in an open, uncontrolled 12-month study.[65] Response to treatment was evaluated by owner questionnaire, urinalysis findings and cystoscopy. Episodes of owner-reported signs of lower urinary tract disease were eliminated in nine of 15 (60%) cats. Somnolence, weight gain and decreased grooming were reported. Cystoscopic appearance of underlying bladder lesions did not change yet cystic uroliths were detected in four cats (4/15 or 27%) during the first six months of observation. Although the authors considered the uroliths to be coincidental or due to increased bladder capacity or incomplete emptying of the bladder, misdiagnosis or misclassification of interstitial cystitis must also be considered. Cystic uroliths are an exclusion criterion for interstitial cystitis.

VIRAL INFECTION

Viral infections have been implicated as causative agents in lower urinary tract disease based on the isolation of feline cell-associated herpesvirus, feline calicivirus and syncytia-

Table 21-12. Urine acidifying and alkalinizing pet food ingredients.

Protein acidifying ingredients
Poultry meal
Corn gluten meal
Other acidifying ingredients
Ammonium chloride*
Calcium chloride
Calcium sulfate
dl-methionine
Phosphoric acid
Alkalinizing ingredients
Calcium carbonate
Potassium citrate
Magnesium oxide

*Not approved in the United States as a food additive.

forming virus from cats with hematuria and dysuria alone or in combination with urethral obstruction.[66] However, other laboratories using routine techniques to isolate viruses have not duplicated these findings in cats with naturally occurring lower urinary tract disease. There are several possible reasons why investigators have been unable to isolate these viruses in subsequent studies: the causative virus is highly cell-associated, has a latent phase or urine inhibits growth in vitro. Although standard cell culture inoculation methods with urine were negative for virus, investigators could experimentally induce bovine herpesvirus type 4 (BHV-4) infections in feline urinary bladders using tissue explantation techniques. However, the pathogenic role of BHV-4 in FLUTD remains unclarified because antibodies have been found in clinically normal cats and antibodies have not been found in clinical cases.[66] It would be valuable to revisit the question of viral etiology in lower urinary tract disease using newer polymerase chain reaction methods for virus detection and identification. Polymerase chain reaction methods allow detection of minuscule quantities of viral nucleic acid in a wide variety of tissues and body fluids.

Key Nutritional Factors

By definition, interstitial cystitis is not amenable to nutritional therapy; therefore, the focus of this section is on nutritional management of urinary precipitates. In its simplest form, the initiation and growth of urinary precipitates involve a chemical precipitation of dissolved ions or molecules from a solution that is supersaturated with precipitate-forming components. The degree of supersaturation or undersaturation of urine with regard to these components influences the probability of precipitates forming. In turn, the urinary concentration of these components is influenced by nutritional factors.

The urinary precipitates of primary concern in FLUTD are struvite (magnesium ammonium phosphate) and calcium oxalate. Some nutritional factors (e.g., urinary pH) have opposing effects on the probability of struvite and calcium oxalate formation. Consequently, the goal is to achieve balance in reducing the likelihood of struvite and calcium oxalate formation. See sidebar "Less Common Urolith Types" for diagnostic and key nutritional factors for uncommon feline uroliths.

WATER

The percent of water in cat foods varies. In general, dry foods are less than 10% water and moist foods are greater than 72% water. The volume of water consumed each day by a cat in a thermoneutral environment depends to a large extent on the composition and quantity of food ingested. The volume of water drunk increases as the moisture content of the food decreases; however, cats fed dry foods usually have lower total water intake than those fed moist foods.[67]

The solute load of the food also influences water consumption; urea is a major contributor to the renal solute load. Increasing the protein content of food increases the solute load; therefore, foods with higher protein content are associated with higher water intake. The metabolism of energy substrates yields endogenous water. The daily volume of endogenously produced water is small (approximately 10 to 15%) compared with the total daily water intake.[68] Fats provide the most water per gram and carbohydrates provide the most water per calorie. When glycogen is oxidized, additional water is released during glycogen mobilization. The amount of water generated differs slightly depending on the source of fat, chain length and degree of saturation. Proteins vary more than fats in the range of endogenous water produced. Because they lead to greater water intake and subsequent higher urine volume, moist foods are recommended in the management of calcium oxalate and struvite urolithiasis.

SPECIFIC FOOD FACTORS

Urinary pH

The kidneys eliminate the acid that is produced each day by metabolism and food. Therefore, to define the "normal" urinary pH, it is necessary to consider the "normal" or habitual diet. The diet of feral house cats has been well studied.[69] On a volume basis, the gastric content of feral cats is approximately 90% small mammals, such as mice and rats. The average urinary pH is approximately 6.3 when cats are fed a normal diet of rat carcasses.[70]

Blood pH is normally maintained within a narrow range by extracellular and intracellular buffering processes and respiratory and renal regulatory mechanisms. Chemical buffering and respiratory compensation protect against abrupt deviations in body pH; however, the kidneys provide longer-term defense against acid and alkali deviations. This process occurs continuously as endogenous acids are generated. The kidneys must conserve bicarbonate in the glomerular filtrate and regenerate bicarbonate degraded by the reaction with metabolic acids in order to maintain normal plasma bicarbonate levels. The kidneys can increase the amount of net acid excretion in urine and generate bicarbonate in response to exogenous acid loads. Urinary organic anion excretion parallels changes in urinary bicarbonate. Urinary organic anions (e.g., citrate and α-ketoglutarate) increase in response to an alkali load and decrease in response to an acid load.[71]

Normally, the kidneys synthesize urinary ammonia and thus ammonium almost exclusively. Ammonia is derived from glutamine and other amino acids in the proximal tubule cells. Adaptive changes in renal ammonia production occur in response to changes in systemic acid-base balance. More ammonia is produced and urinary ammonium ion concentration is increased with chronic metabolic acidosis. The kidneys excrete hydrogen ions (H^+) in the form of titratable acid and ammonium ions. The acidification process is an integrated function that occurs at several nephron segments. The proximal convoluted tubules reabsorb most of the filtered bicarbonate and add ammonia to the tubule fluid. Residual bicarbonate is titrated with filtered buffers (conjugate bases) to form titratable acid in the cortical collecting tubules. There is also a parallel bicarbonate secretory mechanism. The medullary collecting ducts decrease urinary pH and trap ammonia as ammonium. Ammonia exists in two forms in aqueous solution, nonionized ammonia (NH_3) and the monovalent cation ammonium (NH_4^+). Nonionized ammonia is lipid soluble and readily traverses cell membranes in the direction determined by the concentration gradient. At the pH of renal tubular fluid, hydrogen ions avidly combine with ammonia to form ammonium. The ionized form is not lipid soluble; consequently, the ammonium is trapped within the tubular lumen and is excreted in the form of neutral salts (e.g., NH_4Cl).

Bicarbonate resorption in the proximal tubules is effected primarily by neutral Na^+/H^+ exchange, which is driven by the lumen-to-cell sodium gradient. Hydrogen ions secreted into the lumen of the proximal convoluted tubule combine with filtered bicarbonate to form carbonic acid. Carbonic acid, catalyzed by membrane-bound carbonic anhydrase, is broken down to carbon dioxide and water. At equilibrium, dissolved carbon dioxide equilibrates with the gas phase (i.e., the respiratory gas in the pulmonary alveoli). Dissolved carbon dioxide diffuses into the cell and combines with hydroxyl ions. Newly formed bicarbonate and reabsorbed sodium are added to the blood in the process. The net result is the excretion of hydrogen ions and the replenishment of bicarbonate. If a short-term (three to five days) acid load is encountered, the kidneys respond by increasing titratable acid and ammonium excretion.

Physiologic limits for urinary pH in cats are 8.5 to 5.5. Reduction in urinary pH from the upper to lower end of this range changes the ratio of NH_4^+/NH_3 from 3.4:1 to 3,400:1. Thus, acidifying foods increase the urinary concentration of ammonium ions, one component of struvite. However, this increase is more than offset by an even greater decrease in anionic phosphate concentration, another component of struvite, as the urinary pH decreases from 8.5 to 5.5.

The effect of a food on urinary pH is the net effect of its constituent nutrients. Dietary acid is derived from several nutrients (Table 21-12).[72] (See sidebars "Estimating the Effect of Food on Urinary pH" and "Interpreting Urinary pH Test Results.") Sulfuric acid is formed when sulfur-containing amino acid residues of proteins (e.g., methionine and cysteine) are oxidized to sulfate. In general, animal-source protein ingredients contain more sulfur-containing amino acid residues than do plant-source proteins. The quantity of sulfuric acid generated is reflected by the amount of sulfate in the urine.[30]

Phosphorus has strong effects on acid-base balance, depending on its chemical form. Inorganic phosphorus can be ingested as phosphoric acid, monobasic and dibasic or anionic phosphate. Phosphoric acid is used in cat foods to enhance palatability, either separately or as a component of topically applied animal digests. Phosphoric acid has a strong acidifying effect. Monobasic phosphate is also acidifying, dibasic phosphate has little effect on urinary pH[73] and anionic phosphate is alkalizing. At the physiologic pH of 7.4, inorganic phosphorus from phospholipids, phosphoproteins and nucleic acids generates dibasic and monobasic phosphate at a ratio of 1:4, thus its acidifying effect is nearly as strong as that of monobasic phosphate.[74]

The effect of other inorganic cations depends on their pKa and to some extent on their absorption from the intes-

Estimating the Effect of Food on Urinary pH

Several important effects of food on acid-base balance can be described by anion-cation balance (ACB). Calculation of a food's ACB has been evaluated as a practical method for predicting the effect of a food on urinary pH. This method does not consider the differential absorption of cations and anions from the gastrointestinal tract nor the possible different valences of phosphorus. In this method, the ACB is calculated from the concentrations of alkaline and acid compounds in the food, expressed as mmol/kg dry matter, using the formula: ACB = 49.9 (Ca) + 82.3 (Mg) + 43.5 (Na) + 25.6 (K) – 64.6 (P) – 13.4 (Met) – 16.6 (Cys) – 28.2 (Cl).

Key: ACB = anion-cation balance, Ca = calcium, Mg = magnesium, K = potassium, Na = sodium, P = phosphorus, Met = methionine, Cys = cysteine, Cl = chloride (in g/kg dry matter). Factors take into account atomic/molecular weight and valence (2 for phosphorus).

Synonyms for ACB are anion-cation gap, dietary base excess or dietary undetermined anions. The last synonym is a very good description of a positive ACB. Under practical conditions, those accompanying anions of the "alkaline" compounds of the formula (Ca, Mg, K, Na) that are not listed on the "acid" side of the formula are likely to represent carbonates, oxides or organic anions, all of which have an alkalizing effect. In the case of a negative ACB, the acidifying effect may result from direct effects (i.e., phosphorus, sulfur-containing amino acids) or from the accompanying chloride cation (e.g., ammonium).

This method was evaluated in a study involving 10 commercial foods (moist and dry) and several additives. Feeding trials involved four to six cats per trial. Cats were fed the foods for two days and urine was collected for at least five days. During the eight hours after feeding, urinary pH was measured immediately after urination and urine excreted during the reminder of the day was tested the following morning. There was a highly significant correlation between ACB of the food and the mean urinary pH. In the amounts used in this study, the addition of calcium carbonate and calcium lactate significantly increased urinary pH; dibasic calcium phosphate and ascorbic acid had no effect; and calcium chloride, ammonium chloride and phosphoric acid decreased urinary pH (Table 1). A follow-up study confirmed the results. This study showed that with stepwise reduction of ACB, urinary pH decreased proportionally until an ACB of -400 to -500 mmol/kg dry matter was reached, after which no further reduction of urinary pH occurred.

Table 1. Correlation between calculated food base excess and urinary pH when selected ingredients are added to cat foods.

Additives	Amounts (g/kg dry matter)	Urinary pH	Calculated base excess
Control	na*	7.35	na
Calcium carbonate	25.0	8.40	697
Calcium lactate	62.5	8.23	646
Ammonium chloride	12.5	6.53	14
Phosphoric acid	2.5	6.42	32

*na = not applicable.

BIBLIOGRAPHY

Kienzle E, Schuknecht A, Meyer H. Influence of food composition on the urine pH in cats. Journal of Nutrition 1991; 121: S87-S88.

Kienzle E, Wilms-Eilers S. Struvite diet in cats: Effect of ammonium chloride and carbonates on acid base balance of cats. Journal of Nutrition 1994; 124: 265S-269S.

Opitz B, Kienzle E. The use of anion-cation gap in nutrition consultation (abstract). In: Proceedings. European Society of Veterinary and Comparative Nutrition, Munich, Germany, 1997: 34.

FLUTD

Table 21-13. Recommended levels of selected nutrients in commercial foods used for calcium oxalate urolith prevention in cats.

Nutrients	% DM	Caloric basis (per 100 kcal)
Calcium	0.5-0.8	0.11-0.20 g
Phosphorus	0.5-0.7	0.10-0.16 g
Sodium	0.1-0.4	0.03-0.10 g
Magnesium	0.04-0.10	18-20 mg

Key: DM = dry matter.

Table 21-14. Recommended levels of selected nutrients in commercial foods used for struvite urolith prevention in cats.

Nutrients	% DM	Caloric basis (per 100 kcal)
Phosphorus	0.5-0.9	0.11-0.24 g
Sodium	0.2-0.6	0.06-0.11 g
Magnesium	0.04-0.10	9-24 mg

Key: DM = dry matter.

Table 21-15. Recommended levels of selected nutrients in commercial foods used for struvite urolith dissolution in cats.

Nutrients	% DM	Caloric basis (per 100 kcal)
Phosphorus	0.5-0.8	0.11-0.17 g
Sodium	0.7-0.9	0.15-0.18 g
Magnesium	0.04-0.06	9-12 mg

Key: DM = dry matter.

Interpreting Urinary pH Test Results

Although calculation of anion-cation balance may roughly estimate urinary pH, the only well-accepted method of comparing foods is to feed the food to a group of cats and compare urinary pH. Most cat food manufacturers provide urinary pH test data for their products; however, there is no standard urinary pH testing protocol. Consequently, it is important to know the protocol used to measure urinary pH before comparing results from different laboratories.

tine in relation to their accompanying cations. Mineral salts vary in their effect on urinary pH and thus are potential acid or base sources. Oxides and carbonates are alkalizing. Differences in absorption of the cation and anion portion of a salt are important. Intestinal absorption of calcium and magnesium is relatively low; however, absorption of accompanying anions can be high and influence urinary pH. Nonmetabolizable anions (e.g., chloride, phosphate and sulfate) absorbed in excess of their accompanying cations are acidifying. For example, ammonium chloride, calcium chloride and calcium sulfate decrease urinary pH, and magnesium oxide and calcium carbonate increase urinary pH.

Carbohydrates, fat and the sulfur- and phosphorus-free residues of protein have little effect on acid-base-balance if they are fully oxidized to water and carbon dioxide. However, organic acids produced from intermediary metabolism products formed from partial oxidation of carbohydrates or fats (e.g., lactate during anaerobic exercise or β-hydroxybutyrate during ketosis) have a marked acidifying effect. The organic acids generated contribute to net acid production when conjugate bases are excreted in the urine as negatively charged organic anions. The net amount of hydrogen ion contributed by organic acids can be estimated by measuring the amount of organic anions in the urine. Healthy cats fed a balanced diet are unlikely to produce considerable amounts of organic acids from carbohydrate, fat or sulfur- and phosphorus-free protein residues; therefore, it is unlikely that their acid-base-balance is affected by these nutrients.

Organic acids (e.g., ascorbic acid, lactic acid or citric acid) can be fully oxidized in intermediary metabolism. Consequently they have little effect on urinary pH, unless they are excreted in the urine. Most organic acids are rather weak; therefore, marked renal excretion is necessary to affect urinary pH. For example, ascorbic acid in doses less than 1,000 mg/kg body weight did not significantly affect urinary pH of cats fed a balanced diet.[47] By comparison, the conjugated bases of organic acids may change acid-base balance. They take up hydrogen ions during oxidation to water and carbon dioxide. Thus, calcium and magnesium salts containing conjugated bases of organic acids can be as strongly alkalizing as the corresponding carbonates or oxides.

Ammonium and positively charged cationic amino acids (e.g., lysine and arginine) release hydrogen ions when they are transformed into neutral products. Hydrochloric acid is generated if their accompanying anion is chloride. The acidifying effect is obvious.

Urinary pH is not a direct function of acid excretion. Urinary buffer systems can modify the effect of acid intake on urinary pH. Small changes in the acid load of the diet lead to much greater changes in urinary pH when the phosphorus intake of cats is decreased.[75]

Although decreasing urinary pH theoretically increases urinary ammonium concentration, the same change in urinary pH decreases anionic phosphate levels in urine. Thus as urine becomes more acidic, precipitation of struvite becomes less likely. The risk reduction for struvite crystal formation becomes clinically important as the mean daily urinary pH declines to about 6.4.

For most cats less than about seven years of age, the ideal mean daily urinary pH is between 6.1 and 6.4.[76] Urinary pH less than 6.1 may reflect systemic acidosis that may be accompanied by hypercalciuria. Urinary pH values above 6.4 favor struvite precipitation. A slightly higher urinary pH target (i.e., 6.6 to 6.8) may be beneficial for cats at greater risk for calcium oxalate urolith formation because of their age or other risk factors.

Magnesium

For struvite precipitates to form, the urine must be supersaturated with magnesium, ammonium and anionic phosphate. Avoiding excess dietary magnesium intake can reduce the urinary concentration of magnesium. Excess magnesium is present in some commercial cat foods because they contain ingredients high in magnesium (e.g., high-ash meat and bone, fish and poultry meals). Foods recommended for prevention of struvite precipitation should meet the nutritional allowance for magnesium but avoid excess.

Magnesium is an inhibitor of calcium oxalate crystal formation in vitro; therefore, low urinary magnesium concentrations have been suggested as a potential risk factor in the formation of calcium-containing uroliths. At physiologic concentrations of magnesium, in vitro studies demonstrated that magnesium decreased the rate of nucleation and growth of struvite crystals.[77,78] The effect of higher levels of magnesium supplementation has been studied in an experimental model of calcium oxalate nephrolithiasis in which rats received 1% ethylene glycol in drinking water.[49] Magnesium oxide was administered at 200 and 500 mg/100 g food. At a dose of 200 mg/100 g food for two weeks, magnesium oxide did not alter calcium oxalate deposition in the kidney; however, calcium oxalate deposition in the kidney was decreased at the higher dose of 500 mg/100 g food. Human clinical studies of the efficacy of magnesium supplementation on the recurrence of calcium oxalate uroliths have yielded conflicting results.[79,80]

The proposed mechanisms of action of magnesium supplementation include increased urinary pH, increased urinary excretion of citrate and formation of magnesium oxalate complexes in urine. Magnesium oxalate is more soluble than calcium oxalate. The high excretion of magnesium in urine and the formation of magnesium oxalate in theory reduce the concentration of oxalate available for precipitation as calcium oxalate. Tables 21-13, 21-14 and 21-15 list magnesium recommendations in foods for calcium oxalate prevention, struvite prevention and struvite dissolution, respectively.

Phosphorus

Varying dietary phosphorus levels can alter urinary phosphate concentrations in cats, thereby influencing the likelihood of urinary struvite precipitates. Urinary phosphate can exist in several states. Anionic phosphate (PO_4^{3-}) is the important form in precipitation and dissolution of struvite. Urinary concentration of anionic phosphate is reversibly influenced by pH as explained above. Thus as urine becomes more acidic, anionic phosphate is converted to monobasic and dibasic phosphate, thereby reducing the concentration of anionic phosphate available for incorporation in struvite precipitates. As the urine becomes more alkaline, the reaction proceeds in the opposite direction and the concentration of anionic phosphate increases.

In cats, increased levels of dietary phosphorus decrease urinary excretion of calcium. The inhibitory effect of dietary phosphorus on calcium and magnesium absorption can be explained by formation of insoluble calcium-magnesium-phosphate complexes in the lumen of the intestine. Formation of these complexes decreases the concentration of soluble calcium and magnesium, thereby decreasing the availability of these minerals for absorption. The inhibitory effect of dietary phosphorus on urinary excretion was greater in rats than in cats.[29] This finding might be due to the fact that the absorption coefficient for calcium is lower in cats than in rats, making phosphorus-related changes more difficult to detect.[29]

Increasing dietary levels of phosphorus in the form of $NaH_2PO_4 \cdot 2H_2O$ caused a decrease in urinary pH and urinary concentration of calcium and magnesium and increased urinary phosphorus concentration. High dietary intake of phosphorus decreased plasma phosphorus concentrations and creatinine clearance.[29]

The intake of magnesium and calcium influences urinary phosphate concentration. Rats fed a very low-phosphorus food (0.07% dry matter [DM]) had marked hypercalciuria.[81] Feeding rats this very low level of phosphorus for one week resulted in urine highly supersaturated with calcium oxalate and containing large amounts of calcium oxalate crystals. Adult maintenance cat foods contain at least 0.5% DM phosphorus. Tables 21-13, 21-14 and 21-15

Table 21-16. Calcium-rich foods that should be avoided in cats at risk for calcium oxalate urolithiasis.*

Food items	Serving sizes	Calcium (mg)
Low-fat yogurt	1 cup (8 oz)	415
Whole milk	1 cup (8 oz)	291
Cheese	1 oz	200-270
Ice cream or ice milk	1 cup (8 oz)	176
Cottage cheese, creamed	1 cup (8 oz)	136
Broccoli, cooked	1 large stalk	88

*Mineral supplements and some commercial cat foods contain much more calcium than these foods, emphasizing the need for a thorough, complete dietary history.

list phosphorus recommendations in foods for calcium oxalate prevention, struvite prevention and struvite dissolution, respectively.

Calcium

Excess dietary calcium should be avoided to prevent recurrence of calcium oxalate uroliths. The most important sources of excess calcium are commercial foods and mineral supplements containing high calcium levels. High intake of dietary calcium may lead to hypercalciuria and urolith formation in patients with intestinal hyperabsorption of calcium. However, severe calcium restriction can cause negative calcium balance and may contribute to hyperoxaluria.

Intestinal absorption of calcium occurs primarily in the duodenum. Transport of calcium across the gut is vitamin D-dependent and saturable. Calcium availability varies markedly and may be influenced by nondietary and dietary factors. Generally, calcium absorption from the gut is inversely proportional to dietary intake. In other words, absorption is high from low-calcium foods and low from high-calcium foods. Other dietary factors such as vitamin D, sucrose, fructose, glucose, xylose, dietary fiber, oxalic acid, phytic acid, protein and phosphorus reportedly affect calcium availability. The role of individual dietary factors in dogs and cats consuming mixed meals is difficult to assess. Age, estrogen status, pregnancy, disease and medications influence calcium availability in human beings.

Table 21-16 lists calcium-rich foods that should be avoided in homemade diets and in treats. In addition to foods naturally high in calcium, a number of different foods and beverages (e.g., breads and breakfast cereals) are fortified with calcium. The amount of calcium added to these foods is listed on the product label.

Another potential unrecognized source of excess dietary calcium is vitamin-mineral supplements, especially specific calcium supplements. A wide variety of calcium supplements are available over the counter. These supplements differ in the amount of elemental calcium provided. Calcium carbonate, for example, contains 40% calcium (by weight), whereas calcium lactate and calcium gluconate contain 13 and 9% calcium, respectively. There is little information available about the relative availability of calcium from different supplements. Calcium supplements differ not only in their calcium content but also in solubility.

In human patients eating oxalate-rich foods, increasing dietary calcium intake prevents dietary hyperoxaluria.[31] This finding is presumably due to decreased intestinal absorption of oxalate. However, women taking calcium supplements had a 79% increased risk of calcium oxalate uroliths.[82] The increased risk associated with calcium supplements may be due to the timing of ingestion. If not

Table 21-17. Levels of selected nutrients in commercial products used in feline patients with lower urinary tract disease.*

	Protein	Fat	Phosphorus	Calcium	Magnesium	Urinary pH**
Struvite urolith dissolution						
Hill's Prescription Diet Feline s/d, moist	41.7	33.8	0.52	0.62	0.04	5.9-6.1
Hill's Prescription Diet Feline s/d, dry	34.6	25.9	0.82	0.71	0.05	5.9-6.1
Leo Specific Struvil FSW, moist	48.7	32.5	0.52	0.65	0.05	<6.3
Leo Specific Struvil FSD, dry	33.7	28.8	0.49	0.60	0.05	<6.3
Struvite urolith prevention						
Hill's Prescription Diet Feline c/d-s, moist	43.3	21.7	0.51	0.63	0.06	6.2-6.4
Hill's Prescription Diet Feline c/d-s, dry	34.6	16.3	0.67	0.87	0.05	6.2-6.4
Hill's Prescription Diet Feline w/d, moist	41.1	16.6	0.55	0.63	0.05	6.2-6.4
Hill's Prescription Diet Feline w/d, dry	39.2	9.5	0.85	1.04	0.07	6.2-6.4
Iams Eukanuba Urinary Formula Low pH/O, moist	39.6	20.8	na	na	0.10	5.9-6.3
Iams Eukanuba Urinary Formula Low pH/O, dry	34.8	16.9	na	na	0.11	5.9-6.3
Leo Specific Precal FCW, foil pack	57.6	31.6	0.67	0.78	0.04	<6.4
Leo Specific Precal FCD, dry	33.9	25.1	0.62	0.73	0.05	<6.4
Medi-Cal Feline Preventive formula, moist	46.7	31.1	1.06	1.10	0.05	Acid
Medi-Cal Feline Preventive formula, dry	33.4	22.9	0.71	0.83	0.07	Acid
Purina CNM UR-Formula, moist	41.4	16.5	0.82	0.88	0.05	Mean 6.1
Purina CNM UR-Formula, dry	35.4	11.6	0.84	1.12	0.08	Mean 6.1
Select Care Control Formula, moist	50.9	33.3	1.05	1.14	0.10	6.0-6.8
Select Care Control Formula, dry	33.3	22.6	0.75	0.87	0.08	6.0-6.7
Waltham S/O Control pHormula/pH Control, moist	41.1	44.2	1.16	0.95	0.10	6.3-6.5
Waltham S/O Control pHormula/pH Control, dry	36.5	19.7	0.88	0.70	0.06	6.3-6.5
Whiskas Feline Low pH Control Diet, moist	44.8	39.3	0.65	0.80	0.08	Mean 6.3
Whiskas Feline Low pH Control Diet, dry	38.3	18.9	1.03	1.02	0.08	Mean 6.1
Calcium oxalate urolith prevention						
Hill's Prescription Diet Feline c/d-oxl, moist	41.6	19.7	0.55	0.67	0.09	6.6-6.8
Hill's Prescription Diet Feline c/d-oxl, dry	34.2	16.7	0.66	0.80	0.08	6.6-6.8
Hill's Prescription Diet Feline g/d, moist	35.1	19.4	0.54	0.66	0.08	6.4-6.6
Hill's Prescription Diet Feline g/d, dry	33.4	18.9	0.55	0.51	0.05	6.4-6.6
Hill's Prescription Diet Feline k/d, moist	28.3	41.1	0.57	0.57	0.04	6.6-6.9
Hill's Prescription Diet Feline k/d, dry	28.1	27.4	0.61	0.78	0.05	6.6-6.9
Iams Eukanuba Urinary Formula Moderate pH/O, moist	41.3	21.7	na	na	0.11	6.3-6.9
Iams Eukanuba Urinary Formula Moderate pH/O, dry	35.2	17.0	na	na	0.12	6.3-6.9
Select Care Control Formula, moist	50.9	33.3	1.05	1.14	0.10	6.0-6.8
Select Care Control Formula, dry	33.3	22.6	0.75	0.87	0.08	6.0-6.7
Waltham S/O Control pHormula/pH Control, moist	41.1	44.2	1.16	0.95	0.10	6.3-6.5
Waltham S/O Control pHormula/pH Control, dry	36.5	19.7	0.88	0.70	0.06	6.3-6.5

Key: na = information not published by manufacturer.
*This list represents products with the largest market share and for which published information is available.
Manufacturers' published values; nutrients expressed as % dry matter.
**Protocols for measuring urinary pH may vary.

taken with meals, calcium supplements may lead to increased urinary calcium excretion without decreasing oxalate absorption in the GI tract. Table 21-13 lists calcium recommendations in foods for calcium oxalate prevention.

Sodium

Most factors that promote natriuresis tend to increase urinary calcium excretion. Calcium and sodium are reabsorbed at common sites in the renal tubules. Excessive dietary sodium intake may be a risk factor for hypercalciuria and calcium oxalate urolithiasis in dogs and cats. Excessive quantities of dietary sodium should be avoided in patients with recurrent calcium oxalate uroliths. Hypercalciuric people who form calcium-containing uroliths appear to have a proportionally greater increase in urinary calcium excretion than non-urolith formers. Increasing dietary sodium intake from 140 to 310 mmol/day increased urinary calcium excretion by 34% and decreased urinary citrate by 10%.[83] However, urinary calcium and sodium excretion was not correlated in healthy people with low dietary calcium intake.[84] Tables 21-13, 21-14 and 21-15 list sodium recommendations in foods for calcium oxalate prevention, struvite prevention and struvite dissolution, respectively.

Protein

During the last century the predominant urolith type in people in the United States has shifted from struvite to cal-

cium oxalate.[85] Cross-cultural studies have shown a shift from struvite to calcium oxalate uroliths with increasing industrialization.[86] The reason for the increased incidence of calcium oxalate in these human populations is unknown; however, dietary habits are thought to play a major role. Nutritional epidemiologic studies have emphasized the role of increased dietary intake of animal protein. This link seems plausible for the following reasons: the amount of animal protein in the diet correlates with industrialization, and dietary protein increases calcium, uric acid and possibly oxalate excretion and decreases urinary pH.

A high-protein diet reportedly increases urinary calcium excretion in dogs.[87] The 24-hour urinary calcium excretion was almost doubled when dogs were fed a food containing 31% DM protein compared with a food containing 10% DM protein. The type of protein, duration of protein intake and phosphorus intake influence the effect of protein on calcium.

Animal proteins are rich in sulfur-containing amino acids. Sulfur-containing amino acids are metabolized to sulfate and thus may reduce urinary pH and increase urinary calcium and uric acid concentrations. The hypocalciuric effect of phosphorus may vary depending on the form of phosphorus. Excess dietary protein should be avoided by feeding a food that contains 30 to 45% DM protein.

Other Food Factors

OXALATE

In people, most urinary oxalate is derived from metabolic pathways; approximately 40% is derived from the metabolism of ascorbate and the remainder from the conversion of glycolate, glycine and hydroxyproline. These latter substances are found primarily in dietary protein. Under normal circumstances, the pathways for metabolism of ascorbate to oxalate are saturated so that an increase in dietary ascorbic acid intake does not increase urinary excretion of oxalate. However, in certain individuals increased ascorbic acid intake results in increased oxalate excretion. Vitamin B_6 (pyridoxine) is a cofactor in the interconversion of glycine and glyoxylate. Pyridoxine deficiency results in increased formation and urinary excretion of oxalate.

Excessive dietary intake of oxalate is unlikely in companion animals because foods high in oxalate are not likely to be major components of the overall diet. The following foods are considered high-oxalate foods: sugar (in large quantities), chocolate, beets, beet greens, spinach, Swiss chard, rhubarb, whole soybeans, leeks, citrus pulp, wheat germ, sweet potatoes, raspberries, beans, carrots, celery, oranges, squash, corn and potatoes.[35] These ingredients are not commonly used in cat foods.

VITAMIN D

Calcium absorption occurs primarily in the duodenum, and transport is vitamin D-dependent. The metabolically active form of vitamin D (1,25-dihydroxycholecalciferol) is produced when the precursor undergoes hydroxylation in the proximal tubular cells of the kidneys. The primary actions of the active form of vitamin D are: 1) stimulation of intestinal calcium absorption, 2) inhibition of PTH synthesis, 3) inhibition of more active vitamin D synthesis in the kidneys and 4) facilitation of osteoclastic bone resorption. PTH, hypophosphatemia, growth hormone, estrogen and prolactin increase renal synthesis of 1,25-dihydroxycholecalciferol. Hyperphosphatemia, hypercalcemia and damage to the kidneys decrease renal synthesis of 1,25-dihydroxycholecalciferol. The AAFCO dietary allowance for vitamin D for adult cats is 500 to 10,000 IU/kg food.[88] However, cats at risk for calcium oxalate urolithiasis and those with hypercalcemia associated with calcium oxalate urolithiasis should be fed foods that do not exceed 5,000 IU/kg of food. Dietary supplements containing vitamin D should also not be fed to at-risk cats.

POTASSIUM

Transient negative potassium balance has been reported to occur in adult cats receiving long-term dietary acidification (i.e., for struvite urolith prevention) with phosphoric acid and ammonium chloride.[89,90] Potassium balance returned to normal by the end of both studies.

Potassium affects ammonia synthesis. Acute increases in potassium concentration suppress ammonia synthesis. Chronic potassium depletion stimulates ammonia synthesis at the same site as chronic metabolic acidosis. Acidifying foods, therefore, should have potassium levels in excess of the AAFCO minimum allowance of 0.6% (DMB).[88]

FAT

Higher fat foods can be advantageous because the increased energy density reduces overall mineral intake, including magnesium. Compared with protein and carbohydrate, fat provides the highest metabolic water contribution. Alternatively,

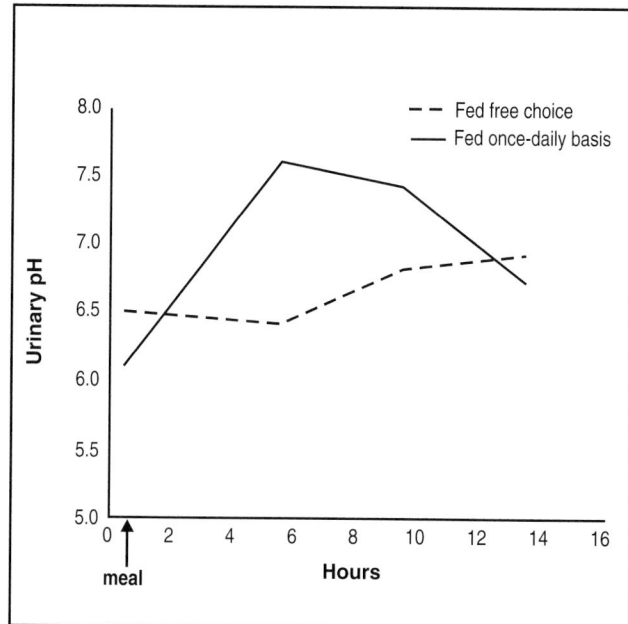

Figure 21-13. Mean urinary pH of cats fed a commercial food either free choice (ad libitum) or once daily. Note how once-daily feeding results in a significant increase in urinary pH (i.e., postprandial alkaline tide). (Adapted from Taton DF, Hamar D, Lewis LD. Evaluation of ammonium chloride as a urinary acidifier in the cat. Journal of the American Veterinary Medical Association 1984; 184: 433-436.)

foods with increased fat content will contribute to obesity, if they are not fed in a controlled manner. Obesity has been identified in some studies as a risk factor for FLUTD.[91] Foods with 8 to 25% DM fat can routinely be fed, depending on the cat's body condition and the desired energy density of the food.

FIBER

Certain dietary fiber sources bind calcium in the small intestine and may reduce the amount of calcium absorbed from the gut. (See Table 2-7.) Adding fiber to the current food or using a commercial fiber-enhanced food has been advocated by some for cats with persistent hypercalcemia and/or recurrent calcium oxalate urolithiasis. Anecdotal reports suggest that moderate levels of crude fiber (9 to 12% DMB) may be useful in these patients.

Assess the Food(s)

Food for cats with lower urinary tract disease should be evaluated for all the key nutritional factors described above. Levels of magnesium, calcium and phosphorus and information about the urinary pH are not required on the guaranteed or typical analysis of pet food labels and usually are not listed. Levels of these nutrients and urinary pH produced by feeding a particular food must be obtained by contacting the manufacturer or consulting published product information (Table 21-17).

Other sources of key nutritional factors include treats, supplements and human food offered as treats or part of the pet's daily intake. Commercial cat treats and processed human foods may have very high levels of minerals, such as phosphorus.

Product claims (e.g., low magnesium) may help in evaluating a food. (See sidebar "Regulatory Claims Related to Low Magnesium, Low Ash and Urinary Tract Health.") In the United States, a food with a "low magnesium" claim

Regulatory Claims Related to Low Magnesium, Low Ash and Urinary Tract Health

The United States Food and Drug Administration, Center for Veterinary Medicine (FDA CVM) has issued guidelines for pet food companies to establish the following claims: "reduces urinary pH," "low magnesium" and "improves urinary tract health." The FDA CVM suggests that submissions requesting permission to make "reduces urinary pH" or "improves urinary tract health" claims include supportive utility data demonstrating efficacy (i.e., the ability of the food to produce an appropriately acidic urine compared with a nonacidifying control food) and safety data.

A food with a label claim such as "helps maintain urinary tract health" is low in magnesium and produces an appropriately acidic urine. The FDA CVM has promulgated guidelines for protocols to support urinary tract health claims. The guidelines focus on prevention of struvite urinary precipitates, but do not address the question of calcium oxalate precipitate formation.

The guidelines suggest safety studies for a minimum of six months. These studies should include physical examinations and the following observations: food consumption, body weight measurements, urinalyses (including sediment examinations), serum biochemistry and blood gas analyses and mineral (calcium, phosphorus, magnesium and potassium) balance studies. Foods claiming to promote urinary tract health and reduce urinary pH must be nutritionally complete and balanced, as demonstrated by the Association of American Feed Control Officials (AAFCO) feeding protocols. It is noteworthy that the "improves urinary tract health" claim focuses on documentation of safety, urine acidification and restricted dietary intake of magnesium and does not in any way address the issue of calcium oxalate urolith formation.

The guideline for a low-magnesium claim is a magnesium level guaranteed less than 0.12% dry matter (using the maximum magnesium and maximum water guarantee). The magnesium must also be less than 25 mg/100 kcal, with energy content based on the AAFCO-approved calculation method or an actual digestibility study. Analysis of multiple batches is required.

In 1985, the Canadian Veterinary Medical Association (CVMA) established a "low ash" cat food certification program based on nutrient content of low-magnesium/pH-controlled cat foods. The required nutrient standards on a dry matter basis are as follows: 1) ash—no more than 6%, 2) magnesium levels—no more than 1.0% and no less than 0.05%, 3) magnesium levels—no more than 20 mg/100 kcal digestible energy and 4) an average resting urinary pH of 6.5 or less, and an average postprandial pH peak less than 7.03.

In July 1995, labeling of veterinary therapeutic foods in Europe (termed "dietetic pet foods") became strictly regulated. (See Chapter 5.) European regulations require only certain indications for therapeutic foods, termed "Particular Nutritional Purposes." Indications permitted for FLUTD include: 1) dissolution of struvite uroliths, 2) reduction of struvite urolith recurrence, 3) reduction of oxalate urolith recurrence, 4) reduction of urate urolith recurrence and 5) reduction of cystine urolith recurrence. Essential nutritional characteristics of the corresponding foods and specific label declarations must be met.

---

contains a maximum of 0.12% DM magnesium or 25 mg magnesium/100 kcal metabolizable energy.

Assess the Feeding Method

The method of feeding can influence urinary pH. Ingestion of food stimulates secretion of gastric acid and a temporary net acid loss from the body. This alkalization of urine is referred to as the postprandial alkaline tide. Specifically, the alkaline tide is caused by the secretion of bicarbonate into the blood by parietal cells of the stomach. This alkali load produces a transient bicarbonaturia that increases urinary pH unless offset by absorption of acidifying ingredients. When offered food free choice, most cats will eat small amounts every few hours, resulting in a smaller but more prolonged alkaline tide than with meal feeding. The smaller alkaline urinary pH excursions observed with free-choice feeding reduce the likelihood of struvite precipitate formation (Figure 21-13). However, free-choice feeding may be associated with obesity, which in turn is a risk factor for FLUTD.

▮ FEEDING PLAN

By definition, idiopathic cystitis is not amenable to nutritional therapy; therefore, the focus of this section is on nutritional management of urinary precipitates. However, idiopathic cystitis represents a risk factor for formation of urethral plugs. Feeding strategies designed to minimize struvite crystalluria may be appropriate for male cats at risk for plug formation.

Select a Food(s)

After a presumptive diagnosis of struvite urolithiasis has been made, a decision regarding surgical or medical therapy with a struvite calculolytic food is required. Treatment with a struvite calculolytic food is contraindicated in growing kittens, reproducing queens and patients with renal failure, metabolic acidosis, hypokalemia, hypertension or congestive heart failure. Surgery may be contraindicated if patient factors increase the risk of general anesthesia or adverse surgical outcomes. Because cystotomy does not necessarily remove all uroliths and because of high recurrence rates, multiple surgeries may be required.[92] The size and the number of uroliths influence the rate of dissolution, but do not determine ultimate success. In theory, medical dissolution may slow resolution of UTI or produce obstructive uropathy. Fortunately, these adverse sequelae are rare.

If a patient has a history of forming both struvite and calcium oxalate uroliths, the food should be selected to reduce the likelihood of calcium oxalate formation (i.e., less acidifying). The rationale for favoring formation of struvite over calcium oxalate is that struvite uroliths usually can be dissolved medically whereas calcium oxalate uroliths generally require surgical removal. Clients should be encouraged to feed only foods with key nutritional factors appropriate for the cat's urolith type. Other foods, treats and supplements may alter the key nutritional factors and increase the risk of recurrence. Clients who own cats that form calcium oxalate crystals and uroliths should be cautioned about grocery brand foods with urinary tract health claims. Such foods are formulated for healthy cats to avoid struvite crystals and uroliths. Feeding such foods may increase the risk for development of calcium oxalate uroliths in at-risk cats.

The Key Nutritional Factors—Feline Lower Urinary Tract Disease table summarizes the key nutritional factors for cats with struvite and calcium oxalate crystals and uroliths. Nutrient content of foods for affected cats should be compared with this list to determine if discrepancies exist between the ideal profile and the product under consideration. In many cases, it will be necessary to contact the manufacturer or review published information to determine the levels of some nutrients. A new food should be selected if discrepancies exist between the patient's current food and the Key Nutritional Factors table. Table 21-17 lists selected foods marketed for cats with specific urinary tract problems.

Determine a Feeding Method

The feeding method selected should consider concurrent problems such as obesity. Although free-choice feeding minimizes the postprandial alkaline tide, it may lead to excessive consumption of calories and contribute to obesity. If moist food is used to increase water consumption and thus reduce the urinary concentration of crystal-forming elements, free-choice feeding is not feasible.

▮ REASSESSMENT

Urinary pH measurements and urinalyses, including microscopic sediment examination, should be conducted periodically. The time of day markedly influences urinary pH. Samples obtained early in the morning, before food is offered, tend to be more acidic, whereas samples obtained within several hours of eating tend to be more alkaline (because of the postprandial alkaline tide). When interpreting the urinary pH of a spot or random sample, it is necessary to consider when the sample was collected relative to the time of eating. When evaluating the effect of a food change on urinary pH it is necessary to standardize time of collection relative to the time of eating. See Figures 21-14 and 21-15 for algorithms to assist in monitoring patients with FLUTD.

Recurrence of uroliths appears to be quite variable (Table 21-18). In general, it is possible for struvite uroliths to recur within weeks to months. Calcium oxalate, calcium phosphate and ammonium urate uroliths tend to recur within months rather than weeks after removal.[93] In two

retrospective studies, recurrence rates ranged from 11 to 37%.[27,94] The mineral composition of the recurrent urolith was not specified in one study.

Interpretation of recurrence and interval until recurrence should be based on a number of factors. Were all uroliths removed from the urinary tract at the time of surgery?[92] Did nonabsorbable suture materials left exposed in the lumen of the bladder during surgery provide a nidus for precipitation of crystalline material? What diagnostic methods were used to detect recurrence? How often was the patient evaluated for recurrence? Did the owner comply with recommendations to decrease the likelihood of recurrence? Has infection with a urease-producing microorganism persisted or recurred? Has an underlying anatomic defect gone uncorrected?

Recurrence rates for calcium oxalate uroliths in human patients without any form of preventive management are 10% at one year, 33% at five years and 50% at 10 years.[95] Current preventive management in people consists of increased fluid intake and avoidance of foods rich in calcium and oxalate. Other measures include treatment with thiazide diuretics, pyridoxine, potassium citrate, orthophosphate and allopurinol.

Medical protocols for dissolution of calcium oxalate uroliths in cats are not available. Therefore, there is a need for an integrated nutritional, medical and surgical approach. If urocystoliths are small enough to pass through the urethra, an alternative to cystotomy is voiding urohydropropulsion.[11] Because the urethra is smaller in males than in females, voiding urohydropropulsion is generally more successful in queens than in toms. Voiding urohydropropulsion is usually ineffective in cats with uroliths lodged in the urethra. Excessive manual compression of the bladder in cats with UTI can cause vesicoureteral reflux of infected urine.

In selected situations, periodic monitoring of venous blood gases for evidence of chronic metabolic acidosis is recommended. These situations include reduced renal function or the concurrent use of an acidifying food and a urinary acidifier. Recently, a handheld analyzer (I-STAT[b]) developed for human bedside testing was introduced to the veterinary market. This portable analyzer uses a test cartridge to measure blood gases on whole blood specimens of about 0.1 ml.

Drug-Nutrient Interactions

The use of urinary acidifiers in conjunction with an acidifying food is not recommended. With continued acid loading, renal excretion of acid increases but does not quite equal the acid intake, resulting in a positive acid

Table 21-18. Summary of biologic behavior—feline lower urinary tract diseases.*

Clinical findings	Spontaneous recovery	Sequelae	Recurrence
Interstitial cystitis	Yes	None	Yes
Bacterial infection	Yes	Struvite formation if urease positive, ascending pyelonephritis	Rare, perineal urethrostomy complications
Uroliths	Rare (spontaneous passage)	Urinary tract infection	Frequent, but variable
Urethral plugs	Rare	Postrenal azotemia	Frequent and unpredictable (iatrogenic?)

*Adapted from Lulich JP, Osborne CA, Kruger JM. Biologic behavior of feline lower urinary tract disease. Veterinary Clinics of North America: Small Animal Practice 1996; 26: 207-215.

FLUTD

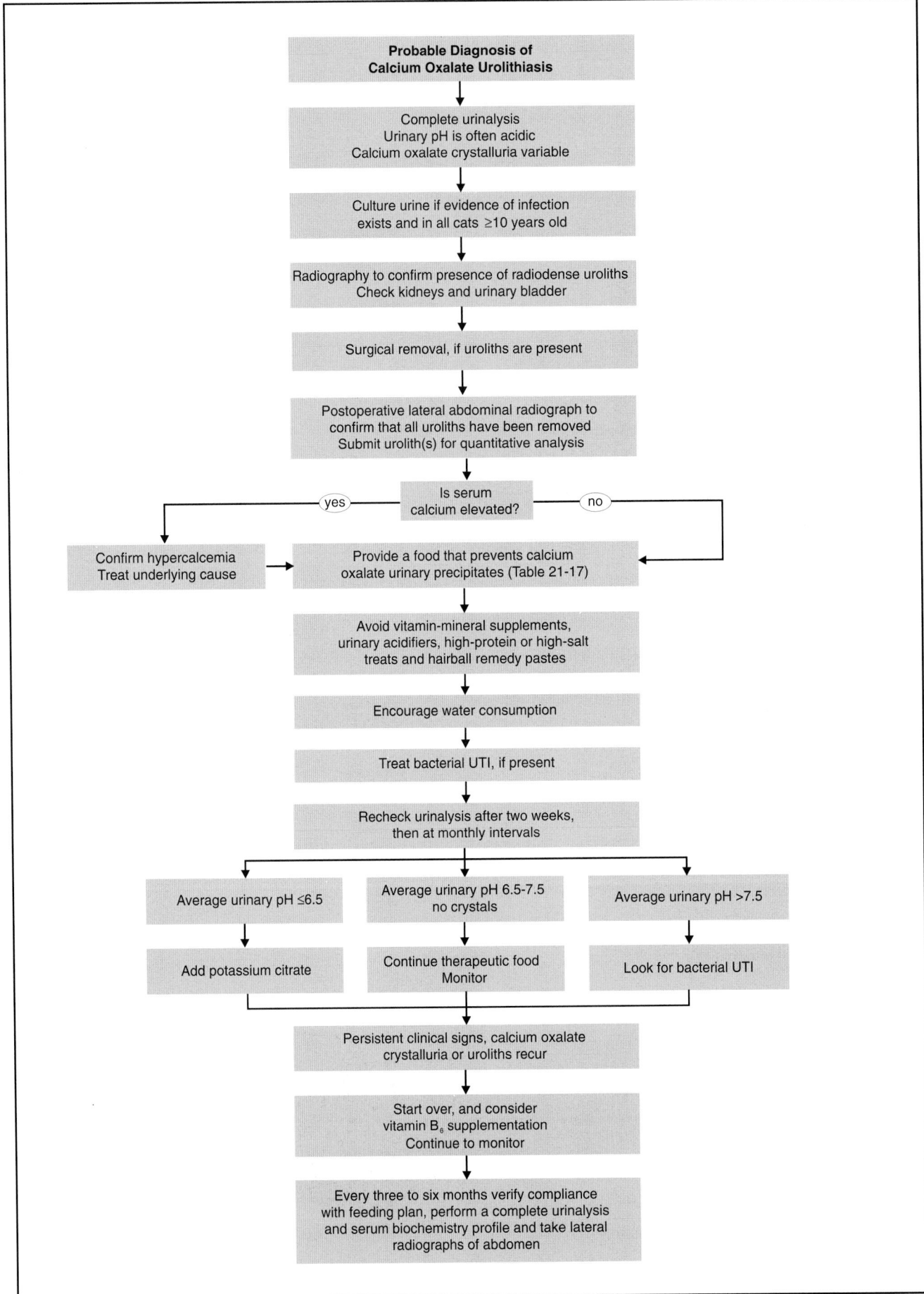

Figure 21-14. Algorithm for management and reassessment of cats with calcium oxalate urolithiasis.

FLUTD

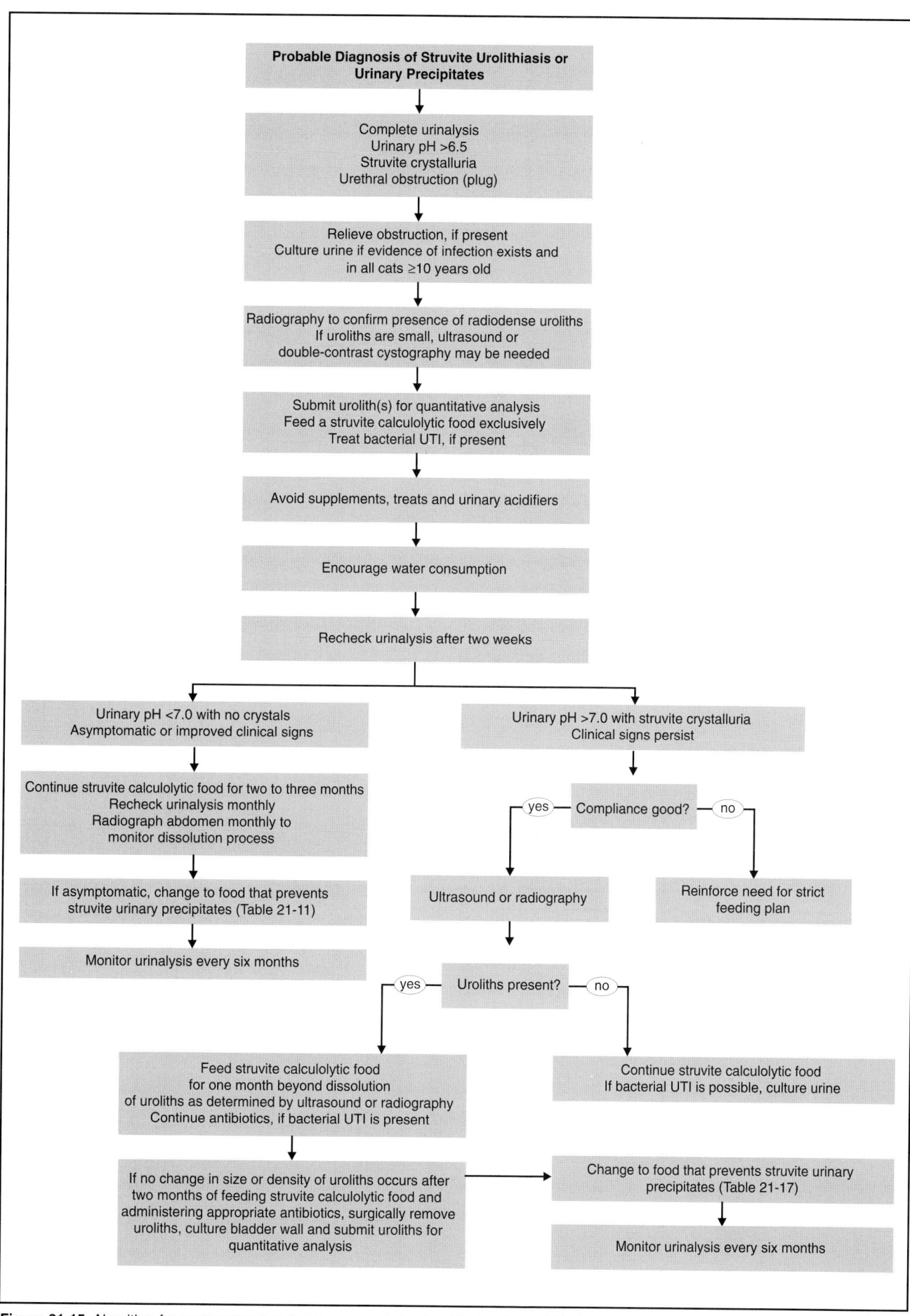

Figure 21-15. Algorithm for management and reassessment of cats with struvite urolithiasis.

balance (i.e., metabolic acidosis). Overacidification leading to metabolic acidosis is more likely in young cats and cats with renal insufficiency. Supplemental acidifiers may be considered if nonacidifying foods are used or if the food is ineffective. The lack of convincing evidence that urinary acidification alone prevents recurrence of idiopathic lower urinary tract disease and the many adverse effects of overacidification preclude the widespread use of urinary acidifiers for nonobstructive lower urinary tract disease in cats.

Although thiazide diuretics may be beneficial in minimizing urinary calcium excretion in people and dogs, no data have been provided to prove their efficacy in cats with calcium oxalate uroliths. Because thiazide diuretics may be associated with adverse effects such as dehydration, hypokalemia and hypercalcemia, their routine use in cats is not recommended, pending further investigation. Drugs that promote hypercalciuria should also be avoided in patients with calcium oxalate uroliths. This precludes routine administration of furosemide or glucocorticoids to these patients.

Investigators have detected sulfadiazine and/or its metabolites in uroliths and a urethral plug from cats with lower urinary tract disease.[96] Factors that predispose cats to precipitation of sulfonamides and/or their metabolites in the urinary tract include administration of high doses of these drugs for prolonged periods, acidic urine and highly concentrated urine.

Most patients with sulfadiazine-associated uroliths had a history of long-term empirical treatment with a combination of sulfadiazine and trimethoprim for suspected bacterial UTIs. Some cats were concomitantly given drugs or foods designed to acidify urine. In two cats, sulfadiazine and/or its metabolites were the only crystalline components detected in the uroliths. Sulfadiazine metabolites were also observed mixed with ammonium acid urate in one cat and in a shell that covered a sterile struvite urolith in another cat.[17] Based on these findings, sulfadiazine should not be used to empirically treat lower urinary tract signs, especially in cats known to: 1) have uroliths, 2) be at increased risk for metabolic uroliths and 3) form acidic and/or highly concentrated urine.

ACKNOWLEDGMENT

The authors and editors thank Dr. Ellen Kienzle, Ludwig-Maximilians-Universitat, Munich, Germany, and Dr. C. A. Tony Buffington, The Ohio State University, Columbus, USA, for their review and suggested revisions to this chapter.

ENDNOTES & REFERENCES

ENDNOTES
a. pH Testr 1. Oakton Model 35624-00.
b. Sensor Devices, Inc., Waukesha, WI, USA.

REFERENCES
1. Lawler DF, Sjolin DW, Collins JE. Incidence rates of feline lower urinary tract disease in cats in the United States. Feline Practice 1985; 15: 13-16.
2. Willeberg P. Epidemiology of naturally occurring feline urological syndrome. Veterinary Clinics of North America: Small Animal Practice 1984; 14: 455-469.
3. Foster SJ. The "urolithiasis" syndrome in male cats: A statistical analysis of the problems with clinical observations. Journal of Small Animal Practice 1967; 8: 207.
4. Osborne CA, Kruger JM, Johnston GR, et al. Feline lower urinary tract disorders. In: Ettinger SJ, ed. Textbook of Veterinary Internal Medicine, 2nd ed. Philadelphia, PA: WB Saunders Co, 1989; 2057-2082.
5. Morris Animal Foundation, Denver, CO, March 1998. Animal health survey.
6. Osborne CA, Kruger JM, Lulich JP. Feline lower urinary tract disorders: Definition of terms and concepts. Veterinary Clinics of North America: Small Animal Practice 1996; 26: 169-179.
7. Bartges JW. Lower urinary tract disease in geriatric cats. In: Proceedings. Fifteenth Annual Veterinary Medical Forum, American College of Veterinary Internal Medicine, Lake Buena Vista, FL, 1997: 322-324.
8. Buffington CAT, Chew DJ. Intermittent alkaline urine in a cat fed an acidifying diet. Journal of the American Veterinary Medical Association 1996; 209: 103-104.
9. Osborne CA, Lulich JP, Thumchai R, et al. Diagnosis, medical treatment, and prognosis of feline urolithiasis. Veterinary Clinics of North America: Small Animal Practice 1996; 26: 589-627.
10. Johnston GR, Feeney DA, Rivers WJ, et al. Diagnostic imaging of the feline lower urinary tract. Veterinary Clinics of North America: Small Animal Practice 1996; 26: 401-415.
11. Lulich JP, Osborne CA, Carlson M, et al. Nonsurgical removal of uroliths in dogs and cats by voiding urohydropropulsion. Journal of the American Veterinary Medical Association 1993; 203: 660-663.
12. Bovee KC, McGuire T. Qualitative and quantitative analysis of uroliths in dogs: Definitive determination of chemical type. Journal of the American Veterinary Medical Association 1984; 185: 983-987.
13. Ruby AL, Ling GV. Methods of analysis of canine uroliths. Veterinary Clinics of North America: Small Animal Practice 1986; 16: 293-302.
14. Ulrich LK, Bird KA, Koehler LA, et al. Urolith analysis: Submission, methods, and interpretation. Veterinary Clinics of North America: Small Animal Practice 1996; 26: 393-400.
15. Bartges JW. Lower urinary tract disease in older cats: What's common, what's not. Veterinary Clinical Nutrition 1996; 3: 57-62.
16. Osborne CA, Lulich JP, Thumcai R, et al. Feline urolithiasis: Etiology and pathophysiology. Veterinary Clinics of North America: Small Animal Practice 1996; 26: 217-232.
17. Osborne CA, Kruger JM, Lulich JP, et al. Disorders of the feline lower urinary tract. In: Osborne CA, Finco DR, eds. Canine and Feline Nephrology and Urology. Baltimore, MD: Williams & Wilkins, 1995; 625-680.
18. Thumchai R, Lulich JP, Osborne CA, et al. Epizootiologic evaluation of urolithiasis in cats: 3,498 cases (1982-1992). Journal of the American Veterinary Medical Association 1996; 208: 547-551.
19. Kirk CA, Ling GV, Franti CE, et al. Evaluation of factors associated with development of calcium oxalate urolithiasis in cats. Journal of the American Veterinary Medical Association 1995; 207: 1429-1434.
20. Curhan GC, Willett WC, Rimm EB, et al. Family history and risk of kidney stones. Journal of the American Society of Nephrology 1997; 8: 1568-1573.
21. Lulich JP, Osborne CA. Overview of diagnosis of feline lower urinary tract disorders. Veterinary Clinics of North America: Small Animal Practice 1996; 26: 339-352.
22. Kruger JM, Osborne CA, Goyal SM, et al. Clinical evaluation of cats with lower urinary tract disease. Journal of the American Veterinary Medical Association 1991; 199: 211-216.
23. Buffington CAT, Chew DJ, Kendall MS, et al. Clinical evaluation of cats with non-obstructive lower urinary tract disease: 109 cases (1993-1995). Journal of the American Veterinary Medical Association 1997; 210: 45-50.
24. Osborne CA, Lulich JP, Bartges JW, et al. Canine and feline urolithiasis: Relationship of etiopathogenesis to treatment and prevention. In: Osborne CA, Finco DR, eds. Canine and Feline Nephrology and Urology. Baltimore, MD: Williams & Wilkins, 1995; 798-888.
25. Rhodes DC, Hinsman E, Rhodes JA, et al. Urinary Tamm-Horsfall glycoprotein concentrations in normal and urolithiasis-affected male cats determined by an ELISA. Journal of the American Veterinary Medical Association 1992; 39: 621-634.
26. Osborne CA, Kruger JM, Lulich JP. Feline matrix-crystalline urethral plugs: A unifying hypothesis of causes. Journal of Small Animal Practice 1992; 33: 172-177.

27. Ling GV. Urinary stone disease. In: Lower Urinary Tract Diseases of Dogs and Cats: Diagnosis, Medical Management, Prevention. St Louis, MO: Mosby, 1995; 168.

28. Sauer LS, Hamar D, Lewis LD. Effect of dietary mineral composition on urinary mineral concentration and excretion. Feline Practice 1985; 15: 10-26.

29. Pastoor FJH. Interactions of dietary minerals in the cat. PhD Thesis, University of Utrecht; The Netherlands, 1993; 23-44.

30. Lemann JJ, Relman AS. The relation of sulfur metabolism to acid-base balance and electrolyte excretion: The effects of dl-methionine in normal man. Journal of Clinical Investigation 1959; 38: 2215-2223.

31. Pak CYC. Hyperoxaluric calcium nephrolithiasis. In: Resnick MI, Pak CYC, eds. Urolithiasis: A Medical and Surgical Reference. Philadelphia, PA: WB Saunders Co, 1990; 65.

32. Archer HE, Dormer AE, Scowen EF, et al. Studies on the urinary excretion of oxalate by normal subjects. Clinical Sciences 1957; 16: 405-411.

33. Chadwick VS, Modha K, Dowling RH. Mechanism of hyperoxaluria in patients with ileal dysfunction. New England Journal of Medicine 1973; 289: 172-176.

34. Knickelbein RG, Aronson PS, Dobbins JW. Oxalate transport by anion exchange across rabbit ileal brush border. Journal of Clinical Investigation 1986; 77: 170-175.

35. Oxalosis and Hyperoxaluria Foundation, 24815 144th Place SE, Kent, WA 98402.

36. Sestili MA. Possible adverse effects of vitamin C and ascorbic acid. Seminars in Oncology 1983; 10: 299-304.

37. Menon M, Koul H. Calcium oxalate nephrolithiasis. Journal of Clinical Endocrinology and Metabolism 1992; 74: 703-707.

38. Bai SC, Sampson DA, Morris JG, et al. Vitamin B_6 requirement of growing kittens. Journal of Nutrition 1989; 119: 1020-1027.

39. Gershoff SN, Faragalla FF, Nelson DA, et al. Vitamin B_6 deficiency and oxalate nephrocalcinosis in the cat. American Journal of Medicine 1959; 27: 72-80.

40. McKerrell RD, Blakemore WF, Heath MF, et al. Primary hyperoxaluria (L-glyceric aciduria) in the cat: A newly recognized inherited disease. Veterinary Record 1989; 125: 31-34.

41. Weinman DJ, Frankfurt SJ, Ince A, et al. Renal tubular transport of organic acids. Journal of Clinical Investigation 1978; 61: 801-806.

42. Andersson H, Bosaeus I. Hyperoxaluria in malabsorptive states. Urology International 1981; 36: 1-9.

43. Rudman D, Dedonis JL, Fountain MT, et al. Hypocitraturia in patients with gastrointestinal malabsorption. New England Journal of Medicine 1980; 303: 657-661.

44. Pak CYC, Ohate M, Laurence EC, et al. The hypercalciurias: Causes, parathyroid functions and idiopathic criteria. Journal of Clinical Investigation 1974; 54: 387-400.

45. Parks JH, Coe FL. A urinary calcium-citrate index for the evaluation of nephrolithiasis. Kidney International 1986; 30: 85-90.

46. Pak CYC. Hypocitraturic calcium nephrolithiasis. In: Resnick MI, Pak CYC, eds. Urolithiasis: A Medical and Surgical Reference. Philadelphia, PA: WB Saunders Co, 1990; 91.

47. Maiwald E, Kienzle E. Effect of vitamin C on urine pH in cats (abstract). In: Proceedings. European Society of Veterinary and Comparative Nutrition, Munich, Germany, 1997: 36.

48. Simpson DP. Citrate excretion: A window on renal metabolism. American Journal of Physiology 1983; 244: F223-F234.

49. Khan SR, Shevock PN, Hackett RL. Magnesium oxide administration and prevention of calcium oxalate nephrolithiasis. Journal of Urology 1993; 149: 412-416.

50. Nakagawa Y, Ahmed M, Hall SL, et al. Isolation from human calcium oxalate renal stones of nephrocalcin, a glycoprotein inhibitor of calcium oxalate growth: Evidence that nephrocalcin from patients with calcium oxalate nephrolithiasis is deficient in γ-carboxyglutamic acid. Journal of Clinical Investigation 1987; 79: 1782-1787.

51. Hess B, Nakagawa Y, Coe FL. Molecular abnormality of Tamm-Horsfall glycoprotein in calcium oxalate nephrolithiasis. American Journal of Physiology 1991; 260: F569-F578.

52. Osborne CA, Polzin DJ, Kruger JM, et al. Relationship of nutritional factors to the cause, dissolution, and prevention of feline uroliths and urethral plugs. Veterinary Clinics of North America: Small Animal Practice 1989; 19: 561-581.

53. Osborne CA, Caywood DD, Johnston GR, et al. Perineal urethrostomy versus dietary management in prevention of lower urinary tract disease. Journal of Small Animal Practice 1991; 32: 296-305.

54. Gregory CR, Vasseur PB. Long-term examination of cats with perineal urethrostomy. Veterinary Surgery 1983; 12: 210-212.

55. Griffin DW, Gregory CR, Kitchell RL. Preservation of striated-muscle urethral sphincter function with use of a surgical technique for perineal urethrostomy in cats. Journal of the American Veterinary Medical Association 1989; 194: 1057-1060.

56. Osborne CA, Johnston GR, Kruger JM, et al. Etiopathogenesis and biologic behavior of feline vesicourachal diverticula. Veterinary Clinics of North America: Small Animal Practice 1987; 17: 697-733.

57. Osborne CA, Kroll RA, Lulich JP, et al. Medical management of vesicourachal diverticula in 15 cats with lower urinary tract disease. Journal of Small Animal Practice 1989; 30: 608-612.

58. Buffington CAT, Blaisdell JL, Binns SP, et al. Decreased urine glycosaminoglycan excretion in cats with interstitial cystitis. Journal of Urology 1996; 155: 1801-1804.

59. Buffington CAT, Chew DJ, Hubler M, et al. Does interstitial cystitis occur in cats? In: Bonagura JD, ed. Current Veterinary Therapy XII. Philadelphia, PA: WB Saunders Co, 1995; 1009-1011.

60. Buffington CAT, Chew DJ, DiBartola SP. Interstitial cystitis in cats. Veterinary Clinics of North America: Small Animal Practice 1996; 26: 317-326.

61. Gao X, Buffington CAT, Au JLS. Effect of interstitial cystitis on drug absorption from urinary bladder. Journal of Pharmacology and Experimental Therapeutics 1994; 271: 818-823.

62. Osborn S, Chew DJ, Buffington CA, et al. Cystoscopic identification of glomerulations in cats with idiopathic cystitis (abstract). Journal of Veterinary Internal Medicine 1994; 8: 169.

63. Buffington CA, Rogers QR, Morris JG. Effect of diet on struvite activity product in feline urine. American Journal of Veterinary Research 1990; 51: 2025-2030.

64. Hokenfellner M, Nunes L, Schmidt RA, et al. Interstitial cystitis: Increased sympathetic innervation and related neuropeptide synthesis. Journal of Urology 1992; 147: 587-591.

65. Chew DJ, Buffington CAT, Kendall MS, et al. Amitriptyline treatment for severe recurrent idiopathic cystitis in cats. Journal of the American Veterinary Medical Association 1998; 213: 1282-1286.

66. Kruger JM, Osborne CA. The role of viruses in feline lower urinary tract disease. Journal of Veterinary Internal Medicine 1990; 4: 71-78.

67. Gaskell CJ. The role of fluid in the feline urological syndrome. In: Burger IH, Rivers JPW, eds. Nutrition of the Dog and Cat. Cambridge, UK: Cambridge University Press, 1989; 353-356.

68. DiBartola SP, Chew DJ, Horton ML. Cystinuria in a cat. Journal of the American Veterinary Medical Association 1991; 198: 102-104.

69. Coman BJ, Brunner H. Food habits of the feral house cat in Victoria. Journal of Wildlife Management 1972; 36: 848-853.

70. Vondruska JF. The effect of rat carcass diet on the urinary pH of the cat. Companion Animal Practice–Feline Nutrition; August 1987: 5-9.

71. Packer RK, Curry CA, Brown KM. Urinary organic anion excretion in response to dietary acid and base loading. Journal of the American Society of Nephrology 1995; 5: 1624-1629.

72. Halperin ML, Jungas RL. Metabolic production and renal disposal of hydrogen ions. Kidney International 1983; 24: 709-713.

73. Kienzle E, Schuknecht A, Meter H. Influence of food composition on the urine pH of cats. Journal of Nutrition 1991; 121: S87-S88.

74. Langendorf H. Säure-Basen-Gleichgewicht und chronisch acidogene und alkalogene Ernährung. Darmstadt, Germany: Dr.-Dietrich-Steinkopff-Verlag, 1963.

75. Kienzle E, Thielen C, Pessinger C. Investigations on phosphorus requirements of adults cats (abstract). Journal of Nutrition 1998; 125: 2598S-2600S.

76. Colloquium on urology. Feline Practice 1997; 25 5/6 (Suppl.): 31-32.

77. Kohri K, Garside J, Blacklock NJ. The role of magnesium in calcium oxalate urolithiasis. British Journal of Urology 1988; 61: 107-115.

78. Li MK, Blacklock NJ, Garside J. Effects of magnesium on calcium oxalate crystallization. Journal of Urology 1985; 133: 123-125.

79. Johansson G, Backman U, Danielson B, et al. Biochemical and clinical effects of the prophylactic treatment of renal calcium stones with magnesium hydroxide. Journal of Urology 1980; 124: 770-774.

80. Ettinger B, Citron JT, Livermore B, et al. Chlorthalidone reduces calcium oxalate calculus recurrence but magnesium hydroxide does not. Journal of Urology 1988; 139: 679-684.

81. Werness PG, Knox FG, Smith LH. Low phosphate diet in rats: A model for calcium oxalate urolithiasis. In: Smith LH, Robertson WG, Finlayson B, eds. Urolithiasis: Clinical and Basic Research. New York, NY: Plenum, 1981; 731-734.

82. Curhan GC, Willett WC, Speizer FE, et al. A prospective study of dietary and supplemental calcium and the risk of kidney stones in women (abstract). In: Proceedings. American Society of Nephrology, San Diego, CA, 1995: 946.

83. Kok DJ, Iestra JA, Doorenbos J, et al. The effects dietary excesses in animal protein and in sodium on the composition of and the crystallization kinetics of calcium oxalate monohydrate in urine of healthy men. Journal of Clinical Endocrinology and Metabolism 1990; 71: 861-867.

84. Dawson-Hughes B, Fowler S, Dalsky G, et al. Sodium excretion influences calcium homeostasis in elderly men and women. Journal of Nutrition 1996; 126: 2107-2112.

85. Goldfarb S. Diet and nephrolithiasis. Annual Review of Medicine 1994; 45: 235-243.

86. Samuel CT, Kasidas GP. Biochemical investigations in renal stone formers. Annals of Clinical Biochemistry 1995; 32: 112-122.

87. Bartges JW, Osborne CA, Felice LJ, et al. Diet effect on activity product ratios of uric acid, sodium urate, and ammonium urate in urine formed by healthy beagles. American Journal of Veterinary Research 1995; 56: 329-333.

88. Association of American Feed Control Officials. Official Publication, 1999.

89. Fettman MJ, Cable JM, Hamar DH, et al. Effect of dietary phosphoric acid supplementation on acid-base balance and mineral and bone metabolism in adult cats. American Journal of Veterinary Research 1992; 53: 2125-2135.

90. Ching S, Norrdin RW, Fettman MJ, et al. Trabecular bone remodeling and bone mineral density in the adult cat during chronic dietary acidification with ammonium chloride. Journal of Bone and Mineral Research 1990; 5: 547-556.

91. Scarlett JM, Donoghue S. Obesity in cats: Prevalence and prognosis. Veterinary Clinical Nutrition 1996; 3: 126-132.

92. Lulich JP, Osborne CA, Polzin DJ, et al. Incomplete removal of canine and feline urocystoliths by cystotomy (abstract). Journal of Veterinary Internal Medicine 1993; 7: 124.

93. Lulich JP, Osborne CA, Kruger JM. Biologic behavior of feline lower urinary tract diseases. Veterinary Clinics of North America: Small Animal Practice 1996; 26: 207-215.

94. Bohonowych RO, Parks JL, Greene RW. Features of cystic calculi in a hospital population. Journal of the American Veterinary Medical Association 1978; 173: 301-303.

95. Coe FL, Flavus MJ. Nephrolithiasis. In: Brenner BM, Rector FC Jr, eds. The Kidney, 4th ed. Philadelphia, PA: WB Saunders Co, 1991; 1728-1767.

96. Osborne CA, Lulich JP, Ulrich L, et al. Pharmacologic treatment and uroliths–Cause or cure. In: Proceedings. Sixteenth Annual Veterinary Medical Forum, American College of Veterinary Internal Medicine, San Diego, CA, 1998: 650-651.

■ CASE 21-1

Obstructive Uropathy in a Cat

John M. Kruger, DVM, PhD
Diplomate ACVIM (Internal Medicine)
College of Veterinary Medicine
Michigan State University
East Lansing, Michigan, USA

Assess the Animal

A four-year-old, castrated male, mixed-breed cat was examined for acute dysuria, pollakiuria and stranguria. The cat had one previous episode of obstructive uropathy approximately 18 months earlier. No other historical problems were identified.

Physical examination revealed that the cat was depressed, lethargic and approximately 5% dehydrated. Temperature was normal. Heart and respiratory rates were increased. The cat weighed 6.4 kg and was considered overweight (body condition score 4/5). Palpation of the urinary tract revealed a firm painful over-distended urinary bladder. A small plug of cream-colored sabulous material was obstructing the urethral lumen at the level of the external urethral orifice.

Analysis of a urine sample collected by cystocentesis revealed moderately concentrated urine with a neutral pH, struvite crystalluria and findings typical of inflammation (i.e., hematuria, pyuria and proteinuria). Aerobic bacteria were not detected by quantitative urine culture. Results of a hemogram were within normal limits. A serum biochemistry profile revealed mild azotemia. Venous blood gas measurement identified a mild metabolic acidosis. Survey abdominal radiographs revealed increased amounts of intra-abdominal fat and an over-distended urinary bladder.

Assess the Food(s) and Feeding Method

The cat had been fed a dry commercial maintenance food free choice. That food was supplemented with a small amount of moist commercial maintenance food (one tablespoon, once daily). The cat had unlimited access to fresh water.

Questions

1. What are potential causes of urethral obstruction in male cats?
2. What differences exist between uroliths and urethral plugs?
3. What are risk factors for formation of struvite crystals?
4. Can urethral plugs be dissolved by dietary management?
5. What is the comparative value of perineal urethrostomy vs. medical therapy in prevention of recurrent urethral obstruction due to struvite-containing urethral plugs?

Answers and Discussion

1. Urethral obstruction may be caused by one or more intramural, mural or extramural abnormalities located at one or more sites. In a prospective study of urethral obstruction in 51 male cats, investigators identified crystalline-matrix urethral plugs in 59% of cats. However, urethroliths were identified in 12% of cats and a specific cause could not be identified in 29% of affected cats. Other possible causes of urethral obstruction include sloughed tissue fragments originating from the bladder or urethra, acquired urethral strictures, prostatic lesions, urethral neoplasms, periurethral neoplasms, congenital urethral anomalies and functional urethral obstruction (e.g., reflex dyssynergia).

2. There are distinct physical and probable etiopathogenic differences between feline uroliths and urethral

plugs. Therefore, these terms should not be used synonymously. Uroliths are highly organized polycrystalline concretions composed primarily of minerals (organic and inorganic crystalloids) and smaller quantities of nonmineral matrix. In contrast, most feline urethral plugs are composed of relatively large quantities of matrix mixed with mineral crystals. However, some urethral plugs are composed primarily of matrix, some consist of sloughed tissue, blood and/or inflammatory reactants and a few are composed primarily of aggregates of crystalline minerals. In general, feline crystalline-matrix urethral plugs appear as cylindrical concretions that conform to the diameter of the urethra and vary from a few mm to several centimeters. They are usually soft, friable, easily compressed and have no visible organized external structure. Urethral plugs contain varying quantities of minerals in proportion to large quantities of matrix. Struvite is the most common mineral type identified in feline urethral plugs. However, a variety of different mineral types (e.g., calcium oxalate, ammonium urate, calcium phosphate) have been identified in urethral plugs of cats, suggesting that multiple risk factors are involved in their formation.

The matrix component of feline urethral plugs is less well defined. Studies in cats and other species suggest that matrix is heterogeneous and may be composed of mucoproteins, albumin, globulins, cells (e.g., erythrocytes, leukocytes, epithelial cells and spermatozoa) and microorganisms (e.g., bacteria and viruses).

One hypothesis suggests that formation of matrix by infectious or noninfectious/inflammatory agents in cats with concomitant crystalluria of any type may lead to formation of matrix-crystal urethral plugs. Crystalluria per se is unlikely to cause production of large quantities of matrix because classic uroliths, which are composed of at least 90% crystalline material, contain relatively little matrix.

3. Risk factors associated with formation of struvite crystals found in urethral plugs are probably similar to those associated with mineral formation in classic struvite uroliths. Factors of major therapeutic importance include dietary factors affecting urine magnesium concentration and urinary pH and factors associated with infection of the urinary tract with urease-producing microorganisms.

4. In general, the immediate need to remove urethral plugs within hours precludes attempts to induce their dissolution over a period of days or weeks. However, it is often possible to repulse urethral plugs into the bladder lumen. Although urethral plugs contain markedly greater quantities of matrix than do classic uroliths, medical protocols effective in inducing sterile struvite urolith dissolution would probably also be effective in dissolving the struvite crystalline component of urethral plugs located in the bladder lumen. However, such therapy may not result in dissolution of plug matrix. In addition, it must be emphasized that calcium oxalate, calcium phosphate and ammonium urate crystals have been identified in some naturally occurring feline urethral plugs.

Attempts to dissolve struvite crystals with urinary acidifiers or foods designed to promote formation of acidic urine should not be initiated in cats with

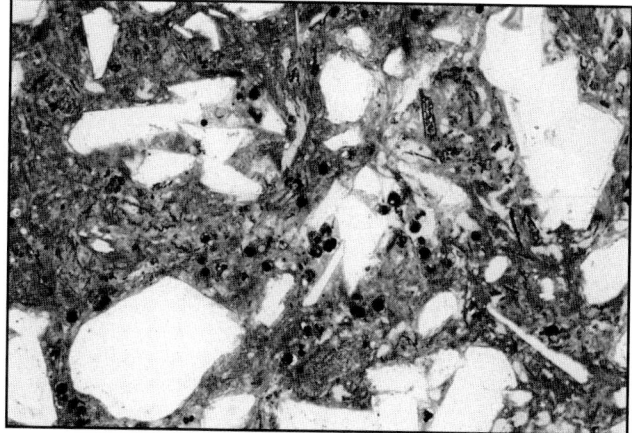

Figure 1. Photomicrograph of a urethral plug removed from a four-year-old, castrated male, mixed-breed cat with obstructive uropathy. Note spaces previously occupied by struvite crystals surrounded by large quantities of amorphous matrix containing white blood cells (toluidine blue stain; 100X original magnification).

postrenal azotemia. The metabolic sequela of urethral obstruction, particularly severe metabolic acidosis, should be corrected before pharmacologic agents or foods designed to acidify urine are used.

5. Perineal urethrostomies can minimize recurrent obstruction of the penile urethra of patients unresponsive to nonsurgical therapeutic and prophylactic management. In a prospective study of 30 cats with struvite crystalline-matrix urethral plugs, perineal urethrostomy and dietary management were equally effective in their ability to prevent recurrent urethral obstruction. However, 16 episodes of bacterial urinary tract infection developed in nine cats with perineal urethrostomies; bacterial urinary tract infections were not observed in cats treated only with dietary management. Further, staphylococcal-induced struvite urocystoliths developed in two cats with perineal urethrostomies. These observations emphasize the fact that perineal urethrostomies may be associated with significant short-term and long-term complications. Localization of the site(s) and cause(s) of urethral obstruction is especially important if urethrostomy is considered.

Progress Notes

To further characterize the composition of the urethral plug and identify potential etiopathologic factors, a portion of the urethral plug was obtained and submitted for light and electron microscopic examination and quantitative mineral analysis. Light microscopic evaluation of the urethral plug revealed that it was composed of numerous unorganized crystals, occasional white blood cells and large quantities of amorphous matrix (Figure 1). Electron microscopy did not reveal any specific etiologic agents. Subsequent quantitative mineral analysis revealed that the crystalline component of the plug was composed of 100% struvite.

Urethral patency was reestablished with a combination of procedures that included: 1) gentle massage of the distal urethra followed by gentle compression of the urinary bladder, 2) partial decompression of the bladder by cystocentesis and 3) flushing of the urethral lumen with sterile 0.9% saline solution. After urine flow was restored, particulate material in the urinary bladder was removed by lavage of the bladder lumen with sterile saline solution. Because the large quantity of urine precipitates in the bladder lumen represented a potential risk factor for reobstruction, a sterile indwelling red-rubber urinary catheter was placed and connected to a closed sterilized drainage system. Systemic fluid and acid-base imbalances associated with obstructive uropathy were corrected over a 24-hour period by intravenous administration of lactated Ringer's solution.

Gross hematuria gradually subsided over 48 hours. The indwelling urinary catheter was removed and the cat was observed for signs of reobstruction. Aerobic bacteria were not detected on follow-up quantitative culture of urine collected via the indwelling catheter before its removal.

The cat was fed a commercial veterinary therapeutic food designed to promote dissolution of the struvite crystal component of the urethral plug (Prescription Diet Feline s/d[a]). When the cat was discharged from the hospital, its owner was instructed to feed the food in sufficient quantity to maintain stable body weight (approximately 320 kcal [1,339 kJ]; 2/3 cup). Analysis of a urine sample collected 20 days after initiation of dietary therapy revealed a pH of 6.0 and no evidence of crystalluria. After approximately three weeks of calculolytic therapy, the food was changed to a commercial veterinary therapeutic food that has lower energy density, decreased fat, increased fiber, reduced magnesium concentration and that produces a normal acidic urine (Prescription Diet Feline w/d[a]). Therapeutic goals were to: 1) promote formation of acidic urine (pH 6.2 to 6.4) at approximately four to eight hours after feeding, 2) reduce or eliminate struvite crystalluria and 3) promote gradual weight reduction. Therapeutic efficacy was monitored by serial urinalyses and physical examinations. Over the next several months the cat lost about 1.2 kg and remained free of signs of lower urinary tract disease. The quantity of food was adjusted to maintain a stable body weight of 5 kg.

Endnote

a. Hill's Pet Nutrition, Inc., Topeka, KS, USA.

Bibliography

Kruger JM, Osborne CA, Goyal SM, et al. Clinical evaluation of cats with lower urinary tract disease. Journal of the American Veterinary Medical Association 1991; 199: 211-216.

Osborne CA, Caywood DD, Johnston GR, et al. Perineal urethrostomy versus dietary management in prevention of lower urinary tract disease. Journal of Small Animal Practice 1991; 32: 296-305.

Osborne CA, Kruger JM, Lulich JP. Feline matrix-crystalline urethral plugs: A unifying hypothesis of causes. Journal of Small Animal Practice 1992; 33: 172-177.

CASE 21-2

Recurrent Urolithiasis in a Himalayan Cat

Timothy A. Allen, DVM
Diplomate ACVIM (Internal Medicine)
Hill's Science and Technology Center
Topeka, Kansas, USA

Carl A. Osborne, DVM, PhD
Diplomate ACVIM (Internal Medicine)
College of Veterinary Medicine
University of Minnesota
St. Paul, Minnesota, USA

Assess the Animal

A five-year-old, neutered male Himalayan cat was examined for a six-week history of pollakiuria, stranguria, licking the penis and gross hematuria. Multiple urocystoliths (bladder uroliths) had been removed one year earlier. The uroliths had been given to the owner at that time and not submitted for analysis. The current clinical signs had not improved after treatment with an oral antimicrobial agent (sulfadiazine/trimethoprim).

Physical examination revealed a thin 3-kg cat (body condition score [BCS] 2/5) with a contracted painful bladder and inflamed penis. Evaluation of these problems included a complete blood count (normal), serum biochemistry profile (normal), urinalysis (red color, proteinuria, hematuria, pH = 6.5, no crystals visualized), urine culture (negative) and abdominal radiographs. Multiple radiodense uroliths were found in the urinary bladder. The owner still had the previously removed uroliths, which were submitted for quantitative analysis. These uroliths were composed of 100% calcium oxalate (monohydrate and dihydrate).

Assess the Food(s) and Feeding Method

The cat ate a variety of commercial dry and moist cat foods before the urocystoliths were removed one year ago. After surgery, the food was changed to a commercial dry veterinary therapeutic food (Prescription Diet Feline c/d-s[a]) formulated to avoid excesses of magnesium and phosphorus and to allow production of a normal acidic urine. These nutritional attributes are important for prevention of struvite crystalluria. This food was offered free choice.

Questions

1. Why were no crystals identified in urine from this patient?
2. What is the probable composition of the recurrent uroliths in this cat?
3. How should this cat be treated and how can recurrence of urolithiasis be minimized?

Answers and Discussion

1. Crystals were not seen in the urine sample because the urine was not supersaturated with crystal-forming substances at the time the sample was collected and examined. This finding suggests an absence of the typical combination of factors that lead to the initiation, nucleation, growth and aggregation of crystals. Some factors that influence the variable presence of crystals include time since the last meal, how concentrated or dilute the urine is, how the urine sample is

handled after collection, fluctuations in urinary pH and differences between the food consumed at home vs. in the hospital.

2. The urocystoliths are probably composed of calcium oxalate, based on the signalment of the animal (calcium oxalate occurs more commonly in neutered male, middle-aged cats with a higher prevalence in Burmese, Himalayan and Persian breeds) and clinical findings (i.e., aciduria, radiodense uroliths and analysis of the previous uroliths).

3. Medical protocols to promote dissolution of calcium oxalate uroliths in cats are unavailable. Urocystoliths small enough to pass through the urethra may be removed by voiding urohydropropulsion. Very small urocystoliths may be retrieved with the aid of a urinary catheter. Surgery is the only practical alternative for removal of larger calcium oxalate uroliths.

Following urolith removal, medical protocols should be considered to minimize urolith recurrence. In general, medical therapy should be formulated in a stepwise fashion, with the initial goal of reducing urine concentration of calculogenic substances.

A food that avoids excess levels of protein, calcium and sodium chloride and does not promote formation of acidic urine (e.g., Prescription Diet Feline c/d-oxl[a]) should be considered to help minimize recurrence of calcium oxalate uroliths in this cat. In addition to not promoting acidic urine (target urinary pH = 6.6 to 6.8), the food should contain citrate that is excreted in the urine to help inhibit formation of calcium oxalate crystals. The food should not contain restricted or increased levels of phosphorus or magnesium. The food should contain fiber to bind calcium in the gastrointestinal tract and decrease calcium absorption. Excessive intake of vitamin D (which promotes intestinal absorption of calcium) and ascorbic acid (a precursor of oxalate) should be avoided by not offering vitamin supplements. The food should be adequately fortified with vitamin B_6 (pyridoxine) because pyridoxine deficiency promotes endogenous production and subsequent urinary excretion of oxalic acid. Commercial foods contain more than adequate levels of pyridoxine; however, homemade foods might be deficient if they are not supplemented. The veterinary therapeutic food fed between the two episodes of urolithiasis is appropriate for helping reduce struvite precipitates in the urinary tract. Because some of the key nutritional factors for prevention of calcium oxalate precipitates are opposed to those for struvite (e.g., urinary pH), that food is inappropriate for a cat with calcium oxalate uroliths and should be discontinued. Selection of appropriate foods for managing urolithiasis is critically dependent on an accurate diagnosis of the mineral type.

Other preventive measures include increasing urine volume and maintaining dilute urine by feeding moist (canned) rather than dry food. Drugs (e.g., furosemide, glucocorticoids) that may increase hypercalciuria should be avoided. Although hydrochlorothiazide diuretics may be beneficial in minimizing urinary calcium excretion in people and dogs, no data have been provided to indicate their efficacy in cats with calcium oxalate uroliths. Serial monitoring (e.g., radiographs, urinalyses, serum biochemistry profiles) should be performed to detect underlying metabolic problems and to detect recurrent uroliths when they are small enough to be removed by nonsurgical techniques.

Progress Notes

Radiographs were reviewed to ensure that radiodense nephroliths were not overlooked. The urocystoliths were removed via cystotomy. Because the number of uroliths could not be determined from the pre-surgery radiographs, postsurgical radiographs were taken to confirm that all of the uroliths had been removed. Taking radiographs after surgery is important because failure to remove all urocystoliths during surgery is common and may result in recurrence of clinical signs despite preventive measures. A moist veterinary therapeutic food was prescribed (Prescription Diet Feline c/d-oxl) that provided the appropriate nutritional benefits discussed above. Because the cat was thin (BCS 2/5), the daily energy requirement (DER) was estimated to be 1.4 x the resting energy requirement at the ideal weight of 4 kg (DER = 265 kcal [1,109 kJ]). The owners were instructed to divide the amount of food supplying the DER (1.25 cans/day) into two daily feedings and monitor the food intake closely until optimal weight was achieved.

Serial monitoring consisted of periodic urinalyses (with emphasis on urine specific gravity, urinary pH, crystalluria and evidence of urinary tract infection), survey radiographs and serum biochemistry profiles (serum calcium and electrolytes). Initially, routine urinalyses were performed every two to four weeks and the owners were carefully interviewed to assess compliance with feeding recommendations.

Endnote

a. Hill's Pet Nutrition, Inc., Topeka, KS, USA.

Bibliography

Osborne CA, Lulich JP, Thumachi R. Feline calcium oxalate uroliths. In: Bonagura JD, ed. Current Veterinary Therapy XII. Philadelphia. PA: WB Saunders Co, 1995; 989-992.

Gastrointestinal and Exocrine Pancreatic Disease

Deborah J. Davenport
Rebecca L. Remillard
Kenny W. Simpson
Guy L. Pidgeon

*". . . food should be . . . frequently administered,
for food soothes the soul."*
Aretaeus, the Cappadocian

ASSESSMENT

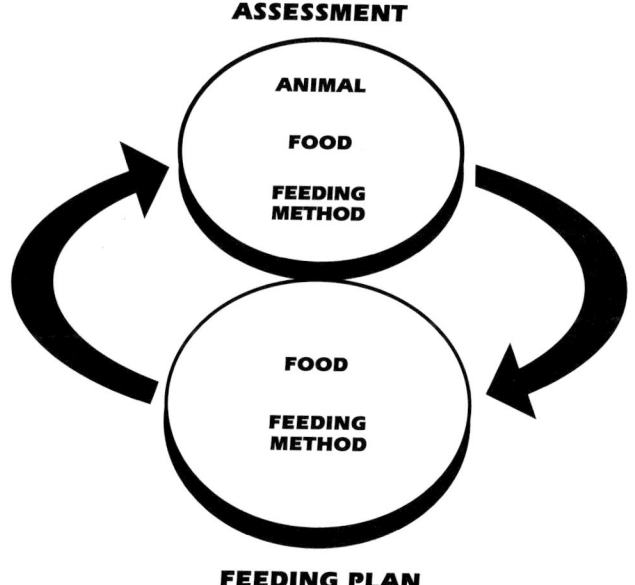

FEEDING PLAN

Note: The reader is referred to Chapter 1 for a detailed discussion of the iterative process of clinical nutrition.

INTRODUCTION

"What should I feed?" is one of the most common queries addressed by veterinarians managing gastrointestinal (GI) and exocrine pancreatic disorders in dogs and cats. Owners of affected pets often intuitively understand that the feeding plan plays an important role in the treatment of their animals and expect guidance regarding specific foods and nutrients to avoid or change in their pet's diet.

Many GI and exocrine pancreatic diseases are amenable to dietary manipulation (Table 22-1). Altering food ingredients, nutrient profiles, food form and feeding method can be powerful tools in managing GI and exocrine pancreatic diseases. Veterinarians should recognize that drug therapy instituted without concomitant dietary therapy often yields less than desirable results in the long-term management of most GI diseases. Occasionally, foods or ingredients may function as diagnostic tools in evaluating patients with GI and pancreatic disorders.

A multitude of factors, including trophic hormones, adequate blood flow, neurologic input and nutrient composition of digesta, are involved in maintaining intestinal integrity (mass and function). Nutrients and ingredients can positively or negatively affect the bowel (Table 22-2). Malnutrition profoundly affects the bowel; effects include decreased pancreatic enzyme production and secretion, intestinal mucosal atrophy and reduced gastric emptying rates. The resultant diarrhea and malassimilation further exacerbate the malnutritive state.[1] In addition, starvation can markedly affect bowel immune response and mucosal integrity.

Discussion of the nutritional management of patients with GI tract and exocrine pancreatic disease can be organized in

KEY WORDS & TERMS—GI & EXOCRINE PANCREATIC DISEASE*

Butyrate
Constipation
Cricopharyngeal achalasia
Diarrhea
Dyschezia
Endoscopy
Exocrine pancreatic insufficiency
Fiber
Flatulence
Gastric dilatation-volvulus
Gastroesophageal junction

Gliadin
Glutamine
Gluten
Hematemesis
Hematochezia
Ileus
Inflammatory bowel disease
Lactose
Lymphangiectasia
Malabsorption
Malassimilation

Maldigestion
Megaesophagus
Melena
Pancreatitis
Regurgitation
Short bowel syndrome
Small intestinal bacterial overgrowth
Steatorrhea
Trypsin-like immunoreactivity
Vomiting

Key words and terms are defined in the Glossary.

KEY POINTS—GI & EXOCRINE PANCREATIC DISEASE

1. Owners of pets affected with gastrointestinal (GI) disease often intuitively understand that the feeding plan plays an important role in the treatment of their animals and expect guidance regarding specific foods and nutrients to avoid or change in their pet's diet.
2. The first objective in managing patients with acute or chronic GI disorders should be to correct dehydration and electrolyte and acid-base imbalances, if present.
3. Vomiting and diarrhea have a myriad of causes and feeding plans vary according to the underlying condition. When a specific cause of acute vomiting or diarrhea is unknown, then feeding plans as outlined for acute gastroenteritis are most appropriate.
4. Dehydration is a frequent problem in dogs and cats with GI disorders. Whenever possible, fluid balance should be maintained via oral consumption of fluids. However, parenteral fluid administration is often needed for dehydrated patients and those unable or unwilling to drink adequate amounts of water.
5. Swallowing disorders are often profoundly debilitating due to malnutrition (i.e., lack of adequate food intake) and recurrent pulmonary infections resulting from aspiration.
6. Foods of differing consistency should be used to determine the best texture for individual patients with swallowing disorders.
7. Because dietary antigens are suspected to play a role in chronic gastritis, chronic colitis and inflammatory bowel disease, some authors recommend the use of "hypoallergenic" or elimination foods for patients with these conditions.
8. Solids and liquids higher in caloric density and fat levels are emptied more slowly from the stomach than similar foods with lower caloric density and fat levels.
9. Bland foods are often recommended for patients with gastritis. The term "bland" is most often applied to easily digested/absorbed or "nonirritating" foods.
10. Considerable effort has been expended over the last 20 years to identify the cause or causes of gastric dilatation-volvulus (GDV). Despite these efforts, no definitive cause for the syndrome has been identified. However, a number of predisposing and precipitating risk factors have been demonstrated through epidemiologic studies.
11. There are no known nutrients of particular concern for dogs with increased risk for GDV. There are, however, a number of prudent feeding management recommen-

dations that should be made to owners of high-risk, large-breed dogs.
12. Foods containing gel-forming soluble fibers should be avoided in patients with gastric emptying and motility disorders because they increase the viscosity of ingesta and slow gastric emptying.
13. The ideal food for patients with gastric emptying disorders has a liquid or semi-liquid consistency. Cold meals slow gastric emptying. Therefore, food should be offered between room and body temperature. Refrigerated or frozen foods should be warmed before being fed.
14. Acute gastroenteritis is one of the most common illnesses of dogs and cats.
15. Glutamine is the preferred respiratory fuel for enterocytes and is a conditionally essential amino acid during intestinal recovery.
16. The electrolyte composition of gastric and intestinal secretions differs from that of extracellular fluids; therefore, loss of gastric and intestinal secretions may result in serum electrolyte abnormalities. Dogs and cats with vomiting and diarrhea may have low, normal or high serum sodium, potassium and chloride concentrations. The derangement that predominates in a particular animal depends on the severity of the disease, nutritional status and site of disease process.
17. In comparison to processes involved with other macronutrients, fat digestion and absorption is relatively complex and may be disrupted in patients with GI disease.
18. Beneficial effects of dietary fiber in patients with GI disorders include: 1) modifying gastric emptying, 2) normalizing intestinal motility and intestinal transport rate, 3) buffering toxins in the GI lumen, 4) binding or holding excess water, 5) supporting growth of normal GI microflora, 6) buffering gastric acid and 7) altering viscosity of GI luminal contents.
19. The term "highly digestible" is not defined in a regulatory sense. However, the term has generally been reserved for products with protein digestibility >87% and fat and carbohydrate digestibility >90%.
20. Withholding all oral intake of food and water for 24 to 48 hours is the first step in the feeding plan for patients with acute gastroenteritis. After this period, animals should be offered small amounts of water or ice cubes every few hours. If water is well tolerated,

Continued on next page.

Continued from previous page.

small amounts of food can be offered several times (six to eight times) per day.

21. Short bowel syndrome is a malabsorptive state that often develops after massive resection of the small intestine but is uncommon in domestic animals.

22. Small intestinal bacterial overgrowth (SIBOG) may develop anytime normal host defenses are impaired. Loss of gastric acid secretion, normal intestinal peristalsis and interdigestive ("housekeeper") motility, the ileocolic valve or local IgA production can result in SIBOG.

23. The clinical utility of fructooligosaccharides (FOS) and other oligosaccharides in the treatment of SIBOG remains unproven.

24. Increased levels of dietary medium-chain triglycerides have theoretical advantages over long-chain triglycerides for the treatment of some forms of GI disease.

25. Wheat-sensitive enteropathy, also termed gluten-sensitive enteropathy, is a chronic small bowel disorder recognized primarily in Irish setter dogs. The disorder is a hypersensitivity to gliadin, a glycoprotein found in many grains including wheat, barley, rye, buckwheat and oats. Gliadin is not found in rice, corn or potatoes.

26. Lactose intolerance results from a relative or absolute deficiency of the enzyme lactase. Unabsorbed lactose induces an osmotic diarrhea when it reaches the colon.

27. Reports suggest that many patients with irritable bowel syndrome improve clinically when the fiber content of the diet is increased.

28. Maintaining normal hydration status and encouraging water intake are important in managing patients with chronic constipation.

29. Excessive flatus is a chronic objectionable problem that occurs often in dogs and less commonly in cats. Changing the sources of protein, carbohydrate or fiber in the food may benefit individual animals.

30. The primary nutritional factor in the management of exocrine pancreatic insufficiency is food digestibility. The use of highly digestible foods works with the addition of pancreatic enzyme preparations to the food.

31. Feeding a high-fat food, treat or table food has often been associated with the onset of acute pancreatitis.

32. The goal of dietary management of patients with pancreatitis is to decrease stimuli to pancreatic secretion and, thus, prevent pancreatic autodigestion, while providing adequate nutrient levels to support tissue repair and recovery.

GI & PANCREAS

KEY NUTRITIONAL FACTORS—GI & EXOCRINE PANCREATIC DISEASE

Table 22-6 lists key nutritional factors for dogs with swallowing disorders.

Table 22-9 lists key nutritional factors for patients with gastritis and/or gastroduodenal ulceration.

Table 22-14 lists key nutritional factors for patients with gastric motility/emptying disorders.

Table 22-20 lists key nutritional factors for patients with acute enteritis.

Table 22-23 lists key nutritional factors for patients with inflammatory bowel disease.

Table 22-25 lists key nutritional factors for patients with lymphangiectasia/protein-losing enteropathy.

Table 22-27 lists key nutritional factors for patients with short-bowel syndrome.

Table 22-28 lists key nutritional factors for patients with small intestinal bacterial overgrowth.

Table 22-32 lists key nutritional factors for patients with acute and chronic colitis.

Table 22-37 lists key nutritional factors for patients with exocrine pancreatic insufficiency.

many ways. This chapter assumes the reader has identified the major clinical problem(s) of the patient as dysphagia (i.e., oropharyngeal disease), regurgitation (i.e., esophageal disease), vomiting (i.e., many causes including primary gastric, intestinal and pancreatic disease), small bowel diarrhea, large bowel diarrhea, constipation or flatulence. Rather than concentrate on these clinical problems, this chapter discusses specific GI tract and exocrine pancreatic diseases thus allowing formulation of better feeding plans for individual patients.

The outline for this chapter is as follows: sections include assessment and feeding plans for: 1) oral, pharyngeal and esophageal disorders, 2) gastric disorders, 3) small intestinal disorders, 4) colonic and rectal disorders and 5) exocrine pancreatic disorders (Table 22-1).

Vomiting and diarrhea, in particular, have a myriad of causes and feeding plans vary according to the underlying condition. When a specific cause of acute vomiting or diarrhea is unknown, then feeding plans as outlined for acute gastroenteritis are most appropriate. When a specific cause of chronic small bowel diarrhea is not identified, then feeding plans as outlined for exocrine pancreatic insufficiency are most appropriate. Finally, when a specific cause of

Table 22-1. Gastrointestinal and exocrine pancreatic diseases amenable to dietary management.

Mouth
Inflammatory disorders (stomatitis, radiation-induced mucositis)
Physical abnormalities (trauma, neoplasia, congenital malformations)
Pharynx and esophagus
Inflammatory disorders (esophagitis)
Motility disorders (cricopharyngeal achalasia, megaesophagus)
Obstructive disorders (vascular ring anomalies, strictures, neoplasia)
Stomach
Gastric dilatation/gastric dilatation-volvulus
Gastric motility/emptying disorders
Gastritis
Gastroduodenal ulceration
Small intestine
Acute enteritis
Inflammatory bowel disease
Intestinal neoplasia
Lymphangiectasia
Protein-losing enteropathy
Short bowel syndrome
Small intestinal bacterial overgrowth
Wheat-sensitive enteropathy
Large intestine
Colitis
Constipation
Flatulence
Irritable bowel syndrome
Perianal fistula
Pancreas
Exocrine pancreatic insufficiency
Pancreatitis

Table 22-2. Potential dietary influences on the gastrointestinal tract.*

Food may alter:
Absorption
Cellular turnover rate
Luminal ammonia concentration
Luminal volatile fatty acid content
Microflora
Motility
Secretory rate
Villous height
Food may be a source of:
Chemical/bacterial toxins
Dietary antigens
Food may correct:
Nutritional deficiencies

*Modified from Guilford WG. Feline gastrointestinal tract disease. In: Wills JM, Simpson KW, eds. The Waltham Book of Clinical Nutrition of the Dog & Cat. London, UK: Pergamon Press, 1994; 221-238.

Performing Dietary Trials in Patients with Gastrointestinal Disease

Nutritional therapies are extremely useful for treating gastrointestinal (GI) disease in dogs and cats. Several commercial and homemade foods are available to practitioners and pet owners for this purpose. Unfortunately, there is no historical or clinical finding that will predict the success of a specific food type. Therefore, selection of the most appropriate food for an individual patient is often based on results of a dietary trial.

Dietary trials are easily performed in most clinical and home settings. Oral food consumption is preferred for managing GI diseases, except in those rare situations in which the animal is intolerant of enteral feeding.

After the veterinarian identifies those foods to be included in the trial, selection of the initial test food is often based on clinical experience and the animal's nutritional history. In general, foods that have been used unsuccessfully in the past to manage the patient should be avoided. Typically, highly digestible GI or elimination foods are good first choices for patients with gastric or small intestinal disorders. Fiber-enhanced foods are often the initial selection when large bowel signs predominate.

No other foods, supplements, table foods or treats should be offered during the dietary trial. Dietary trials are most useful if continued for at least seven to 10 days. In certain settings (e.g., adverse reactions to food), trials lasting two to 12 weeks may be necessary to determine efficacy. (See Chapter 14.) Successful dietary trials are marked by partial or complete resolution of clinical signs.

BIBLIOGRAPHY
Batt RM, Burrows CF. Canine gastrointestinal tract disease. In: Wills JM, Simpson KW, eds. The Waltham Book of Clinical Nutrition of the Dog & Cat. Oxford, UK: Pergamon Press, 1994; 189-220.

Guilford WG, Center SA, Strombeck DR, et al, eds. Strombeck's Small Animal Gastroenterology, 3rd ed. Philadelphia, PA: WB Saunders Co, 1996.

Guilford WG. Feline gastrointestinal tract disease. In: Wills JM, Simpson KW, eds. The Waltham Book of Clinical Nutrition of the Dog & Cat. Oxford, UK: Pergamon Press, 1994; 221-238.

Remillard RL, Thatcher CD. Dietary and nutritional management of gastrointestinal diseases. Veterinary Clinics of North America: Small Animal Practice 1989; 19: 797-817.

---

chronic large bowel diarrhea is not identified, then feeding plans outlined for colitis are most appropriate.

Each patient should be seen as an individual variant of the norm; therefore, multiple dietary manipulations should be considered as needed for any one patient. (See sidebar "Performing Dietary Trials in Patients with Gastrointestinal Disease.") Because of the diverse nature of GI disorders and exocrine pancreatic conditions, a number of food types may be appropriate. (See sidebar "Food Types Useful in the Management of Gastrointestinal and Exocrine Pancreatic Disease.") Nutrient profiles should be considered as *starting points* on a continuum of possible nutrient concentrations that can be adjusted for each patient as needed. All too often, relative terms such as "low" vs. "high" are used without stating the point of reference. The reference point should be the current food(s) that the owner feeds. Changes include increases or decreases, usually in 5 to 10% increments, of nutrient concentrations relative to the previous food.

ORAL DISORDERS

Clinical Importance

The oral cavity is susceptible to a number of acquired and congenital disorders. In comparison to the incidence of dental disease, however, these conditions are relatively uncommon. Chapter 16 discusses dental disease in detail.

Food Types Useful in the Management of Gastrointestinal and Exocrine Pancreatic Disease

GASTROINTESTINAL FOODS

Several commercial veterinary therapeutic foods have been specially formulated for managing gastrointestinal (GI) disease in dogs and cats. Typically, these products are highly digestible and have consistent ingredient and nutrient profiles.

The term highly digestible is not defined in a regulatory sense. However, highly digestible has generally been reserved for products with protein digestibility >87% and fat and carbohydrate digestibilities >90%. The average digestibility coefficients for popular commercial foods are 78 to 81%, 77 to 85% and 69 to 79% for crude protein, crude fat and carbohydrate (nitrogen-free extract [NFE]), respectively. Commercial veterinary therapeutic foods formulated for GI disease usually contain highly refined meat and carbohydrate sources to increase digestibility.

Carbohydrates make up the largest nonwater fraction of foods formulated for managing GI diseases. Carbohydrate digestibility of pet foods is influenced by source and processing. Dogs digest most properly cooked starches very well, including starch components in corn, rice, barley and wheat. Other starches, including potato and tapioca, are less digestible, particularly when inadequately cooked. Although cats also efficiently digest carbohydrates, some clinicians feel that cats with small bowel disorders are less tolerant of dietary carbohydrate than dogs with similar causes of malassimilation.

Recent research has identified a link between particle size and carbohydrate digestibility of moist foods. As a result, carbohydrate ingredients (e.g., rice, corn, etc.) should be chopped or ground before they are incorporated into moist foods. These findings probably do not apply to extruded dry products. In fact, other studies have demonstrated almost complete ileal carbohydrate digestibility in dogs consuming extruded grains.

The requirements for many macro- and microminerals in the face of GI disease are not well understood. However, sodium, potassium and B-vitamin losses are expected with vomiting and diarrhea. Therefore, foods formulated for managing GI diseases should contain sodium, potassium and B vitamins in excess of maintenance allowances. Patients with fat malabsorption are at risk for developing fat-soluble vitamin deficiencies. Highly digestible foods formulated for feeding steatorrheic patients should, therefore, be fortified with fat-soluble vitamins.

It is unusual for GI foods to contain crude fiber levels greater than 5% dry matter (DM) because fiber reduces dry matter digestibility and decreases pancreatic enzymatic activity in vitro. More recently, manufacturers of some highly digestible commercial veterinary therapeutic foods have added small amounts (<5% DM) of soluble or mixed fibers because short-chain fatty acids produced by intestinal microbial fermentation of fiber may positively affect the intestinal mucosa.

Veterinarians recommend GI foods most often for managing acute gastroenteritis or malassimilation associated with small bowel disease or exocrine pancreatic insufficiency. The utility of highly digestible foods has been demonstrated through anecdotal reports and by the use of such foods in clinical trials involving animals with spontaneous and experimental exocrine pancreatic insufficiency. Some gastroenterologists also recommend these foods for patients with certain colonic disorders to reduce exposure of the colonic mucosa to ingesta. This therapeutic strategy has been suggested for management of inflammatory colitides and constipation.

FIBER-ENHANCED FOODS

Commercial veterinary therapeutic foods contain varying levels and sources of fiber. Based on the combined knowledge obtained from research in people, ongoing research in dogs and cats and clinical experience, fiber is beneficial in managing many large and some small bowel diseases.

Soluble fibers (e.g., pectins and gums) increase the viscosity of intestinal contents, which delays gastric emptying and slows small bowel transit time. Viscosity markedly affects the extent of intraluminal mixing of digesta and digestive enzymes, which can shift sites of absorption and subsequently the rate of nutrients entering the bloodstream. Bacteria in the colon ferment soluble fiber to short-chain fatty acids, including acetic, propionic and butyric acids. Colonocytes apparently use butyrate, whereas propionic and acetic acids are absorbed. Short-chain fatty acids are nutritive to the colonic mucosa and foster normal colonic flora while discouraging pathogenic flora. These properties result in an acidic colonic pH and increased colonic bacterial numbers, colonic mucosal mass and fecal dry matter and water content. Soluble fiber may bind and decrease macronutrient absorption and decrease protein digestibility. Certain fiber types, especially gels and gums, may be of benefit in GI disease because they bind toxins and irritating bile acids. This binding effect prevents these substances from further damaging the intestinal mucosal surface.

Insoluble fiber is primarily composed of cellulose and structural polysaccharides that are relatively resistant to digestion and that ferment slowly, increase intestinal residue and normalize intestinal transit time. These fibers have little or no effect on gastric emptying, mineral absorption or colonic microflora unless fed in high concentrations (>20% DM). One of the most profound effects of fiber on the GI tract is the normalization of gut motility, particularly in the stomach, proximal small bowel and colon. This effect appears to be greatest for insoluble fibers such as cellulose. In general, increasing the insoluble fiber content of the food resolves or modulates most cases of colitis. There are several plausible mechanisms by which insoluble fiber controls large bowel diarrhea. Undigested residues absorb water and increase bacterial mass, which increases fecal bulk. Fecal bulk provides physical intraluminal stimulation to re-establish neuromuscular-endocrine coordinations and normalize intestinal transit times. Fecal bulk increases intestinal residue, which absorbs toxins and offending agents.

RESTRICTED- AND MODERATE-FAT FOODS

In general, dietary fat is more digestible than soluble carbohydrate and protein and provides 2.25 times more calories by weight. Average fat digestibility in commercial dog food is approximately 90%. Average fat digestibility of commercial cat foods ranges from 74 to 91%. Patients with GI or pancreatic disease may not tolerate high-fat foods (>25% DM), which may contribute to diarrhea and steatorrhea. Foods containing moderate amounts of fat (12 to 15% DM for dogs and 15 to 22% DM for cats) are generally tolerated and have sufficient caloric density for most patients. Commercial veterinary therapeutic foods containing less than 10% DM fat need to be fed in larger volumes to meet the patient's caloric requirement. Some patients may not tolerate this volume of food.

Continued on next page.

Continued from previous page.

Restricted-fat foods are often recommended for patients with gastroenteritis in which the complex process of fat digestion and absorption may be disrupted. Unabsorbed fat in the bowel lumen may cause secretory diarrhea. Dietary fat should be reduced when fat maldigestion or malabsorption is present due to exocrine pancreatic insufficiency or reduced bowel surface area. The latter occurs in short bowel syndrome and other conditions in which the intestinal villus surface area is markedly reduced by inflammation, infectious agents, neoplasia or surgery. For example, intestinal malabsorption of fat is seriously impaired in primary and secondary lymphangiectasia. Fat restriction is also useful in small intestinal bacterial overgrowth in which many of the side effects of the condition can be ameliorated by removing the inciting cause of the secretory diarrhea.

ELIMINATION FOODS

Elimination foods are most often recommended for patients with GI signs due to suspected food intolerance or food hypersensitivity. Chapter 14 discusses adverse food reactions and elimination foods in more detail.

GLUTEN- AND GLIADIN-FREE FOODS

Several potential antigens are found in flour when cereal grains are processed. One polypeptide, gliadin, is found in wheat, barley, rye, buckwheat and oat flours. Gliadin is responsible for gluten-sensitive enteropathies in people and dogs. Homologous gliadin polypeptides are not present in whole grains and flours produced from rice and corn.

In people, gluten-induced enteropathy or celiac disease is an important malabsorptive disorder. An analogous condition, termed wheat-sensitive enteropathy, has been identified in Irish setter dogs and is suspected to affect dogs of other breeds as well. Affected animals develop small bowel diarrhea due to malabsorption secondary to villous atrophy. Gluten- and gliadin-free foods are most commonly recommended for managing dogs suspected of having wheat-sensitive enteropathy. In most cases, withdrawal of the offending gliadin antigen from the diet results in resolution of the villous atrophy and clinical signs.

MONOMERIC FOODS

Monomeric foods are water-soluble, liquid foods containing nutrients in their simplest absorbable form. Nitrogen is most commonly provided by a mixture of di- and tripeptides and/or individual amino acids. Fats are present as triglycerides or as fatty acids. Carbohydrates are generally present as mono- or disaccharides. Minerals and vitamins are present to meet human requirements. These foods minimize GI and pancreatic secretions and allow nutrient usage with minimal requirements for digestion. In addition, the small size of nitrogen sources (i.e., amino acids, dipeptides and tripeptides) in monomeric products ensures delivery of a truly "hypoallergenic" food. Monomeric foods should be considered for patients with severe malabsorption or short bowel syndrome and in initial refeeding of patients with acute pancreatitis. In addition, these foods may provide "bowel rest" for patients with severe inflammatory

bowel disease. Monomeric foods are often unpalatable and are not well accepted by dogs or cats. Thus, these foods are usually administered for several days via indwelling feeding tubes. Chapter 12 lists monomeric foods (Table 12-8).

BIBLIOGRAPHY
Bartges JW, Anderson WH. Dietary fiber. Veterinary Clinical Nutrition 1997; 4(1): 25-28.

Bissett SA, Guilford WG, Lawoko CR, et al. Effect of food particle size on carbohydrate assimilation assessed by breath hydrogen testing in dogs. Veterinary Clinical Nutrition 1997; 4: 82-95.

Buddington RK, Chen JW, Diamond JM. Dietary regulation of intestinal brush-border sugar and amino acid transport in carnivores. American Journal of Physiology 1991; 261: R793-R801.

Burrows CF, Kronfeld DS, Banta CA, et al. Effects of fiber on digestibility and transit time in dogs. Journal of Nutrition 1982; 112: 1726-1732.

Dimski DS, Buffington CA. Dietary fiber in small animal therapeutics. Journal of the American Veterinary Medical Association 1991; 199: 1142-1146.

Gurr MI, Asp NG. Dietary Fibre. ILSI Europe Concise Monograph Series. Brussels, Belgium: International Life Science Institute Press, 1994; 15.

Jamikorn UA, Harmon DL, Davenport DJ, et al. Fermentability of selected fibers by dog and cat fecal microflora (abstract). In: Proceedings. Annual Meeting. American Society of Animal Science, Indianapolis, IN, July 1999.

Kendall PT, Burger IH, Smith PM. Methods of estimation of the metabolizable energy of cat food. Feline Practice 1985; 15: 38-44.

Kendall PT, Holmes DW, Smith PM. Methods of prediction of the digestible energy content of dog foods from gross energy value, proximate analysis and digestible nutrient content. Journal of the Science of Food and Agriculture 1982; 3: 823-828.

Kendall PT. Comparable evaluation of apparent digestibility in dogs and cats. Proceedings of the Nutrition Society 1981; 40: 45a.

Kienzle E. Carbohydrate metabolism in the cat. 1. Activity of amylase in the gastrointestinal tract of the cat. Journal of Animal Physiology and Animal Nutrition 1993; 69: 92-101.

Kienzle E. Carbohydrate metabolism in the cat. 2. Digestion of starch. Journal of Animal Physiology and Animal Nutrition 1993; 69: 102-114.

Lewis LD, Boulay JP, Chow FHC. Fat excretion and assimilation by the cat. Feline Practice 1979; 9: 46-49.

Morris JG, Trudell J, Pencovic T. Carbohydrate digestion by the domestic cat (*Felis catus*). British Journal of Nutrition 1977; 37: 365-373.

National Research Council. Nutrient Requirements of Dogs. Washington, DC: National Academy Press, 1985; 1-79.

Schunemann C, Muhlum A, Junker S, et al. Prececal and postileal digestibility of various starches and pH values and organic acid content of digesta and feces. Advances in Animal Physiology and Animal Nutrition 1989; 19: 44-58.

Sherding RG, ed. Diseases of the intestines. In: The Cat: Diseases and Clinical Management. New York, NY: Churchill Livingstone, 1989; 955-1006.

Washabau RJ, Buffington CA, Strombeck DR. Evaluation and management of carbohydrate malassimilation. In: Kirk RW, ed. Current Veterinary Therapy IX. Philadelphia, PA: WB Saunders Co, 1986; 889-892.

Wolter R. Total digestibility and ileal digestibility of foods with a high level of starch from corn and tapioca in the dog. PhD Thesis. Alfort National Veterinary School, University of Alfort, Maisons-Alfort, France, 1993.

Among the common conditions affecting the oral cavity are inflammatory lesions and physical abnormalities such as neoplasia, trauma and congenital malformations (e.g., cleft palate).

Acquired inflammatory lesions of the oral cavity and tongue are uncommon in dogs and cats. These conditions include eosinophilic granuloma complex, lymphoplasmacytic stomatitis, labial granuloma and mucositis due to radiation therapy of the head and neck. Infectious oral disorders (e.g., candidiasis or fusospirochetal infections) are very rare and usually occur in immunocompromised animals. Oral neoplasia is the fourth most common cancer of dogs and cats.[1] Trauma to the oral cavity may arise from fights among animals, falls (high-rise syndrome), motor vehicle accidents, chemical and electrical burns and penetrating foreign bodies. Oral congenital anomalies such as cleft palate are uncommon but may have nutritional causes (e.g., copper deficiency in pregnant queens) or profound consequences due to malnutrition and secondary aspiration pneumonia in growing animals.

Assessment

Assess the Animal

HISTORY AND PHYSICAL EXAMINATION

Dogs and cats with oral disease have variable clinical signs depending on the type and location of the lesions. Animals may exhibit dysphagia or pain associated with eating. Owners may report excessive salivation, oral hemorrhage, halitosis and reluctance to eat. In some cases, careful questioning of the owner will reveal ingestion of foreign bodies or caustic materials or a history of trauma. Puppies or kittens with congenital anomalies such as cleft palate may be presented to veterinarians for ineffectual suckling, poor weight gain and coughing or gagging following attempts at nursing.

Sedation may be required to facilitate examination of the oropharynx and tongue. Various conditions may present with specific signs. Congenital defects may be noted in the soft or hard palate. Epulides originate from periodontal stroma and are most commonly located in the gingiva near the incisor teeth and appear as pedunculated or smooth, nonulcerated masses. Odontogenic tumors (e.g., ameloblastoma and odontoma) are typically expansile, slow-growing odontogenic masses that often form in the incisor region. Malignant tumors (e.g., squamous cell carcinoma, malignant melanoma and fibrosarcoma) grow rapidly and are characterized by early invasion of the gingiva and bone. Pets with suspected oral or tonsillar tumors should be carefully evaluated for peripheral lymphadenopathy.

Lymphoplasmacytic stomatitis in cats is characterized by raised, erythemic cobblestone-like lesions at the glossopalatine arches (Figure 22-1), whereas feline eosinophilic granuloma complex manifests as ulcers, plaques and granulomas on the maxillary lips, tongue and palate. In dogs, inflammatory lesions are most often present on the tongue or palatine and labial mucosa.

Head trauma in pets often results in mandibular symphyseal fractures, maxillary fractures, displaced teeth and separation of the hard palate. These injuries may result in reluctance or inability to eat.

Chemical, electrical and thermal burns are characterized by ulceration and necrosis of affected tissues. Animals with oral burns may suffer life-threatening consequences such as pulmonary edema or cardiogenic shock.

LABORATORY AND OTHER CLINICAL INFORMATION

Laboratory values are often unremarkable in animals with oral disease and generally reflect underlying conditions when present. Leukocytosis and a polyclonal hyperglobulinemia are frequent findings in cats with lymphoplasmacytic stomatitis. Radiography is often of value in cases with suspected trauma to assess the extent of bony

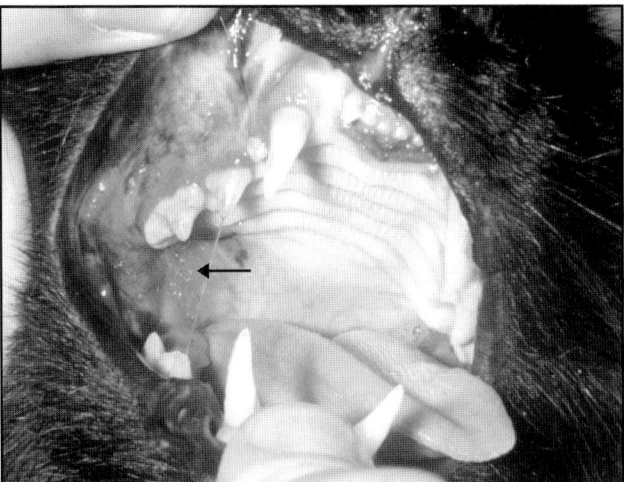

Figure 22-1. Severe lymphoplasmacytic gingivitis and stomatitis in a cat. Note the raised, cobblestone-like lesions (arrow) at the right glossopalatine arch. (Courtesy Dr. Michael Leib, Virginia-Maryland Regional College of Veterinary Medicine, Blacksburg, VA.)

injury. Radiography is invaluable for tumor staging in patients with oral neoplasia. Generally, both skull and thoracic films are evaluated. In addition, thoracic films allow assessment of aspiration pneumonia in young animals with cleft palate. Diagnosis of lesions within the oral cavity often requires biopsy and histopathologic examination.

RISK FACTORS

Age and breed are risk factors for several oral disorders. Young animals are more likely to present with congenital and traumatic lesions, whereas older dogs and cats are more likely to suffer from oral neoplasia and inflammatory disorders. Animals undergoing radiation therapy of the head and neck for cancer are susceptible to radiation-induced mucositis. (See sidebar "Feeding Patients Undergoing Radiation Therapy.") In addition, certain breeds are predisposed to various oral disorders (Table 22-3).

ETIOPATHOGENESIS

Pets with oral disease often exhibit dysphagia or reluctance to eat resulting in malnutrition. Often this nutritional state is compounded by inflammatory, traumatic or neoplastic processes. The etiology of oral inflammatory lesions such as lymphoplasmacytic stomatitis and faucitis, and eosinophilic granuloma complex is unknown. Lymphoplasmacytic stomatitis in cats has been theorized to be an aberrant immunologic response to antigenic stimuli. Various bacterial, viral, periodontal, dietary and immune factors have been implicated. There is a strong association between this disorder and infection with feline immunodeficiency virus (FIV) or calicivirus.[2] Approximately 50% of cats with FIV infection and 60% of cats with feline calicivirus infection have chronic oral disease.[2] These findings do not prove causality, however. The response of some cats with the disorder to radical extraction of teeth and the isolation of antibodies to plaque bacteria (*Actinobacillus* and *Bacteroides* spp) from affected cats also suggest the potential of a "plaque intolerance."[2]

KEY NUTRITIONAL FACTORS

Water

Dehydration is a frequent problem in dogs and cats with oral disorders that interfere with consumption of water. Whenever possible, fluid balance should be maintained via oral consumption of fluids. However, parenteral fluid administration is often needed for dehydrated patients and those unable or unwilling to drink adequate amounts of water.

Energy

A relatively high fat concentration is helpful in meeting the patient's caloric requirement in a small volume of food relative to lower fat foods. Foods with energy densities in excess of 4.5 kcal/g (18.8 kJ/g) dry matter (DM) for dogs and 5 kcal/g (20.9 kJ/g) DM for cats are recommended.

Food Form

The veterinarian or owner should experiment with foods of differing consistency. Often liquid foods or slurries made from moist pet food and water are more readily accepted. A dilute consistency is often associated with less discomfort and is less likely to accumulate in oral lesions or adhere to surgical sites within the oral cavity.

Table 22-3. Breed-associated oral disorders.

Disorders	Breeds
Cleft palate	Brachycephalic dogs and cats
Epulides	Boxer
Gingivitis/stomatitis	Maltese dog
	Siberian husky
Lymphoplasmacytic stomatitis	Abyssinian cat
	Burmese cat
	Himalayan cat
	Maltese cat
	Persian cat
	Siamese cat
Neoplasia	Cocker spaniel
	German shepherd dog
	German shorthaired pointer
	Golden retriever
	Weimaraner

Feeding Patients Undergoing Radiation Therapy

Dogs and cats undergoing radiation therapy for oral and nasal tumors often develop mucositis within the third week of a four- to five-week therapeutic protocol. This inflammation of the oral mucosa is painful; therefore, most animals will stop eating during this time but will drink voluntarily. A change in food form from moist or dry to a liquid is necessary for most animals to continue consuming at least their daily resting energy requirement. Most patients will consume variable quantities of a palatable chilled liquid veterinary therapeutic food during this time even if they won't consume a mixture of their regular food and water. Mixing the liquid with the patient's regular food one week before the expected onset of mucositis allows acclimation to the liquid food. Patients usually voluntarily consume their regular food as the mucositis resolves.

Some patients stop eating and drinking voluntarily when they develop mucositis. These animals require intravenous administration of fluids and nutrition. Discontinuing radiation therapy for a few days is also beneficial. Nasogastric or orogastric feeding tubes are not appropriate, whereas pharyngeal or esophageal feeding tubes may be useful if placed in advance and if they are not in the field to be irradiated. (See Appendix V.) Most patients recover quickly from mucositis (i.e., within three to four days) and consume food and water again, eliminating the need for a gastrostomy tube. Radiation treatments can usually then be continued uneventfully.

BIBLIOGRAPHY

Ogilvie GK, Moore AS, eds. Nutritional support. Managing the Veterinary Cancer Patient: A Practice Manual. Trenton, NJ: Veterinary Learning Systems, 1995; 124-137.

Assess the Food(s) and Feeding Method

The energy density of the patient's food should be compared with the levels described above. Underweight patients may need a nutrient profile similar to that found in a growth or recovery-type formula to regain normal body condition. In addition, the food should be suitable for any other conditions present that are amenable to dietary management.

Because the feeding method is often altered in patients with oral disease, a thorough assessment should include verification of the feeding method currently being used. Items to consider include feeding frequency, amount fed, how the food is offered, access to other food sources including table food and who feeds the animal. All of this information should have been gathered when the history of the animal was obtained.

Feeding Plan

The goals of dietary management for patients with oral disease are to provide adequate nutrition while minimizing discomfort to the pet and enhancing resolution of the oral lesions.

Select a Food(s)

Foods should be energy dense (≥4.5 kcal/g [18.8 kJ/g] DM for dogs and >5 kcal/g [20.9 kJ/g] DM for cats) and in a form that is easily ingested and less irritating to the oral mucosa (e.g., moist foods, gruels or slurries). Animals with extensive oral injuries or inflammation of the oral cavity may benefit from foods designed for assisted feeding or recovery. (See Chapter 12.) Animals with oral neoplasia may benefit from foods specifically formulated for patients with cancer. (See Chapter 25.)

Determine a Feeding Method

Animals with oral disease should initially be fed several small meals daily if they are able and willing to consume food voluntarily. After each meal, the oral cavity should be flushed with water to remove particulate matter adhered to the oral mucous membranes. In many cases, tube-feeding methods are preferred until oral discomfort is reduced and voluntary food consumption resumes. (See Chapter 12 and Appendix V for additional information about tube feeding.)

Reassessment

Body condition scores and hydration status should be evaluated to determine adequacy of food and water consumption. Assisted feeding should be instituted if oral feeding is not adequate to maintain body weight and condition (Chapter 12).

PHARYNGEAL AND ESOPHAGEAL DISORDERS

Clinical Importance

Compared with vomiting and diarrhea, swallowing disorders are relatively uncommon in dogs and cats. However, these conditions are often profoundly debilitating due to malnutrition (i.e., lack of adequate food intake) and recurrent pulmonary infections resulting from aspiration. Pharyngeal and esophageal disorders most commonly encountered include: 1) motility disorders (e.g., cricopharyngeal achalasia, megaesophagus), 2) inflammatory disorders (e.g., esophagitis, gastroesophageal reflux) and 3) obstructive lesions (e.g., vascular ring anomalies, stricture, foreign body).

Assessment

Assess the Animal

HISTORY AND PHYSICAL EXAMINATION

Congenital pharyngeal and esophageal disorders are typically diagnosed in young animals soon after weaning. Rarely, dogs with congenital malformations of the aortic arches, also known as vascular ring anomalies, may present with late-onset regurgitation as adults.[1,2] Acquired pharyngeal and esophageal disease can affect dogs and cats of any age.

Owners of dogs with dysphagia due to pharyngeal disease typically report coughing or gagging as the dog chews and swallows its food. The hallmark of esophageal disorders is regurgitation. (See sidebar "Regurgitation vs. Vomiting.") Additional clinical signs include ptyalism, gurgling esophageal noises, halitosis and apparent pain on swallowing. The frequency of regurgitation is variable. Owners may report immediate postprandial regurgitation of undigested food, water or saliva or describe signs manifested several hours after feeding. Affected dogs and cats often have a voracious appetite despite regurgitation. Dyspnea, coughing, exercise intolerance and syncope may be referable to severe respiratory compromise associated with aspiration pneumonia.

Esophageal disorders are frequently associated with neuromuscular diseases and endocrinopathies. Owners may describe weakness or incoordination and many dogs have a history of recurrent skin and coat problems associated with hypothyroidism.

Poor body condition is often evident (body condition score [BCS] 1/5 or 2/5). Body condition should be monitored closely during reassessment and the BCS should be recorded. Young animals with congenital megaesophagus, vascular ring anomalies or cricopharyngeal achalasia are often stunted in comparison to litter mates.

Auscultatory findings often indicate secondary aspiration pneumonia and may include crackles and prominent bronchovesicular sounds. Dogs with active respiratory disease may be febrile and manifest a mucopurulent nasal discharge.

A complete neurologic examination should be performed on an adult dog with a swallowing disorder because acquired megaesophagus is often associated with neuromuscular disorders. Signs of lower motor neuron

---

Regurgitation vs. Vomiting

Differentiating regurgitation from vomiting is important in distinguishing esophageal from lower gastrointestinal disease. Characteristics of vomiting include expulsion of digested and bile-stained food and retching with involuntary abdominal contractions. Gastric contents are often highly acidic, which may be reflected in the pH of the vomitus. However, vomiting often involves reflux of bicarbonate-rich fluid into the stomach from the duodenum, which buffers gastric acid. The vomited material may then have a neutral or near-neutral pH.

Regurgitation involves less forceful casting-up of tubular, bile-free, undigested food. Mucoid secretions mixed with the undigested food will usually have a pH of 6.5 to 7.0. Copious salivation may also be a confusing sign; it may be a primary sign of esophageal diseases (e.g., foreign body) or it may be part of the nausea that often accompanies vomiting.

BIBLIOGRAPHY

Roudebush P, Jones BD, Vaughan RW. Medical aspects of esophageal disease. In: Jones BD, Liska WD, eds. Canine and Feline Gastroenterology. Philadelphia, PA: WB Saunders Co, 1986; 57.

Twedt DC. Diseases of the esophagus. In: Ettinger SJ, Feldman EC, eds. Textbook of Veterinary Internal Medicine, 4th ed. Philadelphia, PA: WB Saunders Co, 1995; 1124-1142.

Willard MD. Diseases of the stomach. In: Ettinger SJ, Feldman EC, eds. Textbook of Veterinary Internal Medicine, 4th ed. Philadelphia, PA: WB Saunders Co, 1995; 1143-1168.

---

disease may provide evidence of a generalized polymyopathy, polyneuropathy or neuromuscular junctionopathy.

LABORATORY AND OTHER CLINICAL INFORMATION

A complete blood count may provide evidence of aspiration pneumonia and some sense of the severity of infection. In chronically affected patients, serum protein and albumin concentrations may provide an indication of nutritional status. Additionally, other serum biochemical abnormalities may provide evidence for an underlying disorder (e.g., hypoadrenocorticism, hypothyroidism).

Radiography is a vital diagnostic aid for evaluating dogs and cats with suspected swallowing and esophageal disorders. Survey films may provide definitive information in cases of megaesophagus and esophageal foreign bodies (Figure 22-2). Radiographic findings in dogs and cats with megaesophagus include a dilated, air-filled esophagus. In the case of vascular ring anomalies, characteristic esophageal dilatation proximal to the heart base can be identified. Thoracic radiography also allows the clinician to assess the patient for aspiration pneumonia. Additionally, thoracic films may reveal a cranial thoracic mass. Thymoma and thymic lymphosarcoma have been associated with secondary acquired megaesophagus and generalized inflammatory myopathies.

The esophagram offers additional diagnostic information, especially in cases of obstructive lesions, esophagitis and esophageal hypomotility without megaesophagus (Figure 22-3). When coupled with fluoroscopy, an esophagram allows sensitive evaluation of the swallow reflex and esophageal motility (Figure 22-4).

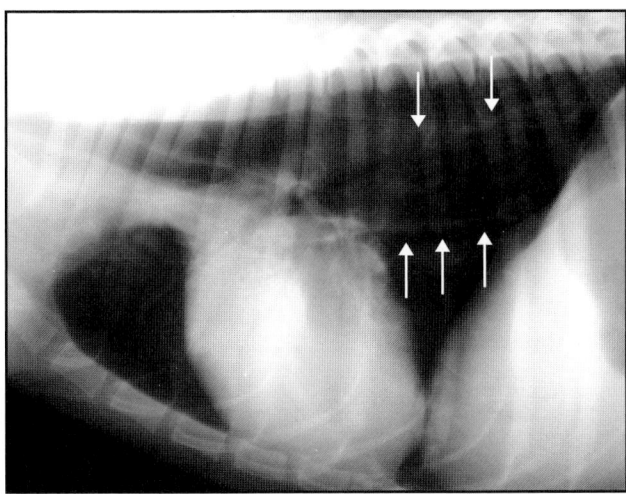

Figure 22-2. Lateral thoracic radiograph demonstrating esophageal dilatation in a dog with acquired megaesophagus. The arrows depict the dorsal and ventral margins of the dilated esophagus. (Courtesy Dr. Joanne Burns, Veterinary Imaging Services, Topeka, KS.)

Figure 22-3. Ventrodorsal thoracic radiograph with a positive-contrast esophagram demonstrating an esophageal stricture due to a persistent right aortic arch in a puppy. Note the narrowed esophageal lumen at the base of the heart (arrow) and dilatation of the esophagus on either side of the obstruction.

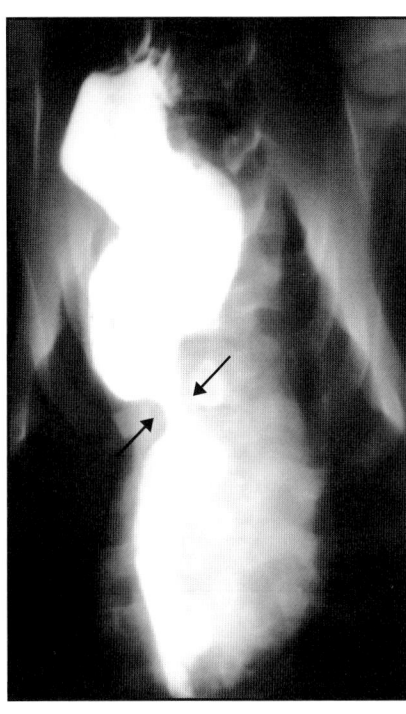

Esophagoscopy is a valuable tool for evaluating dogs and cats with suspected obstructive, neoplastic or inflammatory lesions of the esophagus and pharynx (Figure 22-5). This tool allows visualization of the entire area and collection of tissue specimens for microbiologic and histopathologic examination, if indicated. Additionally, in cases of esophageal foreign bodies or strictures, the flexible endoscope can provide definitive treatment of the lesion. Foreign bodies can be retrieved using a variety of forceps, whereas esophageal strictures are best managed with endoscopic bougienage, balloon dilatation or both procedures.[3]

Acquired megaesophagus can occur secondary to several neuromuscular disorders such as myasthenia gravis, dysautonomia, hypothyroidism, hypoadrenocorticism, systemic lupus erythematosus and other causes of gener-

alized myopathy or neuropathy.[4-8,a] Consult internal medicine and gastroenterology textbooks for a more complete discussion of the diagnosis of these disorders.

Intraluminal esophageal manometry and esophageal scintigraphy are specialized tests that offer dynamic assessment of esophageal motility and pressure.[9,10] The ability to evaluate each phase of the swallowing process allows localization of motility defects to the cricopharynx, esophageal body or gastroesophageal junction. Because anesthetic agents depress esophageal motility, these studies must be performed on awake dogs.[11]

RISK FACTORS

Swallowing disorders are exceedingly rare in cats. In dogs, risk factors for swallowing disorders are primarily breed and age related. Several breeds appear to be predisposed to the development of congenital disorders such as cricopharyngeal achalasia, congenital megaesophagus and vascular ring anomalies (Table 22-4).

There does not seem to be any gender predisposition for idiopathic acquired swallowing disorders. The condition, however, occurs more often in large-breed dogs.[12] One report indicated that Great Dane, golden retriever, German shepherd and Irish setter dogs are at risk for the disease.[7] Middle-aged to older dogs are more likely to develop myasthenia gravis and other neuromuscular disorders resulting in esophageal disease. Nearly 90% of dogs with focal or generalized myasthenia gravis develop megaesophagus.[13] In addition, those breeds predisposed to endocrinopathies (e.g., hypothyroidism and hypoadrenocorticism) are at risk for development of megaesophagus as a manifestation of their disease. Also, it has been reported that dogs with laryngeal paralysis, another neuromuscular condition, are also at risk for development of megaesophagus.[7] In certain areas (e.g., northeastern United States), exposure to lead has been linked to cases of secondary acquired megaesophagus.

ETIOPATHOGENESIS

Pharyngeal and esophageal disorders can generally be attributed to one of three basic pathophysiologic mechanisms: aberrant motility, obstructive lesions or inflammatory degenerative conditions (Table 22-5).[14]

Aberrant Motility

Cricopharyngeal achalasia is characterized by asynchrony of the swallowing reflex. In this condition, the cricopharyngeal muscle fails to relax in coordination with pharyngeal muscle contractions, thus preventing passage of a food bolus from the oropharynx to the esophagus.

Historically, dogs with megaesophagus were presumed to have esophageal achalasia. In this condition, the lower esophageal sphincter fails to relax as esophageal peristaltic activity delivers food to the gastroesophageal junction. However, lower esophageal sphincter pressure is normal and activity is synchronous with esophageal motility in dogs with congenital and acquired megaesophagus. These findings led to the recognition that megaesophagus is a disorder within the body of the esophagus.[9] The work of several investigators suggests that the efferent pathway in many dogs with megaesophagus is functional, whereas the afferent pathway is dysfunctional.[15-17] Using intraluminal balloon distention, Washabau demonstrated that dogs with idiopathic megaesophagus have a defect in their afferent neural pathway.[18] These findings have clinical

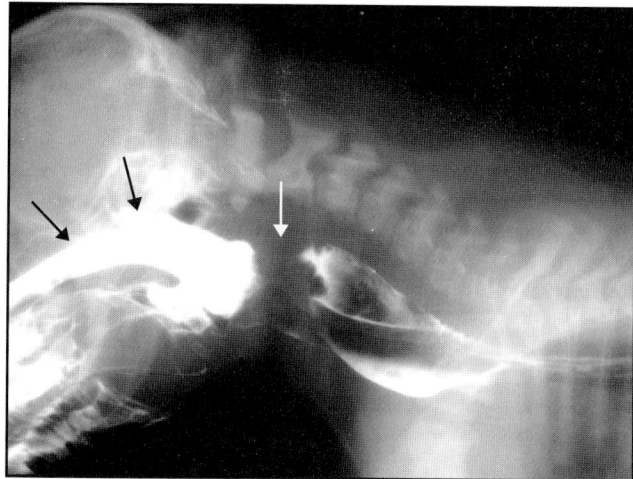

Figure 22-4. Cricopharyngeal achalasia in a cocker spaniel puppy presented for dysphagia. A barium swallow (Left) demonstrated that the cricopharyngeal region (white arrow) did not relax normally during swallowing, which resulted in reflux of barium into the naso- pharynx (black arrows). Only a small amount of barium entered the esophagus. The puppy had a difficult time swallowing liquids as shown by regurgitation of milk back through the nose (Right). (Courtesy Dr. Philip Roudebush, Topeka, KS.)

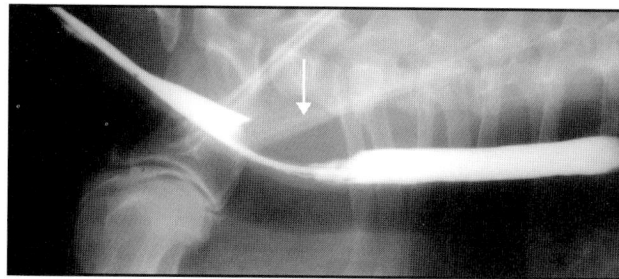

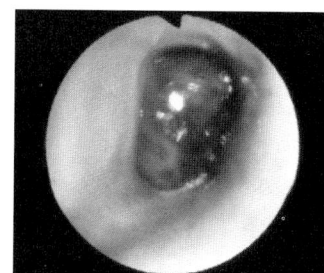

Figure 22-5. Positive-contrast esophagram (Left) from a 12-year-old mixed-breed dog presented for worsening regurgitation. A filling defect is noted in the dorsal wall of the esophagus (arrow). Endoscopy demonstrated a mass lesion (Right) that was confirmed by examination of biopsy specimens as a squamous cell carcinoma. This lesion developed at the site of an acquired esophageal stricture secondary to an episode of postsurgical gastroesophageal reflux. (Courtesy Dr. Michael Leib, Virginia-Maryland Regional College of Veterinary Medicine, Blacksburg, VA.)

GI & PANCREAS

implications because they suggest that foods containing more bulk or prepared in larger boluses may have the capacity to stimulate esophageal motility in mildly affected animals. (See sidebar "Swallowing Reflex.")

Obstructive Lesions

Persistent right aortic arch is the most common vascular ring anomaly recognized in dogs and cats.[2] This anomaly results in constriction of the esophagus at the level of the heart base by the right fourth aortic arch and the ligamentum arteriosum. Esophageal dilatation develops proximal to the vascular ring, leading to regurgitation. Esophageal motility defects may persist if the obstructive lesion is not surgically corrected soon after detection.

Esophageal obstruction due to stricture formation may occur as a consequence of recurrent or severe esophageal injury. Strictures occur most commonly due to esophageal foreign bodies or as a sequelae to gastroesophageal reflux.

Inflammation/Degeneration

Esophagitis arises most often as a consequence of gastroesophageal reflux or foreign body ingestion. The gastroesophageal junction (GEJ) serves as a barrier preventing reflux of gastric contents including pepsin and hydrochloric acid into the lumen of the esophagus. Postprandially, GEJ pressure increases in response to neu-

ral and hormonal stimuli. Certain GI hormones, including gastrin, pancreatic polypeptide, motilin and substance P increase GEJ pressure, whereas others (i.e., secretin, cholecystokinin) reduce GEJ pressure. Dietary influences on the GEJ pressure are presumably mediated via GI hormone release. High-protein meals increase GEJ pressure through gastrin release, whereas high-fat foods reduce GEJ pressure via cholecystokinin release.

Certain sedative agents, including acepromazine, xylazine and diazepam reduce GEJ and may predispose an animal to reflux esophagitis following anesthetic episodes.[11,19] Iatrogenic esophagitis may occur as a sequela to nasoesophageal intubation when the feeding tube crosses the GEJ resulting in incompetence of the sphincter.[20] Occasionally, consumption of irritative substances such as strong acids or alkalis may cause serious esophagitis.

KEY NUTRITIONAL FACTORS

Key nutritional factors for patients with swallowing disorders are listed in Table 22-6 and discussed below. Animals with swallowing disorders are often debilitated and growth of very young animals is often stunted. In addition to the key nutritional factors discussed here,

Table 22-4. Breed-associated disorders of the pharynx and esophagus.

Conditions	Breeds
Cricopharyngeal achalasia	Cocker spaniel
Congenital megaesophagus	Chinese Shar-Pei
	Fox terrier
	German shepherd dog
	Great Dane
	Irish setter
	Labrador retriever
	Miniature schnauzer
	Newfoundland
	Siamese cat
	Wire-haired terrier
Idiopathic acquired megaesophagus	German shepherd dog
	Golden retriever
	Great Dane
	Irish setter
Vascular ring anomalies	Boston terrier
	English bulldog
	German shepherd dog
	Irish setter
	Labrador retriever
	Poodle

Table 22-5. Mechanisms of pharyngeal and esophageal disorders.

Mechanisms	Disorders
Aberrant motility	Congenital megaesophagus
	Cricopharyngeal achalasia
	Dysautonomia
	Endocrinopathies (hypothyroidism, hypoadrenocorticism)
	Idiopathic megaesophagus
	Infectious diseases (canine distemper)
	Myasthenia gravis
	Paraneoplastic syndromes (lymphosarcoma, thymoma)
	Polymyopathies
	Polyneuropathies
	Secondary megaesophagus
	Toxin ingestion (lead)
Inflammatory conditions	Foreign body esophagitis
	Pharyngitis
	Reflux esophagitis
Obstructive lesions	Foreign bodies
	Neoplasia
	Spirocerca lupi granulomas
	Strictures
	Vascular ring anomalies

other nutritional factors may be important depending on the lifestage and body condition of the animal.

Energy and Fat

In patients with motility and obstructive disorders, a relatively high fat concentration is helpful in meeting the patient's caloric requirement in a small volume of food relative to lower fat foods. Foods with greater than 25% DM fat and energy densities in excess of 4.8 kcal/g (20.1 kJ/g) DM are recommended. However, a lower fat content (<15% DM) is a better option for cases of esophagitis with gastric reflux. High dietary fat delays gastric emptying and reduces lower esophageal sphincter pressure, which promotes reflux of food and gastric secretions into the esophagus.[21]

Protein

Protein is required in amounts adequate for tissue repair and to support growth in young animals. Additionally, dietary protein may play an important role in

reducing episodes of gastroesophageal reflux because protein stimulates an increase in gastroesophageal sphincter pressure. This effect is linked to dietary protein's stimulatory effect on gastrin and gastric acid secretion.[22] By increasing the lower esophageal sphincter pressure, episodes of gastroesophageal reflux are decreased, thus limiting the potential for further esophageal injury or aspiration pneumonia. For these reasons, dietary protein content should exceed 25% DM.

Food Form

Foods of differing consistency should be used to determine the best texture for individual patients. A liquid or gruel consistency is usually best for animals with cricopharyngeal achalasia, esophageal obstructive lesions and/or esophagitis. Esophageal performance may improve in animals with megaesophagus when the swallowing reflex is maximally stimulated by the texture of dry foods or when moist foods are formed into large boluses. Dry food or boluses of moist food may act as a stimulus (secondary peristalsis) to any remaining normal esophageal tissue and, therefore, are the form of choice. Gruels or liquids may not stimulate secondary peristalsis, thereby increasing the risk of aspiration pneumonia.

Assess the Food(s) and Feeding Method

The nutrient profile of the patient's current food should be compared with the key nutritional factors described above (Table 22-6). Increasing the energy, fat and protein concentration relative to the current food(s) is often necessary for patients with poor body condition.

Patients with swallowing disorders often require specialized feeding methods because the current feeding protocol of one to three meals per day fed in a bowl on the floor is rarely appropriate. The key tools of nutritional management in these cases are a change in food form and a change in the feeding method.

Feeding Plan

The goals of dietary management for patients with megaesophagus are to minimize regurgitation, avoid secondary aspiration pneumonia and to provide adequate nutrition to regain or maintain proper body weight and condition.

Select a Food(s)

OBSTRUCTIVE LESIONS AND ABERRANT MOTILITY

Feeding a high-calorie (≥4.5 kcal/g [≥18.8 kJ/g] DM), high-fat (≥25% DM), high-protein (≥25% DM) balanced growth or recuperative food is appropriate for most patients with megaesophagus, cricopharyngeal achalasia or obstructive lesions. The food consistency that best promotes flow through the esophagus to the stomach is determined in each case by trial and error. However, gruels often work well, which necessitates using foods with high water content (>80%). Highly digestible (dry matter digestibility ≥90%), calorically dense moist foods are made with ingredients that blenderize easily with water. For example, meat ingredients containing connective and bone tissue do not blenderize as easily as skeletal muscle and organ protein sources. Therefore, using nutrient-dense products made from highly digestible ingredients is

Swallowing Reflex

In animals with simple stomachs, deglutition is a sequential, complex, coordinated action that transports food and liquid from the oral cavity to the stomach. It has been divided into three phases: oropharyngeal, esophageal and gastroesophageal.

The oropharyngeal phase begins with the formation of a bolus in the mouth and ends as the bolus passes through the cricopharyngeal area. Following passage of the bolus, the upper esophageal sphincter contracts to close the upper esophagus and to initiate the esophageal phase of swallowing.

The esophageal phase of deglutition begins with the arrival of the bolus in the cranial esophagus. This phase encompasses passage of the bolus from the cranial esophagus to the gastroesophageal junction (GEJ). Four sequences of events that might occur during the esophageal phase have been described.

1. A swallow is followed immediately by an esophageal peristaltic wave, which progresses uninterrupted to the GEJ (primary peristalsis).
2. The bolus remains in the proximal esophagus until a second or third swallow occurs, then a peristaltic wave carries the combined boluses to the GEJ (primary peristalsis).
3. A bolus temporarily pauses in the proximal esophagus, then a stimulated peristaltic wave carries it to the GEJ (secondary peristalsis).
4. Several boluses accumulate in the proximal esophagus, then a stimulated peristaltic wave carries them to the GEJ (secondary peristalsis).

Direct stimulation of the esophageal wall by a bolus initiates a second peristaltic wave (secondary peristalsis). Progression of primary or secondary peristaltic contractions depends on the presence, size and location of the bolus in the esophagus. In the absence of a bolus, peristalsis in the esophagus does not follow the act of swallowing. In the thoracic esophagus, contractions are facilitated by, but do not depend on a bolus. Thus, two mechanisms are involved in the regulation of esophageal contraction: 1) a central regulatory mechanism (swallowing center) in the brainstem and 2) afferent nerve impulses that originate in the esophagus in the presence of a bolus.

The lower esophageal sphincter (LES) is not a true anatomic sphincter, but rather a physiologic high-pressure zone. This zone is found in the most distal portion of the esophagus and separates the esophagus from the stomach. The LES is the functional term used for this region, but many authors use the anatomic term GEJ. During peristalsis, the LES relaxes and allows the bolus to pass into the stomach (gastroesophageal phase). A prevalent misunderstanding is that LES relaxation and opening are synonymous. Relaxation and opening of the LES are related but distinct events. LES opening is a passive mechanical event affected by the force of an oncoming bolus, whereas LES relaxation occurs as an active reflex process mediated neurologically. The average canine LES begins to relax several seconds before the esophageal pressure wave peaks in the distal esophagus. Even if the LES opens and closes normally, synchronization of LES with the esophageal wave is still required for normal passage of a bolus.

The GEJ is the only area of the gastrointestinal tract in which luminal structures having opposite cavitary pressures are in continuity. Mechanical factors and intrinsic LES tone serve as the major control mechanisms to prevent reflux of gastric contents. Whatever external force or positive pressure is applied to the stomach is also exerted on the terminal abdominal esophagus; therefore, no pressure gradient occurs between the stomach and thoracic esophagus. Other mechanical factors that prevent gastroesophageal reflux include: 1) interdigitating gastric rugal folds, 2) focal thickening of the distal esophageal muscle coat, 3) oblique implantation of the distal esophagus into the stomach and 4) the flap-like cardiac incisura, which is pushed against the GEJ by the enlarging gastric fundus. Gastrin and other gastrointestinal hormones at pharmacologic doses appear to increase LES tone. Whether these hormones function to increase LES tone when released physiologically during normal food ingestion is still speculative.

BIBLIOGRAPHY

Roudebush P, Jones BD, Vaughan RW. Medical aspects of esophageal disease. In: Jones BD, Liska WD, eds. Canine and Feline Gastroenterology. Philadelphia, PA: WB Saunders Co, 1986; 57.

more likely to meet the nutrient requirements of the patient in the smallest volume possible. Recommending larger cans of calorically dense cat food can help reduce the volume and cost of feeding a large dog.

INFLAMMATORY CONDITIONS

Foods with lower levels of dietary fat (<15% DM) are recommended for managing patients with esophagitis and gastroesophageal reflux. Higher dietary fat levels may precipitate gastroesophageal reflux by delaying gastric emptying and reducing lower esophageal sphincter pressure. Increased dietary protein (≥25% DM) enhances lower esophageal sphincter tone.

Determine a Feeding Method

Small-volume, frequent meals are recommended when feeding animals with swallowing disorders. Gruel-type foods are often necessary because the liquid form is more amenable to gravity fill of the stomach. Feeding a high-calorie food to a patient in an upright position and maintaining this position for 20 to 30 minutes after feeding provides ample time for gravitational flow of the food through the esophagus to the stomach. Upright feeding can be accomplished by several methods. The most common technique is to elevate the food bowl so that the dog or cat has to sit down or stand on its hind legs to eat. Pets can be trained to eat on stairs or from a counter or stool. Alternatively, small dogs and cats can be cradled in an upright position in the owner's arms while eating (Figure 22-6). Large dogs have been trained to lie in sternal recumbency on a inclined board for the required period of time. Several companies manufacture devices to facilitate upright feeding (Figure 22-7).

In some animals, upright feeding is not adequate to control regurgitation or is impractical because of the pet's temperament or the owner's schedule. In those cases, placement of a gastrostomy or enterostomy tube is recommended to bypass the esophagus entirely. Nasoesophageal, nasogastric and esophagostomy tubes are not appropriate in this situation. Patients with ongoing signs of malnutrition at presentation should receive a large-bore gastrostomy feeding tube, if possible, and immediate alimentation via the tube until adequate oral intake can be achieved. Gastrostomy tubes have been used successfully for long periods to maintain the nutritional status of dogs with

Table 22-6. Key nutritional factors for dogs with swallowing disorders.*

Disorders	Energy (kcal/g)	Energy (kJ/g)	Fat (%)	Protein (%)
Esophagitis/gastroesophageal reflux	<4.0	<16.7	<15	≥25
Motility disorders	≥4.5	≥18.8	≥25	≥25
Obstructive disorders	≥4.5	≥18.8	≥25	≥25

*Nutrients expressed on a dry matter basis.

megaesophagus. A permanent button-type gastrostomy tube should be considered in cases in which owners are willing to feed their pet long term via gastrostomy tube. Some clinicians prefer feeding via enterostomy tube because of the potential for gastroesophageal reflux and recurrent aspiration. Readers are referred to Chapter 12 and Appendix V for additional details regarding these assisted-feeding techniques. Owners should be made aware that regurgitation will not completely cease even if all food and water is administered through the gastrostomy tube. Many animals will continue to regurgitate fluid, which is most likely salivary secretions. However, the likelihood of aspiration pneumonia is reduced greatly.

Pharyngeal and esophageal tissues heal slowly and are susceptible to secondary bacterial infections. Therefore, surgeons have traditionally recommended to withhold oral feedings of regular pet foods for three to four days for patients with inflammation, trauma or surgery to these tissues. Patients with no history or evidence of malnutrition may be safely held off food for two to three days if necessary, but should receive nutrition by the fourth day. Dietary goals in these patients are to provide adequate nutrition to the patient using foods that minimize irritation and trauma to sensitive pharyngeal and esophageal tissues.

Concurrent Therapy

The feeding plan is often used in conjunction with other therapeutic modalities including surgery (e.g., cricopharyngeal myotomy, esophageal stricture, vascular ring anomaly, esophageal foreign bodies), bougienage (e.g., esophageal stricture), endoscopy (e.g., foreign body removal) and drugs (e.g., antibiotics, prokinetic agents, corticosteroids, antacids, H_2-receptor blockers, mucosal protective agents).

Reassessment

Nutritional reassessment of patients with swallowing disorders includes: 1) monitoring changes in body weight and condition, 2) evaluating owner compliance in delivering the daily food dosage to the patient, 3) determining the extent of ongoing dysphagia or regurgitation and 4) monitoring resolution of other concurrent disease processes (e.g., pneumonia, myopathies, endocrinopathies). Daily food dosage should be adjusted as indicated by changes in the patient's body weight and condition.

■ GASTRIC DISORDERS

Vomiting is the hallmark of gastric disorders in dogs and cats. (See sidebar "Hairballs.") Vomiting may be acute or chronic with a long list of possible etiologies.[1] Vomiting requires a forceful coordinated musculoskeletal effort to eject food from the stomach to the mouth.

Dietary goals are to meet the nutritional requirements of the patient with foods that minimize gastric irritation, promote gastric emptying and normalize gastric motility. In most vomiting cases of less than 48 hours' duration, withholding water for 24 hours and food for 24 to 48 hours generally controls the episode. The patient's regular food should then be gradually reintroduced in small frequent meals over two to three days. Episodes of acute vomiting that occur for longer than three days and cases of chronic vomiting (i.e., persisting longer than 21 days) with signs of malnutrition require more intensive nutritional and medical management.

Gastritis and Gastroduodenal Ulceration

Clinical Importance

Gastritis is one of the most common causes of vomiting in dogs and cats.[2] The prevalence of gastritis in the pet population is unknown but is thought to be high because many different insults can result in gastric mucosal inflammation (Table 22-7). In one survey, 9% of research beagles had histologic evidence of gastritis in the absence of clinical signs.[3]

The prevalence of GI ulcer disease in dogs and cats is low compared with the prevalence reported in people. The infrequent diagnosis of GI ulceration is possibly due to the absence of clinical signs in many cases. In experimental studies involving dogs, extensive gastroduodenal ulceration existed with only mild clinical signs.[4]

Assessment

ASSESS THE ANIMAL

History and Physical Examination
The patient history is often adequate to provide a presumptive diagnosis of gastritis. Owners should be questioned closely about the potential for toxin exposure (e.g., lead, arsenic) and foreign body ingestion (e.g., bones, coins, garbage) by the animal. A history of nonsteroidal antiinflammatory drug (NSAID) administration provides a presumptive diagnosis of drug-induced GI erosions or ulcerations. The veterinarian should query the owner specifically about the use of over-the-counter agents, such as aspirin and ibuprofen.

Vomiting is the most common presenting complaint for dogs with acute or chronic gastritis. Typically, owners report intermittent vomiting of food or bile-stained fluid. Fresh or digested blood appearing as "coffee grounds" may be present in the vomitus. Associated signs may include diarrhea, abdominal pain and melena.

Physical examination is often unremarkable in dogs and cats with gastritis or GI ulcerations. Reduced skin turgor and tacky mucous membranes indicate dehydration. In long-term cases, weight loss and poor body condition may be noted. Pallor and weakness may be present in patients with significant GI blood loss. Other findings may reflect the underlying cause of gastritis (e.g., cutaneous masses or hepatosplenomegaly associated with mastocytosis).

Laboratory and Other Clinical Information

Routine hematology, serum biochemistry profiles and urinalyses help rule out metabolic causes of gastritis. These tests readily identify renal disease, hepatopathies and hypoadrenocorticism. The hematocrit and hemogram are useful in assessing severity and chronicity of gastric disease. Inflammatory leukograms may be identified in animals with neoplasia, perforated GI ulcers, inflammatory bowel disease and phycomycosis. Eosinophilia may indicate parasitism or eosinophilic gastritis. In cats, extreme eosinophilia is suggestive of the hypereosinophilic syndrome or systemic mastocytosis. Identification of circulating mast cells is generally diagnostic for mast cell tumors.

Fecal examinations for parasites and occult blood are important screening tests. Parasites are an unlikely cause of gastritis but should be considered. Gastric parasites such *Ollulanus tricuspis* or *Physaloptera* spp are more readily identified in vomitus or gastric juice. The accuracy of fecal occult blood testing has been confirmed in dogs consuming dry foods.[4,5] Moist meat-based foods often yield false-positive results. Both the modified guaiac and orthotoluidine tests are sensitive and specific for detecting occult blood in feces.[5]

Imaging modalities such as survey and contrast radiography and ultrasonography offer noninvasive diagnostic techniques for evaluating pets with gastritis or GI ulceration. Survey radiography may be useful in the diagnosis of radiopaque foreign bodies. Abnormalities in renal size or shape may suggest renal insufficiency as the cause of gastritis. Hepatosplenomegaly in cats is suggestive of systemic mastocytosis or alimentary lymphosarcoma. Free air in the abdomen is diagnostic for viscus rupture associated with a perforated GI ulcer and indicates the need for immediate exploratory surgery.

Contrast radiographic examinations may be useful. Iodinated contrast agents[a] should be used if GI perforation is suspected. Otherwise, barium sulfate is the contrast agent of choice for GI studies because of its superior ability to coat the GI mucosa. More complete descriptions of radiographic findings in gastric disease are available.[6]

Endoscopic examination is the most sensitive test for detection of gastritis and gastroduodenal ulcerative disease. Gastric fluid can be collected for parasitic and microbiologic examination. Endoscopic evaluation allows for the identification of mucosal and submucosal hemorrhages, erosions and ulcers (Figure 22-8). Most important, endoscopic procedures allow collection of multiple gastric and duodenal biopsy specimens.

Risk Factors

Older animals are more likely to be suffering from metabolic or neoplastic causes of gastritis. Older dogs receiving NSAIDs for management of osteoarthritis are at risk for gastritis and gastroduodenal ulceration. Younger dogs and cats and unsupervised pets are more likely to suffer from gastritis secondary to foreign bodies or dietary indiscretion. A number of breed-associated causes of gastritis have been recognized (Table 22-8). Dachshunds,

miniature schnauzers, toy poodles and other small and toy breeds are most commonly affected with hemorrhagic gastroenteritis.[7] Several breeds are at risk for chronic gastritis including the basenji, Ludenhund and Drentse patrijshond.[8]

Etiopathogenesis

Acute Gastritis and Gastroduodenal Ulceration

Several metabolic disorders have been associated with the development of acute gastritis and GI ulceration. Uremia may result in diffuse GI tract hemorrhage. GI erosions and ulcers are thought to result from the effects of uremic toxins on the gut mucosa. Additionally, increased circulating concentrations of gastrin have been identified in patients with uremia.[9] Hypergastrinemia promotes hyperacidity.

Liver disease is a common cause of GI ulcerations, which may be manifested as hematemesis. The pathogenesis of mucosal ulceration associated with hepatopathies is multifactorial and associated coagulopathies may worsen clinical manifestations. Potential mechanisms include altered gastric blood flow due to portal hypertension, delayed epithelial turnover, gastric hyperacidity and

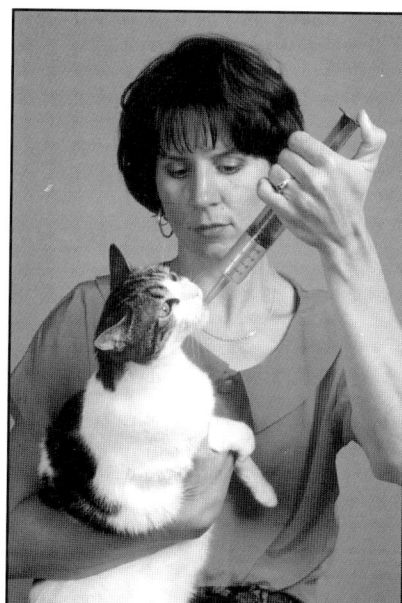

Figure 22-6. Upright feeding position that can be used for cats and small dogs with megaesophagus.

Figure 22-7. Feeding device that can be used to maintain an upright feeding position for patients with megaesophagus.

Hairballs

Hairballs occur commonly in cats because of their normal grooming behavior and sharp barbs on the tongue that enhance hair ingestion. Cats with longer, thicker coats and those with fastidious grooming behavior usually have more problems with hairballs. Swallowed hair initially accumulates as loose aggregates or more compacted, soft aggregates mixed with mucus. Hairballs are periodically regurgitated from the oropharynx or esophagus or vomited from the stomach, or they pass into the intestinal tract where they are voided in the feces. Owners observe periodic gagging, retching and regurgitation or vomiting of hair and mucus (usually not containing food or bile). Hairballs are often tubular (Figure 1).

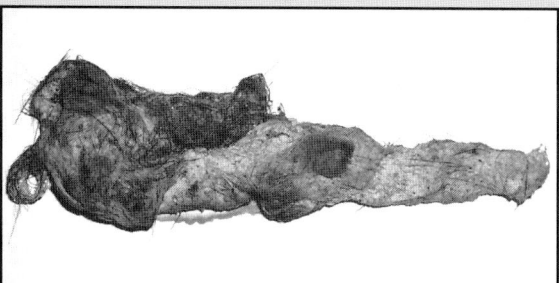

Figure 1. Hairball regurgitated by a cat. Note the typical cylindrical shape.

Trichobezoars are harder concretions within the stomach or intestines formed of hair, mucus and other material. Trichobezoars probably begin as simple aggregates of hair but progress to larger and harder concretions. They are less common in cats than typical hairballs but they are more likely to cause severe clinical signs. Trichobezoars are a common cause of anorexia in pet rabbits. (See Chapter 28.) Large trichobezoars may obstruct pyloric outflow or the intestines. Large trichobezoars must be removed via surgery or endoscopy.

How cats eliminate aggregates of hair is probably similar to how they eliminate the pelts of small mammals that are ingested as part of a natural diet. Cats that hunt frequently may be seen vomiting the pelts of voles, mice, small rabbits and other mammals. This may be a protective mechanism for eliminating less digestible portions of prey.

Although hairballs do not usually cause significant clinical disease, their associated clinical signs are a nuisance for many cat owners. Various laxatives, lubricants, treats and foods are available for routine management of these problems. Laxatives and lubricants should be used intermittently because large daily doses may interfere with normal digestion and nutrient absorption. Frequent regurgitation or vomiting of hairballs (every day) with or without diarrhea, weight loss, anorexia or abdominal pain usually indicates an underlying problem (e.g., gastric motility defect or lymphoplasmacytic enteritis). Cats with severe or frequent clinical signs should be evaluated more extensively with diagnostics including hematology, serum biochemistry profiles, radiography and upper gastrointestinal endoscopy.

BIBLIOGRAPHY
Pedersen NC. Feline Husbandry: Diseases and Management in the Multiple-Cat Environment. Goleta, CA: American Veterinary Publications Inc, 1991; 303.

Table 22-7. Potential causes of gastritis and/or gastroduodenal ulceration.

Adverse reactions to food
  Food allergy (hypersensitivity)
  Food intolerance
Dietary indiscretion
  Chemicals
  Foreign bodies
  Garbage toxicosis
  Gluttony
  Heavy metal toxicosis
  Plants
Drug administration
  Corticosteroids
  Nonsteroidal antiinflammatory agents
Idiopathic gastritis
Infectious agents
  Fungi
  Parasites
  Spiral bacteria
Inflammatory bowel disease
Neoplasia
  Gastrinoma
  Mastocytosis
  Primary gastric neoplasia
Reduced gastric blood flow
  Disseminated intravascular coagulopathy
  Neurologic disorders
  Sepsis
  Shock
Reflux gastritis
Systemic disease
  Hypoadrenocorticism
  Liver disease
  Renal disease

hypergastrinemia. Experimental evidence suggests that hypergastrinemia is a less important mechanism than previously suspected.[10]

Experimentally induced and spontaneous gastritis and gastroduodenal ulcerations have been reported to occur in dogs in conjunction with the use of a variety of NSAIDs including aspirin, indomethacin, naproxen, ibuprofen, phenylbutazone, flunixin meglumine, piroxicam, sulindac and meclofenamic acid.[4,11-13] The ulcerogenicity of NSAIDs is attributed to inhibition of the enzyme cyclooxygenase in the prostaglandin synthesis pathway, resulting in the loss of the gastric protective effects of prostacyclin and prostaglandin E.[13]

Stress ulcerations are poorly defined entities in veterinary patients. However, gastroduodenal ulcerations have been noted in companion animals in conjunction with severe burns, heat stroke, multiple trauma, head injuries and spinal cord disorders. In addition, hypovolemic shock and sepsis may be complicated by development of GI ulcers.

Gastrin-producing pancreatic tumors, histamine-producing tumors (e.g., mast cell tumors, basophilic leukemia) and a pancreatic polypeptide-producing pancreatic tumor have been associated with gastric or duodenal ulceration in dogs and cats. Ulcers in these animals were thought to be induced by persistent gastric hyperacidity stimulated by gastrin, histamine or pancreatic polypeptide.

Chronic Gastritis

The etiopathogenesis of chronic gastritis in dogs and cats is not fully understood. In some cases, an underlying etiology such as parasitism or a metabolic disorder (e.g., uremia, liver disease) can be identified. In most cases, however, an immune-mediated response is hypothesized to be responsible for inflammatory infiltrates within the gastric mucosa. Experimentally, chronic gastritis can be produced in dogs via mucosal irritants, systemic administration of gastric juices or prenatal thymectomy.[14-17] Each of these disturbs oral tolerance. Chronic idiopathic gastritis is probably a subset of the inflammatory bowel disease syndrome or may arise as an adverse reaction to food antigens. Readers are referred to the Small Intestinal Disorders section below and Chapter 14 for a more complete discussion of the pathogenesis of inflammatory bowel disease and adverse reactions to food.

Once present, gastric inflammation interferes with gastric motility and gastric reservoir function leading to vomiting. Nutrients including proteins are lost through the inflamed mucosal surface.

Key Nutritional Factors

Key nutritional factors for patients with gastritis and gastroduodenal ulceration are listed in Table 22-9 and discussed in detail below.

Water

Water is the most important nutrient for patients with acute vomiting because of the potential for life-threatening dehydration due to excessive fluid loss and inability of the patient to replace those losses. Moderate to severe dehydration should be corrected with appropriate parenteral fluid therapy rather than using the oral route.

Minerals

Gastric and intestinal secretions differ from extracellular fluids in electrolyte composition, so their loss can result in systemic electrolyte abnormalities. Dogs and cats with vomiting and diarrhea may have low, normal or high serum sodium, potassium and chloride concentrations. The derangement that predominates in a particular animal depends on the severity of the disease, nutritional status, site of the disease process, etc. For these reasons, serum electrolyte concentrations are helpful in tailoring the fluid therapy and nutritional management of these patients. Mild hypokalemia, hypochloremia and either hypernatremia or hyponatremia are the electrolyte abnormalities most commonly associated with acute vomiting and diarrhea.

Total body depletion of potassium is a predictable consequence of severe or chronic GI disease because the potassium concentration of both gastric and intestinal secretions is high. Hypokalemia in association with GI disease will be particularly profound if losses are not matched by sufficient intake of potassium.

Electrolyte disorders should be corrected initially with appropriate parenteral fluid and electrolyte therapy. Foods for patients with acute gastroenteritis should contain levels of sodium, chloride and potassium above the minimum allowances for normal dogs and cats. Recommended levels of these nutrients are 0.35 to 0.5% DM sodium, 0.50 to 1.3% DM chloride and 0.80 to 1.1% DM potassium.

Protein

Because dietary antigens are suspected to play a role in chronic gastritis, some authors recommend the use of "hypoallergenic" or elimination foods for patients with chronic idiopathic gastritis.[18] In certain cases, elimination foods may be used successfully without pharmacologic intervention. Mild to moderate chronic gastritis may respond to dietary management alone. Ideal elimination foods should: 1) avoid protein excess, 2) have high protein digestibility (≥87%)

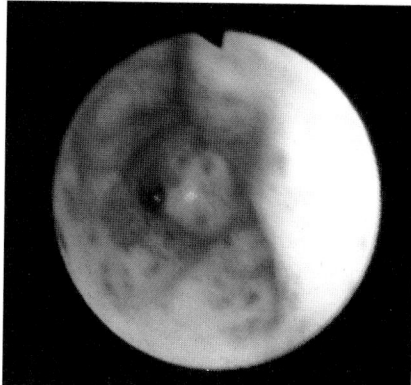

Figure 22-8. Endoscopic appearance of antral gastritis in a dog with chronic vomiting. Note the multiple hemorrhagic erosive lesions of the gastric mucosa. (Courtesy Dr. Michael Leib, Virginia-Maryland Regional College of Veterinary Medicine, Blacksburg, VA.)

Table 22-8. Breed-associated gastric disorders.

Disorders	Breeds
Chronic hypertrophic gastritis	Basenji
	Drentse patrijshond
	Lundehund
Chronic hypertrophic pyloric gastropathy	Lhaso apso
	Maltese dog
	Pekinese
	Shih Tzu
Gastric dilatation-volvulus	Basset hound
	Doberman pinscher
	Gordon setter
	Great Dane
	Irish setter
	Saint Bernard
	Weimaraner
Hemorrhagic gastroenteritis	Dachshund
	Miniature schnauzer
	Toy poodle
Pyloric stenosis	Boston terrier
	Boxer
	Siamese cat

and 3) contain a limited number of novel protein sources to which the animal has never been exposed. Elimination foods are discussed in more detail in Chapter 14.

Fat

Solids and liquids higher in caloric density and fat levels are emptied more slowly from the stomach than similar foods with lower caloric density and fat levels. Fat in the duodenum stimulates the release of cholecystokinin, which delays gastric emptying. Foods with less than 15% DM fat are probably appropriate for dogs with gastritis and those with less than 22% DM fat for cats.

Other Nutritional Factors

Vitamins and Minerals

Iron, copper and B-vitamin supplementation may be of benefit in patients with gastroduodenal ulceration and GI blood loss. The use of hematinics is indicated in patients with nonregenerative, microcytic/hypochromic anemias attributable to iron deficiency. Hematinics are probably not necessary in most animals that receive blood transfusions.

Acid Load

Alkalemia should be expected if the vomiting patient loses hydrogen and chloride ions in excess of sodium and bicarbonate. Hypochloremia perpetuates the alkalosis by increasing renal bicarbonate reabsorption. Mild alkalemia is common, but profound alkalemia is more likely to occur with pyloric or upper duodenal obstruction rather than with acute gastritis.

Acidemia may occur in vomiting patients if the vomited gastric fluid is relatively low in hydrogen and chloride ion content (e.g., during fasting) or if there is concurrent loss of intestinal sodium and bicarbonate. Severe acid-base disorders are best corrected with appropriate parenteral fluid and electrolyte therapy. Foods for patients with acute vomiting and diarrhea should avoid excess dietary acid load. Foods that normally produce alkaline urine are less likely to be associated with acidosis.

ASSESS THE FOOD(S) AND FEEDING METHOD

Levels of the key nutritional factors should be evaluated in foods currently fed to patients with gastritis and compared with recommended levels (Table 22-9). Information from this aspect of assessment is essential for making any changes to foods currently provided. Changing to a more appropriate food is indicated if key nutritional factors in the current food do not match recommended levels.

A thorough assessment should include verification of the feeding method currently used. Items to consider include feeding frequency, amount fed, how the food is offered, access to other food and who feeds the animal. All of this information should have been gathered when the history of the animal was obtained. If the animal has a normal BCS (3/5), the amount of food previously fed (energy basis) was probably appropriate.

Feeding Plan

The first objective in managing acute or chronic gastritis should be to correct dehydration and electrolyte and acid-base imbalances, if present. The dietary goals are to provide a food that meets the patient's nutrient requirements, allows normalization of gastric motility and function and controls vomiting. In most cases of acute vomiting, initial fasting for 24 to 48 hours, with parenteral fluid administration, either reduces or resolves vomiting by simply removing the effects of undigested food and the offending agents from the GI tract. Chronic vomiting cases generally require a more detailed diagnostic and therapeutic (i.e., medical and nutritional) approach.

Table 22-9. Key nutritional factors for patients with gastritis and/or gastroduodenal ulceration.*

Factors	Recommended levels
Acid load	Avoid excess dietary acid
Chloride	0.50 to 1.3%
Fat	<15% for dogs
	<22% for cats
Potassium	0.80 to 1.10%
Protein**	Limit dietary protein to one or two sources
	Use protein sources to which animal has not been exposed previously
	16 to 20% for dogs
	30 to 45% for cats
	Protein digestibility ≥87%
Sodium	0.35 to 0.50%

*Nutrients expressed on a dry matter basis.
**Protein is a key factor for patients with chronic idiopathic gastritis.

SELECT A FOOD(S)

Food selection for vomiting patients should be based on the key nutritional factors described in Table 22-9. In general, veterinary therapeutic foods formulated for the management of GI disease (Table 22-10) or adverse reactions to food (Table 14-5) contain appropriate levels of key nutritional factors.

Bland foods are often recommended for veterinary patients with gastritis. This recommendation probably originated from physicians' recommendation for people recovering from GI upsets to consume bland foods. The term "bland" is poorly defined, but it is most often applied to easily digested/absorbed and nonirritating, nonspicy foods. If that is the accepted definition, most pet foods would fall within this category. The use of topical digests on dry foods may be construed as potentially irritating because many digests contain high concentrations of reactive amines.[19] The term bland is not a useful recommendation to pet owners; instead specific ingredients or nutrients to avoid should be clearly stated.

DETERMINE A FEEDING METHOD

Two feeding methods have been described for patients with acute gastric disorders. The more classic feeding method for patients with acute gastritis begins by discontinuing oral intake of food and water for 24 to 48 hours. After this period, animals should be offered small amounts of water or ice cubes every few hours. If water is well tolerated, small amounts of food can be offered several times (i.e., six to eight times) a day. If the pet eats food without vomiting, the amount fed is gradually increased over three to four days until the animal is receiving its estimated daily energy requirement (DER) in two to three meals per day. Food should be withdrawn and offered again after a few hours if the animal begins to vomit during this period.

In some cases, refeeding may be complicated by persistent vomiting. In such cases, metoclopramide or antiemetic agents are recommended (Table 22-11). Rarely, some animals may require parenteral feeding. (See Chapter 12.)

The second approach, feeding through vomiting, has been a successful alternative to "nothing per os" (NPO) therapy in some vomiting patients. Pregnant women suffering hyperemesis reported feeling less nausea and preferred the placement of a nasogastric tube with slow frequent self feeding of small liquid meals to eating small regular meals or NPO therapy.[20] A possible explanation for the continued vomiting is that the normal motility pattern throughout the length of the bowel cannot be re-established without strong intraluminal stimulation. In fact, vomiting and mucosal atrophy probably perpetuate bowel dysfunction. Feeding restarts normal patterns of motility beginning in the esophagus and food probably re-establishes motility patterns as it passes down the bowel. The physical presence of food and nutrients serves as mechanical and chemical stimuli to the intestine, which in turn releases endogenous and hormonal secretions to re-establish normal bowel motility and function.

Simply refeeding dogs (orally) and cats (via nasoesophageal tube) with protracted vomiting (i.e., lasting more than seven days) has successfully stopped vomiting without antiemetic drugs.[b] Feedings are continued even though the patient may vomit. Most cases of protracted vomiting cease within 24 hours of administering liquid food. These patients are then offered small frequent meals of a highly digestible, moderate-fat food 24 hours after the last episode of vomiting (Table 22-10).

Concurrent Therapy

Nutritional management is often used in conjunction with other therapeutic modalities including parenteral fluids, antacids, H_2-receptor antagonists, cytoprotective drugs, prostaglandin E_2 analogues, antibiotics and anthelmintics (Table 22-11). (See sidebar "Herbal Remedies for Gastrointestinal Disorders.")

Reassessment

Nutritional reassessment of patients with gastritis or gastroduodenal ulcers includes monitoring changes in body weight and condition and determining the extent of vomiting. Daily food dosage should be adjusted as indicated by changes in body weight and condition.

If vomiting persists in the face of appropriate medical and nutritional therapy, different foods should be tried. (See sidebar "Performing Dietary Trials in Patients with Gastrointestinal Disease.") If anemia was identified as a problem in pets with GI ulcers, reassessment of the hemogram is recommended to ensure adequate repletion of iron and copper. In addition, frequent monitoring of fecal occult blood loss is advisable.

Gastric Dilatation/Gastric Dilatation-Volvulus

Clinical Importance

Gastric dilatation (GD) is distention of the stomach with a mixture of air, food and fluid. GD often occurs intermittently, usually in young dogs, particularly as a result of overeating or some other dietary indiscretion. Gastric dilatation-volvulus (GDV) is characterized by rotation of the stomach on its mesenteric axis, entrapping gastric contents and compromising vascular supply to the stomach, spleen and pancreas. Acute GDV is a medicosurgical emergency with high morbidity and mortality. Rarely, chronic, intermittent GDV may occur associated with a partial (i.e., <90 degree) rotation of the stomach.

GDV most commonly affects large-breed, deep-chested dogs and has been estimated to affect 40,000 to 60,000 dogs annually.[21] GDV accounted for 3.4% of deaths of military dogs based on necropsy findings.[22] A review of data from the Veterinary Medical Database, Purdue University, West Lafayette, IN, suggests a 1,500% increase in the frequency of GDV from 1964 to 1974 within cases presented to veterinary teaching hospitals.[23]

Assessment

ASSESS THE ANIMAL

History and Physical Examination

Clinical signs of GD include nausea, belching and vomiting. Conversely, there may be no effort to vomit, but instead lethargy, reluctance to move and grunting sounds with respiratory effort. The onset of GDV is usually acute and often occurs at night or in the early morning. Owners often report some precipitating stressful event. Boarding, hospitalization, travel and participation in shows have been associated with GDV. Affected dogs exhibit restless-

ness, progressive abdominal distention with tympany, abdominal pain, hypersalivation and repeated, nonproductive attempts to vomit. Occasionally, owners will find affected dogs dead or in shock.

Chronic GDV is a rare manifestation of the syndrome. Dogs present with intermittent, progressive signs including vomiting, inappetence and weight loss. Periods of illness are interspersed with periods of normalcy. If untreated, these dogs often progress to acute GDV.

The most prominent sign of GD and GDV is abdominal distention. In some dogs, concurrent splenomegaly may be identified by abdominal palpation. Clinical manifestations of cardiovascular shock, including tachycardia, delayed capillary refill time, pallor and weak pulses may be present.

Laboratory and Other Clinical Information

Laboratory assessment of patients with GDV or GD should include a complete blood count, serum biochemistry profile, urinalysis and blood gas analysis. The complete blood count often reflects stress and can provide early evidence for disseminated intravascular coagulopathy, if thrombocytopenia is present. If faced with thrombocytopenia, a complete coagulation panel is recommended before surgery.

Hypokalemia is common in patients with GDV and should be managed with intravenous potassium supplementation because hypokalemia can potentiate cardiac dysrhythmias. Metabolic acidosis, metabolic alkalosis, respiratory acidosis and mixed acid-base disorders have been reported to occur in dogs with GDV.[24] Routine use of alkalinizing fluids and sodium bicarbonate, therefore, is not recommended.

Radiography is critical to the diagnosis of GD and GDV. Dorsoventral and right lateral views should be evaluated to distinguish simple GD from GDV (Figure 22-9). In most cases, gastric rotation is clockwise (i.e., with the dog in a dorsoventral position) and ranges from 90 to 360 degrees. Other significant findings may include splenomegaly and free abdominal air, which indicates gastric rupture.

Electrocardiograph recordings should be monitored in patients with GDV pre- and postoperatively because cardiac dysrhythmias occur in approximately half of patients.[25] The distended, malpositioned stomach compresses the caudal vena cava and portal vein resulting in cardiovascular compromise. Reduction in venous return and cardiac output leads to myocardial ischemia and cardiovascular shock. Cardiac dysrhythmias, gastric necrosis and multiple organ ischemia are potential consequences if gastric decompression is not performed expeditiously. Generally, dysrhythmias are ventricular in origin and can be life-threatening.

Risk Factors

Considerable effort has been expended over the last 20 years in attempts to identify the cause or causes of GD and GDV. Despite these efforts, no definitive cause for the syndrome has been identified. However, a number of predisposing and precipitating risk factors have been demonstrated through epidemiologic studies (Table 22-12).

These conditions occur most frequently in large-breed, deep-chested dogs, but may occur rarely in smaller dogs and in cats. A number of breeds including the Great Dane, Irish setter, Gordon setter, Weimaraner, Saint Bernard, Doberman pinscher and basset hound appear to be at risk. Other large breeds, notably the retriever breeds, have

Table 22-10. Ingredients and nutrient profiles of selected commercial pet foods used in patients with gastrointestinal disease.*

Products	Protein	Fat	Soluble carbo-hydrate	Crude fiber	Energy density (kcal/g)	Ingredient comments
Moist canine products						
Hill's Prescription Diet Canine i/d	25.9	14.0	52.6	0.7	1.31	Contains soy fiber
Leo Specific Digest CIW	24.4	14.7	48.9	4.2	1.31	Contains vegetable fiber
Iams Eukanuba Low-Residue Adult/Canine						
Medi-Cal Canine Gastro Formula	22.1	12.3	na	1.7	1.15	
Purina CNM Canine EN-Formula	30.5	13.8	48.9	0.9	1.19	22 to 34% of fat from MCT
Select Care Canine Sensitive Formula	22.1	12.3	58.2	1.7	1.24	Contains FOS
Waltham/Pedigree Canine Low Fat	33.8	6.9	49.7	2.4	1.01	
Dry canine products						
Hill's Prescription Diet Canine i/d	26.3	13.8	52.1	1.2	3.85	Contains soy fiber
Iams Eukanuba Low-Residue Adult/Canine	26.0	10.9	57.0	2.1	3.98	Contains beet pulp and FOS
Iams Eukanuba Low-Residue Puppy	34.5	23.1	37.2	2.0	4.64	Contains beet pulp and FOS
Leo Specific Digest CID	27.5	14.3	51.6	1.1	4.01	Contains vegetable fiber
Medi-Cal Canine Gastro Formula	23.4	11.7	na	2.0	3.46	
Purina CNM Canine EN-Formula	25.8	11.7	55.1	1.1	3.79	22 to 34% of fat from MCT
Select Care Canine Sensitive Formula	23.4	11.7	56.2	2.0	3.46	Contains FOS
Waltham/Pedigree Canine Low Fat	24.1	5.4	na	0.4	3.30	
Moist/semi-moist feline products						
Hill's Prescription Diet Feline i/d	40.6	20.1	30.1	1.6	1.06	Contains soy fiber
Iams Eukanuba Low-Residue Adult/Feline	45.3	18.5	34.0	2.4	0.95	Contains beet pulp, FOS and MOS
Leo Specific Dermil FDW	34.7	34.7	23.2	1.5	1.41	Contains vegetable fiber
Medi-Cal Feline HYPOallergenic/Gastro Formula	35.5	25.6	na	1.65	1.07	Contains pheasant and duck as animal protein sources
Purina CNM Feline EN-Formula	41.9	17.0	32.1	1.1	2.75	Contains vegetable gums
Waltham/Whiskas Feline Selected Protein	38.2	29.0	21.7	2.9	1.36	
Dry feline products						
Hill's Prescription Diet Feline i/d	39.9	20.1	31.9	1.3	3.90	Contains soy fiber
Iams Eukanuba Low-Residue Adult/Feline	36.2	16.0	41.0	2.3	3.92	Contains beet pulp, FOS and MOS
Medi-Cal Feline HYPOallergenic/Gastro Formula	29.8	13.6	na	1.6	3.66	
Select Care Feline Neutral Formula	27.7	13.6	51.2	1.6	3.29	Contains FOS, beet pulp, rice bran, duck, potato
Waltham/Whiskas Feline Selected Protein	33.3	12.2	42.2	3.3	3.34	Contains capelin as animal protein source

Key: na = information not published by manufacturer, FOS = fructooligosaccharide, MOS = mannooligosaccharide, MCT = medium-chain triglycerides.
*This list represents products with the largest market share and for which published information is available. Manufacturers' published values. Nutrients expressed as % dry matter; energy expressed as fed. To convert to kJ/g multiply kcal by 4.184.

Table 22-11. Pharmacologic agents useful in managing gastritis, gastroduodenal ulceration and gastric motility/emptying disorders.

Antacids	Give as needed
Antiemetic agents	
Chlorpromazine	0.2 to 0.5 mg/kg body weight, PO, SC, IM every six to eight hours
Prochlorpromazine	0.5 mg/kg body weight, PO, SC, IM every six to eight hours
Antihistamines	
Diphenhydramine	2 to 4 mg/kg body weight, PO
Dimenhydrinate	25 to 50 mg PO per dog or 12.5 mg PO per cat
Antiprostaglandin agent	
Misoprostol	1 to 3 µg/kg body weight, PO every eight to 12 hours (dogs)
H_2-receptor blockers	
Cimetidine	5 to 10 mg/kg body weight, PO, SC every six to eight hours
Ranitidine	1 to 4 mg/kg body weight, PO, SC, IV every eight to 12 hours
Prokinetic agents	
Metoclopramide	0.2 to 0.4 mg/kg body weight, IM, SC every eight hours or 1.0 mg/kg body weight/day as a constant IV infusion
Cisapride	0.25 to 0.5 mg/kg body weight, PO every eight hours
Proton pump inhibitors	
Omeprazole	0.7 to 2.0 mg/kg body weight, PO every 24 hours (dogs)
Sucralfate	1 g/25 kg body weight, PO every six to eight hours

Key: PO = per os, SC = subcutaneously, IM = intramuscularly, IV = intravenously.

much smaller odds ratios. Recent attempts to assess the GDV risk in individual breeds demonstrated a lifetime incidence of 25% in Irish setters and a risk of 10% in Great Danes by the age of 2.6 years.[23]

Within breeds, certain anatomic and conformational factors increase the risk of GDV.[26] Increased adult body size compared with breed standards and a specific type of thoracic conformation as determined radiographically appear to be related to the incidence of GDV. A chest depth-width ratio greater than 1.5 is associated with increased risk for developing GDV in certain breeds.[27-29] Recently, dogs with GDV were found to have elongated hepatogastric ligaments as compared with control dogs of similar breeds.[30] It has been hypothesized that the longer

Herbal Remedies for Gastrointestinal Disorders

Herbal remedies have become a major factor in human health care. Various botanicals have become household words, and sales of herbal remedies are increasing dramatically. As herbs move out of health food stores and into mainstream supermarkets, drug stores and even pet stores, use of these products in pets will also increase.

A wide variety of herbal or botanical products are advocated for patients with gastrointestinal (GI) disorders, including individuals with diarrhea, vomiting, constipation, stomatitis, colitis and flatus. There are also long lists of herbs and botanicals that are described as "gastrointestinal agents." Although today's herbal remedies exhibit varying degrees of therapeutic value, most have not been investigated thoroughly for safety and efficacy. It is beyond the scope of this textbook to list all the herbal and botanical remedies that may have use in pets. Interested readers are referred to books listed in the Bibliography for further information about human herbal remedies that might be used in pets with GI disorders.

BIBLIOGRAPHY

Bisset NG, ed. Herbal Drugs and Phytopharmaceut-icals. Stuttgart, Germany: Medpharm GmbH Scientific Publishers, 1994.

Blumenthal M. The Complete German Commission E Monographs: Therapeutic Guide to Herbal Medicines, 1998.

Huang KC. The Pharmacology of Chinese Herbs, 2nd ed. Boca Raton, FL: CRC Press Inc, 1999.

McGuffin M, Hobbs C, Upton R, et al, eds. Botanical Safety Handbook. Boca Raton, FL: CRC Press Inc, 1997.

Null G. The Clinician's Handbook of Natural Healing. New York, NY: Kensington Publishing Corp, 1997.

Physician's Desk Reference for Herbal Medicines. Montvale, NJ: Medical Economics Co, 1998.

Tyler VE. Herbs of Choice: The Therapeutic Use of Phytomedicinals. New York, NY: The Haworth Press, 1994.

length of the hepatogastric ligament allows increased gastric mobility. There does not appear to be an age predisposition for GD or GDV, but both occur more commonly in middle-aged dogs. The syndrome is also more common in male dogs.[31] Other dog-related risk factors include a nervous or fearful temperament and being underweight. A retrospective study identified intestinal lesions consistent with inflammatory bowel disease in approximately 25% of dogs with GDV.[32]

Several dietary risk factors have been identified in one or more epidemiologic studies.[26,31,33,34] Feeding only one meal a day, feeding only one type of food, rapid eating, episodes of overeating, consumption of large volumes of water, postprandial exercise and a food particle diameter less than 30 mm have been implicated. In a recent case-control study, factors that appeared to decrease the risk of GDV were the inclusion of moist food or table foods as part of the diet.[31]

In the past, consumption of dry dog food, unmoistened dry food, nutritional supplements and cereal- or soy-based foods were incriminated as dietary risk factors for GDV.

More recent epidemiologic studies have not found these factors to increase risk of GDV. In a European study of GDV cases, 40% of patients were consuming dry food, 26% ate moist food and 25% received fresh meat diets.[35] Attempts to reproduce GDV by dietary manipulation have been unsuccessful. In one study, researchers found no difference in gastric motility or emptying in large-breed dogs fed either a moist, meat-based food free of soybean meal or a dry, extruded, cereal-based food containing soybean meal with and without moistening.[36] A similar study evaluating Irish setters fed either a commercial dry food or a meat and bone mixture again showed no difference in gastric emptying or gastric acid secretion between diet types.[37] These investigators concluded that most large dogs are fed dry cereal-based food for reasons of cost and convenience, and that these foods may have been wrongly incriminated as a predisposing factor in GDV.[36]

Etiopathogenesis

A single cause of GDV will probably not be found. GDV is more likely a condition that arises because of the interaction of two or more risk factors. The gastric distention manifested in GDV is associated with an as yet uncharacterized functional or mechanical gastric outflow obstruction. This obstruction results in loss of the normal means for removing air from the stomach (i.e., eructation, vomiting and gastroduodenal flow). In some dogs, gastric volvulus apparently develops as a consequence of gastric distention, but, in others, gastric volvulus may precede the dilatation.

Gas in the stomach of dogs with GDV is primarily atmospheric air, which differs greatly in composition from the gas produced by bacterial fermentation.[38] For that reason, aerophagia is believed to be the primary source of gastric gas in dogs with GDV. In some cases, carbon dioxide concentrations in the trapped stomach air approached 10%.[38] The most likely source for this gas is the interaction between gastric acid and bicarbonate secretions. Normally, swallowed air is eructated and does not accumulate in excessive quantities. It has been hypothesized that dogs with GDV have defective eructation mechanisms. In one study, esophageal motility abnormalities were observed in 60% of dogs with GDV.[39] It is possible that such abnormalities are linked to defective eructation complicated by the anatomic relationship of the stomach and esophagus in deep-chested, large dogs, which also may interfere with effective eructation of air.[40] Aerophagia increases with rapid food consumption, excitement, stress and exercise; thus, controlling these factors is recommended in high-risk dogs.

Hypergastrinemia is present in dogs with acute GDV and persists after treatment and recovery, suggesting that dogs with GDV have a pre-existing hypergastrinemia.[41] Gastrin increases gastroesophageal junction pressure and some investigators have postulated that hypergastrinemia may be a factor in the pathogenesis of GDV.[41] However, further investigations revealed no relationship between the degree of gastric distention and the magnitude of plasma gastrin increase.[42] Others suggest that hypergastrinemia in dogs with GDV is a result of the syndrome rather than a cause.[43]

Key Nutritional Factors

There are no known nutrients of particular concern for dogs with an increased risk for GDV. There are, however, a number of prudent feeding management recommenda-

GI & PANCREAS

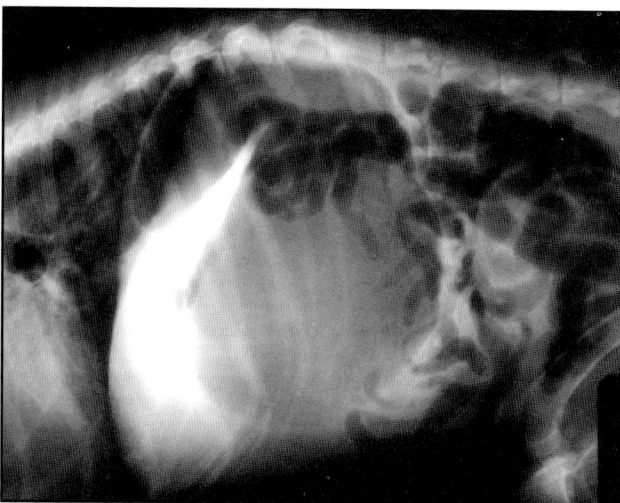

Figure 22-9. Lateral abdominal radiograph from a nine-year-old neutered male Doberman pinscher with a 180-degree gastric dilatation-volvulus. (Courtesy Dr. Joanne Burns, Veterinary Imaging Services, Topeka, KS.)

Table 22-12. Risk factors for canine gastric dilatation-volvulus.*

Eating only one meal per day
Excluding moist food, table food and treats from the diet
Exclusive feeding of one food type
Exercising more than two hours per day
Fearful, nervous or aggressive temperament
Feeding food with a mean particle size <5 mm
Increased chest or abdominal depth:width ratio
Increased adult weight, based on breed standards
Increasing age
Large or giant breed status
    Great Dane, weimaraner, Saint Bernard, Gordon setter,
    Irish setter, standard poodle, basset hound, Doberman pinscher,
    Old English sheepdog, German shorthaired pointer
Lean body condition (body condition score ≤2/5)
Male gender
Purebred status
Rapid eating
Stressful events (boarding in kennel or travel)

*Adapted from Glickman LT, Glickman NW, Schellenberg DB, et al. Multiple risk factors for the gastric dilatation-volvulus syndrome in dogs: A practitioner/owner case-control study. Journal of the American Animal Hospital Association 1997; 33: 197-204. Theyse LFH, Van Den Brom WW, Van Sluijs FJ. Diet and other risk factors for gastric dilatation-volvulus in Great Danes. Journal of Veterinary Surgery 1997; 26: 260.

tions for owners of high-risk, large-breed dogs. These will be discussed below. The key nutritional factors for postoperative patients are similar to those for patients with acute gastritis. Readers should refer to that section for appropriate recommendations.

ASSESS THE FOOD(S) AND FEEDING METHOD

Because no specific key nutritional factors have been established for GD and GDV, foods appropriate for the patient's current lifestage and activity level should be provided. Key nutritional factors for normal dogs are found in Chapter 9. If key nutritional factors in the current food do not match the recommended levels described in Chapter 9, then changing to a more appropriate food is indicated.

Because feeding methods are often altered in postoperative patients and patients at risk for GD and GDV, a thorough assessment should include verification of the feeding

method currently being used. Items to consider include feeding frequency, amount fed, how the food is offered, access to other food, relationship of feeding to exercise and who feeds the animal. All of this information should have been gathered when the history of the animal was obtained. If the animal has a normal BCS (3/5), the amount of food it was fed previously (energy basis) was probably appropriate.

Feeding Plan

Without early diagnosis and appropriate treatment, GDV is usually fatal. Initial management includes cardiovascular stabilization (i.e., treatment of shock and cardiac dysrhythmias), gastric decompression (i.e., orogastric intubation, gastric trocarization), surgery (i.e., gastric repositioning and permanent gastropexy) and appropriate postsurgical care. The feeding plan is implemented as part of a prevention strategy or after rapid, aggressive emergency management.

SELECT A FOOD(S)

For prevention purposes, foods should be chosen that are appropriate for the dog's lifestage and activity level. (See Chapter 9.) In the postoperative period, foods should be used that provide levels of the key nutritional factors outlined for acute gastritis (Tables 22-9 and 22-10).

DETERMINE A FEEDING METHOD

It would appear prudent to recommend feeding a dog at risk for GDV two to three times per day in an environment that decreases competitive eating. If the dog typically eats too fast, placing large balls or rocks in the food bowl or feeding the dog from a muffin tin may slow consumption of food and decrease aerophagia. Feeding a mixture of moist and dry food appears to reduce the risk of GDV.[31] Alternatively, feeding foods with particle sizes greater than 30 mm is also thought to reduce the risk of GDV.[34] Although no definitive link between exercise and GDV has been found, limiting exercise within three to four hours of eating (normal gastric emptying time) is prudent. The Morris Animal Foundation Canine Bloat Panel recommends avoiding vigorous exercise one hour before and two hours after feeding.[44] (See sidebar "Recommendations from the 1990 Morris Animal Foundation Panel on Bloat in Dogs.")

Postoperative patients are best fed small meals frequently. Judicious use of antiemetics and/or metoclopramide in conjunction with continuous feeding may allow adequate caloric intake by patients with persistent vomiting. If tube gastrostomy was chosen as the method of permanent gastropexy, this indwelling catheter should be used for feeding. (See Chapter 12.)

Reassessment

Postoperative patients should be monitored closely for cardiac dysrhythmias, coagulopathies, surgical dehiscence, electrolyte and acid-base abnormalities and infections. After the patient is discharged, the owner should monitor its appetite, activity level and attitude. Rechecks should include body weight and body condition assessment. Food dosages should be adjusted to maintain the dog at ideal body condition. The ultimate marker of success in GDV patients is the prevention of recurrent disease. Rarely, GD will develop in dogs that have had a gas-

Recommendations from the 1990 Morris Animal Foundation Panel on Bloat in Dogs

The following measures may reduce the incidence and recurrence of acute gastric dilatation-volvulus ("bloat"). These measures are especially important when managing purebred dog kennels and individual pet animals of the most susceptible breeds.

1. Large dogs should be fed two or three times daily, rather than once a day, and at times when the owner can observe postfeeding behavior.
2. Owners of susceptible breeds should be aware of prodromal signs (i.e., actions from the dog that signal abdominal discomfort). These signs include evidence of abdominal fullness after meals, whining, pacing, getting up and lying down, stretching, looking at the abdomen, anxiety and unproductive attempts to vomit. Animals with these signs should be examined by a veterinarian as soon as possible.
3. Owners of susceptible breeds should establish a good working relationship with their local veterinarian and should discuss emergency measures in the event of bloat, including administration of antacids (e.g., Mylanta[a] and Di-Gel[b]), passing a stomach tube or piercing the abdomen with a hypodermic needle to relieve bloat.
4. Water should be available to dogs at all times, but should be limited immediately after feeding if overconsumption is a problem.
5. Vigorous exercise, excitement and stress should be avoided one hour before and two hours after meals. Walking, however, is permissible because it may help stimulate normal gastrointestinal function.
6. Food changes should be made gradually over three to five days.
7. Susceptible dogs should be fed individually and, if possible, in a quiet location.
8. Special attention should be paid to the above measures after animals return home from veterinary hospitals and boarding facilities.
9. Dogs that have survived bloat are at increased risk for future episodes; therefore, prophylaxis in the form of preventive surgery or medical management should be discussed with the veterinarian.

ENDNOTES
a. Stuart Pharmaceuticals, Wilmington, DE, USA.
b. Schering-Plough, Corp. Madison, NJ, USA.

BIBLIOGRAPHY
Morris Animal Foundation. Report of the Panel on Bloat in Dogs. Englewood, CO, 1990.

---

tropexy. Any episode of dilatation and precipitating factors should be reported and evaluated.

Gastric Motility/Emptying Disorders

Clinical Importance

Gastric motility disorders arise from conditions that directly or indirectly disrupt three of the basic functions of the stomach: 1) storage of ingesta, 2) mixing and dispersion of food particles and 3) timely expulsion of gastric contents into the duodenum. Table 22-13 outlines a number of primary and secondary causes of gastroparesis reported to occur in dogs and cats. The importance of these disorders in the general pet population is unknown, but primary gastric motility disorders are probably rare.

Assessment

ASSESS THE ANIMAL

History and Physical Examination
Delayed gastric emptying due to any cause results in vomiting. Owners may report vomiting of undigested or partially digested food more than 12 hours after the pet eats. The onset of clinical signs may be gradual in acquired cases of chronic hypertrophic pyloric gastropathy or acute in the case of foreign body ingestion. Clinical signs may have been present since weaning in dogs and cats with congenital pyloric stenosis.

Weight loss and poor body condition are often present in chronic cases. Other manifestations may include intermittent gastric bloating, nausea, partial or complete inappetence and belching. Occasionally, patients will present with unrelenting or projectile vomiting; complete gastric outflow obstruction should be suspected in such cases.

Physical examination findings are often unremarkable beyond evidence of weight loss. Body condition should be assessed and used as a reassessment tool. Gastric distention and tympany may be evident in some cases. Patients with unrelenting vomiting may present with dehydration, depression and malaise. In rare cases, severe electrolyte abnormalities resulting from persistent vomiting may manifest as weakness.

Laboratory and Other Clinical Information
Hematologic and serologic findings in animals with gastroparesis or gastric obstruction are nonspecific and may be more reflective of an underlying disorder. Chronic, persistent vomiting may precipitate dehydration and electrolyte (hypokalemia, hypochloremia) and acid-base abnormalities. Prerenal azotemia is common. Hypochloremic metabolic alkalosis with paradoxical aciduria may be present in dogs and cats with complete pyloric outflow obstruction.

Survey abdominal radiographs are often of benefit when evaluating dogs and cats with gastric motility disorders. Typical findings include a stomach distended by fluid, air or food. The presence of food in the stomach 12 to 18 hours after the last meal is evidence of an emptying disorder. Occasionally, gastric wall thickening may be recognized on survey radiographs. Rarely, extraluminal masses causing pyloric obstruction may be identified.

GI contrast studies confirm delayed gastric emptying. If liquid contrast media (i.e., barium sulfate) remains in the stomach for more than four hours in dogs or 30 minutes in cats, gastroparesis or mechanical obstruction should be suspected.[6] Liquid contrast media, however, is not representative of a typical meal. For that reason, feeding barium

Figure 22-10. Lateral and ventrodorsal abdominal radiographs from a 11-year-old neutered female fox terrier with projectile vomiting demonstrating use of barium-impregnated spheres. A gastric emptying disorder was confirmed because the spheres were detected in the pyloric antrum 16 hours postadministration. (Courtesy Dr. Grant Guilford, Massey University, New Zealand.)

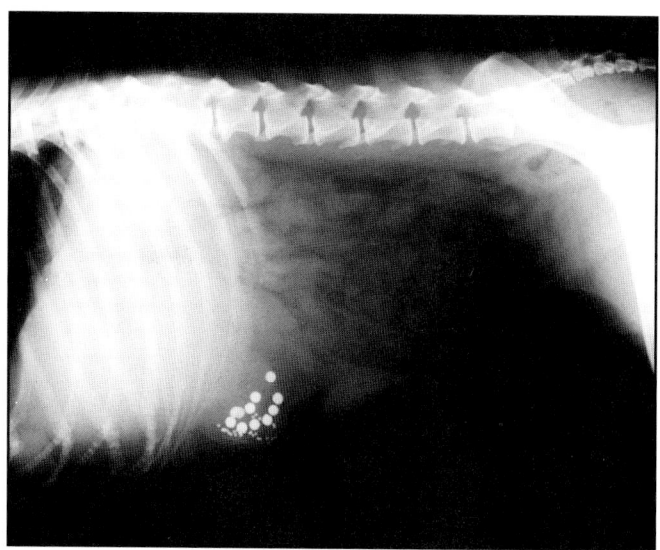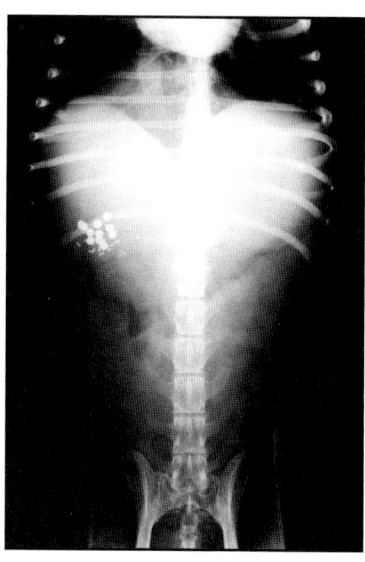

Figure 22-11. Endoscopic view of retained food in the stomach of a 12-year-old neutered female Scottish terrier presented for chronic intermittent vomiting. Food was found in the stomach 20 hours after consumption of a meal, which confirms delayed gastric emptying.

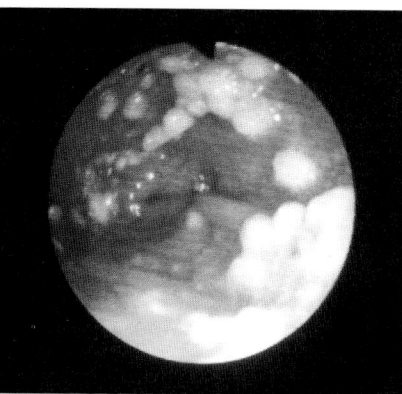

Figure 22-12. Gastroscopic photograph demonstrating hyperplastic mucosal folds (arrow) typical of chronic hypertrophic gastropathy in a 13-year-old neutered male Shih Tzu. (Courtesy Dr. Mike Matz, Southwest Veterinary Specialty Center, Tucson, AZ.)

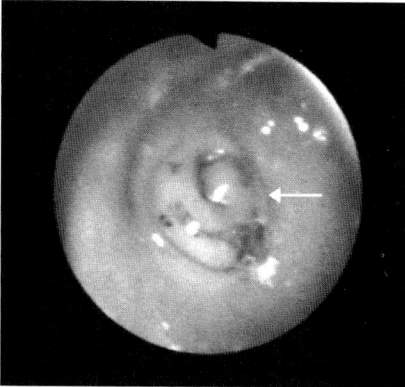

mixed with food or administering radiopaque particles (BIPS)[c] mixed with food more completely assesses gastric function (Figure 22-10).[45] GI contrast studies may also identify thickened gastric walls, intraluminal foreign bodies and extraluminal masses.

Gastric emptying disorders may first be suspected at the time of upper GI endoscopy. Food in the stomach after a 12- to 18-hour fast is good evidence of the condition (Figure 22-11). In some cases, endoscopic findings may be diagnostic. Chronic hypertrophic pyloric gastropathy, for example, has a typical endoscopic appearance, including hyperplastic mucosal folds surrounding the pylorus, pro-

tuberance of the pylorus and polyps (Figure 22-12).[46] In the case of antropyloric or proximal duodenal foreign bodies, endoscopy can be both diagnostic and curative.

Fluoroscopy and nuclear scintigraphy can also be useful diagnostic modalities in patients with delayed gastric emptying by allowing assessment of gastric emptying rate. Ultrasonography may be useful in the evaluation of pyloric masses and extraluminal sources of pyloric compression.[47]

Risk Factors
Several breeds are associated with gastric motility disorders (Table 22-8). Congenital pyloric stenosis is most often encountered in brachycephalic dogs and Siamese cats. Chronic hypertrophic pyloric gastropathy usually affects small purebred middle-aged dogs such as the Lhasa apso, Maltese, Shih Tzu and Pekingese.[48] Young animals are more at risk for gastric foreign bodies, whereas older pets are more likely to have neoplastic lesions that may obstruct gastric outflow.

Etiopathogenesis
Gastric motility disorders may arise from functional or mechanical obstruction of gastric outflow. Functional disorders of gastric emptying arise from abnormal or asynchronous gastric motility. Myenteric neuronal or gastric smooth muscle function or antropyloroduodenal coordination may be impaired.

A number of benign and malignant anatomic lesions of the stomach and proximal duodenum may result in mechanical gastric outflow obstruction (Table 22-13). The most common of these is chronic hypertrophic pyloric gastropathy, which refers to an acquired hypertrophic mucosal or muscular lesion of the pyloric antrum. In addition, congenital pyloric stenosis occurs in young dogs and cats as a consequence of benign muscular hypertrophy of the pylorus. Certain gastric and proximal duodenal neoplasms and granulomatous conditions (e.g., pythiosis, eosinophilic gastritis) can also result in pyloric obstruction.

Key Nutritional Factors
Key nutritional factors are listed in Table 22-14 and are discussed in detail below.

Water
Dehydration is a common problem in animals with persistent vomiting. Dehydration should be corrected with

appropriate parenteral fluid therapy. Thereafter, water should be available free choice. Water should be offered at a temperature between room and body temperature. Colder water should be avoided because cold water and food delay gastric emptying.

Energy

Animals with chronic vomiting are often underweight due to long-standing, inadequate caloric intake. Energy density of the food should be moderate (3.5 to 4.0 kcal/g [14.6 to 16.7 kJ/g] DM) to ensure intake of sufficient energy with small amounts of food. Higher energy densities may help affected animals regain or maintain body weight and condition, but would require higher dietary fat levels. As discussed below, increased levels of dietary fat adversely affect gastric emptying and should be avoided.

Minerals

Abnormalities in serum electrolyte concentrations, especially potassium, sodium and chloride, are common in animals with chronic vomiting and can adversely affect gastric motility and emptying. Initial abnormalities should be corrected with appropriate parenteral fluid therapy. Thereafter, the food should contain levels of minerals appropriate for the animal's lifestage.

Fat

Solids and liquids higher in caloric density and fat levels are emptied more slowly than similar foods with lower caloric density and fat. Fat in the duodenum stimulates release of cholecystokinin, which delays gastric emptying. Foods with less than 15% (dogs) or less than 22% (cats) DM fat are probably appropriate for patients with gastric emptying or motility disorders.

Fiber

Many grocery brand moist foods contain gelling agents such as gums or hydrocolloids to enhance the aesthetic characteristics of the food. Foods containing gel-forming soluble fibers should be avoided in patients with gastric emptying and motility disorders because they increase the viscosity of ingesta and slow gastric emptying.[49-51]

Food Form and Temperature

Liquids are emptied from the stomach more quickly than solids due to lower digesta osmolality. Water is emptied most quickly, whereas liquids containing nutrients are emptied more slowly. High-osmolality fluids are emptied more slowly than dilute fluids. Solids and liquids high in fat are the slowest to be emptied from the stomach.[52]

The ideal food for patients with gastric emptying disorders has a liquid or semi-liquid consistency. Cold meals slow gastric emptying. Therefore, food should be offered between room and body temperature. Refrigerated or frozen foods should be warmed before being fed.

ASSESS THE FOOD(S) AND FEEDING METHOD

The energy density, food form and levels of fat and minerals should be assessed in the current food and compared with the recommendations outlined in the key nutritional factors section (Table 22-14). Most importantly, the food should be complete and balanced for the current lifestage of the animal. The food may not need to be altered for patients with mild disease or few clinical signs.

Patients with gastric motility disorders often require specialized feeding methods; the current feeding protocol is rarely appropriate. A thorough assessment should include

Table 22-13. Potential causes of gastric emptying disorders in dogs and cats.

Functional obstruction (abnormal motility)
Primary motility defects
  Gastric ulcers
  Idiopathic asynchronous motility
  Idiopathic hypomotility
  Infectious gastroenteritis
  Postoperative ileus
Secondary motility defects
  Drug therapy
    Anticholinergics
    Narcotic analgesics
  Electrolyte disturbances
    Hypercalcemia
    Hypocalcemia
    Hypokalemia
    Hypomagnesemia
  Inflammation
    Acute pancreatitis
    Peritonitis
  Metabolic disorders
    Diabetes mellitus
    Hepatic encephalopathy
Mechanical obstruction
Congenital or acquired antral pyloric hypertrophy
Extraluminal compression
Gastric or duodenal foreign bodies
Gastric or duodenal granulomatous lesions
Gastric or duodenal neoplasia or polyps

verification of the feeding method currently used. Items to consider include feeding frequency, amount fed, how the food is offered, access to other food, relationship of feeding to exercise and who feeds the animal. All of this information should have been gathered when the history of the animal was obtained. If the animal has a normal BCS (3/5), the amount of food fed previously was probably appropriate.

Feeding Plan

Dehydration, electrolyte and acid-base abnormalities and gastric outflow obstruction should be corrected with appropriate fluid therapy and surgical intervention before the feeding plan is initiated. For dogs or cats with functional gastric motility disorders, several prokinetic agents are available (Table 22-11) and should be considered if dietary management alone is insufficient to control clinical signs.

SELECT A FOOD(S)

Liquid or semi-liquid foods with restricted levels of fat may promote gastric emptying and should be used initially in patients with gastric motility or emptying disorders. A liquid or semi-liquid consistency can be obtained by adding water to a moist veterinary therapeutic food (Table 22-10). Alternatively, liquid enteral products containing restricted levels of fat may be used (Tables 12-7 and 12-8).

Feeding lower fat foods means that larger or more frequent meals are required to meet the animal's DER. Larger meals may promote more vomiting. Therefore, each animal should be managed individually and the optimal fat level determined according to the patient's ability to tolerate meal size and maintain optimal body condition.

DETERMINE A FEEDING METHOD

Foods should be offered at a temperature between room and body temperature. Frequent small meals (at least three per day) are preferred. In some cases of complete pyloric

Table 22-14. Key nutritional factors for patients with gastric motility/emptying disorders*

Factors	Recommended levels
Energy density	3.5 to 4.0 kcal/g
	14.6 to 16.7 kJ/g
Fat	<15% for dogs
	<22% for cats
Fiber	Avoid foods with gel-forming fiber sources
Food form	Liquid or semi-liquid consistency
Food temperature	Offer foods between room and body temperature
Minerals	Appropriate for current lifestage

*Nutrients expressed on a dry matter basis.

outflow obstruction, parenteral nutritional support may be necessary to meet the animal's needs before surgical alleviation of the obstruction. This is indicated when the patient's body condition is poor (BCS of 1/5 or 2/5) and the patient is deemed at increased risk for postsurgical complications.

Most patients can be fed using a feeding method similar to that used for normal pets if normal gastric function is restored after surgery. The best feeding method will need to be individualized for each patient and determined by trial and error based on remaining gastric function.

Reassessment

Body weight and condition should be assessed every two to four weeks. Presence or absence of vomiting should be documented. If vomiting continues, the food or feeding pattern should be altered. Dividing the daily food intake into additional meals may also increase GI tolerance. Use of prokinetic agents (e.g., metoclopramide, cisapride) should be considered if vomiting persists despite implementation of these therapeutic strategies.

Gradual attempts to normalize the feeding regimen can be made if the animal is doing well on the recommended therapy. Feeding more solid foods and larger, less frequent meals are more convenient for the pet owner.

The prognosis for dogs and cats with gastric motility disorders varies with the underlying cause. Mechanical obstructions can often be managed effectively through surgical or endoscopic (e.g., foreign body retrieval) means, resulting in an excellent prognosis.[48] Occasionally, dogs and cats with long-standing gastric outflow obstruction with gastric distention may have residual gastric motility abnormalities.[53] These animals may benefit from the use of prokinetic agents.

SMALL INTESTINAL DISORDERS

Disorders of the small intestine are frequently encountered in veterinary practice. A number of acute and chronic enteropathies are recognized (Tables 22-15 and 22-16) (See sidebar "Small Intestinal Neoplasia.") and must be distinguished from diseases of other organ systems resulting in GI signs. Typical clinical manifestations of small intestinal disease include diarrhea, weight loss, poor body condition, vomiting, borborygmus and flatulence.

Diarrhea is defined as a change in the frequency, consistency or volume of bowel movements and stools.

Diarrhea is the most common manifestation of small intestinal disease. The diarrhea associated with small intestinal conditions differs from that typically associated with large intestinal disorders (Table 22-17).

Mechanisms of Diarrhea

An understanding of normal gut physiology and the common pathophysiologic mechanisms responsible for diarrhea in companion animals allows for a rational approach to evaluation and treatment of patients with small intestinal disorders. There are four major mechanisms for diarrhea: 1) osmotic, 2) altered mucosal permeability, 3) abnormal motility and 4) secretory.[1]

Osmotic Diarrhea

Osmotic diarrhea, also referred to as diarrhea of malabsorption, is the most common cause of diarrhea in dogs and cats.[1] Osmotic diarrhea may occur in conjunction with other pathophysiologic processes. The presence of unabsorbed nutrients (solutes) in the bowel results in passive diffusion of water into the gut lumen. (See sidebar "Disaccharide Intolerance.") This process continues until the osmolality of the intestinal chyme is approximately that of plasma. Osmotic diarrhea may occur as a result of maldigestion, malabsorption, administration of osmotic laxatives and overeating. Clinical manifestations of osmotic diarrhea include passage of large volumes of fluid or soft stools. Stools may appear greasy if steatorrhea is present. The diarrhea usually resolves following a 24- to 36-hour fast.

Diarrhea Due to Altered Mucosal Permeability

Altered mucosal permeability (i.e., exudative diarrhea) is another common cause of diarrhea in dogs and cats. The large or small bowel may be affected. The intestinal permeability barrier is composed of epithelial tight junctions, mucosal lymphatics and capillaries and the local immune system. Failure of any one of these components can result in diarrhea. GI diseases that result in erosions, ulcerations and mucosal inflammation or infiltration are potential causes of gut permeability changes and diarrhea. Diarrhea associated with increased gut permeability may present as a protein-losing enteropathy (i.e., hypoproteinemia, hypoalbuminemia, weight loss). Fresh and/or melenic blood may be present in the stool. Fecal examination may reveal inflammatory cells. Often these diarrheas do not completely resolve if food is withheld.

Diarrhea Due to Abnormal GI Motility

Diarrhea may be associated with deranged GI motility. It is often difficult to determine whether abnormal GI motility is a primary entity or a secondary consequence of another disorder. In general, deranged GI motility is not a common cause of small bowel diarrhea in dogs and cats. The most common motility derangement is rapid intestinal transit associated with a decreased frequency of rhythmic segmental contractions, also termed ileus. The reduction in segmental contractions results in a "pipe" effect with little resistance to ingesta flow. Ileus may occur in conjunction with infiltrative diseases, severe abdominal pain, parvoviral enteritis or may develop postoperatively. In many cases, iatrogenic ileus complicates the management of animals treated inappropriately with anticholinergic agents. Increased frequency of peristaltic contractions is probably not an important cause of diarrhea in companion animals. However, it may play a role in the irritable bowel syndrome. (See text below.) A reduction in peristaltic or interdigestive motility may result in small intestinal bacterial overgrowth. Response to dietary manipulation is variable.

Secretory Diarrhea

Secretory diarrhea is relatively uncommon in companion animals vs. people (cholera is the prototypical example) and food animal species. Crypt epithelial cells produce intestinal fluid, whereas enterocytes lining the villous tips are responsible for absorption. Normally, absorption exceeds intestinal secretion. Most secretagogue effects are mediated via a second messenger (e.g., cyclic AMP, cyclic GMP, calmodulin). Secretagogues include GI hormones, bacterial enterotoxins, certain pharmacologic agents, deconjugated bile acids and hydroxy fatty acids. Clinical manifestations of secretory diarrhea are often extreme. Patients have large volumes of fluid diarrhea and often become dehydrated rapidly. Generally, fasting is not successful in alleviating clinical signs.

Acute Enteritis

Clinical Importance

Acute gastroenteritis is one of the most common illnesses of dogs and cats. A number of infectious, toxic and dietary factors can trigger the sudden onset of vomiting and diarrhea (Tables 22-7 and 22-15). This section addresses the diagnosis and management of veterinary patients with an acute onset of diarrhea.

Assessment

ASSESS THE ANIMAL

History and Physical Examination

Patients are usually presented for the sudden onset of diarrhea, vomiting or both signs. In many cases, the owner will report that the pet is depressed and has a poor appetite. The number and character of the defecations should be assessed. Large fluid stools are typical of small bowel disorders. Melenic or hemorrhagic stools may indicate a potentially life-threatening disorder (Table 22-18).

Careful attention should be paid to the dietary history. Diet-induced diarrhea is relatively common; therefore, a recent change to a moist high-fat or meat-based food may be the source of the animal's diarrhea.[a,b] Often, it is possible to elicit a history of dietary indiscretion, feeding table foods over a holiday, or access to garbage, carrion or abrasive materials. Cats that hunt birds may have been exposed to *Salmonella* spp and dogs eating raw salmon are at risk for salmon poisoning.[2,3]

Feeding uncooked meat in homemade foods and racing greyhound rations is linked to bacterial enteritis. Greyhound diets often contain raw ground beef and have been identified as fomites for salmonellosis and colibacillosis.[4] Incorporation of raw poultry in foods has been linked to campylobacteriosis and salmonellosis.[5] Readers are referred to Chapter 7 for more information about foodborne gastroenteric illnesses.

Table 22-15. Potential causes of acute small bowel diarrhea in dogs and cats.

Dietary
Dietary indiscretion
Foreign bodies
Garbage toxicity
Infectious agents
Bacteria
  Campylobacter spp
  Clostridium spp
  Escherichia coli
  Salmonella spp
  Staphylococcus spp
  Yersinia spp
Parasites
  Helminths (roundworms, hookworms)
  Protozoa (*Giardia lamblia*, coccidia)
Rickettsia
  Salmon poisoning
Viruses
  Canine distemper
  Coronavirus
  Panleukopenia
  Parvovirus
  Rotavirus
Miscellaneous
Hemorrhagic gastroenteritis
Toxin or drug induced
Chemotherapeutic agents
Digoxin
Heavy metals
Laxatives (magnesium oxide, lactulose)
Nonsteroidal antiinflammatory drugs

Table 22-16. Potential causes of chronic small bowel diarrhea in dogs and cats.

Dietary
Adverse reactions to food
  Food allergy (hypersensitivity)
  Lactose intolerance
Infectious agents
Bacteria
  Campylobacter spp
  Salmonellosis
  Small intestinal bacterial overgrowth
Fungi
  Histoplasmosis
  Pythiosis
Parasites
  Helminths (roundworms, hookworms)
  Protozoa (coccidia, *Giardia lamblia*)
Inflammatory bowel disease
Eosinophilic gastroenteritis
Lymphocytic enteritis
Lymphoplasmacytic enteritis
Suppurative gastroenteritis
Miscellaneous
Juvenile diarrhea of cats
Neoplasia
APUD cell tumors
Lymphosarcoma
Mast cell tumor

Key: APUD = amine precursor uptake and decarboxylation.

Other husbandry issues are also important. Records of vaccinations and anthelmintic treatments should be scrutinized. Questions should be asked about the health of other pets and people in the household. A positive answer to inquiries raises the likelihood that an infectious organism is involved.

Often, affected dogs and cats are depressed and dehydrated. Typically, the diarrhea is most consistent with

Table 22-17. Characteristics of small and large bowel diarrhea.

Characteristics	Small bowel	Large bowel
Blood in feces	Melena	Hematochezia
Fecal quality	Loose, watery, "cow-pie"	Loose to semi-formed, "jelly-like"
Fecal volume	Large quantities	Small quantities
Frequency of defecation	Normal to slightly increased	Increased
Malaise	May be present	Rare
Mucus in feces	Usually absent	Usually present
Steatorrhea	May be present	Absent
Tenesmus	Absent	Usually present
Urgency	Absent	Usually present
Vomiting	May be present	Uncommon
Weight loss	May be present	Rare

Small Intestinal Neoplasia

Lymphosarcoma and adenocarcinoma are the most common intestinal tumors recognized in companion animals. Adenocarcinomas occur most commonly in the jejunum and ileum of cats and in the duodenum and colon of dogs. Lymphosarcoma arising from gut-associated lymphoid tissue is the most common extranodal form. A number of other tumor types occur, including mastocytoma, leiomyosarcoma, leiomyoma and carcinoid tumors, but are less common. The diffuse nature of lymphosarcoma often results in malabsorption and malnutrition and provides the greatest opportunity for dietary therapy.

Nutritional support is of critical importance in managing patients with intestinal neoplasia. Providing optimal nutrition helps the clinician return the patient to ideal body condition, provides some protection against the toxic side effects of antineoplastic chemotherapy and improves the patient's quality of life. (See Chapter 25.) As with many small bowel disorders, use of highly digestible foods is recommended with nutrient levels adjusted for each patient as tolerated.

In cases of intestinal neoplasia, assisted-feeding techniques (enteral or parenteral) may be required initially to meet nutritional, fluid and electrolyte needs as the patient recovers from surgery or receives chemotherapy. In particular, one of the authors (DJD) believes that early nutritional support (i.e., parenteral or enteral) in debilitated cats is very advantageous in the initial management of gastrointestinal lymphosarcoma. Parenteral administration of nutrients can be added to oral intake to fully meet the patient's requirements. Re-establishing normal intestinal function and stimulating adaptation should begin as soon as the patient tolerates oral food intake.

Multiple (i.e., six to eight) small meals per day are recommended in a form best tolerated by the patient. Occasionally, a liquid form of the food may be necessary for patients undergoing various forms of treatment.

BIBLIOGRAPHY

Davenport DJ. Gastrointestinal lymphosarcoma. In: August JR, ed. Consultations in Feline Internal Medicine. Philadelphia, PA: WB Saunders Co, 1991; 419-424.

Ogilvie GK, Moore AS, eds. Gastrointestinal tumors. Managing the Veterinary Cancer Patient: A Practice Manual. Trenton, NJ: Veterinary Learning Systems, 1995; 349-361.

Ogilvie GK, Moore AS, eds. Nutritional support. Managing the Veterinary Cancer Patient: A Practice Manual. Trenton, NJ: Veterinary Learning Systems, 1995; 124-137.

Withrow SJ, MacEwen, eds. Small Animal Clinical Oncology, 2nd ed. Philadelphia, PA: WB Saunders Co, 1996.

small bowel disease (Table 22-17). Occasionally, animals may present with signs reflective of both small and large bowel involvement. Abdominal discomfort may be recognized on palpation. Patients should be carefully evaluated for evidence of septic shock. Animals exhibiting systemic signs of illness such as fever and congested mucous membranes in addition to GI signs should be treated more aggressively.

Laboratory and Other Clinical Information

Because there are many potential causes of acute gastroenteritis, achieving a definitive diagnosis can be difficult. It is more important to determine whether the animal's condition is self-limiting or if it is potentially life-threatening. This decision, based on historical and physical findings, is critical. Some factors suggest a potentially life-threatening condition: 1) abdominal pain, 2) dehydration, 3) depression, 4) fecal leukocytes, 5) fever and 6) melena or hematochezia. Cases of a serious nature should be pursued aggressively with the use of hematology, serum biochemistry profiles, urinalyses and fecal examinations for parasites and other infectious pathogens. Abdominal films or GI contrast radiographs are recommended to rule out obstruction. Self-limiting cases are usually approached more conservatively. Diagnostics are often limited to assessment of hydration status (i.e., packed cell volume, total protein concentration and body weight) and thorough examination of feces for evidence of parasites and bacterial pathogens (e.g., spores of *Clostridium* spp).

Risk Factors

Risk factors for acute gastroenteritis include age, breed, immune status and environment. Young animals are more susceptible to a variety of infectious pathogens including parasites, viruses and bacteria. Several canine breeds (e.g., Chinese Shar-Pei, German shepherd dog, beagle) may have IgA deficiency; therefore, these dogs may be more susceptible to development of a number of GI conditions, including giardiasis and small intestinal bacterial overgrowth (Table 22-19).[6,7] Likewise, immunocompromised animals are at risk for contracting viral or bacterial enteritides. Several conditions including cancer, diabetes mellitus, feline leukemia and immunodeficiency virus infections may result in deranged immune function. Hemorrhagic gastroenteritis is reported most commonly in miniature schnauzers and dachshunds, toy poodles and other toy and small dogs.[8]

Environment also plays an important role in exposure to pathogens. Dogs and cats kept in unsanitary or overcrowded conditions are much more likely to develop infectious enteropathies. In addition, animals kept in poorly con-

Disaccharide Intolerance

Lactose intolerance is the most common carbohydrate intolerance in people and possibly in dogs and cats. Lactose intolerance results from a relative or absolute deficiency of the enzyme lactase. If brush border lactase fails to hydrolyze lactose into galactose and glucose, the unabsorbed sugar will induce an osmotic diarrhea when it reaches the colon. In addition, colonic bacteria ferment lactose, producing organic acids, hydrogen and carbon dioxide, resulting in flatulence and pain.

The intestinal brush border mucosa and the disaccharidase enzymes that it contains (i.e., lactase, sucrase, maltase and α-dextrinase) are often lost due to enteritis from any cause. These enzymes are essential for digestion of disaccharides (i.e., lactose, sucrose, maltose and α-dextrins) and subsequent absorption of their constituent monosaccharides. As mentioned above, unabsorbed disaccharides result in an osmotic diarrhea in the colon.

Often, one to two weeks are needed to restore intestinal lactase and sucrase brush border disaccharidase activity after the cause for their loss is corrected. Diarrhea may, therefore, occur during this period with the ingestion of carbohydrates requiring disaccharidase digestion. For example, jejunal and ileal lactase and sucrase activity were significantly less in piglets fed nothing per os; however, maltase activity in the jejunum and ileum was not different from that of enterally fed piglets after four weeks. Therefore, during and for several days after a diarrheic episode, foods containing maltodextrins should be fed but not those containing lactose and sucrose.

Inadequate intestinal disaccharidase activity is also the mechanism responsible for causing diarrhea after excessive milk consumption. Puppies and kittens normally have small but adequate amounts of intestinal lactase. After weaning age, lactase decreases to about 10% of peak activity in dogs and cats, and continued consumption of milk does not alter the decline in lactase activity. Diarrhea occurs if more lactose is consumed than the animal can digest. Bitch's milk contains only 3.1% lactose and queen's milk 4.2% vs. cow's and goat's milk (4.5 to 5%). This difference explains why puppies and kittens commonly have diarrhea when given cow's or goat's milk as a milk replacer.

Healthy adult dogs and cats may also develop diarrhea when fed milk. Adult dogs and cats have low levels of brush border lactase activity compared with levels present in preweaning animals and levels of other disaccharidases. Most newborn mammals have negligible maltase and sucrase activities, which develop during the first few weeks of life; however, lactase activity is high at birth and decreases with age. In one study, dogs developed diarrhea while consuming more than 1g of lactose/kg body weight, an amount equivalent to about 20 ml milk/kg body weight or three-fourths cup of milk for a 10-kg dog. Thus, milk-based enteral diets and milk drinks for dogs and cats are commonly treated with enzymes (β-galactosidase) to hydrolyze lactase. However, this increases the osmolality of the product, which may cause diarrhea.

Altered intestinal disaccharidase activity also is hypothesized to be one of the factors responsible for diarrhea subsequent to rapid change in foods and feeding methods. Lactase and sucrase are diet-inducible enzymes, whereas, maltase is not. Several days are required for intestinal disaccharidase enzyme activity to respond to a change in dietary carbohydrates.

BIBLIOGRAPHY

Hill FWG, Kelly DF. Naturally occurring intestinal malabsorption in the dog. American Journal of Digestive Disease 1974; 19: 649-665.

Jackson WD, Grand RJ. The human intestinal response to enteral nutrients: A review. Journal of the American College of Nutrition 1991;10: 500-509.

Kretchmer AO. Lactose and lactase. Scientific American 1972; 227: 70-78.

Meyer H, Kienzle E, Hannes M, et al. Nutrition in dogs with hydrolyzed milk. Klientierpraxis 1984; 29: 301-308.

Remillard RL, Dudgeon DL, Yardley J. Atrophied small intestinal responses to oral feedings of milk (abstract). Journal of Nutrition 1998; 128: 2727S-2729S.

Remillard RL, Guerino F, Dudgeon DL, et al. Effects of intravenous glutamine and limited enteral feedings in piglets: Amelioration of small intestinal disuse atrophy. Journal of Nutrition 1998; 128: 2723S-2726S.

Solomons NW, Guerro AM, Torun B. Effective in vivo hydrolysis of milk lactose by beta-galactosidases in the presence of solid foods. American Journal of Clinical Nutrition 1985; 41: 222-227.

Ulshen MH, Lecce JG, Stiles AD, et al. Effects of nursing on growth and development of small bowel mucosa in newborn piglets. Pediatric Research 1991; 30: 337-341.

trolled environments have higher risk for exposure to high-fat table foods, garbage and toxins. Dogs in particular fall prey to indiscriminate eating. Consumption of rotten garbage, decomposing carrion or abrasive materials (e.g., hair, bones, rocks, plastic, aluminum foil) can result in severe enteritis. Poor husbandry practices including inadequate parasite control, overcrowding and poor vaccination measures also put pets at risk for acute gastroenteritis.

Etiopathogenesis

In acute gastroenteritis, diarrhea may occur as a result of any or all of the four mechanisms of diarrhea described above. Many viral organisms and cancer chemotherapeutic agents destroy intestinal villi. Consequently, diarrhea may occur due to altered gut permeability and/or osmotic mechanisms. Additionally, ileus may arise as a consequence of abdominal pain in pets with parvoviral enteritis.

Finally, bacterial pathogens may elaborate enterotoxins that serve as potent secretogogues.

Small bowel atrophy begins within days in the absence of luminal stimulation. Atrophy, the small intestinal response to disuse, occurs in several species with simple stomachs, including foals,[9] cats,[10] dogs[11] and pigs[12] and is similar mor-

Table 22-18. Clinical signs associated with life-threatening rather than self-limiting acute gastroenteritis.

Dehydration
Depression
Abdominal pain
Fever
Melena or hematochezia
Fecal leukocytes

Table 22-19. Breed-associated small intestinal disorders.

Eosinophilic gastroenteritis	German shepherd dog
	Irish setter
Hemorrhagic gastroenteritis	Dachshund
	Miniature schnauzer
Immunoproliferative small intestinal disease	Basenji
	Ludenhund
Intestinal adenocarcinoma	Siamese cat
Lymphoplasmacytic enteritis	German shepherd dog
	Chinese Shar-Pei
	Soft-coated wheaten terrier
	Domestic shorthaired cat
Parvoviral enteritis	Doberman pinscher
	Rottweiler
	Labrador retriever (black)
Small intestinal bacterial overgrowth	German shepherd dog
	Beagle
Lymphangiectasia	Yorkshire terrier
	Golden retriever
	Dachshund
	Basenji (IPSID)
	Ludenhund (IPSID)
Wheat-sensitive enteropathy	Irish setter

Key: IPSID = immunoproliferative small intestinal disease.

Table 22-20. Key nutritional factors for patients with acute enteritis.*

Factors	Recommended levels
Chloride	0.50 to 1.3%
Crude fiber	0.5 to 15% (see text)
Digestibility	≥87% for protein and ≥90% for fat and soluble carbohydrate
Energy density	3.5 to 4.0 kcal/g
	14.6 to 16.7 kJ/g
Fat	12 to 15% for dogs
	15 to 22% for cats
Potassium	0.80 to 1.1%
Protein	Suitable for lifestage
Sodium	0.35 to 0.50%

*Nutrients expressed on a dry matter basis.

phologically. The hallmarks of small bowel atrophy are decreased villus height (about 50% in the jejunum and 25% in the ileum) with an overall reduced absorptive surface area and brush border enzyme activity.[13,14]

Food in the lumen of the small bowel stimulates intestinal integrity (mass and function) by several mechanisms. Ingested nutrients present mechanical and chemical stimuli to the intestine, increasing intestinal secretory and endocrine activity. The type and amount of ingested nutrients mechanically alter the mucosal cell mass by affecting the rate of stem cell division and the rate of mucosal cell renewal. Gastric, duodenal and pancreatobiliary secretions, which normally accompany eating, digestion and absorption, promote mucosal structure and function.[15,16] Refeeding the atrophied small bowel should be done bearing in mind the altered function of the small bowel. Limited enteral feeding of milk (i.e., 2 ml/kg body weight, per os, twice daily) to piglets, providing only 10% of the resting energy requirement (RER), resulted in sig-

nificantly greater jejunal lactase and sucrase activities with taller villi and deeper crypts vs. findings in animals fed NPO.[17]

Glutamine is the preferred respiratory fuel for enterocytes. Glutamine is a conditionally essential amino acid necessary during intestinal recovery to stimulate DNA synthesis and increase mucosal mass.[18] In dogs, there is an increased intestinal requirement for glutamine during the immediate postoperative phase (i.e., less than seven days). Glutamine uptake returns to normal later during the recovery phase (i.e., more than 10 days postsurgery).[19,20]

Key Nutritional Factors

Key nutritional factors for patients with acute enteritis are listed in Table 22-20 and are discussed in detail below.

Water

Water is the most important nutrient in patients with acute vomiting and diarrhea because of the potential for life-threatening dehydration due to excessive fluid loss and inability of the patient to replace those losses. Moderate to severe dehydration should be corrected with appropriate parenteral fluid therapy rather than using the oral route.

Oral fluid therapy is typically reserved for patients with minor fluid deficits or to supply maintenance fluid requirements. Oral rehydration solutions have been commonly used in people and production animals with acute diarrhea. Use of oral rehydration solutions has also been advocated in dog and cats.[21] Oral rehydration solutions contain glucose, amino acids and electrolytes in addition to water. The physiologic basis for these solutions is the coupled transport of sodium and glucose and other actively transported small organic molecules.[22] The maximum uptake of water and electrolytes occurs when the ratio of carbohydrate to sodium approaches 1:1.[22] Recently, an oral rehydration solution containing rice carbohydrate-based glucose polymers developed by the World Health Organization has been licensed for the small animal market (Table 22-21). Such solutions are most useful in secretory diarrheas, which are uncommon in small animals. However, oral rehydration solutions can be useful as an alternate fluid source, if readily consumed by the patient.

Minerals

The electrolyte composition of gastric and intestinal secretions differs from that of extracellular fluids; therefore, loss of gastric and intestinal secretions may result in systemic electrolyte abnormalities. Dogs and cats with vomiting and diarrhea may have low, normal or high serum sodium, potassium and chloride concentrations. The derangement that predominates in a particular animal depends on the severity of the disease, nutritional status, site of the disease process, etc. For these reasons, serum electrolyte concentrations are helpful in tailoring the fluid therapy and nutritional management of these patients. Mild hypokalemia, hypochloremia and either hypernatremia or hyponatremia are the electrolyte abnormalities most commonly associated with acute vomiting and diarrhea.

Depletion of total body potassium is a predictable consequence of severe or chronic GI disease because the potassium concentration of both gastric and intestinal secretions is high. Hypokalemia in association with GI disease will be particularly profound if losses are not matched by sufficient intake of potassium in food.

Table 22-21. Selected commercial oral rehydration solutions available for use in dogs and cats.

Products (manufacturers)	Nutrient content (mEq/l)								Comments
	Na	K	Cl	Mg	Ca	P	Citrate	ME (kcal/l)	
Electramine (Vitae Inc.)	69.8	15.4	69.7	–	–	–	–	–	Contains glycine
Ritrol (Nutramax Labs)	90	20	–	tr	tr	0	30	165	Rice-based WHO formula, mOsm/l = 270, contains glutamine
Pedigree/Whiskas Electrolyte Instant Fluid (Waltham)	40	20	40	–	0	0	9	197	Contains glycine, maltodextrins
Pedialyte Solution (Ross Laboratories)	45	20	35	–	–	–	30	3	
Ricelyte Oral (Mead Johnson)	50	25	45	–	–	–	34	4.2	–
Resol Solution (Wyeth-Ayerst)	50	20	50	4	4	5	34	2.5	–
Rehydralyte Solution (Ross)	75	20	65	–	–	–	30	3	–
Biolyte (Pharmacia/Upjohn)	134	22.8	75.8	6.6	–	–	–	–	–

Key: mEq/l = milliequivalents per liter, ME = metabolizable energy, WHO = World Health Organization, tr = trace.

Electrolyte disorders should be corrected initially with appropriate parenteral fluid and electrolyte therapy. Foods for patients with acute gastroenteritis should contain levels of sodium, chloride and potassium above the minimum allowances for normal dogs and cats. Recommended levels of these nutrients are 0.35 to 0.50% DM sodium, 0.50 to 1.3% DM chloride and 0.80 to 1.1% DM potassium.

Fat

In comparison to processes involved with other macronutrients, fat digestion and absorption are relatively complex and may be disrupted in patients with GI disease. Ingestion of a fatty meal decreases gastroesophageal tone, slows gastric emptying and is a potent stimulus for pancreatic secretion.

On the other hand, dietary fat is a concentrated source of calories; higher fat foods allow smaller amounts of food to be ingested to meet the patient's DER. This is an important consideration in many patients because limiting the amount of food entering the GI tract helps control clinical signs. Fat also improves the palatability of food, which is important in patients with nausea.

For these reasons, foods for patients with acute gastroenteritis and many other GI diseases should contain moderate amounts of fat. Recommended dietary fat levels are 12 to 15% on a dry matter basis (DMB) for dogs and 15 to 22% DMB for cats.

Energy

Energy density of the food should be moderate (3.5 to 4.0 kcal/g [14.6 to 16.7 kJ/g] DM) to ensure intake of sufficient energy with small amounts of food. Foods with higher energy densities may help restore or maintain body weight and condition in these patients but would require higher dietary fat levels. As discussed above, however, increased levels of dietary fat delay gastric emptying and therefore should usually be avoided.

Fiber

Although dietary fiber predominantly affects the large bowel of dogs and cats, fiber can also affect gastric, small intestinal and pancreatic structure and function. Beneficial effects of dietary fiber include: 1) modifying gastric emptying, 2) normalizing intestinal motility and intestinal transport rate, 3) buffering toxins in the GI lumen, 4) binding or holding excess water, 5) supporting growth of normal GI microflora, 6) buffering gastric acid and 7) altering viscosity of GI luminal contents. Dietary fiber also adds nondigestible bulk and decreases the dry matter digestibility of the food.

Various types and levels of dietary fiber have been advocated for patients with acute gastroenteritis. The traditional approach is to recommend very low-fiber foods (<1% DM crude fiber) to enhance dry matter digestibility and provide "low residue" in the GI tract. One of the authors (DJD) recommends small amounts (0.5 to 5% DM crude fiber) of a mixed (i.e., soluble/insoluble) fiber type in conjunction with a highly digestible food. Another of the authors (RLR) has had success using moderate levels (10 to 15% DM crude fiber) of insoluble fiber. Each of these strategies can be successful in managing selected patients with acute gastroenteritis and other GI disorders.

Digestibility

The term "highly digestible" is not defined in a regulatory sense. However, the term has generally been reserved for products with protein digestibility ≥87%, and fat and carbohydrate digestibility ≥90%. The average digestibility coefficients for popular commercial dog and cat foods are 78 to 81%, 77 to 85% and 69 to 79% for crude protein, crude fat and nitrogen-free extract (NFE, carbohydrate), respectively.[23,24] Commercial veterinary therapeutic foods formulated for patients with GI disease (Table 22-10) usually contain meat and carbohydrate sources that have been highly refined to increase digestibility. Meat ingredients in many veterinary therapeutic foods are usually composed of muscle and organ sources rather than meat and bone meals. Typical meat/animal source ingredients in commercial GI foods include egg, cottage cheese, chicken and ground beef.

Carbohydrates make up the largest non-water fraction (i.e., 60 to 80% DM) of commercial and homemade foods formulated for managing patients with GI diseases. In pet foods, carbohydrate digestibility is influenced by source and processing. Dogs digest most properly cooked starches very well including corn, rice, barley and wheat.[25,26] Other starches (i.e., potato and tapioca) are less digestible, especially when inadequately cooked.[27-31] Cats, despite their obligate carnivorous nature, also efficiently digest carbohydrates. However, some veterinarians think that cats with small bowel disorders are less tolerant of dietary carbohydrate than dogs with similar causes of malassimilation.[32-35]

Recent work has identified a link between particle size and carbohydrate digestibility in moist foods.[36] These findings support chopping or grinding carbohydrate ingredients (e.g., rice, corn, etc.) before they are incorporated into moist foods. These findings are probably not applicable to extruded dry products because the extrusion process allows for a more complete cook than the canning process. In fact, other studies have demonstrated almost complete ileal carbohydrate digestibility in normal dogs consuming extruded grains.[37]

In general, dietary fat is more digestible than soluble carbohydrates and protein. The digestibility of fat in average commercial dog foods is approximately 90%.[38] The average digestibility of fat in commercial cat foods ranges from 74 to 91%.[39,40]

Digestibility of protein, carbohydrates and fat in foods for patients with acute GI disease should be high because normal digestion and absorption of nutrients are often compromised. Moderate amounts of fiber decrease the dry matter digestibility of the overall food; however, digestibility of the nonfiber nutrients is usually unaffected.[37]

Other Nutritional Factors
Glutamine

Glutamine is considered a conditionally essential nutrient for pets with severe GI disorders. As the preferred energy substrate for enterocytes, glutamine is necessary for maintaining gut mucosal integrity.[18,41] Commercial and homemade pet foods containing meat ingredients provide glutamine. Unfortunately, an analytical method for determining glutamine levels in foods is not widely available, making selection of foods based on glutamine content impossible.[42] Glutamine intake can be increased by orally administering a 2% solution of glutamine in water; 0.5 g of glutamine per kg body weight should be provided daily. Many pets will readily consume a glutamine solution, or these solutions can be administered by dose syringe or indwelling feeding tubes. Such dosing regimens have been used for treating dogs with parvoviral enteritis. Alternatively, commercial liquid or moist homogenized enteral foods enhanced with glutamine may be offered (Table 12-8).

Acid Load

Acidemia is common in pets with diarrhea because fluid secreted in the caudal small intestine and large intestine contains bicarbonate concentrations higher than those in plasma and sodium in excess of chloride ions. The acidosis is compounded in some patients by development of hypovolemia (i.e., severe dehydration). Severe acid-base disorders are best corrected with appropriate parenteral fluid therapy. Foods for patients with acute vomiting and diarrhea should avoid excess dietary acid load and preferably contain buffering salts (e.g., potassium gluconate and calcium carbonate). Ideally, foods that normally produce a urinary pH greater than 6.8 should be selected.

ASSESS THE FOOD(S) AND FEEDING METHOD

Levels of the key nutritional factors should be evaluated in foods currently fed to patients with acute gastroenteritis and compared with recommended levels (Table 22-20). Information from this aspect of assessment is essential for making any changes to foods currently provided. Changing to a more appropriate food is indicated if key nutritional factors in the current food do not match recommended levels.

A thorough assessment should include verification of the feeding method currently used. Items to consider include feeding frequency, amount fed, how the food is offered, access to other food and who feeds the animal. All of this information should have been gathered when the history of the animal was obtained. If the animal has a normal BCS (3/5), the amount of food previously fed (energy basis) was probably appropriate.

Feeding Plan

The first objective in managing acute gastroenteritis should be to correct dehydration and electrolyte, glucose and acid-base imbalances, if present. The dietary goals are to provide a food that meets the patient's nutrient requirements and allows normalization of intestinal motility and function. Medical therapy may include antibiotics, nonsteroidal antiinflammatory agents (e.g., flunixin meglumine), anti-endotoxin sera and anthelmintics.

SELECT A FOOD(S)

There are several plausible dietary strategies for managing small bowel diarrhea and they may be attempted in any order. The traditional approach is to first feed a highly digestible, low-residue food with moderate levels of fat (12 to 15% DMB for dogs, 15 to 22% DMB for cats). Small amounts (≤5%) of soluble or mixed fiber sources may be included in such foods. Including fiber at these levels does not usually impair digestibility or increase fecal volume. This approach can be accomplished by feeding a variety of commercial veterinary therapeutic foods formulated for GI disease (Table 22-10) or homemade foods (Table 6-8). Foods for puppies and kittens with GI disease should also meet the nutritional requirements for growth.

One of the authors (RLR) prefers to increase dietary fiber content to normalize intestinal motility, water balance and microflora. Fiber has several physiologic characteristics that are beneficial in managing small bowel diarrhea. Moderate amounts of dietary fiber (10 to 15 % DMB) adds nondigestible bulk, which buffers toxins, holds excess water and, perhaps more important, provides intraluminal stimuli to re-establish the coordinated actions of hormones, neurons, smooth muscles, enzyme delivery, digestion and absorption. Fiber normalizes transit time through the small bowel, which means fiber slows a hypermotile state, but also improves a hypomotile state to re-establish normal peristaltic action. Table 22-22 lists selected fiber-enhanced commercial foods.

In cases of protracted small bowel disuse (i.e., greater than seven days), a third strategy may be used. This strategy involves initially feeding small amounts of a monomeric liquid food containing maltodextrins and glutamine (Table 12-8). This type of initial feeding may ease the transition to other foods. Feeding puppies recovering from parvoviral enteritis a monomeric liquid food containing maltodextrins and glutamine reduces nausea and vomiting, and subsequently eases the transition to feeding other commercial veterinary therapeutic foods.[c]

DETERMINE A FEEDING METHOD

Withholding all oral intake of food and water for 24 to 48 hours is the first step in the feeding method for patients with acute gastroenteritis. After this period, animals should be offered small amounts of water or ice cubes every few hours. If water is well tolerated, small amounts of food can be offered several times (i.e., six to eight times) a day. If the pet can eat food without episodes of diarrhea or vomiting, the amount fed can be increased over three to

Table 22-22. Fiber sources and nutrient profiles of selected fiber-enhanced commercial pet foods used in patients with gastrointestinal disease.*

	Protein	Fat	Crude fiber	Fiber source(s)
Moist canine products				
Hill's Prescription Diet Canine r/d	25.3	6.9	26.1	Soybean mill run, cellulose
Hill's Prescription Diet Canine w/d	16.5	12	13.5	Cellulose
Leo Specific CRW	31.6	8.9	17.8	Vegetable fiber
Medi-Cal Canine Fibre Formula	24.7	7.9	15.9	Cellulose
Medi-Cal Canine Weight Control/Geriatric	21.8	10.8	6.1	Cellulose, vegetable gum
Purina CNM Canine OM-Formula	44.1	8.4	19.2	Pea fiber, beet pulp
Select Care Canine Hifactor Formula	24.8	9	15	Cellulose, guar gum
Waltham/Pedigree Canine High Fiber	29.8	8	10.3	Vegetable fiber
Dry canine products				
Hill's Prescription Diet Canine r/d	24.6	8.6	23.7	Peanut hulls, soybean mill run
Hill's Prescription Diet Canine w/d	16.7	6.9	16.8	Peanut hulls
Leo Specific CRD	24.4	5.6	8.9	Vegetable fiber
Medi-Cal Canine Fibre Formula	23.7	9.8	15.8	Peanut hulls, rice hulls
Medi-Cal Canine Weight Control/Geriatric	20	8.5	5.9	Oat hulls
Purina CNM Canine DCO-Formula	25.3	11.3	7	Beet pulp, pea fiber
Purina CNM Canine GL-Formula	28.9	10.5	9	Pea bran
Purina CNM Canine OM-Formula	22.8	6	14.1	Pea fiber, soybean hulls
Select Care Canine Hifactor Formula	25.7	10.8	14.7	Peanut hulls, rice hulls
Waltham/Pedigree Canine High Fiber	21.7	8.3	5	Wheat bran, cellulose, guar gum
Moist feline products				
Hill's Prescription Diet Feline r/d	36.2	7.7	29.8	Cellulose
Hill's Prescription Diet Feline w/d	41.1	16.6	12.3	Cellulose
Leo Specific FRW	42.1	9.3	18.7	Vegetable fiber
Medi-Cal Feline Fibre Formula	40.2	14.4	8.6	Cellulose, vegetable gum
Medi-Cal Feline Weight Control	40.2	17.7	4.7	Cellulose, vegetable gum
Select Care Feline Hifactor Formula	34.1	16.1	7.2	Cellulose, guar gum
Dry feline products				
Hill's Prescription Diet Feline r/d	37.7	8.4	16.7	Cellulose
Hill's Prescription Diet Feline w/d	39.2	9.5	9	Cellulose
Leo Specific FRD	37	7.1	19	Vegetable fiber
Medi-Cal Feline Fibre Formula	34.1	13.8	7.3	Cellulose
Medi-Cal Feline Weight Control	34.4	12.3	4.7	Pea fiber, beet pulp
Purina CNM Feline OM-Formula	37	7.7	11.5	Oat fiber, soybean hulls
Select Care Feline Hifactor Formula	38.2	12.9	5	Pea fiber, beet pulp
Select Care Feline Weight Formula	36.2	12.2	3.6	Beet pulp, cellulose

Key: na = information not published by manufacturer.
*This list represents products with the largest market share and for which published information is available. Manufacturers' published values. Nutrients expressed as % dry matter.

four days until the animal is receiving its estimated DER in two to three meals per day. During this period, if the animal begins to vomit, food should be withdrawn and offered again after several hours. As discussed above, monomeric liquid foods can also be offered.

Refeeding may be complicated by persistent vomiting in some cases of parvoviral enteritis; some puppies develop gastroparesis and may require prokinetic drugs to facilitate feeding. In such cases, intravenous infusion of metoclopramide (at a rate of 1.0 mg/kg body weight/day) is recommended. Alternatively, metoclopramide can be administered to well-hydrated patients subcutaneously or intramuscularly at a dose of 0.5 mg/kg body weight q8h. Some animals may require parenteral feeding. (See Chapter 12.)

Reassessment

The prognosis for recovery in most cases of acute gastroenteritis is good. Body weight should be recorded daily until recovery is complete. Changes in body weight from day to day usually reflect changes in hydration status rather than loss or gain of body tissue. Further diagnostic testing is warranted if vomiting or severe diarrhea persists.

Dogs and cats presenting with multiple or recurrent episodes of small bowel diarrhea require further diagnos-

tic work-up and, most probably, a combination of dietary and medical therapies. Parasitic causes, however, should be ruled out or treated empirically before pursuing further diagnostics. The diagnostic approach to patients with chronic small bowel diarrhea is beyond the scope of this chapter; readers are referred to internal medicine and gastroenterology texts for more information.

Inflammatory Bowel Disease

Clinical Importance

The term inflammatory bowel disease (IBD) refers to a group of chronic, idiopathic GI disorders. Each is characterized by inflammatory infiltrates within the lamina propria of the GI tract. Currently, IBD is considered the most common cause of chronic diarrhea and vomiting in dogs and cats.[43] The generic term, IBD, encompasses lymphoplasmacytic enteritis, lymphocytic gastroenterocolitis, eosinophilic gastroenterocolitis, segmental granulomatous enterocolitis, suppurative enterocolitis and histiocytic colitis. Specific types are categorized on the basis of the type of inflammatory cells found in the lamina propria. The lymphoplasmacytic form is probably the most common type of IBD.[44]

The severity of the condition varies from relatively mild clinical signs to life-threatening protein-losing enteropathies. In particular, the basenji and Ludenhund breeds may present with a very severe variant that has been termed immunoproliferative small intestinal disease.[45-47]

Inflammatory infiltrates may involve the stomach, small bowel and colon. In cats, the stomach and small bowel are affected most often. In dogs, IBD is common in the small and large bowel. In many cases, multiple segments of the bowel are involved and clinical signs may be mixed, reflecting the broad distribution of mucosal lesions.

Assessment

ASSESS THE ANIMAL

History and Physical Examination

The most common clinical signs in dogs and cats with IBD are chronic vomiting, diarrhea and weight loss. The predominant GI sign varies with the portion or portions of bowel affected. Vomiting tends to be the predominant clinical sign when the stomach and proximal duodenum are affected. Loose, fluid or steatorrheic stools are most common when the small intestine is involved. Diarrhea marked by tenesmus, mucus and small scanty stools is noted with colonic lesions. Clinical signs may be intermittent or persistent. Clinical signs tend to increase in frequency and intensity as IBD progresses. The presence of systemic signs is also variable. Some animals present with a history of depression, malaise and inappetence. Others are alert and active at the time they are examined.

The frequency and character of the vomitus and stools are important. At times, vomiting will be temporally related to food intake and the vomitus will contain food particles. In other cases, animals may vomit only fluid or froth. Vomiting hairballs is a typical finding in cats and suggests that the stomach is affected. Owners should be questioned closely about the appearance of the vomited material. Dark black or coffee grounds material suggests gastric ulceration. The diarrhea may be small or large bowel in origin. Again, the color of the stools should be assessed to determine the presence of GI bleeding.

Physical examination findings in dogs and cats with IBD are variable. Many animals have no abnormalities. Others present only with evidence of weight loss and poor body condition. Weight loss may be severe in long-standing cases. Mild to moderate peripheral lymphadenopathy may be detected in rare cases of IBD. This finding is most often recognized in cats with eosinophilic gastroenteritis and hypereosinophilic syndrome, which is characterized by multi-systemic eosinophilic infiltrates.[48]

On occasion, thickened loops of bowel may be detected by abdominal palpation. This finding is more easily detected in cats. A segmental thickening of bowel is consistent with eosinophilic gastroenteritis in cats or granulomatous enteritis in dogs. This finding should also be distinguished from intestinal intussusceptions, foreign bodies, histoplasmosis and neoplastic lesions. Occasionally, animals with IBD present with abdominal pain, which is suggestive of gastroduodenal ulceration.[49,50]

Evidence of hemorrhage or hypoproteinemia may be noted in very severe cases. A vitamin K-dependent coagulopathy may develop in animals with marked steatorrhea. At times, IBD may result in a protein-losing enteropathy. When severe, hypoalbuminemia and external manifestations of hypoproteinemia (i.e., pitting edema, ascites) may be present. Surprisingly, some animals with protein-losing enteropathy may present with only mild or no diarrhea.

Laboratory and Other Clinical Information

Laboratory findings in patients with IBD are often nonspecific. Hematologic findings are variable and may include blood loss anemia, anemia of chronic disease and/or eosinophilia. In cats with eosinophilic gastroenteritis and hypereosinophilic syndrome, eosinophil counts may exceed 100,000/μl.[48] Patients with chronic diarrhea should be assessed with serum biochemistry profiles and urinalyses to determine the systemic effects of the GI disorder and to rule out concurrent disease. Electrolyte abnormalities, including hypokalemia, may be identified. Hypoproteinemia and hypoalbuminemia may be recognized in severe cases with protein-losing enteropathy. Prerenal azotemia may be present in dehydrated patients. In cats, IBD may be associated with pancreatitis and hepatitis.[51] In such cases, increased hepatic enzyme activities, hyperamylasemia, hyperlipasemia and hyperbilirubinemia may be noted. IBD is often associated with a protein-losing nephropathy in soft-coated wheaten terriers. Varying degrees of azotemia and proteinuria are common in these cases.[52,53]

Fecal examinations are very important in the evaluation of patients with chronic diarrhea. Multiple fecal examinations using concentration techniques are necessary to rule out parasitism. Qualitative and quantitative fecal fat examinations assess fat absorption capacity. Marked steatorrhea usually indicates severe infiltrative disease.

Radiographic findings in IBD are usually nonspecific and nondiagnostic. Occasionally, thickened bowel loops are detected.

Endoscopic abnormalities in IBD include mucosal granularity, hyperemia, friability and inability to visualize colonic submucosal blood vessels.[49] Multiple biopsy specimens should be collected from several bowel segments even if the endoscopic appearance is normal because histologic changes may be present despite a normal appearance.[49,54,55]

The definitive diagnosis of IBD is based on histopathologic examination of biopsy specimens (Figure 22-13) collected by endoscopic or surgical techniques.[56] Histologic grading systems have been proposed to allow objective assessment of intestinal biopsy specimens.[49,54,57] Despite the use of formal classification schemes, interpretation of histologic changes can be difficult when the lesions are mild or suggest lymphosarcoma.[56] The latter finding is a serious concern in cases of lymphoplasmacytic enteritis and lymphocytic enteritis.

Recently, quantification of mucosal inflammatory markers found in colonic lavage fluid (e.g., IgG, nitrite) has been suggested for evaluation of dogs with suspected IBD.[58] This technique holds particular promise for monitoring response to treatment.

Risk Factors

There does not appear to be an age or gender predisposition for any of the forms of IBD. The condition usually arises in adult dogs and cats, but has been diagnosed in puppies and kittens (i.e., less than six months of age). In people, there is a well-recognized familial tendency toward IBD.[59] A genetic influence has also been recognized in veterinary medicine (Table 22-19). Certain dog breeds appear to be at risk for various forms of IBD: 1) the German shepherd dog, Chinese Shar-Pei and soft-coated wheaten terrier for lymphoplasmacytic enteritis, 2) the German shepherd dog and Irish setter for eosinophilic gastroenteritis, 3) the boxer and French bulldog for ulcerative colitis and 4) the basenji and Ludenhund for immunoproliferative enteropathy.

The environment may also play an important role in IBD. Animals maintained in overcrowded, contaminated quarters are at risk for development of parasite infections, viral and bacterial enteritis and small intestinal bacterial overgrowth, which have been hypothesized to play a role in the pathogenesis of IBD. The role of parasites in the pathogenesis of IBD is poorly understood; however, occult parasitism has been suggested as a cause for these disorders. For example, in German shepherd dogs, visceral larval migrans has been linked to eosinophilic gastroenteritis.[60] In cats, feline infectious peritonitis has been associated with granulomatous and suppurative enterocolitis.[61] In addition, small intestinal bacterial overgrowth has been reported in association with lymphoplasmacytic infiltrates and enteritis.[62]

Etiopathogenesis

Despite intensive study by veterinary and medical researchers, the pathophysiology of inflammatory bowel disorders is not completely understood.[59,63] The disorder is undoubtedly immune-mediated, yet the pathogenesis of the various forms of IBD is poorly defined. The fundamental pathway for the development of IBD involves hypersensitivity. However, the underlying cause for hypersensitivity reactions is unknown. Two related theories have been espoused. The first speculates that IBD patients develop a defect in the intestinal mucosal barrier. This loss of mucosal integrity results in increased gut permeability and hypersensitivity responses to antigens that are normally tolerated (Figure 22-14).[43] (See sidebar "Wheat-Sensitive Enteropathy.") Alternatively, IBD may result from aberrant immunologic responses to luminal antigens. It is hypothesized that defects in gut-associated lymphatic tissue (GALT) suppressor function may predispose patients to development of hypersensitivity to normally tolerated luminal antigens (Figures 22-15, 14-2, 14-3 and 14-4).[43] Parasites, pathogenic organisms, normal gut flora and dietary antigens may all serve as the substrate for these immunologic reactions. Both potential pathways culminate in release of inflammatory mediators. These substances may then further damage the intestinal mucosal surface and set up a vicious cycle of inflammation and loss of barrier function.

Mucosal inflammatory infiltrates are responsible for the clinical manifestations of IBD. Mucosal inflammation disrupts normal absorptive processes resulting in malabsorption and osmotic diarrhea. Altered gut permeability can result in leakage of fluid, protein and blood into the gut lumen. Malabsorbed fats, carbohydrates and bile acids result in secretory diarrhea. Inflammatory mediators may also directly trigger intestinal secretion and mucus production by goblet cells. Mucosal inflammatory infiltrates may alter intestinal and colonic motility patterns, a mechanism attributed to the influence of prostaglandins and leukotrienes on smooth muscle. Inflammation of the proximal bowel (stomach and small bowel) may stimulate visceral afferent receptors that trigger vomiting. Delayed gastric emptying associated with gastroparesis or ileus may exacerbate vomiting.

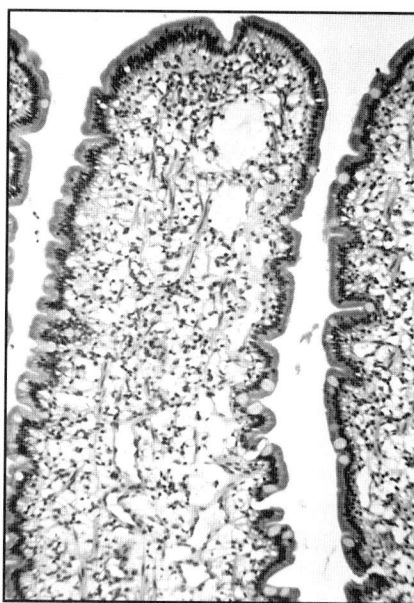

Figure 22-13. Photomicrograph of an intestinal villus showing typical monocellular infiltrates recognized in lymphoplasmacytic enteritis (original magnification 400X).

Key Nutritional Factors

Key nutritional factors for patients with IBD are listed in Table 22-23 and discussed in more detail below.

Water

Dehydration is a frequent problem in patients with IBD. Reduced water consumption is often aggravated by fluid losses from vomiting and/or diarrhea. Whenever possible, fluid balance should be maintained via oral consumption of fluids. However, dehydrated patients and those with persistent vomiting often need parenteral fluid administration.

Minerals

Serum electrolyte concentrations should be assessed regularly to allow early detection of abnormalities as vomiting and diarrhea persist. Hypokalemia is particularly common in patients with IBD. Thus, foods containing 0.85 to 1.1% DM potassium are preferred for dogs and cats with IBD. Initially, potassium levels should be restored with intravenous potassium supplementation.

Energy and Fat

Energy-dense foods are preferred for managing patients with chronic enteropathies. Calorie-dense products allow the clinician to provide smaller volumes of food at each meal, which minimizes GI stretch and secretions. Unfortunately,

Table 22-23. Key nutritional factors for patients with inflammatory bowel disease.*

Factors	Recommended levels
Crude fiber	0.5 to 15% (see text)
Digestibility	≥87% for protein and ≥90% for fat and soluble carbohydrate
Energy density	3.5 to 4.0 kcal/g
	14.6 to 16.7 kJ/g
Fat	12 to 15% for dogs
	15 to 22% for cats
Potassium	0.85 to 1.1%
Protein	Limit dietary protein to one or two sources
	Use protein sources to which animal has not been exposed previously
	16 to 20% for dogs
	30 to 45% for cats

*Nutrients expressed on a dry matter basis.

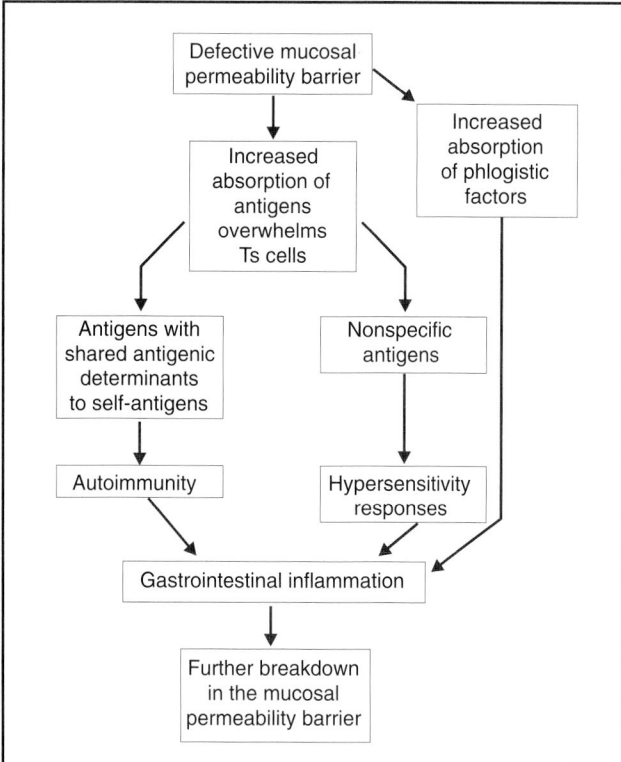

Figure 22-14. A defect in the mucosal permeability barrier has been proposed as a cause of inflammatory bowel disease. (Adapted from Guilford WG. Idiopathic inflammatory bowel diseases. In: Guilford WG, Center SA, Strombeck DR, et al, eds. Strombeck's Small Animal Gastroenterology, 3rd ed. Philadelphia, PA: WB Saunders Co, 1996; 457.)

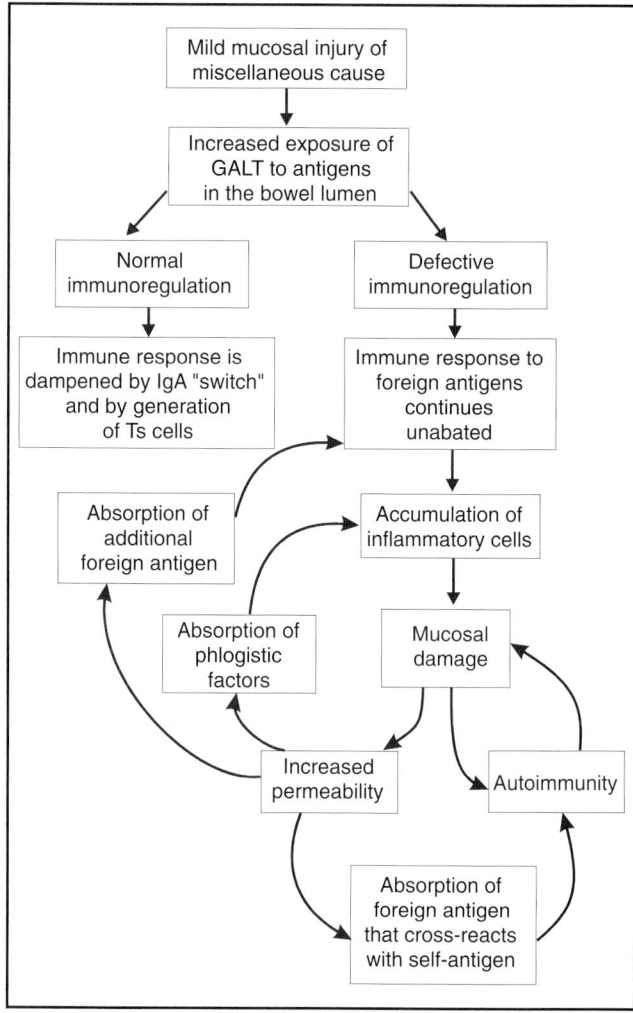

Figure 22-15. A defect in the suppressor function of the gut-associated lymphoid tissue (GALT) has been proposed as a cause of inflammatory bowel disease. (Adapted from Guilford WG. Idiopathic inflammatory bowel diseases. In: Guilford WG, Center SA, Strombeck DR, et al, eds. Strombeck's Small Animal Gastroenterology, 3rd ed. Philadelphia, PA: WB Saunders Co, 1996; 453.)

energy-dense foods are also high in fat. High-fat foods may contribute to osmotic diarrhea and GI protein losses, which complicate IBD. Thus, it is often advantageous to initially provide a food with moderate energy density (3.5 to 4 kcal/g [14.6 to 16.7 kJ/g] DM) and fat levels (12 to 15% DMB for dogs and 15 to 22% DMB for cats). More energy-dense foods with higher fat levels can be offered if the patient tolerates these nutrient levels.

There appears to be a difference in how dogs and cats are able to tolerate dietary fat in the face of GI disease. Normal cats can tolerate much higher concentrations of dietary fat than dogs.[40] Anecdotal information suggests that foods with increased fat content may actually benefit cats with small bowel disease.[64] Controlled evaluations are needed to confirm these observations.

Protein

Protein malnutrition may occur in dogs and cats with IBD due to fecal losses. Recommended dietary protein intake will be discussed in more detail in the following section about protein-losing enteropathies. Protein should be provided at levels sufficient for the appropriate lifestage for patients without excessive GI protein loss. High biologic value, highly digestible (≥87%) protein sources should be used.

Because dietary antigens are suspected to play a role in the pathogenesis of IBD, some authors recommend the use of "hypoallergenic" or elimination foods.[65-68] In some cases, elimination foods may be used successfully without pharmacologic intervention. Mild to moderate feline lymphoplasmacytic enteritis, canine lymphoplasmacytic colitis

and canine eosinophilic gastroenteritis are more likely to respond to dietary management alone. Ideal elimination foods should: 1) avoid protein excess, 2) have high protein digestibility (≥87%) and 3) contain a limited number of novel protein sources to which the animal has never been exposed. Chapter 14 discusses elimination foods in more detail. The suspected pathogenesis of IBD involves an increase in gut permeability; therefore, the use of "sacrificial" dietary antigens in the treatment of IBD has been suggested.[43] (See sidebar "Sacrificial Proteins in Inflammatory Bowel Disease.")

The evidence regarding the efficacy of elimination foods in people with IBD is conflicting.[69] Although specific foods provoking symptoms may be identified in as many as 80% of human patients with Crohn's disease, double-blind rechallenges suggest that food hypersensitivity may be identified consistently in fewer than 10%.[69] Similarly, positive reactions to food antigens applied topically to the gastric mucosa (i.e., gastroscopic food sensitivity test) have been recognized in canine patients with IBD.[70-72] Gastroscopic food sensitivity test findings, however, often do not correlate with the results of provocative diet challenges or clinical responses.[71,d] A protein hydrolysate-based elimination diet has been used successfully in refractory canine IBD cases.[55]

Fiber

Feeding small quantities of soluble or mixed fiber sources to people with IBD has been advocated.[59] In fact, short-chain fatty acid and butyrate enemas induce clinical improvement in people with ulcerative colitis.[73,74] A number of substrates including beet pulp, soy fiber, inulin and fructooligosaccharides have been demonstrated by in vitro fermentation to produce volatile fatty acids that may be beneficial in IBD involving the distal small intestine and colon.[75-78] These fibers are usually incorporated at rates of 1 to 5% DM in commercial products.

Digestibility

Feeding highly digestible (dry matter digestibility ≥90%) foods provides several advantages in the management of dogs and cats with IBD. Nutrients from low-residue foods are more completely absorbed in the proximal gut. Further, low-residue foods are associated with: 1) reduced osmotic diarrhea due to fat and carbohydrate malabsorption, 2) reduced production of intestinal gas due to carbohydrate malabsorption and 3) decreased antigen loads because smaller amounts of protein are absorbed intact. Ideal foods for IBD patients are free of lactose to avoid the complication of lactose intolerance.

The use of monomeric liquid foods and total parenteral nutrition to provide a period of "bowel rest" for people and animals with IBD is controversial.[79] Bowel rest has been recommended as a means of reducing or eliminating antigenic stimuli while minimizing GI secretions. The greatest benefit appears to be for those human patients with Crohn's disease.[80,81] Monomeric feedings provide energy and nitrogen in a readily available, nonantigenic form. Monomeric liquid foods are also supplemented with glutamine. Parenteral nutrition does not appear to provide any advantage over monomeric diets and is not recommended except in those patients unable to tolerate enteral feeding.[63] Bowel rest may theoretically worsen GI mucosal lesions by depriving mucosal epithelial cells of nutrients such as glutamine and short-chain fatty acids.[69] Veterinary experience with parenteral feeding and monomeric and hydrolysate-based foods in the management of IBD is limited.[55,68] Most often, these therapies have been used in refractory cases in which other therapeutic modalities have failed.

Other Nutritional Factors

Vitamins

Adequate intake of water-soluble and fat-soluble vitamins is critical for patients with IBD. In many cases, the limited stores of water-soluble vitamins have been depleted by diarrheic losses and the large fluid flux through the animal. Thiamin deficiency, in particular, occurs commonly and can profoundly affect appetite. Loss of fat-soluble vitamins can be significant in patients with steatorrhea (e.g., vitamin K-deficient coagulopathies may occur in patients with IBD). Initially, parenteral administration of vitamins may be necessary. Dietary intake is often sufficient when the disease responds to treatment and fat absorption is re-established.

Zinc

Zinc deficiency is well recognized in people as a complication of IBD.[82] The small intestine is the primary site of zinc homeostasis and there are several potential mecha-

nisms for zinc deficiency in IBD (Table 22-24). Dietary zinc intake should be assessed if dogs and cats with IBD have poor coat quality or dermatitis.

N-3 Fatty Acids

N-3 fatty acids (omega-3 fatty acids) derived from fish oil or other sources have been hypothesized to have a ben-

---

Wheat-Sensitive Enteropathy

Wheat-sensitive enteropathy is a chronic small bowel disorder recognized primarily in Irish setter dogs. The condition, also termed gluten-sensitive enteropathy, is comparable to celiac disease of people. The disorder results from a hypersensitivity to gliadin, a glycoprotein found in many grains including wheat, barley, rye, buckwheat and oats. Gliadin is not found in rice, corn or potatoes.

Affected dogs usually develop clinical signs by six months of age, including weight loss, failure to thrive and chronic, intermittent small bowel diarrhea.

There are no consistent laboratory findings in dogs with wheat-sensitive enteropathy. The results of intestinal function tests such as D-xylose absorption and serum folate/cobalamin concentrations are often normal. Intestinal biopsy can be a useful diagnostic aid. Typical histopathologic findings include partial villous atrophy and intraepithelial lymphocyte infiltration.

Diagnosis of this condition is usually based on signalment, history and response to a therapeutic food trial. Clinical signs usually resolve within two to four weeks after gliadin-containing grains are eliminated from the food. Definitive diagnosis can be made if the clinical signs recrudesce upon re-exposure to gliadin-containing foods or purified gluten.

The pathogenesis of gluten- or wheat-sensitive enteropathy is not completely understood. Hypersensitivity to gliadin has been theorized to develop in dogs due to an age-related delay in expression of a brush border peptidase (i.e., aminopeptidase N) or to increased intestinal permeability. (See Chapter 14.)

The feeding plan includes eliminating all sources of gliadin from the diet including commercial foods, homemade foods, table foods, commercial treats, supplements and chewable medications containing wheat, barley, rye, buckwheat or oats as ingredients. The carbohydrate portion of the food should be composed of potatoes, rice or corn.

Affected dogs should be fed to meet their daily energy requirement. Young growing dogs should be fed foods suitable for growth, whereas adult and geriatric dogs should receive foods suitable for their lifestage and lifestyle.

BIBLIOGRAPHY

Batt RM, Carter MW, McLean L. Morphological and biochemical studies of a naturally occurring enteropathy in the Irish setter dog; A comparison with coeliac disease in man. Research in Veterinary Science 1984; 37: 339-346.

Daminet SC. Gluten-sensitive enteropathy in a family of Irish setters. Canadian Veterinary Journal 1996; 37: 745-747.

Hall EJ, Batt RM. Development of wheat-sensitive enteropathy in Irish setters: Biochemical changes. American Journal of Veterinary Research 1990; 51: 983-989.

Hall EJ, Batt RM. Development of wheat-sensitive enteropathy in Irish setters: Morphologic changes. American Journal of Veterinary Research 1990; 51: 978-982.

eficial effect in controlling mucosal inflammation in IBD. There is some clinical evidence that dietary supplementation with these fatty acids can modulate the generation and biologic activity of inflammatory mediators. (See Chapter 26.) Diets supplemented with fish oil have been used in a limited number of human trials with mixed results.[83-87] Although use of n-3 fatty acids warrants further consideration in veterinary medicine, there is no well-established effective dose for dogs and cats. A reasonable starting dose estimated from human and animal trials is approximately 175 mg (range 50 to 300 mg) n-3 fatty acids/kg body weight/day. (See Chapter 26 for additional information about the use of n-3 fatty acids in inflammatory disorders.)

ASSESS THE FOOD(S) AND FEEDING METHOD

Levels of key nutritional factors should be evaluated in foods currently being fed to patients with IBD and compared with recommended levels (Table 22-23). Key nutritional factors include water, minerals (especially potassium), energy density, fat, protein, fiber and digestibility. Information from this aspect of assessment is essential for making any changes to foods currently provided. Changing to a more appropriate food is indicated if key nutritional factors in the current food do not match recommended levels.

A thorough assessment should include verification of the feeding method currently being used. Items to consider include feeding frequency, amount fed, how the food is offered, access to other food and who feeds the animal. All of this information should have been gathered when the history of the animal was obtained. If the animal has an ideal BCS (3/5), the amount of food previously fed (energy basis) was probably appropriate. If the animal has poor body condition (BCS of 1/5 or 2/5), the amount of food previously fed may have been inappropriate or significant malassimilation may be occurring due to IBD.

Feeding Plan

The justification for nutritional management of IBD is twofold. First, dietary factors may contribute to the initiation or perpetuation of the disease. Second, malabsorption and malnutrition are common sequelae to IBD.

Dietary intervention should be aimed at controlling clinical signs while providing adequate nutrients to meet requirements and compensate for ongoing losses through the GI tract. Some dogs and cats with IBD may require only dietary manipulation. In other cases, dietary therapy is better used in concert with pharmacologic agents. Antibiotics (e.g., tylosin, tetracycline, metronidazole), anthelmintics (e.g., fenbendazole) and immunosuppressive agents (e.g., corticosteroids, azathioprine, cyclophosphamide) are often used for managing IBD.

SELECT A FOOD(S)

Food selection should focus on foods that reduce intestinal irritation/inflammation and normalize intestinal motility. Three types of foods may be useful in managing diarrhea associated with IBD: 1) highly digestible, low-residue foods formulated for GI disease, 2) fiber-enhanced foods and 3) elimination foods. Unfortunately, no physical examination finding, laboratory test result or historical fact will dictate which method will be successful in any one patient. Dietary trials are often needed to find which food type works best.

The most commonly used strategy is to feed a highly digestible, low-residue GI food with moderate levels of fat (i.e., 12 to 15% DMB for dogs, 15 to 22% DMB for cats). This can be accomplished by feeding a variety of commercial veterinary therapeutic foods (Table 22-10) or homemade foods (Table 6-8).

A second approach is to increase dietary fiber content to normalize intestinal motility, water balance and

---

Sacrificial Proteins in Inflammatory Bowel Disease

Oral tolerance is difficult to maintain in the inflammatory milieu; therefore, animals with inflammatory bowel disease (IBD) are at risk for becoming rapidly sensitive to undigested food proteins entering the lamina propria. This theoretical concern has led to the concept of feeding a "sacrificial protein" source. The first novel protein fed to patients in the early phase of therapy is referred to as a sacrificial protein because it is being offered when the bowel is inflamed and the mucosal barrier porous. The dietary protein source is then changed after the first six weeks of therapy. For animals receiving concurrent prednisone therapy, this diet change is made just before the prednisone dose is decreased from the immunosuppressive to the antiinflammatory range, by which time it is hoped that the mucosal inflammation has been controlled and the mucosal barrier has markedly recovered. As a result, the second dietary protein source is less likely to result in acquired food hypersensitivity and delayed recovery from IBD. The benefit to this recommendation is currently under investigation. This type of nutritional management is likely to be of most value in those animals in which IBD has resulted from a transient injury to the gut-associated lymphoid tissue or the mucosal barrier (e.g., from a viral infection) rather than those in which IBD is due to an inherent (i.e., permanent) defect in these structures.

Grant Guilford, BSVSC, PhD
Diplomate ACVIM (Internal Medicine)
Massey University
New Zealand

Table 22-24. Potential causes of zinc deficiency in patients with inflammatory bowel disease.*

Decreased absorption
  Intestinal inflammation
  Supplemental iron and/or copper
  Surgical resection of distal duodenum
Inadequate dietary intake
  Anorexia
  High fiber or phytate intake
  Parenteral nutrition
Increased losses
  Chronic blood loss
  Increased metabolism
Increased requirements
  Growth
  Lactation
  Pregnancy
  Wound healing

*Adapted from Hendricks KM, Walker A. Zinc deficiency in inflammatory bowel disease. Nutrition Reviews 1988; 46: 401-408.

microflora. Fiber has several physiologic characteristics that are beneficial in managing small bowel diarrhea. Moderate levels of dietary fiber (10 to 15% DMB) add nondigestible bulk, which buffers toxins, holds excess water and, perhaps more important, provides intraluminal stimuli to re-establish the coordinated actions of hormones, neurons, smooth muscles, enzyme delivery, digestion and absorption. Fiber normalizes transit time through the small bowel, which means fiber slows a hypermotile state, but also improves a hypomotile state to re-establish normal peristaltic action. Table 20-22 lists selected fiber-enhanced commercial foods.

The third dietary option in IBD cases is the use of an elimination food with a limited number of highly digestible, novel protein sources. Commercial veterinary therapeutic foods (Table 14-5) or homemade foods that contain novel protein sources often combine lamb, rabbit, venison, duck or fish with a highly digestible or novel carbohydrate source. All other possible dietary sources of protein and carbohydrate should be eliminated including treats, snacks, table foods, vitamin-mineral supplements and chewable/flavored medications. Clinical signs should abate within the first three weeks of strict dietary management (e.g., feeding only the novel ingredient food). After signs abate, owners may add individual specific ingredients previously fed in an effort to identify the allergen. Clinical GI signs may recur within 12 hours after the offending ingredient is fed.

DETERMINE A FEEDING METHOD

Initially the IBD patient should be fed multiple small meals per day as indicated by animal acceptance and tolerance for the food. Meal size can be increased and meal frequency can be reduced as tolerated by the patient after the clinical signs have been successfully managed for several weeks.

Reassessment

Regaining or maintaining optimal body weight and condition, normal activity level, a positive attitude and absence of clinical signs are measures of successful dietary and medical management. The feeding method and amount fed can be adjusted as needed to maintain body weight and condition.

The prognosis for IBD varies with the specific entity present, severity of the condition at the time of presentation and owner compliance. The hypereosinophilic form of eosinophilic gastroenteritis in cats and immunoproliferative enteropathy and histiocytic colitis in dogs may be refractory to treatment.[45,48,88] Likewise, response to therapy may be poor when animals present late in the course of disease and with evidence of protein-losing enteropathy.

In most cases, judicious use of dietary and medical regimens controls the disease. Often, medical measures can be withdrawn after three to six months; thereafter, animals maintain remission with appropriate foods. In some cases, however, pharmacologic treatment may be required for the life of the animal.

The most common causes for failure to respond include noncompliance on the part of the owner and failure of the clinician to tailor a program incorporating both dietary and pharmacologic measures for each patient.[43] On occasion, treatment failures occur because of misdiagnosis of alimentary lymphosarcoma or progression of IBD to lym-

phosarcoma. This progression has been reported to occur in dogs and cats.[89]

Lymphangiectasia and Protein-Losing Enteropathies

Clinical Importance

Lymphangiectasia is a chronic enteropathy characterized by abnormalities of the intestinal lymphatic system. The condition may occur as a primary lymphatic defect or secondarily as a consequence of severe intestinal infiltrative disease (e.g., IBD, alimentary lymphosarcoma, immunoproliferative enteropathy, fungal enteritis). Lymphangiectasia is the most common cause of protein-losing enteropathy (PLE) in dogs and cats. However, PLE is a relatively rare manifestation of diarrheic disorders in dogs and cats.

Assessment

ASSESS THE ANIMAL

History and Physical Examination

Typically, signs of lymphangiectasia are insidious in onset and follow a waxing and waning course over several weeks to months before becoming flagrant. The clinical manifestations of lymphangiectasia are generally attributable to the loss of lymph constituents (i.e., albumin, lymphocytes, fat) or to underlying enteric disease. Many patients present with chronic intermittent diarrhea or vomiting; however, not all patients have GI signs. Progressive weight loss, often in the face of good appetite, is a consistent finding in long-standing cases. Excessive protein loss from leaky intestinal lymphatics results in hypoalbuminemia and loss of colloidal oncotic pressure. External manifestations of hypoalbuminemia may include pitting edema, ascites and pleural effusion. In some cases, chylous effusions of the abdomen, subcutis or thoracic cavity may occur in conjunction with primary or congenital lymphangiectasia.[90-92] These findings probably represent multi-systemic lymphatic defects.

Physical examination findings may be unremarkable in dogs and cats with PLE. Patients with severe hypoproteinemia may present with dyspnea and abdominal enlargement due to accumulation of fluid in the thoracic or abdominal cavities, respectively. Pitting edema of the limbs may be noted. Body condition assessment should be performed because many animals are underweight at the time of presentation.

Laboratory and Other Clinical Information

A consistent pattern of laboratory results can be identified in many dogs with PLE. Panhypoproteinemia (i.e., hypoglobulinemia and hypoalbuminemia) and hypocholesterolemia are classic findings and reflect the loss of lymphatic constituents into the gut lumen. Occasionally, when PLE arises as a consequence of chronic inflammatory enteropathies, hypergammaglobulinemia will be present as well. In lymphangiectasia, lymphopenia is an important finding that can be used to differentiate this condition from other causes of PLE.[93] Other common laboratory findings include the anemia of chronic disease, a stress leukogram and hypocalcemia. Hypocalcemia may be present due to malabsorption of calcium and/or vitamin D

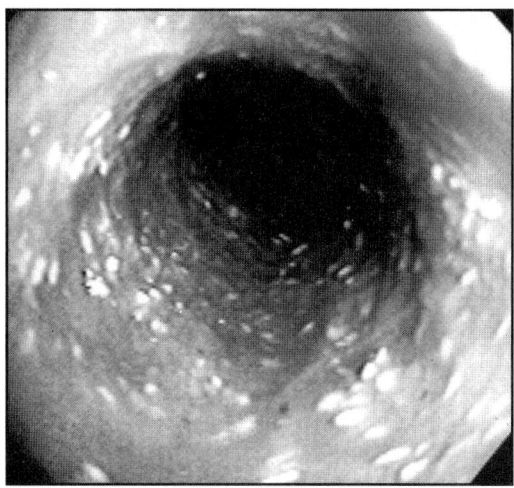

Figure 22-16. Endoscopic view of lymphangiectasia in the duodenum of a three-year-old Yorkshire terrier with diarrhea. Note the raised, white miliary structures along the mucosal surface. These structures are grossly dilated lacteals (intestinal lymphatics) filled with chylomicron-rich fluid. (Courtesy Dr. Chris Ludlow, Veterinary Internal Medicine Specialists of Kansas City, Kansas City, MO.)

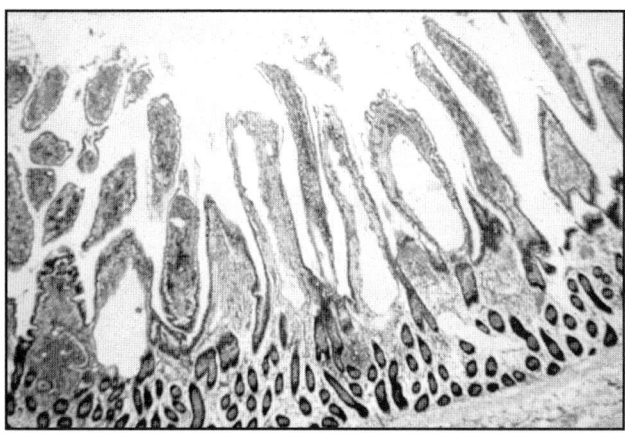

Figure 22-17. Photomicrograph of an intestinal biopsy specimen from a patient with lymphangiectasia. Note the distended intestinal lacteals (original magnification 100X). (Courtesy Dr. Lois Roth, Angell Memorial Animal Hospital, Boston, MA.)

or to a decrease in the protein-bound calcium fraction. Symptomatic hypocalcemia is rare; therefore, ionized calcium levels should be assessed before initiating intravenous calcium supplementation.

Typical intestinal function tests (i.e., D-xylose absorption tests, fecal fat determinations, breath hydrogen tests) yield inconsistent results and are of little value for assessing patients with lymphangiectasia and other types of PLE. Newer tools, such as measuring fecal α-1-protease inhibitor, may become useful diagnostic tools in the future.

Endoscopic examination of patients with suspected PLE or lymphangiectasia can be helpful. Mucosal granularity and glistening white patches, which indicate dilated lacteals may be noted (Figure 22-16). Endoscopy also provides a noninvasive route for obtaining intestinal biopsy specimens. A definitive diagnosis of lymphangiectasia and other types of PLE is made through histologic demonstration of characteristic mucosal lesions. In lymphangiectasia, these lesions include dilated, chyle-engorged lacteals and submu-

cosal lymphatics (Figure 22-17). Often, mucosal edema is present. In some cases, lipogranulomas may be identified adjacent to intestinal and mesenteric lymphatics. The pathogenesis of these lipogranulomas is unknown, but they are hypothesized to result from extravasation of chyle into perilymphatic tissue. The potential for surgical dehiscence should be considered before full-thickness intestinal biopsy specimens are collected from patients with PLE. Thus, samples obtained by endoscopy or per oral suction biopsy capsule are preferred. Full-thickness biopsy specimens should be obtained only if a diagnosis cannot be made based on results of endoscopic examination and evaluation of biopsy specimens collected by that procedure.

Risk Factors

Several breeds appear to be at risk for development of lymphangiectasia. Primary lymphatic lesions appear to be most common in Yorkshire terriers, golden retrievers and dachshunds. Lymphangiectasia secondary to severe mucosal inflammatory infiltrates is a common sequela to immunoproliferative enteropathy in basenjis.[45-47] PLE often occurs in conjunction with a protein-losing nephropathy in soft-coated wheaten terriers.[53]

Etiopathogenesis

Normally, plasma proteins are lost into the GI lumen daily. This loss is attributed to protein leakage at the time of villous tip extrusion. Typically, these plasma proteins are re-assimilated through digestive and absorptive processes. Certain GI disorders can disturb protein balance. Intestinal protein loss can be accelerated when the mucosal barrier is disrupted or disorders interfere with lymphatic drainage. Altered intestinal lymphatic drainage results in reflux of protein-rich lymph into the gut lumen. When the intestinal mucosa is damaged, excess protein can be lost through exudation or hemorrhage. Hypoproteinemia develops in either case after protein losses exceed compensatory synthesis.

Intestinal lymphangiectasia can arise as a primary disorder of the lymphatic system or secondary to chronic IBD. Severe inflammatory infiltrates and lipogranulomas can obstruct lymphatic drainage. Normally, the intestinal lymphatics transport absorbed fats from enterocytes to the venous circulation via the thoracic duct. Lacteals become distended with chyle if lymphaticovenous flow is impaired. Overdistended lacteals rupture and release intestinal lymph (containing protein, lymphocytes, fat and cholesterol) into the lumen. In some patients with primary lymphangiectasia, the lymphatic defects are not limited to the GI tract. In these animals, abnormal lymph flow may result in chylothorax, chylous abdominal effusions and subcutaneous chyle accumulations.[90-92]

Key Nutritional Factors

Key nutritional factors for patients with lymphangiectasia and other types of PLE are listed in Table 22-25 and discussed in detail below.

Fat

The key factor in dietary management of primary and secondary lymphangiectasia is controlling dietary fat. In most pet food products, long-chain triglycerides (LCT) compose approximately 90% of dietary fat. After digestion and lymphatic absorption, LCT provide a major stimulus for intestinal lymph flow. (See Chapter 2 for a discussion of fat digestion and absorption.) LCT are absorbed as chylomicrons and are transported from the mucosal epithelium via lacteals to the thoracic duct and into the systemic circulation. LCT absorption increases both lymph protein content and lymph flow two- to threefold for four to six hours postprandially.[94] The protein content of lymph tends to increase with dietary fat content.[94] Limiting fat intake (i.e., <10% DMB for dogs and <15% DMB for cats) minimizes lymph flow, reduces lacteal and lymphatic distention and minimizes protein loss.

Unfortunately, foods with dietary fat restriction have a lower caloric density. Many animals with PLE are cachectic. Animals fed low-fat foods must consume larger volumes of food to meet caloric needs. If the patient continues to lose weight, adding medium-chain triglycerides (MCT) may be necessary (Table 22-26). MCT are water-soluble, do not require micellarization for absorption, are absorbed directly across enterocytes into the portal vasculature and do not affect lymph flow. However, MCT oil does not contain the essential fatty acids required by dogs and cats, has been linked to hepatic lipidosis in cats,[95] may decrease diet palatability and unabsorbed portions cause diarrhea. (See sidebar "Medium-Chain Triglycerides.")

Protein

Foods fed to animals with PLE should contain high biologic value proteins to replace depleted tissue proteins. Protein content should be adequate to meet the needs of the patient and should be tailored to the species and age of the animal. In general, in excess of 25% DM protein is recommended for dogs and in excess of 35% DM protein for cats. Feeding high-protein or all-meat foods without other dietary alterations has not been successful.[96,97] If severe IBD is the underlying cause of PLE, the use of a low-fat, elimination food containing reduced numbers of highly digestible, novel protein sources should also be considered. (See the Inflammatory Bowel Disease section.)

Fiber

Foods containing high levels of insoluble fiber (>15%) are not routinely recommended for the dietary management of intestinal lymphangiectasia. However, there are cases in the veterinary literature in which a high-fiber (20% DM crude fiber) food was successfully fed because of the food's particularly low fat content.[93,98-100] Dietary fiber binds digestive enzymes and bile acids, decreases pancreatic secretion of lipase and reduces pancreatic enzyme activity. Insoluble fiber, through these mechanisms, decreases intraluminal fat digestion and micelle formation, which selectively inhibits long-chain fatty acid absorption.[99] Therefore, fiber may play a secondary role in reducing long-chain fatty acid absorption and decreasing lymphatic flow and subsequent lymph fluid losses.

However, moderate- and high-fiber (>15% DM crude fiber) foods may be detrimental in managing patients with lymphangiectasia. MCT may need to be added to foods with low energy density in order for some patients to maintain good body condition. The assumption that the "rough" texture of fiber might mechanically traumatize the intestinal mucosa has not been supported by clinical evidence.[68] Low-fat (<10% DMB), low-fiber (<5% crude fiber DMB) veterinary therapeutic foods are available and may be of value in the management of primary and acquired lymphangiectasia. (See Table 13-4.)

Digestibility

Feeding highly digestible (dry matter digestibility ≥90%) foods provides several advantages for managing lymphangiectasia in dogs and cats. Nutrients in low-residue foods are more completely absorbed in the proximal gut. Further, low-residue foods are associated with: 1) reduced osmotic diarrhea due to fat and carbohydrate malabsorption, 2) reduced production of intestinal gas due to carbohydrate malabsorption and 3) decreased antigen loads because smaller amounts of protein are absorbed intact.

Other Nutritional Factors

Vitamin and mineral supplementation is rarely necessary when feeding commercially prepared foods. Dogs and cats usually have body stores of vitamins A, D, E and K to last for several months. However, parenteral supplementation with fat-soluble vitamins may be needed if marked steatorrhea persists. Fat-soluble vitamin supplementation is warranted in cases of long-term fat malabsorption. It is simple and cost effective to administer 1 ml of a vitamin A, D and E product,[e] divided into two intramuscular sites, which should supply fat-soluble vitamins for approximately three months.

Patients with fat malabsorption fed foods containing higher levels of fat may have increased divalent cation losses (i.e., calcium, magnesium, zinc and copper) because of intraluminal saponification. Calcium supplementation is generally not needed because serum calcium levels usually increase in conjunction with serum albumin concentrations. However, intravenous calcium supplementation should be instituted if hypocalcemic tetany develops. Supplementation with other minerals should also be based on evidence of deficiency rather than given pro forma.

ASSESS THE FOOD(S) AND FEEDING METHOD

Levels of key nutritional factors in foods currently fed to patients with lymphangiectasia or PLE should be evaluated and compared with recommended levels (Table 22-25). Key nutritional factors include fat, protein, fiber and digestibility. Information from this aspect of assessment is essential for making any changes to foods currently pro-

Table 22-25. Key nutritional factors for patients with lymphangiectasia/protein-losing enteropathy.*

Factors	Recommended levels
Crude fiber	0.5 to 15% (see text)
Digestibility	≥87% for protein, fat and soluble carbohydrate
Fat	<10% for dogs
	<15% for cats
Protein	>25% for dogs
	>35% for cats

*Nutrients expressed on a dry matter basis.

Table 22-26. Summary of digestion and absorption of long-chain and medium-chain triglycerides.

Characteristics	Long-chain triglycerides	Medium-chain triglycerides
Digestion		
Hydrolysis by gastric lipase	Slow	Fast
Hydrolysis by pancreatic lipase	Fast	Very fast
Luminal transport		
Paracellular absorption	None	Some
Re-esterification and chylomicron formation	Yes	No
Requires bile acid micellarization	Yes	No
Transport route from gut	Lymphatics	Portal blood
Water solubility of essential fatty acids	Low	High

GI & PANCREAS

Medium-Chain Triglycerides

Triacylglycerides (TAG) are the most common form of fat found in foods and stored in body fat depots. TAG are primarily composed of long-chain fatty acids (i.e., 16 to 24 carbons long). Medium-chain triglycerides (MCT) are eight to 10 carbons long and are normally minor constituents of the diet. Increased levels of dietary MCT have theoretical advantages over long-chain triglycerides (LCT) for the treatment of some forms of gastrointestinal disease.

The most striking difference between MCT and LCT is the former are more water soluble than the latter. MCT are normally absorbed by mechanisms independent of those used by LCT. MCT are hydrolyzed more rapidly in the gut, absorbed at a faster rate, are not re-esterified to glycerol in enterocytes and are primarily transported from the gut via the portal vein directly to the liver. Some MCT also appear to be incorporated in chylomicrons and transported to some degree in the thoracic duct.

MCT may have a place in the nutritional management of patients with defects in intraluminal hydrolysis of fat (e.g., decreased pancreatic lipase, decreased bile salts), fat malabsorption or defective lymphatic transport of fat (lymphangiectasia). MCT are prepared commercially by hydrolysis and fractionation of coconut oil to create an oil (MCT Oil[a]) that contains approximately 67% caprylic acid (C8) and 23% capric acid (C10). The oil provides 8.3 kcal/g (34.7 kJ/g); one tablespoon (15 ml) weighs 14 g and provides 115 kcal (481 kJ). The oil can be included in homemade recipes or used to supplement commercial foods. Empiric recommendations are to provide 25 to 30% of calories as MCT.

MCT are also available as part of a nutritionally complete formula for human infants and children (Portagen[a]). This dry powder is composed of corn syrup solids, MCT oil, casein, sucrose, corn oil, soy lecithin, vitamins and minerals. Caloric distribution is 14% protein, 40% fat and 46% carbohydrate. The fat content is 95% MCT. The powder is mixed with water to produce a solution providing 1 kcal (4.2 kJ) per ml. Alternatively, the powder can be included in a home-made food or mixed with a commercial pet food.

Potential side effects of MCT in foods for patients with gastrointestinal disease include poor diet acceptance, vomiting and osmotic diarrhea. These products are expensive and are generally unpalatable for most patients.

ENDNOTE
a. Mead Johnson Nutritionals, Evansville, IN, USA.

BIBLIOGRAPHY
Bach A, Babayan V. Medium chain triglycerides: An update. American Journal of Clinical Nutrition 1982; 36: 950-962.

Delafosse B, Viale J, Pachiaudi C, et al. Long- and medium-chain triglycerides during parenteral nutrition in critically ill patients. American Journal of Physiology 1997; 272: E550-E555.

Johnson RC, Cotter R. Metabolism of medium-chain triglyceride lipid emulsion. Nutrition International 1986; 2: 150-158.

MacDonald ML, Anderson BC, Rogers QR, et al. Essential fatty acid requirements of cats: Pathology of essential fatty acid deficiency. American Journal of Veterinary Research 1984; 45: 1310-1317.

Odle J. New insights into the utilization of medium-chain triglycerides by the neonate: Observations from a piglet model. Journal of Nutrition 1997; 127: 1061-1067.

Sikkema DA, McLoughlin MA, Birchard SJ, et al. Effect of dietary fat on thoracic duct lymph volume and composition in dogs (abstract). Journal of Veterinary Internal Medicine 1993; 7: 119.

Swift L, Hill JO, Peters JC, et al. Medium chain fatty acids: Evidence for incorporation into chylomicron triglyceride in humans. American Journal of Clinical Nutrition 1990; 52: 834-836.

Ulshen MH, Lecce JG, Stiles AD, et al. Effects of nursing on growth and development of small bowel mucosa in newborn piglets. Pediatric Research 1991; 30: 337-341.

vided. Changing to a more appropriate food is indicated if key nutritional factors in the current food do not match recommended levels.

Because the feeding method is often altered for patients with lymphangiectasia and PLE, a thorough assessment should include verification of the feeding method currently being used. Items to consider include feeding frequency, amount fed, how the food is offered, access to other food and who feeds the animal. All of this information should have been gathered when the history of the animal was obtained.

Feeding Plan

The goal of therapy for patients with lymphangiectasia or PLE is to decrease the enteric loss of plasma protein. In some cases, dietary manipulation alone is adequate. In others, concurrent medical management is necessary.

SELECT A FOOD(S)

A food containing low fat, moderate fiber and high carbohydrate and protein should be fed for at least several weeks. In general, fat should be restricted to less than 10% DMB for dogs and less than 15% DMB for cats; however, some cases may require levels as low as 5 to 7% DM

fat. Commercially prepared foods formulated for weight control (Table 13-4) or home-prepared foods (Table 6-5) may be suitable. MCT oil (9 kcal/ml) should be added to the diet to increase caloric density if patients are unable to maintain optimal body weight and condition. This supplement; however, should be used with caution, introduced gradually and should not exceed 25% of the caloric requirement. Dietary protein levels should exceed 25% DMB for dogs and 35% DMB for cats. Some cases of PLE may require additional protein. Dogs may be fed a low-fat (<10% DMB) cat food that has a higher protein (>35% DMB) content and nutrient density than comparable dog food. Protein may also be added in the form of cooked egg whites. Egg whites contain protein of the highest biologic value and are a useful supplement for some animals with PLE.

DETERMINE A FEEDING METHOD

Initially, patients with lymphangiectasia or PLE should be fed multiple small meals per day as indicated by animal acceptance and tolerance for the food. Meal size can be increased again as tolerated by the patient after the clinical signs have been successfully managed for several weeks. In long-standing cases in which the patient is hospitalized and in poor body condition, the patient should be given a parenteral solution containing calories, protein and essential micronutrients. (See Chapter 12.) Calories can also be easily administered peripherally to dogs and cats using an isomolar 20% lipid solution piggybacked with standard fluid therapy at volumes sufficient to meet the patient's RER.[f]

Concurrent Therapy

Immunosuppressive therapy as described for IBD is indicated when lymphangiectasia or PLE occurs as a consequence of mucosal inflammatory infiltrates. In addition to quieting the underlying enteric lesions, corticosteroid therapy has the added advantage of controlling the inflammatory lesions of lymphangiectasia, lymphangitis and lipogranulomas.

When hypoalbuminemia is severe, plasma or dextran infusions may be necessary to restore colloidal oncotic pressure. In general, aggressive nutritional support will be more successful than plasma transfusions in restoring normoalbuminemia. Plasma transfusions may, however, benefit those patients with hypercoagulability resulting from panhypoproteinemia; plasma serves as a rich source of coagulation factors and antithrombin III.

Reassessment

Initially, patients with PLE should be reassessed weekly following discharge from the hospital. Each re-examination should include assessment of body weight and condition. Biweekly assessment of serum albumin and calcium concentrations and lymphocyte counts are useful. In addition, serial radiography can be used to assess the resolution of abdominal or thoracic effusion.

If the patient's condition is improving, dietary therapy should continue until the underlying enteropathy is resolved. Failing that, dietary manipulation should continue for the lifetime of the pet. Over time, it may be possible to increase dietary fat intake; however, this should be done cautiously and only for patients having difficulty maintaining ideal body weight or those manifesting evidence of essential fatty acid deficiency.

Short Bowel Syndrome

Clinical Importance

Short bowel syndrome is a malabsorptive state that often develops after massive resection of the small intestine.[101] Short bowel syndrome is an important clinical entity in people but is uncommon in domestic animals. This difference probably reflects the relative frequency at which predisposing conditions occur. Short bowel syndrome is an important potential complication of extensive intestinal resection.[102] A number of intestinal conditions may warrant the removal of large segments of the bowel, including intussusception, volvulus, infarction, neoplasia, entrapment, linear foreign bodies and fungal infections (pythiosis). To date, the clinical condition has been described only in dogs, but may be expected to occur in cats undergoing similar surgical procedures. The syndrome is characterized by malabsorption due to lack of gut surface area resulting in weight loss, diarrhea and malnutrition. Short bowel syndrome may occur whenever large segments of the small intestine (≥70%) are excised.[103]

Assessment

ASSESS THE ANIMAL

History and Physical Examination

Dogs with short bowel syndrome typically develop diarrhea one or more days after a large portion of the small bowel was resected. The diarrhea may be intermittent or persistent. Stools range from soft, cow-pie consistency to explosive, watery diarrhea. In long-standing cases, the patient may have weight loss, polyphagia and evidence of malnutrition.

Occasionally, animals present weeks to months after surgery with small bowel diarrhea, flatulence and borborygmus. Often, a delayed onset of clinical signs is associated with small intestinal bacterial overgrowth, which can develop as a sequela to resection of the ileocolic valve.

Physical examination findings are usually unremarkable. Body condition assessment may demonstrate poor body condition (BCS 1/5 or 2/5). Most animals are bright, alert and active with a good appetite.

Laboratory and Other Clinical Information

Hematologic and biochemical findings are variable, often reflecting the underlying condition that led to the bowel resection. Hypoproteinemia and hypoalbuminemia may be present in long-term cases. Mild, normocytic, normochromic nonregenerative anemia may be recognized as a consequence of chronic disease. Animals in which the ileum has been resected may have microcytic anemia consistent with that caused by cobalamin deficiency.

Radiographic findings are usually not helpful. Contrast films may demonstrate rapid transit of ingesta from the stomach to the colon. Contrast radiography can also be used to estimate the length of bowel remaining. In normal dogs, the small intestinal length is approximately four times the distance from the crown of the head to the rump. The percentage of small intestine remaining can be calculated by comparing the length of bowel remaining to this standard.[103]

Risk Factors

Puppies and young adult dogs are most likely to suffer from GI conditions that may require extensive small bowel resection. GI conditions that may require resection include intestinal intussusception, volvulus, pythiosis or histoplasmosis, neoplasia and foreign bodies. Larger breeds, especially the German shepherd dog, are more likely to suffer from intussusception and mesenteric volvulus.

Etiopathogenesis

A surgeon may be faced with the need to resect a large portion of the small intestine in the management of a number of obstructive small intestinal diseases. Generally, the potential for the syndrome exists any time 70% or more of the small bowel is resected.[103] Remarkably, dogs with as little as 30 to 40 cm and cats with 18 to 20 cm of residual small intestine may achieve nutritional autonomy.[102,103] Short bowel syndrome arises due to a lack of sufficient mucosal absorptive surface area. The reduced gut surface results in incomplete digestion and absorption of nutrients. Unabsorbed nutrients in the gut lumen lead to osmotic diarrhea. In addition, unabsorbed bile acids and fatty acids may result in secretory diarrhea in the large bowel.

Massive intestinal resection causes morphologic and functional adaptation in the remaining small bowel. Adaptation is stimulated by: 1) exposure to luminal nutri-

GI & PANCREAS

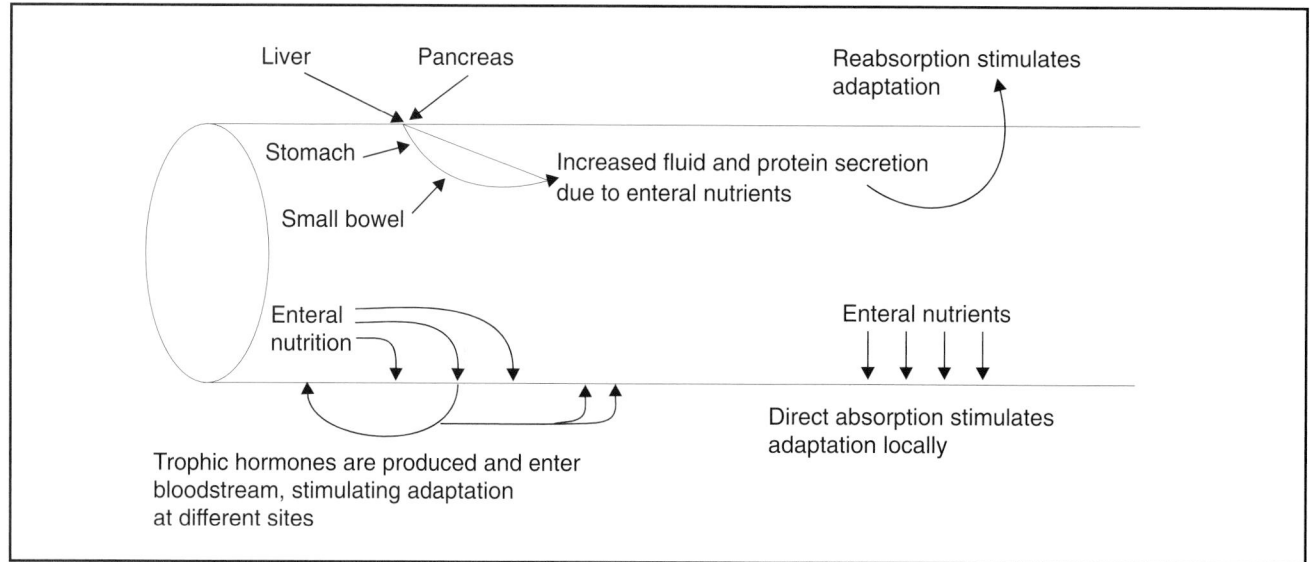

Figure 22-18. Schematic representation of the pathways by which enteral nutrients stimulate intestinal adaptation. (Adapted from Vanderhoff JA, Langnas AN. Short-bowel syndrome in children. Gastroenterology 1997; 113: 1767-1778.)

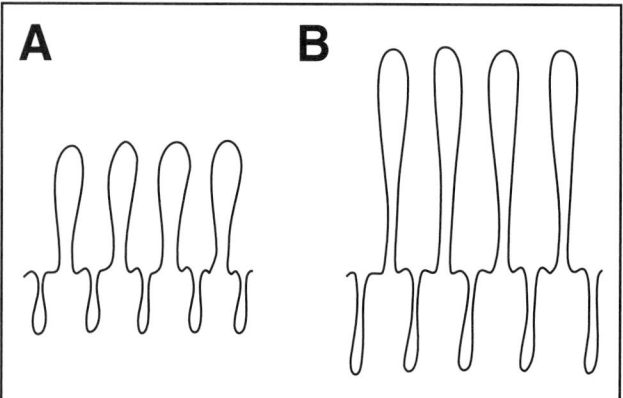

Figure 22-19. Diagrammatic comparison of normal (A) and adapted (B) gastrointestinal epithelium in patients with short-bowel syndrome. Note the increased villus length and crypt depth. Increased muscle mass may also be observed. (Adapted from Vanderhoff JA, Langnas AN. Short-bowel syndrome in children and adults. Gastroenterology 1997; 113: 1767-1778.)

ents, 2) endogenous GI secretions, 3) trophic effects of gut hormones, especially epidermal growth factor, enteroglucagon and gastrin, 4) intraluminal polyamines, 5) neural factors and 6) changes in blood flow to the remaining bowel (Figure 22-18).[104] During adaptation, the intestine dilates and hyperplasia occurs in both villi and crypts; however, the absorptive capacity of individual enterocytes does not change.[105,106] Therefore, the net increase in absorptive function in the remaining small bowel occurs because of increased total surface area.

In general, jejunal resections are tolerated better than removal of the ileum or the ileocolic valve. An intact ileum markedly enhances fluid, bile acid, cobalamin and electrolyte resorption. Loss of the ileocolic valve removes the physical barrier that separates the profuse bacterial flora of the colon from the relatively sparse population of the small bowel. Loss of the valve predisposes patients to development of small intestinal bacterial overgrowth.

Over time, the colon may begin to play an important role in maintaining nutritional homeostasis in patients with short bowel syndrome.[107,108] Following massive small bowel resection, colonic fermentation of malabsorbed carbohydrate may provide significant calories in the form of short-chain fatty acids. Short-chain fatty acids also promote mucosal hyperplasia. The mechanisms that lead to intestinal adaptation are not completely understood. However, a number of GI hormones including enteroglucagon, gastrin, cholecystokinin and secretin are involved as are other pancreatobiliary secretions. Intraluminal foodstuffs including protein, protein hydrolysates, fats and glutamine stimulate release of these substances. Thus, intestinal adaptation appears to rely on exposure of the remnant bowel to intraluminal nutrients.

Intestinal adaptation is marked by enterocyte hyperplasia and increases in bowel diameter, villous height, crypt depth and number of enterocytes per length of the villous/crypt unit (Figure 22-19). Ideally, these physical changes will increase the bowel's absorptive capacity. Mucosal changes begin to occur within one to two days and can result in a fourfold increase in mucosal surface area within 14 days, if intraluminal nutrients are provided.[109]

Key Nutritional Factors

Key nutritional factors for patients with short bowel syndrome are listed in Table 22-27 and discussed in more detail below.

Digestibility

Because this is a malassimilative condition, highly digestible foods (dry matter digestibility ≥90%) are recommended. The use of monomeric foods has been investigated in people with the syndrome; however, clinical evidence suggests that these foods are no more effective than polymeric foods.[110] In addition, use of monomeric foods has been associated with villous atrophy.[110,111] Polymeric foods are preferred because of their cost and palatability.

Energy and Fat

There are sound reasons for including fat in foods for patients with short bowel syndrome. Dogs and cats readily use most fats and oils of either animal or plant origin; therefore, fat should be included in the food for animals with short bowel syndrome up to the point of causing steatorrhea. Dietary fat levels of 10 to 15% DMB in dogs and 15 to 22% DMB in cats are often tolerated. Intraluminal fat is probably the most influential nutrient in stimulating small bowel adaptation. Fat exerts profound effects on enterocyte growth, villus morphology, mucosal enzyme activity and segmental absorptive functions.[112] Fat also slows gastric emptying of digesta, which may better match nutrient load and digestive capabilities in the small bowel.

Many dogs with a long-standing short bowel syndrome are underweight at the time of evaluation.[102,103] Therefore, energy-dense foods (>4.5 kcal/g [>18.8 kJ/g] DM) are recommended.

Replacing 50 to 75% of dietary fat with MCT improves nutritional status in human patients with short bowel syndrome.[113] (See sidebar "Medium-Chain Triglycerides.") Unfortunately, use of MCT in veterinary patients is limited due to cost, poor palatability and poor GI tolerance. For these reasons, it is uncommon for MCT to be incorporated in excess of 30% of calories in homemade foods and 10% of calories in commercial foods. Whether MCT in foods are beneficial at these levels is unknown.

Fiber

Insoluble fiber (10 to 15% DMB) has been successfully used in refeeding patients with short bowel syndrome and is thought to help modulate intestinal motility and better control fecal water. Maintaining intraluminal bulk stimulates the adaptive process through the release of GI trophic factors, including enteroglucagon, gastrin, cholecystokinin, secretin and other pancreatobiliary secretions.

Soluble fiber in foods may benefit animals with short bowel syndrome via modulation of intestinal transit rate, absorption of intestinal water and production of short-chain fatty acids, which stimulate mucosal hyperplasia. Gel-forming fibers (e.g., pectin, gums) may slow gastric emptying rates.[114-116] Fermentable fiber supplementation (e.g., pectin) increases gut mass and colonic villous length, resulting in increased capacity for water reabsorption.[117,118] Additionally, patients that have undergone ileal resection do not absorb bile acids well, which may cause secretory diarrhea. In such cases, dietary intake of moderately fermentable fibers (e.g., beet pulp or soy fiber) may bind bile salts. Some manufacturers add 1 to 5% DM soluble fiber to veterinary therapeutic foods formulated to manage GI disease.

Other Nutritional Factors

Fructooligosaccharides

Fructooligosaccharides (FOS) have been proposed for use in the management of dogs with small intestinal bacterial overgrowth and, therefore, may be useful in cases of short bowel syndrome in which the ileocolic valve has been resected. However, clinical utility of these ingredients remains unproven in dogs and cats.

Vitamins

Fat-soluble vitamins are malabsorbed in many cases of steatorrhea. Although commercial foods are supplemented with fat-soluble vitamins, fat-soluble vitamins may need to be administered intramuscularly until intestinal adaptation occurs.

If the distal ileum is absent, cobalamin deficiency will develop because this portion of the bowel is solely responsible for B_{12} absorption. In such cases, parenteral supple-

Table 22-27. Key nutritional factors for patients with short bowel syndrome.*

Factors	Recommended levels
Carbohydrate	Lactose free
Digestibility	≥87% for protein and ≥90% for fat and soluble carbohydrate
Energy	>4.5 kcal/g
	>18.8 kJ/g
Fat	10 to 15% for dogs
	15 to 22% for cats
Fiber	0.5 to 15% (see text)

*Nutrients expressed on a dry matter basis.

mentation of B_{12} is necessary. When short bowel syndrome is complicated by small intestinal bacterial overgrowth, bacterial usage of vitamin B_{12} may exacerbate cobalamin deficiency.

Glutamine

Glutamine is the preferred respiratory fuel for enterocytes[18,41] and enteral administration of 2% glutamine solutions may be beneficial to patients with short bowel syndrome.[119] Research in short-term (one-week) rat models has shown that adding glutamine to intravenous nutritional solutions reduces some aspects of disuse intestinal atrophy and enhances intestinal immune function.[120-122] Glutamine administered intravenously for six to seven days prevents decreased intestinal weight, DNA content, villus height,[123] and sucrase and lactase activities[124] in adult rats that were fed parenterally. However, administering glutamine in foods[125] and intravenous solutions[13,126] to research animals for more than one week has not been shown to improve intestinal morphology. Glutamine may be a conditionally essential amino acid only during early periods of physiologic stress to stimulate DNA synthesis and increase mucosal mass early in recovery.[127] For example, rats undergoing abdominal radiation and fed glutamine orally for the following eight days had significant increases in jejunal villous numbers and height and an increase in the number of mitoses per crypt. Non-irradiated control rats fed the same glutamine-enriched diet had no significant increase in mucosal cell activity.[128]

Soluble Carbohydrates

The soluble carbohydrate fraction of the selected food should be highly digestible (≥90%). Lactose-containing ingredients should be avoided because extensive small bowel resection results in loss of lactase and other brush border disaccharidases.

ASSESS THE FOOD(S) AND FEEDING METHOD

Levels of key nutritional factors should be evaluated in foods currently fed to patients with short bowel syndrome and compared with recommended levels (Table 22-27). Key nutritional factors include food digestibility, energy density and fat and fiber levels. Information from this aspect of assessment is essential for making any changes to foods currently provided. Changing to a more appropriate food is indicated if key nutritional factors in the current food do not match recommended levels.

Because the feeding method is often altered in patients with short bowel syndrome, a thorough assessment should include verification of the feeding method currently used. Items to consider include feeding frequency, amount fed, how the food is offered, access to other food, relationship of feeding to exercise and who feeds the animal. All of this information should have been gathered when the history of the animal was obtained. If the animal has a normal BCS (3/5), the amount of food previously fed (energy basis) was probably appropriate.

In contrast to feeding methods commonly used for healthy animals (i.e., once or twice daily), patients with short bowel syndrome usually require multiple smaller meals per day to improve digestibility and prevent intestinal overload. The amount of food may need to be increased to help animals regain or maintain ideal body condition.

Feeding Plan

The goals of medical and nutritional therapy for patients with short bowel syndrome are to provide adequate nutritional support during the period of intestinal adaptation and to stimulate adaptive changes that increase function in the remaining bowel segments. Diarrhea should be controlled as soon as possible because most pet owners will not tolerate persistent diarrhea. Changes required in the feeding management of short bowel syndrome are primarily determined by function of the remaining small intestine. Trophic factors such as growth hormone, glutamine and fiber stimulate intestinal hyperplasia.[129] The feeding plan is often used in conjunction with other medical therapy. Drugs commonly used in patients with short bowel syndrome include opiate antidiarrheal agents (e.g., loperamide, diphenoxylate), antibiotics (e.g., tetracycline, tylosin) and bile salt binding agents (e.g., cholestyramine).

SELECT A FOOD(S)

Parenteral nutritional support is often required initially to meet nutritional, fluid and electrolyte needs as patients with short bowel syndrome recover from surgery or to re-establish a positive nutritional intake after chronic malnutrition. Parenteral administration of nutrients can be used in conjunction with oral refeeding to meet the patient's requirements. Re-establishing normal intestinal function and stimulating adaptation should begin as soon as the patient tolerates oral food intake. Experimentally, intestinal adaptation did not occur in dogs with short bowel syndrome fed parenterally.[130] Intestinal adaptation depends on using the remnant bowel, and not "bowel rest."

Refeeding should begin with a highly digestible, low-residue food formulated for managing GI disease (Table 22-10). Such foods meet the RER of the patient in a reasonable volume of food and stimulate adaptation of remaining small bowel segments. Dry foods may be preferred because they may increase gastric retention time; it takes longer to lower the digesta osmolality of dry foods vs. moist foods.

Soluble or mixed fibers are also recommended to modulate intestinal transit and promote mucosal hyperplasia. Typically, products containing 1 to 5% DM crude fiber are well tolerated.

A liquid monomeric food containing glutamine and soluble fiber can be mixed with dry food during the first few days of recovery (Table 12-8). Such foods contain nutrients in readily absorbable forms and glutamine to fuel enterocyte hyperplasia.

DETERMINE A FEEDING METHOD

Multiple (i.e., six to eight) small meals per day are recommended during the period of intestinal adaptation. In some cases, parenteral nutritional support should be considered as an interim feeding method until the animal can meet its needs orally. Parenteral feeding should be considered if the patient continues to lose weight despite consumption of adequate calories. Parenteral infusion rates should be calculated to meet the patient's entire caloric needs. (See Chapter 12.) Total parenteral nutrition can be withdrawn gradually as intestinal function recovers and enteral feeding provides at least 70% of the patient's caloric needs. As mentioned above, intestinal adaptation did not occur in experimental dogs with short bowel syndrome when they were fed only parenterally.[130] Oral feedings or enteral infusions of glutamine-containing diets should continue throughout the parenteral feeding period to facilitate intestinal adaptation.

Reassessment

Weekly determination of body weight and condition and stool evaluations are useful tools for assessing dogs with short bowel syndrome. Medical remedies mentioned above should be considered if dietary therapy alone does not sufficiently improve stool quality and maintain body weight. Well-compensated patients should be evaluated immediately if a decline in body condition is noted. This presentation suggests concurrent GI disease or the onset of small intestinal bacterial overgrowth in dogs without an ileocolic valve.

The prognosis for recovery from short bowel syndrome is variable and cannot be based solely on the extent of resection.[103] The patient's preoperative condition, the functional integrity of the remnant bowel, degree of intestinal adaptation and the site of the resection are also important.[103] For example, secondary complications (i.e., small intestinal bacterial overgrowth and large bowel diarrhea due to bile acid overload) may be avoided if the ileocolic valve can be preserved. In cases of surgical excision of intestinal neoplasia, adjuvant cytotoxic chemotherapy may be detrimental to remaining mucosa. In general, intestinal adaptation occurs in most dogs within one to two months and diarrhea may resolve in that time.[131] However, adaptation may continue for years; thus, stool quality may improve with time. In the meantime, the veterinarian and owner must work closely together to ensure optimal postoperative care.

Small Intestinal Bacterial Overgrowth

Clinical Importance

Small intestinal bacterial overgrowth (SIBOG), a diarrheic disorder characterized by excessive numbers of small intestinal bacteria, has received much attention in recent years.[132-136] Although the incidence of SIBOG is unknown, some authors have suggested that it is present in as many as 50% of dogs with chronic small bowel diarrhea.[137]

Assessment

ASSESS THE ANIMAL

History and Physical Examination

Affected dogs usually present with a history of weight loss and intermittent small bowel diarrhea. Borborygmus and flatulence are also common complaints.

Physical examination findings are often unremarkable. Poor body condition (BCS 1/5 or 2/5) and unthriftiness may be present if the condition is long-standing.

Laboratory and Other Clinical Information

The gold standard for diagnosing SIBOG is quantitative aerobic and anaerobic culture of undiluted duodenal juice. Samples can be collected via endoscopy or direct needle aspiration at surgery.[135,138] In dogs and cats, the small intestine normally contains a relatively sparse bacterial flora compared with the densely populated oral cavity and large bowel. Historically, the accepted upper limit for small intestinal bacterial flora has been 10^5 colony forming units (CFU) per ml based on work done before 1984.[139] More recent studies have demonstrated that the small bowel of healthy dogs may contain bacteria in excess of 10^5 CFU/ml.[136,140,141] Normal cats also have small intestinal bacterial counts in excess of 10^5 CFU/ml.[138,142] These findings suggest that laboratories should establish their own control or reference ranges for duodenal juice using their sampling and microbiologic techniques. Further, quantitative microbiology is cumbersome, invasive and not readily available to practitioners. Therefore, a number of other diagnostic modalities have been explored.

Other tests useful in diagnosing SIBOG include serum folate and cobalamin concentrations, breath hydrogen measurements (with or without lactulose administration) and intestinal permeability tests. Determination of fasting serum folate and cobalamin concentrations is a rapid, noninvasive and simple method for evaluating dogs with suspected SIBOG. Folate and cobalamin analyses have been useful in an experimental model of SIBOG[143] and in naturally occurring cases.[133,144,145] However, these assays have low sensitivity and specificity.[62,133] Serum folate and cobalamin concentrations can be influenced by diet. An analytical survey of commercial foods performed in 1994 revealed a wide range of dietary folate levels.[140] Serum folate and cobalamin concentrations obtained from healthy dogs consuming foods containing high folate and cobalamin levels often exceed the upper limits of the reference ranges established for these vitamins.[140,145] The influence of food on folate and cobalamin concentrations is responsible in part for the poor sensitivity of these assays for the diagnosis of SIBOG.

Breath hydrogen and intestinal permeability tests are nonspecific tools useful for evaluating animals with suspected small intestinal disease. These tests are most commonly available at referral centers and veterinary teaching hospitals.

Response to therapy with antibiotics should not be overlooked as an effective diagnostic tool. A therapeutic trial may be particularly useful in situations when quantitative cultures are not possible due to lack of expertise, expense or anesthetic considerations.

Risk Factors

A number of risk factors have been identified for SIBOG. German shepherd dogs appear to be predisposed to this enteropathy[132,139] possibly because of IgA deficiency.[6,7,132] Exocrine pancreatic insufficiency is also a predisposing factor for SIBOG, and this condition can complicate management of exocrine pancreatic insufficiency.[146]

Investigators have hypothesized that kenneled dogs (especially beagles) may be more likely to have duodenal fluid bacterial counts in excess of 10^5 CFU/ml.[147,8] Kennel-housed beagles, German shepherd dogs, Yorkshire terriers and poodles have subsequently been found to have increased counts.[132,136,140] Quantitative counts in these apparently healthy dogs have ranged up to 10^8 CFU/ml. Potential causes for abnormal bacterial counts in kennel-housed dogs include environment (i.e., cleanliness), coprophagia and breed-specific characteristics (e.g., IgA deficiency).

Etiopathogenesis

SIBOG can develop any time normal host defenses are impaired. Loss of gastric acid secretion, normal intestinal peristalsis and interdigestive ("housekeeper") motility, the ileocolic valve or local IgA production can result in SIBOG. In people, intestinal stasis is the most common cause of SIBOG; however, this entity is far less common in dogs.

Key Nutritional Factors
Digestibility

Feeding highly digestible (dry matter digestibility ≥90%) foods provides several advantages for managing dogs with SIBOG. Nutrients from these low-residue foods are more completely absorbed in the proximal gut. Highly digestible foods are also associated with reduced osmotic diarrhea due to fat and carbohydrate malabsorption and reduced production of intestinal gas due to carbohydrate malabsorption. The ideal food for SIBOG patients is lactose free to avoid the complication of lactose intolerance due to loss of brush border disaccharidases.

Energy and Fat

Energy-dense foods are preferred for managing patients with chronic enteropathies. Calorie-dense products allow the clinician to provide smaller volumes of food at each meal, which minimizes GI stretch and secretions. Unfortunately, energy-dense foods are also high in fat. High-fat foods may contribute to osmotic diarrhea and GI protein losses, which complicate SIBOG. Therefore, it is often advantageous to initially provide a food with moderate energy density (3.5 to 4 kcal/g [14.6 to 16.7 kJ/g] DM) that contains moderate levels of fat (10 to 15% DMB for dogs and 15 to 22% DMB for cats). Higher fat and more energy-dense foods can be offered if the patient tolerates these nutrient levels.

Other Nutritional Factors

FOS have been proposed for use in managing dogs with SIBOG. These nondigestible sugars are thought to promote beneficial bacteria at the expense of bacterial pathogens.[148,149] (See sidebar "Oligosaccharides.") When FOS was fed (1.0% as fed) to a group of German shepherd dogs with asymptomatic SIBOG, total bacterial counts were reduced within the duodenum.[150] However, this reduction was smaller than the change in bacterial numbers demonstrated within the same dogs at different sampling intervals. Therefore, the clinical utility of FOS and other oligosaccharides in the treatment of SIBOG remains unproven.

ASSESS THE FOOD(S) AND FEEDING METHOD

Levels of key nutritional factors should be evaluated in foods currently fed to patients with SIBOG and compared

GI & PANCREAS

Table 22-28. Key nutritional factors for patients with small intestinal bacterial overgrowth.*

Factors	Recommended levels
Digestibility	≥90%
Fat	10 to 15% for dogs
	15 to 22% for cats
Energy	3.5 to 4.0 kcal/g
	14.6 to 16.7 kJ/g

*Nutrients expressed on a dry matter basis.

Oligosaccharides

Oligosaccharides are naturally-occurring carbohydrates found in some fruits, vegetables and grains. Structurally, oligosaccharides are sugar polymers that contain up to six sugars. Oligosaccharides containing fructose are termed fructooligosaccharides (FOS). Those that contain mannose are termed mannanoligosaccharides or MOS and so on. Typically found in low concentrations in foods, these complex carbohydrates can also be manufactured for commercial purposes using microbial or plant-derived enzymatic digestion of sugars.

Oligosaccharides resist digestion by mammalian digestive enzymes. Thus, they are classified as fibers or resistant starches. Because they resist digestion, oligosaccharides enter the large bowel in an intact form where they are readily fermented by certain colonic bacteria such as *Bifidobacterium* and *Bacteroides* spp. Based on in vitro studies, the fermentability of oligosaccharides is intermediate between that of cellulose and lactulose. Other organisms such as lactobacilli, eubacteria and clostridia do not readily use oligosaccharides. This preferential fermentation pattern suggests dietary supplementation with oligosaccharides may be of benefit in fostering beneficial gut bacteria.

The addition of oligosaccharides to pet foods has been studied with variable results. The inclusion of FOS at 0.75% (dry matter basis) did not influence the duodenal flora of healthy cats quantitatively or qualitatively. However, the fecal flora of cats was affected, resulting in increased numbers of lactobacilli and reduced numbers of *Escherichia coli*. Similar findings have been reported to occur in healthy cats consuming another oligosaccharide (i.e., lactosucrose). The clinical significance of these findings is unknown.

Investigators studied FOS supplementation in a group of healthy German shepherd dogs thought to have small intestinal bacterial overgrowth. In these dogs, the inclusion of FOS at 1.0% (as fed) was associated with changes in duodenal bacterial flora. However these changes were of less magnitude than normal dog variability for these parameters. Again, the clinical significance of these findings is unknown.

In some species, MOS derived from yeast cell walls binds to intestinal pathogens such as *Salmonella* spp. MOS inhibits attachment of salmonella to the intestinal mucosa by preferentially binding lectins. This effect has not been demonstrated to occur in companion animals to date.

BIBLIOGRAPHY

Sparkes AH, Papasouliotis K, Sunvold G, et al. Bacterial flora in the duodenum of healthy cats and effect of dietary supplementation with fructooligosaccharides. American Journal of Veterinary Research 1998; 59: 431-435.

Sparkes AH, Papasouliotis K, Sunvold G, et al. Effect of dietary supplementation with fructooligosaccharides on fecal flora of healthy cats. American Journal of Veterinary Research 1998; 59: 436-440.

Terada A, Hara H, Kato S, et al. Effect of lactosucrose (4G-B-D-galactosucrose) on faecal flora and faecal putrefactive products of cats. Journal of Veterinary Medical Science 1993; 55: 291-295.

Willard MD, Simpson RB, Delles EK, et al. Effects of dietary supplementation of fructooligosaccharides on small intestinal bacterial overgrowth in dogs. American Journal of Veterinary Research 1994; 55: 654-659.

with recommended levels (Table 22-28). Key nutritional factors include food digestibility, energy density and fat content. Information from this aspect of assessment is essential for making any changes to foods currently provided. Changing to a more appropriate food is indicated if key nutritional factors in the current food do not match recommended levels.

Because the feeding method is often altered in patients with SIBOG, a thorough assessment should include verification of the feeding method currently being used. Items to consider include feeding frequency, amount fed, how the food is offered, access to other food and who feeds the animal. All of this information should have been gathered when the history of the animal was obtained. If the animal has a normal BCS (3/5), the amount of food previously fed was probably appropriate.

Feeding Plan

The feeding plan is often used in conjunction with other medical therapy. Underlying causes of SIBOG (e.g., partial intestinal obstruction) should be identified and treated before specific medical and dietary therapy is instituted. Antibiotic therapy is usually required for effective management of SIBOG. Antibiotic selection should be based on culture and antimicrobial sensitivity testing of specific pathogens identified in duodenal aspirates. Tetracycline or tylosin should be used if no pathogen is isolated.

SELECT A FOOD(S)

Commercial veterinary therapeutic foods that are highly digestible and designed for patients with GI disease are recommended for patients with SIBOG (Table 22-10). Many of these foods contain moderate levels of dietary fat and energy density. Young growing dogs with SIBOG should receive a food that meets the optimal levels of key nutritional factors for growth. (See Chapter 9.)

DETERMINE A FEEDING METHOD

Ideally, patients with SIBOG should be fed multiple small meals per day as indicated by animal acceptance and tolerance for the food. Meal size can be increased as tolerated by the patient after clinical signs have been successfully managed for several weeks.

Reassessment

Owners of affected animals should be queried regarding frequency of diarrhea, borborygmi and flatus. Body weight and condition should be evaluated frequently to assess resolution of malabsorption. In general, SIBOG can be managed effectively with a combination of medical (e.g., antibiotic) and nutritional therapy.

LARGE INTESTINAL DISORDERS
Colitis
Clinical Importance

Colitis is a common disorder of dogs and cats. A number of infectious, toxic, inflammatory and dietary factors can trigger the sudden onset of large bowel diarrhea (Tables 22-29 and 22-30). This section addresses the diagnosis and management of veterinary patients with acute and chronic colitis.

Currently, IBD is thought to be the most common cause of chronic large bowel diarrhea in dogs and cats.[1] The generic term, IBD, encompasses lymphoplasmacytic enterocolitis, lymphocytic enterocolitis, eosinophilic enterocolitis, segmental granulomatous enterocolitis, suppurative enterocolitis and histiocytic colitis. Specific types are categorized based on the type of inflammatory cells found in the lamina propria. Most authors think that the lymphoplasmacytic form occurs most commonly.[2] The severity of the condition varies from relatively mild clinical signs to life-threatening PLE. The boxer breed may present with an especially severe variant termed histiocytic or ulcerative colitis.[3]

Assessment

ASSESS THE ANIMAL

History and Physical Examination

The most common clinical sign in dogs and cats with acute or chronic colitis is large bowel diarrhea characterized by tenesmus, dyschezia, urgency and passage of mucus and blood (Table 22-17). Clinical signs may be intermittent or persistent. The clinical signs tend to increase in frequency and intensity as colitis progresses. The presence of systemic signs is also variable. Some animals present with a history of depression, malaise and inappetence; however, most are alert and active when examined. Hemorrhagic stools indicate a potentially life-threatening disorder (Table 22-18).

When evaluating colitis cases, careful attention should be paid to the dietary history. Diet-induced diarrhea is common; a recent change to a moist high-fat or meat-based food may be the source of the animal's diarrhea.[a,b] Often, it is possible to elicit a history of dietary indiscretion, feeding table foods over a holiday or access to garbage, carrion or abrasive materials.

Other husbandry issues are also important (e.g., Records of anthelmintic treatments should be scrutinized.). The likelihood that an infectious organism is involved is increased if other animals or people in the household are similarly affected.

Dogs and cats with acute colitis may be depressed and dehydrated and may exhibit pain on abdominal palpation. Patients should be carefully evaluated for evidence of septic shock. Those animals with systemic signs of illness (i.e., fever and congested mucous membranes) in addition to GI signs should be treated more aggressively.

Physical examination findings vary in dogs and cats with chronic colitis. Many animals have no abnormalities. Rarely, dogs and cats with colitis present with weight loss and poor body condition. In such cases, serious infiltrative colonic disorders (e.g., histoplasmosis, neoplasia or histiocytic colitis) should be suspected.

On occasion, thickened loops of bowel may be detected by abdominal palpation, especially in cats. Segmental thickening of bowel is consistent with eosinophilic gastroenterocolitis in cats and granulomatous enteritis in dogs.[4] This finding should also be distinguished from intussusceptions, foreign bodies, histoplasmosis and neoplastic lesions.

Laboratory and Other Clinical Information

Because there are many potential causes of acute colitis, achieving a definitive diagnosis can be difficult. In acute cases, it is most important to determine whether the animal's condition is self-limiting or potentially life-threatening. This determination, based on historical and physical findings is critical. Some factors suggest a potentially life-threatening condition (Table 22-18). Cases of a serious nature should be pursued aggressively with diagnostics (i.e., hematology, serum biochemistry profiles, urinalyses and fecal examinations for parasites and other infectious pathogens). Self-limiting cases are usually approached more conservatively. Diagnostics are often limited to assessing hydration status (i.e., packed cell volume, total protein concentration and body weight) and thorough examination of feces for parasites and bacterial pathogens (e.g., spores of *Clostridium* spp).

Laboratory findings in patients with chronic colitis are often nonspecific. Hematologic findings are variable and may include blood loss anemia, anemia of chronic disease

Table 22-29. Potential causes of acute large bowel diarrhea in dogs and cats.

Dietary
Dietary indiscretion
Foreign bodies
Garbage toxicity
Drugs
Cyclophosphamide
Doxorubicin
Infectious agents
Bacteria
   Campylobacter spp
   Clostridium spp
   Salmonella spp
Parasites
   Giardia lamblia
   Trichuris vulpis
Viruses
   Panleukopenia
   Parvovirus
Miscellaneous
Hemorrhagic gastroenteritis

Table 22-30. Potential causes of chronic large bowel diarrhea in dogs and cats.

Infectious causes
Parasitic
   Giardia lamblia
   Trichuris vulpis
Bacteria
   Campylobacter spp
   Salmonella spp
Viral
   Feline immunodeficiency virus
   Feline leukemia virus
Fungal
   Histoplasmosis
   Pythiosis
Inflammatory bowel disease
Eosinophilic colitis
Lymphocytic colitis
Lymphoplasmacytic colitis
Suppurative colitis
Dietary
Adverse reactions to food
   Food allergy (hypersensitivity)
   Food intolerance
Neoplasia
Adenocarcinoma
Adenoma/polyps
Lymphosarcoma
Mast cell tumor

GI & PANCREAS

and/or eosinophilia. Serum biochemistry profiles and urinalyses should be performed on samples from patients with chronic diarrhea to assess the systemic affect of the GI disorder and to rule out concurrent disease. Electrolyte abnormalities, including hypokalemia, may be identified. Hypoproteinemia and hypoalbuminemia may be recognized in severe cases of PLE. Dehydrated patients may have prerenal azotemia.

Fecal examinations are very important in the evaluation of patients with chronic large bowel diarrhea. Multiple fecal parasite examinations using concentration techniques are necessary to rule out parasitism.

Endoscopic abnormalities in chronic colitis may include mucosal granularity, hyperemia, increased friability and inability to visualize colonic submucosal blood vessels.[5] Multiple biopsy specimens should be collected from multiple bowel segments. Even if these areas appear normal endoscopically, histologic changes may still be present.[5-7] The definitive diagnosis of IBD is based on histopathologic examination of endoscopic or surgical biopsy specimens.[8]

Risk Factors

The risk factors for acute colitis include age, breed, immune status and environment. Young animals are more susceptible to a variety of infectious pathogens including parasites, viruses and bacteria. Likewise, immunocompromised animals are at risk for contracting viral and bacterial enteritides. Hospitalization and administration of cancer chemotherapeutic drugs are associated with nosocomial infection with *Clostridium*[9] and *Campylobacter*[10] species.

Environment also plays an important role in exposure to pathogens. Dogs and cats kept in unsanitary or overcrowded conditions are much more likely to develop infectious enteropathies. In addition, animals kept in poorly controlled environments have a higher risk for exposure to high-fat table foods, garbage and toxins. Dogs in particular eat indiscriminately. Consumption of rotten garbage, decomposing carrion and abrasive materials (e.g., hair, bones, rocks, plastic, aluminum foil) can result in severe colitis. Poor husbandry practices including inadequate parasite control and overcrowding also put pets at risk for acute colitis.

Table 22-31. Breed-associated colonic disorders.

Disorders	Breeds
Flatulence	Brachycephalic dogs and cats
Hemorrhagic gastroenteritis	Dachshund, miniature schnauzer, toy poodle
Irritable bowel syndrome	Working breeds, toy breeds
Ulcerative colitis	Boxer, French bulldog

Table 22-32. Key nutritional factors for patients with acute and chronic colitis.*

Factors	Recommended levels
Chloride	0.5 to 1.3%
Digestibility	≥87% for protein and ≥90% for fat and soluble carbohydrate
Fat	10 to 15% for dogs
	12 to 22% for cats
Fiber	0.5 to 15%
Potassium	0.8 to 1.1%
Protein	Consider elimination foods
Sodium	0.35 to 0.50%

*Nutrients expressed on a dry matter basis.

There does not appear to be an age or gender predisposition for any of the forms of IBD. Certain breeds appear to be at risk for specific colonic disorders (Table 22-31). For example, the boxer breed is linked to histiocytic colitis.[11] Other breeds at risk for chronic inflammatory colonopathies include German shepherd dogs and French bulldogs.[1]

Etiopathogenesis

The four mechanisms of diarrhea were described earlier. In acute colitis, diarrhea may occur as a result of altered gut permeability or osmotic mechanisms. In addition, many of the bacterial pathogens elaborate enterotoxins that serve as potent secretogogues.

Despite intensive study by veterinary and medical researchers, the pathophysiology of IBD is not completely understood.[12,13] See the previous section about IBD for a more complete discussion.

Histiocytic colitis, also termed ulcerative or boxer colitis, is characterized by infiltration of the lamina propria with PAS-positive histiocytes. Some authors have suggested that the presence of these macrophages indicates an infectious etiology. However, to date no organisms have been consistently identified in tissues from affected animals.[3]

Key Nutritional Factors

Key nutritional factors for acute and chronic colitis are listed in Table 22-32 and discussed in more detail below.

Water

Water is the most important nutrient in patients with acute large bowel diarrhea because of the potential for life-threatening dehydration due to excessive fluid losses and inability of the patient to replace those losses. Moderate to severe dehydration should be corrected with appropriate parenteral fluid therapy rather than using the oral route.

Minerals

Potassium depletion is a predictable consequence of severe and chronic enteric diseases because the potassium concentration of intestinal secretions is high. Hypokalemia in association with colitis will be particularly profound if losses are not matched by sufficient dietary intake of potassium.

Electrolyte disorders should be corrected initially with appropriate parenteral fluid and electrolyte therapy. Foods for patients with acute gastroenteritis should contain levels of sodium, chloride and potassium above the minimum allowances for normal dogs and cats. Recommended levels of these nutrients are 0.35 to 0.50% DM sodium, 0.50 to 1.3% DM chloride and 0.80 to 1.1% DM potassium.

Fat

Compared with the processes involved with other macronutrients, fat digestion and absorption are relatively complex and may be disrupted in patients with GI disease. The action of bacterial flora on unabsorbed fats in the colon resulting in hydroxy fatty acid production is an important cause of large bowel diarrhea. Thus, foods for patients with colitis and many other GI diseases often contain low to moderate amounts of fat (i.e., 10 to 15% DMB for dogs and 15 to 22% DMB for cats). However, dogs and cats digest fat very efficiently and the process is rarely disrupted except in malassimilative disorders. Therefore, colitis patients can be fed foods containing higher concentrations of fat when greater caloric density is required.

Protein

Protein should be provided at levels sufficient for the appropriate lifestage of colitis patients unless a protein losing enteropathy is present. High biologic value, highly digestible (≥87%) protein sources are preferred.

Some authors recommend the use of elimination foods because of the suspected role of dietary antigens in the pathogenesis of chronic colitis.[14-16] In some cases, elimination foods may be used successfully without pharmacologic intervention. Mild to moderate lymphoplasmacytic and eosinophilic colitis are the forms most likely to respond to dietary management.[15,17] Chapter 14 discusses elimination foods in more detail. The suspected pathogenesis of IBD involves an increase in gut permeability; therefore, the use of "sacrificial" dietary antigens has been suggested in the treatment of IBD.[1] (See sidebar "Sacrificial Proteins in Inflammatory Bowel Disease.")

Digestibility

Feeding highly digestible (dry matter digestibility ≥90%) foods provides several advantages for managing dogs and cats with long-standing inflammatory colitis. Nutrients from low-residue foods are more completely absorbed from the proximal gut. Low-residue foods are associated with: 1) reduced osmotic diarrhea due to fat and carbohydrate malabsorption, 2) reduced production of intestinal gas due to carbohydrate malabsorption and 3) decreased antigen loads because smaller amounts of protein are absorbed intact.

Fiber

Dietary fiber predominantly affects the large bowel of dogs and cats. Beneficial effects of dietary fiber include: 1) normalizing colonic motility and transit time, 2) buffering toxins in the GI lumen, 3) binding or holding excess water, 4) supporting growth of normal GI microflora, 5) providing fuel for colonocytes and 6) altering viscosity of GI luminal contents.

Various types and levels of dietary fiber have been advocated for use in patients with colitis. Some veterinarians recommend very low-fiber foods (<1% DM crude fiber) to enhance dry matter digestibility and reduce quantities of ingesta presented to the colon. One of the authors (DJD) recommends small amounts (1 to 5% DM crude fiber) of a mixed (i.e., soluble/insoluble) fiber type in conjunction with a highly digestible food. Other authors (RLR) have had success using moderate levels (10 to 15% DM crude fiber) to high levels[18] of insoluble fiber. All three strategies have been used successfully in managing patients with colitis.

Some authors have suggested that feeding insoluble or slowly fermentable fibers is detrimental to the management of colonopathies; these suggestions are based on the results of a small, uncontrolled feeding trial comparing cellulose-containing foods with foods containing beet pulp.[19] However, larger, controlled trials incorporating pre-study histopathology and electron microscopic examination of tissues have not identified any negative effects of slowly fermentable fiber on the colon.[20,21,c] In fact, many clinicians select foods enhanced with insoluble fiber as their first food option in the management of acute and chronic colitis.[22,23,d]

Feeding soluble or mixed fiber sources in small quantities to human patients with chronic inflammatory colitis has been advocated.[12] In fact, short-chain fatty acid and butyrate enemas induce clinical improvement in patients with ulcerative colitis.[24,25] Several substrates including beet pulp, soy fiber, inulin and FOS have been demonstrated by in vitro fermentation to produce volatile fatty acids that

may be beneficial in inflammatory colonopathies.[26-29] Manufacturers of commercial products usually incorporate these fibers at 1 to 5% DMB.

Other Nutritional Factors

Acid Load

Acidemia is common in patients with acute large bowel diarrhea because fluid secreted in the caudal small intestine and large intestine contains bicarbonate concentrations higher than those in plasma and sodium in excess of chloride ions. Hypovolemia (i.e., severe dehydration) compounds the acidosis in some patients. Severe acid-base disorders are best corrected with appropriate parenteral fluid therapy. Foods for patients with colitis should normally produce an alkaline urinary pH. These foods preferably contain buffering salts such as potassium gluconate and calcium carbonate.

N-3 Fatty Acids

N-3 fatty acids derived from fish oil or other sources may have a beneficial effect in controlling mucosal inflammation in patients with chronic inflammatory colitis. There is some clinical evidence that dietary n-3 fatty acid supplementation may modulate the generation and biologic activity of inflammatory mediators. See Chapter 26 and the earlier section about IBD for additional information.

Vitamins

Folic acid supplementation is recommended for patients receiving long-term sulfasalazine therapy.[30]

ASSESS THE FOOD(S) AND FEEDING METHOD

Levels of key nutritional factors in foods currently fed to patients with colitis should be evaluated and compared with recommended levels (Table 22-32). Information from this aspect of assessment is essential for making any changes to foods currently provided. Changing to a more appropriate food is indicated if key nutritional factors in the current food do not match recommended levels.

A thorough assessment should include verification of the feeding method currently being used. Items to consider include feeding frequency, amount fed, how the food is offered, access to other food and who feeds the animal. All of this information should have been gathered when the history of the animal was obtained. In cases in which colitis is caused by exposure to garbage or inappropriate amounts or types of foods, avoiding foods other than the pet's regular food is recommended and will often prevent further occurrences. If the animal has a normal BCS (3/5), the amount of food previously fed (energy basis) was probably appropriate.

Feeding Plan

Initially, the objectives for managing acute colitis should be to correct dehydration and electrolyte, glucose and acid-base imbalances, if present. Medical therapy may include antibiotics, anthelmintics or motility modifying agents (e.g., loperamide).

The dietary goal is to provide a food that meets the patient's nutrient requirements and allows normalization of colonic motility and function, and fecal water balance. In most cases of acute large bowel diarrhea, initial fasting for 24 to 48 hours, with access to water, either reduces or resolves the diarrhea by simply removing the effects of unabsorbed food and offending agents from the colon.

GI & PANCREAS

Often, the patient's previous food can be gradually reintroduced over several days.

In chronic colitis, dietary intervention should be aimed at controlling clinical signs while providing adequate nutrients to meet requirements and compensate for ongoing losses through the GI tract. Optimal management of some dogs and cats with chronic colitis may require only dietary manipulation. In other cases, dietary therapy is better used in concert with pharmacologic agents. Antibiotics (e.g., metronidazole, tylosin), anthelmintics, antiinflammatory agents (e.g., sulfasalazine) and immunosuppressive agents (e.g., corticosteroids, azathioprine, cyclophosphamide) are often used to manage chronic colitis. Lifelong dietary therapy is often required to control clinical signs in long-standing colitis cases.

SELECT A FOOD(S)

Withholding food for one to two days and then reintroducing a homemade or commercial veterinary therapeutic GI-type or fiber-enhanced food is often palliative in managing acute colitis. After feeding the highly digestible or fiber-enhanced food for another three to four days, the pet's regular food may be reintroduced over another three-day period. Further work-up is recommended if colitis recurs when the regular food is reintroduced.

Three types of food can be used to manage chronic colitis and they may be attempted in any order: 1) highly digestible, low-residue foods formulated for GI disease, 2) fiber-enhanced foods and 3) elimination foods. There is no physical examination finding, laboratory test or historical fact to predict which method will be successful in any one patient. Dietary trials are often needed to determine which food type works best for individual patients.

In chronic colitis, one option is to feed a highly digestible, low-residue food with moderate levels of fat and minerals. A variety of low-residue commercial veterinary therapeutic foods are available (Table 22-10); alternatively, homemade foods can be prepared (Table 6-8). Foods for puppies and kittens should also meet the nutritional requirements for growth.

Another approach in chronic colitis is to increase dietary fiber content to normalize intestinal motility, water balance and microflora. Fiber has several physiologic characteristics that aid in managing large bowel diarrhea. Moderate levels of dietary fiber (10 to 15% DMB) add nondigestible bulk that buffers toxins, holds excess water and, perhaps more important, provides intraluminal stimuli to re-establish the coordinated actions of hormones, neurons, smooth muscles, enzyme delivery, digestion and absorption. Fiber normalizes transit time through the large bowel. Table 22-22 lists selected fiber-enhanced commercial foods.

A third option in chronic colitis is to use an elimination food with a limited number of highly digestible, novel protein sources. Commercial veterinary therapeutic foods (Table 14-5) and homemade foods that contain novel protein sources are often formulated from lamb, rabbit, venison, duck or fish and a highly digestible or unusual carbohydrate source. All other possible dietary sources of protein and carbohydrate should be eliminated including treats, snacks, table foods, vitamin-mineral supplements and chewable/flavored medications.

DETERMINE A FEEDING METHOD

The feeding method for patients with acute colitis begins by withholding all oral intake of food for 24 to 48 hours. After this period, animals should be offered small amounts of food several times (i.e., six to eight times) a day. If the pet tolerates food without a recurrence of diarrhea, the amount fed can be increased over three to four days until the animal is receiving its estimated DER in two to three meals per day.

Initially, chronic colitis patients should be fed multiple small meals per day as indicated by animal acceptance and tolerance for the food. Meal size can be increased and meal frequency can be decreased as tolerated by the patient after clinical signs have been successfully managed for several weeks.

Reassessment

The prognosis for recovery in most cases of acute colitis is good. Bouts of acute colitis often resolve within two to four days with conservative medical and nutritional management. Body weight should be recorded daily until recovery is complete. Changes in body weight from day to day usually reflect changes in hydration status rather than loss or gain of lean or adipose tissue. Further diagnostic testing is warranted if vomiting or severe diarrhea persists.

Weekly recordings of body weight and condition and stool evaluations are useful in assessing patients with chronic colitis. Regaining or maintaining optimal body weight and condition, normal activity level, a positive attitude and absence of clinical signs are measures of successful dietary/medical management. The feeding method and amount fed can be adjusted as needed to maintain body weight and condition. Additional medical therapies should be considered if dietary therapy alone fails to improve stool quality and maintain body weight.

Dogs and cats presenting with multiple or recurrent episodes of large bowel diarrhea require further diagnostic work-up and, most probably, a combination of dietary and medical therapies; however, parasitic causes should be ruled out or treated empirically before pursuing further diagnostics.

Irritable Bowel Syndrome in Dogs

Clinical Importance

Irritable bowel syndrome (IBS) is a poorly defined functional bowel disorder of people and animals believed to be caused by GI dysmotility. IBS, also called spastic colitis or nervous colon, is one of the most common GI complaints in human medicine with random population surveys indicating 15 to 20% of adults are affected.[31,32] This disorder is thought to occur far less commonly in pets; however, it has been reported to account for 5 to 17% of large bowel disorders in dogs.[33,34] IBS has not been recognized in cats.

Assessment

ASSESS THE ANIMAL

History and Physical Examination

Dogs with IBS have chronic, intermittent bouts of diarrhea that are predominantly large bowel in character. Frequent, small-volume, fluid stools containing mucus are reported. Occasionally, explosive bouts of diarrhea and flatus may occur, often in association with abdominal pain. Dyschezia, tenesmus and, rarely, hematochezia may be seen. Some dogs have abdominal pain that is relieved by eating, eructation or defecation. Borborygmus, belching and flatus are frequent complaints in IBS. Typically, signs are variable and may change from bout to bout.

In many cases, GI signs can be linked to identifiable stressors. A thorough history may elicit such stress-causing variables as showing, work, owner anxiety, boarding in a kennel and changes in the home environment (e.g., new spouse, child, pet, house or apartment).

Generally, dogs with IBS are in good physical condition and do not exhibit the weight loss or poor body condition often associated with organic GI disorders. Affected dogs may exhibit discomfort during abdominal palpation if examined during an acute episode of GI distress. Rectal examination may reveal mucoid stools.

Laboratory and Other Clinical Information

Results of routine laboratory tests are usually within normal limits. IBS was previously considered a diagnosis of exclusion. Recently, a consistent set of diagnostic criteria has been established for people based on numerous epidemiologic and pathophysiologic investigations (Table 22-33).[35] Unfortunately, clinical criteria have not been standardized in dogs. At this time, the diagnosis of IBS is applied to those dogs with the clinical signs and history described above in which other, more common organic causes have been ruled out. Radiography and colonoscopy are rarely useful in the diagnosis of IBS; findings are usually within normal limits.

Risk Factors

As discussed above, psychological and physical stress appear to play an important role in IBS. Dogs with nervous, excitable temperaments and behavioral disorders such as separation anxiety seem predisposed to IBS. Working and toy-breed dogs are more commonly affected.

Etiopathogenesis

The etiology of IBS is not clearly defined; however, balloon distention, manometric and motility studies in people suggest disordered GI motility and visceral hyper-responsiveness to stimuli. Comparable pathophysiologic research has not been performed in dogs.

The relationship of stress to the myoelectric and motility abnormalities present in IBS is not completely understood (Table 22-34). However, psychological stress can trigger hypermotility. In addition, the effect of central nervous system neuropeptides (e.g., cholecystokinin, serotonin, acetylcholine, vasoactive intestinal peptide and substance P) on GI motility and visceral sensitivity is now recognized.[36] For example, cholecystokinin infusions promote colonic hypermotility and abdominal pain in patients with IBS.

Key Nutritional Factors
Fiber

Reports suggest that many patients with IBS improve clinically when the fiber content of the diet is increased.[2,33,37,38] Increasing dietary fiber alters fecal water content, colonic motility and intestinal transit rate, all of which may benefit patients with IBS. Either fiber sources can be added to typical foods or the patient can be fed fiber-enhanced veterinary therapeutic foods (Table 22-22) to increase dietary fiber intake. High-fiber breakfast cereals can be used to increase the patient's fiber intake. (See Chapter 2, Case 2-1). Fermentable fibers such as psyllium husks (e.g., Metamucil[c]) can be added to a typical or GI food at a rate of 1 to 6 tsp per meal. Soluble fiber typical-

Table 22-33. Diagnostic criteria for the irritable bowel syndrome in people.*

Abdominal pain or discomfort, relieved by defecation and/or associated with a change in stool frequency and/or consistency
Altered stool form
Altered stool frequency
Altered stool passage
An irregular pattern of defecation at least 25% of the time
Bloating or feeling of abdominal distention
Continuous or recurrent symptoms for at least three months
Passage of mucus

*Adapted from Thompson WG, Creed F, Brossman DA, et al. Functional bowel disease and abdominal pain. Gastroenterology International 1992; 5: 75-91.

Table 22-34. Myoelectric and motility abnormalities prominent in people with irritable bowel syndrome.*

Clustered contractions in the small bowel
Delayed but prolonged colonic hypermotility in response to ingestion of food, particularly fats
Increased colonic motility and abdominal pain in response to cholecystokinin
Increased colonic motor activity in response to low concentrations of bile acids
Increased frequency of basal electrical rhythm
Lowered gastroesophageal sphincter pressure
Pronounced colonic hypermotility in response to cholinergic agents
Small bowel transit rate is faster when diarrhea is predominant
Small bowel transit rate is slower when constipation is predominant
Spastic response to rectal distention

*Adapted from Guilford WG. Motility disorders of the bowel. In: Guilford WG, Center SA, Strombeck DR, et al, eds. Strombeck's Small Animal Gastroenterology, 3rd ed. Philadelphia, PA: WB Saunders Co, 1996; 533.

ly improves stool quality, but does not alter the underlying pathophysiologic and motility abnormalities thought to be involved in IBS. The use of wheat bran for managing IBS has been described, but has been unsuccessful in the hands of the authors. Commercial foods containing small amounts of soluble fiber (1 to 5%) or moderate amounts of insoluble fiber (i.e., 10 to 15%) have been used successfully.[2,3,33,37]

ASSESS THE FOOD(S) AND FEEDING METHOD

Levels of crude fiber should be evaluated in foods currently fed to patients with IBS. Information from this aspect of assessment is essential for making any changes to foods currently provided. Changing to a more appropriate food is indicated if levels of crude fiber in the food currently provided do not match recommended levels.

Because the feeding method may be altered in patients with IBS, a thorough assessment should include verification of the feeding method currently being used. Items to consider include feeding frequency, amount fed, how the food is offered, access to other food and who feeds the animal. All of this information should have been gathered when the history of the animal was obtained. If the animal has a normal BCS (3/5), the amount of food previously fed (energy basis) was probably appropriate.

Feeding Plan

The feeding plan should be used in conjunction with efforts to decrease the frequency of events that seem to trigger the problem. Reasonable efforts should be made to identify and eliminate specific stressors. Psychotropic and

Table 22-35. Drugs associated with constipation.*

Antacids
Anticholinergics
Anticonvulsants (phenytoin)
Antidepressants
Barium sulfate
Bismuth subsalicylate
Diuretics
Hematinics
Opiates
Sucralfate

*Dimski DS. Constipation: Pathophysiology, diagnostic approach and treatment. Seminars in Veterinary Medicine and Surgery: Small Animal 1989; 4: 247-254.

GI antispasmodic agents may be beneficial in some cases. The feeding plan alone may not eliminate the problem but it may reduce the frequency and severity of clinical signs.

SELECT A FOOD(S)

IBS is managed most successfully by feeding a food with increased levels of insoluble fiber. Most commercial grocery and specialty brand dog foods contain less than 5% DM crude fiber. Additional fiber can be added to the diet by using fiber supplements or commercial fiber-enhanced foods. It is prudent to increase the fiber concentration in increments of 5% per week until clinical signs improve or resolve. High levels of fiber added to regular pet foods may make the food unpalatable and unbalanced. Alternatively, there are many balanced commercial pet food products offering a wide variety of fiber combinations and concentrations (Table 22-22). Some clinicians successfully manage IBS by gradually adding psyllium husk fiber to highly digestible GI foods.[2,33,37] Recommended doses range from 1 to 6 tsp of psyllium husk fiber per meal.

DETERMINE A FEEDING METHOD

Foods other than those determined to control the clinical signs should be strictly avoided for dogs in which recurring bouts are initiated by diet changes or exposure to garbage or table foods. Feeding once or twice a day is usually sufficient. Feeding three to four meals per day may be necessary in some cases to minimize the amount of ingesta passing into the large bowel at one time.

Reassessment

Regular body weight and condition assessment and stool evaluations are useful for monitoring patients with IBS. Well-compensated patients should be evaluated immediately if a change or decline in condition is noted. Maintaining optimal body weight and condition, normal activity level, a positive attitude and absence of clinical signs are measures of successful dietary and medical management. The feeding method and amount fed can be adjusted as needed to maintain body weight and condition. Additional medical therapy should be considered if dietary therapy alone is not sufficient to improve stool quality and maintain body weight and condition.

Constipation/Megacolon

Clinical Importance

Classically, the term constipation is applied to those patients that pass stools infrequently or exhibit tenesmus in association with defecation. Because it is difficult to obtain accurate information about the defecation habits of pets, constipation is difficult to define in veterinary patients. Constipation appears to be far less common in veterinary medicine than in human medicine. In human medicine, it is the number one GI complaint, accounting for more than 2 million physician visits each year in the United States.[39] Constipation is a clinical sign, not a disease; multiple disorders can result in constipation.

Obstipation is severe constipation that requires medical therapy for relief. Megacolon refers to dilatation of the colon and is usually seen as a consequence of severe chronic constipation or neurogenic disorders. Feline idiopathic megacolon is thought to result from long-standing constipation and/or an underlying innervation defect. A similar condition occurs rarely in dogs. Although relatively uncommon, idiopathic megacolon is a frustrating, recurring problem that often results in euthanasia of the affected animal.

Assessment

ASSESS THE ANIMAL

History and Physical Examination

Animals with megacolon are usually examined for constipation or obstipation. Affected animals exhibit tenesmus, dyschezia and abdominal pain. Chronically constipated animals often exhibit weight loss, inappetence, vomiting, depression and a poor coat.

Owners of constipated pets should be queried about medications their pet is receiving. A number of commonly used drugs are associated with constipation in people and pets (Table 22-35).

Depression and dehydration may be noted at physical examination. Abdominal palpation often reveals colonic distention and the presence of dry hard feces. Digital rectal examination may also reveal dry hard feces.

Most constipated pets do not require diagnostic evaluation beyond a careful history and physical examination and the appropriate exclusion of systemic and GI causes.

Risk Factors

The use of opioid narcotics for pain moderation or control of GI transit time has long been recognized to cause constipation. Several other commonly used medications, including barium sulfate, bismuth subsalicylate and anticonvulsants, also have constipating effects.

Dietary indiscretion is frequently associated with constipation in dogs. Consumption of bones, rocks and clay may trigger an episode. Although not generally prone to dietary indiscretion, cats may develop constipation as a consequence of trichobezoar formation.

Perineal and perianal disorders (e.g., perineal hernias, perianal fistulas and anal sacculitis) often predispose pets to constipation because of the pain associated with defecation. (See sidebar "Dietary Management of Perianal Fistulas in Dogs.") Suppression of defecation results in increased fecal retention time, increased water absorption and inspissated feces. Orthopedic disorders may have a similar effect if the animal experiences pain when it assumes the defecation stance. Improperly healed pelvic fractures may reduce the size of the pelvic inlet and obstruct the colon externally.

Etiopathogenesis

The colon is innervated by the parasympathetic nervous system and intrinsic myenteric and submucosal

Dietary Management of Perianal Fistulas in Dogs

The perianal fistula syndrome is a frustrating problem for pet owners and veterinarians. Although uncommon, this condition is often refractory to treatment and may lead to elective euthanasia. The etiology of perianal fistulas is unknown. Physical factors such as breed (e.g., German shepherd dog), low tail set, anal gland inflammation and fecal contamination of the perineum may be predisposing factors. Some authors have hypothesized that perianal fistulas are analogous to ulcerative proctitis in people. This condition, part of the human inflammatory bowel disease constellation, is thought to be immune mediated. Reports of the successful use of immunosuppressive drugs, including prednisone and cyclosporine, and elimination foods in dogs lend credence to the idea that the condition is immune-mediated.

Dietary treatments for perianal fistula patients are highly case specific. There is no physical examination finding, laboratory test result or historical fact that can predict which dietary maneuver will succeed in a particular patient. The feeding plan is used in conjunction with other therapy such as drying agents, antibiotics, immunosuppressive agents and stool softeners. In many cases, surgical resection of necrotic, inflamed tracts is necessary. A number of procedures have been used including cryotherapy, chemical cautery, electrocautery, tail amputation and radical excision. Interested readers are referred to surgical texts for more information.

Some cases of canine perianal fistula are managed successfully by increasing the insoluble fiber content of the food. If the current food contains less than 5% dry matter (DM) crude fiber, insoluble fiber is the first treatment of choice because it increases fecal bulk, decreases intracolonic pressure and improves transit time. However, it is prudent to increase the dry matter fiber concentration in increments of 5% per week until clinical signs resolve; increasing fiber intake too rapidly may result in pain and obstipation.

Another successful approach in some cases is to use a lower residue food containing a mixed fiber source. Low-residue foods may contain either little or no (<1% DM) crude fiber or use predominately soluble or fermentable fiber (<5% DM total dietary fiber).

Elimination foods have been suggested for managing dogs with perianal fistulas. This approach was used successfully in 18 of 27 (67%) dogs also receiving immunosuppressive doses of corticosteroids. See Chapter 14 for more information about elimination foods.

Some investigators have speculated that n-3 fatty acids derived from fish oil or other sources may have a beneficial effect in controlling inflammation associated with perianal fistulas. Dietary n-3 fatty supplementation has been used successfully in trials involving people with ulcerative colitis and proctitis. Results of these trials suggest that dietary n-3 fatty acid supplementation should be considered for dogs with perianal fistulas. See the section on inflammatory bowel disease and Chapter 26 for more information about n-3 fatty acid administration.

Some dogs with perianal fistulas may benefit from small, frequent meals in conjunction with exercise to encourage more frequent defecation.

Determination of body weight and condition and stool evaluations are useful for assessing patients with perianal fistulas. Patients should be evaluated immediately if a change or decline in body weight or condition is noted. Regaining or maintaining optimal body weight and condition, normal activity level, a positive attitude and absence of clinical signs are measures of successful management. Feeding method and amount fed can be adjusted as needed to maintain body weight and condition as tolerated by the patient. If dietary therapy alone is insufficient to improve stool quality and maintain body weight, additional medical or surgical therapy should be considered. Unfortunately, recurrence is common and prolonged medical therapy and multiple surgeries may be necessary. Many affected dogs are eventually euthanatized because of client frustration with repeated bouts of the disease.

BIBLIOGRAPHY

Day MJ, Weaver BMQ. Pathology of surgically resected tissue from 305 cases of anal furunculosis in the dog. Journal of Small Animal Practice 1992; 33: 583-589.

Harkin KR, Walshaw R, Mullaney TP. Association of perianal fistula and colitis in the German shepherd dog: Response to high dose prednisone and dietary therapy. Journal of the American Animal Hospital Association 1996; 32: 515-520.

Matthews KA, Ayres SA, Tano CA, et al. Cyclosporine treatment of perianal fistulas in dogs. Canadian Veterinary Journal 1997; 38: 39-41.

Scarff DH. Perianal sinus: A medical disease? Waltham Focus 1998; 8: 28-31.

GI & PANCREAS

---

plexuses. Destruction or damage to either pathway results in reduced colonic motility and potentiates constipation.

Normal colonic motility involves both propulsive and nonpropulsive patterns. Food and somatic activity stimulate propulsive contractions, which serve to move colonic contents distally. Nonpropulsive motility, also termed rhythmic segmentation, mixes colonic contents and promotes absorption of water and electrolytes.

Dehydration and electrolyte imbalances may induce constipation. Dehydration enhances colonic water absorption and leaves a dry, hard fecal mass. Electrolyte disturbances (e.g., hyponatremia, hypokalemia, hypocalcemia and hypercalcemia) may alter colonic muscular activity resulting in constipation.

Constipation may result from mechanical obstruction caused by intraluminal or extraluminal masses, rectal strictures and narrow pelvic outlets (e.g., improperly healed pelvic fractures). Additionally, a number of neurologic disorders may result in reduced colonic motility. These include cauda equina syndrome, dysautonomia (Key-Gaskell syndrome) and diabetic or hypothyroid polyneuropathy. The constipating effect of narcotic analgesics is well known but poorly understood. Postulated mechanisms include increased intestinal lack of water, increased rhythmic segmentation and delayed colonic transit.

Key Nutritional Factors
Water

Water is a key nutrient that is often overlooked in constipated animals. Maintaining normal hydration status is important in managing patients with chronic constipation. Methods should be used to encourage water intake. These include ensuring multiple bowls of potable water are available in prominent locations in the pet's environment, feeding moist rather than dry forms of foods, adding small

Table 22-36. Laxatives.

Bulk-forming laxatives
Natural (psyllium, pumpkin, wheat bran, gums)
Synthetic (methylcellulose, polycarbophil)
Emollient/lubricant laxatives
Dioctyl sodium succinate
Mineral oil
Hyperosmolar laxatives
Glycerin
Lactulose
Polyethylene glycol
Sorbitol
Saline laxatives
Magnesium citrate
Magnesium hydroxide
Magnesium sulfate
Sodium phosphate
Stimulant laxatives
Aloe
   Cascara sagrada
   Senna
   Castor oil
Anthraquinones
Diphenylmethanes
   Phenolphthalein
   Bisacodyl

amounts of flavoring substances such as bouillon or broth to water sources and offering ice cubes as treats or snacks.

Fiber

Many patients with constipation improve clinically when the fiber content of the diet is increased. Increasing dietary fiber alters fecal water content, colonic motility and intestinal transit rate, all of which may benefit patients with constipation. Nonfermentable (i.e., insoluble), moderately fermentable and highly fermentable (i.e., soluble) fiber sources have been advocated for management of constipation.[40] Fiber sources can be added to typical foods or the patient can be fed fiber-enhanced veterinary therapeutic foods (Table 22-22) to increase dietary fiber intake.

A number of gel-forming fibers have been recommended as an aid in managing constipation in people[41] and domestic animals.[40] These fibers, whether added or incorporated into food, swell to form emollient gels and facilitate passage of fecal matter. Pumpkin and psyllium husk fiber are not typically incorporated into commercial pet foods but can be used as supplements.

Flatulence and abdominal cramping are potential side effects to using these fermentable, bulk-forming fibers. These side effects can be reduced by a gradual transition to fiber supplementation, slowly increasing the level of added fiber until efficacy is achieved with minimal side effects. Such fibers should be added at no more than 5% of the total diet because soluble fibers can significantly reduce the availability of minerals, including zinc, calcium, iron and phosphorus.[42-44] (See Chapter 2.)

Occasionally, an animal may develop megacolon, constipation or flatulence while being fed moderate- or high-fiber (>15% DM crude fiber) foods. The prudent recommendation in such cases is to decrease the fiber content by 5% DMB, reassess the patient and then decrease the fiber content again if necessary. This situation occurs more commonly in older overweight and obese cats consuming dry, high-fiber (>20% DM crude fiber), low-calorie foods for weight control than in cats being treated for constipation with fiber.

Digestibility

In situations in which colonic motility patterns are completely abolished (e.g., severe megacolon in cats), fiber-enhanced foods are no longer able to stimulate colonic motility and may actually contribute to obstipation. In this situation, changing to a food with high digestibility (dry matter digestibility ≥90%) and high energy density (>4.0 kcal/g [>16.7 kJ/g] DM) will provide adequate calories with a marked reduction in fecal mass. These types of food can markedly reduce the burden of home management (i.e., administering stool softeners and enemas) for pet owners. In such cases, fecal production is reduced to such an extent that owners can generally remove feces via cleansing enemas once or twice weekly. In many cases, this food transition is made as the owner considers the surgical option of subtotal colectomy.

ASSESS THE FOOD(S) AND FEEDING METHOD

Levels of crude fiber and dry matter digestibility should be evaluated in foods currently fed to patients with constipation. Information from this aspect of assessment is essential for making any changes to foods currently provided. Changing to a more appropriate food is indicated if levels of crude fiber or digestibility of the current food do not match recommended levels.

Because the feeding method may be altered in patients with constipation, a thorough assessment should include verification of the feeding method currently being used. Items to consider include feeding frequency, amount fed, how the food is offered, access to other food and who feeds the animal. All of this information should have been gathered when the history of the animal was obtained. If the animal has a normal BCS (3/5), the amount of food previously fed (energy basis) was probably appropriate.

Feeding Plan

Initial management of chronic constipation includes owner education, encouraging increased water intake, dietary changes and judicious use of laxatives and enemas. Obstipation often requires multiple cleansing enemas with or without mechanical removal of impacted feces before dietary changes are instituted.

Surgery may be necessary to remove the affected portion of the bowel in cases of idiopathic megacolon. In most cases, subtotal colectomy with ileorectal or cecocolic-rectal anastomosis is the treatment of choice.

SELECT A FOOD(S)

Constipation is often managed successfully by feeding a food with higher insoluble fiber levels. Most commercial grocery and specialty brand dog foods contain less than 5% DM crude fiber. Additional fiber can be added to the diet by using fiber supplements or feeding commercial fiber-enhanced foods. It is prudent to increase the fiber concentration in increments of 5% per week until clinical signs improve or resolve. Consult the sidebar "Two Methods of Titrating Dietary Fiber Content" for practical information about gradually increasing dietary fiber intake.

High levels of fiber added as a supplement to regular pet foods may make the food unpalatable and unbalanced. Alternatively, there are many balanced commercial pet food products offering a wide variety of fiber combinations and concentrations (Table 22-22).

Two Methods of Titrating Dietary Fiber Content

CASE EXAMPLE

A 10-lb cat fed a grocery store brand moist food with 2% crude fiber on a dry matter basis (DMB) has been presented repeatedly for constipation over the past eight months; however, this week the cat presents with obstipation. The cat is diagnosed as having a megacolon. Therefore, increasing the fiber content of the diet should prove useful, but it should be done gradually. Adding fiber to the diet should be done incrementally to get the most favorable stool bulk to match the remaining ability of the colon to successfully move fecal material (i.e., titrating to effect). Increasing the fiber content 5 to 10% every seven to 14 days is a reasonable rate. The cat has been fed a low-fiber (<5%) food, so it is advisable to begin with a 5 to 10% dietary fiber combination. The cat can be re-evaluated in seven to 10 days and the fiber content increased to 10 to 15% for another two weeks if needed. The cat can be evaluated again in seven to 10 days, and the fiber content increased to 15 to 20% for another two weeks if needed.

METHOD 1

Almost any fiber concentration can be achieved by combining veterinary therapeutic diets (Tables 1 and 2). The calculations are simpler if done on a DMB and when products of the same form are mixed (i.e., dry with dry or moist with moist). Moist foods increase the water content of digesta and feces, which may help in managing constipation.

METHOD 2

Up to 10% fiber can be added to the current food without compromising its overall nutrient balance. In some cases, the desired bulk effect can be obtained by continuing to feed the patient a highly palatable, low-fiber moist food but incrementally adding a high-fiber component. Canned pumpkin is compared to a high-fiber breakfast cereal in Table 3.

Adding a high-fiber cereal has several advantages over feeding canned pumpkin. A smaller volume of cereal, relative to the pumpkin, will significantly increase fiber intake (Table 4). Cereal also contributes other nutrients in addition to fiber. Pumpkin adds 90 g of water per 100 g added, but contains insufficient quantities of all other nutrients.

Table 1. Fiber concentrations of selected veterinary therapeutic foods.

Products	Form	Crude fiber (%)
Prescription Diet Feline i/d*	Moist	1.6
Prescription Diet Feline w/d*	Moist	12.3
Prescription Diet Feline r/d*	Moist	29.8

*Hill's Pet Nutrition, Inc., Topeka, KS, USA.

Table 2. Combinations of selected veterinary therapeutic foods (moist foods) provide varying fiber levels.

Food combinations*	Crude fiber (%)
100% Feline i/d	1.6
75% Feline i/d + 25% Feline w/d	4.3
50% Feline i/d + 50% Feline w/d	7.0
25% Feline i/d + 75% Feline w/d	9.6
100% Feline w/d	12.3
75% Feline w/d + 25% Feline r/d	16.7
50% Feline w/d + 50% Feline r/d	21.1
25% Feline w/d + 75% Feline r/d	25.4
100% Feline r/d	29.8

*Hill's Pet Nutrition, Inc., Topeka, KS, USA.

Table 3. Fiber content of selected foods.

Fiber component	Dry matter (%)	Fiber (%)*	Fiber (%)**
Fiber One cereal***	97	49.4	48.0
Pumpkin, canned	10	28.0	2.8

*Dry matter basis.
**As fed basis.
***General Mills Sales, Minneapolis, MN, USA.

Table 4. The effect of adding a high-fiber dry cereal vs. canned pumpkin to foods.

Desired final crude fiber (%)*	Fiber One cereal**	Pumpkin
3.2	4 g or 1 tsp	60 g or 4 Tbs
5.6	9 g or 2 tsp	150 g or 10 Tbs
8.0	14 g or 1 Tbs	232 g or 15 Tbs
10.4	20 g or 4 tsp	318 g or 21 Tbs

*Dry matter basis.
**General Mills Sales, Minneapolis, MN, USA.

Patients with severe megacolon and some patients with constipation may need foods with high dry matter digestibility and high energy density. Homemade foods (See Chapter 6.) or commercial veterinary therapeutic foods for stress/recovery (Tables 12-7 and 12-9) may be fed to affected patients.

DETERMINE A FEEDING METHOD

In some cases, smaller more frequent meals may aid colonic motility patterns. Dogs should be walked immediately after feeding; both mild exercise and the gastrocolic reflex will often result in defecation during the immediate postprandial period. Feeding three to four meals per day also minimizes the amount of ingesta entering the large bowel at one time. As discussed above, water intake should be encouraged and multiple bowls of potable water should be available at all times.

DIET INTERACTIONS WITH MEDICAL THERAPY

Medical therapies for mild to moderate constipation include enemas, stool softeners, laxatives (Table 22-36) and colonic motility modifiers (e.g., cisapride[f] 0.25 mg/kg body weight, t.i.d. to q.i.d.). A number of poorly absorbed carbohydrates may prove useful as laxatives. These sugars, including polyethylene glycol, sorbitol, lactulose and lactitol are hydrolyzed to fatty acids by the colonic microflora. The metabolites of these sugars exert osmotic pressure and draw fluid into the colon lumen. Additionally, laxative therapy may occasionally be needed to promote fecal hydration and lubrication.

Reassessment

Assessment of body weight and condition and stool evaluations are useful for monitoring patients with constipation. Well-compensated patients should be evaluated immediately if a change or decline in condition is noted. Regaining or maintaining optimal body weight and condition, normal activity level, a positive attitude and absence of clinical signs are measures of successful dietary management. The feeding method and amount fed can be adjusted as needed to maintain body weight and condition. Additional medical therapies should be considered if dietary therapy alone is not sufficient to improve stool quality and maintain body weight. Although treatment is highly case specific, many cases can eventually be managed with diet alone after initial medical therapies are tapered.

Flatulence

Clinical Importance

Flatulence is excessive formation of gases in the stomach or intestine, but the term is often used inappropriately. Excessive flatulence is usually associated with noticeable flatus, belching, borborygmus, or a combination of these signs. Flatus, rather than flatulence, is gas expelled through the anus. Belching is the noisy voiding of gas from the stomach through the mouth. Borborygmus is a rumbling noise caused by the propulsion of gas through the intestines.

Excessive flatus is a chronic objectionable problem that occurs often in dogs and less commonly in cats. Although belching and borborygmus are rarely chief complaints of pet owners, routine questioning may elicit their presence. Flatus, belching and borborygmus occur in normal pets but often develop as a consequence of small intestinal or colonic disorders. At times, flatus is the primary reason pet owners seek veterinary advice.

Assessment

ASSESS THE ANIMAL

Pet owners often describe an increase in frequency of belching, flatus or an objectionable odor associated with flatus. At times, it may be possible to elicit a history of dietary change or dietary indiscretion in association with flatus. Occasionally, belching and flatus develop in conjunction with other GI signs including weight loss, diarrhea and steatorrhea. This type of history is very suggestive of an underlying small intestinal disorder.

In most cases, physical examination findings are unremarkable in dogs and cats with flatulence. Animals may be in poor body condition if objectionable flatus occurs secondary to an underlying GI condition.

Laboratory testing is usually not indicated. However, further evaluation is in order if concomitant GI signs are present. Readers are referred to earlier discussions of small and large bowel disorders for further information.

Risk Factors

Excessive aerophagia is a risk factor for flatulence and is seen with brachycephalic, working and sporting canine breeds and aggressive and competitive eating behaviors. Dietary indiscretion and ingestion of certain pet food ingredients may be risk factors for certain individuals.

Etiopathogenesis

Gas in the GI tract is normal and may be derived from three sources: air swallowing, intraluminal production and diffusion from the blood (Figure 22-20).

The rate of excretion of gas per rectum varies greatly in people and animals. Excretion rates in people range from 400 to 1,500 ml/day (mean 705 ml/day). People, eating their usual diet, passed gas per rectum an average of eight to 10 times per day with an upper normal limit of 20 times per day.[45] The amount and frequency of gas passed per rectum has not been studied in normal pet animals

and those pets whose owners have complained of problems with flatulence.

Swallowed air is thought to contribute the most to gas in the digestive tract. This may be the cause of flatus commonly seen in many brachycephalic breeds. Vigorous exercise and rapid and competitive eating situations may exacerbate aerophagia.

A large amount of gas is formed from bacterial fermentation of poorly digestible carbohydrates and fibers in the colon. Fiber-containing foods contribute to flatus indirectly through reduced dry matter digestibility. Many fibers used in pet foods are fermented by colonic microflora and may contribute to flatus directly. Foods that contain large amounts of nonabsorbable oligosaccharides (e.g., raffinose, stachyose and verbascose) are likely to produce large amounts of intestinal gas.[46] Dogs and cats lack the digestive enzymes needed to split these sugars into absorbable monosaccharides. Therefore, *Clostridium* spp and other bacteria in the colon ferment these sugars producing hydrogen and carbon dioxide. Soybeans, beans and peas contain large quantities of nonabsorbable oligosaccharides. Diseases that cause maldigestion or malabsorption are often associated with excessive flatus because excessive amounts of malassimilated substrates are delivered to the colon where bacterial fermentation occurs. Flatus may be present in animals with lactose intolerance.

The interaction between hydrochloric acid and alkaline food and saliva produces carbon dioxide in the stomach. Carbon dioxide also enters the GI tract through diffusion from the blood.

As much as 99% of flatus is composed of odorless gases (i.e., nitrogen, oxygen, carbon dioxide, hydrogen and methane).[45] The residual 1% is composed of odoriferous gases including ammonia, hydrogen sulfide, indole, skatole, volatile amines and short-chain fatty acids.[45] These gases contribute the objectionable odors associated with flatus. Spoiled food and many dietary substances including onions, spices and high-protein ingredients increase production of odoriferous gases.

Key Nutritional Factors

Digestibility

Digestibility, especially of the carbohydrate fraction of food, is an important nutritional factor in patients with excessive flatulence. Foods with high digestibility (dry matter digestibility ≥90%) are recommended for patients with objectionable flatus.

Food Ingredients

Certain protein, carbohydrate and fiber ingredients or levels may affect flatus production in individual animals. Of the numerous foods alleged to enhance flatus in people, baked beans is the only natural food that has been carefully studied. A diet deriving half of its calories from pork and beans increased flatus elimination in people from a basal level of 15 to 176 ml/hour.[47]

Changing the sources of protein or carbohydrate in the food may benefit some individual animals.[48] For example, changing from a commercial dry food that contains corn, chicken meal and soybean meal to a dry food that contains lamb meal, rice and barley may be helpful. Fiber-enhanced foods may contribute to excessive flatus in some patients. The lactose content of food and treats (e.g., cheese, ice cream, milk) may be a factor in adult dogs and cats, especially those with lactase deficiency. A series of dietary tri-

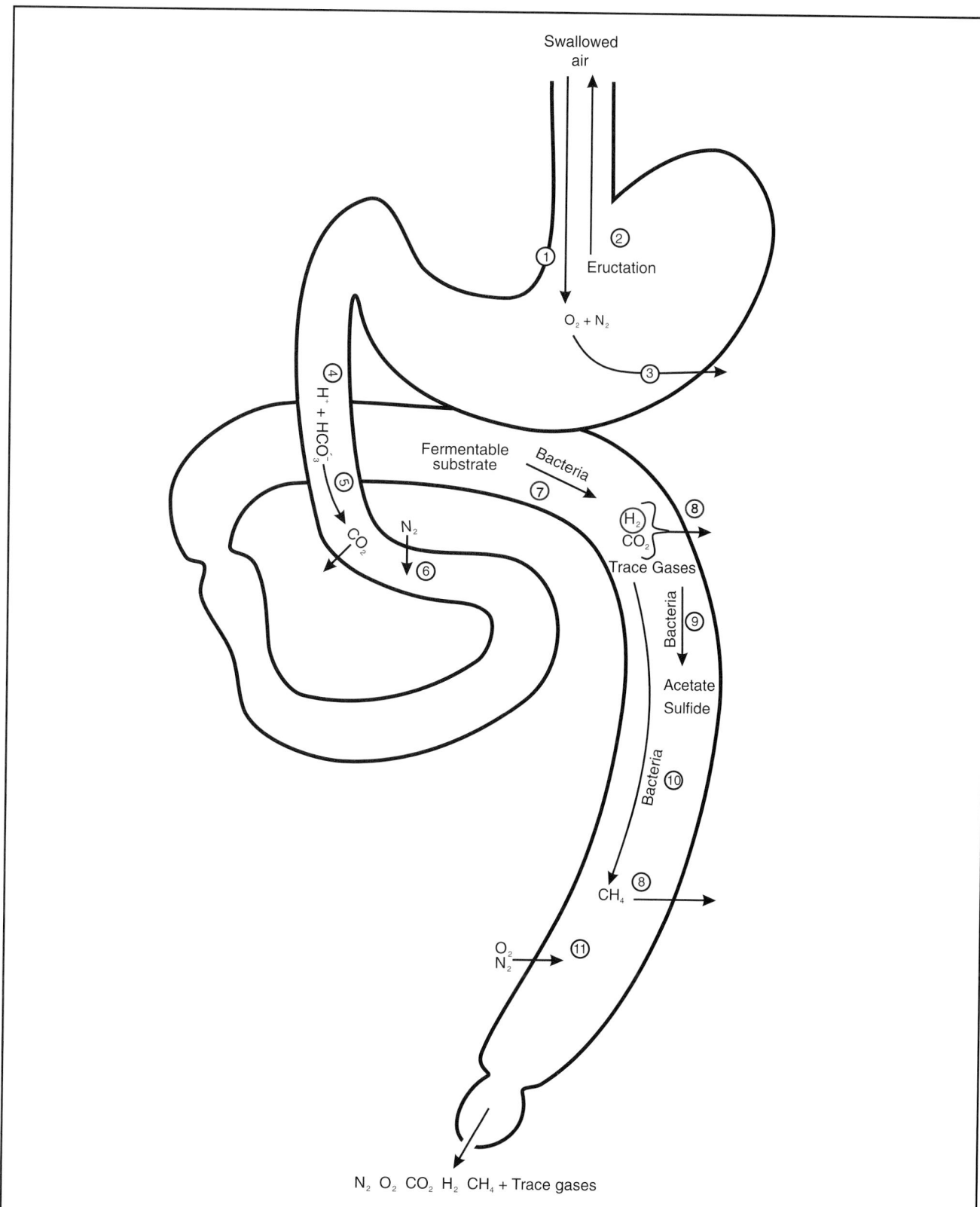

Figure 22-20. Physiology of gas production and removal from the intestinal tract. Air is swallowed (1) and a sizable fraction is then eructated (2). The oxygen (O_2) component of the swallowed air diffuses into the blood (3). The reaction of acid and bicarbonate in the duodenum (4) yields carbon dioxide (CO_2) that rapidly diffuses into the blood (5), whereas nitrogen (N_2) diffuses into the duodenum (6) down the gradient established by CO_2 production. In the large intestine, malabsorbed ingesta and mucus are fermented by bacteria releasing trace gases (some of which are odiferous), CO_2 and H_2 (7). A fraction of the bacterial gases are absorbed into the blood perfusing the large intestine (8). H_2 is also consumed by bacteria in the process of reducing sulfate to sulfide and converting CO_2 to acetate (9). In addition, H_2 is consumed by methanogens (bacteria) in the process of reducing CO_2 to CH_4 (10). Nitrogen and oxygen (11) diffuse from the blood into the large intestine lumen down a gradient created by the production of gas by bacteria. The net result of all of the aforementioned processes determines the composition and rate of excretion of gas per rectum. (Adapted from Strocchi A, Levitt MD. Intestinal gas. In: Feldman M, Scharschmidt BF, Sleisenger MH, eds. Gastrointestinal and Liver Disease, 6th ed. Philadelphia, PA: WB Saunders Co, 1998; 153-159.)

als is often successful in finding a food that lessens flatulence in individual pets.

ASSESS THE FOOD(S) AND FEEDING METHOD

Obtaining a thorough dietary history is of paramount importance in evaluating animals with flatulence. Specific foods, major food ingredients, treats, supplements and opportunities for dietary indiscretion should be evaluated.

A thorough assessment should include verification of the feeding method currently being used. Items to consider include feeding frequency, amount fed, how the food is offered, access to other food, relationship of feeding to exercise and who feeds the animal. All of this information should have been gathered when the history of the animal was obtained. If the animal has a normal BCS (3/5), the amount of food previously fed (energy basis) was probably appropriate.

Feeding Plan

Dietary management of flatulence is primarily concerned with decreasing intestinal gas production by bacterial fermentation of undigested food. Changes in the feeding plan can be used in conjunction with other therapy. Recently, commercial products have been introduced that claim to reduce flatulence. These products contain α-galactosidase and reduce flatulence by improving digestion of nonabsorbable carbohydrates. Anecdotal reports suggest that these products may be beneficial in some dogs. Cats may find the strongly salty taste of the compounds objectionable.

SELECT A FOOD(S)

In general, animals with excessive flatulence will benefit from highly digestible foods. Foods that are high in fermentable and nonfermentable fiber should be avoided. Changing to a food that does not contain soybean meal or that contains different protein and carbohydrate sources benefits some animals. In addition, vegetarian-based foods containing strongly flavored, sulfur-containing vegetables should be avoided. In some cases, reducing dietary protein content alleviates flatulence. In most cases, vitamin-mineral supplements should be avoided because these products may increase intestinal microbial activity.

The initial recommendation is to feed a highly digestible food in small frequent meals. This protocol will reduce food residues available for bacterial fermentation in the large intestine and should reduce gas production.

DETERMINE A FEEDING METHOD

Reducing aerophagia is important in the control of flatulence in dogs, especially in brachycephalic breeds. Feed several small meals daily in an effort to discourage rapid eating and gulping of air. Feeding in a quiet, isolated location will eliminate competitive eating and reduce aerophagia.

Reassessment

Patients should be evaluated for evidence of malassimilation if the methods outlined above are not successful in reducing or controlling flatulence. Relapses in animals that have been controlled often indicate dietary indiscretion.

The prognosis for control of flatulence is good in most cases. However, owners should be educated about normal intestinal gas production and should not expect complete cessation of flatulence.[49]

PANCREATIC DISORDERS

Exocrine Pancreatic Insufficiency

Clinical Importance

Malassimilation is failure of nutrients to pass across the intestinal wall in quantities sufficient to maintain body weight and condition.[1] Malassimilation is divided pathophysiologically into maldigestive and malabsorptive diseases. Malabsorption occurs with diseases that alter the structure and function of the small intestinal mucosa including the lymphatics. (See Small Intestinal Disorders section above.) Maldigestion occurs with defects in intraluminal digestion and may result from gastric, pancreatic or biliary dysfunction. Exocrine pancreatic insufficiency (EPI) refers to a partial or complete deficiency of pancreatic enzymes and is the most common cause of maldigestion in dogs.[2] Occurring most commonly in young dogs as a congenital anomaly, EPI may also develop as a sequela to acute and chronic pancreatitis.[2] EPI is rare in cats but has been reported in both the juvenile and acquired forms.[3]

Assessment

ASSESS THE ANIMAL

History and Physical Examination

Affected dogs and cats have a history of chronic small bowel diarrhea, weight loss and failure to thrive.[4] Pets with EPI defecate frequently (six to 10 bowel movements per day) and stools are typically voluminous, greasy, foul smelling and pale in color. When stained with Sudan III and examined microscopically, fat droplets are readily identified in such feces (Figure 22-21). Polyphagia, borborygmus, pica and coprophagia are often reported. Vomiting and polydipsia occur less commonly.[4]

Affected dogs and cats generally have a normal appearance except for poor body condition (BCS 1/5 or 2/5) and poor coat quality. Animals with pancreatic atrophy will be stunted in comparison to unaffected litter mates or breed standards. Severely affected patients may have hemorrhages due to a vitamin K-deficient coagulopathy.[5]

Laboratory and Other Clinical Information

A presumptive diagnosis of EPI is often based on the signalment and patient history. Definitive diagnosis is achieved by radioimmunoassay of serum trypsin-like immunoreactivity (TLI). Low fasting TLI values (<2.5 µg/l) are indicative of EPI.[6-8] This sensitive, specific, easy to perform serologic assay has replaced older tests including the bentiromide-PABA challenge, assay of fecal proteolytic activity, x-ray film digestion test and oral fat challenges. TLI is a measure of serum trypsin and trypsinogen concentrations. Trypsinogen leaks out of pancreatic acini in trace amounts in healthy animals (normal canine serum TLI values = 5.0 to 35.0 µg/l, normal feline serum TLI values = 17.0 to 50.0 µg/l). In EPI, pancreatic acinar atrophy and fibrosis result in reduced serum TLI values. Serum amylase, isoamylase and lipase concentrations are of no value in diagnosing EPI due to pancreatic atrophy. These tests may be of benefit when EPI occurs in conjunction with pancreatitis.[9]

Risk Factors

EPI due to pancreatic acinar atrophy is most common in young, large-breed dogs. German shepherd dogs and rough-coated collies appear to have a genetic predisposition to pancreatic acinar atrophy; however, any breed can be affected.[2] Siamese cats also appear to be at risk.[a]

Acquired EPI may occur as a consequence of severe or recurrent pancreatic inflammation and resultant fibrosis. Thus, risk factors for acquired EPI are the same as for pancreatitis.

Etiopathogenesis

Juvenile EPI results from atrophy of pancreatic acinar tissue rather than from congenital hypoplasia. This atrophy is idiopathic with minimal evidence of inflammation. One report suggests that histopathologic evidence of atrophy is present before the onset of clinical signs, which usually develop when patients are six to 18 months old.[10] Clinical signs do not develop until 85 to 90% of functional exocrine tissue is lost.[1] In the juvenile form of EPI, endocrine function is usually normal and diabetes mellitus does not develop. In rare cases, EPI and diabetes mellitus may occur concurrently in young dogs and cats.[11,12]

The acquired form of EPI arises as a consequence of the inflammation and fibrosis of end-stage chronic pancreatitis.[13] Diabetes mellitus may develop concurrently because pancreatic islet cells are similarly affected. EPI occurs rarely as a consequence of pancreatic adenocarcinoma or cholecystoduodenostomy.[2]

Several mechanisms are responsible for the severe nutrient malassimilation that occurs in EPI. Most important, the deficiency of pancreatic enzymes results in a failure of intraluminal digestion and inability of the patient to effectively use nutrients. In addition, intestinal mucosal enzyme activity is impaired in both experimental and naturally occurring EPI.[14] Impaired mucosal enzyme function results in abnormal sugar, amino acid and fatty acid transport. The cause for the intestinal mucosal abnormality is unknown but is suspected to result from the absence of trophic pancreatic secretions and concurrent small intestinal bacterial overgrowth (SIBOG).

Dogs with EPI commonly have SIBOG[15-17] because they lack the antibacterial factors present in pancreatic secretions and have changes in immunity secondary to malnutrition. In addition, many German shepherd dogs with EPI also have IgA deficiency.[18,19] Bacterial overgrowth contributes to malnutrition in EPI by destroying exposed brush border enzymes and consuming unabsorbed intraluminal nutrients. In addition, bacterial hydroxylation of fatty acids may exacerbate fat malabsorption and contribute to osmotic and secretory diarrhea.

Diarrhea in EPI is usually characterized as osmotic. Distal ileal and colonic microflora ferment undigested sugars and fats, releasing osmotically active particles. These particles drive an efflux of fluid into the gut lumen, which overwhelms the colonic capacity for water reabsorption. Additionally, hydroxy fatty acids formed from bacterial metabolism of undigested fats can trigger secretory diarrhea.

Key Nutritional Factors

Key nutritional factors for patients with EPI are listed in Table 22-37 and discussed in detail below.

Digestibility

The primary nutritional factor in the management of EPI is food digestibility. The use of highly digestible foods (dry matter digestibility ≥90%) works with the addition of pancreatic enzyme preparations to the food. In one study, the combination of a highly digestible commercial veterinary

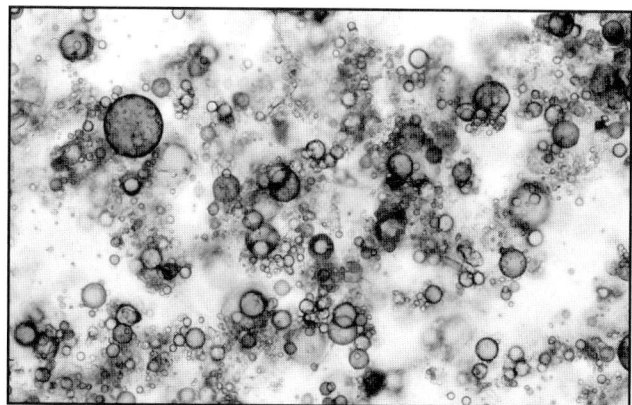

Figure 22-21. Feces stained with Sudan stain demonstrating increased amounts of fat (note globules) typical of exocrine pancreatic insufficiency. (Courtesy Dr. Robert Sherding, College of Veterinary Medicine, The Ohio State University, Columbus.)

Table 22-37. Key nutritional factors for patients with exocrine pancreatic insufficiency.*

Factors	Recommended levels
Digestibility	≥87% for protein and ≥90% for fat and soluble carbohydrate
Fat	10 to 15% for dogs
	15 to 22% for cats
Fiber	<2%

*Nutrients expressed on a dry matter basis.

therapeutic food plus pancreatic enzymes provided more metabolizable energy to dogs with EPI than a grocery brand food with pancreatic enzyme supplementation.[20] Further studies in naturally occurring EPI cases also demonstrated the benefits of feeding highly digestible foods.[21,22]

Highly digestible veterinary therapeutic foods contain meat and carbohydrate sources that have been highly refined to increase digestibility. Typical ingredients in such commercial foods include egg, cottage cheese and muscle and organ meats. Carbohydrates in highly digestible foods are primarily starches of corn, rice, barley and wheat, which are well digested if properly cooked.

Fat

Steatorrhea is the most prominent clinical sign in patients with EPI. As discussed above, feeding a highly digestible food in conjunction with pancreatic enzyme supplementation is more effective than simply decreasing the fat content of the current food.[20,22] Overall fat digestion of a highly digestible food with added pancreatic enzymes can exceed 70%.[20] The addition of medium-chain triglycerides (MCT) to the diet may increase caloric intake; however, MCT decreases diet palatability, which may decrease caloric intake and thus be counterproductive. Addition of MCT is unnecessary in most cases. (See sidebar "Medium-Chain Triglycerides.")

Fiber

Foods for patients with EPI should contain very little fiber (<2% DMB). Decreasing the fiber content from 4% to less than 1% in a study of people with EPI decreased both fecal weight and fat excretion by one-third and reduced bloating and flatus.[23]

Other Nutritional Factors
Vitamins

Micronutrients should be considered in the dietary management of patients with malassimilation. In EPI, the lack of pancreatic lipase results in failed solubilization and absorption of fat-soluble vitamins. The fat-soluble vitamins A and D may be initially administered intramuscularly (1 ml divided into two intramuscular sites every three months), if GI fat absorption remains impaired. Vitamin E supplementation is beneficial when serum concentrations are very low. Clinically, vitamin K deficiency has been described.[5] Severe hemorrhage may occur when vitamin K stores are depleted because of the vitamin's pivotal role in the post-translational carboxylation of coagulation factors. Parenteral supplementation of vitamin K_1 is recommended (5 to 20 mg, q12h) if coagulopathies are detected in dogs or cats with EPI.

Folate and cobalamin are also of concern. Dogs and cats with EPI have low serum cobalamin concentrations.[14] Several mechanisms may play a role in the development of cobalamin deficiency in EPI. The absence of pancreatic bicarbonate secretion may reduce the intestinal luminal pH and the affinity of cobalamin for intrinsic factor.[24] In addition, it is suspected that a pancreatic rather than a gastric intrinsic factor may be necessary for ileal absorption of cobalamin in dogs.[24] Finally, when SIBOG is present, the proximal gut microflora may consume dietary cobalamin before it can be absorbed.[25,26] If serum levels of cobalamin are low, parenteral supplementation is recommended (100 to 250 µg, intramuscularly or subcutaneously, every seven days for several weeks) until serum cobalamin concentration is normalized.[14]

Serum folate levels are elevated in most dogs with EPI probably due to SIBOG and bacterial elaboration of folate.[14] Serum folate concentration may be decreased, however, in dogs with EPI and concurrent enteropathies involving the ileum.[14] In such cases, parenteral supplementation of folate is recommended until the ileal pathology is resolved. Folate deficiency inhibits pancreatic exocrine function in rats.[27]

ASSESS THE FOOD(S) AND FEEDING METHOD

Levels of key nutritional factors should be evaluated in foods currently fed to patients with EPI and compared with recommended levels (Table 22-37). Key nutritional factors include food digestibility, fat and fiber. Information from this aspect of assessment is essential for making any changes to foods currently provided. Changing to a more appropriate food is indicated if key nutritional factors in the food currently provided do not match recommended levels.

Because the feeding method is often altered in patients with EPI, a thorough assessment should include verification of the feeding method currently being used. Items to consider include feeding frequency, amount fed, how the food is offered, access to other food and who feeds the animal. All of this information should have been gathered when the history of the animal was obtained.

Patients with EPI usually should be fed multiple small meals per day with pancreatic enzyme supplementation to improve digestibility.

Feeding Plan

Dietary management is an essential component in the medical management of patients with maldigestive diseases. Dietary intake should meet the patient's nutrient needs in a form that promotes nutrient absorption. The organs of the GI tract have very large reserve capacities and the small intestine has a very large and efficient absorptive area. About 90% of the pancreas must be dysfunctional before clinical signs of maldigestion are seen.[1] Consequently, patients with clinical signs of maldigestion have very little digestive capacity remaining.

SELECT A FOOD(S)

Commercial veterinary therapeutic foods that are highly digestible and designed for patients with GI disease are listed in Table 22-10 and are recommended for patients with EPI. Feeding these foods to patients with EPI often allows smaller amounts of pancreatic enzyme preparations to be used, which results in significant cost savings for pet owners, especially those with large-breed dogs. Foods for young, growing dogs with EPI should also meet the optimal levels of key nutritional factors for growth. (See Chapter 9.)

DETERMINE A FEEDING METHOD

Patients presenting with signs of malnutrition due to chronic maldigestion should be given parenteral nutritional support during the diagnostic work-up. Parenteral nutrition in the management of these patients is primarily supportive, may be essential in the initial stages of case management and improves the patient's attitude and disposition. Parenteral nutrition also improves caloric, nitrogen and micronutrient balances in veterinary patients, thereby decreasing risks associated with diagnostic procedures including exploratory surgery. Continued administration of parenteral nutrition (more than three days) is necessary in debilitated patients as a supportive procedure until nutrients can be adequately absorbed. Parenteral nutrition can be performed at most practices in a manner similar to other fluid therapies. (See Chapter 12.)

At home, feeding two to three times daily helps prevent dietary overload and osmotic diarrhea. Underweight patients should be fed in excess of DER until ideal body weight and condition (3/5) are reached. Even after patients reach ideal body weight, it may be necessary to offer DER plus 20% to allow for the persistent degree of malabsorption in patients with EPI. Pancreatic enzymes should be added immediately before feeding. (See below.)

DIET-DRUG INTERACTIONS

In addition to dietary management, effective treatment of EPI requires oral administration of pancreatic enzymes. Most often, pancreatic enzymes are supplied as dried, powdered extracts of bovine or porcine pancreas (Table 22-38). Lipase activity of pancreatic enzyme preparations varies markedly. As a general rule, the more expensive preparations are the more effective lipase preparations. If available, raw pancreas can be fed successfully.[21] Raw pancreas can be frozen for several months without losing enzyme activity. Dogs should receive 100 g of freshly thawed, chopped pancreas, whereas 30 to 90 g of chopped pancreas can be fed per meal to cats. Tablets, capsules and enteric-coated preparations are not recommended.

Bacterial lipase preparations isolated from *Burkholderia plantarii* are in development. These preparations appear to resist acidity and proteases. Both powdered and liquid bacterial lipases have been used successfully in dogs with experimental EPI.[28]

Pancreatic enzyme supplementation for dogs should be initiated at a dose of 2 tsp of powdered pancreatic extract (or crushed tablets) per 20 kg body weight at each meal. For cats, a starting dose of 1 tsp should be administered with each meal.[28] Enzymes should be mixed with food immedi-

Table 22-38. Enzyme preparations used in patients with exocrine pancreatic insufficiency.*

Products (manufacturers)	Lipase	Protease	Amylase	How supplied
Viokase-V Powder (Fort Dodge)	57,000	285,000	428,000	Powder
Viokase-V Tablets (Fort Dodge)	9,000	57,000	64,000	Tablets
Viokase Powder (Robins)	16,800	70,000	70,000	Powder
Pancrezyme Powder (Daniels Pharmaceuticals)	61,000	330,000	440,000	Powder
Pancrezyme Tablets (Daniels Pharmaceuticals)	9,000	57,000	64,000	Tablets
Pancrease MT4 Capsules (McNeil)	4,000	12,000	12,000	Enteric coated microtablets
Pancrease MT10 Capsules (McNeil)	10,000	30,000	30,000	Enteric coated microtablets
Pancrease Capsules (McNeil)	4,000	25,000	20,000	Enteric coated microspheres
Pancreatic Plus Powder (Butler)	71,400	388,000	460,000	Powder
Pancreatic Plus Tablets (Butler)	9,000	57,000	64,000	Tablets
Pancrelipase Capsules (Geneva)	4,000	25,000	20,000	Enteric coated pellets

*Enzymatic contents (IU) per capsule, tablet or tsp of powder (2.8 g).

ately before the meal is fed. Owners may be able to decrease the dose of pancreatic enzymes based on their pet's response. Most dogs require at least 1 tsp of enzymes per meal.[14]

Antacids or H_2-receptor blockers have been recommended in the therapeutic regimen to reduce gastric acid-induced destruction of orally administered enzymes. This practice, however, is costly and does not increase efficacy of pancreatic enzyme supplementation.[2] Concurrent oral administration of sodium bicarbonate or bile salts and pre-incubation of the meal with pancreatic enzymes are also unnecessary.[2,14] In one study, adding digestive enzymes to food 20 to 30 minutes before feeding did not improve the response to dietary management.[29]

Oral antibiotics may be necessary to resolve clinical signs in dogs and cats with concurrent SIBOG. Tetracycline (20 mg/kg body weight, per os, t.i.d. for 21 days) is most often recommended for this purpose; however, metronidazole (10 to 20 mg/kg body weight, per os, every 24 hours for seven to 14 days) may be more effective if SIBOG with anaerobic organisms is suspected.

Concurrent diabetes mellitus in EPI cases must be managed with insulin. Unfortunately, the fiber-enhanced foods often recommended for diabetic pets are contraindicated for those with EPI.[30] Dietary management of patients with concurrent diabetes mellitus and EPI often requires a modified profile of key nutritional factors. In many cases, foods containing 10 to 15% DM fat, 50 to 55% DM complex, soluble carbohydrate and 5 to 10% total dietary fiber can be used.

Reassessment

Clinical signs usually resolve within two to three days with proper dietary therapy, and weight gain is evident by five to 10 days. Successfully managed canine cases of EPI are recognized by weight gain (0.5 to 1 kg per week) and improved body condition and stool consistency. The food and enzyme dose should be re-evaluated if less satisfactory results are obtained. Often, the initial dose of enzymes is inadequate and must be increased. Every effort should be made to rule out concurrent small bowel disease (e.g., eosinophilic gastroenteritis, lymphoplasmacytic enteritis, SIBOG) when clinical response is unsatisfactory.

Well-compensated patients should be evaluated immediately if a change or decline in condition is noted. Feeding more food than expected may be necessary to compensate for decreased digestibility and to maintain optimal body weight and condition. Regaining or maintaining optimal body weight and condition, normal activity level, a positive attitude and absence of clinical signs are measures of successful dietary management.

Acute and Chronic Pancreatitis

Clinical Importance

Pancreatitis has been recognized as a clinical entity in dogs for more than a century.[31] In dogs, acute pancreatitis is an important differential diagnosis for vomiting and abdominal pain. Because of difficulties in diagnosis, pancreatitis is a less common diagnosis in cats. However, based on recent clinical reports, recognition of feline pancreatitis is apparently increasing.[32-35]

Assessment

ASSESS THE ANIMAL

History and Physical Examination

Dogs with pancreatitis most often present with acute vomiting. Vomiting may be sporadic and mild or very severe. Other clinical signs include abdominal pain, depression, anorexia, fever and diarrhea. Icterus and pale stools may be reported if pancreatic inflammation and edema are severe enough to result in common bile duct obstruction. If present, diarrhea is usually of large bowel origin because the transverse colon passes dorsal to the pancreas and is susceptible to local inflammation at that site.

An episode of dietary indiscretion has often occurred during the 24 hours before the onset of vomiting. Consumption of high-fat table food is commonly related by the owner. Occasionally, the onset of clinical signs is preceded by administration of drugs associated with pancreatitis. Corticosteroids, in particular, have been linked to pancreatitis in dogs.[31]

Cats with pancreatitis have highly variable clinical signs. In some cats, the disease may mimic the typical canine presentation (i.e., acute vomiting, lethargy, anorexia, diarrhea and abdominal pain). In others, a more indolent, smoldering course occurs, resulting in a mild chronic illness.[34] In some cats, pancreatitis may be linked to diabetes mellitus and clinical signs may include polydipsia/polyuria and weight loss.[34] In others, hepatic lipidosis or cholangiohepatitis may occur concurrently.[32,36]

Depression, fever and dehydration may be the most prominent physical examination findings. Abdominal palpation may elicit splinting and discomfort that can be localized to the right cranial quadrant. Icterus, shock and coagulopathies may be detected in severe cases.

Clinical manifestations are variable in chronic pancreatitis. Weight loss and poor body condition may be the only signs noted in cats. An abnormal thickening or hardness of the falciform fat pad may be palpated in some cats, suggesting saponification and fat necrosis.

Laboratory and Other Clinical Information

The laboratory diagnosis of acute and chronic pancreatitis can be very frustrating. Diagnosis is hampered by the poor specificity of available laboratory tests and the inaccessibility of tissue for cytologic or histopathologic examination. Serum amylase and lipase activities are the most commonly used laboratory tests for the diagnosis of pancreatitis in dogs and cats. Unfortunately, these tests are not very specific because they are influenced by a number of other disease conditions (e.g., renal failure, dehydration, hyperlipidemia). In addition, the short half-life of amylase and lipase often precludes their use as diagnostic aids unless the patient is presented promptly after the onset of clinical signs. If present, hyperamylasemia and hyperlipasemia should be considered supportive of a diagnosis of pancreatitis, if azotemia and hyperlipidemia are not present.

Serum TLI concentration has been suggested as a diagnostic aid for evaluating dogs and cats with suspected pancreatitis. Because TLI is specifically pancreatic in origin, high serum TLI concentrations may prove a more reliable indicator of clinical pancreatitis than high amylase or lipase activities.[37]

A complete blood cell count, serum biochemistry profile and urinalysis should be done for any dog or cat suspected to have pancreatitis to rule out other potential causes for the clinical signs. Additionally, these tests may aid in the diagnosis of concurrent medical conditions such as diabetes mellitus, hepatic lipidosis, interstitial nephritis and cholangiohepatitis. An inflammatory leukogram is typically identified in patients with pancreatitis. A degenerative left shift may indicate severe necrotic pancreatitis. If thrombocytopenia is noted on the hemogram, a complete coagulation screen should be performed to rule out disseminated intravascular coagulation.

Table 22-39. Risk factors for pancreatitis in dogs and cats.

Breed
  Briard
  Himalayan cat
  Miniature schnauzer
  Sheltie
Diet
  Dietary indiscretion
  High-fat, low-protein foods
Drug administration
  Azathioprine
  Corticosteroids
  L-asparaginase
  Organophosphate insecticides (cats)
Fasting hyperlipidemia
Gender
  Castrated males
  Spayed females
Hepatobiliary disease
  Feline suppurative cholangiohepatitis
Hypercalcemia
  Hyperparathyroidism
  Intravenous calcium infusion
Increasing age
Intervertebral disk disease
Ischemia or reperfusion
  Postgastric dilatation-volvulus
Obesity

Imaging can be useful for diagnosing pancreatitis in dogs and cats. Findings consistent with pancreatic inflammation on survey abdominal radiographs may include haziness and widening of the gastroduodenal angle in the right cranial quadrant. Often, segmental gas distention of the proximal duodenum is noted. Ultrasonography may reveal fluid-filled cysts or abscesses within the pancreatic parenchyma and can be used to guide needle aspiration of pancreatic masses.[38]

Risk Factors

Several risk factors have been associated with pancreatitis in dogs and cats (Table 22-39). Most animals with these risk factors, however, do not develop pancreatitis.

An association has been made between hyperlipidemia and acute pancreatitis in dogs and people, which has led to speculation that disturbances in lipid metabolism may be involved.[31] The exact relationship is not known in dogs or cats and information is often extracted from human cases. In people and pets, hyperlipidemia is thought to precede and cause the development of pancreatitis; however, it can also be evident during and after such episodes.[31] The rate of hyperlipidemia in people with pancreatitis has been estimated between 3 and 12% when alcoholics are not included in the case study. The incidence of hyperlipidemia has not been established in dogs or cats with pancreatitis, but is generally thought to be high. In a retrospective study of fatal acute pancreatitis in dogs, 26% of patients were hyperlipidemic.[39] However, experimentally induced pancreatitis in dogs has not resulted in lipemia or hypertriglyceridemia.[40,41] Hypertriglyceridemia is present in some but not all naturally occurring cases of canine pancreatitis as determined by serum lipid and electrophoretic patterns.[41,42] Most people with pancreatitis do not have hyperlipidemia; however, those that do and who are not alcoholics more often have a known pre-existing hyperlipoproteinemia type I and V, more specifically hypertriglyceridemia. Similarly, several pet breeds are considered to be predisposed to pancreatitis (e.g., miniature schnauzers, briards, Shetland sheepdogs, Siamese cats) because they are commonly hypertriglyceridemic. (See Chapter 24.)

Feeding a high-fat (>20% DMB) food, treat or table food has often been associated with the onset of acute pancreatitis. Experimentally, feeding high-fat, low-protein foods was associated with the development of pancreatitis and hepatic lipidic changes in dogs.[43,44] The most widely repeated explanation for the association between hypertriglyceridemia and acute pancreatitis is that hydrolysis of serum triglycerides by lipase within the pancreatic microvasculature releases free fatty acids locally. Free fatty acids cause microthrombi and/or bind with calcium to cause further capillary damage, which, in turn, releases more pancreatic lipase.[45] Consumption of calorically dense, high-fat foods also contributes to obesity in pets. Obesity is also considered a risk factor for pancreatitis. In a recent report, 43% of dogs with acute pancreatitis were considered overweight or obese.[39]

Pancreatitis has been associated with hypercalcemia in several dogs with hyperparathyroidism and in a dog receiving a calcium infusion.[31] Experimentally, elevated ionized calcium concentrations can induce pancreatitis in cats.[46] The pathophysiologic mechanism for pancreatitis in association with hypercalcemia has not been elucidated.[31]

Drug-induced pancreatitis in people is very common; alcohol consumption is recognized as the most common cause of the disease. Reports of drug-induced pancreatitis in companion animals are rare. Anecdotal reports suggest that corticosteroids are the most common drug associated with pancreatitis in dogs. Pancreatitis is common in dogs with hyperadrenocorticism and in dogs receiving corticosteroids for management of intervertebral disk disease.[47] Experimentally, corticosteroids increase the sensitivity of dispersed acinar cells to cholecystokinin and stimulate proliferation of the pancreatic ductular epithelium.[31] Evidence is lacking for a role of corticosteroids in the development of pancreatitis in cats.

Ischemia and reperfusion injury have been linked to acute pancreatitis.[14,31] Hypovolemic shock, GDV and abdominal trauma have been reported to precede acute pancreatitis.[14,31] In addition, abdominal surgery marked by inept manipulation of the pancreas can result in pancreatitis.[14,31]

Etiopathogenesis

Acute pancreatitis is the sudden onset of inflammation of the pancreatic acinar tissue. Typically, the primary histopathologic lesion is edema. After resolution, there is usually no residual pancreatic lesion. However, in more severe cases, the pancreatic lesion may become hemorrhagic or may progress to necrosis (Figure 22-22). Mortality is high in acute necrotizing pancreatitis. Acute edematous or hemorrhagic pancreatitis may occur as a singular or recurrent event in dogs and cats.

Pancreatitis occurs as a consequence of intracellular pancreatic acinar enzymatic activation and resultant autodigestion of the pancreas. In the normal pancreas, safeguards ensure that harmful pancreatic enzymes are not activated until they reach the intestinal lumen (Table 22-40).[48] Pancreatic enzymes are synthesized in endoplasmic reticuli, modified in Golgi apparatuses and stored in zymogen granules within acinar cells. Evidence suggests that intracellular pancreatic enzyme activation occurs as a result of abnormal zymogen activation. Normally, zymogens and lysosomes are segregated intracellularly. In pancreatitis, lysosomes containing proteases fuse with zymogen granules (Figure 22-23).[31] The lysosomal contents (e.g., proteases such as cathepsin B) activate trypsinogen. In addition, the acidic environment of lysosomes interferes with self-regulating trypsin inhibitors stored with pancreatic enzymes in zymogen granules.

Cholecystokinin and acetylcholine are widely recognized as the principal physiologic mediators of pancreatic enzyme secretion.[31] Normally, these substances initiate fusion of zymogen granules with the acinar cell membrane. Hyperstimulation of the pancreas with supraphysiologic doses of cholecystokinin appears to cause pancreatitis in experimental animals by interfering with the intracellular movement of zymogens resulting in fusion of zymogens and lysosomes.[31] The lysosomal enzyme cathepsin B is then thought to activate trypsinogen and precipitate pancreatitis.[31] Pancreatic duct obstruction also appears to facilitate fusion of zymogens and lysosomal enzymes. Foods that are high in fat and protein (particularly the amino acid arginine) stimulate production and release of cholecystokinin, gastrin and secretin.[31] Organophosphate insecticides and intravenous calcium infusions are hypothesized to cause hyperstimulation via cholecystokinin.[31]

Bile acid and enteric reflux into the pancreatic duct can also activate pancreatic enzymes interstitially (i.e., within the pancreatic duct system and interstitium).[31] This mech-

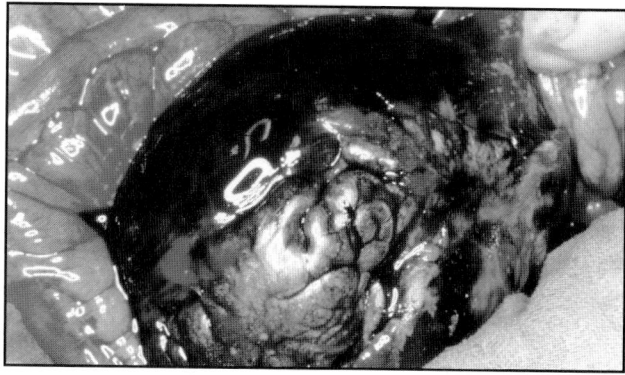

Figure 22-22. Intraoperative photograph of a dog with acute necrotizing pancreatitis. (Courtesy Dr. Dan Smeak, College of Veterinary Medicine, The Ohio State University, Columbus.)

Table 22-40. Protection against autodigestion.*

Enterokinase, produced by the duodenal brush border, is required for activation of proenzymes.
Pancreatic enzymes are synthesized as proenzymes (zymogens).
Serum protease inhibitors bind free trypsin.
The pancreas secretes a trypsin inhibitor in pancreatic juice that binds free trypsin.
Zymogens and lysosomal enzymes are stored in different intracytoplasmic membranes.

*Modified from Stewart AF. Pancreatitis in dogs and cats: Cause, pathogenesis, diagnosis and treatment. Compendium on Continuing Education for the Practicing Veterinarian 1994; 16: 1423-1431.

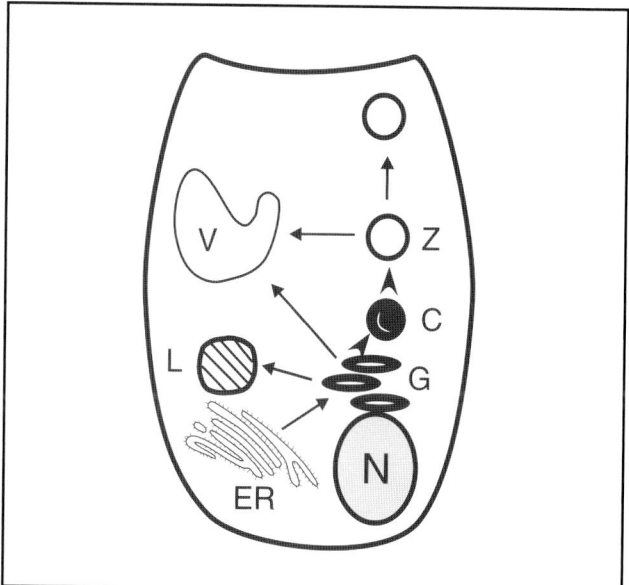

Figure 22-23. Schematic representation of zymogen and lysosomal fusion in acute pancreatitis. Digestive and lysosomal enzymes are synthesized in the rough endoplasmic reticulum (ER) and transferred to the Golgi apparatus (G) next to the nucleus (N). Normally, digestive and lysosomal enzymes are separated. Digestive enzymes are concentrated in zymogen granules within acinar cells and lysosomal enzymes are stored separately in lysosomes (L). Digestive enzymes are concentrated in condensing vacuoles (C) and in zymogen granules (Z) that fuse with luminal-plasma membranes. Hyperstimulation of the pancreas results in mixing of lysomal and digestive enzymes in large vacuoles (V). (Adapted from Simpson KW. Current concepts of the pathogenesis and pathophysiology of acute pancreatitis in the dog and cat. Compendium on Continuing Education for the Practicing Veterinarian 1993; 15: 247-254.)

anism is thought to be involved in the development of pancreatitis in cats in conjunction with suppurative cholangiohepatitis and enteritis.[31] The anatomic configuration of the common bile duct and pancreatic duct in cats facilitates this mechanism. Experimentally, free fatty acids generated by the action of lipase on triglycerides damage acinar cell membranes, releasing lecithin, which causes marked necrosis of acinar cells when converted to lysolecithin by phospholipase A_2.[31]

Regardless of the initiating cause, active pancreatic enzymes (trypsin, phospholipase, collagenase and elastase) and inflammatory mediators are released into the pancreatic tissues and blood vessels. These factors apparently activate coagulation, fibrinolytic, kinin and complement cascades.[31] Circulating defense mechanisms include α_1-antitrypsin and α_2-macroglobulin, which bind to active enzymes to contain local damage and prevent systemic damage.[31] After these defenses are overwhelmed, increased pancreatic permeability leads to fluid loss into the pancreas and the abdomen, a decline in pancreatic blood flow and an increase in the local concentrations of pancreatic enzymes and inflammatory mediators.[31] Large numbers of leukocytes migrate to the inflamed pancreas and serve as a source of free radicals, inflammatory mediators and enzymes.[31] This vicious, self-perpetuating cycle may ultimately lead to thrombosis of pancreatic blood vessels and pancreatic necrosis. Systemic complications may develop, including hypovolemic shock and disseminated intravascular coagulation.

Chronic pancreatitis is less commonly recognized in companion animals vs. people in whom alcohol can serve as a constant stimulus for smoldering acinar inflammation. Some authors suggest that chronic mild interstitial pancreatitis is the most common form of pancreatitis recognized in cats.[14] Histopathologic examination of tissues from dogs and cats with chronic pancreatitis reveals irreversible fibrotic changes resulting from the persistent inflammatory condition. Both chronic and recurrent pancreatitis may result in acquired EPI.

Key Nutritional Factors

Water
Water is the most important nutrient in patients with acute vomiting because of the potential for life-threatening dehydration due to excessive fluid loss and inability of patients to replace those losses. Moderate to severe dehydration should be corrected with appropriate parenteral fluid therapy rather than using the oral route.

Protein
Free amino acids (i.e., phenylalanine, tryptophan and valine) in the duodenum are a strong stimulus for pancreatic secretion, in fact, more so than fat.[49] Therefore, excess dietary protein should be avoided, while providing adequate protein for recovery and tissue repair. Protein levels (DMB) of 15 to 30% for dogs and 30 to 45% for cats are appropriate.

Fat
Obese and hypertrigylceridemic patients recovering from pancreatitis should receive low-fat foods (<10% DMB). Other patients can be fed moderate-fat foods (10 to 15% DMB). The most clinically relevant form of hypertriglyceridemia in veterinary patients is hyperchylomicronemia because triacylglycerides make up 84 to 89% of the lipids in chylomicrons. (See Chapter 24.) Plasma chy-

lomicrons are derived from two sources. Large (12-carbon) triglycerides are present for a few hours after ingestion of dietary fat, whereas smaller triglycerides, secreted from the liver, are always present and independent of dietary fat.

ASSESS THE FOOD(S) AND FEEDING METHOD

Levels of protein and fat should be evaluated in foods currently fed to patients with pancreatitis and compared with recommended levels. Information from this aspect of assessment is essential for making any changes to foods currently provided. Changing to a more appropriate food is indicated if protein and fat levels in the food currently fed do not match recommended levels.

Because the feeding method is often altered in patients with pancreatitis, a thorough assessment should include verification of the feeding method currently being used. Items to consider include feeding frequency, amount fed, how the food is offered, access to other food sources including table food and garbage and who feeds the animal. All of this information should have been gathered when the history of the animal was obtained. In cases in which acute pancreatitis is associated with eating garbage or other inappropriate foods (most often during a holiday), strict avoidance of foods other than the pet's regular food is recommended.

Feeding Plan

The goals of dietary management of patients with pancreatitis are to decrease stimuli to pancreatic secretion (and thus prevent pancreatic autodigestion) and still provide adequate nutrient levels to support tissue repair and recovery. Acute hemorrhagic or necrotizing pancreatitis should be considered a medical emergency. Initially, appropriate parenteral fluid therapy should be provided to correct dehydration and electrolyte and acid-base disturbances. Oral food intake stimulates pancreatic secretions by several mechanisms. Likewise, the physical presence of food in the stomach stimulates gastrin, which in turn stimulates pancreatic secretion. Therefore, NPO therapy is the initial treatment of choice.

Therapy used in conjunction with the feeding plan includes plasma transfusions, nasogastric suctioning of gastric secretions and air, anticholinergic agents, somatostatin analogues (octreotide), antibiotics and surgical exploration of the abdomen for extirpation or drainage of pancreatic abscesses or pseudocysts.

SELECT A FOOD(S)

Small amounts of water, ice cubes, oral rehydration solutions or monomeric foods can be offered after vomiting and abdominal discomfort subside. Monomeric foods are water-soluble, liquid foods containing nutrients in their simplest absorbable form. Thus, nutrients in these foods minimally stimulate pancreatic secretion.[50] Some monomeric products also contain glutamine to stimulate enterocyte hyperplasia after several days of NPO therapy, which may have induced intestinal mucosal atrophy. In general, 1 to 2 ml/kg body weight q.i.d. are well tolerated and rarely induce vomiting.

If liquids are well tolerated for one to two days, solid food may be slowly reintroduced. Highly digestible, commercial veterinary therapeutic foods designed for patients with GI disease are often used initially (Table 22-10).

These foods also contain moderate levels of protein and fat. If vomiting recurs, NPO therapy should be reinstituted and feeding attempted again after 12 to 24 hours. A veterinary therapeutic food formulated for patients with GI diseases should be fed for another seven to 10 days before reintroducing the patient's regular food, if it is to be used at all.

Low-fat (<10% DM fat) foods are often used if obesity or hyperlipidemia was a contributing factor (Table 22-22). High-fat commercial foods (>20% DM fat), table foods and snacks should be avoided. It may be necessary to remind clients of this around the holiday season, when many owners fall prey to the desire to share family meals with pets.

DETERMINE A FEEDING METHOD

Discontinuing oral intake of food and water (NPO) is the cornerstone of initial therapy for acute pancreatitis. Factors that would normally stimulate pancreatic secretions (GI distention and hormone release [gastrin, secretin, cholecystokinin]) are reduced when food and water are withheld. Most patients respond within two to four days. After vomiting and abdominal discomfort resolve or lessen in severity, liquids and food can be reintroduced gradually over several days. Normal feeding methods can be reintroduced after several days without clinical signs, unless dietary indiscretion or inappropriate foods or feeding methods initially contributed to the problem.

After three days of the NPO protocol, patients with severe pancreatitis should receive enteral or parenteral nutritional support. The method deemed most desirable is the least invasive, supports the patient nutritionally and minimally stimulates pancreatic secretions.

Protracted cases of pancreatitis often require parenteral nutrition to meet the patient's energy, protein, electrolyte and B-vitamin requirements while minimizing pancreatic secretions. (See Chapter 12.) Parenteral administration of nutritional solutions (including lipid) has been associated with pancreatic atrophy; so pancreatic stimulation is minimal or nonexistent.[51,52] Intravenous administration of nutrients to support pancreatic patients through a five- to 14-day course of vomiting is possible, safe and economical in most practices. (See Chapter 12.) The authors have found parenteral solutions to be of particular benefit in managing pancreatitis in cats, especially when complicated by hepatic disorders, IBD or interstitial nephritis.[32,36]

Selection of parenteral solutions for feeding patients with pancreatitis is controversial because of the association between hyperlipidemia and pancreatitis. Some authors suggest that selection of parenteral solutions be based on amino acid and dextrose content only, whereas others advocate the use of lipid solutions in the admixture if the patient is not hyperlipidemic. People with pancreatitis have a decreased capacity to oxidize glucose, peripheral resistance to insulin and hyperglycemia. Administering glucose as the sole nonprotein energy source perpetuates hyperglycemia and increases the risk of hepatic steatosis.[53] Lipids in total nutrient admixtures (See Chapter 12.) have been used successfully in dogs and cats with pancreatitis.[b] Lipid emulsions administered intravenously are synthetic 0.5-µm chylomicrons that appear to be well used by rats, people and dogs with pancreatitis.[54-57] People with pancreatitis and concurrent hypertriglyceridemia or hyperlipoproteinemia type I and V are not given lipids intravenously until the levels of these parameters have decreased.[53] Plasma lipid data from dogs

with naturally occurring pancreatitis are sparse; however, not all canine patients with pancreatitis are hypertriglyceridemic.[41,42] Therefore, serum triglyceride levels should be assessed before lipids are administered intravenously. Although isolated cases of pancreatitis in people have been linked to lipid infusion, these cases are considered rare and were complicated by concurrent diseases such as alcoholism and IBD.[58] Second, respiratory quotients in people with pancreatitis are between 0.76 and 0.91, indicating mixed fuel (glucose and lipid) usage. Finally, adding fat to dextrose infusions improves nitrogen balance.[59] Although respiratory quotients have not been measured in dogs and cats with pancreatitis, lipid administration is well tolerated, most likely because the liver would be using endogenous fat stores if lipid were not supplied exogenously as in people.

Placing a jejunostomy tube and bypassing the stomach and duodenum should also be considered in prolonged cases of pancreatitis. These tubes are best placed when patients must undergo general anesthesia and abdominal surgery for other reasons.[60] Studies have demonstrated the efficacy of nasojejunal feeding in people with mild and complicated acute pancreatitis.[61,62] Jejunal feedings in people and dogs stimulate pancreatic secretion no more than parenteral feedings.[63,64] In veterinary patients, however, a practical technique for nasojejunal feeding has not been developed; thus, jejunal feeding requires abdominal surgery. For that reason, some clinicians prefer parenteral feeding of patients with chronic, refractory pancreatitis.

Monomeric liquid foods infused directly into the duodenum of dogs stimulate some pancreatic output, whereas oral administration of the same monomeric foods stimulated a greater volume of pancreatic secretion.[51] If jejunal tube feeding is selected, a liquid food supplemented with glutamine to maintain intestinal integrity that minimally stimulates the pancreas and meets the patient's RER is most suitable. Directly infusing a readily absorbable monomeric liquid food (vs. a polymeric product) into the jejunum should also reduce pancreatic secretions because whole nutrients elicit a greater response from the pancreas than monomeric nutrient forms. Monomeric liquid foods may be infused into the jejunum by slow continuous gravity drip (1 to 2 ml/kg body weight/hour) or, preferably, by an enteral pump. This rate of enteral feeding meets the RER of most patients and precludes other forms of nutritional support until oral intake is possible. If patients tolerate this rate of administration, solid food in small frequent meals may be given for several days in addition to the liquid feedings. Liquid feedings may cease and the number of oral meals per day can be increased when solid food is well tolerated.

Reassessment

Hospitalized patients with pancreatitis should be assessed frequently. Assessment of body weight and condition are recommended to ensure adequate hydration and caloric intake, if instituted. Electrolyte and acid-base status should be monitored to assess adequacy of therapy. Certain laboratory parameters (leukogram and serum concentrations of amylase, lipase, TLI and bilirubin) are helpful markers of progress. However, the patient's attitude, appetite and presence or absence of vomiting and abdominal pain are often the most important predictors of progress. In addition, it is imperative that sera be evaluated for triglyceride concentration initially and then monitored daily for lipemia. It is important to distinguish between lipemia from endogenous sources vs. exogenous fat emulsions when parenteral nutrition is administered.

Discharged patients should be re-evaluated in a number of weeks. If a low-fat, high-fiber food was recommended to control obesity or hyperlipidemia, body weights should be recorded and serum triglyceride concentration determined (or inspected visually for lipemia) to assess compliance with the dietary management program. Regaining or maintaining optimal body weight and condition, normal activity level and absence of clinical signs are measures of successful dietary management.

■ ENDNOTES & REFERENCES

Introduction Reference

1. Guilford WG. Nutritional management of gastrointestinal diseases. In: Guilford WG, Center SA, Strombeck DR, et al, eds. Strombeck's Small Animal Gastroenterology, 3rd ed. Philadelphia, PA: WB Saunders Co, 1996; 889-910.

Oral Disorders References

1. Theilen GH, Madewell BR, eds. Tumors of the digestive tract. In: Veterinary Cancer Medicine, 2nd ed. Philadelphia, PA: Lea & Febiger, 1987; 499-535.
2. DeBowes LJ. Evaluation and management of oral disease. In: August JR, ed. Consultations in Feline Internal Medicine 3. Philadelphia, PA: WB Saunders Co, 1997; 53-61.

Pharyngeal and Esophageal Disorders Endnote & References

ENDNOTE
a. Davenport DJ, Ware W, The Ohio State University, Columbus. Unpublished data. 1986.

REFERENCES
1. Fingeroth JM, Fossum TW. Late-onset regurgitation associated with persistent right aortic arch in two dogs. Journal of the American Veterinary Medical Association 1987; 191: 981-983.
2. Muldoon MM, Birchard SJ, Ellison GW. Long-term results of surgical correction of persistent right aortic arch in dogs: 25 cases (1980-1994). Journal of the American Veterinary Medical Association 1997; 210: 1761-1763.
3. Weyrauch EA, Willard MD. Esophagitis and benign esophageal strictures. Compendium on Continuing Education for the Practicing Veterinarian 1998; 20: 203-211.
4. Dewey CW, Shelton GD, Bailey CS, et al. Neuromuscular dysfunction in five dogs with acquired myasthenia gravis and presumed hypothyroidism. Progress in Veterinary Neurology 1995; 6: 117-123.
5. Shelton GD. Myasthenia gravis—1000 cases later (abstract). In: Proceedings. Fourteenth Annual Veterinary Medical Forum, American College of Veterinary Internal Medicine, San Antonio, TX, 1996: 658.
6. Shelton GD. Pathogenesis of canine megaesophagus: Neuromuscular disorders. In: Proceedings. Fourteenth Annual Veterinary Medical Forum, American College of Veterinary Internal Medicine, San Antonio, TX, 1996: 581-582.
7. Gaynor AR, Shofer FS, Washabau RJ. Risk factors for acquired megaesophagus in dogs. Journal of the American Veterinary Medical Association 1997; 211: 1406-1412.
8. Bartges JW, Nelson DL. Reversible megaesophagus associated with atypical primary hypoadrenocorticism in a dog. Journal of the American Veterinary Medical Association 1992; 201: 889-891.
9. Rogers WA, Fenner WR, Sherding RG. Electromyographic and esophagomanometric findings in clinically normal dogs and in dogs with idiopathic megaesophagus. Journal of the American Veterinary Medical Association 1979; 174: 181-183.
10. Taillefer R, Jadliwalla M, Pellerin E, et al. Radionuclide esophageal transit in detection of esophageal motor dysfunction: Comparison with motility studies (manometry). Journal of Nuclear Medicine 1990; 31: 1921-1926.
11. Strombeck DR, Harrold D. Effects of atropine, acepromazine, meperidine, and xylazine on gastroesophageal sphincter pressure in the dog. American Journal of Veterinary Research 1985; 46: 963-965.
12. Leib MS, Hall RL. Megaesophagus in the dog. II. Clinical aspects. Compendium on Continuing Education for the Practicing Veterinarian 1984; 6: 11-17.
13. Shelton GD, Willard MD, Cardinet GH, et al. Acquired myasthenia gravis: Selective involvement of esophageal, pharyngeal and facial muscles. Journal of Veterinary Internal Medicine 1990; 4: 281-284.
14. Twedt DC. Diseases of the esophagus. In: Ettinger SJ, Feldman EC, eds. Textbook of Veterinary Internal Medicine, 4th ed. Philadelphia, PA: WB Saunders Co, 1995; 1124-1142.
15. Tan BJK, Diamant N. Assessment of the neural defect in a dog with idiopathic megaesophagus. Digestive Diseases and Sciences 1987; 32: 76-85.
16. Holland CT, Satchell PM, Farrow BR. Oesophageal compliance in naturally occurring canine megaesophagus. Australian Veterinary Journal 1993; 70: 414-420.
17. Holland CT, Satchell PM, Farrow BR. Vagal afferent dysfunction in naturally occurring canine esophageal motility disorders. Digestive Diseases and Sciences 1994; 39: 2090-2098.
18. Washabau RJ. Canine megaesophagus: Pathogenesis and therapy. In: Proceedings. Tenth Annual Veterinary Medical Forum, American College of Veterinary Internal Medicine, San Diego, CA, 1992: 671-673.
19. Hall JA, Magne ML, Twedt DC. Effect of acepromazine, diazepam, fentanyl-droperidol and oxymorphone on gastroesophageal sphincter pressure in healthy dogs. American Journal of Veterinary Research 1987; 48: 556-557.
20. Lantz GC, Cantwell HD, Van Vleet JF, et al. Pharyngostomy tube induced esophagitis in the dog: An experimental study. Journal of the American Animal Hospital Association 1983; 19: 207-212.
21. Washabau RJ, Hall JA. Diagnosis and management of gastrointestinal motility disorders in dogs and cats. Compendium on Continuing Education for the Practicing Veterinarian 1997; 19: 721-737.
22. Guilford WG. Nutritional management of gastrointestinal diseases. In: Guilford WG, Center SA, Strombeck DR, et al, eds. Strombeck's Small Animal Gastroenterology, 3rd ed. Philadelphia, PA: WB Saunders Co, 1996; 889-910.

Gastric Disorders Endnotes & References

ENDNOTES
a. Gastrografin. Squibb Diagnostics, New Brunswick, NJ, USA.
b. Remillard RL. Personal obervation. 1998.
c. BIPS. Med-ID, Grand Rapids, MI, USA.

REFERENCES
1. Tams TR. Vomiting, regurgitation, and dysphagia. In: Ettinger SJ, Feldman EC, eds. Textbook of Veterinary Internal Medicine, 4th ed. Philadelphia, PA: WB Saunders Co, 1995; 103-110.
2. Van der Gaag I. The histological appearance of peroral gastric biopsies in clinically healthy and vomiting dogs. Canadian Journal of Veterinary Research 1988; 52: 67-74.
3. Hottendorf GH, Hirth RS. Lesions of spontaneous subclinical disease in beagle dogs. Veterinary Pathology 1974; 11: 240-258.
4. Dow SW, Rosychuk RAW, McChesney AE, et al. Effects of flunixin and flunixin plus prednisone on the gastrointestinal tract of dogs. American Journal of Veterinary Research 1990; 51: 1131-1138.
5. Gilson SD, Parker BB, Twedt DC. Evaluation of two commercial test kits for detection of occult blood in feces of dogs. American Journal of Veterinary Research 1990; 51: 1385-1387.
6. Moon M, Myer W. Gastrointestinal contrast radiology in small animals. Seminars in Veterinary Medicine and Surgery: Small Animal 1986; 1: 121-143.
7. Guilford WG, Strombeck DR. Acute hemorrhagic enteropathy (hemorrhagic gastroenteritis: HGE). In: Guilford WG, Center SA, Strombeck DR, et al, eds. Strombeck's Small Animal Gastroenterology, 3rd ed. Philadelphia, PA: WB Saunders Co, 1996; 433-435.

8. Slappendel RJ, van der Gaag I, van Ness JJ, et al. Familial stomato-cytosis-hypertrophic gastritis (FSHG), a newly recognized disease in the dog (Drentse patrijshond). Veterinary Quarterly 1997; 13: 30-40.

9. Thornhill JA. Control of vomiting in the uremic patient. In: Kirk RW, ed. Current Veterinary Therapy VIII. Philadelphia, PA: WB Saunders Co, 1983; 1022-1025.

10. Booth DM. Serum gastrin levels in dogs with progressive liver disease (abstract). In: Proceedings. Eighth Annual Veterinary Medical Forum, American College of Veterinary Internal Medicine, Washington, DC, 1990; 1124.

11. Lipowitz AJ, Boulay JP, Klausner JS. Serum salicylate concentrations and endoscopic evaluation of the gastric mucosa in dogs after oral administration of aspirin-containing products. American Journal Veterinary Research 1986; 47: 1586-1589.

12. Wallace MS, Zawie DA, Garvey MS. Gastric ulceration in the dog secondary to the use of nonsteroidal antiinflammatory drugs. Journal of the American Animal Hospital Association 1990; 26: 467-472.

13. Davenport DJ. Hematemesis: Diagnosis and treatment. In: Kirk RW, Bonagura JD, eds. Current Veterinary Therapy XI. Philadelphia, PA: WB Saunders Co, 1992; 132-137.

14. Smith WO, Joel W, Wolf S. Experimental atrophic gastritis associated with inhibition of parietal cells. Transactions of the Association of American Physicians 1958; 71: 306-311.

15. Hennes AR, Sevelius H, Lewellyn T, et al. Atrophic gastritis in dogs. Archives of Pathology 1962; 73: 281-287.

16. Krohn KJE, Finlayson NDC. Inter-relations of humoral and cellular immune responses in experimental canine gastritis. Clinical and Experimental Immunology 1973; 14: 237-245.

17. Fukuma K, Sakaguchi S, Kuribayashi K, et al. Immunologic and clinical studies on murine experimental autoimmune gastritis induced by neonatal thymectomy. Gastroenterology 1988; 94: 274-283.

18. Guilford WG. Effect of diet on inflammatory bowel diseases. Veterinary Clinical Nutrition 1997; 4: 58-61.

19. Guilford WG, Roudebush P, Rogers Q. The histamine content of commercial pet foods. New Zealand Veterinary Journal 1994; 42: 201-204.

20. MacBurney M. Feeding through vomiting in pregnant women suffering hyperemesis using a naso-gastric tube with a slow frequent self feeding of small liquid meals. In: Gottschlich M, Matatese L, Shronts E, eds. Nutrition Support Dietetics Core Curriculum. Rockville, MD: Aspen Publishers, 1993.

21. Lantz G, Badylak S, Hiles M, et al. Treatment of reperfusion injury in dogs with experimentally induced gastric dilatation-volvulus. American Journal of Veterinary Research 1992; 53: 1594-1598.

22. Jennings P. Epidemiology of gastric dilatation-volvulus in the military working dog program. Military Medicine 1992; 157: 369-371.

23. Glickman L. Epidemiology of gastric dilation-volvulus in dogs. In: Proceedings. Twenty-first Congress of the World Small Animal Veterinary Association, Jerusalem, Israel, 1996; 81-82.

24. Muir W. Acid-base and electrolyte disturbances in dogs with gastric dilatation-volvulus. Journal of the American Veterinary Medical Association 1987; 181: 229-231.

25. Muir W. Gastric dilatation-volvulus in the dog, with the emphasis on cardiac arrhythmias. Journal of the American Veterinary Medical Association 1982; 180: 739-742.

26. Glickman L, Glickman N, Perez C, et al. Analysis of risk factors for gastric dilatation and dilatation-volvulus in dogs. Journal of the American Veterinary Medical Association 1994; 204: 1465-1471.

27. Glickman LT, Emerick T, Glickman N, et al. Radiological assessment of the relationship between thoracic conformation and the risk of gastric dilatation-volvulus in dogs. Journal of Veterinary Radiology and Ultrasound 1996; 37: 174-180.

28. Schaible RH, Zeich J, Glickman NW, et al. Predisposition to gastric dilatation-volvulus in relation to genetics of thoracic conformation in Irish setters. Journal of the American Animal Hospital Association 1997; 33: 379-383.

29. Schellenberg D, Yi Q, Glickman NW, et al. Influence of thoracic conformation and genetics on the risk of gastric dilatation-volvulus in Irish setters. Journal of the American Animal Hospital Association 1998; 34: 64-73.

30. Hall JA, Willer RL, Seim HB, et al. Gross and histologic evaluation of hepatogastric ligaments in clinically normal dogs and dogs with gastric dilatation-volvulus. American Journal of Veterinary Research 1995; 56: 1611-1614.

31. Glickman LT, Glickman NW, Schellenberg DB, et al. Multiple risk factors for the gastric dilatation-volvulus syndrome in dogs: A practitioner/owner case-control study. Journal of the American Animal Hospital Association 1997; 33: 197-204.

32. Braun L, Lester S, Kuzma AB, et al. Gastric dilatation-volvulus in the dog with histological evidence of preexisting inflammatory bowel disease: A retrospective study of twenty-three cases. Journal of the American Animal Hospital Association 1996; 32: 287-290.

33. Elwood CM. Risk factors for gastric dilatation in Irish setter dogs. Journal of Small Animal Practice 1998; 39: 185-190.

34. Theyse LFH, van de Brom WE, van Sluijs FJ. Small size of food particles and age as risk factors for gastric dilatation volvulus in Great Danes. Veterinary Record 1998; 143: 48-50.

35. Nagel M-L, Neumann W. Magen dilatation-volvulus-syndrom beim hund. Der Prakitsche Tierazt 1992; 73: 871-876.

36. Burrows C, Bright R, Spencer C. Influence of dietary composition on canine gastric emptying and motility–Potential role in acute gastric dilatation. American Journal of Veterinary Research 1985; 46: 2609-2612.

37. Van Kruiningen H, Wojan LD, Stake PE, et al. The influence of diet and feeding frequency on gastric function in the dog. Journal of the American Animal Hospital Association 1987; 23: 145-153.

38. Caywood D, Teague HD, Jackson DA, et al. Gastric gas analysis in the canine gastric dilatation-volvulus syndrome. Journal of the American Animal Hospital Association 1977; 13: 459-462.

39. Van Sluijs FJ, Wolvekamp WTC. Abnormal esophageal motility in dogs with recurrent gastric dilatation-volvulus (abstract). Veterinary Surgery 1993; 22: 250.

40. Guilford WG. Gastric dilatation, gastric dilatation-volvulus and chronic gastric volvulus. In: Guilford WG, Center SA, Strombeck DR, et al, eds. Strombeck's Small Animal Gastroenterology, 3rd ed. Philadelphia, PA: WB Saunders Co, 1996; 303-317.

41. Leib M, Wingfield WE, Twedt DC, et al. Plasma gastrin-immunoreactivity in dogs with acute gastric dilatation-volvulus. Journal of the American Veterinary Medical Association 1984; 185: 205-208.

42. Leib M, Wingfield WE, Twedt DC, et al. Gastric distention and gastrin in the dog. American Journal of Veterinary Research 1985; 46: 2011-2015.

43. Hall J, Twedt D, Curtis C. Relationship of plasma gastrin immunoreactivity and gastroesophageal sphincter pressure in clinically normal dogs and in dogs with previous gastric dilatation-volvulus. American Journal of Veterinary Research 1989; 50: 1228-1232.

44. Morris Animal Foundation. Report of the Panel on Bloat in Dogs. Englewood, CO, 1990.

45. Sparkes AH, Papasouliotis K, Barr FJ. Reference ranges for gastrointestinal transit of barium-impregnated polyethylene spheres in healthy cats. Journal of Small Animal Practice 1997; 38: 340-343.

46. Leib MS, Saunders GK, Moon ML, et al. Endoscopic diagnosis of chronic hypertrophic pyloric gastropathy in dogs. Journal of Veterinary Internal Medicine 1993; 7: 335-341.

47. Biller DS, Partington BP, Miyabayashi T, et al. Ultrasonographic appearance of chronic hypertrophic pyloric gastropathy in the dog. Journal of Veterinary Radiology and Ultrasound 1994; 35: 30-33.

48. Matthieson D, Walter M. Surgical treatment of chronic hypertrophic pyloric gastropathy in 45 dogs. Journal of the American Animal Hospital Association 1986; 22: 241-246.

49. Russell J, Bass P. Canine gastric emptying of fiber meals: Influence of meal viscosity and antroduodenal motility. American Journal of Physiology 1985; 249: G662-G667.

50. Prove J, Ehrlein HJ. Motor function of gastric antrum and pylorus for evacuation of low and high viscosity meals in dogs. Gut 1982; 23: 150-156.

51. Sandhu KS, El Samahi MM, Mena I, et al. Effect of pectin on gastric emptying and gastroduodenal motility in normal subjects. Gastroenterology 1987; 92: 486-492.

52. Fleming CR. Physiology of the gastrointestinal tract: As applied to patients receiving tube enteral nutrition. In: Rombeau JL, Rolandelli RH, eds. Clinical Nutrition: Enteral and Tube Feeding. Philadelphia. PA: WB Saunders Co, 1997; 12-22.

53. Leib MS. Diseases of the stomach. In: Leib MS, Monroe WE, eds. Practical Small Animal Internal Medicine. Philadelphia, PA: WB Saunders Co, 1997; 653-684.

Small Intestinal Disorders Endnotes & References

ENDNOTES

a. Davenport DJ. Unpublished data. 1996.

b. Remillard RL. Personal observation. 1996.

c. Remillard RL. Personal experience. 1998.

d. Davenport DJ. Unpublished data. 1991.

GI & PANCREAS

e. Vital E-A+D containing 100 IU of D and 300 IU of alpha-tocopherol per ml. Schering-Plough Animal Health Corp., Kenilworth, NJ, USA.
f. Remillard RL. Unpublished data. 1998.
g. Williams DA, School of Veterinary Medicine, Purdue University, West Lafayette, IN. Personal communication. 1993.

REFERENCES

1. Moon HW. Mechanisms in the pathogenesis of diarrhea: A review. Journal of the American Veterinary Medical Association 1978; 172: 443-448.
3. Scott FW. *Salmonella* implicated as a cause of song bird fever. Feline Health Topics 1988; 3: 5.
3. Hibler SC, Greene CE. Rickettsial infections in dogs. III. Salmon disease complex and hemobartonellosis. Compendium on Continuing Education for the Practicing Veterinarian 1986; 8: 251-258.
4. Chengappa MM, Staats J, Oberst RD, et al. Prevalence of *Salmonella* in raw meat used in diets of racing greyhounds. Journal of Veterinary Diagnostic Investigation 1993; 5: 372-377.
5. Davenport DJ. *Campylobacter* enteritis. In: Kirk RW, ed. Current Veterinary Therapy X. Philadelphia, PA: WB Saunders Co, 1989; 944-948.
6. Batt R, Barnes A, Rutgers HC, et al. Relative IgA deficiency and small intestinal bacterial overgrowth in German shepherd dogs. Research in Veterinary Science 1991; 50: 106-111.
7. Whitbread TJ, Batt RM, Garthwaite G. Relative deficiency of serum IgA in the German shepherd dog: A breed anomaly. Research in Veterinary Science 1984; 37: 350-352.
8. Guilford WG, Strombeck DR. Acute hemorrhagic enteropathy (hemorrhagic gastroenteritis: HE). In: Guilford WG, Center SA, Strombeck DR, et al, eds. Strombeck's Small Animal Gastroenterology, 3rd ed. Philadelphia, PA: WB Saunders Co, 1996; 433-435.
9. Oikawa M, Kaneko M, Yoshikawa T. Villous hypoplasia of the small intestine in neonatal foals. Zentralblatt Fur Veterinarmedizin. Reihe A 1992; 39: 121-129.
10. Lippert AC, Faulkner JE, Evans AT, et al. Total parenteral nutrition in clinically normal cats. Journal of the American Veterinary Medical Association 1989; 194: 669-676.
11. Remillard RL, Thatcher CD. Parenteral nutrition support in the small animal patient. Veterinary Clinics of North America: Small Animal Practice 1989; 19: 1287-1306.
12. Schulman RJ. Effect of different total parenteral nutrition fuel mixes on small intestinal growth and differentiation in the infant miniature pig. Gastroenterology 1988; 95: 85-92.
13. Remillard RL, Guerino F, Dudgeon DL, et al. Effects of intravenous glutamine and limited enteral feedings in piglets: Amelioration of small intestinal disuse atrophy. Journal of Nutrition 1998; 128: 2723S-2726S.
14. Levine GM, Dere JJ, Steiger E, et al. Role of oral intake in maintenance of gut mass and disaccharide activity. Gastroenterology 1974; 67: 975-982.
15. Yamada T. Gut hormone release induced by food ingestion. American Journal of Clinical Nutrition 1985; 42: 1033-1039.
16. Castillo RO, Feng JL, Stevenson DK, et al. Regulation of intestinal ontogeny by intraluminal nutrients. Journal of Pediatric Gastroenterology and Nutrition 1990; 10: 199-205.
17. Remillard RL, Dudgeon DL, Yardley J. Atrophied small intestinal responses to oral feedings of milk (abstract). Journal of Nutrition 1998; 128: 2727S-2729S.
18. Windmueller HG, Spaeth AE. Uptake and metabolism of plasma glutamine by the small intestine. Journal of Biological Chemistry 1974; 249: 5070-5079.
19. Souba WW, Klimberg VS, Plumley DA, et al. The role of glutamine in maintaining a healthy gut and supporting the metabolic response to injury and infection. Journal of Surgical Research 1990; 48: 383-391.
20. Souba WW, Roughneed PT, Goldwater DL, et al. Postoperative alterations in interorgan glutamine exchange in enterectomized dogs. Journal of Surgical Research 1987; 42: 117-125.
21. Zenger E, Willard MD. Oral rehydration therapy in companion animals. Companion Animal Practice 1989; 19: 6-10.
22. Avery ME, Snyder JD. Oral therapy for acute diarrhea: The underused simple solution. New England Journal of Medicine 1990; 323: 891-894.
23. Kendall PT, Holmes DW, Smith PM. Methods of prediction of the digestible energy content of dog foods from gross energy value, proximate analysis and digestible nutrient content. Journal of the Science of Food and Agriculture 1982; 3: 823-828.
24. Kendall PT. Comparable evaluation of apparent digestibility in dogs and cats. Proceedings of the Nutrition Society 1981; 40: 45a.
25. Walker JA, Harmon DL, Gross KL, et al. Evaluation of nutrient utilization in the canine using the ileal cannulation technique. Journal of Nutrition 1994; 124: 2672S-2676S.

26. Bissett SA, Haslett SJ, Sunvold GD. Comparison of wheat, potato, corn and rice assimilation in dogs with diarrhea using breath hydrogen tests. Veterinary Clinical Nutrition 1998; 5: 4-9.
27. Wolter R. Total digestibility and ileal digestibility of foods with a high level of starch from corn and tapioca in the dog. PhD Thesis. University of Alfort, France, 1993.
28. Schunemann VC, Muhlum A, Junker S, et al. Prececal and postileal digestibility of various starches and pH values and organic acid content of digesta and feces. Advances in Animal Physiology and Animal Nutrition 1994; 19: 44-58.
29. Baker DH, Czarnecki-Maulden GL. Comparative nutrition of cats and dogs. Annual Review of Nutrition 1991; 11: 239-263.
30. Kienzle E. Carbohydrate metabolism in the cat. 2. Digestion of starch. Journal of Animal Physiology and Animal Nutrition 1993; 69: 102-114.
31. Morris JG, Trudell J, Pencovic T. Carbohydrate digestion by the domestic cat (*Felis catus*). British Journal of Nutrition 1977; 37: 365-373.
32. Buddington RK, Chen JW, Diamond JM. Dietary regulation of intestinal brush-border sugar and amino acid transport in carnivores. American Journal of Physiology 1991; 261: R793-R801.
33. Kienzle E. Carbohydrate metabolism of the cat. 1. Activity of amylase in the gastrointestinal tract of the cat. Journal of Animal Physiology and Animal Nutrition 1993; 69: 92-101.
34. Sherding RG. Diseases of the intestines. In: The Cat: Diseases and Clinical Management. New York, NY: Churchill Livingstone, 1989; 955-1006.
35. Washabau RJ, Buffington CA, Strombeck DR. Evaluation and management of carbohydrate malassimilation. In: Kirk RW, ed. Current Veterinary Therapy IX. Philadelphia, PA: WB Saunders Co, 1986; 889-892.
36. Bissett SA, Guilford WG, Lawoko CR, et al. Effect of food particle size on carbohydrate assimilation assessed by breath hydrogen testing in dogs. Veterinary Clinical Nutrition 1997; 4: 82-95.
37. Harmon DL, Walker JA, Silvio JM, et al. Nutrient digestibility in dogs fed fiber-containing diets. Veterinary Clinical Nutrition 1999; 6: 6-10.
38. National Research Council. Nutrient Requirements of Dogs. Washington, DC: National Academy of Sciences, 1985; 1-79.
39. Kendall PT, Burger IH, Smith PM. Methods of estimation of the metabolizable energy of cat food. Feline Practice 1985; 15: 38-44.
40. Lewis LD, Boulay JP, Chow FHC. Fat excretion and assimilation by the cat. Feline Practice 1979; 9: 46-49.
41. Windmueller HG, Spaeth AE. Identification of ketone bodies and glutamine as the major respiratory fuels in vivo for post-absorptive rat small intestine. Journal of Biological Chemistry 1978; 253: 69-76.
42. Kuhn KS, Stehle P, Furst P. Glutamine content of protein and peptide-based enteral products. Journal of Parenteral and Enteral Nutrition 1996; 20: 292-295.
43. Guilford WG. Idiopathic inflammatory bowel diseases. In: Guilford WG, Center SA, Strombeck DR, et al, eds. Strombeck's Small Animal Gastroenterology, 3rd ed. Philadelphia, PA: WB Saunders Co, 1996; 451-486.
44. Leib MS. Diseases of the intestines. In: Leib MS, Monroe WE, eds. Practical Small Animal Internal Medicine. Philadelphia, PA: WB Saunders Co, 1997; 685-760.
45. Breitschwerdt EB. Immmunoproliferative enteropathy of basenjis. Seminars in Veterinary Medicine and Surgery: Small Animal 1992; 7: 153-161.
46. Flesja K, Yri T. Protein-losing enteropathy in the Lundenhund. Journal of Small Animal Practice 1977; 18: 11-23.
47. Williams DA. Gastroenteropathy in Norwegian Lundehunds in the USA (abstract). In: Proceedings. Fifteenth Annual Veterinary Medical Forum, American College of Veterinary Internal Medicine, Lake Buena Vista, FL, 1997: 661.
48. Moore RP. Feline eosinophilic enteritis. In: Kirk RW, ed. Current Veterinary Therapy VIII. Philadelphia, PA: WB Saunders Co, 1983; 791-793.
49. Jergens AE, Moore FM, Haynes JS, et al. Idiopathic inflammatory bowel disease in dogs and cats: 84 cases (1987-1990). Journal of the American Veterinary Medical Association 1992; 201: 1603-1608.
50. Jergens AE. Feline idiopathic inflammatory bowel disease. Compendium on Continuing Education for the Practicing Veterinarian 1992; 14: 509-518.
51. Weiss DJ, Gagne JM, Armstrong PJ. Relationship between inflammatory hepatic disease and inflammatory bowel disease, pancreatitis, and nephritis in cats. Journal of the American Veterinary Medical Association 1996; 209: 1114-1116.

52. Vaden SL, Sellon RK, Spaulding KA, et al. Early manifestations of protein losing enteropathy and nephropathy in soft coated wheaten terriers (abstract). Canine Practice 1998; 23: 42-43.

53. Littman MP, Giger U. Familial protein-losing enteropathy (PLE) and/or protein-losing nephropathy (PLN) in soft-coated wheaten terriers (abstract). Journal of Veterinary Internal Medicine 1990; 4: 133.

54. Roth L, Leib MS, Davenport DJ, et al. Comparisons between endoscopic and histologic evaluation of the gastrointestinal tract in dogs and cats: 75 cases (1984-1987). Journal of the American Veterinary Medical Association 1990; 196: 635-638.

55. Marks SL, LaFlamme DP. Dietary trial in dogs with inflammatory bowel disease utilizing a hydrolyzed protein diet. In: Proceedings. Purina Nutrition Forum, St. Louis, MO, 1998: 7.

56. Wilcock B. Endoscopic biopsy interpretation in canine or feline enterocolitis. Seminars in Veterinary Medicine and Surgery: Small Animal 1992; 7: 162-171.

57. Yamasaki K, Suematsu H, Takahashi T. Comparison of gastric and duodenal lesions in dogs and cats with and without lymphocytic-plasmacytic enteritis. Journal of the American Veterinary Medical Association 1996; 209: 95-97.

58. Gunawardana S, Jergens AE, Ahrens FA, et al. Colonic nitrite and immunoglobulin G concentrations in dogs with inflammatory bowel disease. Journal of the American Veterinary Medical Association 1997; 211: 318-321.

59. Fiocchi C. Inflammatory bowel disease: Etiology and pathogenesis. Gastroenterology 1998; 115: 182-205.

60. Hayden DW, van Kruiningen HJ. Eosinophilic gastroenteritis in German shepherd dogs and its relationship to visceral larva migrans. Journal of the American Veterinary Medical Association 1973; 162: 379-384.

61. Leib MS, Sponenberg DP, Wilcke JR, et al. Suppurative colitis in a cat. Journal of the American Veterinary Medical Association 1986; 188: 739-741.

62. Rutgers HC. SIBOG–More common than you think. In: Proceedings. Fourteenth Annual Veterinary Medical Forum, American College of Veterinary Internal Medicine, San Antonio, TX, 1996: 348-349.

63. Hanauer SB. Inflammatory bowel disease. New England Journal of Medicine 1996; 334: 841-848.

64. Guilford WG. Nutritional management of gastrointestinal diseases. In: Guilford WG, Center SA, Strombeck DR, et al, eds. Strombeck's Small Animal Gastroenterology, 3rd ed. Philadelphia, PA: WB Saunders Co, 1996; 889-910.

65. Nelson RW, Dimperio ME, Long GG. Lymphocytic-plasmacytic colitis in the cat. Journal of the American Veterinary Medical Association 1984; 184: 1133-1135.

66. Nelson RW, Stookey LJ. Nutritional management of idiopathic chronic colitis in the dog. Journal of Veterinary Internal Medicine 1988; 2: 133-137.

67. Davenport DJ, Leib MS, Roth L. Progression of lymphocytic plasmacytic enteritis to lymphosarcoma in three cats. In: Proceedings. Seventh Annual Conference, Veterinary Cancer Society, Madison, WI, 1987: (Suppl.).

68. Guilford WG. Motility disorders of the bowel. In: Guilford WG, Center SA, Strombeck DR, et al, eds. Strombeck's Small Animal Gastroenterology, 3rd ed. Philadelphia, PA: WB Saunders Co, 1996; 532-539.

69. Husain A, Korzenik JR. Nutritional issues and therapy in inflammatory bowel disease. Seminars in Gastrointestinal Disease 1998; 9: 21-30.

70. Vaden SL, Davenport DJ, Hammerberg B, et al. Gastroscopic food sensitivity testing and oral challenge in soft-coated wheaten terriers with protein-losing enteropathy and/or nephropathy (abstract). In: Proceedings. Sixteenth Annual Veterinary Medical Forum, American College of Veterinary Internal Medicine, San Diego, CA, 1998: 695.

71. Guilford WG, Strombeck DR, Rogers Q, et al. Development of gastroscopic food sensitivity testing in dogs. Journal of Veterinary Internal Medicine 1994; 8: 414-422.

72. Elwood CM, Rutgers HC, Batt RM. Gastroscopic food sensitivity testing in 17 dogs. Journal of Small Animal Practice 1994; 35: 199-203.

73. Harig JM, Soergel KH, Komorowski RA, et al. Treatment of diversion colitis with short-chain-fatty acid irrigation. New England Journal of Medicine 1989; 320: 23-28.

74. Breuer RI, Buto SK, Christ ML, et al. Rectal irrigation with short-chain fatty acids for distal ulcerative colitis. Preliminary report. Digestive Diseases and Sciences 1991; 36: 185-187.

75. Sunvold GD, Fahey GC Jr, Merchen NR, et al. Dietary fiber for dogs: IV. In vitro fermentation of selected fiber sources by dog fecal inoculum and in vivo digestion and metabolism of fiber-supplemented diets. Journal of Animal Science 1995a; 73: 1099-1109.

76. Sunvold GD, Fahey GC Jr, Merchen NR, et al. Dietary fiber for cats: In vitro fermentation of selected fiber sources by cat fecal inoculum and in vivo utilization of diets containing selected fiber sources and their blends. Journal of Animal Science 1995b; 73: 2329-2339.

77. Sunvold GD, Fahey GC Jr, Merchen NR, et al. In vitro fermentation of selected fibrous substrates by dog and cat fecal inoculum: Influence of diet composition on substrate organic matter disappearance and short-chain fatty acid production. Journal of Animal Science 1995c; 73: 1110-1122.

78. Jamikorn UA, Harmon DL, Davenport DJ, et al. Fermentability of selected fibers by dog and cat fecal microflora (abstract). Annual Meeting. American Society of Animal Science, Indianapolis, IN, July 1999.

79. Griffiths AM, Ohlsson A, Sherman PM, et al. Meta-analysis of enteral nutrition as a primary treatment of active Crohn's disease. Gastroenterology 1995; 108: 1056-1067.

80. Lewis JD, Fisher RL. Nutrition support in inflammatory bowel disease. Medical Clinics of North America 1994; 78: 1443-1456.

81. Jeejeebhoy KN. Nutritional aspects of inflammatory bowel disease. In: Kirsner JB, Shorter RG, eds. Inflammatory Bowel Disease, 4th ed. Baltimore, MD: Williams & Wilkins, 1995; 734-749.

82. Hendricks KM, Walker A. Zinc deficiency in inflammatory bowel disease. Nutrition Reviews 1988; 46: 401-408.

83. Belluzzi A, Brignola C, Campieri M, et al. Effect of an enteric-coated fish-oil preparation on relapses in Crohn's disease. New England Journal of Medicine 1996; 334: 1557-1560.

84. Mate J, Castanos R, Garcie-Samaniego J, et al. Does dietary fish oil maintain the remission of Crohn's disease: A study case control (abstract). Gastroenterology 1991; 100: A228.

85. Lorenz-Meyer H, Bauer P, Nocolay C, et al. Omega-3 fatty acids and low carbohydrate diet for maintenance of remission in Crohn's disease. A randomized controlled multicenter trial. Scandinavian Journal of Gastroenterology 1996; 31: 778-785.

86. Lorenz R, Weber PC, Szimnau P, et al. Supplementation with n-3 fatty acids from fish oil in chronic inflammatory bowel disease–A randomized, placebo-controlled, double blinded cross-over trial. Journal of Internal Medicine 1989; 225 (Suppl. 731): 225-232.

87. Stenson WF, Cort DC, Rodgers J, et al. Dietary supplementation with fish oil in ulcerative colitis. Annals of Internal Medicine 1992; 116: 609-614.

88. Van Kruiningen HJ. Granulomatous colitis of boxer dogs: Comparative aspects. Gastroenterology 1967; 53: 114-122.

89. Davenport DJ. Gastrointestinal lymphosarcoma. In: August JR, ed. Consultations in Feline Internal Medicine 1. Philadelphia, PA: WB Saunders Co, 1991; 419-423.

90. Fossum TW, Hay WH, Boothe HW, et al. Chylous ascites in three dogs. Journal of the American Veterinary Medical Association 1992; 200: 70-76.

91. Fossum TW, Hodges CC, Scruggs DW, et al. Generalized lymphangiectasia in a dog with subcutaneous chyle and lymphangioma. Journal of the American Veterinary Medical Association 1990; 197: 231-236.

92. Fossum TW, Sherding RG, Zack PM, et al. Intestinal lymphangiectasia associated with chylothorax in two dogs. Journal of the American Veterinary Medical Association 1987; 190: 61-64.

93. Tams TR, Twedt DC. Canine protein-losing gastroenteropathy syndrome. Compendium on Continuing Education for the Practicing Veterinarian 1981; 3: 105-118.

94. Simmonds WJ. The effect of fluid, electrolytes and food intake on thoracic duct flow in unanesthetized rats. Anest J Exp Biol 1954; 32: 285-300.

95. MacDonald ML, Anderson BC, Rogers QR, et al. Essential fatty acid requirements of cats: Pathology of essential fatty acid deficiency. American Journal of Veterinary Research 1984; 45: 1310-1317.

96. Finco DR, Duncan JR, Schall WD, et al. Chronic enteric disease and hypoproteinemia in nine dogs. Journal of the American Veterinary Medical Association 1973; 163: 262-271.

97. Matteeuws D, DeRick A, Thoonen H, et al. Intestinal lymphangiectasia in a dog. Journal of Small Animal Practice 1974; 15: 757-761.

98. Erickson SL. Dietary management of canine lymphangiectasia. Veterinary Medicine 1988; 83: 282-286.

99. Remillard RL. Dietary management of intestinal lymphangiectasia. In: Proceedings. Seventh Annual Veterinary Medical Forum, American College of Veterinary Internal Medicine, San Diego, CA, 1989: 357-358.

100. Sherding RD. Canine intestinal lymphangiectasia. In: Proceedings. Fifth Annual Veterinary Medical Forum, American College of Veterinary Internal Medicine, San Diego, CA, 1987: 679-682.

GI & PANCREAS

101. Vanderhoof JA, Langnas AN. Short-bowel syndrome in children and adults. Gastroenterology 1997; 113: 1767-1778.
102. Yanoff SR, Willard MD. Short bowel syndrome in dogs and cats. Seminars in Veterinary Medicine and Surgery: Small Animal 1989; 4: 226-231.
103. Yanoff SR, Willard MD, Boothe HW, et al. Short-bowel syndrome in four dogs. Veterinary Surgery 1992; 21: 217-222.
104. Chan MF, Klein S. Short-bowel syndrome. In: Rombeau JL, Rolandelli RH, eds. Clinical Nutrition: Enteral and Tube Feeding. Philadelphia, PA: WB Saunders Co, 1997; 575-587.
105. Williamson RCN, Chir M. Intestinal adaptation: Structural, functional and cytokinetic changes. New England Journal of Medicine 1978; 298: 1393-1402.
106. Dowling RH. Update on intestinal adaptation. Triangle 1988; 27: 149-164.
107. Aghdassi E, Plapler H, Kurian R, et al. Colonic fermentation and nutritional recovery in rats with massive small bowel resection. Gastroenterology 1994; 107: 637-642.
108. Nightingale JMD, Lennard-Jones JE, Gertner DJ, et al. Colonic preservation reduces need for parenteral therapy. Gut 1992; 33: 1493-1497.
109. Vanderhoof JA, Langnas AN, Pinch LW, et al. Short bowel syndrome. Journal of Pediatric Gastroenterology and Nutrition 1992; 14: 359-370.
110. McIntyre PB, Fitchew M, Lennard-Jones JE. Patients with a high jejunostomy do not need a special diet. Gastroenterology 1986; 91: 25-33.
111. Levy E, Frileux P, Sandrucci S, et al. Continuous enteral nutrition during the early adaptive stage of the short bowel syndrome. British Journal of Surgery 1998; 75: 549-553.
112. Lentze MJ. Intestinal adaptation in short-bowel syndrome. European Journal of Pediatrics 1989; 148: 294-299.
113. Bochenek W, Rodgers JB, Balint JA. Effects of changes in dietary lipids on intestinal fluid loss in the short bowel syndrome. Annals of Internal Medicine 1970; 72: 205-213.
114. Russell J, Bass P. Canine gastric emptying of fiber meals: Influence of meal viscosity and antroduodenal motility. American Journal of Physiology 1985; 249: G662-G667.
115. Prove J, Ehrlein HJ. Motor function of gastric antrum and pylorus for evacuation of low and high viscosity meals in dogs. Gut 1982; 23: 150-156.
116. Sandhu KS, El Samahi MM, Mena I, et al. Effect of pectin on gastric emptying and gastroduodenal motility in normal subjects. Gastroenterology 1987; 92: 486-492.
117. Sales TRA, Torres HOG, Couto CMF, et al. Intestinal adaptation in short bowel syndrome without tube feeding or home parenteral nutrition: Report of four consecutive cases. Nutrition 1998; 14: 508-512.
118. Koruda MJ, Rolandelli MR, Settle RG, et al. The effect of a pectin-supplemented elemental diet on intestinal adaptation to massive small bowel resection. Journal of Parenteral and Enteral Nutrition 1986; 10: 343-350.
119. Frankel WL, Zhang W, Afonso J, et al. Glutamine enhancement of structure and function in transplanted small intestine in the rat. Journal of Parenteral and Enteral Nutrition 1993; 17: 47-55.
120. Burke DJ, Alverdy JA, Aoys E, et al. Glutamine-supplemented total parenteral nutrition improves gut immune function. Archives of Surgery 1989; 124: 1396-1399.
121. Alverdy JA, Aoys E, Weiss-Carrington P, et al. The effect of glutamine-enriched TPN on gut immune cellularity. Journal of Surgical Research 1992; 52: 34-38.
122. Jacobs DO, Evans DA, Mealy K, et al. Combined effects of glutamine and epidermal growth factor on the rat intestine. Surgery 1989; 104: 358-364.
123. O'Dwyer ST, Smith RJ, Hwang TL, et al. Maintenance of small bowel mucosa with glutamine-enriched parenteral nutrition. Journal of Parenteral and Enteral Nutrition 1989; 13: 579-585.
124. Grant JP, Snyder PJ. Use of L-glutamine in total parenteral nutrition. Journal of Surgical Research 1988; 44: 506-513.
125. Vanderhoof JA, Blackwood DJ, Mohammadpour H, et al. Effects of oral supplementation of glutamine on small intestinal mucosal mass following resection. Journal of the American College of Nutrition 1992; 11: 223-227.
126. Scott TE, Moellman JR. Intravenous glutamine fails to improve gut morphology after radiation injury. Journal of Parenteral and Enteral Nutrition 1992; 16: 440-444.
127. Lacey JM, Wilmore DW. Is glutamine a conditionally essential amino acid? Nutrition Reviews 1990; 48: 297-309.
128. Klimberg VS, Salloum RM, Kasper M, et al. Oral glutamine accelerates healing of the small intestine and improves outcome after whole abdominal radiation. Archives of Surgery 1990; 125: 1040-1045.
129. Byrne TA, Morrissey TB, Nattakom TV, et al. Growth hormone, glutamine, and a modified diet enhance nutrient absorption in patients with severe short bowel syndrome. Journal of Parenteral and Enteral Nutrition 1995; 19: 296-302.
130. Feldman EJ, Dowling RH, McNaughton J, et al. Effect of oral versus intravenous nutrition on intestinal adaptation after small bowel resection in the dog. Gastroenterology 1976; 70: 712-719.
131. Guilford WG, Strombeck DR. Miscellaneous disorders of the bowel, abdomen, and anorectum. In: Guilford WG, Center SA, Strombeck DR, et al, eds. Strombeck's Small Animal Gastroenterology, 3rd ed. Philadelphia, PA: WB Saunders Co, 1996; 503-518.
132. Willard MD, Simpson RB, Fossum TW, et al. Characterization of naturally developing small intestinal bacterial overgrowth in 16 German shepherd dogs. Journal of the American Veterinary Medical Association 1994; 204: 1201-1206.
133. Simpson KW. Small intestinal bacterial overgrowth in the dog. In: Proceedings. North American Veterinary Conference, Orlando, FL, 1994: 259-260.
134. Johnston KL. Small intestinal bacterial overgrowth. Purina Research Report 1999: 1-4.
135. Davenport DJ. Small intestinal bacterial overgrowth–Need for a new definition? In: Proceedings. Fourteenth Annual Veterinary Medical Forum, American College of Veterinary Internal Medicine, San Antonio, TX, 1996: 346-347.
136. Davenport DJ, Ludlow CL, Hunt JH, et al. Effect of sampling method on quantitative duodenal culture in dogs: Endoscopy vs. permucosal aspiration (abstract). Journal of Veterinary Internal Medicine 1994; 8: A37.
137. Rutgers HC, Batt RM, Elwood CM, et al. Small intestinal bacterial overgrowth in dogs with chronic intestinal diseases. Journal of the American Veterinary Medical Association 1995; 206: 187-193.
138. Papasouliotis K, Sparkes AH, Werrett G, et al. Assessment of the bacterial flora of the proximal part of the small intestine in healthy cats, and the effect of the sample collection method. American Journal of Veterinary Research 1998; 59: 48-51.
139. Batt RM, Needham JR. Bacterial overgrowth associated with a naturally occurring enteropathy in the German shepherd dog. Research in Veterinary Science 1983; 35: 42-46.
140. Davenport DJ, Ching RJW, Hunt JH, et al. The effect of dietary levels of folate and cobalamin on the serum concentration of folate and cobalamin in the dog. Journal of Nutrition 1994; 124 (Suppl.): 2559S-2562S.
141. Ludlow CL, Davenport DJ. Small intestinal bacterial overgrowth. In: Bonagura JD, ed. Current Veterinary Therapy XIII. Philadelphia, PA: WB Saunders Co, In press.
142. Johnston K, Lamport A, Batt RM. An unexpected bacterial flora in the proximal small intestine of normal cats. Veterinary Record 1993; 132: 362-363.
143. Davenport DJ. Clinicopathologic parameters of a surgical model of small intestinal bacterial overgrowth (SIBOG) in the dog and evaluation of the usefulness of a PABA-cholic conjugate in the detection of SIBOG in the dog. Master's Thesis. The Ohio State University, Columbus. 1986.
144. Batt RM, Morgan JO. Role of serum folate and vitamin B12 concentrations in the differentiation of small intestinal abnormalities in the dog. Research in Veterinary Science 1982; 32: 17-22.
145. Williams DA. Evaluation of radioassay methods for analysis of canine serum cobalamin and folate (abstract). Journal of Veterinary Internal Medicine 1991; 6: 120.
146. Williams DA, Batt RM, McLean L. Bacterial overgrowth in the duodenum of dogs with exocrine pancreatic insufficiency. Journal of the American Veterinary Medical Association 1987; 191: 201-206.
147. Batt RM, Hall EJ, McLean L, et al. Small intestinal bacterial overgrowth and enhanced intestinal permeability in healthy beagles. American Journal of Veterinary Research 1992; 53: 1935-1940.
148. Fishbein L, Oku M, Gough M. Fructooligosaccharide: A review. Veterinary and Human Toxicology 1988; 30: 104-107.
149. Hidaka M, Hirayama M, Tokunaga T, et al. The effects of undigested fructooligosaccharides on intestinal microflora and various physiological functions on human health. In: Furda I, Brine CJ, eds. New Developments in Dietary Fiber. New York, NY: Plenum Press, 1990; 105-117.
150. Willard MD, Simpson RB, Delles EK, et al. Effects of dietary supplementation of fructooligosaccharides on small intestinal bacterial overgrowth in dogs. American Journal of Veterinary Research 1994; 55: 654-659.

Large Intestinal Disorders Endnotes & References

ENDNOTES

a. Davenport DJ. Unpublished data. 1996.
b. Remillard RL. Personal observation. 1996.
c. Kappel L. Louisiana State University, Baton Rouge. Personal communication. 1998.
d. Remillard RL. Unpublished data. 1999.
e. Proctor & Gamble, Cincinnati, OH, USA.
f. Propulsid. Janssen Pharmaceutica, Inc., Titusville, NJ, USA.

REFERENCES

1. Guilford WG. Idiopathic inflammatory bowel diseases. In: Guilford WG, Center SA, Strombeck DR, et al, eds. Strombeck's Small Animal Gastroenterology, 3rd ed. Philadelphia, PA: WB Saunders Co, 1996; 451-486.
2. Leib MS. Diseases of the intestines. In: Leib MS, Monroe WE, eds. Practical Small Animal Internal Medicine. Philadelphia, PA: WB Saunders Co, 1997; 685-760.
3. Leib MS, Matz ME. Diseases of the large intestine. In: Ettinger SJ, Feldman EC, eds. Textbook of Veterinary Internal Medicine, 4th ed. Philadelphia, PA: WB Saunders Co, 1995; 1232-1260.
4. Moore RP. Feline eosinophilic enteritis. In: Kirk RW, ed. Current Veterinary Therapy VIII. Philadelphia, PA: WB Saunders Co, 1983; 791-793.
5. Jergens AE, Moore FM, Haynes JS, et al. Idiopathic inflammatory bowel disease in dogs and cats: 84 cases (1987-1990). Journal of the American Veterinary Medical Association 1992; 201: 1603-1608.
6. Roth L, Leib MS, Davenport DJ, et al. Comparisons between endoscopic and histologic evaluation of the gastrointestinal tract in dogs and cats: 75 cases (1984-1987). Journal of the American Veterinary Medical Association 1990; 196: 635-638.
7. Marks SL, LaFlamme DP. Dietary trial in dogs with inflammatory bowel disease utilizing a hydrolyzed protein diet. In: Proceedings. Purina Nutrition Forum, St. Louis, MO, 1998: 7.
8. Wilcock B. Endoscopic biopsy interpretation in canine or feline enterocolitis. Seminars in Veterinary Medicine and Surgery: Small Animal 1992; 7: 162-171.
9. Twedt DC. Clostridium perfringens associated enterotoxicosis in dogs. In: Kirk RW, Bonagura JD, eds. Current Veterinary Therapy XI. Philadelphia, PA: WB Saunders Co, 1992; 602-604.
10. Davenport DJ. Campylobacter enteritis. In: Kirk RW, ed. Current Veterinary Therapy X. Philadelphia, PA: WB Saunders Co, 1989; 944-948.
11. Van Kruiningen HJ. Granulomatous colitis of boxer dogs: Comparative aspects. Gastroenterology 1967; 53: 114-122.
12. Fiocchi C. Inflammatory bowel disease: Etiology and pathogenesis. Gastroenterology 1998; 115: 182-205.
13. Hanauer SB. Inflammatory bowel disease. New England Journal of Medicine 1996; 334: 841-848.
14. Nelson RW, Dimperio ME, Long GG. Lymphocytic-plasmacytic colitis in the cat. Journal of the American Veterinary Medical Association 1984; 184: 1133-1135.
15. Nelson RW, Stookey LJ. Nutritional management of idiopathic chronic colitis in the dog. Journal of Veterinary Internal Medicine 1988; 2: 133-137.
16. Guilford WG. Effect of diet on inflammatory bowel diseases. Veterinary Clinical Nutrition 1997; 4: 58-61.
17. Davenport DJ, Leib MS, Roth L. Progression of lymphocytic plasmacytic enteritis to lymphosarcoma in three cats. In: Proceedings. Seventh Annual Conference, Veterinary Cancer Society, Madison, WI, 1987: (Suppl.).
18. Dennis JS, Kruger JM, Mullaney TP. Lymphocytic/plasmacytic colitis in cats: 14 cases (1985-1990). Journal of the American Veterinary Medical Association 1993; 202: 313-318.
19. Reinhart GA, Moxley RA, Clemens ET. Source of dietary fiber and its effects on colonic microstructure, function and histopathology of beagle dogs. Journal of Nutrition 1994; 124: 2701S-2703S.
20. Campbell SL. Commercial diets do not affect the colonic ultrastructure of normal dogs. Masters Thesis. Virginia Polytechnic Institute and State University, Blacksburg, VA, 1993.
21. Leib MS. Effect of commercial diets on the endoscopic and histological appearance of the colon of normal dogs. Journal of the American Animal Hospital Association 1992; 28: 527-532.
22. Leib MS. Plasmacytic-lymphocytic colitis in dogs. In: Kirk RW, ed. Current Veterinary Therapy X. Philadelphia, PA: WB Saunders Co, 1989; 939-943.
23. Leib MS, Matz ME. Diseases of the large intestine. In: Ettinger SJ, Feldman EC, eds. Textbook of Veterinary Internal Medicine, 4th ed. Philadelphia, PA: WB Saunders Co, 1995; 1232-1260.
24. Harig JM, Soergel KH, Komorowski RA, et al. Treatment of diversion colitis with short-chain-fatty acid irrigation. New England Journal of Medicine 1989; 320: 23-28.
25. Breuer RI, Buto SK, Christ ML, et al. Rectal irrigation with short-chain fatty acids for distal ulcerative colitis: Preliminary report. Digestive Diseases and Sciences 1991; 36: 185-187.
26. Sunvold GD, Fahey GC Jr, Merchen NR, et al. Dietary fiber for dogs: IV. In vitro fermentation of selected fiber sources by dog fecal inoculum and in vivo digestion and metabolism of fiber-supplemented diets. Journal of Animal Science 1995a; 73: 1099-1109.
27. Sunvold GD, Fahey GC Jr, Merchen NR, et al. Dietary fiber for cats: In vitro fermentation of selected fiber sources by cat fecal inoculum and in vivo utilization of diets containing selected fiber sources and their blends. Journal of Animal Science 1995b; 73: 2329-2339.
28. Sunvold GD, Fahey GC Jr, Merchen NR, et al. In vitro fermentation of selected fibrous substrates by dog and cat fecal inoculum: Influence of diet composition on substrate organic matter disappearance and short-chain fatty acid production. Journal of Animal Science 1995c; 73: 1110-1122.
29. Jamikorn UA, Harmon DL, Davenport DJ, et al. Fermentability of selected fibers by dog and cat fecal microflora (abstract). Annual Meeting. American Society of Animal Science, Indianapolis, IN, July 1999.
30. Linn FV, Peppercorn MA. Drug therapy for inflammatory bowel disease. Part I. American Journal of Surgery 1992; 164: 85-89.
31. Jones R, Lydeard S. Irritable bowel syndrome in the general population. British Medical Journal 1992; 304: 87-90.
32. Talley NJ, Weaver AL, Zinsmeister AR, et al. Onset and disappearance of gastrointestinal symptoms and functional gastrointestinal disorders. American Journal of Epidemiology 1992; 136: 165-177.
33. Guilford WG. Motility disorders of the bowel. In: Guilford WG, Center SA, Strombeck DR, et al, eds. Strombeck's Small Animal Gastroenterology, 3rd ed. Philadelphia, PA: WB Saunders Co, 1996; 532-539.
34. Henroteaux M. Results of an endoscopic study of colitis in dogs: Predominance of idiopathic colitis. Annals of Med Vet 1990; 134: 389-392.
35. Zighelboim J, Talley NJ. What are functional bowel disorders? Gastroenterology 1993; 104: 1196-1201.
36. Tache Y, Garrick T, Raybould H. Central nervous system action of peptides to influence gastrointestinal motor function. Gastroenterology 1990; 98: 517-528.
37. Leib MS, Saunders GK, Willard MD, et al. Fiber-responsive large bowel diarrhea. In: Proceedings. Fifteenth Annual Veterinary Medical Forum, American College of Veterinary Internal Medicine, Lake Buena Vista, FL, 1997: 319-321.
38. Tams TR. Irritable bowel syndrome. In: Kirk RW, Bonagura JD, eds. Current Veterinary Therapy XI. Philadelphia, PA: WB Saunders Co, 1992; 604-608.
39. Sweeney M. Constipation: Diagnosis and treatment. Home Care Provider 1997; 2: 250-255.
40. Dimski DS. Constipation: Pathophysiology, diagnostic approach, and treatment. Seminars in Veterinary Medicine and Surgery: Small Animal 1989; 4: 247-254.
41. Wald A. Evaluation and management of constipation. Clinical Perspectives in Gastroenterology 1998; 1: 106-115.
42. Wedekind K, Walker L, Hancock J, et al. Bioavailability of zinc and calcium is affected by certain fiber sources (abstract). Federation of American Societies for Experimental Biology Journal 1995; 9: A450.
43. Wedekind K, Walker L, Beyer S, et al. Bioavailability of iron is affected by certain fiber sources in chicks and in puppies (abstract). Trace Elements in Man and Animals 1996; 9: A20.
44. Wedekind K, Beyer S, Titgemeyer E. Bioavailability of phosphorus is affected by certain fiber sources (abstract). Federation of American Societies for Experimental Biology Journal 1996; 10: A524.
45. Strocchi A, Levitt MD. Intestinal gas. In: Feldman M, Scharschmidt BG, Sleisenger MH, eds. Gastrointestinal and Liver Disease, 6th ed. Philadelphia, PA: WB Saunders Co, 1997; 153-160.
46. Levitt MD. Intestinal gas production–Recent advances in flatology. New England Journal of Medicine 1980; 302: 1474-1475.
47. Steggerda FR. Gastrointestinal gas following food consumption. Annals of the New York Academy of Science 1968; 150: 57-66.
48. Suarez FL, Springfield J, Furne J, et al. Gas production in humans ingesting a soybean flour derived from beans naturally low in oligosaccharides. American Journal of Clinical Nutrition 1999; 69: 135-139.

GI & PANCRFAS

49. Cho S. The Gas We Pass: The Story of Farts. Brooklyn, NY: Kane/Miller Book Publishers, 1994.

Pancreatic Disorders Endnotes & References

ENDNOTES

a. Davenport DJ, The Ohio State University, Columbus. Unpublished data. 1985.
b. Remillard RL. Personal experience. 1999.

REFERENCES

1. Jacobs RM, Norris AM, Lumsden JH, et al. Laboratory diagnosis of malassimilation. Veterinary Clinics of North America: Small Animal Practice 1989; 19: 951-977.
2. Williams DA. Exocrine pancreatic insufficiency. In: Ettinger SJ, Feldman EC, eds. Textbook of Veterinary Internal Medicine, 4th ed. Philadelphia, PA: WB Saunders Co, 1994; 1372-1392.
3. Williams DA. Feline exocrine pancreatic insufficiency. In: Bonagura JD, ed. Current Veterinary Therapy XII. Philadelphia, PA: WB Saunders Co, 1994; 732-735.
4. Raiha M, Westermarck E. The signs of pancreatic degenerative atrophy in dogs and the role of external factors in the etiology of the disease. Acta Veterinaria Scandinavica 1989; 30: 447-452.
5. Perry LA, Williams DA, Pidgeon GL. Exocrine pancreatic insufficiency with associated coagulopathy in a cat. Journal of the American Animal Hospital Association 1991; 27: 109-114.
6. Williams DA, Batt RM. Sensitivity and specificity of radioimmunoassay of serum trypsin-like immunoreactivity for the diagnosis of canine exocrine pancreatic insufficiency. Journal of the American Veterinary Medical Association 1988; 192: 195-201.
7. Williams DA, Batt RM. Diagnosis of canine exocrine pancreatic insufficiency by the assay of serum trypsin-like immunoreactivity. Journal of Small Animal Practice 1983; 24: 583-588.
8. Steiner JM, Williams DA. Feline trypsin-like immunoreactivity in feline exocrine pancreatic disease. Compendium on Continuing Education for the Practicing Veterinarian 1996; 18: 543-547.
9. Meyer DJ, Williams DA. Diagnosis of hepatic and exocrine pancreatic disorders. Seminars in Veterinary Medicine and Surgery: Small Animal 1992; 7: 275-284.
10. Westermarck E, Batt RM, Vaillant C, et al. Sequential study of pancreatic structure and function during development of pancreatic acinar atrophy in a German shepherd dog. American Journal of Veterinary Research 1993; 54: 1088-1094.
11. Sherding RG. Canine exocrine pancreatic insufficiency. Compendium on Continuing Education for the Practicing Veterinarian 1979; 1: 816-820.
12. Boari A, Williams DA, Famigli-Bergamini P. Observations on exocrine pancreatic insufficiency in a family of English setter dogs. Journal of Small Animal Practice 1994; 35: 247-250.
13. Watson PJ. Exocrine pancreatic insufficiency as end state of pancreatitis in five dogs (abstract). In: Proceedings. Annual Meeting. European Society of Veterinary Internal Medicine, Brussels, Belgium, 1995: 64.
14. Williams DA. The pancreas. In: Guilford WG, Center SA, Strombeck DR, et al, eds. Strombeck's Small Animal Gastroenterology, 3rd ed. Philadelphia, PA: WB Saunders Co, 1996; 381-411.
15. Williams DA, Batt RM, McLean L. Bacterial overgrowth in the duodenum of dogs with exocrine pancreatic insufficiency. Journal of the American Veterinary Medical Association 1987; 191: 201-206.
16. Westermarck E, Myllys V, Aho M. Effect of treatment on the jejunal and colonic bacterial flora of dogs with exocrine pancreatic insufficiency. Pancreas 1993; 8: 559-562.
17. Simpson KW, Batt RM, Jones D, et al. Effects of exocrine pancreatic insufficiency and replacement therapy on the bacterial flora of the duodenum in dogs. American Journal of Veterinary Research 1990; 51: 203-206.
18. Batt R, Barnes A, Rutgers HC, et al. Relative IgA deficiency and small intestinal bacterial overgrowth in German shepherd dogs. Research in Veterinary Science 1991; 50: 106-111.
19. Whitbread TJ, Batt RM, Garthwaite G. Relative deficiency of serum IgA in the German shepherd dog: A breed anomaly. Research in Veterinary Science 1984; 37: 350-352.
20. Pidgeon G. Effect of diet on exocrine pancreatic insufficiency in dogs. Journal of the American Veterinary Medical Association 1982; 281: 232-235.

21. Westermarck E, Wiberg M, Junttila J. Role of feeding in the treatment of dogs with pancreatic degenerative atrophy. Acta Veterinaria Scandinavica 1990; 31: 325-331.
22. Westermarck E, Junttila JT, Wiberg ME. Role of low dietary fat in the treatment of dogs with exocrine pancreatic insufficiency. American Journal of Veterinary Research 1995; 56: 600-605.
23. Dutta SK, Hlasko J. Dietary fiber in pancreatic disease: Effect of high fiber diet on fat malabsorption in pancreatic insufficiency and in vitro study of the interaction of dietary fiber with pancreatic enzymes. American Journal of Clinical Nutrition 1985; 41: 517-525.
24. Simpson K, Morton D, Batt R. Effect of exocrine pancreatic insufficiency on cobalamin absorption in dogs. American Journal of Veterinary Research 1989; 50: 1233-1236.
25. Batt RM, Morgan JO. Role of serum folate and vitamin B12 concentrations in the differentiation of small intestinal abnormalities in the dog. Research in Veterinary Science 1982; 32: 17-22.
26. Williams DA. Evaluation of radioassay methods for analysis of canine serum cobalamin and folate (abstract). Journal of Veterinary Internal Medicine 1991; 6: 120.
27. Balaghi M, Wagner C. Folate deficiency inhibits pancreatic amylase secretion in rats. American Journal of Clinical Nutrition 1995; 61: 90-96.
28. Suzuki A, Mizumoto A, Sarr MG, et al. Bacterial lipase and high-fat diets in canine exocrine pancreatic insufficiency: A new therapy of steatorrhea? Gastroenterology 1997; 112: 2048-2055.
29. Pidgeon G. Malassimilation syndrome: Maldigestion/malabsorption. In: Kirk RW, ed. Current Veterinary Therapy VII. Philadelphia, PA: WB Saunders Co, 1980; 930-935.
30. Remillard RL, Thatcher CD. Dietary and nutritional management of gastrointestinal diseases. Veterinary Clinics of North America: Small Animal Practice 1989; 19: 797-817.
31. Simpson KW. Current concepts of the pathogenesis and pathophysiology of acute pancreatitis in the dog and cat. Compendium on Continuing Education for the Practicing Veterinarian 1993; 14: 247-254.
32. Akol KG, Washabau RJ, Saunders HM, et al. Acute pancreatitis in cats with hepatic lipidosis. Journal of Veterinary Internal Medicine 1993; 7: 205-209.
33. Hill RC, Van Winkle TJ. Acute necrotizing pancreatitis and acute suppurative pancreatitis in the cat. A retrospective study of 40 cases (1976-1989). Journal of Veterinary Internal Medicine 1993; 7: 25-33.
34. Steiner JM, Williams DA. Feline pancreatitis. Compendium on Continuing Education for the Practicing Veterinarian 1997; 19: 590-602.
35. Hines BL, Salisbury SK, Jakovljevics S, et al. Pancreatic pseudocyst associated with chronic-active necrotizing pancreatitis in a cat. Journal of the American Animal Hospital Association 1996; 32: 147-152.
36. Weiss DJ, Gagne JM, Armstrong PJ. Relationship between inflammatory hepatic disease and inflammatory bowel disease, pancreatitis, and nephritis in cats. Journal of the American Veterinary Medical Association 1996; 209: 1114-1116.
37. Simpson KW, Batt RM, McLean L, et al. Circulating concentrations of trypsin-like immunoreactivity and activities of lipase and amylase after pancreatic duct ligation in dogs. American Journal of Veterinary Research 1989; 50: 629-632.
38. Salisbury SK, Lantz GC, Nelson RW, et al. Pancreatic abscess in dogs: Six cases (1978-1986). Journal of the American Veterinary Medical Association 1988; 193: 1104-1108.
39. Hess RS, Saunders M, Van Winkle TJ, et al. Clinical, clinicopathologic, radiographic, and ultrasonographic abnormalities in dogs with fatal acute pancreatitis: 70 cases (1986-1990). Journal of the American Veterinary Medical Association 1998; 213: 665-670.
40. Bass VD, Hoffman WE, Dorner L. Normal canine lipid profiles and effects of experimentally induced pancreatitis and hepatic necrosis on lipids. American Journal of Veterinary Research 1976; 37: 1355-1357.
41. Whitney MS, Boon D, Rebar AH, et al. Effects of acute pancreatitis on circulating lipids in dogs. American Journal of Veterinary Research 1987; 48: 1492-1497.
42. Rogers WA, Donavan EF, Kociba GJ. Lipids and lipoproteins in normal dogs and in dogs with secondary hyperlipoproteinemia. Journal of the American Veterinary Medical Association 1975; 166: 1092-1101.
43. Lindsay S, Entenman C, Chaikoff IL. Pancreatitis accompanying hepatic disease in dogs fed a high fat, low protein diet. Archives of Pathology 1948; 45: 635-638.
44. Goodhead B. Importance of nutrition in the pathogenesis of experimental pancreatitis in the dog. Archives of Surgery 1971; 103: 724-728.

45. Havel RJ. Pathogenesis, differentiation and management of hyper-lipidemia. Advances in Internal Medicine 1969; 15: 117-150.

46. Frick TW, Hailemariam S, Heitz PU, et al. Acute hypercalcemia induces acinar cell necrosis and intraductal protein precipitates in the pancreas of cats and guinea pigs. Gastroenterology 1990; 98: 1675-1681.

47. Moore RW, Withrow SJ. Gastrointestinal hemorrhage and pancreati-tis associated with intervertebral disk disease in the dog. Journal of the American Veterinary Medical Association 1982; 180: 1443-1447.

48. Stewart AF. Pancreatitis in dogs and cats: Cause, pathogenesis, diag-nosis and treatment. Compendium on Continuing Education for the Practicing Veterinarian 1994; 16: 1423-1431.

49. Go VLW, Hofmann AF, Summerskill WFJ. Pancreozymin assay in man based on pancreatic enzyme secretion: Potency of specific amino acids and other digestive products. Journal of Clinical Investigation 1970; 49: 1558-1564.

50. Green GM, Guan D. Intact proteins vs. amino acid mixtures on pan-creatic enzyme secretion and intraluminal protease activity. In: Bounous G, ed. Uses of Elemental Diets in Clinical Situations. Boca Raton, FL: CRC Press, Inc, 1993; 1-10.

51. Relly GA, Nahrwold DL. Pancreatic secretion in response to an ele-mental diet and intravenous hyperalimentation. Surgery, Gynecology and Obstetrics 1976; 143: 87-91.

52. Betzhold J, Howard L. Enteral nutrition and gastrointestinal dis-ease. In Rombeau JL, Caldwell MD, eds. Clinical Nutrition; Enteral Nutrition and Tube Feeding. Philadelphia, PA: WB Saunders Co, 1986; 338-361.

53. Helton WS. Intravenous nutrition in patients with acute pancreatitis. In: Rombeau JL, Caldwell MD, eds. Clinical Nutrition; Parenteral Nutrition, 2nd ed. Philadelphia, PA: WB Saunders Co, 1993; 442-461.

54. Raasch RH, Hak LJ, Benaim V, et al. Effect of intravenous fat emul-sion on experimental acute pancreatitis. Journal of Parenteral and Enteral Nutrition 1983; 7: 254-256.

55. Silberman H, Dixon NP, Eisenberg D. The safety and efficacy of a lipid-based system of parenteral nutrition in acute pancreatitis. American Journal of Gastroenterology 1982; 77: 494-497.

56. Kawaura Y, Sata H, Fidatani G, et al. The therapy of acute pancre-atitis through intravenous hyperalimentation with fat emulsions. In: Proceedings. Asia Pacific Congress of Gastroenterology, Singapore 1976: 682-658.

57. Zieve L. Relationship between acute pancreatitis and hyperlipi-demia. Medical Clinics of North America 1968; 52: 1493-1500.

58. Wolfe BM, Ney DM. Lipid metabolism in parenteral nutrition. In: Rombeau JL, Caldwell MD, eds. Clinical Nutrition; Parenteral Nutrition. Philadelphia, PA: WB Saunders Co, 1986; 72-99.

59. Sitzmann JV, Steinborn PA, Zinner MJ, et al. Total parenteral nutrition and alternate energy substrates in treatment of severe acute pancre-atitis. Surgery, Gynecology and Obstetrics 1989; 168: 311-317.

60. Swann HM, Sweet DC, Michel K. Complications associated with use of jejunostomy tubes in dogs and cats: 40 cases (1989-1994). Journal of the American Veterinary Medical Association 1997; 210: 1764-1767.

61. McClave SA, Greene LM, Snider HL, et al. Comparison of the safe-ty of early enteral vs. parenteral nutrition in mild acute pancreati-tis. Journal of Parenteral and Enteral Nutrition 1997; 21: 14-20.

62. Kudsk KA, Campbell SM, O'Brien T, et al. Postoperative jejunal feedings following complicated pancreatitis. Nutrition in Clinical Practice 1990; 5: 14-17.

63. Ragins H, Levenson SM, Singer R, et al. Intrajejunal administration of an elemental diet at neutral pH avoids pancreatic stimulation. American Journal of Surgery 1973; 126: 606-614.

64. Cassim MM, Allardyce DB. Pancreatic secretions in response to jejunal feedings of elemental diet. Annals of Surgery 1974; 180: 228-231.

GI & PANCREAS

CASE 22-1

Acute Vomiting in an Irish Setter

Michael S. Leib, DVM, MS
Diplomate ACVIM (Internal Medicine)
Virginia-Maryland Regional College of
Veterinary Medicine
Blacksburg, Virginia, USA

Assess the Animal

A seven-year-old neutered female Irish setter was exam-ined for vomiting and retching of two hours' duration. The dog vomited approximately 20 times during the hour before presentation, producing small amounts of phlegm each time. Earlier in the morning the dog had escaped from the yard and wandered freely. No previous gastroin-testinal (GI) problems were reported by the owner.

Physical examination revealed a 28-kg dog with normal body condition (body condition score [BCS] 3/5) and a firm distended abdomen. Vital signs (mucous membrane color, pulse rate and strength, capillary refill time, respira-tory rate) were normal. Abdominal radiographs revealed a dilated stomach that was full of ingesta but appeared to be in its normal position. The ingesta contained a large amount of calcified material.

A tentative diagnosis of gastric dilatation was made and emergency treatment instituted. An orogastric tube was easily passed into the stomach but only a small amount of gas, fluid and nonspecific debris was recovered. Total decompression was not achieved even after warm water lavage. Intravenous fluids and a sedative were adminis-tered; gastric lavage with suction was continued. Large pieces of a plastic bag were removed and the lavaged gas-tric contents contained a large amount of shellfish debris.

Sufficient decompression was still not obtained; therefore, an exploratory celiotomy was performed.

During surgery, the stomach was found to be in a nor-mal position and a gastrotomy was performed. A large vol-ume of shrimp and crab legs was removed and the stom-ach was lavaged with saline solution. The stomach was sutured closed and attached to the abdominal wall using a modified gastropexy technique. The abdomen was closed routinely and recovery from anesthesia was uneventful.

Assess the Food(s) and Feeding Method

The dog was normally fed a combination of a commer-cial dry grocery brand dog food mixed with various com-mercial moist grocery brand dog foods and table foods. This food combination was offered in the early evening when the owner returned home from work. Water was available free choice.

Questions

1. What are risk factors for gastric dilatation (GD) and gastric dilatation-volvulus (GDV) in dogs?
2. Outline a feeding plan (foods and feeding method) for this patient.

Answers and Discussion

1. Several risk factors for development of GD and GDV have been identified. These risk factors include large-breed (i.e., Great Dane, weimaraner, Saint Bernard, Gordon setter, Irish setter, standard poodle, Newfoundland, basset hound, Doberman pinscher), purebred dog, older age (mean six to seven years old),

heavier body weight (greater than 23 kg), rapid eating, feeding less moist dog food, feeding once daily rather than multiple times daily, feeding less table foods, feeding fewer snacks, gulping water, excessive belching or flatulence, esophageal motility disorders, previous GI disease (e.g., inflammatory bowel disease) and personality (fearful or aggressive vs. happy and easy-going). Other risk factors for GDV identified in Irish setter dogs included feeding a single food form, recent car journey (i.e., within preceding 24 hours), recent time in a boarding kennel (within preceding 24 hours), a history of aerophagia and thin body condition (BCS 1/5 or 2/5).

2. Dietary indiscretion obviously played an important role in development of GD in this dog and should be avoided. However, strategies to avoid other dietary risk factors for GD and GDV should also be considered, including offering a highly digestible food in multiple small meals. Meals should be avoided in association with exercise or traveling in a motor vehicle. Multiple small meals may also help eliminate rapid eating and significant aerophagia. Excessive or recurrent belching, flatus, vomiting, regurgitation and diarrhea may indicate underlying GI disease and warrant further diagnostic evaluation before implementing a feeding plan.

Progress Notes

The dog was offered a small amount of water and a moist highly digestible commercial veterinary therapeutic food

(Prescription Diet Canine i/d[a]) the day following surgery. The amounts of water and food were gradually increased over the next couple of days. The dog was released to the owner's care with instructions to continue the therapeutic food in an amount to meet the daily energy requirement at home (1.6 x resting energy requirement = 1,450 kcal [6.07 MJ]). The food was to be offered in three separate meals (one and one-fourth cups each meal) during the day (morning, immediately after work, late evening before bed). The owner was warned about the increased risk of GDV in Irish setter dogs, the potential for a fatal outcome, associated clinical signs and the need for emergency treatment if the problem recurred. Restricted exercise and avoiding rides in a motor vehicle in close association with meals were suggested. The owner was advised to make all attempts to avoid dietary indiscretion. Three months following surgery, the owner reported the dog was normal and doing well.

Endnote

a. Hill's Pet Nutrition Inc., Topeka, KS, USA.

Bibliography

Elwood CM. Risk factors for gastric dilatation in Irish setter dogs. Journal of Small Animal Practice 1998; 39: 185-190.

Glickman LT, Glickman NW, Perez CM, et al. Analysis of risk factors for gastric dilatation and dilatation-volvulus in dogs. Journal of the American Veterinary Medical Association 1994; 204: 1465-1471.

Leib MS, Blass CE. Acute gastric dilatation in the dog: Various clinical presentations. Compendium on Continuing Education for the Practicing Veterinarian 1984; 6: 707-712.

■ CASE 22-2

Chronic Diarrhea in an Irish Setter

Michael S. Leib, DVM, MS
Diplomate ACVIM (Internal Medicine)
Virginia-Maryland Regional College of
  Veterinary Medicine
Blacksburg, Virginia, USA

Assess the Animal

A two-and-one-half-year-old neutered female Irish setter was examined for a five-month history of worsening diarrhea. Initially, the dog produced one abnormal stool every four or five days but now had two abnormal stools daily. Diarrhea was accompanied by tenesmus, hematochezia and excess fecal mucus. Hookworm ova were found in a fecal flotation; however, therapy with an appropriate anthelmintic did not improve the clinical signs. No other parasites or ova were identified in three additional fecal flotations. The owner reported no obvious weight loss.

The dog was obtained as a stray after being hit by a car more than a year ago. It sustained an acetabular fracture that was managed conservatively. Three other dogs and four cats housed with this dog were clinically normal. The dog lived inside and was well supervised in a fenced yard.

Physical examination was normal except for the healed pelvic fracture noted on rectal palpation. Rectal mucosa felt normal and there was no evidence of sublumbar lym-

phadomegaly or intraluminal masses. Body weight was 30 kg with normal body condition (body condition score [BCS] 3/5).

Assess the Food(s) and Feeding Method

Both a commercial dry grocery brand food (Ken-L-Ration Biskit[a]) and a commercial dry veterinary therapeutic food (Prescription Diet Canine i/d[b]) had been fed during the previous five months. No difference in the diarrhea was noted when the dog ate either food. Table food and other snacks were not offered. Water was available free choice.

Questions

1. Prepare a list of differential diagnoses for this patient.
2. Outline a diagnostic plan for this dog.

Answers and Discussion

1. The following conditions should be strongly considered: lymphoplasmacytic colitis (inflammatory large bowel disease), irritable bowel syndrome, histiocytic ulcerative colitis, neoplasia and whipworm infection. Idiopathic colitis or inflammatory bowel disease involving the colon is a common diagnosis made after biopsy specimens are obtained from dogs with chronic large bowel diarrhea and examined microscopically.

The cause is unknown. The causes of irritable bowel syndrome are poorly understood but the disorder may result from psychological influences on the colon resulting in abnormal motility and signs of large bowel diarrhea. This dog was introduced into the household as a stray. Although the dog seemed to interact well with the seven other household pets, the large number of animals may have caused stress that contributed to the diarrhea. Histiocytic ulcerative colitis has been seen most commonly in boxers but can occur in other breeds. It is much less common than lymphoplasmacytic colitis. Neoplasia would be uncommon in a dog of this age although colonic lymphosarcoma may occur in young dogs. Whipworm infection is still possible despite the negative fecal evaluations for parasites. Other causes of chronic large bowel diarrhea include *Giardia* infection, eosinophilic colitis, cecal inversion, bacterial infection (*Yersinia* spp, *Salmonella* spp, others), histoplasmosis, pythiosis and prototothecosis. These disorders should only be considered after exclusion of the more likely diagnoses listed above.

2. The diagnostic plan for this dog should include the following: fecal flotation with zinc sulfate, complete blood count, serum biochemistry profile, urinalysis and colonoscopy with collection of multiple mucosal biopsy specimens. The laboratory database will evaluate the dog's anesthetic risk and identify systemic diseases that may produce chronic diarrhea. However, the history and physical examination make systemic disease unlikely. Flexible colonoscopy allows visualization and biopsy of the entire colonic mucosa. Although four routine fecal flotations only identified hookworm ova on one occasion, this procedure is not sensitive for identification of *Giardia* cysts. *Giardia* infection commonly produces small bowel diarrhea but can occasionally cause large bowel signs. Zinc sulfate flotation or formol-ether sedimentation is necessary to identify *Giardia* cysts in feces. Whipworms shed ova intermittently; therefore, infection may be present despite multiple negative fecal examinations.

Progress Notes

Two fecal flotations using zinc sulfate failed to identify *Giardia* cysts or other parasite ova. Results of the complete blood count, serum biochemistry profile and urinalysis were normal except for mild eosinophilia (2,200/μl). The cecum, ascending, transverse and majority of the descending colon were normal during endoscopic examination. A small 0.5-cm bleeding erosion was noted 15 cm from the anus. Biopsy specimens were obtained from the ascending and transverse colon, from three normal appearing areas in the descending colon and from the eroded area 15 cm from the anus. Microscopically, the eroded region had mucosal ulceration and moderate mucosal infiltration with plasma cells and lymphocytes. All other biopsy specimens had moderate lymphoplasmacytic infiltration into the mucosa. Final diagnosis was lymphoplasmacytic colitis.

Further Questions

1. Outline a feeding plan for this dog.
2. What other therapy should be considered for this patient?

Answers and Discussion

1. Several different types of foods can be used in patients with large bowel disease. One strategy involves using a highly digestible, low-residue food to minimize the amount of ingesta entering the colon. Another strategy uses foods with moderate levels of fiber to alter colonic motility, increase production of volatile fatty acids and control pathogen growth by helping maintain normal colonic pH. A final strategy uses an elimination ("hypoallergenic") food to decrease the amount of potential antigens absorbed by the colon. Ideal elimination foods have moderate levels of protein (i.e., avoid protein excess); have reduced numbers of novel, highly digestible protein sources; and avoid excess food additives and biogenic amines. (See Chapter 14.) A combination of these dietary strategies can also be tried. Although the etiopathogenesis of lymphoplasmacytic colitis is unknown, limiting exposure of the colonic mucosa to potential antigens is considered an important part of the feeding plan. Use of an elimination food is often the first choice in these cases. Access to table food, snacks and food for other household pets should be avoided. Therapeutic trials with several different food types and careful monitoring are necessary for optimal case management. The food should be fed in an appropriate amount for the animal's body condition and activity level. For this dog, the daily energy requirement was estimated to be 1.6 x resting energy requirement (1,550 kcal [6.49 MJ]).

2. Medical management of chronic colitis also includes antiinflammatory and immunosuppressive drugs (mesalamine, sulfasalazine [sulfapyridine and mesalamine], olsalazine, prednisone, azathioprine) and antimicrobial agents (metronidazole, sulfasalazine, tylosin, other antibiotics). Changing the environment to alleviate stressful situations may also benefit some patients in which irritable bowel syndrome is a complicating factor.

Progress Notes

The dog was fed a commercial dry veterinary therapeutic food (Prescription Diet Canine d/d Rice and Egg[b]) for six weeks (i.e., an elimination food). The dog was fed two cups twice daily. The owner reported only two bouts of diarrhea during this period. The dog was eating the food readily and maintaining normal body weight and condition.

Flexible colonoscopy was again performed. Friable, granular mucosa was observed around the ileocolic junction and in the descending colon. Erosions were not seen. Histopathologic evaluation of biopsy specimens revealed moderate lymphoplasmacytic colitis with an increased eosinophilic component compared with specimens from previous biopsy sites. The feeding plan was not changed but therapy with sulfasalazine[c] (1 g, t.i.d.) was instituted. Although clinical signs were eliminated, tear production gradually decreased over the next six months. Keratoconjunctivitis sicca is a common side effect of prolonged therapy with sulfa drugs. The dose of sulfasalazine was tapered and increased tear production occurred but intermittent diarrhea also returned. Therapy with oral prednisone was initiated (40 mg every 24 hours) and the dose slowly tapered. Oral administration of 10 mg prednisone every 48 hours in conjunction with the feeding plan controlled most of the clinical signs. Stressful circumstances still caused intermittent diarrhea.

Endnotes

a. Quaker Oats, Chicago, IL, USA.
b. Hill's Pet Nutrition Inc., Topeka, KS, USA.
c. Azulfidine. Pharmacia, Dublin, OH, USA.

Bibliography

Leib MS. Chronic diarrhea in a dog. Veterinary Medicine Report 1989; 1: 346-350.

Leib MS, Matz ME. Diseases of the intestines. In: Leib MS, Monroe WE, eds. Practical Small Animal Internal Medicine. Philadelphia, PA: WB Saunders Co, 1997; 685-760.

Nelson RW, Stookey LJ, Kazaxcos E. Nutritional management of idiopathic chronic colitis in the dog. Journal of Veterinary Internal Medicine 1988; 2: 133-137.

■ CASE 22-3

Chronic Diarrhea in a Cat

Deborah J. Davenport, DVM, MS
Diplomate ACVIM (Internal Medicine)
Hill's Science and Technology Center
Topeka, Kansas, USA

Assess the Animal

A 10-year-old castrated male domestic shorthair cat was examined for a three-month history of intermittent diarrhea. The owner described the feces as being abnormal three to five times per week; feces were usually fluid to semi-formed and occasionally black. No tenesmus or blood or mucus in the feces had been noted. The cat had not vomited although the owner felt that its appetite had decreased in the last few days. The cat lived in an apartment and no other animals were in the household.

Physical examination was normal except for mild accumulation of dental calculus and a somewhat "doughy" abdomen. Body weight was 4.4 kg with normal body condition (body condition score [BCS] 3/5). The medical record indicated that a body weight of 4.6 kg was recorded six months previously.

Diagnostic evaluation included a complete blood count (mild eosinophilia, 1,170/µl), serum biochemistry profile (normal), urinalysis (normal), serum T_4 concentration (normal), zinc sulfate fecal flotation (negative for *Giardia* cysts but positive for coccidia ova) and a Sudan black stain for fecal fat (positive). Two weeks of treatment with sulfadimethoxine for coccidiosis improved the diarrhea.

The owner returned with the cat six weeks after completion of sulfadimethoxine treatment because the diarrhea had worsened. The cat was thinner (BCS 2/5) and weighed 3.8 kg. Feces were soft and still positive for fat; however, fecal flotation was negative for coccidia and other parasites. A complete blood count revealed more severe eosinophilia (3,500/µl).

Endoscopic examination of the upper gastrointestinal (GI) tract revealed a normal esophagus and stomach but a coarse, granular, friable mucosa in the duodenum. Histopathologic examination of biopsy specimens collected during endoscopy revealed a normal esophagus, mild lymphoplasmacytic infiltration of the stomach and severe lymphoplasmacytic infiltration in the duodenum. Diagnosis was inflammatory bowel disease (lymphoplasmacytic gastroenteritis).

Assess the Food(s) and Feeding Method

The cat was fed a commercial dry grocery brand cat food. The food and water were offered free choice.

Questions

1. Outline a feeding plan for this cat.
2. What other medical therapy can be used in this patient?

Answers and Discussion

1. Several different types of foods may benefit patients with inflammatory bowel disease. One strategy involves using a highly digestible, low-residue food in conjunction with medical management to control inflammation. (See Question 2.) Another strategy uses foods with mild to moderate levels of fiber to alter intestinal motility in conjunction with medical management. A final strategy uses an elimination ("hypoallergenic") food to decrease mucosal exposure to potential antigens. Although the etiopathogenesis of inflammatory bowel disease is unknown, limiting exposure of the GI mucosa to potential antigens is considered an important part of the feeding plan. Use of an elimination food is often the first choice in these cases although a combination of various dietary strategies can also be tried. Access to table food and snacks should be avoided. Therapeutic trials with several different food types and careful monitoring are necessary for optimal case management. The food should be fed in an appropriate amount for the animal's body condition and activity level. For this cat, the daily energy requirement (DER) was estimated to be 1.4 x resting energy requirement for an ideal body weight of 4.5 kg (DER = 290 kcal [1.21 MJ]).

2. Medical therapy is indicated along with dietary management in most moderate to severe cases of inflammatory bowel disease. Mild to moderate cases may respond to dietary management alone. Although clinical remission can be obtained in some cases without medical therapy, many gastroenterologists believe that remission will be more rapid, complete and prolonged if the patient is given a short course of antiinflammatory drugs. The rationale for this recommendation is that the more rapidly intestinal inflammation can be controlled, the more rapidly the intestinal permeability barrier will be restored and the less exposure the animal will have to intestinal luminal antigens, including the antigens in the new food. A large variety of medications have been used in cats with this condition including oral corticosteroids, parenteral corticosteroids (i.e., nonresponsive patients with severe disease), azathioprine, cyclophosphamide, metronidazole, tylosin, miscellaneous antibiotics and motility modifiers.

Progress Notes

The owner was offered several therapeutic options but elected to try an elimination food alone. The cat was started on a commercial moist veterinary therapeutic food (Prescription Diet Feline d/d[a]) that contained highly digestible ingredients (lamb and rice) to which the cat had not been exposed previously. The food was offered as two meals per day (one-fourth of a 14.25-oz can twice daily). Four weeks later, the owner reported that the diarrhea had resolved completely and the cat weighed 4.2 kg. The feeding plan was continued.

The cat did well for more than a year; however, lethargy, vomiting and weight loss were noted 16 months after the initial diagnosis of inflammatory bowel disease.

Physical examination revealed a thin cat (body weight 3.5 kg, BCS 2/5) with palpably thickened bowel loops. Persistent eosinophilia and elevated liver enzyme activity were present. Evaluation of intestinal biopsy specimens obtained endoscopically revealed GI lymphosarcoma. The cat was euthanatized at the owner's request.

Endnote

a. Hill's Pet Nutrition Inc., Topeka, KS, USA.

Bibliography

Dimski DS. Therapy of inflammatory bowel disease. In: Bonagura JD, ed. Current Veterinary Therapy XII. Philadelphia, PA: WB Saunders Co, 1995; 723-728.

CASE 22-4

Acute Diarrhea in a Young Cat

Deborah J. Davenport, DVM, MS
Diplomate ACVIM (Internal Medicine)
Hill's Science and Technology Center
Topeka, Kansas, USA

Assess the Animal

A six-month-old intact male domestic shorthair kitten was examined for acute onset of vomiting, watery diarrhea, anorexia and lethargy. The kitten had been found as a stray two months previously and vaccination status was unknown. The kitten lived in a barn and the owners were concerned that it had been poisoned. There was a dog that lived in the house and several horses on the property. None of these animals were ill.

Physical examination revealed a depressed, dehydrated cat. Excessive amounts of fluid and gas were palpable in the intestinal tract. Abdominal palpation stimulated vomiting; the vomitus was clear fluid with flecks of blood. Body weight was 2.5 kg and the cat appeared thin (body condition score [BCS] 2/5).

Evaluation included a fecal flotation (negative), complete blood count (leukopenia) and serum biochemistry profile (normal except for changes associated with dehydration). A tentative diagnosis of feline panleukopenia due to feline parvovirus infection was made.

Treatment included aggressive intravenous fluid therapy to correct dehydration and systemic antibiotics. The kitten improved clinically within a few days and the leukocyte count returned to normal. The kitten began drinking water and eating small amounts of a moist homogenized recovery formula (Prescription Diet Canine/Feline a/d[a]). There was no further vomiting but diarrhea continued. The feces were no longer watery but were semi-formed and voluminous.

Assess the Food(s) and Feeding Method

The kitten was fed a commercial dry grocery brand food formulated for growing cats (Purina Kitten Chow[b]). The food and water were available free choice in the barn. The kitten had access to other animal feed (commercial dry dog food, grain mixture for the horses) but had never been seen eating these foods.

Questions

1. What is the likely cause for the persistent diarrhea?
2. What are the key nutritional factors for this patient?
3. Outline a feeding plan for this kitten.

Answers and Discussion

1. Feline parvovirus infection destroys intestinal crypt cells in the jejunum and ileum. This results in shortened, blunt intestinal villi and also malabsorption. Villi will normally regrow very quickly after viremia resolves and crypt cells are re-established. However, some cats have a prolonged recovery period with chronic enteritis and diarrhea. This may occur because villi are slow to recover or because of concurrent parasite, viral or bacterial infection. The recovery food may also contain excessive amounts of fat (29% DM fat) for the recovering gastrointestinal (GI) tract.
2. Key nutritional factors for patients with infectious enteritis include water, electrolytes, acid load, fat, energy, fiber and digestibility.

   Water. Water is the most important nutrient for patients with acute vomiting or diarrhea because of the potential for life-threatening dehydration due to excessive fluid loss and inability of the patient to replace losses. Oral fluid therapy is reserved for cats with minor fluid deficits or to supply maintenance fluid requirements.

   Electrolytes. Hypokalemia, hypochloremia and either hypernatremia or hyponatremia are the electrolyte abnormalities most commonly associated with acute vomiting and diarrhea. Electrolyte disorders should be corrected initially with appropriate parenteral fluid therapy. Foods for cats with acute gastroenteritis should contain levels of sodium, chloride and potassium above the minimum allowances for normal kittens and adult cats.

   Acid load. Acidemia is common in patients with diarrhea and severe dehydration. Severe acid-base disorders are best corrected with appropriate parenteral fluid therapy. Foods for cats with acute vomiting and diarrhea should avoid excess dietary acid load.

   Fat/energy. Dietary fat is a concentrated source of calories; higher fat foods allow smaller amounts of food

GI & PANCREAS

to be ingested to meet the cat's daily energy requirement (DER). This is important for many patients with GI disease because limiting the amount of food entering the GI tract helps control clinical signs. Fat also helps improve the palatability of food, which is important in patients with nausea. For these reasons, foods for cats with acute gastroenteritis should contain moderate amounts of fat (i.e., 15 to 22% dry matter).

Fiber. Dietary fiber is beneficial because it: 1) modifies gastric emptying, 2) normalizes intestinal motility, 3) buffers toxins in the GI lumen, 4) binds or holds excess water, 5) supports growth of normal GI microflora, 6) buffers gastric acid and 7) alters viscosity of GI luminal contents. Cats with gastroenteritis may benefit from small amounts (i.e., crude fiber <5% dry matter) of a mixed (i.e., soluble/insoluble) fiber type in conjunction with a highly digestible food.

Digestibility. Digestibility of foods for cats with acute gastroenteritis should be high (dry matter digestibility ≥90%) because normal digestion and absorption of nutrients is often impaired.

3. Small amounts of water and food should be gradually reintroduced to the kitten. The food should reflect the nutrient profile discussed above. Veterinary therapeutic foods designed for patients with GI disease have appropriate nutrient levels and usually have high digestibility. Levels of nutrients in these products are also usually appropriate for growing cats. The DER should reflect the needs of a growing cat (i.e., at least 2.5 x resting energy requirement or 360 kcal [1.51 MJ]).

Progress Notes

Multiple fecal flotations were negative for intestinal parasites. A fecal culture was negative for bacterial pathogens. Tests for feline leukemia and feline immunodeficiency virus infection were negative. A commercial moist veterinary therapeutic food (Prescription Diet Feline i/d[a]) was mixed with the recovery food (approximately 50:50) and gradually introduced to the kitten. Feline i/d is highly digestible, contains a mixed fiber source and is formulated to meet the nutritional needs of kittens. The cat readily ate this mixture for two days in the hospital and was sent home with the dry formula of Feline i/d (three-fourths cup daily to be increased as the cat grew and gained weight). Semi-formed feces persisted for several weeks but then gradually returned to normal. The food was changed to a commercial dry product appropriate for adult cats when the cat was neutered at nine months of age.

Endnotes

a. Hill's Pet Nutrition Inc., Topeka, KS, USA.
b. Ralston Purina Co., St. Louis, MO, USA.

Bibliography

Pollock RVH, Postorino NC. Feline panleukopenia and other enteric viral diseases. In: Sherding RG, ed. The Cat: Diseases and Clinical Management, 2nd ed. New York, NY: Churchill Livingstone, 1994; 479-487.

■ CASE 22-5

Anorexia in a German Shepherd Crossbred Dog

Philip Roudebush, DVM
Diplomate ACVIM (Internal Medicine)
Hill's Science and Technology Center
Topeka, Kansas, USA

Assess the Animal

A five-year-old neutered male German shepherd crossbred dog was examined on an emergency basis for an acute onset of anorexia and depression. The owners found the dog outside hiding under a large shrub. The dog seemed lethargic and refused food and water when they were offered. Past clinical problems included multiple seizures, hyperlipidemia and recurrent superficial staphylococcal pyoderma. The dog was receiving phenobarbital for seizures and had just completed six weeks of therapy with cephalexin for superficial pyoderma.

Physical examination revealed a very depressed, febrile (rectal temperature 40.0°C [104.0°F]) dog. Pain was elicited when the cranial abdomen was palpated and the dog vomited a small amount of clear liquid. Oral mucous membranes were brick-red. The dog was overweight (body condition score [BCS] 4/5, body weight 45 kg).

Blood was drawn for a complete blood count and serum biochemistry profile. Therapy for shock was initiated with intravenous fluids, antibiotics and corticosteroids. Results of diagnostic studies included leukocytosis with a marked left shift (Table 1, Day 1) and very lipemic serum. Fluid therapy and antibiotics were continued through the night.

Intermittent vomiting continued. The next morning, abdominal radiographs were taken. Loss of serosal detail in the cranial abdomen consistent with focal fluid accumulation or peritonitis was noted. Results of a complete blood count were still consistent with severe inflammation (Table 1, Day 2) and the serum was still lipemic. Results of a serum biochemistry profile included increased serum amylase and lipase activities and increased liver enzyme activity (Table 1, Day 2). Fluid recovered by abdominal lavage was evaluated cytologically. The abdominal lavage fluid contained many nondegenerative neutrophils with no evidence of bacteria. Pancreatitis with nonseptic peritonitis was diagnosed.

Assess the Food(s) and Feeding Method

The dog was fed a commercial dry premium brand dog food free choice plus a variety of leftover food from the owner's meals.

Questions

1. What are potential complications of pancreatitis?
2. What are the key nutritional factors for this patient?
3. Outline a short-term (i.e., next few days) and long-term (i.e., next several months) treatment and feeding plan for this dog.

Table 1. Selected laboratory parameters from a dog with pancreatitis.

Parameters	Day 1	Day 2	Day 6	Day 107	Day 121	Day 154	Reference values
Packed cell volume (%)	68	57	53	45	45	56	37-55
Total white blood cells (cells/μl)	20,900	22,500	12,900	12,500	10,800	26,200	8,000-17,000
Total segmented neutrophils (cells/μl)	9,614	9,450	11,868	8,750	7,236	19,388	3,600-13,100
Total band neutrophils (cells/μl)	5,852	8,775	258	0	1,944	1,834	0-400
Total juvenile neutrophils (cells/μl)	1,254	112	0	0	0	0	0
Amylase (IU/l)	ND	1,608	563	897	2,340	2,640	350-1,200
Lipase (U/l)	ND	107	133	64	ND	260	0-100
ALT (IU/l)	ND	99	77	42	ND	120	0-75
Alkaline phosphatase (IU/l)	ND	333	309	30	ND	757	0-80

Key: ND = not done, ALT = alanine aminotransferase.

Answers and Discussion

1. Life-threatening complications of pancreatitis include shock, pulmonary edema, cardiac dysrhythmias, peritonitis, sepsis, disseminated intravascular coagulopathy, hepatic lipidosis (cats) and extrahepatic bile duct obstruction. Other complications include diabetes mellitus and exocrine pancreatic insufficiency.

2. Key nutritional factors for patients with pancreatitis include water, minerals, protein and fat. Aggressive intravenous fluid therapy to correct water, electrolyte and acid-base deficits is a cornerstone of successful treatment for pancreatitis. Potassium supplementation in fluids is often indicated because of potassium losses in vomitus. Dietary protein and fat are the major stimuli for pancreatic secretions; therefore, excessive levels should be avoided. Excess dietary fat should also be avoided in animals with hyperlipidemia.

3. Initially, oral food and water are withheld for three to five days to minimize pancreatic secretions and help control vomiting. Parenteral fluid therapy is used to correct fluid deficits and electrolyte and acid-base disturbances and to meet maintenance water requirements. Colloids (e.g., dextrans, hetastarch) may be needed initially to maintain blood volume and pancreatic microcirculation. After replacement of deficits, additional fluids are given to match the patient's maintenance requirements and ongoing losses. Drug therapy usually includes corticosteroids (only in shock), antiemetics, antibiotics and analgesics. Food and water are gradually introduced in multiple small feedings while clinical signs, especially vomiting, are monitored. Foods for patients with pancreatitis should avoid excessive levels of protein and fat, and contain balanced levels of other nutrients. Some clinicians suggest using a bland, low-protein, low-fat, high-carbohydrate food such as cooked rice for the initial few days of feeding. Parenteral nutritional support should be considered if clinical signs persist beyond five days. (See Chapter 12.) Long-term use of foods that avoid excess dietary fat (i.e., <10% dry matter fat) may be especially important in this overweight dog with a history of hyperlipidemia. (See Chapter 24.)

Progress Notes

Intravenous fluids, antibiotics and phenobarbital were continued for several days. The dog apparently felt much better by the sixth day of hospitalization and the peripheral inflammatory response was improved (Table 1, Day 6). No vomiting had occurred for 24 hours and the dog readily ate cooked rice. The dog continued to improve and was released to the owner's care four days later.

A commercial low-fat, moderate-fiber veterinary therapeutic food (Prescription Diet Canine w/d[a]) was dispensed for use at home. The dog began eating this food during its last two days in the hospital. The daily energy requirement (DER) was calculated to achieve mild weight loss (1.2 x resting energy requirement for an ideal body weight of 39 kg) while supporting recovery from pancreatitis and peritonitis. DER = 1,500 kcal (6.28 MJ), which was met by feeding three and one-half cups of food twice daily. The owners were asked to eliminate table food and other snacks from the diet.

Three months later, the dog was examined for recurrent pyoderma. Blood parameters were normal and the serum was not lipemic (Table 1, Day 107). The dog's weight remained stable. Antibiotics were dispensed, oral phenobarbital was continued and DER was reduced to 1,250 kcal (5.23 MJ) (two and two-thirds cups of food twice daily). Two weeks later, the dog developed anorexia, vomiting and mild abdominal pain after eating fried chicken. Serum was lipemic and blood parameters were consistent with recurrent pancreatitis (Table 1, Day 121). Five days of therapy with intravenous fluids, antibiotics and nothing per os resulted in clinical improvement. The dog was released to the owner's care with instructions to strictly follow the previously developed feeding plan.

A month later, the dog was again examined for anorexia, vomiting, icterus and severe cranial abdominal pain. Laboratory parameters were consistent with pancreatitis and bile duct obstruction (Table 1, Day 154). Exploratory celiotomy revealed severe, chronic, fibrosing pancreatitis with entrapment and compression of the extrahepatic bile duct. The fibrotic portion of the pancreas was excised and the gallbladder was attached to the duodenum (cholecystoduodenostomy). The dog recovered uneventfully from anesthesia and surgery and was released from the hospital seven days later. The low-fat, moderate-fiber food was fed for the next three years until the dog died from other causes. Significant weight loss did not occur but body weight was stabilized at 43 kg and there was no evidence of hyperlipidemia or further pancreatitis.

Endnote

a. Hill's Pet Nutrition Inc., Topeka, KS, USA.

Bibliography

Williams DA. Acute pancreatitis. In: Kirk RW, Bonagura JD, eds. Current Veterinary Therapy XI. Philadelphia, PA: WB Saunders Co, 1992; 631-639.

GI & PANCREAS

CASE 22-6

Vomiting in a Labrador Retriever Crossbred Dog

Douglas Brum, DVM
Angell Memorial Animal Hospital
Boston, Massachusetts, USA

Assess the Animal

An 18-month-old neutered male Labrador retriever crossbred dog was examined for a 12-hour period of vomiting. The dog had no previous medical problems. The night before presentation, the dog ate a rawhide chew and began to vomit several hours later. The vomitus initially contained undigested food but then rapidly changed to a more liquid consistency. The dog weighed 22.3 kg (body condition score [BCS] 3/5) and was extremely depressed and weak. Rectal body temperature was 37.2°C (99°F). Mucous membranes were pale gray and the capillary refill time was three seconds. The heart rate was 180 beats/min. and femoral pulses were fair to poor. The dog's abdomen was tense and extremely painful. Significant clinical pathologic abnormalities included hyperglycemia (glucose 217 mg/dl, normal 65 to 110), thrombocytopenia (19.0 x $10^3/\mu l$, normal 122 to 475) with clotting dysfunction (i.e., prolonged prothrombin time [8.7 sec., normal 4.5 to 7.6] and activated partial thromboplastin times [19.8 sec., normal 10.3 to 17.0]). Changes consistent with a small intestinal obstruction were apparent radiographically.

Exploratory celiotomy performed within two hours of presentation revealed a mesenteric volvulus involving the jejunum. Most of the jejunum was purple to black due to occlusion of mesenteric vessels. Resection of all questionable bowel was performed resulting in a final anastomosis of the remaining 10 cm of proximal jejunum to the ileum. The duodenum, pancreatic/bile duct, ileum and ileocecal junction were preserved.

Assess the Food(s) and Feeding Method

The dog was normally fed a commercial dry grocery brand food (Purina Dog Chow[a]) once daily. Water was available free choice. Treats, snacks and table foods were given to the dog occasionally.

Questions

1. What preoperative, intraoperative and postoperative care is important for this dog?
2. What complications might occur subsequent to intestinal resection in this patient?
3. What are the key nutritional factors and feeding plan for this dog?

Answers and Discussion

1. Most dogs with mesenteric volvulus present in hypovolemic or endotoxic shock and therefore require immediate aggressive fluid therapy and broad-spectrum antibiotics preoperatively. Rapid surgical intervention is required in cases of small bowel obstruction. Intraoperative blood loss and hemorrhage due to coagulopathies may complicate recovery. Postoperative

concerns include fluid losses, electrolyte imbalances, infection control and caloric intake. These problems can be addressed through aggressive fluid therapy, electrolyte replacement, continued broad-spectrum antibiotics and assisted feeding.
2. Short bowel syndrome often occurs when a large portion of the small intestine is removed, resulting in maldigestion and malabsorption causing diarrhea, steatorrhea, malnutrition and weight loss. The remaining length of small intestine will hypertrophy and absorptive capability will significantly increase; however, the functional capacity of the remaining intestine is difficult to predict and varies from case to case. Generally, complete adaptation takes months.
3. The key nutritional factors for this dog in the immediate postoperative days are water, electrolytes, energy and protein. (See Chapter 12.) Longer-term management of dogs with short bowel syndrome includes providing nutritional support to the patient until the intestine adapts, the diarrhea is controlled and weight can be maintained. A highly digestible food fed in small frequent feedings (i.e., six to eight meals/day) is recommended. Food characteristics should be individually modified to meet each patient's specific needs. Eventually, the patient may be fed its normal or similar food.

Progress Notes

The packed cell volume decreased to 19% during surgery; therefore, the dog was given one unit (500 ml) of packed red cells and one unit (50 ml) of fresh frozen plasma during surgery. Postoperatively, the dog had large amounts of bloody diarrhea, became hypoproteinemic and continued to have significant fluid losses through vomiting and diarrhea.

Crystalloid solutions supplemented with potassium were administered in quantities sufficient to meet fluid requirements and replace ongoing losses. The dog was given a parenteral mixture designed to meet daily fluid, electrolyte, resting energy and protein requirements. This mixture was administered via a peripheral catheter for the first five days after surgery. (See Chapter 12.) After four days, the vomiting had resolved and a nasoesophageal tube (8 Fr.) was placed for a continuous infusion of a commercial liquid monomeric food (Peptamen[b]). This homogenized food contains protein, carbohydrates and fat in small, readily absorbable forms, has a caloric density of 1 kcal (4.2 kJ)/ml and contains glutamine. To meet the daily energy requirement of this dog, 720 ml of the monomeric food were infused via nasoesophageal tube continuously over 24 hours. This liquid food accounted for approximately 720 ml of the patient's daily water requirement, thus infusion of the intravenous crystalloid fluid was appropriately reduced.

After seven days in the hospital, the patient was discharged with instructions for the owner to feed a mixture of a commercial moist growth food (Science Diet Canine Growth[c]), the monomeric liquid food and small amounts of a moist high-fiber veterinary therapeutic food (Prescription Diet Feline r/d[c]). The moist growth food (521 kcal/can [2.18 MJ/can]) provided a nutrient-dense, highly digestible food to promote nutrient absorption and weight gain or maintenance. The monomeric food provided nutrients that were immediately absorbable with little or no digestion, and was to be used in decreasing amounts as the remaining small bowel adapted. Feline r/d (30% dry matter fiber) was used in small amounts to help control the diarrhea. Initially, the dog went home with instructions for the owner to feed 250 kcal (1.05 MJ) of the monomeric liquid food with each half can (260 kcal [1.09 MJ]) of the growth formula and to add 2 Tbs of the high-fiber veterinary therapeutic food as needed to manage diarrhea. This mixture was offered every two to three hours for the first week and then less frequently as the dog tolerated larger meals. The proportions of these foods were varied over the next several weeks, depending on the dog's appetite, body weight/condition and stool quality.

The dog's body weight and condition declined initially; however, as stool quality gradually improved, the body weight and condition improved so that the dog was essentially normal eight weeks after surgery. The dog was fed the moist growth food only until its weight stabilized. After six months, the dog was fed a commercial dry maintenance-type food (Science Diet Canine Maintenance[c]) free choice. Four years postoperatively, the dog continues to do well, maintains a normal weight of 22.7 kg (BCS 3/5) and has reasonably normal stools. The dog is eating two meals a day.

Endnotes

a. Ralston Purina Co., St Louis, MO, USA.
b. ClinTec, Chicago, IL, USA.
c. Hill's Pet Nutrition Inc., Topeka, KS, USA.

Bibliography

Shealy PM, Henderson RA. Canine intestinal volvulus. A report of nine new cases. Veterinary Surgery 1992; 21: 15-19.

Yanoff SR, Willard MD, Boothe HW, et al. Short-bowel syndrome in four dogs. Veterinary Surgery 1992; 21: 217-222.

CASE 22-7

Regurgitation in a Collie

Deborah J. Davenport, DVM, MS
Diplomate ACVIM (Internal Medicine)
Hill's Science and Technology Center
Topeka, Kansas, USA

Assess the Animal

A six-year-old, neutered female collie dog was examined for regurgitation and coughing of two weeks' duration. The owners had first noticed what they described as vomiting two weeks earlier. Further questioning confirmed that the problem was probably regurgitation because the process involved casting-up of undigested food in a tubular form with little or no force, rather than forceful expulsion of digested food with retching and involuntary abdominal contractions. Soft coughing and a mucoid nasal discharge began about a week after the onset of regurgitation. The dog was also somewhat lethargic.

Physical examination revealed a quiet, thin (body condition score [BCS] 2/5), mildly febrile (39.1°C [102.5°F]), 23-kg dog with an increased respiratory rate (45 breaths/min.). Slight mucopurulent discharge was noted in both external nares. Low-pitched, coarse crackles were heard over the entire lung field, but were loudest in the ventral half of the thorax. The coat appeared dry and lusterless. When this finding was mentioned to the owners, they confirmed that a change in coat quality had occurred more than a year ago.

Initial diagnostic evaluation included a complete blood count (neutrophilic leukocytosis), serum biochemistry profile (normal), urinalysis (normal), fecal flotation (whipworm ova) and thoracic radiographs (changes consistent with megaesophagus and mild bronchopneumonia).

Further testing was done to rule out secondary or acquired causes of megaesophagus. A thorough neurologic examination failed to reveal neurologic deficits. Tests for myasthenia gravis (i.e., acetylcholine receptor antibody test) and lead toxicosis were negative. A positive-contrast esophagram revealed no evidence of strictures, granulomas, foreign bodies, neoplasia or extraesophageal compression.

Results of a thyroid screening panel included decreased serum concentrations of total thyroxine (T_4) and free T_4, and increased serum concentrations of thyrotropin (TSH).

The tentative diagnosis was hypothyroidism, megaesophagus and aspiration pneumonia.

Assess the Food(s) and Feeding Method

The dog was normally fed a dry specialty brand food twice daily mixed with a small amount of various moist grocery brand foods. A homemade mixture of chicken and rice had also been offered during the past week in an effort to control the regurgitation.

Questions

1. What are the key nutritional factors to consider for this patient?
2. Outline an appropriate feeding plan (foods and feeding method) for this dog.

Answers and Discussion

1. Key nutritional factors for patients with megaesophagus and other swallowing disorders include energy, fat, protein and food form. Animals with swallowing disorders are often debilitated and underweight because of inadequate food intake and secondary aspiration pneumonia. A relatively high-fat (>15% dry matter [DM] fat), energy-dense (>5.0 kcal/g [20.9 kJ/g] DM) food helps meet the patient's caloric requirement in small volumes of food. Protein is required in amounts adequate to support tissue repair and help reduce episodes of gastroesophageal reflux. Dietary protein should generally exceed 25% (dry matter basis). The food form may influence esophageal motility and subsequent clinical signs. Esophageal performance in animals with congenital or acquired esophageal dilatation may improve when the swallowing reflex is maximally stimulated by the texture of coarse, dry foods. Dry food boluses may

stimulate any remaining normal esophageal tissue; therefore, dry foods are the form of choice because gruels may increase the risk of aspiration pneumonia.

2. The goals of dietary management for patients with megaesophagus are to minimize regurgitation, avoid secondary aspiration pneumonia and provide adequate nutrition to regain or maintain proper body weight and condition. In this case, the feeding plan was used in conjunction with thyroid hormone replacement and treatment of the aspiration pneumonia. (See Progress Notes below.) The acquired esophageal motility defect may or may not be reversible. A high-fat, high-calorie recuperative or growth-type food is appropriate for this dog. The food should be given in small-volume, frequent meals and offered so the dog eats in an upright position. The food consistency and feeding method that best promote flow through the esophagus to the stomach in individual patients are often determined by trial and error.

Progress Notes

Thyroid hormone replacement therapy was started using 0.6 mg per day of oral synthetic levothyroxine sodium[a] (L-thyroxine). The pneumonia was treated with one injection of enrofloxacin (Baytril[b]) followed by oral enrofloxacin tablets (68 mg, b.i.d.) for three weeks. The whipworm infection was treated with a broad-spectrum anthelmintic (Drontal Plus[b]). The food was changed to a commercial dry veterinary therapeutic food (Prescription Diet Canine a/d[c]) designed for stress and recovery. This food has high fat levels (25% dry matter), high energy density (4.8 kcal/g [20.1 kJ] dry matter) and

moderate protein levels (38.1% dry matter) to support recovery and weight gain. Daily energy requirement was estimated to be 1,400 kcal (5.86 MJ) for an ideal body weight of 27 kg. The food was given in small, frequent meals and offered from a bowl placed on the edge of a table.

The coughing and nasal discharge gradually improved so the antibiotic was discontinued. Regurgitation continued but gradually lessened in frequency. Radiographs six weeks later revealed no evidence of aspiration pneumonia, but the megaesophagus was still evident. Body weight (26.5 kg) and body condition (BCS 3/5) had improved. The food was changed to the commercial dry specialty brand food originally fed to the dog but it was offered from an elevated position. This feeding plan successfully reduced the regurgitation to a few episodes per week.

Endnotes

a. Soloxine. Daniels Pharmaceuticals Inc., St Petersburg, FL, USA.
b. Baytril. Bayer Animal Health, Shawnee, KS, USA.
c. Hill's Pet Nutrition Inc., Topeka, KS, USA.

Bibliography

Guilford WG, Strombeck DR. Diseases of swallowing. In: Guilford WG, Center SA, Strombeck DR, et al, eds. Strombeck's Small Animal Gastroenterology, 3rd ed. Philadelphia, PA: WB Saunders Co, 1996; 211-238.

Jaggy A, Oliver JE. Neurologic manifestations of thyroid disease. Veterinary Clinics of North America: Small Animal Practice 1994; 24: 487-494.

Peterson ME, Melian C, Nichols R. Measurement of serum total thyroxine, triiodothyronine, free thyroxine and thyrotropin concentrations for diagnosis of hypothyroidism in dogs. Journal of the American Veterinary Medical Association 1997; 211: 1396-1402.

▌ CASE 22-8

Constipation in a Domestic Shorthair Cat

Deborah J. Davenport, DVM, MS
Diplomate ACVIM (Internal Medicine)
Hill's Science and Technology Center
Topeka, Kansas, USA

Assess the Animal

A six-year-old, neutered male domestic shorthair cat was examined for tenesmus and apparent constipation. The owners had noticed the cat making multiple unproductive attempts to defecate in the litter box. The cat was also seen sitting in the litter box for prolonged periods without making attempts to urinate or defecate. Two other cats in the household were normal. The owners cleaned the litter box daily and noticed both normal and dry, hardened feces. Because the cat had been constipated in the past, the owners were giving a flavored petrolatum product (Laxatone[a]) each day by mouth.

Physical examination revealed a normal-appearing, 3.5-kg cat with normal body condition (body condition score [BCS] 3/5). Abdominal palpation elicited a painful response and the entire colon was distended with firm feces.

Warm tap water and mineral oil enemas were given to the cat; some of the fecal material was subsequently passed. The cat was anesthetized and warm tap water was

infused into the colon while the remaining fecal material was manually expressed by abdominal palpation. The cat was discharged the same day with instructions for the owners to increase the amount of flavored petrolatum given each day by mouth.

Ten days later, the cat was re-examined for similar problems. Abdominal radiographs revealed a markedly distended colon impacted with feces. No foreign material, mass lesions, healed pelvic fractures or spinal abnormalities were noted radiographically. The fecal material was removed via enemas and manual extraction. A tentative diagnosis of chronic constipation and possible megacolon was made.

Assess the Food(s) and Feeding Method

All of the cats in the house were fed a commercial dry specialty brand adult cat food free choice. Canned tuna or a variety of commercial moist grocery brand foods were offered once or twice weekly as a treat. Water was available free choice although all three cats liked to drink from faucets and toilet bowls.

Questions

1. What are the key nutritional factors to consider for this patient?
2. Outline an appropriate feeding plan (foods and feeding method) for this cat.

3. What other therapy can be used in conjunction with the feeding plan?

Answers and Discussion

1. The key nutritional factor for this patient is dietary fiber. Fiber is classified as a bulk-forming laxative although it has many other properties. Fiber's beneficial effects in treating animals with constipation include increasing fecal water content, increasing intestinal motility, altering intestinal transit rate and increasing frequency of defecation.

2. Fiber supplements such as psyllium husk fiber (Metamucil[b] powder, 1 to 4 tsp/meal), wheat bran (1 to 2 Tbs/meal) or pumpkin (1 to 4 Tbs/meal) can be added to moist foods. Alternatively commercial, fiber-enhanced foods can make up part or all of the diet. This cat will need to be fed separately from other cats in the household. Several smaller meals during the day rather than one large meal may be beneficial and will be similar to the free-choice feeding method used previously.

3. Therapy for chronic constipation includes: 1) removing impacted feces, 2) administering laxatives, 3) administering prokinetic agents and 4) performing surgery. Laxatives are classified as bulk laxatives (dietary fiber), emollient laxatives (dioctyl sodium sulfosuccinate), lubricant laxatives (mineral oil, petrolatum), hyperosmotic laxatives (lactulose, magnesium salts, polyethylene glycols) and stimulant laxatives (bisacodyl). All these may be used in cats with mild to moderate constipation, but they should be avoided in cases with functional or mechanical bowel obstruction (obstipation). Studies suggest that stimulating colonic smooth muscle contraction may improve colonic motility in cats with idiopathic dilated megacolon. In vitro studies have shown that cisapride[c] stimulates propulsive motility in the colon, and anecdotal experience suggests that cisapride also effectively stimulates colonic propulsive motility in cats with mild to moderate idiopathic constipation. Cats with long-standing obstipation and megacolon are not likely to improve with dietary, laxative and prokinetic therapy alone. Subtotal colectomy should be considered in these cases.

Progress Notes

Metamucil (0.5 tsp) was added to the moist food and offered to the cat daily in addition to the regular commercial dry food fed free choice. The moist food plus fiber supplement made up approximately half of the daily food intake. Little improvement was noted after one month. The cat was then exclusively fed a commercial moist veterinary therapeutic food (Prescription Diet Feline w/d[d]) with moderate fiber levels (12.3% dry matter crude fiber). There was some improvement after a month with increased frequency of defecation and moister feces. However, constipation remained an intermittent problem. Cisapride, 2.5 mg, twice daily per os, was added to the therapeutic protocol and the cat had only occasional problems with constipation thereafter.

Endnotes

a. EVSCO Pharmaceuticals, Buena, NJ, USA.
b. Procter & Gamble, Cincinnati, OH, USA.
c. Propulsid. Janssen Pharmaceutica, Inc., Titusville, NJ, USA.
d. Hill's Pet Nutrition, Inc., Topeka, KS, USA.

Bibliography

DeNovo RC, Bright RM. Chronic feline constipation/obstipation. In: Kirk RW, Bonagura JD, eds. Current Veterinary Therapy XI. Philadelphia, PA: WB Saunders Co, 1992; 619-626.

Washabu RJ, Hasler AH. Constipation, obstipation and megacolon. In: August JR, ed. Consultations in Feline Internal Medicine 3. Philadelphia, PA: WB Saunders Co, 1997; 104-112.

GI & PANCREAS

CASE 22-9

Chronic Diarrhea in a German Shepherd Crossbred Dog

Jörg M. Steiner, Drmedvet
Diplomate ACVIM (Internal Medicine) and ECVIM (Companion Animal)
College of Veterinary Medicine
Texas A&M University
College Station, Texas, USA

Assess the Animal

A two-and-one-half-year-old neutered male German shepherd crossbred dog was examined for chronic diarrhea, polyphagia and weight loss of six months' duration. The feces were characteristic of small bowel disorders: watery to semi-formed consistency, clay-colored, large volumes passed two to three times per day, no melena or hematochezia and only small amounts of mucus. Body weight had decreased over the past six months from 34 kg to 22 kg and body condition was now poor (body condition score [BCS] 1/5). The dog's coat was dull and brittle.

Diagnostic evaluation included a complete blood count (normal), serum biochemistry profile (normal except for mild elevations in liver enzyme activity), urinalysis (normal), direct fecal smear and fecal flotation for parasites (negative), fecal stain for fat (positive) and testing for serum concentrations of canine trypsin-like immunoreactivity (TLI), cobalamin and folate. Serum canine TLI concentration was decreased (0.6 mg/l, normal 5 to 35), serum cobalamin concentration was decreased (150 ng/l, normal 225 to 1,680) and serum folate concentration was increased (23.4 mg/l, normal 6.7 to 17.4).

Assess the Food(s) and Feeding Method

The dog had been fed several commercial dry foods free choice during the past six months. A veterinary therapeutic food (Limited Ingredient Diet: Canine Whitefish and Potato[a]) had been fed for the last two months as an elimination trial for suspected food allergy. The dog was fed five cups per day (1,645 kcal [6.88 MJ]).

Questions

1. What is the tentative diagnosis?
2. What are the key nutritional factors for this dog?
3. Outline a feeding plan (foods and feeding method) for this patient.
4. What ancillary therapy is indicated to complement the feeding plan?

Answers and Discussion

1. A history of chronic diarrhea, steatorrhea and weight loss in a young German shepherd dog strongly suggests exocrine pancreatic insufficiency (EPI) or another cause of malassimilation (i.e., maldigestion or malabsorption). The decreased serum TLI concentration confirms that EPI is present. Mild increases in hepatic enzyme activity are often seen in patients with EPI. Liver disease does not need to be evaluated further unless hepatic enzyme activity continues to increase or if response to therapy is suboptimal. The decreased serum cobalamin concentration and increased serum folate concentration are consistent with small intestinal bacterial overgrowth. Increased numbers of many species of bacteria generate large quantities of folate, which is available for absorption via specific carriers in the proximal small intestine. In contrast, most bacteria compete for available intraluminal cobalamin and thereby reduce its uptake in the distal small intestine. Bacterial overgrowth in the small intestine commonly occurs as a secondary problem associated with EPI. The poor coat probably reflects protein-calorie malnutrition and essential fatty acid deficiency.

2. Key nutritional factors to consider in patients with EPI include food digestibility and fat, fiber and vitamin content. The use of highly digestible foods (dry matter digestibility ≥90%) in conjunction with pancreatic enzyme supplements provides more metabolizable energy to dogs with EPI than use of foods with average digestibility and comparable supplementation. Although steatorrhea due to fat malassimilation is a prominent sign in patients with EPI, fat restriction is not necessary. Moderate dietary fat levels in conjunction with pancreatic enzyme supplementation are more effective than simply decreasing the fat content of the food. Some forms of dietary fiber impair pancreatic enzyme activity in vitro and may have similar effects in animals. Therefore, excess dietary fiber should be avoided (<2% dry matter [DM] crude fiber) in these patients. Fat-soluble vitamins, cobalamin and folate are also nutrients of concern in patients with EPI and bacterial overgrowth. Patients with malassimilation may develop deficiencies in one or more fat-soluble vitamins. Clinical signs of vitamin K deficiency (vitamin K-responsive coagulopathy) have been described in patients with EPI. Several mechanisms may play a role in cobalamin deficiency including alterations in intestinal luminal pH, decreased levels of intrinsic factor and small intestinal bacterial overgrowth. Serum folate concentrations are often elevated in EPI patients with small intestinal bacterial overgrowth but may be decreased in patients with concurrent enteropathies.

3. Dogs with EPI should be fed commercial or homemade foods that are highly digestible, moderate in fat and low in fiber. Tables 22-10 and 6-8 list such foods. The initial daily energy requirement (DER) should be estimated as 2 x resting energy requirement using an ideal body weight of 34 kg (DER = 2,180 kcal [9.12 MJ]). The DER should be adjusted based on weekly assessments of fecal quality, body weight and body condition. Parenteral administration of fat-soluble and B-complex vitamins is also appropriate.

4. Pancreatic enzyme supplementation is necessary using either dried pancreatic extracts (1 tsp/10 kg body weight with meal) or raw bovine or porcine pancreas (60 g/10 kg body weight with meal). Powdered extracts are usually preferred to tablets and capsules. The amount can be gradually decreased to find the minimum effective dose after clinical improvement occurs. Broad-spectrum antimicrobial therapy is appropriate for most cases of small intestinal bacterial overgrowth; oral oxytetracycline or tylosin is often recommended. However, small intestinal bacterial overgrowth is often self-limiting in patients with EPI if dietary alterations and pancreatic enzyme supplementation are successful in controlling clinical signs. Small intestinal bacterial overgrowth is clinically significant in some patients with EPI, so recovery will not be complete unless antimicrobial therapy is given.

Progress Notes

The food was changed to a commercial dry veterinary therapeutic food that was highly digestible, moderate in fat and low in fiber (Prescription Diet Canine i/d[b]). Two tsp of dried pancreatic extract (Pancrezyme[c]) were mixed thoroughly with two cups of slightly moistened food (750 kcal [3.14 MJ]). This mixture was fed three times daily.

The dog ate this mixture well and the diarrhea gradually decreased over the next six to eight weeks. Body weight increased, body condition improved and the dog's coat became shinier and less brittle as stool quality improved. A body weight of 31 kg and BCS of 3/5 were reached approximately 12 weeks after initiating therapy. At that time the dosage of dried pancreatic extract was reduced to 1.5 tsp with each meal and plans were made to further reduce the dosage if clinical signs did not return.

Endnotes

a. Innovative Veterinary Diets, Newport, KY, USA.
b. Hill's Pet Nutrition, Inc., Topeka, KS, USA.
c. Daniels Pharmaceuticals Inc., St Petersburg, FL, USA.

Bibliography

Pidgeon G. Effect of diet on exocrine pancreatic insufficiency in dogs. Journal of the American Veterinary Medical Association 1982; 281: 232-235.

Williams DA. Exocrine pancreatic disease. In: Ettinger SJ, Feldman EC, eds. Textbook of Veterinary Internal Medicine, 4th ed. Philadelphia, PA: WB Saunders Co, 1994; 1372-1392.

Williams DA. Small intestinal bacterial overgrowth. In: Guilford WG, Center SA, Strombeck DR, et al, eds. Strombeck's Small Animal Gastroenterology, 3rd ed. Philadelphia, PA: WB Saunders Co, 1996; 370-373.

CHAPTER 23

Hepatobiliary Disease

Philip Roudebush

Deborah J. Davenport

Donna S. Dimski

"Let us celebrate that great maroon snail, whose back nestles in the dome
of the diaphragm like some blind wise slave, crouching above its colleague viscera,
secret, resourceful, instinctive."
Richard Selzer (Notes on the Art of Surgery)

LIVER DISEASE

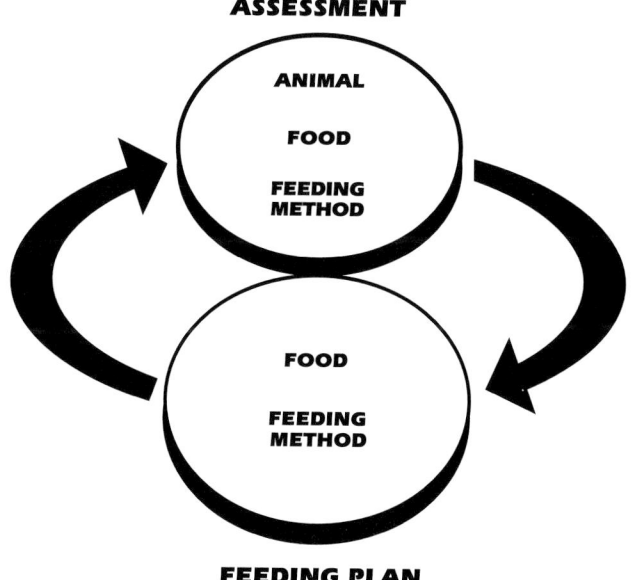

ASSESSMENT

FEEDING PLAN

Note: The reader is referred to Chapter 1 for a detailed discussion of the iterative process of clinical nutrition.

INTRODUCTION

Among the most challenging problems in medicine are those that involve failure of a metabolically active organ, such as the liver. The normal liver carries out an estimated 1,500 essential biochemical functions.[1] In addition to its role in drug metabolism, the removal of environmental and endogenous noxious substances and synthesis of important substances (e.g., albumin and blood clotting factors), the liver plays a key role in digestion and metabolism of foods/nutrients. The liver influences nutritional status through its elaboration of bile salts and central role in intermediary metabolism of protein (amino acids), carbohydrate, fat and vitamins. Table 23-1 lists selected hepatic functions that influence nutrient digestion and metabolism.

The liver has tremendous storage capacity, functional reserve and regenerative capabilities. All of these functions protect the body from profound metabolic alterations. However, these same characteristics complicate the clinical recognition of serious liver disease. Consequently, hepatobiliary disease must be severe or associated with cholestasis before clinical signs and/or laboratory tests reveal or confirm its presence. As a result, the patient is often suffering profound metabolic alterations by the time an appropriate feeding plan is implemented.

Malnutrition is a common finding in patients with advanced hepatic disease and is an independent risk factor for predicting clinical outcome in human patients with chronic hepatic disease.[2] Significant weight loss occurred in 14%,[3] mild to moderate steatorrhea in 50% and deficiency of fat-soluble vitamins occurred in 40% of human

KEY WORDS & TERMS—HEPATOBILIARY DISEASE*

Ammonia
Aromatic amino acid(s)
Ascites
Branched-chain amino acid(s)
Cholangiohepatitis
Cholangitis
Cholecystitis
Cholelithiasis
Cholestasis

Cirrhosis
Copper-associated hepatotoxicosis
Copper chelating agents
Fibrosis
Glucose intolerance
Hepatic encephalopathy
Hepatic lipidosis
Hepatitis
Hepatocyte

Hepatopathy
Hyperammonemia
Microhepatica
Portal hypertension
Portosystemic shunt (acquired and
  congenital)
Urea cycle

Key words and terms are defined in the Glossary.

KEY POINTS—HEPATOBILIARY DISEASE

1. The normal liver carries out an estimated 1,500 essential biochemical functions.
2. The liver has tremendous storage capacity, functional reserve and regenerative capabilities.
3. Hepatobiliary disease, despite its relatively uncommon occurrence, causes significant morbidity and mortality if not diagnosed early and managed appropriately.
4. Altered (delayed) drug metabolism may be the first evidence of liver disease recognized by pet owners and veterinarians. Prolonged recovery from anesthesia or sedation is a common finding in dogs and cats with liver disease.
5. Neurobehavioral signs of hepatic encephalopathy develop in young animals with congenital portosystemic vascular anomalies and in animals with severe acquired liver insufficiency.
6. Alterations in liver and abdominal size are common in dogs and cats with hepatobiliary disorders, though not all these changes are detectable on routine physical examination.
7. Albumin commonly has been used as an indicator of liver function, but it is a nonspecific marker because its concentration reflects hepatic synthesis, rate of degradation, pathologic excretion and volume of distribution.
8. Cytologic or histopathologic tissue examination is essential for definitive diagnosis of hepatobiliary diseases.
9. Obese cats and those with prolonged anorexia of any cause are at increased risk for hepatic lipidosis.
10. Alterations in nitrogen metabolism are one of the most prominent biochemical changes in chronic liver failure. Hyperammonemia is a common finding and probably results from a combination of factors.
11. Feline hepatic lipidosis is a well-recognized syndrome characterized by the accumulation of excess triacylglycerides in hepatocytes with resulting cholestasis and hepatic dysfunction.
12. Bedlington terriers often develop copper storage disease and a subsequent hepatopathy. The role of copper in hepatic diseases in other dog breeds is less clear.
13. Portosystemic shunts are vascular communications between the portal and systemic venous systems. The communication usually occurs between the portal vein and caudal vena cava and allows access of portal blood to the systemic circulation without first passing through the liver. Congenital portosystemic vascular shunts are most common.
14. Chronic hepatitis (sometimes called chronic active hepatitis) in dogs is a poorly defined group of clinico-pathologic entities characterized by parenchymal necrosis, particularly piecemeal and/or bridging necrosis, with lymphoplasmacytic inflammation.
15. Portal hypertension (i.e., a persistent increase in portal venous pressure) can be considered a "homeostatic" response to chronic fibrosis, cirrhosis and altered hepatic lobular architecture.
16. A large amount of taurine is localized in the bile acid pool.
17. The use of L-carnitine supplements or L-carnitine-supplemented foods seems appropriate in obese cats undergoing weight reduction and may also benefit cats with hepatic lipidosis.
18. Copper intake can be controlled in dogs with copper-associated hepatotoxicosis by feeding one of a few commercial veterinary therapeutic foods or homemade foods.
19. In addition to dietary changes, treatment of hepatic copper toxicosis involves use of zinc and copper chelating agents.
20. Because lipid peroxidation has been implicated in the pathogenesis of copper toxicosis and other forms of chronic hepatitis, use of supplemental vitamin E, vitamin C and other antioxidants may be beneficial.
21. The protein requirement of patients with portosystemic vascular shunts has been roughly estimated from a nutritional study in adult dogs with surgically created shunts: approximately 14 to 16% protein calories (15 to 20% dry matter [DM] protein) for dogs and 26 to 30% protein calories (30 to 35% DM protein) for cats.
22. Avoiding excess dietary sodium chloride is necessary in animals with ascites, portal hypertension or significant hypoalbuminemia.
23. Foods with increased dietary fiber levels may be of benefit to patients with hepatobiliary disease.
24. Hypokalemia is dangerous because it may exacerbate expression of hepatic encephalopathy. Foods for dogs and cats with liver disease should be potassium replete (i.e., >0.8% DM potassium), and potassium supplementation should be considered.
25. Vitamin K becomes important in animals with chronic liver disease, prolonged cholestasis or evidence of excessive bleeding.
26. Patients with hepatobiliary disease may benefit from multiple daily feedings rather than one or two large meals.
27. Despite extensive investigation, the pathogenesis of hepatic encephalopathy has yet to be elucidated. There are probably multiple factors underlying the disorder.

KEY NUTRITIONAL FACTORS—HEPATOBILIARY DISEASE

Factors	Associated conditions	Dietary recommendations
Energy/fat	Feline hepatic lipidosis Cholangitis/cholangiohepatitis Copper-associated hepatotoxicosis Portosystemic vascular shunt Chronic hepatitis and cirrhosis	Provide adequate daily energy intake Use foods with energy density >4.0 kcal/g dry matter Use foods with 15 to 30% fat (dry matter basis) in dogs and 20 to 40% fat (dry matter basis) in cats Fat intake may need to be restricted in patients with steatorrhea
Protein	Feline hepatic lipidosis Cholangitis/cholangiohepatitis Copper-associated hepatotoxicosis Portosystemic vascular shunt Chronic hepatitis and cirrhosis	Cats: provide foods with 30 to 45% protein (dry matter basis) Dogs: provide foods with 15 to 30% protein (dry mater basis) Animals with hepatic encephalopathy often need lower dietary protein levels to control clinical signs
Taurine	Feline hepatic lipidosis Cholangitis/cholangiohepatitis	Provide foods with 2,500 to 5,000 ppm taurine (dry matter basis) Supplement homemade foods or human enteral products with 250 to 500 mg taurine per day
Potassium	Feline hepatic lipidosis Cholangitis/cholangiohepatitis	Provide adequate dietary potassium Use foods with 0.8 to 1.0% potassium (dry matter basis)
Copper	Copper-associated hepatotoxicosis	Avoid excess dietary copper Use foods with ≤5.0 ppm copper (dry matter basis) Do not use supplements containing copper Avoid foods with high copper content (See Table 23-7.)
Zinc	Copper-associated hepatotoxicosis	Give supplemental zinc: 50 to 100 mg elemental zinc, per os, twice daily
Antioxidant vitamins	Copper-associated hepatotoxicosis Chronic hepatits and cirrhosis	Give supplemental antioxidant vitamins Vitamin E: 400 to 500 IU, per os, daily Vitamin C: 500 to 1,000 mg, per os, daily
Carnitine	Feline hepatic lipidosis	Give supplemental carnitine: 250 to 500 mg, per os, daily
Sodium chloride	Portal hypertension (ascites)	Avoid excess dietary sodium chloride Dogs: use foods with 0.1 to 0.25% sodium (dry matter basis) and 0.25 to 0.40% chloride (dry matter basis) Cats: use foods with 0.2 to 0.35% sodium (dry matter basis) and 0.30 to 0.45% chloride (dry matter basis)
Fiber	Portosystemic vascular shunt Chronic hepatitis and cirrhosis	Provide increased levels of fermentable fiber Use foods with total dietary fiber of 3 to 8% (dry matter basis)
Arginine	Most liver diseases	Provide increased levels of dietary arginine Dogs: provide foods with 1.2 to 2.0% arginine (dry matter basis) Cats: provide foods with 1.5 to 2.0% arginine (dry matter basis)

LIVER DISEASE

patients with nonalcoholic cirrhosis.[4] Food intake was normal and was unrelated to the degree of malnutrition, suggesting that factors other than decreased food intake are involved in the malnutrition of human patients with hepatic disease. Potential causes of malnutrition in animals with hepatic disease include: 1) anorexia, nausea and vomiting, 2) impaired nutrient digestion, absorption and metabolism, 3) increased energy requirements and 4) accelerated protein catabolism with impaired protein synthesis.[5]

The complex relationship between nutrition and the liver is reflected by the magnitude of the difficulties encountered in managing patients with compromised hepatic function. Malnutrition adversely affects hepatocellular function and structure.[3] The liver is unique because it derives much of its nutrient blood supply from a vein and not an artery.[6] The portal vein provides 70 to 75% of total hepatic blood flow.[7] Portal venous blood is nutrient rich in the absorptive state but oxygen poor. The hepatic artery provides about 25 to 30% of blood flow with oxy-

gen-rich blood.[7] Hepatotropic factors in portal venous and arterial blood modulate the functional and structural integrity of the liver.[8] Concentrations of several hormones, including insulin, glucagon, glucocorticoids, thyroid hormones, parathyroid hormone, calcitonin, α- and β-adrenergic agents, and insulin-like growth factors I and II, increase after hepatic injury or resection and may affect the ensuing hepatic regenerative growth.[9]

Unlike most terminally differentiated cells, hepatocytes in adult liver retain the capacity to proliferate. After partial (70%) hepatectomy, compensatory hyperplasia begins within minutes of resection and is typically completed within two weeks in rats and in less than one month in people.[10,11] The management of many hepatic diseases should thus be predicated on using this capacity to maximum advantage.[12]

Nutritional management of hepatobiliary disease is usually directed at clinical manifestations of the disease rather than the specific cause itself. The goals of nutritional management for hepatobiliary disease include:

1) maintaining normal metabolic processes, 2) correcting electrolyte disturbances, 3) avoiding toxic by-product accumulation and 4) providing substrates to support hepatocellular repair and regeneration.[13]

Table 23-1. Major hepatobiliary functions related to nutrient digestion and metabolism.

Metabolic functions
Converts glucose to glycogen and triacylglycerides during absorptive state
Converts glycogen to glucose in postabsorptive period
Synthesizes glucose from glucogenic precursors such as glycerol and amino acids in postabsorptive period (gluconeogenesis)
Transforms amino acids (transamination and deamination), synthesizes nonessential amino acids as needed for metabolism
Synthesizes triacylglycerols and secretes them as lipoproteins
Synthesizes and releases cholesterol into blood
Forms ketones from degraded fatty acids during fasting
Synthesizes urea from degraded amino acids (sole site in body)
Synthesizes plasma albumin and fibrinogen
Biliary functions
Synthesizes bile salts from cholesterol, which are secreted into bile for lipid emulsification and absorption in the small intestine
Secretes a bicarbonate-rich solution to help neutralize acid in the duodenum
Secretes plasma cholesterol into bile
Conjugates and excretes bilirubin in bile
Detoxifies substances by biotransformation before biliary excretion
Excretes endogenous and foreign organic molecules in bile
Storage functions
Stores glucose as glycogen and triacylglycerides
Stores vitamins, particularly A but also D, E, K, B_{12} and to a lesser extent other B vitamins
Stores minerals such as iron, copper, manganese and zinc
Stores blood, especially with pressure increases in the hepatic vein or posterior vena cava
Endocrine functions
Activates (partial) vitamin D by dehydroxylation
Converts thyroxine to triiodothyronine
Secretes IGF-1 in response to growth hormone
Metabolizes (deactivates) and excretes hormones
Miscellaneous functions
Removes bacteria and food antigens that regularly cross the intestinal epithelial barrier (Kupffer cells of mononuclear-macrophage system in the sinusoids)

CLINICAL IMPORTANCE

The prevalence of hepatobiliary disease is unknown due to variable factors involved in how liver disease is reported in the veterinary literature. Among the factors involved in this variation are clinical vs. biopsy vs. necropsy findings, geographic differences and when the study was conducted. There was a lower prevalence of feline hepatic lipidosis before 1980 and there are few reports of non-icteric gallbladder or biliary tract disease before routine use of ultrasonography as a diagnostic tool. Many hepatic lesions are not due to primary liver disease. In such cases, lesions represent a toxic insult or altered circulation compromising hepatic function. Table 23-2 summarizes hepatic diseases or lesions commonly recognized in dogs and cats.

Primary hepatic neoplasms are uncommon in dogs and cats comprising only 0.8 and 2.3% of all neoplasms in these species.[14] Metastases to the liver are much more common; 7 to 36% of all dogs with cancer had hepatic involvement at necropsy.[14] In cats, the incidence of nonhemolymphatic primary liver tumors is 1.5 to 2.3%.[14] There are no data about the prevalence of hepatic metastases in cats with neoplasia.

A recent report did not include liver disease in a list of the 25 most common diagnoses made in dogs or cats seen in private veterinary practices in the United States.[15] Although the combined prevalence of hepatobiliary disease is small compared with the prevalence of other gastrointestinal (GI) disorders, hepatobiliary disease has increased clinical significance because the liver plays a central role in maintaining normal metabolic homeostasis. Hepatobiliary disease, despite its relatively uncommon occurrence, causes significant morbidity and mortality if not diagnosed early and managed appropriately.

ASSESSMENT

Assess the Animal

History and Physical Examination

Patients with acquired hepatobiliary disease usually display vague clinical signs early in the disease process

Table 23-2. Hepatic diseases and lesions commonly recognized in dogs and cats.

Canine necropsy (%)*	Feline necropsy (%)*	Feline biopsy (%)**	Canine/feline biopsy***
Hepatitis (18)	Hepatitis (22.9)	Lipidosis (49)	Steroid hepatopathy
Metastatic neoplasia (13.9)	Nonspecific hepatopathy (13.5)	Inflammatory liver disease (26)	Neoplasia
Steroid-induced hepatopathy (11.8)	Metastatic neoplasia (12.8)	Neoplasia (10)	Hepatitis (dogs)
Passive congestion (9.1)	Lipidosis (11.0)	Vacuolar changes (4)	Cholangiohepatitis (cats)
Necrosis (8.1)	Passive congestion (10.7)	Portal vascular anomalies (3)	Lipidosis (cats)
Nonspecific hepatopathy (7.2)	Necrosis (9.9)	Toxic hepatopathy (2)	Focal necrosis
Portosystemic vascular shunt (5.7)	Atrophy (3.8)	Miscellaneous disorders (6)	Cholestasis
Vacuolar hepatopathy (5.6)	Portosystemic vascular shunt (2.5)		Cirrhosis
Fibrosis (4.1)	Miscellaneous disorders (12.9)		Passive congestion
Lipidosis (3.9)			
Primary neoplasia (3.8)			
Cirrhosis (2.3)			
Miscellaneous disorders (6.5)			

*Strombeck DR, Guilford WG, eds. Pathogenesis and incidence of hepatic disease. In: Small Animal Gastroenterology, 2nd ed. Davis, CA: Stonegate Publishing, 1990; 526-527.
**Armstrong PJ, Weiss DJ, Gagne JM. Inflammatory liver disease. In: August JR, ed. Consultations in Feline Internal Medicine 3. Philadelphia, PA: WB Saunders Co, 1997; 68-78.
***Descending order of prevalence. Richter KP. Diseases of the liver. In: Tams TR, ed. Handbook of Small Animal Gastroenterology. Philadelphia, PA: WB Saunders Co, 1996; 409.

Table 23-3. Clinical signs associated with hepatobiliary disease.*

Early signs	Major bile duct occlusion	Severe hepatic insufficiency	Portosystemic vascular anomaly
Anorexia	Anorexia	Anorexia	Stunted body size
Vomiting	Vomiting/hematemesis	Vomiting/hematemesis	Abnormal behavior (lethargy)
Diarrhea/constipation	Diarrhea/constipation	Diarrhea/constipation	Diarrhea/constipation
Weight loss	Weight loss	Weight loss	Weight loss
Pyrexia	Pyrexia	Pyrexia	Pyrexia
No jaundice	Jaundice within 72 hours	Jaundice as disease advances	No jaundice
Polydipsia/polyuria	Polydipsia	Polydipsia/polyuria	Polydipsia/polyuria
Clear to yellow urine	Orange urine	Clear to orange urine	Clear urine
Iris normal color	Iris normal color	Iris normal color	Copper-colored iris (cats)
	Bleeding tendencies	Bruising/bleeding tendencies	Normal blood clotting
	Acholic (pale) feces	Brown to melenic feces	Brown feces
	Melenic feces if bleeding	Green feces	Melena
	Hepatomegaly (firm, rounded borders)	Hepatomegaly (cats)	Microhepatica
	Ascites (if >6 weeks)	Normal to microhepatica (dogs)	
		Ascites	Ascites (rare)
		Edema (rare in cats)	Edema does not occur
		Hepatic encephalopathy	Hepatic encephalopathy
		Urinary tract obstruction (uroliths)	Urinary tract obstruction (uroliths)
		Ptyalism (cats)	Enlarged kidneys
			Cryptorchid (dogs)

*Adapted from Center SA. Pathophysiology, laboratory diagnosis, and diseases of the liver. In: Ettinger SJ, Feldman EC, eds. Textbook of Veterinary Internal Medicine, 4th ed. Philadelphia, PA: WB Saunders Co, 1995; 1267.

(Table 23-3). However, jaundice appears within the first 72 hours in animals with major bile duct obstruction.[16] Animals with congenital portovascular anomalies may also develop clinical signs associated with hepatic encephalopathy in the first several months of life.[16] Demonstration of certain metabolic uroliths (i.e., ammonium urate and other purine uroliths) may also indicate underlying liver disease such as portosystemic vascular shunts. (See Chapter 20.)

GI abnormalities common in patients with hepatobiliary disease include anorexia, vomiting and diarrhea.[16] Anorexia and ptyalism (hypersalivation) are especially common in cats (Figure 23-1). Hematemesis suggests GI ulceration, a complication of hepatobiliary disease. The anorexia, GI disturbances and metabolic alterations associated with liver disease often contribute to chronic weight loss. Other common clinical signs of hepatobiliary disease include: 1) polydipsia and polyuria, 2) intermittent pyrexia, 3) icterus of the sclera, mucous membranes and skin, 4) pigmented urine (bilirubinuria), 5) changes in abdominal configuration due to hepatomegaly and/or ascites (Figure 23-2), 6) stunted or small body stature (Figure 23-3) and 7) excessive bleeding (i.e., hemorrhages of the skin and mucous membranes, melena, hematuria).[16] Bleeding tendencies develop due to malabsorption of vitamin K in patients with extrahepatic bile duct obstruction or failure of procoagulant synthesis.[16] Subclinical blood clotting abnormalities may become clinically evident during liver biopsy procedures or surgery.

Altered (delayed) drug metabolism may be the first evidence of liver disease recognized by the owner or veterinarian. Prolonged recovery from anesthesia or sedation is a common finding in dogs and cats with liver disease.[16]

Neurobehavioral signs of hepatic encephalopathy develop in young animals with congenital portosystemic vascular anomalies and in animals with severe acquired liver insufficiency. This manifestation of liver disease is uncommon; however, typical signs include aggression (cats) (Figure 23-4), aimless wandering, manic barking (dogs), ataxia, lethargy, episodic weakness, ptyalism (cats

especially), altered consciousness (disorientation, stupor or rarely coma), head pressing (Figure 23-5), sudden blindness, circling, pacing and seizures.[16] As with other metabolic encephalopathies, these signs may be episodic and often can be historically linked to meals, dietary changes, GI hemorrhage or some other causal event.

Alterations in liver and abdominal size are common in dogs and cats with hepatobiliary disorders, though these changes are not always detected on routine physical exam-

LIVER DISEASE

Figure 23-1. A 14-year-old Persian cat with ptyalism due to liver disease.

ination.[16] The normal liver can be difficult to palpate in dogs and cats and the edges are normally sharp, not rounded. In cats, most acquired hepatic disorders are associated with hepatomegaly that can be detected by abdom-

inal palpation. Hepatomegaly is also readily detected in dogs. On the other hand, reduced liver size is difficult to detect in both dogs and cats. Hepatomegaly may be caused by passive venous congestion, diffuse inflammation, nodular hyperplasia and infiltration by fat, glycogen or neoplastic cells. Pain on palpation of the liver usually indicates acute liver disease but must be differentiated from pain arising from the pancreas, stomach or spleen. Abdominal enlargement associated with ascites usually develops slowly and insidiously. Small amounts of effusion may go undetected, whereas moderate to severe abdominal effusion may be readily noted.

Changes in fecal color and consistency are noted in some patients.[16] Pale, tan or gray acholic feces may be observed when bile flow is obstructed (as with either intrahepatic or extrahepatic cholestasis). Feces become dark green or green-orange when large quantities of bilirubin pigments enter the intestinal tract as occurs with hemolytic or prehepatic jaundice. Significant upper GI bleeding results in melena.

Laboratory Evaluation

It is beyond the scope of a nutrition textbook to discuss the plethora of laboratory tests and imaging techniques (i.e., radiography, nuclear medicine, ultrasound) used to detect and confirm hepatobiliary disease and their interpretation. The reader is referred to small animal internal medicine and GI texts for these details. However, routine tests that may help establish parameters for developing a feeding and reassessment plan will be summarized.

Liver disease is often discovered during routine hematologic, urine and serum biochemistry screening tests. Hematologic changes may include anemia, abnormal erythrocyte morphology, reduced platelet numbers or function, and detection of icteric or lipemic plasma.[16-18] A regenerative anemia caused by blood loss due to GI hemorrhage and/or a bleeding diathesis may by present. More commonly, a nonregenerative anemia is found and is associated with chronic disease, chronic blood loss, malnutri-

Figure 23-2. A domestic shorthair cat with abdominal enlargement due to liver disease and ascites. (Photograph courtesy Dr. Susan Johnson, The Ohio State University, Columbus.)

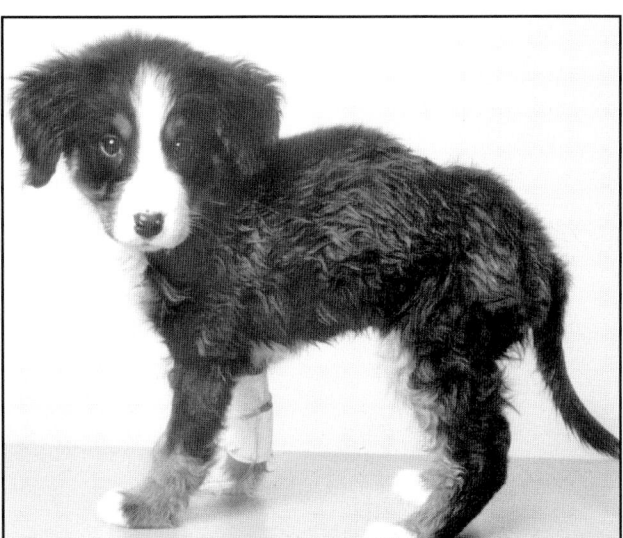

Figure 23-3. A 12-week-old Bernese mountain dog with stunted growth and poor body condition associated with a congenital portosystemic shunt (patent ductus venosus).

Figure 23-4. An eight-month-old Himalayan cat with clinical signs of aggression associated with hepatic encephalopathy due to a congenital portosystemic shunt.

tion and reduced erythrocyte survival.[16,17] Target cells, poikilocytes and spur cells, Heinz bodies (cats) and microcytosis are erythrocytic abnormalities seen in animals with liver disease.[16-18] Erythrocyte microcytosis is associated with both acquired and congenital portosystemic vascular shunts in dogs. A recent study suggested that cats with acute or chronic cholangiohepatitis had higher segmented and band neutrophil counts than cats with lymphocytic portal hepatitis.[19]

The liver is the primary site for synthesis, degradation and regulation of plasma proteins.[16,17] Total protein concentration reflects overall protein balance, but does not provide as much information as albumin and globulin concentration measurements. Albumin has been used commonly as an indicator of liver function, but it is a nonspecific marker because its concentration reflects hepatic synthesis, rate of degradation, pathologic excretion (e.g., urine, GI tract, draining cutaneous lesions) and volume of distribution. Hyperglobulinemia is common in animals with acquired liver disease and may be great enough to mask hypoalbuminemia if only total serum protein concentration is evaluated.[16,17]

Liver enzymes typically included in serum biochemistry profiles include alanine aminotransferase (ALT, formerly SGPT), alkaline phosphatase (ALP), gamma-glutamyl transferase (GGT) and aspartate aminotransferase (AST, formerly SGOT). Increased serum liver enzyme activity is common in small animal patients and not necessarily associated with significant liver disease.[16,17] Enzyme activity can increase as a result of induction, reversible and irreversible changes in cellular membranes, hepatocellular injury and/or biliary injury. Increased liver enzyme activity lacks specificity and provides no indication of functional capabilities of the liver. Cats with chronic cholangiohepatitis have higher ALT activities and total bilirubin concentrations than cats with lymphocytic portal hepatitis.[19] Mild increases in liver enzyme activity (i.e., one-and-one-half-fold to twofold normal) in an otherwise normal animal should be evaluated again in two to four weeks. If liver enzyme activity remains abnormal, liver function tests are indicated.

A number of liver function tests have been used in veterinary medicine including: 1) Bromsulphalein (BSP) dye clearance, 2) serum bile acid concentration, 3) glucagon tolerance test, 4) ammonia tolerance test, 5) resting plasma ammonia concentration and 6) caffeine clearance.[16,17] Of these, fasting and postprandial serum bile acid determinations and ammonia tolerance testing are the ones used most often in clinical practice. Liver function studies such as serum bile acid concentrations are used to: 1) identify occult liver disease, 2) assess liver function when there is increased liver enzyme activity, 3) determine whether a liver biopsy is warranted and 4) monitor response to therapy.[20,21]

Normal blood coagulation depends on production of plasma coagulation factors by the liver. Blood coagulation tests should always be performed in patients with significant liver disease before liver biopsy or surgery. Even if there are no clinical signs of excessive bleeding, coagulation test results are frequently abnormal. In one study, plasma coagulation factor abnormalities occurred in more than half of dogs with naturally occurring hepatic disease.[22]

Imaging the Liver

Routine imaging of the hepatobiliary system includes abdominal radiography and ultrasonographic imaging.[23,24]

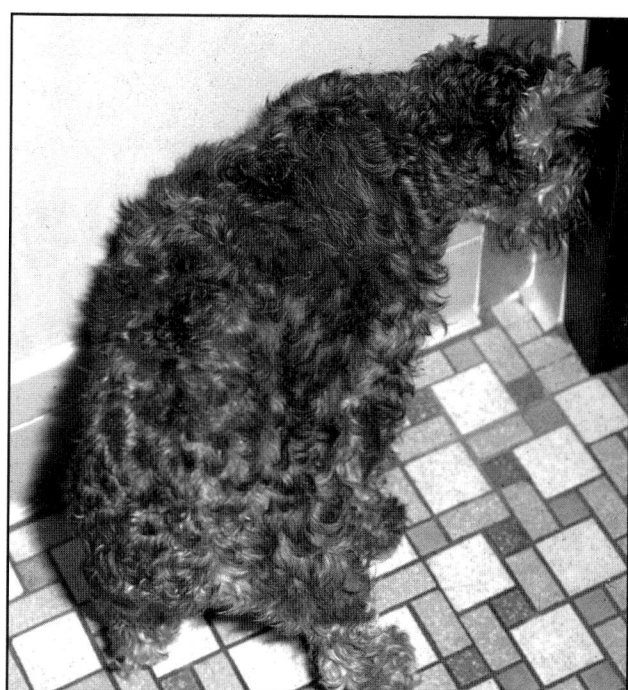

Figure 23-5. A miniature schnauzer with head pressing due to hepatic encephalopathy as a result of chronic hepatitis and cirrhosis.

The most important features evident during radiographic assessment of the liver are alterations in its size, position and shape and variation in density. The general criteria that have been used to estimate liver size are the position of the stomach axis as determined by the angle of the gas shadow with the rib margins and the position of the caudoventral tip of the liver shadow in relation to the costal arch.[23,24] However, these criteria are quite variable because of differences in thoracic conformation, respiratory phases and patient positioning. Blunting or rounding of the liver margins suggests diffuse hepatomegaly. Irregular or bumpy liver margins indicate hepatic neoplasia, regenerative nodules, hepatic cysts or other focal lesions. Detection of gas in the common bile duct, gallbladder or hepatic ducts is significant and may indicate anaerobic infection, recent surgery, gastroenteritis or paralytic ileus. Radiodense mineralized lesions may represent choleliths (gallstones) or dystrophic mineralization within hepatic parenchyma as a sequela to various hepatic diseases.

Contrast radiography can be used to evaluate the liver and portal blood flow.[25] In general, cholecystography and hepatic arteriography are limited to referral centers. Several techniques have been described for portal venography that are useful in private veterinary practices. Portograms are indicated in dogs and cats with suspected congenital or acquired portosystemic vascular shunts. Contrast radiography has been replaced, in most cases, by ultrasonography and nuclear scintigraphy.

Hepatic ultrasonography is useful for initial disease identification and then as a method for monitoring disease progression.[23,26-29] Ultrasonography can be used to detect and differentiate focal and diffuse liver disorders. Ultrasonic examination of the hepatobiliary system should include systematic evaluation of the hepatic parenchyma, portal and hepatic veins, gallbladder and biliary system. Ultrasonography is highly operator-dependent and imaging expertise takes time to develop. Readers are referred to diagnostic imaging textbooks and manuals for detailed descriptions and classifications of hepatic lesions identified by ultrasonography.[26-29]

Nuclear imaging procedures (e.g., hepatic scintigraphy) are used to assess the liver and confirm portosystemic vascular shunting. These techniques are usually only available at referral centers.

Liver Biopsy

Cytologic or histopathologic tissue examination is essential for definitive diagnosis of hepatobiliary disease.[16,30,31] Exceptions include patients with congenital por-

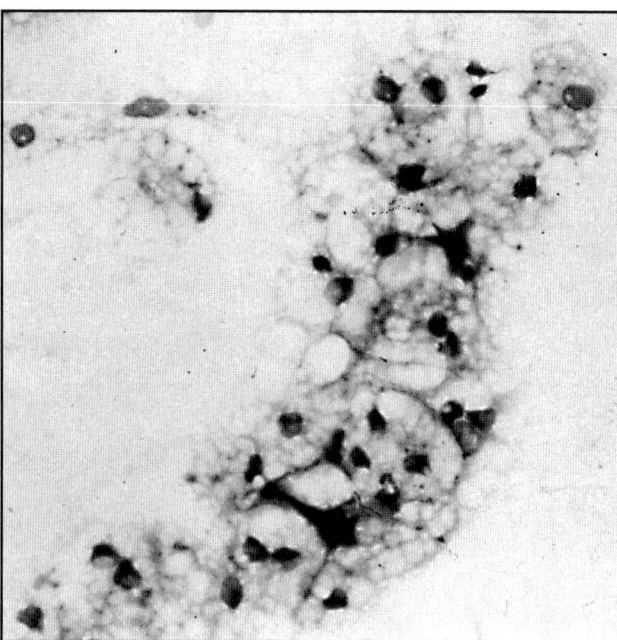

Figure 23-6. A cytologic specimen obtained by fine-needle aspiration of the liver from a cat with hepatic lipidosis. Note the lipid-laden hepatocytes. (Photograph courtesy Dr. Joseph Taboada, Louisiana State University, Baton Rouge.)

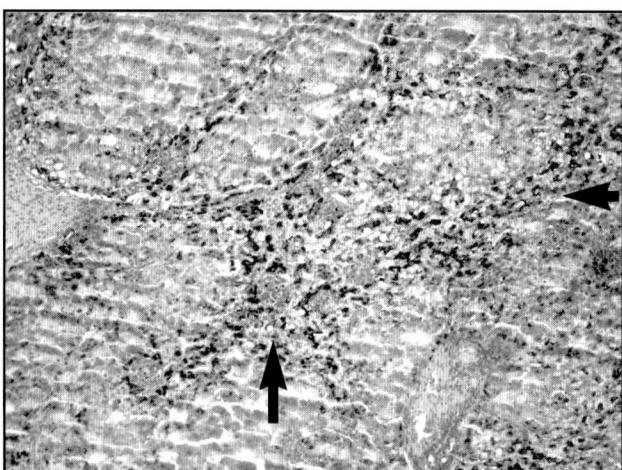

Figure 23-7. Photomicrograph of a liver biopsy specimen from a Doberman pinscher with chronic hepatitis. Note the accumulation of copper (arrows) as detected with rubeanic acid stain. In such cases, the hepatic copper content should be determined by quantitative methods.

tosystemic vascular anomalies, which are confirmed with liver function tests, ultrasonography, portography and/or nuclear scintigraphy. Liver biopsy is an invasive procedure that must be carefully considered before implementation. Common options for securing liver tissue include ultrasonographic-guided needle biopsy, laparoscopic needle or pinch biopsy and celiotomy for wedge biopsy.[16] If a needle procedure is used, a minimum of three and optimally five to seven samples should be collected. The advantage of fine-needle aspiration cytology is decreased risk (Figure 23-6). However, a representative sample may not be obtained with this technique. Liver tissue should be submitted for histopathologic and cytologic evaluation, aerobic and anaerobic bacterial cultures and copper quantification when copper toxicosis is suspected. Specific stains for collagen, lipid, copper, iron and infectious agents may be required (Figure 23-7).

Hepatic copper content can be determined using fresh or formalin-fixed liver tissue.[30,32] Most laboratories need 1 g or less of tissue for analysis. The normal copper content of canine hepatic tissue is debated.[33-36] Generally, canine hepatic copper concentrations of 400 to 1,000 µg/g dry weight (DW) or less are considered normal. Concentrations from 1,000 to 2,000 µg/g DW may be either a cause or an effect of chronic liver disease. Hepatic copper concentrations greater than 2,000 µg/g DW are often associated with copper toxicosis.

Risk Factors

Although any dog breed can be affected by chronic hepatitis and cirrhosis, certain breeds are predisposed to these disorders.[33] These include: 1) Bedlington terriers (copper-associated hepatotoxicosis), 2) West Highland white terriers, Skye terriers and Doberman pinschers (chronic hepatitis) and 3) American and European cocker spaniels, standard poodles, Labrador retrievers and Scottish terriers (idiopathic cirrhosis). German shepherd dogs are predisposed to idiopathic hepatic fibrosis. Purebred dogs are at increased risk for portosystemic vascular shunts, especially miniature schnauzers, Irish wolfhounds and Yorkshire terriers. Extrahepatic vascular shunts usually occur in cats and small-breed dogs, whereas large-breed dogs are more likely to have an intrahepatic vascular shunt. In general, inflammatory hepatopathies are more common in females, whereas congenital liver disease is more common in males.

The age at onset of clinical signs may be helpful in differentiating congenital from acquired liver disease. Dogs with congenital portosystemic vascular shunts usually develop clinical signs within the first six months of life; most dogs are less than two years old when congenital portosystemic shunts are diagnosed.[37] However, congenital vascular shunts are not diagnosed in some dogs until they are five to 10 years old.[37] Cats are generally older than dogs when diagnosed with shunts.[37] Acquired portosystemic vascular shunts secondary to liver disease and portal hypertension occur in animals of any age.

Obese cats and those with prolonged anorexia (from any cause) are at increased risk for hepatic lipidosis. Unvaccinated animals are at risk for infectious viral hepatitis. Exposure to wildlife, livestock and asymptomatic carriers is a risk factor for leptospirosis. Bacterial hepatitis is associated with omphalitis (neonates), septicemia, peritonitis, pancreatitis, trauma and immunosuppressive disorders (secondary to diabetes mellitus, hyperadrenocorticism, etc.). Pancreatitis, extrahepatic bile duct obstruction and inflammatory bowel disease are risk factors for cholangiohepatitis in cats.[38]

The liver is a target for a wide array of chemicals and biologic substances because of its metabolic and detoxifying functions. Animals less than 16 weeks old may have immature hepatic enzyme function for metabolism and excretion of potentially hepatotoxic drugs.[39] Table 23-4 lists drugs, chemicals and biologic substances that are clinically important causes of liver disease in dogs and cats.

Etiopathogenesis

Metabolic Alterations in Hepatocellular Dysfunction

Hepatocellular dysfunction is responsible for a number of metabolic disturbances that alter usage of various nutrients by the body (Table 23-5). Changes in protein, carbohydrate and fat metabolism are particularly prominent in the fasting state.[5,40-44] Attempts to correct these alterations by manipulating nutrient supply represent an important strategy in the management of patients with significant hepatic disease.

Impaired hepatic metabolism and storage may result in vitamin and mineral deficiencies. A combination of these metabolic and storage problems usually exists in patients with hepatic disease, and each problem should be considered before appropriate dietary therapy is begun.

CARBOHYDRATE ALTERATIONS

The liver plays a key role in the usage of the major monosaccharides glucose, fructose and galactose.[44] Glucose can be used for energy production or to synthesize other substrates (e.g., amino acids, fatty acids), or it can be stored as glycogen. Liver glycogen can be readily mobilized when glucose is in demand. Hepatic glycogen can normally meet glucose needs (primarily for the brain) for 24 to 36 hours.[17]

In human patients with hepatic cirrhosis, glycogen stores are more rapidly depleted (in 10 to 12 hours), which results in premature protein catabolism to supply amino acids for gluconeogenesis.[45] Gluconeogenesis, the production of glucose from amino acids, glycerol or lactate, is carried out only in the liver and the renal cortex. Glycolysis is the only pathway by which glucose can be oxidized anaerobically

Table 23-4. Clinically relevant hepatotoxins for dogs and cats.

Drugs
Acetaminophen
Amoxicillin/clavulanic acid
Carprofen
Ciprofloxacin
Diazepam
Diethylcarbamazine
Diethylcarbamazine-oxibendazole
Glucocorticoids
Griseofulvin
Halothane
Isoniazid
Ketoconazole
Mebendazole
Megestrol acetate
Methimazole
Methotrexate
Methoxyflurane
Methyltestosterone
Oxibendazole
Phenobarbital
Phenylbutazone
Phenytoin
Primidone
Sulfasalazine
Tetracycline
Thiacetarsamide
Trimethoprim-sulfa

Chemicals and biologic substances
Aflatoxin
Blue-green algae
Cycad seeds
Gossypol
Heavy metals
Pennyroyal oil
Phenols

Table 23-5. Metabolic alterations in hepatic failure.*

Alterations	Mechanisms
Hyperglucagonemia	Portosystemic shunting
	Impaired hepatic degradation
	Increased plasma aromatic amino acid levels
	Hyperammonemia
Hyperinsulinemia	Increased peripheral insulin resistance
	Decreased insulin to glucagon ratio
	Impaired hepatic degradation
Increased plasma epinephrine and cortisol levels	Impaired hepatic degradation
Decreased liver and muscle carbohydrate stores	Accelerated glycogenolysis
	Impaired glycogenesis
Increased gluconeogenesis	Hyperglucagonemia
Hyperglycemia (fasting and postprandial)	Portosystemic shunting
	Increased gluconeogenesis
	Decreased insulin-dependent glucose uptake
	Decreased insulin-hepatic glycolysis
Increased plasma aromatic amino acid levels	Decreased hepatic clearance and incorporation into proteins
	Increased release into the circulation
Decreased plasma branched-chain amino acid levels	Hyperinsulinemia and excessive uptake
	Increased usage as an energy source
Increased plasma methionine, glutamine, asparagine and histidine levels	Decreased hepatic clearance

*Adapted from Marks SL, Rogers QR, Strombeck DR. Nutritional support in hepatic disease. Part I. Metabolic alterations and nutritional considerations in dogs and cats. Compendium on Continuing Education for the Practicing Veterinarian 1994; 16: 972.

LIVER DISEASE

Ammonia Metabolism and the Urea Cycle

Excretion of excess ammonia is necessary for life; therefore, animals have developed different approaches to this problem. Mammals use the urea cycle as an ammonia disposal mechanism.

UREA SYNTHESIS

Urea is synthesized in the liver via the urea cycle (Figure 1). The initial step in urea production is synthesis of carbamoyl phosphate from bicarbonate and ammonia. Carbamoyl phosphate synthetase I catalyzes carbamoyl phosphate formation in mitochondria. This reaction requires free Mg^{++} and magnesium adenine triphosphate, the rate-limiting enzyme of the urea cycle.

Next, citrulline is formed from carbamoyl phosphate and ornithine. Ornithine transcarbamoylase, another mitochondrial enzyme, catalyzes this reaction. This step is followed by the cytosolic portion of the urea cycle, beginning with a reaction catalyzed by argininosuccinate synthetase that combines citrulline with aspartate, a second nitrogen donor, to form argininosuccinate. Argininosuccinate is cleaved to arginine and fumarate via the action of argininosuccinate lyase. Finally arginine is cleaved by arginase to form urea and ornithine. Urea is released into the circulation and ornithine reenters the urea cycle.

THE UREA CYCLE IN NONCARNIVOROUS ANIMALS

In noncarnivorous mammals (i.e., herbivores and omnivores), the urea cycle is controlled by the activities of constituent enzymes, which in turn are controlled by the substrates they act upon. Additionally, during periods of normal protein intake, most enzymes involved in urea synthesis in noncarnivorous animals operate only at 20 to 50% capacity, allowing for adaptation to high- or low-protein foods. These mechanisms conserve nitrogen during periods of food deprivation, but slow the response time for ammonia detoxification after ingestion of a high-protein meal.

The amino acid intermediates used in the urea cycle (i.e., ornithine, citrulline and arginine) are formed within the cycle itself and are provided by dietary sources of amino acids. In noncarnivorous mammals, amino acids for the urea cycle can be synthesized via alternative pathways; for example, rats can synthesize ornithine via proline or glutamate, a process that doesn't occur in obligate carnivores. Therefore, noncarnivorous animals can better adapt to foods containing protein of lower quality that may not contain all of the amino acids required for urea cycle function or foods that vary in protein content over time.

THE UREA CYCLE IN CARNIVOROUS ANIMALS

In contrast to noncarnivorous animals, carnivores (e.g., cats and ferrets) have not developed adaptive mechanisms to conserve nitrogen during periods of low protein intake. Only minimal changes in enzymatic activity are seen in cats fed either high- or low-protein foods. Thus, urea cycle enzymes act continuously, independent of dietary protein intake. Because enzymatic activity is constant, carnivores control the urea cycle via concentrations of urea cycle intermediates, which allows for rapid detoxification of ammonia.

Carnivores are also unable to synthesize ornithine from proline and glutamate. Therefore, ornithine for the urea cycle must be synthesized exclusively from arginine. Although a small amount of arginine can be synthesized from citrulline in the kidney, the high activity of hepatic arginase dictates that arginine for the urea cycle be supplied primarily from food. To illustrate this point, adult cats and ferrets develop hyperammonemia and hepatic encephalopathy when fed foods devoid of arginine.

GLUTAMINE SYNTHESIS

Glutamine synthesis is the second primary mechanism by which mammals can metabolize excess ammonia. Hepatic

Continued on next page.

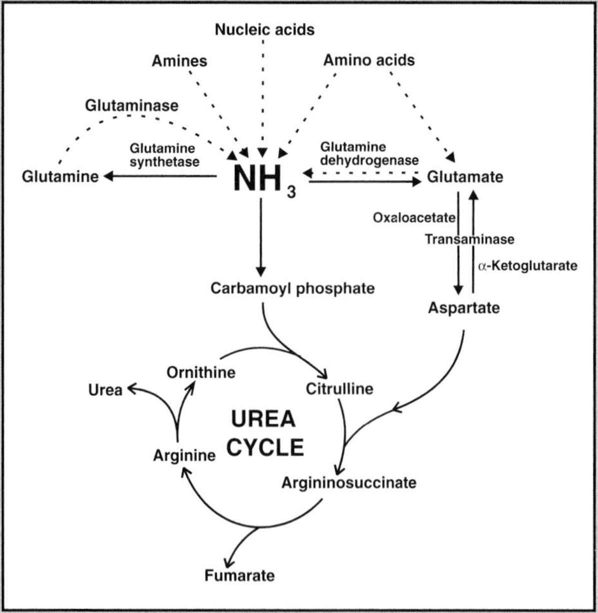

Figure 1. General scheme of hepatic ammonia metabolism, illustrating the pathways of ammonia usage (solid arrows) and ammonia formation (broken arrows). (Adapted from Ampola MG. The urea cycle: Enzymes and defects. In: Arias IM, Boyer JL, Fausto N, et al, eds. The Liver: Biology and Pathobiology, 3rd ed. New York, NY: Raven Press, 1994; 366.)

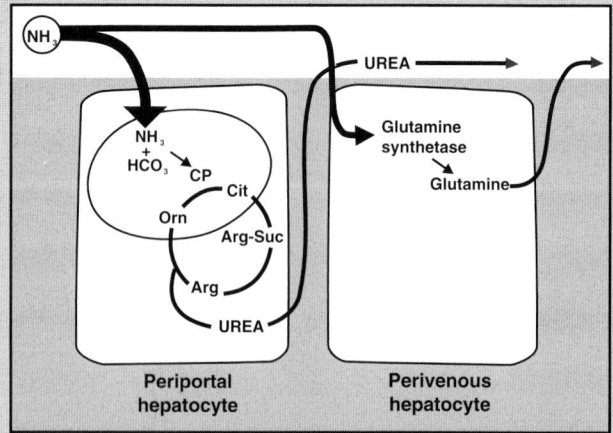

Figure 2. The scavenger role of perivenous hepatocytes. Most ammonia is metabolized to urea in the periportal hepatocytes. Ammonia not metabolized to urea is metabolized to glutamine by the perivenous hepatocytes (catalyzed by glutamine synthetase). This prevents ammonia from entering the systemic circulation and allows for uncoupling of urea production, which may be useful in acid-base regulation. Key: CP = carbamoyl phosphate, Cit = citrulline, Arg-Suc = argininosuccinate, Arg = arginine, Orn = ornithine. (Adapted from Dimski DS. Ammonia metabolism and the urea cycle: Function and clinical implications. Journal of Veterinary Internal Medicine 1994; 8: 75.)

glutamine synthetase is compartmentalized in a small area surrounding the centrilobular vein; thus, perivenous cells serve as "scavengers" for any ammonia that has not been converted to urea by the periportal hepatocytes (Figure 2). Approximately one-third of the total ammonia from portal blood is detoxified by glutamine synthesis, although this percentage varies depending on the acid-base status.

The glutamine synthetase pathway is a high-affinity system, ensuring that ammonia does not reach the systemic circulation in toxic concentrations. In contrast, urea production is a low-affinity, high-capacity system for detoxifying ammonia. Thus, glutamine synthesis acts as a back-up system for ammonia detoxification, allowing urea production to be decreased as required for acid-base regulation, while preventing hyperammonemia.

BIBLIOGRAPHY
Dimski DS. Ammonia metabolism and the urea cycle: Function and clinical implications. Journal of Veterinary Internal Medicine 1994; 8: 73-78.

with production of ATP. Regulation of glycolysis in the liver is highly integrated with that of gluconeogenesis, lipogenesis, glycogen synthesis and glycogenolysis. (See Chapter 2.)

Fasting hypoglycemia is uncommon in patients with liver disease because euglycemia can be maintained with as little as one-fourth to one-third of normal liver parenchymal mass.[46] However, hepatogenic hypoglycemia can occur in dogs with cirrhosis, congenital portosystemic vascular anomalies, fulminant hepatic failure, septicemia and extensive hepatic neoplasia.[17]

Glucose intolerance is more common than hypoglycemia in people with severe hepatic dysfunction. As many as 80% of human cirrhotic patients have this abnormality.[46] The importance and causes of glucose intolerance in dogs and cats with liver disease are poorly documented. Hyperglycemia has been observed in some dogs with cirrhosis and portosystemic vascular shunts and in some cats with hepatic lipidosis and cholangitis or cholangiohepatitis.[17] Hyperglucagonemia has been suggested to occur in dogs with cirrhosis that develop an uncommon necrotizing skin disorder (i.e., superficial necrolytic dermatitis, hepatocutaneous syndrome). This disorder is characterized by skin erosions and ulcerations with alopecia, exudation and thick adherent crusts on the footpads and around mucocutaneous junctions.[47] Affected dogs also have depressed plasma amino acid concentrations.

PROTEIN AND AMINO ACID ALTERATIONS

The liver synthesizes the majority of circulating plasma proteins. The most abundant is albumin, which represents 55 to 60% of the total plasma protein pool.[17] Albumin serves as a binding and carrier protein for hormones, amino acids, steroids, vitamins, calcium and fatty acids, as well as exogenous compounds, drugs, toxins, etc. Albumin also helps maintain normal plasma oncotic pressure. The other proteins synthesized and secreted by the liver are usually glycosylated proteins (i.e., glycoproteins) that function in hemostasis, protease inhibition, transport and ligand binding. Hypoalbuminemia, edema, ascites and increased bruising/bleeding tendencies result from decreased plasma protein production due to liver disease.[17]

Protein regulatory events in the liver include amino acid storage and deamination of amino acids for intermediary metabolism. Generally, the essential amino acids (including the aromatic amino acids [AAA], but not the branched-chain amino acids [BCAA]) and some of the nonessential amino acids are degraded in the liver.[17,48] In dogs and other omnivores, the activities of key degradative enzymes are typically down-regulated when minimal dietary protein is eaten to ensure amino acid availability for protein synthesis. Then, the activities of these key metabolic enzymes rapidly increase when excess dietary protein is ingested. This down-regulation does not occur in carnivores such as cats. (See Chapter 11.) Amino acids not required for protein synthesis are deaminated and oxidized or will be converted to carbohydrate and lipid. In this way, the liver plays an important role in energy balance and regulation of plasma concentrations of important amino acids. (See Chapter 2.)

The deamination of amino acids is linked to carbohydrate and lipid metabolism via a number of common intermediates. These intermediates (e.g., pyruvate, fumarate, succinyl-CoA, oxaloacetate and acetyl-CoA) are entry points for amino acid carbon skeletons into the tricarboxylic acid (TCA or Krebs) cycle after deamination. (See Chapter 2.) Intermediates are used primarily for energy production, gluconeogenesis and storage of excess dietary energy as triacylglycerides.

Alterations in nitrogen metabolism are one of the most prominent biochemical changes in chronic liver failure. Hyperammonemia is a common finding and probably results from a combination of factors including: 1) active amino acid deamination and gluconeogenesis, 2) bacterial degradation of protein in the gut, 3) impaired or inadequate ureagenesis and 4) inadequate delivery of ammonia to the liver because of portosystemic vascular shunting.[17,49] (See sidebar "Ammonia Metabolism and the Urea Cycle.")

Plasma amino acid concentrations may be altered in patients with liver disease.[17,50-54] Plasma amino acid concentrations differ depending on the type of hepatic failure present. In health, the AAA (i.e., tyrosine, phenylalanine and tryptophan) are efficiently extracted from the portal circulation and metabolized by the liver. Reduced liver function is associated with an increase in circulating levels of AAA because of continued mobilization of amino acids for gluconeogenesis and impaired hepatic AAA metabolism.[17,50] The plasma concentrations of BCAA (i.e., leucine, isoleucine and valine) and most other amino acids metabolized in peripheral tissues are reduced because of an increased rate of usage by muscle and adipose tissue.[17,50] The molar ratio between BCAA and the AAA (i.e., BCAA:AAA) in healthy dogs usually ranges between 3.0 to 4.0. This ratio is often reduced to 1.0 or less in dogs with portosystemic vascular anomalies and chronic hepatitis.[17,51-53] Conversely, massive acute hepatic necrosis in dogs has been found to cause an increase in the plasma con-

LIVER DISEASE

centrations of all amino acids except arginine.[50] Increased circulating catecholamine, insulin and glucagon concentrations are thought to contribute to the altered amino acid metabolism seen in patients with liver disease.[17,51]

Alterations in plasma amino acid profiles may also play a role in the pathogenesis of hepatic encephalopathy.[55,56] The characteristic amino acid profile described above formed the basis for the initial development of BCAA-enriched solutions used for nutritional support of human patients with chronic hepatic disease and hepatic encephalopathy.

LIPID ALTERATIONS

Lipid metabolic processes in the liver include: 1) fatty acid and triacylglyceride synthesis, 2) phospholipid and cholesterol synthesis, 3) lipoprotein metabolism and 4) bile salt synthesis. Fatty acids are synthesized in the liver from carbohydrate precursors by conversion of these precursors to acetyl-CoA. Fatty acids are generally stored in the liver as triacylglycerides. After hepatic glycogen

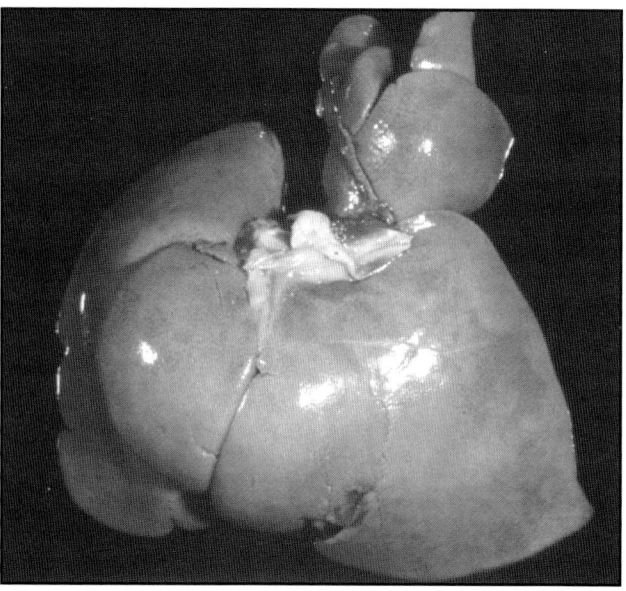

Figure 23-8. An enlarged, pale yellow liver from a cat with hepatic lipidosis.

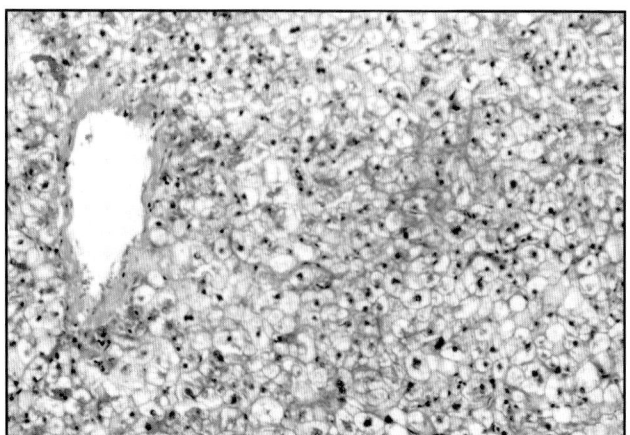

Figure 23-9. Photomicrograph of a liver specimen from a cat with hepatic lipidosis. Hepatocytes containing lipid appear empty with an inconspicuous nucleus when processed routinely with formalin fixation and hematoxylin and eosin stain.

stores are depleted, fatty acids are mobilized from adipose tissue and their rate of hepatic oxidation increases. The ketone bodies produced are an important energy source for peripheral tissues (i.e., brain, skeletal muscle) and serve to decrease the rate of glucose usage.

The liver is a site for β-oxidation of fatty acids, producing energy from fatty acid substrates. (See Chapter 2.) Carnitine functions to transport long-chain fatty acids across the inner mitochondrial membrane into the mitochondrial matrix for β-oxidation. The liver is also a major site of cholesterol synthesis from acetyl-CoA. Cholesterol is found throughout the body as a structural component of cell membranes, a substrate for synthesis of steroid hormones and is important in the liver as the precursor for bile acid synthesis. The liver secretes lipoprotein particles and is an essential organ for their uptake and metabolism.

The composition of plasma lipids and lipoproteins is altered in patients with liver disease. These abnormalities are associated with changes in lipoprotein and cholesterol synthesis, lecithin-cholesterol acyltransferase deficiency, defective lipolysis, abnormal recognition and uptake of lipoproteins by the liver and regurgitation of biliary lipids into plasma.[17] Obstructive jaundice may lead to hypercholesterolemia and hypertriglyceridemia.[17] Hypocholesterolemia has been recognized in animals with portosystemic vascular anomalies and acquired hepatic insufficiency.[17] Hypotriglyceridemia has been recognized in dogs with portosystemic shunts and hepatic necrosis.[17] Little is known about changes in lipoprotein fractions in dogs and cats with liver disease.

VITAMIN AND MINERAL ALTERATIONS

The liver serves as a storage reservoir for certain vitamins and minerals. Vitamin A can be stored in quantities sufficient for several months. The other fat-soluble vitamins (D, E and K) and vitamin B_{12} are also stored in the liver. The rest of the B vitamins are found in high concentration in hepatic tissue, but the liver is not generally considered a storage reservoir. Iron from dietary sources and from erythrocyte degradation is sequestered in hepatic tissue. Copper, manganese, selenium and zinc are trace elements normally present in high concentrations in the liver. (See Chapter 2.)

Changes may occur in the patterns of storage and availability of all of these micronutrients in patients with significant liver disease. Malabsorption and alterations in hepatic blood flow may decrease availability and liver concentrations of certain vitamins and minerals. An adequate supply of B-complex vitamins is essential for the liver to perform a myriad of metabolic activities.

Common Hepatobiliary Diseases

FELINE HEPATIC LIPIDOSIS

Feline hepatic lipidosis is a well-recognized syndrome characterized by accumulation of excess triacylglycerides in hepatocytes with resulting cholestasis and hepatic dysfunction (Figures 23-8 and 23-9).[57-61] Many cats with idiopathic hepatic lipidosis are obese and often present with a history of prolonged anorexia after a stressful event. The biochemical mechanisms responsible for inducing hepatic lipidosis during fasting are not completely understood.[57,62,63] Potential causes include protein deficiency, excessive peripheral lipolysis, excessive lipogenesis, inhibition of lipid oxidation and inhibition of the synthesis and secretion of very low-densi-

Hepatic Encephalopathy

The term hepatic encephalopathy refers to the complex neurologic and behavior disturbances that may occur in people and animals with either congenital portocaval vascular shunts or advanced acquired liver disease. A number of conditions can trigger hepatic encephalopathy in animals with compensated liver disease, including azotemia, constipation, use of sedatives and anesthetics, gastrointestinal bleeding, hypokalemia, alkalosis and high-protein meals.

Despite extensive investigation, the pathogenesis of hepatic encephalopathy has yet to be elucidated. Hepatic encephalopathy is probably multifactorial in origin. Four theories currently exist for the pathogenesis of this disorder. They include: 1) ammonia as the putative neurotoxin, with or without synergistic toxins, 2) alteration in monoamine neurotransmitters as a result of perturbed aromatic amino acid metabolism, 3) alteration in amino acid neurotransmitters, γ-aminobutyric acid (GABA) and/or glutamate and 4) increased cerebral concentrations of an endogenous benzodiazepine-like substance. Other theories no longer believed tenable include lack of a brain protective factor, depletion of cerebral energy, false neurotransmitters and alterations in the blood-brain barrier. Interested readers are referred to review articles that describe these potential pathophysiologic mechanisms in more detail. (See Bibliography.)

Ammonia has been implicated in the pathogenesis of hepatic encephalopathy since the late nineteenth century. However, the importance of the role of ammonia in the disorder is debated. On balance, ammonia appears to play a role in hepatic encephalopathy, but its precise effect on cerebral function and importance in the pathogenesis remain undetermined. A number of other toxins may act synergistically to cause cerebral dysfunction in patients with hepatic encephalopathy including mercaptans (e.g., methanethiol), short-chain fatty acids, phenols, bile salts and other molecules.

Hyperammonemia and decreased serum urea nitrogen concentrations may also reflect decreased urea cycle function due to decreased hepatic perfusion. Fasting hyperammonemia was present in 88% and low serum urea nitrogen concentration was present in 39% of dogs with congenital portosystemic vascular shunts indicating disruption of normal urea cycle function. Fasting hyperammonemia was found in 9 of 9 cats with congenital portosystemic vascular shunts. Correction of impaired hepatic blood flow may improve urea cycle function. Most dogs and cats will have normal or markedly improved plasma ammonia concentrations subsequent to surgical ligation of a congenital shunt.

Profound alterations in the plasma concentrations of many amino acids have been reported to occur in people and dogs with hepatic encephalopathy. However, the precise relationship of altered amino acid metabolism to the mechanism of cerebral dysfunction in patients with hepatic encephalopathy remains undetermined. Plasma amino acid abnormalities also occur in people and dogs with chronic liver disease that do not have encephalopathic clinical signs.

Methionine may precipitate encephalopathic signs when fed or supplemented in high amounts to patients with portosystemic shunts. Levels of methionine found typically in commercial or homemade foods should not be harmful although excess supplementation (e.g., giving DL-methionine as a urinary acidifier) should be avoided.

Cats develop hepatic encephalopathy if fed foods deficient in arginine. Cats affected with hepatic lipidosis have low serum arginine concentrations. Because animal-origin protein is generally rich in arginine, most commercial cat foods and foods for stress and recovery are well fortified with this amino acid. Homemade vegetable-based foods and human enteral foods used in cats with encephalopathic clinical signs should be supplemented with arginine. Arginine levels in food should always be above the minimum dietary allowance for adult maintenance (>0.5% dry matter [DM] in dogs, >1.0% DM in cats). A dietary arginine level of 1.2 to 2.0% DM in dogs and 1.5 to 2.0% DM in cats seems appropriate for most patients with liver disease.

Although the precise neurochemical basis of hepatic encephalopathy has still not been elucidated, its development is a severe complication of hepatobiliary disease and should be managed aggressively and appropriately. The encephalopathy is often fully reversible with amelioration of the underlying liver disease.

BIBLIOGRAPHY

Blaxter AC, Holt PE, Pearson GR, et al. Congenital portosystemic shunts in the cat: A report of nine cases. Journal of Small Animal Practice 1988; 29: 631-645.

Johnson CA, Armstrong PJ, Hauptman JG. Congenital portosystemic shunts in dogs: 46 cases (1979-1986). Journal of the American Veterinary Medical Association 1987; 191: 1478-1483.

Maddison JE. Hepatic encephalopathy: Current concepts of the pathogenesis. Journal of Veterinary Internal Medicine 1992; 6: 341-353.

Riordan SM, Williams R. Treatment of hepatic encephalopathy. New England Journal of Medicine 1997; 337: 473-479.

Taboada J, Dimski DS. Hepatic encephalopathy: Clinical signs, pathogenesis and treatment. Veterinary Clinics of North America: Small Animal Practice 1995; 25: 337-355.

ty lipoproteins. The prognosis for this life-threatening disorder has improved dramatically during the past several years as a result of long-term enteral feeding (i.e., three to eight weeks or longer).[57,61,64] Resolution of hepatic lipidosis associated with pancreatitis, infection and the use of drugs depends on the success of treating the underlying disorder.[60]

COPPER-ASSOCIATED HEPATOTOXICOSIS IN DOGS

Bedlington terriers often develop copper storage disease and a subsequent hepatopathy. The disease is somewhat similar to Wilson's disease in people.[65] It is caused by an inherited autosomal recessive trait that results in impaired biliary excretion of copper.[66,67] The frequency of the copper toxicosis gene in the Bedlington terrier breed has been estimated in England and the United States.[68] These estimates suggest that about 25% of Bedlington terriers are affected and another 50% are carriers.

Homozygous recessive individuals invariably accumulate hepatotoxic levels of copper by two to four years of age.[65,69,70] Without treatment, affected dogs develop liver disease and die, usually between three to seven years of age.[65,69,70] It has become possible to distinguish affected, homozygous normal and carrier dogs in some Bedlington terrier pedigrees using DNA markers.[68]

Hepatic mitochondria are important intracellular targets of hepatic copper toxicosis. Functional abnormalities of mitochondria associated with oxidative injury (i.e., lipid peroxidation) have been documented to occur in people, rats and Bedlington terriers with copper-induced

LIVER DISEASE

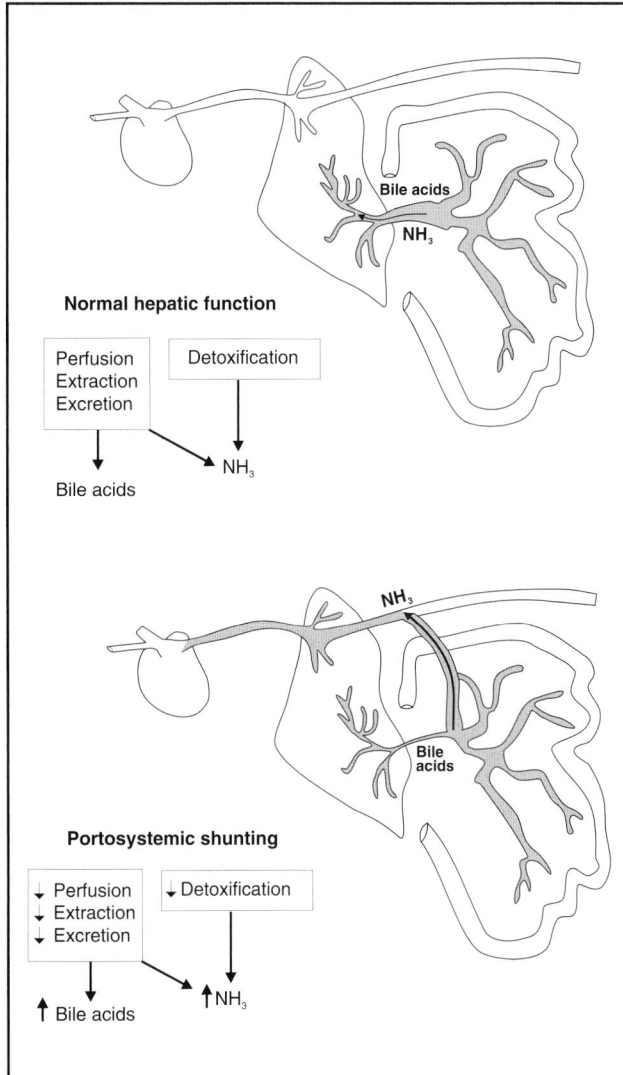

Figure 23-10. The effect of portosystemic shunting on hepatic extraction of bile acids and ammonia. (Adapted from Center SA. Hepatic vascular diseases. In: Guilford WG, Center SA, Strombeck DR, et al, eds. Strombeck's Small Animal Gastroenterology, 3rd ed. Philadelphia, PA: WB Saunders Co, 1996; 805, 813.)

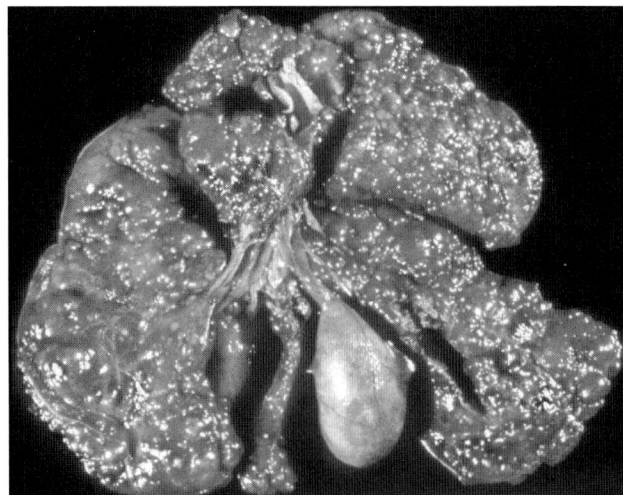

Figure 23-11. Cirrhotic liver from an eight-year-old female Doberman pinscher with chronic hepatitis. (Photograph courtesy Dr. Susan Johnson, The Ohio State University, Columbus.)

hepatic injury.[71,72] Oxidative injury and abnormal hepatic mitochondrial respiration may be involved in the pathogenesis of copper toxicosis. This theory forms the basis for using vitamin E and other antioxidants as potential therapeutic agents.

Multifocal centrilobular hepatitis first appears in Bedlington terriers when hepatic copper concentrations exceed approximately 2,000 ppm (μg/g) DW.[69,70] Copper levels greater than 3,000 ppm DW result in widespread hepatic necrosis in some dogs. Postnecrotic cirrhosis develops if the dog survives the episode of massive necrosis.

The role of copper in hepatic diseases observed in other dog breeds is less clear. This includes chronic hepatitis and cirrhosis seen in breeds such as West Highland white terriers, Skye terriers, Kerry blue terriers, cocker spaniels, Doberman pinschers and others.[73] Some investigators and clinicians theorize that elevated hepatic copper concentrations precede the liver disease,[32,36,74,75] whereas others contend that the excess hepatic copper resulted from faulty copper excretion caused by chronic cholestasis.[62,76,77] A third group theorizes that elevated hepatic copper levels are antecedent to the disease and are incidental to disease progression.[34,35,78] The liver diseases in these dogs are distinct from copper toxicosis in Bedlington terriers in that hepatic copper concentrations are generally lower and do not increase with age. Further studies are needed to document the specific cause of elevated hepatic copper concentrations in non-Bedlington terrier dogs and the role, if any, of copper in the initiation and progression of hepatic injury in these breeds.

PORTOSYSTEMIC VASCULAR SHUNTS

Portosystemic shunts are vascular communications between the portal and systemic venous systems.[37] The communication usually occurs between the portal vein and caudal vena cava and allows access of portal blood to the systemic circulation without first passing through the liver (Figure 23-10). Congenital portosystemic vascular shunts are most common. They represent anomalous embryonal vessels that occur as single intrahepatic or extrahepatic shunts.[25,29,37] Acquired portosystemic vascular shunts form in response to portal hypertension caused by fibrosis and chronic cirrhosis. Multiple extrahepatic shunts are typically seen.

Clinical signs of hepatic encephalopathy usually predominate as a result of inadequate hepatic clearance of enterically derived toxins and altered liver function. (See sidebar "Hepatic Encephalopathy.") Ammonium urate and other purine uroliths also occur in some animals because of high urinary excretion of ammonia and uric acid. (See Chapter 20.) Stunted growth or failure to gain weight may occur in young animals with congenital shunts.

CHRONIC HEPATITIS AND CIRRHOSIS IN DOGS

Chronic hepatitis (sometimes termed chronic active hepatitis) in dogs is a poorly defined group of clinicopathologic entities characterized by parenchymal necrosis, particularly piecemeal and/or bridging necrosis, with associated lymphoplasmacytic inflammation.[30,78,79] Chronic hepatitis is a syndrome in dogs with many causes; it is not a specific disease entity. The presence of lymphoplasmacytic inflammation suggests an immune-mediated mechanism and autoantibodies have been recognized in dogs with chronic hepatitis.[80,81] However, the target cell or struc-

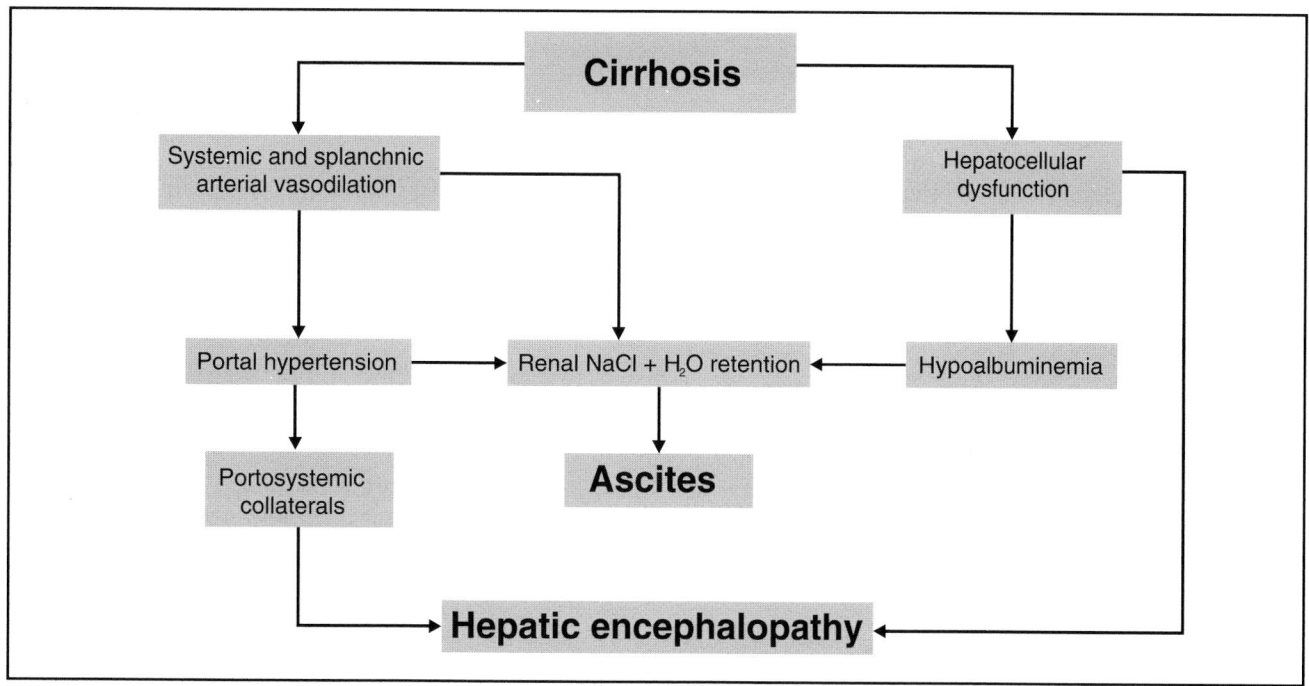

Figure 23-12. Interrelationships between the complications of cirrhosis. (Adapted from Abrams GA, Fallon MB. Cirrhosis of the liver and its complications. In: Andreoli TTE, Bennett JC, Carpenter CCJ, et al, eds. Cecil Essentials of Medicine, 4th ed. Philadelphia, PA: WB Saunders Co, 1997; 341.)

ture of the immune reaction has not been identified.[78] The insidious onset contributes to the poor understanding of the pathogenesis and the advanced stage of the disease when it is recognized in most patients.

Hepatic fibrosis is an accumulation of extracellular collagen and connective tissue within the liver.[62] Fibrosis develops as a sequela to a single episode of massive hepatic necrosis or chronic hepatic parenchymal damage and inflammation. Hepatic cirrhosis is fibrosis with regenerative nodules (Figure 23-11).[30] Fibrosis and regenerative nodules impair hepatic blood and bile flow, thus perpetuating hepatocellular injury.

Steatorrhea occurs in approximately 40% of human patients with hepatic cirrhosis and is related to decreased delivery of bile salts into the intestinal lumen, impaired intestinal capacity for absorption of long-chain fatty acids,[82] interference with lipid absorption resulting from antibiotic therapy (e.g., neomycin), and in some cases, concurrent exocrine pancreatic insufficiency.[83] Steatorrhea may occur in dogs with chronic hepatitis and cirrhosis, but appears to be uncommon.

CHOLANGITIS/CHOLANGIOHEPATITIS IN CATS

Cholangitis (i.e., inflammation of the biliary ducts, especially the intrahepatic ducts) and cholangiohepatitis (i.e., inflammation of the biliary ducts and liver) are common feline liver diseases.[19,38,84] Three histopathologic types are generally recognized: 1) suppurative, 2) lymphocytic and 3) lymphoplasmacytic. Bacterial infection (*Escherichia coli* and anaerobes are most common) occurs in many cases with suppurative inflammation, whereas immunologic mechanisms are probably involved in the lymphocytic and lymphoplasmacytic types. The suppurative form may precede the other two forms. The endpoint of these clinical entities is often cirrhosis.

Many cats with these conditions also have sludged or inspissated bile, which causes partial or complete biliary obstruction.[38,84] Concurrent cholecystitis, pancreatitis, extrahepatic bile duct obstruction and inflammatory bowel disease are common in affected cats.[38,84]

PORTAL HYPERTENSION

Portal hypertension (i.e., a persistent increase in portal venous pressure) can be considered a "homeostatic" response to chronic fibrosis, cirrhosis and altered hepatic lobular architecture.[85] Portal venous blood flow is gradually increased to maintain normal perfusion in hepatic lobules in which vascular resistance is increased due to fibrosis. Eventually, portal venous pressure may exceed systemic venous pressure and portosystemic shunts may develop. Shunting nutritionally depletes the liver and substrates are not delivered to the liver for degradation and metabolism; hepatic encephalopathy may result.

Increased vascular resistance within the liver also impairs lymphatic flow and results in ascites (Figure 23-12).[17,85] Peritoneal fluid accumulation decreases intravascular volume and systemic venous pressure, further aggravating portal hypertension. Retention of sodium, chloride and water occurs because of pathophysiologic mechanisms similar to those in patients with congestive heart failure.[86] (See Chapter 18.)

BILE DUCT OBSTRUCTION

Extrahepatic bile duct obstruction is associated with a number of conditions (Table 23-6). Cholestasis associated with occlusion of the major bile ducts leads to serious hepatobiliary injury within a few weeks.[87] Obstructed bile flow and the resulting stagnation of bile acids and other compounds injures cell membranes and organelles. Bacterial cholecystitis may develop due to biliary reflux of intestinal bacteria or lymphohematogenous dissemination. Biliary

Table 23-6. Causes of extrahepatic bile duct obstruction.*

Cholelithiasis
Cholecystitis (choledochitis)
Neoplasia
    Bile duct adenocarcinoma
    Pancreatic adenocarcinoma
    Lymphosarcoma
    Local tumor invasion
Malformation (polycystic liver disease)
Parasitic (trematode infection)
Extrinsic compression
    Lymph nodes
    Pancreatic mass
    Entrapment in diaphragmatic hernia
Fibrosis or stricture
    Blunt trauma
    Peritonitis
    Pancreatitis
    Iatrogenic (postsurgical)

*Adapted from Center SA. Diseases of the gallbladder and biliary tree. In: Guilford WG, Center SA, Strombeck DR, et al, eds. Strombeck's Small Animal Gastroenterology, 3rd ed. Philadelphia, PA: WB Saunders Co, 1996; 870.

injury is associated with cytokine-mediated inflammation and free radical injury. Long-term changes include biliary epithelial hyperplasia, cholangitis, multifocal parenchymal necrosis, fibrosis and cirrhosis.[87] Coagulopathies associated with vitamin K deficiency may develop within three weeks.

Key Nutritional Factors

The specific nutrient requirements of pets with various naturally occurring hepatobiliary diseases are poorly understood or documented. Most nutritional recommendations for these patients are based on understanding normal hepatic function, studies in animals with experimentally induced disease, results in human patients with comparable diseases and clinical experience. The wide range of hepatobiliary diseases and differing severity also mean that one nutrient profile will not be adequate for all patients.

Despite these challenges, general recommendations for key nutritional factors can be made that will benefit most patients with hepatobiliary disorders. The following section will discuss these key factors in more detail and outline specific recommendations for the most common hepatobiliary disorders.

Feline Hepatic Lipidosis

ENERGY

Provision of adequate daily energy intake is the cornerstone of successful medical management of cats with hepatic lipidosis.[57,62,64,88,89] An adequate supply of energy is needed to: 1) prevent catabolism of amino acids for energy, 2) inhibit peripheral lipolysis and 3) avoid excess energy consumption, which will promote hepatic triacylglyceride accumulation. Cats with hepatic lipidosis are often fed commercial veterinary therapeutic products via assisted-feeding techniques. (See Chapter 12 and Appendix V.) Foods containing 25 to 40% dry matter (DM) fat and energy densities equal to or in excess of 4.4 kcal/g (18.4 kJ/g) DM are well tolerated by most cats and result in clinical improvement when fed in appropriate amounts. The daily energy requirement (DER) for cats with hepatic lipidosis should be at least the resting energy requirement (RER)

for ideal body weight when cats are managed in the hospital and 1.1 to 1.2 x RER when managed at home.

PROTEIN

Protein and its constituent amino acids are important in cats with hepatic lipidosis. Cats are less efficient in sparing protein during fasting than other animals. As such, protein deficiency is thought to play a major role in the development of feline idiopathic hepatic lipidosis. In cats with hepatic lipidosis, signs of protein malnutrition include hypoalbuminemia, anemia, muscle wasting and negative nitrogen balance.[63,90] Specific amino acids (e.g., methionine and arginine) become limiting during fasting in obese cats.[63] Protein or amino acid deficiency may induce lipid accumulation in the liver by limiting lipoprotein synthesis needed for normal hepatic lipid metabolism and transport.[63] Protein supplementation at only one-fourth of the daily requirement (22 g protein/day) significantly reduces lipid accumulation in the liver and promotes positive nitrogen balance during long-term fasting in obese cats.[64]

Cats with hepatic lipidosis will usually tolerate moderate amounts of dietary protein unless they are suffering from concurrent hepatic encephalopathy, which is uncommon. Commercial veterinary therapeutic foods containing 30 to 45% DM protein are well tolerated by affected cats and have been used successfully in many cases.

POTASSIUM

Hypokalemia may develop due to inadequate potassium intake, vomiting, polydipsia and polyuria, magnesium depletion and concurrent chronic renal failure. In one study, hypokalemia was present in 19 of 66 cats (29%) with severe hepatic lipidosis.[59] Hypokalemia was significantly related to nonsurvival in this group of cats. Hypokalemia is dangerous because it may prolong anorexia and exacerbate expression of hepatic encephalopathy. Foods for cats with hepatic lipidosis should be potassium replete (0.8 to 1.0% DM potassium), or potassium supplementation (2 to 6 mEq potassium gluconate per day) should be considered.

CARNITINE

Food and biosynthesis by the liver are the primary sources of carnitine for animals. Carnitine transports long-chain fatty acids across the inner mitochondrial membrane into the mitochondrial matrix for β-oxidation. Carnitine also removes potentially toxic acyl groups from cells and equilibrates ratios of free CoA/acetyl-CoA between the mitochondria and cytoplasm.

Obesity is a risk factor for feline hepatic lipidosis and several studies have investigated the relationship between carnitine, weight loss in obese cats and feline hepatic lipidosis. Jacobs and colleagues found that mean concentrations of carnitine in plasma, liver and skeletal muscle were significantly greater in cats with idiopathic hepatic lipidosis than in control cats.[91] These findings suggest that systemic carnitine deficiency does not appear to contribute to the pathogenesis of feline idiopathic hepatic lipidosis. However, other studies have shown that feline foods supplemented with L-carnitine benefit obese cats undergoing rapid weight loss. Armstrong and colleagues showed that dietary L-carnitine supplementation protected obese cats from hepatic lipid accumulation during caloric restriction and rapid weight loss.[92] Center and colleagues showed that foods supplemented with L-carnitine can safely facilitate rapid weight loss in privately owned obese cats.[93,94] Based on these studies, the use of L-carnitine supplements or L-carnitine supplemented foods seems appropriate for obese cats undergoing weight reduction.

L-carnitine supplementation may also benefit cats with hepatic lipidosis.[62] One author has recommended a dose of L-carnitine for cats with hepatic lipidosis of 250 to 500 mg per day.[62] Others have found that lower doses (7 to 14 mg/kg body weight) also result in beneficial effects in weight loss, obesity prevention and in cats with hepatic lipidosis.[a]

Copper-Associated Hepatotoxicosis in Dogs

ENERGY

Providing adequate daily energy intake is important in managing patients with copper toxicosis. An adequate supply of energy is needed to allow protein synthesis and prevent tissue catabolism that generates ammonia. The exact caloric needs of affected patients have not been determined, but they would be expected to be similar to those for other patients treated at home (1.4 to 1.8 x RER) or in the hospital (1.0 to 1.2 x RER). Patients with clinical evidence of hepatic encephalopathy should have energy partitioned between carbohydrates and fat as discussed under portosystemic vascular shunts.

PROTEIN

Most dogs with copper toxicosis develop clinical manifestations of liver disease during adulthood (two to six years of age). Protein requirements have not been established for these dogs but would be expected to be similar to those for other adult dogs (15 to 30% DM). Patients with evidence of hepatic encephalopathy will often need more restricted dietary protein levels.

COPPER

Avoiding excessive copper intake is important in those animals in which serious hepatic injury has not yet occurred. A minimum dietary copper requirement has been established as 2.9 ppm available copper (dry matter basis [DMB]) for growth.[95] A minimum dietary copper allowance of 7.3 ppm (DMB) for growth and adult maintenance has been established for typical dog foods.[96] Studies have shown that Bedlington terriers achieve copper balance when consuming approximately 0.4 mg copper per day.[97] All this information suggests that foods for dog with suspected or confirmed copper-associated hepatotoxicosis should have not more than 5.0 ppm copper (DMB) from an available copper source.

Copper intake can be controlled by feeding selected commercial veterinary therapeutic foods or homemade foods. Dogs should not be fed supplements containing copper or table foods that have a high copper content (Table 23-7). Certain fiber sources (See Table 2-7.) and minerals in food (See Figure 2-21.) inhibit copper absorption. The appropriate levels of these nutrients in foods for patients with copper toxicosis have not be investigated. Zinc supplementation is important for blocking copper absorption and is discussed below.

ZINC

Treatment of hepatic copper toxicosis involves use of zinc and copper chelating agents such as D-penicillamine or tri-

Table 23-7. Copper content of selected foods.

Foods with very high* to high copper content
Cocoa
Heart
Kidney
Legumes
Liver*

Mushrooms
Nuts
Shellfish*
Skeletal muscle (meat)

Foods low in copper
Cheese
Cottage cheese
Rice
Tofu

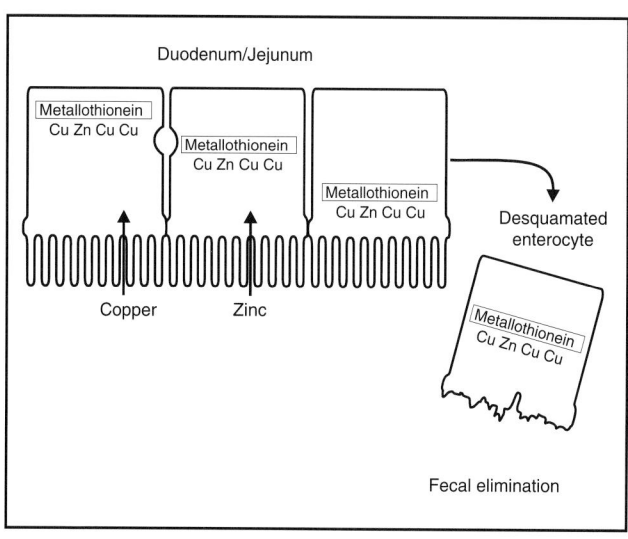

Figure 23-13. Diagrammatic representation of zinc and copper interaction in the intestine. Copper hepatotoxicosis is often treated with zinc supplementation. Zinc appears to induce synthesis of intestinal metallothionein, which has greater affinity for copper than for zinc. Metallothionein binds zinc and copper making them unavailable for systemic absorption. The metals are excreted in the feces with desquamated enterocytes. (Adapted from Center SA. Pathophysiology of liver disease: Normal and abnormal function. In: Guilford WG, Center SA, Strombeck DR, et al, eds. Strombeck's Small Animal Gastroenterology, 3rd ed. Philadelphia, PA: WB Saunders Co, 1996; 596, 599.)

entine.[98,99] Chelating agents bind to copper and increase its excretion in urine. Unlike chelating agents, zinc is thought to act by blocking intestinal absorption of copper. Animal and human studies have shown that zinc induces synthesis of intestinal metallothionein, which has greater affinity for copper than for zinc.[100-102] In enterocytes, metallothionein acts as an intracellular ligand binding zinc, copper, mercury and cadmium to form mercaptides, thereby rendering them unavailable for systemic absorption. Thus, the metals are excreted in the feces with desquamated epithelial cells (Figure 23-13). In human patients with Wilson's disease, intestinal metallothionein concentrations were significantly elevated during zinc therapy when compared with the concentrations in patients not receiving zinc therapy.[101,102] A marked increase in intestinal metallothionein levels was observed in two human patients within a few days after zinc treatment was initiated. This finding was accompanied by suppression of copper

LIVER DISEASE

uptake.[101,102] Discontinuation of zinc therapy was associated with progressive decreases in intestinal metallothionein concentrations and increased copper uptake.

Zinc acetate has been recommended and used most often as a source of elemental zinc.[99] Zinc sulfate, zinc methionine and zinc gluconate are also available. A loading dose of 100 mg elemental zinc per os twice daily is given for three months and the dose is then decreased to 50 mg twice daily. The zinc should be given separate from meals unless nausea and vomiting occur. In those cases, zinc can be given with a small amount of food. Reduced hepatic copper concentrations, decreased hepatic enzyme activity and improved hepatic histologic features were noted after two years of zinc therapy in a small number of affected dogs.[99]

ANTIOXIDANT VITAMINS

Because lipid peroxidation has been implicated in the pathogenesis of copper toxicosis, use of supplemental vitamin E, vitamin C and other antioxidants may be beneficial. No specific dosage of vitamins E and C have been documented to be safe and efficacious in dogs with liver disease. However, 400 to 500 IU vitamin E and 500 to 1,000 mg vitamin C given per os daily have been recommended in dogs with inflammatory liver disease.[73]

Portosystemic Vascular Shunts

ENERGY

Providing adequate daily energy intake is important for managing patients with portosystemic vascular shunts. An adequate supply of energy is needed to allow protein synthesis and prevent tissue catabolism that generates ammonia. The exact caloric needs of these patients have not been determined but would be expected to be similar to those for other patients treated at home (1.4 to 1.8 x RER) or in the hospital (1.0 to 1.2 x RER). Young animals with congenital shunts may be stunted or underweight. DER calculations for these animals should be based on ideal weight rather than current body weight. (See Table 1-7.)

The sources of energy in the food or foods may be important for patients with portosystemic shunts. Experimental studies suggest that feeding foods with a high carbohydrate component is advantageous.[103] Providing at least 30 to 50% of dietary calories in the form of easily digested, complex soluble carbohydrate (e.g., corn, rice, wheat, barley) may help avert encephalopathic clinical signs.[37]

Fat is an important source of calories. Only a minor decrease in fat digestibility (i.e., 92 to 85%) occurred in dogs with experimentally created portosystemic shunts.[104] Other studies showed that dogs with experimental shunts tolerate foods containing 20 to 25% DM fat.[37] Moderate dietary fat intake (15 to 30% DM fat for dogs and 20 to 40% DM fat for cats) seems appropriate for portosystemic shunt patients unless fat malabsorption (i.e., steatorrhea) is evident.

PROTEIN

The protein requirement of patients with portosystemic vascular shunts has been roughly estimated from a nutritional study in adult dogs with surgically created shunts.[104] This study showed that ingestion of 2.11 g crude protein/kg body weight/day with an 80% or greater availability was adequate to maintain body protein reserves without producing hepatic encephalopathy. In the absence of other data, this recommendation for dietary protein intake

seems appropriate. This equates to approximately 14 to 16% protein calories (15 to 20% DM protein) for dogs and 25 to 30% protein calories (30 to 35% DM protein) for cats. These levels of dietary protein are approximately twice the minimum protein requirement for adult dogs and cats. Some animals with hepatic encephalopathy may need lower levels of dietary protein in conjunction with medical therapy to control clinical signs of neurotoxicity.

In addition to the absolute amount of protein fed, the amino acid profile and digestibility are important for optimal protein usage. Amino acids from poor-quality protein sources will be deaminated and metabolized to a greater extent than amino acids from higher-quality protein sources and will exacerbate hyperammonemia. Poorly digested proteins may be degraded by intestinal bacteria and add to the body's ammonia burden.

The importance of the dietary protein source has been studied in human patients with hepatic encephalopathy and in several experimental studies in dogs with portosystemic vascular shunts.[37] Vegetable and dairy protein sources have produced the best results in maintaining positive nitrogen balance with minimal encephalopathic signs in human patients with liver disease.[105-107] Foods using soybean meal averted encephalopathic signs in dogs with experimentally created shunts.[94,108,109] In addition, dairy products (especially cottage cheese) have been frequently recommended for use in homemade foods for dogs and cats with portosystemic shunts and chronic hepatic insufficiency.[37,89] The amino acid composition of these protein sources is not significantly different from that of meat sources, suggesting that other food factors such as digestibility and levels of soluble carbohydrate and fermentable fiber are important. Fermentable carbohydrates increase microbial nitrogen fixation, reduce ammonia production and absorption and promote colonic evacuation.[37]

The abnormal plasma amino acid profile in patients with hepatic disease can be improved by feeding a protein with an amino acid composition high in BCAA and low in AAA. However, a causal relationship between a deranged BCAA-AAA ratio in plasma and cerebrospinal fluid and hepatic encephalopathy remains unproved. The deranged BCAA-AAA ratio associated with portosystemic shunting correlates better with the severity of shunting and hepatic insufficiency than with the presence or absence of hepatic encephalopathy.[37,56,110] Although formulating and using foods to minimize development of this adverse ratio have long been recommended, it is not clear whether the recommendation provides a benefit to people and dogs.[110] In contrast, feeding a food with moderate protein restriction (rather than providing a theoretically optimal amino acid balance) prevents weight loss and development of neurologic signs in dogs with portosystemic shunts.[104]

Parenteral and enteral supplemental formulas designed to normalize circulating amino acid concentrations have been evaluated in numerous clinical trials involving people with portosystemic encephalopathy. These formulas contain reduced levels of AAA and increased levels of BCAA. Despite the large number of investigations, it is difficult to analyze the data because of marked differences in study designs, lack of randomization and variation in formulas used.[48,111-113] Because formulas enriched with BCAA are very expensive, use of such formulas can be justified only in patients with hepatic failure that are unable to tolerate adequate protein from standard enteral or parenteral products.

Chronic Hepatitis and Cirrhosis

ENERGY

Providing adequate daily energy intake is important in managing patients with chronic hepatitis. An adequate supply of energy is needed to allow protein synthesis and prevent tissue catabolism that generates ammonia. The exact caloric needs of affected patients have not been determined, but would be expected to be similar to those for other patients treated at home (1.4 to 1.8 x RER) or in the hospital (1.0 to 1.2 x RER). Patients with clinical evidence of hepatic encephalopathy should have energy partitioned between carbohydrates and fat as discussed under portosystemic vascular shunts.

PROTEIN

Protein and its constituent amino acids are important in patients with chronic hepatitis and/or cirrhosis. Hypoalbuminemia, which reflects depleted body stores and reduced protein synthesis, is a frequent and serious problem in patients with chronic liver disease. Protein plays a leading role in hepatic regeneration; therefore, patients with liver disease require adequate protein intake to remain anabolic and support regeneration of hepatocytes. On the other hand, dietary protein restriction may be important in patients with end-stage cirrhosis, hyperammonemia and hepatic encephalopathy. Protein, or more accurately, nitrogen excess, is a major contributor to neurotoxic precursors formed when amino acids are metabolized to ammonia. For patients with liver disease, the goal is to provide adequate dietary protein to support hepatic regeneration while avoiding excess dietary protein that might contribute to hepatic encephalopathy.

Most dogs and cats with chronic hepatitis develop clinical problems during adulthood. Protein requirements have not been established for these animals, but would be expected to be similar to those for other adult dogs (15 to 30% DM) or cats (30 to 45% DM). Patients with evidence of hepatic encephalopathy will often need restricted dietary protein levels as discussed under portosystemic vascular shunts.

ANTIOXIDANT VITAMINS

Because lipid peroxidation may be involved in the pathogenesis of some forms of acute liver injury[114] and chronic hepatitis, use of supplemental vitamin E, vitamin C and other antioxidants may be beneficial. No specific dosages of vitamins E and C have been documented to be safe and effective for dogs with liver disease. However, 400 to 500 IU vitamin E and 500 to 1,000 mg vitamin C given per os daily have been recommended for dogs with inflammatory liver disease.[73]

Cholangitis/Cholangiohepatitis in Cats

Key nutritional factors for cats with cholangitis and cholangiohepatitis are similar to those outlined for cats with hepatic lipidosis.

Portal Hypertension

ENERGY AND PROTEIN

Portal hypertension usually occurs secondary to chronic hepatitis and cirrhosis. See the energy and protein recommendations in that section for more specific information.

SODIUM AND CHLORIDE

Excessive dietary sodium chloride should not be given to animals with ascites, portal hypertension and/or significant hypoalbuminemia. Sodium chloride restriction as recommended for patients with renal and cardiac failure is appropriate. Recommended dietary levels are 0.10 to 0.25% DM sodium for dogs and 0.20 to 0.35% DM sodium for cats. Optimal chloride levels have not been established, but are typically 1.5 times sodium levels.

Bile Duct Obstruction

Most patients with bile duct obstruction are candidates for exploratory celiotomy and corrective surgery. Parenteral or enteral assisted feeding is often used before and after surgery, while the patient recovers. (See Chapter 12.) Appropriate adult maintenance-type foods are generally indicated after recovery. Patients with concurrent pancreatitis, exocrine pancreatic insufficiency or inflammatory bowel disease may require a food with an altered nutrient profile. (See Chapter 22.)

Other Nutritional Factors

Fat

The role of dietary fat in patients with hepatic disease has not been specifically determined. Dietary lipids are beneficial because they have a protein-sparing effect, reduce carbohydrate intolerance, augment fat-soluble vitamin absorption, enhance palatability and are an important source of energy and essential fatty acids.

A minor decrease in fat digestibility (i.e., from 92 to 85%) was found in dogs with experimentally created portosystemic vascular shunts.[104] Clinically significant impaired fat digestion may occur in animals with biliary disease and/or cholestasis. A number of studies have shown that dogs with experimental lesions do well on foods containing 20 to 35% DM fat.[37] Human patients with portal hypertension associated with cirrhosis may develop fat malabsorption.[115]

There seems to be no reason for routinely restricting dietary fat in dogs and cats with liver disease. Dietary fat levels of 15 to 30% DM for dogs and 20 to 40% DM for cats are probably appropriate for most patients with liver disease that do not have evidence of significant cholestasis or fat malassimilation (i.e., steatorrhea). One of two different situations may be occurring if steatorrhea is a problem in a patient with hepatobiliary disease. First, the patient may have concurrent disease that is contributing to fat malassimilation, such as exocrine pancreatic insufficiency. Second, the patient may have significant bile duct obstruction and may be a candidate for an exploratory celiotomy.

Medium-chain triglycerides (MCT; i.e., carbon chain lengths less than 12) have theoretical advantages over long-chain triglycerides (LCT) for the treatment of GI and some forms of hepatobiliary disease.[116] MCT may be more easily hydrolyzed and absorbed than LCT; however, these advantages have yet to be proved. Caloric supplementation with MCT is useful for malnourished human cirrhotic patients with steatorrhea and those with advanced cholestatic hepatic disease.[117] Results of controlled clinical trials using MCT in animals with cirrhotic or cholestatic liver disease have not been reported.

Increased dietary levels of n-3 fatty acids may benefit animals with inflammatory liver disease. See Chapter 26 for information about the use of fatty acids to modify inflammatory diseases.

Fiber

Foods with increased dietary fiber levels may benefit patients with hepatobiliary disease. Dietary fiber reduces the availability and production of nitrogenous wastes in the GI tract. Although highly digestible foods were previously advocated in an effort to maximize digestion and absorption and reduce colonic residues considered a major source of encephalopathic toxins, this practice is now not recommended. Increased amounts of fermentable fiber encourage nitrogen fixation by enteric bacteria, resulting in reduced quantities of nitrogenous substances available for absorption. Increased dietary fiber is also thought to bind noxious bile acids, endotoxins and other bacterial products. Dietary fiber is also useful in maintaining euglycemia (See Chapter 24.) and altering the pH of colonic contents. Commercial and homemade foods with low dietary fiber levels can be supplemented with psyllium husk fiber (1 tsp per 5 to 10 kg body weight, added to each meal).

Taurine

In dogs and cats, taurine is synthesized primarily in the liver and bile salts are exclusively conjugated with taurine. Compared to cats, dogs have a high capacity to synthesize taurine and dietary taurine is not essential in most instances. Food-induced bile salt excretion into the gut can result in significant loss of taurine, particularly when normal enterohepatic recycling is interrupted. In cats, taurine synthesis is limited and dietary taurine is essential. Therefore, assurance of adequate taurine nutriture is important in animals with enterohepatic circulation abnormalities and possibly in liver disease. In certain species, taurine also stimulates the synthesis and turnover of bile independent of its role as a bile acid conjugate. Taurine appears to aid in choleresis in dogs and possibly cats. This role may explain the observation that taurine can prevent cholestasis in certain models of liver disease. Most commercial cat foods and foods for stress and recovery are well fortified with this amino acid. However, homemade and human enteral foods fed to cats should be supplemented with taurine (250 to 500 mg/day). Providing a source of taurine is important for cats with hepatic lipidosis.

Iron

Iron deficiency may occur in patients with GI ulceration and hemorrhage associated with chronic hepatitis, portal hypertension or bile duct obstruction. Microcytosis, an erythrocyte abnormality associated with iron deficiency, also develops in dogs with portosystemic vascular shunts despite adequate iron stores.[16,37] Iron supplementation is indicated when serum iron concentrations are low, hypochromia is recognized or gastroenteric bleeding or another source of chronic blood loss is recognized.[33] Iron supplementation of homemade foods is usually necessary.

On the other hand, iron loading by hepatocytes and Kupffer cells has been recognized in some animals with inflammatory liver diseases. Iron is a potent catalyst of oxidative processes and iron-associated hepatic injury may involve lipid peroxidation of membranes and organelle damage.[62] Foods for dogs with chronic hepatitis and those with secondary hemosiderosis documented by evaluation of liver biopsy specimens should avoid excessive iron levels. Iron levels of 80 to 140 ppm (DMB) meet the dietary allowance without providing excessive intake.[96] Injectable or oral supplements containing iron should be avoided in these patients.

Zinc

There is much evidence suggesting that zinc deficiency is prevalent in people with hepatic disease.[118] Urea synthetic capacity is thought to be reduced in zinc-deficient patients because of decreased hepatic ornithine transcarbamoylase activity and increased muscle glutamine synthetase activity.[5] Zinc deficiency could thus adversely affect multiple aspects of ammonia metabolism.[119] Foods should contain more than 200 mg/kg DM zinc, or the food should be supplemented with zinc gluconate (3 mg/kg body weight/day) or zinc sulfate (2 mg/kg body weight/day) divided into three doses.[5] Zinc supplementation in patients with copper-associated hepatotoxicosis was discussed previously.

Potassium

Hypokalemia may develop because of inadequate potassium intake, vomiting, hyperaldosteronism, polydipsia and polyuria, magnesium depletion and administration of loop diuretics (e.g., furosemide) for managing ascites. Hypokalemia is dangerous because it may exacerbate anorexia and expression of hepatic encephalopathy. Foods for dogs and cats with liver disease should be potassium replete (i.e., 0.8 to 1.0% DM potassium), or potassium supplementation should be considered.

Vitamins

Vitamin deficiencies are common in patients with chronic hepatic disease. Deficient dietary intake and malabsorption are the principal causes for vitamin deficiency, although decreased storage, metabolic defects and increased requirements also may be involved.[5]

Deficiency of water-soluble vitamins may occur due to inadequate intake, vomiting and urinary losses. Hepatic concentrations of folate, riboflavin, nicotinamide, pantothenic acid, pyridoxine and vitamin B_{12} are decreased in people with cirrhosis.[120] Commercial pet foods usually contain sufficient quantities of water-soluble vitamins to meet the needs of most patients with liver disease. Supplementation with water-soluble vitamins is indicated in patients: 1) receiving aggressive diuretic therapy for ascites, 2) with profound polydipsia and polyuria, 3) with prolonged anorexia and 4) eating homemade foods.

Vitamin K becomes important in animals with chronic liver disease, those with prolonged cholestasis and those with evidence of excessive bleeding. Abnormal blood coagulation tests and excessive bleeding reflect impaired hepatic synthesis of clotting factors and/or a consumptive coagulopathy. Patients with chronic liver disease may be vitamin-K deficient or unable to convert vitamin K_1 to its active form. Vitamin K stores in the liver are limited and can be rapidly depleted when dietary sources are inadequate or lipid malabsorption is severe. Abnormal blood coagulation tests in many patients with liver disease will return to normal after parenteral administration of vitamin K_1 (1 to 5 mg/kg body weight/day, given intramuscularly or subcutaneously) for several days. This therapy is often given before liver biopsy or surgical procedures.

Assess the Food(s)

Table 23-8 lists general recommendations for foods to use in patients with hepatobiliary disease. For specific diseases, the quantities of the key nutritional factors in the current food should be determined. This evaluation usually includes energy density, protein, taurine (cats), crude fat, soluble carbohydrate (nitrogen-free extract [NFE]), sodium, chloride, potassium and crude fiber. The nutrient quantities can then be compared with those recommended for most patients with hepatobiliary disease (Table 23-9).

Other important nutrients to consider in some patients with hepatobiliary disease include water-soluble vitamins, iron, copper, zinc, vitamin E, vitamin K and carnitine. The food should be balanced for the appropriate species and age, especially for cats and young animals with congenital hepatopathies. Nutrient quantities are especially important to consider in patients with hepatic encephalopathy.

Crude protein, crude fat and crude fiber quantities in the food can be estimated from the guaranteed or typical analysis on the product label. More detailed nutrient information must be obtained by contacting the manufacturer or consulting published information.

Assess the Feeding Method

It may not always be necessary to change the feeding method when managing a patient with hepatobiliary disease; however, a thorough assessment includes verification that an appropriate feeding method is being used. Items to consider include feeding route, amount fed, how the food is offered, access to other food and who feeds the animal. All of this information should have been gathered when the patient history was obtained. If the animal has normal body condition (body condition score 3/5), the amount of food previously fed (energy basis) was probably appropriate.

FEEDING PLAN

The universal goals for dietary management of hepatobiliary disorders include maintaining metabolic balance while providing nutrients for healing and regeneration of damaged tissue. Other important objectives include: 1) correcting and preventing malnutrition, 2) reducing the need for hepatic "work," 3) avoiding production of hepatotoxic and neurotoxic compounds and 4) eliminating the underlying cause of hepatic disease. The goals of therapy in patients with hepatic encephalopathy also include: 1) recognizing and correcting precipitating causes of encephalopathy (e.g., GI bleeding and constipation) and 2) reducing intestinal production and absorption of neurotoxins.

Select a Food(s)

A wide variety of foods are typically used or recommended for patients with hepatic disease. These include

Table 23-8. General recommendations for foods used in patients with hepatobiliary disease.

Avoid excess dietary protein*
  Restricted amounts of protein compared to regular
    commercial foods
  High-quality protein
  High protein digestibility (>85%)
Moderate levels of dietary fat
Highly digestible, moderate levels of soluble carbohydrate
High energy density
Highly palatable
Increased levels of fermentable fiber
Increased potassium levels
Increased zinc levels
Avoid excess or deficient dietary iron levels (dogs)
Avoid excess dietary copper levels (dogs)
Avoid excess dietary sodium and chloride levels
Increased B vitamin, vitamin E, vitamin C and vitamin K levels
Increased arginine levels
Increased taurine levels (especially cats)
Increased carnitine levels

*Especially in patients with hepatic encephalopathy.

Table 23-9. Recommended levels of key nutritional factors for patients with hepatobiliary disease.*

Nutritional factors	Dogs	Cats
Protein (%)**	15-30	30-45
Fat (%)	15-30	20-40
Soluble carbohydrate (%)	45-55	30-40
Total dietary fiber (%)***	3-8	3-8
Energy (kcal/g)†	>4.0	>4.0
Arginine (%)	1.2-2.0	1.5-2.0
Taurine (ppm)	–	2,500-5,000
Sodium (%)	0.1-0.25	0.20-0.35
Chloride (%)	0.25-0.40	0.30-0.45
Potassium (%)	0.8-1.0	0.8-1.0

*Nutrients expressed on a dry matter basis.
**Protein levels may need to be decreased in patients with hepatic encephalopathy.
***Total dietary fiber is different from crude fiber and is more accurate for measuring levels of fermentable fiber.
†To convert to kJ/g multiply kcal by 4.184.

commercial veterinary therapeutic foods (Table 23-10) and homemade foods.[89,121] (See Tables 6-4 and 6-7.) Commercial veterinary therapeutic foods designed for patients with renal disease were often recommended for patients with hepatobiliary disease. Recently, commercial veterinary therapeutic foods designed specifically for patients with hepatic disease have become available (Table 23-10). Foods designed for assisted feeding and recovery are often used in cats with hepatic lipidosis or inflammatory liver disease.

Although the total protein content of some veterinary therapeutic foods is lower than that of regular commercial pet foods, protein quality and digestibility are usually high. Many of these foods should provide adequate protein to support hepatic function and hepatocyte repair and regeneration while avoiding higher protein levels that increase hepatic workload and might exacerbate hyperammonemia and hepatic encephalopathy. These foods are also balanced and contain appropriate amounts of other key nutritional factors (e.g., fat, carbohydrates, minerals and vitamins). Short-term discontinuation of protein intake or further reduction of protein intake may be necessary in patients with severe liver failure and hepatic encephalopathy.

Table 23-10. Levels of key nutrients in selected commercial products used in patients with hepatobiliary disease.*

Moist canine products	Protein (%)	Fat (%)	Carbohydrate (%)	Energy (kcal/g)	Potassium (%)	Sodium (%)	Chloride (%)	Copper (ppm)
Hill's Prescription Diet Canine k/d	14.8	27.8	50.7	4.7	0.33	0.22	0.42	5.5
Hill's Prescription Diet Canine l/d	17.8	24.1	50.4	4.4	0.91	0.19	0.62	4.8
Hill's Prescription Diet Canine u/d	11.5	27.2	57.3	5.1	0.39	0.25	0.43	3.4
Leo Specific Renil CKW	18.7	16.9	56.4	4.5	0.94	0.15	0.50	3.8
Leo Specific Uremil CUW	13.1	18.4	61.0	4.6	0.96	0.14	0.57	2.8
Medi-Cal Canine Reduced Protein	16.8	21.8	na	na	na	0.24	na	na
Pedigree Canine Hepatic Support	16.3	11.3	64.8	3.9	0.83	0.13	na	5.0
Purina CNM Canine NF-Formula	16.5	27.4	50.4	4.7	0.72	0.24	0.43	10.3
Select Care Canine Modified Formula	16.8	21.8	41.7	na	0.96	0.24	na	na
Waltham/Pedigree Canine Low Protein	17.4	30.8	47.2	5.1	0.3	0.36	na	26.6
Dry canine products								
Hill's Prescription Diet Canine k/d	14.6	19.5	61.5	4.5	0.32	0.19	0.37	16.4
Hill's Prescription Diet Canine l/d	17.8	24.0	51.0	4.4	0.90	0.19	0.68	5.0
Hill's Prescription Diet Canine u/d	9.3	20.6	64.6	4.9	0.62	0.24	0.45	3.5
Iams Eukanuba Kidney Formula-Early Stage	21.0	14.5	57.4	4.3	0.71	0.53	1.34	na
Iams Eukanuba Kidney Formula-Advanced Stage	15.5	15.2	64.3	4.8	0.6	0.51	1.44	na
Leo Specific Renil CKD	14.7	19.6	58.7	4.7	0.99	0.14	0.54	3.9
Medi-Cal Canine Reduced Protein	14.9	19.7	na	na	na	0.28	na	na
Pedigree Canine Hepatic Support Diet	17.8	12.2	63.3	4.2	0.9	0.13	na	6.0
Purina CNM Canine NF-Formula	15.9	15.7	62.8	4.4	0.86	0.22	0.57	12.1
Select Care Canine Modified Formula	14.4	19.7	61.1	4.2	0.88	0.28	na	na
Waltham/Pedigree Canine Low Protein	17.8	10.6	68.2	4.2	0.78	0.26	na	9.1

Moist feline products	Protein (%)	Fat (%)	Carbohydrate (%)	Energy (kcal/g)	Potassium (%)	Sodium (%)	Chloride (%)	Taurine (%)
Hill's Prescription Diet Canine/Feline a/d	45.7	28.7	16.5	5.5	0.96	0.78	0.81	0.52
Hill's Prescription Diet Feline k/d	28.8	40.0	23.9	5.1	0.95	0.18	0.25	0.52
Hill's Prescription Diet Feline l/d	31.8	23.4	36.9	4.4	0.96	0.22	0.86	0.52
Iams Eukanuba Maximum-Calorie/Canine & Feline	44.0	41.8	7.8	5.9	1.06	0.32	0.79	0.26
Leo Specific Renil FUW	34.9	39.7	15.9	5.6	0.83	0.28	0.44	0.28
Medi-Cal Feline Reduced Protein	36.4	45.5	na	na	na	na	na	na
Purina CNM Feline CV-Formula	42.5	26.8	23.1	4.9	1.33	0.2	1.09	0.31
Purina CNM Feline NF-Formula	31.1	29.5	30.6	5.2	0.96	0.16	0.45	0.45
Select Care Modified Formula	35.0	53.0	4.3	na	1.00	0.23	na	na
Waltham/Whiskas Feline Low Protein	34.5	51.0	7.6	5.8	0.99	0.33	na	na
Dry feline products								
Hill's Prescription Diet Feline k/d	28.2	27.8	38.8	4.6	0.64	0.28	0.33	0.16
Hill's Prescription Diet Feline l/d	31.7	23.2	37.6	4.4	0.90	0.28	0.63	0.50
Iams Eukanuba Maximum-Calorie/Feline	44.2	29.6	19.1	5.4	0.91	0.54	1.06	0.22
Leo Specific Renil FKD	25.4	25.9	39.5	2.8	1.44	0.21	1.03	0.14
Purina CNM NF-Formula	30.8	12.9	50.6	4.3	0.88	0.2	0.64	0.18
Select Care Modified Formula	28.3	22.1	4.1	4.4	0.92	0.27	na	na
Waltham/Whiskas Feline Low Protein	26.1	22.2	na	na	0.89	0.22	na	na

*This list represents products with the largest market share and for which published information is available.
Manufacturers' published values; expressed on dry matter basis.
na = information not available.

Determine a Feeding Method

Sick, anorectic and severely malnourished patients with hepatobiliary disease should be hospitalized to initiate supportive care and assisted-feeding techniques. Early tube feeding via nasogastric or gastrostomy tube remains the cornerstone of therapy for feline patients with hepatic lipidosis and all other anorectic patients with liver disease. See Chapter 12 and Appendix V for details about foods and enteral feeding techniques commonly used in dogs and cats. Patients that are eating enough food to meet their DER can usually be managed at home.

The DER of patients with hepatobiliary disease is similar to the DER for hospitalized animals and normal adult dogs and cats at home. Force feeding of moist food and appetite stimulants can be used to ensure caloric intake, but these strategies often fail to meet the pet's caloric requirements and frustrate the owner and pet. Appetite stimulants such as anabolic steroids and benzodiazepine derivatives should be used cautiously in patients with hepatic disease, because of the potential for hepatotoxicity.[122]

Many animals may develop learned aversion to the foods they are offered if GI disturbances accompany liver disease. This is the classic scenario in cats with hepatic lipidosis. Cats that refuse to eat a food they associate with nausea may continue to avoid that food even after a complete recovery. Tube feeding is therefore preferable in cats with hepatic lipidosis and should be started immediately after a diagnosis is made. Such an approach is preferred to offering several commercial foods and possibly having the cat develop an aversion to them. The prognosis for feline hepatic lipidosis is influenced largely by the ability of the

Table 23-11. General therapy for patients with heptobiliary disease.*

Fluid therapy	
Maintain hydration	Give appropriate parenteral fluid therapy
Prevent hypokalemia	Add KCl to maintenance fluids
	Use potassium-replete food or potassium supplement
Maintain acid-base balance	Avoid alkalosis in patients with hepatic encephalopathy
Prevent or control hypoglycemia	Add dextrose to parenteral fluids as needed
Nutritional support	
Maintain caloric intake	Ensure that DER is being met; if not, begin assisted feeding
Provide adequate vitamins and minerals	Use complete and balanced food
	Add B vitamins to fluids or give as injection
Modify feeding plan to control complications	See specific complications below
Control of hepatic encephalopathy	
Modify food and prevent formation and absorption of enteric toxins	Avoid excess dietary protein
	Use retention enemas q6h containing neomycin and lactulose or povidone iodine solution
	Give neomycin or metronidazole and lactulose orally
Control gastrointestinal hemorrhage	Treat GI parasites, treat gastric ulcers, avoid drugs that exacerbate GI hemorrhage (e.g., aspirin, glucocorticoids)
Correct metabolic imbalances	See fluid therapy above
Avoid drugs or therapies that exacerbate hepatic encephalopathy	Do not administer sedatives, analgesics, anesthetics, diuretics, stored blood or methionine-containing products
Control seizures	Use appropriate anticonvulsant drugs (e.g., phenobarbital, potassium bromide)
Control infection	Give systemic antimicrobials (see below)
Control ascites and edema	Avoid excess dietary sodium chloride
	Administer diuretics (e.g., furosemide, spironolactone)
	Paracentesis for relief of dyspnea only
Control coagulation defects and anemia	Give vitamin K_1 parenterally
	Give fresh plasma or blood transfusion as needed
Control gastrointestinal ulceration	Give H_2 blockers (e.g., cimetidine, ranitidine) or cytoprotective agents (e.g., sucralfate)
Control infection and endotoxemia	Give systemic antibiotics (e.g., penicillin, ampicillin, cephalosporins, aminoglycosides)
	Give intestinal antibiotics (e.g., neomycin)
	Give toxin binders (e.g., cholestyramine)
Manage cholestasis	Give bile "altering" or choleretic drugs (e.g., ursodiol)
	Surgically correct extrahepatic bile duct obstruction

Key: DER = daily energy requirement.
*Adapted from Johnson SE, Sherding RG. Diseases of the liver and biliary tract. In: Birchard SJ, Sherding RG, eds. Manual of Small Animal Practice. Philadelphia, PA: WB Saunders Co, 1994; 730.

veterinarian or owner to aggressively meet the caloric requirements of the cat via enteral feeding.

Multiple daily feedings rather than one or two large meals may benefit patients with hepatobiliary disease. Multiple meals may minimize the release of free fatty acids from adipose tissue, improve digestibility and reduce the quantity of ingesta at any one time that enters the large intestine where bacterial fermentation occurs. Studies involving people with hepatic failure have shown that nitrogen balance can be improved if the food is divided into small, frequent meals, including a snack at bedtime.[123] Nauseated patients may also better tolerate multiple small meals.

ADJUNCTIVE THERAPY

Dietary therapy is only beneficial when performed in conjunction with proper medical and surgical management of the specific hepatobiliary disease involved. Medical management often includes use of antimicrobials, diuretics, antiinflammatory agents, immunomodulators, nonabsorbable disaccharides and bile "altering" agents (Table 23-11). In acute hepatic failure, correction of fluid and electrolyte imbalances and treatment of other complications such as metabolic acidosis, excessive bleeding, hypotension, hypoglycemia, cardiac dysfunction, renal failure, cerebral edema and infections take precedence

over nutritional support. Surgical management includes ligation of portosystemic vascular shunts, correction of bile duct obstruction and removal of focal liver masses.

Nonabsorbable Disaccharides

Administration of lactulose is considered one of the treatments of choice for hepatic encephalopathy.[124] Lactulose is a synthetic disaccharide that is hydrolyzed by colonic bacteria principally to lactic and acetic acids (Figure 23-14). Lactulose probably exerts its beneficial effects by: 1) lowering colonic pH with subsequent trapping of ammonia, 2) inhibiting ammonia generation by colonic bacteria through a process known as catabolite repression, 3) increasing intestinal transit rate due to its cathartic properties and 4) suppressing bacterial and intestinal ammonia generation by providing a carbohydrate source.[124] The dosage required to achieve these goals varies greatly, with a range of 2.5 to 25 ml, three times daily for dogs and 1.0 to 3.0 ml, three times daily for cats.[124] The dosage should be reduced if watery diarrhea develops.

Lactulose also is highly effective when added to enema fluid (composed of 30% lactulose and 70% water) and given as a retention enema. Approximately 20 to 30 ml/kg body weight are infused and retained in the colon for 20 to 30 minutes before evacuation.[124] Lactulose requires intestinal bacteria for activation; neomycin and other antibiotics, however, inhibit bacterial growth. Despite this

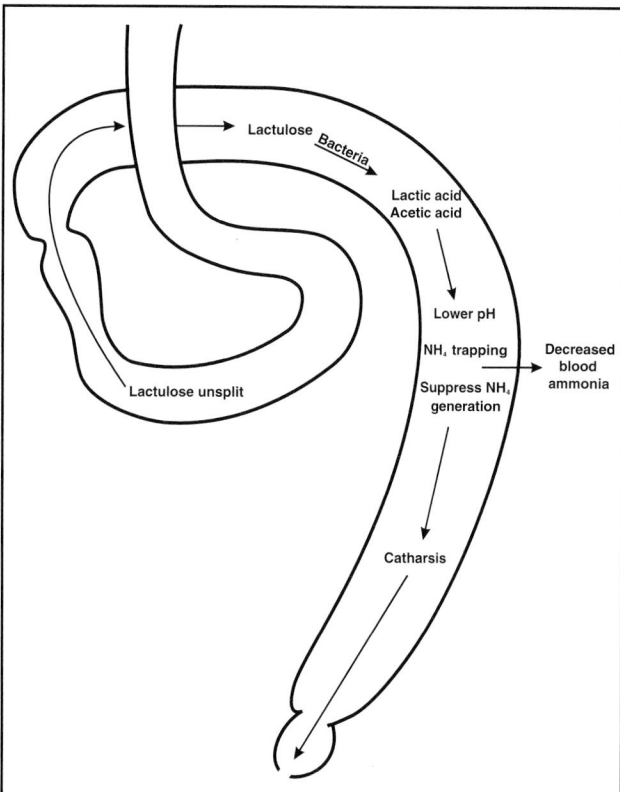

Figure 23-14. Lactulose therapy for treatment of hepatic encephalopathy. Intact lactulose reaches the colon where bacteria convert it to organic acids, which affect ionization of ammonia in the colon and reduce ammonia absorption. An increase in colonic transport rate (catharsis) may also occur. (Adapted from Sherlock S. Diseases of the Liver and Biliary System, 8th ed. Boston, MA: Blackwell Scientific Publications, 1989; 131.

antagonism, lactulose and neomycin have been used simultaneously with additive or synergistic effect.[125]

Copper Chelating Agents

Treatment of hepatic copper toxicosis is clearly indicated for Bedlington terriers with subclinical or clinical liver disease. Some investigators advocate treatment for other breeds of dogs with chronic hepatitis and cirrhosis in which copper accumulation is documented by liver histopathology and/or elevated hepatic copper concentrations (generally greater than 1,000 to 2,000 ppm DW).[33]

Treatment of hepatic copper toxicosis usually involves use of zinc and copper chelating agents such as D-penicillamine or trientine (Figure 23-15).[73,98,99] Zinc blocks copper absorption, as discussed earlier under key nutritional factors. Chelating agents bind to copper and increase its excretion in urine. D-penicillamine, the copper chelating agent most frequently recommended for use in dogs, should be given at a dosage of 10 to 15 mg/kg body weight twice daily, on an empty stomach.[70] Vomiting is the most common side effect in dogs, but can be alleviated by giving the agent more frequently in reduced doses. D-penicillamine therapy also has been associated with pyridoxine deficiency in people.[126] However, this problem has not been recognized in dogs.

Trientine[b] (2,2,2-tetramine) is another chelating agent. In a clinical trial, chelation results with trientine (10 to 15 mg/kg body weight, per os, twice daily) were comparable to those of D-penicillamine and fewer side effects were noted.[127] Modification of 2,2,2-tetramine to 2,3,2-tetramine increases potency as a copper chelating agent. Use of 2,3,2-tetramine in affected Bedlington terriers reduced liver copper concentrations significantly after 200 days of treatment at a dose of 15 mg/kg body weight.[98] This drug is not commercially available but can be obtained from chemical supply companies in the form of N,N'-bis(2-aminoethyl)-1,3-propanediamine and prepared as a salt for oral administration.

Long-term concurrent use of chelating agents and zinc may be counterproductive.[100] However, during initial treatment of symptomatic human patients, physicians have recommended a combination of a chelating agent and zinc for four to six months, then switching to zinc alone for maintenance.[100] This same approach can be used in canine patients.

Vitamins

Parenteral vitamin K_1 administration may benefit patients: 1) with chronic liver disease and prolonged cholestasis (i.e., more than two weeks), 2) with clinical evidence of increased bleeding tendencies (i.e., bruising, overt hemorrhage) and 3) undergoing surgical or liver biopsy procedures. Vitamin supplements that contain vitamin K should always be added to homemade foods.

Patients with chronic liver disease, those with polydipsia and polyuria, those receiving diuretics and those with anorexia lasting more than one week may benefit from parenteral administration of B vitamins. Levels of B-complex vitamins in commercial foods are usually adequate, but vitamin supplements that contain B vitamins should always be added to homemade foods.

Vitamin E and vitamin C can be given as antioxidant supplements for patients with inflammatory liver disease. Initial doses of 400 to 500 IU vitamin E and 500 to 1,000 mg vitamin C given per os daily have been recommended for dogs with inflammatory liver disease.[73]

■ REASSESSMENT

The owner and veterinarian should monitor the appetite, body weight and body condition of the patient, while observing the frequency and severity of GI disturbances (i.e., vomiting, diarrhea), icterus and neurobehavioral signs. One of the most important clinical findings is improvement in the animal's attitude and activity level. This finding is highly correlated with nutritional success. Serial laboratory evaluations (every few days to weeks) of serum liver enzyme activity, serum concentrations of bilirubin, bile acids and potassium and blood ammonia concentrations are also useful. Serial hepatic biopsy specimens (every few months) can be evaluated for hepatic copper concentrations and assessment of inflammatory hepatopathies. Body weight, abdominal configuration and ultrasonography can be used to monitor patients with ascites.

Enteral feeding tubes often can be removed from cats with hepatic lipidosis and/or cholangiohepatitis after several weeks or months of assisted feeding. Enteral tubes are usually removed after the cat has shown clinical improvement and has begun eating two-thirds to three-fourths of its normal DER on its own. Many patients can be fed foods

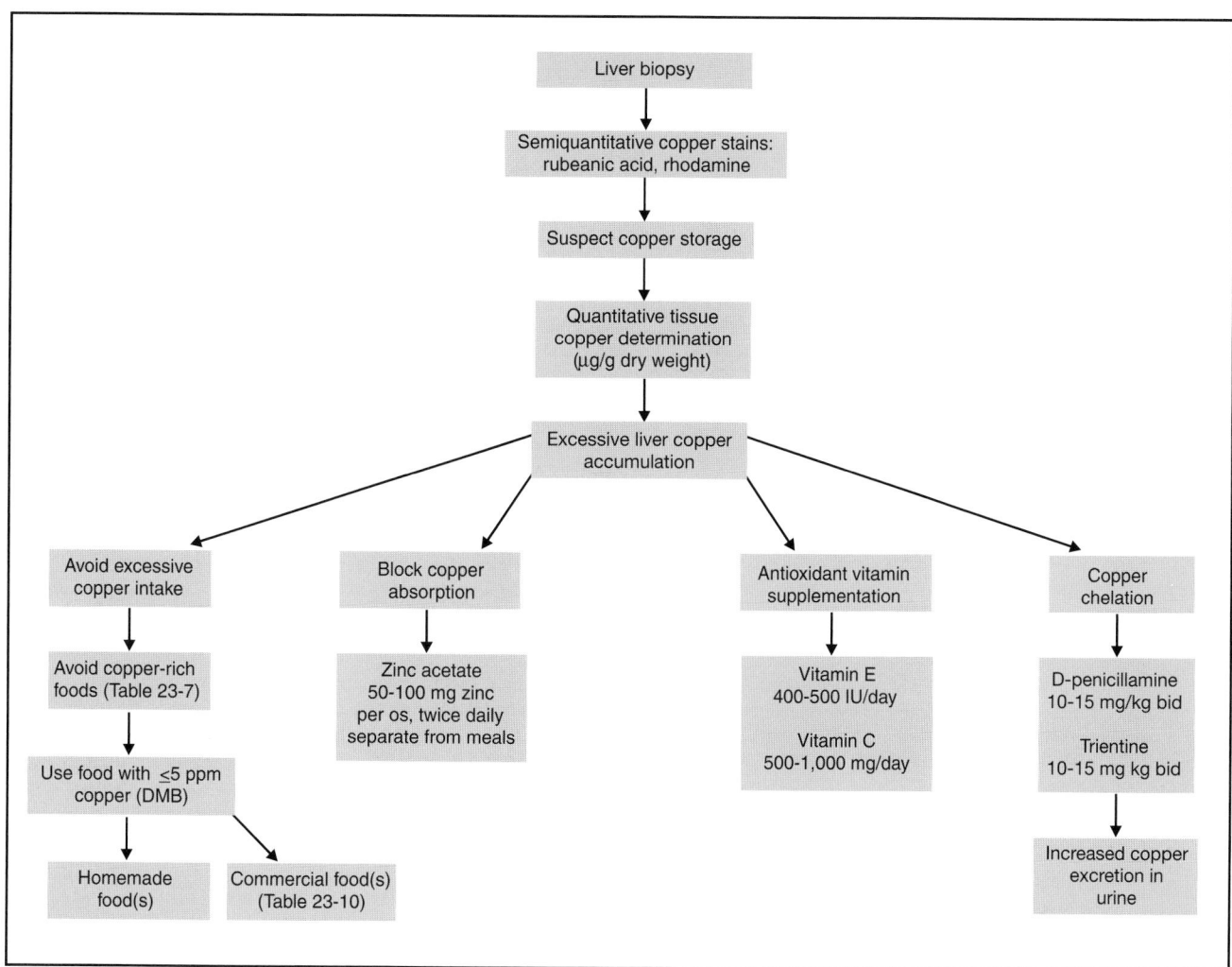

Figure 23-15. Algorithm for treating copper hepatotoxicosis in dogs. (Adapted from Center SA. Chronic liver diseases. In: Guilford WG, Center SA, Strombeck DR, et al, eds. Strombeck's Small Animal Gastroenterology, 3rd ed. Philadelphia, PA: WB Saunders Co, 1996; 749.)

for maintenance of normal adult animals after hepatobiliary disease is resolved. These include patients that have recovered from an acute hepatic insult or hepatic lipidosis and patients that have undergone successful repair of portosystemic shunts.

Vomiting is often a problem in patients with hepatobiliary disease, especially cats with hepatic lipidosis or hepatic encephalopathy. Small frequent meals, continuous tube feeding and antiemetics may be helpful. More aggressive medical treatment of hepatic encephalopathy may also be needed. Long-term administration of lactulose and/or neomycin for management of hepatic encephalopathy may lead to nutrient malabsorption secondary to altered intestinal transit time and suppressed bacterial flora activity.

■ ENDNOTES & REFERENCES

ENDNOTES

a. Géraldine Blanchard, Ecole Nationale Vétérinaire d'Alfort, Paris, France. Personal communication. 1999.

b. Cuprid. Merck & Company, Inc., Rahway, NJ, USA.

REFERENCES

1. Zakim D. Pathophysiology of liver disease. In: Smith LH, Thier SO, eds. Pathophysiology: The Biological Principles of Disease, 2nd ed. Philadelphia, PA: WB Saunders Co, 1985; 1253-1298.

2. Qiao ZK, Halliday ML, Coates RA, et al. Relationship between liver cirrhosis, death rate and nutritional factors in 38 countries. International Journal of Epidemiology 1988; 17: 414-418.

3. O'Keefe SF, El-Zayadi AR, Carraher TE, et al. Malnutrition and immunocompetence in patients with liver disease. Lancet 1980; 2: 615-617.

4. Morgan AG, Kelleher J, Walker BE, et al. Nutrition in cryptogenic cirrhosis and chronic aggressive hepatitis. Gut 1976; 17: 113-118.

5. Marks SL, Rogers QR, Strombeck DR. Nutritional support in hepatic disease. Part I. Metabolic alterations and nutritional considerations in dogs and cats. Compendium on Continuing Education for the Practicing Veterinarian 1994; 16: 971-978.

6. Anderson WD, Anderson BG. Atlas of Canine Anatomy. Philadelphia, PA: Lea & Febiger, 1994; 697-703.

7. Center SA, Strombeck DR. Liver: Normal structure and function. In: Guilford WG, Center SA, Strombeck DR, et al, eds. Strombeck's Small Animal Gastroenterology, 3rd ed. Philadelphia, PA: WB Saunders Co, 1996; 540-552.

8. Diehl AM. Nutrition, hormones, metabolism, and liver regeneration. Seminars in Liver Disease 1991; 11: 315-320.

9. Bucher NLR, Malt RA. Regeneration of Liver and Kidney. Boston, MA: Little, Brown and Co, 1971; 143-176.

10. Higgins GM, Anderson RM. Experimental pathology of the liver: Restoration of the liver by the white rat following partial surgical removal. Archives of Pathology 1931; 12: 186-202.

11. Francavilla A, Panella C, Polimeno L, et al. Hormonal and enzymatic parameters of hepatic regeneration in patients undergoing major liver resections. Hepatology 1990; 12: 1134-1138.

12. Bauer JE, Schenck PA. Nutritional management of hepatic disease. Veterinary Clinics of North America: Small Animal Practice 1989; 19: 513-526.

13. Blackburn GL, O'Keefe SJD. Nutrition in liver failure. Gastroenterology 1989; 97: 1049-1051.

14. Hammer AS, Sikkema DA. Hepatic neoplasia in the dog and cat. Veterinary Clinics of North America: Small Animal Practice 1995; 25: 419-425.

15. Lund EM, Armstrong PJ, Kirk CA, et al. Health status and population characteristics of dogs and cats examined at private veterinary practices in the United States. Journal of the American Veterinary Medical Association 1999; 214: 1336-1341.

16. Center SA. Pathophysiology, laboratory diagnosis, and diseases of the liver. In: Ettinger SJ, Feldman EC, eds. Textbook of Veterinary Internal Medicine, 4th ed. Philadelphia, PA: WB Saunders Co, 1995; 1261-1312.

17. Center SA. Pathophysiology of liver disease: Normal and abnormal function. In: Guilford WG, Center SA, Strombeck DR, et al, eds. Strombeck's Small Animal Gastroenterology, 3rd ed. Philadelphia, PA: WB Saunders Co, 1996; 553-632.

18. Dial SM. Clinicopathologic evaluation of the liver. Veterinary Clinics of North America: Small Animal Practice 1995; 25: 257-273.

19. Gagne JM, Armstrong PJ, Weiss DJ, et al. Clinical features of inflammatory liver disease in cats: 41 cases (1983-1993). Journal of the American Veterinary Medical Association 1999; 214: 513-516.

20. Bostwick DR, Meyer DJ. Bilirubin and bile acids in the diagnosis of hepatobiliary disease. In: Bonagura JD, ed. Current Veterinary Therapy XII. Philadelphia, PA: WB Saunders Co, 1995; 736-740.

21. Center SA, Erb HN, Joseph SA. Measurement of serum bile acids concentrations for diagnosis of hepatobiliary disease in cats. Journal of the American Veterinary Medical Association 1995; 207: 1048-1054.

22. Badylak SF, Dodds WJ, Van Vleet JF. Plasma coagulation factor abnormalities in dogs with naturally occurring hepatic disease. American Journal of Veterinary Research 1983; 44: 2336-2340.

23. Partington BP, Biller DS. Hepatic imaging with radiology and ultrasound. Veterinary Clinics of North America: Small Animal Practice 1995; 25: 305-335.

24. Pechman RD. The liver and spleen. In: Thrall DE, ed. Textbook of Veterinary Diagnostic Radiology, 3rd ed. Philadelphia, PA: WB Saunders Co, 1998; 458-466.

25. Moon ML. Diagnostic imaging of portosystemic shunts. Seminars in Veterinary Medicine and Surgery: Small Animal 1990; 5: 120-126.

26. Barr F. Diagnostic Ultrasound in the Dog and Cat. Oxford, UK: Blackwell Scientific Publications, 1990; 21-45.

27. Nyland TG, Mattoon JS, Wisner ER. Ultrasonography of the liver. In: Nyland TG, Mattoon JS, eds. Veterinary Diagnostic Ultrasound. Philadelphia, PA: WB Saunders Co, 1995; 52-73.

28. Partington BP, Biller DS. Liver. In: Green RW, ed. Small Animal Ultrasound. Philadelphia, PA: Lippincott-Raven Publishers, 1996; 105-130.

29. Lamb CS. Ultrasonography of portosystemic shunts in dogs and cats. Veterinary Clinics of North America: Small Animal Practice 1998; 28: 725-753.

30. Meyer DJ. Hepatic pathology. In: Guilford WG, Center SA, Strombeck DR, et al, eds. Strombeck's Small Animal Gastroenterology, 3rd ed. Philadelphia, PA: WB Saunders Co, 1996; 633-653.

31. Kerwin SC. Hepatic aspiration and biopsy techniques. Veterinary Clinics of North America: Small Animal Practice 1995; 25: 275-291.

32. Thornburg LP, Beissenherz M, Dolan M, et al. Histochemical demonstration of copper-associated protein in the canine liver. Veterinary Pathology 1985; 22: 327-332.

33. Center SA. Chronic liver diseases. In: Guilford WG, Center SA, Strombeck DR, et al, eds. Strombeck's Small Animal Gastroenterology, 3rd ed. Philadelphia, PA: WB Saunders Co, 1996; 705-765.

34. Thornburg LP, Rottinghaus G, McGowan M, et al. Hepatic copper concentrations in purebred and mixed-breed dogs. Veterinary Pathology 1990; 27: 81-88.

35. Thornburg LP, Rottinghaus G, Dennis G, et al. The relationship between hepatic copper content and morphologic changes in the liver of West Highland white terriers. Veterinary Pathology 1996; 33: 656-661.

36. Thornburg LP, Polley D, Dimmit R. The pathogenesis of copper-associated liver disease in dogs. Canine Practice 1985; 12: 33-38.

37. Center SA. Hepatic vascular diseases. In: Guilford WG, Center SA, Strombeck DR, et al, eds. Strombeck's Small Animal Gastroenterology, 3rd ed. Philadelphia, PA: WB Saunders Co, 1996; 802-833.

38. Armstrong PJ, Weiss DJ, Gagne JM. Inflammatory liver disease. In: August JR, ed. Consultations in Feline Internal Medicine 3. Philadelphia, PA: WB Saunders Co, 1997; 68-78.

39. Short CR. Drug disposition in neonatal animals. Journal of the American Veterinary Medical Association 1984; 184: 1161-1162.

40. McCullough AJ, Tavill AS. Disordered energy and protein metabolism in liver disease. Seminars in Liver Disease 1991; 11: 265-277.

41. Latfi R, Killam RW, Dudrick SJ. Nutritional support in liver failure. Surgical Clinics of North America 1991; 71: 567-578.

42. Bauer JE. Nutrition and liver function: Nutrient metabolism in health and disease. Compendium on Continuing Education for the Practicing Veterinarian 1986; 8: 923-931.

43. Bauer JE. Hepatic disease, nutritional therapy, and the metabolic environment. Journal of the American Veterinary Medical Association 1996; 209: 1850-1854.

44. Chang EB, Sitrin MD, Black DB. Gastrointestinal, Hepatobiliary, and Nutritional Physiology. Philadelphia, PA: Lippincott-Raven Publishers, 1996; 245-263.

45. Owen OE, Reichle FA, Mozzoli MA, et al. Hepatic, gut, and renal substrate flux rates in patients with hepatic cirrhosis. Journal of Clinical Investigation 1981; 68: 240-252.

46. Zakim D. Metabolism of glucose and fatty acids by the liver. In: Zakim D, Boyer TD, eds. Hepatology: A Textbook of Liver Disease, 2nd ed. Philadelphia, PA: WB Saunders Co, 1982; 65-96.

47. Gross TL, Ihrke PJ, Walder EJ. Superficial necrolytic dermatitis. Veterinary Dermatopathology. St Louis, MO: Mosby-Year Book, 1992; 46-48.

48. Skeie B, Kvetan V, Gil KM, et al. Branch-chain amino acids: Their metabolism and clinical utility. Critical Care Medicine 1990; 18: 549-571.

49. Dimski DS. Ammonia metabolism and the urea cycle: Function and clinical implications. Journal of Veterinary Internal Medicine 1994; 8: 73-78.

50. Strombeck DR, Rogers QR. Plasma amino acid concentrations in dogs with hepatic disease. Journal of the American Veterinary Medical Association 1978; 173: 93-96.

51. Strombeck DR, Harrold D, Rogers QR, et al. Plasma amino acids, glucagon, and insulin concentrations in dogs with nitrosamine-induced hepatic disease. American Journal of Veterinary Research 1983; 44: 2028-2036.

52. Strombeck DR, Harrold D, Rogers QR. Effects of catecholamines and ammonia on plasma and brain amino acids in dogs. American Journal of Physiology 1984; 247: E276-E283.

53. Rutgers C, Stradley RP, Rogers WA. Plasma amino acid analysis in dogs with experimentally induced hepatocellular and obstructive jaundice. American Journal of Veterinary Research 1987; 48: 696-702.

54. Aguirre A, Yoshimura N, Westman T, et al. Plasma amino acid concentrations in dogs with two experimental forms of liver damage. Journal of Surgical Research 1974; 16: 339-345.

55. Fischer JE, Funovics JM, Aguirre A, et al. The role of plasma amino acids in hepatic encephalopathy. Surgery 1975; 78: 276-290.

56. Maddison JE. Hepatic encephalopathy: Current concepts of the pathogenesis. Journal of Veterinary Internal Medicine 1992; 6: 341-353.

57. Biourge V, MacDonald MJ, King L. Feline hepatic lipidosis: Pathogenesis and nutritional management. Compendium on Continuing Education for the Practicing Veterinarian 1990; 12: 1244-1258.

58. Biourge V, Pion P, Lewis J, et al. Spontaneous occurrence of hepatic lipidosis in a group of laboratory cats. Journal of Veterinary Internal Medicine 1993; 7: 194-197.

59. Center SA, Crawford MA, Guida L, et al. A retrospective study of 77 cats with severe hepatic lipidosis: 1975-1990. Journal of Veterinary Internal Medicine 1993; 7: 349-359.

60. Cornelius LM, Jacobs G. Feline hepatic lipidosis. In: Kirk RW, ed. Current Veterinary Therapy X. Philadelphia, PA: WB Saunders Co, 1989; 869-873.

61. Dimski DS, Taboada J. Feline idiopathic hepatic lipidosis. Veterinary Clinics of North America: Small Animal Practice 1995; 25: 357-373.

62. Center SA. Hepatic lipidosis, glucocorticoid hepatopathy, vacuolar hepatopathy, storage disorders, amyloidosis and iron toxicity. In: Guilford WG, Center SA, Strombeck DR, et al, eds. Strombeck's Small Animal Gastroenterology, 3rd ed. Philadelphia, PA: WB Saunders Co, 1996; 766-782.

63. Biourge V, Groff JM, Fisher C, et al. Nitrogen balance, plasma free amino acid concentrations and urinary orotic acid excretion during long-term fasting in cats. Journal of Nutrition 1994; 124: 1094-1103.

64. Biourge V, Massat B, Groff JM, et al. Effects of protein, lipid, or carbohydrate supplementation on hepatic lipid accumulation during rapid weight loss in obese cats. American Journal of Veterinary Research 1994; 55: 1406-1415.

65. Hultgren BD, Stevens JB, Hardy RM. Inherited, chronic, progressive hepatic degeneration in Bedlington terriers with increased copper concentrations: Clinical and pathologic observations and comparison with other copper-associated liver diseases. American Journal of Veterinary Research 1986; 47: 365-377.

66. Su L-C, Ravanshad S, Owens CA, et al. A comparison of copper-loading disease in Bedlington terriers and Wilson's disease in humans. American Journal of Physiology 1982; 243: G226-G230.

67. Su L-C, Owens CA, Zollman PE, et al. A defect of biliary excretion in copper-laden Bedlington terriers. American Journal of Physiology 1982; 243: G231-G236.

68. Yuzbasiyian-Gurkan V, Blanton SH, Cao Y, et al. Linkage of a microsatellite marker to the canine copper toxicosis locus in Bedlington terriers. American Journal of Veterinary Research 1997; 58: 23-27.

69. Twedt DC, Sternlieb I, Gilbertson SR. Clinical, morphologic and chemical studies on copper toxicosis of Bedlington terriers. Journal of the American Veterinary Medical Association 1979; 175: 269-275.

70. Twedt DC. Copper hepatotoxicity in dogs: Pathophysiology, diagnosis and therapy. In: Proceedings. Ninth Annual Veterinary Medical Forum, American College of Veterinary Internal Medicine, Washington, DC, 1990: 169-172.

71. Sokol RJ, Deveraux MW, O'Brien K, et al. Abnormal hepatic mitochondrial respiration and cytochrome C oxidase activity in rats with long-term copper overload. Gastroenterology 1993; 105: 178-187.

72. Sokol RJ, Twedt DC, McKim JM, et al. Oxidant injury to hepatic mitochondria in patients with Wilson's disease and Bedlington terriers with copper toxicosis. Gastroenterology 1994; 107: 1788-1798.

73. Rolfe DS, Twedt DC. Copper-associated hepatopathies in dogs. Veterinary Clinics of North America: Small Animal Practice 1995; 25: 399-417.

74. Thornburg LP, Rottinghaus G, Koch J, et al. High liver copper levels in two Doberman pinschers with sub-acute hepatitis. Journal of the American Animal Hospital Association 1984; 20: 1003-1005.

75. Thornburg LP, Shaw D, Dolan M, et al. Hereditary copper toxicosis in West Highland white terriers. Veterinary Pathology 1986; 23: 148-154.

76. Haywood S, Rutgers HC, Christian MK. Hepatitis and copper accumulation in Skye terriers. Veterinary Pathology 1988; 25: 408-414.

77. Johnson GF, Zawie DA, Gilbertson SR, et al. Chronic active hepatitis in Doberman pinschers. Journal of the American Veterinary Medical Association 1982; 180: 1438-1442.

78. Thornburg LP. Histomorphological and immunohistochemical studies of chronic active hepatitis in Doberman pinschers. Veterinary Pathology 1998; 35: 380-385.

79. Speeti M, Eriksson J, Saari S, et al. Lesions of subclinical Doberman hepatitis. Veterinary Pathology 1998; 35: 361-369.

80. Weiss DJ, Armstrong PJ, Mruthyunjaya A. Anti-liver membrane protein antibodies in dogs with chronic hepatitis. Journal of Veterinary Internal Medicine 1995; 9: 267-271.

81. Andersson M, Sevelius E. Circulating autoantibodies in dogs with chronic liver disease. Journal of Small Animal Practice 1992; 33: 389-394.

82. Malagelada JR, Pihl O, Linscher WG. Impaired absorption of micellar long chain fatty acids in patients with alcoholic cirrhosis. American Journal of Digestive Diseases 1974; 19: 1016-1020.

83. Lee SP, Lai KS. Exocrine pancreatic function in hepatic cirrhosis. American Journal of Gastroenterology 1976; 65: 244-248.

84. Day DG. Feline cholangiohepatitis complex. Veterinary Clinics of North America: Small Animal Practice 1995; 25: 375-385.

85. Johnson SE. Portal hypertension. Part I. Pathophysiology and clinical consequences. Compendium on Continuing Education for the Practicing Veterinarian 1987; 9: 741-748.

86. Martin P-Y, Gines P, Schrier RW. Nitric oxide as a mediator of hemodynamic abnormalities and sodium and water retention in cirrhosis. New England Journal of Medicine 1998; 339: 533-541.

87. Center SA. Diseases of the gallbladder and biliary tree. In: Guilford WG, Center SA, Strombeck DR, et al, eds. Strombeck's Small Animal Gastroenterology, 3rd ed. Philadelphia, PA: WB Saunders Co, 1996; 860-888.

88. Biourge V. Nutrition and liver disease. Seminars in Veterinary Medicine and Surgery: Small Animal 1997; 12: 34-44.

89. Marks SL, Rogers QR, Strombeck DR. Nutritional support in hepatic disease. Part II. Dietary management of common liver disorders in dogs and cats. Compendium on Continuing Education for the Practicing Veterinarian 1994; 16: 1287-1295.

90. Barsanti J, Jones B, Spano J, et al. Prolonged anorexia associated with hepatic lipidosis in three cats. Feline Practice 1977; 7: 52-57.

91. Jacobs G, Cornelius L, Keene B, et al. Comparison of plasma, liver, and skeletal muscle carnitine concentrations in cats with idiopathic hepatic lipidosis and in healthy cats. American Journal of Veterinary Research 1990; 51: 1349-1351.

92. Armstrong PJ, Hardie EM, Cullen JM, et al. L-carnitine reduces hepatic fat accumulation during rapid weight reduction in cats (abstract). In: Proceedings. Tenth Annual Veterinary Medical Forum, American College of Veterinary Internal Medicine, San Diego, CA, 1992: 810.

93. Center SA, Reynolds AP, Harte J, et al. Metabolic influence of oral L-carnitine during a rapid 18-week weight loss program in obese cats (abstract). In: Proceedings. Fifteenth Annual Veterinary Medical Forum, American College of Veterinary Internal Medicine, Lake Buena Vista, FL, 1997: 665.

94. Center SA, Reynolds AP, Harte J, et al. Clinical effects of rapid weight loss in obese pet cats with and without supplemental L-carnitine (abstract). In: Proceedings. Fifteenth Annual Veterinary Medical Forum, American College of Veterinary Internal Medicine, Lake Buena Vista, FL, 1997: 665.

95. National Research Council. Nutrient Requirements of Dogs. Washington, DC: National Academy Press, 1985.

96. Association of American Feed Control Officials. Official Publication, 1999.

97. Brewer GJ, Schall WD, Padgett GA, et al. The role of genetic and dietary factors in zinc therapy in copper toxicosis in dogs. Morris Animal Foundation Progress Report, September 1989.

98. Twedt DC, Hunsaker HA, Allen KGD. Use of 2,3,2-tetramine as a hepatic copper chelating agent for treatment of copper hepatotoxicosis in Bedlington terriers. Journal of the American Veterinary Medical Association 1988; 92: 52-58.

99. Brewer GJ, Dick RD, Schall W, et al. Use of zinc acetate to treat copper toxicosis in dogs. Journal of the American Veterinary Medical Association 1992; 201: 564-568.

100. Brewer GJ. Zinc in the treatment of Wilson's disease: How it works (Letter to the Editor). Gastroenterology 1993; 104: 1568.

101. Friedman LS. Zinc in the treatment of Wilson's disease: How it works (Letter to the Editor). Gastroenterology 1993; 104: 1568.

102. Yuzbasiyian-Gurkan V, Grider A, Nostrant T, et al. Treatment of Wilson's disease with zinc: X. Intestinal metallothionein induction. Laboratory Clinical Medicine 1992; 120: 380-386.

103. Zieve L, Zieve FJ. The dietary prevention of hepatic coma in Eck fistula dogs: Ammonia and the carbohydrate to protein ratio. Hepatology 1987; 7: 196-198.

104. Laflamme DP, Allen SW, Huber TL. Apparent dietary protein requirement of dogs with portosystemic shunt. American Journal of Veterinary Research 1993; 54: 719-723.

105. Uribe M. Treatment of portal systemic encephalopathy: The old and new treatments. In: Grisolia S, ed. Cirrhosis, Hepatic Encephalopathy, and Ammonium Toxicity. New York, NY: Plenum Press, 1990; 235-253.

106. Bianchi GP, Marchesini G, Fabbri A, et al. Vegetable versus animal protein diet in cirrhotic patients with chronic encephalopathy: A random crossover comparison. Journal of Internal Medicine 1993; 233: 385-392.

107. Weber FL, Minco D, Fresard KM, et al. Effects of vegetable diets on nitrogen metabolism in cirrhotic subjects. Gastroenterology 1985; 89: 538-544.

108. Thompson JSD, Schafer DR, Haun J, et al. Adequate diet prevents hepatic coma in dogs with Eck fistulas. Surgical Gynecology and Obstetrics 1986; 162: 126-130.

LIVER DISEASE

109. Schaeffer MC, Rogers QR, Buffington CA, et al. Long-term biochemical and physiologic effects of surgically placed portosystemic shunts in dogs. American Journal of Veterinary Research 1986; 47: 346-355.

110. Meyer HP. Chronic hepatic encephalopathy: Studies into the pathogenesis and treatment in the dog. PhD Thesis. State University of Utrecht, The Netherlands, 1998.

111. Morgan MY. Branched chain amino acids in the management of chronic liver disease: Facts and fantasies. Journal of Hepatology 1990; 11: 133-141.

112. Ericksson LS, Conn HO. Branched-chain amino acids in the management of hepatic encephalopathy: An analysis of variants. Hepatology 1989; 10: 228-246.

113. Naylor CD, O'Rourke K, Detsky AS, et al. Parenteral nutrition with branched-chain amino acids in hepatic encephalopathy: A meta-analysis. Gastroenterology 1989; 97: 1033-1042.

114. Scalfani L, Shimm P, Edelman J, et al. Protective effect of vitamin E in rats with acute liver injury. Journal of Parenteral and Enteral Nutrition 1986; 10: 184-187.

115. Linscher WG. Metabolism in cirrhosis. American Journal of Clinical Nutrition 1979; 23: 488-492.

116. Guilford WG. Nutritional management of gastrointestinal diseases. In: Guilford WG, Center SA, Strombeck DR, et al, eds. Strombeck's Small Animal Gastroenterology, 3rd ed. Philadelphia, PA: WB Saunders Co, 1996; 889-910.

117. Munoz SJ. Nutritional therapies in liver disease. Seminars in Liver Disease 1991; 11: 278-291.

118. Riggio O, Merli M, Capocaccia L. The role of zinc in the management of hepatic encephalopathy. In: Bengtsson F, Jeppsson F, eds. Progress in Hepatic Encephalopathy. Boca Raton, FL: CRC Press Inc, 1991; 303-312.

119. Mullen KD, Weber FL. Role of nutrition in hepatic encephalopathy. Seminars in Liver Disease 1991; 11: 292-304.

120. Leevy CM, Thompson A, Baker H. Vitamins and liver injury. American Journal of Clinical Nutrition 1982; 35: 56-72.

121. Michel KE. Nutritional management of liver disease. Veterinary Clinics of North America: Small Animal Practice 1995; 25: 485-501.

122. Wilson JD. Androgens. In: Goodman LS, Gillman A, Rall TW, et al, eds. The Pharmacological Basis of Therapeutics, 8th ed. New York, NY: Pergamon Press, 1990; 1413-1430.

123. Swart GR, Zillikens MC, van Vuure JK, et al. Effect of a late evening meal on nitrogen balance in patients with cirrhosis of the liver. British Medical Journal 1989; 299: 1202-1203.

124. Hardy RM. Hepatic encephalopathy. In: Kirk RW, Bonagura JD, eds. Current Veterinary Therapy XI. Philadelphia, PA: WB Saunders Co, 1992; 639-645.

125. Weber FL Jr, Fresard KM, Lally BR. Effects of lactulose and neomycin on urea metabolism in cirrhotic subjects. Gastroenterology 1982; 82: 213-217.

126. Jaffe I, Altman K, Merryman P. The antipyridoxine effects of penicillamine in man. Journal of Clinical Investigation 1964; 43: 1869-1873.

127. Allen KGD, Twedt DC, Hunsaker HA. Tetramine cupruretic agents: A comparison in dogs. American Journal of Veterinary Research 1987; 48: 28-30.

CASE 23-1

Intermittent Vomiting in a Miniature Schnauzer

Deborah J. Davenport, DVM, MS
Diplomate ACVIM (Internal Medicine)
Hill's Science and Technology Center
Topeka, Kansas, USA

Assess the Animal

A three-and-one-half-year-old, neutered female miniature schnauzer was examined for a two-year course of intermittent vomiting. The vomitus rarely contained food and was usually described as a yellow or clear fluid. No diarrhea had been noted. The owners reported that the dog became depressed and lethargic during these vomiting episodes. Antiemetic treatment by another veterinarian had partially controlled the vomiting. Laboratory evaluation, abdominal radiographs and gastrointestinal (GI) contrast radiography four and six months before admission revealed no abnormalities.

Physical examination revealed a thin, nervous dog (body condition score [BCS] 1/5; body weight 7.1 kg). No other abnormalities were noted (Figure 1).

A complete blood count revealed erythrocyte microcytosis (i.e., decreased mean corpuscular volume) without hypochromia or anemia. Abnormal results of a serum biochemistry profile included a low serum urea nitrogen level (7 mg/dl, normal 10 to 25 mg/dl), hypoproteinemia (total protein 5.9 g/dl, normal 6.0 to 7.2 g/dl), hypoalbuminemia (2.4 g/dl, normal 3.0 to 4.5 g/dl) and mildly increased alkaline phosphatase activity (125 IU/l, normal 10 to 75 IU/l). Bilirubinuria and many ammonium biurate crystals were found on urinalysis. The stomach appeared cranially displaced on abdominal radiographs, which suggested microhepatica (small liver).

The clinical, laboratory and radiographic changes suggested the presence of a portosystemic shunt. An ammonia tolerance test demonstrated elevated baseline and challenge blood ammonia levels. In an effort to confirm and categorize the type of portosystemic shunting, splenoportography and cranial mesenteric angiography were performed. Contrast medium was injected into a mesenteric vein and into the splenic pulp. Both injections demonstrated a single large shunt between the portal system and the caudal vena cava external to the liver (Figure 2). Only

Figure 1. A three-and-one-half-year-old, neutered female miniature schnauzer with chief complaints of intermittent vomiting, depression and lethargy with weight loss and poor body condition.

minimal circulation within the liver was demonstrated. The final diagnosis was a portocaval shunt with intermittent episodes of hepatic encephalopathy.

Surgical ligation of the shunt was recommended based on detectable hepatic portal blood flow and the extrahepatic location of the portocaval anastomosis. At the owners' request, the procedure was scheduled for three weeks later.

Assess the Food(s) and Feeding Method

Several dietary changes had been made over the past two years in an effort to control the intermittent vomiting. The most recent food was a commercial dry veterinary therapeutic food for GI problems (Prescription Diet Canine i/d[a]). This food was offered in multiple small meals throughout the day.

Questions

1. What are the key nutritional factors to consider for this dog during the next three weeks?
2. Outline a treatment and feeding plan for this patient before surgery.

Answers and Discussion

1. Key nutritional factors to consider in animals with portosystemic shunts include energy, protein and carbohydrate. Providing adequate daily energy intake is the cornerstone of successful medical management of dogs with hepatobiliary disease, especially underweight animals such as this patient. With respect to protein, the goal is to provide adequate dietary protein to support hepatic regeneration while avoiding excess that might contribute to hepatic encephalopathy. The amount of protein needed by patients with portosystemic vascular shunts has been roughly estimated from a study in dogs with surgically created shunts. This study showed that ingestion of 2.11 g crude protein/kg body weight/day with an 80% or greater availability is adequate to maintain body protein reserves without producing hepatic encephalopathy. The protein should be high quality (i.e., high biologic value) and easily assimilated. Feeding a food with a high carbohydrate to protein component was shown to be advantageous to dogs with experimentally created shunts.

2. A commercial or homemade food that avoids excess dietary protein while providing adequate non-protein calories from fat and carbohydrate is recommended. Foods formulated for renal failure and liver patients generally meet these criteria. The daily energy requirement (DER) should be initially calculated at 1.2 to 1.4 x resting energy requirement (RER) for the estimated ideal body weight (10 kg). Administration of nonabsorbable disaccharides (e.g., lactulose) is also recommended in patients with hepatic encephalopathy. Colonic bacteria hydrolyze lactulose to lactic and acetic acids. Lactulose seems beneficial for several reasons. It: 1) lowers colonic pH with subsequent trapping of ammonium ions, 2) inhibits ammonia generation by colonic bacteria and 3) increases intestinal transit rate via cathartic properties. Neomycin and other aminoglycoside antibiotics can also be used to decrease ammonia production by inhibiting intestinal bacteria.

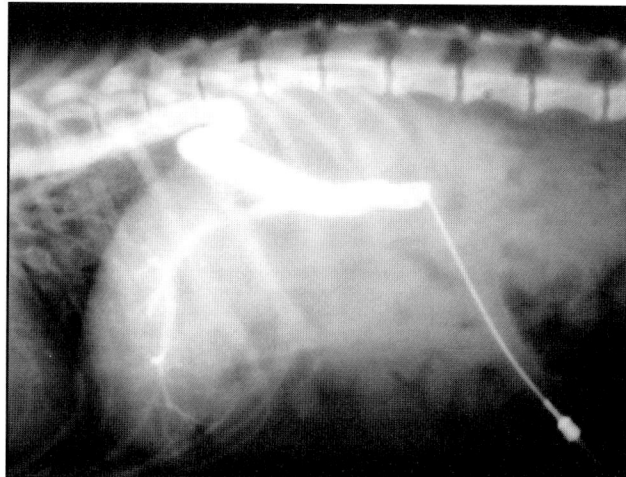

Figure 2. A lateral radiograph showing the results of an injection of positive-contrast medium into a mesenteric vein. A large vascular shunt is communicating from the portal vasculature to the caudal vena cava.

Progress Notes

The food was changed to a commercial dry veterinary therapeutic product (Prescription Diet Canine k/d[a]) that contained reduced levels of high-quality and easily digested protein while providing a good source of non-protein calories (14.6% dry matter [DM] protein, 19.5% DM fat, 61.5% DM soluble carbohydrate). DER was calculated to be 1.2 x RER for an estimated optimal body weight of 10 kg (DER = 440 kcal [1.84 MJ]). The food was to be offered in at least three separate meals throughout the day. Additional therapy consisted of oral lactulose syrup[b] (10 ml, three times daily).

Three weeks later, the dog had gained 1.2 kg body weight. The owners reported a marked decrease in the number of vomiting episodes and periods of lethargy and depression. No new physical findings were noted. The hypoproteinemia, hypoalbuminemia and ammonium biurate crystalluria persisted. Results of clotting studies done before surgery were normal. During surgery, an anastomotic vessel was easily visualized at the level of the right kidney. This vessel was partially ligated. The dog was released from the hospital five days later with instructions for the owners to continue feeding the veterinary therapeutic food and administering lactulose, as described before surgery.

The dog was reassessed one month later. Body weight had increased to 8.6 kg, the BCS was 2/5 and the owners reported no episodes of malaise or vomiting. The serum urea nitrogen, total protein and albumin concentrations were normal, and ammonium biurate crystals were absent from the urine. Abdominal radiographs showed an increase in liver size. Because of the apparent return of normal hepatic function and size, the owners were instructed to change the food to a regular adult maintenance product (25% DM protein, 15.4% DM fat, 53.3% DM soluble carbohydrate) and discontinue the lactulose. The food dosage was continued at 1.2 x RER (440 kcal [1.84 MJ]).

Five months later the dog was examined again. Body weight was 10 kg with a BCS of 3/5. The owners reported that the higher protein food had not precipitated any clinical signs. No changes in food(s) or feeding methods were recommended.

Endnotes

a. Hill's Pet Nutrition, Inc., Topeka, KS, USA.
b. Cholac. Alra Laboratories, Gurnee, IL, USA.

Bibliography

Center SA. Hepatic vascular diseases. In: Guilford WG, Center SA, Strombeck DR, et al, eds. Strombeck's Small Animal Gastroenterology, 3rd ed. Philadelphia, PA: WB Saunders Co, 1996; 802-846.

Laflamme DP, Allen SW, Huber TL. Apparent dietary protein requirement of dogs with portosystemic shunt. American Journal of Veterinary Research 1993; 554: 719-723.

■ CASE 23-2

Vomiting in a Miniature Poodle

Philip Roudebush, DVM
Diplomate ACVIM (Internal Medicine)
Hill's Science and Technology Center
Topeka, Kansas, USA

Assess the Animal

A seven-year-old male miniature poodle was examined for lethargy, excessive panting, elevated liver enzyme activity and intermittent vomiting of six weeks' duration. The vomitus was usually yellow foam or partially digested food. Elevated liver enzyme activity was noted on laboratory work obtained by the referring veterinarian (Table 1, Days 0 and 12). A two-week course of oral amoxicillin failed to improve the patient's problems. The dog received a single 2-mg intramuscular injection of triamcinolone[a] for generalized pruritus. The lethargy, panting and vomiting were first noted shortly thereafter.

Physical examination revealed a bright, alert dog that weighed 5 kg, appeared slightly overweight (body condition score [BCS] 4/5) and panted continuously. Other findings included a few subcutaneous lipomas, mild periodontal disease, hepatomegaly, bilateral lenticular sclerosis, right patellar luxation and no evidence of testicles in the scrotum. The owners were given the dog as a young puppy and denied that it had been castrated.

Evaluation of these problems included a complete blood count (mild leukocytosis), heartworm check (negative), serum biochemistry profile (normal except for elevated liver enzyme activity [Table 1, Day 19]), urinalysis (normal), fecal flotation (hookworms) and abdominal radiographs. Survey abdominal radiographs revealed an extremely enlarged liver that displaced the axis of the stomach dorsocaudally and displaced the small bowel caudally. A positive-contrast gastrointestinal (GI) series using barium demonstrated a segment of terminal jejunum or ileum with an abnormal mucosal pattern. The prothrombin time and activated partial thromboplastin time were normal. Examination of a fine-needle aspirate of the liver revealed vacuolar changes in hepatocytes consistent with steroid hepatopathy. An anthelmintic was administered for the hookworm infection.

The dog was reexamined one week later for an ACTH response test with determination of resting and post-ACTH plasma cortisol concentrations. An exploratory celiotomy was also planned to obtain liver and intestinal biopsy specimens and remove the retained testicles.

The resting cortisol concentration was subnormal and failed to increase after intramuscular administration of ACTH gel (Table 1, Day 19). During surgery, a diffusely enlarged, pale liver with rounded margins was noted; biopsy specimens were obtained from the liver, distal small intestine and colon; the retained testicles were identified and removed. Histopathologic examination of these specimens revealed diffuse testicular atrophy, normal intestinal structure except for mild dilatation of lacteals and multifocal hepatic vacuolar change consistent with steroid hepatopathy.

The tentative diagnosis was secondary hypoadrenocorticism and hepatopathy associated with parenteral administration of corticosteroids.

Assess the Food(s) and Feeding Method

The dog was normally fed a combination of commercial grocery brand moist dog food mixed with broiled chicken and cottage cheese. The commercial food and table food were mixed in approximately a 50:50 ratio. An unspecified amount of this mixture was offered twice daily. The dog preferred to drink either ice water or ice tea.

Questions

1. What are the key nutritional factors to consider for this patient?
2. Outline a feeding plan for this dog including food(s) and feeding method.
3. What other therapy should be considered?
4. How should this dog be monitored for response to therapy?

Answers and Discussion

1. The key nutritional factors for patients with mild to moderate hepatic disease expected to be self-limiting include energy, protein and fat. The food should con-

Table 1. Laboratory data from a miniature poodle with steroid hepatopathy.

Parameters	Day 0	Day 12	Day 19	Day 56	Day 110	Day 142	Day 214	Reference values
Alkaline phosphatase (IU/l)	4,990	4,960	3,080	>400	313	106	26	10-80
Alanine aminotransferase (IU/l)	1,380	1,600	1,450	>500	184	236	45	10-70
Cortisol, resting (µg/dl)	na	na	0.3	<1.0	1.8	1.4	12.3	0.5-4.0
Cortisol, post ACTH (µg/dl)	na	na	0.5	<1.0	1.9	1.7	17.5	8.0-20.0

Key: na = information not available.

tain appropriate amounts of these key nutrients and other essential nutrients based on the animal's current lifestage. (See Chapter 9.) Dramatic changes are not necessary in the nutrient levels of food(s) for patients with mild to moderate hepatic disease and no evidence of hepatic failure, portosystemic vascular shunts, ascites or hepatic encephalopathy.

2. A commercial dog food formulated for older dogs (i.e., senior or geriatric food) would be appropriate for this patient. Such a food would be more balanced and avoid the probable excess protein and fat provided by the current diet of 50% moist commercial grocery brand food and 50% chicken and cottage cheese. The daily energy requirement (DER) should be calculated to maintain current body weight until the liver disease has resolved. The food and water should be offered in multiple small meals throughout the day to help control nausea and vomiting.

3. Antibiotics can be used for a short time after surgery to prevent bacterial infection. Physiologic doses of oral hydrocortisone may be given to alleviate glucocorticoid deficiency (and control clinical signs such as lethargy and vomiting) while not exacerbating the liver disease. The patient should also avoid stressful environmental situations because it cannot respond normally to these events.

4. Serum liver enzyme activity and plasma cortisol concentrations (resting and post-ACTH) should be monitored every two months until they return to normal. The clinical signs of lethargy, vomiting and hepatomegaly should resolve as biochemical parameters improve.

Progress Notes

The dog made an uneventful recovery from surgery and was discharged to the owners' care three days later. Oral ampicillin was started before surgery and continued for 10 days. Other than the single triamcinolone injection, no other sources of exogenous corticosteroids were identified.

In the hospital, the dog began eating a moist specialty brand dog food formulated for senior dogs (Science Diet Canine Senior[b]). This food was nutritionally balanced compared with the combination of commercial dog food, chicken and cottage cheese offered at home. The DER was estimated to be 1.2 to 1.4 x resting energy requirement (RER) for an ideal weight of 4.5 kg (250 to 290 kcal [1.0 to 1.2 MJ]; two-thirds to three-fourths can daily). The food was offered in small frequent meals throughout the day. The owners were also instructed to add water to the food or warm the food in a microwave oven if it was necessary to encourage acceptance.

No other treatment was given because the secondary hypoadrenocorticism and steroid hepatopathy were expected to resolve as the effects of the injectable triamcinolone decreased over the next several months. Recheck examinations over the next six months documented clinical improvement and gradual reduction in liver enzyme activity (Table 1, Days 56 to 214). Plasma cortisol concentrations returned to near normal by Day 214. The dog remained normal for the next three years before it died from complications of immune-mediated thrombocytopenia.

Endnotes

a. Vetalog Parenteral. Solvay Animal Health, Mendota Heights, MN, USA.
b. Hill's Pet Nutrition, Inc., Topeka, KS, USA.

Bibliography

Center SA. Vacuolar hepatopathy/glucocorticoid hepatopathy. In: Guilford WG, Center SA, Strombeck DR, et al, eds. Strombeck's Small Animal Gastroenterology, 3rd ed. Philadelphia, PA: WB Saunders Co, 1996; 782-788.

CASE 23-3

Anorexia and Icterus in a Domestic Shorthair Cat

Rebecca L. Remillard, PhD, DVM
Diplomate ACVN
Angell Memorial Animal Hospital
Boston, Massachusetts, USA

Assess the Animal

A six-year-old neutered female domestic shorthair cat was referred for a one-month history of weight loss and a week-long history of vomiting, icterus and anorexia. The cat was kept exclusively indoors. The family had relocated to the state two months before the cat was presented to the referring veterinarian. The referring veterinarian treated the cat with intravenous fluids.

Physical examination revealed a depressed, cachectic cat (body weight 3.1 kg, body condition score [BCS] 1/5). The cat's mucous membranes, sclera, inner pinnae, lips and nose were icteric. Mild hepatomegaly was detected by abdominal palpation. Dehydration (approximately 5%)

Table 1. Laboratory data from a domestic shorthair cat with icterus.

Parameters	Day 1	Day 15	Reference values
Packed cell volume (%)	27.5	31.7	30-45
Hemoglobin (g/dl)	9.2	10	10-15
Glucose (mg/dl)	150	89	70-110
Total protein (g/dl)	5.9	7.2	6.5-7.7
Albumin (g/dl)	2.2	2.4	2.5-4.0
Alanine aminotransferase (IU/l)	264	80	10-33
Alkaline phosphatase (IU/l)	110	45	14-43

was evident based on abnormal skin turgor and tacky mucous membranes.

Results of a complete blood count were consistent with a stress leukogram and mild microcytic normochromic anemia. Results of a serum biochemistry profile included hyperbilirubinemia, elevated liver enzyme activities, mild hyperglycemia, hypoproteinemia, hypoalbuminemia and mild hypokalemia (Table 1). Urinalysis results were normal except for marked bilirubinuria. A blood coagulation profile revealed slightly prolonged prothrombin time (13.4 seconds, normal 8.5 to 10.5 seconds). Vitamin K_1 therapy was started (phytonadione, 5 mg/kg body weight, subcutaneously, q12h).

Ultrasonographic evaluation of the liver revealed hepatomegaly with a diffuse increase in echogenicity and no evidence of intrahepatic masses. Hepatic tissue was obtained by ultrasonographic-guided needle biopsy. The hepatic tissue was brown, soft and floated in 10% formalin. Cytologic evaluation revealed an increased number of bile casts, increased amount of bilirubin within hepatocytes and all hepatocytes contained vacuoles filled with lipid. These findings were interpreted as hepatocyte lipid accumulation and cholestasis. Histopathologic evaluation of the liver specimen revealed similar changes. Bacterial culture of a portion of the liver biopsy specimen was negative. A diagnosis of feline hepatic lipidosis was made.

Assess the Food(s) and Feeding Method

Historically, since the cat was neutered at nine months of age, it had been slightly overweight (BCS 4/5). Therefore, for several years the cat had been fed a dry commercial specialty brand food with a reduced caloric density (Science Diet Feline Maintenance Light[a]). The food was offered free choice. The exact amount of food consumed by the cat over the last month was unknown but markedly less than normal. A 4-lb bag of food usually lasted a month, but the owners had not purchased a new bag within the last two months. During the past week, the referring veterinarian had been giving vitamin-B supplements and force feeding an unknown amount of a commercial recovery food (Prescription Diet Canine/Feline a/d[a]) per os. The cat was still vomiting three to four times per day.

Questions

1. Outline an appropriate fluid and feeding plan (food, amount and method of administration) for this cat.
2. In addition to the fluid and feeding plan, what other medical therapy may be appropriate for cats with idiopathic hepatic lipidosis?
3. How should the patient's response to therapy be monitored?

Answers and Discussion

1. Severe dehydration and electrolyte and acid-base disturbances should be corrected with appropriate parenteral fluid therapy before initiating the feeding plan. The single most effective means of treating feline patients with hepatic lipidosis is providing fluid and nutritional support with assisted feeding. This is most easily accomplished using liquid foods administered through a nasoesophageal tube or homogenized/blended foods administered by gastrostomy tube. (See Chapter 12.) These tubes are well tolerated by cats and help ensure adequate caloric intake and, if necessary, owners can continue feeding the cat at home. A variety of commercial liquid and blended enteral products have been used successfully in patients with hepatic lipidosis.

   Energy requirements, and therefore the daily amount of food, should be calculated to meet the resting energy requirement (RER) for the cat's current body weight. The amount of food should be divided into multiple small feedings (four to six meals daily). Most cats can initially tolerate at least 30-ml bolus feedings and can be given 50- to 80-ml meals after a few days of refeeding. However, vomiting cats, especially those that have not eaten for weeks, may not tolerate bolus feedings initially, but will tolerate continuous rate infusion of a liquid food.

   Vitamin K_1 therapy should be used in cats with abnormal coagulation tests. Some clinical investigators have advocated L-carnitine supplementation for improving recovery based on results in experimental models of feline hepatic lipidosis. At the present time there are no clinical studies demonstrating the effectiveness of carnitine supplementation in cats with naturally occurring disease.

2. Vomiting is a common complication of enteral feeding in cats and can be managed with antiemetic drugs given 15 to 30 minutes before each feeding. Cats with hepatic lipidosis rarely develop hepatic encephalopathy. If they do, lactulose, enemas and oral antibiotics may also be needed. Cats that do not eat voluntarily may be given appetite stimulants.

3. The amount of food given each day should be carefully recorded to ensure that an appropriate caloric intake is being achieved. Complications of tube feeding should be monitored. These include epiphora (nasoesophageal tubes), displacement of the tube, vomiting, diarrhea and infection at the site of gastrostomy tube placement. Clinical improvement in the hospital is marked by decreasing icterus, serum bilirubin concentrations, liver enzyme activities and improved activity and mental attitude. Long-term weight gain, improved body condition and a return of normal appetite indicate improvement. In general, one to three weeks of assisted feeding are necessary, but some patients may require three to seven months of tube feeding. Many patients can be managed at home until normal appetite returns. At home, food and water should be readily available and offered before each tube feeding. Decreasing the amount fed or discontinuing the number of daily tube feedings is recommended when the cat begins to show interest in food again. The feeding tube may be removed when the cat voluntarily consumes an amount equal to its RER for two to three consecutive days.

Progress Notes

An intravenous catheter and nasoesophageal tube were placed the day of hospital admission. The cat was given fluid and nutritional therapy concurrently with vitamin K_1 therapy as diagnostic procedures were performed. Because the cat was still vomiting three to four times per day, a liquid food (CliniCare Feline[b] containing 1 kcal [4.2 kJ]/ml) was given by continuous rate infusion. The cat's RER was 163 kcal (682 kJ)/day [70(3.1)$^{0.75}$]. Fluid requirements were 200 ml/day (3.1 x 60 ml/kg body weight + 5% + ongoing losses). Therefore, the cat initially received 163 ml of liquid food via nasoesophageal tube and 37 ml of Plasmalyte A (with 30 mEq KCl/l), intravenously per day. Dehydration and hypokalemia were corrected, and vomiting ceased by Day 2 of hospitalization. The cat tolerated the continuous rate infusion given by nasoesophageal tube, and its prothrombin time returned to within normal limits after four treatments with vitamin K_1.

A gastrostomy tube (G-tube) was placed on Day 3 of hospitalization. Twelve hours after the tube was placed, the cat began receiving 30-ml bolus feedings of a blended commercial veterinary recovery food (Prescription Diet Canine/Feline a/d) (2 cans plus 50 ml water = 1 kcal/ml). The cat had no problems with the G-tube or the blended food and was discharged to the owners' care on Day 4 with instructions to offer the cat food (Science Diet Feline Maintenance[a]) first and, if the cat did not voluntarily eat, to then feed 55 ml of the blended recovery food followed by a 12-ml water flush, three times daily. This feeding regimen provided the cat with 165 kcal (690 kJ) and 200 ml of water daily.

The owners returned with the cat 11 days later. The G-tube was in place, body weight was 3.3 kg and the cat was more alert with less intense icterus. A complete blood count showed no evidence of anemia. The serum biochemistry profile revealed normoglycemia, increased serum total protein and albumin concentrations and decreased serum total bilirubin concentration. The liver enzyme activities had almost returned to normal (Table 1). The cat was still not eating spontaneously; therefore, an appetite stimulant (cyproheptadine[c]) was prescribed (2 mg per os, twice daily). The cat continued to receive 80 ml of the blended food twice daily via the G-tube. The cat began eating the adult maintenance-type food spontaneously after four days of receiving the appetite stimulant. The G-tube was removed three days after the cat began eating voluntarily and the recommendation was made to continue feeding the maintenance-type food free choice until the cat achieved an ideal BCS (3/5) and body weight (approximately 5.0 kg). The owners were instructed to monitor the cat's appetite, body weight and body condition closely and, after the cat had achieved an optimal BCS, to change the feeding method from free choice to meal feeding a specific quantity of food (approximately one-fourth cup, twice daily) to maintain optimal body weight and condition.

Endnotes

a. Hill's Pet Nutrition Inc., Topeka, KS, USA.
b. Abbott Laboratories, North Chicago, IL, USA.
c. Periactin. Merck & Company, Inc., Rahway, NJ, USA.

Bibliography

Center SA, Crawford MA, Guida L, et al. A retrospective study of 77 cats with severe hepatic lipidosis: 1975-1990. Journal of Veterinary Internal Medicine 1993; 7: 349-359.

Center SA. Hepatic lipidosis. In: Guilford WG, Center SA, Strombeck DR, et al, eds. Strombeck's Small Animal Gastroenterology, 3rd ed. Philadelphia, PA: WB Saunders Co, 1996; 766-782.

CASE 23-4

Polyuria/Polydipsia in a Doberman Pinscher[a]

Philip Roudebush, DVM
Diplomate ACVIM (Internal Medicine)
Hill's Science and Technology Center
Topeka, Kansas, USA

Assess the Animal

A five-year-old neutered female Doberman pinscher was examined for polyuria and polydipsia. The dog's history was uneventful except for treatment of a recurrent interdigital cyst. Physical examination was normal. Body weight was 28.6 kg with a body condition score (BCS) of 3/5. The dog had weighed 32 kg during an examination five months earlier. Blood was obtained for a complete blood count and serum biochemistry profile. Urine was obtained for a urinalysis.

Results of the complete blood count were normal. Serum biochemistry profile abnormalities included elevated liver enzyme activity (Table 1, Day 1). Results of the urinalysis were normal except for dilute urine (specific gravity = 1.005). Radiographs of the abdomen were normal except for a small liver silhouette.

Liver specimens were obtained using an ultrasound-guided biopsy needle. Histopathologic changes were consistent with moderate, diffuse, subacute hepatitis. Most of the inflammatory cells were neutrophils and macrophages. Macrophages and some hepatocytes contained focal accumulation of granular pigment. Special stains were positive for accumulating copper, but the quantity of copper was not determined. Bacterial culture of one of the biopsy specimens recovered a coagulase-negative *Staphylococcus* species. This organism was considered normal flora or an opportunistic pathogen. The *Staphylococcus* spp was sensitive to most commonly available antibiotics except ampicillin.

Assess the Food(s) and Feeding Method

The dog was normally fed four cups of a dry specialty brand dog food (Iams Minichunks[b]) once daily in the evening.

Table 1. Body weight and selected laboratory values from a Doberman pinscher with hepatitis.

Parameters	Day 1	Day 49	Day 73	Day 108	Day 164	Day 288	Day 314	Day 350	Reference values
Body weight (kg)	28.6	28.4	27.3	30.5	30.5	30	29.5	na	na
Glucose (mg/dl)	101	120	95	109	85	132	114	155	60-115
Urea nitrogen (mg/dl)	6	2.5	5	10	5	4.1	3.3	11.6	10-25
Creatinine (mg/dl)	1.2	1.3	2.1	0.5	1.4	1	1	1	0.5-1.2
Total protein (g/dl)	6.4	6.9	6.6	6.6	7.4	6.8	6.7	na	5.5-7.2
Albumin (g/dl)	2.2	3.1	2.8	2.8	3	2.7	2.7	2.7	3.0-4.5
Total bilirubin (mg/dl)	0	1.2	2.3	0.4	0.4	0.4	0.2	0.4	0.0-0.6
Alkaline phosphatase (IU/l)	2,655	2,579	1,447	500	215	494	425	541	8.0-75
Alanine aminotransferase (IU/l)	1,080	707	747	417	158	115	136	155	6.0-70

Key: na = information not available.

Questions

1. What is the most likely diagnosis for this patient?
2. Outline an appropriate feeding plan for this dog.
3. In addition to the feeding plan, what other medical therapy is appropriate for this patient?
4. How should the response to therapy be monitored?

Answers and Discussion

1. Middle-aged female Doberman pinscher dogs may develop an aggressive form of chronic hepatitis. Affected dogs may present in fulminant hepatic failure, or the disorder may be detected early based on elevated serum enzyme activity found on routine screening biochemistry profiles. Dogs with advanced liver disease present with weight loss, anorexia, polydipsia/polyuria, icterus, ascites, bleeding tendencies, severe depression and/or signs of hepatic encephalopathy. Dogs presenting in reasonable condition when first examined survive longer. These dogs are typically bright and responsive, have minimal weight loss and do not have ascites or hepatic encephalopathy. Typical serum biochemistry findings include hypoalbuminemia, elevated liver enzyme activity, elevated fasting bile acid concentrations, prolonged coagulation tests and hyperbilirubinemia.

   Histopathologic features of chronic hepatitis in Doberman pinschers include variable degrees of degeneration and necrosis of periportal hepatocytes and mixed inflammatory cell infiltrates. Portal fibrosis may be mild to severe; hepatic cirrhosis occurs in severely affected dogs. The livers of affected dogs have moderately increased copper and increased iron concentrations. The role of copper in this disease is not understood but may be associated with cholestasis. Iron accumulation may be associated with hepatic necrosis, hemorrhage and inflammation. Excessive copper and iron accumulation may aggravate ongoing hepatic inflammation.

2. General recommendations for the nutritional management of patients with chronic hepatitis include feeding foods that are energy dense, contain adequate levels of potassium, avoid excess levels of protein, copper, iron, sodium and chloride and contain some fermentable fiber. These goals can be met with either commercial veterinary therapeutic or homemade foods. Highly palatable, energy-dense foods offered in multiple small meals throughout the day may help overcome the nausea and gastrointestinal (GI) complications often associated with liver disease.

3. Definitive medical management of dogs affected with chronic hepatitis is not well established. Medical therapy often includes antibiotics, antiinflammatory and immunosuppressive drugs (e.g., prednisone, azathioprine), choleretic or bile "altering" agents (e.g., ursodeoxycholic acid), vitamin E and other antioxidants, zinc supplementation and copper chelating agents (i.e., D-penicillamine, tetramine). Diuretics may be needed for patients with severe ascites. Hepatic encephalopathy should be treated with further reduced protein intake, oral antibiotics, lactulose and retention enemas (Table 23-11).

4. Patients with chronic hepatitis should be monitored frequently (i.e., every few months) with serial physical examinations, body weight and body condition determinations and serum biochemistry profiles that include measurement of albumin concentration and liver enzyme activity. The owner should also be encouraged to document the amount of food eaten daily. If treatment is successful, the dog will maintain body weight, body condition and serum albumin concentrations, have gradually reduced liver enzyme activity and remain alert and active. Serial liver biopsy specimens (i.e., every six to nine months) can also be used to monitor pathologic changes and quantify hepatic copper concentrations.

Progress Notes

The dog was given 500 mg cephalexin, per os, twice daily for the possible secondary bacterial hepatitis. The food was changed to a veterinary therapeutic food that avoids excess levels of protein, sodium, chloride, copper and iron (Prescription Diet Canine u/d[c]). The daily energy requirement (DER) was estimated to be 1.4 to 1.6 x resting energy requirement (RER) for an ideal body weight of 32 kg (DER = 1,440 to 1,650 kcal [6.02 to 6.90 MJ]). The DER was met by feeding 4 to 5 cups of dry Canine u/d daily.

Evaluation six and 10 weeks later revealed slightly reduced liver enzyme activity, continued weight loss and mild hyperbilirubinemia (Table 1, Days 49 and 73). The dog was alert and active but not eating well according to the owner. The dietary management was not changed, but more aggressive therapy for liver inflammation and copper accumulation was initiated. This therapy consisted of a bile altering agent (ursodeoxycholic acid, ursodiol[d], 300 mg per os, daily with food), prednisone (30 mg per os, once daily for two weeks and then 30 mg every other day), vitamin E (400 IU per os, daily) and zinc gluconate (100 mg elemental zinc per os, twice daily).

Further evaluation one month and three months later (Table 1, Days 108 and 164) revealed an alert, active dog that had gained weight. The owner reported that the dog seemed to be doing well. Dietary management and medical therapy were continued.

Eighteen weeks later (Day 288) the dog was examined for vomiting, diarrhea and fever. Two other dogs at home were also affected with the same clinical signs. Viral gastroenteritis was suspected. Liver enzyme activity remained increased but lower than the original values (Table 1, Day 288). A liver biopsy was recommended to assess the extent of hepatitis, fibrosis and copper accumulation but was declined by the owner. Therapy was not changed.

One month later, the dog was examined because the owner was concerned about weight loss. Mild weight loss was documented, but the dog's serum biochemistry parameters remained stable (Table 1, Day 314). Therapy was not changed. Five weeks later the dog was presented in a comatose state. Serum biochemistry parameters were not significantly changed from previous values (Table 1, Day 350); however, a resting blood ammonia concentration was elevated (367 μg/dl, normal 0 to 98 μg/dl). Hepatic encephalopathy was diagnosed. The dog was euthanatized at the owner's request.

Endnotes

a. Thanks to Dr. Roy L. Davis, Red Bridge Animal Clinic, Kansas City, MO, USA, for providing the information about this patient.

b. The Iams Co., Dayton, OH, USA.

c. Hill's Pet Nutrition Inc., Topeka, KS, USA.

d. Actigall. CibaGeneva Pharmaceuticals, Summit, NJ, USA.

Bibliography

Center SA. Chronic hepatitis in the Doberman pinscher. In: Guilford WG, Center SA, Strombeck DR, et al, eds. Strombeck's Small Animal Gastroenterology, 3rd ed. Philadelphia, PA: WB Saunders Co, 1996; 742-743.

Speeti M, Eriksson J, Saari S, et al. Lesions of subclinical Doberman hepatitis. Veterinary Pathology 1998; 35: 361-369.

Strombeck DR, Miller LM, Harrold D. Effects of corticosteroid treatment on survival time in dogs with chronic hepatitis: 151 cases (1977-1985). Journal of the American Veterinary Medical Association 1988; 193: 1109-1113.

Thornburg LP. Histomorphological and immunohistochemical studies of chronic active hepatitis in Doberman pinschers. Veterinary Pathology 1998; 35: 380-385.

CASE 23-5

Increased Hepatic Enzyme Activities in a Bedlington Terrier

David C. Twedt, DVM
Diplomate ACVIM (Internal Medicine)
College of Veterinary Medicine and Biomedical Sciences
Colorado State University
Fort Collins, Colorado, USA

Assess the Animal

A one-and-one-half-year-old female Bedlington terrier (Figure 1) was evaluated because a littermate had recently been diagnosed with copper-associated hepatotoxicity. A serum biochemistry profile obtained by the referring veterinarian identified an abnormal alanine aminotransferase (ALT) activity of 161 IU/l (reference range 10 to 120 IU/l). The dog was considered to be normal by the owner and a physical examination was unremarkable. The dog weighed 6.6 kg and had normal body condition (body condition score [BCS] 3/5).

Another serum biochemistry profile confirmed an elevated ALT of 189 IU/l. Serum protein and bile acid concentrations, and clotting times were normal suggesting adequate hepatic function. The liver was grossly normal when biopsy specimens were collected at laparoscopy. Evaluation of the biopsy specimens revealed mild focal hepatic necrosis with many hepatocytes containing golden brown granules. These granules stained positive for copper using rhodamine copper stain (Figure 2). Hepatic copper quantitation was 4,901 µg/g dry weight liver (normal reference 120 to 400 µg/g dry weight liver). A diagnosis of inherited copper hepatotoxicity was made.

Assess the Food(s) and Feeding Method

The diet was currently a mixture of a commercial dry grocery brand dog food (Purina Dog Chow[a]) and various commercial moist grocery brand foods with occasional table foods. The foods were mixed together at each meal so that approximately two-thirds of the volume came from dry food and one-third from moist food. The exact daily caloric intake was unknown. The patient was eating approximately the same amount of food and there had been no change in body weight during the last year.

Questions

1. What are the key nutritional factors to consider in this patient?

2. What nutritional supplements might benefit patients with copper hepatotoxicity?

Answers and Discussion

1. Key nutritional factors to consider in patients with copper-associated hepatoxicosis include energy, protein, copper, zinc and antioxidant vitamins. Providing

Figure 1. A one-and-one-half-year-old female Bedlington terrier affected with inherited copper hepatotoxicity.

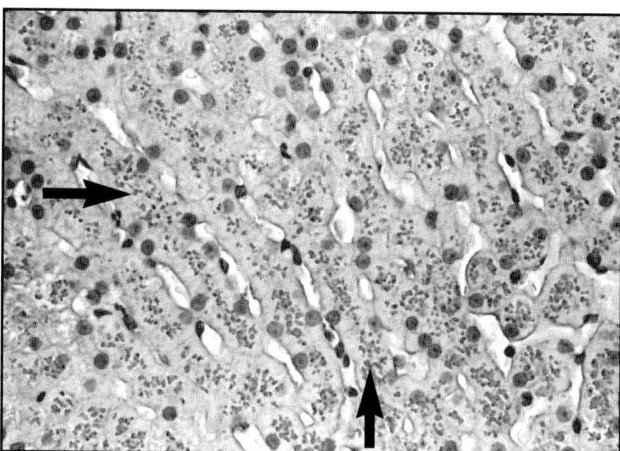

Figure 2. A photomicrograph of a liver specimen from a Bedlington terrier. Granules located in hepatocytes (arrows) stained positive for copper (rhodamine copper stain).

LIVER DISEASE

adequate daily energy intake is important to allow protein synthesis and prevent tissue catabolism that generates ammonia. The exact caloric needs of these patients have not been determined but would be expected to be similar to those of other dogs of similar age and body condition.

Most dogs with copper toxicosis develop clinical problems or liver disease is detected during adulthood (i.e., two to six years of age). Protein requirements have not been established for these dogs, but they would be expected to be similar to those of other adult dogs (15 to 30% dry matter [DM]). Patients with evidence of hepatic encephalopathy will often need more restricted dietary protein levels.

Foods low in copper are recommended for affected dogs that accumulate hepatic copper. Restriction of dietary copper as the primary therapy probably does little to lower abnormal hepatic copper concentrations in diseased dogs. Copper-restricted foods alone have a very minimal effect in causing a net depletion of hepatic copper.

It is difficult to limit dietary copper intake because commercial dog foods contain supplemental copper to meet or exceed dietary allowances established by the Association of American Feed Control Officials (AAFCO) or similar regulatory agencies. The AAFCO minimum allowance is 7.3 ppm copper (dry matter basis [DMB]) or 2.1 mg copper/1,000 kcal (4.18 MJ) metabolizable energy. Most commercial dog foods exceed these levels of copper. These levels are appropriate for normal dogs but are excessive for dogs with copper-associated liver disease. For affected Bedlington terriers, foods with less than 5 ppm DM copper from available sources are appropriate. A few commercial veterinary therapeutic foods have low copper levels (Table 23-10).

Homemade foods can be prepared that do not contain excess copper. (See Table 6-7.) These foods should exclude liver, shell fish, organ meats and cereals because of their high copper content. Vitamin-mineral supplements that do not contain a copper source are recommended. Treats and table food containing copper should also be avoided.

Decreasing the copper content of the food decreases the amount of copper that is absorbed through the intestine and enters the liver. Foods with low copper levels appear to be most useful for managing young dogs diagnosed with an inherited hepatic copper accumulation defect.

2. Oral zinc supplementation decreases intestinal absorption of copper. Zinc induces the increased synthesis of an intestinal mucosal metal-binding protein metallothionein. Copper that enters the intestine binds tenaciously to metallothionein, blocking the transfer of copper to the animal. The copper-metallothionein complex is lost in the feces during normal intestinal epithelial cell turnover.

Studies suggest that zinc supplementation will prevent copper accumulation and may actually decrease hepatic copper stores in affected patients. This "decoppering" method, however, is a slow process. Therefore, patients with high concentrations of hepatic copper should first receive copper chelating agents to reduce copper levels. In the author's experience,

zinc supplementation alone may not be adequate for maintaining affected Bedlington terriers.

Zinc supplementation (i.e., as acetate, sulfate, gluconate or methionine) given at a dose of 5 to 10 mg/kg body weight every 12 hours has been recommended. Alternatively, 200 mg of elemental zinc given orally for several months for induction, then lowered to a maintenance dose of 100 mg daily, may be used. Serum zinc concentrations should be monitored with the goal of approximately doubling the serum zinc concentrations. Zinc should not be given with meals.

There is also evidence from experimental studies that increased concentrations of hepatic copper catalyze hepatocellular oxidative damage and that therapeutic levels of antioxidants have protective properties. Vitamin E (d-α-tocopherol 200 to 400 IU/day) may be used as adjunct therapy. Vitamin C (ascorbic acid) has been suggested by some to decrease hepatic copper concentrations. However, this practice is not recommended because vitamin C promotes increased oxidative damage in the presence of high copper concentrations.

Progress Notes

A low-copper homemade food was recommended, but the owner wanted to continue feeding the dog commercial foods. No major changes to the current feeding plan were made other than eliminating table foods. The estimated daily energy requirement (DER) was 1.6 x resting energy requirement (RER) = 430 kcal (1.8 MJ). The foods were divided into equal portions and fed twice daily. A copper chelating agent, penicillamine[b] (125 mg, twice daily), was also given before meals.

Evaluation at six months found that the liver enzyme activities had returned to the normal reference range. A second liver biopsy was performed 12 months after therapy was instituted. The hepatic copper concentration had declined to 3,900 µg/g dry weight liver, and mild fibrosis, vacuolar degeneration and hepatic copper in centrolobular hepatocytes were evident histologically. Penicillamine therapy was continued.

An elective ovariohysterectomy was performed four years after the onset of penicillamine therapy and a liver biopsy specimen was obtained at that time. Both hepatic histology and hepatic copper concentration (125 µg/g liver) were normal. The penicillamine was discontinued and therapy with zinc gluconate (100 mg, twice daily, for a two-month induction period, followed by 50 mg, twice daily) and vitamin E (200 IU, twice daily) was instituted. Serum zinc concentrations were maintained between 200 and 300 g/ml, which was considered in the therapeutic range. Liver enzyme activities were evaluated at six-month intervals and were normal for three years. At that point, serum ALT concentrations began to increase and remained consistently abnormal when evaluated at six-month intervals for 18 months (i.e., ALT concentrations were 196, 275 and 278 IU/l, respectively). Zinc supplementation was thought not to be maintaining the patient. Therefore, a liver biopsy was suggested to obtain a specimen for evaluation of hepatic copper concentration. The owner declined the biopsy. Zinc therapy was discontinued and penicillamine therapy was re-instituted. The dog was also fed a homemade food, which probably had a lower copper con-

Table 1. Homemade food for a Bedlington terrier with copper hepatotoxicosis.

Ingredients*	Amounts (g)	
Long grain brown rice, cooked	192	
Cottage cheese, 4% fat	71	
Margarine	8	
Calcium carbonate	1	
Iodized "lite" salt (KCl/NaCl)	1.7	(1/2 tsp)
Brewer's yeast	1	
Other supplements**		

*Provides 350 kcal (1.46 MJ).
**Each day: 175 IU vitamin D, 28 mg iron, 8 µg vitamin B_{12}.

tent than the commercial foods that were being fed (Table 1). Vitamin-mineral supplements without copper were prescribed and the owner added small quantities of cooked ground beef, chicken or eggs to the basic homemade food recipe. One year following the change to the homemade food and reintroduction of penicillamine therapy, the ALT concentrations returned to the normal reference range.

Further Discussion

This case demonstrates that inherited copper hepatotoxicity can be managed and progression can be stopped by reducing hepatic copper concentrations, if the disease is detected early. The apparent failure of zinc therapy in this case suggests that therapy with copper chelating agents should be instituted in Bedlington terriers with this disease. Penicillamine and trientine[c] are both effective copper chelating agents. It remains unknown whether a low-copper food in conjunction with zinc therapy would have been beneficial in this case. Combination chelating agent and zinc therapy, essentially attacking the problem by two different mechanisms is intriguing, but there are no objective studies evaluating this form of therapy. It is possible that penicillamine may chelate zinc in the GI tract making both drugs less effective.

Endnotes

a. Ralston Purina Co., St Louis, MO, USA.

b. Cuprimine. Merck & Company, Inc., Rahway, NJ, USA.

c. Syprine. Merck & Company, Inc., Rahway, NJ, USA.

Bibliography

Brewer GJ, Dick RD, Schall W. Use of zinc acetate to treat copper toxicosis in dogs. Journal of the American Veterinary Medical Association 1992; 201: 564-568.

Guilford WG. Nutritional management of gastrointestinal tract diseases. In Proceedings. Tenth Annual Veterinary Medical Forum, American College of Veterinary Internal Medicine, San Diego, CA, 1992: 66-69.

Rolfe DS, Twedt DC. Copper-associated hepatopathies in dogs. Veterinary Clinics of North America: Small Animal Practice 1995; 25: 399-416.

LIVER DISEASE

CHAPTER 24

Endocrine and Lipid Disorders

Steven C. Zicker
Richard B. Ford
Richard W. Nelson
Claudia A. Kirk

"Nothing in life is to be feared. It is only to be understood."
Marie Curie

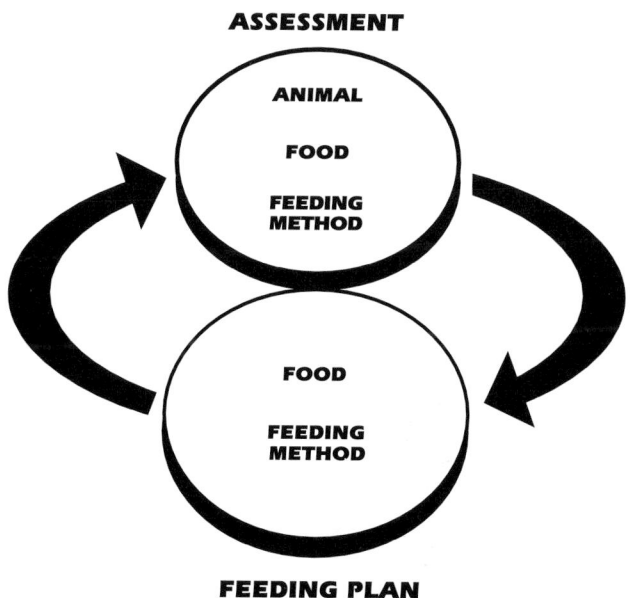

ASSESSMENT

ANIMAL

FOOD

FEEDING METHOD

FOOD

FEEDING METHOD

FEEDING PLAN

Note: The reader is referred to Chapter 1 for a detailed discussion of the iterative process of clinical nutrition.

INTRODUCTION

Energy metabolism is the conversion of ingested chemical energy (food) into other biosynthetic products (proteins, fat, carbohydrates), heat or waste products. Cofactors (minerals), coenzymes (vitamins), hormones, physiologic/nutritional state and disease may affect the flux and direction of metabolic processes. In addition, the quantity and type of energy supplying nutrients ingested may influence their own metabolic fate.

Several levels of control may be present in cells to regulate the flux of nutrients into, within and between tissues. The controls imposed upon different tissues or cells may slow down, speed up or completely inhibit the flux of a nutrient through a cell. Potential schemes for regulation include: 1) control of transmembrane transport, 2) presence or absence of functional proteins such as enzymes or hormone receptors (genetic expression), 3) subcellular compartmentalization of enzymes and 4) modulation of appropriate enzyme rates. Several brief examples may help define the above mechanisms.

Regulation via transmembrane transport: cells may use simple diffusion, facilitated diffusion or active transport to acquire nutrients. The last two may be subject to allosteric and genetic regulation. The result is regulation of flux into cells.

Regulation via genetic expression: skeletal muscle does not express glucose-6-phosphatase or glucagon receptors. Therefore, although skeletal muscle has ample glycogen it does not contribute to glucose release to the bloodstream as does the liver.

KEY WORDS & TERMS—ENDOCRINE AND LIPID DISORDERS*

Cholesterol	Hyperglycemia	Lipemia
Diabetes insipidus	Hyperlipidemia	Lipoprotein
Diabetes mellitus	Hypoglycemia	Non-insulin dependent diabetes
Epinephrine	Hypothyroidism	mellitus (NIDDM)
Futile cycling	Insulin	Thyrotoxicosis
Glucagon	Insulin-dependent diabetes	Thyroxine (T_4)
Glucocorticoids	mellitus (IDDM)	Triacylglyceride (triglyceride)
Growth hormone	Insulin-secreting beta-cell tumor	Triiodothyronine (T_3)

Key words and terms are defined in the Glossary.

KEY POINTS—ENDOCRINE AND LIPID DISORDERS

1. The degree to which any key nutritional factor affects management of diabetes mellitus depends to a large extent on the efficacy of primary disease control through insulin or other pharmacologic treatment, and accurate diagnosis of confounding disease processes.

2. In insulin-dependent diabetes mellitus (IDDM), beta cells of the pancreas are progressively destroyed and lose their ability to secrete insulin.

3. Non-insulin-dependent diabetes mellitus (NIDDM) is characterized by insulin resistance at the peripheral tissues and/or dysfunctional beta cells and is referred to as a relative insulin deficiency.

4. IDDM may affect dogs of all ages, genders and breeds, but is more common in the four- to 14-year-old age group, with females affected twice as often as males. NIDDM accounts for approximately one in five cases of diabetes mellitus in dogs.

5. Obesity increases the risk for NIDDM in cats by fourfold.

6. For most animals, feeding at the daily energy requirement (DER) for ideal body weight in conjunction with adequate pharmacologic control of diabetes mellitus will achieve desired body weight.

7. For obese diabetic animals, a conservative weight-loss protocol may need to be instituted after medical problems are stabilized.

8. Increased urine output associated with diabetes mellitus will increase obligatory loss of electrolytes such as sodium, potassium, chloride, calcium and phosphorus.

9. Dietary modification, in conjunction with insulin therapy, is an effective adjunct in the control of diabetes mellitus in dogs and cats. In general, foods with decreased fat, moderate fiber, moderate protein and low levels of simple sugars should be recommended.

10. Including moderate amounts (approximately 8 to 17% of dry matter) of insoluble or mixed insoluble and soluble dietary fiber aids nutritional management of IDDM and NIDDM in dogs and cats.

11. Feeding must be coordinated with the time frame of exogenously administered insulin.

12. Commercial dry foods are preferred in patients with diabetes mellitus because semi-moist and moist-dry forms are often high in simple carbohydrates, and commercial moist foods may contain higher levels of protein and simple carbohydrates.

13. Multiple small meals (three to six) throughout the day may be better than a single meal for patients with insulin-secreting beta-cell neoplasia.

14. Hyperthyroidism is primarily a disease of cats.

15. Commercial moist, semi-moist and dry foods that meet AAFCO minimum nutrient levels for adult maintenance are recommended for hyperthyroid animals.

16. Animals with hypothyroidism often are overweight, in poor body condition and have poor skin and coat quality.

17. Successful treatment of primary disease processes (i.e., exogenous thyroid administration) in hypothyroidism will usually result in some weight loss when energy is provided at the calculated DER for ideal body weight.

18. The clinical importance of hyperlipidemia in companion animal medicine is related to four facts: 1) lipemic serum may positively or negatively interfere with quantitative analyses of other serum analytes, 2) hyperlipidemia in fasted (>12 hours) dogs or cats is abnormal and should be addressed as a significant clinical finding, 3) hyperlipidemic patients are at risk for developing significant clinical illness and 4) specific dietary and/or drug intervention can eliminate or at least diminish the morbidity associated with hyperlipidemia.

19. Several endocrine, renal and hepatic diseases variably alter lipoprotein metabolism resulting in either hypertriglyceridemia or hypercholesterolemia (e.g., diabetes mellitus, protein-losing nephropathy, hyperadrenocorticism, hypothyroidism).

20. Long-term dietary management of dogs and cats with lipemia is indicated only after secondary causes of hypertriglyceridemia have been ruled out.

21. Because chylomicrons are exclusively of dietary origin, restriction of dietary fat is the first and most important line of therapy for dogs and cats with primary hypertriglyceridemia. Foods containing less than 12% fat (dry matter basis) are most commonly recommended for life-long nutritional therapy.

22. Hypercholesterolemia, without hypertriglyceridemia, is not known to pose a significant health threat to affected dogs or cats.

23. The goals of dietary therapy in hyperlipidemia are to achieve a clear serum sample, total triglyceride concentration less than 500 mg/dl and negative chylomicron test.

KEY NUTRITIONAL FACTORS—ENDOCRINE AND LIPID DISORDERS

Disorders	Factors	Dietary recommendations
Diabetes mellitus	Water	Fresh, clean water should be available at all times
	Energy	In obese animals, restrict energy intake to achieve weight loss
		Timing of meals (energy intake) must be coordinated with administration of exogenous insulin
	Soluble carbohydrate	Limit the amount of simple sugars and provide food with complex carbohydrates
		Dogs: complex carbohydrates 50 to 55% of food (dry matter basis)
		Cats: complex carbohydrates 20 to 40% of food (dry matter basis)
	Dietary fiber	Provide a food with increased amounts of dietary fiber
		Dogs and cats: dietary fiber 8 to 17% of food (dry matter basis)
		Provide a food with moderate to low amounts of fat
	Fat	Dogs and cats: dietary fat <20% (dry matter basis)
		Provide a food with moderate amounts of protein
	Protein	Dogs: crude protein 15 to 25% (dry matter basis)
		Cats: crude protein 28 to 45% (dry matter basis)
Hypothyroidism	Energy/fat	If the animal is obese, provide a food with decreased fat and energy density
Hyperthyroidism	Water	Fresh, clean water should be available at all times
	Energy	In underweight animals, provide increased energy and dietary fat
	Protein	In underweight animals, provide increased dietary protein unless renal function is compromised
Hyperlipidemia	Triglyceride	Restrict dietary fat (<12% dry matter basis)
		Add lipid-reducing drugs (fibrates) if dietary management alone is unsuccessful in controlling hyperlipidemia

Regulation via subcellular compartmentalization: long-chain fatty acid catabolism occurs in mitochondria and transport into the matrix from the cytosol is tightly regulated. This process is advantageous because synthesis occurs in the cytosol and this physical separation prevents futile cycling.

Regulation via enzymatic modulation: enzymes may be modulated by metabolite concentrations via allosteric means (much like a dimmer switch), covalent modification (like an on-off switch) or adaptive mechanisms (altered amount of enzyme via genetic expression). The last two are usually achieved via hormone signals in response to environmental or nutritional stimuli. These stimuli modify flux through metabolic pathways.

Several disease states that alter energy metabolism are discussed in this chapter. These diseases manifest their clinical signs by altering subcellular homeostasis. As discussed above, this may occur at one of several different levels and can be quite complex. This chapter focuses on specific interactions of nutrition with endocrine and lipid disorders and how nutritional therapy may be used to affect their management.

DIABETES MELLITUS

Diabetes mellitus describes an alteration in cellular transport and metabolism of glucose. Certain tissues (e.g., skeletal muscle, adipose tissue and cardiac muscle) depend on insulin stimuli for transport of glucose into their cytosol. In diabetes mellitus, these cells either never receive the signal or do not interpret it properly. General pathophysiologic mechanisms suggested include: 1) insufficient insulin release from the pancreas, 2) lack of insulin receptors (down regulation) and 3) inability of a normal number of insulin receptors to transduce the signal (Table 24-1).[1]

Table 24-1. Possible causes of diabetes mellitus in dogs and cats.*

Concurrent illness (hyperadrenocorticism, acromegaly)
Drugs (glucocorticoids, progestins)
Genetics
Immune-mediated insulitis
Infection
Islet amyloidosis
Obesity
Pancreatitis

*Adapted from Feldman EC, Nelson RW, eds. Diabetes mellitus. Canine and Feline Endocrinology and Reproduction, 2nd ed. Philadelphia, PA: WB Saunders Co, 1996; 340.

Classification

Diabetes mellitus has been classified historically by a variety of schemes. The following scheme has been proposed for people with diabetes mellitus: 1) insulin-dependent diabetes mellitus (IDDM or type I), 2) non-insulin-dependent diabetes mellitus (NIDDM or type II), 3) secondary diabetes mellitus (type S), 4) impaired glucose tolerance (e.g., gestational diabetes) (type IGT) and 5) previous abnormality of glucose tolerance (type PrevAGT).[2] Treatment regimen and complication rates can differ markedly among the different diabetic classifications. For the purposes of this textbook, only IDDM and NIDDM are considered.

In IDDM, beta cells of the pancreas are progressively destroyed and lose their ability to secrete insulin. Approximately 75% of the beta cells must be destroyed before insulin secretion is inadequate to maintain normal glucose tolerance.[3] IDDM is characterized by insulinopenia and dependence on exogenous insulin administration for treatment.

NIDDM is characterized by insulin resistance at the peripheral tissues and/or dysfunctional beta cells.[4] NIDDM has been referred to as a relative insulin deficiency because

Table 24-2. Differential diagnosis for hyperglycemia in dogs and cats.*

Acromegaly
Diabetes mellitus
Diestrus (bitch)
Drug therapy (glucocorticoids, progestogens, megesterol acetate)
Exocrine pancreatic insufficiency
Glucose-containing fluids
Hyperadrenocorticism
Hyperthyroidism (cats)
Laboratory error
Pancreatitis
Pheochromocytoma
Renal insufficiency
Stress

*Adapted from Feldman EC, Nelson RW, eds. Diabetes mellitus. Canine and Feline Endocrinology and Reproduction, 2nd ed. Philadelphia, PA: WB Saunders Co, 1996; 349.

the amount of insulin actually secreted by the beta cells may be increased, decreased or normal. The concentration of glucose in serum is thus determined by the relative response of peripheral tissues to the secreted insulin, which is usually blunted. Patients with NIDDM may be misdiagnosed with IDDM depending on the severity of beta-cell dysfunction and peripheral insulin resistance. NIDDM patients may not be totally dependent on administration of exogenous insulin to maintain glucose homeostasis.

Assessment

Assess the Animal

HISTORY

Dogs and cats with diabetes mellitus are usually examined because of polyuria, polydipsia, polyphagia, weight loss and diminished activity. Care should be taken to differentiate between polyphagia from underfeeding compared to polyphagia associated with disease (true polyphagia). Less commonly, complaints of blindness (dogs), rear-limb weakness (cats) and lethargy (dogs and cats) may be identified. If diabetic ketoacidosis (DKA) develops, affected animals are often examined for vomiting, weakness, anorexia and coma. DKA may be precipitated by infection, severe stress, hypokalemia, hypomagnesemia, renal failure, drugs that decrease insulin secretion, drugs that cause insulin resistance or inadequate fluid intake.[5] Subclinical diabetes mellitus may only become more noticeable to owners when another disease process precipitates clinical signs associated with DKA. Concurrent disease is common in diabetic dogs and cats and may prompt diabetes mellitus to manifest itself or be a consequence of the diabetic state. Therefore, assessment is important in developing a management protocol.[1,6]

PHYSICAL EXAMINATION

Body condition scores (BCS) for diabetic dogs and cats range from emaciated (BCS 1/5) to obese (BCS 5/5) depending on the severity and duration of disease. Weight loss is thought to be more severe in animals with IDDM compared with that of patients with NIDDM. Weight loss, which becomes obvious with time, is a hallmark sign of diabetes mellitus. Other physical findings may include lethargy, unkempt coats (cats), hepatomegaly, cataracts (dogs), icterus (cats), rear-limb weakness (cats) and dehydration.[6,7]

DIAGNOSTIC TESTING

Hemograms

Results of complete blood counts are usually within normal ranges in uncomplicated cases of diabetes mellitus. An increase in packed cell volume may be present in dogs and cats with DKA due to decreased extracellular water attributable to osmotic diuresis. Leukocytosis or shifts of white cell morphology to more immature types may indicate an underlying infectious process that is confounding the diagnosis of uncomplicated diabetes mellitus.

Serum Biochemistry Profiles

The most consistent and requisite feature of diabetes mellitus is persistent fasting hyperglycemia and glucosuria in the absence of other disease processes. Hyperglycemia, however, may be caused by other disease or physiologic states and drugs (Table 24-2). A thorough assessment may help identify the underlying cause of hyperglycemia. Repetitive determination of serum glucose concentrations may be required in cats to differentiate diabetes mellitus from stress hyperglycemia. A diagnosis of DKA is established if ketonuria is present with systemic metabolic acidosis.

Other commonly identified abnormalities include increased serum concentrations of cholesterol and triglycerides. Increased serum concentrations of urea nitrogen and creatinine may be present when dehydration becomes severe enough to impair renal diffusion (prerenal azotemia). Electrolyte and acid-base alterations are more common in animals with DKA and include: 1) hyponatremia, 2) hypokalemia, 3) hypocalcemia, 4) hypomagnesemia, 5) hypophosphatemia and 6) hypochloremia. A shift in acid-base balance towards metabolic acidosis with a compensatory respiratory alkalosis may occur.

Increased activity of alanine aminotransferase (ALT) in serum may be present in cases in which hepatic lipidosis has resulted in hepatocellular damage. Activity of serum alkaline phosphatase (ALP) may also be increased. Increased serum ALP activity is primarily associated with hepatomegaly and biliary stasis; however, pancreatic inflammation resulting in extrahepatic biliary obstruction may also be present. Less commonly, serum concentrations of bile acids and total bilirubin may be elevated.

Dogs and cats with diabetes mellitus may present with concurrent exocrine pancreatic insufficiency or pancreatitis.[8] Increased activity of amylase and lipase in serum may indicate pancreatitis; however, the correlation of these two enzyme activities with pancreatitis is variable and is especially poor in cats. Other disease processes may also result in increased activity of these enzymes in serum.

Other Biochemical Tests

Determination of insulin concentration in serum is not routinely performed in suspected cases of diabetes mellitus. A reliable radioimmunoassay must be used when measuring serum insulin, especially in cats. Insulin exhibits variance in the primary amino acid sequence between species; therefore, the test methodology must be validated for each species. Serum insulin concentrations, when they are determined, may be high, normal or low. Concentrations of insulin greater than 15 µU/ml may indicate the presence of functional beta cells. Conversely, concentrations of insulin less than 10 µU/ml do not preclude the possibility of functional beta cells. Serum trypsin-like immunoreactivity can be used to help differentiate pancreatitis (increased activity) from exocrine pancreatic insufficiency (decreased activity). (See Chapter 22.)

Serum thyroid-hormone concentrations are usually normal in diabetic dogs and cats. However, both hypothyroidism and hyperthyroidism may be associated with insulin resistance and can occur in conjunction with diabetes mellitus. As such, evaluation of thyroid function may be useful in patients with diabetes mellitus that is difficult to control with insulin and dietary intervention. (See Case 24-2.) Care must be exercised in interpretation of serum T_4 concentrations in sick dogs and cats because concentrations of thyroxine (T_4) may be falsely low in poorly regulated cases of diabetes mellitus. This alteration is presumed to be attributable to the euthyroid sick syndrome.[9]

Urinalyses

Urine specific gravity is typically greater than 1.025 in diabetic dogs and cats. Urine specific gravity less than 1.015 should increase suspicion for concurrent disorders, such as renal insufficiency or hyperadrenocorticism. Glucosuria is a hallmark finding in untreated diabetic dogs and cats. Lack of glucosuria rules out overt diabetes mellitus as the cause of polyuria and polydipsia. Other common urinalysis findings include ketonuria, proteinuria and changes consistent with urinary tract infection (i.e., bacteriuria and pyuria). Proteinuria may result from either bacterial infection or glomerulosclerosis secondary to basement membrane damage from the primary disease process.

RISK FACTORS

Most dogs diagnosed with diabetes mellitus have the IDDM classification type. IDDM may affect dogs of all ages, genders and breeds, but is more common in the four- to 14-year-old age group, with females affected twice as often as males. Breeds apparently at higher risk include keeshounds, pulis, Cairn terriers, miniature pinschers and poodles. Breeds apparently at lower risk include cocker spaniels, German shepherd dogs, collies, Pekingese, rottweilers and boxers.[10] These risk factors insinuate that a genetic component may be involved in development of disease. NIDDM is less common in dogs than cats but still accounts for approximately one in five cases.[11]

IDDM and NIDDM may affect cats of any age; however, they are diagnosed more commonly in cats older than six years. In contrast to findings in dogs, diabetes mellitus occurs predominately in neutered male cats and is usually of the NIDDM type. There has been no breed predilection determined as of yet in cats;[12] however, obesity increases the risk for NIDDM in cats by fourfold.[13]

ETIOPATHOGENESIS

Insulin Physiology

Insulin is produced in the beta cells of the endocrine pancreas and is released in response to increased concentrations of glucose in plasma. Active insulin is a dipeptide that is linked by disulfide bonds between cysteine amino acid side chains. Insulin is first synthesized as proinsulin in beta cells and is subsequently processed by a cleavage step that produces C-peptide and active insulin.[14]

Active insulin released into the bloodstream normally interacts at target tissues via cell surface receptors specific for insulin. Most tissues have insulin receptors but some (e.g., skeletal and cardiac muscle and adipose tissue) depend more on insulin for the acquisition of glucose and amino acids than others, and are classified as insulin-

dependent tissues.[15,16] For example, brain tissue has insulin receptors, but is quite capable of transporting glucose intracellularly without the help of hormonal stimuli; therefore, it is considered an insulin-independent tissue.

Insulin receptors in liver and fat cells consist of two alpha and two beta units. The alpha unit provides the binding site for insulin and the beta unit is a transmembrane protein. Insulin receptors appear to transduce the signal by either receptor/insulin complex aggregation and internalization, or via a tyrosine kinase/autophosphorylation reaction that does not require internalization of the complex. The insulin signal then acts intracellularly to increase or decrease specific metabolic pathways such as glycolysis and gluconeogenesis. The insulin signal also increases uptake of glucose into insulin-dependent cells via translocation of the GLUT4 transport protein to the cell surface membrane from the cytosol.[17] GLUT4 is one of five glucose transport proteins and is expressed only in insulin-dependent tissues.[18]

Insulin-Dependent Diabetes Mellitus

The etiology of IDDM in dogs and cats is not well understood but is probably multifactorial in origin. Genetics, immune-mediated disease, inflammatory conditions, infections, exogenous drugs, body condition, concurrent disease and pancreatic beta-cell degeneration have all been suggested as possible etiologies (Table 24-1). Immune-mediated insulitis may play a role in development of IDDM in dogs. In one study, beta-cell specific antibodies were identified in approximately 50% of diabetic dogs studied.[19]

Non-Insulin-Dependent Diabetes Mellitus

NIDDM is classically characterized by insulin resistance or beta-cell dysfunction. A number of models in other species have been proposed to account for the observed dysfunction including decreased GLUT4 expression or responsiveness in target tissues,[20,21] leptin protein deficiency in mice,[22] hepatic overproduction of glucose[23] and many others. NIDDM in cats is often characterized by deposition of amylin in pancreatic beta islet cells.[24] Whether amylin is a primary factor in beta-cell dysfunction or secondary to

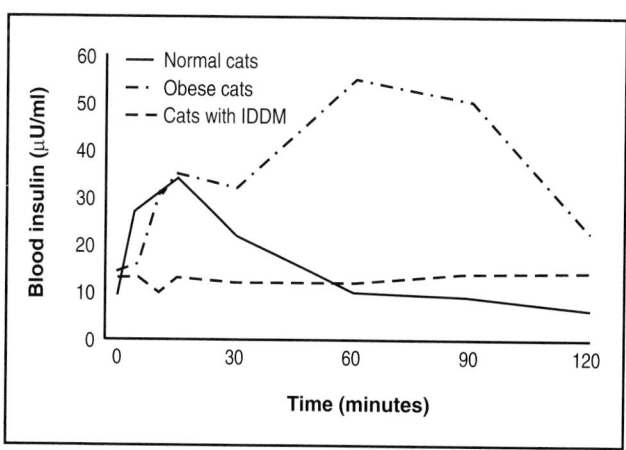

Figure 24-1. Mean blood insulin concentrations following the intravenous injection of 0.5 g glucose/kg body weight in normal cats, extremely obese cats and cats with IDDM. The insulin secretory pattern in obese cats is similar to that of people with NIDDM. (Adapted from Nelson RW. Disorders of the endocrine pancreas. In: Ettinger SJ, ed. Textbook of Veterinary Internal Medicine, 3rd ed. Philadelphia, PA: WB Saunders Co, 1989; 1676.)

overstimulation of beta cells in response to peripheral insulin resistance is not known.[25] In addition, prolonged elevation of plasma glucose in cats (i.e., glucose toxicity) causes hydropic degeneration of beta cells[26] and decreased pancreatic insulin secretion.[27] NIDDM in dogs and cats appears to be associated with obesity and possibly subsequent down regulation of peripheral insulin receptors, as in people (Figure 24-1).[10,25,28]

KEY NUTRITIONAL FACTORS

Key nutritional factors consist of nutrients of concern and other factors such as food type and digestibility. This section emphasizes key nutritional factors that have significant variance in commercial foods and markedly affect management of diabetes mellitus. The degree to which any of these factors affects management of diabetes mellitus depends to a large degree on the efficacy of primary disease control through insulin or other pharmacologic treatment.

Water

Increased water loss due to osmotic diuresis from glucose, and ketone bodies if DKA is present, must be compensated. Generally, a source of potable water is recommended in amounts sufficient to meet the increased water requirement. This is usually accomplished via free-choice access to water. Dehydrated patients and those with DKA may require parenteral fluid administration. Caution should be observed with type and rate of fluid replacement because of electrolyte perturbations. Rapid replacement of fluid loss with hypotonic solutions may lead to water intoxication and cerebral edema.[29]

Energy

Animals with diabetes mellitus display a classic clinical picture of polyphagia with weight loss. This dichotomy may be attributable to inappropriate hormonal signals that result in poor cellular use of glucose and amino acids with concomitant urinary loss of nutrients. Before making recommendations for daily energy requirement (DER), it is important to emphasize that clinical response of animals with diabetes mellitus to dietary manipulation depends on the level of control of the primary disease process and the presence or absence of concurrent disease. For example, if weight loss or weight gain is a continuing problem, it may be due to poorly controlled diabetes mellitus or concurrent disease such as thyroid disorders (dogs and cats), lymphoplasmacytic enteritis (cats) or hyperadrenocorticism (dogs), rather than inappropriate calculation of DER. Consistent re-evaluation and owner education are important tools in adjusting food dose and managing diabetes mellitus.

The basal metabolic rate (BMR) may actually be decreased in animals with poorly controlled diabetes mellitus because of the euthyroid sick syndrome. Caution should therefore be taken to avoid over diagnosis of true hypothyroidism in light of the prevalence of euthyroid sick syndrome. Hyperthyroidism is rare in dogs but may occur in some cats with diabetes mellitus.

For most animals (BCS 2/5 to 4/5), feeding at the DER for ideal body weight in conjunction with adequate control of diabetes mellitus will achieve desired body weights. It is best to calculate a DER, as a multiple of resting energy requirement (RER), based on the standard formulas for normal animals. (See Chapter 1.) For neutered dogs, a factor of 1.6 x RER and for intact dogs, a factor of 1.8 x RER are good initial estimates of DER. For neutered cats, a factor of 1.2 x RER and a factor of 1.4 x RER for intact cats are appropriate starting points. All animals should be reevaluated regularly with food doses adjusted as indicated based on body condition.

For obese diabetic animals, a conservative weight-loss protocol may need to be instituted after medical problems are stabilized. Calculation of DER for ideal body weight is a good initial estimate for calculation of food doses. Frequent monitoring and readjustment should be the norm rather than the exception in weight-loss programs for animals with concurrent disease such as diabetes mellitus. Animals that are too lean may need to be fed a food with less than 10% crude fiber to increase food energy density to a level where body weight is increased.

Protein

Diabetic animals may have increased loss of amino acids in urine attributable to inappropriate or inadequate hormonal signals and renal glomerulopathy. It is important to provide protein quantity and quality that will meet the requirements of diabetic animals in the face of increased amino aciduria while avoiding excess protein content that may enhance renal damage or contribute to excessive insulin secretion. Protein should be approximately 15 to 25% of the food on a dry matter basis (DMB) for dogs and greater than 28% of the food on a DMB for cats, with a true protein digestibility greater than 85%.

Soluble Carbohydrate

Glucose is one of the most potent secretagogues of insulin in healthy subjects. The composition and quantity of carbohydrates in foods for management of diabetes mellitus in people is controversial. (See sidebar "Next Generation Foods for Diabetes Mellitus.") Diets containing up to

Table 24-3. Effect of feeding insoluble dietary fiber to dogs and cats with diabetes mellitus.*

	Mean daily insulin dose (U/kg/day)	Mean fasting blood glucose (mg/dl)	Mean blood glucose/24 hrs (mg/dl)	Mean urine glucose excretion (g/24 hrs)	Mean glycosylated hemoglobin (%)
Dog food**					
Low-fiber food (1% DM)	1.9 ± 0.6	247 ± 99	246 ± 100	9.3 ± 14.0	6.9 ± 1.8
High-fiber food (13% DM)	1.7 ± 0.5	164 ± 69	184 ± 71	2.8 ± 3.3	5.9 ± 1.4
Cat food**					
Low-fiber food (1% DM)	1.2 ± 0.7	328 ± 153	285 ± 131	Not done	2.7 ± 0.8
High-fiber food (12% DM)	1.0 ± 0.6	191 ± 118	182 ± 99	Not done	2.1 ± 0.4

Key: DM = dry matter.
*Nelson R, Duesberg C, Ford S, et al. Dietary insoluble fiber and glycemic control of diabetic dogs (abstract). In: Proceedings. Twelfth Annual Veterinary Medical Forum, American College of Veterinary Internal Medicine, San Francisco, CA, 1994: 993. Nelson R, Scott-Moncrief C, DeVries S, et al. Dietary insoluble fiber and glycemic control of diabetic cats (abstract). In: Proceedings. Twelfth Annual Veterinary Medical Forum, American College of Veterinary Internal Medicine, San Francisco, CA, 1994: 996.
**By the parameters shown here, dogs and cats eating the higher fiber food had better glycemic control than comparable animals eating the low-fiber food.

80% carbohydrate have been recommended for diabetic people.[30] Some details about the effect of carbohydrate composition have been investigated in management of diabetes mellitus in dogs and cats; however, absolute quantities have not been fully evaluated.

The use of fructose in foods for cats with diabetes mellitus should be avoided. Cats do not appear to metabolize fructose, which leads to fructose intolerance, polyuria and potential renal damage.[31] Fructose may be found in commercial semi-moist foods, as a humectant in the form of sucrose, or high-fructose corn syrup. The potential effects of fructose in foods for dogs with diabetes mellitus have not been evaluated.

Fiber

There is evidence to support the hypothesis that feeding foods with moderate amounts of fiber, substituted for starch, has a positive effect on glycemic control in dogs and cats (Table 24-3). The amount of crude fiber in commercial pet foods ranges from 0.4 to 30% DMB. Crude fiber analytical methods detect some soluble but primarily insoluble fiber types. Dogs eating foods with an insoluble fiber content of 10 to 15% cellulose DMB and more than 50% digestible carbohydrate had significantly better glycemic control than dogs fed the same food without insoluble fiber.[32] Cats fed a food with 12% insoluble fiber also had increased glycemic control.[33]

Addition of soluble fiber (13% DMB) to foods also increased glycemic control in dogs; however, coat and fecal quality were altered clinically.[34] Soluble fiber may be partially fermented to short-chain fatty acids and then used as energy by colonocytes or absorbed into the blood. These steps decrease the amount of carbohydrate in the bloodstream and do not require insulin for assimilation.

Although an ideal fiber content has not been established, it is evident that including moderate amounts (approximately 8 to 17% DMB) of insoluble or mixed insoluble and soluble dietary fiber aids nutritional management of IDDM and NIDDM in dogs and cats. There appears to be no difference between soluble and insoluble fiber effects in dogs.[1] Some soluble fibers and mixtures of soluble/insoluble fibers may decrease small intestinal digestion of certain nutrients without affecting total tract digestibility.[35] Caution should be exercised with use of either fiber type in the management of diabetes mellitus because hyperglycemia inhibits the gastrocolic response, which may predispose to constipation.[36] In addition, increased fiber levels may trap water in the GI tract; therefore, water balance may need to be more closely monitored in animals with poorly controlled diabetes mellitus fed foods with moderate fiber levels.

Food Type

Semi-moist foods tend to have a hyperglycemic effect compared to dry foods because they contain increased levels of simple carbohydrates and other ingredients used as humectants (e.g., propylene glycol) (Figure 24-2). Semi-moist foods should be avoided in dogs and cats with diabetes mellitus.

Fat

Abnormalities of lipid metabolism are manifested in diabetic dogs and cats via increased serum concentrations of triglycerides, cholesterol or both. In addition, concurrent pancreatitis is common in dogs and cats with diabetes mellitus. Therefore, excess dietary fat should be avoided in diabetic dogs and cats (Table 24-4).[1]

Next Generation Foods for Diabetes Mellitus

Current recommendations for carbohydrate intake in people with diabetes mellitus presumes that all carbohydrates have a similar glycemic response. However, in select studies, the effect of carbohydrates on glycemic response has been shown to differ markedly. The effect of carbohydrate composition depends on a variety of factors such as carbohydrate type, matrix in which the carbohydrate is found, the type of processing the carbohydrate has undergone and total amount of carbohydrate consumed. For example, in people, sucrose is approximately equal in glycemic index to starches in breads and rice.

Starches that resist intestinal hydrolysis (resistant starches) show promise for better control of postprandial glycemia in people and may prove useful in diabetic dogs and cats.

BIBLIOGRAPHY

Fields M, Lewis CG, Lure MD. Responses of insulin to oral glucose and fructose loads in marginally copper-deficient rats fed starch or fructose. Nutrition 1996; 12: 524-528.

Franz MJ, Horton ES, Bantle JP, et al. Nutrition principles for the management of diabetes and related complications. Diabetes Care 1994; 5: 490-501.

Raben A, Tagliabue A, Christensen NJ, et al. Resistant starch: The effect on postprandial glycemia, hormonal response, and satiety. American Journal of Clinical Nutrition 1994; 60: 544-551.

Table 24-4. Nutritional recommendations for diabetic dogs and cats.*

Nutrients	Dogs	Cats
Carbohydrate	50 to 55	20 to 40
Crude fiber**	10 to 15	10 to 15
Fat	<20	<20
Protein***	15 to 25	28 to 45

*Nutrients expressed on a % dry matter basis.
**Crude fiber underestimates the soluble and total dietary fiber content of foods. See text and Chapter 2 for details.
***Animals with renal failure should receive protein levels at the low end of the range.

Omega-3 Fatty Acids

A major purported benefit of omega-3 (n-3) fatty acids in the treatment of people with diabetes mellitus is the decreased incidence of atherosclerotic disease.[37] At present, the recommendation of fish oil (enhanced with n-3 fatty acids) for management of IDDM is more accepted than for NIDDM in people. The dose of fish oil, diet composition and type of diabetes have resulted in confounding results. Administration of supplemental n-3 fatty acids to diabetic people generally increased high-density lipoprotein concentrations, improved blood viscosity, reduced triglyceride levels and reduced blood pressure. However, reports of reduced glycemic control, increased apolipoprotein B levels and increased low-density lipoprotein levels with concomitant increases in cholesterol concentrations have dampened enthusiasm for the use of n-3 fatty acids in diabetic people.[37] Because atherosclerotic disease is not as much of a concern in dogs and cats, the beneficial effects of n-3 fatty acids in lieu of potential loss of glycemic control may not be warranted.

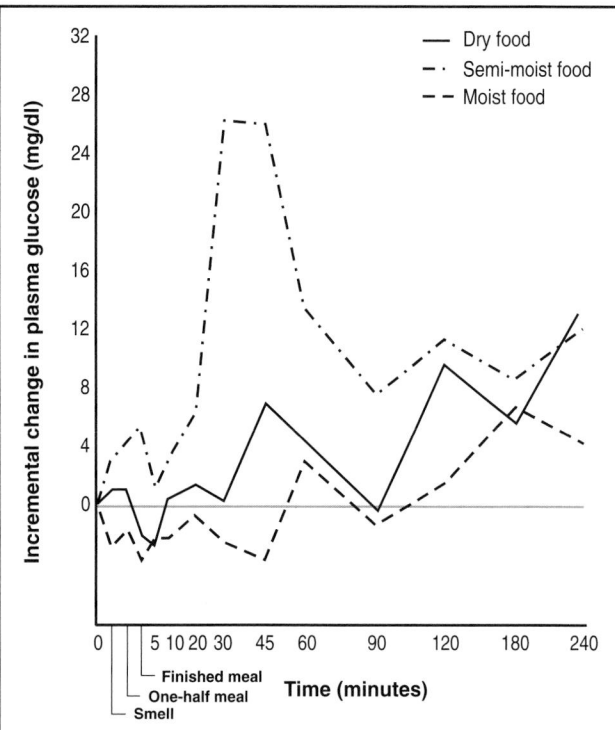

Figure 24-2. Changes in postprandial plasma glucose concentrations in healthy dogs fed commercial dry, semi-moist or moist dog food. Each dog consumed 50 kcal/kg body weight. Results are expressed as means compared with respective time-0 values. Note the profound increase in plasma glucose concentrations that follow consumption of semi-moist foods, which makes them an inappropriate food form for diabetic animals. (Adapted from Holste LC, Nelson RW, Feldman EC, et al. Effect of dry, soft moist, and canned dog foods on postprandial blood glucose and insulin concentrations in healthy dogs. American Journal of Veterinary Research 1989; 50: 987.)

Macrominerals

Increased urine output associated with diabetes mellitus increases obligatory loss of electrolytes such as sodium, potassium, chloride, calcium and phosphorus. Dogs and cats with diabetes mellitus may have whole body phosphorus deficits despite normal or high serum phosphorus concentrations. One-fourth of dogs and nearly half of cats with DKA have hypophosphatemia when initially examined.[1] Diabetic ketoacidosis will also hasten loss of cations (sodium, potassium, calcium, magnesium) because ketone bodies possess weak acid properties.

Diabetes mellitus may lead to depletion of body magnesium stores via osmotic diuresis, especially when hyperglycemia is poorly controlled.[38,39] In addition, treatment of DKA may result in shifts of magnesium into intracellular compartments further decreasing serum magnesium concentrations. Magnesium is essential in glucose homeostasis at several different levels including as: 1) a cofactor in several enzymes of the glucose oxidation pathway, 2) a cofactor in glucose transport systems across plasma membranes, 3) a modulator of energy transfer from high-energy phosphate bonds and 4) having a possible role in the release of insulin. However, it is generally accepted that magnesium depletion is a result rather than a cause of diabetes mellitus; therefore, alleviation of signs of diabetes mellitus would not be expected with dietary repletion of magnesium. Generally, treatment of diabetes mellitus, which results in good glycemic control, corrects magnesium deficiency if the patient is fed a typical commercial pet food. In some cases of diabetes mellitus with severe magnesium depletion, supplemental magnesium may be required as part of the treatment regimen.[40]

It is necessary to replace depleted electrolytes to achieve normal homeostasis. No studies have been performed to establish recommended levels of minerals in foods for animals with diabetes mellitus. Dogs and cats without renal impairment should be fed foods with adequate amounts of phosphorus to avoid and replace whole body phosphorus deficits. However, excess dietary phosphorus should be avoided in animals with renal impairment. Diabetic cats fed foods with low magnesium content

Table 24-5. Selected commercial pet foods used in patients with diabetes mellitus.*

Products	Protein	Fat	Crude fiber**	Carbohydrate
Dry canine products				
Hill's Prescription Diet Canine w/d	16.7	12.0	16.8	55.2
Iams Eukanuba Glucose-Control	29.3	8.1	2.9	53.1
Purina CNM DCO-Formula	25.3	12.4	7.6	47.8
Select Care Canine Hifactor Formula	25.7	10.8	14.7	41.8
Waltham/Pedigree Canine High Fibre Diet	21.3	8.2	4.9	59.1
Moist canine products				
Hill's Prescription Diet Canine w/d	16.5	12.0	13.5	53.9
Select Care Canine Hifactor Formula	24.8	90	15.0	41.0
Waltham/Pedigree Canine High Fibre Diet	29.8	8.0	10.3	45.0
Dry feline products				
Hill's Prescription Diet Feline w/d	39.2	9.5	9.0	36.5
Purina CNM OM-Formula	37.0	7.7	11.5	36.3
Select Care Feline Hifactor Formula	38.2	12.9	5.0	38.3
Moist feline products				
Hill's Prescription Diet Feline w/d	41.1	16.6	12.3	23.7
Select Care Feline Hifactor Formula	34.1	16.1	7.2	36.3

*Products with the largest market share for which published information was available.
**Crude fiber underestimates the soluble and total dietary fiber content of foods. See Chapter 2 for details.
All nutrients expressed on % dry matter basis.

Trace Minerals and Vitamins in Diabetes Mellitus

Changes in trace mineral nutrition status associated with diabetes mellitus have been evaluated in multiple species. The role of zinc in diabetes mellitus is controversial; however, it may affect insulin release from the pancreas, glucose tolerance and insulin resistance through changes in insulin binding and activity. Zinc appears to have biphasic activity; low concentrations enhance insulin secretion and activity whereas higher levels reverse this effect. Whole body zinc stores are often low in patients with diabetes mellitus.

Chromium has been proven to be an essential trace element and is thought to have a role in glucose homeostasis. Chromium has no known enzymatic cofactor function, but it may exist as a complex with nicotinic acid and amino acids to form a "glucose tolerance factor" that may aid insulin action. Chromium supplementation may improve glucose tolerance in malnourished subjects and subjects with poor glucose tolerance. Chromium supplements given to diabetic people have mostly proven ineffective in improving glycemic control; however, efficacy may vary on a case-by-case basis and chromium may prove beneficial in some individuals. At present, there is no reliable method to detect marginal chromium deficiency. Cats may display some gastrointestinal side effects when supplemental chromium is administered.

Manganese deficiency has been associated with perturbations in insulin secretion and carbohydrate and lipid metabolism, including impaired glucose usage in laboratory animals; however, its importance in the etiopathogenesis of diabetes is controversial. Repletion of manganese in deficient animals restores normal glucose tolerance and improves insulin secretion. However, treatment of diabetic subjects with manganese supplements had no impact on glycemic control; therefore, it is inferred that manganese deficiency is not a major factor in the pathophysiology of diabetes mellitus.

Iron overload can cause glucose intolerance due to pancreatic damage secondary to hemochromatosis. Overall, iron status does not seem to play a role in diabetes mellitus. Other trace element deficiencies such as vanadium and selenium have been associated with changes in glucose tolerance or insulin-like activity. Vanadium administered to healthy cats caused vomiting and diarrhea but also lowered blood glucose levels in one diabetic cat. Selenium appears to play no role in the development or manifestation of diabetes mellitus.

Substantiation of trace mineral benefits in diabetic dogs and cats has been confounding. Improvement with supplementation appears to occur on a case-by-case basis. In general, until otherwise proven, providing a food with microminerals supplied according to Association of American Feed Control Officials (AAFCO) recommendations for the appropriate lifestage should suffice for most animals with diabetes mellitus.

Diabetes mellitus may increase or decrease vitamin balance (Table 1). Conversely, vitamin status may affect the development and manifestations of diabetes mellitus. Much of the investigative work in this area is controversial and needs to be clarified. In general, foods that contain AAFCO recommended levels of vitamins for adult maintenance should meet most of the altered requirements induced by diabetes. In some cases of diabetes mellitus, it may be necessary to supplement the food with exogenous B vitamins.

Diabetic osteopenia is fairly well-documented in people and has a rational paradigm. Diabetes mellitus may lead to hypomagnesemia, which leads to decreased parathyroid hormone secretion and action, which then results in decreased formation of 1,25-dihydroxyvitamin D_3. Insulin deficiency further impairs formation of 1,25-dihydroxyvitamin D_3. The resultant impaired ability to enhance calcium absorption and retention in the face of hypercalciuria leads to calcium depletion.

Vitamin A homeostasis and status may influence development and control of diabetes mellitus. However, studies have yielded conflicting results; therefore, the effect of vitamin A on diabetes mellitus remains clouded. Most commercial pet foods provide abundant vitamin A.

Table 1. Micronutrient status in people with diabetes mellitus.*

Minerals	IDDM	NIDDM
Chromium	Normal to increased	Normal
Copper	Normal	Normal to increased
Iron	Normal	Normal
Manganese	Normal to decreased	Increased
Selenium	Increased	?
Zinc	Decreased	Decreased
Vitamins		
1,25 DHCC	Decreased	Normal
Thiamin	Normal	Normal
Vitamin A	Decreased?	Normal
Vitamin B$_{12}$	Normal to decreased	Normal
Vitamin B$_6$	Normal to decreased	Normal to decreased
Vitamin C	Normal to decreased	Normal to decreased
Vitamin E	Increased	Increased

Key: IDDM = insulin-dependent diabetes mellitus, NIDDM = non-insulin-dependent diabetes mellitus, 1,25 DHCC = 1,25-dihydroxycholecalciferol.
*Adapted from Mooradian AD, Morley JE. Micronutrient status in diabetes mellitus. American Journal of Clinical Nutrition 1987; 45: 877.

BIBLIOGRAPHY

Driscoll HK, Chertow BS, Jelic TM, et al. Vitamin A status affects the development of diabetes and insulitis in BB rats. Metabolism 1996; 45: 248-253.

Keen CL, Zidenberg-Cherr S. Manganese. In: Ziegler EE, Filer LJ, eds. Present Knowledge in Nutrition, 7th ed. Washington, DC: ILSI Press, 1996; 334-343.

Mooradian AD, Morley JE. Micronutrient status in diabetes mellitus. American Journal of Clinical Nutrition 1987; 45: 877-895.

Nielson FH. Other trace elements. In: Ziegler EE, Filer LJ, eds. Present Knowledge in Nutrition, 7th ed. Washington, DC: ILSI Press, 1996; 353-377.

Plotnick AN, Greco DS, Crans DS, et al. Oral vanadium compounds: Preliminary studies on toxicity in normal cats and hypoglycemic potential in diabetic cats (abstract). In: Proceedings. Thirteenth Annual Veterinary Medical Forum, American College of Veterinary Internal Medicine, Lake Buena Vista, FL, 1995: 996.

Stoecker BJ. Chromium. In: Ziegler EE, Filer LJ, eds. Present Knowledge in Nutrition. Washington, DC: ILSI Press, 1996; 344-352.

Tuitoek PJ, Lakey JRT, Rajotte RV, et al. Strain variation in vitamin A (retinol) status of streptozotocin-induced diabetic rats. International Journal of Vitamin and Nutrition Research 1996; 66: 101-105.

should be monitored carefully to avoid magnesium depletion. In general, foods that meet Association of American Feed Control Officials (AAFCO) recommendations for adult maintenance should supply adequate amounts of macrominerals to compensate for the increased losses described above. Diabetes mellitus may also affect micromineral and vitamin status. (See sidebar "Trace Minerals and Vitamins in Diabetes Mellitus.")

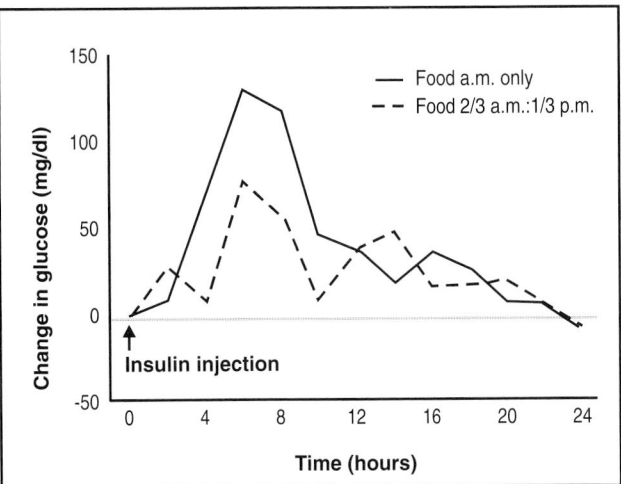

Figure 24-3. Mean change in blood glucose concentrations in eight dogs with insulin-dependent diabetes mellitus (IDDM) fed 66 kcal/kg body weight of a commercial moist dog food. A fixed amount of NPH insulin was administered to each dog at 8:00 a.m. Food was given either in one meal at 8:00 a.m. or in two meals at 8:00 a.m. (two-thirds of the food) and 6:00 p.m. (one-third of the food). Note the reduction in the mean blood glucose excursion merely by feeding multiple rather than one meal daily. (Adapted from Nelson RW. Disorders of the endocrine pancreas. In: Ettinger SJ, ed. Textbook of Veterinary Internal Medicine, 3rd ed. Philadelphia, PA: WB Saunders Co, 1989; 1694.)

Figure 24-4. This nine-year-old, neutered male domestic longhair cat presented for polydipsia, polyuria, polyphagia and weight loss. The initial diagnoses were diabetes mellitus and concurrent hyperthyroidism. The cat was treated with methimazole for the hyperthyroidism; however, the diabetes mellitus persisted. The diabetes mellitus was controlled with a combination of oral glipizide and a veterinary therapeutic food containing low-fat and moderate fiber levels. Methimazole therapy was continued.

Assess the Food(s)

Levels of the key nutritional factors should be evaluated in foods currently being fed to diabetic animals. Key nutritional factors include the amount of energy consumed and dietary levels of protein, soluble carbohydrate, fiber and fat. Amounts and levels of key nutritional factors should be compared to those established for diabetic dogs and cats. (See Table 24-4 and Key Nutritional Factors—Endocrine and Lipid Disorders.) Information from this aspect of assessment is essential for making any changes to foods currently provided. If key nutritional factors in the current food(s) do not match the recommended levels, then changing to a more appropriate food is indicated. Table 24-5 lists selected commercial foods often fed to patients with diabetes mellitus.

Assess the Feeding Method

It is imperative that feeding methods complement pharmaceutical treatment protocols. Insulin is usually administered in conjunction with meals; therefore, thorough evaluation is required to assess whether any modifications to the feeding plan may be necessary. This is especially true when considering concurrent disease and physiologic changes associated with aging or response to treatment.

Treatment and Feeding Plan

Treatment for diabetes mellitus usually involves a combination of commonly available options. Treatment with injectable insulin or oral sulfonylurea agents has been the mainstay of pharmacologic intervention for uncomplicated diabetes mellitus.[1] Nutritional intervention is the major nonpharmacologic treatment modality in diabetes mellitus. NIDDM in cats may resolve with appropriate dietary treatment and proper case management (Figure 24-4). Efficacy of dietary treatment depends to a great degree on the ability to manage the primary disease via medical treatment options.

Exercise should be constant from day to day because large variations in activity level may affect glycemic control. Food changes should be accompanied by concurrent monitoring to assess if glycemic control has been affected. In general, increasing fiber levels increases glycemic control and decreasing fiber content decreases glycemic control. Changes in food/fiber may result in the need to adjust the insulin dose by up to 20%.[a] If the weight of the animal changes, in either planned or unplanned fashion, then reassessment should take place at least every two weeks because the insulin dosage may need to be readjusted with changes in body weight. It is also important to control concurrent disease processes via appropriate therapy.

Feeding Plan for IDDM

Dietary modification, in conjunction with insulin therapy, has been shown to be an effective adjunct in the control of diabetes mellitus in dogs and cats. The model for dietary management of diabetes mellitus is inferred from human nutrition and research in dogs and cats. In general, foods with decreased fat, moderate fiber, moderate protein and low levels of simple sugars have been recommended. Concerns have been raised about the composition of carbohydrate in cat foods because cats have a different capacity to metabolize carbohydrates than dogs.[41]

The energy intake of diabetic animals must be assessed in relation to body condition. A number of diabetic animals may present in obese body condition, which necessitates implementation of a dietary plan to achieve weight loss. (See Chapter 13.) In other cases, feeding a food with moderate to high levels of fiber may pose problems for maintenance of current weight in thin patients. In such cases, feeding an increased quantity of food above the calculated maintenance requirement or slightly increasing the fat content of foods may prove useful. Increasing food dose may not result in increased weight gain if diabetes is poorly controlled.

Feeding must be coordinated with the time frame of the exogenously administered insulin. This coordination of feeding and maximal insulin activity minimizes postprandial hyperglycemia and maximizes food usage (Figure 24-3). Ideally, several small meals given at regular intervals throughout the day with and following insulin administration result in minimal hyperglycemia.[42,43] Generally, for animals receiving once-a-day insulin, half of the caloric requirement is fed at the time of exogenous insulin administration and the other half eight to 10 hours later. If insulin is given twice daily, half of the caloric requirement should be fed with each injection. It may be beneficial to offer a small snack between feedings. The food should be divided into four or more smaller meals for animals with poor glycemic control to aid in maintaining serum glucose concentrations within an acceptable range.[42,43] Food should be offered just before insulin administration to avoid insulin-induced hypoglycemia. Commercial foods often used in patients with IDDM are listed in Table 24-5.

Feeding Plan for NIDDM

The nutritional plan for NIDDM is similar to that for IDDM. Many cats with NIDDM are obese; therefore, caloric restriction may be a requisite part of dietary management. Care must be taken to avoid rapid weight loss that may predispose to hepatic lipidosis. Loss of 0.5 to 1% of initial body weight per week is considered safe. (See Chapter 13.) Hepatic lipidosis does not seem to be a weight-loss concern for dogs. Sulfonylurea agents may induce vomiting in cats; therefore, food may need to be offered a few hours before drug administration to ensure nutrient absorption.

Feeding Plan for Diabetic Ketoacidosis

Intensive care and intravenous fluid administration are not required if the animal is bright, alert and well-hydrated. Administration of short- or intermediate-acting insulin can be initiated in conjunction with feeding recommendations similar to those for IDDM and NIDDM. Some DKA animals may require in-hospital intensive care. Goals are to correct dehydration, electrolyte disorders (hypokalemia, hypophosphatemia, hyponatremia, hypochloremia, hypomagnesemia), ketonuria and acidosis while initiating a feeding plan. Nutritional recommendations are similar to those for IDDM and NIDDM after the animal is stabilized.

Reassessment

Clinical Signs

Response to treatment can be assessed through careful questioning of the owner of the diabetic pet. Favorable response to treatment may be indicated by decreased water intake, decreased urination, decreased food intake, achievement of weight goals and a generalized increased thriftiness. Continuation of polyuria, polydipsia, polyphagia and inability to achieve weight goals are unfavorable responses. Veterinary reassessment should take place every three to four months if the animal is stable and doing well. If the animal is symptomatic, veterinary reassessment should take place every one to two weeks until it is stable.

Body Weight and Condition

Achievement of weight goals can be measured through assessing body condition and weight. These measurements may also provide insight about the degree of glycemic control and the presence of other disease processes, especially in cases in which adjustments in food dose do not produce expected changes in body condition. Animals should be weighed once every two weeks and have body condition assessed at least once monthly. The owner should be encouraged to keep a chart of body weights and BCS. It may take several months to achieve weight-loss goals in obese animals. A loss of 10% body weight in already thin animals indicates a need for reassessment of the dietary and pharmacologic regimens.

Food Intake

Food intake, with maintenance of body weight, should decrease in animals with a favorable response to exogenous insulin administration. This response is caused by increased nutrient usage associated with hormonal treatment. If animals are anorectic or have depressed food intake, the relative palatability of the food may be poor and another food should be tried after ruling out medical causes. It is especially important to monitor food intake in cats because prolonged anorexia is a risk factor for hepatic lipidosis.[44]

Urine Glucose and Ketones

Most owners can monitor urine glucose and ketones. A decrease in urinary ketone bodies and glucose signals a favorable response to treatment. In well-controlled diabetes mellitus, no ketone bodies should be present in the urine. Several urinalyses should be performed throughout the day to assess control of glycemia. Ideally, urine should be free of glucose for the majority of the tests. Moderate amounts of glucose and any ketone bodies indicate a need to reassess insulin treatment or evaluate for concurrent disease.

Biochemistry Profiles

The biochemistry profile should return to normal with well-controlled diabetes and adequate nutritional intake. The primary exception is hyperglycemia that may or may not be present depending on when the blood sample is obtained in relation to insulin administration. Abnormalities of biochemical constituents in the face of controlled diabetes mellitus should be evaluated as separate disease entities.

Serial Blood Glucose Curves

Serial determination of the temporal response of blood glucose concentration to insulin over 12 to 24 hours during the management of diabetes mellitus may prove useful in adjusting insulin dosage. The ideal response is to have a glucose nadir around 100 to 125 mg/dl and to maintain glucose concentration below 250 mg/dl for the majority of the curve. Details on adjustment and in-depth analysis of serial glucose curves are given elsewhere.[1]

Serial determination of glucose curves, although useful, has limited application in clinical practice. Stress and unfamiliarity of subjects with clinic surroundings often confound results of glucose curves. Cats are especially prone to stress-induced hyperglycemia. Therefore, use of serial glucose curves in this species may be limited. Nonetheless, serial glucose curves provide information, when appropriately interpreted, for adjustment of insulin dosage in many subjects.[1]

Glycosylated Hemoglobin and Fructosamine

Measurement of glycated proteins (e.g., hemoglobin and serum proteins [fructosamine]) is a common method of monitoring glycemic control in people. Glucose binds nonenzymatically and irreversibly to different proteins. The percentage of glycated protein depends on the concentration of glucose in serum and the half-life of the protein. Glucose bound to hemoglobin (glycosylated hemoglobin) is the most commonly used indicator of glycemic control in people, providing an index of glycemic control during the life span of red blood cells (70 to 90 days). Glycated serum proteins (fructosamine) are similarly used to indicate glycemic control for the 10 to 15 days before testing.

Commercial automated testing for glycated proteins in dogs and cats has not proven reliable. Affinity chromatography results specific for canine and feline glycosylated proteins have been determined; however, values vary between laboratories. Nevertheless, careful determination of fructosamine or glycated hemoglobin using species-specific testing methods have yielded useful results to help interpret glycemic control in cats and dogs.[1,45-48]

In addition to altered metabolism, some complications of diabetes mellitus are associated with the above aberrant glycosylation of proteins. Hyperglycemia, which induces non-enzymatic glycosylation of body proteins, results in physiologic dysfunction in target proteins. Common complications include cataract formation in dogs, neuropathy in cats, basement membrane disease, nephropathy, weight loss, DKA and recurrent infections in both species.[49] Increased monitoring should be performed to avoid these serious complications when situations with increased stress (e.g., holidays, boarding.), unplanned food indiscretions and concurrent disease are present.

■ INSULIN-SECRETING TUMORS

Clinical Importance

The prevalence of insulin-secreting beta-cell tumors (insulinoma) in dogs and cats is not accurately known; however, clinicians classify occurrences as uncommon in dogs and rare in cats. Although there is no proven breed predisposition, certain breeds of dogs are thought to be affected more commonly including boxers, fox terriers, German shepherd dogs and Irish setters.[50] In one study, the mean age of dogs at time of diagnosis was 9.5 years, with a range of three to 14 years and no gender predilection.[50] Clinical signs are attributable to excessive insulin secretion from insulin-secreting beta-cell tumors. The inciting cause of insulin-secreting beta-cell neoplasia is unknown.

Assessment

Assess the Animal

HISTORY AND PHYSICAL EXAMINATION

Clinical signs of insulin-secreting beta-cell tumors may be subtle to owners but are usually related to recurrent hypoglycemia. Dogs may be symptomatic for one to six months, with some clinical signs reported to be present for more than one year. Signs associated with hypoglycemia include lethargy, weakness, syncope, seizures, and in severe cases, coma. Seizure activity is more common than syncope and coma. Signs of hypoglycemia are often episodic because normal compensatory counter-regulatory mechanisms (e.g., catecholamine or glucagon release) increase concentrations of blood glucose when hypoglycemia is encountered.[51] Signs may last for a few seconds to minutes depending on the lag interval and the magnitude of counter-regulatory mechanisms.[50]

A strong association exists between development of clinical signs and food deprivation, exercise, excitement and eating. The association with excitement, exercise and food deprivation is attributable to increased glucose consumption, relative to food intake.[50] The association with eating is due to hyper-responsiveness of insulinomas to external stimuli such as food intake. Therefore, postprandial hypoglycemia may occur two to six hours after eating from excessive insulin secretion in response to a normal meal.

Recent and past dietary history should be evaluated, including methods of feeding, interval of feeding, quantity of food and type of food. The relationship of clinical signs to time of feeding should be thoroughly evaluated in dogs with a potential diagnosis of insulinoma. Intake of snacks, scraps and water should be evaluated for completeness. If possible, ingredient formulation from commercially prepared and homemade foods should be obtained to aid in assessment of dietary changes needed, if any. If caloric density and quantity of food provided are known, daily caloric intake should be determined and compared to energy requirements.

Dietary histories of dogs with insulinomas may be unremarkable; however, the association of eating with subsequent clinical signs, or control of signs by increasing the frequency of feeding, may be noted by some owners. Animals fed one large meal per day may be more likely to develop signs than animals fed several small meals throughout the day.

Physical examination of dogs with insulin-secreting beta-cell tumors is often normal because visible and palpable abnormalities are rare. However, in some cases peripheral neuropathies causing proprioceptive deficits, depressed placing reflexes and muscle atrophy may be present.[52] The pathogenesis of these neuropathies is subject to debate.[50] Weight gain attributable to anabolic effects of insulin may be noted in some cases.

LABORATORY AND OTHER DIAGNOSTIC TESTS

Confirmation of insulin-secreting beta-cell tumors requires identification of fasting hypoglycemia coupled with inappropriate insulin secretion for the degree of hypoglycemia observed. However, differential diagnoses for hypoglycemia are extensive and may be generalized into categories such as endocrine, hepatic, substrate and miscellaneous (Table 24-6). Extensive laboratory work may be necessary to differentiate these diseases.

Hypoglycemia is the only consistent finding in dogs with insulin-secreting beta-cell tumors (serum glucose less than 60 mg/dl). The average serum glucose concentration in 71 dogs with insulinomas was 46 mg/dl, with a range of 15 to 78 mg/dl.[50] A normal serum glucose concentration does not rule out insulinoma. Food deprivation for eight hours induced hypoglycemia in 31 of 35 trials. Almost all dogs with insulin-secreting beta-cell neoplasia develop hypoglycemia within 12 hours of food deprivation.

Other abnormalities that may occur in the serum biochemistry analysis include hypoalbuminemia, hypophosphatemia, hypokalemia and increased alkaline phosphatase and alanine aminotransferase activity.[53] Increased hepatic enzyme activity is nonspecific and may confuse the diagnosis with primary hepatic disease. Results of urinalyses and complete blood counts are usually within normal limits.

Identifying hyperinsulinemia in conjunction with hypoglycemia is the gold standard for confirming a diagnosis of insulin-secreting beta-cell tumors. The protocol requires simultaneous determination of serum glucose and insulin concentrations when the serum glucose concentration is less than 60 mg/dl (preferably less than 50 mg/dl). Animals may need to be deprived of food for four to 12 hours to achieve the appropriate serum glucose concentration. Serum glucose concentrations may be estimated hourly by strip chemistry technology. When concentrations approach approximately 40 mg/dl, a serum sample should be submitted for measurement of glucose and insulin levels. A serum insulin concentration greater than 20 µU/ml with a corresponding serum glucose concentration less than 60 mg/dl strongly supports a diagnosis of insulin-secreting beta-cell tumor. An insulin concentration less than 5 µU/ml is inconsistent with insulin-secreting beta-cell tumors. Serum concentrations of insulin between 10 and 20 µU/ml (normal range) are consistent with a diagnosis of an insulin-secreting beta-cell tumor, if other causes of hypoglycemia have been ruled out.[50]

Radiographic evaluation of insulin-secreting beta-cell tumors is usually unremarkable because of the small size of the tumors. Ultrasonography has proven more useful in establishing a diagnosis in dogs with appropriate clinical signs. However, ultrasonographic detection is not without difficulty; in one study, histologic-confirmed tumors were successfully identified by ultrasound antemortem in only 27% of dogs.[50] Identification of a pancreatic mass via ultrasound or exploratory celiotomy, with or without methylene blue staining, confirms the diagnosis (Figure 24-5).[54]

KEY NUTRITIONAL FACTORS

Carbohydrates

Simple carbohydrates, such as glucose, are more potent secretagogues of insulin than are starch or fibers (complex carbohydrates). Simple carbohydrates, therefore, should be avoided in foods for animals with insulin-secreting beta-cell neoplasia because of their greater insulin secretagogue activity. Carbohydrates in complex form (e.g., starch) are preferred because they may be more slowly digested. Soluble fiber may be fermented to short-chain fatty acids, which have limited secretagogue potential.

Table 24-6. Differential diagnosis for fasting hypoglycemia.*

Endocrine
Excess insulin or insulin-like factors
    Extrahepatic tumor producing and secreting insulin-like
        substances
    Iatrogenic insulin overdose
    Insulin-producing islet cell tumor
Growth hormone deficiency
    Hypopituitarism affecting several tropic hormones
        (ACTH, GH)
    Monotropic growth hormone deficiency
Cortisol deficiency
    Hypoadrenocorticism
    Hypopituitarism
    Isolated ACTH deficiency
Hepatic
Congenital
    Glycogen storage diseases
    Vascular shunts
Acquired
    Chronic fibrosis (cirrhosis)
    Hepatic necrosis (toxins, infectious agents)
    Vascular shunts
Substrate
Extrapancreatic tumors that use large quantities of glucose
Fasting hypoglycemia of pregnancy
Puppy hypoglycemia = ketonemia (alanine deficiency?)
Severe malnutrition
Severe polycythemia
Uremia
Miscellaneous
Artifacts
Drugs (sulfonylurea, etc.)

Key: ACTH = adrenocorticotropic hormone, GH = growth hormone.
*Adapted from Feldman EC, Nelson RW, eds. Beta-cell neoplasia: Insulinoma. Canine and Feline Endocrinology and Reproduction, 2nd ed. Philadelphia, PA: WB Saunders Co, 1996; 427.

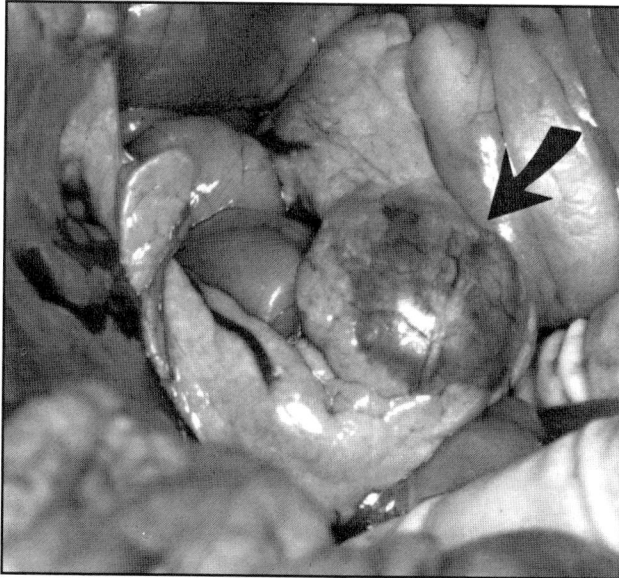

Figure 24-5. Picture of an insulin-secreting beta-cell tumor from an 11-year-old, neutered female Labrador retriever-cross dog with clinical signs related to hypoglycemia (intermittent weakness, seizures). Inappropriate hyperinsulinemia (serum glucose concentration 37 mg/dl, serum insulin concentration 46 µU/ml) was documented and the tumor (arrow) identified at surgery. Complete removal resulted in reestablishment of euglycemia, which lasted approximately six months at which time clinical signs related to hypoglycemia recurred.

However, fiber (soluble and insoluble) decreases the glycemic index and may not be appropriate for dogs with insulin-secreting beta-cell tumor.

The role of carbohydrates in the dietary management of dogs with insulinomas needs to be further investigated; however, the following general recommendations can be made: 1) avoid moist or semi-moist foods high in simple sugars, or rapidly digestible starch, 2) reduce crude fiber to less than 5%

Table 24-7. Nutrient recommendations for dogs and cats with insulin-secreting beta-cell tumor.*

Nutrients	Dogs	Cats
Carbohydrate	Avoid excess levels of simple carbohydrates	Avoid excess levels of simple carbohydrates
Crude fiber	<5	<5
Fat	20 to 25	25 to 30
Protein	15 to 25	28 to 45

*Nutrients expressed on a % dry matter basis.

Table 24-8. Etiology of hypothyroidism in dogs.*

Primary hypothyroidism
Lymphocytic thyroiditis
Idiopathic atrophy
Follicular cell hyperplasia (dyshormonogenesis)
Neoplastic destruction
Iatrogenic
Antithyroid medication
Radioactive iodine treatment
Surgical removal

Secondary hypothyroidism
Defective TSH molecule
Defective TSH-follicular cell receptor interaction
Iatrogenic
Drug therapy (glucocorticoids)
Hypophysectomy
Radiation therapy
Pituitary malformation
Hypoplasia of pars distalis
Pituitary cyst
Pituitary destruction
Neoplasia
Pituitary thyrotropic cell suppression
Euthyroid sick syndrome
Naturally acquired hyperadrenocorticism

Tertiary hypothyroidism
Congenital hypothalamic malformation
Acquired destruction of hypothalamus
Abscess
Granuloma
Hemorrhage
Inflammation
Neoplasia
Defective TRH molecule
Defective TRH-thyrotroph receptor interaction

Congenital hypothyroidism
Circulating thyroid hormone transport defects
Deficient dietary iodine intake
Dyshormonogenesis (iodine organification defect)
Ingestion of goitrogens
Thyroid gland dysgenesis
Aplasia
Ectasia
Hypoplasia

Key: TRH = thyrotropin-releasing hormone, TSH = thyroid-stimulating hormone.
*Adapted from Feldman EC, Nelson RW, eds. Hypothyroidism. Canine and Feline Endocrinology and Reproduction, 2nd ed. Philadelphia, PA: WB Saunders Co, 1996; 71.

of the dry matter, 3) minimize the carbohydrate proportion of the food and 4) when carbohydrates are fed, maximize the proportion of complex, nonfiber carbohydrates (i.e., starch).

Protein

Amino acids are also secretagogues of insulin, especially arginine and leucine.[55] It is unknown if high- or low-protein foods, or proportions of amino acids in the food, have a major effect on the management of insulinomas in dogs. Low-protein foods administered to young rats significantly decreased insulin secretion from isolated pancreatic beta islet cells.[56] Therefore, foods for animals with insulinomas should contain adequate but not excessive amounts of protein (15 to 25% DM for dogs, 28 to 45% DM for cats).

Energy

Insulin secretion enhances the uptake and storage of glucose and amino acids to insulin-sensitive tissues such as skeletal and adipose tissue. Thus, animals with insulin-secreting beta-cell tumor may have adequate daily energy intake but the flux of energy throughout the body may be dysregulated resulting in excessive adipose and muscle tissue consumption. The rapid turnover of glucose through the blood pool and misdirection to inappropriate tissues (muscle, adipose), may predispose to low energy supply to nervous tissue, which has no substantial reserve of energy. Therefore, dietary goals for energy management revolve around modulating the flux of energy through the different compartments so that nervous tissue is never deprived: 1) feed at DER (reassess frequently), 2) provide multiple small meals each day to maintain a constant energy intake and 3) counsel clients to have a sucrose solution ready if neurologic signs develop due to energy deprivation.[50]

Fat

The liver is the major organ responsible for fat synthesis and maintenance of glucose homeostasis via gluconeogenesis and glycogenolysis. The high concentration of insulin in serum enhances hepatic fat synthesis from amino acids and glucose and fat deposition in adipose tissue. The primary source of fuel for the liver is fatty acids, and under the influence of glucagon, fatty acids actually stimulate hepatic gluconeogenic pathways. Although speculative, it may be possible that foods with lower protein and carbohydrate and higher fat content may actually benefit management of insulinomas by delaying gastric emptying and decreasing insulin secretion via the above metabolic pathways.

Assess the Food(s)

Foods being fed should be evaluated for levels of carbohydrate, protein, energy, fiber and fat. Protein, fat and crude fiber levels can be estimated from the guaranteed or typical analysis on the product label; however, levels of carbohydrate and energy density must be obtained by contacting the manufacturer or obtaining published product information. Levels of these key nutritional factors in current foods should be compared to recommended levels (Table 24-7). Commercial foods with excessive levels of simple carbohydrates (semi-moist or moist-dry forms) should be avoided.

Assess the Feeding Method

It may not always be necessary to change the feeding method when managing animals with insulin-secreting beta-cell neoplasia; however, it is important to ascertain current feeding practices and provide clients with a rational plan when change is indicated. Thorough evaluation warrants compilation of all feeding methods currently in place as well as potential for change. This is especially true when considering concurrent disease, owner constraints and physiologic changes associated with aging. Multiple small meals throughout the day may be better than a single meal for patients with insulin-secreting beta-cell neoplasia.

Treatment and Feeding Plan

Surgical exploration with removal or debulking of insulin-secreting beta-cell neoplasia appears to offer the best chance for a cure. Long-term medical management is required if the mass is diffuse or can't be resected completely. The primary medical therapy is dietary management; however, pharmacologic intervention with glucocorticoids, diazoxide, somatostatin, phenytoin, alloxan, propranolol or combination therapy may prove beneficial. The reader is referred elsewhere for specific information about pharmacologic intervention.[50]

The food recommended for animals with insulin-secreting beta-cell tumors should be low in total carbohydrates, moderate to high fat and moderate to low protein. The carbohydrates should contain minimal fiber levels. Foods should be highly digestible with the possible exception of complex carbohydrates, which may be of more benefit if they slightly resist digestion (Table 24-7). Commercial dry foods are preferred because semi-moist and moist-dry forms are often high in simple carbohydrates, and commercial moist foods may contain higher levels of both protein and simple carbohydrates.

Energy intake should be calculated for each patient. The total daily caloric intake should be divided into three to six equal feedings that can be administered throughout the day. If the patient shows signs of hypoglycemia (seizures), but is still capable of eating, a snack or small meal should be made available. Small amounts of corn syrup or honey may be applied to the gums of animals with seizures especially if offering a meal is ill advised because of the danger of aspiration. Small, frequent meals should be provided after the animal is capable of eating on its own.

Reassessment

The owner can monitor response to therapy by observing clinical signs. Lack of lethargy, weakness, seizures and coma indicate adequate control. Recurrence of clinical signs under nonstress conditions may indicate growth or metastasis of the tumor or inappropriate compliance and/or treatment. Periodic monitoring of serum glucose concentrations in the hospital setting may indicate the degree of therapeutic success. In almost all cases of medical management, the prognosis is poor to guarded with a survival expectancy in dogs of 12 to 24 months.[57]

■ DISORDERS OF THE THYROID GLAND

Clinical Importance

Hyperthyroidism is primarily a disease of cats with the first clinical reports appearing in the late 1970s and early 1980s.[58,59] Disease prevalence has been estimated at one in 300 from necropsy findings.[60] The prevalence of the disease appears to be increasing; cases in one hospital increased from three per month to 22 per month over a 12-year period.[61]

In dogs, hyperthyroidism is only found with thyroid neoplasia.[62] However, most thyroid neoplasia in dogs tends to be nonfunctional compared to the functional type found in cats. About 10% of dogs with thyroid neoplasia exhibit hyperthyroidism attributable to functional thyroid tumors.[62]

Hypothyroidism is primarily a problem of dogs and rarely observed in cats. The most common cause of hypothyroidism in dogs is classified as primary (causes within the gland); however, extra-thyroidal causes have been identified (Table 24-8). No overall incidence has been reported; however, hypothyroidism is considered the most commonly diagnosed endocrinopathy in dogs. Cases of hypothyroidism in cats are typically congenital or iatrogenic resulting from treatment of hyperthyroidism.

Assessment

Assess the Animal

The goals of animal assessment in patients with suspected thyroid disease are: 1) establish the diagnosis of hyper- or hypothyroidism, 2) identify concurrent disease,

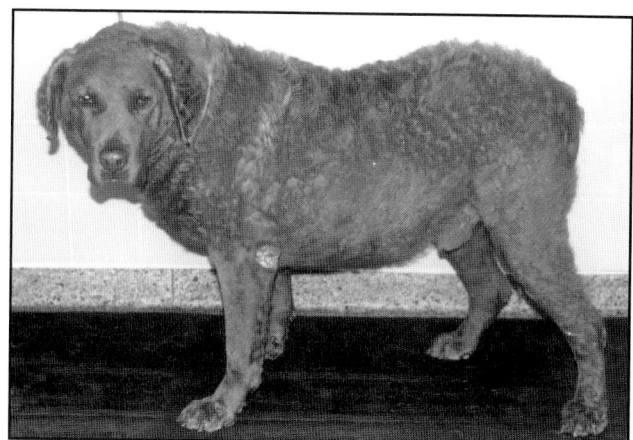

Figure 24-6. An eight-year-old male Chesapeake Bay retriever with hypothyroidism. Note the poor coat, lethargic appearance, myxedema of the face and drooping eyelids. (Reprinted with permission from Feldman EC, Nelson RW, eds. Hypothyroidism. Canine and Feline Endocrinology and Reproduction, 2nd ed. Philadelphia, PA: WB Saunders Co, 1996; 79.)

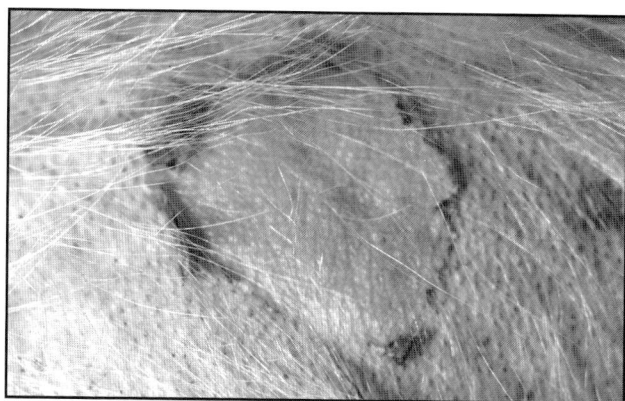

Figure 24-7. Alopecia and seborrhea in an English setter with hypothyroidism.

Table 24-9. Clinical signs associated with hypothyroidism and hyperthyroidism.

Clinical signs	Hypothyroidism	Hyperthyroidism
Appetite	Normal to decreased	Increased to decreased
Behavior	Lethargy, mental dullness, inactivity, cold intolerance	Nervous, hyperactive to lethargic, excess vocalization, aggressive, heat intolerance
Coat	Dry/sparse (endocrine alopecia), seborrhea	Dry/greasy/patchy alopecia/unkempt
Eyes	Normal or corneal lipid deposits, corneal ulceration/uveitis	Normal
Heart rate/rhythm	Normal to decreased with possible dysrhythmias	Increased with possible dysrhythmias
Neck	Normal/mass	Normal/mass
Neuromuscular	Seizures, ataxia, circling, vestibular signs, weakness, knuckling, facial nerve paralysis	Weakness, tremors, ventroflexion of head, muscle wasting
Respiratory	Normal	Panting, respiratory distress, dysphonia (dogs)
Skin	Hyperpigmentation	Normal
Stools	Constipation to diarrhea	Bulky to diarrhea
Thirst	Normal to decreased	Increased
Urine	Normal	Excess urination
Vomiting	No	Possible
Weight	Normal to increased	Normal to decreased
Other	Reproductive dysfunction, poor growth	Reproductive dysfunction

Table 24-10. Differential diagnosis for hyperthyroidism.*

Nonthyroid endocrine disease
  Acromegaly (rare)
  Diabetes insipidus (rare)
  Diabetes mellitus
  Hyperadrenocorticism (rare)
Renal disease
Heart disease
  Congestive cardiomyopathy
  Hypertrophic cardiomyopathy
  Idiopathic dysrhythmia
Gastrointestinal disease
  Cancer
  Diffuse gastrointestinal disorders
  Inflammatory
  Pancreatic exocrine insufficiency
Hepatopathy
  Cancer
  Inflammatory
Pulmonary disease

*Adapted from Feldman EC, Nelson RW, eds. Feline hyperthyroidism (thyrotoxicosis). Canine and Feline Endocrinology and Reproduction, 2nd ed. Philadelphia, PA: WB Saunders Co, 1996; 135.

3) assess body condition for specific dietary recommendations and 4) identify inciting causes, if possible.

HISTORY AND PHYSICAL EXAMINATION

Clinical signs of excessive or insufficient thyroid activity are numerous and may be confused with other disease processes (Tables 24-9 and 24-10). The appearance of clinical signs may be insidious with some being more distinctive than others. A complete physical and laboratory examination is necessary to achieve a precise diagnosis. All body systems should be examined and evaluated individually and in the context of the overall disease process. Typically, hyperthyroidism is a disease of older cats with a mean age of 12 to 14 years,[63] although cats as young as two years of age have been treated for hyperthyroidism.[b] No gender or breed predilection has been established for hyperthyroid cats.[64] Some canine breeds appear to be at increased risk for hypothyroidism; however, there is no documented gender predilection.

Dietary history of animals with hyperthyroidism usually includes polyphagia due to increased cellular metabolism. However, it is not uncommon to see decreased appetite following a prolonged period of polyphagia. Decreased appetite is usually associated with weakness, muscle wasting and severe weight loss.

Hypothyroidism may be confused with several other diseases because there is no specific abnormality other than thyroid dysfunction (Table 24-10). Hypothyroidism is usually associated with signs related to decreased cellular metabolism. Occasionally, iodine deficiency has been identified as a cause of hypothyroidism in dogs; however, most commercial dog foods contain adequate iodine.[9] No other associations with dietary history have been reported as causes of hypothyroidism in dogs. However, selenium deficiency may influence thyroid status because deiodinase I and possibly deiodinase II are selenoproteins.

Animals with hypothyroidism often are overweight, in poor body condition and have poor skin and coat conditions (Figures 24-6 and 24-7). Hyperthyroid animals are typically underweight and often have muscle wasting. However, in either instance, animals may be within normal weight ranges depending on how advanced the disease process is when recognized. The presence of concurrent diseases may influence these parameters and careful examination may reveal other abnormalities that may not be noted by owners.

LABORATORY AND OTHER DIAGNOSTIC TESTING

The primary purpose of laboratory testing is to establish a diagnosis of hyper- or hypothyroidism and screen the animal for concurrent disease. Any number of abnormalities may be present in individual animals; however, clinical studies have enumerated common changes (Table 24-11). Specific diagnostics for thyroid dysfunction should be performed if thyroid disease is still consistent with and suspected from results of the initial screening.

Serum Thyroid Concentrations

Thyroid hormones in blood (total T_4 or triiodothyronine [T_3]) may exist either bound to carrier proteins or free in the water fraction of serum (free T_4 or T_3). Determination of total T_4 concentrations has proven more useful than total T_3 levels for differentiating hyperthyroidism in cats. Free T_4 concentrations (by dialysis) should be determined to substantiate disease in cases in which total T_4 values are nondiagnostic, but hyperthyroidism is still suspected.[65]

Findings in dogs with thyroid neoplasms depend on the type of neoplasm and extent of proliferation or destruction of normal thyroid tissue within the gland. In dogs, mea-

Table 24-11. Laboratory findings in animals with hypothyroidism and hyperthyroidism.

Laboratory tests	Hypothyroidism	Hyperthyroidism
Biochemical analysis	Increased cholesterol, triglyceride, ALT (mild), ALP (mild) and CK (mild, variable) values	**Cats:** increased ALT, ALP, creatinine, urea nitrogen, glucose, bilirubin and phosphate values **Dogs:** mild increases in urea nitrogen, liver enzyme and possibly calcium values
Cardiac diagnostics	Bradycardia, inverted T waves	**Cats:** tachycardia, PVCs, hypertrophic cardiomyopathy **Dogs:** normal
Complete blood count	Normocytic, normochromic, nonregenerative anemia with leptocytes possible	**Cats:** erythrocytosis, leukocytosis, lymphopenia, eosinopenia, increased MCV **Dogs:** mild, normocytic, normochromic, non-regenerative anemia
Imaging	Normal/thyroid mass, metastatic lesions, thoracic or abdominal effusion	Normal or cardiac/respiratory abnormalities
Urinalysis	Normal to nonspecific increase in white blood cells	**Cats:** increased or decreased specific gravity, glucosuria, signs of inflammation **Dogs:** normal

Key: MCV = mean corpuscular volume, ALT = alanine aminotransferase, ALP = serum alkaline phosphatase, PVC = premature ventricular contraction, CK = creatine kinase.

surement of total T_4 or T_3 is considered sufficient for diagnosis and has revealed that hyperthyroidism is present in about 10% of thyroid neoplasms.[62] The remaining thyroid neoplasms in dogs cause either euthyroid (55%) or hypothyroid (35%) characteristics.

An appropriate diagnosis of hypothyroidism may be made through thyroid-function testing, clinical signs and response to trial thyroid-hormone administration. In theory, low concentrations of thyroid hormone should be associated with a diagnosis of hypothyroidism. However, hypothyroid dogs without neoplasia of the thyroid gland are usually not definitively diagnosed by determination of concentrations of total T_4 or T_3 in serum due to the considerable overlap of the concentration of these two hormones between euthyroid and hypothyroid animals. Measurement of free T_4 in serum has the same interpretative dilemma as total T_4 and is considered not as reliable. In addition, a small percentage of hypothyroid dogs have normal T_4 levels in the face of antithyroid hormone antibodies, which further clouds diagnostic accuracy of thyroid-hormone tests.[66,67] Concentrations of these hormones should be interpreted in conjunction with clinical and physical signs to arrive at an educated assessment of thyroid status.[9]

Serum TSH

Determination of thyroid-stimulating hormone (TSH) concentration is considered the gold standard for diagnosing hypothyroidism in people. In general, elevated concentrations of TSH indicate primary hypothyroidism. Secondary and tertiary hypothyroidism are indicated by concentrations of TSH within a normal range and decreased to normal serum T_4 concentrations. Assays for canine TSH are available and appear quite promising in diagnosis of hypothyroidism. In addition, TSH testing in conjunction with baseline thyroid-hormone concentrations in blood appears to be a sensitive and specific method to diagnose canine hypothyroidism in preliminary studies.[68,69]

Thyroid-Hormone (T_3) Suppression Test

This test is used to distinguish euthyroid from mildly hyperthyroid cats in cases in which T_4 and fT_4 (free T_4) values are nebulous. The T_3 suppression test is based on the theory that TSH is suppressed by increasing concen-

trations of thyroid hormones in normal cats. TSH secretion is suppressed and T_4 and T_3 concentrations are increased in hyperthyroid cats because of autonomous secretion. In this test, T_3 is administered orally, three times per day for seven treatments, while T_4 concentrations are determined before and after T_3 administration. T_4 concentrations will not be suppressed in hyperthyroid cats but will be suppressed in normal cats.[64]

Sodium Pertechnetate

This test is used to identify functional thyroid tissue in dogs and cats. Radioactive sodium pertechnetate is infused intravenously and uptake by thyroid tissue is assessed by scintillation scan. Sodium pertechnetate uptake is useful for diagnosing unilateral compared to bilateral disease, extrathyroidal tissue, metastasis and thyroid-tumor activity in cats with hyperthyroidism. In dogs, pertechnetate uptake may identify the extent of a thyroid tumor if the tumor takes up the radionuclide. However, pertechnetate uptake does not correlate well with metastatic potential or the thyroid-functional status of thyroid tumors in dogs.

ETIOPATHOGENESIS

Normal Thyroid Function

The thyroid gland is the site of thyroid-hormone synthesis and is regulated by integration of cortical and substrate feedback signals (Figure 24-8).[9,70] The thyroid gland concentrates iodide under the influence of TSH for thyroid-hormone synthesis. Iodide anions undergo peroxidation and linkage to tyrosine residues, which are components of larger acceptor proteins (i.e., primarily thyroglobulin). Excess absorbed iodine is eliminated primarily in urine; however, unabsorbed amounts may be found in feces.[70]

Tyrosine residues attached to thyroglobulin may be either monoiodinated (monoiodotyrosine [MIT]) or diiodinated (diiodotyrosine [DIT]) and subsequent dimerization results in formation of the iodothyronines, T_3 and T_4. Thyroglobulin is subsequently processed so that T_4, and to a much lesser degree T_3, are eventually released into the bloodstream. All T_4 and approximately 20% of T_3 found in serum are produced directly by the thyroid gland; 99% of these hormones are bound to serum proteins.[70] The portion of T_4 and T_3 partitioned into serum, and not associated with protein, is often called free or fT_4 and fT_3. Some biologically inactive mono- and diiodotyrosines (MIT, DIT) and intact thyroglobulin may be released into the circulation. Reverse T_3 (rT_3) is another inactive thyroid metabolite found in serum and is formed from the deiodination of T_4.

T_3, the more active form of thyroid hormone, is primarily produced from thyroxine via deiodinase enzymes in target tissues. Deiodinase I, a selenoprotein, is located primarily in the kidneys and liver.[71] Deiodinase I prefers rT_3 as a substrate, releasing DIT; therefore, it may be important in the deactivation process of thyroid hormone. Deiodinase I also has activity for T_4, producing active T_3; however, this is an order of magnitude less than the rT_3 affinity. The T_3 produced by the liver may be released into the general circulation to exert its biologic activity. The exact physiologic importance of deiodinase I in the liver has yet to be elucidated.[71]

The enzyme deiodinase II is specific for production of T_3 from T_4 and is found in low concentrations in most cells including those of the brain, skin, muscle and placenta.[71,72]

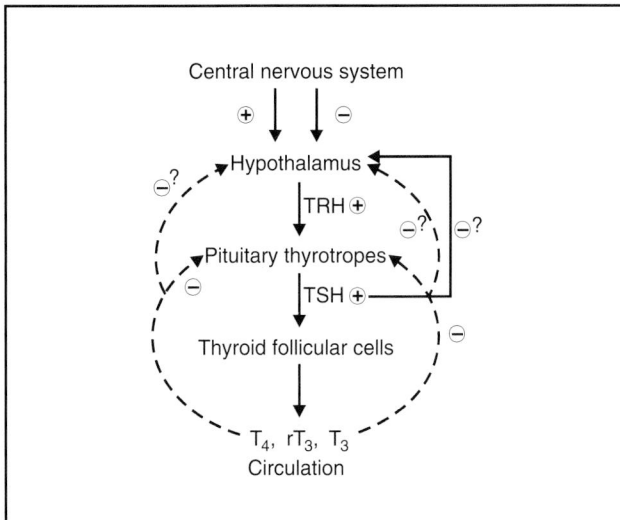

Figure 24-8. Schematic of the hypothalamic-pituitary-thyroid axis. Key: TRH = thyrotropin-releasing hormone, TSH = thyroid-stimulating hormone (thyrotropin), T_4 = thyroxine, T_3 = 3,5,3'-triiodothyronine, rT_3 = reverse T_3, $\oplus$ = stimulation, $\ominus$ = inhibition.

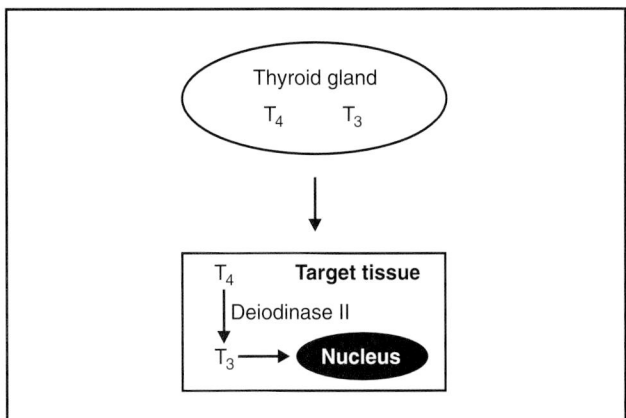

Figure 24-9. Deiodinase II enzyme is found in low concentrations in most cells and is responsible for the intracellular production of T_3 from T_4. The production of T_3 and subsequent nuclear binding is probably the major physiologic route of thyroid action.

Deiodinase II is responsible for the intracellular production of T_3, which may subsequently be moved to the nucleus of these cells (Figure 24-9). Production of T_3 and subsequent nuclear binding is probably the major physiologic route of thyroid action. Preliminary evidence suggests deiodinase II is a selenoprotein.[73]

The major route of thyroid hormone action is thought to be via a nuclear interaction at peripheral tissues. As a result, cells increase consumption and production of energy and exert hormonal effects for normal growth and development of skeletal and neural tissues. The exact mode of this action has yet to be elucidated; however, it is thought to involve the key enzymatic controls of carbohydrate, fat and protein metabolism. In addition, investigators have proposed a possible uncoupling of oxidative phosphorylation and modulation of Na/K-ATPase activity at the cellular membrane.[9,70]

Hypothyroidism in dogs can be divided into primary, secondary, tertiary and congenital causes. Primary hypothyroidism is by far the most prevalent form, comprising approximately 95% of all cases.[9,74] The two most common causes of primary hypothyroidism in dogs are lymphocytic thyroiditis and idiopathic follicular atrophy (Table 24-8).

RISK FACTORS

Feline Hyperthroidism

No definitive risk factors have been identified for the apparent increased prevalence of hyperthyroidism in cats. Whether the increased prevalence is real or not is subject to question. Several reasons have been suggested for the apparent increase including increased owner awareness, increased popularity of cats as house pets, increased longevity, environmental factors and increased diagnostic skills of veterinarians.[64]

Nutritional factors have been readily suggested as potential inducing agents.[63] Cats fed moist foods were apparently at significantly higher risk of hyperthyroidism than those fed dry or semi-moist foods.[63] Most commercially prepared cat foods contain adequate amounts of iodine, with measured levels ranging from three to 100 times recommended amounts.[75,76] Variability in iodine intake has resulted in iodine-induced hyperthyroidism in people (Jodbasedow syndrome).[77,78] In addition, deficient or excessive iodine intake in homemade or poorly formulated foods may also be goitrogenic.[63] Other goitrogenic compounds may be unknowingly included in the production process of commercial foods or in homemade foods (Table 24-12).[64,79] Because several goitrogenic compounds are metabolized via hepatic glucuronidation, which is a limiting pathway in cats, they may contribute to hyperthyroidism.[64] None of the above nutritional factors has been proven to be involved in the apparent increased prevalence of hyperthyroidism in cats.

Other non-nutritional risk factors suggested, but not proven, have included circulating thyroid stimulators similar to the immunoglobulins produced with Grave's disease in people. Growth factors (e.g., platelet-derived factors, epidermal growth factors and insulin-like growth factors) stimulate thyroid-cell proliferation and may effect the gland via autocrine or paracrine activity. Finally, it is possible that selection of an oncogene that promotes hyperthyroidism has occurred with the continuous inbreeding of domestic cats.[64]

Canine Hyperthyroidism

The risk factors for development of hyperthyroidism in dogs are similar to those for cats. Iodine deficiency or excess, chronic stimulation of thyroid-hormone production, goitrogenic substances in the environment or food, ionizing radiation and gene abnormalities have all been suggested as possible etiologies. No definitive cause has yet been identified.

Canine Hypothyroidism

The potential risk factors and causes of hypothyroidism in dogs are numerous. There appears to be a breed predilection with purebred medium- to large-breed dogs being more commonly represented. This finding may indicate a genetic predisposition. Iodine deficiency seems unlikely as a potential inciting agent because commercial dog foods usually contain adequate iodine. However, selenium metabolism and status may need to be investigated because deiodinase I and possibly deiodinase II are selenoproteins.

KEY NUTRITIONAL FACTORS

Water

Cats and dogs with hyperthyroidism often exhibit polyuria and polydipsia. Therefore, a readily available source of potable water is recommended for free-choice access. Animals with hypothyroidism usually do not display increased requirements for water.

Energy

Uncompensated hyperthyroid animals are usually in an increased metabolic, energy-deficit state. Treatment of the primary disease usually results in equilibration of energy requirements to what is expected for age and physiologic status. Therefore, primary emphasis should be directed at regulation of the disease process rather than nutritional intervention. Provision of DER at the calculated ideal body weight of the animal should result in rapid return to normal body weight if primary disease processes are controlled.

Animals with untreated hypothyroidism usually have a decreased metabolic rate and use fewer calories than normal. Treatment of primary disease is most important to normalize metabolic processes and is a prerequisite to successful nutritional intervention, especially if weight loss is necessary. After primary disease treatment has been instituted, DER should be calculated based on ideal body weight, which will usually result in some normalization of weight. If obesity is severe then a conservative weight-reduction program may be instituted. (See Chapter 13.) Failure of nutritional intervention to normalize weight most often results from inadequate primary disease control or lack of owner compliance.

Protein

Hyperthyroid animals are in a hypercatabolic state and may exhibit signs of protein wasting and deficiency. Increased protein intake may be needed during the recovery period to replenish body protein. However, hyperthyroidism is frequently associated with renal failure, which should prompt a complete evaluation of renal function before feeding higher protein foods. (See Chapter 19.)

Hypothyroid animals do not have an increased need for protein and may even have a decreased need if not fully compensated by exogenous thyroid supplementation. In general, foods that meet AAFCO nutrient allowances are adequate. Excess dietary protein should be avoided if renal disease is present. (See Chapter 19.)

Fat

Hyperthyroid animals may have decreased fat stores because they are in an increased metabolic state. Treat-

Table 24-12. Goitrogenic factors in foods and the environment.*

Nutrients or food types
Cabbage (goitrin)
Canned foods
Cassava (linamarin)
Cyanides
Excess iodine
Iodine deficiency
Millet
Rutabagas
Sweet potatoes
Turnips
Seaweed
Various beans (including soybeans)

Environmental
Polychlorinated biphenyls (fish-containing foods)
Pesticides
Phthalates
Polyphenols (fish-containing foods)
Propylthiouracil (drug)
Resorcinols (fish-containing foods)

*Epidemiologic associations and risk factors.

ment of primary disease and use of a food that meets AAFCO nutrient allowances for the desired physiologic state should result in rapid normalization of body weight. If severe wasting of body mass has occurred, the fat content of foods may be increased to achieve higher energy density and enhance weight gain.

Hypothyroid animals usually are in a state of decreased metabolism and therefore often have excessive body stores of fat. Animals with obesity, hyperlipidemia and hypercholesterolemia may benefit from restricted fat intake to near AAFCO minimum allowances.

Fiber

Foods with mild to moderate amounts of fiber (3 to 17% DM) may be useful in management of obesity associated with hypothyroidism. In addition, increased fiber levels may help manage hyperlipidemia. Foods with moderate- to high-fiber levels (8 to 23% DM) should be avoided in animals with poor body condition.

Macrominerals

Because hyperthyroidism may result in macromineral abnormalities (i.e., phosphorus, potassium, sodium, calcium), it is best to avoid foods with excess (all-purpose foods) or deficient levels. Decreased sodium chloride intake may benefit some cases in which hypertension and cardiac disease are primary problems. (See Chapter 18.) Foods that exceed AAFCO minimum nutrient allowances should suffice in most cases.

Trace Minerals

Iodine may be excessive or deficient in different states of thyroid disease. Iodine intake should be thoroughly evaluated to determine adequacy. In addition, animals with hypothyroidism may have decreased absorption of iron from the gastrointestinal tract resulting in microcytic hypochromic anemia. Iron nutrition of these patients should receive special attention during the recovery phase of treatment. Selenium status may also be assessed because deiodinase I and possibly deiodinase II are selenoproteins and a deficiency may alter thyroid metabolism. However, established reference values for selenium evaluation in dogs and cats have not been validated. Generally, foods that meet AAFCO minimum allowances for trace minerals are adequate; however, commercial products vary greatly in trace mineral nutriture.

Assess the Food(s)

Information from assessing the food is essential for making any changes to foods currently fed. This information, in conjunction with assessment of the animal, leads to development of a rational, total nutritional plan. After complete assessment of the animal and current food is completed, the following steps should take place: 1) establish nutritional requirements and key nutritional factors, 2) critically compare the current nutrient supply with recommended key nutritional factors and 3) identify deficiencies between key nutritional factors and current intake.

Assess the Feeding Method

It may not always be necessary to change the feeding method when managing animals with hyperthyroidism or hypothyroidism. However, a thorough evaluation includes verification that an appropriate feeding method is being used. Any deviations from ideal feeding methods should be identified and changes made as required.

Treatment and Feeding Plan

The success of nutritional management of hypothyroidism and hyperthyroidism depends to a great degree on the effectiveness of medical/surgical treatment for the primary disease. Three modes of treatment are generally accepted for hyperthyroidism in cats: 1) long-term anti-thyroid medication, 2) surgical thyroidectomy and 3) radioactive iodine.[80]

The mainstay of treatment for primary hypothyroidism is administration of exogenous thyroid supplements (sodium levothyroxine). Known goitrogenic substances should be removed from the food(s) and environment, if possible (Table 24-12). Secondary and tertiary hypothyroidism may require additional therapy (e.g., glucocorticoids or cobalt teletherapy).[9]

Hypothyroidism

Animals with hypothyroidism range from normal weight to obese. Successful treatment of primary disease processes will usually result in some weight loss when energy is provided at the calculated DER for ideal body weight. However, in some cases, a weight-loss program may need to be instituted. A food low in fat (less than 17% DM), higher in fiber (8 to 23% DM) and adequate in protein (20% DM for dogs, 28 to 45% DM for cats) is recommended. (See Chapter 13.) Special attention should be paid to mineral status because certain fibers may interfere with the absorption of these nutrients, which may already be in low reserve.

The amount of food required/offered to attain adequate weight loss should follow the guidelines in Chapter 13. Numerous small meals may be necessary to alleviate owner concerns about providing inadequate energy. However, one to two daily feedings containing an appropriate quantity of energy are probably sufficient to achieve adequate results.

Hyperthyroidism

Foods adequate in energy, protein and palatability are recommended for hyperthyroid animals. Commercial moist, semi-moist and dry foods that meet AAFCO minimum nutrient allowances for adult maintenance should suffice. Commercially prepared maintenance-type foods may be mixed with growth-type formulas to achieve higher protein and fat intakes, if needed, during the convalescent period.[64] However, growth foods may add excessive sodium and phosphorus possibly complicating concurrent renal disease or primary cardiac disease.

Animals will usually return to normal body weight if provided energy at the calculated DER for ideal body weight. Small amounts in several feedings may need to be fed during recovery. Two daily feedings are adequate once an animal resumes normal eating behavior.

Reassessment

Patient response to treatment may be assessed in a variety of ways. The simplest method is via owner observation of clinical signs, bimonthly body weight charting and monitoring food intake. Return to normal activity, size and appearance generally indicates successful response to treatment. No change in clinical signs, weight or activity necessitates reevaluation of the treatment and diagnosis.

Evaluation of basal thyroid-hormone concentration in serum is another way of assessing response to treatment. Evaluation of thyroid-hormone concentrations may shed new information on owner compliance and response to treatment.

■ OTHER ENDOCRINE DISORDERS

Several other endocrine diseases of small animals may benefit from adjunct nutritional therapy. No specific recommendations have been established for these disorders but some pragmatic suggestions can be made.

Hypoadrenocorticism

Hypoadrenocorticism (Addison's disease) presents as a mineralocorticoid deficiency with subsequent hyponatremia, hypochloremia and hyperkalemia. Deficiency of aldosterone results in dehydration and hypovolemia with resultant prerenal azotemia. In addition, a mild acidosis may result from impaired ability to reabsorb bicarbonate and chloride ions from the renal tubules. Other abnormalities may include low serum albumin concentrations possibly attributable to malabsorption.[81]

Animals with hypoadrenocorticism should be managed medically to stabilize clinical signs and alleviate metabolic abnormalities. Initially, fluid replacement may be necessary with crystalloid solutions administered intravenously. After stabilization, the animal should have free access to an ample source of potable water and an appropriate food.

Foods high in potassium (more than 1% DM) should be avoided until the disease process is well-controlled. Subsequent to good medical control, foods containing adequate sodium and chloride levels and highly digestible protein should be fed.[82] Foods that contribute to acidosis (e.g., high sulfur amino acid content or low dietary cation-anion ratios) should be avoided because a mild acidosis may already exist. In general, foods that meet AAFCO minimum nutrient allowances for maintenance should be adequate, although anecdotal reports of positive response to salt supplementation are noted. Energy needs should be adjusted as needed according to the body condition of the individual animal.

Animals undergoing treatment for hypoadrenocorticism may develop iatrogenic hyperadrenocorticism.[81] Resulting clinical signs include obesity, polyuria/polydipsia, hypertriglyceridemia, hypercholesterolemia and poor body condition. Animals that develop these signs should be fed according to the next section.

Hyperadrenocorticism

Hyperadrenocorticism (Cushing's syndrome) is characterized by excessive circulating concentrations of cortisol. The excessive concentrations may be from endogenous or exogenous sources. The resulting clinical signs are typical of cortisol action including polydipsia, polyuria, polyphagia, hepatomegaly, panting, obesity with weight redistribution to the abdomen and muscle wasting.[83] Accurate diagnosis of primary disease and any underlying disorders (e.g., hypertension, pancreatitis and diabetes mellitus) is important to successful resolution. Treatment should focus on alleviation of high circulating levels of cortisol and management of secondary and underlying disease processes.

An adequate source of potable water should be available to sustain animals until polyuria/polydipsia resolves. Because cortisol stimulates lipolysis and increases circulating concentrations of cholesterol and triglycerides, recommending a food lower in fat (less than 12% DM) and moderate in crude fiber (8 to 17% DM) is reasonable. In addition, a food low in fat and moderate in fiber may aid in weight loss and control of mild hyperglycemia (glucose concentrations between 120 and 180 mg/dl) in dogs with glucocorticoid-induced carbohydrate intolerance. Protein should be highly digestible (greater than 85%) and meet AAFCO recommendations for adult maintenance to compensate for muscle wasting associated with this disease. Cortisol may also affect mineral (i.e., increased calcium excretion) and vitamin metabolism; therefore, a food that meets AAFCO allowances for adult dogs should be used. Foods that avoid excessive levels of sodium and chloride are recommended if hypertension is present. (See Chapter 18.)

Acromegaly

Acromegaly is a disorder of growth hormone secretion. Growth hormone is released from the pituitary gland under the influence of hypothalamic signals. Growth hormone may then act at distant tissues in anabolic fashion via liver-secreted insulin-like growth factor 1 (IGF-1) or in catabolic fashion via direct action of growth hormone and cortisol.[84]

Several stimuli may affect secretion of growth hormone; however, in acromegaly, concentrations of growth hormone and IGF-1 in the circulation are increased. Increased concentrations of IGF-1 lead to proliferation of bone cartilage and soft tissues and organomegaly. The antagonistic effects of growth hormone result in anti-insulin effects that may lead to diabetes mellitus.

Because acromegaly may lead to clinical diabetes mellitus, dietary therapy should be aimed at the goals discussed in the section on diabetes mellitus. In general, foods with moderate fiber (8 to 17% DM), low levels of simple sugars (avoid semi-moist foods), low fat (less than 12% DM) and adequate highly digestible protein (greater than 85% digestibility) are recommended. An ample supply of potable water should be available. Energy needs should be adjusted as needed according to the body condition of the individual animal.

Diabetes Insipidus

Diabetes insipidus may be central, nephrogenic or psychogenic. There are usually no major metabolic abnormalities other than excessive polydipsia and polyuria. Mild electrolyte abnormalities may be present and are attributed to concomitant loss with polyuria. The etiology of diabetes insipidus is unclear in dogs and cats.[85] Differentiation of psychogenic diabetes insipidus from the other forms via a modified water-deprivation test is important for water allowance recommendations.[85]

Nutrient and energy requirements are similar to those for adult maintenance and should be met by foods that meet AAFCO recommendations. Avoiding excessive salt intake may be beneficial in management of central and nephrogenic diabetes insipidus. Foods should be supplied in an amount necessary to meet the DER to support the ideal body weight of the animal. A continuous source of potable water is necessary in cases of central and nephrogenic diabetes insipidus. Gradual limitation of water intake between 60 to 80 ml/kg body weight/24 hours often resolves polyuria and polydipsia in psychogenic diabetes insipidus. Decreases of no more than 10% of free-choice water intake per week are recommended until the normal intake is achieved.

DISORDERS OF LIPID METABOLISM

Hyperlipidemia (also called hyperlipoproteinemia) refers to a disturbance of lipid metabolism that results in an elevated concentration of blood lipids, particularly triglycerides and/or cholesterol. In the fasted state, hyperlipidemia is an abnormal laboratory finding that represents either accelerated synthesis or retarded degradation of lipoproteins.[1] Among dogs and cats, the most common, clinically important type of hyperlipidemia is characterized by an excess concentration of triglycerides in blood, a condition referred to as hypertriglyceridemia.[2,3] The serum and plasma of affected animals typically appear milky white and turbid, or lipemic. In cases of extreme hypertriglyceridemia, the patient's serum can be so lipemic that it is opaque, or lactescent (Figure 24-10).

Hypercholesterolemia refers to an excess concentration of cholesterol in blood. Most of the circulating cholesterol in dogs and cats is carried on high-density lipoprotein (HDL), the smallest lipoprotein.[2,4,5] Because HDL particles are small and do not refract light, patients with extreme cholesterol elevations will not have lipemic serum unless the triglyceride concentration is also elevated.

The clinical importance of hyperlipidemia in companion animal medicine centers around four facts: 1) lipemic serum may positively or negatively interfere with quantitative analyses of other serum analytes, 2) hyperlipidemia in fasted (greater than 12 hours) dogs or cats is abnormal and should be addressed as a significant clinical finding, 3) hyperlipidemic patients are at risk for developing significant clinical illness, including at least one potentially fatal disease (i.e., acute pancreatitis) and 4) specific dietary and/or drug intervention can eliminate or at least diminish the morbidity associated with hyperlipidemia.

ENDOCRINE AND LIPID

Assessment

Assess the Animal

HISTORY AND PHYSICAL EXAMINATION

The major clinical manifestations of hyperlipidemia include intermittent vomiting, diarrhea and abdominal discomfort and seizures in dogs; cutaneous xanthomata (Figure 24-11) and peripheral neuropathy in cats and lipid

Figure 24-10. Blood samples from a Doberman pinscher dog with hypothyroidism and severe lipemia. The picture on the left was taken immediately after the sample was drawn. Note that the lipid content is so high that even in black and white photography the blood has a "tomato soup" appearance. The blood sample on the right was allowed to separate forming a "cream layer" of triglyceride-rich chylomicrons on top.

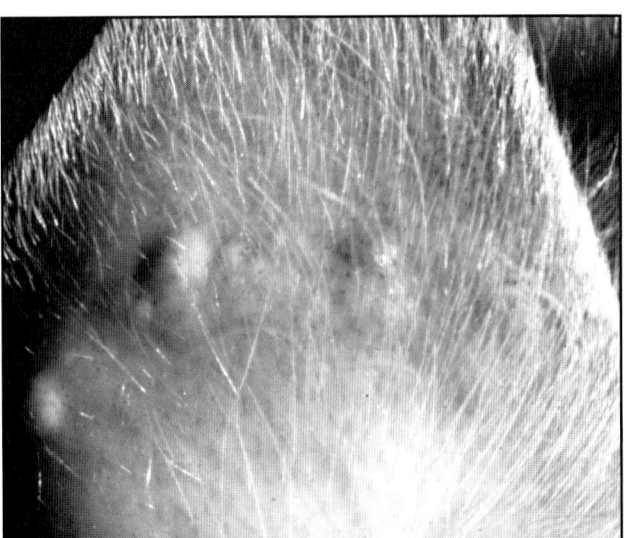

Figure 24-11. Xanthomas on the pinna of a cat with hyperlipidemia. Xanthomas are tumors composed of lipid-laden foam cells, which are histiocytes containing cytoplasmic lipid material. These lesions resolved with use of a low-fat, high-fiber food.

keratopathies (Figure 24-12) and lipemia retinalis in dogs and cats (Figure 24-13). Some hyperlipidemic dogs and cats do not manifest clinical signs but are considered to be at risk for developing overt signs in the future. Atherosclerosis is a rare manifestation of hyperlipidemia in dogs and cats as opposed to people.

Dogs with Hyperlipidemia

Table 24-13 lists the clinical signs associated with hypertriglyceridemic states in dogs. The presenting complaints most often associated with hypertriglyceridemia are vague and intermittent but usually center around vomiting and diarrhea. Accompanying signs include non-localizing abdominal discomfort and occasional pain, accompanied by a transient decrease in appetite. The owner may report that signs are episodic, lasting a few hours to a few days, and may resolve spontaneously with fasting. Abdominal distention is occasionally reported. There appears to be no gender predilection. Affected dogs are generally four years of age and older although younger dogs may be affected.

On physical examination, dogs may appear lethargic and may or may not manifest abdominal pain. Clinical signs and history are compatible with acute pancreatitis; however, abdominal radiographs, ultrasound and laboratory evidence supporting a diagnosis of pancreatitis are typically lacking. The term pseudopancreatitis has been suggested to describe the clinical manifestations associated with hypertriglyceridemia.[2,3]

Lipemia retinalis, a condition characterized by the appearance of pale pink retinal arterioles and venules, is an incidental finding seen on funduscopic examination of lipemic dogs and cats (Figure 24-13). This condition does not affect vision. Laboratory analysis of affected animals will verify extreme hypertriglyceridemia, typically greater than 1,000 mg/dl.

Sustained hypertriglyceridemia is a principal risk factor among people and dogs for the development of acute pancreatitis.[1,3,6-10] Dogs with acute abdominal pain and vomiting should be evaluated for hyperchylomicronemia at the time of presentation and during the recovery phase when food intake is restored.

Hypertriglyceridemia should also be considered in patients presenting with a history of seizures. A small number of patients, many of them miniature schnauzers, diagnosed with idiopathic epilepsy have elevated fasting triglyceride concentrations and lipemic serum.[11,12] In some dogs, dietary therapy has successfully reduced blood triglyceride levels and eliminated seizures without concomitant use of anticonvulsant drugs. Interestingly, seizures associated with hyperlipidemia are not necessarily associated with other signs typically attributed to hyperlipidemia (e.g., vomiting and diarrhea).

Although owners of hypertriglyceridemic dogs rarely express concern about their pet's inactivity or lethargy at the time of initial presentation, several owners have remarked how their pet's activity level increased as a result of lowering circulating triglyceride levels.[a]

Cats with Hyperlipidemia

Clinical signs reported to occur in hyperlipidemic cats are quite different than those reported to occur in dogs (Table 24-13). The most common clinical finding in affected cats is cutaneous xanthoma, a painless, raised lesion caused by an accumulation of lipid-laden macrophages or foam cells in the skin (Figure 24-11).[13-15] Xanthomas are most likely to occur over bony prominences and areas of skin subject to direct injury.

Xanthomata may also occur in other tissues such as liver, spleen, kidney, heart, skeletal muscle and intestines. Uniquely, xanthomata can form at the point where spinal nerves emerge through the vertebral foramina,[16] the point at which nerves and vascular tissue are subject to mild injury associated with the movement of adjacent vertebrae. Peripheral neuropathy caused by neuronal xanthoma is characterized by motor paralysis. Signs vary depending on the specific nerves involved. Horner's syndrome, tibial nerve paralysis and radial nerve paralysis have been reported most often.[15,16] In cases in which mixed motor and sensory nerves have been affected, sensation to painful stimuli was retained.

Lipemia retinalis is more common in cats than dogs (Figure 24-13). Other ocular manifestations of hyperchylomicronemia in cats are uncommon but include iridocyclitis, arcus lipoides corneae and lipemic aqueous and lipid keratopathy (Figure 24-12). These lesions are thought to occur subsequent to existing ocular disease in lipemic cats.[15,17]

LABORATORY EVALUATION

Veterinarians assessing a dog or cat for hyperlipidemia should submit serum or plasma rather than whole blood. (See sidebar "Handling Lipemic Samples.") Samples for cholesterol and triglyceride determinations can be refrigerated or frozen for several days without significant effect.

The presence of excess triglycerides, particularly if associated with retention of chylomicrons, is an important source of either positive (falsely increased) or negative (falsely decreased) interference for analytes determined by colorimetric methods.[9] The effect of lipemia on individual analytes is variable and depends on the degree of lipemia, the analyte being measured and the analytic method used. Lipemia also causes in vitro hemolysis, a phenomenon induced by the effect of lipid on erythrocyte membrane fragility, which may also induce interference when performing laboratory profiles.[18] The extent to which in vitro hemolysis affects determination of hemoglobin and hematocrit values has not been established. The amount of red-cell hemolysis appears to be proportional to the length of time red cells are in contact with the lipemic serum and the degree of lipemia. The type and extent of interference induced by lipemia varies from one laboratory to another, depending on the analytical instrumentation and methodologies used. Visual inspection of the patient's serum provides valuable physical evidence about the presence or absence of an excessive concentration of triglycerides. In fasting patients (i.e., 24-hour fast or longer), lipemia or lactescent serum denotes hypertriglyceridemia and is usually associated with triglyceride concentrations in excess of 2,000 mg/dl (canine normal = 50 to 150 mg/dl, feline normal = 50 to 100 mg/dl). A diagnosis of hypertriglyceridemia should be based on laboratory determination of serum triglycerides in uncleared serum. By laboratory methods used in North America, serum triglyceride concentrations greater than 500 mg/dl are abnormal for fasted dogs and cats. Although a correlation has not been observed between triglyceride concentrations and the severity of clinical signs, dogs with a triglyceride concentration of 1,000 mg/dl or higher are at risk for developing

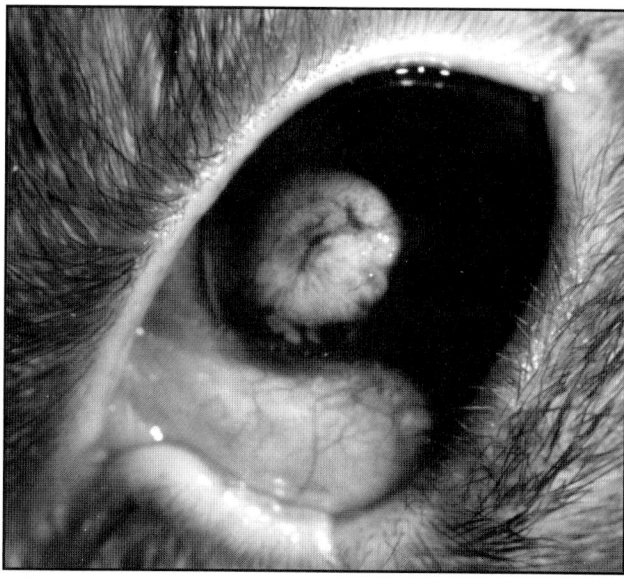

Figure 24-12. Lipid keratopathy in a rabbit. Note the white lipid accumulation in the corneal stroma. Corneal vascularization may precede or follow lipid deposition. Lipid keratopathy has been described in several species including human beings, rabbits, cats and dogs.

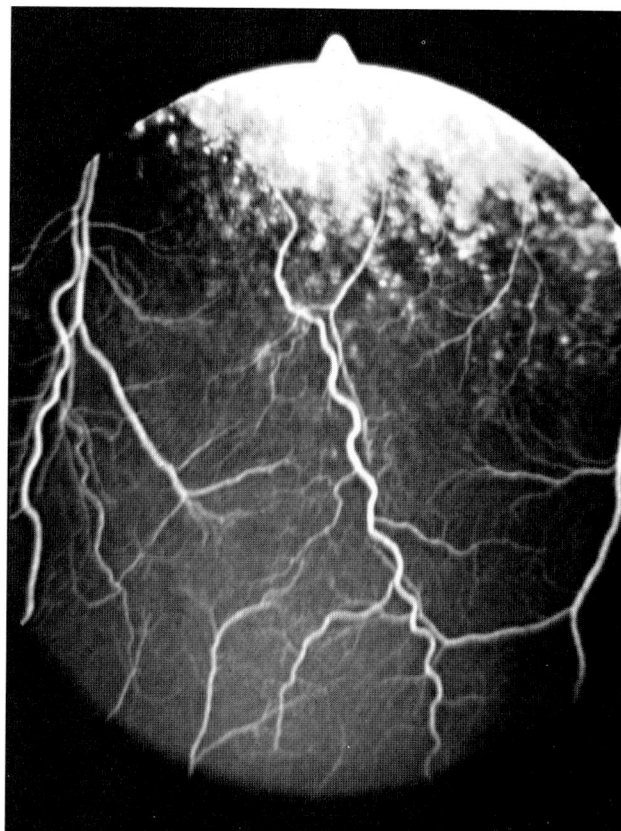

Figure 24-13. Lipemia retinalis in a cat with hyperlipidemia. Note the white, milky appearance of the retinal blood vessels.

clinical signs and, as such, are candidates for dietary intervention.[6,12,19] Maintaining triglyceride levels less than 500 mg/dl in lipemic (familial) patients may be difficult with nutritional management alone. A more reasonable target range for dietary control is 500 to 1,000 mg/dl postprandially. Further, clinical signs of hypertriglyceridemia appear to be uncommon in patients with postprandial triglyceride levels less than 1,000 mg/dl.

Significant hyperlipidemia characterized by lipemic serum and hypertriglyceridemia has been observed as an incidental finding in fasted adult dogs and cats. The

Handling Lipemic Samples

Submission of lipemic blood to a commercial laboratory necessitates knowing how the sample will be processed. Because of the interference induced by lipemia, some laboratories will simply reject lipemic samples. Many laboratories, however, will attempt to clear lipemic serum (by removing chylomicrons) before performing any biochemical assays. Unfortunately, there is neither a standardized method of clearing lipemic serum nor do commercial laboratories consistently report whether or not an attempt was made to clear the sample. For veterinarians, however, knowledge of the fact that a lipemic sample was cleared before determining the triglyceride concentration is critical in making reasonable interpretations. Although clearing a lipemic sample eliminates interference associated with chylomicrons, it effectively eliminates a critical element of clinical information (i.e., that the patient is hypertriglyceridemic).

Ideally, two aliquots of a serum sample from a lipemic patient should be submitted simultaneously. One sample, if effectively cleared, can be used to perform routine biochemical testing, including triglyceride levels. Determining triglyceride concentrations in the second, lipemic (uncleared) sample documents the true extent of triglyceride excess, serves as an important baseline value for assessing response to therapy and can, when compared to the triglyceride value in the cleared sample, characterize the nature of the hyperlipidemia.

Table 24-13. Clinical signs and diseases associated with hypertriglyceridemia in dogs and cats.

Dogs
Abdominal discomfort*
Acute pancreatitis
Behavioral (lethargy, inactivity)
Crystalline stromal dystrophy (especially cavalier King Charles spaniels)
Cushing's syndrome
Fasting lipemia (six to 12 hours)
Intermittent diarrhea*
Intermittent vomiting*
Lipemia retinalis
Lipemic aqueous
Lipid corneal dystrophy/arcus lipoides corneae
Seizures

Cats
Cutaneous xanthomata
Lipemia retinalis
Lipid keratopathy
Peripheral nerve paralysis
   Horner's syndrome
   Tibial nerve paralysis
   Radial nerve paralysis
Splenomegaly

*These clinical signs may occur concomitantly in the same patient. The collective term used to describe these signs is "pseudopancreatitis."

absence of clinical signs at the time of presentation does not justify ignoring the significance of the lipemia. Because of the risks associated with hypertriglyceridemia, normal patients with persistent lipemia should be managed in the same manner as those presenting with clinical signs.

Hyperchylomicronemia is confirmed in fasted dogs with lipemic serum, hypertriglyceridemia (in uncleared serum) greater than 500 mg/dl and a positive chylomicron test. Clinical signs are not prerequisite for diagnosis nor for recommending therapeutic intervention. However, therapy in dogs that do not have associated signs is generally reserved for those having fasting hypertriglyceridemia on two consecutive samples two to four weeks apart.

Chylomicrons will normally appear in the serum of dogs and cats within 30 minutes to one hour after ingestion of a meal containing fat. This finding is associated with a transient (i.e., six to 12 hours) increase in serum triglycerides after which triglyceride levels rapidly return to baseline values. Physiologic hyperlipidemia is easily excluded from consideration if the patient is known to have fasted throughout the 12-hour period before blood collection. In normal, postprandial animals, serum turbidity is associated with a modest elevation of serum triglycerides (from 150 to 400 mg/dl) that typically returns to normal within 10 hours.

Lipoprotein Electrophoresis

Lipoprotein electrophoresis (LPE) has been used as a means of characterizing abnormalities in lipid metabolism.[3,8,20] The value of LPE has been in question in human medicine for several years and is justifiably questioned in veterinary medicine. Compared to the quantitative assays currently available, LPE appears to have limited value in the clinical evaluation of lipid disorders in dogs and cats.

The Chylomicron Test

Knowing that the patient has fasting lipemia provides immediate evidence of hypertriglyceridemia. The lipid disorder may be further characterized by performing a simple, in-hospital test for the presence of chylomicrons. The lipemic serum, separated from red cells, is refrigerated and allowed to stand undisturbed for six to 12 hours. Chylomicrons, if present, will float to the surface of the sample forming an opaque "cream layer" over a clear infranatant (Figure 24-14). This finding suggests a disorder of chylomicron metabolism, the most common form of hyperlipidemia in dogs. If the sample remains turbid, but doesn't form a cream layer, retention of very low-density lipoproteins (VLDL), rather than chylomicrons, is suggested. This finding also suggests that the hyperlipidemia is secondary to an underlying disorder. In some dogs, particularly poorly regulated diabetics, a cream layer may form over turbid, lipemic serum suggesting retention of chylomicrons and VLDL.[6,19]

RISK FACTORS

Familial (primary) hyperchylomicronemia in cats has been reported as an autosomal recessive trait limited to certain lines of cats. The trait is thought to be present in mixed-breed cats throughout much of the world; therefore, clinically affected cats appear sporadically. Certain dog breeds, most notably miniature schnauzers, are also at increased risk of clinical illness associated with hypertriglyceridemia characterized by the inability to degrade chylomicrons. Though not definitively proven, these disorders are generally accepted to be caused by a familial trait.

Results of a limited survey of healthy adult dogs suggested that primary hypercholesterolemia might occur within some families of Doberman pinschers and rottweilers.[a]

Secondary risk factors (i.e., particularly endocrine disorders, certain drugs and possibly certain diets leading to hyperlipidemia) are known to occur but have not been well-studied. For example, profound fasting hypertriglyceridemia occurs inconsistently in dogs with unregulated diabetes mellitus. Clinical signs associated with excess triglyceride concentrations typically include vomiting, diarrhea and abdominal discomfort. Approximately 30% of untreated hypothyroid dogs and from 25 to 30% of untreated dogs with pituitary-dependent hyperadrenocorticism have an excess serum cholesterol concentration. However, the relationship between clinical signs, if any, and the hyperlipidemia has not been established.

In some animals, drugs are known to either decrease lipoprotein degradation or increase lipoprotein production, thereby causing hyperlipidemia. For example, dogs receiving long-term phenobarbital therapy for regulation of idiopathic epilepsy may develop hypercholesterolemia. The clinical significance is unknown and may, in fact, be related to thyroid-hormone production or activity. Cats receiving megestrol acetate may secondarily develop diabetes mellitus, which may culminate in altered lipoprotein lipase activity and hyperchylomicronemia.

ETIOPATHOGENESIS

Normal Lipid Metabolism

Lipoproteins

Cholesterol and triglycerides are hydrophobic molecules; therefore, they cannot circulate in the aqueous milieu of blood without being incorporated into complex, spherical macromolecules called lipoproteins.[1,19,21-23] The water-soluble outer coat of the lipoprotein is comprised of phospholipids, non-esterified (free) cholesterol and several unique proteins called apolipoproteins (Figure 24-15). Cholesterol, in the form of cholesterol esters, and triglycerides are carried within the nonpolar core of spherical lipoprotein macromolecules. Abnormally high concentrations of cholesterol or triglycerides, as measured in routine biochemical assays, actually reflect increased synthesis or decreased degradation of lipoproteins.

Apolipoproteins

It is well-recognized that the apolipoproteins (commonly referred to as apoproteins), contained within the outer coat of lipoproteins, bind to specific enzymes or transport proteins on cell membranes.[1,19,24] Thus, they are responsible for directing the lipoprotein to various sites of metabolism. Several apoproteins have been recognized in dogs and cats. Abnormalities or deficiencies in specific apoproteins are likely to be responsible for altered lipoprotein metabolism that culminates in hyperlipidemia.

Apoprotein C-II (also called apo C-II) (Figure 24-15) activates lipoprotein lipase and is very much involved in triglyceride metabolism during the postprandial period. An inherited deficiency in apo C-II is one of the proposed mechanisms responsible for hyperchylomicronemia in dogs.

Classes of Lipoproteins

Four major lipoprotein classes in dogs and cats can be separated by preparative nonionic precipitation and ultracentrifugation: 1) chylomicrons, 2) very low-density lipoproteins (VLDL), 3) low-density lipoproteins (LDL) and 4) high-density lipoproteins (HDL).[4,6,25] A comprehensive lipoprotein profile consists of determining the concentration (mg/dl) of triglycerides and cholesterol in each lipoprotein class. Through lipoprotein profiling, it is possible to categorize hyperlipidemic patients according to lipoprotein phenotype, facilitate diagnosis of primary and

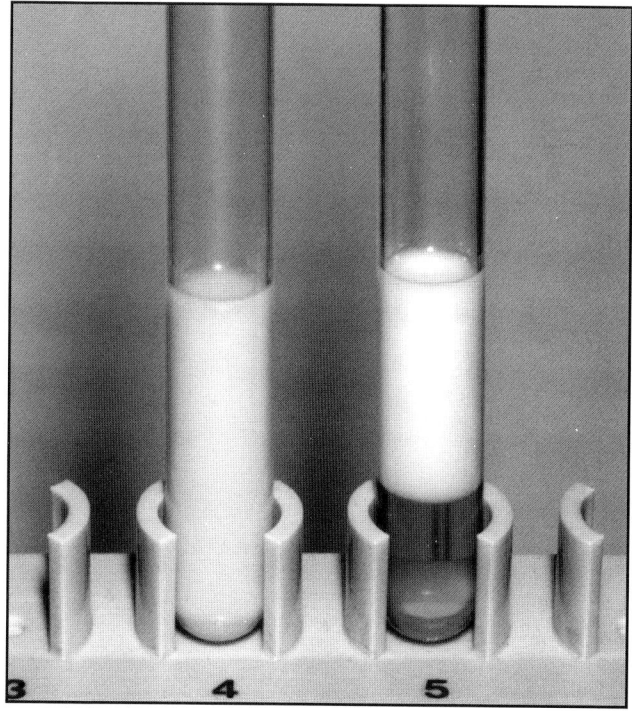

Figure 24-14. The positive chylomicron test. The lactescent serum in both tubes was obtained from a dog with hypertriglyceridemia. The sample on the left is the serum immediately after separation from the red blood cells whereas the sample on the right was allowed to stand undisturbed for 10 hours. The so-called "cream layer" is comprised of triglyceride-rich chylomicrons. (Reprinted with permission from Ford RB. Canine hyperlipidemia. In: Ettinger SJ, Feldman EC, eds. Textbook of Veterinary Internal Medicine, 4th ed. Philadelphia, PA: WB Saunders Co, 1995; 1417.)

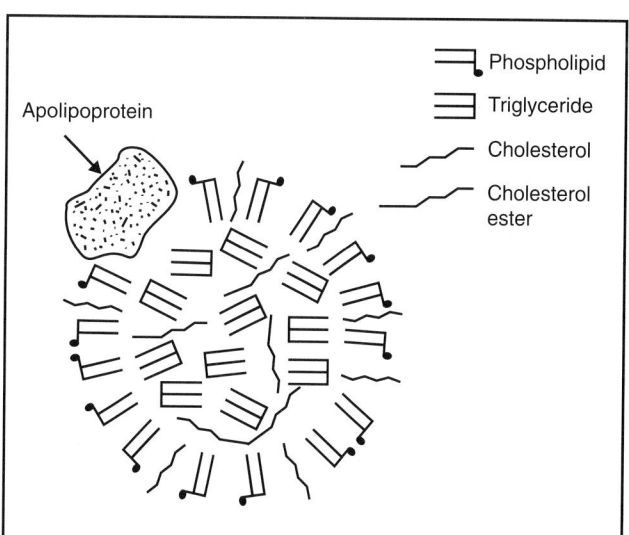

Figure 24-15. Diagram illustrating the composition and structure of lipoproteins. Cholesterol and triglycerides comprise much of the lipoprotein core and are present in varying proportions. (Adapted from Brody T, ed. Nutritional Biochemistry. New York, NY: Academic Press Inc, 1994; 276.)

secondary lipid disorders and even prescribe therapy. Unfortunately, uniform standards for performing lipoprotein profiles are not commercially available. On the other hand, laboratory determinations of total cholesterol and triglycerides are routinely available and can be used to make sound diagnostic and therapeutic decisions.

Chylomicrons

The largest and least dense lipoprotein particles are chylomicrons. These large, triglyceride-rich lipoprotein complexes are responsible for the transport of dietary fat (triglycerides) from the small intestine via the lymphatics and general circulation to various sites of metabolism. Appearing in plasma within one hour after consumption of a fat-containing meal, chylomicrons can be visually confirmed as turbid or cloudy serum, a finding that corresponds to a transient (i.e., six to 12 hours postprandial), physiologic hypertriglyceridemia. A cream layer comprised of chylomicrons may form over a clear infranatant if serum is allowed to stand undisturbed for six to 10 hours.

In dogs, and probably cats, only about 10% of the lipid contained in chylomicrons is cholesterol (cholesterol ester). After a meal, hypertriglyceridemia is associated with transient increases in serum cholesterol that may exceed the normal reference range.

Chylomicrons transport fat to the capillaries of adipose tissue and skeletal muscle where they are exposed to the enzyme lipoprotein lipasacyl. The enzyme, once activated by apo C-II, hydrolyzes triglycerides into glycerol and free fatty acids. What remains of the chylomicron is a remnant particle, rich in cholesteryl esters, that subsequently delivers cholesterol to the liver.[21,22,26,27] Chylomicron hydrolysis is normally complete within six to 12 hours following a meal, after which the plasma will again become clear.

Fasting hyperchylomicronemia is an abnormal condition resulting from decreased clearance of chylomicrons in the circulation. It is recognized in dogs, cats and people. Although clinical manifestations recognized in dogs are quite different from those in cats, hyperchylomicronemia is the most common lipid disorder recognized in companion animals.

Very Low-Density Lipoproteins

Produced in the liver and containing a predominance of triglycerides, VLDL are transported to tissue capillaries where they are catabolized by lipoprotein lipase in the same manner as chylomicrons.[1,27] Retention of VLDL, and the resulting hypertriglyceridemia, occurs frequently in dogs with insulin-dependent diabetes mellitus. Although serum turbidity is manifest in the fasted patient, a cream layer will not separate when the sample is left undisturbed, even when refrigerated.

Low-Density Lipoproteins

Like VLDL, LDL are responsible for transporting endogenously synthesized lipids (especially cholesterol) from the liver to target tissues. Subsequent to the hydrolysis of VLDL and the removal of triglycerides from its core, a short-lived intermediate-density lipoprotein is ultimately processed by hepatic lipase to form LDL. Delivery of LDL to peripheral tissues is facilitated by the interaction of the structural protein of LDL with a specific receptor, called the LDL receptor. In people, approximately 70% of total cholesterol is carried within LDL, which is sometimes referred to as the atherogenic lipoprotein.[5] However, most cholesterol in dogs and cats is carried on HDL.

High-Density Lipoproteins

Newly formed HDL, secreted by the liver and the intestine, binds with unesterified cholesterol released from peripheral tissues during normal cellular turnover.[1,25-27] The conversion process from nascent HDL to mature, spherical HDL particles is mediated by the enzyme lecithin-cholesterol acyltransferase (LCAT).[1,26] As members of the antiatherogenic lipoprotein family, HDLs are recognized for their ability to remove excess cholesterol from tissues and transport it to the liver.

A number of subgroups of HDL have been recognized in people (HDL_2 and HDL_3)[1] and dogs (HDL_1 and HDL_2).[5,11,12] In both dogs and cats, a large HDL molecule (HDL_1) is formed as HDL acquires free cholesterol and expands under the influence of LCAT. However, the actual role of HDL subgroups in predicting or diagnosing disease in animals has not been defined. Because commercial laboratories do not routinely isolate HDL subgroups, subgroup analyses in veterinary medicine have not been found to have immediate application in clinical practice.

CLASSIFICATION OF HYPERLIPIDEMIC STATES

Hyperlipidemic states can be classified as postprandial, familial or acquired. Familial hyperlipidemia, also called primary hyperlipidemia, refers to those defects in lipoprotein metabolism that are known or suspected to be inherited. Fasting lipemia is frequently recognized in miniature schnauzers and is believed to be linked to a familial defect in chylomicron metabolism. Feline hyperchylomicronemia is the only hyperlipidemic state proven to be familial.[13-16]

Acquired hyperlipidemia, also called secondary hyperlipidemia, refers to an excess concentration of lipid in blood resulting from an underlying disease in which normal lipoprotein metabolism is markedly altered. Several endocrine diseases alter lipid metabolism leading to secondary hyperlipidemia. For example, insulin-deficient states alter carbohydrate and lipid metabolism. Animals with insulin-dependent diabetes mellitus may have either hypertriglyceridemia or hypercholesterolemia. Hyperadrenocorticism, renal disease and hypothyroidism are variably associated with secondary hyperlipidemia.[2,7,20,25,28,29]

In clinical practice, it is not unusual to encounter a patient with both primary and secondary hyperlipidemia. A miniature schnauzer presented with diabetes mellitus is likely to have extreme elevations in serum triglycerides and lactescent serum. From the clinician's perspective, hyperlipidemia, whether primary or secondary, can be associated with undesirable clinical effects. The ability to recognize the signs associated with hyperlipidemia and to make appropriate dietary or therapeutic recommendations becomes fundamental to the management of these cases.

Postprandial Hyperlipidemia

Triglycerides are the predominant dietary fat present in pet food. Subsequent to consuming a meal, dogs and cats will experience transient, physiologic hyperlipidemia characterized by increased triglyceride concentration (circulating chylomicrons) and, depending on the amount of fat consumed, serum turbidity (lipemia). However, postprandial hyperlipidemia does not necessarily imply that a disorder of lipid or lipoprotein metabolism exists. In normal dogs and cats, postprandial hyperlipidemia normally persists from six to 12 hours after a meal. Even when a high-fat food is consumed, serum triglyceride levels are not expected to exceed 500 mg/dl in normal animals. In dogs and cats, hyperlipidemia associated with serum triglyceride levels greater than 1,000 mg/dl, whether fasted or not, is likely to result from an underlying disorder of lipid metabolism.[2] Because chylomicrons carry only a fraction of circulating cholesterol, consumption of a meal has little impact on cholesterol during the six- to 12-hour postprandial period.

Postprandial hyperlipidemia, although physiologic, must be distinguished from intrinsic causes (primary or secondary). Confirming that a hyperlipidemic patient has fasted for 10 to 12 hours before collection of blood effectively excludes a recent meal as the cause for increased blood lipids and, therefore, justifies further evaluation in an attempt to determine the source of the hyperlipidemic state.

Canine Familial Hyperchylomicronemia

Hypertriglyceridemia, particularly that associated with retention of chylomicrons, is the most prevalent lipid disorder recognized in dogs and cats and is associated with the greatest health risk.[3,30] In dogs, the precise mechanism has not been elucidated; however, this disorder of lipoprotein metabolism is believed to be caused by either the lack of lipoprotein lipase activity or the absence of apo C-II.[1,21,26,29] Several reports have been published suggesting that miniature schnauzers are predisposed to primary or familial hyperlipidemia.[2,3,11,12,30] Although it is not definitively known that hyperlipidemia is an inherited disorder of miniature schnauzers, there appears to be a higher than expected prevalence of hypertriglyceridemia in the breed.[3,a] Several other purebred and mixed-breed dogs have been identified as having fasting hyperchylomicronemia with significant clinical illness, but have no detectable underlying disease.

Canine Idiopathic Hypercholesterolemia

Results of a limited survey of healthy, adult dogs suggested that primary hypercholesterolemia might occur within some families of Doberman pinschers and rottweilers.[6] A relationship between the presence of peripheral corneal dystrophy, regarded by some ophthalmologists as containing cholesterol, and excess serum cholesterol concentration (greater than 300 mg/dl) is of noteworthy interest. Lipoprotein profiles of affected dogs demonstrate elevations of LDL-cholesterol.[a] To date, no studies have demonstrated whether or not administration of cholesterol-lowering drugs would either decrease the cholesterol concentration of hypercholesterolemic dogs or cause regression of the corneal dystrophy. Dietary management with a low-fat veterinary therapeutic food was successful in treatment of bilateral lipid keratopathy in one dog.[31]

Occasionally, extreme elevations of cholesterol will be discovered incidentally in healthy, adult dogs with normal triglyceride values. The clinician is justified in evaluating the patient for evidence of an underlying disorder, such as diabetes mellitus or hyperadrenocorticism. However, in some dogs, hypercholesterolemia cannot be explained. Unless clear evidence of underlying disease exists, treatment specifically intended to lower serum cholesterol does not appear to be warranted.

Feline Inherited Hyperchylomicronemia

In 1983,[14] a primary, genetic disorder of young New Zealand cats was found to alter chylomicron metabolism. Cats that had inherited this disorder developed a form of hyperlipidemia similar to that reported to occur in miniature schnauzers.

Secondary Disorders of Lipid Metabolism

Considering the prevalence of metabolic diseases that affect lipid metabolism, it is possible that secondary hyperlipidemia affects more animals than primary hyperlipidemia. Several endocrine diseases, as well as renal and hepatic diseases, variably alter lipoprotein metabolism resulting in either hypertriglyceridemia or hypercholesterolemia.

Diabetes Mellitus

Hyperlipidemia secondary to diabetes mellitus in dogs and cats may be characterized by hypertriglyceridemia and moderate hypercholesterolemia.[2,6,25] In insulin-deficient states, clearance of chylomicrons is impaired due to insufficient activation of lipoprotein lipase in vascular endothelial cells by insulin.[1] Examination of lipid profiles of diabetic dogs reveals lipemia, an increase in both chylomicrons and VLDL and a corresponding increase in triglyceride concentration. In some diabetic dogs, excess serum cholesterol concentrations will be present independent of hypertriglyceridemia. In one study, diabetic dogs did not have cholesterol levels significantly different from those of a control population.[25] LDL-cholesterol, on the other hand, was increased presumably as a result of increased LDL synthesis. The clinical significance of this finding is unknown.

Although a relationship between the quality of glucose regulation and serum triglyceride levels has been recognized in people, it is not known whether a similar relationship exists in dogs and cats. Lipemia retinalis in dogs and cutaneous xanthomatosis in cats are associated clinical findings that may be apparent among insulin-dependent diabetics, particularly those with severe hypertriglyceridemia. The hyperlipidemia associated with diabetes mellitus usually improves or resolves as glycemic control is achieved.

Diabetic dogs with excess serum triglyceride concentrations appear to be at risk for developing acute pancreatitis or pseudopancreatitis. Dietary fat restriction can be expected to lower the serum triglyceride concentration and may facilitate glycemic regulation in dogs receiving insulin.

Protein-Losing Nephropathy

Hyperlipidemia, characterized by increased serum cholesterol or triglyceride levels, may be detected in patients with proteinuria due to glomerulonephritis or amyloidosis. An inverse relationship between elevated blood lipids/lipoproteins and decreased plasma albumin concentration has been reported to occur in patients with nephrotic syndrome. The actual pathogenesis whereby the hyperlipidemia develops is complex and appears to be due to a combination of factors involving altered metabolism of lipoproteins.[32] Hypercholesterolemia occurs inconsistently in dogs with heavy proteinuria. The lipoprotein profile of dogs and cats with nephrotic syndrome has not yet been characterized. The influence of hyperlipidemia on morbidity and mortality in nephrotic syndrome is unknown.

Hyperadrenocorticism

Hypercholesterolemia has been recognized in dogs with hyperadrenocorticism (Cushing's syndrome) without concomitant diabetes mellitus.[6,7,25] Affected dogs have clear serum, increased plasma cholesterol and LDL-cholesterol levels, but no discrete clinical signs specifically attributable to the excess cholesterol. In a limited study of adult dogs confirmed to have hyperadrenocorticism, only 30% were hypercholesterolemic.[a] There appears to be little diagnostic value to performing lipid determinations in dogs suspected of having endogenous cortisol excess. However, monitoring changes in a given patient's cholesterol profile may have prognostic value in dogs undergoing treatment.

Hypothyroidism

Hypercholesterolemia is present in up to two-thirds of hypothyroid dogs and is believed to result from impaired LDL clearance from the general circulation. It has been suggested that an absolute T_3 deficiency may lead to an increased hepatic cholesterol pool. In turn, LDL-receptor activity is down-regulated preventing excess sterol accumulation in the liver.[25] Atherosclerotic-type arterial lesions have occasionally been reported.[7] This finding has led to the suggestion that cholesterol be included in an initial diagnostic

screening for hypothyroidism. However, superior laboratory tests are available for evaluating thyroid disease in cats and dogs and should be considered before serum cholesterol evaluation. Therapy should be directed towards correcting the thyroid-hormone deficiency. Although hypothyroid people may experience decreased cholesterol levels after thyroid-replacement therapy is started, there is no apparent value in monitoring cholesterol in affected dogs.

KEY NUTRITIONAL FACTORS

Chylomicrons are exclusively of dietary origin; therefore, the amount and type of dietary fat is of primary

Table 24-14. Selected commercial foods used in patients with hyperlipidemia.[*]

Products	kcal/kg (DM*)	MJ/kg (DM)	% kcal or kJ from fat**	Fat (%) DM	Crude fiber % DM
Dry canine products					
Hill's Prescription Diet Canine r/d	2,966	12.4	24.0	8.4	23.5
Hill's Prescription Diet Canine w/d	3,216	13.5	23.0	8.8	16.8
Hill's Science Diet Canine Maintenance Light	3,293	13.8	23.0	9.0	14.8
Iams Eukanuba Reduced Fat Formula	4,306	18.0	23.0	10.0	4.4
Iams Less Active	4,281	17.9	28.0	12.5	5.6
Iams Eukanuba Restricted-Calorie	4,053	17.0	15.0	6.6	1.9
Leo Specific Finess CRD	3,633	15.2	14.6	5.6	8.9
Medi-Cal Canine Weight Control/Geriatric	3,434	14.4	na	8.3	5.9
Medi-Cal Canine Fibre Formula	3,078	12.9	na	10.1	15.8
Purina Fit & Trim	3,100	13.0	17.4	7.4	10.8
Purina O.N.E. Reduced Calorie Formula	3,623	15.2	20.4	8.9	3.1
Purina ProPlan Reduced Calorie Formula	3,638	15.2	24.1	9.7	2.7
Purina CNM-OM Formula	2,783	11.6	17.7	6.0	15.2
Quaker Cycle Lite	3,217	13.5	24.3	10.1	4.8
Select Care Canine Hifactor Formula	3,278	13.7	28.0	10.8	14.7
Waltham/Pedigree Calorie Control/Low Calorie	3,500	14.6	22.7	8.9	1.8
Moist canine products					
Hill's Prescription Diet Canine r/d	3,000	12.6	24.0	8.3	21.2
Hill's Prescription Diet Canine w/d	3,114	13.0	31.0	12.5	12.2
Hill's Science Diet Canine Maintenance Light	3,540	14.8	22.0	9.6	10.5
Iams Less Active (Beef & Liver Formula)	5,416	23.1	40.0	20.5	4.5
Leo Specific Finess CRW (foil pack)	3,511	14.7	23.0	8.9	17.7
Medi-Cal Canine Weight Control	na	na	na	12.3	6.1
Medi-Cal Canine Fibre Formula	3,309	13.8	na	7.9	15.9
Purina CNM OM Formula	2,478	10.4	28.1	8.4	19.2
Quaker Cycle Lite	3,904	16.3	41.6	18.7	8.4
Select Care Canine Hifactor Formula	3,077	12.9	25.0	9.0	15.0
Waltham/Pedigree Calorie Control/ Low Calorie	3,662	15.4	36.5	16.9	2.1
Dry feline products					
Hill's Prescription Diet Feline r/d	3,277	13.7	24.0	9.1	14.6
Hill's Prescription Diet Feline w/d	3,531	14.8	23.0	9.3	7.9
Hill's Science Diet Feline Maintenance Light	3,523	14.7	22.0	9.0	8.5
Iams Eukanuba Restricted-Calorie	4,352	18.2	23.0	10.3	2.1
Iams Less Active Formula	4,437	18.6	29.0	13.6	3.3
Leo Specific Finess FRD	3,290	13.8	na	7.2	18.7
Medi-Cal Feline Weight Control	3,831	16.0	na	12.3	3.8
Medi-Cal Feline Fibre Control	2,813	11.8	na	13.8	7.3
Purina CNM-OM Formula	3,034	12.7	26.9	7.7	11.5
Purina ProPlan Cat Reduced Calorie Formula	4,118	17.2	23.4	9.4	2.5
Select Care Feline Hifactor Formula	3,778	15.8	29.0	12.9	5.0
Select Care Feline Weight Formula	3,800	15.9	27.0	12.2	3.6
Whiskas Feline Calorie Control	3,389	14.2	na	8.9	4.4
Moist feline products					
Hill's Prescription Diet Feline r/d	3,236	13.5	24.0	9.1	17.3
Hill's Prescription Diet Feline w/d	3,327	15.6	38.0	16.6	12.3
Hill's Science Diet Feline Maintenance Light	3,550	14.9	29.0	12.1	9.2
Leo Specific Finess FRW (foil pack)	3,458	14.5	25.8	9.3	18.7
Medi-Cal Feline Weight Control	3,873	16.2	na	17.7	5.5
Medi-Cal Feline Fibre Formula	3,391	14.2	na	14.4	8.6
Select Care Feline Hifactor Formula	3,857	16.1	36.0	16.1	7.2
Waltham/Whiskas Feline Calorie Control/Low Calorie	3,904	16.3	50.0	24.0	2.1

Key: na = information not published by manufacturer.
*From manufacturers' published information, or calculated from manufacturers' published as fed values.
**From manufacturers' published information, or calculated using energy factors of 4 kcal/g for nitrogen free extract and crude protein and 9 kcal/g for crude fat.

importance. Foods containing less than 12% fat (DMB) are most commonly recommended. Other key nutritional factors (e.g., fiber) should be considered in patients with secondary hyperlipidemia and underlying diseases such as diabetes mellitus (See previous sections in this chapter.) and protein-losing nephropathy. (See Chapter 19.)

Assess the Food(s)

The food is the single most important element in the management of primary hyperlipidemia, particularly in hypertriglyceridemic patients. If the hyperlipidemic patient's current food contains more than 12% DM fat, then a dietary change should be considered. Table 24-14 lists commercial foods that are commonly recommended for these patients. Table 6-5 gives a low-fat homemade food recipe. Depending on their underlying disease, dogs and cats with secondary hyperlipidemia may benefit from lower fat foods that also meet recommendations for other key nutritional factors. As an example, protein is important in patients with protein-losing nephropathy and water, soluble carbohydrate and fiber are important in patients with diabetes mellitus.

Assess the Feeding Method

It may not always be necessary to change the feeding method when managing a patient with hyperlipidemia, but a thorough assessment includes verification that an appropriate feeding method is being used. Items to consider include feeding route, amount fed, how the food is offered, access to other food and who feeds the animal. All of this information should have been gathered when the history of the animal was obtained. If the dog or cat has a normal BCS (3/5), the amount of food it was fed previously (energy basis) was probably appropriate. Dogs and cats with hyperlipidemia due to diabetes mellitus benefit from a feeding protocol that matches their insulin therapy.

Feeding Plan

Long-term dietary management of dogs and cats with lipemia caused by primary hypertriglyceridemia is indicated only after secondary causes of hypertriglyceridemia have been ruled out. The approach to treating any patient with secondary hypertriglyceridemia centers around managing the underlying disease; an appropriate response to the medication should include resolution of the lipemia. Concurrent disorders may also influence the key nutritional factors and lead to other food and feeding method choices. The patient's BCS and body weight should be recorded before initiating therapy because these become important parameters to monitor during reassessment.

Select a Food(s)

Because chylomicrons are exclusively of dietary origin, restriction of dietary fat is the first and most important line of therapy for dogs and cats with primary hypertriglyceridemia. Several foods are available at reasonable cost to pet owners, an important consideration because many cases necessitate life-long nutritional therapy.

Foods containing less than 12% fat (DMB) should be used. Table 24-14 summarizes the nutrient content of various commercial foods that avoid excess dietary fat and may be used in hyperlipidemic dogs or cats. The foods listed in Table 24-14 represent appropriate recommendations for dogs and cats

with hypercholesterolemia that have clinical signs associated with, or caused by, their hyperlipidemic state. Hypercholesterolemia without hypertriglyceridemia is not known to pose a significant health threat to affected dogs or cats. Because most dogs and cats with elevated cholesterol levels have a metabolic disease (e.g., diabetes mellitus or hypothyroidism), an attempt should be made to diagnose and treat the specific underlying disorder before recommending dietary therapy.

When recommending long-term dietary therapy, it is important to understand that the desired response to a particular food will vary from one animal to another.

Determine a Feeding Method

The method of feeding is often not altered in the nutritional management of lipid disorders. If a new food is fed, the amount to feed can be determined from the product label or other supporting materials. The food dosage may need to be changed if the fat level in the food is reduced, because the caloric density of the new food will probably differ from that of the previous food (i.e., the caloric density will usually be lower). If body weight and condition are optimal, the dosage of the new food should reflect the amount of kcal or kJ consumed by the animal previously. The food dosage is usually divided into two or more meals per day.

Good compliance is necessary for effective clinical nutrition. Enabling compliance includes limiting access to other foods and knowing who feeds the animal. If the dog or cat comes from a household with multiple pets, access to other pets' food should be denied (e.g., a dog with hyperlipidemia eating cat food).

Medical Management of Secondary Hyperlipidemic States

Hyperlipidemic states associated with a primary underlying disorder (e.g., diabetes mellitus or hyperadrenocorticism) can cause clinical signs in dogs and cats indistinguishable from those caused by primary hyperlipidemic states. Accurate diagnosis and treatment of the underlying disorder should resolve the hyperlipidemia and any associated signs. However, dietary therapy as outlined above should still be implemented. Dogs and cats with clinical signs associated with persistent hyperlipidemia, whether primary or secondary, should benefit from low-fat dietary therapy as long as optimal weight is maintained.

Reassessment

The effect of dietary therapy on hyperlipidemic patients is best determined three to four weeks after the feeding plan is initiated. Reassessment includes reviewing the client's assessment of the patient's response, documenting body weight and condition and evaluating the extent outward manifestations (i.e., ocular or cutaneous lesions) have resolved. Laboratory assessment involves: 1) collecting a blood sample from a fasted animal (10 to 12 hours), 2) evaluating the appearance of the serum for lipemia, 3) determining the triglyceride level in uncleared serum and 4) performing a chylomicron test. The veterinary health care team should assess the client's compliance with the outlined feeding plan. Feeding high-fat snacks and treats and access to other pet foods, even infrequently, can markedly increase circulating triglyceride levels in affected patients.

The goals of dietary therapy are to achieve a: 1) clear serum sample, 2) total triglyceride concentration less than 500 mg/dl

Medical Management of Primary Hyperlipidemia

Although dietary therapy is recommended as the initial means of managing primary hypertriglyceridemia, up to 10% of dogs with idiopathic hyperlipidemia are unresponsive to dietary fat restriction and may require pharmacologic supplementation. A variety of medical treatments for reducing lipid levels in dogs and cats have been recommended. However, the efficacy and pharmacokinetics of these treatments in animals have not been well-researched. Further, cost, dosage and toxicity are factors that must be considered when recommending long-term drug therapy to manage primary hyperlipidemic states.

FIBRATES

Gemfibrozil is the most commonly recommended drug to lower serum triglyceride levels in dogs and cats when dietary management fails. The drug is administered to dogs at doses ranging from 200 mg/day, orally, to 150 to 300 mg every 12 hours. The dosage of gemfibrozil for cats is 7.5 to 10 mg/kg body weight every 12 hours. Side effects in cats and dogs appear to be minimal; however, recent reports have suggested a long-term cancer risk associated with its use in people.

DIETARY SUPPLEMENTS

Marine fish oils are rich in n-3 (omega-3) fatty acids, which effectively decrease production of triglyceride-rich VLDL. Marine fish oils have been recommended as the first line of medical treatment for idiopathic hypertriglyceridemia in dogs. Suggested doses range from 10 to 30 mg/kg to 200 mg/kg body weight. Experience with marine fish oils is limited and most reported successes are based on anecdotal reports.

Dietary fiber and massive doses of nicotinic acid (niacin) have also been recommended for reducing serum cholesterol concentrations in people and thereby reducing the risk of coronary artery disease. There is no known value in using nicotinic acid to manage primary hyperlipidemic states in dogs and cats. Fat-restricted foods may or may not contain increased levels of dietary fiber.

Dietary supplementation with aged garlic extract has beneficial effects on the lipid profile and blood pressure of moderately hypercholesterolemic human patients. The effect of garlic extracts on hyperlipidermic animals has not been investigated.

STATINS

The 3-hydroxy-3-methylglutaryl coenzyme A (HMG CoA) reductase inhibitors, commonly referred to as "statins," effectively reduce hepatic cholesterol synthesis and enhance excretion of LDL-cholesterol from the circulation. Because of their ability to reduce the risk of coronary artery disease, the HMG CoA reductase inhibitors are the preferred class of drug prescribed to manage hypercholesterolemia in people. Although these drugs are generally well-tolerated by dogs, the actual therapeutic advantage associated with lowering circulating levels of LDL-cholesterol is unknown. Dogs and cats normally have very low levels of LDL-cholesterol. Specific dosages for dogs and cats have not been reported.

BILE ACID SEQUESTRANTS

The bile acid sequestrants, categorized as ion exchange resins, effectively reduce serum cholesterol concentrations through their ability to reduce enterohepatic circulation of bile salts and enhance cholesterol excretion. Cholestyramine has been recommended for dogs with persistent idiopathic hypercholesterolemia at dosages of 1 to 2 g every 12 hours. However, the associated side effects, principally gastrointestinal discomfort and diarrhea, combined with the fact that actually reducing serum cholesterol levels may not resolve clinical signs, limits the clinical value of these drugs.

BIBLIOGRAPHY

Harris WS. Pharmacologic management of hyperlipidemias. In: Proceedings. Fourteenth Annual Veterinary Medical Forum, American College of Veterinary Internal Medicine, San Antonio, TX, 1996: 63-64.

Steiner M, Khan AH, Holbert D, et al. A double-blind crossover study in moderately hypercholesterolemic men that compared the effect of aged garlic extract and placebo administration on blood lipids. American Journal of Clinical Nutrition 1996; 64: 866-870.

Watson TDG. Diagnosis and management of hyperlipidemia in dogs and cats. In: Proceedings. Fourteenth Annual Veterinary Medical Forum, American College of Veterinary Internal Medicine, San Antonio, TX, 1996: 65-66.

and 3) negative chylomicron test. A reasonably acceptable goal is slight serum turbidity, a triglyceride concentration less than 1,000 mg/dl and an incomplete cream layer at the top of the sample. Unless weight loss is desired, the patient's body weight and BCS should be the same as it was before the feeding plan was initiated.

Some patients remain profoundly hyperlipidemic despite excellent owner compliance in feeding a fat-restricted food. The reason is still unknown. However, these animals should continue to receive a low-fat food; human table food should not be fed. The patient should be reassessed in one to two months. If a demonstrable reduction in fasting serum triglyceride concentrations hasn't occurred, drug therapy should be added to the dietary therapy. Drug therapy for patients with primary hypertriglyceridemia has included clofibrate, niacin, gemfibrozil and dietary supplementation with n-3 polyunsaturated fatty acids from fish oils.[33-36,a] (See sidebar "Medical Management of Primary Hyperlipidemia.")

Patients that lose a significant amount of weight (more than 1% of body weight per week) should receive gradually increasing amounts of the recommended low-fat food until desired weight can be maintained. Most dogs and cats with primary hyperlipidemia will experience a marked reduction in serum triglyceride and cholesterol concentrations if daily fat intake is decreased through exclusive feeding of a fat-restricted food. In addition, amelioration or elimination of clinical signs can be expected within two weeks (dogs with pseudopancreatitis) to as long as three months (cats with cutaneous xanthomata) after therapy with a low-fat food is implemented.

■ ENDNOTES & REFERENCES

Endocrine Disorders

ENDNOTES

a. Nelson RW. Unpublished data.
b. Turrell JE, Veterinary Oncology Specialties, Pacifica, CA, USA. Personal communication. 1997.

REFERENCES

1. Feldman EC, Nelson RW. Diabetes mellitus. In: Canine and Feline Endocrinology and Reproduction, 2nd ed. Philadelphia, PA: WB Saunders Co, 1996; 339-391.

2. Stogdale L. Definition of diabetes mellitus. Cornell Veterinarian 1986; 76: 156-174.

3. Porte D Jr. β-cells in type II diabetes mellitus. Diabetes 1991; 40: 166-180.

4. Hales CN. The pathogenesis of NIDDM. Diabetologia 1994; 37 (Suppl 2): S162-S168.

5. Nichols R, Crenshaw KL. Complications and concurrent disease associated with diabetic ketoacidosis and other severe forms of diabetes mellitus. Veterinary Clinics of North America: Small Animal Practice 1995; 25: 617-624.

6. Plotnick AN, Greco DS. Diagnosis of diabetes mellitus in dogs and cats. Veterinary Clinics of North America: Small Animal Practice 1995; 25: 563-570.

7. Feldman EC, Nelson RW. Diabetic ketoacidosis. In: Canine and Feline Endocrinology and Reproduction, 2nd ed. Philadelphia, PA: WB Saunders Co, 1996; 392-421.

8. Williams DA, Minnich F. Canine exocrine pancreatic insufficiency–A survey of 640 cases diagnosed by assay of serum trypsin-like immunoreactivity (abstract). Journal of Veterinary Internal Medicine 1990; 4: 123.

9. Feldman EC, Nelson RW, eds. Hypothyroidism. In: Canine and Feline Endocrinology and Reproduction, 2nd ed. Philadelphia, PA: WB Saunders Co, 1996; 68-117.

10. Hoenig M. Pathophysiology of canine diabetes. Veterinary Clinics of North America: Small Animal Practice 1995; 25: 553-561.

11. Robertson KA, Feldman EC, Polonsky K. Spontaneous diabetes mellitus in 24 dogs: Incidence of type I versus type II disease (abstract). In: Proceedings. Seventh Veterinary Medical Forum, American College of Veterinary Internal Medicine, San Diego, CA, 1989: 1036.

12. Crenshaw KL, Peterson ME. Pretreatment clinical and laboratory evaluation of cats with diabetes mellitus: 104 cases (1992-1994). Journal of the American Veterinary Medical Association 1996; 209: 943-949.

13. Scarlett JM. The skinny on feline obesity. Cornell University, College of Veterinary Medicine. Catwatch vol. 1 No. 9, November 1997.

14. Muench KH. Protein synthesis: Translation and posttranslational modification. In: Devlin TM, ed. Textbook of Biochemistry with Clinical Correlations, 2nd ed. New York, NY: John Wiley & Sons, 1986; 737-764.

15. Harris RA. Carbohydrate metabolism I: Major metabolic pathways and their control. In: Devlin TM, ed. Textbook of Biochemistry with Clinical Correlations, 2nd ed. New York, NY: John Wiley & Sons, 1986; 261-328.

16. Granner DK. Hormones of the pancreas. In: Murray RK, Granner DK, Mayes PA, et al, eds. Harper's Biochemistry, 21st ed. San Mateo, CA: Appleton & Lange, 1988; 547-563.

17. Thorens B, Charron MJ, Lodish HF. Molecular physiology of glucose transporters. Diabetes Care 1990; 13: 209-218.

18. James DE, Brown R, Navarro J, et al. Insulin-regulatable tissues express a unique insulin sensitive glucose transport protein. Nature 1988; 333: 183-185.

19. Hoenig M, Dawe DL. A qualitative assay for beta cell antibodies. Preliminary results in dogs with diabetes mellitus. Veterinary Immunology and Immunopathology 1992; 32: 195-203.

20. Garvey WT, Maianu L, Huecksteadt TP, et al. Pretranslational suppression of GLUT4 transports causes insulin resistance in type II diabetes. Journal of Clinical Investigation 1991; 87: 1072-1081.

21. Eriksson J, Koranyi L, Bourey R, et al. Insulin resistance in type 2 (non-insulin-dependent) diabetic patients and their relatives is not associated with a defect in the expression of the insulin-responsive glucose transporter (GLUT4) gene in human skeletal muscle. Diabetologia 1992; 35: 143-147.

22. Wolf GW. Leptin: The weight-reducing plasma protein encoded by the obese gene. Nutrition Reviews 1996; 54: 91-93.

23. DeFronzo RA. The triumvirate: Beta cell, muscle, liver. A collusion responsible for NIDDM. Diabetes 1988; 37: 667-687.

24. Johnson KH, Hayden DW, O'Brian TD, et al. Spontaneous diabetes mellitus-islet amyloid complex in adult cats. American Journal of Pathology 1986; 125: 416-419.

25. Lutz TA, Rand JS. Pathogenesis of feline diabetes mellitus. Veterinary Clinics of North America: Small Animal Practice 1995; 25: 527-552.

26. Dohan FC, Lukens FDW. Lesions of the pancreatic islets produced in cats by administration of glucose. Science 1947; 105: 183.

27. Rand JS. Understanding feline diabetes. In: Proceedings. Fourteenth Annual Veterinary Medical Forum, American College of Veterinary Internal Medicine, San Antonio, TX, 1996: 82-83.

28. Panciera DL, Thomas CB, Eicker WS, et al. Epizootiologic patterns of diabetes mellitus in cats: 333 cases (1980-1986). Journal of the American Veterinary Medical Association 1990; 197: 1504-1508.

29. Schaer M. Diabetic hyperosmolar nonketotic syndrome in a cat. Journal of the American Animal Hospital Association 1975; 11: 42-45.

30. Brunzell JD, Lerner RL, Hazzard WR, et al. Improved glucose tolerance with high carbohydrate feeding in mild diabetes. New England Journal of Medicine 1971; 284: 521-524.

31. Kienzle E. Blood sugar levels and renal sugar extraction after the intake of high carbohydrate diets in cats. Journal of Nutrition 1994; 125: 2563S-2567S.

32. Nelson RW, Duesberg CA, Ford SL, et al. Effect of dietary insoluble fiber on control of glycemia in dogs with naturally acquired diabetes mellitus. Journal of the American Veterinary Medical Association 1998; 212: 380-386.

33. Nelson RW, Scott-Moncrief C, DeVries S, et al. Dietary insoluble fiber and glycemic control of diabetic cats (abstract). Journal of Veterinary Internal Medicine 1994; 8: 165.

34. Nelson RW, Ihle SL, Lewis LD, et al. Effects of dietary fiber supplementation on glycemic control in dogs with alloxan induced diabetes mellitus. American Journal of Veterinary Research 1992; 52: 2060-2066.

35. Muir HE, Murray SM, Fahey GC, et al. Nutrient digestion by ileal cannulated dogs as affected by dietary fibers with various fermentation characteristics. Journal of Animal Science 1996; 74: 1641-1648.

36. Sims MA, Hasler WL, Chey WD, et al. Hyperglycemia inhibits mechanoreceptor-mediated gastrocolonic responses and colonic peristaltic reflexes in healthy humans. Gastroenterology 1995; 108: 350-359.

37. Nettleton JA. Omega-3 fatty acids in other diseases: Diabetes. In: Omega-3 Fatty Acids and Health. New York, NY: Chapman & Hall, 1995; 287-298.

38. Mooradian AD, Morley JE. Micronutrient status in diabetes mellitus. American Journal of Clinical Nutrition 1987; 45: 877-895.

39. Shils ME. Magnesium. In: Ziegler EE, Filer LJ, eds. Present Knowledge in Nutrition. Washington, DC: ILSI Press, 1996; 256-264.

40. Senior DF. Fluid therapy, electrolytes and acid-base control. In: Ettinger SJ, Feldman EC, eds. Textbook of Veterinary Internal Medicine, 4th ed. Philadelphia, PA: WB Saunders Co, 1995; 294-311.

41. Maskell IE, Graham P. Endocrine disorders. In: Wills JM, Simpson KW, eds. The Waltham Book of Clinical Nutrition of the Dog & Cat. Tarrytown, NY: Elsevier, 1994; 373-394.

42. Ihle SL. Nutritional therapy for diabetes mellitus. Veterinary Clinics of North America: Small Animal Practice 1995; 25: 585-597.

43. Nelson RW. Dietary therapy for diabetes mellitus. Compendium on Continuing Education for the Practicing Veterinarian 1988; 10: 1387-1392.

44. Barsanti JA, Jones BD, Spano JS, et al. Prolonged anorexia associated with hepatic lipidosis in three cats. Feline Practice 1977; 7: 52-57.

45. Elliot DE, Nelson R, Reusch C, et al. Glycosylated hemoglobin and fructosamine concentrations in diabetic cats (abstract). Journal of Veterinary Internal Medicine 1995; 9: 180.

46. Crenshaw KL, Peterson ME, Moroff SD, et al. Serum fructosamine concentration as an index of glycemia in cats with diabetes mellitus and stress hyperglycemia (abstract). Journal of Veterinary Internal Medicine 1995; 9: 180.

47. Thoresen SI, Bredal WP. Clinical usefulness of fructosamine measurements in diagnosing and monitoring feline diabetes mellitus. Journal of Small Animal Practice 1996; 37: 64-68.

48. Reusch C, Hoyer-Ott M. Zur Bedeutung der Fructosamin-Bestimmung in der überwachung des Diabetes mellitus; I.) Untersuchungen bei gesundenü und diabetischein katzen sowi bei katzen mit sogenannter stresshyperglykämie. Kleinterpraxis 1995; 40: 95-100.

49. Munana KR. Long-term complications of diabetes mellitus, Part I: Retinopathy, nephropathy, neuropathy. Veterinary Clinics of North America: Small Animal Practice 1995; 25: 715-730.

50. Feldman EC, Nelson RW, eds. Beta-cell neoplasia: Insulinoma. In: Canine and Feline Endocrinology and Reproduction, 2nd ed. Philadelphia, PA: WB Saunders Co, 1996; 422-441.

51. Cryer PE, Gerich JE. Glucose counterregulation, hypoglycemia, and intensive insulin therapy in diabetes mellitus. New England Journal of Medicine 1985; 313: 232-241.

52. Braund KG, Steiss JE, Amling KA, et al. Insulinoma and subclinical peripheral neuropathy in two dogs. Journal of Veterinary Internal Medicine 1987; 1: 86-90.

ENDOCRINE
AND LIPID

53. Leifer CE, Peterson ME, Matus RE. Insulin-secreting tumor: Diagnosis and medical and surgical management in 55 dogs. Journal of the American Veterinary Medical Association 1986; 188: 60-64.

54. Smeak DD, Fingeroth JM, Bilbrey SA. Intravenous methylene blue as a specific stain for primary and metastatic insulinoma in a dog. Journal of the American Animal Hospital Association 1988; 24: 478-480.

55. Curry DL, Morris JG, Rogers QR, et al. Dynamics of insulin and glucagon secretion by the isolated perfused cat pancreas. Comparative Biochemistry and Physiology 1982; 72: 333-338.

56. Tse EO, Gregoire FM, Magrum LJ, et al. A low protein diet lowers islet insulin secretion but does not alter hyperinsulinemia in obese Zucker (fa/fa) rats. Journal of Nutrition 1995; 125: 1923-1929.

57. Caywood DD, Klausner JS, O'Leary TP, et al. Pancreatic insulin-secreting neoplasms: Clinical, diagnostic and prognostic features in 73 dogs. Journal of the American Animal Hospital Association 1988; 24: 577-584.

58. Peterson ME, Johnson GF, Andrews LK. Spontaneous hyperthyroidism in the cat (abstract). In: Proceedings. Veterinary Medical Forum, American College of Veterinary Internal Medicine, 1979: 108.

59. Holzworth J, Theran P, Carpenter JL. Hyperthyroidism in the cat: Ten cases. Journal of the American Veterinary Medical Association 1980; 46: 345-353.

60. Ferguson D. Pathogenesis of feline hyperthyroidism. In: August JR, ed. Consultations in Feline Internal Medicine, 2nd ed. Philadelphia, PA: WB Saunders Co, 1993; 133-143.

61. Broussard JD, Peterson ME, Fox PR. Changes in clinical and laboratory findings in cats with hyperthyroidism from 1983-1993. Journal of the American Veterinary Medical Association 1995; 206: 302-305.

62. Feldman EC, Nelson RW, eds. Canine thyroid tumors and hyperthyroidism. In: Canine and Feline Endocrinology and Reproduction, 2nd ed. Philadelphia, PA: WB Saunders Co, 1996; 166-185.

63. Scarlett JM. Epidemiology of thyroid diseases of dogs and cats. Veterinary Clinics of North America: Small Animal Practice 1994; 24: 477-486.

64. Feldman EC, Nelson RW, eds. Feline hyperthyroidism (thyrotoxicosis). In: Canine and Feline Endocrinology and Reproduction, 2nd ed. Philadelphia, PA: WB Saunders Co, 1996; 118-165.

65. Peterson ME. Update on hyperthyroidism in cats. In: Proceedings. Thirteenth Annual Veterinary Medical Forum, American College of Veterinary Internal Medicine, Lake Buena Vista, FL, 1995: 135-139.

66. Nachreiner RF, Refsal KR. The Michigan State University thyroid function profile. Canine Practice 1997; 22: 45-46.

67. Nelson RW. Use of baseline thyroid hormone concentrations for diagnosing canine hypothyroidism. Canine Practice 1997; 22: 39-40.

68. Ramsey I, Herrtage M. Distinguishing normal, sick, and hypothyroid dogs using total thyroxine and thyrotropin concentrations. Canine Practice 1997; 22: 43-44.

69. Scott-Moncrieff JC. Serum canine thyrotropin concentrations in experimental and spontaneous canine hypothyroidism. Canine Practice 1997; 22: 41-42.

70. Kaptein EM, Hays MT, Ferguson DC. Thyroid hormone metabolism: A comparative evaluation. Veterinary Clinics of North America: Small Animal Practice 1994; 24: 431-463.

71. Larsen PR, Berry MJ. Nutritional and hormonal regulation of thyroid deiodinases. Annual Review of Nutrition 1995; 15: 323-352.

72. Freake HC, Oppenheimer JH. Thermogenesis and thyroid function. Annual Review of Nutrition 1995; 15: 263-291.

73. Davey JC, Becker KB, Schneider MJ, et al. Cloning of a cDNA for the type II iodothyronine deiodinase. Journal of Biological Chemistry 1995; 270: 26786-26789.

74. Panciera DL. Canine hypothyroidism. Part I. Clinical findings and control of thyroid hormone secretion and metabolism. Compendium on Continuing Education for the Practicing Veterinarian 1990; 12: 689-701.

75. Mumma RO, Rashid KA, Shane BS, et al. Toxic and protective constituents in pet foods. American Journal of Veterinary Research 1986; 47: 1633-1637.

76. Johnson LA, Ford HC, Tartellin MF, et al. Iodine content of commercially-prepared foods. New Zealand Veterinary Journal 1992; 40: 18-20.

77. Skare S, Frey HMM. Iodine induced thyrotoxicosis in apparently normal thyroid glands. Acta Endocrinologica 1980; 94: 332-336.

78. Fradkin JE, Wolff J. Iodine-induced thyrotoxicosis. Medicine 1983; 62: 1-20.

79. Sartelet H, Serghat S, Lobstein A, et al. Flavonoids extracted from Fonio millet (*Digitaria exilis*) reveal potent antithyroid properties. Nutrition 1996; 12: 100-106.

80. Kintzer PP. Considerations in the treatment of feline hyperthyroidism. Veterinary Clinics of North America: Small Animal Practice 1994; 24: 577-585.

81. Melian C, Peterson ME. Diagnosis and treatment of naturally occurring hypoadrenocorticism in 42 dogs. Journal of Small Animal Practice 1996; 37: 268-275.

82. Association of American Feed Control Officials. Official Publication, 1999.

83. Feldman EC, Nelson RW, eds. Hyperadrenocorticism (Cushing's Syndrome). In: Canine and Feline Endocrinology and Reproduction, 2nd ed. Philadelphia, PA: WB Saunders Co, 1996; 187-265.

84. Feldman EC, Nelson RW, eds. Disorders of growth hormone. In: Canine and Feline Endocrinology and Reproduction, 2nd ed. Philadelphia, PA: WB Saunders Co, 1996; 38-66.

85. Feldman EC, Nelson RW, eds. Water metabolism and diabetes insipidus. In: Canine and Feline Endocrinology and Reproduction, 2nd ed. Philadelphia, PA: WB Saunders Co, 1996; 2-37.

Lipid Disorders

ENDNOTE
a. Ford RB. Unpublished observation. April 1994.

REFERENCES
1. Brown MS, Goldstein JL. The hyperlipoproteinemias and other disorders of lipid metabolism. In: Braunwald E, Isselbacher KJ, Petersdorf RG, et al, eds. Harrison's Principles of Internal Medicine, 11th ed. New York, NY: McGraw-Hill, 1987; 1650-1661.

2. Ford RB. Clinical management of lipemic patients. Compendium on Continuing Education for the Practicing Veterinarian 1996; 18: 1053-1065.

3. Ford RB. Idiopathic hyperchylomicronemia in miniature schnauzers. Journal of Small Animal Practice 1993; 34: 488-492.

4. Mahley RW, Weisgraber KH. Canine lipoproteins and atherosclerosis I. Isolation and characterization of plasma lipoproteins from control dogs. Circulation Research 1974; 35: 713-721.

5. Mahley RW, Weisgraber KH, Innerarity T. Canine lipoproteins and atherosclerosis II. Characterization of the plasma lipoprotein associated with atherogenic and nonatherogenic hyperlipidemia. Circulation Research 1974; 35: 722-733.

6. Armstrong PJ, Ford RB. Hyperlipidemia. In: Kirk RW, ed. Current Veterinary Therapy X. Philadelphia, PA: WB Saunders Co, 1989; 1046-1050.

7. DeBowes LJ. Lipid metabolism and hyperlipoproteinemia in dogs. Compendium on Continuing Education for the Practicing Veterinarian 1987; 9: 727-731.

8. Sanfey H, Cameron JL. Pancreatitis and hyperlipemia. In: Berk JE, ed. Gastroenterology, 4th ed. Philadelphia, PA: WB Saunders Co, 1985; 4055-4071.

9. Whitney MS, Boon GD, Rebar AH, et al. Effects of acute pancreatitis on circulating lipids in dogs. American Journal of Veterinary Research 1987; 48: 1492-1497.

10. Williams DA. Exocrine pancreatic disease. In: Ettinger SJ, Feldman EC, eds. Textbook of Veterinary Internal Medicine, 4th ed. Philadelphia, PA: WB Saunders Co, 1995; 1372-1392.

11. Rogers WA, Donovan EF, Kociba GJ. Idiopathic hyperlipoproteinemia in dogs. Journal of the American Veterinary Medical Association 1975; 166: 1087-1099.

12. Rogers WA, Donovan EF, Kociba GJ. Lipids and lipoproteins in normal dogs and dogs with secondary hyperlipoproteinemia. Journal of the American Veterinary Medical Association 1975; 166: 1092-1100.

13. Jones BR, Watson TDG. In: Proceedings. Specialist Session on Lipid Disorders. British Small Animal Veterinary Association Annual Congress, Birmingham, UK, 1995.

14. Jones BR, Wallace A, Harding DRK, et al. Occurrence of idiopathic, familial hyperchylomicronaemia in a cat. Veterinary Record 1983; 112: 543-547.

15. Jones BR. Feline hyperlipidemia. In: Ettinger SJ, Feldman EC, eds. Textbook of Veterinary Internal Medicine, 4th ed. Philadelphia, PA: WB Saunders Co, 1995; 1410-1414.

16. Jones BR. Inherited hyperchylomicronaemia in the cat. Journal of Small Animal Practice 1993; 34: 493-499.

17. Crispin SM. Ocular manifestations of hyperlipoproteinemia. Journal of Small Animal Practice 1993; 34: 500-506.

18. Allerman AR. The effects of hemolysis and lipemia on serum biochemical constituents. Veterinary Medicine 1990; 85: 1272-1284.

19. Chapman MJ. Animal lipoproteins: Chemistry, structure, and comparative aspects. Journal of Lipid Research 1980; 21: 789-853.

20. Whitney MS. Evaluation of hyperlipidemias in dogs and cats. Seminars in Veterinary Medicine and Surgery: Small Animal 1992; 7: 292-300.

21. Schaefer EJ, Levy RI. Pathogenesis and management of lipoprotein disorders. New England Journal of Medicine 1985; 312: 1300-1310.

22. Weinberg RB. Lipoprotein metabolism: Hormonal regulation. Hospital Practice 1987; 22: 223-243.

23. Watson TDG, Barrie J. Lipoprotein metabolism and hyperlipidaemia in the dog and cat: A review. Journal of Small Animal Practice 1993; 34: 479-487.

24. Naito HK. The clinical significance of apolipoprotein measurements. Journal of Clinical Immunoassay 1986; 9: 11-20.

25. Barrie J, Watson TDG, Stear MJ, et al. Plasma cholesterol and lipoprotein concentration in the dog: The effect of age, breed, gender and endocrine disease. Journal of Small Animal Practice 1993; 34: 507-712.

26. Gotto AM. Lipoprotein metabolism and the etiology of hyperlipidemia. An update: Pharmacologic approaches to the hyperlipidemias. Hospital Practice 1988 (Suppl. 1); 23: 4-13.

27. Eckel RH. Lipoprotein lipase. New England Journal of Medicine 1989; 16: 1060-1068.

28. Rogers WA. Lipemia in the dog. Veterinary Clinics of North America: Small Animal Practice 1977; 7: 637-640.

29. Zerbe CA. Canine hyperlipidemias. In: Kirk RW, ed. Current Veterinary Therapy IX. Philadelphia, PA: WB Saunders Co, 1986; 1045-1053.

30. Ford RB. Canine hyperlipidemia. In: Ettinger SJ, Feldman EC, eds. Textbook of Veterinary Internal Medicine, 4th ed. Philadelphia, PA: WB Saunders Co, 1995; 1414-1419.

31. Linton LL, Moore CP, Collier LL. Bilateral lipid keratopathy in a boxer dog: Cholesterol analyses and dietary management. Progress in Veterinary and Comparative Ophthalmology 1994; 3: 9-14.

32. Bernard DB. Metabolic abnormalities in nephrotic syndrome: Pathophysiology and complications. In: Brenner BM, Stein JH, eds. Contemporary Issues in Nephrology, vol 9: Nephrotic Syndrome. New York, NY: Churchill Livingstone, 1982; 87-120.

33. Logas D, Beale KM, Bauer JE. Potential clinical benefits of dietary supplementation with marine-life oil. Journal of the American Veterinary Medical Association 1991; 199: 1631-1636.

34. Levy RI. Currently available lipid-lowering agents. An update: Pharmacologic approaches to the hyperlipidemias. Hospital Practice 1988 (Suppl. 1); 23: 14-21.

35. Schaefer EJ. When and how to treat the dyslipidemias. Hospital Practice 1988; 23: 69-84.

36. Watson TDG. Diagnosis and management of hyperlipidemia in dogs and cats. In: Proceedings. Fourteenth Annual Veterinary Medical Forum, American College of Veterinary Internal Medicine, San Antonio, TX, 1996: 65-66.

CASE 24-1

Polyuria/Polydipsia in a Cat

Richard W. Nelson, DVM
Diplomate ACVIM (Internal Medicine)
School of Veterinary Medicine
University of California, Davis
Davis, California, USA

Assess the Animal

A six-year-old, neutered female domestic shorthair cat was examined for polyuria and polydipsia of two weeks' duration, lethargy and anorexia. The cat remained indoors at all times and had been overweight for several years.

Physical examination revealed an alert, hydrated cat. Body weight was 4.8 kg with a body condition score (BCS) of 5/5. The optimal body weight was estimated to be 3.5 kg. The abdomen was tense when palpated but non-painful. The borders of the liver were palpable beyond the margins of the rib cage and the bladder was distended. The coat had a greasy appearance with slight dander.

Results of a complete blood count were normal. Abnormal serum biochemistry profile results included increased glucose (398 mg/dl, reference interval = 70 to 110 mg/dl) and cholesterol (416 mg/dl, reference interval = 90 to 250 mg/dl) concentrations. Urinalysis revealed glucosuria and a urine specific gravity of 1.019. The tentative diagnoses were diabetes mellitus and obesity.

Assess the Food(s) and Feeding Method

The cat was normally fed a commercial specialty brand dry cat food (Science Diet Feline Maintenance[a]) free choice and one can of a commercial grocery brand "gourmet" cat food (Fancy Feast Chunk Chicken Feast[b]) twice daily. Table 1 lists nutrient levels in these foods. The gourmet food contained approximately 85 kcal (356 kJ) per can. Water was available free choice. The cat's appetite has always been very good until yesterday.

Questions

1. What factors may have predisposed this cat to developing diabetes mellitus?
2. What key nutritional factors should be considered for this patient?
3. Outline an appropriate feeding plan (foods and feeding method) for this cat.
4. How should this patient be monitored?

Answers and Discussion

1. Obesity is a known risk factor for development of non-insulin-dependent diabetes mellitus (NIDDM), especially in cats. NIDDM may occur in obese animals subsequent to down regulation of peripheral insulin receptors, as occurs in people.
2. The key nutritional factors for patients with uncomplicated diabetes mellitus are water, energy, fat and fiber.

Table 1. Nutrient levels in foods fed to a diabetic cat.

Nutrients (DMB)	Dry specialty brand food*	Moist grocery brand food**
Crude fat (%)	23.0	34.0
Crude fiber (%)	1.0	0.4
Energy (kcal/g)	4.5	4.9
NFE (%)	37.0	5.3
Protein (%)	33.8	50.8

Key: DMB = dry matter basis, NFE = nitrogen-free extract.
*Science Diet Feline Maintenance, Hill's Pet Nutrition, Inc., Topeka, KS, USA.
**Fancy Feast Chunk Chicken Feast, Friskies Petcare Co, Glendale, CA, USA.

Dietary minerals and vitamins may also be important in patients with some forms of diabetes mellitus (ketoacidosis) and those with prolonged polydipsia and polyuria. Water should always be available free choice and in abundant amounts. The amount of energy and source of energy substrates (e.g., avoid simple sugars and fat) are also important. Energy for this patient is best supplied by complex carbohydrates and protein. Excess dietary fat should also be avoided as part of a weight-reduction program. (See Chapter 13.) Increased dietary fiber helps reduce the caloric density of the food and helps maintain glycemic control in conjunction with medical management.

3. The goals of dietary management for this cat include: 1) reducing weight to improve or eliminate peripheral insulin resistance and other metabolic abnormalities, 2) providing consistent daily energy intake and 3) minimizing postprandial fluctuations in serum glucose concentrations. The cat should be fed a food that contains lower energy density, lower fat and higher crude fiber levels than the foods currently being offered. The amount of food should be divided and offered at least twice daily immediately after treatment with insulin or oral hypoglycemic agents. Daily food dosage should be calculated for optimal body weight. Many well-regulated overweight diabetic cats lose weight when fed at optimal body weight. An energy calculation of 1.2 x resting energy requirement (RER) for the estimated optimal body weight is a reasonable starting point.

4. Response to treatment can be assessed through careful owner observation. Favorable response to treatment is indicated by decreased water intake, decreased urination, decreased food intake (in animals that exhibit polyphagia), achievement of weight goals and a generalized increased thriftiness. Unfavorable responses include continuation of polyuria, polydipsia, polyphagia and inability to achieve weight goals. If the animal is stable and doing well then veterinary reassessment should take place every three to four months. If the animal is symptomatic then veterinary reassessment should take place every one to two weeks until stable.

Achievement of weight goals can be measured through BCS and body weight. Cats should be weighed and have body condition assessed at least once a month. A chart of body weight and BCS may be kept by the owner. Weight loss will usually take six to 12 months to occur. (See Chapter 13.) A loss of 10% body weight in already thin animals indicates a need for reassessment of the dietary regimen and diabetic regulation.

Maintenance of body weight with a reduction in food intake should occur in polyphagic animals responding favorably to exogenous insulin administration. This response occurs due to increased nutrient usage associated with hormonal treatment. If animals exhibit anorexia or depressed food intake then the relative palatability of the food may be poor and another food should be tried after ruling out medical causes. It is especially important to monitor food intake in cats because prolonged anorexia can lead to hepatic lipidosis.

Abnormalities in the serum biochemistry profile should return to normal with well-controlled diabetes and adequate nutritional intake. The major exception to this is hyperglycemia, which may or may not be present depending on when the blood sample is obtained in relation to when insulin is administered. Abnormalities of biochemical constituents in the face of controlled diabetes mellitus should be evaluated as separate disease entities.

Progress Notes

An oral hypoglycemic sulfonylurea drug (glipizide[c]) was chosen (5 mg per os, twice daily) because the owners did not want to give insulin injections. The food was changed to a commercial moist veterinary therapeutic food (Prescription Diet Feline w/d[a]) that was lower in fat (16.6% dry matter [DM]) and energy (3.64 kcal/g, 15.2kJ/g), and higher in crude fiber (12.3% DM) than the previous foods. Soluble carbohydrate (nitrogen-free extract, NFE) content of the new food was 23.7% DM. The daily food amount was divided into two meals and offered 30 minutes after the drug treatment each morning and evening. Total daily energy intake was initially calculated at 1.2 x RER for a body weight of 3.5 kg (210 kcal/day, 880 kJ/day).

The cat lost weight over the next six months. It reached a body weight of 3.8 kg (BCS 3/5) and glipizide was eventually discontinued because normal glucose tolerance was maintained with dietary management alone. The lower fat, higher fiber food was continued but the amount fed was increased (190 kcal/day, 795 kJ/day) to maintain optimum body weight and condition.

Endnotes

a. Hill's Pet Nutrition, Inc., Topeka, KS, USA.
b. Friskies Petcare Co, Glendale, CA, USA.
c. Glucotrol. Roerig Division, Pfizer Inc., New York, NY, USA.

Bibliography

Kirk CA, Feldman EC, Nelson RW. Diagnosis of naturally acquired type-I and type-II diabetes mellitus in cats. American Journal of Veterinary Research 1993; 54: 463-467.

Nelson RW, Feldman EC, Ford SL, et al. Effect of an orally administered sulfonylurea, glipizide, for treatment of diabetes mellitus in cats. Journal of the American Veterinary Medical Association 1993; 203: 821-827.

CASE 24-2

Insulin Resistance in a Labrador Retriever

Richard W. Nelson, DVM
Diplomate ACVIM (Internal Medicine)
School of Veterinary Medicine
University of California, Davis
Davis, California, USA

Assess the Animal

A five-year-old, 39-kg, castrated male, Labrador retriever was admitted to a referral institution because of difficulty in controlling diabetes mellitus. Insulin-dependent diabetes mellitus (IDDM) had been diagnosed one year before referral. The dog had initially responded well to 25 IU of beef/pork NPH insulin administered once daily. During the two months before referral, the dog developed pro-

Table 1. Nutrient levels in foods fed to a diabetic dog.

Nutrients (DMB)	Dry grocery brand food*	Moist grocery brand food**	Dry veterinary therapeutic food***
Crude fat (%)	13.3	21.8	6.9
Crude fiber (%)	4.3	1.1	16.8
Energy (kcal/g)	3.7	4.4	3.2
Protein (%)	24.8	39.7	16.7
Soluble carbohydrate (%)	52.2	28.3	55.2

Key: DMB = dry matter basis.
*Alpo Beef Flavored Dinner. Friskies Petcare Co, Glendale, CA, USA.
**Cycle Adult. Friskies Petcare Co, Glendale, CA, USA.
***Prescription Diet Canine w/d. Hill's Pet Nutrition, Inc., Topeka, KS, USA.

gressively worsening polyuria and polydipsia despite receiving 50 IU of insulin once daily. No other abnormalities were reported by the owner or referring veterinarian.

The dog was alert and responsive with normal temperature, pulse and respiratory rate. Abnormalities identified included obesity (body condition score 5/5), hepatomegaly and a dry lusterless coat. The estimated optimal body weight was approximately 32 kg.

Abnormalities of the serum biochemistry profile included hyperglycemia, preprandial lipemia, hypercholesterolemia and increased alanine aminotransferase activity. Urinalysis revealed glucosuria, bacteriuria and a urine culture isolated *Escherichia coli*. Abdominal ultrasonography and thoracic radiographs were unremarkable. An initial blood glucose curve revealed persistent hyperglycemia at all time points (greater than 300 mg/dl).

Assess the Food(s) and Feeding Method

The dog was being fed a mixture of commercial moist and dry food twice daily. One can of a grocery brand dog food (Cycle Adultᵃ) mixed with one to two cups of a dry grocery brand dog food (Alpo Beef Flavored Dinnerᵃ) was offered at the time of the insulin injection in the morning. A second portion of the same dry and moist food mixture was offered eight hours later. Table 1 lists nutrient levels in these foods. The dog was eating approximately 1,600 to 1,800 kcal/day (6.69 to 7.53 MJ).

Questions

1. What factors may be contributing to the apparent insulin resistance in this dog?
2. What are the key nutritional factors that should be considered in this patient?
3. Outline an appropriate feeding plan (food and feeding method) for this dog.
4. What concurrent therapy should be used in this patient?

Answers and Discussion

1. Insulin resistance exists whenever normal concentrations of insulin produce a less than normal biologic response. Proposed mechanisms for insulin resistance include: 1) an abnormal insulin molecule, 2) increased insulin degradation, 3) insulin antibodies, 4) insulin-receptor antibodies, 5) high circulating levels of counterregulatory hormones, 6) insulin-receptor defects (altered numbers or affinity) and 7) postreceptor defects. In diabetic dogs and cats, insulin resistance has been arbitrarily defined to exist when therapeutic doses

of insulin exceed 2.0 to 2.5 units/kg body weight per day. Conditions that can contribute to insulin resistance include obesity, hyperadrenocorticism, acromegaly (excess growth hormone), hyperthyroidism (cats), hypothyroidism, renal failure, liver disease, bacterial infections, pregnancy and anti-insulin antibodies.

2. The key nutritional factors for patients with uncomplicated diabetes mellitus are water, energy, fat and fiber. Water should always be available free choice and in abundant amounts. The amount of energy and source of energy substrates (e.g., avoid simple sugars) are also important. Excess dietary fat should be avoided as part of a weight-reduction program. Increased dietary fiber helps reduce caloric density of the food and helps maintain glycemic control in conjunction with medical management.

3. The goals of dietary management in this dog include: 1) decrease obesity, which may improve or eliminate peripheral insulin resistance and other metabolic abnormalities, 2) provide consistent daily energy intake and 3) minimize postprandial fluctuations in serum glucose concentrations. The dog should be fed a food that contains lower energy density, lower fat and higher crude fiber levels than the foods currently being offered. The amount of food should be divided and offered at least twice daily immediately after treatment with insulin. Daily food dosage should be calculated; a starting energy calculation of 1.0 x resting energy requirement (RER) for the estimated optimal body weight is a reasonable starting point.

4. The bacterial urinary tract infection may be contributing to insulin resistance and should be eliminated with appropriate antimicrobial therapy. The beef/pork insulin should also be changed to another insulin type in case anti-insulin antibodies are contributing to the problem.

Progress Notes

The urinary tract infection was treated with oral cefadroxilᵇ for 10 days and the insulin was changed to 55 IU recombinant human Lente insulinᶜ every 12 hours, subcutaneously. The food was changed to a commercial dry veterinary therapeutic food that was lower in fat, higher in soluble carbohydrates and higher in dietary fiber (Prescription Diet Canine w/dᵈ) than the current foods (Table 1). The estimated daily energy requirement for weight loss was 1,000 kcal/day (4.18 MJ); this was met by feeding 2.25 cups twice daily shortly after insulin administration.

Reassessment one month later showed that insulin continued to be ineffective despite increasing the dose to 60

IU every 12 hours, subcutaneously. The owner reported recent lethargy, weakness and excessive shedding in addition to continuing polyuria and polydipsia. Results of serum biochemistry analysis, urinalysis, blood glucose curves and a complete blood count had not changed from those values at the initial presentation. Baseline serum thyroxine concentration was low (0.6 µg/dl, reference = 1.5 to 3.5 µg/dl) and decreased to 0.5 µg/dl four hours following administration of 200 µg of thyrotropin-releasing hormone (TRH). Hypothyroidism with insulin resistance, diabetes mellitus and obesity became the working diagnoses. Levothyroxine sodium[e] (0.8 mg, per os, every 12 hours) was initiated and the insulin dosage was reduced (30 IU, subcutaneously, every 12 hours). The feeding plan was unchanged.

Over the next three months the insulin dosage was stabilized at 28 IU, subcutaneously, every 12 hours. The dog's activity level and coat improved. A weight loss of 5 kg was attained as well. Abnormalities in the serum biochemistry profile were alleviated except for the hyperglycemia. Serum thyroxine concentration six hours after levothyroxine administration was 4.8 µg/dl (normal = 1.5 to 3.5 µg/dl).

Additional Comments

Diabetes mellitus in dogs is most often insulin-dependent. When conventional therapy fails to work, other disease processes should be considered as well as other modalities of treatment for diabetes control. The use of a low-fat, high-fiber food in this case was beneficial for weight reduction and maintaining glycemic control. Weight reduction should follow the guidelines established in Chapter 13.

Endnotes

a. Friskies Petcare Co, Glendale, CA, USA.
b. Cefa-Tabs., Fort Dodge Laboratories, Fort Dodge, IA, USA.
c. Humulin L. Eli Lilly & Co, Indianapolis, IN, USA.
d. Hill's Pet Nutrition, Inc., Topeka, KS, USA.
e. Soloxine. Daniels Pharmaceuticals, St. Petersburg, FL, USA.

Bibliography

Nelson RW. Insulin resistance in diabetic dogs and cats. In: Bonagura JD, ed. Current Veterinary Therapy XII. Philadelphia, PA: WB Saunders Co, 1995; 390-393.

Peterson ME, Sampson GR. Insulin and insulin syringes. In: Bonagura JD, ed. Current Veterinary Therapy XII. Philadelphia, PA: WB Saunders Co, 1995; 387-390.

■ CASE 24-3

Episodic Diarrhea in a Mixed-Breed Dog

Richard B. Ford, DVM
Diplomate ACVIM (Internal Medicine)
School of Veterinary Medicine
North Carolina State University
Raleigh, North Carolina, USA

Assess the Animal

A seven-year-old, female, mixed-breed dog was initially examined for a four-month history of episodic diarrhea accompanied by lethargy and a decreased appetite. The owner reported that the frequency of the episodes had gradually increased to once weekly over the last two months. Clinical signs would spontaneously resolve within 24 to 48 hours.

The initial physical examination revealed an active, alert dog. Abdominal palpation was unremarkable and well-tolerated. The dog weighed 11.8 kg and appeared thin (body condition score 2/5) although the owner had not reported weight loss.

A presumptive diagnosis of dietary intolerance was made and empiric treatment with a veterinary therapeutic food for management of gastrointestinal disease was initiated. Ten days later the dog was examined for significant lethargy and abdominal discomfort. The owner indicated that the dog had eaten nothing during the past 24 hours but did drink water. Soft feces were noted occasionally. Abdominal palpation was associated with discomfort; however, the source of the abdominal pain could not be localized.

Results of an abdominal radiograph, urinalysis and fecal flotation for intestinal parasites were normal. Blood collected for analysis was profoundly lipemic and moderately hemolyzed. Test results were obtained from a commercial laboratory on the following day. Results of a complete blood count were normal. Abnormal serum biochemistry profile results included hypocalcemia (8.5 mg/dl, normal 9.2 to 11.2 mg/dl). Serum cholesterol (278 mg/dl) and triglyceride (96 mg/dl) concentrations were normal.

Assess the Food(s) and Feeding Method

The dog was normally fed a combination of dry and moist commercial grocery store brand foods with occasional snacks. The food was offered once a day. The dog's diet had been consistent for several years until the change 10 days ago to a moist veterinary therapeutic food (Prescription Diet Canine i/d[a]) designed for the management of gastrointestinal disorders.

Questions

1. Why is the serum triglyceride concentration normal in a patient with lipemia?
2. What is the tentative diagnosis in this patient?
3. What is an appropriate feeding plan (food[s] and feeding method) for this dog?

Answers and Discussion

1. In an attempt to avoid lipid interference with other biochemical assays, many commercial laboratories will use ultracentrifugation to clear chylomicrons before performing any tests on a lipemic serum sample. This process removes excess triglycerides before testing. Thus, the triglyceride concentration reported by the laboratory may be normal. Simply observing a lipemic sample in a fasted (six to 12 hours) animal is sufficient clinical evidence to document hypertriglyceridemia.

The low-serum calcium concentration was probably an artifact due to interference from the lipemia.

2. The predominant cause of hyperlipidemia in dogs is excess concentrations of triglyceride-rich chylomicrons. Thus, canine hyperchylomicronemia (hypertriglyceridemia) is the most likely diagnosis, after the clinician has observed the serum sample and confirmed the presence of lipemia by observation (i.e., a cream layer denoting hyperchylomicronemia) or measuring triglyceride levels (i.e., levels exceeding 500 mg/dl). Fasting lipemia can be a significant clinical problem associated with episodic diarrhea, inappetence, abdominal discomfort and occasional vomiting. The collective term to describe this syndrome is "pseudopancreatitis." The rapid worsening of clinical signs justifies expanding the differential diagnosis to include pancreatitis, hypoadrenocorticism, neoplasia and primary intestinal disease (e.g., inflammatory bowel disease, etc.). Additional endocrine testing may be indicated to rule out secondary causes of hyperlipidemia.

3. For any patient with fasting hyperlipidemia, regardless of the cause, food with a fat content less than 12% dry matter is recommended. (See Table 24-14.) Foods designed for empiric management of gastrointestinal disorders often have a fat content that exceeds this recommendation. Multiple small meals rather than one large meal per day may be helpful in patients with gastrointestinal signs.

Progress Notes

After fasting hypertriglyceridemia (hyperchylomicronemia) was confirmed, the initial treatment prescribed was limited to fat restriction. Dry Prescription Diet Canine w/d[a] was recommended because of its palatability and low-fat content (approximately 6.9% on a dry matter basis). The owner was advised that: 1) dietary management is the most reasonable, economical means of controlling this potentially serious condition, 2) dietary fat restriction

Table 1. Serum triglyceride levels before and after three weeks of treatment with a low-fat veterinary therapeutic food.*

Initial level	2,350 mg/dl**
Three-week level	477 mg/dl**

*Prescription Diet Canine w/d. Hill's Pet Nutrition, Inc., Topeka, KS, USA.
**Uncleared specimen.

would be a life-long requirement, if treatment were successful and 3) even a single high-fat meal (e.g., eating from the trash) could acutely exacerbate clinical signs and cause pancreatitis.

The patient was reexamined after consuming the veterinary therapeutic food for three weeks to assess dietary compliance and serum triglyceride levels. A fasting (overnight) blood sample was collected. The serum triglyceride (uncleared) concentration was determined and compared to that obtained during the initial examination (Table 1).

Results suggested excellent dietary control of the hyperlipidemic state and good dietary compliance. Specific drug intervention was deemed unnecessary at the time the patient was re-checked. However, the owner was advised that although the risk of serious illness (pancreatitis) had been markedly reduced, follow-up examinations twice yearly, including fasting triglyceride measurements, would be a prudent course to follow.

Endnote

a. Hill's Pet Nutrition, Inc., Topeka, KS, USA.

Bibliography

Ford RB. Canine hyperlipidemia. In: Ettinger SJ, Feldman EC, eds. Textbook of Veterinary Internal Medicine, 4th ed. Philadelphia, PA: WB Saunders Co, 1995; 1414-1419.

ENDOCRINE AND LIPID

CHAPTER 25

Cancer

Gregory K. Ogilvie

Stanley L. Marks

"Cancer, unlike politics and religion, is not a topic of controversy. No one is for it."
S. Mooney, 1989

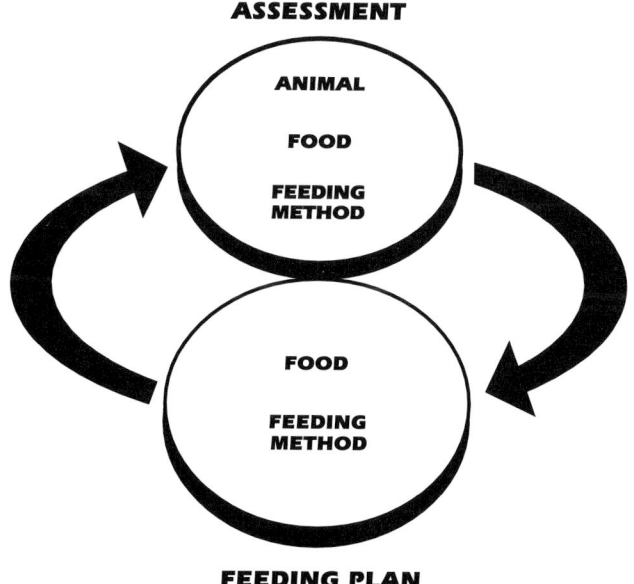

ASSESSMENT

ANIMAL

FOOD

FEEDING METHOD

FOOD

FEEDING METHOD

FEEDING PLAN

Note: The reader is referred to Chapter 1 for a detailed discussion of the iterative process of clinical nutrition.

CLINICAL IMPORTANCE

Cancer is one of the most common causes of nonaccidental death of dogs and cats.[1,2] One study documented the cause of death in a series of more than 2,000 necropsy cases.[2] In that study, 45% of dogs that lived to 10 years or older died of cancer. Overall, 23% of pets examined at necropsy died of cancer.

Cats have the largest number of different retroviruses of any companion animal. Retroviral infections in cats produce a wide spectrum of diseases, including cancer. Retroviruses are considered the most common infectious cause of morbidity and mortality in the feline population.[3] The overall prevalence (number of diagnosed cases/year) of feline leukemia virus infection in the United States is between 1 and 3%.[3] The prevalence is less than 1% in single-cat households and as great as 30% in multi-cat households. The prevalence in sick cats is 11.5%.[3]

The overall prevalence of cancer in pets also appears to be increasing.[4] The prevalence is increasing for a variety of reasons, but is, in part, related to the fact that pets are living longer. Practicing veterinarians will more frequently diagnose and manage pets with cancer because of this increased prevalence.

Cancer is also a common and serious disease for people. Many pet owners have had cancer or will have a personal experience in which cancer affects themselves, a family member or an acquaintance. This fact suggests that veterinarians and health care teams should approach pets with cancer and their owners in a positive, compassionate and knowledgeable manner. These owners are also able to understand the impor-

KEY WORDS & TERMS—CANCER*

Anaerobic metabolism	Glutamine	Micronutrient
Arginine	Glycine	Phenylalanine
Cancer cachexia	Hyperinsulinemia	Protease inhibitor
Docosahexaenoic acid	Hyperlactatemia	Resting energy expenditure
Eicosanoids	Indirect calorimetry	Retinoids
Eicosapentaenoic acid	L-asparaginase	Tyrosine

Key words and terms are defined in the Glossary.

KEY POINTS—CANCER

1. Cancer cachexia is an involuntary weight loss that occurs in the presence of adequate nutritional intake.
2. The metabolic alterations associated with cancer occur before clinical evidence of weight loss.
3. Animals with cancer cachexia have a decreased quality of life and their survival time is markedly shorter than that of animals with the same diseases without cachexia.
4. Dogs (and probably cats) with a wide variety of cancers have significant elevations in lactic acid and insulin levels that increase markedly when dextrose is administered intravenously or foods high in easily digestible carbohydrates are fed.
5. Nutritional support of cancer patients maximizes healing, decreases side effects of chemotherapy, ameliorates the metabolic alterations induced by cancer and prolongs the disease-free interval and survival.
6. Placing feeding tubes and providing enteral nutritional support should always be considered for cancer patients. Placement of feeding tubes at the time of surgery is convenient and allows both short- and long-term nutritional management of patients. It is far easier to prevent development of cancer cachexia than return a patient with cancer cachexia to a more normal state.
7. Most cats and dogs suffering from the early stages of cancer appear normal to their owners and veterinarians; however, they have detectable metabolic changes such as hyperlactatemia, hyperinsulinemia and alterations in

blood amino acid profiles.
8. Until further information is known about the effects of hyperlactatemia on critically ill animals with cancer, glucose- and lactate-containing fluids should generally be avoided.
9. Foods high in carbohydrates can increase the total amount of lactate produced and increase the need for the host to use energy inappropriately for conversion of lactate to glucose. This metabolic pathway causes long-term detrimental effects in animals with cancer.
10. Arginine, in large doses, exerts numerous beneficial effects on the immune system.
11. Surgery, radiation therapy and chemotherapy may adversely affect nutritional status. The malnutrition that results from treatment assumes even more importance because many cancer patients are already debilitated from their disease.
12. In cancer patients, a large proportion of the daily energy requirement should come from dietary fat because tumor cells have difficulty using fats and loss of body fat accompanies cachexia.
13. Increased levels of dietary n-3 fatty acids may benefit cancer patients by inhibiting tumors and enhancing immune function.
14. Reassessment of cancer patients should include monitoring effects of cancer on the animal, treatment and nutritional management on the tumor and treatment and nutritional support on the patient.

tance of nutrition in cancer patients and how proper feeding can enhance the quality and length of life for pets with cancer.

Proper nutritional support can reduce or prevent toxicoses associated with cancer therapy and ameliorate the metabolic alterations induced by cancer. In addition, there is growing evidence that specific nutrients can be used to treat the malignant disease directly or indirectly. This chapter will focus on the nutritional management of patients with cancer rather than on nutritional strategies to prevent cancer.

■ ASSESSMENT

Assess the Animal

History and Physical Examination

For convenience, metabolic and clinical alterations in cancer patients have been described in four phases (Table 25-1).[5-15] The first phase is a preclinical "silent" phase in

which patients do not exhibit clinical signs of disease. Most dogs and cats in the early stages of cancer often appear normal to their owners and veterinarians. As the underlying malignancy progresses, owners often state that their pet seems to be "slowing down" or aging more rapidly, or is less active and less willing to engage in normal activities. Despite normal clinical appearances, patients in Phase 1 have detectable metabolic changes such as hyperlactatemia, hyperinsulinemia and alterations in blood amino acid profiles.

The second phase is a clinical phase in which patients begin to exhibit anorexia, lethargy and early evidence of weight loss. These patients are more likely to exhibit side effects associated with chemotherapy, radiation therapy, immunotherapy and surgery. The third phase (cancer cachexia) is an accentuated form of the second phase characterized by marked debilitation, weakness and biochemical evidence of negative nitrogen balance such as hypoalbuminemia. In this phase, cancer patients begin to lose body carbohydrate and fat stores. Vomiting, diarrhea, weakness,

KEY NUTRITIONAL FACTORS—CANCER

Factors	Associated conditions	Dietary recommendations
Carbohydrate (NFE)	Altered carbohydrate metabolism Hyperlactatemia Hyperinsulinemia Glucose intolerance	Avoid excess dietary soluble carbohydrate NFE <25% of dry matter or <20% of metabolizable energy of the food

Protein	Altered protein metabolism
	Lower plasma amino acid
	  concentrations
	Loss of lean muscle mass
	  (cachexia)
	Altered immune function
	Impaired wound healing
		Avoid protein deficiency
		Provide dietary protein in excess of adult requirements
		Dogs: protein = 30 to 45% of dry matter or 25 to 40% of metabolizable energy of the food
		Cats: protein = 40 to 50% of dry matter or 35 to 45% of metabolizable energy of the food

Fat	Altered lipid metabolism Altered blood lipid profiles Loss of body fat accumulation (cachexia) Reduced tumor cell use of fat	Provide a large proportion of energy from fat Fat = 25 to 40% of dry matter or 50 to 65% of metabolizable energy of the food

Fatty acids	n-3 fatty acids inhibit
	  tumorigenesis
	n-3 fatty acids influence cytokine
	  production
	n-3 fatty acids reduce serum lactate
	  concentrations
		Provide foods with increased levels of n-3 fatty acids (>5.0% dry matter)
		Provide foods with an n-6:n-3 ratio <3.0

Arginine	Promotes wound healing Enhances immune function Inhibits tumorigenesis	Provide foods with arginine levels >2% (dry matter basis)

lethargy and weight loss are clinical signs reported by owners of dogs and cats with end-stage cancer.

A fourth phase (recovery or remission) occurs in those patients undergoing treatment with apparent elimination of their disease. Metabolic alterations persist in some patients despite elimination or control of the cancer via chemotherapy, radiation or surgery. In some individuals, the therapy itself may cause changes that affect the feeding plan. Animals may develop food aversions at any time because of treatment-induced alterations in taste and smell.

Clinical staging of cancer is performed by assessing the tumor size, depth of tumor invasion, presence of tumor in regional lymph nodes and by identifying tumors in distant sites. This information is used to stage tumors by the TNM system: T (tumor size and/or invasion), N (nodal involvement) and M (distant metastasis). Tumor staging may correlate with clinical behavior in certain types of cancer and, in the future, may help determine whether a tumor will respond to nutritional management. In general, body condition scoring is the most practical tool for monitoring the overall nutritional effects of cancer and cancer treatment in dogs and cats. (See Chapter 1.)

Most cancers are thought to arise through the process of multi-step carcinogenesis.[16] (See sidebar "Causes of Cancer.")

Laboratory and Other Clinical Information

Laboratory evaluation of total lymphocyte count, hematocrit and serum albumin and urea nitrogen concentrations can be helpful to further evaluate nutritional status. The use of these parameters, however, is limited because hypoalbuminemia and lymphopenia have many causes unrelated to cancer. Albumin also has a relatively

long half-life (eight days in normal dogs) and is slow to respond to changes in nutritional status. Body weight becomes an insensitive index in patients with severe intestinal malassimilation with marked hypoalbuminemia and ascites. Clearly, no single "gold standard" test exists for determining a cancer patient's nutritional status. Plasma amino acid profiles and serum lactate concentra-

Table 25-1. Phases of clinical and metabolic alterations in cancer patients.

	Clinical changes	Metabolic changes
Phase 1	Preclinical, silent phase No obvious clinical signs	Hyperlactatemia Hyperinsulinemia Altered blood amino acid profiles

Phase 2	Early clinical signs
	Anorexia
	Lethargy
	Mild weight loss
	More susceptible to
	  side effects from
	  chemotherapy, etc.
		Similar metabolic changes

Phase 3	Cachexia
	Anorexia
	Lethargy
	More susceptible to
	  side effects from
	  chemotherapy, etc.
		Similar changes but more
		  profound

Phase 4	Recovery
	
	Remission
		Metabolic changes may
		  persist
		Changes secondary to
		  surgery, chemotherapy
		  or radiation therapy

tions have not been used clinically to date to assess the nutritional status of veterinary cancer patients.

In certain tumors, grading the degree of malignancy histologically predicts biologic behavior. Tumor grading is somewhat subjective, but pathologists often evaluate several features to assign a grade, including: 1) degree of differentiation, 2) mitotic index, 3) degree of cellular or nuclear polymorphism, 4) invasiveness, 5) stromal reaction and 6) lymphoid response.[17] Tumor grade may correlate with survival, metastatic rate, disease-free interval or with frequency or speed of local recurrence. Not only can a prognosis be determined based on tumor grade, but treatment may be modified to apply more aggressive therapies to higher grade tumors.

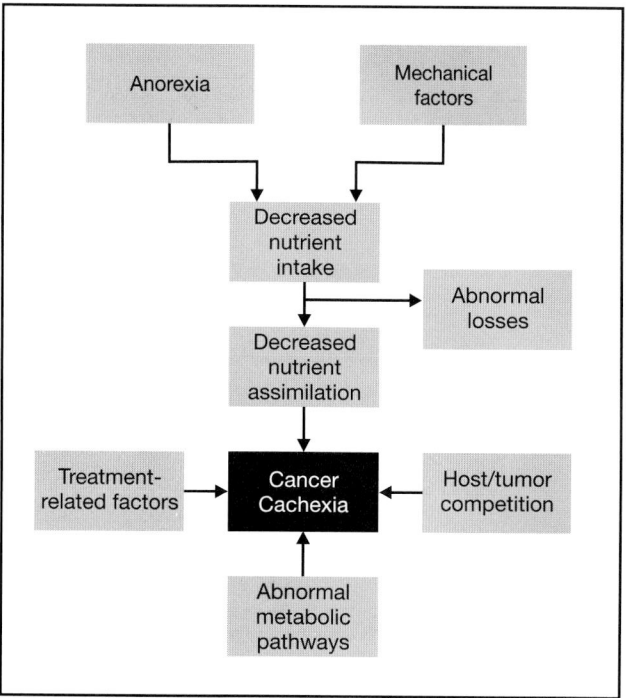

Figure 25-1. Mechanisms of cancer cachexia.

Nutritional Effects of Cancer

Cancer cachexia, a common manifestation of a wide variety of malignancies in people, dogs and cats, is a complex paraneoplastic syndrome that includes progressive weight loss that occurs even in the face of apparently adequate nutritional intake.[5-9] People with cancer cachexia have decreased quality of life, decreased response to therapy and shortened survival time when compared with those with similar diseases but not exhibiting clinical or biochemical signs associated with this condition.[5-12] Increasing evidence suggests that metabolic alterations are a significant problem in most canine and feline cancer patients.[5-7]

The metabolic alterations associated with cancer occur before any overt clinical signs associated with cachexia are ever identified. The end-stage of cancer cachexia is weight loss that is due not only to primary effects of the tumor, such as compression or infiltration of the alimentary tract, but also may be related to: 1) therapy (e.g., chemotherapy-induced anorexia, nausea or vomiting) or 2) alteration of metabolic pathways composing this paraneoplastic syndrome (Figure 25-1).[5-7] Many tumor-bearing animals have altered metabolism, which necessitates special methods for delivering nutrients and specific types of fluid and nutrient support.[5-15,18-20]

CARBOHYDRATE METABOLISM

Carbohydrate metabolism is dramatically altered in dogs with cancer. Metabolic alterations are suspected to occur in cats but have not been proved. Altered metabolism occurs because tumors preferentially metabolize glucose for energy by anaerobic glycolysis, forming lactate as an end product.[6,21] The host must then expend energy to convert lactate to glucose by the Cori cycle, resulting in a net energy gain by the tumor and a net energy loss by the host.[19,21-23] Abnormalities have been documented in peripheral glucose disposal, hepatic gluconeogenesis, insulin effects and whole body glucose oxidation and turnover.[18-20]

Altered carbohydrate metabolism occurs in dogs with lymphoma but without clinical evidence of cachexia. Following a 90-minute intravenous glucose tolerance test,

---

Causes of Cancer

There are three basic steps in multi-step carcinogenesis that ultimately lead to generation of a cancer cell from a normal cell: 1) initiation, 2) promotion and 3) progression. Initiating agents induce permanent and irreversible changes in the DNA of affected cells. Promoting agents cause reversible tissue and cellular changes up to development of the first autonomous tumor cell. Promoting action generally occurs over a long latency period and requires nearly continuous exposure to the promoting agent. Progressing agents convert initiated cells, or cells undergoing promotion, into cells that exhibit the malignant phenotype, capable of developing into a mature neoplasm.

Multi-step carcinogenesis occurs through five basic pathways; more than one pathway may be involved in the generation of a particular tumor. The five carcinogenesis pathways are: 1) heritable, 2) passive, 3) biologic, 4) chemical and 5) physical.

Although no breed-specific genetic alterations have been found to predispose domestic pets to develop neoplastic disease, certain breeds of dogs have a higher incidence of cancer than others. These breeds include boxers, German shepherd dogs, Scottish

terriers and golden retrievers. Siamese cats appear to be at more risk than other feline breeds.

Point mutations, chromosomal translocations and gene amplification occur as spontaneous events in any dividing cell population. These changes accumulate over a lifetime, possibly explaining why many cancers arise in mature or aged individuals.

The most common biologic agents capable of inducing cancer are retroviruses, DNA tumor viruses and some parasites.

Many different chemical compounds, some naturally occurring and some synthetic, are capable of inducing malignant neoplasia. In most cases, chemical carcinogens require repeated administration or exposure to demonstrate an effect.

Physical carcinogens include ultraviolet radiation, ionizing radiation and foreign materials.

BIBLIOGRAPHY
London CA, Vail DM. Tumor biology. In: Withrow SJ, MacEwen EG, eds. Small Animal Clinical Veterinary Oncology. Philadelphia, PA: WB Saunders Co, 1996; 16-31.

serum lactate and insulin concentrations were significantly higher when compared with control values (Figures 25-2 and 25-3).[24] The hyperlactatemia and hyperinsulinemia did not improve when these dogs achieved remission with doxorubicin chemotherapy.[20] These metabolic alterations also occur in dogs with nonhematopoietic malignancies (e.g., osteosarcoma, mammary adenocarcinoma and pulmonary bronchogenic adenocarcinoma).[24] The hyperlactatemia and hyperinsulinemia associated with these cancers did not improve when a subset of dogs had their tumors completely surgically excised. The same metabolic alterations are suspected to occur in cats.

Investigators are beginning to understand the clinical significance of altered carbohydrate metabolism. In one study, researchers documented exacerbation of hyperlactatemia in dogs with lymphoma by infusing lactated Ringer's solution (Figure 25-4).[19] In that study, blood lactate concentrations of relatively healthy, well-hydrated dogs with lymphoma were compared with those of control dogs. Blood lactate concentrations in dogs with lymphoma dogs were significantly elevated before, during and after lactated Ringer's solution was infused at a relatively modest rate (4.125 ml/kg body weight/hr). This lactated Ringer's-induced increase in lactate concentration may create an additional metabolic burden, requiring the host to convert lactate back to glucose, further exacerbating energy demands.

This finding may be even more important for septic, critically ill cancer patients that require more intensive fluid therapy. One could assume that glucose-containing fluids may increase hyperlactatemia as shown during glucose tolerance tests. Until further information is known about the effects of hyperlactatemia on critically ill animals with cancer, glucose- and lactate-containing fluids should generally be avoided.

Foods high in carbohydrate also appear to increase the total amount of lactate produced when fed to dogs with lymphoma. Mean blood glucose, lactate and insulin concentrations obtained during food tolerance testing were often higher in dogs fed a high-carbohydrate, low-fat food (9% fat, 58% carbohydrate on a dry matter basis) compared to those fed a low-carbohydrate, high-fat food (37% fat, 14% carbohydrate on a dry matter basis).[25] However, although there was a positive initial response to chemotherapy, there was no difference in the duration of remission between the two groups.

PROTEIN METABOLISM

Human cancer patients have decreased body muscle mass, decreased skeletal protein synthesis and altered nitrogen balance. These patients concurrently have increased skeletal protein breakdown, liver protein synthesis and whole body protein synthesis for tumor growth.[21-23] Tumors often preferentially use amino acids for energy.[21-23,26-30] The use of amino acids by tumors for energy becomes clinically significant when protein degradation exceeds intake. This imbalance can alter immune response, gastrointestinal (GI) function and surgical wound healing.[27,28]

In one study, cancer-bearing dogs had significantly lower plasma concentrations of threonine, glutamine, glycine, valine, cystine and arginine and significantly higher concentrations of isoleucine and phenylalanine than did normal control dogs.[15] The results were the same for different types of tumors. Alterations in plasma amino

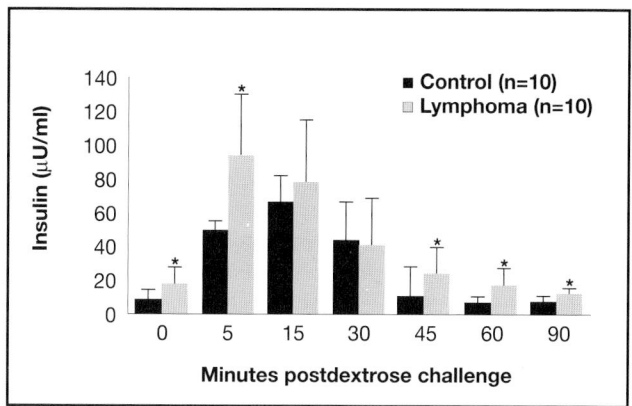

Figure 25-2. Serum insulin concentrations from dogs with and without lymphoma before and after intravenous administration of 500 mg glucose/kg body weight. Asterisks indicate values from dogs with lymphoma that differ significantly ($p<0.001$) from control dog values obtained at the same time. (Adapted from Vail DM, Ogilvie GK, Wheeler SL, et al. Alterations in carbohydrate metabolism in canine lymphoma. Journal of Veterinary Internal Medicine 1990; 4: 307.)

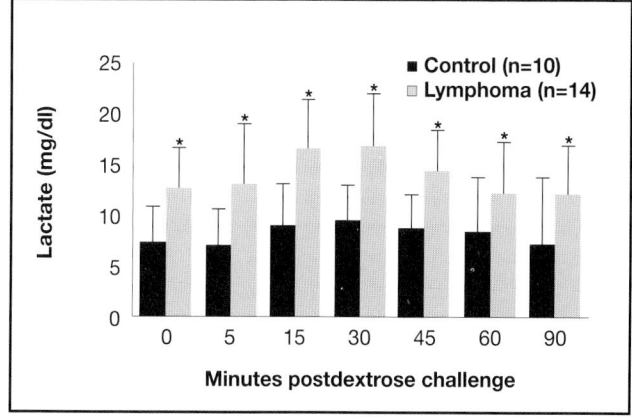

Figure 25-3. Serum lactate concentrations from dogs with and without lymphoma before and after intravenous administration of 500 mg glucose/kg body weight. Asterisks indicate values from dogs with lymphoma that differ significantly ($p<0.001$) from control dog values taken at the same time. (Adapted from Vail DM, Ogilvie GK, Wheeler SL, et al. Alterations in carbohydrate metabolism in canine lymphoma. Journal of Veterinary Internal Medicine 1990; 4: 307.)

acid profiles do not normalize after tumors are surgically removed. This finding suggests that cancer induces long-lasting changes in protein metabolism that may be due to elaboration of specific cytokines such as tumor necrosis factor or toxhormone. It is hypothesized that these changes also occur in cats.

Arginine, a dibasic amino acid, is an essential amino acid for cats and is considered to be a conditionally essential amino acid for dogs. Arginine is synthesized endogenously in the kidney from gut-derived citrulline and is converted by the enzyme arginase into ornithine and urea. Arginine has potent secretagogue effects on several endocrine and neuroendocrine glands. Intravenous administration of arginine induces secretion of growth hormone, prolactin, insulin, glucagon, insulin-like growth factor-1, pancreatic polypeptide, somatostatin and catecholamines.[31] Arginine, given in large doses, exerts numerous beneficial effects on the immune system, particularly on thymus-dependent and T-cell-dependent immune reac-

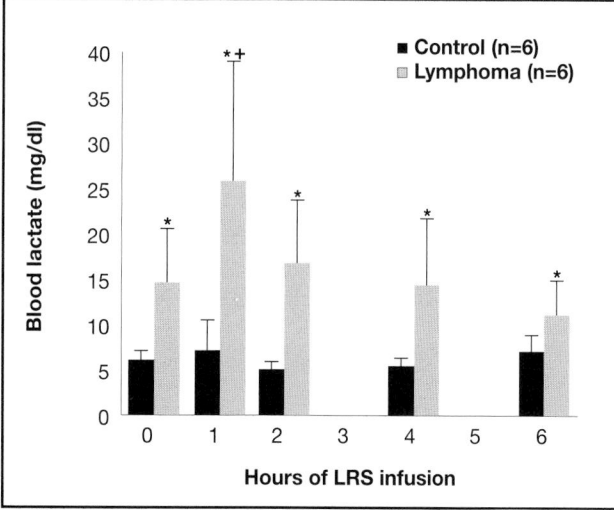

Figure 25-4. Blood lactate concentrations from dogs with and without lymphoma before and during intravenous infusion of lactated Ringer's solution (LRS). Asterisks indicate values from dogs with lymphoma that differ significantly (p<0.05) from control dog values obtained at the same time. Plus signs indicate values that differ significantly (p<0.05) from pre-infusion baseline values within the same test group. (Adapted from Vail DM, Ogilvie GK, Fettman MJ, et al. Exacerbation of hyperlactatemia by infusion of lactated Ringer's solution in dogs with lymphoma. Journal of Veterinary Internal Medicine 1990; 4: 228-232.)

tions. The exact mechanism whereby arginine stimulates T-cell function is unknown. In addition to its positive effects on immune function, arginine may also influence tumor growth, metastatic rate and survival time in patients with cancer. (See sidebar "Amino Acids and Cancer.")

LIPID METABOLISM

Loss of body fat accounts for the majority of weight loss in patients with cancer cachexia, although protein loss also occurs. Thus, it is not surprising that animals and people with cancer have marked abnormalities in lipid metabolism.[32-38] The decreased lipogenesis and increased lipolysis observed in people and rodents with cancer cachexia result in increased blood concentrations of free fatty acids, very low-density lipoproteins, triglycerides, plasma lipoproteins and hormone-dependent lipoprotein lipase activity, whereas concentrations of endothelial-derived lipoprotein lipase decrease.[34]

Lipid profiles have been evaluated in dogs with lymphoma to determine if alterations similar to those reported in other species are present.[35] In contrast to healthy control dogs, dogs with lymphoma had significantly higher concentrations of cholesterol associated with very low-density lipoprotein, total triglycerides as well as the triglyceride concentrations associated with very low-density lipoprotein (VLDL-TG), low-density lipoprotein and high-density lipoprotein (HDL-TG). Significantly lower concentrations of cholesterol associated with high-density lipoprotein (HDL-CH) were also noted. HDL-TG and VLDL-TG concentrations from dogs with lymphoma were significantly increased above pretreatment values after remission was lost. Additionally, dogs developed overt signs of cancer cachexia. These abnormalities did not normalize when clinical remission was obtained.

The clinical significance of the previously mentioned lipid parameters in dogs with lymphoma is unknown.

However, abnormalities in lipid metabolism have been linked to a number of clinical problems including immunosuppression, which correlates with decreased survival in affected people.[21,34,39]

In contrast to how tumor cells use carbohydrates and proteins, some tumor cells have difficulty using lipids as a fuel source, while host tissues continue to oxidize lipids for energy.[36] This finding has led to the hypothesis that foods relatively high in fat may benefit animals with cancer compared with foods relatively high in carbohydrates.

Omega-3 (n-3) fatty acids inhibit tumorigenesis and cancer spread in animal models, and form the basis for work in prevention and treatment of cancer in people.[40-43] Omega-3 fatty acids (eicosapentaenoic acid, docosahexaenoic acid) generally have an inhibitory effect on tumor growth. Metastases are enhanced by omega-6 (n-6) fatty acids (linoleic acid, γ-linolenic acid). In vivo studies have shown that eicosapentaenoic acid has selective tumoricidal action without harming normal cells.[40-50] Omega-3 fatty acids reduce radiation-induced damage to pig skin.[51] This effect appears to be specific for healthy nonmalignant cells.

Eicosapentaenoic acid decreases protein degradation without altering protein synthesis; the net effect is anti-cachectic.[52] Foods with high n-3 fatty acid concentrations ameliorate endotoxin-induced lactic acidosis in guinea pigs.[53] This finding may be of clinical importance because hyperlactatemia is a common problem in dogs with lymphoma. Administration of n-3 fatty acids reduced secretion of tumor necrosis factor alpha (TNF-α), interleukin-1β (IL-1β), interleukin-1α (IL-1α) and interleukin-2.[52-57] This may be especially important because IL-1 and TNF are important mediators of cachexia and may act as tumor growth factors.[52-57]

ENERGY EXPENDITURE

Cancer cachexia may be partly due to negative energy balance secondary to decreased energy intake or altered energy expenditure.[58,59] Many investigators have found alterations in basal metabolic rate (BMR) and resting energy requirement (RER) that were associated with altered carbohydrate, protein and lipid metabolism in human patients with cancer cachexia.[58,59]

Because the thyroid gland and its constitutive hormones are intimately involved in the control of energy homeostasis,[60,61] investigators have speculated that perturbations in thyroid function or thyroid hormone concentrations play a role in altering energy states in tumor-bearing individuals. In one study, researchers compared thyroid hormone concentrations in dogs with cancer (with and without chronic weight loss) with those in nontumor-bearing dogs (with and without chronic weight loss).[62] Diminished serum concentrations of T_4, T_3 and free T_3 occurred proportional to the degree of weight loss, regardless of tumor-bearing status. Apparently, these reductions in hormone concentrations are related to the abnormal nutritional state or severity of illness rather than to a tumor-related phenomenon.

Energy expenditure and caloric requirements are increased in tumor-bearing animals and people when compared with values in healthy individuals.[63-67] Several studies have evaluated energy expenditure in dogs with lymphoma and non-hematopoietic malignancies (e.g., carcinomas and sarcomas) and compared those values with values in healthy, client-owned dogs.[24,68] These studies found no significant differences in energy expenditure (and presumably caloric requirements) in dogs with a wide range of malignancies when compared with healthy, client-owned dogs. This finding suggests that, in general, dogs with cancer and no evidence of weight loss do not have energy requirements higher than those of apparently healthy dogs without cancer. Further, these parameters do not change significantly in dogs with cancer when the tumor is removed surgically.[69]

These findings suggest that daily energy requirement (DER) in animals with uncomplicated cancer are similar to those of normal animals. However, complications of cancer and cancer treatment, such as sepsis, may significantly alter the energy requirement in individual patients.

Nutritional Effects of Cancer Treatment

Besides the effects of cancer itself, various modalities used to treat cancer (radiation, chemotherapy and surgery, used alone or in combination) may adversely affect nutritional status. The malnutrition that results from treatment assumes even more importance given that many cancer patients are already debilitated from their disease. Anticancer therapy may produce only mild, transient nutritional disturbances, such as mucositis, or it may lead to severe, permanent nutritional problems, as in small bowel resection or in disabilities of mastication and swallowing after head and neck surgery or radiation. In general, problems should be anticipated, feeding tubes placed and animals fed earlier to lessen the toxic effects of treatment.

SURGERY

Surgery is used in the treatment of cancer in an attempt to remove tumors or alleviate clinical signs (e.g., intestinal or urinary obstruction). Nutritional problems that may develop depend on the surgical location and type of procedure performed (Table 25-2). Preliminary studies in dogs also suggest that the metabolic alterations associated with cancer persist even after the tumor is removed surgically.[24] In general, feeding tubes (gastrostomy, jejunostomy) should be placed at the time of surgery to avoid subsequent anesthesia and to allow early feeding.

Radical surgery of the head and neck may lead to significant malnutrition by altering normal eating mechanisms. Although some of these changes are temporary, many patients have permanent difficulty with chewing, swallowing and risk of aspiration. Proactive placement of gastrostomy tubes (See Appendix V.) during head and neck surgery will facilitate enteral feeding during the immediate postoperative period. These tubes may be used for long-term enteral feeding of some cancer patients. (See Chapter 12.)

The nutritional sequelae of gastric and intestinal resection are directly related to the site and extent of resection and to the individual functions of the various segments. The ability of various segments of the small intestine to increase absorptive capabilities over a period of several months prevents major clinical problems after small bowel resection unless resection is massive. With massive resection, malabsorption (short bowel syndrome) becomes the primary nutritional problem. (See Chapter 22.) In people, colon surgery is usually well-tolerated and the large water and electrolyte losses in the early postoperative period decrease rapidly after surgery.

Table 25-2. Effects of surgery on cancer patients that may have nutritional implications.

Cancer sites	Surgical procedures	Possible nutritional problems
Head, neck, tongue	Mandibulectomy Maxillectomy Glossectomy	Difficulty prehending, chewing and swallowing food
Esophagus	Esophagectomy, with or without reconstruction	Dysphagia Regurgitation
Stomach	Gastrectomy, partial or complete	Altered gastic emptying Diarrhea
Small intestine	Resection	Malabsorption Diarrhea Intestinal obstruction
Large intestine	Colectomy, partial or complete	Fluid and electrolyte imbalances
Pancreas, liver	Pancreatectomy Cholecystectomy Cholecystoduo-denostomy	Diabetes mellitus Maldigestion

Table 25-3. Effects of chemotherapy on cancer patients that may have nutritional implications.

Stomatitis, glossitis, pharyngitis	Diarrhea
Alterations in smell or taste	Constipation
Decreased appetite	Nausea
Food aversions	Vomiting

Table 25-4. Effects of radiation therapy on cancer patients that may have nutritional implications.

Treatment areas	Acute effects	Chronic effects
Head and neck	Mucositis of mouth, tongue, esophagus	Dry mouth Dental disease Alterations in smell Alterations in taste
Thorax	Esophagitis	Esophageal fistula Esophageal stricture
Abdomen	Nausea, vomiting Enteritis, diarrhea Malabsorption	Intestinal obstruction Fistula formation Chronic enteritis

CHEMOTHERAPY

Chemotherapeutic agents may contribute to malnutrition through a variety of direct and indirect mechanisms, including: 1) anorexia, 2) nausea, 3) vomiting, 4) mucositis, 5) organ injury (toxicosis) and 6) food aversions (Table 25-3). These problems should be anticipated and feeding tubes placed before therapy. Early feeding lessens the adverse effects of therapy. Chemotherapeutic agents affect normal and malignant cells but have the greatest effect on rapidly proliferating cells such as epithelial cells of the GI tract. The degree to which GI function is affected depends on the chemotherapeutic agent, drug dosage, duration of treatment, rate of metabolism and the individual animal's susceptibility.

Small bowel villous damage is a major side effect of some chemotherapeutic agents and may be greatly intensified when radiation therapy is given concurrently. The rapid renewal rate of the alimentary tract epithelium usually means that clinical problems from drug-induced mucositis are short-lived.

CANCER

Nausea and vomiting commonly accompany the administration of many anticancer drugs. Alterations in smell and taste are reported to occur in people and may occur in animals. Side effects experienced during chemotherapy make it difficult for some patients to consume optimal amounts of food.

Corticosteroids such as prednisone are used in chemotherapeutic protocols for some cancers, most

---

Amino Acids and Cancer

METHIONINE AND ASPARAGINE

Certain tumor cell lines require methionine for growth. Replacement of methionine with its precursor, homocysteine, locks these tumor cells into late S and G2 phases of the cell cycle. Because certain cancer chemotherapeutic agents are cell-cycle specific, the percentage of tumor cells sensitive to chemotherapy increases, improving the therapeutic index. Asparagine is essential for tumor cell growth in lymphoma. Treatment of dogs and cats with L-asparaginase has induced complete remissions in up to 80% of dogs and cats with lymphoma.

TYROSINE AND PHENYLALANINE

Tyrosine and phenylalanine restriction has been reported to suppress melanoma cell growth in tissue cultures and in rodent tumor models. The administration of tyrosine and phenylalanine increased the survival of melanoma tumor-bearing mice and increased the effectiveness of levodopa against melanoma.

ARGININE AND GLUTAMINE

Arginine and glutamine may have specific therapeutic value. Adding arginine to parenteral solutions decreases tumor growth and metastatic rate in rodent cancer models. Increased dietary arginine, in conjunction with increased dietary n-3 fatty acid intake, influences clinical signs, quality of life and survival time in dogs with cancer. In a group of dogs receiving chemotherapy for lymphoma, food supplemented with arginine and n-3 fatty acids resulted in elevations in plasma arginine and eicosapentaenoic and docosahexaenoic acid levels. Plasma levels of arginine and n-3 fatty acids were positively correlated with survival time. Similarly, in dogs undergoing radiation therapy for nasal carcinomas, plasma levels of arginine, eicosapentaenoic and docosahexaenoic acid were positively correlated with quality of life and negatively correlated with inflammatory mediators and mucositis in irradiated areas.

Glutamine is an essential precursor for nucleotide biosynthesis and is the most important oxidative fuel for enterocytes. Supplementation of enteral preparations with glutamine is beneficial in several animal models of intestinal injury by improving intestinal morphometry, reducing bacterial translocation, enhancing local immunity and improving survival. Glutamine has only recently been recognized as a conditionally essential amino acid in certain pathophysiologic states. Glutamine is added to most human enteral formulas.

One study using a feline model of methotrexate-induced intestinal injury failed to demonstrate a beneficial role for glutamine supplementation to an amino acid-based purified food. (See sidebar "Novel Foods, Ingredients and Cancer.") Additional studies are warranted to determine whether glutamine supplementation of commercially available foods containing intact protein sources improves intestinal integrity during chemotherapy administration to dogs and cats with cancer.

GLYCINE

Some amino acids may decrease the toxicity associated with chemotherapy. For example, glycine reduces cisplatin-induced nephrotoxicity.

BIBLIOGRAPHY

Alverdy JC. Effects of glutamine-supplemented diets on immunology of the gut. Journal of Parenteral and Enteral Nutrition 1990; 14: 109S-113S.

Anderson CR, Ogilvie GK, LaRue SM, et al. Effect of fish oil and arginine on acute effects of radiation injury in dogs with nasal tumors: A double-blind, randomized study (abstract). Veterinary Cancer Society/American College of Veterinary Radiology Meeting, Chicago, IL, December 1997.

Asselin BL, Ryan D, Frantz CN, et al. In vitro and in vivo killing of acute lymphoblastic leukemia cells by L-asparaginase. Cancer Research 1989; 49: 4363-4369.

Barbul A, Sisto DA, Wasserkrug HL, et al. Arginine stimulates lymphocyte immune response in healthy human beings. Surgery 1981; 90: 244-251.

Burke D, Alverdy JC, Aoys E, et al. Glutamine-supplemented total parenteral nutrition improves gut immune function. Archives of Surgery 1989; 124: 1396-1400.

Fox AD, Kripke SA, DePaula J, et al. Effect of glutamine-supplemented enteral diet on methotrexate-induced enterocolitis. Journal of Parenteral and Enteral Nutrition 1988; 12: 325-331.

Heyman SN, Rosen S, Silva P, et al. Protective action of glycine in cisplatin nephrotoxicity. Kidney International 1991; 40: 273-279.

Marks SL, Cook AK, Reader R, et al. Glutamine supplementation of an amino acid-based purified diet fails to improve intestinal mucosal integrity following methotrexate-induced enteritis in cats. From: Marks SL. Dietary modulation of methotrexate-induced enteritis in cats. PhD Dissertation, University of California, Davis, 1996.

Meadows GG, Oeser DE. Response by B16 melanoma-bearing mice to varying levels of phenylalanine and tyrosine. Nutrition Report International 1983; 28: 1073-1088.

Meadows GG, Pierson HF, Abdallah RM, et al. Dietary influence of tyrosine and phenylalanine on the response of B16 melanoma to carbidopa levodopa methyl ester chemotherapy. Cancer Research 1982; 42: 3056-3065.

Ogilvie GK, Fettman MJ, Mallinckrodt CH, et al. Effect of fish oil and arginine on remission and survival of dogs with lymphoma: A double-blind, randomized study. Cancer 1998; (Accepted for publication).

Sheng-Long YE, Istafan NW, Driscoll DF, et al. Tumor and host response to arginine and branched chain amino acid enriched total parenteral nutrition. Cancer 1992; 69: 261-270.

Souba WW. Glutamine and cancer. Annals of Surgery 1993; 218: 715-728.

Souba WW, Klimberg VS, Hautamaki RD, et al. Oral glutamine reduces bacterial translocation following abdominal radiation. Journal of Surgical Research 1990; 48: 1-5.

Stern PH, Hoffman RM. Enhanced in vitro selective toxicity of chemotherapeutic agents for human cancer cells based on a metabolic defect. Journal of the National Cancer Institute 1986; 76: 629-634.

Tachibana K, Mukai K, Hirauka I, et al. Evaluation of the effect of arginine enriched amino acid solution on tumor growth. Journal of Parenteral and Enteral Nutrition 1985; 9: 428-434.

Windmueller HG, Spaeth AG. Respiratory fuels and nitrogen metabolism in vivo in small intestine of fed rats. Quantitative importance of glutamine, glutamate, and aspartate. Journal of Biological Chemistry 1980; 255: 107-112.

Xu D, Lu Q, Thirstrup C, et al. Elemental diet-induced bacterial translocation and immunosuppression is not reversed by glutamine. Journal of Trauma 1993; 35: 821-824.

notably lymphoma. High doses or prolonged therapy with corticosteroids causes profound polydipsia and polyuria and increased losses of water-soluble vitamins.

RADIATION

Although fewer than 10% of the patients seen in one of the author's (GKO) oncology practice receive radiation therapy, animals receiving treatment may have complica-

---

Vitamins and Cancer

Retinoids, β-carotene, vitamin C and vitamin E all appear to influence the growth and metastasis of cancer cells by a variety of mechanisms. Some of these mechanisms include selected receptor-mediated antiproliferative activities. These vitamins have been reported to bind their cytosolic receptors followed by translocation of the bound complex to the nucleus where the receptors mediate gene regulation. Other effects result from antioxidant, hormone-like and immunomodulator capabilities.

RETINOIDS

"Retinoids" refer to the entire group of naturally occurring and synthetic vitamin A derivatives, including retinol, retinal and retinoic acid. Retinoids appear to have the potential for regulating cancer cells either alone or in combination with other agents. Specific studies in human and veterinary medicine suggest that retinoids alone or with other agents can be effective for the treatment of certain types of malignancies. The synthetic retinoids, isotretinoin and etretinate, have been used successfully in some dogs with intracutaneous cornifying epitheliomas, other benign skin tumors, cutaneous lymphoma, solar-induced squamous cell carcinoma and associated preneoplastic lesions. The retinoids promote cellular differentiation and may enhance the susceptibility of neoplastic cells to chemotherapy and radiation therapy.

VITAMIN C

Vitamin C (ascorbic acid) has been reported to inhibit nitrosation reactions and prevent chemical induction of cancers of the esophagus and stomach. Processed foods high in nitrates and nitrites, such as bacon and sausage, are often supplemented with vitamin C to reduce the carcinogenic capability of the resultant nitrosamines.

Ascorbic acid may be one therapeutic alternative for overcoming drug resistance in some cancer cells. Studies suggest that an ascorbic acid-sensitive mechanism may be involved in drug resistance to vincristine in certain cancer cell lines. Despite the extensive amount of vitamin C research, few direct data exist proving its efficacy in dogs and cats.

VITAMIN E

Vitamin E (α-tocopherol) can also inhibit nitrosation reactions. Vitamin E also has a broad capacity to inhibit mammary tumor carcinogenesis and colon carcinogenesis in rodents. Research indicates that vitamin E influences a variety of cell functions including free-radical scavenging, which can prevent oxidative damage that leads to cell death.

In addition to its anticancer properties, vitamin E may potentially convey therapeutic efficacy against certain malignancies. Vitamin E has been reported to have antiproliferative activity, which involves the binding of the vitamin to salicylic receptors, followed by translocation to the nucleus where DNA binds on the domains of receptors that mediate gene regulatory events. Retrovirus-induced tumorigenesis involves transformation of normal cells into tumor cells. Evidence suggests that vitamin E may normalize the immune system by interacting with macrophages and T lymphocytes to inhibit retroviral-induced infections.

BIBLIOGRAPHY

Bertram JS, Kolonel LN, Meyskens FL. Rationale and strategies for chemoprevention of cancer in humans. Cancer Research 1987; 47: 3012-3018.

Boutwell RK. An overview of the role of diet and nutrition in carcinogenesis. In: Nutrition, Growth and Cancer. New York, NY: Alan R. Liss, Inc, 1988.

Branda RF. Effects of folic acid deficiency on tumor cell biology. In: Jacobs MM, ed. Vitamins and Minerals in the Prevention and Treatment of Cancer. Boca Raton, FL: CRC Press Inc, 1991; 167-185.

Chance WT, Balasubramainiam A, Sheriff S, et al. Possible role of neuropeptide Y in experimental cancer anorexia. In: Jacob MM, ed. Diet and Cancer: Markers, Prevention and Treatment. New York, NY: Plenum Press, 1993; 109-134.

Hong WK, Lipman SM, Itri LM, et al. Prevention of secondary primary tumors with isotretinoin in squamous cell carcinoma of the head and neck. New England Journal of Medicine 1990; 323: 796-805.

Kline K, Cochran GS, Sanders BG. Growth inhibitory effects of vitamin E succinate on retrovirus-transformed tumor cells in vitro. Nutrition and Cancer 1990; 14: 27-35.

Kline K, Rao A, Romach EH, et al. Vitamin E effects on retrovirus-induced immune dysfunction. Annals of the New York Academy of Science 1990; 58: 294.

Kline K, Sanders BG. Modulation of immune suppression and enhanced tumorigenesis in retrovirus tumor challenged chickens treated with vitamin E. In Vivo 1989; 3: 161-185.

Lamm DL, Riggs DR, Shriver JS, et al. Megadose vitamins in bladder cancer: A double blind clinical trial. Journal of Urology 1994; 151: 21-26.

Li J, Sartorelli CA. Synergistic induction of the differentiation of WEH1-38 D+ myelomonocytic leukemia cells by retinoic acid and granulocyte colony-stimulating factor. Leukemia Research 1992; 16: 571-577.

Micronutrients, nonnutritive dietary factors and cancer. In: Reddy BS, Cohen LA, eds. Diet, Nutrition, and Cancer: A Critical Evaluation, vol II. New York, NY: CRC Press Inc, 1986.

Mirvish SS. Effects of vitamins C and E on N-nitroso compound formation, carcinogenesis, and cancer. Cancer 1986; 58: 1842-1855.

National Academy of Sciences. Diet and Health: Implications for Reducing Chronic Disease Risk. Washington, DC: National Academy Press, 1989.

Ogilvie GK, Vail DM. Advances in nutritional therapy for the cancer patient. Veterinary Clinics of North America: Small Animal Practice 1990; 20: 969-989.

Pirisi L, Batova A, Jenkins GR, et al. Increased sensitivity of human keratinocytes immortalized by human papillomavirus type 16 DNA to growth control by retinoids. Cancer Research 1992; 52: 187-192.

Quillin P. An overview of the link between nutrition and cancer. In: Quillin P, Williams RM, eds. Adjuvant Nutrition Cancer Treatment. Arlington Heights, IL: Cancer Treatment Foundation, 1993; 1-17.

Weisburg JH. Interactions of nutrients in oncogenesis. American Journal of Clinical Nutrition 1991; 53: 2265-2271.

White SD, Rosychuk RA, Scott KV, et al. Use of isotretinoin and etretinate for the treatment of benign cutaneous neoplasia and cutaneous lymphoma in dogs. Journal of the American Veterinary Medical Association 1993; 202: 387-391.

CANCER

Minerals and Cancer

Minerals that have been suggested as being important in patients with cancer, include selenium, iron and zinc. Optimal levels of specific minerals for cancer prevention and treatment have not been established for pet animals.

SELENIUM

Selenium has been one of the most heavily studied minerals associated with the development of cancer. Low serum selenium levels have been observed in human patients with gastrointestinal cancer. In rodents, dietary supplementation with selenium inhibits colon, mammary gland and stomach carcinogenesis.

IRON

Iron transferrin and ferritin have been linked to cancer risk and cancer cell growth. Lung, colon, bladder and esophageal cancer in people have been highly correlated with increased serum iron concentrations and increased transferrin saturation. Because many tumor cells require iron for growth, it has been suggested that the increased use of iron by the tumor depresses serum iron levels in human cancer patients. Mice with low levels of iron have slow tumor growth compared to those with normal iron levels.

ZINC

In people, low levels of zinc in blood and diseased tissue have been observed in esophageal, pancreatic and bronchial cancer. Zinc deficiency appears to enhance carcinogenesis in laboratory animals.

BIBLIOGRAPHY

Ip C. Factors influencing the anticarcinogenic efficacy of selenium in dimethylbenzanthracene-induced mammary tumorigenesis in rats. Cancer Research 1981; 41: 2638-2644.

Jacobs MM, Griffin AC. Effects of selenium on chemical carcinogenesis: Comparative effects on antioxidants. Biological Trace Element Research 1979; 1: 2-21.

Jacobs MM, Jansson B, Griffin AC. Inhibitory effects of selenium on 1,2-dimethylhydrazine and methylazoxymethanol acetate induction of colon tumors. Cancer Letters 1977; 2: 133-144.

Ogilvie GK, Vail DM. Metabolic alterations and nutritional therapy for the veterinary cancer patient. In: Withrow SJ, MacEwen EG, eds. Clinical Veterinary Oncology. Philadelphia, PA: WB Saunders Co, 1996.

Shamberger RJ, Rukovena E, Longfield AK, et al. Antioxidants and cancer. I. Selenium in the blood of normal and cancer patients. Journal of the National Cancer Institute 1973; 50: 867-887.

Torti FM, Torti SV. Cytokines, iron homeostasis and cancer. In: Jacobs MM, ed. Diet and Cancer: Markers, Prevention, and Treatment. New York, NY: Plenum Press, 1993; 237-245.

tions that affect food intake. The complications of radiation vary according to the region of the body radiated, dose, fractionation and associated antitumor therapy such as surgery or chemotherapy. Complications may develop acutely during radiation or become chronic and progress even after radiation therapy has been completed (Table 25-4).

Radiation to the head and neck affects the oral mucosa and salivary secretions. Saliva production decreases in conjunction with an increase in saliva viscosity, when the salivary glands are in the field of radiation. In addition to causing mouth dryness (xerostomia) and impairing swallowing, the decrease in salivation alters the oral bacterial flora, which in turn may promote dental disease and stomatitis. In people, the thick, scant secretions may also create a feeling of nausea.[70]

The mucosa of the mouth and oropharynx is sensitive to radiation, which can produce a sore mouth or throat, painful ulcerations, bleeding or even chronic radiation ulcers. Radionecrosis of oral tissue may result from the combination of trauma and infection superimposed on highly radiated tissues. Radiation damage alters or suppresses taste and smell sensations and affects sensitivity to food texture and temperature. In people, taste returns gradually within two to four months after radiation therapy is completed, but may take up to one year. Alterations in smell and taste undoubtedly occur in animals but have not been well-documented. These changes create a potentially serious situation because patients are often already anorectic and undernourished.

Radiation to the thoracic area induces esophagitis and dysphagia. These lesions and signs usually disappear after cessation of therapy. Tumor necrosis, however, may produce delayed complications such as ulceration, fistula formation and obstruction from fibrosis and stricture.

Abdominal or pelvic radiation may alter intestinal function. Patients receiving upper abdominal radiation may experience nausea and vomiting whereas those receiving radiation to the lower abdomen often experience diarrhea due to intestinal mucosal damage, loss of villi and accompanying malabsorption. Acute radiation enteritis usually disappears after therapy is discontinued. However, late effects of abdominal radiation may occur months to years after completion of radiation therapy and are manifested as intestinal obstruction, fistula formation and chronic enteritis.[71]

Radiation therapy in animals is usually performed on five successive days per week with patients restrained by general anesthesia, which presents an opportunity to place a feeding tube. (See Appendix V.) This treatment schedule requires careful planning of the feeding method to ensure that patients eat their required amount of food each day.

Unless nutritional intervention is provided, many patients lose weight during radiation therapy. Enteral feeding is indicated if oral feeding becomes impossible or food intake is inadequate. (See Chapter 12.)

Risk Factors

Numerous studies have outlined risk factors of certain nutrients and their relationship to the development of cancer. For example, decreased fiber and increased fat have been most commonly incriminated as causal factors for the development of a wide variety of malignant conditions of the GI tract, breast and urinary bladder in people.

To date, few data exist regarding the relationship between diet and cancer in pet animals. One exception is a study by Sonnenschein and colleagues.[72] This group conducted a case-controlled study of nutritional factors and canine breast cancer. Neither a high-fat diet nor obesity one year before diagnosis increased the risk of breast cancer. However, the risk of breast cancer among neutered dogs was significantly reduced in dogs that had been thin at nine to 12 months of age. Among intact dogs, the risk associated with being thin at nine to 12 months of age was reduced, but not significantly. Results of this study suggest that nutritional factors resulting in altered body composition early in life may be important in canine breast cancer.

Key Nutritional Factors

Alterations in carbohydrate, lipid and protein metabolism precede obvious clinical disease and cachexia in cancer patients. These metabolic alterations may persist in patients with clinical remission or apparent recovery from their cancer. Key nutritional factors in cancer patients include soluble carbohydrate, fat, fatty acids, energy, protein and a few specific amino acids, notably arginine. (See Key Nutritional Factors—Cancer.)

Carbohydrates may be poorly used because of peripheral insulin resistance. Feeding high levels of carbohydrate may lead to hyperglycemia, glucosuria, hyperosmolarity, hepatic dysfunction and respiratory insufficiency. In addition, foods high in carbohydrate may increase the total amount of lactate produced. Carbohydrates should supply no more than 20% and preferably 10% of the DER (soluble carbohydrate less than 25% dry matter).

A large proportion of the daily ME requirement should come from dietary fat because tumor cells have difficulty using fats and loss of body fat accompanies cachexia. Dietary fat should provide 50 to 65% of the calories or 25 to 40% of the dry matter in the food(s). Increased levels of dietary n-3 fatty acids (greater than 5.0% dry matter) may benefit cancer patients, according to studies that link n-3 fatty acids to tumor inhibition and immune enhancement.

Dietary protein should exceed levels normally used for maintenance of adult animals because cancer patients have altered protein metabolism and often suffer loss of lean muscle mass (cachexia). Dietary protein should provide 25 to 40% of the ME (30 to 45% dry matter) in dogs and 35 to 45% of the ME (40 to 50% dry matter) in cats. The minimum effective level of dietary arginine for cancer patients is unknown, but, based on work in other species, it is appropriate to provide more than 2% arginine (dry matter basis).

Other Nutritional Factors

Several vitamins, minerals and novel foods and ingredients have also received considerable attention in cancer prevention and therapy. (See sidebars "Vitamins and Cancer," "Minerals and Cancer," "Amino Acids and Cancer," "Novel Foods, Ingredients and Cancer.")

Assess the Food(s)

One of the first steps in evaluating the cancer patient with weight loss or anorexia is to obtain an accurate dietary history that clearly defines the patient's food(s), food intake and feeding methods. Evaluation of a food's guaranteed analysis can provide an estimate of the crude protein, crude fat and carbohydrate content of the food after the nutrients have been converted to a dry matter or energy basis. (See Chapter 1.) The manufacturer can also be contacted to obtain information about the energy density, protein, fat, fatty acid and soluble carbohydrate content of the food(s). Appendices L and M list nutrient profiles of some commercial pet foods and treats. Foods containing less than 30% protein calories and more than 40% carbohydrate calories should be avoided in cancer patients. This includes most commercial dry pet foods. Table 25-5 lists selected commercial foods that have been recommended for cancer patients.

Many debilitated or cachectic animals are fed home-cooked foods by their owners to enhance palatability and food intake. Because these foods are frequently formulated by owners, they are often unbalanced (low calcium, abnormal calcium-phosphorous ratio, deficient minerals and vitamins) or are too low in protein and energy to maintain cancer patients. (See Chapter 6.)

Rodents and people with cancer who consume foods that contain 30 to 50% of nonprotein calories as fat have increased nitrogen and energy balance and increased weight gain. In addition, higher fat foods are associated with slower tumor growth and improved glucose tolerance. Although the ideal foods for dogs and cats with cancer are unknown, several general conclusions can be made.

Lean body mass decreases during catabolic illnesses such as cancer inasmuch as amino acids are redistributed for: 1) hepatic acute-phase-reactant protein synthesis, 2) support of the cellular immune response, 3) provision of gluconeogenetic substrate and 4) direct oxidation as a fuel source. Current recommendations for protein or amino acid alimentation in dogs and cats with increased metabolic needs are between 30 to 45% of the ME.

Some tumor cells have difficulty using lipids as a fuel source vs. carbohydrates and proteins. In contrast, host tissues continue to oxidize lipids for energy. This phenomenon has led to the hypothesis that foods relatively high in fat may be of benefit to animals with cancer when compared with foods high in easily digestible carbohydrates. Fat should supply 50 to 65% of the daily ME requirement for cancer-bearing dogs and cats.[73]

Major developments have occurred in understanding the role of eicosanoids in the pathophysiology of illness and injury. There is also evidence that dietary fatty acid composition clearly affects eicosanoid metabolism.[74] Foods enriched with fish oils are high in n-3 fatty acids, the precursors to trienoic prostaglandins (e.g., PGE_3) and pentanoic leukotrienes (e.g., LTB_5). Alteration of arachidonic acid metabolism has great implications for modification of the immune response following injury and cancer.[75] In addition, n-3 fatty acids inhibit tumorigenesis and cancer spread in animal models and are being evaluated for their role in cancer prevention and treatment in human and veterinary patients.

Assess the Feeding Method

Careful assessment of the feeding method is important to determine whether the animal is receiving its caloric requirement and if it is able to prehend, masticate, swallow and assimilate its food. Calculation of the patient's DER, determination of the energy density of the food, careful measurement of the amount of food eaten by the animal and body condition scoring will help establish whether cancer patients with weight loss are actually receiving sufficient calories and nutrients.

RER is calculated for the current body weight and typical factors are used to establish an estimated DER. (See Chapter 1.) Hospitalized patients should eat enough food to at least meet their estimated RER. Patients at home should eat enough food to meet their estimated DER (RER x appropriate factor). Enteral or parenteral feeding techniques are indicated if hospitalized patients are unable to eat their estimated RER. (See Chapter 12 and Appendix V.) If hospitalized patients are eating their estimated RER and patients at home are eating their estimated DER, then frequent monitoring of body weight and body condition is indicated.

FEEDING PLAN

Nutritional support of the cancer patient must be individualized. Nutritional therapy should be undertaken with the overall prognosis of the patient clearly in mind so that the aggressiveness of dietary intervention (e.g., supportive, adjunctive, definitive) can be appropriately adjusted. Owners of cancer patients should be educated about the integral part nutrition plays in the total management of their pet's disease. Dietary modification depends on the extent of disease, anorexia, nausea, weight loss and consequences of treatment.

Some underweight animals with cancer will stabilize at a less than optimal body condition score (BCS) (2/5 rather than 3/5). It may be difficult to achieve weight gain in these patients; therefore, the goal should change to maintaining this leaner body condition. (See Chapter 12, Accomodation.)

Select a Food(s)

It is naive to believe that a single nutrient or set of nutrients will be effective for the treatment and prevention of all cancers. However, altered metabolism documented in cancer patients and clinical studies performed to date suggest that modifying nutrient intake may help reverse the adverse effects of cancer.

Several commercial veterinary therapeutic foods and moist specialty foods provide key nutrients in appropriate levels (Table 25-5). However, only once commercial food (Prescription Diet Canine n/d[a]) has been shown to improve the longevity and quality of life of selected canine patients with cancer.[76] It is important to consider feeding cancer patients food(s) with an appropriate nutrient profile. (See Key Nutritional Factors—Cancer.) Many pets eat commercial dry foods that are usually higher in soluble carbohydrates (greater than 50% dry matter) and lower in fat (less than 20% dry matter) and protein (25 to 40% dry matter) than optimal.

Determine a Feeding Method

The enteral route of feeding is the preferred route of nutritional support because it is easier, less expensive and more physiologic than parenteral administration. In addition, enteral feeding improves mucosal thickness, stimulates gut trophic hormones and stimulates IgA production. Enhancing the palatability of food is the simplest means of increasing voluntary intake (Figure 25-5). A food can sometimes be made more palatable by adding flavor enhancers or heating the food to improve its aroma and mouth feel.

If dietary manipulation fails and the patient is capable of ingesting food, drug therapy can be attempted before offering food. Administration of a benzodiazepine derivative (diazepam or oxazepam) or cyproheptadine increases appetite transiently; however, these drugs are unreliable for ensuring adequate caloric intake. Benzodiazepine derivatives are contraindicated in patients with severely reduced hepatic function, especially when signs of hepatic encephalopathy are present. In addition, the appetite-stimulating properties of these agents appear to wane with time when used in sick animals. Megestrol acetate causes weight gain and increased appetite in people with cancer. The clinical benefit of this drug in veterinary patients remains to be determined. Controlled studies with human cancer patients have revealed that cyproheptadine, corticosteroids and nandrolone decanoate have little to no

Table 25-5. Nutrient profiles of selected commercial pet foods that can be used in cancer patients.*

Products	Protein	Fat	Carbohydrate	n-3 fatty acids	Arginine
Canine products					
Hill's Prescription Diet Canine/Feline a/d, moist	45.7	28.7	17.4	2.6	2.05
Hill's Prescription Diet Canine a/d, dry	38.1	25.0	29.2	0.83	2.12
Hill's Prescription Diet Canine n/d, moist	37.2	32.1	21.5	7.3	3.1
Iams Eukanuba Maximum-Calorie/Canine, dry	40.1	29.0	22.7	0.9	na
Iams Eukanuba Maximum-Calorie/Feline, dry	44.2	29.6	19.1	0.93	na
Iams Eukanuba Maximum-Calorie/Canine & Feline, moist	44.0	41.9	7.8	0.79	na
Purina Feline CV-Formula, moist	42.5	26.8	23.1	na	na
Feline products					
Hill's Prescription Diet Canine/Feline a/d, moist	45.7	28.7	17.4	2.6	2.05
Hill's Prescription Diet Feline p/d, moist	48.8	31.5	11.2	0.43	2.67
Iams Eukanuba Maximum-Calorie/Feline, dry	44.2	29.6	19.1	0.93	na
Iams Eukanuba Maximum-Calorie/Canine & Feline, moist	44.0	41.9	7.8	0.79	na
Purina Feline CV-Formula, moist	42.5	26.8	23.1	na	na
Select Care Feline Development Formula, moist	48.0	32.2	12.1	na	na

Key: na = Information is not published by the manufacturer.
*Nutrients are expressed on % dry matter basis.
Values were obtained from manufacturers' published information.

Novel Foods, Ingredients and Cancer

PROTEASE INHIBITORS

Much information suggests that soybean-derived Bowman-Birk inhibitor can inhibit or suppress carcinogenesis in vivo and in vitro. Extracts of the Bowman-Birk inhibitor suppress carcinogenesis in several animal model systems, including colon- and liver-induced carcinogenesis in mice, anthracene-induced cheek pouch carcinogenesis in hamsters, lung tumorigenesis in mice and esophageal carcinogenesis in rats. Bowman-Birk inhibitor concentration inhibits metastases and weight loss associated with radiation-induced thymic lymphoma in mice. Irradiated rodents treated with dietary Bowman-Birk inhibitor have fewer deaths, lower average grade of lymphoma and larger fat stores than controls. In addition, various soy products produce dramatic protection against methotrexate (MTX)-induced enterotoxicity in rodent models.

One study was performed using a feline model of MTX-induced enteritis to determine the impact of purified foods containing intact protein sources (soybean protein or casein) or crystalline amino acids on intestinal structure and function. Cats receiving a commercially available (complex) food served as the control group. MTX administration was associated with severe enterotoxicity manifested by vomiting and diarrhea, especially in cats receiving the crystalline amino acid and casein-based purified foods. Cats receiving the casein-based purified food had the largest decrease in total white blood cell (WBC) and platelet counts, the greatest villous atrophy (Figure 1) and the highest incidence of positive mesenteric lymph node and hepatic bacterial cultures (50% and 33%, respectively). Cats fed the soybean protein-based purified food had the least villous atrophy (Figure 2) and a significantly smaller magnitude of reduction in WBC counts

compared with cats receiving the crystalline amino acid (Figure 3) and casein-based purified foods. Feeding complex (Figure 4) and soybean protein-based foods was also associated with the greatest secretagogue activity on plasma cholecystokinin (CCK) concentrations after ingestion of the respective meals, compared with concentrations in cats receiving the amino acid and casein-based purified foods. This study showed an association between feeding a soybean protein-based purified food and improved intestinal integrity. These findings might be associated with a greater secretagogue effect in stimulating trophic gut hormones such as CCK. In contrast, the casein-based purified food was associated with increased morbidity, villous atrophy, increased bacterial translocation, and decreased secretagogue activity on CCK. Additional studies may determine the underlying mechanism of protection and the exact compound(s) responsible for soybean protein's protective effects.

GARLIC

Epidemiologic studies have suggested a correlation between high garlic consumption and reduced risk of cancer. Garlic, garlic extracts and several thioalkyl compounds inhibit the activation of carcinogens and carcinogen-induced aberrations in the cell nucleus. Garlic extracts have an anti-promotion effect in animals exposed to carcinogens. Further, garlic exerts direct cytolytic effects against cultured human breast cancer cells and human melanoma cells. The concentrations of garlic used in these studies to arrest cancer cell growth had no effect on normal cells.

Pretreatment with garlic protects rodents against subsequent induction of tumors by a variety of carcinogens. There are no studies demonstrating the safety and efficacy of garlic for the prevention or treatment of cancer in people, dogs and cats.

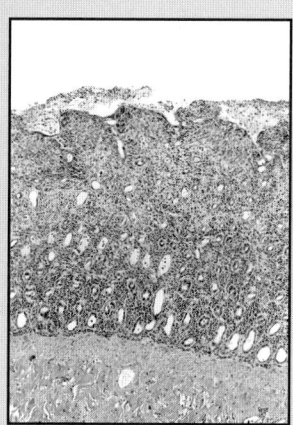

Figure 1.

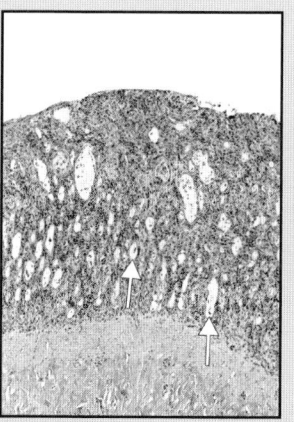

Figure 2.

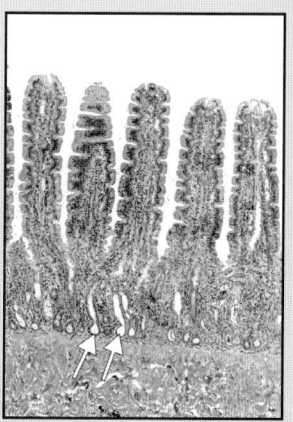

Figure 3.

Figure 4.

Figure 1. Distal duodenal section obtained 72 hours postmethotrexate administration from a cat fed a casein-based purified diet. The villi are severely blunted and fused with multifocal ulceration. Crypt loss is marked and the remaining crypts are severely dilated.

Figure 2. Proximal duodenal section obtained 72 hours postmethotrexate administration from a cat fed a soybean protein-based purified diet. Villi have normal architecture and crypts are moderately dilated.

Figure 3. Proximal duodenal section obtained 72 hours postmethotrexate administration from a cat fed a purified diet containing free amino acids. Villi are completely effaced. The surface is covered with an intermittent layer of attenuated enterocytes. Crypts are severely dilated and distorted (arrows).

Figure 4. Distal duodenal section obtained 72 hours postmethotrexate administration from a cat fed a commercial food containing intact protein sources. Villi have normal architecture. Crypts in the lamina propria are moderately dilated (arrows).

(Figures 1 to 4 Adapted from: Marks SL. Dietary modulation of methotrexate-induced enteritis in cats. PhD Dissertation, University of California, Davis, 1996.)

Continued on next page.

Continued from previous page.

BIBLIOGRAPHY

Billings PC, Habres JM, Kennedy AR. Inhibition of radiation-induced transformation of C3H10T1/2 cells by specific protease substrates. Carcinogenesis 1990; 11: 329-332.

Funk MA, Baker DH. Effect of soy products on methotrexate toxicity in rats. Journal of Nutrition 1991; 121: 1684-1692.

Kennedy AR. Effects of protease inhibitors and vitamin E in the prevention of cancer. In: Prasad KN, Meyskens FL, eds. Nutrients and Cancer Prevention. Clifton, NJ: The Humana Press Inc, 1990; 79-98.

Marks SL, Reader R, Backus RC, et al. Dietary soybean protein helps maintain intestinal mucosal integrity in cats with methotrexate-induced enteritis. In: Marks SL. Dietary modulation of methotrexate-induced enteritis in cats. PhD Dissertation, University of California, Davis, 1996.

McAnena OJ, Harvey LP, Bonau RA, et al. Alteration of methotrexate toxicity in rats by manipulation of dietary components. Gastroenterology 1987; 92: 354-360.

Messadi DV, Billings PC, Shklar G, et al. Inhibition of oral carcinogenesis by a protease inhibitor. Journal of the National Cancer Institute 1986; 76: 447-452.

St. Clair W, Billings P, Carew J, et al. Suppression of DMH-induced carcinogenesis in mice by dietary addition of the Bowman-Birk protease inhibitor. Cancer Research 1990; 50: 580-586.

Wargovich MJ, Sumiyoshi H, Baer A, et al. Chemoprevention of GI cancer in animals by naturally occurring organosulfur compounds in allium vegetables. In: Jacobs MM, ed. Vitamins and Minerals in the Prevention and Treatment of Cancer. Boca Raton, FL: CRC Press Inc, 1991.

Weed H, McGandy RB, Kennedy AR. Protection against dimethyl-hydrazine-induced adenomatous tumors of the mouse colon by the dietary addition of an extract of soybeans containing the Bowman-Birk protease inhibitor. Carcinogenesis 1985; 6: 1239-1241.

Witschi H, Kennedy AR. Modulation of lung tumor development in mice with the soybean-derived Bowman-Birk protease inhibitor. Carcinogenesis 1989; 10: 2275-2277.

impact on improving food intake, body weight and clinical outcome.[77-79] A deficiency of B vitamins is associated with anorexia and may occur in some cancer patients fed unbalanced homemade foods or patients that have decreased food intake.

Enteral-feeding techniques should be considered if these appetite-stimulating efforts fail or if long-term nutritional support (more than several days) is required. Enteral feeding via nasoesophageal intubation, esophagostomy tubes or gastrostomy tube is the most reliable and efficient method for ensuring adequate alimentation. (See Chapter 12.) In many situations, it is best to proactively place an enteral feeding device during surgery or before radiation therapy is initiated. Examples include placing a gastrostomy tube in patients with oral tumor resections or before radiation treatment to the nose, oral cavity or neck.

Parenteral nutrition should be reserved for animals that are unable to assimilate nutrients or those with intractable vomiting. An example is a patient with GI lymphoma that is stabilized with parenteral nutrition until remission is obtained with chemotherapy (Case 25-1). The enteral route can then be used. Parenteral nutrition in human cancer patients is a controversial subject, with a large number of clinical trials failing to document significant benefit with respect to nutritional parameters, survival or tumor response.[80,81]

REASSESSMENT

Reassessment of cancer patients should include monitoring the effects of: 1) cancer on the animal, 2) treatment and nutritional management on the tumor and 3) treatment and nutritional support on the patient. The overall effects of cancer, cancer treatment and nutritional management on the animal are best assessed by comparing the current body weight and BCS with previous assessments. The patient's appetite should be assessed and the daily caloric intake monitored closely. Improvements in body weight sand condition are important indicators that overall treatment and feeding plans are adequate. Clinical staging of the cancer can be repeated to assess the specific tumor response to treatment. Appropriate modifica-

tions to the feeding plan should be made as the patient's status changes.

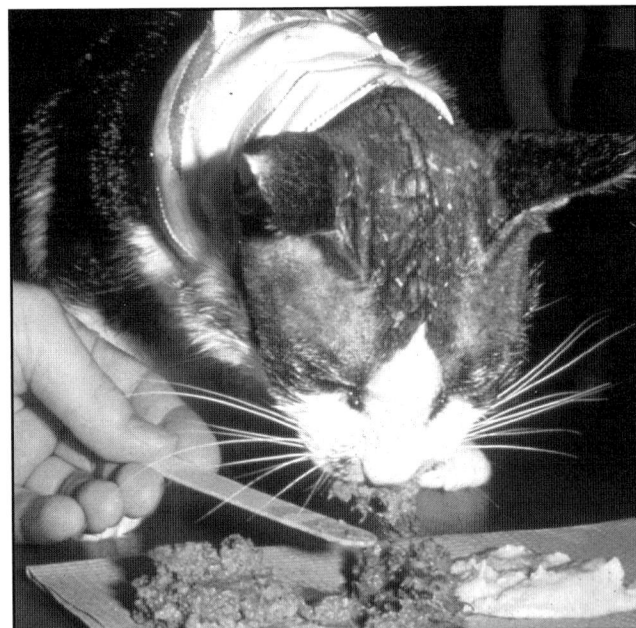

Figure 25-5. Methods to encourage food consumption (including feeding a variety of highly palatable aromatic foods, uniformly warming the food to just below body temperature and administering chemical stimulants) can be tried before enteral support is initiated. (Adapted from Ogilvie GK. Alterations in metabolism and nutritional support for veterinary cancer patients: Recent advances. Compendium on Continuing Education for the Practicing Veterinarian 1993; 15: 925-937.)

ENDNOTE & REFERENCES

ENDNOTE

a. Hill's Pet Nutrition, Inc., Topeka, KS, USA.

REFERENCES

1. Morris Animal Foundation. Animal health survey. Englewood, CO, 1991.
2. Bronson RT. Variation in age at death of dogs of different sexes and breeds. American Journal of Veterinary Research 1982; 43: 2057-2059.

3. Macy DW. Hematopoietic tumors. In: Withrow SJ, MacEwen EG, eds. Small Animal Clinical Oncology. Philadelphia, PA: WB Saunders Co, 1996; 432-451.

4. Dorn CR. Epidemiology of canine and feline tumors. Journal of the American Animal Hospital Association 1976; 12: 307-312.

5. Ogilvie GK, Vail DM. Metabolic alterations and nutritional therapy for the veterinary cancer patient. In: Withrow SJ, MacEwen EG, eds. Small Animal Clinical Veterinary Oncology. Philadelphia, PA: WB Saunders Co, 1996; 117-128.

6. Ogilvie GK, Vail DM. Unique metabolic alterations associated with cancer cachexia in the dog. In: Kirk RW, Bonagura JD, eds. Current Veterinary Therapy XI. Philadelphia, PA: WB Saunders Co, 1992; 433-438.

7. Ogilvie GK, Moore AS. Nutritional support. In: Managing the Veterinary Cancer Patient: A Practice Manual. Trenton, NJ: Veterinary Learning Systems, 1995; 124-127.

8. Shein PS, Kisner D, Haller D, et al. Cachexia of malignancy. Cancer 1976; 43: 2070-2076.

9. Ogilvie GK, Moore AS. Nutritional management. In: Managing the Veterinary Cancer Patient: A Practice Manual. Trenton, NJ: Veterinary Learning Systems, 1995; 44-96.

10. Theologides A. Cancer cachexia. Cancer 1979; 43: 2004-2012.

11. Buzby GP, Steinberg JJ. Nutrition in cancer patients. Symposium on Surgical Nutrition 1981; 61: 691-699.

12. Landel AM, Hammond WG, Mequid MM. Aspects of amino acid and protein metabolism in cancer-bearing states. Cancer 1985; 55: 230-237.

13. Bray GA, Campfield LA. Metabolic factors in the control of energy stores. Metabolism 1975; 24: 99-117.

14. Vail DM, Ogilvie GK, Wheeler SL. Metabolic alterations in patients with cancer cachexia. Compendium on Continuing Education for the Practicing Veterinarian 1990; 12: 381-387.

15. Ogilvie GK, Vail DM. Advances in nutritional therapy for the cancer patient. Veterinary Clinics of North America: Small Animal Practice 1990; 20: 969-985.

16. London CA, Vail DM. Tumor biology. In: Withrow SJ, MacEwen EG, eds. Small Animal Clinical Veterinary Oncology. Philadelphia, PA: WB Saunders Co, 1996; 16-31.

17. Powers BE. The pathology of neoplasia. In: Withrow SJ, MacEwen EG, eds. Small Animal Clinical Veterinary Oncology. Philadelphia, PA: WB Saunders Co, 1996; 4-15.

18. Vail DM, Ogilvie GK, Wheeler SL, et al. Alterations in carbohydrate metabolism in canine lymphoma. Journal of Veterinary Internal Medicine 1990; 4: 8-11.

19. Vail DM, Ogilvie GK, Fettman MJ, et al. Exacerbation of hyperlactatemia by infusion of lactated Ringer's solution in dogs with lymphoma. Journal of Veterinary Internal Medicine 1990; 4: 228-232.

20. Ogilvie GK, Vail DM, Wheeler SJ. Effect of chemotherapy and remission on carbohydrate metabolism in dogs with lymphoma. Cancer 1992; 69: 233-238.

21. Heber D, Byerley LO, Chi J, et al. Pathophysiology of malnutrition in the adult cancer patient. Cancer 1986; 58: 1867-1873.

22. Bozzetti F, Pagnoni AM, Del Vecchio M. Excessive caloric expenditure as a cause of malnutrition in patients with cancer. Surgery Gynecology and Obstetrics 1980; 150: 229-234.

23. Dempsey DT, Mullen JL. Macronutrient requirements in the malnourished cancer patient. Cancer 1985; 55: 290-294.

24. Ogilvie GK, Walters LM, Salman MD, et al. Alterations in carbohydrate metabolism in dogs with non-hematopoietic malignancies. American Journal of Veterinary Research 1997; 58: 277-281.

25. Ogilvie GK, Walters LM, Salman MD, et al. Treatment of dogs with lymphoma with adriamycin and a diet high in carbohydrate or high in fat. Cancer 1992; 69: 233-238.

26. Chory ET, Mullen JL. Nutritional support of the cancer patient: Delivery systems and formulations. Surgical Clinics of North America 1986; 66: 1105-1120.

27. Langstein HN, Norton JA. Mechanisms of cancer cachexia. Hematology/Oncology Clinics of North America 1991; 5: 103-123.

28. Kurzer M, Meguid MM. Cancer and protein metabolism. Surgical Clinics of North America 1986; 66: 969-1001.

29. Teyek JA, Bistrian BR, Hehir DJ, et al. Improved protein kinetics and albumin synthesis by branched chain amino acid-enriched total parenteral nutrition in cancer cachexia. Cancer 1986; 58: 147-157.

30. Oram-Smith JC, Stein TP. Intravenous nutrition and tumor host protein metabolism. Journal of Surgical Research 1977; 22: 499-503.

31. Barbul A. Arginine: Biochemistry, physiology, and therapeutic implications. Journal of Parenteral and Enteral Nutrition 1986; 10: 227-238.

32. Chlebowski RT, Heber D. Metabolic abnormalities in cancer patients: Carbohydrate metabolism. Surgical Clinics of North America 1986; 66: 957-968.

33. Dewys WD. Pathophysiology of cancer cachexia: Current understanding and areas of future research. Cancer Research 1982; 42: 722-726.

34. McAndrew PF. Fat metabolism and cancer. Surgical Clinics of North America 1986; 66: 1003-1012.

35. Ogilvie GK, Ford RD, Vail DM, et al. Alterations in lipoprotein profiles in dogs with lymphoma. Journal of Veterinary Internal Medicine. 1994; 8: 62-66.

36. Shein PS, Kisner D, Haller D, et al. The oxidation of body fuel stores in cancer patients. Annals of Surgery 1986; 204: 637-642.

37. Tisdale MJ, Brennan RA, Fearon KC. Reduction of weight loss and tumour size in a cachexia model by a high fat diet. British Journal of Cancer 1987; 56: 39-43.

38. Daly JM, Lieberman M, Goldfine J, et al. Enteral nutrition with supplemental arginine, RNA and omega-3 fatty acids: A prospective clinical trial (abstract). Journal of Parenteral and Enteral Nutrition 1991; 15: 19S.

39. Souba WW. Glutamine and cancer. Annals of Surgery 1993; 218: 715-728.

40. Lowell JA, Parnes HL, Blackburn GL. Dietary immunomodulation: Beneficial effects on carcinogenesis and tumor growth. Critical Care Medicine 1990; 18: S145-S148.

41. Ramesh G, Das UN, Koratkar R, et al. Effect of essential fatty acids on tumor cells. Nutrition 1992; 8: 343-347.

42. Dippenaar N, Booyenes J. The reversibility of cancer: Evidence that malignancy in melanoma cells is gamma linolenic acid deficiency dependent. South Africa Medical Journal 1982; 62: 505-507.

43. Begin ME, Ellis G, Das UN, et al. Differential killing of human carcinoma cells supplemented with n-3 and n-6 polyunsaturated fatty acids. Journal of the National Cancer Institute 1986; 77: 2053-2057.

44. Begin ME, Das UN, Ellis G, et al. Selective killing of human cancer cells by polyunsaturated fatty acids. Prostaglandins and Leukotrienes in Medicine 1985; 19: 177-182.

45. Plumb JA, Luo W, Kerr DJ. Effect of polyunsaturated fatty acids on the drug sensitivity of human tumor cell lines resistant to either cisplatin or doxorubicin. British Journal of Cancer 1993; 67: 728-733.

46. Mengeaud V, Nano JL, Fournel S, et al. Effects of eicosapentaenoic acid, gamma-linolenic acid and prostaglandin E1 on three human colon carcinoma cell lines. Prostaglandins, Leukotrienes and Essential Fatty Acids 1992; 47: 313-319.

47. Pascale AW, Ehringer WD, Stillwell W, et al. Omega-3 fatty acid modification of membrane structure and function. II. Alteration by docosahexaenoic acid of tumor cell sensitivity to immune cytolysis. Nutrition and Cancer 1993; 19: 147-157.

48. Jenski LJ, Sturdevant LK, Ehringer WD, et al. Omega-3 fatty acid modification of membrane structure and function. I. Dietary manipulation of tumor cell susceptibility to cell and complement mediated lysis. Nutrition and Cancer 1993; 19: 135-146.

49. Roush GC, Pero RW, Powell J, et al. Modulation of the cancer susceptibility measure, adenosine diphosphate ribosyl transferase (ADPRT), by differences in N-3 and N-6 fatty acids. Nutrition and Cancer 1991; 16: 197-207.

50. Holian O, Nelson R. Action of long-chain fatty acids on protein kinase C activity: Comparison of omega-6 and omega-3 fatty acids. Anticancer Research 1992; 12: 975-980.

51. Hopewell JW, Robbins MEC, van den Aardweg GJMJ, et al. The modulation of radiation-induced damage to pig skin by essential fatty acids. Cancer Research 1992; 3: 703-727.

52. Beck SA, Smith KL, Tisdale MJ. Anticachectic and antitumor effect of eicosapentaenoic acid and its effect on protein turnover. Cancer Research 1991; 51: 6089-6093.

53. Pomposelli JJ, Flores EA, Blackburn GL, et al. Diets enriched with n-3 fatty acids ameliorate lactic acidosis by improving endotoxin-induced tissue hypoperfusion in guinea pigs. Annals of Surgery 1989; 213: 166-176.

54. Kumar GS, Das UN, Kumar KV, et al. Effect of n-6 and n-3 fatty acids on the proliferation of human lymphocytes and their secretion of TNF-α and IL-2 in vitro. Nutrition Research 1992; 12: 815-823.

55. Endres S, Ghorrani R, Kelly VE, et al. The effect of dietary supplementation with n-3 polyunsaturated fatty acids on the synthesis of

interleukin-1 and tumor necrosis factor by mononuclear cells. New England Journal of Medicine 1989; 320: 265-271.

56. Gelin J, Moldawer LL, Lonnroth C, et al. Role of endogenous tumor necrosis factor-α and interleukin-1 for experimental tumor growth and the development of cancer cachexia. Cancer Research 1991; 51: 415-421.

57. Orosz P, Echtenacher B, Falk W, et al. Enhancement of experimental metastasis by tumor necrosis factor. Journal of Experimental Medicine 1993; 177: 1391-1398.

58. Lawson DH, Richmond A, Nixon DW, et al. Metabolic approaches to cancer cachexia. Annual Review of Nutrition 1982; 2: 277-301.

59. Dempsey DT, Feurer ID, Knox LS, et al. Energy expenditure in malnourished GI cancer patients. Cancer 1984; 53: 1265-1273.

60. Premachandra BN, Perlstein IB, Williams K. Circulating and tissue thyroid hormones in relation to hormone action: Pathophysiologic significance. In: Fatherby K, Palde Druyter SB, eds. Hormones in Normal and Abnormal Human Tissues, vol 2. Berlin, NY, 1981; 282-287.

61. Sestoft L. Metabolic aspects of the calorigenic effect of thyroid hormone in mammals. Clinical Endocrinology 1980; 13: 489-506.

62. Vail DM, Panciera D, Ogilvie GK. Thyroid hormone concentrations in conditions of chronic weight loss in dogs with special reference to cancer cachexia. Journal of Veterinary Internal Medicine 1994; 8: 122-127.

63. Dempsey DT, Knox LS, Mullen JL, et al. Energy expenditure in malnourished patients with colorectal cancer. Archives of Surgery 1986; 121: 789-795.

64. Hansell DT, Davies JWL, Burns HJG. The relationship between resting energy expenditure and weight loss in benign and malignant disease. Annals of Surgery 1986; 203: 240-243

65. Fredrix EWHM, Wouters EFM, Soeters PB, et al. Resting energy expenditure in patients with non-small cell lung cancer. Cancer 1991; 68: 1616-1621.

66. Zyliez Z, Schwantje O, Wagener DJT, et al. Metabolic response to enteral food in different phases of cancer cachexia in rats. Oncology 1990; 47: 87-91.

67. Delarue J, Lerebours E, Tilly H, et al. Effect of chemotherapy on resting energy expenditure in patients with non-Hodgkin's lymphoma. Cancer 1990; 65: 2455-2459.

68. Walters LM, Ogilvie GK, Fettman MJ, et al. Repeatability of energy expenditure measurements in normal dogs by indirect calorimetry. American Journal of Veterinary Research 1993; 54: 1881-1885.

69. Ogilvie GK, Walters LM, Salman MD, et al. Effect of anesthesia and surgery on energy expenditure determined by indirect calorimetry in dogs with malignant and non-malignant conditions. Journal of the American Veterinary Medical Association 1996; 57: 1463-1467.

70. Ross BT. The impact of radiation therapy on the nutrition status on the cancer patient: An overview. In: Bloch AS, ed. Nutrition Management of the Cancer Patient. Rockville, MD: Aspen Publishers, 1990; 173-180.

71. Kokal WA. The impact of antitumor therapy on nutrition. Cancer 1985; 55: 273-278.

72. Sonnenschein EG, Glickman LT, Goldschmidt MH, et al. Body conformation, diet, and risk of breast cancer in pet dogs: A case-control study. American Epidemiology 1991; 133: 694-703.

73. Donoghue S. Nutritional support of hospitalized patients. Veterinary Clinics of North America: Small Animal Practice 1989; 19: 475-495.

74. Hwang DH, Carroll AE. Decreased formation of prostaglandin derived from arachidonic acid by dietary linolenate in rats. American Journal of Clinical Nutrition 1980; 33: 590-597.

75. Kelley VE, Ferretti A, Izui S, et al. A fish oil diet rich in eicosapentaenoic acid reduces cyclooxygenase metabolites and suppresses lupus in MRL-1 pr mice. Journal of Immunology 1985; 134: 1914-1919.

76. Canine Cancer (monograph). Hill's Pet Nutrition, Inc, Topeka, KS, 1998.

77. Kardinal CG, Loprinzi CL, Schaid DJ, et al. A controlled trial of cyproheptadine in cancer patients with anorexia and/or cachexia. Proceedings of the American Society of Clinical Oncology 1990; 9: 325.

78. Chlebowski RT, Herrold J, Ali I, et al. Influence of nandrolone decanoate on weight loss in advanced non-small cell lung cancer. Cancer 1986; 58: 183-186.

79. Willcox JC, Cou J, Shaw J, et al. Prednisolone as an appetite stimulant in patients with cancer. British Medical Journal 1984; 288: 27-31.

80. McGeer AJ, Detsky AS, O'Rourke K. Parenteral nutrition in cancer patients undergoing chemotherapy: A meta-analysis. Nutrition 1990; 6: 478-483.

81. Chlebowski RT. Nutritional support of the medical oncology patient. Hematology/Oncology Clinics of North America 1991; 5: 147-160.

■ CASE 25-1

Diarrhea and Weight Loss in a Gordon Setter

Stanley L. Marks, BVSc, PhD
Diplomate ACVIM (Internal Medicine, Oncology)
and ACVN
School of Veterinary Medicine
University of California, Davis
Davis, California, USA

Assess the Animal

A seven-year-old, 23-kg, intact male Gordon setter was examined for anorexia, lethargy, diarrhea and weight loss of six weeks' duration. Physical examination revealed a depressed, cachectic dog (body condition score 1/5). The remainder of the physical examination was unremarkable except for mild dehydration (5%). Abnormal results of a complete blood count, serum biochemistry profile and urinalysis included hypoalbuminemia (2.1 g/dl, normal 2.8 to 3.5) and hypoglobulinemia (2.3 g/dl, normal 3.0 to 3.5). Thoracic and abdominal radiographs were normal. Intestinal lymphoma was confirmed based on histopathologic evaluation of biopsy specimens taken from the small intestine during flexible endoscopy of the upper gastrointestinal tract.

The cachexia was likely due to a combination of diminished caloric intake, malassimilation and altered metabolism secondary to malignancy (Table 1). The anorexia was probably associated with the intestinal lymphoma, secondary abdominal pain and hyperlactatemia. The dehydration and lethargy were probably secondary to the underlying problems causing cachexia.

Assess the Food(s) and Feeding Method

The dog was normally fed one cup of a dry specialty brand food twice daily (810 kcal [3.39 MJ]) with occasional table foods. The food had the following nutrient profile (dry matter basis):

Protein = 29%

Crude fat = 19%

Crude fiber = 3.5%

Calcium = 1.6%

Phosphorus = 1.3%

Sodium = 0.4%

Chloride = 0.5%

Potassium = 0.6%

Magnesium = 0.1%

NFE (carbohydrate) = 44%.

Questions

1. What indices can be used to assess this dog's nutritional status in the face of severe cachexia?
2. What are the types and amounts of macronutrients that should be fed to this dog?
3. What is this patient's caloric requirement?
4. What food(s) and feeding method should be used in this dog?

Answers and Discussion

1. Because anthropometric measurements are usually not performed in dogs and cats, nutritional status is determined by a thorough history and physical examination. Laboratory evaluation of total lymphocyte counts, hematocrit and serum albumin and urea nitrogen concentrations can be helpful to further evaluate nutritional status. The use of these parameters is limited because hypoalbuminemia and lymphopenia have many causes unrelated to nutritional status. Albumin also has a relatively long half-life (eight days in normal dogs) and is slow to respond to changes in nutritional status. In the face of severe intestinal malassimilation with marked hypoalbuminemia and ascites, body weight becomes an insensitive index. Body condition assessment is the best means of assessing nutritional status of patients with cancer.

2. Some tumor cells preferentially use carbohydrates and protein, but have difficulty using lipids. Host tissues can continue to oxidize lipids for energy. This phenomenon has led to the hypothesis that foods relatively high in fat benefit animals with cancer compared with foods high in easily digested carbohydrates. Dietary carbohydrates should be reduced to limit the tumor from metabolizing glucose for energy by anaerobic glycolysis with the formation of lactate as an end product. Fluid therapy to correct dehydration should avoid fluids containing lactate. High concentrations of carbohydrate may result in peripheral lactate production and energy loss by futile cycling through the Cori cycle. Other complications of excess dietary carbohydrate include hyperglycemia, hyperosmolar states, excess CO_2 production and hepatic steatosis. An appropriate formulation for supporting canine cancer patients contains 30 to 45% protein calories, 50 to 65% fat calories and less than 20% carbohydrate calories.

3. The estimated resting energy requirement (RER) for this dog at its current weight is RER = $70(BW_{kg})^{0.75}$ or 735 kcal (3.08 MJ). Daily energy requirement (DER) would be approximately 1,000 kcal (4.15 MJ) (1.35 x RER). This amount could be increased if activity level were higher or if weight gain was being promoted.

4. Although the cure for intestinal lymphoma remains elusive, it is clear that adequate, aggressive nutritional support is a key adjuvant to the treatment plan for cancer patients with chronic diarrhea. The enteral route is the preferred route of nutritional support because it is easier, less expensive and more physiologic than parenteral administration. However, some animals are temporarily unable to assimilate nutrients administered into the gastrointestinal tract because of functional (severe malassimilation secondary to intestinal lymphoma), anatomic (short bowel syndrome) or mechanical (ileus or obstruction) reasons.

Patients with intractable vomiting or diarrhea, severe malabsorption and severe pancreatitis may also benefit from parenteral nutrition (PN). PN is indicated in this dog because of the absence of available functional bowel to digest and absorb sufficient nutrients to promote recovery. It is well-documented, however, that animals receiving long-term PN develop intestinal mucosal atrophy, bacterial translocation and reduced concentrations of secretory IgA.

Because enteral feeding improves mucosal thickness, stimulates gut trophic hormones and stimulates IgA production, partial enteral feeding via nasoesophageal intubation is recommended. PN can be used to supply the bulk of the dog's energy and protein requirements, whereas enteral feeding can be used to help maintain intestinal mucosal integrity and limit bacterial translocation. Nasoesophageal tubes are an excellent first choice for the short-term (i.e., less than 10 days) enteral feeding of most critically ill dogs and cats. One disadvantage of nasoesophageal tubes is their small diameter (3- to 8-Fr. tubes), necessitating the use of a liquid enteral formula.

Treatment and Feeding Plan

PN was initiated on Day 2 of hospitalization at a rate of 20 ml/hr (50% of the estimated DER). The rate was increased to 40 ml/hr on Day 3 of hospitalization. The parenteral solution consisted of 8.5% crystalline amino acids, 20% lipid, 50% dextrose and B-complex vitamins. Body weight, attitude, rectal temperature and concentrations of serum total protein, glucose and electrolytes were monitored to allow for early recognition and management of complications. A multi-drug approach to treat lymphoma was started on Day 2 of hospitalization.

Nasoesophageal feeding was instituted on Day 3 using an energy-dense (1.3 kcal/ml, 5.44 kJ/ml) commercial enteral formula (Prescription Diet Canine/Feline a/d[a]) that contains high levels of protein (45.7% dry matter), fat (28.7% dry matter), glutamine (6.6% dry matter), arginine (2.1% dry matter) and n-3 fatty acids (2.6% dry matter). The enteral formula was tube-fed four times daily (50 ml per feeding) to supply 20% of the dog's estimated caloric requirement. Although low-fat foods are better tolerated in a variety of gastrointestinal disorders, the multiple small feedings and slow rate of administration were felt to abrogate this concern. The dog was receiving its DER on Day 4 of hospitalization through the combined use of enteral and parenteral routes. No complications were observed with the feeding regimen. The dog appeared brighter and had gained 1.1 kg of body weight.

The dog gained an additional 1.5 kg of body weight over the next four days of hospitalization and its attitude and diarrhea continued to improve. On Day 8 of hospitalization, the PN administration rate was decreased to 20 ml/hr (50% of estimated caloric requirement). In place of the nasoesophageal feedings, small frequent feedings of a moist commercial veterinary therapeutic food (Prescription Diet Canine n/d[a]) were given to meet 50% of the dog's caloric requirement. The dog was discharged 10 days after initial hospitalization following discontinuation of parenteral feeding. The moist veterinary therapeutic food was continued at home. DER was increased to 1,300 kcal (5.44 MJ).

The dog continued to do well throughout the rest of the induction period (six weeks), and was seen weekly for physical examinations, complete blood counts and chemotherapy administration. Apart from continued mild nonregenerative anemia, and mild neutropenia on Day 31, the dog maintained in complete remission and showed no adverse effects to chemotherapy. The dog had gained 6 kg of body weight at the end of the induction period (Day 45) and its body condition score had improved to 2/5. Reassessment on Day 180 revealed a bright, alert and responsive dog that appeared to be in complete remission.

Further Discussion

It is imperative that a cancer patient's response to dietary therapy be evaluated and modified if needed. The DER can vary by as much as 20% between different dogs with the same body weight and catabolic insult. Thus, the patient's caloric intake may need to be increased or decreased depending on body weight and condition. Long-term administration of chemotherapeutic agents such as prednisone or other immunosuppressive therapy

Table 1. Nutritional problems associated with gastrointestinal neoplasia.

Anorexia with progressive weight loss and dehydration
Taste changes causing reduced food intake
Alterations in fat, carbohydrate and protein metabolism
Intestinal malabsorption associated with:
Protein-losing enteropathy
Electrolyte and fluid loss

could further worsen malnutrition and predispose patients to significant infective complications.

Endnote

a. Hill's Pet Nutrition, Inc., Topeka, KS, USA.

Bibliography

Matus RE. Chemotherapy of lymphoma and leukemia. In: Kirk RW, ed. Current Veterinary Therapy X. Philadelphia, PA: WB Saunders Co, 1989; 482-488.

■ CASE 25-2

Chronic Vomiting in a Cat

Gregory K. Ogilvie, DVM
Diplomate ACVIM (Internal Medicine, Oncology)
College of Veterinary Medicine and
 Biomedical Sciences
Colorado State University
Fort Collins, Colorado, USA

Assess the Animal

A 10-year-old, neutered female domestic shorthair cat was examined for persistent vomiting of 10 days' duration. The vomiting occurred most commonly after meals, was projectile at times and was becoming more frequent. Two months earlier, another veterinarian removed an "abscessed lymph node" found during an exploratory celiotomy that was performed to determine the cause of intermittent vomiting. Histopathology was not performed on the excised lymph node.

The cat appeared very depressed, slightly dehydrated and was breathing slowly (10 breaths/min.). Dried vomitus was adhered to its lower jaw and chest. Rectal temperature was 38.8°C (102°F). The pulse rate was 180/min. Mucous membranes were tacky and pale pink. Body weight was 3 kg and the body condition score was 2/5.

A complete blood count, serum biochemistry profile, urinalysis, chest and abdominal radiographs and feline leukemia virus and feline immunodeficiency virus tests were performed. Results of these tests were negative or within normal limits except for the following values: hypoalbuminemia (2.1 g/dl, normal 2.8 to 3.5), hypochloremia (109 mEq/l, normal 118 to 125), hyponatremia (120 mEq/l, normal 147 to 156), hypokalemia (3.0 mEq/l, normal 4.0 to 4.5) and metabolic alkalosis (bicarbonate 39 mEq/l, normal 17 to 24). A dilated stomach and proximal duodenum were noted on radiographs. Very lit-

tle abdominal fat was present. A tentative diagnosis of proximal gastrointestinal obstruction was made.

The metabolic problems were treated with intravenous fluids (0.9% NaCl with 40 mEq KCl/l) in anticipation of an exploratory celiotomy. A "napkin ring" stricture of the proximal duodenum was surgically resected. Intraoperative cytology and subsequent histopathology confirmed a diagnosis of intestinal lymphosarcoma.

Assess the Food(s) and Feeding Method

The cat was normally fed a commercial dry specialty brand cat food formulated for adult cats. The food was offered free choice.

Questions

1. Why is nutritional management important for recovery of this cat?
2. What short-term and long-term feeding methods should be used in this patient?
3. Chemotherapy is indicated in this cat to control systemic disease. Can nutritional therapy be used to manage adverse effects of chemotherapy?

Answers and Discussion

1. Hypoalbuminemia, reduced fat mass and less than ideal body condition indicate significant malnutrition in this patient. Cancer cachexia is associated with slow wound healing, decreased immune response, increased toxicity from chemotherapy and decreased survival. Nutritional support of cancer patients maximizes healing, decreases side effects of chemotherapy and prolongs the disease-free interval and survival.
2. Feeding tubes and enteral nutritional support should always be considered in cancer patients undergoing surgery. Placement of feeding tubes at the time of

surgery is convenient and allows both short- and long-term nutritional management of the patient. It is far easier to prevent development of cancer cachexia than to return a patient with cancer cachexia to a more normal state. Feeding tubes are also convenient to ensure that medications (e.g., antiemetics, antibiotics) are administered without the need for central venous access. Chemotherapy, radiation therapy and cachexia are associated with poor wound healing in cancer patients. Because of these factors, gastrostomy tubes may be associated with higher complication rates such as leakage and development of peritonitis. Esophagostomy tubes may be preferred in these types of patients for enteral nutritional support. (See Appendix V.)

3. Well-controlled studies in human cancer patients show that adequate nutritional support is associated with decreased toxicity from chemotherapy. Although similar studies have not been performed using dogs and cats, it is likely that side effects of chemotherapy would also be minimized in animals receiving appropriate food(s) in adequate amounts.

Progress Notes

Both a jejunostomy and an esophagostomy tube were placed during surgery. Within 24 hours after surgery, feeding was started with a commercial human liquid food (Osmolite HN[a]) supplemented with protein (Promod[a]). Chemotherapy was started for lymphoma even though no obvious disease was found outside the intestinal tract. The cat was treated initially with cyclophosphamide, vincristine, prednisone and doxorubicin at the time of suture removal.

As soon as vomiting subsided (one week after surgery), jejunostomy tube feeding was discontinued and feeding through the esophagostomy tube was initiated. Metoclopramide was given via the tubes as needed to control further vomiting. After four weeks, the cat had gained weight and was able to maintain improved body condition with voluntary oral feeding of a veterinary enteral product (Prescription Diet Canine/Feline a/d[b]). The Canine/Feline a/d was continued for three months during chemotherapy. The original dry specialty food was fed when chemotherapy was discontinued. The cat has remained in clinical remission for three years.

Endnotes

a. Ross Laboratories, Columbus, OH, USA.
b. Hill's Pet Nutrition, Inc., Topeka, KS, USA.

CHAPTER 26

Use of Fatty Acids in Inflammatory Disease

William D. Schoenherr
Philip Roudebush
William S. Swecker

"Food is an important part of a balanced diet."
Fran Lebowitz

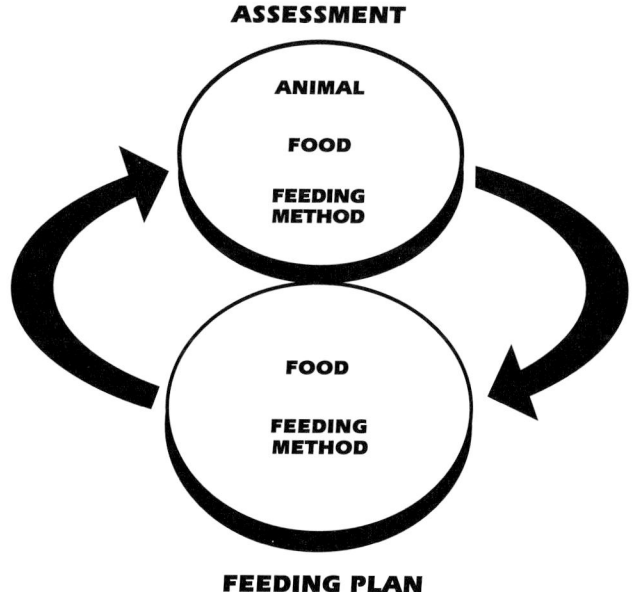

ASSESSMENT

ANIMAL

FOOD

FEEDING METHOD

FOOD

FEEDING METHOD

FEEDING PLAN

Note: The reader is referred to Chapter 1 for a detailed discussion of the iterative process of clinical nutrition.

■ INTRODUCTION

Regulation of the immune system is extremely complex. We are only starting to understand how the immune system coordinates the body's response to a disease or invading pathogen. However, even with our incomplete understanding, we can modulate the immune system.

Immunomodulation designates either suppression or augmentation of an immune response. Suppressing function of the immune system is important in cases of excessive inflammation or immune-mediated disease. Augmenting the immune response is helpful when increased resistance to disease is required. Nutrition plays an important role in modulation of the animal's immune system.

The majority of scientific literature about the interaction between nutrition and the immune system correlates the effects of nutrient deficiency and modulation of an immune response. These studies have evaluated deficiencies of protein, energy, the fat-soluble vitamins A, D and E, the B-complex vitamins, vitamin C and the minerals selenium, iron, zinc and copper and their relationship to immune dysfunction. Undoubtedly, the nutritional status of the animal plays an important role in resistance mechanisms against disease-causing organisms and may influence the outcome of disease in infected animals.

Most recently, researchers have concentrated efforts on evaluating the impact that specific fatty acids have on modulation of the immune system. This chapter will concentrate on the role of dietary fatty acids in modulation of inflammatory disease of the skin and musculoskeletal sys-

KEY WORDS & TERMS—INFLAMMATORY DISEASE*

Alpha-linolenic acid
Arachidonic acid
Arthritis (osteoarthritis)
Cyclooxygenase (pathway)
Cytokine
Dihomogammalinolenic acid
Docosahexaenoic acid

Eicosanoid
Eicosapentaenoic acid
Gamma-linolenic acid
Immunomodulation
Immunonutrition
Leukotriene
Linoleic acid

Lipoxygenase (pathway)
n-3 (omega-3) fatty acid
n-6 (omega-6) fatty acid
Polyunsaturated fatty acid (PUFA)
Prostaglandin
Pruritus

*Key words and terms are defined in the Glossary.

KEY POINTS—INFLAMMATORY DISEASE

1. The term immunomodulation is used to designate suppression or augmentation of the immune response.
2. Dietary polyunsaturated fatty acids (PUFA) serve as substrates that may be metabolized to form important biologically active compounds.
3. The two most important series of PUFA are the n-6 series (the first double bond located at the sixth carbon atom) and the n-3 series (the first double bond located at the third carbon atom).
4. Many marine plants, especially algae, elongate chains and add double bonds to α-linolenic acid to yield n-3 PUFA; their transfer through the food chain to fish accounts for the abundance of eicosapentaenoic acid (EPA; 20:5n-3) and docosahexaenoic acid (DHA; 22:6n-3) in certain marine fish oils.
5. The proportion of different types of fatty acids in cell membranes can be changed by altering the composition of fatty acids consumed by the animal.
6. Changing the type of fatty acids available to cells, including cells of the immune system (e.g., lymphocytes or monocytes), modifies the fatty acid composition of the membrane phospholipids of those cells. A change in cell function is apparent after the membrane fatty acid composition changes.
7. The amounts and types of eicosanoids synthesized are determined by the availability of the fatty acid precursor released from the membrane, and by the activities of cyclooxygenase and lipoxygenases.
8. Macrophages are the most significant source of eicosanoids because they possess both cyclooxygenase and lipoxygenase enzymes, and also are subject to eicosanoid's regulatory effects.
9. Alteration of macrophage eicosanoid production will modulate immune function.
10. Consumption of fish oil with n-3 PUFA or oils high in α-linolenic acid results in production of fewer proinflammatory eicosanoids and larger amounts of anti-inflammatory eicosanoids, thereby reducing the

immunologic response to an inflammatory episode. Consequently, the change in type of eicosanoid production and the subsequent alteration in cytokine production can reduce inflammation by eicosanoid-mediated effects. This premise is the basis for using these fatty acids for treatment of chronic inflammatory conditions.
11. Inflammatory skin diseases, especially allergic dermatoses, are common and important clinical entities.
12. Twenty to 50% of dogs with allergic pruritus will improve with modification in fatty acid intake if secondary bacterial and yeast infections are controlled. Synergistic effects have been documented between fatty acids and other antipruritic agents such as antihistamines and glucocorticoids.
13. Arthritis (osteoarthritis) is the most common form of joint and musculoskeletal disease affecting dogs, but is relatively uncommon in cats.
14. Dietary manipulation of n-6 and n-3 fatty acids to abate the production of certain prostaglandins in the inflammatory process has been evaluated in people with rheumatoid arthritis, but there has been little reported research using companion animals with arthritis.
15. Fatty acid levels in the diet can be modified by changing the food, adding a supplement or doing both.
16. In many cases, fatty acid supplements contain much lower concentrations of fatty acids than concentrations already found in the foods being consumed by the animal. It may be more appropriate and convenient to change the animal's food to one with higher concentrations of appropriate fatty acids than to add a fatty acid supplement to the animal's current food.
17. Laboratory and clinical studies in a number of species have established an initial dose of 50 to 250 mg of total n-3 fatty acids per kg body weight per day as a reasonable starting point for patients with inflammatory disease.

tem. These concepts may have broader application to modulation of inflammatory disease in other organ systems, as well. The reader is referred to other sources for a discussion of the broader aspects of immunonutrition. (See sidebar "Immunonutrition.")

This chapter is organized as follows: 1) a review of the role of polyunsaturated fatty acids (PUFA) in inflammation, 2) how the inflammatory response is modulated by

altering dietary fatty acids, 3) clinical importance and assessment of the animal with inflammatory skin disease, 4) use of fatty acids as antipruritic agents, 5) clinical importance and assessment of the animal with arthritis, 6) use of fatty acids for arthritis, 7) assessment of the food(s) and feeding methods in patients with dermatitis or arthritis and 8) development of feeding plans for these patients.

KEY NUTRITIONAL FACTORS—INFLAMMATORY DISEASE

Factors	Associated conditions	Dietary recommendations
Polyunsaturated fatty acids	Dermatitis Pruritus Arthritis Other inflammatory diseases	Provide additional dietary levels of specific n-6 (gamma-linolenic acid [GLA]) or n-3 (alpha-linolenic acid [ALA], eicosapentaenoic acid [EPA], docosahexaenoic acid [DHA]) fatty acids. GLA is provided in supplements containing borage oil, black currant oil or evening primrose oil. ALA is provided in supplements or foods with flax, flax oil or linseed oil. EPA and DHA are provided in supplements or foods with fish meal or fish oil. Supplements or foods should initially provide 50 to 250 mg total n-3 fatty acids/kg body weight/day.

THE ROLE OF PUFA IN INFLAMMATION

All mammals synthesize fatty acids de novo up to palmitic acid (16:0), which may be elongated to stearic acid (18:0) and converted into oleic acid (18:1). Plants, unlike mammals, can insert additional double bonds into oleic acid and produce the PUFA linoleic acid (LA, 18:2n-6) and α-linolenic acid (ALA, 18:3n-3). Both LA and ALA are considered essential fatty acids because animals cannot synthesize them from other series of fatty acids; thus, they must be supplied by the diet.

Dietary PUFA serve as substrates that may be metabolized to form important, biologically active compounds. To produce those metabolites, a number of cells contain a group of enzymes that desaturate, elongate and oxygenate fatty acids.

All PUFA are categorized based on the position of the first double bond in the structure from the terminal end (Figure 26-1). The two most important PUFA series are the n-6 series (the first double bond is located at the sixth carbon atom) and the n-3 series (the first double bond is located at the third carbon atom).

In the n-6 series, linoleic acid can be desaturated to yield γ-linolenic acid (GLA, 18:3n-6), which is elongated to dihomo-γ-linolenic acid (DGLA, 20:3n-6) and ultimately desaturated again to produce arachidonic acid (AA, 20:4n-6) in the animal (Figure 26-2).

Many marine plants, especially algae, elongate chains and add double bonds to ALA to yield n-3 PUFA with 20 and 22 carbon atoms and five or six double bonds (Figure 26-2). Formation of these long-chain n-3 PUFA by marine algae and their transfer through the food chain to fish account for the abundance of eicosapentaenoic acid (EPA, 20:5n-3) and docosahexaenoic acid (DHA, 22:6n-3) in certain marine fish oils.

Eicosanoid Production from Fatty Acids

Fatty acids have diverse functions in cells but their principal roles are as energy sources and as membrane constituents. In current theories of cell membrane structure, it is hypothesized that most of the phospholipid present in the membrane takes the form of a bimolecular sheet with fatty acid chains in the interior of the bilayer (the "fluid mosaic" model).[1] The proportion of different types of fatty acids in cell membranes can be changed by altering the composition of fatty acids consumed by the animal. Modifying the fatty acid composition of the cell membrane

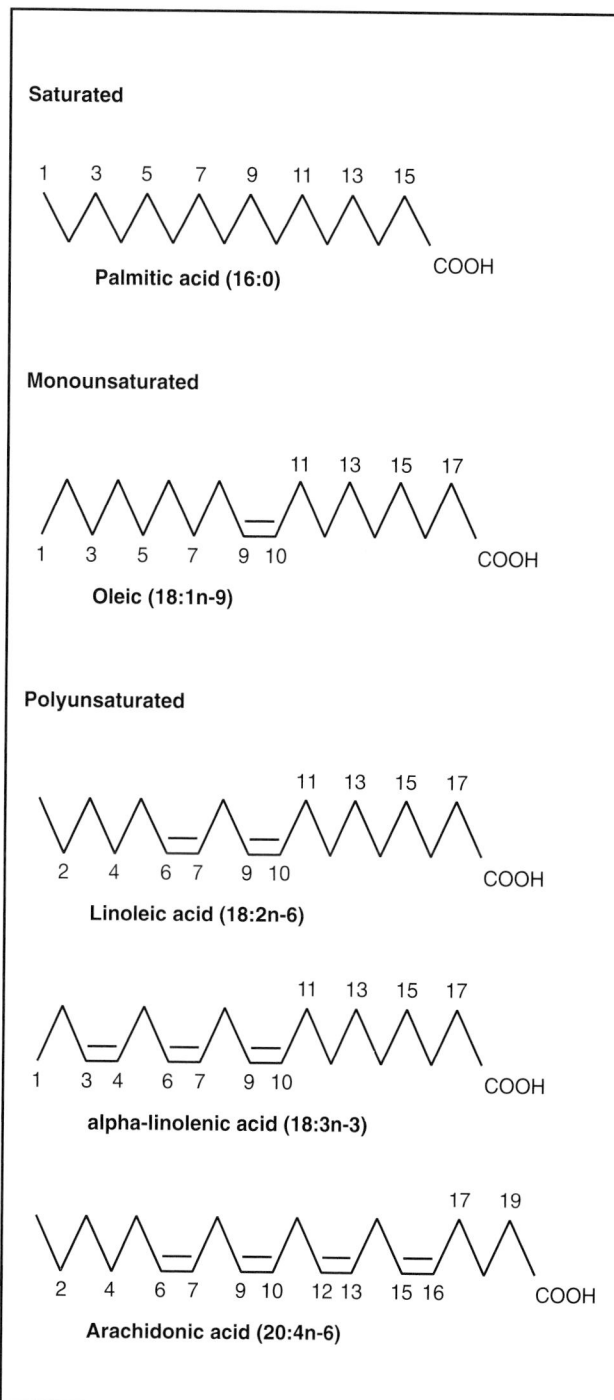

Saturated

Palmitic acid (16:0)

Monounsaturated

Oleic (18:1n-9)

Polyunsaturated

Linoleic acid (18:2n-6)

alpha-linolenic acid (18:3n-3)

Arachidonic acid (20:4n-6)

Figure 26-1. Chemistry and nomenclature of fatty acids.

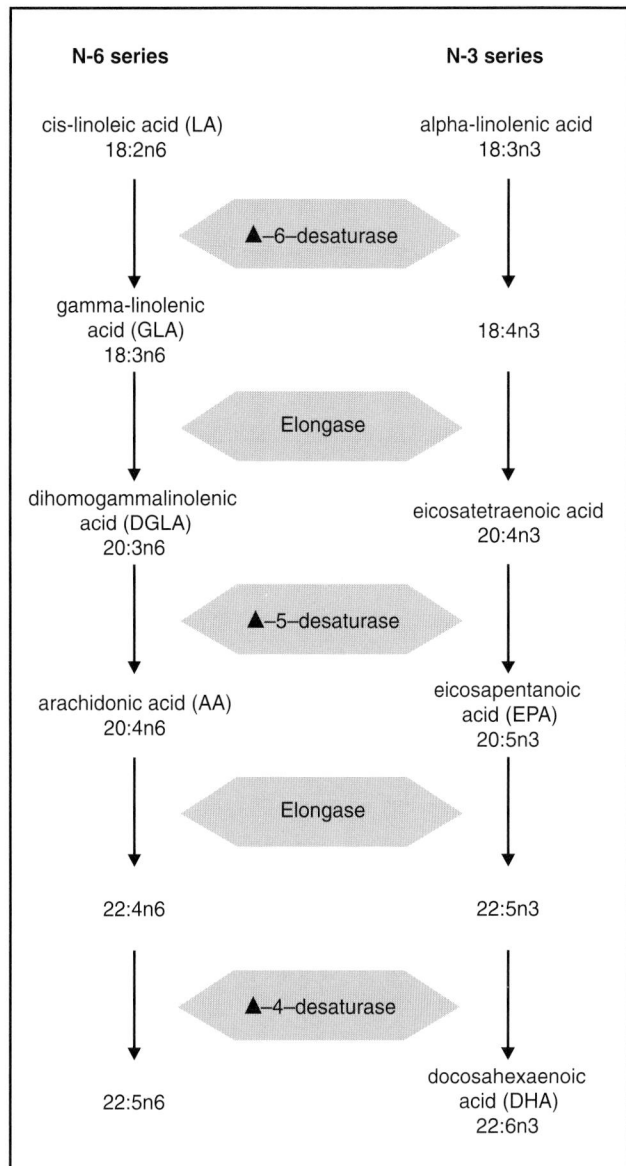

Figure 26-2. Metabolic transformations of two major unsaturated fatty acid families by desaturation and elongation.

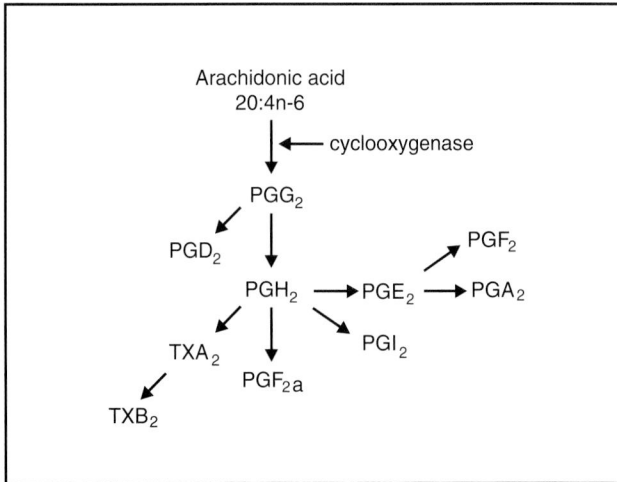

Figure 26-3. Arachidonic acid metabolism by the cyclooxygenase cascade. Key: TX = thromboxane, PG = prostaglandin.

changes membrane fluidity. Both the fatty acid composition of membrane phospholipids and the fluidity of the membrane affect membrane activities.[2]

Certain membrane fatty acids also have specific roles in the regulation of cell functions. For example, AA, GLA and EPA act as precursors for the synthesis of eicosanoids, an important group of immunoregulatory molecules that function as local hormones and mediators of inflammation. Changing the type of fatty acids available to cells, including cells of the immune system (e.g., lymphocytes and monocytes), modifies the fatty acid composition of the membrane phospholipids of those cells. A change in cell function is apparent after the membrane fatty acid composition changes.[3]

Eicosanoids are a family of 20-carbon oxygenated derivatives of GLA, AA and EPA, and include prostaglandins (PG) and thromboxanes (TX), which together are termed prostanoids, and leukotrienes (LT), lipoxins (LX), hydroperoxyeicosatetraenoic acids (HPETE) and hydroxyeicosatetraenoic acids (HETE).

Eicosanoid synthesis begins with metabolism of GLA, EPA or AA by one of two enzyme systems: 1) cyclooxygenase, which yields PG and TX (Figure 26-3) or 2) the 5-, 12- or 15-lipoxygenases, which yield LT, LX, HPETE and HETE (Figure 26-4).[4] The amounts and types of eicosanoids synthesized are determined by the availability of the fatty acid precursor released from the membrane, and by the activities of cyclooxygenase and the lipoxygenases.[5]

In most conditions the principal precursor for these compounds is AA, although GLA and EPA compete with AA for the same enzyme systems. The eicosanoids derived from AA appear to be more common in normal physiologic circumstances. This finding is explained by the higher content of AA than GLA or EPA in most membrane phospholipids, and a lower specificity of cyclooxygenase for GLA and EPA than for AA. The eicosanoids produced from AA are proinflammatory as compared to eicosanoids formed from GLA or EPA and may result in pathologic conditions when produced in excessive amounts.[4,6]

The major products of the cyclooxygenase cascade formed from AA are the proinflammatory 2-series PG and TX, PGE$_2$ and TXA$_2$. Aspirin and nonsteroidal anti-inflammatory drugs (NSAIDs) primarily inhibit the cyclooxygenase cascade. The n-3 PUFA also competitively inhibit oxygenation of AA by cyclooxygenase. Ingestion of fish oils containing n-3 PUFA decreases membrane AA levels because n-3 PUFA replace AA in the substrate pool and decrease the capacity to synthesize eicosanoids from AA.[6-10]

The products derived from AA through the lipoxygenase pathway are the proinflammatory 4-series LT: LTB$_4$, LTC$_4$, LTD$_4$, LTE$_4$, 12 HETE and 15 HETE (Figure 26-5). In contrast, eicosanoids derived from GLA and EPA promote minimal to no inflammatory activity. LTB$_5$ and 15 HETE are products derived from EPA via the lipoxygenase pathway that inhibit production of LTB$_4$.[6-10]

EPA gives rise to the 3-series PG and TX and the 5-series LT (Figure 26-5). The eicosanoids produced from EPA do not always have the same biologic properties as the analogues produced from AA. For example, LTB$_5$ is less active than LTB$_4$ with regard to chemotactic and aggregatory properties in neutrophils and PGE$_3$ is a less potent inhibitor of lymphocyte proliferation than PGE$_2$ (Figure 26-6). DGLA also competes with AA for cyclooxygenase and, therefore, decreases production of cyclooxygenase products from AA and favors production of the 1-series PG and TX (Figure 26-6).

GLA is readily converted to DGLA (Figure 26-2) and increases the production of the 1-series PG and 15-hydroxy-DGLA. PGE$_1$ inhibits mobilization of AA from the membrane phospholipid stores restricting eicosanoid production from AA, and 15-hydroxy-DGLA reduces conversion of AA to its 5- and 12-lipoxygenase metabolites.[11] GLA is an intermediate in the formation of AA from LA and increasing dietary GLA might lead to an increase in tissue levels of AA. The Δ-5 desaturation step, which converts DGLA to AA, is a rate-limiting step and is quite slow in animals.[12] No change or a small increase in tissue AA levels is found when GLA is fed; however, DGLA tissue levels increase in relation to dietary levels of GLA.

Modulation of Immune Response and Inflammation by Fatty Acids

Macrophages are the most significant source of eicosanoids (PG, TX, LT and HETE) because they possess cyclooxygenase and lipoxygenase enzymes, and are subject to regulatory effects of both enzyme systems. Macrophages modulate the intensity and duration of inflammatory and immune responses. Alteration of macrophage eicosanoid production modulates immune function.[7,13-16]

AA is the major PUFA in membrane phospholipids of macrophages and lymphocytes.[17] The response of tissue that is irritated or injured is inflammation, a mechanism by which tissue protects itself immunologically. In brief, phospholipases act on phospholipids of cell membranes to release fatty acids. AA, the fatty acid in greatest concentration, is released and converted into eicosanoids, which mediate inflammation.

Four AA-derived leukotrienes and one PG play a central role in the inflammatory process. LTB$_4$ stimulates neutrophil and eosinophil chemotaxis and increases vascular permeability. LTC$_4$, LTD$_4$ and LTE$_4$ encourage smooth muscle contraction and increase vascular permeability. PGE$_2$ inhibits T and B lymphocyte proliferation, reduces cytokine production and limits natural killer (NK) cell activity. Increased production of LT and PGE$_2$ has been reported in many chronic inflammatory diseases.[18] Figure 26-7 summarizes the effects of AA-derived eicosanoids on lymphocyte functions and cytokine production.[19]

Consumption of fish oil with n-3 PUFA or oils high in the n-6 fatty acid GLA (e.g., evening primrose oil, borage oil and black currant oil) results in replacement of AA in the macrophage membrane with EPA or DGLA. The result is production of fewer AA-derived eicosanoids and more EPA- or GLA-derived eicosanoids, thereby reducing the immunologic response to an inflammatory episode.[13,20-24] Consequently, changing the type of eicosanoid production and the subsequent alteration in cytokine production can reduce inflammation by eicosanoid-mediated effects.[11,20-25] This premise is the basis for using EPA or GLA for treatment of chronic inflammatory conditions.

Immunonutrition

A detailed discussion of immunonutrition is beyond the scope of this chapter. Readers interested in learning more about nutritional modulation of the immune response (besides the role of dietary fatty acids discussed in this chapter) should refer to the following articles and textbooks.

Beisel WR. History of nutritional immunology: Introduction and overview. Journal of Nutrition 1992; 122: 591-596.

Bendich A, Chandra RK, eds. Micronutrients and Immune Functions. New York, NY: New York Academy of Sciences, 1990.

Bowers TL. Nutrition and immunity. Part 1: Overview and influence of macronutrients. Veterinary Clinical Nutrition 1997; 4(2): 45-50.

Bradley J, Xu X. Diet, age and the immune system. Nutrition Reviews 1996; 54: S43-S50.

Burkholder WJ, Swecker WS. Nutritional influences on immunity. Seminars in Veterinary Medicine and Surgery: Small Animal 1990; 5: 154-166.

Halliwell B. Antioxidants and human disease–A general introduction. Nutrition Reviews 1997; 55: S44-S52.

Langseth L. Oxidants, Antioxidants, and Disease Prevention. Washington, DC: ILSI Press, 1995.

Munoz C, Schlesinger L, Cavaillon JM. Interaction between cytokines, nutrition and infection. Nutrition Research 1995; 15: 1815-1844.

Scrimshaw NS, SanGiovanni JP. Synergism of nutrition, infection and immunity: An overview. American Journal of Clinical Nutrition 1997; 66: 464S-477S.

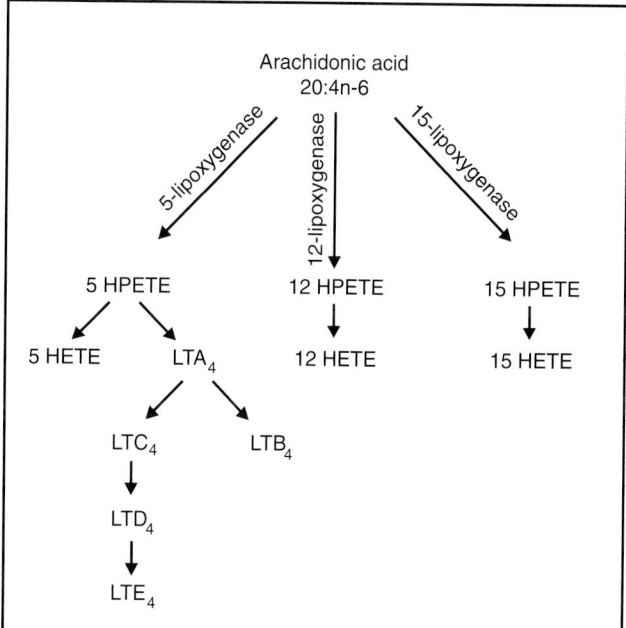

Figure 26-4. Arachidonic acid metabolism by the lipoxygenase pathway. Key: HPETE = hydroperoxyeicosatetraenoic acid, HETE = hydroxyeicosatetraenoic acid, LT = leukotriene.

■ INFLAMMATORY SKIN DISEASE
Clinical Importance

Surveys and textbooks suggest that skin disorders are the most common reason for patient visits to veterinary hospitals.[26] Surveys also indicate that 15 to 25% of all small animal practice activity is involved with the diagnosis and treatment of skin and coat problems.[26]

The most commonly diagnosed canine skin disorders are allergy (flea-bite hypersensitivity, atopy), skin cancer, bacterial pyoderma, seborrhea, parasitic dermatoses, adverse reactions to food (food hypersensitivity or food intolerance), immune-mediated dermatoses and endocrine

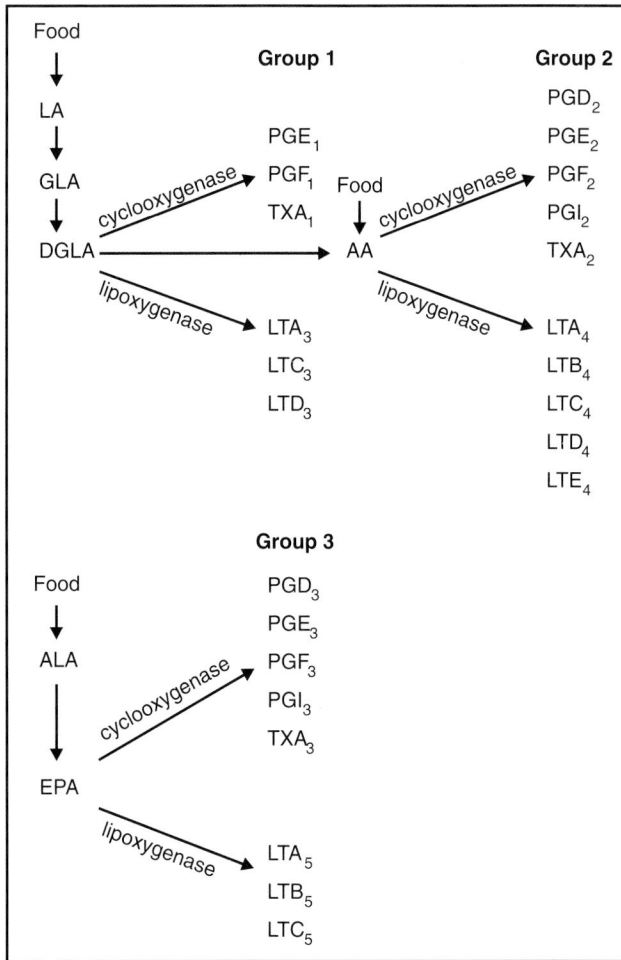

Figure 26-5. Polyunsaturated fatty acid metabolism by the lipoxygenase pathway. Key: LA = linoleic acid, GLA = γ-linolenic acid, DGLA = dihomo-γ-linolenic acid, ALA = α-linolenic acid, EPA = eicosapentaenoic acid, PG = prostaglandin, LT = leukotriene, TX = thromboxane.

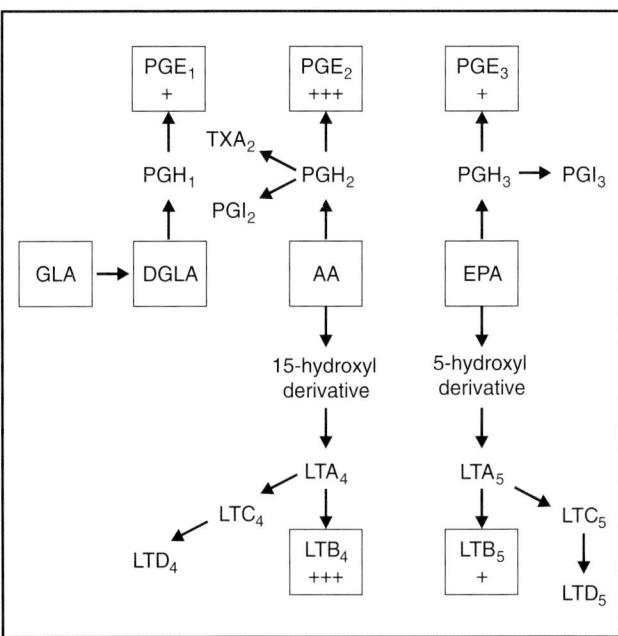

Figure 26-6. Potential effects of n-3 and n-6 PUFAs on inflammation. Key: LA = linoleic acid, GLA = γ-linolenic acid, DGLA = dihomo-γ-linolenic acid, AA = arachidonic acid, EPA = eicosapentaenoic acid, PG = prostaglandin, LT = leukotriene, TX = thromboxane, (+++ = strongly proinflammatory, + = weakly proinflammatory.

dermatoses.[27,28] The most common feline skin disorders are abscesses, parasitic dermatoses, allergy (flea-bite hypersensitivity, atopy), papulocrustous (miliary) dermatitis, eosinophilic granuloma complex, fungal infections, adverse reactions to food, psychogenic dermatoses, seborrheic conditions, neoplastic tumors and immune-mediated dermatoses.[28,29] These data confirm that inflammatory skin diseases, especially allergic dermatoses, are common and important clinical entities.

Assessment

Assess the Animal

HISTORY AND PHYSICAL EXAMINATION

Numerous skin diseases have an inflammatory component. However, dietary fatty acid therapy has been used primarily in patients with allergic skin disease or patients with pruritus or (papulocrustons (miliary) dermatitis for which a specific cause has not been identified.

Pruritus is the most common historical feature of allergic skin disease in dogs and cats. Clinical signs reportedly first occur in most dogs and cats with atopy between six months and three years of age.[26,30] Lesions of canine atopy usually involve the muzzle, periocular region, pinnae and external ear canals, paws, axillae, groin and abdomen. Although the face and paws are most commonly involved, many animals will have generalized pruritus by the time they are examined. Chronic licking, rubbing, chewing or scratching can result in alopecia, lichenification, hyperpigmentation, scaling and excoriation. Other common lesions in atopic dogs include papules and erythematous macules, secondary superficial pyoderma, secondary *Malassezia* dermatitis, chronic otitis externa and seborrhea.

Atopic cats are most commonly described with symmetric alopecia, miliary dermatitis, eosinophilic plaques, indolent ulcer of the lip, pruritus of the head and neck with excoriations or generalized pruritus.[26,31] Atopic cats are pruritic, but many are secretive and groom or traumatize themselves without the owner's knowledge.

Cats with miliary dermatitis have numerous small erythematous papules with adherent brownish crusts and various degrees of alopecia and pruritus.[26,31] These lesions can usually be palpated over the dorsal lumbar and cervical regions long before they are visualized. Feline miliary dermatitis is most commonly a manifestation of flea allergy, but may occur with other ectoparasite infestations, dermatophytosis, bacterial folliculitis, adverse food reactions, atopy, drug eruptions and immune-mediated skin disease.

Canine flea-bite hypersensitivity is characterized by a pruritic, papular dermatitis.[26] Flea bites induce an initial papule that may then form a crust. Chronic pruritus may lead to alopecia, lichenification, severe crusting and hyperpigmentation. Lesions are typically confined to the dorsal lumbosacral area, caudomedial thighs, ventral abdomen and flanks. Pyotraumatic dermatitis ("hot spots"), secondary bacterial pyoderma and secondary seborrhea are common in chronic cases. The presence of otitis externa, severe pedal pruritus or facial pruritus strongly suggests concurrent atopy or adverse food reaction.

There are numerous insects besides fleas and arachnids in the normal dog and cat environment that can stimulate hypersensitivity reactions. Blackfly, deerfly, horsefly, mosquito, red ant, black ant and tick bites may all contribute to allergic skin disease in dogs and cats.[30] The primary clinical sign is pruritus, although an erythematous maculopapular dermatitis may be present.[26] Nodules and papules induced by mosquito bites are usually found on the bridge of the nose and pinnae of cats. Stable flies occasionally induce a granulomatous reaction, producing nodules or plaques and varying degrees of alopecia on the pinnae. Ticks may induce nodules due to granuloma formation at the site of attachment. Acute-onset nasal dermatitis has also been observed in dogs; pruritic papules and nodules are found on the bridge of the nose.

Adverse reactions to food mimic other allergic diseases. The clinical features and management of adverse food reactions are described in detail in Chapter 14.

LABORATORY AND OTHER CLINICAL INFORMATION

Skin biopsy and histopathology can be used to confirm the presence of inflammatory skin disease. Chronic hyperplastic dermatitis is a common histopathologic reaction pattern seen in dogs with chronic allergy.[32] The predominant types of inflammatory cells may suggest the specific allergic disease. However, many chronic dermatoses have similar histopathologic features, making specific diagnosis difficult.

Two methods of allergy testing are available to practitioners. Intradermal testing has been performed for many years. More recently, in vitro tests for detection of allergen-specific IgE have become commercially available.

Intradermal testing is the most widely accepted method for making a definitive diagnosis of canine atopic disease and for selecting allergens for hyposensitization.[26,30] Intradermal allergy tests detect the presence of allergen-specific IgE fixed to the surface of mast cells in the dermis, as well as assess the ability of IgE to fix allergen and cause mast cell degranulation and subsequent vasodilatation. In a well-controlled study using allergen mixes, 59% of dogs responded to hyposensitization that was formulated on the basis of intradermal testing results.[33]

Intradermal allergy testing has several disadvantages. Negative intradermal results occur in some dogs strongly suspected to have atopy. Antiinflammatory and antihistamine drugs must be withdrawn before testing to prevent false-negative results. The test cannot be performed on dogs with generalized dermatitis. Shaving of the coat and sedation are usually required. Intradermal allergy testing is time-consuming and not cost-effective when performed infrequently. Most intradermal testing is performed at dermatologic referral centers because of these disadvantages. Intradermal testing for food hypersensitivity is unreliable in animals with dermatologic disease. (See Chapter 14.)

In vitro allergy tests measure serum concentrations of allergen-specific IgE and avoid many of the disadvantages of intradermal allergy tests.[34] In vitro allergy tests require only a serum sample; so they are readily available to private practitioners and can be used on animals with generalized dermatitis. Laboratories use several different techniques to detect circulating IgE levels, including a radioallergosorbent test (RAST), enzyme-linked immunosorbent assay (ELISA) or liquid-phase enzyme immunoassay (EIA). Problems with in vitro testing include poor reproducibility and a high false-positive rate.[35] Preliminary results suggest that more than 60% of atopic dogs respond

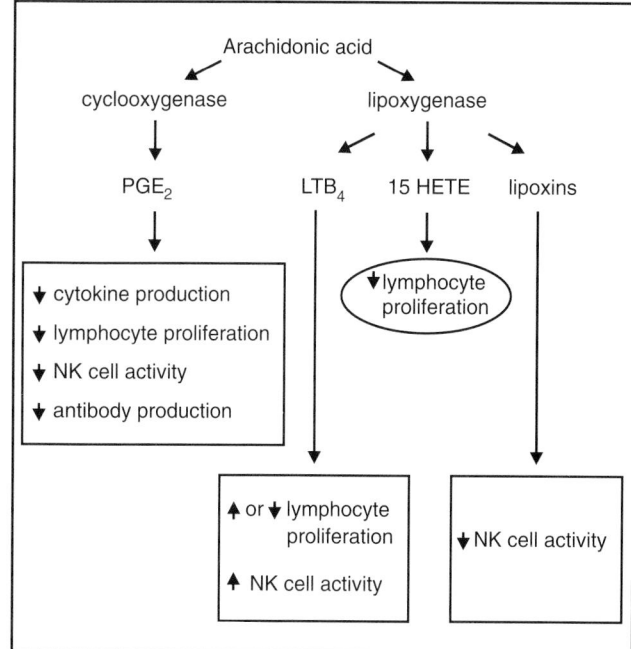

Figure 26-7. Regulation of immune cell function by arachidonic acid-derived eicosanoids. Key: PG = prostaglandin, LT = leukotriene, HETE = hydroxyeicosatetraenoic acid, NK = natural killer.

to hyposensitization formulated on the basis of in vitro results.[36,37] In vitro testing is also available for confirmation of flea-allergic dermatitis[38] but is unreliable for diagnosis of food hypersensitivity. (See Chapter 14.)

Controversy continues over whether intradermal or in vitro testing is the better method for confirming a diagnosis of atopy and for selecting allergens for hyposensitization. Further, long-term studies are needed to evaluate responses of allergic animals to hyposensitization based on both types of testing.

RISK FACTORS

Atopy is an inherited predisposition to the development of IgE antibodies to environmental allergens, resulting in allergic disease. Although the exact mode of inheritance is unknown, strong breed predilection and familial involvement in dogs indicate a genetically determined cause. Canine breeds reported to be predisposed to atopy include the Cairn terrier, West Highland white terrier, Scottish terrier, wire-haired fox terrier, Boston terrier, Sealyham terrier, Lhasa apso, Dalmatian, pug, Irish setter, English setter, golden retriever, Labrador retriever, boxer, miniature schnauzer, English bulldog, Bichon Frise, Chinese Shar-Pei, Shih Tzu, German shepherd dog, Belgian Tervuren, beauceron and cocker spaniel.[26,30,36] However, canine atopy may be seen in any breed, including mixed breeds. Breed predisposition has not been reported for atopic cats.[26]

Hypersensitivity requires environmental exposure to flea, other biting insect or arachnid allergens. Depending on the offending allergen, these cases may be seasonal in temperate climates; worse clinical signs occur during warm weather. The onset of clinical signs may be historically correlated with an increase in insect or arachnid numbers in the environment.

USE OF FATTY ACIDS AS ANTIPRURITIC AGENTS

The use of fatty acids as antipruritic agents in dogs and cats has been the subject of numerous studies and considerable debate. The inflammation and dermatitis associated with allergic skin disease may be partially caused by abnormal essential fatty acid metabolism and inappropriate eicosanoid synthesis.[39] A unique feature of skin is that it lacks Δ-6- and Δ-5-desaturase enzyme activity, and thus is incapable of making AA from LA or EPA from ALA (Figure 26-2).[40] Skin can elongate GLA to DGLA and EPA to DHA. Normal dogs metabolize dietary sources of ALA to EPA and DHA elsewhere in the body. These fatty acids are then incorporated into the skin.[41]

DGLA, EPA and DHA in cutaneous cellular membranes may decrease inflammation through competition with AA for metabolic enzymes or because of the antiinflammatory nature of the eicosanoids produced.[39] The rationale for specifically administering products high in GLA is that GLA can be incorporated into the skin, where it is rapidly elongated to DGLA. Because skin lacks desaturase enzymes, DGLA is not further metabolized to arachidonic acid. As a result, DGLA competes with AA for metabolic enzymes. Thus there is a decrease in AA-derived eicosanoids and an increase in the antiinflammatory eicosanoids PGE_1 via the cyclooxygenase cascade and 15-HETE via the lipoxygenase pathway.

ALA is an n-3 PUFA that is metabolized to EPA and DHA, and incorporated into the skin of normal dogs.[41] Findings suggest that atopic dermatitis in human beings is associated with a deficiency of Δ-6-desaturase activity, which prevents the rapid conversion of ALA to EPA and DHA in atopic individuals.[42,43] Comparable studies using atopic dogs and cats have not been published. However, one study suggested that subsets of atopic dogs exist with different fatty acid metabolic capabilities.[44]

The use of fatty acids for treating atopy and chronic pruritus has been extensively studied in dogs.[44-58] Unfortunately, most of these studies have been uncontrolled, nonblinded clinical trials using low doses of fatty acids for short periods (Table 26-1). In these studies, 0 to more than 75% of pruritic animals had degrees of clinical improvement. The three, well-controlled clinical studies using placebos and high doses of fatty acids for six weeks or more showed decreased pruritus in 0 to more than 50% of the patients.[54,56,57] Dogs that did not have decreased pruritus still showed improvement in other clinical signs, including less erythroderma and skin edema. The benefit of fatty acid supplementation is maximized in dogs if other contributing diseases such as adverse reactions to food, flea hypersensitivity, bacterial pyoderma and *Malassezia* dermatitis are controlled. Overall, it is probably safe to inform clients that up to 50% of dogs with allergic pruritus will improve with modification in fatty acid intake, if secondary bacterial and yeast infections are controlled. Synergistic effects have been documented between fatty acids and other antipruritic agents such as antihistamines and glucocorticoids.[26,49,51]

The use of fatty acids for management of allergic skin disease and papulocrustous (miliary) dermatitis in cats has been reported.[59-62] More than 50% of allergic cats may improve, based on the results of uncontrolled, nonblinded clinical trials published to date (Table 26-1).

ARTHRITIS

The term arthritis has been used in a broad sense to cover a number of well-defined pathologic entities, but, defined simply, it is inflammation of a joint. Arthritis is classified into two broad categories for clinical diagnosis: 1) the degenerative types of arthritis, in which degradation of the articular cartilage is a prominent feature and 2) the inflammatory arthropathies, in which an obvious synovitis is the main pathologic feature.[63]

Osteoarthritis is the most common form of arthritis recognized in people and most veterinary species.[64,65] It gener-

Table 26-1. Summary of clinical studies using fatty acid supplementation in dogs and cats with dermatologic disease.

Reference number	Number of animals	Type of trial	Duration of therapy	Control of pruritus (%)*	Control of clinical signs**
Dogs with pruritus					
44	18	Open	8 weeks	48	
45	45	Open	7 days	22	
46	93	Open	NR	35	
47	10	Open	9 weeks	0	+
48	33	Open	NR	94	
49	43	Open	7 days	0	
50	28	Open	12 weeks	NR	+
51	30	Open	14 days	27	
52	20	DB	14 days	25	
53	23	Open	14 days	22	
54	35	DBPC	9 weeks	0	+
55	21	DB	8 weeks	76	+
56	10	DBPC	8 weeks	0	+
57	16	DBPC	6 weeks	56	+
58	28	Open	8 weeks	50	
Cats with skin disease					
59	8	Open	6 weeks	75	+
60	11	Open	12 weeks	100	+
61	14	Open	12 weeks	78	+
62	28	Open	6 weeks	57	

Key: NR = not reported, DB = double blind, DBPC = double blind, placebo controlled, Open = nonblinded.
*Percentage of animals in which good to excellent pruritus control was reported.
**A + symbol indicates that improvement in clinical signs other than pruritus was noted (e.g., less erythroderma, less edema).

ally is a slowly progressive disease, and is characterized by two main pathologic processes: degeneration of articular cartilage, with loss of proteoglycan and collagen, and proliferation of new bone. In addition, a variable inflammatory response occurs within the synovial membrane.[63]

Inflammatory arthropathies are classified as infective, immune-based or crystal-induced.[63] The most common category of the noninfective inflammatory arthritides in people and dogs is immune-based. Of these, rheumatoid arthritis is the most prevalent form. Rheumatoid arthritis is an immune-based arthritis characterized by chronic inflammation and synovitis associated with distortion of normal tissue architecture, degradation of the extracellular matrix and inadequate repair.

Clinical Importance

Arthritis (osteoarthritis) is the most common form of joint and musculoskeletal disease affecting dogs but is relatively uncommon in cats. Preliminary results of the National Companion Animal Study (40,000 dogs) revealed that arthritis was the eighth most common diagnosis in dogs seven to 10 years old and the fourth most common diagnosis in dogs more than 10 years old.[66] Arthritis was clinically evident in 3% of all dogs over 10 years old. The prevalence of osteoarthritis in pets is likely to increase with increasing life spans.

Assessment

Assess the Animal

HISTORY AND PHYSICAL EXAMINATION

Osteoarthritis is characterized by the gradual development of joint pain, stiffness and limitation of motion. Clinical signs may be exacerbated by exercise, obesity, long periods of recumbency and cold, damp weather. Dogs may have a history of joint trauma (fracture, luxation, ligament injury) or developmental disorders (patellar luxation, fragmented coronoid process, hip dysplasia, osteochondrosis, etc.).

The earliest sign noted by the owner is a loss of normal performance, often manifested as a pet's reluctance to jump or climb stairs.[63] Temporary stiffness after rest is also an early sign of joint disease and is frequently present in osteoarthritis before the onset of overt lameness. Only in advanced cases of osteoarthritis is stiffness a problem for prolonged periods of time. Stiffness is invariably accompanied by obvious lameness. Other clinical signs of arthritis include reduced range of motion, crepitus, joint swelling, joint instability and pain.

LABORATORY AND OTHER CLINICAL INFORMATION

Radiography remains the primary diagnostic modality for suspected cases of osteoarthritis. Radiographic changes may be seen in soft and mineralized tissues. In early osteoarthritis, radiographic changes may be minimal or absent. The earliest radiographic sign of osteoarthritis is usually increased periarticular soft tissue opacity associated with synovial effusion. New bone, in the form of periarticular osteophytes, becomes radiographically apparent within a few weeks of the onset of osteoarthritis. New bone may be deposited in the subchondral region (subchondral sclerosis) and appears as an increased radiopacity of the subchondral bone. Table 26-2 lists other radiographic features of osteoarthritis. A radiographic diagnosis of osteoarthritis should be based on full consideration of all these features.

Table 26-2. Radiographic features of arthritis.

Synovial effusion and periarticular soft tissue swelling
Osteophyte formation
Subchondral bone sclerosis
Attrition of subchondral bone
Bone remodeling
Reduction in joint space
Subluxation
Intraarticular and periarticular soft tissue mineralization
Subchondral cyst formation

Arthrocentesis and synovial fluid analysis can be used to support a diagnosis of degenerative joint disease. A slightly higher number of mononuclear cells is seen, generally fewer than 2,000 cells/ml. Large numbers of neutrophils are likely due to underlying immune-mediated or infectious arthritis. Synovial fluid can be submitted for bacterial culture and antimicrobial sensitivity testing. Biopsy of synovial tissue is helpful in ruling out other arthritides and neoplasia.

Coombs, antinuclear antibody (ANA) and rheumatoid factor tests help rule out immune-mediated disease whereas serum titers help rule out borreliosis, ehrlichiosis and other rickettsial infections.

RISK FACTORS

Working dogs, athletic dogs and obese animals place more stress on their joints and are more likely to incur injury (fracture, luxation, ligament injury) and degenerative joint disease. Some dogs are at risk for developmental orthopedic diseases (hip dysplasia, osteochondrosis) that cause arthritis. (See Chapter 17.) Infective arthritis (bacterial, spirochetal, rickettsial, protozoal, fungal) and immune-based arthritides (rheumatoid, systemic lupus erythematosus, idiopathic polyarthritis) may mimic degenerative joint disease and carry their own set of risk factors.

USE OF FATTY ACIDS FOR ARTHRITIS

In most inflammatory arthritides, prostaglandins are the active agent involved in the inflammation process. Diverting prostaglandin production from the inflammatory 2-series (PGE$_2$) to the less inflammatory 1- or 3-series (PGE$_1$ or PGE$_3$) may benefit patients (e.g., reduce inflammation and joint stiffness). Dietary manipulation of n-6 and n-3 fatty acids to abate production of certain prostaglandins in the inflammatory process has been evaluated in people with rheumatoid arthritis, but there has been little research reported on the use of these fatty acids in companion animals.

A consistent response to dietary fatty acid manipulation has been observed in studies of people with rheumatoid arthritis. Numerous well-designed clinical studies evaluating dietary supplementation with n-3 and n-6 PUFA have been conducted. The anticipated antiinflammatory effects were accompanied by reduced active synovitis in most trials. Table 26-3 summarizes major studies in various species.[67-86]

In 16 of the 20 trials reported in Table 26-3, a positive response was found in those patients or animals whose diet was supplemented with GLA, EPA or DHA. The degree of positive response varied based on the length of treatment, dosage, number of patients or animals and severity of disease. The only study with negative results was an early rat study[70] in which animals had an increased incidence of collagen-induced arthritis when fed a food supplemented with fish oil. Overall, arthritic animals treated with various fatty acid regimens improved clinically.

The most encouraging studies have been conducted in the last few years.[83-86] In these long-term (six months to one year), double-blind, controlled studies, human patients were given various fish oil or EPA/DHA regimens in addition to physician-prescribed nonsteroidal antiinflammatory drugs. In each trial, patients receiving the fish oil or EPA/DHA regimens were able to reduce or discontinue drug usage without experiencing pain or joint stiffness. Patient-assessed and physician-assessed pain scores were reduced for the fish oil or EPA/DHA treatment groups when compared with the control groups. The ability of patients to reduce or discontinue drug usage appeared to be related to fish oil or EPA/DHA dosage and length of treatment.

Many problems remain to be solved before these dietary supplements can be recommended as standard treatment for arthritides in dogs or cats. The only canine study[81] was a compilation of observations of dog owners who perceived improvement in their pets' arthritic clinical signs when their dogs were treated with fatty acids for various dermatologic problems. In this preliminary study, 13 of 22 dogs with chronic, intercurrent hip arthritis had noticeable improvement in clinical signs of arthritis during treatment with a fatty acid supplement for a two-week period. Though encouraging, better controlled studies in dogs with more objective measures of improvement need to be considered to validate the findings of this experiment and to confirm the results from the human tests.

Assess the Food(s)

Patients with dermatitis or arthritis may benefit from changes in dietary fatty acid intake. The most common modification is to increase n-3 fatty acid intake and/or increase intake of GLA, an n-6 fatty acid. Table 26-4 lists typical pet food ingredients and supplements with their associated fatty acids.

Fatty acid levels in the overall diet can be modified by changing the food(s), adding a supplement or doing both. Initially, the essential fatty acid levels in the current food(s) should be assessed. Unfortunately, information about fatty acid concentrations in commercial pet foods is difficult to obtain. This information is not typically found in guaranteed or typical analysis statements on pet food labels and is often not published by the manufacturer. The manufacturer should be contacted directly to obtain information about fatty acid concentrations in specific products. Table 26-5 contains information about fatty acid concentrations in selected commercial dog foods. Comparable data for cat foods are lacking.

If the animal is given a supplement, the fatty acid concentrations in the supplement should also be determined. Most supplements marketed to improve in skin and coat list the fatty acid concentrations on the product label or in published technical information. Table 26-5 contains information about fatty acid concentrations in selected commercial fatty acid supplements.

In many cases, fatty acid supplements contain much lower concentrations of fatty acids than concentrations already found in the food(s) being consumed by the animal (Table 26-5). Thus, it may be more appropriate and convenient to change the animal's food to one with higher concentrations of appropriate fatty acids rather than adding a fatty acid supplement to the animal's current food. In some cases, changing the food(s) and simultaneously adding a fatty acid supplement may be appropriate.

It is important to remember that the optimal concentrations and ratios of fatty acids have not been established for normal animals or dogs and cats with clinical disease. Trial and error with various food and supplement combinations may be needed in an individual animal to achieve the best clinical response.

Other nutrients such as zinc, magnesium, biotin, pyridoxine, vitamin E and vitamin C are important cofactors in fatty acid metabolic pathways. Most commercial pet foods have adequate levels of these nutrients; routine supplementation would not be expected to improve clinical response. Many fatty acid supplements contain additional amounts of these cofactor nutrients.

Assess the Feeding Method

It may not always be necessary to change the feeding method when managing a patient with dermatitis or

Table 26-3. Summary of studies using fatty acid treatment for arthritis.

Reference number	Number of subjects	Species	Type of arthritis	Duration of therapy	Improvement in arthritis
67	NR	Rat	AAM	6 weeks	Yes
68	20	Human beings	RA	12 weeks	No
69	10	Human beings	RA	3 weeks	No
70	NR	Rat	CIAM	6 weeks	No
71	NR	Mouse	CIAM	9 weeks	Yes
72	37	Human beings	RA	12 weeks	Yes
73	40	Human beings	RA	14 weeks	Yes
74	12	Human beings	RA	6 weeks	Yes
75	15	Human beings	RA	18 months	Yes
76	23	Human beings	RA	12 weeks	Yes
77	9	Human beings	RA	12 weeks	No
78	32	Human beings	RA	6 months	Yes
79	67	Human beings	RA	16 weeks	Yes
80	43	Human beings	RA	6 months	Yes
81	25	Dog	NR	2 weeks	Yes
82	51	Human beings	RA	12 weeks	Yes
83	90	Human beings	RA	52 weeks	Yes
84	64	Human beings	RA	52 weeks	Yes
85	90	Human beings	RA	52 weeks	Yes
86	66	Human beings	RA	30 weeks	Yes

Key: NR = not reported, AAM = adjuvant arthritis model, RA = rheumatoid arthritis, CIAM = collagen-induced arthritis model..

arthritis, but a thorough assessment includes verification that an appropriate feeding method is being used. Items to consider include feeding route, amount fed, how the food is offered, access to other food and who feeds the animal. All of this information should have been gathered when the history of the animal was obtained. If the animal has a normal body condition score (3/5), the amount of food previously fed (energy basis) was probably appropriate.

and/or fish oil as major ingredients. Dietary GLA concentrations can be increased by using a supplement with evening primrose, borage or black currant oil. Most com-

Table 26-4. Fatty acids found in pet food ingredients and supplements.

Fatty acids	Ingredient/supplement
Linoleic acid (n-6)	Vegetable oils (soy oil, corn oil, safflower oil, canola oil, etc.)
	Grains (corn, soybeans)
Gamma-linolenic acid (GLA, n-6)	Black currant oil
	Borage oil
	Evening primrose oil
Alpha-linolenic acid (ALA, n-3)	Flax
	Flax (linseed) oil
Eicosatetraenoic acid (EPA, n-3)	Fish meal
	Cold water marine oils
Docosahexaenoic acid (DHA, n-3)	Fish meal
	Cold water marine oils

FEEDING PLAN

Select a Food or Supplement

Dietary n-3 fatty acid concentrations can be increased by using a supplement (usually a cold water marine oil) or changing to food(s) that contains flaxseed, fish meal

Table 26-5. The total essential fatty acid intake for a 10-kg dog eating 600 kcal (2,510 kJ) per day of selected commercial foods or being given one of the selected supplements.*

Foods	Food consumed (g)	Total n-6 consumed (mg)	Total n-3 consumed (mg)**
Hill's Science Diet Canine Maintenance, dry	155	5,179	529
Hill's Science Diet Canine Light, dry	216	7,488	777
Hill's Science Diet Canine Senior, dry	169	5,662	575
Hill's Science Diet Canine Maintenance Lamb Meal & Rice, dry	154	5,081	798
Hill's Science Diet Canine Active, dry	130	6,760	650
Hill's Prescription Diet Canine d/d Rice & Egg, dry	148	5,039	563
Hill's Prescription Diet Canine d/d Rice & Salmon, dry	150	4,050	1,350
Hill's Prescription Diet Canine d/d Rice & Duck, dry	164	5,576	656
Hill's Prescription Diet Canine d/d Lamb & Rice, moist	432	2,633	647
Hill's Prescription Diet Canine d/d Whitefish & Rice, moist	542	5,962	1,030
Hill's Prescription Diet Canine/Feline a/d, moist	472	6,230	2,832
Iams Eukanuba Response Formula, dry	147	2,353	441
Iams Eukanuba Response Formula, moist	476	9,381	1,285
Iams Eukanuba Nutritional Recovery, dry	129	5,418	1,058
Iams Eukanuba Nutritional Recovery, moist	300	6,690	810
Iams Puppy, dry	140	4,900	280
Iams Less Active, dry	171	4,446	342
NutroMax, dry	140	5,460	280
NutroMax Special, dry	158	3,634	158
Purina Dog Chow, dry	158	3,160	158
Purina Puppy Chow, dry	158	2,844	158
Purina Fit 'N Trim, dry	182	3,002	182
Purina HiPro, dry	158	3,160	158
Purina ProPlan Reduced Calorie, dry	182	3,640	182
Purina CNM LA-Formula dry	166	1,680	1,680
Supplements			
DermCaps Regular	1 capsule	402	42
DermCaps ES	1 capsule	368	125
DermCaps 100s	1 capsule	402	252
DermCaps Liquid	1 ml	621	65
DermCaps ES Liquid	1 ml	375	130
Dermega III Regular	1 capsule	310	63
Dermega III Extra Strength	1 capsule	412	172
EFA-Caps	1 capsule	10	75
EFA-Caps HP	1 capsule	30	160
EFA-Z Plus	1/4 oz	3,410	83
Palavite	10-g scoop	492	95
Pet-Derm OM Regular	1 capsule	14	135
Pet-Derm OM Extra Strength	1 capsule	28	270
Pet-Derm OM Liquid	2 ml	28	270
Palamega	1 tablet	95	105
3V Caps Skin Formula for Small & Medium Breeds	1 capsule	0	171
3V Caps Skin Formula for Medium & Large Breeds	1 capsule	0	300
3V Caps Skin Formula for Large & Giant Breeds	1 capsule	0	417
3V Caps Skin Formula Liquid	1 ml	0	185

*Adapted from Roudebush P, Bloom PB, Jewell DJ. Consumption of essential fatty acids in selected commercial dog foods compared with dietary supplementation (abstract). In: Proceedings. Annual Members Meeting AAVD & ACVD, Nashville, TN, 1997: 10-11.
**Laboratory and clinical studies in a number of species have established a daily dosage for total n-3 fatty acids that seems to be a reasonable starting point in patients with inflammatory disease. An initial dose of 50 to 250 mg of total n-3 fatty acids/kg body weight/day seems to be effective in a large number of studies.

INFLAMMATORY DISEASE

mercial pet foods already exceed the n-6 essential fatty acid requirement for linoleic acid by using vegetable oil and/or vegetable ingredients in their formula.

It is clear that dietary fatty acid levels well above those needed to avoid fatty acid deficiency benefit some animals with arthritis, allergic skin disease and chronic pruritus. What is less clear are answers to the following questions: 1) which fatty acid or combination of fatty acids is most effective, 2) what ratio of n-6 to n-3 fatty acids is optimal, 3) what absolute amount of n-6 and n-3 fatty acids is appropriate in normal animals and what amount is effective in animals with clinical disease, 4) what levels of other nutrients (vitamins, trace minerals) are needed to allow fatty acid therapy to be effective and 5) what level of total dietary fat is needed to optimize fatty acid metabolism and clinical efficacy.

Although definitive answers to these questions are lacking, laboratory and clinical studies in a number of species have established a daily dosage for total n-3 fatty acids that seems to be a reasonable starting point in patients with inflammatory disease. An initial dose of 50 to 250 mg of total n-3 fatty acids (ALA, EPA and/or DHA) per kg body weight per day seemed to be effective in a large number of studies.[a,b,21,24,57,73,85-90] This total dose can be supplied through a combination of appropriate foods and supplements (Table 26-5). Further studies using dogs and cats should help refine the most effective dose, type, ratio and time periods for fatty acid therapy.

The risks and side effects of high levels of dietary fatty acids are few. Soft feces, overt diarrhea, flatulence and oral malodor ("fishy breath") are most commonly noted at levels of fatty acid supplementation used in most patients. These risks and side effects are outweighed by the possibility that fatty acid supplements will allow practitioners to reduce or eliminate the use of nonsteroidal anti-inflammatory drugs in arthritis cases or discontinue corticosteroid therapy for pruritic dogs and cats. The veterinary community will need to confirm the benefits of fatty acid supplementation for inflammatory diseases in dogs and cats in well-designed, controlled studies.

Determine a Feeding Method

Other than supplementation, the method of feeding is often not altered in the nutritional management of dermatitis or arthritis. If a new food or supplement is fed, the amount to feed can be determined from the product label or other supporting materials. The food dosage may need to be changed if the caloric density of the new food differs from that of the previous food. The food dosage is usually divided into two or more meals per day. The food dosage and feeding method should be altered if the animal's body weight and condition are not optimal.

For clinical nutrition to be effective, there needs to be good client compliance. Enabling compliance includes limiting the patient's access to other foods and knowing who feeds the animal. If the animal comes from a multiple-pet household, it should be determined whether the pet with dermatitis or arthritis has access to the other pets' food.

REASSESSMENT

Fatty acid-responsive diseases usually respond to dietary changes or supplementation over several weeks to several months. Once a dietary change or supplement has been started, the patient should be examined every four weeks for significant improvement in pruritus, skin erythema or lameness. Some patients may not respond for several months or may need concurrent therapy with antihistamines, topical agents (medicated shampoo), corticosteroids or nonsteroidal antiinflammatory agents.

ENDNOTES & REFERENCES

ENDNOTES

a. Logas DB, Veterinary Dermatology Center, Winter Park, FL, USA. Personal communication. September 1997.

b. Schoenherr WD. Unpublished data. September 1997.

REFERENCES

1. Singer SJ, Nicholson GL. The fluid mosaic model of the structure of cell membranes. Science 1972; 175: 720-731.

2. Adams DA, Freauff SJ, Erickson KL. Biophysical characterization of dietary lipid influences on lymphocytes. In: Kabana J, ed. Pharmacological Role of Lipids, vol. 2. Champaign, IL: American Oil Chemists Society, 1985.

3. Johnson M, Carey F, McMillan RM. Alternative pathways of arachidonate metabolism: Prostaglandins, thromboxane and leukotrienes. In: Campbell PN, Marshall RD, eds. Essays in Biochemistry. New York, NY: Academic Press Inc, 1983; 40-141.

4. Sigal E. The molecular biology of mammalian arachidonic acid metabolism. American Journal of Physiology 1991; 260: L13-L28.

5. Sumida C, Graber R, Nunez E. Role of fatty acids in signal transduction: Modulators and messengers. Prostaglandins, Leukotrienes and Essential Fatty Acids 1993; 48: 117-122.

6. Lands WEM. N-3 fatty acids as precursors for active metabolic substances: Dissonance between expected and observed events. Journal of Experimental Medicine 1989; 225: 1-20.

7. Lokesh BR, German JB, Kinsella JE. Differential effect of docosahexaenoic acid and eicosapentaenoic acid on suppression of lipoxygenase pathway in peritoneal macrophages. Biochimica et Biophysica Acta 1988; 958: 99-107.

8. Lokesh BR, Kinsella JE. Modulation of prostaglandin synthesis in mouse peritoneal macrophages by enrichment of lipids with either eicosapentaenoic or docosahexaenoic acids in vitro. Immunobiology 1987; 175: 406-419.

9. Broughton KS, Whelan J, Hardardottir I, et al. Effect of increasing the dietary (n-3) to (n-6) polyunsaturated fatty acid ratio on murine liver and peritoneal cell fatty acids and eicosanoid formation. Journal of Nutrition 1991; 121: 155-164.

10. Croft LD, Beilin LJ, Legge FM, et al. Effects of diet enriched in eicosapentaenoic or docosapentaenoic acids on prostanoid metabolism in the rat. Lipids 1987; 22: 647-650.

11. Horrobin DF, Manku MS. Clinical biochemistry of essential fatty acids. In: Horrobin DF, ed. Omega-6 essential fatty acids: Pathophysiology and roles in clinical medicine. New York, NY: Alan R Liss, 1990; 21-53.

12. Manku MS, Morse-Fisher N, Horrobin DF. Changes in human plasma essential fatty acid levels as a result of administration of linoleic acid and gamma-linoleic acid. European Journal of Clinical Nutrition 1988; 42: 55-60.

13. Meydani SN, Endres S, Woods MM, et al. Oral (n-3) fatty acid supplementation suppresses cytokine production and lymphocyte proliferation: Comparison between young and older women. Journal of Nutrition 1991; 121: 547-555.

14. Hwang D. Essential fatty acids and the immune response. Federation of American Societies for Experimental Biology Journal 1989; 3: 2052-2061.

15. Magrum LJ, Johnston PV. Modulation of prostaglandin synthesis in rat peritoneal macrophages with omega-3 fatty acids. Lipids 1983; 18: 514-521.

16. Lokesh BR, Black JM, German JB, et al. Docosahexaenoic acid and other dietary omega-3 polyunsaturated fatty acids suppress leukotriene synthesis by mouse peritoneal macrophages. Lipids 1988; 23: 968-972.

17. Stossel TP, Mason RJ, Smith AL. Lipid peroxidation by human blood phagocytes. Journal of Clinical Investigation 1974; 54: 638-645.

18. Goodwin JS, Ceuppens J. Regulation of the immune response by prostaglandins. Journal of Clinical Immunology 1983; 3: 295-315.

19. Calder PC. Effects of fatty acids and dietary lipids on cells of the immune system. Proceedings of the Nutrition Society 1996; 55: 127-150.

20. Calder PC, Bond JA, Harvey DJ, et al. Uptake of saturated and unsaturated fatty acids into macrophage lipids and their effect upon macrophage adhesion and phagocytosis. Biochemical Journal 1990; 269: 807-814.

21. Endres S, Ghorbani R, Kelley EV, et al. The effect of dietary supplementation with n-3 polyunsaturated fatty acids on the synthesis of interleukin-1 and tumor necrosis factor by mononuclear cells. New England Journal of Medicine 1989; 320: 265-271.

22. Endres S, Meydani SN, Ghorbani R, et al. Dietary supplementation with n-3 fatty acids suppresses interleukin-2 production and mononuclear cell proliferation. Journal of Leukocyte Biology 1993; 54: 599-603.

23. Baldie G, Kaimakamis D, Rotondo D. Fatty acid modulation of cytokine release from human monocytic cells. Biochimica et Biophysica Acta 1993; 1179: 125-133.

24. Lee TH, Hoover RL, Williams JD, et al. Dietary enrichment with eicosapentaenoic and docosahexaenoic acids in human subjects impairs in vitro neutrophil and monocyte function and leukotriene generation. New England Journal of Medicine 1985; 312: 1217-1224.

25. Watson J, Madhok R, Wijelath E, et al. Mechanism of action of polyunsaturated fatty acids in rheumatoid arthritis. Biochemical Society Transactions 1990; 18: 284-285.

26. Scott DW, Miller WH, Griffin CE. Small Animal Dermatology, 5th ed. Philadelphia, PA: WB Saunders Co, 1995.

27. Sischo WM, Ihrke PJ, Franti CE. Regional distribution of 10 common skin diseases in dogs. Journal of the American Veterinary Medical Association 1989; 195: 752-756.

28. Scott DW, Paradis M. A survey of canine and feline skin disorders seen in a university practice. Canadian Veterinary Journal 1990; 31: 830-835.

29. Nesbitt GH. Incidence of feline skin disease: A survey. In: Proceedings. Annual Members Meeting AAVD & ACVD, Las Vegas, NV, 1982.

30. Griffin CE, Kwochka KW, MacDonald JM, eds. Current Veterinary Dermatology. St Louis, MO: Mosby-Year Book, 1993.

31. Sousa CA. Exudative, crusting and scaling dermatoses. Veterinary Clinics of North America: Small Animal Practice 1995; 25: 813-832.

32. Gross TL, Ihrke PJ, Walder EJ, eds. Veterinary Dermatopathology. St Louis, MO: Mosby-Year Book, 1992; 68-70.

33. Willemse A, Van den Brom WE, Rijnberk A. Effect of hyposensitization on atopic dermatitis in dogs. Journal of the American Veterinary Medical Association 1984; 184: 1277-1280.

34. Codner EC, Griffin CE. Serologic allergy testing for dogs. Compendium on Continuing Education for the Practicing Veterinarian 1996; 18: 237-248.

35. Codner EC, Lessard P. Comparison of intradermal allergy test and enzyme-linked immunosorbent assay in dogs with allergic skin disease. Journal of the American Veterinary Medical Association 1993; 202: 739-743.

36. Anderson RK. The diagnosis of atopic disease—Intradermal or in vitro testing? Journal of Veterinary Allergy and Immunology 1993; 1: 23-28.

37. Sousa CA, Norton AL. Advances in methodology for diagnosis of allergic skin disease. Veterinary Clinics of North America: Small Animal Practice 1990; 20: 1419-1427.

38. Cook CA, Stedman KE, Frank GR, et al. The in vitro diagnosis of flea bite hypersensitivity: Flea saliva vs. whole flea extracts (abstract). In: Proceedings. Third World Congress of Veterinary Dermatology, Edinburgh, Scotland, 1996: 170.

39. White PD. Essential fatty acids: Use in management of canine atopy. Compendium on Continuing Education for the Practicing Veterinarian 1993; 15: 451-457.

40. Campbell KL. Fatty acid supplementation and skin disease. Veterinary Clinics of North America: Small Animal Practice 1990; 20: 1475-1486.

41. Campbell KL, Roudebush P. Effects of four diets on serum and cutaneous fatty acids, transepidermal water losses, skin surface lipids, hydration and condition of the skin and haircoat of dogs (abstract). In: Proceedings. Annual Members Meeting AAVD & ACVD, Santa Fe, NM, 1995: 80-81.

42. Manku MS, Horrobin DF, Morse NL. Reduced levels of prostaglandin precursors in the blood of atopic patients: Defective delta-6-desaturase function as a biochemical basis for atopy. Prostaglandins 1982; 9: 615-628.

43. Manku MS, Horrobin DF, Morse NL. Essential fatty acids in the plasma phospholipids of patients with atopic eczema. British Journal of Dermatology 1984; 110: 643-648.

44. Scott DW, Miller WH, Reinhart GA, et al. Effect of an omega-3/omega-6 fatty acid containing commercial lamb and rice diet on pruritus in atopic dogs: Results of a single-blinded study. Canadian Journal of Veterinary Research 1997; 61: 145-153.

45. Scott DW, Buerger RG. Nonsteroidal anti-inflammatory agents in the management of canine pruritus. Journal of the American Animal Hospital Association 1988; 24: 425-428.

46. Miller WH, Griffin CE, Scott DW, et al. Clinical trial of DVM DermCaps in the treatment of allergic skin disease in dogs: A non-blinded study. Journal of the American Animal Hospital Association 1989; 25: 163-168.

47. Lloyd DH, Thomsett LR. Essential fatty acid supplementation in the treatment of canine atopy: A preliminary study. Veterinary Dermatology 1989; 1: 41-44.

48. Lloyd DH. Essential fatty acids and skin disease. Journal of Small Animal Practice 1989; 30: 207-212.

49. Scott DW, Miller DH. Nonsteroidal management of canine pruritus: Chlorpheniramine and fatty acid supplement (DVM DermCaps) in combination, and the fatty acid supplement at twice the manufacturer's recommended dosage. Cornell Veterinarian 1990; 80: 381-387.

50. Scarff D, Harvey R, McEwan N. A multicentre placebo-controlled practitioner study to investigate the effect of evening primrose oil in canine atopic dermatosis (abstract). In: VonTschnarner C, Halliwell REW, eds. Advances in Veterinary Dermatology, vol. 1, Philadelphia, PA: Bailliere Tindall, 1990; 481.

51. Paradis M, Lemay S, Scott DW. The efficacy of clemastine (Tavist), a fatty acid-containing product (DVM Derm Caps) and the combination of both in the management of canine pruritus. Veterinary Dermatology 1991; 2: 17-20.

52. Scott DW, Miller WH, Decker GA, et al. Comparison of the clinical efficacy of two commercial fatty acid supplements (EfaVet & DVM DermCaps), evening primrose oil and cold water marine fish oil in the management of allergic pruritus in dogs: A double blinded study. Cornell Veterinarian 1992; 82: 319-329.

53. Miller WH, Scott DW, Wellington JR. Investigation on the antipruritic effects of ascorbic acid given alone or in combination with a fatty acid supplement to dogs with allergic skin disease. Canine Practice 1992; 17: 11-13.

54. Scarff DH, Lloyd DH. Double blind, placebo-controlled, crossover study of evening primrose oil in the treatment of canine atopy. Veterinary Record 1992; 131: 97-99.

55. Bond R, Lloyd DH. A double-blind comparison of olive oil and a combination of evening primrose oil and fish oil in the management of canine atopy. Veterinary Record 1992: 131: 558-560.

56. White PD. Effects of gamma linolenic acid supplementation on serum and cutaneous fatty acid profiles and cutaneous eicosanoids in normal and atopic dogs. A double-blind, placebo-controlled, crossover study (abstract). In: Proceedings. Second World Congress of Veterinary Dermatology, Montreal, Canada, 1992: 32-33.

57. Logas D, Kunkle GA. Double-blinded crossover study with marine oil supplementation containing high-dose eicosapentaenoic acid for the treatment of canine pruritic skin disease. Veterinary Dermatology 1994; 5: 99-104.

58. Schick RO, Schick MP, Reinhart GA. Efficacy of an omega-3 fatty acid adjusted diet in pruritic dogs (abstract). In: Proceedings. European Society of Veterinary Dermatology, Barcelona, Spain, 1995: 245.

59. Harvey RG. Management of feline miliary dermatitis by supplementing the diet with essential fatty acids. Veterinary Record 1991; 128: 326-329.

60. Harvey RG. A comparison of evening primrose oil and sunflower oil for the management of papulocrustous dermatitis in cats. Veterinary Record 1993; 133: 571-573.

61. Harvey RG. Effect of varying proportions of evening primrose oil and fish oil on cats with crusting dermatosis (miliary dermatitis). Veterinary Record 1993; 133: 208-211.

62. Miller WH, Scott DW, Wellington JR. Efficacy of DVM Derm Caps/Liquid in the management of allergic and inflammatory dermatoses of the cat. Journal of the American Animal Hospital Association 1993; 29: 37-40.

63. Bennett D, May C. Joint diseases of dogs and cats. In: Ettinger SJ, Feldman EC, eds. Textbook of Veterinary Internal Medicine, 4th ed. Philadelphia, PA: WB Saunders Co, 1995; 2053-2059.

64. Ball J, Sharp J. Osteoarthritis. In: Scott JT, ed. Copeman's Textbook of the Rheumatic Diseases. Edinburgh, Scotland: Churchill Livingstone, 1978; Chapter 25.

65. Rose RJ. The intra-articular use of sodium hyaluronate for the treatment of osteoarthritis in the horse. New Zealand Veterinary Journal 1979; 27: 5-8.

66. Lund E, Armstrong J, Kolar L, et al. Companion animal top ten: Disease prevalence in private practice. In: Proceedings. Fourteenth Veterinary Medical Forum, American College of Veterinary Internal Medicine, San Antonio, TX, 1996: 131.

67. Kunkel SL, Ogawa H, Ward PA, et al. Suppression of chronic inflammation by evening primrose oil. Progress in Lipid Research 1981; 20: 885-888.

68. Hansen TM, Lerche A, Kassis V, et al. Treatment of rheumatoid arthritis with prostaglandin E_1 precursors cis-linoleic acid and gamma-linoleic acid. Scandinavian Journal of Rheumatology 1983; 12: 85-88.

69. Jantti J, Isomaki H, Laitinen O, et al. Linoleic acid treatment in inflammatory arthritis. International Journal of Clinical Pharmacology, Therapy and Toxicology 1983; 23: 89-91.

70. Prickett JD, Trentham DE, Robinson DR. Dietary fish oil augments the induction of arthritis in rats immunized with Type II collagen. Journal of Immunology 1984; 132: 725-729.

71. Leslie CA, Gonnerman WA, Ullman MD, et al. Dietary fish oil modulates macrophage fatty acids and decreases arthritis susceptibility in mice. Journal of Experimental Medicine 1985; 162: 1336-1349.

72. Kremer JM, Michalek AV, Lininger L, et al. Effects of manipulation of dietary fatty acids on clinical manifestations of rheumatoid arthritis. Lancet 1985; 1: 184-187.

73. Kremer JM, Jubiz W, Michalek A, et al. Fish-oil fatty acid supplementation in active rheumatoid arthritis. Annals of Internal Medicine 1987; 106: 497-503.

74. Sperling RI, Weinblatt M, Robin JL, et al. Effects of dietary supplementation with marine fish oil on leukocyte lipid mediator generation and function in rheumatoid arthritis. Arthritis and Rheumatism 1987; 30: 988-997.

75. Belch JJF, Ansell D, Madhok R, et al. Effects of altering dietary essential fatty acids on requirements for non-steroidal anti-inflammatory drugs in patients with rheumatoid arthritis: A double blind placebo controlled study. Annals of the Rheumatic Diseases 1988; 47: 96-104.

76. Cleland LG, French JK, Betts WH, et al. Clinical and biochemical effects of dietary fish oil supplements in rheumatoid arthritis. Journal of Rheumatology 1988; 15: 1471-1475.

77. Jantti J, Nikkari T, Solakivi T, et al. Evening primrose oil in rheumatoid arthritis: Changes in serum lipids and fatty acids. Annals of the Rheumatic Diseases 1989; 48: 124-127.

78. Kremer JM, Lawrence DA, Jubisz W, et al. Dietary fish oil and olive oil supplementation in patients with rheumatoid arthritis; Clinical and immunological effects. Arthritis and Rheumatism 1990; 33: 810-820.

79. van der Tempel H, Tulleken JE, Limbuerg JE, et al. Effects of fish oil supplementation in rheumatoid arthritis. Annals of the Rheumatic Diseases 1990; 49: 76-80.

80. Kjeldsen-Kragh J, Lund JA, Riise T, et al. Dietary omega-3 fatty acid supplementation and naproxen treatment in patients with rheumatoid arthritis. Journal of Rheumatology 1992; 19: 1531-1536.

81. Miller WH, Scott DW, Wellington JR. Treatment of dogs with hip arthritis with a fatty acid supplement. Canine Practice 1992; 17(6): 6-8.

82. Nielsen GL, Faarvang KL, Thomsen BS, et al. The effects of dietary supplementation with n-3 polyunsaturated fatty acids in patients with rheumatoid arthritis: A randomized, double blind trial. European Journal of Clinical Investigation 1992; 22: 687-691.

83. Skoldstam L, Borjesson O, Kjallman A, et al. Effect of six months of fish oil supplementation in stable rheumatoid arthritis. A double blind, controlled study. Scandinavian Journal of Rheumatology 1992; 21: 178-185.

84. Lau CS, Morley KD, Belch JJF. Effects of fish oil supplementation on non-steroidal anti-inflammatory drug requirement in patients with mild rheumatoid arthritis—A double blind placebo controlled study. British Journal of Rheumatology 1993; 32: 982-989.

85. Geusens P, Wouters C, Nijs J, et al. Long-term effects of omega-3 fatty acid supplementation in active rheumatoid arthritis—A 12-month double blind, controlled study. Arthritis and Rheumatism 1994; 37: 824-829.

86. Kremer JM, Lawrence DA, Petrillo GF, et al. Effects of high-dose fish oil on rheumatoid arthritis after stopping nonsteroidal anti-inflammatory drugs. Clinical and immune correlates. Arthritis and Rheumatism 1995; 38: 1107-1114.

87. Hawthorne AB, Daneshmend TK, Hawkey CJ, et al. Treatment of ulcerative colitis with fish oil supplement: A prospective 12 month randomized controlled trial. Gut 1992; 33: 922-928.

88. Vaughn DM, Reinhart GA. Evaluation of dietary n-6 to n-3 fatty acid ratios on leukotriene B synthesis in dog skin and neutrophils. Veterinary Dermatology 1994; 5: 163-173.

89. Lorenz R, Weber PC, Szimnau P, et al. Supplementation with n-3 fatty acids from fish oil in chronic inflammatory bowel disease—A randomized, placebo-controlled, double blinded cross-over trial. Journal of Internal Medicine 1989; Suppl 731: 225-232.

90. Stenson WF, Cort DC, Rodgers J, et al. Dietary supplementation with fish oil in ulcerative colitis. Annals of Internal Medicine 1992; 116: 609-614.

■ CASE 26-1

Pruritus and Seborrhea in a Wire-Haired Fox Terrier

Kevin P. Byrne, DVM
Diplomate ACVD
School of Veterinary Medicine
University of Pennsylvania
Philadelphia, Pennsylvania, USA

Assess the Animal

A four-and-one-half-year-old, castrated male wire-haired fox terrier was examined for a two-year history of pruritus, oily coat and red skin bumps. Initially, the problems had been seasonal (occurring in the summer), but this year they did not clear up during the winter months. The pruritus had been responsive to oral prednisone. Physical examination revealed diffuse mild seborrhea oleosa with moderate erythema and scaling. These lesions were worse on the dorsum. Hypotrichosis with pustules and crusts were also found on the dorsum and in the axillae. Interdigital erythema was also present. The dog weighed 14 kg and had a body condition score of 4/5.

The initial evaluation of these problems included skin scrapings (negative) and interdigital skin cytology (no abnormal findings). Diagnosis was superficial bacterial pyoderma with seborrheic dermatitis and possible underlying allergic disease. Treatment was initiated with an oral antibiotic (cephalexin, 250 mg, t.i.d.), an antiseborrheic/antibacterial shampoo (twice weekly baths), and a six-week dietary elimination trial using a combination of commercial moist and dry therapeutic foods containing venison and potato.[a]

Six weeks later the dog weighed 13.5 kg and the owner reported a 50% improvement in the pruritus. Examination revealed no visible signs of bacterial pyoderma but erythema persisted in the axillary and interdigital areas.

Assess the Foods and Feeding Method

The dog was normally fed a mixture of various dry and moist commercial grocery brand foods supplemented with occasional table foods (rice, potatoes, pasta) and various commercial biscuit snacks. The commercial venison and potato veterinary therapeutic foods were used for six weeks as part of a dietary elimination trial. The owners were instructed not to feed any other commercial foods, table foods or snacks during this trial.

Questions

1. What additional diagnostic tests would be helpful in this patient?
2. What dietary changes may help manage the pruritus and dermatitis in this patient?

Answers and Discussion

1. Underlying allergic disease due to atopy, flea allergy or food allergy could cause the pruritus, dermatitis and seborrhea seen in this patient and predispose the dog to secondary pyoderma. Atopy can be ruled out with intradermal and in vitro allergy testing. There was no evidence of flea infestation. The clinical improvement was probably due to elimination of the superficial bacterial pyoderma.

2. Supplementing the current food with fatty acids or changing to another food with higher fatty acid levels may benefit this patient. Fatty acid therapy alone is rarely successful in controlling moderate to severe pruritus in most patients with skin disease, but may be effective when used concurrently with other therapies. A synergistic effect between fatty acid and antihistamine administration has been documented in some clinical trials involving allergic dogs.

Progress Notes

Intradermal skin testing was positive for a few weed antigens. Blood was drawn for in vitro (ELISA) allergy testing. Positive reactions were found to house dust mites, several trees, several grasses and several weeds, including ragweed. The probable diagnosis was atopy with secondary superficial pyoderma and seborrhea. Treatment was initiated with an antihistamine (hydroxyzine, 25 mg, t.i.d.) and a fatty acid supplement[b] (1 capsule twice daily with food) that delivered 500 mg of eicosapentaenoic acid (EPA) daily in addition to the fatty acids in the food. Bathing with the shampoo was continued.

Eight weeks later the owners reported some improvement in the level of pruritus, but evidence of self-induced alopecia persisted (barbered hairs on the dorsal lumbar region). The skin was also erythematous; salivary staining was evident in these areas. The bathing, fatty acid supplementation and hydroxyzine administration were continued. Hyposensitization injections were started using allergens identified by the ELISA performed two months earlier. The veterinary therapeutic foods were fed until they were gone (about two weeks). At that time, the owner began feeding the dry and moist grocery store brand foods fed previously.

The owner reported significant improvement eight weeks later. There were no areas of visible erythema on the skin, but salivary staining persisted on all four feet. There was mild oiliness and scale accumulation on the dorsum. Bathing, hydroxyzine administration, hyposensitization injections and fatty acid supplementation were continued.

Further Discussion

The optimal dose of n-3 fatty acids and γ-linolenic acid for control of inflammation and pruritus has not been established. The levels of these fatty acids in the grocery brand foods the patient was eating were unknown. The venison and potato veterinary therapeutic foods provided approximately 50 mg of n-3 fatty acids per day to the patient. The supplement provided an additional 500 mg of EPA, which markedly increased total n-3 intake. This dosing level may have been enough additional n-3 fatty acids (36 to 40 mg EPA/kg body weight) to benefit this patient. The clinical improvement was probably attributable to the combination of all therapies used in this dog.

Endnotes

a. IVD Limited Ingredient Diets. Nature's Recipe Pet Foods, Corona, CA, USA.
b. 3V Caps Skin Formula. DVM Pharmaceuticals, Miami, FL, USA.

Bibliography

Scott DW, Miller WH, Griffin CE. Small Animal Dermatology, 5th ed. Philadelphia, PA: WB Saunders Co, 1995; 211-218.

Paradis M, Scott DW. Nonsteroidal therapy for canine and feline pruritus. In: Kirk RW, Bonagura JD, eds. Current Veterinary Therapy XI. Philadelphia, PA: WB Saunders Co, 1992; 563-566.

Roudebush P, Bloom PB, Jewell DJ. Consumption of essential fatty acids in selected commercial dog foods compared to dietary supplementation (abstract). In: Proceedings. Thirteenth Annual Members Meeting AAVD & ACVD, Nashville, TN, 1997: 10-11.

INFLAMMATORY DISEASE

CHAPTER 27

Dietary Effects on Drug Metabolism

Martin J. Fettman
Robert W. Phillips

"Too far East is West."
English proverb

INTRODUCTION

When the effects of veterinary pharmaceuticals are evaluated and standardized doses are determined, researchers typically use relatively healthy, fasted animals that have been maintained on foods with acceptable nutrient balance. However, in clinical settings, animals receiving a drug often have variable food intake or specific nutrient imbalances, or they must be given a drug in conjunction with a meal, or some combination of these factors may be in play. Prior dietary composition and nutritional health may greatly affect drug absorption, distribution, metabolism, efficacy and toxicity (Table 27-1). Concurrent food intake also may markedly affect drug availability and pharmacokinetics (Table 27-2).

Practicing veterinarians must be acquainted with the effects diet can have on drug metabolism in order to anticipate adjustments in the food or drug dose, properly time administration of drugs and allow for changes in the margin for error between efficacy and toxicity of pharmaceutical agents.

GENERAL TYPES OF FOOD AND DRUG INTERACTIONS

Food-drug interactions that occur as a result of the physical form or chemical properties of food may lead to drug binding, precipitation, inactivation or ionization, which alters gastrointestinal (GI) absorption. These interactions may occur in vitro after mixing the drug with food to make administration more convenient, to enhance palatability or to reduce GI irritation. Another concern is adsorption of drugs to synthetic surfaces of the equipment used for nutrient and drug administration (e.g., food containers, feeding syringes, tubing for assisted feeding). Physiochemical interactions may occur in vivo, whereby drug absorption from the GI tract is decreased because of chelation by dietary fiber or minerals, or increased because of favorable changes in ionization or solvent partitioning.

Metabolic Interactions

Both nutrient and non-nutrient substances in foods can alter the metabolism of absorbed drugs. Nutrients are nourishing ingredients of food. Non-nutrient substances are chemicals without metabolic value, including naturally occurring phytochemicals and synthetic chemicals added inadvertently or purposely to food. Protein and energy malnutrition can alter the synthesis of plasma proteins, affecting drug distribution and pharmacokinetics. Individual dietary lipid, carbohydrate, protein, vitamin and mineral levels can effect changes in xenobiotic-metabolizing enzymes, resulting in altered clearance, circulating concentrations and resultant therapeutic efficacy. Naturally occurring non-nutrient food ingredients and added synthetic preservatives may similarly alter pharmacokinetics and apparent drug effectiveness.

Indirect Physiologic Effects

The rate and extent of drug elimination are also affected by changes in blood flow and drug delivery to the principal organs of metabolism for that particular agent. Thus, postprandial alterations in blood flow to the liver may affect drug clearance from the portal and systemic circula-

KEY WORDS & TERMS—DIETARY EFFECTS ON DRUG METABOLISM*

Antacid	Drug toxicity	Non-nutrient
Antioxidant	Enterohepatic cycling	Nutraceutical
Availability	Flavoprotein	Nutrient
Biotransformation	Hydrophilic	Organonitrile
Cholecalciferol	Kwashiorkor	Partitioning
Choleretic	Lipophilic	Pharmaceutical
Cruciferous plants	Lipotrope	Pharmacokinetics
Cytoprotective agents	Macronutrient	Phase I metabolism
Drug absorption	Metabolic phenotype	Phase II metabolism
Drug conjugation	Micronutrient	Phytochemical
Drug distribution	Microsomal mixed-function oxidase	Thyroglobulin
Drug efficacy	system	Xenobiotic
Drug metabolism	Mutagenicity	

*Key words and terms are defined in the Glossary.

KEY POINTS—DIETARY EFFECTS ON DRUG METABOLISM

1. Published drug doses do not account for nutrient-drug interactions.
2. Published drug doses are based on ideal body weight and composition.
3. Physical and chemical interactions between foods and drugs can reduce drug availability.
4. Nutrient and non-nutrient food ingredients can alter rates of drug metabolism.
5. Some foods can be used to facilitate drug administration and absorption.
6. Some nutrients can be used to minimize adverse effects of drugs or to potentiate their action.
7. Analysis of apparent treatment failure should include evaluation of food composition and timing of feeding.
8. Anorexia is the most important diet-related threat to drug efficacy.
9. The risks associated with adverse interactions between diet "supplements" and prescribed drugs usually outweigh their usefulness.
10. Supplementation with specific nutrients by prescription may be indicated to facilitate the actions of certain drugs.
11. Obesity significantly alters the pharmacokinetics of many drugs.
12. Changes in body weight or composition during the course of an illness may alter the pharmacokinetics, efficacy and toxicity of prescribed medications.

tion, and altered blood flow to the kidneys may change the rate of urinary elimination. Likewise, changes in functional morphology or pathology due to specific nutrient deficiencies or excesses can affect drug clearance.

GENERAL EFFECTS OF FOOD AND DRUG INTERACTIONS

Ameliorating Potential Adverse Effects

The composition and volume of food consumed can modify the degree of GI irritation caused by concurrently administered oral drugs. Enteral and parenteral fluid intake can augment drug absorption and distribution and protect against renal damage induced by nephrotoxic agents. Supplementation with specific nutrients may prevent deficiencies secondary to adverse drug effects on nutrient absorption and metabolism.

Potentiating Drug Action

Specific nutrients can increase drug effects by facilitating GI absorption, improving drug distribution or decreasing drug metabolism and excretion. Further, some nutrients

may be necessary for optimal drug effects (e.g., arginine for nitric oxide production, cysteine for nitroglycerin action and carnitine for optimal activity of cardiac glycosides).

Impaired Drug Action

Impaired drug action is the adverse effect most often considered when evaluating nutrient-drug interactions that impair therapeutic efficacy. These adverse effects may result from inadequate amounts of the drug reaching the site of action, or nutrient interference with the drug's action. Drug action may be impaired for variable periods of time after food composition and feeding behavior are altered, if target cell receptor numbers or affinity are suppressed or long-lived biotransforming enzyme systems have been induced.

Adverse Side Effects

Pathologic reactions to nutrient-induced changes in drug distribution and metabolism can be of greater immediate consequence than loss of disease control following impaired drug action. Drug metabolism and excretion routes may be altered, resulting in accumulation of toxic quantities of the agent itself or the products of its biotransformation. This phenomenon is similar in principle to adverse interactions between concurrently administered drugs, but may be more difficult to identify because mental recollection and written records of nutrient intake are not usually as complete as for administration of pharmaceutical agents.

EFFECTS OF NUTRIENTS ON DRUG ABSORPTION

General Observations

The absorption of orally administered drugs may be: 1) decreased, 2) delayed, 3) unaffected or 4) enhanced by the concomitant consumption of food (Figure 27-1 and Tables 27-2 to 27-4). This interaction depends on the physical and chemical nature of the food and the drug, including such things as meal size and type, the formulation in which the drug is administered, the order in which the food and drug are ingested and the interval between their consumption.[1]

Any food can reduce drug absorption by creating a barrier that prevents dispersion of the drug and dissolution of the active agent in GI luminal contents. Drugs are better absorbed in dilute vs. concentrated solution because of greater dissolution and more rapid gastric emptying. In people, absorption of erythromycin stearate is reduced by approximately one-half when taken with food or a small fluid volume, as compared with a large fluid volume.[2] Absorption of acetylsalicylic acid (aspirin), cephalexin, metronidazole, digoxin, hydralazine and cimetidine are similarly affected.[2]

Alternatively, food does not affect absorption of other drugs in people, including erythromycin estolate, oxazepam, propylthiouracil and enteric-coated aspirin granules in caplet form.[2] In fact, food enhances the absorption of certain drugs (e.g., erythromycin ethylsuccinate, nitrofurantoin, hydrochlorothiazide and diazepam).[2] The rate and quantity of drug and nutrient delivery are important, as evidenced by studies of hydralazine absorption. A bolus of nutrients impairs hydralazine uptake whereas a constant infusion over several hours does not.[3] Total hydralazine absorption, however, is similar in both cases, although absorption is delayed by a bolus meal.

Studies of penicillin absorption in dogs after oral administration have yielded conflicting results. In a study of greyhounds receiving 20 mg/kg body weight ampicillin or amoxicillin per os with no food, moist food or dry food, ampicillin absorption was impeded 60 to 80% by feeding, whereas amoxicillin absorption was unaffected.[4] In a more recent study involving a variety of breeds, absorption was impaired about 30% when ampicillin (20 mg/kg body weight) was administered immediately or two hours after feeding a dry food as compared with ampicillin adminis-

tered to fasting dogs or one hour before feeding.[5] Absorption of ampicillin (20 mg/kg body weight) administered immediately after feeding a moist food was similarly impaired, whereas administration two hours after feeding a moist food had a lesser effect on absorption.

In a comparative study of different penicillin preparations given to dogs, peak plasma concentrations of ampicillin, amoxicillin, penicillin V, phenethicillin and cloxacillin were decreased 40 to 50% by feeding immediately before drug administration; however, time to maximal concentrations was increased 0.5 to 1.5 hours only for ampicillin and amoxicillin.[6] From these studies, it is recommended that ampicillin be given to fasted dogs and at least one hour before feeding to ensure adequate drug absorption.

Table 27-1. Factors affecting the disposition of drugs that can be influenced by foods.

Absorption
GI transit time
GI luminal environment
Enterocyte function
Electrochemical gradient across the GI mucosa
pH gradient across the GI mucosa

Distribution
Drug-binding proteins
Blood cells that bind or metabolize drugs

Metabolism
Site of metabolism
    Organ
    Tissue
    Cell type
    Cell organelle
Biotransformation pathways
    Phase I oxidative vs. phase II conjugative pathways
Cofactors required for metabolism
    Vitamins
    Minerals
    Reducing agents
Non-nutrient enzyme inducers
    Phytochemicals
    Synthetic contaminants
    Preservatives

Excretion
Route of excretion
    Biliary
    Fecal
    Mammary
    Pulmonary
    Renal
    Salivary
    Sweat
Electrochemical gradient across mucosa of excretory organs
Rate of excretion

Table 27-2. Pharmaceutical attributes that determine the effects of nutrients on drug absorption.

Attribute	Examples
Physiochemical properties	Lipophilic or hydrophilic
Drug formulation	Tablet, capsule or liquid
Meal type	Volume, temperature, moisture
Drug dose	Amount and concentration
Route of administration	By mouth, by gastric tube, etc.
Order of administration	Pre- vs. postprandial
Time interval between food and drug administration	Phase of digestion
Owner/patient compliance	Mixing drugs and food for ease of administration

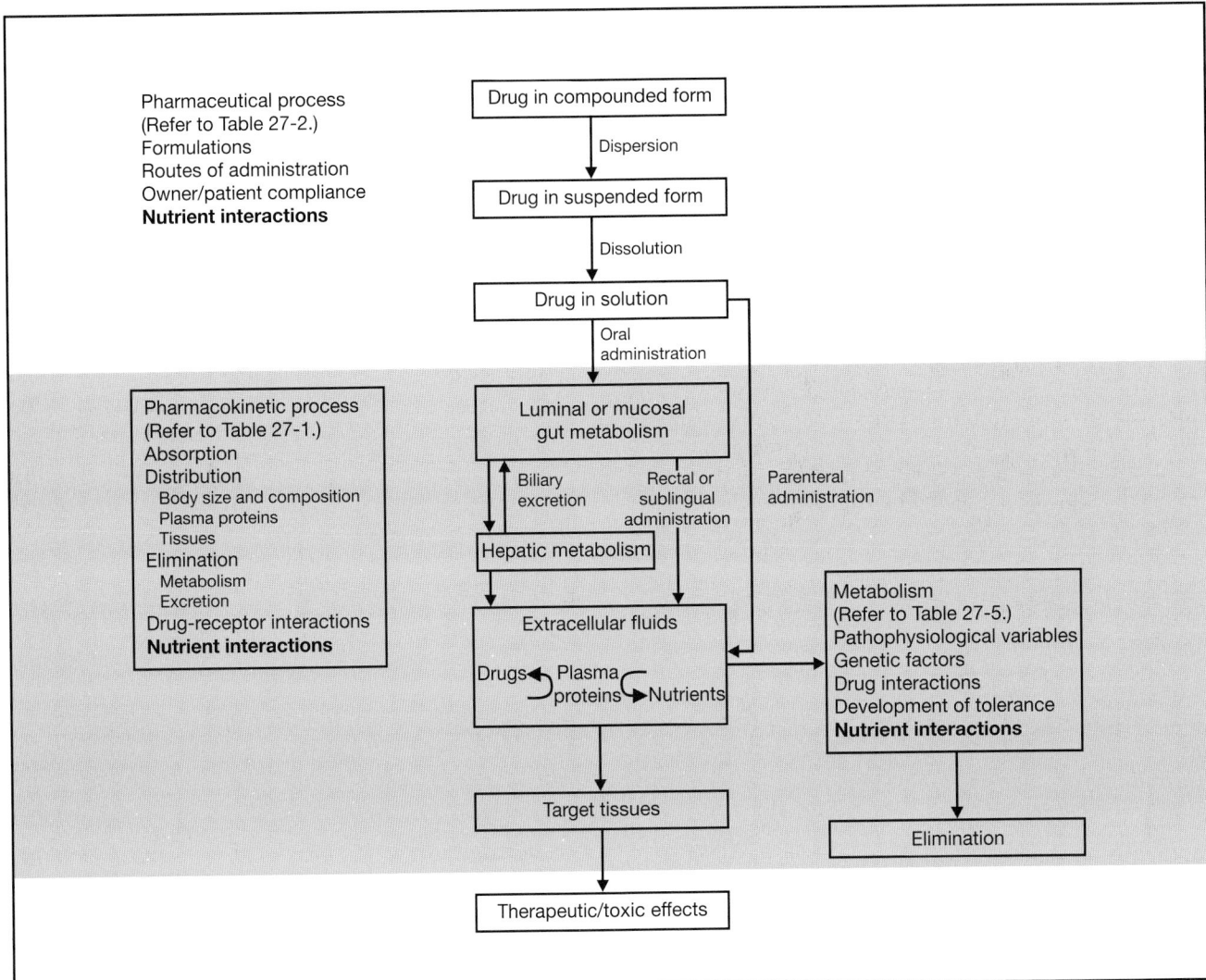

Figure 27-1. Determinants of drug absorption, distribution, metabolism and excretion that may be modified by nutrient interactions. (Adapted from Grahame-Smith DG, Aronson JK. In: The Oxford Textbook of Clinical Pharmacology and Drug Therapy. Oxford, UK: Oxford University Press, 1985.)

Table 27-3. Examples of drugs whose absorption may be affected by concomitant food consumption.*

Enhanced absorption	Reduced absorption	Delayed absorption
α-tocopherol	Amoxicillin	Acetaminophen
Carbamazepine	Ampicillin	Aspirin
Chlorothiazide	Antipyrine	Atenolol
Diazepam	Astemizole	Cefaclor
Dicoumarol	Captopril	Cephalexin
Erythromycin	Cephalexin	Cephradine
Griseofulvin	Chlorpromazine	Cimetidine
Hydrochlorothiazide	Erythromycin stearate	Digoxin
Labetalol	Isoniazid	Furosemide
Lithium	Ketoconazole	Glipizide
Mebendazole	Levodopa	Hydralazine
Metoprolol	Lincomycin	Ibuprofen
Nitrofurantoin	Methacycline	Metronidazole
Phenytoin	Methyldopa	Piroxicam
Propoxyphene	Nafcillin	Quinidine
Propranolol	Penicillamine	Sulfonamides
Riboflavin	Penicillins	Theophylline
Spironolactone	Phenobarbital	
Sulfamethoxydiazine	Propantheline	
	Quinolones	
	Rifampin	
	Tetracyclines	
	Warfarin	

*Modified from Williams L, Davis JA, Lowenthal DT. Medical Clinics of North America 1993; 77: 815-829.

Physical Incompatibilities

Specific nutrients (e.g., dietary fiber) can impede drug absorption across the GI mucosa by adsorbing the agent or increasing the unstirred water layer on the mucosal surface.[7] Some of these interactions are predictable, based on the behavior of fiber in binding substances such as bile acids or decreasing the absorptive rate of solutes such as monosaccharides. Psyllium mucilloid decreases the absorption of riboflavin, β-carotene, iron, zinc and other trace elements.[1]

Both nutritive and non-nutritive cytoprotective agents adsorb drugs and inhibit their absorption. For example, sucralfate binds tetracycline, phenytoin, cimetidine, digoxin and levothyroxine.[8,9] Antacids (e.g., aluminum hydroxide) can precipitate tetracyclines, iron salts, warfarin, digoxin, quinidine, phenothiazines, indomethacin, isoniazid, sulfadiazine, prednisone and levothyroxine.[1,10] Mineral supplements, including iron salts such as ferrous sulfate can decrease the absorption of methyldopa, penicillamine, tetracycline, levothyroxine and quinolone antibiotics.[1,11] Calcium salts and calcium-containing foods (e.g., milk, 1 to 2 mg calcium/ml) can precipitate insoluble tetracycline chelates.[12] Foods of plant origin may contain phytic acid, which inhibits zinc and calcium absorption, and tannins, which inhibit iron uptake. Gelatinization of liquid drug formulations following mixing with enteral formulas has been observed for certain expectorants, elixirs, syrups, concentrates and suspensions.

The potential binding of pharmaceutical agents to equipment used for administration should also be considered. Adsorption of vitamin A and drugs such as phenytoin and insulin to plastic polymers used in nasogastric, gastrostomy and enterostomy tubing has been reported.[13,14] Further, precipitation or gelatinization of drugs by nutrients can block feeding tubes.

Physical Factors Affecting GI Absorption of Drugs

The cephalic phase of digestion is normally initiated by the perception, visualization, smell and taste of food. This phenomenon contributes to normal GI motility, secretion, digestion and absorption of food and pharmaceutical agents. For example, when acetaminophen is administered by nasogastric tube postoperatively, its absorption is significantly reduced compared with its absorption following oral administration.[15] Decreased GI motility due to stress, pain, luminal obstruction and postsurgical ileus may also contribute to reduced absorption.

Commercial moist and dry foods similarly affect gastric emptying; however, solid food may decrease the emptying of liquids and liquids may decrease the rate and pattern of solid emptying.[16,17] Specific dietary components that affect the rate of GI transit can also alter oral drug assimilation. In dogs, meals containing cellulose or wheat bran increase the frequency of postprandial contractions; yet, only cellulose decreases duodenojejunal flow and prolongs transit time.[18] However, bran increases mixing and onward propulsion of ingesta. Addition of guar gum induces continuous low-amplitude contractions in dogs, increases jejunal flow, but still increases transit time because of water adsorption and luminal distention. Soluble fibers (e.g., methylcellulose) increase luminal viscosity, resulting

Table 27-4. Timing of drug administration relative to feeding.

Examples of drugs that should be administered after a fast to facilitate GI absorption (About one hour before or three hours after a meal).

Antibacterials
Macrolides

Erythromycin	Tylosin

Penicillins

Amoxicillin	Hetacillin
Ampicillin	Methicillin
Carbenicillin	Nafcillin
Cloxacillin	Oxacillin
Dicloxacillin	Penicillin

Sulfonamides

Sulfadiazine	Sulfabromomethazine
Sulfadimethoxine	Sulfachloropyridazine
Sulfamerazine	Sulfaethoxypyridazine
Sulfamethazine	Sulfaquinoxaline
Sulfisoxazole	Tetroxoprim
Sulfathiazole	Trimethoprim

Tetracyclines (except doxycycline)

Chlortetracycline	Oxytetracycline
Minocycline	Tetracycline

Chelating agents
Penicillamine

Laxatives
Bisacodyl

Examples of drugs that should be administered with food to minimize gastric irritation.

Antibacterials

Isoniazid	Nitrofurantoin
Metronidazole	Sulfasalazine

Anticonvulsants

Phenytoin	Primidone
Phenobarbital	

Antiinflammatory agents

Aspirin	Naproxen
Indomethacin	Phenylbutazone

Diuretics

Azetazolamide	Triamterene
Thiazides	

Phenothiazines

Acepromazine	Promazine
Chlorpromazine	Triflupromazine
Prochlorperazine	Trimeprazine

Examples of drugs that should be administered with large amounts of water to facilitate their action and to prevent dehydration.

Laxatives
Aluminum, calcium and magnesium salts
Methylcellulose
Psyllium

in delayed gastric emptying and increased thickness of the unstirred water layer.[7] Thus, both delivery of drug to the intestine and contact with the mucosal surface are impeded.

Addition of fat to a meal changes intragastric distribution of solid material, induces segmental changes in antral and pyloric motility and retards gastric emptying.[19] Intraduodenal instillation of dilute glucose solutions at a rate in excess of approximately 2 kcal (8.4 kJ)/min., regardless of tonicity, stimulates both phasic and tonic pyloric contractions, thereby inhibiting gastric emptying and delaying oral drug absorption. Propranolol and metoprolol are affected in this manner.[20,21] Enterohepatic cycling of drugs (e.g., doxycycline) may be affected by rate of passage and by portal blood flow and hepatic metabolism.

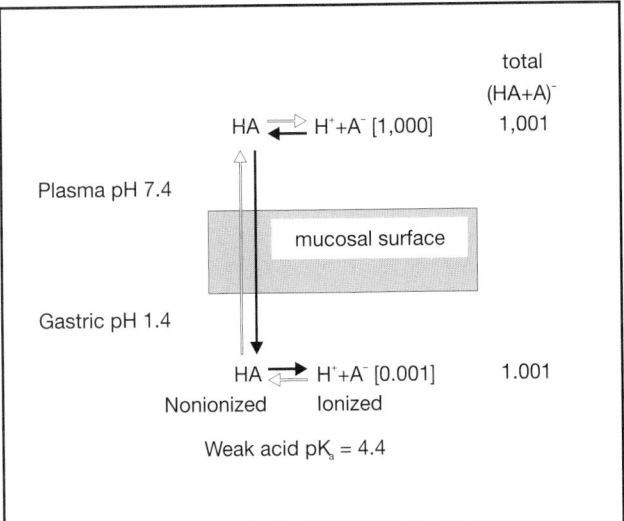

Figure 27-2. Influence of pH on the distribution of a weak acid between gastric contents and blood plasma across the gastric mucosa. The nonionized form of the drug predominates at low pH following gastric acid release. Only the nonionized form has sufficient lipid solubility to diffuse across the gastric mucosa. The ratio of ionized to nonionized drug may be calculated from the Henderson-Hasselbalch equation, and is determined by the pH on either side of the mucosa relative to the pKa of the drug. Dietary factors that increase or decrease gastric acid secretion will promote or inhibit acidic drug absorption. (Adapted from Benet LZ, Kroetz DL, Sheiner LB. The dynamics of drug absorption, distribution, and elimination. In: Hardman JA, Limbird LE, eds. Goodman and Gilman's The Pharmacological Basis of Therapeutics, 9th ed. New York, NY: McGraw-Hill, 1996.)

Table 27-5. Dietary factors that may affect drug metabolism and excretion (principally through induction of phase I biotransformation).

Macronutrients	Micronutrients	Non-nutrients
Protein	Vitamins	Antioxidants (BHA, BHT)
Carbohydrate	Minerals	Coumarins
Fat	Essential fatty acids	Flavonoids
Fiber		Indoles
		Methylxanthines
		Organonitriles
		Phenols
		Pyrolysis by-products
		Terpenoids

Examples of drugs whose metabolism and excretion is altered by these dietary factors

Acetaminophen	Morphine
Allopurinol	Oxazempam
Aminophylline	Penicillin
Cefoxitin	Pentobarbital
Chloramphenicol	Phenobarbital
Chloroquine	Phenytoin
Diazepam	Prednisolone
Estradiol	Propranolol
Hexobarbital	Theophylline
Isoniazid	Zoxazolamine
Meperidine	

Chemical Factors Affecting GI Absorption of Drugs

Beyond the effects of drug binding or precipitation, specific nutrients may compete for absorption by the intestinal mucosa. For instance, phenytoin absorption is impaired by concurrent administration of the B vitamins folic acid and pyridoxine.[1] Concurrent food intake and particular food ingredients can alter gastric or intestinal pH, thereby altering drug dissolution, ionization and absorption. In addition to the effect of milk calcium content on tetracycline absorption, milk can increase gastric pH, inducing premature dissolution of enteric-coated tablets, resulting in gastric irritation, altered absorption or both.

Gastric acid secretion associated with food ingestion can assist in the dissolution and ionization of alkaline drugs. Gastric acid secretion, however, limits the rate of absorption of alkaline drugs, while promoting the absorption of dissolved, unionized acidic drugs (Figure 27-2). The subsequent release of bicarbonate-rich pancreatic secretions promotes ionization of acidic drugs, but facilitates absorption of dissolved, unionized alkaline drugs. Release of hydrochloric acid in the stomach typically leads to alkalinization of the blood and the postprandial "alkaline tide," establishing an ionization gradient that can affect diffusion of ionizable compounds across the GI mucosa.

By affecting the food's acidification potential, dietary cation-anion balance can alter mineral absorption and drug availability through changes in ionization. Concurrent consumption of fats can affect drug absorption, depending on the polarity and lipid solubility of the individual agent. For example, it has been well-documented that lipid-soluble vitamins and the antifungal agent griseofulvin are better absorbed when taken with whole milk or a fatty meal.[1] High-fat foods may promote the absorption of nitrofurantoin, chlorothiazide and riboflavin by delaying gastric emptying, which facilitates dissolution in the stomach before passage into the small intestine for uptake.[1]

■ TRANSPORT FROM THE GI TRACT TO THE SITE OF ACTION OR METABOLISM

Dietary factors that affect blood flow will alter the rate of delivery of absorbed drugs to their site of action or metabolism. Dehydration not only may reduce GI blood flow and absorption, but may also reduce the absorbed drug's subsequent delivery to or removal from particular tissues. Hypovolemia and reduced tissue perfusion may result in target tissue doses below the effective concentration. Decreased blood flow may reduce hepatic extraction for metabolism and excretion. Decreased urine formation may increase drug accumulation and toxicity in various organs; aminoglycoside accumulation in the renal proximal tubules is a common example. Other dietary ingredients may affect cardiac output (methylxanthines), renal blood flow (protein) or intestinal reperfusion following ischemia (antioxidants), thereby altering drug distribution.

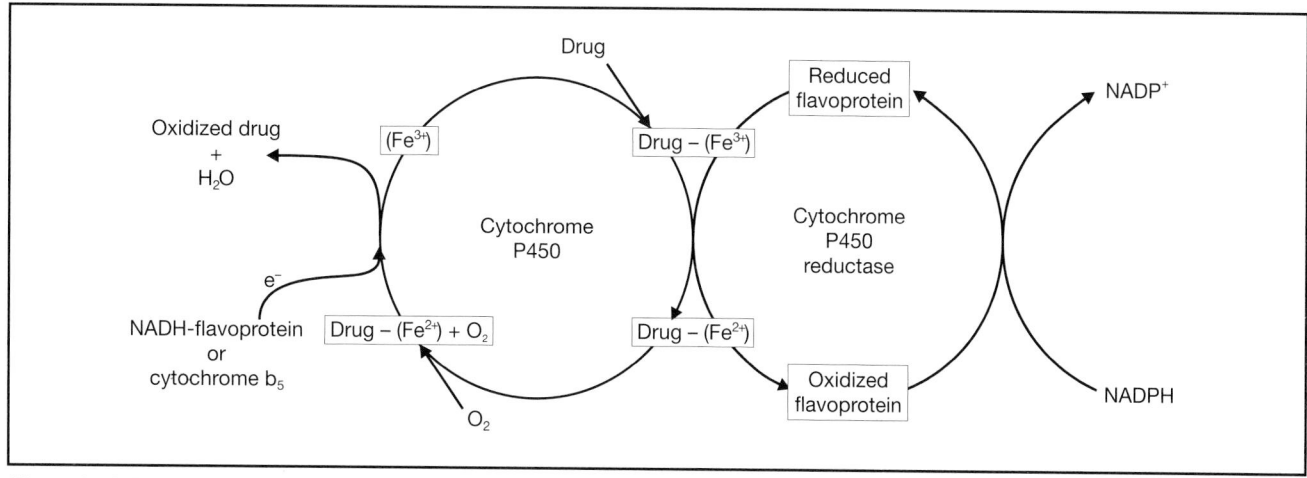

Figure 27-3. The hepatic phase I microsomal mixed function oxidase system for drug metabolism. (Adapted from Benet LZ, Sheiner LB. Pharmacokinetics: The dynamics of drug absorption, distribution, and elimination. In: The Pharmacological Basis of Therapeutics, 7th ed. New York, NY: McGraw-Hil,1985.) Key: Fe = iron, $NADP^+$ = the oxidized form of nicotinamide-adenine dinucleotide phosphate, NADPH = the reduced form of NADP.

Like many metabolites and hormones, drugs may be transported in the blood in the free form or bound to plasma proteins. Thus, changes in nutritional status that affect plasma protein synthesis will likely affect drug binding and distribution. For example, hypoalbuminemia due to low dietary protein quantity or quality can affect the distribution of antibiotics, barbiturates, cardiac glycosides and analgesics. Drugs and nutrients may influence one another's disposition because binding to plasma proteins is competitive. High postprandial free fatty acid levels can displace anionic compounds from cationic binding sites on plasma proteins. Drugs and nutrients that are competitively transported into erythrocytes may be similarly affected. This effect has been documented for the interaction between folic acid and the loop diuretics furosemide and ethacrynic acid.[1] Dietary factors that influence acid-base metabolism can alter blood pH and intraerythrocytic pH, thereby affecting drug ionization, protein binding and cell uptake.

DIETARY EFFECTS ON DRUG METABOLISM

The clearance of many drugs from the circulation depends on their biotransformation in the liver, kidneys and other organs with xenobiotic-metabolizing enzymes (Table 27-5).[12,22] For drugs that are metabolized rapidly, extraction is determined principally by organ blood flow. For example, the rate-limiting step for clearance of indocyanine green and sulfobromophthalein sodium is hepatic blood flow. For drugs that are metabolized relatively slowly, clearance from the circulation is determined primarily by the quantity and affinity of enzymes responsible for their metabolism.

Hepatic drug metabolism occurs through two predominant biotransformation pathways: 1) phase I (oxidation, reduction and hydrolysis) and 2) phase II (glutathione or glucuronide conjugation, acetylation and sulfation). Phase I reactions are catalyzed principally by a family of cytochrome P450 enzymes in the microsomal mixed function oxidase system. Phase I reactions alter the functional

groups of a compound (Figure 27-3). Phase II reactions are catalyzed by families of glutathione-S-transferase, glucuronyl transferase and N-acetyltransferase isoenzymes. Phase II reactions result in conjugation and altered water solubility (Figure 27-4). The outcome of phase I and II reactions is reduced pharmacologic activity and enhanced drug excretion. In some cases, phase I reactions may increase the activity or toxicity of drugs, whereas phase II reactions may alter the tissue distribution and subsequent target organs for toxicity or mutagenicity of the drug's metabolites.[23,24]

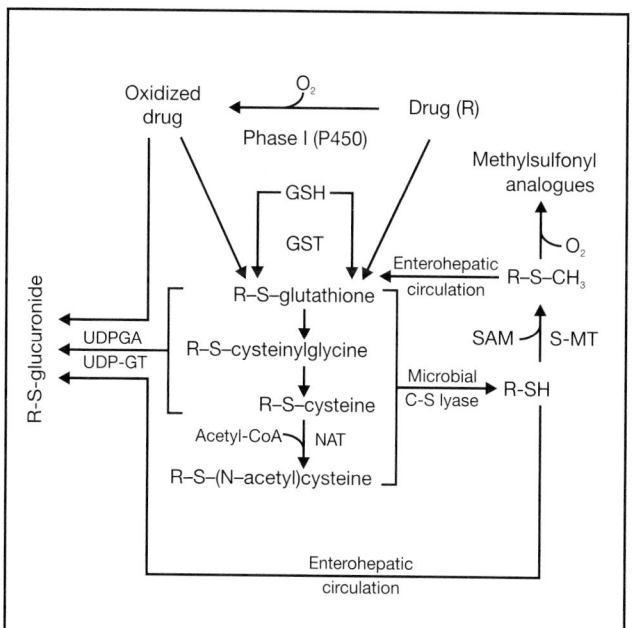

Figure 27-4. The hepatic phase II biotransformation system for drug metabolism. (Adapted from Fettman MJ, Butler RN, McMichael AJ, et al. Metabolic phenotypes and colorectal neoplasia. Journal of Gastroenterology and Hepatology 1991; 6: 81-90.) Key: P450 = cytochrome P450, GSH = reduced glutathione, GST = glutathione-S-transferase, acetyl-CoA = acetyl-coenzyme A, NAT = N-acetyltransferase, UDPGA = uridine diphosphoglucuronic acid, UDP-GT = UDP-glucuronyl transferase, SAM = S-adenosyl-methionine, S-MT = S-methyltransferase.

Macronutrient Effects on Drug Metabolism

Inappetence due to disease is a common cause of decreased macronutrient intake that can affect drug action. Further, changes in the macronutrient composition of the diet can significantly alter hepatic drug metabolism.

Dietary Protein Intake

In experimental studies in rats, low dietary protein intake reduced the metabolism and increased the toxicity of pentobarbital, strychnine and zoxazolamine.[23] The activities of the mixed function oxidase enzymes flavoprotein reductase and cytochrome b_5 are decreased by dietary protein restriction. Inducibility of cytochrome P450 by phenobarbital in rats is also decreased by feeding less dietary protein.[25]

High-protein, (e.g., 44 vs. 10% of kcal, as fed) low-carbohydrate foods (e.g., 35 vs. 70% of kcal, as fed) enhance the hepatic metabolism and excretion of many different drugs in people, including acetaminophen, oxazepam, theophylline, propranolol and estradiol.[25-27] Conversely, consumption of protein restricted foods for as few as 10 days significantly decreases elimination of these drugs.

Certain essential amino acids may stimulate hepatic protein synthesis and thereby induce the hepatic mixed function oxidase system. Sulfur-containing amino acids can promote hepatic drug metabolism by increasing glutathione synthesis and subsequent conjugation reactions.[28] Starvation can reduce the activity of glutathione-S-transferase and the synthesis of glutathione for conjugation; events that also participate in the development of fasting hyperbilirubinemia.

Dietary protein-related changes in renal blood flow and renal tubular transport can simultaneously affect the clearance of drugs eliminated in urine.[29] Increased dietary protein intake in dogs increases the elimination of gentamicin and reduces the potential for nephrotoxicity, presumably by stimulating renal blood flow.[30,31] In people, low-protein diets decrease the hepatic metabolism of allopurinol to oxypurinol, and decrease renal excretion of oxypurinol.[32] The pharmacokinetics of allopurinol and oxypurinol in dogs do not appear to be affected by dietary protein.[33]

Dietary Carbohydrate Intake

High carbohydrate intake in laboratory animals depresses oxidative drug metabolism.[26] High dietary fructose, glucose and sucrose levels increase barbiturate-sleeping time and decrease in vitro metabolism of barbiturates in mice.[25] Parenteral glucose has the same effect in dogs and cats; thus, high dietary intake of these carbohydrates would likely modify barbiturate responses in these species as well. Supplemental carbohydrate administration in rats increases liver weight, hepatic fat and glycogen deposition, but decreases hepatic mixed function oxidase activities. Carbohydrate feeding in rats can similarly decrease the microsomal activation of carcinogens such as benzo(a)pyrene and aflatoxin B_1.

In people, long-term consumption of high-carbohydrate diets depresses antipyrine and theophylline clearance.[25] The proposed mechanism involves inhibition of the synthesis of d-aminolevulinic acid synthetase, a key enzyme in the synthesis of heme for cytochrome P450.[23] However, carbohydrate is also required for UDP-glucuronyl transferase activity for glucuronidation of oxidized drug metabolites; short-term deprivation of carbohydrates can decrease rates of conjugation. This, too, contributes to the hyperbilirubinemia of fasting.

Dietary Fat Intake

In addition to the effects of dietary fat intake on drug absorption and plasma protein binding, lipid intake can affect hepatic xenobiotic-metabolizing enzyme activities.[25] Foods deficient in essential fatty acids result in decreased rates of drug metabolism. Dietary lipids have been reported to be essential for optimal induction of P450 enzymes by phenobarbital. Rats fed a 20% corn oil diet for four days had twofold increases in the activities of several hepatic P450 isoenzymes (P450 2, 2A1, 2B1, 2C11, 2E1 and 3A) as compared with enzyme activities in rats fed a fat-free diet.[34] However, there is an inverse relationship between lung P450 2B1 activity and dietary fat intake. In one study in which rats were fed 6% dietary lipid for 40 days as coconut, peanut, corn or fish oil, cytochrome P450 and epoxide hydrolase activities were highest in the fish-oil group.[35] In this same study, UDP-glucuronyl transferase type I activity was increased by fish oil or corn oil supplementation, but reduced by coconut oil.

In another study, rats fed 10% dietary lipid for two weeks as soybean oil, lard or fish oil were exposed to pentachlorobenzene (PECB). Blood concentrations of the metabolite pentachlorophenol were highest and tissue concentrations of PECB were lowest after feeding fish oil.[36]

Fish oils are high in polyunsaturated fatty acids, particularly of the n-3 family (eicosapentaenoic and docosahexaenoic acids), but contain relatively less n-6 fatty acids than other sources. Effects of fish oil supplementation may be due to: 1) altered cell and organelle membrane fluidity, 2) increased propensity towards oxidative damage and/or 3) specific induction of enzyme synthesis. In people, the degree of dietary fatty acid saturation has had little effect on oxidation of antipyrine or theophylline; however, the principal cytochrome P450 isoenzyme, 3A4, is sensitive to microsomal membrane characteristics.[25] A dietary deficiency of labile methyl donors (e.g., choline or methionine) increases spontaneous and chemically induced hepatocarcinogenesis in rats because of decreased microsomal enzyme activity.[37] Lipotrope deficiency also impairs methylation of DNA and RNA; however, a considerable portion of microsomal lipid can be removed in vitro without adversely affecting P450 activity.

Effects of Feeding Route

The route of nutrient administration may also affect hepatic drug metabolism. Decreased hepatic clearance of indocyanine green in pigs fasted for 12 days is returned to normal after enteral feeding for 12 days.[38] However, intravenous feeding with an identical formula did not improve hepatic clearance despite similar weight gains. Hepatic hydroxylation of pentobarbital and demethylation of meperidine by rats are significantly impaired following seven days of parenteral feeding with a formula that otherwise maintains hepatic drug clearance when administered enterally.[39] Lipid-free total parenteral nutrition depresses hepatic phase I and II conjugative drug metabolism. Parenteral lipid-free nutrition for 10 days in rats decreased the hepatic activities of cytochrome P450 oxidase, p-nitroanisole demethylase and p-nitrophenol glutathione-S-transferase by one-half.[40] Thus, the intake of macronutrients, composition of the food and route of nutritional support interact to modify drug metabolism.

Micronutrient Effects on Drug Metabolism

Dietary Vitamin Intake

The hepatic mixed function oxidase system requires several vitamins.[22,41] Niacin and riboflavin participate directly as the principal components of the electron carriers $NADP^+$, NAD^+, FAD and FMN, which are coenzymes for cytochrome P450 reductase, DT-diaphorase and NADH-cytochrome b_5 reductase.[22] Dietary deficiency can lead to a generalized decrease in total P450 and associated monooxygenase activities.[23,42]

Folate deficiency blocks the induction of cytochrome P450 by phenobarbital, and pyridoxine (vitamin B_6) deficiency may alter cysteine conjugate b-lyase activity.[23] Excessive dietary folate can antagonize methotrexate activity, whereas increased pyridoxine intake can increase the metabolism of levodopa, thereby reducing its effectiveness. Thiamin deficiency increases the levels of cytochrome P450 2E1, NADH-P450 reductase and cytochrome b_5, but decreases the oxidation of N-nitrosodimethylamine, acetaminophen, aminopyrine, ethylmorphine, zoxazolamine and benzo(a)pyrene.[22]

The antioxidant vitamins (A, C and E) are required for normal membrane synthesis and stability. Vitamin A deficiency decreases hepatic mixed function oxidase system activity and depresses oxidation of aminopyrine, ethylmorphine, aniline, benzo(a)pyrene and 7-ethoxycoumarin.[22] Vitamin C deficiency decreases NADPH-P450 reductase activity and prolongs the half-life of antipyrine, acetaminophen and salicylamide. Vitamin E deficiency decreases microsomal metabolism of ethylmorphine, codeine and benzo(a)pyrene.[22] Effects of vitamin E deficiency occur without decreases in cytochrome P450 activity, and probably relate to the antioxidant properties of tocopherol, which may prevent oxidative damage to membrane lipids. Vitamins A and D are substrates for cytochrome P450 and can competitively block the metabolism of other P450 substrates.

Dietary Mineral Intake

Many minerals modulate hepatic drug metabolism. Iron is required for heme synthesis in cytochromes and for metal ion-catalyzed oxidative reactions.[24] Iron deficiency results in decreased metabolism of hexobarbital and aminopyrine.[22] Selenium is a cofactor for glutathione peroxidase; selenium deficiency may promote oxidative damage to the microsomal system. Hypothyroidism resulting from iodide deficiency increases flavoprotein synthesis and cytochrome P450 oxidative activity.[43] Deficiencies of zinc, magnesium and potassium decrease drug metabolism, whereas high concentrations of heavy metals (e.g., cobalt and cadmium) may block heme synthesis and thereby lower cytochrome P450 levels.[22]

Non-Nutrient Effects on Drug Metabolism

Non-nutrient dietary factors can profoundly influence drug metabolism by inducing the activity of many hepatic biotransformation enzymes.[25] Phenols (e.g., hydroxycinnamic, dihydroxycinnamic and ferulic acids) are antioxidants that block chemical carcinogenesis. Methylxanthines, including caffeine, theobromine and theophylline, competitively bind to cytochrome P450 to block oxidation of other compounds. Coumarin derivatives in vegetables and fruits induce glutathione-S-transferase activity. Organonitriles (1-cyano-2-hydroxy-3-butene, 1-cyano-3,4-epithiobutane, 1-cyano-3,4-epithiobutane) and indole derivatives (indole-3-carbinol, 3,3'-diindolmethane, indole-3-acetonitrile) in cruciferous plants (e.g., broccoli, cauliflower and cabbage) increase hepatic and renal glutathione concentrations and induce hepatic and renal glutathione-S-transferase activities.[28]

Excessive organonitrile exposure induces hepatic and renal toxicity, which may impair drug metabolism, whereas small amounts may have anti-carcinogenic properties.[25,28] Flavonoids and terpenoids from citrus fruits can either induce or block cytochrome P450-related oxidative reactions, and can exert mutagenic or anti-tumorigenic effects, depending on the dose administered.[25] Flavonoids in grapefruit juice can significantly prolong the half-life of dihydropyridine calcium channel blockers (e.g., nifedipine, felodipine and nisoldipine).

Butylated hydroxytoluene (BHT) and butylated hydroxyanisole (BHA) are added to certain processed food products to inhibit lipid oxidation.[25] These food additives competitively inhibit cytochrome P450-related oxidases, but induce other enzymes, including glutathione-S-transferase, glucuronyl transferase, DT-diaphorase and quinone reductase. In some experimental systems, they have demonstrated anti-carcinogenic properties, presumably by blocking activation of chemical carcinogens.[44] In other systems, a hydroperoxide derivative has been shown to have a tumor-promoting effect.[45] Polycyclic hydrocarbons and related pyrolysis products of charbroiling are reported to increase cytochrome P450 oxidase activities and to increase the clearance of such drugs as theophylline, bufaralol, acetaminophen, tacrine and warfarin.[25] Induction of cytochrome P450 hydroxylase can lead to activation of arylamine and heterocyclic amines, which are also consumed with food, and have been linked to stimulation of carcinogenesis.

DIETARY EFFECTS ON DRUG EXCRETION

Following P450 hydroxylation, heterocyclic amines may subsequently undergo N-acetylation, the metabolic phenotype and activity of which affects the organ and route of excretion of the metabolite.[46] If there is "slow" N-acetyltransferase activity, most of the hydroxylated amine undergoes hepatic glucuronidation and is returned to the blood for excretion in the urine. In people, so called "slow acetylators" are predisposed to urinary bladder cancer. Those individuals with "fast" N-acetyltransferase activity appear to be predisposed to colorectal cancer, presumably through preferential colonocytic metabolism to mutagenic arylamides and acetoxyarylamines. Thus, metabolic phenotype as determined by genetics, or from enzyme induction due to dietary effects, can influence the site, route and rate of drug excretion.

Because many of the drugs excreted by the kidneys undergo active transport by anion- or cation-specific mechanisms in the renal tubular epithelium, their elimination can be altered through competitive inhibition by other charged solutes. Pharmacologically, this effect has been purposely employed by the co-administration of probenecid with penicillins to block elimination by the anion-specific renal tubular transport mechanism. Nutritionally, this effect may result from consumption of divalent cations (e.g., calcium and magnesium), which decrease renal tubular transport and accumulation of aminoglycosides such as gentamicin.[47-50] As a result, urinary elimination of the antibiotic is increased and nephrotoxicity thereby reduced.

Further, dietary alterations in urinary pH can affect the ionization and trapping of drugs secreted into the tubular lumina. The relatively common practice of formulating commercial feline foods to promote urinary acidification in the prevention and treatment of lower urinary tract diseases (e.g., struvite crystalluria and urolithiasis) may also affect the elimination of pharmaceutical agents excreted in the urine.[51]

Food ingredients that stimulate bile, fecal or urine flow may affect the excretion of drugs by these routes. For example, dietary fats with choleretic properties will enhance the excretion of drug metabolites in the bile and the return of enterohepatically recycled drugs such as doxycycline. Salts of divalent cations (e.g., magnesium oxide and magnesium hydroxide) can exert a laxative effect that may increase fecal elimination of poorly absorbed oral drugs and enterohepatically recycled drugs. High dietary salt content and other naturally occurring diuretics, including active loop diuretics, can enhance the excretion of drugs and their metabolites in urine.

■ BENEFICIAL EFFECTS OF NUTRIENTS ON DRUG ACTION

The presence of food need not impair drug absorption, and within limits may be indicated to facilitate safe GI uptake of drugs (Table 27-4). Food may prevent GI irritation, modify drug-induced nausea or delay drug uptake, increasing the ultimate amount of drug absorbed (Table 27-6). For example, food can promote gastric acid secretion to enhance the uptake of an acidic drug such as aspirin, while simultaneously protecting the mucosa from irritation by the drug.

Consumption of food can minimize nausea induced by the concurrent administration of hypertonic salt and carbohydrate solutions. In people, micronized preparations of phenytoin are actually better absorbed in the fed rather than the fasted state.[13] In other cases, dietary supplementation with a specific nutrient may be indicated to counteract adverse drug side effects, to prevent drug-induced nutrient imbalances or to potentiate therapeutic effects.

Provision of Nutrients to Prevent Drug-Induced Imbalances

Additional energy and protein may be indicated to combat alterations in drug metabolism associated with prolonged decreases in food intake. A critical example would be

the provision of nutrients during enteral- or parenteral-assisted feeding of patients incapable of voluntary food consumption. Effects of individual nutrient deficiencies have already been described. In addition, studies of prolonged starvation and of kwashiorkor in people have demonstrated significant reductions in the metabolism of numerous drugs by both phase I and phase II hepatic biotransformation systems.[25] These drugs include chloroquine, isoniazid, penicillin, chloramphenicol, tobramycin and cefoxitin. In addition, hypoalbuminemia-related decreases in drug binding alter the clearance of cloxacillin, streptomycin, sulfamethoxazole, sulfadiazine, digoxin, thiopentone and phenylbutazone.[1] Malnutrition-related decreases in renal blood flow and glomerular filtration rate have caused gentamicin toxicity.

Most commercial pet foods are adequately fortified with micronutrients; therefore, supplementation is not necessary unless a homemade food is fed, nutrient intake is decreased or a specific medical indication for prescription of a nutrient as a "nutraceutical" exists. Vitamin supplementation may be indicated to counteract the effects of drugs that specifically antagonize vitamin absorption or function. These include: 1) the use of folacin to manage deficiency induced by folic acid antagonists such as methotrexate, 2) vitamin K vs. antagonists in the coumarin family, 3) tocopherol, retinol and/or ascorbic acid to counter losses due to oxidative drug damage, 4) cholecalciferol for deficiency induced by anticonvulsants such as phenytoin, 5) thiamin to replace that lost to thiaminase activity in raw fish and 6) B vitamins to replace those lost following antibiotic-induced alterations in the GI microflora.

Specific minerals may also become deficient because of binding or precipitation in the GI tract, or following enhanced fecal losses due to laxatives or urinary loss due to diuretics. Urinary electrolyte losses due to loop diuretics can lead to significant physiologic abnormalities. Trace elements such as zinc may bind to fiber or be precipitated by phytates. Oral calcium supplements may block iron absorption. Excessive use of antacids, laxatives and binding resins can result in macroelement deficiencies.

Glutathione precursors (e.g., cysteine or N-acetylcysteine) may be indicated to counter the oxidative damage induced by pharmaceutical agents such as the: 1) analgesic acetaminophen, 2) urinary antiseptic methylene blue, 3) injectable anesthetic propofol and 4) antitumor agent doxorubicin.[28] Oxidative damage resulting from administration of oxidized lipid supplements or excessive use of n-3 fatty acid sources may also necessitate treatment with glutathione precursors or antioxidant vitamins.

Provision of additional water may be indicated for the prevention or treatment of renal damage resulting from nephrotoxic drug administration. Examples of drugs whose administration should routinely be coupled to increased water intake include cisplatin, aminoglycosides, nonsteroidal antiinflammatory drugs, analgesics and diuretics.

Provision of Nutrients to Enhance Drug Effects

Certain nutrients may be prescribed to facilitate a drug's intended effect or to synergistically promote the target physiologic functions. Additional energy or protein can generally facilitate therapeutic drug effects by promoting optimal distribution and hepatic biotransformation activities. These additions will tend to normalize pharmacoki-

Table 27-6. Examples of the effects of nutrients on drug action.

Beneficial effects	Examples
Enhanced GI drug absorption	Fatty foods enhance absorption of griseofulvin
Prevention of undesirable drug effects	Foods minimize nausea induced by metronidazole
Enhancement of desirable drug effects	Water enhances laxative effects of psyllium
Improved drug metabolism	Enteral feeding supports metabolism of cefoxitin
Altered drug excretion	Protein promotes renal excretion of gentamicin
Detrimental effects	**Examples**
Impaired GI drug absorption	Food interferes with absorption of ampicillin
Antagonism of desirable drug effects	Folate opposes chemotherapeutic effects of methotrexate
Potentiation of undesirable drug effects	Potassium increases potential toxicity of captopril
Impaired drug metabolism	Fish oil enhances hepatic oxidation of phenobarbital
Altered drug excretion	Calcium increases urinary excretion of gentamicin

netics to ensure the individual patient's dose response may more closely approximate the anticipated response.

Providing adequate energy and protein to patients receiving exogenous thyroid hormones plays an integral role in the physiologic response to that supplementation.[43] Undernutrition may result in reduced synthesis of thyroid-binding plasma proteins and subsequent changes in thyroid pharmacokinetics. Reductions in energy or protein intake suppress target tissue monodeiodination of thyroxine to the physiologically active triiodothyronine. Triiodothyronine levels decrease within 24 hours of fasting or caloric restriction, and may decline by 40 to 50% within three days. Should fasting induce increased adrenal glucocorticoid secretion, depressed target tissue triiodothyronine receptor levels may also be observed. Although these reductions in target-cell responsiveness to thyroid hormones represent an appropriate adaptation to conserve energy during starvation, the effect on exogenous thyroid hormone pharmacotherapy may be undesirable.

It is important to maintain a regular feeding schedule and consistent food for animals with diabetes mellitus to stabilize intermediary metabolism. The administration of exogenous insulin to insulin-dependent diabetics and the administration of oral hypoglycemic agents to non-insulin-dependent diabetics should be timed relative to feeding. For both forms of diabetes mellitus, specific dietary formulations are indicated to: 1) modulate GI carbohydrate uptake, 2) meet protein requirements without adversely affecting renal function and 3) moderate overall lipid metabolism to prevent ketoacidosis. (See Chapter 24.)

Dietary intake of specific minerals that modulate hormonal axes should be considered, including calcium and phosphorus intake when cholecalciferol is administered for chronic renal failure, and sodium and potassium when mineralocorticoids are replaced in hypoadrenocorticism. The trace minerals chromium and vanadium may improve glucose tolerance and facilitate management of diabetics with insulin or oral hypoglycemic agents.[52,53] Specific n-3 fatty acid therapy may be used to potentiate the effects of anti-inflammatory drugs, anticoagulants and antineoplastic agents.[54] Arginine may be provided to improve nitric oxide production and to enhance immune function,[55] glutamine to promote enterocyte metabolism,[56] cysteine to enhance glutathione synthesis,[57] carnitine to improve digoxin responsiveness in congestive heart failure[58] and antioxidant vitamins to protect against oxidative damage. Specific clinical management approaches using trace nutrients are presented in Chapters 25 and 26.

Dietary fiber may be indicated along with drug therapy for a number of diseases. Increased dietary fiber intake has proved beneficial in the treatment of insulin-dependent and non-insulin-dependent diabetes mellitus by moderating GI carbohydrate absorption. Fermentable dietary fiber increases colonic short-chain fatty acid concentrations and decreases luminal pH. As a result, these fibers may be used as the primary treatment for canine and feline colitis or as an ancillary therapy to sulfasalazine or metronidazole treatment. Soluble fibers (e.g., psyllium mucilloid) may act in this way in conjunction with other antidiarrheal treatments, or as stool softeners for use with laxatives to treat constipation.[59] Hepatic cytochrome P450 concentrations and UDP-glucuronyl transferase activities appear to be altered by the type and quantity of fiber in the food.[60]

Dietary buffers may be indicated in conjunction with other therapies for chronic renal failure to correct metabolic acidosis or to facilitate activity of replacement pancreatic enzymes in exocrine pancreatic disease. They may be used to enhance alkaline drug absorption from the GI tract and to promote acidic drug excretion in the urine. Alkalinization of the urine has been used clinically to reduce the ionization, renal accumulation and toxicity of aminoglycosides.[61] Finally, buffers (e.g., sodium bicarbonate, aluminum hydroxide) can be used with H_2-receptor antagonists (e.g., cimetidine, ranitidine) or as laxatives (e.g., magnesium oxide, magnesium hydroxide).

ADVERSE EFFECTS OF NUTRIENTS ON DRUG ACTION

In addition to ameliorating undesirable effects on drug absorption or metabolism, specific nutrients may antagonize desired drug effects (Table 27-6). Excess caloric intake will complicate weight management in obese patients. Excess protein intake can adversely affect renal handling of drugs by increasing renal blood flow and drug excretion, or by promoting intraglomerular hypertension and reducing glomerular filtration in chronic renal failure. High protein intake can increase the hepatic metabolism of drugs such as the methylxanthines, resulting in reduced therapeutic efficacy.

High mineral intake can complicate drug therapy of specific disorders: 1) sodium and hypertension, 2) potassium and hypoadrenocorticism, 3) magnesium and feline lower urinary tract disease and 4) phosphorus and chronic renal failure.

Excessive dietary intake of iodine can lead to a para-doxical "iodine toxicosis goiter" through what is referred to as the "Wolff-Chaikoff effect." As iodide accumulation by the thyroid gland increases, so does iodination of tyrosyl residues of thyroglobulin. However, very high iodine levels appear to cause auto-inhibition of iodide organification and thyroglobulin proteolysis, leading to thyroid hormone deficiency. This phenomenon has been observed in foals born to mares that received excessive iodine supplementation during gestation, as well as in other species.[62,63]

Naturally occurring non-nutritive dietary factors that may influence drug responses include methylxanthines, which may complicate aminophylline therapy, histamine in certain types of fish, which may interfere with antihistamine treatment and tyramine in chicken livers and aged cheeses, which confound the action of monoamine oxidase inhibitors. Alcohols and antioxidants added to certain nutrient sources as preservatives and humectants may have adverse effects as well. Benzoic acid and benzoyl alcohol in commercial fluid and drug preparations, propylene glycol in semi-moist commercial cat food and onion powder in commercial human baby foods may induce oxidative erythrocyte damage and Heinz body anemia in cats.[64-67] These substances are no longer commonly used in commercial product manufacturing.

EFFECTS OF OBESITY ON DRUG METABOLISM

Although complicated by the metabolic effects of overnutrition during weight gain or restricted food intake during weight loss, numerous studies have documented a significant effect of obesity on drug metabolism in people and other animals.[68] Changes in the apparent volume of distribution have been observed because of alterations in the quantity of body fat. Obesity increases the volume distribution of lipophilic drugs such as alprazolam, carbamazepine, diazepam, methotrexate, oxazepam, sufentanil and vancomycin. Obesity decreases the volume distribution of polar compounds including acetaminophen, ciprofloxacin, furosemide, gentamicin, isoniazid, sulfisoxazole and tolbutamide.[69-77]

Drug clearance may be affected following changes in hepatic microsomal enzyme induction, as well as alterations in the predominant pathways used for phase II conjugation reactions. Several investigations have demonstrated enhanced biotransformation of volatile anesthetics in obese patients, resulting in increased production of the reactive intermediates typically responsible for organ toxicity.[78] Enhanced hepatic oxidative metabolism of halothane in obese people has resulted in increased serum levels of fluoride and bromide ions; the former is associated with increased hepatotoxicity. Half-life elimination of triazolam is prolonged in obese subjects, and clearance following oral administration is reduced, presumably because of decreases in first-pass hepatic extraction.

Drug toxicity may be enhanced when the dose administered is based on total body mass, but distribution is restricted to lean body mass, resulting in higher plasma drug concentrations and greater exposure to susceptible organs.[79,80] Obese rats appear to be at increased risk for gentamicin and furosemide nephrotoxicity by this mecha-nism.[79,80] Susceptibility to the toxic affects of these drugs remains even when the dose is decreased to reflect lean body mass and to equalize drug exposure. Studies of acetaminophen toxicity in rats have shown that when obese animals are dosed according to fat-free mass, toxicity is increased because of a metabolic shift toward less sulfation and more glucuronidation.[81] Obesity likewise appears to increase drug glucuronidation in people. Further, target organs may be predisposed to drug toxicity by pre-existing obesity-related lesions such as hepatic lipidosis.

Obesity increases steroid hormone clearance in people because of enhanced aromatization and interconversion of androgens to estrogens by adipose tissue.[70] Prednisolone and methylprednisolone succinate clearance in obese people is also increased, although potential contributions by increased cardiac output, hepatic blood flow, liver size and hydrolysis by extrahepatic carboxyesterases have not been resolved. On the other hand, methylprednisolone clearance appears to be decreased, suggesting that obesity may affect specific oxidative pathways very differently.[70]

Although similar studies have not been conducted in companion animals, certain generalizations can be made. Obesity will result in changes in the effective dose administered for drugs given according to total body weight, whether it is increased because of poor lipid solubility or decreased because of lipophilicity. Drug dose or dosing interval may need to be adjusted to maintain therapeutic effect and protect against toxicity. Alterations in body composition concurrent with drug administration may have significant effects on clinical efficacy and margin of safety, and must be considered whenever a patient's body weight changes markedly.[71]

SUMMARY

Quantitatively and qualitatively, ingested nutrients have major effects on the biologic activity of pharmacologic agents. This is true not just for orally administered drugs in the GI tract, but also for drugs administered parenterally. Ingested nutrients may modify hepatic and renal metabolic processes, thus altering the action of parenterally administered drugs. Inappetence associated with many chronic diseases may significantly modify drug absorption, metabolism and action.

Specific macronutrients and micronutrients not only support normal physiologic processes necessary for drug delivery and action, but may also modify specific metabolic processes integral to drug activity. For instance, dietary protein must be sufficient to ensure adequate plasma protein synthesis and maintenance of plasma volume for the delivery and action of most systemically administered drugs. Dietary protein may also specifically affect the hepatic metabolism of some drugs, the renal elimination of others and the modification by target tissues of yet others. Specific amino acids can play a role in drug metabolism and action as well. Food is a major modulator of drug activity and food-drug interrelationships must be considered when designing treatment regimens.

Because few studies to determine the effects of food on drug metabolism have been conducted in dogs and cats, it is difficult to delineate specific feeding recommendations for drugs commonly used in veterinary practice. However, it is important to consider potential nutrient-drug interactions whenever the expected action of a prescribed drug is not seen in an individual patient. One may alter the dosing schedule relative to meals or adjust the dietary composition or dose to correct overt nutrient imbalances. Alternatively, one may determine circulating drug concentrations to detect changes in pharmacokinetics and to establish the need for a change in drug type or dose. It is clear that a standardized food, consistent feeding schedule and balanced nutrient intake are prerequisites to successful pharmacologic management of disease.

REFERENCES

1. Roe DA. In: Diet and Drug Interactions. New York, NY: Van Nostrand Reinhold, 1989.

2. Toothaker RD, Welling PG. The effect of food on drug bioavailability. Annual Review of Pharmacology and Toxicology 1980; 20: 173-199.

3. Semple HA, Koo W, Tam YK, et al. Interactions between hydralazine and oral nutrients in humans. Therapeutic Drug Monitoring 1991; 13: 304-308.

4. Watson ADJ, Egerton JR. Effect of feeding on plasma antibiotic concentrations in greyhounds given ampicillin and amoxicillin by mouth. Journal of Small Animal Practice 1977; 18: 779-786.

5. Kung K, Hauser BR, Wanner M. Effect of the interval between feeding and drug administration on oral ampicillin absorption in dogs. Journal of Small Animal Practice 1995; 36: 65-68.

6. Watson ADJ, Emslie DR, Martin ICA, et al. Effect of ingesta on systemic availability of penicillins administered orally in dogs. Journal of Veterinary Pharmacology and Therapeutics 1986; 9: 140-149.

7. Reppas C, Meyer JH, Sirois PJ, et al. Effect of hydroxypropyl-methylcellulose on gastrointestinal transit and luminal viscosity in dogs. Gastroenterology 1991; 100: 1217-1223.

8. Havrankova J, Lahaie R. Levothyroxine binding by sucralfate. Annals of Internal Medicine 1992; 117: 445-446.

9. McCarthy DM. Sucralfate. New England Journal of Medicine 1991; 325: 1017-1025.

10. Liel Y, Sperber AD, Shany S. Nonspecific intestinal adsorption of levothyroxine by aluminum hydroxide. American Journal of Medicine 1994; 97: 363-365.

11. Campbell NR, Hasinoff BB, Stalts H, et al. Ferrous sulfate reduces thyroxine efficacy in patients with hypothyroidism. Annals of Internal Medicine 1992; 117: 1010-1013.

12. Williams L, Davis JA, Lowenthal DT. The influence of food on the absorption and metabolism of drugs. Medical Clinics of North America 1993; 77: 815-829.

13. Fleisher D, Sheth N, Kou JH. Phenytoin interaction with enteral feedings administered through nasogastric tubes. Journal of Parenteral and Enteral Nutrition 1990; 14: 513-516.

14. Spence RK, Camishion RC. Bioavailability of medication delivered via nasogastric tube is decreased in the immediate postoperative period. American Journal of Surgery 1995; 169: 430-432.

15. Elfant AB, Levine SM, Peikin SR, et al. Ferrous sulfate reduces thyroxine efficacy in patients with hypothyroidism. Annals of Internal Medicine 1992; 117: 1010-1013.

16. Burrows CF, Bright RM, Spencer CP. Influence of dietary composition on gastric emptying and motility in dogs: Potential involvement in acute gastric dilatation. American Journal of Veterinary Research 1985; 46: 2609-2612.

17. Horowitz M, Maddox A, Bochner M, et al. Relationships between gastric emptying of solid and caloric liquid meals and alcohol absorption. American Journal of Physiology 1989; 257: G291-G298.

18. Bueno L, Praddaude F, Fioramonti J, et al. Effect of dietary fiber on gastrointestinal motility and jejunal transit time in dogs. Gastroenterology 1981; 80: 701-707.

19. Heddle R, Collins PJ, Dent J, et al. Motor mechanisms associated with slowing of the gastric emptying of a solid meal by an intraduodenal lipid infusion. Journal of Gastroenterology and Hepatology 1989; 4: 437-447.

20. Chow HH, Lalka D. Pharmacokinetics of d-propranolol following oral, intra-arterial and intraportal administration: Contrasting effects of oral glucose pretreatment. Biopharmaceutics and Drug Disposition 1993; 14: 217-231.

21. Heddle R, Fone D, Dent J, et al. Stimulation of pyloric motility by intraduodenal dextrose in normal subjects. Gut 1988; 29: 1349-1357.

22. Anderson KE, Kappas A. Dietary regulation of cytochrome P450. Annual Review of Nutrition 1991; 11: 141-167.

23. Guengerich FP. Effects of nutritive factors on metabolic processes involving bioactivation and detoxication of chemicals. Annual Review of Nutrition 1984; 4: 207-231.

24. Parke DV, Ioannides C. The role of nutrition in toxicology. Annual Review of Nutrition 1981; 1: 207-234.

25. Guengerich FP. Influence of nutrients and other dietary materials on cytochrome P450 enzymes. American Journal of Clinical Nutrition 1995; 61 (Suppl.): 651S-658S.

26. Fagan TC, Walle T, Oexmann MJ, et al. Increased clearance of propranolol and theophylline by high-protein compared with high-carbohydrate diet. Clinical Pharmacology and Therapeutics 1987; 41: 402-406.

27. Pantuck EJ, Pantuck CB, Kappas A, et al. Effects of protein and carbohydrate content of diet on drug conjugation. Clinical Pharmacology and Therapeutics 1991; 50: 254-258.

28. Fettman MJ. Comparative aspects of glutathione metabolism affecting individual susceptibility to oxidant injury. Compendium on Continuing Education for the Practicing Veterinarian 1991; 13: 1079-1091.

29. Park GD, Spector R, Kitt TM. Effect of dietary protein on renal tubular clearance of drugs in humans. Clinical Pharmacokinetics 1989; 17: 441-451.

30. Behrend EN, Grauer GF, Greco DS, et al. Effects of dietary protein conditioning on gentamicin pharmacokinetics in dogs. Journal of Veterinary Pharmacology and Therapeutics 1994; 17: 259-264.

31. Grauer GF, Greco DS, Behrend EN, et al. Effects of dietary protein conditioning on gentamicin-induced nephrotoxicosis in healthy male dogs. American Journal of Veterinary Research 1994; 55: 90-97.

32. Berlinger WG, Park GD, Spector R. The effect of dietary protein on the clearance of allopurinol and oxypurinol. New England Journal of Medicine 1985; 313: 771-776.

33. Bartges JW, Osborne CA, Felice LJ, et al. Influence of two diets on pharmacokinetic parameters of allopurinol and oxypurinol in healthy beagles. American Journal of Veterinary Research 1997; 58: 511-515.

34. Yoo JSK, Smith TJ, Ning SM, et al. Modulation of the levels of cytochromes P450 in rat liver and lung by dietary lipid. Biochemical Pharmacology 1992; 43: 2535-2542.

35. Mounie J, Faye B, Magdalou J, et al. Modulation of UDP-glucuronyltransferase activity in rats by dietary lipids. Journal of Nutrition 1986; 116: 2034-2043.

36. Umegaki K, Ikegami S, Ichikawa T. Fish oil enhances pentachlorobenzene metabolism and reduces its accumulation in rats. Journal of Nutrition 1995; 125: 147-153.

37. Rogers AE. Methyl donors in the diet and responses to chemical carcinogens. American Journal of Clinical Nutrition 1995; 61 (Suppl.): 659S-665S.

38. Waters B, Kudsk KA, Jarvi EJ, et al. Effect of route of nutrition on recovery of hepatic organic anion clearance after fasting. Surgery 1994; 115: 370-374.

39. Knodell RG, Steele NM, Cerra FB, et al. Effects of parenteral and enteral hyperalimentation on hepatic drug metabolism in the rat. Journal of Pharmacology and Experimental Therapeutics 1984; 229: 589-597.

40. Raftogianis RB, Franklin MR, Glainsky RE. The depression of hepatic drug conjugation reactions in rats after lipid-free total parenteral nutrition administered via the portal vein. Journal of Parenteral and Enteral Nutrition 1995; 19: 303-309.

41. Yang CS, Brady JF, Hong JY. Dietary effects on cytochromes P450, xenobiotic metabolism and toxicity. Federation of American Societies for Experimental Biology Journal 1992; 6: 737-744.

42. Catz CS, Juchau MR, Yaffe SJ. Effects of iron, riboflavin and iodide deficiencies on hepatic drug metabolizing enzyme systems. Journal of Pharmacology and Experimental Therapeutics 1970; 174: 197-205.

43. Danforth E, Burger AG. The impact of nutrition on thyroid hormone physiology and action. Annual Review of Nutrition 1989; 9: 201-227.

44. DeLong MJ, Prohaska HJ, Talalay P. Tissue-specific induction patterns of cancer-protective enzymes in mice by tert-butyl-4-hydroxyanisole and related substituted phenols. Cancer Research 1985; 45: 546-551.

DRUG METABOLISM

45. Guyton KZ, Bhan P, Kuppusamy P, et al. Free radical-derived quinone methide mediates skin tumor promotion by butylated hydroxytoluene hydroperoxide: Expanded role for electrophiles in multistage carcinogenesis. Proceedings of the National Academy of Sciences 1991; 88: 946-950.

46. Fettman MJ, Butler RN, McMichael AJ, et al. Metabolic phenotypes and colorectal neoplasia. Journal of Gastroenterology and Hepatology 1991; 6: 81-90.

47. Brinker KR, Bulger RE, Dobyan DC, et al. Effect of potassium depletion on gentamicin nephrotoxicity. Journal of Laboratory and Clinical Medicine 1981; 98: 292-301.

48. Quarum ML, Houghton DC, Gilbert DN, et al. Increasing dietary calcium moderates experimental gentamicin nephrotoxicity. Journal of Laboratory and Clinical Medicine 1984; 103: 104-114.

49. Schumacher J, Wilson RC, Spano JS, et al. Effect of diet on gentamicin-induced nephrotoxicosis in horses. American Journal of Veterinary Research 1991; 52: 1274-1278.

50. Wong NLM, Magil AB, Dirks JH. Effect of magnesium diet in gentamicin-induced acute renal failure in rats. Nephron 1989; 51: 84-88.

51. Fettman MJ, Coble JM, Hamar DW, et al. Effect of dietary phosphoric acid supplementation on acid-base balance and mineral and bone metabolism in adult cats. American Journal of Veterinary Research 1992; 53: 2125-2135.

52. Anderson RA, Polansky MM, Bryden NA, et al. Supplemental chromium effects on glucose, insulin, glucagon, and urinary chromium losses in subjects consuming controlled low-chromium diets. American Journal of Clinical Nutrition 1991; 54: 909-916.

53. Boden G, Chen X, Ruiz J, et al. Effects of vanadyl sulfate on carbohydrate and lipid metabolism in patients with non-insulin dependent diabetes mellitus. Metabolism 1996; 45: 1130-1135.

54. Meydani SN. Effect of (n-3) polyunsaturated fatty acids on cytokine production and their biological function. Nutrition 1996; 12: S8-S14.

55. Kirk SJ, Barbul A. Role of arginine in trauma, sepsis, and immunity. Journal of Parenteral and Enteral Nutrition 1990; 14: 226S-229S.

56. Hall JC, Heel K, McCauley R. Glutamine. British Journal of Surgery 1996; 83: 305-312.

57. Sellke FW, Tomanek RJ, Harrison DG. L-cysteine selectively potentiates nitroglycerin-induced dilation of small coronary microvessels. Journal of Pharmacology and Experimental Therapeutics 1991; 258: 365-369.

58. Pepine CJ. The therapeutic potential of carnitine in cardiovascular disorders. Clinical Therapeutics 1991; 13: 2-21.

59. Fettman MJ. Potential benefits of psyllium mucilloid supplementation of oral replacement formulas for neonatal calf scours. Compendium on Continuing Education for the Practicing Veterinarian 1992; 14: 247-255.

60. Nugon-Boudon L, Roland N, Flinois JP, et al. Hepatic cytochrome P450 and UDP-glucuronosyl transferase are affected by five sources of dietary fiber in germ-free rats. Journal of Nutrition 1996; 126: 403-409.

61. Brown SA, Riviere JE. Comparative pharmacokinetics of aminoglycoside antibiotics. Journal of Veterinary Pharmacology and Therapeutics 1991; 14: 1-35.

62. Drew B, Barber WP, Williams DG. The effect of excess dietary iodine on pregnant mares and foals. Veterinary Record 1975; 97: 93-95.

63. Driscoll J, Hintz HF, Schryver MF. Goiter in foals caused by excessive iodine. Journal of the American Veterinary Medical Association 1978; 173: 858-859.

64. Bedford PGC, Clarke EGC. Suspected benzoic acid poisoning in the cat. Veterinary Record 1971; 88: 599-601.

65. Wilkie DA, Kirby R. Methemoglobinemia associated with dermal application of benzocaine cream in a cat. Journal of the American Veterinary Medical Association 1988; 192: 85-86.

66. Christopher MM, Perman V, Eaton JW. Contribution of propylene glycol-induced Heinz body formation to anemia in cats. Journal of the American Veterinary Medical Association 1989; 194: 1045-1056.

67. Kaplan AJ. Onion powder in baby food may induce anemia in cats. Journal of the American Veterinary Medical Association 1995; 207: 1405.

68. Reidenberg MM. Obesity and fasting–Effects on drug metabolism and drug action in man. Clinical Pharmacology and Therapeutics 1977; 22: 729-733.

69. Ducharme MP, Slaughter RL, Edwards DJ. Vancomycin pharmacokinetics in a patient population: Effect of age, gender, and body weight. Therapeutic Drug Monitoring 1994; 16: 513-518.

70. Dunn TE, Ludwig EA, Slaughter RL, et al. Pharmacokinetics and pharmacodynamics of methylprednisolone in obesity. Clinical Pharmacology and Therapeutics 1991; 49: 536-549.

71. Caraco Y, Zylber-Katz E, Berry EM, et al. Significant weight reduction in obese subjects enhances carbamazepine elimination. Clinical Pharmacology and Therapeutics 1992; 51: 501-506.

72. Abernethy DR, Greenblatt DJ, Divoll M, et al. The influence of obesity on the pharmacokinetics of oral alprazolam and triazolam. Clinical Pharmacokinetics 1984; 9: 177-183.

73. Shum L, Jusko WJ. Theophylline disposition in obese rats. Journal of Pharmacology and Experimental Therapeutics 1984; 228: 380-386.

74. Yuk J, Nightingale CH, Sweeney K, et al. Pharmacokinetics of nafcillin in obesity. Journal of Infectious Diseases 1988; 157: 1088-1089.

75. Fleming RA, Eldridge RM, Johnson CE, et al. Disposition of high-dose methotrexate in an obese cancer patient. Cancer 1991; 68: 1247-1250.

76. Schwartz AE, Matteo RS, Ornstein E, et al. Pharmacokinetics of sufentanil in obese patients. Anesthesia and Analgesia 1991; 73: 790-793.

77. Allard S, Kinzig M, Boivin G, et al. Intravenous ciprofloxacin disposition in obesity. Clinical Pharmacology and Therapeutics 1993; 54: 368-373.

78. Bentley JB, Vaughan RW, Gondolfi AJ, et al. Halothane biotransformation in obese and nonobese patients. Anesthesiology 1982; 57: 94-97.

79. Corcoran GB, Salazar DE, Chan HH. Obesity as a risk factor in drug-induced organ injury. III. Increased liver and kidney injury by furosemide in the obese overfed rat. Toxicology and Applied Pharmacology 1989; 98: 12-24.

80. Corcoran GB, Salazar DE. Obesity as a risk factor in drug-induced organ injury. IV. Increased gentamicin nephrotoxicity in the obese overfed rat. Journal of Pharmacology and Experimental Therapeutics 1989; 248: 17-22.

81. Corcoran GB, Wong BK. Obesity as a risk factor in drug-induced organ injury: Increased liver and kidney damage by acetaminophen in the obese overfed rat. Journal of Pharmacology and Experimental Therapeutics 1987; 241: 921-927.

■ CASE 27-1

Epilepsy in a Dachshund

Lauren Trepanier, DVM
Diplomate ACVIM (Internal Medicine)
School of Veterinary Medicine
University of Wisconsin-Madison
Madison, Wisconsin, USA

Assess the Animal

An 11-year-old, neutered female dachshund weighing 10 kg was presented for evaluation of poorly controlled seizures. Idiopathic epilepsy had been diagnosed when the dog was six months old. The dog had received phenobarbital, phenytoin or a combination of both drugs for the past nine years. During the past few months, the dog had been having clusters of seizures each month, despite treatment with phenobarbital. Trough serum phenobarbital concentrations (20.4 μg/ml) were within the therapeutic range (15 to 45 μg/ml).

The results of physical and neurologic examinations were normal. The dog's body condition was 3/5. Serum biochemistry analysis revealed increases in liver enzyme activity (alkaline phosphatase, gamma-glutamyl transferase) and abnormal preprandial and postprandial bile acid concentrations. Abdominal ultrasonography revealed mild hepatomegaly with normal hepatic echogenicity. Two small cystic calculi were evident in the urinary bladder.

The presumptive diagnosis was subclinical anticonvulsant-associated hepatopathy. Treatment was initiated with another anticonvulsant, potassium bromide (20 mg/kg body weight, per os, q24h), to control the seizures and allow the dose of phenobarbital to be reduced. The dog had no seizures during the two months after initiation of potassium bromide treatment. Serum bromide concentration had reached 1,100 mg/l (therapeutic range 1,000 to 2,000 mg/l). Alkaline phosphatase and gamma-glutamyl transferase activities had decreased markedly.

On re-examination one month later, the dog was still free from seizures, but had persistent cystic calculi. In the past, the dog had been treated for recurrent struvite crystalluria and cystic calculi with antibiotics and a veterinary therapeutic food. A struvite calculolytic food (Prescription Diet Canine s/d[a]) and antibiotic (Clavamox[b]) were prescribed. Two weeks later, the dog had a cluster of five seizures over a 36-hour period.

Assess the Food(s) and Feeding Method

For the past three years, the dog had been fed a moist veterinary therapeutic food (Prescription Diet Canine c/d[a]) that contains reduced levels of struvite precursor substances and produces an acidic urinary pH. These nutritional characteristics help keep struvite crystalluria and urolithiasis from recurring. Because of the recurrent cystic calculi, the food was changed two weeks ago to a moist veterinary therapeutic food (Prescription Diet Canine s/d[a]) shown to help dissolve struvite uroliths. Nutrient profiles of the two foods are summarized in Table 1.

Questions

1. What potential food-drug interactions could be causing the recent increased seizure activity in this dog?
2. What other diagnostic tests should be performed in this patient?
3. How should the treatment and feeding plan be modified?

Answers and Discussion

1. The most likely food-drug interaction in this dog is between the potassium bromide anticonvulsant and the dietary chloride load. Bromide is excreted slowly, but almost exclusively by the kidneys. The amount of bromide excreted depends on the total body halide (i.e., fluorine, chlorine, bromine, iodine) concentration. Bromide and chloride compete for renal tubular reabsorption. An increase in chloride load, in the form of dietary sodium chloride or ammonium chloride, will markedly increase urinary excretion of bromide in several species, including dogs. In addition, high-chloride foods fed experimentally to dogs will significantly shorten the elimination half-life of bromide and lead to decreases in serum bromide concentrations. The veterinary therapeutic food being fed to the dog to help dissolve the cystic uroliths contains increased levels of sodium chloride to increase urine volume thereby decreasing the concentration of struvite-forming constituents in the urine.
2. Serum bromide concentrations can be measured to determine whether therapeutic levels are being maintained. In this patient, the serum bromide concentration the day after

Table 1. Nutrient profiles of veterinary therapeutic foods fed to the patient.

Nutrient (% DMB)	Canine c/d, canned[a]	Canine s/d, canned[a]
Protein	22.8	7.6
Fat	23.9	26.2
Carbohydrate (NFE)	48.4	58.5
Crude fiber	0.6	2.7
Calcium	0.63	0.28
Phosphorus	0.48	0.10
Potassium	0.51	0.48
Magnesium	0.07	0.02
Sodium	0.29	1.28
Chloride	0.65	2.41

the seizures was 410 mg/l, which was much lower than the concentration measured one month earlier (1,100 mg/l) and below the normal therapeutic range (1,000 to 2,000 mg/l). The anticonvulsant dosage or formulation had not been changed, and the owner was adamant that doses of potassium bromide had not been missed.

3. Because high chloride intake enhances bromide elimination and may have reduced the serum bromide concentration, the owner was instructed to discontinue feeding the moist calculolytic food and to resume feeding the moist struvite-preventive food, with the lower chloride content. The dog was fed to maintain a weight of 10 kg (520 kcal [2.18 MJ]; 1.1 cans/day).

Seven weeks after being fed the lower chloride food again and with daily potassium bromide treatment (20 mg/kg body weight), the dog's serum bromide concentration was 990 mg/l. If a change to a higher chloride food or a food of unknown chloride content is necessary, serum bromide concentrations should be monitored frequently during the weeks to months after the dietary change, and the dosage of potassium bromide should be adjusted as needed to maintain therapeutic bromide concentrations. Eradication of urinary tract infection and monitoring urinary pH to ensure that the urine is continuously acidic are required for successful treatment and prevention of struvite urolithiasis. Serial radiographs and urinalyses should be performed to monitor the cystic uroliths. Surgical removal of uroliths may be indicated if they persist, increase in size or cause clinical problems.

Progress Notes

Serum bromide concentrations remained stable between 1,200 and 1,250 mg/l over the next 21 months. Seizures were not observed since the cluster of seizures that occurred after the change to the high-chloride food.

Endnotes

a. Hill's Pet Nutrition, Inc, Topeka, KS, USA.
b. Pfizer Animal Health, West Chester, PA, USA.

Bibliography

Shaw N, Trepanier LA, Center SA, et al. High dietary chloride content associated with loss of therapeutic serum bromide concentrations in an epileptic dog. Journal of the American Veterinary Medical Association 1996; 208: 234-236.

Trepanier LA, Babish JG. Effect of dietary chloride content on the elimination of bromide by dogs. Research in Veterinary Science 1995; 58: 252-255.

CASE 27-2

Hyperadrenocorticism in a Dachshund

Philip Roudebush, DVM
Diplomate ACVIM (Internal Medicine)
Hill's Science and Technology Center
Topeka, Kansas, USA

Assess the Animal

An eight-year-old neutered female dachshund was examined for chronic dermatitis. The owners reported a slowly progressive, non-pruritic dermatopathy and polydipsia and polyuria of three to four months' duration. The dermatitis had been treated with antibiotics and griseofulvin with no response. To the owners' knowledge, the dog had received no corticosteroids.

Physical examination revealed an alert, active 10-kg dog with normal body condition (3/5), a dry coat and a "pot-bellied" appearance. The abdomen was distended and totally devoid of hair. The skin on the abdomen was markedly thinned. Bilateral alopecia and hyperpigmentation were evident on the dorsum, extending from the shoulders to the flank. Focal, circumscribed plaques with peripheral erythema were present in the inguinal and axillary regions. The remainder of the physical examination was normal.

Diagnostic evaluation included a complete blood count (lymphopenia, eosinopenia), serum biochemistry profile (hypercholesterolemia 1,414 mg/dl, normal 125 to 250) and increased alkaline phosphatase activity (491 IU/l, normal less than 50 IU), urinalysis (dilute urine with hematuria and bacteriuria) and thoracic and abdominal radiographs (calcification of subcutaneous tissues along the back). Subsequent urine culture yielded large numbers of *Escherichia coli*. Histologic evaluation of skin biopsy specimens confirmed calcinosis cutis. Water consumption in the hospital exceeded 120 ml/kg body weight/24 hours (normal = 40 to 60 ml/kg body weight).

The tentative diagnosis was pituitary-dependent hyperadrenocorticism with secondary calcinosis cutis and bacterial urinary tract infection. Hyperadrenocorticism was confirmed by excessive plasma cortisol response to intramuscular injection of ACTH gel (cortisol, pre 27 µg/dl and cortisol, two hours postACTH 60.0 µg/dl; normal pre cortisol 0.5 to 4.0 µg/dl and postACTH 8.0 to 20.0 µg/dl).

Assess the Food(s) and Feeding Method

The dog was fed a combination of a commercial grocery store brand dry food and a grocery store brand moist food. The dry food was available free choice and the moist food was fed once daily in the morning.

Question

1. Mitotane[a] (o,p'-DDD) was used to treat the hyperadrenocorticism in this patient. What food-drug interactions would be important to consider in the treatment and feeding plans?

Table 1. Availability of mitotane in dogs when given in various vehicles.*

Dogs	Dosage method	Maximum plasma drug concentration (mg/l)
Normal	Tablets, fasting	0.4
	Pure drug in emulsion	11.0
	Ground tablets in oil with food	15.4
	Tablets in food	13.0
Hyperadrenocorticism	Tablets in food	24.5

*Adapted from Watson ADJ, Rijnberk A, Moolenaar AJ. Systemic availability of o,p'-DDD in normal dogs, fasted and fed, and in dogs with hyperadrenocorticism. Research in Veterinary Science 1987; 43: 160-165.

Answer and Discussion

1. Mitotane is a commonly used drug for treatment of canine hyperadrenocorticism. Mitotane exerts a direct cytotoxic effect on the adrenal cortex, resulting in selective, progressive necrosis and atrophy of the zonae fasciculata and reticularis.

The efficacy of mitotane therapy in patients with hyperadrenocorticism can be improved markedly by dosing with food. Studies have shown that the systemic availability of mitotane is very poor when intact tablets are administered to fasting dogs, whereas availability is much better from intact or powdered tablets given with food (Table 1). Mitotane is soluble in fat but poorly soluble in water. The presence of dietary fat during drug administration could assist in dissolution and absorption of lipophilic drugs such as mitotane. Based on these studies, mitotane should always be administered with meals.

The interaction between food and drug probably explains some of the variation in response of pituitary-dependent hyperadrenocorticism patients to mitotane, in relation to the time required to gain initial control with daily administration and the efficacy of weekly maintenance doses. Failure to administer the drug with food may contribute to the apparent "resistance" to the effects of the drug seen in some dogs with hyperadrenocorticism.

Interactions between drugs and ingested food are common. The most common outcome is reduced or delayed absorption of the drug, although absorption is sometimes increased or unaffected by food. In many instances the changes in drug availability are modest and their clinical significance is not great. However, the substantial effect of food on mitotane availability is almost certainly clinically important and should be considered when prescribing adrenolytic therapy with this drug.

Clinical signs that owners should monitor include the dog's attitude, appetite and water intake. A common, early adverse sign of mitotane toxicity is diminished appetite, which usually occurs before other adverse clinical signs develop such as vomiting, weakness and complete anorexia. Therefore, the owners should observe the appetite closely before administration of the daily mitotane dose. If the food is consumed rapidly, the owner should administer the mitotane immediately after the dog finishes the meal. If the food is consumed slowly or not at all, the owners should contact the veterinarian before administering the drug.

Progress Notes

Therapy was initiated at home with an induction or loading dose of mitotane (42 mg/kg body weight/day for seven to 10 days). One 500-mg tablet was given each day following the morning meal of moist food. The dog ate the morning meal rapidly over the next 10 days; mitotane was administered each day. By Day 10 of treatment, daily water consumption had decreased from more than 120 ml/kg body weight/day to 31 ml/kg body weight/day. Daily mitotane administration was stopped and weekly therapy initiated. The dog was also treated with sulfisoxazole for the concurrent cystitis.

Endnote

a. Lysodren. Bristol-Myers Oncology Division, Evansville, IN, USA.

Bibliography

Peterson ME, Kintzer PP. Medical treatment of pituitary-dependent hyperadrenocorticism: Mitotane. Veterinary Clinics of North America: Small Animal Practice 1997; 27: 255-272.

Kintzer PP, Peterson ME. Mitotane (o,p'-DDD) treatment of 200 dogs with pituitary-dependent hyperadrenocorticism. Journal of Veterinary Internal Medicine 1991; 5: 182-190.

Watson ADJ, Rijnberk A, Moolenaar AJ. Systemic availability of o,p'-DDD in normal dogs, fasted and fed, and in dogs with hyperadrenocorticism. Research in Veterinary Science 1987; 43: 160-165.

DRUG METABOLISM

SECTION V

Feeding Small Mammals, Reptiles and Birds

CHAPTER 28

Feeding Small Exotic Mammals

James W. Carpenter

Christine M. Kolmstetter

"All the thoughts of a turtle are turtles, and of a rabbit, rabbits."
The Natural History of Intellect, 1893

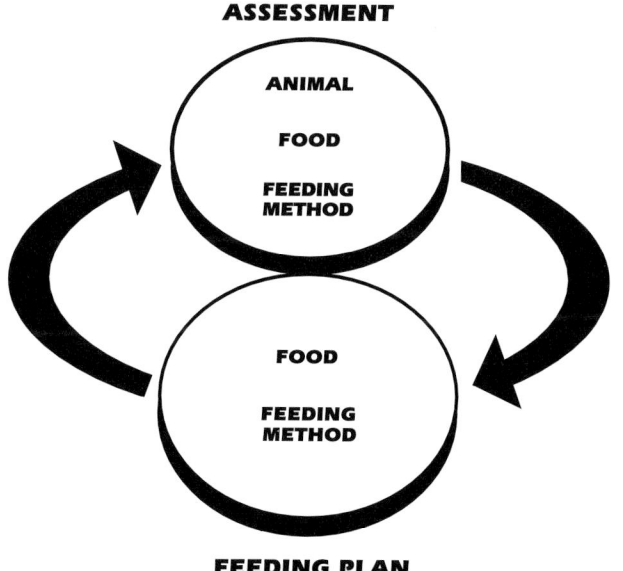

ASSESSMENT

ANIMAL

FOOD

FEEDING METHOD

FOOD

FEEDING METHOD

FEEDING PLAN

Note: The reader is referred to Chapter 1 for a detailed discussion of the iterative process of clinical nutrition.

INTRODUCTION

Ferrets, rabbits and rodents are popular pets that are often presented to veterinarians for advice about their care, including diet and feeding management and treatment of medical disorders. Each species presents nutritional challenges. Dietary management of ferrets, rabbits and rodents may be modified by lifestage, level of physical activity and state of health. Owners may need advice about feeding healthy pets to meet needs for maintenance, growth, reproduction or stress. Patients may present with disorders caused by an imbalanced diet or improper feeding practices. In addition, nutritional support is used for rehabilitation of debilitated animals. This chapter covers the nutritional needs of healthy pet ferrets, rabbits and rodents and those with common disease processes. Appendix R summarizes feeding and care of orphaned and injured mammalian wildlife.

Dietary management begins with assessment of the animal, food and feeding method. A feeding plan is formulated based on the results of this assessment. (See Chapter 1.) Although data are lacking for specific exotic species, assessment is similar to that for other mammals. It begins with a thorough history of the animal, including diet, husbandry and environment. Physical examination includes recording body weight and assessing body condition, using body condition scores.

Details on body condition scoring systems are unavailable for most small mammals; however, a five-point system (where 1 = cachectic, 3 = optimal and 5 = obese) can be applied to all species. Body condition scores qualita-

KEY WORDS & TERMS—SMALL EXOTIC MAMMALS*

Anorexia	Gastric stasis	Mustelid
Cecotrope	Hindgut fermenter	Open-rooted teeth
Cecotrophy	Kit	Pregnancy toxemia
Coprophagy	Lagomorph	Rodent
Diastema	Malocclusion	Scurvy
Enterotoxemia	Mucoid enteropathy	Trichobezoar

*Key words and terms are defined in the Glossary.

KEY POINTS—SMALL EXOTIC MAMMALS

1. Ferrets require highly digestible foods containing large amounts of protein and fat, and therefore, may be fed commercial foods (preferably dry) manufactured for cats, mink or ferrets.
2. To ensure high biologic value and maintain high food digestibility, most dietary protein for ferrets should originate from animal-based ingredients, with minimal plant-source ingredients.
3. Growing and lactating ferrets should be fed foods formulated for growth and reproduction.
4. Cecotropes are produced by rabbits during the night and early morning and are consumed directly from the anus to provide the animal with additional protein and microbially synthesized B-complex vitamins.
5. High-fiber diets for rabbits promote intestinal motility, help prevent gastric stasis and subsequent formation of trichobezoars (hairballs), provide nutrition for intestinal microorganisms and minimize susceptibility to enteritis.
6. Anorexia is a common clinical presentation of pet rabbits and frequently results from malocclusion of teeth or from trichobezoars.
7. Trichobezoars and gastric stasis in rabbits can usually be prevented by feeding a high-fiber diet, minimizing stress and boredom and grooming the animal frequently.

8. Some cases of mucoid enteropathy and enterotoxemia in rabbits appear to be dietary related.
9. The preferred diet for pet rabbits is a high-fiber pelleted food, supplemented with loose hay (mixed grass hay, timothy hay or grass clippings) fed free choice and judicious amounts of leafy greens and fresh vegetables.
10. Because the rabbit's intestinal microflora is sensitive to abrupt changes in osmolarity, pH and other factors, food changes should be introduced gradually.
11. Rodents are identified by their four prominent, continuously erupting incisor teeth. Canine teeth are absent.
12. Most rodents are coprophagic; their feces are an important source of B-complex vitamins and protein.
13. Anorexia, weight loss and dehydration are common clinical problems in pet rodents and are frequently the result of improper husbandry.
14. Guinea pigs are unable to synthesize vitamin C. Hypovitaminosis C secondary to improper diet is a common clinical problem.
15. Chinchillas should be fed a diet high in fiber.
16. Enteritis, often secondary to a diet too low in fiber, is a common problem in hamsters and carries a guarded prognosis.
17. Gerbils, rats and mice should be fed a dry rodent food, free choice.

tively assess amounts of body fat and muscle. Excessive loss of body fat suggests starvation (due to husbandry, diet or disease), whereas excessive loss of muscling suggests advanced starvation, forced inactivity or altered metabolic states (often due to disease).

Other factors may become part of the overall assessment. Small mammals, for example, can also be evaluated for the condition of their skin and fur and their behavior and attitude. As for other species, serum biochemistry profiles are of limited use in nutritional assessment.

DOMESTIC FERRETS

Husbandry

The domestic or European ferret (*Mustela putorius furo*) is a member of the family Mustelidae, order Carnivora. Other mustelids include the mink (*Mustela vison*), skunk (*Mephitis* spp, *Spilogale* spp) and weasel (*Mustela* spp).[1]

Pet ferrets were domesticated from the wild European polecat and were probably brought to North America by English settlers 300 years ago.[2] Two variations are recognized, based on coloration: 1) the wild (or fitch) ferret is pale yellow buff with a black mask, legs and tail and 2) the albino ferret is white with pink eyes.

Ferrets have become increasingly popular as companion animals due to their small size, ease of care and maintenance and inquisitive personality.[1] In recent years, ferrets also have been used extensively as laboratory animals. Although the size of the pet ferret population in the United States is unknown, estimates are as high as eight to 12 million.[a] General texts and articles on husbandry and medicine are useful introductions to these popular pets.[1-6]

Key Nutritional Factors

Ferrets are carnivores; they thrive on highly digestible foods containing large amounts of protein and fat, with minimal soluble carbohydrate and fiber. Thus, pet ferrets may be fed commercial foods manufactured for cats or mink. Both types of products appear to be adequate for all lifestages of ferrets. Commercial foods marketed specifically for ferrets mirror the formulations known to be successful in mink and cats.[7,8] Guidelines for cat foods may be used when assessing the completeness and balance of foods intended for ferrets.[8] (See Appendix J.)

Protein and Amino Acids

Ferrets require foods containing 32 to 38% protein (dry matter basis [DMB] and metabolizable energy [ME] basis). These levels correspond to label guaranteed analyses of about 29 to 34% for dry and about 7 to 8.5% for moist cat food.

Specific amino acid requirements are unknown for ferrets, but are assumed to be similar to requirements for cats. For example, young ferrets fed a single meal of an arginine-free food developed hyperammonemia, as do young cats.[9] Likewise, cats and other strict carnivores need the high biologic value of proteins found in meat. To ensure high biologic value and maintain high food digestibility, dietary protein for ferrets should originate primarily from animal-based ingredients (poultry meal, meat by-products, eggs).

Fat and Fatty Acids

Ferrets thrive when fed commercial foods containing 20 to 30% fat (DMB). These levels correspond to label guaranteed analyses of about 18 to 27% for dry and 5 to 8% for moist cat food.

Specific fatty acid requirements are unknown, but it is assumed that ferrets require linoleic and arachidonic acids. The former is abundant in vegetable oils, whereas the latter is abundant in animal-based ingredients (especially nervous tissue). Fatty acid requirements should be met by providing meat-based commercial cat or mink foods.

Soluble Carbohydrates and Fiber

Other strictly carnivorous species, such as cats and mink, have no dietary requirement for carbohydrates, including fiber. Glucose is provided by hepatic gluconeogenesis, using amino acids. Dietary fiber may play a role in weight control and reduction and in certain gastrointestinal disorders.

The simple, short digestive tract of strict carnivores dictates hydrolysis of most dietary fuels, with little or no hindgut fermentation of fiber. Generally, foods with added fiber should not be fed to healthy ferrets and those in above-maintenance physiologic states, such as growth and lactation, but those foods may be considered for patients with fiber-responsive disorders.

Energy

Metabolic rates for mustelids vary, but generally those with a long thin body shape, short fur, strict carnivorous behavior and high activity (e.g., ferrets and mink) have high metabolic rates, hence high caloric needs, relative to other mustelids (e.g., skunks) or mammals (e.g., cats) with different body shapes and activity levels.[10] Seasonal metabolic cycles complicate predictions of energy needs. Generally, autumn (shortening daylight) signals fat deposition and weight gain, whereas spring (lengthening daylight) signals fat mobilization and weight loss.[11]

Table 28-1. Average daily metabolizable energy (ME) intakes for ferrets at maintenance (M) and above-maintenance states, based on the recommendation of 200 to 300 kcal ME/kg body weight. For this table, 250 kcal/kg was used. Much variation between individuals should be expected.*

Body weight (g)	Daily energy intake (kcal ME)				
	M	**1.5M**	**2M**	**2.5M**	**3M**
200	50	75	100	125	150
300	75	112	150	188	225
400	100	150	200	250	300
500	125	188	250	312	375
600	150	225	300	375	450
700	175	262	350	438	525
800	200	300	400	500	600
900	225	338	450	562	675
1,000	250	375	500	625	750
1,200	300	450	600	750	900
1,400	350	525	700	875	1,050
1,600	400	600	800	1,000	1,200
1,800	450	675	900	1,125	1,350
2,000	500	750	1,000	1,250	1,500
2,200	550	825	1,100	1,375	1,650

*To convert to kJ, multiply kcal by 4.184.

Ferrets reportedly consume 200 to 300 kcal (837 to 1,255 kJ) ME/kg body weight daily for adult maintenance (Table 28-1).[6] This amount equals about one-half to three-fourths cup of dry cat food containing about 400 kcal (1,674 kJ) ME per cup (standard 8-oz. measuring cup). This is about three times greater than the food intake of an average cat.

Energy needs increase for growth and reproduction (Table 28-1). Caloric requirements may be met by increased intake of an adult maintenance food or by consumption of a food with increased caloric density. Increasing food intake works to a point, but foods with higher caloric density should be offered in demanding situations. Thus, growing and lactating ferrets should be fed cat foods formulated for growth and reproduction. (See Appendix J.)

A ration with a caloric density of about 5.0 kcal/g (20.9 kJ/g) dry matter (DM) has been recommended for ferrets.[6] Generally, dry cat foods contain 4.0 to 5.0 kcal ME/g (16.7 to 20.9 kJ ME/g) DM, or about 360 to 450 kcal ME/100 g (about 1 cup) (1,506 to 1,883 kJ ME/100 g). Moist cat foods contain 4.0 to 5.0 kcal ME/g (16.7 to 20.9 kJ ME/g) DM, or about 360 to 450 kcal ME/400 g (about one 13-oz. can) (1,506 to 1,883 kJ ME/400 g). Dry foods are generally preferred for ferrets because their texture may help prevent periodontal disease.

Obesity is uncommon in ferrets, but may occur in later years as activity decreases. Most ferrets, therefore, are fed successfully by free-choice access to commercial cat or mink dry food with judicious additions of snacks. Food intake should be regulated for overweight ferrets.

Vitamins and Minerals

Dietary guidelines for cats and mink have been established by controlled comparative trials and thus are followed for pet ferrets because of limited research data in this species (Appendix J). Most published accounts suggest that ferrets require vitamins and minerals in amounts similar to other carnivores. For example, research suggests that ferrets grow well when fed calcium (0.6 to 0.8% DM) and phosphorus (0.4 to 1.0% DM) in ranges fed to other mammalian carnivores.[12] Unlike cats, however, ferrets absorb ß-carotene (the plant-based precursor of vitamin A).[13] Despite this interesting finding, foods for pet ferrets should contain preformed vitamin A (e.g., retinyl palmitate) and should not rely on carotenoids.

Generally, deficiencies of specific vitamins and minerals are unlikely to occur in ferrets fed commercial foods formulated for cats, ferrets or mink. Deficiencies are more likely to occur in ferrets fed poorly formulated homemade foods. Imbalanced homemade foods for carnivores are most likely to be deficient in calcium and iodine. Both nutrients are deficient in common ingredients such as meats, most dairy products, rice and vegetables. Homemade foods should contain sources of calcium (bone meal, calcium carbonate) and iodine (iodized salt, kelp). Chapter 6 contains recipes for balanced homemade foods for cats that may be given to owners who insist on cooking for their ferrets.[14]

Deficiencies may also occur when excessive amounts of table food or supplements are added to commercial cat, ferret and mink foods. Supplementation with table foods or single ingredients above about 10% of DM may create an imbalance in previously balanced foods. For example, adding large amounts of corn oil reduces protein and other essential nutrients to deficient levels (on an energy basis). Deficiencies may also arise when large amounts of calcium are added to balanced foods because excess calcium interferes with absorption of trace minerals such as zinc and copper.

Vitamin and mineral toxicities may occur in ferrets overdosed with commercial supplements (e.g., chewable vitamin-mineral preparations given as treats) or with specific ingredients (e.g., vitamin A intoxication from an all-liver diet).

Special Nutritional Needs

Kits from six weeks (weaning) to about 14 weeks of age require a soft, moist food. Dry cat food (formulated for all lifestages or for growth and reproduction) soaked with water is generally adequate for growth.[15] Goat's milk added to softened cat food has been recommended for slow-growing kits.[15] Ferrets achieve 90% of their adult size by 14 weeks of age, thus food consumption is very high.

Pregnant and lactating ferrets also require above-maintenance levels of food. Generally, pregnant animals need about twice the maintenance level, whereas animals at peak lactation need three to four times the maintenance amounts.

Food intake varies seasonally. Under natural lighting conditions, ferrets eat more and gain weight in the fall in preparation for the cold winter months.[15] As the photoperiod increases in the spring, ferrets tend to lose most of their body fat, thereby preparing them for summer heat. Weight cycling may occur at other times as a result of unnatural photoperiods.[15]

Selected Nutritional Diseases

Although the prevalence of nutrient deficiencies and toxicities in ferrets is largely unknown, specific diet-related problems are rarely seen in practice. Like dogs and cats, some ferrets with dermatologic problems respond to dietary supplementation with fatty acids (See Chapters 15 and 26.), but direct causal links between diet and disease remain to be established.

Anecdotal reports suggest that some, but not all, ferrets with dermatologic problems may respond to adding meat or liver to their usual diet of commercial cat food. This finding suggests that ferrets may be responding to arachidonic acid in meat or perhaps additional protein. When feeding liver, care must be taken to avoid inducing vitamin A toxicosis. Generally, no more than 30 g of liver should be added per 800 kcal (3,347 kJ).

Ferrets fed excessive dietary fat risk protein deficiency. Protein deficiency manifests as slow growth in the young, low conception rates and failed lactation in breeding females and impaired immunity and generalized unthriftiness in ferrets of all ages. The problem may be corrected by feeding a commercial cat food.

Commercial foods appear to provide adequate levels of vitamins and minerals for ferrets. Most published reports of clinical problems have occurred in large breeding operations or under laboratory conditions.

Vitamin E deficiency results in yellow discoloration of body fat, hemolytic anemia, anorexia and a progressively impaired gait leading to paralysis.[6] Affected young growing kits are found dead or depressed, cry when handled and are reluctant to move. Diffuse firm swellings under the skin and prominent subcutaneous lumps in the inguinal areas are clinical manifestations of the deficiency.[6] This disease has been termed yellow fat disease, fatty degeneration of the liver and steatitis. It results from feeding foods containing high levels of polyunsaturated fatty acids with inadequate vitamin E.[6] Diagnosis is based on the clinical signs and a history of feeding a food containing high levels of polyunsaturated fatty acids, deficient levels of vitamin E or both.

Thiamin deficiency resulting from feeding fish containing thiaminase has been reported to occur on ferret farms in New Zealand.[6] The disease was seen in weanling animals and adults. Clinical signs included anorexia and lethargy followed by dyspnea, prostration and convulsions.

Zinc toxicosis has also been reported to occur in ferrets on farms in New Zealand.[6] The toxicosis resulted from excessive intake of zinc, that had leached from galvanized feeding pans and water dishes. Presumptive zinc toxicosis was based on clinical signs (anemia, posterior weakness and lethargy), gross pathology, histologic examination of the kidney and liver and demonstration of elevated levels of zinc in these tissues.

Copper toxicosis has been reported to occur in sibling pet ferrets.[16] Signs referred to liver disease; tissue copper concentrations confirmed the diagnosis. A genetic predisposition to copper toxicosis was proposed.

Ferrets also can develop lower urinary tract disease similar to that seen in domestic cats. Suggestions for prevention mirror the recommendations for feline lower urinary tract disease (See Chapter 21.), but the disease in ferrets is not as well-documented.

Feeding Plan

Foods for ferrets should be formulated for strict carnivores—mink, cats or specifically for ferrets. Protein and fat levels should preferably be 32 to 38% and 20% DM, respectively. Commercial foods should generally contain more animal-based than plant-based ingredients, to ensure high digestibility, palatability and protein quality.

Foods may be fed free choice, unless the ferret is overweight. Because of their high metabolic rate, ferrets consume more calories, hence more food, than cats.

Healthy ferrets should not be fed high-fiber foods. Dietary fiber, though, may play a role in weight control and in fiber-responsive disorders.

Other dietary recommendations for ferrets include:

• Vitamin and mineral supplements are generally unnecessary for healthy ferrets fed well-formulated commercial cat or mink foods. Supplementing foods that are already balanced increases the risk of creating an imbalance and secondary deficiencies or intoxications.

• It is common practice to feed ferrets commercial cat food supplemented with table foods such as cooked meat, fish, poultry, eggs or fresh liver.[3,4] Foods containing lactose or simple sugars should be avoided to prevent digestive upset. Fruits and vegetables may be offered in limited quantities; ferrets will not digest the fiber in these foods. Some fruit and vegetable treats preferred by ferrets include cucumbers, green peppers, bananas, raisins and melons.[5] A rule of thumb is to offer a ferret no more than one teaspoon per day of any treat.[5]

• Dry foods are generally recommended for ferrets because they may help keep the animal's teeth and gums in good condition, cost less and are easier to store and feed than moist foods.

• Ferrets do not need to eat mice or other rodents.

• Because hairballs occasionally occur in ferrets, feline hairball laxatives may be given to susceptible individuals every other day, following label dosage recommendations for cats.[5] (See Chapter 22.)

• Bones should be avoided to prevent obstructions in the oral cavity and gastrointestinal tract.

• Fresh water, in either a bowl or drinking bottle, should be available free choice.

RABBITS

Husbandry

The domestic rabbit (*Oryctolagus cuniculus*) (order Lagomorpha) is a descendent of the old world rabbit of western Europe and northwestern Africa.[17] It has become a popular pet, resulting in an increased demand for veterinary care for this species. Although domestic rabbits are used for commercial meat and fur production, teaching and biomedical research, exhibition by rabbit fanciers and as outdoor pets, most now are probably household pets. As pets, rabbits are small, relatively easy to care for, fastidious, quiet mannered and can be litter box trained.

As noted by their dental formula (I2/1, C0/0, P3/2, M3/3), lagomorphs can be distinguished from rodents by the presence of two pairs of upper incisor teeth. The smaller, second upper incisor teeth are directly behind the first and lack a cutting edge. Rabbit teeth are all open-rooted (continuously growing). Malocclusion and overgrowth are most likely to occur with the incisor teeth (Figure 28-1), which grow 10 to 12 cm a year throughout life, although malocclusion and overgrowth of the molar teeth may also occur.[18]

As herbivorous hindgut fermenters, rabbits have a gastrointestinal system resembling that of horses.[19] Both species possess a noncompartmentalized stomach and a large cecum. The simple stomach has thin walls and indistinctly separated glandular and nonglandular areas. The

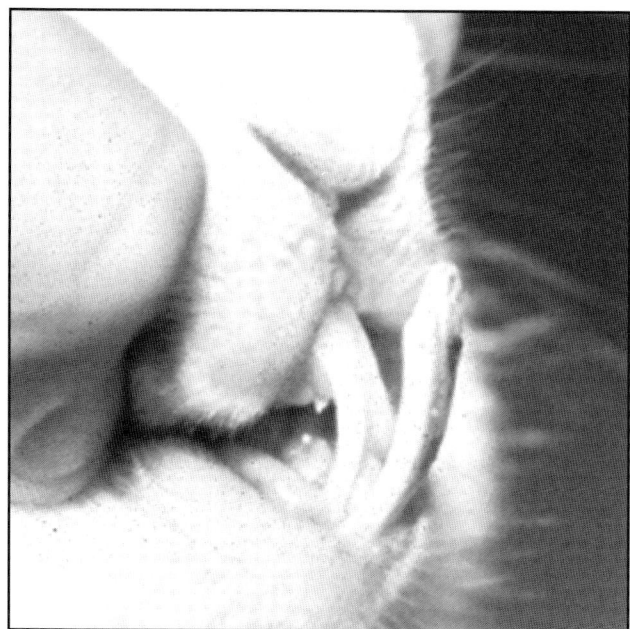

Figure 28-1. Overgrown, maloccluded incisor teeth frequently result in malnutrition or anorexia in rabbits.

Table 28-2. Average daily metabolizable energy intakes for rabbits at maintenance (M) and above-maintenance states.* Much variation between individuals should be expected.

Body weight (kg)	Daily energy intake (kcal ME)**				
	M	Growth	Early gestation	Late gestation	Lactation
1.4	129	258	174	258	387
1.6	142	284	192	284	426
1.8	156	312	211	312	468
2.0	168	336	227	336	504
2.3	187	374	252	374	561
2.5	199	398	269	398	597
2.7	211	422	285	422	633
3.0	228	456	308	456	684
3.2	239	478	323	478	717
3.4	250	500	338	500	750
3.6	261	522	352	522	783
4.1	288	576	389	576	864
4.5	309	618	417	618	927
5.4	354	708	478	708	1,062
6.4	402	804	543	804	1,206
7.3	444	888	599	888	1,332

*Adapted from Tobin G. Small pets—Food types, nutrient requirements and nutritional disorders. Manual of Companion Animal Nutrition & Feeding. London, UK: British Small Animal Veterinary Association, 1996; 208-225.
**To convert to kJ, multiply kcal by 4.184.

terminal ileum expands and forms a thin-walled sacculus rotundus. Large amounts of lymphatic tissue are located in the wall of the sacculus, giving it a "honeycomb" external appearance. The cecum is very large (perhaps about 10-fold the stomach capacity) and thin walled, occupying much of the abdominal cavity. Antiperistaltic action moves small particles and solubles into the cecum, where cellulose is digested and fermented. The gastrointestinal transit time is four to five hours.

Instead of chewing cud for improved digestion, as would ruminants, rabbits use coprophagy. Cecotropes (specialized fecal pellets produced in the cecum) are excreted during the night and early morning as clusters of grapelike material and are consumed (cecotrophy) directly from the anus. Cecotropes contain twice the protein (25 to 30% DM) of usual fecal pellets, more B vitamins and much less fiber.[20] Cecotrophy is particularly important for efficient digestion of forage proteins. The process also provides the animal with microbially synthesized B-complex vitamins, microbial protein and small quantities of volatile fatty acids. The pH of the rabbit's stomach is extremely acidic (<2.0), which may neutralize large amounts of bacteria ingested with cecotropes.

The most clinically relevant feature, however, of the rabbit's gastrointestinal system may be that the myoelectrical initiation of peristalsis does not occur in the stomach, but rather in the distal duodenum or jejunum. This feature allows hair to accumulate in the stomach and may account for the common occurrence of gastric trichobezoars in rabbits (Figures 28-2 to 28-4).[21]

Key Nutritional Factors

Energy

Daily caloric needs for maintenance of healthy adult rabbits are estimated to be $100(BW_{kg})^{0.75}$ (Table 28-2).[20] Thus, a healthy adult rabbit weighing 4 kg consumes almost 300 kcal/day (1,255kJ). Because energy needs relate to metabolic body size, smaller breeds require a higher caloric intake per unit of body weight.

Daily energy needs increase for growth (190 to $210[BW_{kg}]^{0.75}$), early gestation ($135[BW_{kg}]^{0.75}$), late gestation ($200[BW_{kg}]^{0.75}$) and lactation ($300[BW_{kg}]^{0.75}$) (Table 28-2).[20] Thus, there are two- to threefold increases in energy needs; therefore, food consumption correspondingly increases during growth and lactation.[22,23] Energy needs also increase in cold environmental temperatures.

Production rabbits often adjust feed intake to meet energy needs, when appropriate feed is available. Pet rabbits, however, occasionally overeat and risk obesity.

Protein and Fat

Rabbits require 13 to 18% DM dietary crude protein (Table 28-3). Research suggests that 13% is adequate for maintenance, 15 to 16% for maximum growth and 18% for gestating or lactating does. These levels are allowable minimums determined for laboratory and production rabbits and do not take into account optimal protein levels for household pets, or protein needs for stressed or sick rabbits. Generally, though, healthy house rabbits should thrive at these levels if maintained in comfortable surroundings.

Rabbits require adequate amounts of relatively high-protein, high-quality foods, which is achieved by efficient use of plant proteins, such as those found in alfalfa and clover (Table 28-4). Low-protein foods and nonprotein nitrogen are used poorly. Bacterial protein from the lower bowel contributes little to the amino acid needs of growing rabbits, but may benefit adults fed poor-quality protein at maintenance.

Rabbits require no added dietary fat. Most foods contain 2 to 5% fat, which is sufficient (Table 28-3).

Soluble Carbohydrates and Fiber

Rabbits need a minimum of 12 to 16% dietary crude fiber. The low end of the range, 12%, has been recommended for lactating does, 14% for growth and gestation and 15 to 16% for maintenance (Table 28-3).[24] These levels are minimums established for production rabbits; higher fiber levels may benefit pets.

Adequate insoluble dietary fiber is important for rabbit health. In studies, growth rates were reduced in young rabbits fed low-fiber foods. Growth rates of production rabbits are optimal when foods containing 10 to 15% crude fiber DMB are fed. Enteritis is more common in rabbits fed less than 10% crude fiber.[19] Fiber promotes intestinal motility, provides nutrition for intestinal microorganisms and minimizes susceptibility to enteritis. Cecal fermentation of fiber produces volatile fatty acids (acetate, butyrate and proprionate), which are absorbed and used for energy. Volatile fatty acids aid in the control of pathogenic organisms by helping to maintain a low cecal pH. Foods with adequate fiber help to prevent obesity and hair chewing (Table 28-4).[22]

Table 28-3. Requirements of selected nutrients for rabbits.*

Nutrients (DMB)	Growth (4-12 wks)	Lactation	Gestation	Maintenance	Does and litters fed one food
Crude protein (%)	15	18	18	13	17
Amino acids					
Methionine + cystine (%)	0.5	0.6	–	–	0.55
Lysine (%)	0.6	0.75	–	–	0.7
Crude fiber (%)	14	12	14	15-16	14
Digestible energy (kcal/kg)**	2,500	2,700	2,500	2,200	2,500
Fat (%)	3	5	3	3	3
Minerals					
Calcium (%)	0.5	1.1	0.8	0.6	1.1
Phosphorus (%)	0.3	0.8	0.5	0.4	0.8
Vitamins					
A (IU/kg)	6,000	12,000	12,000	–	10,000
D (IU/kg)	900	900	900	–	900
E (ppm)	50	50	50	50	50

Key: DMB = dry matter basis.
*Adapted from Cheeke PR. Rabbits. In: Pond WG, Church DC, Pond KR, eds. Basic Animal Nutrition and Feeding. New York, NY: John Wiley & Sons, 1995; 451-459.
**To convert to kJ, multiply kcal by 4.184.

Vitamins

A dietary supply of vitamins A, D and E is an integral part of rabbit nutrition. Bacteria in the gut synthesize B vitamins in adequate quantities. Thus, addition of B vitamins to commercial foods may be unnecessary, though it often occurs. The adequacy of vitamin K synthesis in the gut is questionable; therefore, manufacturers often add this fat-soluble vitamin to commercial foods.

Because vitamins A and E are readily destroyed by oxidation, food preparation and storage methods should prevent losses from excess light and heat. Foods containing more than 30% alfalfa meal may provide sufficient vitamin A in the form of the precursor ß-carotene.[25] Deficiency may occur, however, if old (more than one year postharvest) alfalfa is fed.

Table 28-3 lists recommended levels of dietary vitamin A for production rabbits. Recommendations for pet rabbits include 7,000 IU vitamin A/kg food, 40 mg vitamin E/kg food and 2 mg vitamin K/kg food.[20]

Minerals

Calcium requirements for rabbits appear to be similar to those for other species (e.g., 0.5 to 1.0% DM [Table 28-3]). Rabbits absorb calcium very efficiently and the excess is excreted in urine, rather than in the bile as typically occurs in other species.[19] Interestingly, rabbits have a higher than normal serum calcium level (12 to 13 mg/dl) compared to other mammals. These physiologic rarities (shared by horses) have led some investigators to suggest that excess dietary calcium (found in such foods as alfalfa hay) may harm rabbits. These assumptions may appear to be incorrect for healthy rabbits. Table 28-5 lists calcium and phosphorus contents of commonly fed forages.

Most rabbit foods contain adequate calcium because formulations include alfalfa meal, which averages about 1.4% calcium, 0.2% phosphorus and at least 300 IU vitamin D_2 (ergocalciferol) per g (DM).[26] Prolonged intake of high-calcium foods (4% DM) may cause calcification of soft tissues such as the aorta and kidneys; hypervitaminosis D most likely exacerbates the effect because it aids calcium absorption.[19] Feeding a food (i.e., possibly a diet lower in alfalfa or alfalfa meal) containing 0.5% calcium prevents soft tissue calcification.

Special Nutritional Needs

The energy requirements of production rabbits fed free choice have been met by feeding dry foods containing 2.2 kcal/g (9.2 kJ/g) of food during maintenance, 2.5 kcal/g (10.5 kJ/g) of food during growth and gestation and 2.7 kcal/g (11.3 kJ/g) during lactation.[24] Alternatively, energy

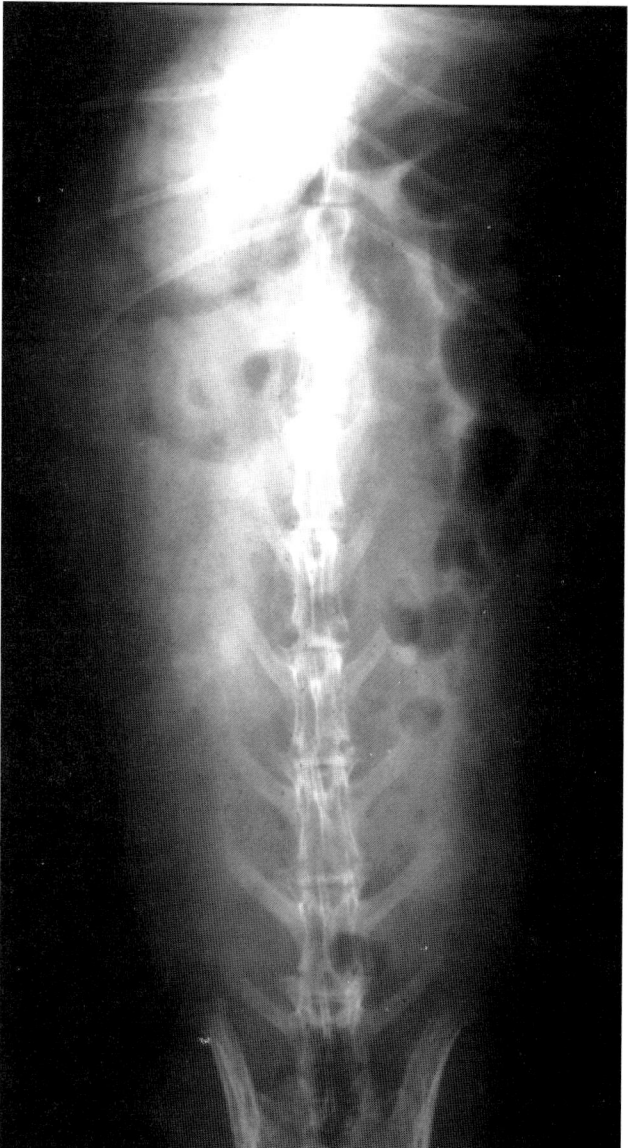

Figure 28-2. A ventrodorsal radiograph of the abdomen of a rabbit with a gastric trichobezoar. Note the tubular distention of the stomach. (Reprinted with permission from Veterinary Medicine 1995; 90: 365-372.)

goals may be met by feeding a single pelleted commercial rabbit food (hence a single energy density, often about 2.5 kcal/g [10.5 kJ/g] DM) and the intake of food, instead of the food itself, is varied to meet above-maintenance needs.

Ideally, specific foods could be used for different functions: creep, starter, grower, finisher, lactation and mainte-

Table 28-4. Protein and fiber contents (dry matter basis) of forages commonly fed to rabbits.*

Forage	Crude protein (%)	Cellulose (%)	Hemicellulose (%)	Lignin (%)	ADF** (%)	Crude fiber (%)
Alfalfa hay	14	26	12	12	39	32
Alfalfa meal	18	24	–	11	35	26
Clover hay	16	26	9	10	–	29
Orchard grass hay	8	39	27	9	45	37
Timothy hay	9	33	31	5	36	31

*United States—Canadian Tables of Feed Composition, 3rd revision. Washington, DC: National Academy Press, 1982.
**ADF = acid detergent fiber.

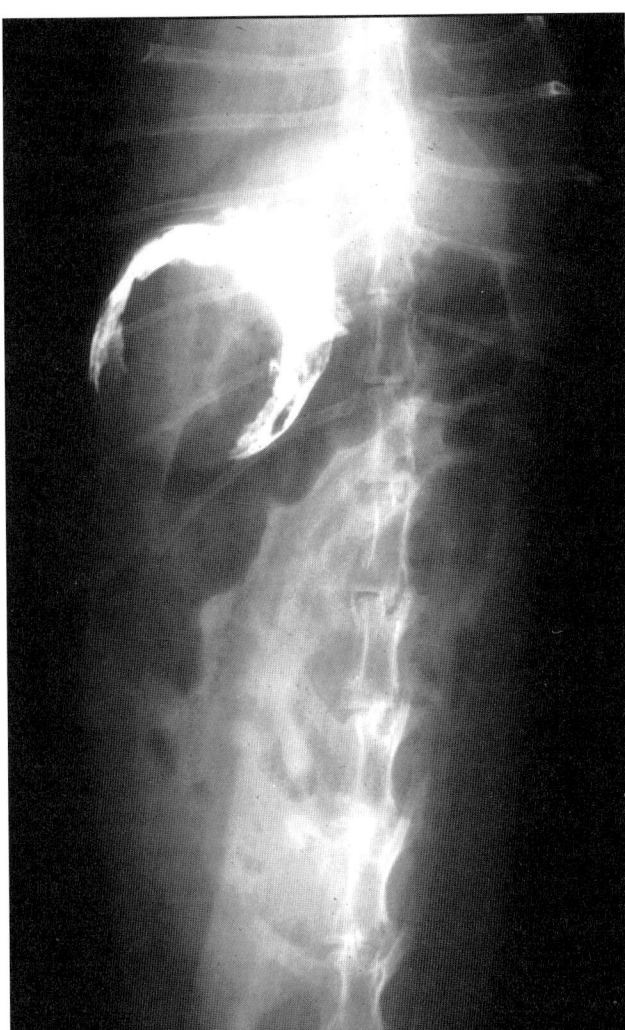

Figure 28-3. A ventrodorsal radiograph of the abdomen of the rabbit in Figure 28-2 following a barium swallow. Note the contrast outlining the mass filling the gastric lumen. (Reprinted with permission from Veterinary Medicine 1995; 90: 365-372.)

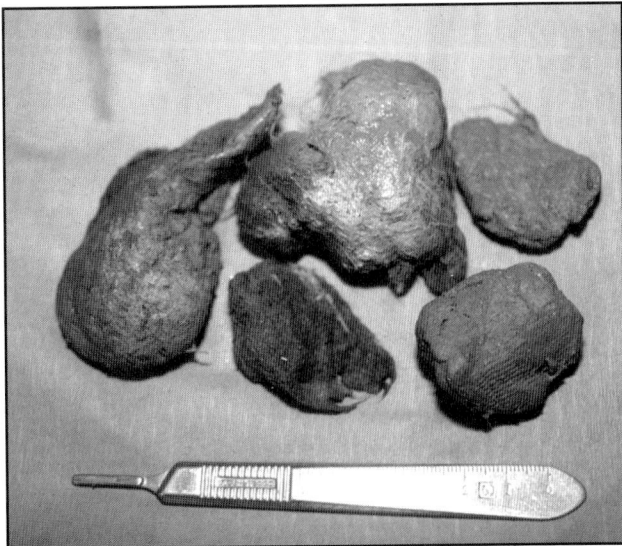

Figure 28-4. The gastric trichobezoar removed in pieces from the rabbit in Figures 28-2 and 28-3 weighed 102 g. Trichobezoars are frequently associated with feeding a low-fiber food. (Reprinted with permission from Veterinary Medicine 1995; 90: 365-372.)

nance.[19] In most instances, however, commercial rabbit producers find it impractical to use more than one food. Thus, a single commercial pellet is typically fed to the entire rabbit colony. Adjustments for increased consumption of food above normal must be made for pregnant and lactating animals. Similar techniques may be used for pet rabbits.

Compared with many other mammals, rabbits have a high water intake. Rabbits drink about 120 ml/kg body weight daily,[19] and even more during lactation and in hot weather.

Selected Nutritional Diseases

Although nutrient requirements of rabbits have been summarized,[19,24,25,27-29] data about specific requirements are limited. However, the major nutritional problems of rabbits are not specific nutrient deficiencies or imbalances, but rather disturbances in digestive tract function (enteric disease) associated with dietary factors[19] or with malocclusion of the teeth.

Malocclusion

Anorexia is a common clinical presentation of pet rabbits. Malocclusion of the teeth is a likely cause. Because rabbit incisor teeth are open-rooted, a developmental defect in the normal appositional anatomy precludes normal wear; thus, overgrowth of the teeth occurs (Figure 28-1). Overgrown incisor teeth may limit or prevent prehension of food and can traumatize the oral mucosa. A complete physical examination of rabbits should always include an evaluation of the oral cavity, including the molar teeth.[21] Maloccluded incisor teeth need to be trimmed every four to six weeks.

Rabbit molar and premolar teeth may also occasionally be maloccluded. Maloccluded molars should be floated with a fine file or their sharp points clipped off with a rongeur.

Trichobezoars

Another common cause of anorexia in rabbits is gastric obstruction by a trichobezoar (Figures 28-2 to 28-4). Hairballs are common incidental findings in rabbit necropsies, even among short-haired breeds. The rabbit's inability to vomit and the small pyloric lumen predispose it to hair accumulation in the stomach. A definitive diagnosis can be difficult. Occasionally, the stomach can be palpated in the cranial abdomen as a large, doughy mass. Survey radiography may reveal an enlarged stomach with displaced intestines. Contrast radiography may aid the diagnosis.

Feeding fresh pineapple juice (10 ml/day) (which contains the enzyme bromelain), papaya tablets (which contain papain) or proteolytic enzymes (e.g., Viokase[b]) have been reported to aid breakdown and passage of trichobezoars.[21] Although there is no evidence that bromelain or papain can degrade hair, they may help dissolve the proteinaceous matrix that binds trichobezoars together.[21] Strategies for treating trichobezoars have been previously reported.[21] Hairballs or gastric stasis in rabbits can generally be prevented by feeding adequate dietary fiber (>14% DM crude fiber), minimizing stress and boredom and grooming the animal frequently.[30]

Mucoid Enteropathy

Pet rabbits are also commonly presented with diarrhea, for which there are several differential diagnoses. Mucoid enteropathy is a gastrointestinal disorder that is paradoxically characterized by constipation and diarrhea,[21] and by anorexia, lethargy, weight loss, cecal impaction and excessive production of mucus in the digestive tract.[31] The cause of mucoid enteropathy is still under investigation, but the disease appears to be caused by changes in cecal pH that result from disruptions in the normal cecal flora.[31,32] It is likely that it occurs secondary to microbial alterations caused by hyperacidic cecal pH.[31] A food containing about 20% crude fiber seems to maintain an optimal cecal pH to prevent changes in the normal microbial flora.

Mucoid enteropathy generally occurs in young rabbits, typically those just beyond weaning age (seven to 14 weeks).[32] It is rarely encountered in rabbitries that feed a high-fiber ration and avoid grains, simple carbohydrates and excesses of fats and proteins. Treatment includes feeding a high-fiber food (alfalfa hay) or syringe feeding a vegetable baby food.[32] In some cases, metoclopramide stimulates gastric emptying and apparently improves cecal activity. Fluid therapy to correct fluid and electrolyte imbalances is a priority to counteract losses that accompany the diarrhea.[21] Other treatment recommendations have been previously reported.[21]

Enterotoxemia

Rabbits, particularly those recently weaned, are sensitive to foods high in sugars and starches.[21] Feeding these foods has been associated with at least some cases of enterotoxemia. Nutritional counseling, therefore, is an important part of rabbit medicine, especially because many rabbit owners think lettuce and carrots are an appropriate diet for their animals.

Obesity

Many household rabbits have limited opportunities for exercise with almost unlimited access to palatable foods. Therefore, obesity is common in pet rabbits.

Because rabbits vary widely in body size, optimal body weights are difficult to estimate. Frequent weighing of each rabbit and recording the results in the medical record are important components of a preventive medicine program. Owners can be shown gradual increases in their rabbit's weight and the need for intervention. Systems for body condition scoring have not been published for rabbits and would be a welcome addition to preventive medicine programs.

Because rabbits use fiber efficiently, obesity may even occur when feeding high-fiber foods. However, weight control may be achieved by limiting the quantity of food offered. The amount of food offered should be reduced gradually, perhaps 10% every two weeks, until a level is achieved that maintains weight and body condition at a desired level.

Vitamin Deficiency and Toxicosis

Although B-complex vitamins and vitamin K are synthesized by cecal microbes and obtained by the rabbit via cecotrophy, manufacturers may add all of the essential vitamins to commercial foods. The requirement for vitamin

Table 28-5. Calcium, phosphorus and vitamin D_2 contents (dry matter basis) of forages commonly fed to rabbits.*

Forages	Calcium (%)	Phosphorus (%)	Vitamin D_2 (IU/g)
Alfalfa hay	1.3	0.2	1,411
Alfalfa meal	1.4	0.2	–
Clover hay	1.5	0.3	1,914
Orchard grass hay	0.4	0.4	–
Timothy hay	0.5	0.2	1,930

*United States—Canadian Tables of Feed Composition, 3rd revision. Washington, DC: National Academy Press, 1982.

D may be low because rabbits readily absorb calcium and phosphorus.[24]

Signs of vitamin D toxicosis include progressive emaciation and weakness, loss of appetite, diarrhea and paralysis. Soft tissues (i.e., liver, kidneys, artery walls and muscle) may become extensively calcified.[24]

Vitamin A deficiency and excess may lead to reproductive disturbances. Low conception rates, fetal resorption, low survival of newborn kits and hydrocephalus in fetuses occur with toxic levels. Toxicosis is generally associated with adding synthetic vitamin A to foods that contain high levels of good-quality alfalfa.[24] Vitamin A-deficient rabbits exhibit poor growth, leg deformities, increased susceptibility to disease (e.g., enteritis) and hydrocephalus.[24]

Little information is available about the vitamin E requirements of rabbits. Signs of deficiency include muscular dystrophy, with paralysis of the hind legs, and reproductive failure.[24]

Feeding Plan

The preferred food for pet rabbits is a commercial, high-fiber (at least 12 to 16% DM) pelleted food containing 13 to 18% crude protein, fed at the rate of one-fourth cup/2.3 kg body weight, divided into two daily meals.[24,33] Some rabbits thrive, however, when pellets are offered free choice. Rabbits may be fed in this manner unless overeating and obesity become problems or an adequate amount of loose hay is not consumed.

Pellets should be supplemented with loose hay (mixed grass hay, timothy hay or dried grass clippings) that is provided free choice.[33] Alfalfa hay can be offered throughout the growth stages, but then should be discontinued because it contains higher than needed protein and calcium levels.

The diet may be supplemented with judicious amounts of leafy greens (romaine lettuce, kale, mustard greens, carrot tops, parsley and dandelion greens) and fresh vegetables (carrots, broccoli, green peppers, cauliflower and cabbage). In addition, rabbits may be fed a small amount (up to one tablespoon/2.3 kg body weight) of fresh fruit (strawberries, other berries, apples) daily or several times per week. Amounts of these palatable snacks should be limited, because all are nutritionally incomplete and may cause an imbalance in the diet (Table 28-6). Rabbits should not receive sugary treats or crackers and bread, which can cause abnormal fermentation in the gut and an overgrowth of certain bacteria resulting in serious, often fatal diarrhea.

Other dietary recommendations for rabbits include:
- Because the rabbit's intestinal microflora/intestinal

Table 28-6. Energy and nutrient contents of foods commonly fed as snacks to rabbits and rodents.*

Food items	Weight (g)	Water (%)	Energy kcal/g** (As fed)	(DMB)	Protein	Fat	Carbohydrate	Fiber	Ca	P
Lettuce, romaine	100	94	0.18	3.0	36	7	50	11	1.1	0.4
Spinach, raw	100	91	0.26	2.9	36	3	48	7	1.0	0.6
Mung bean sprouts, raw	100	89	0.35	3.2	31	2	54	6	0.1	0.5
Summer squash, 1/2 cup	100	94	0.18	3.0	17	2	65	9	0.4	0.4
Blueberries, 1 cup	145	85	0.51	3.4	4	2	80	12	0.1	0.1
Strawberries, 1 cup	149	92	0.28	3.5	6	4	77	6	0.2	0.2
Apple, no skin, 1 medium	128	84	0.51	3.2	1	2	86	4	tr	tr
Banana, 1 medium	114	74	0.82	3.2	4	2	86	2	tr	tr
Cantaloupe, 1 cup	160	90	0.32	3.2	8	2	79	4	0.1	0.2

Key: DMB = dry matter basis, tr = trace.
*Nutrients expressed as % dry matter, except water and as fed energy.
**To convert to kJ, multiply kJ by 4.184.

factors may be sensitive to abrupt changes in osmolarity, pH and other factors, food changes should be introduced gradually (over four to five days). For some rabbits with sensitive gastrointestinal tracts, food changes may need to be made over a 10-day period.[18] This is especially true for four- to 12-week-old rabbits. Current and new feeds should be mixed 75:25 to begin the conversion. Quantities of the new food can then be increased gradually every few days.

• High-energy foods may increase susceptibility to mucoid enterotoxemia.

• Pellets should be refrigerated to reduce nutrient degradation and spoilage.

• Clean fresh water should be available at all times.

RODENTS

Introduction

The approximately 1,700 species of rodents in existence today represent over one-half of the total species of living mammals. The order Rodentia is divided into three suborders (sciuromorph, myomorph and hystricomorph), based primarily on variations in the origin of the masseter muscle. The word rodent originates from the Latin verb "rodere," to gnaw. Rodents are identified by their four prominent continuously erupting (hypsodontic) incisor teeth, which are frequently orange or yellow. Canine teeth are absent, and a gap, or diastema, exists between the incisor and cheek teeth. All rodents have six upper and six lower molar teeth, which may be either open- or closed-rooted, depending on the species. The presence or absence of premolar teeth is also species dependent.

Understanding rodent dentition is important because malocclusion and overgrowth of open-rooted teeth are common clinical problems, with sequelae such as weight loss, malnutrition and oral mucosal ulcerations. Normal gnawing behavior occurs when a rodent holds an object, frequently with the assistance of the forefeet, against the immobile upper incisor teeth and then shears with lateral to medial movements of the lower incisor teeth and jaw. During the gnawing process, the rodent moves the lower jaw forward, allowing apposition of incisor teeth but preventing occlusion and abrasion of cheek teeth. By withdrawing the cheek into the diastema, the rodent can compartmentalize the gnawed material into the cranial portion of the oral cavity, thus allowing for lengthy periods of gnawing without necessarily having to swallow the gnawed material. During the chewing process, the lower jaw moves caudally to bring upper and lower cheek teeth into apposition. The complex muscles and anatomic variations in the associated skull bones, which allow for such specialized jaw movements, are a primary means of classifying rodent species.

Although veterinarians may be presented with some very unusual pet rodents for examination, diagnosis and treatment of health problems, the most commonly seen pet rodents are the guinea pig (*Cavia porcellus*), chinchilla (*Chinchilla laniger*), hamster (multiple species), Mongolian gerbil (*Meriones unguiculatus*), rat (*Rattus norvegicus*) and mouse (*Mus musculus*). Rodents are intelligent, are relatively inexpensive to purchase and maintain and require little space. Unfortunately, however, owners are frequently unaware of specific husbandry requirements until problems resulting from conditions such as improper caging, poor nutrition and water deprivation become evident. A thorough history about husbandry practices can provide invaluable clues to the clinician when trying to address an owner's concerns.

Cage Requirements

A critical aspect of rodent husbandry is proper caging. This requirement must be considered when assessing suspected nutritional problems. Inadequate housing, poorly positioned food or water dispensers, dirty cages and a stressful environment can contribute to problems such as anorexia and dehydration. A variety of cages are available in pet stores, and one must be selected carefully, keeping in mind the characteristics of the species it will house. In general, cages must be escape-proof and predator-proof, provide adequate ventilation, minimize the possibility of trauma, have mounted sipper bottles and provide adequate floor space.

Cages can be constructed of metal, glass or plastic. Wood should not be used for caging rodents because it can be gnawed and is difficult to disinfect. Environmental enrichment such as running wheels, tunnels, hide boxes and bedding should be provided, again keeping in mind the behavioral characteristics of the particular animal. Solid flooring is preferred to wire because it minimizes potential limb trauma and pododermatitis; however, it is more difficult to keep clean. Wire flooring can be used successfully if it is of proper mesh size and a portion of the cage contains solid flooring.

Bedding should be nonabrasive, nontoxic, clean, absorbent, inedible, dust-free and capable of being made into nests. Various medical problems have been associated with some frequently used bedding materials. Cedar shavings have been associated with dermatopathies and pulmonary and hepatic changes. Pine may affect hepatic enzymes. Hardwood shavings such as aspen and shredded nontoxic paper are the most commonly recommended bedding materials. Gerbils, hamsters and mice apparently prefer larger amounts of bedding than do guinea pigs, chinchillas and rats.[35] Frequency of cage cleaning and replacement of bedding varies with the type of rodent and size of cage.

Common Aspects of Rodent Nutrition

Although little research has concerned pet rodents specifically, the popularity of rodents as laboratory animals has led to extensive nutritional study. Nutrient requirements for laboratory rodents serve as initial guides to the nutrient requirements of pet rodents (Table 28-7).[36]

Coprophagy

Most rodents are coprophagous and fecal pellets are frequently ingested directly from the anus. Generally lighter, softer feces (cecotrophs) are selectively ingested. These feces are produced in the cecum and contain important B-complex vitamins and protein. Young rodents ingest maternal feces, thereby inoculating their own intestinal tracts with autochthonous flora.[37,38]

Anorexia, Weight Loss and Dehydration

Clinical problems related to anorexia, weight loss, dehydration or a combination of these factors are frequently observed in pet rodents. Common etiologies include husbandry-related factors such as food and/or water deprivation, inability to reach or manipulate food or water utensils, inappropriate diet, sudden dietary changes, poor hygiene, overcrowding, inadequate temperatures and other environmental stressors.[35]

Careful and tactful questioning by the clinician is necessary for the client to realize or admit to the presence and significance of inadequate husbandry practices. If possible, the client should bring the rodent and its entire cage to the veterinary visit for a more thorough assessment of the animal's environment.

Following a complete physical examination, basic diagnostic studies such as biochemistry profiles, complete blood counts, radiographs and fecal examinations should be conducted whenever possible to rule out malocclusion, gastrointestinal disease and other primary disease problems. Fecal culture and abdominal ultrasound are also often useful.

The prognosis for an anorectic, dehydrated rodent with significant weight loss is guarded. Supportive care includes administering oral, subcutaneous and/or intraperitoneal fluids and offering a variety of sweetened foods or treats to encourage food intake. Many rodents will also tolerate gentle force-feeding. Pelleted rodent feed may be blenderized with water and appropriate supplements such as yogurt, vegetable baby food or both. Alternatively, liquid enteral products formulated for people or pets may be fed without supplementation.

Feeding is best accomplished by wrapping the animal gently in a towel, placing the feeding syringe into the diastema, expressing small volumes into the oral cavity and allowing the animal to swallow. One-ml syringes can be used to feed mice, and 3- to 10-ml catheter-tipped syringes to feed larger rodents. Owners can be shown how to feed their pets at home; however, they must be able to recognize when the animal is responsive enough to allow force feeding, to minimize potential problems with aspiration. Small meals should be fed several times throughout the day.

Malocclusion

Malocclusion is another common clinical problem in pet rodents. The incisor teeth are usually involved, although the cheek teeth may also be maloccluded depending on the species. Etiologies include genetic, dietary, infectious and traumatic factors. Overgrown teeth can result in tongue and oral ulcers, ptyalism, anorexia and weight loss. An oral examination is an important but often difficult component of a rodent physical examination. An otoscope may help visualize cheek teeth, but the examination may necessitate sedation. Skull radiographs are also useful in assessing severe malocclusion and tooth root abscesses.

Inhalant anesthesia, preferably isoflurane, administered through a face mask, is adequate for short dental procedures, such as trimming incisor teeth. The animal is masked down and the mask is removed when the animal attains an appropriate level of anesthesia. Its mouth is held open with gauze strips around the upper and lower incisor teeth, and the incisor teeth are cut quickly, preferably with a high-speed dental drill. A variable-speed, rotary power tool with a circular cutting blade (Dremel Moto-Tool[c]) can also be used. Care should be used not to injure the tongue and surrounding tissues. Sharp clippers may be used to trim the teeth of smaller rodents; anesthesia usually isn't necessary. However, teeth may split or shatter with this method. Inhalant anesthesia via face mask is impractical for lengthier dental procedures on cheek teeth, which may require clipping with bone rongeurs.[39,40] Injectable anesthesia may be required for these procedures because small rodents are very difficult to intubate.

Rodents with chronic malocclusion problems may need teeth trimming every few months. Owners should monitor the animals for anorexia and drooling. Breeding of rodents with malocclusion problems should be discouraged.

Guinea Pigs

Husbandry

The domestic guinea pig belongs in the Caviidae family, which consists of short-tailed or tailless rodents that have one pair of mammary glands, four digits on the forefeet and three digits on the hindfeet. The most commonly seen breeds are: 1) the shorthair or English, which has very uniform short hair, 2) the Abyssinian, which has a coat arranged in whorls or rosettes and 3) the Peruvian, which can have a coat several inches long. Various coat colors and multicolored patterns also exist for each of these species. Pet guinea pigs live for five to seven years and weigh 450 to 750 g. Gestation averages 68 days and litter size ranges from two to four young.[37,41]

Table 28-7. Estimated nutrient requirements of laboratory rodents.* Some of these values were determined by rigorous comparative trials, others by examination of foods known to suffice for specific species. The data presented here are intended to be used only as starting points. The literature cited should be consulted for more details.

Nutrient	Rats M**	Rats Above M**	Mice Above M	Gerbils Above M	Hamsters
Protein as casein (%)***	4.2	12	12.5-18	16-25	15.0
Fat (%)	5.0	5	5	5-20	5
Digestible energy (kcal/kg)†	3,800	3,800	–	–	4.2
L-amino acids					
Arginine (%)	–	0.6	0.3	–	0.76
Asparagine (%)	–	0.4	–	–	–
Glutamic acid (%)	–	4.0	–	–	–
Histidine (%)	0.08	0.3	0.2	–	0.40
Isoleucine (%)	0.31	0.5	0.4	–	0.89
Leucine (%)	0.18	0.75	0.7	–	1.39
Lysine (%)	0.11	0.70	0.4	–	1.20
Methionine (%)	0.23	0.60	0.5	–	0.32
Phenylalanine-tyrosine (%)	0.18	0.80	0.4	–	0.83
Proline (%)	–	0.40	–	–	–
Threonine (%)	0.18	0.50	0.4	–	0.70
Tryptophan (%)	0.05	0.15	0.1	–	0.34
Valine (%)	0.23	0.60	0.5	–	0.91
Nonessential (%)	0.48	0.50	–	–	–
Minerals					
Calcium (%)	–	0.50	0.4	0.6-0.8	0.59
Chloride (%)	–	0.05	–	0.2-0.8	–
Magnesium (%)	–	0.04	0.05	0.1-0.2	0.06
Phosphorus (%)	–	0.40	0.4	0.3-0.4	0.30
Potassium (%)	–	0.36	0.2	0.7-0.9	0.61
Sodium (%)	–	0.05	–	0.2-0.4	0.15
Sulfur (%)	–	0.03	–	–	–
Chromium (mg/kg)	–	0.30	2.0	–	–
Copper (mg/kg)	–	5.00	4.5	0.4-4.0	1.6
Fluoride (mg/kg)	–	1.00	–	0-11	0.024
Iodine (mg/kg)	–	0.15	0.25	1-37	1.6
Iron (mg/kg)	–	35.00	25.00	130-470	140
Manganese (mg/kg)	–	50.00	45.00	3-45	3.65
Selenium (mg/kg)	–	0.10	–	–	0.1
Zinc (mg/kg)	–	12.00	30.00	0-8	9.2
Vitamins					
A (IU/kg)	–	4,000	500	18,000-32,000	–
D (IU/kg)	–	1,000	150	2,000-3,250	2,484
E (IU/kg)	–	30	20	9-1,200	3
K (mcg/kg)	–	50	3,000	–	4,000
Choline (mg/kg)	–	1,000	600	750-3,000	2,000
Folic acid (mg/kg)	–	1	0.5	100-1,800	2
Niacin (mg/kg)	–	20	10	22-90	90
Pantothenate (mg/kg)	–	8	10	25-60	40
Riboflavin (mg/kg)	–	3	7	4-20	15
Thiamin (mg/kg)	–	4	5	4-22	20
B_6 (mg/kg)	–	6	1	4-22	6
B_{12} (mcg/kg)	–	50	10	0.18	10

*Clark JD, Olfert ED. Rodents (Rodentia). In: Fowler ME, ed. Zoo and Wild Animal Medicine. Philadelphia, PA: WB Saunders Co, 1986; 728-733.
**M = maintenance; healthy, non-stressed adults in comfortable surroundings. Above M = ill or stressed adults and growing, pregnant or lactation animals.
***Minimum protein requirements were determined with animals fed purified and semi-purified diets containing casein as a protein source. For animals fed commercial diets comprised of complex ingredients and relatively lower digestibilities, dietary protein should be higher.
†To convert to kJ, multiply kcal by 4.184.

Guinea pigs are herbivores with simple stomachs. Their teeth are open-rooted and erupt continuously. The dental formula is 1I/1, C0/0, P1/1 and M3/3. Guinea pigs have a long digestive tract with a gastric emptying time of approximately two hours and a total gastrointestinal transit time from eight to 20 hours. Normal gastrointestinal flora consists primarily of *Lactobacillus* and occasionally *Streptococcus* spp, yeast and soil bacteria.[38,42] Much of the digestive process occurs in the cecum, which is a thin-walled sac divided into numerous lateral pouches by smooth muscle bands (taenia coli). The cecum is normally found on the central and left side of the abdomen and may contain as much as 65% of the gastrointestinal contents.[43] Guinea pigs are coprophagous.

Special Nutritional Needs

Guinea pigs, people and other primates are unable to synthesize vitamin C (ascorbic acid) because they lack the enzyme L-gluconolactone oxidase, which is needed to convert glucose to ascorbic acid. Adequate dietary supplementation is, therefore, critical to prevent hypovitaminosis C (scurvy), as detailed below. (See Feeding Plan.)

Guinea pigs display behavioral characteristics that influence their overall nutritional status. For example, they are extremely susceptible to stressful situations such as inadequate housing, moving into a new household or different cage and changing feeding schedules. Stressed guinea pigs may become anorectic and lose weight.

Proper housing accommodations can be provided by an open-topped enclosure at least 10 inches high, with a floor space of at least 101 square inches for an adult animal, and twice this floor space for a breeding sow. Either solid or wire flooring can be used. Wire flooring allows for feces and urine to drop to the bottom of the cage. However, it may cause foot injuries and subsequent pododermatitis. Wire flooring should consist of a rectangular mesh 75 by 12 mm. At least a portion of the cage should have a solid bottom.[39] Solid floors with a substrate of shredded paper or hardwood shavings generally require more frequent cleaning but are preferable for pet guinea pigs.

Because guinea pigs are easily startled, the cage should be placed in a quiet area in the home to minimize exposure to sudden movements and loud noises. Ideally, a relatively constant temperature between 18 to 24°C (65 to 75°F), and a humidity between 40 and 70% should be maintained.[42] Elevated temperatures may cause heat stress. A cool, damp environment can predispose guinea pigs to respiratory diseases.

Additional behavioral characteristics of guinea pigs include their tendency to contaminate food and water dishes with excreta. Sipper bottles are preferred to minimize contamination of drinking water. However, guinea pigs can pass ingesta into sipper tubes. Guinea pigs also play with the end of the sipper tube and cause leaks, resulting in wet bedding and an empty water bottle. Food and water utensils should be cleaned and soiled bedding removed daily.

Any changes in access to food and water should be made gradually, over five to 10 days. Owners should be cautioned to monitor their pets for signs of anorexia and decreased water intake when husbandry changes are made.[44]

Common Nutritional Disorders

HYPOVITAMINOSIS C

Although quality commercial guinea pig foods are formulated with adequate vitamin C, hypovitaminosis C (scurvy) is still a common clinical problem because of this nutrient's lability during storage. Also, feeding guinea pigs rabbit food without providing additional vitamin C may cause scurvy. Because guinea pigs are incapable of storing vitamin C, scurvy appears within one to two weeks after a vitamin C deficient food is fed. Death usually occurs within three weeks.[20]

Guinea pigs with scurvy present with anorexia, weight loss, an unkempt appearance and gingivitis. Animals are reluctant to move because of joint and muscle pain. Discomfort is apparent when limbs are palpated. Ascorbic acid is required for normal collagen formation; therefore, deficiencies primarily affect the musculoskeletal system. Sequelae include enlarged costochondral junctions, hemorrhage into muscles and joints and abnormalities in epiphyseal growth centers with subsequent pathologic fractures. Secondary infections, delayed wound healing and

diarrhea may also be present. Subclinical vitamin C deficiency should be considered in any guinea pig presented with generalized illness. Young animals and pregnant sows are affected most severely.[40,44]

Diagnosis of vitamin C deficiency is based on the history and clinical signs. Radiographs may reveal skeletal changes.

Treatment involves oral or parenteral supplementation with 50 to 100 mg vitamin C/kg body weight until clinical signs resolve.[39] Owners can supplement the diet with liquid pediatric vitamin C products obtained over-the-counter from pharmacies and supermarkets. (Appropriate dietary supplements are discussed in the Feeding Plan section.) Anorectic and dehydrated animals should receive supportive care such as fluids and forced alimentation as discussed in the Introduction to Rodents section. Client education about dietary requirements of guinea pigs plays a critical role in preventing this disease.

PREGNANCY TOXEMIA

Pregnancy toxemia occurs primarily in obese, anorectic, stressed guinea pigs. Genetics may also play a role. Clinical signs occur within about five days (before and after) of parturition and include lethargy, ruffled coat, anorexia, prostration, muscle spasms and death.

Diagnostic tests may reveal hypoglycemia (perhaps hyperglycemia when near death), hyperlipidemia, ketonemia, hyperkalemia, hyponatremia, hypochloremia, proteinuria and urinary pH less than five.

Supportive care includes administration of fluids, 5% glucose given orally or intravenously, corticosteroids and antibiotics. Cesarean section may be attempted to save the fetuses. Prognosis, however, is poor and treatment is generally unsuccessful. Preventing obesity in sows (preferably a body weight less than 500 g), providing a good food, minimizing stress and monitoring for anorexia will reduce the risk of pregnancy toxemia.[38]

CECAL IMPACTION

Low fiber intakes (perhaps <10% DM crude fiber) predispose guinea pigs to cecal impaction. Prevention is best accomplished by providing adequate long-stem fiber in the form of chopped grass hay. Hay should be offered free choice, even when fiber-containing guinea pig pellets are fed.

SOFT TISSUE CALCIFICATION

Guinea pigs are reportedly susceptible to a syndrome involving calcification of soft tissues, especially in the forelimbs. The syndrome is thought to be related to dietary levels of calcium, phosphorus, magnesium, potassium and vitamin D.[20] Means of prevention are unknown, but efforts should be made to restrict use of supplements and to keep vitamin D levels below 2,000 IU/kg food DM.[20]

Feeding Plan

FEEDING ADULTS

Guinea pigs are strict herbivores and should be maintained on a food specifically labeled for the species. Commercial dry rabbit food, although similar in appearance, should not be used because it is inadequate in protein and more importantly, in vitamin C.

Vitamin C

Adequate dietary vitamin C levels are critical for overall good health, and although commercial guinea pig foods are formulated with approximately 800 mg vitamin C/kg DM, low vitamin C intake is still a common problem due to the vitamin's lability. Heat, moisture and contact with metals hasten its deterioration during storage. Ideally, guinea pig pellets should be stored at 22°C (72°F) and should be used within 90 days of milling.[39] Consumers may have difficulty determining how long the product has been on the shelf at the time of purchase because: 1) the milling date is frequently not stated on the food container and 2) many pet stores buy feed in bulk and then repackage product for resale. Owners should therefore be encouraged to buy food in small quantities from a reputable pet store that has relatively high turnover of food products, and to store the food properly at home.

Guinea pigs require approximately 10 mg vitamin C/kg body weight daily for maintenance and 30 mg/kg body weight daily for gestation. If the freshness of guinea pig pellets is unknown, 200 mg/ml vitamin C can be added to the drinking water. However, the half-life of this nutrient in clean, fresh water is only 24 hours, and shorter if organic debris is present or if metal containers are used. Vitamin C can also be given orally on a daily basis using human pediatric vitamin C formulations.[39] Food can also be supplemented with vitamin C by daily feeding of small amounts of vegetables high in vitamin C (e.g., red or green peppers, tomatoes, spinach and asparagus). Excess ingested vitamin C is excreted rapidly in the urine, with 80% of the ingested amount being eliminated in three days. Fresh vegetables should be thoroughly rinsed to minimize potential pesticide contaminants and bacterial pathogens such as *Salmonella* spp.[45]

Protein, Fiber and Water

Commercial guinea pig pellets contain approximately 20% crude protein and 9 to 18% crude fiber, DMB. For an adult guinea pig, average daily food consumption is 6 g/100 g body weight and average daily water consumption is 10 ml/100 g body weight.[45] Because guinea pigs are such fastidious eaters, owners should be discouraged from frequently changing brands of food to prevent anorexia. Small amounts of high-quality timothy or grass hay may also be offered. Oral lesions may occur if the hay is too coarse. Secondary infection of these lesions with beta-hemolytic *Streptococcus* spp can lead to cervical lymphadenitis and abscess formation. Owners who allow their guinea pigs access to the yard should also be forewarned about possible herbicide/pesticide exposure. Overgrazing on lush lawns or fresh grass clippings can also result in diarrhea.

FEEDING NEONATES

Newborn guinea pigs are precocious, with teeth, a full coat and open eyes. Birth weights vary from 60 to 100 g. Neonates weighing less than 50 to 60 g rarely survive. Birth weight is related to genetic characteristics and maternal nutritional status, and is directly proportional to gestation length and inversely proportional to litter size. Neonatal guinea pigs remain close to the sow but generally will not nurse for the first 12 to 24 hours and, therefore, should not be force fed during this time. Neonates usually begin eating solid food at four to five days of age (i.e., guinea pig chow softened with cow's milk or water). If several lactating sows are present, the young may nurse alternately among them. In this case, the smaller piglets must be monitored to ensure that they nurse adequately.

Weaning age varies from 14 to 28 days when body weight reaches 150 to 200 g. Average daily weight gain should be 2.5 to 3.5 g until 60 days of age.[38]

Chinchillas

Husbandry

Chinchillas belong in the Chinchillidae family and are closely related to guinea pigs. Chinchillas originate from the rocky slopes of the South American Andes, where they were nearly hunted to extinction in the early part of this century because of their prized pelts. A small group of chinchillas brought to the United States at that time were successfully bred in captivity and are progenitors for the majority of today's pet population.

Chinchilla breeds are characterized by their coat color, which in the wild is a smoky blue-gray. Other color variations represent mutations. The normal coat is thick and soft, an attribute that often masks problems such as weight loss. Adult chinchillas weigh from 400 to 600 g and have an average life span of 10 years, with a maximum up to 20 years. The average gestation period is 111 days, and average litter size is two, with a range of one to six. The dental formula is I1/1, C0/0, P1/1, M3/3. All teeth are open-rooted. Incisor teeth grow 6.2 to 7.6 cm per year.[46]

Chinchillas are hindgut fermenters and have a very long alimentary tract, measuring more than 3.5 m in adult animals. The proximal colon is sacculated and communicates with the large thin-coiled cecum. The longer distal colon is smooth.[47] Chinchillas are coprophagic.

Proper housing is a critical factor for a chinchilla's overall well-being. The animal's native environment includes a relatively low temperature and humidity and a sloping, hard, rocky habitat that requires that chinchillas jump from one crevice to another. Chinchillas should therefore be housed in a large (minimum of 1,650 cm² floor area per animal), multilevel cage in order to accommodate normal, active behavior. If wire mesh flooring is used, the mesh size should be small enough to prevent leg entrapment. Some areas of solid flooring should be provided to minimize foot lesions. The optimal temperature range is 16 to 21°C (60 to 70°F). Temperatures as low as 0°C (32°F) can be tolerated if the animal has been acclimated. Temperatures greater than 27°C (80°F) can result in heatstroke, particularly in the presence of high humidity.

Chinchillas are fastidious groomers and should be provided with a dust bath for a short time each day. Keeping the dust bath dish in the cage continuously results in fecal contamination of the dish and subsequently of the coat. Dust can be obtained commercially and consists of a mixture of 9:1 silver sand to Fuller's earth.[46,48]

Because chinchillas are hindgut fermenters, they have complex digestive processes for fermenting fiber in the food. Any disruption of these processes can result in diarrhea, constipation, mucoid enteritis, bloat, intussusception and rectal prolapse. Inappropriate foods and sudden food changes are common causes of such problems. Inappropriate foods include those that contain high levels of simple carbohydrates and protein or not enough fiber. Such foods alter cecal fermentation processes with subsequent changes in pH, motility and flora, resulting in enteritis. Any change in the normally gram-positive gastrointestinal flora can lead to overgrowth of bacteria such as *Escherichia coli* and *Clostridium, Proteus* and *Pseudomonas* spp. Therefore, antibiotics such as the beta-lactams, clindamycin, lincomycin and erythromycin should be avoided. Other causes of enteritis include *Salmonella* spp, *Giardia lamblia, Cryptosporidium* spp, coccidia and nematodes.[46-48] Unfortunately, the exact cause of gastroenteritis frequently remains undetermined, thus subsequent treatment is symptomatic, including administration of fluids, dietary changes (adding fiber) and appropriate antibiotics.

There are few documented integumentary disorders of chinchillas directly associated with specific nutrients. Fatty acid deficiency leads to a poor coat, skin flaking and possibly cutaneous ulcers. Zinc deficiency can result in alopecia.[49]

Feeding Plan

FEEDING ADULTS

Specific nutrient requirements for chinchillas have not been well established. With the exception of being placentophagic, chinchillas are considered to be strict herbivores and subsist in the wild on shrubs and grasses. Controversy exists among various authors as to what type of feeding plan is most suitable for captive animals. However, all recommendations reflect a high overall dietary fiber requirement. Experts generally agree that good nutritional status can be achieved by feeding a combination of pellets and free-choice, good-quality grass or timothy hay. Commercially available chinchilla pellets are preferred to guinea pig and rabbit pellets because of formulation and size differences. Because chinchillas often use their forefeet to hold their food, the shape and size of the pellets affect ease of food handling and amount of wastage. On a dry matter basis, pellets should consist of 18 to 20% crude protein, 15 to 35% crude fiber and 4% fat.

Only one to two tablespoons of pellets should be fed per day, because overfeeding may cause enteritis. Treats such as fresh fruits, vegetables and nuts can be offered occasionally but should compose less than 10% of the total diet.[46,50] Fresh water in clean sipper bottles should always be available.

FEEDING NEONATES

Newborn chinchillas are precocious and weigh from 30 to 50 g. They generally begin eating pelleted food at one week of age, and are completely weaned by six to eight weeks. Orphaned neonates can be hand-reared or fostered onto other chinchillas, and can survive independently after two to three weeks of age. Two reportedly successful hand-feeding formulas vary markedly. One is a mixture of one part unsweetened condensed milk and two parts water. The other is a mixture of one-half water, one-half evaporated milk, with glucose added to achieve a final concentration of 25%.[47,51]

Hamsters

Husbandry

Hamsters are rodents in the Cricetidae family. There are many species of hamsters. The most commonly seen are the golden or Syrian hamster (*Mesocricetus auratus*), the Chinese hamster (*Cricetulus griseus*) and the dwarf hamster (*Phodopus sungorus*). Hamsters are not native to the United States. They were introduced into this country in 1938 for research purposes.

Although hamster species vary markedly, male and female adults weigh 85 to 130 g and 95 to 150 g, respectively. Females tend to be larger and more aggressive than males. Life spans are relatively short and average from 18 to 24 months. The gestation period is 15 to 16 days. Litter size ranges from five to nine. Young are born without hair, with eyes and ears closed, but with erupted incisor teeth. The dental formula is I1/1, C0/0, P0/0, M3/3. Incisor teeth grow throughout life, but molar teeth are closed-rooted. Hamsters possess large cheek pouches that are used to transport and store food. When alarmed, hamsters will also temporarily store their young in these pouches. The stomach is divided into glandular and nonglandular portions. The nonglandular forestomach is lined with keratinized epithelium and is the site of pregastric fermentation.[52,53] Like rabbits and many rodents, hamsters are coprophagic.

Hamsters are nocturnal animals. Although they are not true hibernators, hamsters enter a period of "pseudohibernation" from which they can be aroused when exposed to shorter day lengths and temperatures below 4.4°C (40°F). In the wild, hamsters are solitary animals that live in burrows. Hamsters are very active at gnawing and escape by chewing through cages or by pushing open cage lids. Subsequent ingestion of inappropriate household items can lead to serious gastrointestinal problems. Therefore, proper caging, as with other rodents, is a critical factor to the overall well-being of these animals.

Cages for adult hamsters should have a floor space of at least 125 cm² and a height of at least 15 cm. The traditional slotted metal food hoppers that are placed on top of the cage and frequently used for rats and mice are generally inappropriate for hamsters. The flat face of these pets makes it difficult for them to retrieve food items. If slotted metal food hoppers are used, the slots should be at least 7/16 in. wide. Clean water in a sipper bottle should always be available and the bottle should be placed low enough for the hamster to reach. The recommended environmental temperatures for hamsters are 18.3 to 21.1°C (65 to 70°F). Relative humidity should be between 30 and 70%.[54,55]

Acute enteric diseases are common problems among hamsters, especially weanlings. Underlying causes often remain unknown, but stress, inadequate food and improperly positioned feeders are often contributing factors. Processed food should have a minimum of 8% crude fiber to prevent diarrhea. *Campylobacter* spp are thought to be the causative agent of proliferative ileitis diarrhea or "wet tail;" however, *Escherichia coli, Clostridium* spp or *Bacillus* spp may also be involved. Rapid weight loss, dehydration and staining of the perineal region are present clinically. Other possible sequelae include intestinal blockage, prolapse and intussusception. Administration of inappropriate antibiotics (e.g., penicillin, ampicillin, lincomycin and bacitracin) can result in overgrowth of *Clostridium difficile* and a subsequent fatal enterocolitis.[55]

The prognosis for hamsters presenting with signs of enteritis is generally guarded. Treatment involves supportive care such as administration of fluids subcutaneously or intraperitoneally, appropriate antibiotics (e.g., trimethoprim sulfadiazine, chloramphenicol or enrofloxacin) and oral bismuth salicylate. Hamsters with enteritis should be hand-fed and placed in a warm environment.

Few reports document specific nutrient deficiencies in hamsters. Generalized alopecia and skin problems have been associated with low protein levels (less than 16%) and with deficiencies in pantothenic acid, riboflavin, pyridoxine, niacin, fatty acids and copper. Vitamin E deficiency can lead to muscular weakness, ocular secretions and death. Hamsters fed foods high in polyunsaturated fat are more susceptible to vitamin E deficiency and subsequent muscular dystrophy.[49,55]

Feeding Plan

Specific nutrient requirements for hamsters have not been well established. In the wild, hamsters are omnivorous, ingesting a variety of plants, seeds, fruits and meats. Pelleted rodent foods that provide 16 to 20% crude protein appear to provide good growth rates, whereas those containing 8 to 12% crude protein appear to be inadequate. Hamsters tend to ingest fruits, nuts, cereals and prepackaged "rodent treats" preferentially to the more nutritionally balanced commercial dry rodent foods; therefore, these items should be provided in limited quantities. Adult food consumption averages 15 to 20 g/day.[55]

Pregnant and lactating females have markedly increased food consumption. A one-week supply of food should be placed in the cage at about Day 13 of gestation to minimize disturbances during parturition. Food should be placed on the cage floor rather than in a hopper to minimize the dam's distraction with food gathering, which may result in neglect of the young. This practice also allows easier access to food for pups as they approach weaning. Pups should also have easy access to the water bottle and they should be observed closely to ensure that they can pull hard enough on the sipper tube to obtain water. Neonatal hamsters are altricial, and have birth weights from 2 to 3 g. Young begin gnawing on solid food at seven to 10 days of age and are weaned around 21 days. Weaning weights average 35 g. Attempts at hand raising or cross-fostering of orphaned hamster neonates onto other rodent species are generally unsuccessful.[54]

Gerbils

Husbandry

Gerbils are rodents in the Cricetidae family. The Mongolian gerbil is the most common pet species. A frequent color pattern is agouti or brown, but other color variations such as black, white and cinnamon also exist. Gerbils are social, burrowing animals native to the desert regions of central Asia. As pets, they are generally friendly and easily handled. Because of their water conservation mechanisms, they produce only a few drops of urine daily and are, therefore, virtually odor free. Adult gerbils weigh from 55 to 100 g and have a life span of three to four years. Gerbils generally form monogamous pairs, which is unique among rodents. Gestation length is 24 to 26 days, with a litter size of four to seven. Neonates are altricial. Approximately half of the pet gerbil population exhibits spontaneous, convulsive seizures that are induced by strange environments or excitement. Fatalities are uncommon and anticonvulsant therapy has not been recommended.[42,56]

Gerbils can be housed as described for hamsters. They also actively gnaw, so cages need to be escape-proof. Adult gerbils should be provided with a minimum floor space of 230 cm² with sides at least 15 cm high. Temperatures should be maintained between 18 to 29°C (65 to 85°F) and humidity levels between 30 and 50%. Gerbils do not tolerate high temperatures and their coat appears greasy under conditions of high humidity.[54]

Diarrhea can result from food changes, contaminants or deprivation and protozoal or bacterial infections, such as salmonellosis. Treatment is symptomatic as described for hamsters, because the specific etiology frequently remains undetermined.

Specific nutrient deficiencies are uncommon in gerbils fed commercial dry rodent food. Animals maintained on high-fat foods such as excessive amounts of sunflower seeds develop hypercholesterolemia with excess fat deposits throughout the body. However, atherosclerosis does not appear to occur under these conditions, which has made gerbils important in cardiac disease research. Weanling animals are especially susceptible to malnutrition and dehydration as a result of poor accessibility to food and water.[54]

Feeding Plan

In the wild, gerbils feed on plants, seeds and insects. In captivity, they should be fed a commercial dry rodent food offered free choice. Gerbils will ingest seeds preferentially, which results in a diet high in fat and low in calcium. Gerbils generally eat about eight meals per day, with a total food consumption of 5 to 8 g. Because they eat frequent small meals, rapid weight loss occurs if food quantities are limited. Clean water in easily accessible sipper bottles should always be available. Young gerbils generally begin eating solid food at 14 to 16 days of age and are weaned at 20 to 26 days. Dry rodent food can be softened with water for weanlings.[56]

Rats

Husbandry

The common pet rat belongs in the Muridae family and originated in central Asia. Adult female and male rats weigh from 250 to 300 g and 450 to 520 g, respectively. The average life span ranges from 2.5 to 3.5 years. The gestation period is 21 to 23 days, and litter size ranges from six to 12. The rat's dental formula is I1/1, C0/0, P0/0, M3/3. Incisor teeth erupt continuously, but molar teeth are permanently rooted. Rats have a divided stomach, a large cecum, no gallbladder and a gastrointestinal transit time of 12 to 24 hours.

A variety of cages, usually plastic or metal, are available in pet stores. General guidelines for optimal caging were discussed previously. (See Rodents, Cage Requirements.) Cages need to be made escape-proof because rats are adept at chewing through cages, lifting lids and opening small cage doors. Adult rats should be provided with a minimum of 250 cm² of floor space and a cage height of 18 cm. Ambient temperatures should be 18 to 27°C (65 to 80°F), with an optimum temperature of 22°C (72°F). Relative humidity should be maintained at 40 to 70%.[57,58]

Although various nutrient deficiencies have been produced in experimental rats and are described in detail in the literature, they are uncommon in pet animals fed commercial dry rodent food. Protein deficiencies probably are most common and can result in anemia, cataracts, poor growth and impaired reproduction.

Feeding Plan

Rats should be fed a commercial dry rodent food, offered free choice. They are primarily nocturnal feeders. Adult rats consume approximately 10 g of food/100 g of body weight. Treats should not exceed 10% of food intake. Dietary fiber content should be at least 5% to minimize problems with diarrhea. On a dry matter basis, crude protein requirements are approximately 10% for maintenance and 20% for growth and reproduction. Young rats are weaned at 21 days of age at which time body weight ranges from 40 to 50 g.[42,58]

Mice

Husbandry

The mouse belongs in the Muridae family and originated in Asia. Average life span is 1.5 to 3 years and adult weight ranges from 20 to 40 g. Gestation lasts 19 to 21 days, with litter sizes ranging from 10 to 12. The dental formula is I1/1, C0/0, P0/0, M3/3. Only the incisor teeth are open-rooted. Gastrointestinal transit time is eight to 14 hours.[42,59]

Cage requirements are similar to those described for rats. (See Rodents, Cage Requirements.) Floor space per adult mouse should be at least 97 cm², and 390 cm² for a breeding female. Ambient temperatures should be maintained in the range of 18 to 29°C (65 to 85°F), with an average of 22°C (72°F). Humidity can range from 30 to 70%.[60]

Feeding Plan

Mice should be fed a clean, fresh, commercial dry rodent food. Optimal nutrient requirements have not been established and probably vary markedly among various strains of mice. The literature suggests that foods containing 17 to 24% protein, 5% or less fat and 2.5% fiber result in adequate performance levels. Mineral requirements are unknown. Adult mice ingest 4 to 5 g of food daily. Young mice generally begin eating dry food at 10 days of age and are weaned at 21 days.[42,60] Clean, fresh water in sipper bottles should always be available.

ENDNOTES & REFERENCES

ENDNOTES

a. American Ferret Association. Personal communication, 1996.

b. Fort Dodge Laboratories, Overland Park, KS, USA.

c. Dremel. Racine, WI, USA.

REFERENCES

1. Carpenter JW, Harms CA, Harrenstien L. Biology and medicine of the domestic ferret: An overview. Journal of Small Exotic Animal Medicine 1994; 2: 151-162.

2. Fox JG, ed. Taxonomy, history, and use. In: Biology and Diseases of the Ferret. Philadelphia, PA: Lea & Febiger, 1988; 3-13.

3. Bernard SL, Gorham JR, Ryland LM. Biology and diseases of ferrets. In: Fox JG, Cohen BJ, Loew FM, eds. Laboratory Animal Medicine. Orlando, FL: Academic Press Inc., 1984; 386-397.

4. Ryland LM, Bernard SL. A clinical guide to the pet ferret. Compendium on Continuing Education for the Practicing Veterinarian 1983; 5: 25-32.

5. Brown SA. Husbandry, handling and diagnostic procedures for ferrets. In: Proceedings. Annual Meeting of American Animal Hospital Association, Seattle, WA, 1993; 66-78.

6. McLain DE, Thomas JA, Fox JG. Nutrition. In: Fox JG, ed. Biology and Diseases of the Ferret. Philadelphia, PA: Lea & Febiger, 1988; 135-152.

7. National Research Council. Nutrient Requirements of Mink and Foxes, 2nd ed. Washington, DC: National Academy of Sciences, 1982.

8. Association of American Feed Control Officials. Official Publication, 1999.

9. Deshmukh DR, Rusk CD. Effects of an arginine-free diet on urea cycle enzymes in young and adult ferrets. Enzyme 1989; 41: 168-174.

10. Knudsen KL, Kilgore DL. Temperature regulation and basal metabolic rate in the spotted skunk, Spilogale putorius. Comparative Biochemistry and Physiology 1990; 97A: 27-33.

11. Robbins CT. Wildlife Feeding and Nutrition, 2nd ed. New York, NY: Academic Press Inc., 1993; 114-161.

12. Edfors CH, Ullrey DE, Aulerich RJ. Effects of dietary calcium concentration and calcium-phosphorus ratio on growth and selected plasma and bone measures in young European ferrets (Mustela putorius furo). Journal of Zoo Wildlife Medicine 1990; 21: 185-191.

13. Ribaya-Mercado JD, Holmgren SC, Fox JG, et al. Dietary beta-carotene absorption and metabolism in ferrets and rats. Journal of Nutrition 1989; 119: 665-668.

14. Donoghue S, Kronfeld DS. Home-made diets. In: Wills JM, Simpson KW, eds. Waltham Book of Clinical Nutrition of the Dog & Cat. Oxford, UK: Pergamon Press, 1994; 445-449.

15. Morton C, Morton F. Ferrets. Hauppauge, NY: Barron's Educational Series, 1985; 43-45.

16. Fox JG, Zeman DH, Mortimer JD. Copper toxicosis in sibling ferrets. Journal of the American Veterinary Medical Association 1994; 205: 1154-1156.

17. Fox RR. Taxonomy and genetics. In: Manning PJ, Ringler DH, Newcomer CE, eds. The Biology of the Laboratory Rabbit, 2nd ed. San Diego, CA: Academic Press Inc., 1994; 1-26.

18. Harkness JE, Wagner JE. The Biology and Medicine of Rabbits and Rodents, 3rd ed. Philadelphia, PA: Lea & Febiger, 1989; 9-19.

19. Cheeke PR. Nutrition and nutritional diseases. In: Manning PJ, Ringler DH, Newcomer CE, eds. The Biology of the Laboratory Rabbit, 2nd ed. San Diego, CA: Academic Press Inc., 1994; 321-333.

20. Tobin G. Small pets–Food types, nutrient requirements and nutritional disorders. Manual of Companion Animal Nutrition & Feeding. London, UK: British Small Animal Veterinary Association, 1996; 208-225.

21. Gentz EJ, Harrenstien LA, Carpenter JW. Dealing with gastrointestinal, genitourinary, and musculoskeletal problems in rabbits. Veterinary Medicine 1995; 90: 365-372.

22. Harkness JE. Rabbit husbandry and medicine. Veterinary Clinics of North America: Small Animal Practice 1987; 17: 1019-1044.

23. Collins BR. Common diseases and medical management of rodents and lagomorphs. In: Jacobson ER, Kollias GV Jr, eds. Contemporary Issues in Small Animal Practice 1988; 9: 261-316.

24. Cheeke PR. Rabbits. In: Pond WG, Church DC, Pond KR, eds. Basic Animal Nutrition and Feeding. New York, NY: John Wiley & Sons, 1995; 451-459.

25. Fraser CM. Nutrition: Rabbits. In: The Merck Veterinary Manual. Rahway, NJ: Merck & Co, 1991; 1277-1278.

26. United States—Canadian Tables of Feed Composition, 3rd revision. Washington, DC: National Academy Press, 1982.

27. Cheeke PR. Rabbit Feeding and Nutrition. Orlando, FL: Academic Press Inc., 1987; 88, 147.

28. Cheeke PR, Patton NM, Lukefahr SD, et al. Rabbit Production. Danville, IL: The Interstate Printers & Publishers, 1987; 131-194, 249.

29. Lebas F. Nutrition of rabbits. In: Wiseman J, ed. Feeding of Non-ruminant Livestock. London, UK: Butterworth & Co, 1987; 63-69.

30. Carpenter JW, Mashima TY, Gentz EJ, et al. Caring for rabbits: An overview and formulary. Veterinary Medicine 1995; 90: 340-364.

31. Lelkes L, Chang C-L. Microbial dysbiosis in rabbit mucoid enteropathy. Laboratory Animal Science 1987; 37: 757-764.

32. Jenkins JR. Another look at mucoid enteritis. Veterinary Forum 1993; July: 54-55.

33. Jenkins JR. Nutrition and nutrition-related diseases of rabbits. Journal of Small Exotic Animal Medicine 1991; 1: 12-14.

34. Clark JD, Olfert ED. Rodents (Rodentia). In: Fowler ME, ed. Zoo and Wild Animal Medicine. Philadelphia, PA: WB Saunders Co, 1986; 728-733.

35. Harkness JE. Biology and husbandry—Comparative aspects. In: A Practitioner's Guide to Domestic Rodents. Lakewood, CO: AAHA Professional Library Series, 1993; 3-8.

36. National Research Council. Nutrient Requirements of Laboratory Animals, 3rd ed. Washington, DC: National Academy Press Inc., 1978.

EXOTIC MAMMALS

37. Clark JD. Biology and diseases of other rodents. In: Fox JG, Cohen BJ, Loew FM, eds. Laboratory Animal Medicine. Orlando, FL: Academic Press Inc., 1984; 183-205.

38. Manning PJ, Wagner JE, Harkness JE. Biology and diseases of guinea pigs. In: Fox JG, Cohen BJ, Loew FM, eds. Laboratory Animal Medicine. Orlando, FL: Academic Press Inc., 1984; 149-177.

39. Quesenberry KE. Guinea pigs. Veterinary Clinics of North America: Small Animal Practice 1994; 24: 67-87.

40. Harkness JE, Wagner JE, eds. Specific diseases and conditions. In: The Biology and Medicine of Rabbits and Rodents. Baltimore, MD: Williams & Wilkins, 1995; 171-317.

41. Anderson LC. Guinea pig husbandry and medicine. Veterinary Clinics of North America: Small Animal Practice 1987; 17: 1045-1059.

42. Harkness JE, Wagner JE, eds. Biology and husbandry. In: The Biology and Medicine of Rabbits and Rodents. Baltimore, MD: Williams & Wilkins, 1995; 13-73.

43. Richardson VCG. Diseases of domestic guinea pigs. In: Price CJ, Bedford PGC, Sutton JB, eds. Library of Veterinary Practice. Oxford, UK: Blackwell Scientific Publications, 1992; 49-60.

44. Peters LJ. The guinea pig: An overview. In: Johnston DE, ed. Exotic Animal Medicine in Practice. The Compendium Collection, vol I. Trenton, NJ: Veterinary Learning Systems, 1991; 15-27.

45. Harkness JE. Biology and husbandry—Guinea pigs. In: A Practitioner's Guide to Domestic Rodents. Lakewood, CO: AAHA Professional Library Series, 1993; 11-14.

46. Hoefer HL. Chinchillas. Veterinary Clinics of North America: Small Animal Practice 1994; 24: 103-111.

47. Williams CSF. Chinchillas. In: Practical Guide to Laboratory Animals. St. Louis, MO: CV Mosby Co, 1979; 3-11.

48. Jenkins JR. Husbandry and common diseases of the chinchilla. Journal of Small Exotic Animal Medicine 1992; 2: 15-17.

49. Scott D, Miller W, Griffin C, eds. Small Animal Dermatology. Philadelphia, PA: WB Saunders Co, 1995; 1129-1165.

50. Harkness JE. Biology and husbandry—Chinchillas. In: A Practitioner's Guide to Domestic Rodents. Lakewood, CO: AAHA Professional Library Series, 1993; 29-32.

51. Kraft H. Diseases of Chinchillas. Neptune City, NJ: TFH Publications, 1987; 77-90.

52. Battles AH. The biology, care and diseases of the Syrian hamster. In: Johnston DE, ed. Exotic Animal Medicine in Practice. The Compendium Collection, vol I. Trenton, NJ: Veterinary Learning Systems, 1991; 5-14.

53. Van Hoosier GL, Ladiges WC. Biology and diseases of hamsters. In: Fox JG, Cohen BJ, Loew FM, eds. Laboratory Animal Medicine. Orlando, FL: Academic Press Inc., 1984; 124-145.

54. Wagner JE, Farrar PL. Husbandry and medicine of small rodents. Veterinary Clinics of North America: Small Animal Practice 1987; 17: 1061-1087.

55. Harkness JE. Biology and husbandry—Hamsters. In: A Practitioner's Guide to Domestic Rodents. Lakewood, CO: AAHA Professional Library Series, 1993; 15-18.

56. Harkness JE. Biology and husbandry—Gerbils. In: A Practitioner's Guide to Domestic Rodents. Lakewood, CO: AAHA Professional Library Series, 1993; 19-20.

57. Kohn DF, Barthold SW. Biology and diseases of rats. In: Fox JG, Cohen BJ, Loew FM, eds. Laboratory Animal Medicine. Orlando, FL: Academic Press Inc., 1984; 91-120.

58. Harkness JE. Biology and husbandry—Rats. In: A Practitioner's Guide to Domestic Rodents. Lakewood, CO: AAHA Professional Library Series, 1993; 21-24.

59. Jacoby RO, Fox JG. Biology and diseases of mice. In: Fox JG, Cohen BJ, Loew FM, eds. Laboratory Animal Medicine. Orlando, FL: Academic Press Inc., 1984; 31-88.

60. Harkness JE. Biology and husbandry—Mice. In: A Practitioner's Guide to Domestic Rodents. Lakewood, CO: AAHA Professional Library Series, 1993; 25-28.

CASE 28-1

Anorexia in a Guinea Pig

Christine M. Kolmstetter, DVM
College of Veterinary Medicine
University of Tennessee
Knoxville, Tennessee, USA

Assess the Animal

A one-year-old female Peruvian guinea pig was examined for a two-week history of anorexia and decreased activity. The volume and consistency of the feces were normal. The owner had purchased the guinea pig at two months of age; no other pets were in the household. The animal was housed in a 30-gallon aquarium that contained a shredded paper substrate. The aquarium was located in a quiet area in the living room. The animal was handled daily. No recent changes in environment or husbandry had occurred, and there was no history of trauma.

Physical examination revealed a bright, alert, thin guinea pig with a dull coat. The incisor and cheek teeth and oral mucosa appeared normal. The animal was reluctant to move. Although the guinea pig's joints were not palpably swollen, the animal seemed uncomfortable when the elbow and hock joints were gently flexed and extended. Abdominal palpation was normal.

Assess the Food(s) and Feeding Method

Commercial dry guinea pig food and fresh water in a sipper bottle were provided free choice.

Questions

1. What other questions should be included in the dietary history?
2. What is this patient's most likely nutritional problem?
3. What further diagnostic tests should be offered to the client?
4. What treatment should be recommended?

Answers and Discussion

1. The owner should be questioned about the source of the commercial dry guinea pig food, its length and manner of storage in the home and what other food items were consumed by the guinea pig. This question revealed that, for the sake of convenience, the owner purchased several bags of food at a local discount grocery store. This supply lasted for two to three months.
2. Hypovitaminosis C is the most likely nutritional problem, based on the history and clinical signs.
3. A complete blood count, serum biochemistry profile and whole body radiographs would reveal the extent of the disease and help disclose other underlying problems that might be present.
4. This patient's food should be supplemented with oral or injectable vitamin C. The client should be educated about proper nutrition and other aspects of husbandry at this time.

CHAPTER 29

Feeding Reptiles

Scott Stahl

Susan Donoghue

"In the parched path I have seen the good lizard
(one drop of crocodile) meditating."
Frederico Garcia Lorca, 1921

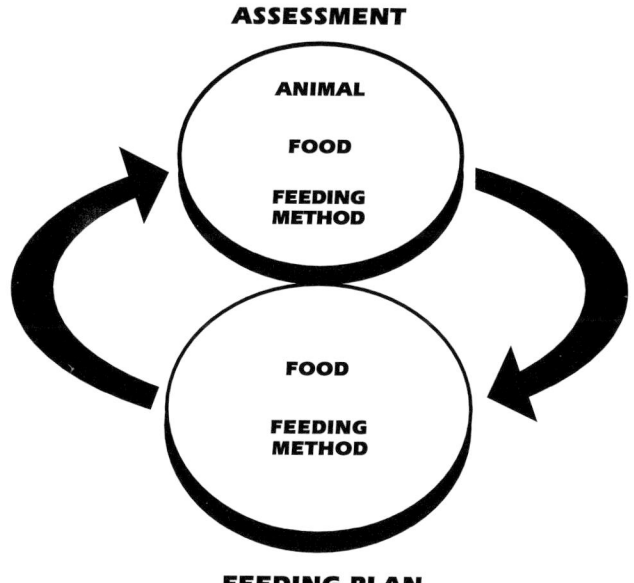

ASSESSMENT

ANIMAL

FOOD

FEEDING METHOD

FOOD

FEEDING METHOD

FEEDING PLAN

Note: The reader is referred to Chapter 1 for a detailed discussion of the iterative process of clinical nutrition.

INTRODUCTION

Diversity among the more than 6,500 species of reptiles challenges a veterinarian's ability to know the feeding management, estimate the nutritional requirements and recommend appropriate diets for every species presented in practice. With the exception of field studies on free-living reptiles, nutritional research is limited. Thus, recommendations are based on knowledge of natural diets, feeding histories, clinical experience and principles of comparative nutrition.

Identification of different species becomes easier with experience, but is often complicated because owners may know only a common name for their reptile. Common names can be colloquial or assigned to more than one species. Therefore, misidentification of a patient may result in serious errors in nutritional recommendations. Reference texts help identify species and provide information about natural history and diet.[1-8] This information can guide recommendations for habitat, including requirements for temperature, light, humidity, substrate, furnishings and social interaction. Failure to provide a suitable environment can lead to stress, causing negative effects on food intake and metabolic status of the patient.

For purposes of clinical nutrition, reptiles may be grouped into herbivores, omnivores and carnivores according to broad generalizations about their natural diet (Table 29-1). These distinctions serve as initial guides for making recommendations about diet and feeding management.

REPTILES

KEY WORDS & TERMS—FEEDING OF REPTILES*

Body condition
Carnivorous reptiles
Chelonians
Dysecdysis
Ectothermic
Endothermic
Enophthalmos
Fuzzy mice
Gout

Herbivorous reptiles
Heterothermic
Hyperkeratinization
Hypervitaminosis A
Hypovitaminosis A
Invertebrate prey
Metabolic bone disease
Metabolic rate
Nitrogen

Omnivorous reptiles
Pinkie mice
Sarcopenia
Squamous metaplasia
Thiaminase
Uric acid
Uricemia
Vertebrate prey

*Key words and terms are defined in the Glossary.

KEY POINTS—FEEDING OF REPTILES

1. With the exception of field studies using free-living reptiles, nutritional research is limited. Thus, dietary recommendations for reptiles are based on knowledge of natural diets and feeding histories, clinical experience and principles of comparative nutrition.
2. For purposes of clinical nutrition, reptiles may be grouped into herbivores, omnivores and carnivores according to broad generalizations about natural diet. These distinctions serve as initial guides for detecting nutritional disorders and for making recommendations about diet and feeding management.
3. For reptiles, nutritional disorders are often due to errors in husbandry; thus, history taking should include specific questions about management, diet and feeding plans.
4. Many signs of malnutrition may be evident during the physical examination and should be noted in the patient's record. Examples include corneal and conjunctival disease, respiratory infection, enophthalmos and dysecdysis.
5. Patients may also be scored for body condition (fat:lean ratio, degree of emaciation or fat loss) and muscle wasting (cachexia, sarcopenia, protein depletion).
6. Diagnostic testing helps assess nutritional and overall health status. This is especially important because reptiles, like birds, attempt to hide their illnesses.
7. Because reptiles do not use energy to maintain body temperature, they require fewer calories than do birds and mammals. Metabolic rates for reptiles relate to metabolic body size—the smaller the animal, the greater its metabolic rate per unit body weight. Metabolic rates in reptiles average about one-fourth those of mammals.
8. For carnivorous reptiles, exogenous fuel sources are primarily fat and protein; intake of carbohydrate, including fiber, is minimal.
9. For herbivorous reptiles, exogenous fuel sources are primarily carbohydrate and protein. Dietary fat is usually less than 10% of dry matter.
10. Neonatal prey fed to smaller carnivorous and omnivorous reptiles may lack sufficient calcium and fat-soluble vitamins.
11. Invertebrates are routinely "dusted" with powdery vitamin-mineral supplements to supply calcium and other nutrients lacking in the diet. Dusting is quantitatively risky; it may induce nutrient toxicities if overdone, deficiencies if underdone and poor intake because calcium salts and many vitamins are unpalatable.
12. Domestic fruits and vegetables available from grocery stores are lower in nutritional value (especially protein and fiber) than fruits and plants consumed in the wild.
13. Fruits contain mostly water, fructose and small amounts of fiber. Additions of even small amounts of fruit markedly dilute the calories, nutrients and fiber provided by greens.
14. Diet-related nutritional deficiencies in carnivorous reptiles include calcium deficiency from unsupplemented invertebrates or muscle meat, vitamin A deficiency from iceberg lettuce and muscle meat, and thiamin (vitamin B_1) and tocopherol (vitamin E) deficiencies from fish that contain thiaminases and high levels of polyunsaturated fatty acids.
15. Common problems in herbivorous reptiles include multiple deficiencies (especially calcium deficiency) from unsupplemented produce and protein deficiency from diets containing large amounts of fruit.
16. Metabolic bone disease is probably the most common nutritionally related disease seen in lizards, especially green iguanas. This disease is caused by dietary deficiency of calcium, excess of dietary phosphorus, deficiency of vitamin D_3 or a combination of factors.
17. Hypovitaminosis A is probably the most common nutritional disease of chelonia. These animals are typically fed unsupplemented iceberg lettuce, hamburger or other foods deficient in vitamin A.

ASSESSMENT

Assess the Animal

Signalment

Examination of the patient begins with the signalment. After the reptile presented has been properly identified by species, its age and gender should be estimated. Consider its stage of growth, reproductive status and degree of health, because these factors affect dietary recommendations. For example, certain species of aquatic turtles (e.g., the common sliders often kept as pets) change from eating a primarily carnivorous diet to eating a more herbivorous diet with maturity. Thus, feeding recommendations may differ for juvenile and adult reptiles.

Table 29-1. Foods and fuel sources vary in reptiles, depending on the carnivorous, omnivorous or herbivorous nature of the species.*

Common pets	Carnivores	Omnivores	Herbivores
	Snakes	Box turtles	Most tortoises
	Aquatic turtles	Bearded dragons	*Iguana* spp
	Most monitors, tegus	Day geckos	*Uromastyx* spp
	Most lizards	Forest-dwelling tortoises	*Corucia zebrata*
	Leopard geckos	Anoles	
	Chameleons	Blue-tongued skinks	
Foods	Mealworms	Slugs	Greens
	Flies	Snails	Fruits
	Crickets	Crickets	Vegetables
	Mice	Fruits	Clover
	Fish	Vegetables	Dandelions
	Rats	Greens	Grasses
Dietary contents (% kcal metabolizable energy)			
Protein	25-60	15-40	15-35
Fat	30-60	5-40	<10
Carbohydrate	<10	20-75	55-75

*Adapted from Donoghue S, Langenberg J. Nutrition. In: Mader DR, ed. Reptile Medicine and Surgery. Philadelphia, PA: WB Saunders Co, 1996; 148-174.

Nutritional needs for reproductively active reptiles tend to be greater than for nonreproductive reptiles. This is especially true for females that need energy for development of ovarian follicles, oviductal eggs and embryos and require calcium for egg laying (often multiple clutches in a breeding season). However, some reptiles may become anorectic during phases of reproduction. For example, male snakes may refuse food during courtship and copulation or during times that seasonally correlate with these activities (e.g., ball pythons may not eat during the "dry season"). Likewise, females may not accept food while gravid. Therefore, for reproductively active reptiles, consider recommending heavier feeding during nonreproductive periods to compensate for subsequent nutritional demands.

The nutritional requirements for sick reptiles may also differ from those of healthy reptiles.[9] The overall health status of the patient dictates the need for a change from a traditional diet. Typically, the clinician should recommend foods with greater nutrient digestibility and availability.[9]

History

For reptiles, nutritional disorders are often caused by errors in husbandry; thus, history taking should include specific questions about management. First, a general history is obtained.[7,10] Pertinent information includes the patient's origin (e.g., private breeder, importer, pet shop), whether the patient was born in captivity or caught in the wild, length of ownership, whether there are other reptiles in the home and the disease history for the patient and the entire reptile collection.

The history should include specific questions about husbandry (Table 29-2).

A dietary history allows the veterinarian to assess the animal's intake of energy and nutrients, and may provide information about the animal's clinical condition and behavior. It also may help in the early detection of nutritional problems before they become serious clinical disorders. Dietary histories may be complex for some reptiles (e.g., iguanas and tortoises) that consume a mix of different foods, including salads and supplements.

One goal of a dietary history is to obtain information on all available foods offered to the patient. Foods that may be intentionally offered include commercial foods, home-made salads, snacks, treats and supplements. Foods may also be available unintentionally, such as houseplants for iguanas and tortoises that free range in homes.

Attention should be given to the quality and wholesomeness (absence of potential pathogens) of the food, cleanliness of feeding utensils and the skills and reliability of those responsible for feeding. The veterinarian should also determine whether the reptile has appropriate access to water.

It is best to query those directly responsible for feeding the reptile and not to rely on second-hand information. For complicated feeding programs involving a wide variety of foods, it may be best to ask owners to complete seven- to 10-day diaries, listing all foods offered and estimates of amounts consumed. For both written and oral dietary histories, care must be taken to avoid influencing responses by owners.

When obtaining a dietary history, include specifics about: 1) diet—what is fed, how often and how much, how the food is prepared, where the food is placed in the habitat, when the food is removed and which foods the reptile actually consumes, 2) supplementation—are supplements used, what type, how are they offered, how often, does the animal eat the food when the supplement is offered and 3) water—how is water offered, frequency of water changes and has the owner observed the animal drinking.

Table 29-2. Husbandry questions for reptile owners.

Housing
Type and size of habitat
Location (indoors, outdoors)
Description of cage substrate and furniture
Presence of cage mates
Frequency of and routine for cleaning
Temperature
Type of heating (radiant, ventral sources)
Positioning of heat in cage
Measured temperature ranges within habitat (should be gradients of temperature)
Safety precautions used to prevent thermal injury
Light
Type of lighting provided (incandescent, fluorescent, natural sunlight)
Light filtered by glass or Plexiglas (these filter out ultraviolet light)
Positioning of light source
Length of light cycle

For carnivorous reptiles, dietary histories should concern type, source and health of the prey offered and the frequency of feeding. Look for problems with over- or underfeeding, offering malnourished prey, feeding only or mostly invertebrate prey, failure to provide additional supplementation, etc.

For herbivorous reptiles, dietary histories should especially concern the sources of protein, calcium and fiber. Another concern is whether commercially prepared foods are being diluted by excessive amounts of fruits or vegetables. For those patients fed mixed salads, look for sources of protein (romaine lettuce, legumes), calcium (calcium carbonate), fiber (crumbled hay cubes or fresh grasses). For commercial foods, check labels for ingredients.

Physical Examination

Initially, observe the undisturbed patient from a distance. Posture, respiratory rate and movement, activity level, agility, strength and symmetry should be noted and compared with the results of the hands-on examination.

After the reptile is appropriately restrained, it may be evaluated physically. The physical examination should be consistent and follow a similar pattern with each patient. This process reduces the likelihood that something will be overlooked. A typical approach is to start at the head and work caudally.

Many signs of malnutrition may be evident during the examination and should be noted in the patient's record. Examples include corneal and conjunctival abnormalities and respiratory disease, which may indicate hypovitaminosis A. Enophthalmos may suggest dehydration or ination and cachexia. Abnormal color in the oral cavity may be due to anemia or icterus. (Note: This finding may be misleading in the bearded dragon, *Pogona vitticeps*, for example, which naturally has yellow oral mucous membranes.) Increased amounts of mucus in the mouth may indicate hypovitaminosis A. Dysecdysis (abnormal shedding) may suggest dehydration or hypo- or hypervitaminosis A.

After a thorough physical examination, the reptile should be weighed. Patients may also be scored for body condition (fat:lean ratio, degree of emaciation or fat loss) and muscle wasting (cachexia, sarcopenia, protein depletion). (See Chapter 1.) Average weights and morphometrics have not been established for reptiles, but in-house ranges can be established at a practice.

A general guide for reptiles (and mammals) is that an acute loss of 10% or chronic loss of 20% of body weight indicates the need for nutritional intervention. Body weight, however, provides limited quantitative data about lean body mass. All weight loss, even in healthy reptiles, is accompanied by loss of lean and adipose tissue. Losses of body fat and tissue protein will be accelerated in ill reptiles and those recovering from surgery. Muscle wasting is typically characterized clinically by loss of muscle mass and body weight. Protein catabolism results in cumulative losses of skeletal muscle mass and eventually loss of function of enzyme systems. Tissue proteins usually continue to be depleted during initial recovery from illness and surgery. Weight gain immediately after illness or surgery typically represents water and fat replacement whereas tissue protein is restored later.

Diagnostic Testing

In addition to a thorough physical examination, diagnostic testing helps assess nutritional and overall health status.

This is especially important because reptiles, like birds, attempt to hide their illnesses. Diagnostic tests such as hematology and serum biochemistry analyses may be helpful.

Reptile blood is fragile. It is best preserved with heparin and should be processed immediately.[11,12] Reptiles tend to have lower normal hematocrit values than other companion animals. Blood samples should be processed in-house or sent to a commercial clinical laboratory that specializes in reptile blood analyses. This is important to obtain consistently accurate total white blood cell and differential counts. Experienced laboratory technicians can describe the morphology of the cells (i.e., toxic, degranulating, shrunken), which can be just as valuable as the white blood cell total and differential counts. Serial samples are helpful for assessing progression of disease and health status.

Kidney disease is common in reptiles; however, uric acid levels may be affected by the most recent meal eaten by the reptile and may not be a sensitive indicator of renal function. In many cases, elevated serum phosphorus and subsequent decreased serum calcium values (usually in an inverse ratio of phosphorus to calcium) may indicate renal disease much earlier than elevated uric acid concentrations.

Deficiencies of calcium and vitamin D are common in reptiles. Radiographs can be a valuable tool to evaluate quality and density of bones. Additionally, radiography and ultrasonography are useful in assessing fat reserves and evaluating reproductive status of females.

Key Nutritional Factors

Reptiles differ from mammalian and avian patients in the metabolism of energy and nitrogen. These differences affect water balance, intake of essential nutrients, prevalence of diet-related diseases and causes of mortality. This section discusses the key nutritional factors that affect reptiles as well as common diseases caused by nutrient excesses and deficiencies.

ENERGY

Reptiles are ectothermic and heterothermic. Their body temperature depends on ambient environmental temperatures, rather than on internal metabolism, and varies with fluctuating temperatures. This effect of ambient temperature on body temperature affects metabolic rate (hence caloric needs), activity (e.g., food procurement) and digestion. In most cases, reptiles maintain an appropriate core body temperature if provided with a sufficient temperature gradient within their habitat. However, temperatures that are too cold will limit food consumption and impair digestion. Temperatures that are too hot will lead to excessive stress, decreased food intake and weight loss.

Because energy is not used to maintain body temperature, reptiles require fewer calories than birds and mammals. Metabolic rates in reptiles relate to metabolic body size—the smaller the animal, the greater its metabolic rate per unit body weight. The metabolic rates of reptiles average about one-fourth those of mammals. Energy requirements increase with eating, activity, reproduction, growth, protein synthesis (i.e., wound healing) and certain disorders (Table 29-3). Daily energy intakes should be calculated by multiplying the metabolic rate by a factor (i.e., 1.1 to 2.5) that accounts for activity and other conditions that increase metabolic rate. Unlike birds and mammals, energy requirements for reptiles do not increase with cold ambient temperatures. Estimates of daily calorie intakes

Table 29-3. Estimates of standard metabolic rate (MR) in kcal/day and fractional increases for feeding and activity for reptiles at 30°C (86°F).*

Body weight (g)	MR	1.1 MR	1.25 MR	1.5 MR	2.0 MR	2.5 MR
5	0.54	0.6	0.68	0.81	1.08	1.4
10	0.92	1.0	1.2	1.4	1.8	2.3
15	1.3	1.4	1.6	1.9	2.6	3.2
20	1.6	1.7	2.0	2.4	3.2	4.0
25	1.9	2.0	2.3	2.8	3.8	4.8
30	2.2	2.4	2.7	3.2	4.4	5.5
40	2.7	3.0	3.4	4.0	5.4	6.8
50	3.2	3.5	4.0	4.8	6.4	8
75	4.4	4.8	5.4	6.5	8.8	11
100	5.4	6.0	6.8	8.2	11	14
125	6.4	7.1	8.1	9.7	13	16
150	7.4	8.2	9.3	11	15	18
175	8.4	9.2	10	12	17	21
200	9.3	10	12	14	19	23
250	11	12	14	16	22	28
300	13	14	16	19	26	32
350	14	16	18	21	28	35
400	16	17	20	24	32	40
450	17	19	22	26	34	42
500	19	21	23	28	38	48
600	22	24	27	32	44	55
700	24	27	30	36	48	60
800	27	30	34	40	54	68
900	30	32	37	44	60	75
1,000	32	35	40	48	64	80
1,250	38	42	47	57	76	95
1,500	44	48	55	66	88	110
1,750	49	54	62	74	98	122
2,000	54	60	68	82	108	135
2,500	65	71	81	97	130	162
3,000	74	82	93	112	148	185
3,500	84	92	105	126	168	210
4,000	93	102	116	140	186	232
4,500	102	112	127	153	204	255
5,000	110	122	138	166	220	275
6,000	127	140	159	191	254	318
7,000	143	157	179	215	286	358
8,000	159	174	198	238	318	398
9,000	174	191	217	261	348	435
10,000	188	207	236	283	376	470
15,000	257	283	322	386	514	642
20,000	321	353	402	482	642	802
25,000	382	420	477	572	764	955
30,000	439	483	549	659	878	1,098
40,000	548	603	685	822	1,096	1,370
50,000	651	716	813	976	1,302	1,628

*MR = 32(BW$_{kg}$)$^{0.77}$ where MR = standard metabolic rate in kcal/day and BW = body weight in kg. To convert to kJ, multiply kcal by 4.184.
Adapted from Donoghue S, Langenberg J. Nutrition. In: Mader DR, ed. Reptile Medicine and Surgery. Philadelphia, PA: WB Saunders Co, 1996; 148-174.

are generally derived from experimental studies using a limited number of species, field work on species not often seen in practice and on clinical experiences of knowledgeable herpetoculturists.[8,9]

Fuel use varies with the feeding ecology of the species. Generally, assumptions can be made based on the species' food preferences. For carnivores (e.g., snakes, most monitors and many aquatic turtles), exogenous fuel sources are fat (providing 8.5 to 9 kcal/g [35.6 to 37.7 kJ/g]) and protein (providing 3.7 to 4 kcal/g [15.5 to 16.7 kJ/g]). Intake of carbohydrate, including fiber, is minimal (Table 29-1). Rates of gluconeogenesis are likely to stay relatively high in these species.

For herbivores (e.g., tortoises, green iguanas, prehensile tail skinks [*Corucia zebrata*] and spiny tail lizards [*Uromastyx* spp]), exogenous fuel sources are primarily carbohydrate (about 3.5 kcal/g [14.6 kJ/g]) and protein (about 3.5 kcal/g [14.6 kJ/g]). Dietary fat (providing about 8.5 kcal/g [35.6 kJ/g]) is usually less than 10% of

dry matter (Table 29-1). Fermentation of fiber in the lower bowel of herbivores yields short-chain fatty acids that are also used for energy (perhaps providing about 2 kcal/g [8.4 kJ/g] of fiber).

Energy Deficiency and Excess

Low calorie intake leads to underweight and cachectic conditions. Ribs and vertebral processes are prominent or palpable in underweight snakes and lizards. Some exhibit longitudinal folds of skin along the lateral body wall. Thin turtles and tortoises lack heft. Poor body condition may be caused by: 1) improper husbandry, 2) stress, 3) improper temperature, 4) inappropriate diets or too little food and 5) underlying diseases that affect appetite and metabolism.

Excessive caloric intake leads to rapid growth in juveniles and overweight and obese conditions in adults. Especially at risk are those species with a sedentary nature, such as large snakes and lizards. Also at risk are reptiles kept in small habitats and fed high-fat foods, such as aquatic turtles main-

REPTILES

tained in small tanks. Treatment includes decreasing caloric intake and increasing activity. For example, an obese aquatic turtle that is fed commercial pellets daily can, instead, be fed pellets only three times per week and be offered greens on the other days of the week. Tank size should also be increased to encourage activity.

WATER

All captive reptiles should have access to fresh water. Proper delivery of water is important. Turtles and snakes generally drink from bowls. Some lizards such as anoles, chameleons and day geckos lap up droplets sprayed or dripped onto foliage. Other lizards, such as iguanas and monitor lizards learn to drink from bowls and smaller reptiles from lids (e.g., plastic caps for pet food cans). Some reptiles may reject water held in plastic containers, presumably because of odor or taste. A switch to glass, ceramic or

Table 29-4. Purine content varies in foods. Low-purine and potentially acidic foods should be selected and high-purine and alkaline foods should be avoided for reptiles predisposed to gout.*

High-purine foods
Anchovies
Asparagus
Brains
Kidney
Liver
Mince meats
Mushrooms
Sardines
Low-purine foods
Breads
Cereals
Cheese
Eggs
Fats
Fruits
Milk
Most vegetables
Nuts
Potentially acidic foods
Brazil nuts
Breads
Cereals
Cheese
Corn
Cranberries
Lentils
Meats
Plums
Prunes
Rice
Walnuts
Potentially alkaline foods
Almonds
Beet greens
Beets
Chard
Chestnuts
Coconut
Dairy
Dandelion
Fruits**
Kale
Molasses
Mustard greens
Spinach
Turnip greens

*Adapted from Donoghue S, Langenberg J. Nutrition. In: Mader DR, ed. Reptile Medicine and Surgery. Philadelphia, PA: WB Saunders Co, 1996; 148-174.
**Except plums, prunes and cranberries.

stainless steel bowls usually corrects the situation. Tortoises and some snakes soak in large, shallow bowls. Soaking enhances water uptake and stimulates excretion.

Desert animals require less water than temperate and tropical species. Some species receive enough water from food to meet requirements. Empirically, daily parenteral doses of water for rehydration are 10 to 25 ml/kg body weight.[11]

Water-Related Problems

Water is critically important for reptiles and relates to many of the diseases seen in practice, such as gout and dysecdysis. Aquatic species are at less risk for dehydration, but water quality is critical for these animals. Routine water analyses may be important for maintaining health in aquatic reptiles.[9] Water should be fresh for all species. Bacterial counts and culture can be included in routine water analyses. The method of providing water to reptiles will influence the humidity in the environment.

Clinical impressions suggest that inadequate humidity may contribute to dehydration, stress and dysecdysis. Likewise, excessive humidity may contribute to skin infections and hyperkeratinization.

NITROGEN

Lizards and snakes excrete mostly uric acid. Aquatic turtles tend to excrete more ammonia and urea than uric acid, whereas terrestrial tortoises excrete relatively more uric acid.[13] Excretory patterns are clinically important because of difficulties in maintaining positive water balance and the prevalence of dehydration in reptiles.

Dehydration is common, especially in sick reptiles. It may result from water provided in improper form or anorexia, or may occur secondary to disease. Uricotelic species require large amounts of water to sustain normal excretion. Dehydration in these species may result in urinary stasis, hyperuricemia and gout, a disease characterized by deposition of urate crystals in soft tissues and joints. Prevention is based on maintaining adequate hydration. Purines may be restricted by reducing protein levels. Restriction of purines is feasible by avoiding high-purine foods such as liver (Table 29-4).

Many reptiles appear to have marked protein requirements. Those that are strict carnivores naturally consume diets consisting of 30 to 60% protein (metabolizable energy [ME] basis). Herbivorous reptiles consume less protein, but optimal ranges remain to be defined. Feeding trials in green iguanas suggested that dietary protein levels of about 28% (dry matter basis [DMB]) are needed for optimal growth.[14,15]

OTHER NUTRIENTS

Intake of nutrients varies with feeding habits. For large carnivorous reptiles, vertebrate prey are assumed to be "complete and balanced" packages that contain all of the essential nutrients. However, neonatal prey (e.g., pinkie [newborn] mice) that are fed to smaller carnivores and omnivores, may lack sufficient calcium and fat-soluble vitamins.[16] In adult prey, calcium, phosphorus and magnesium are provided by bone, most trace minerals and vitamins by liver and kidneys, iodine by thyroid glands and zinc by the pancreas. The protein quality is high. Calories are provided almost entirely by fat and protein, and carbohydrate sources are limited to the intestinal content of the prey (Table 29-5).

Invertebrate prey also contain much fat and protein but lack a calcium-rich skeleton (Table 29-6). The chitinous (amino-cellulose) exoskeleton of most invertebrates con-

Table 29-5. Caloric and nutrient content of vertebrate prey.

Food items (g)	Water (%)	Energy (kcal/g)* (As fed)	Energy (kcal/g)* (DMB)	Protein (% kcal)	Fat (% kcal)	NFE (% kcal)	Calcium (mg/kcal)	Phosphorus (mg/kcal)
Mouse, adult (27)	65	1.7	4.8	48	47	5	5.0	3.6
Mouse, pup (1.5)	81	0.8	4.2	57	40	3	3.8	3.7
Mouse, pup (4)	71	1.7	5.9	29	69	2	2.4	2.2
Rat, adult (330)	66	1.6	4.7	55	43	2	4.4	3.2
Chick, day old (40)	73	1.3	4.8	52	44	4	2.7	2.0
Atlantic herring (100)	69	1.8	5.7	39	58	3	na	1.4
Atlantic smelt (100)	77	1.0	4.3	63	31	6	3.2	4.4

Key: NFE = nitrogen-free extract (soluble carbohydrate), DMB = dry matter basis, na = not available.
*To convert to kJ, multiply kcal by 4.184.

Table 29-6. Caloric and nutrient content of invertebrate prey.

Food items	Water (%)	Energy (kcal/g)* (As fed)	Energy (kcal/g)* (DMB)	Protein (% kcal)	Fat (% kcal)	NFE (% kcal)	Calcium (mg/kcal)	Phosphorus (mg/kcal)
Gryllus domesticus (house cricket)	68	1.0	3.1	40	54	6	0.3	2.7
Acheta domestica (commercial cricket)	62	1.9	4.8	50	44	6	0.2	2.6
Tenebrio molitor (mealworm larvae)	58	2.1	5.0	37	60	3	0.1	1.2
Galleria mellonella (waxworm larvae)	63	2.1	5.7	27	73	0	0.1	0.9
Musca domestica (fly larvae)	70	1.5	4.9	48	44	8	0.1	na
Lumbricus terrestris (earthworm)	84	0.5	3.1	73	13	14	Variable	Variable

Key: NFE = nitrogen-free extract (soluble carbohydrate), DMB = dry matter basis, na = not available.
*To convert to kJ, multiply kcal by 4.184.

tains nonprotein nitrogen. The digestibility of this chitin is questionable.[9]

Invertebrates are routinely "dusted" with powdery vitamin-mineral supplements to supply calcium and other nutrients lacking in the diet. Dusting can be problematic; it may induce nutrient toxicities if excessive and create deficiencies if too little is provided. Additionally, some reptiles will refuse foods that have been dusted because calcium salts and many vitamins are unpalatable.

Domestic fruits and vegetables available from grocery stores are lower in nutritional value (especially protein and fiber) than fruits and plants consumed in the wild. Among domestic produce, higher protein levels are found in greens (e.g., romaine lettuce, collard greens and spinach), alfalfa and mung-bean sprouts, mushrooms and bamboo shoots. Domestic produce rarely provides enough protein, calcium and fiber, or adequate levels of trace minerals and vitamins to support growth and reproduction in reptiles; therefore, produce needs supplementation (Table 29-7).[9]

Fruits are consumed readily by herbivorous reptiles, probably because of the bright colors, sweet taste and moist texture. However, fruits contain mostly water, fructose and small amounts of fiber. Additions of even small amounts of fruit can markedly dilute the calories, nutrients and fiber provided by greens.

NUTRIENT DEFICIENCIES AND EXCESSES

With the exception of those species consuming whole prey, many reptiles suffer from deficiencies and excesses of nutrients. Common among many species are deficiencies of calcium and vitamin D_3.

Vitamin D_3 is problematic. Limited research data, anecdotal evidence and clinical impressions suggest that, at least in some species, dermal synthesis of 1,25-dihydroxycholecalciferol may be more efficient than gastrointestinal absorption of dietary vitamin D_3. Thus, exposure to natural sunlight or ultraviolet (full spectrum) lighting may be critical for adequate vitamin D_3 synthesis in some reptile species. Interactions between vitamin D, calcium and

phosphorus, and secondary interactions with vitamin A and several trace minerals, complicate nutritional requirements. For now, general recommendations include consistent but not excessive supplementation of diets (except when feeding whole vertebrate prey) with both calcium and vitamin D_3, exposure to full-spectrum lights and, whenever possible, exposure to direct sunlight.

Diet-related nutritional deficiencies in carnivores include calcium deficiency from feeding primarily unsupplemented invertebrates or muscle meat, vitamin A deficiency from feeding primarily iceberg lettuce and muscle meat, and thiamin (vitamin B_1) and tocopherol (vitamin E) deficiency from feeding fish containing thiaminases and high levels of polyunsaturated fatty acids.

Common problems in herbivores include multiple deficiencies—especially calcium deficiency—from feeding unsupplemented produce and protein deficiency from feeding diets containing large amounts of fruit.

Oversupplementation may potentially lead to toxic intakes of vitamins A and D, phosphorus, selenium, iodine and other trace minerals. Some nutrient interactions may occur in reptiles. For example, excess dietary calcium may interfere with the absorption of zinc and copper, and affect the thyroidal uptake of iodine.

Metabolic Bone Disease

Metabolic bone disease is probably the most common nutritionally related disease seen in lizards, especially green iguanas. This disease is caused by a dietary deficiency of calcium, excess of dietary phosphorus, deficiency of vitamin D_3 or a combination of these factors. Clinical signs include soft mandibular and maxillary bones, deformed or fractured bones, muscle tremors, poor growth, spinal deviations and paralysis.[11] The disease is most commonly seen in young, growing lizards and adults maintained indoors. Metabolic bone disease is also common in chelonians (tortoises and turtles). Clinical signs include a soft carapace and plastron, improper shell growth and fractured limbs.[11] Treatment includes dietary correction and provision of natural sunlight or full-spectrum ultravi-

Table 29-7. Caloric and nutrient content of produce on a % dry matter basis.

Food items	Weight (g)	Water (%)	Energy (kcal/g*) (As fed)	DMB	Protein	Fat	NFE	Fiber	Calcium	Phosphorus
Romaine lettuce	100	94	0.18	3.0	36	7	50	11	1.1	0.4
Spinach (raw)	100	91	0.26	2.9	36	3	48	7	1.0	0.6
Dandelion greens (raw)	100	86	0.44	3.1	18	5	61	11	1.2	0.4
Alfalfa sprouts (raw)	100	88	0.39	3.2	37	4	39	12	0.3	0.8
Bamboo shoots (canned, 1 cup)	133	94	0.18	3.0	28	1	51	13	0.2	0.2
Vegetables (mixed, frozen, 2/3 cup)	100	83	0.47	2.8	16	2	68	7	0.1	0.3
Mushrooms (raw, 10 small)	100	90	0.27	2.7	30	6	49	9	0.1	1.3
Sweet potato (1 large)	180	64	0.82	2.8	5	1	84	2	0.1	0.2
Apple (no skin, 1 medium)	128	84	0.51	3.2	1	2	86	4	tr	tr
Banana (1 medium)	114	74	0.82	3.2	4	2	86	2	tr	tr
Cantaloupe (1 cup)	160	90	0.32	3.2	8	2	79	4	0.1	0.2
Strawberries (1 cup)	149	92	0.28	3.5	6	4	77	6	0.2	0.2

Key: NFE = nitrogen-free extract (soluble carbohydrate), DMB = dry matter basis, tr = trace.
*To convert to kJ, multiply kcal by 4.184.

olet light. For severe cases, parenteral injections of calcium, vitamin D_3 and calcitonin may be necessary.[7,9,17-19]

Hypovitaminosis A

Deficiency of vitamin A occurs in lizards fed unsupplemented produce and insects. It is characterized by squamous metaplasia, which causes shedding problems, stomatitis, palpebral edema, conjunctivitis and respiratory disease.[11] Secondary bacterial infections are also common. Treatment includes vitamin A supplementation, parenterally and orally, and dietary correction.

Hypovitaminosis A is likely the most common nutritional disease of chelonia. These animals are typically fed unsupplemented iceberg lettuce, hamburger or other foods deficient in vitamin A. Squamous metaplasia results in palpebral edema and respiratory disease. Common clinical findings include conjunctivitis, nasal discharge, wheezing and stridor.[11] Additionally, respiratory disease may cause water turtles to swim in a lopsided fashion due to fluid buildup in one lung. Secondary bacterial infections are common. Poor skin and shell quality may also be noted.

Treatment of hypovitaminosis A includes dietary correction and oral administration of vitamin A (200 to 300 IU/kg body weight). Secondary bacterial infections are treated with an appropriate antibiotic. Dietary vitamin A should be increased (2,000 to 10,000 IU/kg diet dry matter).

Fat-Soluble Vitamin Toxicities

Oversupplementation with fat-soluble vitamins may result in renal disease, hepatic disease and metastatic calcification. The exact requirements of vitamins A and D_3 are currently unknown, but excessive amounts may cause problems in lizards. Clinical signs are consistent with multiple organ failure. The most common example is seen in green iguanas maintained on commercial dog and/or cat food. Renal failure and metastatic calcification of major vessels typically occur. Treatment in most cases involves attempts to reverse organ damage through supportive care, especially fluid therapy. Additionally, calcitonin[a] may be used (2 IU/kg body weight, given intramuscularly q24h) to help reverse metastatic calcification.[8,19]

Tortoises and box turtles are very sensitive to injections of vitamin A. When given parenterally, these drugs may cause sloughing of the skin, resulting in severe skin ulceration.[8,11] These preparations are best given orally. Treatment

for vitamin toxicity in most cases is supportive care and removal of the vitamin source.

Although commercially prepared foods may occasionally be involved, the excessive use of vitamin supplements is more commonly the cause of vitamin toxicities.

Thiamin Deficiency

Thiamin deficiency is seen occasionally in garter snakes and water snakes fed frozen fish exclusively. Thiaminases, found in many species of fish, deplete available thiamin. Thiamin-deficient snakes typically present with neurologic disease characterized by ataxia, seizures, twisting and rolling. Treatment involves changing the diet to include fresh fish, insects and mice scented with fish, and medicating with oral or parenteral thiamin hydrochloride (25 mg/kg body weight, per os or intramuscularly).[8]

Assess the Food(s)

Foods appropriately balanced with carbohydrates, proteins, fats, vitamins, minerals and water are essential for all reptiles. Care of captive reptiles must address good nutrition at several levels; the daily satisfaction and health of the reptile as well as the long-term contributions to growth, maturation, defense against disease and reproductive health—the hallmark of good nutrition.

Three methods of providing nutrients and achieving these objectives are commonly used: 1) commercially prepared foods, 2) homemade mixed foods or 3) a combination of commercial and homemade foods, with or without supplements.

Commercially Prepared Foods

Reptiles may be fed commercially prepared foods formulated for the species or the most similar domestic animal. There is little scientific literature about the nutrient requirements of reptiles. However, several reports provide some insight into the levels of dietary nutrients required to result in a nutritionally adequate diet.[20] These reports make it possible to formulate prepared foods with a high probability of nutritional adequacy for some reptilian species.

Testing protocols for nutritional adequacy have not yet been established for reptile foods, as they have been for commercially prepared canine and feline foods. As the use of commercially prepared reptile foods becomes more widespread, testing protocols for nutritional adequacy will be established and required.

Commercially prepared foods offer many benefits, including nutrient balance and convenience. A moist, extruded or pelleted food will supply all the nutrients in one particle or form. Thus, the probability of producing a nutritional imbalance by feeding a commercially prepared food is much less than when reptiles are fed individual human foods prepared by uninformed owners. See Appendix S for a listing of selected foods with their guaranteed analyses.

If commercially prepared food is offered, examine the label for nutrient information or guarantees. The primary nutrients of concern depend on whether the reptile is carnivorous, omnivorous or herbivorous. Protein, fat, soluble carbohydrate, fiber, vitamin and mineral levels should be appropriate for the individual reptile. Label space does not allow for detailed nutrient information. Therefore, the manufacturer should be contacted for additional nutritional information. When purchasing or recommending commercial herbivore foods, read labels with extreme care. Some may contain low levels of antibiotics and other growth promotants that have unpredictable and potentially deleterious effects on reptiles. Regardless of the type of food fed, a sample can be submitted to a commercial laboratory for analysis. (See Appendix U for a listing of laboratories.) Consult the laboratory in advance to determine the sample size needed, preservation techniques recommended and shipping instructions.

Compare the nutrient levels of the commercial food to those recommended in this chapter to determine if there are any gaps in the nutrient profile. If the food doesn't meet recommended nutrient levels, the owner should change or supplement the diet. The food should not be fed if its label contains no nutrient information and the manufacturer does not provide nutrient levels in other promotional literature or is unavailable to answer questions by phone.

Commercial forages for herbivorous reptiles include legumes, primarily alfalfa, which can be pelleted, cubed and chopped. Unfortunately, most tortoises and herbivorous lizards show limited interest in alfalfa-based meals, eating these items only when disguised with fresh produce or when no other foods are available.

Hay can be purchased from feed stores and farms. Chopped and cubed hay is sold in pet shops and feed stores. Care should be taken to avoid prolonged storage of these products because about half the vitamin A activity from β-carotene is lost from hay within a year of cutting.

Hay-based pellets range from 12 to 28% (DMB) crude protein and 14 to 19% crude fiber (DMB). Some success has been noted in the use of hay-based pellets as bedding for juvenile herbivorous reptiles. Although these products are safe if wholesome, pellets can mold quickly and the reptile may then be at risk to develop respiratory disease and digestive upset.

Some commercially prepared foods marketed specifically for iguanas are variable in content. Look for products with at least 18% crude protein in the dry matter. Pellets may be soaked in water or fruit juice before feeding. Wet pellets may mold, so they should be offered fresh daily.

Some commercially prepared foods marketed specifically for aquatic species are sold as complete diets and are made from fish and crustacean meals, plant-based ingredients and various additives. Some manufacturers fail to add essential vitamins and minerals. Processes used in extrusion and pelleting involve high temperatures that partially destroy labile vitamins. (See Chapter 4.) Mineral and vitamin content of fish meals vary with the species, season of harvest and processing. Examine labels and products carefully. Some foods may not be adequate to sustain growth or even maintenance of carnivorous reptiles. However, the alternative homemade diet is often less desirable.

Protein in dog and cat foods ranges from 16 to 40% of ME; many pet foods provide more than 22% of ME from protein and more than 25% of ME from fat. These protein levels are likely to be adequate for carnivorous reptiles.

Herbivores generally suffer digestive upset when dietary fat exceeds about 12%. Herbivorous reptiles are unlikely to thrive on diets containing more than 12% fat, which limits the use of commercial pet foods to the "light" varieties. Light varieties often contain higher levels of fiber, which is favorable for herbivores.

Homemade Diets

A wide variety of homemade foods have been suggested for reptiles. Although homemade foods may provide adequate nourishment, most reptile owners are unwilling to devote the time necessary to properly prepare these diets. Additionally, owners must be willing to regularly observe which food components are being consumed to prevent reptiles from developing or reverting to preferential selection of specific ingredients. Considering these factors, well-formulated commercially prepared foods are a better alternative for most captive reptiles.

Supplements

Supplements are marketed as containing primarily vitamins and minerals in various amounts. Few if any supply all vitamins and minerals known to be essential for domestic species including reptiles. The tendency is to leave out those that are unpalatable or expensive. Until more work is done on reptile nutrition, no one product should be relied upon to supply all essential nutrients to captive reptiles. Better value may be achieved by using a broad-spectrum micronutrient product designed for people or domestic animals. These products may be used for reptiles, but care must be taken to provide vitamin D_3 (not vitamin D_2) and to avoid overdosage.[9] A general mammalian guideline that may also be useful in assessing reptile supplements is vitamins A:D:E should be present in a ratio approximating 100:10:1. A review of the nutrient content of many of the commonly used supplements for reptiles has been published.[9] If a commercially prepared food constitutes more than 50% of total dietary intake, supplements are contraindicated.

Although calcium is often included in commercial vitamin-mineral supplements, it is rarely present in quantities sufficient to meet requirements for reptiles fed mixed salads or invertebrates. Additional calcium may be provided as limestone (38% calcium), or as calcium salts—carbonate (40% calcium), lactate (18% calcium) and gluconate (9% calcium). Calcium and phosphorus are supplied in bone meal (24% calcium, 12% phosphorus) and dicalcium phosphate (18 to 24% calcium, 18% phosphorus). Bone meal tablets vary in size. A small (aspirin size) tablet weighs 0.75 g and provides about 180 mg calcium and 90 mg phosphorus. Products vary, so labels should be read carefully. Powdered calcium supplements can be dusted on salads and tablet forms can be crushed and mixed with food.

Assess the Feeding Method

It may not always be necessary to change the feeding method when managing reptile patients; however, a vet-

REPTILES

erinarian should verify that an appropriate feeding method is being used. Items to consider include feeding route, amount fed, how the food is offered and who feeds the reptile. All of this information should be gathered when the nutritional history is obtained. If the reptile has normal body condition and weight, the amount of food previously fed (on an energy basis) was probably appropriate.

FEEDING PLAN

The advantages and disadvantages of feeding reptiles commercially prepared and homemade foods were discussed above. If an individual reptile is healthy and exhibits no signs of deficiency disease, the owner probably is feeding the reptile appropriately and there is no need to change the food.

Although some prepared foods have been available for only a limited time, the overall nutritional quality of commercially prepared foods is rapidly improving as manufacturers consider new scientific information when they prepare their formulations. As commercially prepared foods become more widely used, many of the diet-induced diseases currently observed by veterinarians will become of historical interest only, just as they have for other companion pets.

Lizards

Lizard species (Sauria) may be herbivorous, omnivorous or carnivorous. Lizards that are carnivorous may consume either invertebrate or vertebrate prey, or both. Gastrointestinal morphology reflects feeding behavior. Thus, herbivorous lizards have hindguts adapted for fermentation of dietary fiber, and carnivorous lizards have relatively short and simple intestinal tracts suited for hydrolysis in the small intestine.

Herbivores

The green iguana (*Iguana iguana*) is the most common herbivorous lizard seen in veterinary practice. These large, arboreal, diurnal lizards originate from Central and South America and require tropical temperatures (approximately 32°C [90°F]) and humidity (approximately 90% relative humidity). With proper care, green iguanas may live 10 to 15 years in captivity. However, mistakes in husbandry and diet often lead to an early demise.

Other herbivorous lizards include prehensile tail skinks (*Corucia* spp) and chuckwallas (*Sauromalus* spp). Others, such as spiny tailed lizards (*Uromastyx* spp) and rock iguanas (*Cyclura* spp), use hindgut fermentation and are often classified as herbivores, but also are known to consume invertebrate prey.

Diets for herbivorous lizards should include leafy greens such as romaine lettuce and collard greens, mustard greens and endive, dandelion and clover. Vegetables such as green beans, okra, carrots, yellow squash, zucchini and commercial thawed frozen mixed vegetables can make up a small fraction, perhaps 10 to 20%, of the diet.

Spinach, cabbage, peas, potatoes and beet greens contain oxalates that bind calcium and trace minerals, inhibiting their absorption. Trace mineral deficiencies may result if the diet is composed primarily of these foods and mineral intakes are marginal. Goitrogens are found in cabbage, kale, mustard and other cruciferous plants. Large intakes of these foods with marginal iodine intake may lead to hypothyroidism. Small

amounts of these oxalate-containing and goitrogenic vegetables may still be fed safely as part of the diet.

Fruits can be used as "treats" or as a very small portion of the diet. Palatable choices include papaya, mango, cantaloupe, grapes and oranges.

Commercially prepared foods may constitute a significant portion of the diet (i.e., up to 50 to 60%). See Appendix S for a listing of selected foods. Treats and other nutritionally imbalanced foods should constitute no more than 10% of the diet.

If commercially prepared foods are used for 50% or more of the diet, additional supplementation is usually unnecessary. Homemade diets of vegetables and fruits should be supplemented. Several recipes have been published.[8,9] Juveniles should be fed bite-sized foods, once or twice daily. Adults should be fed daily or every other day. These diurnal lizards should be offered food at a time that correlates with their need to bask and thermoregulate to allow efficient digestion of food.

Omnivores

Some of the most common omnivorous lizards presented to veterinary practitioners include bearded dragons (*Pogona* spp), blue-tongued skinks (*Tiliqua* spp), water dragons (*Physignathus* spp) and plated lizards (*Gerrhosaurus* spp). In captivity, these omnivores consume prey (often invertebrates) or a meat-based, commercially prepared food mixed with fruits and vegetables.

A commercially prepared food should make up 60 to 75% of the total diet. The remaining portion may include invertebrates such as crickets, meal worms, wax worms, sweepings (insects found by gently sweeping grasses with a net; counsel clients to make sure no pesticides have been used on the grass), earthworms, snails and slugs (especially for skinks). Other prey include small vertebrates, such as newborn and fuzzy mice, adult mice and rats and chicks. Cooked eggs may also be included as a protein source. Dog food (moist and dry), primate biscuits and trout food can be fed. Cat food is appropriate (up to 50 to 60% of the diet) for blue-tongued and pink-tongued skinks; however, these foods should be fed cautiously to other omnivorous lizards to prevent risks from overfeeding a high-fat food.

Fresh greens and produce may make up the rest of the diet. Palatable foods include leafy vegetables, squash, carrots, green beans, alfalfa sprouts and thawed frozen mixed vegetables. Fruits should include melon, papaya and oranges.

Nutritionally adequate, commercially prepared foods are available for omnivorous lizards. However, because no long-term feeding trials have been reported, performance of lizards should be monitored to ensure that they are thriving.

In general, the more varied the overall diet, the less supplementation is necessary. If 50% or more of the diet includes dog food, monkey biscuits, cat food or complete omnivore foods, no supplementation is necessary. Otherwise, supplementation of produce and dusting of invertebrates are recommended.

Carnivores

The most common carnivorous lizards kept in captivity are monitors (*Varanus* spp), tegus (*Tupinambis* spp) and Gila monsters and beaded lizards (*Heloderma* spp). These animals eat whole prey items (vertebrate [Figure 29-1] and invertebrate), but some also will eat cooked meat and eggs and commercial pet food. Feeding cooked meat and eggs is recommended to avoid exposure to potential pathogenic bacteria such as *Salmonella* spp.

Commercially prepared foods are available for monitors and tegus. As with any dietary regimen, the reptiles should be monitored for any dietary-related disease. Supplementation is rarely necessary for adult carnivorous lizards if they are eating whole vertebrate prey items or commercially prepared food or a variety of foods. A calcium and vitamin D_3 supplement can be used twice weekly for juveniles fed a diet of newborn mice and insects.

Insectivorous lizards kept in captivity include species of geckos (Gekkonidae and Eublepharidae), old-world chameleons (*Chamaeleo* spp), water dragons (*Physignathus* spp), anoles (*Anolis* spp), small skinks (Scincidae), monitors (*Varanus* spp), girdle-tailed lizards (*Cordylus* and *Pseudocordylus* spp), lacertas (Lacertidae), basilisks (*Basiliscus* spp), collared lizards (*Crotaphytus* spp), sailfin dragons (*Hydrosaurus* spp), ameivas (*Ameiva* spp) and swifts (*Sceloporus* spp). These species thrive on a wide variety of well-fed and well-supplemented insects such as crickets, meal worms, wax-moth larvae, king meal worms, cockroaches and fruit flies (for juveniles). Other insects and worms when available, include butterworms, grasshoppers, earthworms, flies, fly larvae and sweepings.

Insects can be fed a relatively balanced diet to "gut load" them before they are fed to lizards. A variety of whole diets can be used to feed insects including psittacine pellets, tropical fish flakes and commercial invertebrate "gut loading" foods. Also, insects can be fed vegetables that have a high precursor vitamin A content such as collard greens, kale, romaine and red-leaf lettuce, grated carrots and sweet potatoes.[21] Invertebrates should be dusted with a calcium supplement and a multivitamin supplement before they are fed to the reptile. (See Supplements.) Calcium supplement can be used daily for young growing reptiles and three to four times weekly for adults. Multivitamin supplements (which should contain some preformed vitamin A) should be used less frequently (i.e., once or twice weekly).[21]

Prey should be of the appropriate size for the lizard. A general guide is for prey length to be less than the width of the lizard's head. Insects that are too large may bite the lizard or, if swallowed, cause it to regurgitate. Generally, only enough prey to be consumed at one feeding should be offered. Excessive numbers of insects may cause stress or injury to the lizards.

Juveniles should be fed daily. Adults can be fed every second or third day.

Occasionally, larger and adult species of insectivorous lizards can be fed newborn, fuzzy or adult mice. The mice should make up no more than about 25% of the diet.

Several small lizard species, such as anoles and day geckos, readily accept fruit-flavored baby foods and yogurt. Basilisks, sailfin dragons and water dragons may accept a small amount of fruit. These soft foods provide a convenient medium for supplementation of calcium, vitamins and trace minerals.

Fresh water should always be available for lizards. Large soaking bowls should be provided for some species, such as water dragons and water monitors, Nile and Dumeril's monitors, sailfin lizards and basilisks. Misting the environment daily may help increase humidity for tropical species. Chameleons and some smaller species of lizards (e.g., anoles) usually won't drink from standing water. It is usually necessary to visually stimulate these lizards with drip

Figure 29-1. Monitor lizards are carnivorous. This large monitor (*Varanus giganteus*) awaits a pre-killed rat to be dropped into its enclosure.

systems, air bubbling systems or by misting the trees and plants in their environment to encourage drinking. These reptiles can also be placed on a clothes-drying rack or large plant, such as a *Ficus* spp, and placed under a spray of water in a shower, in order to simulate a rain shower and encourage drinking.

Some of the desert species (e.g., *Uromastyx* lizards and chuckwallas) need only small water bowls for drinking; however, they may benefit from being soaked in a warm water bath once or twice weekly. Water sources may harbor bacteria so bowls must be kept meticulously clean. Routine disinfection is recommended. Vitamin-mineral supplements should not be added to water sources because they may reduce palatability and result in increased bacterial populations.

Snakes: Serpentes

Snakes that Eat Mammalian and Avian Prey

Most of the snakes seen by private practitioners feed on mammals. Boids (pythons and boas), rat and corn snakes (*Elaphe* spp) and gopher, bull and pine snakes (*Pituophis* spp) are some of the more common snakes presented to veterinarians. Their diet consists of rats, mice, gerbils, rabbits and young chicks. These prey items should be fed a high-quality, complete ration to provide adequate nutrition for snakes.

Trauma associated with feeding live prey is common. Therefore, training snakes to eat stunned, dead or thawed frozen prey is preferred. These reptiles are attracted to prey by the smell, the heat radiating from the prey item and by movement. To help encourage snakes to eat dead food, the prey item should be warm when offered. It can also be wiggled with a long pair of forceps. Eventually, even stubborn snakes become accustomed to eating dead prey.

Frozen rodents should be thawed rapidly in very hot water to minimize intestinal bacterial bloom. Caution

REPTILES

Figure 29-2. Hog-nosed snakes typically feed on amphibians, such as toads, in the wild. In captivity, they can be tricked into eating toad-scented mice. This young Western hog-nosed snake is eating a mouse backwards.

should be used when feeding chicks or other birds to snakes because of potential exposure to salmonella. Boiling chicks before feeding may reduce the risk.

Some snakes are finicky feeders. For example, ball pythons prefer gerbils (which are found in their native habitat) or brown or black rodents, rather than white laboratory rodents.

Supplementation is not necessary when feeding whole vertebrate prey. The only exception is with long-term feeding of newborn mice, which may be deficient in calcium. Allowing newborn mice to obtain milk from the mother for a day or two improves their calcium content. Also, dipping newborn mice in a liquid calcium supplement increases dietary calcium content. Feeding fuzzy mice also improves calcium content. Obese rodents and those that have been frozen for more than six months may have reduced vitamin content.

Snakes that are housed together should be separated for feeding to minimize injuries to each other and to help identify which snake has eaten. If two or more snakes attack the same prey, one snake may inadvertently eat or injure the other.

Feeding frequency varies, depending on the species of snake. Generally, young growing snakes should be fed every five to seven days. Mature, adult snakes may be fed weekly, biweekly or even monthly.

Snakes that Eat Reptiles, Amphibians and Fish

Some snakes feed on ectotherms, including amphibians, fish, crayfish and other reptiles. Snakes that eat these prey items include king snakes (*Lampropeltis* spp), indigo snakes (*Drymarchon* spp), water snakes (*Nerodia* spp), hog-nosed snakes (*Heterodon* spp), ring-necked snakes (*Diadophis* spp) and garter snakes (*Thamnophis* spp). The prey should be frozen for at least three days to minimize exposure to parasites; many of the prey are intermediate hosts to reptile parasites. Freezing may eliminate nematode parasites; however, it will not usually eliminate bacteria and protozoa. Regular fecal examinations and dewormings may be necessary to control protozoal parasites.

Ectotherm snakes should be trained to eat rodents. Initially, rodents can be scented with a more typical prey item. For example, a hog-nosed snake that typically eats toads and frogs in the wild can be encouraged to eat a rodent whose fur has been rubbed with a toad or frog to impart a familiar scent

(Figure 29-2). Eventually, most of these snakes will accept rodents as their primary diet. Supplementation is usually unnecessary if a portion of the diet is made up of rodents.

Snakes that eat other snakes in the wild (e.g., king snakes) should be housed alone to prevent cage-mate predation.

Insectivorous Snakes

Insect-eating snakes typically seen by veterinarians include green snakes (*Opheodrys* spp), worm snakes (*Carphophis* spp), ring-necked snakes (*Diadophus* spp), brown snakes (*Storeria* spp) and other primarily fossorial snakes. Additionally, some ectotherm snakes eat insects, especially as juveniles.

A variety of worms and insects should be offered, including crickets, mealworms, earthworms, nightcrawlers and wax-moth larvae. Insects should be fed a complete diet before they are fed to snakes. Insects should be dusted with a calcium and vitamin supplement weekly. Some of the larger snakes in this group may be weaned onto pinkie mice for added nutrition. Pinkies can be supplemented by dipping them into a liquid calcium supplement.

Many of these snakes also feed on very small amphibians, such as salamanders, tadpoles and frogs. As with feeding ectotherm snakes, cold-blooded prey items should be frozen for at least three days to minimize parasitic infections.

For all snakes, fresh water should be provided at all times. Water bowls should be cleaned and disinfected regularly. A water container that is large enough for soaking should be provided. Vitamin-mineral supplements should not be added to the water. Palatability may be reduced and bacteria in the water may feed on the supplements resulting in a bacterial bloom.

Turtles and Tortoises: Chelonia

Carnivorous Turtles

The most common carnivorous turtles seen by veterinarians are water turtles, such as snapping turtles (*Chelydra* spp), mata mata turtles (*Chelys* spp) and alligator snapping turtles (*Macrochelys* spp). These turtles usually eat only while in water. They can be fed in their regular aquatic environment or, better yet, in a separate water-filled tank. This practice decreases the amount of fecal material and decaying food in their aquarium, thereby reducing water quality problems.

Most aquatic turtles are fed commercial turtle or fish pellets. See Appendix S for a listing of selected commercial foods for tortoises and turtles. Trout food comes in several sized pellets. Large pellets tend to float well and are attractive to large turtles, whereas smaller pellets tend to sink quickly but are readily accepted by juveniles and small turtles. Trout food may be difficult for reptile owners to find because it is usually only available by special order from feed stores. It is typically sold only in 50-lb bags. Veterinarians who see a large number of reptiles may want to purchase the food, separate it into smaller amounts (store it in a freezer) and make it available to clients who own turtles.

Fish (e.g., goldfish, minnows and guppies) are also fed to aquatic turtles and are available as feeder fish from pet stores. Smelt, mackerel and other oily fish should be fed in limited quantities because their high polyunsaturated fatty acid content may lead to vitamin E deficiency and steatitis. Also, fish may contain thiaminases. Feeding wild-caught fish should also be discouraged because they may be intermediate hosts for reptile parasites. Amphibians (e.g., tadpoles and frogs) can also be fed but they too are safest if captive-born. Crayfish are not recommended because they may harbor the bacterium *Beneckia chitonvora*, which has been implicated in shell diseases of turtles.[22]

Other food items include earthworms, snails, slugs, beetles, grasshoppers, moths, crickets, mealworms, giant mealworms, wax worms and other insects. Wild-caught prey should be free of insecticides and pesticides.

Carnivorous turtles may occasionally consume leafy vegetables or fruits, which can be fed as treats. Vitamin-mineral supplementation is not necessary if turtles eat a variety of commercial foods. Cuttlebone may be added as a calcium supplement for juveniles.

Figure 29-3. Box turtles are omnivorous. This Eastern box turtle is eating a commercial turtle ration with added chopped fruit.

Omnivorous Aquatic Turtles

The most common omnivorous water turtles seen by veterinarians are red-eared sliders (*Trachemys* spp), painted turtles (*Chrysemys* spp), Reeves turtles (*Chinemys* spp), diamondback terrapins (*Malaclemys* spp), map turtles (*Graptemys* spp) and river cooters (*Pseudemys* spp). Many omnivorous water turtles are primarily carnivores as juveniles and become more herbivorous as they age. The carnivorous portion of the diet is the same as described for carnivorous water turtles and should make up between 75 and 100% of the diet for juveniles and about 50% of the diet for adults. A wide variety of vegetables should be offered to round out the diet.

Generally, vegetables that float are preferable because turtles can nibble on them throughout the day. Favorites include greens such as romaine lettuce, collard greens, endive, Swiss chard and kale. Fruits tend to disintegrate in water. Supplementation of the diet is usually unnecessary if the diet is varied and includes commercial foods.

Box Turtles

Some of the most popular box turtles include the eastern box turtle (*Terrapene carolina carolina*), the ornate box turtle (*Terrapene ornata ornata*), the three-toed box turtle (*Terrapene carolina triunguis*) and the Asian box turtle (*Cuora* spp).

Box turtles are primarily omnivorous, although some species such as the Asian box turtle are more carnivorous. Box turtles tend to eat more animal protein as juveniles and become more omnivorous as they mature. The carnivorous portion of the diet is similar to that described for water turtles and should include a wide variety of invertebrates such as earthworms, slugs, mealworms and wax worms.

Commercial box turtle foods, low-fat dog food, trout food, primate biscuits and small amounts of cat food add variety and nutritional balance to the diet. Fruits and vegetables will be more readily accepted as box turtles mature, but should be offered at all ages (Figure 29-3). Box turtles seem most interested in eating red, orange and yellow foods. They tend to favor strawberries, tomatoes, raspberries and blueberries. These fruits can be used to entice turtles to eat. Red food dye can be used to convince stubborn animals to try different and more balanced foods.

Water for box turtles should always be available in a shallow, heavy bowl or dish to allow the turtle to enter the water without spilling the contents. Additionally, box turtles should be soaked in a warm water bath once or twice weekly for approximately 30 minutes. Vitamin-mineral supple-

ments should not be placed in water sources because they may reduce palatability and may increase bacterial growth.

Herbivorous Tortoises

The most common tortoises seen by veterinarians are California desert tortoises (*Gopherus agassizii*), leopard tortoises (*Geochelone pardalis*), South American red-footed tortoises (*Geochelone carbonaria*), yellow-footed tortoises (*Geochelone denticulata*), Greek tortoises (*Testudo graeca*), hingeback tortoises (*Kinexys* spp) and gopher tortoises (*Gopherus polyphemus*). Most tortoises are strictly herbivorous, although a few accept meat-based foods. All use hindgut fermentation.

The basic diet for most tortoises includes a staple of leafy vegetables, such as collard greens, romaine lettuce, parsley, leaf lettuce, dandelion greens, turnip greens and Swiss chard. Dandelion and clover are excellent forages. These should make up 60 to 70% of the diet. Avoid feeding excessive quantities of produce containing oxalates (e.g., spinach) and goitrogens (e.g., kale). Commercially prepared foods for tortoises and iguanas work well for the other 30 to 40% of the diet because they supply protein, vitamins and minerals not present in vegetables.

Timothy hay, alfalfa hay and pellets and grass clippings may be offered to increase the fiber content of the diet. The remainder of the diet may include small amounts of fruits and vegetables.

For juvenile tortoises, foods should be finely chopped into small, manageable pieces to increase consumption. To minimize ingestion of cage and enclosure substrate, food should be offered on flat trays or plates that the juveniles can climb onto. Tortoises are often unable to eat from bowls or raised feeders.

Produce should be supplemented with calcium, vitamins and trace minerals. Usually, diets are supplemented twice weekly for hatchlings and once every seven to 10 days for adults. Supplementation may be unnecessary if 50% or more of the tortoise's diet is comprised of commercial food.

Many tortoises will not drink from water bowls, so all tortoises should be soaked in a tub or large bowl of warm water (up to the plastron) for 15 to 20 minutes to encourage drinking and excretion. Generally, tropical species should be soaked twice weekly, whereas desert species may need to be soaked only once a week. Hatchlings should be soaked daily.

ENDNOTE & REFERENCES

ENDNOTE

a. Calcimar. Rorer Pharmaceutical Corporation, Fort Washington, PA, USA.

REFERENCES

1. Obst FJ, Richter K, Jacob U. Atlas of Reptiles and Amphibians for the Terrarium. Neptune City, NJ: TFH Publications, 1988.
2. Mattison C. The Care of Reptiles and Amphibians in Captivity, 2nd ed. New York, NY: Sterling Publishing Co, 1987.
3. Zimmerman E. Breeding Terrarium Animals. Neptune City, NJ: TFH Publications, 1986.
4. Rossi JV. Snakes of the United States and Canada. Malabar, FL: Krieger Publishing, 1992.
5. de Vosjoli P. The Lizard Keeper's Handbook. Lakeside, CA: Advanced Vivarium Systems, 1994.
6. de Vosjoli P. General Care and Maintenance of Popular Tortoises. Lakeside, CA: Advanced Vivarium Systems, 1996.
7. Boyer TH. Metabolic bone disease. In: Mader DR, ed. Reptile Medicine and Surgery. Philadelphia, PA: WB Saunders Co, 1996; 385-392.
8. Frye FL. A Practical Guide for Feeding Captive Reptiles. Malabar, FL: Krieger Publishing Co, 1991; 61.
9. Donoghue S, Langenberg J. Nutrition. In: Mader DR, ed. Reptile Medicine and Surgery. Philadelphia, PA: WB Saunders Co, 1996; 148-174.
10. Divers S. Basic reptile husbandry, history taking and clinical examination. In Practice 1996; 18: 51-65.
11. Frye FL. Biomedical and Surgical Aspects of Captive Reptile Husbandry. Malabar, FL: Krieger Publishing Co, 1991; 52-53.
12. Bolten AB, Jacobson ER, Bjorndal KA. Effects of anticoagulant and auto-analyzer on blood biochemical values of loggerhead sea turtles (*Caretta caretta*). American Journal of Veterinary Research 1992; 53: 2224-2227.
13. Schmidt-Nielsen K. Animal Physiology, 4th ed. Cambridge, UK: Cambridge University Press, 1990; 382-384.
14. Donoghue S. Growth of juvenile green iguanas (*Iguana iguana*) fed four diets. Journal of Nutrition 1994; 124: 2626S-2629S.
15. Donoghue S. Dietary protein requirements of pet green iguanas (*Iguana iguana*). In: Proceedings. Waltham International Symposium, Orlando, FL, 1997: 108.
16. Douglas TC, Pennino M, Dierenfeld ES. Vitamins E and A, and proximate composition of whole mice and rats used as feed. Comparative Biochemistry and Physiology 1994; 107: 419-424.
17. Rossi J. A practical and effective treatment for metabolic bone disease in the green iguana. In: Proceedings. North American Veterinary Conference, Orlando, FL, 1992: 707.
18. Mader DR. Use of calcitonin in green iguanas, *Iguana iguana*, with metabolic bone disease. Bulletin of the Association of Reptilian and Amphibian Veterinarians 1993; 3: 41.
19. Barten SL. The treatment of iatrogenic hypercalcemia in iguanas with synthetic calcitonin. In: Proceedings. North American Veterinary Conference, Orlando, FL, 1995: 765.
20. Allen ME, Oftedal OT, Baer DJ, et al. Nutritional studies with the green iguana. In: Proceedings. Eighth Dr. Scholl Conference on Nutrition of Captive Wild Animals, Lincoln Park Zoological Gardens, Chicago, IL, 1989: 73-81.
21. Stahl SJ. Captive management, breeding, and common medical problems of the veiled chameleon (*Chamaeleo calyptratus*). In Proceedings. Association of Reptilian and Amphibian Veterinarians, Houston, TX, 1997: 29-40.
22. Boyer TH, Boyer DM. Aquatic turtle care. Bulletin of the Association of Reptilian and Amphibian Veterinarians 1992; 2: 13-17.

CASE 29-1

Swollen Eyes and Respiratory Difficulty in a Box Turtle

Scott Stahl, DVM
Diplomate ABVP (Avian)
Pender Veterinary Clinic
Fairfax, Virginia, USA

Susan Donoghue, VMD
Diplomate ACVN
Nutrition Support Services
Pembroke, Virginia, USA

Assess the Animal

An adult, female Eastern box turtle (*Terrepene carolina carolina*) weighing 357 g was presented for examination. The turtle had a carapace length of 125 mm, and a plastron length of 121 mm. The turtle had been caught and maintained in captivity for one year. It was kept indoors during the winter in a 20-gallon aquarium with one other female Eastern box turtle. In the late spring, it was placed in an outdoor enclosure. The outside environment contained a small wooded area, weeds, grass and leaves. Open areas in the enclosure allowed exposure to sunlight. One male and two other female box turtles also lived in this outdoor enclosure. The turtle was observed laying a clutch of eggs one month earlier.

The owner presented the turtle because its eyes were swollen and sometimes sealed shut. Congestion was noted and mucus bubbled from the turtle's nares. The turtle was anorectic and lethargic.

Physical examination revealed bilaterally swollen eyelids with conjunctivitis and purulent discharge. Visual inspection of the corneas was difficult due to swelling. Mucus was present in both nares, and congestion and mucus were noted in the oral cavity. Increased upper respiratory noises were heard. Skin and shell quality were normal. Body weight was fair.

A culture was taken of the mucus in the nares. A diagnosis of hypovitaminosis A and secondary bacterial conjunctivitis and rhinitis was made based on the historical information and physical examination findings.

Assess the Food(s) and Feeding Method

The turtle's diet for the previous year consisted of a variety of fruits, such as apples, bananas, strawberries, and earthworms and insects found in the outdoor enclosure. The owner had not used any supplements for several months, but previously had used a multivitamin supplement.

Questions

1. What nutrient problems should be suspected based on the dietary history?
2. What should be the initial treatment be for this turtle?
3. What long-term changes should be made in the diet?

Answers and Discussion

1. The current diet was probably deficient in vitamin A and other vitamins and minerals, such as calcium. Earthworms are generally a nutritious dietary item, but the fruits offered provided only trace amounts of calcium and inadequate supplementation was provided. Additionally, not feeding a complete food, such as

commercial box turtle, trout or dog food as a part of the diet contributed to the problem.

2. The patient was soaked in a warm water bath for 20 minutes then placed in an incubator at 29°C (85°F) and fluid therapy was initiated (20 ml/kg body weight of lactated Ringer's solution given epicoelomically). Vitamin A (200 to 300 IU/kg body weight) was given orally. The turtle was started on enrofloxacin[a] (5 mg/kg body weight, q48h) administered into the musculature of the front legs. One or two gentamicin ophthalmic drops were placed in each eye twice daily.[b]

3. The patient's diet was changed to include foods with higher vitamin A content. A variety of vegetables and fruits, and a commercial box turtle food were provided.

Progress Notes

The following day, the box turtle was soaked in a warm water bath for 15 minutes. Afterward, purulent material was gently removed from the periocular tissues with an eye rinse.[c] Gentamicin ophthalmic drops were placed in both eyes. The patient was then tube fed an enteral diet[d] placed directly into the stomach with a curved metal feeding tube. The following day, the enrofloxacin, gentamicin drops and the warm water bath were repeated.

The turtle was sent home with a two-week course of parenteral enrofloxacin and gentamicin drops. The owner was instructed to apply a vitamin A eye preparation[e] to the eyes daily for 14 days and soak the turtle daily for 15 to 20 minutes. Changes in the diet were recommended and the owner was encouraged to offer food immediately following the soaks.

At a follow-up visit two weeks later, the owner said the turtle had begun to eat well and was much more active. Upon physical examination, the eyes were open and markedly less swollen (Figure 1) and no nasal discharge was present. Culture results of the nasal discharge taken earlier revealed *Pseudomonas aeruginosa*. This organism was sensitive to enrofloxacin and gentamicin. The oral

Figure 1. An Eastern box turtle that presented initially for bilaterally swollen eyelids and conjunctivitis with purulent discharge.

dose of vitamin A was repeated, and enrofloxacin, gentamicin and vitamin A drops were continued for another seven days.

Endnotes

a. Baytril. Bayer Corporation, Agricultural Division, Animal Health, Shawnee Mission, KS, USA.
b. Gentocin Durafilm. Schering-Plough Animal Health, Union, NJ, USA.
c. Dacriose Solution. Ciba Vision Ophthalmics, Atlanta, GA, USA.
d. Ensure Liquid Nutrition. Ross Laboratories, Columbus, OH, USA.
e. Turtle Eye Clear. Tetra Terafauna, Morris Plains, NJ, USA.

Bibliography

Boyer TH. Hypovitaminosis A and Hypervitaminosis A. In: Mader DR, ed. Reptile Medicine and Surgery. Philadelphia, PA: WB Saunders Co, 1996; 382-385.

Frye FL. Biomedical and Surgical Aspects of Captive Reptile Husbandry. Malabar, FL: Krieger Publishing Co, 1991; 52-53.

CASE 29-2

Lethargy and Bone Swelling in an Green Iguana

Scott Stahl, DVM
Diplomate ABVP (Avian)
Pender Veterinary Clinic
Fairfax, Virginia, USA

Susan Donoghue, VMD
Diplomate ACVN
Nutrition Support Services
Pembroke, Virginia, USA

Assess the Animal

An 18-month-old green iguana (*Iguana iguana*) was purchased from a local pet store as a farm-raised juvenile and had been in the owner's possession for one year. The iguana was examined for anorexia of 10 days' duration, a swollen mouth and lethargy.

The iguana was housed in a 20-gallon aquarium with indoor/outdoor carpeting, a branch, plastic plant, water bowl and food bowl. A large "hot rock" provided heat. No artifical lighting was provided, but the cage was placed near a window. The iguana was housed alone; the owner had no other reptiles. The iguana had no history of illness and had never been examined by a veterinarian.

The iguana was generally depressed. Its color was a dull yellow-green. At 253 g and 8 inches (snout to vent length) the animal appeared stunted. Under optimal conditions, it should have been three or four times heavier and markedly longer (i.e., 12 to 14 inches). The mandibular bones were severely swollen, the right side significantly more so than the left. Yellow-brown dried material was present along the exposed mandibular mucous membranes. The right forearm, left tibia and right and left femurs were enlarged. The muscle mass over the rear limbs and tailbase was poor. Results of abdominal palpation were normal. The patient exhibited muscle tremors and fasciculations when handled. It was unable to lift its body off the ground to ambulate but would try to slide along the ground.

Radiographs were taken to assess the skeletal system. The right radius and ulna were fractured, but the fractures

REPTILES

appeared old (i.e., callous formation). Poor cortical bone density was evident on all long bones and the mandibular and maxillary bones.

A diagnosis of metabolic bone disease was made based on the clinical history, physical examination and radiographic findings.

Assess the Food and Feeding Method

The patient had been raised on a diet of red-tipped and iceberg lettuce, peas, corn, carrots, apples and strawberries. It was fed daily and was offered two or three of these items at a time. The food was always chopped into small pieces and sometimes dusted with a "reptile vitamin." The owner did not know the name of the supplement, only that it came in a yellow container. The supplement hadn't been used for months. Fresh water was always available.

Questions

1. What nutrient problems should be suspected based on the dietary history?
2. What is the initial treatment for metabolic bone disease?
3. What should be the long-term feeding plan?
4. What other husbandry recommendations should be made?

Answers and Discussion

1. The iguana has been fed a diet low in calcium and high in phosphorus, with poor and inconsistent calcium and vitamin supplementation. The iguana has not been exposed to natural sunlight or ultraviolet light, probably leading to vitamin D_3 deficiency. Sunlight through a glass window does not provide ultraviolet exposure. Other nutrient deficiencies are likely, too.
2. Initially the patient was placed in an incubator at approximately 31°C (88°F). Warm lactated Ringer's solution was given intracoelomically (20 ml/kg body

weight). Eight hours later, vitamin D (1,000 IU vitamin D/kg body weight, intramuscularly) and a calcium-containing solution[a] (0.5 ml/kg body weight, subcutaneously) were given. The iguana was kept overnight in the incubator. The following day, fluid therapy was repeated and an enteral nutritional product[b] was administered orally (50% of metabolic requirement, e.g., 5.5 kcal [23 kJ] or 5.5 ml of the liquid enteral product [Table 29-3]) using a 14-Fr. red rubber urinary catheter. The iguana was started on an oral calcium supplement (1 mg/kg body weight).[c]
3. The iguana's diet was changed to include a wider variety of calcium-rich vegetables. Supplementation included calcium carbonate sprinkled onto the greens, and once weekly sprinkling of a vitamin D_3-containing product onto the greens. Recommendations included placing a full-spectrum fluorescent bulb within 12 to 18 inches of the patient.
4. Iguanas are diurnal basking lizards and must be provided with radiant heat. A temperature gradient should be provided in their environment. The upper end of the temperature range should be 31 to 35°C (88 to 95°F). A "hot rock" does not provide adequate heat for an iguana. A clamp lamp with an incandescent light bulb was placed at one end of the aquarium to keep the hot end of the cage between 31 and 33.5°C (88 and 92°F). In addition, a hide box was provided to help minimize stress and branches were removed to prevent falls until the patient's bones strengthened.

Progress Notes

The iguana's owner was instructed to slowly feed the enteral nutritional product with a syringe (5 to 10 kcal [21 to 42 kJ] daily in small divided doses). The patient was also soaked daily in a warm water bath. The iguana was given the oral calcium supplement (1 ml/kg body weight, b.i.d.) for 30 days.

The iguana returned in one week for a follow-up examination. The owner reported that the iguana was readily accepting the enteral nutritional product and was more alert and active. Upon physical examination, the mandible seemed firmer and the patient was much more responsive. Calcitonin[d] was administered intramuscularly (50 IU/kg body weight). The patient's diet was switched from the enteral product to moistened commercial iguana food. Small meatball-shaped pellets were fed (four to five pieces were fed one or two times daily, depending on the iguana's appetite). Additionally, two tablespoons of chopped dark green leafy vegetables (e.g., collard greens, kale, romaine lettuce) were offered daily. Oral calcium was continued.

The iguana returned weekly for calcitonin injections and a second injection of vitamin D. Three weeks later, a follow-up examination revealed stronger, firmer mandibular and maxillary bones and reduced swelling and increased strength in the long bones. The iguana was able to lift its body off the ground to ambulate. It was eating commercial food vigorously and also eating some of the greens. The owner reported that the iguana was spending time basking and had become more active. The oral calcium supplement was reduced to once daily dosing.

A recheck one month later revealed that the iguana was able to move normally (Figure 1). The mandibular and maxillary bones were firm and the patient's appetite

Figure 1. An 18-month-old iguana that presented initially with anorexia, lethargy and a swollen mouth. The iguana's growth had been severely stunted and it had markedly swollen mandibular bones.

was dramatically improved. Rechecks were recommended at three-month intervals over the next year to prevent relapses.

Endnotes

a. Calphosan Solution. Glenwood Inc., Tenafly, NJ, USA.
b. Ensure Liquid Nutrition. Ross Laboratories, Columbus, OH, USA.
c. Neo-Calglucon. Sandoz, East Hanover, NJ, USA.
d. Miacalcin. Schering-Plough, Kenilworth, NJ, USA.

Bibliography

Boyer TH. Metabolic bone disease. In: Mader DR, ed. Reptile Medicine and Surgery. Philadelphia, PA: WB Saunders Co, 1996; 385-392.

Mader DR. Use of calcitonin in green iguanas, *Iguana iguana*, with metabolic bone disease. Bulletin of the Association of Reptilian and Amphibian Veterinarians 1993; 3: 41.

Rossi J. A practical and effective treatment for metabolic bone disease in the green iguana. In: Proceedings. North American Veterinary Conference, Orlando FL, 1992: 707.

■ CASE 29-3

Anorexia and Lethargy in a Green Iguana

Connie J. Orcutt, DVM
Diplomate ABVP (Avian)
Angell Memorial Animal Hospital
Boston, Massachusetts, USA

Assess the Animal

A two-year-old female green iguana weighing 1.6 kg was presented for anorexia and lethargy of six days' duration. The owner obtained the iguana 18 months ago. The iguana was housed in a 75-gallon aquarium with another iguana. The aquarium was heated with a heating pad under the tank and a 220-watt infrared heat lamp. Ultraviolet-B light was provided by an artificial light source; however, the owner couldn't specify how long the source was provided daily.

When examined, the iguana was lethargic, but moved when stimulated. The overall skin coloration was dark and dull. A firm mass was palpated in the caudodorsal coelomic cavity; deep palpation elicited a response from the patient. The patient's long bones were palpably normal. The mandible was firm and non-compressible.

Abnormal results of a complete blood count and serum biochemistry profile included a heterophilic leukocytosis, hyperproteinemia, marked hyperphosphatemia, hyperuricemia and marked increases in creatine kinase levels and aspartate aminotransferase activity. Radiographs demonstrated bilaterally symmetric soft tissue opacities in the caudodorsal coelomic cavity; these opacities were thought to be the patient's kidneys. A sonogram revealed enlarged hyperechoic kidneys bilaterally.

Assess the Food(s) and Feeding Method

The iguana's diet consisted of a variety of vegetables including greens, broccoli and dandelions as well as an unspecified commercial iguana food, which made up approximately 50% of the total diet. Fruit was given occasionally. The owner had been supplementing the diet with a vitamin-mineral supplement twice daily for several months.

Questions

1. What nutritional problems are suggested by the diet? Could any of these explain the iguana's clinical signs?
2. What is the pathophysiology of the biochemical abnormalities? What is the significance of the abnormalities found by imaging?

3. How can this condition by treated?

Answers and Discussion

1. The owner has been providing large amounts of vitamin D_3 in the form of the vitamin-mineral supplement and the commercially prepared iguana food. Vitamin D_3 is essential for calcium uptake from the intestinal tract; however, it can be toxic when given in large amounts. Either hypervitaminosis D or hypocalcemia could be responsible for the lethargy and anorexia exhibited by the patient.
2. Hyperproteinemia may be due to dehydration. Hyperuricemia and hyperphosphatemia indicate some degree of renal failure. The increase in aspartate aminotransferase activity and elevated creatine kinase value indicate either muscle degeneration and/or hepatic damage. Renomegaly and pain elicited when the kidneys were palpated are signs consistent with nephrosis. The increased opacity in the region of the kidneys seen radiographically and by ultrasound is consistent with mineralization of the renal parenchyma. The combination of these findings is suggestive of renal failure secondary to hypervitaminosis D.
3. Excessive supplementation with vitamin D_3 allows large amounts of calcium to be absorbed from the intestinal tract. The resulting soft tissue mineralization, however, can be widespread and severe. End-stage renal failure is generally unresponsive to treatment; however, diuresis may provide short-term palliative treatment.

Progress Notes

The iguana was diuresed with a mixture of 0.9% saline, 2.5% dextrose and lactated Ringer's solution administered intracoelomically for two days. Unfortunately, the patient died on Day 3. Results of a necropsy examination revealed moderate tubular nephrosis and severe degeneration with mineralization and necrosis of the heart and skeletal muscles. The final diagnosis was vitamin D toxicosis. Vitamin D_3 and calcium metabolism are still not well-elucidated in iguanas and vitamin D_3 requirements have not been established. It is unclear how well vitamin D_3 is absorbed in these animals. The risk of oversupplementation can be avoided by providing exposure to adequate amounts of ultraviolet-B light, thus allowing the body to form its own vitamin D_3 instead of giving oral supplementation.

REPTILES

CHAPTER 30

Feeding Passerine and Psittacine Birds

George V. Kollias

Heidi Wearne Kollias

"Of all forms of life birds are the most beautiful, most musical, most admired, most watched and most defended. Without them much of our world would seem ominously lifeless and silent."

Roger Tory Peterson

ASSESSMENT

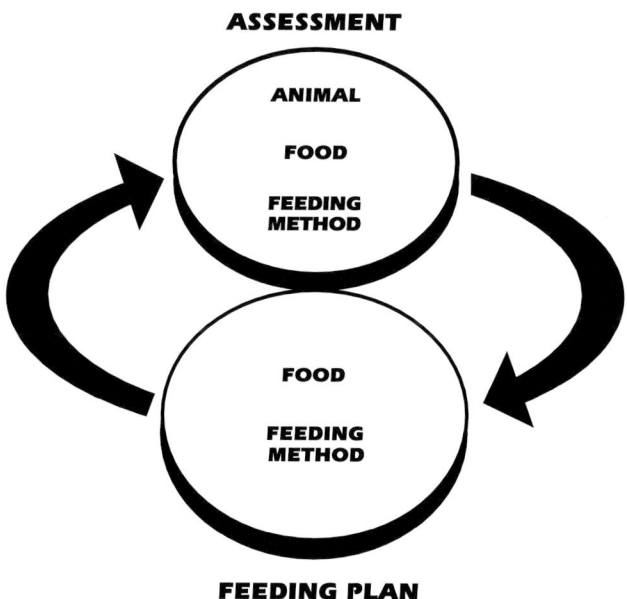

ANIMAL

FOOD

FEEDING METHOD

FOOD

FEEDING METHOD

FEEDING PLAN

Note: The reader is referred to Chapter 1 for a detailed discussion of the iterative process of clinical nutrition.

INTRODUCTION

One avian medicine reference states that 75% of the medical problems seen in companion and aviary birds have at least a partial nutritional basis.[1] Dietary-induced deficiencies and excesses may lead to immune dysfunction, increased susceptibility to infectious diseases and metabolic and biochemical derangements that manifest clinically as nutritional secondary hyperparathyroidism, thyroid hyperplasia (dysplasia), hemochromatosis and a variety of other problems.

Dietary-induced diseases frequently occur in companion and aviary psittacine and passerine birds for several reasons. First, until recently, specific nutritional requirements for these birds were unknown. Thus, investigators and veterinary practitioners tended to extrapolate the well-known nutrient needs of poultry to other avian species. Although these nutrient needs generally apply, specific nutritional differences of domestic chickens and other avian species have been reported. For example, riboflavin deficiency in broiler chicks manifests itself clinically as "curled-toe paralysis," which is not observed in cockatiel chicks. Cockatiels lack pigmentation (achromatosis) in their primary feathers as a result of riboflavin deficiency.[2] Although differences of this type exist experimentally, many prepared foods overcome these differences by supplying levels of nutrients well in excess of the minimum requirement for chickens.

Second, and more important, many people think that all-seed diets (particularly diets composed of only one seed type, such as millet or sunflower) and diets com-

KEY WORDS & TERMS—FEEDING PASSERINE AND PSITTACINE BIRDS*

Apterylae
Cere
Choana
Cloaca
Hemochromatosis
Molt (moult)

Passerine
Pecten
Pododermatitis
Powder down
Premaxilla
Propatagium

Psittacine
Squamous metaplasia
Thyroid hyperplasia
Xanthine oxidase

Key words and terms are defined in the Glossary.

KEY POINTS—FEEDING PASSERINE AND PSITTACINE BIRDS

1. The specific nutritional requirements for most species of captive non-domestic birds are unknown.
2. The clinical manifestations of specific nutrient deficiencies in psittacine and passerine birds differ from those reported for domestic poultry.
3. The addition of excessive amounts of fruits and vegetables to the diets of companion birds dilutes key nutrients present in nutritionally balanced commercially prepared foods.
4. The types of seeds present in most commercial mixes are not native to areas where most pet birds originate.
5. Although seed mixtures can supply nutrients such as fats, carbohydrates and some minerals, they are frequently deficient in vitamins A, D and K.
6. Seeds and other foods play important roles in initiat-

ing courtship and reproductive behavior in many species of psittacine and passerine birds.
7. Birds are not able to preferentially balance their diets when offered a variety of food items.
8. Small, white caseous nodules around the choanae and other areas of the oral pharynx may be associated with hypovitaminosis A in companion birds.
9. Many of the foods commonly fed to companion birds are composed primarily of carbohydrates and fats.
10. The major benefits of commercially prepared foods are nutrient balance and convenience for the owner.
11. Conversion of a pet bird's diet to a completely new, balanced food may take from weeks to months, depending on the degree and length of habituation.

posed of or heavily supplemented with fruits, vegetables and other human foods are complete foods for birds. In reality, most commercially available seeds are deficient in certain limiting nutrients (e.g., specific amino acids, vitamins and trace and macrominerals such as calcium and sodium). Also, seeds are not the primary or natural diet of most species of companion birds. For example, one study revealed that when given the opportunity, the endangered Puerto Rican parrot (*Amazona vittata*) consumed seven species of fruits, seeds and leaves (new foliage), the fruiting structures of 44 species of trees (in addition to bark) and seven species of canopy vines.[3] Thus, seeds compose only a small part of their total diet in the wild.

Additionally, evidence suggests that increased protein may be needed during certain points in the reproductive cycle. In the wild, insects supply these increased needs. It is difficult for bird owners to meet these special needs feeding only seed mixtures.

But, perhaps the most common cause of dietary-induced diseases in companion birds is the practice of adding fruits and vegetables sold for human consumption to commercially prepared foods or supplemented seed mixtures. The most readily available fruits and vegetables contain primarily water, carbohydrates and fiber. They are severely deficient in protein, vitamins and minerals[4] when compared to the nutrient recommendations for psittacine and passerine birds.[5] Thus, fruits and vegetables primarily dilute key nutrients present in nutritionally balanced commercially prepared foods. Birds often preferentially eat fruits and vegetables because of their high water content instead of dry extruded or pelleted foods and seed mixtures. In fact, birds often select food items based on water

content, texture, color or taste, rather than nutrient content,[6] resulting in very imbalanced nutrient intakes.

This common feeding practice leads directly to the third reason captive birds develop nutritional deficiencies, which is the tendency of individual birds to select specific food items from a variety of offerings. Because malnourished birds often tend to overeat the food items presented to them, it is unclear whether this is a cause or an effect of malnutrition. It does lead to the popular misconception that birds are able to preferentially balance their diets. As a result, individual birds may become habituated or fixated on a specific food item (e.g., sunflower, safflower or millet seeds, or grapes or oranges). Yet these specific items are usually deficient in several essential nutrients.

This chapter summarizes assessment criteria and feeding plans for healthy birds commonly kept as pets. Additional information for feeding pet and wild birds is found in Appendix N (Body Weights of Birds), Appendix O (Foods for Caged and Aviary Birds) and Appendix Q (Feeding Orphaned and Injured Birds).

■ ASSESSMENT

Assess the Animal

Signalment

Veterinary practitioners and their health care teams should become familiar with the most common psittacine and passerine species. Psittacine birds are members of the order Psittaciformes (parrots and parakeets). Passerine birds belong to the order Passeriformes, which includes finches, sparrows, buntings, mynahs, canaries and serins.

Estimation of age and sex is important in nutritional assessment. Like dogs and cats, birds have different requirements with varying age and function. Immature psittacine and passerine species characteristically have dull-colored feathers. Beak color varies with age in some species. If adults are dark-billed, immature birds of the same species may have light-colored bills. If adults have pale beaks, those of juveniles are generally dark or have dark markings at the base of the beak. Immature passerine birds are particularly difficult to identify until they go through their first or second molt.

Iris color may help in estimating the age of some species. Young psittacine birds have brown or dark irides. The iris color of macaws fades to gray within one year, appears white from one to three years, then turns yellow in mature birds. The iris color of Amazon parrots may change to red-orange as birds mature. African grey parrots' irides lighten from brown through gray to white. The irides of both genders of immature Moloccan cockatoos (and most all-white cockatoos) are brown; mature males have red irides and mature females have dark brown irides.

History

Because the clinical manifestations of malnutrition in birds are quite variable the history and physical examination are very important (Table 30-1). Before a bird is presented at the veterinary hospital, the client should be instructed to:

1. Bring the bird in its own cage.
2. Not clean the cage.
3. Empty the water dish.
4. Remove all grit (if used) from the cage.
5. Cover the cage and wrap it with a blanket in cold weather.
6. Remove all cage furniture if the bird is weak or injured.
7. Bring any medications and vitamin-mineral supplements the bird has been offered.
8. Bring a sample of the foods offered daily (e.g., seed mixtures, pelleted or extruded food) and a list of fruits, vegetables or other foods regularly fed.

The history should include general questions such as: 1) the origin of the bird, 2) length of ownership, 3) housing arrangements, 4) type of heat and humidity provided, 5) light sources used (e.g., ultraviolet, full spectrum, fluorescent, natural, etc.), 6) exposure to other birds, 7) foods and supplements normally fed, for how long and in what quantities, 8) the owner's assessment of the presenting condition (including changes in food and water consumption, droppings, environment and behavior) and 9) information relative to previous treatment by the owner or another veterinarian.

The history for a newly acquired bird (owned for less than 10 months) will often include exposure to infectious diseases (viral, mycoplasmal, bacterial and mycotic) as a result of contact with other birds in a pet shop, aviary or quarantine facility. These problems are among the most difficult to accurately diagnose and treat. Other problems commonly associated with a newly acquired bird include acute malnutrition, trauma, parasitism (hematogenous, gastrointestinal and respiratory), intoxications and secondary immunosuppression associated with one or a combination of the above.

Birds owned for more than 10 months can be considered to be from an "uncontaminated" environment unless other birds frequently immigrate and emigrate from the household or collection. Individual birds not exposed to other birds for this period may have chronic malnutrition of dietary origin. Veterinarians can improve or help to resolve these problems by making sound dietary recommendations.

Physical Examination

GENERAL EXAMINATION

Observation of the patient in its cage or aviary environment is important. The condition of the cage may indicate the type of human/animal bond (e.g., concern or lack thereof). First observe the bird at a distance (nonthreatening). A healthy bird should appear alert and attentive. Tame birds generally appear relaxed and calm. Some birds vocalize and are very active during examination (macaws, Amazon parrots, African grey parrots and conures). Abnormalities include fluffing of the feathers, head tucking, rhythmic movement of the tail, frequent blinking, lethargy and falling asleep on the examination table.

Trunk and limb asymmetry and skeletal deformities are obvious if the veterinarian is familiar with normal conformation. Drooping wing(s) may indicate paresis or injury. Restlessness, shifting of body weight or favoring one leg may suggest discomfort or dysfunction from pain or injury. Dysequilibrium may be associated with spinal malformation, toxin ingestion, head injury or metabolic derangement affecting the central nervous system that may be associated with malnutrition, especially inadequate intake of calcium or B-complex vitamins. Only minimal restraint should be used during the physical examination.

ORAL EXAMINATION

The oral cavity should have a neutral odor. Causes of a foul-smelling oral cavity include bacterial pharyngitis, sinusitis or digestive disorders that may be exacerbated by diet or malnutrition. Normal oral epithelium is shiny and has uniform color. Some psittacine and passerine birds (cockatoos, Amazon parrots and macaws) have darkly pigmented oral epithelium, whereas others have a pink oral mucosa.

White caseous lesions on or below the mucosa may suggest inflammatory changes secondary to squamous metaplasia associated with hypovitaminosis A. These types of lesions also may be observed with poxvirus infection, candidiasis, trichomoniasis and coliform abscesses. Sick birds often accumulate mucus in the mouth, under the premaxilla and tongue. Birds that recover from hypovitaminosis A and viral infections may have scar formation around the choanae, or the normal papillae on the choanal borders may be blunted or absent.

Tongue characteristics vary with the species. Psittacine birds normally have a smooth-surfaced, symmetric, thick and fleshy tongue with a thick layer of epithelium near the tip. The color varies from pink to black depending on the species. Passerine birds have a rigid tongue with a whitish or light gray tip. Unilateral swelling of the tongue may indicate abscess formation.

BEAK AND CERE EXAMINATION

The beak is normally smooth, uniformly colored with a deep sheen. Abnormal, rapid beak growth may be associated with malnutrition, specific viral disease (psittacine beak and feather disease virus), obesity or hepatopathy. Budgerigars with rapid beak growth often have reddish-black discoloration on the anterior margin of the premaxilla. Twisted beaks (mostly seen in fledglings) are often associated with malnutrition, systemic disease, feeding trauma or genetic-based malformation. Psittacine birds require branches or hard wood to chew on for beak conditioning. Cuttlebones and mineral blocks are inadequate for this pur-

Table 30-1. Clinical manifestations of malnutrition in birds.*

Systems	Physical or clinical manifestations
Pansystemic or generalized	Immune suppression (lack of infectious disease resistance) Polyphagia/obesity Epithelial hyperplasia or metaplasia (skin, respiratory, gastrointestinal) Poor growth Low body weight Subcutaneous edema (vitamin E/selenium deficiency) Behavioral changes Hypocalcemia Polyuria/polydipsia Gout
Integumentary 　Skin	Exfoliative dermatitis Pododermatitis Dryness Pruritus Poor wound healing Uropygial gland hypertrophy and duct obstruction
Beak	Excessive or abnormal beak growth, dryness, epithelial exfoliation
Feathers	Color or pigment changes (depigmentation, hyperpigmentation, melanosis) Abnormal markings in feathers ("stress lines") Molting abnormalities Retained feather sheaths Brittle frayed feathers Feather picking Lack of development of contour feathers Curling of feathers
Gastrointestinal 　Oral pharynx	Generalized epithelial alterations White (caseous-appearing) plaques involving the oral mucosa Mucosal ulceration Salivary gland abscessation
Crop	Secondary crop stasis or impaction Regurgitation Lithiasis
Esophagus, proventriculus, 　　ventriculus	Altered motility, mucosal erosion, regurgitation Koilin abnormalities (erosion, dysgenesis)
Small and large bowel	Diarrhea Enteritis (e.g., clostridial infections secondary to high-sugar diets) Malabsorption
Liver	Hepatopathies (e.g., fatty liver syndrome)
Pancreas	Pancreatic atrophy
Respiratory	Generalized epithelial alterations Partial or complete upper or lower airway obstruction causing dyspnea (rhinal cavity, sinuses, syrinx) Serous nasal discharge
Eyes	Serous ocular discharge Lacrimal duct obstruction (epiphora) secondary to epithelial debris accumulation Palpebrae (eyelid) paresis or paralysis
Central and peripheral 　nervous and neuromuscular	Behavioral changes (e.g., aggression, cannibalism, self mutilation) Seizures (salt toxicity, hypothiaminosis, hypocalcemia, vitamin E deficiency) Cervical paralysis (folic acid deficiency) Abnormal gait, "jerky leg movements" (pyridoxine deficiency) Syncope (hypoglycemia, hypocalcemia) Muscular weakness/paresis (vitamin E deficiency, hyponatremia)
Musculoskeletal	Pathologic fractures (metabolic bone disease) Slipped tendon (deficiency of manganese, biotin, pantothenic and/or folic acid in some species) Limb deformities (valgus/varus deformities involving long bones) Hock (tibiotarsal/tarsometatarsal) joint enlargement
Urogenital	Gout Epithelial hyperplasia/metaplasia (renal and/or ureteral obstruction) Endocrinopathy affecting fertility/reproductive performance Egg binding (endocrine or neuromuscular in origin)
Hematopoetic	Hemorrhagic diathesis (vitamin E deficiency) Anemia Coagulopathy (vitamin K deficiency, hepatopathy)
Endocrine	Goiter (thyroid dysplasia) due to iodine deficiency

*Adapted from MacWhirter P. Malnutrition. In: Ritchie BW, Harrison GJ, Harrison LR, eds. Avian Medicine: Principles and Applications. Lake Worth, FL: Wingers Publishing,1994; 842-861. Kollias GV. Diets, feeding practices, and nutritional problems in psittacine birds. Veterinary Medicine 1995; 90: 29-39.

pose. In fact, cuttlebones should *not* be recommended for beak conditioning or as a nutritional supplement. A flaky or rough-looking beak may be associated with malnutrition, lack of proper chewing or systemic disease. The beak should also be examined for fractures, dislocations and erosive lesions that may result from bacterial, fungal or viral infections (e.g., psittacine beak and feather disease).

The cere, a soft cutaneous appendage containing the nares, should normally be firm and smooth and should lack flakes and debris. The nares should be evenly placed in relationship to the cere and should be bilaterally symmetric in size and shape. Change in diameter may indicate past or present respiratory infections or neoplasia. Nasal discharge is abnormal and may be indicated by staining of the feathers above the cere.

EYE AND EAR EXAMINATION

The eyes are best examined with the aid of transillumination externally and from inside the oral cavity. Birds have the ability to voluntarily control pupil size, thus pupillary constriction in response to light is not an accurate indication of vision. A menace response should be present bilaterally.

Symmetry, position and mobility of the globes should be noted. If conjunctivitis is present, culture and sensitivity testing should be done along with a detailed nutritional history. The cornea should be smooth and shiny. Any irregularities should be investigated by staining with fluorescein dye. The anterior chamber of the eye should be examined with indirect or direct ophthalmoscopy. The iris should be flat and thin and have a freely moving pupillary border. Clarity of the lens should be determined when the pupil is dilated.

A normal fundic examination should reveal an evenly reflective, avascular retina. The pecten, a heavily pigmented pleated vascular structure, extends from the optic disk into the vitreous.

The ears normally are free of exudate and debris. Epithelial debris often accumulates in the external auditory meatus of birds as a sign of malnutrition.

SKIN AND FEATHER EXAMINATION

Injuries and other problems involving the wings are common in birds. Examination should include complete palpation of both wings. Twisted, brittle and deformed wing feathers may be associated with malnutrition, genetics, trauma or a combination of causes. Abnormal feathering is associated with a variety of problems and diseases; malnutrition is the most common cause.

Large areas of feather loss may result from self-mutilation secondary to dermatitis, suggesting possible nutritional and/or systemic disease. The wing web (propatagium) should be evaluated for signs of dermatitis and trauma. The feathers often have to be displaced away from the featherless tracts (apterylae) to examine the skin over the head, dorsum, wings, upper legs and abdomen. Dry exfoliating skin may indicate nutritional problems or a very dry environment.

Primary dermatologic problems in birds are rare; most problems are secondary to trauma or systemic diseases, including malnutrition. Skin overlying cervical and abdominal regions can be assessed for elasticity in an attempt to crudely determine hydration and nutritional status in young birds and to a lesser extent in older birds. The skin of the feet and legs should be shiny and have a uniform scaled pattern.

Malnutrition can cause smooth, worn and ulcerated palmar surfaces of the feet. Pododermatitis, with or without ulcer formation, is often associated with improper perches and is exacerbated by malnutrition (e.g., hypovitaminosis A).

Overgrowth of the claws often accompanies beak lesions and is associated with metabolic and nutritional disorders, especially in lories, finches, budgerigars, canaries and Amazon parrots. Some species, such as Frill canaries, normally have long claws.

Contour feathers should adhere tightly together, appear homogeneous and have a bright sheen. The eclectus parrot, however, characteristically has loose, hair-like feathers. The wing and tail feathers should be transilluminated to allow examination for mites, color abnormalities, structural damage and vane abnormalities (e.g., holes).

Feather lice and mite infestations are common in newly imported birds. Feather picking and mutilation occur commonly in psittacine birds but only occasionally in passerine species. Frequent causes include boredom, stress (change in the owner/bird routine), systemic diseases and improper diet.

Feathers of psittacine birds overlying the rump, thigh and crest areas should be examined for signs consistent with viral beak and feather disease. Powder down (a powdery white substance) is present on the feathers of white cockatoo species, African grey parrots and cockatiels. Powder down is a normal finding.

Soiled feathers around the vent may indicate disease of the urogenital or gastrointestinal system. Protrusion of the cloacal mucosa may be associated with mucosal hyperplasia, cloacal papillomas, uterine prolapse (associated with egg binding), irritation due to masturbation, straining due to low intestinal obstruction or inflammation.

REGIONAL PALPATION

After examination of the skin and feathers, the intermandibular space should be palpated for swelling (e.g., abscess formation) that may occur secondary to hypovitaminosis A in psittacine birds. The crop should normally be partially filled with food. A fluid-filled crop is an abnormal finding, except in recently fed chicks. Normally, the ventral borders of the liver are barely evident. Caudally, the ventriculus is palpable between the right and left acetabulum.

The keel or pectoral musculature, a reservoir for large quantities of glycogen, should be palpated as an indicator of overall body condition. No body condition scoring system has been developed for birds. Besides palpation, body weight (mass) is the best criterion. Appendix N has adult weight ranges for most avian species.

CARDIOPULMONARY EXAMINATION

Cardiopulmonary examination includes auscultation of the sinuses, trachea and thoracic and abdominal air sacs using a pediatric stethoscope. Normally, only the gentle rush of air should be heard. Audible sounds on inspiration and expiration indicate respiratory disease. Abnormal sounds (e.g., clicking, rattling, wheezing, squeaking and honking) may be associated with hepatopathies, respiratory parasites (air sac mites in passerine birds), malnutrition-induced air sac and tracheal epithelial debris and endocrine disease (e.g., thyroid dysplasia).

Birds normally respire with their mouths closed. Open-mouthed breathing may result from: 1) anxiety (stress),

Table 30-2. Nutrition recommendations for avian foods.*

Nutrient	Psittacine Minimum	Psittacine Maximum	Passerine Minimum	Passerine Maximum
Gross energy (kcal/kg)**	3,200	4,200	3,500	4,500
Total protein (%)	12.0		14.0	
Linoleic acid (%)	1.0		1.0	
Amino acids				
Lysine (%)	0.65		0.75	
Methionine (%)	0.30		0.35	
Methionine + cystine (%)	0.50		0.58	
Arginine (%)	0.65		0.75	
Threonine (%)	0.40		0.46	
Vitamins (fat soluble)				
Vitamin A activity (total) (IU/kg)	8,000		8,000	
Vitamin D_3 (IU/kg)	500	2,000	1,000	2,500
Vitamin E (ppm)	50		50	
Vitamin K (ppm)	1.0		1.0	
Vitamins (water soluble)				
Thiamin (ppm)	4.0		4.0	
Riboflavin (ppm)	6.0		6.0	
Niacin (ppm)	50.0		50.0	
Pyridoxine (ppm)	6.0		6.0	
Pantothenic acid (ppm)	20.0		20.0	
Biotin (ppm)	0.25		0.25	
Folic acid (ppm)	1.50		1.50	
Vitamin B_{12} (ppm)	0.01		0.01	
Choline (ppm)	1,500		1,500	
Minerals				
Calcium (%)	0.30	1.20	0.50	1.20
Phosphorus (%)	0.30		0.50	
Calcium:phosphorus ratio	1.0:1.0	2.0:1.0	1.0:1.0	2.0:1.0
Potassium (%)	0.40		0.40	
Sodium (%)	0.12		0.12	
Chlorine (%)	0.12		0.12	
Magnesium (ppm)	600		600	
Trace minerals				
Manganese (ppm)	65.0		65.0	
Iron (ppm)	80.0		80.0	
Zinc (ppm)	50.0		50.0	
Copper (ppm)	8.0		8.0	
Iodine (ppm)	0.40		0.40	
Selenium (ppm)	0.10		0.10	

*Adapted from The Exotic Bird Nutrition Expert Panel Report, Nutrition and Management Committee of the Association of Avian Veterinarians, 1996.
**To convert to kJ, multiply kcal by 4.184.

2) hyperthermia, 3) compensation for a plugged nostril, 4) anemia, 5) lung, tracheal and air sac disease, 6) abdominal masses and ascites that compress air sacs and 7) excessive handling and excitement. A bird's respiratory rate should return to normal one to two minutes posthandling; if not, cardiopulmonary dysfunction may be present. Auscultation is of value to assess heart rate and rhythm, but murmurs are rarely heard.

Laboratory and Other Clinical Information

Laboratory data can help in the assessment of avian patients. However, veterinary diagnostic laboratories and practices generally do not offer the expertise necessary to provide reproducible laboratory results unless there is an individual on the staff who has taken a special interest in avian clinical laboratory medicine. A detailed description of avian laboratory evaluations is beyond the scope of this chapter (See sidebar "Pet Bird References."); however, a few clinical chemistry tests with nutritional implications deserve special comment.

Nitrogen excretion in birds involves the conversion of purines to uric acid via the enzyme xanthine oxidase. Renal tubular water resorption is highly variable in birds (60 to 99%). Avian kidneys are often involved in a number of primary (e.g., renal gout) and secondary diseases (e.g., bacterial enteritis, acute chlamydiosis) because of their relatively large size (approximately 1% of body weight) and the associated renal portal system. There is no single best test to assess renal function. Single plasma uric acid levels are a relatively insensitive indicator of renal tubular damage. Consequently, plasma creatine values, blood gas analysis, urinalyses in polyuric birds and/or serial plasma uric acid determinations must be used to diagnose and predict the outcome of avian renal disease.

Normal avian serum glucose levels are much higher than those of mammals with equivalent body surface area. Glucose values range from 550 to 600 mg/dl in hummingbirds to 140 to 180 mg/dl in ostriches. Stress associated with handling can rapidly elevate serum glucose levels.

Table 30-3. Commercially prepared foods and dietary supplements for pet birds.*

Manufacturers	Addresses and phone numbers	Product names and descriptions
Rolf C. Hagen, Inc.	50 Hampden Rd. PO Box 634 Mansfield, MA 02048 (508) 339-0269/ FAX (508) 339-9454	Tropican High Performance Diets; extruded granular foods and fortified seed diets; breeder and hand-rearing formula; high-performance and maintenance foods; vitamin, mineral and amino acid supplements
HBD International, Inc.	220 Congress Park Dr. Delray Beach, FL 33445 (561) 279-4233/ FAX (561) 279-4235	Adult Lifetime Formula, High Potency Formula; extruded bird foods (breeder and maintenance); hand-rearing formula (trainer bird available to assist in food conversion)
Kaytee Products, Inc.	521 Clay Street PO Box 230 Chilton, WI 53104 (800) 529-8331 FAX (920) 849-4734	Forti-diets; fortified seed foods (contain vitamins, minerals and protein granules in seed mixes); nutritional supplements and treats
Lafeber Co.	24981 N. 1400 East Road Cornell, IL 61319 (800) 842-6445 or (815) 358-2301 FAX (800) 932-3341 or (815) 358-2352 Canada: (800) 345-6596	Avi-Era Diets; pelleted and granular complete adult foods; fortified seed cakes; hand-rearing formula; nutritional support formulas for gavage feeding; medicated pellets; vitamin and nutritional supplements
Nekton USA, Inc.	14405 60th St. North Clearwater, FL 34602 (813) 530-3500	Nekton-S, Nekton-MSA; trace mineral, vitamin, and amino acid supplements for a variety of avian species
Premium Nutritional Products, Inc./ZuPreem	PO Box 2094 Mission, KS 66202 (800) 345-4767/ FAX (913) 722-6226	ZuPreem Fruit Blend and Avian Maintenance; extruded breeding foods for psittacine and passerine birds
Roudybush Foods	3075 Alhambra Dr. Suite 103 Cameron Park, CA 95682 (800) 326-1726/ FAX (530) 676-9585	Roudybush Special Diets (acute care, intestinal care, kidney care, liver care, proventricular dilation care, reducing care); pellets and crumbles for maintenance and breeding food
Ziegler Brothers, Inc.	PO Box 95 Gardners, PA 17324 (717) 677-6181 or (800) 841-6800 FAX (717) 677-6826	Hand-rearing formulas; pellets and crumbles for breeding, growth and maintenance foods; medicated pellets

*Additional information about commercial bird foods is found in Appendix O.

Assess the Food(s)

The patient history should minimally include a list of foods offered daily. In addition, clients should be encouraged to provide a sample of any commercially prepared foods they feed.

If the food offered is commercially prepared, examine the label for nutrient information or guarantees. The primary nutrients of concern are protein and calcium. Many foods commonly fed to companion birds are composed primarily of carbohydrates and fat. The label of an acceptable commercially prepared food should list a protein guarantee of at least 12%. From the list of ingredients on the label, determine if a source of calcium is included in the food. Seeds commonly contain more phosphorus than calcium. Thus, an added calcium source, such as calcium carbonate, dicalcium phosphate, bone meal, ground limestone or ground oyster shells, helps balance the calcium phosphorus ratio of bird foods. Regardless of the type of food fed, a sample can be submitted to a commercial laboratory for analysis. (See Appendix U for a listing of laboratories.) Consult the laboratory in advance to determine the sample size needed, preservation techniques recommended and shipping instructions.

Pet Bird References

A clinical nutrition textbook cannot adequately discuss all the important aspects of avian husbandry and clinical medicine. Readers with a specific interest in avian husbandry and clinical evaluation of pet birds are referred to a number of excellent references that emphasize these aspects of avian care. A few of the more widely available references are listed here.

Altman RB, Clubb SL, Dorrestein GM, et al. Avian Medicine and Surgery. Philadelphia, PA: WB Saunders Co, 1997.

Beynon PH, Forbes NA, Lawton MPC. Manual of Psittacine Birds. Ames, IA: British Small Animal Veterinary Association and Iowa State University Press, 1996.

Ritchie BW, Harrison GJ, Harrison LR. Avian Medicine: Principles and Applications. Lake Worth, FL: Wingers Publishing, 1994.

Rosskopf WJ, Woerpel RW. Diseases of Cage and Aviary Birds, 3rd ed. Baltimore, MD: Williams & Wilkins, 1996.

Rupley AE. Manual of Avian Practice. Philadelphia, PA: WB Saunders, 1997.

Seminars in Avian and Exotic Pet Medicine (published quarterly). WB Saunders Co.

Compare the nutrient levels of the food to those recommended in Table 30-2 to determine if there are any gaps in the nutrient profile. Complete nutrient levels of foods can sometimes be found on the label, in sales materials or from the manufacturer. The food is acceptable if its nutrient levels meet or exceed those levels in Table 30-2. If not, recommend that the owner select a food that meets these recommended levels.

The food should not be used for long-term feeding if its label contains no nutrient information or is just a list of ingredients such as seeds or dried fruit. The following discussion describes common strategies used to feed birds. In some instances, it can be very difficult to determine whether an individual bird receives levels of nutrients recommended in Table 30-2.

Foods appropriately balanced with carbohydrates, proteins, fats, vitamins, minerals and water are essential for all birds. Stewardship of confined birds must address good nutrition at several levels: the daily satisfaction and health of the bird as well as the long-term contributions to growth, maturation, defense against disease and reproductive health—the hallmark of good nutrition.

Three methods of providing nutrients and achieving these objectives are commonly used: 1) commercially prepared foods, 2) seeds and seed mixtures and 3) homemade mixed foods.

Commercially Prepared Foods

The benefits of using commercially prepared, nutritionally complete foods become obvious when the feeding of birds kept as companions is compared with the feeding of other companion animals. Prepared foods supply more than 90% of the nutrients for companion dogs and cats in North America and can contribute markedly to the health of these animals. The gradual transition from diets composed primarily of human food, including table scraps, to commercially prepared complete and balanced foods for dogs and cats has taken about 50 years. The same transition will undoubtedly occur in a much shorter time for pet birds as the number and quality of products available increase.

The major benefits of commercially prepared foods are nutrient balance and convenience. Manufacturers commonly formulate commercial foods using sound scientific principles following established nutrient recommendations (Table 30-2).[5] Although adherence to these recommendations and ingredient quality may vary among manufacturers, an extruded or pelleted diet supplies all the nutrients in one particle. Such formulations help prevent alteration of nutrient balance by uninformed owners who feed imbalanced seeds or human foods, or by birds that consume different quantities of imbalanced foods that are fed separately.

A potential disadvantage of feeding commercial foods is that testing protocols for nutritional adequacy have not yet been established for avian foods, as they have been for commercial canine and feline foods. Still, the probability of producing a nutritional imbalance by feeding a commercial avian food is much less than when seeds or human foods prepared by uninformed owners are fed to birds. As the use of commercial avian foods becomes more widespread, testing protocols will be established.

Seeds and Seed Mixtures

Seeds are a popular, convenient, inexpensive method of providing nutrients to companion birds. But they are not necessarily the best or even the most natural food for pet birds. A recent renaissance in the pet bird food industry has taken into account the long forgotten holistic views of habitats and natural history of many avian species. Interesting facts have come to light. Food selection in birds is predominantly a learned behavior. Nestling birds accept the appropriate foods brought to them by their parents and once fledged observe where and how to obtain these foods for themselves. In a pet industry where captive breeding and isolation of companion birds are the norm, individual birds have little or no experience with their natural environment or natural food sources and may not have the opportunity to observe feeding behaviors of other birds. Although hundreds of years of domestication in some species have altered feeding behaviors, the associated physiology of nutrient assimilation and use have not changed markedly. The types of seeds present in most commercial mixes are not native to areas where most pet bird species originate. Although seeds may have been used opportunistically in the wild, they would not have been available in large quantities. Considering all these facts, seeds are no more of a "natural" food than any other method of providing nutrients for companion birds.

Other disadvantages of all seed diets are that the diet can be altered easily by uninformed owners or birds can consume certain seed types, avoiding others, resulting in an imbalanced nutrient intake. With these disadvantages in mind, seeds are much less desirable than commercially prepared foods for feeding companion birds.

As mentioned, seeds are a common element in many pet bird diets. A well-balanced seed mixture can supply essential nutrients such as fats, carbohydrates and some minerals. However, seeds are rarely, if ever, an appropriate sole nutritional source because they provide inadequate levels of protein, vitamins and minerals. There are numerous commercially available seed mixtures that vary greatly in type and quality. Individual seed types are also sold in most stores, thus formulating seed mixtures is a common practice. The availability of individual seed types promotes nutrient imbalance when uninformed owners create a mixture based primarily on the price and physical appearance of the seeds. Thus, creation or use of homemade seed mixtures should be discouraged.

Commercial mixtures for a particular group of birds may vary greatly in seed types and proportions from one company to another, indicating the lack of scientific sophistication involved in preparing seed mixture diets. Seed mixtures may contain protein, vitamin and mineral supplements in pellet or crumble form. This is the manufacturer's attempt to overcome the nutrient imbalances inherent in a seeds-only diet. The assumption is that birds will consume all of the seeds and supplement pellets, and thus have a nutritionally balanced diet. Unfortunately, this assumption is not always reality. If seed mixtures containing supplements are used to feed confined birds, the owner should be advised to leave the food in front of the bird until the entire mixture has been eaten before giving the bird more of the mixture. This practice will ensure that the bird consumes the entire diet, not a nutritionally imbalanced, isolated segment. Because individual birds may not accept some components of a supplemented seed mixture, consuming them irregularly or not at all, an imbalanced nutrient intake is much more likely to occur when

Table 30-4. Special nutritional needs of emberizids (order Passiformes, family Emberizidae).*

Genus and species	Common names	Special nutritional needs**
Emberzia tahapisi	Cinnamon-breasted rock bunting	Canary seed mix, mealworms, ant eggs, weed seeds, milk-soaked bread needed in breeding season
Emberzia hortulana	Ortolan bunting	Same as *E. tahapisi*
Sicalis flaveola	Saffron or Brazilian saffron finch	Need an abundance of insects and some greens in breeding season, in addition to that listed for *E. tahapisi*
Sicalis luteola	Yellow grassquit or little saffron finch	In addition to canary seed mix, insects and greens are required
Tiaris canora	Cuban grassquit or Cuban finch	Same as *S. luteola*
Tiaris olivacea	Yellow-faced grassquit or olive finch	Honeycomb regularly; canary seed mix, ant eggs, hard-boiled egg, insects, mealworms, leaf lice, little spiders, greens (chickweed, etc.), tropical seed varieties
Lophospingus pusillus	Black-crested finch or pygmy cardinal	Live foods (e.g., insects, mealworms) needed during breeding season
Sporophilia lineola	Lined seedeater	Same as *L. pusillus*
Sporophila albigularis	White-throated seedeater	Canary seed mix, greens, small mealworms and fruits (apples and bananas are essential)
Volatina jacarina	Blue-black grassquit or jacarina finch	Same as *S. albigularis*
Rhodospingus cruentus	Crimson or rhodospingus finch	Same as *S. albigularis*
Paroaria dominicana	Red-crowned Dominican or Pope cardinal	Live food recommended in addition to canary seed mix as for *S. albigularis*
Paroaria capitata	Yellow-billed cardinal	Must offer a variety of foods in order to prevent this species from eating only seeds; diet should consist of live food, fruits (berries, apples, oranges, greens [chickweed]), small mealworms, ant eggs and canary seed mix
Passerina lelancheri	Orange-bellied, orange-breasted or rainbow bunting	Canary seed mix, insects, canary color foods or pine and spruce twigs to maintain brilliant coloration

*Adapted from Burgmann PM. Feeding Your Pet Bird. New York, NY: Barron's Educational Series, 1993. Lint KC, Lint AM. Feeding Cage Birds—A Manual of Diets for Aviculture. New York, NY: Blanford Press, 1988; 133-175. Vriends MM. Simon and Schuster's Guide to Pet Birds. New York, NY: Simon and Schuster, 1984; 104-118. Woolham F. Diets. In: The Handbook of Aviculture. New York, NY: Blanford Press, 1987; 15-23.
**In addition to commercial foods, these dietary "supplements" or additions are thought to be necessary to stimulate courtship and reproductive behavior or to prevent self mutilation or feather picking by providing environmental/behavioral enrichment.

Table 30-5. Special nutritional needs of fringillids (order Passeriformes, family Fringillidae).*

Genus and species	Common names	Special nutritional needs**
Fringilla coelebs	Chaffinch	Need live insects, supplemental commercial softbill diet, sprouted seeds (rape, turnip, radish) and canary seed mixture in breeding season
Serinus serinus	European serin	Additional small seeds (e.g., lettuce, spray millet, etc.)
Serinus alario	Black-headed canary or alario finch	Varied seed mixture needed to induce breeding
Serinus mozambicus	Yellow-eyed or green singing finch, yellow-fronted canary	Canary seed mix, insect diet, greens
Serinus leucopygia	White-rumped, Layard's seedeater or gray singing finch	Feed the same as *S. mozambicus*
Serinus canaria	Wild canary, island canary	Feed the same as *S. mozambicus*
Carduelis carduelis	European goldfinch	In addition to the basic finch diet, thistle seeds, other seeds, insects and other invertebrates
Carduelis (chloris) chloris	Greenfinch	Canary seed mix, rape seed, small sunflower seed, some hemp, linseed, teasel and greens

*Adapted from Burgmann PM. Feeding Your Pet Bird. New York, NY: Barron's Educational Series, 1993. Lint KC, Lint AM. Feeding Cage Birds—A Manual of Diets for Aviculture. New York, NY: Blanford Press, 1988; 133-175. Vriends MM. Simon and Schuster's Guide to Pet Birds. New York, NY: Simon and Schuster, 1984; 120-130. Woolham F. Diets. In: The Handbook of Aviculture. New York, NY: Blanford Press, 1987; 15-23.
**In addition to commercial foods, these dietary "supplements" or additions are thought to be necessary to stimulate courtship and reproductive behavior or to prevent self mutilation or feather picking by providing environmental/behavioral enrichment.

a supplemented seed mixture is the sole dietary form fed.

Bird owners feed a variety of live foods as supplements to seeds and seed mixtures. When research showed that even strict seed-eaters opportunistically eat insects as a protein source at certain periods in their reproductive cycle and to improve their condition for migration, insect foods became commercially available. Insect supplements are particularly appropriate for Pekin robins, Indian white eyes, shamas, waxbills and cardinals. Live food must be supplied for other species, most notably chaffinch, avadavats and all Phloceids.

White worms (*Enchytraes* larvae) are available commercially and can be kept for long periods much like earthworms in a cool, damp moss and leaf litter substrate. These worms are especially useful to provide when parent birds are brooding and feeding their young. Ant pupae, which bird fanciers have relied on heavily for their avian diets, are now available commercially in large outlets and by mail order. Water shrimp (*Daphnia* spp) are relished by some species and greatly enhance red pigments in their plumage. Aphids that feed on members of the rose family concentrate the same pigments and may be more appropriate for small passerine birds. Moth larvae, commonly known as waxworms, and beetle larvae, called mealworms, supply extra protein and fat, especially at the onset of the breeding season. Care should be taken to restrict the intake of these insects or birds will rapidly gain weight and become obese.

Most true insect-eating birds remove the heads of larvae before the larvae are ingested. Clients should be instructed to remove the head capsules before feeding such larvae, if it is observed that the bird does not perform this function. This practice removes a largely indigestible chitinous mass from entering the gastrointestinal tract and eliminates the possibility that a live larvae could burrow through the crop wall or cause gastrointestinal obstruction.

Table 30-6. Special nutritional needs of waxbills and allies (order Passeriformes, family Estrildidae).*

Genus and species	Common names	Special nutritional needs**
Pytillia melba	Melba finch or crimson-faced waxbill, green winged pytilia	Need a rich variety of insects and small seeds to prevent hatchling rejection
Estrilda melpoda	Orange-cheeked waxbill	Require small insects for maintenance and breeding
Estrilda rhodopyga	Crimson or rosy-rumped waxbill	Require insects all year, especially during breeding season
Estrilda astrild	Common or St. Helene waxbill	Insects and soaked seeds are essential
Estrilda caerulescens	Red-tailed lavender, lavender waxbill	Ant eggs, fine cut mealworms, white worms, greens (lettuce, endive, chicory, chickweed)
Uraeginthus bengalus	Red-cheeked cordon bleu	Live food important, especially for breeding (aphids, ant eggs and spiders)
Uraeginthus angolensis	Blue-breasted cordon bleu, Angolan cordon bleu or blue-breasted waxbill	Feed the same as U. bengalus
Granatina (U.) granatina	Violet-eared waxbill	In addition to small seeds (grass seeds, spray millet) live food is essential all year for behavioral enrichment
Lagonosticta senegala	Red-bellied firefinch	When chicks are hatched, extra amounts of live food, greens and egg foods are essential for feeding the chicks
Amandava formosa	Green avadavat	Some live food is essential year round
Amandava amandava	Strawberry finch or red avadavat	Some live food is essential year round
Amandava subflava	Golden-breasted or zebra waxbill	Some live food is essential year round
Padda oryzivora	Java sparrow or rice bird	Basic passerine seed mix and greens for breeding
Longchura ferruginosa	Black-headed chestnut or chestnut-bellied munia or black-headed nun	Insects, weed seeds, basic passerine seed mix, greens, canary-chick rearing food and bread soaked in milk during breeding season
Longchura malacca	Black-headed munia or pearl-headed silverbill	Same as L. ferruginosa
Longchura caniceps	Gray-headed munia or pearl-headed silverbill	Same as L. ferruginosa
Longchura punctulata	Scaly-breasted munia, spice bird or spice finch	Same as L. ferruginosa
Longchura malabarica	Indian silverbill or white-throated munia	Same as L. ferruginosa
Longchura striata var. domestica	Bengalese	Same as L. ferruginosa
Longchura castaneothorax	Chestnut-breasted finch or munia	Same as L. ferruginosa
Neochimia modesta	Cherry or plum-headed finch	Ripe and half-ripe seeds, berries, greens and a variety of live foods are necessary
Taeniopytia bichenovii	Bicheno's or double-barred finch	Same as N. modesta
Taeniopygiaa guttata	Zebra finch	Same as N. modesta
Poephilia acuticauda	Long-tailed finch	Same as N. modesta
Poephilia cincta	Black-throated or parson finch	In addition to small ripe and half-ripe seeds, insects, greens, soaked white bread, soaked and germinated seeds and cuttlefish bone are essential
Poephilia personata	Masked finch	Same as P. cincta
Chloebia gouldiae	Gouldian finch	During molting these birds must be supplied with protein-rich foods, vitamins and minerals, soaked and recently sprouted seeds. Avoid white millet in this species
Neochimia ruficauda	Star finch	During the breeding season, provide a rich variety of insects, seeds, greens and commercial egg and rearing foods

*Adapted from Burgmann PM. Feeding Your Pet Bird. New York, NY: Barron's Educational Series, 1993. Lint KC, Lint AM. Feeding Cage Birds—A Manual of Diets for Aviculture. New York, NY: Blanford Press, 1988; 133-175. Vriends MM. Simon and Schuster's Guide to Pet Birds. New York, NY: Simon and Schuster, 1984; 130-180. Woolham F. Diets. In: The Handbook of Aviculture. New York, NY: Blanford Press, 1987; 15-23.
**In addition to commercial foods, these dietary "supplements" or additions are thought to be necessary to stimulate courtship and reproductive behavior or to prevent self mutilation or feather picking by providing environmental/behavioral enrichment.

Homemade Mixed-Food Diets

A wide variety of homemade mixed-food diets have been suggested as alternatives for birds that will not accept commercially prepared foods or seed mixtures even with added fruits and vegetables.[7-11] These diets can result in excellent feathering and appropriate body mass for the species, with no discernible signs of nutritional deficiency, if prepared carefully from scientifically developed recipes. These diets often contain varying amounts of ingredients such as seeds, nuts, cooked eggs, low-fat yogurt or cheese, vegetables, fruits, grains, bread, pasta, multigrain cereals, legumes, seed mixes, pelleted or extruded psittacine diets, vitamin supplements and calcium supplements. When converting birds to a new homemade diet, have the client offer a mixture containing all the ingredients at one time. This practice usually prevents preferential selection of certain ingredients. Although larger parrots have difficulty eating small seeds such as milo or oat groats, a seed mixture containing 30% hulled safflower, 30% milo, 30% oat groats and 10% peanuts works well for smaller birds.

Although homemade mixed-food diets may provide adequate nourishment, most companion bird owners are unwilling to devote the time necessary to adequately prepare these diets. Additionally, owners must be willing to regularly observe which food components are being consumed to prevent birds from developing or reverting to preferential selection of specific ingredients.

Water

Although feeding a well-balanced food is essential, it is easy to overlook the single most important dietary component: water. As with all animals, water is absolutely essential for birds. Water acts as a food carrier and aids in digestion. Some foods are high in water content, but others require free water for efficient digestion and absorption. Some avian species are more physiologically adept at extracting water from their foods. Budgerigars in the wild, for example, are capable of absorbing sufficient water from seeds and green foods to allow them to go without water for many days. This observation, however, is not an experiment to be undertaken by the pet owner. Birds should never go for more than a few hours without access to fresh clean water. Studies have shown that canaries will die within 48 hours if water is withheld.

Water makes up more than 50% of a bird's body weight. (In young birds, the percentage may be even higher.) Blood and lymph are largely composed of water. Further, because birds have no sweat glands, water intake plays an important role in thermoregulation. Breeding females may require increased amounts of water for egg production and for heat regulation while incubating eggs.

Water should be provided in containers that are easily accessible but not located in a place that can collect feces, feathers, food particles, etc. For this reason, water bowls should be attached to the wall of enclosures, near or above food bowls. They should not be so large as to invite bathing.

Assess the Feeding Method

It may not always be necessary to change the feeding method when managing an avian patient, but a thorough assessment includes verification that an appropriate feeding method is being used. Items to consider include feeding route, amount fed, how the food is offered and who feeds the bird. All of this information should have been gathered when the history of the bird was obtained. If the bird has normal body condition, the amount of food it was fed previously (energy basis) was probably appropriate.

FEEDING PLAN

Select a Food(s)

The advantages and disadvantages of feeding birds commercially prepared foods, seeds and seed mixtures and homemade mixed foods were discussed above. If an individual bird is healthy and exhibits no signs of deficiency disease, the owner probably is feeding the bird appropriately and there is no need to change the food. In general, however, fewer deficiency diseases will result from feeding a complete, nutritionally balanced food that meets the nutrient levels listed in Table 30-2.

Although some prepared foods have been available for only a limited time, the overall nutritional quality of commercial foods is rapidly improving as manufacturers use new scientific information to create their formulations. As commercially prepared foods become more widely used, many of the diet-induced diseases currently observed by avian veterinarians will become of historical interest only, just as they have for other companion pets.

Table 30-3 lists some of the widely available commercially prepared complete and specialized avian foods. Owners should be encouraged to experiment with different prepared foods if their bird does not accept a particular product. Often a bird will readily accept an alternative form, shape or formulation of a complete food. When changing the diet of a bird from seeds or fresh human foods to a commercially prepared complete food, the previous foods should be eliminated or substantially restricted to encourage consumption of the complete avian food.

Tables 30-4 through 30-8 list foods that meet the special nutritional or behavioral needs of passerine birds. In addition to commercial foods, these dietary "supplements" or additions are thought to be necessary to stimulate courtship and reproductive behavior or to prevent self mutilation or feather picking by providing environmental/behavioral enrichment. Table 30-9 lists homemade mixed-food diets for psittacine birds.

Determine the Feeding Method

Because of the convenience, most owners offer food free choice with additional food added to the bowl as needed. When a seed mixture or homemade diet is offered free choice, it is unknown how much and what components the bird actually consumes. Therefore, the owner may not realize that the bird has not eaten for 24 to 48 hours.

Owners who feed prepackaged seeds, seed mixtures or treats for birds often assume that the product is nutritionally complete and the bird will eat all parts of the product. Both of these assumptions are often incorrect. To correct or avoid these problems, bird owners should offer a nutritionally complete prepared food at regular intervals as a part of the total diet.

Feeding Intervals

An ideal strategy is to ensure that food is offered to companion birds for one to two hours, two or three times

Table 30-7. Special nutritional needs of weavers, wydahs and queleas (order Passiformes, family Ploceidae).*

Genus and species	Common names	Special nutritional needs**
Ploceus cucullatus	Rufous-necked, black-headed, village weaver or vitelline-masked weaver	Live food is essential, in addition to millets, white grass, weed seeds and grains (oats and wheat) for breeding
Ploceus vitellinus	Half-masked or Zesser-masked weaver	Same as *P. cucullatus*
Ploceus intermedius	Masked weaver	Same as *P. cucullatus*
Ploceus phillippinus	Baya weaver	Same as *P. cucullatus*
Euplectus afra	Napoleon weaver, yellow-crowned or golden bishop	Live food is essential, as are small seeds, fruits and greens (See *Ploceus* spp)
Euplectus hordeacea	Blackwinged bishop, crimson-crowned bishop	Same as *P. cucullatus, E. afra*
Euplectus orix	Grenadier weaver or red bishop	Same as *P. cucullatus, E. afra*
Euplectus progne	Long-tailed willow bird, giant wydah	Same as *P. cucullatus, E. afra*
Euplectus ardens	Red-collared willow bird or wydah	Same as *P. cucullatus, E. afra*

*Adapted from Burgmann PM. Feeding Your Pet Bird. New York, NY: Barron's Educational Series, 1993. Lint KC, Lint AM. Feeding Cage Birds—A Manual of Diets for Aviculture. New York, NY: Blanford Press, 1988; 133-175; Vriends MM. Simon and Schuster's Guide to Pet Birds. New York, NY: Simon and Schuster, 1984; 182-190. Woolham F. Diets. In: The Handbook of Aviculture. New York, NY: Blanford Press, 1987; 15-23.
**In addition to commercial foods, these dietary "supplements" or additions are thought to be necessary to stimulate courtship and reproductive behavior or to prevent self mutilation or feather picking by providing environmental/behavioral enrichment.

Table 30-8. Special nutritional needs of babblers and starlings (order Passeriforme, family Timaliidae and family Sturnidae).*

Genus and species	Common names	Special nutritional needs**
Leitothrix lutea	Red-billed leiothrix or Pekin robin	Dead, dried or live insects are essential for breeding
Gracula religiosa	Hill mynah	Must be offered a commercial or formulated low-iron food to prevent hemochromatosis; during breeding requires insects and fruit low in or devoid of iron

*Adapted from Kollias GV. Diets, feeding practices, and nutritional problems in psittacine birds. Veterinary Medicine 1995; 90: 29-39. Burgmann PM. Feeding Your Pet Bird. New York, NY: Barron's Educational Series, 1993. Lint KC, Lint AM. Feeding Cage Birds—A Manual of Diets for Aviculture. New York, NY: Blanford Press, 1988; 133-175.
**In addition to commercial foods, these dietary "supplements" or additions are thought to be necessary to stimulate courtship and reproductive behavior or to prevent self mutilation or feather picking by providing environmental/behavioral enrichment.

daily. The food should be removed during the interim periods, although this is not standard practice for most owners or care providers. Offering food at specific times during the day creates a bond between the owner and bird. This feeding regimen also increases the probability that an owner will examine the contents of the food and water bowls to determine exactly what and how much was consumed and whether the bowls require cleaning.

Changing Foods

Unless commercially prepared nutritionally complete foods are fed, birds fed free choice may develop a habituation to a single type of food (monophagism). This fixation may result in single or multiple nutrient deficiencies. After a deficiency occurs, the owner is faced with changing the food. This can be a formidable challenge depending on the age and species of the bird. Changing foods is generally easier with younger birds and with smaller parrots such as cockatiels and conures. Cockatoos, macaws and African grey parrots are more resistant to change. Most passerine birds switch to new foods easily.

Totally changing the diet should not be attempted if the bird is sick or under stress (e.g., recent acquisition, change in environment, exposure to temperature extremes, molting etc.). Conversion to a new balanced food may take from weeks to months depending on the degree and length of habituation. Ninety percent of healthy cockatiels can been converted to a new food within seven days.

A variety of strategies can be used to convert birds to a new food. If one of these approaches is unsuccessful, an alternate one should be tried.

1. Gradually add the new food to the current diet, increasing the amount of the new food over days to weeks. Remember that texture and color are important; therefore, adding a food that the bird really likes (e.g., brown sugar, carrots) may make the conversion much easier.
2. Unless the new food is extruded or pelleted, warming or cooling the food may make a difference in acceptance. The food should be warmed to no hotter than 40.6°C (105°F). Microwaves should be used cautiously because the interior of the food may be much hotter than the exterior. Alternatively, food can be cooled to refrigerator temperatures (2 to 4°C [35 to 40°F]).
3. Try offering the bird a soft food such as baby cereal, fruits or vegetables, cooked oatmeal or cream of wheat. Birds like the texture of these foods. Then gradually add a prepared diet to these mixtures.
4. If a bird is hand-trained or hand-reared, feeding outside the cage is often helpful. Alternatively, place the new food item in the cage at strategic locations (e.g., by a mirror or favorite toy or attach the food item to the cage bars).
5. Have the owner eat what you want the bird to eat. Some birds mimic their owners by eating foods they see their owners eat.
6. Begin feeding a new food every other day. For larger birds, remove the seeds on that day. If a smaller bird (e.g., a budgerigar, canary or finch) has not eaten the new food by the late afternoon, offer seeds to prevent hypoglycemia overnight. Alternate-day feedings will also prevent excessive weight loss. Increase feedings to four, then five, then seven days a week.
7. Remove all seeds before retiring for the night. In the morning, offer a commercially prepared complete food

Table 30-9. Homemade mixed-food diets for psittacine birds.*

Diet 1	20-30% seeds and nuts 20-30% dark green, yellow and orange vegetables 10-15% fruit (avoid excess apples and bananas, which have little nutritional value and may contain excessive phosphorus) 20-30% pelleted or extruded psittacine food, which is added to the mixture after thawing and immediately before feeding Much of this diet can be made in advance and frozen in small portions
Diet 2	30% small- or large-parrot seed mix 20% cooked brown rice, dark multigrain bread, pasta and multigrain cereals 15% frozen or fresh vegetables, such as peas, carrots and squash 15% legumes, such as cooked kidney and pinto beans 20% pelleted or extruded psittacine food, which is added to the mixture after thawing and immediately before feeding Much of this diet can be made in advance and frozen in small portions
Diet 3	45% grains, breads and cereal group (whole wheat bread, cooked brown rice, seed mixture) 45% fresh vegetables (broccoli, endive, carrots, pumpkin, winter squash, collard greens, sweet potato) and fruits (limit quantities of papaya, cantaloupe and apricots to 5% of total fruit) 5% from the protein and fat group, including hard-cooked or scrambled eggs and peanuts or other mature legumes (e.g., navy or kidney beans) 5% dairy group (for calcium and protein) Use low-fat, nonlactose dairy products, such as low-fat yogurt, cottage cheese and hard cheese; other sources of calcium (although not as good as food sources) may include cuttlebone, oyster shell and mineral blocks; larger psittacine birds may ignore these items or destroy rather than consume them
Diet 4	24% cooked long grain rice 25% cooked kidney beans 24% frozen whole kernel corn 24% pelleted or extruded psittacine diet (total soft diet = 96.63%) Approximately 2% powdered vitamin supplement 1-4% calcium supplement (total supplements = 3.37%) This diet is formulated based on wet weight. Small portions can be frozen (excluding the pelleted or extruded diet) and used as needed. Pay particular attention to food hygiene because these foods decompose fairly rapidly.

*Some species of psittacine birds, such as lorries, have specific dietary requirements for fruit or nectar that differ from those of more common species of New World parrots. When fruit or nectar is used, percentages in the diet should be based on relative proportions by volume, not on a dry or wet weight basis. Avoid including avocado because it is toxic to small psittacine birds. Adapted from Ullrey DE, Allen MR, Baer DJ. Formulated diets versus seed mixtures for Psittacines. Journal of Nutrition 1991; 121: S193-S205. Kollias GV. Diets, feeding practices, and nutritional problems in psittacine birds. Veterinary Medicine 1995; 90: 29-39.

with new food items instead of the seed. Do not add seed until noon. This strategy presents no danger to the birds because the previous seed(s) are available later in the day.

The bird's physical condition and body weight should be monitored during the conversion period to prevent starvation. Keep in mind that most birds eating all seeds or "junk food" (e.g., potato chips, peanuts, candy) may be overweight or even obese. If a bird loses excessive body condition during the conversion period, as determined through weighing, it may refuse to eat the previously fed food. Gavage or tube feeding for one to three days will be required to stimulate the bird to eat.

All of these strategies have been successful in enticing companion psittacine birds to eat a more balanced food(s). Occasionally, however, individual birds cannot be converted. These birds may require specialized water and food supplements to overcome serious vitamin and mineral deficiencies. In some cases when conversion is unsuccessful, the bird may need to be hospitalized away from the owner. At the hospital, a rigorous dietary protocol can be implemented that may be successful once the behavioral influences of the owner are eliminated.

In multiple-bird households, owners will have an easier time converting birds to a new food if at least one bird has been converted and the other birds can observe it eating the new food. HBD International will provide an "instructor" bird to assist in food conversion if all other methods are unsuccessful (See Table 30-3 or Appendix O for address).

Client education is crucial to the success of food conversion, especially with companion birds. Owners should be advised to be persistent and patient during this process.

REFERENCES

1. MacWhirter P. Malnutrition. In: Ritchie BW, Harrison GJ, Harrison LR, eds. Avian Medicine: Principles and Application. Lake Worth, FL: Wingers Publishing, Inc, 1994; 842-861.
2. Grau CR, Roudybush TE. Protein requirements of growing cockatiels. In: Proceedings. Western Poultry Disease Conference, Salt Lake City, UT, 1985: 107-108.
3. Snyder NFR. Movements and food. In: The Parrots of Luquillo: Natural History and Conservation of the Puerto Rican Parrot. Los Angeles, CA: Western Foundation of Vertebrate Zoology, 1987; 67-93.
4. Nutrient Content of Foods, USDA Agricultural Handbook No. 8, Washington, DC.
5. Exotic Bird Nutrition Expert Panel Report, Nutrition and Management Committee of the Association of Avian Veterinarians, 1996.
6. Ullrey DE, Allen MR, Baer DJ. Formulated diets versus seed mixtures for Psittacines. Journal of Nutrition 1991; 121: S193-S205.
7. Kollias GV. Diets, feeding practices, and nutritional problems in psittacine birds. Veterinary Medicine 1995; 90: 29-39.
8. Burgmann PM. Feeding Your Pet Bird. New York, NY: Barron's Educational Series, Inc, 1993.
9. Lint KC, Lint AM. Feeding Cage Birds–A Manual of Diets for Aviculture. New York, NY: Blanford Press, 1988; 133-175.
10. Vriends MM. Simon and Schuster's Guide to Pet Birds. New York, NY: Simon and Schuster, 1984; 104-118, 130-180, 182-190.
11. Woolham F. Diets. In: The Handbook of Aviculture. New York, NY: Blanford Press, 1987; 15-23.

BIRDS

SECTION VI

Appendices

Glossary

Index

Appendices

Jacques Debraekeleer, DVM

Introduction to Appendices

The primary objective of the appendices is to provide readers with quick reference tables containing unit conversions, energy calculations, feeding guides and other data relating to nutrition, nutritional assessment and nutritional management of animals. The emphasis here is on practical rather than 100% complete information.

Appendix A contains conversion tables that can be used to interconvert units regularly found in the literature but not commonly used in all countries. Appendix B contains common abbreviations and many of the abbreviations used in this edition of *Small Animal Clinical Nutrition*. It also lists a series of names and abbreviations of veterinary and commercial associations and selected official institutions.

The appendices also provide practical information about nutrition and the nutritional assessment of pets at different lifestages. For example, Appendix E provides data about puppies and kittens during the postnatal period, and Appendix K compares the composition of common milk replacers with milk from bitches and queens. Appendices F through I list feeding guides and body weights or body types of growing and adult dogs and cats.

The appendices listing nutrient levels of selected commercial foods are not intended to be a complete overview of the pet food market. Rather, they provide a representative sample of the different types of food available for dogs, cats and birds. Specific manufacturers can be contacted for the same information and for product updates.

Appendices P through S will help veterinary practitioners provide optimal nutritional care for injured and orphaned wild animals until specialized help is found. These appendices also provide nutritional information for small and less common pets, such as small rodents and some reptiles.

I would like to thank all those who helped collect the information in these appendices and the companies that were willing to provide information about their products. Special thanks go to Dr. Mark L. Morris, Jr., for his advice and Dr. Philip Roudebush for his regular assistance.

Jacques Debraekeleer, DVM

Appendix A
*Conversion Tables**

Table A-1. Conversions to and from metric measures.
Table A-2. Comparison between US and imperial systems.
Table A-3. Conversion of conventional units to SI units.
Table A-4. Temperature conversions.
Table A-5. Equivalent values and conversion factors.
Table A-6. Wine measures.
Table A-7. Percent, ppm and ppb.
Table A-8. Energy conversion units.
Table A-9. Vitamins A, D and E: Conversions from international units to equivalent activity.
Bibliography

*See Appendix B for a list of abbreviations.

Table A-1. Conversions to and from metric measures.

Imperial/US to metric				Metric to imperial/US			
Weights							
1	gr (grain)	64.8	mg	1	g	15.43	gr
1	oz (avoirdupois)	28.35	g	1	g	0.0353	oz
1	lb (avoirdupois)	453.6	g	1	g	0.0022	lb
1	lb	0.454	kg	1	kg	2.2	lb
1	ton (short)	907.2	kg	1	kg	0.0011	short ton
1	ton	0.907	ton	1	ton	1.1	ton
Dosages							
1	mg/lb	2.2	mg/kg	1	mg/kg	0.454	mg/lb
1	kcal/lb	2.2	kcal/kg	1	kcal/kg	0.454	kcal/lb
Volumes							
US							
1	fl oz	29.57	ml	1	l	33.82	fl oz
1	cup	0.237	l	1	l	4.221	cup
1	pt	0.473	l	1	l	2.114	pt
1	qt	0.946	l	1	l	1.057	qt
1	gal	3.785	l	1	l	0.264	gal
Imperial							
1	fl oz	28.41	ml	1	l	35.20	fl oz
1	cup	0.284	l	1	l	3.520	cup
1	pt	0.568	l	1	l	1.760	pt
1	qt	1.136	l	1	l	0.88	qt
1	gal	4.546	l	1	l	0.22	gal
Linear measures							
1	in	2.54	cm	1	cm	0.394	in
1	ft	30.48	cm	1	m	3.28	ft
1	yd	91.44	cm	1	m	1.094	yd
1	mi	1.61	km	1	km	0.62	mi
Area							
1	in²	6.45	cm²	1	cm²	0.155	in²
1	ft²	929	cm²	1	m²	10.764	ft²
1	yd²	0.836	m²	1	m²	1.196	yd²
1	acre	0.405	ha	1	ha	2.47	acres
1	mi²	2.59	km²	1	km²	0.386	mi²

Table A-2. Comparison between US and imperial systems.

	Imperial				US		
1	fl oz	28.42	ml	1	fl oz	29.57	ml
1	cup	10	fl oz	1	cup	8	fl oz
1	pt	20	fl oz	1	pt	16	fl oz
1	qt	40	fl oz	1	qt	32	fl oz
1	gal*	160	fl oz	1	gal**	128	fl oz
1	gal*	4	qt	1	gal**	4	qt
1	gal*	4.55	l	1	gal**	3.78	l

*1 gal (imperial) = 4 qt = 8 pt = 16 cups = 160 oz = 4.55 l.
**1 gal (US) = 4 qt = 8 pt = 16 cups = 128 oz = 3.78 l.

Table A-3. Conversion of conventional units to SI units.*

Chemical constituents	Conventional units	x	Factors	=	SI units
Acetoacetate	mg/dl		97.95		µmol/l
Acetone	mg/dl		172.2		µmol/l
ACTH	pg/ml		0.2202		pmol/l
Alanine	mg/dl		112.20		µmol/l
Albumin	g/dl		10.0		g/l
α-aminobutyric acid	mg/dl		96.97		µmol/l
α-tocopherol (vitamin E)	mg/dl		23.22		µmol/l
Ammonia (as NH_3)	µg/dl		0.5872		µmol/l
Ammonia (as NH_4)	µg/dl		0.5543		µmol/l
Arginine	mg/dl		57.40		µmol/l
Ascorbic acid (vitamin C)	mg/dl		56.78		µmol/l
Asparagine	mg/dl		75.69		µmol/l
Bicarbonate	mEq/l		1.0		mmol/l
Bile acids (total)	µg/ml		2.547		µmol/l
Bilirubin	mg/dl		17.1		µmol/l
Bromsulphalein (BSP)	mg/dl		11.93		µmol/l
Calcium	mg/dl		0.250		mmol/l
Calcium (ionized)	mEq/l		0.500		mmol/l
Carotenes	µg/dl		0.01863		µmol/l
Ceruloplasmin	mg/dl		10.0		mg/l
Chloride	mEq/l		1.0		mmol/l
Cholecalciferol (vitamin D_3)	ng/ml		2.599		nmol/l
Cholesterol	mg/dl		0.02586		mmol/l
Citrulline	mg/dl		57.08		µmol/l
Cobalamin (vitamin B_{12})	pg/ml		0.7378		pmol/l
Cobalamin (vitamin B_{12})	ng/dl		7.378		pmol/l
Cobalt	µg/dl		0.1697		µmol/l
Copper	µg/dl		0.1574		µmol/l
Cortisol	µg/dl		27.59		nmol/l
CO_2 pressure (pCO_2)	mm Hg		0.1333		kPa
CO_2 total	mEq/l		1.0		mmol/l
Creatinine	mg/dl		88.4		µmol/l
Creatinine clearance	ml/min		0.01667		ml/s
Cystine	mg/dl		41.61		µmol/l
Enzymes**	U/l		16.67		nkat/l
Fibrinogen	mg/dl		0.01		g/l
Folate	ng/ml		2.266		nmol/l
Fructose	mg/dl		55.51		µmol/l
GGT (γ-glutamyltransferase)	IU/l		1.0		U/l
Glucose	mg/dl		0.05551		mmol/l
Glutamic acid	mg/dl		67.97		µmol/l
Glutamine	mg/dl		68.42		µmol/l
Glycine	mg/dl		133.2		µmol/l
Haptoglobin	mg/dl		0.01		g/l
Hematocrit	%		0.01		fraction of 1
Hemoglobin	g/dl		10.0		g/l
Histidine	mg/dl		64.45		µmol/l
β-hydroxybutyrate	mg/dl		96.05		µmol/l
Hydroxyproline	mg/dl		76.26		µmol/l
IgA, IgG, IgM	mg/dl		0.01		g/l
Insulin	µU/ml		7.175		pmol/l
Iodine	µg/dl		78.8		nmol/l
Iron	µg/dl		0.1791		µmol/l
Isoleucine	mg/dl		76.24		µmol/l
Lactate	mg/dl		0.111		mmol/l
Lead	µg/dl		0.04826		µmol/l
Leucine	mg/dl		76.24		µmol/l
Lysine	mg/dl		68.40		µmol/l

(Continued on next page.)

Table A-3. Conversion of conventional units to SI units.* (Continued from previous page.)

Chemical constituents	Conventional units	x	Factors	=	SI units
Magnesium	mg/dl		0.4114		mmol/l
Manganese	μg/dl		0.182		μmol/l
Mercury	μg/l		4.985		nmol/l
Methemoglobin	g/dl		10.0		g/l
Methionine	mg/dl		67.02		μmol/l
Molybdenum	μg/dl		0.1042		μmol/l
Myoglobin	mg/dl		0.5848		μmol/l
Nitrogen	mg/dl		0.7138		mmol/l
O_2 pressure (pO_2)	mm Hg		0.1333		kPa
Ornithine	mg/dl		75.67		μmol/l
Osmolality	mOsm/kg		1.0		mmol/kg
Phenylalanine	mg/dl		60.54		μmol/l
Phosphorus	mg/dl		0.3229		mmol/l
Potassium	mEq/l		1.0		mmol/l
Progesterone	ng/ml		3.18		nmol/l
Proline	mg/dl		86.86		μmol/l
Protein	g/dl		10.0		g/l
Pyridoxine (vitamin B_6)	ng/ml		5.982		nmol/l
Pyruvate	mg/dl		113.6		μmol/l
RBC count	$10^6/mm^3$		1.0		$10^{12}/l$
Retinol (vitamin A)	μg/dl		0.03491		μmol/l
Riboflavin (vitamin B_2)	μg/dl		26.57		nmol/l
Selenium	μg/dl		0.1266		μmol/l
Serine	mg/dl		95.16		μmol/l
Sodium	mEq/l		1.0		mmol/l
Taurine	mg/dl		79.91		μmol/l
Testosterone	ng/ml		3.467		nmol/l
Threonine	mg/dl		83.95		μmol/l
Thyroxine (T_4)	μg/dl		12.87		nmol/l
Transferrin	mg/dl		0.01		g/l
Triglycerides	mg/dl		0.01129		mmol/l
Triiodothyronine (T_3)	ng/dl		0.01536		nmol/l
Tryptophan	mg/dl		48.97		μmol/l
Tyrosine	mg/dl		55.19		μmol/l
Urate (uric acid)	mg/dl		59.48		μmol/l
Urea	mg/dl		0.1665		mmol/l
Urea nitrogen (BUN, SUN)	mg/dl		0.714		mmol/l
Urea nitrogen (BUN, SUN)	mg/dl		0.357		mmol urea/l
Urobilinogen	mg/dl		16.9		μmol/l
Valine	mg/dl		85.36		μmol/l
Vitamin A (retinol)	μg/dl		0.03491		μmol/l
Vitamin B_2 (riboflavin)	μg/dl		26.57		nmol/l
Vitamin B_6 (pyridoxine)	ng/dl		5.982		nmol/l
Vitamin C (ascorbic acid)	mg/dl		56.78		μmol/l
Vitamin D_3 (cholecalciferol)	ng/dl		2.599		nmol/l
Vitamin E (α-tocopherol)	mg/dl		23.22		μmol/l
WBC count	$10^3/mm^3$		1.0		$10^9/l$
WBC differential	cells/mm^3		1.0		10^6 cells/l
Xylose	mg/dl		0.06661		mmol/l
Zinc	μg/dl		0.153		μmol/l

*SI is the abbreviation of the French "Système International." It has been used in France since 1961 and has been adopted by most countries. Many scientific journals have also adopted the system to overcome the chaos arising from the use of different units. In addition, quantitating the amount of a substance in moles (SI units) rather than in grams may also confer a scientific advantage, allowing for an easier understanding of molecular relationships. This table lists the constituents of most interest in practice, when reading research papers or when dealing with nutrition.

**There is no general agreement nor recommendation for the use of katal (1 kat = 1 mol/sec) in place of the widely used international unit (1 U = 1 μmol/min). The U/l should be used for all enzyme activities.

Table A-4. Temperature conversions.*

°C	°F	°C	°F	°C	°F	°C	°F	°C	°F
0	32.0	10	50.0	20	68.0	30	86.0	40	104.0
1	33.8	11	51.8	21	69.8	31	87.8	41	105.8
2	35.6	12	53.6	22	71.6	32	89.6	42	107.6
3	37.4	13	55.4	23	73.4	33	91.4	43	109.4
4	39.2	14	57.2	24	75.2	34	93.2	44	111.2
5	41.0	15	59.0	25	77.0	35	95.0	45	113.0
6	42.8	16	60.8	26	78.8	36	96.8	46	114.8
7	44.6	17	62.6	27	80.6	37	98.6	47	116.6
8	46.4	18	64.4	28	82.4	38	100.4	48	118.4
9	48.2	19	66.2	29	84.2	39	102.2	49	120.2
								50	122.0

*When you know the Fahrenheit temperature, subtract 32 and multiply by 5/9 to obtain °C. When you know the Celsius temperature, multiply by 9/5 then add 32 to obtain °F.

Table A-5. Equivalent values and conversion factors.

Volumes

1	gtt*	0.05	ml		1	cup**	16	Tbs
1	tsp	5	ml		1	ml	20	gtt
1	dsp	8	ml		1	cup**	236.6	ml
1	Tbs	15	ml		1	cup***	284.2	ml

Weights

1	oz	437.5	gr†		1	g	1,000	mg
1	lb	16	oz		1	kg	1,000	g
1	ton (short)	2,000	lb		1	ton (metric)	1,000	kg

Linear measures

1	in	2.54	cm		1	mm	1,000	µm
1	ft	12	in		1	cm	10	mm
1	yd	3	ft		1	dm	10	cm
1	mi	1,760	yd		1	m	100	cm
					1	km	1,000	m

Area

1	ft²	144	in²		1	cm²	100	mm²
1	yd²	9	ft²		1	m²	10,000	cm²
1	acre	4,840	yd²		1	are	100	m²
1	mi²	640	acres		1	ha	100	ares
					1	km²	100	ha

Temperature††

-459.67	°F	0	K		-273.15	°C	0	K
32	°F	273.15	K		0	°C	273.15	K
212	°F	373.15	K		100	°C	373.15	K

*Official dropper size for water at 15°C.
**US cup.
***Imperial cup.
†gr = grains.
††See Table A-4 for temperature conversions from °C to °F and vice versa.

Table A-6. Wine measures.

Wines	Regions	ml	Bottles
Wine glass	–	60	–
Bottle	Standard	750	–
	Alsace	720	–
	Champagne	800	–
	Edelzwicker (Alsace)	1,000	–
Magnum	All	1,500	2
Marie-Jeanne	Bordeaux	2,250	3
Jéroboam	Burgundy/Champagne	3,000	4
Double magnum	Bordeaux	3,000	4
Réhoboam	Burgundy/Champagne	4,500	6
Jéroboam	Bordeaux	4,500	6
Methuselah	Burgundy/Champagne	6,000	8
Impériale	Bordeaux	6,000	8
Salmanazar	Burgundy/Champagne	9,000	12
Balthazar	Burgundy/Champagne	12,000	16
Nebuchadnezzar	Burgundy/Champagne	15,000	20
Fillette angevine	–	350	–
Pot beaujolais	–	450	–
Quart	Champagne	200	–
Demi	Champagne	400	–
Médium	Champagne	600	–

Table A-7. Percent, ppm and ppb.

Percent	ppm	ppb
µg/0.1 mg	1 µg/g	1 ng/g
mg/0.1 g	1 mg/kg	1 µg/kg
g/100 g	0.4545 mg/lb	0.4545 µg/lb
kg/100 kg	1 g/ton (1,000 kg)	1 mg/ton (1,000 kg)
g/0.22 lb	1 kg/1,000 ton	
ml/100 ml		
l/hl		
cm/m		
m²/a		

Table A-8. Energy conversion units.

Kilocalorie	kcal	1,000 cal	4.184 kJ
Kilojoule	kJ	1,000 joule	0.239 kcal
Megajoule	MJ	1,000 kJ	239.0 kcal

Conversion from:	To:	
mg/MJ	mg/100 kcal	÷ 2.39
mg/100 kcal	mg/MJ	x 2.39
g/MJ	mg/100 kcal	÷ 0.00239
mg/100 kcal	g/MJ	x 0.00239
mg/100 kcal	g/100 kcal	÷ 1,000
g/100 kcal	mg/100 kcal	x 1,000
mg/MJ	g/MJ	÷ 1,000
g/MJ	mg/MJ	x 1,000

Table A-9. Vitamins A, D and E: Conversions from international units to equivalent activity.*

Vitamins	Units	Substances	
Vitamin A	1 IU	0.300 µg of crystalline retinol (vitamin A alcohol)	0.550 µg of vitamin A palmitate
Vitamin A	1 RE*	1 µg of crystalline retinol (vitamin A alcohol)	6 µg of β-carotene 12 µg of other provitamin A carotenoids
Provitamin A	1 IU	0.6 µg β-carotene	1.2 µg of other provitamin A carotenoids
Vitamin D	1 IU	0.025 µg of crystalline vitamin D_3	
Vitamin E	1 IU	1 mg of synthetic racemic α-tocopherol acetate = dl-α-tocopherol acetate = all racemic α-tocopherol acetate	

1 mg of synthetic racemic α-tocopherol = 1 mg of synthetic racemic α-tocopherol	= 1.1 IU of vitamin E
1 mg of naturally occurring α-tocopherol = d-α-tocopherol = RRR-tocopherol	= 1.49 IU of vitamin E
1 mg of naturally occurring α-tocopherol acetate = d-α-tocopherol acetate	= 1.36 IU of vitamin E

*On pet food labels and tables with daily nutrient allowances for pets, the vitamins A, D and E are expressed in international units (IU). These units reflect the activity of these vitamins, not their amounts. United States Pharmacopeia Units (USP) are equivalent to IU. In human foods, retinol equivalent (RE) is often used for vitamin A activity.

BIBLIOGRAPHY

1. Debuigne G. Dictionaire des Vins Larousse. Paris, France: Librairie Larousse, 1969; 75.

2. Kaneko JJ, ed. Appendixes. In: Clinical Biochemistry of Domestic Animals, 4th ed. San Diego, CA: Academic Press Inc, 1989; 877-901.

3. Laposata M. SI unit conversion table. In: New England Journal of Medicine SI Unit Conversion Guide. Boston, MA: New England Journal of Medicine Books, 1992; 53-107.

4. The Council of the Royal Pharmaceutical Society of Great Britain. Vitamin A substances. In: Reynolds JEF, ed. Martindale the Extra Pharmacopeia, 30th ed. London, UK: The Pharmaceutical Press, 1993; 1050-1052.

5. McDonald P, Edwards RA, Greenhalgh JFD, et al. Energy metabolism. In: Animal Nutrition, 5th ed. Harlow (Essex), UK: Longman Scientific & Technical, 1995; 179-180.

6. McDonald P, Edwards RA, Greenhalgh JFD, et al. Vitamins. In: Animal Nutrition, 5th ed. Harlow (Essex), UK: Longman Scientific & Technical, 1995; 66-96.

7. McDowell LR. Vitamin A IV—Analytical procedures. In: Vitamins in Animal Nutrition—Comparative Aspects to Human Nutrition. San Diego, CA: Academic Press Inc, 1989; 15.

8. McDowell LR. Vitamin D IV—Analytical procedures. In: Vitamins in Animal Nutrition—Comparative Aspects to Human Nutrition. San Diego, CA: Academic Press Inc, 1989; 59-60.

9. McDowell LR. Vitamin E III—Chemical structure and properties. In: Vitamins in Animal Nutrition—Comparative Aspects to Human Nutrition. San Diego, CA: Academic Press Inc, 1989; 94-96.

10. Rico AG, Braun JP, Benard P. Introduction du système international d'unités en chimie clinique. Le Point Véterinaire 1978; 6(30): 77-78.

11. Plumb DC. Appendix. In: Veterinary Drug Handbook. White Bear Lake, MN: PharmaVet Publishing, 1971; 651-676.

12. Ready Reference Guide. In: Fraser CM, ed. The Merck Veterinary Manual, 6th ed. Rahway, NJ: Merck & Co, Inc, 1986; 905-914.

13. Robinson J, ed. The Oxford Companion to Wine. Oxford, UK: Oxford University Press, 1994; 141.

14. Zak R. Measures. In: Basic Factors for Basic Science. New York, NY: Raven Press, 1990; 222-228.

Appendix B

Abbreviations

Table B1. General abbreviations.
Table B-2. Metric prefixes.
Table B-3. Abbreviations used to express allowances, requirements, food content or food intake.
Table B-4. Greek and Latin numerical prefixes.
Table B-5. Abbreviations used in prescription writing.
Bibliography

Table B-1. General abbreviations.*

°C	degrees Celsius (centigrade)	D-	dextrorotatory
°F	degrees Fahrenheit	DE	digestible energy
µosm	microosmol	DER	daily energy requirement
AAA	aromatic amino acid	DEXA	dual energy x-ray absorptiometry
ACB	anion-cation balance	DIT	diiodotyrosine
ACT	activated clotting time	DKA	diabetic ketoacidosis
ADF	acid detergent fiber	dl	deciliter
ADH	antidiuretic hormone	DM	dry matter
ADP	adenosine diphosphate	% DM	percent dry matter
AEE	acid ether extract	DMB	dry matter basis
AHA	acetohydroxamic acid	DNA	deoxyribonucleic acid
AIDS	acquired immunodeficiency syndrome	DW	dry weight
ALP	alkaline phosphatase	EAA	essential amino acid
ALT	alanine aminotransferase	EDTA	ethylenediaminetetraacetic acid
AMP	adenosine monophosphate	EE	ether extract
APR	activity product ratio	EFA	essential fatty acid
ARF	acute renal failure	e.g.	for example
AST	aspartate aminotransferase	ELISA	enzyme-linked immunosorbent assay
ATP	adenosine triphosphate	EPI	exocrine pancreatic insufficiency
BCAA	branched-chain amino acid	ERR	energy requirement of running
BCS	body condition score	E/T	total essential amino acid content
BEE	basal energy expenditure	FA	fatty acid
BER	basal energy requirement	FAD	flavin-adenine dinucleotide
BHA	butylated hydroxyanisole	$FADH_2$	reduced form of FAD
BHT	butylated hydroxytoluene	Fe	iron
BHV	bovine herpesvirus	FE	fecal energy
BMR	basal metabolic rate	FeLV	feline leukemia virus
BSA	body surface area	FFA	free fatty acid
BSP	Bromsulphalein	FIV	feline immunodeficiency virus
BUN	blood urea nitrogen	fl oz	fluid ounce
BV	biologic value (of protein); blood volume	FLUTD	feline lower urinary tract disease
BW	body weight	FOS	fructooligosaccharide
BW_{kg}	body weight in kilograms	Fp	flavoprotein
C	carbon, canine tooth	Fr	French
CaOx	calcium oxalate	fru	fructose
CBC	complete blood count	fT_3	free T_3
cc	cubic centimeter	fT_4	free T_4
CCK	cholecystokinin	G-6-P	glucose-6-phosphate
CEJ	cementoenamel junction	GABA	γ-aminobutyric acid
CF	crude fiber	gal	galactose
CFU	colony forming unit	GALT	gut-associated lymphoid tissue
CHO	carbohydrate	GD	gastric dilatation
CK	creatine kinase	GDV	gastric dilatation-volvulus
Cl	chlorine, chloride	GE	gross energy
CM	chylomicron	GEJ	gastroesophageal junction
cm	centimeter	GFR	glomerular filtration rate
CNS	central nervous system	GGT	γ-glutamyltransferase
Co	cobalt	GI	gastrointestinal
CO_2	carbon dioxide	glu	glucose
CO_3	carbonate	GMP	guanosine monophosphate
CP	crude protein	GPD	gaseous product of digestion
Cr	chromium	gr	grain
CRF	chronic renal failure	GRAS	generally recognized as safe
Cr-P	creatine phosphate	GTF	glucose tolerance factor
CS	chemical score	GTP	guanosine triphosphate
CSF	cerebrospinal fluid	H	hydrogen
CV	coefficient of variation	h	hour
d	day, distance		

(Continued on next page.)

Table B-1. General abbreviations.* (Continued from previous page.)

Hct	hematocrit	NH_3	ammonia
Hg	mercury	NH_4	ammonium
Hgb	hemoglobin	NPO	nothing per os
HI	heat increment of food	NPR	net protein ratio
H_2O	water	NPU	net protein utilization
HP	heat production	NSAID	nonsteroidal antiinflammatory drug
HPLC	high-performance liquid chromatography	O_2	oxygen
HSL	hormone-sensitive lipase	OTC	over the counter
I	iodine, incisor tooth	oz	ounce
IBD	inflammatory bowel disease	P	phosphorus, premolar tooth
IBS	irritable bowel syndrome	PCV	packed cell volume
IDDM	insulin-dependent diabetes mellitus	PER	protein efficiency ratio
i.e.	that is	Pi	inorganic orthophosphate
IgA	immunoglobulin A	pK	negative logarithm of ionization constant (K)
IgE	immunoglobulin E	PLE	protein losing enteropathy
IGF	insulin-like growth factor	PLN	protein losing nephropathy
IgG	immunoglobulin G	PLP	pyridoxal phosphate
IgM	immunoglobulin M	PMP	pyridoxamine phosphate
IFN	international feed name	PN	parenteral nutrition
IM	intramuscular(ly)	PO_4	phosphate
IP	intraperitoneal(ly)	ppb	parts per billion
IU	international unit	ppm	parts per million
IV	intravenous(ly)	PPi	inorganic pyrophosphate
K	potassium	PTH	parathyroid hormone
kcal	kilocalorie(s), Calorie(s)	PUFA	polyunsaturated fatty acid
kg	kilogram	q	every
kJ	kilojoule	RBC	red blood cell
L-	levorotatory	RBP	retinol binding protein
l	liter	RDA	recommended dietary/daily allowance
lb	pound	RE	retinol equivalent, retained energy
LCAT	lecithin cholesterol acyltransferase	REE	resting energy expenditure
LC-NEFA	long-chain NEFA	RER	resting energy requirement
LCT	long-chain triacylglyceride	RNA	ribonucleic acid
LDL	low-density lipoprotein	RNV	relative nutritive value
LES	lower esophageal sphincter	RPV	relative protein value
LPE	lipoprotein electrophoresis	RQ	respiratory quotient = $\dot{V}CO_2/\dot{V}O_2$
M	molar tooth	RSS	relative supersaturation
m	meter	RTA	renal tubular acidosis
m^2	meter squared	rT_4	reverse T_4
MAG	monoacylglyceride	S	sulfur
MAP	magnesium ammonium phosphate	SC or SQ	subcutaneous(ly)
max	maximum	SCFA	short-chain fatty acid
mcg or µg	microgram	SIBOG	small intestinal bacterial overgrowth
MCH	mean corpuscular hemoglobin	SNGFR	single nephron GFR
MCHC	mean corpuscular hemoglobin concentration	SO_4	sulfate
MCT	medium-chain triglyceride	spp	species
MCV	mean corpuscular volume	SSA	sulfosalicylic acid
ME	metabolizable energy	SUN	serum urea nitrogen
mEq/l	milliequivalent per liter	T_3	triiodotyrosine
MER	maintenance energy requirement	T_4	thyronine
mg	milligram	TAG	triacylglyceride
Mg	magnesium	TBHQ	tert-butyl-hydroquinone
min	minute, minimum	TLI	trypsin-like immunoreactivity
MIT	monoiodotyrosine	TCA	tricarboxylic acid
MJ	megajoule	TDN	total digestible nutrients
ml	milliliter	TEE	total energy expenditure
mm	millimeter	TG	triglyceride
mM	millimolar	TPP	thiamine pyrophosphate
mol wt	molecular weight	TNA	total nutrient admixture
mOsm	milliosmol	TNTC	too numerous to count
mosm/l	milliosmol per liter	TPN	total parenteral nutrition
MPG	mercaptopropionyl	TSH	thyroid-stimulating hormone
MTX	methotrexate	UDP	uridine diphosphate
N	nitrogen	UE	urine energy
Na	sodium	UPC	urine protein-creatinine ratio
NAD	nicotinamide-adenine dinucleotide	UTI	urinary tract infection
NADH	reduced form of NAD	UTP	uridine triphosphate
NDF	neutral detergent fiber	$\dot{V}CO_2$	rate of carbon dioxide production
NE	net energy	VFA	volatile fatty acid
NEFA	nonesterified fatty acid	VLDL	very low-density lipoprotein
NE_m	net energy for maintenance	$\dot{V}O_2$	rate of oxygen consumption
NE_p	net energy for production	WBC	white blood cell
NIDDM	non-insulin-dependent diabetes mellitus	wt	weight
NFE	nitrogen-free extract		

*Many of the words and terms in this table are defined in the Glossary. Words not found in the Glossary can be found in medical dictionaries.

APPENDIX B

Table B-2. Metric prefixes.

M	mega-	10^6	m	milli-	10^{-3}
k	kilo-	10^3	μ	micro-	10^{-6}
d	deci-	10^{-1}	n	nano-	10^{-9}
c	centi-	10^{-2}	p	pico-	10^{-12}

Table B-3. Abbreviations used to express allowances, requirements, food content or food intake.

% DM	% dry matter (% of nutrient present in the food after all water is removed, thus moisture = 0%)
mg/kg	milligrams per kilogram
IU/kg	international units per kilogram
mg/kg DM	milligrams per kilogram dry matter
IU/kg DM	international unit per kilogram dry matter
Unit/100 kcal ME	mg, g or IU per 100 kilocalories metabolizable energy
Unit/100 kcal DE	mg, g or IU per 100 kilocalories digestible energy
Unit/MJ ME	mg, g or IU per megajoule of metabolizable energy
Unit/MJ DE	mg, g or IU per megajoule of digestible energy
Percent calories	calories from a specific nutrient as % of total energy delivered by the food assuming the nutrient is completely used for energy (used for protein, fat and carbohydrate)
per BW$_{kg}$	per kg body weight
per kg$^{0.75}$	per kg metabolic weight

Table B-4. Greek and Latin numerical prefixes.

English	Greek	Latin	English	Greek	Latin
One	mono-	uni-	Nine	ennea-	novem-
Two	di-	bi-	Ten	deka-	decem-
Three	tri-	ter-	Eleven	endeka-	undecem-
Four	tetra-	quadri-	Twelve	dodeka-	duodecem-
Five	penta-	quinque-	Twenty	eicosa-	viginti-
Six	hexa-	sexa-	Hundred	hecto-	cent-
Seven	hepta-	septa-	Thousand	kilo-	milli-
Eight	octa-	octo-	Half	hemi-	semi-

Table B-5. Abbreviations used in prescription writing.

Abbreviations	Latin	English	Abbreviations	Latin	English
ā	ante	before	o.d.	omnie die	daily
aa.	ana	of each	PO	per os	by mouth
a.c.	ante cibum	before meals	OS	oculus sinister	left eye
AD	auris dextra	right ear	OU	oculus uterque	both eyes
ad lib	ad libitum	as desired	p.r.n.	pro re nata	according to circumstances
amp	ampula	ampule	pil	pilula	pill
aq.	aqua	water	pv.	pulvis	powder
AS	auris sinistra	left ear	p.	post	after
AU	aures unitas	both ears	p.c.	post cibum	after food
b.i.d.	bis in die	twice a day	q.	quaque	each, every
c.	cum	with	q. 3 h.	quaque 3 hora	every 3 hours, etc.
C.	congius	gallon	q.i.d.	quarter in die	4 times a day
cap.	capula	capsule	q.s.	quantum suffICit	as much as needed
disp	–	dispense	qq hor	quoque hora	each hour
div.	divide	divide	s	sine	without
dos.	dosis	dose	s.i.d.	semel in die	once a day
eq. pts.	equalis partes	equal parts	s.o.s.	si opus sit	if necessary
et	et	and	Sig. or S.	signa	write on the label, directions for use
ft.	fiat	make	sol.	solutio	solution
gtt(s)	gutta(e)	drop(s)	ss	semisse	half
h.	hora	hour	stat.	statim	immediately
h.s.	hora somni	at bedtime	susp	–	suspension
haust.	haustus	drench	t.i.d.	ter in die	3 times a day
M.	misce	mix	tab.	tabella	tablet
n.r.	non repetatur	not to be renewed	Tbs	–	tablespoon (15 ml)
no.	numero	number	tsp	–	teaspoon (5 ml)
O.	octarius	pint	Ut dict	ut dictum	as directed
OD	oculus dexter	right eye			

BIBLIOGRAPHY

1. Eckhoff GA. A guide to abbreviations used in writing prescriptions. Conference on Drug Usage by the Practitioner, Iowa State University, Ames. November 17-19, 1976. Veterinary Medicine/Small Animal Clinician 1977; 72: 535.

2. General considerations in nutrition. In: Mellentin RW, ed. Gaines Basic Guide to Canine Nutrition, 4th ed. White Plains, NY: General Foods Corp, 1977; 1-14.

3. Plumb DC. Appendix. In: Veterinary Drug Handbook. White Bear Lake, MN: PharmaVet Publishing, 1971; 651-676.

4. Abbreviations and symbols. In: Fraser CM, ed. The Merck Veterinary Manual, 6th ed. Rahway, NJ: Merck & Co, Inc, 1986; ix.

5. Zak R. Measures. In: Basic Factors for Basic Science. New York, NY: Raven Press, 1990; 222-228.

6. Zak R. The roots of science. In: Basic Factors for Basic Science. New York, NY: Raven Press, 1990; 1-9.

7. Anhang. In: Roche Lexikon Medizin, Hoffman-La Roche and Urban & Scwarzenberg, 1993; 1833-1837.

8. Beaton GH. Criteria of an adequate diet. In: Shils ME, Young VR, eds. Modern Nutrition in Health and Disease, 7th ed. Philadelphia, PA: Lea & Febiger, 1988; 649-665.

9. Food and Nutrition Board, USA. How should the recommended dietary allowances be revised? A concept paper from the Food and Nutrition Board. Nutrition Reviews 1994; 52: 216-219.

10. Harper AE. Dietary standards and dietary guidelines. In: Brown ML, ed. Present Knowledge in Nutrition, 6th ed. Washington, DC: International Life Science Institute Nutrition Fouindation, 1990; 491-501.

Appendix C
Food Energy Calculations

Table C-1. Calculation of gross energy.
Table C-2. Calculation of digestible energy.
Table C-3. Calculation of metabolizable energy.
Table C-4. Calculation of metabolizable energy (modified Atwater values).
Table C-5. Calculation of metabolizable energy of moist cat foods.
Bibliography

Table C-1. Calculation of gross energy.

		kcal					kJ	
Protein	x	5.65			Protein	x	23.64	
Fat	x	9.40			Fat	x	39.33	
NFE	x	4.15			NFE	x	17.36	
Crude fiber	x	4.15			Crude fiber	x	17.36	
kcal ME/100 g			Sum		kJ ME/100 g			Sum

Key: NFE = nitrogen-free extract, GE = gross energy.

Table C-2. Calculation of digestible energy.

		kcal						kJ		
Protein	x	% digestibility	x	5.65		Protein	x	% digestibility	x	23.64
Fat	x	% digestibility	x	9.40		Fat	x	% digestibility	x	39.33
NFE	x	% digestibility	x	4.15		NFE	x	% digestibility	x	17.36
kcal ME/100 g			Sum			kJ ME/100 g				Sum

Key: NFE = nitrogen-free extract, DE = digestible energy.

Table C-3. Calculation of metabolizable energy.

		kcal*						kJ*		
Protein	x	% digestibility	x	4.40		Protein	x	% digestibility	x	18.41
Fat	x	% digestibility	x	9.40		Fat	x	% digestibility	x	39.33
NFE	x	% digestibility	x	4.15		NFE	x	% digestibility	x	17.36
kcal ME/100 g			Sum			kJ ME/100 g				Sum

Key: nitrogen-free extract, ME = metabolizable energy.
*The difference between digestible and metabolizable energy involves the energy derived from protein. On average, an estimated 1.25 kcal/g (5.23 kJ/g) protein is lost in the urine as urea in dogs.

Table C-4. Calculation of metabolizable energy (modified Atwater values).

		kcal				MJ	
Protein	x	3.5		Protein	x	0.15	
Fat	x	8.5		Fat	x	0.36	
NFE	x	3.5		NFE	x	0.15	
kcal ME/100 g		Sum		MJ ME/kg		Sum	

Key: nitrogen-free extract, ME = metabolizable energy.

AAFCO publishes Table C-4 (kcal); Table C-4 (MJ) is derived from Table C-4 (kcal) using appropriate conversion factors. Table C-4 (kcal) is based on Table C-3 (kcal), using an average digestibility of 80% for protein, 90% for fat and 85% for NFE (carbohydrate). These tables list values of metabolizable energy (ME) that are reasonably accurate for foods of average digestibility. High-fiber foods may be less digestible; therefore, the real ME may be lower than the calculated ME. These tables may underestimate the energy density of highly digestible foods.

Although Table C-4 (kcal) was developed for dog foods, it is also used for cat foods, and is recognized as the official method to calculate ME for dog and cat foods in the United States. Table C-4 (MJ) has been adopted as the official method to calculate the energy density of dietetic foods for weight reduction and convalescence in dogs (all types of food) and cats (foods with moisture content of less than 14%), but is subject to change.

Table C-5. Calculation of metabolizable energy of moist cat foods.

kcal ME/100 g = % CP x 3.9 + % EE x 7.7 + % NFE x 3.0 − 5

MJ ME/kg = % CP x 0.1632 + % EE x 0.3222 + % NFE x 0.1255 − 0.2092

Key: CP = crude protein, EE = ether extract, NFE = nitrogen-free extract.

The metabolizable energy calculated using Table C-5 may be more accurate for moist cat foods than the method used in Table C-4. The second equation in Table C-5 has been adopted by the European Union as the official method to calculate the energy density of feline dietetic foods intended for weight reduction and convalescence with a moisture content of more than 14%, but is subject to change.

BIBLIOGRAPHY

1. Official Publication. Association of American Feed Control Officials, 1999.
2. Commission Directive 95/10/EC. Official Journal of The European Communities 22.4.1995, No. L91/39-40.
3. Kendall PT, Burger IH, Smith PM. Methods of estimation of the metabolizable energy content of cat foods. Feline Practice 1985; 15: 38-44.
4. National Research Council. Nutrient Requirements of Cats. Washington, DC: National Academy Press, 1986; 3, 43.
5. National Research Council. Nutrient Requirements of Dogs. Washington, DC: National Academy Press, 1985; 2.

Appendix D

Allometric and Zoometric Tables

I. Introduction
   Table D-1. Metabolic weight (BW$^{0.75}$) of dogs and cats.
   Table D-2. Metabolic rate for animals of different taxonomic groups.
II. Body surface area of cats and dogs
   Table D-3. Body surface area of cats.
   Table D-4. Body surface area of dogs.
III. Equations used to calculate energy requirements of adult cats and dogs
   Table D-5. Equations for calculating resting energy requirement of cats and dogs.
   Table D-6. Equations for calculating daily energy requirement for maintenance of adult dogs.
   Table D-7. Equations for calculating daily energy requirement using factors to account for breed variation, activity, physiologic state and illness.

Bibliography

I. Introduction

Metabolic functions, drug dosages and energy requirements do not always correlate linearly with body weight (BW), but are more closely related to BW raised to some power, such as metabolic weight or body surface area (BSA). This finding is particularly true for dogs, in which the adult BW varies from less than 2 kg to more than 70 kg. This Appendix includes tables that convert BW to BSA, and different equations for calculating energy requirements of dogs and cats.

Body weights of nonobese adult cats vary only two- to threefold. Exact allometric considerations used to adjust nutritional requirements are, therefore, not very important. Nevertheless, different equations exist, but the differences are more related to activity than to differences in body size and shape.

Table D-1. Metabolic weight (BW$^{0.75}$) of dogs and cats.*

Body weights		Metabolic weights	Body weights		Metabolic weights
kg	lb	BW$^{0.75}$	kg	lb	BW$^{0.75}$
1	2.2	1.000	41	90.2	16.203
2	4.4	1.682	42	92.4	16.498
3	6.6	2.280	43	94.6	16.792
4	8.8	2.828	44	96.8	17.084
5	11.0	3.344	45	99.0	17.374
6	13.2	3.834	46	101.2	17.663
7	15.4	4.304	47	103.4	17.950
8	17.6	4.757	48	105.6	18.236
9	19.8	5.196	49	107.8	18.520
10	22.0	5.623	50	110.0	18.803
11	24.2	6.040	51	112.2	19.084
12	26.4	6.447	52	114.4	19.364
13	28.6	6.846	53	116.6	19.643
14	30.8	7.238	54	118.8	19.920
15	33.0	7.622	55	121.0	20.196
16	35.2	8.000	56	123.2	20.471
17	37.4	8.372	57	125.4	20.745
18	39.6	8.739	58	127.6	21.017
19	41.8	9.100	59	129.8	21.288
20	44.0	9.457	60	132.0	21.558
21	46.2	9.810	61	134.2	21.827
22	48.4	10.158	62	136.4	22.095
23	50.6	10.503	63	138.6	22.362
24	52.8	10.843	64	140.8	22.627
25	55.0	11.180	65	143.0	22.892
26	57.2	11.514	66	145.2	23.156
27	59.4	11.845	67	147.4	23.418
28	61.6	12.172	68	149.6	23.680
29	63.8	12.497	69	151.8	23.941
30	66.0	12.819	70	154.0	24.200
31	68.2	13.138	71	156.2	24.459
32	70.4	13.454	72	158.4	24.717
33	72.6	13.768	73	160.6	24.974
34	74.8	14.080	74	162.8	25.230
35	77.0	14.390	75	165.0	25.486
36	79.2	14.697	76	167.2	25.740
37	81.4	15.002	77	169.4	25.994
38	83.6	15.305	78	171.6	26.246
39	85.8	15.606	79	173.8	26.498
40	88.0	15.905	80	176.0	26.750

*Metabolic weight (BW$^{0.75}$) can be calculated by cubing BW$_{kg}$ and then taking its square root twice.

Table D-2. Metabolic rate (RER) for animals of different taxonomic groups.*

kcal ME/24 hours			(Sub)classes or orders
129	x	$kg^{0.75}$	Passeriformes
78	x	$kg^{0.75}$	Other birds
70	x	$kg^{0.75}$	Placental mammals
48	x	$kg^{0.75}$	Marsupialia
10	x	$kg^{0.75}$	Reptiles at optimal temp. (37°C)

*Adapted from Dorrestein 1991 and 1993.

II. Body surface area of cats and dogs

Body surface area (BSA) is used by some investigators and clinicians to calculate energy needs, fluid requirements and some drug dosages. The formula used to calculate BSA is:

$$\frac{K_m \times BW^{0.67}}{100}$$

Where K_m for cats = 10.4 and K_m for dogs = 10.1. Body weight (BW) is measured in kg. BSA is expressed in m^2.

Table D-3. Body surface area (BSA) of cats.

Body weights		BSA
kg	lb	m^2
1	2.2	0.10
2	4.4	0.17
3	6.6	0.22
4	8.8	0.26
5	11.0	0.30
6	13.2	0.34
7	15.4	0.38

Table D-4. Body surface area (BSA) of dogs.

Body weights		BSA	Body weights		BSA
kg	lb	m^2	kg	lb	m^2
1	2.2	0.10	36	79.2	1.10
2	4.4	0.16	37	81.4	1.12
3	6.6	0.21	38	83.6	1.14
4	8.8	0.25	39	85.8	1.16
5	11.0	0.30	40	88.0	1.18
6	13.2	0.33	41	90.2	1.20
7	15.4	0.37	42	92.4	1.22
8	17.6	0.40	43	94.6	1.24
9	19.8	0.44	44	96.8	1.26
10	22.0	0.47	45	99.0	1.28
11	24.2	0.50	46	101.2	1.30
12	26.4	0.53	47	103.4	1.32
13	28.6	0.56	48	105.6	1.33
14	30.8	0.59	49	107.8	1.35
15	33.0	0.61	50	110.0	1.37
16	35.2	0.64	51	112.2	1.39
17	37.4	0.67	52	114.4	1.41
18	39.6	0.69	53	116.6	1.43
19	41.8	0.72	54	118.8	1.44
20	44.0	0.74	55	121.0	1.46
21	46.2	0.77	56	123.2	1.48
22	48.4	0.79	57	125.4	1.50
23	50.6	0.82	58	127.6	1.51
24	52.8	0.84	59	129.8	1.53
25	55.0	0.86	60	132.0	1.55
26	57.2	0.89	61	134.2	1.57
27	59.4	0.91	62	136.4	1.58
28	61.6	0.93	63	138.6	1.60
29	63.8	0.95	64	140.8	1.62
30	66.0	0.98	65	143.0	1.63
31	68.2	1.00	66	145.2	1.65
32	70.4	1.02	67	147.4	1.67
33	72.6	1.04	68	149.6	1.68
34	74.8	1.06	69	151.8	1.70
35	77.0	1.08	70	154.0	1.72

III. Equations used to calculate energy requirements of adult cats and dogs

Several equations have been proposed over the years to calculate the resting energy requirement (RER) and the daily energy requirement (DER) of cats and dogs. Most often RER and DER are calculated as a function of metabolic weight ($BW_{kg}^{0.75}$). The accu-

racy of these equations has occasionally been questioned, and several alternative equations have been proposed. Tables D-5 and D-6 compare several of the different equations. It is unrealistic to expect that any equation will precisely calculate the specific energy requirements for all cats or dogs. The equation based on $BW_{kg}^{0.75}$ is widely accepted and easy to use.

Table D-5. Equations for calculating resting energy requirement of cats and dogs.

BW	$70 \times BW^{0.75}$* kcal ME	$0.293 \times BW^{0.75}$ MJ ME	$70 + 30 \times BW$** kcal ME	$0.29 + 0.126 \times BW$ MJ ME
5	234	0.98	220	0.92
10	394	1.65	370	1.55
20	662	2.77	670	2.80
30	897	3.75	970	4.06
40	1,113	4.66	1,270	5.31
60	1,509	6.31	1,870	7.82

Key: BW = body weight in kilograms, ME = metabolizable energy.
*Adapted from Kleiber 1961.
**Adapted from NRC 1985.

Table D-6. Equations for calculating daily energy requirement for maintenance of adult dogs.

				kcal ME				
BW	1.6 x RER $112 \times BW^{0.75}$*	$140 + 60 \times BW$**	$132 \times BW^{0.75}$***	$100 \times BW^{0.88}$†	$162 \times BW^{0.64}$††	$1,500 \times BSA$†††	$98 \times BW^{0.75}$‡	$121 \times BW^{0.75}$‡‡
5	374	440	441	412	454	443	328	405
10	630	740	742	759	707	704	551	680
20	1,059	1,340	1,248	1,396	1,102	1,117	927	1,144
30	1,436	1,940	1,692	1,995	1,428	1,464	1,256	1,551
40	1,781	2,540	2,100	2,569	1,717	1,774	1,559	1,925
60	2,415	3,740	2,846	3,671	2,226	2,325	2,113	2,609

				MJ ME				
BW	1.6 x RER $0.47 \times BW^{0.75}$*	$0.59 + 0.25 \times BW$**	$0.552 \times BW^{0.75}$***	$0.418 \times BW^{0.88}$†	$0.678 \times BW^{0.64}$††	$6.28 \times BSA$†††	$0.41 \times BW^{0.75}$‡	$0.506 \times BW^{0.75}$‡‡
5	1.57	1.84	1.85	1.72	1.90	1.85	1.37	1.69
10	2.64	3.10	3.11	3.17	2.96	2.94	2.31	2.84
20	4.43	5.61	5.22	5.84	4.61	4.68	3.88	4.78
30	6.01	8.12	7.08	8.35	5.98	6.13	5.26	6.47
40	7.45	10.63	8.78	10.75	7.18	7.42	6.52	8.03
60	10.10	15.65	11.91	15.36	9.31	9.73	8.84	10.89

Key: ME = metabolizable energy, BW = body weight in kilograms, BSA = body surface area, MJ = megajoules, RER = resting energy requirement.
*See Chapters 1 and 2.
**Adapted from NRC 1985.
***Adapted from NRC 1974.
†Adapted from NRC 1985.
††Adapted from Burger and Johnson 1991.
†††Adapted from Hill 1993.
‡Adapted from Männer 1991.
‡‡Adapted from Kienzle and Rainbird 1991 (DE was converted to ME).

Table D-7. Equations for calculating daily energy requirement (DER) using factors to account for breed variation, activity, physiologic state and illness.*

kcal ME/day = (156 x BW$^{0.667}$) x k_1 x k_2 x k_3 x k_4 or MJ ME/day = (0.653 x BW$^{0.667}$) x k_1 x k_2 x k_3 x k_4

Body weights		DER	
kg	lb	156 x BW$^{0.667}$	0.653 x BW$^{0.667}$
5	11	456	1.91
10	22	725	3.03
20	44	1,151	4.81
30	66	1,508	6.31
40	88	1,827	7.64
60	132	2,394	10.02

Breed	k_1	Activity	k_2	Physiologic state	k_3	Illness, stress	k_4
Husky	0.8	Sedentary	0.8	Old	0.9	Forced	0.6-0.8
Beagle	0.9	Neutered	0.8	Postweaning	2.0	immobilzation	
Great Dane	1.1	Nervous	1.2	Last 1/3 of	1.5	Basic surgery	1.2
		Hyperactive	1.2	pregnancy		Sepsis	1.2-1.5
				Peak lactation	3.0-3.5	Severe trauma	1.2-2.0

Key: ME = metabolizable energy, BW = body weight in kilograms, k_1 = breed-specific variation, k_2 = activity, k_3 = physiologic state, or lifestage, k_4 = illness and stress.
*Paragon B-M. Personal communication. November 1996.

BIBLIOGRAPHY

1. Burger IH, Johnson JV. Dogs large and small: The allometry of energy requirements within a single species. Journal of Nutrition 1991; 121: S18-S21.

2. Burger IH. Energy needs of companion animals: Matching food intakes to requirements throughout the life cycle. Journal of Nutrition 1994; 124: 2584S-2593S.

3. Dorrestein GM. Problemen bij en aanbevelingen voor de behandeling van bijzondere gezelschapsdieren. Tijdschrift voor Diergeneeskunde 1993; 118: 4-7.

4. Dorrestein GM. The pharmacokinetics of avian therapeutics. Veterinary Clinics of North America: Small Animal Practice 1991; 21: 1241-1264.

5. Henness AM, Theilen GH, Madewell BR, et al. Use of drugs based on square meters of body surface area. Journal of the American Veterinary Medical Association 1977; 171: 1076-1077.

6. Hill RC. A rapid method of estimating maintenance energy requirement from body surface area in inactive adult dogs and cats. Journal of the American Veterinary Medical Association 1993; 202: 1814-1816.

7. Kienzle E, Rainbird A. Maintenance energy requirement of dogs: What is the correct value for the calculation of metabolic body weight in dogs? Journal of Nutrition 1991; 121: S39-S40.

8. Kirkwood JK. The influence of size on the biology of the dog. Journal of Small Animal Practice 1985; 26: 97-110.

9. Kittleson MD, Knowlen GG. Positive inotropic drugs in heart failure. In: Kirk RW, ed. Current Veterinary Therapy IX. Philadelphia, PA: WB Saunders Co, 1986; 323-328.

10. Kleiber M. Body size and metabolic rate. In: The Fire of Life. John Wiley & Sons, 1961; 212.

11. Lewis LD, Morris ML Jr, Hand MS. Nutrients. In: Small Animal Clinical Nutrition III. Topeka, KS: Mark Morris Associates, 1987; 1-1—1-25.

12. Männer K. Energy requirement for maintenance of adult dogs. Journal of Nutrition 1991; 121: S37-S38.

13. National Research Council. Nutrient Requirements of Dogs. Washington, DC: National Academy Press, 1985; 2-38.

14. National Research Council. Tables. Nutrient Requirements of Dogs. Washington, DC: National Academy Press, 1985; 44-45.

15. Paragon B-M. Personal communication. November 1996.

16. Rainbird AL, Kienzle E. Untersuchungen zum Energiebedarf des Hundes in Abhängigkeit von Rassezugehörigkeit und Alter. Kleintierpraxis 1989; 35: 149-158.

17. Rivers JPW, Burger IH, eds. Allometric considerations in the nutrition of dogs. In: Nutrition of the Dog and Cat. Cambridge, UK: Cambridge University Press, 1989; 67-112.

18. Rosenthal RC. Chemotherapy. In: Ettinger SJ, Feldman EC, eds. Textbook of Veterinary Internal Medicine, 4th ed. Philadelphia, PA: WB Saunders Co, 1995; 473-484.

Appendix E

Data for Neonatal, Pediatric and Orphaned Puppy and Kitten Care

I.   Data for neonatal and pediatric care
II. Orphaned puppy and kitten care
Bibliography

I. Data for neonatal and pediatric care

Table E-1. Litter sizes and birth weights of selected canine breeds.*

Breeds**	Average litter sizes	Birth weights (g)
Airedale terrier	9	300
Appenzell mountain dog	10	465
Australian silky terrier	3	—
Bernese mountain dog	5	445
Borzoi	9	450
Boxer	8	440
Cavalier King Charles spaniel	4	230
Chihuahua	2-3	140
Chow chow	6	460
Dachshund	4	215
Dalmatian	5-6	—
Doberman pinscher	7	410
English bulldog	7	295
English cocker spaniel	6	230
English springer spaniel	11	375
Fox terrier	3	260
French bulldog	5	215
German shorthaired pointer	7-8	415
German shepherd	6	445
Great Pyrenees	≥5	705
Hovawart	11	435
Irish terrier	6	270
Labrador retriever	5	450
Maltese	3	155
Miniature dachshund	3	210
Miniature pinscher	3	—
Miniature poodle	2-3	165
Miniature schnauzer	4	155
Newfoundland	7	595
Norwich terrier	5	225
Papillon	3	120
Pekingese	2-3	—
Pomeranian	2	—
Pug	3	—
Rottweiler	7	—
Saint Bernard	7	640
Scottish terrier	5	240
Shetland sheepdog	4-5	260
Shih Tzu	2-3	—
Sloughi	3	670
Standard schnauzer	6	285
Yorkshire terrier	5	95

*Because of the very large variation in adult body weight of dogs and number of puppies per litter, there is no direct relationship between birth weight and the body weight of the mother. Puppies from the largest breeds weigh approximately 1% of the bitch's weight, whereas a Chihuahua puppy averages 6.4% of its mother's body weight. Adapted from References 6, 16 and 26.
**Breeds listed here are those for which data were available.

Table E-2. Normal physiologic values for neonatal puppies and data for neonatal care.

Birth weight	Individual Total litter BW at 8-10 days of age	1-6.5% of mother's weight 12-14% of mother's weight 2x birth weight	
Daily weight gain	Week 1 Weeks 2-4 Weeks 5-10 >10 weeks	8% (5-10%) 5% (3.5-6%) 2 g/kg adult BW 2-4 g/kg adult BW	
Body temperature		°C	°F
	24 hr after birth Weeks 1-2 Weeks 2-4 >4 weeks	35.5 ± 0.8 34.5-37.2 36.0-37.8 37.8-38.3	96 ± 1.4 94-99 97-100 97-101
Heart rate	Weeks 1-2 Weeks 3-4 Weeks 5-6 Week 7 Weeks 8-12	230-240 beats/min 210-220 beats/min 195 beats/min 185 beats/min 165-175 beats/min	
Respiratory rate	At birth	15-35/min	
Shivering reflex develops	—	6-8 days	
Eyes	Eyes open Visual following of moving objects Recognition of owner and mother	10-14 days 3-4 weeks 4-5 weeks	
Ears	Open Reaction to auditory stimuli	12-17 days 3-4 weeks	
Locomotion	Stepping movements with forelimbs Stepping movements with pelvic limbs Ability to stand Steady gait Walking and running	5-6 days 7-10 days 10 days 3 weeks 4 weeks	
Micturition and defecation	Voluntary control	16-21 days	
Activated sleep	Muscle tic disappears	4 weeks	
Descent of testicles	—	18-45 days	
Urine specific gravity	—	1.006-1.007	
Optimal environmental temperature			
Pup's immediate environment or incubator for orphans			
		°C	°F
	Week 1 Week 2 Week 3 Weeks 4-12	29-32 26-29 23-26 23	84-90 79-84 73.4-79 73.4
Measured in the environment around the litter			
	Week 1	24-27	75-81
Daily energy requirement (orphans)		kcal/kg BW	kJ/kg BW
	Week 1 Week 2 Week 3 Week 4	13-15 15-20 20 ≥20	55-60 65-85 85 ≥85
Water requirement	—	180 (130-220) ml/BW$_{kg}$/day	
Eating solid food	—	4-5 weeks	
Teeth eruption			
	Deciduous teeth	Incisors Canines Premolars	3-4 weeks 3 weeks 4-12 weeks
	Permanent teeth Canines Premolars Molars	Incisors 4-6 months 4-6 months 5-7 months	3-5 months
Body water	At birth	80%	
Fat reserves	At birth At 2 weeks At 1 month Nonobese adult dogs	1-2% 10% 17% 22-23%	

Table E-3. Normal physiologic values for neonatal kittens and data for neonatal care.

Litter size	—	Average: 3-5 (1-7) kittens
Body weight	Birth weight Weeks 1-2 Weeks 3-4	90-120 g Double Triple
Daily weight gain	Weeks 1-4	Average: 10-13 g/day
Body temperature	24 hr after birth End of Week 1	33.3-35.5°C (92-96°F) 36.6°C (98°F)
Heart rate	Weeks 0-4	>220 beats/min
Respiration rate	Weeks 1-2	15-35 breaths/min
Shivering reflex develops	—	Week 1
Eyes	Eyelids open Pupillary light response	8 (5-14) days 24 hr after eyelids separate
Ears	Reaction to auditory stimuli External ear canals open Development of functional hearing	3 days 6-14 days (completely open by 17 days) 21 days
Locomotion	Forelimbs start to support weight Ability to stand Sitting Walking unsteadily Start climbing	3-4 (1-10) days 10 (5-25) days 20 days 21-22 days 31 (22-40) days
Micturition and defecation	Voluntary control	3 weeks

Optimal environmental temperature
Kitten's immediate environment or incubator for orphans

		°C	°F
	Week 1	32-34	89.5-93
	Week 2	27-29	81-84
	Week 3	24-27	75-81
	Weeks 4-12	24	75

Measured in the environment around the litter

		°C	°F
	Week 1	24-27	75-81

Energy requirements	At birth At 4 weeks	380 kcal/kg 250 kcal/kg
Eating solid food	—	28-50 days
Teeth eruption Deciduous teeth	Incisors Canines Premolars	2-3 weeks 3-4 weeks 3-6 weeks
Permanent teeth	Incisors Canines Premolars Molars	3-4 months 4-5 months 4-6 months 4-5 months

II. Orphaned puppy and kitten care

Puppies and kittens may be considered orphaned if they lack sufficient maternal care for survival from birth to weaning. Several physiologic needs normally provided by the mother must be met to ensure survival of neonates: heat, humidity, nutrition, immunity, elimination, sanitation, security and social stimulation. In orphaned puppies and kittens, these needs must be met by a foster bitch, foster queen or the caregiver. Most orphans can be raised successfully with proper care and nutrition.

Physical Environment

Puppies and kittens should be housed in warm draft-free enclosures. Incubators are ideal, particularly for newborns. Pet carriers, shoe boxes or cardboard boxes are suitable substitutes. The bedding should be soft, absorbent and warm. Thread-free cloth, fleece and shavings are appropriate and help puppies and kittens feel secure as they snuggle into them.

Neonates demonstrate a certain degree of poikilothermy and are unable to regulate body temperatures well during the first four weeks of life. Puppies and kittens huddle together close to their mother, which generates an optimal microclimate, protects them against changes in environmental temperature and decreases the rate of heat loss. Orphans cannot seek protection near their mother and are more sensitive to suboptimal environmental conditions.

Without the mother, neonates can quickly become hypothermic, which leads to circulatory failure and death. Artificial heat should provide age-optimal environmental temperatures (Tables E-2 and E-3). It is best to set the heating source to establish a gradation of heat in the nest box. A gradation of environmental temperatures allows neonates to move toward or away from the heat source as needed to avoid hyperthermia, which can be as detrimental as hypothermia. Puppies and kittens can rapidly become dehydrated secondary to overheating. Maintaining humidity near 50% helps reduce water loss and maintains the moisture and health of mucous membranes.

Social Environment

To fulfill non-nutritional nursing needs, hand-reared puppies and kittens often nurse other littermates in the nest box. To avoid skin trauma related to excessive nursing, puppies and kittens can be housed individually or separated by dividers. Although beneficial for alleviating problems due to non-nutritive nursing, separation of the litter reduces temperature and humidity in the immediate environment and social stimulation by littermates. Social stimulation can be provided by brief but regular handling. The stress associated with regular handling increases neural development and improves weight gain in kittens. Kittens raised without social stimulation develop abnormal behavior patterns (i.e., kittens reduce normal exploratory behavior and become more suspicious and aggressive as adults). Similar changes may occur in puppies. Peer contact can compensate for maternal deprivation. Therefore, benefits of separating neonates must be weighed against the potential for development of abnormal behavior and increased risk for hypothermia. Puppies and kittens should interact with littermates as much as possible until weaning.

General Husbandry

Puppies and kittens obtain passive systemic immunity from colostrum and passive local immunity from continued ingestion of bitch's/queen's milk. If possible, neonates should receive colostrum or bitch's/queen's milk within the first 12 to 16 hours of birth. This is particularly critical for puppies and kittens fed only milk replacers because they lack systemic and local immune protection.

Normally the umbilical cord will be severed by the mother. If not, it should be cut to 1.5 in. (3.5 to 4 cm) and an appropriate topical antiseptic applied. Orphaned puppies and kittens are at greater risk for infectious disease; thus, sanitary husbandry practices are important. To reduce risk for diseases, puppies and kittens should not be exposed to older animals or grouped within multiple litters. Feeding equipment and bedding should be kept clean and sanitized. Caretakers should wash their hands before handling neonates and after stimulating elimination.

Puppies and kittens cannot voluntarily urinate or defecate until about three weeks of age. Until that time they rely on the mother to stimulate the urogenital reflex to initiate elimination. Caretakers should stimulate puppies and kittens after feeding by gently swabbing the perineal region with a warm moistened cotton ball or cloth (Figure E-1).

Often puppies or kittens within a litter look similar; therefore, it may be difficult to tell them apart when hand rearing, especially in large litters. Different colored nail polish can be painted on the claws to help differentiate individuals; paint a different paw for each separate animal (e.g., blue front left paw, blue right rear paw, pink right front paw, etc.).

Assessment

Orphaned puppies and kittens should be thoroughly evaluated when first seen. A careful physical examination of the neonate(s) and mother, if available, should

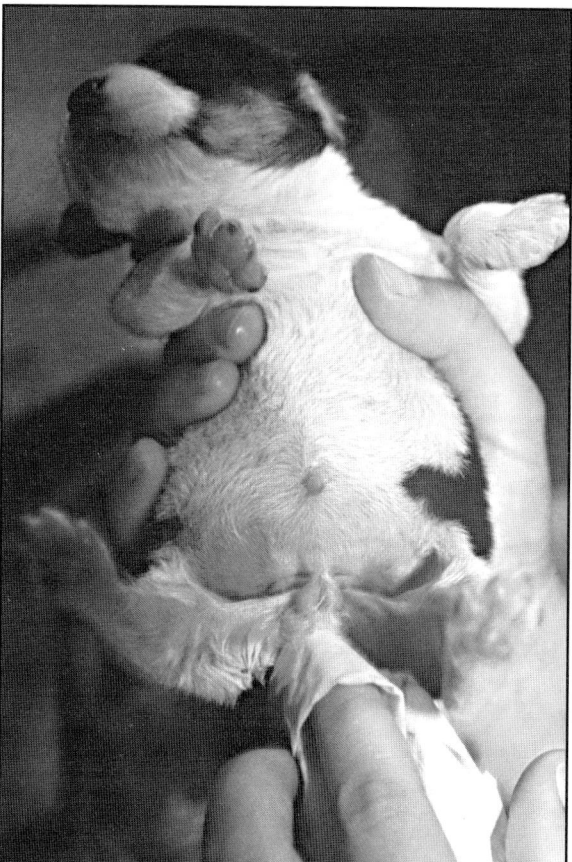

Figure E-1. After each meal, the abdomen and anogenital region of puppies and kittens should be swabbed with warm, moistened cotton or gauze to mimic licking by the mother. This will stimulate urination and defecation.

be performed to detect the potential cause for abandonment. Particular attention should be given to detect common problems such as hypothermia, hypoglycemia, dehydration and congenital defects. The current nutritional and hydration status should also be noted. Puppies or kittens fostered onto another mother should be supervised initially to detect any behavioral problems between the foster parent, its young and the orphan(s). The puppies or kittens should be immediately accepted and allowed to nurse. Watch for signs of rejection or impending cannibalism by the mother.

Key Nutritional Factors
Energy

Table E-4 summarizes the estimated energy requirements of neonatal puppies and kittens. A very common mistake is to underestimate the energy requirements of neonates. But in the beginning, it is better not to overfeed to avoid diarrhea. In most cases, it is best to follow label recommendations on commercial products or feed based on caloric calculations.

Table E-4. Recommendations for energy intake of orphaned kittens and puppies.*

Ages	kcal ME/100 g BW	kJ ME/100 g BW
Week 1	13-15	55-60
Week 2	15-20	65-85
Week 3	20	85
Week 4	≥20	≥85

*Adapted from Mundt et al 1981, Schaeffers-Ockens 1993, Sheffy 1978, Baines 1981, Hoskins 1990, Monson 1987.

Energy requirements of newborn puppies and kittens are about 24 kcal (100 kJ) metabolizable energy (ME)/100 g BW. (See Table E-2 for specific energy requirements based on age.) In general, kittens less than one week old will eat a volume equal to 10 to 15% of their body weight as milk or milk replacer and a volume equal to 20 to 25% of their body weight between Weeks 1 to 4. This is a reasonable target if the caloric content of the food is unknown.

Water

Water is one of the most important nutrients in orphan feeding. A normal puppy needs about 60 to 100 ml of fluid per pound body weight per day (130 to 220 ml/kg body weight). On average, orphaned puppies (and probably kittens) should receive about 180 ml/kg body weight to make orphan feeding successful. Water should be given until 180 ml/kg body weight is reached if the milk replacer doesn't provide this much water at the recommended dilution.

Digestibility

Dry matter digestibility of milk for bitches and queens is very high (>95%). Digestibility of milk replacer formulas should be high (>90%) to allow for smaller quantities to be fed and avoid diarrhea.

Other Nutritional Factors

The preferred nutrient profile of milk, commercial milk replacers and homemade replacer formulas for nursing puppies and kittens should be similar to that of milk from bitches and queens. (See Appendix K.) Values recommended by the Association of American Feed Control Officials (AAFCO) for growth should be followed when the concentration of nutrients in maternal milk is unknown. (See Appendix J.)

It is essential that commercial milk replacers and homemade replacer formulas have adequate protein and essential amino acid content. The arginine and histidine levels in the formula are particularly important. Deficiency of these amino acids can cause cataract development in neonates and contribute to anorexia and poor growth.

Milk replacers are often fortified with iron at concentrations higher than those found in bitch's or queen's milk. Orphaned puppies and kittens, especially low birth-weight neonates born with low iron reserves, may benefit from iron intakes higher than those normally found in milk. The additional iron supports hematopoiesis and helps avoid anemia sometimes observed in three- to four-week-old neonates.

High osmolality should be avoided because it may cause hyperosmolar diarrhea and potentiate dehydration. High osmolarity may delay gastric emptying and predispose to regurgitation, vomiting and aspiration during the next meal, if the stomach is not completely empty. The osmolality of bitch's and queen's milk is approximately 569 mOsm/kg and 329 mOsm/kg, respectively.

Food Form

Foods should be liquid until puppies and kittens are three to four weeks of age when semi-solid to solid foods may be introduced.

Feeding Plan

Success of orphan rearing depends on how well the caregiver fulfills the daily routine of hygienic measures, strict feeding schedules and all the aspects of care normally done by the bitch or queen. These measures are vital for the survival of puppies and kittens early in life.

Hygiene

Hygienic measures must be more stringent for orphaned puppies and kittens because they may have received less colostrum and be more susceptible to infections than other neonates.
- Feeding materials (e.g., bottles and nipples) should be cleaned thoroughly and boiled in water between uses.
- Ingredients for homemade milk replacers should be fresh and refrigerated until used.
- Never prepare more milk replacer than can be used in 24 hours and refrigerate.
- Formulas should be discarded after one hour at room temperature.
- At least twice a week, orphans should be washed gently with a soft moistened cloth to simulate cleaning by the dam's tongue.

Select a Milk or Milk Replacer

Foods used to feed orphans may consist of bitch's/queen's milk, commercial milk replacer or homemade replacer formulas. Bitch's/queen's milk is the food of choice and will provide nutrients in the proper levels for nursing puppies and kittens. Rarely is bitch's or queen's milk available in sufficient quantities to hand raise orphans. Commercial milk replacers are generally preferred although several homemade formulas have proved sufficient. (See Appendix K.) In one study, kittens fed either a commercial or homemade milk replacer had higher weight gains than kittens fed by the queen.

Commercial and homemade milk replacers should closely mimic the profile of bitch's or queen's milk. Unsupplemented ruminant milk may be used as a base for homemade formulas but does not meet the nutritional needs of puppies or kittens. There is also no nutritional benefit to using goat's milk over cow's milk. Appendix K compares the nutrient profile of bitch's and queen's milk with that of cow's milk, various milk replacers, homemade replacer formulas and milk from other species.

Determine a Feeding Method
Fostering

The optimal means of feeding orphaned or rejected puppies or kittens is to foster them to another lactating bitch or queen. Fostering is the least labor intensive, provides optimal nutrition, reduces mortality, improves immune status, usually provides an optimal physical environment and promotes normal social development of the puppy or kitten. Unlike large animals, bitches and queens readily accept additional puppies and kittens during lactation. If several foster mothers are available, it is best to place orphans in litters with fewer than 14 days age difference. Larger puppies and kittens often crowd out smaller individuals if the age discrepancy is too large. This situation can be managed by supervised feeding until the orphans can fend for themselves. Unfortunately, foster mothers are not normally available and alternative techniques must be used.

Partial Orphan Rearing

Puppies and kittens that cannot be successfully raised by the bitch or queen for reasons of health, poor lactation performance or too large of a litter, may be left with the mother but given supplemental feeding to support nutritional needs. Supplemental food may be given by hand feedings, timed feedings using a surrogate bitch/queen or puppies/kittens reared in a communal situation. Partial orphan rearing can be done by splitting the litter into two groups of equal number and size. One group is allowed to stay with the mother while the other is taken away and fed milk replacer. The groups are exchanged three to four times daily. It is important to feed the group that is separated from the mother before it is returned to the mother. As a result, the group just placed with the dam will be less inclined to nurse immediately. It is better to supplement all the puppies or kittens in the litter rather than just a few. The advantages of partial orphan rearing are similar to those of fostering. In addition, continued access to the mother can help stimulate milk production and mothering behaviors. Like foster mothers, surrogate mothers are rarely available. Further, rejection and cannibalism must be closely monitored. Partial orphan rearing may also be necessary to assist the efforts of foster mothers.

Hand Feeding

The most common method of raising orphaned puppies and kittens is hand feeding. Orphans are typically fed by eye dropper, syringe, bottles or stomach tubes.

Bottle Feeding. Bottle feeding is the preferred method for vigorous puppies and kittens with good sucking reflexes (Figures E-2 and E-3). Bottle feeding has the advantage that neonates will suck until they are satiated and reject the milk or formula when full. However, bottle feeding can be time consuming, especially with large litters.

Most puppies and kittens will readily suck small pet nursers available in pet stores (Figure E-4). Feeding bottles for dolls or bottles with nipples for premature human infants are alternatives. The nipple opening should only allow one drop at a time to fall from the nipple when the bottle is inverted. A horizontal slit made with a razor blade instead of a round hole may make it easier for neonates to obtain milk or formula. Milk should be sucked—never squeezed—from the bottle. Too rapid flow may lead to aspiration of milk and pneumonia and/or death.

Puppies and kittens should normally be held in a horizontal position with the head in a natural position (Figure E-2). This posture reduces the risk of aspiration. Although some puppies may prefer a different position during feeding (Figure E-3), careful observation is necessary because the risk of aspiration is increased.

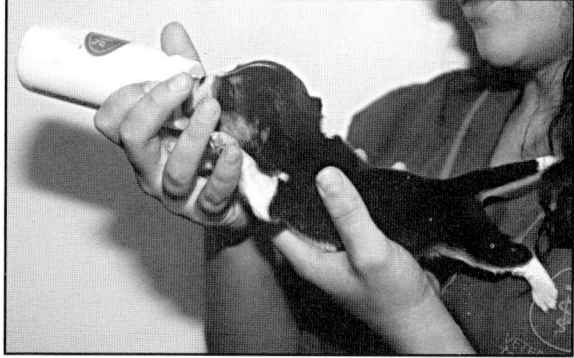

Figure E-2. This is the preferred position for bottle feeding kittens and puppies. This position mimics the normal nursing position and decreases the likelihood of aspiration.

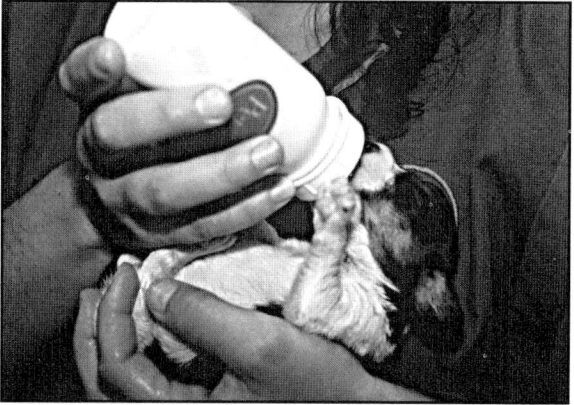

Figure E-3. Some neonates prefer different positions for bottle feeding. This puppy prefers nursing in dorsal recumbency. Close observation is required because this position may predispose to aspiration.

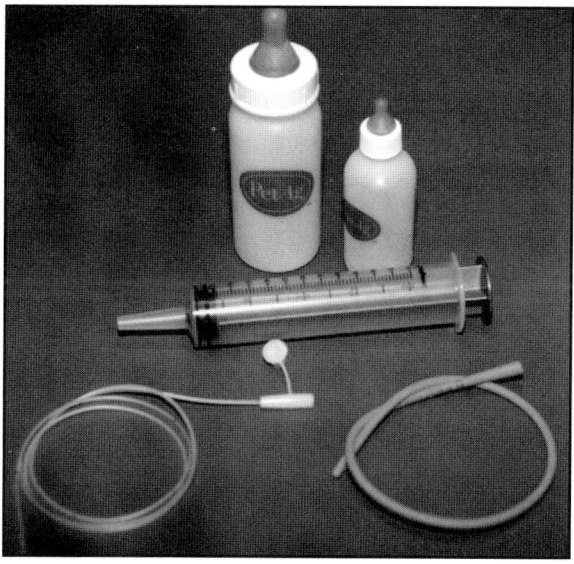

Figure E-4. Various bottles and feeding tubes can be used for hand feeding orphaned puppies and kittens. Examples of commercial pet nursing bottles and feeding tubes are shown here.

Tube Feeding. Puppies and kittens that are weak or suckle poorly may need to be tube fed. Tube feeding is quicker than bottle feeding and is often used when several orphans must be cared for by the same person(s). Bottle feeding allows puppies and kittens to control the amount of food intake, whereas tube

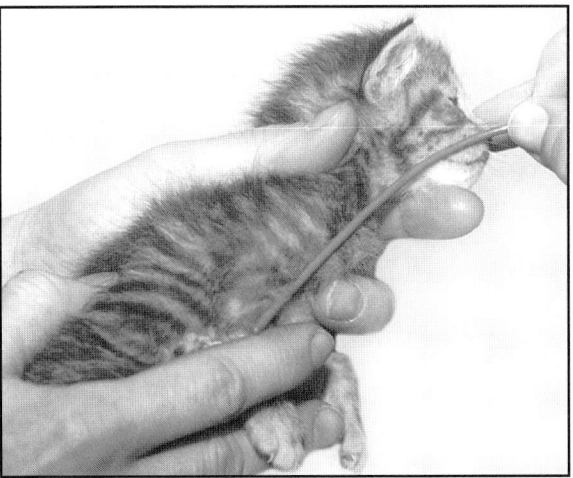

Figure E-5. Feeding tubes should be premeasured and marked at a spot approximately 75% of the distance from the nose to the last rib. This placement will ensure the tube tip is in the distal esophagus.

Figure E-6. Puppies and kittens should be held horizontally in the palm of the hand for tube feeding.

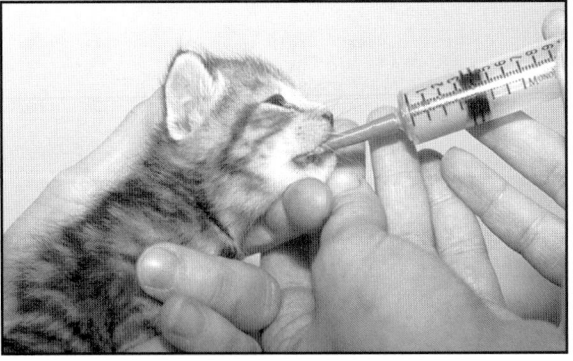

Figure E-7. A lubricated tube is gently advanced to the premeasured mark and warm formula is administered over several minutes. The tube should be withdrawn and repositioned if resistance or struggling is encountered.

feeding bypasses this control mechanism. Infant feeding tubes (5 to 8 Fr.) or soft urethral or intravenous catheters may be used (Figure E-4).

The tube should be lubricated and placed in the lower esophagus, which is approximately 75% of the distance from the nose to the last rib (Figure E-5). It is best to measure and mark the tube with an indelible marker or a piece of tape before insertion. Recheck measurements every few days to account for the rapidly changing size of the puppy or kitten. The orphan should normally be placed in a horizontal position with the head in a natural position (Figure E-6).

The mouth can be opened using the same hand that steadies the head. Gently advance the tube to the premeasured mark. If resistance is encountered or the animal suddenly struggles, the tube may be in the trachea. It should be removed and repositioned into the esophagus. Do not feed until proper placement is assured. After the tube is placed, attach the feeding syringe and slowly administer the warmed formula (over about one to two minutes) (Figure E-7). The stomach may be palpated to determine the degree of distention. Administration should be stopped if the stomach becomes taut or resists formula flow. Continuation of feeding may result in overdistention and regurgitation. If regurgitation occurs, withdraw the tube and discontinue feeding until the next meal.

Feeding Schedule. Orphans should be fed a minimum of four times daily, although feeding every two to four hours is preferred for very young neonates and weak individuals and every four to six hours for older puppies and kittens. In normal circumstances, one- to two-week-old puppies and kittens will usually obtain more than 90% of their normal daily intake in four to five meals. Milk replacer should be warmed to 38°C (100°F) and delivered slowly.

Cold foods, rapid feeding rate or overfeeding may result in regurgitation, aspiration, bloating and diarrhea. Review and correct the feeding methods if untoward signs develop. If diarrhea is observed, food volume should be reduced or diluted with water, then gradually returned to levels to meet caloric requirements over successive feedings. It is better to underfeed than overfeed neonatal puppies and kittens.

Strict hygiene of feeding equipment and formula as described above are especially important with hand feeding.

Reassessment

Orphaned puppies or kittens should be evaluated daily for the first two weeks of life. They should remain normally hydrated, sleep quietly between feedings and gain weight at a rate similar to bitch- or queen-raised neonates. Alertness, eagerness to suckle, general behavior, body temperature (i.e., temperature of skin and lower limbs), body weight and stool character should be recorded daily or more often if neonates appear weak or listless.

Orphan rearing permits precise measurement of food intake. In nursing puppies, weight gains reportedly range from 1 g body weight/2 to 5 g of milk intake during the first weeks of life. It is realistic to expect orphaned puppies to gain about the same. Kittens should grow about 100 g/week.

If puppies or kittens do not thrive when fed a commercial milk replacer or homemade replacer, the nutrient content should be compared with mother's milk. (See Appendix K.) The dilution recommended by the manufacturer should also be checked. In some cases, it may be necessary to switch to another formula.

Puppies or kittens with rectal temperatures less than 35°C (95°F) should not be fed milk formula. At this temperature the sucking reflex is usually absent and normal gut motility has ceased. Neonates should first be warmed slowly after receiving a warm solution of 2.5% glucose by subcutaneous injection (1 ml/30 g body weight).

BIBLIOGRAPHY—DATA FOR NEONATAL AND PEDIATRIC CARE

1. Beaver BV. Behavior development and behavioral disorders. In: Hoskins JD, ed. Veterinary Pediatrics: Dogs and Cats from Birth to Six Months. Philadelphia, PA: WB Saunders Co, 1990; 19-28.

2. Björck G. Care and feeding of the puppy in the postnatal and weaning period. In: Anderson RS, ed. Nutrition and behaviour in dogs and cats. Proceedings. First Nordic Symposium on Small Animal Veterinary Medicine, Oslo, Norway,. September 15-18, 1982, Oxford, UK: Pergamon Press, 1984; 25-33.

3. Breazile JE. Neurologic and behavioral development in the puppy. Veterinary Clinics of North America: Small Animal Practice 1978; 8: 31-45.

4. Harvey CE, Emily PP. Function, formation and anatomy of oral structures in carnivores. In: Small Animal Dentistry. St. Louis, MO: Mosby-Year Book, Inc, 1993; 1-18.

5. Hoskins JD. Clinical evaluation of the kitten: From birth to eight weeks of age. Compendium on Continuing Education for the Practicing Veterinarian 1990; 12: 1215-1225, 1232.

6. Kaiser G. Die reproduktionsleistung der haushunde in ihrer beziehung zur körpergröße und zum gewicht der rassen III. Teil Zeitschrift für Tierzüchtg Züchtgsbiologie 1971; 88: 316-340.

7. Kienzle E, Meyer H, Dammers C, et al. Milchaufnahme, gewichtentwicklung, milchverdaulichkeit, sowie energie- und nährstoffretention bei saugwelpen. Fortschritte in der Tierphysiologie und Tierernährung (Advances in Animal Physiology and Animal Nutrition) 1985; 16: 27-50.

8. Kirkwood JK. The influence of size on the biology of the dog. Journal of Small Animal Practice 1985; 26: 97-110.

9. Loveridge GG. Verschiedene einflußfaktoren auf das wachstum von katzenwelpen (Some factors affecting kitten growth). Ernährung, Fehlernährung und Diätetik bei Hund und Katze. In: Proceedings. International Symposium, Hannover, Germany, September 3-4, 1987; 115-118.

10. Lüerssen D. Daten zum descensus testis des hundes. Kleintierpraxis 1990; 35: 407-410.

11. Meyer H, Dammers C, Kienzle E. Körperzusammensetzung neugeborener welpen und nährstoffbedarf trägender hündinnen. Fortschritte in der Tierphysiologie und Tierernährung (Advances in Animal Physiology and Animal Nutrition) 1985; 16: 7-25.

12. Meyer H, Stadtfeld G. Investigations on the body and organ structure of dogs. In: Anderson RS, ed. Nutrition of the Dog and Cat. Oxford, UK: Pergamon Press, 1980; 15-30.

13. Mosier JE. The puppy from birth to six weeks. Veterinary Clinics of North America: Small Animal Practice 1978; 8: 79-100.

14. Mundt H-C, Thomée A, Meyer H. Zur energie- und eiweißversorgung von saugwelpen über die muttermilch. Kleintierpraxis 1981; 26: 353-360.

15. Oftedal OT. Lactation in the dog: Milk composition and intake by puppies. Journal of Nutrition 1984; 114: 803-812.

16. Okkens AC, Hekerman TWM, de Vogel JWA, et al. Influence of litter size and breed on variation in length of gestation in the dog. Veterinary Quarterly 1993; 15: 160-161.

17. Rauchfuss R. Untersuchungen über die körperzusammensetzung neugeborener hundewelpen unterschiedlich großer rassen. Inaugural Dissertation, Hannover, Germany, 1978.

18. Root MV, Johnston SD, Olson PN. Estrus length, pregnancy rate, gestation and parturition lengths, litter size, and juvenile mortality in the domestic cat. Journal of the American Animal Hospital Association 1995; 31: 429-433.

19. Schroeder GE, Smith GA. Food intake and growth of German shepherd puppies. Journal of Small Animal Practice 1994; 35: 587-591.

20. Shaefers-Okkens AC. Pediatrie. Handout at the Post University Course, Gent, Belgium, January 14, 1993.

21. Shaefers-Okkens AC. Voorjaarsdagen, Amsterdam, The Netherlands. Personal communication. April 24-26, 1992.

22. Siegal M. Kittens and disorders. In: Mordicai S, ed. The Cornell Book of Cats. New York, NY: Villard Books, 1991; 41-47.

23. Stadtfeld G. Untersuchungen über die körperzusammensetzung des hundes. Inaugural Dissertation. Hannover, Germany, 1978.

24. Trautvetter E, Pagel E-B, Skrodzki M, et al. Änderungen der herzschlagzahlen beim hundewelpen in den ersten zwölf lebenswochen. Berliner Münchner Tierärztliche Wochenschrift 1990; 103: 229-232.

25. Vondruska JF. Diagnosis of pregnancy in cats. Veterinary Medicine/Small Animal Clinician 1983; 78: 1225-1230.

26. Wong WT, Lee MKC. Some observations on the population and natal patterns among purebred dogs in Malaysia. Journal of Small Animal Practice 1985; 26: 111-119.

BIBLIOGRAPHY—ORPHANED PUPPY AND KITTEN CARE

1. Adkins Y, Zicker SC, Lepine A, et al. Protein and nutrient composition of cat milk throughout lactation (abstract). Federation of American Societies for Experimental Biology Journal 1995; 9: 1019.

2. Baines FM. Milk substitutes and the hand rearing of puppies and kittens. Journal of Small Animal Practice 1981; 22: 555-578.

3. Goldblum OM, Holzman IR, Fisher SE. Intragastric feeding in the neonatal dog: Its effect on intestinal osmolality. American Journal of Diseases of Children 1981; 135: 631-633.

4. Greco DS. The physical examination. In: Hoskins JD, ed.Veterinary Pediatrics: Dogs and Cats from Birth to Six Months. Philadelphia, PA: WB Saunders Co, 1990; 1-7.

5. Ha YH, Milner JA, Corbin JE. Arginine requirements in immature dogs. Journal of Nutrition 1978; 108: 203-210.

6. Hoskins JD, ed. Nutrition and nutritional disorders. In: Veterinary Pediatrics: Dogs and Cats from Birth to Six Months. Philadelphia, PA: WB Saunders Co, 1990; 473-486.

7. Jean-Blain C. Allaitement et sevrage du chiot. Revue de Médecine Vétérinaire 1973; 124: 1255-1268.

8. Kienzle E, Landes E. Aufzucht verwaister Jungtiere Teil I: Indikationsstellung und Zusammensetzung der Muttermilch. Kleintierpraxis 1995; 40: 681-685.

9. Kienzle E, Landes E. Aufzucht verwaister Jungtiere Teil II: Herstellung von Milchaustauschern und praktische Durchführung dermutterlosen Aufzucht. Kleintierpraxis 1995; 40: 687-700.

10. Lawler DF, Evans RH. Nutritional and environmental considerations in neonatal medicine. In: Kirk RW, ed. Current Veterinary Therapy X. Philadelphia, PA: WB Saunders Co, 1989; 1325-1333.

11. Lawler DF. Canine and feline periparturient problems. In: Small Animal Reproduction and Pediatrics, Purina Specialty Review, Pro Visions 1991; 21-51.

12. Mapletoft RJ, Schutte AP, Coubrough RI, et al. The perinatal period of dogs. Nutrition and management in the hand-rearing of puppies. Journal of the South African Veterinary Medical Association 1974; 45: 183-189.

13. Monson WJ. Orphan rearing of puppies and kittens. Veterinary Clinics of North America: Small Animal Practice 1987; 17: 567-576.

14. Pibot P, Jean-Blain C. Allaitement artificiel et sevrage du chiot. Recueil de Médecine Vétérinaire 1989; 165: 567-575.

15. Sheffy BE. Nutrition and nutritional disorders. Veterinary Clinics of North America: Small Animal Practice 1978; 8: 7-29.

16. Vainisi SJ, Edelhauser HF, Wolf ED, et al. Nutritional cataracts in timber wolves. Journal of the American Veterinary Medical Association 1981; 179: 1175-1180.

Appendix F
Body Weights and Feeding Guides for Growing Dogs and Cats

I. Introduction

This appendix: 1) provides an initial guide for calculating the daily food intake for growing dogs and cats and 2) lists the approximate body weights of puppies and kittens at different ages.

Because all animals are individuals and requirements vary with environmental conditions, breed and activity, a single table cannot predict the precise energy requirements of all animals, particularly during growth, when requirements change rapidly. Therefore, all feeding guides are only approximations, and quantities of food provided should be adjusted to maintain optimal body weight and condition. Feeding guides on pet food labels may recommend amounts that differ from the intake levels suggested here. Pet owners should be advised of this information.

II. Growing dogs

Tables F-1 through F-9 provide a guide for calculating daily food intakes for growing dogs and are tools for nutritional assessment of puppies. Table F-1 provides equations for calculating daily energy requirements of growing puppies. Tables F-2 to F-9 list the adult body weights of dogs (i.e., 1 to 70 kg) with the expected body weight and energy requirement at different ages. The expected body weights listed for puppies at different ages can be used to evaluate growth rate. A body weight markedly lower than listed values may suggest malnutrition or disease. Alternatively, puppies that are considerably

heavier than expected from the table values may be growing too fast. This information is particularly important for large- and giant-breed puppies, which are predisposed to developmental orthopedic disease when overfed. (See Chapter 17.) Overfeeding during growth may also predispose to obesity later in life. Because the following tables are not breed specific and not tailored to individual dogs, they should be used as a starting point only and interpreted in relation to physical examination and body condition findings.

Example

A three-month-old male Labrador retriever puppy is presented for vaccinations. The owner asks for recommendations about nutrition and care during the growth period. The estimated adult body weight is 32 kg (70.4 lb). (See Appendix G.) The veterinarian informs the client about the increased risk of obesity and skeletal disorders such as osteochondrosis in Labrador retrievers and that the risks may be lessened by feeding a food with moderate calcium levels and relatively restricted energy levels, fed in meal-restricted fashion. The puppy weighs 10.5 kg (23.1 lb). Table F-4 indicates that at three months of age, the expected body weight of a 32-kg adult dog is about 11.3 kg (24.9 lb).

According to Table F-4, this three-month-old puppy should receive about 1,328 kcal [5.56 MJ]/day. Because a lower energy intake may be beneficial (i.e., reduce risks of developmental orthopedic disease and obesity), the practitioner recommended an energy intake based on the puppy's current body weight (about 1,225 kcal [5.13 MJ]/day) (Table F-4). The amount fed can always be increased to supply 1,328 kcal [5.56 MJ]/day, based on the puppy's body condition. The veterinarian further explained that the puppy will reach normal adult size despite the energy restriction.

Two months later the owner presented the puppy for evaluation of occasional lameness. Physical examination revealed slight radius curvus of the left front leg with lateral deviation of the metacarpus. The puppy weighed 20.5 kg (45.1 lb). Table F-6 indicates that at five months of age this puppy should only weigh about 18.3 kg (40.3 lb). The puppy's current weight is not appreciably different from the value given in Table F-6; however, Tables F-2 through F-9 only provide rough reference points. A weight of 20.5 kg is 12% more than expected, and keep in mind that two months earlier, the puppy weighed less than its expected weight; therefore, the puppy has been growing at a higher rate than is probably ideal.

The veterinarian, therefore, questioned the client about the amount of food provided and the feeding method. No additional calcium was provided to the complete growth food that was recommended at three months of age. However, the owner admitted that she felt guilty about the small amounts of food the dog received and that a friend had recommended feeding the puppy free choice. The food contains 3.80 kcal metabolizable energy/g and a 20-lb bag lasts 18 to 19 days. The puppy therefore consumes 480 to 505 g/day or 1,820 to 1,920 kcal/day (7.6 to 8.0 MJ/day). Ideally, at four to five months of age this puppy should only receive about 1,530 kcal/day (6.4 MJ/day). The feeding method used led to 20 to 25% overfeeding, which predisposes to developmental orthopedic disease.

Table F-2. Approximate daily energy requirements of puppies at one month of age, based on current and mature body weights.*

Adult BW (kg)	Current BW (kg)	DER (MJ)	DER (kcal)	Adult BW (kg)	Current BW (kg)	DER (MJ)	DER (kcal)
1	0.2	0.26	61		(Continued from below)		
2	0.3	0.33	79	36	2.5	1.49	356
3	0.5	0.40	96	37	2.6	1.52	363
4	0.6	0.47	112	38	2.6	1.55	370
5	0.8	0.53	127	39	2.7	1.58	377
6	0.9	0.59	140	40	2.7	1.60	383
7	1.0	0.64	152	41	2.8	1.63	390
8	1.1	0.68	164	42	2.8	1.66	397
9	1.2	0.73	174	43	2.9	1.69	403
10	1.2	0.77	184	44	2.9	1.72	410
11	1.3	0.81	194	45	3.0	1.74	416
12	1.4	0.85	203	46	3.0	1.77	423
13	1.4	0.89	212	47	3.1	1.80	430
14	1.5	0.93	221	48	3.1	1.82	436
15	1.6	0.96	230	49	3.2	1.85	442
16	1.6	1.00	238	50	3.2	1.88	449
17	1.7	1.03	246	51	3.2	1.90	455
18	1.7	1.06	254	52	3.3	1.93	461
19	1.8	1.09	261	53	3.3	1.96	468
20	1.8	1.12	268	54	3.4	1.98	474
21	1.9	1.15	275	55	3.4	2.01	480
22	1.9	1.17	281	56	3.4	2.03	486
23	2.0	1.20	287	57	3.5	2.06	492
24	2.0	1.22	292	58	3.5	2.09	499
25	2.1	1.25	298	59	3.6	2.11	505
26	2.1	1.27	304	60	3.6	2.14	511
27	2.2	1.29	309	61	3.7	2.15	515
28	2.2	1.32	315	62	3.7	2.17	519
29	2.3	1.34	320	63	3.8	2.19	524
30	2.3	1.36	325	64	3.8	2.21	528
31	2.3	1.38	330	65	3.9	2.23	532
32	2.4	1.40	335	66	3.9	2.24	536
33	2.4	1.42	340	67	4.0	2.26	540
34	2.4	1.44	344	68	4.0	2.28	545
35	2.5	1.46	349	69	4.1	2.30	549
(Continued next column)				70	4.1	2.31	553

Key: BW = body weight, DER = daily energy requirement, kcal = kilocalories, MJ = megajoules.
*Adapted from Gesellschaft für Ernährungsphysiologie Empfehlungen für die Versorgung mit Energie. In: Ausschuß für Bedarfsnormen. Energie- und Nährstoffbedarf Nr. 5 Hunde. Frankfurt/Main, Germany: DLG Verlag, 1989; 32-44. Gesellschaft für Ernährungsphysiologie Grunddaten für die Berechnung des Energie- und Nährstoffbedarfs. In: Ausschuß für Bedarfsnormen. Energie- und Nährstoffbedarf Nr. 5 Hunde. Frankfurt/Main, Germany: DLG Verlag, 1989; 9-31.

Table F-1. Energy requirements of puppies.*

Up to 50% of adult body weight (4 to 5 months of age)	3.0 x resting energy requirement*
Between 50 and 80% of adult body weight	2.5 x resting energy requirement
Between 80 and 100% of adult body weight	2.0 x resting energy requirement

*Resting energy requirement = $70(BW_{kg})^{0.75}$ in kcal = $293(BW_{kg})^{0.75}$ in kJ.

Table F-3. Approximate daily energy requirements of puppies at two months of age, based on current and mature body weights.*

Adult BW (kg)	Current BW (kg)	DER (MJ)	DER (kcal)	Adult BW (kg)	Current BW (kg)	DER (MJ)	DER (kcal)
1	0.3	0.37	89		(Continued from below)		
2	0.6	0.53	126	36	7.1	3.93	939
3	0.9	0.67	159	37	7.3	3.98	952
4	1.2	0.80	190	38	7.4	4.04	965
5	1.5	0.92	220	39	7.6	4.09	977
6	1.7	1.04	249	40	7.7	4.14	990
7	2.0	1.16	276	41	7.8	4.19	1,002
8	2.2	1.26	301	42	7.9	4.24	1,014
9	2.3	1.36	325	43	8.0	4.29	1,025
10	2.5	1.45	347	44	8.2	4.34	1,037
11	2.7	1.57	374	45	8.3	4.39	1,048
12	2.9	1.68	401	46	8.4	4.43	1,059
13	3.1	1.79	427	47	8.5	4.48	1,070
14	3.3	1.89	452	48	8.6	4.52	1,081
15	3.5	2.00	477	49	8.7	4.57	1,092
16	3.7	2.10	502	50	8.8	4.61	1,102
17	3.9	2.20	526	51	8.9	4.66	1,113
18	4.1	2.30	549	52	9.0	4.70	1,123
19	4.2	2.39	572	53	9.1	4.74	1,133
20	4.4	2.49	594	54	9.2	4.78	1,143
21	4.6	2.59	618	55	9.2	4.82	1,152
22	4.8	2.68	642	56	9.3	4.86	1,162
23	5.0	2.78	665	57	9.4	4.90	1,171
24	5.2	2.88	688	58	9.5	4.94	1,180
25	5.3	2.97	711	59	9.5	4.98	1,189
26	5.5	3.07	733	60	9.6	5.01	1,198
27	5.7	3.16	755	61	9.7	5.04	1,205
28	5.9	3.25	777	62	9.8	5.07	1,212
29	6.0	3.34	799	63	10.0	5.10	1,218
30	6.2	3.44	821	64	10.1	5.12	1,224
31	6.4	3.52	842	65	10.2	5.15	1,231
32	6.5	3.61	864	66	10.3	5.18	1,237
33	6.7	3.70	885	67	10.4	5.20	1,243
34	6.8	3.79	906	68	10.6	5.23	1,249
35	7.0	3.88	926	69	10.7	5.25	1,255
(Continued next column)				70	10.8	5.28	1,261

Key: BW = body weight, DER = daily energy requirement, kcal = kilocalories, MJ = megajoules.
*Adapted from Gesellschaft für Ernährungsphysiologie Empfehlungen für die Versorgung mit Energie. In: Ausschuß für Bedarfsnormen. Energie-und Nährstoffbedarf Nr. 5 Hunde. Frankfurt/Main, Germany: DLG Verlag, 1989; 32-44. Gesellschaft für Ernährungsphysiologie Grunddaten für die Berechnung des Energie- und Nährstoffbedarfs. In: Ausschuß für Bedarfsnormen. Energie- und Nährstoffbedarf Nr. 5 Hunde. Frankfurt/Main, Germany: DLG Verlag, 1989; 9-31.

Table F-4. Approximate daily energy requirements of puppies at three months of age, based on current and mature body weights.*

Adult BW (kg)	Current BW (kg)	DER (MJ)	DER (kcal)	Adult BW (kg)	Current BW (kg)	DER (MJ)	DER (kcal)
1	0.5	0.50	120		(Continued from below)		
2	0.9	0.74	178	36	12.5	6.05	1,447
3	1.4	0.96	230	37	12.7	6.14	1,468
4	1.8	1.16	278	38	13.0	6.23	1,489
5	2.3	1.35	324	39	13.2	6.32	1,509
6	2.6	1.55	371	40	13.4	6.40	1,530
7	3.0	1.74	415	41	13.7	6.48	1,549
8	3.4	1.91	457	42	13.9	6.56	1,569
9	3.7	2.08	497	43	14.1	6.64	1,588
10	4.0	2.24	536	44	14.3	6.72	1,607
11	4.4	2.41	577	45	14.5	6.80	1,625
12	4.7	2.58	617	46	14.7	6.88	1,643
13	5.1	2.75	657	47	14.9	6.95	1,661
14	5.4	2.91	695	48	15.1	7.02	1,679
15	5.8	3.07	733	49	15.2	7.10	1,696
16	6.1	3.22	771	50	15.4	7.17	1,713
17	6.4	3.38	807	51	15.6	7.24	1,730
18	6.8	3.53	843	52	15.7	7.31	1,746
19	7.1	3.68	879	53	15.9	7.37	1,762
20	7.4	3.82	913	54	16.0	7.44	1,778
21	7.7	3.97	950	55	16.2	7.50	1,793
22	8.1	4.12	986	56	16.3	7.57	1,808
23	8.4	4.27	1,021	57	16.4	7.63	1,823
24	8.8	4.42	1,057	58	16.6	7.69	1,838
25	9.1	4.57	1,092	59	16.7	7.75	1,852
26	9.4	4.71	1,126	60	16.8	7.81	1,866
27	9.7	4.86	1,161	61	17.0	7.84	1,874
28	10.1	5.00	1,195	62	17.2	7.87	1,882
29	10.4	5.14	1,229	63	17.4	7.90	1,889
30	10.7	5.28	1,262	64	17.5	7.93	1,896
31	11.0	5.42	1,295	65	17.7	7.96	1,904
32	11.3	5.56	1,328	66	17.9	7.99	1,911
33	11.6	5.69	1,361	67	18.1	8.02	1,917
34	11.9	5.83	1,393	68	18.2	8.05	1,924
35	12.3	5.96	1,425	69	18.4	8.08	1,931
(Continued next column)				70	18.6	8.10	1,937

Key: BW = body weight, DER = daily energy requirement, kcal = kilocalories, MJ = megajoules.
*Adapted from Gesellschaft für Ernährungsphysiologie Empfehlungen für die Versorgung mit Energie. In: Ausschuß für Bedarfsnormen. Energie-und Nährstoffbedarf Nr. 5 Hunde. Frankfurt/Main, Germany: DLG Verlag, 1989; 32-44. Gesellschaft für Ernährungsphysiologie Grunddaten für die Berechnung des Energie- und Nährstoffbedarfs. In: Ausschuß für Bedarfsnormen. Energie- und Nährstoffbedarf Nr. 5 Hunde. Frankfurt/Main, Germany: DLG Verlag, 1989; 9-31.

Table F-5. Approximate daily energy requirements of puppies at four months of age, based on current and mature body weights.*

Adult BW (kg)	Current BW (kg)	DER (MJ)	(kcal)	Adult BW (kg)	Current BW (kg)	DER (MJ)	(kcal)
1	0.6	0.59	141		(Continued from below)		
2	1.2	0.89	213	36	17.2	7.09	1,694
3	1.8	1.16	278	37	17.5	7.22	1,725
4	2.4	1.41	338	38	17.9	7.34	1,755
5	3.0	1.65	395	39	18.2	7.47	1,784
6	3.5	1.90	453	40	18.6	7.59	1,814
7	4.1	2.13	509	41	18.9	7.71	1,843
8	4.6	2.35	561	42	19.2	7.83	1,871
9	5.0	2.56	612	43	19.5	7.95	1,899
10	5.5	2.76	660	44	19.9	8.06	1,927
11	6.0	2.98	712	45	20.2	8.18	1,955
12	6.5	3.19	762	46	20.5	8.29	1,982
13	7.0	3.40	812	47	20.8	8.40	2,009
14	7.5	3.60	860	48	21.0	8.52	2,035
15	8.0	3.80	908	49	21.3	8.62	2,061
16	8.5	4.00	955	50	21.6	8.73	2,087
17	9.0	4.19	1,001	51	21.9	8.84	2,113
18	9.5	4.38	1,047	52	22.1	8.94	2,138
19	9.9	4.57	1,092	53	22.4	9.05	2,162
20	10.4	4.75	1,136	54	22.6	9.15	2,187
21	10.9	4.91	1,175	55	22.9	9.25	2,211
22	11.3	5.07	1,213	56	23.1	9.35	2,235
23	11.8	5.23	1,250	57	23.3	9.45	2,258
24	12.2	5.38	1,287	58	23.6	9.55	2,282
25	12.7	5.54	1,323	59	23.8	9.64	2,304
26	13.1	5.69	1,359	60	24.0	9.74	2,327
27	13.5	5.84	1,395	61	24.2	9.80	2,343
28	14.0	5.98	1,430	62	24.4	9.87	2,359
29	14.4	6.13	1,464	63	24.7	9.93	2,374
30	14.8	6.27	1,498	64	24.9	10.00	2,389
31	15.2	6.41	1,532	65	25.1	10.06	2,404
32	15.6	6.55	1,565	66	25.3	10.12	2,419
33	16.0	6.69	1,598	67	25.5	10.18	2,433
34	16.4	6.82	1,631	68	25.6	10.24	2,448
35	16.8	6.96	1,663	69	25.8	10.30	2,461
	(Continued next column)			70	26.0	10.36	2,475

Key: BW = body weight, DER = daily energy requirement, kcal = kilocalories, MJ = megajoules.
*Adapted from Gesellschaft für Ernährungsphysiologie Empfehlungen für die Versorgung mit Energie. In: Ausschuß für Bedarfsnormen. Energie-und Nährstoffbedarf Nr. 5 Hunde. Frankfurt/Main, Germany: DLG Verlag, 1989; 32-44. Gesellschaft für Ernährungsphysiologie Grunddaten für die Berechnung des Energie- und Nährstoffbedarfs. In: Ausschuß für Bedarfsnormen. Energie- und Nährstoffbedarf Nr. 5 Hunde. Frankfurt/Main, Germany: DLG Verlag, 1989; 9-31.

Table F-6. Approximate daily energy requirements of puppies at five months of age, based on current and mature body weights.*

Adult BW (kg)	Current BW (kg)	DER (MJ)	(kcal)	Adult BW (kg)	Current BW (kg)	DER (MJ)	(kcal)
1	0.7	0.56	135		(Continued from below)		
2	1.4	0.89	212	36	20.2	6.97	1,666
3	2.1	1.17	280	37	20.7	7.13	1,704
4	2.8	1.44	344	38	21.1	7.29	1,741
5	3.5	1.69	404	39	21.6	7.44	1,779
6	4.1	1.93	462	40	22.0	7.60	1,815
7	4.7	2.16	517	41	22.5	7.75	1,852
8	5.3	2.38	570	42	22.9	7.90	1,888
9	5.9	2.59	620	43	23.4	8.05	1,924
10	6.5	2.80	668	44	23.8	8.20	1,959
11	7.1	3.00	716	45	24.2	8.34	1,994
12	7.7	3.19	762	46	24.6	8.49	2,029
13	8.3	3.38	807	47	25.1	8.63	2,064
14	8.9	3.56	851	48	25.5	8.78	2,098
15	9.4	3.74	894	49	25.9	8.92	2,132
16	10.0	3.92	936	50	26.3	9.06	2,165
17	10.6	4.09	978	51	26.7	9.20	2,199
18	11.1	4.26	1,018	52	27.1	9.34	2,232
19	11.6	4.43	1,058	53	27.4	9.47	2,264
20	12.2	4.59	1,096	54	27.8	9.61	2,297
21	12.7	4.75	1,136	55	28.2	9.75	2,329
22	13.3	4.91	1,174	56	28.6	9.88	2,361
23	13.8	5.07	1,212	57	28.9	10.01	2,393
24	14.3	5.23	1,249	58	29.3	10.14	2,424
25	14.8	5.38	1,286	59	29.7	10.27	2,455
26	15.4	5.53	1,323	60	30.0	10.40	2,486
27	15.9	5.68	1,358	61	30.3	10.48	2,506
28	16.4	5.83	1,394	62	30.7	10.57	2,525
29	16.9	5.98	1,428	63	31.0	10.65	2,545
30	17.4	6.12	1,463	64	31.4	10.73	2,564
31	17.9	6.26	1,497	65	31.7	10.80	2,582
32	18.3	6.40	1,530	66	32.0	10.88	2,601
33	18.8	6.54	1,563	67	32.3	10.96	2,619
34	19.3	6.68	1,596	68	32.6	11.03	2,637
35	19.7	6.81	1,628	69	32.9	11.11	2,655
	(Continued next column)			70	33.3	11.18	2,673

Key: BW = body weight, DER = daily energy requirement, kcal = kilocalories, MJ = megajoules.
*Adapted from Gesellschaft für Ernährungsphysiologie Empfehlungen für die Versorgung mit Energie. In: Ausschuß für Bedarfsnormen. Energie- und Nährstoffbedarf Nr. 5 Hunde. Frankfurt/Main, Germany: DLG Verlag, 1989; 32-44. Gesellschaft für Ernährungsphysiologie Grunddaten für die Berechnung des Energie- und Nährstoffbedarfs. In: Ausschuß für Bedarfsnormen. Energie- und Nährstoffbedarf Nr. 5 Hunde. Frankfurt/Main, Germany: DLG Verlag, 1989; 9-31.

Table F-7. Approximate daily energy requirements of puppies at six months of age, based on current and mature body weights.*

Adult BW (kg)	Current BW (kg)	DER (MJ)	DER (kcal)	Adult BW (kg)	Current BW (kg)	DER (MJ)	DER (kcal)
1	0.8	0.59	142			*(Continued from below)*	
2	1.6	0.96	229	36	23.3	7.57	1,809
3	2.4	1.28	305	37	23.9	7.74	1,851
4	3.2	1.57	375	38	24.5	7.92	1,892
5	4.0	1.84	441	39	25.0	8.09	1,934
6	4.7	2.11	504	40	25.6	8.26	1,974
7	5.5	2.36	565	41	26.2	8.43	2,015
8	6.2	2.60	622	42	26.7	8.60	2,055
9	6.8	2.83	677	43	27.3	8.77	2,095
10	7.5	3.05	730	44	27.8	8.93	2,135
11	8.2	3.27	781	45	28.4	9.10	2,174
12	8.9	3.48	832	46	28.9	9.26	2,213
13	9.6	3.68	880	47	29.4	9.42	2,252
14	10.2	3.88	928	48	30.0	9.59	2,291
15	10.9	4.08	974	49	30.5	9.75	2,329
16	11.5	4.27	1,020	50	31.0	9.90	2,367
17	12.2	4.45	1,064	51	31.5	10.06	2,405
18	12.8	4.63	1,108	52	32.0	10.22	2,443
19	13.4	4.81	1,150	53	32.5	10.38	2,480
20	14.0	4.99	1,192	54	33.0	10.53	2,517
21	14.6	5.16	1,234	55	33.6	10.68	2,554
22	15.3	5.34	1,276	56	34.0	10.84	2,590
23	15.9	5.51	1,317	57	34.5	10.99	2,626
24	16.5	5.68	1,357	58	35.0	11.14	2,663
25	17.1	5.85	1,397	59	35.5	11.29	2,698
26	17.7	6.01	1,437	60	36.0	11.44	2,734
27	18.3	6.17	1,475	61	36.5	11.54	2,757
28	18.9	6.33	1,513	62	37.1	11.63	2,781
29	19.4	6.49	1,551	63	37.6	11.73	2,804
30	20.0	6.65	1,588	64	38.1	11.83	2,827
31	20.6	6.80	1,625	65	38.7	11.92	2,849
32	21.1	6.95	1,661	66	39.2	12.02	2,872
33	21.7	7.10	1,697	67	39.7	12.11	2,895
34	22.2	7.25	1,732	68	40.3	12.20	2,917
35	22.8	7.39	1,767	69	40.8	12.30	2,939
		(Continued next column)		70	41.3	12.39	2,961

Key: BW = body weight, DER = daily energy requirement, kcal = kilocalories, MJ = megajoules.
*Adapted from Gesellschaft für Ernährungsphysiologie Empfehlungen für die Versorgung mit Energie. In: Ausschuß für Bedarfsnormen. Energie- und Nährstoffbedarf Nr. 5 Hunde. Frankfurt/Main, Germany: DLG Verlag, 1989; 32-44. Gesellschaft für Ernährungsphysiologie Grunddaten für die Berechnung des Energie- und Nährstoffbedarfs. In: Ausschuß für Bedarfsnormen. Energie- und Nährstoffbedarf Nr. 5 Hunde. Frankfurt/Main, Germany: DLG Verlag, 1989; 9-31.

Table F-8. Approximate daily energy requirements of puppies at seven months of age, based on current and mature body weights.*

Adult BW (kg)	Current BW (kg)	DER (MJ)	DER (kcal)	Adult BW (kg)	Current BW (kg)	DER (MJ)	DER (kcal)
1	0.9	0.57	137			*(Continued from below)*	
2	1.7	0.92	219	36	24.7	7.08	1,693
3	2.6	1.21	289	37	25.3	7.22	1,724
4	3.4	1.48	353	38	25.9	7.34	1,755
5	4.2	1.72	411	39	26.5	7.47	1,786
6	4.9	1.96	469	40	27.1	7.60	1,816
7	5.7	2.19	525	41	27.7	7.72	1,846
8	6.4	2.41	577	42	28.3	7.85	1,875
9	7.1	2.62	627	43	28.8	7.97	1,904
10	7.8	2.82	675	44	29.4	8.09	1,933
11	8.6	3.04	727	45	30.0	8.21	1,962
12	9.3	3.25	777	46	30.6	8.33	1,990
13	10.0	3.45	826	47	31.1	8.44	2,018
14	10.7	3.65	873	48	31.7	8.56	2,046
15	11.4	3.85	920	49	32.2	8.67	2,073
16	12.1	4.04	965	50	32.8	8.79	2,100
17	12.8	4.22	1,010	51	33.3	8.90	2,127
18	13.5	4.41	1,053	52	33.8	9.01	2,154
19	14.2	4.59	1,096	53	34.4	9.12	2,180
20	14.8	4.76	1,138	54	34.9	9.23	2,206
21	15.5	4.93	1,177	55	35.4	9.34	2,232
22	16.1	5.09	1,216	56	35.9	9.44	2,257
23	16.8	5.24	1,253	57	36.5	9.55	2,282
24	17.4	5.40	1,291	58	37.0	9.65	2,307
25	18.1	5.55	1,327	59	37.5	9.76	2,332
26	18.7	5.70	1,363	60	38.0	9.86	2,357
27	19.3	5.85	1,398	61	38.5	9.97	2,382
28	20.0	6.00	1,433	62	39.1	10.07	2,407
29	20.6	6.14	1,467	63	39.7	10.17	2,431
30	21.2	6.28	1,501	64	40.2	10.28	2,456
31	21.8	6.42	1,534	65	40.8	10.38	2,481
32	22.4	6.55	1,567	66	41.3	10.48	2,505
33	23.0	6.69	1,599	67	41.9	10.58	2,529
34	23.5	6.82	1,631	68	42.4	10.68	2,553
35	24.1	6.95	1,662	69	43.0	10.78	2,577
		(Continued next column)		70	43.5	10.88	2,600

Key: BW = body weight, DER = daily energy requirement, kcal = kilocalories, MJ = megajoules.
*Adapted from Gesellschaft für Ernährungsphysiologie Empfehlungen für die Versorgung mit Energie. In: Ausschuß für Bedarfsnormen. Energie-und Nährstoffbedarf Nr. 5 Hunde. Frankfurt/Main, Germany: DLG Verlag, 1989; 32-44. Gesellschaft für Ernährungsphysiologie Grunddaten für die Berechnung des Energie- und Nährstoffbedarfs. In: Ausschuß für Bedarfsnormen. Energie- und Nährstoffbedarf Nr. 5 Hunde. Frankfurt/Main, Germany: DLG Verlag, 1989; 9-31.

Table F-9. Approximate daily energy requirements of puppies at 12 months of age, based on current and mature body weights.*

Adult BW (kg)	Current BW (kg)	DER (MJ)	DER (kcal)	Adult BW (kg)	Current BW (kg)	DER (MJ)	DER (kcal)
1	1.0	0.55	132		*(Continued from below)*		
2	2.0	0.93	222	36	30.5	7.78	1,859
3	3.0	1.26	301	37	31.3	7.93	1,895
4	4.0	1.56	373	38	32.1	8.08	1,930
5	5.0	1.85	441	39	32.8	8.22	1,965
6	5.9	2.13	509	40	33.6	8.37	2,000
7	6.9	2.40	573	41	34.4	8.51	2,035
8	7.8	2.65	634	42	35.1	8.66	2,069
9	8.6	2.90	692	43	35.9	8.80	2,103
10	9.5	3.13	748	44	36.6	8.94	2,136
11	10.5	3.36	803	45	37.4	9.08	2,169
12	11.4	3.59	857	46	38.1	9.21	2,202
13	12.4	3.81	910	47	38.8	9.35	2,235
14	13.3	4.03	962	48	39.6	9.48	2,267
15	14.3	4.24	1,013	49	40.3	9.62	2,299
16	15.2	4.45	1,064	50	41.0	9.75	2,330
17	16.2	4.66	1,113	51	41.7	9.88	2,362
18	17.1	4.86	1,162	52	42.4	10.01	2,393
19	18.1	5.06	1,210	53	43.1	10.14	2,424
20	19.0	5.26	1,258	54	43.8	10.27	2,454
21	19.8	5.45	1,302	55	44.6	10.40	2,485
22	20.6	5.63	1,345	56	45.2	10.52	2,515
23	21.4	5.80	1,387	57	45.9	10.65	2,545
24	22.2	5.97	1,428	58	46.6	10.77	2,574
25	22.9	6.14	1,468	59	47.3	10.89	2,603
26	23.7	6.30	1,507	60	48.0	11.01	2,633
27	24.4	6.46	1,545	61	48.7	11.15	2,666
28	25.1	6.62	1,582	62	49.5	11.29	2,699
29	25.8	6.77	1,619	63	50.2	11.43	2,732
30	26.5	6.92	1,655	64	50.9	11.57	2,765
31	27.2	7.07	1,690	65	51.7	11.70	2,797
32	27.8	7.21	1,724	66	52.4	11.84	2,830
33	28.5	7.35	1,758	67	53.1	11.97	2,862
34	29.1	7.49	1,791	68	53.9	12.11	2,894
35	29.8	7.63	1,823	69	54.6	12.24	2,926
(Continued next column)				70	55.3	12.38	2,958

Key: BW = body weight, DER = daily energy requirement, kcal = kilocalories, MJ = megajoules.
*Adapted from Gesellschaft für Ernährungsphysiologie Empfehlungen für die Versorgung mit Energie. In: Ausschuß für Bedarfsnormen. Energie- und Nährstoffbedarf Nr. 5 Hunde. Frankfurt/Main, Germany: DLG Verlag, 1989; 32-44. Gesellschaft für Ernährungsphysiologie Grunddaten für die Berechnung des Energie- und Nährstoffbedarfs. In: Ausschuß für Bedarfsnormen. Energie- und Nährstoffbedarf Nr. 5 Hunde. Frankfurt/Main, Germany: DLG Verlag, 1989; 9-31.

III. Growing cats

Tables F-10 and F-11 provide an initial guide for calculating food intake of growing kittens if a client chooses not to feed her kitten free choice. These tables can also help assess food intake when conducting a dietary history or evaluating the growth rate of kittens. Table F-10 lists equations for calculating the daily energy requirements of growing kittens. Table F-11 lists the body weight of kittens at different ages. The values listed are only averages; therefore, the body weight of individual kittens may be lower or higher. The approximate energy requirements at different ages are given per kg body weight and as total daily energy requirements. The requirements per kg body weight can be used when the current body weight of a kitten is markedly different from the weights listed in the table.

Table F-10. Energy requirements of kittens.*

Up to 50% of adult body weight (about four months of age)	3.0 x resting energy requirement*
Between 50 and 70% of adult body weight (about six months of age)	2.5 x resting energy requirement
Between 70 and 100% of adult body weight (about nine to 12 months of age)	2.0 x resting energy requirement

*Resting energy requirement = $70(BW_{kg})^{0.75}$

Table F-11. Approximate body weights and energy requirements of kittens.*

	Female kittens**			Age (months)		Male kittens**		
BW_{kg}	kcal/BW_{kg}	kcal/day	kJ/day		BW_{kg}	kcal/BW_{kg}	kcal/day	kJ/day
0.11	250	28	115	Birth	0.12	250	29	122
0.4	240	96	402	1	0.5	240	115	482
0.7	210	147	615	2	1.0	210	210	879
1.0	200	200	834	3	1.5	200	300	1,255
1.5	175	263	1,098	4	2.0	175	350	1,464
1.8	145	261	1,092	5	2.6	145	377	1,577
2.1	135	284	1,186	6	3.0	135	405	1,695
2.3	120	276	1,155	7	3.4	120	408	1,707
2.5	110	278	1,164	8	3.7	110	402	1,680
2.7	100	270	1,130	9	3.9	100	394	1,648
2.8	95	262	1,097	10	4.1	95	390	1,630
2.9	90	259	1,084	11	4.3	90	387	1,619
3.0	85	255	1,067	12	4.5	85	383	1,600

Key: BW = body weight, kcal = kilocalories, kJ = kilojoules.
*Adapted from Bibliography Sources 3 to 7.
**Females represent the lower end of the range, whereas males represent the upper end.

BIBLIOGRAPHY

1. Gesellschaft für Ernährungsphysiologie Empfehlungen für die Versorgung mit Energie. In: Ausschuß für Bedarfsnormen. Energie- und Nährstoffbedarf Nr. 5 Hunde. Frankfurt/Main, Germany: DLG Verlag, 1989; 32-44.

2. Gesellschaft für Ernährungsphysiologie Grunddaten für die Berechnung des Energie und Nährstoff-bedarfs. In: Ausschuß für Bedarfsnormen. Energie- und Nährstoffbedarf Nr. 5 Hunde. Frankfurt/Main, Germany: DLG Verlag, 1989; 9-31.

3. Data on file. Hill's Pet Nutrition, Inc., Topeka, KS, USA.

4. Holme DW. Practical use of prepared foods for dogs and cats. In: Edney ATP, ed. Dog & Cat Nutrition. Oxford, UK: Pergamon Press, 1982; 47-59.

5. Loveridge GG. Verschiedene Einflußfaktoren auf das Wachstum von Katzenwelpen (Some factors affecting kitten growth). In: Ernährung, Fehlernährung und Diätetik bei Hund und Katze. In: Proceedings. International Symposium, Hannover, Germany, September 3-4, 1987: 115-118.

6. National Research Council. Nutrient Requirements of Cats. Washington, DC: National Academy Press, 1986; 3-28.

7. Rainbird AL. Feeding throughout life. In: Edney ATP, ed. Dog & Cat Nutrition, 2nd ed. Oxford, UK: Pergamon Press, 1988; 75-96.

8. Hedhammar Å, Wu F-M, Krook L, et al. Overnutrition and skeletal disease: An experimental study in growing Great Dane dogs. Cornell Veterinarian 1974; 64: 9-160.

9. Kealy RD, Olsson SE, Monti KL, et al. Effects of limited food consumption on the incidence of hip dysplasia in growing dogs. Journal of the American Veterinary Medical Association 1992; 210: 857-863.

10. Meyer H, Zentek J. Über den Einfluß einer unterschiedlichen Energieversorgung wachsender Doggen auf Körpermasse und Skelettentwicklung 1. Mitteilung: Körpermasseentwicklung und Energiebedarf. Journal of Veterinary Medicine A 1992; 39: 130-141.

Appendix G
Feeding Guides for Mature Dogs and Cats

I. Introduction

Standards for energy intake are average requirements of population groups; therefore, the energy requirements of half the population may be less and half may be more than the recommended energy intake. Consequently, recommendations for energy intake in the following tables and on packaging materials of commercially prepared foods are only starting points. Each animal should be monitored individually, and food intake should be adapted to maintain optimal body weight and condition.

II. Feeding guides for dogs

Table G-1. Summary of daily energy requirements of dogs based on lifestage.

Lifestages	x RER	kcal/kg$^{0.75}$*	MJ/kg$^{0.75}$
RER	1.0	70	0.293
Obese prone	1.4	100	0.42
Neutered	1.6	112	0.47
Intact	1.8	125	0.525
Moderate work	3.0	210	0.88
Heavy work	4.0-8.0	280-560	1.17-2.35

Key: RER = resting energy requirement, kcal = kilocalories,
kg = kilograms, MJ = megajoules.
*Metabolic weight (kg$^{0.75}$) can be calculated by cubing body weight and then taking its square root twice.

Table G-2. Daily energy requirements of adult dogs in kilocalories metabolizable energy (kcal ME/kg$^{0.75}$).

Body weights kg	lb	RER 70 kcal/kg$^{0.75}$	Obese prone 100 kcal/kg$^{0.75}$ 1.4 x RER	Neutered 112 kcal/kg$^{0.75}$ 1.6 x RER	Intact 125 kcal/kg$^{0.75}$ 1.8 x RER
1	2.2	70	100	112	125
2	4.4	118	168	188	210
3	6.6	160	228	255	285
4	8.8	198	283	317	354
5	11.0	234	334	374	418
6	13.2	268	383	429	479
7	15.4	301	430	482	538
8	17.6	333	476	533	595
9	19.8	364	520	582	650
10	22.0	394	562	630	703
11	24.2	423	604	676	755
12	26.4	451	645	722	806
13	28.6	479	685	767	856
14	30.8	507	724	811	905
15	33.0	534	762	854	953
16	35.2	560	800	896	1,000
17	37.4	586	837	938	1,047
18	39.6	612	874	979	1,092
19	41.8	637	910	1,019	1,138
20	44.0	662	946	1,059	1,182
21	46.2	687	981	1,099	1,226
22	48.4	711	1,016	1,138	1,270
23	50.6	735	1,050	1,176	1,313
24	52.8	759	1,084	1,214	1,355
25	55.0	783	1,118	1,252	1,398
26	57.2	806	1,151	1,290	1,439
27	59.4	829	1,184	1,327	1,481
28	61.6	852	1,217	1,363	1,522
29	63.8	875	1,250	1,400	1,562
30	66.0	897	1,282	1,436	1,602
31	68.2	920	1,314	1,471	1,642
32	70.4	942	1,345	1,507	1,682
33	72.6	964	1,377	1,542	1,721
34	74.8	986	1,408	1,577	1,760
35	77.0	1,007	1,439	1,612	1,799
36	79.2	1,029	1,470	1,646	1,837
37	81.4	1,050	1,500	1,680	1,875
38	83.6	1,071	1,531	1,714	1,913
39	85.8	1,092	1,561	1,748	1,951
40	88.0	1,113	1,591	1,781	1,988
41	90.2	1,134	1,620	1,815	2,025
42	92.4	1,155	1,650	1,848	2,062
43	94.6	1,175	1,679	1,881	2,099
44	96.8	1,196	1,708	1,913	2,135
45	99.0	1,216	1,737	1,946	2,172
46	101.2	1,236	1,766	1,978	2,208
47	103.4	1,257	1,795	2,010	2,244
48	105.6	1,277	1,824	2,042	2,280
49	107.8	1,296	1,852	2,074	2,315
50	110.0	1,316	1,880	2,106	2,350
52	114.4	1,356	1,936	2,169	2,421
54	118.8	1,394	1,992	2,231	2,490
56	123.2	1,433	2,047	2,293	2,559
58	127.6	1,471	2,102	2,354	2,627
60	132.0	1,509	2,156	2,415	2,695
62	136.4	1,547	2,209	2,475	2,762
64	140.8	1,584	2,263	2,534	2,828
66	145.2	1,621	2,316	2,593	2,894
68	149.6	1,658	2,368	2,652	2,960
70	154.0	1,694	2,420	2,710	3,025
72	158.4	1,730	2,472	2,768	3,090
74	162.8	1,766	2,523	2,826	3,154
76	167.2	1,802	2,574	2,883	3,218
78	171.6	1,837	2,625	2,940	3,281
80	176.0	1,872	2,675	2,996	3,344

Key: RER = resting energy requirement, kcal = kilocalories, kg = kilograms, lb = pounds.

Table G-3. Daily energy requirements of active adult dogs in kilocalories metabolizable energy (kcal ME/kg$^{0.75}$).

Body weights		Light work 140 kcal/kg$^{0.75}$ 2.0 x RER	Moderate work 210 kcal/kg$^{0.75}$ 3.0 x RER	Heavy work	
kg	lb			280 kcal/kg$^{0.75}$ 4.0 x RER	560 kcal/kg$^{0.75}$ 8.0 x RER
1	2.2	140	210	280	560
2	4.4	235	353	471	942
3	6.6	319	479	638	1,277
4	8.8	396	594	792	1,584
5	11.0	468	702	936	1,872
6	13.2	537	805	1,073	2,147
7	15.4	602	904	1,205	2,410
8	17.6	666	999	1,332	2,664
9	19.8	727	1,091	1,455	2,910
10	22.0	787	1,181	1,575	3,149
11	24.2	846	1,268	1,691	3,382
12	26.4	903	1,354	1,805	3,611
13	28.6	958	1,438	1,917	3,834
14	30.8	1,013	1,520	2,027	4,053
15	33.0	1,067	1,601	2,134	4,268
16	35.2	1,120	1,680	2,240	4,480
17	37.4	1,172	1,758	2,344	4,688
18	39.6	1,223	1,835	2,447	4,894
19	41.8	1,274	1,911	2,548	5,096
20	44.0	1,324	1,986	2,648	5,296
21	46.2	1,373	2,060	2,747	5,494
22	48.4	1,422	2,133	2,844	5,689
23	50.6	1,470	2,206	2,941	5,881
24	52.8	1,518	2,277	3,036	6,072
25	55.0	1,565	2,348	3,130	6,261
26	57.2	1,612	2,418	3,224	6,448
27	59.4	1,658	2,487	3,317	6,633
28	61.6	1,704	2,556	3,408	6,816
29	63.8	1,750	2,624	3,499	6,998
30	66.0	1,795	2,692	3,589	7,178
31	68.2	1,839	2,759	3,679	7,357
32	70.4	1,884	2,825	3,767	7,534
33	72.6	1,928	2,891	3,855	7,710
34	74.8	1,971	2,957	3,942	7,885
35	77.0	2,015	3,022	4,029	8,058
36	79.2	2,058	3,086	4,115	8,230
37	81.4	2,100	3,150	4,201	8,401
38	83.6	2,143	3,214	4,285	8,571
39	85.8	2,185	3,277	4,370	8,739
40	88.0	2,227	3,340	4,454	8,907
41	90.2	2,268	3,403	4,537	9,074
42	92.4	2,310	3,465	4,620	9,239
43	94.6	2,351	3,526	4,702	9,403
44	96.8	2,392	3,588	4,784	9,567
45	99.0	2,432	3,649	4,865	9,730
46	101.2	2,473	3,709	4,946	9,891
47	103.4	2,513	3,770	5,026	10,052
48	105.6	2,553	3,830	5,106	10,212
49	107.8	2,593	3,889	5,186	10,371
50	110.0	2,632	3,949	5,265	10,530
52	114.4	2,711	4,067	5,422	10,844
54	118.8	2,789	4,183	5,578	11,155
56	123.2	2,866	4,299	5,732	11,464
58	127.6	2,942	4,414	5,885	11,770
60	132.0	3,018	4,527	6,036	12,073
62	136.4	3,093	4,640	6,187	12,373
64	140.8	3,168	4,752	6,336	12,671
66	145.2	3,242	4,863	6,484	12,967
68	149.6	3,315	4,973	6,630	13,261
70	154.0	3,388	5,082	6,776	13,552
72	158.4	3,460	5,191	6,921	13,842
74	162.8	3,532	5,298	7,065	14,129
76	167.2	3,604	5,405	7,207	14,414
78	171.6	3,675	5,512	7,349	14,698
80	176.0	3,745	5,617	7,490	14,980

Key: RER = resting energy requirement, kcal = kilocalories, kg = kilograms, lb = pounds.

Table G-4. Daily energy requirements of adult dogs in megajoules metabolizable energy (MJ ME/kg$^{0.75}$).

Body weights		RER 0.293 MJ/kg$^{0.75}$	Obese prone 0.42 MJ/kg$^{0.75}$ 1.4 x RER	Neutered 0.47 MJ/kg$^{0.75}$ 1.6 x RER	Intact 0.525 MJ/kg$^{0.75}$ 1.8 x RER
kg	lb				
1	2.2	0.29	0.42	0.47	0.53
2	4.4	0.49	0.71	0.79	0.88
3	6.6	0.67	0.96	1.07	1.20
4	8.8	0.83	1.19	1.33	1.48
5	11.0	0.98	1.40	1.57	1.76
6	13.2	1.12	1.61	1.80	2.01
7	15.4	1.26	1.81	2.02	2.26
8	17.6	1.39	2.00	2.24	2.50
9	19.8	1.52	2.18	2.44	2.73
10	22.0	1.65	2.36	2.64	2.95
11	24.2	1.77	2.54	2.84	3.17
12	26.4	1.89	2.71	3.03	3.38
13	28.6	2.01	2.88	3.22	3.59
14	30.8	2.12	3.04	3.40	3.80
15	33.0	2.23	3.20	3.58	4.00
16	35.2	2.34	3.36	3.76	4.20
17	37.4	2.45	3.52	3.93	4.40
18	39.6	2.56	3.67	4.11	4.59
19	41.8	2.67	3.82	4.28	4.78
20	44.0	2.77	3.97	4.44	4.97
21	46.2	2.87	4.12	4.61	5.15
22	48.4	2.98	4.27	4.77	5.33
23	50.6	3.08	4.41	4.94	5.51
24	52.8	3.18	4.55	5.10	5.69
25	55.0	3.28	4.70	5.25	5.87
26	57.2	3.37	4.84	5.41	6.04
27	59.4	3.47	4.97	5.57	6.22
28	61.6	3.57	5.11	5.72	6.39
29	63.8	3.66	5.25	5.87	6.56
30	66.0	3.76	5.38	6.02	6.73
31	68.2	3.85	5.52	6.17	6.90
32	70.4	3.94	5.65	6.32	7.06
33	72.6	4.03	5.78	6.47	7.23
34	74.8	4.13	5.91	6.62	7.39
35	77.0	4.22	6.04	6.76	7.55
36	79.2	4.31	6.17	6.91	7.72
37	81.4	4.40	6.30	7.05	7.88
38	83.6	4.48	6.43	7.19	8.04
39	85.8	4.57	6.55	7.33	8.19
40	88.0	4.66	6.68	7.48	8.35
41	90.2	4.75	6.81	7.62	8.51
42	92.4	4.83	6.93	7.75	8.66
43	94.6	4.92	7.05	7.89	8.82
44	96.8	5.01	7.18	8.03	8.97
45	99.0	5.09	7.30	8.17	9.12
46	101.2	5.18	7.42	8.30	9.27
47	103.4	5.26	7.54	8.44	9.42
48	105.6	5.34	7.66	8.57	9.57
49	107.8	5.43	7.78	8.70	9.72
50	110.0	5.51	7.90	8.84	9.87
52	114.4	5.67	8.13	9.10	10.17
54	118.8	5.84	8.37	9.36	10.46
56	123.2	6.00	8.60	9.62	10.75
58	127.6	6.16	8.83	9.88	11.03
60	132.0	6.32	9.05	10.13	11.32
62	136.4	6.47	9.28	10.38	11.60
64	140.8	6.63	9.50	10.63	11.88
66	145.2	6.78	9.73	10.88	12.16
68	149.6	6.94	9.95	11.13	12.43
70	154.0	7.09	10.16	11.37	12.71
72	158.4	7.24	10.38	11.62	12.98
74	162.8	7.39	10.60	11.86	13.25
76	167.2	7.54	10.81	12.10	13.51
78	171.6	7.69	11.02	12.34	13.78
80	176.0	7.84	11.23	12.57	14.04

Key: RER = resting energy requirement, MJ = megajoules, kg = kilograms, lb = pounds.

Table G-5. Daily energy requirements of active adult dogs in megajoules metabolizable energy (MJ ME/kg$^{0.75}$).

Body weights		Light work 0.585 MJ/kg$^{0.75}$ 2.0 x RER	Moderate work 0.88 MJ/kg$^{0.75}$ 3.0 x RER	Heavy work	
kg	lb			1.17 MJ/kg$^{0.75}$ 4.0 x RER	2.35 MJ/kg$^{0.75}$ 8.0 x RER
1	2.2	0.59	0.88	1.17	2.35
2	4.4	0.98	1.48	1.97	3.94
3	6.6	1.33	2.01	2.67	5.35
4	8.8	1.65	2.49	3.31	6.63
5	11.0	1.96	2.94	3.91	7.84
6	13.2	2.24	3.37	4.49	8.99
7	15.4	2.52	3.79	5.04	10.09
8	17.6	2.78	4.19	5.57	11.15
9	19.8	3.04	4.57	6.08	12.18
10	22.0	3.29	4.95	6.58	13.19
11	24.2	3.53	5.32	7.07	14.16
12	26.4	3.77	5.67	7.54	15.12
13	28.6	4.01	6.02	8.01	16.05
14	30.8	4.23	6.37	8.47	16.97
15	33.0	4.46	6.71	8.92	17.87
16	35.2	4.68	7.04	9.36	18.76
17	37.4	4.90	7.37	9.80	19.63
18	39.6	5.11	7.69	10.22	20.49
19	41.8	5.32	8.01	10.65	21.34
20	44.0	5.53	8.32	11.07	22.18
21	46.2	5.74	8.63	11.48	23.00
22	48.4	5.94	8.94	11.89	23.82
23	50.6	6.14	9.24	12.29	24.63
24	52.8	6.34	9.54	12.69	25.43
25	55.0	6.54	9.84	13.08	26.22
26	57.2	6.74	10.13	13.47	27.00
27	59.4	6.93	10.42	13.86	27.78
28	61.6	7.12	10.71	14.24	28.54
29	63.8	7.31	11.00	14.62	29.30
30	66.0	7.50	11.28	15.00	30.06
31	68.2	7.69	11.56	15.37	30.81
32	70.4	7.87	11.84	15.74	31.55
33	72.6	8.05	12.12	16.11	32.29
34	74.8	8.24	12.39	16.47	33.02
35	77.0	8.42	12.66	16.84	33.74
36	79.2	8.60	12.93	17.20	34.46
37	81.4	8.78	13.20	17.55	35.18
38	83.6	8.95	13.47	17.91	35.89
39	85.8	9.13	13.73	18.26	36.60
40	88.0	9.30	14.00	18.61	37.30
41	90.2	9.48	14.26	18.96	38.00
42	92.4	9.65	14.52	19.30	38.69
43	94.6	9.82	14.78	19.65	39.38
44	96.8	9.99	15.03	19.99	40.06
45	99.0	10.16	15.29	20.33	40.74
46	101.2	10.33	15.54	20.67	41.42
47	103.4	10.50	15.80	21.00	42.09
48	105.6	10.67	16.05	21.34	42.76
49	107.8	10.83	16.30	21.67	43.43
50	110.0	11.00	16.55	22.00	44.09
52	114.4	11.33	17.04	22.66	45.41
54	118.8	11.65	17.53	23.31	46.71
56	123.2	11.98	18.01	23.95	48.00
58	127.6	12.29	18.49	24.59	49.28
60	132.0	12.61	18.97	25.22	50.55
62	136.4	12.93	19.44	25.85	51.81
64	140.8	13.24	19.91	26.47	53.06
66	145.2	13.55	20.38	27.09	54.30
68	149.6	13.85	20.84	27.71	55.53
70	154.0	14.16	21.30	28.31	56.75
72	158.4	14.46	21.75	28.92	57.96
74	162.8	14.76	22.20	29.52	59.17
76	167.2	15.06	22.65	30.12	60.36
78	171.6	15.35	23.10	30.71	61.55
80	176.0	15.65	23.54	31.30	62.73

Key: RER = resting energy requirement, MJ = megajoules, kg = kilograms, lb = pounds.

Daily energy requirements of pregnant bitches

Energy requirements during gestation are the sum of the energy needed for normal adult maintenance of a non-pregnant dog (daily energy requirement [DER]) plus what is needed to accrete fetal and maternal tissue. Because accretion of fetal and maternal tissue is minimal during the first 35 days of gestation, the increase in energy requirement only becomes significant from the sixth week on. However, it is better to increase the food intake progressively starting at Week 5. This allows the bitch to build reserves for the last week of gestation, during which food intake is compromised by abdominal fill. During gestation, DER is estimated as 1.9 x RER (132 kcal ME/kg$^{0.75}$ or 550 kJ ME/kg$^{0.75}$).

Table G-6. Summary of daily energy requirements of pregnant bitches based on week of gestation.*

Weeks of gestation	Total DER (kcal ME/day)	Total DER (kJ ME/day)
1-4	DER**	DER**
5	DER + 18 kcal ME/kg BW	DER + 75 kJ ME/kg BW
6-8	DER + 36 kcal ME/kg BW	DER + 150 kJ ME/kg BW
9	DER + 18 kcal ME/kg BW	DER + 75 kJ ME/kg BW

Key: DER = daily energy requirement, kcal = kilocalories, ME = metabolizable energy, kJ = kilojoules, BW = body weight.
*Gesellschaft für Ernährungsphysiologie Empfehlungen für die Versorgung mit Energie. In: Ausschuß der Bedarfsnormen der Gesellschaft für Ernährungsphysiologie Energie- und Nährstoffbedarf (Energy and Nutrient Requirements), No. 5 Hunde/Dogs. Frankfurt/Main, Germany: DLG Verlag, 1989; 32-44.
**During gestation, DER is estimated 1.9 x RER (132 kcal ME/kg$^{0.75}$ or 550 kJ ME/kg$^{0.75}$).

Table G-7. Daily energy requirements of pregnant bitches in kilocalories metabolizable energy.*

Body weights kg	lb	Weeks 1-4	Week 5	Weeks 6-8	Week 9
1	2.2	132	150	168	150
2	4.4	222	258	294	258
3	6.6	301	355	409	355
4	8.8	373	445	517	445
5	11.0	441	531	621	531
6	13.2	506	614	722	614
7	15.4	568	694	820	694
8	17.6	628	772	916	772
9	19.8	686	848	1,010	848
10	22.0	742	922	1,102	922
11	24.2	797	995	1,193	995
12	26.4	851	1,067	1,283	1,067
13	28.6	904	1,138	1,372	1,138
14	30.8	955	1,207	1,459	1,207
15	33.0	1,006	1,276	1,546	1,276
16	35.2	1,056	1,344	1,632	1,344
17	37.4	1,105	1,411	1,717	1,411
18	39.6	1,154	1,478	1,802	1,478
19	41.8	1,201	1,543	1,885	1,543
20	44.0	1,248	1,608	1,968	1,608
21	46.2	1,295	1,673	2,051	1,673
22	48.4	1,341	1,737	2,133	1,737
23	50.6	1,386	1,800	2,214	1,800
24	52.8	1,431	1,863	2,295	1,863
25	55.0	1,476	1,926	2,376	1,926
26	57.2	1,520	1,988	2,456	1,988
27	59.4	1,563	2,049	2,535	2,049
28	61.6	1,607	2,111	2,615	2,111
29	63.8	1,650	2,172	2,694	2,172
30	66.0	1,692	2,232	2,772	2,232
31	68.2	1,734	2,292	2,850	2,292
32	70.4	1,776	2,352	2,928	2,352
33	72.6	1,817	2,411	3,005	2,411
34	74.8	1,859	2,471	3,083	2,471
35	77.0	1,899	2,529	3,159	2,529
36	79.2	1,940	2,588	3,236	2,588
37	81.4	1,980	2,646	3,312	2,646
38	83.6	2,020	2,704	3,388	2,704
39	85.8	2,060	2,762	3,464	2,762
40	88.0	2,100	2,820	3,540	2,820

(Continued on next page.)

Table G-7. Daily energy requirements of pregnant bitches in kilocalories metabolizable energy.* (Continued from previous page.)

Body weights		kcal ME per day			
kg	lb	Weeks 1-4	Week 5	Weeks 6-8	Week 9
42	92.4	2,178	2,934	3,690	2,934
44	96.8	2,255	3,047	3,839	3,047
46	101.2	2,332	3,160	3,988	3,160
48	105.6	2,407	3,271	4,135	3,271
50	110.0	2,482	3,382	4,282	3,382
52	114.4	2,556	3,492	4,428	3,492
54	118.8	2,629	3,601	4,573	3,601
56	123.2	2,702	3,710	4,718	3,710
58	127.6	2,774	3,818	4,862	3,818
60	132.0	2,846	3,926	5,006	3,926
62	136.4	2,917	4,033	5,149	4,033
64	140.8	2,987	4,139	5,291	4,139
66	145.2	3,057	4,245	5,433	4,245
68	149.6	3,126	4,350	5,574	4,350
70	154.0	3,194	4,454	5,714	4,454
72	158.4	3,263	4,559	5,855	4,559
74	162.8	3,330	4,662	5,994	4,662
76	167.2	3,398	4,766	6,134	4,766
78	171.6	3,465	4,869	6,273	4,869
80	176.0	3,531	4,971	6,411	4,971

Key: kcal = kilocalories, ME = metabolizable energy, kg = kilograms, lb = pounds.
*Gesellschaft für Ernährungsphysiologie Empfehlungen für die Versorgung mit Energie. In: Ausschuß für bedarfsnormen der Gesellschaft für Ernährungsphysiologie Energie- und Nährstoffbedarf (Energy and Nutrient Requirements), No. 5 Hunde/Dogs. Frankfurt/Main, Germany: DLG Verlag, 1989; 32-44.

Table G-8. Daily energy requirements of pregnant bitches in megajoules metabolizable energy.*

Body weights		MJ ME per day			
kg	lb	Weeks 1-4	Week 5	Weeks 6-8	Week 9
1	2.2	0.55	0.63	0.70	0.63
2	4.4	0.93	1.08	1.23	1.08
3	6.6	1.26	1.48	1.71	1.48
4	8.8	1.56	1.86	2.16	1.86
5	11.0	1.85	2.22	2.60	2.22
6	13.2	2.12	2.57	3.02	2.57
7	15.4	2.38	2.90	3.43	2.90
8	17.6	2.63	3.23	3.83	3.23
9	19.8	2.87	3.55	4.23	3.55
10	22.0	3.11	3.86	4.61	3.86
11	24.2	3.34	4.16	4.99	4.16
12	26.4	3.56	4.46	5.37	4.46
13	28.6	3.78	4.76	5.74	4.76
14	30.8	4.00	5.05	6.11	5.05
15	33.0	4.21	5.34	6.47	5.34
16	35.2	4.42	5.62	6.83	5.62
17	37.4	4.62	5.90	7.18	5.90
18	39.6	4.83	6.18	7.54	6.18
19	41.8	5.03	6.46	7.89	6.46
20	44.0	5.22	6.73	8.24	6.73
21	46.2	5.42	7.00	8.58	7.00
22	48.4	5.61	7.27	8.92	7.27
23	50.6	5.80	7.53	9.26	7.53
24	52.8	5.99	7.80	9.60	7.80
25	55.0	6.17	8.06	9.94	8.06
26	57.2	6.36	8.32	10.28	8.32
27	59.4	6.54	8.58	10.61	8.58
28	61.6	6.72	8.83	10.94	8.83
29	63.8	6.90	9.09	11.27	9.09
30	66.0	7.08	9.34	11.60	9.34
31	68.2	7.26	9.59	11.93	9.59
32	70.4	7.43	9.84	12.25	9.84
33	72.6	7.60	10.09	12.57	10.09
34	74.8	7.78	10.34	12.90	10.34
35	77.0	7.95	10.58	13.22	10.58
36	79.2	8.12	10.83	13.54	10.83
37	81.4	8.29	11.07	13.86	11.07
38	83.6	8.45	11.31	14.18	11.31
39	85.8	8.62	11.56	14.49	11.56
40	88.0	8.78	11.80	14.81	11.80

(Continued on next page.)

Table G-8. Daily energy requirements of pregnant bitches in megajoules metabolizable energy.* (Continued from previous page.)

| Body weights | | MJ ME per day | | | |
kg	lb	Weeks 1-4	Week 5	Weeks 6-8	Week 9
42	92.4	9.11	12.27	15.44	12.27
44	96.8	9.44	12.75	16.06	12.75
46	101.2	9.76	13.22	16.68	13.22
48	105.6	10.07	13.69	17.30	13.69
50	110.0	10.38	14.15	17.92	14.15
52	114.4	10.69	14.61	18.53	14.61
54	118.8	11.00	15.07	19.14	15.07
56	123.2	11.31	15.52	19.74	15.52
58	127.6	11.61	15.98	20.34	15.98
60	132.0	11.91	16.43	20.94	16.43
62	136.4	12.20	16.87	21.54	16.87
64	140.8	12.50	17.32	22.14	17.32
66	145.2	12.79	17.76	22.73	17.76
68	149.6	13.08	18.20	23.32	18.20
70	154.0	13.37	18.64	23.91	18.64
72	158.4	13.65	19.07	24.50	19.07
74	162.8	13.93	19.51	25.08	19.51
76	167.2	14.22	19.94	25.66	19.94
78	171.6	14.50	20.37	26.24	20.37
80	176.0	14.77	20.80	26.82	20.80

Key: MJ = megajoules, ME = metabolizable energy, kg = kilograms, lb = pounds.
*Gesellschaft für Ernährungsphysiologie Empfehlungen für die Versorgung mit Energie. In: Ausschuß für Bedarfsnormen der Gesellschaft für Ernährungsphysiologie Energie- und Nährstoffbedarf (Energy and Nutrient Requirements), No. 5 Hunde/Dogs. Frankfurt/Main, Germany: DLG Verlag, 1989; 32-44.

Daily energy requirements of lactating bitches

Bitches should be fed free choice during lactation. However, bitches with small litters may be meal fed in at least three daily meals. The energy requirement of a lactating bitch includes energy for adult maintenance and the energy needed to produce milk. During the first five weeks of lactation, milk production, and therefore energy requirement for milk production, is primarily related to the number of puppies. The following

table is only a starting point for energy requirement. The quantity of food and therefore the energy needed must be adapted to each individual bitch. As a rule of thumb, during peak lactation, bitches need 132 kcal (550 kJ) ME per kg$^{0.75}$ for adult maintenance (1.9 x RER), plus 25% of this amount should be added for each puppy. When a bitch has only one or two puppies, the additional energy needed for milk production may increase to 30 to 50% per puppy.

Table G-9. Daily energy requirements for lactation.

Number of puppies	DER
1	3 x RER
2	3.5 x RER
3-4	4 x RER
5-6	5 x RER
7-8	5.5 x RER
≥9	≥6 x RER

Key: DER = daily energy requirement, RER = resting energy requirement.

III. Feeding guides for cats

Table G-10. Summary of daily energy requirements of adult cats in kilocalories metabolizable energy.*

| Body weights | | RER | Intact | Neutered | Linear formula |
kg	lb	70 kcal/kg$^{0.75}$	100 kcal/kg$^{0.75}$ 1.4 x RER	85 kcal/kg$^{0.75}$ 1.2 x RER	65 kcal/kg BW
2	4.4	118	168	143	130
3	6.6	160	228	194	195
4	8.8	198	283	240	260
5	11.0	234	334	284	325
6	13.2	268	383	326	390
7	15.4	301	430	366	455
8	17.6	333	476	404	520
9	19.8	364	520	442	585
10	22.0	394	562	478	650

Key: DER = daily energy requirement, RER = resting energy requirement, kg = kilograms, lb = pounds, kcal = kilocalories, BW = body weight.
*Daily energy requirements of obese-prone cats may be close to RER, whereas active cats may need up to 90 kcal/kg body weight.

Table G-11. Summary of daily energy requirements of adult cats in kilojoules metabolizable energy.*

Body weights		RER	Intact	Neutered	Linear formula
kg	lb	293 kJ/kg$^{0.75}$	410 kJ/kg$^{0.75}$ 1.4 RER	350 kJ/kg$^{0.75}$ 1.2 x RER	272 kJ/kg BW
2	4.4	493	690	589	544
3	6.6	668	935	798	816
4	8.8	829	1,160	990	1,088
5	11.0	980	1,371	1,170	1,360
6	13.2	1,123	1,572	1,342	1,632
7	15.4	1,261	1,764	1,506	1,904
8	17.6	1,394	1,950	1,665	2,176
9	19.8	1,522	2,130	1,819	2,448
10	22.0	1,648	2,306	1,968	2,720

Key: DER = daily energy requirement, RER = resting energy requirement, kg = kilograms, lb = pounds, kJ = kilojoules, BW = body weight.
*Daily energy requirements of obese-prone cats may be close to RER, whereas active cats may need up to 375 kJ/kg body weight.

Daily energy requirements of pregnant queens

Daily energy requirements of pregnant queens increase progressively from about 90 kcal (375 kJ) metabolizable energy/kg body weight to more than 100 kcal (420 kJ) metabolizable energy/kg body weight.

Table G-12. Daily energy requirements of pregnant queens.

Body weights		kcal ME/day		kJ ME/day	
kg	lb	90 kcal/kg BW	100 kcal/kg BW	375 kJ/kg BW	kJ/kg BW
2	4.4	180	200	750	840
3	6.6	270	300	1,125	1,260
4	8.8	360	400	1,500	1,680
5	11.0	450	500	1,875	2,100
6	13.2	540	600	2,250	2,520
7	15.4	630	700	2,625	2,940
8	17.6	720	800	3,000	3,360
9	19.8	810	900	3,375	3,780
10	22.0	900	1,000	3,750	4,200

Key: kcal = kilocalories, ME = metabolizable energy, kJ = kilojoules, kg = kilograms, lb = pounds, BW = body weight.

Daily energy requirements of lactating queens

From about Week 4 on, the energy requirements of lactating queens include energy intake by kittens. The following tables are only starting points; the caloric requirements for some queens may even be higher. Therefore, queens should be fed free choice during lactation. At least three daily meals should be provided if the queen is meal fed.

Table G-13. Summary of daily energy requirements of lactating queens.*

Weeks of lactation	DER
Weeks 1-2	RER + 30% per kitten
Week 3	RER + 45% per kitten
Week 4	RER + 55% per kitten
Week 5	RER + 65% per kitten
Week 6	RER + 90% per kitten

Key: DER = daily energy requirement, RER = resting energy requirement.
*National Research Council. Nutrient Requirements of Cats. Washington, DC: National Academy Press, 1986; 41.

Table G-14. Daily energy requirements of lactating queens in kilocalories metabolizable energy/day based on number of kittens.*

Weeks of lactation	Body weights kg	lb	Number of kittens One	Two	Three	Four	Five	Six
1	3	6.6	180	230	275	325	370	370
	4	8.8	240	305	375	430	495	495
	5	11.0	300	380	460	540	620	620
2	3	6.6	200	250	300	350	400	400
	4	8.8	265	330	400	470	535	535
	5	11.0	330	415	500	585	670	670
3	3	6.6	215	280	350	415	480	480
	4	8.8	290	375	465	550	640	640
	5	11.0	360	470	580	690	800	800
4	3	6.6	235	320	400	485	570	570
	4	8.8	310	424	535	650	760	760
	5	11.0	390	530	670	810	950	950
5	3	6.6	252	350	450	550	650	750
	4	8.8	335	470	600	735	870	1,000
	5	11.0	420	585	750	915	1,085	1,250
6	3	6.6	270	408	545	685	820	960
	4	8.8	360	545	730	910	1,095	1,280
	5	11.0	430	680	910	1,140	1,370	1,600

*National Research Council. Nutrient Requirements of Cats. Washington, DC: National Academy Press, 1986; 41.

Table G-15. Daily energy requirements of lactating queens in megajoules metabolizable energy/day based on number of kittens.*

Weeks of lactation	Body weights kg	lb	Number of kittens One	Two	Three	Four	Five	Six
1	3	6.6	0.76	0.96	1.16	1.36	1.56	1.56
	4	8.8	1.01	1.27	1.54	1.81	2.08	2.08
	5	11.0	1.26	1.59	1.93	2.26	2.60	2.60
2	3	6.6	0.83	1.04	1.26	1.47	1.68	1.68
	4	8.8	1.11	1.39	1.68	1.96	2.25	2.25
	5	11.0	1.38	1.74	2.09	2.45	2.81	2.81
3	3	6.6	0.91	1.18	1.46	1.73	2.01	2.01
	4	8.8	1.21	1.58	1.94	2.31	2.68	2.68
	5	11.0	1.51	1.97	2.43	2.89	3.35	3.35
4	3	6.6	0.98	1.33	1.68	2.04	2.39	2.39
	4	8.8	1.31	1.78	2.25	2.71	3.18	3.18
	5	11.0	1.63	2.22	2.81	3.39	3.98	3.98
5	3	6.6	1.06	1.47	1.89	2.30	2.73	3.14
	4	8.8	1.41	1.96	2.51	3.07	3.63	4.19
	5	11.0	1.76	2.45	3.14	3.83	4.54	5.23
6	3	6.6	1.13	1.71	2.29	2.86	3.44	4.02
	4	8.8	1.51	2.28	3.05	3.82	4.59	5.36
	5	11.0	1.80	2.85	3.81	4.77	5.73	6.70

*National Research Council. Nutrient Requirements of Cats. Washington, DC: National Academy Press, 1986; 41.

BIBLIOGRAPHY

1. Gesellschaft für Ernährungsphysiologie Empfehlungen für die Versorgung mit Energie. In: Ausschuß für Bedarfsnormen der Gesellschaft für Ernährungsphysiologie Energie- und Nährstoffbedarf (Energy and Nutrient Requirements), No. 5 Hunde/Dogs. Frankfurt/Main, Germany: DLG Verlag, 1989; 32-44.
2. Lewis LD, Morris ML Jr, Hand MS. Nutrients. In: Small Animal Clinical Nutrition III. Topeka, KS: Mark Morris Associates, 1987; 1-1-1-2.
3. Meyer H, Kienzle E, Dammers C. Milchmenge und Milchzusammensetzung bei der Hündin sowie Futteraufnahme und Gewich-tsenwicklung ante und post partum. Fortschritte in der Tierphysiologie und Tierernährung (Advances in Animal Physiology and Animal Nutrition) 1985; 16: 51-72.
4. National Research Council. Nutrient Requirements of Dogs. Washington, DC: National Academy Press, 1985.
5. National Research Council. Nutrient Requirements of Cats. Washington, DC: National Academy Press, 1986.
6. Ontko JA, Phillips PH. Reproduction and lactation studies with bitches fed semi-purified diets. Journal of Nutrition 1958; 65: 211-218.

Appendix H
Canine Body Weights and Height at Withers

Table H-1. Body weights in kilograms and height at withers in centimeters of selected canine breeds.
Table H-2. Body weights in pounds and height at withers in inches of selected canine breeds.
Bibliography

This appendix provides ranges of body weights and heights at the withers of dogs. These measurements are generally considered as breed standards. These data provide an initial indication about whether an animal is over- or underweight, and can assist in determining the target body weight for obese and growing animals. Because there is much variation among dogs within a breed, the following values cannot be considered as the optimal body weight for an individual dog. Body weight should be related to height at the withers and body condition.

Table H-1. Body weights in kilograms and height at withers in centimeters of selected canine breeds.

Breeds	Body weights (kg)		Height at withers (cm)	
	Females	Males	Females	Males
Affenpinscher	3	4	23	28
Afghan hound	23	27	60-65	65-72.5
Ainu dog	na	na	41-47.5	49-52.5
Airedale terrier	19	25	55-58	58-60
Akita	34	46	60-65	65-70
Alaskan malamute	34	57	57.5-65	62.5-70
American cocker spaniel	11	12.5	34-36	36-39
American Eskimo dog				
Toy	na	na	22.5	30
Miniature	na	na	>30	37.5
Standard	na	na	>37.5	47.5
American water spaniel	11-18	13.5-20.5	37.5-45	37.5-45
Anatolian shepherd dog	41-59	50-64	70-77.5	72.5-80
Anglo-French hound				
Small	22	25	47.5	55
Great	30	32	60	67.5
Appenzell mountain dog	22	25	46-50	55-58
Ariegeois	30	30	52.5-57.5	55-60
Artois hound	18	24	52	59
Australian cattle dog	16	20	42.5-47.5	45-50
Australian kelpie	13.5	13.5	50	50
Australian shepherd	na	na	45-52.5	50-57.5
Australian terrier	6.5	6.5	25	27.5
Basenji	10	11	40	43
Basset hound	18	27	32.5	37.5
Beagle	12	14	32.5	38
Beagle harrier	20	20	42.5	47.5
Bearded collie	18	27	50-52.5	52.5-55
Beauce shepherd (Beauceron)	30	38	60-68	63-70
Bedlington terrier	8	10.5	37.5-41	40-44
Belgian shepherd dog				
Groenendael	28	28	56-60	60-65
Laekenois	28	28	56-60	60-65
Malinois	28	28	56-60	60-65
Tervuren	28	28	56-60	60-65
Bergamasco	26-32	32-38	55	60
Bernese mountain dog (Berner Sennenhund)	4-45	50	57.5-65	62.5-70
Bichon frisé	na	na	23	28
Billy	25	30	57.5-62.5	60-65
Bloodhound (St. Hubertus dog)	36-45.5	41-50	57.5-62.5	62.5-67.5
Bolognese	2.5	4	25-27.5	27.5-30
Bordeaux dog (medium = doguins)	35-40	38-45	na	na
Bordeaux dog (large = dogues)	>40	>45	Smaller than male	58-66
Border collie	13.5	20.5	45-52.5	47.5-55
Border terrier	5-6.4	6-7	25	25
Borzoi	25-41	34-48	≥65	≥70

(Continued on next page.)

Table H-1. Body weights in kilograms and height at withers in centimeters of selected canine breeds. (Continued from previous page.)

Breeds	Body weights (kg)		Height at withers (cm)	
	Females	Males	Females	Males
Boston terrier				
Lightweight class	na	≤6.8	na	na
Middleweight class	na	≤9.0	na	na
Heavyweight class	na	≤11.4	na	na
Bourbonnais setter	18	26	52.5	na
Bouvier des Ardennes	na	na	40-46	42-48
Bouvier des Flandres	27-35	35-40	53-66	61-69
Boxer	24	32	53-59	56-63
Brazilian guard dog	40.5	45	60	74
Briard	34	34	55-64	58-68
Brittany spaniel	13.5	18	44	51
Brussels griffon (Petit Brabançon)	2.2	≤5.5	17.5	22
Bulldog	18-23	23-25	na	na
Bullmastiff	40-54.5	50-59	60-65	62.5-67.5
Bull terrier	23.5	28	52.5	55
Cairn terrier	6	7.5	24	30
Canaan dog	18	25	49	59
Cao de Castro Laboreiro	20-30	30-40	52-57	56-60
(Portuguese watchdog)				
Catalonian shepherd	20-30	30-40	43-48	45-50
Cavalier King Charles spaniel	5	8	30	33
Chesapeake Bay retriever	25-32	29.5-36	52.5-60	57.5-65
Chihuahua	≤2.7	≤2.7	16	20
Chinese crested dog	≤5.5	≤5.5	22.5-30	27.5-32.5
Chow chow	20	32	42.5-50	47.5-55
Clumber spaniel	25-32	32-38.5	42.5-47.5	47.5-50
Collie (rough and smooth)	20-30	25-34	55-60	60-65
Coonhound				
Black and tan coonhound	25-34	27-36	57.5-62.5	62.5-67.5
Redbone coonhound	25-34	27-36	57.5-62.5	62.5-67.5
Coton deTulear	5.5	7	25	30
Curly-coated retriever	32	36	57.5-62.5	62.5-67.5
Czesky terrier	6	9	27.5	35
Dachshund				
Miniature (UK)	4.5	4.5	na	na
Miniature (USA)	≤5	≤5	na	na
Standard (UK)	9.0	12	na	na
Standard (USA)	7.3	14.5	na	na
Dalmatian	22.7	27	47.5	57.5
Dandie Dinmont terrier	8	11	20	27.5
Deerhound (Scottish)	30-43	38.5-50	≥70	75-80
Doberman pinscher	29	40	60-65	65-70
Dogue de Bordeaux	54	65	69	75
Dupuy setter	na	na	64-65	66-67.5
Dutch shepherd	30	30	54-61	57.5-62.5
Elkhound (Norwegian elkhound)	20	25	49	51
English cocker spaniel	12-14.5	12.5-15.5	37.5-40	40-42.5
English setter	18	31.5	60	62.5
English springer spaniel	18	22.5	47.5	50
English toy spaniel (King Charles)	3.5	6.5	25	25
Entlebuch mountain dog	25	30	50	50
Eskimo dog	25-41	30-50	50-60	57.5-67.5
Estrela mountain dog	27-41	34-48	50-60	57.5-67.5
Eurasier	18-26	23-32	48-56	52-60
Field spaniel	16	25	42.5	45
Finnish spitz	11.3	16	39-45	44-50

(Continued on next page.)

Table H-1. Body weights in kilograms and height at withers in centimeters of selected canine breeds. (Continued from previous page.)

Breeds	Body weights (kg)		Height at withers (cm)	
	Females	Males	Females	Males
Flat-coated retriever	25-34	25-36	55-59	57.5-61
Foxhound				
American foxhound	na	na	52.5-60	55-62.5
English foxhound	29.5	32	52.5-60	55-62.5
Fox terrier (smooth and wire)	6.8-7.7	7-8.2	≤39	≤39
French bulldog	8	13	30	30
French hound	27	28	61-67.5	61-71
French setter	27	27	60	60
French spaniel	20	25	52.5-57.5	55-60
German hunt terrier	7-8	9-10	40	40
German pointer (Deutscher Vorstehund)				
German shorthaired pointer	20.5-27	25-32	52.5-57.5	57.5-62.5
German wirehaired pointer	20.5-29	25-34	55-60	60-65
German shepherd dog	32	43	55-60	60-65
German spaniel	20	30	39-44	39-49
German spitz				
Small (Kleinspitz)	2.9	3.0	22.5	27.5
Standard (Mittelspitz)	11.3	11.3	29	32.5
Glen of Imaal terrier	16	16	35	35
Golden retriever	25-29.5	29.5-34	54-56	57.5-60
Gordon setter	20.5-32	25-36	57.5-65	60-67.5
Great Dane	55	80	72 (min.)	80 (min.)
Great Gascony blue	32	35	59-64	62.5-70
Greater Swiss mountain dog	na	na	59-67.5	64-71
Greenland dog	≥30	≥30	55	60
Greyhound	27-29.5	29.5-32	67.5-70	70-75
Griffon Vendéen				
Petit basset	11.5	16	32.5	37.5
Basset	18	20	37.5	42.5
Briquet	16	24	50	55
Grand	30	35	60	65
Hamiltonstövare	23	27	45-56	49-59
Hanover hound	38	45	Smaller than male	50-60
Harlequin pinscher	na	na	30	35
Harrier	22	27	47.5	52.5
Havanese	3	5.5	25	26
Hovawart	25-35	30-40	55-65	60-70
Hungarian coarse-haired vizsla	na	na	52.5-59	56-64
Hungarian greyhound	22.5-27	27-32	na	na
Hungarian Kuvasz	≤50	≤50	65-69	70-74
Ibizan hound	20.5	23	56-65	59-69
Iceland dog	na	na	38-44	42-48
Irish red and white setter	18	32	59	67.5
Irish setter	27.2	31.7	57.5-62.5	67.5
Irish terrier	11	12	45	45
Irish water spaniel	20.5-26	25-29.5	52.5-57.5	55-60
Irish wolfhound	≥48	≥54	≥75	≥80
Italian greyhound	2.5	4.5	32	38
Italian segugio	18	28	47.5-55	52.5-57.5
Italian setter	25	40	na	na
Italian spinone	28-32	32-37	57.5-64	59-69
Jämthund	na	na	52.5-57.5	57.5-62.5
Japanese chin	1.8	3.2	20	27.5
Japanese fighting dog	45	91	≥59	≥59
Japanese spitz	5.9	5.9	Smaller than male	30-35
Japanese terrier	na	na	30	37.5
Jura hound	na	na	44	55
Keeshond	25	30	42.5	45
Kerry blue terrier	na	15-18	44-47.5	45-49

(Continued on next page.)

Table H-1. Body weights in kilograms and height at withers in centimeters of selected canine breeds. (Continued from previous page.)

Breeds	Body weights (kg)		Height at withers (cm)	
	Females	Males	Females	Males
Komondor	36-50	45-68	≥64	≥69
Kooikerhondje	9	11	37.5	37.5
Kromfohrländer	12	12	37.5	45
Kuvasz (Hungarian shepherd)	32-41	45-52	65-70	70-75
Labrador retriever	25-32	29.5-36	54-59	56-61
Lakeland terrier	7	7.7	34	36
Lancashire heeler	3.5	5.4	25	30
Lapland spitz	20	20	39-44	44-49
Lapponian herder	≤30	≤30	43-48	48-55
Leonberger	36.3	68	65-75	73-80
Lhasa apso	na	na	Smaller than male	25
Löwchen	2	4	20	35
Maltese	1.8	2.7	25	25
Manchester terrier				
Toy (American-bred)	≤3.2	≤3.2	na	na
Toy (English toy terrier)	≤5.4	≤5.4	25	30
Standard (American-bred)	≥5.5	≤7.3	na	na
Standard (open classes)	≥7.3	≤10	37.5	40
Maremma sheepdog	30-40	35-45	60-68	65-73
Mastiff	75	90	≥69	≥75
Mexican hairless dog	na	na	40	50
Miniature bull terrier	4.5	18	25	35
Miniature pinscher	4.5	4.5	25	31
Mudi	8	13	35	47.5
Münsterlander				
Small	15	17	47.5	55
Large	25	25-30	57.5	60
Neapolitan mastiff	50	70	60-68	64-72
Newfoundland	50-55	60-69	65	70
Nivernais griffon	23	25	Smaller than male	52.5-57.5
Norfolk terrier	5	5.5	22.5	25
Norwegian buhund	12	18	Smaller than male	42.5-45
Norwich terrier	4.5	5.4	≤25	≤25
Nova Scotia duck tolling retriever	16.5	23	42.5	52.5
Old English sheepdog (bobtail)	25	30	≥52.5	≥55
Otterhound	30-45	34-52	57.5-65	60-67.5
Papillon	1.5	5	20	27.5
Parson Jack Russell terrier	na	na	30-32.5	32.5-35
Pekingese	3-5	3.6-6.5	na	na
Pharaoh hound	na	na	52.5-60	57.5-62.5
Picardy shepherd	23	32	50-60	55-65
Pinscher	na	na	42.5	47.5
Pointer	20-29.5	25-34	57.5-65	62.5-70
Poitevin	30	30	62.5	70
Polish lowland sheepdog	na	na	40-46	42.5-50
Pomeranian	1.5	3.2	27.5	27.5
Poodle				
Toy	na	na	≤25	≤25
Miniature	5	5	>25	37.5
Standard	20	32	>37.5	na
Porcelaine	25	28	52.5-55	55-57.5
Portuguese setter	na	na	47.5-55	51-60
Portuguese water dog	16-23	19-27	42.5-52.5	50-57.5
Pudelpointer	25	32	≥60	≥60
Pug	6.5	8	25	30
Puli (Hungarian puli)	10-13	13-15	36-40	40-44
Pumi	8	13	32.5	44
Pyrenean mastiff	55	70	Smaller than male	69-79

(Continued on next page.)

Table H-1. Body weights in kilograms and height at withers in centimeters of selected canine breeds. (Continued from previous page.)

Breeds	Body weights (kg)		Height at withers (cm)	
	Females	Males	Females	Males
Pyrenean mountain dog (Great Pyrenees)	38.5-45	45.5-55	62.5-72.5	67.5-80
Pyrenean shepherd	8	13.5	38-50	39-50
Rafeiro do alentejo	35-45	40-45	64-70	66-74
Rhodesian ridgeback	32	38.5	60-65	62.5-67.5
Rottweiler	40	50	55-62.5	60-67.5
Rumanian shepherd dog	50	50	63.5	65
Saint Bernard	50	90.5	≥65	≥70
Saint-Germain setter (St-G. Braque)	18	26	na	na
Saluki	13	30	≥54	58-70
Samoyed	17-25	20-30	47.5-53	53-59
Schapendoes (Dutch sheepdog)	na	na	40-47	43-50
Schipperke				
Small type	3	5	25-30	27.5-32.5
Large type	5.4	8.2	25-30	27.5-32.5
Schnauzer				
Miniature	5	6.8	30	35
Standard	15	18	45-46	46-50
Giant (Riesenschnauzer)	30	35	60-65	65-70
Scottish terrier	8-9.5	8.5-10	≥25	≥25
Sealyham terrier	8-9	10-11	26	30 (max.)
Shar-Pei	18	25	45	50
Shetland sheepdog (sheltie)	na	na	32.5	40
Shiba Inu	9	13.6	34-39	36-41
Shih Tzu	4	8	22.5	26
Siberian husky	16-22.5	20-27	50-55	53-60
Sicilian hound	10-12	12-14	42.5-45	45-50
Silky terrier (Australian)	3.6	4.5	22.5	25
Skye terrier	11.5	11.5	24	25
Sloughi	20	27	58	75
Soft-coated wheaten terrier	13.5-16	16-18	42.5-45	45-47.5
Spanish greyhound (Galgo Espanol)	27	30	Smaller than male	64-69
Spanish mastiff	50	60	Smaller than male	65-70
Stabyhoun	15	20	na	≤47.5
Staffordshire bull terrier	11-15	13-17	35	40
Staffordshire terrier (American)	na	na	42.5-45	45-47.5
Sussex spaniel	16	20	32.5	37.5
Swedish vallhund	11.4	16	30-32.5	32.5-34.4
Swiss scent hound (Laufhunde)	na	na	44	55
Tahltan bear dog	6.8	6.8	30	40
Tawny brittany basset	na	na	32.5	42.5
Tibetan mastiff	≥82	≥82	≥60	≥65
Tibetan spaniel	4	6.8	25	25
Tibetan terrier	8	13.6	35	42
Vizsla (Hungarian vizsla)	20	30	52.5-58	56-60
Weimaraner	32	38	57.5-62.5	62.5-67.5
Welsh corgi				
Cardigan	11.4-15.5	13.6-17	26	31
Pembroke	10-12.7	10-13.6	25	30
Welsh springer spaniel	16	20	42.5-45	45-47.5
Welsh terrier	9	9.5	Smaller than male	37.5
West Highland white terrier	7	10	25	27.5
Whippet	13	13	45-52.5	47.5-55
Wirehaired pointing griffon	23	27	50-55	55-60
Yorkshire Terrier	≤3.5	≤3.5	22.5	22.5

Key: na = information not available.

Table H-2. Body weights in pounds and height at withers in inches of selected canine breeds.

Breeds	Body weights (lb)		Height at withers (inches)	
	Females	Males	Females	Males
Affenpinscher	6.5	9	9	11
Afghan hound	50	60	24-26	26-29
Ainu dog	na	na	16.5-19	19.5-21
Airedale terrier	42	55	22-23	23-24
Akita	75	101	24-26	26-28
Alaskan malamute	75	126	23-26	25-28
American cocker spaniel	24	28	13.5-14.5	14.5-15.5
American Eskimo dog				
Toy	na	na	≥9	≥12
Miniature	na	na	>12	15
Standard	na	na	>15	19
American water spaniel	25-40	30-45	15-18	15-18
Anatolian shepherd dog	90.5-130	110-141	28-31	29-32
Anglo-French hound				
Small	49	55	19	22
Great	66	71	24	27
Appenzell mountain dog	48.5	55	18.5-20	22-23
Ariegeois	66	66	21-23	22-24
Artois hound	40	53	20.8	23.8
Australian cattle dog	35	45	17-19	18-20
Australian kelpie	30	30	20	20
Australian shepherd	na	na	18-21	20-23
Australian terrier	14	14	10	11
Basenji	22	24	16	17
Basset hound	40	60	13	15
Beagle	26.5	31	13	15
Beagle harrier	44	44	17	19
Bearded collie	40	60	20-21	21-22
Beauce shepherd (Beauceron)	66	85	24-27	25-28
Bedlington terrier	17	23	15-16.5	16-17.5
Belgian shepherd dog				
Groenendael	62	62	22-24	24-26
Laekenois	62	62	22-24	24-26
Malinois	62	62	22-24	24-26
Tervuren	62	62	22-24	24-26
Bergamasco	57-70	70-84	22	24
Bernese mountain dog (Berner Sennenhund)	88-100	110	23-26	25-28
Bichon frisé	na	na	9	11
Billy	55	66	23-25	24-26
Bloodhound (St. Hubertus dog)	80-100	90-110	23-25	25-27
Bolognese	5.5	9	10-11	11-12
Bordeaux dog (medium = doguins)	77-88	84-99	na	na
Bordeaux dog (large = dogues)	>88	>99	Smaller than male	23-26.5
Border collie	30	45	18-21	19-22
Border terrier	11.5-14	13-15.5	10	10
Borzoi	55-90	75-105	≥26	≥28
Boston terrier				
Lightweight class	na	≤15	na	na
Middleweight class	na	≤20	na	na
Heavyweight class	na	≤25	na	na
Bourbonnais setter	40	57	21	21
Bouvier des Ardennes	na	na	16-18.5	17-19
Bouvier des Flandres	60-77	77-88	21-26.5	24.5-27.5
Boxer	53	70	21-23.5	22.5-25
Brazilian guard dog	89	99	24	29.5
Briard	75	75	22-25.5	23-27
Brittany spaniel	30	40	17.5	20.5
Brussels griffon (Petit Brabançon)	5	≤12	7	8

(Continued on next page.)

Table H-2. Body weights in pounds and height at withers in inches of selected canine breeds. (Continued from previous page.)

Breeds	Body weights (lb)		Height at withers (inches)	
	Females	Males	Females	Males
Bulldog	40-50	50-55	na	na
Bullmastiff	88-120	110-130	24-26	25-27
Bull terrier	52	62	21	22
Cairn terrier	13	16	9.5	12
Canaan dog	40	55	19.5	23.5
Cao de Castro Laboreiro (Portuguese watchdog)	44-66	66-88	21-23	22-24
Catalonian shepherd	44-66	66-88	17-19	18-20
Cavalier King Charles spaniel	10	18	12	13
Chesapeake Bay retriever	55-70	65-80	21-24	23-26
Chihuahua	≤6	≤6	6.3	8
Chinese crested dog	≤12	≤12	9-12	11-13
Chow chow	44.5	70	17-20	19-22
Clumber spaniel	55-70	70-85	17-19	19-20
Collie (rough and smooth)	44-65	55-75	22-24	24-26
Coonhound				
Black and tan coonhound	55-75	60-80	23-25	25-27
Redbone coonhound	55-75	60-80	23-25	25-27
Coton deTulear	12	15	10	12
Curly-coated retriever	70	80	23-25	25-27
Czesky terrier	13	20	11	14
Dachshund				
Miniature (UK)	10	10	na	na
Miniature (USA)	≤11	≤11	na	na
Standard (UK)	20	26	na	na
Standard (USA)	16	32	na	na
Dalmatian	50	59.5	19	23
Dandie Dinmont terrier	18	24	8	11
Deerhound (Scottish deerhound)	66-95	85-110	≥28	30-32
Doberman pinscher	64	88	24-26	26-28
Dogue de Bordeaux	119	143	27.5	30
Dupuy setter	na	na	25.5-26	26.5-27
Dutch shepherd	≥66	≥66	21.5-24.5	23-25
Elkhound	44	55	19.5	20.5
English cocker spaniel	26.5-32	27.5-34	15-16	16-17
English setter	40	70	24	25
English springer spaniel	40	50	19	20
English toy spaniel (King Charles)	8	14	10	10
Entlebuch mountain dog	55	66	20	20
Eskimo dog	55-90	66-110	20-24	23-27
Estrela mountain dog	60-90	75-105	20-24	23-27
Eurasier	40-57	51-71	19-22.5	21-24
Field spaniel	35	55	17	18
Finnish spitz	25	35	15.5-18	17.5-20
Flat-coated retriever	55-75	55-80	22-23.5	23-24.5
Foxhound				
American foxhound	na	na	21-24	22-25
English foxhound	65	70	21-24	22-25
Fox terrier (smooth and wire)	15-17	16-18	≤15.5	≤15.5
French bulldog	18	29	12	12
French hound	60	62	24.5-27	24.5-28.5
French setter	60	60	24	24
French spaniel	44	55	21-23	22-24
German hunt terrier	16-18	19.5-22	16	16
German pointer (Deutscher Vorstehund)				
German shorthaired pointer	45-60	55-70	21-23	23-25
German wirehaired pointer	45-64	55-75	22-24	24-26
German shepherd dog	70	95	22-24	24-26
German spaniel	44	66	15.5-17.5	15.5-19.5

(Continued on next page.)

Table H-2. Body weights in pounds and height at withers in inches of selected canine breeds. (Continued from previous page.)

Breeds	Body weights (lb)		Height at withers (inches)	
	Females	Males	Females	Males
German spitz				
Small (Kleinspitz)	6.4	6.6	9	11
Standard (Mittelspitz)	25	25	11.5	13
Glen of Imaal terrier	35	35	14	14
Golden retriever	55-65	65-75	21.5-22.5	23-24
Gordon setter	45-70	55-80	23-26	24-27
Great Dane	121	176	≥29	≥32
Great Gascony blue	71	77	23.5-25.5	25-28
Greater Swiss mountain dog	na	na	23.5-27	25.5-28.5
Greenland dog	≥66	≥66	22	24
Greyhound	60-65	65-70	27-28	28-30
Griffon Vendéen				
Petit basset	25	35	13	15
Basset	40	44	15	17
Briquet	35	53	20	22
Grand	66	77	24	26
Hamiltonstövare	50	60	18-22.5	19.5-23.5
Hanover hound	84	99	Smaller than male	20-24
Harlequin pinscher	na	na	12	14
Harrier	48	60	19	21
Havanese	7	12	10	10.5
Hovawart	55-77	66-88	22-26	24-28
Hungarian coarse-haired vizsla	na	na	21-23.5	22.5-25.5
Hungarian greyhound	50-60	60-70	na	na
Hungarian Kuvasz	≤110	≤110	26-27.5	28-29.5
Ibizan hound	45	50	22.5-26	23.5-27.5
Iceland dog	na	na	15-17.5	17-19
Irish red and white setter	40	70	23.5	27
Irish setter	60	70	23-25	27
Irish terrier	25	27	18	18
Irish water spaniel	45-58	55-65	21-23	22-24
Irish wolfhound	≥105	≥120	≥30	≥32
Italian greyhound	5.5	10	13	15
Italian segugio	39	62	19-22	21-23
Italian setter	55	88	na	na
Italian spinone	62-70	71-82	23-25.5	23.5-27.5
Jämthund	na	na	21-23	23-25
Japanese chin	4	7	8	11
Japanese fighting dog	100	200	≥23.5	≥23.5
Japanese spitz	13	13	Smaller than male	12-14
Japanese terrier	na	na	12	15
Jura hound	na	na	17.5	22
Keeshond	55	66	17	18
Kerry blue terrier	na	33-40	17.5-19	18-19.5
Komondor	80	100-150	≥25.5	≥27.5
Kooikerhondje	20	24	15	15
Kromfohrländer	26	26	15	18
Kuvasz (Hungarian shepherd)	70-90	99-110	26-28	28-30
Labrador retriever	55-70	65-80	21.5-23.5	22.5-24.5
Lakeland terrier	15	17	13.5	14.5
Lancashire heeler	8	12	10	12
Lapland spitz	44	44	15.5-17.5	17.5-19.5
Lapponian herder	≤66	≤66	17-19	19-22
Leonberger	80	150	26-30	29-32
Lhasa Apso	na	na	Smaller than male	10
Löwchen	4	9	8	14
Maltese	4	6 (≤7)	10	10

(Continued on next page.)

Table H-2. Body weights in pounds and height at withers in inches of selected canine breeds. (Continued from previous page.)

Breeds	Body weights (lb)		Height at withers (inches)	
	Females	Males	Females	Males
Manchester terrier				
Toy (American-bred)	na	≤7	na	na
Toy (English toy terrier)	na	≤12	10	12
Standard (American-bred)	≥12	≤16	na	na
Standard (open classes)	≥16	≤22	15	16
Maremma sheepdog	66-88	77-99	24-27	26-29
Mastiff	165	198	≥27.5	≥30
Mexican hairless dog	na	na	16	20
Miniature bull terrier	10	40	10	14
Miniature pinscher	10	10	10	12.5
Mudi	18	29	14	19
Münsterlander				
Small	33	37	19	22
Large	55	55-66	23	24
Neapolitan mastiff	110	154	24-27	25.5-29
Newfoundland	110-120	132-152	26	28
Nivernais griffon	50	55	Smaller than male	21-23
Norfolk terrier	11	12	9	10
Norwegian buhund	26	40	Smaller than male	17-18
Norwich terrier	10	12	na	≤10
Nova Scotia duck tolling retriever	36	51	17	21
Old English sheepdog (bobtail)	55	66	≥21	≥22
Otterhound	65-100	75-115	23-26	24-27
Papillon	3.3	11	8	11
Parson Jack Russell terrier	na	na	12-13	13-14
Pekingese	7-11	8-14.3	na	na
Pharaoh hound	na	na	21-24	23-25
Picardy shepherd	50	70	20-24	22-26
Pinscher	na	na	17	19
Pointer	45-65	55-75	23-26	25-28
Poitevin	66	66	25	28
Polish lowland sheepdog	na	na	16-18.5	17-20
Pomeranian	3	7	11	11
Poodle				
Toy	na	na	≤10	≤10
Miniature	11	11	>10	15
Standard	44.5	70	>15	na
Porcelaine	55	62	21-22	22-23
Portuguese setter	na	na	19-22	20.5-24
Portuguese water dog	35-50	42-60	17-21	20-23
Pudelpointer	55	70	≥24	≥24
Pug	14	18	10	12
Puli (Hungarian puli)	22-28.5	28.5-33	14.5-16	16-17.5
Pumi	17.5	28.5	13	17.5
Pyrenean mastiff	121	154.5	Smaller than male	27.5-31.5
Pyrenean mountain dog (Great Pyrenees)	85-99	100-121	25-29	27-32
Pyrenean shepherd	18	30	15-20	15.5-20
Rafeiro do alentejo	77-99	88-99	25.5-28	26.5-29.5
Rhodesian ridgeback	70	85	24-26	25-27
Rottweiler	88	110	22-25	24-27
Rumanian shepherd dog	110	110	25	26
Saint Bernard	110	200	≥26	≥28
Saint-Germain setter (St-G. Braque)	40	57	na	na
Saluki	29	66	≥22	23-28
Samoyed	37-55	44-66	19-21	21-23.5
Schapendoes (Dutch sheepdog)	na	na	16-19	17-20

(Continued on next page.)

Table H-2. Body weights in pounds and height at withers in inches of selected canine breeds. (Continued from previous page.)

| Breeds | Body weights (lb) | | Height at withers (inches) | |
	Females	Males	Females	Males
Schipperke				
Small type	7	11	10-12	11-13
Large type	11	18	10-12	11-13
Schnauzer				
Miniature	11	15	12	14
Standard	33	40	18-18.5	18.5-20
Giant (Riesenschnauzer)	66	77	24-26	26-28
Scottish terrier	18-21	19-22	10	na
Sealyham terrier	18-20	23-24	10.5	≤12
Shar-Pei	40	55	18	20
Shetland sheepdog (sheltie)	na	na	13	16
Shiba Inu	20	30	13.5-15.5	14.5-16.5
Shih Tzu	9	18	9	10.5
Siberian husky	35-50	44-60	20-22	21-24
Sicilian hound	22-26	26-30	17-18	18-20
Silky terrier (Australian)	8	10	9	10
Skye terrier	25	na	9.5	10
Sloughi	45	60	23	30
Soft-coated wheaten terrier	30-35	35-40	17-18	18-19
Spanish greyhound	60	66	Smaller than male	25.5-27.5
Spanish mastiff	110	132	Smaller than male	26-28
Stabyhoun	33	44	na	19 (max.)
Staffordshire bull terrier	24-34	28-38	14	16
Staffordshire terrier (American)	na	na	17-18	18-19
Sussex spaniel	35	45	13	15
Swedish vallhund	25	35	12-13	13-14
Swiss scent hound (Laufhunde)	na	na	17.5	22
Tahltan bear dog	15	15	12	16
Tawny brittany basset	na	na	13	17
Tibetan mastiff	≥180	≥180	≥24	≥26
Tibetan spaniel	9	15	10	10
Tibetan terrier	18	30	14	17
Vizsla (Hungarian vizsla)	44	66	21-23	22.5-24
Weimaraner	70	85	23-25	25-27
Welsh corgi				
Cardigan	25-34	30-38	10.5	12.5
Pembroke	22-28	22-30	10	12
Welsh springer spaniel	35	45	17-18	18-19
Welsh terrier	20	21	Smaller than male	15-15.5
West Highland white terrier	15	22	10	11
Whippet	28	28	18-21	19-22
Wirehaired pointing griffon	50	60	20-22	22-24
Yorkshire terrier	≤8	≤8	9	9

Key: na = information not available.

BIBLIOGRAPHY

1. Asselbergs CC, Beer-Schell A, Bosch B, et al. Rasgroepen en rasbeschrijvingen. In: Handboek Kynologie. Zaventem, Belgium: Bohn-Stafleu-Van Loghum, 1994.

2. Breed Standards (Card Deck). American Kennel Club. Raleigh, NC, 1996.

3. Fiorone F, Gondrexon-Ives Browne A. Elseviers Groot Rashonden Boek. Amsterdam, The Netherlands: Elsevier, 1971.

4. Hand MS, Armstrong PJ, Allen TA. Obesity: Occurrence, treatment, and prevention. Veterinary Clinics of North America: Small Animal Practice 1989; 19: 447-474.

5. Lewis LD, Morris ML Jr, Hand MS. Obesity. In: Small Animal Clinical Nutrition III. Topeka, KS: Mark Morris Associates, 1987; 6-1.

6. Meyer H. Tabellenanhang-Tabelle I. Lebendmasse, Nachkommenzahl und Geburtsmasse in verschiedener Hunderassen. In: Ernährung des Hundes, 2nd ed. Stuttgart, Germany: Eugen Ulmer Verlag, 1990; 283-284.

7. Meeus C, Sarewitz E, eds. In: The Illustrated Encyclopedia of Dog Breeds. Edison, NJ: The Wellfleet Press, 1994.

Appendix I
Body Types of Cats

Data about body weights of different cat breeds are not available. Therefore, Appendix I gives body types as an alternative to the body weight and height ranges given for dogs in Appendix H. Purebred cats have two extreme body types: "oriental" and "cobby" (Table I-1).

The oriental type is often described in breed standards as lithe, elegant and fine-boned. This type has tapered lines or is streamlined. In most breeds of this type, the body is slim, almost tubular, or serpentine, with a firm musculature. The head is small and wedge-shaped. Cats with this body type are light-built; adults seldom weigh more than 4 kg (8.8 lb). Terms such as svelte, slim or foreign are also used to indicate the oriental type. Siamese cats represent the oriental body type (Figure I-1).

Cobby refers to heavy, strongly built cats. These cats are described as low-lying, short-legged, compact and broad-chested (Figure I-2). They have large shoulders, a large trunk and a shorter tail. The cobby body type is typified by American and European shorthair cats. Generally, these cats are larger than the oriental types. For example, an adult noncastrated male can weigh more than 5 kg (11 lb).

Table I-1 provides some typical examples of these two feline types. Many cats do not really belong to either group, but have a modified, moderate or intermediate build. Inheritance of body type is polygenic, generating an almost continuous variation. Even within a specific type, some breeds are slightly less cobby or less oriental than other breeds. Moreover, the word foreign is sometimes used to describe breeds that are slightly less oriental. For example, the Russian blue is sometimes called foreign as opposed to oriental. The American curl and Egyptian mau are sometimes called semi-foreign because they weigh less than the cobby type. The Scottish fold is referred to as semi-cobby because its body type is between cobby and semi-foreign.

A few breeds do not match any of these groups. Typically they are strongly built cats that are larger than the cobby type. Examples are the Maine coon cat, the ocicat and the Norwegian forest cat. An average Maine coon male weighs about 7 kg (15.5 lb) and an average female weighs about 5 kg (11 lb.) Adult ocicats have an average body weight between 5.5 and 7 kg (12 and 15.5 lb). The Norwegian forest cat (Norsk Skaukatt), a unique Scandinavian breed, resembles the Maine coon cat.

Table I-1. Feline body types.

Oriental or svelte build	Cobby build
Siamese	American shorthair
Colorpoint shorthair	American wirehair
Balinese	Burmese
Oriental shorthair	British shorthair
Oriental longhair	Chartreux
Singapura	Cornish rex
English Havana brown	European shorthair
Javanese	Exotic shorthair
Russian blue*	Himalayan
	(Persian colorpoint)
	Kashmir
	Persian

*Less oriental.

Figure I-1. The Siamese represents the oriental body type.

Figure I-2. An example of a cat with a cobby build.

BIBLIOGRAPHY

1. Caras R, ed. Harper's Illustrated Handbook of Cats, 6th ed. New York, NY: Harper Collins Publishers Inc, 1993; 24-29.
2. Siegal M, ed. The Cornell Book of Cats. New York, NY: Villard Books, 1991; 17-38.
3. Wright M, Walters S, Bruin S. Katten, 2nd ed. Amsterdam, The Netherlands: Het Spectrum, 1987.

Appendix J
Nutrient Requirements and Allowances for Dogs and Cats

I. Introduction

When recommending a food or evaluating nutrient intake, a clear distinction must be made between nutrient requirements and recommendations for daily intake (RDI), also referred to as recommended daily allowances (RDA).

Requirements reflect the minimum average level of intake of a nutrient, which, over time, is sufficient to maintain the desired physiologic functions of animals in a population. The National Research Council (NRC) has established minimum requirements, which were last published in 1985 for dogs and in 1986 for cats (Tables J-1 to J-3).

Recommended daily allowance or recommended daily intake is the level of intake of a nutrient or food component that appears to be adequate to meet the known nutritional needs of practically all healthy individuals. It reflects the minimum requirement plus a safety margin for differences in availability and for nutrient interactions.

Assessing an animal's nutritional status and subsequently developing a nutritional recommendation can be categorized into two different modes that highlight the differences between the concepts of nutrient requirements and nutrient allowances. When one is asked to give a nutritional recommendation for an individual animal the approach will be different from when an animal needs to be assessed for its nutritional status.

When asked to make a nutritional recommendation for an individual animal, one should ensure that the nutrient intake or level in the food is sufficient to meet the needs of practically all healthy animals in the representative population (or lifestage). Recommendations for a particular animal must by definition exceed the requirements of almost all individuals in the specified group. When asked to recommend a prepared food for healthy pets, one can refer to the nutrient profiles published by the Association of American Feed Control Officials (AAFCO) (Tables J-4 to J-9).

When formulating (homemade) foods, it is often more practical to use recommendations that express the daily intake of nutrients (per kg body weight or per kg metabolic weight). Such data have been published in the German literature over the past decade (Tables J-20 to J-23).

In addition to the data as published originally, Tables J-1 to J-9 and J-12 to J-17 provide the same data converted to nutrient levels per 100 g dry matter, per 100 kcal metabolizable energy (ME) and per MJ ME.

(Editors' note: The following tables do not necessarily reflect the author's and editors' recommendations, which can be found in Chapters 9 and 11.)

II. Minimum nutrient requirements (NRC)

Although the NRC publications were intended to serve as a guide to formulate diets, they did not account for nutrient availability. Some of the requirements were based on studies in which nutrients were delivered by highly purified ingredients, where digestibility was not compromised by interactions between dietary constituents or by the effects of processing. Therefore, most values listed in the 1985 edition of Nutrient Requirements of Dogs and 1986 edition of Nutrient Requirements of Cats, published by NRC, are minimum requirements of essential nutrients and not recommended allowances. (See Bibliography Sources 14 and 15).

Table J-1. Minimum nutrient requirements of growing dogs. (Adapted from National Research Council. Nutrient Requirements of Dogs. Washington, DC: National Academy Press, 1985.)

Nutrients	Units	Per kg BW*	Per 100 kcal**	Per MJ**	Units	DM***
Protein†						
Arginine	mg	274	137	327	%	0.48
Histidine	mg	98	49	117	%	0.17
Isoleucine	mg	196	98	234	%	0.34
Leucine	mg	318	159	380	%	0.56
Lysine	mg	280	140	335	%	0.49
Methionine-cystine	mg	212	106	253	%	0.37
Phenylalanine-tyrosine	mg	390	195	466	%	0.68
Threonine	mg	254	127	304	%	0.44
Tryptophan	mg	82	41	98	%	0.14
Valine	mg	210	105	251	%	0.37
Dispensable amino acids	mg	3,414	1,707	4,080	%	5.97
Fat	g	2.7	1.35	3.23	%	4.7
Linoleic acid	mg	540	270	645	%	0.95
Minerals						
Calcium	mg	320	160	382.4	%	0.56
Phosphorus	mg	240	120	286.8	%	0.42
Potassium	mg	240	120	286.8	%	0.42
Sodium	mg	30	15	35.9	%	0.05
Chloride	mg	46	23	55.0	%	0.08
Magnesium	mg	22	11	26.3	%	0.04
Iron	mg	1.74	0.87	2.1	mg/kg	30.5
Copper	mg	0.16	0.08	0.2	mg/kg	2.8
Manganese	mg	0.28	0.14	0.3	mg/kg	4.9
Zinc	mg	1.94	0.97	2.3	mg/kg	34
Iodine	µg	32	16	38	mg/kg	0.6
Selenium	µg	6	3	7.2	mg/kg	0.11
Vitamins						
Vitamin A	IU	202	101	241.4	IU/kg	3,535
Vitamin D	IU	22	11	26.3	IU/kg	385
Vitamin E††	IU	1.2	0.6	1.4	IU/kg	21
Vitamin K†††	–	–	–	–	–	–
Thiamin	µg	54	27	64.5	mg/kg	0.95
Riboflavin	µg	100	50	119.5	mg/kg	1.75
Pantothenic acid	µg	400	200	478	mg/kg	7.00
Niacin	µg	450	225	537.8	mg/kg	7.88
Pyridoxine	µg	60	30	71.7	mg/kg	1.05
Folic acid	µg	8	4	9.6	mg/kg	0.14
Biotin†††	–	–	–	–	–	–
Vitamin B_{12}	µg	1.0	0.5	1.2	µg/kg	18
Choline	mg	50	25	59.8	g/kg	0.88

Key: BW = body weight, kcal = kilocalories, MJ = megajoules, DM = dry matter.
*Based on an average 3-kg growing beagle puppy consuming 600 kcal metabolizable energy (ME)/day.
**Metabolizable energy.
***Presumes an energy density of 3.5 kcal ME/g dry matter.
†Quantity sufficient to supply minimum amounts of available indispensable and dispensable amino acids specified below.
††Requirement depends on an intake of polyunsaturated fatty acids (PUFA) and the presence of other antioxidants. A fivefold increase may be required under conditions of high PUFA intake.
†††Dogs have a metabolic requirement for vitamin K and biotin; however, a dietary requirement was not demonstrated when natural ingredients were fed.

Table J-2. Minimum nutrient requirements of adult dogs. (Adapted from National Research Council. Nutrient Requirements of Dogs. Washington, DC: National Academy Press, 1985.)

Nutrients	Units	Per kg BW*	Per 100 kcal**	Per MJ**	Units	DM***
Protein†						
Arginine	mg	21	28	68	%	0.10
Histidine	mg	22	30	71	%	0.10
Isoleucine	mg	48	65	155	%	0.23
Leucine	mg	84	113	271	%	0.40
Lysine	mg	50	67	161	%	0.24
Methionine-cystine	mg	30	40	97	%	0.14
Phenylalanine-tyrosine	mg	86	116	277	%	0.41
Threonine	mg	44	59	142	%	0.21
Tryptophan	mg	13	18	42	%	0.06
Valine	mg	60	81	193	%	0.28
Dispensable amino acids	mg	1,266	1,706	4,078	%	5.97
Fat	g	1	1.35	3.2	%	4.7
Linoleic acid	mg	200	270	644	%	0.94
Minerals						
Calcium	mg	119	160.4	383.3	%	0.56
Phosphorus	mg	89	119.9	286.7	%	0.42
Potassium	mg	89	119.9	286.7	%	0.42
Sodium	mg	11	14.8	35.4	%	0.05
Chloride	mg	17	22.9	54.8	%	0.08
Magnesium	mg	8.2	11.1	26.4	%	0.04
Iron	mg	0.65	0.9	2.1	mg/kg	30.7
Copper	mg	0.06	0.08	0.2	mg/kg	2.8
Manganese	mg	0.10	0.13	0.3	mg/kg	4.7
Zinc	mg	0.72	1.0	2.3	mg/kg	34
Iodine	µg	12	16	38.7	mg/kg	0.6
Selenium	µg	2.2	3.0	7.1	mg/kg	0.104
Vitamins						
Vitamin A	IU	75	101	242	IU/kg	3,538
Vitamin D	IU	8	11	26	IU/kg	377
Vitamin E††	IU	0.5	0.7	1.6	IU/kg	24
Vitamin K†††	–	–	–	–	–	–
Thiamin	µg	20	27	64	mg/kg	0.94
Riboflavin	µg	50	67.4	161	mg/kg	2.36
Pantothenic acid	µg	200	270	644	mg/kg	9.43
Niacin	µg	225	303	725	mg/kg	10.61
Pyridoxine	µg	22	30	71	mg/kg	1.04
Folic acid	µg	4	5.4	13	mg/kg	0.19
Biotin†††	–	–	–	–	–	–
Vitamin B$_{12}$	µg	0.5	0.7	1.6	µg/kg	24
Choline	mg	25	34	80.5	g/kg	1.18

Key: BW = body weight, kcal = kilocalories, MJ = megajoules, DM = dry matter.
*Based on an average 10-kg adult dog consuming 742 kcal metabolizable energy (ME)/day.
**Metabolizable energy.
***Based on 3.5 kcal ME/g dry matter.
†Quantity sufficient to supply minimum amounts of available indispensable and dispensable amino acids specified below.
††Requirement depends on an intake of polyunsaturated fatty acids (PUFA) and the presence of other antioxidants. A fivefold increase may be required under conditions of high PUFA intake.
†††Dogs have a metabolic requirement for vitamin K and biotin, but a dietary requirement was not demonstrated when natural ingredients were fed.

Table J-3. Minimum nutrient requirements of growing cats. (Adapted from National Research Council. Nutrient Requirements of Cats. Washington, DC: National Academy Press, 1986.)

Nutrients	Units	DM*	Units	Per 100 kcal**	Per MJ**
Protein*	%	24	g	4.8	11.5
Arginine	%	1	mg	200	478
Histidine	%	0.3	mg	60	143
Isoleucine	%	0.5	mg	100	239
Leucine	%	1.2	mg	240	574
Lysine	%	0.8	mg	160	382
Methionine-cystine	%	0.75	mg	150	359
Methionine	%	0.4	mg	80	191
Phenylalanine-tyrosine	%	0.85	mg	170	406
Phenylalanine	%	0.4	mg	80	191
Taurine†	mg	40	mg	8	19
Threonine	%	0.7	mg	140	335
Tryptophan	%	0.15	mg	30	72
Valine	%	0.6	mg	120	287
Fat††					
Linoleic acid	%	0.5	mg	100	239
Arachidonic acid	mg	20	mg	4	10
Minerals					
Calcium	%	0.8	mg	160	382
Phosphorus	%	0.6	mg	120	287
Potassium†††	%	0.4	mg	80	191
Sodium	%	0.05	mg	10	24
Chloride	%	0.19	mg	38	91
Magnesium	%	0.04	mg	8	19
Iron	mg/kg	80	mg	1.6	3.8
Copper	mg/kg	5.0	mg	0.1	0.2
Iodine	mg/kg	0.35	mg	0.01	0.017
Zinc	mg/kg	50	mg	1.0	2.4
Manganese	mg/kg	5.0	mg	0.1	0.24
Selenium	mg/kg	0.1	µg	2	5
Vitamins					
Vitamin A	IU/kg	3,333	IU	67	159
Vitamin D	IU/kg	500	IU	10	24
Vitamin E‡	IU/kg	30	IU	0.6	1.4
Vitamin K‡‡	µg/kg	100	µg	2.0	5
Thiamin	mg/kg	5	µg	100	239
Riboflavin	mg/kg	4	µg	80	191
Pyridoxine	mg/kg	4	µg	80	191
Niacin	mg/kg	40	µg	800	1,912
Pantothenic acid	mg/kg	5	µg	100	239
Folic acid‡‡	mg/kg	0.8	µg	16	38
Biotin‡‡	µg/kg	70	µg	1.4	3
Vitamin B$_{12}$	µg/kg	20	µg	0.4	1
Choline‡‡‡	g/kg	2.4	mg	48	115

Key: kcal = kilocalories, MJ = megajoules, DM = dry matter.
*Presumes an energy density of 5.0 kcal metabolizable energy/g dry matter.
**Metabolizable energy.
***This level may not be high enough, based on research reported in 1987, particularly for processed foods.
†Assuming that all the minimum essential amino acid requirements are met.
††No requirement for fat is known apart from the need for essential fatty acids, and as a carrier for fat-soluble vitamins. Some fat usually enhances palatability.
†††The minimum potassium requirement increases with protein intake.
‡This minimum should be adequate for a moderate- to low-fat diet. It may increase three- to fourfold with a diet high in polyunsaturated fatty acids, especially when fish oil is present.
‡‡These vitamins may not be required unless antimicrobial agents or antivitamin compounds are present in the diet.
‡‡‡Choline is not essential in the diet but if this quantity of choline is not present, the methionine requirement should be increased to provide the same quantity of methyl groups.

III. National certification systems
United States (Association of American Feed Control Officials)

Whereas the NRC strives to provide the minimum nutrient requirements for cats and dogs, the Canine and Feline Nutrition Expert Subcommittees (CNE and FNE) of AAFCO have established practical standard nutrient profiles for dog and cat foods based on commonly used ingredients. These profiles now serve as the "recognized authority on animal nutrition" for cat and dog foods, as the term is applied in AAFCO pet food regulations. Under these regulations, nutritional adequacy of pet foods can be established for a designated lifestage (growth, reproduction, adult maintenance or all lifestages) either by reference to the AAFCO Nutrient Profile or by successfully passing the minimum feeding protocol for the designated lifestage. In the first case, the food must contain levels of nutrients that fall within the minimum and maximum levels as detailed in Tables J-4 to J-9. For-

mulating foods accordingly allows a company to make the following label claim: "Food X" is formulated to meet the nutritional levels established by the AAFCO Dog (or Cat) Food Nutritional Profiles for "Lifestage A."

The fact that a pet food is formulated to meet the profile criteria should not deter or discourage manufacturers from conducting appropriate feeding trials to demonstrate nutritional adequacy. This recommendation is especially important because pet foods with the same guaranteed analysis may vary in digestibility and nutritional adequacy. Pet foods that successfully pass the minimum AAFCO feeding protocols for a particular lifestage (See description of test protocols, Tables J-10 and J-11.) can state the following on the label: Animal feeding tests using AAFCO procedures substantiate that "Food Y" provides complete and balanced nutrition for "Lifestage B." See Chapter 5 for examples of how to interpret label claims on pet foods.

Table J-4. AAFCO nutrient profiles for dog foods: Minimum nutrient allowances for growth and reproduction.* (Adapted from the Association of American Feed Control Officials. Official Publication, 1999.)

Nutrients	Units	DM**	Units	Per 100 kcal***	Per MJ***
Protein	%	22.0	g	6.3	15
Arginine	%	0.62	mg	177	423
Histidine	%	0.22	mg	63	150
Isoleucine	%	0.45	mg	129	307
Leucine	%	0.72	mg	206	492
Lysine	%	0.77	mg	220	526
Methionine-cystine	%	0.53	mg	151	362
Phenylalanine-tyrosine	%	0.89	mg	254	608
Threonine	%	0.58	mg	166	396
Tryptophan	%	0.20	mg	57	137
Valine	%	0.48	mg	137	328
Fat	%	8.0	g	2	5
Linoleic acid	%	1.0	mg	286	683
Minerals					
Calcium†	%	1.0	mg	286	683
Phosphorus†	%	0.8	mg	229	546
Potassium	%	0.6	mg	171	410
Sodium	%	0.3	mg	86	205
Chloride	%	0.45	mg	129	307
Magnesium	%	0.04	mg	11	27
Iron	mg/kg	80	mg	2.3	5.5
Copper	mg/kg	7.3	mg	0.2	0.5
Manganese	mg/kg	5.0	mg	0.14	0.3
Zinc	mg/kg	120	mg	3.4	8.2
Iodine	mg/kg	1.5	µg	42.9	102
Selenium	mg/kg	0.11	µg	3.14	7.5
Vitamins					
Vitamin A	IU/kg	5,000	IU	143	341.4
Vitamin D	IU/kg	500	IU	14.3	34.1
Vitamin E	IU/kg	50	IU	1.4	3.4
Thiamin	mg/kg	1.0	µg	28.6	68.3
Riboflavin	mg/kg	2.2	µg	62.9	150.2
Pantothenic acid	mg/kg	10	µg	285.7	682.9
Niacin	mg/kg	11.4	µg	325.7	778.5
Pyridoxine	mg/kg	1.0	µg	28.6	68.3
Folic acid	mg/kg	0.18	µg	5.1	12.3
Vitamin B_{12}	µg/kg	22	µg	0.6	1.5
Choline	g/kg	1.2	mg	34	81.9

Key: kcal = kilocalories, MJ = megajoules, DM = dry matter.
*Table J-6 lists maximum nutrient levels for all lifestages.
**Presumes an energy density of 3.5 kcal metabolizable energy/g dry matter. Rations with an energy density greater than 4.0 kcal/g should be corrected for energy density.
***Metabolizable energy.
†The calcium-phosphorus ratio should be between 1:1 and 2:1.

Table J-5. AAFCO nutrient profiles for dog foods: Minimum nutrient allowances for adult maintenance.* (Adapted from the Association of American Feed Control Officials. Official Publication, 1999.)

Nutrients	Units	DM**	Units	Per 100 kcal***	Per MJ***
Protein	%	18.0	g	5.1	12
Arginine	%	0.51	mg	146	348
Histidine	%	0.18	mg	51	123
Isoleucine	%	0.37	mg	106	253
Leucine	%	0.59	mg	169	403
Lysine	%	0.63	mg	180	430
Methionine-cystine	%	0.43	mg	123	294
Phenylalanine-tyrosine	%	0.73	mg	209	498
Threonine	%	0.48	mg	137	328
Tryptophan	%	0.16	mg	46	109
Valine	%	0.39	mg	111	266
Fat	%	5.0	g	1	3
Linoleic acid	%	1.0	mg	286	683
Minerals					
Calcium†	%	0.6	mg	171	410
Phosphorus†	%	0.5	mg	143	341
Potassium	%	0.6	mg	171	410
Sodium	%	0.06	mg	17	41
Chloride	%	0.09	mg	26	61
Magnesium	%	0.04	mg	11	27
Iron	mg/kg	80	mg	2.3	5.5
Copper	mg/kg	7.3	mg	0.2	0.5
Manganese	mg/kg	5.0	mg	0.14	0.3
Zinc	mg/kg	120	mg	3.4	8.2
Iodine	mg/kg	1.5	µg	43	102
Selenium	mg/kg	0.11	µg	3.1	7.5
Vitamins					
Vitamin A	IU/kg	5,000	IU	143	341
Vitamin D	IU/kg	500	IU	14	34
Vitamin E	IU/kg	50	IU	1.4	3.4
Thiamin	mg/kg	1.0	µg	29	68
Riboflavin	mg/kg	2.2	µg	63	150
Pantothenic acid	mg/kg	10	µg	286	683
Niacin	mg/kg	11.4	µg	326	778
Pyridoxine	mg/kg	1.0	µg	29	68
Folic acid	mg/kg	0.18	µg	5.1	12
Vitamin B$_{12}$	µg/kg	22	µg	0.6	1.5
Choline	g/kg	1.2	mg	34	82

Key: kcal = kilocalories, MJ = megajoules, DM = dry matter.
*Table J-6 lists maximum nutrient levels for all lifestages.
**Presumes an energy density of 3.5 kcal metabolizable energy/g dry matter. Rations with an energy density greater than 4.0 kcal/g should be corrected for energy density.
***Metabolizable energy.
†The calcium-phosphorus ratio should be between 1:1 and 2:1.

Table J-6. AAFCO nutrient profiles for dog foods: Maximum nutrient allowances for all lifestages.* (Adapted from the Association of American Feed Control Officials. Official Publication, 1999.)

Nutrients	Units	DM*	Units	Per 100 kcal**	Per MJ**
Minerals					
Calcium	%	2.5	mg	714	1,707
Phosphorus	%	1.6	mg	457	1,093
Magnesium	%	0.3	mg	86	205
Iron	mg/kg	3,000	mg	86	205
Copper	mg/kg	250	mg	7.1	17
Zinc	mg/kg	1,000	mg	28.6	68
Iodine	mg/kg	50	µg	1,429	3,414
Selenium	mg/kg	2	µg	57	137
Vitamins					
Vitamin A	IU/kg	250,000	IU	7,143	17,072
Vitamin D	IU/kg	5,000	IU	143	341
Vitamin E	IU/kg	1,000	IU	28.6	68

Key: kcal = kilocalories, MJ = megajoules, DM = dry matter.
*Presumes an energy density of 3.5 kcal metabolizable energy/g dry matter. Rations with an energy density greater than 4.0 kcal/g should be corrected for energy density.
**Metabolizable energy.

Table J-7. AAFCO nutrient profiles for cat foods: Minimum nutrient allowances for growth and reproduction. Table J-9 lists maximum nutrient allowances for all lifestages. (Adapted from the Association of American Feed Control Officials. Official Publication, 1999.)

Nutrients	Units	DM*	Units	Per 100 kcal**	Per MJ**
Protein	%	30	g	7.5	18
Arginine	%	1.25	mg	312.5	747
Histidine	%	0.31	mg	77.5	185
Isoleucine	%	0.52	mg	130	311
Leucine	%	1.25	mg	312.5	747
Lysine	%	1.2	mg	300	717
Methionine-cystine	%	1.1	mg	275	657
Methionine	%	0.62	mg	155	370.5
Phenylalanine-tyrosine	%	0.88	mg	220	526
Phenylalanine	%	0.42	mg	105	251
Threonine	%	0.73	mg	182.5	436
Tryptophan	%	0.25	mg	62.5	149
Valine	%	0.62	mg	155	370.5
Fat*	%	9	g	2.25	5.4
Linoleic acid	%	0.5	mg	125	299
Arachidonic acid	%	0.02	mg	5	12.0
Minerals					
Calcium	%	1.0	mg	250	597.5
Phosphorus	%	0.8	mg	200	478
Potassium	%	0.6	mg	150	358.5
Sodium	%	0.2	mg	50	119.5
Chloride	%	0.3	mg	75	179
Magnesium†	%	0.08	mg	20	48
Iron††	mg/kg	80	mg	2	5
Copper††† (canned)	mg/kg	5	µg	125	299
Copper††† (extruded)	mg/kg	15	µg	375	896
Iodine	mg/kg	0.35	µg	8.8	21
Zinc	mg/kg	75	mg	1.9	4.5
Manganese	mg/kg	7.5	µg	187.5	448
Selenium	mg/kg	0.1	µg	2.5	6
Vitamins					
Vitamin A	IU/kg	9,000	IU	225	538
Vitamin D	IU/kg	750	IU	19	45
Vitamin E‡	IU/kg	30	IU	0.75	2
Vitamin K‡‡	mg/kg	0.1	µg	2.5	6
Thiamin‡‡‡	mg/kg	5	µg	125	299
Riboflavin	mg/kg	4	µg	100	239
Pyridoxine	mg/kg	4	µg	100	239
Niacin	mg/kg	60	µg	1,500	3,585
Pantothenic acid	mg/kg	5	µg	125	299
Folic acid	mg/kg	0.8	µg	20	48
Biotin§	mg/kg	0.07	µg	1.75	4
Vitamin B$_{12}$	µg/kg	20	µg	0.5	1
Choline§§	g/kg	2.4	mg	60	143
Taurine (extruded)	%	0.1	mg	25	60
Taurine (canned)	%	0.2	mg	50	119.5

Key: kcal = kilocalories, MJ = megajoules, DM = dry matter.

*Presumes an energy density of 4 kcal metabolizable energy/g dry matter. Rations with energy densities greater than 4.5 kcal/g should be corrected for energy density. Rations with energy densities less than 4.0 kcal/g should not be corrected for energy density.

**Metabolizable energy.

***Although a true requirement for fat per se has not been established, the minimum level was based on recognition that fat is a source of essential fatty acids and a carrier for fat-soluble vitamins, and it enhances palatability and supplies adequate caloric density.

†If the mean urinary pH of cats fed free choice is not less than 6.4, the risk of struvite urolithiasis increases as the magnesium content of the food increases.

††Because of very poor availability, iron from carbonate and oxide sources that are added to the food should not be considered in determining the minimum nutrient level.

†††Because of very poor availability, copper from oxide sources that are added to the food should not be considered in determining the minimum nutrient level.

‡Add 10 IU vitamin E above the minimum level/g fish oil/kg of food.

‡‡Vitamin K does not need to be added unless the food contains more than 25% fish on a dry matter basis.

‡‡‡Because processing may destroy up to 90% of the thiamin in a food, allowances in formulation are made to ensure the minimum nutrient level is met after processing.

§Biotin does not need to be added unless the food contains antimicrobial or antivitamin compounds.

§§Methionine may be substituted for choline as a methyl donor at a rate of 3.75 parts for one part choline by weight, when methionine exceeds 0.62%.

Table J-8. AAFCO nutrient profiles for cat foods: Minimum nutrient allowances for adult maintenance. Table J-9 lists maximum nutrient allowances for all lifestages. (Adapted from the Association of American Feed Control Officials. Official Publication, 1999.)

Nutrients	Units	DM*	Units	Per 100 kcal**	Per MJ**
Protein	%	26.0	g	6.5	16
Arginine	%	1.04	mg	260.0	621
Histidine	%	0.31	mg	77.5	185
Isoleucine	%	0.52	mg	130	311
Leucine	%	1.25	mg	312.5	747
Lysine	%	0.83	mg	208	496
Methionine-cystine	%	1.10	mg	275	657
Methionine	%	0.62	mg	155	370.5
Phenylalanine-tyrosine	%	0.88	mg	220	526
Phenylalanine	%	0.42	mg	105	251
Threonine	%	0.73	mg	182.5	436
Tryptophan	%	0.16	mg	40.0	96
Valine	%	0.62	mg	155	370.5
Fat***	%	9.0	g	2.25	5.4
Linoleic acid	%	0.5	mg	125	299
Arachidonic acid	%	0.02	mg	5	12.0
Minerals					
Calcium	%	0.6	mg	150	358.5
Phosphorus	%	0.5	mg	125	299
Potassium	%	0.6	mg	150	358.5
Sodium	%	0.2	mg	50	119.5
Chloride	%	0.3	mg	75	179
Magnesium[†]	%	0.04	mg	10	24
Iron[††]	mg/kg	80	mg	2	5
Copper[†††]	mg/kg	5	µg	125	299
Iodine	mg/kg	0.35	µg	8.8	21
Zinc	mg/kg	75	mg	1.9	4.5
Manganese	mg/kg	7.5	µg	187.5	448
Selenium	mg/kg	0.1	µg	2.5	6
Vitamins					
Vitamin A	IU/kg	5,000	IU	125	299
Vitamin D	IU/kg	500	IU	13	30
Vitamin E[‡]	IU/kg	30	IU	0.75	2
Vitamin K[‡‡]	mg/kg	0.1	µg	2.5	6
Thiamin[‡‡‡]	mg/kg	5.0	µg	125	299
Riboflavin	mg/kg	4.0	µg	100	239
Pyridoxine	mg/kg	4.0	µg	100	239
Niacin	mg/kg	60	µg	1,500	3,585
Pantothenic acid	mg/kg	5.0	µg	125	299
Folic acid	mg/kg	0.8	µg	20	48
Biotin[§]	mg/kg	0.07	µg	1.75	4
Vitamin B_{12}	µg/kg	20	µg	0.5	1
Choline[§§]	g/kg	2.4	mg	60	143
Taurine (extruded)	%	0.10	mg	25	60
Taurine (canned)	%	0.20	mg	50	119.5

Key: kcal = kilocalories, MJ = megajoules, DM = dry matter.
*Presumes an energy density of 4 kcal metabolizable energy/g dry matter. Rations with energy densities greater than 4.5 kcal/g should be corrected for energy density. Rations with energy densities less than 4.0 kcal/g should not be corrected for energy density.
**Metabolizable energy.
***Although a true requirement for fat per se has not been established, the minimum level was based on recognition that fat is a source of essential fatty acids and a carrier for fat-soluble vitamins, and it enhances palatability and supplies adequate caloric density.
[†]If the mean urinary pH of cats fed free choice is not less than 6.4, the risk of struvite urolithiasis increases as the magnesium content of the food increases.
[††]Because of very poor availability, iron from carbonate and oxide sources that are added to the food should not be considered in determining the minimum nutrient level.
[†††]Because of very poor availability, copper from oxide sources that are added to the food should not be considered in determining the minimum nutrient level.
[‡]Add 10 IU vitamin E above the minimum level/g fish oil/kg of food.
[‡‡]Vitamin K does not need to be added unless the food contains more than 25% fish on a dry matter basis.
[‡‡‡]Because processing may destroy up to 90% of the thiamin in the diet, allowances in formulation are made to ensure the minimum nutrient level is met after processing.
[§]Biotin does not need to be added unless the food contains antimicrobial or antivitamin compounds.
[§§]Methionine may be substituted for choline as a methyl donor at a rate of 3.75 parts for one part choline by weight, when methionine exceeds 0.62%.

Table J-9. AAFCO nutrient profiles for cat foods: Maximum nutrient allowances for all lifestages.* (Adapted from the Association of American Feed Control Officials. Official Publication, 1999.)

Nutrients	Units	DM*	Units	Per 100 kcal**	Per MJ**
Methionine	%	1.5	mg	375	896
Zinc	mg/kg	2,000	mg	50	120
Vitamin A	IU/kg	750,000	IU	18,750	44,814
Vitamin D	IU/kg	10,000	IU	250	598

Key: kcal = kilocalories, MJ = megajoules, DM = dry matter.
*Presumes an energy density of 4 kcal metabolizable energy/g dry matter. Rations with energy densities greater than 4.5 kcal/g should be corrected for energy density. Rations with energy densities less than 4.0 kcal/g should not be corrected for energy density.
**Metabolizable energy.

AAFCO Feeding Protocols for dog and cat foods
General

To participate in feeding tests, dogs and cats shall be selected on a statistically sound basis. The results are then compared to those from a control group, a historical colony average or to reference values published by AAFCO (absolute method).

Controls

Breed and gender distribution must be the same as in the test group, and the minimum number of animals is the same as the minimum number requested for the test animals.

Diet and feeding parameters

During the test, animals shall receive the test food as their sole source of nourishment. The same formulation shall be fed throughout the test. The animals shall be fed ad libitum or based on energy needs. Fresh water shall be provided ad libitum. Diets fed to the control group or to dogs/cats in the determination of the historical colony, must have successfully passed the minimum feeding protocols for the respective lifestage.

Clinical observations and measurements

- Daily food consumption should be measured and recorded.
- Individual body weights should be recorded at the beginning, weekly and at the end of the test.
- Hemoglobin, packed cell volume, serum alkaline phosphatase and serum albumin values (and whole blood taurine levels for cats) shall be recorded at the end of the test.
- All animals shall be given a complete physical examination by a veterinarian at the beginning and the end of the test. They shall be evaluated for general health, body and hair coat condition and comments shall be recorded.
- A number of animals, not to exceed 25% of those starting the test, may be removed for non-nutritional reasons or poor food intake (only during the first two weeks). Reason for removal and data already collected must be recorded.
- A necropsy shall be conducted on any animal which dies during the test, and findings recorded.
- Reproducing animals: In addition to the above, the following should be recorded: 1) queen's or bitch's body weight within 24 hours after delivery, 2) puppies' or kittens' body weight within 24 hours after birth, weekly and at the end of the test, 3) litter size, at birth, at one day after birth and at the end of the test, and 4) stillbirth and congenital abnormalities.

Table J-10. AAFCO Feeding Protocols for dog foods. (Adapted from the Association of American Feed Control Officials. Official Publication, 1999.)

Lifestages	No. of dogs required	Age	Minimum duration of test
Adult maintenance	≥8	At least one year old	26 weeks
Growth	≥8 from three different bitches	Weaned and at a maximum of eight weeks old	10 weeks
Pregnancy/lactation	≥8 bitches	At least one year old	Begin at or before estrus and continue until the puppies are four weeks old

Table J-11. AAFCO Feeding Protocols for cat foods. (Adapted from the Association of American Feed Control Officials. Official Publication, 1999.)

Lifestages	No. of cats required	Age	Minimum duration of test
Adult maintenance	≥8	At least one year old	26 weeks
Growth	≥8 from three different queens	Weaned and at a maximum of nine weeks old	10 weeks
Pregnancy/lactation	≥8 queens	At least one year old	Begin at or before estrus and continue until the kittens are six weeks old

Canada (Canadian Veterinary Medical Association)

- The Canadian Veterinary Medical Association (CVMA) developed a program to certify pet foods and to monitor those foods to ensure that they continue to meet the standards for composition and digestibility. The primary target is commercial pet food sold in "over-the-counter" markets.

The requirements for CVMA certification follow:

- Food samples are analyzed for composition and digestibility. The nutrient profile of the food must meet the CVMA nutritional standards for the corresponding species and lifestage (Tables J-12 to J-17).

- The food must support the lifestage for which it is intended, by passing a feeding trial successfully, using the AAFCO protocol.
- Production plants are inspected for good manufacturing practices.

After fulfilling all the steps in the program, a company is authorized to have a seal printed on the label, with the following statement: "Certified by the Canadian Veterinary Medical Association to meet its nutritional standards."

Once certified, foods are subject to ongoing monitoring.

Table J-12. CVMA nutrient standards for certified dog foods: Minimum standards for adult dogs.* (Adapted from the Pet Food Certification Program. Canadian Veterinary Medical Association, 1993.)

Nutrients	Units	DM**	Units	Per 100 kcal***	Per MJ***
Protein	%	22	g	6.3	15
Fat[†]	%	5	g	1.4	3
Linoleic acid	%	1	mg	286	683
Minerals					
Calcium	%	1.1	mg	314	751
Phosphorus	%	0.9	mg	257	615
Potassium	%	0.6	mg	171	410
Sodium chloride	%	1.1	mg	314	751
Magnesium	%	0.04	mg	11	27
Iron	mg/kg	60	mg	1.7	4
Copper[††]	mg/kg	7.3	mg	0.2	0.5
Manganese	mg/kg	5	mg	0.14	0.34
Zinc[†††]	mg/kg	120	mg	3.4	8
Iodine	mg/kg	1.54	μg	44	105
Vitamins					
Vitamin A	IU/kg	5,000	IU	143	341
Vitamin D	IU/kg	500	IU	14	34
Vitamin E	IU/kg	50	IU	1.4	3.4
Thiamin	mg/kg	1.0	μg	29	68
Riboflavin	mg/kg	2.2	μg	63	150
Pantothenic acid	mg/kg	10	μg	286	683
Niacin	mg/kg	11.4	μg	326	778
Pyridoxine	mg/kg	1.0	μg	29	68
Folic acid	mg/kg	0.18	μg	5	12
Biotin	mg/kg	0.10	μg	3	7
Vitamin B_{12}	μg/kg	22	μg	0.6	1.5
Choline	g/kg	1.2	mg	34	82

Key: kcal = kilocalories, MJ = megajoules, DM = dry matter.
*Table J-14 lists suggested upper nutrient limits.
**Presumes an energy density of 3.5 kcal metabolizable energy/g dry matter.
***Metabolizable energy.
[†]Quantity sufficient to supply the minimum amount of essential fatty acids.
[††]Canadian Veterinary Journal 1987; 28: 744-745.
[†††]Recommended allowance based on research in other species.

Table J-13. CVMA nutrient standards for certified dog foods: Other lifestages.* (Adapted from the Pet Food Certification Program. Canadian Veterinary Medical Association, 1993.)

Lifestage/nutrients	Units	DM**	Units	Per 100 kcal***	Per MJ***
Puppies					
Protein	%	28	g	8	19
Fat	%	9	g	2.6	6
Linoleic acid	%	2	mg	571	1,366
Reproduction					
Protein	%	25	g	7.1	17
Fat	%	15	g	4.9	11.6
Crude fiber (max.)	%	5	g	1.4	3.4
Geriatrics					
Protein (min.)	%	18	g	5.1	12.3
Fat	%	5	g	1.4	3.4

Key: kcal = kilocalories, MJ = megajoules, DM = dry matter.
*Table J-14 lists suggested upper nutrient limits.
**Presumes an energy density of 3.5 kcal metabolizable energy/g dry matter.
***Metabolizable energy.

Table J-14. CVMA nutrient standards for certified dog foods: Suggested upper limits. (Adapted from the Pet Food Certification Program. Canadian Veterinary Medical Association, 1993.)

Nutrients	Units	DM*	Units	Per 100 kcal**	Per MJ**
Protein	%	55	g	15.7	38
Fat	%	50	g	14.3	34
Minerals					
Calcium***	%	4	mg	1,143	2,731
Iron	mg/kg	1,500	mg	42.9	102
Selenium	mg/kg	10	µg	286	683
Vitamins					
Vitamin A	IU/kg	37,100	IU	1,060	2,533
Vitamin D	IU/kg	4,000	IU	114	273
Vitamin E	IU/kg	1,000	IU	28.6	68
Vitamin K	IU/kg	2,000	IU	57	137
Thiamin	mg/kg	1,000	µg	28,571	68,287
Riboflavin	mg/kg	44	µg	1,257	3,005
Pantothenic acid	mg/kg	2,000	µg	57,143	136,575
Pyridoxine	mg/kg	50	µg	1,429	3,414
Biotin	mg/kg	1	µg	28.6	68
Vitamin B$_{12}$	µg/kg	7,800	µg	223	533
Vitamin C	g/kg	10	mg	286	683

Key: kcal = kilocalories, MJ = megajoules, DM = dry matter.
*Presumes an energy density of 3.5 kcal metabolizable energy/g dry matter.
**Metabolizable energy.
***Studies have shown, however, that even lower levels of calcium can cause skeletal deformities in growing dogs and levels over 2% dry matter should be avoided. (Hazewinkel HAW. Influences of different calcium intakes on calcium metabolism and skeletal development in young Great Danes. Doctorate Thesis, Faculty of Veterinary Medicine, University of Utrecht, Utrecht, The Netherlands, May 30, 1985.)

Table J-15. CVMA nutrient standards for certified cat foods: Minimum standards for adult cats.* (Adapted from the Pet Food Certification Program. Canadian Veterinary Medical Association, 1993.)

Nutrients	Units	DM**	Units	Per 100 kcal***	Per MJ***
Protein†	%	28	g	7.0	17
Taurine	mg/kg	1,000	mg	25.0	60
Fat††	%	9	g	2.3	5
Linoleic acid	%	1	mg	250	598
Arachidonic acid	mg/kg	100	mg	2.5	6
Minerals					
Calcium	%	1.0	mg	250	598
Phosphorus	%	0.8	mg	200	478
Potassium	%	0.3	mg	75	179
Sodium chloride	%	0.5	mg	125	299
Magnesium	%	0.05	mg	13	30
Iron	mg/kg	100	mg	2.5	6.0
Copper	mg/kg	5	mg	0.13	0.3
Manganese	mg/kg	10	mg	0.25	0.6
Zinc	mg/kg	75	mg	1.9	4.5
Iodine	mg/kg	1	µg	25	60
Selenium	mg/kg	0.1	µg	2.5	6.0
Vitamins					
Vitamin A	IU/kg	10,000	IU	250.0	597.5
Vitamin D	IU/kg	1,000	IU	25.0	60
Vitamin E†††	IU/kg	80	IU	2.0	5
Thiamin	mg/kg	5	mg	0.13	0.3
Riboflavin	mg/kg	5	mg	0.13	0.3
Pantothenic acid	mg/kg	10	mg	0.25	0.6
Niacin	mg/kg	45	mg	1.13	2.7
Pyridoxine	mg/kg	4	mg	0.10	0.24
Folic acid	mg/kg	1	µg	25	60
Biotin	mg/kg	0.05	µg	1.3	3
Vitamin B_{12}	µg/kg	20	µg	0.5	1.2
Choline	g/kg	2	mg	50.0	120

Key: kcal = kilocalories, MJ = megajoules, DM = dry matter.
*Table J-17 lists suggested upper nutrient limits.
**Presumes an energy density of 4 kcal metabolizable energy/g dry matter.
***Metabolizable energy.
†Quality equivalent to that derived from unprocessed mammalian, avian or fish muscle. Processing may decrease protein quality and necessitate higher concentrations.
††Quantity sufficient to supply the minimum amount of essential fatty acids.
†††Higher levels may be necessary when large concentrations of unsaturated lipids, such as tuna oil, are included in the diet.

Table J-16. CVMA nutrient standards for certified cat foods: Other lifestages.* (Adapted from the Pet Food Certification Program. Canadian Veterinary Medical Association, 1993.)

Lifestage/nutrients	Units	DM**	Units	Per 100 kcal***	Per MJ***
Kittens					
Protein	%	35	g	8.75	21
Fat	%	17	g	4.25	10.2
Linoleic acid	%	2	mg	500	1,195
Arachidonic acid	%	0.1	mg	25	60
Reproduction					
Protein	%	35	g	8.75	21
Fat	%	20	g	5	12
Low magnesium/pH controlled					
Ash (max.)	%	6	g	1.5	3.6
Magnesium†	%	0.05-0.1	mg	12.5-25	30-60
Average daily urinary pH	max.	6.5			
Postprandial urinary pH	max.	7.0			

Key: kcal = kilocalories, MJ = megajoules, DM = dry matter.
*Table J-17 lists suggested upper nutrient limits.
**Presumes an energy density of 4 kcal metabolizable energy/g dry matter.
***Metabolizable energy.
†Magnesium level/100 kcal digestible energy shall be no more than 20 mg.

Table J-17. CVMA nutrient standards for certified cat foods: Suggested upper limits. (Adapted from the Pet Food Certification Program. Canadian Veterinary Medical Association, 1993.)

Nutrients	Units	DM*	Units	Per 100 kcal**	Per MJ**
Protein	%	55	g	13.8	33
Fat	%	50	g	12.5	30
Minerals					
Calcium***	%	4	mg	1,000	2,390
Iron	mg/kg	1,500	mg	37.5	90
Selenium	mg/kg	10	µg	250	598
Vitamins					
Vitamin A	IU/kg	87,000	IU	2,175	5,198
Vitamin D	IU/kg	10,000	IU	250	598
Vitamin E	IU/kg	1,000	IU	25	60
Vitamin K	IU/kg	2,000	IU	50	120
Thiamin	mg/kg	5,000	µg	125,000	298,757
Riboflavin	mg/kg	100	µg	2,500	5,975
Pantothenic acid	mg/kg	2,000	µg	50,000	119,503
Pyridoxine	mg/kg	50	µg	1,250	2,988
Biotin	mg/kg	1	µg	25	60
Vitamin B$_{12}$	µg/kg	6,000	µg	150	359
Vitamin C	g/kg	10	mg	250	598

Key: kcal = kilocalories, MJ = megajoules, DM = dry matter.
*Presumes an energy density of 4 kcal metabolizable energy/g dry matter.
**Metabolizable energy.

Japan (Fair Competition Code)

The Fair Competition Code (FCC) guides and protects consumers in their selection of pet foods, with regard to quality and nutritional adequacy and helps prevent unjustifiable claims. The claim "Total Nutrition Food" or similar terms can be used if the:

- Typical analysis of a product meets or exceeds the nutrient levels published by the Japanese Fair Trade Commission (Tables J-18 and J-19). The label can then claim: "This product has been proven to satisfy the standard for 'Total Nutrition Food' as a result of analytical tests accepted by the Pet Food Fair Trade Association."
- Food successfully passed a feeding test for the lifestage for which it is intended. The label can claim: "This product has been proven to be 'Total Nutrition Food' as a result of feeding tests accepted by the Pet Food Fair Trade Association."

The tests required are basically the same as the AAFCO feeding tests in the USA.

Table J-18. Minimum nutrition standards for dog foods in Japan. (Adapted from The Fair Competition Code, 1991.)

Nutrients	Units	DM*	Units	Per 100 kcal	Per MJ
Protein	%	22	g	6.3	15
Fat	%	5	g	1.4	3
Linoleic acid	%	1	mg	286	683
Minerals					
Calcium	%	1.1	mg	314	751
Phosphorus	%	0.9	mg	257	615
Sodium chloride	%	1.1	mg	314	751
Vitamins					
Vitamin A	IU/kg	5,000	IU	143	341
Thiamin	mg/kg	1.0	µg	29	68
Riboflavin	mg/kg	2.2	µg	63	150
Biotin	mg/kg	0.1	µg	3	7

Key: kcal = kilocalories, MJ = megajoules, DM = dry matter.
*Metabolizable energy. Values per 100 kcal were calculated based on an energy density of 3.5 kcal metabolizable energy/g dry matter.

Table J-19. Minimum nutrition standards for cat foods in Japan. (Adapted from The Fair Competition Code, 1991.)

Nutrients	Units	DM*	Units	Per 100 kcal	Per MJ
Protein	%	28	g	7.0	17
Fat	%	9	g	2.3	5
Linoleic acid	%	1	mg	250	598
Minerals					
Calcium	%	1.0	mg	250	598
Phosphorus	%	0.8	mg	200	478
Sodium chloride	%	0.5	mg	125	299
Vitamins					
Vitamin A	IU/kg	10,000	IU	250	597.5
Vitamin E	IU/kg	80	IU	2.0	5
Thiamin	mg/kg	5.0	µg	125	299
Riboflavin	mg/kg	5.0	µg	125	299
Taurine	mg/kg	0.1	µg	2.5	6

Key: kcal = kilocalories, MJ = megajoules, DM = dry matter.
*Metabolizable energy. Values per 100 kcal were calculated based on an energy density of 4.0 kcal metabolizable energy/g dry matter.

IV. Other recommendations for daily nutrient intake

Assessing nutrition can be done in two ways: 1) the nutrient profile of a food can be compared to the recommended nutrient profile for its intended life cycle or 2) the animal's daily nutrient intake per kg body weight or per $kg^{0.75}$ can be assessed. The latter is the most practical approach for assessing treats and formulating a homemade food. Tables J-20 to J-23 provide recommendtions for daily nutrient intake per kg body weight or per $kg^{0.75}$.

Table J-20. Recommendations for daily nutrient intake of growing dogs. (Adapted from Ausschuβ für Bedarfsnormen der Geselschaft für Ernährungsphysiologie, 1989; 20-21, 54. The lower figure refers to large breeds [60 kg]; the higher to toy and small breeds.)

Nutrients	Units	Age (months)				
		2	3	4	5-6	7-12
Protein*						
Digestible protein (average)	g/kg BW	6.5	5.5	4.5	4	3.5
Digestible protein (average)	$g/kg^{0.75}$	9	8.5	8	7.5	6.5
Fat						
Linoleic acid	$g/kg^{0.75}$	0.27				
Minerals						
Calcium	mg/kg BW	390-585	400-525	355-420	240-305	120-145
Phosphorus	mg/kg BW	205-300	190-245	170-195	130-160	80-90
Sodium	mg/kg BW	129	95	76	64	54
Potassium	mg/kg BW	127	91	75	65	57
Magnesium	mg/kg BW	23	29	25	20	16
Iron	mg/kg BW	1.2-3	4.4-4.8	4.4-4.8	4.4-4.8	4.4-4.8
Copper	mg/kg BW	0.24-0.5	0.24-0.5	0.24-0.5	0.24-0.5	0.24-0.5
Zinc	mg/kg BW	1.1-3.7	3.2-4.1	3.2-4.1	3.2-4.0	1.3-1.7
Manganese	mg/kg BW	0.02	0.08-0.11	0.08-0.11	0.07-0.08	0.07-0.08
Iodine	mg/kg BW	0.025	0.025	0.025	0.025	0.025
Selenium	mg/kg BW	0.005	0.005	0.005	0.005	0.005
Vitamins						
Vitamin A	IU/kg BW	200	200	200	200	200
Vitamin D	IU/kg BW	2	2	20	2	2
Vitamin E	IU/kg BW	1.2	1.2	1.2	1.2	1.2
Thiamin	µg/kg BW	55	55	55	55	55
Riboflavin	µg/kg BW	100	100	100	100	100
Pantothenic acid	µg/kg BW	400	400	400	400	400
Niacin	µg/kg BW	450	450	450	450	450
Pyridoxine	µg/kg BW	60	60	60	60	60
Biotin	µg/kg BW	4	4	4	4	4
Folic acid	µg/kg BW	8	8	8	8	8
Vitamin B$_{12}$	µg/kg BW	1	1	1	1	1

Key: BW = body weight.
*Biologic value of approximately 70.

Table J-21. Recommendations for daily nutrient intake of adult dogs. (Adapted from Ausschuß für Bedarfsnormen der Geselschaft für Ernährungsphysiologie, 1989; 20-21, 54. The lower figure refers to large breeds [60 kg]; the higher to toy and small breeds.)

Nutrients	Units	Adult maintenance	Gestation > 30 days	Lactation No. puppies <4	Lactation No. puppies 4-6	Lactation No. puppies >6
Protein*						
Digestible protein	g/kg$^{0.75}$	4.3-5.0	7 (6.0-8.5)	9-12	13-21	15-24
Digestible protein	g/kg BW		Adult maintenance + 1.3 g/kg BW			
Fat						
Linoleic acid	g/kg$^{0.75}$	0.27				
Carbohydrate			Min. 20% of energy			
Minerals						
Calcium	mg/kg BW	100**	165	250	425	495
Phosphorus	mg/kg BW	75	120	175	290	335
Sodium	mg/kg BW	50***	60	75	105	115
Potassium	mg/kg BW	55***	65	87	125	140
Magnesium	mg/kg BW	15**	18	20	30	35
Iron	mg/kg BW	1.4	6.8	1.8	2.4	2.6
Copper	mg/kg BW	0.1	0.16	0.35	0.67	0.76
Zinc	mg/kg BW	0.9	1.3	2	3.2	3.7
Manganese	mg/kg BW	0.07	0.08	0.09	0.12	0.13
Iodine	mg/kg BW	0.015	0.025	0.025	–	–
Selenium	mg/kg BW	0.0025	0.005	0.005	–	–
Vitamins						
Vitamin A	IU/kg BW	75	200	200	200	200
Vitamin D	IU/kg BW	10	20	20	20	20
Vitamin E	IU/kg BW	0.5	1.2	1.2	1.2	1.2
Thiamin	µg/kg BW	20	55	55	55	55
Riboflavin	µg/kg BW	50	100	100	100	100
Pantothenic acid	µg/kg BW	200	400	400	400	400
Niacin	µg/kg BW	200	450	450	450	450
Pyridoxine	µg/kg BW	20	60	60	60	60
Biotin	µg/kg BW	2	4	4	4	4
Folic acid	µg/kg BW	4	8	8	8	8
Vitamin B$_{12}$	µg/kg BW	0.5	1	1	1	1

Key: BW = body weight.
*Biologic value of approximately 70.
**Can be 20 to 30% lower than the recommended intake without risk of deficiency.
***Can be 50% lower than the recommended intake without risk of deficiency.

Table J-22. Recommendations for daily nutrient intake of growing cats. (Adapted from Meyer H, Heckötter E. III. Empfehlungen zur Versorgung der Katze mit Energie und Nährstoffen. In: Meyer H, ed. Futterwerttabellen für Hunde und Katzen. Hannover, Germany: Schlütersche Verlaganstalt, 1986; 12-14.)

Nutrients	Units	Age (weeks) 10	Age (weeks) 20	Age (weeks) 30	Age (weeks) 40
Protein					
Digestible protein	g/kg BW	14	9.5	6.5	5.0
Digestible protein	g/kg$^{0.75}$	14	11	9.0	7.5
Minerals					
Calcium	mg/kg BW	150	150	150	150
Phosphorus	mg/kg BW	130	130	130	130
Potassium	mg/kg BW	120	120	120	120
Sodium	mg/kg BW	100	100	100	100
Magnesium	mg/kg BW	20	20	20	20
Chloride	mg/kg BW	150	150	150	150
Iron	mg/kg BW	2	2	2	2
Copper	mg/kg BW	0.25	0.25	0.25	0.25
Zinc	mg/kg BW	2.5	2.5	2.5	2.5
Manganese	mg/kg BW	0.2	0.2	0.2	0.2
Iodine	mg/kg BW	0.15	0.15	0.15	0.15
Selenium	mg/kg BW	0.005	0.005	0.005	0.005
Vitamins					
Vitamin A	IU/kg BW	1,000-1,500	1,000-1,500	1,000-1,500	1,000-1,500
Vitamin D	IU/kg BW	20	20	20	20
Vitamin E	mg/kg BW	4	4	4	4
Thiamin	µg/kg BW	200	200	200	200
Riboflavin	µg/kg BW	100	100	100	100
Pantothenic acid	µg/kg BW	400	400	400	400
Niacin	µg/kg BW	1,200	1,200	1,200	1,200
Pyridoxine	µg/kg BW	100	100	100	100
Biotin	µg/kg BW	2-4	2-4	2-4	2-4
Folic acid	µg/kg BW	20	20	20	20

Key: BW = body weight.

Table J-23. Recommendations for daily nutrient intake of adult cats. (Adapted from Meyer H, Heckötter E. III. Empfehlungen zur Versorgung der Katze mit Energie und Nährstoffen. In: Meyer H, ed. Futterwerttabellen für Hunde und Katzen. Hannover, Germany: Schlütersche Verlaganstalt, 1986; 12-14.)

Nutrients	Units	Adult maintenance	Pregnancy*	Lactation
Protein				
Digestible protein	g/kg BW	4.5	6.5	15
Digestible protein	g/kg$^{0.75}$	6.5	9.0	21
Taurine**	mg/kg BW	20**	–	–
Fat				
Linoleic acid	mg/kg BW	250	–	–
Arachidonic acid	mg/kg BW	3	–	–
Minerals				
Calcium	mg/kg BW	80	110	250
Phosphorus	mg/kg BW	70	100	230
Potassium	mg/kg BW	80	110	260
Sodium	mg/kg BW	80	110	260
Magnesium	mg/kg BW	12	18	28
Chloride	mg/kg BW	120	170	400
Iron	mg/kg BW	1.5	2.1	2.0
Copper	mg/kg BW	0.1	0.15	0.3
Zinc	mg/kg BW	1.0	1.4	3.3
Manganese	mg/kg BW	0.1	0.14	0.3
Iodine	mg/kg BW	0.05	0.06	0.16
Selenium	mg/kg BW	0.002	0.005	0.005
Vitamins				
Vitamin A	IU/kg BW	500-700	1,000-2,000	1,000-2,000
Vitamin D	IU/kg BW	10	20	20
Vitamin E	mg/kg BW	2	4	4
Thiamin	μg/kg BW	100	300	300
Riboflavin	μg/kg BW	50	100	100
Pantothenic acid	μg/kg BW	200	400	400
Niacin	μg/kg BW	800	1,200	1,200
Pyridoxine	μg/kg BW	80	100	100
Biotin	μg/kg BW	2-4	2-4	2-4
Folic acid	μg/kg BW	20	20	20

Key: BW = body weight.
*Second half of pregnancy.
**Research results reported in 1986 indicate that this level may not be high enough, particularly for processed foods and perhaps for cooked foods.

BIBLIOGRAPHY

1. Association of American Feed Control Officials. Official Publication, 1999; 122-144.

2. Ausschuß für Bedarfsnormen der Gesellschaft für Ernährungsphysiologie Energie-und Nährstoffbedarf (Energy and Nutrient Requirements). No. 5 Hunde/Dogs. Frankfurt, Germany: DLG Verlag, 1989.

3. Beaton GH. Criteria of an adequate diet. In: Shils ME, Young VR, eds. Modern Nutrition in Health and Disease, 7th ed. Philadelphia, PA: Lea & Febiger, 1988; 649-665.

4. Canadian Veterinary Medical Association. Nutrient standards for the CVMA Pet Food Certification Program. Canadian Veterinary Journal 1987; 28: 744-745.

5. Canadian Veterinary Medical Association. Pet Food Certification Program 1995. Canadian Veterinary Medical Association. Ottawa, Ontario, Canada, 1993; 1-20.

6. Fair Competition Code regarding representations on pet foods. Japan Fair Trade Commission Notification No. 25, October 22, 1991.

7. Food and Nutrition Board USA. How should the recommended dietary allowances be revised? A concept paper from the Food and Nutrition Board. Nutrition Reviews 1994; 52: 216-219.

8. Harper AE. Dietary standards and dietary guidelines. In: Brown ML, ed. Present Knowledge in Nutrition, 6th ed. Washington, DC: International Life Sciences Institute, 1990; 491-501.

9. Hazewinkel HAW. Influences of different calcium intakes on calcium metabolism and skeletal development in young Great Danes. Doctorate Thesis, Faculty of Veterinary Medicine, University of Utrecht, Utrecht, The Netherlands, May 30, 1985.

10. Huber Th, Wilson RC, McGarity SA. Variation in digestibility of dry dog foods with identical label guaranteed analysis. Journal of the American Animal Hospital Association 1986; 22: 571-575.

11. Meyer H, Heckötter E. III. Empfehlungen zur Versorgung der Katze mit Energie und Nährstoffen. In: Meyer H, ed. Futterwerttabellen für Hunde und Katzen. Hannover, Germany: Schlütersche Verlaganstalt, 1986; 12-14.

12. National Research Council. Introduction. In: Nutrient Requirements of Dogs. Washington, DC: National Academy Press, 1985a; 1.

13. National Research Council. Preface. In: Nutrient Requirements of Cats. Washington, DC: National Academy Press, 1986a; iii.

14. National Research Council. Tables. In: Nutrient Requirements of Cats. Washington, DC: National Academy Press, 1986b; 42.

15. National Research Council. Tables. In: Nutrient Requirements of Dogs. Washington, DC: National Academy Press, 1985b; 44-45.

16. Sheffy BE. The 1985 revision of the National Research Council nutrient requirements of dogs and its impact on the pet food industry. In: Burger IH, Rivers JPW, eds. Nutrition of the Dog and Cat. Cambridge, UK: Cambridge University Press, 1989; 11-34.

Appendix K
Comparative Analysis of Milks and Milk Replacers

I. Introduction

This appendix compares the composition of dog and cat milk with that of infant formulas for puppies and kittens (homemade and processed) at the recommended concentration. The appendix also compares milk composition of selected species.

Milk provides nutrition (fluids, energy and balanced nutrition) until the offspring is able to eat solid food. Colostrum transfers immunity. In addition, the milk of most species investigated thus far contains growth factors such as epidermal growth factor, insulin-like growth factors I and II, insulin and other peptide growth factors such as nerve growth factors and transforming growth factor. These growth factors exert trophic effects on the gastrointestinal tract, liver, spleen, pancreas and lungs, and convey important regulatory signals to developing offspring. These factors may protect against gastrointestinal viral infections and stimulate recovery from such infections. Insulin may play a role in gut closure after intake of colostrum via luminal or humoral effects on enterocytes. The concentration of these growth factors is much higher in colostrum than in mature milk.

II. Comparative analysis of queen's milk, bitch's milk and milk replacers for kittens and puppies

Table K-1. Nutrient content of milk replacers compared with that of queen's milk/100 g of milk, as fed.*

Nutrients	Units**	Queen's milk***	Feline Milk Substitute Instant Diet —powder (Waltham)†	Just Born Kittens —powder (Farnam)††	Just Born Kittens —liquid (Farnam)††	KMR —powder (PetAg)††	Milkodog —powder (Vétoquinol)††	Whiskas Cat Milk —liquid (Pedigree)††
Dilution†††	na	na	1 + 4	1 + 1	na	1 + 2	1 + 2	na
Moisture	g	79	80.8	51.8	78.4	67.4	67.8	84.0
Dry matter	g	21	19.2	48.2	21.6	32.6	32.2	16.0
Crude protein	g	7.5	8.3	17.5	8.1	14.5	10.0	4.5
Arginine	mg	430	na	745	310	623	323	110
Taurine	mg	10	60	5	<10	13.3	<3.3	40
Fat	g	8.5	5.3	10.2	5.4	9.08	8.0	3.5
Linoleic acid (C18:2)	g	≥1.3	na	4.98	1.22	3.67	0.33	0.07
Arachidonic acid (C20:4)	mg	≥110	na	5	<10	10	6.7	<10
Carbohydrate								
NFE	g	na	4.4	17.2	6.8	6.8	12.2	7.0
Lactose	g	4.0	3.7	10.8	4.9	5.4	11.6	<0.2
Crude fiber	g	na	0	0.15	0.1	0.2	0.13	0.1
Minerals								
Total ash	g	0.6	1.2	3.15	1.2	2.1	1.9	1.0
Calcium	mg	180	220	450	200	370	283	130
Phosphorus	mg	162	180	485	200	290	257	130
Sodium	mg	90	100	240	110	220	130	96
Potassium	mg	103	140	610	170	267	383	180
Magnesium	mg	9	16	60	30	23	24.7	15
Copper	mg	0.11	0.3	1.5	0.6	0.3	0.03	<0.1
Iron	mg	0.35	2.4	11.5	5.0	1.3	0.4	1.3
Energy								
ME‡	kcal	121	102	208	98	151	146	70
ME‡	kJ	505	425	871	410	634	610	292
Osmolarity	mOsm/kg	329	na	551	376	618	569	667

Key: na = not available, NFE = nitrogen-free extract, ME = metabolizable energy, mOsm = milliosmoles.
*This table gives the composition at the dilution recommended by the manufacturer for powdered formulas.
**g/100 g = %.
***Adkins et al 1997, Keen et al 1982, Kienzle et al 1995a, Remillard et al 1993, Sturman 1993. (See Bibliography.)
†Manufacturers' data.
††Based on analyses conducted by Woodson-Tenent Laboratories, June 1996.
†††The first number represents the milk powder, the second represents the added water (e.g., 1 + 2 = one part of powder plus two parts of water).
‡Calculated based on modified Atwater values: crude protein and NFE x 3.5 kcal/g, fat x 8.5 kcal/g.

Table K-2. Nutrient content of milk replacers compared with that of queen's milk/100 kcal metabolizable energy.*

Nutrients	Units	Queen's milk	Feline Milk Substitute Instant Diet —powder (Waltham)	Just Born Kittens —powder (Farnam)	Just Born Kittens —liquid (Farnam)	KMR —powder (PetAg)	Milkodog —powder (Vétoquinol)	Whiskas Cat Milk —liquid (Pedigree)
Crude protein	g	6.25	8.2	8.4	8.2	9.5	6.8	6.4
Fat	g	7.1	5.2	4.9	5.5	6.0	5.5	5.0
Linoleic acid (C18:2)	mg	>1.1	na	2,391	1,245	2,426	229	100
Carbohydrate								
NFE	g	na	4.4	8.3	7.0	4.5	8.4	10.0
Lactose	g	3.3	3.7	5.2	5.0	3.6	8.0	<0.3
Minerals								
Total ash	g	0.5	1.2	1.5	1.2	1.4	1.3	1.4
Calcium	mg	150	217	216	204	244	195	186
Phosphorus	mg	135	177	233	204	192	176	186
Sodium	mg	75	98	115	112	145	89	138
Potassium	mg	85.8	138	293	173.5	176	263	258
Magnesium	mg	7.5	16	29	30.6	15.4	17	21.5
Copper	mg	0.09	0.3	0.7	0.6	0.2	0.023	<0.1
Iron	mg	0.29	2.4	5.5	5.1	0.8	0.3	1.9

Key: na = not available, NFE = nitrogen-free extract.
*The nutrient levels per 100 kcal metabolizable energy in Table K-2 were calculated from the nutrient and energy levels in Table K-1.

Table K-3. Nutrient content of milk replacers compared with that of bitch's milk/100 g of milk, as fed.*

Nutrients	Units**	Bitch's milk***	Canine Milk Substitute Instant Diet—powder (Waltham)†	Esbilac—liquid (PetAg)††	Esbilac—powder (PetAg)††	Just Born—powder (Farnam)††	Milkodog—powder (Vétoquinol)††	Mother's Helper—powder (Lambert Kay)††	Mother's Helper—liquid (Lambert Kay)††	Nuturall—powder (VPL)††	Welpi Dog—powder (ASID Bonz)††
Dilution†††	na	na	1 + 4	na	1 + 2	1 + 1	1 + 2	1 + 2	na	1 + 1	1 + 2
Moisture	g	77.3	80.8	85.2	67.7	52.4	67.8	67.6	85.0	51.9	68.0
Dry matter	g	22.7	19.2	14.8	32.3	47.6	32.2	32.4	15.0	48.1	32.0
Crude protein	g	7.5	6.6	5.1	11.25	14.7	10.0	11.7	4.8	14.7	9.6
Arginine	mg	420	na	250	660	640	323	663	220	600	360
Fat	g	9.5	7.8	5.1	13.1	15.3	8.0	13.6	6.1	15.7	6.0
Linoleic acid (C18:2)	g	1.11	0.6	2.59	1.46	8.38	0.33	2.31	0.91	8.02	0.42
Carbohydrate											
NFE	g	3.8	3.5	3.5	5.7	13.9	12.2	5.1	3.0	13.8	10.8
Lactose	g	3.3	2.7	2.8	4.3	6.2	11.6	1.0	3.3	6.45	13.0
Crude fiber	g	na	0	0.2	0.1	0.25	0.13	0.17	0.3	0.15	0.1
Minerals											
Total ash	g	1.2	1.3	1.0	2.2	3.5	1.9	1.8	0.8	3.7	2.2
Calcium	mg	240	220	140	427	710	283	200	140	685	327
Phosphorus	mg	180	180	110	353	635	257	263	110	600	270
Sodium	mg	80	80	63	93	225	130	117	47	235	137
Potassium	mg	120	140	150	357	480	383	350	130	555	420
Magnesium	mg	11	16	14	12.7	26.0	24.7	16.7	17	25	27
Copper	mg	0.33	0.3	0.2	0.73	0.65	0.03	0.23	0.1	0.65	0.37
Iron	mg	0.7	3.0	1.1	1.8	10.0	0.4	2.2	1.1	10.5	0.67
Energy											
ME‡	kcal	146##	111	74	171	230	146	175	80	234	123
ME‡	kJ	610##	465	307	715	963	610	730	332	980	513
Osmolarity	mOsm/kg	569	na	276	347	846	525	332	279	858	569

Key: na = not available, NFE = nitrogen-free extract, ME = metabolizable energy, mOsm = milliosmoles.
*This table gives the composition at the dilution recommended by the manufacturer for powdered products.
**g/100 g = %
***Anderson 1991, Gesellschaft für Ernährungsphysiologie 1989, Kienzle et al 1985, Meyer et al 1985, Mundt et al 1981, Oftedal 1984, Rüsse 1961.
†Manufacturers' data.
††Based on analysis by Woodson-Tenent Laboratories, June 1996.
†††The first number is the milk powder, the second the water (e.g.,1 + 2 = one part of powder plus two parts of water).
‡Calculated based on modified Atwater values: crude protein and NFE x 3.5 kcal/g, fat x 8.5 kcal/g.
##Kienzle et al 1985, Meyer et al 1985, Mundt et al 1981, Oftedal 1984. (See Bibliography.)

Table K-4. Nutrient content of milk replacers compared with that of bitch's milk/100 kcal metabolizable energy.*

Nutrients	Units	Bitch's milk**	Canine Milk Substitute Instant Diet —powder (Waltham)	Esbilac —liquid (PetAg)	Esbilac —powder (PetAg)	Just Born —powder (Farnam)	Milkodog —powder (Vétoquinol)	Mother's Helper —powder (Lambert Kay)	Mother's Helper —liquid (Lambert Kay)	Nuturall —powder (VPL)	Welpi Dog —powder (ASID Bonz)
Protein	g	5.2	5.9	6.9	6.6	6.4	6.8	6.7	6.1	6.3	7.8
Arginine	mg	288	na	340	387	278	222	381	277	257	294
Fat	g	6.4	7.0	7.0	7.7	6.7	5.5	7.8	7.7	6.7	4.9
Linoleic acid (C18:2)	g	0.76	0.58	3.53	0.86	3.64	0.23	1.32	1.15	3.43	0.34
Carbohydrate											
NFE	g	2.6	3.15	4.8	3.4	6.0	8.4	2.94	3.74	5.9	8.8
Lactose	g	2.3	2.43	3.8	2.5	2.7	8.0	0.57	4.13	2.76	10.8
Crude fiber	g	na	0.0	0.3	0.06	0.1	0.1	0.1	0.4	0.06	0.08
Minerals											
Total ash	g	0.82	1.2	1.3	1.3	1.5	1.3	1.0	1.0	1.6	1.8
Calcium	mg	164	198	191	250	309	195	115	176	293	266
Phosphorus	mg	123	162	150	207	276	176	151	139	257	220
Sodium	mg	55	72	86	55	98	89	67	59	101	111
Potassium	mg	82	126	204	209	209	263	201	164	238	342
Magnesium	mg	7.5	14.5	19	7.4	11.3	16.9	9.6	21.4	10.7	22
Copper	mg	0.23	0.27	0.27	0.4	0.3	0.023	0.1	0.1	0.3	0.30
Iron	mg	0.48	2.7	1.5	1.1	4.3	0.3	1.3	1.4	4.5	0.54

Key: NFE = nitrogen-free extract.
*The nutrient levels per 100 kcal metabolizable energy in Table K-4 were calculated from the nutrient and energy levels in Table K-3.

Table K-5. Homemade milk replacers for puppies.

Recipe 1*		Recipe 2**		Recipe 1 (modified)	
Skim milk	43.8 g	Cow's milk†	800 ml	Skim milk	64 g
Low-fat curd***	40 g	Half cream††	200 ml	Low-fat curd***	15 g
Egg yolk (2/3)	10 g	Bone meal	6 g	One egg yolk	15 g
Vegetable oil	6 g	Citric acid	4 g	Vegetable oil	3 g
Vitamin-mineral mix	0.2 g	One egg yolk	15 g	Vitamin-mineral mix	2.5 g
		Vitamin A	2,000 IU	$CaCO_3$	0.5 g

*Kienzle 1985, 1991, 1995. (See Bibliography.)
**Björk 1984, Baines 1981. (See Bibiliography.)
***Do not use cottage cheese because it may increase the risk of clotting in the neonate's stomach.
†3% fat.
††12% fat (i.e., half cream in the UK).

Table K-6. Homemade milk replacers for kittens.

Recipe 1*		Recipe 2**	
Skim milk	70 g	One whole egg, fresh	15 g
Low-fat curd***	15 g	Protein supplement	25 g
Lean beef hash	8 g	Milk, sweetened, condensed	17 ml
Egg yolk (1/5)	3 g	Corn oil	7 ml
Vegetable oil	3 g	Water	250 ml
Lactose	0.8 g		
Vitamin-mineral mix	0.2 g		
Total	100 g	**Total**	310 g

*Kienzle 1991. (See Bibliography.)
**Remillard et al 1993. (See Bibliography.)
***Do not use cottage cheese because it may increase the risk of clotting in the neonate's stomach.

Table K-7. Comparisons between homemade milk replacers for puppies and kittens and bitch's and queen's milk.*

Nutrients	Units**		Puppies				Kittens	
		Bitch's milk	Recipe 1***	Recipe 2***	Recipe 1 modified†	Queen's milk	Recipe 1***	Recipe 2
Moisture	g	77.3	76.6	85.3	79.9	79.3	83.1	86.4
Dry matter	g	22.7	23.4	14.7	20.1	20.7	16.9	13.6
Crude protein	g	7.5	9.9	3.5	7.5	7.5	7.1	6.4
Fat	g	9.5	9.5	5.5	8.1	8.6	4.4	3.4
NFE	g	3.8	3.3	4.6	3.5	4	4.7	2.9
Ash	g	1.2	0.8	0.7	1.3	0.6	0.8	0.7
Calcium	mg	240	92.6	290	287	180	96.2	109
Phosphorus	mg	180	177	200	186	162	126	109
Sodium	mg	80	32	50	34	90	33.5	90
Potassium	mg	127	96	150	110	103	117	113
Copper	mg	0.33	0.03	na	0.05	0.11	0.03	0.2
Iron	mg	0.7	0.68	na	0.95	0.35	0.6	3.5
Zinc	mg	0.95	0.79	na	1.01	na	0.7	1.9
ME††	kcal	146	130	80	110	121	80	62
ME††	kJ	610	544	335	460	506	335	260

Key: NFE = nitrogen-free extract, ME = metabolizable energy.
*From Meyer et al 1986, Watt et al 1975. (See Bibliography.)
**g/100 ml or g/100 g = %.
***Calculated before addition of the vitamin-mineral mix.
†Calculated based on the addition of 2.5 g Pecutrin (Bayer).
††Calculated except for bitch's milk, for which the actual energy density was known from the literature.

III. Conclusions and recommendations

- When raising orphaned puppies or kittens, the nutrient profile of the milk replacer should approximate the profile of dam's milk as closely as possible. This can be done reasonably well with a good infant formula.
- Orphans ideally should receive colostrum during the first 24 to 36 hours after birth for adequate transfer of immunoglobulins.
- Most growth factors (which are also present in cow's milk) may be destroyed during the processing of infant formulas.
- The energy density of the milk replacer should be adequate at the recommended dilution. If the energy density is too low, the neonate's intake capacity may be exceeded, and despite a high volume of intake, neonates may not gain weight and may actually lose weight. Affected neonates may start vocalizing and become restless. During the first week of life, the capacity of milk intake is limited to about 10 to 15 ml per feeding.
- The other important role of milk is hydration of neonates. Very concentrated formulas may not provide enough water and predispose the neonate to dehydration. Therefore, it is important that neonates receive about 180 ml of water per kg body weight per day. The milk replacer should provide this amount of water at the recommended dilution. If not, water should be added. It is better to switch to another brand if the energy density becomes insufficient with further dilution. Further dilution may predispose neonates to hypoglycemia.

- Hypertonic solutions (≥ 700 mOsm/kg H_2O) may delay gastric emptying in young puppies and predispose them to vomiting. High osmolality may also increase the risk of diarrhea. Therefore, the osmolality of milk replacers should not exceed that of bitch's milk.
- Most artificial milk formulas are prepared with cow's milk as a base. Cow's milk is low in arginine compared with bitch's and queen's milk and may predispose neonates to cataract development.
- Taurine is low in some milk replacers for kittens.
- All homemade preparations and milk replacer dilutions should be refrigerated and used within 24 hours after preparation.
- Egg whites should not be used in homemade formulas because they predispose neonates to diarrhea.
- Cottage cheese should be avoided; however, curd can be used, especially in milk replacers for kittens. Casein micelles in cow's milk are larger than those in bitch's or queen's milk. In addition, queen's milk is high in albumin compared with casein. Curd contains coagulated casein, and the micelles are not dissolved, but kept in suspension. This decreases the risk of hard coagula formation in the stomach.
- Cream is not a desirable fat source because fat from cow's milk contains high concentrations of short- and medium-chain fatty acids, whereas bitch's milk and queen's milk are rich in linoleic acid.
- For these reasons, it is best to wean neonates as early as possible and feed them a balanced and highly digestible food for growing dogs or cats. (See Chapters 9 and 11 for more information.)

IV. Composition of milk from selected species

Table K-8. Composition of milk from selected species.

Species	DM (g)	Protein (g)	Fat (g)	Sugars (g)*	Ash (g)	Ca (mg)	P (mg)	Na (mg)	K (mg)	Mg (mg)	Cu (mg)	Fe (mg)	Zn (mg)	kcal (per 100 ml)	Source**
						per 100 g or 100 ml***					per liter				
Primates															
Baboon	14	1.5	4.5	7.8	0.3	na	na	na	na	na	na	na	na	na	26
Rhesus monkey	15.4	2.3	4.6	7.9	na	na	na	na	na	na	1	1.2	2	na	26
Human being	12.6	1.63	3.75	7.0	0.2	25.5	14.1	26.7	60.2	3.3	0.2-0.4	0.3-0.9	1-3	61	3,12,24
Ursidae															
Brown bear	31.9	9.2	17.1	2.2	1.5	na	na	na	na	na	na	na	na	na	26
Black bear	37.6	7.0	25.1	3.0	na	na	na	na	na	na	na	na	na	na	26
Canidae															
Arctic fox	28.6	11.1	13.5	3.0	1.0	na	na	na	na	na	na	na	na	na	26
Red fox	18.1	6.7	5.8	4.6	0.9	na	na	na	na	na	na	na	na	na	26
Domestic dog	22.7	7.5	9.5	3.8	1.2	240	180	80	120	11	3.3	7.3	7-12	146	Table K-3
Mustelidae															
Striped skunk	30.6	9.9	13.8	3.0	na	na	na	na	na	na	na	na	na	na	26
Ferret	na	6.9	9.7	3.8	na	na	na	na	na	na	na	na	na	na	26
American mink	21.7	5.6	7.3	4.5	1.0	na	na	na	na	na	na	na	na	na	26
Felidae															
African lion	26.8	11.8	8.7	3.2	na	na	na	na	na	na	na	na	na	na	26
Domestic cat	20.7	7.5	8.6	4.0	0.6	180	162	90	103	9	0.8-1.4	3-4	5-7	120	Table K-1
Equidae															
Ass	10.8	1.7	1.8	5.9	0.4	na	na	na	na	na	na	na	na	na	26
Zebra	11.3	1.6	2.2	7.0	0.4	na	na	na	na	na	0.2-1.0	2-4	2-3	na	26
Przewalski horse	10.5	1.6	1.5	6.7	0.3	na	na	na	na	na	0.2	na	na	na	26
Horse (domestic)	10.5	2.0	1.4	6.7	0.4	103	65	na	na	na	0.2-0.4	0.3-0.8	1-3	na	26
Camelidae															
Bactrian camel	15.2	4.3	4.3	na	0.9	na	na	na	na	na	na	na	na	na	26
Dromedary	13.6	3.6	4.5	5.0	0.7	na	na	na	na	na	na	na	na	na	26
Cervidae															
Red deer	21.1	7.1	8.5	4.5	1.4	na	na	na	na	na	na	na	na	na	26
Reindeer	26.3	9.5	10.9	3.4	1.3	na	na	na	na	na	na	na	na	na	26
Bovidae															
Cow	13.0	3.3	3.7	5.0†	0.7	115	95	40	145	12	0.05-0.2	0.2-0.6	4-5	74	3,6,16,26
Goat	12.0	2.9	3.8	4.7	0.8	na	na	na	na	na	0.1-0.2	0.3-0.4	3-6	na	6,26
Sheep	18.2	4.1	7.3	5.0	0.8	192	100	na	na	na	0.2-0.4	0.4-0.6	1-2	na	6,26
Suidae															
Sow	19	6	8	4	0.9	210	150	na	na	na	0.6-1.0	1-3	4-6	na	6,19
Rodents															
Golden hamster	22.6	9.4	4.9	4.9	na	na	na	na	na	na	na	na	na	119	16,26
Mouse	40.8	12.5	27.0	2.6	na	na	na	na	na	na	1-2	15	10-17	na	6,26
Rat	na	9.4	12.0	3.2	na	na	na	na	na	na	1-2	3-6	5-10	159	6,26
Guinea pig	17.5	6.3	5.7	4.8	0.8	na	na	na	na	na	0.4-0.6	0.8	4	na	6
Chinchilla	23.5	7.3	11-16	1.7	1.0	na	na	na	na	na	na	na	na	175	6,16,26
Rabbit	31.0	11.5	15.0	1-2	1.8	610	380	100	240	na	1	2-4	2-4	206	6,16,26
Insectivores															
Hedgehog	32.2	12.6	12.6	2.0	na	287	213	88	183	na	2.6	52	30	190	16

Key: DM = dry matter, Ca = calcium, P = phosphorus, Na = sodium, K = potassium, Mg = magnesium, Cu = copper, Fe = iron, Zn = zinc, na = not available.
*Most of which is lactose.
**See Bibliography for source numbers.
***g/100 g or g/100 ml = %.
†4.6 g lactose.

BIBLIOGRAPHY

1. Adkins Y, Zicker SC, Lepine A, et al. Changes in nutrient and protein composition of cat milk throughout lactation. American Journal of Veterinary Research 1997; 58: 370-375.

2. Andersen AC. Puppy production to weaning age. Journal of the American Veterinary Medical Association 1957; 130: 151-158.

3. Anderson RS, Carlos GM, Robinson IP, et al. Zinc copper, iron and calcium concentrations in bitch milk. Journal of Nutrition 1991; 121: S81-S82.

4. Association of American Feed Control Officials. Official Publication, 1999.

5. Atkinson S, Alston-Mills B, Lönnerdal B, et al. Major minerals and ionic constituents in human and bovine milk. In: Jensen RG, ed. Handbook of Milk Composition. San Diego, CA: Academic Press Inc, 1995; 592-622.

6. Baines FM. Milk substitutes and the hand rearing of puppies and kittens. Journal of Small Animal Practice 1981; 22: 555-578.

7. Björck G. Care and feeding of the puppy in the postnatal and weaning period. In: Anderson RS, ed. Nutrition and Behaviour in Dogs and Cats. Proceedings. First Nordic Symposium on Small Animal Veterinary Medicine, Oslo, Norway, September 15-18, 1982. Oxford, UK: Pergamon Press, 1984; 25-33.

8. Carroll EJ. Lactation. In: MacDonald LE, ed. Veterinary Endocrinology and Reproduction, 2nd ed. Philadelphia, PA: Lea & Febiger, 1975.

9. Cartwright GE, Wintrobe MM, Buschke RH, et al. Anemia, hypoproteinemia, and cataracts in swine fed casein hydrolysate or zein: Comparison with pyridoxine-deficiency anemia. Journal of Clinical Investigation 1945; 24: 268-277.

10. Casey CE, Smith A, Zhang P. Microminerals in human and animal milks. In: Jensen RG, ed. Handbook of Milk Composition. San Diego, CA: Academic Press Inc, 1995; 622-674.

11. Davidson MG, Nasisse MP. Ocular diseases of the young dog and cat. In: Proceedings. Kal Kan Forum 1986: 4-10.

12. Davis TA, Nguyen HV, Garcia-Bravo R, et al. Amino acid composition of the milk of some mammalian species changes with stage of lactation. British Journal of Nutrition 1994; 72: 845-853.

13. Donovan SM, Odle J. Growth factors in milk as mediators of infant development. Annual Reviews in Nutrition 1994; 14: 147-167.

14. Dzieye J, Brooks D. Canine cataracts. Compendium on Containing Education for the Practicing Veterinarian 1983; 5: 81-87.

15. Gesellschaft für Ernährungsphysiologie, Grunddaten für die Berechnung des Energie und Nährstoff-bedarfs. In: Ausschuß für Bedarfsnormen. Energie- und Nährstoffbedarf Nr. 5 Hunde. Frankfurt/Main, Germany: DLG Verlag, 1989; 19.

16. Glaze MB, Blanchard GL. Nutritional cataracts in a Samoyed litter. Journal of the American Animal Hospital Association 1983; 19: 951-954.

17. Goldblum OM, Holzman IR, Fisher SE. Intragastric feeding in the neonatal dog. American Journal of Diseases of Children 1981; 135: 631-633.

18. Hall WK, Bowles LL, Sydenstricher VP, et al. Cataracts due to deficiencies of phenylalanine and of histidine in the rat: A comparison with other types of cataracts. Journal of Nutrition 1948; 36: 277-295.

19. Halliday JA, Bell K, McKenzie H, et al. Feline whey proteins: Identification, isolation and initial characterization of a-lactalbumin, b-lactoglobulin and lysozyme. Comparative Biochemistry and Physiology 1990; 958: 773-779.

20. Halliday JA, Bell K, Shaw DC. Feline and canine milk lysozymes. Comparative Biochemistry and Physiology 1993; 1068: 859-865.

21. Jenness R, Sloan RE. The composition of milk of various species—A review. Dairy Science Abstracts 1970; 32: 599-614.

22. Jensen RG, Newburg DS. Bovine milk lipids. In: Jensen RG, ed. Handbook of Milk Composition. San Diego, CA: Academic Press Inc, 1995; 543-575.

23. Johnson AH. The composition of milk. In: Webb BH, Johnson AH, Johnson JA, eds. Fundamentals of Dairy Chemistry, 2nd ed. Westport, CT: AVI Publishing Co, 1974; 1-57.

24. Johnson CA, Grace JA, Probst MR. The effect of maternal illness on perinatal health. Veterinary Clinics of North America: Small Animal Practice 1987; 17: 555-566.

25. Johnson CA, Grace JA. Care of newborn puppies and kittens. In: Proceedings. Kal Kan Forum 1987: 9-16.

26. Johnston SD, Raksil S. Fetal loss in the dog and cat. Veterinary Clinics of North America: Small Animal Practice 1987; 17: 535-554.

27. Keen CL, Lönnerdal B, Clegg MS, et al. Developmental changes in composition of cats' milk: Trace elements, minerals, protein, carbohydrate and fat. Journal of Nutrition 1982; 112: 1763-1769.

28. Keen CL, Lönnerdal B, Clegg M. Developmental changes in composition of rat milk: Trace elements, minerals, protein, carbohydrate and fat. Journal of Nutrition 1981; 111: 226-236.

29. Kienzle E. Raising of motherless puppies and kittens. In: Proceedings. World Small Animal Veterinary Association Congress. Vienna, Austria, 1991: 240-242.

30. Kienzle E, Kamphues J. Gesundheitsstörungen bei Katzenwelpen nach Einsatz ungeeigneter Milchaustauscher. Kleintierpraxis 1991; 36: 264-268.

31. Kienzle E, Landes E. Aufzucht verwaister Jungtiere Teil I: Indikationsstellung und Zusammenseztung der Muttermilch. Kleintierpraxis 1995; 40: 633-685.

32. Kienzle E, Landes E. Aufzucht verwaister Jungtiere Teil II: Herstellung von Milchaustauschern und praktische Durchführung der mutterlosen Aufzucht. Kleintierpraxis 1995; 40: 687-728.

33. Kienzle E, Meyer H, Dammers C, et al. Milchaufnahme, Gewichtentwicklung, Milchverdaulichkeit, sowie Energi- und Nährstoff- retention bei Saugwelpen. Fortschritte in der Tierphysiologie und Tierernährung (Advances in Animal Physiology and Animal Nutrition) 1985; 16: 27-50.

34. Lewis LD, Morris ML Jr, Hand MS. Orphan feeding and care. In: Small Animal Clinical Nutrition III. Topeka, KS: Mark Morris Associates, 1987; 3-18-3-19.

35. Mapletoft RJ, Schutte AP, Coubrough RI, et al. The perinatal period of dogs–Nutrition and management in the hand-rearing of puppies. Journal of the South African Veterinary Medical Association 1974; 45: 183-189.

36. Martin CL, Chambreau T. Cataract production in experimentally orphaned puppies fed a commercial replacement for bitch's milk. Journal of the American Animal Hospital Association 1982; 18: 115-119.

37. Meyer H, Kienzle E, Dammers C. Milchmenge und Milchzusammensetzung bei der Hündin sowie Futteraufnahme und Gewichtsenwicklung ante und post partum. Fortschritte in der Tierphysiologie und Tierernährung (Advances in Animal Physiology and Animal Nutrition) 1985; 16: 51-72.

38. Monson WJ. Is cataract development in orphaned puppies a nutritional problem? Pet-Ag Division information sheet. Elgin, IL, 1983.

39. Monson WJ. Orphan rearing of puppies and kittens. Veterinary Clinics of North America: Small Animal Practice 1987; 17: 567-576.

40. Morris JG, Rogers QR. Metabolic basis for some of the nutritional peculiarities of the cat. In: Edney ATB, ed. Recent Advances in Feline Nutrition. Journal of Small Animal Practice 1982; 23: 599-613.

41. Mosier JE. The puppy from birth to six weeks. Veterinary Clinics of North America: Small Animal Practice 1978; 8: 79-100.

42. Mosier JE. Appendix. Veterinary Clinics of North America: Small Animal Practice 1978; 8 :155.

43. Mundt H-C, Thomée A, Meyer H. Zur Energie-und Eiweißversorgung von Saugwelpen über die Muttermilch. Kleintierpraxis 1981; 26: 353-360.

44. National Research Council. Nutrient Requirements of Cats. Washington, DC: National Academy Press, 1996.

45. National Research Council. Nutrient Requirements of Dogs. Washington, DC: National Academy Press, 1995.

46. Neville MC, Jensen RG. The physical properties of human and bovine milks. In: Jensen RG, ed. Handbook of Milk Composition. San Diego, CA: Academic Press Inc, 1995; 81-85.

47. Neville MC. Volume and caloric density of human milk. In: Jensen RG, ed. Handbook of Milk Composition. San Diego, CA: Academic Press Inc, 1995; 99-113.

48. Newburg DS, Neubauer SH. Carbohydrates in milks: Analysis, quantities, and significance. In: Jensen RG, ed. Handbook of Milk Composition. San Diego, CA: Academic Press Inc, 1995; 273-349.

49. Oftedal OT, Iverson SJ. Comparative analysis of nonhuman milks. In: Jensen RG, ed. Handbook of Milk Composition. San Diego, CA: Academic Press Inc, 1995; 749-855.

50. Oftedal OT. Lactation in the dog: Milk composition and intake by puppies. Journal of Nutrition 1984; 114: 803-812.

51. Poffenbarger EM, Olson PN, Chandler ML, et al. Use of adult dog serum for colostrum in the neonatal dog. American Journal of Veterinary Research 1991; 52: 1221-1224.

52. Poston GA, Rils RC, Rumsey GL, et al. The effect of supplement dietary amino acids, minerals and vitamins on salmonoid fed cataractogenic diet. Cornell Veterinarian 1977; 67: 472-509.

53. Remillard RL, Pickett JP, Thatcher CD, et al. Comparison of kittens fed queen's milk with those fed milk replacers. American Journal of Veterinary Research 1993; 54: 901-907.

54. Reynolds HY, Johnson JS. Quantitation of canine immunoglobulins. Journal of Immunology 1970; 105: 698-703.

55. Rubin LF. Atlas of Veterinary Ophthalmoscopy. Philadelphia, PA: Lea & Febiger, 1974.

56. Rüsse I. Die Laktation der Hündin. Zentralblatt für Veterinär Medizin Reihe A 1961; 8: 252-281.

57. Schaefers-Okkens AC. Pediatrie Post University Course. Gent, Belgium, January 14, 1993.

58. Strohbehn-Enelstad J. Supportive treatment for diseases of neonatal puppies. Veterinary Medicine/Small Animal Clinician 1982; 77: 1215-1217.

59. Swaisgood HE. Protein and amino acid composition of bovine milk. In: Jensen RG, ed. Handbook of Milk Composition. San Diego, CA: Academic Press Inc, 1995; 464-468.

60. Taylor TJ, Graham DL. A compilation of data on feline nutrient requirements. Iowa State Veterinarian 1971; 3: 144-148.

61. Vainisi SJ, Edelhauser HF, Wolf ED, et al. Nutritional cataracts in timber wolves. Journal of the American Veterinary Medical Association 1981; 179: 1175-1180.

62. Von Sallman L, Reid ME, Grimes PA, et al. Tryptophan-deficiency cataracts in guinea pigs. Archives of Ophthalmology 1959; 62: 662-672.

63. White M, Hathaway M, Dayton W, et al. IGF-1 levels in mammary secretions and serum of dogs (abstract). In: Proceedings. Thirteenth Annual Veterinary Medical Forum, American College of Veterinary Internal Medicine. Lake Buena Vista, Florida, 1995: 1001.

64. Widdowson EM. Food, growth and development in the suckling period. In: Graham-Jones O, ed. Canine and Feline Nutritional Requirements. Oxford, UK: Pergamon Press, 1964; 1-16.

Appendix L
Nutrient Profiles of Commercial Dog and Cat Foods

I. Cat foods

Table L-1. Moist grocery brand cat foods. This table lists products with a large market share and for which information is available. Grocery brands are those pet foods traditionally sold in grocery outlets and in some pet superstores.*

Foods	Moisture	kcal/g	Protein	Fat	NFE	Crude fiber	Ca	P	K	Na	Cl	Mg
Associate Wholesale Grocers Best Choice Tuna for Cats**	75.8	3.62	77.2	9.3	3.6	0.4	1.32	0.95	1.07	1.03	1.65	0.13
Friskies Alpo Cat Food with Chicken & Rice***	76.9	4.90	45.0	38.5	1.3	2.34	1.52	1.26	1.07	0.83	1.57	0.08
Friskies Alpo Tuna Treat**	71.1	3.90	76.9	14.7	0.0	0.4	1.66	1.56	1.14	0.69	1.31	0.10
Friskies Beef & Liver Dinner***	75.5	4.85	46.5	36.5	3.5	2.23	2.14	1.38	0.97	1.17	1.79	0.07
Friskies Turkey & Giblets Dinner***	75.7	4.91	47.0	36.7	4.0	1.35	1.82	1.41	0.92	0.91	1.78	0.07
Friskies Fancy Feast Chunky Chicken Feast***	75.6	4.88	50.8	34.0	5.3	0.4	2.54	1.76	0.79	0.93	1.09	0.07
Friskies Fancy Feast Flaked Tuna Feast***	73.9	3.83	61.3	14.9	11.5	1.9	1.76	1.23	na	0.81	na	0.10
Friskies Fancy Feast Savory Salmon Feast***	75.8	4.18	56.8	24.5	3.4	1.7	2.47	1.99	1.27	0.50	1.20	0.11
Friskies Fancy Feast Tender Liver & Chicken Feast**	76.4	5.07	55.0	36.9	0.3	1.27	0.76	1.14	1.06	0.47	0.80	0.07
Friskies Fancy Feast Turkey & Giblets Feast***	76.0	4.73	55.9	32.0	1.5	1.7	0.96	1.31	1.14	0.44	1.08	0.08
Friskies Kitten Formula, Cat Food Turkey Formula***	75.2	4.81	51.5	34.8	1.4	1.7	1.81	1.65	1.04	0.50	1.04	0.08
Friskies Kitten Formula, Ocean Whitefish Formula***	77.0	3.89	65.2	17.8	2.6	0.9	3.00	2.52	1.67	0.81	1.50	0.14
Friskies Senior Canned Cat Food Turkey & Giblets in Gravy***	76.6	4.68	48.8	32.0	7.4	1.7	1.08	1.25	1.90	0.39	0.59	0.08
Friskies Special Diet, Canned Turkey & Giblets Dinner***	77.6	4.85	48.6	34.4	6.2	1.4	0.89	0.95	1.17	0.98	2.10	0.08
Heinz 9 Lives Plus Salmon in Gravy**	77.0	3.81	62.5	12.9	15.2	0.9	0.65	0.78	0.48	1.00	1.65	0.08
Heinz 9 Lives Plus Turkey & Giblets Dinner**	76.8	4.32	42.0	28.9	11.3	0.9	2.67	2.20	0.99	2.07	2.63	0.12
Heinz Amoré Tuna Favorites, Tuna or Shrimp Entree**	74.4	3.73	75.5	11.2	3.6	0.8	1.44	0.94	1.21	0.82	1.33	0.16
Heinz Kozy Kitten Fish Dinner**	74.3	4.33	38.0	24.6	26.0	3.5	1.55	1.20	1.09	0.30	0.39	0.19
Kal Kan Optimum with Ocean Whitefish**	77.4	5.08	37.4	41.3	7.3	1.8	2.74	2.25	0.75	0.84	0.66	0.13
Kal Kan Sheba with Savory Duck in Meaty Juices**	82.1	4.23	63.1	23.2	1.3	2.2	2.18	1.40	1.17	1.12	1.23	0.09
Kal Kan Sheba with Turkey in Meaty Juices**	82.6	4.29	60.3	25.3	0.7	2.3	2.18	1.32	1.26	0.97	1.09	0.09
Kal Kan Whiskas Choice Cuts in Sauce with Beef & Chicken**	81.6	4.15	44.8	22.2	20.0	1.1	2.18	1.90	0.65	1.47	1.36	0.09
Kal Kan Whiskas Kitty Stew**	79.3	4.86	51.4	33.3	6.7	1.0	1.06	1.54	0.96	0.77	0.67	0.08
Pedigree Katkins†	84.0	3.88	36.3	30.6	13.9	2.0	2.60	1.70	na	0.60	na	0.09
Pedigree Katkins Chunks†	78.0	4.05	30.5	27.0	33.2	1.4	1.60	1.50	na	1.00	na	0.06
Pedigree Kitekat†	85.0	3.80	37.3	29.3	14.0	2.0	2.20	1.50	na	0.7	na	0.10
Pedigree Kitekat Chunks†	79.0	3.76	34.2	22.4	31.8	1.4	2.10	2.00	na	1.2	na	0.07
Pedigree Sheba†	82.0	3.78	62.2	18.2	6.1	1.7	1.30	1.30	na	1.1	na	0.07
Pedigree Whiskas Fine Cuts***	82.0	4.11	47.8	30.7	6.2	1.7	1.90	1.90	na	1.30	na	0.10
Pedigree Whiskas Kitten***	81.0	4.21	50.5	29.7	6.2	2.1	1.70	1.50	na	0.80	na	0.06
Pedigree Whiskas Select Cuts***	80.0	3.70	38.5	20.1	30.2	1.5	1.40	1.60	na	1.2	na	0.07
Pedigree Whiskas Supermeat***	83.0	3.94	48.2	27.1	8.3	2.4	1.40	1.60	na	0.90	na	0.08
Ralston Purina Tender Beef Dinner**	74.0	4.64	43.9	29.3	17.4	0.8	1.77	1.42	0.96	0.58	1.04	0.09
Ralston Purina Tuna Dinner**	75.8	4.18	50.4	20.7	18.9	0.4	1.69	1.41	1.12	0.62	1.24	0.10
Average nutrient content of moist grocery brand cat foods	**77.9**	**4.29**	**51.2**	**26.6**	**9.7**	**1.5**	**1.77**	**1.51**	**1.08**	**0.88**	**1.28**	**0.09**
Range of nutrient contents of moist grocery brand cat foods	71.1-85.0	3.62-5.08	30.5-77.2	9.3-41.3	0-33.2	0.4-3.5	0.65-3.0	0.78-2.52	0.48-1.67	0.3-2.07	0.39-2.63	0.06-0.19

Key: NFE = nitrogen-free extract, Ca = calcium, P = phosphorus, K = potassium, Na = sodium, Cl = chloride, Mg = magnesium, na = not available.
*Nutrients, except for moisture, are expressed as % dry matter. Energy is expressed in kcal metabolizable energy/g dry matter. Kilocalories of metabolizable energy are either declared by the manufacturer or calculated based on modified Atwater values: protein = 3.5 kcal/g, fat = 8.5 kcal/g, NFE = 3.5 kcal/g. To convert to kJ, multiply kcal by 4.184.
**Analyses conducted in December 1995 and June 1996 by an independent laboratory (Woodson-Tenent Laboratories, Inc., Des Moines, IA, USA).
***Manufacturers' data.
†Data from Henderson AJ, ed. The Henston Small Animal Veterinary Vade Mecum, 15th ed. Peterborough, UK: Veterinary Business Development Ltd, 1996; 101-104.

Table L-2. Dry grocery brand cat foods. This table lists products with a large market share and for which information is available. Grocery brands are those pet foods traditionally sold in grocery outlets and in some pet superstores.*

Foods	Moisture	kcal/g	Protein	Fat	NFE	Crude fiber	Ca	P	K	Na	Cl	Mg
Friskies Alpo Dry Cat Food Gourmet Dinner**	8.3	3.70	33.3	10.7	46.3	2.3	1.04	1.16	0.60	0.60	0.94	0.12
Friskies Dry Cat Food Ocean Fish Flavor***	8.3	3.70	35.7	11.2	42.8	2.2	1.31	1.32	0.62	0.61	0.96	0.13
Friskies Fancy Feast Savory Salmon Flavor***	7.1	4.17	34.9	19.3	37.4	2.2	1.39	1.13	0.62	0.21	0.71	0.07
Friskies Fancy Feast Turkey & Giblets Flavor***	6.6	4.16	34.9	19.1	37.6	2.1	1.34	1.07	0.62	0.21	0.72	0.07
Friskies Kitten Formula Dry Cat Food***	8.3	3.70	39.0	11.5	38.7	2.1	1.78	1.45	0.70	0.46	0.68	0.13
Friskies Premium Chef's Blend 4 Delicious Flavors Dry Cat Food**	5.6	3.75	34.0	11.9	44.2	2.6	1.27	1.47	0.54	0.49	0.68	0.12
Friskies Premium Chef's Blend Dry Cat Food***	8.3	3.63	36.2	10.0	43.3	2.3	1.34	1.35	0.59	0.62	0.89	0.14
Friskies Senior Dry Cat Food***	8.5	3.74	32.5	10.4	49.1	2.8	1.20	0.93	0.59	0.26	0.90	0.11
Friskies Senior Dry Cat Food with Lamb Meal, Rice and Barley***	8.3	3.65	31.3	9.3	50.4	2.7	1.26	1.19	0.60	0.30	0.58	0.14
Friskies Special Diet Dry Cat Food***	8.3	4.01	33.4	16.5	41.2	2.0	1.18	1.07	0.76	0.31	0.87	0.09
Heinz 9 Lives Plus Tuna & Egg**	6.7	3.72	33.2	10.8	46.7	1.8	1.33	1.33	0.66	0.34	0.71	0.12
Heinz Kozy Kitten Dry Gulf Fish & Shrimp Flavor**	7.2	3.59	31.8	8.9	49.0	3.5	1.35	1.05	0.79	0.29	0.47	0.18
Kal Kan Whiskas Original Crave Recipe**	7.1	3.66	32.3	10.4	46.9	2.6	1.31	1.25	0.73	0.62	0.84	0.14
Pedigree Brekkies†	7.5	3.59	32.2	8.5	51.4	2.7	1.20	1.10	na	0.80	na	0.10
Pedigree Whiskas Cocktail†	7.5	3.66	41.7	8.3	43.1	1.6	1.00	1.10	na	0.90	na	0.07
Pedigree Whiskas Crunch†	7.5	3.58	20.4	5.8	67.7	2.7	1.10	0.90	na	0.50	na	0.05
Ralston Purina Alley Cat Poultry & Seafood Flavors**	6.1	3.82	36.8	14.6	36.9	4.1	1.43	1.18	0.85	0.44	0.65	0.18
Ralston Purina Cat Chow***	8.5	3.70	37.1	13.2	40.3	1.6	1.72	1.34	0.78	0.32	na	0.13
Ralston Purina Cat Chow Mature***	8.5	3.54	36.8	9.7	44.5	1.8	1.38	1.09	0.82	0.35	na	0.12
Ralston Purina Cat Chow Special Care**,***	7.5	4.36	34.1	14.6	44.9	1.0	0.99	0.94	0.84	0.30	1.08	0.08
Ralston Purina Deli Cat**	8.4	3.86	37.3	13.0	41.5	1.4	1.20	1.08	0.93	0.37	0.68	0.14
Ralston Purina Kit 'N Kaboodle**	6.8	3.81	35.1	12.6	43.1	2.3	1.34	1.08	0.92	0.40	0.80	0.14
Ralston Purina Kitten Chow***	8.5	3.72	41.0	13.8	35.5	1.8	1.54	1.46	0.80	0.33	na	0.14
Ralston Purina Meow Mix Chicken! Turkey! Salmon! Flavors**	6.3	3.80	37.0	12.4	41.4	1.5	1.37	1.22	0.95	0.52	1.10	0.13
Ralston Purina O.N.E. Chicken and Rice Formula for Cats***	8.5	4.59	34.4	15.5	42.6	1.4	1.15	0.96	0.85	0.22	na	0.07
Ralston Purina O.N.E. Chicken and Rice Formula for Kittens***	8.5	4.73	39.1	18.4	33.8	1.4	1.21	1.09	0.86	0.33	na	0.11
Average nutrient content of dry grocery brand cat foods	**7.6**	**3.84**	**34.8**	**12.3**	**43.9**	**2.17**	**1.30**	**1.17**	**0.74**	**0.43**	**0.79**	**0.12**
Range of nutrient contents of dry grocery brand cat foods	**5.6-8.5**	**3.54-4.73**	**20.4-41.7**	**5.8-19.3**	**33.8-67.7**	**1-4.1**	**0.99-1.78**	**0.9-1.47**	**0.54-0.95**	**0.21-0.9**	**0.47-1.1**	**0.05-0.18**

Key: NFE = nitrogen-free extract, Ca = calcium, P = phosphorus, K = potassium, Na = sodium, Cl = chloride, Mg = magnesium, na = not available.
*Nutrients, except for moisture, are expressed as % dry matter. Energy is expressed in kcal metabolizable energy/g dry matter. Kilocalories of metabolizable energy are either declared by the manufacturer or calculated based on modified Atwater values: protein = 3.5 kcal/g, fat = 8.5 kcal/g, NFE = 3.5 kcal/g. To convert to kJ, multiply kcal by 4.184.
**Analyses conducted in December 1995 and June 1996 by an independent laboratory (Woodson-Tenent Laboratories, Inc., Des Moines, IA, USA).
***Manufacturers' data.
†Data from Henderson AJ, ed. The Henston Small Animal Veterinary Vade Mecum, 15th ed. Peterborough, UK: Veterinary Business Development Ltd, 1996; 101-104.

Table L-3. Moist specialty brand cat foods. This table lists products with a large market share and for which information is available. Specialty brands are premium and super premium foods traditionally sold in pet stores, pet superstores or veterinary hospitals.*

Foods	Moisture	kcal/g	Protein	Fat	NFE	Crude fiber	Ca	P	K	Na	Cl	Mg
Eagle Pet Products Eagle Pack Beef & Liver***	76.5	5.02	46.8	36.2	8.51	1.7	1.11	1.02	0.72	0.60	na	0.09
Eagle Pet Products Eagle Pack Chicken, Rice & Lamb***	73.1	4.90	39.4	33.1	19.7	1.1	1.08	0.86	1.04	0.82	na	0.09
Eagle Pet Products Eagle Pack Poultry & White Fish***	77.4	5.22	45.6	38.9	8.41	0.9	1.19	1.02	0.66	0.49	na	0.10
Hill's Prescription Diet Feline g/d***	75.8	4.36	35.1	19.4	37.2	3.3	0.66	0.54	0.74	0.29	0.57	0.08
Hill's Prescription Diet Feline p/d***	71.1	4.85	48.8	31.5	11.2	0.5	1.10	0.90	0.90	0.51	0.91	0.09
Hill's Science Diet Feline Growth Tuna***	74.0	4.63	44.2	28.8	18.1	1.5	1.00	0.85	1.31	0.50	1.77	0.08
Hill's Science Diet Feline Growth***	69.6	5.43	49.0	36.2	6.9	0.6	1.09	0.95	0.76	0.56	0.88	0.09
Hill's Science Diet Feline Maintenance Beef ***	75.6	4.50	45.2	25.4	19.9	2.9	0.94	0.78	0.86	0.33	0.84	0.05
Hill's Science Diet Feline Maintenance Light***	75.6	3.80	45.1	14.8	27.3	7.0	0.70	0.57	0.78	0.33	0.80	0.06
Hill's Science Diet Feline Maintenance Liver & Chicken***	75.6	4.39	45.2	25.0	20.7	2.3	0.94	0.82	0.82	0.38	0.90	0.04
Hill's Science Diet Feline Maintenance Seafood***	75.6	4.38	45.2	25.4	20.0	2.6	0.93	0.70	0.86	0.42	0.72	0.08
Hill's Science Diet Feline Maintenance Tuna***	73.4	4.47	43.3	23.8	26.7	1.5	0.80	0.68	1.40	0.50	1.70	0.07
Hill's Science Diet Feline Maintenance Turkey***	75.6	4.58	45.2	25.4	20.7	2.5	0.82	0.82	0.82	0.30	0.75	0.07
Hill's Science Diet Feline Senior Beef***	75.0	4.16	40.8	20.4	28.4	5.2	0.64	0.68	0.72	0.32	0.65	0.06
Hill's Science Diet Feline Senior Tuna***	73.0	4.27	40.0	20.0	33.3	1.4	0.80	0.63	1.40	0.40	1.80	0.07
Hill's Science Diet Feline Senior Turkey***	75.0	4.16	40.8	20.4	27.6	5.2	0.68	0.68	0.76	0.32	0.88	0.06
Iams Beef Formula***	76.1	5.75	47.2	31.7	14.8	0.8	1.17	1.04	0.88	0.29	0.59	0.06
Iams Catfish Formula***	75.6	5.70	49.4	30.3	13.4	1.3	1.15	0.98	0.90	0.29	0.57	0.07
Iams Chicken Formula***	75.5	5.77	46.9	31.8	14.1	1.2	1.10	1.02	0.81	0.29	0.61	0.07
Iams Lamb & Rice Formula***	74.1	5.63	45.6	32.0	14.1	2.2	1.20	1.08	0.85	0.39	0.85	0.05
Iams Less Active for Cats Chicken & Rice Formula***	75.6	4.93	44.3	19.7	27.9	1.2	1.15	1.11	1.64	0.45	0.82	0.10
Iams Less Active for Cats Fish & Rice Formula***	75.8	4.44	44.2	17.8	30.6	0.8	1.40	1.12	1.40	0.45	0.74	0.09
Iams Ocean Fish Formula***	76.7	5.86	46.1	32.2	13.3	2.2	1.16	1.03	1.07	0.43	0.73	0.10
Iams Turkey Formula***	74.9	5.48	48.1	33.4	11.8	1.1	0.99	0.88	0.84	0.28	0.56	0.07
Nature's Recipe Select Balance Feline Adult Formula***	71.0	4.48	42.4	27.6	23.5	1.4	0.69	0.69	na	0.34	na	0.10
Nature's Recipe Select Balance Feline Reduced Activity Formula***	75.0	4.15	48.0	18.0	26.4	2.3	0.68	0.68	na	0.52	na	0.08
Nature's Recipe Select Balance Kitten Formula***	71.0	4.51	45.5	29.3	15.9	1.7	1.45	1.24	na	0.41	na	0.10
Nutro California Chicken Supreme**	80.6	4.50	58.1	26.6	5.99	0.5	1.08	0.98	0.83	1.34	1.96	0.06
Nutro Lamb & Turkey**	76.5	4.64	55.8	29.9	3.92	0.9	1.96	1.36	0.64	0.90	1.58	0.07
Nutro Salmon/Whitefish**	77.4	4.51	55.8	26.9	7.92	0.4	1.42	1.06	0.84	1.06	1.81	0.07
Nutro Veal Pate**	78.9	4.31	59.2	26.2	0.38	1.0	3.47	2.18	0.57	0.71	0.66	0.09
Pedigree Veterinary Plan 65/38***	85.4	4.45	42.5	35.6	9.6	1.4	1.85	1.78	1.10	0.98	na	0.10
Pedigree Veterinary Plan 75/34***	83.8	4.63	39.5	40.1	8.6	1.2	1.05	0.99	1.05	0.80	na	0.10
Pedigree Veterinary Plan 80/39***	81.4	4.30	43.0	33.3	10.8	1.6	1.08	1.08	0.86	0.91	na	0.16
Pedigree Veterinary Plan 100/40***	78.1	4.57	46.1	37.4	3.7	1.4	1.42	1.37	0.87	0.68	na	0.08
Average nutrient content of moist specialty brand cat foods	75.9	4.74	45.9	28.2	16.9	1.9	1.14	0.98	0.93	0.52	0.99	0.10
Range of nutrient contents of moist specialty brand cat foods	69.6-85.4	3.80-5.86	35.1-59.2	14.8-40.1	0.38-37.2	0.4-7.0	0.64-3.47	0.54-2.18	0.57-1.64	0.28-1.34	0.56-1.96	0.04-0.16

Key: NFE = nitrogen-free extract, Ca = calcium, P = phosphorus, K = potassium, Na = sodium, Cl = chloride, Mg = magnesium, na = not available.
*Nutrients, except for moisture, are expressed as % dry matter. Energy is expressed in kcal metabolizable energy/g dry matter. Kilocalories of metabolizable energy are either declared by the manufacturer or calculated based on modified Atwater values: protein = 3.5 kcal/g, fat = 8.5 kcal/g. To convert to kJ, multiply kcal by 4.184.
**Analyses conducted in December 1995 and June 1996 by an independent laboratory (Woodson-Tenent Laboratories, Inc., Des Moines, IA, USA).
***Manufacturers' data.

Table L-4. Dry specialty brand cat foods. This table lists products with a large market share and for which information is available. Specialty brands are premium and super premium foods traditionally sold in pet stores, pet superstores or veterinary hospitals.*

Foods	Moisture	kcal/g	Protein	Fat	NFE	Crude fiber	Ca	P	K	Na	Cl	Mg
Diamond Maintenance***	8.4	4.25	33.2	16.8	41.2	3.0	0.88	0.76	0.65	0.27	0.61	0.11
Diamond Professional***	8.5	4.67	37.4	23.2	29.8	2.6	1.13	0.99	0.66	0.38	0.66	0.10
Eagle Pet Products Eagle Pack Cat/Kitten Pack***	6.9	4.37	34.8	22.6	35.1	1.8	1.29	0.75	0.67	0.43	na	0.06
Eagle Pet Products Eagle Pack Maintenance Pack***	8.0	3.88	34.6	13.2	44.2	2.2	1.20	0.87	0.65	0.43	na	0.09
Hill's Prescription Diet Feline g/d***	7.5	4.23	33.4	18.9	41.9	1.4	0.51	0.55	0.75	0.34	0.68	0.05
Hill's Prescription Diet Feline p/d***	7.5	4.44	36.1	23.7	32.8	1.1	1.24	0.94	0.69	0.43	0.88	0.08
Hill's Science Diet Feline Growth***	7.5	4.95	37.1	26.8	29.1	1.2	1.30	0.96	0.64	0.35	0.71	0.11
Hill's Science Diet Feline Maintenance***	7.5	4.76	33.8	23.0	36.9	1.0	0.85	0.74	0.67	0.32	0.76	0.07
Hill's Science Diet Feline Maintenance Light***	9.0	3.60	40.7	9.0	38.0	6.8	0.96	0.79	0.68	0.30	0.72	0.06
Hill's Science Diet Feline Senior***	8.0	4.04	33.7	16.3	41.6	2.5	0.87	0.68	0.88	0.29	0.94	0.08
Iams Cat Food***	7.0	4.82	35.5	24.0	32.4	1.8	1.14	1.01	0.75	0.31	0.58	0.09
Iams Eukanuba Cat Food Chicken & Rice***	7.5	5.10	37.7	23.7	29.8	2.1	1.03	0.92	0.94	0.55	1.06	0.10
Iams Eukanuba Cat Food Lamb & Rice***	7.5	5.07	37.7	23.7	29.7	2.1	1.03	0.92	0.80	0.39	0.77	0.10
Iams Kitten Food***	7.3	4.94	37.7	24.9	29.9	1.5	1.28	1.02	0.97	0.65	0.54	0.10
Iams Less Active for Cats***	7.7	4.28	32.4	16.6	43.3	2.0	1.09	0.92	0.76	0.32	0.65	0.09
Iams Natural Lamb & Rice for Cats***	7.0	4.84	35.4	24.3	31.4	1.8	1.12	0.99	0.97	0.47	1.00	0.10
Iams Ocean Fish & Rice for Cats***	6.9	4.46	36.4	24.8	30.6	1.6	1.15	1.04	0.86	0.30	0.74	0.10
Nature's Recipe Select Balance Feline Adult Formula***	8.0	4.05	34.8	20.1	38.0	1.6	1.02	0.83	na	0.41	na	0.09
Nature's Recipe Select Balance Feline Reduced Activity Formula***	8.0	3.68	34.5	9.78	46.7	3.3	0.91	0.86	na	0.38	na	0.09
Nature's Recipe Select Balance Kitten Formula***	8.0	4.15	38.0	22.3	31.5	1.6	1.08	1.03	na	0.51	na	0.10
Nutro Max Cat Adult***	8.5	4.29	36.1	21.9	33.3	2.2	1.09	1.04	0.50	0.61	0.47	0.08
Nutro Max Cat Lite***	10.0	3.70	37.2	11.9	39.6	4.4	1.11	1.07	0.50	0.37	0.43	0.08
Nutro Max Kitten***	8.9	4.33	41.2	23.6	25.3	2.5	1.32	1.21	0.66	0.64	0.48	0.11
Nutro's Natural Choice Cat***	8.2	4.05	33.6	16.9	41.2	1.4	1.20	0.80	0.04	0.58	0.44	0.10
Nutro's Natural Choice Kitten***	9.0	4.15	35.7	19.5	35.4	1.8	1.37	1.10	0.68	0.66	0.51	0.10
Pedigree Veterinary Plan 300/34***	10.3	3.34	29.0	9.5	53.1	2.7	1.09	1.01	0.52	0.45	na	0.12
Pedigree Veterinary Plan 300/38***	9.5	3.31	31.3	7.7	50.5	4.4	1.22	1.12	0.61	0.52	na	0.13
Pedigree Veterinary Plan 320/39***	9.5	3.54	33.7	10.5	47.3	1.7	1.34	1.26	0.45	0.50	na	0.12
Pedigree Veterinary Plan 330/40***	8.7	3.61	36.3	12.7	41.9	1.9	1.19	1.12	0.48	0.49	na	0.12
Pedigree Whiskas Advance Formula 8-Plus†	8.0	4.46	35.9	25.0	31.0	1.6	1.10	0.98	na	0.98	na	0.09
Pedigree Whiskas Advance Formula Adult†	8.0	4.29	34.8	22.8	32.6	2.2	1.10	0.98	na	0.87	na	0.09
Pedigree Whiskas Advance Formula Kitten/Growth†	8.0	4.51	35.9	26.1	29.9	1.6	1.10	0.91	na	0.87	na	0.09
Pedigree Whiskas Advance Formula Less Active†	8.0	3.91	30.4	15.2	44.6	2.2	1.10	0.98	na	0.87	na	0.09
Ralston Purina Pro Plan Cat Adult***	7.5	4.71	34.2	16.6	42.2	1.4	0.97	0.94	0.82	0.25	na	0.07
Ralston Purina Pro Plan Cat Growth***	7.5	5.00	36.5	22.7	33.3	1.2	1.08	1.06	0.86	0.39	na	0.10
Ralston Purina Pro Plan Cat Lite Formula***	7.5	4.12	34.8	9.4	47.6	2.5	1.06	0.91	0.86	0.26	na	0.07
Ralston Purina Pro Plan Turkey & Barley Formula for Cats***	8.0	4.44	35.8	18.9	36.0	2.4	1.25	1.09	0.88	0.33	na	0.11
Royal Canin Felinotechnique Fit32***	8.0	4.19	34.8	14.1	41.3	2.7	1.14	1.03	0.65	0.38	0.71	0.09
Royal Canin Felinotechnique Kitten34***	8.0	4.57	37.0	21.7	31.5	2.7	1.30	1.09	0.65	0.38	0.71	0.09
Royal Canin Felinotechnique Senior28***	8.0	4.78	30.4	25.0	36.2	2.7	0.98	0.65	0.87	0.38	0.76	0.09
Royal Canin Felinotechnique Sensible33***	8.0	4.95	35.9	23.9	30.4	2.7	1.09	1.03	0.65	0.38	0.65	0.09
Royal Canin Felinotechnique Slim37***	8.0	3.80	40.2	10.9	37.2	4.4	1.30	1.09	0.65	0.43	0.71	0.09
Average nutrient content of dry specialty brand cat foods	**8.1**	**4.28**	**35.3**	**18.5**	**37.4**	**2.4**	**1.10**	**0.95**	**0.70**	**0.46**	**0.69**	**0.09**
Range of nutrient contents of dry specialty brand cat foods	**6.9-10.3**	**3.31-5.10**	**29-41.2**	**7.7-26.8**	**25.3-53.1**	**1.0-6.8**	**0.51-1.37**	**0.55-1.26**	**0.04-0.97**	**0.25-0.98**	**0.43-1.06**	**0.05-0.13**

Key: NFE = nitrogen-free extract, Ca = calcium, P = phosphorus, K = potassium, Na = sodium, Cl = chloride, Mg = magnesium, na = not available.

*Nutrients, except for moisture, are expressed as % dry matter. Energy is expressed in kcal metabolizable energy/g dry matter. Kilocalories of metabolizable energy are either declared by the manufacturer or calculated based on modified Atwater values: protein = 3.5 kcal/g, fat = 8.5 kcal/g, NFE = 3.5 kcal/g. To convert to kJ, multiply kcal by 4.184.

**Analyses conducted in December 1995 and June 1996 by an independent laboratory (Woodson-Tenent Laboratories, Inc., Des Moines, IA, USA).

***Manufacturers' data.

†Data from Henderson AJ, ed. The Henston Small Animal Veterinary Vade Mecum, 15th ed. Peterborough, UK: Veterinary Business Development Ltd, 1996; 101-104.

II. Dog foods

Table L-5. Moist grocery brand dog foods. This table lists products with a large market share and for which information is available. Grocery brands are those pet foods traditionally sold in grocery outlets and in some pet superstores.*

Foods	Moisture	kcal/g	Protein	Fat	NFE	Crude fiber	Ca	P	K	Na	Cl	Mg
Friskies Alpo Chopped with Chicken***	76.6	4.69	42.8	33.0	11.0	2.9	2.67	1.64	1.47	0.39	0.62	0.18
Friskies Alpo Chunky with Beef**	75.6	4.84	46.4	33.8	9.84	1.6	1.39	1.03	1.23	0.53	0.94	0.15
Friskies Alpo Chunky with Liver**	76.8	4.36	49.9	25.5	12.7	1.7	2.15	1.51	1.29	0.65	1.03	0.16
Friskies Alpo Prime Cuts Gourmet Dinner**	79.1	4.10	44.2	19.5	25.5	0.9	1.40	1.07	0.94	1.21	1.50	0.07
Friskies Gourmet Cuts with Beef & Liver***	77.3	4.19	46.3	20.3	24.2	0.4	1.28	0.93	1.76	0.97	1.98	0.20
Friskies Mighty Dog Beef***	76.2	5.03	48.5	39.2	0.14	2.08	1.74	1.48	1.15	0.74	0.48	0.09
Friskies Mighty Dog Gourmet Dinner**	73.7	5.37	40.1	45.2	3.57	0.4	2.16	1.75	0.95	0.80	1.03	0.09
Friskies Mighty Dog Senior Turkey & Rice Dinner***	76.8	4.60	36.9	30.1	21.3	1.7	2.97	1.87	1.08	0.27	0.33	0.12
Heinz Cycle Adult***	81.5	4.37	36.6	17.2	34.8	1.8	1.16	0.94	0.97	1.23	0.81	0.11
Heinz Cycle Lite***	79.2	4.08	26.7	13.0	43.3	7.5	1.04	0.94	1.08	0.79	0.52	0.16
Heinz Cycle Puppy***	77.9	4.43	40.3	23.1	24.4	2.1	1.30	1.06	1.33	0.82	0.88	0.12
Heinz Cycle Senior***	81.4	5.05	26.9	17.2	45.6	2.0	1.01	0.82	1.00	0.78	0.63	0.10
Heinz Ken-L Ration Original Chunky Beef**	74.3	3.98	46.2	19.5	20.1	3.1	1.44	1.32	1.71	1.17	0.97	0.21
Heinz King Kuts Chicken & Beef**	77.6	4.12	46.4	20.7	21.2	0.9	1.43	1.20	1.11	1.25	1.91	0.09
Heinz Skippy Chunks in Gravy with Beef**	79.9	3.98	44.0	17.7	26.8	3.5	1.05	0.90	1.29	0.60	0.70	0.20
Kal Kan Pedigree Beef Choice**	81.5	4.18	40.5	22.5	24.2	1.1	1.84	1.51	0.65	2.22	2.54	0.09
Kal Kan Pedigree Choice Cuts with Beef & Liver**	79.3	4.17	40.6	23.3	21.9	1.0	2.27	1.79	0.68	2.22	2.61	0.10
Kal Kan Pedigree Chopped Combo**	79.5	4.78	40.2	37.9	4.23	1.5	4.09	2.43	1.07	0.83	0.58	0.10
Kal Kan Pedigree Select Dinners (Cesar with Beef in Aspic)**	82.0	4.28	59.6	24.2	4.00	2.2	1.39	1.39	1.22	1.28	1.06	0.08
Kal Kan Pedigree Select Dinners (Cesar with Chicken & Liver in Aspic)**	81.2	4.56	57.6	29.1	2.02	2.1	1.17	1.44	1.06	1.38	0.96	0.07
Kal Kan Pedigree with Chunky Chicken**	78.7	5.21	37.6	42.7	7.56	1.4	2.7	1.69	0.80	0.66	0.56	0.09
Pedigree Bounce†	81.0	4.53	36.3	26.8	27.2	1.1	1.3	1.1	na	0.2	na	0.09
Pedigree Bounce Super Chunks†	78.0	4.41	29.0	26.6	32.6	1.8	2.1	1.8	na	1.0	na	0.07
Pedigree Cesar†	84.0	4.62	53.0	30.0	5.6	1.3	1.5	1.7	na	0.9	na	0.09
Pedigree Chappie†	77.0	3.52	25.7	6.1	59.1	0.1	1.9	1.3	na	0.2	na	0.10
Pedigree Chum†	81.0	4.68	33.2	32.6	22.1	2.1	2.2	1.2	na	0.8	na	0.1
Pedigree Chum Junior†	80.0	5.15	34.5	39.5	17.0	2.0	0.9	1.0	na	0.6	na	0.07
Pedigree Chum Puppy Food†	78.0	5.18	38.8	39.1	14.7	1.8	1.2	1.1	na	0.4	na	0.06
Pedigree Chum Tender Bites†	80.0	4.70	51.0	32.0	4.8	2.1	1.3	1.5	na	0.9	na	0.09
Pedigree Pal†	80.0	4.35	35.7	26.0	25.0	1.0	1.7	1.4	na	0.2	na	0.09
Average nutrient content of moist grocery brand dog foods	78.8	4.5	41.2	27.1	19.9	1.84	1.73	1.36	1.14	0.87	1.08	0.11
Range of nutrient contents of moist grocery brand dog foods	73.7-84	3.52-5.37	25.7-59.6	6.1-45.2	0.14-59.1	0.1-7.5	0.9-4.09	0.82-2.43	0.65-1.76	0.2-2.22	0.33-2.61	0.06-0.21

Key: NFE = nitrogen-free extract, Ca = calcium, P = phosphorus, K = potassium, Na = sodium, Cl = chloride, Mg = magnesium, na = not available.
*Nutrients, except for moisture, are expressed as % dry matter. Energy is expressed in kcal metabolizable energy/g dry matter. Kilocalories of metabolizable energy are either declared by the manufacturer or calculated based on modified Atwater values: protein = 3.5 kcal/g, fat = 8.5 kcal/g, NFE = 3.5 kcal/g. To convert to kJ, multiply kcal by 4.184.
**Analyses conducted in December 1995 and June 1996 by an independent laboratory (Woodson-Tenent Laboratories, Inc., Des Moines, IA, USA).
***Manufacturers' data.
†Data from Henderson AJ, ed. The Henston Small Animal Veterinary Vade Mecum, 15th ed. Peterborough, UK: Veterinary Business Development Ltd, 1996; 90-95.

Table L-6. Dry grocery brand dog foods. This table lists products with a large market share and for which information is available. Grocery brands are those pet foods traditionally sold in grocery outlets and in some pet superstores.*

Foods	Moisture	kcal/g	Protein	Fat	NFE	Crude fiber	Ca	P	K	Na	Cl	Mg
Friskies Alpo Beefy Dinner***	8.3	3.64	24.1	10.9	53.5	2.9	1.92	1.33	0.65	0.59	0.87	0.21
Friskies Alpo Dry Dog Food with Lamb Meal, Rice & Barley***	6.5	3.95	26.7	15.5	48.5	2.3	1.49	1.33	0.60	0.58	0.91	0.17
Friskies Come 'N Get It Dry Dog Food***	8.3	3.70	23.9	11.9	52.8	2.9	1.90	1.31	0.65	0.59	0.86	0.21
Friskies Field Trial Bite Size***	7.0	3.73	23.8	12.9	51.6	3.9	1.49	1.15	0.90	0.29	0.42	0.27
Heinz Cycle Adult***	8.9	3.91	26.5	13.1	52.2	2.9	1.00	0.77	0.79	0.33	0.58	0.14
Heinz Cycle Lite***	9.2	3.40	21.0	7.8	55.5	9.9	1.14	0.84	0.94	0.12	0.42	0.13
Heinz Cycle Puppy***	7.0	4.24	31.0	19.4	39.4	2.0	1.74	1.26	1.08	0.39	1.07	0.11
Heinz Cycle Senior***	9.6	3.67	21.6	9.4	62.1	2.9	0.80	0.62	0.63	0.09	0.60	0.13
Heinz Ken-L Ration Gravy Train Beef Flavor**	8.5	3.76	23.7	10.5	58.1	2.0	0.95	0.79	0.81	0.33	0.46	0.15
Kal Kan Pedigree Mealtime Lamb & Rice**	8.8	3.96	24.6	13.9	54.8	1.8	0.86	0.81	0.53	0.52	0.80	0.11
Kal Kan Pedigree Mealtime Rice & Vegetables**	8.4	3.74	23.2	11.5	55.7	2.0	1.79	1.20	0.45	0.51	0.74	0.13
Kal Kan Pedigree Mealtime Small Bites**	8.4	3.74	22.9	11.2	56.7	2.2	1.50	1.11	0.49	0.51	0.75	0.13
Pedigree Chum Complete†	8.0	3.78	25.5	11.7	54.0	1.6	1.4	1.3	na	0.53	na	0.10
Pedigree Chum Complete Junior†	6.0	3.87	27.6	13.1	51.3	2.2	0.90	0.90	na	0.90	na	0.09
Pedigree Chum Complete Puppy†	7.5	4.10	31.7	13.3	39.9	2.2	1.40	1.10	na	0.38	na	0.10
Ralston Purina Chuck Wagon Stampede**	6.8	3.82	26.4	12.2	53.0	1.7	1.24	1.00	0.61	0.49	0.87	0.12
Ralston Purina Dog Chow***	10.1	4.04	23.5	13.5	53.4	2.2	1.1	0.89	0.66	0.33	0.76	0.15
Ralston Purina Fit & Trim**,***	8.5	3.10	15.3	7.4	60.4	10.7	1.03	0.71	0.78	0.23	0.45	0.17
Ralston Purina Grrravy**	6.8	3.76	25.7	12.9	50.5	3.3	1.60	1.08	0.87	0.48	0.63	0.19
Ralston Purina Hi Pro**,***	8.5	4.08	30.2	11.8	49.7	1.9	1.31	0.93	0.52	0.42	0.63	0.14
Ralston Purina Kibbles and Chunks**	11.4	3.80	26.4	12.3	52.5	2.0	1.41	1.11	0.54	0.38	0.60	0.12
Ralston Purina Mainstay**	6.9	3.52	19.3	11.0	54.5	7.0	1.43	1.05	0.61	0.37	0.57	0.17
Ralston Purina Nutrient Management Dog Food***	8.5	4.22	28.0	11.4	52.3	1.5	1.16	0.93	0.60	0.37	na	na
Ralston Purina Nutrient Management Puppy Food***	8.5	4.32	31.5	12.6	47.0	1.5	1.31	1.04	0.66	0.35	na	na
Ralston Purina O.N.E. Adult Formula**,***	8.0	4.49	29.9	18.7	42.6	1.6	1.48	1.07	0.61	0.50	0.62	0.09
Ralston Purina O.N.E. Lamb & Rice Formula***	7.5	4.55	29.1	17.9	43.5	1.6	1.19	0.97	0.58	0.52	na	na
Ralston Purina O.N.E. Lamb & Rice Formula for Puppies***	7.5	4.70	31.1	18.9	40.0	1.7	1.30	1.05	0.54	0.45	na	na
Ralston Purina O.N.E. Lite Formula***	8.5	3.54	18.2	8.9	63.7	3.1	1.36	0.98	0.61	0.38	na	na
Ralston Purina Puppy Chow***	8.5	4.03	29.5	11.5	50.6	1.8	1.31	0.94	0.60	0.40	na	na
Ralston Purina Senior***	8.0	3.50	18.2	8.5	61.5	5.9	1.20	0.78	0.71	0.29	na	na
Wafcol 20†	6.5	3.67	21.4	6.4	61.0	4.3	1.4	0.96	na	0.47	na	0.03
Wafcol Energy Plus†	6.5	3.82	26.7	10.7	49.2	4.3	2.35	1.6	na	0.51	na	0.05
Average nutrient content of dry grocery brand dog foods	8.0	3.88	25.3	12.3	52.2	3.1	1.36	1.03	0.67	0.43	0.66	0.14
Range of nutrient contents of dry grocery brand dog foods	6-11.4	3.10-4.70	15.3-31.7	6.4-19.4	39.4-63.7	1.5-10.7	0.80-2.35	0.62-1.6	0.45-1.08	0.09-0.9	0.42-1.07	0.03-0.27

Key: NFE = nitrogen-free extract, Ca = calcium, P = phosphorus, K = potassium, Na = sodium, Cl = chloride, Mg = magnesium, na = not available.

*Nutrients, except for moisture, are expressed as % dry matter. Energy is expressed in kcal metabolizable energy/g dry matter. Kilocalories of metabolizable energy are either declared by the manufacturer or calculated based on modified Atwater values: protein = 3.5 kcal/g, fat = 8.5 kcal/g, NFE = 3.5 kcal/g. To convert to kJ, multiply kcal by 4.184.

**Analyses conducted in December 1995 and June 1996 by an independent laboratory (Woodson-Tenent Laboratories, Inc., Des Moines, IA, USA).

***Manufacturers' data.

†Data from Henderson AJ, ed. The Henston Small Animal Veterinary Vade Mecum, 15th ed. Peterborough, UK: Veterinary Business Development Ltd; 1996; 90-95.

Table L-7. Moist specialty brand dog foods. This table lists products with a large market share and for which information is available. Specialty brands are premium and super premium foods traditionally sold in pet stores, pet superstores or veterinary hospitals.*

Foods	Moisture	kcal/g	Protein	Fat	NFE	Crude fiber	Ca	P	K	Na	Cl	Mg
AVCA Pet Nutrition Select Balance Canine Adult Formula***	72.0	4.37	30.4	23.2	36.7	3.1	1.13	0.95	na	0.24	na	na
Eagle Pet Products Eagle Pack Beef & Rice***	72.7	4.77	44.3	30.0	19.1	0.7	1.36	1.14	0.88	0.73	na	na
Eagle Pet Products Eagle Pack Chicken & Rice***	71.0	4.80	36.6	32.1	22.8	1.0	1.59	1.14	0.76	0.62	na	na
Eagle Pet Products Eagle Pack Lamb & Rice***	73.6	4.85	32.6	34.1	23.1	1.5	1.89	1.25	0.98	0.87	na	na
Eagle Pet Products Eagle Pack Liver & Rice***	72.8	4.71	46.7	29.0	17.3	1.1	1.32	1.18	0.85	0.70	na	na
Eagle Pet Products Eagle Pack Puppy Dinner***	73.8	4.69	40.1	28.6	24.4	0.8	1.56	1.07	0.88	0.73	na	na
Hill's Prescription Diet Canine g/d***	73.0	4.12	18.9	10.7	64.1	1.9	0.63	0.41	0.78	0.22	0.84	0.07
Hill's Prescription Diet Canine p/d***	70.0	4.72	30.0	28.0	33.3	1.0	1.30	1.13	0.60	0.47	0.77	0.13
Hill's Science Diet Canine Active Formula/Performance***	72.1	4.97	30.1	25.8	36.9	1.1	0.93	0.72	0.65	0.47	1.03	0.08
Hill's Science Diet Canine Growth***	70.0	4.14	29.3	23.0	39.0	1.3	1.33	1.00	0.83	0.40	0.79	0.13
Hill's Science Diet Canine Growth Beef & Rice Formula***	76.4	4.39	29.2	22.4	37.7	3.2	1.10	0.97	0.93	0.38	1.12	0.11
Hill's Science Diet Canine Growth Beef & Vegetable Formula***	76.3	4.36	29.1	22.4	37.8	3.1	1.06	0.97	0.84	0.38	1.03	0.11
Hill's Science Diet Canine Light***	74.0	3.28	18.1	9.6	60.0	7.7	0.58	0.50	0.62	0.31	0.58	0.12
Hill's Science Diet Canine Maintenance Beef***	76.4	4.33	25.4	15.8	52.8	1.0	0.59	0.51	0.94	0.25	0.91	0.10
Hill's Science Diet Canine Maintenance Beef & Chicken***	75.8	4.03	24.8	15.7	54.1	0.8	0.61	0.62	0.66	0.29	0.69	0.08
Hill's Science Diet Canine Maintenance Beef & Rice Formula***	79.3	4.07	25.1	15.0	50.7	3.6	0.63	0.53	0.87	0.24	0.95	0.10
Hill's Science Diet Canine Maintenance Beef & Vegetable***	79.8	4.07	24.8	15.3	50.6	3.7	0.64	0.50	0.79	0.25	0.79	0.10
Hill's Science Diet Canine Maintenance Chicken Formula***	75.7	4.01	24.7	16.5	53.4	0.9	0.64	0.66	0.62	0.23	0.52	0.10
Hill's Science Diet Canine Maintenance Turkey***	75.4	4.23	24.4	15.9	54.4	0.8	0.65	0.65	0.61	0.26	0.51	0.10
Hill's Science Diet Canine Senior Beef***	75.8	4.11	19.4	16.1	59.2	1.3	0.61	0.54	0.70	0.17	0.59	0.08
Hill's Science Diet Canine Senior Chicken Formula***	75.4	3.93	18.6	15.9	59.4	1.6	0.65	0.57	0.65	0.24	0.50	0.11
Hill's Science Diet Canine Senior Turkey***	76.0	4.15	19.1	15.8	59.7	1.2	0.63	0.51	0.62	0.25	0.68	0.08
Iams Beef Formula***	75.2	4.98	39.5	27.4	25.1	2.4	1.01	0.85	0.85	0.44	0.65	0.12
Iams Chicken Formula***	75.5	5.23	40.6	28.7	23.2	1.8	1.72	1.31	1.06	0.57	0.49	0.08
Iams Less Active Beef & Liver Formula***	76.7	4.95	41.2	20.2	30.5	1.3	1.12	0.94	1.42	0.43	0.73	0.09
Iams Less Active Chicken & Rice Formula***	76.6	4.79	41.9	18.0	32.1	1.3	1.50	1.20	1.54	0.43	0.90	0.13
Iams Puppy Formula***	68.1	4.59	46.9	28.5	13.5	2.5	1.51	1.32	1.19	0.60	1.19	0.09
Iams Turkey Formula***	75.2	5.01	38.8	28.5	24.6	2.6	1.29	1.09	1.13	0.64	0.52	0.08
Nature's Recipe Select Balance Canine Lamb & Rice Formula***	72.5	4.70	34.6	30.9	24.0	1.5	1.89	1.05	na	0.62	na	na
Nature's Recipe Select Balance Canine Puppy***	72.0	4.38	32.1	25.0	31.1	2.9	2.12	1.36	na	0.50	na	na
Nature's Recipe Select Balance Canine Reduced Activity Formula***	75.1	3.43	20.0	10.0	53.2	11.0	0.76	0.68	na	0.24	na	na
Pedigree Veterinary Plan 80/26***	81.5	4.32	28.1	16.8	44.3	1.1	1.46	1.14	1.73	0.54	na	0.08
Pedigree Veterinary Plan 90/21***	78.6	4.21	22.0	18.7	48.1	2.8	1.26	0.98	1.64	0.42	na	0.08
Pedigree Veterinary Plan 100/29***	77.0	4.35	31.7	25.2	28.7	3.5	1.43	1.30	1.30	0.65	na	0.14
Pedigree Veterinary Plan 130/33***	71.5	4.56	37.5	24.2	28.8	2.8	1.58	1.30	0.77	0.42	na	0.08
Superior Brands Dr. Ballard Maintenance Beef & Barley**	78.9	4.44	43.6	25.4	21.4	1.0	1.47	1.04	0.71	1.28	1.28	0.07
Superior Brands Dr. Ballard Maintenance Chicken & Rice**	81.0	4.21	43.4	20.8	26.3	1.1	1.31	1.10	0.63	1.42	1.63	0.07
Superior Brands Dr. Ballard Maintenance Lamb & Rice**	79.8	4.34	41.1	25.3	21.5	0.5	2.72	0.99	0.54	1.39	1.54	0.09
Superior Brands Dr. Ballard Maintenance Turkey & Barley**	78.0	4.64	46.5	29.3	14.7	0.1	1.46	1.18	0.68	1.55	1.77	0.07
Average nutrient content of moist specialty brand dog foods	75.1	4.42	32.1	22.1	36.9	2.1	1.21	0.93	0.89	0.53	0.88	0.10
Range of nutrient contents of moist specialty brand dog foods	68.1-81.5	3.28-5.23	18.1-46.9	9.6-34.1	13.5-64.1	0.1-11.0	0.58-2.72	0.41-1.36	0.54-1.73	0.17-1.55	0.49-1.77	0.07-0.14

Key: NFE = nitrogen-free extract, Ca = calcium, P = phosphorus, K = potassium, Na = sodium, Cl = chloride, Mg = magnesium, na = not available.
*Nutrients, except for moisture, are expressed as % dry matter. Energy is expressed in kcal metabolizable energy/g dry matter. Kilocalories of metabolizable energy are either declared by the manufacturer or calculated based on modified Atwater values: protein = 3.5 kcal/g, fat = 8.5 kcal/g, NFE = 3.5 kcal/g. To convert to kcal, multiply kcal by 4.184.
**Analyses conducted in December 1995 and June 1996 by an independent laboratory (Woodson-Tenent Laboratories, Inc., Des Moines, IA, USA).
***Manufacturers' data.

Table L-8. Dry specialty brand dog foods. This table lists products with a large market share and for which information is available. Specialty brands are premium and super premium foods traditionally sold in pet stores, pet superstores or veterinary hospitals.*

Foods	Moisture	kcal/g	Protein	Fat	NFE	Crude fiber	Ca	P	K	Na	Cl	Mg
Diamond High Protein***	8.4	4.25	28.7	20.2	39.1	3.5	1.54	1.25	0.76	0.38	0.60	0.19
Diamond Lamb, Rice & Turkey Formula***	8.2	4.09	25.5	15.5	46.4	3.5	1.62	1.20	0.76	0.33	0.69	0.26
Diamond Lite Formula***	10.0	3.76	17.8	8.9	62.2	4.4	0.68	0.76	0.52	0.14	0.28	0.14
Diamond Maintenance***	8.2	4.02	23.1	13.7	50.9	3.6	1.63	1.24	0.73	0.37	0.66	0.19
Diamond Professional***	8.4	4.50	33.2	22.3	33.1	2.8	1.58	1.38	0.79	0.38	0.74	0.14
Diamond Puppy Food***	8.1	4.53	34.4	22.3	32.2	2.7	1.34	1.12	0.78	0.59	0.66	0.14
Eagle Pet Products Eagle Pack Kennel Pack***	7.4	3.94	28.1	16.3	44.7	3.4	1.73	1.19	0.63	0.55	na	na
Eagle Pet Products Eagle Pack Lite Pack***	8.6	3.39	18.8	8.9	56.7	7.6	1.64	0.88	0.68	0.39	0.89	0.15
Eagle Pet Products Eagle Pack Maintenance Pack***	8.2	3.83	22.0	13.3	54.5	2.9	1.42	0.98	0.66	0.58	na	na
Eagle Pet Products Eagle Pack Natural Pack***	7.7	3.70	25.1	13.2	48.5	3.5	1.84	1.41	0.69	0.61	0.90	0.14
Eagle Pet Products Eagle Pack Power Pack***	6.5	4.20	32.8	21.7	34.2	3.2	2.03	1.18	0.63	0.43	na	na
Eagle Pet Products Eagle Pack Premium Select***	8.4	3.88	25.0	16.5	45.5	3.4	1.64	0.98	0.68	0.51	0.88	0.12
Eagle Pet Products Eagle Pack Puppy Pack***	6.9	4.05	30.7	18.6	37.4	3.3	1.93	1.29	0.67	0.61	na	na
Hill's Prescription Diet Canine g/d***	8.0	3.95	18.7	10.9	66.1	1.0	0.61	0.40	0.61	0.18	0.53	0.05
Hill's Prescription Diet Canine p/d***	7.5	4.51	31.8	22.7	34.4	2.9	1.73	1.19	0.79	0.34	0.53	0.13
Hill's Prescription Diet Canine p/d Large Breed***	7.5	3.46	29.4	9.2	47.5	8.3	0.90	0.70	0.65	0.35	0.72	0.11
Hill's Science Diet Canine Active Formula/Performance***	7.5	4.52	30.5	27.0	35.0	2.0	0.99	0.75	0.61	0.39	0.80	0.09
Hill's Science Diet Canine Growth***	7.5	4.26	29.3	19.2	41.2	2.6	1.44	1.16	0.70	0.51	0.77	0.15
Hill's Science Diet Canine Large Breed Growth***	7.5	3.75	29.7	10.6	51.6	2.4	1.01	0.80	0.64	0.35	0.77	0.12
Hill's Science Diet Canine Light***	9.0	3.05	18.7	9.6	50.1	16.9	0.73	0.57	0.78	0.22	0.46	0.15
Hill's Science Diet Canine Maintenance***	8.0	4.22	25.0	15.4	53.3	1.7	0.72	0.65	0.65	0.28	0.45	0.13
Hill's Science Diet Canine Senior***	8.0	3.86	18.5	10.7	63.8	3.0	0.60	0.55	0.63	0.17	0.54	0.11
Hill's Science Diet Lamb Meal & Rice Canine Growth***	7.5	4.95	29.1	19.9	41.0	2.1	1.70	1.16	0.61	0.39	0.83	0.09
Hill's Science Diet Lamb Meal & Rice Canine Maintenance***	8.0	4.25	22.6	15.9	53.6	2.3	1.08	0.80	0.62	0.28	0.63	0.10
Iams Chunks***	8.0	4.17	29.8	17.8	42.3	2.9	1.51	1.10	0.89	0.60	0.54	0.11
Iams Eukanuba Adult Maintenance Formula***	8.0	4.71	28.5	18.4	45.3	2.2	1.20	0.92	0.89	0.60	0.70	0.10
Iams Eukanuba Large Breed Puppy Formula***	8.6	4.53	29.6	17.2	44.9	2.1	0.98	0.82	0.63	0.24	0.80	0.09
Iams Eukanuba Medium Breed Puppy Formula***	6.9	4.60	32.8	20.5	37.1	2.7	1.28	1.00	0.86	0.33	0.77	0.12
Iams Eukanuba Natural Lamb & Rice***	6.9	4.42	26.2	16.7	48.4	2.2	1.29	1.02	0.92	0.63	0.54	0.12
Iams Eukanuba Natural Lamb & Rice Formula for Puppies***	7.4	4.46	29.9	17.3	43.7	2.4	1.30	1.03	0.80	0.53	0.65	0.10
Iams Eukanuba Premium Performance***	7.8	4.83	34.0	23.0	35.1	1.9	1.30	1.00	0.87	0.60	0.65	0.11
Iams Eukanuba Reduced Fat***	7.5	4.19	21.3	10.5	61.4	2.0	0.97	0.76	0.78	0.50	0.54	0.05
Iams Eukanuba Senior Maintenance Formula***	7.9	4.58	29.3	12.8	48.5	2.3	1.51	0.95	0.68	0.40	0.54	0.12
Iams Eukanuba Small Breed Puppy Formula***	7.5	4.86	36.2	23.9	31.5	1.9	1.41	1.08	0.86	0.74	0.71	0.10
Iams Eukanuba Weaning Diet***	7.5	4.86	36.2	23.9	31.5	1.9	1.41	1.08	0.86	0.74	0.74	0.09
Iams Lamb Meal & Rice for Puppies***	7.7	4.44	29.3	16.3	40.8	3.4	1.94	1.54	0.89	0.70	1.17	0.20
Iams Less Active***	7.6	4.17	22.2	12.5	56.5	2.8	1.14	0.85	0.78	0.37	0.54	0.13
Iams Minichunks***	8.0	4.17	29.8	17.8	42.3	2.9	1.51	1.10	0.89	0.60	0.54	0.11
Iams Natural Lamb Meal & Rice***	8.0	3.95	25.1	14.2	46.3	4.2	1.85	1.57	1.01	0.65	1.23	0.23
Iams Puppy***	8.1	4.66	32.1	19.9	38.7	2.8	1.37	1.04	0.87	0.71	0.71	0.12
Iams Senior***	8.0	4.23	27.5	12.0	51.9	2.5	1.13	0.90	0.75	0.27	0.52	0.12
Nature's Recipe Select Balance Canine Adult Formula***	8.0	3.97	25.0	14.7	51.9	3.0	0.85	0.83	na	0.34	na	na
Nature's Recipe Select Balance Canine Lamb & Rice Formula***	8.0	4.30	29.4	17.9	40.0	4.0	1.85	1.30	na	0.58	na	na
Nature's Recipe Select Balance Canine Puppy Formula***	8.0	4.13	30.4	19.0	40.2	2.7	1.30	1.06	na	0.42	na	na
Nature's Recipe Select Balance Canine Reduced Activity***	8.0	3.30	19.0	5.4	57.1	13.0	0.62	0.55	na	0.33	na	na
Nutro Max & Max Mini***	8.9	4.03	29.1	18.8	40.5	3.4	1.62	1.31	0.55	0.38	0.46	0.11
Nutro Max Puppy***	8.8	4.08	32.6	20.3	34.6	4.3	1.67	1.38	0.71	0.55	0.59	0.13
Nutro Max Special***	9.7	3.58	19.4	9.8	59.0	4.7	1.27	1.04	0.48	0.30	0.34	0.11
Nutro's Natural Choice Adult***	9.2	3.85	27.4	13.8	49.0	3.0	1.54	1.38	0.55	0.39	0.33	0.10
Nutro's Natural Choice Lite***	9.9	3.42	16.8	7.8	62.0	4.4	0.83	0.67	0.48	0.32	0.36	0.12

(Continued on next page.)

Table L-8. Dry specialty brand dog foods. This table lists products with a large market share and for which information is available. Specialty brands are premium and super premium foods traditionally sold in pet stores, pet superstores or veterinary hospitals.* (Continued from previous page.)

Foods	Moisture	kcal/g	Protein	Fat	NFE	Crude fiber	Ca	P	K	Na	Cl	Mg
Nutro's Natural Choice Plus***	8.9	4.17	32.2	20.0	38.4	1.8	1.64	1.36	0.69	0.55	0.57	0.12
Nutro's Natural Choice Puppy***	9.0	3.89	29.0	15.6	44.3	3.5	1.56	1.43	0.71	0.55	0.60	0.11
Pedigree Chum Advance Formula Activity Plus†	8.0	4.28	34.8	21.7	32.1	2.7	1.20	0.90	na	0.22	na	0.10
Pedigree Chum Advance Formula Adult Supreme†	8.0	4.11	28.3	17.4	44.0	2.7	1.70	1.20	na	0.22	na	0.09
Pedigree Chum Advance Formula Junior Plus†	8.0	4.20	30.4	19.6	39.1	2.7	0.98	0.82	na	0.22	na	0.10
Pedigree Chum Advance Formula Light Menu†	8.0	3.57	19.6	6.5	64.1	2.2	1.60	1.40	na	0.22	na	0.09
Pedigree Chum Advance Formula Puppy Supreme†	8.0	4.34	34.8	22.8	31.0	2.7	1.20	0.87	na	0.22	na	0.09
Pedigree Veterinary Plan 330/26***	9.7	3.65	23.3	7.8	57.4	3.9	1.14	1.11	0.70	0.42	na	0.22
Pedigree Veterinary Plan 340/21***	10.2	3.79	19.7	10.6	60.9	3.0	0.90	0.87	0.56	0.39	na	0.17
Pedigree Veterinary Plan 360/29***	8.3	3.93	28.9	13.6	49.8	1.7	1.09	0.98	0.55	0.48	na	0.11
Pedigree Veterinary Plan 380/33***	7.5	4.11	33.8	17.8	39.4	1.8	1.43	1.20	0.76	0.61	na	0.13
Ralston Purina Pro Plan Dog Adult***	7.5	4.41	29.7	19.2	43.2	1.6	1.30	1.07	0.54	0.40	na	0.11
Ralston Purina Pro Plan Dog Growth***	7.5	4.54	31.9	19.5	40.0	2.0	1.35	1.03	0.65	0.51	na	0.11
Ralston Purina Pro Plan Dog Lite***	7.5	3.63	15.9	9.6	65.5	2.7	1.41	0.95	0.58	0.37	na	0.09
Ralston Purina Pro Plan Dog Performance***	7.5	4.71	34.1	21.6	36.9	1.5	1.12	0.83	0.63	0.43	na	0.09
Ralston Purina Pro Plan Natural Turkey & Barley Dog***	8.5	4.39	27.7	18.0	45.7	2.2	1.20	0.96	0.66	0.33	na	0.07
Ralston Purina Pro Plan Natural Turkey & Barley Puppy***	7.5	4.54	30.7	19.6	40.5	2.1	1.24	1.03	0.65	0.38	na	na
Royal Canin A2***	8.0	4.72	38.0	27.2	23.9	2.7	1.74	1.09	0.65	0.38	0.82	0.11
Royal Canin AD32***	8.0	4.67	34.8	21.7	33.2	2.7	1.47	1.09	0.71	0.38	0.82	0.11
Royal Canin HE30***	8.0	4.44	32.6	17.4	39.1	2.7	1.41	0.98	0.65	0.38	0.82	0.11
Royal Canin LA23***	8.0	4.00	25.0	8.7	55.4	4.4	1.30	0.65	0.65	0.38	0.71	0.11
Royal Canin Maxi Adult 1 (GR26)***	8.0	4.50	28.3	17.4	45.1	2.7	1.20	0.76	na	na	na	0.11
Royal Canin Maxi Adult 2 (SGR26)***	8.0	4.49	28.3	17.4	44.8	3.3	0.87	0.65	na	na	na	0.11
Royal Canin Maxi Junior (AGR36)***	8.0	4.30	39.1	15.2	34.2	2.7	1.63	1.25	0.71	0.38	0.82	0.11
Royal Canin MD25***	8.0	4.24	27.2	13.0	49.5	2.7	1.20	0.92	0.65	0.38	0.82	0.11
Royal Canin Medium Adult 1 (AM25)***	8.0	4.26	27.2	13.0	50.2	2.7	1.20	0.92	0.71	0.38	0.82	0.11
Royal Canin Medium Adult 2 (SM25)***	8.0	4.27	27.2	13.0	48.9	3.3	0.87	0.65	na	na	na	0.11
Royal Canin Medium Junior (AM32)***	8.0	4.67	34.8	21.7	33.2	2.7	1.47	1.09	0.71	0.38	0.82	0.11
Royal Canin Mini Adult 1 (PR27)***	8.0	4.48	29.4	17.4	43.5	2.7	1.30	0.98	na	na	na	0.11
Royal Canin Mini Adult 2 (SPR27)***	8.0	4.49	29.4	17.4	43.7	3.3	0.87	0.65	na	na	na	0.11
Royal Canin Mini Junior (APR33)***	8.0	4.67	35.9	21.7	32.1	2.7	1.30	1.09	na	na	na	0.11
Royal Canin ST35***	8.0	4.48	38.0	27.2	23.9	2.7	1.74	1.09	0.65	0.38	0.82	0.11
Sunshine Nurture Adult Light*	7.3	3.24	26.0	9.6	43.3	15.2	1.07	0.80	0.58	0.40	0.57	0.15
Sunshine Nurture Bite Sized Adult**	8.1	4.03	29.0	16.0	47.1	2.6	0.89	0.71	0.66	0.34	0.67	0.12
Sunshine Nurture Lamb Meal & Rice**	6.5	3.87	25.9	14.5	49.3	3.3	1.41	0.95	0.47	0.34	0.60	0.17
Sunshine Nurture Puppy Growth**	6.2	4.10	31.9	18.0	41.5	2.5	1.28	0.81	0.62	0.36	0.74	0.11
Superior Brands Dr. Ballard Great Performance**	6.0	4.50	34.1	26.0	31.3	1.2	1.84	1.19	0.79	0.36	0.93	0.09
Superior Brands Dr. Ballard Oven Bake Lamb & Rice**	6.0	4.22	29.1	19.3	44.6	1.3	1.10	0.89	0.78	0.40	0.99	0.11
Superior Brands Dr. Ballard Oven Bake Maintenance**	6.0	4.25	26.9	20.1	45.7	1.2	1.22	0.90	0.79	0.38	1.00	0.09
Superior Brands Dr. Ballard Oven Bake Senior**	7.8	4.07	25.7	15.9	51.9	1.6	0.72	0.66	0.77	0.37	1.01	0.08
Wafcol Puppy Food†	6.5	3.71	28.5	8.6	49.2	5.3	2.35	1.6	na	0.51	na	0.05
Wafcol Vegetarian†	6.5	3.66	21.4	8.6	55.6	8.6	1.4	0.96	na	0.47	na	0.03
Wafcol Veteran†	6.5	3.74	17.1	8.6	62.0	5.3	1.6	1.5	na	0.21	na	0.04
Average nutrient content of dry specialty brand dog foods	7.9	4.17	28.1	16.3	45.1	3.3	1.33	1.01	0.70	0.42	0.69	0.12
Range of nutrient contents of dry specialty brand dog foods	6-10.2	3.05-4.95	15.9-39.1	5.4-27.2	23.9-66.1	1.0-16.9	0.6-2.35	0.40-1.6	0.47-1.01	0.14-0.74	0.28-1.23	0.03-0.26

Key: NFE = nitrogen-free extract, Ca = calcium, P = phosphorus, K = potassium, Na = sodium, Cl = chloride, Mg = magnesium, na = not available.
*Nutrients, except for moisture, are expressed as % dry matter. Energy is expressed in kcal metabolizable energy/g dry matter. Kilocalories of metabolizable energy are either declared by the manufacturer or calculated based on modified Atwater values: protein = 3.5 kcal/g, fat = 8.5 kcal/g, NFE = 3.5 kcal/g. To convert to kJ, multiply kcal by 4.184.
**Analyses conducted in December 1995 and June 1996 by an independent laboratory (Woodson-Tenent Laboratories, Inc., Des Moines, IA, USA).
***Manufacturers' data.
†Data from Henderson AJ, ed. The Henston Small Animal Veterinary Vade Mecum, 15th ed. Peterborough, UK: Veterinary Business Development Ltd, 1996; 90-95.

III. Manufacturers' index

Associate Wholesale Grocers Inc.,
  Kansas City, KS, USA
Diamond Pet Foods, Meta, MO, USA
Eagle Pet Products, Inc., Mishawaka, IN, USA
Friskies Pet Care Co., Glendale, CA, USA
Heinz Co., Newport, KY, USA
Hill's Pet Nutrition, Inc., Topeka, KS, USA
Kal Kan Foods Inc., Vernon, CA, USA
Nature's Recipe Pet Foods, Inc., Newport, KY, USA
Nutro Products Inc., City of Industry, CA, USA
Pedigree Petfoods, Melton Mowbray, UK
Ralston Purina Co., St Louis, MO, USA
Royal Canin, Aimargues, France
Sunshine Pet Foods, Red Bay, AL, USA
Superior Brands Co., Glendale, CA, USA
The Iams Company, Dayton, OH, USA
Wafcol Ltd., Stockport, UK

Appendix M
Nutrient Profiles of Treats and Snacks

I. Introduction

In the United States, up to 86% of dog owners and about 68% of cat owners regularly give treats to their animals. In 1995, canine treat sales totaled $516 million in the United States. Grocery stores carry an average of 57 and mass merchandisers about 54 different items. Treats for dogs represent 9% of the total pet food market in the United States, and about 6.4% in the United Kingdom.

Giving several treats per day can markedly affect a pet's daily cumulative caloric intake and alter the nutritional adequacy of the diet. A 7-kg (15.4-lb) adult dog receiving two snacks per day may become 30% overweight in one year, unless comparable calories are withheld from the daily food intake. A growing large-breed puppy may double its calcium intake if it receives many daily snacks. Thus, a dietary history should always include specific questions about treats, including the brand, size and number of treats given daily. This information is critical when specific nutritional problems must be ruled out (e.g., skeletal problems in large-breed puppies, adverse reactions to food and obesity). When a dog or cat is affected by disease, such as urolithiasis, diabetes mellitus, heart failure or renal disease, dietary restrictions should be followed rigorously and treats should be carefully selected or even banned. Of particular concern are caloric density, protein, calcium, phosphorus, sodium, magnesium and urinary pH.

This appendix lists the nutrient profiles of some of the leading brands of treats and snacks in Europe and North America. The information contained here is often unavailable from other sources. Because 65 to 90% of pet owners share foods from the table with their pets, analyses of table foods often given as treats are also provided.

Tables M-1, M-4, M-6 and M-8 can be used while taking a dietary history. These tables list the nutrient content per treat, making it easy to calculate how a particular treat affects total daily nutrient levels.

Tables M-3, M-5, M-7 and M-9 provide the nutrient profile of the same treats on a dry matter basis. Although concerns may arise about one particular nutrient, the entire nutritional profile should be considered before recommending a particular treat. The ideal treat should match the nutrient profile of the food or diet that is recommended for the lifestage or disease of the pet. Because the veterinary health care team has no control over how many treats the owner is going to give, it is best to base recommendations on the nutrient profile given as % dry matter.

The nutrients of concern for a particular pet's lifestage or disease should be considered before a recommendation is made. (See respective chapters.) The treat should be considered inappropriate if one of those nutrients is significantly above or below the generally recommended level. Treats may be inappropriate if all or several of the nutrients of concern are even marginally different from recommended levels.

Moreover, one must bear in mind that not all treats are complete foods; therefore, the number of treats given daily and the size of the treat are variables that influence the recommendation. A treat that only weighs 0.25 g, but has a high phosphorus level (% dry matter), may not really be contraindicated in chronic renal disease, if only one or two treats are given daily. However, a treat weighing 20 g with the same phosphorus level may be unacceptable for the same animal.

Veterinarians should also consider the size of the dog. It may be appropriate to give two treats to a large dog, but the same number and size of treats may be unacceptable for small dogs.

II. Commercial treats and human foods often used as treats for cats

Table M-1. Commercial treats for cats on a nutrient content/treat basis. This list represents products with a large market share and for which information is available.

Treats	Weight (g)	kcal ME*	DM (g)	Protein (g)	Fat (g)	NFE (g)	Crude fiber (g)	Ca (mg)	P (mg)	K (mg)	Na (mg)	Cl (mg)	Mg (mg)
Heinz Pounce Treats for Cats with Tuna**	1.5	3.7	1	0.3	0.1	0.4	0	1.35	11.3	16.4	9.2	21.9	1.2
Pedigree Whiskas Kitbits with Rabbit & Turkey***	0.4	1.1	0.3	0.1	0	0.13	0	7.8	5.2	2	5	6.3	0.24
Ralston Purina Whisker Lickin's Kluckers Chicken-Flavored**	1.1	2.9	0.7	0.3	0.1	0.2	0	9	10.7	5.9	6.2	8.5	0.7
Thomas Cork Hartz Treatsters Chicken Flavour***	0.25	0.8	0.2	0.1	0	0.1	0	6.1	3.8	2.1	2.1	3.2	0.38

Key: kcal = kilocalories, ME = metabolizable energy, DM = dry matter, NFE = nitrogen-free extract, Ca = calcium, P = phosphorus, K = potassium, Na = sodium, Cl = chloride, Mg = magnesium.
*Kcal metabolizable energy calculated based on modified Atwater values: protein = 3.5 kcal/g, fat = 8.5 kcal/g, NFE = 3.5 kcal/g dry matter.
To convert to kJ, multiply kcal by 4.184.
**Analyses conducted in December 1995 by an independent laboratory (Woodson-Tenent Laboratories, Inc., Des Moines, IA, USA).
***Analyses conducted in June 1996 by an independent laboratory (Woodson-Tenent Laboratories, Inc., Des Moines, IA, USA).

Table M-2. Magnesium and energy content of selected treats and snacks for cats.

Treats/snacks	Weight (g/snack)	kcal ME (per snack)	Magnesium (mg/snack)	Magnesium (mg/100 kcal ME)
Commercial treats				
Heinz Pounce Treats for Cats with Tuna*	1.5	3.7	1.2	32
Pedigree Whiskas Kitbits with Rabbit & Turkey**	0.4	1.1	0.24	21
Ralston Purina Whisker Lickin's Kluckers Chicken-Flavored*	1.1	2.9	0.7	24
Thomas Cork Hartz Treatsters Chicken Flavour**	0.25	0.8	0.38	48
North American snacks*				
Cheese				
Cheddar cheese	28.4	105	12.8	12.2
Fruit				
Apples (pared)	34.5	18.3	1.7	9.3
Apples (not pared)	34.5	17.4	2.8	16.1
Raisins	0.25	0.7	0.1	12.9
Ice cream				
Ice cream (10% fat)	66.5	119	9.3	7.8
Ice cream (12% fat)	66.5	128	9.3	7.3
European snacks*				
Biscuits				
Boudoir (lady finger)	6	20	0.2	1.0
Dry biscuit (average)	5	20	0.9	4.5
Speculoos	8	35	1.2	3.4
Speculoos (all wheat)	8	33	6.4	19.4
Cheese				
Gouda	10	32	3.0	9.4
Fruit				
Dates (dried)	7	18.6	3.5	18.8
Raisins (dried)	0.25	0.6	0	6.7
Meat (cold cuts)				
Pâté de foie (liver pâté)	10	33	1	3.0
Salami (1 slice)	10	43	1.9	4.4
Saucisson (average) (1 slice)	10	36	0.7	1.94

*Analyses conducted in December 1995 by an independent laboratory (Woodson-Tenent Laboratories, Inc., Des Moines, IA, USA).
**Analyses conducted in June 1996 by an independent laboratory (Woodson-Tenent Laboratories, Inc., Des Moines, IA, USA).
***Based on Bibliography Sources 4, 6, 8 and 10.

Table M-3. Commercial treats for cats on a nutrient level/100 g dry matter basis. This list represents products with a large market share and for which information is available.*

	Moisture	kcal ME	Protein	Fat	NFE	Crude fiber	Ca	P	K	Na	Cl	Mg
Heinz Pounce Treats for Cats with Tuna**	34.4	375	32.9	13.6	41.2	0.6	1.4	1.1	1.7	0.9	2.2	0.12
Pedigree Whiskas Kitbits with Rabbit & Turkey***	22.1	356	33.5	10.6	42.4	1.5	2.5	1.7	0.7	1.6	2	0.08
Ralston Purina Whisker Lickin's Kluckers Chicken-Flavored**	30.9	397	43.5	17	28.7	1.3	1.2	1.5	0.8	0.9	1.2	0.09
Thomas Cork Hartz Treatsters Chicken Flavour***	8.4	340	35.2	8.5	41.4	3.1	2.6	1.7	0.9	0.9	1.4	0.16

Key: kcal = kilocalories, ME = metabolizable energy, DM = dry matter, NFE = nitrogen-free extract, Ca = calcium, P = phosphorus, K = potassium, Na = sodium, Cl = chloride, Mg = magnesium.
*Nutrients, except for moisture, are expressed as % dry matter. Energy is expressed as kcal metabolizable energy/100 g dry matter. Kilocalories metabolizable energy calculated based on modified Atwater values: protein = 3.5 kcal/g, fat = 8.5 kcal/g, NFE = 3.5 kcal/g dry matter.
To convert to kJ, multiply kcal by 4.184.
**Analyses conducted in December 1995 by an independent laboratory (Woodson-Tenent Laboratories, Inc., Des Moines, IA, USA).
***Analyses conducted in June 1996 by an independent laboratory (Woodson-Tenent Laboratories, Inc., Des Moines, IA, USA).

III. Commercial treats for dogs

Table M-4. Commercial treats for dogs on a nutrient content/treat basis. This list represents products with a large market share and for which information is available.

Treats	Weight (g)	kcal ME*	DM (g)	Protein (g)	Fat (g)	NFE (g)	Crude fiber (g)	Ca (mg)	P (mg)	K (mg)	Na (mg)	Cl (mg)	Mg (mg)
Friskies Chew-eez Beef Hide Treats, Original and Beef Basted Flavors†	20	60.6	17.4	14.7	1.0	0.2	0.5	116	na	na	120	180	na
Heinz 100% Natural Treats Ken-L Ration**	7.6	25.9	7.1	1.3	0.5	4.9	0.1	17	49	48	41	67	15
Heinz Meaty Bone Medium**	18.2	64.2	16.8	2.3	1.8	11.7	0.4	8	55	71	116	191	20
Heinz Original Jerky Treats**	6.8	21.9	5.1	2	1.3	1.1	0.1	35	35	71	140	214	7
Heinz Pup-Peroni Jerky Snack Sticks Ken-L Ration**	6.6	21.3	5.2	1.8	1	1.9	0.1	55	44	59	73	106	7
Heinz Snausages Beef Flavor Ken-L Ration**	6.6	17.4	4.7	1.5	0.6	2	0.1	61	46	98	44	115	7
Hill's Prescription Diet Treats†	4	11.8	3.7	0.67	0.3	2.0	0.6	22	17	28	4	13	5
Hill's Science Diet Canine Adult Treats†	5	16.9	4.6	1.1	0.5	2.6	0.3	29	29	28.5	10.5	33	4
Hill's Science Diet Canine Growth Treats†	5	16.8	4.6	1.2	0.5	2.3	0.3	63.5	52.5	28	15	32.5	4.4
Hill's Science Diet Canine Senior Treats†	5	16.2	4.6	0.8	0.4	2.8	0.4	30	28.5	28	7	22	4.5
Hill's Science Diet Canine Light Treats†	5	14.8	4.6	0.8	0.3	2.7	0.6	29	28.5	38	11	28	6.6
Iams Biscuits Original Large†	42.5	137	39.1	11.1	2.8	21.7	1.3	510	383	259	64	136	55
Iams Biscuits Original Small†	9.5	31	8.7	2.5	0.6	4.9	0.3	114	86	58	14	30	12
Nabisco Milk-Bone Small**	5	16.4	4.7	1.1	0.3	2.8	0.1	71	54	30	21	27	7
Pedigree Chum Markies***	11.8	38.2	10.6	1.5	1.3	6.2	0.2	426	148	32	79	117	na
Pedigree Chum Maxi Biscrok***	19.5	61.5	18.1	2.5	1.3	11.8	0.3	646	184	53	123	203	na
Pedigree Chum Rask Large†	92	269	76.4	29.2	2.3	35.2	2.8	na	na	na	na	na	na
Pedigree Chum Rask Medium†	64	187	53.1	20.3	1.6	24.5	1.9	na	na	na	na	na	na
Pedigree Chum Schmackos with Beef***	8.4	25.5	7.1	2.5	0.9	2.7	0.2	73	64	97	173	251	na
Pedigree Chum Tandem with Beef & Chicken***	3.9	9.7	2.8	0.7	0.3	1.4	0.1	68	16	20	36	51	na
Ralston Purina Beggin Strips Original Bacon Flavor**	10.3	28.8	8	1.7	0.6	5.2	0.1	44	49	33	65	92	11
Ralston Purina Biscuits Medium**	10.2	36.8	9.6	2.5	1.3	4.9	0.2	114	106	91	29	43	21
Ralston Purina Bonz Steak Bone Shaped**	20.4	65.7	18.2	3.1	1.3	12.5	0.3	241	155	86	53	84	24
Spillers Latz BONZO Kleine Lieblings-Knochen***	11.4	38.4	10.4	1.9	1.1	6.3	0.2	148	55	51	109	184	na
Stewart Fiber Formula Dog Large Biscuits†	28.4	73.6	25.5	4.1	0.8	14.7	4.9	176	105	na	20	na	na
Stewart Fiber Formula Dog Medium Biscuits†	10.1	26.2	9.1	1.5	0.3	5.2	1.7	63	37	na	7	na	7.6
Stewart Lambmeal & Rice Formula Dog Biscuits†	1.5	5.2	1.35	0.12	0.11	1.09	0.02	4	2.6	na	3	na	na
Veterinary Medical Diets Medi-Treats†	4.5	13.5	4.2	0.7	0.3	2.9	0.2	30	14.5	na	7.7	na	na

Key: kcal = kilocalories, ME = metabolizable energy, DM = dry matter, NFE = nitrogen-free extract, Ca = calcium, P = phosphorus, K = potassium, Na = sodium, Cl = chloride, Mg = magnesium, na = not available.
*Kilocalories metabolizable energy calculated based on modified Atwater values: protein = 3.5 kcal/g, fat = 8.5 kcal/g, NFE = 3.5 kcal/g dry matter. To convert to kJ, multiply kcal by 4.184.
**Analyses conducted in December 1995 by an independent laboratory (Woodson-Tenent Laboratories, Inc., Des Moines, IA, USA).
***Analyses conducted in June 1996 by an independent laboratory (Woodson-Tenent Laboratories, Inc., Des Moines, IA, USA).
†Information published by manufacturer.

Table-M-5. Commercial treats for dogs on a nutrient level/100 g dry matter basis. This list represents products with a large market share and for which information is available.*

Treats	Moisture	kcal ME	Protein	Fat	NFE	Crude fiber	Ca	P	K	Na	Cl	Mg
Friskies Chew-eez Beef Hide Treats, Original and Beef Basted Flavors†	13	349	84.5	5.7	1.1	2.9	0.67	na	na	0.69	1.03	na
Heinz 100% Natural Treats Ken-L Ration**	6.5	364	18.5	6.9	68.8	1.6	0.2	0.7	0.7	0.6	0.9	0.21
Heinz Meaty Bone Medium**	7.9	383	13.8	10.5	70	2.5	0.1	0.3	0.4	0.7	1.1	0.12
Heinz Original Jerky Treats**	24.7	427	38.7	25.6	21.3	2.1	0.7	0.7	1.4	2.7	4.2	0.13
Heinz Pup-Peroni Jerky Snack Sticks Ken-L Ration**	21.5	411	34.4	19.3	36.1	2	1.1	0.9	1.2	1.4	2.1	0.13
Heinz Snausages Beef Flavor Ken-L Ration**	28.5	369	32.2	12.3	43.2	1	1.3	1	2	1	2	0.15
Hill's Prescription Diet Treats†	6.5	364	18.5	6.9	68.8	1.6	0.24	0.68	0.67	0.58	0.94	0.21
Hill's Science Diet Canine Adult Treats†	8	367	22.8	10.4	56.6	6	0.6	0.6	0.6	0.2	0.7	0.08
Hill's Science Diet Canine Growth Treats†	8	365	25.9	11.6	50.1	5.5	1.4	1.1	0.6	0.3	0.7	0.10
Hill's Science Diet Canine Senior Treats†	8	353	18.2	8.8	61.2	7.7	0.7	0.6	0.6	0.2	0.5	0.10
Hill's Science Diet Canine Light Treats†	8	322	18.2	6.6	57.8	12.4	0.6	0.6	0.8	0.2	0.6	0.14
Iams Biscuits Original Large†	8	353	28.3	7.1	55.4	3.3	1.3	1	0.7	0.2	0.4	0.14
Iams Biscuits Original Small†	8	353	28.3	7.1	55.4	3.3	1.3	1	0.7	0.2	0.4	0.14
Nabisco Milk-Bone Small**	6.3	350	23.6	6.8	60	3	1.5	1.1	0.6	0.4	0.6	0.15
Pedigree Chum Markies***	10.2	401	14.3	12.4	58.6	1.6	4	1.4	0.3	0.8	1.1	na
Pedigree Chum Maxi Biscrok***	7.6	341	14	7.4	65.4	1.4	3.6	1	0.3	0.7	1.1	na
Pedigree Chum Schmackos with Beef***	15.5	359	35.4	12.2	37.5	2.8	1	0.9	1.4	2.4	3.5	na
Pedigree Chum Tandem with Beef & Chicken***	29.7	350	26.3	9.9	49.7	3	2.5	0.6	0.7	1.3	1.9	na
Ralston Purina Beggin Strips Original Bacon Flavor**	22.8	363	21.2	7.1	65.4	1.8	0.6	0.6	0.4	0.8	1.2	0.14
Ralston Purina Biscuits Medium**	5.9	384	26.4	13.2	51.3	2.6	1.2	1.1	1	0.3	0.5	0.22
Ralston Purina Bonz Steak Bone Shaped**	10.9	362	16.9	7.4	68.5	1.8	1.3	0.9	0.5	0.3	0.5	0.14
Spillers Latz BONZO Kleine Lieblings-Knochen***	8.7	369	18.5	10.8	60.6	2.2	1.4	0.5	0.5	1.1	1.8	na
Stewart Fiber Formula Dog Medium & Large Biscuits†	10	288	16.1	3.2	57.5	19	0.7	0.4	na	0.1	na	na
Stewart Lambmeal & Rice Formula Dog Biscuits†	10	385	8.6	8.5	80.4	0.9	0.3	0.2	na	0.23	na	0.06
Veterinary Medical Diets Medi-Treats†	7.0	320	15.3	7.4	69.1	4.1	0.72	0.34	na	0.18	na	na

Key: kcal = kilocalories, ME = metabolizable energy, DM = dry matter, NFE = nitrogen-free extract, Ca = calcium, P = phosphorus, K = potassium, Na = sodium, Cl = chloride, Mg = magnesium, na = not available.

*Nutrients, except for moisture, are expressed as % dry matter. Energy is expressed as kcal metabolizable energy/100 g dry matter. Kilocalories metabolizable energy calculated based on modified Atwater values: protein = 3.5 kcal/g, fat = 8.5 kcal/g, NFE = 3.5 kcal/g dry matter. To convert to kJ, multiply kcal by 4.184.

**Analyses conducted in December 1995 by an independent laboratory (Woodson-Tenent Laboratories, Inc., Des Moines, IA, USA).

***Analyses conducted in June 1996 by an independent laboratory (Woodson-Tenent Laboratories, Inc., Des Moines, IA, USA).

†Information published by manufacturer.

IV. Nutrient content of human foods often used as treats

Table-M-6. Nutrient content of human foods often used as animal treats in North America on a nutrient content/treat basis.*

Foods	Weight (g)	kcal ME**	DM (g)	Protein (g)	Fat (g)	NFE (g)	Crude fiber (g)	Ca (mg)	P (mg)	K (mg)	Na (mg)	Mg (mg)
Cheese												
American cheese (pasteurized) (1 oz.)	28.4	97.2	17	6.6	8.5	0.5	na	198	219	22.7	322	na
Cheddar cheese (1 oz.)	28.4	105	17.9	7.1	9.1	0.6	na	213	136	23.2	199	12.8
Chocolate												
Bitter baking chocolate	28.4	167	27.7	3	15	8.1	0.7	22.1	109	235	1.1	82.8
Bittersweet chocolate	28.4	150	27.8	2.2	11.3	13.2	0.5	16.4	80.5	174	0.9	na
Cadbury plain milk chocolate	28.4	142	28.1	2.2	9.2	16.1	0.1	64.6	65.5	109	26.6	16.4
Chocolate chips	10.5	46.2	10.2	0.6	2.2	7.3	0	4.1	12	14.1	42.1	na
Hershey's plain milk chocolate	43.9	220	43.6	3.4	14.2	25	0.2	100	102	169	41.3	25.5
Fruit												
Apples (not pared)	34.5	17.4	5.1	0.1	0.1	4.7	0.2	2.1	3.5	38	0.3	2.8
Apples (pared)	34.5	18.3	5.4	0.1	0.2	4.7	0.3	2.4	3.5	38	0.3	1.7
Raisins	0.3	0.7	0.2	0	0	0.2	0	0.2	0.3	1.9	0.1	0.1
Ice cream												
Ice cream (10% fat)	66.5	119	24.5	3	7.1	13.8	na	99.1	76.5	120	41.9	9.3
Ice cream (12% fat)	66.5	128	25.2	2.7	8.3	13.7	na	81.8	65.8	74.5	26.6	9.3
Meat												
Bologna	23	64.4	10.1	2.8	6.3	0.3	na	1.6	29.4	52.9	299	na
Frankfurter	66.5	189	29.5	8.3	18.4	1.2	na	4.7	88.4	146	731	na
Others												
Brownies with nuts (homemade)	35	162	31.5	2.3	10.9	17.6	0.24	14.3	51.7	66.4	87.7	na
Oreo	9.3	41.5	9	0.3	2	6.7	na	na	na	16.7	56.7	na
Peanut butter	5.3	30.2	5.2	1.5	2.6	0.8	0.1	3.3	21.6	35.5	32.2	na
Popcorn	6	20.9	5.8	0.8	0.3	4.5	0.1	0.7	24.4	na	0.2	na
Popcorn (with fat and salt)	9	37.8	8.7	0.9	2	5.2	0.2	0.7	19.4	na	175	na
Potato chips (1 oz.)	28.4	149	27.8	1.5	11.3	13.7	0.5	11.3	39.4	320	284	na
Pretzels (1 oz.)	28.4	95.6	27.1	2.8	1.3	21.4	0.1	6.2	37.1	36.9	476	na

Key: kcal = kilocalories, ME = metabolizable energy, DM = dry matter, NFE = nitrogen-free extract, Ca = calcium, P = phosphorus, K = potassium, Na = sodium, Cl = chloride, Mg = magnesium, na = not available.
*Based on Bibliography Sources 4 and 10.
**Kilocalories metabolizable energy calculated based on modified Atwater values: protein = 3.5 kcal/g, fat = 8.5 kcal/g, NFE = 3.5 kcal/g dry matter. To convert to kJ, multiply kcal by 4.184.

APPENDIX M

Table M-7. Nutrient content of human foods often used as animal treats in North America on a nutrient level/100 g dry matter basis.*

Foods	Moisture	Energy (kcal ME)	Protein	Fat	NFE	Crude fiber	Ca	P	K	Na	Mg
Cheese											
American cheese (pasteurized)	40.0	571	38.7	50	3.2	na	1.2	1.3	0.1	1.9	na
Cheddar cheese	37.0	585	39.7	51.1	3.3	na	1.2	0.8	0.1	1.1	0.1
Chocolate											
Bitter baking chocolate	2.3	601	11.0	54.3	29.1	2.6	0.1	0.4	0.9	na	0.3
Bittersweet chocolate	1.8	538	8.0	40.4	47.4	1.8	0.1	0.3	0.6	na	na
Cadbury plain milk chocolate	0.9	505	7.8	32.6	57.3	0.4	0.2	0.2	0.4	0.1	0.06
Chocolate chips	2.7	452	5.6	21.6	71.2	0.4	0	0.1	0.1	0.4	na
Hershey's plain milk chocolate	0.9	505	7.8	32.6	57.3	0.4	0.2	0.2	0.4	0.1	0.06
Fruit											
Apples (not pared)	85.1	339	1.3	2.0	90.6	4.0	0	0.1	0.7	0	0.06
Apples (pared)	84.4	340	1.3	3.9	86.5	6.4	0.1	0.1	0.7	0	0
Raisins	18.0	339	3.0	0.2	93.3	1.1	0.1	0.1	0.9	0	0
Ice cream											
Ice cream (10% fat)	63.2	486	12.2	28.8	56.5	na	0.4	0.3	0.5	0.2	0
Ice cream (12% fat)	62.1	508	10.6	33	54.4	na	0.3	0.3	0.3	0.1	0
Meat											
Bologna	56.2	639	27.6	62.8	2.5	na	0	0.3	0.5	3	na
Frankfurters	55.6	641	28.2	62.2	4.1	na	0	0.3	0.5	2.5	na
Others											
Brownies with nuts (homemade)	9.8	515	7.2	34.7	55.7	0.8	0.1	0.2	0.2	0.3	na
Oreo	3.6	461	3.7	22.2	74.1	na	na	na	0.2	0.6	na
Peanut butter	1.8	581	28.3	50.3	15.6	1.9	0.1	0.4	0.7	0.6	na
Popcorn (plain)	4.0	362	13.2	5.2	77.6	2.3	1.7	0	0.4	na	na
Popcorn (with fat and salt)	3.1	434	10.1	22.5	59.2	1.8	0	0.2	na	2.0	na
Potato chips**	1.8	536	5.4	40.5	49.3	1.6	0	0.1	1.2	1.0	na
Pretzels**	4.5	353	10.3	4.7	79.2	0.3	0	0.1	0.1	1.7	na

Key: kcal = kilocalories, ME = metabolizable energy, DM = dry matter, NFE = nitrogen-free extract, Ca = calcium, P = phosphorus, K = potassium, Na = sodium, Cl = chloride, Mg = magnesium, na = not available.
*Based on Bibliography Sources 4 and 10. Nutrients, except for moisture, are expressed as % dry matter. Energy is expressed as kcal metabolizable energy/100 g dry matter. Kilocalories metabolizable energy calculated based on modified Atwater values: protein = 3.5 kcal/g, fat = 8.5 kcal/g, NFE = 3.5 kcal/g dry matter. To convert to kJ, multiply kcal by 4.184.
**Sodium content varies and may be higher than the levels listed here.

Table M-8. Nutrient content of human foods often used as animal treats in Europe on a nutrient content/treat basis.*

Foods	Weight (g)	kcal ME**	DM (g)	Protein (g)	Fat (g)	NFE (g)	Crude fiber (g)	Ca (mg)	P (mg)	K (mg)	Na (mg)	Cl (mg)	Mg (mg)
Biscuits													
Boudoir (lady finger)	6	20	5.5	0.4	0.2	4.8	0	1.4	5.3	6.3	3.0	na	0.2
Dry biscuit (average)	5	20	5	0.3	0.6	4	0	1.6	4.2	8	11.6	na	0.9
Petit beurre	8	30	7.9	0.5	0.8	6.2	0	na	na	na	na	na	na
Speculoos	8	35	7.9	0.4	1.5	5.8	0	1.3	5.3	6.4	27	na	1.2
Speculoos (all wheat)	8	33	7.9	0.5	1.3	5.5	0.3	2	17	18.4	22.4	na	6.4
Cheese													
Camembert	10	26	4.9	2.5	2.0	0.1	0	60	30	11	79	na	na
Gouda	10	32	5.8	2.5	2.7	0	0	92	52	12	60	na	3
Gruyère	10	40.5	6.8	2.9	3.5	0.1	0	90	60	10	50	na	na
Parmesan	10	38	7.4	4	2.7	0.2	0	100	90	12.5	100	na	na
Chocolate													
Fondant (bitter)	25	109	25	1.4	6.8	13.5	1.7	12.5	37.5	100	2.5	na	25
Milk chocolate (bittersweet)	25	118	25	2	7.4	13.9	na	50	50	100	25	na	13.8
White chocolate	25	122	25	2	7.3	15.2	na	na	na	na	na	na	na
Fruit													
Dates (dried)	7	18.6	5.7	0.14	0	5.2	0.5	5	4.3	42.5	0.7	na	3.5
Raisins (dried)	0.3	0.6	0.2	0	0	0.17	0	0.1	0.3	2	0.1	na	0
Meat (cold cuts)													
Pâté de foie (liver pâté)	10	33	5.1	1.2	3.3	0.3	0	2	15	8	80	na	1
Salami (one slice)	10	43	6.8	1.9	4.2	0.1	0	2.8	16.7	30	152	na	1.9
Saucisson (average) (one slice)	10	36	5.4	1.4	3.6	0.2	0	2.5	15.4	18.3	102	na	0.7

Key: kcal = kilocalories, ME = metabolizable energy, DM = dry matter, NFE = nitrogen-free extract, Ca = calcium, P = phosphorus, K = potassium, Na = sodium, Cl = chloride, Mg = magnesium, na = not available.
*Based on Bibliography Sources 6 and 8.
**Kilocalories metabolizable energy calculated based on modified Atwater values: protein = 3.5 kcal/g, fat = 8.5 kcal/g, NFE = 3.5 kcal/g dry matter. To convert to kJ, multiply kcal by 4.184.

Table M-9. Nutrient content of human foods often used as animal treats in Europe on a nutrient level/100 g dry matter basis.*

Foods	Moisture	Energy (kcal ME)	Protein	Fat	NFE	Crude fiber	Ca	P	K	Na	Mg
Biscuits											
Boudoir (lady finger)	5.9	369	8.1	4.14	87.1	0	0	0.1	0.1	0.1	0
Dry biscuit (average)	1	406	6.7	12.1	80.0	0	0	0.1	0.2	0.2	0
Petit beurre	1	378	5.7	10.1	77.8	0	na	na	na	na	na
Speculoos	1	437	5.5	19.2	72.8	0	0	0.1	0.1	0.3	0
Speculoos (all wheat)	1	411	6.6	17	69.7	4	0	0.2	0.2	0.3	0.1
Cheese											
Camembert	51	533	51	40.8	2.0	0	1.2	0.6	0.2	1.6	na
Gouda	42	552	42.9	47.2	0	0	1.6	0.9	0.2	1.0	0.1
Gruyère	32	592	42.7	51.5	1.5	0	1.3	0.9	0.2	0.7	na
Parmesan	26	509	54.1	36.5	2.7	0	1.4	1.2	0.2	1.4	na
Chocolate											
Fondant (bitter)	0	438	5.5	27	54	6.6	0.1	0.2	0.4	0	0.1
Milk chocolate (bittersweet)	0	473	7.8	29.5	56	0	0.2	0.2	0.4	0.1	0.1
White chocolate	0	488	8	29	61	0	na	na	na	na	na
Fruit											
Dates (dried)	20	328	2.5	0	91.3	9.4	0.1	0.1	0.8	0	0.1
Raisins (dried)	16	292	3	0.7	78.8	6.4	0	0.1	0.9	0	0
Meat (cold cuts)											
Pâté de foie (liver pâté)	49	651	23.7	64.1	6.5	0.4	0	0.3	0.2	1.6	0
Salami (one slice)	32	628	27.4	61.8	1.9	0	0	0.3	0.4	2.2	0
Saucisson (average) (one slice)	46	671	25.9	66.7	3.7	0	0.1	0.3	0.3	1.9	0

Key: kcal = kilocalories, ME = metabolizable energy, DM = dry matter, NFE = nitrogen-free extract, Ca = calcium, P = phosphorus, K = potassium, Na = sodium, Cl = chloride, Mg = magnesium, na = not available.
*Based on Bibliography Sources 6 and 8. Nutrients, except for moisture, are expressed as % dry matter. Energy is expressed as kcal metabolizable energy/100 g dry matter. Kilocalories metabolizable energy calculated based on modified Atwater values: protein = 3.5 kcal/g, fat = 8.5 kcal/g, NFE = 3.5 kcal/g. To convert to kJ, multiply kcal by 4.184.

V. Manufacturers' index

Heinz Pet Products, Newport, KY, USA
Hill's Pet Nutrition, Inc., Topeka, KS, USA
Nabisco Inc., East Hanover, NJ, USA
Pedigree Petfoods, Melton Mowbray, UK
Ralston Purina Co., St Louis, MO, USA
Friskies Latz, Euskirchen, Germany
Stewart Pet Products Ltd., South Bend, IN, USA
Thomas Cork SM Ltd., Nottingham, UK
Veterinary Medical Diets Inc., Guelph, Ontario,
  Canada

BIBLIOGRAPHY

1. Campbell WE. Effects of training, feeding regimens, isolation, and physical environment on canine behavior. Modern Veterinary Practice 1986; 239-241.

2. Harlow J. US Petfood Market Trends. In: Proceedings. Petfood Forum. Chicago, IL, April 15-17, 1996: 257-312.

3. Anonymous. Essais sans suite. No. 107. Médecine et Nutrition 1991; 27: 248.

4. Pennington JAT. In: Food Values of Portions Commonly Used, 15th ed. New York, NY: Harper & Row, 1989.

5. PFMA Profile. The Pet Food Manufacturers' Association, UK 1993.

6. Randoin L, Le Gallic P, Dupuis Y, et al. Tables de composition des aliments. Institut Scientifique d'Hygiène Alime. Malakoff, France: LT Editions J. Lanore, 1990.

7. Slater MR, Robinson LE, Zoran DL, et al. Diet and exercise patterns in pet dogs. Journal of the American Veterinary Medical Association 1995; 207: 186-190.

8. Table Belge de Composition des Aliments. Brussels, Belgium: NUBEL, 1992.

9. Voith VL. Attachment of people to companion animals. Veterinary Clinics of North America: Small Animal Practice 1985; 15: 289-295.

10. Watt BK, Merill AL, et al. Composition of Foods. Agriculture Handbook No. 8. Agriculture Research Service, United States Department of Agriculture, 1975.

Appendix N
Body Weights of Selected Species of Birds

Introduction

This appendix can be used for calculating energy requirements and food and water intake for selected species of caged and aviary birds. Wild birds are included where data are available. Therefore, this guide also serves as a reference for these wild birds and related species of comparable size. However, this table is only a reference guide; individual wild birds should be weighed at the outset of a feeding program and then weekly until the estimated optimal body condition is reached. Moreover, for some species, there is either a broad range of body weights or different references provided different values. Table N-1 lists both values with their respective references when such discrepancies occur.

Table N-1. Names and adult body weights of selected species of birds.

Popular names	Scientific names	Body weights
Anseriformes		
Canada goose	*Branta candensis*	3.5-4.5 kg
Domestic duck	*Anas platyrhynchos* (var. dom.)	2-3.5 kg
Goose (domestic)	*Anser anser* (var. dom.)	4-5 kg
Mallard duck	*Anas platyrhynchos*	1.75 kg
Galliformes		
Bobwhite quail	*Colinus virginianus*	~150 g
Domestic fowl	*Gallus gallus*	1.75-4 kg
Japanese quail (miniature quail)	*Coturnix coturnix japonica*	18-42 g
Pheasant	*Phasianus colchicus*	1.2 kg
Turkey (domestic)	*Meleagris gallopavo* (var. dom.)	4-15 kg
Turkey (wild)	*M. gallopavo*	4 kg
Gruiformes		
Crowned crane	*Balearica pavonina*	3.5-4.0 kg
Columbiformes		
Collared turtle dove	*Streptopelia decaocto*	150-220 g
Diamond dove	*Geopelia cuneata*	25-50 g
Stock dove	*Columba oenus*	240-300 g
Pigeons (rock dove)	*Columba livia*	
Light breeds	–	250-300 g
Medium-size breeds (racing pigeons)	–	380-450 g
Heavy breeds	–	up to 1,000 g
Psittaciformes		
Amazon species	*Amazona* spp	350-400 g
Blue-crowned Amazon	–	740 (618-998) g
Blue-fronted Amazon	*A. aestiva*	432 (275-510) g
Double yellow-headed Amazon	*A. ochrocephala oratrix*	568 (463-694) g
Hispanolian Amazon	*A. ventralis*	268 g
Mealy Amazon	*A. farinosa*	600-685 g
Mexican red-headed Amazon	*A. viridigenalis*	360 (343-377) g
Orange-winged Amazon	*A. amazonica*	440-470 g
Yellow-fronted Amazon	*A. ochrocephala ochrocephala*	260-460 g
Yellow-naped Amazon	*A. ochrocephala auropalliata*	596 (476-795) g
Budgerigar	*Melopsittacus undulatus*	30-60 g
Cockatiels	*Nymphicus hollandicus*	80-140 g
Cockatoos		300-800 g
Bare-eyed cockatoo	*Cacatua sanguinea*	331 g
Citron cockatoo	*C. sulphurea cintrinocristata*	283-514 g
Goffin's cockatoo	*C. goffini*	221-386 g
Leadbeater's cockatoo (Major Mitchell's)	*C. leadbeateri*	423 (381-474) g
Moluccan cockatoo	*C. moluccensis*	808 (640-1,025) g
Palm (goliath) cockatoo	–	990-1,057 g
Rose-breasted cockatoo	*C. roseicapilla*	299 (281-390) g
Sulfur-crested cockatoo (greater)	*C. galerita galerita*	806 (608-1,200) g
Sulfur-crested cockatoo (lesser)	*C. sulphurea*	303 (251-412) g
Triton cockatoo	*C. galerita triton*	559 g
Umbrella cockatoo	*C. alba*	552 (458-756) g
Conures (various species)		80-100 g
Blue-crowned conure	*Aratinga acuticaudata haemorrhous*	84-96 g
Jandaya conure	–	118-128 g
Queen of Bavaria (conure)	–	250-275 g

(Continued on next page.)

Table N-1. Names and adult body weights of selected species of birds. (Continued from previous page.)

Popular names	Scientific names	Body weights
Lovebirds (various species)	*Agapornis* spp	40-70 g
Macaws	*Ara* spp	650-750 g
Blue and gold macaw	*A. ararauna*	1,021 (892-1,294) g
Buffon macaw	*A. ambigua*	1,080-1,534 g
Green-winged macaw	*A. chloroptera*	1,179 (1,058-1,529) g
Hyacinth macaw	*Anodorhynchus hyacinthus*	9 lb*
Hyacinth macaw		1,355 (1,185-1,529) g**
Military macaw	*Ara militaris*	788 (774-1,065) g
Red-fronted macaw	*A. rubrogenys*	458 g
Scarlet macaw	*A. macao*	1,103 (1,058-1,464) g
Yellow-collared macaw	*A. auricollis*	223-308 g
Parakeets		
Australian parakeet	–	30-110 g
Bourke's parakeet	–	40 (35-43) g
Kakariki parakeet	–	35-56 g
Pennant's parakeet	*Platycercus elegans*	180-200 g
Princess of Wales parakeet	–	108 (102-129) g
Red-crowned parakeet	–	60-75 g
Red-rumped parakeet	–	65 (62-69) g
Parrots	*Psittacus* spp	
African grey parrot	*P. erithacus*	300-400 g
Blue-headed pionus	*Pionus menstruus*	238-278 g
Eclectus parrot	*Lorius roratus*	432 (347-524) g
Senegal parrot	*Piocephalus senegalus*	125-150 g
Apodiformes		
Humming birds	Trochilidae (family)	2.5-5 g
Passeriformes		
Canary	*Serinus canarius*	20 (12-30) g
Cardinal	*Pyrrhuloxia* spp	~40 g
Goldbreasted (zebra waxbill)	*Amandava subflava*	7 g
Goldfinch	*Carduelis carduelis*	15-20 g
Greater Indian hill mynah	*Gracula religiosa*	150-260 g
Greenfinch	*Chloris chloris*	15-20 g
House sparrow	*Passer domesticus*	25-30 g
Java rice sparrow	–	20 g
Java sparrow	*Padda oryzivora*	7-12 g
Pekin robin	*Leiothrix lutea*	17 g
Robin (American)	*Turdus migratorius*	50 g
Robin (European)	*Erithacus rubecula*	20-30 g
Society finch	*Lonchura domestica*	10-16 g
Starling	*Sturnus vulgaris*	70-80 g
Zebra finch	*Phoephila guttata*	10-16 g
Raptors		
American kestrel	*Falco spaverius*	100 g
Bald eagle (female)	*Haliaetus leucocephalus*	3,000 g
Bald eagle (male)	–	5,000 g
Harris hawk	*Parabuteo unicinctus*	574-1,000 g
Hawks (Swainson's rough-legged)		1,000-1,500 g
Merlin	*Falco columbarius aesalon*	200 g
Osprey	–	1,500 g
Peregrine falcon (female)	*Falco peregrinus*	750 g
Peregrine falcon (male)	–	500 g
Red-tailed hawk	*Butea jamaicensis*	1,000 (698-1,350) g
Sharpy (female)		150 g
Sparrow hawk	*Accipiter nisus*	150-300 g
Owls		
Great horned owl	*Bubo virginianus*	1,800-1,900 g
Long-eared owl	*Asio otus*	350 g
Saw-whet	–	60 g
Short-eared owl	*Asio flammeus*	350 g
Snowy owl	*Nyctea scandiaca*	1,800-1,900 g

*Adapted from Bibliography Sources 2 and 5.
**Adapted from Bibliography Sources 4 and 7.

BIBLIOGRAPHY

1. Altman RB, Clubb SL, Dorrestein GM, et al, eds. Avian Medicine and Surgery. Philadelphia, PA: WB Saunders Co, 1997; 918-928, 1027-1028.

2. Arnall L, Keymer IF. Weights, heart rates, etc. In: Bird Diseases. London, UK: Ballière Tindall, 1975; 482.

3. Carpenter JW, Mashima TY, Rupiper DJ. Biological and physiological values of selected avian species. In: Exotic Animal Formulary. Manhattan, KS: Graystone Publications, 1996; 158-159.

4. Devriese L. Ziekten van Siervogels en Duiven, 2nd ed. Gent, Belgium: Rijksuniversiteit Gent, 1985; 52.

5. Exotic Animals: A Veterinary Handbook. Trenton, NJ: Veterinary Learning Systems, 1995; 121-125, 131-135.

6. Fowler ME. Care of orphaned wild animals. Veterinary Clinics of North America: Small Animal Practice 1979; 9: 447-471.

7. Turner T. First aid for cage birds. In Practice 1985; 5: 76-81.

Appendix O
Foods for Caged and Aviary Birds

Table O-1. Guaranteed analyses of selected commercial foods for adult psittacine birds.
Table O-2. Guaranteed analyses of selected commercial foods for psittacine birds with increased nutrient demands.
Table O-3. Guaranteed analyses of selected commercial foods for finches and canaries.
Table O-4. Guaranteed analyses of selected commercial foods for pigeons and doves.
Table O-5. Guaranteed analyses of selected commercial foods for birds with special needs.
Table O-6. Recommendations for hand feeding baby psittacine birds.
Table O-7. Guaranteed analyses of formulas for hand feeding or tube feeding.
Table O-8. Manufacturers of bird foods.
Table O-9. Common and scientific names of bird seeds.
Bibliography

Table O-1. Guaranteed analyses (% as fed) of selected commercial foods for adult psittacine birds.*

Products	Food types	Moisture	Protein	Fat	Fiber
Large and medium psittacine birds					
Harrison's Bird Diets Adult Lifetime Formula Coarse Grind	Extruded	10	15	5.5	6.5
Kaytee Products Exact Original All Parrot & Large Conure Daily Diet	Extruded	12	15	6	5
Kaytee Products Exact Parrot & Large Conure Rainbow	Extruded	12	15	6	5
Kaytee Products Exact Parrot & Large Conure Rainbow Chunky	Extruded	12	15	6	5
Kaytee Products Fiesta Parrot Food	Seed based	12	15	12	15
Kaytee Products Forti-Diet-Nutritionally Fortified Parrot Food	Seed based	12	16	12	18
Kaytee Products Safflower Select Parrot Food	Seed based	12	16	12	16
Lafeber's Premium Daily Diet	Pelleted	10.5	14	4	2
Lake's Unlimited Avian Maintenance Diet	Pelleted	10	12	4.5	5
Mazuri Purina Mills 56A8 Mazuri Parrot Maintenance	Extruded	na	15	5	6
Premium Nutritional Products ZuPreem Avian Maintenance	Extruded	10	14	4	2.5
Premium Nutritional Products ZuPreem Fruit Blend	Extruded	10	14	4	2.5
Rolf C. Hagen Tropican Lifetime Maintenance Formula	Extruded	8	14	9	4.5
Small psittacine birds					
Harrison's Bird Diets Adult Lifetime Formula Fine Grind	Extruded	10	14	5	4.5
Harrison's Bird Diets Adult Lifetime Mash	Mash	10	15	4.2	5
Kaytee Products Exact Cockatiel Rainbow	Extruded	12	14	5	5
Kaytee Products Exact Original Cockatiel Daily Diet	Extruded	12	14	5	5
Kaytee Products Exact Original Parakeet Daily Diet	Extruded	12	14	5	5
Kaytee Products Fiesta Cockatiel Food	Seed based	12	16	12	12
Kaytee Products Fiesta Parakeet Food	Seed based	12	15	6	10
Kaytee Products Forti-Diet-Nutritionally Fortified Cockatiel Food	Seed based	2	15	9	14
Kaytee Products Forti-Diet-Nutritionally Fortified Parakeet Food	Seed based	12	14	4	8
Kaytee Products Safflower Select Cockatiel Food	Seed based	12	15.5	8	14
Lafeber's Premium Daily Diet	Pelleted	10.5	14	4	2
Lake's Unlimited Avian Maintenance Diet	Pelleted	10	12	4.5	5
Mazuri Purina Mills 56A6 Mazuri Small Bird Maintenance	Extruded	na	14.5	5	5
Premium Nutritional Products ZuPreem Avian Maintenance	Extruded	10	14	4	2.5
Premium Nutritional Products ZuPreem Fruit Blend	Extruded	10	14	4	2.5
Rolf C. Hagen Tropican Lifetime Maintenance Formula	Extruded	8	14	9	4.5

Key: na = not available.
*Moisture = maximum moisture, protein = minimum crude protein, fat = minimum crude fat, fiber = maximum crude fiber.

Table O-2. Guaranteed analyses (% as fed) of selected commercial foods for psittacine birds with increased nutrient demands (baby birds, growing birds, debilitated or depleted birds and molting birds).*

Products	Food types	Moisture	Protein	Fat	Fiber
Large and medium psittacine birds					
Harrison's Bird Diets High Potency Coarse Grind	Extruded	10	18	11	6.5
Harrison's Bird Diets High Potency Mash	Mash	10	20	14	8
Harrison's Bird Diets Juvenile Formula Hand Feeding Mix	Pelleted	10	18	11	4
Kaytee Products Exact Hand Feeding Formula for Macaws	Extruded	10	19	12	5
Lake's Unlimited Avian Special Needs Diet	Pelleted	10	17	5	5
Mazuri Purina Mills 56A9 Mazuri Parrot Breeder	Extruded	na	19.5	6.5	4.5
Rolf C. Hagen Day One Baby Bird and Special Care Formula	Powdered	8	24	12	na
Rolf C. Hagen Tropican Breeding Diet	Extruded	8	22	9	3.5
Rolf C. Hagen Tropican Breeding Mash	Mash	9	22	11	3.5
Small psittacine birds					
Harrison's Bird Diets High Potency Formula Fine Grind	Extruded	10	20	12	5
Harrison's Bird Diets High Potency Mash	Mash	10	20	14	8
Harrison's Bird Diets Juvenile Formula	Powdered	10	18	11	4
Kaytee Products Exact Hand Feeding Formula for Baby Birds	Extruded	10	22	8	5
Lake's Unlimited Avian Special Needs Diet	Pelleted	10	17	5	5
Mazuri Purina Mills 56A7 Mazuri Small Bird Breeder	Extruded	na	18	6.5	4.5
Rolf C. Hagen Day One Baby Bird and Special Care Formula	Powdered	8	24	12	0
Rolf C. Hagen Tropican Breeding Diet	Extruded	8	22	9	3.5
Rolf C. Hagen Tropican Breeding Mash	Mash	9	22	11	3.5

Key: na = not available.
*Moisture = maximum moisture, protein = minimum crude protein, fat = minimum crude fat, fiber = maximum crude fiber.

Table O-3. Guaranteed analyses (% as fed) of selected commercial foods for finches and canaries.*

Products	Food types	Moisture	Protein	Fat	Fiber
EFFEM GmbH Trill	Seed based	na	19	26.1	42.9
EFFEM GmbH Trill Breeding Diet	Seed based	na	19.7	5.9	62.1
Harrison's Bird Diets Adult Lifetime Mash	Mash	10	15	4.2	5
Harrison's Bird Diets High Potency Mash	Mash	10	20	14	8
Kaytee Products Exact Canary/Finch Rainbow	Extruded	12	15	6	5
Kaytee Products Exact Original Canaries/Finches Daily Diet	Extruded	12	15	6	5
Kaytee Products Forti-Diet-Nutritionally Fortified Finch Food	Seed based	12	14	5.5	9
Kaytee Products Forti-Diet-Nutritionally Fortified Canary Food	Seed based	12	17	14	7
Lafeber's Premium Daily Diet	Pelleted	10.5	14	4	2
Lake's Unlimited Avian Maintenance Diet	Pelleted	10	12	4.5	5
Lake's Unlimited Avian Special Needs Diet	Pelleted	10	17	5	5
Mazuri Purina Mills 56A6 Mazuri Small Bird Maintenance	Extruded	na	14.5	5	5
Mazuri Purina Mills 56A7 Mazuri Small Bird Breeder	Extruded	na	18	6.5	4.5
Premium Nutritional Products ZuPreem Avian Maintenance	Extruded	10	14	4	2.5
Premium Nutritional Products ZuPreem Fruit Blend	Extruded	10	14	4	2.5

Key: na = not available.
*Moisture = maximum moisture, protein = minimum crude protein, fat = minimum crude fat, fiber = maximum crude fiber.
Exotic finches may have increased requirements and may benefit from foods that have increased amounts of protein and fat.

Table O-4. Guaranteed analyses of selected commercial foods for pigeons and doves.*

Products	Food types	Moisture	Protein	Fat	Fiber
Harrison's Bird Diets Adult Lifetime Formula Fine Grind	Extruded	10	14	5	4.5
Harrison's Bird Diets High Potency Mash	Mash	10	20	14	8
Kaytee Products Breeding & Conditioning (No. 6 Plus)	Seed based	12	16	4	5.5
Kaytee Products Dove Food	Seed based	12	12	2.5	6
Kaytee Products Economy Pigeon	Seed based	12	13	2.5	3.5
Kaytee Products Flying Pigeon (No. 5 Plus)	Seed based	12	15	2.5	4.5
Kaytee Products High Energy Racing Pigeon	Seed based	12	16	8	7
Kaytee Products Hi-Protein Race & Show Conditioning Pigeon Pellets (No. 6 Plus)	Pelleted	12	20	3.5	5
Kaytee Products Hi-Value Breeding Pigeon Pellets (No. 4 Plus)	Pelleted	12	16	3.5	4
Kaytee Products Valley Trift No.1	Seed based	12	12.5	2.5	4

*Moisture = maximum moisture, protein = minimum crude protein, fat = minimum crude fat, fiber = maximum crude fiber.

Table O-5. Guaranteed analyses (% as fed) of selected commercial foods for birds with special needs.*

Products	Food types	Moisture	Protein	Fat	Fiber
Soft-billed birds (low-iron formulas)**					
Harrison's Bird Diets Adult Lifetime Low Iron Formula	Extruded	10	14	6	4
Reliable Protein Products Softbilled Bird-Fare	Soft moist	45	20	7	6
Fruit and nectar eaters***					
Harrison's Bird Diets Adult Lifetime Formula Fine Grind† (L)	Extruded	10	14	5	4.5
Harrison's Bird Diets Adult Lifetime Low Iron Formula† (A)	Extruded	10	14	6	4
Harrison's Bird Diets Adult Lifetime Mash	Mash	10	15	4.2	5
Harrison's Bird Diets High Potency Formula Fine Grind† (L)	Extruded	10	20	12	5
Harrison's Bird Diets High Potency Low Iron Formula† (A)	Extruded	na	na	na	na
Flamingos, cranes, ibis					
Mazuri Purina Mills 5644 Mazuri Flamingo Complete	Extruded	na	19	5	4
Mazuri Purina Mills 5645 Mazuri Flamingo Breeder	Extruded	na	34	5	7
Mazuri Purina Mills 5646 Mazuri Crane Diet	Extruded	na	20	5	4
Reliable Protein Products Flamingo-Fare	Soft moist	45	25	8	4
Zeigler Brothers Crane	Soft moist	na	24	5	6
Waterfowl, ducks, swan, geese, sea ducks					
Mazuri Purina Mills 5640 Mazuri Waterfowl Breeder	Extruded	na	17	2.5	6
Mazuri Purina Mills 5641 Mazuri Waterfowl Starter	Extruded	na	20	3	6.5
Mazuri Purina Mills 5642 Mazuri Waterfowl Maintenance, Disks	Extruded	na	14	3	4.5
Mazuri Purina Mills 5681 Mazuri Sea Duck Diet	Extruded	na	21.5	5	4.5

Key: na = not available, L = specifically for lories, A = all birds with special needs, including lories.
*Moisture = maximum moisture, protein = minimum crude protein, fat = minimum crude fat, fiber = maximum crude fiber.
**Toucans, mynahs, hornbills, birds of paradise and other birds known to be susceptible to hemochromatosis should receive formulas containing less than 100 ppm iron.
***Lories, toucans, humming birds, flowerpeckers, birds of paradise, white-eyes and honey creepers. In addition to commercial food, a variety of diced fresh, ripe fruit and fruit juice should be provided. Avocado is potentially toxic for smaller birds.
†For lories, soak one tablespoon of product with two tablespoons of water and one-half teaspoon of corn syrup.

Table O-6. Recommendations for hand feeding baby psittacine birds.

Ages	Dilutions (% solids)	No. daily feedings
Day 1	10	Every 2 hours*
Day 2	12	5-6
Day 3	15	5-6
Day 4	18	5-6
Day 5	20	5-6
Days 6-7	23-25	5-6
Week 2	23-30	4-5
Weeks 3-5	23-30	3
Weeks 6-8	23-30	2
Older than 8 weeks	na	Usually eating solid food

Key: na = not applicable.
*Between 6 a.m. and 12 p.m.

Table O-7. Guaranteed analyses (% as fed) of formulas for hand feeding or tube feeding.*

Products	Food types	Moisture	Protein	Fat	Fiber	kcal/g
Harrison's Bird Diets High Juvenile Formula	Pelleted	10	18	11	4	na
Harrison's Bird Diets High Potency Mash	Mash	10	20	14	8	na
Kaytee Products Exact Hand Feeding Formula for Baby Birds	Extruded	10	22	8	5	na
Lafeber's Emerald II	Powdered	na	18.5	na	na	3.4
Reliable Protein Products Avian-Fare	Soft moist	45	26	8	5	na
Rolf C. Hagen Day One Baby Bird and Special Care Formula	Powdered	8	24	12	0	na
Rolf C. Hagen Tropican Breeding Mash	Mash	9	22	11	3.5	na

Key: na = not available.
*Moisture = maximum moisture, protein = minimum crude protein, fat = minimum crude fat, fiber = maximum crude fiber.

Table O-8. Manufacturers of bird foods.

Bird Ranch Diets
20833 Roscoe Ave.
Canoga Park, CA 91306

EFFEM GmbH
Postfach 1280
D-27 281 Verden/Aller
Germany
Fax: 49-4231-944-650

Harrison's Bird Diets
HBD International, Inc.
220 Congress Park Drive, Suite 232
Delray Beach, FL 33445
561-279-4233 or 1-800-745-7329
Fax: 561-279-4235
http://www.hbdintl.com

Kaytee Products, Inc.
P.O. Box 230
Chilton, WI 53014
800-KAYTEE-1 (800-529-8331)
Fax: 920-849-4734

Lafeber Company
24981 N. 1400 East Road
Cornell, IL 61319
800-842-6445 or 815-358-2301 (USA)
800-345-6596 (Canada)
Fax: 800-932-3341 or 815-358-2352 (USA)
http://www.lafeber.com

Lake's Unlimited, Inc.
639 Stryker Ave.
St. Paul, MN 55107
800-634-2473 or 612-290-0606
Fax: 612-290-0526

Marion Zoological Scenic Birdfoods
13803 Industrial Park Blvd.
Plymouth, MN 55441
800-327-7974 or 612-559-3305
Fax: 612-559-0789

Mazuri Purina Mills, Inc.
P.O. Box 66812
St. Louis, MO 63166-6812
800-227-8941 or 314-768-4592
Fax: 314-768-4894

Premium Nutritional Products, Inc.
P.O. Box 2094
Mission, KS 66202
800-345-4767
Fax: 913-722-6226

Pretty Bird International, Inc.
P.O. Box 177
5810 Stacy Trail
Stacy, MN 55079
800-356-5020 or 651-462-1799
Fax: 800-311-6646

Reliable Protein Products, Inc.
44-489 Town Center Way
Suite D, PMB 505
Palm Desert, CA 92260
760-321-7533
Fax: 760-321-0395

Rolf C. Hagen, Inc.
P.O. Box 490
Riguad, Québec J0P 1P0
Canada

USA: R.C. Hagen Corp. 50 Hampton Rd.
Mansfield, MA 02048
508-339-9531
Fax: 508-339-6973

UK: R.C. Hagen Ltd. Castleford, W. Yorkshire WF10
5QH

France: R.C. Hagen S.A. F-94387 Bonneuil-sur Marne
Germany: Weltweit Import-Export, D-2081 Holm
Spain: ICA, Apartado de Correos 75, Barbera del Valles,
Barcelona

Roudybush Foods
3075 Alhambra Dr.
Suite 103
Cameron Park, CA 95682
800-326-1726
Fax: 530-676-9585

SC Ranch
P.O. Box 745
Poway, Ca 92064

Zeigler Brothers, Inc.
P.O. Box 95
Gardners, PA 17324
800-841-6800 or 717-677-6181
Fax: 717-677-6826

Table O-9. Common and scientific names of bird seeds.

Common names	Scientific names
Almonds	*Prunus dulcis*
Anise seed	*Pimpinella anisum*
Beechnuts	*Fagus* spp
Brazil nuts	*Bertholletia excelsa*
Buckwheat	*Fagopyrum esculentum*
Canary (grass) seed	*Phalaris canariensis*
Caraway seed	*Carum carvi*
Cashew nuts	*Anacardium occidentale*
Corn	*Zea mays*
English walnuts	*Juglans regia*
False flax seed	*Camelina sativa*
Fennel seed	*Foeniculum vulgare*
Flax seed	*Linum usilatissimum*
Gold of pleasure	*Camelina sativa*
Hazelnuts	*Corylus* spp
Hemp seed	*Cannabis sativa*
Lettuce seed	*Lactuca sativa*
Macadamia nuts	*Macadamia* spp
Millet (common or proso)	*Panicum milioceum*
Millet (spray or foxtail)	*Setaria italica*
Milo (grain sorghum)	*Sorghum bicolor*
Niger	*Guizotia abyssinica*
Oat groats	*Avena sativa*
Pea	*Pisum* spp
Pecans	*Carya illinoensis*
Pinon nuts	*Pinus edulis*
Pistachio nuts	*Pistacia vera*
Poppy seed	*Papaver somniferum*
Pumpkin seed	*Cucurbita* spp
Rape seed	*Brassica rapa*
Rice	*Oryza sativa*
Safflower seed	*Carthamus tinctorius*
Sesame seed	*Sesamum indicum*
Squash seed	*Cucurbita* spp
Sunflower seed	*Helianthus annuus*
Teazle seed	*Dipsacus* spp
Wheat	*Triticum vulgare*

BIBLIOGRAPHY

1. Allen KL. Hand-raising psittacines. In: Rosskopf WJ Jr, Woerpel RW, eds. Diseases of Cage and Aviary Birds, 3rd ed. Baltimore, MD: Williams & Wilkins, 1996; 54-56.

2. André J-P. La consultation des psittacidés. Le Point Vétérinaire 1996; 28: 23-29.

3. Arnall L, Keymer IF, eds. Nutrition and metabolism. In: Bird Diseases. London, UK: Ballière Tindall, 1975; 71-82.

4. Clubb SL. Psittacine pediatrics, husbandry and medicine. In: Altman RB, Clubb SL, Dorrestein GM, et al, eds. Avian Medicine and Surgery. Philadelphia, PA: WB Saunders Co, 1997; 73-95.

5. Cooper JE. Feeding exotic and pocket pets. Journal of Small Animal Practice 1990; 31: 482-488.

6. Devriese L. Ziekten van Siervogels en Duiven, 2nd ed. Gent, Belgium: Rijksuniversiteit Gent, 1985; 119-128.

7. Hargis AM, Stauber E, Casteel S, et al. Avocado (Persea americana) intoxication in caged birds. Journal of the American Veterinary Medical Association 1989; 194: 64-66.

8. Kollias GV. Diets, feeding practices, and nutritional problems in psittacine birds. Veterinary Medicine 1995; 90: 29-39.

9. Lafeber TJ. Physical examination, laboratory and medication techniques, and hospitalization procedures for cage birds. In: Kirk RW, ed. Current Veterinary Therapy III. Philadelphia, PA: WB Saunders Co, 1968; 349-357.

10. Taylor M. Basic pet bird husbandry and nutrition. In: Proceedings. Eastern States Veterinary Conference, Orlando, FL, 1991: 569-573.

11. Taylor EJ, Nott HMR, Earle KE. The nutrition of the canary (*Serinus canarius*) Journal of Nutrition 1994; 124: 2636S-2637S.

12. Ullrey DE, Allen ME, Baer DJ. Formulated diets versus seed mixtures for psittacines. Journal of Nutrition 1991; 121: S193-S205.

13. Ullrey DE, Allen ME. Formulated diets versus seed mixtures for psittacines. In: Proceedings. Eastern States Veterinary Conference, Orlando, FL, 1991: 576-577.

14. Vogel K. Hygiene der Futterung. In: Die Taube Taubenkrankheiten, 2nd ed. Berlin, Germany: VEB Deutscher Lanwirtschaftsverlag, 1970; 31-34.

15. Zwart P, Dorrestein GM, van der Hage MH. Krankheiten von Großpapageien: Ein praxisbezogener Überblick. Kleintierpraxis 1989; 34: 573-577.

Appendix P
Centers for Wildlife Protection and Rehabilitation

Introduction

Many people want to help diseased or injured animals, and veterinary practitioners often receive calls about young animals found on the ground or in a nest in the absence of their parents. Most young animals found alone, however, have not actually been deserted by their parents. The first step is to determine if the young animal is truly orphaned. Wild mothers may not return to their young if people or their pets are gathered around the nest or burrow. On the other hand, young animals can be handled and safely placed back in nests, because a wild animal will not desert its young due to the of the odor of human beings. Young animals have been successfully returned to their parents up to 48 hours after being found. Many wild animals are anemic, dehydrated, hypothermic and/or hypoproteinemic when found.

The protocol for dealing with an orphaned or injured wild animal should be as follows:
1. Eliminate immediate life-threatening conditions, such as hemorrhage, hypoxia or shock.
2. Establish a normal body temperature.
3. Treat dehydration.
4. Diagnose and treat disease or injury.
5. Nourish the animal and establish a feeding regimen.
6. Meet behavioral needs.
7. Establish the long-term disposition of the animal by determining its potential for rehabilitation to the wild.

When handling wildlife, always remember that animals may be a source of zoonotic diseases. They also can be dangerous, and might bite despite the fact that they are badly injured and apparently stuporous.

The care of orphaned wild animals is a challenging task. The ultimate goal of wildlife rehabilitation is to return the animal to a suitable environment as soon as it is able to survive. Adult animals are the least likely to accept life in captivity and may be under constant stress. They often refuse to eat or adapt to captive diets, whereas infant animals adapt to captivity more readily.

In addition, wild animals are often protected by different laws or acts. In many countries, people are not allowed to keep wild animals, including hand-raised orphans. Therefore, an animal must be transferred to a licensed wildlife rehabilitation agency for ongoing care until it can be released to the wild again.

The responsibility of people and nonspecialized veterinarians is to provide primary care and nutrition until the animal can be transported to a specialized institution or clinic. The following institutes can be contacted to obtain legal information about recuperating wildlife and addresses of rehabilitation centers and other qualified persons.

UNITED STATES

The National Wildlife Rehabilitators Association
14 North 7th Ave.
St. Cloud, MN 56303-4766
320-259-4086

The Southeastern Raptor Rehabilitation Center (SERRC)
College of Veterinary Medicine
Contact: Joseph L. Shelnutt, Executive Director
Auburn University 36849-5523
Auburn, AL 36831-1107
Tel. center: 334-844-6025
After hours: 334-844-4690
e-mail: shelnjl@vetmed.auburn.edu

U.S. Fish and Wildlife Services
Region 1 (WA, OR, ID, NV, CA, HI)
Bridgett Tuerler
U.S. Fish and Wildlife Service
911 N.E. 11th Ave.
Portland, OR 97232-4181
503-872-2715

Region 2 (AZ, NM, TX, OK)
Kamile McKeever
U.S. Fish and Wildlife Service
Migratory Bird Permits Division
P.O. Box 709
Albuquerque, NM 87103-0709
505-248-7882

Region 3 (MN, IA, MO, WI, IL, IN, MI, OH)
Marlys Bulander
U.S. Fish and Wildlife Service
Migratory Bird Permit Office, Region 3
Bishop Henry Whipple Federal Building
1 Federal Drive
Fort Snelling, MN 55111-4056
612-713-5436

Region 4 (AR, LA, MS, AL, GA, FL, NC, SC, TN, KY)
Carmen Simonton
U.S. Fish and Wildlife Service
P.O. Box 49208
Atlanta, GA 30359
404-679-7049

Region 5 (WV, VA, PA, MD, DE, NJ, NY, CT, RI, MA, VT, NH, ME)
David Dobias
Migratory Bird Permit Office
U.S. Fish and Wildlife Service
P.O. Box 779
Hadley, MA 01035-0779
413-253-8643

Region 6 (CO, WY, KS, NE, UT, ND, SD, MT)
Chris Olsen
Migratory Bird Permit Office
U.S. Fish and Wildlife Service
P.O. Box 25486, DFC
Denver, CO 80225
303-236-8171

Region 7 (AK)
Steve Kendall
U.S. Fish and Wildlife Service
1011 East Tudor Road
Anchorage, AK 99503
907-786-3693

The International Wildlife Rehabilitation Council
4437 Central Place, Suite B4
Suisun, CA 94585
707-864-1761
Fax: 707-864-3106

BELGIUM
Coördinatiecentrum KBVBV
Veeweidestraat 43-45
B-1070 Brussel
02-521.28.50
Fax: 02-527.09.89

FRANCE
Ligue pour la Protection des Oiseaux (L.P.O.)
Corderie Royale-BP.263
F-17305 Rochefort Cedex
546.82.12.34
Fax: 543.83.95.86

GRAND-DUCHE de LUXEMBOURG
Lëtzebuerger Natur-a Vulleschutzliga (L.N.V.L.)
Ligue Luxembourgeoise Protection Nature et Oiseaux (L.L.P.N.O.)
Rue de Bettembourg
L-1899 Kockelscheuer
352-29.04.04
Fax: 352-29.05.04

THE NETHERLANDS
Nederlandse Vereniging tot Bescherming van de Vogels
16c Driebergseweg
3708 JB Zeist
030-693.77.00

SWITZERLAND
Schweizer Vogelschutz SVS
Postfach-CH
Zürich
01-463.72.71
Fax: 01-461.47.78

BIBLIOGRAPHY

1. Porter SL. Raising orphaned wildlife. In: Proceedings. North American Veterinary Conference, Orlando, FL, 1993: 813-815.
2. Pokras M, Porter S. An introduction to nonavian wildlife emergencies. Veterinary Clinics of North America: Small Animal Practice 1994; 24: 187-206.
3. Porter SL. Wildlife medicine I. In: Proceedings. North American Veterinary Conference, Orlando, FL, 1993; 808-810.
4. Fowler ME. Care of orphaned wild animals. Veterinary Clinics of North America: Small Animal Practice 1979; 9: 447-471.

Appendix Q
Feeding Orphaned and Injured Birds

I. Introduction

Fledgling birds may fall or be blown from the nest. Such birds may fail to feed, become weak and die without human intervention. However, when people find a bird in the absence of its parents, whether it be on the ground or in a nest, it is often better to convince them to return the bird to the place where it was found, and observe it for a while to see if it has been abandoned or not. Young songbirds such as robins, blue jays, mocking birds and sparrows are often found on the ground. These fledglings are just learning to fly and will continue to be fed by their parents unless threatened by a dog, cat or person.

This appendix provides practical recommendations for nutritional support of orphaned and injured birds until more specialized help is found. Young raptors in particular must be transferred immediately to a licensed wildlife rehabilitator (See Appendix P.) because there is a significant risk of improper imprinting.

In general, wild birds have nutritional requirements similar to those of pet birds. The feeding recommendations in Chapter 30 for normal pet birds can be used to generate feeding plans for many wild birds.

II. Energy requirements

The daily energy requirements of most captive birds vary from 1 to 2 x resting energy requirement (RER) depending on activity and housing. The daily energy requirements of passerine birds range from 1.25 to 7.2 x RER. It is often appropriate to initially feed an amount of food that supplies the RER (Table Q-1) and gradually increase the amount as needed to maintain body condition.

Table Q-1. Resting energy requirements of birds.*

Bird types	kcal/kg$^{0.75}$	kJ/kg$^{0.75}$
Passerine birds**	129	540
Non-passerine birds***	78	326
Seabirds	90	377

*Appendix N lists body weights of selected bird species.
**At a mean core temperature of 42°C (107.6°F).
***At a mean core temperature of 40°C (104°F).

III. Rehydration and drinking

Most captured birds, especially passerines, are in various states of dehydration, hypothermia and hypoglycemia. These problems should be corrected before starting normal feeding.

Rehydration
- Oral rehydration is less stressful than other routes; however, it can only be done safely when the bird is normothermic, conscious and standing or perching.
- As a rule, most birds can tolerate 1.5 to 2.5 ml of fluid per 100 g body weight. In general, birds with a crop have a larger capacity than birds without a crop (Table Q-2).
- Fluids can be administered every six to eight hours and the quantity given can be increased progressively.
- Warm the solution to 38 to 39°C (100.4 to 102°F) before administration to help prevent hypothermia.
- Oral administration of 5% dextrose can rapidly and effectively restore fluid deficits. Other suitable solutions are lactated Ringer's and Hartmann's solution.
- Fluid requirements increase during hot weather. Distressed birds also have increased requirements

Table Q-2. Maximum suggested fluid volume for gavage in selected species of birds.

Species	Amounts (ml/bird)*
Canary	0.25-0.5
Budgerigar	1-2
Lovebird	2-3
Cockatiel	3-6
Falcon	10
Parrot (depending on size)	5-10
African grey parrot	15-35
Tawny owl	15
European buzzard	20
Cockatoo	20-40

*Fluids can be given every six to eight hours (three to four times daily).

due to increased respiratory water loss. However, stressed and critically ill birds only tolerate small volumes of fluid given at increased intervals.

Drinking

- Most birds cannot suck (pigeons are exceptions); therefore, water must be spooned up to the beak or tongue and allowed to trickle down the pharynx when the bird's head is raised.
- Waterfowl have the highest requirement for water.
- Healthy fruit-eating birds, such as mynahs and lorikeets, seldom need to drink when receiving their natural food.
- Raptors have a relatively low water consumption when eating whole prey.
- Seed-eating birds need to drink more because their natural food is relatively low in water. When insufficient water is available for seed-eating birds, food intake decreases and death may occur within days. For example, pigeons drink about 10 ml/100 g body weight (approximately 50 ml/day); canaries and small passerine birds may drink about two to five times more per unit of body weight than pigeons, depending on ambient temperature.
- Because young birds do not drink, their food must contain sufficient water to meet daily requirements.

IV. General feeding methods

Changing foods can be challenging, especially for sick birds and those undergoing stress, such as a change in environment.

Color and texture of food

- Color and texture may influence the bird's interest in the food more than taste and nutrient content. Bright-colored objects, such as marbles, can be placed in the food container to encourage eating.
- Psittacine and fruit-eating birds may like the texture of soft foods such as baby cereal, fruits and vegetables, cooked oatmeal and mashes made from cereals.

Presentation of food

The way food is presented is equally important.

- Certain waterfowl will select their food only in relation to water.
- Birds may be encouraged to consume food pellets if the pellets are placed on newspaper or brown paper. As the bird pecks at one pellet, or moves about on the paper, the surrounding pellets move and make noise, which interests the bird.

- Birds of prey often hold out for "real meat" and refuse to eat prepared products. It may take two or three weeks to convert a meat-oriented animal to a commercial product.
- Most birds prefer food to be warmed up (maximum about 40°C [104°F]); however, others prefer food cooled to refrigerator temperatures (2 to 4°C [36 to 39°F]).

Tube feeding tips

- Ill birds often refuse to eat in captivity and may have to be force-fed to prevent further weakening.
- A liquid food or gruel can be administered through a soft catheter or a stainless steel ball-tipped feeding cannula connected to a syringe. A lacrimal catheter can be used for small birds. Five-Fr. infant feeding tubes have been recommended for birds the size of canaries, budgerigars and finches, 10-Fr. catheters for birds the size of cockatiels or medium-size parrots and 15-Fr. catheters for birds the size of large parrots. A metallic protective pod is necessary to prevent larger birds from breaking the catheter or cannula.
- Table Q-3 lists commercial formulas for tube feeding birds.
- It is important to use proper technique to avoid aspiration pneumonia. The head must be held and extended and the neck stretched. The bird should be held vertically to prevent reflux of food. The catheter or cannula should be introduced from the left side of the beak and advanced over the tongue into the esophagus (situated on the right side). Introducing catheters from the right side creates an immediate danger of aspiration pneumonia. At the slightest resistance, the catheter should be withdrawn and the procedure started again. The thin esophageal wall can be perforated easily and depositing food subcutaneously can be detrimental to the bird.
- Food should be injected very slowly into the crop, which should be filled but not overfilled. As a rule, 1.5 to 3 ml can be given per 100 g body weight, and repeated two to four times daily (Table Q-4). Adult birds should be fed smaller amounts at frequent intervals because they have small crops. The volume of food may be increased as the crop adapts.
- Immediately after each feeding, the bird should be quietly placed in its cage to decrease stress and the risk of regurgitation.
- During feeding, constantly observe the back of the oropharynx to ensure that the food does not enter into the mouth. The catheter must be withdrawn and the airway cleaned if the crop fills and food refluxes into the oropharynx.
- Weak and debilitated birds should be given an oral electrolyte solution two to three times during the first 24 hours before liquid food is administered.
- If possible, birds should be given a formula with low lactose levels.
- Meat- and carrion-eating birds, such as raptors and crows, should receive a commercial liquid or blenderized moist food for dogs or cats.
- Before administration, the food should be warmed to about 30 to 35°C (86 to 95°F).

Table Q-3. Formulas for tube feeding birds.*

Products	Manufacturers	Comments
Lafeber's Emeraid I	Lafeber Company, Cornell, IL	Source of mono-, di- and trisaccharides, easily dissolved in water for gavage.
Lafeber's Emeraid II	Lafeber Company, Cornell, IL	Primarily from rice flour and dried whole egg (crude protein: 18.5% DM, 3.4 kcal/g DM [14.2 kJ]).
High Potency Mash or Juvenile Formula	Harrison's Bird Diets, Inc., Delray Beach, FL	Mix 1 part of formula with 2 to 6 parts of hot water. Feed lukewarm.
Day One Baby Bird and Special Care Formula	Rolf C. Hagen, Inc., Québec, Canada	Mix 1 part of formula with 4 to 5 parts water.
Milk-free soy isolate (human) infant formulas	Several	Appropriate for tube feeding seed-eating birds. Mix 1 part powder with 1 part water.
Liquid or semi-liquid diets for dogs or cats	Several	Works well for short-term enteral feeding of most birds. Should not be given to fruit and nectar eaters.

Key: DM = dry matter.
*See Table O-7 for more information.

Table Q-4. Volumes for tube feeding birds.

Species	Body weights (g)	Amounts (ml/bird)	Frequencies (x daily)
Small finch	10-16	0.1-0.3	6
Canary and finch	20	0.25-0.5	2-4
Budgerigar	35-60	0.5-1.5	2-4
Parakeet	40-110	1-3	2-3
Cockatiel	80-140	2-4	2-4
Conure	80-250	2.5-5	4
Sulfur-crested cockatoo	250-300	6-12	2-3
Amazon parrot	300-600	5-14	2-3
Small parrot	na	5-8	2-4
Medium-large parrot	na	8-12	2-4
African grey parrot	300-500	10-14	2-3
Cockatoo	300-800	8-15	2-4
Mollucan cockatoo	1,000-1,500	20-40	2-3
Macaw	450-1,200	10-30	2-4

Key: na = not available.

V. Feeding orphaned birds
Introduction
- Clients should be advised that orphan feeding is extremely demanding and mortality can be high.
- Many baby birds are dehydrated when found and should be warmed first and given an oral electrolyte or glucose solution.
- In general, nidifugous birds (e.g., galliformes and many anseriformes) are able to eat on their own and don't pose a problem, if kept warm and fed a starter meal for chicks or a concentrated food for birds.

Practical feeding tips
- Most birds have an excellent gaping reflex and open their mouth readily.
- If the bird does not gape immediately, its mouth can be gently pried open. However, this technique should be avoided whenever possible because of the risk of fracturing the mandibula. Most baby birds respond quickly and can be trained in a short time to accept hand-feeding.
- A bird can be encouraged to open its beak by gently tapping on the nest cup, on its bill or on the feathers around it. In many cases, only noise around the nest will stimulate the bird to gape for food. Therefore, it may be useful to make a soft whistling or chirping noise, or to tap on the side of the nest at each feeding time. It is important to use the same stimulus consistently.
- Many young birds start gaping when food on a tooth pick is moved in front of their bill.
- When the bird opens its mouth, food should be placed far back over the tongue.
- A forceps, a toothpick, the flattened end of a Q-Tip, a tongue depressor (trimmed to appropriate size and rounded) or a small paintbrush (rinsed and disinfected with chlorhexidine) makes an excellent device for placing small bits of food in a bird's mouth.
- It is necessary to wait for the bird to swallow before offering more food.
- In general, one should continue to feed until the bird stops gaping. However, do not feed so much that the crop is packed full at each feeding. It is better to provide more frequent but smaller meals.
- After each bit of food is given, a liberal amount of water should follow to ease the passage of food through the esophagus and help supply the daily water needs.
- When food from the previous meal is still present in the crop, no additional food should be given to

avoid fermentation in the crop (sour crop). Over-feeding may also result in crop atony or impaction.
- If the crop retains food, it can be flushed with small amounts of commercially prepared strained applesauce baby food.
- Gruels should be fed warm, around 40°C (104°F). Offering food below 38°C (100°F) may result in poor acceptance, whereas the risk of thermal trauma to the crop increases when the food is served at temperatures above 42°C (108°F).
- The moisture content of the food should be optimal. After the first week of life, the food should contain approximately 30% solids.
- Gruels should be thoroughly homogenized to prevent separation of solids from water.
- Gruels that are too thick, contain too much fat or are fed at too low temperature may cause delayed emptying of the crop.
- Failure to raise orphans is frequently caused by failure to supply adequate energy rather than overfeeding.
- The number of daily feedings varies with age, size and species of bird. As a rule, the crop should be allowed to empty completely before the next feeding. Most naked nestlings (e.g., most passerines)

require food every 10 to 20 minutes over a 12- to 14-hour period during the first 10 days of life. Fully feathered nestlings can be offered a food mixed with meal worms in a shallow dish.
- Most feathered fledglings require food every 45 to 90 minutes, depending on age and species.
- Although they can do without feedings every two hours at night, baby birds should be fed late in the evening and first thing in the morning.
- People should keep detailed daily records of the bird's body weight, food consumption, numbers of daily feedings and crop emptying patterns.

Handling and practical husbandry tips
- One must take into account that young wild birds may get the wrong "imprinting" when raised in absence of their congeners. This is very important for birds that must be placed back in their natural environment.
- For most birds, imprinting takes place between the second or third week and the sixth week of age. Imprinting occurs between Days 1 and 10 for galliforme and other nidifugous birds. For birds of prey, imprinting occurs between Weeks 3 and 6.

Table Q-5. Feeding frequency for orphaned wild birds.

Age of chicks	Number of feedings
Days 0-4	Every 10-15 min. from 6 a.m. to 10 p.m.
Days 4-10	Every 15-20 min. from 6 a.m. to 10 p.m.
Days 10-14	Every 45-60 min. from 6.30 a.m. to 9.30 p.m.
After Day 14	Every 60-90 min. from 7 a.m. to 9 p.m.

Table Q-6. Ambient temperature for nestling birds.

Age characteristics	Song birds	Psittacine birds
Naked nestling	27.0-32.0°C (80-90°F)	32.0-34.5°C (90-94°F)
Covered with down	26.5-29.5°C (80-85°F)	32.0-34.5°C (86-90°F)
Feathered fledgling	21.0-27.0°C (70-80°F)	na

Key: na = not available.

VI. Feeding recommendations for selected birds
Injured adults
- Because of their higher RERs, passerine birds are more susceptible to hypoglycemia and should not be fasted.
- The order of passerine birds is very diversified, and comprises granivorous (seed-eating), nectivorous (nectar-eating), frugivorous (fruit-eating), insectivorous, carnivorous and omnivorous species. Therefore, it is impossible to make one recommendation for all passerine birds.
- Seed-eating birds with a large crop and highly developed muscular gizzard can ingest large amounts of seed when food is abundant and retain food until the next source is found.
- Most adult songbirds will do well when fed a commercially prepared complete food for passerine birds as a basal diet. A moist dog food can be substituted temporarily.

- Supplements to the basal food for passerine birds should be adapted to each suborder or family.
- Although most passerine birds accept fruit and seeds, live food should always be given, including flies, maggots, worms, larvae, beetles, butterflies, snails and slugs, cockroaches or spiders.
- Insectivorous birds can progressively adapt to eat non-live food. This practice can be encouraged by mixing live meal worms or other insects in their food.
- Fruit eaters should receive a variety of diced fresh, sweet, ripe fruit and fruit juice in addition to a soaked commercial food for passerines or soft-billed birds.
- Some fruit- and nectar-eating birds require vitamin C.
- Toucans, mynahs, hornbills, birds of paradise and other birds susceptible to hemochromatosis should receive soft-bill pellets containing less than 100

ppm of iron. Hemochromatosis also occurs in captive wild passerine birds such as crows, starlings and blackbirds. Because ascorbic acid may increase the availability of iron, fruits rich in ascorbic acid (e.g., citrus, kiwi) are not recommended.

Orphans

• Songbirds less than one week old that have no pinfeathers are extremely difficult to raise.

• Most passerine birds can be raised on a commercial food for baby birds, a formula consisting of 1 part hard-boiled egg yolk and 1 part Gerber's High Protein Cereal mixed with warm water or a moist dog food with moderate protein content (20 to 30% dry matter [DM]) and moderate fat content (10 to 15% DM) as a basal diet.

• Although live insects are often recommended, it is safer to feed fresh, dead insects to orphaned insectivorous birds.

Table Q-7. Specific recommendations for selected orphaned birds.

Species	Adult bird recommendations	Development at hatching*	Orphaned bird recommendations
Ciconiiformes Herons, egrets, bitterns	na	na	First 10 to 14 days of life: minced or ground skinned, whole rodents. Older than 14 days: chopped small rodents or fresh or recently thawed fish fed at a rate of 30 to 60% of body weight daily. Supplement with vitamin E and thiamin when fish is fed.
Galliformes Pheasant, quail, grouse, turkey	Commercial gamebird or chicken food	Precocial	Commercial gamebird, turkey or chicken starter and growing ration supplemented with insects and hard-boiled egg yolk. Allow grit.
Gruiformes Whooping crane (*Grus americana*), sandhill crane (*Grus canadensis*)	In general, cranes adapt well to captivity and will eat a commercial food.**	na	A mixture of commercial poultry food and ground rodents or a commercial crane food given freely with water.
Coots, gallinules, rail	na		Typically fussy eaters; additional force-feeding may be necessary. Commercial poultry, gamebird or waterfowl foods supplemented with insects, minced rodents or aquatic vegetables.
Columbiformes Pigeons, doves	Commercial food for domestic pigeons***	Altricial and psilopaedic	Easy to raise. Ideally a foster should be obtained from a local pigeon breeder. Pigeons do not gape, but put their beak into their parent's beak to obtain food. They should be force-fed every half hour until about 10 days of age (crop half full at a time). Feed a mixture containing equal amounts of chicken starter and wild bird seed made to a slurry with water or milk. (Warm mash with milk until bird is 5 weeks old).
Caprimulgiformes Nighthawks, nightjars, whippoorwill	na	Altricial and psilopaedic	Mash for baby birds or feed moist dog food. Mix 1:1 with insects (e.g., crickets, grubs, wax worms or mealworms). Nighthawks require prolonged force-feeding. Handle carefully to avoid mandibular fractures, because of the mandible's mid-shaft hinge.
Apodiformes Hummingbirds	1 tsp evaporated milk, 1 tsp honey, 1 cup water. Supplement with sweet, ripe fruit or canned baby food (fruit).	Altricial	80 g white cane sugar, 5 g protein supplement,† 457 ml water. The feeding response of hummingbird chicks is triggered by the insertion of the parent's bill into the mouth. Therefore, feed with a special eyedropper or Pasteur pipette. Feed one drop every 20 to 30 minutes.
Piciformes Flickers, woodpeckers	Insectivorous frugivores can temporarily survive on a commercial food for passerine birds supplemented with leaves, fruits and berries.	na	Feed 60-70% mash for baby birds or feed moist dog food, 10-20% baby cereal, 20% berries. Supplement with insects and worms.

(Continued on next page.)

APPENDIX Q

Table Q-7. Specific recommendations for selected birds. (Continued from previous page.)

Species	Adult bird recommendations	Development at hatching*	Orphan bird recommendations
Passeriformes **_Granivores_** Finches, chickadees, juncos	Commercial food for passerine birds supplemented with leaves, fruits, roots and invertebrates (e.g., insects, grubs). Granivorous passerine birds probably need grit.	Altricial and psilopaedic	Mash for baby birds or feed moist dog food. To accustom birds to eating seeds 20% of overall diet should be seeds by Day 10. Feed every half-hour during the day.
Ground insectivores Robins, thrushes, towhees	Commercial food for passerine birds supplemented with earthworms, white worms or other grubs.	Altricial and psilopaedic	Mash for baby birds or feed moist dog food. Mix 1:1 with earthworms or white worms. Feed every half-hour during the day.
Aerial insectivores Flycatchers, kingbirds, phoebes, swallows, swifts, wrens	Flycatchers are almost entirely insectivorous and catch insects during flight. They may need to be hand-fed insects.	Altricial and psilopaedic	Mash for baby birds or feed moist dog food. Mix 1:1 with insects (e.g., dried flies, crickets, grubs, wax worms or mealworms). Feed small bites every 20 to 30 minutes.
Insectivorous omnivores Blackbirds, mockingbirds, orioles, tanagers, thrashers, warblers	Commercial food for passerine birds supplemented with leaves, fruits and a variety of invertebrates.	Altricial and psilopaedic	Mash for baby birds or feed moist dog food. Mix 1:1 with insects (e.g., fresh, thawed crickets) or earthworms. Feed every half-hour during the day.
Insectivorous frugivores Waxwings	Commercial food for passerine birds supplemented with leaves, fruits and berries.	na	Feed 60-70% mash for baby birds or feed moist dog food, 10-20% baby cereal, 20% berries. Supplement with insects and worms.
Omnivores Crows, jays, grackles, shrikes	Moist dog food supplemented leaves, fruits, roots and a variety of invertebrates. Shrikes impale their prey (insects) on plant spikes or other pointed objects. In captivity, they need to be provided with thorns or spikes to ensure food intake.	Altricial and psilopaedic	Mash for baby birds or feed moist dog food. Supplement with up to 10% lean hamburger. Also add crickets, flies, grubs, small pieces of fruit or Gerber's strained fruit. Crows can be raised on moist dog food. Feed every half-hour during the day.

Key: na = not available.
*Altricial = Birds that are hatched with their eyes closed and have few or no feathers. The young are helpless at hatching and require complete parental care for some time. Psilopaedic = Naked at hatching. Precocial = Young are well-developed at hatching, covered with down and are able to move about and feed themselves.
**See Table O-5.
***See Table O-4.
†Gevral Protein (Lederle) or Super Hydramin powder (Nion).

Table Q-8. Homemade foods that may be substituted for live or insectile foods.*

Mixture 1	Mixture 2
70 g fine biscuit meal or baby rusk	50 g fine biscuit meal or baby rusk
10 g dried whole milk	25 g dried flies or shrimp meal
10 g wheat germ	25 g animal fat
10 g whitefish meal	25 g ant "eggs" (i.e., pupae)
5 g dried yeast	25 g whole cooked egg (0.5 egg)
1 tsp vegetable oil	25 g honey
1 tsp cod liver oil	25 g wheat germ
0.5 tsp cod liver oil	

*Adapted from Bibliography Source 2.

VII. Feeding recommendations for raptors

- Birds of prey may try to escape and/or harm themselves. Handling and housing requires knowledge of the bird's specific temperament.
- Preparation for release into the wild must be done by specialized rehabilitators.

Injured adult raptors

- Injured raptors (birds of prey) are often found starving; therefore, they should be warmed and rehydrated with an electrolyte glucose solution before starting the feeding plan. Raptors should be tube fed before their natural food is reintroduced.

- Owls, hawks, vultures and eagles can be fed raw rodents, chopped chicken or raw chicks.
- Raptors should not receive all meat; a mixture containing meat, hair and feathers and bones is better suited to the nutritional needs of raptors.
- Chopped whole laboratory mice can be fed and decrease the risk of introducing pathogens. A commercial food for raptors can be fed and supplemented with meat if necessary for acceptance (e.g., Birds of Prey-Fare: moisture 45%, protein 24%, fat 10%, fiber 3% [Reliable Protein Products, Inc., 44-489 Town Center Way, Suite D, PMB 505, Palm Desert, CA 92260, 760-321-7533, Fax: 760-321-0395]).

- Birds of prey often hold out for "real meat" and refuse to eat prepared products. This problem can be overcome by initially feeding small prey that is still moving or attaching the food to a stick and moving the food in front of the bird.
- The daily energy requirement of captive raptors is 109 kcal/kg$^{0.68}$ (456 kJ).
- Small birds of prey (100 to 200 g) require about 18 to 25% of their body weight in food each day, whereas large raptors (800 to 1,200 g) only require 6 to 11%.

Orphaned raptors

- Orphaned raptors generally react when a small piece of meat or a large insect is moved in front of their beak, or when the prey touches the feathers around the beak.
- Later, young predators will accept food when it is put under their foot; however, they may have to be force-fed initially.
- Baby raptors require special feeding techniques. Because of their special needs and potential for improper imprinting, young raptors must be transferred to a licensed wildlife rehabilitator immediately.
- Ground or minced, skinned and beheaded adult rodents or plucked day-old cockerels or quail rolled in bone meal (for falcons) may be fed during the first two to 10 days of life.
- Thereafter, fur and feathers can be fed in moderation with chopped whole animals until the bird is forming pellets well; then allow free access to food.
- After 18 days whole animals can be given. The size and number depend on the size of the bird.

Table Q-9. Feeding frequency for orphaned raptors.

Ages (days)	Frequencies (daily)
0-5	8-10 times
6-9	4-7 times
10-21	4 times
21-50	Twice
≥51	Once (hawks morning, owls evening)

Table Q-10. Natural prey of raptors.

Accipiters	Prey
Red-tailed hawks	Mice, rats, rabbits, snakes
Golden eagles	Rats, rabbits, gophers
Bald eagles	Fish, rodents, birds
Kites	
Black-shouldered kites	Mice
Everglade kites	Snails
Falcons	
Kestrels	Mice, crickets, small birds, lizards
Merlins	Mice, small birds
Prairie falcons	Birds, mice
Peregrine falcons	Birds
Osprey	Fish

VIII. Feeding recommendations for waterfowl

Water

- Waterfowl (anseriformes) naturally spend most of their life on water and water intake also occurs through the skin. Water should be sprinkled over captive birds when the environmental relative humidity drops below 40%.
- Altering the taste of water with drugs or use of plastic containers should be avoided.
- Cool drinking water should be available (below 15°C [59°F]). Water intake decreases and birds contaminate the water when the water temperature increases above 18 to 20°C (64.5 to 68°F) (e.g., birds drinking from containers exposed to the sun). Waterfowl need lots of water especially during warm weather.
- Because of their unique renal structure, waterfowl drink large amounts of water to eliminate waste. Insufficient water intake may lead to renal disturbances, especially in geese.
- Geese and ducks immerse their beaks completely under water before tilting their head back to swallow. If the animal can soak only the tip of its beak, it will not drink enough. The water container should be placed at the level of the bird's back to prevent dehydration.
- When force-feeding waterfowl, approximately 1 liter of water per kg body weight is needed daily.

Food

Adult waterfowl

- A commercially prepared food for waterfowl is appropriate.
- A moist dog food with a moderate protein content (15 to 20% dry matter) may be used to temporarily feed ducks and other water birds.
- Geese are herbivores; their natural food, therefore, should be rich in fresh grass.
- All adult waterfowl should have access to grit.

Orphaned waterfowl

- Waterfowl are precocial.
- Commercial duck, gamebird or turkey starter and grower mash, supplemented with fresh aquatic vegetables are appropriate.
- Feed free choice with water.
- All orphaned waterfowl should have access to grit.

IX. Feeding recommendations for seabirds

- The key is to provide a variety of fresh whole fish, including skull and bones (minerals), liver (vitamins) and gonads (fat).
- Live moving fish may stimulate feeding. Wiggling a dead fish with a forceps or dropping it from above to make a splash may help stimulate feeding.
- Adding warm cod liver oil may stimulate food intake in albatross, petrels and shearwaters.
- Some birds may only feed when in water.
- It may be necessary to force-feed injured birds with food and water if they can't feed naturally.
- Orphaned shore birds generally do well when fed crustaceans, worms and insects. Commercial dog food is an acceptable alternative.

Table Q-11. Specific feeding recommendations for seabirds.

Species	Where food is captured	Predominant food items*	Alternatives*	Orphans**
Gaviiformes (divers and loons)				
Xantus' murrelet	Subsurface	Plankton	Fish larvae: anchovies rockfish, saury	na
Arctic loon, common murre	Subsurface only	Fish, squid	na	na
Podicipedifores				
Western grebe	Subsurface only	Fish, squid	na	na
Procellariiformes				
Black-footed albatross, Northern fulmar	Surface only (dipping)	Fish, squid, carrion	Neustonic squid, offal	na
Phalarope spp, storm petrels	Surface	Neuston	Insects, fish eggs, small crustaceans	na
Shearwaters	Surface and midwater	Fish, squid, carrion	Surface and mid-water fish, squid	na
Pelecaniformes				
Cormorants	Subsurface only	Fish, squid	na	Altricial and psilopaedic White-bait fish (may need to add thiamin and multivitamins, especially vitamin E). It may be necessary to close the bill and milk or massage the fish down the bird's throat. Feed every 30 to 60 minutes.
Brown pelican	Surface	Epipelagic fish	Anchovies	Same as comments above.
Anseriformes				
Scoters	Bottom feeder	Invertebrates	Mollusks, nereids, herring eggs	na
Charadriiformes				
Arctic tern, coastal tern	Surface	Epipelagic fish	na	Precocial Omnivores that do well when fed a mixture of dog food, ground or minced rodents, insects and fish.
Gulls	Surface only (dipping)	Fish, squid, carrion	Surface fish, squid offal, carrion, insects	Same as comments above.
Pigeon Guillemot	Subsurface only	Fish, squid	na	Same as comments above.
Others				
Pomarine jaeger	Pursue weaker birds until they drop their prey	Fish, squid	Epipelagic fish	na

Key: na = not available.
*Epipelagic fish = surface fish. Neuston/neustonic = aggregate of minute aquatic organisms that float in the surface film of a body of water.
**Altricial = Birds that are hatched with their eyes closed and have few or no feathers. The young are helpless at hatching, and require complete parental care for some time. Psilopaedic = Naked at hatching. Precocial = Young are well-developed at hatching, covered with down and are able to move about and feed themselves.

BIBLIOGRAPHY

1. Abou-Madi N, Kollias GV. Avian fluid therapy. In: Kirk RW, Bonagura JD, eds. Current Veterinary Therapy XI. Philadelphia, PA: WB Saunders Co, 1992; 1154-1159.
2. Altman RB, Clubb SL, Dorrestein GM, et al, eds. Avian Medicine and Surgery. Philadelphia, PA: WB Saunders Co, 1997; 27-44, 73-95, 232-252, 867-885, 887-909, 910-917, 973-991.
3. Arnall L, Keymer IF. Nutrition and metabolism. In: Bird Diseases. London, UK: Ballière Tindall, 1975; 71-82.
4. Asterino R. Diseases and care of wild passerines. In: Rosskopf WJ Jr, Woerpel RW, eds. Diseases of Cage and Aviary Birds, 3rd ed. Baltimore, MD: Williams & Wilkins, 1996; 965-980, 981-1001, 1007-1027.
5. Campbell TW. Raptor rehabilitation in the private veterinary hospital. In: Exotic Animals: A Veterinary Handbook. Trenton, NJ: Veterinary Learning Systems, 1995; 121-125.
6. Carpenter JW, Mashima TY, Rupiper DJ. Exotic Animal Formulary. Manhattan, KS: Graystone Publications, 1996; 163-165, 290-293.
7. Carrère J. Nutrition des palmipèdes et maladies de la nutrition. Bulletin des GTV September 1988; 5: 53-63.
8. Castets M. Elevage et habitat des palmipèdes. Bulletin des GTV September 1988; 5: 17-51.
9. Clipsham R. Psittacine pediatrics. In: Proceedings. Eastern States Veterinary Conference, Orlando, FL, 1991: 557-559.
10. Clubb SL. Psittacine neonatology. In: Kirk RW, Bonagura JD, eds. Current Veterinary Therapy XI. Philadelphia, PA: WB Saunders Co, 1992; 1142-1145.
11. Cooper JE. Feeding exotic and pocket pets. Journal of Small Animal Practice 1990; 31: 482-488.
12. Cooper JE. Hospitalizing raptors. In: Proceedings. North American Veterinary Conference, Orlando, FL, 1997: 673-674.
13. Devriese L. Ziekten van siervogels en duiven, 2nd ed. Gent, Belgium: Rijksuniversiteit, 1985.
14. Dolphin RE, Olsen DE. The feeding and care of orphan birds. Veterinary Medicine/Small Animal Clinician 1977; 12: 1868-1869.
15. Earle KE, Clarke NR. The nutrition of the budgerigar (*Melopsittacus undulatus*). Journal of Nutrition 1991; 121: S45-S46.
16. Ensley P. Caged bird medicine and husbandry. Veterinary Clinics of North America: Small Animal Practice 1979; 9: 499-525.
17. Evans RH. Care and feeding of orphan mammals and birds. In: Kirk RW, ed. Current Veterinary Therapy IX. Philadelphia, PA: WB Saunders Co, 1986; 775-787.
18. Fowler ME. Care of orphaned wild animals. Veterinary Clinics of North America: Small Animal Practice 1979; 9: 447-471.
19. Kirkwood JK. Energy requirements for maintenance and growth of wild mammals, birds and reptiles. Journal of Nutrition 1991; 121: S29-S34.

20. Kollias GV. Diets, feeding practices, and nutritional problems in psittacine birds. Veterinary Medicine 1995; 90: 29-39.

21. Meij BP, Lumeij JT. Biotechniek en lichamelijk onderzoek bij vogels. Deel 2. Dier-en-Arts 1990; 4: 68-74.

22. Mikaelian I, Wœhrlé A. Eléments de thérapeutique des oiseaux sauvages et de compagnie. Le Point Vétérinaire 1992; 23: 83-92.

23. Miller EA. Medical update: Caring for orphaned wild birds. Veterinary Technician 1996; 5: 328-330.

24. Porter SL. Raising orphan wildlife. In: Proceedings. North American Veterinary Conference, Orlando, FL, 1993: 813-815.

25. Porter SL. Wildlife medicine I. In: Proceedings. North American Veterinary Conference, Orlando, FL, 1993: 808-810.

26. Porter SL. Wildlife medicine II. In: Proceedings. North American Veterinary Conference, Orlando, FL, 1993: 810-812.

27. Quesenberry KE. Avian nutritional support. In: Kirk RW, Bonagura JD, eds. Current Veterinary Therapy XI. Philadelphia, PA: WB Saunders Co, 1992; 1160-1163.

28. Quesenberry KE. Avian pediatrics. In: Proceedings. North American Veterinary Conference, Orlando, FL, 1992: 655-656.

29. Sedgewick CJ. Allometric scaling and emergency care: The importance of body size. In: Fowler ME, ed. Zoo & Wild Animal Medicine: Current Therapy 3. Philadelphia, PA: WB Saunders Co, 1993; 34-37.

30. Taylor M. Basic pet bird husbandry and nutrition. In: Proceedings. Eastern States Veterinary Conference, Orlando, FL, 1991: 569-573.

31. Taylor EJ, Nott HMR, Earle KE. The nutrition of the canary (*Serinus canarius*). Journal of Nutrition 1994; 124: 2636S-2637S.

32. Turner T. First aid for cage birds. In Practice 1985; 5: 76-81.

33. Ullrey DE, Allen ME, Baer DJ. Formulated diets versus seed mixtures for psittacines. Journal of Nutrition 1991; 121: S193-S205.

34. Vogel K. Die Taube Taubenkrankheiten, 2nd ed. Berlin, Germany: VEB Deutscher Landwirtschaftsverlag, 1970; 31-34.

35. Wolf P, Kamphues J. Die Futter–und Wasseraufnahme bei Kanarien–Einflußfaktoren und Abhängigkeiten. Kleintierpraxis 1992; 37: 545-552.

36. Zwart P, Dorrestein GM, van der Hage MH. Krankheiten von Großpapageien: Ein praxisbezogener Überblick. Kleintierpraxis 1989; 34: 573-577.

Appendix R
Feeding Orphaned and Injured Mammalian Wildlife

I. Introduction

This appendix provides practical recommendations for nutritional support of orphaned and injured mammals, until more specialized help is found. After immediate support is provided, the animal should be transferred to a licensed wildlife rehabilitator for ongoing care until it can be released to the wild again. Medical treatment is beyond the scope of this appendix.

II. Energy requirements

Orphans often fail to thrive due to inadequate energy and water intake. Newly rescued animals should be fed small quantities of food to ease the transition to the new food. Providing enough food to meet the animal's resting energy requirement (RER) (Table R-1) is a good initial goal. The amount fed can be increased gradually. The daily energy requirement of most captive mammals varies from 1 to 2 x RER, depending on activity and housing.

Whenever possible, body weights are provided in this appendix to allow quick calculation of food intake. However, individual animals should always be weighed before starting nutritional support and frequently thereafter because changes in body weight are important in evaluating results.

Because of their high metabolic rate, very small mammals should be force-fed if they do not eat for more than 12 hours. If tube feeding is necessary, up to 3 ml of an enteral product/100 g body weight can be administered per feeding. See Chapter 12 for enteral feeding products.

Table R-1. Resting energy requirements of mammals.*

Mammal type	kcal/kg$^{0.75}$	kJ/kg$^{0.75}$
Placental mammals	70	294
Marsupial mammals	49	205

*At normal body temperature.

III. Rehydration and drinking

Many animals are anemic, dehydrated and hypothermic when found. These problems should be corrected before normal feeding is started.

- Daily maintenance fluid requirements for most adult mammals are 35 to 40 ml/kg body weight (16 to 18 ml/lb).
- Neonates have increased fluid requirements (two to three times more than adults). As a rule, one can start with about 10 ml of water/100 g body weight.
- Fluid requirements of very young animals are met with milk (or milk replacer). When more liquid is needed, additional nursing, further dilution of milk with water or intubation may be necessary.
- Fluid requirements increase during hot weather and when animals are distressed. Diseases that cause fever, vomiting or diarrhea can increase fluid requirements two to five times.
- Dehydration must be corrected as early as possible, particularly in orphaned neonates. If moderate dehydration is present (about 7%), rehydration can be accomplished by oral gavage with a warm electrolyte solution or lactated Ringer's solution.
- A successful regimen for adults is to give 40 to 55 ml/kg body weight (18 to 25 ml/lb) of replacement fluid by stomach tube in two or three divided doses. This regimen should be repeated every 12 to 24 hours until rehydration is complete.

IV. General recommendations for orphaned mammalian wildlife

- Many orphans are too young to thermoregulate. Thus, maintenance of normothermia is one of the most important objectives in rearing wild neonatal mammals until the age of three to four weeks. They should be kept at an environmental temperature of 29 to 35°C (84 to 95°F).
- Hypothermic neonates should be warmed up progressively before being fed. They should be warmed in a warm-water bath at 38 to 40.5°C (100 to 105°F), gently massaged and dried immediately with a hairdryer.
- Daily maintenance fluid requirements (about 100 ml/kg body weight/day) must also be met until the animal is fed a milk replacer.
- The milk replacer should always be fed at body temperature.
- Exact information about requirements is lacking for most species. Start feeding progressively, but avoid overfeeding. Dilute the recommended formula as follows for the first few feedings: one-third formula at the recommended dilution + two-thirds water. Then dilute the formula 50/50 to be at 100% at the recommended dilution after 24 to 48 hours. Overfeeding often causes more serious problems than underfeeding (e.g., bloating, diarrhea).
- Restrict the quantity per feeding to avoid aspiration pneumonia. Respect the animal's comfortable stomach capacity (4 to 6 ml/100 g for most small mammals).
- The daily energy requirements of young growing mammals may vary from two to four times the RER (Table R-1).
- Neonates must be allowed to suckle from a "natural position."
- For most small mammals, except lagomorphs, stomach capacity averages 40 to 60 ml/kg body weight.
- Defecation and micturition must be stimulated in the same way as is done with orphaned puppies and kittens.
- Milk replacers for dogs and cats often do not match the nutrient profile of mother's milk for many wild animals. Therefore, it may be necessary to use a different dilution than recommended for puppies or kittens, add cream or lactose or mix different milk replacers in specific proportions as indicated for some species (Tables R-4, R-7 and R-10). The milk formulas in Table R-2 are compatible with one another and can be mixed in various proportions and diluted with warm water to obtain a formula that best matches the milk of the species. (See Appendix K.)
- A starting point for daily milk intake for orphaned mammals is 20 to 30% of body weight for carnivores and rodents, and 20% of body weight for opossums and armadillos.

Table R-2. Nutrient content (as fed basis) of milk replacers for orphaned wildlife.*

Nutrients	Milk Matrix 20/14	Milk Matrix 20/20	Milk Matrix 23/30	Milk Matrix 25/13	Milk Matrix 30/55**	Milk Matrix 33/40	Milk Matrix 42/25	KMR	Esbilac
kcal (GE)	432	448	496	420	625	578	507	512	585
MJ (GE)	1.81	1.87	2.08	1.76	2.62	2.42	2.12	2.14	2.45
Moisture (%)	5.0	5.3	4.5	5.4	3.6	2.1	2.7	3.0	3.0
Protein (%)	20.6	20.0	23.9	25	31.7	34.0	43.4	43.0	34.0
Fat (%)	16.0	20.0	30.0	14.6	55.0	42.9	29.0	26.0	43.0
NFE (carbohydrate) (%)	51.6	47.2	34.8	48.0	2.7	15.6	18.6	22.0	15.0
Crude fiber (%)	0.0	0.0	0.0	0.0	0.0	0.0	0.0	0.0	0.0
Ash (%)	6.8	7.5	6.8	7.0	7.0	5.4	6.3	6.4	5.4
Calcium (%)	1.00	0.76	1.13	0.56	1.09	1.16	1.32	1.01	1.02
Phosphorus (%)	0.80	0.64	0.52	0.57	0.75	0.80	1.00	0.89	0.76
Sodium (%)	0.51	0.61	0.33	0.59	0.57	0.43	0.45	na	na
Potassium (%)	1.30	1.76	1.54	1.85	0.81	0.64	0.71	na	na
Magnesium (mg/100 g)	95	130	76	120	88	62	70	na	na
Copper (mg/100 g)	2.8	1.4	2.2	2.0	1.0	1.3	1.4	na	na
Iron (mg/100 g)	10.8	11.4	11.0	11.0	11.0	4.2	4.4	na	na
Zinc (mg/100 g)	8.7	10.0	12.3	10.2	6.0	7.9	8.0	na	na

Key: GE = gross energy, NFE = nitrogen-free extract, na = not available.
*Manufacturers' data.
**Multi-Milk (PetAg) is the same as Milk Matrix 30/55. Both are low in carbohydrate and contain only traces of lactose. They can be used interchangeably. Information obtained from the manufacturer.

V. Feeding recommendations for selected mammalian wildlife species

Canids such as coyotes, foxes and wolves, and procyonids such as raccoons have nutritional requirements similar to those of domestic dogs. The general feeding recommendations outlined in Chapter 9 for normal dogs can be used in these species. Felids such as ocelots, lynxes and bobcats, and mustelids such as ferrets, mink, badgers, skunks, weasels and wolverines have nutritional recommendations similar to those of domestic cats. The general feeding recommendations outlined in Chapter 11 for normal cats can be used in these species. Wild rodents such as rabbits, beavers, squirrels and woodchucks have nutritional requirements similar to those of rodents kept as pets. The general feeding recommendations outlined in Chapter 28 for pet rodents can be used in these species. The reader is referred to the bibliography and textbooks on wildlife biology and medicine for more detailed discussions of husbandry of individual species.

Table R-3. Feeding adult wild carnivores.

Species	Adult body weights	Foods
Canidae		
Coyote *(Canis latrans)*	9-12 kg	Commercial dog food
Fox *(Vulpes* spp) (red fox, gray fox)	4-9 kg	Commercial dog food
Wolf	23-57 kg	Commercial dog food
Felidae		
Ocelot *(Felis pardalis)*	11.4-34 kg	ZuPreem* Feline Diet, or a commercial cat food
Mountain lion	36-100 kg	ZuPreem Feline Diet, or a commercial cat food
Lynx	11-23 kg	ZuPreem Feline Diet, or a commercial cat food
Margay *(Felis wiedi)*	≤9 kg	ZuPreem Feline Diet, or a commercial cat food
Bobcat	7-11 kg	ZuPreem Feline Diet, or a commercial cat food
Mustelidae		
Ferret *(Mustella putorius furo)*	0.9-2.0 kg (male)	Complete ferret food, or a commercial cat food
North American black-footed ferret *(Mustella nigripes)*	0.45-1.35 kg (female)	
American mink *(Mustella vison)*	na	Complete ferret food or mink food, or a commercial cat food
Badger	7-9 kg	Complete ferret food, or a commercial cat food
Ermine *(Mustella erminea)*	100 g	Complete ferret food, or a commercial cat food
Skunk *(Mephitis* spp)	0.75-2.5 kg	Moist dog or cat food supplemented with banana, apple, grape and egg
Weasel *(Mustella frenata)*	—	Complete ferret food, or a commercial cat food
Wolverine *(Gulo gulo)*	40 kg	Complete ferret food, or a commercial cat food
Procyonidae		
Raccoon *(Procyon lotor)*	15-22 kg	Moist dog food supplemented with banana or other fruit, and egg or meat
Cacomistle (ring-tailed cat) *(Bassariscus astutus)*	0.85-1.1 kg	Moist dog or cat food

*Premium Nutritional Products, Mission, KS, USA.

Table R-4. Feeding orphaned wild carnivores.*

Species	Birth weights	Feeding frequencies	Amounts per feeding	Milk formulas**	Weaning foods/ remarks
Canidae					
Coyote *(Canis latrans)*	na	q4-6h	na	Puppy milk replacer	Puppy food
Fox *(Vulpes* spp) (red fox, gray fox)	na	q4	na	Puppy or kitten milk replacer	Puppy food with or without 10% ground whole rodents
Wolf	600 g	q2h	15-20 ml	Puppy milk replacer	Puppy food supplemented with grubs and insects
Felidae					
Mountain lion	560 g	q2h during daytime	13-30 ml	Kitten milk replacer	Kitten food
Lynx	140 g	q2h during daytime	5-8 ml	Kitten milk replacer	Kitten food
Bobcat	na	q4-5h	na	Kitten milk replacer	Kitten food
Mustelidae					
Ferret	10 g	na	na	Multi-Milk or kitten milk replacer plus cream	High-protein (≥35%), high-fat (25%) kitten food
Badger	400 g	q4-6h	20 ml	15 g KMR + 10 g Multi-Milk + 75 g water	Dog or cat food supplemented with rodents or kitten milk replacer
Mink	na	3-5 times daily	na	Kitten milk replacer and/or Multi-Milk	Mink or kitten food, supplemented with grubs, insects or ground whole rodents
Skunk	na	q4h	na	15 g KMR + 10 g Multi-Milk + 75 g water or kitten milk replacer or Multi-Milk	Mink, puppy or kitten food, with grubs and insects
Weasel	na	3-6 times daily	na	Puppy or kitten milk replacer	Mink or kitten food, with grubs, insects or ground whole rodents
Procyonidae					
Raccoon	125 g	3-5 times daily	na	10 g Esbilac + 20 g Milk Matrix 23/30 + 100 g water or puppy or kitten milk replacer	Moist puppy or mink food, supplemented with a variety of vegetables
Cacomistle	na	q3h	na	Puppy milk replacer	Puppy or kitten food
River otter	na	3-5 times daily	na	Kitten milk replacer	Mink, puppy or kitten food supplemented with ground whole rodents

Key: na = not available.
*Appendix K lists milk replacers.
**Animals should be fed in a sitting position.

Table R-5. Guaranteed/average analyses of commercial foods for wild carnivores.*

Products	Moisture	Protein	Fat	NFE	Fiber	Ca	P
Kaytee Products Forti-Diet Ferret Food**	12	35	18	na	4	na	na
Mazuri Purina Mills 5635 Mazuri Omnivore Zoo Feed A**	na	25	6	na	5	na	na
Mazuri Purina Mills 5M22 Mazuri Omnivore Zoo Feed B**	na	24	8	na	6	na	na
Mazuri Purina Mills 5M08 Mazuri Ferret Food**	na	38	20.5	na	4	na	na
Mazuri Purina Mills 5M52 Mazuri Exotic Canine Food**	na	28.5	18	na	4	na	na
Performance Foods Totally Ferret**	10	36	22	na	1.5	na	na
Premium Nutritional Products ZuPreem Feline Diet***	62.2	16.8	15.7	2.0	0.8	0.46	0.38
Premium Nutritional Products ZuPreem Ferret Diet**	10	40	21	na	3	na	na
Premium Nutritional Products ZuPreem Omnivore Diet***	8	21.7	6.3	53	4.8	0.96	0.83

Key: na = not available.
*Manufacturers' data. Nutrients expressed as % as fed.
**Guaranteed analysis. Moisture = max. % moisture, protein = min. % protein, fat = min. % fat, fiber = max. % crude fiber, Ca = min. % calcium, P = min. % phosphorus.
***Average analysis. Protein = crude protein, fat = crude fat, NFE = nitrogen-free extract, fiber = crude fiber, Ca = calcium, P = phosphorus.

Table R-6. Feeding adult wild rodents and lagomorphs.

Species	Foods
True or European rabbit (*Oryctolagus cuniculus*)*	Commercially prepared rabbit pellets. Adequate intake of coarse, nondigestible fiber is essential. Foods for hamsters and rats are not appropriate for rabbits.
American cottontail rabbit (*Sylvilagus* spp)	Commercially prepared rabbit pellets. Adequate intake of coarse, nondigestible fiber is essential. Oats, barley, green leafy vegetables, beets and small amounts of stale bread, fruit and leftovers from the table may be given to hares and rabbits. Grass hay (timothy hay) may be offered free choice. Alfalfa hay is higher in protein and calcium and is better reserved for growing, reproducing and malnourished rabbits. Sugar beets and excessive amounts of green leafy vegetables may cause diarrhea and should be avoided. See other comments above for rabbits.
Hare (*Lepus* spp)	Commercially prepared rabbit pellets. Adequate intake of coarse, nondigestible fiber is essential.
Squirrel	Sweet feed, sweet potatoes, dark green leafy vegetables, rodent or rabbit pellets.

*Body weight 1 to 9 kg.

Other important points to remember when feeding adult wild rodents and lagomorphs include:
• Rodents may be encouraged to consume food pellets by offering them on newspaper or a brown paper bag.
• Many rodents are nocturnal feeders.
• Leporidae (rabbits and hares) are monogastric herbivores; coprophagy is essential for adequate intake of amino acids and vitamins A, D and B complex.

• Water is often neglected. Wild rodents that eat enough greens only need a minimal amount of water; however, in captivity they need to drink. The average water intake of a rabbit eating pellets should be approximately 10% of body weight.
• Anorectic rabbits can be syringe fed the following mixture: blenderized rabbit pellets, fruit, vegetable baby food and baby cereals mixed with water, Isocal or Isocal HCN (Mead-Johnson Nutritionals, Evansville, IN, USA). A 5-Fr. nasogastric tube can be used in some instances.

Table R-7. Feeding orphaned rodents and lagomorphs.

Species	Birth weights (g)	Feeding positions	Feeding frequencies	Feeding amounts (ml)	Milk formulations*	Weaning foods
Domestic rabbit	60-100	Tube feed	q3-4h	na	Puppy milk replacer; after baby rabbits open their eyes, supplement with a gruel of rodent pellets and milk replacer	Rabbit pellets, fresh grass clippings, dandelion leaves, clover, etc.
Cottontail rabbit	na	Tube feed	q2h	2-3 ml	20 g KMR + 40 g Multi-Milk + 100 g water or puppy milk replacer	Rabbit pellets, fresh grass clippings, dandelion leaves, clover, etc.
Jack rabbit (hare)	na	Tube feed	2-6 times daily	5-15 ml	20 g KMR + 40 g Multi-Milk + 100 g water or puppy milk replacer	Rabbit pellets
Beaver	na	na	q3h	na	80 g water + 30 g Multi-Milk + 10 g Milk Matrix 23/30 or evaporated milk, undiluted	Rodent or rabbit food, selected shrubs, twigs, branches
Chinchilla	35-50	na	q3h	na	Evaporated milk diluted 1:1	na
Hamster	2	na	q2h	na	Evaporated milk diluted 1:1	na
Guinea pig	90	na	4-8 times daily	na	Evaporated milk diluted 1:1, need vitamin C daily	Rodent food plus vitamin C, selected shrubs, twigs, branches
Muskrat	na	Sitting	3-6 times daily	na	Puppy milk replacer plus Multi-Milk	Rodent or rabbit food
Nutria	na	Sitting	3-5 times daily	na	Puppy milk replacer plus cream	Rabbit or rodent food
Ground squirrel (gopher)	na	Sitting	q2h	na	Puppy milk replacer or Multi-Milk or evaporated milk diluted 1:1	Rodent food
Porcupine	na	na	q3h	na	Evaporated milk, undiluted	na
Tree squirrel**	na	Sitting	3-6 times daily	na	Puppy milk replacer plus cream	Switch progressively to a laboratory rodent food, supplement with broccoli, sweet potatoes, green leafy vegetables
Woodchuck/other marmots	na	na	3-5 times daily	na	Puppy milk replacer or Multi-Milk	Rodent or rabbit food

Key: na = not available.
*Appendix K lists milk replacers.
**Offer a gruel made from baby cereal or dry puppy food and milk replacer in a shallow dish after baby squirrels open their eyes.

Table R-8. Guaranteed analyses (as fed basis) of commercial foods for wild rodents and lagomorphs.*

Rabbit products	Moisture	Protein	Fat	Fiber	Ca	P
Kaytee Products Exact Pet Rabbit Food Rainbow	12	14	3	6-20	0.6	0.35
Kaytee Products Fiesta Rabbit Food	12	15	5	12.5-15	0.6-1.1	0.4
Kaytee Products Forti-Diet Rabbit Food	12	17	3	15-18	0.6-1.1	0.4
Squirrel products						
Kaytee Products Squirrel Food	12	10	8	10	na	na
Hare and other lagomorph products						
Mazuri Purina Mills 5652 Mazuri Lagomorph Diet	na	16	2	18	na	na
General						
Mazuri Purina Mills 5663 Mazuri Rodent Diet	na	23	6.5	4	na	na

Key: na = not available.
*Moisture = max. % moisture, protein = min. % protein, fat = min. % fat, fiber = max. % crude fiber, Ca = min. % calcium, P = min. % phosphorus.

Table R-9. Feeding adult wild insectivores and marsupials.

Species	Body weights	Foods	Remarks
Armadillo and anteaters	5-6.5 kg	Commercial food for insectivores (e.g., Reliable Protein Products Insectivore-Fare) or moist dog food supplemented with active, cultured yogurt provided as a thick gruel. A more diluted gruel is better to make the transition from the natural food in recently captured animals. Fruits (ripe bananas, oranges, limes and avocados) as treats.	Natural food: in addition to insects, they readily consume various fruits and animal protein sources.
Hedgehogs and tenrecs African hedgehog *(Atelerix albiventris)* European hedgehog *(Erinaceus europeus)* Miniature hedgehog *(Echinops telfairi)*	250-600 g 400-1,200 g	Commercial food for insectivores such as hedgehogs or commercial dog food. Supplement as a treat or mix with food: insects, earthworms, mealworms, shrimp, crickets and newborn mice, chopped raw meat, liver or heart, milk, eggs, cottage cheese, small amounts of diced fruit (e.g., bananas, raisins) and vegetables, seeds, pine nuts and small roots.	Natural food: a variety of insects and small vertebrates Water should be placed in flat stable bowls. Food should be offered in the evening.
Virginian opossum *(Didelphis marsupialis virginiana)*	3 kg	Homogenized laboratory mice or commercial moist dog food.	na

Key: na = not available.

Table R-10. Feeding orphaned insectivores and marsupials.

Species	Birth weights	Feeding frequencies	Feeding amounts (ml)	Milk formulations*	Weaning foods
Armadillo and anteaters	na	q2h	8 ml	Puppy milk replacer or Multi-Milk	Kitten or puppy food
Hedgehogs	na	3-5 times daily	na	15 g KMR + 20 g Multi-Milk + 70 g water; hedgehog sucklings have no lactase activity, and milk of hedgehogs contains almost no lactose. A puppy milk replacer can be used.	Puppy food
Virginian opossum**	56 g	q2h	1-2 ml	100 g water + 15 g Milk Matrix 23/30 + 15 g Milk Matrix 30/55 or puppy milk replacer	Kitten or puppy food

Key: na = not available.
*Appendix K lists milk replacers.
**Opossums pose special problems because the semi-permanent mouth-to-nipple attachment in the pouch of the mother does not require a good sucking reflex. Very young opossums should be tube fed until their eyes are opened and then progressively offered a gruel of milk replacer and moist puppy food with a moderate fat level.

VI. Manufacturers of commercial foods for mammalian wildlife

Kaytee Products, Inc.
521 Clay Street
P.O. Box 230
Chilton, WI 53014
800-KAYTEE1 (800-529-8331)
Fax: 414-849-4734

Mazuri Purina Mills, Inc.
P.O. Box 66812
St. Louis, MO 63166-6812
314-768-4592
Fax: 314-768-4644

Performance Foods, Inc.
3001 Industrial Lane
Unit 4
Broomfield, CO 80020
303-410-1101

Premium Nutritional Products, Inc.
P.O. Box 2094
Mission, Kansas 66202
800-345-4767
Fax: 913-722-6226

Reliable Protein Products, Inc.
44-489 Town Center Way
Suite D, PMB 505
Palm Desert, CA 92260
760-321-7533
Fax: 760-321-0395

BIBLIOGRAPHY

1. Anderson LC. Guinea pig husbandry and medicine. Veterinary Clinics of North America: Small Animal Practice 1987; 17: 1045-1060.
2. Bell JA. Ensuring proper nutrition in ferrets. Veterinary Medicine 1996; 91: 1098-1103.
3. Bell JA. Ferret nutrition and diseases associated with inadequate nutrition. In: Proceedings. North American Veterinary Conference, Orlando, FL, 1993: 719-720.
4. Besch-Williford CL. Biology and medicine of the ferret. Veterinary Clinics of North America: Small Animal Practice 1987; 17: 1155-1183.
5. Carpenter JW, Mashima TY, Rupiper DJ. Hedgehogs. In: Exotic Animal Formulary. Manhattan, KS: Graystone Publications, 1996; 181-187.
6. Carpenter JW, Mashima TY, Rupiper DJ. Appendix 49. Check list for the care of sick, injured, or orphaned wild animals. In: Exotic Animal Formulary. Manhattan, KS: Graystone Publications, 1996; 285-286.
7. Carpenter JW, Mashima TY, Rupiper DJ. Appendix 50. Recommended diets and weaning considerations for orphaned wild mammals. In: Exotic Animal Formulary. Manhattan, KS: Graystone Publications, 1996; 287-289.
8. Cooper JE. Feeding exotic and pocket pets. Journal of Small Animal Practice 1990; 31: 482-488.
9. Evans RH. Care and feeding of orphan mammals and birds. In: Kirk RW, ed. Current Veterinary Therapy IX. Philadelphia, PA: WB Saunders Co, 1986; 775-787.
10. Evans RH. Rearing orphaned wild mammals. Veterinary Clinics of North America: Small Animal Practice 1987; 17: 755-783.
11. Fowler ME. Care of orphaned wild animals. Veterinary Clinics of North America: Small Animal Practice 1979; 9: 447-471.
12. Harkness JE. Rabbit husbandry and medicine. Veterinary Clinics of North America: Small Animal Practice 1987; 17: 1019-1044.
13. Harkness JE. Small rodents. Veterinary Clinics of North America: Small Animal Practice 1994; 24: 89-102.
14. Hillyer EV. Approach to the anorectic rabbit. In: Proceedings. North American Veterinary Conference, Orlando, FL, 1992: 715-716.
15. Hillyer EV. Pet rabbits. Veterinary Clinics of North America: Small Animal Practice 1994; 24: 25-65.
16. Hoefer HL. Hedgehogs. Veterinary Clinics of North America: Small Animal Practice 1994; 24: 113-119.
17. Isenbügel E, Baumgartner RA. Diseases of the hedgehog. In: Fowler ME, ed. Zoo & Wild Animal Medicine: Current Therapy 3. Philadelphia, PA: WB Saunders Co, 1993; 294-302.
18. Kirkwood JK. Energy requirements for maintenance and growth of wild mammals, birds and reptiles. Journal of Nutrition 1991; 121: S29-S34.
19. Landes E, Struck S, Meyer H. Digestive tract and digestibility of different feedstuffs in hedgehogs (abstract). In: Proceedings. Sixth Annual Congress of the European Society of Veterinary Internal Medicine, Veldhoven, The Netherlands, September 1996; 26.
20. McLain DE, Thomas JA, Fox JG. Nutrition. In: Fox JG, ed. Biology and Diseases of the Ferret. Philadelphia, PA: Lea & Febiger, 1988; 135-152.
21. Miller RM. Exotic carnivores. Veterinary Clinics of North America: Small Animal Practice 1979; 9: 569-580.
22. Miller SA. Exotics: Care and treatment of hedgehogs and tenrecs. Veterinary Technician 1996; 332-335.
23. Oglesbee BL. Emergency medicine for pocket pets. In: Bonagura JD, ed. Current Veterinary Therapy XII. Philadelphia, PA: WB Saunders Co, 1995; 1328-1331.
24. Okerman L. Voeding. In: Ziekten van konijnen Een handleiding voor Dierenartsen, Gent, Belgium: Rijksuniversiteit 1985; 15-17.
25. Pokras M, Porter S. An introduction to nonavian wildlife emergencies. Veterinary Clinics of North America: Small Animal Practice 1994; 24: 187-206.
26. Porter SL. Wildlife medicine I. In: Proceedings. North American Veterinary Conference, Orlando, FL, 1993: 808-810.
27. Porter SL. Wildlife medicine II. In: Proceedings. North American Veterinary Conference, Orlando, FL, 1993: 810-812.
28. Porter SL. Raising orphan wildlife. In: Proceedings. North American Veterinary Conference, Orlando, FL, 1993: 813-815.
29. Quesenberry KE. Ferrets–Basic approach to veterinary care. In: Hillyer EV, Quesenberry KE, eds. Ferrets, Rabbits, and Rodents: Clinical Medicine and Surgery. Philadelphia, PA: WB Saunders Co, 1997; 14-25.
30. Rosenthal K. Ferrets. Veterinary Clinics of North America: Small Animal Practice 1994; 24: 1-23.
31. Sedgewick CJ, Martin JC. Concepts of veterinary practice in wild mammals. Veterinary Clinics of North America: Small Animal Practice 1994; 24: 175-185.
32. Sedgewick CJ. Allometric scaling and emergency care: The importance of body size. In: Fowler ME, ed. Zoo & Wild Animal Medicine: Current Therapy 3. Philadelphia, PA: WB Saunders Co, 1993; 34-37.
33. Wagner JE, Farrar PL. Husbandry and medicine of small rodents. Veterinary Clinics of North America: Small Animal Practice 1987; 17: 1061-1087.
34. Wallach JD. Nutrition of exotic pets. Veterinary Clinics of North America: Small Animal Practice 1979; 9: 405-414.

Appendix S
Feeding Orphaned and Injured Amphibians and Reptiles

I. Amphibians
    Table S-1. Body weights of selected amphibians.
II. Reptiles
    Table S-2. Feeding recommendations for selected tortoises and turtles.
    Table S-3. Guaranteed analyses of selected commercial foods for reptiles.
    Table S-4. Guaranteed analyses of selected commercial supplements for reptiles.
III. Manufacturers of commercial foods for amphibians and reptiles.
Endnotes
Bibliography

Poikilothermic (ectothermic) animals such as reptiles and amphibians must be kept at a specific temperature to function well. The range of temperatures within which a species functions optimally is called the preferred optimal temperature range. A chain of events that often results in death (maladaptation syndrome) may occur at temperatures outside this range. Metabolism increases with high environmental temperatures, and the animal may be unable to eat enough food to maintain body weight. Amphibians and reptiles may refuse to eat when temperatures are low.

I. Amphibians
Practical recommendations
- Temperate species of salamanders should be kept between 10 and 16°C (50 to 61°F). Temperatures above 20°C (68°F) should be avoided.
- Tropical species of salamanders do best in environments with very high humidity and temperatures between 15 and 20°C (59 to 68°F). Temperatures above 23°C (73.4°F) should be avoided.
- Temperate species of frogs should be kept between 15 and 25°C (59 to 77°F).
- Temperatures for tropical species of frogs should be kept between 25 and 30°C (77 to 86°F).

Nutrition
- Adult amphibians are almost exclusively carnivorous, whereas larvae may be carnivorous, herbivorous or omnivorous.
- Many species only accept live, moving food. They can be fed a variety of live prey such as crickets, fruit flies, meal worms, earthworms and tubifex worms.
- Large frogs and toads also consume neonatal mice and rats.
- Aquatic salamanders can be fed tubifex worms, water fleas, fresh water shrimps, insect larvae and earthworms. However, some earthworms (manure worms) sold as fish bait are toxic to salamanders.
- If accepted, ZuPreem Monitor and Tegu Diet[a] and dry dog, cat or fish foods are also appropriate for feeding amphibians.
- Ideally, a wide variety of foods should be offered.

Commercial foods for Amphibia
- In the United States, at least one complete food for healthy adult Amphibia is available: 5634 Mazuri Amphibian Feed[b] This food is a soft-moist 5-mm pellet, with the following guaranteed analysis: protein 43%, fat 15% and crude fiber 3%.
- Tube feeding, using Emeraid II[c] or Repto-Min[d] should be implemented when animals refuse to eat. The amount of food provided per 24 hours should not exceed 2% of body weight.

Table S-1. Body weights of selected amphibians.

Common names	Genus and species	Body weights (g)
Leopard frog	*Rana pipiens*	25-46
American bullfrog	*Rana catesbeiana*	225-305
Cuban tree frog	*Hyla septentrionalis*	28-35
Tiger salamander	*Ambystoma tigricum*	35

II. Reptiles
- Many reptiles will not drink voluntarily from a container of water. Therefore, water must be supplied by droplet or by mist-gun application onto foliage. Reptiles can then lap up moisture as they would following rainfall. Lizards especially may need this means of providing water.
- Foods should be mixed thoroughly to prevent finicky eaters from refusing certain foods or ingredients.
- Young animals should be fed twice a day.
- Anorexia in reptiles is often the result of too frequent handling and/or an improper environmental temperature.
- Some variation between day and night is desirable. Most reptiles can be kept at day temperatures between 26 and 32°C (79 to 90°F) and night temperatures between 22 to 28°C (72 to 82°F). To allow for optimal thermoregulation, a thermal gradient should always be provided within the same enclosure with a cooler area at background temperature (night temperatures) and a hot spot (day temperatures).

- The resting energy requirement (RER) of reptiles depends on body temperature. At a mean core temperature of 37°C (98.6°F) the RER is 5 to 10 kcal/kg$^{0.75}$ (21 to 42 kJ/kg$^{0.75}$).

Chelonians (turtles and tortoises)

- Complete commercial foods manufactured for turtles and tortoises are the safest and easiest way for lay people to feed their pets. Dry dog food or monkey biscuits can be given temporarily to omnivorous and herbivorous tortoises until more specialized help is found.

Tortoises

- Terrestrial tortoises are primarily herbivorous and have adapted to eating plant material such as fresh leafy vegetables, fruits and nontoxic flowers.
- Adults tortoises may eat about 5% of their body weight daily.
- All tortoises eat during the day.
- Young animals should be fed twice a day.
- The appetite of tortoises can be influenced by the color, odor and movements of the prey.
- As a general rule, tortoises should obtain most of their calories from carbohydrate sources (75%), with about 12.5% coming from protein and about 12.5% from fat.
- Food for herbivorous tortoises should contain at least 12% crude fiber, with the ideal range being 20 to 30%. They should receive a variety of fruits and vegetables, supplemented with multivitamins and minerals. If no forage is available, fiber sources should be added, such as chopped alfalfa hay, ground alfalfa pellets or rabbit pellets.
- Most tortoises have to submerge their head to drink. They can also obtain some water from dew or raindrops on plants.
- Ideally, multiple water stations should be provided for tortoises.

Turtles and terrapins

- Aquatic turtles should be fed in water.
- Most fresh water turtles and terrapins are omnivorous, and will usually consume earthworms, crustaceans, small fish, mouse pups, meat and commercially prepared cat foods, as well as algae and green leafy vegetables, such as romaine lettuce, watercress, pond weeds, etc.
- Some aquatic turtles are carnivorous and eat fish as well as other vertebrate and invertebrate prey.

Table S-2. Feeding recommendations for selected tortoises and turtles.

Species (common names)	Habitats	Adult sizes	Eating habits
Terrestrial tortoises			
Geochelone carbonaria (redfoot tortoise)	South American savannas	na	Herbivorous with supplemental invertebrates and meats. Redfoot tortoises like more fruit than most other species of tortoises.
Geochelone denticulata (yellowfoot tortoise)	South American rain forest	Body weight: 9-11.5 kg	Herbivorous with supplemental invertebrates and meats. Yellowfoot tortoises like more fruit than most other species of tortoises.
*Testudo graeca** (Greek spur-thighed tortoise)	Northern Africa, Middle East, Southern Europe	Length: 15-20 cm	Herbivorous
*Testudo hermanni** (Hermann's tortoise)	Southern Europe	Length: 13-30 cm	Herbivorous
Testudo horsefieldi (Russian tortoise)	European grasslands	na	Herbivorous with supplemental invertebrates and meats. Russian tortoises should receive more dark leafy greens than fruit.
Aquatic turtles			
*Chelus fimbriatus** (Matamata)	Guinea and the Amazon	na	Provide live fish
Chelydra serpentina (common snapping turtle)	United States	Length: 38-50 cm Body weight: 25 kg	Carnivorous
Emys orbicularis (European fresh water turtle)	Southern Europe, France, Northern Africa	Length: 13-18 cm	Carnivorous, has to be fed in water
Graptemys kohni (map turtle)	Southeast United States	Length: 25 cm	Carnivorous (invertebrates, fish and meats) supplemented with pond weeds, algae or other greens (e.g., watercress). Mollusks and insects are indispensable for youngsters.

(Continued on next page.)

Table S-2. Feeding recommendations for selected tortoises and turtles. (Continued from previous page.)

Species (common names)	Habitats	Adult sizes	Eating habits
Terrestrial tortoises			
Kinosternon leucostomum spurelli	United States	na	Carnivorous (mollusks and insects)
Mauremys leprosa	Southern Europe, Northern Africa	Length: 20 cm	Carnivorous
Pseudemys scripta elegans (Florida turtle or cooters)	Southeastern United States, Mexico	na	Adults are omnivores that eat invertebrates, fish and meats and pond weeds, algae and other greens (e.g., watercress). Juveniles are carnivorous.
Semi-aquatic turtles			
Terrapene carolina (American box turtle)	United States, Mexico	Length: 15-25 cm	Omnivorous: diet includes invertebrates (e.g., earthworms and slugs), meat, pond weeds and algae, with supplemental fish. Access to water is essential, despite a more terrestrial lifestyle.

Key: na = not available.
*Protected species. Other species listed above may also be protected; however, information was not available.

Lizards

- Lizards may be insectivores, carnivores or herbivores. Dry dog food can be fed temporarily to all three types until more specialized help is found.
- Insectivorous lizards accept crickets and mealworm larvae.
- Herbivorous lizards eat fruits, vegetables supplemented with multivitamins and minerals and fiber sources, such as chopped alfalfa or ground alfalfa pellets.
- Carnivorous lizards accept freshly killed vertebrate prey such as mice, rats and chicks.

Snakes

- The daily energy requirement (DER) of captive snakes at 28°C (82.4°F) is about 11 kcal/kg$^{0.75}$ (45 kJ/kg$^{0.75}$).
- All snakes are carnivorous and eat live vertebrate prey including fish, amphibians and earthworms. They also accept freshly killed vertebrate prey such as mice, rats and chicks. Most snakes will accept dead rodents, but some only eat moving (live) food.
- Care must be taken when live food is offered because some rodents may attack snakes. Therefore, snakes should not be left unattended with aggressive live prey (e.g., mice, rats).
- A moist cat or dog food can be a good alternative for short-term feeding.

Table S-3. Guaranteed analyses of selected commercial foods for reptiles.*

	Moisture	Protein	Fat	Fiber
Tortoises				
Kaytee Products Kaytee Land Turtle & Tortoise Food	12	14	4	10
Mazuri Purina Mills 5M21 Mazuri Tortoise Diet	na	15	3	18
Aquatic turtles				
Kaytee Products Kaytee Aquatic Turtle Food	12	35	10	5
Reliable Protein Products Reptile-Fare	45	20	6	5
Tetra Werke Tetra Young Turtle Food (Repto Min "New")	9	38	1.5	2
Iguanas and plant-eating lizards				
Kaytee Products Kaytee Adult Iguana	12	12.5	3	12
Kaytee Products Kaytee Juvenile Iguana	12	19	3	10
Mazuri Purina Mills 5M35 Mazuri Iguana Diet	na	25	2.5	18
Premium Nutritional Products ZuPreem Iguana Diet	78	5	0.5	3.5
Carnivorous lizards and snakes				
Premium Nutritional Products ZuPreem Monitor and Tegu Diet	78	10	6	1
Other				
Mazuri Purina Mills 5175 Mazuri Alligator Diet	na	45	8	3
Tetra Werke Tetra Repto Min	8	38	5	2
Tetra Werke Tetra Terra Fauna Repto Life	6	27	5.5	1

Key: na = not available.
*Moisture = maximum % moisture, protein = minimum % crude protein, fat = minimum % crude fat, fiber = maximum % crude fiber.

Table S-4. Guaranteed analyses of selected commercial supplements for reptiles.*

	Ca (%)	P (%)	Mg (%)	Vitamin A (IU)	Vitamin D (IU)	Vitamin E (mg)	Pantothenic acid (mg)	Menadione (mg)	Vitamin C (mg)	Zn (mg)	Cu (mg)	Mn (mg)	I (mg)
Tetra Werke Tetra Terra Fauna Reptical Concentrated Reptile Supplement	32-37	6.5	na	25,680	3,850	11	20	10	na	na	na	na	na
Tetra Werke Tetra Terra Fauna Reptovit or Tetra Reptovit Land Reptiles	9.1	8.3	1.1	50,000	1,250	110	na	na	na	300	70	30	na
Tetra Werke Tetra Repto Fauna Reptisol Herbivore Reptiles	na	na	na	100,000	8,000	na	110	na	1,000	na	na	na	na
Tetra Werke Tetra Terra Fauna Vitalife	4.6-4.9	0.8	0.02	220,264	11,454	1,057	na	na	396	76	28	70	8

Key: Ca = calcium, P = phosphorus, Mg = magnesium, Zn = zinc, Cu = copper, Mn = manganese, I = iodine.
*Calcium, phosphorus and magnesium are guaranteed percentages, vitamins and trace elements are minimum amounts per 100 g.

Tube feeding reptiles
Herbivorous tortoises and iguanas
- Herbivorous tortoises and iguanas can be tube fed small quantities of puréed or blenderized fresh carrots, Swiss chard, peas, frozen-thawed mixed vegetables, creamed corn or soaked alfalfa pellets milled for rabbits or guinea pigs. Freshly blended apples or strained apple sauce also may be fed.
- Canned herbivore foods such as ZuPreem Iguana Diet[a] can be used after blenderizing with water.

Omnivorous and carnivorous reptiles
Tube feed twice or more weekly using a formula that contains sufficient animal protein, such as:
- Canned food for carnivorous reptiles such as ZuPreem Monitor and Tegu Diet[a].
- Liquid foods for dogs or cats.
- Canned dog or cat food.
- Gamebird chow or strained infant meat mixtures that are easy to blenderize.

Canned foods and infant meat mixtures should be blenderized with water to make a slurry that is passed through a strainer.

III. Manufacturers of commercial foods for amphibians and reptiles

Kaytee Products, Inc.
P.O. Box 230
Chilton, WI 53014
800-KAYTEE-1 (800-529-8331)
Fax: 414-849-4734

Lafeber Company
24981 N. 1400 East Road
Cornell, IL 61319
800-842-6445 or 815-358-2301 (USA)
800-345-6596 (Canada)
Fax: 800-932-3341 or 815-358-2352 (USA)

Mazuri Purina Mills, Inc.
P.O. Box 66812
St. Louis, MO 63166-6812
800-227-8941 or 314-768-4592
Fax: 314-768-4644

Premium Nutritional Products, Inc.
P.O. Box 2094
Mission, KS 66202
800-345-4767
Fax: 913-722-6226

Reliable Protein Products, Inc.
44-489 Town Center Way, Suite D, PMB 505
Palm Desert, CA 92260
760-321-7533
Fax: 760-321-0395

Tetra Werke, GmbH
Dr. rer. nat. Ulrich Baensch GmbH
Herrenteich 78, D-49324 Melle (Germany)
P.O. Box 1580, D-49304 Melle (Germany)
5422-105.273
Fax: 5422-105.429.85

ENDNOTES

a.   Premium Nutritional Products, Inc., Mission, KS, USA.

b.   Mazuri Purina Mills, St. Louis, MO, USA.

c.   Lafeber Company, Cornell, IL, USA.

d.   Tetra Werke, GmbH, Melle, Germany.

BIBLIOGRAPHY

1.   Allen ME, Ullrey DE. Nutritional husbandry of amphibians and reptiles. In: Proceedings. Eastern States Veterinary Conference, Orlando, FL, 1991: 607-608.

2.   Campbell TW. Husbandry concerns for pet reptiles. Exotic Animals: A Veterinary Handbook. Trenton, NJ: Veterinary Learning Systems, 1995; 144-146.

3.   Carpenter JW, Mashima TY, Rupiper DJ. Exotic Animal Formulary. Manhattan, KS: Graystone Publications, 1996; 31-89, 285-286.

4.   Cavignaux R. Les principales tortues rencontrées en consultation. Le Point Vétérinaire 1996; 28: 41-42.

5.   Cooper JE. Feeding exotic and pocket pets. Journal of Small Animal Practice 1990; 31: 482-488.

6.   Crawshaw GJ. Amphibian medicine. In: Kirk RW, Bonagura JD, eds. Current Veterinary Therapy XI. Philadelphia, PA: WB Saunders Co, 1992; 1219-1230.

7.   Donoghue S, Langenberg J. Nutrition. In: Mader DR, ed. Reptilian Medicine and Surgery. Philadelphia, PA: WB Saunders Co, 1996; 148-174.

8.   Firmin Y. La consultation des tortues. Le Point Vétérinaire 1996; 28 (6/7): 31-40.

9.   Fowler ME. Care of orphaned wild animals. Veterinary Clinics of North America: Small Animal Practice 1979; 9: 447-471.

10. Frye FL. Reptile medicine and husbandry. Veterinary Clinics of North America: Small Animal Practice 1979; 9: 415-428.

11. Jacobson ER. Snakes. Veterinary Clinics of North America: Small Animal Practice 1993; 23: 1179-1212.

12. Kirkwood JK. Energy requirements for maintenance and growth of wild mammals, birds and reptiles. Journal of Nutrition 1991; 121: S29-S34.

13. Mautino M, Page CD. Biology and medicine of turtles and tortoises. Veterinary Clinics of North America: Small Animal Practice 1993; 23: 1251-1270.

14. Page CD, Mautino M. Clinical management of tortoises. In: Proceedings. Eastern States Veterinary Conference, Orlando, FL, 1991: 604-606.

15. Pokras M, Porter S. An introduction to nonavian wildlife emergencies. Veterinary Clinics of North America: Small Animal Practice 1994; 24: 187-206.

16. Porter SL. Raising orphan wildlife. In: Proceedings. North American Veterinary Conference, Orlando, FL, 1993: 813-815.

17. Porter SL. Wildlife medicine I and II. In: Proceedings. North American Veterinary Conference, Orlando, FL, 1993: 808-812.

18. Raphael BL. Amphibians. Veterinary Clinics of North America: Small Animal Practice 1993; 23: 1271-1286.

19. Sedgewick CJ. Allometric scaling and emergency care: The importance of body size. In: Fowler ME, ed. Zoo & Wild Animal Medicine: Current Therapy 3. Philadelphia, PA: WB Saunders Co, 1993; 34-37.

20. Wallach JD. The mechanics of nutrition of exotic pets. Veterinary Clinics of North America: Small Animal Practice 1979; 9: 405-414.

21. Walshaw SO. Reptilian management and medical care. In: Exotic Animals: A Veterinary Handbook. Trenton, NJ: Veterinary Learning Systems, 1995; 147-154.

22. Wright KM. Husbandry and nutrition of tortoises. In: Proceedings. North American Veterinary Conference, Orlando, FL, 1997; 767-769.

Appendix T
Nutrient Content of Human Foods

Introduction
Bibliography

Introduction

This appendix can be used to quickly assess or formulate homemade foods. The nutrient contents listed below are averages from different sources. In addition, the nutrient content of a food may vary from day to day and in different regions. Differences may be relatively large due to variation in the type of ground a crop is grown in, the method of analysis, the harvest time and methods of preparation and storage time. Unless the food is a specific brand, the composition of the same food items (e.g., vegetables, meats and pastas) is very similar in European and North American references.

Table T-1. Nutrient content of common protein sources.*

	Moisture	ME** (kcal)	(kJ)	Protein	Fat	NFE	Fiber	Ca	P	Na	K	Mg	Serving size***
Meats													
Chicken													
Fryers, raw meat, without skin	77.2	107	448	19.3	2.7	0.0	0.0	0.01	0.20	0.06	0.29	na	na
Fryers, light meat, raw, without skin	77.2	101	423	20.5	1.5	0.0	0.0	0.01	0.22	0.05	0.32	0.02	na
Fryers, dark meat, raw, without skin	77.3	112	469	18.1	3.8	0.0	0.0	0.01	0.19	0.07	0.25	na	na
Fryers, raw giblets	78.4	103	431	17.5	3.1	0.1	0.0	0.01	0.22	na	na	na	na
Fryers, raw wings	73.5	146	611	18.5	7.4	0.0	0.0	0.01	0.20	na	na	na	na
Fryers, fried wings	52.6	268	1,121	29.0	14.8	2.7	0.0	0.01	0.24	na	na	na	na
Hens and cocks, light meat, raw, without skin	71.7	133	556	23.4	3.7	0.0	0.0	0.01	0.22	0.05	0.32	0.03	na
Hens and cocks, dark meat, raw, without skin	71.2	154	644	20.2	7.5	0.0	0.0	0.01	0.19	0.07	0.25	0.02	na
Hens and cocks, raw giblets	66.8	191	799	18.6	11.6	1.8	0.0	0.02	0.21	na	na	na	na
Turkey													
Light meat, raw, without skin	73.0	116	485	24.6	1.2	0.0	0.0	na	na	0.05	0.32	na	na
Dark meat, raw, without skin	73.6	128	536	20.9	4.3	0.0	0.0	na	na	0.08	0.31	na	na
Raw, total edible	64.2	218	912	20.1	14.7	0.0	0.0	na	na	na	na	na	na
Duck													
Domesticated, raw meat, without skin	68.8	165	690	21.4	8.2	0.0	0.0	0.01	0.29	0.07	0.29	na	na
Raw, total edible	54.3	326	1,364	16.0	28.6	0.0	0.0	0.01	0.18	na	na	na	na
Beef													
Ground beef, raw, lean	68.3	179	749	20.7	10.0	0.0	0.0	0.01	0.19	na	na	0.02	na
Raw, regular	60.2	268	1,121	17.9	21.2	0.0	0.0	0.01	0.16	na	0.24	0.02	na
Chuck cuts, raw, lean	70.3	158	661	21.3	7.4	0.0	0.0	0.01	0.21	na	na	0.02	na
Raw, total edible	60.8	257	1,075	18.7	19.6	0.0	0.0	0.01	0.19	na	na	0.02	na
Lamb													
Composite of cuts, raw, lean	62.5	247	1,033	16.8	19.4	0.0	0.0	0.01	0.15	na	na	0.02	na
Raw, regular	61.0	263	1,100	16.5	21.3	0.0	0.0	0.01	0.15	na	na	0.02	na
Raw, fat	56.3	310	1,297	15.4	27.1	0.0	0.0	0.01	0.14	na	na	na	na
Pork													
Composite of cuts, total edible raw, fat class (28% fat, 72% lean)	52.6	346	1,448	14.6	31.4	1.5	0.0	0.01	0.16	na	na	na	na
Composite of cuts, total edible raw, medium fat class (23% fat, 77% lean)	56.3	308	1,289	15.7	26.7	0.0	0.0	0.01	0.18	na	na	0.02	na
Composite of cuts, total edible raw, thin class (19% fat, 81% lean)	59.5	276	1,155	16.7	22.7	0.0	0.0	0.01	0.19	na	na	na	na
Composite of cuts, lean raw, average	69.0	174	728	19.1	10.2	0.0	0.0	0.01	0.22	na	na	0.02	na
Horse													
Raw, lean meat	74.0	135	565	19.0	4.5	0.0	0.0	0.01	0.13	0.04	0.29	0.02	na
Rabbit													
Raw, meat	70.0	162	678	21.0	8.0	0.0	0.0	0.02	0.35	0.04	0.39	na	na
Venison													
Raw, lean meat	74.0	126	527	21.0	4.0	0.0	0.0	0.01	0.25	na	na	na	na
Fish													
Cod, raw	81.2	78	326	17.6	0.3	0.0	0.0	0.01	0.19	0.07†	0.38	0.03	na
Halibut, raw	76.5	100	418	20.9	1.2	0.0	0.0	0.01	0.21	0.05††	0.45	0.02	na
Mackerel, raw (average)	68.5	175	732	20.5	9.8	0.0	0.0	0.01	0.26	na	na	0.03	na
Salmon, raw	63.6	217	908	22.5	13.4	0.0	0.0	0.08	0.19	na	na	na	na
Sardines, raw	70.7	160	669	19.2	8.6	0.0	0.0	0.03	0.22	na	na	na	na

(Continued on next page.)

Table T-1. Nutrient content of common protein sources.* (Continued from previous page.)

	Moisture	ME** (kcal)	(kJ)	Protein	Fat	NFE	Fiber	Ca	P	Na	K	Mg	Serving size***
Fish (continued)													
Sardines, in oil (solids and liquid)	50.6	311	1,301	20.6	24.4	0.6	0.0	0.35	0.43	0.51	0.56	na	na
Trout, raw	66.3	195	816	21.5	11.4	0.0	0.0	na	na	na	na	na	na
Tuna, raw	71.0	139	582	25.0	3.6	0.0	0.0	na	na	0.04††	na	na	na
Shrimp, raw	78.2	91	381	18.1	0.8	1.5	0.0	0.06	0.17	0.14	0.22	na	na
Other animal products													
Kidneys													
Beef, raw	75.9	130	544	15.4	6.7	0.9	0.0	0.01	0.22	0.18	0.23	na	na
Calf, raw	77.4	113	473	16.6	4.6	0.1	0.0	na	na	na	na	na	na
Pork, raw	77.8	106	444	16.3	3.6	1.1	0.0	0.01	0.22	0.12	0.18	na	na
Lamb, raw	77.7	105	439	16.8	3.3	0.9	0.0	0.01	0.22	0.20	0.23	na	na
Heart													
Beef, raw, lean	77.5	108	452	17.1	3.6	0.7	0.0	0.05	0.20	0.09	0.19	0.02	na
Calf, raw	76.2	124	519	15.0	5.9	1.8	0.0	0.003	0.16	0.09	0.21	na	na
Pork, raw	77.4	113	473	16.8	4.4	0.4	0.0	0.003	0.13	0.05	0.11	na	na
Lamb, raw	71.6	162	678	16.8	9.6	1.0	0.0	0.011	0.25	na	0.16	na	na
Chicken, raw	74.3	134	561	18.6	6.0	0.1	0.0	0.004	0.16	0.08	0.16	na	na
Turkey, raw	71.3	171	715	16.2	11.2	0.2	0.0	na	na	0.07	0.24	na	na
Liver													
Beef, raw	69.7	140	586	19.9	3.8	5.3	0.0	0.01	0.35	0.14	0.28	0.01	na
Calf, raw	70.7	140	586	19.2	4.7	4.1	0.0	0.01	0.33	0.07	0.28	0.02	na
Lamb, raw	70.8	136	569	21.0	3.9	2.9	0.0	0.01	0.35	0.05	0.20	0.01	na
Pork, raw	71.6	131	548	20.6	3.7	2.6	0.0	0.01	0.36	0.07	0.26	0.02	na
Chicken, raw	72.2	129	540	19.7	3.7	2.9	0.0	0.01	0.24	0.07	0.17	na	na
Turkey, raw	70.4	138	577	21.2	4.0	2.9	0.0	na	na	0.06	0.16	na	na
Goose, raw	66.9	182	761	16.5	10.0	5.4	0.0	na	na	0.14	0.23	na	na
Rumen													
Beef, cleaned	80.0	121	506	12.0	7.0	0.5	0.0	0.02	0.04	0.02	0.04	0.02	na
Beef, uncleaned	72.0	147	615	20.0	5.0	0.6	1.1	0.12	0.13	0.05	0.10	0.04	na
Dairy and egg products													
Milk													
Whole	87.4	65	272	3.5	3.5	4.9	0.0	0.12	0.09	0.05	0.14	0.01	244 g/8-oz cup
Skim	90.5	36	151	3.6	0.1	5.1	0.0	0.12	0.10	0.05	0.15	0.01	245 g/8-oz cup
Dried, whole	2.0	502	2,100	26.4	27.5	38.2	0.0	0.91	0.71	0.41	1.33	0.10	na
Dried, nonfat	3.0	363	1,519	35.9	0.8	52.3	0.0	1.31	1.02	0.53	1.75	0.14	68 g/8-oz cup
Canned, evaporated, unsweetened	73.8	137	573	7.0	7.9	9.7	0.0	0.25	0.21	0.12	0.30	0.03	249 g/8-oz cup
Whey, dried	4.5	349	1,460	12.9	1.1	73.5	0.0	0.65	0.59	na	na	na	na
Buttermilk													
Fluid, cultured (from skim milk)	90.5	36	151	3.6	0.1	5.1	0.0	0.12	0.10	0.13	0.14	0.01	245 g/8-oz cup
Dried	2.8	387	1,619	34.3	5.3	50.0	0.0	1.25	0.97	0.51	1.61	na	7 g/Tbs
Yogurt													
From whole milk	88.0	62	259	3.0	3.4	4.9	0.0	0.11	0.09	0.05	0.13	na	227 g/8-oz cup
From partially skimmed milk	89.0	50	209	3.4	1.7	5.2	0.0	0.12	0.09	0.05	0.14	na	na
Cottage cheese													
Creamed	78.9	103	431	12.5	4.5	2.7	0.0	0.06	0.13	0.40	0.08	0.01	210 g/8-oz cup‡
Low fat (1% fat)	82.5	73	305	12.4	1.0	27.4	0.0	0.06	0.13	0.41	0.08	0.01	226 g/8-oz cup
Low fat (2% fat)	79.3	90	377	13.8	2.0	3.6	0.0	0.07	0.15	0.41	0.10	0.01	226 g/8-oz cup

(Continued on next page.)

Table T-1. Nutrient content of common protein sources.* (Continued from previous page.)

	Moisture	ME** (kcal)	(kJ)	Protein	Fat	NFE	Fiber	Ca	P	Na	K	Mg	Serving size***
Cheeses													
Cheddar (American cheese)	37.0	398	1,665	25.0	32.2	2.1	0.0	0.75	0.48	0.70	0.08	0.05	1 in³ = 17 g
Gouda	42.0	346	1,448	24.9	27.4	0.0	0.0	0.92	0.52	0.60	0.12	0.03	na
Camembert (US)	52.2	299	1,251	17.5	24.7	1.8	0.0	0.11	0.18	na	0.11	na	na
Camembert (France)	51.0	284	1,188	25.0	20.0	1.0	0.0	0.60	0.30	0.79	0.11	na	na
Parmesan	29.5	393	1,644	38.0	26.0	2.3	0.0	1.20	0.90	0.90	0.14	0.05	na
Eggs													
Whole	73.7	163	682	12.9	11.5	0.9	0.0	0.05	0.21	0.12	0.13	0.01	50 g/large egg
White	87.6	51	213	10.9	tr	0.8	0.0	0.01	0.02	0.15	0.14	0.01	33 g/egg
Dried whole	4.1	592	2,477	47.0	41.2	4.1	0.0	0.19	0.80	0.43	0.46	0.04	5 g/Tbs
Vegetables													
Soy													
Soybean flour, high fat	8.0	380	1,590	41.2	12.1	31.1	2.2	0.24	0.65	tr	1.78	0.27	85 g/8-oz cup
Soybean flour, low fat	8.0	356	1,490	43.4	6.7	34.1	2.5	0.26	0.63	tr	1.86	0.29	88 g/8-oz cup
Soybean milk, liquid	92.4	33.0	138	3.4	1.5	2.2	0.0	0.02	0.05	0.01	0.14	0.02	240 g/8-oz cup
Soybean milk, powder	4.2	429	1,795	41.8	20.3	27.8	0.2	0.28	na	na	na	na	na
Others													
Baker's yeast	71.0	111	464	16.0	1.2	9.0	0.3	0.03	0.61	0.03	0.65	0.06	na

Key: ME = metabolizable energy, kcal = kilocalories, kJ = kilojoules, NFE = nitrogen-free extract, Ca = calcium, P = phosphorus, Na = sodium, K = potassium, Mg = magnesium, tr = trace, g = grams, Tbs = tablespoon (15 ml), in³ = cubic inches, na = not available.

*All nutrients are expressed on a percent as fed or as is basis unless otherwise noted.
**Metabolizable energy per 100 g as fed.
***g/serving.
†Some fish are treated with brine, in which case the sodium content is markedly increased. Sodium levels of cod treated with brine may approach 0.26%.
††Some fish are treated with brine, in which case the sodium content is markedly increased. Sodium levels of halibut treated with brine may approach 0.36%.
†††Some fish are treated with brine, in which case the sodium content is markedly increased. Sodium levels of tuna treated with brine may approach 0.44%.
‡One rounded tablespoon = 28 g.

Table T-2. Essential amino acid content of common protein sources.*

	Protein	Arg	Isoleu	Leu	Lys	Met	Cys	Phe	His	Thr	Trp	Val
Meats and fish												
Beef	20	1.34	1.02	1.60	1.82	0.54	0.26	0.90	0.60	0.92	0.26	1.06
Chicken	21	1.30	0.97	1.58	1.89	0.57	0.27	0.95	0.40	0.88	0.23	1.01
Lamb	18	1.10	0.83	1.30	1.77	0.47	0.23	0.68	0.40	1.13	0.23	0.86
Pork	15	0.89	0.68	1.05	1.44	0.41	0.20	0.57	0.50	0.65	0.17	0.72
Cod, raw	17.6	1.07	0.82	1.45	1.46	0.53	0.19	0.70	0.52	0.78	0.20	0.92
Halibut, raw	20.9	1.29	0.96	1.69	1.91	0.62	0.22	0.81	0.61	0.91	0.23	1.07
Tuna, raw	25	1.40	1.08	1.90	2.14	0.69	0.25	0.91	0.69	1.02	0.26	1.20
Other animal products												
Beef stomach	15	1.05	0.63	1.01	1.20	0.36	0.20	0.57	0.40	0.65	0.20	0.75
Heart	17	1.09	0.88	1.55	1.46	0.37	0.27	0.78	0.40	0.78	0.22	0.95
Kidney	16	0.90	0.67	1.25	1.31	0.34	0.22	0.80	0.40	0.67	0.21	0.90
Liver	20	1.06	0.86	1.56	1.70	0.48	0.28	1.00	0.50	0.86	0.26	1.16
Dairy and egg products												
Casein	84.4	3.50	5.75	8.84	7.17	2.82	0.31	4.83	2.60	3.93	1.08	6.73
Cottage cheese												
Creamed	12.5	0.57	0.73	1.28	1.0	0.38	0.12	0.67	0.41	0.55	0.14	0.77
1% fat	12.4	0.56	0.73	1.27	1.0	0.37	0.11	0.67	0.41	0.55	0.14	0.77
2% fat	13.8	0.63	0.81	1.41	1.11	0.41	0.13	0.74	0.46	0.61	0.15	0.85
Curd (skim)	36	1.28	2.24	3.43	2.72	0.86	0.31	1.70	0.90	1.61	0.49	2.40
Egg white	11	0.59	0.62	0.90	0.64	0.39	0.20	0.64	0.24	0.53	0.20	0.86
Egg yolk	16	1.15	0.93	1.36	1.15	0.42	0.26	0.64	0.36	0.90	0.29	1.10
Skim dry milk	36	1.28	2.24	3.43	2.72	0.86	0.31	1.70	0.90	1.61	0.49	2.40
Whole egg	13	0.79	0.73	1.08	0.81	0.42	0.23	0.66	0.26	0.66	0.23	0.98
Whole egg, dried	48	3.02	3.06	4.05	2.94	1.44	1.07	2.66	1.10	2.29	0.76	3.42
Whole milk	3.5	0.14	0.2	0.36	0.29	0.10	0.04	0.19	0.09	0.18	0.05	0.26
Vegetables												
Soybean meal with hulls	44	3.08	2.34	3.46	2.80	0.61	0.67	2.17	1.13	1.74	0.61	2.16
Soybean meal without hulls	50	3.41	2.43	3.73	3.09	0.69	0.74	2.46	1.22	1.92	0.67	2.50
Soybeans	34	2.58	1.95	3.11	2.08	0.64	0.65	2.15	0.91	1.63	0.49	1.93
Others												
Baker's yeast	16	0.73	0.89	1.30	1.23	0.29	0.14	0.77	0.40	0.82	0.15	1.0

Key: Arg = arginine, Isoleu = isoleucine, Leu = leucine, Lys = lysine, Met = methionine, Cys = cysteine, Phe = phenylalanine, His = histidine, Thr = threonine, Trp = tryptophan, Val = valine.
*Protein and amino acids are expressed in percent as fed or as is. Amino acids are expressed as percent of the food item not as percent of protein.

Table T-3. Nutrient content of common fat sources.*

	Moisture	ME** (kcal)	(kJ)	Protein	Fat	NFE	Fiber	Ca	P	Na	K	Mg	Serving size***
Vegetable sources													
Avocado	74.0	167	699	2.1	16.4	4.7	1.6	0.01	0.04	0.0	0.60	na	173 g/medium size
Flaxseed	7.2	496	2,075	19.8	38.7	17.2	14.4	0.25	0.55	na	0.70	0.35	
Margarine	15.5	720	3,012	0.6	81.0	0.4	0.0	0.02	0.02	0.99†	0.02†	na	16 g/Tbs
Peanut butter	1.7	589	2,464	25.2	50.6	187.0	1.8	0.06	0.38	0.61	0.63	0.17	na
Peanuts (roasted)	1.8	582	2,435	26.2	48.7	17.9	2.7	0.07	0.41	0.01	0.70	0.18	na
Pecans	3.4	687	2,874	9.2	71.2	12.3	2.3	0.07	0.19	tr	0.60	0.14	na
Animal sources													
Butter	15.5	716	2,996	0.6	81	0.4	0.0	0.02	0.02	0.99††	0.02	0.002	na
Beef, separable fat	15.2	736	3,079	5.8	78.8	0.0	0.0	0.003	0.05	na	na	na	na
Cheddar cheese	37.0	398	1,665	25.0	32.2	2.1	0.0	0.75	0.48	0.70	0.08	0.05	na
Chicken, fryers, raw skin	66.3	223	933	16.1	17.1	0.0	0.0	0.01	0.17	na	na	na	na
Chicken, fryers, fried skin	32.5	419	1,753	28.3	28.9	9.1	0.0	0.01	0.19	na	na	na	na
Cream, heavy whipping	56.6	352	1,473	2.2	37.6	3.1	0.0	0.08	0.06	0.03	0.09	0.01	na
Egg yolk, fresh	51.1	348	1,456	16.0	30.6	0.6	0.0	0.14	0.57	0.05	0.10	1.5	17 g/egg
Pork, separable fat	12.4	770	3,222	3.5	83.7	0.0	0.0	0.002	0.01	0.07	0.28	na	na
Sardines, canned, solids and liquid	50.6	311	1,301	20.6	24.4	0.6	0.0	0.35	0.43	0.51	0.56	na	na
Tuna, canned, solids and liquid	52.6	288	1,205	24.2	20.5	0.0	0.0	0.01	0.29	0.80	0.30	na	na
Whole milk	87.4	65	272	3.5	3.5	4.9	0.0	0.12	0.09	0.05	0.14	0.01	na

Key: ME = metabolizable energy, kcal = kilocalories, kJ = kilojoules, NFE = nitrogen-free extract, Ca = calcium, P = phosphorus, Na = sodium, K = potassium, Mg = magnesium, tr = trace, g = grams, Tbs = tablespoons (15 ml), na = not available.
*All nutrients are expressed on a percent as fed or as is basis unless otherwise noted.
**Metabolizable energy/100 g as is.
***g/serving.
†Values apply to salted margarine. Unsalted margarine contains less than 0.01% of either sodium or potassium.
††Values apply to salted butter. Unsalted butter contains about 0.02% sodium, whereas some salted butter may contain up to 1.5% sodium.

Table T-4. Fat and fatty acid composition of common fat sources.

	ME* per 100 g		Total fat**	Linoleic acid***	Arachidonic acid***	α-linolenic acid***	MCT***	Other***
	(kcal)	(kJ)	(%)	(%)	(%)	(%)	(%)	
Fats								
Beef tallow†	870	3,640	97	2	0.8	0.6	na	na
Beef, separable fat, raw	736	3,079	79.0	2.2	na	na	na	na
Butter†	716	2,996	81.0	2.5	0.95	0.7	5.7	na
Chicken fat	900	3,766	100	19	0.75	1.3	1	na
Lard†	902	3,774	100	10	1.7	1	na	na
Margarine, hydrogenated††	720	3,012	81	14	na	na	1	na
Margarine (liquid oil)	720	3,012	81	29	na	na	na	na
Mutton fat	856	3,582	97	4	na	1.3	na	na
Pork, separable fat, raw	770	3,222	83.7	8	na	na	na	n-6/n-3 ratio: 4 to 1 in muscle fat
Oils†††								
Black currant seed oil	900	3,766	100	48	na	13	na	Total n-6: 77-87%, n-6/n-3 ratio: 5 to 1
Canola oil (rapeseed oil)	900	3,766	100	14-22	na	7-10	na	n-6/n-3 ratio: 2.2 to 1
Coconut oil (coconut milk)	900	3,766	100	2	na	na	55	na
Corn oil	900	3,766	100	55	na	1	na	na
Cottonseed oil	900	3,766	100	53	na	0.5	na	na
Linseed (flax) oil	900	3,766	100	16	na	53	na	na
Menhaden (fish) oil	900	3,766	100	25	na	na	na	n-3: EPA 15%, DHA 9%
Oat oil	900	3,766	100	45	na	0.2	na	na
Olive oil	900	3,766	100	10	na	1	na	na
Palm oil	900	3,766	100	10	na	1	na	na
Palm kernel oil	900	3,766	100	2	na	≥50	na	na
Peanut oil	900	3,766	100	30	2.2	1.5	na	na
Rice bran oil	900	3,766	100	32	na	1.1	na	na
Safflower oil	900	3,766	100	76	na	0.5	na	na
Sesame seed oil	900	3,766	100	42	na	0.2	na	na
Soybean oil	900	3,766	100	54	na	7	na	n-6/n-3 ratio: 7.7 to 1
Soybean oil, hardened	900	3,766	100	26	na	na	na	na
Sunflower seed oil	900	3,766	100	66	na	0.5	na	na
Walnut oil	900	3,766	100	na	0.6	10	na	na
Wheat germ oil	900	3,766	100	na	na	7	na	na
Other fat sources								
Avocado	167	699	16.4	2	na	na	na	na
Cheddar cheese	398	1,665	32.2	1	na	0.4	na	na
Chicken, fryers, raw skin	223	933	17.1	3	na	na	na	na
Chicken, fryers, fried skin	419	1,753	28.9	5	na	na	na	na
Cream, heavy, whipping	352	1,473	37.6	1	na	na	na	na
Egg, yolk, fresh	348	1,456	30.6	2	0.15	2	na	na
Egg, whole, hard cooked	na	na	11.5	1	na	na	na	na
Flaxseed	496	2,075	38.7	5.6	na	19.4	na	Total n-6: 19.8
Peanut butter	589	2,464	50.6	14	na	na	na	na
Peanuts, roasted, shelled	582	2,435	48.7	14	na	na	na	na
Pecans, shelled	687	2,874	71.2	14	na	na	na	na
Sardines, in oil (solids and liquid)	311	1,301	24.4	na	na	na	na	na
Tuna, in oil (solids and liquid)	288	1,205	20.5	8	na	na	na	na
Whole milk‡	65	272	3.5	na	na	0.1	na	na

Key: ME = metabolizable energy, kcal = kilocalories, kJ = kilojoules, MCT = medium-chain triglycerides, na = not available, EPA = eicosapentaenoic acid, DHA = docosahexaenoic acid.
*Metabolizable energy/100 g as is.
**% fat expressed on an as fed or as is basis.
***% of total fatty acids.
†1 tablespoon = about 15 g.
††1 tablespoon = about 11 g.
†††1 tablespoon of most oils = about 14 g, which supplies about 125 kcal ME; 1 teaspoon = about 4.6 g, which supplies about 42 kcal.
‡1cup = 240 g.

Table T-5. Nutrient content of common carbohydrate and fiber sources.*

	Moisture	ME (kcal)	ME (kJ)	Protein	Fat	NFE	Fiber	Ca	P	Na	K	Mg	Serving size***
Vegetable sources													
Beans, common													
Canned, solids and liquid (red)	76.0	90	377	5.7	0.4	16.4	0.9	0.03	0.11	0.0	0.26	na	na
Raw, white or red (average)	11.1	338	1,414	14.6	1.5	61.0	4.2	0.13	0.41	0.02	1.06	0.16	na
Carrots													
Canned, solids and liquid	91.8	28	117	0.6	0.2	6.5	0.6	0.03	0.02	0.24	0.12	na	na
Canned, drained solids	91.2	30	126	0.8	0.3	6.7	0.8	0.03	0.02	0.24	0.12	na	155 g/8-oz cup
Fresh, raw	88.2	42	176	1.1	0.2	9.7	1.0	0.04	0.04	0.05	0.34	0.02	na
Green beans													
Canned, solids and liquid	92.0	21	88	1.0	0.1	4.2	0.6	0.03	0.02	0.24	na	na	na
Raw, fresh	89.0	39	163	2.4	0.2	7.0	1.4	0.07	0.04	0.0	0.26	0.03	na
Green peas													
Canned, solids and liquid	82.6	66	276	3.5	0.3	11.0	1.5	0.02	0.07	0.24	0.10	na	na
Canned, drained solids	77.0	88	368	4.7	0.4	14.5	2.3	0.03	0.08	0.24	0.10	0.02	170 g/8-oz cup
Raw	78.0	84	351	6.3	0.4	12.4	2.0	0.03	0.12	0.0	0.32	0.04	156 g/8-oz cup
Potatoes													
Boiled, after paring	82.8	65	272	1.9	0.1	14.0	0.5	0.01	0.04	0.0	0.29	na	na
Boiled, in skin	79.8	76	318	2.1	0.1	16.6	0.5	0.01	0.05	0.0	0.41	0.03	na
Flour	7.6	351	1,469	8.0	0.8	78.3	1.6	0.03	0.18	0.03	1.59	na	180 g/8-oz cup
French fried	44.7	274	1,146	4.3	13.2	35.0	1.0	0.02	0.11	0.01	0.85	na	na
Spinach													
Cooked, boiled, drained	92.0	23	96	3.0	0.3	3.0	0.6	0.09	0.04	0.05	0.32	na	180 g/8-oz cup
Raw	90.7	26	109	3.2	0.3	3.7	0.6	0.09	0.05	0.07	0.47	0.09	56 g/8-oz cup
Cereals and breads													
Bagels	29.1	296	1,238	10.9	2.5	56.2	na	0.04	0.07	0.36	0.07	0.02	55 g/bagel
Barley, pearled	11.1	349	1,460	8.2	1.0	78.3	0.5	0.02	0.19	0.0	0.16	0.04	na
Breads													
White	35.6	270	1,130	8.7	3.2	50.3	0.2	0.08	0.10	0.51	0.11	0.02	25 g/slice
Whole wheat	36.4	243	1,017	10.5	3.0	46.1	1.7	0.10	0.23	0.53	0.27	0.08	28 g/slice
Buckwheat													
Flour, light	12.0	347	1,452	6.4	1.2	79.0	0.5	0.01	0.09	na	0.32	0.05	98 g/8-oz cup
Whole grain	11.0	335	1,402	11.7	2.4	63.0	9.9	0.11	0.28	na	0.45	0.23	na
Corn, flour	12.0	368	1,540	7.8	2.6	76.1	0.7	0.01	0.16	tr	0.09	0.02	117 g/8-oz cup
Flakes (breakfast cereal)	3.0	393	1,644	7.4	0.5	85.8	2.5	0.01	0.05	0.30†	0.09	0.02	28 g/8-oz cup
Meal (whole ground)	12.0	362	1,515	9.0	3.4	74.5	1.0	0.02	0.22	tr	0.25	0.11	122 g/8-oz cup
Corn (maize)													
Corn starch	12.0	362	1,515	0.3	tr	87.5	0.1	0.0	0.0	0.0	0.0	0.0	na
Oats, whole grain	12.0	332	1,389	11.5	4.7	60.0	10.2	0.06	0.40	0.0	0.44	0.15	na
Oatmeal, cooked	86.5	55	230	2.0	1.0	9.5	0.2	0.01	0.06	0.22	0.06	na	250 g/8-oz cup
Oatmeal, dry	8.3	390	1,632	14.2	7.4	67.0	1.2	0.05	0.40	0.0	0.35	0.11	233 g/8-oz cup
Pastas													
Macaroni, spaghetti, cooked	63.6	148	619	5.0	0.5	30.0	0.1	0.01	0.07	0.0	0.08	0.02	na
Macaroni, spaghetti, dry	10.4	369	1,544	12.5	1.2	74.9	0.3	0.03	0.16	0.0	0.20	0.05	na

(Continued on next page.)

APPENDIX T

Table T-5. Nutrient content of common carbohydrate and fiber sources.* (Continued from previous page.)

	Moisture	ME** (kcal)	(kJ)	Protein	Fat	NFE	Fiber	Ca	P	Na	K	Mg	Serving size***
Rice													
Brown, raw	12.0	360	1,506	7.5	1.9	67.5	0.9	0.03	0.22	0.01	0.21	0.09	na
Brown, cooked, with salt	70.3	119	498	2.5	0.6	25.2	0.3	0.01	0.07	0.28	0.07	na	185 g/8-oz cup
Long grain, cooked with salt	73.4	106	444	2.1	0.1	23.2	0.1	0.02	0.06	0.36	0.04	0.01	na
Long grain, parboiled, dry	10.3	369	1,544	7.4	0.3	81.1	0.2	0.06	0.20	0.01	0.15	na	175 g/8-oz cup
White, cooked, with salt	72.6	109	456	2.0	0.1	24.1	0.1	0.04	0.10	0.37	0.03	na	112 g/8-oz cup
White, polished, raw	12.0	363	1,519	6.7	0.4	80.1	0.3	0.02	0.09	0.01	0.09	0.03	na
Rye													
Flour, light	11.0	357	1,494	9.4	1.0	77.5	0.4	0.02	0.19	na	0.20	0.07	102 g/8-oz cup
Whole grain	11.0	334	1,397	12.1	1.7	71.4	2.0	0.04	0.38	na	0.47	0.12	na
Wheat, whole grain	12.8	331	1,383	11.7	2.1	69.6	2.1	0.04	0.48	0.0	0.39	0.16	na
Cream of wheat (farina)													
Cooked	89.5	42	176	1.3	0.1	8.7	tr	0.0	0.01	0.14	0.01	0.0	235 g/8-oz cup
Dry	10.3	371	1,552	11.4	0.9	76.6	0.4	0.02	0.11	0.0	0.08	0.03	11 g/Tbs
Wheat bran	11.5	213	891	16.0	4.6	52.8	9.1	0.12	1.28	0.01	1.12	0.49	3.5 g/Tbs
Wheat flour (whole)	12.0	333	1,393	13.3	2.0	68.7	2.3	0.04	0.37	0.0	0.37	0.11	125 g/8-oz cup
Wheat germ	11.5	363	1,519	26.6	10.9	44.2	2.5	0.07	1.12	0.0	0.83	0.34	na
Fruits													
Apples													
Not pared	84.4	58	243	0.2	0.6	13.5	1.0	0.01	0.01	0.0	0.11	0.01	138 g/apple
Pared	85.1	54	226	0.2	0.3	13.5	0.6	0.01	0.01	0.0	0.11	0.01	128 g/apple
Apricots													
Canned, solids and liquid-juice pack	84.1	54	226	1.0	0.2	13.2	0.4	0.02	0.02	0.0	0.36	0.01	28 g/half
Dried	25	260	1,088	5.0	0.5	63.5	3.0	0.07	0.11	0.03	0.98	0.06	3.5 g/half
Raw	85.3	51	213	1.0	0.2	12.2	0.6	0.02	0.02	0.0	0.28	0.01	35 g/apricot
Bananas, raw	75.7	85	356	1.1	0.2	21.7	0.5	0.01	0.03	0.0	0.37	0.03	114 g/banana
Blackberries, raw	84.5	58	243	1.2	0.9	8.8	4.1	0.03	0.02	0.0	0.17	0.03	144 g/8-oz cup
Blueberries, raw	83.2	62	259	0.7	0.5	13.8	1.5	0.02	0.01	0.0	0.08	0.01	145 g/8-oz cup
Cherries													
Sour, raw	83.7	58	243	1.2	0.3	14.1	0.2	0.02	0.02	0.0	0.19	0.01	na
Sweet, raw	80.4	70	293	1.3	0.3	17.0	0.4	0.02	0.02	0.0	0.19	0.01	6.8 g/cherry
Dates, natural, dry	22.5	274	1,146	2.2	0.5	70.6	2.3	0.06	0.06	0.0	0.65	0.06	8.3 g/date
Figs													
Dried	23.0	274	1,146	4.3	1.3	63.5	5.6	0.13	0.08	0.03	0.64	0.07	18.7 g/fig
Raw	77.5	80	335	1.2	0.3	19.1	1.2	0.04	0.02	0.0	0.19	0.02	50 g/fig
Grapes													
American types	81.6	69	289	1.3	1.0	15.1	0.6	0.02	0.01	0.0	0.16	0.01	92 g/8-oz cup
European types	81.4	67	280	0.6	0.3	16.8	0.5	0.01	0.02	0.0	0.17	0.01	160 g/8-oz cup
Nectarines, raw	81.8	64	268	0.6	tr	16.7	0.4	0.0	0.02	0.01	0.29	0.01	136 g/nectarine
Oranges, peeled	86.0	49	205	1.0	0.2	11.7	0.5	0.04	0.02	0.0	0.20	0.01	120-140 g/orange
Peaches													
Canned, solids and liquid-juice pack	87.2	45	188	0.6	0.1	11.2	0.4	0.01	0.02	0.0	0.21	0.01	248 g/8-oz cup
Raw	89.1	38	159	0.6	0.1	9.1	0.6	0.01	0.02	0.0	0.20	0.01	87 g/peach
Pears													
Canned, solids and liquid-juice pack	87.3	46	192	0.3	0.3	11.0	0.8	0.01	0.01	0.0	0.13	0.01	248 g/8-oz cup
Raw, including skin	83.2	61	255	0.7	0.4	13.9	1.4	0.01	0.01	0.0	0.13	0.01	166 g/pear

(Continued on next page.)

Table T-5. Nutrient content of common carbohydrate and fiber sources.* (Continued from previous page.)

	Moisture	ME** (kcal)	(kJ)	Protein	Fat	NFE	Fiber	Ca	P	Na	K	Mg	Serving size***
Pineapple													
Raw	85.3	52	218	0.4	0.2	13.3	0.4	0.02	0.01	0.0	0.15	0.01	na
Canned, solids and liquid-juice pack	84.0	58	243	0.4	0.1	14.8	0.3	0.02	0.01	0.0	0.15	0.01	250 g/8-oz cup
Prunes, dried, softened	28.0	255	1,067	2.1	0.6	65.8	1.6	0.05	0.08	0.01	0.69	0.04	8.4 g/prune
Raisins, natural	18.0	289	1,209	2.5	0.2	76.5	0.9	0.06	0.10	0.03	0.76	0.04	150 g/8-oz cup

Key: ME = metabolizable energy, kcal = kilocalories, kJ = kilojoules, NFE = nitrogen-free extract, Ca = calcium, P = phosphorus, Na = sodium, K = potassium, Mg = magnesium, tr = trace, g = grams, Tbs = tablespoons (15 ml), na = not available.

*All nutrients are expressed on a percent as fed or as is basis unless otherwise designated.

**Metabolizable energy/100 g as is.

***g/serving.

†Low-sodium breakfast cereal is available with about 0.01% sodium.

Table T-6. Nutrient content of selected mineral sources.*

	Moisture (%)	Ca (%)	P (%)	Na (%)	K (%)	Mg (%)	Cl (%)	Ca/P ratio	Weight (g/tsp)
Mineral sources									
Bone meal	10	≥28	≥13	0.5	na	0.7	0.0	2.1	4
Calcium carbonate	0	36-39	na	na	na	na	na	na	5
Tums tablets** contain 0.50 g calcium carbonate per tablet = 200 mg calcium									
Tums Extra tablets** contain 0.75 g calcium carbonate per tablet = 300 mg calcium									
Tums Ultra tablets** contain 1.0 g calcium carbonate per tablet = 400 mg calcium									
Dicalcium phosphate powder	20.9	23	18	na	na	na	na	1.3	4
Salt (NaCl)	0	0	0	39.3	0	0	60.7	0	4
Lite salt (50% NaCl/50% KCl)	0	0	0	17.3	29.4	0	53.3	0	5
Salt substitute (potassium chloride)	0	0	0	0	52.4	0	47.6	0	5

Key: Ca = calcium, P = phosphorus, Na = sodium, K = potassium, Mg = magnesium, Cl = chloride, g = grams, tsp = teaspoons, na = not available.
*All nutrients are expressed on a percent as fed or as is basis. (See Chapter 2.)
**SmithKline-Beecham, Pittsburg, PA, USA.

Table T-7. Purine content of selected foods.*

Foods highest in purines (250-825 mg/100 g as fed)	
Anchovies (363 mg/100 g)	Mackerel
Kidney (beef: 200 mg/100 g)	Meat extracts (160-400 mg/100 g)
Game meats	Sardines (295 mg/100 g)
Gravies	Scallops
Herring	Sweat breads (825 mg/100 g)
Liver (calf/beef: 233 mg/100 g)	
Foods high in purines (50-150 mg/100 g as fed)	
Asparagus	Meat soups and broths
Whole grain breads and cereals	Mushrooms
Cauliflower	Oatmeal
Eel	Poultry: chicken, duck, turkey
Fish	Shellfish: crab, lobster, oysters
Legumes: beans, lentils, peas	Spinach
Meat: beef, lamb, pork, veal	Wheat germ and bran
Foods low in purines (0-50 mg/100 g as fed)	
Breads and cereals, except whole grain	Milk
Cheese	Nuts
Eggs	Sugars, syrups, sweets
Fats	Vegetables, except those listed above
Fish (roe)	Vegetable and cream soups
Fruits	

*Purines are normally formed in the body during the metabolic breakdown of nucleoproteins. Although the total protein intake may be more important than the type of protein, it is preferable to select protein sources that are relatively low in purine precursors for dietary management of urate urolithiasis.

Table T-8. Gluten-containing and gluten-free foods.*

Gluten-containing grains	Gluten-free grains and products
Barley (hordeins)	Corn, corn flour, corn meal, cornstarch
Buckwheat	Gluten-free wheat starch
Oats (avenins)	Beans and bean flour
Rye (secalin, prolamines)	Potatoes and potato flour
Wheat (gliadin)	Rice and rice flour
	Soybeans and soy flour

*See Chapters 14 and 22 for more information about gluten.

BIBLIOGRAPHY

1. Galli C, Simopoulos AP, eds. Dietary w-3 and w-6 Fatty Acids: Biological Effects and Nutritional Essentiality. New York, NY: Plenum Press, 1989; 21-55, 213-218, 309-315, 389-390.

2. Gesellschaft für Ernährungsphysiologie Grunddaten für die Berechnung des Energie- und Nährstoffbedarfs. In: Ausschuß für Bedarfsnormen. Energie- und Nährstoffbedarf Nr. 5 Hunde. Frankfurt, Germany: DLG Verlag, 1989.

3. Holland B, Welch AA, Unwin ID, et al, eds. In: The Composition of Foods, McCance and Widdowson's 5th Revised & Extended Edition. Cambridge, UK: The Royal Society of Chemistry and Ministry of Agriculture, Fisheries and Food, 1991.

4. Mead JF, Alfin-Slater RB, Howton DR, et al. Distribution of fatty acids in the tissue lipids. In: Lipids: Chemistry, Biochemistry, and Nutrition. New York, NY: Plenum Press, 1986; 69-81.

5. Menke K-H, Huss W. Tierernährung und Futtermittelkunde. Stuttgart, Germany: Verlag Eugen Ulmer, 1987.

6. Meyer H, Heckötter E. Futterwerttabellen für Hunde und Katzen. Hannover, Germany: Schlütersche Verlaganstalt und Druckerei, 1986.

7. National Research Council. Nutrient Requirements of Cats. Washington, DC: National Academy Press, 1986.

8. National Research Council. Nutrient Requirements of Dogs. Washington, DC: National Academy Press, 1985.

9. Pennington JAT. Food Values of Portions Commonly Used, 15th ed. New York, NY: Harper & Row, Publishers, 1989.

10. Randoin L, Le Gallic P, Dupuis Y, et al. Tables de composition des aliments Institut Scientifique d'Hygiène Alimentaire, 6th ed. Malakoff, France: LT Editions J. Lanore, 1990.

11. Table Belge de Composition des Aliments. Brussels, Belgium: NUBEL, 1992.

12. Watt BK, Merrill AL. Composition of Foods–Raw, Processed, Prepared. Agriculture Handbook No 8. Washington, DC: Agricultural Research Service USDA, 1975.

13. Ziegler EE, Filer LJ Jr, eds. Present Knowledge in Nutrition, 7th ed. Washington, DC: ILSI Press, 1996; 44-66.

Appendix U
Food Analytical and Toxicology Laboratories

Introduction

This appendix lists laboratories where samples can be sent for analysis of homemade and commercial pet foods and ingredients. Analyses can be performed to confirm the nutritional adequacy of a homemade recipe or to check a food suspected of being deficient in or containing excessive levels of specific nutrients.

The toxicology laboratories listed here can help rule out rare cases of food poisoning (bacterial or toxic substances) due to contamination of homemade or commercial foods.

Four types of laboratories are listed.

- Food analysis laboratories: Laboratories that perform complete nutrient analyses of pet foods and ingredients.
- Food analysis and toxicology laboratories: Laboratories where samples can be sent for nutrient analysis and for detection of toxic substances in foods or ingredients.
- Toxicology laboratories: Laboratories where samples are analyzed for toxic substances in foods or ingredients.
- Feeding trial laboratories: Laboratories that conduct feeding trials such as Association of American Feed Control Officials feeding trials, digestibility studies, etc.

Table U-1. Canadian food analytical and toxicology laboratories.

Food Analyses
Agri-Food Laboratories
Unit 1, 503 Imperial Road North
Guelph, Ontario N1H 6T9
800-265-7175
519-837-1600
Fax: 519-837-1242

Industrial Laboratories of Canada, Inc.
95 Townline Road
Tillsonburg, Ontario N4G 4H3
519-842-6447
Fax: 519-688-0644

Feeding Trials
Ontario Nutro Laboratory
855 St. David Street North
Fergus, Ontario N1M 2L1
519-843-5669
Fax: 519-843-5676

Toxicology Laboratories
Toxicology Laboratory O.S. Longman Building
6906 116th Street
Edmonton, Alberta T6H 4P2
403-427-2270

University of Guelph
Animal Health Laboratory
P.O. Box 3612
Guelph, Ontario N1G 2W5
519-823-8800
Fax: 519-821-8072

Table U-2. United States food analytical laboratories.

Arizona
Agri-Data Systems, Inc.
21620 N. 19th Ave., Suite A-10
Phoenix, AZ 85027
602-582-3888
Fax: 602-582-2916

California
ANRESCO, Inc.
1370 Van Dyke Avenue
San Francisco, CA 94124
415-822-1100
Fax: 415-822-6615

McIntosh Laboratories
2292 Trade Zone Boulevard
San Jose, CA 95131-1801
408-946-3935
Fax: 408-946-7376

Michelson Laboratories, Inc.
6280 Chalet Drive
Los Angeles, CA 90040
310-928-0553
Fax: 310-927-6625

Illinois
Center for Microanalysis of Materials
Materials Research Laboratory
University of Illinois at Urbana-Champaign
104 S. Goodwin Avenue
Urbana, IL 61801
217-333-1370
Fax: 217-244-8544

Gabriel Laboratories, Ltd.
1421 N. Elston
Chicago, IL 60622
773-486-2123
Fax: 773-486-0004

Meat Industry Laboratories, Inc.
1950 N. Persian Road
Chicago, IL 60609
773-523-7017
Fax: 773-523-9588

Northland Laboratories
1810 Frontage Road Bldg. 7
Northbrook, IL 60062
847-272-8700
Fax: 847-272-2348

Northview Laboratories, Inc.
1880 Holste Road
Northbrook, IL 60062
847-564-8181
Fax: 847-564-8269

Suburban Laboratories, Inc.
4140 Litt Drive
Hillside, IL 60162
708-544-3260
Fax: 708-544-8587

Tox Monitor Laboratories, Inc.
33 West Chicago Avenue
Oak Park, IL 60302
708-345-6970
Fax: 708-383-0591

Indiana
B.F.C. Industries
Midwest Labs
1711 W. Dewey St.
Bremen, IN 46506
219-546-5560
Fax: 219-546-5517

Iowa
Iowa Testing Laboratories, Inc.
Hwy. 17 North
Eagle Grove, IA 50533
P.O. Box 188
Eagle Grove, IA 50533
515-448-4741
Fax: 515-448-3402

Kansas
Wenger Manufacturing, Inc.
714 Main
Sabetha, KS 66534
P.O. Box 130
Sabetha, KS 66534
913-284-2133
Fax: 913-284-3771

Kentucky
Microbac Laboratories, Inc.
1121 W. Broadway
Louisville, KY 40203
502-589-6019
Fax: 502-589-0539

Massachusetts
Shuster Laboratories
5 Hayward Street
Quincy, MA 02171
617-328-7600
Fax: 617-770-0957

Michigan
Neugen Corp.
620 Lesher Place
Lansing, MI 48912
517-372-9200
Fax: 517-372-0108

(Continued on next page.)

Table U-2. United States food analytical laboratories.* (Continued from previous page.)

Minnesota
Medallion Laboratories
9000 Plymouth Avenue
Minneapolis, MN 55427
612-540-4453
Fax: 612-540-4010

Minnesota Valley Testing Laboratories, Inc.
1126 N. Front Street
New Ulm, MN 56073
507-354-8517
Fax: 507-359-2890

Missouri
ABC Analytical Bio-Chemistry Laboratories, Inc.
P.O. Box 1097
Columbia, MO 65205
573-474-8579
Fax: 573-443-9033

Environmental Analysis, Inc.
Highway 67
Florissant, MO 63033
314-921-4488
Fax: 314-921-4494

ITS Doty Laboratories, Inc.
Central Technologies
1435 Clay Street
North Kansas City, MO 64116
P.O. Box 7498
North Kansas City, MO 64116
816-471-8580
Fax: 816-471-7842

Ralston Analytical Laboratories
Checkerboard Square
St. Louis, MO 63164
800-423-6832
Fax: 314-982-1078

Nebraska
Harris Laboratories, Inc.
621 Rose Street
Lincoln, NE 68502
P.O. Box 80837
Lincoln, NE 68501
402-476-2811
Fax: 402-476-7598

Midwest Laboratories, Inc.
13611 B Street
Omaha, NE 68144
402-334-7770
Fax: 402-334-9121

New York
NE DHIA
Forage Analysis Laboratory
NY State College of Veterinary Medicine
730 Warren Rd.
Ithaca, NY 14850-9877
607-253-3000

New York Testing Laboratories, Inc.
84 Kean Street
West Babylon, NY 11074
516-491-3800
Fax: 516-491-4142

Oneida Research Services, Inc.
One Halsey Road
Whitesboro, NY 13492
315-736-3050
Fax: 315-736-2460

North Carolina
Southern Testing and Research Laboratories, Inc.
3809 Airport Drive
Wilson, NC 27896
919-237-4175
Fax: 919-237-9341

Ohio
Hill Top Research, Inc.
P.O. Box 429501
Cincinnati, OH 45242
514-831-3114
Fax: 514-831-1217

Microbiological Laboratories, Inc.
9593 Page Road
Streetsboro, OH 44241
330-626-2264

Owens-Illinois
One SeaGate
Toledo, OH 43666
419-247-5000
Fax: 419-247-2839

Oklahoma
Standard Testing and Engineering Company
3400 N. Lincoln
Oklahoma City, OK 73105
405-528-0541
Fax: 405-528-0559

Oregon
Food Quality Analysts, Inc.
6400 S.W. Canyon Court
Suite 80
Portland, OR 97221
503-297-3636
Fax: 503-297-3738

(Continued on next page.)

Table U-2. United States food analytical laboratories. (Continued from previous page.)

Pennsylvania
Lancaster Laboratories
2425 New Holland Pike
Lancaster, PA 17601
717-656-2301
Fax: 717-656-2681

Microbac
4850 McKnight Road
Pittsburgh, PA 15237
412-931-5851
Fax: 412-931-0473

Texas
Industrial Laboratories
3001 Cullen Street
Fort Worth, TX 76107
817-332-2259

Maxim Technologies
222 Cavalcade Boulevard
Houston, TX 77249
P.O. Box 8768
Houston, TX 77249-8768
713-692-9151
Fax: 713-696-6307

Virginia
Environmental Systems Service, Ltd.
500 Stone Street
Bedford, VA 24523
P.O. Box 736
Bedford, VA 24523
540-586-5413
Fax: 540-586-5530

Washington
Laucks Testing Laboratories, Inc.
940 South Harney Street
Seattle, WA 98108
206-767-5060
Fax: 206-767-5063

Wisconsin
Covance Laboratories America, Inc.
3301 Kinsman Boulevard
Madison, WI 53707
P.O. Box 7454
Madison, WI 53707-7545
608-241-4471
Fax: 608-241-7227

Commercial Testing Laboratory, Inc.
514 Main Street
Colfax, WI 54730
P.O. Box 526
Colfax, WI 54730
715-962-3121
Fax: 715-962-4030

Industrial Toxicology Laboratory
West Allis Memorial Hospital
8901 W. Lincoln Avenue
West Allis, WI 53227
414-328-7940
Fax: 414-328-8560

Table U-3. United States food analytical and toxicology laboratories.

Woodson-Tenent Laboratories, Inc.
Corporate Headquarters
1331 Union Ave., Suite 1500
Memphis, TN 38104
P.O. Box 2135
Memphis, TN 38101
901-272-7511
Fax: 901-272-2926

North Little Rock, Arkansas
312 North Hemlock
North Little Rock, AR 72114
P.O. Box 5341
North Little Rock, AR 72119
501-374-5181
Fax: 501-374-0713

Gainesville, Georgia
Atlas Circle
Gainesville, GA 30501
P.O. Box 1097
Gainesville, GA 30501
404-536-5909
Fax: 404-536-6909

Des Moines, Iowa
3507 Delaware Ave.
Des Moines, IA 50313
P.O. Box 1292
Des Moines, IA 50305
515-265-1461
Fax: 515-266-5453

Goldston, North Carolina
West 902 Highway
Goldston, NC 27252
P.O. Box 367
Goldston, NC 27252
919-837-2121
Fax: 919-837-2174

Dayton, Ohio
313 East Helena
Dayton, OH 45404
P.O. Box 164
Dayton, OH 45404
513-222-4179
Fax: 513-222-7401

Memphis, Tennessee
345 Adams Avenue
Memphis, TN 38103
P.O. Box 2135
Memphis, TN 38101
901-525-6333
Fax: 901-529-9106

Table U-4. United States toxicology laboratories.

California
California Veterinary Diagnostic Laboratory System
School of Veterinary Medicine
University of California, Davis
P.O. Box 1770
Davis, CA 95617
916-752-8709
Fax: 916-752-8709

California Veterinary Diagnostic Laboratory System
University of California, Tulare Branch
18830 Road 112
Tulare, CA 93274
209-688-7543
Fax: 209-606-4231

Colorado
Veterinary Diagnostic Laboratory
300 W. Drake Road
Fort Collins, CO 80523
970-491-1281
Fax: 970-491-0320

Connecticut
University of Connecticut
Department of Pathobiology
Diagnostic Testing Services
61 N. Eagleville Road
P.O. Box U-89
Storrs, CT 06269-3203
203-486-3736
Fax: 203-486-2794

Florida
Florida Department of Agriculture
Animal Disease Laboratory
P.O. Box 420460
Kissimmee, FL 34742-0460
407-846-5200
Fax: 407-846-5204

Toxin Technology, Inc.
7165 Curtiss Ave.
Sarasota, FL 34231
813-925-2032
Fax: 813-925-2130

Georgia
University of Georgia
Diagnostic Assistance Laboratory
University of Georgia
College of Veterinary Medicine
Athens, GA 30602-7383
706-542-5915
Fax: 706-542-5977

University of Georgia
Veterinary Diagnostic and Investigation Laboratory
P.O. Box 1389
Tifton, GA 31793
912-386-3340
Fax: 912-386-7128

Idaho
University of Idaho
Department of Food Science and Toxicology
Moscow, ID 83843
208-885-7081
Fax: 208-285-1715

Illinois
Illinois Department of Agriculture
Animal Disease Laboratory
Shattue Road
Centralia, IL 62801
618-532-6701
Fax: 618-532-1195

Illinois Department of Agriculture
Animal Disease Laboratory
1455 Windish Drive
Galesburg, IL 61402
P.O. Box 2100X
Galesburg, IL 61402-2100
309-344-2451
Fax: 309-344-7358

University of Illinois
Veterinary Diagnostic Laboratories
College of Veterinary Medicine
2001 South Lincoln Ave.
Urbana, IL 61801
P.O. Box U
Urbana, IL 61801
217-333-1620
Fax: 217-333-4628

Indiana
Purdue University
Animal Disease Diagnostic Laboratory
School of Veterinary Medicine
1175 ADDL
West Lafayette, IN 47907-1175
765-494-7440
Fax: 765-494-9181

Iowa
Iowa State University
Veterinary Diagnostic Laboratory
College of Veterinary Medicine
Ames, IA 50011
515-294-1950
Fax: 515-294-3564

(Continued on next page.)

Table U-4. United States toxicology laboratories. (Continued from previous page.)

Kansas
Kansas State University
Veterinary Diagnostic Laboratory
1800 Denison
Manhattan, KS 66506
913-532-5650
Fax: 913-532-4481

Kentucky
Murray State University
Breathitt Veterinary Center
P.O. Box 2000
Hopkinsville, KY 42241-2000
502-886-3959
Fax: 502-886-4295

University of Kentucky
Livestock Disease Diagnostic Center
1429 Newtown Pike
Lexington, KY 40511
606-253-0571
Fax: 606-255-1624

Louisiana
Veterinary Medical Diagnostic Laboratory
1909 S. Stadium Drive
Baton Rouge, LA 70803
P.O. Box 16570 A
Baton Rouge, LA 70803
504-346-3193
Fax: 504-346-3390

Massachusetts
Tufts University
Division of Diagnostic Labs
200 Westboro Road
North Grafton, MA 01536
508-839-7900
Fax: 508-839-7999

Michigan
Animal Health Diagnostic Laboratory
Michigan State University
P.O. Box 30076
Lansing, MI 48909-7576
517-353-0635
Fax: 517-353-5096

Neogen Corporation
620 Lesher Place
Lansing, MI 48912
517-372-9200
800-234-5333
Fax: 517-372-9004

Minnesota
University of Minnesota
Minnesota Veterinary Diagnostic Laboratory
1943 Carter Avenue
St. Paul, MN 55201
612-625-8787
Fax: 612-624-8707

Mississippi
Mississippi Department of Agriculture
Mississippi Veterinary Diagnostic Laboratory
P.O. Box 4389
Jackson, MS 39296
601-354-6089
Fax: 601-354-6097

Missouri
University of Missouri
Veterinary Medical Diagnostic Laboratory
P.O. Box 6023
Columbia, MO 65205
573-882-6811
Fax: 573-882-1411

Romer Labs, Inc.
1301 Stylemaster Drive
Union, MO 63084
573-583-8600
Fax: 573-583-6553

Montana
State of Montana Animal Health Division
Diagnostic Laboratory
P.O. Box 997
Bozeman, MT 59771-0997
406-994-4885
Fax: 406-994-6344

Nebraska
University of Nebraska
Veterinary Diagnostic Center
P.O. Box 830907
Lincoln, NE 68583-0907
402-472-1434
Fax: 402-472-3094

New York
Cornell University
Veterinary Diagnostic Laboratory
NY State College of Veterinary Medicine
P.O. Box 5786
Ithaca, NY 14853-5786
607-253-3900
Fax: 607-253-3943

(Continued on next page.)

Table U-4. United States toxicology laboratories. (Continued from previous page.)

North Carolina
North Carolina Department of Agriculture
Rollins Animal Disease Diagnostic Lab
P.O. Box 12223
Cameron Village Station
Raleigh, NC 27605
919-733-3986
Fax: 919-733-0454

North Dakota
North Dakota State University
Veterinary Diagnostic Laboratory
Van Es Hall
Fargo, ND 58105
701-237-7511
Fax: 701-237-7514

Ohio
Ohio Department of Agriculture
Division of Animal Health
8995 E. Main Street
Reynoldsburg, OH 43068
614-866-6361
Fax: 614-575-2068

Oklahoma
Oklahoma Animal Disease Diagnostic Laboratory
Oklahoma State University
P.O. Box 7001
Stillwater, OK 74078
405-744-6623
Fax: 405-744-8612

Oregon
Oregon State University
Veterinary Diagnostic Laboratory
P.O. Box 429
Corvallis, OR 97339
541-737-3261
Fax: 541-737-6817

Pennsylvania
Pennsylvania Department of Agriculture
Bureau of Animal Industry Laboratory
2305 N. Cameron
Harrisburg, PA 11710
717-787-2103
Fax: 717-772-2780

South Dakota
South Dakota State University
Animal Disease Diagnostic Laboratory
P.O. Box 2175
Brookings, SD 57007
605-688-5172
Fax: 605-688-6003

Texas
Texas A & M University
Veterinary Medical Diagnostic Laboratory
P.O. Box 3200
Amarillo, TX 79106
806-353-7478
Fax: 806-359-0636

Texas Veterinary Medical Diagnostic Laboratory
P.O. Drawer 3040
College Station, TX 77841-3040
409-845-9000
Fax: 409-845-1794

Washington
Washington State University
Animal Disease Diagnostic Laboratory
P.O. Box 2037
Pullman, WA 99165
509-335-9696
Fax: 509-335-7424

Wisconsin
Industrial Toxicology Laboratory
West Allis Memorial Hospital
8901 W. Lincoln Avenue
West Allis, WI 53227
414-328-7940
Fax: 414-328-8560

Wisconsin Department of Agriculture
Wisconsin Animal Health Laboratory
6101 Mineral Point Road
Madison, WI 53705
608-266-6687
Fax: 608-267-0636

Wyoming
Wyoming State Veterinary Laboratory
1174 Snowy Range Road
Laramie, WY 82070
307-742-6638
Fax: 307-742-2156

Table U-5. United States feeding trial laboratories.

Alabama
Pet Specialties, Inc.
P.O. Drawer 807
Hanceville, AL 35077
205-352-4194
Fax: 205-352-9708

Illinois
Boebel Research Center
21796 W. Highway 176
Mundelein, IL 60060
847-566-5200

Michigan
Covance Research Products, Inc.
6321 S. 6th Street
Kalamazoo, MI 49009
616-375-0482
Fax: 616-375-8403

Pennsylvania
Summit Ridge Farms
RD 1, Box 131
Susquehanna, PA 18847
570-756-2656
Fax: 570-756-2826

White Eagle Laboratories, Inc.
2003 Lower State Road
Doylestown, PA 18901
215-348-3868
Fax: 215-348-5081

Table U-6. European food analyses and toxicology laboratories.

Austria
Food Analyses
Veterinär Medizinische Universität
Institute für Ernährung
Veterinärplatz 1
Josef Baumgasse 1
A-1210 Wien
01-250.77.32.00
Fax: 01-250.77.32.90

Austria
Toxicology
Veterinär Medizinische Universität
Institut für Bacteriologie
Veterinärplatz 1
A-1210 Wien
01-250.77.21.06

Belgium
Food Analyses and Toxicology
Laboratorium ECCA NV
Klaartestraat 24
B-9052 Zwijnaarde
09-222 48 43
Fax: 09-221 72 83

SGS Agrilab NV
Haven 407
Polderdijkweg 16
B-2030 Antwerpen
03-545 87 75
Fax: 03-545 87 79

Czech Republic
Food Analyses
SVÚ Praha
Sídlištní 24
165 03 Praha 6-Lysolaje
02-344 600
Fax: 02-344 291

Denmark
Food Analyses
Steins Laboratorium A/S
Olof Palmes Allé 13A
8200 Århus N
8610-8070
Fax: 8610-8889

Statens Veterinære Serumlaboratorium
Bülowsvej 27
1790 København V
3530 0100
Fax: 3136 1735

Finland
Food Analyses and Toxicology
Plant Production Inspection Centre
Agricultural Chemistry Department
P.O. Box 83
Fin-01301 Vantaa

France
Food Analyses and Toxicology
EEB
Rue du Professeur Vèzes
F-333000 Bordeaux
56.01.84.03
Fax: 57.87.11.63

LAA
12, rue des Beaux Soleils
F-95523 Cergy Pontoise
B.P. 205-OSNY
F-95523 Cergy Pontoise
1-34.41.61.61
Fax: 1-30.32.83.71

Lab. Analyse UCAAB
B.P. N° 19
F-02402 Château Thierry
23.84.80.23
Fax: 23.83.39.27

Germany
Food Analyses
Institut Fresenius
Im Maisel 14
D-65232 Taunusstein-Neuhof
P.O. Box 1261
D-65232 Taunusstein-Neuhof
06128-744-252
Fax: 01628-744-201

Greece
Food Analyses and Toxicology
Center of Veterinary Foundations of Athens
Institute of Toxicology-Department of Microbiology
25 Neapoleos St.
153 41 AG. Paraskevi
01-639 13 78
Fax: 01-639 94 77

Toxicology
National Foundation of Agriculture Research
Veterinary Institute of Infectious and Parasitic
Diseases-Department of Toxicology
66, 26th October St.
546 27 Thessaloniki
031-55 20 24-9
Fax: 031-55 20 23

(Continued on next page.)

Table U-6. European food analyses and toxicology laboratories. (Continued from previous page.)

The Netherlands
Food Analyses and Toxicology
S/G Nutrilab B.V.
Laboratorium voor Onderzoek en Advies
Burgstraat 12 Postbus 7
4283 ZG Giessen
0183-44 63 05
Fax: 0183-44 25 97

TNO-CIVO-Institutes
TNO-Voeding
Utrechtseweg 48
3700AJ Zeist
P.O. Box 360
3700 AJ Zeist
030-694 41 44
Fax: 030-696 26 73

Norway
Food Analyses and Toxicology
Norwegian Institute for Food and
Environmental Analysis
P.O. Box 174, Økern
N-0609 Oslo
023-17 26 50
Fax: 023-17 26 51

Slovak Republic
Food Analyses
UKSUP
Letná 1
40 01 Košice
095-622 24 25
Fax: 095-622 905 48

Slovenia
Food Analyses
Veterinary Faculty
Department of Nutrition Hygiene and Pathology
1115 Ljubljana-p.p. 25
Gerbiceva 60
061-1258 292
Fax: 061-218 005

Sweden
Food Analyses and Toxicology
Statens Veterinärmedicinska Anstalt
Fodermedellaboratoriet
Ulls väg 2 B
750 07 Uppsala
018-674000
Fax: 018-309162

Svelab
Box 143
191 22 Sollentuna
08-623 53 00
Fax: 08-623 53 10

Analycen
Box 905
531 19 Lidköping
0510-887 00
Fax: 0510-228 69

Agrolab Scandinavia AB
Box 9024
291 09 Kristianstad
044-244 810

Turkey
Food Analyses
U.Ü. Veteriner Fak.
c/o Prof. H. Yavuz
Department of Animal Nutritional Diseases
Görülde kampüsü
16059 Bursa
Fax: 0224-442.80.69

United Kingdom
Food Analyses and Toxicology
Dr Bernard Dyer and Partners (1948), Ltd.
73-77 Bermondsey Street
London SE1 3XF
0171-378 1414
Fax: 0171-403.8208

Table U-7. Japanese food analyses and toxicology
laboratories.

Japan Food Research Laboratories
52-1 Motoyoyogi-cho Shibuya-ku
Tokyo 151-0062
03-3469 7131
Fax: 03-3469 7009

Appendix V

Assisted-Feeding Techniques

Introduction

This appendix describes various enteral feeding techniques and thus complements Chapter 12 (Assisted Feeding in Hospitalized Patients: Enteral and Parenteral Nutrition). Techniques described here include syringe feeding, nasoesophageal tube place-ment, pharyngostomy tube placement, esophagosto-my tube placement and gastrostomy tube placement. The Bibliography includes sources that can be con-sulted for further discussion of these and other enter-al feeding techniques such as enterostomy tube placement.

Syringe feeding

Patients are often fed a liquid or moist homogenized product by syringe on a short-term basis. For dogs, the syringe tip is placed between the molar teeth and cheek with the head held in a normal or lowered position (Figure V-1). For cats, the syringe tip is placed between the four canine teeth (Figure V-2). The patient may choose to swallow the liquid or allow it to flow out of the mouth by gravity. Some patients refuse to swallow the liquid or food; therefore, force feeding may increase the risk of aspiration. Syringe feeding should be discon-tinued if the patient does not swallow food voluntarily.

Figure V-1. Syringe-feeding technique for administering liquid or moist homogenized foods to dogs.

Figure V-2. Syringe-feeding technique for administering liquid or moist homogenized foods to cats.

Nasoesophageal tube placement

Nasoesophageal tubes are generally used for three to seven days, but are occasionally used longer (weeks). Polyurethane tubes (6 to 8 Fr., 90 to 100 cm) with or without a weighted tip and silicone feeding tubes (3.5 to 10 Fr., 20 to 105 cm) may be placed in the caudal esophagus or stomach. The preferred placement of all tubes originating cranial to the stomach is in the caudal esophagus to minimize gastric reflux and subsequent esophagitis. An 8-Fr. tube will pass through the nasal cavity of most dogs; a 5-Fr. tube is more comfortable in cats.

The length of tube to be inserted is determined by measuring from the nasal planum along the side of the animal to the caudal margin of the last rib (Figure V-3). A piece of adhesive tape is wrapped over the tube at this point or an indelible marker is used to mark how far the tube should be inserted. Tape will also provide a tab to secure the tube. The tip of

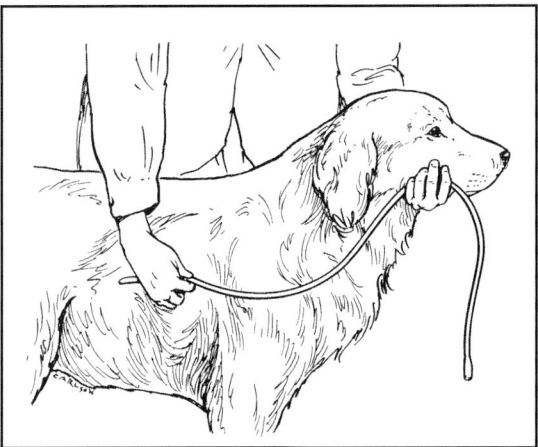

Figure V-3. The length of tube to insert is determined by measuring from the nose to the last rib. Marking the tube at three-quarters of the distance between the last rib and the nose will place the end of the tube in the caudal esophagus. This location is marked with an indelible marker or a piece of adhesive tape. Tape can also serve as a suture tab to secure the tube.

the tube should be positioned in the caudal esophagus. The animal's nose is desensitized by placing a few drops of topical anesthetic (2% lidocaine or 0.5% proparacaine) into a nostril and tilting the head upward for a few seconds. The tip of the tube is lubricated with a water-soluble lubricant or 2 to 5% lidocaine ointment/jelly before passage.

To pass the tube, direct the tip in a caudoventral, medial direction into the ventrolateral aspect of the external nares. The head is generally held in a normal static position. As soon as the tip of the catheter reaches the medial septum at the floor of the nasal cavity in dogs, the external nares are pushed dorsally, which opens the ventral meatus, ensuring passage of the tube into the oropharynx (Figure V-4). To aid passage, the proximal end of the tube is lifted as the nose is pushed upward (Figure V-4). In cats, because of the lack of a well-developed alar fold, the tube can be inserted initially in a ventromedial direction and continued directly into the oropharynx. The tube is inserted until the adhesive tape tab is reached (Figure V-5).

To evaluate proper tube placement, 3 to 15 ml of sterile water or saline solution may be injected through the tube and the animal evaluated for coughing (Figure V-6). A lateral radiograph may be taken of the neck to confirm the tube is placed in the caudal esophagus (i.e., over the larynx). After confirmation of position, the tube is secured with either sutures or glue. The first tape tab is secured to the skin just lateral to the external nares. A second tape tab is secured to the skin on the dorsal nasal midline, just rostral to the level of the eyes. An Elizabethan collar is used in most animals to prevent inadvertent removal of the tube (Figure V-7).

Complications of nasoesophageal intubation include epistaxis, lack of tolerance of the procedure and inadvertent removal of the tube by the animal. Incidence of tube removal by the animal has been reported to be as high as 50% even with use of collars. Nasoesophageal tubes should not be used in vomiting patients or those with respiratory disease.

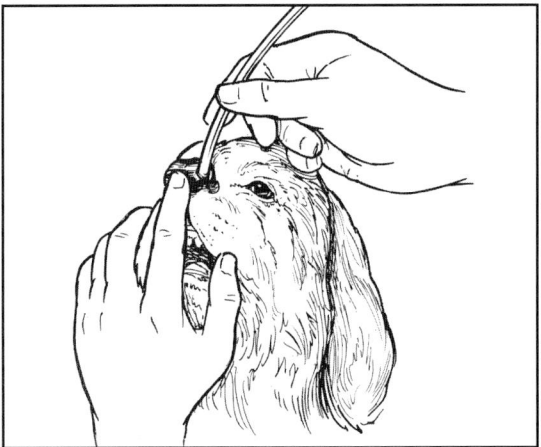

Figure V-4. The external nares are pushed dorsally and the proximal end of the tube is lifed to facilitate passage of the tube into the ventral nasal meatus.

Figure V-5. The tube is inserted until the indelible mark or adhesive tape tab is reached. Sutures or glue are used to secure the tape tab to the skin.

(Continued on next page.)

(Continued from previous page.)

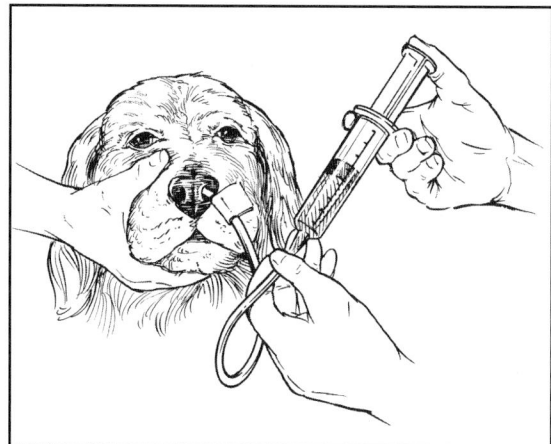

Figure V-6. A test injection of sterile water or saline solution is made to ensure proper tube placement.

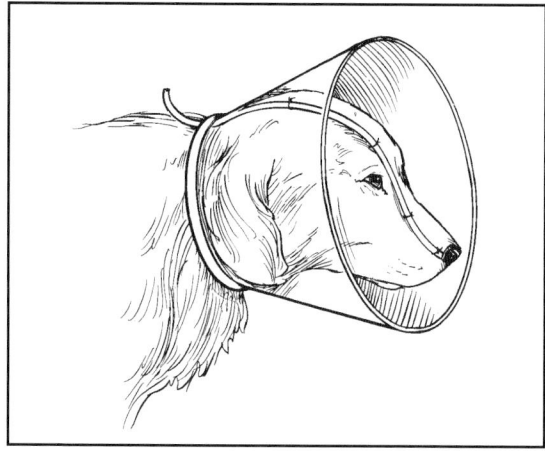

Figure V-7. Securing the tube at several locations by suturing or gluing tape tabs to the skin and applying collars will help decrease inadvertent removal of the tube by the animal.

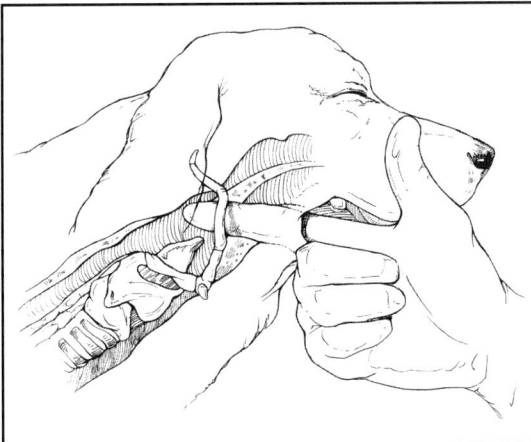

Figure V-8. A finger is used to find the optimal exit site for the pharyngostomy tube. The tube should exit the pharyngeal wall as far as caudally and dorsally as possible.

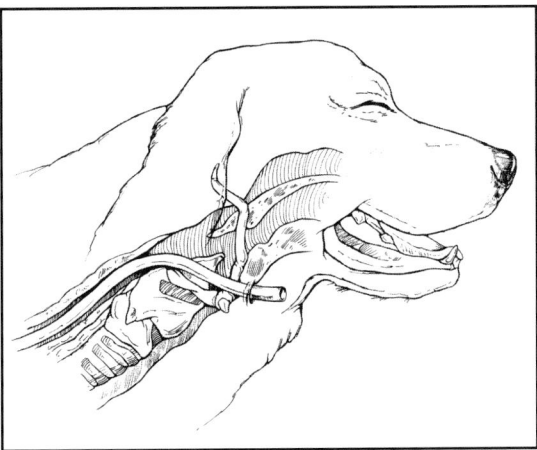

Figure V-9. Proper placement of a pharyngostomy tube with the tube exiting dorsal and caudal to the larynx.

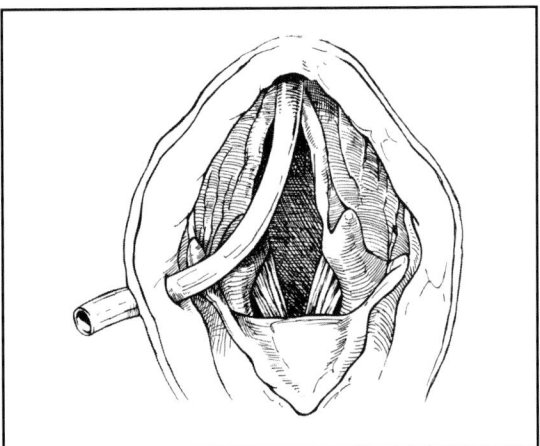

Figure V-10. Inappropriate positioning of a pharyngostomy tube, as depicted here, causes the tube to course over the laryngeal opening and to interfere with movement of the epiglottis. This placement can lead to serious airway obstruction. The tube should exit the pharyngeal wall as far caudally and dorsally as possible.

Pharyngostomy tube placement

In some instances, a pharyngostomy tube is used to bypass the nose and mouth of an animal requiring nutritional support (e.g., in cases of facial trauma) or when nasoesophageal tubes are not tolerated. Pharyngostomy tubes have been largely replaced by esophagostomy tubes or gastrostomy tubes placed percutaneously.

The animal is anesthetized, intubated and positioned in lateral recumbency. The area caudal to the mandible on either side is prepared for aseptic surgery. A 14- to 18-Fr. polyvinylchloride tube is premeasured as described in Figure V-3, except that the tube exit site will be caudal to the mandible.

With the mouth held open with a speculum, palpate the hyoid apparatus with one finger. The tube exit site must be carefully planned to avoid interfering with laryngeal opening and epiglottic movement. The tube should exit as far caudally and dorsally along the lateral pharyngeal wall as possible. The finger inside the mouth locates the hyoid apparatus and protrudes from the pharyngeal wall laterally at the selected exit site (Figure V-8). Alternatively, forceps can be used to bulge the pharyngeal wall laterally. The finger locates the pulsating carotid artery, ensuring that it will be avoided, while providing a target for the tunneling forceps. A 1-cm skin incision is made over the bulging pharyngeal wall. Long, curved forceps are used to bluntly tunnel caudally through the tissues from outside to inside. Blunt dissection prevents injury to nearby nerves, carotid artery and jugular vein. Forceps are used to grasp one end of the feeding tube so it exits through the dissection site while the other end is passed down the esophagus (Figure V-9). The tube is then secured to the skin with tape and sutures.

Complications include airway obstruction, tube displacement, damage to cervical nerves and blood vessels and infection at the exit site. Placing the tube exit site caudal to the hyoid apparatus or use of very large diameter tubes is much more likely to result in airway obstruction or aspiration (Figure V-10). The animal should be observed frequently for signs of respiratory embarrassment as it recovers from anesthesia. Frequent inspection and cleansing of the tube entrance/exit site help prevent skin infection. These tubes should not be used in vomiting patients or those with respiratory disease.

Esophagostomy tube placement

Several techniques have been described for mid-cervical placement of esophagostomy tubes in dogs and cats. The animal receives light general anesthesia while an esophagostomy tube is placed. The entire lateral cervical region from the ventral midline to near the dorsal midline is clipped and aseptically prepared for surgery.

In one technique, appropriately sized, curved Kelly, Carmalt or similar forceps are inserted into the pharynx and then into the proximal cervical esophagus. The tip of the forceps is turned laterally and pressure is applied in an outward direction, thereby tenting up the cervical tissue so that the instrument tip can be seen and palpated externally. A small skin incision, just large enough to accommodate the feeding tube, is made over the tip of the forceps. In small dogs and cats, the tip of the forceps is forced bluntly through the esophagus. In larger dogs, a deeper incision is made to allow passage of the tip of the forceps through the esophagus. The tube is premeasured as described in Figure V-3 so that the distal tip resides in the mid to caudal esophagus. The distal tip of the tube is grasped with forceps, pulled into the esophagus and out through the mouth, turned around and redirected into the esophagus. The tube is then secured with tape and sutures. A light circumferential bandage containing antibiotic-impregnated gauze is then placed at the exit site.

Another technique uses a percutaneous feeding tube applicator (ELD Gastrostomy Tube Applicator[a]) (Figure V-11).

Reported complications of tube esophagostomy for nutritional support include tube displacement due to vomiting or scratching by the animal and skin infection around the exit site.

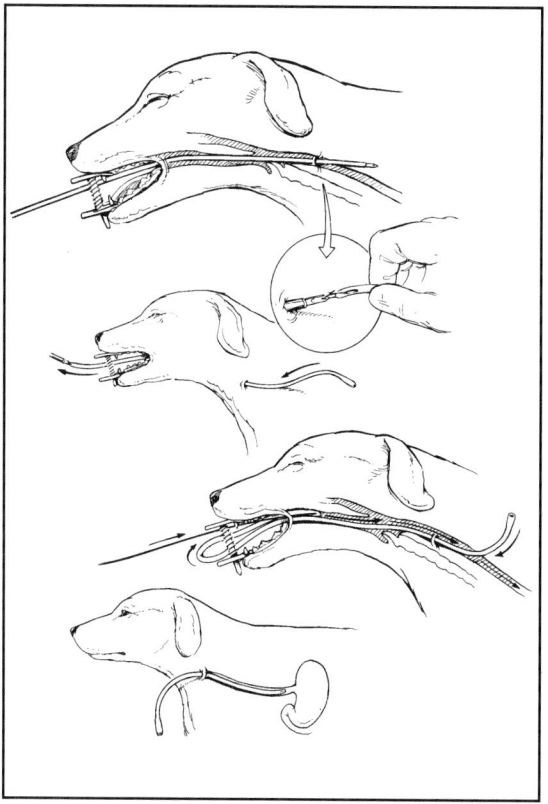

Figure V-11. Insertion of a percutaneous feeding tube applicator into the midcervical esophagus. The distal tip is palpated and an incision is made through the skin and subcutaneous tissue over the tip of the applicator. The trocar is advanced through the esophageal wall and directed through the incision. The distal end of the feeding tube is secured to the eyelet of the trocar with suture material. (See also Figure V-23.) The applicator and attached feeding tube are retracted into the esophagus and out the mouth. The feeding tube is redirected into the esophagus for final placement. A wire stylet can be inserted into the feeding tube if necessary to ease placement in the esophagus.

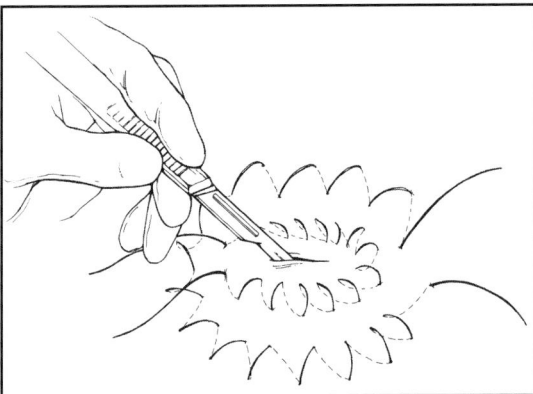

Figure V-12. Two full-thickness pursestring sutures are placed concentrically around the selected gastrostomy site to help invert the stomach around the tube. A stab incision is made in the center of the suture pattern for tube placement.

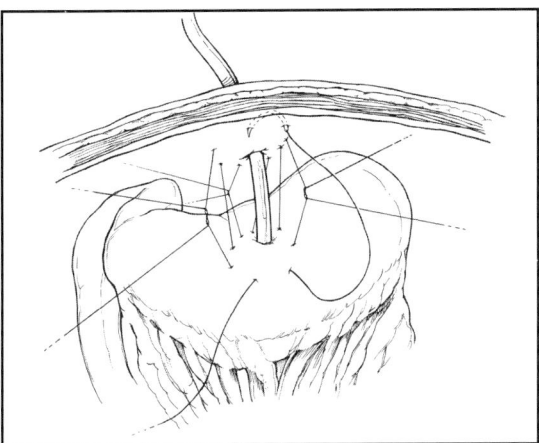

Figure V-13. The stomach is sutured to the abdominal wall with four preplaced mattress sutures (or a simple continuous pattern). These sutures should include the strong abdominal fascia and the gastric submucosa. Tightening the loops brings the gastric serosa and omentum snugly in contact with the peritoneum.

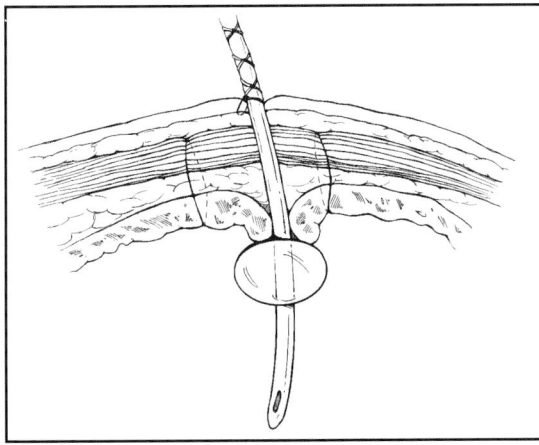

Figure V-14. A mushroom-tip Pezzer catheter or one with an inflatable bulb is placed in the stomach. After the gastropexy sutures are placed, gentle traction is applied on the external end of the tube to ensure this area of the stomach is adjacent to the abdominal wall.

Surgical gastrostomy tube placement

A limited left flank celiotomy for gastrostomy tube placement provides an alternative when endoscopic or blind gastrostomy techniques are not performed. A gastrostomy tube may also be inserted when a celiotomy is performed for other reasons. General anesthesia is administered and the left flank is aseptically prepared for surgery. The prepared left paracostal area is draped and a 2- to 3-cm incision is made through the skin and subcutaneous tissue. The incision is made just caudal and parallel to the last rib, with its dorsal limit just below the ventral edge of the paravertebral epaxial musculature. The incision should be extended ventrally so that the intraperitoneal rather than the retroperitoneal space is accessed. The incision should be long enough to permit insertion of one or two fingers and a tissue forceps.

The greater curvature of the stomach is located and an Allis or Babcock tissue forceps is used to grasp and exteriorize the stomach through the incision. A stomach tube may be passed by an assistant and the stomach dilated with 10 to 15 ml of air/kg body weight if difficulty is encountered locating the stomach. Exteriorizing the stomach through a small flank incision can be difficult, especially in larger, deep-chested canine breeds. The left lateral aspect of the gastric body or the caudal aspect of the fundus is selected for the ostomy site. Two pursestring sutures are placed around the selected ostomy site (Figure V-12). A stab incision is made through the ostomy site, the tube is inserted into the stomach and the pursestring sutures are tied snugly. Tube sizes 14 to 22 Fr. are usually adequate.

The tube may exit the body wall through a separate stab wound or the original incision. The stomach is then fixed to the abdominal wall where the tube enters the peritoneum using a continuous suture pattern circling the gastrostomy tube placement (Figure V-13). After the gastropexy sutures are placed, gentle traction is applied to the external end of the tube to ensure the stomach is adjacent to the abdominal wall (Figure V-14). The tube is secured to the skin using sutures or glue.

Potential risks with this procedure are the same as with any celiotomy and include wound infection, peritonitis and dehiscence. Pressure necrosis of the stomach may also occur if excessive tension is placed on the pursestring sutures. Wrapping the intraperitoneal tube with the omentum should contain leakage to a localized site. A layer of greater omentum can also be placed over the ostomy site before the stab incision is made into the stomach.

Percutaneous gastrostomy tube placement with gastropexy using a large-bore stiff plastic stomach tube has also been described. This technique is less invasive than the technique described here and may be more convenient for some veterinary practitioners. See the Fossum reference in the Bibliography for further details.

Percutaneous gastrostomy tube placement

There are two basic techniques for percutaneous placement of gastrostomy tubes. One technique uses an endoscope, whereas the other involves a "blind," nonendoscopic approach using a gastrostomy tube placement device or applicator. The advantages of percutaneous vs. surgical gastrostomy tube placement are ease and speed of placement, lower cost and less tissue trauma.

Percutaneous endoscopic gastrostomy tubes

Percutaneous endoscopic gastrostomy (PEG) tubes are inserted with the aid of general anesthesia. The patient is placed in right lateral recumbency and an area of the left flank extending 4 to 6 inches caudal to the last rib is surgically prepared. Figures V-15 to V-21 describe tube placement technique in detail. Landmarks for feeding tube placement are usually 1 to 2 cm caudal to the last rib and one-third the distance from the ventral border of the epaxial musculature to the ventral midline. Commercial 20-Fr. Pezzer catheter assembly kits[b] are now available for small animal patients and provide cost-effective, convenient materials for PEG tube placement (Figure V-18).

Following insertion, the tube is usually incorporated into a light bandage, with the free end brought to a convenient position for feeding. PEG tubes should be left in place for a minimum of five to seven days. Firm adhesions between the gastric serosa and the peritoneum have been reported to form within 48 to 72 hours of PEG tube placement in healthy dogs but do not reliably form in healthy cats. Adhesion formation may also be variable in undernourished animals.

The stomach should be empty when the tube is removed. Sedation or anesthesia is not generally required for tube extraction. Tubes are removed by exerting firm traction on the tube, while simultaneously applying counter-pressure around the exit site (Figure V-22). An alternative method of removal, suitable for dogs weighing more than 10 kg, is to cut the catheter off flush with the skin, leaving the catheter tip to be passed in the feces. The resulting gastrocutaneous fistula usually heals rapidly.

Complications of PEG tube placement include vomiting, peristomal skin infection, cellulitis and pressure necrosis at the tube exit site.

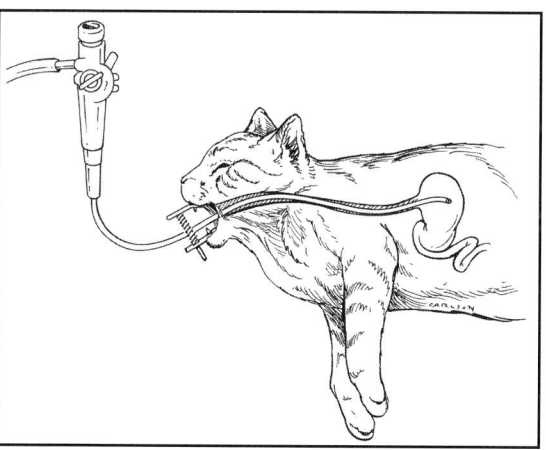

Figure V-15. The animal is positioned in right lateral recumbency and an endoscope is introduced. The stomach is insufflated with air so that the gastric wall comes in contact with the body wall and the spleen is displaced caudally.

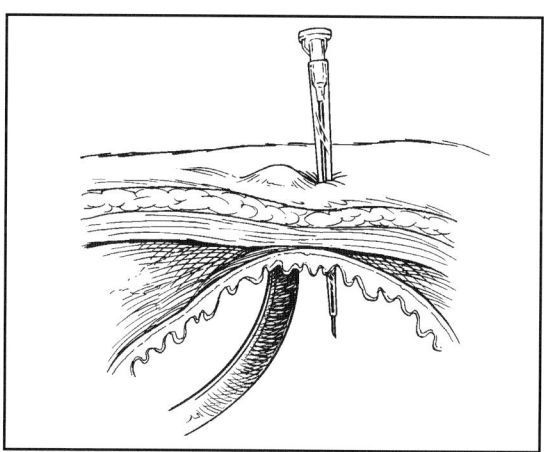

Figure V-16. The lighted tip of the endoscope will be seen pressing outward against the abdominal wall. A large-bore needle or over-the-needle intravenous catheter is inserted into the stomach adjacent to the endoscope tip.

(Continued on next page.)

(Continued from previous page.)

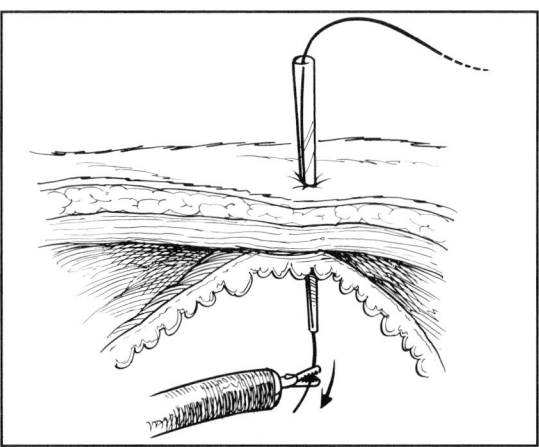

Figure V-17. Nylon suture is advanced through the needle or catheter until it can be grasped with endoscopic retrieval forceps. The suture material is pulled out through the mouth as the endoscope is withdrawn.

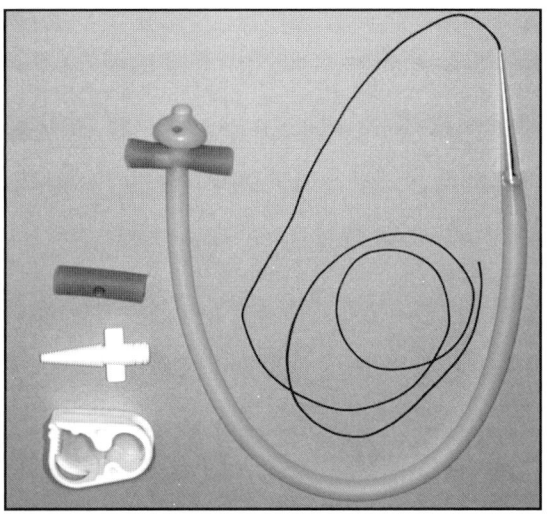

Figure V-18. Commercial 20-Fr. Pezzer catheter assembly kits[b] provide the most convenient materials for PEG tube placement. The catheter guide is already secured to the free end of the feeding tube in commercial kits.

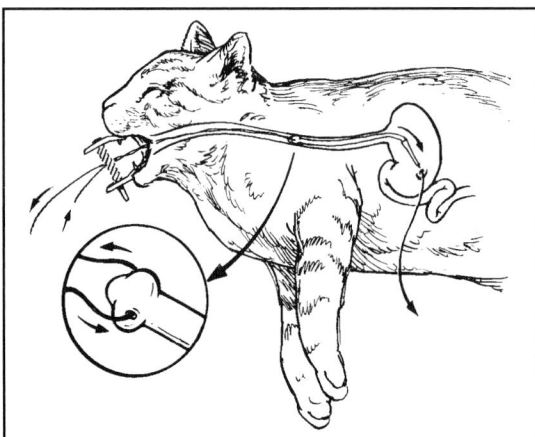

Figure V-19. The lubricated catheter is drawn down the esophagus as the suture exiting the body wall is pulled. A second "safety" suture is placed through the openings in the mushroom-tip feeding tube (insert) and exits the mouth. This safety suture is used to retrieve the feeding tube from the stomach if problems occur during the placement procedure.

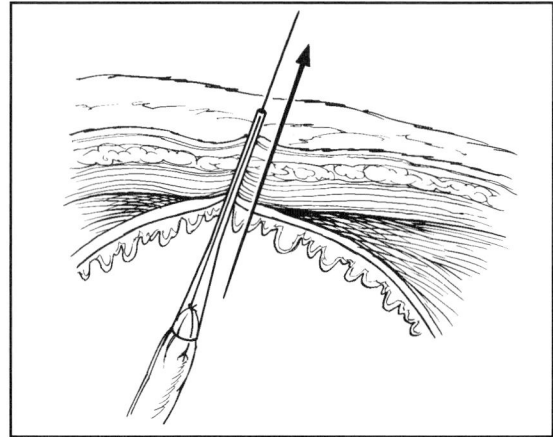

Figure V-20. Resistance will be encountered when the catheter tip guide contacts the body wall. Steady traction and firm application of counter-pressure to the body wall will allow the guide tip to emerge through the skin (arrow). A small skin incision (2 to 3 mm) at the point of exit may help.

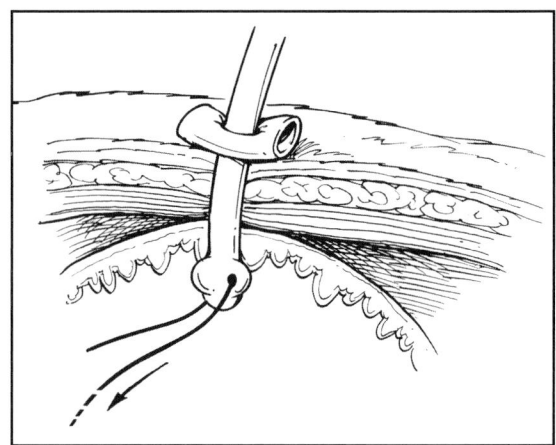

Figure V-21. Gentle traction is used to bring the stomach and abdominal wall into loose contact. A rubber flange is fitted down the tube and a piece of tape attached to prevent tube slippage. The tube is not usually sutured or glued to the skin. The safety suture is removed via the mouth (arrow) after the feeding tube is secured.

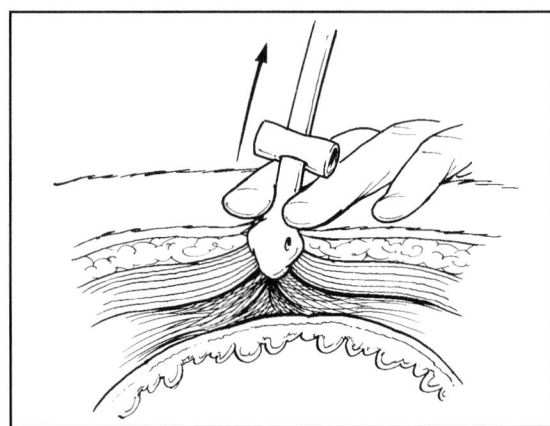

Figure V-22. PEG tubes are usually removed by traction. The mushroom tip will usually collapse as it pulls through the abdominal wall. The resulting gastrocutaneous fistula usually heals rapidly.

Percutaneous nonendoscopic gastrostomy tubes

Percutaneous gastrostomy techniques have been developed to allow convenient, cost-effective placement of feeding tubes without relying on availability of relatively expensive endoscopes. One nonendoscopic technique uses a commercial feeding tube applicator device[a] (Figure V-23) as previously described in the esophagostomy tube section. The other nonendoscopic technique uses a commercial gastrostomy tube placement device[c] (Figure V-24) pressed against the stomach wall. Use of either device allows suture material to be placed through the body wall into the stomach and retrieved through the mouth, and a gastrostomy tube to be inserted as described for PEG tube placement.

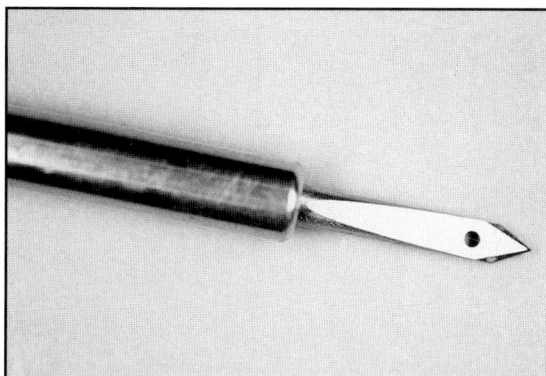

Figure V-23. A commercial gastrostomy tube applicator[a] can be used for percutaneous nonendoscopic gastrostomy tube placement in dogs and cats. The rigid outer tube encloses a trocar that can be pushed through the stomach and abdominal wall. A suture is placed through the small hole in the trocar tip, pulled into the stomach and then pulled antegrade out through the mouth. See Figure V-11 for use of this device in esophagostomy tube placement.

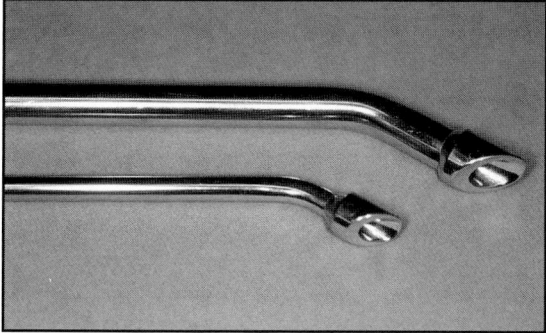

Figure V-24. Commercial gastrostomy tube placement devices in various lengths and diameters can be used for percutaneous nonendoscopic gastrostomy tube placement in dogs and cats.

ENDNOTES

a. Jorgensen Laboratories, Inc., Loveland, CO, USA.
b. Mill-Rose Laboratories, Inc., Mentor, OH, USA.
c. Cook Instruments Inc., Spencer, IN, USA.

BIBLIOGRAPHY

1. Abood SK, Buffington CA. Improved nasogastric intubation technique for administration of nutritional support in dogs. Journal of the American Veterinary Medical Association 1991; 199: 577-579.

2. Armstrong PJ, Hand MS, Frederick GS. Enteral nutrition by tube. Veterinary Clinics of North America: Small Animal Practice 1990; 20: 237-275.

3. Bright RM, DeNovo RC, Jones JB. Use of a low-profile gastrostomy device for administering nutrients in two dogs. Journal of the American Veterinary Medical Association 1995; 207: 1184-1186.

4. Crowe DT, Devey JJ. Esophagostomy tubes for feeding and decompression: Clinical experience in 29 small animal patients. Journal of the American Animal Hospital Association 1997; 33: 393-403.

5. Crowe DT, Downs MO. Pharyngostomy complications in dogs and cats and recommended technical modifications: Experimental and clinical investigations. Journal of the American Animal Hospital Association 1986; 22: 493-503.

6. Crowe DT. Clinical use of an indwelling nasogastric tube for enteral nutrition and fluid therapy in the dog and cat. Journal of the American Animal Hospital Association 1986; 22: 675-682.

7. DeBowes LJ, Coyne B, Layton CE. Comparison of French-Pezzer and Malecot catheters for percutaneously placed gastrostomy tubes in cats. Journal of the American Veterinary Medical Association 1993; 202: 1963-1965.

8. Devitt CM, Seim HB. Clinical evaluation of tube esophagostomy in small animals. Journal of the American Animal Hospital Association 1997; 33: 56-60.

9. Fossum TW, ed. Postoperative care of the surgical patient. In: Small Animal Surgery. St Louis, MO: Mosby-Year Book, Inc, 1997: 64-85.

10. Mauterer JV, Abood SK, Buffington CA, et al. New technique and management guidelines for percutaneous nonendoscopic tube gastrostomy. Journal of the American Veterinary Medical Association 1994; 205: 574-579.

AAFCO see Association of American Feed Control Officials.

abrasion (dental) excessive wear of the teeth due to contact with an external source.

absolute basis the quantity of nutrient needed by an animal in a 24-hour period; usually expressed as grams per kilogram body weight.

absorption the uptake of substrates into or across tissues.

acceptability/acceptance a food with enough gustatory and sensory appeal to allow the animal to eat enough to maintain body weight.

achromotrichia loss of normal hair color.

acquired pellicle an acellular organic, thin protein film deposited on tooth surfaces.

action level an FDA enforcement guideline that identifies the level of a contaminant that the agency believes adulterates a food product.

activity product the product of the chemical activities of two ionic materials, which is a mathematical expression used to estimate the degrees of saturation (that is undersaturation, supersaturation and oversaturation).

activity product ratio an ex vivo test that quantitatively measures the propensity to form urinary precipitates by determining the relative supersaturation of a test urine sample before and after incubation with purified seed crystals.

acute 1. a disease or clinical syndrome having a rapid onset, a short duration and pronounced clinical signs. 2. in toxicology, a single exposure or a continuous exposure that lasts less than 24 hours.

acute disease a disease having severe clinical signs and a course of 12 to 24 hours.

acute pyotraumatic dermatitis skin inflammation resulting from a dog or cat biting or scratching at a part of its body in an attempt to alleviate some painful stimulus or itch. Called also acute moist dermatitis or hot spot.

acute renal failure abrupt and sustained inability of the kidneys to regulate water and solute balance with rapid deterioration of renal function resulting in azotemia.

additive substances purposely put into foods to give them some desirable characteristic: color, flavor, texture, stability or resistance to spoilage.

ad libitum feeding at pleasure or performed with freedom; refers usually to providing an animal unlimited access to food or water. Called also free-choice feeding.

adverse reaction to food a clinically abnormal response to an ingested food or food additive.

advisory level a non-binding FDA guideline designed to advise the industry as to the maximum level of a particular contaminant that the agency believes to be "safe."

aerobic requires air or free oxygen to live and grow.

afterload the impedance to ventricular emptying; one determinant of cardiac output.

aging the progressive changes that occur after maturity in various organs that lead to decreased ability of an organism to meet the demands of the environment.

aldosterone the main mineralocorticoid secreted by the adrenal gland, the principal biologic activity of which is regulation of electrolyte and water balance by promoting the retention of sodium (and, therefore, water) and the excretion of potassium.

alopecia absence of hair from skin where it normally is present.

alpha-linolenic acid common name for an n-3 18-carbon polyunsaturated fatty acid with three double bonds. Chemically defined as all cis 9,12,15-octadecatrienoic acid (18:3n-3). Abbreviated commonly as ALA.

alveolar process the compact and cancellous bony structure that surrounds and supports the teeth.

amino acid(s) any organic compound containing an amino ($-NH_2$) and a carboxyl ($-COOH$) group that serves as a building block for proteins.

ammonia a colorless alkaline gas, NH_3, with a pungent odor and acrid taste, that is soluble in water. Ammonia is an end product of protein metabolism.

ammonium urate urolithiasis formation of uroliths composed primarily of ammonium urate with resultant clinical signs.

anabolic/anabolism the constructive phase of cellular metabolism in which simple molecules are assembled in stepwise reactions into more complex nutrient substances (carbohydrates, fats and proteins) by living cells.

anaerobic able to live and grow in the complete lack of air or free oxygen.

anaerobic metabolism metabolism that occurs in the absence of molecular oxygen.

anaerobic threshold the workload at which anaerobic metabolism becomes an important part of energy production and lactate begins to accumulate in the blood.

anagen the phase of the hair cycle during which hair is synthesized.

anagen defluxion sudden loss of hair due to an unusual event (e.g., antimitotic drugs, infectious disease, metabolic disease) that interferes with anagen, resulting in abnormalities of the hair follicle and hair shaft.

analyte(s) a substance(s) undergoing analysis.

angiotensin any of a family of polypeptide vasopressor hormones formed by the catalytic action of renin on angiotensinogen; angiotensin I is a relatively inactive precursor of angiotensin II; angiotensin II is a powerful vasopressor, a direct stimulator of sodium reabsorption and a stimulator of aldosterone release from the adrenal cortex.

angiotensin-converting enzyme (ACE) a peptidase enzyme found chiefly in the lung that converts the decapeptide angiotensin I to the octapeptide angiotensin II.

anorexia lack or loss of appetite; with **complete anorexia**, the patient eats nothing, whereas with **partial anorexia**, the patient eats some food but less than that required to meet resting energy requirement.

anosmia the inability to smell.

antacid a nutrient or non-nutrient substance that neutralizes acid; usually an orally administered compound used to safeguard gastrointestinal mucosa against damage by gastric acid.

anthropomorphic attributing human-based perceptions to the pet's needs or preferences.

antioxidant 1. a nutrient or non-nutrient substance that either prevents formation of, or quenches, free radicals. 2. one of many synthetic or natural substances added to a food to prevent or delay its deterioration via oxidation by either combining with free radicals or by scavenging oxygen.

apical   toward the root or apex of the tooth.

apterylae   featherless tracts in the skin of birds; feathers normally develop in rows or tracts called pterylae.

arachidonic acid   common name for an n-6 20-carbon polyunsaturated fatty acid with four double bonds from which prostaglandins, thromboxane and leukotrienes are derived; essential fatty acid for cats and some other species. Chemically defined as all cis 5,8,11,14-eicosatetraenoic acid (20:4n-6). Abbreviated commonly as AA.

arginine   an essential amino acid that is a key intermediate in the urea cycle, which is the major metabolic pathway that detoxifies nitrogenous wastes, such as ammonia. Arginine is also involved in formation of nitric oxide in the body, which helps regulate blood flow.

arginine vasopressin (AVP)   a hormone secreted by the pituitary gland that has vasopressor activity and influences resorption of water by the kidney tubules resulting in concentration of urine. Called also antidiuretic hormone (ADH).

aromatic amino acid(s)   the amino acids tyrosine, phenylalanine and tryptophan, which are characterized structurally by having a benzene ring.

arthritis (osteoarthritis)   disorder of movable joints characterized by deterioration of articular cartilage, osteophyte formation and bone remodeling, changes in periarticular tissues and low-grade inflammation.

ascites   abnormal accumulation of serous fluid within the peritoneal cavity, which may result in distention of the abdomen.

as fed basis   concentration of a nutrient in the food as it is fed to the animal; the nutrient concentration is adjusted to include the water content of the food.

ash   the incombustible inorganic residue remaining after incineration; generally the mineral content of food.

aspic   binder made from carageenen or other gums creating a jelly-like consistency.

Association of American Feed Control Officials (AAFCO)   agency that develops official pet food regulations for the United States.

atopy   a genetic predisposition toward the development of hypersensitivity (allergic) reactions against common environmental antigens such as pollen, molds, house dust mites, etc.

atrial natriuretic peptide/factor (ANP/ANF)   a peptide hormone found in cardiomyocytes of the atria that is thought to play a role in the regulation of blood pressure and blood volume.

attrition (dental)   excessive wear of the teeth due to tooth to tooth contact during mastication.

Atwater values   theoretical gross energy values for protein (4 kcal/g), carbohydrate (4 kcal/g) and fat (9 kcal/g).

availability (bioavailability)   the degree to which a drug or nutrient becomes available to the target tissue after administration or consumption.

azotemia   presence of abnormally high concentration of urea, creatinine and other nonprotein nitrogenous substances in the blood.

bacillus   a rod-shaped bacterial cell.

balance   see balanced food, ration or diet.

balanced food, ration or diet   1. one that provides an animal with the proper amounts and proportions of all the nutrients needed for a 24-hour period; avoids deficiencies and excesses. 2. all non-energy nutrients in the food are in proper concentration to the energy density of that food.

basal energy requirement (BER)   the energy requirement for a normal animal in a thermoneutral environment, awake but with no movement (resting) and in a postabsorptive (fasting) state.

behavior   the way in which an animal behaves or performs; blend of inherited (species-specific) and learned components.

beta-oxidation   an energy-yielding catabolism of fatty acids that occurs within the mitochondrial space.

bioavailability   see availability.

biotransformation   the series of chemical alterations of a compound (e.g., a drug) occurring within the body, as by enzymatic activity. Drug biotransformation may produce products that have effects different from those of the parent drug.

body condition score   an assessment of an animal's relative proportions of muscle and fat using both visual assessment and palpation, and comparing the animal under examination with a sterotyped animal on a chart.

body weight   an objective measure of the weight of an animal usually expressed as grams, kilograms, ounces or pounds.

bone remodeling   the process by which bone is restructured in response to physiologic cues. This process is controlled by hormonal, biomechanical and nutrient inputs and achieved through osteoclastic resorption and osteoblastic formation of new bone.

brachycephalic   skull type characterized as short and wide.

branched-chain amino acid(s)   the amino acids isoleucine, valine and leucine, which are characterized structurally as having an alkyl side chain, each with a methyl group branch.

brand name   the name by which products of a given company are identified; usually conveys the overall image of a product.

bring-down/cooling leg   final phase of the canning process in which the cans are cooled with 18-25°C water prior to labeling.

bring-up leg   initial phase of the canning process in which the cans are heated to temperatures of 80 to 100°C with hot water.

buccal   anatomic term referring to the tooth surface towards the cheek.

bulk ingredients   ingredients that are delivered in large quantities, i.e., rail cars, truckloads and "supersacks."

burst   an area of the principal display panel of a product label that is designed to highlight information or provide specific information in a visually impactful manner.

butyrate   a short-chain fatty acid produced by digestion and catabolism of dietary fibers by gut microflora; important source of energy for colonocytes.

cachexia   a profound and marked state of general ill health and malnutrition.

calcitonin   a peptide hormone produced in the C-cells of the thyroid gland in response to increases in plasma calcium concentrations.

calcium oxalate urolithiasis   formation of uroliths composed primarily of calcium and oxalate with resultant clinical signs.

calcium phosphate urolithiasis   formation of uroliths composed primarily of calcium and phosphate with resultant clinical signs.

calculolytic food   a food that when fed produces undersaturation of urine with calculogenic minerals such that uroliths are dissolved.

calculus (tartar) mineralized plaque that forms a hard shell on tooth surfaces.

caloric density energy per unit weight of food; usually expressed as kcal or kJ of metabolizable energy per gram of food or gram of food dry matter.

Canadian Veterinary Medical Association (CVMA) the organization that represents the veterinary profession in Canada.

cancer cachexia severe malnutrition and body wasting that occurs in patients with cancer.

canine behavior profiles typical behavior characteristics of purebred dogs that can be used to select a dog breed that suits an owner's environment, lifestyle and preferences.

canine hip dysplasia an abnormal development of the hip joint manifested by varying degrees of laxity of surrounding soft tissues, instability of the joint and malformation of the femoral head and acetabulum with osteoarthritis.

Canine Nutrition Expert (CNE) subcommittee a group of canine nutrition experts organized by AAFCO to develop nutrient profile guidelines for commercial dog foods.

canning a process of preserving high moisture food products. Metal cans are filled, sealed and cooked at high temperatures for the amount of time necessary to achieve commercial sterility.

carbohydrate an aldehyde or ketone derivative of a polyhydric alcohol; so named because the hydrogen and oxygen are usually in proportion to form water $(CH_2O)_n$. The most important carbohydrates are starches, sugars, celluloses and gums.

carbohydrate threshold the workload at which carbohydrate becomes a major energy substrate (30 to 50% $\dot{V}O_2$ max), but energy metabolism is still completely aerobic.

cardiac cachexia severe body wasting that occurs with chronic heart failure.

cardiac glycosides a group of compounds occurring in certain plants (e.g., *Digitalis*) having a characteristic action on the contractile force and electrical activity of the heart.

cardiac output the volume of blood pumped by the left ventricle per unit of time; usually expressed as liters (milliliters) per minute.

caries (dental) demineralization of tooth enamel with subsequent destruction of organic materials caused by the action of microorganisms on carbohydrates.

carnitine a water-soluble, vitamin-like quaternary amine found in high concentrations in mammalian cardiac and skeletal muscle.

carnivore any animal that eats primarily animal flesh.

carnivorous reptiles those members of the class *Reptilia* that eat primarily foodstuffs from animals.

carrion the decaying flesh of a body.

catabolic/catabolism the destructive phase of cellular metabolism in which complex nutrient substances (carbohydrates, fats and proteins) are degraded in stepwise reactions into simpler, smaller end products by living cells.

catagen the brief portion of the hair cycle in which hair growth (anagen) stops and resting (telogen) begins.

cecotrope specialized fecal pellets produced in the cecum and excreted during the night and early morning as clusters of grape-like material; rabbits and other species consume these pellets as an important part of the diet.

cecotrophy consumption of cecotropes.

Center for Veterinary Medicine (CVM) the section of the Food and Drug Administration charged with the primary responsibility for ensuring the safety of animal feeds and animal drugs used in the United States.

central proteins visceral proteins of which there are two types: constitutive such as albumin and transferrin, and acute-phase reactants such as globulins and ferritin.

cere the fleshy appendage lying across the base of the beak of birds containing the nares.

cervical (dental) at the neck of the tooth, the cementoenamel junction.

chelonians member of the order *Chelonia*; includes tortoises, terrapins, turtles and sea turtles.

choana the opening between the nasal cavity and the nasopharynx; plural choanae.

cholangiohepatitis inflammation of the biliary ducts and liver.

cholangitis inflammation of the biliary ducts, especially the intrahepatic ducts.

cholecalciferol vitamin D_3, a fat-soluble vitamin; the form of vitamin D produced de novo in animals by ultraviolet activation of 7-dehydrocholesterol.

cholecystitis inflammation of the gallbladder.

cholelithiasis the presence or formaton of gallstones.

choleretic an agent that stimulates bile production by the liver.

cholestasis stoppage or suppression of bile flow, due to intrahepatic or extrahepatic causes.

cholesterol a steroid alcohol in animal fats and oils, found in bile, brain tissue, milk, egg yolk, myelin sheaths of nerve fibers, the liver, kidneys and adrenal glands.

chondrocyte a mature cartilage cell embedded in a lacuna within the cartilage matrix.

chronic 1. a disease or clinical syndrome having a long duration. 2. in toxicology, a continuous exposure that exceeds 24 hours.

chronic disease a disease persisting for a long time, the period is undefined and varies with circumstances; usually more than one week. Also, a long-standing disease with little or slow progression.

chronic interstitial nephritis renal lesions characterized by mononuclear cell infiltration of the interstitium, loss of tubules, cortical and medullary fibrosis, tubular and glomerular atrophy or sclerosis and decreased renal function.

chronic progressive renal failure after a critical point is reached, a common pathway for progressive renal damage is activated, which relentlessly and irrepressibly impairs renal function, regardless of underlying cause.

chronic renal failure abnormal state that results from extensive irreversible reduction in the number of functional nephrons.

cirrhosis liver disease characterized pathologically by loss of normal microscopic lobular architecture with fibrosis and nodular regeneration.

cloaca a common passage for fecal, urinary and reproductive discharges in birds and most lower vertebrates.

closed registry databank of animal phenotypic information; an example is a registry to certify individual animals as free of radiographic evidence of hip dysplasia.

Clostridium botulinum rod-shaped, thermophilic, spore-forming, anaerobic bacterium that produce a potent neuroparalytic exotoxin responsible for botulism.

coenzyme an organic nonprotein molecule, frequently a derivative of a water-soluble vitamin, that is required by certain enzymes to produce their reactions.

cofactor a substance or compound with which another must unite in order to function.

colloid solution a solution containing particles larger than crystalloid molecules that resists diffusion; the particles are dispersed but not large enough to settle out by gravity.

colostrum the thick, milky fluid secreted by the mammary gland for several days before and after parturition. Colostrum contains antibodies and contributes to passive immunity.

commercial sterility the point at which processed canned foods are completely free of pathogenic microorganisms of public health significance.

compounding 1. the procedure for weighing and blending all of the ingredients in a recipe or formula in preparation for extrusion or retort cooking. 2. mixing two or more parenteral nutrient solutions into one bag.

compound urolith(s) urolith with a nucleus composed of one mineral type and a shell of a different mineral type.

conditionally essential nutrient a nonessential nutrient that becomes an essential nutrient when certain physiologic and pathophysiologic conditions result in relative deficiency.

Confédération des Industries Agro-Alimentaires de l' UE (CIAA) trade association for manufacturers of human foods and drinks in Europe.

congenital defects abnormalities of structure or function that are present at birth.

congenital renal disease renal disease present at birth that may be genetically determined or may result from exposure to adverse environmental factors during development.

congestive heart failure the form of heart failure characterized by pulmonary and/or systemic venous congestion associated with sodium chloride and water retention.

constipation infrequent or difficult evacuation of feces.

contaminant an agent that contaminates.

contaminate the addition of an agent (contaminant) that makes a food unfit for consumption.

cooker/mixer a device that serves the dual function of mixing raw ingredients together while beginning the cooking process; usually used in manufacture of commercial moist foods.

copper-associated hepatotoxicosis chronic liver disease associated with abnormal, excessive copper accumulation; autosomal recessive trait in Bedlington terrier dogs.

copper chelating agents agents that bind to copper and increase its excretion in urine; D-penicillamine and trientine are examples.

coprophagy ingestion of feces.

coronal (dental) toward the tooth crown.

cor pulmonale right ventricular enlargement due to pulmonary hypertension secondary to disease of pulmonary blood vessels.

crevicular pertaining to the gingival crevice or sulcus; e.g., crevicular fluid.

cricopharyngeal achalasia motor dysfunction of the cricopharyngeal sphincter in which a failure of relaxation prevents the food bolus from entering the esophagus during swallowing.

cruciferous plant any plant of the family *Cruciferae* such as mustard, cress, broccoli, cauliflower, rape, kale, chou moellier or canola.

crude fat method of expressing fat as determined by a specific analytical procedure that estimates the lipid content of a food using an ether extraction technique.

crude fiber method of expressing fiber as determined by a specific analytical procedure that represents the organic residue that remains after plant material has been treated with dilute acid and alkali solutions; this technique usual-

ly underestimates the level of true dietary fiber in the product because crude fiber primarily consists of hemicellulose and cellulose but fails to include pectins and gums.

crude protein method of expressing protein resulting as determined by a specific analytical procedure that estimates protein content by measuring nitrogen.

crust a layer of solid matter that forms when dried exudate, serum, pus, blood, cells, scales or medications adhere to the skin surface.

crystal a naturally produced angular solid of definite form with systematically arranged units, usually evenly spaced on a lattice.

crystallization the formation of crystals; conversion to a crystalline form.

crystallization inhibitors substances found in urine that inhibit mineral crystallization or aggregation.

crystallization promoters substances found in urine that promote mineral crystallization or aggregation.

crystalloid solution a solution that contains particles smaller than colloid molecules and passes readily through animal membranes.

crystalluria microscopic stones (microliths) formed as a result of precipitation of minerals and other metabolites in urine.

CVMA Pet Food Certification Program a program of pet food certification in Canada developed and administered by the Canadian Veterinary Medical Association.

cyclooxygenase pathway cellular pathway in which arachidonic acid is converted to prostaglandins and thromboxanes.

cystine urolithiasis formation of uroliths composed primarily of cystine with resultant clinical signs.

cystinuria excretion of excessive amounts of the nonessential amino acid cystine in urine. Possibly associated with excretion of other amino acids in urine.

cystitis inflammation of the urinary bladder.

cystocentesis puncture of the urinary bladder for the purpose of obtaining an uncontaminated urine sample.

cytokine compound synthesized by activated cells of the immune system that enhances the proliferation and differentiation of other cells in the immune system in response to immune stimulation.

cytoprotective agents substance that guards against cellular damage; usually an orally administered, non-absorbable compound used to safeguard gastrointestinal mucosa.

daily energy requirement (DER) the total daily energy requirement of an animal; normally calculated by multiplying resting energy requirement by a factor that represents age, neuter status, activity, reproductive status, etc.

deficiency 1. a lack or defect. 2. a range of nutrient concentrations at which physiologic function is consistently and reproducibly impaired.

degenerative joint disease diarthroidal joint disorders characterized by progressive deterioration of articular cartilage; osteoarthrosis, osteoarthritis or secondary joint disease.

dental substrate material that accumulates on the tooth surface such as pellicle, plaque, calculus and materia alba.

dermis the layer of the skin underlying the epidermis.

designator terminology appearing on the principal display panel of a pet food label that clearly identifies the food for animal consumption ("dog food" or "for cats"). Called also the statement of intent.

developmental orthopedic disease bone and joint disease caused by alterations in endochondral ossification during growth and differentiation of bone and supporting soft tissues.

diabetes insipidus central diabetes insipidus is a metabolic disorder attributable to deficient quantities of antidiuretic hormone (ADH, vasopressin) released or produced resulting in failure of tubular reabsorption of water in the kidney; marked polydipsia and polyuria are clinical signs.

diabetes mellitus a broadly applied term used to denote several clinical syndromes that have in common an alteration in the cellular transport and metabolism of glucose.

diarrhea abnormal increase in the frequency, fluidity or volume of feces resulting from excessive fecal water content.

diastema the space or cleft in the dental arch between the incisors and canines and cheek teeth. Called also interdental space. A large diastema is characteristic of rodents.

dietary history in a clinical examination, the collection and recording of facts about the foods, water, snacks and treats fed to an animal and the feeding methods employed.

dietary indiscretion adverse reactions resulting from such behaviors as gluttony, pica or ingestion of indigestible material.

dietetic pet food the official term in Europe that describes those pet foods sold by veterinarians for management or prevention of specific diseases.

digest 1. the physiologic process of converting food into chemical substances that can be absorbed and assimilated. 2. a generic term for a class of flavor enhancers. Meat or poultry tissue/organs are "digested" with acids or enzymes that breakdown protein and/or fats creating new compounds. Digests can be either liquid or dry forms.

digestibility the percentage of the food's gross nutrient content released following mechanical and chemical digestive processes. Digestibility is influenced by both food characteristics and the digestive efficiency of the host.

digestible energy (DE) the energy remaining after the energy lost in feces is subtracted from gross energy.

digestible protein the protein remaining after the protein lost in feces is subtracted from protein in food.

dihomogammalinolenic acid common name for an n-6 20-carbon polyunsaturated fatty acid with three double bonds. Chemically defined as all cis 8,11,14-eicosatrienoic acid (20:3n-6). Abbreviated commonly as DGLA.

diphyodont having two dentitions, a deciduous and a permanent.

docosahexaenoic acid common name for an n-3 22-carbon polyunsaturated fatty acid with six double bonds. Chemically defined as all cis 4,7,10,13,16,19-docosahexaenoic acid (22:6n-3). Abbreviated commonly as DHA.

drug absorption the act of taking up drugs by the body by specific chemical or molecular action.

drug conjugation the joining of a drug with a natural substance of the body to form a product for elimination from the body.

drug distribution the process by which a drug is delivered to tissues distant from the site of absorption.

drug efficacy the ability of a drug to produce its intended effects.

drug metabolism the process by which a drug is chemically altered by the body's tissues following absorption and distribution.

drug toxicity the ability of a drug to produce undesirable or deleterious effects.

dryer a large machine built for the purpose of removing moisture from pet food kibbles with dry heated air during manufacture.

dry matter food residue after it has been heated to a constant weight and all of the moisture in the sample has been removed.

dry matter basis expression of nutrient content of food or the requirements of an animal on a moisture-free basis.

dry matter, energy basis defined expression of the nutrient content of a food on a moisture-free basis at a defined caloric concentration.

dry mix the combination of all dry ingredients that make up a recipe or formula.

duration see exercise duration.

dyschezia difficult or painful defecation.

dysecdysis abnormal shedding of the skin of reptiles, usually associated with malnutrition, dehydration or poor environment (too cold, too dry).

dysuria painful or difficult urination.

eating behavior behavior exhibited when eating food.

ectothermic the regulation of body temperature by the external environment rather than by internal metabolism, with thermoregulation accomplished by behavioral means; i.e., the animal seeks an appropriate environmental temperature.

EFA-responsive dermatoses a variety of skin diseases that are not due to essential fatty acid (EFA) deficiency but seem to respond to high levels of dietary essential fatty acids.

eicosanoid(s) a family of compounds derived from arachidonic acid (e.g., prostaglandins, leukotrienes, thromboxanes and lipoxins) that have various metabolic functions in animals.

eicosapentaenoic acid common name for an n-3 20-carbon polyunsaturated fatty acid with five double bonds. Chemically defined as all cis 5,8,11,14,17-eicosapentaenoic acid (20:5n-3). Abbreviated commonly as EPA.

elemental liquid food see monomeric liquid food.

endocardiosis an idiopathic degenerative disease of the atrioventricular (AV) valves that leads to valvular insufficiency. Called also chronic acquired degenerative valvular disease.

endoscopy visual inspection of any cavity of the body by means of an endoscope.

endothermic thermoregulation accomplished by internal heat production.

endotoxin a toxic substance (usually cell wall material of gram-negative bacteria) that is released following disruption of the cell.

endurance exercise exercise that is long in duration, usually several hours, and relies primarily on aerobic metabolism.

energy the ability to do work; all activities of the body require energy and all needs are met by the consumption of food containing energy in chemical form.

energy basis concentration of a nutrient in food expressed per unit of energy, usually per 100 kcal or 1 megajoule of metabolizable energy.

energy density see caloric density.

enophthalmos backward displacement of the eye into the orbit.

enrobe the process of coating commercial dry pet food with either liquids or powders; e.g., fat and flavor enhancers.

enrober rotating drum-like device that evenly coats dry pet foods.

enteral feeding use of the upper alimentary tract (mouth, esophagus, stomach, small intestine) as a route for assisted feeding of patients.

enterohepatic cycling the process by which a substance, either native or foreign to the body, undergoes recirculation between the intestine and liver, via the portal venous system and biliary tract.

enterotoxemia a condition characterized by toxins in the blood produced in the intestines.

enterotoxin a bacterial toxin that has specificity for intestinal cells.

epidermis the outermost and avascular layer of the skin.

epinephrine a hormone produced by the adrenal gland that aids in the regulation of the sympathetic nervous branch of the autonomic nervous system; powerful vasopressor that increases heart rate and cardiac output, increases glycogenolysis and release of glucose from the liver.

essential amino acid(s) amino acid(s) required for protein synthesis that cannot be synthesized by animals and must be obtained in the food; arginine, histadine, isoleucine, leucine, lysine, methionine, phenylalanine, threonine, tryptophan, valine, taurine (cats).

essential fatty acid(s) (EFA) polyunsaturated, long-chain fatty acid(s) necessary for normal body function that cannot be synthesized de novo by mammals and must be obtained from the food.

ethoxyquin highly effective synthetic antioxidant approved for use in pet foods.

European Commission (EC) the main legislative body of the European Union; makes proposals for directives and legislation, and monitors the application of treaties and decrees.

European Economic Community (EEC) an economic association first established in 1958 to abolish barriers to free trade among member nations and adopt common import duties on goods from other countries. The name of the EEC was changed to Economic Community (EC) with the Treaty of Maastricht in 1992.

European Union (EU) same as the Economic Community (see European Economic Community). The EU currently includes 15 countries: Austria, Belgium, Denmark, Finland, France, Germany, Greece, Ireland, Italy, Luxembourg, the Netherlands, Portugal, Spain, Sweden and the United Kingdom.

exercise performance of physical activity characterized by muscle contraction and energy expenditure.

exercise duration the length of time of exercise. Exercise duration and intensity dictate caloric requirement and preferred substrate type.

exercise energy requirement (EER) energy expended for muscular activity.

exercise frequency how often exercise is performed; i.e., times per day or week.

exercise intensity the amount of work done (or energy used) per unit time, often expressed as a percentage of $\dot{V}O_2$ max. Low intensity is up to 30% $\dot{V}O_2$ max; high intensity is >75% $\dot{V}O_2$ max.

exercise training consistent performance of some type of exercise with the purpose of producing a measurable effect on body systems used in that type of exercise. Intensity, duration and frequency must be great enough to produce a measurable effect on the systems being trained.

exocrine pancreatic insufficiency inability of the pancreas to produce and secrete adequate amounts of digestive enzymes resulting in maldigestion, steatorrhea, weight loss and an unthrifty appearance.

exotoxin a toxic substance formed by certain species of bacteria and found outside the bacterial cell.

exposure an actual or suspected contact with an organism or substance.

extrudate dough-like material cooked in an extruder under pressure and heat before forming and cutting. Cutting the strands of extrudate into short pieces as they exit the extruder forms kibbles.

extruder primary cooking/forming machine in the manufacture of dry and semi-moist pet foods and snacks. The extruder is made up of a cylindrical multi-segmented barrel that contains the screw(s) and shaping die.

facial (dental) anatomic term referring to the tooth surface towards the lip or cheek; subdivided into labial and buccal surfaces.

familial nephropathy renal disease that occurs in related animals with a higher frequency than would be expected by chance.

fat 1. the adipose or fatty tissue of the body. 2. neutral fat; a triacylglyceride that contains three fatty acids attached to glycerol by an ester linkage.

fatty acid(s) any straight-chain monocarboxylic acid, especially those occurring in fats; generally classified as **saturated fatty acids**, those with no double bonds; **monounsaturated fatty acids**, those with one double bond; and **polyunsaturated fatty acids (PUFA)**, those with multiple double bonds.

Fédération Européenne de l'Industrie des Aliments pour Aminaux Familiers (FEDIAF) trade association representing the pet food industry in Europe.

feeding behavior behavior exhibited when obtaining or eating food.

feeding method how foods are fed to an animal including the feeding route, amount fed and how the food is offered (when, where, by whom and how often).

feeding trial a timed, variable-controlled period of food intake that measures a characteristic or biologic effect of the food.

feline lower urinary tract disease (FLUTD) disease in cats recognized by hematuria, dysuria, pollakiuria and/or urethral obstruction; these signs may result from a variety of etiologies such as infection, urolithiasis, neoplasia, neurogenic disorders, inflammatory conditions and anatomic defects.

Feline Nutrition Expert (FNE) subcommittee a group of feline nutrition experts organized by AAFCO to develop nutrient profiles for commercial cat foods.

feline urologic syndrome (FUS) a historical term used to describe the clinical state that accompanies lower urinary tract disease in cats.

fermentation the anaerobic enzymatic conversion of organic compounds, especially carbohydrates, to simpler compounds such as volatile fatty acids. An essential part of the digestion that occurs in the colon and cecum.

fiber that portion of ingested foodstuffs that cannot be broken down by intestinal enzymes of mammals and, therefore, passes through the small intestine undigested. It is composed of cellulose, hemicellulose, gums, pectin and other undigestible carbohydrates.

fibrosis accumulation of extracellular collagen and connective tissue.

filler/sealer a high-speed machine used in the canning process to fill and seal cans.

fines very small particles of dry pet foods found at the bottom of the container (e.g., bag).

finicky an ingestive behavior requiring highly palatable food offerings or frequent flavor changes for adequate acceptability and food consumption.

flag an area of the principal display panel on a pet food label that is designed to highlight information or provide specific information in a visually impactful manner.

flatulence excessive formation of gases in the stomach or intestine; flatus is gas expelled through the anus.

flavoprotein a conjugated protein containing a flavin nucleotide.

flavor rotation a feeding practice consisting of frequent changes of flavors or varieties to increase consumption.

food addiction an extension of the term finicky in which all foods and flavors except one have become unacceptable.

food additive a substance purposely incorporated in food to provide desirable characteristics, including color, flavor, texture, stability or resistance to spoilage.

food allergy an acute or chronic adverse food reaction due to an immunologic reaction resulting from ingestion of a food or food additive. Called also food hypersensitivity.

food anaphylaxis a classic, acute allergic (hypersensitivity) reaction to food or food additives with systemic consequences such as respiratory distress, vascular collapse and urticaria.

Food and Drug Administration (FDA) the federal government body with primary responsibility for regulating foods, food additives, drugs and cosmetics in the United States.

food dosage the amount of a given food required by an animal to meet its nutritional requirements.

food idiosyncrasy an abnormal response that resembles food allergy, but does not involve immune mechanisms; a type of food intolerance.

food intolerance a non-immunologic, abnormal physiologic response to a food or food additive.

food poisoning an adverse effect caused by the direct action of a food or food additive on the host without the involvement of immune mechanisms. Called also food toxicosis.

food-restricted meal feeding a method of feeding animals whereby a specific amount of food is fed at specific intervals throughout the day.

free-choice feeding unlimited access to food throughout the day. Called also ad libitum feeding.

frequency see exercise frequency.

furcation (dental) the normal anatomic space where a tooth root or roots join the tooth crown.

futile cycling two opposing reactions, using different enzymatic processes, that when summed result in the net hydrolysis of ATP, loss of energy as heat and no net change of substrate.

Future Directions for Veterinary Medicine report issued in 1989 by the Pew National Veterinary Education Program that identified emerging trends in veterinary medicine and veterinary education in the United States.

fuzzy mice one- to two-week-old haired mice used as prey for captive reptiles.

GALT (gut-associated lymphoid tissue) lymphoid tissue associated with the gut including the tonsils, Peyer's patches, and lamina propria of the gastrointestinal tract.

gamma-linolenic acid common name for an n-6 18-carbon polyunsaturated fatty acid with three double bonds. Chemically defined as all cis 6,9,12-octadecatrienoic acid (18:3n-6). Abbreviated commonly as GLA.

gastric dilatation-volvulus a syndrome of gastric dilatation leading to volvulus seen most often in deep-chested, large- and giant-breed dogs; usually fatal unless recognized and treated early. Called also bloat.

gastric stasis reduced stomach motility leading to retention of gastric contents.

gastroesophageal junction anatomic region where the esophagus enters the stomach; lower esophageal sphincter is the functional term used for this region.

gelatinization cooking of starch by rupturing the starch granules under conditions of moisture and heat.

generic pet food non-branded pet foods emphasizing "lowest cost."

geriatric cats cats 12 years old and older that typically have outward signs of aging.

geriatric dogs dogs nine to 12 years old or older, depending on breed, that typically have outward signs of aging.

geriatrics the branch of medicine dealing with the problems of aging and diseases of older animals.

gestation the period of development of the young in viviparous animals from the time of ovum fertilization to birth.

giant-breed dogs dogs with adult body weights in excess of 50 kg.

gingiva(e) the portion of the oral mucosa that covers the alveolar processes and the cervical portions of the teeth. Subdivided into the attached and free gingiva.

gingival margin the coronal rim of the free gingival tissue.

gingival recession loss of gingiva resulting in loss of gingival attachment.

gingival sulcus the normal space between the free gingival margin and the tooth.

gingivitis inflammation of the gingivae or gum tissue.

gliadin a glutamine- and proline-rich polypeptide found in some cereal flours and thought to contain a toxic factor responsible for causing gluten-sensitive enteropathy in susceptible people (celiac disease) and dogs.

glomerular capillary hypertension critical intraglomerular hemodynamic factor responsible for promoting glomerular injury.

glomerular hyperfiltration reducing renal mass increases single nephron glomerular filtration rate (SNGFR) in surviving nephrons. Increased SNGFR is accompanied by intraglomerular hemodynamic changes that increase flux of plasma proteins through the mesangium. The presence of these proteins stimulates mesangial cell proliferation and matrix production and eventually leads to glomerulosclerosis.

glomerulations raised network of blood vessels visible during cystoscopic examination of human patients with interstitial cystitis.

glomerulopathy any disease of the renal glomeruli.

glucagon a polypeptide hormone secreted by the pancreas (alpha cells of the islets) in response to hypoglycemia or to stimulation by growth hormone. It increases blood glucose concentration by stimulating glycogenolysis in the liver.

glucocorticoids any corticoid substance (hormone of the adrenal cortex or other natural or synthetic compound with similar activity) that increases gluconeogenesis, raising the concentration of liver glycogen and blood glucose; examples include cortisol, cortisone and corticosterone.

glucokinase an enzyme that in the presence of ATP catalyzes glucose to glucose-6-phosphate; similar to hexokinase but active at much higher glucose concentrations.

glucose intolerance the impaired cellular uptake or metabolism of glucose caused by certain metabolic or receptor abnormalities; may lead to delayed glucose disappearance, hyperglycemia, hyperinsulinemia or abnormal patterns of insulin secretion in response to a glucose load.

glutamine a five-carbon amino acid that plays a key metabolic role in the citric acid cycle, transamination reactions, the antioxidant glutathione and as a folic acid cofactor. Glutamine is a conditionally essential nutrient.

gluten   the protein of wheat, barley and other cereal grains, which gives dough its tough elastic character; gluten is a mixture of gliadin and glutenin.

glycine   a nonessential amino acid postulated to be a neurotransmitter in the central nervous system.

glycoprotein   a class of compounds consisting of a protein conjugated to a carbohydrate.

gonadectomy   removal of the testes or ovaries.

gout   a disorder of uric acid metabolism characterized by hyperuricemia and deposition of urates in and around the joints.

grease out   migration of fat through the inner liner of the package leaving a grease stain on the outside of the package.

grocery pet food   nationally or regionally branded pet foods emphasizing palatability and available for purchase in grocery outlets.

gross energy (GE)   the total potential energy of a foodstuff determined by measuring the total heat produced when the food is burned in a bomb calorimeter.

growing cats   young cats less than 10 to 12 months old that are in the active stage of growth and maturation.

growing dogs   young dogs less than 14 months old that are in the active stage of growth or maturation.

growth hormone   a peptide secreted by the pituitary gland that directly influences protein, carbohydrate and lipid metabolism, and controls the rate of skeletal and visceral growth.

guaranteed analysis   that portion of the pet food label that lists or guarantees certain minimum or maximum levels of nutrients.

gustation   the sense of taste.

hair cycle   the cycle of events associated with hair growth, which consists of a growing period (anagen), a resting period (telogen) and a transitional period (catagen) between these two stages.

halitosis   oral malodor, foul breath.

headspace   the air space between the product and package in moist or dry pet foods.

health maintenance   see wellness.

heart disease   numerous anatomic and physiologic abnormalities of the heart or great vessels that may or may not become clinically significant.

heart failure   the set of extracardiac signs resulting from the inability of the heart to deliver enough blood to the peripheral tissues to meet metabolic demands of the body for nutrients.

heat labile   destroyed by temperatures achieved by normal cooking.

hedonics   the branch of psychology that deals with pleasurable and unpleasurable experiences.

hematemesis   vomiting of blood.

hematochezia   fresh blood adherent to feces.

hematuria   blood in urine.

hemochromatosis   severe abnormal accumulation of iron in hepatic parenchymal cells and other organs of certain birds (mynahs, hornbills, birds of paradise) resulting in anorexia, weight loss, hepatomegaly, ascites, dyspnea and sudden death.

hepatic encephalopathy   the complex neurologic and behavior disturbances that may occur with either congenital portacaval vascular shunts or advanced acquired liver disease.

hepatic lipidosis   abnormal accumulation of lipids in the liver.

hepatitis   inflammation of the liver.

hepatocyte   a liver cell.

hepatopathy   any disease of the liver.

herbivore   any animal that eats primarily plants and plant products.

herbivorous reptiles   those members of the class *Reptilia* that eat primarily foodstuffs from plants.

heterothermic   animals with a wide range of body temperatures that reflect environmental temperatures.

hexokinase   an enzyme that catalyzes the transfer of a high-energy phosphate group of ATP to a hexose sugar, usually D-glucose, producing D-glucose-6-phosphate.

hindgut fermenter   those animals that digest and assimilate their food primarily through fermentation in the cecum and large intestine.

homeostasis   a tendency to stability in the normal body states (internal environment) of the organism.

humectant   a substance that adds or retains moisture; e.g., propylene glycol, high fructose corn syrup and glycerine.

hunger   1. a craving for food. 2. a localized subjective sensation, assumed to occur in animals, caused by emptiness and a resulting hypermotility of the stomach.

hydrophilic   strong affinity for water.

hygroscopic   a material that has a high affinity to absorb moisture.

hyperammonemia   a metabolic disorder marked by elevated concentrations of ammonia or ammonium ions in blood.

hypercalcitoninism   excessive secretion of calcitonin and the resultant changes. Hypercalcitoninism may contribute to the pathophysiology of developmental orthopedic disease in some dogs.

hypercalciuria   excretion of excessive amounts of calcium in urine.

hyperglycemia   elevated concentrations of blood glucose.

hyperinsulinemia   persistently elevated levels of blood insulin.

hyperkeratinization   excessive development of epidermal keratin.

hyperkeratosis   increased thickness of the stratum corneum (horny layer of the skin).

hyperlactatemia   elevated concentrations of blood lactate; this phenomenon occurs in many patients with cancer because of altered carbohydrate metabolism.

hyperlipidemia   a general term for elevated concentrations of any or all lipids in the blood.

hyperoxaluria   excretion of excessive amounts of urinary oxalates.

hyperparathyroidism   abnormally increased activity of the parathyroid gland with excessive secretion of parathyroid hormone (parathormone), which may be primary or secondary. Secondary nutritional hyperparathyroidism is usually due to inadequate calcium intake.

hyperplasia (skin)   increased thickness of the noncornified epidermis due to increased numbers of epidermal cells.

hypertension (systemic)   sustained abnormally high blood pressure that may be associated with end organ changes, such as retinal hemorrhage.

hypervitaminosis A   a condition produced by ingestion or injection of excessive amounts of vitamin A; most commonly observed in cats and reptiles.

hypoglycemia   an abnormally decreased concentration of blood glucose.

hypotension   persistently lowered blood pressure.

hypothyroidism   the clinical syndrome resulting from a deficiency of thyroxine.

hypovitaminosis A   a condition produced by ingestion of insufficient amounts of vitamin A; usually associated with squamous metaplasia of epithelium and frequently observed in reptiles and birds eating unbalanced diets.

idiopathic cystitis   a term applied to cats with non-obstructive, chronic, recurrent lower urinary tract signs that have met inclusion and exclusion criteria adapted from interstitial cystitis in human beings.

ileus   1. obstruction of the intestines. 2. dilatation of intestines associated with inhibition of bowel motility. Called also adynamic ileus.

immunomodulation   the suppression or augmentation of an immune response.

immunonutrition   the practice of using nutrients for immunomodulation.

incidence   the proportion of individuals that develop the condition of interest over a defined period of time. Incidence refers to only new cases and thus reflects the risk of becoming a case during a defined time period.

indirect calorimetry   calculation of heat production by measuring the respiratory exchange of oxygen and carbon dioxide. Calorimetry is important in measuring and understanding the factors that influence energy requirements.

inflammatory bowel disease   a group of heterogeneous disorders in which mucosal inflammation of the stomach, small intestine and/or colon is found without evidence of other disorders; most commonly causes chronic vomiting or diarrhea in dogs and cats.

information panel   the part of the pet food label immediately contiguous to the principal display panel that contains important information about the product such as the ingredient statement, guaranteed or typical analysis, feeding directions, etc.

ingredient   a raw or processed agricultural commodity, or other nutrient source, used in food compounding.

ingredient statement   the list of food ingredients on the product label. The information found in the statement will vary depending on the country where the food is sold.

insulin   a peptide hormone formed from proinsulin in the beta cells of the pancreatic islets and secreted into the blood in response to an increase in blood glucose or amino acid concentrations. Insulin promotes storage of glucose and uptake of amino acids in insulin-sensitive tissues, increases protein and lipid synthesis and inhibits lipolysis and gluconeogenesis.

insulin-dependent diabetes mellitus (IDDM)   diabetes mellitus caused by an absolute deficiency of insulin; successful management requires administration of exogenous insulin or drugs that promote insulin secretion. Called also Type I diabetes mellitus in people.

insulin-secreting beta-cell tumor   a tumor of the beta cells of the pancreatic islets, which usually causes clinical signs associated with profound hypoglycemia due to excessive or inappropriate insulin secretion. Called also functional insulinoma.

intensity   see exercise intensity.

intermediary metabolism   the various chemical reactions involved in the transformation of food molecules into essential cellular building blocks.

intermediate exercise   exercise that lasts a few minutes to a few hours.

interstitial cystitis   term used in human medicine for patients, usually women, with lower urinary tract symptoms, including bladder pain and severe urgency, of chronic duration (>9 months) and unknown etiology when more common and objective conditions have been excluded.

invertebrate prey   animals (without endoskeletons) typically fed to reptiles and birds such as insects, worms, larvae, spiders, ant eggs, snails, slugs, etc.

iterative process   repetitive process.

keratin   a highly stable, fibrous protein containing disulfide bonds.

keratinization   the complex process by which a mitotically active cell in the basal layer of the epidermis becomes a dead keratinized cell in the superficial layer of the epidermis.

key nutritional factors   includes nutrients of concern and other food characteristics that have relevance to specific disease treatment or prevention goals.

kibble   extruded, formed, individual pieces of dry pet food.

kilocalorie (kcal)   one calorie is the energy needed to raise the temperature of 1 g water from 14.5 to 15.5°C. 1 kcal = 1,000 calories = 4.184 kJ.

kilojoule (kJ)   one kilojoule equals 107 ergs or the energy expended when 1 kg is moved 1 meter by 1 newton. 1kJ = 0.239 kcal.

kit   a newborn ferret, fox or mink.

Kjeldahl's method (test)   a method of determining the amount of nitrogen in an organic compound, which is then used to estimate crude protein content.

Km   Michaelis-Menten constant.

kwashiorkor   a syndrome in people produced by severe protein deficiency.

labial (dental)   anatomic term referring to the tooth surface towards the lip.

labile protein(s)   a small protein store (3% of body protein) readily lost or gained from the body in the adaptive response to starvation and repletion.

lactation   1. the secretion of milk by the mammary glands. 2. the period of time during which the dam lactates.

lactose   a sugar derived from milk, which on hydrolysis yields glucose and galactose.

lagomorph   hares and rabbits; members of the order *Lagomorpha*.

lamination   a laminar structure or arrangement.

large-breed dogs   dogs with adult body weights of 25 to 50 kg.

L-asparaginase   an enzyme that catalyzes the reaction L-asparagine + H_2O = L-aspartate + NH_3. This reaction occurs in mammalian and bacterial cells. The enzyme is used clinically in the treatment of human and animal cancers.

lead product   the member of a product family that has undergone nutritional adequacy testing; manufacturers of other members of the product family can make similar nutritional claims with limited testing.

lean body mass   the active metabolic fraction of the body exclusive of stored fat.

learned aversion   avoidance of a particular food because its previous intake was associated with an unpleasant experience (e.g., burned mouth or nausea).

leukotriene(s)   arachidonic acid metabolites produced predominantly by granulocytes, which mediate many of the inflammatory phenomena characteristic of immediate hypersensitivity reactions.

lifestage nutrition adapting the nutrient profile of the food to the specific requirements of the animal, which optimizes the nutritional plan, foods and feeding methods for the individual physiologic stages of an animal's life (growth, reproduction, adulthood, old age).

lingual (dental) anatomic term referring to the mandibular tooth surface towards the tongue.

linoleic acid common name for an n-6 18-carbon polyunsaturated fatty acid with two double bonds. Chemically defined as cis cis 9,12-octadecadienoic acid (18:2n-6). Abbreviated commonly as LA.

lipemia an excess of fat or lipid in the blood.

lipid any of a heterogeneous group of fats and fat-like substances that are water insoluble and extractable by nonpolar solvents such as alcohol, ether, benzene, etc.

lipophilic strong affinity for fats.

lipoproteins any of the macromolecular complexes that transport lipids in the blood. They consist of a core of hydrophobic lipids covered by a layer of phospholipids and apoproteins that make the complex water soluble.

lipotrope a nutrient or non-nutrient substance, that may prevent or correct disorders of hepatic lipid processing and/or hepatic lipidosis by hastening removal or decreasing the deposit of fat in the liver.

lipoxygenase pathway a pathway in which arachidonic acid is converted to leukotrienes and lipoxins.

liquid diets foods with greater than 90% moisture.

lymphangiectasia dilatation of lymphatic vessels; intestinal lymphangiectasia results in leakage of protein from intestinal villi (protein-losing enteropathy) with resulting hypoproteinemia, diarrhea, edema, ascites and weight loss.

macromineral those minerals required by animals in grams per day amounts.

macronutrient an essential nutrient that has a minimum daily requirement or allowance in milligrams, grams or kilograms per day.

maintenance energy requirement (MER) the energy requirement of a moderately active adult animal in a thermoneutral environment. It includes energy needed for obtaining, digesting and absorbing food in amounts to maintain body weight as well as energy for spontaneous activity.

malabsorption impaired intestinal absorption of nutrients from food.

malassimilation the inability of the gastrointestinal tract to take up one or more ingested nutrients whether due to faulty digestion (maldigestion) or to impaired intestinal mucosal transport (malabsorption).

maldigestion incomplete digestion of food as occurs with exocrine pancreatic insufficiency.

malnutrition abnormal nutrition; includes nutritional excesses and deficiencies.

malocclusion abnormal occlusion of teeth.

materia alba a soft mixture of salivary proteins, dead cells, food debris and miscellaneous matter that accumulates on tooth surfaces.

matrix the nondialyzable organic portion of uroliths that remains after crystalline components have been dissolved with mild solvents.

mature milk nutrient fluid secreted by the mammary gland starting several days after parturition.

megaesophagus generalized esophageal dilatation resulting from an aperistaltic esophagus secondary to a neuromuscular disorder.

melanin a wide range of pigments that are chiefly responsible for the coloration of skin and hair.

melena black, tarry feces resulting from digested blood.

metabolic acidosis condition that occurs when the balance between the addition of hydrogen ions to body fluids and their excretion by the kidney is disrupted.

metabolic body size see metabolic weight.

metabolic bone disease a range of bone diseases associated with metabolic disorders; e.g., renal secondary hyperparathyroidism, nutritional secondary hyperparathyroidism, rickets, osteoporosis.

metabolic food reaction an adverse reaction to a food or food additive as a result of the effect of the substance on the metabolism of the host (e.g., lactase deficiency).

metabolic phenotype a category of metabolic activity to which an individual may be assigned based on xenobiotic biotransformation capacity.

metabolic rate the rate of energy metabolism in the body. The basal metabolic rate is the rate of energy consumption by the body when it is completely at rest.

metabolic water water in the body derived from chemical reactions during metabolism of nutrients.

metabolic weight the body weight of an animal in kilograms raised to the three-quarters power (body weight$^{0.75}$) derived from the relationship between metabolism and size; provides a basis upon which to compare metabolism among species, breeds and animals of differing sizes.

metabolism the sum of all the physical and chemical processes by which organic substances are produced.

metabolizable energy (ME) energy available to the animal after energy from feces, urine and combustible gases has been substracted.

metabolizable protein protein available to the animal after protein from feces and urine has been subtracted.

metastable solution a solution, such as urine, that has the capacity to retain more of a compound in solution than would be predicted by knowledge of its true solubility in water.

microbe single cell organisms capable of causing disease in people and animals including bacteria, rickettsiae, protozoa and fungi.

microhepatica a smaller than normal liver.

micromineral those minerals required by an animal in the diet in milligrams per day amounts.

micronutrient an essential nutrient that has a minimum daily requirement or allowance in micrograms or less per day.

microsomal mixed-function oxidase system the enzymatic system responsible for phase I, cytochrome P450-dependent xenobiotic metabolism; predominantly located in the liver, but also in the kidneys, intestines and lungs.

mineral inorganic solid crystalline chemical element.

minimum nutrient requirements minimum nutrient intake that will maintain normal function.

Ministries of Agriculture administrative departments that are responsible for the implementation of European Union directives and regulations in their respective countries, which deal with animal health and disease prevention, and quality of animal products, plants and plant materials.

modified Atwater values theoretical metabolizable energy values for protein (3.5 kcal/g), carbohydrate (3.5 kcal/g) and fat (8.5 kcal/g).

modular liquid food a food with greater than 90% moisture that contains predominantly one nutrient.

molt (moult) the replacement of all feathers, typically following breeding and often preceding migration of birds. Molting in most birds follows a regular sequence within each feather tract.

monadic feeding test a feeding trial that tests the acceptance of a single food.

monomeric liquid food a food with greater than 90% moisture with nutrients in a simplified compounded form. Sometimes incorrectly called elemental food.

morbidity a diseased condition or state.

morphometry the measurement of body forms; e.g., limb length, pelvic circumference.

mortality 1. the quality of being mortal. 2. death as a statistic.

mouth feel the oral sensation as influenced by food temperature, viscosity, stickiness, kibble size/shape and particle brittleness.

mucoid enteropathy an enterotoxin-induced secretory diarrhea of rabbits, of unknown cause, characterized by watery diarrhea with abdominal distention.

mustelid a member of the *Mustelidae* family of carnivores including ferret, weasel, mink, wolverine, badger, skunk, sea otter, otter and ermine.

mutagenicity the property of being able to induce genetic mutation.

n-3 fatty acid shorthand notation that numbers the first double bond from the methyl terminal carbon atom of a fatty acid. Called also omega-3 fatty acid.

n-6 fatty acid shorthand notation that numbers the first double bond from the methyl terminal carbon atom of a fatty acid. Called also omega-6 fatty acid.

National Companion Animal Study a large companion animal epidemiologic study conducted by the Center for Companion Animal Health at the University of Minnesota.

National Research Council (NRC) a private, nonprofit organization that evaluates and compiles research done by others. The NRC functions as the working arm of the National Academy of Sciences, the National Academy of Engineers and the Institute of Medicine in the United States.

natriuresis excretion of increased amounts of sodium in the urine relative to intake; may occur in certain disease states or following therapy with certain drugs such as diuretics.

natural foods foods wholly composed of ingredients completely devoid of artificial or manmade substances including but not limited to synthetic flavors, colors, preservatives or other additives.

neonatal period pertaining to the period immediately after birth; the duration varies depending on the ability of the animal to survive without its dam but is usually several weeks.

neophobia reluctance or refusal to change from an established food to another one.

nephrocalcinosis precipitation of calcium salts in the tubulointerstitium of the kidney. Recognized histologically by the deposition of stainable calcium salts in the kidney.

net weight a declaration of the net quantity of contents; usually expressed as ounces, pounds, grams or kilograms on food labels.

nidus point of origin or focus of a morbid process; e.g., a urolith.

nitrogen a chemical element that constitutes four-fifths of common air, occurs in proteins and amino acids and is, thus, present in all living cells.

nonessential amino acid(s) amino acid(s) required for protein synthesis but which are synthesized in adequate quantities by animals from other amino acids and are not specifically required in the food.

non-insulin-dependent diabetes mellitus (NIDDM) diabetes mellitus characterized by insulin resistance at the peripheral tissues and/or dysfunctional beta cells in the pancreatic islets; referred to as a relative insulin deficiency because the amount of insulin actually secreted may be increased, decreased or normal. Called also Type II diabetes mellitus in people.

non-nutrient a chemical without metabolic value.

nucleation the initial event in the formation of uroliths, which is characterized by the appearance of submicroscopic molecular aggregates of crystalloids.

nutraceutical derived from the combination of "nutrients" and "pharmaceuticals," and the concept that specific substances may be prescribed in the treatment or prevention of a disease; often inplies the administration of nutrients in amounts that exceed their known dietary requirement.

nutrient a metabolically useful component of food; may be essential or nonessential.

nutrient allowances (dogs and cats) nutrient levels that are adequate to meet the known nutrient needs of almost all healthy dogs and cats. Allowances usually exceed minimum requirements because they include safety factors that compensate for food nutrient availability variances due to ingredient and processing variables and for individual differences in nutrient requirements within dog and cat populations.

nutrient profile the array and quantity of specific nutrients in food.

nutrient-responsive dermatoses a wide variety of skin disorders that are not due to a dietary nutrient deficiency but which respond to specific nutrient supplementation.

nutrients of concern nutrients of particular importance for managing specific diseases and/or to optimize normal physiologic processes such as growth, gestation, lactation and physical work.

nutrition(al) adequacy statement the statement on a pet food label that describes the type of animal for which the product is intended (growing animal, adult, reproducing female, etc.) and how the claim is substantiated. Called also product descriptor.

nutrition(al) claim nutrition statements appearing on the principal display panel of pet food labels; examples include "100% Nutritious" or "100% Complete Nutrition."

nutritional risk factors those nutrients, nutrient levels, foods and feeding methods that increase the risk for certain diseases in animals.

nutrition counseling providing advice about appropriate foods and feeding methods for an individual animal or group of animals.

obesity an increase in body weight as the result of an excessive accumulation of fat; obese individuals weigh 20% or more than optimal body weight.

oligosaccharides carbohydrates that yield only a small number of monosaccharides upon hydrolysis.

omnivore any animal eating both plant and animal foods.

omnivorous reptiles those members of the class *Reptilia* that eat foodstuffs from both animals and plant materials.

open registry databank of genetic history for any animal breed, individual and for specific genetic diseases.

open-rooted teeth teeth having persistently open apices that grow for the life of the tooth and with no distinct root structure; continuously growing teeth. Lagomorphs and rodents have this type of tooth structure.

oral malodor see halitosis.

oral tolerance an immunologic response consisting of the development of specific nonreactivity of the gastrointestinal lymphoid tissue to a given antigen that in other circumstances can induce cell-mediated or humoral immunity.

organic foods foods with ingredients from cereals or grains grown with fertilizers or pesticides of animal or vegetable origin (not synthetic) and ingredients from animals that were not treated with hormones.

organonitrile an organic compound containing the -CN moiety; a characteristic component of cruciferous plants.

orthokeratosis a form of hyperkeratosis in which the cells do not have nuclei.

osmolality a property of a solution that depends on the concentration of the solute per unit of solvent.

osmolarity a property of a solution that depends on the concentration of osmotically active particles in solution.

osteochondritis dissecans (OCD) a specific form of osteochondrosis in which the cartilage flap above the lesion is released into the joint and perpetuates the cycle of joint disease.

osteochondrosis a disruption in endochondral ossification that results in focal lesions of growth cartilage.

overnutrition an excess of a nutrient or nutrients that results in a pathologic lesion or response.

overweight an excessive increase in adipose tissue (fat); overweight individuals weigh 10 to 19% more than optimal body weight.

oxidative potential propensity to oxidize.

palatability the relative preference for two foods as measured by standardized methods.

palatal (dental) anatomic term referring to the maxillary tooth surface towards the palate.

pancreatitis inflammation of the pancreas.

parakeratosis a form of hyperkeratosis in which the cells have nuclei.

parathyroid hormone (PTH) a peptide hormone released from the parathyroid gland in response to decreased concentrations of calcium in blood, which is important in calcium homeostasis. Called also parathormone.

parenteral administered by some other route than the alimentary canal.

parenteral nutrition administration of nutritional support by some route other than the alimentary canal; typical routes include intravenous, intraosseous and intraperitoneal. **Partial parenteral nutrition** meets only part of the patient's nutritional requirements and often supplements nutrition by the enteral route, whereas **total parenteral nutrition** meets all the patient's nutritional requirements.

paronychia inflammation involving the folds of tissue surrounding the toe nail.

partial anorexia see anorexia.

partial orphan rearing use of enteral feedings with milk replacers to supplement nursing; most often used when the bitch or queen produces insufficient milk for the entire litter.

partial parenteral nutrition see parenteral nutrition.

partitioning 1. dividing into parts. 2. the process by which a drug becomes distributed between different interfacing compartments as affected by ionization or solvent affinity.

passerine birds belonging to the order *Passeriformes*; includes 5,000 or more perching birds such as finches, sparrows, buntings, mynahs, canaries and serins.

Pearson square a simplified box method of determining the relative proportions of two ingredients required to achieve a particular intermediate nutrient concentration.

pecten a comb or comb-like structure in birds.

percent body fat (%BF) the percentage of the body weight that is adipose tissue (fat).

periodontal disease any pathologic process that affects the periodontium.

periodontal ligament a structure composed primarily of connective tissue fibers located between the cementum and the alveolar bone.

periodontitis gingivitis plus inflammation/destruction of the supporting periodontium (cementum, periodontal ligament, alveolar bone).

periodontium the structures that surround and support the tooth; gingivae, cementum, periodontal ligament and alveolar bone.

peripheral protein(s) skeletal muscle protein(s).

pesticide a substance that prevents, destroys, mitigates or repels any pest.

Pet Food Institute (PFI) the national trade organization of dog and cat food manufacturers in the United States.

pharmaceutical 1. pertaining to pharmacy or drugs. 2. a medicinal drug.

pharmacokinetics the action of drugs in the body over a period of time, including the processes of absorption, distribution, localization in tissues, biotransformation and excretion.

pharmacologic food reaction an adverse reaction to a food or food additive as a result of a naturally derived or added chemical that produces a drug-like or pharmacologic effect in the host.

phase I metabolism the process of xenobiotic modification through oxidation, reduction, and/or hydrolysis by the cytochrome P-450 enzyme system.

phase II metabolism the process of xenobiotic modification through glutathione or glucuronide conjugation, acetylation, and/or sulfation by enzymatic systems.

phenylalanine an essential amino acid.

phytin/phytate/phytic acid forms of organic phosphorus, presumably inositol hexaphosphate, occurring in plant proteins.

phytochemical a chemical derived from plants.

pica craving and eating unnatural articles of food or foreign materials; a depraved appetite.

pinkie mice hairless neonatal (newborn) mice used as prey for captive reptiles.

plaque (dental) soft, sticky organic deposit on the tooth surfaces, composed primarily of bacteria and salivary glycoproteins.

pododermatitis inflammation of the skin of the foot.

pollakiuria abnormally frequent urination.

polymeric liquid food a food with a moisture content greater than 90% containing nutrients in a macro compounded form.

polyunsaturated fatty acid a fatty acid carbon chain that contains more than one double bond. Abbreviated commonly as PUFA.

portal hypertension a persistent increase in portal venous pressure.

portosystemic shunt single or multiple blood vessel abnormalities, intrahepatic or extrahepatic in location, that result in venous blood from the intestine bypassing the liver.

postprandial occurring after meals. Called also postcibal.

powder down powdery white substance normally found on feathers of white cockatoo species, African grey parrots and cockatiels.

power work done per unit time (the rate of doing work); metabolic power is energy turnover per unit time.

ppb part per billion.

ppm part per million.

preference feeding test a feeding trial that tests two foods side by side for comparative choice preferences between the pair.

pregnancy toxemia in guinea pig sows, particularly obese ones, uteroplacental ischemia in late pregnancy, causing lethargy, anorexia and rapid death.

preload ventricular end-diastolic volume; one determinant of cardiac output.

premaxilla a bone in the upper jaw of birds that serves as the major supporting structure for the beak.

premium pet food a market category of foods featuring high quality ingredient and processing standards.

preprandial occurring before meals.

preservative substances added to foods to protect or retard decay, discoloration or spoilage under normal conditions of use or storage.

prevalence the proportion of animals evaluated possessing a condition of interest at a given point in time; analogous to a "snapshot" of old and new cases and, thus, reflects the risk of being a case at a given time.

principal display panel the part of the product label that is most likely to be displayed, shown or examined under customary conditions of display at retail sale.

private label pet food a market category featuring a retailer's "own house" branding.

product family a group of pet foods from the same manufacturer that have similar characteristics (same process category such as dry or moist; same intended purpose such as adult maintenance or growth; similar nutrient profile) but vary in some ingredients. A family usually includes a lead product and various flavor variations of this product.

product identity the primary means by which a specific pet food is identified by the consumer; usually includes a product name but may also include a manufacturer's name and/or a brand name.

product vignette a vignette, graphic or pictorial representation of a product on a pet food label.

propatagium the web of skin that makes up the wing membrane of birds in front of the elbow that stretches from shoulder to carpus.

proportional morbidity the proportion of hospitalized animals with the condition of interest.

prostaglandin one of a group of hormone-like substances produced from long-chain polyunsaturated fatty acids.

protease inhibitor a drug that inhibits the enzymes that split the interior peptide bonds in proteins.

protein any of a group of complex organic compounds that contain carbon, hydrogen, oxygen, nitrogen and sometimes sulfur, the characteristic element being nitrogen, and which are the principal constituents of the protoplasm of all cells. All proteins have a common property; their structure includes simple units, amino acids.

protein calories the percentage of calories in food that are contributed by protein.

protein-calorie malnutrition a clinical syndrome produced by severe protein and energy deficiency, character-ized by retarded growth, changes in skin and hair pigment, edema, anemia and pathologic changes of internal organs. Referred to as kwashiorkor when it occurs in people.

proteinuria presence of protein in the urine; implies the presence of excessive quantities, generally greater than 400 mg/dog/24 hours, >30 mg/kg body weight/24 hours or a urine protein to creatinine ratio >2.0.

provitamin a precursor of a vitamin; a substance from which the animal can form vitamins.

pruritus itching.

psittacine birds belonging to the order *Psittaciformes*; the parrots and parakeets.

purine urolithiasis formation of uroliths composed primarily of salts of uric acids (ammonium and sodium urate) and less commonly xanthine with resultant clinical signs.

pyelonephritis inflammation of the kidney and renal pelvis, usually septic.

queen a mature, intact female cat used for breeding or one presently lactating.

rancidity the auto-oxidation of fats and oils in foods that produces peroxides, hydroperoxides, aldehydes and free oxygen radicals that create off odors and flavors and destroy fat-soluble vitamins.

recommended dietary allowances (RDAs) nutrient levels that are adequate to meet the known nutritional needs of almost all healthy people.

regurgitation 1. a backward flowing, as the casting up of undigested food. 2. backward flowing of blood into the heart or between the chambers of the heart when a valve is malfunctioning.

relative body weight (RBW) an animal's current weight divided by its estimated optimal weight, usually expressed as a whole number or percentage.

renal disease any damage to the kidney, location and extent not specified. Because of the large functional reserve of the kidney, the term renal disease should not be used synonymously with the terms renal failure or uremia. Quantitative information about renal function or dysfunction is not implied by the use of this term. Renal disease may affect glomeruli, tubules, blood vessels and/or supporting tissue; e.g., interstitial tissue.

renal insufficiency decrease in renal function; e.g., decreased glomerular filtration rate.

renal osteodystrophy bone disease observed with chronic renal failure.

renal secondary hyperparathyroidism increased levels of parathyroid hormone (PTH) associated with renal dysfunction. Factors involved include phosphorus retention, hypocalcemia, calcitriol deficiency and skeletal resistance to PTH.

renin a proteolytic enzyme synthesized, stored and secreted by the kidney; plays a role in regulation of blood pressure and blood volume by catalyzing conversion of the plasma glycoprotein angiotensinogen to angiotensin I.

renolith urolith located in the kidney, usually the renal pelvis.

resistant starch a fraction of starch found in foods that potentially resists digestion in the small intestine; may have functions similar to those of fibers.

resorptive lesion (dental) caries-free resorption of the tooth structure commonly seen at the cementoenamel junction. Called also neck lesion or cervical line lesion.

respiratory quotient the ratio of the volume of carbon dioxide given off by the body tissues to the volume of oxygen absorbed by them.

resting energy expenditure   see resting energy requirement.

resting energy requirement (RER)   the energy requirement for a normal but unfasted animal at rest in a thermoneutral environment; includes energy needed for digestion, absorption and metabolism of food and recovery from previous physical activity.

retinoid-responsive dermatoses   a variety of skin disorders and diseases that are not due to vitamin A deficiency but appear to respond to high levels of natural or synthetic vitamin A administration.

retinoids   the group of naturally occurring and synthetic vitamin A derivatives.

retort   the cooking and sterilizing machine used in the manufacture of canned foods. Retorts use steam and pressure to achieve commercial sterility and are found in batch or hydrostatic designs.

rickets   a condition caused by deficiency of vitamin D, especially during growth, characterized by a disturbance in normal bone ossification.

risk factor management   detection and management of health risk factors as part of a wellness program.

risk factors   those genetic, environmental or nutritional factors that increase the likelihood of disease.

rodent   a member of the order *Rodentia* including rats and mice and allied species.

saprophytic   grows in decomposing organic matter.

sarcopenia   abnormal loss of lean muscle mass.

satiety   being in a state of satiation; the full satisfaction of desire to eat and drink.

saturated solution   holding all of a solute that can be held in solution by a solvent; saturation is the state of being saturated.

scale   an accumulation of loose fragments of the horny layer of the skin.

scurvy   the disease caused by nutritional deficiency of ascorbic acid (vitamin C).

self feeding   see free-choice feeding or ad libitum feeding.

senior cats   cats between ages 7 and 11 years with an increased risk for age-related disease; may or may not have obvious physical or behavioral characteristics of aging.

senior dogs   dogs between ages 5 and 11 years, depending on the breed, with an increased risk for age-related disease; may or may not have obvious physical or behavioral characteristics of aging.

shelf life   functional life of a product. A product with poor shelf life spoils or becomes rancid prematurely.

short bowel syndrome   a malabsorptive disorder resulting from massive resection of the small bowel, the degree and kind of malabsorption depends on the site and extent of the resection.

short-chain fatty acid(s)   fatty acids containing two to six carbon atoms that are products of microbial metabolism, primarily in the large intestine or rumen; acetic, proprionic and butyric acids are the major examples.

silica urolithiasis   formation of uroliths composed primarily of silica with resultant clinical signs.

small intestinal bacterial overgrowth   a syndrome of malabsorption causing chronic or recurring diarrhea believed to be due to abnormally large populations of bacteria in the small intestine.

socialization   the process of familiarization between animals in a group and, in companion animals, between the animal and people.

specialty pet food   a segment of premium pet foods available in limited, non-grocery distribution.

species-specific behaviors   those inherited behavioral traits that are unique to a species.

spin-out   larger ingredient particles forced towards the outer edges of a canned food matrix during can filling due to low viscosity.

spore   an inactive resting, resistant form of a bacterial cell.

sprint exercise   high-intensity activity that can be sustained less than two minutes.

squamous metaplasia   epithelial changes in animals (often birds and reptiles) usually associated with hypovitaminosis A that result in lesions in the oropharynx, conjunctiva and respiratory tract.

stain   discoloration of the tooth or of tooth-accumulated materials (e.g., pellicle, plaque, calculus).

starch   1. any of a group of polysaccharides of the general formula $(C_6H_{10}O_5)_n$, composed of a long-chain polymer of glucose in the form of amylose and amylopectin; it is the chief storage form of energy in plants. 2. a preparation consisting of the granules separated from the mature grain of corn or wheat, or from potato tubers, occurring as irregular white masses or fine powder.

statement of calorie content   the calorie content found on pet food labels in the United States; the statement is based on kilocalories of metabolizable energy on an as fed basis and is expressed as kcal per kg of product.

statutory statement   the mandatory declarations that form a separate and distinct portion of the information panel of pet food labels in Europe.

steatorrhea   excessive amounts of fat in the feces; the feces are bulky, greasy, malodorous and pale in color.

sterilization leg   primary cooking and sterilization period in the manufacture of canned pet food. During this phase, the product becomes commercially sterile.

stomatitis   inflammation of the oral soft tissues.

struvite urolithiasis   formation of uroliths composed primarily of magnesium ammonium phosphate with resultant clinical signs.

subgingival   below the free gingival margin.

supersaturated solution   a solution that is more saturated with a substance at a given temperature than would be normally expected.

supplement   a concentrated nutrient source that is added to a basic diet for treating a real or perceived nutrient imbalance.

supragingival   above the free gingival margin.

systems review   in a clinical examination, the thorough review of all body systems using a complete history, physical examination and extended laboratory database.

table food   foods normally consumed by people that are given to animals as a portion of their diet.

taurine   a beta-sulfonic amino acid; an essential amino acid for cats.

telogen   the phase of the hair cycle when the hair is not actively growing but is retained in the follicle as a dead or club hair that is subsequently lost.

telogen defluxion   hair loss associated with a stressful event (e.g., pregnancy, severe illness, surgery) that causes the abrupt, premature cessation of growth of many anagen hair follicles and the synchronization of these hair follicles in catagen, then in telogen.

thermic effect of food (TEF)   the obligatory cost in energy of digesting and absorbing food.

thermoneutral zone the environmental temperature zone in which metabolic heat production by the animal is minimal. Called also comfort zone or zone of minimal metabolism.

thermoregulation the physiologic process controlling the balance between heat production and heat loss in the body to maintain body temperature.

thiaminase an enzyme that catalyzes the splitting of thiamin into a pyrimidine and a thiazole derivative. It is present in some plants (bracken) and in some species of fish so that foods containing these materials are likely to be deficient in thiamin.

thyroglobulin an iodine-containing glycoprotein found in the colloid of the follicles of the thyroid gland; the iodinated tyrosine moieties of thyroglobulin form the active hormones thyroxine and triiodothyronine, which are released into the blood on proteolysis of thyroglobulin.

thyroid hyperplasia abnormal increase in size of the thyroid gland caused by formation and growth of new normal thyroid cells. Called also goiter.

thyrotoxicosis a morbid condition due to overactivity of the thyroid gland.

thyroxine (T4) a hormone of the thyroid gland that contains iodine and is a derivative of the amino acid tyrosine. The chemical name is tetraiodothyronine. Thyroxine influences metabolic rate, growth and development, nutrient metabolism, reproduction and resistance to infection.

time-restricted meal feeding a method of feeding animals whereby an unlimited amount of food is offered for a specific amount of time, usually for five to 10 minutes, at specific intervals throughout the day.

tolerance 1. the ability to endure an agent without ill effects. 2. the maximum legal limit of a drug or pesticide residue in an edible animal tissue, raw agricultural commodity or processed food.

tom(cat) an intact male cat typically used for breeding.

total dietary fiber that portion of ingested food that cannot be broken down by intestinal enzymes and juices and, therefore, passes through the small intestine and colon undigested. Dietary fiber is not to be confused with "crude fiber" measurements that usually underestimate actual total dietary fiber levels in food.

total nutrition admixture (TNA) a solution used for parenteral administration containing amino acids, lipids, dextrose, vitamins and minerals.

total parenteral nutrition see parenteral nutrition.

toxicity 1. the quality of being poisonous. 2. a range of nutrient concentrations at which pharmacotoxicologic effects occur.

toxin any poisonous substance of microbial, vegetable or animal origin.

training see exercise training.

treat small rewards of food not intended to be major contributors to total daily nutrient intake.

triacylglyceride (TAG) a compound consisting of three molecules of fatty acid esterified to glycerol; it is a neutral fat synthesized from carbohydrates for storage in animal adipose cells. Called also triglyceride.

trichobezoar a hairball; a concretion within the stomach or intestines formed of hairs.

trichography/trichogram a diagnostic technique performed by plucking hairs from the skin and examining them under a microscope.

triglyceride see triacylglyceride.

triiodothyronine (T3) an organic iodine-containing thyroid hormone with several times the biologic activity of thyroxine.

trypsin-like immunoreactivity (TLI) an immunoassay that detects both trypsinogen and trypsin; serum TLI concentration is both highly sensitive and specific for the diagnosis of exocrine pancreatic insufficiency.

tumor necrosis factor (TNF) a cytokine produced by macrophages that has many biologic functions; one form of TNF is involved in metabolic responses associated with body wasting.

tyrosine nonessential amino acid that is synthesized metabolically from phenylalanine; it is a precursor of thyroid hormones, catecholamines and melanin.

undernutrition improper nutrition due to inadequate food supply or failure to ingest, assimilate or use any or all of the necessary food elements.

undersaturated solution a solution that contains sufficiently low concentrations of crystalloids to permit dissolution of additional quantities of the crystalloid.

United States Department of Agriculture (USDA) the federal department with primary responsibility for domestic food production including grain and slaughterhouse inspection, animal disease prevention and control, supervision of animal vaccine manufacturers and inspection of imported foods.

universal product code (UPC) the number and bar code on a pet food label that identify the product for sales and tracking purposes.

urate a salt of uric acid.

urea cycle a cyclic series of reactions that produce urea, a major route for removal of ammonia produced in the metabolism of amino acids in the liver and kidney.

urease an enzyme that catalyzes the decomposition of urea to ammonia and carbon dioxide.

uremia literally defined as urine in blood or presence of abnormal quantities of urine constituents in blood. The term is used to indicate clinical signs associated with retention of abnormal blood concentrations of substances normally eliminated in the urine. Although uremia is always accompanied by azotemia and renal failure, azotemia and renal failure may or may not be associated with uremia.

uremic syndrome constellation of clinical signs brought about by renal failure; e.g., lethargy, anorexia, gastroenteritis, anemia and osteodystrophy.

urethral plugs obstructing material in the urethra of cats that is soft, compressible, cylindrical or shapeless, white or tan and consists of large amounts of matrix and variable amounts of crystalline components.

urge incontinence inability to control urination with involuntary passage of urine.

uric acid the end product of purine metabolism in many but not all species of animals.

uricemia excessive amounts of uric acid in the blood.

urinary acidifier a drug or substance used to increase urine acidity.

urinary pH the measure of the degree to which urine is acidic or alkaline. When referring to pet foods, the average urine pH values produced by a group of animals eating a specific food.

urine the fluid containing water and waste products that is excreted by the kidneys.

urocystolith urolith located in the urinary bladder.

urohydropropulsion a technique used to dislodge uroliths obstructing the urethra.

urolith polycrystalline concretions that typically contain more than 90% organic or inorganic crystalloids and less than 10% organic matrices.

urolithiasis the formation of urinary stones anywhere in the urinary tract from less soluble crystalloids of urine.

vasoactive amines amines that cause vasodilation and increased small vessel permeability; e.g., histamine, serotonin and others.

vegan a person who eats a diet that does not contain animal ingredients or foods.

vegetarian a person who eats a meatless diet.

vertebrate prey animals with endoskeletons typically fed to reptiles, such as rats, mice, gerbils, rabbits, young chicks, fish, toads, frogs, etc.

veterinary therapeutic pet food pet foods having specific nutrient characteristics and balances to treat or provide adjunct medical support in nutritionally responsive clinical conditions.

virulence the ability of a microbe to invade a host and cause disease.

vitamer any of a number of compounds that possess a given vitamin activity; there are niacin vitamers, pyridoxine vitamers, A vitamers, D vitamers, etc.

vitamin a general term for a number of unrelated organic substances that are essential in small amounts for normal metabolism.

vitamin E-responsive dermatoses a variety of skin disorders and diseases that are not due to vitamin E deficiency but appear to respond to high levels of supplemental vitamin E.

$\dot{V}O_2$ oxygen consumption; a measure of workload or exercise intensity.

$\dot{V}O_2$ max maximal oxygen consumption. Workload is frequently expressed as a percentage of $\dot{V}O_2$ max and work done above this level has a significant anaerobic component.

vomiting forcible ejection of stomach contents through the mouth. Called also emesis.

water a combination of hydrogen and oxygen (H_2O) that is vital to life.

weaning the act of separating the young from the dam that they have been nursing.

wellness concepts and programs that attempt to promote health in an individual or group; in contrast to focusing on diagnosis, treatment or management of disease.

work the result of a force acting against a resistance to produce motion. The amount of work done and energy used are the same for the exercising animal.

workload expected work done per unit time, synonymous with exercise intensity.

World Health Organization (WHO) an agency of the United Nations that is devoted to attainment of the highest level of health by all peoples of the world.

xanthine a purine compound found in most body tissues and fluids; a precursor of uric acid.

xanthine oxidase enzyme that catalyzes the conversion of hypoxanthine to xanthine and xanthine to uric acid.

xanthine oxidase inhibitor a drug, such as allopurinol, that is used to decrease production of uric acid and reduce serum and urine uric acid concentrations.

xenobiotic any substance, harmful or not, that is foreign to the animal's biologic system.

xerosis abnormal dryness, as of the skin (xerosis cutis).

zinc-responsive dermatoses a variety of skin disorders and diseases that respond to dietary changes or zinc supplements.

Page numbers followed by t denote tables; those followed by f denote figures; those followed by s denote sidebars; and those followed by c denote cases.

Appetite stimulants, in hospitalized patients, 370t
Arachidonic acid, metabolism, 909-911, 910f, 911f
Arginine, 49t, 57
recommendations for renal disease, 587-588
requirement in cats, 300
use in hospitalized patients, 365s
use in patients with cancer, 889t, 891-892, 894s
use in patients with hepatobiliary disease, 813t
Arginine vasopressin (AVP), 533, 535-537, 569-570
Aromatic amino acids (See Amino acids)
Arthritis
assessment of, 915
clinical importance of, 915
use of fatty acids as treatment for, 915-916
Ascites, 816f, 825, 825f
Ascorbic acid (See Vitamin C)
As fed basis, conversion steps, 6t
Ash, 24f
protein:ash ratio in selected pet food ingredients, 141t
Assessment, as part of iterative process
of the animal, 3-8
of the feeding method, 11-14
of the food(s), 9-11
of hospitalized patients, 354-367
Assisted feeding (See Enteral feeding, Parenteral feeding)
Atopy
assessment of, 912-913
risk factors for, 913
use of fatty acids as treatment for, 914, 914t
ATP, 27, 27f, 28f, 29, 29f, 264t, 265, 265f
Atrial natriuretic factor (peptide), 533-538
Atwater calorie factors,
Aversion, food, 296s, 593
Azotemia, 548, 566t, 568 (See Renal disease/failure)

B

B$_1$, vitamin (See Thiamin)
B$_2$, vitamin (See Riboflavin)
B$_6$, vitamin (See Pyridoxine)

B$_{12}$, vitamin (See Cobolamin)
Bacillus cereus, 189, 197-198c
Balanced diet, 12-13, 13s, 16s
Barley, 53t, 58t, 138t, 139f, 139, 141f, 172t, 1129t
Basal energy expenditure (See Basal energy requirement)
Basal energy requirement (BER), 31, 32t
Basal metabolic rate (BMR), 1009t (See also Basal energy requirement)
Beef, ground
comparison to cat nutrient requirements, 297t
comparison to dog nutrient requirements, 218t
nutrient content of, 218t
Beet pulp, 43, 43f, 46t, 48t, 757t
Begging, in dogs, 227s
Belching (See Flatulence)
Beta-carotene, 83-84
Bile duct obstruction, 825-826, 826t, 829
Bioflavonoids, 95
Biogenic amines, in food, 189-190, 438-439
Biologic dose-response curve, 23f
Biologic value (protein), 54s, 58t
Biotin
deficiency of, 106-107c
structure, metabolism and sources of, 92
Birds, pet
adult body weights of, 1092-1093t
assessment of, 980-984
assessment of foods for, 985-989
changing foods for, 990-991
commercial foods for, 985t, 1094-1096t
commonly prepared foods for, 985t, 986-989
feeding intervals for, 989-990
feeding plans for, 989-991
hand-feeding recommendations for, 1096t
homemade mixed-food diets for, 989, 991t
manifestations of malnutrition in, 982t
nutrient recommendations for, 984t
popular and scientific names of, 1092-1093t
seed and seed mixtures for, 986-988, 1098t
special nutritional needs of passerine birds, 987-988t
water for, 989
Birds, wild
adult body weights, 1092-1093t
feeding orphaned and injured, 1101-1109
popular and scientific names of, 1092-1093t
Birth weights
of cats, 1014t
of dogs, 1012-1013t
Bitch's milk, 238t, 331t, 1066-1067t
Black currant oil, 917t, 1128t
Blended foods, for hospitalized patients, 374
Bloat (See Gastric dilatation-volvulus)
Blood glucose (See Hypoglycemia, Hyperglycemia, Diabetes mellitus)
Blood pressure (See also Hypertension)
measurement of, 532, 571
regulation of, 541
Body condition score
assessment in large growing dogs, 516t
assessment in obesity, 405-406
methods in cats, 5f
methods in dogs, 4f
Body surface area, 1009t
Body types, of cats, 1047

Appendices Directory